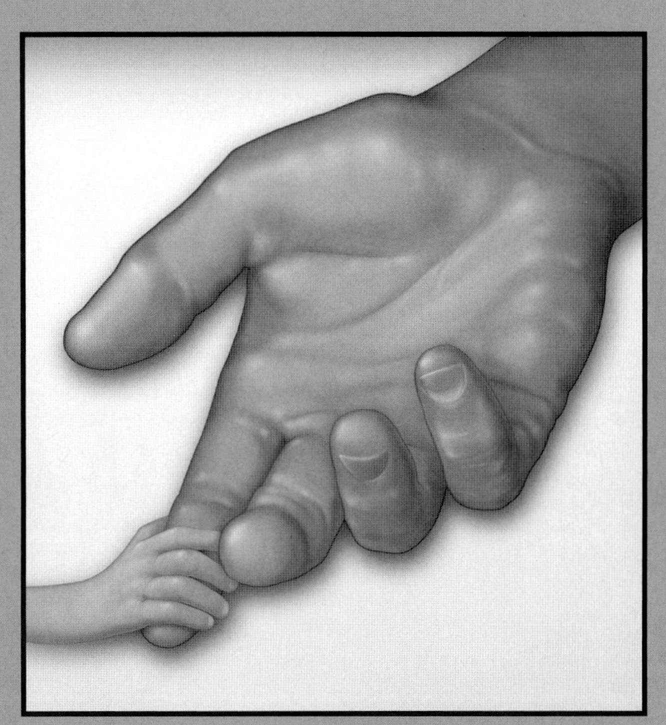

Pediatric Surgery

Pediatric Surgery

SIXTH EDITION

VOLUME TWO

Jay L. Grosfeld, MD
Lafayette Page Professor and Chairman Emeritus
Department of Surgery, Indiana University School of Medicine
Surgeon-in-Chief and Director of Pediatric Surgery Emeritus, Riley Hospital for Children
Indianapolis, Indiana

James A. O'Neill, Jr., MD
John Clinton Foshee Distinguished Professor of Surgery
Former Chairman, Section of Surgical Sciences, Former
Chairman, Department of Surgery, Surgeon-in-Chief Emeritus
Vanderbilt University Medical Center
Nashville, Tennessee

Arnold G. Coran, MD
Professor of Pediatric Surgery
University of Michigan Medical School
Former Surgeon-in-Chief
C.S. Mott Children's Hospital
Ann Arbor, Michigan

Eric W. Fonkalsrud, MD
Professor and Emeritus Chief of Pediatric Surgery
David Geffen School of Medicine at UCLA
Department of Surgery
Los Angeles, California

Anthony A. Caldamone, MD, FAAP
Associate Editor, Urology Section
Professor of Surgery (Urology) and Pediatrics
Brown University School of Medicine
Chief of Pediatric Urology, Hasbro Children's Hospital
Providence, Rhode Island

MOSBY
ELSEVIER

1600 John F. Kennedy Blvd.
Ste 1800
Philadelphia, PA 19103-2899

PEDIATRIC SURGERY

ISBN-13: 978-0-323-02842-4
ISBN-10: 0-323-02842-X
Volume 1 PN 999603772X
Volume 2 PN 9996037789

Notice

Knowledge and best practice in this field are constantly changing. As new research and experience broaden our knowledge, changes in practice, treatment and drug therapy may become necessary or appropriate. Readers are advised to check the most current information provided (i) on procedures featured or (ii) by the manufacturer of each product to be administered, to verify the recommended dose or formula, the method and duration of administration, and contraindications. It is the responsibility of the practitioner, relying on their own experience and knowledge of the patient, to make diagnoses, to determine dosages and the best treatment for each individual patient, and to take all appropriate safety precautions. To the fullest extent of the law, neither the Publisher nor the Editors assumes any liability for any injury and/or damage to persons or property arising out or related to any use of the material contained in this book.

The Publisher

Library of Congress Cataloging-in-Publication Data
Pediatric surgery.— 6th ed. / edited by Jay L. Grosfeld ... [et al.].
p. ; cm.
Includes bibliographical references and index.
ISBN-13: 978-0-323-02842-4 ISBN-10: 0-323-02842-X
1.Children—Surgery. I. Grosfeld, Jay L.
[DNLM: 1. Surgical Procedures, Operative—Child. 2. Surgical Procedures, Operative—Infant. WO 925 P371 2006]
RD137.P42 2006
617.9′8- -dc22 2005049600

ISBN-13: 978-0-323-02842-4
ISBN-10: 0-323-02842-X

Acquisitions Editor: Judith Fletcher
Senior Developmental Editor: Janice Gaillard
Publishing Services Manager: Tina K. Rebane
Senior Project Manager: Linda Lewis Grigg
Design Direction: Gene Harris
Cover Designer: Gene Harris

Printed in USA

Last digit is the print number: 9 8 7 6 5 4 3 2

To our wives
Margie, Susan, Peggy, and Susi.
To our children and grandchildren for giving
us the time and providing the sensitivity
and support to prepare these volumes.
To children everywhere who have suffered
from congenital and acquired surgical conditions
and have provided the experience and inspired us.

Contributors

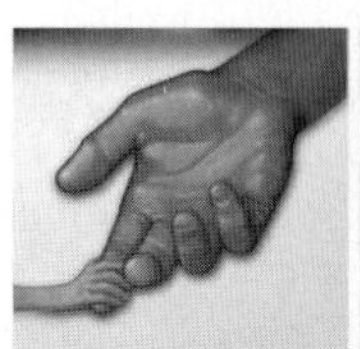

Mark C. Adams, MD, FAAP
Professor of Urology and Pediatrics, Vanderbilt University School of Medicine; Pediatric Urologist, Monroe Carell Jr. Children's Hospital at Vanderbilt, Nashville, Tennessee
Magaureter and Prune-Belly Syndrome

N. Scott Adzick, MD
C. Everett Koop Professor of Pediatric Surgery, University of Pennsylvania School of Medicine; Surgeon-in-Chief, The Children's Hospital of Philadelphia, Philadelphia, Pennsylvania
Cysts of the Lungs and Mediastinum

Craig T. Albanese, MD
Professor of Surgery, Pediatrics, and Obstetrics and Gynecology, and Chief, Division of Pediatric Surgery, Department of Surgery, Stanford Hospital & Clinics, Stanford; John A. and Cynthia Fry Gunn Director of Surgical Services, Lucile Packard Children's Hospital at Stanford, Palo Alto, California
Necrotizing Enterocolitis

Fred Alexander, MD
Associate Professor of Surgery, Cleveland Clinic Lerner School of Medicine of Case Western Reserve University; Staff Surgeon, Cleveland Clinic Foundation, Cleveland, Ohio
Crohn's Disease

R. Peter Altman, MD
Professor of Surgery, Columbia University College of Physicians and Surgeons; Surgeon-in-Chief, Morgan Stanley Children's Hospital of New York Presbyterian, New York, New York
The Jaundiced Infant: Biliary Atresia

Richard J. Andrassy, MD
Denton A. Cooley Professor and Chairman, Department of Surgery, University of Texas Medical School at Houston; Executive Vice President of Clinical Affairs and Associate Dean for Clinical Affairs, University of Texas at Houston, Houston, Texas
Rhabdomyosarcoma

Walter S. Andrews, MD
Professor of Surgery, University of Missouri–Kansas City School of Medicine; Director, Transplantation Program, Children's Mercy Hospital, Kansas City, Missouri
Gallbladder Disease and Hepatic Infections

Harry Applebaum, MD
Clinical Professor of Surgery, David Geffen School of Medicine at UCLA; Head, Division of Pediatric Surgery, Kaiser Permanente Medical Center, Los Angeles, California
Duodenal Atresia and Stenosis—Annular Pancreas

Marjorie J. Arca, MD
Assistant Professor of Surgery, Medical College of Wisconsin; Attending Surgeon, Children's Hospital of Wisconsin, Milwaukee, Wisconsin
Atresia, Stenosis, and Other Obstructions of the Colon

Robert M. Arensman, MD
Professor of Surgery, Louisiana State University School of Medicine; Attending Surgeon, Ochsner Clinic Foundation, New Orleans, Louisiana
Gastrointestinal Bleeding

James B. Atkinson, MD
Professor and Chief, Division of Pediatric Surgery, Department of Surgery, David Geffen School of Medicine at UCLA, Los Angeles, California
Liver Tumors

Richard G. Azizkhan, MD, PhD(Hon)
Professor of Surgery and Pediatrics, Lester Martin Chair of Pediatric Surgery, and Vice Chair, Department of Surgery, University of Cincinnati College of Medicine; Surgeon-in-Chief and Director, Division of Pediatric Surgery, Cincinnati Children's Hospital Medical Center, Cincinnati, Ohio
Teratomas and Other Germ Cell Tumors

Anwar Baban, MD
Laboratory of Molecular Genetics, Gaslini Children's Hospital, Genoa, Italy
Hirschsprung's Disease and Related Neuromuscular Disorders of the Intestine

Douglas C. Barnhart, MD, MSPH
Assistant Professor, Departments of Surgery and Pediatrics, University of Alabama at Birmingham School of Medicine; Attending Surgeon, The Children's Hospital of Alabama, Birmingham, Alabama
Biopsy Techniques for Children with Cancer

Robert H. Bartlett, MD
Professor of Surgery, University of Michigan Medical School, Ann Arbor, Michigan
Extracorporeal Life Support for Cardiopulmonary Failure

Laurence S. Baskin, MD
Professor of Urology, University of California, San Francisco, School of Medicine; Chief, Pediatric Urology, UCSF Children's Hospital at UCSF Medical Center, San Francisco, California
Hypospadias

Spencer W. Beasley, MB, ChB, MS
Clinical Professor of Pediatrics and Surgery, Christchurch School of Medicine and Health Sciences, University of Otago; Chief of Child Health Services, Division of Child Health, and Clinical Director, Paediatric Surgery, Christchurch Hospital, Christchurch, New Zealand
Torticollis

Michael L. Bentz, MD, FAAP, FACS
Professor of Surgery, Pediatrics, and Plastic Surgery, and Chairman, Division of Plastic Surgery, University of Wisconsin School of Medicine and Public Health; Chief of Plastic Surgery, University of Wisconsin Hospital and Clinics, Madison, Wisconsin
Hand, Soft Tissue, and Envenomation Injuries

Victor E. Boston, MD, FRCSI, FRCSEng, FRCSEd
Honorary Senior Lecturer, Department of Surgery, The Queen's University of Belfast Faculty of Medicine; The Royal Belfast Hospital for Sick Children, Belfast, Northern Ireland
Ureteral Duplication and Ureteroceles

Scott C. Boulanger, MD, PhD
Assistant Professor of Surgery, Division of Pediatric Surgery, University of Mississippi Medical Center School of Medicine, Jackson, Mississippi
Inguinal Hernias and Hydroceles

Edward L. Bove, MD
Professor of Surgery, University of Michigan Medical School; Head, Section of Cardiac Surgery, C.S. Mott Children's Hospital, Ann Arbor, Michigan
Congenital Heart Disease and Anomalies of the Great Vessels

Mary L. Brandt, MD
Professor and Vice Chair, Michael E. DeBakey Department of Surgery, Baylor College of Medicine, Texas Children's Hospital, Houston, Texas
Disorders of the Breast

John W. Brock III, MD
Professor of Urologic Surgery, Vanderbilt University School of Medicine; Director, Pediatric Urology, Vanderbilt Medical Center; Surgeon in Chief, Monroe Carell Jr. Children's Hospital at Vanderbilt, Nashville, Tennessee
Bladder Exstrophy

Rebeccah L. Brown, MD
Assistant Professor of Clinical Surgery and Pediatrics, University of Cincinnati College of Medicine; Associate Director of Trauma Services, Cincinnati Children's Hospital Medical Center, Cincinnati, Ohio
Genitourinary Tract Trauma

Marybeth Browne, MD
Surgical Resident, McGaw Medical Center of Northwestern University, Chicago, Illinois
Gastrointestinal Bleeding

Terry L. Buchmiller, MD
Formerly Assistant Professor of Surgery, Weill Medical College of Cornell University of New York, New York; Currently Assistant Professor of Surgery, Harvard Medical School; Assistant in Surgery, Children's Hospital Boston, Boston, Massachusetts
The Jaundiced Infant: Biliary Atresia

Ronald W. Busuttil, MD, PhD
Professor and Executive Chairman, Department of Surgery, David Geffen School of Medicine at UCLA; Chief, Division of Liver and Pancreas Transplantation, Dumont-UCLA Liver Cancer Center; Director, Pfleger Liver Institute, UCLA Medical Center, Los Angeles, California
Liver Transplantation

Michelle S. Caird, MD
Lecturer, Department of Orthopaedic Surgery, Alfred Taubman Health Care Center, University of Michigan, Ann Arbor, Michigan
Musculoskeletal Trauma

Anthony A. Caldamone, MD, FAAP
Professor of Surgery (Urology) and Pediatrics, Brown University School of Medicine; Chief of Pediatric Urology, Hasbro Children's Hospital, Providence, Rhode Island
Renal Infection, Abscess, Vesicoureteral Reflux, Urinary Lithiasis, and Renal Vein Thrombosis

Darrell A. Campbell, Jr., MD
Professor of Surgery, University of Michigan Medical School; Chief of Clinical Affairs, University of Michigan Health System, Ann Arbor, Michigan
Renal Transplantation

Donna A. Caniano, MD
Professor of Surgery and Pediatrics, The Ohio State University College of Medicine and Public Health; Surgeon-in-Chief, Children's Hospital, Columbus, Ohio
Ethical Considerations

Michael G. Caty, MD
Associate Professor of Surgery and Pediatrics, University at Buffalo School of Medicine and Biomedical Science; Surgeon-in-Chief, Women and Children's Hospital of Buffalo, Buffalo, New York
Adrenal Tumors

Dai H. Chung, MD
Associate Professor of Surgery and Pediatrics, The University of Texas Medical Branch School of Medicine at Galveston; Chief, Section of Pediatric Surgery, UTMB Children's Hospital, Galveston, Texas
Burns

Robert E. Cilley, MD
Professor of Surgery and Pediatrics, Penn State College of Medicine; Chief, Division of Pediatric Surgery, Milton S. Hershey Medical Center, Hershey, Pennsylvania
Disorders of the Umbilicus

Paul M. Colombani, MD
Professor of Surgery, Pediatrics, and Oncology, and Robert Garrett Professor of Surgery, Johns Hopkins University School of Medicine; Chief, Division of Pediatric Surgery, Johns Hopkins Medicine; Pediatric Surgeon-in-Charge, Johns Hopkins Hospital, Baltimore, Maryland
Surgical Implications Associated with Bone Marrow Transplantation

Joel D. Cooper, MD
Professor of Surgery, University of Pennsylvania School of Medicine; Chief, Division of Thoracic Surgery, Hospital of the University of Pennsylvania, Philadelphia, Pennsylvania
Lung Transplantation

Arnold G. Coran, MD
Professor of Pediatric Surgery, University of Michigan Medical School, Ann Arbor, Michigan
Nutritional Support; Congenital Anomalies of the Esophagus; Hirschsprung's Disease and Related Neuromuscular Disorders of the Intestine; Abnormalities of the Female Genital Tract

Robin T. Cotton, MD
Professor of Otolaryngology, University of Cincinnati School of Medicine; Director, Pediatric Otolaryngology–HNS, Cincinnati Children's Hospital Medical Center, Cincinnati, Ohio
Lesions of the Larynx, Trachea, and Upper Airway

Michael C. Dalsing, MD
Professor of Surgery and Director, Section of Vascular Surgery, Indiana University School of Medicine, Indianapolis, Indiana
Venous Disorders in Childhood

Alan Daneman, MBBCh, BSc, FRANZCR, FRCPC
Professor of Radiology, University of Toronto Faculty of Medicine; Staff Radiologist, Hospital for Sick Children, Toronto, Ontario, Canada
Intussusception

Andrew M. Davidoff, MD
Associate Professor, Department of Surgery and Pediatrics, University of Tennessee School of Medicine; Chief, Division of General Pediatric Surgery, St. Jude Children's Research Hospital, Memphis, Tennessee
Principles of Pediatric Oncology, Genetics of Cancer, and Radiation Therapy

Richard S. Davidson, MD
Associate Professor, University of Pennsylvania School of Medicine; Attending Surgeon, Children's Hospital of Philadelphia and Shrener's Hospital, Philadelphia
Musculoskeletal Trauma

Romano T. DeMarco, MD
Assistant Professor of Urologic Surgery, Division of Pediatric Urology, Vanderbilt University School of Medicine, Nashville, Tennessee
Bladder Exstrophy

Daniel A. DeUgarte, MD
Pediatric Surgery Fellow, University of Michigan Medical School and C.S. Mott Children's Hospital, Ann Arbor, Michigan
Liver Tumors

Eric Devaney, MD
Assistant Professor of Surgery, University of Michigan Medical School; Attending Surgeon, C.S. Mott Children's Hospital, Ann Arbor, Michigan
Congenital Heart Disease and Anomalies of the Great Vessels

William Didelot, MD
Professor of Pediatric Orthopaedics, Indiana University School of Medicine; Staff Surgeon, Riley Hospital for Children, Indianapolis, Indiana
Major Congenital Orthopedic Deformitites

John W. DiFiore, MD
Clinical Assistant Professor of Surgery, Case School of Medicine; Staff Pediatric Surgeon, Children's Hospital at Cleveland Clinic, Cleveland, Ohio
Respiratory Physiology and Care

Patrick A. Dillon, MD
Assistant Professor of Surgery, Washington University in St. Louis School of Medicine; Attending Surgeon, St. Louis Children's Hospital, St. Louis, Missouri
Gastrointestinal Tumors

Peter W. Dillon, MD
Professor of Surgery and Pediatrics, Penn State College of Medicine; Vice Chair, Department of Surgery, and Chief, Division of Pediatric Surgery, Penn State Children's Hospital, Hershey, Pennsylvania
Congenital Diaphragmatic Hernia and Eventration

Patricia K. Donahoe, MD
Marshall K. Bartlett Professor of Surgery, Harvard Medical School; Director, Pediatric Surgical Research Laboratories and Chief, Pediatric Surgical Services Emerita, Massachusetts General Hospital, Boston
Ambiguous Genitalia

James C. Y. Dunn, MD, PhD
Assistant Professor of Surgery, David Geffen School of Medicine at UCLA; Attending Surgeon, Mattel Children's Hospital at UCLA, Los Angeles, California
Appendicitis

Simon Eaton, BSc, PhD
Senior Lecturer in Pediatric Surgery and Metabolic Biochemistry, Department of Pediatric Surgery, Institute of Child Health, University College London, London, United Kingdom
Neonatal Physiology and Metabolic Considerations

Martin R. Eichelberger, MD
Professor of Surgery and Pediatrics, George Washington University School of Medicine and Health Sciences; Director, Emergency Trauma, Burn Service, and Senior Attending, Pediatric Surgery Service, Children's National Medical Center; President and CEO, Safe Kids Worldwide, Washington, DC
Accident Victims and Their Emergency Management

Sigmund H. Ein, MDCM, FRCSC, FAAP, FACS
Associate Professor of Surgery, Adjunct Clinical Faculty, Department of Surgery, University of Toronto Faculty of Medicine; Honorary Staff Surgeon, Division of General Surgery, The Hospital for Sick Children, Toronto; Courtesy Staff, Department of Surgery, Lakeridge Health Corporation, Oshawa, Ontario, Canada
Intussusception

Carolyn Ells, RTT, PhD
Assistant Professor of Medicine, McGill University Faculty of Medicine; Clinical Ethicist, Sir Mortimer B. Davis Jewish General Hospital, Montreal, Quebec, Canada
Ethical Considerations

Barry L. Eppley, MD, DMD
Professor of Plastic Surgery, Indiana University School of Medicine, Indianapolis, Indiana
Cleft Lip and Palate

Mary E. Fallat, MD
Professor of Surgery, and Director, Division of Pediatric Surgery, University of Louisville; Chief of Surgery, Kosdir Children's Hospital, Louisville, Kentucky
Ovarian Tumors

Diana L. Farmer, MD
Professor of Clinical Surgery, Pediatrics and Obstetrics, Gynecology, and Reproductive Medicine, University of California, San Francisco, School of Medicine; Surgeon-in-Chief, UCSF Children's Hospital, San Francisco, California
Cysts of the Lungs and Mediastinum

Douglas G. Farmer, MD
Associate Professor of Surgery, David Geffen School of Medicine at UCLA; Director, Intestinal Transplantation, Dumont-UCLA Transplant Center, Los Angeles, California
Liver Transplantation; Intestinal Transplantation

Steven J. Fishman, MD
Professor of Surgery, Harvard University Medical School; Senior Associate in Surgery, Children's Hospital Boston, Boston, Massachusetts
Vascular Anomalies: Hemangiomas and Malformations

Alan W. Flake, MD
Professor of Surgery and Obstetrics and Gynecology, University of Pennsylvania School of Medicine; Director, Children's Institute for Surgical Science, The Children's Hospital of Philadelphia, Philadelphia, Pennsylvania
Molecular Clinical Genetics and Gene Therapy

Robert P. Foglia, MD
Associate Professor of Surgery and Division Chief, Pediatric Surgery, Washington University in St. Louis School of Medicine; Surgeon-in-Chief, St. Louis Children's Hospital, St. Louis, Missouri
Gastrointestinal Tumors

Eric W. Fonkalsrud, MD
Professor of Surgery, David Geffen School of Medicine at UCLA; Emeritus Chief of Pediatric Surgery, UCLA Medical Center, Los Angeles, California
Ulcerative Colitis; Lymphatic Disorders

Henri R. Ford, MD
Vice-Chair and Visiting Professor of Surgery, Keck School of Medicine of USC; Surgeon-in-Chief and Vice President, Surgery, and Medical Director, Burtie Green Bettingen Surgery Center, Children's Hospital Los Angeles, Los Angeles, California
Sepsis and Related Considerations

Stephanie M. P. Fuller, MD
Clinical Fellow, Division of Cardiothoracic Surgery, The Children's Hospital of Philadelphia and Thomas Jefferson University Hospital, Philadelphia, Pennsylvania
Heart Transplantation

Victor F. Garcia, MD
Professor of Surgery, University of Cincinnati College of Medicine; Director of Trauma Services, Cincinnati Children's Hospital Medical Center, Cincinnati, Ohio
Genitourinary Tract Trauma; Bariatric Surgery in Adolescents

John M. Gatti, MD
Assistant Professor of Surgery and Urology, University of Missouri–Kansas City School of Medicine; Director of Minimally Invasive Urology, Children's Mercy Hospital of Kansas City, Kansas City, Missouri
Abnormalities of the Urethra, Penis, and Scrotum

Michael W. L. Gauderer, MD
Professor of Surgery and Pediatrics (Greenville), University of South Carolina School of Medicine, Columbia; Adjunct Professor of Bioengineering, Clemson University, Clemson; Chief, Division of Pediatric Surgery, Children's Hospital, Greenville Hospital System, Greenville, South Carolina
Stomas of the Small and Large Intestine

James D. Geiger, MD
Associate Professor of Surgery, University of Michigan Medical School; Staff Surgeon, C.S. Mott Children's Hospital, Ann Arbor, Michigan
Biopsy Techniques for Children with Cancer

Keith E. Georgeson, MD
Professor of Surgery, University of Alabama at Birmingham School of Medicine; Chief of Pediatric Surgery, The Children's Hospital of Alabama, Birmingham, Alabama
Gastroesophageal Reflux Disease

Cynthia A. Gingalewski, MD
Assistant Professor of Surgery and Pediatrics, George Washington University School of Medicine and Health Science; Pediatric Surgeon, Children's National Medical Center, Washington, DC
Other Causes of Intestinal Obstruction

Kenneth I. Glassberg, MD
Professor of Urology, Columbia University College of Physicians and Surgeons; Director, Division of Pediatric Urology, Morgan Stanley Children's Hospital of New York–Presbyterian, New York, New York
Renal Agenesis, Dysplasia, and Cystic Disease

Philip L. Glick, MD, MBA
Professor of Surgery, Pediatrics, and Obstetrics and Gynecology, University of Buffalo School of Medicine and Biomedical Sciences; Executive Director, Miniature Access Surgery Center (MASC), Women and Children's Hospital of Buffalo, Buffalo, New York
Inguinal Hernias and Hydroceles

Sherilyn A. Gordon, MD
Assistant Professor of Surgery, Division of Liver and Pancreas Transplantation, David Geffen School of Medicine at UCLA, Los Angeles, California
Intestinal Transplantation

Tracy C. Grikscheit, MD
Senior Fellow in Pediatric Surgery, Children's Hospital and Regional Medical Center and University of Washington School of Medicine, Seattle, Washington
The Impact of Tissue Engineering in Pediatric Surgery

Jay L. Grosfeld, MD
Lafayette Page Professor of Pediatric Surgery Emeritus, Indiana University School of Medicine; Surgeon-in-Chief Emeritus, Riley Hospital for Children, Indianapolis, Indiana
Neuroblastoma; Jejunoileal Atresia and Stenosis; Abnormalities of the Female Genital Tract

Angelika C. Gruessner, MS, PhD
Associate Professor of Surgical Science, University of Minnesota Medical School, Minneapolis, Minnesota
Pancreas and Islet Cell Transplantation

Rainer W. G. Gruessner
Professor of Surgery, University of Minnesota Medical School, Minneapolis, Minnesota
Pancreas and Islet Cell Transplantation

Philip C. Guzzetta, Jr., MD
Professor of Surgery and Pediatrics, George Washington University School of Medicine and Health Sciences; Interim Chief of Pediatric Surgery, Children's National Medical Center, Washington, DC
Nonmalignant Tumors of the Liver

Carroll M. Harmon, MD, PhD,
Associate Professor of Surgery, University of Alabama at Birmingham School of Medicine; Attending Surgeon, Children's Hospital, Birmingham, Alabama
Congenital Anomalies of the Esophagus

Michael R. Harrison, MD
Professor of Surgery, Pediatrics, and Obstetrics, Gynecology, and Reproductive Sciences, University of California, San Francisco, School of Medicine; Director, Fetal Treatment Center, UCSF Children's Hospital and Medical Center, San Francisco, California
The Fetus as a Patient

Andrea A. Hayes-Jordan, MD
Assistant Professor of Surgery and Pediatrics, University of Texas Medical School at Houston and M.D. Anderson Cancer Center; Pediatric Surgeon, Memorial Hermann Children's Hospital and M.D. Anderson Cancer Center, Houston, Texas
Lymph Node Disorders

Stephen R. Hays, MD, MS, FAAP
Assistant Professor of Anesthesiology and Pediatrics, Vanderbilt University School of Medicine; Director, Pediatric Pain Services, Vanderbilt Children's Hospital, Nashville, Tennessee
Pediatric Anesthesia

John H. Healey, MD
Professor of Orthopaedic Surgery, Weill Medical College of Cornell University; Chief of Orthopaedic Surgery, Memorial Sloan-Kettering Cancer Center, New York, New York
Bone Tumors

W. Hardy Hendren III, MD, FACS, FAAP, FRCS (Irel&Engl), FRCPS(Glasgow), DSc(Drexel), MD(HonCausa) Université Aix Marseilles
Robert E. Gross Distinguished Professor of Surgery, Harvard Medical School; Chief of Surgery Emeritus, Children's Hospital Boston; Honorary Surgeon, Massachusetts General Hospital, Boston, Massachusetts
Megaureter and Prune-Belly Syndrome

Bernhard J. Hering, MD
Assistant Professor of Surgery, University of Minnesota Medical School; Associate Director, Diabetes Institute for Immunology and Transplantation, University of Minnesota Medical Center, Fairview, Minneapolis, Minnesota
Pancreas and Islet Cell Tranplantation

David N. Herndon, MD
Professor of Surgery and Pediatrics and Jesse H. Jones Distinguished Chair in Burn Surgery, University of Texas Medical Branch School of Medicine at Galveston; Chief of Staff and Director of Research, Shriners Burns Hospital, Galveston, Texas
Burns

Ronald B. Hirschl, MD
Professor of Surgery, University of Michigan Medical School; Head, Section of Pediatric Surgery, and Surgeon-in-Chief, C.S. Mott Children's Hospital, Ann Arbor, Michigan
Extracorporeal Life Support for Cardiopulmonary Failure

George W. Holcomb III, MD, MBA
Katharine Berry Richardson Professor of Surgery, University of Missouri–Kansas City School of Medicine; Surgeon-in-Chief, Children's Mercy Hospital, Kansas City, Missouri
Gallbladder Disease and Hepatic Infections

Charles B. Huddleston, MD
Professor of Surgery, Washington University in St. Louis School of Medicine; Chief, Pediatric Cardiothoracic Surgery, and Surgical Director, Lung Transplant Program, St. Louis Children's Hospital, St. Louis, Missouri
Lung Transplantation

Raymond J. Hutchinson, MS, MD
Professor of Pediatrics, University of Michigan Medical School; Director of Clinical Services, Pediatric Hematology/Oncology, C.S. Mott Children's Hospital, Ann Arbor, Michigan
Surgical Implications of Hematologic Disease

John M. Hutson, MD(Monash), MD(Melb), FRACS, FAAP(Hon)
Professor of Pediatric Surgery, Department of Pediatrics, University of Melbourne Faculty of Medicine, Melbourne; Director of General Surgery, Royal Children's Hospital, Parkville, Victoria, Australia
Undescended Testis, Torsion, and Varicocele

Thomas Inge, MD, PhD
Associate Professor of Surgery and Pediatrics, University of Cincinnati College of Medicine; Surgical Director, Comprehensive Weight Management Program, Cincinnati Children's Hospital Medical Center, Cincinnati
Bariatric Surgery in Adolescents

Vincenzo Jasonni, MD
Professor of Pediatric Surgery, University of Genoa Medical School; Surgeon-in-Chief and Chair of Pediatric Surgery, Gaslini Children's Hospital, Genoa, Italy
Hirschsprung's Disease and Related Neuromuscular Disorders of the Intestine

Nishwan Jibri, MD
Department of Pediatric Surgery, Gaslini Children's Hospital, Genoa, Italy
Hirschsprung's Disease and Related Neuromuscular Disorders of the Intestine

Byron D. Joyner, MD
Associate Professor of Urology, University of Washington School of Medicine; Residency Director, University of Washington Urology Program, and Faculty/Staff, Children's Hospital and Regional Medical Center, Seattle, Washington
Ureteropelvic Junction Obstruction

Martin Kaefer, MD
Associate Professor, Department of Urology, Indiana University School of Medicine; Pediatric Urologist, Riley Children's Hospital, Indianapolis, Indiana
Disorders of Bladder Function

Henry K. Kawamoto, Jr., MD, DDS
Clinical Professor of Surgery, Department of Surgery, Division of Plastic Surgery, David Geffen School of Medicine at UCLA; Director, Craniofacial Surgery, UCLA Medical Center, Los Angeles, California
Craniofacial Anomalies

Robert M. Kay, MD
Associate Professor of Orthopedic Surgery, Keck School of Medicine of USC; Orthopedic Surgeon, Children's Hospital Los Angeles, Los Angeles, California
Bone and Joint Infections

Kosmas Kayes, MD
Staff Surgeon, Riley Hospital for Children and St. Vincent Children's Hospital, Indianapolis, Indiana
Major Congenital Orthopedic Deformities

Mark L. Kayton, MD
Assistant Member, Memorial Sloan-Kettering Cancer Center; Assistant Attending Surgeon, Division of Pediatric Surgery, Memorial Hospital, New York, New York
Surgical Implications Associated with Bone Marrow Transplantation

Robert E. Kelly, Jr., MD, FACS, FAAP
Associate Professor of Clinical Surgery and Pediatrics, Eastern Virginia Medical School, Children's Hospital of the King's Daughters, Norfolk, Virginia
The Nuss Procedure for Pectus Excavatum [Chapter 59]

Stephen S. Kim, MD
Assistant Professor of Surgery, University of Washington School of Medicine; Attending, Division of Pediatric Surgery, Children's Hospital and Regional Medical Center, Seattle, Washington
Necrotizing Enterocolitis

Michael D. Klein, MD
Arvin I. Philippart Chair and Professor of Surgery, Wayne State University School of Medicine; Surgeon-in-Chief, Children's Hospital of Michigan, Detroit, Michigan
Congenital Defects of the Abdominal Wall

Giannoula Klement, MD
Instructor in Pediatrics (Hematology-Oncology), Harvard University Medical School; Assistant in Pediatrics, Children's Hospital Boston, Boston, Massachusetts
Vascular Anomalies: Hemangiomas and Malformations

Matthew J. Krasin, MD
Assistant Member and Radiation Oncologist, St. Jude Children's Research Hospital, Memphis, Tennessee
Principles of Pediatric Oncology, Genetics of Cancer, and Radiation Therapy

Thomas M. Krummel, MD, FACS
Professor in Surgery, Stanford University School of Medicine; Service Chief, Surgery, Stanford Hospital & Clinics, Stanford; Susan B. Ford Surgeon-in-Chief, Lucile Packard Children's Hospital at Stanford, Palo Alto, California
New and Emerging Surgical Technologies and the Process of Innovation

Jean-Martin Laberge, MD, FRCSC, FACS
Professor of Surgery, McGill University Faculty of Medicine; Director, Division of Pediatric General Surgery, The Montreal Children's Hospital, Montreal, Quebec, Canada
Infections and Diseases of the Lungs, Pleura, and Mediastinum

Ira S. Landsman, MD
Associate Professor of Anesthesiology and Pediatrics, Vanderbilt University School of Medicine; Director, Division of Pediatric Anesthesia, Vanderbilt Children's Hospital, Nashville, Tennessee
Pediatric Anesthesia

Michael P. La Quaglia, MD
Professor of Surgery, Weill Medical College of Cornell University; Chief, Pediatric Surgical Service, Memorial Sloan-Kettering Cancer Center, New York, New York
Hodgkin's Disease and Non-Hodgkin's Lymphoma

Stanley T. Lau, MD
Pediatric Surgery Fellow, Women and Children's Hospital of Buffalo, Buffalo, New York
Adrenal Tumors

Steven L. Lee, MD
Regional Pediatric Surgeon, Kaiser Permanente, Los Angeles Medical Center, Los Angeles, California
Duodenal Atresia and Stenosis—Annular Pancreas

Joseph L. Lelli, Jr., MD
Assistant Professor of Surgery, Wayne State Medical School; Pediatric Surgeon, The Children's Hospital of Michigan, Detroit, Michigan
Polypoid Diseases of the Gastrointestinal Tract

Marc A. Levitt, MD
Assistant Professor of Surgery and Pediatrics, University of Cincinnati College of Medicine; Associate Director, Colorectal Center for Children, Cincinnati Children's Hospital Medical Center, Cincinnati, Ohio
Anorectal Malformations

Harry Lindahl, MD, PhD
Lecturer in Pediatrics, University of Helsinki School of Medicine; Chief of Pediatric Surgery, Hospital for Children and Adolescents, Helsinki; University Central Hospital, Helsinki, Finland
Esophagoscopy and Diagnostic Techniques

Thom E. Lobe, MD
Professor of Surgery and Pediatrics, University of Tennessee School of Medicine, Memphis, Tennessee; Pediatric Surgeon, Blank Children's Hospital, Des Moines, Iowa
Other Soft Tissue Tumors

Randall T. Loder, MD
Garceau Professor of Orthopaedic Surgery, Indiana University School of Medicine; Director of Pediatric Orthopaedics, Riley Hospital for Children, Indianapolis, Indiana
Amputations in Children

Thomas G. Luerssen, MD
Professor of Neurological Surgery, Indiana University School of Medicine; Chief, Pediatric Neurosurgery Service, Riley Hospital for Children, Indianapolis, Indiana
Central Nervous System Injuries

Jeffrey R. Lukish, MD
Associate Professor of Surgery and Pediatrics, Uniformed Services University of the Health Sciences F. Edward Hébert School of Medicine, Bethesda, Maryland; Chief, Division of Pediatric Surgery, and Attending Pediatric Surgeon, The National Naval Medical Center and Walter Reed Army Medical Center, Washington, DC
Accident Victims and Their Emergency Management

Dennis P. Lund, MD
Chairman, Division of General Surgery, University of Wisconsin-Madison, and Surgeon-in-Chief, UW Children's Hospital, Madison, Wisconsin
Alimentary Tract Duplications

Mary Beth Madonna, MD
Assistant Professor of Surgery, Northwestern University Feinberg School of Medicine; Attending Surgeon, Children's Memorial Hospital and John H. Stroger, Jr. Hospital of Cook County, Chicago, Illinois
Gastrointestinal Bleeding

John C. Magee, MD
Associate Professor of Surgery, University of Michigan Medical School; Director, Adult and Pediatric Renal Transplantation, and Director, Pediatric Liver Transplantation, University of Michigan Health System, Ann Arbor, Michigan
Renal Transplantation

Giuseppe Martucciello, MD
Associate Professor of Pediatric Surgery, Faculty of Medicine, University of Genoa, Genoa, and University of Pavia, Pavia; Director, and Surgeon-in-Chief, Department of Pediatric Surgery, IRCCS Scientific Institute Policlinico San Matteo, Pavia, Italy
Hirschsprung's Disease and Related Neuromuscular Disorders of the Intestine

Stephen J. Mathes, MD
Professor of Surgery and Head, Division of Plastic and Reconstructive Surgery, University of California, San Francisco, School of Medicine, San Francisco, California
Congenital Defects of the Skin, Connective Tissues, Muscles, Tendons, and Hands

Eugene D. McGahren III, MD
Associate Professor of Surgery and Pediatrics, University of Virginia School of Medicine; Pediatric Surgeon, University of Virginia Health System, Charlottesville, Virginia
Laryngoscopy, Bronchoscopy, and Thoracoscopy; Ascites

Leslie T. McQuiston, MD, FAAP
Staff Pediatric Urologist, Urology Associates of North Texas, Cook Children's Hospital, Fort Worth, Texas
Renal Infection, Abscess, Vesicoureteral Reflux, Urinary Lithiasis, and Renal Vein Thrombosis

Peter Metcalfe, MD, FRCSC
Pediatric Urology Fellow, Indiana University School of Medicine and Riley Hospital for Children, Indianapolis, Indiana
Incontinent and Continent Urinary Diversion

Alastair J. W. Millar, MBChB(Cape Town), FRCS, FRACS, FCS(SA), DCh
Honorary Professor, Paediatric Transplantation and Hepatopancreaticobiliary Surgery, University of Birmingham; Consultant, Paediatric Liver and Intestinal Transplantation and Hepatopancreaticobiliary Surgery, Birmingham Children's Hospital, Birmingham, United Kingdom
Caustic Strictures of the Esophagus

Eugene Minevich, MD, FACS, FAAP
Assistant Professor of Surgery, Cincinnati Children's Hospital Medical Center, Cincinnati, Ohio
Structural Disorders of the Bladder, Augmentation

Edward P. Miranda, MD
Professor of Surgery, Division of Plastic Surgery, University of California, San Francisco, School of Medicine, San Francisco, California
Congenital Defects of the Skin, Connective Tissues, Muscles, Tendons, and Hands

Michael E. Mitchell, MD
Professor of Urology, University of Washington School of Medicine; Chief, Pediatric Urology, Children's Hospital and Regional Medical Center, Seattle, Washington
Ureteropelvic Junction Obstruction

Takeshi Miyano, MD, PhD
Professor, Department of Pediatric Surgery, Juntendo University School of Medicine; Director, Juntendo University Hospital, Tokyo, Japan
The Pancreas

Delora Mount, MD, FACS, FAAP
Assistant Professor of Surgery and Pediatrics, University of Wisconsin School of Medicine and Public Health; Chief of Pediatric Plastic Surgery, University of Wisconsin Hospital and Clinics; Director, Craniofacial Anomalies Clinic, American Family Children's Hospital, Madison, Wisconsin
Hand, Soft Tissue, and Envenomation Injuries

Pierre Mouriquand, MD
Professor of Pediatric Urology, Claude-Bernard University Medical School; Head, Department of Pediatric Urology, Debrousse Hospital, Lyon, France
Renal Fusions and Ectopia

Noriko Murase, MD
Associate Professor of Surgery, University of Pittsburgh School of Medicine, Pittsburgh, Pennsylvania
Principles of Transplantation

J. Patrick Murphy, MD
Professor of Surgery, University of Missouri–Kansas City School of Medicine; Chief, Urology Section, Children's Mercy Hospital of Kansas City, Kansas City, Missouri
Abnormalities of the Urethra, Penis, and Scrotum

Saminathan S. Nathan, MD
Director, Musculoskeletal Oncology Service, Department of Orthopaedics, National University Hospital, Singapore, Singapore
Bone Tumors

Kurt D. Newman, MD
Professor of Surgery and Pediatrics, George Washington University School of Medicine and Health Sciences; Surgeon-in-Chief, Children's National Medical Center; Executive Director, Joseph E. Robert, Jr. Center for Surgical Care, Washington, DC
Lymph Node Disorders

Alp Numanoglu, MD, FCS(SA)
Senior Lecturer in Paediatric Surgery, University of Cape Town School of Child and Adolescent Health; Senior Specialist, Department of Paediatric Surgery, Red Cross Children's Hospital, Institute of Child Health, Cape Town, South Africa
Caustic Strictures of the Esophagus

Donald Nuss, MB, ChB, FRCS(C), FACS, FAAP
Professor of Clinical Surgery and Pediatrics, Eastern Virginia Medical School; Children's Hospital of the King's Daughters, Norfolk, Virginia
The Nuss Procedure for Pectus Excavatum [Chapter 59]

Richard Ohye, MD
Assistant Professor of Surgery, University of Michigan Medical School; Surgical Director, Pediatric Cardiac Transplantation, and Director, Pediatric Cardiovascular Surgery Fellowship Program, C.S. Mott Children's Hospital, Ann Arbor, Michigan
Congenital Heart Disease and Anomalies of the Great Vessels

Keith T. Oldham, MD
Professor of Surgery, Medical College of Wisconsin; Surgeon-in-Chief, Children's Hospital of Wisconsin, Milwaukee, Wisconsin
Atresia, Stenosis, and Other Obstructions of the Colon

James A. O'Neill, Jr., MD, MA(Hon)
J.C. Foshee Professor and Chairman Emeritus, Section of Surgical Sciences, Vanderbilt University School of Medicine; Surgeon-in-Chief Emeritus, Vanderbilt University Medical Center, Nashville, Tennessee
Choledochal Cyst; Bladder and Cloacal Exstrophy; Conjoined Twins; Arterial Disorders

Evelyn Ong, MBBS, BSc, FRCS(Eng)
Joint Royal College of Surgeons of England/British Association of Paediatric Surgeons Research Fellow; Department of Paediatric Surgery, Institute of Child Health, University College London; Clinical Research Fellow, Great Ormond Street Hospital for Children NHS Trust, London, United Kingdom
Neonatal Physiology and Metabolic Considerations

William L. Oppenheim, MD
Professor of Orthopedic Surgery, David Geffen School of Medicine at UCLA; Director of Pediatric Orthopedics, UCLA Medical Center; Consultant, Shriners Hospital of Los Angeles, Los Angeles, California
Bone and Joint Infections

H. Biemann Othersen, Jr., MD
Professor of Surgery and Pediatrics and Emeritus Head, Division of Pediatric Surgery, Medical University of South Carolina College of Medicine; Attending Surgeon, MUSC Children's Hospital, Charleston, South Carolina
Wilms' Tumor

Mikki Pakarinen, MD, PhD
Consultant Pediatric Surgeon, Hospital for Children and Adolescents, University of Helsinki Medical Faculty, Helsinki, Finland
Other Disorders of the Anus and Rectum, Anorectal Function

Keshav Pandurangi, MD
Vascular Surgery Fellow, Indiana University School of Medicine, Indianapolis, Indiana
Venous Disorders in Childhood

Richard H. Pearl, MD, FACS, FAAP, FRCSC
Professor of Surgery and Pediatrics,University of Illinois College of Medicine at Peoria; Surgeon-in-Chief, Children's Hospital of Illinois, Peoria, Illinois
Abdominal Trauma

Alberto Peña, MD
Professor of Surgery and Pediatrics, University of Cincinnati College of Medicine; Director, Colorectal Center for Children, Cincinnati Children's Hospital Medical Center, Cincinnati, Ohio
Anorectal Malformations

Rafael V. Pieretti, MD
Chief, Section of Pediatric Urology, Department of Pediatric Surgery, Massachusetts General Hospital, Boston, Massachusetts
Ambiguous Genitalia

Agostino Pierro, MD, FRCS(Eng), FRCS(Ed), FAAP
Nuffield Professor of Paediatric Surgery and Head of Surgery Unit, Institute of Child Health, University College London; Consultant Paediatric Surgeon, Great Ormand Street Hospital for Children NHS Trust, London, United Kingdom
Neonatal Physiology and Metabolic Considerations

William P. Potsic, MD, MMM
Professor of Otorhinolaryngology–Head and Neck Surgery, University of Pennsylvania School of Medicine; Director, Division of Otolaryngology, and Vice Chair for Clinical Affairs, The Children's Hospital of Philadelphia, Philadelphia, Pennsylvania
Otolaryngologic Disorders

Pramod S. Puligandla, MD, MSc, FRCSC
Assistant Professor of Surgery and Pediatrics, McGill University Faculty of Medicine; Attending Staff, Division of Pediatric Surgery and Pediatric Critical Care Medicine, The Montreal Children's Hospital of the McGill University Health Center, Montreal, Quebec, Canada
Infections and Diseases of the Lungs, Pleura, and Medistinum

Devin P. Puapong, MD
Senior Surgical Resident, Kaiser Permanente Medical Center, Los Angeles,California
Duodenal Atresia and Stenosis—Annular Pancreas

Prem Puri, MS, FRCS, FRCS(Edin), FACS
Professor of Paediatrics, University College Dublin; Consultant Paediatric Surgeon and Director of Research, Children's Research Centre, Our Lady's Hospital for Sick Children, Crumlin, Dublin, Ireland
Intestinal Neuronal Dysplasia

Judson G. Randolph, MD
Professor of Surgery Emeritus, George Washington University School of Medicine and Health Sciences; Former Surgeon-in-Chief, Children's National Medical Center, Washington, DC
A Brief History of Pediatric Surgery

Frederick J. Rescorla, MD
Professor of Surgery, Indiana University School of Medicine; Surgeon-in-Chief, Riley Hospital for Children, Indianapolis, Indiana
The Spleen

Jorge Reyes, MD
Professor of Surgery, University of Washington School of Medicine; Chief, Division of Transplant Surgery, University of Washington Medical Center, Seattle, Washington
Principles of Transplantation

Richard R. Ricketts, MD
Professor of Surgery, Emory University School of Medicine; Chief, Division of Pediatric Surgery, Children's Health Care of Atlanta at Egleston, Atlanta, Georgia
Mesenteric and Omental Cysts

Richard C. Rink, MD
Robert A. Garrett Professor of Pediatric Urologic Research and Professor of Urology, Indiana University School of Medicine; Chief, Pediatric Urology, Riley Hospital for Children, Indianapolis, Indiana
Incontinent and Continent Urinary Diversion

Risto J. Rintala, MD
Professor of Pediatric Surgery, University of Helsinki Medical Faculty; Chief, General Pediatric Surgery, Hospital for Children and Adolescents, Helsinki, Finland
Other Disorders of the Anus and Rectum, Anorectal Function

Albert P. Rocchini, MD
Professor of Pediatrics and Director of Pediatrics Cardiology, University of Michigan Redical School; Director of Pediatric Cardiology, University of Michigan Hospital, Ann Arbor
Neonatal Cardiovascular Physiology and Care

Heinz Rode, M Med(Chir), FCS(SA), FRCS(Edin)
Professor of Paediatric Surgery, University of Cape Town School of Child and Adolescent Health; Head of Pediatric Surgery, Red Cross Children's Hospital, Institute of Child Health, Cape Town, South Africa
Caustic Strictures of the Esophagus

Bradley M. Rodgers, MD
Professor of Surgery and Pediatrics, University of Virginia School of Medicine; Chief, Division of Pediatric Surgery, Department of Surgery, University of Virginia Medical Center; Chief, Children's Surgery, UVA Children's Hospital, Charlottesville, Virginia
Laryngoscopy, Bronchoscopy, and Thoracoscopy

A. Michael Sadove MD, MS
James Harbaugh Professor of Surgery (Plastic), Indiana University School of Medicine; Chief of Plastic Surgery, Riley Hospital for Children, Indianapolis; Chairman of Surgery, Clarian North Medical Center, Carmel, Indiana
Cleft Lip and Palate

Bob H. Saggi, MD
Assistant Professor of Surgery, Department of Surgery, Division of Immunology and Organ Transplantation, University of Texas Medical School at Houston; Staff Surgeon, Memorial Hermann Hospital, Houston, Texas
Liver Transplantation

Arthur P. Sanford, MD
Assistant Professor of Surgery, The University of Texas Medical Branch School of Medicine at Galveston; Staff Physician, Shriners Burns Hospital, Galveston, Texas
Burns

L. R. Scherer III, MD
Associate Professor of Clinical Medicine, Indiana University School of Medicine; Director of Trauma, Riley Hospital for Children, Indianapolis, Indiana
Peptic Ulcer and Other Conditions of the Stomach

Jay J. Schnitzer, MD, PhD
Associate Professor of Surgery, Harvard Medical School; Associate Visiting Surgeon, Massachusetts General Hospital, Boston, Massachusetts
Ambiguous Genitalia

Marshall Z. Schwartz, MD
Professor of Surgery and Pediatrics, Drexel University College of Medicine; Director, Pediatric Surgery Research Laboratory, and Surgical Director, Pediatric Renal Transplantation, St. Christopher's Hospital for Children, Philadelphia, Pennsylvania
Hypertrophic Pyloric Stenosis

Robert C. Shamberger, MD
Robert E. Gross Professor of Surgery, Harvard Medical School; Chief, Department of Surgery, Children's Hospital Boston, Boston, Massachusetts
Congenital Chest Wall Deformities

Nina L. Shapiro, MD
Associate Professor of Surgery/Pediatric Otolaryngology, David Geffen School of Medicine at UCLA; Attending Surgeon, UCLA Medical Center, Los Angeles, California
Salivary Glands

Curtis A. Sheldon, MD
Professor, University of Cincinnati College of Medicine; Professor and Director (Pediatric Urology), Cincinnati Children's Hospital Medical Center, Cincinnati, Ohio
Structural Disorders of the Bladder, Augmentation

Stephen J. Shochat, MD
Professor of Surgery and Pediatrics, University of Tennessee School of Medicine; Surgeon-in-Chief and Chairman, Department of Surgery, St. Jude Children's Research Hospital, Memphis, Tennessee
Tumors of the Lung

Michael A. Skinner, MD
Associate Professor of Surgery and Pediatric Surgery, Duke University School of Medicine, Durham, North Carolina
Surgical Diseases of the Thyroid and Parathyroid Glands

C. D. Smith, MD, MS
Associate Professor of Surgery and Pediatrics, Medical University of South Carolina College of Medicine; Attending, Division of Pediatric Surgery, MUSC Medical Center, Charleston, South Carolina
Cysts and Sinuses of the Neck

Jodi L. Smith, MD, PhD
Assistant Professor of Neurological Surgery, Department of Neurological Surgery, Indiana University School of Medicine; Pediatric Neurosurgeon, Riley Hospital for Children, Indianapolis, Indiana
Management of Neural Tube Defects, Hydrocephalus, Refractory Epilepsy, and Central Nervous System Infections

Samuel D. Smith, MD
Professor of Surgery, University of Arkansas for Medical Sciences College of Medicine; Chief of Pediatric Surgery, Arkansas Children's Hospital, Little Rock, Arkansas
Disorders of Intestinal Rotation and Fixation

Charles L. Snyder, MD
Associate Professor of Surgery, University of Missouri–Kansas City School of Medicine, Kansas City, Missouri; Clinical Assistant Professor of Surgery, University of Kansas School of Medicine, Kansas City, Kansas; Director of Clinical Research, The Children's Mercy Hospital, Kansas City, Missouri
Meckel's Diverticulum

Lewis Spitz, MBChB, MD(Hon), PhD, FRCS, FRCPCH, FAAP(Hon), FCS(SA)(Hon)
Emeritus Nuffield Professor of Pediatric Surgery, Institute of Child Health, University College London; Consultant Paediatric Surgeon, Great Ormond Street Hospital, London, United Kingdom
Esophageal Replacement

Thomas L. Spray, MD
Professor of Surgery, University of Pennsylvania School of Medicine; Chief, Division of Cardiothoracic Surgery, and Alice Langdon Warner Endowed Chair in Pediatric Cardiothoracic Surgery, The Children's Hospital of Philadelphia, Philadelphia, Pennsylvania
Heart Transplantation

Thomas E. Starzl, MD, PhD
Distinguished Service Professor of Surgery, University of Pittsburgh School of Medicine; Director Emeritus, Thomas E. Starzl Transplantation Institute, Pittsburgh, Pennsylvania
Principles of Transplantation

Charles J. H. Stolar, MD
Professor of Surgery and Pediatrics, Columbia University College of Physicians and Surgeons; Chief, Pediatric Surgery, Morgan Stanley Children's Hospital of New York–Presbyterian, New York, New York
Congenital Diaphragmatic Hernia and Eventration

Phillip B. Storm, MD
Assistant Professor of Neurosurgery, University of Pennsylvania School of Medicine; Attending Neurosurgeon, Hospital of the University of Pennsylvania and The Children's Hospital of Philadelphia, Philadelphia, Pennsylvania
Brain Tumors

Steven Stylianos, MD
Professor of Surgery, University of Miami Leonard M. Miller School of Medicine; Chief, Department of Pediatric Surgery, Miami Children's Hospital, Miami, Florida
Abdominal Trauma

Wendy T. Su, MD
Fellow, Pediatric Surgical Service, Memorial Sloan-Kettering Cancer Center, New York, New York
Hodgkin's Disease and Non-Hodgkin's Lymphoma

Riccardo Superina, MD, CM, FRCSC, FACS
Professor of Surgery, Northwestern University, Director, Transplant Surgery, Children's Memoral Hospital, Chicago, Illinois
Portal Hypertension

David E. R. Sutherland, MD, PhD
Professor of Surgery, University of Minnesota Medical School; Head, Transplant Division, and Director, Diabetes Institute for Immunology and Transplantation, University of Minnesota Medical Center, Fairview, Minneapolis, Minnesota
Pancreas and Islet Cell Transplantation

Leslie N. Sutton, MD
Professor of Neurosurgery, University of Pennsylvania School of Medicine; Chairman, Division of Pediatric Neurosurgery, The Children's Hospital of Philadelphia, Philadelphia, Pennsylvania
Brain Tumors

Edward P. Tagge, MD
Professor of Surgery and Pediatrics, Division of Pediatric Surgery, Medical University of South Carolina College of Medicine; Attending Surgeon, MUSC Children's Hospital, Charleston, South Carolina
Wilms' Tumor

Daniel H. Teitelbaum, MD
Professor of Surgery, University of Michigan Medical School; Pediatric Surgeon, C.S. Mott Children's Hospital, Ann Arbor, Michigan
Nutritional Support; Hirschsprung's Disease and Related Neuromuscular Disorders of the Intestine

Claire L. Templeman, MD
Assistant Professor of Clinical Gynecology and Surgery, Keck School of Medicine at USC; Pediatric Surgeon, Children's Hospital Los Angeles, Los Angeles, California
Ovarian Tumors

Gonca Topuzlu Tekant, MD
Associate Professor of Pediatric Surgery, Istanbul University School of Medicine; Pediatric Surgeon, Cerrahpasa Medical Faculty, Istanbul, Turkey
Gastroesophageal Reflux Disease

Joseph J. Tepas III, MD
Professor of Surgery and Pediatrics, University of Florida College of Medicine; Staff Physician, Shands Jacksonville, Jacksonville, Florida
Vascular Injuries

Patrick B. Thomas, MD
Pediatric Surgery Fellow, Texas Children's Hospital, Baylor College of Medicine, Houston, Texas
Wilms' Tumor

Dana Mara Thompson, MD, MS
Associate Professor of Otorhinolaryngology, Mayo Graduate School of Medicine; Attending, Otorhinolaryngology Department, Mayo Clinic, Rochester, Minnesota
Lesions of the Larynx, Trachea, and Upper Airway

Juan A. Tovar, MD, PhD
Professor of Surgical Pediatrics, Department of Pediatrics, Universidad Autonoma de Madrid; Head, Department of Pediatric Surgery, Hospital Universitario LaPaz, Madrid, Spain
Disorders of Esophageal Function

Jeffrey S. Upperman, MD, MA
Assistant Professor of Surgery, Keck School of Medicine of USC; Attending Surgeon, Children's Hospital Los Angeles, Los Angeles, California
Sepsis and Related Considerations

Joseph P. Vacanti, MD
John Homans Professor of Surgery, Harvard Medical School; Chief, Pediatric Surgery, Massachusetts General Hospital, Boston, Massachusetts
The Impact of Tissue Engineering in Pediatric Surgery

Dennis W. Vane, MD, MS, MBA
Professor of Surgery, University of Vermont College of Medicine; Chair, Pediatric Surgery, and Vice-Chair, Clinical Affairs, Department of Surgery, Fletcher Allen Health Care, Burlington, Vermont
Child Abuse and Birth Injuries

Mirjana Vustar, MD
Assistant Professor of Anesthesiology and Pediatrics, Vanderbilt University School of Medicine; Director, Pediatric Anesthesia Education, Vanderbilt Children's Hospital, Nashville, Tennessee
Pediatric Anesthesia

Brad W. Warner, MD
Professor of Surgery and Pediatrics, University of Cincinnati College of Medicine; Attending Surgeon and Director of Surgical Research, Division of Pediatric General and Thoracic Surgery, Cincinnati Children's Hospital Medical Center, Cincinnati, Ohio
Short-Bowel Syndrome

Thomas R. Weber, MD
Professor of Surgery, Saint Louis University School of Medicine; Director, Pediatric Surgery, Cardinal Glennon Children's Hospital, St. Louis, Missouri
Esophageal Rupture and Perforation

David E. Wesson, MD
Professor of Surgery and Chief, Division of Pediatric Surgery, Baylor College of Medicine; Chief, Pediatric Surgery Service, Texas Children's Hospital, Houston, Texas
Thoracic Injuries

Karen W. West, MD
Professor of Surgery, Indiana University School of Medicine; Director of ECMO, Riley Hospital for Children, Indianapolis, Indiana
Primary Peritonitis

Ralph F. Wetmore, MD
Professor of Otorhinolaryngology–Head and Neck Surgery, University of Pennsylvania School of Medicine; Senior Surgeon, The Children's Hospital of Philadelphia, Philadelphia, Pennsylvania
Otolaryngologic Disorders

Eugene Wiener, MD
Professor, Department of Surgery (Pediatric), University of Pittsburgh School of Medicine; Executive Vice President and Chief Medical Officer, Children's Hospital of Pittsburgh, Pittsburgh, Pennsylvania
Testicular Tumors

Jay M. Wilson, MD
Associate Professor of Surgery, Harvard Medical School; Attending, Children's Hospital Boston, Boston, Massachusetts
Respiratory Physiology and Care

Russell K. Woo, MD
Instructor in Surgery, Department of Surgery, Stanford University School of Medicine; Staff Physician, Stanford Hospital and Clinic, Stanford, and Lucile Packard Children's Hospital at Stanford, Palo Alto, California
New and Emerging Surgical Technologies and the Process of Innovation

Hsi-Yang Wu, MD
Assistant Professor of Urology, University of Pittsburgh School of Medicine; Director of Pediatric Urology Research, Children's Hospital of Pittsburgh, Pittsburgh, Pennsylvania
Testicular Tumors

Elizabeth Yerkes, MD
Assistant Professor of Urology, Feinberg School of Medicine at Northwestern University; Attending Urologist, Children's Memorial Hospital, Chicago, Illinois
Incontinent and Continent Urinary Diversion

Daniel G. Young, MBChB, FRCS(Edin, Glasg), DTM&H
Honorary Senior Research Fellow, University of Glasgow; Former Head (Retired), Department of Surgical Pediatrics, Royal Hospital for Sick Children, Glasgow, United Kingdom
A Brief History of Pediatric Surgery

Moritz M. Ziegler, MD
Professor of Surgery, Division of Pediatric Surgery, University of Colorado School of Medicine; Surgeon-in-Chief, The Children's Hospital, Denver, Colorado
Meconium Ileus

The senior editors (from left to right): James A. O'Neill, Jr., Jay L. Grosfeld, Arnold G. Coran, and Eric W. Fonkalsrud.

Preface

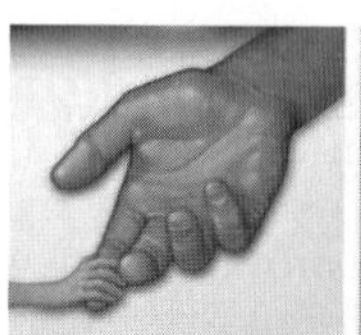

The first edition of ***Pediatric Surgery*** was published by Year Book Medical Publishers in 1962, with Drs. Kenneth Welch, William Mustard, Mark Ravitch, Clifford Benson, and William Snyder serving as the initial Editorial Board. The project was conceived to meet the need for a comprehensive work on pediatric surgery, with the heaviest concentration focused in the traditional fields of general, thoracic, and urologic surgery. Numerous contributors participated in the development of this new textbook that would for the next 44 years be known worldwide as the leading comprehensive resource in the field of children's surgery. Four additional editions of the textbook have been published since that time.

It has been 8 years since the fifth edition of the book was published in 1998. In the interim, we have experienced a veritable explosion of new scientific information, characterized by the elucidation of the human genome, development of tissue engineering, and introduction of other new technologies that have clearly impacted methods of diagnosis and how we treat our patients.

The sixth edition has an international flair and contains 133 chapters prepared by contributors from the United States, Canada, Europe, Asia, Australia, New Zealand, and Africa. It was the intent of the editors to include expert contributors with a significant or unique experience in their respective areas of interest so that all of the chapters would comply with the goal of providing current and practical information that was very well referenced in a modern comprehensive and authoritative text. A significant number of new authors and coauthors participated in this effort. Among the new contributions is a chapter concerning the history of pediatric surgery, providing a brief background of the origins of our profession in the United Kingdom, United States, and Asia. Other new chapters include material on molecular clinical genetics and gene therapy, the impact of tissue engineering in pediatric surgery, new and emerging technologies in surgical science, principles of pediatric oncology/genetics and radiation therapy, small bowel transplantation, and adolescent bariatric surgery.

All the other chapters were significantly changed, updated, and often expanded with the addition of numerous recent references. Some examples include the current status of the fetus as a patient; congenital chest wall deformities, which now includes up-to-date information on the Nuss procedure; pediatric anesthesia; ethical and legal considerations; the genetics of Hirschsprung disease; new information on short bowel syndrome (i.e., the Step procedure); and the inclusion of minimally invasive surgical techniques (laparoscopy, thoracoscopy) embedded within each chapter where appropriate.

Other major revisions and updated material are included. In Part I: neonatal physiology and metabolic considerations, respiratory physiology and care, neonatal cardiovascular physiology and care, extracorporeal life support and cardiopulmonary failure, sepsis and related conditions, hematologic disorders, and nutrition; Part II: trauma (including burn care); Part III: major tumors of childhood; Part IV: organ transplantation (liver, lung, heart, pancreas, kidney, and surgical implications of bone marrow transplantation), which was also reorganized and updated with the new protocols and information regarding contemporary care techniques and outcomes; Part V: conditions affecting the head and neck; Part VI: thoracic conditions (including esophageal atresia and tracheoesophageal fistula, along with various other esophageal conditions, lung cysts, congenital diaphragmatic hernia, and others); Part VII: a very wide spectrum of common congenital and acquired abdominal conditions (including hernias, abdominal wall defects, intestinal atresia, meconium ileus, Hirschsprung's disease, anorectal malformations, duplications, inflammatory bowel disease, biliary atresia, choledochal cyst, pancreatic conditions, spleen, portal hypertension and others); Part VIII: genitourinary disorders; and Part IX: special areas of pediatric surgery (conjoined twins, congenital heart disease, hand and soft tissue, orthopedic, neurologic, and vascular disorders). Many of the chapters are well illustrated and enhanced with the use of charts, tables, radiographic images, photographs of gross pathology and histology, and operative techniques.

The Editorial Board for the sixth edition is composed of Drs. Jay L. Grosfeld, James A. O'Neill, Jr., Eric W. Fonkalsrud, and Arnold G. Coran. All four were members of the editorial group for the fifth edition. The initial editorial responsibility for chapter assignments was evenly distributed among the four senior editors. We are grateful to Dr. Anthony A. Caldamone, who ably served as the section editor for Part VIII, genitourinary disorders. Dr. Grosfeld served as chairman of the board and, as lead editor, was the final reviewer of the entire manuscript. We are indebted to the editors who preceded us in the prior five editions who set the standard that we have tried to uphold for the sixth edition of *Pediatric Surgery*.

The editors wish to thank our administrative assistants and secretaries Karen Jaeger, Donna Bock, Gale Fielding, Cheryl Peterson, and Carol Simmons, who in addition to their usual responsibilities, were willing to support us in completing this effort. We recognize this would not have been accomplished without them and appreciate their many contributions. We also express our sincere appreciation and thanks to many contributors from around the world who have played an important role in the preparation of the sixth edition. We are grateful for their willingness to share their knowledge and expertise and for complying with the specified format of the textbook in a timely manner that allowed us to meet production deadlines.

We are also grateful to the Elsevier/Mosby publishing staff for their support and cooperation in maintaining a high standard in the development and preparation of the sixth edition. We wish to recognize Ms. Janice Gaillard, Senior Developmental Editor, and Faith Voit, Freelance Editor, who prepared the manuscript for production; Judith Fletcher, Publishing Director; and Ms. Linda Grigg, Senior Project Manager, who guided this book throughout the production process.

The photograph of the senior editors was taken in April 2005 during a meeting of the American Surgical Association. The editors have viewed their work in preparing the sixth edition of *Pediatric Surgery* as a labor of love, and we express our hope that the textbook will provide a valued special resource to practicing pediatric surgeons, those in training, and other professionals who care for infants and children. It is our hope that this textbook will serve as a resource that will benefit future generations of children affected with surgical illness thoughout the world.

THE EDITORS

Contents

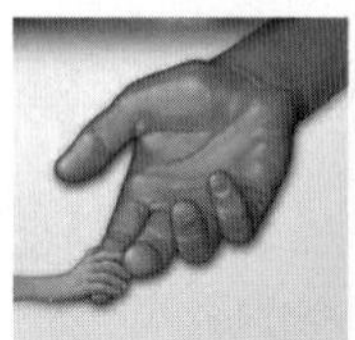

VOLUME ONE

VOLUME TWO

Color Plates

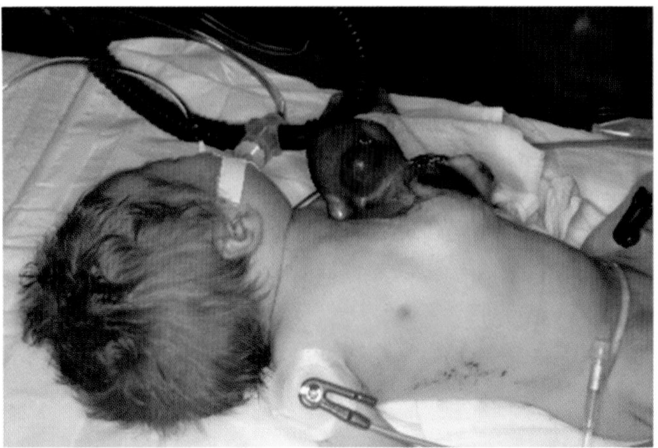

Figure 73–2 Ectopia cordis.

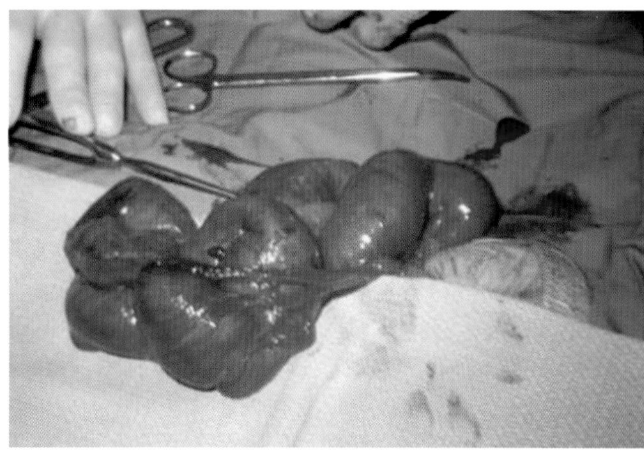

C

Figure 80–5 *C,* At laparotomy a volvulus was observed with multiple intestinal atresias due to complicated meconium ileus. The infant had cystic fibrosis.

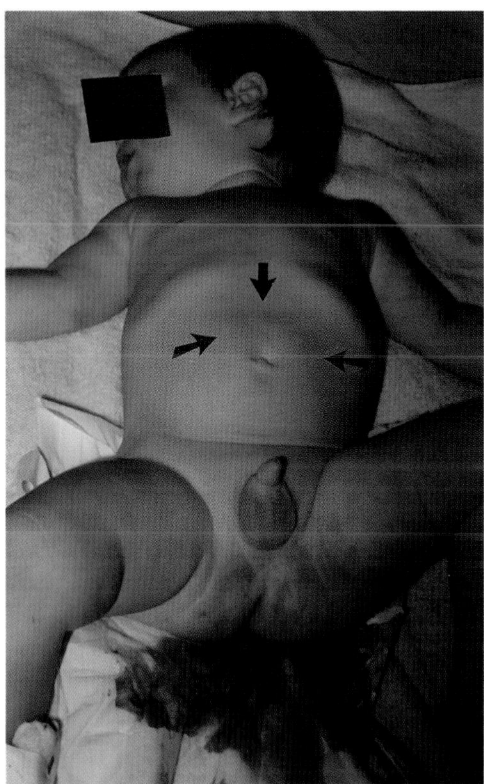

Figure 83–4 Pale, lethargic infant with intussusception and the classic currant jelly stool. Note the epigastric mass (*arrows*).

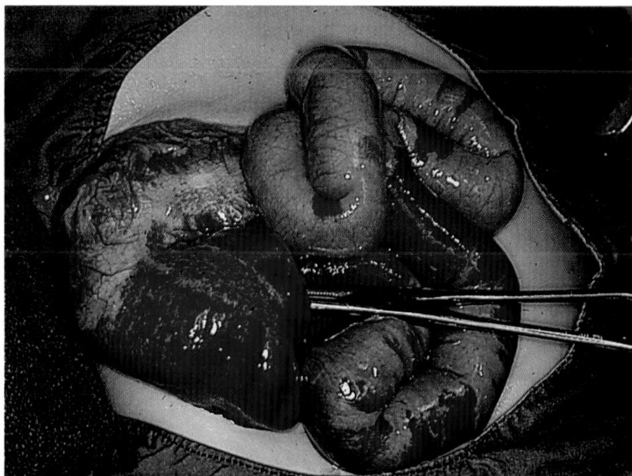

Figure 83–24 Ileocolic intussusception incompletely reduced. The cecum and ascending colon are congested and full. Note the partially reduced, congested, but viable terminal ileum.

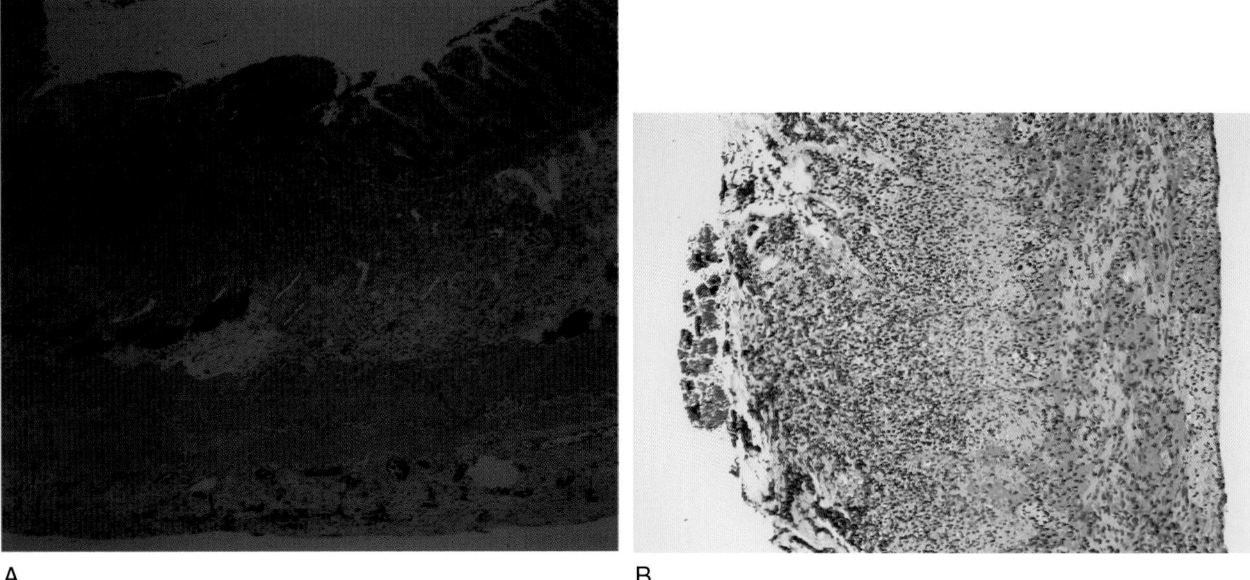

Figure 92–1 *A,* Histologic section demonstrating early necrotizing enterocolitis with inflammation and pneumatosis intestinalis in the submucosa (hematoxylin-eosin stain, ×150). *B,* Histologic section demonstrating advanced necrotizing enterocolitis with transmural necrosis and loss of villus and crypt architecture (hematoxylin-eosin stain, ×150).

Figure 93–1 Bear claw deformity in Crohn's colitis.

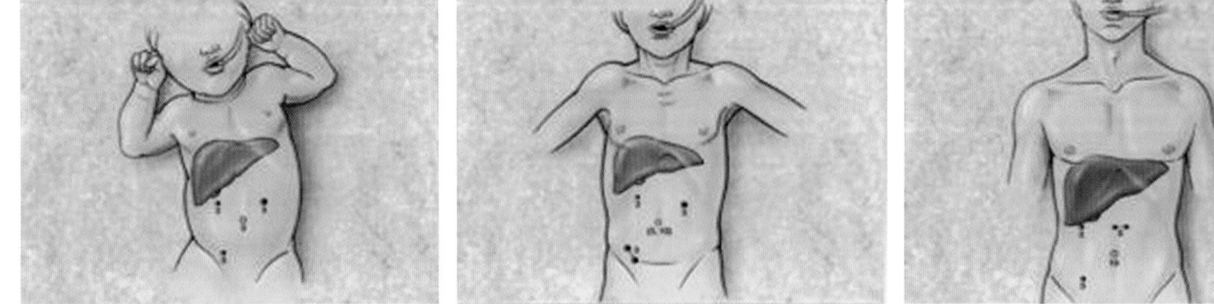

Figure 105–5 Placement of the cannulas and instruments in patients undergoing laparoscopic cholecystectomy depends on the patient's age and size. In an infant, 3- and 5-mm ports/instruments can be utilized. Also, the ports/instruments should be separated as much as possible to create an adequate working space for the operation (*left*). In a prepubertal child, the port/instruments should be widely spaced as well. A 3-mm instrument can often be used in the surgeon's left hand. In younger patients in this age range, a 5-mm umbilical cannula may be possible. However, for most patients, a 10-mm umbilical cannula is necessary to extract the gallbladder through this incision (*middle*). In a teenager, the port placement more closely resembles that seen in adults (*right*).

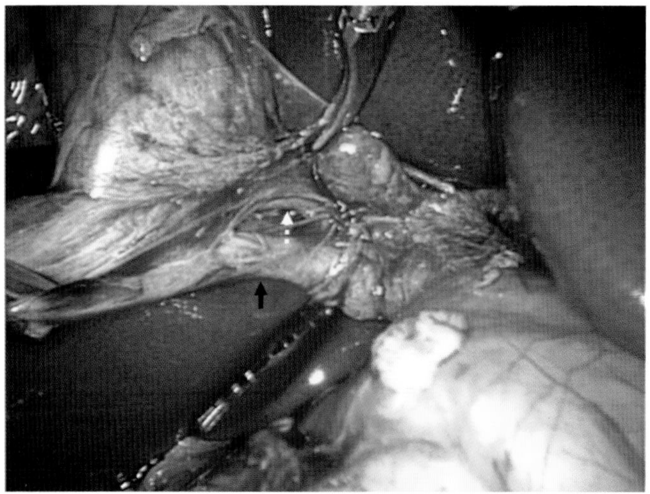

Figure 105–6 During the initial stages of the laparoscopic cholecystectomy, it is vitally important to retract the infundibulum directly lateral so as to create a 90-degree angle between the cystic duct (*solid arrow*) and common duct. Note the cystic artery (*dotted arrow*) cephalad to the cystic duct.

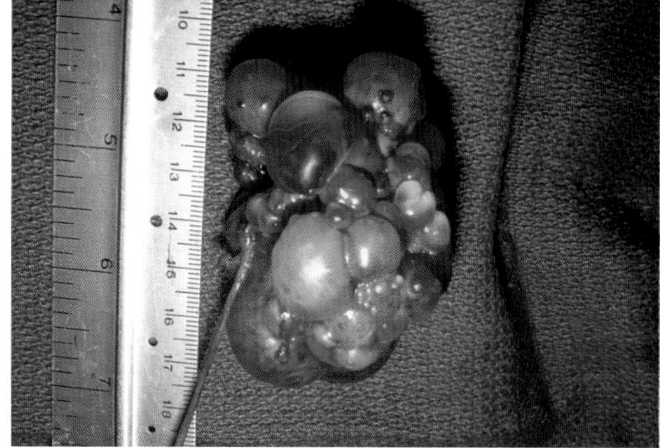

Figure 109–3 Typical multicystic kidney with atretic ureter. Note the "bunch of grapes" appearance. (From Shah SH, Glassberg KI: Multicystic dysplastic kidney disease. In Gearhart JP, Rink RC, Moriquand PDE [eds]: Pediatric Urology. Philadelphia, WB Saunders, 2001, p 279.)

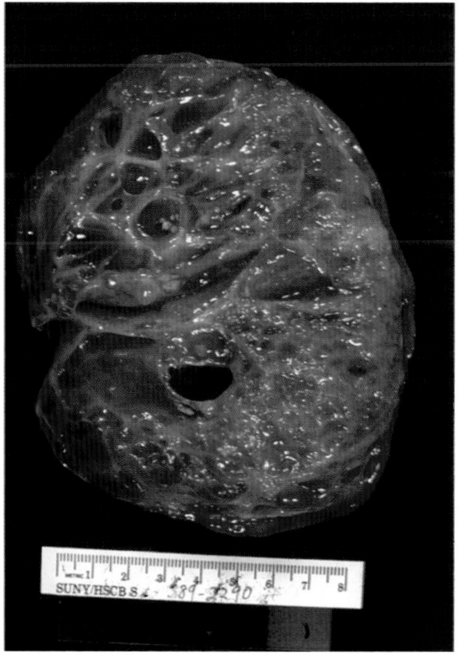

C

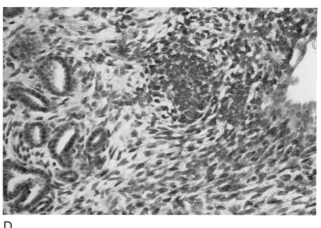

D

Figure 109–9 *C,* Cross section of the mass reveals noncommunicating loculations. *D,* On microscopy, nests of blastema cells with tubular elements are seen between the loculi, findings typical of multilocular cyst with partially differentiated Wilms' tumor.

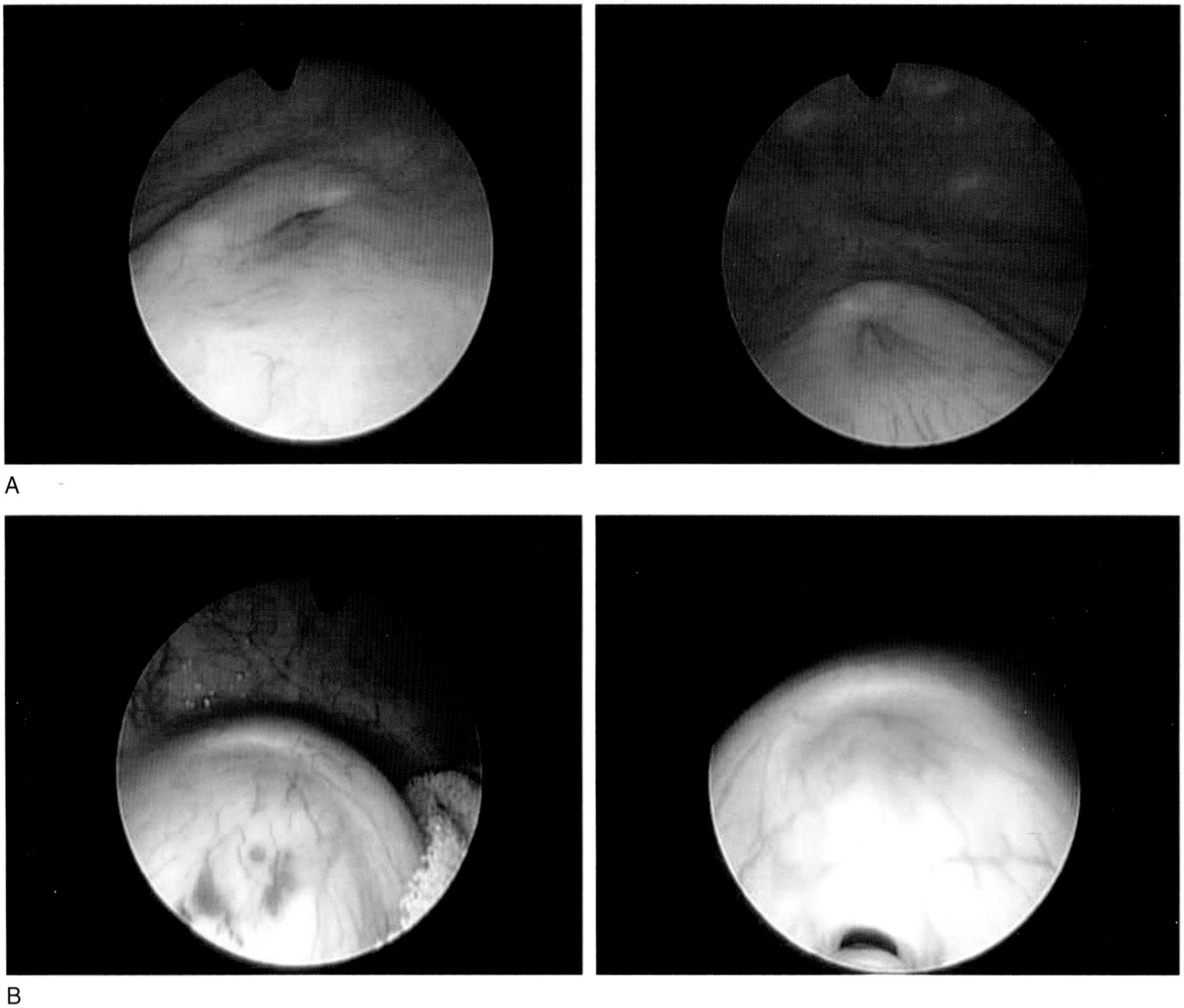

A

B

Figure 112–13 Endoscopic injection. *A,* Left and right ureteral orifices before injection. *B,* Left and right ureteral orifices demonstrating the crescent appearance after injection.

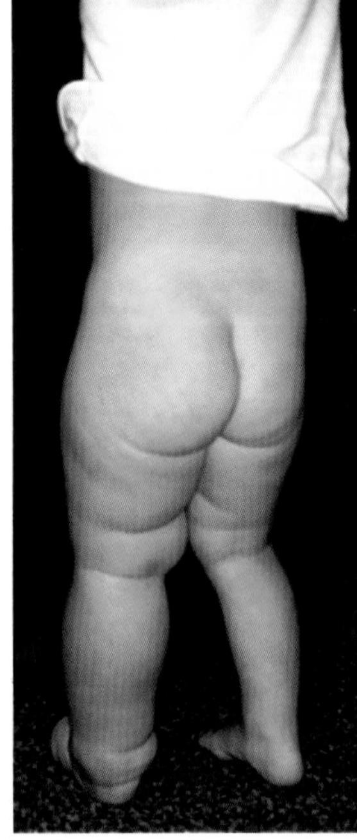

Figure 132-3 Klippel-Trenaunay syndrome. Note unilateral limb hypertrophy, edema, and limb-length discrepancy.

Part VII

ABDOMEN

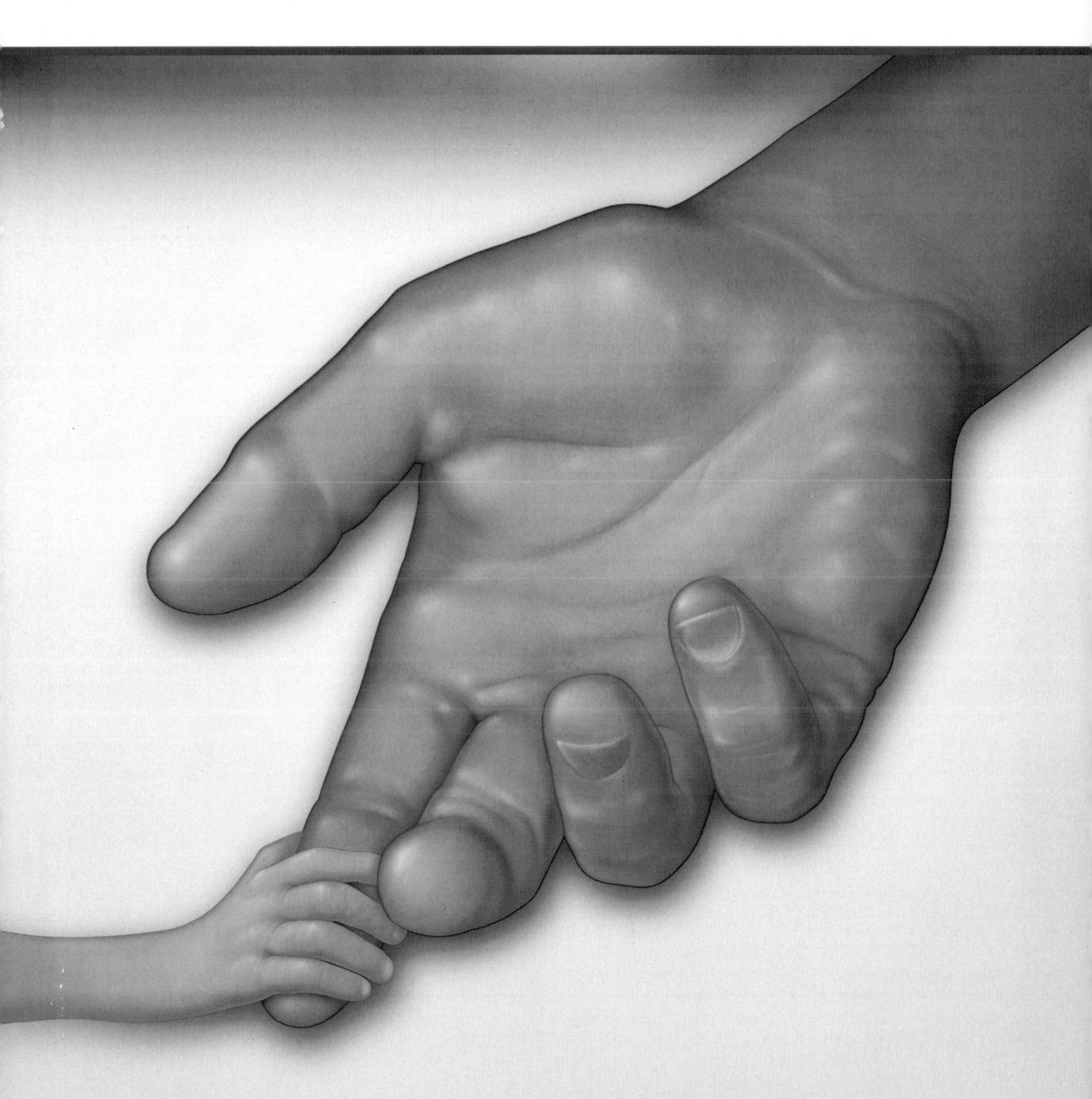

Chapter 72

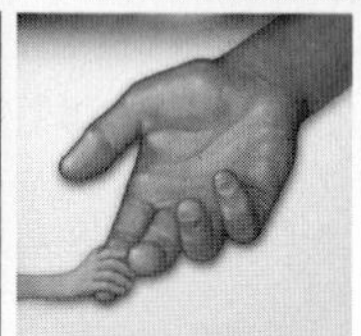

Disorders of the Umbilicus

Robert E. Cilley

HISTORY

Umbilical malformations have been depicted in art and sculpture since the antiquities, but the developmental basis for these abnormalities was not recognized until the late 19th century. Surgical textbooks, such as that by von Bergmann in 1904, clearly describe the embryology responsible for persistence of the vitellointestinal duct as a fistula, sinus, or cyst.[105] The symptoms of fecal drainage ("congenital umbilical anus") and prolapse of the intestine were well known. The surgeon was advised to avoid pitfalls such as excision of an "umbilical tumor" that exposed two intestinal lumens because it would indicate that the vitellointestinal remnant had been excised in excess back to the ileum. An umbilical polyp representing a persistent remnant of the duct was referred to as an "enteroteratoma."

Surgical management has changed little in the past 100 years. Interestingly, then as now, granulomas of the umbilical cord were treated by silver nitrate cauterization. The embryologic basis of developmental abnormalities of the urachus was similarly recognized, and their surgical treatment was described much as it is today. The natural history of spontaneous resolution of most umbilical hernias was also understood at the end of the 19th century. External compression was often recommended, and the importance of preservation of the appearance of the umbilicus rather than excision was noted. Repair of umbilical abnormalities was recognized as formidable in small children, and little is known of the true operative morbidity and mortality in the hands of the surgical pioneers who first attempted their correction.

The most complete work on the umbilicus is the classic text by Cullen, which was published in 1916.[31] This encyclopedic work is still the most definitive work on the subject. Cullen's curiosity was originally stimulated by a case of cancer at the umbilicus, and it inspired him to explore the entire topic of umbilical pathology. He stated, "The study of the umbilicus, which in the beginning had seemed so unimportant, became so fascinating that I covered most of the literature on the subject."[31]

The vital functions of the umbilicus in utero and the structures that pass through it in normal development contrast with its lack of physiologic importance after birth. Its psychological importance throughout life is attested to by individuals who have endured surgical loss of their umbilicus. Pediatric surgeons are the first to be consulted whenever there is an unusual finding of the umbilicus in newborns and older children. Umbilical herniorrhaphy is among the more commonly performed operations in childhood. In addition, the umbilicus serves as a portal of entry for most laparoscopic procedures, and it may be used as an intestinal or urinary stoma site. Cannulation of its vessels, either in their native location or transposed surgically, provides vascular access in neonates. The umbilicus is considered to be aesthetically important,[28] and it may be an object of display and adornment. Exposure of the umbilicus is commonplace, as is the use of jewelry and piercings to enhance its appearance.

NORMAL EMBRYOLOGY

The classic description of the formation of the umbilicus indicates that the abdominal wall forms by a combination of lateral infolding and ventral flexion of the disk-shaped trilaminar embryo that begins in the fourth gestational week. However, the actual growth of the embryo does not truly involve "bending" and "folding" of structures but rather represents differential growth of tissues. Initially, the amnion is located in a dorsal direction, whereas the yolk sac occupies a ventral position. The embryo is attached to the chorion, the forerunner of the placenta, by a connecting stalk composed of extraembryonic mesoderm in which the umbilical vessels develop and into which the allantois grows (Fig. 72-1A). The yolk sac maintains its ventral position but is divided into intracoelomic and extracoelomic portions (Fig. 72-1B). The intracoelomic portion, derived from the roof of the yolk sac, becomes the primitive alimentary canal and maintains a connection with the extracoelomic portion through the vitelline or omphalomesenteric duct. This connection is normally lost by the fifth to seventh week of gestation.[31,42] Persistence of this connection, as a remnant of either the developing alimentary tract or the accompanying vitelline vessels, accounts for some of the abnormalities described in this chapter.

Early in the third week of gestation, a diverticulum called the allantois forms from the posterior wall of the

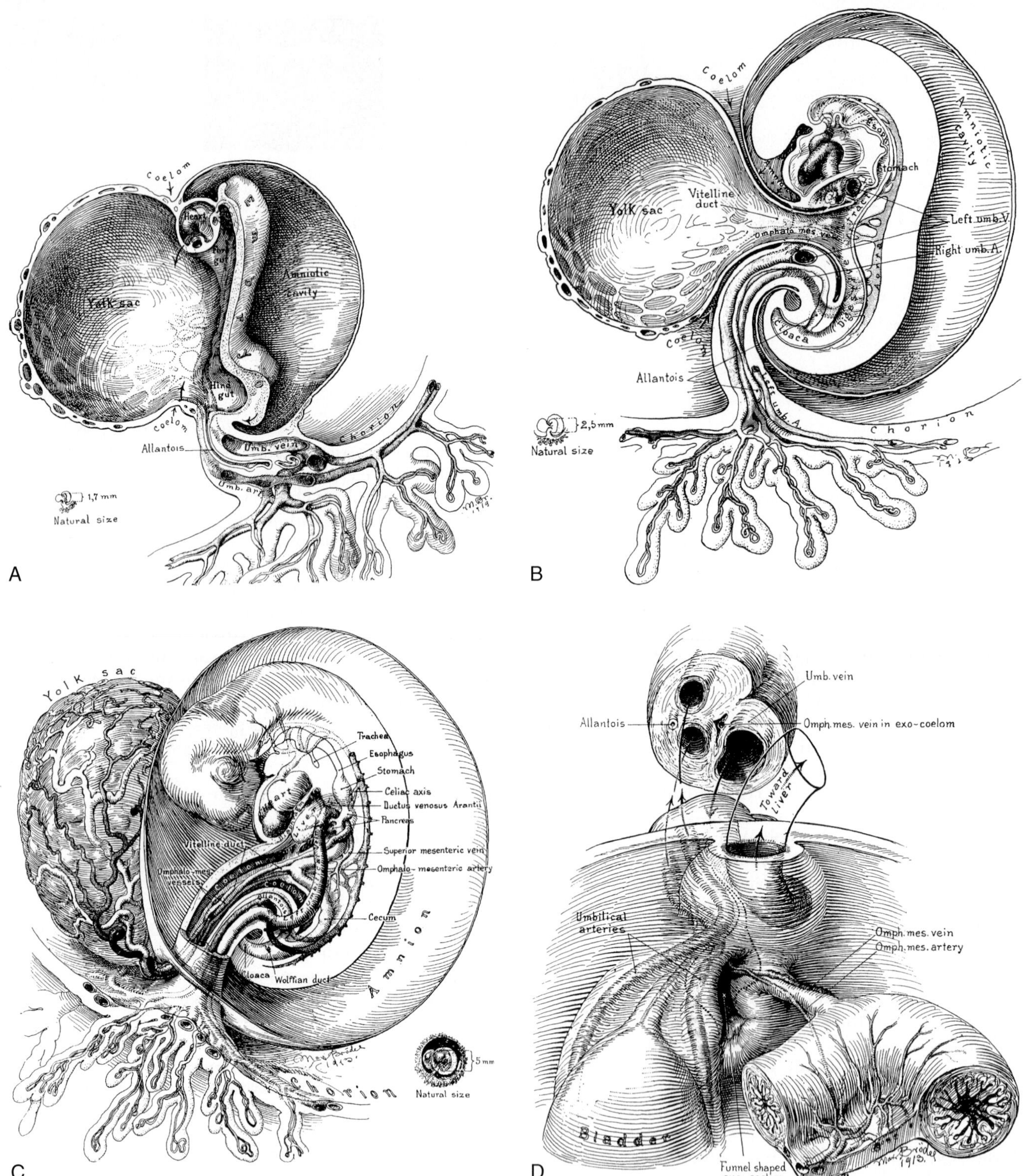

Figure 72–1 *A,* A 1.7-mm embryo (third week). The primitive gut is not yet separate from the yolk sac. The amniotic cavity can be seen dorsally. The umbilical vessels develop in the extraembryonic mesoderm and connect the embryo to the developing placenta. *B,* A 2.5-mm embryo (fourth week). Infolding and flexion of the embryo draws the amnion around the body. The vitelline duct is part of the developing umbilical cord. (From Cullen TS: Embryology, Anatomy, and Diseases of the Umbilicus Together with Diseases of the Urachus. Philadelphia, WB Saunders, 1916.) *C,* A 5-mm embryo (fifth week) demonstrating a complete umbilical cord. The vitelline duct connection between the yolk sac and the alimentary tract is lost between the fifth and seventh weeks. *D,* A 45-mm embryo (10 weeks) viewed from inside. The intestines, which were extraembryonic coelomic (i.e., within the umbilical cord) between the 6th and 10th weeks, have returned to the peritoneal cavity.

TABLE 72-1 Fate of Structures Related to the Developing Umbilicus

Structure	Fate	Remnants, Pathologic Condition
Urachus (connects the bladder to the allantois)	Obliterates	Median umbilical ligament, patent urachus, sinus, cyst
Omphalomesenteric duct (connects the midgut to the yolk sac)	Obliterates	Meckel's diverticulum, patent omphalomesenteric duct, sinus, cyst, bands, polyp
Omphalomesenteric arteries	Most regress; fuse to form the celiac, superior mesenteric, and inferior umbilicus	Dominant artery may accompany Meckel's diverticulum, fibrous band to the mesenteric arteries
Omphalomesenteric veins	Plexus around the duodenum becomes the superior mesenteric and portal vein (contribution from both the left and right vein)	Preduodenal portal vein if the ventral portion of the plexus persists
Umbilical arteries	Obliterate after birth	Lateral umbilical ligaments
Umbilical veins	Right obliterates; left returns placental blood to the inferior vena cava through the ductus venosus	Falciform ligament

yolk sac and extends into the connecting stalk of the embryo (Fig. 72-1A and B). The allantois serves as a reservoir for the developing renal system in lower vertebrates but has no known role in human development; it remains rudimentary as the transitory extraembryonic portion of the urachus. As the distal hindgut, or cloaca, partitions into the urogenital sinus ventrally and the anorectal canal dorsally, the developing bladder remains connected by the urachus to the allantois within the body stalk (Fig. 72-1D). The urachus is derived wholly from the developing bladder and may persist in various forms, which accounts for the abnormalities described later.

As the embryo develops, the amnion is drawn around it to surround the embryo and cover all the developing umbilical cord structures, including the allantois, umbilical vessels, vitelline duct, and primitive mesenchymal tissue (Wharton's jelly) (Fig. 72-1C). During the period of rapid intestinal growth between the 6th and 10th weeks of gestation, the developing midgut is extracoelomic. As the body wall continues to develop, the intestines are incorporated into the coelomic cavity and intestinal rotation and fixation progress. The fibromuscular umbilical ring continues to contract and is usually closed by the time of birth (Fig. 72-1D). Persistence of the fascial opening as an umbilical hernia occurs frequently and is most commonly seen in premature infants. Unlike other abdominal wall defects, umbilical hernias have a clear tendency to resolve without specific treatment as a result of the ongoing development of tissues at the umbilical ring after birth. The fate of the structures that relate to the development of the umbilicus is shown in Table 72-1.

THE UMBILICUS AT BIRTH

Modern obstetric practice uses plastic clamps that are placed a few centimeters from the umbilical skin during cord division at the time of delivery. Topical antimicrobials, such as triple dye, bacitracin, silver sulfadiazine, povidone-iodine, chlorhexidine, hexachlorophene, alcohol, salicylic sugar powder, green clay powder, silver-benzyl-peroxide powder, or 1% basic fuchsin, may be applied to the cord after birth.[89,90] All these agents are effective in reducing bacterial colonization rates, and their use is recommended when adequate cord care cannot be guaranteed. These agents may affect cord separation time, some cause discoloration, and repeated use of iodine-containing antimicrobials may result in systemic absorption of iodine and suppression of thyroid function. In developed countries, dry cord care, without the application of topical antibiotics, in association with routine soap and water bathing and meticulous hand washing practices is as effective as topical agents in reducing infection.[126]

Intestinal injury may result from injudicious placement of an umbilical cord clamp when an unrecognized small hernia of the umbilical cord (i.e., a small omphalocele) is present. Abdominal wall defects that relate to the umbilicus (i.e., gastroschisis and omphalocele) are covered in Chapter 73.

The normal time for separation of the umbilical cord after birth ranges from 3 days to 2 months.[120] Antimicrobial treatment may prolong cord separation by decreasing leukocyte infiltration. Delayed separation of the umbilical cord has been associated with heritable neutrophil mobility defects and widespread infections that are often lethal.[51] The abnormal neutrophils lack a membrane glycoprotein, which results in abnormal attachment, chemotaxis, and phagocytosis.[120] Although persistence of umbilical cord attachment beyond 3 weeks of age has been suggested to be a sign of such immunologic abnormalities, recent studies that have included more than 600 newborns have demonstrated the range of normal newborn cord separation to be broad (3 to 67 days), with a mean of 14 to 15 days.[84,120] In these studies, nearly 10% of normal newborns underwent cord separation after 3 weeks of age, thus indicating that delayed cord separation is not a reliable indicator of immunologic disease. If prolonged cord separation is associated with umbilical infection, leukocyte adhesion deficiency disorders should be suspected and an immunologic evaluation performed.[45,53,90]

After separation of the cord, the umbilicus may have many appearances. A normal umbilicus is characterized by a depression in which may be found the *mamelon* (a central eminence that contains the remnants of the solid portion of the umbilical cord) and the *cicatrix* (dense scar where the intraembryonic and extraembryonic coelom were in continuity). The *cushion* is the slightly raised margin that surrounds the umbilical depression. Cullen described more than 60 "normal" configurations of the umbilicus.[31]

UMBILICAL ABNORMALITIES

Acquired

Umbilical Granuloma

After cord separation, a small mass of granulation tissue may develop at the base. These granulomas consist of true granulation tissue with fibroblasts and abundant capillaries; the granulomas range in size from 1.0 mm to approximately 1.0 cm. The surface often has a pedunculated appearance. Umbilical granulomas may be treated by cauterization with one or more applications of silver nitrate until the area epithelializes. Alternatively, the granuloma may be excised and silver nitrate or absorbable hemostatic material applied.[80] If the mass does not respond to cauterization, a true umbilical polyp or sinus tract must be suspected (see later).

Umbilical Infections

Although modern perinatal practice has dramatically reduced the incidence of omphalitis, infections of the umbilicus still occur with alarming morbidity and mortality, particularly in Third World countries. Rigorous asepsis, hand washing, and cord care (either dry cord care or topical antimicrobials) have reduced the incidence of umbilical infections to less than 1% in hospitalized newborns.[72] Before the institution of such practices, the mortality rate for omphalitis was 65%. The primary pathogens implicated in these infections were *Staphylococcus aureus* and *Streptococcus pyogenes*. Currently, gram-negative bacteria play an important role in the pathogenesis of umbilical infections. Severe infections are often polymicrobial. Omphalitis may be manifested as a purulent umbilical discharge or periumbilical cellulitis. Delivery at home, low birth weight, use of umbilical catheters, and septic delivery are risk factors. Tetanus infection occurs on rare occasion. Intravenous antibiotic therapy is effective in eradicating most infections. Omphalitis is a common problem in developing countries, where it accounts for more than a quarter of neonatal hospital admissions.[4,101]

Cellulitis may progress to fasciitis, and such progression may be subtle. Signs of necrotizing fasciitis include abdominal distention, tachycardia, purpura, blistering, pyrexia, hypothermia, leukocytosis, and progression of cellulitis despite antibiotic therapy. Bacteriologic cultures demonstrate polymicrobial flora.[16] Necrotizing fasciitis and umbilical gangrene may be lethal and require immediate wide surgical debridement for patient survival.[63,66,72,79,94,95,106] Excision should be performed immediately on recognition; all infected skin, fat, and fascia should be excised back to viable, bleeding abdominal wall musculature. The umbilicus is obligatorily excised. Excision of preperitoneal tissue, including the umbilical vessels and urachal remnant, may be critically important to achieve eradication of the infection because these tissues harbor invasive bacteria and may provide a route for the progressive spread of infection seen after less extensive surgical debridement.[63] The defect may require a temporary prosthetic patch for closure, but ultimate fascial closure and umbilical reconstruction may leave an acceptable appearance. Hyperbaric oxygen therapy has been advocated as adjuvant therapy, but it is not of proven benefit.[95] The overall reported mortality associated with necrotizing fasciitis in collected series is 81%.[63,66,72,79,94,95,106]

Umbilical drainage resulting from chronic infection of umbilical remnants, such as umbilical artery remnants, has also been reported.[21] Excision and debridement are curative. Omphalitis can result in necrosis and breakdown of the umbilical stump with spontaneous evisceration within the first 2 months of life and may be associated with portal venous thrombosis and subsequent extrahepatic portal hypertension.

Congenital

Omphalomesenteric Remnants

Remnants of the vitelline or omphalomesenteric duct account for a wide variety of umbilical abnormalities that may require surgical correction.[76] These remnants include fistulas, sinus tracts, cysts, mucosal remnants, and congenital bands. Typical variations of the pathologic varieties are illustrated in Figure 72-2A to F.[31,60,77]

If the vitelline duct is patent from the terminal ileum to the umbilicus, fecal umbilical drainage will be noted (Fig. 72-3A). Although this event is dramatic to parents, the problem is immediately recognizable on examination, and parents may be reassured that prompt surgical correction is simple and curative. Prolapse of the proximal and distal ileum through the patent duct has a characteristic appearance. Although contrast injections are of interest, they do not change the surgical approach (Fig. 72-3B). Anatomically unusual conditions, such as an unexpected origin of the vitelline duct from the appendix, will be recognized at the time of surgery.[29,125] Unless another, more serious medical condition exists, a patent vitelline duct should be excised promptly. A mechanical intestinal preparation is not needed, although we customarily stop formula feeding and administer a preoperative dose of oral antibiotics. Perioperative intravenous antibiotics are also given. The operation may be performed through the umbilicus itself or via exposure through an inferior circumumbilical incision. Additional abdominal incisions are not usually required. Full exploration and identification of all umbilical structures, including one vein, two arteries, and the urachal remnant, are indicated. The vitelline duct is traced to the ileum and divided. The ileum is closed, and care must be taken to control any dominant vitelline

A B C

D E F

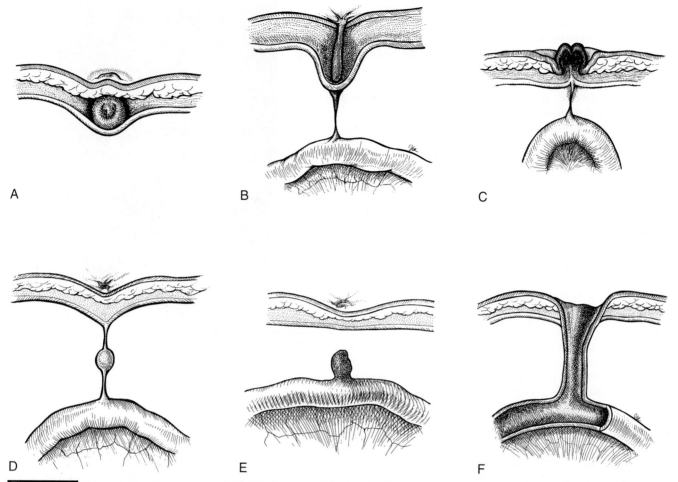

Figure 72-2 Various vitelline duct remnants. *A,* Umbilical cyst containing intestinal tissue. *B,* Umbilical sinus with a band. *C,* Umbilical polyp covered with intestinal mucosa. *D,* Fibrous band containing a cyst. *E,* Meckel's diverticulum. *F,* Patent vitelline duct. Other varieties and combinations exist.

vessels that may be present. After the fascia is closed, umbilicoplasty is performed.

Small duct remnants and sinuses may have less characteristic drainage. Injection of contrast material may be helpful in delineating the nature of the problem in these instances, but surgical exploration remains the definitive diagnostic test. It is important that a full exploration be performed and that all umbilical structures, including the intraperitoneal undersurface of the umbilicus, be visualized to identify and remove any bands attached to

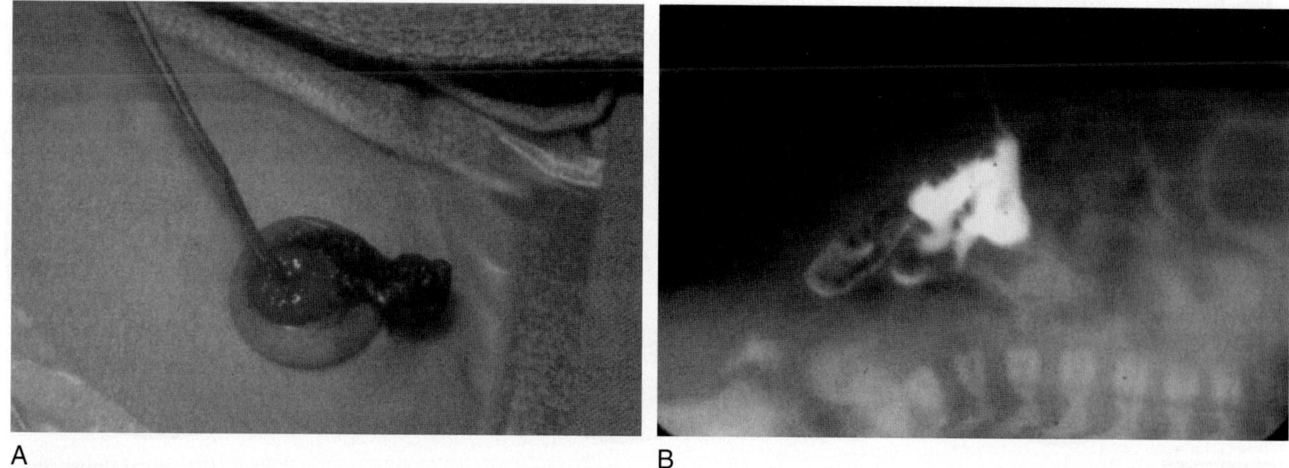

Figure 72-3 *A,* This photo of a newborn demonstrates probe patency of a vitelline duct into the ileum. *B,* A radiograph with contrast medium injected into a patent vitelline duct demonstrates filling of the small intestine. Studies of this sort are not usually necessary.

the small intestine. If a Meckel diverticulum is attached to a vitelline band discovered at exploration, it is excised. Cystic remnants of the vitelline duct may become infected and cause acute symptoms, even in older individuals. If an abscess has formed, it may require surgical drainage; excision of any remnant may be accomplished at a later time. The vitelline duct or any remnant attachments between the abdominal wall and the intestine may cause angulation, volvulus, or herniation of intestinal loops, thereby resulting in mechanical intestinal obstruction. The nature of the obstruction will be discovered during laparotomy.

Rarely, spontaneous regression of a patent vitelline duct may occur.[58,65] In one case, the defect was documented by a fistulogram shortly after birth, but it was not operated on until the patient was 3 months of age. At that time, only a Meckel diverticulum was found, but it had no connection to the umbilicus, thus indicating that some regression had occurred in the interim.

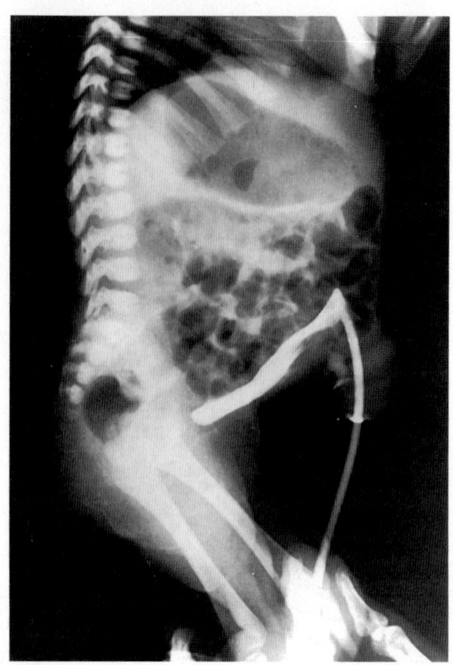

Figure 72-5 Radiograph with contrast medium injected into a patent urachus demonstrates filling of the bladder. (From Jona JZ: Umbilical anomalies. In Raffensberger JG [ed]: Swenson's Pediatric Surgery, 5th ed, Norwalk, Conn, Appleton & Lange, 1990. Used with permission.)

Urachal Remnants

Various abnormalities of the urachus have been described.[6,31,82] The typical abnormalities are depicted in Figure 72-4. A patent urachus is associated with drainage of urine from the umbilicus. Clear drainage from the umbilicus should always raise suspicion of a patent urachus, particularly if an ammoniac rash is present. Although the definitive anatomy is discovered during laparotomy, frank drainage of urine from the umbilicus requires an investigation of the urinary tract to look for bladder outlet obstruction in which the urachus is functioning as a relief valve (Fig. 72-5).[56] Such conditions are rare. A patent urachus may be approached either through the umbilicus or through an infraumbilical incision. It is important to identify all the umbilical structures for a definitive diagnosis. The patent urachus is ligated and transected at the level of the bladder; broad-based connections are closed in two layers with absorbable sutures.

Urachal sinuses may give rise to umbilical drainage or be discovered on examination. Urachal cysts most often cause

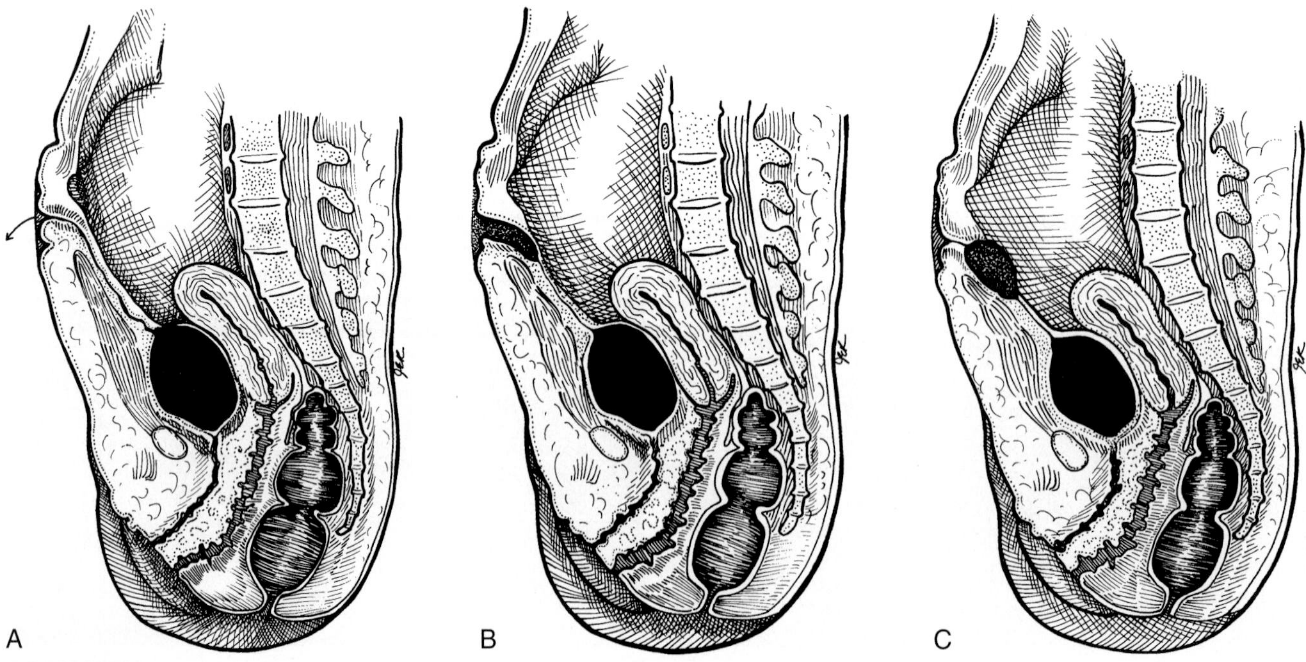

Figure 72-4 Various urachal remnants. *A,* Patent urachus with communication between the bladder and umbilicus. *B,* Urachal sinus. *C,* Urachal cyst, which is usually associated with infection.

an infection manifested as a painful mass localized between the umbilicus and the suprapubic area. Ultrasonography or computed tomography may be helpful to confirm the diagnosis. Other unusual manifestations have been reported, including a lateral mass.[14] The urachus has also been described as exiting from the midline below the umbilicus.[30,86] In addition, a patent urachus may be one of the causes of a giant umbilical cord in the newborn.[83] When a urachal cyst becomes infected and develops into an abscess, drainage of the acute process is required. After the abscess is drained, complete healing may take place. It is unknown whether subsequent laparotomy to remove any residual cyst remnants is necessary.

Urachal remnants may cause complications later in life. Abnormal epithelium, including colonic, small intestine, and squamous, may be present in incidentally removed urachal remnants.[113] The fate of these tissues is unknown, but many different malignant tumors have been reported to originate from the urachus. A partial list of tumors in adults arising from the urachus is shown in Table 72-2. Pediatric tumors, including rhabdomyosarcoma and neuroblastoma, may originate from urachal remnants as well.[24,122]

Pain plus retraction of the umbilicus during micturition has been described as a sign of a urachal anomaly.[61,93] Resection of the urachal remnant is curative.

Diagnostic imaging, including ultrasound, contrast injections, computed tomography, and magnetic resonance imaging, may occasionally be helpful in diagnosing and treating umbilical abnormalities.[12] An infant with umbilical discharge caused by both a persistent urachus and an omphalomesenteric duct has been reported.[70]

Umbilical Dysmorphology

A single umbilical artery may occur in conjunction with many syndromes and is associated with congenital abnormalities in a third of cases. Such abnormalities include trisomy 18 and renal and cardiac anomalies. Children with dysmorphic features may have characteristic findings that aid in diagnosis. Minor abnormalities that lack medical significance can nonetheless provide insight into the nature and timing of dysmorphologic events that occur during development.[41] Commonly, dermatoglyphics, hair patterning, auricular shape, and genital configuration are part of such observations. Minor abnormalities of the configuration of the umbilicus may be useful in the classification of dysmorphologic findings. For example, an umbilicus that is situated unusually high on the abdominal wall at the level of the lower rib cage and is very flat and poorly epithelialized indicates Robinow's syndrome, which is also characterized by a flat facial profile, mesomelic shortening, and genital hypoplasia. If the umbilicus is broad and prominent with a large stalk and redundant periumbilical skin, Rieger's syndrome should be suspected, especially if these umbilical abnormalities occur in conjunction with goniodysgenesis and hypodontia. If the umbilicus is prominent with a button-like central portion in a deep longitudinally oriented ovoid depression or very flat with radiating branches of the cicatrix, Aarskog's syndrome, a condition classically characterized by short stature, facial dysplasia, syndactyly, and genital anomalies, is indicated.[111]

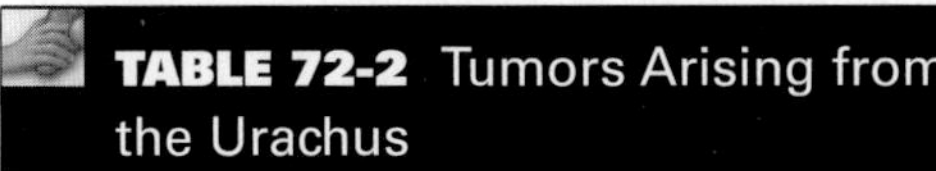

TABLE 72-2 Tumors Arising from the Urachus

Adenocarcinoma
Transitional cell carcinoma
Squamous cell carcinoma
Mucinous (cyst) adenocarcinoma
Malignant fibrous histiocytoma
Fibrosarcoma
Pleomorphic sarcoma
Yolk sac tumor
Inflammatory pseudotumor
Villous adenoma (premalignant)

Other Congenital and Acquired Pathologic Conditions of the Umbilicus

Suprapubic dermoid sinuses usually extend from the skin overlying the pubis and pass over the superior surface of the bladder to the umbilicus alongside the urachus.[43,87] The embryologic origin of such a sinus tract remains unclear, although it may be a variant of a dorsal urethral duplication.

Children with bladder and cloacal exstrophy may have an omphalocele or a low-set umbilicus incorporated into the upper portion of the open bladder plate, along with diastasis of the lower abdominal wall musculature and diastasis of the symphysis pubis.[75] Variants of exstrophy include superior vesicointestinal fissure, duplicate exstrophy, and pseudoexstrophy, in which the bladder is intact and only the musculoskeletal abnormalities are present.

Numerous unusual protrusions have been described at the umbilicus. Ectopic pancreatic tissue, including islets, is best explained by the pluripotential nature of cells of the vitelline duct.[19] Abnormal portions of liver connected to the main lobes of the liver have been described and probably represent entrapment by closure of the umbilical ring.[97] A giant, 10-cm hamartoma originating from the umbilicus without intra-abdominal involvement has been excised without incident.[23] The appendico-omphalic explanation of a fistula between the appendix and the umbilicus was noted earlier ("Omphalomesenteric Remnants"). Entrapment of the appendix in the umbilicus, such as in a small omphalocele, may also explain some fistulas from the appendix to the umbilicus.[13,57] Keloid formation has been observed after umbilical cord separation.[39] A giant umbilical cord may contain urachal remnants and ectatic vessels and may mask a small omphalocele. Care should be exercised during application of the cord clamp whenever the appearance of the cord is abnormal.

The umbilicus may be affected by any disease of hair-bearing skin, including dermatoses and infections. It may be the site of ectopic tissue, including endometriosis, as well as numerous primary and metastatic tumors, in addition to those of urachal origin (see Table 72-2). Many acquired

TABLE 72-3 Acquired Conditions of the Umbilicus

Condition	Comment	Source
Dermatoses	Seborrheic dermatitis, psoriasis, herpes gestationis, Fabry's disease	Powell 1988[91]
Foreign body reactions	Starch, talc, inserted objects	Powell 1988
Omphalith	Concretion of keratinous and sebaceous material	Powell 1988
Pilonidal disease	Related to hair-bearing sinus tracts	Steck 1965,[104] Sroujieh 1989,[103] Gupta 1990[46]
Infections	Bacterial, fungal, viral, parasitic	Powell 1988
Endometriosis	Ectopic endometrial tissue	Powell 1988, Franklin 1990[40]
Benign tumors	Nevi, pyogenic granuloma, inclusion cysts, hemangioma, dermatofibroma, neurofibroma, granular cell tumor, teratoma, desmoid tumor, lipoma	Powell 1988
Malignant tumors, primary	Melanoma, urachal adenocarcinoma, squamous cell carcinoma, basal cell carcinoma, sarcoma	Shetty 1990,[98] Powell 1988, Cornil 1967[26]
Malignant tumors, metastatic	Stomach, pancreas, endometrium, ovary, cervix, colon, small intestine, gallbladder, lung, prostate, breast, unknown	Shetty 1990
Enteric fistulas	Originate from Crohn's disease, perforated appendicitis, other such visceral perforations as colon, gallbladder	Park 1991,[88] Veloso 1989,[114] Burchell 1989[18]
Psychiatric disorders	Symbolic vagina	Waltzer 1974[117]
Miscellaneous disorders	Perforation from a ventriculoperitoneal shunt; infections, dermatoses, and granulation tissue from piercing	Bryant 1988,[17] Lena 1994[69]

pathologic conditions of the umbilicus are summarized in Table 72-3.

Umbilical piercing is common and may present dilemmas in management. Trauma surgeons should be familiar with the opening mechanisms of body piercings to facilitate radiology studies and as needed for emergency procedures.[59] Removal of the piercing device is not necessarily recommended if infection occurs.[118] Local infections can be treated by warm compresses and antibiotic ointment. If infection persists, oral antibiotics are prescribed. The site is cleansed with antibiotic soap and the jewelry rotated and left in place to allow drainage. Infections that require surgical drainage or debridement are rare.

Umbilical Lint

Umbilical lint collects as a direct result of the whorled umbilical hair acting on clothing-derived material. Hair encircles the umbilicus and the keratin scales overlap with their bases pointing toward the hair follicle. This arrangement imposes direction on the random movement of the clothing lint that occurs when the material rubs back and forth across the abdomen with body movement. The periumbilical hairs act in a ratchet-like fashion to move the lint into the depths of the umbilicus. Umbilical lint does not form in the absence of umbilical hair, and the color of the lint is that of the clothes worn.

UMBILICAL HERNIA

Anatomy

At birth, the umbilicus is surrounded by a dense fascial ring that represents a defect in the linea alba. The umbilical opening is reinforced by strongly attached remnants of the umbilical arteries and urachus in an inferior direction and the more weakly attached umbilical vein in a superior direction. A layer of fascia (Richet's fascia) derived from the transversalis fascia supports the base of the umbilicus. The peritoneum forms an intact undersurface of the umbilical ring, and skin overlies the umbilicus after the cord has separated. When the supporting fascia of the umbilical defect is weak or absent, a direct hernia results (Fig. 72-6).[121] An umbilical hernia in children is surrounded by the dense fascia of the umbilical ring through which a peritoneal sac attached to the overlying skin protrudes. The umbilical ring continues to close over time and the fascia of the umbilical defect strengthens, which accounts for the spontaneous resolution of this defect in most children.

An indirect umbilical hernia has also been described in which the peritoneal contents herniate from a point immediately superior to the umbilical ring. The hernia follows the umbilical canal along the umbilical vein, the

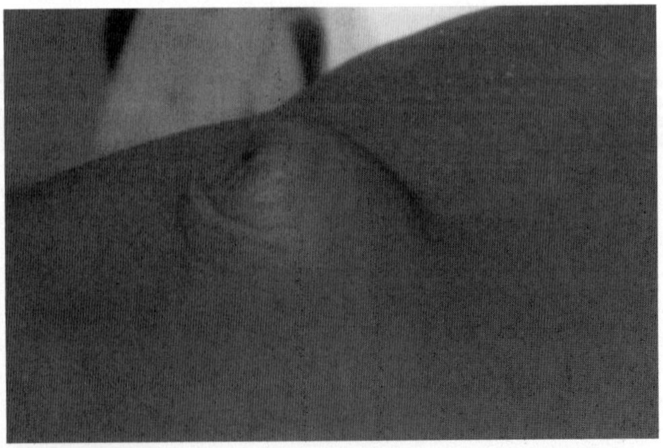

Figure 72-6 This photo of a 5-year-old girl shows the typical appearance of an umbilical hernia.

linea alba in an anterior direction, and a thin layer of preperitoneal fascia in a posterior direction.[11] This form of herniation has been suggested to cause proboscoid hernias in children; in this defect, the umbilical cicatrix is displaced progressively in an inferior direction as the hernia enlarges. This defect may also be responsible for umbilical hernias in some adults.

The umbilical hernia of childhood is distinguished from a "hernia of the umbilical cord," in which there is a defect in the peritoneum, as well as an open fascial defect at the umbilicus. Intestines herniate into the substance of the umbilical cord itself and are covered only by amnion. A hernia of the umbilical cord is, in effect, a small omphalocele.

Incidence and Natural History

There is no doubt a molecular basis for umbilical ring closure.[109] Genetic heterogeneity accounts for the presence of an open umbilical ring in some children at the time of birth, whereas in others, the ring is closed at the time of cord separation. Unlike inguinal and epigastric hernias, which have no real tendency to close after term, the umbilical ring is programmed to continue closure in many children for weeks, months, or years after birth.

Umbilical hernias in childhood occur with equal frequency in boys and girls. Numerous reports document a high incidence in African and African American infants.[17,35,116] The umbilical ring is open throughout most of gestation but becomes progressively smaller as gestation progresses. Most umbilical hernias in infants are recognized after cord separation in the first few weeks of life, and almost all are noted by 6 months of age. Most undergo spontaneous closure during the first 3 years of life. Umbilical defects are found in many premature infants after cord separation. Although umbilical hernias are commonly found in low-birth-weight infants (75% of infants weighing less than 1500 g), most will resolve.[115] The lack of accurate longitudinal studies of children with umbilical defects does not allow definitive conclusions to be drawn about their natural history.[96] Umbilical hernias with a small ring diameter (<1.0 cm) are more likely to close spontaneously and close sooner than those with a large ring diameter (>1.5 cm). The diameter of the umbilical defect is prognostically important, whereas the length of the protrusion is not. Some umbilical hernias that are present at 5 years of age will close spontaneously without an operation.[47,52] The relationship between umbilical hernias that become symptomatic later in life and childhood umbilical defects is unknown. The protruding portion of the hernia generally remains unchanged while the fascial ring closes until it is too small to admit any contents into the hernia sac. The hernia thus tends to disappear abruptly.[52] Umbilical hernias are commonly observed in patients with Down syndrome, trisomy 18, trisomy 13, mucopolysaccharidoses, and congenital hypothyroidism. Umbilical defects (hernia or omphalocele) are part of the Beckwith-Wiedemann syndrome. Incarceration of intestine or omentum, strangulation, perforation, evisceration, and pain are rare events in the natural history of umbilical hernias in children. The most difficult task of the pediatric surgeon is to convince the family that observation alone will be successful in most cases and that an operation is not indicated for their child, especially in infancy. It is helpful to teach the parents to monitor the size of the defect relative to the size of one of their fingers.

Uncorrected umbilical hernias can become symptomatic at any time in life. Rupture and evisceration are very rare but can occur.[2,102] Incarceration is rare, but the small bowel is most commonly affected when it does occur. Conditions that increase intra-abdominal pressure increase the likelihood of complications. Repair of umbilical hernias in patients with ascites is hazardous. Umbilical hernias may also become symptomatic during pregnancy, and if incarceration occurs, surgery is required. Unusual contents of umbilical hernias include uterine fibroids and endometrial elements.[33,124]

Surgical Indications

Although repair of childhood umbilical hernias has been advocated to prevent the complication of incarceration in adults, the relationship between the two events is unclear.[67,78] Rare events, such as incarceration requiring reduction, strangulation, perforation, and evisceration, are absolute indications for surgery. In the absence of these absolute indications, persistence and appearance are relative indications for operative repair in developed countries. Infants with giant proboscoid hernias in whom the umbilical ring does not narrow during serial observations may be considered for repair in the first 2 years of life. Typical umbilical hernias should be observed at least until age 2. If there is no improvement in the size of the umbilical ring, consider repair. Ample evidence supports the decision to postpone repair until later in childhood. Large defects (>1.5 cm) that persist past the age of 5 should be repaired. Evidence-based guidelines are lacking, and the decision may be individualized on the basis of such considerations as family history, parental desires, and local practices. The appearance of a hernia often drives families to insist that the hernia be repaired. In less developed parts of the world, it may be appropriate to actively observe umbilical hernias, with surgery reserved for those with complications such as incarceration.[3,73]

If the child has a tender umbilical mass, the hernia may be reduced by milking the air out of the incarcerated loop of intestine and applying firm, steady pressure on the incarcerated mass. Admitting a patient for observation to rule out peritonitis and performing the operation the next day are appropriate. If the incarceration resists reduction, an emergency procedure is warranted. In an infant with an inguinal hernia and a concomitant umbilical hernia, the umbilical hernia should generally be left alone because it will probably close spontaneously.

Surgical Technique, Results, and Complications

Procedures described for the repair of umbilical hernias in children range from multiple layers of closure after opening the peritoneum to closed techniques in which the peritoneal sac is inverted or treated like an inguinal hernia sac and ligated with sutures.[7,10] Absorbable and nonabsorbable sutures have been advocated. The redundant skin of a large defect may be left in place and improves in appearance over time. Some have advocated excision of the skin and reconstruction when a large proboscoid hernia is present (see later). However, the fundamental technique of umbilical hernia repair has changed little since the 1953 description by Gross.[44] Secure closure of the fascia, usually in a transverse fashion, and preservation of the appearance of the umbilicus are common to all repairs. Strapping and taping of the defects have been discredited.[100,121]

Repair of an umbilical hernia is performed as an outpatient procedure with the patient under general anesthesia. Local anesthesia may be infiltrated into the wound before or after the procedure, but paraumbilical infiltration avoids distortion of tissues by the anesthetic.[27] Administration of local anesthesia before the incision conforms to the principles of preemptive analgesia. An infraumbilical skin crease incision is made (Fig. 72-7). Subcutaneous dissection is performed to circumscribe the sac. The sac is transected and may be dissected from the undersurface of the umbilical skin, but extensive and time-consuming dissection is unnecessary. Leaving a small remnant of the peritoneal sac on the undersurface of the umbilical skin causes no complications. The sac may be trimmed to a strong fascial edge or simply folded inward to allow placement of interrupted absorbable sutures in a transverse orientation. To ensure accurate placement of sutures, they are tied only after placement is complete. A second layer of closure is unnecessary. Inversion of the umbilical skin is maintained with fine absorbable dermal suture between the underside of the umbilicus and the midportion of the fascial closure. The skin is closed with intradermal absorbable sutures and covered with a small dressing that applies adequate pressure.

Although infection predisposes to recurrence of the hernia, such complications are rare. Visceral injuries are possible but should not occur if the fascial edges are kept in view during the procedure.

USE OF THE UMBILICUS

Cannulation of the umbilical arteries and umbilical vein is commonly performed in sick neonates and provides a convenient means for intravascular access and monitoring. Associated risks are related to infection, vascular thrombosis, and direct injury from catheters.[22] The umbilicus is

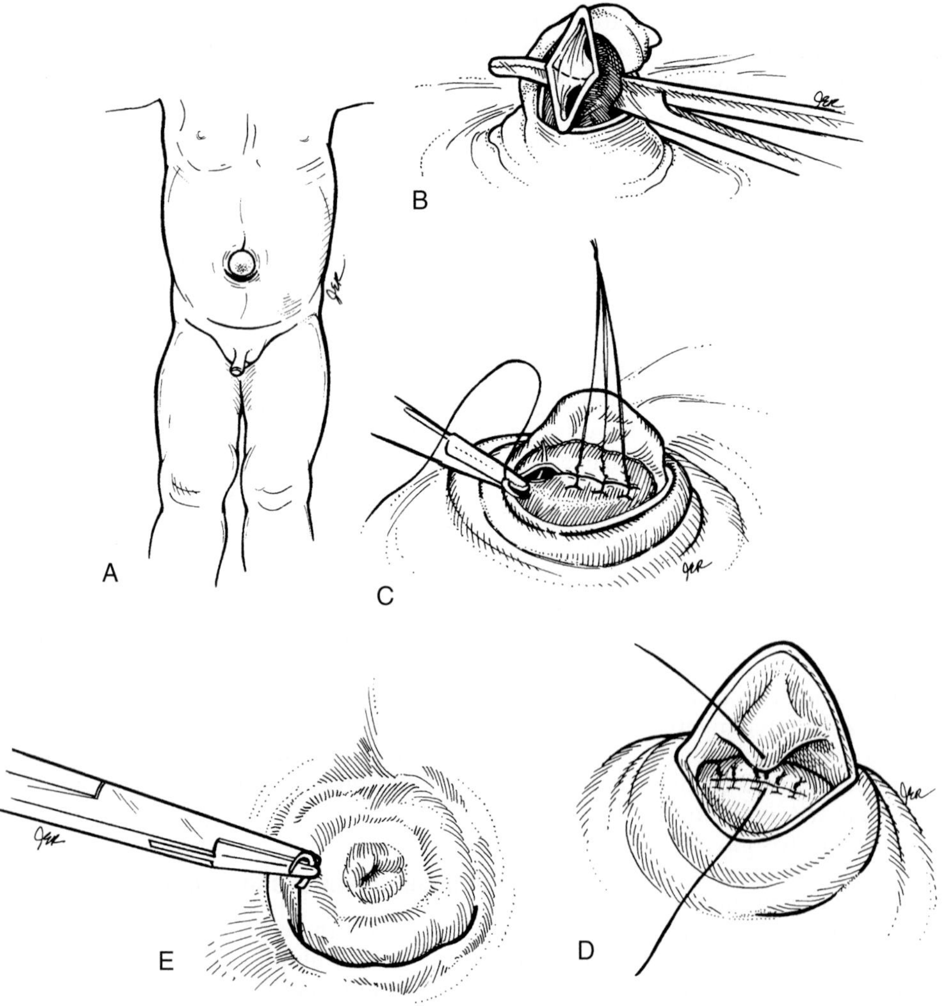

Figure 72-7 Repair of an umbilical hernia. *A,* An infraumbilical, curvilinear incision is marked. *B,* The sac is encircled and opened. *C,* The fascia is closed transversely. *D,* A tacking suture is placed between the undersurface of the umbilical skin and the fascia. *E,* Final result.

frequently used as the entry site for laparoscopic equipment. The center of the umbilicus may be opened and the fascial ring probed and spread for access in infants, small children, and those with a shallow umbilicus. This technique leaves almost no detectable incision. In patients with a deep umbilicus, a separate infraumbilical incision may be preferable. The umbilical port is most often used as the primary site for placement of the viewing camera. Closure of the fascial defect after removal of the port is necessary to reduce the risk for formation of a hernia. The umbilicus has also been used to mask the abdominal incision used for pyloromyotomy in cases of hypertrophic pyloric stenosis.[38] This approach results in an almost undetectable scar.

The umbilicus can also be used as a stoma site.[20] No studies have compared the complication rate for intestinal stomas brought out of the umbilicus with those brought out from other locations in the abdominal wall; however, complications of umbilical stomas were reported by one study to be common.[37] After closure, the umbilicus is reconstructed and a nearly normal appearance is achieved. We have used the umbilicus as a temporary ostomy site and have found it satisfactory. Though providing no physiologic benefit, it leaves the patient with one less obvious incision site.

The umbilicus has also been used as an exit site for urinary diversion. In premature infants, a temporary cutaneous vesicostomy brought out of the umbilicus functions well and can be closed with excellent cosmetic results.[1] Intestinal conduits for urinary diversion have also been brought out of the umbilicus.[15]

RECONSTRUCTION AND PRESERVATION OF THE UMBILICUS

The umbilicus is aesthetically important, and its absence can be distressing to patients. The appearance of the umbilicus should be acceptable to the patient and family. A T-shaped or oval umbilicus with a superior hood may be the most aesthetically appealing configuration for females.[28] A very broad or protruding umbilicus may be perceived to be less acceptable. One of the goals of all umbilical surgical procedures is to maintain or restore as normal an appearance as possible. Standard umbilical hernia repair produces minimal distortion of the umbilicus and generally results in a satisfactory appearance. Omphalomesenteric and urachal remnants can usually be excised through the umbilicus as noted earlier. After laparoscopy via the umbilicus, if the umbilical skin is secured to the fascial closure, a satisfactory umbilical depression is maintained.

Umbilicoplasty for Giant Hernias with Redundant Skin

When large hernias (giant proboscoid hernias) are repaired, the redundant skin results in an unnatural appearance. Some improvement may occur with the passage of time, but a broad, flat, protruding configuration may persist. Reconstruction by a variety of techniques may improve the immediate and long-term appearance.[8,9,25,54,92,110] We have found the "tripartite umbilicoplasty" based on the technique described by Reyna et al. to be satisfactory for immediate reconstruction of giant umbilical hernias.[92] None of these techniques has been widely adopted and shown to be superior in long-term follow-up, however.

Umbilicoplasty for Abdominal Wall Defects

The umbilicus may be retained or reconstructed during the repair of abdominal wall abnormalities. The structures of the umbilical cord may be incorporated into a reconstruction of the umbilicus, or a neo-umbilicus may be fashioned.[50,64,68,81,85,112,119]

In gastroschisis and omphalocele, fascial repair may be performed through the circular skin defect that remains after the umbilical structures have been excised. This is the case for both primary and staged closures. The circular skin defect may then be closed with an intradermal purse-string suture that is incorporated into the middle of the fascial closure (Fig. 72-8).[64] Even if the fascial defect is enlarged for the application of a Silastic chimney, the lower portion of the defect can be closed in a similar circular fashion to create the appearance of an umbilicus.[50] Others have advocated preservation of the umbilicus in the repair of abdominal wall defects and leaving the umbilical remnants in place in continuity with the skin closure.[81,112,119] The umbilicus is abnormally located in all children with bladder exstrophy and is often associated with a small omphalocele defect. It may be transposed more cephalad at the time of bladder closure to create a more normal appearance.[48] In children with prune-belly syndrome, the umbilicus may be preserved on a vascularized pedicle and located appropriately after the removal of excess skin.[34]

Reconstruction of an Absent Umbilicus

In some circumstances a new umbilicus must be constructed when it is absent as a result of previous surgical removal. The normal location for the umbilicus is at the level of the iliac crests, overlying the third or fourth lumbar vertebrae. Umbilical reconstruction should create a round or oval depression with steep walls that is centrally fixed to the abdominal wall fascia. Some umbilical reconstructions tend to flatten over time. Tubularized skin reconstructions may be more durable and may also mimic the "cushion" or slightly raised area that surrounds the umbilical depression. Many techniques have been proposed to reconstruct an absent umbilicus.* They vary considerably in their complexity, but none have proved superior in long-term follow-up. Several techniques have been specifically described to reconstruct an absent umbilicus after exstrophy repair.[36,48,49,108]

*References 5, 32, 55, 62, 64, 71, 74, 85, 99, 107, 123.

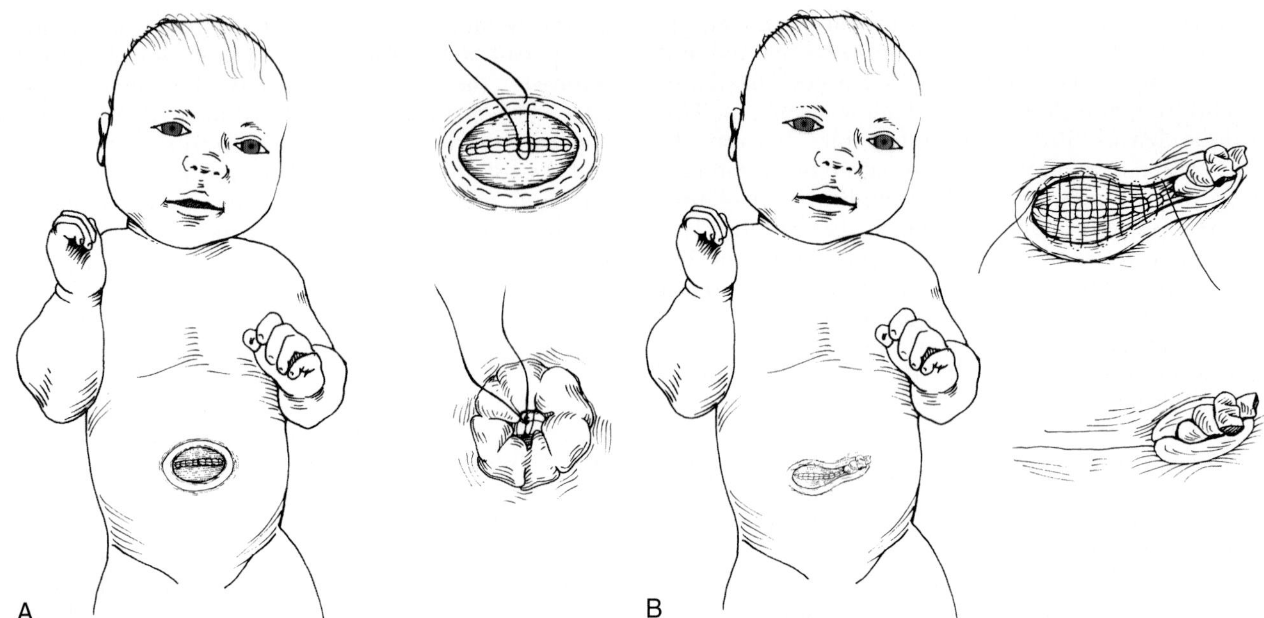

Figure 72–8 Technique of umbilicoplasty after excision of the cord structures or when a procedure is performed through the umbilicus (e.g., surgical repair of gastroschisis or a small omphalocele, excision of an omphalomesenteric remnant through the umbilical ring, excision of a urachal remnant through the umbilicus). *A,* Child with gastroschisis after fascial closure. Placement of a circumferential purse-string dermal suture is shown. Note that the suture passes through the fascia. *B,* Retention of the umbilical cord after repair of gastroschisis.

REFERENCES

1. Adzick NS, Harrison MR, Glick PL, et al: Temporary cutaneous umbilical vesicostomy in premature infants with urethral obstruction. J Pediatr Surg 1986;21:171-172.
2. Ahmed A, Ahmed M, Nmadu PT: Spontaneous rupture of infantile umbilical hernia: Report of three cases. Ann Trop Paediatr 1998;18:239-241.
3. Ameh EA, Chirdan LB, Nmadu PT, et al: Complicated umbilical hernias in children. Pediatr Surg Int 2003;19:280-282.
4. Ameh EA, Nmadu PT: Major complications of omphalitis in neonates and infants. Pediatr Surg Int 2002;18:413-416.
5. Bartsich SA, Schwartz MH: Purse-string method for immediate umbilical reconstruction. Plast Reconstr Surg 2003; 112:1652-1655.
6. Begg RD: The urachus: Its anatomy, histology and development. J Anat 1930;64:170-183.
7. Benjamin B, Vinocur CD, Wagner CW, et al: A closed technique for umbilical hernia repair. Surg Gynecol Obstet 1987;164:473-474.
8. Billmire DF: A technique for the repair of giant umbilical hernia in children. J Am Coll Surg 2002;194:677-680.
9. Blanchard H, St-Vil D, Carceller A, et al: Repair of the huge umbilical hernia in black children. J Pediatr Surg 2000; 35:696-698.
10. Blodgett JB: Transumbilical repair of congenital umbilical hernia. Surg Gynecol Obstet 1941;72:632-634.
11. Blumberg NA: Infantile umbilical hernia. Surg Gynecol Obstet 1980;150:187-192.
12. Boothroyd AE, Cudmore RE: Ultrasound of the discharging umbilicus. Pediatr Radiol 1996;26:362-364.
13. Borgna-Pignatti C, Andreis IA, Bettili G, Zamboni G: Delayed separation of an appendix-containing umbilical stump. J Pediatr Surg 1995;30:1717-1718.
14. Boyle G, Rosenberg HK, O'Neill JA: An unusual presentation of an infected urachal cyst. Review of urachal anomalies. Clin Pediatr (Phila) 1988;27:130-134.
15. Braren V, Workman CH, Johns OT, et al: Use of the umbilical area for placement of a urinary stoma. Surg Gynecol Obstet 1979;148:543-546.
16. Brook I: Microbiology of necrotizing fasciitis associated with omphalitis in the newborn infant. J Perinatol 1998; 18:28-30.
17. Bryant MS, Bremer AM, Tepas JJ 3rd, et al: Abdominal complications of ventriculoperitoneal shunts. Case reports and review of the literature. Am Surg 1988;54:50-55.
18. Burchell MC: Spontaneous umbilical fistula in Crohn's disease. Report of a case. Dis Colon Rectum 1989;32: 621-623.
19. Caberwal D, Kogan SJ, Levitt SB: Ectopic pancreas presenting as an umbilical mass. J Pediatr Surg 1977;12: 593-599.
20. Cameron GS, Lau GY: The umbilicus as a site for temporary colostomy in infants. J Pediatr Surg 1982;17: 362-364.
21. Choi SO, Park WH, Kang JS: Purulent umbilical drainage from infection of left umbilical artery associated with open umbilicoperitoneal communication. J Pediatr Surg 1988; 23:382-383.
22. Cilley RE: Arterial access in infants and children. Semin Pediatr Surg 1992;1:174-180.
23. Cilley RE: Giant hamartoma protruding from the umbilicus in a newborn. Unpublished data.
24. Clapuyt P, Saint-Martin C, De Batselier P, et al: Urachal neuroblastoma: First case report. Pediatr Radiol 1999;29: 320-321.
25. Cone JB, Golladay ES: Purse-string skin closure of umbilical hernia repair. J Pediatr Surg 1983;18:297.
26. Cornil C, Reynolds CT, Kickham CJ: Carcinoma of the urachus. J Urol 1967;98:93-95.
27. Courreges P, Poddevin F, Lecoutre D: Para-umbilical block: A new concept for regional anaesthesia in children. Paediatr Anaesth 1997;7:211-214.
28. Craig SB, Faller MS, Puckett CL: In search of the ideal female umbilicus. Plast Reconstr Surg 2000;105:389-392.

29. Crankson SJ, Ahmed GS, Palkar V: Patent omphalomesenteric duct of the vermiform appendix in a neonate: Congenital appendicoumbilical fistula. Pediatr Surg Int 1998;14:229-230.
30. Crawford RA, Sethia KK, Fawcett DP: An unusual presentation of a urachal remnant. Br J Urol 1989;64:315-316.
31. Cullen TS: Embryology, Anatomy, and Diseases of the Umbilicus Together with Diseases of the Urachus. Philadelphia, WB Saunders, 1916.
32. de Lacerda DJ, Martins DM, Marques A, et al: Umbilicoplasty for the abdomen with a thin adipose layer. Br J Plast Surg 1994;47:386-387.
33. Ehigiegba AE, Selo-Ojeme DO: Myomectomy in pregnancy: Incarcerated pedunculated fibroid in an umbilical hernia sac. Int J Clin Pract 1999;53:80.
34. Ehrlich RM, Lesavoy MA: Umbilicus preservation with total abdominal wall reconstruction in prune-belly syndrome. Urology 1993;41:231-232.
35. Evans AG: The comparative incidence of umbilical hernias in colored and white infants. J Natl Med Assoc 1941;33: 158-160.
36. Feyaerts A, Mure PY, Jules JA, et al: Umbilical reconstruction in patients with exstrophy: The kangaroo pouch technique. J Urol 2001;165:2026-2027.
37. Fitzgerald PG, Lau GY, Cameron GS: Use of the umbilical site for temporary ostomy: Review of 47 cases. J Pediatr Surg 1989;24:973.
38. Fitzgerald PG, Lau GY, Langer JC, et al: Umbilical fold incision for pyloromyotomy. J Pediatr Surg 1990;25: 1117-1118.
39. Ford T, Widgerow AD: Umbilical keloid: An early start. Ann Plast Surg 1990;25:214-215.
40. Franklin RR, Navarro C: Extragenital endometriosis. Prog Clin Biol Res 1990;323:289-295.
41. Friedman JM: Umbilical dysmorphology. The importance of contemplating the belly button. Clin Genet 1985;28: 343-347.
42. Gray SW, Skandalakis JE: The bladder and urethra. In Gray SW, Skandalakis JE (eds): Embryology for Surgeons: The Embryological Basis for the Treatment of Congenital Defects. Philadelphia, WB Saunders, 1972, pp 519-552.
43. Groff DB: Suprapubic dermoid sinus. J Pediatr Surg 1993; 28:242-243.
44. Gross RE: The Surgery of Infancy and Childhood: Its Principles and Techniques. Philadelphia, WB Saunders, 1953, pp 423-427.
45. Guneser S, Altintas DU, Aksungur P, et al: An infant with severe leucocyte adhesion deficiency. Acta Paediatr 1996; 85:622-624.
46. Gupta S, Sikora S, Singh M, et al: Pilonidal disease of the umbilicus—a report of two cases. Jpn J Surg 1990;20: 590-592.
47. Hall DE, Roberts KB, Charney E: Umbilical hernia: What happens after age 5 years? J Pediatr 1981;98:415-417.
48. Hanna MK: Reconstruction of umbilicus during functional closure of bladder exstrophy. Urology 1986;27:340-342.
49. Hanna MK, Ansong K: Reconstruction of umbilicus in bladder exstrophy. Urology 1984;24:324-326.
50. Harmel RP Jr: Primary repair of gastroschisis with umbilicoplasty. Surg Gynecol Obstet 1985;160:464-465.
51. Hayward AR, Harvey BA, Leonard J, et al: Delayed separation of the umbilical cord, widespread infections, and defective neutrophil mobility. Lancet 1979;1:1099-1101.
52. Heifetz CJ, Bilsel ZT, Gaus WW: Observations on the disappearance of umbilical hernias in infancy and childhood. Surg Gynecol Obstet 1963;116:469-473.
53. Hung CH, Cheng SN, Hua YM, et al: Leukocyte adhesion deficiency disorder: Report of one case. Acta Paediatr Taiwan 1999;40:128-131.
54. Ikeda H, Yamamoto H, Fujino J, et al: Umbilicoplasty for large protruding umbilicus accompanying umbilical hernia: A simple and effective technique. Pediatr Surg Int 2004; 20:105-107.
55. Itoh Y, Arai K: Umbilical reconstruction using a cone-shaped flap. Ann Plast Surg 1992;28:335-338.
56. Jona JZ: Umbilical anomalies. In Raffensberger JG (ed): Swenson's Pediatric Surgery, 5th ed. Norwalk, CT, Appleton & Lange, 1990, pp 193-195.
57. Kadzombe E, Currie AB: Neonatal fistula from the appendix to the umbilicus. J Pediatr Surg 1988;23: 1059-1060.
58. Kamii Y, Zaki AM, Honna T, et al: Spontaneous regression of patient omphalomesenteric duct: From a fistula to Meckel's diverticulum. J Pediatr Surg 1992;27:115-116.
59. Khanna R, Kumar SS, Raju BS, et al: Body piercing in the accident and emergency department. J Accid Emerg Med 1999;16:418-421.
60. Kittle CF, Jenkins HP, Dragstedt LR: Patent omphalomesenteric duct and its relation to the diverticulum of Meckel. Arch Surg 1947;54:10-36.
61. Knoll LD, Pustka RA, Anderson JR, et al: Periumbilical pain secondary to persistent urachal band. Urology 1988; 32:526-528.
62. Korachi A, Oudit D, Ellabban M: A simplified technique for umbilical reconstruction. Plast Reconstr Surg 2004;114: 619-621.
63. Kosloske AM, Bartow SA: Debridement of periumbilical necrotizing fasciitis: Importance of excision of the umbilical vessels and urachal remnant. J Pediatr Surg 1991;26: 808-810.
64. Krummel TM, Sieber WK: Closure of congenital abdominal wall defects with umbilicoplasty. Surg Gynecol Obstet 1987;165:168-169.
65. Kurzbart E, Zeitlin M, Feigenbaum D, et al: Rare spontaneous regression of patent omphalomesenteric duct after birth. Arch Dis Child Fetal Neonatal Ed 2002;86:F63.
66. Lally KP, Atkinson JB, Woolley MM, et al: Necrotizing fasciitis. A serious sequela of omphalitis in the newborn. Ann Surg 1984;199:101-103.
67. Lassaletta L, Fonkalsrud EW, Tovar JA, et al: The management of umbilical hernias in infancy and childhood. J Pediatr Surg 1975;10:405-409.
68. Lee SL, DuBois JJ, Greenholz SK, et al: Advancement flap umbilicoplasty after abdominal wall closure: Postoperative results compared with normal umbilical anatomy. J Pediatr Surg 2001;36:1168-1170.
69. Lena SM: Pierced navels are troublesome. CMAJ 1994;150: 646-647.
70. Lizerbram EK, Mahour GH, Gilsanz V: Dual patency of the omphalomesenteric duct and urachus. Pediatr Radiol 1997;27:244-246.
71. Marconi F: Reconstruction of the umbilicus: A simple technique. Plast Reconstr Surg 1995;95:1115-1117.
72. Mason WH, Andrews R, Ross LA, et al: Omphalitis in the newborn infant. Pediatr Infect Dis J 1989;8:521-525.
73. Meier DE, OlaOlorun DA, Omodele RA, et al: Incidence of umbilical hernia in African children: Redefinition of "normal" and reevaluation of indications for repair. World J Surg 2001;25:645-648.
74. Miller MJ, Balch CM: "Iris" technique for immediate umbilical reconstruction. Plast Reconstr Surg 1993;92: 754-756.
75. Mitchell W, Venable D, Patel AJ: Pseudoexstrophy. Urology 1993;41:134-136.
76. Moore TC: Omphalomesenteric duct malformations. Semin Pediatr Surg 1996;5:116-123.
77. Moore TC: Omphalomesenteric duct anomalies. Surg Gynecol Obstet 1956;103:569-580.

78. Morgan WW, White JJ, Stumbaugh S, et al: Prophylactic umbilical hernia repair in childhood to prevent adult incarceration. Surg Clin North Am 1970;50:839-845.
79. Moss RL, Musemeche CA, Kosloske AM: Necrotizing fasciitis in children: Prompt recognition and aggressive therapy improve survival. J Pediatr Surg 1996;31:1142-1146.
80. Nagar H: Umbilical granuloma: A new approach to an old problem. Pediatr Surg Int 2001;17:513-514.
81. Nagaya M, Ando H, Tsudo M, et al: Preservation of the umbilical cord at the primary fascial closure in infants with gastroschisis. J Pediatr Surg 1993;28:1471-1472.
82. Nix JT, Menville JG, Albert M, et al: Congenital patent urachus. J Urol 1958;79:264-273.
83. Nobuhara KK, Lukish JR, Hartman GE, et al: The giant umbilical cord: An unusual presentation of a patent urachus. J Pediatr Surg 2004;39:128-129.
84. Novack AH, Mueller B, Ochs H: Umbilical cord separation in the normal newborn. Am J Dis Child 1988;142:220-223.
85. Park S, Hata Y, Ito O, et al: Umbilical reconstruction after repair of omphalocele and gastroschisis. Plast Reconstr Surg 1999;104:204-207.
86. Park WH, Choi SO: An unusual urachal sinus with external opening in the midline suprapubic area. J Pediatr Surg 2003;38:E18-E20.
87. Park WH, Choi SO, Park KK, et al: Prepubic dermoid sinus: Possible variant of dorsal urethral duplication (Stephens type 3). J Pediatr Surg 1993;28:1610-1611.
88. Park WH, Choi SO, Woo SK, et al: Appendicumbilical fistula as a sequela of perforated appendicitis. J Pediatr Surg 1991;26:1413-1415.
89. Pezzati M, Biagioli EC, Martelli E, et al: Umbilical cord care: The effect of eight different cord-care regimens on cord separation time and other outcomes. Biol Neonate 2002;81:38-44.
90. Pomeranz A: Anomalies, abnormalities, and care of the umbilicus. Pediatr Clin North Am 2004;51:819-827.
91. Powell FC, Su WP: Dermatoses of the umbilicus. Int J Dermatol 1988;27:150-156.
92. Reyna TM, Harris WH Jr, Smith SB: Surgical management of proboscoid herniae. J Pediatr Surg 1987;22:911-912.
93. Rowe PC, Gearhart JP: Retraction of the umbilicus during voiding as an initial sign of a urachal anomaly. Pediatrics 1993;91:153-154.
94. Samuel M, Freeman NV, Vaishnav A, et al: Necrotizing fasciitis: A serious complication of omphalitis in neonates. J Pediatr Surg 1994;29:1414-1416.
95. Sawin RS, Schaller RT, Tapper D, et al: Early recognition of neonatal abdominal wall necrotizing fasciitis. Am J Surg 1994;167:481-484.
96. Shaw A: Disorders of the umbilicus. In Welch KJ, Randolph JG, Ravitch MM, et al (eds): Pediatric Surgery. Chicago, Year Book, 1986, pp 731-739.
97. Shaw A, Pierog S: "Ectopic" liver in the umbilicus: An unusual focus of infection in a newborn infant. Pediatrics 1969;44:448-450.
98. Shetty MR: Metastatic tumors of the umbilicus: A review 1830-1989. J Surg Oncol 1990;45:212-215.
99. Shinohara H, Matsuo K, Kikuchi N: Umbilical reconstruction with an inverted C-V flap. Plast Reconstr Surg 2000; 105:703-705.
100. Sibley WL 3rd, Lynn HB, Harris LE: A twenty-five year study of infantile umbilical hernia. Surgery 1964;55:462-468.
101. Simiyu DE: Morbidity and mortality of neonates admitted in general paediatric wards at Kenyatta National Hospital. East Afr Med J 2003;80:611-616.
102. Singh UK, Singh S, Ojha P, et al: Spontaneous rupture of umbilical hernia in an infant. Indian Pediatr 2000;37: 341-342.
103. Sroujieh AS, Dawoud A: Umbilical sepsis. Br J Surg 1989;76:687-688.
104. Steck WD, Helwig EB: Umbilical granulomas, pilonidal disease and the urachus. Surg Gynecol Obstet 1965;120: 1043-1057.
105. Steinthal AJ: Malformations of the umbilicus and urachus: Faulty closure of the vitello-intestinal duct and its results. In von Bergmann E, von Bruns P, von Mikuliez J, et al (eds): A System of Practical Surgery. Philadelphia, Lea Brothers, 1904, pp 142-149, 593-606.
106. Stunden RJ, Brown RA, Rode H, et al: Umbilical gangrene in the newborn. J Pediatr Surg 1988;23:130-134.
107. Sugawara Y, Hirabayashi S, Asato H, et al: Reconstruction of the umbilicus using a single triangular flap. Ann Plast Surg 1995;34:78-80.
108. Sumfest JM, Mitchell ME: Reconstruction of the umbilicus in exstrophy. J Urol 1994;151:453-454.
109. Suzuki N, Labosky PA, Furuta Y, et al: Failure of ventral body wall closure in mouse embryos lacking a procollagen C-proteinase encoded by *Bmp1*, a mammalian gene related to *Drosophila tolloid*. Development 1996;122:3587-3595.
110. Tamir G, Kurzbart E: Umbilical reconstruction after repair of large umbilical hernia: The "lazy-M" and omega flaps. J Pediatr Surg 2004;39:226-228.
111. Tsukahara M, Fernandez GI: Umbilical findings in Aarskog syndrome. Clin Genet 1994;45:260-265.
112. Uceda JE: Umbilical preservation in omphalocele repair. J Pediatr Surg 1994;29:1412-1413.
113. Upadhyay V, Kukkady A: Urachal remnants: An enigma. Eur J Pediatr Surg 2003;13:372-376.
114. Veloso FT, Cardoso V, Fraga J, et al: Spontaneous umbilical fistula in Crohn's disease. J Clin Gastroenterol 1989;11: 197-200.
115. Vohr BR, Rosenfield AG, Oh W: Umbilical hernia in low birth weight infants (less than 1500 grams). J Pediatr 1977;90:807-808.
116. Walker SH: The natural history of umbilical hernia. A six-year follow up of 314 negro children with this defect. Clin Pediatr (Phila) 1967;6:29-32.
117. Waltzer H: The umbilicus as vagina substitute. A clinical note. Psychoanal Q 1974;43:493-496.
118. Weir E: Navel gazing: A clinical glimpse at body piercing. Can Med Assoc J 2001;164:864.
119. Wesson DE, Baesl TJ: Repair of gastroschisis with preservation of the umbilicus. J Pediatr Surg 1986;21; 764-765.
120. Wilson CB, Ochs HD, Almquist J, et al: When is umbilical cord separation delayed? J Pediatr 1985;107:292-294.
121. Woods GE: Some observations on umbilical hernia in infants. Arch Dis Child 1953;28:450-462.
122. Yokoyama S, Hayashida Y, Nagahama J, et al: Rhabdomyosarcoma of the urachus. A case report. Acta Cytol 1997;41:1293-1298.
123. Yotsuyanagi T, Nihei Y, Sawada Y: A simple technique for reconstruction of the umbilicus, using two twisted flaps. Plast Reconstr Surg 1998;102:2444-2446.
124. Yuen JS, Chow PK, Koong HN, et al: Unusual sites (thorax and umbilical hernia sac) of endometriosis. J R Coll Surg Edinb 2001;46:313-315.
125. Zaidenstein L, Freud E, Schwartz M, et al: Clinical presentation of rare appendiculo-omphalic anomalies. J Pediatr Surg 1995;30:1702-1703.
126. Zupan J, Garner P, Omari AAA: Topical umbilical cord care at birth (Cochrane Review). Cochrane Database Syst Rev 2004;3:CD001057.

Chapter 73

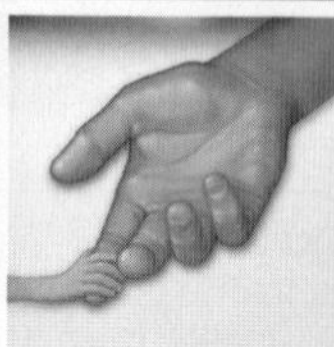

Congenital Defects of the Abdominal Wall

Michael D. Klein

HISTORY

Newborns with abdominal wall defects were reported in the first century AD by Aulus Cornelius Celsus, a Roman physician, and then by Paulus Aegineta in the fifth century.[67] Omphalocele is described in the 16th century printed works of Ambrose Paré,[123] and Lycosthenes may have been the first to describe gastroschisis at about the same time.[103] Taruffi introduced the term *gastroschisis* in 1894.[156] For many years gastroschisis was confused with an omphalocele that had a torn sac.[133] Moore and Stokes are credited with limiting it to the specific clinical entity as we understand it today,[112] although they give credit to earlier authors who used the term, such as Bernstein,[19] but not to the earliest collected series of Massabuau and Guibal.[107] The first successful repair of omphalocele was reported by Hey in 1802.[60] In 1873 Visick described the successful repair of gastroschisis.[166] Ahlfeld[1] in 1899 described painting an omphalocele sac with alcohol to produce an eschar and awaiting contraction and epithelialization. The use of mercurochrome for painting the sac was popularized by Max Grob,[52,53,122] although toxic effects of mercurochrome were described later.[32,46,150] A modern version was introduced by Ein and Shandling, who used an adhesive semipermeable artificial membrane.[45] Olshausen in 1887 first reported skin flap coverage of defects after removal of the membrane,[120] and Gross further demonstrated its effectiveness and popularized the technique.[56] Staged closure of the resultant hernia could be difficult because of failure of the abdominal cavity to grow without the impetus of the intestines within it and because of intestinal adhesions to the skin flaps. For this reason, the skin was sometimes closed over an intact omphalocele sac.[55,105] In 1967 Schuster introduced staged reduction of large omphaloceles with prosthetic material because he noted that the abdominal cavity did not grow with skin closure alone.[142] New techniques continue to be described. The fact that no operative technique has achieved universal success or acceptance is attested to by the many ingenious methods that have been devised, including skin grafting,[73,99] pneumoperitoneum to stretch the abdominal wall in preparation for closure,[119,130] partial hepatectomy,[27,78] lateral relaxing incisions in the fascia,[14] and division of the rectus abdominis muscles.[85]

SPECTRUM OF CLINICAL CONGENITAL ABDOMINAL WALL DEFECTS

The clinically important defects are all umbilical with intact rectus abdominis muscles (Table 73-1). Omphalocele is a large defect (greater than 4 cm) covered by amniotic membrane that contains midgut and other abdominal organs, including the liver and often the spleen and gonad (Fig. 73-1). One unusual form of omphalocele is the cephalic fold defect, or pentalogy of Cantrell, in which the abdominal wall defect is supraumbilical and the heart is in the sac through a defect in the pericardium and the central tendon of the diaphragm.[29] Ectopia cordis thoracis (when the heart is outside the chest with no pericardial covering as opposed to being

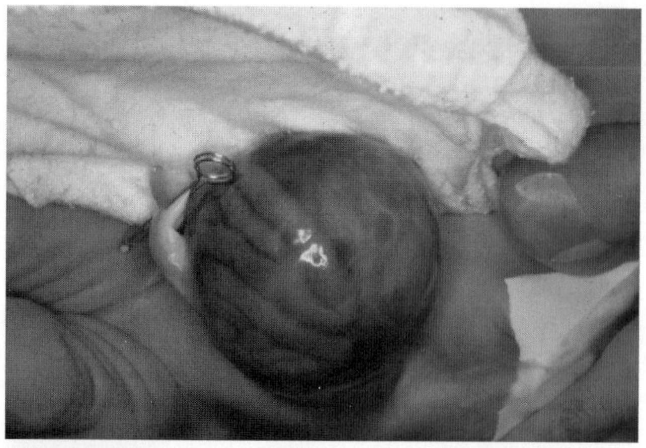

Figure 73–1 Omphalocele.

TABLE 73-1 Comparison of Congenital Abdominal Wall Defects

Defect	Site	Sac	Contents	Frequency	Associated Anomalies	Outcome
Omphalocele—lateral fold	Umbilicus	Yes	Liver, intestine, spleen, gonad	Common	Chromosomal, cardiac	Good (depending on associated anomalies)
Omphalocele— cephalic fold (pentalogy of Cantrell)	Superior umbilicus	Yes	Liver, intestine	Rare	Cardiac, sternal cleft, pericardial defect, central tendon diaphragm defect	Poor
Omphalocele—caudal fold (cloacal exstrophy)	Inferior umbilicus	Yes	Intestine	Rare	Bladder exstrophy, imperforate anus, epispadias	Fair
Umbilical cord hernia	Umbilicus	Yes	Intestine	Unusual	Uncommon	Good
Gastroschisis	Right umbilicus	No	Intestine	Common	Intestinal atresia	Good
Ectopia cordis thoracis	Midline sternum	No	Heart	Rare	Cardiac	Poor

inside the omphalocele sac) might be considered a form of a cephalic fold defect (Fig. 73-2). Another unusual omphalocele is the caudal fold defect, cloacal exstrophy, in which the defect is infraumbilical and accompanied by exstrophy of the bladder and imperforate anus (see Chapter 118). Gastroschisis is less than 4 cm in diameter, has no covering membrane, and usually contains only the midgut with the stomach (Fig. 73-3). Umbilical cord hernia is also less than 4 cm and contains only the midgut, but it is covered by a membrane (Fig. 73-4). Umbilical hernia is distinguished from these anomalies by two features: the defect is covered by normal skin, and it is only rarely present at birth, instead usually becoming apparent in the first weeks or months of life. In the literature before 1970 and in the literature outside pediatric surgery even today, these three forms were often confused, particularly omphalocele and gastroschisis, thus making it difficult to interpret the data.

Infants with congenital abdominal wall muscular deficiency, or prune-belly, syndrome have all the normal layers of the abdominal wall, but very little muscle in the loose areolar tissue. Much of the morbidity is related to similar muscular deficiency in the genitourinary and gastrointestinal tracts (see Chapter 114).

Other abdominal wall defects, often incompatible with life,[97,127,154] have been described in humans,[9,30] including true absence of abdominal wall structures with evisceration of bowel.[49,109]

EMBRYOLOGY

Embryology of the Abdominal Wall

At 3 weeks' gestation the flat cellular disk of the embryo develops four folds that will enclose the body cavities (Fig. 73-5A and B). Two lateral folds form the pleuroperitoneal canals once they meet anteriorly in the midline. The cephalic fold brings down with it the developing heart, which actually began distal to the brain, but now takes its place within the anterior chest wall. It also carries the septum transversum, which continues posteriorly and divides the pleuroperitoneal canals into the pleural and peritoneal cavities. The caudal fold brings with it the developing bladder or allantois, which started off (in the flat disk embryo) distal to the anus. During this process the gut tube has formed along the length of the embryo with a communication at the umbilicus to the yolk sac;

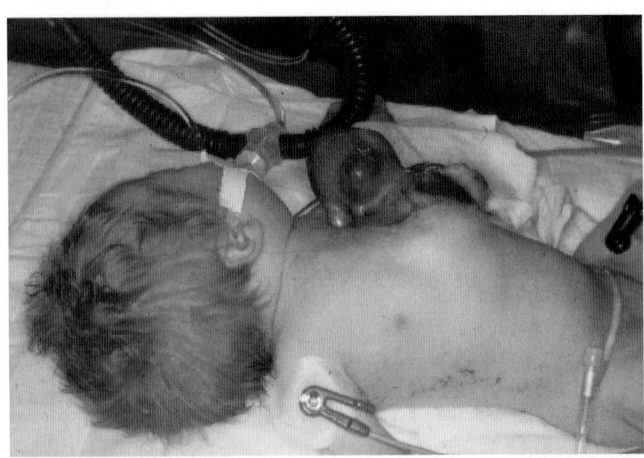
Figure 73-2 Ectopia cordis. *(See color plate.)*

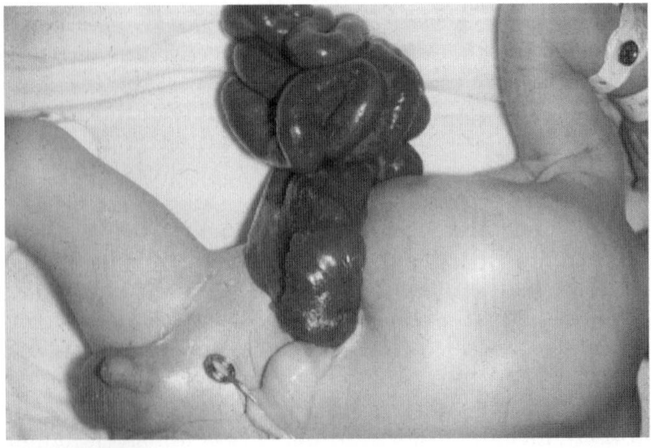
Figure 73-3 Gastroschisis.

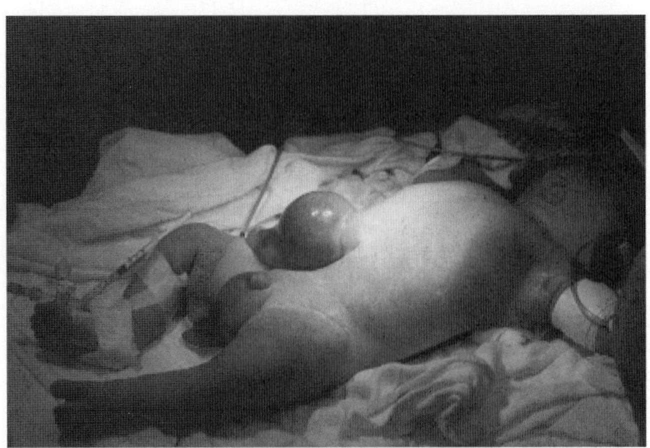

Figure 73–4 Umbilical cord hernia.

the yolk sac will eventually disappear, sometimes leaving a vitelline duct remnant on the distal ileum. At about 5 weeks' gestation, this gut tube will begin to elongate and develop within the umbilical coelom (Fig. 73-5C), a cavity in the body stalk on the anterior surface of the embryo. At about 10 weeks' gestation the gut returns from the space within the umbilical stalk to the peritoneal cavity and undergoes rotation and fixation.

Embryogenesis of the Defects

Omphalocele represents a failure of the body folds to complete their journey.[43] Most omphaloceles are lateral fold defects and are always at the umbilicus. The rectus muscles often insert far apart on the costal margins and for this reason cannot be brought entirely together in a repair. Whatever the insult may be that causes it, this aberration occurs early in embryogenesis and is thus likely to

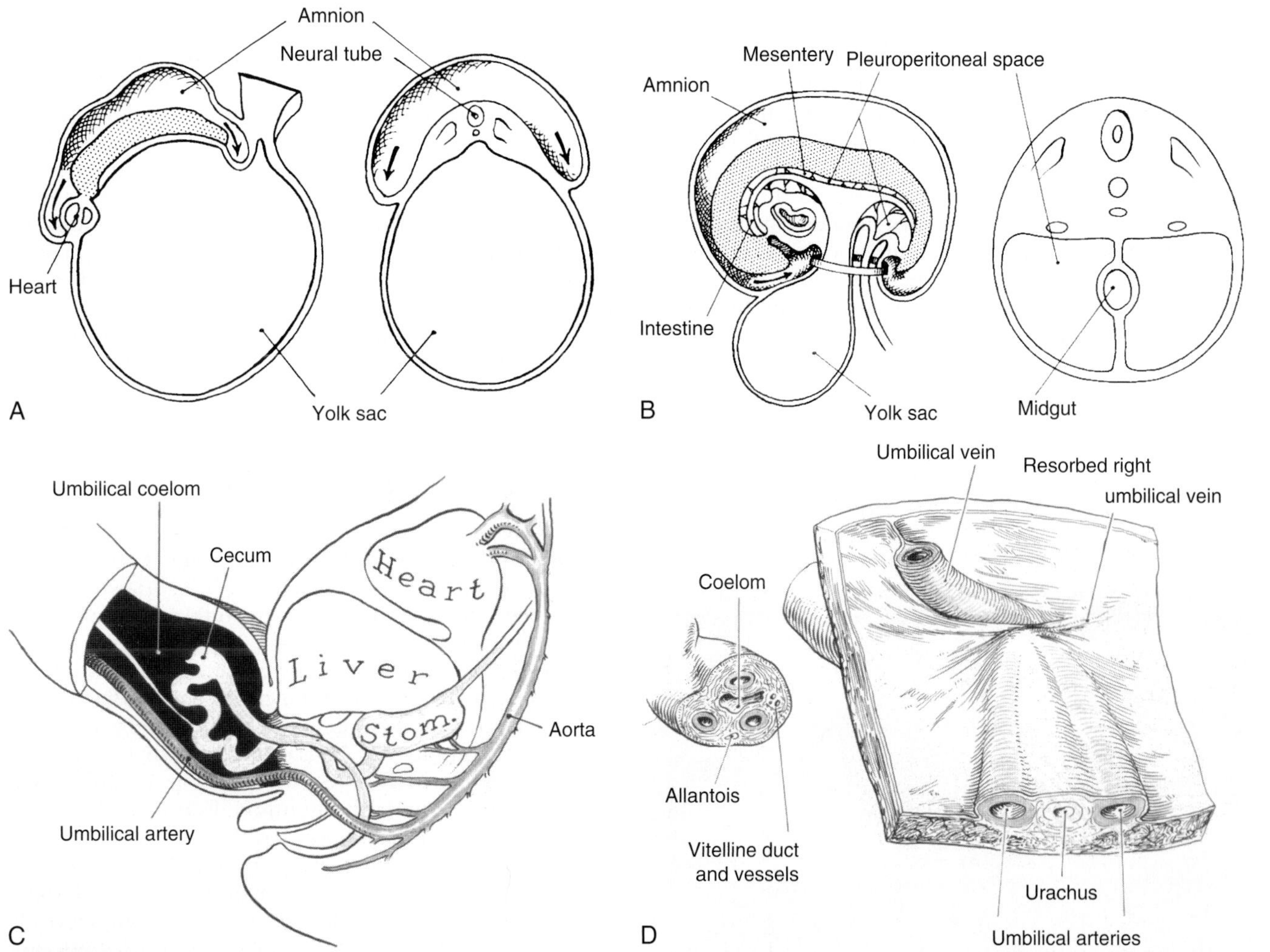

Figure 73–5 Embryology of the abdominal wall. *A,* Two-week embryo as a flat disk before folding to form the body cavities. *B,* At 4 weeks the folding is complete. The gut tube is about to be pinched off the yolk sac. *C,* At 6 weeks the elongating midgut enters the umbilical coelom. *D,* A view from inside the abdominal cavity showing the relatively unsupported right side of the umbilicus as a result of resorption of the right umbilical vein.

affect other organ systems as well, so children with omphalocele frequently have associated anomalies. Cephalic fold defects result in ectopia cordis or the pentalogy of Cantrell, whereas caudal fold defects cause bladder and cloacal exstrophy. Ectopia cordis thoracis may be better explained by mechanical disruption caused by bands formed with rupture of the chorion or yolk sac. These children often have other stigmata of band disruptions such as facial clefts.[70]

Gastroschisis, antenatal exposure of the viscera, is probably caused by failure of the umbilical coelom to develop.[76] The elongating intestine then has no space in which to expand and ruptures out the body wall just to the right of the umbilicus, possibly because the right side of the umbilicus is relatively unsupported as a result of resorption of the right umbilical vein at about 4 weeks' gestation (Fig. 73-5D).[144] Thus, gastroschisis has no covering membrane. In gastroschisis the bowel is usually thickened, matted, edematous, and covered with a fibrinous peel. Some have explained the latter appearance on the basis of the change in amniotic fluid electrolyte composition with the onset of fetal kidney function.[4,79,159,160] There is evidence from studies in animals both that the peel forms in utero[34,102,138] and that it is a postnatal event.[38] Some investigators have related the condition of the bowel to the presence of meconium from the fetus in the amniotic fluid.[116,120] In a recent clinical study, neonates delivered with meconium staining had a fibrinous peel, whereas those without staining had none.[116] Our clinical observation of more than 50 deliveries indicates that the appearance of the bowel is most likely a postnatal event (Fig. 73-6). At the moment of birth, the bowel in gastroschisis is usually quite normal. Twenty minutes later it begins to acquire the characteristic changes. These changes may be due to exposure to air, but more likely they are related to mesenteric venous occlusion at the level of the abdominal wall defect with resultant edema and transudation of proteinaceous fluid.

Umbilical cord hernia is a simple failure of the midgut to return to the peritoneal cavity at 10 to 12 weeks. Thus this defect contains only midgut and is covered by a membrane. Such hernias are much smaller than omphaloceles and have a better outlook. Distinguishing umbilical cord hernia from omphalocele both embryologically and clinically is important in managing patients and reporting results. Margulies[106] first translated the embryologic work of Pernkopf[124] and Politzer and Sternberg[126] into English, which permitted Benson, Penberthy, and Hill[18] to recognize it as a separate clinical entity.

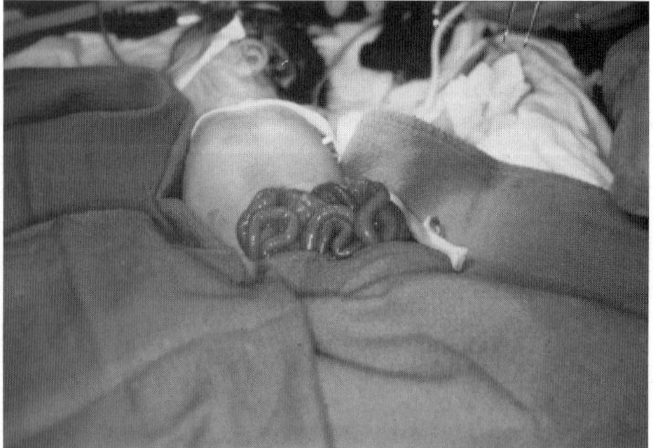

Figure 73-6 Gastroschisis at delivery. The bowel does not appear matted, edematous, and coated with a fibrinous peel.

Alternative explanations for these various defects, especially gastroschisis, have been presented but are not generally accepted. Some have thought that gastroschisis must represent "failure of mesodermalization" with actual absence of abdominal wall components.[66,68] Although such anomalies have been reported, they are usually stillborn monstrosities. Nearly all live-born children with abdominal wall defects have intact abdominal walls with normal muscle layers. Others have reported that some abdominal wall defects are not developmental but acquired as a result of interruption of blood flow at the umbilicus.[63] This explanation does not account for the associated anomalies in some defects, nor the fact that the abdominal wall is really normal in these defects and it is only the umbilical opening that is large and abnormal. One study has implicated cigarette smoking, especially when combined with maternal use of other vasoconstrictive agents.[170] Many early reports state that gastroschisis is an omphalocele with a ruptured or torn sac.[158] The fact that no gastroschisis has so much as a remnant of a sac argues against this.

There are several animal models of abdominal wall defects induced by exogenous agents. Although some of the defects are called omphaloceles in these reports, they really resemble gastroschisis, rachischisis, or an unusual body wall deformity that would be incompatible with life. Such studies raise the issue of whether the apparent increase in incidence of gastroschisis since 1970 might be due to new environmental teratogens.[42] Whereas one investigator found no association between possible teratogens and gastroschisis,[95] others have implicated birth control pills, aspirin,[83,169] and illegal substances.[63]

Genetics and Familial Occurrence

There are rare reports of abdominal wall defects, mainly omphaloceles, occurring in families and even in twins; however, they are not very common.[129,134] No specific genes have been identified with congenital abdominal wall defects, yet they certainly do occur as part of syndromes. Beckwith-Wiedemann syndrome (congenital abdominal wall defect, macroglossia, and hypoglycemia with a propensity for the development of abdominal tumors later in life) is the most common.[17,172] It is remarkable that the abdominal wall defect in Beckwith-Wiedemann syndrome can be any of the three aforementioned entities and yet we presume that they all have a different embryogenesis. Other syndromes involving these defects are OEIS (omphalocele, exstrophy, imperforate anus, and spinal anomalies),[144] Gershoni-Baruch syndrome (omphalocele, diaphragmatic hernia, cardiovascular abnormalities, and radial ray defects), which is probably autosomal recessive,[48] Donnai-Barrow syndrome (diaphragmatic hernia, exomphalos, absent corpus callosum, hypertelorism, myopia, and sensorineural deafness), which is most likely autosomal recessive,[31] and Fryns' syndrome (congenital diaphragmatic hernia, coarse facies, acral hypoplasia, and often omphalocele[8]).[13] OEIS is closely related to caudal fold omphalocele and may be related to a specific gene.[157] Omphalocele is also more likely to be associated with a chromosomal anomaly,[136,175] especially trisomy 13, 18, or 21.[28,131,148]

There is very little clinical suspicion of a genetic role in gastroschisis, but one study found that 6% of patients with gastroschisis had a relative with a similar diagnosis when a careful family history was taken.[161] In a mouse model, gastroschisis has been reported to occur with deletion of the gene for aortic carboxypeptidase-like protein.[90]

ANTENATAL CONSIDERATIONS

Ultrasound

Today, the diagnosis is usually made antenatally by ultrasound (US).[150] Omphalocele can be distinguished from gastroschisis by the presence of a sac and from umbilical cord hernia by the presence of the liver in the defect. The diagnosis allows for antenatal counseling, which given the generally good prognosis, can be reassuring. In a report from 11 European antenatal US registries, the sensitivity for detecting omphalocele was 75% (range, 25% to 100%), and that for gastroschisis was 83% (18% to 100%).[15] The first age at which omphalocele was detected was 18 ± 6 weeks, and gastroschisis, 20 ± 7 weeks. Only 41% of fetuses with omphaloceles detected antenatally were live-born. Twenty-two percent were fetal deaths, and in 37% the pregnancies were terminated. Fifty-nine percent of fetuses with gastroschisis were live-born, with 12% being fetal deaths and 29% terminations.

Antenatal US also detects associated anomalies.[64] In gastroschisis these anomalies are usually intestinal atresias.[10] The frequency of associated cardiac anomalies in omphalocele makes antenatal echocardiography very helpful.[163]

Given the poor outcome of all forms of ectopia cordis, termination could be a reasonable alternative when US demonstrates the heart outside the chest. Some ultrasonographers have attempted to correlate the bowel problems of gastroschisis with the antenatal appearance on US,[11,86,127] but this has not been successful in all centers, including our own recent experience.[5,26]

Routine use of antenatal US in general has not been definitively shown to improve perinatal morbidity or maternal outcome, although there may be some survival benefit for a fetus with a life-threatening anomaly. There may, however, be a cost savings, mainly related to the mother choosing termination of pregnancy. Such has not been the case for either omphalocele or gastroschisis.[165]

Amniotic Fluid and Serum Tests

Elevated alpha fetoprotein (AFP) in both maternal serum and amniotic fluid and elevated amniotic fluid acetylcholinesterase (AChE) have been correlated with abdominal wall defects when there is no myelomeningocele.[114] In a study of 23 pregnancies with gastroschisis and 17 with omphalocele, second-trimester serum AFP was 9.42 times greater than normal in gastroschisis and 4.18 times normal in omphalocele.[137] Another study found elevated amniotic fluid AFP in 100% of pregnancies with gastroschisis and in only 20% of those with omphalocele. AChE was elevated in 80% of pregnancies with gastroschisis and 27% of those with omphaloceles.[162]

OBSTETRIC DELIVERY

Intuitively, it may seem appropriate to deliver these patients by cesarean section to avoid injury to the bowel or tearing of the omphalocele sac, and some reports claim a benefit for cesarean section.[44,93,135] There is also, however, a report of two patients with gastroschisis whose bowel was injured during cesarean section delivery.[40] The more recent obstetric literature finds no benefit of cesarean section.[58,62,94,143,147,153] Some reports even show no benefit with referral of the mother for delivery in a pediatric surgery center.[117,152] One must conclude that the mode of delivery is a decision to be made by the obstetrician on the basis of obstetric indications, not necessarily on the presence of an abdominal wall defect.

The belief that the condition of the bowel in gastroschisis is due to a relatively late (33 weeks) intrauterine event has led some to recommend preterm delivery.[111] Because we think that the condition of the bowel is a postnatal event, we do not believe that it is worth the risks of prematurity. It seems most likely that the good results observed with preterm delivery by planned cesarean section are related to the fact that it allows for immediate repair and avoids the venous congestion of the mesentery and its effect on the intestine. Others have also found no benefit of preterm delivery.[44]

Antenatal intervention has been suggested for gastroschisis, but is as yet unproven. Based on experimental studies indicating that it is amniotic fluid that causes the bowel damage in gastroschisis,[3] physicians in Turkey have performed amniotic fluid exchange in one patient and believed that it was responsible for the normal appearance of the bowel at delivery.[2] Amnioinfusion of normal saline has been used in France for pregnancies with gastroschisis and oligohydramnios, with apparent improvement in the character of the bowel at delivery.[139,167]

Antenatal counseling and coordination with the obstetric team are essential. Because the condition of the bowel in gastroschisis and distention of the bowel and size of the liver in omphalocele are often related to the time between delivery and repair, it is important to make arrangements for repair as soon as possible after delivery.

CLINICAL FEATURES

Omphalocele

Omphalocele is a central abdominal wall defect, usually larger than 4 cm in diameter. It is always covered by a translucent sac from which the umbilical cord extends. The sac may be torn during delivery, but this is unusual. The muscles of the abdominal wall are normal; however, the rectus abdominis muscles insert laterally on the costal margins, thereby creating a depression defect superiorly. The sac usually contains the liver, midgut, and frequently other organs such as the spleen or gonad. Babies with omphalocele are usually full term.

Incidence

Before 1970, omphalocele was the most common of the abdominal wall defects; it is now the second after gastroschisis. The overall incidence is 1 to 2.5 per 5000 live births,[107] with a male preponderance.[28]

Associated Conditions

Conditions associated with omphalocele are listed in Table 73-2. As many as 45% of patients with omphalocele have been reported to have a cardiac abnormality, including ventricular septal defect, atrial septal defect, ectopia cordis, tricuspid atresia, coarctation of the aorta, and persistent pulmonary hypertension of the newborn.[51] Chromosomal abnormalities can be found in up to 40%,[118] and an association with Down's syndrome has also been reported.[131] Patients with omphalocele are more likely to be large for gestational age (macrosomia or greater than 4 kg in birth weight).[168] Musculoskeletal and neural tube defects are also reported in greater than expected incidence.[7,98] Gastroesophageal reflux is more likely, with 43% being affected in one study,[81] and at 1 year of age 33% may have cryptorchidism.[71]

Cephalic Fold Omphalocele (Pentalogy of Cantrell)

The five elements of this pentalogy are remarkably constant.[29] There is a supraumbilical omphalocele, which may contain only the liver or mainly the liver. Through the translucent sac one can often see the heart or a left ventricular diverticulum that has extruded through the diaphragmatic defect. Also present are a lower sternal cleft, a defect in the central tendon of the diaphragm, a defect in the pericardium, and an intracardiac abnormality.

Ectopia Cordis Thoracis

In this rare anomaly the heart has no pericardium and protrudes from between the two halves of the split sternum with the apex pointing up toward the chin. There are usually associated intracardiac anomalies and occasionally other anomalies such as an associated abdominal wall defect that is not part of the pentalogy of Cantrell.

TABLE 73-2 Associated Conditions

Omphalocele	Gastroschisis
Cardiac	Intestinal atresia
Chromosomal	Small for gestational age
Down's syndrome	Premature
Macrosomia	Gastroesophageal reflux
Gastroesophageal reflux	Cryptorchidism
Cryptorchidism	
Musculoskeletal	
Neural tube defects	

Caudal Fold Omphalocele (Cloacal Exstrophy, Vesicointestinal Fissure)

Unlike the cephalic fold defect, the elements of this anomaly are extremely variable. There is usually an infraumbilical omphalocele that seldom contains the liver, exstrophy of the bladder with associated epispadias, diastasis of the pubic rami, and an imperforate anus. The ileum prolapses between the two halves of the exstrophied bladder. The clinical issues are discussed in detail in Chapter 118.

Gastroschisis

In contrast to omphalocele, gastroschisis is a small defect, usually less than 4 cm. It occurs adjacent to the umbilicus just to the right of the cord in all but a few rare instances. Occasionally, a skin bridge may be present between the cord and the defect, but the abdominal wall and its muscles are normal. There is no sac or remnant of a sac. The midgut is herniated through the defect and occasionally a gonad as well. At birth the bowel can appear perfectly normal, but more than 20 minutes after birth, the extruded intestine may be thickened and covered with a fibrinous exudate matted together so that individual loops cannot be distinguished. There have been several reports of gastroschisis with a small remnant of midgut appearing above a defect that has essentially closed, most likely caused by antenatal volvulus.[21,36]

Gastroschisis in the fetus is probably associated with intrauterine distress. Neonates with gastroschisis are more frequently premature and commonly have respiratory problems. Even term babies with gastroschisis are more likely to be small for gestational age[24,25,50] and to have younger mothers.[33]

Incidence

Gastroschisis has become the most common of the abdominal wall defects over the last 30 years.[12,72,108,136] This may be related to the increased incidence of prematurity and the increased survival of premature infants in general or to the fact that it was not until the 1970s that distinction between gastroschisis and omphalocele was regularly made.[76] The incidence is about 2 to 4.9 per 10,000 live births,[12,88,108,132] with a male preponderance.[28]

Associated Conditions

The anomalies associated with gastroschisis are usually related to the midgut, with the most common being intestinal atresia (see Table 73-2).[149] In the first year of life infants with gastroschisis are very likely to have gastroesophageal reflux (16%)[81] and undescended testicle (15%), although the latter often corrects spontaneously.[71,89]

Umbilical Cord Hernia

This uncommon defect is generally small and occurs at the umbilicus, with the umbilicus extending from it. It is covered with a sac and often confused with omphalocele. The differences are that it contains only midgut, never liver, and the abdominal wall above the defect is normal, with the rectus muscles meeting in the midline at the xiphoid. Few associated anomalies are reported with this defect. Like all abdominal defects in which the midgut has not returned to the abdominal cavity before birth to allow for rotation and fixation, these patients have malrotation, although it is not usually a cause of intestinal obstruction.

TREATMENT

Omphalocele

Initial Care

Although the bowel in omphalocele is protected by the sac, surgery is still urgently needed to increase the chance for primary closure. A nasogastric (NG) tube should be placed early to keep the intestines decompressed. A rectal examination aids this with evacuation of meconium. Maintenance of body temperature is especially important (see Chapter 6). Ventilator support and supplemental oxygen should be supplied as needed.

Because of the frequency of associated heart defects, cardiology evaluation and echocardiography are in order, although the results will not delay repair. The most common defect is a ventricular septal defect, which will seldom be symptomatic until the compliance of the newborn ventricles changes during the first week of life to left ventricular predominance.

Intravenous fluids are provided at maintenance rates, best through an upper extremity. If not done at birth, 1 mg of vitamin K should be administered, as well as prophylactic antibiotics. If the defect has been diagnosed antenatally at our center, we repair the defect immediately in the delivery room, as we do for gastroschisis. We believe that this strategy improves the chance for immediate fascial closure.

The value of primary closure has been debated. Some believe that staged closure is so successful that it is preferable to avoid the possible complications of increased abdominal pressure, which include respiratory compromise, decreased venous return with decreased urine output and cardiac output, compromise of the blood supply to the intestine, and acidosis related to kinking of the hepatic veins as the liver is reduced. Nonoperative initial treatment (painting the sac with an antiseptic) is still useful when operative closure is not possible.[82]

Operative Closure

In the operating room the sac and abdomen are prepared with an antiseptic and excess cord is removed. If the patient is hypoxic or unstable, we cannulate and preserve the umbilical artery or vein (or both) for transplantation to the lateral abdominal wall for postoperative monitoring, but this is rarely needed.[47] We always use plastic adhesive edge drapes to preserve heat. We first attempt to reduce the abdominal contents with the sac intact, as a number of reports suggest.[59,74,178] Such reduction is often impossible either because the abdominal cavity is too small or because the sac is adherent to the liver and falciform ligament. We then incise the skin a few millimeters from the sac circumferentially around the defect and elevate skin flaps until the rectus muscles can be identified. At this point the sac is excised with ligation of the umbilical vessels and urachus. Any sac adherent to the liver is divided such that some remnants are left on the liver. If the viscera cannot be reduced, it is helpful to stretch the abdominal wall manually in a posterior-to-anterior direction. The intestine is replaced first and then the liver. The liver effectively holds the intestine in place, and if skin flap closure should be necessary, the secondary operation will be much safer. For primary closure, mattress sutures are placed through all layers of the abdominal wall except the skin. It is important to place these sutures through the rectus abdominis muscles and not just through the midline fascia, which may result in a postoperative hernia. It will not be possible to appose the rectus muscles in the upper portion of the incision because they insert broadly on the costal margin. It is also not necessary because the liver fills this space. Turning anterior rectus fascial flaps to cover this defect has been suggested, but we have not found this to be necessary. It is best to place the abdominal sutures without tying them and then pull alternate sutures to either side to see how the patient will tolerate fascial closure. If the anesthesiologist can ventilate the patient with less than 25 cm H_2O, closure is safe. The skin is closed with a running suture, and in most patients this makes a scar that looks like an umbilicus. In addition, several methods have been described for performing a cosmetic umbilicoplasty at the initial operation.[57,84,92,173] It often suffices to close the skin incision in a subcuticular purse-string fashion with absorbable suture material while taking every second or third bite to the fascia. However, frequently not enough skin is available for most of these procedures. In many cases the skin will have a tenuous vascular supply and appear blanched. Adhesive tape should not be used for a wound dressing.

Other methods have been suggested to determine whether the fascial closure is too tight: a saphenous vein intravenous line that will not drip by gravity or intravesical or NG tube pressure greater than 20 cm H_20.[85,171] If the fascial closure is judged to be too tight, one can consider only skin closure, but in our experience, if the closure is still too tight after the maneuvers suggested, the skin closure will also probably be too tight. In this case the viscera can be covered with a prosthetic silo that will allow slow reduction of the abdominal viscera over a 1-week period. The simplest of these devices is the preformed Silastic chimney with a spring-loaded ring at the bottom, which is placed though the defect beneath the edges of the abdominal wall (Fig. 73-7).[141] It is helpful to suture this ring to the abdominal wall to prevent the ring from extruding as pressure is applied to reduce the viscera. Antibiotic ointment is applied around the edges as a dressing. If this device (or an appropriate size of this device) is not available, one can use 0.007-inch-thick Dacron-reinforced Silastic. We suture one piece to each

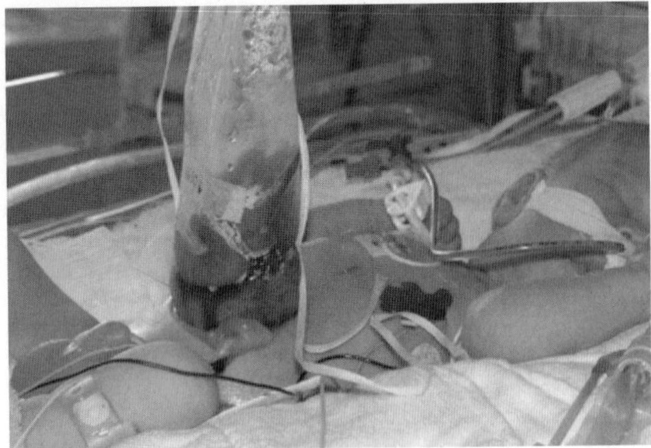

Figure 73-7 Gastroschisis with bowel contained in a preformed Silastic silo.

side of the abdominal wall so that the knots are on the outside and the edges of both the fascia and Silastic face out. We then separately suture up the inferior and superior edges and over the top (Fig. 73-8).

We do not perform a Ladd procedure or appendectomy. If a testicle is present in the sac, it can be placed in the abdominal cavity because in most cases it will be in the scrotum in a year. If an obvious atresia is present, we will bring out a single stoma through normal abdominal wall and wait at least 3 weeks before performing an anastomosis.

Giant omphalocele presents a special problem when the defect is so large that even after staged reduction of the intestinal contents with a Silastic prosthesis, neither fascia nor skin can be brought over the defect. Several techniques have been proposed to deal with this problem, including the use of skin flaps with grafting to the open areas remaining.[177] One group has reported using absorbable mesh to stabilize the defect and then either mobilizing skin flaps or using skin grafts over the granulation tissue that forms.[16] However, intestinal fistula is a risk with this technique. We have tried on several occasions to use Gore-Tex and then place skin flaps or grafts over the Gore-Tex, with failure on each occasion as a result of sepsis and sloughing. However, it has been possible to use flaps or grafts on the granulating surface that occurs after removing the Gore-Tex, and the underlying pseudocapsule seems to stabilize the abdominal wall. The use of tissue expanders in older infants is also appealing.[39]

Postoperative Care

With primary closure, most patients require assisted ventilation initially, but over a period of several days the abdominal wall accommodates the abdominal contents. Intravenous fluids are administered at 150 mL/kg/hr or more to maintain urine output at 1 mL/kg/hr. A central intravenous line is placed for parenteral nutrition. Short-term antibiotics are administered if primary closure has been performed, but antibiotics are continued until completion of staged closure with a prosthesis. The wound is managed with antibiotic ointment and the sutures are removed at 3 weeks. We keep a 10-French sumped NG tube on low intermittent suction until there is evidence of bowel function, including stooling, decreased distention, and reduced NG tube output. The tube is then removed and 12 hours later feedings are begun gradually. It is not unusual for the appearance of bowel function to be delayed. If intestinal function has not resumed in 3 weeks, a small bowel contrast study may be indicated.

If a prosthesis has been used, it is usually appropriate to initiate reduction of the abdominal contents on postoperative day 1. Reduction is accomplished simply by manual manipulation, which can then be secured in many ways: applying long clamps suspended by umbilical tape to the overhead warmer, applying a TIA 90 stapler, running a suture back and forth, or using umbilical cord clamps (Fig. 73-9). A particularly ingenious method is a ringer mechanism described by Sawin et al.,[140] but it is not commercially available. Simply tying the prosthetic sac with umbilical tape leaves a larger circular defect than closing it side to side does. One might even consider adding several sutures to each side outside the prosthesis

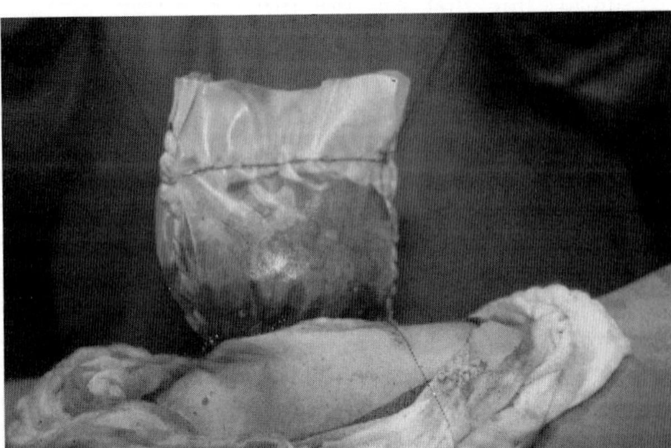

Figure 73-8 Gastroschisis with bowel contained in a hand-sewn Silastic silo.

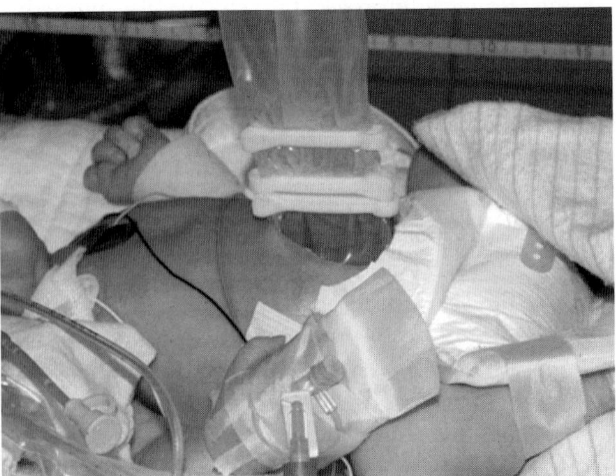

Figure 73-9 Reduction of intestine contained in a preformed Silastic silo.

when it is applied. These sutures can then be tied once the prosthesis is flat to further appose the edges.

Despite Schuster's original hypothesis, it is unlikely that the abdominal wall grows during reduction.[142] It is more likely that the edema of the bowel wall resolves and the intestinal contents are emptied while the abdominal wall is simply stretched.

The several methods of measuring intra-abdominal pressure discussed earlier were originally used to monitor primarily closure and then reduction of a prosthesis. The most important lesson learned from these studies is that we had been reducing the abdominal contents too slowly, usually every other day. It is important to be aggressive. Most often the prosthesis can be removed and the abdominal wall closed in 7 days. If it is not performed by 14 days, the prosthesis may begin to separate from the abdominal wall because it is not incorporated into tissue. Recently, Jona has suggested that active reduction may not be necessary.[69] In his small series no pressure was applied to the silo and the abdominal contents spontaneous reduced by day 8.

If skin flaps have been used, the definitive repair can be done at any time, depending on the patient's general condition. If the intestine begins to grow into a large skin sac instead of stretching the abdominal cavity, an abdominal binder can be used to direct forces inward. When it is time to bring the fascia together, the skin can be dissected off the liver with little trauma other than some mild bleeding that will stop with pressure. If the edges of the muscular abdominal wall cannot be brought together, a prosthetic mesh patch can be used as long as it can be entirely covered by healthy skin. If a part of it must be left exposed, it is unlikely to be incorporated and will become infected or extruded. If one can predict that skin flap closure will not be possible initially, it is probably best to avoid dissecting flaps so that that tissue will be healthier when it is time for the final repair.

If a postoperative hernia occurs, it can usually be repaired at 1 year of age without the use of a prosthetic patch. In occasional patients the hernia resolves spontaneously.

Ectopia Cordis Thoracis and Cephalic Fold Defect

Operative repair of ectopia cordis thoracis and cephalic fold defects is especially challenging. It is difficult to replace the heart in the thoracic cavity without kinking the great vessels or the pulmonary veins. Coverage with soft tissue to gain time can result in cardiac tamponade, so wide intrathoracic dissection around the heart and great vessels has been advocated to increase the space within the chest. In the cephalic fold defect (pentalogy of Cantrell), the sternal cleft and pericardial defect need no special treatment. We have used immediate skin closure of the omphalocele and allowed the patient to grow and have the intracardiac defect treated later. A Gore-Tex patch can then be used to close the central tendon of the diaphragm with no tension so that the heart can extend somewhat into the abdomen. With growth the patch becomes taut and elevates the heart slowly into the chest, which can grow to receive it. The fascia of the abdominal wall is closed once cardiorespiratory stability has been achieved. In ectopia cordis thoracis, it is also important to provide a rigid covering for the heart. This has been performed with rib struts between the sternal halves and with prosthetic material. Reported repairs of these difficult clinical problems emphasize creative use of available tissue and individual anatomic features.[61,91,113]

Caudal Fold Defect

This complex problem is more completely dealt with in Chapter 118. Initial management might consist of closure of the omphalocele and creation of a colostomy. Lund and others have discussed subsequent management.[100]

Gastroschisis

Initial Care

Two features of gastroschisis make initial care somewhat different from that of omphalocele. The patient is frequently premature, and closer attention must be paid to heat preservation, respiratory support, and the large surface area of exposed intestine. The latter is also responsible for increased fluid needs and heat loss. Perhaps the best way to control this problem is to place most of the infant immediately in a plastic drawstring bowel bag to control evaporative heat and fluid loss.[146] Because in most cases the intestine will be perfectly normal immediately after delivery whether the delivery is vaginal or cesarean, the faster the bowel can be reduced, the more likely primary closure can be achieved and the less bowel wall edema and fibrinous coating will accumulate.

We have chosen to deal with this issue by operating immediately after delivery.[35] Because our obstetricians prefer cesarean delivery for all children with abdominal wall defects, we can arrange for the entire pediatric surgical team to be ready in an adjacent operating room.

Operative Technique

Time is taken to wipe the vernix caseosa carefully from most of the baby to facilitate many of the subsequent maneuvers. If there is no immediate respiratory distress, an intravenous line is started, monitoring equipment is applied, and the patient is intubated. While the anesthesiologist is involved with these activities, the surgeon holds the umbilical cord up and, loop by loop, reduces the intestine. In most cases, by the time that the patient is ready for skin preparation, the bowel has been totally reduced. It is helpful to evacuate meconium from the rectum by anal dilatation. Other operative maneuvers and postoperative care are similar to that described for omphalocele. A very satisfactory cosmetic closure can be obtained for gastroschisis by leaving the entire umbilicus intact during the initial stages of the procedure (Fig. 73-10). The vessels and urachus can be divided at the level of the peritoneum after trimming the cord. A subcuticular skin

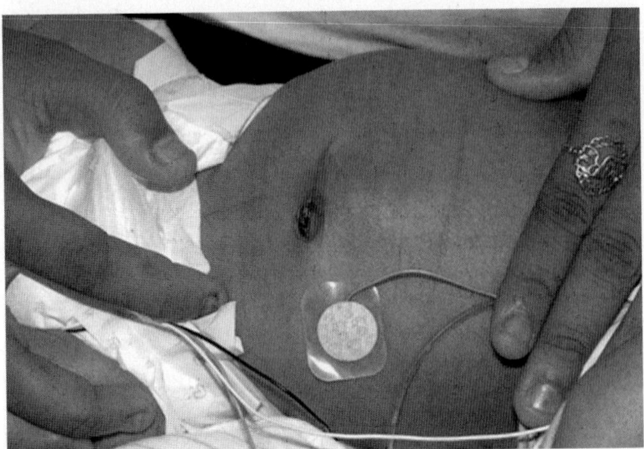

Figure 73-10 Gastroschisis with cosmetic closure obtained by preserving the umbilicus.

closure is then performed with the umbilicus being the left edge of the midportion of the incision, or often the entire incision, because the defect can often be quite small with gastroschisis or umbilical cord hernia.

In several centers the spring-loaded preformed Silastic pouch is frequently placed at the bedside on arrival of the patient.[110,174] Reduction can then be performed also at the bedside, and the patient is taken to the operating room only for final closure. Kidd et al. have found that with this technique, they perform fewer primary closures (34% versus 84%) and have a somewhat longer length of stay (38 days versus 30 days), but the mortality (3% excluding those with lethal associated anomalies) and time until full feeding are no different.[75] They did, however, report fewer ventilator days, infections, strictures, reoperations, and episodes of necrotizing enterocolitis. Bianchi et al. have also shown that waiting several hours to reduce the intestinal mass may not be as deleterious as has been supposed.[22,23]

Umbilical Cord Hernia

This defect is easily reduced by holding the sac upward and gently massaging the bowel into the peritoneal cavity. The fascia can always be closed primarily, and a cosmetic umbilicoplasty is nearly always feasible.

COMPLICATIONS

Complications may be related to prematurity (in gastroschisis), associated anomalies (in omphalocele), gastrointestinal tract anomalies (in gastroschisis), and a closure that is too tight. Mention has already been made of the increased fluid needs and delayed recovery of bowel function. It is important to be prepared to treat the problems of prematurity, including heat loss, respiratory failure, hyperbilirubinemia, hypoglycemia and hyperglycemia, and hypocalcemia. In managing respiratory distress it is important to obtain blood for capillary blood gas analysis from the upper extremities because the lower extremities are likely to be edematous and yield blood that is both lower in oxygen and higher in carbon dioxide than is representative. Patients with gastroschisis and ruptured omphalocele are frequently hypovolemic. Philippart et al. studied fluid resuscitation in patients with both gastroschisis and omphalocele by using muscle pH as an indication of adequate perfusion and resuscitation.[125] They found that all infants needed at least 25% of estimated blood volume during surgery (17 to 80 mL/kg in 45 to 120 minutes) and required 82 to 312 mL/kg in the first 24 hours of life. Urine output is a good monitor of volume in neonates. Treatment of most of the gastrointestinal tract anomalies can be delayed. In omphalocele, the bowel may be normal enough to sustain an anastomosis, but edema accumulates in all tissues and the liver expands with the length of the operation. In both gastroschisis and omphalocele, when necessary, an atresia can be replaced even without a stoma and dealt with 3 to 6 weeks later when the abdominal wall has healed.

A closure that is too tight can lead to ventilatory compromise, decreased venous return and low cardiac output, and oliguria. The remedy is to return the patient to the operating room to remove the fascial sutures and perform skin closure only. One may need to add a prosthesis. If a prosthesis has been used initially, it may be possible to open it at the bedside and reclose it more loosely. In omphalocele, postoperative metabolic acidosis can develop as a result of kinking of the hepatic veins from reduction of the liver. In this case, removal and refashioning of the prosthesis may be necessary.

All these patients tend to have a very slow onset of bowel function, no matter how quickly the defect is reduced or how normal the bowel appears. Bowel function seems to return faster in patients with omphalocele than in those with gastroschisis.[176] We try to be patient and will not perform a contrast study in an infant with no bowel function until 3 weeks have passed.

OUTCOME

Short Term

The survival rate is 90% in most series.[12,155] In a registry study in Texas, the survival rate of infants with gastroschisis was 93% in 1995-1997.[115] In a study from Manchester, a 94% gastroschisis survival rate was obtained.[41] Of the seven patients who died, five died of overwhelming sepsis. Primary fascial closure was achieved in 80%. The median time to feeding was 30 days (range, 5 to 60 days), and the median length of stay was 42 days (range, 11 to 183 days). Those who required a silo or had associated intestinal atresia (8 of 91 patients) required more time until feeding and had a greater length of stay, but no increased mortality.

Survival rates for omphalocele range from 70% to 95%, with most of the mortality being related to the associated cardiac and chromosomal anomalies.[155] Mabogunje and Mahour reported no difference in mortality from omphalocele for birth weight, size of the defect, or type of initial closure.[104] They also reported no significant change in mortality from 1960-1970 (23%) to 1970-1980, when it was 19%. Mortality was mainly related to associated anomalies. For their patients with gastroschisis, survival rates did increase in the more recent decade to 91%, and mortality was attributed to prematurity, bowel complications, and *Candida* sepsis associated with total parenteral nutrition.

There are few survivors of any form of ectopia cordis,[6,65] but Groner does report one normally active 12-year-old who wears a plastic shield to cover the as yet unreconstructed bony defect.[54]

At the Children's Hospital of Michigan in Detroit from 1990 through mid-2004 we treated 128 patients: 78 with gastroschisis (39 male and 39 female), 47 with omphalocele (28 male and 19 female), and 3 with umbilical cord hernia (all female). Mothers of patients with gastroschisis had an average age of 22, and the patients had an average birth weight of 2.5 kg and an average gestational age of 35.3 weeks. Mothers of patients with omphalocele had an average age of 29 years, and the patients had an average birth weight of 2.9 kg and an average gestational age of 36.6 weeks. Antenatal US had been performed in 62% of the mothers of patients with gastroschisis and in 79% of the mothers of patients with omphalocele.

The overall survival rate is 97%, 99% for gastroschisis and 94% for omphalocele, with the mortality being related to associated cardiac and chromosomal anomalies. Postoperative complications were noted in 9% of the patients with gastroschisis (wound problems, volvulus, sepsis, adhesions) and 17% of the patients with omphalocele (delay in tolerating feeding, bowel obstruction, oliguria, hemodynamic instability, metabolic acidosis, and cardiac arrest).

Long Term

In an Austrian study by Lunzer et al.,[101] four of seven survivors with omphalocele had serious associated anomalies (two with Beckwith-Wiedemann syndrome, one with a porencephalic cyst, and one with skeletal defects). These children had handicaps associated only with these anomalies and not with the omphalocele. The three other children are developing normally. One of 11 children with gastroschisis showed signs of mental retardation, and the other 10 are developing normally.

Davies and Stringer interviewed 25 of 35 patients who underwent surgery for gastroschisis between 1972 and 1984 and survived longer than 1 year.[37] Their median age was 16 years. Ninety-six percent were in good health and experienced normal growth, and 35% required further surgery related to gastroschisis, two for small bowel obstruction and three for scar revision. Fifty-seven percent reported that absence of an umbilicus caused them some distress during childhood. In 25 school-aged children with gastroschisis reported by Swartz et al., 7 were held back a grade or enrolled in special classes, but all participated in normal physical activities.[155] Eighty-four percent of these patients reported normal bowel movements. Those with abdominal complaints were usually evaluated as nonspecific or functional. Of 22 patients who required bowel resection at the initial operation, 10 had bowel complications, whereas only 2 of the 68 without a bowel resection had such complications. Ten percent of all patients underwent further surgery for abdominal wall hernia, scar revision, or undescended testis.

In a combined series of omphalocele and gastroschisis reported by Tunell et al., 94 patients had an 88% survival rate.[164] There was long-term follow-up in 61 patients for a mean of 14.2 years. Nineteen needed 31 reoperations, mainly for abdominal wall hernia and intestinal atresia. Eighty percent described their quality of life as good, but 40% were concerned about their height and felt inadequate in sports and social activities. Many also expressed concern about the absence of an umbilicus.

Another combined series with a mean age at follow-up of 8.8 years was reported by Lindham from Sweden.[96] He noted several episodes of bowel obstruction in the first year of life, recurrent abdominal pain without a specific abnormality, and some concern in girls about the scar and the absence of an umbilicus. Growth and development, however, were normal.

In a study by Davies and Stringer, patients with gastroschisis averaged the 32nd percentile for weight at 5 years of age and the 52nd percentile after that.[37] With complicated gastroschisis (such as gastroschisis associated with intestinal atresia), they reached only the 25th percentile. Berseth et al. from Stanford[20] found that most survivors of omphalocele and gastroschisis had poor weight gain. None had gastrointestinal or metabolic problems at 3 years of age based on imaging studies, fecal fat excretion, and serum chemistry. One third had IQ lower than 90, and this was related to the length of hospitalization and nongastrointestinal anomalies.

Koivusalo et al. from Finland sent detailed questionnaires to 75 patients older than 17 years with congenital abdominal wall defects (16 with omphalocele, 11 with gastroschisis) and received a response from 76%.[80] The only illness found more frequently than in the general population was rheumatoid arthritis in 7%. Thirty-seven percent reported some morbidity related to the scar and absence of the umbilicus, 51% had functional gastrointestinal disorders, and 12% had low self-esteem. Still, 88% reported that they were in good health, and their quality of life and educational levels were no different from that of the general population.

Adverse late cardiorespiratory and pulmonary effects are seldom found in patients with either omphalocele or gastroschisis.[176] Many children do express concern later in life about the absence of an umbilicus. Although both the short-term and long-term outlook for patients with ectopia cordis and both cephalic fold and caudal fold omphaloceles is guarded, patients with lateral fold omphalocele, umbilical cord hernia, and gastroschisis have an excellent survival rate and long-term prognosis. Most problems are related to associated conditions, not to the abdominal wall defect or its repair.

REFERENCES

1. Ahlfeld F: Der Alkohol bei der Behandlung inoperabeler Bauchbrüche. Monatsschr Geburtsh Gynäkol 1899;10:124.
2. Aktug T, Demir N, Akgur FM, et al: Pretreatment of gastroschisis with transabdominal amniotic fluid exchange. Obstet Gynecol 1998;91:821.

3. Aktug T, Ucan B, Olguner M, et al: Amnio-allantoic fluid exchange for the prevention of intestinal damage in gastroschisis. III: Determination of the waste products removed by exchange. Eur J Pediatr Surg 1998;8:326.
4. Albert A, Margarit J, Julia V, et al: Morphology and mucosal biochemistry of gastroschisis intestine in urine-free amniotic fluid. J Pediatr Surg 2003;38:1217.
5. Alsulyman OM, Monteiro H, Ouzounian JG, et al: Clinical significance of prenatal ultrasonographic intestinal dilatation in fetuses with gastroschisis. Am J Obstet Gynecol 1996;175:982.
6. Amato JJ, Zelen J, Talwalkar NG: Single stage repair of thoracic ectopia cordis. Ann Thorac Surg 1995;59:518.
7. Ardinger HH, Williamson RA, Grant S: Association of neural tube defects with omphalocele in chromosomally normal fetuses. Am J Med Genet 1987;27:135.
8. Arnold SR, Debich-Spicer DD, Opitz JM, et al: Documentation of anomalies not previously described in Fryns syndrome. Am J Med Genet 2003;116A:179.
9. Arroyo Carrera I, Pitarch V, Garcia MJ, et al: Unusual congenital abdominal wall defect and review. Am J Med Genet 2003;119A:211.
10. Axt R, Quijano F, Boos R, et al: Omphalocele and gastroschisis: Prenatal diagnosis and peripartal management. A case analysis of the years 1989-1997 at the Department of Obstetrics and Gynecology, University of Homburg/Saar. Eur J Obstet Gynecol Reprod Biol 1999;87:47.
11. Babcook CJ, Hedrick MH, Goldstein RB, et al: Gastroschisis: Can sonography of the fetal bowel accurately predict postnatal outcome? J Ultrasound Med 1994;13:701.
12. Baerg J, Kaban G, Tonita J, et al: Gastroschisis: A sixteen-year review. J Pediatr Surg 2003;38:771.
13. Bamforth JS, Leonard CO, Chodirker BN, et al: Congenital diaphragmatic hernia, coarse facies, and acral hypoplasia: Fryns syndrome. Am J Med Genet 1989;32:93.
14. Banfield EE: Congenital omphalocele. Northwest Med 1955;54:258.
15. Barisic I, Clementi M, Hausler M, et al: Evaluation of prenatal ultrasound diagnosis of fetal abdominal wall defects by 19 European registries. Ultrasound Obstet Gynecol 2001; 8:309.
16. Bawazir OA, Wong A, Sigalet DL: Absorbable mesh and skin flaps or grafts in the management of ruptured giant omphalocele. J Pediatr Surg 2003;38:725.
17. Beckwith JB, Wang CI, Donnell GN, et al: Hyperplastic fetal visceromegaly with macroglossia, omphalocele, cytomegaly of adrenal fetal cortex, postnatal somatic gigantism, and other abnormalities: Newly recognized syndrome. Proc Am Pediatr Soc 1964;41:16.
18. Benson CD, Penberthy GC, Hill EJ: Hernia into umbilical cord and omphalocele. Arch Surg 1949;58:833.
19. Bernstein P: Gastroschisis, a rare teratological condition in the newborn. Arch Pediatr 1940;57:505.
20. Berseth CL, Malachowski N, Cohn RB, Sunshine P: Longitudinal growth and late morbidity of survivors of gastroschisis and omphalocele. J Pediatr Gastroenterol Nutr 1982;1:375.
21. Bhatia AM, Musemeche CA, Crino JP: Gastroschisis complicated by midgut atresia and closure of the defect in utero. J Pediatr Surg 1996;31:1288.
22. Bianchi A, Dickson AP: Elective delayed reduction and no anesthesia: 'Minimal intervention management' for gastroschisis. J Pediatr Surg 1998;33:1338.
23. Bianchi A, Dickson AP, Alizai NK: Elective delayed midgut reduction—no anesthesia for gastroschisis: Selection and conversion criteria. J Pediatr Surg 2002;37:1334.
24. Blakelock R, Upadhyay V, Kimble R, et al: Is a normally functioning gastrointestinal tract necessary for normal growth in late gestation? Pediatr Surg Int 1998;13:17.
25. Blakelock RT, Upadhyay V, Pease PW, Harding JE: Are babies with gastroschisis small for gestational age? Pediatr Surg Int 1997;12:580.
26. Brun M, Grignon A, Guibaud L, et al: Gastroschisis: Are prenatal ultrasonographic findings useful for assessing the prognosis? Pediatr Radiol 1996;26:723.
27. Buchanan RW, Cain WL: A case of a complete omphalocele. Ann Surg 1965;143:552.
28. Calzolari E, Volpato S, Bianchi F, et al: Omphalocele and gastroschisis: A collaborative study of five Italian congenital malformation registries. Teratology 1993;47:47.
29. Cantrell JR, Haller JA, Ravitch MM: A syndrome of congenital defects involving the abdominal wall, sternum, diaphragm, pericardium, and heart. Surg Gynecol Obstet 1958; 107:602.
30. Castanon M, Guimaraes L, Tarrado X, et al: Congenital epigastric evisceration: A case report. J Pediatr Surg 2003; 38:1253.
31. Chassaing N, Lacombe D, Carles D, et al: Donnai-Barrow syndrome: Four additional patients. Am J Med Genet 2003;121A:258.
32. Clark JA, Kasselberg AG, Glick AD, O'Neill JA Jr: Mercury poisoning from merbromin (Mercurochrome) therapy of omphalocele: Correlation of toxicologic, histologic, and electron microscopic findings. Clin Pediatr (Phila) 1982; 21:445.
33. Colombani PM, Cunningham MD: Perinatal aspects of omphalocele and gastroschisis. Am J Dis Child 1977; 131:1386.
34. Correia-Pinto J, Tavares ML, Baptista MJ, et al: A new fetal rat model of gastroschisis: Development and early characterization. J Pediatr Surg 2001;36:213.
35. Coughlin JP, Drucker DE, Jewell MR, et al: Delivery room repair of gastroschisis. Surgery 1993;114:822.
36. Davenport M, Haugen S, Greenough A, Nicolaides K: Closed gastroschisis: Antenatal and postnatal features. J Pediatr Surg 2001;36:1834.
37. Davies BW, Stringer MD: The survivors of gastroschisis. Arch Dis Child 1997;77:158.
38. Deans KJ, Mooney DP, Meyer MM, et al: Prolonged intestinal exposure to amniotic fluid does not result in peel formation in gastroschisis. J Pediatr Surg 1999;34:975.
39. De Ugarte DA, Asch MJ, Hedrick MH, et al: The use of tissue expanders in the closure of a giant omphalocele. J Pediatr Surg 2004;39:613.
40. Dinatti LA, Meagher DP Jr, Martinez-Frontanilla LA: "Bucket handle" avulsion of intestine in gastroschisis. J Pediatr Surg 1993;28:840.
41. Driver CP, Bruce J, Bianchi A, et al: The contemporary outcome of gastroschisis. J Pediatr Surg 2000;35:1719.
42. Drongowski RA, Smith RK Jr, Coran AG, et al: Contribution of demographic and environmental factors to the etiology of gastroschisis: A hypothesis. Fetal Diagn Ther 1991;6:14.
43. Duhamel B: Embryology of exomphalos and allied malformations. Arch Dis Child 1963;38:142.
44. Dunn JC, Fonkalsrud EW, Atkinson JB: The influence of gestational age and mode of delivery on infants with gastroschisis. J Pediatr Surg 1999;34:1393.
45. Ein SH, Shandling B: A new nonoperative treatment of large omphaloceles with a polymer membrane. J Pediatr Surg 1978;13:255.
46. Fagan DG, Pritchard JS, Clark TW, Greenwood MR: Organ mercury levels in infants with omphaloceles treated with organic mercurial antiseptics. Arch Dis Child 1977;52:962.
47. Filston HC, Izant RJ: Translocation of the umbilical artery to the lower abdomen: An adjunct to the postoperative monitoring of arterial blood gases in major abdominal wall defects. J Pediatr Surg 1975;10:225.

48. Franceschini P, Guala A, Licata D, et al: Gershoni-Baruch syndrome: Report of a new family confirming autosomal recessive inheritance. Am J Med Genet 2003;122A:174.
49. Fraser N, Crabbe DC: An unusual left-sided abdominal-wall defect. Pediatr Surg Int 2002;18:66.
50. Fries MH, Filly RA, Callen PW, et al: Growth retardation in prenatally diagnosed cases of gastroschisis. J Ultrasound Med 1993;12:583.
51. Gibbin C, Touch S, Broth RE, Berghella V: Abdominal wall defects and congenital heart disease. Ultrasound Obstet Gynecol 2003;21:334.
52. Grob M: Lehrbuch der Kinderchirurgie. Stuttgart, Germany, Georg Thieme Verlag, 1957.
53. Grob M: Conservative treatment of exomphalos. Arch Dis Child 1963;38:148.
54. Groner JI: Ectopia cordis and sternal defects. In Ziegler MM, Azizkhan RG, Weber TR (eds): Operative Pediatric Surgery. New York, McGraw-Hill, 2003, p 279.
55. Gross RE: A new method for surgical treatment of omphaloceles. Surgery 1948;24:277.
56. Gross RE: Omphalocele (umbilical eventration). In Gross RE (ed): The Surgery of Infancy and Childhood. Philadelphia, WB Saunders, 1953, p 406.
57. Harmel RP Jr: Primary repair of gastroschisis with umbilicoplasty. Surg Gynecol Obstet 1985;160:464.
58. Heider AL, Strauss RA, Kuller JA: Omphalocele: Clinical outcomes in cases with normal karyotypes. Am J Obstet Gynecol 2004;190:135.
59. Hendrickson RJ, Partrick DA, Janik JS: Management of giant omphalocele in a premature low-birth-weight neonate utilizing a bedside sequential clamping technique without prosthesis. J Pediatr Surg 2003;38(10):E14.
60. Hey W: Practical Observation in Surgery. London, Cadell & Davis, 1802.
61. Hornberger LK, Colan SD, Lock JE, et al: Outcome of patients with ectopia cordis and significant intracardiac defects. Circulation 1996;94(9 Suppl):II32.
62. How HY, Harris BJ, Pietrantoni M, et al: Is vaginal delivery preferable to elective cesarean delivery in fetuses with a known ventral wall defect? Am J Obstet Gynecol 2000; 182:1527.
63. Hoyme HE, Higginbottom MC, Jones K: The vascular pathogenesis of gastroschisis: Intrauterine interruption of the omphalomesenteric artery. J Pediatr 1981;98:228.
64. Hughes MD, Nyberg DA, Mack LA, et al: Fetal omphalocele: Prenatal US detection of concurrent anomalies and other predictors of outcome. Radiology 1989;173:371.
65. Humpl T, Huggan P, Hormberger LK, McCrindle BW: Presentation and outcomes of ectopia cordis. Can J Cardiol 1999;15:1353.
66. Izant RJ Jr, Brown F, Rothmann BF: Current embryology and treatment of gastroschisis and omphalocele. Arch Surg 1966;93:49.
67. Jarcho J: Congenital umbilical hernia. Surg Gynecol Obstet 1937;65:593.
68. Johnson AH: Omphalocele and related defects. Am J Surg 1967;114:279.
69. Jona JZ: The 'gentle touch' technique in the treatment of gastroschisis. J Pediatr Surg 2003;38:1036.
70. Kaplan LC, Matsuoka R, Gilbert EF, et al: Ectopia cordis and cleft sternum: Evidence for mechanical teratogenesis following rupture of the chorion or yolk sac. Am J Med Genet 1985;21:187.
71. Kaplan LM, Koyle MA, Kaplan GW, et al: Related association between abdominal wall defects and cryptorchidism. J Urol 1986;136:645.
72. Kazaura MR, Lie RT, Irgens LM, et al: Increasing risk of gastroschisis in Norway: An age-period-cohort analysis. Am J Epidemiol 2004;159:358.
73. Kearns JE, Clarke BG: One stage surgical repair of gastroschisis (omphalocele) by cutis graft technic. Plast Reconstr Surg 1950;6:41.
74. Kern HM: New and simplified procedure for repairing omphalocele. Am J Surg 1949;77:783.
75. Kidd JN Jr, Jackson RJ, Smith SD, Wagner CW: Evolution of staged versus primary closure of gastroschisis. Ann Surg 2003; 237:759.
76. Klein MD: Robot-enhanced fetoscopic surgery. J Pediatr Surg 2004;39:1463.
77. Klein MD, Hertzler JH: Congenital defects of the abdominal wall. Surg Gynecol Obstet 1981;152:805.
78. Kleinhaus S, Kauffer N, Boley SJ: Partial hepatectomy in omphalocele repair. Surgery 1968;64:484.
79. Kluck P, Tibboel D, van der Kamp AW, et al: The effect of fetal urine on the development of the bowel in gastroschisis. J Pediatr Surg 1983;18:47.
80. Koivusalo A, Lindahl H, Rintala RJ: Morbidity and quality of life in adult patients with a congenital abdominal wall defect: A questionnaire survey. J Pediatr Surg 2002; 37:1594.
81. Koivusalo A, Rintala R, Lindahl H: Gastroesophageal reflux in children with a congenital abdominal wall defect. J Pediatr Surg 1999;34:1127.
82. Kouame BD, Dick RK, Ouattara O, et al: Therapeutic approaches for omphalocele in developing countries: Experience of Central University Hospital of Yopougon, Abidjan, Cote d'Ivoire. Bull Soc Pathol Exot 2003;96:302.
83. Kozer E, Nikfar S, Costei A, et al: Aspirin consumption during the first trimester of pregnancy and congenital anomalies: A meta-analysis. Am J Obstet Gynecol 2002;187:1623.
84. Krummel TM, Sieber WK: Closure of congenital abdominal wall defects with umbilicoplasty. Surg Gynecol Obstet 1987;165:168.
85. Lacey SR, Carris LA, Beyer AJ 3rd, Azizkhan RG: Bladder pressure monitoring significantly enhances care of infants with abdominal wall defects: A prospective clinical study. J Pediatr Surg 1993;28:1370.
86. Lafer DJ: Rectus muscle transection for visceral replacement. Surgery 1968;63:988.
87. Langer JC, Khanna J, Caco C, et al: Prenatal diagnosis of gastroschisis: Development of objective sonographic criteria for predicting outcome. Obstet Gynecol 1993; 81:53.
88. Laughon M, Meyer R, Bose C, et al: Rising birth prevalence of gastroschisis. J Perinatol 2003;23:291.
89. Lawson A, de la Hunt MN: Gastroschisis and undescended testis. J Pediatr Surg 2001;36:366.
90. Layne MD, Yet SF, Maemura K, et al: Impaired abdominal wall development and deficient wound healing in mice lacking aortic carboxypeptidase-like protein. Mol Cell Biol 2001;21:5256.
91. Leca F, Thibert M, Khoury W, et al: Extrathoracic heart (ectopia cordis). Int J Cardiol 1989;22:221.
92. Lee SL, DuBois JJ, Greenholz SK, Huffman SG: Advancement flap umbilicoplasty after abdominal wall closure: Postoperative results compared with normal umbilical anatomy. J Pediatr Surg 2001;36:1168.
93. Lenke RR, Hatch EI Jr: Fetal gastroschisis: A preliminary report advocating the use of cesarean section. Obstet Gynecol 1986;67:395.
94. Lewis DF, Towers CV, Garite TJ, et al: Fetal gastroschisis and omphalocele: Is cesarean section the best mode of delivery? Am J Obstet Gynecol 1990;163:773.
95. Lindham S: Teratogenic aspects of abdominal wall defects. Z Kinderchir 1983;38:211.
96. Lindham S: Long-term results in children with omphalocele and gastroschisis—a follow-up study. Z Kinderchir 1984;39:164.

97. Lippman O: Ein seltener Fall von Spaltbildung der vorderen Leibenswand, nebst Beitrag zur Enstehung von Bauchspalten. Zentralb Gynakol 1937;61:516.
98. Loder RT, Guiboux JP: Musculoskeletal involvement in children with gastroschisis and omphalocele. J Pediatr Surg 1993;28:584.
99. Lore JM: Omphalocele treated with split-thickness skin graft. N Y State J Med 1963;63:3573.
100. Lund DP, Hendren WH: Cloacal exstrophy: Experience with 20 cases. J Pediatr Surg 1993;28:1360.
101. Lunzer H, Menardi G, Brezinka C: Long-term follow-up of children with prenatally diagnosed omphalocele and gastroschisis. J Matern Fetal Med 2001;10:385.
102. Luton D, de Lagausie P, Guibourdenche J, et al: Influence of amnioinfusion in a model of in utero created gastroschisis in the pregnant ewe. Fetal Diagn Ther 2000;15:224.
103. Lycosthenes C: Prodigiorum ac ostentorum chronicon. Henricum Petri, 1557.
104. Mabogunje OA, Mahour GH: Omphalocele and gastroschisis. Trends in survival across two decades. Am J Surg 1984;148:679.
105. Maguire CH: Surgical management of omphalocele. Arch Surg 1949;59:484.
106. Margulies I: Omphalocele (amniocele). Am J Obstet Gynecol 1945;49:695.
107. Massabuau G, Guibal A: L'éviscération ombilicale congénitale. Arch Mal l'App Difestif 1933;23:129.
108. McDonnell R, Delany V, Dack P, et al: Changing trend in congenital abdominal wall defects in eastern region of Ireland. Ir Med J 2002;95:236.
109. Melikoglu M, Karaguzel G, Ogus M, et al: A gastroschisis-like abdominal wall defect in the left hypochondrium. Case report and literature review. Eur J Pediatr Surg 1998;8:52.
110. Minkes RK, Langer JC, Mazziotti MV, et al: Routine insertion of a Silastic spring-loaded silo for infants with gastroschisis. J Pediatr Surg 2000;35:843.
111. Moore TC, Collins DL, Catanzarite V, et al: Pre-term and particularly pre-labor cesarean section to avoid complications of gastroschisis. Pediatr Surg Int 1999;15:97.
112. Moore TC, Stokes GE: Gastroschisis. Surgery 1953;33:112.
113. Morales JM, Patel SG, Duff JA, et al: Ectopia cordis and other midline defects. Ann Thorac Surg 2000;70:111.
114. Morrow RJ, Whittle MJ, McNay MB, et al: Prenatal diagnosis and management of anterior abdominal wall defects in the west of Scotland. Prenat Diagn 1993;13:111.
115. Nembhard WN, Waller DK, Sever LE, et al: Patterns of first-year survival among infants with selected congenital anomalies in Texas, 1995-1997. Teratology 2001;64:267.
116. Nichol PF, Hayman A, Pryde PG, et al: Meconium staining of amniotic fluid correlates with intestinal peel formation in gastroschisis. Pediatr Surg Int 2004;20:211.
117. Nicholls G, Upadhyaya V, Gornall P, et al: Is specialist centre delivery of gastroschisis beneficial? Arch Dis Child 1993;69:71.
118. Nicolaides KH, Snijders RJ, Cheng HH, et al: Fetal gastrointestinal and abdominal wall defects: Associated malformations and chromosomal abnormalities. Fetal Diagn Ther 1992;7:102.
119. Nissan S: Pneumoperitoneum as aid for second stage repair of omphalocele. Arch Surg 1965;91:839.
120. Olguner M, Akgur FM, Api A, et al: The effects of intraamniotic human neonatal urine and meconium on the intestines of the chick embryo with gastroschisis. J Pediatr Surg 2000;35:458.
121. Olshausen RZ: Zur Therapie der Nabelschnurhernien. Arch Gynakol Berlin 1887;29:443.
122. Paltia V: Omphalocele. Acta Chir Scand 1960;30:119.
123. Paré A: The Workes of That Famous Chirugeon, Book 24, Chapter 66. Th Cotes and R Young, 1634, p 959.
124. Pernkopf E: Die Entwicklung der Form des Magendarmkanales beim Menschen. II Die weitere Auftretens der ersten Dunndarmschlingen. Z Anat Entwgesch 1925;77:1.
125. Philippart AI, Canty TG, Filler RM: Acute fluid volume requirements in infants with anterior abdominal wall defects. J Pediatr Surg 1972;7:553.
126. Politzer G, Sternberg H: Ueber die Entwicklung der ventralen Korperwand und des Nabelstranges beim Menschen. Z Anat Entwgesch 1930;92:279.
127. Pribram E: Anteromedian mero-crania (nosencephalos), combined with hypogastroschisis dextra and malformation of the fingers and toes. Arch Pathol Lab Med 1927; 3:400.
128. Pryde PG, Bardicef M, Treadwell MC, et al: Gastroschisis: Can antenatal ultrasound predict infant outcomes? Obstet Gynecol 1994;84:505.
129. Pryde PG, Greb A, Isada NB: Familial omphalocele: Considerations in genetic counseling. Am J Med Genet 1992;44:624.
130. Ravitch MM: Giant omphalocele: Second stage repair with the aid of pneumoperitoneum. JAMA 1963;185:42.
131. Reddy VN, Aughton DJ, DeWitte DB, Harper CE: Down syndrome and omphalocele: An underrecognized association. Pediatrics 1994;93:514.
132. Reid KP, Dickinson JE, Doherty DA: The epidemiologic incidence of congenital gastroschisis in Western Australia. Am J Obstet Gynecol 2003;189:764.
133. Remensnyder JP: Intrauterine rupture of omphalocele. Surgery 1963;54:681.
134. Rothenberg RE, Barnett T: Omphalocele in siblings. Arch Surg 1957;75:131.
135. Sakala EP, Erhard LN, White JJ: Elective cesarean section improves outcomes of neonates with gastroschisis. Am J Obstet Gynecol 1993;169:1050.
136. Salihu HM, Pierre-Louis BJ, Druschel CM, et al: Omphalocele and gastroschisis in the State of New York, 1992-1999. Birth Defects Res A Clin Mol Teratol 2003; 67:630.
137. Saller DN Jr, Canick JA, Palomaki GE, et al: Second-trimester maternal serum alpha-fetoprotein, unconjugated estriol, and hCG levels in pregnancies with ventral wall defects. Obstet Gynecol 1994;84:852.
138. Santos MM, Tannuri U, Maksoud JG: Alterations of enteric nerve plexus in experimental gastroschisis: Is there a delay in the maturation? J Pediatr Surg 2003;38:1506.
139. Sapin E, Mahieu D, Borgnon J, et al: Transabdominal amnioinfusion to avoid fetal demise and intestinal damage in fetuses with gastroschisis and severe oligohydramnios. J Pediatr Surg 2000;35:598.
140. Sawin R, Glick P, Schaller R, et al: Gastroschisis wringer clamp: A safe, simplified method for delayed primary closure. J Pediatr Surg 1992;27:1346.
141. Schlatter M, Norris K, Uitvlugt N, et al: Improved outcomes in the treatment of gastroschisis using a preformed silo and delayed repair approach. J Pediatr Surg 2003;38:459.
142. Schuster SR: A new method for the staged repair of large omphaloceles. Surg Gynecol Obstet 1967;125:837.
143. Segel SY, Marder SJ, Parry S, et al: Fetal abdominal wall defects and mode of delivery: A systematic review. Obstet Gynecol 2001;98:867.
144. Shanske AL, Pande S, Aref K, et al: Omphalocele-exstrophy-imperforate anus-spinal defects (OEIS) in triplet pregnancy after IVF and CVS. Birth Defects Res A Clin Mol Teratol 2003;67:467.

145. Shaw A: The myth of gastroschisis. J Pediatr Surg 1975; 10:235.
146. Sheldon RE: The bowel bag: A sterile, transportable method for warming infants with skin defects. Pediatrics 1974;53:267.
147. Singh SJ, Fraser A, Leditschke JF, et al: Gastroschisis: Determinants of neonatal outcome. Pediatr Surg Int 2003;19:260.
148. Snijders RJ, Brizot ML, Faria M, et al: Fetal exomphalos at 11 to 14 weeks of gestation. J Ultrasound Med 1995; 14:569.
149. Snyder CL, Miller KA, Sharp RJ, et al: Management of intestinal atresia in patients with gastroschisis. J Pediatr Surg 2001;36:1542.
150. Stanley-Brown EG, Frank JE: Mercury poisoning from application to omphalocele. JAMA 1971;216:2144.
151. Stoll C, Clementi M, Euroscan Study Group: Prenatal diagnosis of dysmorphic syndromes by routine fetal ultrasound examination across Europe. Ultrasound Obstet Gynecol 2003;21:543.
152. Stoodley N, Sharma A, Noblett H, et al: Influence of place of delivery on outcome in babies with gastroschisis. Arch Dis Child 1993;68:321.
153. Strauss RA, Balu R, Kuller JA, et al: Gastroschisis: The effect of labor and ruptured membranes on neonatal outcome. Am J Obstet Gynecol 2003;189:1672.
154. Stroer WFH: Zur Aetiologie der Bauchspalten. Beitr Pathol Anat Allg Pathol 1949;106:302.
155. Swartz KR, Harrison MW, Campbell JR, Campbell TJ: Long-term follow-up of patients with gastroschisis. Am J Surg 1986;151:546.
156. Taruffi G: Storia della Teratologia, vol VII. Bologna, Italy, Regia Tipografia, 1894.
157. Thauvin-Robinet C, Faivre L, Cusin V, et al: Cloacal exstrophy in an infant with 9q34.1-qter deletion resulting from a de novo unbalanced translocation between chromosome 9q and Yq. Am J Med Genet 2004;126A:303.
158. Thomas DF, Atwell JD: The embryology and surgical management of gastroschisis. Br J Surg 1976;63:893.
159. Tibboel D, Raine P, McNee M, et al: Developmental aspects of gastroschisis. J Pediatr Surg 1986;21:865.
160. Tibboel D, Vermey-Keers C, Kluck P, et al: The natural history of gastroschisis during fetal life: Development of the fibrous coating on the bowel loops. Teratology 1986; 33:267.
161. Torfs CP, Curry CJ: Familial cases of gastroschisis in a population-based registry. Am J Med Genet 1993;45:465.
162. Tucker JM, Brumfield CG, Davis RO, et al: Prenatal differentiation of ventral abdominal wall defects. Are amniotic fluid markers useful adjuncts? J Reprod Med 1992;37:445.
163. Tulloh RM, Tansey SP, Parashar K, et al: Echocardiographic screening in neonates undergoing surgery for selected gastrointestinal malformations. Arch Dis Child Fetal Neonatal Ed 1994;70:F206.
164. Tunell WP, Puffinbarger NK, Tuggle DW, et al: Abdominal wall defects in infants. Survival and implications for adult life. Ann Surg 1995;221:525.
165. Vintzileos AM, Ananth CV, Smulian JC, et al: Routine second-trimester ultrasonography in the United States: A cost-benefit analysis. Am J Obstet Gynecol 2000;182:655.
166. Visick C: An umbilical hernia in a newly born child. Lancet 1873;1:829.
167. Volumenie JL, de Lagausie P, Guibourdenche J, et al: Improvement of mesenteric superior artery Doppler velocimetry by amnio-infusion in fetal gastroschisis. Prenat Diagn 2001;21:1171.
168. Waller DK, Keddie AM, Canfield MA, Scheuerle AE: Do infants with major congenital anomalies have an excess of macrosomia? Teratology 2001;64:311.
169. Werler MM, Sheehan JE, Mitchell AA: Maternal medication use and risks of gastroschisis and small intestinal atresia. Am J Epidemiol 2002;155:26.
170. Werler MM, Sheehan JE, Mitchell AA: Association of vasoconstrictive exposures with risks of gastroschisis and small intestinal atresia. Epidemiology 2003;14:349.
171. Wesley JR, Drongowski R, Coran AG: Intragastric pressure measurement: A guide for reduction and closure of the Silastic chimney in omphalocele and gastroschisis. J Pediatr Surg 1981;16:264.
172. Wiedemann HR: Complexe malformatif familial avec hernie ombilicale et macroglossie—un "syndrome nouveau"? J Genet Humaine 1964;13:223.
173. Williams AM, Brain JL: The normal position of the umbilicus in the newborn: An aid to improving the cosmetic results in exomphalos major. J Pediatr Surg 2001;36:546.
174. Wu Y, Vogel AM, Sailhamer EA, et al: Primary insertion of a Silastic spring-loaded silo for gastroschisis. Am Surg 2003;69:1083.
175. Yatsenko SA, Mendoza-Londono R, Belmont JW, et al: Omphalocele in trisomy 3q: Further delineation of phenotype. Clin Genet 2003;64:404.
176. Zaccara A, Iacobelli BD, Calzolari A, et al: Cardiopulmonary performances in young children and adolescents born with large abdominal wall defects. J Pediatr Surg 2003;38:478.
177. Zaccara A, Zama M, Trucchi A, et al: Bipedicled skin flaps for reconstruction of the abdominal wall in newborn omphalocele. J Pediatr Surg 2003;38:613.
178. Zaiem MM: Staged closure of omphalocele major using autogenous sac as supportive material. Saudi Med J 2003; 24(5 Suppl):S57.

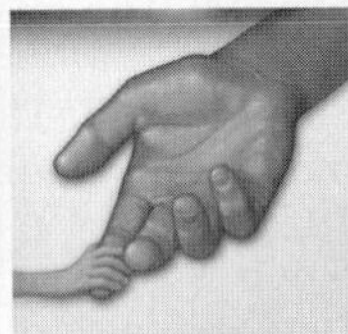

Chapter 74

Inguinal Hernias and Hydroceles

Philip L. Glick and Scott C. Boulanger

HISTORY

Inguinal hernias were recognized at least as far back as 1500 BC. What appears to be an inguinal hernia is depicted on an ancient Greek statuette, and Egyptian writings describe groin bulges elicited by coughing (the Papyrus of Ebers, circa 1552 BC).[57] There is also evidence that surgery for hernias was performed as early as 1200 BC. The Roman physician Celsus is credited with some of the earliest hernia surgeries, done around AD 50.[57] About that same time, Galen described the anatomy of the processus vaginalis; however, he thought that hernias were the result of rupture of the peritoneum, with stretching of overlying muscle and fascia.[57] This may be the origin of the slang term for hernia: "rupture."

Modern hernia surgery began in the 19th century when an accurate understanding of the anatomy of the inguinal canal became available.[57] Richter, Camper, and Scarpa, among others, contributed to the field during this period. Cooper in 1804 described the transversalis fascia as well as the pectineal, or Cooper's, ligament. In 1811 Colles described the reflection of the inguinal ligament, and Cloquet in 1817 observed that the processus vaginalis was rarely closed at birth. With a thorough understanding of inguinal anatomy, modern hernia surgery awaited only the development of aseptic techniques.

In 1870 Lister introduced the concept of antisepsis in surgery, and Halsted began operating with gloves in 1896.[57] Von Mikulicz took this one step further, performing aseptic surgery in 1904. These developments allowed rapid progress to be made in hernia surgery. In 1871 Marcy described an operation still in use by pediatric surgeons today: high ligation of an unopened sac through the external ring and tightening of the internal ring. This technique led to an unacceptably high recurrence rate in adults, however.[87] In 1887 Bassini reported his results using a technique that involved opening of the external oblique muscle, high ligation of the sac, tightening of the external ring, and reconstruction of the posterior inguinal floor.[87] He, along with Halsted, is credited with the development of modern hernia repair.

GENEALOGY OF HERNIA SURGERY (NORTH AMERICAN PERSPECTIVE)

Modern pediatric hernia repair continues to revolve around standard principles: opening the external oblique muscle, exposure of the internal ring, high ligation of the sac, and repair of the anterior wall of the inguinal canal. The details of this seemingly simple operation, however, vary greatly from surgeon to surgeon. In the United States, Ladd and Gross are considered the fathers of pediatric surgery.[38] In their textbook *Abdominal Surgery of Infancy and Childhood,* they provide a clear description of their method of hernia repair,[56] which is essentially that of Ferguson.[31] The steps are as follows: The external oblique muscle and external ring are exposed. The external ring is opened with scissors from the external ring extending proximally. The cremasteric muscles are bluntly separated, and the hernia sac is grasped with forceps and elevated. The hernia sac is then sharply dissected from surrounding structures. The sac is opened, and a gauze-covered finger continues the blunt dissection. The neck of the sac is transfixed with a suture, and the excess sac is excised. The neck of the sac is then sutured under the internal oblique and external oblique muscles using double needles fitted to the ligature, which are then passed backward out through the internal and external obliques. The external oblique is closed by imbrication. The top edge is sutured to the inguinal ligament, and the lower edge is sutured to the upper portion of the external oblique. Scarpa's fascia is then closed, followed by skin closure.

In a recent survey of North American pediatric surgeons, Levitt et al.[61] documented the degree of variability from that technique over the last 60 years. Eighty-one percent of surgeons (640 respondents) could trace their training lineage back to Ladd and Gross, and some aspects of the repair were well preserved. For example, 94% closed Scarpa's fascia, 90% bluntly spread the cremasteric muscles, 81% identified the ilioinguinal nerve, 79% did not inspect the testicle, 78% left the distal sac untouched except to drain fluid, and 65% incised Scarpa's fascia with scissors. Other aspects of the Ladd and Gross repair are no longer practiced, such as inserting a finger into the sac, bluntly dissecting the sac with gauze, and using a postoperative Stiles dressing. The authors proposed that the variations arose from a combination of training, clinical experience, and analysis of the literature. Hernia surgery is the most common operation performed by pediatric surgeons, making it a model for understanding how surgical modifications occur.

INCIDENCE

As stated previously, inguinal hernia repair is the most common operation performed by pediatric surgeons. The percentage of children with inguinal hernias ranges from 0.8% to 4.4%.[12]

Age

Inguinal hernia most commonly presents during the first year of life, with a peak during the first few months. Approximately one third of children are younger than 6 months at the time of operation.[12] The highest incidence of hernia is found in premature infants: 16% to 25%.[79,105] This correlates fairly well with the patency rate of the processus vaginalis; at birth, 80% are patent, and the rate decreases dramatically during the first 6 months of life.[93] However, all indirect hernias, regardless of age at presentation, are likely secondary to failure of the processus vaginalis to close completely during fetal and newborn development.

Sex

Males are much more likely to have hernias, with the reported male-female ratio between 3:1 and 10:1.[12] Although premature infants have a higher incidence of hernia, there does not appear to be a significant gender difference among this group.[11,75,103]

Side

Approximately 60% of hernias are right sided.[83] This is true for males and females. In males, this is possibly the result of the later descent of the right testicle than the left, but this obviously does not explain the observation in females. Bilateral hernias are present in approximately 10% of cases.[83] It has been suggested that patients with left-sided hernias are more likely to develop right-sided hernias than vice versa.[22,64] More recent data suggest that this may not be true, however.[9,37,100]

Family History

Approximately 11.5% of patients have a family history of hernia.[12] There is an increased incidence in twins as well—about 10.6% in male twins and 4.1% in female twins.[3]

EMBRYOLOGY

Indirect inguinal hernias are fundamentally the result of failure of the processus vaginalis to close (Fig. 74-1). The processus vaginalis is an invagination of the peritoneum through the internal ring that can first be identified during the third month of fetal life.[19] Some have suggested that formation of the processus vaginalis is a result of intra-abdominal pressure,[6] whereas others believe that it is an active process.[1,2] The intra-abdominal testis passes through the processus during the seventh to ninth months of gestation, and the processus elongates. Subsequently, the portion of the processus vaginalis lying above the testicle obliterates, closing the internal inguinal ring, while the distal portion persists as the tunica vaginalis. When this fails to occur, patency of the processus vaginalis results, potentially causing an indirect inguinal hernia (if bowel or other organs can enter the processus) or a hydrocele (peritoneal fluid only). In females, the canal of Nuck corresponds to the processus vaginalis and communicates with the labia majora, the female homologue of the scrotum. The canal of Nuck normally closes around the seventh month of gestation, earlier than in males.

The exact timing of closure is uncertain. Studies have suggested that as many as 80% to 100% of infants are born with a patent processus vaginalis and that closure, if it occurs, is most likely within the first 6 months of life.[82,93] After that, the patency rate falls more gradually and plateaus around age 3 to 5 years. It also appears that the left side closes earlier than the right. It is unknown where in the processus (i.e., proximal, middle, or distal) closure begins. After closure, the processus persists as a cord, which subsequently disappears. The high rate of

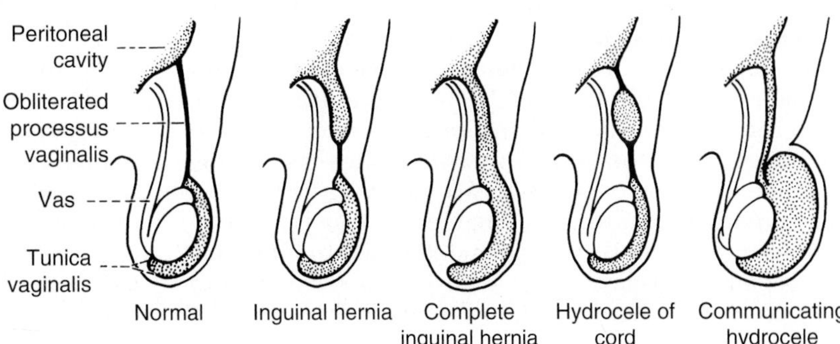

Figure 74–1 The most common variants of hernias and hydroceles arising from failure of complete obliteration of the processus vaginalis.

TABLE 74–1 Factors Contributing to the Development of Congenital Inguinal Hernia

Urogenital
Undescended testis
Exstrophy of bladder
Increased peritoneal fluid
Ascites
Ventriculoperitoneal shunt
Peritoneal dialysis
Increased intra-abdominal pressure
Repair of exomphalos or gastroschisis
Severe ascites (e.g., chylous)
Meconium peritonitis
Chronic respiratory disease
Cystic fibrosis
Connective tissue disorders
Ehlers-Danlos syndrome
Hunter-Hurler syndrome
Marfan's syndrome
Mucopolysaccharidosis

patency associated with undescended testis suggests that closure can occur only after descent of the testicle and that these processes are linked.

The biologic mechanisms that signal and direct the descent of the testicle through the inguinal canal and obliterate the processus are, for the most part, unknown. Androgens appear to play a role, because patency of the processus is common in androgen insensitivity syndrome. However, the processus itself has no androgen receptors. Work from Clarnette and Hutson[19] implicated the genitofemoral nerve and calcitonin gene-related peptide (CGRP) in both testicular descent and obliteration of the processus vaginalis. They suggested that reduced calcitonin gene-related protein release from the genitofemoral nerve prenatally may result in undescended testis, whereas reduced release postnatally may lead to hernias and hydroceles.

Although it is clear that a patent processus vaginalis is a prerequisite for an inguinal hernia, it is not sufficient, and other factors are involved. Table 74-1 provides a list of contributing factors that have been identified.

CLINICAL FEATURES

Inguinal hernias (unless otherwise indicated, the term *inguinal hernia* refers to an indirect inguinal hernia) are generally found by parents at bath time or by pediatricians during well-child examinations. There is typically a history of an intermittent bulge in the groin, labia, or scrotum. It is most often apparent when there is increased intra-abdominal pressure, such as during episodes of crying or straining. When taking the history, it is important to distinguish inguinal hernia from communicating hydrocele, undescended testis, and inguinal adenopathy. Hernias may be discovered at birth, or they may present weeks, months, or even years later, but the defect has been there since birth. This is important to remember when an asymptomatic hernia is found, in terms of the timing of surgery (i.e., not an emergency) and the activities the child should be allowed to participate in while awaiting repair (i.e., no restrictions if asymptomatic).

Hernias are usually asymptomatic. Because hernias often appear during episodes of infant distress, parents often think that the hernia is the cause of the distress. Unfortunately, many of these perceived symptoms persist after the repair. Older children often complain of groin or inguinal discomfort during exercise.

Incarcerated hernias result from entrapment of bowel or other viscera within the hernia sac. Debate continues over whether entrapment occurs at the internal or external ring. Although it can occur at both, entrapment at the level of the internal ring predominates. This can cause intermittent pain and irritability. Subsequently, signs of bowel obstruction result, such as distention, vomiting, and obstipation. If the hernia is not reduced, strangulation may occur, and blood supply to the incarcerated organ may be compromised to the point of infarction. The patient may present with peritonitis at this point. This process can occur in as little as 2 hours. Incarceration occurs most commonly in the first 6 months of life and is relatively rare after age 5 years.

The concern in the young, preverbal population is that their caretakers may not recognize the signs and symptoms of incarceration in a timely manner. We instruct the families of infants with hernias awaiting elective surgery that the differential diagnosis of a crying baby includes needs to be fed, needs a diaper change, needs a nap, and needs an operation (may have an incarcerated hernia), and we instruct the families what to look for (sage advice given to PLG by his senior resident, Dr. Don Nakayama, 1982).

EXAMINATION

To examine for inguinal hernia, the patient is placed supine and undressed on an examining table in a warm room. The examiner first observes the patient for an inguinal mass or asymmetry in the pubic region. The testis should be held in the scrotum with a finger across the top of the scrotum to account for both testes and to sort out true inguinal bulges from retractile testes. If no mass can be identified, an older child should stand and perform a Valsalva maneuver; an infant may be allowed to strain or cry to provoke an inguinal bulge to appear. If a mass is still not present, the spermatic cord can be palpated to determine thickening (silk string sign).[56] This is performed by laying a single finger over the spermatic cord at the level of the pubic tubercle. The finger is lightly rolled over the cord from side to side (Fig. 74-2). A positive sign indicates thicker cord structures within the inguinal canal compared with the normal side. The examiner has the sensation of rubbing two pieces of silk together or the sensation of a plastic bag with a few drops of water in it (plastic baggie sign), but these signs are not completely accurate.

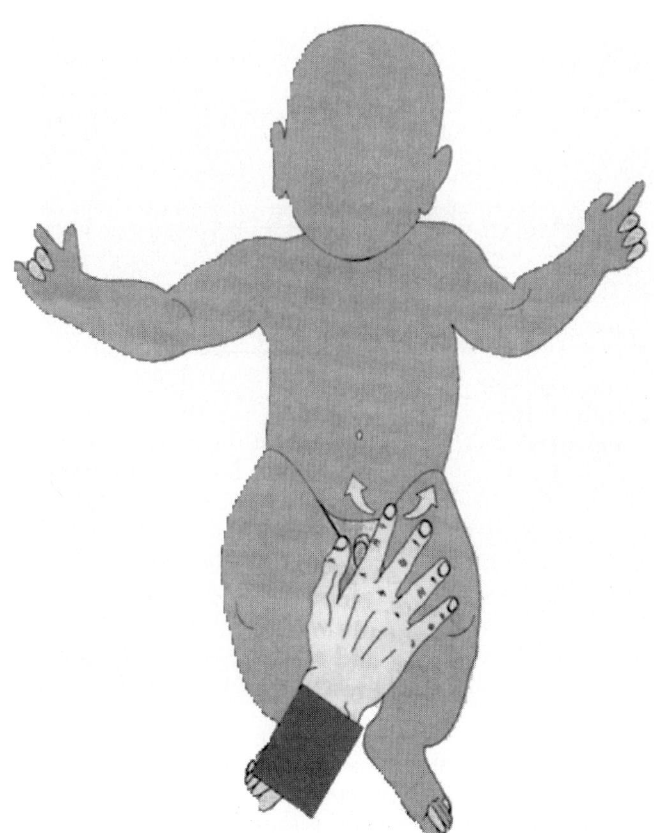

Figure 74-2 Examination for an inguinal hernia. A single finger is laid over and parallel to the inguinal structures, and the finger is rubbed across the cord from side to side at the level of the pubic tubercle.

If a hernia is not demonstrable on physical examination, some surgeons still operate if the hernia was seen previously by a physician or if the parents provide a very good history.[86] However, with parental education, follow-up examinations, and modern radiologic techniques, unnecessary surgery can be avoided in equivocal cases.

RADIOLOGIC INVESTIGATION

In most cases, the diagnosis of an inguinal hernia can be made by history and physical examination alone. However, in a small subset of patients, radiologic testing may be of value. Previously, the technique most commonly used was herniography, but this has now been replaced by groin ultrasonography (US).

Herniography is performed by injecting water-soluble contrast material into the peritoneal cavity via an infraumbilical fluoroscopic-guided injection.[47] Gravity allows the contrast material to pool in the hernia sac, which is identified by plain radiographs taken at 5-, 10-, and 45-minute intervals. Hydroceles can be identified by this technique, and femoral hernias can be differentiated from inguinal hernias. This test is also useful for detecting contralateral hernias or in postoperative patients with recurrent ipsilateral groin symptoms. It has no value, however, for incarcerated hernias, because the neck of the sac is occluded in those cases. Complications of this technique are rare and include intestinal perforation, intramural intestinal hematoma, and allergic reactions to the contrast media.[47,106] Despite this, herniography has not found widespread use.

US has recently gained popularity as an adjunct to the physical examination. It has the advantage of being rapid, noninvasive, and complication free. Chen et al.[17] performed US bilaterally on 244 boys presenting with either unilateral or bilateral hernias. They noted an accuracy of 97% when using 4 mm as the upper limit of the normal diameter of the inguinal canal. In a series of 642 children, Erez et al.[29] noted that an inguinal canal measuring 3.6 ± 0.8 mm preoperatively was associated with normal findings at surgery, whereas a measurement of 4.9 ± 1.1 mm was associated with a patent processus vaginalis and 7.2 ± 2.0 mm or greater was associated with a true hernia. Therefore, with the use of appropriate measurements, US is a reliable tool for diagnosing hernias when there is a good history but an equivocal physical examination, and it is potentially useful for preoperative evaluation of the contralateral groin in patients presenting with unilateral hernias (Fig. 74-3). However, US is not used extensively.

MANAGEMENT

A true inguinal hernia will not resolve spontaneously, so surgical closure is always indicated. Because of the high risk of incarceration, particularly in young infants, repair should be performed expeditiously. Some reports suggest that 90% of complications can be avoided if repair is undertaken within 1 month of diagnosis.[85,107] Most patients can be treated safely in an ambulatory setting. Exceptions include premature infants and older children with significant risk factors such as cardiac or respiratory problems.

Anesthesia

The anesthetic type varies with the patient. Options include general, regional, or local techniques, and the choice depends on several factors, including the patient's age and the presence of significant comorbidities. Most patients receive general anesthesia with endotracheal intubation or laryngeal mask. Healthy full-term infants and older patients are generally given general endotracheal anesthesia, and this has been found to be extremely safe. However, others, particularly premature infants (<36 weeks' gestational age and <60 weeks' gestational age plus chronologic age), require a more varied approach. Regional techniques (spinal, epidural, or caudal anesthesia) are often chosen in these situations, and all are equally effective. A recent review of the Cochrane database found several small trials comparing regional versus general anesthesia.[26] No statistical difference was demonstrable in terms of postoperative apnea or bradycardia, respiratory rate, or postoperative oxygen desaturation. However, the total number of patients enrolled in the trials was only 108.

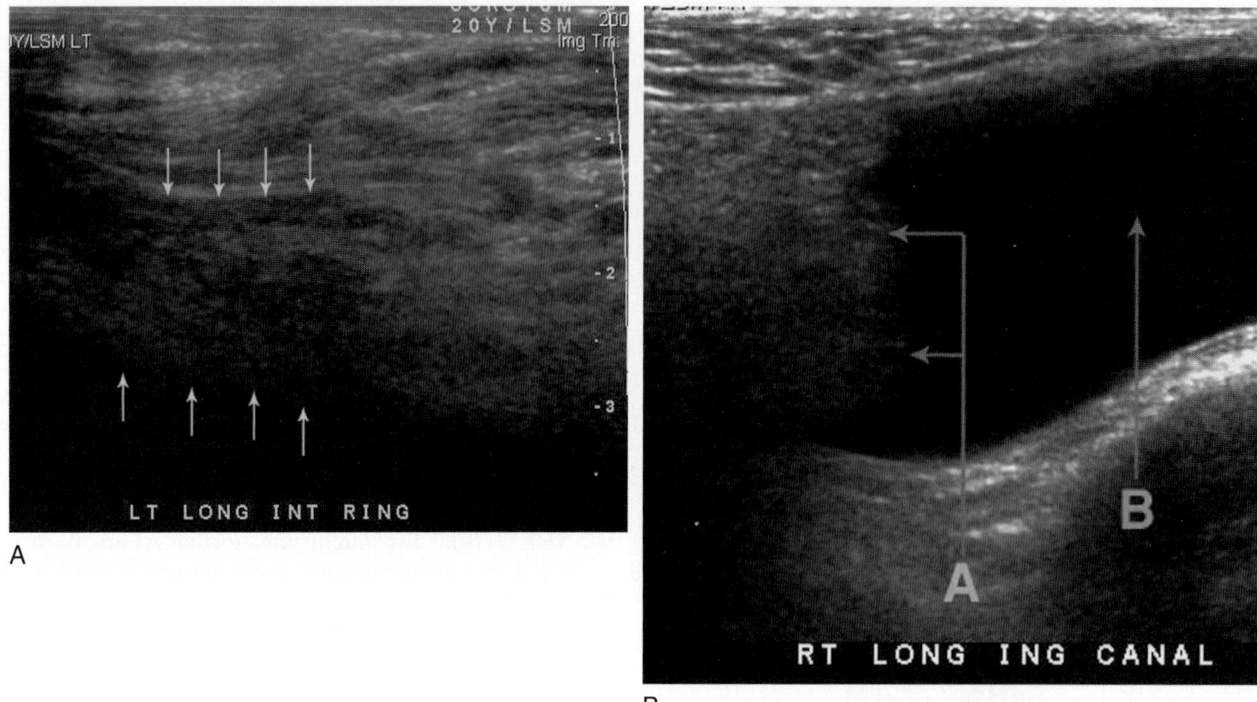

Figure 74–3 Ultrasound examination of the inguinal canal. *A*, No hernia. The arrows outline the normal inguinal canal. The strands are the vas deferens and cord structures. Using Doppler imaging, arterial signals to the scrotum and venous signals to the inferior vena cava would be seen. *B*, Inguinal hernia. The double arrow points to the leading edge of incarcerated viscera. If it were bowel, peristalsis would be evident; if it were omentum, it would not. The single arrow is fluid in the hernia sac.

Postoperative pain control has also been a matter for debate. Caudal blocks are routinely performed in some centers, whereas other centers use local anesthetic instilled in the operative field. A randomized, prospective trial compared instillation of 0.25% bupivacaine without epinephrine (2.5 mg/kg) versus caudal block and found no difference in the level of postoperative pain control.[23] Additionally, instillation of local anesthetic (so-called splash technique) was as effective as injection into the wound.

Age for Overnight Stay

Most full-term infants and older children undergo same-day hernia surgery. The age at which an ex-premature infant can safely have same-day surgery is debatable. One study showed that preterm infants less than 41 to 46 weeks' postconceptual age and with a history of neonatal apnea had a greater risk of postoperative apnea.[62] Another large study, using sophisticated techniques for monitoring postoperative breathing disturbances, found that infants less than 44 weeks' postconceptual age were at increased risk of clinically significant episodes of postoperative apnea.[63] In 1995 a combined analysis from eight prospective studies was performed; the conclusion was that the incidence of postoperative apnea did not drop below 1% (with 95% statistical confidence) until 56 weeks for a 32-week premature infant and 54 weeks for a 34-week premature infant.[25] In our center we prefer to err on the side of caution and routinely use 60 weeks' postconceptual age as the cutoff.

Timing of Surgery

Most surgeons currently recommend repair of the hernia soon after diagnosis.[61] This practice can result in a significant reduction of complications from the hernia and is practicable because of the safety of modern anesthesia. For premature infants, most surgeons now recommend repair before discharge, after the child has attained a weight of about 2 kg. This is in contradistinction to surgical practice up to 1996, when only 33% of surgeons polled would operate on a premature infant.[107] One disadvantage of early surgery in premature infants is that recurrence is more frequent in smaller infants. In Europe a randomized, prospective trial is under way comparing infants repaired at 2.5 kg versus 5 kg.[68]

Technique in Males

The fundamental principle guiding pediatric inguinal hernia repair is high ligation of the sac. A modified Ferguson repair was the procedure of choice of Ladd and Gross.[56] They preferred this type of repair to the Mitchell-Banks repair popular in Great Britain, which was a simple high ligation of the sac via the internal ring without opening the external oblique muscle.[87] In the

Ferguson repair, the external oblique is opened, and reconstruction of the inguinal canal is performed without altering the relationship of the spermatic cord to the inguinal canal. Later we describe our technique for inguinal hernia repair and highlight significant variations (Fig. 74-4).

With the patient in the supine position, the midline pubic tubercle and anterior superior iliac spine are marked. The pubic tubercle is a particularly important landmark because the external ring lies inferior and lateral to it. An incision is made with the medial end just superior and lateral to the pubic tubercle. As children age, the internal ring becomes more lateral, whereas in infants the internal ring and external ring overlap. In older children, the distance between the two increases, necessitating a more laterally placed incision. Making the incision too medial in a child of any age runs the risk of dissection injury to the cord structures as they exit the external ring before finding the inguinal ligament.

The incision is carried down through the dermis to expose the subcutaneous fat or Camper's fascia. Camper's fascia is spread with scissors to expose the more substantial Scarpa's fascia. Care is taken not to injure the inferior epigastric vein, which lies above Scarpa's fascia. Scarpa's fascia is then grasped and cut and spread with scissors to expose the external oblique muscle. Once the external oblique is identified, the inguinal ligament is cleared from lateral to medial by gentle spreading down to the level of the external ring. Care should be taken to stay above the inguinal ligament to avoid injury to the femoral vascular structures. An incision is made in the external oblique along the line of its fibers and extended by spreading with scissors. Straight hemostats can be applied to the cut edges of the external oblique, near the external ring, to facilitate their subsequent identification and closure. The undersurface of the external oblique, superiorly and inferiorly, is cleared off with forceps and a gauze sponge to identify the transversalis fascia, iliofemoral and ilioinguinal nerves, and cremasteric muscle fibers. A small cut is made in the cremasteric, and it is spread open to reveal the hernia sac. The hernia sac is grasped, taking a large, gentle bite of tissue and elevating the cord structures into the wound until an inverted V-shaped opening underneath the sac

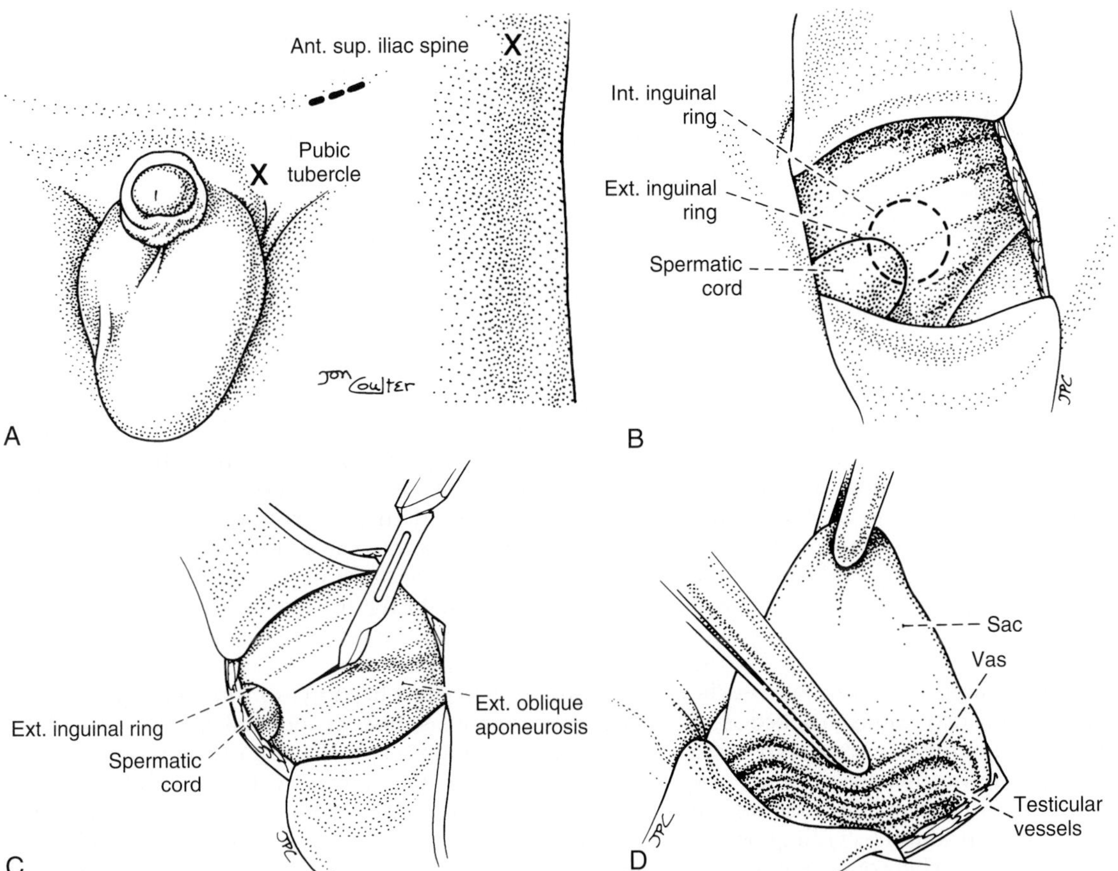

Figure 74-4 Technique of inguinal hernia repair in male children. *A,* The pubic tubercle and anterior superior iliac spine are used as landmarks to place the inguinal incision over the internal ring *(dashes). B,* In infants younger than 1 year, the internal and external rings overlap, and the inguinal canal is short. Often an incision in the external oblique muscle is not necessary to gain access to the internal ring. *C,* In older children, the external oblique aponeurosis is incised lateral to the external ring and over the internal ring. The undersurface of the external oblique is cleared of cremasteric fibers. *D,* The cremasteric muscle is incised and spread with scissors to expose the spermatic cord, which is grasped and elevated. The vas and spermatic vessels are then gently separated from the white hernia sac without touching them.

Continued

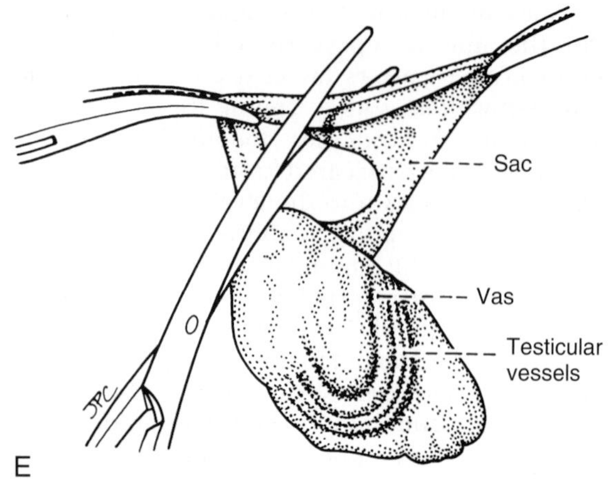

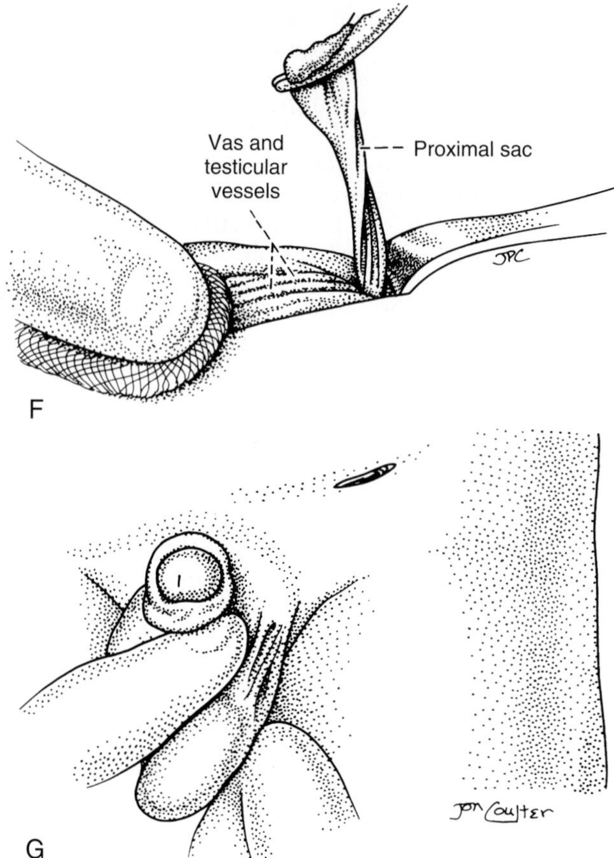

Figure 74–4 Cont'd *E,* The hernia sac is inspected for contents. The empty hernia sac is then sharply divided between clamps. The edges of the distal sac are cauterized, and the distal sac is dropped back into the wound. *F,* The proximal sac is gently dissected to the level of the internal ring, where the preperitoneal fat will be seen. The sac is then twisted on itself, taking care not to incorporate the vas deferens and vessels, and double-ligated. *G,* The testis is pulled back into position in the scrotum, and the spermatic cord is straightened. A standard layered closure is performed with absorbable suture.

is clearly seen. A forceps is placed through this opening. The spermatic fascia is then bluntly opened, and the vas deferens and vessels are dissected away from the sac. The sac is checked for contents, and the vas and vessels are reidentified. Two clamps are then placed across the sac close together, and the sac is divided. The proximal sac is cleaned to the level of the internal ring, twisted on itself, and ligated at the level of the internal ring with monofilament absorbable suture. Ladd and Gross used silk suture to ligate the sac, but we have seen silk sutures "spit out" of the wound years after the original repair and switched to absorbable suture to avoid this problem. The distal sac is not dissected because this may result in ischemic orchitis or postoperative hematoma. Noncommunicating hydroceles may be windowed open but should not be completely removed, for the same reasons. Inspection of the testicle is not mandatory, but if it is done, care must be taken not to damage the normal insertion of the gubernaculum onto the dartos fascia. The testis is then returned to the normal scrotal position by pulling on the scrotal skin and the dartos fascia. The wound is closed in layers. Scarpa's fascia is closed with an interrupted absorbable suture. We prefer a running subcuticular skin closure, but an interrupted closure is equally good. Steri-strips are applied, and an impermeable plastic dressing is placed over the wound to protect it from stool or urine (in diaper-age children). We have abandoned the use of colloidion because of safety issues.

Technique in Females

The surgical repair of hernias in females is somewhat simpler than in males because there is no need to identify and preserve a spermatic cord. The surgical approach to the inguinal canal is the same as in males. The hernia sac is identified and inspected for contents. Often the ovary, tube, or mesosalpinx is contained within the sac (Fig. 74-5). If the sac is empty, it is divided between clamps. The distal sac is dropped back into the wound after the edges have been cauterized. The proximal sac is dissected out to the level of the internal ring, twisted, and double-ligated. We then close the ring with one or two sutures and close the wound in standard fashion.

Before twisting and ligation, we routinely open the sac because as many as 40% of inguinal hernias in females have a sliding component. It is not uncommon for ovary, fallopian tube, or uterus to lie within the wall of the sac and not reduce into the abdominal cavity. If the fallopian tube is not readily visible, some surgeons place traction on the round ligament to identify the tube before ligation of the sac. We do not routinely attach the sac and the round ligament to the conjoint tendon in order to reestablish the normal support for the uterus (Bastionelli maneuver).

If the fallopian tube is identified in the wall of the sac as a sliding hernia, we make no attempt to dissect it off the sac. Rather, we place an external purse-string stitch in the sac above the fallopian tube, invert the sac into the

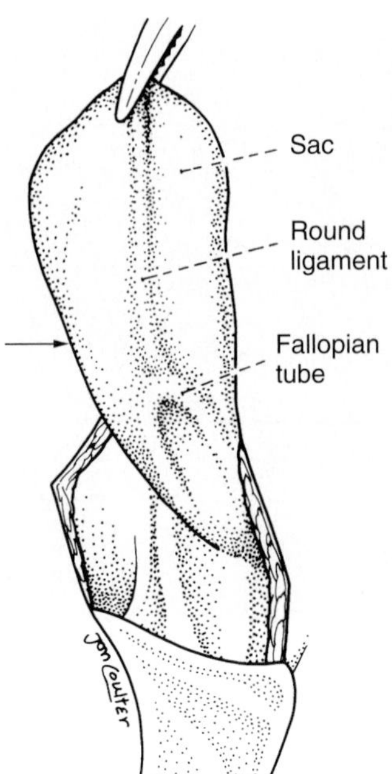

Figure 74–5 Hernia sac in a female. The fallopian tube is often found in the wall of the hernia sac as a sliding hernia and must be identified. If necessary, the hernia sac is opened, and the round ligament is followed to the fallopian tube.

internal ring, and then close the internal ring with one or two sutures, as described by Bevan.[7] Alternatively, the flap procedure described by Goldstein and Potts[92] may be used.

Laparoscopic Repair

Laparoscopic repair of inguinal hernias has been established in adults for a number of years. Stated advantages include less pain and earlier return to work, repair of bilateral hernias through the same ports, and easier repair of recurrent hernias. Disadvantages include increased cost, longer operating time, and a prolonged learning curve. In addition, multiple techniques have been proposed, such as transabdominal repairs and extraperitoneal repairs. For these reasons, most pediatric surgeons consider laparoscopy unnecessary for hernia repair in children because of the small incisions used and the relative ease of repair compared with adults, as well as the minimal pain children experience with the open procedure.

El-Gohary[28] reported a series of laparoscopic hernia repairs in 28 females. In his series, the hernia sac was inverted into the abdominal cavity, and endoscopic loop ties were placed at the base of the inverted sac. Because this technique does not allow exclusion of the cord structures in males, this procedure should be used only in females. Schier[88] reported a series of laparoscopic hernia repairs in 14 females. In his technique, two to three intracorporeally placed Z-stitches were used to close the processus vaginalis.

Montupet and Esposito[71] reported the first successful laparoscopic hernia repair in boys. A purse-string stitch was placed around the neck of the sac, and care was taken to deliberately exclude the vas deferens and spermatic vessels. There were no surgical complications in 45 males, but there were two early recurrences requiring a second laparoscopic repair. In 2000 Schier[89] updated his series and included males. He also altered his technique, using several interrupted sutures rather than Z-stitches to close the sac. This procedure was performed on 129 patients (81 boys), with one early recurrence. More recently, Schier adopted an intracorporeal purse-string stitch in an effort to reduce recurrences.

Other groups have made use of specially designed devices to pass sutures extraperitoneally around the neck of the sac. Lee and Liang[60] reported on 450 patients in whom such a device was used and found a recurrence rate of 0.88%, comparable to open repairs. Prasad et al.[77] reported a small series in which a commercially available curved steel awl was used to assist passage of the sutures.

The technique of laparoscopic hernia repair is still evolving and is troubled by a fairly high recurrence rate. We have stopped performing laparoscopic procedures in males owing to this high recurrence rate and to our concern that the cord structures cannot be visualized and protected as well as with the open technique. However, significant changes in the technique will continue to occur.

Laparoscopic hernia surgery in males is performed with the patient under general anesthesia in the supine position and a nasogastric tube and Foley or straight catheter in place. A 5-mm trocar is placed transumbilically, and a pneumoperitoneum is established. A laparoscopic inspection is then performed. Bilateral or unusual hernias, such as femoral or direct hernias, are easily identified. Two 3-mm stab incisions are made in the right and left lower quadrants, respectively, allowing the trocarless introduction of 3-mm instruments. Placing the ports in this way allows both sides to be addressed easily. A purse-string stitch is placed at the neck of the sac using a laparoscopic 3-mm needle driver. The cord structures are readily identified and excluded from the purse-string stitch. Hematoma formation must be avoided because it will obscure the cord structures as the procedure progresses and may lead to injury. Once the stitch is placed, it is tied intracorporeally. The 3-mm ports do not require suture closure, and the umbilical port is closed with absorbable suture.

As mentioned earlier, several alternative techniques are available. The most straightforward of these may be that of Prasad et al.[77] In their technique, an umbilical port is placed for the camera, and that is the only port used. The level of the internal ring on the abdominal wall skin is determined by palpation, and a small skin incision is made with a knife. Under direct laparoscopic guidance, a purse-string suture is placed through the skin into the peritoneal cavity halfway around the internal ring using an extracorporeal needle driver, and the needle is left in the abdomen. A curved steel awl is then used to come around the other half of the ring through the same skin opening, taking care not to injure the cord structures. The awl is used to grasp the needle and pull it back out, completing the purse-string. The knot is tied extracorporeally, and closure of the internal ring is confirmed laparoscopically.

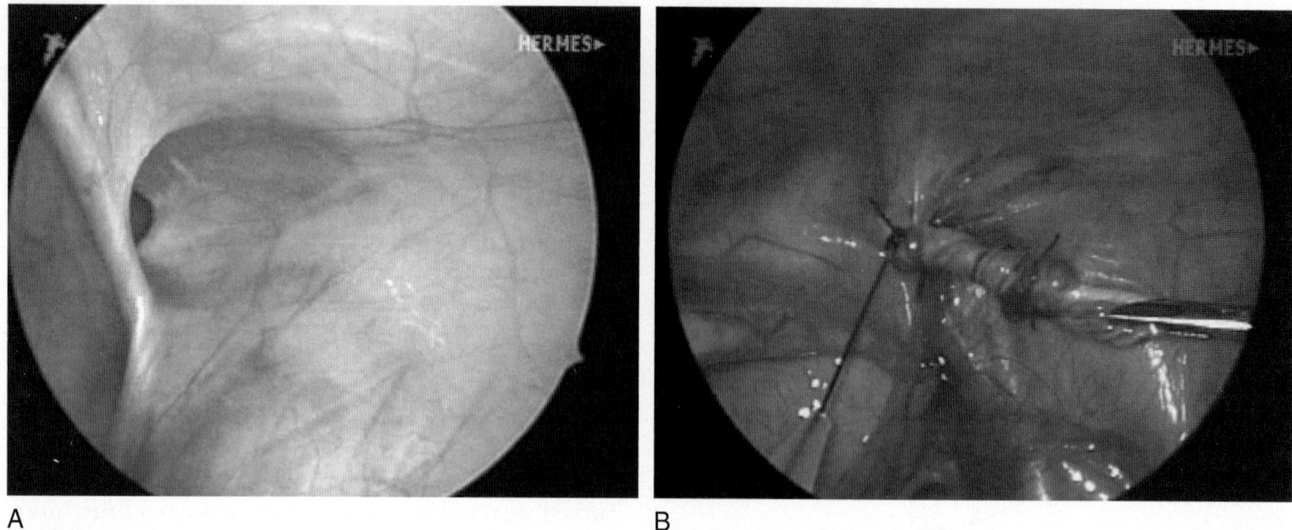

Figure 74-6 Laparoscopic view of the processus vaginalis. *A,* Open processus. *B,* Processus inverted into the peritoneal cavity and ligated with endoloops.

In females we prefer to use a laparoscopic inversion ligation (LIL) technique because there is no need to be concerned about cord structures. Port sites are chosen as for males.[113] A bowel grasping or Maryland clamp is placed into the hernia sac, and the apex is grasped and inverted into the abdominal cavity (Fig. 74-6). The sac is twisted on itself, and two endoloops are placed at the base to ligate the sac. Care is needed to ensure that when twisting the sac, the adnexal structures are not caught up in the high ligation. We have had no recurrences in our series, and surgical complications are quite low.

CONTRALATERAL EXPLORATION

In 1955 Rothenberg and Barnett[82] reported that in children with inguinal hernias, 100% of those younger than 1 year and 68.5% of those older than 1 year had bilateral hernias. Since that report, routine bilateral exploration has been one of the most contentiously debated issues in pediatric hernia surgery. The recent application of laparoscopy to the diagnosis of bilateral hernias has added to the debate.

Because of the high rate of bilateral hernias, Rothenberg and Barnett recommended routine contralateral exploration; however, some of their findings were not true hernias but rather patent processus vaginalis. Although many surgeons supported routine exploration, others noted that there was a high negative exploration rate because not every patent processus develops into a clinical hernia. In addition, routine exploration puts both testicles and both vas deferens at risk. Even so, in a 1981 survey of pediatric surgeons, Rowe and Marchildon[86] found that 80% of surgeons routinely performed contralateral exploration in boys, and 90% did so in girls younger than 1 year. A more recent survey suggests a trend away from routine contralateral exploration: 40% of respondents routinely explore males younger than 2 years, and only 13% routinely explore boys between 2 and 5 years; 39% routinely explore females, and 51% routinely explore premature infants.[61] This survey also highlighted another trend: 24% of surgeons use laparoscopy to investigate the contralateral side.

We believe that routine exploration of the contralateral side results in many unnecessary procedures, needlessly places the contralateral vas and testicle at risk, and is an unwarranted expense. We base that judgment on the fact that although as many as 60% to 80% of infants younger than 1 year and 40% of older children have a patent processus, only about 20% of patients presenting with a unilateral hernia develop a clinical hernia on the other side.[84,86,93] Therefore, one would need to perform approximately 10 operations to prevent two future hernias. Some suggest that the incidence of hernia on the asymptomatic side is as low as 7%. Thus, many surgeons perform selective contralateral exploration based on the sex and age of the patient or the side of the hernia.

Sex

Historically, many surgeons performed bilateral exploration in females primarily because doing so posed very little risk to patients because of the relative rarity of finding reproductive structures in the sac. In their 1981 survey, Rowe and Marchildon[86] reported that 90% of surgeons routinely explored the contralateral groin in girls younger than 1 year. Wiener et al.[107] surveyed surgeons in 1996 and found that 84% performed routine exploration in females younger than 4 years. It appears that this trend is decreasing, because in 2002 Levitt et al.[61] found that only 39% of surgeons performed bilateral exploration in girls younger than 5 years. Despite the rare findings of reproductive structures in the hernia sac, damage to the inguinal floor and the ilioinguinal and iliofemoral nerves is still possible. Because of the lack of follow-up data in the literature, it is difficult to quantify these risks. Still, we know that only about 20% of females with a unilateral hernia will develop a contralateral hernia; thus a large number of explorations would be needed to prevent a few hernias from developing. Chertin et al.[18] recently reviewed 300 females undergoing unilateral hernia repair. In a follow-up ranging from 1 to 4 years, only 8% developed a contralateral hernia, and this was not influenced by age at operation or side of initial hernia.

Age

Based on the findings of Rothenberg and Barnett[82] that 100% of infants younger than 1 year with inguinal hernias have bilateral patent processus vaginalis, many surgeons routinely perform contralateral exploration in infants. In the 2002 survey of surgeons, 51% of respondents stated that they routinely performed contralateral exploration in premature infants, and 40% performed contralateral exploration in boys younger than 2 years.[61] This is considerably lower than the 80% of respondents who routinely explored the contralateral side in boys in the 1981 survey.[86] In a series of 1052 patients followed for up to 11 years, contralateral hernias appeared in 13.1% of boys younger than 1 year and 13.7% of those younger than 2 years.[49] In females, contralateral hernias appeared in 9.6% of patients younger than 1 year and 13.9% of those younger than 5 years. Another recent series looked at 181 infants younger than 1 year undergoing unilateral repair.[4] In a follow-up ranging from 5 to 10 years, 7.7% developed contralateral hernias. Based on these results, it is questionable whether younger children have a significantly higher risk of developing a contralateral inguinal hernia sometime in the future.

Side

It is speculated that right-sided hernias are more common than left-sided ones because the right processus vaginalis closes later. Therefore, patients presenting with left-sided hernias would be more likely to have bilateral hernias than those presenting initially with right-sided hernias. As a result, many surgeons recommended routine exploration in patients presenting with left-sided hernias. McGregor et al.[64] reviewed a 20-year experience and found that 41% of patients with an initial left inguinal hernia later presented with a right hernia, whereas only 14% of patients who initially had a right-sided hernia developed a left hernia. Other series, however, reported much lower rates of contralateral occurrence after left-sided repair. For example, Kemmotsu et al.[50] reviewed 1052 patients who had undergone unilateral repair and found that the side of initial repair did not influence contralateral recurrence. In a meta-analysis, Miltenburg et al.[67] found that with left repair, the risk of contralateral recurrence was 11% higher than with right repair. Overall, it appears that the side of the initial hernia has no bearing on the risk of developing a contralateral hernia.

Alternative Exploration Techniques

In an effort to limit the number of negative contralateral explorations, alternative techniques have been used to determine the patency of the contralateral processus. One of these is diagnostic pneumoperitoneum (the Goldstein test), in which the abdomen is insufflated via the hernia sac and the contralateral groin is palpated for crepitance, indicating a patent processus vaginalis. In a study of 62 patients, 7 (11%) had a positive study.[49] Each underwent exploration and was found to have a contralateral hernia. Of the 55 remaining patients, only three (5%) subsequently developed a clinical hernia. In our opinion, this technique is both safe and reliable; however, others have found it to be unreliable and likely to miss a patent processes. Bakes dilators have been used to probe the contralateral groin, but this technique is often difficult as well as unreliable. Herniograms were discussed previously and are rarely used today. US was also discussed earlier and is fairly sensitive for detecting the presence of a patent processes vaginalis when appropriate size criteria are used.

Laparoscopy

In the early 1990s laparoscopy was introduced as a means of assessing the contralateral groin. Laparoscopy has the advantages of being technically easy and allowing direct visualization of the contralateral internal ring; in addition, the equipment is now widely available. Laparoscopy can be performed in a variety of ways. Perhaps the most common technique is to place a port through the ipsilateral hernia sac to insufflate the abdomen and introduce the camera. Evaluation of the contralateral side is easier with the use of an angled scope (e.g., 70 degrees). Others introduce the camera via an umbilical port or introduce small cameras through an angiocatheter placed through the abdominal wall to give in-line visualization. Also, both flexible and rigid scopes have been used.[35]

Yerkes et al.[111] used laparoscopy to evaluate 627 patients younger than 10 years with unilateral hernias during a 5-year period for the presence of a contralateral patent processus vaginalis (CPPV). Among the patients younger than 1 year, 46% were diagnosed with a CPPV; 39% of those older than 1 year had a CPPV. Geisler et al.[36] evaluated 358 patients aged 1 month to 13 years and determined that the overall incidence of CPPV was 33%. By age, the incidence was as follows: 50% of those younger than 1 year, 45% younger than 2 years, 37% younger than 5 years, and 15% older than 5 years. Pellegrin et al.[76] studied 50 patients and found that the overall incidence of CPPV was 31%; Rescorla et al.[81] reported a 48% overall incidence. Overall, laparoscopy has shown a fairly consistent rate of CPPV, approximately 30% to 45%.

The question becomes, which of these CPPVs will eventually become clinical hernias? The answer is not known and would most likely require a randomized, prospective trial with essentially lifelong follow-up—a practical impossibility. However, Kiesewetter and Parenzan[52] performed routine contralateral exploration in 100 infants younger than 2 years and found a 61% incidence of CPPV; they then closely followed 231 patients who had only unilateral repair and found that 31% went on to develop contralateral hernias, approximately half of what would be expected. Based on this and data from Rowe and Clatworthy,[84] one would expect laparoscopy to decrease the number of unneeded procedures significantly. Opponents of laparoscopy point out that more than half the patients will receive a procedure they do not need (not counting patients with false-negative laparoscopy). Moreover, when factoring in time and equipment, there is a significant increase in cost; however, the advent of reusable equipment has diminished these cost and time factors.

As children age, the rate of CPPV clearly decreases. The question becomes, is there an age after which laparoscopy is no longer valuable? Bhatia et al.[8] studied 101 children between 2 and 8 years old and 171 children younger than 2 years. Among the latter, 38% had CPPV, whereas 20% of the older children had CPPV. In a group of 12 patients older than 8 years, only one was positive for CPPV. The authors concluded that laparoscopy is justified in children older than 2 years but could reach no conclusion about children older than 8 years because of the small sample size. In the study by Geisler et al.,[36] there was a 15% incidence of CPPV in patients older than 5 years. It seems likely that somewhere between 5 and 8 years of age, there is a significant decrease in the utility of laparoscopy.

IRREDUCIBLE HERNIA (INCARCERATION)

Most inguinal hernias are readily reducible into the abdominal cavity. Those that are difficult to reduce are incarcerated. A strangulated hernia occurs when there is vascular compromise of the entrapped viscera, caused by constriction from a tight internal or external ring. Most children progress rapidly to strangulation if the hernia is not reduced.[101] Initially, constriction by the ring leads to venous and lymphatic obstruction and subsequent swelling of the viscera. Arterial compromise follows and, if the process is unchecked, leads to gangrene and perforation of the bowel or other viscera. Strangulation can also damage the testicle by compromising the blood supply, and patients with incarcerated hernias are more likely to have testicular atrophy after hernia repair.

Various series have reported that the incidence of incarceration ranges from 12% to 17% and is similar in boys and girls.[83,98] Incarceration is most likely to occur in the first year of life; the incidence falls off thereafter (Fig. 74-7). In two large series, full-term infants younger than 2 to 3 months old were found to have incarceration rates of 28% to 31%[80,83]; in another report, the rate was 24% in infants younger than 6 weeks old.[69] Interestingly, premature infants were found to have a lower incidence of incarceration compared with full-term infants (13% versus 18%). This may be a result of larger rings and weaker muscle. Also, many of these infants are in neonatal intensive care units under constant surveillance, and incarcerated hernias may be prevented by early reduction or may simply be underreported.

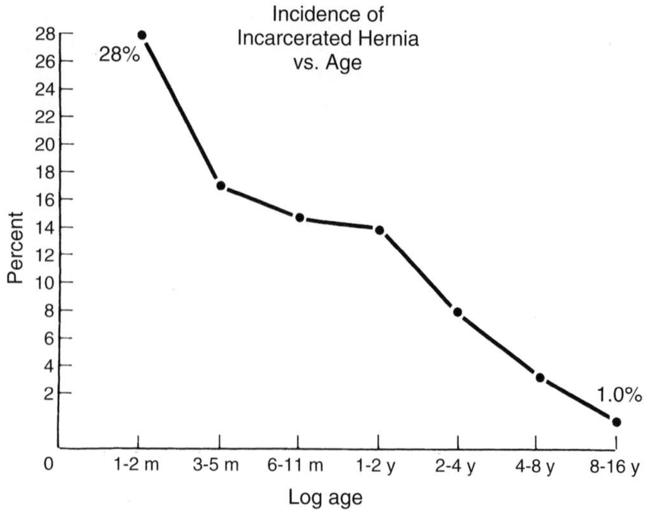

Figure 74–7 Incidence of incarcerated hernia by age. Incarceration is most common during the first year of life; then the incidence drastically decreases.

Diagnosis of Strangulation

If a loop of bowel becomes entrapped in a hernia, the patient often becomes extremely irritable and develops intense pain, followed by signs of obstruction (abdominal distention, vomiting, absence of flatus or stool). A tense, nonfluctuant mass is found in the groin, possibly extending into the scrotum. As the viscera strangulate, the mass becomes more tender. Occasionally the mass transilluminates and may be confused with a hydrocele. Under no circumstances should the mass be aspirated in an attempt to diagnose and treat a supposed hydrocele.

Late signs of strangulation are shock, blood in the stool, and peritonitis. The testes are usually palpable, but they may be large and firm and difficult to distinguish from a testicular torsion. Abdominal radiographs reveal partial or complete bowel obstruction. Bowel gas may also be seen in the scrotum. In uncertain cases, US can be useful to distinguish bowel from hydrocele fluid or a testicular torsion.

Nonoperative Management

In patients without obvious signs of shock or peritonitis, nonoperative management is tried first. In most instances the incarcerated bowel lies anterior to the external ring and is trapped there, so we prefer the following technique (Fig. 74-8): Lay the child down and try to calm him or her without feeding, with the feet elevated if possible. Standing on the ipsilateral side of the child, or at the feet of an infant, place the left index and middle finger on the ipsilateral anterior superior iliac crest and sweep the fingers down along the inguinal canal toward the ipsilateral scrotum, keeping tension on the testicle, inguinal mass, or scrotal skin with the left hand. Constant gentle traction on the scrotum helps align the long axis of the hernia sac with the axis of the inguinal canal. Next, at the level of the ipsilateral internal ring, apply pressure with the right index

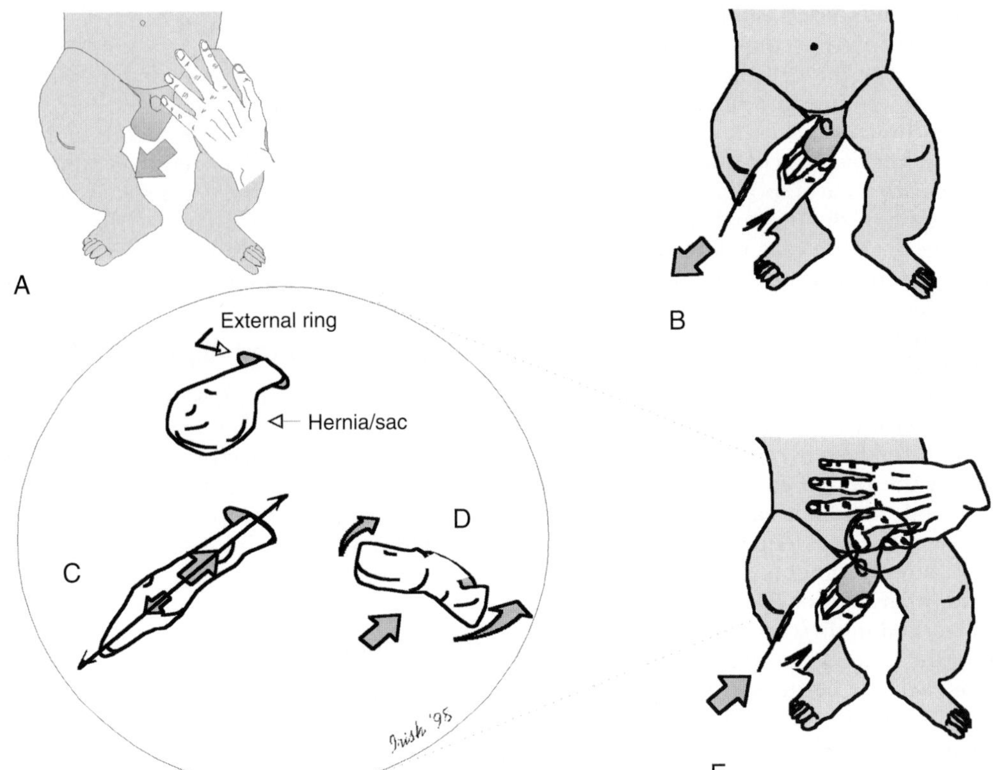

Figure 74–8 Suggested method of reducing an incarcerated inguinal hernia. *A,* Standing on the ipsilateral side of the child or at the feet of an infant, place the left middle and index fingers on the ipsilateral (left in this example) anterior superior iliac spine and sweep them down along the inguinal canal, toward the ipsilateral scrotum. *B,* Keep tension on the testicle, hernia mass, or scrotal skin with the left hand. *C,* Constant, gentle traction on the scrotum helps align the long axis of the hernia with the axis of the inguinal canal. Next, apply pressure with the right index finger and thumb on either side of the hernia neck. *D,* This, along with traction on the scrotum, helps keep the external and internal rings open and prevents the hernia sac from overlapping or being caught on these potential barriers during reduction. *E,* Finally, with the left hand at the apex of the mass, and with constant pressure on the inguinal canal from the right index finger and thumb, walk the fingers slowly up the groin toward the internal ring, keeping constant pressure on the bottom of the hernia contents.

finger and thumb on either side of the hernia neck. This, along with traction on the scrotum, helps align the external and internal rings and keep them open, and it prevents the hernia sac from overlapping or being caught on these potential barriers during reduction. Finally, with the left hand at the apex of the mass, and with constant pressure at the level of the internal ring from the right index finger and thumb, walk the fingers of the left hand slowly up the groin toward the internal ring, keeping constant pressure on the bottom of the hernia contents. This may take several minutes. If successful, the hernia contents will gradually disappear into the internal ring. To be certain that the hernia is reduced, compare the contralateral side. If this technique is unsuccessful or the child has a difficult time tolerating it, sedation may be used. We do not recommend reduction of the bowel under general anesthesia, because injury to the bowel may occur or gangrenous bowel may be placed back into the peritoneal cavity and be unrecognized. Often sedation alone is sufficient to promote spontaneous reduction. Reduction of gangrenous bowel has been reported, however, so we recommend watching the child in the hospital for 24 hours after a difficult reduction.[99] We delay definitive repair of the hernia for at least 24 to 48 hours to let the edema resolve.

Operative Management

When nonoperative management fails or the patient has signs of shock or peritonitis, surgery is indicated. The patient is prepared for surgery in the standard way. Intravenous fluids are initiated, and urine output is monitored. Broad-spectrum antibiotics are given, and if signs of obstruction are present, a nasogastric tube is placed. After adequate resuscitation, the patient is taken to the operating room. If the hernia reduces after general anesthesia is induced but before surgery, the operation should still proceed. Several operative approaches have been advocated for incarcerated hernias, including inguinal and preperitoneal approaches. Laparoscopy can also be useful in the management of incarcerated hernias.

Inguinal Approach

The standard approach to inguinal hernia repair is used, except that the incision is somewhat longer. The external ring is opened, and the hernia sac is identified. If the hernia contents are still present, they are inspected and, if viable, reduced back into the peritoneal cavity. The hernia is then repaired in the standard fashion. If the intestine cannot be reduced, the inferior epigastric vessels are ligated, and a portion of the floor of the inguinal canal is taken down to enlarge the internal ring. A formal floor repair is required in these instances.

If the bowel in the hernia sac is of questionable viability, it can be covered with a warm sponge and reinspected in a few minutes. Again, if the internal ring is constricting, it can be enlarged, taking care not to let the bowel slip back into the peritoneal cavity. If the bowel is determined to be nonviable, it can be resected and primarily reanastomosed through the inguinal incision, through a counterincision through the transversalis fascia (La Roque incision), or through a separate abdominal incision.[55] If the bowel is viable, it is replaced into the peritoneal cavity, and the hernia repair is completed.

Difficulty arises if the hernia contents reduce before they can be inspected, in which case the hernia sac is inspected and opened. If no evidence of bowel infarction is found, such as bowel contents or foul-smelling or blood-stained fluid, many surgeons proceed with repair. Laparoscopy can be used in these instances to determine bowel viability, with the camera placed either in the umbilical position or through the hernia sac. In fact, a camera can be placed at the beginning of the procedure, and the hernia contents can be reduced under laparoscopic visualization.[58] If the contents are viable, a standard hernia repair is performed. If the bowel is questionable, it can be reinspected laparoscopically after the hernia repair. If it is clearly nonviable, the intestine can be brought out through the umbilical port site and resected.

Preperitoneal Approach

Some surgeons prefer a preperitoneal approach to incarcerated hernias. This approach, described in adults by Cheatle[16] in 1921, has been used successfully in children. Kamaledeen and Shanbhogue,[48] in a report of 24 patients, and Turnock et al.,[102] in a report of 12 patients, found the preperitoneal approach easier in terms of reducing the hernia contents and performing the herniotomy. If necessary, the peritoneum can be opened to determine bowel viability.

The preperitoneal approch is performed through a skinfold incision at the level of the anterior superior iliac spine, and a standard gridiron approach is used to reach the preperitoneal plane. The internal ring and the hernia sac are identified lateral to the inferior epigastric vessels. The peritoneum is then opened at the base of the hernia sac, and the contents are inspected. Nonviable bowel can be readily dealt with through this incision. Otherwise, the bowel contents are reduced back into the peritoneal cavity, and the herniotomy is performed. Should the external ring prevent reduction, one can simply dissect superficially to the external oblique muscle down to the external ring and enlarge it. Once the herniotomy is performed, the wound is closed in the standard fashion. This incision resembles an appendectomy scar on the right side, so the parents should be warned of this. This preperitoneal approach can also be performed transperitoneally and is preferred by some surgeons.

Pfannenstiel Approach

Koga et al.[53] recently proposed a Pfannenstiel transperitoneal approach to incarcerated hernias. They perform a Pfannenstiel skin incision followed by a midline fasciotomy. The bowel is reduced and inspected, and if resection is necessary, there is excellent exposure through this incision. The hernia sac can also be easily repaired through this incision. The authors suggest that this approach leaves a cosmetically acceptable scar.

Authors' Preferred Approach

Our preferred approach is to perform laparoscopy through an umbilical port, reduce the hernia contents under laparoscopic visualization, and perform subsequent herniotomy through a standard inguinal incision. There are no reports of complete laparoscopic repair of incarcerated hernias in children.

Incarcerated Ovary

Special mention must be made of the female patient with an asymptomatic incarcerated ovary. Historically, many believed that this incarcerated, mobile, nontender ovary was of long-standing duration and was not at risk for strangulation. Subsequent reports have challenged this idea.[72] The consensus is that these hernias should be repaired as soon as possible.[61]

POSTOPERATIVE COMPLICATIONS

Scrotal Swelling

After hernia repair, and particularly after communicating hydrocele repair, fluid may accumulate in the distal sac, forming a hydrocele. Usually this resolves spontaneously; rarely, aspiration may be necessary. Scrotal hematoma may follow excision of the distal sac.

Iatrogenic Undescended Testicle

Iatrogenic undescended testis after hernia repair is an uncommon but possibly underreported complication. Kiesewetter and Oh[51] reported 2 patients with this abnormality in a series of 248 patients, and Hecker and Ring-Mrozik[44] reported 5 patients in a series of 1957 patients, an incidence of 0.2%. Except in the case of congenital undescended testicle, this abnormality results from failure to replace the testis back in the scrotum at the conclusion of the procedure, or the testis may subsequently become trapped in a retracted location. Orchiopexy is required to correct this problem.

Recurrence

It is difficult to determine the precise incidence of recurrence after indirect inguinal hernia repair because factors such as sex and incarceration are not always clearly defined in reported series. In general, the reported recurrence rate for uncomplicated hernia repair is 0% to 0.8%; this rises to about 15% for premature infants and about 20% after operation for incarcerated hernias. In many series, patients were not contacted for long-term review; therefore, the true incidence is not known and is probably higher than stated. Reports on patients with incarcerated inguinal hernias often do not state whether the initial management was operative or nonoperative.

Many factors associated with the development of primary hernias may predispose to recurrence. For instance, Grosfeld et al.,[41] in a series of 25 patients with ventriculoperitoneal shunts, identified three recurrent inguinal hernias (12%). Incarceration is also an important risk factor for recurrence. Steinau et al.[97] found that in 29 patients (25 boys, 4 girls) with recurrent inguinal hernia, the primary hernia had been incarcerated in 24%; in contrast, a 7.6% incidence of recurrence was reported in 2754 patients without incarceration. Other risk factors were postoperative complications (9.4% recurrence rate) and concomitant diseases and abnormalities.[96] Interestingly, Harvey et al.[43] found that the surgeon's level of experience was not a factor, although technical inadequacies contributed to recurrence. Most recurrent inguinal hernias are indirect and probably result from tearing of a friable sac, failure to dissect the complete sac, a slipped ligature at the neck of the sac, or failure to ligate the sac high enough at the internal ring. Another risk factor for recurrence is prematurity. Several series have reported an increased recurrence rate in premature infants, ranging from 2% to 15%.

Less frequently, a "recurrence" presents as a direct inguinal hernia or as a femoral hernia missed at the first operation. Of the 34 recurrences reported by Steinau et al.,[96] four were direct and one was femoral. In the series reported by Fonkalsrud et al.,[33] 4 of 13 direct inguinal hernias (31%) followed repair of an indirect hernia. A direct hernia that presents after repair of an indirect hernia is either a concomitant hernia not recognized at the initial operation or new pathology caused by damage to the posterior wall of the inguinal canal during the initial dissection. A recurrent hernia in the femoral area is also more likely to be a missed hernia than a true recurrence.

Several large series now exist of laparoscopic inguinal hernia repair in children. Schier[89] reported 403 inguinal hernia repairs on 279 patients and had a recurrence rate of 2.3%. The technique of laparoscopic inguinal hernia repair varies from surgeon to surgeon and is still evolving. Moreover, there is likely to be a learning curve with the laparoscopic technique, so recurrences will probably be more frequent earlier in one's experience. In our experience with laparoscopic hernia repair in males, recurrence rates were quite high; therefore, we do not use this technique in males. However, in females, using the previously described LIL repair, we have had no recurrences.

Injury to the Vas Deferens

Although vas transection may be obvious intraoperatively, accidental operative crush injury to the vas deferens is unlikely to be recognized until adulthood, and even then, only if the injury is bilateral. Vas transections should be immediately repaired with two to three simple monofilament 8-0 absorbable sutures placed with the aid of magnification. Sparkman[94] reported a 1.6% incidence of proven injury to the vas deferens, based on the finding of "segments of the vas deferens" in 5 of 313 hernia sacs from children who had undergone hernia repair. Details of the cases were not published, and no histologic or clinical information is available, however. Walker and Mills[104] found small glandular inclusions in approximately 6% of hernia sacs from prepubertal boys, which they believed to be müllerian duct remnants and not segments of the vas deferens. They emphasized that these structures were of no clinical significance. It is likely that similar structures accounted for some of the findings reported by Sparkman. Perhaps a better estimate is provided by Steigman et al.,[95] who reviewed the histology of hernia sacs submitted from 7314 males undergoing hernia repair over a 14.5-year period. Seventeen cases contained vas deferens (0.23%), 22 had epididymis (0.3%), and 30 had embryonal rests (0.4%). Three sacs (0.04%) contained coexisting vas deferens and epididymis. Partrick et al.[74] found only a 0.13% incidence of vas injury in an analysis of 1494 sacs and argued that the incidence is so low that routine histologic evaluation of the sac is not warranted.

Shandling and Janik[91] demonstrated the vulnerability of the vas during hernia repair. In their experiments, the vas deferens of rats were exposed and grasped with fingers, nontoothed forceps, bulldog vascular clamps, or mosquito hemostats. Serial studies of the vas were done over 6 months, and damage to the vas was found in all manipulations except digital handling. Ceylan et al.[15] demonstrated that stretching of the spermatic cord might also damage the vas and testicle. They applied horizontal stretch force of varying amounts to the spermatic cords of rats. Significant thinning of the smooth muscle layer of the vas was noted with all degrees of stretching, as was testicular atrophy.

The relationship between male fertility and previous inguinal hernia repair is not well defined. Homonnai et al.[46] reported findings in 131 men referred to an infertility clinic who had undergone inguinal hernia repair between the ages of 2 and 35 years. Although 14% of these men had testicular atrophy or abnormal sperm findings that might have been related to the hernia operation, clinical details, such as the incidence of incarceration and the experience of the surgeon, were not reported. Yavetz et al.[110] reviewed 8500 patients referred to an infertility clinic, 565 of whom (6.65%) reported an incidence of inguinal hernia repair with or without testicular atrophy. No correlation was found between age at hernia repair and semen quality following operation.

Operative injury to the vas deferens may result in obstruction of the vas, with diversion of spermatozoa to the testicular lymphatics. This breach of the blood-testis barrier produces an antigenic challenge, with the formation of spermatic autoagglutinating antibodies. In a review of 76 infertile men with spermatic autoagglutinating antibodies, 12 (16%) had had unilateral inguinal hernia repair during childhood.[34] In 10 of these men, the site of the inguinal hernia repair was explored, and in 5 patients, obstruction of the vas deferens was identified. The authors concluded that accidental transection and ligation of the vas can and does occur during inguinal hernia repair in a child and may be a reason for infertility in men. Parkhouse and Hendry[73] reported similar findings. Thus, although these reports do not indicate the incidence of male infertility after inguinal hernia repair, they suggest that an association exists.

Testicular Atrophy

The testicular vessels are vulnerable to operative injury, particularly in small infants, but reports of testicular atrophy after routine hernia repair are rare. Fischer and Mumenthaler[32] and Fahstrom et al.[30] each reported a 1% incidence of testicular atrophy. In these studies, the operative technique varied, and the number of incarcerated hernias was not reported; therefore, this may not reflect the true incidence of testicular atrophy when hernia repair is performed by an experienced surgeon using simple high ligation to obliterate the open sac.

With incarcerated hernia, the blood supply to the testis may be compromised. The incidence of testicular compromise in association with incarcerated inguinal hernia ranges from 2.6% to 5%. The finding of a cyanotic testicle at emergency operation is common, occurring in approximately 11% to 29% of cases. The actual incidence of testicular atrophy as indicated by histologic examination or diminished size at follow-up is much lower, varying from 0% to 19%. Unfortunately, reported series of patients treated with emergency operation consist of small numbers of patients, and the length of follow-up and the criteria for evaluation of the testis vary considerably. Puri et al.,[78] in an analysis of 87 boys with incarcerated hernia treated by nonoperative reduction, found unilateral testicular atrophy in 2 patients (2.3 %). From the available data, we conclude that vascular compromise is common, but the risk of actual infarction is low. Therefore, unless the testis is frankly necrotic, it should not be removed.

Herniated Ovary

The herniated ovary and fallopian tube are also susceptible to vascular compromise as a result of either incarceration or, perhaps more likely, torsion of the ovary within the hernia sac. The reported incidence of strangulation of irreducible ovaries is as high as 32%. Boley et al.[10] reported a 27% strangulation rate in 15 females presenting with incarceration.

Intestinal Injury

With incarcerated hernias, the incidence of intestinal infarction is remarkably low. Between 1960 and 1965, the incidence of intestinal resection in Rowe and Clatworthy's[83] report of 351 patients with incarcerated hernias was 1.4%. A review of three series published since 1978 showed no resections in 221 patients with incarcerated hernias.

Loss of Abdominal Domain

One complication of hernia surgery, particularly in premature infants, that is rarely discussed is postoperative respiratory failure as a result of lost abdominal domain. In giant inguinal hernias, particularly bilateral ones, the majority of intestine can lie within the hernia sac and outside of the peritoneal cavity. If this persists for some time, the intestine can lose its right of abdominal domain. During repair, the intestine is returned to the abdominal cavity, resulting in increased intra-abdominal pressure and respiratory failure. Bascombe et al.[5] reported an ex-premature infant with large bilateral inguinal hernias who required 41 days of mechanical ventilation after repair.

Respiratory failure after inguinal hernia repair is quite common. Gollin et al.[39] found that 34% of premature infants required mechanical ventilation after herniorrhaphy. Increased intra-abdominal pressure as a result of loss of domain may be an unrecognized contributor to this problem. As a result of our experience, we recommend staged repair of large bilateral hernias in the elective setting; with modern techniques, the risk of a second anesthesia is very low. In an emergency setting, such as repair of giant incarcerated hernias, a silo such as that used for abdominal wall defects may be considered to alleviate abdominal compartment pressures and allow the intestine to be slowly returned to the abdomen.

MORTALITY

Mortality associated with inguinal hernia may be related to complications of the hernia or to coexisting risk factors, such as prematurity or cardiac disease. In 1938 Thorndike and Ferguson[101] reported an overall mortality of 2.8% for incarcerated hernias treated between 1927 and 1936. In 1954 Clatworthy and Thompson[21] reported one death in 135 patients treated for incarcerated hernia (0.7%); in a 1970 report from the same institution, there were no deaths among 351 patients treated for incarcerated hernia. Since then, death from incarcerated hernia has become a rarity. The risk is higher when the hernia is strangulated. In the United Kingdom in 1989, five deaths were reported in infants with strangulated hernia. The risk factors identified included age younger than 6 months and lack of pediatric experience on the part of the surgeon and the anesthesiologist.

Operative mortality in premature infants is now rare. In two of the most recent series of premature infants undergoing hernia repair, no deaths were reported in a total of 303 patients.[54,69]

COMPLICATIONS OF LAPAROSCOPIC REPAIR

Laparoscopy has only recently been applied to the repair of pediatric inguinal hernias, making long-term conclusions impossible. However, short-term complications have been reported. Schier et al.[90] reported their combined experience with 933 laparoscopic repairs in 666 children, with a follow-up ranging from 2 months to 7 years. The recurrence rate was 3.4%, but the authors did not break down the incidence of recurrence by age or sex. They also noted four postoperative hydroceles and a "subtle change in testicular position and size" in one male patient. In Schier's[89] personal series of 403 inguinal hernia repairs in 279 children, a recurrence rate of 2.7% was reported over a mean follow-up of 23 months.

As stated earlier, we do not routinely perform laparoscopic hernia repair in males because of the high incidence of recurrence. We perform laparoscopic repair in females using a slightly different technique than that reported in the literature. To date, we have had no recurrences, but the numbers are very small and follow-up is limited.

To date, no series has identified a vas deferens injury or testicular atrophy using the laparoscopic approach. Proponents argue that because the vas and spermatic vessel are easily identified and avoided, this technique should be better at avoiding iatrogenic injury and minimizing postoperative infertility. Given the small patient numbers and the limited follow-up, this remains to be seen, because most vas injuries during open surgery go unrecognized until issues of fertility develop. Therefore, we recommend that laparoscopic repair of pediatric hernias in males be limited to special circumstances, such as recurrent inguinal hernias repaired initially via the groin or an incidental inguinal hernia found during a clean laparoscopic case performed for another reason.

SPECIAL CONSIDERATIONS

Prematurity

It is well established that premature infants have a higher incidence of inguinal hernias and are likely to have a bilateral presentation. The more premature the infant, the higher the incidence of inguinal hernia. Walsh,[105] in a review of 82 infants weighing less than 2000 g, found a 13% incidence of inguinal hernia; 7 of 28 infants (25%) weighing less than 1500 g had inguinal hernias, compared with 4 of 54 infants (7%) weighing more than 1500 g. Rescorla and Grosfeld[80] reviewed 100 infants younger than 2 months old who required inguinal hernia repair; 30% of these infants were premature, and 44% had bilateral hernias. Of 1391 very-low-birth-weight infants (<1500 g) reported by Rajput et al.,[79] 222 (16%) developed inguinal hernias between 28 days and 20 months of age (corrected). Peevy et al.[75] studied 397 newborn infants and found a 9% incidence of inguinal hernias in those weighing between 1000 and 1500 g and a 30% incidence in those weighing 500 to 1000 g. In a small series reported by Harper et al.,[42] among 37 premature infants weighing less than 1000 g, 11 (30%) developed inguinal hernias; 2 of these 11 (18%) were incarcerated. Although the incidence of incarceration is increased in infants and may be as high as 28%, it appears to be lower in premature infants, with a reported incidence of 13% to 18%.

Ventriculoperitoneal Shunts and Peritoneal Dialysis

A significant factor in the development of an inguinal hernia is excess fluid and pressure in the peritoneal cavity; in patients with a patent processus vaginalis, procedures that introduce fluid into the peritoneal cavity may induce a hernia or hydrocele. It is unknown whether the hernia is caused by the physical presence of the fluid or is secondary to increased intra-abdominal pressure. Abnormal neuromuscular function may also be a factor. Moazam et al.[70] reviewed 134 patients who had ventriculoperitoneal shunt procedures; 19.5% of patients with meningomyelocele and 47% of those with intraventricular hemorrhage had hernias; all of the latter were premature, however. Grosfeld et al.[41] found a 14% incidence of inguinal hernia after the insertion of a ventriculoperitoneal shunt; 20% of these patients developed incarceration, and the hernia recurred in 16%. Based on this study, the authors recommended that (1) infants with ventriculoperitoneal shunts be watched closely for the development of clinical inguinal hernias, (2) operation be done promptly after the diagnosis of a hernia because of the increased risk of incarceration, and (3) the contralateral side be explored in the case of a clinical unilateral hernia. Clarnette et al.[20] evaluated 430 patients who underwent ventriculoperitoneal shunt placement; 15% developed inguinal hernias, and hydroceles developed in another 6% of boys. Hernias were bilateral in 47% of boys and 27% of girls. The incidence of subsequent inguinal hernia development closely paralleled the age at which the shunt was performed. In infants shunted during the first few months of life, the incidence was 30%; it fell sharply to 10% in patients shunted after age 1 year. The authors concluded that increased intra-abdominal pressure is the likely cause of these hernias. In addition, they concluded that the incidence of a patent processus vaginalis is 30% in the first few months of life, which supports the likelihood that the processus vaginalis can close during the first year of life.

There is a well-established risk of inguinal hernia in patients on long-term ambulatory peritoneal dialysis, ranging from 7% to 15%. In such cases, the patent processus vaginalis is likely to develop into a frank hernia. Intraoperative herniography is recommended at the time of peritoneal dialysis catheter placement; water-soluble contrast is infused through the catheter, and the patient is placed in a head-up position for 15 minutes. If a patent processus vaginalis is identified, repair is in order. Alternatively, direct laparoscopic visualization of the internal ring can be performed at the time of catheter placement, particularly if the latter is done laparoscopically. Repair can then be performed via an open approach or laparoscopically.

Sliding Hernia

The fallopian tube or mesosalpinx is frequently found in the wall of the hernia sac in girls and is at risk for injury. The operative management has already been discussed.

The appendix may also be found in the wall of a sliding hernia sac. Appendectomy, if it can be done safely, permits high ligation of the sac in the usual way. Alternatively, the sac is ligated distal to the appendix, and the proximal sac, with the appendix, is reduced into the abdominal cavity, with or without purse-string closure, as for a sliding hernia in girls. In an infant, the bladder may lie medially beneath the internal ring and may be pulled down with the hernia sac during dissection. If this is not recognized, high ligation of the hernia sac may include the bladder wall, leading to hematuria, possible necrosis of the bladder wall, and extravasation of urine. This situation can be avoided by careful inspection of the neck of the sac at the time of transfixion. When there is any question about this possibility, the sac should be opened and the contents inspected. Occasionally, the bladder may extend down the medial wall of the sac, representing a true sliding hernia. Shaw and Santulli[92] recommend a flap operation, as in the Goldstein-Potts repair in females, but we simply ligate and divide the sac distal to the bladder, invert the stump, and narrow the internal ring (Bevan repair).[7]

Direct Inguinal Hernia

Direct inguinal hernia was once thought to be extremely rare in children, but the increasing use of laparoscopy has shown it to be somewhat more common than previously believed. In the past, the most common presentation was as a recurrence after repair of an indirect inguinal hernia, probably because the direct hernia was missed at the initial operation or was caused by damage to the floor of the inguinal canal during the first operation. Wright[108] encountered only 19 direct hernias in more than 1600 inguinal hernia operations (1.2%). However, Gorsler and Schier[40] found a 3.9% incidence of direct hernias in 403 inguinal hernias. The diagnosis should be suspected if, when operating on an indirect hernia, a typical sac cannot be found and a fascial defect is found medial to the inferior epigastric vessels. Management is by repair of the transversalis fascia, such as a Bassini repair, or by a Cooper's ligament repair.

Femoral Hernia

Femoral hernias are also rare in children and are often misdiagnosed clinically on examination or at the time of indirect inguinal hernia repair. In Fonkalsrud's[33] review of 5452 patients with inguinal hernias and Burke's[13] review of 5141 patients—a total of 10,593 infants and children—there were 21 patients with femoral hernias (0.2%), ranging in age from 6 weeks to 13 years. The female to male ratio is almost 2:1. The correct preoperative diagnosis was made in 8 of 21 patients (38%). Four had bilateral femoral hernias, and in five patients the hernias were incarcerated.

De Caluwe et al.[27] described 38 patients with femoral hernias over a 20-year period; 4 patients had bilateral femoral hernias. The correct preoperative diagnosis was made in 53%. Of the 18 patients who were misdiagnosed, 7 required a second operation. Whenever intraoperative findings (e.g., failure to find a significant indirect inguinal hernia) do not correlate with the preoperative diagnosis, consideration of a direct inguinal hernia or a femoral hernia should be entertained. Before the availability of pediatric laparoscopy, taking down the inguinal floor and inspecting the inguinal canal were justified in these circumstances. However, with the common availability of laparoscopic equipment, Lee and DuBois[59] advocate diagnostic laparoscopy as an adjunct to hernia repair, particularly in cases of recurrence. They described four patients with presumed recurrence of an indirect inguinal hernia who underwent diagnostic laparoscopy at the second surgery; three of these patients had femoral hernias. They also identified three contralateral femoral hernias.

Wright[109] reported 16 patients with femoral hernias and advocated repair through a femoral (infrainguinal) approach, suturing the inguinal ligament to the pectineal ligament and pectineal fascia. Ceran et al.[14] used a mesh plug successfully in four children, as did Lee and DuBois.[59] We prefer a standard Cooper's ligament repair for first-time explorations and have found the mesh plug useful for patients previously operated on with ipsilateral femoral hernias.

Inherited Disorders of Connective Tissue

Patients with Hunter-Hurler, Ehlers-Danlos, and Marfan's syndromes frequently have inguinal hernias and are prone to recurrence unless the floor of the inguinal canal is repaired in addition to the usual high ligation of the sac. Coran and Eraklis[24] found that 36% of 50 patients with Hunter-Hurler syndrome developed inguinal hernias. The recurrence rate with high ligation alone was 56%, and formal herniorrhaphy was recommended. In adolescents, we recommend high ligation of the indirect sac, followed by tensionless floor repair with mesh.

Cystic Fibrosis

The incidence of inguinal hernia in patients with cystic fibrosis is between 6% and 15%.[45] The incidence of absent vas deferens in the general population is 0.5% to 1%, based on vasectomy studies.[65,112] In those with cystic fibrosis, abnormalities of the vas deferens, ranging from obstruction to complete absence, are invariably present and are usually bilateral. Failure to identify the vas should, therefore, lead to an evaluation for cystic fibrosis. Agenesis of the vas deferens is found in association with renal dysgenesis in patients who do not have cystic fibrosis, so evaluation of the upper urinary tract is recommended in these situations.

Intersex

Rarely, a phenotypic female with a palpable gonad in the labia may be a genetic male with androgen insensitivity syndrome or a true hermaphrodite. If an ovary is encountered in the hernia sac of a female patient, it should be carefully examined for evidence of testicular tissue (ovotestis). Males with androgen insensitivity syndrome do not have fallopian tubes and a uterus, but they do have small testes. Hermaphrodites may have a fallopian tube in the hernia sac, and examination of the gonad reveals an asymmetrical ovotestis. In both situations, if an abnormal gonad is encountered, it should not be removed. Small wedge sections are taken from each pole, the gonad is replaced, and the hernia is repaired. This condition is discussed further in Chapters 121 and 122.

Splenogonadal Fusion

Splenic tissue may be fused to an otherwise normal testis (splenotesticular fusion). Presentation is with a scrotal mass, and the usual preoperative diagnosis is a testicular tumor. Orchiectomy is not necessary; intraoperative frozen section provides the diagnosis and allows preservation of the testis. Spleno-ovarian fusion may also be encountered. Alternatively, splenogonadal fusion may present as an undescended testis or intra-abdominal mass. Laparoscopy has been used to both diagnose and treat this condition.

Adrenal Rests

Ectopic adrenal tissue appearing as a small mass of yellowish tissue in the apex of the hernia sac is not rare. It was found in 10 of 385 operations for inguinal hernia (2.6%), an incidental finding in each case.[66] In another series, the incidence was 0.2% in 1077 sacs analyzed.[74] The adrenal tissue at this site is likely the result of attachment of developing adrenal cells to the testis before descent from the retroperitoneum to the scrotum during fetal development.

Congenital Hydrocele

A hydrocele is a collection of fluid in the space surrounding the testicle between the layers of the tunica vaginalis. Hydroceles may be communicating with the peritoneal cavity (patent processus vaginalis with free flow of fluid) or noncommunicating (usually scrotal in males, with a thin groin). Hydroceles are common in infants and children, and in many cases, they are associated with an indirect inguinal hernia. Hydroceles are often bilateral and have a higher rate of occurrence on the right side. They can vary in size and often get larger during the day while the child is upright and then decrease in size overnight while the child is supine and gravity drains the hydrocele. Occasionally, a hydrocele may extend through the inguinal canal into the retroperitoneum as an abdominoscrotal hydrocele. These are frequently confused with indirect inguinal hernias. A child may also present with a roundish, tense, but painless mass in the upper scrotum or inguinal canal; this is a hydrocele of the cord. Daily fluctuation in the size is indicative of a communicating hydrocele. An acute hydrocele may be secondary to an acute process within the tunica vaginalis or torsion of the testis or its appendages. These are associated with considerable pain and tenderness. Alternatively, an acute hydrocele may be seen concurrent with or following an acute upper respiratory infection or a diarrheal illness, when coughing or straining forces fluid into a previously undetected patent processus vaginalis.

Usually a hydrocele can be distinguished from an inguinal hernia on physical examination. Typically, a nontender cystic swelling of the scrotum that surrounds the testicle and transilluminates is evident. Simple transillumination does not guarantee the diagnosis of a hydrocele, however, because incarcerated gas-filled intestine also transilluminates. Therefore, aspiration should never be attempted for diagnosis. It is usually possible to palpate a thin spermatic cord above the hydrocele. However, this may be difficult in a large hydrocele of the cord or an abdominoscrotal hydrocele.

In the majority of children with congenital hydrocele, the processus vaginalis closes behind the hydrocele (noncommunicating), and the hydrocele typically resolves by age 2 years. Therefore, operation is not recommended in the first 2 years of life unless the hydrocele is communicating or a hernia cannot be ruled out. An exception is a large, tense hydrocele associated with discomfort. Hydroceles that persist beyond 2 years of age or those that arise in an older child require operation. The operation consists of high ligation of the patent processus vaginalis. The distal hydrocele sac is opened and drained, and the open sac is left in place; the edges do not require suturing, as in adult hydrocele operations. Reaccumulation of fluid in the sac is rare and generally resolves spontaneously.

REFERENCES

1. Backhouse K: The gubernaculum testis Hunteri: Testicular descent and maldescent. Ann R Coll Surg Engl 1964; 35:15.
2. Backhouse K, Butler H: The gubernaculum testis of the pig. J Anat 1960;94:208.
3. Bakwin H: Indirect inguinal hernia in twins. J Pediatr Surg 1971;6:165-168.
4. Ballantyne A, Jawaheer G, Munro FD: Contralateral groin exploration is not justified in infants with a unilateral inguinal hernia. Br J Surg 2001;88:720-723.
5. Bascombe D, Caty M, Glick PL: Surgical Rounds 2004; 31:520-522.
6. Bergin WC, Gier HT, Marion GB, Coffman J R: A developmental concept of equine cryptorchism. Biol Reprod 1970;3:82-92.
7. Bevan A: Sliding hernias of the ascending colon and caecum, the descending colon, sigmoid, and the bladder. Ann Surg 1930;92:754.
8. Bhatia AM, Gow KW, Heiss KF, et al: Is the use of laparoscopy to determine presence of contralateral patent processus vaginalis justified in children greater than 2 years of age? J Pediatr Surg 2004;39:778-781.
9. Bock JE, Sobye JV: Frequency of contralateral inguinal hernia in children: A study of the indications for bilateral herniotomy in children with unilateral hernia. Acta Chir Scand 1970;136:707-709.
10. Boley SJ, Cahn D, Lauer T, et al: The irreducible ovary: A true emergency. J Pediatr Surg 1991;26:1035-1038.

11. Boocock GR, Todd PJ: Inguinal hernias are common in preterm infants. Arch Dis Child 1985;60:669-670.
12. Bronsther B, Abrams MW, Elboim C: Inguinal hernias in children—a study of 1000 cases and a review of the literature. J Am Med Womens Assoc 1972;27:522-525.
13. Burke J: Femoral hernia in childhood. Ann Surg 1967; 166:287-289.
14. Ceran C, Koyluoglu G, Sonmez K: Femoral hernia repair with mesh-plug in children. J Pediatr Surg 2002;37: 1456-1458.
15. Ceylan H, Karakok M, Guldur E, et al: Temporary stretch of the testicular pedicle may damage the vas deferens and the testis. J Pediatr Surg 2003;38:1530-1533.
16. Cheatle G: An operation for inguinal hernia. BMJ 1921; 2:1025.
17. Chen KC, Chu CC, Chou TY, Wu CJ: Ultrasonography for inguinal hernias in boys. J Pediatr Surg 1998;33:1784-1787.
18. Chertin B, De Caluwe D, Gajaharan M, et al: Is contralateral exploration necessary in girls with unilateral inguinal hernia? J Pediatr Surg 2003;38:756-757.
19. Clarnette TD, Hutson JM: The genitofemoral nerve may link testicular inguinoscrotal descent with congenital inguinal hernia. Aust N Z J Surg 1996;66:612-617.
20. Clarnette TD, Lam SK, Hutson JM: Ventriculo-peritoneal shunts in children reveal the natural history of closure of the processus vaginalis. J Pediatr Surg 1998;33:413-416.
21. Clatworthy HW, Thompson A: Incarcerated and strangulated inguinal hernia in infants: A preventable risk. JAMA 1954;154:123.
22. Clausen EG, Jake RJ, Binkley FM: Contralateral inguinal exploration of unilateral hernia in infants and children. Surgery 1958;44:735-740.
23. Conroy JM, Othersen HB Jr, Dorman BH, et al: A comparison of wound instillation and caudal block for analgesia following pediatric inguinal herniorrhaphy. J Pediatr Surg 1993;28:565-567.
24. Coran AG, Eraklis AJ: Inguinal hernia in the Hurler-Hunter syndrome. Surgery 1967;61:302-304.
25. Cote CJ, Zaslavsky A, Downes JJ, et al: Postoperative apnea in former preterm infants after inguinal herniorrhaphy: A combined analysis. Anesthesiology 1995;82:809-822.
26. Craven PD, Badawi N, Henderson-Smart DJ, O'Brien M: Regional (spinal, epidural, caudal) versus general anaesthesia in preterm infants undergoing inguinal herniorrhaphy in early infancy. Cochrane Database Syst Rev 2003;CD003669.
27. De Caluwe D, Chertin B, Puri P: Childhood femoral hernia: A commonly misdiagnosed condition. Pediatr Surg Int 2003; 19:608-609.
28. El-Gohary MA: Laparoscopic management of persistent mullerian duct syndrome. Pediatr Surg Int 2003;19: 533-536.
29. Erez I, Rathause V, Vacian I, et al: Preoperative ultrasound and intraoperative findings of inguinal hernias in children: A prospective study of 642 children. J Pediatr Surg 2002; 37:865-868.
30. Fahstrom C, Holmberg L, Johannson H: Atrophy of the testis following operations upon the inguinal region of infants and children. Acta Chir Scand 1963;126:221.
31. Ferguson A: Oblique inguinal hernia: Typical operation for its radical cure. JAMA 1899;33:6.
32. Fischer V, Mumenthaler A: 1st bilaterale herniotomie bei sauglingen unde kleinkindern unit einseitiger Lesitenhernie angezeigt? Helv Chir Acta 1957;4:436.
33. Fonkalsrud E, deLorimier A, Clatworthy HW: Femoral and direct inguinal hernias in infants and children. JAMA 1965; 192:597.
34. Friberg J, Fritjofsson A: Inguinal herniorrhaphy and sperm-agglutinating antibodies in infertile men. Arch Androl 1979;2:317-322.
35. Gardner TA, Ostad M, Mininberg DT: Diagnostic flexible peritoneoscopy: Assessment of the contralateral internal inguinal ring during unilateral herniorrhaphy. J Pediatr Surg 1998;33:1486-1489.
36. Geisler DP, Jegathesan S, Parmley MC, et al: Laparoscopic exploration for the clinically undetected hernia in infancy and childhood. Am J Surg 2001;182:693-696.
37. Given JP, Rubin SZ: Occurrence of contralateral inguinal hernia following unilateral repair in a pediatric hospital. J Pediatr Surg 1989;24:963-965.
38. Glick PL, Azizkhan RG: A Genealogy of North American Pediatric Surgery: From Ladd until Now. St Louis, Quality Medical Publishing, 1997.
39. Gollin G, Bell C, Dubose R, et al: Predictors of postoperative respiratory complications in premature infants after inguinal herniorrhaphy. J Pediatr Surg 1993;28: 244-247.
40. Gorsler CM, Schier F: Laparoscopic herniorrhaphy in children. Surg Endosc 2003;17:571-573.
41. Grosfeld JL, Cooney DR, Smith J, Campbell RL: Intra-abdominal complications following ventriculoperitoneal shunt procedures. Pediatrics 1974;54:791-796.
42. Harper RG, Garcia A, Sia C: Inguinal hernia: A common problem of premature infants weighing 1000 grams or less at birth. Pediatrics 1975;56:112-115.
43. Harvey MH, Johnstone MJ, Fossard DP: Inguinal herniotomy in children: A five year survey. Br J Surg 1985; 72:485-487.
44. Hecker WC, Ring-Mrozik E: [Results of follow-up of operations in pediatric patients with indirect inguinal hernia]. Langenbecks Arch Chir 1987;371:115-121.
45. Holsclaw DS, Shwachman H: Increased incidence of inguinal hernia, hydrocele, and undescended testicle in males with cystic fibrosis. Pediatrics 1971;48:442-445.
46. Homonnai ZT, Fainman N, Paz GF, David MP: Testicular function after herniotomy: Herniotomy and fertility. Andrologia 1980;12:115-120.
47. Jewett TC Jr, Kuhn IN, Allen JE: Herniography in children. J Pediatr Surg 1976;11:451-454.
48. Kamaledeen SA, Shanbhogue LK: Preperitoneal approach for incarcerated inguinal hernia in children. J Pediatr Surg 1997;32:1715-1716.
49. Kapur P, Caty M, Glick P: Pediatric hernias and hydroceles. In Glick P, Irish M, Caty M (eds): The Pediatric Clinics of North America. Philadelphia, WB Saunders, 1998, pp 773-789.
50. Kemmotsu H, Oshima Y, Joe K, Mouri T: The features of contralateral manifestations after the repair of unilateral inguinal hernia. J Pediatr Surg 1998;33:1099-1102.
51. Kiesewetter WB, Oh KS: Unilateral inguinal hernias in children: What about the opposite side? Arch Surg 1980;115:1443-1445.
52. Kiesewetter WB, Parenzan L: When should hernia in the infant be treated bilaterally? JAMA 1959;171:287.
53. Koga H, Yamataka A, Ohshiro K, et al: Pfannenstiel incision for incarcerated inguinal hernia in neonates. J Pediatr Surg 2003;38:E16-E18.
54. Krieger NR, Shochat SJ, McGowan V, Hartman GE: Early hernia repair in the premature infant: Long-term follow-up. J Pediatr Surg 1994;29:978-981.
55. La Roque G: The permanent cure for inguinal and femoral hernia. Surg Gynecol Obstet 1919;29:507.
56. Ladd WE, Gross RE: Abdominal Surgery of Infancy and Childhood. Philadelphia, WB Saunders, 1941.

57. Lau WY: History of treatment of groin hernia. World J Surg 2002;26:748-759.
58. Lavonius MI, Ovaska J: Laparoscopy in the evaluation of the incarcerated mass in groin hernia. Surg Endosc 2000; 14:488-489.
59. Lee SL, DuBois JJ: Laparoscopic diagnosis and repair of pediatric femoral hernia: Initial experience of four cases. Surg Endosc 2000;14:1110-1113.
60. Lee Y, Liang J: Experience with 450 cases of micro-laparoscopic herniotomy in infants and children. Pediatr Endosurg Innov Techn 2002;6:25-28.
61. Levitt MA, Ferraraccio D, Arbesman MC, et al: Variability of inguinal hernia surgical technique: A survey of North American pediatric surgeons. J Pediatr Surg 2002;37: 745-751.
62. Liu L, Cote C, Goudsouzian N, et al: Life threatening apnea in infants recovering from anesthesia. Anesthesiology 1983;56:510.
63. Malviya S, Swartz J, Lerman J: Are all preterm infants younger than 60 weeks postconceptual age at risk for postoperative apnea? Anesthesiology 1993;78:1076.
64. McGregor DB, Halverson K, McVay CB: The unilateral pediatric inguinal hernia: Should the contralateral side be explored? J Pediatr Surg 1980;15:313-317.
65. Michelson L: Congenital anomalies of the vas deferens and epididymis. J Urol 1989;61:384.
66. Michowitz M, Schujman E, Solowiejczyk M: Aberrant adrenal tissue in the wall of a hernial sac. Am Surg 1979;45:67-69.
67. Miltenburg DM, Nuchtern JG, Jaksic T, et al: Meta-analysis of the risk of metachronous hernia in infants and children. Am J Surg 1997;174:741-744.
68. Miserez M: Inguinal hernia repair in a premature infant. J Pediatr Surg 2004;39:252.
69. Misra D, Hewitt G, Potts SR, et al: Inguinal herniotomy in young infants, with emphasis on premature neonates. J Pediatr Surg 1994;29:1496-1498.
70. Moazam F, Glenn JD, Kaplan BJ, et al: Inguinal hernias after ventriculoperitoneal shunt procedures in pediatric patients. Surg Gynecol Obstet 1984;159:570-572.
71. Montupet P, Esposito C: Laparoscopic treatment of congenital inguinal hernia in children. J Pediatr Surg 1999; 34:420-423.
72. Moss RL, Hatch EI Jr: Inguinal hernia repair in early infancy. Am J Surg 1991;161:596-599.
73. Parkhouse H, Hendry W: Vasal injuries during childhood and their effect on subsequent fertility. Br J Urol 1991; 67:91.
74. Partrick DA, Bensard DD, Karrer FM, Ruyle SZ: Is routine pathological evaluation of pediatric hernia sacs justified? J Pediatr Surg 1998;33:1090-1092.
75. Peevy KJ, Speed FA, Hoff CJ: Epidemiology of inguinal hernia in preterm neonates. Pediatrics 1986;77:246-247.
76. Pellegrin K, Bensard DD, Karrer FM, Meagher DP Jr: Laparoscopic evaluation of contralateral patent processus vaginalis in children. Am J Surg 1996;172:602-605.
77. Prasad R, Lovvorn HN 3rd, Wadie GM, Lobe TE: Early experience with needleoscopic inguinal herniorrhaphy in children. J Pediatr Surg 2003;38:1055-1058.
78. Puri P, Guiney EJ, O'Donnell B: Inguinal hernia in infants: The fate of the testis following incarceration. J Pediatr Surg 1984;19:44-46.
79. Rajput A, Gauderer MW, Hack M: Inguinal hernias in very low birth weight infants: Incidence and timing of repair. J Pediatr Surg 1992;27:1322-1324.
80. Rescorla FJ, Grosfeld JL: Inguinal hernia repair in the perinatal period and early infancy: Clinical considerations. J Pediatr Surg 1984;19:832-837.
81. Rescorla FJ, West KW, Engum SA, et al: The "other side" of pediatric hernias: The role of laparoscopy. Am Surg 1997;63:690-693.
82. Rothenberg R, Barnett TM: Bilateral herniotomy in infants and children. Surgery 1955;37:949.
83. Rowe MI, Clatworthy HW: Incarcerated and strangulated hernias in children: A statistical study of high-risk factors. Arch Surg 1970;101:136-139.
84. Rowe MI, Clatworthy HW Jr: The other side of the pediatric inguinal hernia. Surg Clin North Am 1971;51:1371-1376.
85. Rowe MI, Copelson LW, Clatworthy HW: The patent processus vaginalis and the inguinal hernia. J Pediatr Surg 1969;4:102-107.
86. Rowe MI, Marchildon MB: Inguinal hernia and hydrocele in infants and children. Surg Clin North Am 1981;61: 1137-1145.
87. Sachs M, Damm M, Encke A: Historical evolution of inguinal hernia repair. World J Surg 1997;21:218-223.
88. Schier F: Laparoscopic herniorrhaphy in girls. J Pediatr Surg 1998;33:1495-1497.
89. Schier F: Laparoscopic surgery of inguinal hernias in children—initial experience. J Pediatr Surg 2000;35: 1331-1335.
90. Schier F, Montupet P, Esposito C: Laparoscopic inguinal herniorrhaphy in children: A three-center experience with 933 repairs. J Pediatr Surg 2002;37:395-397.
91. Shandling B, Janik J: The vulnerability of the vas deferens. J Pediatr Surg 1981;16:461.
92. Shaw A, Santulli TV: Management of sliding hernias of the urinary bladder in infants. Surg Gynecol Obstet 1967; 124:1314-1316.
93. Snyder W Jr, Greaney E Jr: Inguinal hernia. In Benson C, Mustard W, Ravitch M, et al (eds): Pediatric Surgery. Chicago, Year Book Medical Publishers, 1962, pp 573-587.
94. Sparkman R: Bilateral exploration in inguinal hernia in juvenile patients. Surgery 1962;51:393.
95. Steigman CK, Sotelo-Avila C, Weber TR: The incidence of spermatic cord structures in inguinal hernia sacs from male children. Am J Surg Pathol 1999;23:880-885.
96. Steinau G, Schleef J, Lambertz M, Schumpelick V: [Incidence of contralateral inguinal hernias in infancy and childhood]. Langenbecks Arch Chir 1997;382: 252-256.
97. Steinau G, Treutner KH, Feeken G, Schumpelick V: Recurrent inguinal hernias in infants and children. World J Surg 1995;19:303-306.
98. Stephens BJ, Rice WT, Koucky CJ, Gruenberg JC: Optimal timing of elective indirect inguinal hernia repair in healthy children: Clinical considerations for improved outcome. World J Surg 1992;16:952-956.
99. Strauch ED, Voigt RW, Hill JL: Gangrenous intestine in a hernia can be reduced. J Pediatr Surg 2002;37:919-920.
100. Tackett LD, Breuer CK, Luks FI, et al: Incidence of contralateral inguinal hernia: A prospective analysis. J Pediatr Surg 1999;34:684-687.
101. Thorndike AJ, Ferguson C: Incarcerated inguinal hernia in infancy and childhood. Am J Surg 1938;39:429.
102. Turnock RR, Jones MO, Lloyd DA: Preperitoneal approach to irreducible inguinal hernia in infants. Br J Surg 1994; 81:251.
103. van Zeben-van der Aa TM, Verloove-Vanhorick SP: Inguinal hernias are common in preterm infants. Arch Dis Child 1986;61:99.
104. Walker AN, Mills SE: Glandular inclusions in inguinal hernial sacs and spermatic cords: Mullerian-like remnants confused with functional reproductive structures. Am J Clin Pathol 1984;82:85-89.

105. Walsh S: The incidence of external hernias in premature infants. Acta Paediatr 1962;51:161.
106. White JJ, Haller JA Jr, Dorst JP: Congenital inguinal hernia and inguinal herniography. Surg Clin North Am 1970;50:823-837.
107. Wiener ES, Touloukian RJ, Rodgers BM, et al: Hernia survey of the Section on Surgery of the American Academy of Pediatrics. J Pediatr Surg 1996;31:1166-1169.
108. Wright J: Direct inguinal hernia in infancy and childhood. Pediatr Surg Int 1994;9:161.
109. Wright JE: Femoral hernia in childhood. Pediatr Surg Int 1994;9:167.
110. Yavetz H, Harash B, Yogev L, et al: Fertility of men following inguinal hernia repair. Andrologia 1991;23: 443-446.
111. Yerkes EB, Brock JW 3rd, Holcomb GW 3rd, Morgan WM 3rd: Laparoscopic evaluation for a contralateral patent processus vaginalis: Part III. Urology 1998;51:480-483.
112. Young D: Bilateral aplasia of the vas deferens. Br J Surg 1949;36:417.
113. Zallen, Glick PL: Laparoscopic inversion ligation hernia repair. J Laparoendosc Adv Surg Tech. Submitted for publication.

Chapter 75

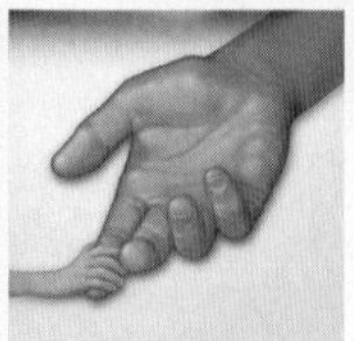

Undescended Testis, Torsion, and Varicocele

John M. Hutson

UNDESCENDED TESTIS

History

The importance of a descended testis has been known since ancient times, but the mechanism of descent remained obscure until 1786 when Hunter dissected the human fetus and found the intra-abdominal testis connected to the inguinoabdominal wall by a ligament called the gubernaculum testis because it appeared to guide the testis to the scrotum.[79]

Embryology

Testicular descent into the low-temperature environment of the scrotum in mammals is a complex multiple-stage process.[190] Up to the time of sexual differentiation in the human fetus at 7 to 8 weeks' gestation the fetal testis and ovary occupy similar positions. The gonadal positions then diverge; the testis remains close to the future inguinal canal, whereas the ovary moves away from the groin. The gonad is held by the cranial suspensory ligament (upper pole) and the gubernaculum (lower pole).

The cranial suspensory ligament, which persists in girls, regresses in boys while the gubernaculum enlarges, especially at its distal end where it is embedded in the inguinal abdominal wall. The inguinal canal forms by condensation of mesenchyme around the gubernaculum to form the inguinal musculature. The mesenchyme of the gubernaculum persists to form a solid cord, which later becomes hollowed out by a diverticulum of peritoneum, the processus vaginalis.[5] The proximal gubernaculum, which is initially attached to the gonad, becomes expanded by growth of the caudal epididymis. The processus vaginalis grows caudad into the gubernacular mesenchyme, partly hollowing out the gubernaculum. The caudal end of the gubernaculum remains solid, but the proximal part is divided into a central column attached to the epididymis and an annular parietal layer within which the cremaster muscle develops. At the start of the third trimester, the caudal end of the gubernaculum bulges beyond the inguinal abdominal wall (Fig. 75-1) and migrates across the pubic region to the scrotum.[70] The processus vaginalis elongates proportionally inside the gubernaculum so that the testis can leave the peritoneal cavity within it (see Fig. 75-1). Scrotal migration of the gubernaculum and the testes is complete by 35 weeks.[70,71] During migration, the gubernaculum is loose within the inguinoscrotal mesenchyme, suggesting enzymatic digestion of the adjacent tissues. After migration is complete, the processus vaginalis becomes secondarily attached to the bottom of the scrotum (see Fig. 75-1).

The different phases of testicular descent are hormonally regulated.[183] The hormones controlling descent and their mechanism of action remain controversial.[71] The early phase of abdominal testicular descent is regulated separately from the migratory inguinoscrotal phase.[80,88] Androgen controls regression of the cranial suspensory ligament of the testis, but regression of this ligament is not essential for testicular descent.[109] Enlargement of the gubernaculum testis is primarily controlled by a nonandrogenic hormone, recently found to be insulin-like factor 3 (Insl3).[128]

Insl3 is made up of two peptide chains linked by a disulfide bond, with homology to relaxin, and it is now recognized to be part of the insulin family of growth factors.[128] Knockout mice with mutated Insl3 were found to have high intra-abdominal testes and an abnormal gubernaculum, consistent with a role of Insl3 in stimulating the "swelling reaction" of the gubernaculum to initiate transabdominal testicular descent.[42,105] Studies both in vivo and in vitro show a primary role for Insl3 in stimulating early gubernacular growth, with secondary roles for testosterone and müllerian-inhibiting substance.[42,105]

Migration of the testis and gubernaculum from the inguinal region of the scrotum is under androgenic control. In instances of complete androgen resistance or gonadotropin deficiency, inguinoscrotal migration is absent.[59] The mechanism of androgenic control of gubernacular migration is unknown, but there is mounting evidence that implicates the genitofemoral nerve. It has

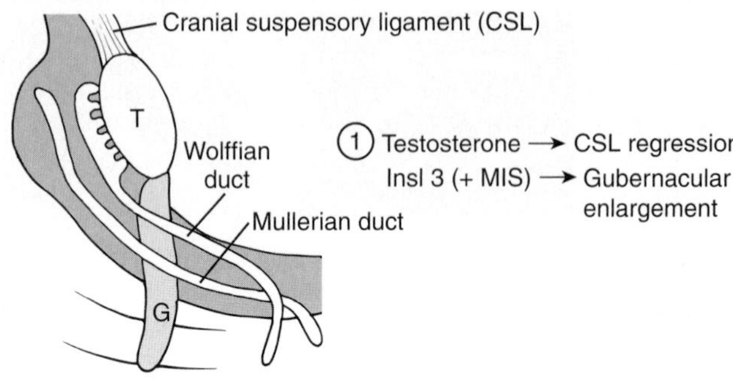

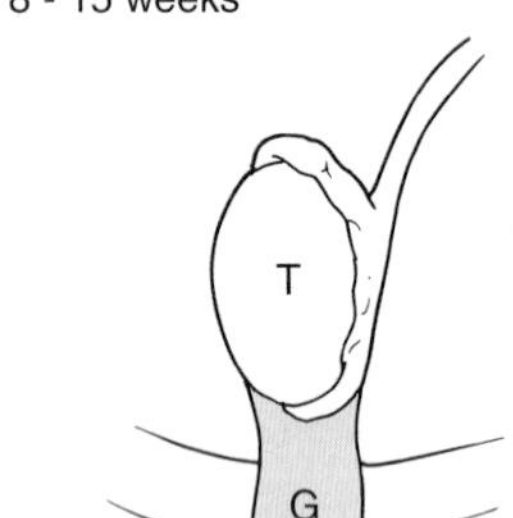

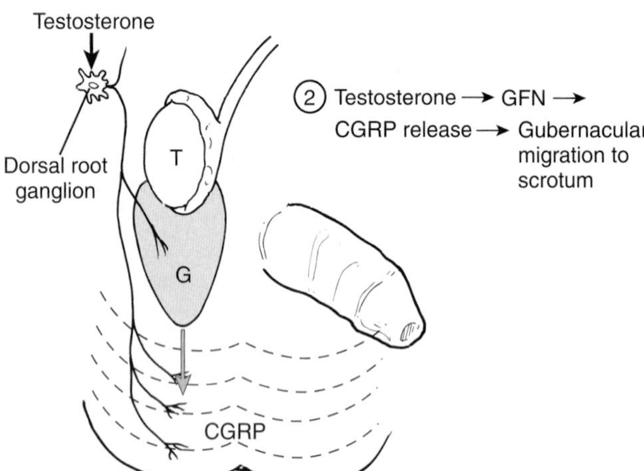

Figure 75–1 Schema showing gubernacular development in the two phases of testicular descent in the human fetus. In the first ("transabdominal") phase at 8 to 15 weeks the testis (T) is held near the inguinal abdominal wall during embryonic growth by enlargement of the gubernaculum (G). This relative change in testicular position compared with the ovary is controlled by testicular hormones, with insulin-like factor 3 (Insl3) the primary hormone possibly augmented by MIS/AMH. The cranial ligament regresses under the action of testosterone. In the second ("inguinoscrotal") phase at 28 to 35 weeks, the gubernaculum migrates by elongation toward the scrotum. This is controlled by testosterone acting on the genitofemoral nerve (GFN) in the dorsal root ganglia to differentiate the sensory fibers to release calcitonin gene-related peptide (CGRP). CGRP controls growth and direction of migration of the rat gubernaculum, and it is hypothesized that it does the same in humans. AMH, antimüllerian hormone; CSL, cranial suspensory ligament; MIS, müllerian-inhibiting substance; GFN, genitofemoral nerve.

been postulated, although as yet unproven, that the sensory branches of the genitofemoral nerve release calcitonin gene-related peptide (CGRP), which may then indirectly control gubernacular migration by stimulation of growth of the gubernacular tip.[81] The physical force for migration of the testis is probably provided by intra-abdominal pressure acting through the patent processus vaginalis. Recent work also implicates the propulsive force of the developing cremaster muscle in the wall of the gubernaculum and its sympathetic nerve supply.[172]

Any anomaly disrupting normal testicular descent leads to cryptorchidism.[84] The complexity of the normal process of descent suggests that causative factors for non-descent are multifactorial. Because most undescended testes are located outside the inguinal canal, the migratory inguinoscrotal phase of testicular descent is probably deranged more commonly. In contrast, the passive anchoring of the gubernaculum in the transabdominal phase is less frequently disrupted, so that intra-abdominal testes are relatively uncommon, occurring in 5% to 10% of cryptorchid boys.[151] In most cases, the undescended testis is located near the neck of the scrotum, just outside or a little lateral to the external inguinal ring, in the superficial inguinal pouch. Abnormalities of gubernacular migration may be related to defects in the migratory mechanism itself or failure of genitofemoral nerve function.[31,88] Defects in the nerve may be caused by deficiency of androgen secretion during the second and third trimester as a result of deficiency of gonadotropin production by the pituitary or the placenta. Recognizable endocrine disorders, such as müllerian-inhibiting substance deficiency or decreased testosterone synthesis or receptor function, also cause failure of testicular descent but are relatively rare. With the recent discovery of Insl3 and its role in transabdominal descent, a search has been made for mutations of the Insl3 gene in undescended testes but only relatively rare cases have been described.[7,51,176]

Undescended testes lying well outside the normal line of descent, such as in the perineum or femoral region, are rare, and their cause is unknown. Hutson and associates[88] suggested that this may be the result of an abnormal location of the genitofemoral nerve with consequent abnormal migration of the gubernaculum to the wrong site. The cause of transverse testicular ectopia also is unknown, but in animal models transverse ectopia can be induced readily by cutting the gubernacular attachment to the testes so that the gonad is no longer required to exit the abdominal cavity through the ipsilateral inguinal canal. Increased gonadal mobility may permit accidental descent through the contralateral inguinal canal.[87] The latter also occurs in boys with persisting müllerian duct syndrome, where the elongated gubernacular cord predisposes to accidental descent down the contralateral inguinal canal.

A number of inherited syndromes are associated with undescended testes. The underlying cause is not known, although many are associated with microcephaly, suggesting the possibility of pituitary hormone or gonadotropin deficiency.[63] Some multiple malformation syndromes are also associated with neurogenic and mechanical anomalies, for example, arthrogryposis multiplex congenita.[45] These disorders may cause cryptorchidism either by external compression of the deformed fetus or by intrinsic neurologic anomalies. Experimental inguinoscrotal compression during testicular descent is associated with undescended testes.[113] Intra-abdominal testes are characteristic of the prune-belly syndrome. The cause of the cryptorchidism is controversial, with thoughts ranging from a mesodermal defect to transient prenatal urinary obstruction.[9,122,132,138] The absence of a processus vaginalis within the inguinal canal and the position of the testes on the posterior surface of the bladder are consistent with an obstructive cause. Ten percent of infants with posterior urethral valves also have cryptorchidism.[102]

Cryptorchidism is common in infants with abdominal wall defects, such as gastroschisis (where the gubernaculum may be ruptured), exomphalos (omphalocele), and exstrophy of the bladder.[96] Undescended testes occur in more than 15% of infants with gastroschisis and at least a third of children with exomphalos or omphalocele.[63,96] Whether this is caused by decreased abdominal pressure or other mechanical effects is not certain, although a role for abdominal pressure has been determined in experimental animals.[3]

Neural tube defects have a high incidence of undescended testes.[103] When there is a myelomeningocele affecting the upper lumbar spinal cord, the incidence of undescended testes is greater than one third. This could be caused either by abdominal wall paralysis and lower-than-normal abdominal pressure or by dysplasia of the genitofemoral nerve motor nucleus at the site of the myelomeningocele.[85]

Separation of the body of the epididymis from the undescended testis is frequently observed.[50,91,100] This is more common in intra-abdominal and high inguinal cryptorchid testis. Whether this is the cause of the cryptorchidism or merely secondary to decreased androgen production in utero occurring simultaneously is not known. Experimental evidence in rodents treated with antiandrogens suggests that in utero androgen deficiency causes epididymal deficiency.[19]

Abnormalities of the vas deferens occur commonly in boys with cryptorchid testes. The impalpable intracanalicular testis may have a vas deferens forming a loop, which protrudes distally through the external inguinal ring. Based on examination of the blood supply of such a long-loop vas, Fowler and Stephens proposed transection of the main testicular vessels to the high undescended testis to permit orchidopexy with testis viability maintained by the redundant vas deferens with its collateral blood supply.[53] Although this operation is less commonly performed as an open one-stage procedure because of the high incidence of atrophy, it is now commonly performed laparoscopically as a one- or two-stage procedure.[141]

Classification of Undescended Testes

Classification of gonadal position in undescended testes is complicated by the mobility of the testis in the tunica vaginalis. *Undescended testis* is best defined as a testis that cannot be manipulated to the bottom of the scrotum without undue tension on the spermatic cord. A normally descended testis resides spontaneously in the lower scrotum even if it was retracted when the patient was first examined. The positions of undescended testes can be divided into those arrested in the line of normal descent and those in truly ectopic positions (Fig. 75-2). The intra-abdominal

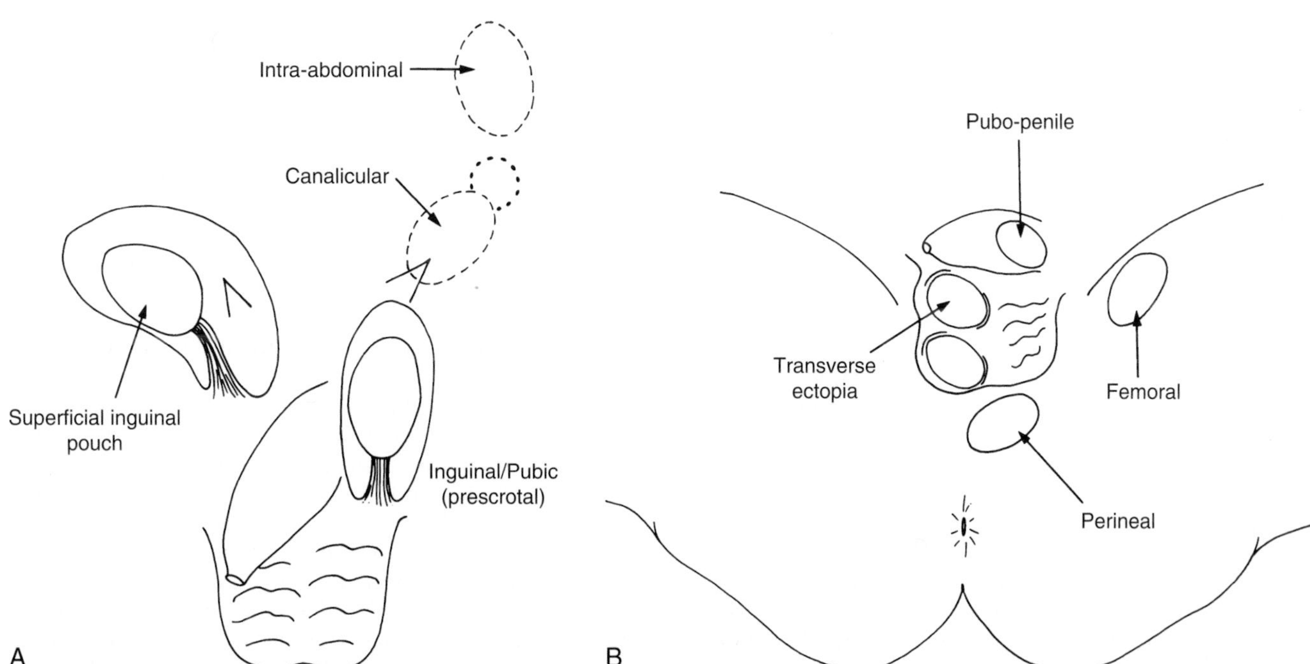

Figure 75–2 The range of positions that may be adopted by undescended testes. *A,* In the line of normal descent (including the controversial superficial inguinal pouch, note that the gubernaculum is attached near the neck of the scrotum in most instances). *B,* True ectopic sites, which are rare. (From Hutson JM, Beasley SW: Descent of the Testis. London, Edward Arnold, 1992.)

testis is usually located within a few centimeters of the internal inguinal ring, with the vas deferens and the testicular vessels traveling extraperitoneally and then entering the testis through a short mesorchium. Such intra-abdominal testes were often difficult to find through extraperitoneal exploration through the inguinal canal but are now relatively easy to identify at laparoscopy.

A canalicular testis is one that lies within the inguinal canal but may be difficult or impossible to palpate because of the overlying musculature. Such gonads may be squeezed out of the inguinal canal and become palpable at the external inguinal ring, so-called emergent testes.

Undescended testes beyond the external ring may lie near the neck of the scrotum or may be lateral and a little above the external inguinal ring in the superficial inguinal pouch, originally described by Browne (see Fig. 75-2).[18] The latter location is rarely an indication of aberrant gubernacular migration because at surgery the gubernacular attachment is nearly always at or near the neck of the scrotum.[50,84] Essentially, the superficial inguinal pouch is the space created by the tunica vaginalis in the groin and is limited superficially by Scarpa's fascia and its deep attachment to the fascia lata just caudad to the inguinal ligament. Whether testes in the superficial inguinal pouch should be labeled as ectopic is controversial, but because the gubernaculum is attached at or near the neck of the scrotum, they seem to be better classified as testes arrested in the line of normal descent.[69] Truly ectopic testes may be located in the perineum, femoral region, pubopenile region, or contralateral hemiscrotum secondary to transverse ectopia.

Retractile Testes

Transient retraction of the testis out of the scrotum is a normal reflex caused by contraction of the cremaster muscle. This muscle functions to regulate the temperature of the testis and to protect it from extrinsic trauma.[161] Retraction occurs as a result of low temperature or stimulation of the cutaneous branch of the genitofemoral nerve (inner thigh).

The normal retractile reflex is weak or absent at birth, and the scrotum is often pendulous. Later in childhood, when androgen levels are low, cremasteric contractility is significantly increased and the cremasteric reflex more pronounced. After 10 years of age, the reflex becomes less pronounced as androgen levels rise with the onset of puberty. The cremasteric reflex and normal retractile testis have been studied by Farrington, who found a high incidence of retractility in the middle of childhood.[48]

At present, there is no consensus about what constitutes a retractile testis.[8] Most clinicians agree that a retractile testis is a descended testis, although careful follow-up is required because it does not always remain descended. The retractile testis probably reflects a normal physiologic response to contraction of the cremaster muscle related to age. Goh and Hutson suggest that so-called retractile testes are, in fact, testes with acquired maldescent.[57] As the distance between the external inguinal ring and the bottom of the scrotum increases with age (from 5 cm in an infant to 10 cm by 10 years of age), it is necessary for the spermatic cord to lengthen for the testis to remain located in the scrotum. Retractile testes may represent acquired maldescent secondary to failure of the spermatic cord to elongate with age, which may be a sequel of excessive contractility of the cremaster muscle in some boys, as in those with cerebral palsy and spastic diplegia.[167]

Ascending Testes

A newly described variant of the retractile testis is the ascending testis.[8,92] In many of these children, long-term follow-up studies have demonstrated that subsequent ascent out of the scrotum later in childhood is often related to delayed descent into the scrotum within the first 3 months after birth. Ascending testes are now being documented by a number of authors.[4,8] The difference between ascending and retractile testes is otherwise not clear, and it may be that they are different names for a similar problem.

Studies suggest that not all undescended testes are present from birth. Many children with cryptorchidism present later in childhood despite attempts at screening in infancy.[40] In addition, on careful questioning of such families, there is often no history of an anomaly at birth or in early childhood.[60]

Acquired cryptorchidism is likely to be secondary to failure of the spermatic cord to elongate in proportion to body growth. Such testes appear to ascend out of the scrotum with increasing age, but measurements of the cord length suggest that this ascent is more apparent than real. This is certainly true in patients with cerebral palsy, in whom acquired cryptorchidism approaches 50% in postpubertal boys with severe spastic diplegia.[167]

Atwell has suggested that ascending or retractile testes may be caused by persistence of the processus vaginalis, which is likely to inhibit elongation of the adjacent vas deferens and testicular vessels.[4] In patients with cerebral palsy in whom the cremaster muscle has proven spasticity, the cause is clearly related to abnormal muscle contraction. In cases in which the testis migrated to the scrotum prenatally and was present within the scrotum in infancy but the position is too high later in childhood, orchidopexy is often successful through a scrotal approach.[13,154]

Incidence of Undescended Testes

In a landmark study in 1964, Scorer found the incidence of undescended testes was 4.3% in infants.[160] By 1 year of age, the incidence had fallen to 0.96%. In 1986, the incidence of cryptorchidism at 1 year of age was 1.58% in British children. The John Radcliffe Hospital Cryptorchidism Study Group found that spontaneous descent occurred postnatally in the first 3 months; beyond that time, it was rare.[92,93] The rate for orchidopexy in England and Wales has effectively doubled in recent decades.[143] Although this difference between the incidence of cryptorchidism and frequency of orchidopexy suggests that some orchidopexies may be unnecessary;

it may also reflect a true increase in the incidence of undescended testes, although this remains controversial.[8] It has been suggested that one explanation of the apparent doubling of orchidopexy rates may be related to acquired ascending or retractile testes.[8] Because the recommended age for surgery for congenital undescended testes has decreased to age 1 or younger, those children with acquired undescended testes are now more readily distinguishable from those children with congenital failure of gubernacular migration.[40]

The frequency of undescended testes is significantly increased in premature infants.[125] When birth weight is less than 1500 g, the incidence of cryptorchidism reaches 60% to 70%.[52] The presumptive cause of this high frequency of cryptorchidism is that normal descent is not completed generally until about 35 weeks' gestation. Most undescended testes in premature infants continue to descend postnatally, so that if such children are examined at 12 weeks beyond their expected normal delivery date, the incidence of cryptorchidism has fallen to more normal levels.

Complications of Cryptorchidism

Controversy persists about whether the testis is primarily abnormal, leading to maldescent, or alternatively is undescended, leading to a secondary abnormality. Evidence now suggests that abnormalities seen postnatally in undescended testes are secondary. Occasional primary abnormalities in the hypothalamic-pituitary-gonadal axis, however, lead to inadequate hormone secretion, maldescent, and primary testicular abnormalities.

Species differences have made investigative studies regarding the effects of undescended testes difficult to evaluate. Many studies concerning cryptorchidism have been carried out on rodents, in which the important developmental aspects of gubernacular migration are complete by the 10th day after birth. The testis, however, does not descend into the scrotum until 2 to 3 weeks in mice or 3 to 4 weeks in rats, at the time of pubertal sexual maturation.[46] Human gubernacular migration and testicular descent occur simultaneously and are normally complete before birth. The effects of undescended testes in the rat, therefore, do not become evident until after puberty.

Temperature Effects

The scrotal testis resides in a specialized low-temperature environment with the pampiniform plexus, scrotal pigmentation, absence of subcutaneous fat, and regulation by temperature-sensitive muscles, such as the cremaster and dartos muscle, all ensuring decreased temperature of the epididymis and gonad. The scrotal testis in the human is maintained at 33°C compared with 34°C to 35°C noted in the inguinal region and 37°C intra-abdominally (Fig. 75-3).[119,171] The physiology of the testis is well adapted to this lower temperature; therefore, in the undescended testis where the ambient temperature is increased the testis undergoes progressive alteration.[190]

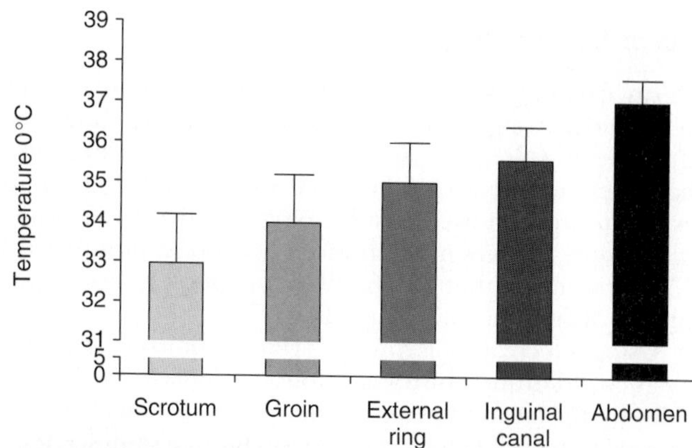

Figure 75-3 The temperature (mean ± standard deviation) of the testis at different levels. (From Hutson JM, Beasley SW: Descent of the Testis. London, Edward Arnold, 1992.)

Endocrine Effects

Corticosteroid pathways in rat testes made cryptorchid by surgical fixation before puberty show no gross abnormalities, indicating that Leydig cells are still functional with cryptorchidism in this model. Measurement of testicular testosterone content in rats made cryptorchid at birth shows no abnormality up to 2 to 3 weeks of age but decreased testosterone production compared with controls after puberty.[47] Gonadotropic regulation of both Leydig and Sertoli cells is abnormal after puberty.[78] The number of Sertoli and Leydig cells, however, remains relatively normal.[12] Functional derangements in Sertoli cells with cryptorchidism have been well documented by de Kretser and Risbridger.[35]

Plasma gonadotropin and testosterone levels have been measured in infants with undescended testes, and the normal postnatal rise in plasma luteinizing hormone (LH) levels and testosterone were found to be significantly lower than normal.[55,147] It is difficult to determine conclusively whether this postnatal androgen deficiency is a primary abnormality or secondary to nondescent.

In a study of premature infants born with a mean gestational age of 30 weeks, there was a persistently high incidence (19%) of undescended testes at 18 months despite some testes descending postnatally.[6] The normal rise in testosterone seen in the second and third month postnatally failed to develop in these premature infants with cryptorchidism. The authors concluded that inadequate stimulation of testosterone by human chorionic gonadotropin (hCG) in utero may contribute to the pathogenesis of undescended testes in this special group. Both plasma testosterone and LH levels were decreased in cryptorchid infants between 1 and 4 months of age.[90] Although androgen levels may be deficient, androgen receptor levels in scrotal skin fibroblasts and testicular biopsy specimens taken at orchidopexy are normal in infants with bilateral cryptorchidism.[17] Serum levels of müllerian-inhibiting substance are normally elevated between 4 and 12 months of age, but in children with cryptorchidism this postnatal rise in müllerian-inhibiting substance levels was inhibited.[187]

Germ Cell Development

Germ cell deficiency in cryptorchidism was previously regarded as congenital.[161] It has been observed, however, that the histology of the testes is initially normal and becomes progressively abnormal with age. Mengle and associates first showed in a histologic study of 752 testicular biopsy specimens in children between 2 months and 15 years of age that the number of spermatogonia per tubule decreased by 3 years of age.[118]

Using electron microscopy, Hadziselimovic and colleagues[65] identified histologic abnormalities in the Leydig cells in the second year of life. More detailed studies showed impaired Leydig cell development in undescended testes in the first 2 to 6 months, whereas the Sertoli and germ cells appeared normal.[64] By the end of the second year of life, nearly 40% of undescended testes had completely lost their germ cells. They concluded that germ cell deficiency in undescended testes is secondary because only 1 infant of nearly 100 younger than 1 year of age lacked all germ cells and because 70% of biopsy specimens in such small infants had normal numbers of germ cells.[62] More recently, Huff and coworkers studied the transformation of neonatal gonocytes to type A spermatogonia, an early postnatal step in development of the germ cells, and documented that this early step in germ cell development is deficient in infants with cryptorchidism.[75-77]

Some authors have proposed that these early stages in germ cell development are controlled by androgens and are hence deficient because of postnatal androgen deficiency.[75] There is some contrary evidence to suggest, however, that müllerian-inhibiting substance may be controlling early postnatal germ cell development.[10,188] Certainly, androgen blockade or deficiency does not prevent gonocytes transforming to type A spermatogonia in neonatal rodents.[189]

Fertility

Fertility is lower in men with a past history of cryptorchidism. In previous generations, it was believed that the undescended testis suffered no adverse changes until after puberty and surgical intervention was not necessary until 12 to 15 years of age.[161] The evidence that germ cell maturation is already abnormal after 6 months of age has led clinicians to appreciate that not only is postnatal degeneration an important issue but also that early intervention may prevent it. In animal studies, it is relatively easy to demonstrate that surgically induced or congenital cryptorchidism causes decreased fertility because of germ cell deficiency after puberty.[98] Paternity rates are not deficient in unilateral cryptorchidism in both animals and humans; but with bilateral cryptorchidism, fertility is significantly impaired.[107,108] Data attempting to correlate fertility rates with timing of surgery are not yet available because there are no long-term studies of children undergoing orchidopexy in the first year of life. Fertility in men with a history of retractile testes remains quite controversial, with some authors describing abnormalities on sperm counts that are not reflected in paternity rates.[131,146,149]

Malignancy

The risk of a testis tumor occurring in men with a past history of cryptorchidism was at one time believed to be 35 to 50 times greater than normal.[182] By using different methods of calculating the relative risk, Woodhouse[185] suggested the actual risk is 5- to 10-fold. When looking at all men with testis tumors, a relative risk for those with a history of unilateral cryptorchidism is 15-fold or 33-fold for bilateral undescended testes, with the risk of cancer being highest with intra-abdominal testes.[11,23,170]

The progressive degeneration of germ cells and dysplasia seen in cryptorchid testes is thought to be related to the increased risk of malignancy.[67] Testis tumors are not common in childhood, and they usually occur at the same age as testis tumors in normally descended testes (i.e., 20 to 40 years). Giwercman and colleagues have speculated that testis tumors may be caused by an intrinsic abnormality in the testis rather than secondary dysplasia.[56] They suggest that carcinoma in situ germ cells are the forerunner of invasive tumors and are, in fact, malignant gonocytes. Such germ cells displaying histologic characteristics of carcinoma in situ can be identified in neonates with dysgenetic testes and ambiguous genitalia. Skakkabaek and associates have described the histologic features of carcinoma in situ and provided strong evidence that these abnormal cells are a prerequisite to invasive testis tumors.[165] They recommend that young men with a past history of cryptorchidism should be offered testicular biopsy to exclude this condition before malignancy occurs.

Inguinal Hernia

The processus vaginalis normally obliterates after descent of the testis in the perinatal period. Undescended testes are associated with a higher incidence of patent processus vaginalis and inguinal hernia, in many cases leading to early surgical intervention because of the risk of incarcerated hernia. A clinically evident hernia present with a cryptorchid testis is an indication for immediate intervention. Most surgeons elect to perform a hernia repair and orchidopexy simultaneously.

Torsion of a Cryptorchid Testis

Previous surgical textbooks quote a high incidence of up to 20% for torsion in unoperated undescended testes.[161] In the past 30 years, however, the trend to earlier surgical intervention has meant that most pediatric surgeons now rarely see torsion in an undescended testis. The mobility of a testis within the tunica vaginalis in the superficial inguinal pouch may predispose to torsion, but the exact frequency is now difficult to determine.[157]

Trauma

Inguinal testes are thought to be at a slightly increased risk of direct trauma, although as with testicular torsion, early surgical intervention has made this a less common problem.[52] The most common clinical cause of trauma in an undescended testis I have seen is in children with cerebral palsy requiring wheelchair restraint. In these children, an inguinal testis may be compressed by the straps of the wheelchair.

Psychological Factors

Cryptorchidism is a major psychological problem because the obvious physical abnormality of the genitalia promotes parental anxiety about subsequent fertility.

Testicular-Epididymal Fusion Abnormality

Abnormal connection between the testis and the epididymis is common in cryptorchidism.[91,100] The risk of abnormal fusion is greater with testes inside the canal or the abdomen than in inguinal testes or those lying at the neck of the scrotum. These abnormalities may be related to underlying androgen deficiency in utero, and in a percentage of these the abnormality may be sufficient to interfere with fertility.

Diagnosis

The aim of the clinical examination is to identify the presence or absence of a palpable gonad and to determine the lowest position that it will sit comfortably without undue tension.[86] The lowest limit of testicular position without tension probably corresponds to the caudal limit of the tunica vaginalis. Examination should be conducted in warm surroundings and with the child relaxed. With the child recumbent on the examination table, the genitalia should be inspected for the appearance of the scrotum and any inguinal swelling suggesting a high testis or an associated hernia. Cranial traction on the suprapubic skin to expose the scrotum often makes testes that are retracted to the upper part of the scrotum conspicuous. The appearance of the scrotum varies dramatically with age, with the neonatal scrotum being thin, pendulous, and flabby compared with the middle of childhood, when the scrotum is small and puckered. If the testis is lying within the scrotum, it is usually visible through the thin scrotal skin. Hypoplasia of the hemiscrotum suggests that the testis has never been within it. A hemiscrotum of normal size is more likely if the testis is retractile or ascending.

The key to locating a suprascrotal testis is to remember that the testis is contained within the tunica vaginalis and is therefore mobile. In addition, the bony landmarks of the inguinal ligament should be identified. To locate a testis in the superficial inguinal pouch, light palpation with the flat of the hand is most effective. If palpation is too hard, this often displaces the testis from under the fingers, so it may be missed. At least 80% to 90% of testes are palpable in the inguinal region or can be squeezed out of the inguinal canal and felt at the external ring by pressing firmly on the abdominal wall laterally near the anterosuperior iliac spine and pressing downward and medially toward the scrotum. Intra-abdominal or intracanalicular testes that cannot be delivered outside the external ring are uncommon. Once the mobile testis has been identified in the groin, one hand of the examiner attempts to push the testis toward the scrotum while the other hand attempts to grasp it through the thin scrotal skin. The aim of this maneuver is to determine the lowest level to which the testis can be manipulated without undue tension. A normally retractile testis should be able to be brought right to the bottom of the scrotum and remain there. The position of the testis at physical examination can be documented by measurement from the pubic tubercle as described by Scorer,[160] although this degree of documentation is usually unnecessary.

The most useful clinical observation is whether the testis can reside in the scrotum spontaneously. Examination of the scrotum in the newborn is easy because the testes are readily visible and palpable when in the scrotum. If the testes can be felt above the scrotum, the child should be reexamined at 3 months of age to see whether there has been delayed descent. If the testis remains out of the scrotum at age 3 months, a confident diagnosis of congenital undescended testis can be made. If the testis has descended within the first 12 weeks, there is a risk that it may re-ascend out of the scrotum later in childhood, and such children are best kept under close observation.

Determining the exact testicular position may be difficult if there is an associated incarcerated inguinal hernia. Once the hernia has been reduced by manual compression, the position of the testis can usually be identified.

The clinical distinction between a normally retractile testis and an undescended testis caused by a congenital or acquired abnormality can be difficult. Useful criteria for distinguishing normally retractile testes are as follows:

1. The testis can be brought fully to the bottom of the scrotum without difficulty.
2. The testis remains in the scrotum after manipulation without immediate retraction.
3. The testis is normal in size.
4. There is a history that the testis resides spontaneously in the scrotum some of the time.

If the testis cannot be palpated in the usual position in the groin near the external inguinal ring, the sites for an ectopic testis should be examined, such as the femoral region and perineum. Truly impalpable testes are relatively uncommon, being variously reported in 5% to 28% of boys with undescended testes.[20,94,156,181] If the testis cannot be palpated, this implies that it is either intra-abdominal (45%) or within the inguinal canal (up to 25%), or alternatively it may be absent (45%). The latter situation is known as the *vanishing testis* and is likely the result of intrauterine torsion of the spermatic cord during migration of the gubernaculum to the scrotum.[39,77,178] This leads to secondary atrophy of the testis, and the contralateral testis is commonly enlarged, which is a useful physical sign.[76,99]

Blind inguinal exploration for the impalpable undescended testis is unlikely to be successful. Numerous imaging techniques have been recommended to identify the position of such a testis.[74] These include abdominal and inguinal ultrasonography, computed tomography (CT), magnetic resonance imaging (MRI), and spermatic venography and arteriography. Laparoscopy recently has become the most common way to identify the position of an intra-abdominal testis and to exclude the possibility of secondary atrophy.[14,123,142] Laparoscopy offers the additional benefit of ligation of the testicular vessels should a two-stage Fowler-Stephens operation be contemplated.[14]

Treatment

Hormone Treatment

Hormone therapy is based on the premise that the undescended testis is caused by deficiency of the hypothalamic-pituitary-gonadal axis and that postnatal treatment can induce the required migration of the gubernaculum.[61] Therapy has been tried with testosterone, hCG, and luteinizing hormone-releasing hormone (LHRH). Direct androgen therapy was abandoned many years ago because excessive doses caused precocious puberty. In the past 10 to 20 years, hCG has been in common use in Europe but less commonly used elsewhere. More recently, LHRH has been tried.

The results of hormone therapy have been mixed and depend on a number of factors. Success rates for treatment range from 10% to 50%.[38,73,148] Children older than 4 years and those with bilateral undescended testes near the scrotal entrance or retractile testes respond most favorably to hCG. Testes in the superficial inguinal pouch, the most common variant of the anomaly, have a low success rate. It has been suggested that the successful cases are due to the fact that most were retractile testes.[148] Christiansen and coworkers[24] reported a 25% success rate with hCG with complete descent, and in a further 25% the position of the testis was improved. On review of their article, however, it is difficult to exclude acquired variants of undescended testis such as retractile or ascending testes. In unilateral undescended testis, which is statistically much more likely to be of congenital origin, only 14% of boys have successful hormonal therapy.

In a randomized, double-blind study comparing hCG and LHRH, Rajfer and coworkers found 6% of boys treated with hCG responded with testicular descent compared with a 19% success rate for LHRH.[148] They concluded that neither hCG nor LHRH was effective in promoting descent of truly undescended testes. A double-blind, placebo-controlled study of LHRH nasal spray in boys with cryptorchid testis showed a 9% success rate with LHRH compared with 8% with placebo treatment.[37,38] A second course of LHRH therapy increased the descent rate to 18%. Young children had the lowest response rate, and LHRH was not useful for impalpable testes.

Some clinicians suggest that hormone therapy diagnoses a retractile testis (which has a high success rate) and thereby avoids surgery. *Acquired* undescended testes with severe retraction or secondary ascent may respond to hCG treatment at levels of 100 IU/kg intramuscularly twice a week for 3 to 4 weeks. Alternatively, LHRH can be given as a nasal spray at 100 mg in each nostril six times a day for 3 to 4 weeks. In my surgical department, hormonal therapy is used rarely, and nearly all children with congenital or acquired cryptorchidism are offered orchidopexy.

Surgical Treatment

Treatment of cryptorchidism is based on the assumption that early intervention will prevent secondary degeneration of the testes caused by high temperature.[190] The scrotal testis is 3°C to 4°C cooler than the intra-abdominal core temperature, which is essential for normal postnatal testicular development.[119] The timing of surgery remains controversial, with some studies suggesting that delayed orchidopexy late in childhood is associated with good results, whereas others show poor results. Studies showing early degeneration of the germ cells in the first 6 to 12 months through to macroscopic atrophy in school-age children all suggest that undescended testes undergo progressive degeneration after birth.[75,101] Although the evidence that early surgery prevents this degeneration sequence is not yet available in humans, it is shown in all animal studies.[129]

For some years, orchidopexy has been recommended in the second year of life, but it is now my practice to recommend orchidopexy at 6 months. This is because the first signs of damage to the testes are identified at about 6 months of age.[75] Orchidopexy in such young children, however, can be challenging. In pediatric surgical centers, it is quite reasonable to perform orchidopexy in the second 6 months of life; however, in centers with less experience in small children, surgery between 18 months and 2 years may be safer. When orchidopexy is done in a pediatric surgical center, a younger age does not increase the risk of complications.[184]

In my clinic I recommend routine examination of all boys at birth with repeat examination at 3 months in those children in whom one or both testes were not descended at birth. If the testis remains undescended at 3 months, the child is best referred for orchidopexy at 6 to 12 months of life or in the second year. When the testis has descended spontaneously in the first 12 weeks, such children are best observed every few years to ensure that they do not develop acquired undescended testes later in childhood. Children presenting with a concomitant inguinal hernia should have immediate orchidopexy done at the same time that the inguinal herniorrhaphy is performed. This is much safer than delaying the orchidopexy after the herniotomy because re-exploration of the inguinal canal in this circumstance has a higher risk of damage to the vas and vessels. In older boys presenting with what is presumed to be acquired maldescent, I recommend that surgery should be offered to these children (or alternatively hormone therapy) once the testis no longer resides spontaneously in the scrotum. This is a controversial recommendation to some.

Orchidopexy is performed as an ambulatory procedure with the child entering the hospital or clinic an hour or so before operation and discharged a few hours later.[82] Topical anesthetic cream is applied to the back of the hand so induction of anesthesia by injection is not painful. Under general anesthesia, a regional or local anesthetic block is performed to provide pain relief for the first few hours postoperatively.

For inguinal undescended testes, a skin crease incision is made over the external ring and extending a little laterally (Fig. 75-4A). The remaining details are shown in Figure 75-4B to N.

A widely patent processus vaginalis is common (up to 70%) and needs to be separated from the vas deferens and the testicular vessels (see Fig. 75-4D). The hernia sac is wrapped around the vessels anteriorly with the vas deferens posteromedial and the vessels posterolateral. In high undescended testes, particularly those found in the

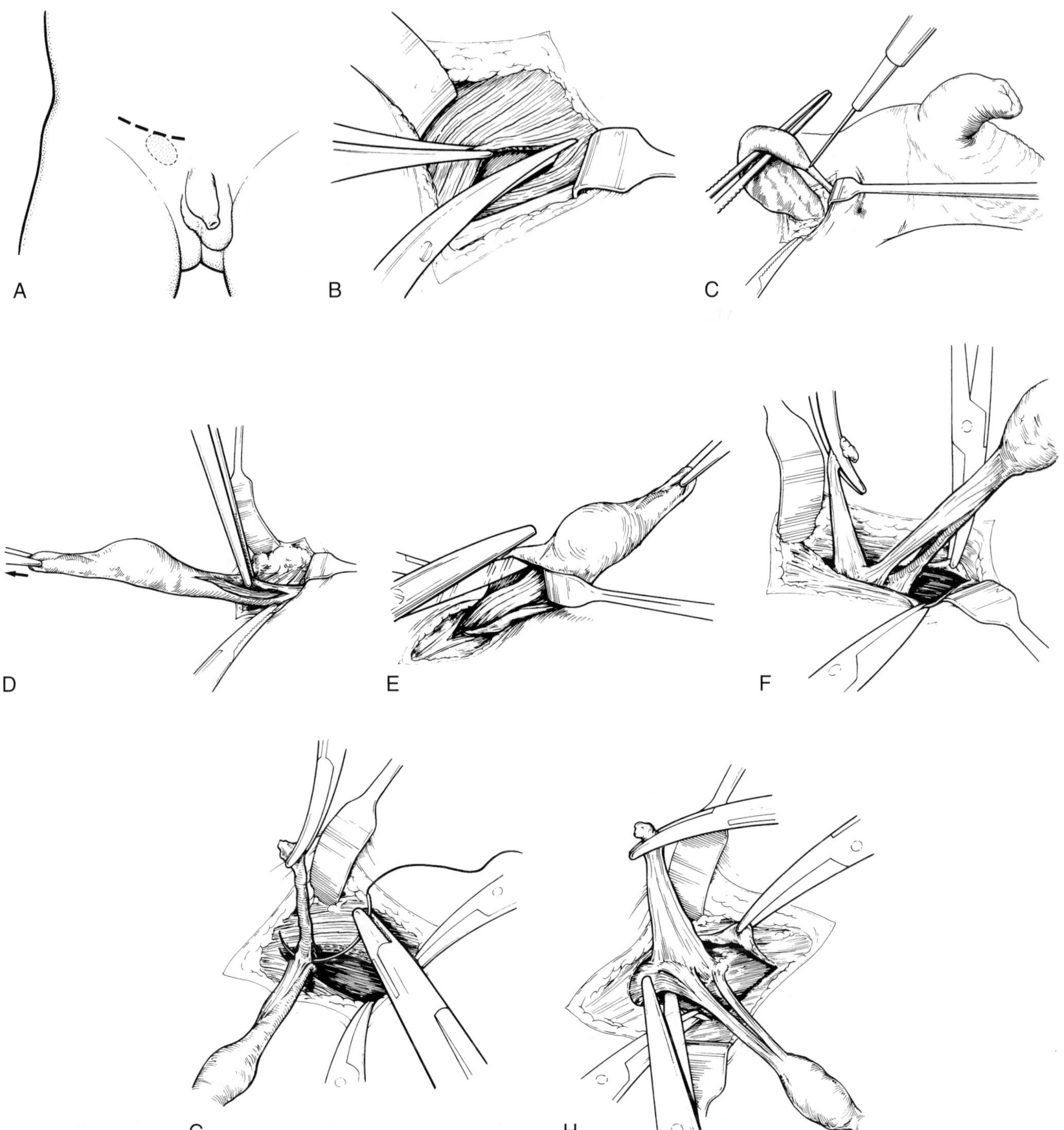

Figure 75–4 *A*, Skin crease incision over external ring and extending laterally. *B*, After dividing Scarpa's fascia, the external oblique aponeurosis is exposed and opened with a scalpel and extended medially toward the external inguinal ring with scissors. Application of mosquito forceps to the edges may facilitate subsequent identification and closure. *C*, A testis in the superficial inguinal pouch or pubic region is easily seen at this point, and it can be picked up so traction on the spermatic cord can permit the distal attachment of the gubernaculum to be identified and divided. In most instances, the gubernaculum is attached just lateral or above the neck of the scrotum. *D*, With traction on the tunica vaginalis, the cremaster muscle fibers are stripped off and any residual processus vaginalis is dissected off the vas and vessels, beginning posteriorly where the free edges of the sac are found. *E*, The vas and vessels are identified separate from the hernial sac and are protected by a small retractor while the sac is clamped and divided. *F*, The anteromedial processus vaginalis is dissected from the posterolateral gonadal vessels up to the internal inguinal ring, where the vas deferens diverges medially. *G*, Transfixion and ligation of the processus vaginalis at the internal ring. Twisting the sac first ensures that the needle does not catch any intraperitoneal structures inadvertently. *H*, Extra length may be achieved by freeing up the lateral side of the gonadal vessels in the retroperitoneal space.

Continued

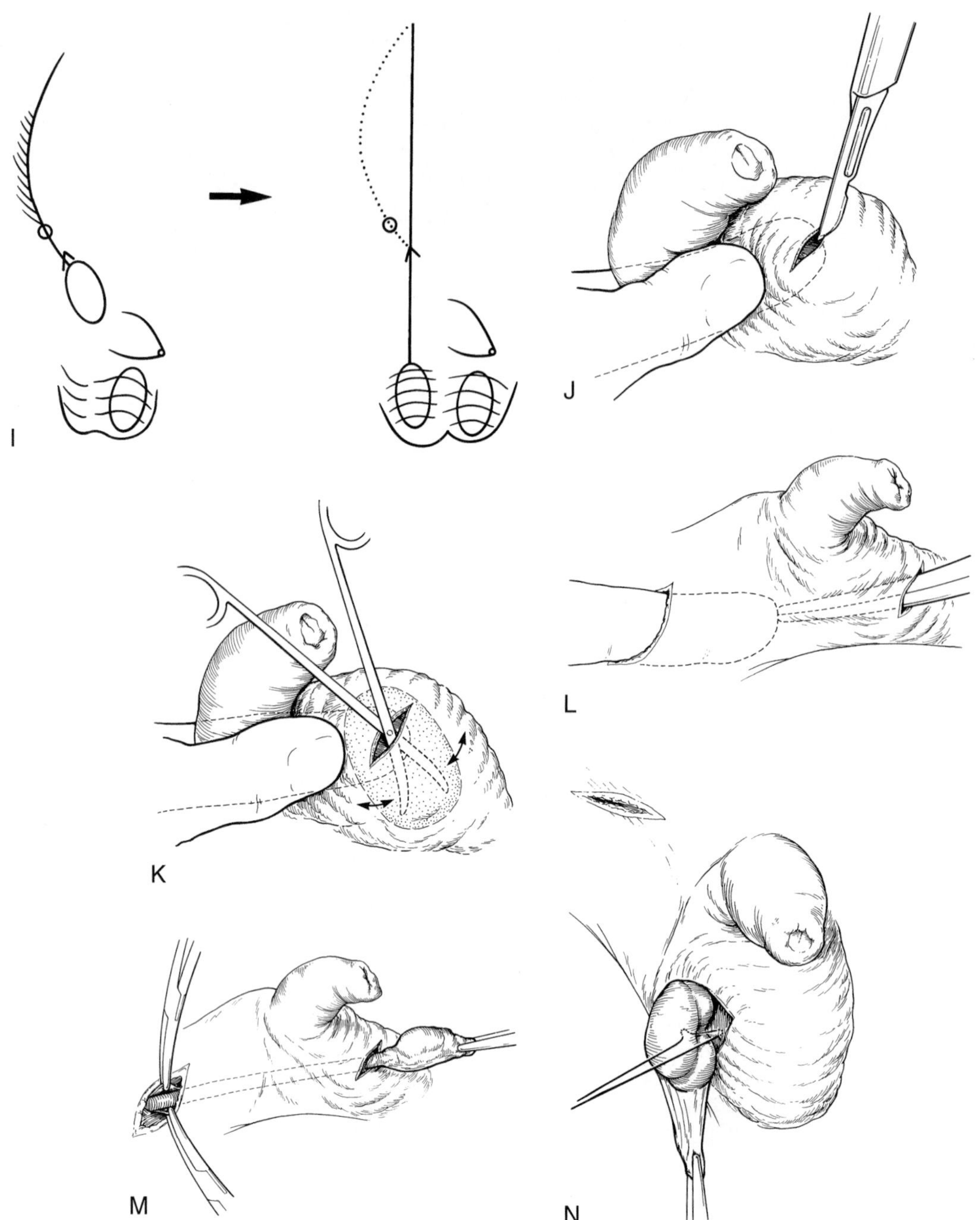

Figure 75–4 Cont'd *I,* Straightening of the path taken by the gonadal vessels may allow the testis to reach the scrotum. *J,* Incising the scrotal skin after blunt finger dissection has created a path to the scrotum from the inguinal incision. Either midline or transverse incisions may be used to gain entrance to the subdartos space; I prefer the latter because there is less bleeding. *K,* A subcutaneous pouch is made in the scrotum by undermining the incision with scissors or artery forceps. Careful attention must be given to hemostasis to avoid a postoperative hematoma. *L,* A fine artery forceps is pushed through the inguinoscrotal fascia, guided by the retreating finger, to connect the two incisions by a small buttonhole. *M,* The forceps grasps the testis, being careful not to twist the cord structures and pulls the testis down to the scrotal incision through the fascial buttonhole into the subdartos pouch. *N,* There may not be tension on the testis, and anchoring is optional. The testis may be sutured to the scrotal septum by a fine suture through the tunica albuginea, or alternatively the opening in the fascial buttonhole can be narrowed with one or two sutures, particularly if there is any tension on the cord structures, so the testis does not retract upward. The scrotal and inguinal incisions are closed in routine fashion. (From Spitz L, Coran AG: Pediatric surgery. In Rob and Smith's Operative Surgery, 5th ed. London, Chapman & Hall, 1995.)

inguinal canal, the hernia sac may completely envelop the testis so that the vas and vessels are inside the sac within a mesorchium. The method of separation of the hernia sac is that employed during routine hernia repair: the sac is stretched over the index finger while round-ended, nontoothed dissecting forceps gently sweep off the other cord structures, taking care not to damage the testicular vessels and vas deferens. En masse separation of the vas deferens and vessels is easier if the sac remains intact. If an opening is made inadvertently, the edges of the peritoneum should be picked up with forceps to maintain extensile exposure. The vas deferens is adherent to the back of the hernia sac, so it must be positively identified before the sac is divided.

Once the cord structures have been separated from the sac, safely identified, and protected, the sac is divided (see Fig. 75-4E). Dissection is continued proximally up to the internal ring, where external peritoneal fat and divergence of the testicular vessels laterally from the vas medially indicates the retroperitoneum (see Fig. 75-4F). The processus vaginalis is then transfixed and ligated at the internal inguinal ring (see Fig. 75-4G).

Further mobilization of the testicular vessels in the retroperitoneal space may be achieved by dividing small fibrous bands laterally that hold the testicular vessels and prevent them being gently stretched to allow the testis to reach the scrotum (see Fig. 75-4H). In older children, straightening the curved path taken by the testicular vessels may effectively lengthen the spermatic cord (see Fig. 75-4I), but this advantage is much less evident in small children. Since the advent of laparoscopy, it can be seen that the testicular vessels actually take a straight path from the abdominal aorta toward the internal inguinal ring and that retroperitoneal dissection is more likely to gain length by allowing greater traction and stretching of the testicular artery rather than by straightening the path taken.

The vas deferens usually has sufficient length to reach the scrotum without any special maneuvers. In difficult cases, however, the inferior epigastric vessels can be divided or the posterior wall of the inguinal canal can be opened medial to the inferior epigastric vessels and the testis taken medially to them. This may give an extra centimeter or so of length to the vas deferens. The method of fixation of the testis in the scrotum is shown in Figure 75-4J to N.

An alternative operation, which is particularly suitable for boys with acquired maldescent, is the transscrotal operation described by Bianchi and Squire[13] and Russinko and colleagues.[154] A transverse incision is made at the neck of scrotum, and the tunica vaginalis is exposed, delivered through the wound, and placed under tension. Loose connective tissue attachments to the spermatic cord are divided to expose the spermatic cord itself. Commonly, there is a residual fibrous strand of the processus vaginalis that is not fully obliterated. Once this fibrous strand has been divided, the vas and vessels stretch out to reach the bottom of the scrotum without difficulty.[25] The testis can be anchored by closing the neck of the scrotum or by suture of the testis to the scrotal septum.

When the testis is located within the inguinal canal or the abdomen, the spermatic cord may have insufficient length to reach the scrotum despite the maneuvers described previously. In this circumstance, the surgeon has a number of choices available. If there is necessary expertise and back-up support, microvascular anastomosis can be performed, with transection of the testicular vessels and reanastomosis to the inferior epigastric artery and vein.[54] This technique requires a high level of experience and skill with the operating microscope so it is not often used. More commonly, if the testis has been dissected but does not reach the scrotum, it can be sutured in the groin at the lowermost point where it reaches comfortably as a first-stage procedure, and a second attempt is made 6 to 12 months later. Success rates for this two-stage orchidopexy have been quoted to be 70% to 90%.[68]

An alternative approach is the Fowler-Stephens procedure in which the testicular vessels are ligated intra-abdominally and the testis swung down on a long-loop vas supplied by collateral circulation from the artery to the vas and some cremasteric vessels (see Fig. 75-7A and B).[53] Radical dissection of the inguinal canal before making the decision to perform a Fowler-Stephens operation may jeopardize its success by damaging the collateral blood supply. This complication can be overcome by performing the Fowler-Stephens operation as a two-stage procedure with initial ligation of the testicular vessels without disturbance to the collateral blood supply; the subsequent second-stage operation then allows the testis to be mobilized on the enlarged collateral vessels from the vas deferens, which then usually reach the scrotum. In follow-up studies of this two-stage procedure researchers report 70% to 90% scrotal position without atrophy.[15,41]

Many surgeons now use laparoscopy for impalpable testes in the inguinal canal and abdomen.[94,142] An immediate orchidopexy should be successful if the testis can be pulled to the opposite internal inguinal ring. A staged Fowler-Stephens operation is also relatively straightforward, and early results are promising. In the first stage, laparoscopic localization of the testis allows a decision to be made about orchidopexy versus orchidectomy, which should be considered if the testis is small or dysgenetic. If orchidopexy is believed warranted, simple ligation of the testicular vessels above the testes can be performed with an endosurgical tie or a clip.[14] Six months later, the testis can then be mobilized on a flap of peritoneum containing the collateral blood supply and swung down through the medial edge of inguinal canal to reach the scrotum. At present, I perform both stages laparoscopically.[157]

Complications of Surgery

In the hands of experienced surgeons and particularly with the routine use of magnification, the risk of complications after orchidopexy should be less than 5% (Table 75-1).[84] Damage to the testicular vessels leading to atrophy is the most feared complication, but this is relatively rare. More subtle damage to the vas deferens leading to occlusion of its lumen and subsequent interference with fertility is a theoretic problem, but its exact frequency is difficult to determine. Hemorrhage in the wound secondary to poor hemostasis occurs occasionally.

The most common complication after orchidopexy, particularly now that many are done in infants, is

TABLE 75-1 Complications of Orchidopexy

Failure of testis to reach scrotum
Secondary atrophy of the testis
Retraction of testis out of scrotum
Occlusion of vas deferens
Hemorrhage
Wound infection

wound infection. Both the inguinal and scrotal incisions are at risk for infection at any age, but, in my experience, scrotal infection is more common in infants. Usually this is of no serious consequence and responds to simple antibiotic treatment or drainage. Secondary ascent of the testis after orchidopexy is an uncommon but important complication caused by inadequate mobilization of the cord or inadequate fixation of the testis within the scrotal pouch. Postoperative lymphedema and vascular congestion of the testis after orchidopexy is a common finding that resolves spontaneously over the first month or two.

After orchidopexy, the child is usually reexamined 1 to 2 weeks later to remove the dressing and assess the short-term outcome. A further follow-up examination is performed 6 to 12 months later to determine whether there has been any significant atrophy or secondary malposition of the testis. The end result and appearance are satisfactory in the majority of instances.

Success rates are higher for those testes that have passed through the external inguinal ring, whereas intracanalicular or abdominal testes have a higher incidence of persisting abnormality after orchidopexy. The intra-abdominal testis may fail to reach the scrotum, at least after a single-stage procedure, or it may be an inadequate gonad subsequently and atrophy. Total infarction of the testis is rare and is reported in 3% of patients with an impalpable testis. A further 15% to 20% have some atrophy after orchidopexy.[1] The risk of atrophy is probably increased if a second operation is required to bring the testis to the scrotum. Exact figures in this subgroup, however, are not available.

The risk of atrophy after orchidopexy is increased if a simultaneous inguinal hernia is performed for incarcerated or strangulated hernia. It is difficult to determine whether the increased rate of atrophy is secondary to compromise of the testicular vessels caused by compression or to the greater dissection required with a large hernia sac. The timing for orchidopexy has therefore been a compromise between the potentially increasing risk of testicular dysplasia with age compared with the potentially increased risk of postoperative atrophy in younger children. Wilson-Storey and colleagues[184] compared 100 infants younger than 2 years of age with 100 toddlers or older children undergoing orchidopexy after age 2 years. They found an incidence of testicular atrophy of 5% in both groups, suggesting that the risk of postoperative atrophy is not directly related to age in pediatric surgical centers.

Fertility

A significant number of studies have evaluated fertility in men after orchidopexy (Table 75-2).[21,106,108,115,134,145,164] Testes initially located beyond the inguinal canal have a good prognosis for fertility, although location does not change outcome for unilateral cases.[107] Interpretation of results is difficult, however, because in most current fertility studies of men the operations were between 6 and 13 of years of age, suggesting that this group includes many acquired variants such as ascending and retractile testes. These latter patients are far less likely to have abnormal fertility because early germ cell maturation would have occurred normally when the testis was in the scrotum during infancy. The histology of ascending testis is reported to be similar to congenitally cryptorchid testes, and histopathology correlates with future fertility potential.[152,153]

An extensive review of the literature has failed to demonstrate any significant improvement in fertility with early operation within the range of 4 to 14 years.[164] Although 27 papers were reviewed, only four reports were recently published and we can no longer extrapolate data from operations done on adolescent patients before the 1950s and 1960s. With advances in knowledge and changes in clinical management in the past 25 years (i.e., earlier surgical intervention), it is inappropriate to compare these older historical studies with the results of current treatment. Whether orchidopexy in infancy ultimately achieves a significantly improved rate of fertility remains to be seen.

TABLE 75-2 Fertility After Orchidopexy

Authors	No. of Patients	Average Age at Operation	Fertility Tests	Fertility: Unilateral	Fertility: Bilateral
Puri et al., 1985	142	7-13	Semen analysis	74	30
Singer et al., 1988	25	6.2	Semen analysis	70	40
Cendron et al., 1989	40	7.0	Paternity	87	33
Kumar et al., 1989	56	7-18+	Paternity	84	60
Okuyama et al., 1989	167	2-5	Semen analysis	95	24
Mandat et al., 1994	135	8.9	Semen analysis	53	26
Lee et al., 2001	51	7.1	Paternity	90	—

Malignancy

At present, there are no accurate data available as to whether orchidopexy in early infancy reduces the risk of subsequent testicular cancer. However, Cortes reports that the risk of malignancy for acquired undescended testes is very low.[30] There will be a lag time between the current trend of orchidopexy in infancy and convincing evidence that this change in the management alters outcome for congenital undescended testes. At this time, all clinicians can do is define those features that appear to affect prognosis. Good prognostic signs include the testis near the neck of the scrotum, ascending or retractile testes, and possibly operation in early infancy. Poor prognosis is associated with primary dysplasia of the testis or epididymis, intra-abdominal or intracanalicular testes, an associated strangulated inguinal hernia, and possibly operation delayed until late childhood or adolescence.

TORSION OF THE TESTIS

Torsion of the testis was first described in 1840 by Delasiauve.[36] The condition was first reported in the newborn by Taylor in 1897,[173] and torsion of a testicular appendage was first described by Colt in 1922.[27] Ombredanne,[136] in 1913, described a lesion that was probably a testicular appendage, although he did not recognize its true nature.

Twisting or torsion of the testis results in occlusion of the gonadal blood supply, which, if unrelieved, leads to necrosis. Although it is not the most common cause of the acute scrotum in childhood, it is certainly the most important (Fig. 75-5). Torsion of the testis usually occurs in a fully descended testis and is a surgical emergency because of the high incidence of gonadal necrosis.

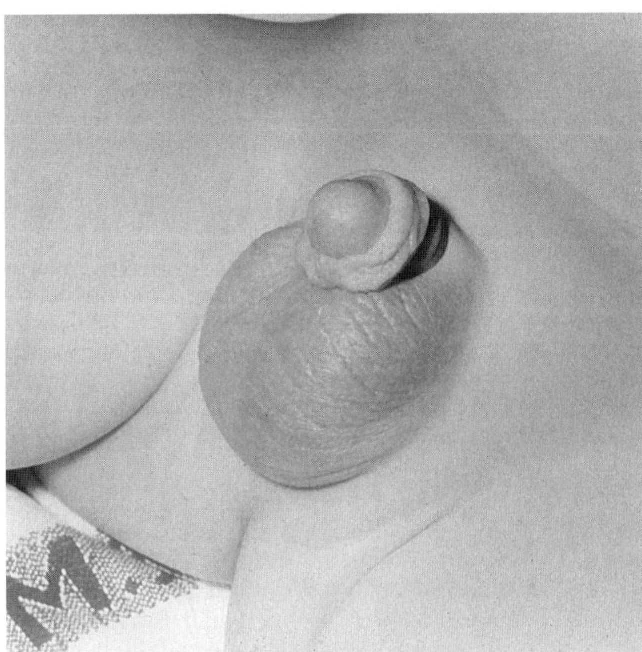

Figure 75-5 Mechanical causes of the acute scrotum present as pain, swelling, and redness confined to the hemiscrotum, as shown in this 1-year-old infant, because the inflammatory reaction is limited by the ipsilateral tunica vaginalis.

Intratunical or intravaginal torsion occurs most commonly and is predisposed to by an abnormally high investment of the spermatic cord by the tunica vaginalis. The long narrow mesorchium allows the testis to lie horizontally rather than be fixed vertically as with the normal testis. In the latter circumstance, the short mesorchium attaches to the full length of the epididymis and allows testicular movement within the tunica vaginalis but prevents complete torsion. The pendulous testis associated with a high investment of the cord has a horizontal lie and allows the testis to be readily twisted by leg movement or cremasteric contractions. A rare variant of intratunical torsion is one in which there is separation between the testis and the epididymis, allowing torsion between these structures. This is likely to be more common in undescended testes.

Extratunical or extravaginal torsion is less common and is confined to the perinatal period. During descent of the gubernaculum and testis into the scrotum, there is a loose areolar plane around these moving structures, which allows the entire testis and spermatic cord to twist.

Beyond the newborn period, testicular torsion is almost always associated with the *bell-clapper* deformity. Trauma and physical activity may be important, as may action of the cremaster muscle.[112] Cremasteric contraction may be either the cause or the effect of torsion. The high incidence of testicular torsion at puberty suggests that sudden enlargement of the testis associated with increased serum testosterone levels may be a predisposing factor.

Torsion of the testis does not always cause necrosis if the number of twists is small or the testis untwists spontaneously. In an experimental dog model, four complete turns of the spermatic cord caused necrosis within 2 hours, whereas one complete turn produced no ischemia in up to 12 hours.[168] In adolescent boys, necrosis is likely after 24 hours of symptoms but may occur after as little as 2 hours.[95,162]

In 1761, Morgagni described the appendix testis, now known as the *hydatid of Morgagni*.[86] This is believed to be an embryologic remnant of the cranial end of the müllerian or paramesonephric duct. It is present in more than 90% of males and varies in size from 1 to 10 mm in diameter. It is the most frequently twisted of the four testicular appendages. The others are the appendix epididymis, which is a remnant of the wolffian duct, the paradidymis, and the vas aberrans. These vestigial structures have a similar histology, being composed of gelatinous and vascular connective tissue covered with a columnar epithelium. The hydatid of Morgagni is usually pedunculated, which predisposes to torsion. The most frequent time for torsion of the testicular appendix is at about 11 years of age. This peak, just before the onset of puberty, may be related to early pubertal stimulation by estrogens.[26,155,166]

Inflammatory conditions of the scrotum are often called epididymo-orchitis, even though the epididymis alone is usually affected before puberty. Epididymitis is rare after puberty, whereas epididymo-orchitis is more common after puberty. The mumps virus has a predilection for the postpubertal but not the prepubertal testis. Epididymitis seen before puberty is usually caused by infection reaching the epididymis by retrograde spread along the vas deferens from the urinary tract. *Escherichia coli* is the common organism, and infections are predisposed to by urinary tract abnormalities or urethral instrumentation. The most common group now suffering epididymo-orchitis in childhood are boys with spina bifida having intermittent catheterization. This is occasionally seen in infants with imperforate anus and rectourethral fistula.

Idiopathic scrotal edema is occasionally confused with torsion of the testis or its appendages. In this condition, there is rapidly developing edema of the scrotum with spread to or from the inguinal region, penis, or perineum. The cause of this edema is not always apparent but may be bacterial cellulitis or a topical allergy.

A rare cause of the acute scrotum, which may be confused with testicular torsion, is fat necrosis. It is characterized by the sudden appearance of tender, often bilateral small lumps within the scrotal skin. The affected boys are often obese, and there may be a history of swimming in cold water.

Clinical Features

Torsion of the testis is common in adolescence, but before puberty torsion of a testicular appendage is more common (Table 75-3). There are two peaks of incidence for torsion of the testis: in the early neonatal period and in adolescent boys aged 13 to 16. In a review of 771 children up to the age of 16 presenting with acute scrotum, 58% had torsion of the testicular appendage and 29% had torsion of the testes. Epididymitis had been diagnosed in 13%, although a significant number of these subsequently turned out to have torsion of a testicular appendage that had not been recognized.[26]

Clinical presentation of testicular torsion is usually heralded by the sudden onset of pain in the testis, lower abdomen, or groin, associated with nausea and vomiting. Occasionally the onset is more gradual without severe pain, leading to delayed diagnosis. A previous history of short-lived, similar pains suggests prior incomplete torsion with spontaneous resolution. A horizontal lie of the testis when the boy stands indicates high investment of the spermatic cord. Unless the testis and the epididymis are necrotic, local palpation is exquisitely painful. The hemiscrotum rapidly becomes red and edematous, and, if untreated, infarction of the testis may give the hemiscrotum a bluish discoloration. The inflammatory signs usually end abruptly at the edge of the hemiscrotum, because this coincides with the limits of the peritoneum, tunica vaginalis. A reactive hydrocele from effusion of edema fluid into the tunica may make the physical signs more difficult to interpret (see Fig. 75-5).

Torsion of a testicular appendage presents with an almost similar history, although often the degree of pain is less severe. A bluish black spot (*blue-dot*) may be seen through the skin at the upper pole of the testis, and palpation of this area causes extreme pain, whereas palpation of the testis itself causes little discomfort. The degree of inflammation of the epididymis is variable with testicular appendage torsion. Once secondary inflammation and edema of the scrotum occur, it may be impossible to distinguish between testicular torsion and torsion of a testicular appendage.

Investigations such as radioisotope scans and Doppler ultrasound have been used to determine whether there is blood flow to the testes in acute scrotum.[133,186] In adolescents beyond pubertal age, such tests may be more useful because the volume of the testis is large enough to allow a reasonably high level of accuracy. Before puberty, however, when the testis is less than 1 or 2 mL in volume, such tests are of lower accuracy and have very limited clinical usefulness. I do not usually perform these studies but immediately explore the scrotum through a small midline scrotal incision.

TABLE 75-3 Causes of Acute Scrotum

Pathology	Frequency	Age at Presentation
Extravaginal torsion of testis	Uncommon	Perinatal
Intravaginal torsion of testis	Common	Anytime, peak at 13-16 yr
Testicular appendage torsion	Very common	Anytime, peak at 11 yr
Epididymitis	Rare	0-6 mo
Mumps orchitis	Uncommon	Only after puberty
Idiopathic scrotal edema	Uncommon	0-5 yr
Fat necrosis of scrotum	Rare	5-15 yr

Treatment

Treatment of the acute scrotum and possible torsion of the testis is immediate operative exploration of the scrotum. A midline incision is made in the scrotum, and the hemiscrotum is opened with diathermy. The edema in the scrotal wall may make identification of the tunica vaginalis difficult. It is easy to recognize once this has been opened by the efflux of hydrocele fluid. The testis is delivered through the incision if there is evidence of torsion of the gonad itself. Where the testis appears normally viable, its upper pole is manipulated into the wound and the twisted hydatid is delivered through the incision and excised. Usually this is a black pea after hemorrhagic infarction. A significant number of hydatids, however, undergo torsion without secondary hemorrhage and appear pale at surgery. These should always be excised and sent for pathologic confirmation of necrosis.

If the testis is twisted, this is untwisted and the viability assessed. In a prepubertal child, this maneuver is usually relatively easy, and circulation returns within a few minutes. In the postpubertal testis, particularly when there has been some secondary hemorrhage, viability may be difficult to determine. In this circumstance, it may be better to observe the testis for several minutes while exploring the contralateral scrotum. The use of a Doppler probe may be helpful to determine if there is testicular blood flow.

The contralateral hemiscrotum should always be explored when torsion of the testis has been found because the anomaly is usually bilateral. It is not sufficient to place a few absorbable sutures between the testis and the scrotal wall. The best technique is to create a window of tunica vaginalis by excising a segment of the tunica and suturing the edges of the defect to the tunica vaginalis with nonabsorbable sutures.[126] This creates permanent fusion of the testicular surface with the connective tissues of the scrotum and creates a new mesorchium. Inadequate fixation with absorbable sutures may result in recurrent torsion.[116,175]

It is controversial whether testes of doubtful viability should be excised or left in situ to see whether they will recover any hormonal function. There is now good evidence that testicular ischemia damages the blood-testis barrier and exposes the child older than 10 years of age to the potential risk of autoimmunization against his own spermatogonia.[145] This potentially serious complication has been recognized because spermatogenesis later in life is poor in men who underwent fixation of ischemic testes in adolescence. The risk of autoimmunization related to ischemia is low in children younger than age 10 because there is no blood-testis barrier then and spermatogenesis has not yet occurred.[120,180] It is my practice, therefore, to leave doubtful testes in situ in children younger than 10. In children older than 10 with an ischemic gonad, I recommend orchidectomy.

Another controversial issue is whether neonates presenting with a dead testis, apparently caused by perinatal torsion, should have the contralateral testis fixed.[34,121] As mentioned previously, perinatal torsion is often caused by torsion of the spermatic cord during testicular descent. A significant percentage of such children, however, also have an unfixed or bell-clapper testis and are therefore at risk of having contralateral torsion. A firm recommendation is difficult to give on this issue, but a strong case can be made for exploration of the contralateral testis and fixation as described for adolescent torsion, especially in an infant younger than a few weeks old. After 3 months of age, secondary adherence of the gubernaculum to the scrotum should have occurred and exploration is less useful.

In adolescents presenting with intermittent recurrent testicular pain, bilateral orchidopexy may be justified, especially if there is a horizontal lie of the testes on clinical examination. Almost one third of adolescents who undergo acute torsion have a history of previous intermittent pain.

VARICOCELE

Dilation of the testicular veins in the pampiniform venous plexus causes a varicocele.[83] The countercurrent heat exchange mechanism in the spermatic cord vessels is disrupted, which leads to an increased temperature of the testis and scrotum. The abnormally high temperature can be detected by thermography and causes progressive dysfunction of the testis and epididymis.[29,190] This may lead to subsequent testicular atrophy and infertility, as first proposed by Tulloch.[177] Testicular atrophy may be significant in adult life but may become evident quite early in adolescence.[144] The incidence of varicocele is 15% among men in general and rises to 20% to 40% in men presenting to infertility clinics. In children younger than age 10 years, varicocele is rare, but by the end of adolescence the incidence has risen to that seen in the adult population.[137] Varicocele may occur in small children with Wilms' tumor, neuroblastoma, or hydronephrotic kidney that causes obstruction of venous return from the testis. Although most cases of varicocele occur on the left, varicocele on the right side is suggestive of a retroperitoneal tumor.

Clinical Presentation

Varicocele presents as a soft, distensible mass in the upper part of the scrotum (Fig. 75-6). In 80% to 90% of cases they present on the left side, with bilateral lesions reported as occurring between 2% and 20% and right-sided lesions between 1% and 7%.[159] In the supine position, a redundant left hemiscrotum and horizontal lie of the left testis may be noted.[32] On standing, the varicocele fills with blood to produce the typical "bag of worms" appearance. The lesion is not usually painful; however, the boy may complain of a dragging sensation.

Varicoceles may be classified by size into grades I to III or small, medium, and large. Small varicocele (grade I) may be evident only during Valsalva maneuver.[127,169] Medium-size varicoceles (grade II) are palpable without Valsalva maneuver, and large varicoceles are visible as a scrotal space-occupying lesion.[174]

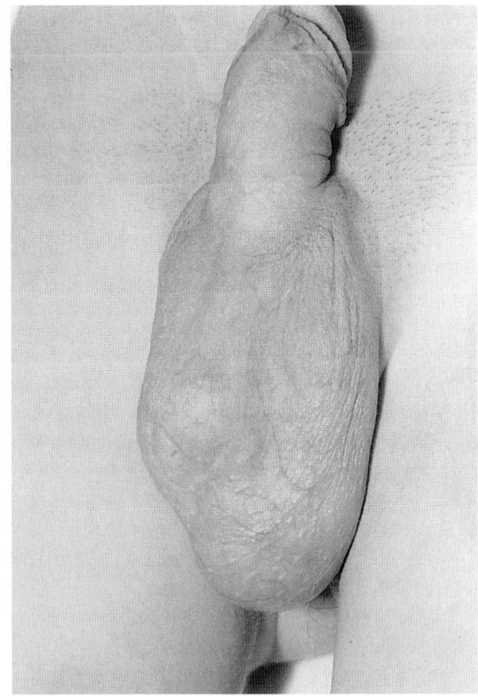

Figure 75-6 A grade III varicocele in a 14-year-old boy is visible as a space-occupying lesion of the left hemiscrotum even in the supine position before surgery. On standing, the dilated vessels fill to produce a "bag of worms."

Etiology

Lack of valves in the left testicular vein is one of the primary factors in the etiology of varicocele. In postmortem examinations, the left testicular vein contains no valves in 40% of specimens compared with absence of valves in only 23% of right spermatic veins, and the right-angle entry of the left spermatic vein into the high-pressure venous system of the left renal vein may predispose to varicocele.[2] When upright, the long pressure column generated in the pampiniform plexus results in poor venous return and varicose distention of the veins. There are a number of other etiologic theories, including disruption of the venous pump created by the coverings of the spermatic cord, compression of the left renal vein between the superior mesenteric artery and the aorta, extrinsic pressure on the left testicular vein by a full sigmoid colon, and vascular spasm at the origin of the left testicular vein caused by adrenaline coming from the left adrenal gland. In a series of 659 patients undergoing spermatic venography, absence of the valves in the left testicular veins was documented in 484 patients.[16] In addition, a further 172 patients with varicocele had valves intact but had reflux of blood into the testicular vein through collaterals draining the left kidney. Renal vein stenosis was identified in 103 patients. The external spermatic vein (cremasteric vein) also has been implicated, because it may be dilated in up to 50% of varicoceles.[22]

Because the testis is supplied by three separate arteries, so is the venous drainage formed by more than one set of veins. Blood reaches the testis via the testicular (or internal spermatic) artery from the abdominal aorta, the deferential artery supplying the vas deferens, and the cremasteric (or external spermatic) artery arising from the external iliac artery and inferior epigastric vessels (Fig. 75-7A). These three vessels form an anastomosis around the caudal epididymis. Blood drains from the testis and epididymis into the pampiniform plexus accompanying the testicular artery. Above the internal inguinal ring, the number of venous channels decreases to one or two and finally coalesces into a single testicular vein entering either the inferior vena cava on the right or the left renal vein; the latter join at a right angle. Retrograde flow in the veins is prevented by the presence of valves. Anastomoses with subsidiary veins occur along the vas deferens to the base of the bladder through the cremasteric and scrotal veins to the saphenous vein (see Fig. 75-7B).

Effects of Varicocele

Varicocele leads to testicular atrophy and subsequent infertility in adult life, probably secondary to abnormally high temperatures.[104] How the excessive temperature actually produces testicular dysfunction, however, is not so clear. A number of abnormalities have been documented in hormonal function and other physiologic parameters of the testis, but whether these are primary or secondary abnormalities is uncertain. This is particularly true for a proposed defect in the hypothalamic-pituitary-gonadal axis. Serum testosterone levels are usually normal, although a subclinical defect in the androgen axis is possible.[28] Leydig cell hypoplasia with high serum follicle-stimulating hormone levels has mostly been reported in adults with established testicular atrophy. Inhibited testicular development during puberty is seen in association with histologic changes that are similar to those seen in adults with infertility caused by varicocele.[110,114,134] Where testicular atrophy is recognizable, an abnormal production of pituitary hormones occurs in response to a gonadotropin-releasing hormone stimulation test.

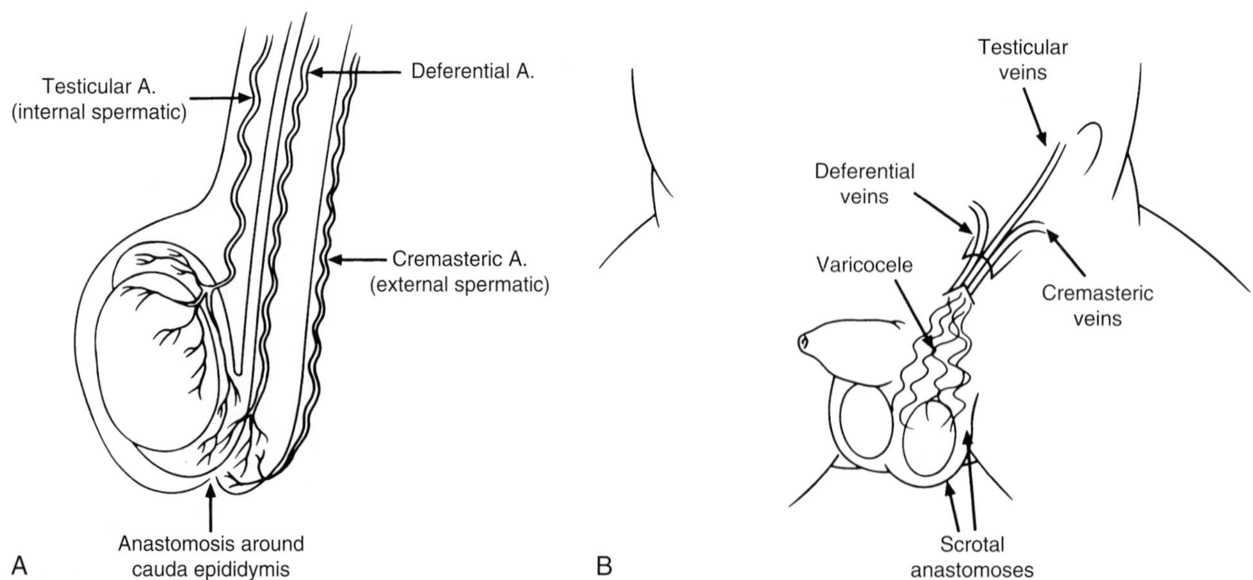

Figure 75-7 *A*, Arterial supply to the testis, epididymis, and vas deferens, with anastomoses around the cauda epididymis. *B*, Venous drainage of the testis, showing the anastomoses with the varicocele. (From Hutson JM: Varicocele and its treatment. Pediatr Surg Int 1995;10:509.)

Indications for Treatment

The criteria for treatment are controversial, with common indications including symptoms such as chronic pain or discomfort, demonstrable atrophy of the testis in adolescence, and subfertility in adults. When there is greater than a 10% difference in gonadal volume on orchidometry, Parrott and Hewatt[140] advocate operation. Nagar and Levran[127] have recommended screening of school boys by physical examination to identify varicoceles at any early stage of development and found varicoceles were present but asymptomatic in 10% of nearly 800 boys examined. They propose that screening enabled the diagnosis to be made at an earlier age and a lower stage of disease. They speculated that this should produce improved future fertility in adults, but this will not be proven for some time. Doppler ultrasound is currently a popular test used in adult infertility clinics to identify subclinical varicoceles.[33] In early adolescence, however, when the testicular volume and blood flow is much less than in adults, the role of Doppler ultrasound is less reliable. Diagnostic or therapeutic testicular venography is currently popular for men with varicocele.[130,158] In young adolescents, general anesthesia is usually required for such a procedure, although a study using therapeutic testicular venography with insertion of spring coils has been described using only local anesthesia.

Operation

The multiple theories of etiology of varicocele have led to a wide range of surgical options (Fig. 75-8). Inguinal exploration has been a standard procedure for many years, with careful ligation of all the venous channels as described by Ivanissevich[89] and by Sayfan and colleagues.[158] Historically, this technique has been associated with a high incidence of secondary hydrocele, accidental ligation of the testicular artery leading to testicular atrophy, and recurrence of the varicocele.[43,58] Poor results in some hands have led to a search for alternative approaches, including microsurgical dissection of the testicular veins, preserving the testicular artery and lymphatics within the spermatic cord. Some authors have suggested identifying the artery or veins intraoperatively so that the artery can be preserved. For this purpose, both Doppler ultrasonography and venography have been used, but the role of these intraoperative investigations remains uncertain.[58,66,111] Antegrade sclerotherapy is also being used in some units.[117]

Shafik and associates have suggested plication of the external spermatic fascia to cause external compression of the pampiniform vessels.[163] This is a simple procedure but does not address the persisting problem of retrograde flow of blood within the testicular veins. One might predict a high frequency of recurrence, although this is not currently known.

Laparoscopic ligation of the testicular vein proximal to the internal ring has gained popularity.[142] Some authors have recommended selective ligation of the venous channels preserving the artery, whereas others have recommended mass ligation of the artery and the veins. Many publications attest to the feasibility of laparoscopic ligation, but long-term follow-up is not available.[43,150]

Palomo first proposed mass ligation of the testicular vessels, including both artery and veins in the retroperitoneum above the internal inguinal ring.[139] The technique has a high success rate with a surprisingly low risk of testicular atrophy as long as the collateral vessels have been preserved.[72,97,140,150] The operation has been available for a long time but has only recently gained popularity. Fear of devascularizing the testis has made many surgeons cautious. As stated in Palomo's publication, however, the blood supply of the testis should be maintained if any two of the three vessels are preserved. Because the cremasteric and deferential vessels are preserved, the collateral arterial supply of the testis should be intact, and no venous channels are accidentally excluded by being mistaken for the testicular artery itself.

Retroperitoneal mass ligation as described by Palomo is my personal choice. I offer the family the option of having the procedure done laparoscopically or by a small open retroperitoneal approach. The laparoscopic method is similar to that described elsewhere in this

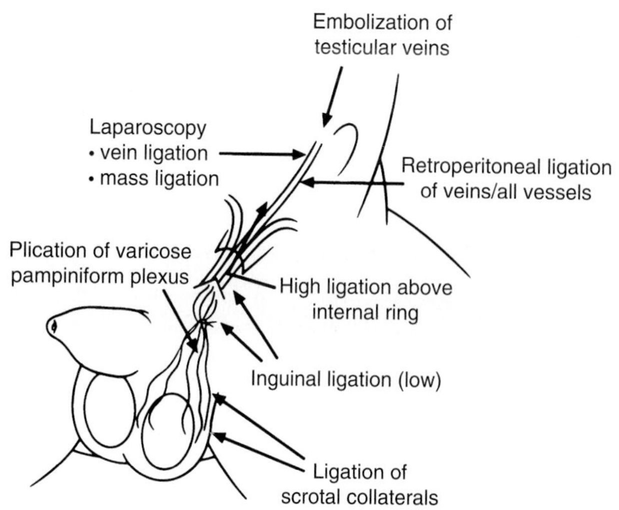

Figure 75-8 The large range of approaches to correction of a varicocele. (From Hutson JM: Varicocele and its treatment. Pediatr Surg Int 1995;10:509.)

book, with a 5-mm telescope port through the umbilicus and two 4-mm ports, one in the left abdomen level with the umbilicus and the other in the hypogastrium. With the surgeon standing on the right side of the operating table and the assistant on the left, the video screen is placed near the left foot. The colon can be displaced readily by tilting the patient. The peritoneum is opened several centimeters away from the internal inguinal ring, and the entire vascular pedicle including artery and all venous channels is ligated in continuity with a 3-0 absorbable suture.

The open procedure is also straightforward and may be done on an ambulatory basis. Under a short general anesthetic, an incision is made in the left iliac fossa medial and just a little below the left anterosuperior iliac spine. This is usually several centimeters away from the internal inguinal ring. The oblique muscles are divided along the line of their fibers just lateral to the rectus abdominis muscle. Once the peritoneum is visualized, it is mobilized medially by pledget and blunt dissection. Using this site of access, the peritoneal cavity is shallow, and medial displacement of the peritoneum immediately exposes the testicular pedicle well below the level of the ureter entering the pelvis. The vascular pedicle is isolated from the overlying peritoneum with a right-angle forceps, and two 3-0 absorbable ligatures are placed in continuity around the pedicle. It is not necessary to divide the testicular pedicle, although this is an option. On removal of the retractors, the peritoneum immediately resumes its normal position, and a few tacking sutures can be placed in the muscle layers and the skin closed with subcuticular sutures in the normal manner. Because this approach does not disturb all the lymphatic drainage of the inguinoscrotal region and leaves collaterals to the cremasteric and deferential vessels intact, the postoperative risk of an acute hydrocele is lower than with other procedures.

Results

The recognized complications of varicocele repair are shown in Table 75-4. The risk of recurrence or persistence of the varicocele is quoted as 5% to 45%.[58] Risk of reactive hydrocele varies between 7% and 39%. The incidence of testicular atrophy, which is one of the most important outcome measures related to this surgery, is rarely reported, so accurate figures are unknown.

Ilioinguinal nerve damage has been reported after inguinal approaches, and genitofemoral nerve injuries have been reported after laparoscopy as well as injury to the vas. Ligation of the veins within the inguinal canal using a modified Ivanissevich procedure has a 16% recurrence, compared with high retroperitoneal selective vein ligation, which has a reported recurrence rate of 11%. They also compared 32 boys treated with mass ligation through the Palomo procedure in which they found no failures and no testicular atrophy after any of the operations. I concur from my own experience that the Palomo operation is the preferred technique. The surgical management of varicocele continues to evolve, but at present the Palomo operation done either by open or laparoscopic approaches holds reasonable promise as having higher success and lower complication rates than previous procedures.

TABLE 75-4 Complications of Varicocele Repair

Recurrence/persistence	5%-45%
Reactive hydrocele	7%-39%
Testicular atrophy	Not known
Ilioinguinal nerve injury	Not known
Injury to vas deferens	Not known

REFERENCES

1. Adamsen S, Bornesson B: Factors affecting the outcome of orchidopexy for undescended testis. Acta Chir Scand 1988;154:529.
2. Ahlberg NE, Bartley O, Chidekel N: Right and left gonadal veins: An anatomical and statistical study. Acta Radiol (Diagn) 1966;4:517.
3. Attah AA, Hutson JM: The role of intra-abdominal pressure in cryptorchidism. J Urol 1993;150:994.
4. Atwell JD: Ascent of the testis: fact or fiction. Br J Urol 1985;57:474.
5. Backhouse KM: Embryology of testicular descent and maldescent. Urol Clin North Am 1982;9:315.
6. Baker BA, Morley R, Lucas A: Plasma testosterone in preterm infants with cryptorchidism. Arch Dis Child 1988; 63:1198.
7. Baker LA, Nef S, Nguyen MT, et al: The insulin-3 gene: Lack of a genetic basis for human cryptorchidism. J Urol 2002;167:2534.
8. Barthold JS, Gonzalez R: The epidemiology of congenital cryptorchidism, testicular ascent and orchiopexy. J Urol 2003;170:2396.
9. Beasley SW, Bettenay F, Hutson JM: The anterior urethra provides clues to the aetiology of prune belly syndrome. Pediatr Surg Int 1988;3:169.
10. Behringer RR, Finegold MJ, Cate RL: Mullerian-inhibiting substance function during mammalian sexual development. Cell 1994;79:415.
11. Benson RC Jr, Beard CM, Kelalis PP, Kurland LT: Malignant potential of the cryptorchid testis. Mayo Clin Proc 1991;66:372.
12. Bergh A, Nikula H, Damber JE, et al: Altered concentrations of gonadotrophin, prolactin and GnRH receptors, and endogenous steroids in the abdominal testes of adult unilaterally cryptorchid rats. J Reprod Fertil 1985;74:279.
13. Bianchi A, Squire BR: Trans-scrotal orchidopexy: Orchidopexy revisited. Pediatr Surg Int 1989;4:189.
14. Bloom DA: Two-step orchiopexy with pelviscopic clip ligation of the spermatic vessels. J Urol 1991;145:1030.
15. Boddy S, Gordon AC, Thomas DF, Browning FS: Experience with the Fowler-Stephens and microvascular procedures in the management of intra-abdominal testes. Br J Urol 1991;68:199.
16. Braedel HU, et al: A possible ontogenic etiology for idiopathic left varicocele. J Urol 1994;151:62.
17. Brown TR, Berkovits GD, Gearheart JP: Androgen receptors in boys with isolated bilateral cryptorchidism. Am J Dis Child 1988;142:933.

18. Browne D: Some anatomical points in operation for undescended testicle. Lancet 1933;1:460.
19. Cain MP, Kramer SA, Tindall DK, Husmann DA: Expression of androgen receptor protein within the lumbar spinal cord during ontologic development and following antiandrogen induced cryptorchidism. J Urol 1994;152:766.
20. Canavese F, Lalla R, Linari A, et al: Surgical treatment of cryptorchidism. Eur J Pediatr 1993;152(Suppl 2):S43.
21. Cendron M, Keating MA, Huff DS, et al: Cryptorchidism, orchiopexy and infertility: A critical long-term retrospective analysis. J Urol 1989;142:559.
22. Chehval MJ, Purcell MH: Varicocelectomy: Incidence of external spermatic vein involvement in the clinical varicocele. Urology 1992;39:573.
23. Chilvers C, Pike MC: Epidemiology of undescended testis. In: Urological and Genital Cancer. Oxford, Blackwell Scientific, 1989.
24. Christiansen P, Muller J, Buhl S, et al: Treatment of cryptorchidism with human gonadotropin releasing hormone. Horm Res 1988;30:187.
25. Clarnette TD, Rowe D, Hasthorpe S, Hutson JM: Incomplete disappearance of the processus vaginalis as a cause of ascending testis. J Urol 1997;157:1889.
26. Clift VL, Hutson JM: The acute scrotum in childhood. Pediatr Surg Int 1989;4:185.
27. Colt GH: Torsion of the hydatid of Morgagni. Br J Surg 1922;9:464.
28. Comhaire F, Vermeulen A: Plasma testosterone in patients with varicocele and sexual inadequacy. J Clin Endocrinol Metab 1975;40:824.
29. Comhaire FH: Vasculature of the testis: Assessment and management of varicocele. In Burger H, de Kretser D (eds): The Testis, 2nd ed. New York, Raven Press, 1989.
30. Cortes D, Thorup J, Petersen BL: Testicular neoplasia in undescended testes of cryptorchid boys-does surgical strategy have an impact on the risk of invasive testicular neoplasia? Turk J Pediatr 2004;46(Suppl):35-42.
31. Costa WS, Sampaio FJ, Favorito LA, Cardoso LE: Testicular migration: Remodelling of connective tissue and muscle cells in human gubernaculum testis. J Urol 2000;167:2171.
32. Coveney EC, Fitzgerald RJ: Varicocele and the horizontal testis: A change in position? J Pediatr Surg 1994;29:452.
33. Cvitanic OA, Cronan JJ, Sigman M, et al: Varicoceles: Postoperative prevalence—a prospective study with color Doppler US. Radiology 1994;287:711.
34. Das S, Singer A: Controversies of perinatal torsion of the spermatic cord: A review, surgery and recommendations. J Urol 1990;143:231.
35. de Kretser DM, Risbridger GP: Changes in Sertoli cell structure and function. In Hutson JM, Beasley SW (eds): The Cryptorchid Testis. Boca Raton, FL, CRC Press, 1989.
36. Delasiauve LJF: Descente tardive du testicule gauche, prisé pour une hernie etranglée. Rev Med Fr Etrang 1840;1:363.
37. De Muinck Keizer-Schrama SMPF: Hormonal treatment of cryptorchidism. Horm Res 1988;30:178.
38. De Muinck Keizer-Schrama SMPF, Hazebroek FWJ, Drop SLS, et al: Double-blind, placebo-controlled study of luteinizing-hormone-releasing hormone nasal spray in treatment of undescended testes. Lancet 1986;1:876.
39. Diamond DA, Caldamone AA, Elder JS: Prevalence of the vanishing testis in boys with a unilateral impalpable testis: Is the side of presentation significant? J Urol 1994;152:502.
40. Donaldson KM, Tong SYC, Hutson JM: Prevalence of late orchidopexy is consistent with some undescended testes being acquired. Indian J Pediatr 1996;63:725.
41. Elder JS: Two-stage Fowler-Stephens orchidopexy in the management of intra-abdominal testes. J Urol 1992; 148:1239.
42. Emmen JM, McLuskey A, Adham IM, et al: Hormonal control of gubernaculum development during testis descent: Gubernaculum outgrowth in vitro requires both insulin-like factor and androgens. Endocrinology 2000;141:4720.
43. Esposito C, Valla JS, Najmaldin A, et al: Incidence and management of hydrocele following varicocele surgery in children. J Urol 2004;171:1271.
44. Esposito C, Monguzzi GL, Gonzalez-Sabin MA, et al: Laparoscopic treatment of pediatric varicocele: A multicenter study of the Italian society of video surgery in infancy. J Urol 2000;163:1944.
45. Fallat ME, Hersh JH, Hutson JM: Theories on the relationship between cryptorchidism and arthrogryposis. Pediatr Surg Int 1992;7:271.
46. Fallat ME, Williams MPL, Farmer PJ, et al: Histologic evaluation of inguinoscrotal migration of the gubernaculum in rodents during testicular descent and its relationship to the genitofemoral nerve. Pediatr Surg Int 1992;7:265.
47. Farrer JH, et al: Impaired testosterone biosynthesis in cryptorchidism. Fertil Steril 1985;44:125.
48. Farrington GH: The position and retractability of the normal testis in childhood with reference to the diagnosis and treatment of cryptorchidism. J Pediatr Surg 1968; 3:53.
49. Favorito LA, Sampaio FJ, Javaroni V, et al: Proximal insertion of gubernaculum testis in normal human fetuses and in boys with cryptorchidism. J Urol 2000;164:792.
50. Favorito LA, Klojda CA, Costa WS, Sampaio FJ: Is there a relationship with anomalous insertions of the distal gubernaculum testis and testicular ectopia? Analysis in human fetuses and patients with cryptorchidism. J Urol 2003;170:554.
51. Ferlin A, Simonato M, Baroloni L, et al: The INSL3-LGR8/GREAT ligand-receptor pair in human cryptorchidism. J Clin Endocrinol Metab 2003;88:4273.
52. Fonkalsrud EW, Mengel W: The Undescended Testis. Chicago, Year Book Medical Publishers, 1981.
53. Fowler R, Stephens FD: The role of testicular vascular anatomy in the salvage of high undescended testes. Aust N Z J Surg 1959;29:92.
54. Frey P, Bianchi A: Microvascular autotransplantation of intra-abdominal testes. Progr Pediatr Surg 1989;23:115.
55. Gendrel D, Roger M, Job J-C: Plasma gonadotropin and testosterone values in infants with cryptorchidism. J Pediatr 1980;97:217.
56. Giwercman A, Muller J, Skakkebaek NE: Cryptorchidism and testicular neoplasia. Horm Res 1988;30:157.
57. Goh DW, Hutson JM: Can undescended testes be acquired? Lancet 1993;341:504.
58. Goldstein M, Gilbert BR, Dicker AP, et al: Microsurgical inguinal varicocelectomy with delivery of the testis: An artery and lymphatic sparing technique. J Urol 1992;148:1808.
59. Grocock CA, Charlton HM, Pike MC: Role of the fetal pituitary in cryptorchidism induced by exogenous maternal oestrogen during pregnancy in mice. J Reprod Fertil 1988; 83:295.
60. Hack WW, Meijer RW, van der Voort-Doedens LM, et al: Natural course of acquired undescended testis in boys. Br J Surg 2003;90:728.
61. Hadziselimovic F (ed): Cryptorchidism: Management and Implications. Berlin, Springer-Verlag, 1983.
62. Hadziselimovic F: Fertility and cryptorchidism. Am J Dis Child 1985;139:963.
63. Hadziselimovic F, Duckell JW, Snyder HM 3rd, et al: Omphalocele, cryptorchidism and brain malformations. J Pediatr Surg 1987;22:854.
64. Hadziselimovic F, Herzog B, Girard J, et al: Cryptorchidism—histology, fertility and treatment. Prog Reprod Biol Med 1984;10:1.

65. Hadziselimovic F, Herzog B, Seguchi H: Surgical correction of cryptorchidism at 2 years: Electron microscopic and morphometric investigations. J Pediatr Surg 1975;10:19.
66. Hart RR, Rushton HG, Belman AB: Intraoperative spermatic venography during varicocele surgery in adolescents. J Urol 1992;148:1514.
67. Haughey BP, Graham S, Brasure J, et al: The epidemiology of testicular cancer in upstate New York. Am J Epidemiol 1989;130:25.
68. Hazebroek FWJ, Molenaar JC: The management of the impalpable testis by surgery alone. J Urol 1992;148:629.
69. Herzog B, Steigert M, Hadziselimovic F: Is a testis located at the superficial inguinal pouch (Denis Browne pouch) comparable to a true cryptorchid testis? J Urol 1992; 148:622.
70. Heyns CF: The gubernaculum during testicular descent in the human fetus. J Anat 1987;153:93.
71. Heyns CF, Hutson JM: Historical review of theories on testicular descent. J Urol 1995;153:754.
72. Hirokawa M, Matsushita K, Iwamoto T, et al: Assessment of Palomo's operative method for fertile varicocele. Andrologia 1993;25:47.
73. Hoorweg-Nijman JJG, Havers HM, Delemarre-van de Waal HA: Effect of human chorionic gonadotrophin (hCG)/ follicle-stimulating hormone treatment versus hCG treatment alone on testicular descent: A double-blind placebo-controlled study. Eur J Endocrinol 1994;130:60.
74. Hrebinko RL, Bellinger MF: The limited role of imaging techniques in managing children with undescended testes. J Urol 1993;150:458.
75. Huff DS, Hadziselimovic F, Snyder HM 3rd, et al: Early postnatal testicular maldevelopment in cryptorchidism. J Urol 1991;146:624.
76. Huff DS, Snyder HM, Hadziselimovic F: An absent testis is associated with contralateral testicular hypertrophy. J Urol 1992;148:627.
77. Huff DS, Wu HY, Snyder HM 3rd, et al: Evidence in favor of the mechanical (intrauterine torsion) theory over the endocrinopathy (cryptorchidism) theory in the pathogenesis of testicular agenesis. J Urol 1991;146:630.
78. Huhtaniemi I, Bergh A, Nikula H, Damber JE: Differences in the regulation of steroidogenesis and tropic hormone receptors between the scrotal and abdominal testes of unilaterally cryptorchid adult rats. Endocrinology 1984; 115:550.
79. Hunter J: A description of the situation of the testis in the foetus, with its descent into the scrotum. In Observations on Certain Parts of the Animal Oeconomy. London, Castle-Street Leicester Square, 1786.
80. Hutson JM: A biphasic model for the hormonal control of testicular descent. Lancet 1985;2:419.
81. Hutson JM, Sasaki Y, Huynh J, et al: The gubernaculum in testicular descent and cryptorchidism. Turk J Pediatr 2004; 46(Suppl):3-6.
82. Hutson JM: Orchidopexy. In Spitz L, Coran AG (eds): Operative Pediatric Surgery, Rob & Smith's Operative Surgery, 6th ed. London, Arnold Chapman, 2006.
83. Hutson JM: Varicocele and its treatment. Pediatr Surg Int 1995;10:509.
84. Hutson JM, Beasley SW: Descent of the Testis. Melbourne, Edward Arnold, 1992.
85. Hutson JM, Beasley SW, Bryan AD: Cryptorchidism in spina bifida and spinal cord transection: A clue to the mechanism of transinguinal descent of the testis. J Pediatr Surg 1988;23:275.
86. Hutson JM, Woodward AA, Beasley SW: Jones' Clinical Paediatric Surgery: Diagnosis and Management, 5th ed. Melbourne, Blackwell Scientific, 1999.
87. Hutson JM, Davidson PM, Reece LA, et al: Failure of gubernacular development in the persistent Mullerian duct syndrome allows herniation of the testes. Pediatr Surg Int 1994;9:544.
88. Hutson JM, Hasthorpe S, Heyns CF: Anatomical and functional aspects of testicular descent and cryptorchidism. Endocr Rev 1996;18:259.
89. Ivanissevich O: Left varicocele due to reflux: Experience with 4,470 operative cases in 42 years. J Int Coll Surg 1960; 34:742.
90. Job JC, Toublanc JE, Chaussain JL, et al: Endocrine and immunological findings in cryptorchid infants. Horm Res 1988;30:167.
91. Johansen TEB: Anatomy of the testis and epididymis in cryptorchidism. Andrologia 1987;19:565.
92. John Radcliffe Hospital Cryptorchidism Study Group: Cryptorchidism: An apparent substantial increase since 1960. BMJ 1986;293:1401.
93. John Radcliffe Hospital Cryptorchidism Study Group: Boys with late descending testes: The source of patients with "retractile" testes undergoing orchidopexy. BMJ 1986; 293:789.
94. Kanemoto K, Hayashi Y, Kojima Y, et al: The management of nonpalpable testis with combined groin exploration and subsequent transinguinal laparoscopy. J Urol 2002; 167:674.
95. Kaplan GW, King CR: Acute scrotal swelling in children. J Urol 1970;104:219.
96. Kaplan LM, Koyle MA, Kaplan GW, et al: Association between abdominal wall defects and cryptorchidism. J Urol 1986;136:645.
97. Kass EJ, Marcol B: Results of varicocele surgery in adolescents: A comparison of techniques. J Urol 1992;148:694.
98. Keel BA, Abney TO: Cryptorchidism-induced changes in spermatogenesis and fertility. In Abney TO, Keel BA (eds): The Cryptorchid Testis. Boca Raton, FL, CRC Press, 1989.
99. Koff S: Does compensatory testicular enlargement predict monorchism? J Urol 1991;146:632.
100. Koff WJ, Scaletscky R: Malformations of the epididymis in undescended testis. J Urol 1990;143:340.
101. Kogan SJ, Tennebaum S, Gill B, et al: Efficacy of orchiopexy at patient age 1 year for cryptorchidism. J Urol 1990;144:508.
102. Kreuger RP, Hardy BE, Churchill BM: Cryptorchidism in boys with posterior urethral valves. J Urol 1980;124:101.
103. Kropp KA, Voeller KKA: Cryptorchidism in meningomyelocele. J Pediatr 1981;99:110.
104. Ku JH, Son H, Kwak C, et al: Impact of varicocele on testicular volume in young men: Significance of compensatory hypertrophy of contralateral testis. J Urol 2002; 168:1541.
105. Kubota Y, Temelcos C, Bathgate RA, et al: The role of insulin 3, testosterone, Mullerian inhibiting substance and relaxin in rat gubernaculum growth. Mol Hum Reprod 2002;8:900.
106. Kumar K, Bremner DN, Brown PW: Fertility after orchiopexy for cryptorchidism: A new approach to assessment. Br J Urol 1989;64:516.
107. Lee PA, Coughlin MT, Bellinger MF: Paternity and hormone levels after unilateral cryptorchidism: Association with pretreatment testicular location. J Urol 2000; 164:1697.
108. Lee PA, Coughlin MT, Bellinger MF: No relationship of testicular size at orchiopexy with fertility in men who previously had unilateral cryptorchidism. J Urol 2001;166:236.
109. Lee SMY, Hutson JM: Effect of androgens on the cranial suspensory ligament and ovarian position. Anat Rec 1999; 225:306.

110. Lipshultz LI, Corriere JN Jr: Progressive testicular atrophy in the varicocele patient. J Urol 1977;117:175.
111. Loughlin KR, Brooks DC: The use of a Doppler probe to facilitate laparoscopic varicocele ligation. Surg Gynecol Obstet 1992;174:326.
112. Lrhorfi H, Manunta A, Rodriquez A, Lobel B: Trauma-induced testicular torsion. J Urol 2002;168:2548.
113. Luthra M, Hutson JM, Stephens FD: Effects of external inguinoscrotal compression on descent of the testis in rats. Pediatr Surg Int 1989;4:403.
114. Lyon RP, Marshall S, Scott MP: Varicocele in childhood and adolescence: Implication in adulthood fertility? Urology 1982;19:641.
115. Mandat KM, Wieczorkiewica B, Gubala-Kacala M, et al: Semen analysis of patients who had orchidopexy in childhood. Eur J Pediatr Surg 1994;4:94.
116. May RE, Thomas WEG: Recurrent torsion of the testis following previous surgical fixation. Br J Surg 1980;67:129.
117. Mazzoni G, Spagnoli A, Lucchetti MC, et al: Adolescent varicocele: Tauber antegrade sclerotherapy versus Palomo repair. J Urol 2001;166:1462.
118. Mengel W, Hienz HA, Sippe WG 2nd, Hecker WC: Studies on cryptorchidism: A comparison of histological findings in the germinative epithelium before and after the second year of life. J Pediatr Surg 1974;9:445.
119. Mieusset R, Fouda PJ, Vaysse P, et al: Increase in testicular temperature in case of cryptorchidism in boys. Fertil Steril 1993;59:1319.
120. Mininberg DT, Chen ME, Witkin SS: Antisperm antibodies in cryptorchid boys. Eur J Pediatr 1993;152(Suppl):S23.
121. Mishriki SF, Winkle DC, Frank JD: Fixation of a single testis: Always, sometimes or never. Br J Urol 1992;69:311.
122. Moerman P, Fryns JP, Goddeeris P, Lauweryns JM: Pathogenesis of the prune belly syndrome: A fractional urethral obstruction caused by prostatic hypoplasia. Pediatrics 1984;73:470.
123. Moore RG, Peters CA, Bauer SB, et al: Laparoscopic evaluation of the nonpalpable testis: A prospective assessment of accuracy. J Urol 1994;151:728.
124. Morgagni GB, cited in Jones PG: Torsion of the testis and its appendages during childhood. Arch Dis Child 1962; 37:214.
125. Morley R, Lucas A: Undescended testes in low birthweight infants. BMJ 1987;295:753.
126. Morse TS, Hollabaugh RS: The "window" orchidopexy for prevention of testicular torsion. J Pediatr Surg 1977; 12:237.
127. Nagar H, Levran R: Impact of active case-finding on the diagnosis and therapy of pediatric varicocele. Surg Gynecol Obstet 1993;177:38.
128. Nef S, Parada LF: Hormones in male sexual development. Genes Dev 2000;14:3075.
129. Nguyen MT, Showalter PR, Timmons CF, et al: Effects of orchiopexy on congenitally cryptorchid insulin-3 knockout mice. J Urol 2002;168:1779.
130. Nieschlag E, Behre HM, Schlingbeider A, et al: Surgical ligation vs. angiographic embolization of the vena spermatica: A prospective randomized study for the treatment of varicocele-related infertility. Andrologia 1993;25:233.
131. Nistal M, Paniagua R: Infertility in adult males with retractile testes. Fertil Steril 1984;41:395.
132. Nunn P, Stephens FD: The triad syndrome: A composite anomaly of the abdominal wall, urinary system and testes. J Urol 1961;86:782.
133. Nussbaum Blask AR, et al: Color Doppler sonography and scintigraphy of the testis: A prospective, comparative analysis in children with acute scrotal pain. Pediatr Emerg Care 2002;18:67.
134. Okuyama A, Koide T, Itatani H, et al: Pituitary-gonadal function in schoolboys with varicocele and indications for varicocelectomy. Eur Urol 1981;7:92.
135. Okuyama A, Nonomura N, Nakamura M, et al: Surgical management of undescended testis: Retrospective study of potential fertility in 274 cases. J Urol 1989;142:749.
136. Ombredanne L: Torsions testiculaires chez les enfants. Bull Mem Soc Chir Paris 1913;38:799.
137. Oster J: Varicocele in children and adolescents. Scand J Urol Nephrol 1971;5:27.
138. Pagon RA, Smith DW, Shephard TH: Urethral obstruction malformation complex: A cause of abdominal muscle deficiency and the "prune belly." J Pediatr 1979; 94:900.
139. Palomo A: Radical cure of varicocele by a new technique: Preliminary report. J Urol 1949;61:604.
140. Parrott TS, Hewatt L: Ligation of the testicular artery and vein in adolescent varicocele. J Urol 1994;152:791.
141. Patil KK, Duffy PG, Woodhouse CR, Ransley PG: Long-term outcome of Fowler-Stephens orchiopexy in boys with prune-belly syndrome. J Urol 2004;171:1666.
142. Peters CA: Laparoscopy in pediatric urology. Curr Opin Urol 2004;14:67.
143. Pike MC, Chilvers C, Peckham MJ: Effect of age at orchidopexy on risk of testicular cancer. Lancet 1986;1:1246.
144. Podesta ML, Gottlieb S, Medel R Jr, et al: Hormonal parameters and testicular volume in children and adolescents with unilateral varicocele: Preoperative and postoperative findings. J Urol 1994;152:794.
145. Puri P, Barton D, O'Donnell B: Prepubertal testicular torsion: Subsequent fertility. J Pediatr Surg 1985;20:598.
146. Puri P, Nixon HH: Bilateral retractile testes—subsequent effects on fertility. J Pediatr Surg 1977;12:563.
147. Raivio T, Toppari J, Kaleva M, et al: Serum androgen bioactivity in cryptorchid and noncryptorchid boys during the postnatal reproductive hormone surge. J Clin Endocrinol Metab 2003;88:2597.
148. Rajfer J, Handelsman DJ, Swerdloff RS, et al: Hormonal therapy of cryptorchidism: A randomised, double-blind study comparing human chorionic gonadotropin and gonadotropin-releasing hormone. N Engl J Med 1986; 314:466.
149. Rasmussen TB, Ingerslev HJ, Hostrup H: Natural history of the maldescended testis. Horm Res 1988;30:164.
150. Riccabona M, Oswald J, Koen M, et al: Optimizing the operative treatment of boys with varicocele: Sequential comparison of 4 techniques. J Urol 2003;169:666.
151. Rozanski TA, Bloom DA: The undescended testis. Urol Clin North Am 1995;22:107.
152. Rusnack SL, Wu HY, Huff DS, et al: The ascending testis and the testis undescended since birth share the same histopathology. J Urol 2002;168:2590.
153. Rusnack SL, Wu HY, Huff DS, et al: Testis histopathology in boys with cryptorchidism correlates with future fertility potential. J Urol 2003;169:659.
154. Russinko PJ, Siddiq FM, Tackett L, Caldomone AA: Prescrotal orchiopexy: An alternative surgical approach for the palpable undescended testis. J Urol 2003; 170:2436.
155. Samnakay N, Cohen RJ, Orford J, et al: Androgen and oestrogen receptor status of the human appendix testis. Pediatr Surg Int 2003;19:520.
156. Saw KC, Eardley I, Dennis MJ, Whitaker RH: Surgical outcomes of orchiopexy: I. Previously unoperated testes. Br J Urol 1992;70:90.
157. Sawchuk T, Costabile RA, Howards SS, Rodgers BM: Spermatic cord torsion in an infant receiving human chorionic gonadotropin. J Urol 1993;150:1212.

158. Sayfan J, Soffer V, Orda R: Varicocele treatment: Prospective randomized trial of 3 methods. J Urol 1992; 148:1447.
159. Saypol DC: Varicocele. Int J Androl 1981;2:61.
160. Scorer CG: The descent of the testis. Arch Dis Child 1964; 39:605.
161. Scorer CG, Farrington GH: Congenital Deformities of the Testis and Epididymis. London, Butterworths, 1971.
162. Sessions AE, Rabinowitz R, Hulbert WC, et al: Testicular torsion: Direction, degree, duration and disinformation. J Urol 2003;169:663.
163. Shafik A, Khalil AM, Saleh M: The fasciomuscular tube of the spermatic cord: A study of its surgical anatomy and relation to varicocele: A new concept for the pathogenesis of varicocele. Br J Urol 1972;44:147.
164. Singer R, Dickerman Z, Sagir M, et al: Endocrinological parameters and cell-mediated immunity post operation for cryptorchidism. Arch Androl 1988;20:153.
165. Skakkebaek NE, Berthelsen JG, Giwercman A, Muller J: Carcinoma in situ of the testis: Possible origin from gonocytes and precursor of all types of germ cell tumors except spermatocytomas. Int J Androl 1987;10:19.
166. Skoglund RW, McRoberts JN, Ragde H: Torsion of testicular appendages: Presentation of 43 new cases and a collective review. J Urol 1970;104:598.
167. Smith JA, Hutson JM, Beasley SW, Reddihough DS: The relationship between cerebral palsy and cryptorchidism. J Pediatr Surg 1989;23:275.
168. Sonda LP, Lapides J: Experimental torsion of the spermatic cord. Surg Forum 1961;12:502.
169. Steckel J, Dicker AP, Goldstein M: Relationship between varicocele size and response to varicocelectomy. J Urol 1993;149:769.
170. Stone JM, Cruickshank DG, Sandeman TF, Matthews JP: Laterality, maldescent, trauma and other clinical factors in the epidemiology of testis cancer in Victoria, Australia. Br J Cancer 1991;64:132.
171. Sutthoff-Lorey G, Waag KL: Die Pra und intraoperative Genebetemperaturmessung bei maldescensus Testis. In Schier F, Waldsschmidt J (eds): Maldescensus Testis. Munich, Zuckschwerdt Verlag, 1990.
172. Tanyel FC: The descent of testis and reason for failed descent. Turk J Pediatr 2004;46(Suppl):7-17.
173. Taylor MR: A case of testicle strangulated at birth: Castration: recovery. BMJ 1897;1:458.
174. Thomas JC, Elder JS: Testicular growth arrest and adolescent varicocele: Does varicocele size make a difference? J Urol 2002;168:1689.
175. Thurston A, Whitaker R: Torsion of testis after previous testicular surgery. Br J Surg 1983;70:217.
176. Tomboc M, Lee PA, Mitwally MF, et al: Insulin-like 3/relaxin like factor gene mutations are associated with cryptorchidism. J Clin Endocrinol Metab 2000;85:4013.
177. Tulloch WS: A consideration of sterility factors in the light of subsequent pregnancies: Subfertility in the male. Trans Edin Obstet Soc 1952;59:29.
178. Turek PJ, Ewalt DH, Snyder HM 3rd, et al: The absent cryptorchid testis: Surgical findings and their implications for diagnosis and etiology. J Urol 1994;151:718.
179. Uehling DT: Fertility in men with varicocele. Int J Fertil 1968;13:58.
180. Urry RL, Carrell DT, Starr NT, et al: The incidence of antisperm antibodies in infertility patients with a history of cryptorchidism. J Urol 1994;151:381.
181. Walker RD: Diagnosis and management of the nonpalpable undescended testicle. AUA Update Series 1992;11:153.
182. Whitaker RH: Neoplasia in cryptorchid men. Semin Urol 1988;6:107.
183. Wilson JD, George FW, Griffin JE: The hormonal control of sexual development. Science 1981;211:1278.
184. Wilson-Storey D, McGenity K, Dickson JAS: Orchidopexy: The younger the better? J R Coll Surg (Edinb) 1990; 35:362.
185. Woodhouse CRJ: Undescended testes. In Long-term Paediatric Urology. Oxford, Blackwell Scientific, 1991.
186. Wu HC, Sun SS, Kao A, et al: Comparison of radionuclide imaging and ultrasonography in the differentiation of acute testicular torsion and inflammatory testicular disease. Clin Nucl Med 2002;27:490.
187. Yamanaka J, Baker M, Metcalfe S, Hutson JM, et al: Serum levels of Mullerian inhibiting substance in boys with cryptorchidism. J Pediatr Surg 1991;26:621.
188. Zhou B, Watts LM, Hutson JM: The effect of Mullerian inhibiting substance (MIS) on germ cell development of the neonatal mouse in vitro. J Urol 1993;150:613.
189. Zhou B: Normal pre-pubertal development of spermatogonia in immature testicular feminized (TFM/y) mice with complete androgen resistance. J Pediatr Surg (in press).
190. Zorgniotti AW (ed): Temperature and environmental effects on the testis. Adv Exp Med Biol 1991;286:199.

Chapter 76

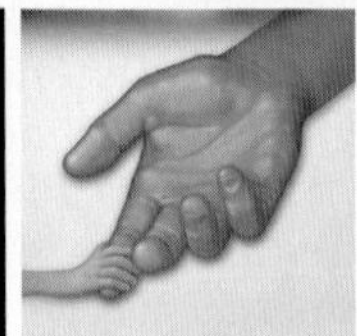

Hypertrophic Pyloric Stenosis

Marshall Z. Schwartz

HISTORY

In 1717, Blair[7] described an infant with postmortem findings consistent with hypertrophic pyloric stenosis. The first complete description of hypertrophic pyloric stenosis was by Hirschsprung in 1888.[23] He believed that this entity was congenital and represented failure of involution of the fetal pylorus and named it *angeborener pylorusstenose* (congenital pyloric stenosis). Dufour and Fredet,[12] in 1908, suggested that surgical correction could be accomplished by splitting the hypertrophied pyloric muscle to the submucosa and closing the muscle transversely. In 1912, Ramstedt[46] suggested that closure of the muscle was not necessary, and the current standard operation was established.

Infantile hypertrophic pyloric stenosis (IHPS) is a common cause of gastric outlet obstruction in infants. The prevalence of IHPS ranges from 1.5 to 4.0 per 1000 live births in white infants but is less prevalent in African American and Asian children.[35] Reports have suggested that the incidence is increasing.[34,39] It is well known that it is more common in boys than girls, with a ratio of approximately 2:1 to 5:1.[35] The occurrence of IHPS has been associated with several variables, including both environmental and familial factors.

IHPS is now thought to be caused by a mechanism other than a developmental defect. In a series of 1000 boys studied by barium swallow immediately after birth, Wallgren[63] found no anatomic abnormalities of the pylorus. Subsequently, IHPS developed in five of these infants. In a similar, but more recent study, 1400 consecutive newborn infants underwent ultrasound (US) measurements of the pylorus, with no abnormalities seen.[48] In nine of these infants, however, IHPS subsequently developed.

ANATOMY AND HISTOLOGY

The gross appearance of the pylorus in IHPS is that of an enlarged, pale muscle mass usually measuring 2 to 2.5 cm in length and 1 to 1.5 cm in diameter (Fig. 76-1). Histologically, there is marked muscle hypertrophy and hyperplasia[43] primarily involving the circular layer and hypertrophy of the underlying mucosa.[22] Immunohistochemical analysis of the hypertrophic muscle reveals an increase in fibroblasts, fibronectin, proteoglycan chondroitin sulfate,[45] desmin,[19] elastin,[42] and collagen.[36] Confocal microscopy identifies abnormally contorted and thickened nerve fibers.[29] The net result of these changes is either partial or complete obstruction of the pyloric channel.

ETIOLOGY

The etiology of IHPS has intrigued investigators for several decades. Despite considerable research attempting to elucidate the etiology of IHPS, no definitive causative factors have been identified. Both genetic and environmental factors seem to play a role in the pathophysiology. Evidence for a genetic predisposition includes variability among races, a clear male preponderance, an increased risk to first-born infants with a positive family history, and certain ABO blood types. Mitchell and Risch studied the familial occurrence patterns of IHPS and noted that it

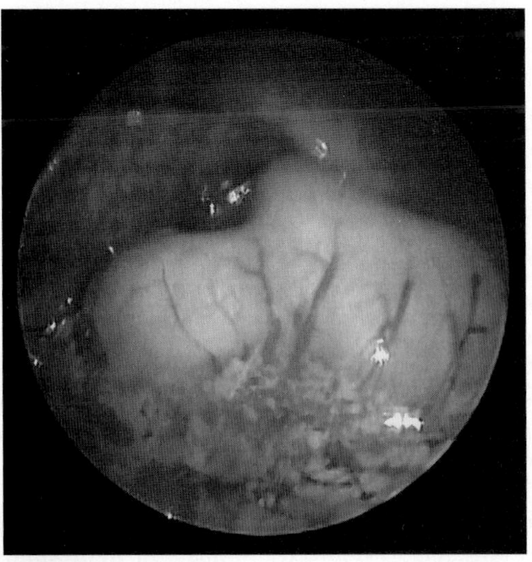

Figure 76–1 Laparoscopic view of a hypertrophied pylorus.

was compatible with either multifactorial threshold inheritance or the effects of multiple interacting loci.[35] Although pyloric stenosis is more common in boys, the risk for IHPS in the offspring of mothers who had pyloric stenosis as a baby is greater than if the father had IHPS. Environmental factors associated with IHPS include the method of feeding (breast-feeding versus formula feeding), seasonal variability, erythromycin exposure, and transpyloric feeding of premature infants.[25,35,47,58]

Another focus has been on alterations in relaxation of the pyloric muscle. One study noted a decrease in ganglion cells in the circular muscle of the pylorus,[4] but a subsequent study found that the ganglion cells were normal in number but appeared to be immature.[14] Zuelzer[67] and Jona[26] did not find any change in number or ultrastructural appearance of the ganglion cells. As new technology and concepts have evolved, additional associations have been described that involve IHPS and gastrointestinal peptides, growth factors, neurotrophins, changes in neural development, and nitric oxide.

Growth Factors and Gastrointestinal Peptides

Over the past several decades numerous gastrointestinal peptides or growth factors have been implicated by direct or indirect methodologies as having a causal relationship, including gastrin, substance P, epidermal growth factor (EGF), transforming growth factor-α (TGF-α), insulin-like growth factor-I, somatostatin, secretin, enteroglucagon, and neurotensin.[10,56] Other peptides have been evaluated for their potential relationship to IHPS. Substance P, a neurotransmitter responsible for enteric muscle contraction, could produce chronic pylorospasm leading to muscle hypertrophy.[60] This peptide is present in higher concentration in the pyloric muscle of patients with IHPS. Shima et al. found an increase in the gene expression of EGF, TGF-α, and insulin-like growth factor-I and an increase in immunostaining for EGF and TGF-α.[40,53,54] Somatostatin, secretin, enteroglucagon, and neurotensin have also been implicated.[10,11,21] However, their role has not been substantiated, and no clear etiologic relationship has been identified.

Neurotrophins, Neural Development, and Nerve Function

Neurotrophins, which are important for nerve differentiation and survival, have been noted to be decreased in IHPS. Further studies have shown that one of the specific receptors for these neurotrophins, the tyrosine kinase A receptor c-kit, is not present in IHPS tissue.[20,61,65] Investigators also identified that the pylorus in IHPS is deficient in glial-derived growth factors, which may be indicative of immature development of the enteric nervous system.[18]

Other techniques have been applied to the evaluation of pyloric innervation. Okazaki et al. used monoclonal antibodies targeted to nerve terminals and neurofilaments.[41] They found a reduced density of both neural elements in patients with IHPS. Kobayashi et al. demonstrated a decrease in nerve-supporting cells in both the circular and longitudinal muscle layers in infants with IHPS.[30] Piotrowska et al. found that muscle biopsy specimens from IHPS patients have decreased numbers of interstitial cells of Cajal, the pacemaker cells for the gastrointestinal tract, and a lack of heme oxygenase-2, which may play a role in communicating between the interstitial cells of Cajal and smooth muscle cells.[44]

Nitric Oxide

Nitric oxide can induce smooth muscle relaxation in the esophagus, stomach, and intestine. It was reasoned that a deficiency of nitric oxide in the pyloric muscle might result in failure of relaxation.[1,57,59] Nicotinamide-adenine dinucleotide phosphate (NADPH) diaphorase (essentially identical to nitric oxide synthase) was measured in biopsy specimens of hypertrophied pyloric muscle wall from IHPS patients. The hypertrophied circular muscle did not demonstrate any NADPH diaphorase activity, but the activity in the longitudinal muscle was normal. The authors concluded that the lack of nitric oxide synthase in pyloric tissue might be responsible for pylorospasm and lead to IHPS.[62]

Thus, at present no definitive cause of IHPS has been elucidated. Whatever the mechanism, it must take into account that the process of IHPS generally occurs several weeks after birth and the circular muscle hypertrophy is transient even without myotomy. It is also apparent that whatever triggers IHPS causes a dramatic change in cellular architecture and function through what may be a broad array of pathways.

CLINICAL FEATURES AND DIFFERENTIAL DIAGNOSIS

The typical clinical finding in an infant with IHPS is the onset of nonbilious vomiting at 2 to 8 weeks of age with a peak occurrence at 3 to 5 weeks. However, IHPS has been diagnosed at birth[66] and even in utero.[27] Initially, the emesis may not be frequent or forceful, but over a period of several days it progresses to nearly every feeding and becomes forceful (projectile). On occasion, there may be blood in the emesis that gives it a brownish discoloration or a coffee-ground appearance as a result of gastritis or esophagitis. Infants with IHPS remain hungry after emesis and are otherwise not ill appearing or febrile. A significant delay in diagnosis leading to severe dehydration, however, results in a lethargic infant. Some infants have diarrhea (starvation stools) and are thought to have gastroenteritis. Approximately 2% to 5% of infants have jaundice from indirect hyperbilirubinemia, which can reach levels as high as 15 to 20 mg/dL. This is believed to be secondary to glucuronyl transferase deficiency.[49] In premature infants, IHPS is generally diagnosed 2 weeks later than in term infants.[58] The emesis may not be projectile and evolves more slowly, which frequently leads to a delay in diagnosis.

Pylorospasm and gastroesophageal reflux may be difficult to differentiate from IHPS without further imaging evaluation. Other medical causes of nonbilious vomiting include gastroenteritis, increased intracranial pressure, and metabolic disorders. Other surgical causes of nonbilious emesis include antral webs, pyloric atresia, duplication cyst of the antropyloric region, and ectopic pancreatic tissue within the pyloric muscle, all far less common than IHPS.

DIAGNOSIS

Nonbilious projectile vomiting, visible peristaltic waves in the left upper part of the abdomen, and hypochloremic, hypokalemic metabolic alkalosis are cardinal features of IHPS. A definitive diagnosis can be made in 75% of infants with IHPS by careful physical examination of the upper part of the abdomen, but this is becoming a lost skill. Frequently, imaging procedures are requested by primary care physicians in lieu of a careful physical examination. To be successful in palpating an enlarged pylorus, the infant must be calm, warm, and cooperative. The use of a pacifier or a small feeding (5% dextrose in water) may be helpful. If the stomach is distended, aspiration with a nasogastric tube facilitates successful palpation of an enlarged pylorus, often referred to as "the olive." With the infant supine and the legs bent to relax the abdominal muscles, the examining hand should be placed on the epigastrium. After the edge of the liver has been identified with the fingertips, gentle pressure deep to the liver and progressing caudally in the midline a third of the distance between the umbilicus and xiphoid should reveal a palpable pylorus if IHPS is present. The examiner should be willing to commit 5 to 15 minutes of uninterrupted time if necessary. One should be able to roll the hypertrophied pylorus under the fingertips to be convinced of the diagnosis. Failure to palpate the pylorus requires further workup to clarify the cause of vomiting. The differential diagnosis includes food allergy, gastroesophageal reflux, antral web, pyloric duplication, and vomiting occasionally accompanying adrenogenital syndrome.

US not only has become the most common initial imaging technique for the diagnosis of IHPS but is also clearly the standard for diagnosing IHPS. Under optimal circumstances, this technique is very reliable. However, it is dependent on the level of experience and expertise of the ultrasonographer. The generally accepted criteria for a positive US study is a pyloric muscle thickness of 3.5 to 4 mm or more and a pyloric channel length of 16 mm or greater (Fig. 76-2).[28] Some centers also determine pyloric diameter and consider more than 14 mm to be abnormal.[28] Lamki et al.[32] reviewed their experience with US and concluded that a muscle thickness of 3 mm should be considered a positive finding for IHPS in infants younger than 30 days. US also obviates the need for radiographs and the associated radiation exposure.

If US is not diagnostic, an upper gastrointestinal (UGI) contrast examination is highly effective in making the diagnosis of IHPS. This study should demonstrate an elongated pyloric channel and indentation on the antral outline, which are indirect findings of pyloric muscle enlargement (Fig. 76-3). If barium does not leave the stomach, it is not possible to confirm the diagnosis of IHPS because pylorospasm can also produce complete gastric outlet obstruction. However, if sufficient time is taken with intermittent fluoroscopy, it should be possible to

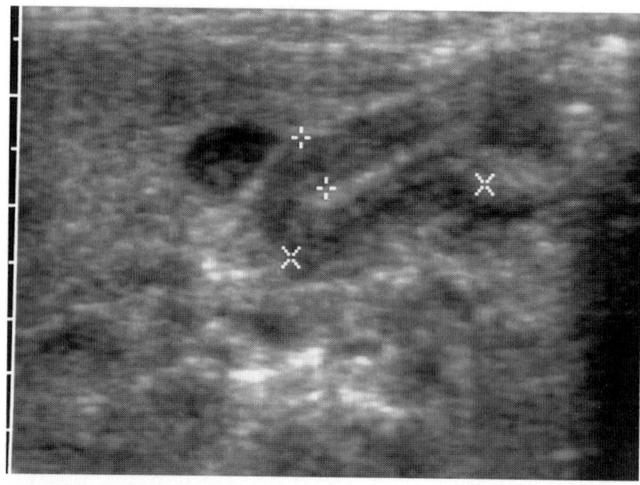

A

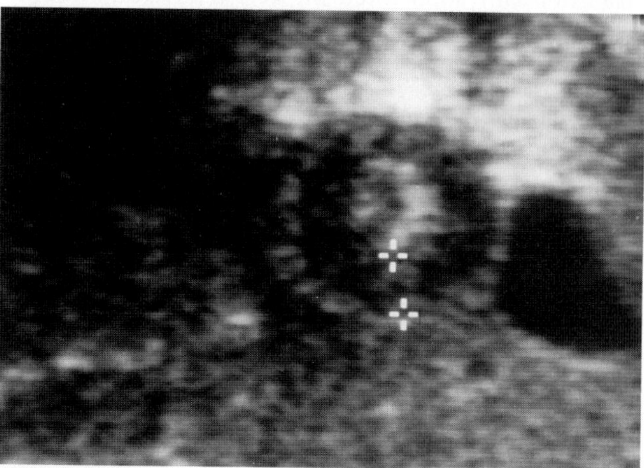

B

Figure 76-2 Ultrasound images of the hypertrophied pylorus in a 5-week-old infant. *A*, A longitudinal view is shown with pyloric length (X-X) measuring 18 mm and pyloric muscle thickness (+-+) measuring 5.2 mm. (Courtesy of Dorothy Bulas, MD.) *B*, Transverse view illustrating muscle thickness (+-+).

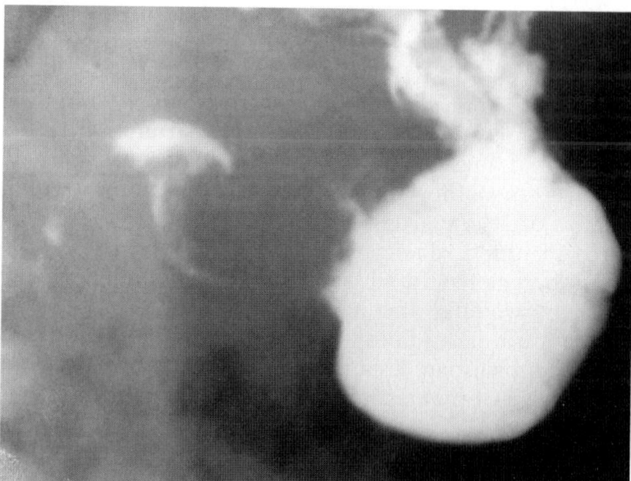

Figure 76-3 Upper gastrointestinal study illustrating an elongated pyloric channel with shoulders proximally as indirect evidence of pyloric muscle hypertrophy. Note the small amount of contrast in the duodenal bulb defining the length of the hypertrophied pylorus.

differentiate between the two entities. It is advisable for the radiologist to aspirate the residual barium from the stomach after termination of the radiographic procedure to avoid perioperative aspiration.

In 1998 our group conducted a survey of practice patterns for the diagnosis of IHPS among pediatric surgeons in community, university, and children's hospitals.[3] The questionnaire was distributed to 487 board-certified pediatric surgeons, with a 69% response rate. Ninety-one percent of the respondents stated that they would not request a further diagnostic test if a pyloric olive was palpable. US was identified as the diagnostic study of choice for an inconclusive physical examination (86% of the time). Finally, 82% of pediatric surgeons would proceed with an operation with a positive US study even if the results of physical examination under anesthesia were negative. The response to this question indicates that US has essentially supplanted physical examination as the diagnostic test of choice for IHPS.[3]

TREATMENT

Preoperative Preparation

It is most important to prepare the infant appropriately and adequately for anesthesia and surgical correction of IHPS. The length of preparation depends on the severity of the fluid and electrolyte abnormalities. Benson and Alpern[6] defined three levels of severity based primarily on the serum carbon dioxide content (slight, <25 mEq/L; moderate, 26 to 35 mEq/L; and severe, >35 mEq/L). In addition to the elevated bicarbonate, hypokalemia, hypochloremia, dehydration, and possibly malnutrition may be present.

Most infants with IHPS do not have complete gastric outlet obstruction and can therefore tolerate their gastric secretions. Oral feedings should be discontinued. A nasogastric tube should not be placed routinely because it removes additional fluid and hydrochloric acid from the stomach, which perpetuates the electrolyte and acid-base imbalance.

Fluid resuscitation should be based on the degree of dehydration and the extent of electrolyte abnormalities. Most infants with IHPS should be able to be resuscitated within a 24-hour period. With severe metabolic and fluid abnormalities, however, aggressive resuscitation can produce rapid fluid and electrolyte shifts, possibly leading to seizures and other complications. Intravenous administration of 5% dextrose in 0.45 normal saline containing 20 to 40 mEq/L of potassium chloride is the optimal resuscitation regimen for fluid and electrolyte replacement. Initially avoiding the addition of potassium chloride in the intravenous fluid while awaiting urine output only delays appropriate treatment. The exception (rare) is knowledge of preexisting renal impairment or evidence of acute renal compromise. Hyponatremia is rarely a problem. Nonetheless, it is common to see normal saline given as an initial bolus. However, there is little rationale for the use of normal saline because it enhances the hypokalemia by dilution and provides an excess amount of sodium. Intravenous therapy should be correlated with the level of dehydration. An initial rate for fluid resuscitation is 1.25 to 2 times the normal maintenance rate until adequate fluid status is achieved. The concentration of potassium chloride in the intravenous fluid should be based on the level of hypokalemia and the rate of infusion while keeping in mind that a potassium chloride concentration exceeding 40 mEq/L is rarely indicated. It is appropriate to monitor urine output and serum electrolytes. Normalizing the serum bicarbonate level (with the goal of decreasing the level below 30 mEq/dL) usually lags behind normalization of fluid volume and serum potassium and chloride. Administration of ammonium chloride or dilute hydrochloric acid is rarely necessary. As noted previously, indirect hyperbilirubinemia with clinical signs of jaundice occurs in a small percentage of infants with IHPS. It is not usually necessary to evaluate the hyperbilirubinemia further. After corrective surgery, the hyperbilirubinemia resolves.

Operative Procedure (Open)

In the operating room, before the induction of anesthesia, it is important to aspirate the stomach. If a barium UGI study has been performed, it is advisable to remove the residual contrast material by gastric irrigation and suctioning to avoid the risk for perioperative aspiration.

The operative procedure of choice remains the Ramstedt pyloromyotomy. This procedure has stood the test of time because it is straightforward, curative, and associated with remarkably low morbidity. The standard approach is a right upper quadrant transverse incision of approximately 2.5 to 3 cm made either over or lateral to the right rectus muscle and just superior to the edge of the liver. The fascial layers are divided transversely over the rectus muscle, and it can be either retracted laterally or split longitudinally in the middle. Several other incisions have been described.[12] A commonly used alternative is a supraumbilical curved skin incision followed by division of the midline fascia superiorly for 1 to 2 cm. The edge of the liver is retracted superiorly to expose the greater curvature of the stomach (near the pylorus), which is grasped with a noncrushing clamp and brought out through the incision. A damp gauze sponge can then be used to grasp the stomach, and with traction inferiorly and laterally, the pylorus can be delivered through the incision. Grasping the duodenum or pylorus directly with forceps can result in injury or perforation of these structures and should therefore be avoided. The serosa on the anterior wall of the hypertrophied pylorus is incised with a scalpel from the area of hypertrophied muscle just distal to the antral-pyloric junction to just proximal to the pyloric vein (Fig. 76-4). I and many others prefer to use the back of a scalpel handle to complete the myotomy by bluntly splitting the hypertrophied muscle down to the submucosa (see Fig. 76-4). Other surgeons prefer the use of a pyloric spreading clamp, such as that described by Benson.[5] It is appropriate to leave a few pyloric muscle fibers intact at the duodenal end to reduce the risk for duodenal perforation. Most incomplete myotomies are a result of failure to extend it far enough proximally onto the antrum. A careful check for a leak

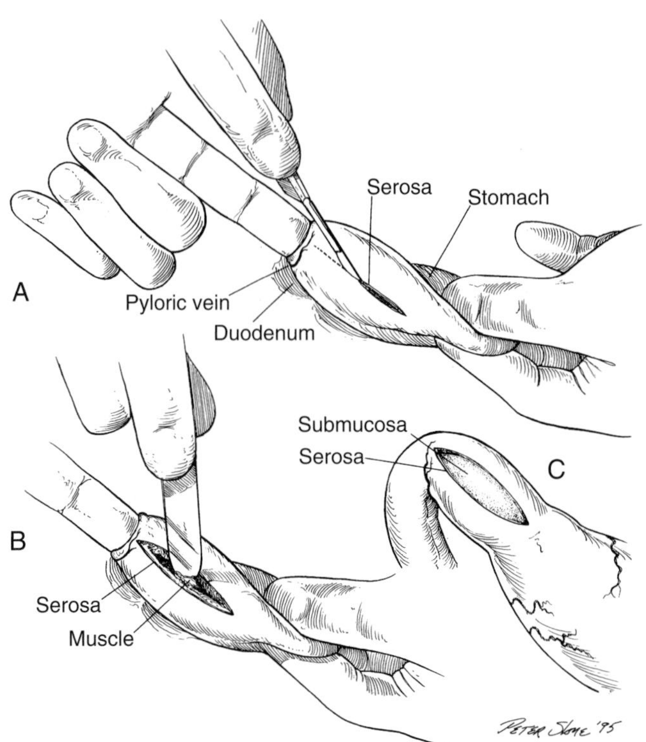

Figure 76–4 Pyloric stenosis, operative technique. *A,* Pylorus delivered from the peritoneal cavity and stabilized between the surgeon's index finger at the duodenal end with the stomach grasped proximally by the assistant. The serosal incision is outlined and begun. *B,* Back of a scalpel handle being used to split the hypertrophied muscle down to the submucosa. *C,* Completed myotomy showing submucosa bulging through the divided muscle.

from the stomach or duodenum should be made before returning the pylorus to the peritoneal cavity. Bleeding from the pyloric muscle edges or submucosal surface is generally venous and almost always stops after returning the stomach and pylorus to the peritoneal cavity.

Entrance into the lumen during pyloromyotomy should be a rare event. If it occurs, the submucosa should be approximated with interrupted fine absorbable suture and a portion of omentum placed over this site. An infrequently needed alternative is to reapproximate the myotomy site, rotate the pylorus 180 degrees, and perform a myotomy on the posterior wall of the pylorus. The fascial layers of the abdominal wall are closed with running absorbable suture. The skin is closed with subcuticular suture and Steri-Strips and covered with Op-Site dressing.

Laparoscopic Procedure

The first description of laparoscopic pyloromyotomy was by Alain et al. in 1991.[2] Since that time there have been numerous publications supporting this approach. As the procedure is currently performed in most centers, the infant is placed supine at the end of the operating table (Fig. 76-5). A 5-mm port is placed in the umbilicus and the abdomen is insufflated with CO_2. Two additional access sites are placed (under direct vision with the camera) in the left and right upper quadrants (Fig. 76-6). After infiltration with a local anesthetic, a No. 11 scalpel blade is used to make a small (3 mm) skin incision, and the muscle is penetrated with an arthrotomy knife. A grasper is placed through the left upper quadrant incision and used to grasp the antrum just proximal to the pylorus. Using the same technique for access, the arthrotomy knife is passed through the right upper quadrant incision. The grasper stabilizes the pylorus, and the arthrotomy knife incises the serosal surface over the hypertrophied pylorus in a fashion similar to what is done during the "open" technique (Fig. 76-7). The blade is retracted and the sheath of the arthrotomy knife is used to initiate splitting of the hypertrophied muscle. The arthrotomy knife is removed, and a pyloric spreader designed for laparoscopic procedures is placed through the right upper quadrant incision. This instrument is used to complete the myotomy (Fig.76-8). At the completion of the myotomy, each side of the divided muscle is grasped and moved in opposite directions to ensure that a complete myotomy has been achieved. Air is then insufflated through a nasogastric tube (typically 60 mL) to check for a leak. If none is seen, the instruments are removed, the CO_2 is evacuated, and the umbilical port is removed. The umbilical fascial defect is closed, and the skin at all three sites is closed with subcuticular suture.

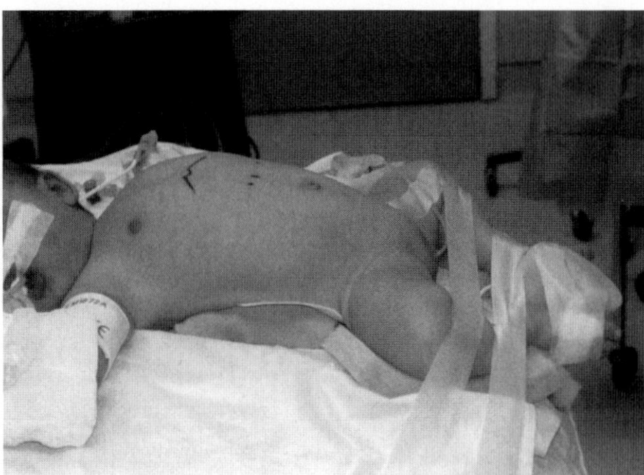

Figure 76–5 Position of the infant on the operating room table for laparoscopic pyloromyotomy.

Comparison of the Open Versus Laparoscopic Approach

Although aesthetics were the initial impetus for developing this procedure, proponents of laparoscopic pyloromyotomy now cite many other benefits, including faster recovery time with quicker return to full feeding, earlier postoperative discharge, a decrease in postoperative emesis, and a decrease in pain.[15] However, advocates of open pyloromyotomy state that recovery time is similar and that the laparoscopic approach has a greater complication rate, including perforation,[9,13,15,55,63] missed perforation,[13]

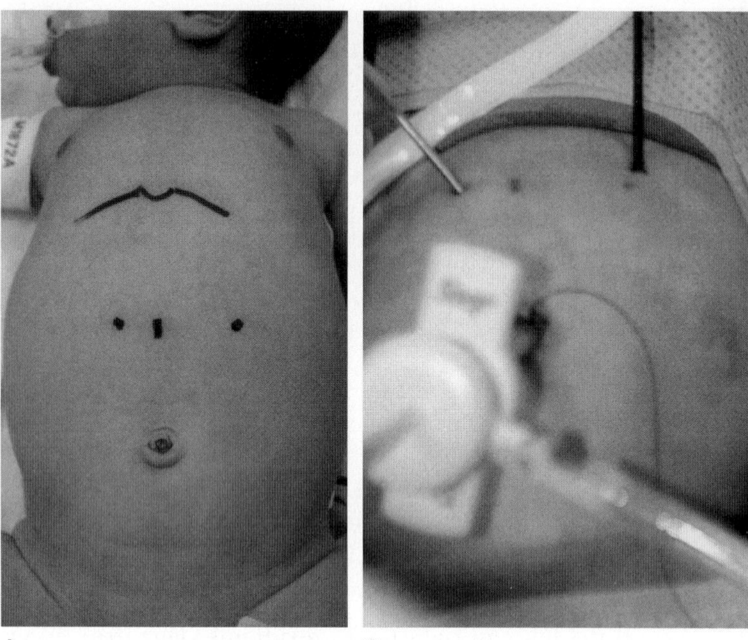

Figure 76-6 Location of "ports" (*A*) and after the instruments and telescope are in place (*B*).

incomplete myotomy,[13,64] an increase in operative time, and increased expense.[9] All the published studies to date have been retrospective and demonstrate a marked degree of variability.

The range for the average time to discharge in the published literature for laparoscopy is similar to that for open procedures. Of the four publications that compare time to discharge between the open procedure and laparoscopy, only one group found statistical significance, and the difference in discharge time was only 4 hours (Table 76-1).[8,9,31,38,51,52,55]

There is wide variation in the incidence of postoperative emesis. The range for laparoscopy was 1% to 68%, whereas for the open procedure it was 25% to 65%, with no statistical significance observed between the open and laparoscopic groups.[8,9,15,17,31]

The average time to establish full feeding in the laparoscopic group ranged from 16 to 32 hours versus 20 to 61 hours for the open procedure (Table 76-2).[8,9,13,15,17] The results are no different if the Fujimoto outlier study is eliminated.[15]

The wound infection rate for both groups was similar and ranged from 0% to 6% in the laparoscopic groups and from 0% to 7% in the open groups. None of these studies identified a significant difference between the groups (Table 76-3).[8,13,15,24,31,38,55]

The operative time was similar for both groups, with laparoscopy taking from 24.3 to 41 minutes and the open

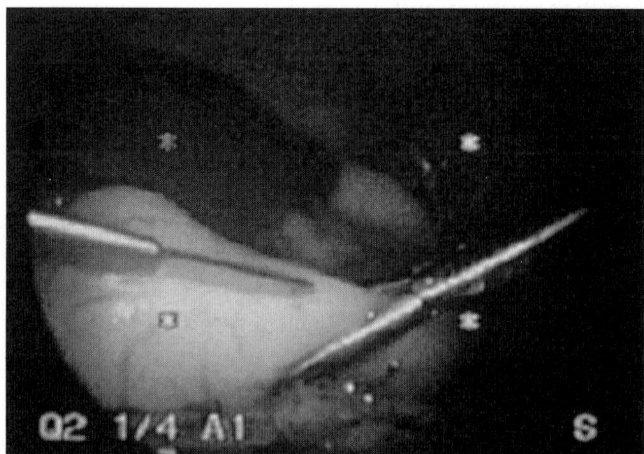

Figure 76-7 View through the laparoscope with the arthrotomy knife being used to incise the serosa over the hypertrophied pylorus.

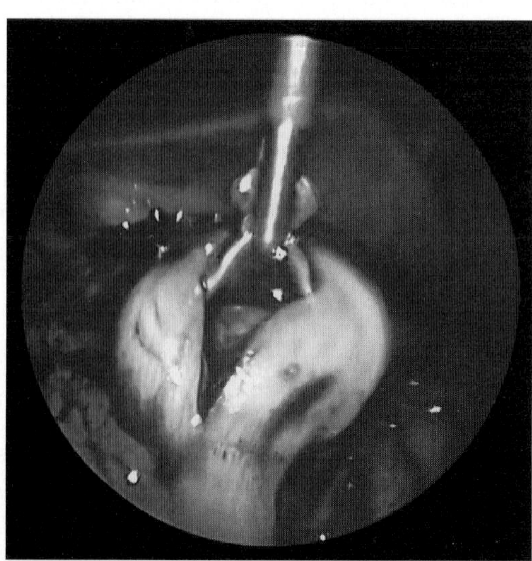

Figure 76-8 Hypertrophied pyloric muscle after being split with the spreader.

TABLE 76-1 Average Length of Stay (Hours)

Author	*N*	Laparoscopic	Open
Kramer WL, et al.	133	61.6	
Caceres M, Liu D	56	60	61.5
Campbell BT, et al.	117	31	28
Shankar KR, et al.*	86		58
Sitsen E, Bax NM, van der Zee DC	72	70	74†
Najmaldin A, et al.	37	28	
Scorpio RJ, et al.	63	44	63
Range		28-70	28-74

*Umbilical approach only.
†$P < .05$.

TABLE 76-2 Average Time to Full Feeding (Hours)

Author	*N*	Laparoscopic	Open
Caceres M, Liu D	56	24.1	27
Campbell BT, et al.	117	19	20
Fujimoto T, et al.*	60	34.8	61.2†
Ford WD, Crameri JA, Holland AJ	84	32	41
Greason KL, et al.	25	19	23
Range		19-35	20-61

*Umbilical approach only.
†$P < .01$.

procedure taking from 18.9 to 32.5 minutes. Yagmurlu et al.[64] (the largest study) showed that laparoscopy was faster by 4.7 minutes on average. Sitsen et al.[55] and Scorpio et al.[51] found that laparoscopy was slower by 14.3 minutes and 13 minutes, respectively, but in each series the smaller number of patients probably indicates less operative experience at the time of the study. The other five comparative studies failed to reach statistical significance (Table 76-4).*

The perforation rate, which includes both duodenal and pyloric injuries, had ranges of 0.4% to 10% for laparoscopic pyloromyotomy and 0% to 6% for the open procedure. Four comparative studies found that laparoscopy had a slightly higher perforation rate, but the differences were not statistically significant (Table 76-5).[9,13,15,31,55,64]

Other factors that have been analyzed include the abdominal wall hernia rate, which in some laparoscopic groups ranged from 4% to 7%,[51,55] interleukin 6, and heat loss. Fujimoto et al. found that interleukin-6 peak levels were significantly lower in the laparoscopy group 24 hours after surgery.[15] They hypothesized that this could indicate a decreased level of stress on the patient. Holland et al. found that laparoscopy tended to decrease the temperature of the infant to a greater degree than the open procedure did, which may have detrimental physiologic effects.[24] These biologic markers indicate subtle differences between the open and laparoscopic procedures, but they may not be clinically significant.

To date all studies in the literature are retrospective. As experience with laparoscopy increases and as the learning curve for the surgeon becomes shorter and the technology continues to improve, application of this technique may become commonplace. The larger laparoscopic studies demonstrate a comparable complication rate, and there may be a decrease in subjective factors such as pain and earlier feeding. Ultimately, the main difference may be the increased cost of laparoscopy. However, for surgeons who have limited exposure or access to laparoscopic techniques and equipment, the "open" Ramstedt pyloromyotomy remains the gold standard with which all other methods should be compared.

*References 8, 9, 13, 15, 17, 31, 38, 51, 52, 55, 64.

Postoperative Management

In the majority of infants, feeding can be started within 4 hours after the surgical procedure. Infants with hematemesis from gastritis may benefit by delaying feeding for an additional 6 to 12 hours after the procedure. A typical feeding schedule is shown in Table 76-6. It is clear that the more aggressive the feeding schedule, the greater the incidence of emesis in the initial postoperative period, but this approach is usually successful and generally allows for earlier hospital discharge.[16] The feeding schedule shown in Table 76-6 is moderately aggressive and allows for hospital discharge approximately 24 hours after the feedings are initiated. In the future, infants may be discharged within 3 or 4 hours after pyloromyotomy, in which case resumption of feeding will be undertaken by the family at home.

Nonoperative Treatment

This approach never gained acceptance in North America but was practiced in the past in some European countries. Although infants with IHPS can be managed with frequent small feedings, this practice necessitates either a prolonged hospital stay or an attentive caregiver at home and may lead to aspiration and malnutrition. It may take months for the hypertrophied muscle to resolve. The occasional mortality led to abandonment of this type of management.

TABLE 76-3 Average Wound Infection Rate

Author	*N*	Laparoscopic	Open
Kramer WL, et al.	133	3%	
Caceres M, Liu D	56	0%	3%
Fujimoto T, et al.*	60	0%	7%
Sitsen E, Bax NM, van der Zee DC	72	6%	3%
Ford WD, Crameri JA, Holland AJ	84	3%	2%
Najmaldin A, et al.	37	0%	
Scorpio RJ, et al.	63	0%	5%
Range		0%-6%	0%-7%

*Umbilical approach only.

TABLE 76-4 Average Operative Time (Minutes)

Author	N	Laparoscopic	Open
Yagmurlu A, et al.	457	24.3*	29
Kramer WL, et al.	133	29	
Caceres M, Liu D	56	36.1	32.5
Campbell BT, et al.	117	38	33
Shankar KR, et al.†	86		30
Fujimoto T, et al.†	60	27.4	31.9
Sitsen E, Bax NM, van der Zee DC	72	33.2	18.9*
Ford WD, Crameri JA, Holland AJ	84	41	28
Greason KL, et al.	25	25.4	26.1
Najmaldin A, et al.	37	29	
Scorpio RJ, et al.	63	40.2‡	27.3
Range		24-41	19-33

*$P < .01$.
†Umbilical approach only.
‡$P < .05$.

COMPLICATIONS

Complications after pyloromyotomy should be minimal if performed by experienced surgeons. Vomiting, frequent in the early postoperative period, is thought to be secondary to gastroesophageal reflux or discoordination of gastric peristalsis or gastric atony and should not be considered a complication. Frequent vomiting persisting beyond 3 to 4 days may suggest an incomplete myotomy or an unsuspected perforation. A postoperative contrast study may demonstrate a leak but is not helpful in evaluating the completeness of the myotomy. It takes several weeks for the radiographic appearance of the pylorus to improve.[50] Persistent and frequent vomiting 1 week beyond the pyloromyotomy may require re-exploration.

OUTCOME

After pyloromyotomy, mortality should be a rare occurrence, and morbidity should be very low. In a large series of infants undergoing open pyloromyotomy, the incidence of perforation was 2.3%, wound-related complications occurred in 1%, and there was one death.[5] More recent series have reported even lower morbidity and mortality.[37]

TABLE 76-5 Average Perforation Rate

Author	N	Laparoscopic	Open
Yagmurlu A, et al.	457	0.40%	3.6%*
Kramer WL, et al.	133	3%	
Campbell BT, et al.	117	8%	4%
Fujimoto T, et al.†	60	3%	0%
Sitsen E, Bax NM, van der Zee DC	72	9%	6%
Ford WD, Crameri JA, Holland AJ	84	10%	6%
Range		0.4%-10%	0%-6%

*$P < .05$.
†Umbilical approach only.

TABLE 76-6 Postpyloromyotomy Feeding Schedule*

Pedialyte, 30 mL orally every 3 hr × 1
Full-strength formula, 30 mL orally every 3 hr × 1
Full-strength formula, 45 mL orally every 3 hr × 2
Full-strength formula, 60 mL orally every 3 hr × 1
Full-strength formula, 75 mL orally every 3 hr × 1
Full-strength formula as desired

*Begin 4 to 6 hours after surgery. For very small infants, the starting feeding volume may be reduced to 15 mL and the schedule stopped at volumes of 60 to 75 mL, which provide an adequate calorie supply. Breast milk can be substituted for formula if appropriate.

As experience with laparoscopic pyloromyotomy increases, outcomes will be similar to those after the open approach. With a somewhat aggressive postoperative feeding schedule, infants should be able to be discharged within 24 hours of pyloromyotomy.

The long-term sequelae from pyloromyotomy are minimal. Ludtke et al.[33] evaluated the presence of gastrointestinal symptoms, measured scintigraphic gastric emptying, and determined pyloric measurements by US in 36 adults 17 to 27 years after pyloromyotomy. Their results were compared with those of age-matched and gender-matched controls. They identified no differences between the postpyloromyotomy group and the control group for the parameters measured.

ACKNOWLEDGMENT

The author wishes to thank David Otterburn, MD, Pediatric Surgery Research Fellow, for his significant assistance in updating this chapter.

REFERENCES

1. Abel RM, Bishop AE, Dore CJ, et al: A quantitative study of the morphological and histochemical changes within the nerves and muscle in infantile hypertrophic pyloric stenosis. J Pediatr Surg 1998;33:682.
2. Alain JL, Grousseau D, Terrier G: Extramucosal pyloromyotomy by laparoscopy. Surg Endosc 1991;5:174.
3. Alavi K, Bauer TL, Wolfson PJ, Schwartz MZ: Pyloromyotomy without palpation: The new standard of care [abstract]? Paper presented at the Annual Meeting of the American Pediatric Surgical Association, Hilton Head, SC, 1998.
4. Belding HD, Kernohan JW: A morphologic study of the myenteric plexus and musculature of the pylorus with special reference to the changes in hypertrophic pyloric stenosis. Surg Gynecol Obstet 1953;97:322.
5. Benson CD: Infantile hypertrophic pyloric stenosis. In Welch KJ, Randolph JG, Ravitch MM, et al (eds): Pediatric Surgery, 4th ed. Chicago, Year Book, 1986.
6. Benson CD, Alpern EB: Preoperative and postoperative care of congenital pyloric stenosis. Arch Surg 1957;75:877.

7. Blair P: On the dissection of a child much emaciated. Phil Trans 1717;30:631.
8. Caceres M, Liu D: Laparoscopic pyloromyotomy: Redefining the advantages of a novel technique. J Soc Laparoendosc Surg 2003;7:123.
9. Campbell BT, McLean K, Barnhart DC, et al: A comparison of laparoscopic and open pyloromyotomy at a teaching hospital. J Pediatr Surg 2002;37:1068.
10. Christofides ND, Mallet E, Ghatei MA, et al: Plasma enteroglucagon and neurotensin in infantile pyloric stenosis. Arch Dis Child 1983;58:52.
11. Dick AC, Ardill J, Potts SR, Dodge JA: Gastrin, somatostatin and infantile hypertrophic pyloric stenosis. Acta Paediatr 2001;90:879.
12. Dufour H, Fredet P: La stenose hypertrophique du pylore chez le nourisson et son traitement chirurgical. Rev Chir 1908;37:208.
13. Ford WD, Crameri JA, Holland AJ: The learning curve for laparoscopic pyloromyotomy. J Pediatr Surg 1997;32:552.
14. Friesen SR, Boley JO, Miller DR: The myenteric plexus of the pylorus: Its early normal development and its changes in hypertrophic pyloric stenosis. Surgery 1956;39:21.
15. Fujimoto T, Lane GJ, Segawa O, et al: Laparoscopic extramucosal pyloromyotomy versus open pyloromyotomy for infantile hypertrophic pyloric stenosis: Which is better? J Pediatr Surg 1999;34:370.
16. Georgeson KE, Corbin TJ, Griffen JW, Breaux CW Jr: An analysis of feeding regimens after pyloromyotomy for hypertrophic pyloric stenosis. J Pediatr Surg 1993;28:1478.
17. Greason KL, Thompson WR, Downey EC, Lo Sasso B: Laparoscopic pyloromyotomy for infantile hypertrophic pyloric stenosis: Report of 11 cases. J Pediatr Surg 1995; 30:1571.
18. Guarino N, Shima H, Oue T, et al: Glial-derived growth factor signaling pathway in infantile hypertrophic pyloric stenosis. J Pediatr Surg 2000;35:835.
19. Guarino N, Shima H, Puri P: Structural immaturity of the pylorus muscle in infantile hypertrophic pyloric stenosis. Pediatr Surg Int 2000;16:282.
20. Guarino N, Yoneda A, Shima H, et al: Selective neurotrophin deficiency in infantile hypertrophic pyloric stenosis. J Pediatr Surg 2001;36:1280.
21. Heine W, Groger B, Litzenberger M, et al: Results of Lambling gastric juice analysis in infants with spastic hypertrophic pyloric stenosis (SHPS). Padiatr Padol 1986; 21:119.
22. Hernanz-Schulman M, Lowe LH, Johnson J, et al: In vivo visualization of pyloric mucosal hypertrophy in infants with hypertrophic pyloric stenosis: Is there an etiologic role? AJR Am J Roentgenol 2001;177:843.
23. Hirschsprung H: Falle von angeborener Pylorus Stenose. J Kinderheilk 1888;27:61.
24. Holland AJ, Ford WD: The influence of laparoscopic surgery on perioperative heat loss in infants. Pediatr Surg Int 1998;13:350.
25. Honein MA, Paulozzi LJ, Himelright IM, et al: Infantile hypertrophic pyloric stenosis after pertussis prophylaxis with erythromycin: A case review and cohort study. Lancet 1999;354:2101.
26. Jona JZ: Electron microscopic observation in infantile hypertrophic pyloric stenosis (IHPS). J Pediatr Surg 1978;13:17.
27. Katz S, Basel D, Brabski D: Prenatal gastric dilatation and infantile hypertrophic pyloric stenosis. J Pediatr Surg 1988; 23:1021.
28. Keller H, Waldermann D, Greiner P: Comparison of preoperative sonography with intraoperative findings in congenital hypertrophic pyloric stenosis. J Pediatr Surg 1987; 22:950.
29. Kobayashi H, Miyahara K, Yamataka A, et al: Pyloric stenosis: New histopathologic perspective using confocal laser scanning. J Pediatr Surg 2001;36:1277.
30. Kobayashi H, O'Briain DS, Puri P: Selective reduction of intramuscular nerve supporting cells in infantile hypertrophic pyloric stenosis. J Pediatr Surg 1994; 29:651.
31. Kramer WL, Van der Bilt JD, Bax NM, et al: Hypertrophic pyloric stenosis in infants: Laparoscopic pyloromyotomy. Ned Tijdschr Geneeskd 2003;147:1646.
32. Lamki N, Athay PA, Round ME, et al: Hypertrophic pyloric stenosis in the neonate—diagnosis criteria revisited. Can Assoc Radiol J 1993;44:21.
33. Ludtke FE, Bertus M, Michalski S, et al: Long-term analysis of ultrasonic features of the antropyloric region 17-27 years after treatment of infantile hypertrophic pyloric stenosis. J Clin Ultrasound 1994;22:299.
34. Mason PF: Increasing infantile hypertrophic pyloric stenosis? Experience in an overseas military hospital. J R Coll Surg Endinb 1991;36:293.
35. Mitchell LE, Risch N: The genetics of infantile hypertrophic pyloric stenosis. Am J Dis Child 1993;147:1203.
36. Miyazaki E, Yamataka T, Ohshiro K, et al: Active collagen synthesis in infantile hypertrophic pyloric stenosis. Pediatr Surg Int 1998;13:237.
37. Murtagh K, Perry P, Corlett M, Fraser I: Infantile hypertrophic pyloric stenosis. Dig Dis 1992;10:190.
38. Najmaldin A, Tan HL: Early experience with laparoscopic pyloromyotomy for infantile hypertrophic pyloric stenosis. J Pediatr Surg 1995;30:37.
39. O'Donoghue JM, Connolly KD, Gallagher MM, et al: The increasing incidence of infantile hypertrophic pyloric stenosis. Ir J Med Sci 1993;162:175.
40. Ohshiro K, Puri P: Increased insulin-like growth factor-I mRNA expression in pyloric muscle in infantile hypertrophic pyloric stenosis. Pediatr Surg Int 1998;13:253.
41. Okazaki T, Yamataka A, Fujiwara T, et al: Abnormal distribution of nerve terminals in infantile hypertrophic pyloric stenosis. J Pediatr Surg 1994;29:655.
42. Oue T, Puri P: Abnormalities of elastin and elastic fibers in infantile hypertrophic pyloric stenosis. Pediatr Surg Int 1999;15:540.
43. Oue T, Puri P: Smooth muscle cell hypertrophy versus hyperplasia in infantile hypertrophic pyloric stenosis. Pediatr Res 1999;45:853.
44. Piotrowska AP, Solari V, Puri P: Distribution of heme oxygenase-2 in nerves and interstitial cells of Cajal in the normal pylorus and in infantile hypertrophic pyloric stenosis. Arch Pathol Lab Med 2003;127:1182.
45. Pueyo Gil C, Oshiro K, Elias Pollina J, et al: Increase of the chondroitin-sulfate proteoglycan, fibronectin and fibroblasts in infantile hypertrophic pyloric stenosis. Cirugia Pediatr 2001;14:103.
46. Ramstedt C: Zur Operation der angeborenen Pylorus Stenose. Med Klin 1912;8:1702.
47. Rasmussen L, Green A, Hansen LP: The epidemiology of infantile hypertrophic pyloric stenosis in a Danish population. Int J Epidemol 1989;18:413.
48. Rollins MD, Shields MD, Quinn RJ, Woolridge MA: Pyloric stenosis: Congenital or acquired. Arch Dis Child 1989; 64:138.
49. Roth B, Statz A, Heinisch HM, Gladtke E: Elimination of indocyanine green by the liver of infants with hypertrophic pyloric stenosis and the icteropyloric syndrome. J Pediatr 1981;99:240.
50. Runstrom G: On the roentgen anatomical appearance of congenital pyloric stenosis during and after the manifest stage of the disease. Acta Pediatr Scand 1939;26:383.

51. Scorpio RJ, Tan HL, Hutson JM: Pyloromyotomy: Comparison between laparoscopic and open surgical techniques. J Laparoendosc Surg 1995;5:81.
52. Shankar KR, Losty PD, Jones MO, et al: Umbilical pyloromyotomy—an alternative to laparoscopy? Eur J Pediatr Surg 2001;11:8.
53. Shima H, Ohshiro K, Puri P: Increased local synthesis of epidermal growth factors in infantile hypertrophic pyloric stenosis. Pediatr Res 2000;47:201.
54. Shima H, Puri P: Increased expression of transforming growth factor-alpha in infantile hypertrophic pyloric stenosis. Pediatr Surg Int 1999;15:198.
55. Sitsen E, Bax NM, van der Zee DC: Is laparoscopic pyloromyotomy superior to open surgery? Surg Endosc 1998;12:813.
56. Spitz L, Zail SS: Serum gastrin levels in congenital hypertrophic pyloric stenosis. J Pediatr Surg 1976;11:33.
57. Subramaniam R, Doig CM, Moore L: Nitric oxide synthase is absent in only a subset of cases of pyloric stenosis. J Pediatr Surg 2001;36:616.
58. Tack ED, Perlman JM, Bower RJ, McAlister WH: Pyloric stenosis in the sick premature infant: Clinical and radiologic findings. Am J Dis Child 1988;142:68.
59. Takahashi T: Pathophysiological significance of neuronal nitric oxide synthase in the gastrointestinal tract. J Gastroenterol 2003;38:421.
60. Tam PK: Observation and perspectives of the pathology and possible aetiology of infantile hypertrophic pyloric stenosis: A histological, biochemical, histochemical and immunocytochemical study. Ann Acad Med Singapore 1985;14:523.
61. Vanderwinden JM, Liu H, DeLaet MH, et al: Study of the interstitial cells of Cajal in infantile hypertrophic pyloric stenosis. Gastroenterology 1996;111:1408.
62. Vanderwinden JM, Mailleux P, Schiffmann SN, et al: Nitric oxide synthase activity in infantile hypertrophic pyloric stenosis. N Engl J Med 1992;327:511.
63. Wallgren A: Preclinical stage of infantile hypertrophic pyloric stenosis. Am J Dis Child 1946;72:371.
64. Yagmurlu A, Barnhart DC, Vernon A, et al: Comparison of the incidence of complications in open and laparoscopic pyloromyotomy: A concurrent single institution series. J Pediatr Surg 2004;39:292.
65. Yamataka A, Fujiwara T, Kato Y, et al: Lack of intestinal pacemaker (c-kit positive) cells in infantile pyloric stenosis. J Pediatr Surg 1996;31:96.
66. Zenn MR, Redo SF: Hypertrophic pyloric stenosis in the newborn. J Pediatr Surg 1993;28:1577.
67. Zuelzer W: Infantile hypertrophic pyloric stenosis. In Welch KJ, Randolph JG, Ravitch MM, et al (eds): Pediatric Surgery, 4th ed. Chicago, Year Book, 1986.

Chapter 77

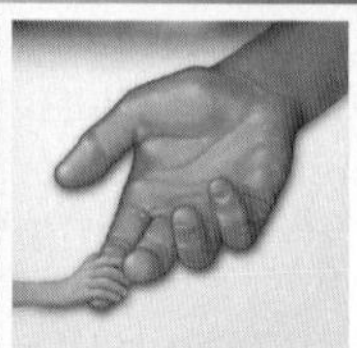

Peptic Ulcer and Other Conditions of the Stomach

L. R. Scherer III

ACUTE AND CHRONIC PEPTIC ULCER

Historically, peptic ulcer disease has been described as the combined action of acid and pepsin on gastrointestinal mucosa. The history of peptic ulcer disease in infants and children dates back to 1826. A collective literature review on peptic ulcers in 243 children was published by Bird and colleagues in 1941.[16] The series consisted of 119 patients who required surgical treatment for peptic ulcer. Ulcers in infants aged 1 to 15 days of age characteristically presented acutely with hemorrhage or perforation without premonitory signs or symptoms. Preschool-aged children, on the other hand, frequently had a prodromal illness before the onset of hemorrhage or perforation. The heterogeneity of the cause of the ulcers was apparently not recognized, and these differences were ascribed to age.

The theories and etiology of peptic ulcer disease remained consistent for the next 45 years. Careful historical information regarding ulcer-like symptoms in children with no other identified causes and eliciting a family history of peptic ulcer disease were common in instances of primary gastroduodenal ulceration.[108,142] In 1984, Marshall and Warren[91] reported a possible bacteriologic cause for primary ulcers. Secondary ulcers were defined as those caused by severe stress or critical illness. This classification of peptic ulcer is used in this chapter in discussing cause, diagnosis, and treatment (Table 77-1).

Epidemiology

Primary Peptic Ulcer Disease

The incidence of peptic ulcer in children is approximately 5.4/100,000 new cases per year.[97] Although the incidence in boys is two to three times higher than that in girls, the sex distribution is similar in infants and very young children. Several predisposing factors have been implicated in the development of peptic ulcer disease in patients of all ages.

Duodenal and prepyloric ulcers behave similarly and are usually associated with higher levels of hydrochloric acid secretion. Ulcers occur more often in patients with blood type O, who have a 30% increased risk for developing duodenal ulcers when compared with those individuals with blood types A, B, and AB. The adult with duodenal ulcer is more likely to be a nonsecretor of ABH blood group substances. This excess of nonsecretors has not been noted in children with peptic ulcer disease.[71] Gastric ulcers (other than those situated in a prepyloric location) occur primarily in younger patients, who often

TABLE 77-1 Classification and Causes of Gastritis and Ulcers in Children

Classification/Category	Etiology
Primary	*Helicobacter pylori*
Secondary	
Excessive acid production	Zollinger-Ellison syndrome Antral G-cell hyperplasia Antral G-cell hyperfunction Systemic mastocytosis Renal failure, hyperparathyroidism
Stress	Infants: traumatic delivery, neonatal sepsis, perinatal asphyxia Children: shock, trauma, sepsis, head injury, burns
Other conditions	Eosinophilic gastroenteritis Ménétrier's disease, hypertrophic gastritis Lymphocytic (varioliform) gastritis Autoimmune (atrophic) gastritis Gastroduodenal Crohn's disease
Drug-related	Nonsteroidal anti-inflammatory drugs, with or without *H. pylori* Aspirin Ethanol (alcohol)

have hyposecretion of acid (but not achlorhydria) and most frequently have type A blood. The ulcer usually is located in the area of the junction of parietal cell mass and the antral mucosa.[72]

The question has been raised as to whether peptic ulcer disease in children is the same condition that presents in adults. A strong familial tendency has been noted. Thirty-three to 56 percent of children with ulcer disease have first- and second-degree relatives with peptic ulcer disease.[58,71,107,129] The incidence of peptic ulcer is also higher in monozygous twins than in dizygous twins. Heritability of peptic ulcer disease has been calculated at 0.91 per first-degree relative for children,[71] a rate considerably higher than the heritability calculation of 0.37 derived for adults. A positive family history for peptic ulcer disease is considered an important characteristic of ulcer disease in children.[108,132] There is a link to primary gastritis and peptic ulceration occurring in children in the presence of *Helicobacter pylori* infection clustering among family members of affected individuals.[28,38] Mucosal inflammation (gastritis) was more frequently observed than ulceration in patients with *H. pylori*–induced injury.[39]

Current evidence indicates that persons younger than 18 years old presenting with peptic ulcer and no other identified causes have a primary gastroduodenal ulceration (see Table 77-1). *H. pylori* colonizes the gastric antrum and has satisfied Koch's postulates as a human pathogen causing primary ulceration and chronic-active gastritis in children.[159] The incidence of *H. pylori* infection is estimated to be 0.5% per year in industrialized countries[52,90] and 3% to 10% per year in developing countries.[121] The route of transmission of *H. pylori* is postulated to be fecal-oral or oral-oral.[4,51] Risk factors associated with *H. pylori* infection in children include familial overcrowding, endemic country of origin, poor socioeconomic level, and ethnicity. Pathologic conditions associated with *H. pylori* infection include chronic superficial gastritis, chronic active gastritis, primary duodenal ulcer, gastric ulcers, Barrett's esophagus, gastric cancer, and MALT lymphoma.[18,69,114,122]

Secondary Peptic Ulcer Disease

Secondary ulcers (stress ulcers) are acute ulcers in children usually associated with major physical or thermal trauma, sepsis, shock, or other critical illness (see Table 77-1). Gastric stress ulcers are usually multiple superficial mucosal erosions found primarily in the fundus of the stomach. The cause of gastrointestinal ulcers has been related to one or a combination of three factors: (1) decreased mucosal blood flow, (2) disruption of the protective mucosal barrier, and (3) intraluminal acidity.[1] Stress ulcers account for 80% of the peptic disease seen during infancy and early childhood.[115] Drug- and chemical-induced ulcers resemble stress ulcers in appearance and distribution. The ulcer that occurs with such intracranial disorders as brain tumors or head injuries, however, is usually a single, deep ulcer that is prone to perforation (Cushing's ulcer). Studies in adults indicate that gastric hypersecretion is not associated with stress ulcers or ulcers resulting from drug ingestion.[88,101] Most Cushing's ulcers, on the other hand, are associated with an increased acid output.[90,116] Secondary ulcers in older children are frequently single and deep (similar to Cushing's ulcer) instead of the usual multiple superficial stress ulcerations seen in the adult. No detailed studies have been done to determine whether gastric hypersecretion is present in children with stress ulcers.

Previously, stress ulcers in children were thought to resemble Cushing's ulcer in adults because they are duodenal, single, and deeply penetrating; in contrast, stress ulcers in adults are multiple and superficial. With the development of pediatric endoscopy, the location of stress ulcers in children was found to be similar to that in adults, mostly occurring in the stomach, but other investigators have observed an equal distribution in the stomach and duodenum.[83] Morden and associates[103] described a series of 10 patients with severe complicated medical illnesses, all of whom had multiple gastric ulcers.

Williams and coworkers[162] described the largest series of stress ulcers in children. The 194 cases consisted primarily of Curling's ulcers associated with serious burn injuries. One hundred of these ulcers were diagnosed clinically; the rest were discovered at autopsy. The ulcer was located in the duodenum in 43 of the 63 cases for which a site was identified. The only clinically significant gastric ulcers in the series were diagnosed after perforation. In a series of 29 patients reported by Grosfeld and colleagues, the distribution of duodenal to gastric lesions was almost equal.[56] All of these ulcers were solitary except for one; in this patient multiple ulcers were found at autopsy. Two children had ulcers secondary to severe burn injury but none had an associated intracranial lesion. In another series of 25 patients with secondary ulcers, the lesions were almost equally distributed between the duodenum and the stomach.[35] The single gastric ulcers in these studies were usually located in the prepyloric region and behaved similarly to duodenal ulcers. Endoscopy has refined the approach to diagnosis and has led to a better understanding of the presentation and course of ulcer disease in children. Currently, more than two thirds of the patients receiving treatment with corticosteroids or nonsteroidal anti-inflammatory drugs (NSAIDs) developed secondary peptic ulcer disease presenting as acute epigastric pain.[106]

Gastric Physiology and Pathophysiology

Aggressive Factors

Acid secretion has been identified in the fetal stomach as early as the 19th week of gestation, and pepsin secretion is present by the 34th week. Term infants can secrete both acid and pepsin.[19] Gastric hyposecretion occurs during the first 5 hours after birth and increases during the next 48 hours when the pH stabilizes to a value of approximately 3.0.[61] The premature infant also can secrete acid and pepsin but not as much as the term infant. Thirty-three percent of premature infants have an alkaline gastric pH, and 20% do not produce acid for 10 days. Many premature infants will maximally produce gastric acid by 4 days.[106] In neonates, the parietal cell mass per unit area is two to three times that found in adults.[124] Infants have a relatively high acid secretion during the first week to 10 days of life (Table 77-2).[61] Maternal gastrin secretion may be

TABLE 77-2 Aggressive and Defensive Factors Involved in the Gastroduodenal Mucosal Balance

Aggressive Factors	Mucosal Defense Factors
Vascular injury: decreased microcirculation	Mucosal circulation: adequate microcirculation
Cancer chemotherapeutic agents	Epithelial cell turnover
Aspirin	Increased bicarbonate secretion
Nonsteroidal anti-inflammatory drugs	Inhibit gastric acid secretion
Infectious agents: cytomegalovirus, herpesvirus	Preserve vascular flow/microcirculation
Systemic stress: increased catecholamines	Restore epithelial cell surface
Increased pepsin secretion	Mucous layer: glycoproteins, glycocalyx
H. pylori	Bicarbonate layer: pH gradient
	Immunoglobulins: IgG, IgA

responsible for both the increased parietal cell mass and the high acid secretion rate. Acid secretion rapidly decreases after about 10 days of age.[2] During the next 4 months, acid and pepsin secretion increase, paralleling weight instead of age throughout childhood.

Elevated levels of gastric acid secretion have been reported in children with peptic ulcer disease. Similar to adult studies, elevated acid secretion is not necessarily useful in identifying the child with peptic ulcer disease. For example, Ghai[50] used the augmented histamine test to study 18 children with peptic ulcer disease and 16 control children. He found no significant increase in basal acid output in patients with an ulcer. The mean maximal and peak acid output increased, but the two groups overlapped; maximal and peak values increased with the patient's age and weight. Robb and coworkers[129] noted a similar relationship of age, weight, and acid secretion but did not observe any difference between the acid secretion in 49 children with duodenal ulcers compared with 30 children with dyspepsia and no ulcer. Nagita and associates[112] measured the diurnal variation of intragastric pH in children with primary peptic ulcer and healthy children. They found that gastric acidity increased with age and approached adult levels by age 14 years. In children with gastric ulcers, the mean pH for all ages was higher than that for the age-matched controls; in children with duodenal ulcers, the mean time during which the pH was less than 2 was greater than in an age-adjusted comparison group.[112]

In 1984, Marshall and Warren[91] reported the successful culture, under microaerophilic conditions, of a novel bacterium *(Helicobacter pylori)* from the antral mucosa of humans (see Table 77-2). Recurrent peptic ulcers in adults may be associated with gastritis that primarily involves the antrum. The accumulation of clinical and laboratory studies provides strong evidence that *H. pylori* fulfills each of Koch's postulates as a cause of chronic active gastritis in humans.[159] *H. pylori* is a highly motile gram-negative, S-shaped rod that produces enzymes such as urease, catalase, and oxidase. The flagella-bearing *H. pylori* organisms require a microaerobic environment for culture, reflecting their environmental niche to navigate through the thick and viscous mucus layer to reach the apical layer of the gastric epithelium.[43] All children infected with *H. pylori* appear to develop chronic-active gastritis. Most have asymptomatic infections that may never lead to clinically evident disease. Theories concerning the mechanism that causes inflammation include the bacterial production of urease and vacuolating cytotoxin. Urease hydrolyzes urea to ammonia and bicarbonate at the gastric mucosal surface. Ammonia can be directly toxic to epithelial cells, and the concomitant increase in the mucosal surface pH may interfere with gastric epithelial function, such as production of mucus.[100] Recently, attention has focused on the vacuolating cytotoxin produced by certain strains of *H. pylori*. This cytotoxin produces vacuoles in the cytoplasm of eukaryotic cells in vitro. The gene *(vac A)* of this cytotoxin has two alleles and is variably expressed among isolates.[127] CagA, a cytotoxic protein, has been isolated in approximately 60% of *H. pylori* isolates and its presence correlates strongly with the expression of the vacuolating cytotoxin.[63] Cytotoxin-producing strains tend to be more virulent than toxin-negative strains. Some researchers now classify the strains into type I (cytotoxin positive) and type II (cytotoxin negative). Type I strains are associated with more severe gastritis or duodenal disease than type II strains.[119]

Cellular injury in the gastric and duodenal epithelium initiates a significant immune response (see Table 77-2). The inflammatory infiltrate in the gastric mucosa includes monocytes, macrophages, and polymorphonuclear and plasma cells.[7,161] Increased levels of inflammatory cytokines have been measured in the inflamed mucosa of infected children. These cytokines include interferon-γ, interleukin-1 (IL-1), IL-2, IL-6, and IL-8.[143]

Defensive Factors

A wide range of clinical and laboratory studies have attempted to clarify the pathogenesis of stress peptic ulcers. The presence of hydrochloric acid is required for ulcer formation even though hypersecretion is not usually present, except with Cushing's ulcer. Most of the factors contributing to the development of stress ulcers reduce the ability of the stomach mucosa to protect itself against acid injury rather than causing an increase in the amount of acid secreted.[147] Investigators generally agree that mucosal ischemia also is implicated in the pathogenesis of stress ulcers (see Table 77-2).[26] Normally, small amounts of hydrogen ion diffuse into the mucosa but are rapidly cleared or neutralized if mucosal blood flow is adequate. Ischemia reduces production of mucus and the capacity for neutralization of acid entering the tissues, leading to an accumulation of hydrogen ions and subsequent mucosal ulceration. The adverse effect of ischemia on energy metabolism may be an additional factor that reduces the ability of the mucosa to defend itself against injury.[95] Intravenous infusion of sodium bicarbonate administered during the experimental production of mucosal injury by hemorrhagic shock has a protective effect. This suggests that the pH of arterial blood perfusing the stomach may also be important in determining the ability of the gastric mucosa to protect itself against acid injury.[27] These findings suggest that ischemia, energy deficits, and systemic acidosis are important factors in the pathogenesis of stress ulcers.

In instances of medication-induced ulcers, the drug disrupts the mucosal permeability barrier.[102] The gastric mucosa cannot contain the hydrogen ion within the lumen, and an ulcer results from an excessive back-diffusion of hydrogen ion into the mucosal cells. A thick mucous gel is secreted from the superficial epithelial cells and mucus cells throughout the stomach. The release of mucus is stimulated by cholinergic agonists, prostaglandins, and inflammatory or immune cytokines. The layer of mucus in the stomach is approximately 20 times the thickness of the surface epithelial cells and is full of charged protein particles. In the normal setting, this mucus provides an effective barrier to the deleterious effects of acid.

Prostaglandins protect against the development of experimentally induced stress ulcers.[98] The mechanism is uncertain but may be related to prostaglandin's stimulation of chloride ion transport out of the cell in exchange for bicarbonate ion, which blocks cyclic adenosine monophosphate (AMP) generation. The available intracellular bicarbonate increases the ability of the cell to buffer acid. Endogenous prostaglandins also have a role in maintaining adequate blood flow to the gastric mucosa and stimulate production of mucus, improving the ability of the mucosa to withstand acid destruction.[130] Corticosteroids and NSAIDs have been implicated as causative agents in peptic ulcer disease. Studies have shown the cytoprotective effect of prostaglandins, the development of ulcers during treatment with NSAIDs and corticosteroids, and a decreased level of prostaglandins in the stomach during treatment; these findings suggest causality in the development of NSAID and corticosteroid-induced peptic ulcers.[106,144] Drugs can cause secondary ulcers by damaging the mucosa and thereby allowing acid-peptic digestion. Aspirin is a common agent associated with medication-induced secondary ulcers. Excessive dosing of another commonly available medication, ferrous sulfate, has also been implicated as a cause of ulcers in children. Evidence concerning corticosteroids as a contributory factor in the development of stress ulcer is contradictory.[29] Although the causal relation of corticosteroid and NSAID therapy to the development of secondary ulcers remains the subject of debate, increasing evidence suggests causality.[106,144] In general, drug-induced ulcers should respond to cessation of the medication and conservative supportive treatment unless complications develop.

TABLE 77-3 Clinical Findings in Primary and Secondary Gastritis and Peptic Ulcer Disease

Disease Entity	Signs and Symptoms
Primary gastritis	Asymptomatic (most common) Recurrent abdominal pain (any location) Epigastric pain Water brash, heartburn (gastroesophageal reflux disease symptoms) Vomiting, nausea, anorexia Iron deficiency anemia Short stature, growth failure (?)
Secondary gastritis	Abdominal pain Upper gastrointestinal blood loss—hematemesis, melena Epigastric pain localization ("crampy") Irritability, change in feeding patterns Fatigue Iron deficiency anemia
Primary peptic ulcer disease	Chronic, recurrent abdominal pain Episodic epigastric pain Vomiting, particularly recurrent Nocturnal awakening Anemia
Secondary peptic ulcer disease	Life-threatening gastrointestinal bleeding Gastric or duodenal perforation Shock Abdominal pain (rare)

Clinical Presentation

The clinical features of primary peptic ulcer disease in children can easily be confused with those of many other disorders; this similarity may inflate the actual incidence of ulcer disease in children (Table 77-3). Clinical symptoms in the infant include refusal of feedings, persistent crying, and vomiting.[72] The risk of a child developing an ulcer may be higher with a positive family history. Several studies present evidence that in an endemic population of infected parents, mothers in particular may play a key role in transmission of *H. pylori* to the child.[132] The diagnosis is often elusive until such complications as perforation or bleeding occur. Vomiting is common in preschool-aged and school-aged children with peptic ulcers. Abdominal pain is recognized with increasing frequency as the child becomes older. The pain is often vague and difficult to describe and may be related to meals or relieved by eating, as is seen in adults.[35,137] In older children and adolescents, the clinical presentation and natural history of peptic ulcers are more comparable to those observed in adults. The ulcers present with epigastric and nocturnal abdominal pain in teenagers with a positive family history of peptic ulceration. In this setting, despite healing of the acute ulceration, the natural history of this *disease process* is for the ulcer to recur. It is now clear that such ulcers are not related to a genetic predisposition to hyperpepsinogenemia but are associated with *H. pylori* infection.[141] Almost all patients with primary peptic ulcer disease present with abdominal pain. Unfortunately, psychogenic, recurrent abdominal pain of childhood, the most common pediatric intestinal disorder, causes nearly identical symptoms.[25] Nocturnal awakening caused by episodes of abdominal pain may differentiate organic from psychogenic origin. Gremse and Shakoor[55] evaluated the predictive values of signs and symptoms of acid-peptic disease in children in whom endoscopy confirmed the diagnosis. Six symptoms correlated significantly with acid-peptic disease: epigastric pain, nocturnal pain, postprandial pain, water brash, weight loss, and a family history of peptic ulcer disease. Only 7% of children with psychogenic recurrent abdominal pain report pain occurring at night compared with 60% of children with peptic ulcer disease. In a study of 110 children with duodenal ulcer, the mean age at diagnosis was 11.3 years; in 46% of children, some symptom of peptic ulcer disease manifested before 10 years of age.[108]

Secondary ulcers are acute. Although the age of patients with secondary ulcers ranges from 1 day to 18 years, most patients are younger than 6 years of age. Secondary peptic ulcers are usually due to noxious agents (e.g., corticosteroids and NSAIDs) or after major stresses (e.g., burns, head injury, systemic illness).[141] In these settings, upper gastrointestinal tract hemorrhage, vomiting, and perforation are frequent presenting features. Diagnosis is therefore more difficult and usually made when a catastrophic event such as hemorrhage or perforation occurs. Gastrointestinal bleeding, the predominant presenting symptom of secondary ulcers, occurs in 92% of patients younger than 6 years of age.[13] The ulcers tend not to recur after healing if either the offending agent or underlying disease predisposing to mucosal ulceration is successfully treated.

Diagnosis

Endoscopic diagnosis followed by treatment with histamine-2 (H_2)-receptor antagonists has changed the presentation and course of acute ulcer disease in children. Before the use of endoscopy in children, patients with peptic ulcer disease frequently presented with an acute surgical abdomen, massive hemorrhage, or perforation; the diagnosis was made at the time of operation or autopsy. The present indications for the early diagnosis of acid-peptic disease are gastrointestinal bleeding, dysphagia, persistent vomiting, and the abdominal pain characterized above.[15] Gastric analysis is not a useful diagnostic test. Secondary ulcer was previously diagnosed by contrast radiologic studies, angiography, laparotomy, and autopsy. The known occurrence of secondary ulcers in association with physiologic stress should lead to the diagnosis before signs and symptoms become catastrophic. Radiologic diagnosis can be difficult in the presence of hemorrhage because blood clots can mask the ulcer; therefore, endoscopy has become the standard for the diagnosis of the acute bleeding ulcer. In one report, endoscopy provided a diagnosis in 85% of children with upper gastrointestinal bleeding compared with 62% using radiologic studies.[153] Angiography can be useful in locating a bleeding ulcer if the rate of bleeding is at least 0.5 mL/min.[44,154]

H. pylori

Invasive Methods: Endoscopy is the method of choice to accurately diagnose peptic ulceration in children. Nodularity in the antrum of the stomach is a specific (but not sensitive) feature indicative of active *H. pylori* infection in children. Biopsy specimens should be taken from the stomach and tested for the presence of *H. pylori* by a variety of techniques, including staining of biopsy sections (silver, Giemsa, Genta, acridine orange) and microscopic evaluation, culture, and testing for the presence of urease activity. In children and teenagers receiving concurrent therapy with a proton pump inhibitor, biopsies should be performed on the body and cardia (and, possibly, transition zones) of the stomach as well as from the antrum to reduce the chances of false-negative results.[34] Follow-up endoscopy is rarely necessary in pediatric populations, except in the setting of peptic ulceration associated with complications (e.g., massive hemorrhage or perforation).

Noninvasive Methods: Infection with *H. pylori* induces a vigorous immune response resulting in the presence of local and systemic antibodies. *H. pylori*-specific IgG antibodies are present in serum, plasma, whole blood, saliva, gastric juice, and urine. The humoral immune response is less vigorous in children. Therefore, the cutoff values established for use in adults to determine the presence or absence of *H. pylori* infection are not appropriate in young children. Increasing concerns have been raised about the utility of testing for antibodies in low-prevalence settings such as is the case for children and adolescents living in developed nations. Although immunoassays are relatively inexpensive and technically easy to perform, those employed in children must first be validated in each country or region, using serum samples obtained from relevant populations.[28] Breath testing using the stable isotope ^{13}C- or radiolabeled ^{14}C-urea as substrate shows great promise as an alternative approach to noninvasively diagnose *H. pylori* infection in adults. However, ^{14}C-labeled substrates should not be used in children and women during their reproductive years. Urea breath testing is accurate in children older than 2 years of age.[23,75] A commercially available stool antigen test has been reported to be highly accurate as a diagnostic test in adults. In contrast to serology, in which antibody titers may remain elevated for months after successful eradication of the organism, the stool antigen test is reported to turn negative within a week after elimination of *H. pylori.* The accuracy of the stool antigen test when used in pediatric populations in a variety of clinical settings validates its usefulness.[75]

Treatment

The treatment of peptic ulcer disease in children is similar to that employed in adults. Antacids and H_2 receptor antagonists (e.g., cimetidine) are the mainstays of medical therapy. Other therapeutic agents include selective anticholinergic agents, proton-pump inhibitors, cytoprotective agents, and anti-infective agents (Table 77-4).

Omeprazole and lansoprazole, proton-pump inhibitors, inhibit the stimulation of gastric acid secretion at the final common pathway (cyclic AMP-adenylate cyclase, H^+-K^+ adenosine triphosphatase inhibition). Therefore, all forms of secretion (histaminergic, gastrinergic, and cholinergic) are blocked. A pediatric dosage of omeprazole, 1 mg/kg/day up to 20 mg/day; or lansoprazole, 0.5 mg/kg/day up to 30 kg then 30 mg daily in children greater than 30 kg, is effective in 95% of patients within 4 weeks.[74] Although omeprazole is well tolerated, side effects include headache, nausea, and abdominal pain.

TABLE 77-4 Three Recommended Combination Eradication Therapies for *H. pylori*-Associated Disease in Children

Medications	Dose	Duration of Treatment
Amoxicillin	50 mg/kg/day	14 days bid
Clarithromycin	15 mg/kg/day	14 days bid
Proton pump inhibitor	1.0 mg/kg/day	1 month bid
Amoxicillin	50 mg/kg/day	14 days bid
Metronidazole	20 mg/kg/day	14 days bid
Proton pump inhibitor	1.0 mg/kg/day	1 month bid
Clarithromycin	15 mg/kg/day	14 days bid
Metronidazole	20 mg/kg/day	14 days bid
Proton pump inhibitor	1.0 mg/kg/day	1 month bid

In children with documented *H. pylori* gastritis or duodenal ulcer, eradication of this microorganism requires the use of standard antimicrobial agents and bismuth preparations (see Table 77-4). The current standard treatment consists of two antibiotics (choosing two of the following): amoxicillin (50 mg/kg/day), clarithromycin (15 mg/kg/day), or metronidazole (20 mg/kg/day) and a proton pump inhibitor. Treatment regimens include twice-daily dosing of antibiotics for 2 weeks and a proton-pump inhibitor for 4 weeks. The use of this triple therapy results in eradication of the infection in more than 80% to 90% of patients.[34,74,75]

Antacids effectively neutralize acid secretion and heal peptic ulcer disease compared with placebo (75% compared with 40%). Unfortunately, compliance is disappointing, and the complications of the medications including diarrhea and constipation are bothersome. Therapy requires antacid administration (0.5 mL/kg) 1 hour before meals, 3 hours after meals, and at bedtime.

Histamine is a stimulant of gastric secretion. H_2 receptors for H_2 are present on the gastric acid–producing parietal cells of the stomach; H_2 receptor antagonists inhibit responses to all secretagogues and thus are effective in suppressing gastric acid secretion. Cimetidine (20 to 40 mg/kg/day) was the first commercially available antagonist. The anti-androgen side effects and the effects on the central nervous system are likely due to the imidazole ring of the compound, which inhibits the cytochrome P450 system of the liver. Ranitidine (2 to 4 mg/kg/day), an H_2 antagonist that lacks an imidazole ring, is six to eight times more potent and is equally effective (85% to 95%) in healing ulcers in 8 weeks. However, a relapse rate of 20% has been reported. Famotidine and nizatidine are other potent antagonists used in adults, but little information regarding their use in children has been reported.

The cytoprotective effect of sucralfate results from a coating action due to the negative charge of the sulfated disaccharide aluminum salt that adheres to the positive protein charge of the injured mucosa. The compound also seems to stimulate mucus production and prostaglandin synthesis, bind bile salts, and neutralize pepsin and acid. The adult dosage is 1 g (1 g/10 mL slurry) four times per day; the childhood dose is 40 to 80 mg/kg/day. Constipation is the only clinically significant side effect.

The E-type prostaglandins, including misoprostol, enprostil, and arbaprostil, are cytoprotective.[106] The mechanism of action that provides protection to the mucosa is related to blocking production of cyclic AMP, stimulation of HCO_3^-, and an increase in mucosal blood flow. The adult dose is 200 µg four times daily, but there is little documented information concerning experience in children.

Surgical Treatment

Historically and presently, surgical management of peptic ulcer disease has been reserved for complications such as perforation, bleeding, obstruction, and intractable pain. Follow-up studies of children with primary ulcer disease treated medically revealed a high rate of recurrence after cessation of treatment throughout childhood and into adult life.[108,125] Increasing numbers of these patients eventually required surgical treatment. Because of the prolonged morbidity reported in medically treated patients, earlier surgical intervention had been recommended.[128] Vagotomy and pyloroplasty rather than gastric resection is recommended as effective treatment, with a minimal effect on subsequent growth and development.[73] In the past decade, highly selective or parietal cell vagotomy has been used extensively in several centers to treat adult patients with peptic disease, but no series has been reported in children. The high recurrence rate observed with this approach (10% to 15%) may be an issue; however, some consider this rate to be acceptable in children because it may cause only minimal disturbance of growth and development while providing a reasonably good long-term outcome.[62]

Bleeding or perforated ulcer that occurs in the first 1 to 2 weeks of life (unassociated with other illness or stress) appears to be an acute ulcer resulting from hypersecretion of acid caused by maternal gastrin. These ulcers are usually complicated by bleeding and often respond to orogastric decompression, accompanied by careful saline lavage to keep blood clots evacuated from the stomach and appropriate volume replacement. Perforation requires prompt surgical intervention employing the simplest method (i.e., a Graham patch) to safely close the defect. If the operation is performed for hemorrhage, simple suture ligation of the ulcer bed should suffice. No evidence suggests that these ulcers recur.

Although the incidence of bleeding and perforation has diminished over the past 2 decades, the complication of chronic obstruction from peptic ulcer disease is unchanged. In a recent 45-year review, Azarow and associates[8] described a persistently high incidence of gastric outlet obstruction requiring surgical intervention. Vagotomy and pyloroplasty or gastroenterostomy were used to relieve the obstructions. Chronic, partial gastric outlet obstruction secondary to a congenital problem, such as a duodenal web[3,79] or hypertrophic pyloric stenosis also can result in peptic ulcers in infants and children. It is important to identify the cause in these instances because the ulcer can be completely relieved by treatment of the distal obstruction.

Zollinger-Ellison Syndrome

The Zollinger-Ellison syndrome is relatively rare in children.[131] The diagnosis may be suggested by the presence of large gastric rugal folds, duodenal dilatation, and edema of the small-bowel mucosa and can be confirmed by an elevated serum gastrin level. The calcium infusion test, reliable in both adults and children, has been used to confirm the diagnosis of hypergastrinemia. Treatment of the Zollinger-Ellison syndrome has traditionally been total gastrectomy unless the primary pancreatic tumor can be completely resected. Some reports suggest that H_2 receptor antagonists or proton-pump inhibitors can eliminate the need for gastrectomy in children.[37] The fact that many of these endocrine tumors may be malignant suggests that a careful evaluation of each case to determine its nature and long-term follow-up after treatment with H_2 receptor antagonists or proton-pump inhibitors is necessary before reliable conclusions about management can be drawn. In addition, occasionally the gastrin-producing tumors may occur in the wall of the duodenum and require resection. The multiple endocrine neoplasia type 1 syndrome may be present in 25% of the cases. Somatostatin receptor scintigraphy is useful in detecting primary and metastatic gastrinomas.

Stress Ulcer

Prevention is the preferred treatment goal for stress ulcers. It has been shown experimentally that, under simulated clinical conditions, development of stress ulcers requires a low gastric pH. The use of prophylactic antacids to maintain the gastric intraluminal pH at a value of 6.0 or greater is effective. Supportive care with improved ventilatory support, maintenance of vascular volume, correction of acid-base imbalance, and nutritional support may also contribute to the ability of the gastric mucosa to withstand acid-peptic injury.

The effectiveness of H_2 receptor antagonists and proton-pump inhibitors for the prevention of stress ulcers is extremely effective.[30,74] An H_2 receptor antagonist is probably indicated in the prevention and treatment of Cushing's ulcers, which are associated with gastric hypersecretion.

When a secondary ulcer presents as bleeding, immediate supportive treatment with balanced salt solution and blood transfusion is frequently adequate. Children who have experienced a major episode of upper gastrointestinal hemorrhage or recurrent bleeding require endoscopy.[164] Endoscopy for bleeding requires greater skill and greater technical demands than do other endoscopic procedures. The endoscopist should have the knowledge and experience not only to identify the source of bleeding but also to control it. Potential interventions include therapeutic injections (of hypertonic NaCl, epinephrine, or absolute ethanol), and cauterization with heater probe, bipolar coagulation, or laser (Nd:YAG or argon). If the endoscopist is not a surgeon, a pediatric surgeon should evaluate the child before emergency endoscopy. The surgeon may then be available to observe the source of hemorrhage and be immediately available for surgical intervention if necessary.

If massive hemorrhage continues or recurs despite drug and endoscopic therapy, surgical control is indicated. Massive hemorrhage has been defined as blood loss in a 24-hour period equal to the total estimated blood volume in infants younger than 2 years of age and as loss equal to half of the estimated blood volume in older children (with 80 mL/kg used as an estimation of total blood volume). This definition correlates with the report of Williams and coworkers,[162] in which no child recovered without surgical management if the rate of blood loss was more than 60% of the estimated total blood volume in 24 hours. The successful use of selective intra-arterial vasopressin to manage bleeding stress ulcer in a child has been reported,[84] but others have not found this to be useful.[57,103] Although bleeding often precedes perforation of a secondary ulcer, perforation can be the initial presentation and requires immediate operation.

The surgical procedures used to treat stress ulcers have ranged from simple closure of a perforation to oversewing of the base of a bleeding ulcer to gastrectomy.[24] As a general rule, these ulcers are not associated with an ulcer diathesis and therefore should respond to the simplest procedure that effectively treats the presenting problem. Because stress ulcers are the result of an underlying disease, recurrence of the ulcer is possible if the underlying problem is unresolved; this fact must therefore be considered when the appropriate operation is being selected. The simplest procedure, plication of the site of perforation or oversewing of the bleeding point, is usually effective. On the other hand, when it is apparent that the underlying problem will remain unresolved for an extended period, a more definitive ulcer procedure may be appropriate. Vagotomy and pyloroplasty are recommended most frequently because they rarely interfere with subsequent growth. Vagotomy and antrectomy may occasionally be necessary to control the bleeding ulcer in patients with extensive burns and intracranial problems.[118] Antrectomy also may be necessary for large perforations that cannot be managed by pyloroplasty, although the possibility of serosal patching to close such large defects should be kept in mind. In adults, even total gastrectomy has been infrequently recommended for treating massive hemorrhage from multiple gastric ulcers. Such a procedure is rarely indicated in children. The surgeon who operates on a child for ulcer disease must remember that the patient must continue to grow and develop; therefore, the simplest, least disruptive procedure should be selected. Evidence suggests that these children do have problems, such as low hemoglobin levels.[157] Experimental evidence comparing the effects of gastrectomy with vagotomy and pyloroplasty on growth and development in miniature swine[120] suggest that vagotomy with pyloroplasty results in less growth disturbance. Follow-up data indicate that vagotomy with pyloroplasty is an effective method of treatment unassociated with substantial long-term problems.[73] In view of the reports of osteoporosis, iron deficiency, and dumping noted in adults who have had various operations for peptic ulcer disease,[89,104] long-term follow-up is essential. There are rare reports of adenocarcinoma occurring in gastric remnants after subtotal gastrectomy.[133] The risk is higher after a Billroth II (gastrojejunostomy) anastomosis. One of our patients developed cancer in the gastric remnant at age 23 years—12 years after a vagotomy and antrectomy for a chronic obstructing duodenal ulcer. Other tumors may arise in the stomach and present with bleeding due to erosion. These include rare cases of gastric teratoma and instances of leiomyosarcoma and gastrointestinal stromal tumors (GIST). These conditions are presented in detail in Chapter 31.

OTHER CONDITIONS OF THE STOMACH

Congenital Gastric Outlet Obstruction

Pyloric Atresia

History

In 1937, a 4-day-old infant died 36 hours after operation for "pyloric stenosis." Autopsy revealed that the obstruction was caused by a complete prepyloric diaphragm. Between 1940 and 1959 successful surgical treatment of complete prepyloric diaphragm was reported and a double diaphragm was noted to occur in preterm and term infants younger than 1 week old.[14] At least six reports have described familial occurrence,[45] and an autosomal recessive mode of inheritance has been suggested.

Embryology and Pathology

The antral and supra-ampullary part of the duodenum develop from the caudal end of the foregut. Atresias in this region occur in the form of webs, membranes, or rarely solid cords (Table 77-5). The cause of antral web and atresia has not been fully elucidated. Numerous proposals have been made to explain the occurrence of this rare anomaly. It is generally believed that intrauterine vascular accidents cause ischemic necrosis and subsequent bowel atresia, but it is unlikely for this to occur in the stomach because the blood supply is abundant. It is also difficult to envisage the possibility of failure of recanalization as has been proposed as a cause of fetal bowel occlusion because there is no firm evidence that such occlusion ever occurs in the stomach. Type I occlusion is more often noted in the duodenum or proximal jejunum.[158] Skandalakis and Gray[146] have postulated that redundancy and slipping of epithelial lining may initiate the formation of an incomplete diaphragm. Sharma and associates[140] also hypothesize this etiology on a small series of acquired mucosal obstruction of the pylorus. Although these explanations appear to be a possible cause of membranous webs, it still remains speculative and definite confirmatory evidence is not currently available. The similarities of the clinicopathologic features in related patients and its occurrence in siblings and cousins, in the absence of teratogenic factors, point to a genetic etiology that is similar in pathology to the familial genetic etiology of infants with pyloric atresia[45] and epidermolysis bullosa.[33,126] One other cause of gastric outlet obstruction with similar embryology is the pyloroduodenal duplication cyst.[60,177]

TABLE 77-5 Classification of Antral and Supra-ampullary Atresias

I. Pyloric
   A. Membrane
   B. Atresia
II. Antral (1.0 cm or more proximal to pylorus)
   A. Membrane
   B. Atresia

Clinical Presentation and Pathophysiology

There is often a maternal history of polyhydramnios. With the frequent use of prenatal ultrasound, polyhydramnios may be observed and the fetal stomach may be distended during the last trimester.[160] The affected infant presents in the first few days of life with nonbilious vomiting and complete gastric outlet obstruction.[40,134] The diaphragm may be perforated, but frequently the lumen is essentially completely obstructed when the aperture is less than 10 mm in size.[13,158] Respiratory problems are common, and dyspnea, tachypnea, cyanosis, and excessive salivation may be presenting findings that may be mistaken for signs of esophageal atresia.[20,81] Examination of the abdomen shows epigastric fullness due to the distended stomach. If diagnosis is delayed, excessive distention of the stomach may lead to perforation. Since the obstruction is proximal to the ampulla of Vater, the passage of a meconium stool may mislead the casual observer.

Diagnosis

Abdominal radiography confirms the clinical diagnosis (Fig. 77-1). It may be necessary to aspirate the stomach

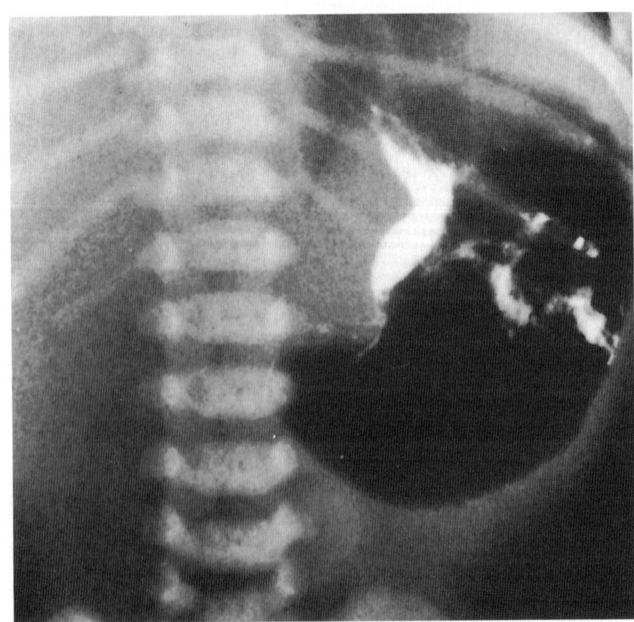

Figure 77-1 Pyloric atresia in a newborn. Air provides excellent contrast. No air extends beyond the pylorus. This child was dehydrated and developed hypochloremic, hypokalemic alkalosis after early postnatal discharge. The anomaly was successfully treated by end-to-end gastroduodenostomy.

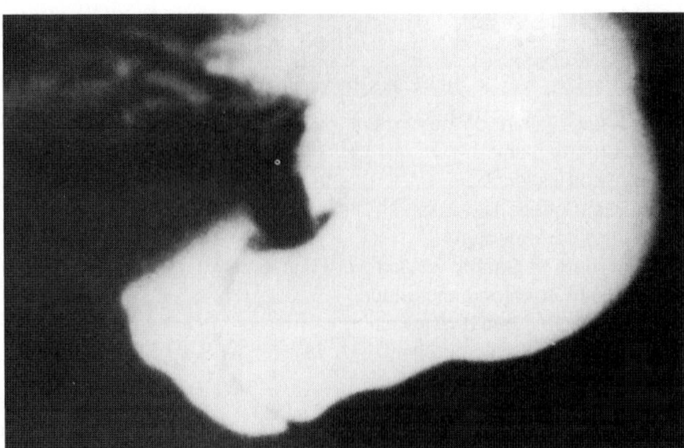

Figure 77-2 Incomplete antral diaphragm in a newborn. This infant had non–bile-stained vomitus shortly after birth. A dilute barium contrast swallow established the diagnosis of an incomplete obstruction. Treatment with a Heineke-Mikulicz pyloroplasty and with excision of the web was successful.

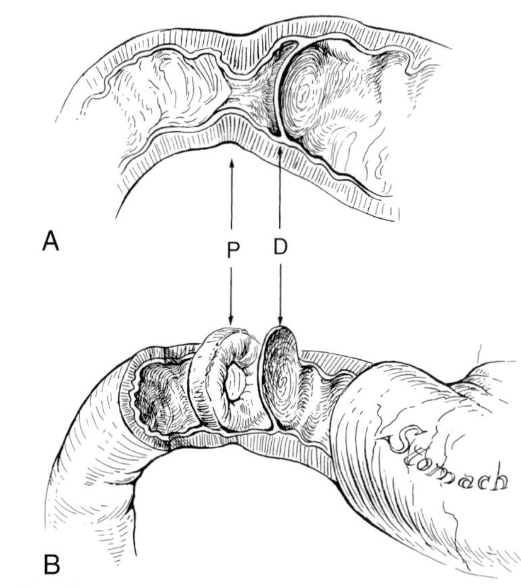

Figure 77-4 Congenital pyloric and prepyloric obstruction. *A*, Prepyloric membrane. *B*, Antral diaphragm. P, pylorus; D, diaphragm.

of liquid contents and re-instill a similar volume of air; injection of contrast material is usually unnecessary. The aspirated material is always nonbilious. Abdominal radiography performed in various positions may be required to establish the correct diagnosis. A single gastric bubble is observed with no air visible beyond the pylorus. With symptoms of nonbilious vomiting, a distended stomach, and air noted distal to the stomach, dilute barium or soluble contrast is required for the diagnosis of an incomplete pyloric membrane (Fig. 77-2).

The difficulty in identifying a pyloric web at laparotomy cannot be overemphasized and the surgeon must create a generous proximal gastrotomy. Haller and Cahill[59] warn against missing a pyloric web in association with a duodenal atresia. They recommend a wide gastrotomy and distal passage of a catheter after excision of the prepyloric diaphragm to identify an associated duodenal diaphragm.

Treatment

Pyloric atresia can usually be recognized at the time of operation; a fibrous cord may join two blind ends (Fig. 77-3). Gastrotomy and distal passage of a catheter may be required to detect membranous obstructions (Fig. 77-4). Excision of a complete or partial diaphragm with Heineke-Mikulicz or Finney pyloroplasty is the most straightforward corrective procedure. In the presence of pyloric atresia with the atretic ends separated by a cord-like or discontinuous segment, gastroduodenostomy is necessary. Dessanti and associates described an anatomic pyloric sphincter reconstruction procedure utilizing the atretic cul-de-sac to perform an end-to-end anastomosis.[36] This procedure replaces the resection of the atretic segment and a side-to-side or end-to-oblique anastomosis because of the size disparity between the stomach and duodenum. A temporary decompression gastrostomy and insertion of a transgastric feeding tube may be useful. Recent advances in endoscopy have stimulated development of alternate treatment strategies, including balloon dilatation, laser web excision, and laser radial incisions of a type I membrane. The number of these cases is few, and long-term follow-up data are limited.

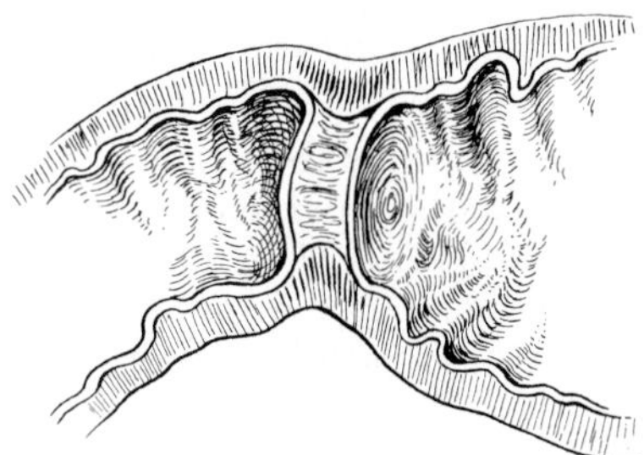

Figure 77-3 Pyloric atresia. The seromuscular layers are uninterrupted. The tissue between the gastric and duodenal mucosa was of two types: fibrous and areolar.

Outcomes

Survival should be anticipated if diagnosis and surgical intervention occur early and if neonatal supportive care is given. Death has been associated with delayed diagnosis[10,79,117] and associated conditions.[123] Fifty-nine cases of congenital pyloric atresia have been reported. A familial occurrence was described in 13 infants in six families; an unexplained high-mortality rate was seen in this familial group. Some familial cases are associated with epidermolysis bullosa.[81,117,150] Junctional epidermolysis bullosa/pyloric atresia syndrome is associated with extremely adverse outcomes due to the risk of sepsis, malabsorption, renal disease, and failure to thrive. Of the 70 cases presented in the medical literature, death occurred in 54 patients by 11 months of age. Of the 16 survivors, all are plagued with complications of epidermal disease ranging from 30 days to 16 years.[33] Pyloric atresia associated with junctional epidermolysis bullosa results from mutations in the *PLEC1* gene. The lethal form is associated with intracellular degradation of beta-4 integrin.

Pyloric Duplication

Duplications of the stomach and pylorus are uncommon, representing less than 3% of alimentary tract duplications. Pyloric duplications are slightly more frequent in girls. They share a common wall with the stomach or pylorus and rarely communicate. Infants present with nonbilious vomiting and weight loss in the first 2 to 3 weeks of life.[31,148] The condition may be mistaken for hypertrophic pyloric stenosis. Occasionally, pyloric duplications present with a palpable mass, further confusing this occurrence with hypertrophic pyloric stenosis. The diagnosis is suggested by ultrasound studies that show a cystic extraluminal mass compressing the gastric outlet. The condition may not be recognized until the time of operation. The procedure of choice is extramucosal excision. Occasionally cyst-gastrostomy may be necessary. Postoperative survival is expected and complications are few. Duplication cysts affecting the stomach usually present later in life. Duplications are covered extensively in Chapter 88.

Volvulus of the Stomach

History

Gastric volvulus was first reported by Berti in 1886. In 1904, Borchardt described the classic triad of acute or localized distention of the epigastrium associated with pain, inability to pass a nasogastric tube, and nonproductive attempts at vomiting. Numerous case reports have been published on adults and children. Gastric volvulus in children is a rare condition; a recent literature review described 51 cases in infants and children.[22] Fifty-two percent were younger than 1 year of age, and 26% were younger than 1 month of age. Bautista-Casasnovas and coworkers[12] reported their 25 year experience with children, confirming the early age of diagnosis of acute volvulus in infants. A more recent review suggests chronic gastric volvulus is encountered more frequently than the acute form; in adults, it is often seen in association with paraesophageal hiatal hernia.[152] Acute gastric volvulus, on the other hand, is a true surgical emergency.

Embryology and Classification

Gastric volvulus is rare because the stomach is held securely in place by the gastrophrenic ligaments, esophageal hiatus, retroperitoneal fixation of the duodenum, short gastric vessels, and gastrocolic ligament. It occurs only when these attachments are lax or absent. Gastric volvulus is occasionally associated with eventration of the diaphragm, diaphragmatic hernia, congenital bands, elongated gastric attachments, or absence of the gastrocolic ligament. Predisposing factors to the abnormal rotation of the stomach can be divided into primary lack of fixation, disorders of anatomy, and abnormalities of adjacent organs.[94,135] They are detailed in Table 77-6.

Acute gastric volvulus is the most frequent presentation in children. Most case reports[11,94,110,139,149] and the largest single institutional[12] study identify neonates and infants younger than 6 months of age as the most common age group of children with acute volvulus of the stomach.

TABLE 77-6 Anatomic Etiology of Gastric Volvulus

- I. Absence, Failure of Attachment, or Elongation of Gastric Fixation
  - A. Gastrosplenic
  - B. Gastrocoloic
  - C. Gastrohepatic
  - D. Greater omentum
- II. Disorders of Gastric Anatomy or Function
  - A. Acute or chronic distention
    - 1. Gastric outlet obstruction
    - 2. Gastric hypomotility
    - 3. Massive aerophagia
  - B. Peptic ulcer disease
  - C. Neoplasm of the stomach
  - D. Hourglass stomach
  - E. Gastric ptosis
- III. Abnormalities of Adjacent Organs
  - A. Diaphragm
    - 1. Hiatal hernia, sliding or paraesophageal
    - 2. Bochdalek's hernia or other congenital defect
    - 3. Diaphragmatic rupture
    - 4. Eventration of the diaphragm
    - 5. Phrenic nerve palsy
  - B. Splenomegaly, polysplenia
  - C. Volvulus of transverse colon
  - D. Malrotation and midgut volvulus
  - E. Dislocation or hypoplasia of the left lobe of the liver

The principal symptoms include crying and colic (90%), nausea and vomiting (67%), and, less frequently, abdominal distention, gastroesophageal reflux, failure to thrive, or recurrent respiratory infections.

Gastric volvulus is classified according to the plane of rotation (Fig. 77-5). In *organoaxial* volvulus, the stomach rotates on its long axis; the greater curvature passes anteriorly but may be displaced posteriorly. In the less common *mesenterioaxial* volvulus, rotation is on an axis from greater to lesser curvature (the pylorus or cardia commonly rotates anteriorly). The opposite rotation may also occur. The torsion may be total, involving the entire stomach, or partial, limited to the pyloric end. The rotating section usually passes anteriorly.

Radiologic Features

Radiographic examination confirms the diagnosis of gastric volvulus and often identifies underlying associated congenital anomalies or defects. The radiographic features of acute volvulus of the stomach include (1) localized massive distention of the upper abdomen; (2) high greater curvature of the stomach (87%); (3) greater curvature crossing the stomach (83%); (4) fixation of the loop regardless of the position of the patient; (5) delimitation of ingested barium at the tapered extremity of the esophagus, the so-called "bird's beak"; (6) possible evidence of a hiatal sacculation or other diaphragmatic herniation; and (7) deviation of the position of the spleen.

Treatment

Gastric volvulus may present acutely and require acute surgical intervention to prevent or limit vascular compromise.

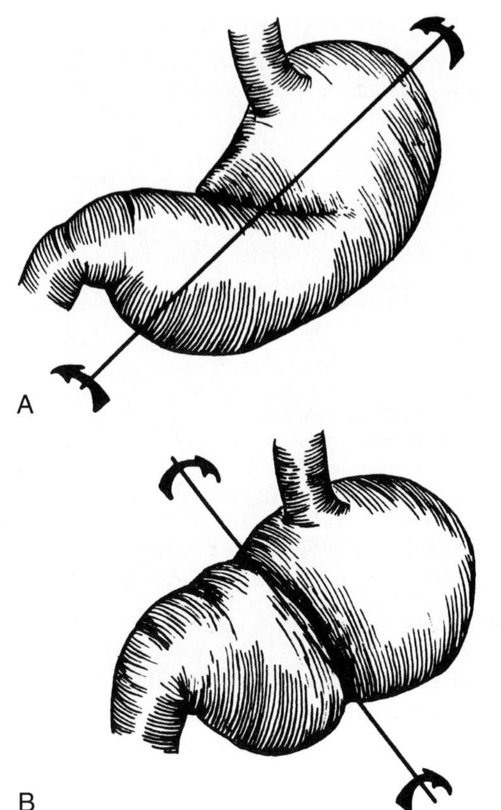

Figure 77-5 Gastric volvulus. *A*, Organoaxial. The greater curvature usually passes forward, as depicted, but may rotate posteriorly. *B*, Mesenterioaxial. The pylorus or the cardia commonly rotates anteriorly, but the opposite may occur. (From Cole BC, Dickinson SJ: Acute volvulus of the stomach in infants and children. Surgery 1971;70:707; with permission.)

Simple decompression with a nasogastric tube may temporize the situation but is inadequate as a long-term treatment. At operation, gastric decompression facilitates reduction. Once normal anatomic relationships have been restored, the site is carefully inspected to identify possible areas of perforation or gangrene. The remainder of the procedure is focused on preventing a recurrence of volvulus and correcting any diaphragmatic defects (hiatal and Bochdalek hernias). In infants and children, gastrostomy or anterior gastropexy is then performed. There are several case reports of successful outcomes using each of these techniques by open or endoscopic repair.[11,12,149] Follow-up of these patients ranges from 1 to 10 years without recurrence. Recurrence despite fixation has also been reported.[152]

Gastric Perforation in the Newborn

Background

Spontaneous gastric perforation in the neonatal period often occurs in infants who require resuscitation or have an episode of hypoxia shortly after birth. Boys are more commonly affected than girls and the reported incidence is 1 in 2900 births. There are two common theories regarding the events leading up to gastric perforation. The first postulates that an ischemic insult associated with perinatal stress results in a hypoxic mucosal injury and progresses to perforation in a few days. The second theory is related to gastric overinflation that may be the result of overaggressive mask resuscitation, accidental esophageal intubation and vigorous insufflation, trauma from passage of an orogastric tube or proximal distention, and perforation due to a distal outlet obstruction from pyloric atresia. Gastric ischemia and perforation may also be observed in premature infants with extensive necrotizing enterocolitis affecting most of the gastrointestinal tract.

History

Perforation of the gastrointestinal tract of the newborn without demonstrable cause, so-called spontaneous perforation, was first reported 1826. In 1943, a neonatal gastrointestinal perforation was closed successfully. In 1964, Lloyd and coworkers[86] reported 61 cases of spontaneous perforation of the gastrointestinal tract in the newborn and called attention to the fact that all of these lesions, regardless of location, were the result of ischemic necrosis. The undesirable side effects of an asphyxial defense mechanism, known as selective circulatory ischemia, activated by perinatal stress, hypoxia, or shock, was implicated as the principal factor causing these lesions.[9,42,155] In 1969, Lloyd[87] reviewed the world literature and found 315 cases of neonatal gastrointestinal perforation qualifying as ischemic lesions. Since then, multiple predisposing factors and causes have been suggested.[5,46,145]

Embryology and Pathology

Although ischemia may be the common denominator, a multifactorial cause is likely, including congenital muscular defect of the gastric wall,[99] bacterial colonization of the gut with pathogenic organisms,[82] the presence of a hyperosmolar luminal substrate such as carbohydrate, immaturity of the immune system,[56] and endothelial injury related to the use of indomethacin.[145] Gregory and colleagues[54] described the association of perinatal stress in 39 of 42 infants with ischemic necrosis of the gut.

The actual mechanisms by which ischemic changes are induced remain uncertain. It is believed that blood is shunted to the heart and the brain at the expense of the peripheral, renal, and mesenteric vascular beds. The reader is referred to the report of Elsner and associates[42] for details concerning the "diving reflex" theory in mammals and in humans. Asphyxia at birth in infants with low Apgar scores is particularly likely to lead to gastrointestinal perforation. Redistribution of blood flow during hypoxia, hypovolemia, or other stress states[156] with shunting away from mesenteric vascular beds is thought to result in microvascular injury[64,65] and subsequent loss of mucosal integrity.[68] Persistence of the ischemic insult, which allows extension of microvascular thrombosis, leads to the transmural necrosis seen in intestinal perforation. The periods of stress and potential mesenteric ischemia may be temporally remote from the recognition of perforation. Indomethacin therapy in low-birth-weight infants also has been implicated in occurrence of gastrointestinal perforations.[53,111,145] The neonate also has an immature immune system, and prematurity is associated with deficiencies in complement, opsonization, phagocyte function, IgA, and IgM and the function of T lymphocytes.[48,93] (Gastrointestinal perforation is covered extensively in Chapter 92.) Isolated gastric perforation usually occurs along the greater curvature between the smooth muscle layers and, as previously noted, has been associated with lactobezoars in premature infants, iatrogenic injury due to overzealous resuscitation with an Ambu bag, inadvertent esophageal intubation, as a result of trauma from the passage of an orogastric tube, and related to unrecognized injury during placement of a percutaneous endoscopic gastrostomy tube in older infants and children.[47,56]

Signs and Symptoms and Diagnosis

The first indication of intestinal perforation usually occurs at 5 to 15 days of life, but spontaneous gastric perforation often occurs at 3 to 5 days of life. Abdominal distention is frequently abrupt and rapidly progressive. Signs of hypovolemia and decreased perfusion are usually present, manifested by tachycardia and lethargy. Respiratory difficulty from massive pneumoperitoneum may be the first sign. Infants born of pregnancies complicated by abruptio placentae, placenta previa, and amnionitis (severe fetal distress) and infants delivered by emergency cesarean section are at increased risk and should be carefully observed.

Although many premature infants at risk have not had feedings initiated, if feedings were started, they should be stopped in infants who were progressing satisfactorily and suddenly refuse feedings or infants who are listless and apathetic and in whom a septic workup is undertaken. Serial abdominal radiographs should be obtained until the cause of the problem is elucidated. Most infants with gastric perforation have evidence of free air on abdominal radiographs (Fig. 77-6). Further evaluation includes measurement of leukocyte and platelet counts and arterial pH and blood gas analysis.

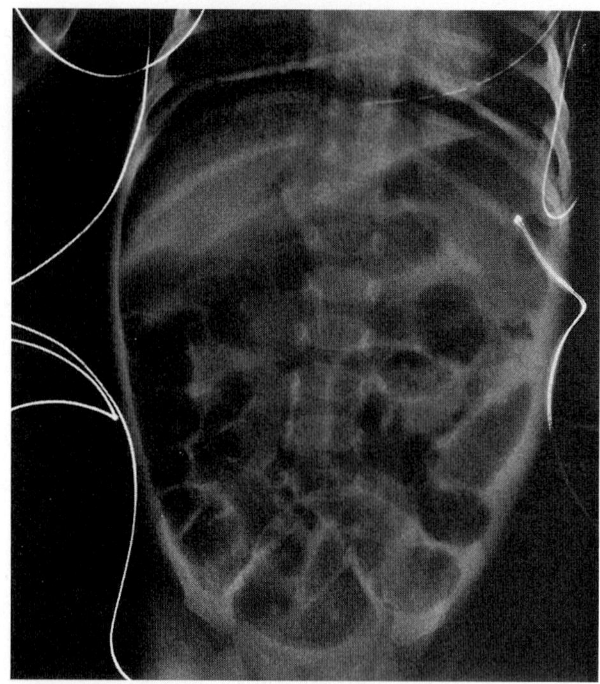

Figure 77–6 Abdominal radiograph in an infant with spontaneous gastric perforation shows free air in the peritoneal cavity.

Treatment

The condition of an infant with gastric perforation can deteriorate rapidly; therefore, early recognition and prompt treatment are essential. This includes rapid fluid resuscitation, blood transfusion, correction of acidosis, administration of antibiotics, orogastric suction, maintenance of body temperature, and performance of only essential diagnostic studies.[85] These infants usually require immediate intubation and ventilatory support. Paracentesis to evacuate the pneumoperitoneum with a blunt needle or plastic catheter may relieve life-threatening respiratory distress due to diaphragmatic elevation during the resuscitation period. If transportation to a tertiary-care neonatal intensive care facility is indicated, resuscitation should begin before transport. The infant should be transported by experienced personnel who can continue the resuscitation en route.

Emergency laparotomy through a transverse, supraumbilical abdominal incision is used. The peritoneal contents should be cultured for aerobic and anaerobic bacterial organisms and fungi. The abdomen should be systematically explored, directed by the location of the greatest amount of peritoneal soilage. Clear gastric contents or slightly bile-tinged fluid often suggests a perforation of the stomach or duodenum. Darkly stained or feculent material suggests a perforation of the small intestine or colon. Perforation sites may be occult; after careful examination of the bowel from the esophageal hiatus to the pelvic floor, exploration of the lesser omental space may be necessary. Looking for bubbles when the abdomen is filled with warm saline has been suggested. Most spontaneous gastric perforations occur along the greater curvature of the stomach distal to the esophagus. Perforation due to a duodenal ulcer in infancy occurs on the anterior wall of the duodenum or near the pyloroduodenal junction, whereas gastric ulcers may perforate along the lesser curvature near the antral-fundic junction. Perforations of the stomach can usually be débrided and closed primarily. If the greater curvature of the stomach is more extensively involved with necrosis, it can be resected and the residual stomach can be turned into a tubular structure using an autostapling device. Occasionally when there is extensive necrosis of the gastric antrum, a partial gastrectomy and gastroenterostomy may be required. A Billroth I procedure (gastroduodenostomy) is preferred. If there are associated ischemic perforations in the small bowel that are discrete and the adjacent bowel is healthy, the perforation may be repaired primarily. If there is extensive necrosis, bowel resection may be necessary. The decision to perform an anastomosis or to exteriorize the residual bowel depends on the level of the perforation and the degree of contamination. Because infants tolerate high intestinal fistulas poorly, it is tempting to perform a primary anastomosis if the ischemia is limited. However, the sick infant's best chance for survival often depends on a short exteriorization procedure. Peritoneal drainage, achieved by the percutaneous placement of a Penrose drain into the peritoneal cavity of very-low-birth-weight neonates with intestinal perforation, was described originally over 25 years ago by Ein and colleagues.[41] Initially, this procedure was recommended as a temporary measure for small, extremely ill infants with perforated necrotizing enterocolitis to drain air and stool, relieve symptoms of abdominal compartment syndrome and sepsis, and allow the infant to better tolerate subsequent laparotomy. Recently, clinicians have recognized a separate subset of premature neonates with bowel perforation in whom the perforation develops spontaneously and is not associated with necrotizing enterocolitis. This so called spontaneous, focal, idiopathic, indomethacin-associated, or isolated intestinal perforation responds well to peritoneal drainage.[5,21,145] This approach cannot be employed in infants with perforation of the stomach because they require prompt operative repair. It is, therefore, important for the clinician to have a high index of suspicion for the presence of a gastric perforation to avoid unnecessary delays in therapy. The topics of necrotizing enterocolitis, idiopathic perforation, and peritoneal drainage are covered extensively in Chapter 92.

Infants with isolated gastric perforation generally receive antibiotics for 7 days. After a period of bowel rest and antibiotics, enteral feedings are started when there is evidence of bowel function and gastric returns through the orogastric tube are clear and of low volume. Many clinicians obtain a contrast swallow before initiating feedings. Upper or lower contrast studies are routinely obtained in those infants who do not tolerate enteral feedings to evaluate for a gastric leak or obstruction.

Outcomes

Current survival for isolated gastric perforation is 75% to 80%: those infants who succumb often have multiple organ dysfunction as a result of their initial insult associated with peritonitis, sepsis, and immature immunologic function. Infants with gastric necrosis associated with extensive necrotizing enterocolitis have a very high morbidity and mortality.[56]

Congenital Microgastria

History

Congential microgastria is a rare condition first reported in the 1800s.[17,32] To date, 43 cases have been reported. The malformation has been frequently associated with other congenital anomalies, including asplenia, malrotation of the intestines, situs inversus, megaesophagus,[66,151] and upper limb anomalies such as radial, ulnar, and thenar hypoplasia (microgastria-limb reduction association).[17,32] Increasing regionalization of the care of infants and children in pediatric hospitals has resulted in increased recognition of this condition.[6,67,136] Reported therapy for microgastria has ranged from conservative dietary manipulation in patients minimally affected to surgical augmentation of the small stomach.

Embryology and Pathology

This is a rare congenital anomaly of the caudal part of the embryologic foregut, characterized by a small, tubular stomach, megaesophagus, and incomplete gastric rotation. The esophageal, gastric, small, and large intestinal mucosa are normal. There are many associated conditions of the gastrointestinal tract, such as nonrotation of the midgut with duodenal bands and asplenia. Situs inversus and asplenia have been reported.[80] Skeletal anomalies, including micrognathia, radial and ulnar hypoplasia, vertebral anomalies, oligodactyly, and hypoplastic nails, are common. Anophthalmia has also been reported.[136]

Because of the associated anomalies in organogenesis, arrest in development is thought to occur between the fourth and the eighth weeks of fetal life. Absence of the gallbladder has also been reported.[113] Massive and persistent reflux into the biliary tract may occur. Patients may have congenital heart disease characterized by a single atrium, a single ventricle, and total anomalous pulmonary venous return into the portal vein.

Clinical Presentation and Pathophysiology

With the more frequent use of prenatal ultrasound, polyhydramnios and a small stomach may be noted late in a pregnancy. Most patients are beyond the neonatal period at the time of diagnosis, frequently have a dilated esophagus with an ill-defined gastroesophageal junction, and are therefore prone to gastroesophageal reflux. The most frequent presenting signs are vomiting, aspiration and pneumonia, and failure to thrive. Malnutrition and developmental delay may result. Diarrhea is common. An incompetent lower esophageal sphincter has been demonstrated in these cases. When coupled with reduced gastric capacity and a dilated esophagus, vomiting, esophageal erosion, and aspiration are common. Although not well studied, it is postulated that malnutrition and diarrhea may result from a small gastric capacity with rapid emptying of acid content. Bacterial overgrowth and a blind loop–like syndrome have been suggested to explain the diarrhea and malnutrition, but results of the Shilling test have been normal.

Diagnosis

Contrast examination of the upper gastrointestinal tract with barium, usually the first study obtained, demonstrates the features just mentioned. Imaging techniques augment the radiographs.[138] Endoscopy has proved difficult and has yielded confusing results. Appropriate cardiac studies are dictated by the specific findings, and asplenia may be demonstrated by examination of the peripheral erythrocytes for Howell-Jolly bodies and by nuclear imaging. If gastroesophageal reflux disease is a clinical feature, manometry and esophageal pH studies may be appropriate. In patients with diarrhea, malnutrition, or growth retardation, intestinal absorption studies may elucidate the cause.

Treatment

Medical treatment should be attempted initially. Continuous or night-time orogastric feedings may allow the patient to grow and the stomach to enlarge so that the patient can then tolerate normal feedings. If gastroesophageal reflux disease develops, prokinetic agents and acid-reducing therapy may improve gastric emptying. Complications of gastroesophageal reflux may require the use of a nasojejunal feeding tube or surgically placed jejunostomy tube. The jejunal feedings supplement the smaller oral feedings, allowing the stomach to enlarge.[109] If the infant's stomach fails to enlarge, several authors have recommended augmenting the stomach capacity by construction of a double-row jejunal reservoir,[49,96,105] and outcomes from early follow-up are encouraging.

REFERENCES

1. Acra SA, Nakagawa N, Ghishan FK: Peptic ulcer diseases in children. Comprehens Ther 1991;17:22-26.
2. Agunod M, Yamaguchi N, Lopez R, et al: Correlative study of hydrochloric acid, pepsin, and intrinsic factor secretion in newborns and infants. J Dig Dis 1969;14:400-414.
3. Airan B, Yadav K, Yadav RV: Congenital incomplete duodenal diaphragm with prediaphragmatic duodenal ulcer. Am J Gastroenterol 1979;72:426-427.
4. Allaker RP, Young KA, Hardie JM, et al: Prevalence of *Helicobacter pylori* at oral and gastrointestinal sites in children: Evidence for possible oral-to-oral transmission. J Med Microbiol 2002;51:312-317.
5. Alpan G, Eyal F, Vinograd I, et al: Localized intestinal perforation after enteral administration of indomethacin in premature infants. J Pediatr 1985;106:277-281.
6. Anderson KD, Guzzetta PC: Treatment of congenital microgastria and dumping syndrome. J Pediatr Surg 1983; 18:747-750.
7. Ashorn M: What are the specific features of *Helicobacter pylori* gastritis in children? Ann Med 1995;27:617-620.
8. Azarow K, Kim P, Shandling B, et al: A 45-year experience with surgical treatment of peptic ulcer disease in children. J Pediatr Surg 1996;31:750-753.
9. Barlow B, Santulli TV: Importance of multiple episodes of hypoxia or cold stress on the development of enterocolitis in an animal model. Surgery 1975;77:687-690.
10. Bar-Maor JA, Nissan S, Nevo S: Pyloric atresia: A hereditary congenital anomaly with autosomal recessive transmission. J Med Genet 1972;9:70-72.
11. Basaran UN, Inan M, Ayhan S, et al: Acute gastric volvulus due to deficiency of the gastrocolic ligament in a newborn. Eur J Pediatr 2002;161:288-290.
12. Bautista-Casasnovas A, Varela-Cives R, Fernandez-Bustillo JM, et al: Chronic gastric volvulus: Is it so rare? Eur J Pediatr Surg 2002;12:111-115.
13. Bell MJ, Keating JP, Ternberg JL, et al: Perforated stress ulcers in infants. J Pediatr Surg 1981;16:998-1002.
14. Bell MJ, Ternberg JL, McAlister W, et al: Antral diaphragm—a cause of gastric outlet obstruction in infants and children. J Pediatr 1977;90:196-202.
15. Benaroch LM, Rudolph CD: Pediatric endoscopy. Semin Gastrointest Dis 1994;5:32-46.
16. Bird C, Limper M, Mayer J: Surgery in peptic ulceration of the stomach and duodenum in infants and children. Ann Surg 1941;114:526.
17. Blank E, Chisolm AJ: Congenital microgastria, a case report with a 26-year follow-up. Pediatrics 1973;51:1037-1041.
18. Blaser MJ, Chyou PH, Nomura A: Age at establishment of *Helicobacter pylori* infection and gastric carcinoma, gastric ulcer, and duodenal ulcer risk. Cancer Res 1995;55:562-565.
19. Boyle JT: Acid secretion from birth to adulthood. J Pediatr Gastroenterol Nutr 2003;37(Suppl 1):S12-S16.
20. Bronsther B, Nadeau MR, Abrams MW: Congenital pyloric atresia: A report of three cases and a review of the literature. Surgery 1971;69:130-136.
21. Camberos A, Patel K, Applebaum H: Laparotomy in very small premature infants with necrotizing enterocolitis or focal intestinal perforation: Postoperative outcome. J Pediatr Surg 2002;37:1692-1695.
22. Cameron AE, Howard ER: Gastric volvulus in childhood. J Pediatr Surg 1987;22:944-947.
23. Canete A, Abunaji Y, Alvarez-Calatayud G, et al: Breath test using a single 50-mg dose of ^{13}C-urea to detect *Helicobacter pylori* infection in children. J Pediatr Gastroenterol Nutr 2003;36:105-111.
24. Chan KL, Tam PK, Saing H: Long-term follow-up of childhood duodenal ulcers. J Pediatr Surg 1997;32:1609-1611.
25. Chelimsky G, Czinn S: Peptic ulcer disease in children. Pediatr Rev 2001;22:349-355.
26. Cheung LY, Chang N: The role of gastric mucosal blood flow and H^+ back-diffusion in the pathogenesis of acute gastric erosions. J Surg Res 1977;22:357-361.
27. Cheung LY, Porterfield G: Protection of gastric mucosa against acute ulceration by intravenous infusion of sodium bicarbonate. Am J Surg 1979;137:106-110.
28. Chong SK, Lou Q, Zollinger TW, et al: The seroprevalence of *Helicobacter pylori* in a referral population of children in the United States. Am J Gastroenterol 2003;98:2162-2168.
29. Conn HO, Blitzer BL: Nonassociation of adrenocorticosteroid therapy and peptic ulcer. N Engl J Med 1976;294: 473-479.
30. Cook DJ, Reeve BK, Guyatt GH, et al: Stress ulcer prophylaxis in critically ill patients: Resolving discordant meta-analyses [see comment]. JAMA 1996;275:308-314.
31. Cooper S, Abrams RS, Carbaugh RA: Pyloric duplications: Review and case study. Am Surg 1995;61:1092-1094.
32. Cunniff C, Williamson-Kruse L, Olney A: Congenital microgastria and limb reduction defects. Pediatrics 1993;91: 1192-1194.
33. Dank JP, Kim S, Parisi MA, et al: Outcome after surgical repair of junctional epidermolysis bullosa-pyloric atresia syndrome: A report of 3 cases and review of the literature. Arch Dermatol 1999;135:1243-1247.
34. Das BK, Kakkar S, Dixit VK, et al: *Helicobacter pylori* infection and recurrent abdominal pain in children. J Trop Pediatr 2003;49:250-252.
35. Deckelbaum RJ, Roy CC, Lussier-Lazaroff J, et al: Peptic ulcer disease: A clinical study in 73 children. Can Med Assoc J 1974;111:225-228.
36. Dessanti A, Iannuccelli M, Dore A, et al: Pyloric atresia: An attempt at anatomic pyloric sphincter reconstruction. J Pediatr Surg 2000;35:1372-1374.
37. Drake DP, Maciver AG, Atwell JD: Zollinger-Ellison syndrome in a child: Medical treatment with cimetidine. Arch Dis Child 1980;55:226-228.
38. Drumm B, Perez-Perez GI, Blaser MJ, et al: Intrafamilial clustering of *Helicobacter pylori* infection. N Engl J Med 1990;322:359-363.
39. Drumm B, Sherman P, Cutz E, et al: Association of *Campylobacter pylori* on the gastric mucosa with antral gastritis in children. N Engl J Med 1987;316:1557-1561.

40. Ducharme JC, Bensoussan AL: Pyloric atresia. J Pediatr Surg 1975;10:149-150.
41. Ein SH, Marshall DG, Girvan D: Peritoneal drainage under local anesthesia for perforations from necrotizing enterocolitis. J Pediatr Surg 1977;12:963-967.
42. Elsner R, Franklin DL, Van Citters RL, et al: Cardiovascular defense against asphyxia. Science 1966;153:941-949.
43. Figura N: Identifiable *Helicobacter pylori* strains or factors important in the development of duodenal ulcer disease. Helicobacter 1997;2(1).
44. Fliegel CP, Herzog B, Signer E, et al: Bleeding gastric ulcer in a newborn infant diagnosed by transumbilical aortography. J Pediatr Surg 1977;12:560-589.
45. Gahukamble DB: Familial occurrence of congenital incomplete prepyloric mucosal diaphragm. J Med Genet 1998; 35:1040-1042.
46. Garland J, Nelson D, Rice T, et al: Increased risk of gastrointestinal perforations in neonates mechanically ventilated with either face mask or nasal prongs. Pediatrics 1985;76:406-410.
47. Gauderer MW: Percutaneous endoscopic gastrostomy—20 years later: A historical perspective. J Pediatr Surg 2001; 36:217-219.
48. Gennari R, Alexander JW, Gianotti L, et al: Granulocyte-macrophage colony-stimulating factor improves survival in two models of gut-derived sepsis by improving gut barrier function and modulating bacterial clearance. Ann Surg 1994;220:68-76.
49. Gerbeaux J, Couvreur J, Vialas M, et al: Congenital absence of the stomach. Ann Pediatr 1971;18:349-356.
50. Ghai O: An assessment of gastric acid secretory response with "maximal" augmented histamine stimulation in children with peptic ulcer. Arch Dis Child 1965;40:77.
51. Goodman KJ, Correa P: The transmission of *Helicobacter pylori:* A critical review of the evidence. Int J Epidemiol 1995;24:875-887.
52. Granquist A, Bredberg A, Sveger T, et al: A longitudinal cohort study on the prevalence of *Helicobacter pylori* antibodies in Swedish children and adolescents. Acta Paediatr 2002;91:636-640.
53. Gray PH, Pemberton PJ: Gastric perforation associated with indomethacin therapy in a pre-term infant. Aust Pediatr J 1980;16:65-66.
54. Gregory JR, Campbell JR, Harrison MW, et al: Neonatal necrotizing enterocolitis: A 10 year experience. Am J Surg 1981;141:562-567.
55. Gremse DA, Shakoor S: Symptoms of acid-peptic disease in children. South Med J 1993;86:997-1000.
56. Grosfeld JL, Molinari F, Chaet M, et al: Gastrointestinal perforation and peritonitis in infants and children: Experience with 179 cases over ten years. Surgery 1996;120:650-655; discussion 655-656.
57. Grosfeld JL, Shipley F, Fitzgerald JF, et al: Acute peptic ulcer in infancy and childhood. Am Surg 1978;44:13-19.
58. Habbick BF, Melrose AG, Grant JC: Duodenal ulcer in childhood: A study of predisposing factors. Arch Dis Child 1968;43:23-27.
59. Haller JA Jr, Cahill JL: Combined congenital gastric and duodenal obstruction: Pitfalls in diagnosis and treatment. Surgery 1968;63:503-506.
60. Hamada Y, Inoue K, Hioki K: Pyloroduodenal duplication cyst: Case report. Pediatr Surg Int 1997;12:194-195.
61. Harada T, Hyman PE, Everett S, et al: Meal-stimulated gastric acid secretion in infants. J Pediatr 1984;104:534-538.
62. Harmon JW, Jordan PH Jr: Verdict on vagotomy. Gastroenterology 1981;81:809-810.
63. Harris PR, Godoy A, Arenillas S, et al: CagA antibodies as a marker of virulence in Chilean patients with *Helicobacter pylori* infection. J Pediatr Gastroenterol Nutr 2003;37:596-602.
64. Harrison MW, Connell RS, Campbell JR, et al: Microcirculatory changes in the gastrointestinal tract of the hypoxic puppy: An electron microscope study. J Pediatr Surg 1975;10:599-608.
65. Harrison MW, Connell RS, Campbell JR, et al: Fine structural changes in the gastro-intestinal tract of the hypoxic puppy: A study of natural history. J Pediatr Surg 1977;12:403-408.
66. Herman TE, Siegel MJ: Imaging casebook: Asplenia syndrome with congenital microgastria and malrotation. J Perinatal 2004;24:50-52.
67. Hochberger O, Swoboda W: Congenital microgastria: A follow-up observation over six years. Pediatr Radiol 1974; 2:207-208.
68. Hopkins GB, Gould VE, Stevenson JK, et al: Necrotizing enterocolitis in premature infants: A clinical and pathologic evaluation of autopsy material. Am J Dis Child 1970;120: 229-232.
69. Hussell T, Isaacson PG, Crabtree JE, et al: The response of cells from low-grade B-cell gastric lymphomas of mucosa-associated lymphoid tissue to *Helicobacter pylori.* Lancet 1993;342:571-574.
70. Idjadi F, Robbins R, Stahl WM, et al: Prospective study of gastric secretion in stressed patients with intracranial injury. J Trauma Inj Infect Crit Care 1971;11:681-688.
71. Jackson RH: Genetic factors in the development of duodenal ulcer in childhood. Gut 1971;12:856-857.
72. Johnson D, L'Heureux P, Thompson T: Peptic ulcer disease in early infancy: Clinical presentation and roentgenographic features. Acta Pediatr Scand 1980;69:753-760.
73. Johnston PW, Snyder WH: Survey of vagotomy and pyloroplasty in infants and children. Am J Surg 1970;120:173-181.
74. Kato S, Ebina K, Fujii K, et al: Effect of omeprazole in the treatment of refractory acid-related diseases in childhood: Endoscopic healing and twenty-four-hour intragastric acidity. J Pediatr 1996;128:415-421.
75. Kato S, Ozawa K, Okuda M, et al: Accuracy of the stool antigen test for the diagnosis of childhood *Helicobacter pylori* infection: A multicenter Japanese study. Am J Gastroenterol 2003;98:296-300.
76. Kato S, Takeyama J, Ebina K, et al: Omeprazole-based dual and triple regimens for *Helicobacter pylori* eradication in children. Pediatrics 1977;100:e3.
77. Kawashima H, Iwanaka T, Matsumoto M, et al: Pyloric stenosis caused by noncystic duodenal duplication and ectopic pancreas in a neonate. J Pediatr Gastroenterol Nutr 1998;27:228-229.
78. Keramidas DC, Voyatzis N: Pyloric atresia: Report of a second occurrence in the same family. J Pediatr Surg 1972; 7:445-446.
79. Keramidas DC, Voyatzis N: Duodenal ulcer associated with incomplete duodenal diaphragm. J Pediatr Surg 1975;10: 837-838.
80. Kessler H, Smulewicz JJ: Microgastria associated with agenesis of the spleen. Radiology 1973;107:393-396.
81. Konvolinka CW, Steward RE Jr: Pyloric atresia. Am J Dis Child 1978;132:903-905.
82. Kosloske AM: Necrotizing enterocolitis in the neonate. Surg Gynecol Obstet 1979;148:259-269.
83. Kumar D, Spitz L: Peptic ulceration in children. Surg Gynecol Obstet 1984;159:63-66.
84. Lerner AG, Meng CH, Schneider KM: Selective intra-arterial vasopressin in the management of stress ulcers in childhood. Pediatrics 1973;51:126-128.
85. Linkner L, Benson C: Spontaneous perforation of the stomach in the newborn. Ann Surg 1959;149:525.
86. Lloyd J, Espiasse E, Bernstein J: Etiology of gastrointestinal perforations in the newborn. Harper Hosp Bull 1964;22:224.
87. Lloyd JR: The etiology of gastrointestinal perforations in the newborn. J Pediatr Surg 1969;4:77-84.

88. Lucas CE, Sugawa C, Riddle J, et al: Natural history and surgical dilemma of "stress" gastric bleeding. Arch Surg 1971;102:266-273.
89. Magnusson B, Hallberg L, Arvidsson B: Iron absorption from food and from ferrous ascorbate: A study in normal subjects, patients with peptic ulcer and patients after partial gastrectomy. Scand J Hematol 1976;26:69-85.
90. Malaty HM, Kim JG, Kim SD, et al: Prevalence of *Helicobacter pylori* infection in Korean children: Inverse relation to socioeconomic status despite a uniformly high prevalence in adults. Am J Epidemiol 1996;143:257-262.
91. Marshall BJ, Warren JR: Unidentified curved bacilli in the stomach of patients with gastritis and peptic ulceration. Lancet 1984;1:1311-1315.
92. Maton PN: Zollinger-Ellison syndrome. Recognition and management of acid hypersecretion. Drugs 1996;52:33-44.
93. Maxson RT, Jackson RJ, Smith SD: The protective role of enteral IgA supplementation in neonatal gut origin sepsis. J Pediatr Surg 1995;30:231-233; discussion 233.
94. McIntyre RC Jr, Bensard DD, Karrer FM, et al: The pediatric diaphragm in acute gastric volvulus. J Am Coll Surg 1994;178:234-238.
95. Menguy R: Role of gastric mucosal energy metabolism in the etiology of stress ulceration. World J Surg 1981; 5:175-180.
96. Menon P, Rao KL, Cutinha HP, et al: Gastric augmentation in isolated congenital microgastria. J Pediatr Surg 2003; 38:E4-E6.
97. Mezoff AG, Balistreri WF: Peptic ulcer disease in children. Pediatr Rev 1995;16:257-265.
98. Miller TA, Jacobson ED: Gastrointestinal cytoprotection by prostaglandins. Gut 1979;20:75-87.
99. Miserez M, Barten S, Geboes K, et al: Surgical therapy and histological abnormalities in functional isolated small bowel obstruction and idiopathic gastrointestinal perforation in the very low birth weight infant. World J Surg 2003;27: 350-355.
100. Mobley HL: The role of *Helicobacter pylori* urease in the pathogenesis of gastritis and peptic ulceration. Aliment Pharmacol Ther 1996;1:57-64.
101. Moody FG, Cheung LY: Stress ulcers: Their pathogenesis, diagnosis, and treatment. Surg Clin North Am 1976;56: 1469-1478.
102. Moody FG, Zalewsky CA, Larsen KR: Cytoprotection of the gastric epithelium. World J Surg 1981;5:153-163.
103. Morden RS, Schullinger JN, Mollitt DL, et al: Operative management of stress ulcers in children. Ann Surg 1982; 196:18-20.
104. Morgan DB, Hunt G, Paterson CR: The osteomalacia syndrome after stomach operations. Q J Med 1970;39:395-410.
105. Moulton SL, Bouvet M, Lynch FP: Congenital microgastria in a premature infant. J Pediatr Surg 1994;29:1594-1595.
106. Mulberg AE, Linz C, Bern E, et al: Identification of nonsteroidal antiinflammatory drug-induced gastroduodenal injury in children with juvenile rheumatoid arthritis. J Pediatr 1993;122:647-649.
107. Murphy MS, Eastham EJ: Peptic ulcer disease in childhood: Long-term prognosis. J Pediatr Gastroenterol Nutr 1987; 6:721-724.
108. Murphy MS, Eastham EJ, Jimenez M, et al: Duodenal ulceration: Review of 110 cases. Arch Dis Child 1987;62: 554-558.
109. Murray KF, Lillehei CW, Duggan C: Congenital microgastria: Treatment with transient jejunal feedings. J Pediatr Gastroenterol Nutr 1999;28:343-345.
110. Mutabagani KH, Teich S, Long FR: Primary intrathoracic gastric volvulus in a newborn. J Pediatr Surg 1999;34: 1869-1871.
111. Nagaraj HS, Sandhu AS, Cook LN, et al: Gastrointestinal perforation following indomethacin therapy in very low birth weight infants. J Pediatr Surg 1981;16:1003-1007.
112. Nagita A, Amemoto K, Yoden A, et al: Diurnal variation in intragastric pH in children with and without peptic ulcers. Pediatr Res 1996;40:528-532.
113. Neifeld JP, Berman WF, Lawrence W, et al: Management of congenital microgastria with a jejunal reservoir pouch. J Pediatr Surg 1980;15:882-885.
114. Newton M, Bryan R, Burnham WR, et al: Evaluation of *Helicobacter pylori* in reflux oesophagitis and Barrett's oesophagus. Gut 1997;40:9-13.
115. Nord KS, Lebenthal E: Peptic ulcer in children: A review. Am J Gastroenterol 1980;73:75-80.
116. Norton L, Greer J, Eiseman B: Gastric secretory response to head injury. Arch Surg 1970;101:200-204.
117. Olsen L, Grotte G: Congenital pyloric atresia: Report of a familial occurrence. J Pediatr Surg 1976;11:181-184.
118. O'Neill JA Jr, Pruitt BA Jr, Moncrief JA: Surgical treatment of Curling's ulcer. Surg Gynecol Obstet 1968;126: 40-44.
119. Orsini B, Ciancio G, Censini S, et al: *Helicobacter pylori* cag pathogenicity island is associated with enhanced interleukin-8 expression in human gastric mucosa. Dig Liver Dis 2000;32:458-467.
120. Othersen HB Jr, Garcia R, Doering EJ: The effect of gastric resections and denervation upon growth in miniature swine. J Pediatr Surg 1973;8:159-163.
121. Parsonnet J: The incidence of *Helicobacter pylori* infection. Aliment Pharmacol Ther 1995;2:45-51.
122. Parsonnet J: *Helicobacter pylori* in the stomach—a paradox unmasked [see comment]. N Engl J Med 1996;335: 278-280.
123. Peltier FA, Tschen EH, Raimer SS, et al: Epidermolysis bullosa letalis associated with congenital pyloric atresia. Arch Dermatol 1981;117:728-731.
124. Polacek MA, Ellison EH: Gastric acid secretion and parietal cell mass in the stomach of a newborn infant. Am J Surg 1966;111:777-781.
125. Puri P, Boyd E, Blake N, et al: Duodenal ulcer in childhood: A continuing disease in adult life. J Pediatr Surg 1978;13:525-526.
126. Puvabanditsin S, Garrow E, Kim DU, et al: Junctional epidermolysis bullosa associated with congenital localized absence of skin, and pyloric atresia in two newborn siblings. J Am Acad Dermatol 2001;44(2 Suppl):330-335.
127. Qiao W, Hu JL, Xiao B, et al: cagA and vacA genotype of *Helicobacter pylori* associated with gastric diseases in Xi'an area. World J Gastroenterol 2003;9:1762-1766.
128. Ravitch MM, Duremides GD: Operative treatment of chronic duodenal ulcer in childhood. Ann Surg 1970;171: 641-646.
129. Robb JD, Thomas PS, Orszulok J, et al: Duodenal ulcer in children. Arch Dis Child 1972;47:688-696.
130. Robert A, Nezamis JE, Lancaster C, et al: Mild irritants prevent gastric necrosis through "adaptive cytoprotection" mediated by prostaglandins. Am J Physiol 1983;245: G113-G121.
131. Rosenlund ML: The Zollinger-Ellison syndrome in children: A review. Am J Med Sci 1967;254:884-892.
132. Rothenbacher D, Winkler M, Gonser T, et al: Role of infected parents in transmission of *Helicobacter pylori* to their children. Pediatr Infect Dis J 2002;21:674-679.
133. Sasaki H, Sasano H, Ohi R, et al: Adenocarcinoma at the esophageal gastric junction arising in an 11-year-old girl. Pathol Int 1999;49:1109-1113.
134. Saw EC, Arbegast NR, Comer TP: Pyloric atresia: A case report. Pediatrics 1973;51:574-577.

135. Scherer L, Haller J: Gastrostomy in infants and children: Gastric volvulus. In Scott HW, Sawyers JL (eds): Surgery of the Stomach, Duodenum, and Small Intestine. Boston, Blackwell Scientific, 1992.
136. Schulz RD, Niemann F: Congenital microgastria occurring in combination with skeletal malformations: New syndrome. Helv Pediatr Acta 1971;26:185-191.
137. Seagram CG, Stephens CA, Cumming WA: Peptic ulceration at the Hospital for Sick Children, Toronto, during the 20-year period 1949-1969. J Pediatr Surg 1973; 8:407-413.
138. Shackelford GD, McAlister WH, Brodeur AE, et al: Congenital microgastria. Am J Roentgenol Rad Ther Nucl Med 1973;118:72-76.
139. Shah A, Shah AV: Laparoscopic gastropexy in a neonate for acute gastric volvulus. Pediatr Surg Int 2003;19: 217-219.
140. Sharma KK, Agrawal P, Toshniwal H: Acquired gastric outlet obstruction during infancy and childhood: A report of five unusual cases. J Pediatr Surg 1997;32:928-930.
141. Sherman P, Czinn S, Drumm B, et al: *Helicobacter pylori* infection in children and adolescents: Working Group Report of the First World Congress of Pediatric Gastroenterology, Hepatology, and Nutrition. J Pediatr Gastroenterol Nutr 2002;35(Suppl 2):S128-S133.
142. Sherman PM: Peptic ulcer disease in children. Diagnosis, treatment, and the implication of Helicobacter pylori. Gastroenterol Clin North Am 1994;23:707-725.
143. Shimizu T, Haruna H, Ohtsuka Y, et al: Cytokines in the gastric mucosa of children with Helicobacter pylori infection. Acta Paediatr 2004;93:322-326.
144. Shimizu T, Yamashiro Y, Yabuta K: Impaired increase of prostaglandin E_2 in gastric juice during steroid therapy in children. J Pediatr Child Health 1994;30:169-172.
145. Shorter N, Liu J, Mooney D, et al: Indomethacin-associated bowel perforations: A study of possible risk factors. J Pediatr Surg 1999;34:442-444.
146. Skandalakis JE, Gray SW (eds): Embryology for Surgeons. Baltimore, Williams & Wilkins. 1994.
147. Skillman JJ, Silen W: Stress ulcers. Lancet 1972;2:1303-1306.
148. Stannard MW, Currarino G, Splawski JB: Congenital double pylorus with accessory pyloric channel communicating with an intraluminal duplication cyst of the duodenum. Pediatr Radiol 1993;23:48-50.
149. Stiefel D, Willi UV, Sacher P, et al: Pitfalls in therapy of upside-down stomach. Eur J Pediatr Surg 2000;10: 162-166.
150. Tan KL, Murugasu JJ: Congenital pyloric atresia in siblings. Arch Surg 1973;106:100-102.
151. Tanaka K, Tsuchida Y, Hashizume K, et al: Microgastria: Case report and a review of the literature. Eur J Pediatr Surg 1993;3:290-292.
152. Tanner NC: Chronic and recurrent volvulus of the stomach with late results of "colonic displacement." Am J Surg 1968;115:505-515.
153. Tedesco FJ, Goldstein PD, Gleason WA, et al: Upper gastrointestinal endoscopy in the pediatric patient. Gastroenterology 1976;70:492-494.
154. Ternberg JL, Koehler PR: The use of arteriography in the diagnosis of the origin of acute gastrointestinal hemorrhage in children. Surgery 1968;63:686-689.
155. Touloukian RJ: Gastric ischemia: The primary factor in neonatal perforation. Clin Pediatr 1973;12:219-225.
156. Touloukian RJ, Posch JN, Spencer R: The pathogenesis of ischemic gastroenterocolitis of the neonate: Selective gut mucosal ischemia in asphyxiated neonatal piglets. J Pediatr Surg 1972;7:194-205.
157. Tsuchida Y, Makino S, Ishida M: A follow-up study of subtotal gastrectomy in infancy and early childhood. J Pediatr Surg 1974;9:499-500.
158. Tunell WP, Smith EI: Antral web in infancy. J Pediatr Surg 1980;15:152-155.
159. Veldhuyzen van Zanten SJ, Sherman PM: Indications for treatment of *Helicobacter pylori* infection: A systematic overview. Can Med Assoc J 1994;150:189-198.
160. Weissman A, Achiron R, Kuint J, et al: Prenatal diagnosis of congenital gastric outlet obstruction. Prenat Diag 1994; 14:888-891.
161. Whitney AE, Emory TS, Marty AM, et al: Increased macrophage infiltration of gastric mucosa in *Helicobacter pylori*-infected children. Dig Dis Sci 2000;45:1337-1342.
162. Williams JW, Pannell WP, Sherman RT: Curling's ulcer in children. J Trauma Inf Infect Crit Care 1976;16:639-644.
163. Wilson SD: The role of surgery in children with the Zollinger-Ellison syndrome. Surgery 1982;92:682-692.
164. Wyllie R, Kay MH: Therapeutic intervention for nonvariceal gastrointestinal hemorrhage. J Pediatr Gastroenterol Nutr 1996;22:123-133.

Chapter 78

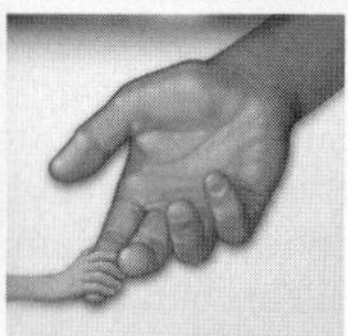

Bariatric Surgery in Adolescents

Victor F. Garcia and Thomas Inge

The increasing prevalence of childhood obesity both in the United States and worldwide constitutes a public health crisis of prodigious proportions.[82,89,222,239] Obesity is a progressive, chronic, and often fatal disease, refractory to currently available medical interventions. It accounts for 400,000 deaths each year and is second only to smoking as a preventable cause of premature death in the United States.[182] Recent analyses suggest that obesity-related decreases in life expectancy predominantly affect age groups younger than previously thought, especially in young black males.[101] In the United States, children are the fastest growing segment of the obese population.[133] Only relatively recently has childhood obesity been widely recognized as more than a social stigma and as having serious immediate and long-term health consequences.[70,268] Childhood and adolescent obesity are independent risk factors for adult morbidity and premature mortality.[106,119] Additionally, obesity is now considered the most pressing nutritional disorder among children and adolescents.[95,161,217] In its extreme, obesity is refractory to even the most intensive conventional approaches to weight loss.[87]

Bariatric surgery currently is the most effective means to achieve durable weight loss and amelioration, if not resolution, of most obesity-related comorbidities in severely obese individuals. It also decreases the long-term mortality of morbidly obese patients.[54,100] The morbidity is between 5% and 11%. The mortality is estimated to be between 0.05% and 0.5%.[49] Experienced centers have shown that weight loss after bariatric surgery is sustained.[136,189,192,204,247] Among adults, the nutritional consequences of the most common bariatric surgical procedures are well defined and effectively managed with supplementation. Among adolescents, however, it is unknown whether the outcome will be the same as in adults or whether there will be unacceptably high degrees of recidivism and long-term nutritional sequelae related to poor compliance or multigenerational ramifications of reduced micronutrient absorption.[209,248] Nonetheless, for the extremely obese adolescent there are no effective nonsurgical treatments. As the number of severely obese children increases and the serious health consequences escalate, surgical weight loss is gaining currency as the only effective means to treat severely obese adolescents.

In this chapter, we provide a conceptual framework and clinical guidelines for adolescent bariatric surgery. The approach borrows heavily from the most successful adult bariatric surgical programs as well as from the "best practices" in treating adolescents with other chronic diseases, such as cystic fibrosis, asthma, and cancer.[131,199,211,215,253]

The basic premise is that the unique physiologic, cognitive, developmental, and psychosocial needs of the adolescent are best managed with a family-centered approach, incorporating behavior modification techniques that have been successful in other chronic models. Given the technical difficulty of bariatric surgery, the complexity of the postoperative management of the patient undergoing bariatric surgery, and the uncertainty about its long-term outcomes in adolescents, regionalization of care with a focus on prospective clinical data collection will be essential to achieving outcomes commensurate with the best adult series. Furthermore, it will accelerate our understanding of the short- and long-term consequences of bariatric surgery among adolescents.

HISTORY OF BARIATRIC SURGERY IN ADOLESCENTS

The earliest report of pediatric bariatric surgery was Randolph and Weintraub's experience with jejunal ileal bypass.[206] Their reported outcomes were similar to those in adults. More specifically, the weight loss was dramatic and sustained and the improvements in quality of life were viewed as excellent. However, the metabolic complications were significant[231] and considered unacceptable by today's standards. Greenstein and Rabner[126] reported a largely favorable experience with vertically banded gastroplasty, concluding that adolescents given extensive dietary counseling can experience the same benefits as adults undergoing a purely restrictive gastric operation. The subsequent reports of bariatric surgery in pediatrics have consisted of small case series of adolescents largely undergoing open and, more recently, laparoscopic Roux-en-Y gastric bypass (RYGBP)[1,10,45,142,205,234,238,243,248] or laparoscopic adjustable gastric band (LAGB).[1,77] The reported outcomes have been good to excellent, with few complications and no procedure-related mortality. As with pediatric laparoscopic cholecystectomy, minimally invasive repair of pectus excavatum, and laparoscopic anti-reflux procedures, bariatric operations among adolescents have not been studied in a prospective and controlled fashion. None of the adolescents who have undergone adjustable gastric banding has been followed for more than 4 years. In a short-term study of adolescents undergoing adjustable gastric banding, median excess weight loss was reportedly 35 kg at 2 years. The band was judged to be safe and effective in this short-term study.[77] The report with the largest and longest follow-up is that of Sugerman and associates,[248] who reported 33 adolescents (mean preoperative body mass index (BMI [weight in kilograms/stature in meters squared] = 52 kg/m^2) who underwent bariatric procedures, primarily gastric bypass. This group had an excess weight loss of 63% (mean BMI = 33 kg/m^2) at 5 years and 56% (mean BMI = 34 kg/m^2) at 10 years after operation. Only 6 of 9 patients who were 14 years after operation could be found. These 6 had maintained 33% of their excess weight loss (mean BMI = 38 kg/m^2)[248]; 15% of the cohort had regained most or all of their overweight, suggesting that recidivism may be just as likely in adolescents as in adults. These data beg several questions—whether adolescents require alternate selection criteria or different postoperative management strategies than adults and whether the long-term nutritional and metabolic outcomes of adolescents will be better or worse than similarly obese adolescents who have undergone bariatric surgery in youth.

In 2001, Garcia and Inge established the first children's hospital–based bariatric surgery program at Cincinnati Children's Hospital Medical Center.[114,142] The bariatric surgery program was integrated into an existing behaviorally based weight management program for children and adolescents. This comprehensive weight management program offers bariatric services to adolescents with intractable clinically severe obesity. Candidates for bariatric surgery are evaluated and subsequently followed by two pediatric bariatric surgeons, a pediatric cardiologist with special expertise in pediatric obesity, advanced practice nurses, dietitians, psychologists, and an exercise physiologist.

THE SCIENCE OF OBESITY

Obesity research is one of most exciting areas of scientific investigation at the nexus of physiology, genetics, neurobiology, endocrinology, molecular biology, and gastrointestinal surgery. In recent years, there has been considerable progress in our understanding of some causes of obesity and the scientific basis for its intractability. Seminal observations have been made regarding the neuroanatomic basis of feeding behavior,[127,145,223] the molecular mechanisms that regulate food intake and energy consumption,[108,109] the genes that influence energy balance,[56,121,228] and the inflammatory component of excess adipose tissue.[272] The delineation of the complex interplay of these systems with environmental, developmental, emotional, and psychological factors incontrovertibly dispels the simplistic notion that "deciding" to eat less and exercise more can control weight. It also provides a basis for the association of obesity with a spectrum of metabolic disorders such as insulin resistance syndrome, polycystic ovary syndrome, and cardiovascular disease.[109] In brief, substantial scientific evidence points to a precise and powerful biologic system that maintains body weight within a narrow range,[109,221] suggesting that severe obesity is not a personal choice but a chronic and highly intractable disease with a continuum of risk.

Energy Expenditure

Living organisms obey the first law of thermodynamics. Therefore, if the amount of energy in is not equivalent to the amount of energy out, weight gain will occur. Over long periods of excess intake, energy is stored in the body as triglyceride. In general, however, body weight remains relatively stable, attesting to the role of subconscious neural systems in modulating fluctuations in energy intake and expenditure to maintain balance. Several studies suggest that the highly heritable regulation of energy expenditure has a significant influence on body weight. Weight loss by a severely obese person is met with a genetically mediated compensatory decrease in energy expenditure, metabolic activity, and an increase in appetite to resist weight change.[157] An adolescent who reduces body weight from 300 to 250 pounds must consume far fewer daily calories to maintain the new reduced weight, as compared with someone with a weight that is stable at 250 pounds. Consequently it is exceedingly difficult for those who lose weight to maintain weight loss.

Genetics

Genes regulate body weight by balancing caloric intake and energy expenditure. Familial aggregation and twin studies have demonstrated that genes contribute to the development of obesity with a heritability index of 0.7 to 0.8, a degree of heritability equivalent to that of height.[6,214] Only about 5% of childhood morbid obesity is a result of a single gene defect, usually in an isoform of the melanocortin receptor, the receptor for α-melanocyte-stimulating hormone.[180] In the remainder of the population, obesity is the result of many genes interacting with environmental factors. There is evidence that genes and metabolic processes that predispose to obesity offered our ancestors a survival advantage in times when food was scarce.[99,151] This may explain the highly variable frequency of obesity in different populations (African Americans, Native Americans, and Hispanics) that once lived under adverse conditions.

Obesity-Induced Inflammation

Obesity and the associated metabolic pathologies are associated with a chronic inflammatory response characterized by abnormal cytokine production, increased acute-phase reactants, and activation of inflammatory signal pathways.[156,265] Overweight and obese children and adults have elevated serum levels of C-reactive protein, interleukin-6, tumor necrosis factor-α, and leptin, all of which are known markers of inflammation and are closely associated with both cardiovascular risk factors and cardiovascular and noncardiovascular causes of death. This may explain the increased risk of diabetes, heart disease, and many other chronic diseases in the obese. It is postulated that the inflammation associated with obesity is causally linked to diseases such as type 2 diabetes, polycystic ovary syndrome, nonalcoholic steatohepatitis, and cardiovascular disease.[31,47,65,137] As obesity develops, an inflammatory response associated with obesity appears to be triggered and predominantly reside in adipose tissue.[137]

The cellular source of these inflammatory changes may be not only adipocytes but also macrophages and perhaps adipocyte precursors. Macrophage infiltration of adipose tissue is characteristic of human obesity.[263,265] Both BMI and average adipocyte size are significant predictors of macrophage accumulation in adipose tissue.[263] Gene expression analysis has shown that fat-infiltrating macrophages are an important source of inflammation in adipose tissue.[272] Adipocytes are also cytokine producers and can activate the complement cascade.[139] Studies over the past decade strongly suggest that inflammatory pathways are critical in the development of insulin resistance and type 2 diabetes mellitus.[137] It is unclear how the inflammatory response is triggered and maintained in obesity and how this results in metabolic disorders.[265] Further elucidation of the relationship between inflammation and metabolic outcomes may lead to valuable mechanistic insights and therapeutic developments. In the interim, surgical weight loss remains the most effective means to ameliorate metabolic consequences of severe obesity.[5,75,76,148,191,192,204]

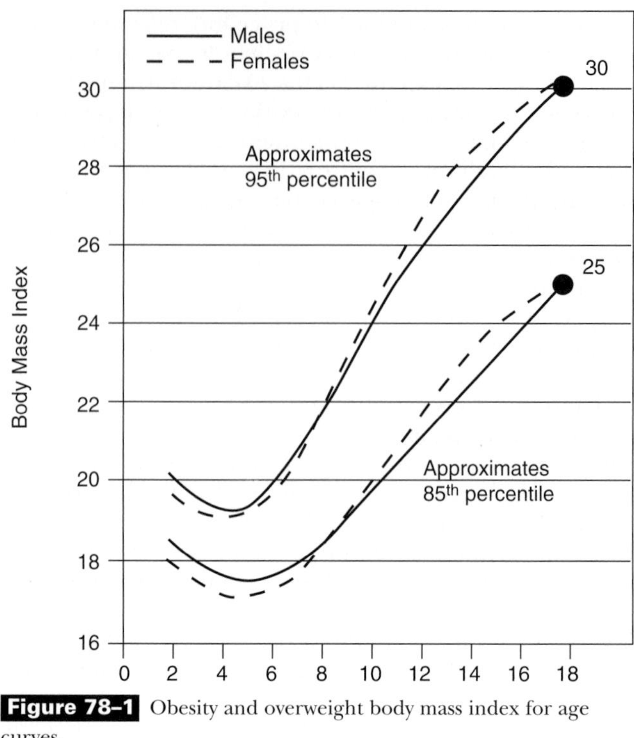

Figure 78–1 Obesity and overweight body mass index for age curves.

DEFINITIONS

Ideally, health-oriented definitions of overweight and obesity should be based on the amount of excess body fat at which health risks increase. The health risks associated with overweight and obesity are part of a continuum and at a given level of adiposity may vary depending on the specific population observed.[141] Indeed, health risks of obesity are different among races. Therefore, it is exceedingly difficult to define precisely what level of adiposity corresponds to an elevated health risk for a particular individual.

Nonetheless, in adults, the level of obesity at which the risk of morbidity increases is determined on an actuarial basis based on BMI.[44,257] BMI is a widely accepted weight for height index that correlates with fat burden. Most clinical and epidemiologic studies examining obesity rely on BMI as an indication of fatness, although it is far from an ideal measure of adiposity. For instance, it is widely recognized that many athletes are over an ideal weight and have elevated BMI. However, they are not obese, because their overweight is due to elevated lean mass. The adult cutoff points most widely used are a BMI of 25 kg/m^2 for overweight and a BMI of 30 kg/m^2 for obesity. Definitions of adult obesity are generally not used for children and adolescents who have not yet completed linear growth, because physiologic changes in fat mass are expected during growth and maturation.[97] For example, at birth the median BMI may be 13 kg/m^2, and BMI increases to 17 kg/m^2 at age 1, decreases to 15 kg/m^2 at age 6, then increases to 21 kg/m^2 at age 20. Of the various methods used to measure excess adiposity in children, BMI is acceptable if one uses percentiles for age and gender to account for the normal changes in BMI occurring with growth and maturation. The 85th and 95th percentiles of BMI for age have been used to define overweight and obesity (Fig. 78-1).[16,17,73]

The 95th percentile definition of obesity in pediatrics is a statistical designation, not a health risk–based definition.[141] It is possible that health risks of obesity are more directly related to central adiposity than to BMI. The fact that some fat depots (e.g., intra-abdominal) are considered more risky than others (e.g., subcutaneous), and the fact that BMI does not convey information about regional fat distribution, is another limitation inherent in using a BMI-based definition of obesity.

ADOLESCENT OBESITY

Epidemiology

Obesity is the most prevalent and serious nutritional disorder in the United States. Nearly 60% of adults are either overweight or obese. Over the past 14 years, the prevalence of adult obesity (BMI > 30 kg/m^2) has increased only 2-fold, whereas the prevalence of BMI greater than 40 kg/m^2 has increased 4-fold, and prevalence of BMI greater than 50 kg/m^2 has increased 5-fold.[245] Over the past 2 decades, there has also been an increase in the prevalence of overweight and obesity in children in the United States.[194] The proportion of children and adolescents who are obese has tripled in the past 3 decades.[193,194] Children are thus the fastest growing segment of the overweight and obese population in this country.[98] This dramatic increase in childhood obesity is also being observed in other countries.[78,110,115,153,169,174,274] Similar to the adult trend, the relative increase in the prevalence of children with extreme obesity is also greater than the increase in children with lesser degrees of obesity.[73]

There are significant ethnic and racial disparities in the prevalence of obesity among boys and girls. Among boys, the highest percentages of overweight occurred among Mexican Americans. Among girls, the highest percentage of overweight occurred among non-Hispanic blacks, followed by Mexican Americans. The lowest percentage of overweight occurred among non-Hispanic white girls.[80,123,244] The prevalence of overweight (= 85th percentile) was about one third higher in black girls than in white girls: 31% versus 22%.[150] The prevalence of obesity (= 95th percentile) in black girls was twice as high as in white girls: 18% versus 8%. An alarming finding in this study was the approximate doubling of the rate of overweight and obesity. By 19 years of age, overweight was present in more than half of black and a third of white girls and more than a third of black girls were obese as compared with one fifth of white girls.[150] The increased susceptibility to obesity among blacks may be related to racial differences in energy balance, because African Americans have lower resting energy expenditure than do whites.[113,152]

Risk Factors

The risk of obesity accumulates with age and is influenced by genetic, biologic, psychological, sociocultural, and environmental factors acting throughout our life span. Recent insights into the fetal, neonatal, and developmental origins of obesity[195] have implications for clinical evaluation of the adolescent candidate for bariatric surgery. There are critical phases in the development of adolescent obesity within the period between preconception and adolescence.[18,22,103,154,179,259] There is epidemiologic evidence linking birth weight and later BMI[198] in childhood[21] and adulthood.[235] Lower birth weight elevates the risk for central obesity[21,43] and insulin resistance.[43] The mechanism for this association is unknown but may be related to the "thrifty genotype or phenotype."[195] Childhood obesity risks are higher for offspring of mothers with diabetes mellitus.[232] Postnatally, longer duration of breast-feeding[117,118] and later onset of adiposity rebound[267] reduce the risk of adolescent overweight. Of all the aforementioned risk factors, low birth weight and high BMI of the adolescent confer the highest risk of chronic obesity.

Obesity in family members is an additional risk factor for adolescent obesity. The odds ratio for persistence of childhood obesity into adulthood is about 3 if one parent or 10 if two parents are obese.[268] This effect is most pronounced in children younger than 10 years. Puberty also is a critical period for the development of obesity.[132] Earlier menarche is seen in obese children. A BMI greater than the 85th percentile is associated with a 2-fold increase in rate of early menarche.[164,262] The risk of obesity persisting into adulthood is far higher among obese adolescents than among overweight younger children.[266,268] Finally, there is a preexisting racial-ethnic disparity in the risk of obesity.[244] Lower socioeconomic groups may be especially vulnerable because of poor diet and limited opportunity for physical activity.[123]

Health Consequences

Adolescent obesity has important health consequences as outlined in Table 78-1. Associated with the rise in the prevalence and severity of pediatric obesity in the United States, there has been an emergence of new or newly identifiable health conditions in children,[71] with onset at a younger age[185,186] and an increased risk for

TABLE 78-1 Health Consequences of Adolescent Obesity

Psychosocial
Poor self-esteem[107,243]
Depression[71,120]
Eating disorders[3,42]
Neurologic
Pseudotumor cerebri[14,55]
Pulmonary
Sleep apnea[8,34,160,270]
Asthma and exercise intolerance[128,259]
Cardiovascular
Dyslipidemia[10,152,257-260]
Hypertension[19,20,24-26,41,188,237]
Coagulopathy
Chronic inflammation[64]
Endothelial dysfunction[5,111,138,255]
Gastrointestinal
Gallstones
Steatohepatitis[183,197,219-221]
Renal
Glomerulosclerosis[4]
Endocrine
Type 2 diabetes mellitus[12,13,79,83,84,89,140]
Insulin resistance[21,26,46,60,81,149]
Metabolic syndrome[60,61,144,265,275]
Precocious puberty[155,262]
Polycystic ovary syndrome[104,163]
Musculoskeletal
Slipped capital femoral epiphysis
Blount's disease
Forearm fractures
Flat feet

adult morbidity and mortality.[185] Childhood obesity also has adverse social and economic consequences.[124,241,260] The persistence of obesity,[129] with 70% to 80% of overweight children becoming obese adults,[70] is of particular concern for certain complications.

The clustering of hypertension, dyslipidemia, chronic inflammation, hypercoagulability, endothelial dysfunction, and hyperinsulinemia, known as insulin resistance syndrome or metabolic syndrome,[116] has been identified in children as young as 5 years of age.[275] The Bogalusa Heart Study noted the correlation of cardiovascular disease risk factors with asymptomatic coronary atherosclerosis. The more severely obese individuals had more advanced lesions.[176,177] A recent report suggests that the metabolic syndrome is far more common among children and adolescents than previously reported and that its prevalence increases directly with the degree of obesity.[264] Each element of the syndrome worsens with increasing obesity, independent of age, gender, and pubertal status.

A prediabetic state, consisting of glucose intolerance and insulin resistance, is highly prevalent among severely obese children, even before clinical diabetes has been diagnosed.[233] Even though formerly considered an "adult onset" disease, type 2 diabetes mellitus now accounts for nearly half of all new pediatric diagnoses of diabetes[90,202] and is thought to be largely the result of the pediatric obesity epidemic. Of particular concern are data from the Centers for Disease Control and Prevention suggesting that 33% of all Americans born in the year 2001 will develop diabetes.[187] For blacks and Hispanics this number rises to nearly 50%.[187] The striking and sobering findings of the United Kingdom Prospective Diabetes Study confirms the progressive nature of type 2 diabetes despite intensive therapy and good glycemic control. The data suggest that the onset of the beta cell dysfunction associated with diabetes occurs well before the development of hyperglycemia and may commence many years before diagnosis of the disease.[77,146,162,256] Other work clearly suggests that type 2 diabetes developing in childhood or early adulthood progresses much more rapidly than in adults[7] and may be more virulent than diabetes that develops later in adulthood.[67] This may be host dependent (i.e., a younger and thus more vulnerable host) or related to the more rapid accumulation of excess central adipose tissue as compared with an adult.

Nonalcoholic steatohepatitis is recognized as a common cause of chronic liver disease in children.[219] This condition is frequently associated with obesity, with 25% of overweight children in one report having abnormally elevated liver function tests.[105] It has been suggested that obesity-related pediatric nonalcoholic steatohepatitis[212] may become a major cause of hepatic failure and a leading indication for liver transplantation in decades to come.[52,53,219,220]

Exercise intolerance, sleep-disordered breathing, and asthma are frequent pulmonary complications of adolescent obesity.[94,216] Asthma and exercise intolerance can also limit physical activity and contribute to further increases in weight.[82] Obstructive sleep apnea (OSA), the most severe manifestation of sleep-disordered breathing, can significantly impair the obese adolescent's health-related quality of life,[229] result in abnormal left ventricular geometry,[9] and put them at increased risk for hyperactivity and learning difficulties.[51] Some have also documented decreased somatic growth and systemic hypertension in children with obstructive sleep apnea.[227] Some work does suggest that obesity in childhood elevates the risk of OSA by four to five times that seen in nonobese children.[216] However, although OSA is a clinically significant problem that correlates directly with BMI, neither the prevalence of OSA in obese children nor the absolute risk of growth and cardiovascular problems has been accurately quantified in the published literature.[227] Anecdotally, in our adolescent patients with obesity related OSA, surgical weight loss has allowed them to avoid tracheostomy. Within 6 months of surgery, a polysomnogram shows no evidence of sleep apnea or sleep-disordered breathing.

Arguably the most prevalent and debilitating consequences of adolescent obesity are psychosocial.[71,242] The psychological stress of social stigmatization imposed on obese children may be as damaging as the medical morbidities.[57] Many obese adolescents have low self-esteem associated with sadness and high-risk behaviors.[242] In a recent inventory of health-related quality of life indices, obese adolescents demonstrated significantly lower quality of life scores than lean children and scores that were comparable to pediatric cancer patients.[229] Overweight has also been associated with lower levels of socioeconomic attainment. Women who were overweight adolescents were less likely to marry and had completed fewer years of school.[124]

The health consequences of childhood obesity are broader in scope, greater in prevalence, and more severe at a given time point in disease progression than previously thought.[12,26,60,83,163,175,237,252,264] BMI thresholds for obesity do not account for the ethnic disparity of disease burden nor the accelerated progression of disease in certain populations of obese adolescents.[84,188,196] The progressively younger age at which adult diseases are recognized in children,[70-72,275] the increasing prevalence of impaired glucose tolerance, insulin resistance, metabolic syndrome, and type 2 diabetes mellitus in younger children,[23,50,90,233,237,275] and the suggestion that childhood-onset type 2 diabetes mellitus may be more virulent than adult-onset diabetes[67] validate concerns about the clinical relevance of the current definitions of obesity in children and about disease burden over time affecting the ability to control these comorbidities.[167,170,225]

ADOLESCENT COGNITIVE DEVELOPMENT: CONCEPTS AND PRINCIPLES RELEVANT TO ADOLESCENT BARIATRIC SURGERY

Cognitive development refers to the development of the ability to think and reason. Around 6 to 12 years of age, children develop the ability to think concretely. Adolescence marks the beginning of more complex thinking. At any given age, adolescents are at varying stages of cognitive and psychosocial development, which more closely correlates with pubertal status than with chronologic age.[251] Additionally, there are gender differences in the attainment of formal operations and identity formation, enabling new levels of intellectual functioning, abstract thinking,[201] and cognitive skills that are critical to providing assent to, and complying with, medical recommendations. Examples of formal operations include thinking about possibilities, hypothetical-deductive reasoning, anticipating events that have not yet happened, thinking about conventional limits, and thinking about thought. Before the attainment of formal operations, the adolescent functions and reasons in concrete operations. At this stage of development, the adolescent problem solving is confined to identifiable objects that are either directly perceived or imagined and mental operations are only possible when they are applied to information from the direct experience. In acquiring formal operations, the adolescent has the ability to reason, think abstractly and logically, form hypotheses, and consider various consequences of behavior. The adolescent who has acquired this ability is better able to consider the consequences of taking or not taking nutritional supplements or of following and adhering to the prescribed protein-sparing diet. Adolescence also is generally regarded as a period of social experimentation, limit testing, risk taking, and egocentrism—all of which predictably add to the challenge of adolescent compliance with desired health behaviors.

The postoperative management of the adolescent bariatric patient requires an assessment of the level of cognitive development and an understanding of the risk-taking propensity of adolescents.[85] It is also important to note that the level of cognitive sophistication differs from adolescent to adolescent and may be independent of chronologic age.[58] The attainment of new mental abilities does not carry with it immediate proficiency in their use nor does education alone enhance cognitive maturity. Enhanced compliance with a vigorous nutritional and lifestyle regimen requires effective education that applies cognitive development theory and also input from peers and family that help the adolescent attain a more realistic appreciation of their own vulnerability.

Compliance

Long-term therapeutic success with bariatric surgery is dependent on compliance with the prescribed dietary, lifestyle, and nutritional supplement regimen. Adolescence is generally viewed as a time of increased experimentation, with a variety of health-related behaviors such as diet and exercise. Expertise with enhancing adherence to preventive health practices and compliance with treatment regimens is critical. Historically, compliance with health recommendations in the adolescent population is disappointingly low, estimated at 40% to 50% for adolescents with chronic medical conditions such as cystic fibrosis, diabetes, and asthma.[32,200] Rand and McGregor found that after bariatric surgery fewer than 20% of adolescents demonstrated perfect compliance with vitamin and mineral supplementation regimens.[205] For adolescents with chronic medical conditions, adherence with rigorous medical and dietary regimens is substantially improved with use of behavioral therapy.[69,93,158,208,271] Unfortunately, there is no clear profile of the psychosocial factors consistently associated with the compliant patient, thus precluding a "cook book" solution for the prevention and management of poor compliance in the adolescent who has undergone bariatric surgery. To enhance adolescent compliance with a lifelong postoperative dietary and nutritional supplement regimen, an adolescent bariatric surgery program should employ professionals capable of assessing levels of cognitive development, personality characteristics such as self-esteem and locus of control, as well as family variables such as cohesiveness and level of effective communication.[58,59] Prior knowledge of these factors may enhance the ability of the bariatric team and the primary care physician to offer useful anticipatory guidance postoperatively. For example, it can be very useful to know when and with whom most non-nutritive calories are consumed so that the team is aware of the periods/people that may increase the adolescent's vulnerability to maladaptive postoperative eating habits.

Adolescent compliance may be enhanced by (1) visual aids; (2) focus on immediate benefit from treatment; (3) participation in self-management; (4) self-monitoring; and (5) self-reinforcement.[207] Adolescent self-management and related strategies encourage independence from the family, an important developmental task of adolescence. With the alterations in eating patterns that are required after bariatric surgery, repetitive reinforcement is needed to facilitate the formation of lifelong health-promoting habits. Patients and their families may require counseling and close follow-up to promote their physical and emotional well-being.

The adolescent bariatric surgery program should build on the best practices of other adolescent disease management programs[210,240] and thus be based on the premise that sustained weight control for the adolescent requires structured family involvement and continued support.

Specific strategies to increase adolescent compliance include education, treatment regimen modification within the social-cultural context of the patient, and enlisting family and peer support (Table 78-2).[58] Some adolescents

TABLE 78-2 Strategies to Improve Postoperative Compliance

- Rehearse the dietary regimen preoperatively to enable problem identification and solving before the surgical intervention.
- Use actual measuring cups, a food scale, and photographs of specific food items that are recommended to enhance the adolescent's ability to follow through with plans.
- Provide the adolescent with a diet diary and exercise diary with form pages to be filled out and practice this preoperatively.
- Provide a list of acceptable food items for every phase of the patient's postoperative recovery (first week, second through fourth week, second through third month, etc.) including the caloric density and protein, carbohydrate, and fat content of the items to encourage label reading.
- Provide a detailed listing of micronutritional supplements needed postoperatively that includes the reason why the supplement is needed and the potential consequences of not taking it.

respond to formalized modes of reinforcement such as contracting.

BARIATRIC SURGERY

Bariatric surgery should be viewed as a surgical discipline and not just a technical procedure. Bariatric patients are a distinct and often problematic cohort with serious and often multiple concurrent comorbidities. They have unique postoperative needs, and in the event of postoperative complications conventional diagnostic approaches often do not work. They require close long-term follow-up, making the transition of the adolescent who undergoes bariatric surgery to adult care an essential component of the clinical care plan.

The majority of bariatric surgery is now performed laparoscopically. Minimally invasive bariatric surgery has significant advantages over open surgery but is one of the most technically difficult operations to perform.[226] The learning curve is steep.[100] Schauer and associates suggest the curve levels off at 100 operations.[224] Laparoscopic skills employed in foregut surgery are not directly transferable to bariatric surgery, and proficiency in minimally invasive surgery may not confer the same level of proficiency in minimally invasive bariatric surgery. Associated with the proliferation in the number of bariatric procedures performed there has been an increase in the mortality and morbidity rates above those published in earlier, more commonly referenced studies.[100,165] Consequently, several societies and associations have developed credentialing criteria and guidelines for bariatric surgery and, most recently, the American Society for Bariatric Surgery has introduced criteria for Centers of Excellence in Bariatric Surgery. Pediatric surgeons pursuing bariatric surgery should at a minimum take a course in bariatric surgery and have their early experience proctored by an experienced laparoscopic bariatric surgeon. Additionally, they must be cognizant of and take into account, during patient selection, characteristics that are recognized as risk factors for perioperative complications and mortality.[49,91,92,125,166,203]

Surgical Options

There are four bariatric procedures in general use: Roux-en-Y gastric bypass (RYGBP; standard, long-limb, and very long-limb Roux); laparoscopic adjustable gastric band (LAGB); vertical banded gastroplasty; and biliopancreatic diversion, with or without duodenal switch. Each has its unique profile of potential complications and nutritional concerns.[40] All of these operations can achieve significant weight loss with improvement or reversal of obesity comorbidities. Each can be performed laparoscopically, which may result in shorter length of hospital stay, shorter convalescence,[92,168,190] and decreased risk of wound complications. When compared with open procedures, laparoscopic bariatric surgery has a higher incidence of intra-abdominal complications.[189] There are ongoing attempts to determine what patient features might predict which particular operation might be best suited to an individual's needs, but none has been prospectively evaluated.[39] For the most part, vertical banded gastroplasty is of historical interest and will not be addressed further. Table 78-3 outlines the percentage of excess weight loss, associated morbidity and mortality, and whether the operations can be revised or reversed.

Roux-en-Y Gastric Bypass

Gastric bypass is chiefly a restrictive procedure that modifies normal appetite signals and is modestly malabsorptive as well. It is the first of the gastric procedures and the most common bariatric procedure performed in the United States. The restrictive component is a small gastric pouch (15 to 20 mL) with a small gastric outlet (1 to 2 cm) that results in early and sustained satiety. Intestinal continuity is reestablished with a gastrointestinal bypass of varying segments of bowel: standard, 75 cm; long limb, 150 cm; and very long limb or distal gastric bypass, 250 cm.[226] The limb can be positioned retrocolic or antecolic, and the gastrojejunal anastomosis can be fashioned with an end-to-end stapler or linear stapler, or it can be hand sewn.[226] We employ the technique described by Higa and colleagues (Fig. 78-2).[135] It has the lowest reported leak rate from the gastrojejunostomy, an independent risk factor for procedure-related mortality.[91,92,226]

In patients with a BMI of 50 kg/m^2 the longer limb bypasses result in weight loss comparable to that seen with the standard gastric bypass in less obese patients. Weight loss (30% to 40% of preoperative weight) occurs over 1 to 2 years, followed by a plateau. Complications include dumping syndrome, gastrojejunal stomal stenosis, marginal ulcers, and internal hernias. This operation

TABLE 78-3 Comparison of Bariatric Procedures

Procedure	Weight Loss (% EBW)	Mortality (%)	Morbidity (%)	Can Be Reversed	Can Be Revised	Durability of Weight Loss
RYGBP	65-70	0.5	5	Yes	Yes	++++
LAGB	47	0.1	5	Yes	Yes	?
VGB	60-65	0.1	5	Yes	Yes	+
BPD ± DS	70	1.5	5	Yes	Yes	++++

RYGBP, Roux-en-Y gastric bypass; LAGB, laparoscopic adjustable gastric band; VGB, vertical banded gastroplasty; BPD ± DS, biliopancreatic diversion with or without duodenal switch; EBW, excess body weight.

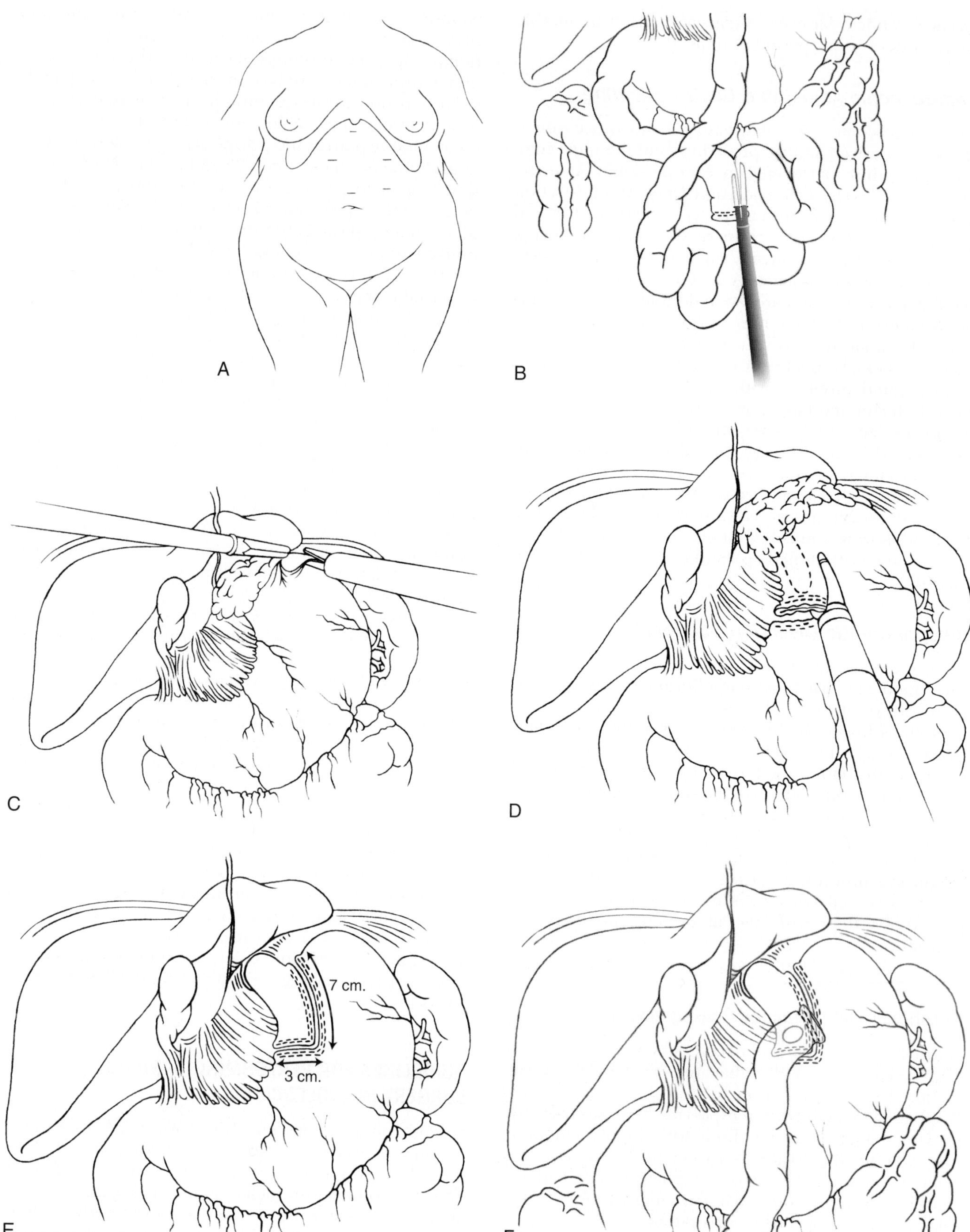

Figure 78–2 Roux-en-Y gastric bypass surgery. *A,* Sites for various laparoscopic ports. *B,* Preparation of the Roux limb. *C,* Mobilization of stomach. *D,* Preparing bypass pouch. *E,* Pouch is 3.0-cm wide and 7.0 cm long. *F,* Gastrojejunal anastomosis.

has been studied for over 14 years and results in durable weight loss over this period of time.[204]

Laparoscopic Adjustable Gastric Banding

The laparoscopic adjustable gastric band procedure is the least invasive bariatric procedure and the most common procedure performed in Europe, Latin America, and Australia. The U.S. Food and Drug Administration approved the use of the Lap Band in 2001. Its use and acceptance in this country is increasing. The laparoscopically placed band creates a small pouch and a small stoma high on the stomach. A port for adjustment of the band is placed in the anterior abdominal wall. Periodic adjustments of the band are critical for a successful outcome. Complications of the Lap Band include gastric prolapse, stomal obstruction, erosion of the band into the stomach, and problems with the access port. The pars flaccida technique has significantly reduced the risk of gastric prolapse.[184,218] A recent review of the literature determined that although the short-term morbidity and mortality risks associated with gastric banding were lower than with gastric bypass, the long-term efficacy of the adjustable gastric band is unproved. Evaluation by randomized controlled trials is recommended to define the merits of the Lap Band compared with gastric bypass.[49]

Biliopancreatic Diversion/Duodenal Switch

Biliopancreatic diversion[230] is widely used in Europe. The duodenal switch is a modification developed by Hess and colleagues.[134] Both are primarily malabsorptive operations involving the creation of a 100- to 150-mL gastric pouch. By dividing the intestine into a long enteric limb anastomosed to a long biliopancreatic limb a common channel 50 to 150 cm from the ileocecal valve is created and toxic problems seen with jejunoileal bypass are avoided. The weight loss is greater with biliopancreatic diversion with a duodenal switch than with the other weight loss procedures. However, the vitamin, nutrient, and protein deficiencies are more common with these procedures than with the aforementioned bariatric procedures.[11]

Nutritional and Metabolic Consequences

Nutritional and metabolic consequences of bariatric surgery have been well delineated.[35-38,74,243,246] There is impaired absorption of iron, folate, calcium, and vitamin B_{12} after all procedures that bypass the lower stomach and proximal small intestine. Even with supplementation, iron, vitamin B_{12}, folate, and calcium deficiencies may occur. Given the known poor compliance among adolescents,[205] certain factors, such as vitamin B_1, folate, and calcium, warrant special consideration.

Folate is specifically needed for the synthesis of DNA and RNA and amino acid interconversion, particularly methylation reactions in the methionine-homocysteine cycle. It is essential for growth, cell differentiation, gene regulation, repair, and host defense.[37,130] Folate deficiency is more prevalent in the general population than previously suggested. Adequate maternal periconceptional folic acid consumption during critical periods of organ formation may reduce the likelihood of neural tube defects, conotruncal structural heart defects, obstructive urinary tract abnormalities, limb defects, facial clefts, and congenital hypertrophic pyloric stenosis. Closure of the neural tube occurs between 26 and 28 days after conception (e.g., 1 to 2 weeks after the first missed menstrual period, before pregnancy is recognized). Folic acid supplementation started after this critical period is therefore unlikely to prevent a neural tube defect.

Maternal folic acid deficiency is also associated with perinatal complications such as low birth weight, prematurity, placental abruption, infarction, and the development of neuroectodermal tumors in children. Folic acid deficiency, suggested by elevated plasma homocysteine, is also associated with cardiovascular diseases, increased risk of dysplasias, and the subsequent development of cancer. Given the protean manifestations of folic acid deficiency, the general recommendation is that all women of childbearing age take folic acid supplementation. In the adolescent who undergoes bariatric surgery, folic acid–supplemented food items (e.g., cereals) may be inadequate. Additional supplementation contained in multivitamins is thus critical; measurement of serum folate and homocysteine concentrations may be useful.[33,74,112,181]

Adolescence is a period of enormous skeletal growth. This period of peak skeletal mineral accretion is a window of opportunity to influence lifelong bone health, both positively and negatively. Variations in calcium nutrition in adolescence may account for as much as 50% of the difference in hip fracture rates in postmenopausal years.[172,173] Although it is generally assumed that the obese adolescent has greater than normal bone mass[159] and is not operating at a disadvantage as it pertains to calcium absorption and risk for fracture or later osteoporosis, that point is debated by some.[86] It is not clear whether the decrease in bone density that occurs after surgical weight loss, combined with potential poor compliance with vitamin D and calcium intake, will put the adolescent bariatric patient at greater risk for fractures later in life. Thus, we consider it essential to closely monitor bone mineral density of adolescents undergoing bariatric surgery, particularly gastric bypass and biliopancreatic diversion.

GUIDELINES FOR PERFORMING BARIATRIC SURGERY IN ADOLESCENCE

Severely obese adolescents who have failed nonsurgical attempts at weight loss and have serious comorbidities should be considered candidates for bariatric surgery. There are others with such extreme obesity that activities of daily living may be severely impaired and in whom the development of health consequences of obesity is inevitable. Figure 78-3 outlines an algorithm for management as proposed by an expert panel of specialists in pediatric obesity.[143] For adolescents who have failed 6 months of attempts at professionally supervised weight

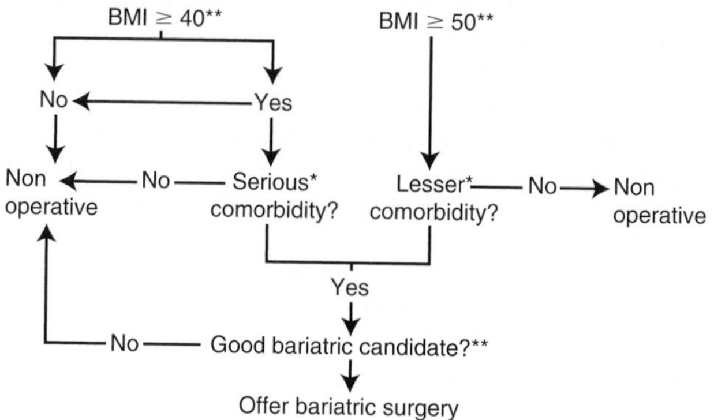

Figure 78-3 Algorithm for management of the obese adolescent. (From Inge TH, Krebs NF, Garcia VF, et al: Bariatric surgery for severely overweight adolescents: Concerns and recommendations. Pediatrics 2004;114:217-223.)

loss, bariatric surgery is a reasonable weight loss option (Table 78-4).

Increasing preoperative weight and male gender are risk factors for procedure-related complications and mortality.[91,92] Given that, vis-à-vis the suggested guidelines, adolescents selected for bariatric surgery *will* be heavier on average than adult bariatric patients. It is important for the surgeon to consider the impact of patient size on the potential for increased risks of the procedure. Some authors have suggested that surgeons who are early in the learning curve should avoid these high-risk patients to reduce complications.[91]

Adolescent bariatric surgery should be performed in centers having a multidisciplinary team capable of providing long-term follow-up and managing the unique

TABLE 78-4 Attributes of Adolescent Bariatric Candidate

- Patient is motivated and has good insight.
- Patient has realistic expectations.
- Family support and commitment is present.
- Patient is compliant with health care commitments.
- Family and patient understand that long-term lifestyle changes are needed.
- Patient agrees to long-term follow-up.
- Decisional capacity is present.
- Weight loss attempts are well documented.
- No major psychiatric disorders are evident that may complicate postoperative regimen adherence.
- No major conduct/behavioral problems are present.
- No substance abuse was noted in preceding year.
- Patient has no plans for pregnancy in upcoming 2 years.

behavioral challenges posed by the adolescent age group. Consistent with the guidelines established by the American Society for Bariatric Surgery and the American College of Surgeons,[249] these teams should include specialists with expertise in adolescent obesity evaluation and management, psychology, nutrition, physical activity instruction, and bariatric surgery. Depending on individual needs, additional expertise in adolescent medicine, endocrinology, pulmonology, gastroenterology, cardiology, orthopedics, and ethics should be readily available. The team approach should include a review process similar to that used in multidisciplinary pediatric oncology and transplant programs. This review should result in culturally sensitive treatment recommendations tailored for the patient and family.

The optimal timing for weight loss surgery for overweight adolescents is unknown and largely influenced by the pressing health needs of the patient. There are growth and maturation factors that need to be considered. Physiologic maturation is generally complete by sexual maturation (Tanner) stage 3 or 4. Skeletal maturation (adult stature) is normally attained by age 13 to 14 in girls and 15 to 16 in boys. Overweight children generally experience accelerated onset of puberty. As a result, they are likely to be taller and have advanced bone age compared with age-matched non-overweight children. If there is uncertainty about whether adult stature has been attained, skeletal maturation (bone age) can be objectively assessed with a radiograph of the hand and wrist. If an individual had attained more than 95% of adult stature, it is unlikely that a bariatric procedure would significantly impair completion of linear growth.

In determining patient suitability, all candidates should undergo a comprehensive psychological evaluation. Goals of this evaluation are (1) to identify psychological stressors or conflict within the family and past/present psychiatric, emotional, behavioral, or eating disorders; (2) to define potential supports and barriers to patient adherence and family readiness for surgery and the required lifestyle changes (particularly if one or both parents are obese); (3) to assess whether there are reasonable outcome expectations; and, most importantly, (4) to determine the level of cognitive and psychosocial development of the adolescent. With the alterations in eating patterns that are required after bariatric surgery, repetitive reinforcement is needed to facilitate the formation of lifelong health-promoting habits. Bariatric surgical programs for this age group should be based on the premise that sustained weight control for the adolescent requires intensive and regular postoperative psychological support. The role of the behavioral therapist depends on the level of intellectual function of the adolescent and includes behavioral rehearsal of regimen components before surgery, the use of behavioral contracts to outline regimen requirements and document the patient's agreement to adhere to them, a plan for patient and parental monitoring of adherence, and contingency reinforcement for adherence. The therapist plays a central role in developing parent-adolescent communication and conflict resolution skills and empirically based behavioral and family interventions, which facilitate the family's management of the patient's new lifestyle.

A stable family environment, with full, unconditional support of all family members is a desirable prerequisite for bariatric surgery in adolescents.

CLINICAL PATHWAY FOR THE MANAGEMENT OF THE ADOLESCENT UNDERGOING BARIATRIC SURGERY

Bariatric surgery reduces the intake and decreases the absorption of food items rich in essential fatty acids, vitamins, and other specific nutrients, the long-term results of which are of legitimate concern and a subject of ongoing inquiry.[15,68,88,102,178,213,273] Major weight loss after bariatric surgery improves reproductive function of severely obese women as well as normalization of gestational weight changes, reduction of fetal macrosomia, and normalization of infant birth weight.[171,270] Nonetheless, poor nutrition during fetal development can result in adult obesity, as suggested by the Dutch famine cohort.[213] Therefore, success in adolescent bariatric surgery requires an expanded definition—not only sustained weight loss but also subsequent normal progression through the remainder of adolescence, adulthood, and eventually uncomplicated reproduction of normal offspring.

The long-term consequences of bariatric surgery performed on adolescents have not been prospectively evaluated. The goals of adolescent bariatric surgery centers and programs should be not only to achieve dramatic and sustained weight loss but also to contribute to the understanding of the most effective operations, risk factors for recidivism, and long-term outcome of adolescents undergoing bariatric surgery. Centers performing adolescent bariatric surgery should pay particular attention to bone mineral density and the ramifications of lifelong decreased vitamin and nutrient absorption on the adolescent and, particularly relevant to reproductive females, their offspring. Progress in this regard will require the implementation of broad-based clinical and basic research programs at these centers. The potential benefits of regionalizing selected, complex surgical procedures such as adolescent bariatric surgery have been well documented.[27-30,48,96,122] Toward this end, adolescent bariatric surgery should be concentrated in centers willing and able to provide comprehensive and extended preoperative and postoperative investigations, including laboratory and diagnostic evaluations. Therefore, the clinical pathway developed by the Comprehensive Weight Management Center at Cincinnati Children's Hospital Medical Center is designed to better characterize the prevalence and resolution of obesity-related complications among adolescents who undergo bariatric surgery as well as provide surveillance for the known and potential consequences of the more popular bariatric surgical procedures performed at a comparatively young age.

Our preoperative panel includes a complete chemistry profile, liver function tests, uric acid, transferrin, iron, folate, lipid profile, urinalysis, electrocardiogram, blood cell count, hemoglobin A_{1C}, fasting blood glucose and fasting insulin, thyroid-stimulating hormone, and a pregnancy test for females. Nondiabetics receive a 2-hour glucose tolerance test. With the exception of the glucose tolerance test, the aforementioned laboratory and diagnostic panels are repeated at 3, 6, 9, and 12 months postoperatively and then yearly. Body composition is assessed with either bioelectrical impedance, for patients weighing in excess of 300 pounds, or dual energy x-ray absorptiometry analysis (DEXA) for patients weighing less than 300 pounds preoperatively and at 3, 6, and 12 months postoperatively. DEXA not only allows for the measurement of rate and relative amounts of fat and lean body mass loss but also provides a quantitative assessment of changes in bone mineral density. This body composition analysis is used to modify dietary plans intended to preserve lean body mass during the period of dramatic weight loss. Evidence suggesting that even as little as a 2 standard deviation change in bone mineral content of the adolescent can significantly increase the risk of osteoporosis and bone fractures in later life underscores the importance of meticulous and extended monitoring of nutrient, vitamin, and mineral absorption.[147] Because of the increased prevalence of abnormal heart geometry[62,63,66] and sleep disorders[9] among obese adolescents compared with nonobese adolescents, candidates for bariatric surgery undergo echocardiography and pediatric-specific polysomnography.

OUR BARIATRIC SURGERY EXPERIENCE

The first comprehensive weight management program in a children's hospital was established in Cincinnati in 2001.[114,142] To date, 66 patients have undergone Roux-en-Y gastric bypass (4 by open laparotomy, 62 laparoscopically). Of the patients followed for 1 year or more, the mean preoperative weight in this cohort was 361 pounds (164 kg), the BMI ranged from 44 to 85 kg/m^2, with a mean of 57 kg/m^2. After 1 year, the mean weight was 222 pounds (101 kg) and BMI ranged from 26 to 58 kg/m^2, with a mean of 35 kg/m^2. This represents a 39% reduction in BMI over the year. Excess weight loss has been 63%. One patient who presented with a BMI of 85 had lost 71 kg at 1 year and has regained 6 kg at the end of his second year postoperatively. There have been no deaths due to the intervention; and although two leaks have occurred, there has been none from the hand-sewn gastrojejunal anastomosis. Both leaks were managed minimally invasively without physiologic compromise of the patients. Preoperative comorbidities of obesity have largely been reversed after gastric bypass. Three patients with type 2 diabetes and 7 patients with OSA have experienced complete remission and no longer require hypoglycemic medications and continuous positive airway pressure. Complications in this initial series have been similar to those observed in similar series with adult patients. One notable exception has been the development of beriberi in two adolescents after gastric bypass,[255] which has prompted the addition of a B-complex vitamin to our regimen. Only a few of our most extremely obese patients have required precautionary, short-term stays in an intensive care unit postoperatively.

Adolescent obesity may represent a disease that is more serious[101] and more difficult to manage[205,248] compared with this disease in adults. We currently lack an understanding of the long-term outcomes (both positive and negative) of bariatric procedures in this population. Thus, centers offering bariatric care to these patients are obligated to critically evaluate outcomes, both positive and potentially negative, by ensuring that a mechanism is in place to carefully collect detailed data regarding comorbidity change and adverse events on all adolescents who undergo surgery. This will help us to better define the role of bariatric procedures in the management of these patients.

CONCLUSION

The obesity epidemic in this country has generated a population of adolescents with the premature onset of adult disease. Clinical and epidemiologic studies have elucidated some of the life course risk factors for the development of childhood and adolescent obesity. Currently, bariatric surgery is the most effective treatment that achieves sustained weight loss and resolves or ameliorates the majority of the associated comorbidities. Success in adolescent bariatric surgery should be defined not only in terms of weight loss and morbidity resolution but also in terms of normal progression through adolescence and adulthood. Toward this goal adolescent bariatric surgery programs should have team members with expertise that increases the likelihood of life-long compliance with complex nutritional and lifestyle regimens, that is, expertise that enables them to assess and meet the unique medical, cognitive, physiologic, and psychosocial needs of the adolescent. The guidelines for bariatric surgery should be conservative, be sensitive to the potential impact on the growth potential of the adolescent, and offer surgery during the time course of the disease that minimizes the risk of procedure-related complications and ensures the greatest likelihood of treating the comorbidities associated with obesity. Adolescent compliance with the strict nutritional and lifestyle regimens required after bariatric surgery may be best managed with a family-centered team that incorporates behavioral strategies to maximize compliance with postoperative dietary and physical activity instructions. Bariatric surgery is an exceedingly complex and technically difficult operation. The relative effects of hospital volume and surgeon volume in terms of procedure-related mortality and outcomes have direct implications for volume-based referral. Given the existent uncertainty about long-term outcomes of bariatric surgery in adolescents, regionalization of care and a national patient database are imperatives, essential to achieving outcomes commensurate with the best adult series and to accelerating our understanding of the short- and long-term consequences of bariatric surgery among adolescents.

REFERENCES

1. Abu-Abeid S, Gavert N, Klausner JM, Szold A: Bariatric surgery in adolescence. J Pediatr Surg 2003;38:1379-1382.
2. Adami GF, Meneghelli A, Scopinaro N: Night eating and binge eating disorder in obese patients. Int J Eat Disord 1999;25: 335-338.
3. Adelman RD, Restaino IG, Alon US, Blowey DL: Proteinuria and focal segmental glomerulosclerosis in severely obese adolescents. J Pediatr 2001;138:481-485.
4. Aggoun Y, Tounian P, Dabbas-Tyan M, et al: [Arterial rigidity and endothelial dysfunction in obese children]. Arch Mal Coeur Vaiss 2002;95:631-635.
5. Albrecht RJ, Pories WJ: Surgical intervention for the severely obese. Baillieres Best Pract Res Clin Endocrinol Metab 1999;13:149-172.
6. Allison DB, Miller RA, Austad SN, et al: Genetic variability in responses to caloric restriction in animals and in regulation of metabolism and obesity in humans. J Gerontol A Biol Sci Med Sci 2001;56(Spec No 1):55-65, 2001.
7. American Diabetes Association: Type 2 diabetes in children and adolescents. Pediatrics 2000;105:671-680.
8. Amin R, Daniels S: Relationship between obesity and sleep-disordered breathing in children: Is it a closed loop? J Pediatr 2002;140:641-643.
9. Amin RS, Kimball TR, Bean JA, et al: Left ventricular hypertrophy and abnormal ventricular geometry in children and adolescents with obstructive sleep apnea. Am J Respir Crit Care Med 2002;165:1395-1399.
10. Anderson AE, Soper RT, Scott DH: Gastric bypass for morbid obesity in children and adolescents. J Pediatr Surg 1980; 15:876-881.
11. Anthone GJ, Lord RV, DeMeester TR, Crookes PF: The duodenal switch operation for the treatment of morbid obesity. Ann Surg 2003;238:618-627; discussion 627-628.
12. Arslanian S: Type 2 diabetes in children: Clinical aspects and risk factors. Horm Res 2002;57(Suppl 1):19-28.
13. Aye T, Levitsky LL: Type 2 diabetes: An epidemic disease in childhood. Curr Opin Pediatr 2003;15:411-415.
14. Balcer LJ, Liu GT, Forman S, et al: Idiopathic intracranial hypertension: Relation of age and obesity in children. Neurology 1999;52:870-872.
15. Barker DJ, Eriksson JG, Forsen T, Osmond C: Fetal origins of adult disease: Strength of effects and biological basis. Int J Epidemiol 2002;31:1235-1239.
16. Barlow SE, Dietz WH: Obesity evaluation and treatment: Expert Committee recommendations. The Maternal and Child Health Bureau, Health Resources and Services Administration and the Department of Health and Human Services. Pediatrics 1998;102:E29.
17. Barlow SE, Dietz WH, Klish WJ, Trowbridge FL: Medical evaluation of overweight children and adolescents: Reports from pediatricians, pediatric nurse practitioners, and registered dietitians. Pediatrics 2002;110:222-228.
18. Bartley M, Blane D, Montgomery S: Health and the life course: Why safety nets matter. BMJ 1997;314:1194-1196.
19. Barton M, Furrer J: Cardiovascular consequences of the obesity pandemic: Need for action. Expert Opin Invest Drugs 2003;12:1757-1759.
20. Bartosh SM, Aronson AJ: Childhood hypertension: An update on etiology, diagnosis, and treatment. Pediatr Clin North Am 1990;46:235-252.
21. Bavdekar A, Yajnik CS, Fall CH, et al: Insulin resistance syndrome in 8-year-old Indian children: Small at birth, big at 8 years, or both? Diabetes 1999;48:2422-2429.
22. Ben-Shlomo Y, Kuh D: A life course approach to chronic disease epidemiology: Conceptual models, empirical challenges and interdisciplinary perspectives. Int J Epidemiol 2002;31:285-293.
23. Berenson GS: Bogalusa Heart Study: A long-term community study of a rural biracial (black/white) population. Am J Med Sci 2001;322:293-300.
24. Berenson GS, Srinivasan SR: Emergence of obesity and cardiovascular risk for coronary artery disease: The Bogalusa Heart Study. Prev Cardiol 2001;4:116-121.

25. Berenson GS, Wattigney WA, Webber LS: Epidemiology of hypertension from childhood to young adulthood in black, white, and Hispanic population samples. Pub Health Rep 1996;111(Suppl 2):3-6.
26. Bhatia V: IAP National Task Force for Childhood Prevention of Adult Diseases: Insulin resistance and type 2 diabetes mellitus in childhood. Indian Pediatr 2004;41:443-457.
27. Birkmeyer JD, Dimick JB: Potential benefits of the new Leapfrog standards: Effect of process and outcomes measures. Surgery 2004;135:569-575.
28. Birkmeyer JD, Dimick JB, Birkmeyer NJ: Measuring the quality of surgical care: Structure, process, or outcomes? J Am Coll Surg 2004;198:626-632.
29. Birkmeyer JD, Finlayson EV, Birkmeyer CM: Volume standards for high-risk surgical procedures: Potential benefits of the Leapfrog initiative. Surgery 2001;130:415-422.
30. Birkmeyer JD, Siewers AE, Finlayson EV, et al: Hospital volume and surgical mortality in the United States. N Engl J Med 2002;346:1128-1137.
31. Black PH: The inflammatory response is an integral part of the stress response: Implications for atherosclerosis, insulin resistance, type II diabetes and metabolic syndrome X. Brain Behav Immun 2003;17:350-364.
32. Borowitz D, Wegman T, Harris M: Preventive care for patients with chronic illness: Multivitamin use in patients with cystic fibrosis. Clin Pediatr 1994;33:720-725.
33. Borson-Chazot F, Harthe C, Teboul F, et al: Occurrence of hyperhomocysteinemia 1 year after gastroplasty for severe obesity. J Clin Endocrinol Metab 1999;84:541-545.
34. Bower CM, Gungor A: Pediatric obstructive sleep apnea syndrome. Otolaryngol Clin North Am 2000;33:49-75.
35. Boylan LM, Sugerman HJ, Driskell JA: Vitamin E, vitamin B-6, vitamin B-12, and folate status of gastric bypass surgery patients. J Am Diet Assoc 1988;88:579-585.
36. Brolin RE, Gorman JH, Gorman RC, et al: Prophylactic iron supplementation after Roux-en-Y gastric bypass: A prospective, double-blind, randomized study. Arch Surg 1998;133: 740-744.
37. Brolin RE, Gorman JH, Gorman RC, et al: Are vitamin B_{12} and folate deficiency clinically important after Roux-en-Y gastric bypass? J Gastrointest Surg 1998;2:436-442.
38. Brolin RE, Gorman RC, Milgrim LM, Kenler HA: Multivitamin prophylaxis in prevention of post-gastric bypass vitamin and mineral deficiencies. Int J Obes 1991;15:661-667.
39. Buchwald H: A bariatric surgery algorithm. Obes Surg 2002;12:733-746; discussion 747-750.
40. Buchwald H: Overview of bariatric surgery. J Am Coll Surg 2002;194:367-375.
41. Buiten C, Metzger B: Childhood obesity and risk of cardiovascular disease: A review of the science. Pediatr Nurs 2000;26:13-18.
42. Burrows A, Cooper M: Possible risk factors in the development of eating disorders in overweight pre-adolescent girls. Int J Obes Relat Metab Disord 2002;26:1268-1273.
43. Byberg L, McKeigue PM, Zethelius B, Lithell HO: Birth weight and the insulin resistance syndrome: Association of low birth weight with truncal obesity and raised plasminogen activator inhibitor-1 but not with abdominal obesity or plasma lipid disturbances. Diabetologia 2000;43:54-60.
44. Calle EE, Thun MJ, Petrelli JM, et al: Body-mass index and mortality in a prospective cohort of U.S. adults. N Engl J Med 1999;341:1097-1105.
45. Capella JF, Capella RF: Bariatric surgery in adolescence: Is this the best age to operate? Obes Surg 2003;13:826-832.
46. Caprio S: Insulin resistance in childhood obesity. J Pediatr Endocrinol Metab 2002;15(Suppl 1):487-492.
47. Chan JC, Cheung JC, Stehouwer CD, et al: The central roles of obesity-associated dyslipidaemia, endothelial activation and cytokines in the Metabolic Syndrome—an analysis by structural equation modelling. Int J Obes Relat Metab Disord 2002;26:994-1008.
48. Chang RK, Klitzner TS: Can regionalization decrease the number of deaths for children who undergo cardiac surgery? A theoretical analysis. Pediatrics 2002;109:173-181.
49. Chapman AE, Kiroff G, Game P, et al: Laparoscopic adjustable gastric banding in the treatment of obesity: A systematic literature review. Surgery 2004;135:326-351.
50. Chen W, Bao W, Begum S, et al: Age-related patterns of the clustering of cardiovascular risk variables of syndrome X from childhood to young adulthood in a population made up of black and white subjects: The Bogalusa Heart Study. Diabetes 2000;49:1042-1048.
51. Chervin RD, Dillon JE, Archbold KH, Ruzicka DL: Conduct problems and symptoms of sleep disorders in children. J Am Acad Child Adolesc Psychiatry 2003;42:201-208.
52. Chitturi S, Farrell GC: Etiopathogenesis of nonalcoholic steatohepatitis. Semin Liver Dis 2001;21:27-41.
53. Chitturi S, Farrell GC, George J: Non-alcoholic steatohepatitis in the Asia-Pacific region: Future shock? J Gastroenterol Hepatol 2004;19:368-374.
54. Christou NV, Sampalis JS, Liberman M, et al: Surgery decreases long-term mortality, morbidity, and health care use in morbidly obese patients. Ann Surg 2004;240:416-423; discussion 423-424.
55. Cinciripini GS, Donahue S, Borchert MS: Idiopathic intracranial hypertension in prepubertal pediatric patients: Characteristics, treatment, and outcome. Am J Ophthalmol 1999;127:178-182.
56. Clement K, Boutin P, Froguel P: Genetics of obesity. Am J Pharmacogenomics 2002;2:177-187.
57. Committee on Nutrition of the American Academy of Pediatrics: Prevention of pediatric overweight and obesity. Pediatrics 2003;112:424-430.
58. Cromer B: Compliance with health recommendations. In Stanford Friedman MF, Schonberg SK, Alderman E (eds): Comprehensive Adolescent Health Care, 2nd ed. New York, Mosby-Year Book, 1998, pp 104-108.
59. Cromer BA, Tarnowski KJ: Noncompliance in adolescents: A review. J Dev Behav Pediatr 1989;10:207-215.
60. Cruz ML, Goran MI: The metabolic syndrome in children and adolescents. Curr Diab Rep 2004;4:53-62.
61. Csabi G, Torok K, Jeges S, Molnar D: Presence of metabolic cardiovascular syndrome in obese children. Eur J Pediatr 2000;159:91-94.
62. Daniels SR, Kimball TR, Morrison JA, et al: Effect of lean body mass, fat mass, blood pressure, and sexual maturation on left ventricular mass in children and adolescents. Statistical, biological, and clinical significance. Circulation 1995;92:3249-3254.
63. Daniels SR, Witt SA, Glascock B, et al: Left atrial size in children with hypertension: The influence of obesity, blood pressure, and left ventricular mass. J Pediatr 2002;141: 186-190.
64. Das UN: Is obesity an inflammatory condition? Nutrition 2001;17:953-966.
65. Das UN: Obesity, metabolic syndrome X, and inflammation. Nutrition 2002;18:430-432.
66. de Simone G, Devereux RB, Daniels SR, et al: Stroke volume and cardiac output in normotensive children and adults: Assessment of relations with body size and impact of overweight. Circulation 1997;95:1837-1843.
67. Dean H, Flett B: Natural history of type 2 diabetes mellitus diagnosed in childhood: Long term follow-up in young adults. Diabetes 2002;51:A24.
68. Delisle H: [Foetal programming of nutrition-related chronic diseases]. Sante 2002;12:56-63.

69. Denzer C, Reithofer E, Wabitsch M, Widhalm K: The outcome of childhood obesity management depends highly upon patient compliance. Eur J Pediatr 2004;163:99-104.
70. Dietz WH: Childhood weight affects adult morbidity and mortality. J Nutr 1998;128(Suppl):411S-414S.
71. Dietz WH: Health consequences of obesity in youth: Childhood predictors of adult disease. Pediatrics 1998; 101:518-525.
72. Dietz WH: Overweight and precursors of type 2 diabetes mellitus in children and adolescents. J Pediatr 2001;138:453-454.
73. Dietz WH: Overweight in childhood and adolescence. N Engl J Med 2004;350:855-857.
74. Dixon JB, Dixon ME, O'Brien PE: Elevated homocysteine levels with weight loss after Lap-Band surgery: Higher folate and vitamin B_{12} levels required to maintain homocysteine level. Int J Obes Relat Metab Disord 2001;25:219-227.
75. Dixon JB, O'Brien PE: Health outcomes of severely obese type 2 diabetic subjects 1 year after laparoscopic adjustable gastric banding. Diabetes Care 2002;25:358-363.
76. Dixon JB, O'Brien PE: Lipid profile in the severely obese: Changes with weight loss after lap-band surgery. Obes Res 2002;10:903-910.
77. Dolan K, Creighton L, Hopkins G, Fielding G: Laparoscopic gastric banding in morbidly obese adolescents. Obes Surg 2003;13:101-104.
78. Dorosty AR, Siassi F, Reilly JJ: Obesity in Iranian children. Arch Dis Child 2002;87:388-391; discussion 388-391.
79. Drake AJ, Smith A, Betts PR, et al: Type 2 diabetes in obese white children. Arch Dis Child 2002;86:207-208.
80. Dwyer JT, Stone EJ, Yang M, et al: Prevalence of marked overweight and obesity in a multiethnic pediatric population: Findings from the Child and Adolescent Trial for Cardiovascular Health (CATCH) study. J Am Diet Assoc 2000;100:1149-1156.
81. Dwyer T, Blizzard L, Venn A, et al: Syndrome X in 8-year-old Australian children: Stronger associations with current body fatness than with infant size or growth. Int J Obes Relat Metab Disord 2002;26:1301-1309.
82. Ebbeling CB, Pawlak DB, Ludwig DS: Childhood obesity: Public-health crisis, common sense cure. Lancet 2002;360: 473-482.
83. Ehtisham S, Barrett TG: The emergence of type 2 diabetes in childhood. Ann Clin Biochem 2004;41:10-16.
84. Ehtisham S, Hattersley AT, Dunger DB, Barrett TG: First UK survey of paediatric type 2 diabetes and MODY. Arch Dis Child 2004;89:526-529.
85. Elkind D: Cognitive development. In Stanford Friedman MF, Schonberg SK, Alderman E (eds): Comprehensive Adolescent Health Care, 2nd ed. St. Louis, Mosby-Year Book, 1998, pp 34-37.
86. Ellis KJ, Shypailo RJ, Wong WW, Abrams SA: Bone mineral mass in overweight and obese children: Diminished or enhanced? Acta Diabetol 2003;40(Suppl 1):S274-277.
87. Epstein LH, Myers MD, Raynor HA, Saelens BE: Treatment of pediatric obesity. Pediatrics 1998;101:554-570.
88. Eriksson J, Forsen T, Osmond C, Barker D: Obesity from cradle to grave. Int J Obes Relat Metab Disord 2003;27:722-727.
89. Fagot-Campagna A: Emergence of type 2 diabetes mellitus in children: Epidemiological evidence. J Pediatr Endocrinol Metab 2000;13(Suppl 6):1395-1402.
90. Fagot-Campagna A, Pettitt DJ, Engelgau MM, et al: Type 2 diabetes among North American children and adolescents: An epidemiologic review and a public health perspective. J Pediatr 2000;136:664-672.
91. Fernandez AZ Jr, DeMaria EJ, Tichansky DS, et al: Experience with over 3,000 open and laparoscopic bariatric procedures: Multivariate analysis of factors related to leak and resultant mortality. Surg Endosc 2004;18:193-197.
92. Fernandez AZ Jr, DeMaria EJ, Tichansky DS, et al: Multivariate analysis of risk factors for death following gastric bypass for treatment of morbid obesity. Ann Surg 2004;239:698-702; discussion 702-703.
93. Fielding D, Duff A: Compliance with treatment protocols: Interventions for children with chronic illness. Arch Dis Child 1999;80:196-200.
94. Figueroa-Munoz JI, Chinn S, Rona RJ: Association between obesity and asthma in 4- to 11-year old children in the UK. Thorax 2001;56:133-137.
95. Filozof C, Gonzalez C, Sereday M, et al: Obesity prevalence and trends in Latin-American countries. Obes Rev 2001;2:99-106.
96. Finlayson EV, Goodney PP, Birkmeyer JD: Hospital volume and operative mortality in cancer surgery: A national study. Arch Surg 2003;138:721-725; discussion 726.
97. Flegal KM: Defining obesity in children and adolescents: Epidemiologic approaches. Crit Rev Food Sci Nutr 1993; 33:307-312.
98. Flegal KM, Troiano RP: Changes in the distribution of body mass index of adults and children in the US population. Int J Obes Relat Metab Disord 2000;24: 807-818.
99. Flodmark CE: Thrifty genotypes and phenotypes in the pathogenesis of early-onset obesity. Acta Paediatr 2002; 91:737-738.
100. Flum DR, Dellinger EP: Impact of gastric bypass operation on survival: A population-based analysis. J Am Coll Surg 2004;199:543-551.
101. Fontaine KR, Redden DT, Wang C, et al: Years of life lost due to obesity. JAMA 2003;289:187-193.
102. Forsen T, Eriksson J, Tuomilehto J, et al: The fetal and childhood growth of persons who develop type 2 diabetes. Ann Intern Med 2000;133:176-182.
103. Fox J: A life course approach to chronic disease epidemiology. BMJ 1998;317:421.
104. Franks S: Adult polycystic ovary syndrome begins in childhood. Best Pract Res Clin Endocrinol Metab 2002;16: 263-272.
105. Franzese A, Vajro P, Argenziano A, et al: Liver involvement in obese children: Ultrasonography and liver enzyme levels at diagnosis and during follow-up in an Italian population. Dig Dis Sci 1997;42:1428-1432.
106. Freedman DS, Dietz WH, Srinivasan SR, Berenson GS: The relation of overweight to cardiovascular risk factors among children and adolescents: The Bogalusa Heart Study. Pediatrics 1999;103:1175-1182.
107. French SA, Story M, Perry CL: Self-esteem and obesity in children and adolescents: A literature review. Obes Res 1995;3:479-490.
108. Friedman JM: The function of leptin in nutrition, weight, and physiology. Nutr Rev 2002;60(Suppl):S1-S14; discussion S68-S84.
109. Friedman JM: A war on obesity, not the obese. Science 2003;299:856-858.
110. Galal OM: The nutrition transition in Egypt: Obesity, undernutrition and the food consumption context. Public Health Nutr 2002;5:141-148.
111. Gallistl S, Sudi KM, Borkenstein M, et al: Correlation between cholesterol, soluble P-selectin, and D-dimer in obese children and adolescents. Blood Coagul Fibrinolysis 2000;11:755-760.
112. Gallistl S, Sudi KM, Erwa W, et al: Determinants of homocysteine during weight reduction in obese children and adolescents. Metabolism 2001;50:1220-1223.
113. Gannon B, DiPietro L, Poehlman ET: Do African Americans have lower energy expenditure than Caucasians? Int J Obes Relat Metab Disord 2000;24:4-13.

114. Garcia VF, Langford L, Inge TH: Application of laparoscopy for bariatric surgery in adolescents. Curr Opin Pediatr 2003;15:248-255.
115. Ghannem H, Darioli R, Limam K, et al: Epidemiology of cardiovascular risk factors among schoolchildren in Sousse, Tunisia. J Cardiovasc Risk 2001;8:87-91.
116. Gidding SS, Bao W, Srinivasan SR, Berenson GS: Effects of secular trends in obesity on coronary risk factors in children: The Bogalusa Heart Study. J Pediatr 1995;127:868-874.
117. Gillman MW: Breast-feeding and obesity. J Pediatr 2002; 141:749-757.
118. Gillman MW, Rifas-Shiman SL, Camargo CA Jr, et al: Risk of overweight among adolescents who were breastfed as infants. JAMA 2001;285:2461-2467.
119. Glanz K, Croyle RT, Chollette VY, Pinn VW: Cancer-related health disparities in women. Am J Public Health 2003;93:292-298.
120. Goodman E, Whitaker RC: A prospective study of the role of depression in the development and persistence of adolescent obesity. Pediatrics 2002;110:497-504.
121. Goran MI: Genetic influences on human energy expenditure and substrate utilization. Behav Genet 1997;27:389-399.
122. Gordon TA, Bowman HM, Tielsch JM, et al: Statewide regionalization of pancreaticoduodenectomy and its effect on in-hospital mortality. Ann Surg 1998;228:71-78.
123. Gordon-Larsen P, Adair LS, Popkin BM: Ethnic differences in physical activity and inactivity patterns and overweight status. Obes Res 2002;10:141-149.
124. Gortmaker SL, Must A, Perrin JM, et al: Social and economic consequences of overweight in adolescence and young adulthood. N Engl J Med 1993;329:1008-1012.
125. Gould JC, Garren MJ, Starling JR: Lessons learned from the first 100 cases in a new minimally invasive bariatric surgery program. Obes Surg 2004;14:618-625.
126. Greenstein RJ, Rabner JG: Is adolescent gastric-restrictive antiobesity surgery warranted? Obes Surg 1995;5:138-144.
127. Grill HJ, Kaplan JM: The neuroanatomical axis for control of energy balance. Front Neuroendocrinol 2002; 23:2-40.
128. Guerra S, Wright AL, Morgan WJ, et al: Persistence of asthma symptoms during adolescence: Role of obesity and age at onset of puberty. Am J Respir Crit Care Med 2004;170:78-85.
129. Guo SS, Wu W, Chumlea WC, Roche AF: Predicting overweight and obesity in adulthood from body mass index values in childhood and adolescence. Am J Clin Nutr 2002;76:653-658.
130. Hall J, Solehdin F: Folic acid for the prevention of congenital anomalies. Eur J Pediatr 1998;157:445-450.
131. Hazzard A, Hutchinson SJ, Krawiecki N: Factors related to adherence to medication regimens in pediatric seizure patients. J Pediatr Psychol 1990;15:543-555.
132. Heald FP, Khan MA: Teenage obesity. Pediatr Clin North Am 1973;20:807-817.
133. Hedley AA, Ogden CL, Johnson CL, et al: Prevalence of overweight and obesity among US children, adolescents, and adults, 1999-2002. JAMA 2004;291:2847-2850.
134. Hess DS, Hess DW: Biliopancreatic diversion with a duodenal switch. Obes Surg 1998;8:267-282.
135. Higa KD, Boone KB, Ho T, Davies OG: Laparoscopic Roux-en-Y gastric bypass for morbid obesity: Technique and preliminary results of our first 400 patients. Arch Surg 2000;135:1029-1033; discussion 1033-1034.
136. Higa KD, Ho T, Boone KB: Laparoscopic Roux-en-Y gastric bypass: Technique and 3-year follow-up. J Laparoendosc Adv Surg Tech A 2001;11:377-382.
137. Hirosumi J, Tuncman G, Chang L, et al: A central role for JNK in obesity and insulin resistance. Nature 2002;420: 333-336.
138. Hirsch S, Pia De la Maza M, Yanez P, et al: Hyperhomocysteinemia and endothelial function in young subjects: Effects of vitamin supplementation. Clin Cardiol 2002;25:495-501.
139. Hotamisligil GS, Shargill NS, Spiegelman BM: Adipose expression of tumor necrosis factor-alpha: Direct role in obesity-linked insulin resistance. Science 1993;259: 87-91.
140. Hotu S, Carter B, Watson PD, et al: Increasing prevalence of type 2 diabetes in adolescents. J Paediatr Child Health 2004;40:201-204.
141. Hubbard VS: Defining overweight and obesity: What are the issues? Am J Clin Nutr 2000;72:1067-1068.
142. Inge TH, Garcia V, Daniels S, et al: A multidisciplinary approach to the adolescent bariatric surgical patient. J Pediatr Surg 2004;39:442-447; discussion 446-447.
143. Inge TH, Krebs NF, Garcia VF, et al: Bariatric surgery for severely overweight adolescents: Concerns and recommendations. Pediatrics 2004;114:217-223.
144. James PT, Rigby N, Leach R: The obesity epidemic, metabolic syndrome and future prevention strategies. Eur J Cardiovasc Prev Rehabil 2004;11:3-8.
145. Jequier E: Leptin signaling, adiposity, and energy balance. Ann NY Acad Sci 2002;967:379-388.
146. Kahn SE: Clinical review 135: The importance of beta-cell failure in the development and progression of type 2 diabetes. J Clin Endocrinol Metab 2001;86:4047-4058.
147. Kalkwarf HJ, Khoury JC, Lanphear BP: Milk intake during childhood and adolescence, adult bone density, and osteoporotic fractures in US women. Am J Clin Nutr 2003; 77:257-265.
148. Karason K, Lindroos AK, Stenlof K, Sjostrom L: Relief of cardiorespiratory symptoms and increased physical activity after surgically induced weight loss: Results from the Swedish Obese Subjects study. Arch Intern Med 2000; 160:1797-1802.
149. Keller KB, Lemberg L: Obesity and the metabolic syndrome. Am J Crit Care 2003;12:167-170.
150. Kimm SY, Barton BA, Obarzanek E, et al: Obesity development during adolescence in a biracial cohort: The NHLBI Growth and Health Study. Pediatrics 2002;110:e54.
151. Kimm SY, Glynn NW, Aston CE, et al: Racial differences in the relation between uncoupling protein genes and resting energy expenditure. Am J Clin Nutr 2002;75: 714-719.
152. Kimm SY, Glynn NW, Aston CE, et al: Effects of race, cigarette smoking, and use of contraceptive medications on resting energy expenditure in young women. Am J Epidemiol 2001;154:718-724.
153. Krassas GE, Tzotzas T, Tsametis C, Konstantinidis T: Prevalence and trends in overweight and obesity among children and adolescents in Thessaloniki, Greece. J Pediatr Endocrinol Metab 2001;14(Suppl 5):1319-1326; discussion 1365.
154. Lacour M, Zunder T, Dettenkofer M, et al: An interdisciplinary therapeutic approach for dealing with patients attributing chronic fatigue and functional memory disorders to environmental poisoning—a pilot study. Int J Hyg Environ Health 2002;204:339-346.
155. Lazar L, Kauli R, Bruchis C, et al: Early polycystic ovary–like syndrome in girls with central precocious puberty and exaggerated adrenal response. Eur J Endocrinol 1995; 133:403-406.
156. Lehrke M, Lazar MA: Inflamed about obesity. Nat Med 2004;10:126-127.
157. Leibel RL, Rosenbaum M, Hirsch J: Changes in energy expenditure resulting from altered body weight. N Engl J Med 1995;332:621-628.

158. Lemanek KL, Kamps J, Chung NB: Empirically supported treatments in pediatric psychology: Regimen adherence. J Pediatr Psychol 2001;26:253-275.
159. Leonard MB, Shults J, Wilson BA, et al: Obesity during childhood and adolescence augments bone mass and bone dimensions. Am J Clin Nutr 2004;80:514-523.
160. Lessell S: Pediatric pseudotumor cerebri (idiopathic intracranial hypertension). Surv Ophthalmol 1992;37:155-166.
161. Levine J, Melanson EL, Westerterp KR, Hill JO: Measurement of the components of nonexercise activity thermogenesis. Am J Physiol Endocrinol Metab 2001; 281:E670-E675.
162. Levy J, Atkinson AB, Bell PM, et al: Beta-cell deterioration determines the onset and rate of progression of secondary dietary failure in type 2 diabetes mellitus: The 10-year follow-up of the Belfast Diet Study. Diabet Med 1998; 15:290-296.
163. Lewy VD, Danadian K, Witchel SF, Arslanian S: Early metabolic abnormalities in adolescent girls with polycystic ovarian syndrome. J Pediatr 2001;138:38-44.
164. Lin-Su K, Vogiatzi MG, New MI: Body mass index and age at menarche in an adolescent clinic population. Clin Pediatr 2002;41:501-507.
165. Livingston EH: Procedure incidence and in-hospital complication rates of bariatric surgery in the United States. Am J Surg 2004;188:105-110.
166. Livingston EH, Huerta S, Arthur D, et al: Male gender is a predictor of morbidity and age a predictor of mortality for patients undergoing gastric bypass surgery. Ann Surg 2002;236:576-582.
167. Long SD, O'Brien K, MacDonald KG Jr, et al: Weight loss in severely obese subjects prevents the progression of impaired glucose tolerance to type II diabetes: A longitudinal interventional study. Diabetes Care 1994;17:372-375.
168. Lujan JA, Frutos MD, Hernandez Q, et al: Laparoscopic versus open gastric bypass in the treatment of morbid obesity: A randomized prospective study. Ann Surg 2004; 239:433-437.
169. Luo J, Hu FB: Time trends of obesity in pre-school children in China from 1989 to 1997. Int J Obes Relat Metab Disord 2002;26:553-558.
170. MacDonald KG Jr, Long SD, Swanson MS, et al: The gastric bypass operation reduces the progression and mortality of non-insulin-dependent diabetes mellitus. J Gastrointest Surg 1997;1:213-220.
171. Marceau P, Kaufman D, Biron S, et al: Outcome of pregnancies after biliopancreatic diversion. Obes Surg 2004; 14:318-324.
172. Matkovic V: Osteoporosis as a pediatric disease: Role of calcium and heredity. J Rheumatol Suppl 1992;33:54-59.
173. Matkovic V, Ilich JZ, Andon MB, et al: Urinary calcium, sodium, and bone mass of young females. Am J Clin Nutr 1995;62:417-425.
174. Matsushita Y, Yoshiike N, Kaneda F, et al: Trends in childhood obesity in Japan over the last 25 years from the national nutrition survey. Obes Res 2004;12:205-214.
175. Matthews DR, Wallace TM: Children with type 2 diabetes: The risks of complications. Horm Res 2002;57(Suppl 1): 34-39.
176. McGill HC Jr, Herderick EE, McMahan CA, et al: Atherosclerosis in youth. Minerva Pediatr 2002;54: 437-447.
177. McGill HC Jr, McMahan CA, Herderick EE, et al: Obesity accelerates the progression of coronary atherosclerosis in young men. Circulation 2002;105:2712-2718.
178. Mi J, Law C, Zhang KL, et al: Effects of infant birthweight and maternal body mass index in pregnancy on components of the insulin resistance syndrome in China. Ann Intern Med 2000;132:253-260.
179. Michels KB: Early life predictors of chronic disease. J Womens Health 2003;12:157-161.
180. Miraglia Del Giudice E, Cirillo G, Nigro V, et al: Low frequency of melanocortin-4 receptor (MC4R) mutations in a Mediterranean population with early-onset obesity. Int J Obes Relat Metab Disord 2002;26:647-651.
181. Misra A: Risk factors for atherosclerosis in young individuals. J Cardiovasc Risk 2000;7:215-229.
182. Mokdad AH, Marks JS, Stroup DF, Gerberding JL: Actual causes of death in the United States, 2000. JAMA 2004; 291:1238-1245.
183. Molleston JP, White F, Teckman J, Fitzgerald JF: Obese children with steatohepatitis can develop cirrhosis in childhood. Am J Gastroenterol 2002;97:2460-2462.
184. Msika S: [Surgery for morbid obesity: 2. Complications. Results of a Technologic Evaluation by the ANAES]. J Chir 2003;140:4-21.
185. Must A, Jacques PF, Dallal GE, et al: Long-term morbidity and mortality of overweight adolescents: A follow-up of the Harvard Growth Study of 1922 to 1935. N Engl J Med 1992;327:1350-1355.
186. Must A, Spadano J, Coakley EH, et al: The disease burden associated with overweight and obesity. JAMA 1999;282: 1523-1529.
187. Narayan KM, Boyle JP, Thompson TJ, et al: Lifetime risk for diabetes mellitus in the United States. JAMA 2003;290: 1884-1890.
188. Nesbitt SD, Ashaye MO, Stettler N, et al: Overweight as a risk factor in children: A focus on ethnicity. Ethn Dis 2004;14:94-110.
189. Nguyen NT, Goldman C, Rosenquist CJ, et al: Laparoscopic versus open gastric bypass: A randomized study of outcomes, quality of life, and costs. Ann Surg 2001; 234:279-289; discussion 289-291.
190. Nguyen NT, Wolfe BM: Laparoscopic versus open gastric bypass. Semin Laparosc Surg 2002;9:86-93.
191. O'Brien PE, Dixon JB: Lap-band: outcomes and results. J Laparoendosc Adv Surg Tech A 2003;13:265-270.
192. O'Brien PE, Dixon JB, Brown W, et al: The laparoscopic adjustable gastric band (Lap-Band): A prospective study of medium-term effects on weight, health and quality of life. Obes Surg 2002;12:652-660.
193. Ogden CL, Carroll MD, Flegal KM: Epidemiologic trends in overweight and obesity. Endocrinol Metab Clin North Am 2003;32:741-760.
194. Ogden CL, Flegal KM, Carroll MD, Johnson CL: Prevalence and trends in overweight among US children and adolescents, 1999-2000. JAMA 2002;288:1728-1732.
195. Oken E, Gillman MW: Fetal origins of obesity. Obes Res 2003;11:496-506.
196. Palaniappan LP, Carnethon MR, Fortmann SP: Heterogeneity in the relationship between ethnicity, BMI, and fasting insulin. Diabetes Care 2002;25: 1351-1357.
197. Palasciano G, Portincasa P, Vinciguerra V, et al: Gallstone prevalence and gallbladder volume in children and adolescents: An epidemiological ultrasonographic survey and relationship to body mass index. Am J Gastroenterol 1989;84:1378-1382.
198. Parsons TJ, Power C, Logan S, Summerbell CD: Childhood predictors of adult obesity: A systematic review. Int J Obes Relat Metab Disord 1999;23(Suppl 8):S1-S107.
199. Partridge AH, Avorn J, Wang PS, Winer EP: Adherence to therapy with oral antineoplastic agents. J Natl Cancer Inst 2002;94:652-661.
200. Phipps S, DeCuir-Whalley S: Adherence issues in pediatric bone marrow transplantation. J Pediatr Psychol 1990; 15:459-475.

201. Piaget J: The Growth of Logical Thinking From Childhood to Adolescence. New York, Basic Books, 1958.
202. Pinhas-Hamiel O, Dolan LM, Daniels SR, et al: Increased incidence of non-insulin-dependent diabetes mellitus among adolescents. J Pediatr 1996;128:608-615.
203. Podnos YD, Jimenez JC, Wilson SE, et al: Complications after laparoscopic gastric bypass: A review of 3464 cases. Arch Surg 2003;138:957-961.
204. Pories WJ, Swanson MS, MacDonald KG, et al: Who would have thought it? An operation proves to be the most effective therapy for adult-onset diabetes mellitus. Ann Surg 1995;222:339-350; discussion 350-352.
205. Rand CS, McGregor AM: Adolescents having obesity surgery: A 6-year follow-up. South Med J 1994;87:1208-1213.
206. Randolph JG, Weintraub WH, Rigg A: Jejunoileal bypass for morbid obesity in adolescents. J Pediatr Surg 1974;9: 341-345.
207. Rapoff M, Barnard MU: Compliance with pediatric medical regimens. In Cramer JA (ed): Patient Compliance in Medical Practice and Clinical Trials. New York, Raven Press, 1991, pp 73-98.
208. Rapoff MA: Assessing and enhancing adherence to medical regimens for juvenile rheumatoid arthritis. Pediatr Ann 2002;31:373-379.
209. Rapoff MA: Commentary: Pushing the envelope: Furthering research on improving adherence to chronic pediatric disease regimens. J Pediatr Psychol 2001;26: 277-278.
210. Rapoff MA, Belmont J, Lindsley C, et al: Prevention of nonadherence to nonsteroidal anti-inflammatory medications for newly diagnosed patients with juvenile rheumatoid arthritis. Health Psychol 2002;21:620-623.
211. Rapoff MA, Purviance MR, Lindsley CB: Educational and behavioral strategies for improving medication compliance in juvenile rheumatoid arthritis. Arch Phys Med Rehabil 1988;69:439-441.
212. Rashid M, Roberts EA: Nonalcoholic steatohepatitis in children. J Pediatr Gastroenterol Nutr 2000;30:48-53.
213. Ravelli AC, van der Meulen JH, Osmond C, et al: Obesity at the age of 50 y in men and women exposed to famine prenatally. Am J Clin Nutr 1999;70:811-816.
214. Ravussin E, Lillioja S, Knowler WC, et al: Reduced rate of energy expenditure as a risk factor for body-weight gain. N Engl J Med 1988;318:467-472.
215. Reddington C, Cohen J, Baldillo A, et al: Adherence to medication regimens among children with human immunodeficiency virus infection. Pediatr Infect Dis J 2000;19:1148-1153.
216. Redline S, Tishler PV, Schluchter M, et al: Risk factors for sleep-disordered breathing in children: Associations with obesity, race, and respiratory problems. Am J Respir Crit Care Med 1999;159:1527-1532.
217. Reitman A, Friedrich I, Ben-Amotz A, Levy Y: Low plasma antioxidants and normal plasma B vitamins and homocysteine in patients with severe obesity. Isr Med Assoc J 2002; 4:590-593.
218. Ren CJ: Controversies in bariatric surgery: Evidence-based discussions on laparoscopic adjustable gastric banding. J Gastrointest Surg 2004;8:396-397; discussion 404-405.
219. Roberts EA: Nonalcoholic steatohepatitis in children. Curr Gastroenterol Rep 2003;5:253-259.
220. Roberts EA: Steatohepatitis in children. Best Pract Res Clin Gastroenterol 16:749-765, 2002.
221. Rosenbaum M, Leibel RL, Hirsch J: Obesity. N Engl J Med 1997;337:396-407.
222. Rosenbloom AL, Joe JR, Young RS, Winter WE: Emerging epidemic of type 2 diabetes in youth. Diabetes Care 1999; 22:345-354.
223. Sainsbury A, Cooney GJ, Herzog H: Hypothalamic regulation of energy homeostasis. Best Pract Res Clin Endocrinol Metab 2002;16:623-637.
224. Schauer P, Ikramuddin S, Hamad G, Gourash W: The learning curve for laparoscopic Roux-en-Y gastric bypass is 100 cases. Surg Endosc 2003;17:212-215.
225. Schauer PR, Burguera B, Ikramuddin S, et al: Effect of laparoscopic Roux-en Y gastric bypass on type 2 diabetes mellitus. Ann Surg 2003;238:467-484; discussion 484-485.
226. Schauer PR, Ikramuddin S: Laparoscopic surgery for morbid obesity. Surg Clin North Am 2001;81:1145-1179.
227. Schechter MS: Technical report: Diagnosis and management of childhood obstructive sleep apnea syndrome. Pediatrics 2002;109:e69.
228. Schonfeld-Warden NA, Warden CH: Uncoupling proteins: A molecular basis for racial differences in energy expenditure (and obesity?). Am J Clin Nutr 2002;75:607-608.
229. Schwimmer JB, Burwinkle TM, Varni JW: Health-related quality of life of severely obese children and adolescents. JAMA 2003;289:1813-1819.
230. Scopinaro N, Adami GF, Marinari GM, et al: Biliopancreatic diversion. World J Surg 1998;22:936-946.
231. Silber T, Randolph J, Robbins S: Long-term morbidity and mortality in morbidly obese adolescents after jejunoileal bypass. J Pediatr 1986;108:318-322.
232. Silverman BL, Rizzo TA, Cho NH, Metzger BE: Long-term effects of the intrauterine environment. The Northwestern University Diabetes in Pregnancy Center. Diabetes Care 1998;21(Suppl 2):B142-B149.
233. Sinha R, Fisch G, Teague B, et al: Prevalence of impaired glucose tolerance among children and adolescents with marked obesity. N Engl J Med 2002;346:802-810.
234. Soper RT, Mason EE, Printen KJ, Zellweger H: Gastric bypass for morbid obesity in children and adolescents. J Pediatr Surg 1975;10:51-58.
235. Sorensen HT, Sabroe S, Rothman KJ, et al: Relation between weight and length at birth and body mass index in young adulthood: Cohort study. BMJ 1997;315:1137.
236. Sorof J, Daniels S: Obesity hypertension in children: A problem of epidemic proportions. Hypertension 2002; 40:441-447.
237. Srinivasan SR, Frontini MG, Berenson GS: Longitudinal changes in risk variables of insulin resistance syndrome from childhood to young adulthood in offspring of parents with type 2 diabetes: The Bogalusa Heart Study. Metabolism 2003;52:443-450; discussion 451-453.
238. Stanford A, Glascock JM, Eid GM, et al: Laparoscopic Roux-en-Y gastric bypass in morbidly obese adolescents. J Pediatr Surg 2003;38:430-433.
239. Steinberger J, Moran A, Hong CP, et al: Adiposity in childhood predicts obesity and insulin resistance in young adulthood. J Pediatr 2001;138:469-473.
240. Stewart KS, Dearmun AK: Adherence to health advice amongst young people with chronic illness. J Child Health Care 2001;5:155-162.
241. Strauss RS: Childhood obesity. Pediatr Clin North Am 2002;49:175-201.
242. Strauss RS: Childhood obesity and self-esteem. Pediatrics 2000;105:e15.
243. Strauss RS, Bradley LJ, Brolin RE: Gastric bypass surgery in adolescents with morbid obesity. J Pediatr 2001;138: 499-504.
244. Strauss RS, Pollack HA: Epidemic increase in childhood overweight, 1986-1998. JAMA 2001;286:2845-2848.
245. Sturm R: Increases in clinically severe obesity in the United States, 1986-2000. Arch Intern Med 2003;163:2146-2148.
246. Sugerman HJ: Bariatric surgery for severe obesity. J Assoc Acad Minor Phys 2001;12:129-136.

247. Sugerman HJ: Gastric bypass surgery for severe obesity. Semin Laparosc Surg 2002;9:79-85.
248. Sugerman HJ, Sugerman EL, DeMaria EJ, et al: Bariatric surgery for severely obese adolescents. J Gastrointest Surg 2003;7:102-108.
249. Surgeons, American College of: Recommendations for Facilities Performing Bariatric Surgery. Bulletin of the American College of Surgeons, No. 85, 2000.
250. Surgery, American Society for Bariatric: Guidelines for Bariatric Surgery. Bulletin of the American College of Surgeons, No. 85, 2000.
251. Taranger J, Engstrom I, Lichenstein H, Svennberg-Redegren I: Somatic pubertal development. Acta Paediatr Scand Suppl 1976;258(Suppl):121-135.
252. Ten S, Maclaren N: Insulin resistance syndrome in children. J Clin Endocrinol Metab 2004;89:2526-2539.
253. Thompson SM, Dahlquist LM, Koenning GM, Bartholomew LK: Brief report: Adherence-facilitating behaviors of a multidisciplinary pediatric rheumatology staff. J Pediatr Psychol 1995;20:291-297.
254. Tounian P, Aggoun Y, Dubern B, et al: Presence of increased stiffness of the common carotid artery and endothelial dysfunction in severely obese children: A prospective study. Lancet 2001;358:1400-1404.
255. Towbin A, Inge TH, Garcia VF, et al: Beriberi after gastric bypass surgery in adolescence. J Pediatr 2004;145:263-267.
256. Turner RC, Cull CA, Frighi V, Holman RR, and for the UK Prospective Diabetes Study Group: Glycemic control with diet, sulfonylurea, metformin, or insulin in patients with type 2 diabetes mellitus: Progressive requirement for multiple therapies (UKPDS 49). JAMA 1999;281: 2005-2012.
257. Van Itallie TB: Health implications of overweight and obesity in the United States. Ann Intern Med 1985;103:983-988.
258. von Mutius E, Schwartz J, Neas LM, et al: Relation of body mass index to asthma and atopy in children: The National Health and Nutrition Examination Study III. Thorax 2001; 56:835-838.
259. Wahlqvist ML: Chronic disease prevention: A life-cycle approach which takes account of the environmental impact and opportunities of food, nutrition and public health policies—the rationale for an eco-nutritional disease nomenclature. Asia Pac J Clin Nutr 2002;11(Suppl 9): S759-S762.
260. Wang G, Dietz WH: Economic burden of obesity in youths aged 6 to 17 years: 1979-1999. Pediatrics 2002;109:E81.
261. Wang Y: Is obesity associated with early sexual maturation? A comparison of the association in American boys versus girls. Pediatrics 2002;110:903-910.
262. Wattigney WA, Srinivasan SR, Chen W, et al: Secular trend of earlier onset of menarche with increasing obesity in black and white girls: The Bogalusa Heart Study. Ethn Dis 1999;9:181-189.
263. Weisberg SP, McCann D, Desai M, et al: Obesity is associated with macrophage accumulation in adipose tissue. J Clin Invest 2003;112:1796-1808.
264. Weiss R, Dziura J, Burgert TS, et al: Obesity and the metabolic syndrome in children and adolescents. N Engl J Med 2004;350:2362-2374.
265. Wellen KE, Hotamisligil GS: Obesity-induced inflammatory changes in adipose tissue. J Clin Invest 2003;112:1785-1788.
266. Whitaker RC: Understanding the complex journey to obesity in early adulthood. Ann Intern Med 2002;136:923-925.
267. Whitaker RC, Deeks CM, Baughcum AE, Specker BL: The relationship of childhood adiposity to parent body mass index and eating behavior. Obes Res 2000;8:234-240.
268. Whitaker RC, Wright JA, Pepe MS, et al: Predicting obesity in young adulthood from childhood and parental obesity. N Engl J Med 1997;337:869-873.
269. Wing YK, Hui SH, Pak WM, et al: A controlled study of sleep related disordered breathing in obese children. Arch Dis Child 2003;88:1043-1047.
270. Wittgrove AC, Jester L, Wittgrove P, Clark GW: Pregnancy following gastric bypass for morbid obesity. Obes Surg 1998;8:461-464; discussion 465-466.
271. Wysocki T, Greco P, Harris MA, et al: Behavior therapy for families of adolescents with diabetes: Maintenance of treatment effects. Diabetes Care 2001;24:441-446.
272. Xu H, Barnes GT, Yang Q, et al: Chronic inflammation in fat plays a crucial role in the development of obesity-related insulin resistance. J Clin Invest 2003;112:1821-1830.
273. Yajnik C: Interactions of perturbations in intrauterine growth and growth during childhood on the risk of adult-onset disease. Proc Nutr Soc 2000;59:257-265.
274. Yarnell JW, McCrum EE, Patterson CC, et al: Prevalence and awareness of excess weight in 13- and 14-year-olds in Northern Ireland using recent international guidelines. Acta Paediatr 2001;90:1435-1439.
275. Young-Hyman D, Schlundt DG, Herman L, et al: Evaluation of the insulin resistance syndrome in 5- to 10-year-old overweight/obese African-American children. Diabetes Care 2001;24:1359-1364.

Chapter 79

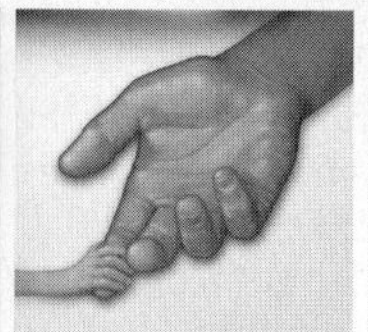

Duodenal Atresia and Stenosis—Annular Pancreas

Harry Applebaum, Steven L. Lee, and Devin P. Puapong

The duodenum is the most common site of neonatal intestinal obstruction, accounting for nearly half of all cases.[16] Although duodenal atresia, stenosis, and annular pancreas were recognized as disease entities as early as the 18th century, successful treatment of congenital high intestinal obstruction was a rare exception well into the 20th century. The first reported case of duodenal atresia is attributed to Calder, in 1733.[12] Cordes, in 1901,[15] described the typical clinical findings associated with this congenital defect, whereas Vidal from France and Ernst from the Netherlands are credited with the first successful surgical repairs, in 1905 and 1914, respectively.[24,84] By 1929, Kaldor was able to identify 250 patients with duodenal atresia reported in the literature, although a review by Webb and Wangensteen, in 1931, revealed only nine survivors.[41,85] In stark contrast, modern surgical management has resulted in greater than 95% survival, with the uncommon mortalities usually related to anomalies of other organ systems.[33]

Historically, when duodenal atresia was encountered in association with trisomy 21 (Down syndrome), a finding in nearly one third of patients, the newborn obstruction was often intentionally left untreated. It was not until the1970s that changing societal and medical ethics led to a universal operative approach for infants born with these paired anomalies.[58,69,82] A gradual decline in the incidence of newborns with duodenal obstruction can be attributed to the increasing ability of perinatologists to determine an abnormal chromosome association early in gestation, leading to elective termination of many of these pregnancies.[14,67,76,83]

The incidence of duodenal atresia has been estimated at 1 in 6000 to 1 in 10,000 births.[28] A recent large review of 18 congenital anomaly registries across Europe identified 64 cases among 670,093 births, or 1 in 10,500.[35] Although no specific genetic abnormality is known to cause duodenal atresia, the number of reports of the anomaly occurring among siblings and among several generations of a family, as well as its frequent association with trisomy 21, suggests that one may be present.[13,29,37,53,57,59,71,83,90]

EMBRYOLOGY

During the third week of embryonic development, gastrulation occurs. The cellular surface of the embryo facing the yolk sac becomes the endoderm, that facing the amniotic sac becomes the ectoderm, while the middle layer becomes the mesoderm. The endoderm gives rise to the gut tube beginning in the fourth week of development. In the sixth week, the gut epithelium proliferates rapidly, resulting in obliteration of the intestinal lumen. The intestine is then gradually recanalized over the next several weeks of development. Errors in recanalization are thought to be the primary cause of duodenal atresia and stenosis. A total failure of recanalization leads to an atresia, whereas a partial failure leads to a stenotic perforate membrane.[6,66,74] This etiology differs from that of intestinal atresias and stenoses in other parts of the bowel, which are thought to result from vascular accidents during the later phases of gestation.[52]

The pancreas begins to develop from the endodermal lining of the duodenum in the fourth week of gestation. Two pouches are formed that develop into a larger dorsal and a smaller ventral pancreatic primordium. The ventral bud then rotates dorsally to fuse with the dorsal bud during the eighth week. If the ventral bud fails to rotate completely, it remains anterior to the duodenum and fusion with the ventral pancreatic primordium results in a ring of pancreatic tissue encircling the duodenum.[6,42,62,66,74]

Approximately half of all infants with duodenal atresia or stenosis will also have a congenital anomaly of another organ system.[5,7,44,65,70,80,87,91] Sweed collated statistics for associated anomalies from a dozen large series of duodenal obstructions and found Down syndrome, annular pancreas, congenital heart disease, and malrotation to be the most common (Table 79-1).[81]

SPECTRUM OF INVOLVED DISORDERS

Several varieties of intrinsic and extrinsic congenital lesions can cause complete (81%) or partial (19%) obstruction

TABLE 79-1 Associated Anomalies (Collected Statistics)

Anomaly	%
Down syndrome	28.2
Annular pancreas	23.1
Congenital heart disease	22.6
Malrotation	19.7
Esophageal atresia/tracheoesophageal fistula	8.5
Genitourinary	8.0
Anorectal	4.4
Other bowel atresia	3.5
Other	10.9
None	45.0

Data from Sweed Y: Duodenal obstruction. In Puri P (ed): Newborn Surgery, 2nd ed, London, Arnold, 2003, p 423.

of the duodenum.[16] The spectrum of abnormalities causing intrinsic obstruction includes imperforate and perforate webs of variable thickness within continuous bowel as well as complete or almost complete bowel discontinuity. Abnormalities causing extrinsic obstruction include annular pancreas, preduodenal portal vein, Ladd's bands, and volvulus.[37,39,43,50,51,54,55,60]

Gray and Skandalakis have grouped the variations of duodenal atresia into three types[32]:

Type 1 (92% of cases)[25]: There is an obstructing septum (web) formed from mucosa and submucosa with no defect in the muscularis. The mesentery is intact. A variant of type 1 duodenal atresia, a "windsock deformity," can occur if the membrane is thin and elongated (Fig. 79-1A). The base of the membrane usually lies in the second portion of the duodenum but balloons out distally, distending the third and fourth portions. Thus, externally the obstruction appears considerably more distal than it actually is.[73]

Type 2 (1% of cases): A short fibrous cord connects the two blind ends of the duodenum. The mesentery is intact (see Fig. 79-1B).

Type 3 (7% of cases): There is no connection between the two blind ends of the duodenum. There is a V-shaped mesenteric defect (see Fig. 79-1C).

In type 1 atresia the obstructing septum may vary in thickness from one to several millimeters. Imperforate septa cause a complete obstruction, whereas those with central perforations cause incomplete obstruction. With perforate septa, the diameter of the opening directly determines the degree of obstruction and is therefore inversely related to the level of symptomatology (Fig. 79-2).[73]

Although intrinsic blockage may occur in almost any portion of the duodenum, it occurs near the juncture of the first and second portions in 85% of cases. The distal portion of the common bile duct often traverses the medial portion of the septum, with the ampulla commonly located on the proximal surface of the obstruction. In rare instances, the distal portion of the duct is bifid, with proximal and distal openings, giving rise to what at first glance appears to be an impossible situation of air and bile distal to a complete congenital obstruction.[9,10]

With an annular pancreas, the ring of pancreatic tissue encircling the duodenum may itself cause an extrinsic partial obstruction. More often, however, a duodenal atresia or stenotic web underlies the annulus and is the actual cause of blockage.[22] The pancreatic ductal anatomy is altered, with major ductal structures traversing the annular portion (Fig. 79-3). The distal duct is often located within the tissue of the underlying intrinsic obstruction, and the ampulla opens onto its surface. In cases where there is no associated intrinsic obstruction, the distal ductal anatomy is normal, and it is not uncommon to make a diagnosis of annular pancreas much later in life during laparotomy for an unrelated condition.[39]

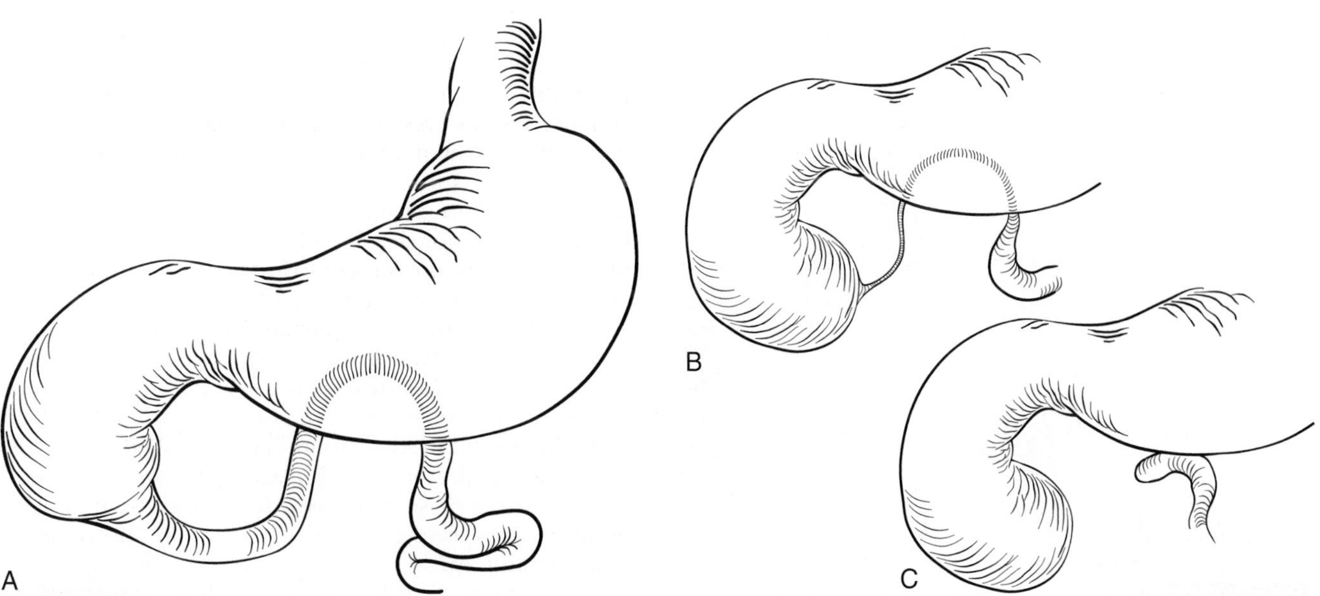

Figure 79-1 *A,* Type I duodenal atresia. *B,* Type II duodenal atresia. *C,* Type III duodenal atresia.

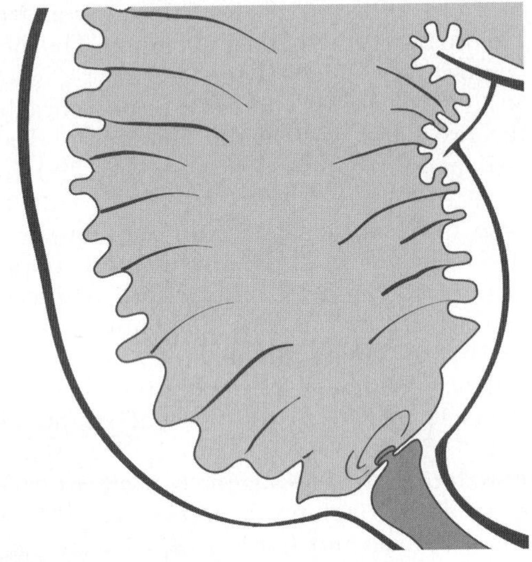

Figure 79-2 Typical duodenal web with central perforation.

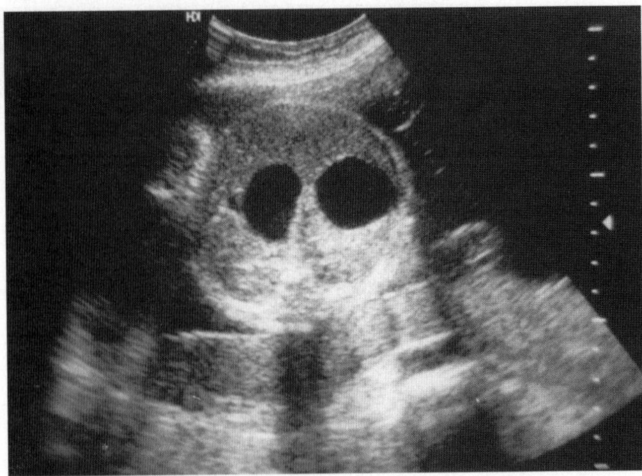

Figure 79-4 Fetal ultrasound showing "double-bubble" sign.

A preduodenal portal vein crosses the anterior surface of the second portion of the duodenum rather than running posterior to it and may cause incomplete obstruction by compression. This rare cause of extrinsic duodenal compression is usually found in infants with complex congenital heart disease.[33,60]

Intestinal malrotation results in Ladd's bands that usually give rise to an extrinsic partial obstruction of the second to third portion of the duodenum. Varying degrees of midgut volvulus—acute, intermittent, or chronic—can occur in these infants, also resulting in obstruction.[75]

CLINICAL PRESENTATION

Advances in prenatal care have allowed the majority of duodenal obstructions, both complete and incomplete, to be detected before birth.[36] Maternal polyhydramnios, noted in 30% to 65% of cases, is an early clue that should lead to further investigation.[16,55] Because polyhydramnios often leads to preterm labor, approximately one half of these infants will be premature. The classic "double bubble" obstructive pattern is usually easily identifiable on fetal ultrasound. The larger of the twin bubbles juxtaposed in the fetal abdomen is the dilated, fluid-filled stomach, whereas the other is the distended proximal duodenum (Fig. 79-4). This study will also occasionally identify an annular pancreas.[63,88]

Repeated bilious emesis is the characteristic clinical feature of almost all newborns with duodenal obstruction. Because of the proximal level of intestinal blockage, the infant does not appear distended, although a subtle upper abdominal fullness may be noted. Placement of a nasogastric tube with a return of greater than 30 mL of fluid is suggestive of an intestinal obstruction. In cases lacking prenatal diagnosis, it is somewhat common for an incorrect initial diagnosis of meconium aspiration to be made. During post-delivery airway suctioning, the tracheal catheter may be inadvertently passed down the esophagus, leading to wrongful interpretation of bilious gastric fluid as tracheal aspirate.

In patients with complete or high-grade duodenal obstruction, a plain radiograph of the abdomen will generally confirm the diagnosis, with a finding of the "double bubble" sign. The lack of more distal intestinal gas is diagnostic of a complete obstruction, whereas the presence of gas indicates a partial obstruction. In situations in which the diagnosis is suspected but the "double bubble" sign is not clearly visible, injection of 30 to 60 mL of air through the nasogastric tube may unmask this characteristic imaging finding (Fig. 79-5).

The recognition of partial obstructions may be considerably delayed if the obstruction is of a relatively minor degree.[28] In this situation it is not uncommon for symptoms to first occur when advancing the infant from formula to solid food, or it may be unmasked much later in infancy, childhood, or, in rare instances, adulthood, when a progressive decrease in motility or impaction of food or a foreign body causes more pronounced symptomatology.[27,56,68]

With characteristic findings of duodenal obstruction on plain abdominal radiographs, it is appropriate to proceed

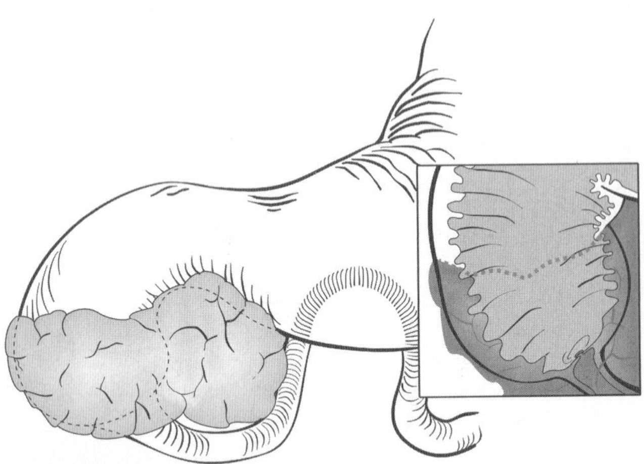

Figure 79-3 Annular pancreas with underlying web causing partial duodenal obstruction.

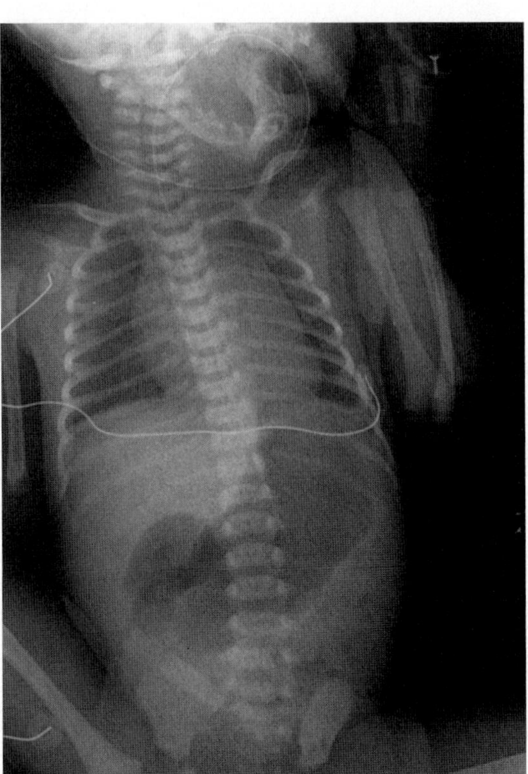

Figure 79-5 Plain abdominal film of newborn with duodenal stenosis (perforated web). Note small amount of air distal to "double bubble." Same finding with lack of distal air would indicate duodenal atresia.

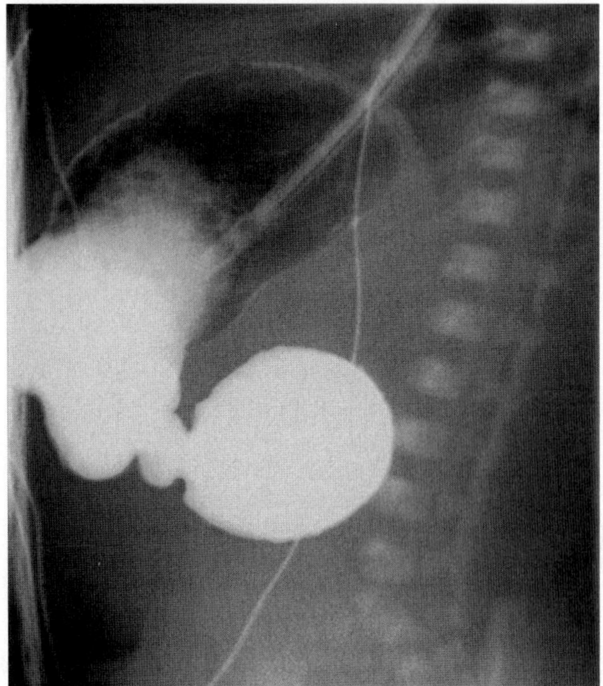

Figure 79-6 Duodenal atresia evident on upper gastrointestinal radiographic contrast study.

directly to operative intervention without obtaining contrast studies. Occasionally, an upper gastrointestinal contrast study may be helpful in differentiating intrinsic duodenal obstruction from midgut volvulus. With intrinsic obstruction, a smooth, rounded end will usually be seen at the level of obstruction in the second portion of the duodenum and a ligament of Treitz may be visible if the obstruction is incomplete (Fig. 79-6). A distal "beaking" effect in the third portion should arouse concern about volvulus and the need for an urgent operation. However, preoperative differentiation of the two anatomic problems is completely unnecessary if the patient is to undergo exploration within a short period of time.[26]

The upper gastrointestinal contrast study is useful for the evaluation of older infants and children with symptoms of chronic partial obstruction.[11] Gastroduodenoscopy may be a helpful diagnostic and sometimes therapeutic tool in these patients.[49,64]

TREATMENT

Neonates with duodenal obstruction are initially managed with nasogastric or orogastric tube decompression and intravenous fluids. Gastrointestinal losses are replaced appropriately, and placement of a peripherally inserted central catheter line for parenteral nutrition is recommended, because feeding is commonly delayed for up to several weeks after repair. Assuming that a diagnosis of midgut volvulus has been reasonably excluded, surgical correction of duodenal obstruction is not urgent. It can take place once the infant is optimized hemodynamically and associated anomalies have been appropriately studied.[44] Pulmonary status and size may preclude early operative intervention in very premature infants, and decompression accompanied by parenteral nutrition may be required for several weeks before undertaking repair.

The operation is best accomplished through a right upper quadrant transverse incision halfway between the liver edge and the umbilicus, carried slightly across the midline. After abdominal exploration, the right colon and hepatic flexure are then mobilized medially to allow full exposure of the proximal duodenum. Eviscerating and positioning the small bowel and colon cephalad and to the left of the incision best achieves access to the third and fourth portions of the duodenum. This maneuver will fully expose the root of the mesentery and ligament of Treitz. Although many patients with high-grade duodenal obstruction will have accompanying malrotation, on closer inspection a number will actually be found to have a pseudo-malrotation, because the underlying grossly dilated duodenum may cause abnormal leftward displacement of the right colon and hepatic flexure. Absence of the ligament of Treitz will be noted in patients with true malrotation.

The entire duodenum is inspected and the probable location and type of the obstruction noted. In a complete or nearly complete obstruction, the proximal duodenum appears as a large, boggy, thickened sphere. In type I cases, diminutive, gasless bowel distal to this point indicates that the obstruction is complete. In type II and III cases, the discontinuity of the bowel will become evident during dissection. In patients with annular pancreas,

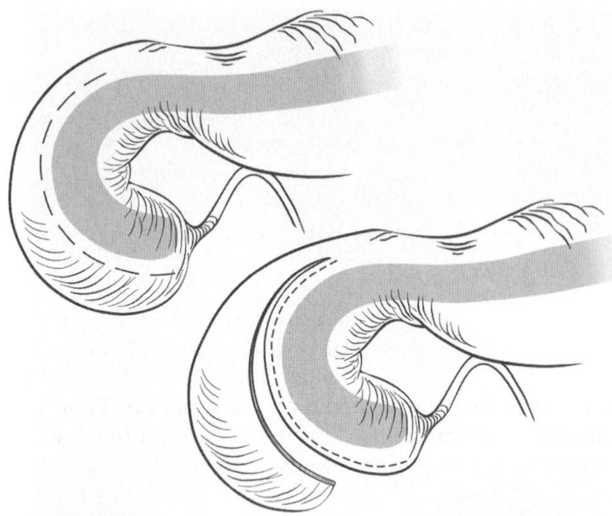

Figure 79-7 Tapering of distended proximal duodenum over dilator.

pancreatic tissue will be seen extending circumferentially around the second portion of the duodenum.

When there is gross dilatation of the proximal segment, a tapering duodenoplasty as the initial part of the procedure may hasten the postoperative return of effective peristalsis.[1,3,19,38,46,77,92] This is accomplished by either suture plication or by resection using a GIA stapler or needle-tip electrocautery and suture closure. The tapering is positioned on the anterior or anterolateral surface to avoid damage to the common bile duct, pancreas, and ampulla (Fig. 79-7).[40] Additionally, division of the ligament of Treitz to help mobilize the distal segment may greatly facilitate an eventual untwisted, tension-free anastomosis.

When there is continuity of the proximal and distal duodenum, it is best to open the distal bowel near the apparent point of obstruction, in a position and direction suitable for a potential bypass. If filmy or thin webs are identified as the cause of the obstruction, they may sometimes be excised rather than bypassed. In this case, the incision is carried over the web into the proximal lumen and the web is excised with cautery. If the ampulla is on the medial aspect of the web, or is not well visualized, excision should include only the lateral portion of the web. The duodenum is closed as a duodenoplasty in a transverse manner, to shorten and widen the bowel overlying the resection to minimize the risk of stenosis. Web excision should only be attempted when the web is thin and when it is clearly the only cause of obstruction.

In almost all situations, a duodenoduodenostomy, joining the bowel just proximal and distal to the obstruction, is the best corrective option. It is the most direct, physiologic repair and, of the available options, has the least potential for later complications. When this procedure is difficult because of patient anatomy, particularly in some small, premature infants, duodenojejunostomy is an alternative choice. A loop of proximal jejunum is chosen that will comfortably reach the proximal duodenal segment and is brought through the mesentery of the right transverse colon in a retrocolic position.

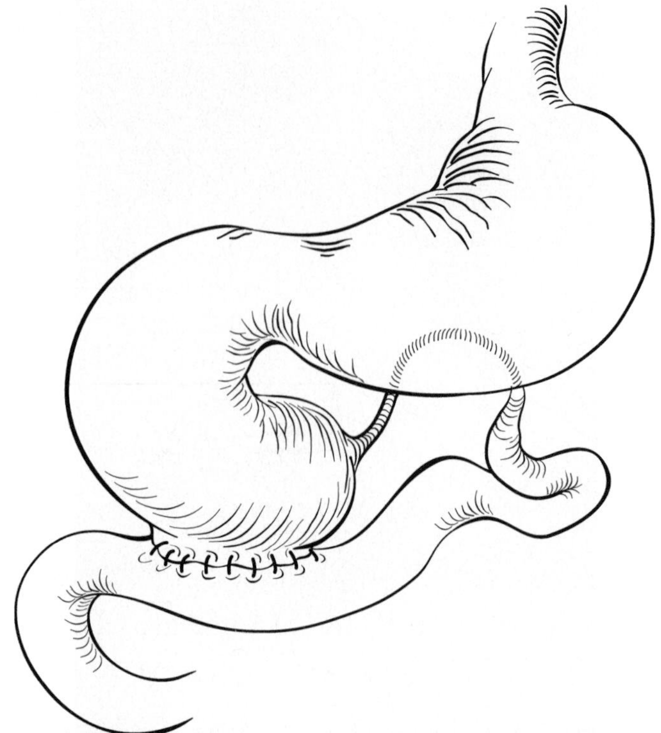

Figure 79-8 Duodenojejunostomy.

Duodenojejunostomy provides postoperative results that are generally equivalent to those obtained with duodenoduodenostomy (Fig. 79-8). Gastrojejunostomy is associated with frequent late complications of marginal ulceration and blind loop syndrome, and therefore should be avoided.

In recent series of patients with duodenal obstruction, duodenoduodenostomy has been the procedure of choice in the great majority of patients (>80%), with duodenojejunostomy used in approximately 10% and web excision in 5% to 10%. Gastrojejunostomy was a rarely chosen option.[8,16,25,34]

When performing a bypass anastomosis, a "diamond anastomosis" (proximal transverse and distal longitudinal incisions) (Fig. 79-9A), first described by Kimura, is preferred over the "simple anastomosis" (proximal and distal longitudinal incisions) (see Fig. 79-9B).[45,47,86] There is evidence that this asymmetrical anastomosis will maintain itself in a more wide-open position and permit earlier transit of duodenal contents.

The antimesenteric incisions in each segment should be 1 to 2 cm in length, depending on the size of the patient, to ensure an adequately patent anastomosis. With type III deformities, the end of the distal segment is spatulated appropriately. Before making the incision in the distal segment, it is useful to inject saline into the lumen while occluding the bowel distally to slightly stretch the wall, thus enabling a technically easier anastomosis. Additionally, a 10 French Foley catheter should be passed proximally into the stomach and distally into the jejunum and pulled back with the balloon inflated, to ensure that no additional web or a windsock deformity is overlooked. Before starting the anastomosis, small ribbon retractors

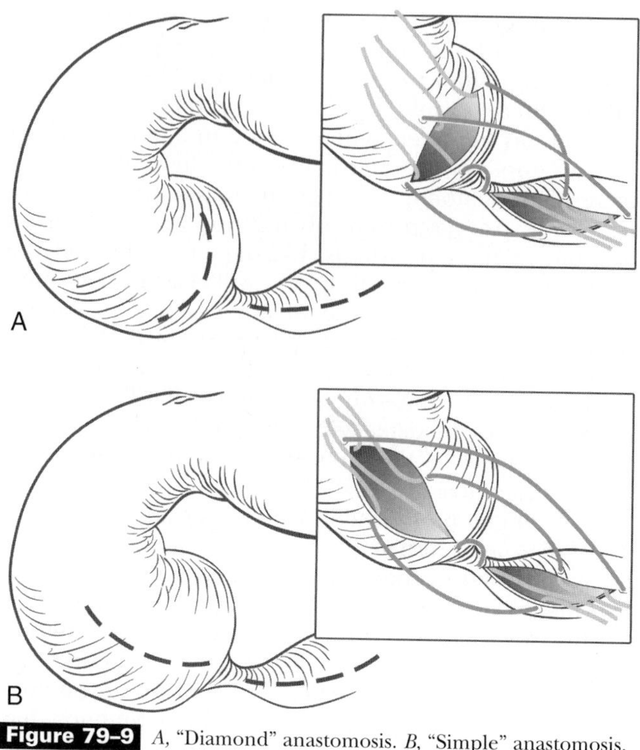

Figure 79–9 *A,* "Diamond" anastomosis. *B,* "Simple" anastomosis.

can be placed in the proximal dilated segment to inspect the point of obstruction and to determine the position of the ampulla of Vater. This anatomic landmark is usually easily visible, even in small premature infants. In most patients, it is found in the proximal segment, adjacent to or on the anteromedial aspect of the stenosis or web. In the remaining patients, it will empty into the distal segment, also adjacent to or on the obstruction.

The diamond anastomosis is constructed by placing initial stay sutures joining the midpoints of each incision to the ends of the other. Placement should anticipate a posterior row of knots inside the lumen and an anterior row on the outside. The posterior row of the anastomosis is constructed using a repeating bisecting technique, to ensure even placement of the sutures and good coaptation of the bowel edges. The anterior row of the anastomosis is then completed in a similar fashion. The anastomosis is checked for patency, and the intestine is returned to the abdominal cavity in its usual position. If the right colon has been extensively mobilized and the ligament of Treitz taken down, or if a malrotation is present, the intestine is replaced with the small bowel on the right and the colon on the left, in the manner of a Ladd's procedure. A nasogastric tube is positioned in the stomach. Although commonly used in the past, gastrostomy tubes are now considered useful only in selected infants who are not expected to feed orally in the near future. Some surgeons routinely position transanastomotic feeding tubes, although their benefit has not been clearly delineated.[4,86]

Congenital obstruction of the distal duodenum at or near the ligament of Treitz presents an especially difficult problem. The long segment of atonic dilated duodenum is difficult to effectively taper, so that the reconstructed bowel and anastomosis are likely to function poorly for a lengthy time period or not at all. In this situation, subtotal removal of the dilated duodenum with preservation of the ampulla is recommended (Fig. 79-10A).[23,48] The anterior wall of the second portion of the duodenum is opened and the ampulla of Vater is located. The ligament of Treitz is taken down and the dilated duodenum is dissected from the pancreas in a retrograde fashion to just distal to the ampulla. The first and second portions of the duodenum are then tapered to near the level of

Figure 79–10 *A,* Mobilization of distal dilated duodenum after division of the ligament of Treitz. *B,* Onlay of normal jejunum after resection of distal duodenum (*note:* oblique resection to preserve ampulla).

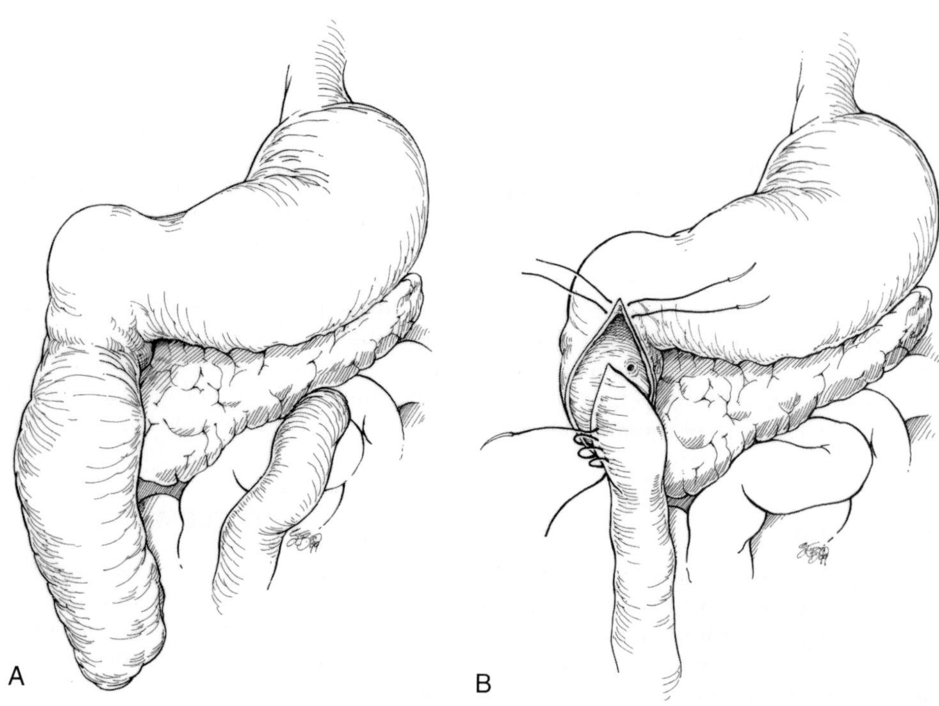

the ampulla, with the resected proximal duodenum removed in continuity with the distal duodenum. The end of the normal jejunum distal to the obstruction is spatulated and anastomosed to the tapered proximal segment (see Fig. 79-10B).

When annular pancreas is encountered in association with duodenal obstruction, bypass is always the procedure of choice. The ring of pancreatic tissue should never be transected because of the major ductal structures that traverse it. Damage to these structures will lead to leakage of pancreatic fluid and/or pancreatitis. An obstructing preduodenal portal vein is bypassed in a similar manner.

There have been several recent reports of successful laparoscopic bypass procedures to correct neonatal duodenal obstruction.[8,31,79] It is currently impossible to compare the long-term outcomes of this technique with those of the classic open approach, because of the limited number of selected patients who have undergone this treatment.

Postoperatively, total parenteral nutrition is continued and nasogastric tube output is monitored. As with other neonatal intestinal procedures, feedings may be started when the volume of the nasogastric output has diminished and its color has lightened and it becomes clear. This stage is commonly reached within several days to a week but may be prolonged. Small feedings are then initiated, with volume and concentration advanced as tolerated. This is a rapid process in most infants, and the majority may be discharged within one to several weeks.

COMPLICATIONS

Intraoperative

There are several intraoperative judgmental and technical pitfalls that will lead to postoperative difficulties.[17] Incorrect identification of the site of obstruction most commonly occurs when a long, floppy web (windsock deformity) is present. The proximally based web fills with gastrointestinal secretions and balloons out into the distal duodenum, distending it and causing the site of obstruction to appear much more distal than it actually is. The unwary surgeon, not recognizing the true attachment of the web, may then construct a bypass anastomosis entirely distal to it. Additionally, on rare occasions, there will be more than one obstruction present. A distal web is easily missed because of the lack of any obvious adjacent proximal dilatation. The careful passage and withdrawal of balloon catheters both proximally into the stomach and distally into the jejunum before starting an anastomosis should prevent both of these situations.[2,11,72]

Postoperative

Prolonged feeding intolerance is the most common complication after surgery to relieve duodenal obstruction. There is a great deal of variability in the time required for a bypass anastomosis or web excision to function adequately. Although a variety of prokinetic agents have been proposed to hasten this process, none has been found to be of any consistent benefit. In general, if no specific difficulties were encountered at the initial procedure, there should be concern if relatively normal function has not been achieved by 2 to 3 weeks. At that time, an upper gastrointestinal series is helpful to search for residual anatomic obstruction, anastomotic stenosis, previously unrecognized obstruction at a different location, or poor peristalsis. Placing small clips on the anastomosis during initial surgery will assist in determining the location and cause of any residual problems. Any decisions as to further surgical procedures should be based on a combined assessment of both imaging studies and clinical gastrointestinal function. Dilated proximal duodenum may be visualized radiographically for at least several months in the presence of a fully functional bypass anastomosis.[78]

If prolonged poor function should occur, the finding of an anatomic obstruction is far less likely than identifying persistently poor peristalsis. Additional simple tapering of the proximal duodenum may suffice to provide adequate additional motility, while subtotal duodenectomy combined with proximal tapering is advisable if the initial obstruction was in the distal duodenum.[48] Once adequate gastrointestinal function has been achieved, further problems may develop but are uncommon.

Late duodenal obstruction may occasionally be noted in older infants and children. This may occur after a seemingly successful neonatal bypass procedure or excision of web or de novo when a diagnosis of partial duodenal obstruction was initially missed. In the former, a piece of fibrous food or a foreign body may become impacted at the site of a partially resected web or relatively narrow anastomosis that was either constructed to an inadequate size, has become strictured over time, or has failed to grow with the child. In the last instance, it may occur at the site of a relatively low-grade stenosis that has become progressively symptomatic because of the development of proximal dilatation and ineffective peristalsis. In others, no persistent anatomic obstruction can be demonstrated after initial surgical correction but poor peristalsis can be demonstrated in an area of persistent, and sometimes increasing, dilatation.[18]

Proximal tapering is often very helpful at this time, either in conjunction with correction of an obviously inadequate initial procedure or often by itself, in situations in which no distinct anatomic narrowing is found.[20,21]

Most of these older infants and children are large enough for full-function upper gastrointestinal endoscopy, which may aid in the diagnosis and may be therapeutic by permitting dilatation of anastomotic strictures or resection of webs.[49,64]

OUTCOMES

Survival of infants with duodenal obstruction has increased from 45% to 95% over the past half century.[30,32,61,89] This dramatic improvement is primarily related to improved diagnosis and surgical and postoperative management, although selective pregnancy termination has likely played a role. Almost all mortality is now related to associated anomalies of other organ systems, primarily those of the heart, lungs, and brain.

REFERENCES

1. Adzick NS, Harrison MR, deLorimier AA: Tapering duodenoplasty for megaduodenum associated with duodenal atresia. J Pediatr Surg 1986;21:311.
2. Akhtar J, Guiney EJ: Congenital duodenal obstruction. Br J Surg 1992;79:133.
3. Alexander F, DiFiore J, Stallion A: Triangular tapered duodenoplasty for the treatment of congenital duodenal obstruction. J Pediatr Surg 2002;37:862.
4. Arnbjornsson E, Larsson M, Finkel Y, Karpe B: Transanastomotic feeding tube after an operation for duodenal atresia. Eur J Pediatr Surg 2002;12:159.
5. Andrassy RJ, Mahour GH: Gastrointestinal anomalies associated with esophageal atresia or tracheoesophageal fistula. Arch Surg 1979;114:1125.
6. Arey LB: Developmental Anatomy: A Textbook and Laboratory Manual of Embryology, 7th ed. Philadelphia, WB Saunders, 1974.
7. Bailey PV, Tracy TFJ, Connors RH, et al: Congenital duodenal obstruction: A 32-year review. J Pediatr Surg 1993;28:92.
8. Bax NM, Ure BM, van der Zee DC, van Tuijl I: Laparoscopic duodenoduodenostomy for duodenal atresia. Surg Endosc 2001;15:217.
9. Bickler SW, Harrison MW, Blank E, Campbell JR: Microperforation of a duodenal diaphragm as a cause of paradoxical gas in congenital duodenal obstruction. J Pediatr Surg 1992;27:747.
10. Boyden EA, Cope JG, Bill AHJ: Anatomy and embryology of congenital intrinsic obstruction of the duodenum. Am J Surg 1967;114:190.
11. Brown RA, Millar AJ, Linegar A, et al: Fenestrated duodenal membranes: An analysis of symptoms, signs, diagnosis, and treatment. J Pediatr Surg 1994;29:429.
12. Calder E: Two examples of children born with preternatural conformation of the guts. Med Essays (Edinburgh) 1733;1:203.
13. Celli J, van Bokhoven H, Brunner HG: Feingold syndrome: Clinical review and genetic mapping. Am J Med Genet 2003;122A:294.
14. Chasen ST, Sharma G, Kalish RB, Chervenak FA: First-trimester screening for aneuploidy with fetal nuchal translucency in a United States population. Ultrasound Obstet Gynecol 2003;22:149.
15. Cordes L: Congenital occlusion of the duodenum. Arch Pediatr 1901;18:401.
16. Dalla Vecchia LK, Grosfeld JL, West KW, et al: Intestinal atresia and stenosis: A 25-year experience with 277 cases. Arch Surg 1998;133:490.
17. Danismend EN, Brown N: Morbidity and mortality in duodenal atresia. Z Kinderchir 1986;41:86.
18. de Lorimier AA: Bowel motility in infants and children born with duodenal atresia and stenosis. J Pediatr Surg 1998;33:950.
19. Dewan LA, Guiney EJ: Duodenoplasty in the management of duodenal atresia. Pediatr Surg Int 1990;5:253.
20. Ein SH, Shandling B: The late nonfunctioning duodenal atresia repair. J Pediatr Surg 1986;21:798.
21. Ein SH, Kim PC, Miller HA: The late nonfunctioning duodenal atresia repair—a second look. J Pediatr Surg 2000;35:690.
22. Elliot GB, Kliman MR, Elliot KA: Pancreatic annulus: A sign or cause of duodenal obstruction. Can J Surg 1968;11:357.
23. Endo M, Ukiyama E, Yokoyama JMK: Subtotal duodenectomy with jejunal patch for megaduodenum secondary to congenital duodenal malformation. J Pediatr Surg 1998; 33:1636.
24. Ernst NP: A case of congenital atresia of the duodenum treated successfully by operation. BMJ 1916;1:1644.
25. Escobar MA, Ladd AP, Grosfeld JL, et al: Duodenal atresia and stenosis: Long-term follow-up over 30 years. J Pediatr Surg 2004;39:867.
26. Eustace S, Connolly B, Blake N: Congenital duodenal obstruction: An approach to diagnosis. Eur J Pediatr Surg 1993;3:267.
27. Ferraris VA, McPhail JF: Adult duodenal web associated with peptic ulcer disease. Surg Gynecol Obstet 1984;158:461.
28. Fonkalsrud EW, DeLorimier AA, Hays DM: Congenital atresia and stenosis of the duodenum: A review compiled from the members of the Surgical Section of the American Academy of Pediatrics. Pediatrics 1969;43:79.
29. Gahukamble DB, Khamage AS, Shaheen AQ: Duodenal atresia: Its occurrence in siblings. J Pediatr Surg 1994; 29:1599.
30. Girvan DP, Stephens CA: Congenital intrinsic duodenal obstruction: A twenty-year review of its surgical management and consequences. J Pediatr Surg 1974;9:833.
31. Gluer S, Petersen C, Ure BM: Simultaneous correction of duodenal atresia due to annular pancreas and malrotation by laparoscopy. Eur J Pediatr Surg 2002;12:423.
32. Gray SW, Skandalakis JE: Embryology for Surgeons: The Embryological Basis for the Treatment of Congenital Defects. Philadelphia, WB Saunders, 1986.
33. Grosfeld JL, Rescorla FJ: Duodenal atresia and stenosis: Reassessment of treatment and outcome based on antenatal diagnosis, pathologic variance, and long-term follow-up. World J Surg 1993;17:301.
34. Grosfeld JL, Ballantine TV, Shoemaker R: Operative management of intestinal atresia and stenosis based upon pathologic findings. J Pediatr Surg 1979;14:368.
35. Haeusler MC, Befghold A, Stoll C, et al: EUROSCAN Study Group: Prenatal ultrasonographic detection of gastrointestinal obstruction: Results from 18 European congenital anomaly registries. Prenat Diagn 2002;22:616.
36. Hancock BJ, Wiseman NE: Congenital duodenal obstruction: The impact of an antenatal diagnosis. J Pediatr Surg 1989;24:1027.
37. Hendricks SK, Sybert VP: Association of annular pancreas and duodenal obstruction—evidence for Mendelian inheritance? Clin Genet 1991;39:383.
38. Hutton KA, Thomas DF: Tapering duodenoplasty. Pediatr Surg Int 1988;3:132.
39. Irving IM: Duodenal atresia and stenosis: Annular pancreas. In Lister J, Irving IM (eds): Neonatal Surgery, London, Butterworths, 1990, p 424.
40. Jona JZ, Belin RP: Duodenal anomalies and the ampulla of Vater. Surg Gynecol Obstet 1976;143:565.
41. Kaldor J: Atresia of the duodenum and duodenal diverticula. Ann Surg 1929;89:6.
42. Kamisawa T, Yuyang T, Egawa N, et al: A new embryologic hypothesis of annular pancreas. Hepatogastroenterology 2001;48:277.
43. Kiernan PD, ReMine SG, Kiernan PC, et al: Annular pancreas: Mayo Clinic experience from 1957 to 1976 with review of the literature. Arch Surg 1980;115:46.
44. Kimble RM, Harding J, Kolbe A: Additional congenital anomalies in babies with gut atresia or stenosis: When to investigate and which investigation. Pediatr Surg Int 1997;12:565.
45. Kimura K, Tsugawa C, Ogawa K, et al: Diamond-shaped anastomosis for congenital duodenal obstruction. Arch Surg 1977;112:1262.

46. Kimura K, Perdzynski W, Soper RT: Elliptical seromuscular resection for tapering the proximal dilated bowel in duodenal or jejunal atresia. J Pediatr Surg 1996;31:1405.
47. Kimura K, Mukohara N, Nishijima E, et al: Diamond-shaped anastomosis for duodenal atresia: An experience with 44 patients over 15 years. J Pediatr Surg 1990;25:977.
48. Kling K, Applebaum H, Dunn J, et al: A novel technique for correction of intestinal atresia at the ligament of Treitz. J Pediatr Surg 2000;35:353.
49. Kokkonen ML, Kalima T, Jaaskelainen J, Louhimo I: Duodenal atresia: Late follow-up. J Pediatr Surg 1988;23:216.
50. Komuro H, Makino S, Tahara K: Choledochal cyst associated with duodenal obstruction. J Pediatr Surg 2000;35:1259.
51. Knechtle SJ, Filston HC: Anomalous biliary ducts associated with duodenal atresia. J Pediatr Surg 1990;25:1266.
52. Lambrecht W, Kluth D: Hereditary multiple atresias of the gastrointestinal tract: Report of a case and review of the literature. J Pediatr Surg 1998;33:794.
53. Lemire EG, Evans JA, Giddins NG, et al: A familial disorder with duodenal atresia and tetralogy of Fallot. Am J Med Genet 1996;66:39.
54. McCollum MO, Jamieson DH, Webber EM: Annular pancreas and duodenal stenosis. J Pediatr Surg 2002;37:1776.
55. Merrill JR, Raffensperger JG: Pediatric annular pancreas: Twenty years' experience. J Pediatr Surg 1976;11:921.
56. Mikaelsson C, Arnbjornsson E, Kullendorff CM: Membranous duodenal stenosis. Acta Paediatr 1997;86:953.
57. Mitchell CE, Marshall DG, Reid WD: Preampullary congenital duodenal obstruction in a father and son. J Pediatr Surg 1993;28:1582.
58. Molenaar JC: The legal investigation of a decision not to operate on an infant with Down's syndrome and a duodenal atresia: A report from the Netherlands. Bioethics 1992;6:35.
59. Moore SW, de Jongh G, Bouic P, et al: Immune deficiency in familial duodenal atresia. J Pediatr Surg 1996;31:1733.
60. Mordehai J, Cohen Z, Kurzbart E, Mares AJ: Preduodenal portal vein causing duodenal obstruction associated with situs inversus, intestinal malrotation, and polysplenia: A case report. J Pediatr Surg 2002;37:E5.
61. Nixon HH, Tawes R: Etiology and treatment of small intestinal atresia: Analysis of a series of 127 jejunoileal atresias and comparison with 82 duodenal atresias. Surgery 1971;69:41.
62. Nobukawa B, Otaka M, Suda K, et al: An annular pancreas derived from paired ventral pancreata, supporting Baldwin's hypothesis. Pancreas 2000;20:408.
63. Norton KI, Tenreiro R, Rabinowitz JG: Sonographic demonstration of annular pancreas and a distal duodenal diaphragm in a newborn. Pediatr Radiol 1992;22:66.
64. Okamatsu T, Arai K, Yatsuzuka M, et al: Endoscopic membranectomy for congenital duodenal stenosis in an infant. J Pediatr Surg 1989;24:367.
65. Pameijer CR, Hubbard AM, Coleman B, Flake AW: Combined pure esophageal atresia, duodenal atresia, biliary atresia, and pancreatic ductal atresia: Prenatal diagnostic features and review of the literature. J Pediatr Surg 2000;35:745.
66. Patten BM: Human Embryology, 3rd ed. New York, McGraw-Hill, 1968.
67. Pinette MG, Egan JF, Wax JR, et al: Combined sonographic and biochemical markers for Down syndrome screening. J Ultrasound Med 2003;22:1185.
68. Pittschieler K, Gentili L: Endoscopic diagnosis of duodenal stenosis. J Pediatr Gastroenterol Nutr 1997;24:359.
69. Randolph JG: The doctor's dilemma in Down's syndrome and duodenal atresia. Hosp Physician 1974;10:23.
70. Ried IS: Biliary tract anomalies associated with duodenal atresia. Arch Dis Child 1973;48:852.
71. Rogers JC, Harris DJ, Holder T: Annular pancreas in a mother and daughter. Am J Med Genet 1993;45:116.
72. Rossello PJ: Congenital duodenal atresia associated with a separate duodenal diaphragm. J Pediatr Surg 1978;13:441.
73. Rowe MI, Buckner D, Clatworthy HW Jr: Wind sock web of the duodenum. Am J Surg 1968;116:444.
74. Sadler T: Langman's Medical Embryology, 9th ed. Philadelphia, Lippincott Williams and Wilkins, 2003.
75. Samuel M, Wheeler RA, Mami AG: Does duodenal atresia and stenosis prevent midgut volvulus in malrotation? Eur J Pediatr Surg 1997;7:11.
76. Schuchter K, Hafner E, Stangl G, et al: The first trimester "combined test" for the detection of Down syndrome pregnancies in 4939 unselected pregnancies. Prenat Diagn 2002;22:211.
77. Sherman JO, Schulten M: Operative correction of duodenomegaly. J Pediatr Surg 1974;9:461.
78. Spigland N, Yazbeck S: Complications associated with surgical treatment of congenital intrinsic duodenal obstruction. J Pediatr Surg 1990;25:1127.
79. Steyaert H, Valla JS, Van Hoorde E: Diaphragmatic duodenal atresia: Laparoscopic repair. Eur J Pediatr Surg 2003; 13:414.
80. Sumner TE, Auringer ST, Cox TD: A complex communicating bronchopulmonary foregut malformation: Diagnostic imaging and pathogenesis. Pediatr Radiol 1997;27:799.
81. Sweed Y: Duodenal obstruction. In Puri P (ed): Newborn Surgery, 2nd ed, London, Arnold, 2003, p 423.
82. Todres ID, Krane D, Howell MC, Shannon DC: Pediatricians' attitudes affecting decision-making in defective newborns. Pediatrics 1977;60:197.
83. Torfs CP, Christianson RE: Anomalies in Down syndrome. Am J Med Genet 1998;77:431.
84. Vidal E: 18e Congrès de chirurgie, Paris: Procès verbaux mémoires et discussion. Assoc Fr Chir 1905;18:739.
85. Webb CH, Wangensteen OH: Congenital intestinal atresia. Am J Dis Child 1931;41:262.
86. Weber TR, Lewis JE, Mooney D, Connors R: Duodenal atresia: A comparison of techniques of repair. J Pediatr Surg 1986;21:1133.
87. Wei JL, Rodeberg D, Thompson DM: Tracheal agenesis with anomalies found in both VACTERL and TACRD associations. Int J Pediatr Otorhinolaryngol 2003;67:1013.
88. Weiss H, Sherer DM, Manning FA: Ultrasonography of fetal annular pancreas. Obstet Gynecol 1999;94:852.
89. Wesley JR, Mahour GH: Congenital intrinsic duodenal obstruction: A twenty-five year review. Surgery 1977; 82:716.
90. Yokoyama T, Ishizone S, Momose Y, et al: Duodenal atresia in dizygotic twins. J Pediatr Surg 1997;32:1806.
91. Young DG, Wilkinson AW: Abnormalities associated with neonatal duodenal obstruction. Surgery 1968;63:832.
92. Young JS, Goco I, Pennell T: Duodenoplasty and reimplantation of the ampulla of Vater for megaduodenum. Am J Surg 1993;59:685.

Chapter 80

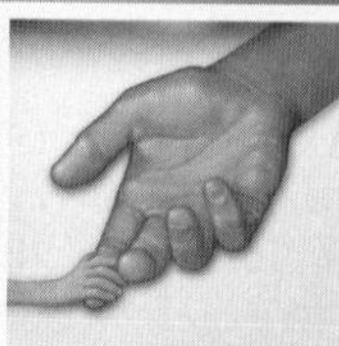

Jejunoileal Atresia and Stenosis

Jay L. Grosfeld

HISTORY

Goeller is credited with the first description of ileal atresia in 1684.[37] Other early observations concerning intestinal atresia were recorded by Calder (1773)[153] and Osiander (1779).[47] Voisin performed an enterostomy for intestinal atresia in 1804, and Meckel published a review of the topic and speculated on its cause in 1812. In 1889, Bland-Sutton[15] proposed a classification of the types of atresia and postulated that intestinal atresia occurred at the sites of *obliterative embryologic events,* such as atrophy of the vitelline duct. In 1894, Wanitschek unsuccessfully attempted the first resection and anastomosis for intestinal atresia.[47] In 1900, Tandler[137] proposed the theory that atresia was related to failure of recanalization (vacuolization) of the solid-cord stage of bowel development. These observations were confirmed by Johnson in 1910.[64] In 1911, Fockens[39] performed the first successful anastomosis for intestinal atresia. In 1912, Spriggs[132] suggested that mechanical accidents, including vascular occlusions, might be responsible for these occurrences. This concept was supported by clinical observations on atresia by Davis and Poynter (1922)[31] and by Webb and Wangensteen (1931).[153] Evans' extensive review (1951)[37] concerning 1498 instances of gastrointestinal atresia documented that a successful result was achieved in only 139 infants. The classic experimental observations of Louw and Barnard (1955)[80] confirming the role of late intrauterine mesenteric vascular accidents as the cause of most jejunoileal atresias laid the foundations for the modern-day understanding and care of these interesting anomalies.

INCIDENCE

Jejunoileal atresia and stenosis is a major cause of neonatal intestinal obstruction. *Atresia* refers to a congenital obstruction caused by complete occlusion of the intestinal lumen and accounts for 95% of cases. *Stenosis* is defined as a partial intraluminal occlusion, resulting in an incomplete intestinal obstruction, and accounts for 5% of jejunoileal obstructions. During the past 2 decades, a better understanding of etiologic factors and impaired intestinal function as well as refinements in pediatric anesthesia, operative technique, and preoperative and postoperative care (especially in the area of nutritional support) have led to a significant improvement in survival.

The incidence of jejunoileal atresia has been reported from as high as 1 in 330 (United States) and 1 in 400 (Denmark) live births to 1 in 1500 live births.[37] In epidemiologic studies, Cragan and colleagues[28,29] and Harris and coworkers[55] observed a higher prevalence of small-bowel atresia in African-American children and among twins. A similar increase in the frequency of jejunal atresia in discordant nonidentical twins was also observed in the Netherlands.[92] A population-based study from Hawaii showed that jejunoileal atresia was more common in Far East Asians than whites.[41] The risk for development of small intestinal atresias is increased after maternal use of pseudoephedrine alone and in combination with acetaminophen and in mothers with migraine headaches receiving ergotamine tartrate and caffeine (Cafergot) during pregnancy.[46,156]

Of 387 cases of intestinal atresia and stenosis treated from 1972 to 2004 at the Riley Children's Hospital in Indianapolis, Indiana, 194 were jejunoileal, 169 were duodenal, and 24 were colonic. Nixon and Tawes,[99] noted a 2:1 ratio in the frequency of jejunoileal to duodenal atresias. In a review of 619 cases of jejunoileal atresia and stenosis from the experience of members of the Surgical Section of the American Academy of Pediatrics, de Lorimier and associates[32] noted that boys and girls were equally affected. Although the mean birth weight in this relatively large group of infants was 2.7 kg (range: 0.9 to 4.8 kg), one third of the infants with jejunal atresia, one fourth of those with ileal atresia, and more than one half of those with multiple atresias were of low birth weight.[32] Infants in whom the atresia is detected on prenatal ultrasound examination are often of low birth weight.[4] Although 30% of infants with duodenal atresia or stenosis have Down syndrome, trisomy 21 is relatively uncommon in patients with jejunoileal atresia. Nixon and Tawes[99] noted only 2 cases of trisomy 21 among 127 cases, and de Lorimier and associates[32] noted only 5 among 619 cases. The only patient of the 194 infants with jejunoileal atresia at the Riley Children's Hospital who had Down syndrome had coexisting duodenal atresia.

ETIOLOGY

The early concepts concerning the cause of jejunoileal atresia were briefly considered in the historical sketch. In 1900, Tandler[137] theorized that intestinal atresia was related to a lack of revacuolization of the solid-cord stage of intestinal development. In 1959, Lynn and Espinas[82] confirmed some of Tandler's observations concerning epithelial plugging. Although mucosal atresia was frequently noted in instances of duodenal atresia, jejunoileal atresia as a result of epithelial plugging was uncommon. Most jejunoileal atresias are separated by a cordlike segment or a V-shaped mesenteric gap defect. Clinical observations by Louw and Barnard,[80] Santulli and Blanc,[121] and Nixon[98] that bile pigments, squames, and lanugo hairs were often found distal to atretic segments strongly suggested that some factors other than epithelial plugging were involved. Fetal bile secretion and the swallowing of amniotic fluid begin in the 11th and 12th weeks of intrauterine life, well after revacuolization of the solid-cord stage. Postmortem observations of vascular abnormalities, such as deficiency in arteriomesenteric arcades, added strength to suspicions that other etiologic factors were involved.

In 1955, Louw and Barnard[80] subjected dog fetuses to ligation of mesenteric vessels and strangulation obstruction late in the course of gestation. Ten to 14 days later, examination of affected fetal intestine demonstrated a variety of atretic conditions similar to those observed clinically in human neonates. These findings strongly suggested that most jejunoileal atresias are the result of a late intrauterine mesenteric vascular catastrophe. Courtois[26] demonstrated that after fetal operations in rabbits, intrauterine intestinal perforation can heal without a trace (with or without evidence of meconium peritonitis) or result in stenosis or atresia. He further observed that if an intestinal loop was isolated, resorption of the loop occurred if its blood supply was poor. Santulli and Blanc,[121] Abrams,[1] Koga and colleagues,[72] and Tovar and associates[144] confirmed these findings in various experimental studies performed on fetal rabbits, sheep, dogs, and chick embryos. Sweeney and associates, in 2001, noted a higher incidence of associated anomalies in infants with jejunal atresia (42%) than ileal atresia (2%) and suggested that some cases of jejunal atresia may arise from a malformative process.[135] Glüer reported the occurrence of jejunoileal atresia in four sets of twins after intra-amniotic injection of dyes and theorized a teratogenic mechanism.[44] In a rat model using doxorubicin (Adriamycin), Gillick and colleagues documented that abnormal development of the notochord in the area of the developing midgut was associated with multiple intestinal atresias.[43]

Frequent clinical instances of intestinal atresia as a result of late intrauterine mesenteric vascular insults such as volvulus, intussusception, internal hernia, and constriction of the mesentery in a tight gastroschisis or omphalocele defect have been observed.[14,50,51,62,74,151] de Lorimier and associates[32] noted evidence of bowel infarction in 42% of 619 cases of jejunoileal atresia. Nixon and Tawes[99] observed macroscopic or microscopic intrauterine peritonitis in 61 of 127 patients with atresia, with an obvious volvulus noted in 44. Murphy[95] noted that 5% of atresias were related to fetal internal hernia. Reports by Santulli and Blanc,[121] Nixon and Tawes,[99] and Okmian and Kovamees[101] document instances of atresia related to bowel incarceration in an omphalocele. Iatrogenic postpartum ileal atresia as a result of umbilical clamping of an occult omphalocele was reported by Vassy and Boles[146] and by Landor and colleagues.[76] Grosfeld and Clatworthy[51] observed the occurrence of jejunal atresia with infarction of the entire midgut in a tight gastroschisis defect. In the American Academy of Pediatrics survey, jejunoileal atresia associated with gastroschisis was observed in 2% of patients.[32] More recently, however, the incidence of gastroschisis complicated by bowel atresia is more common, being noted in 10% to 25% of cases.[45,91,129] In my institution, 28 of 194 cases (14.4%) of jejunoileal atresia were associated with gastroschisis. Intrauterine intussusception is an infrequently reported cause of atresia. Evans' review[37] of 1498 cases recognized only nine examples of atresia associated with intussusception. However, Komuro described intrauterine intussusception as a cause of intestinal atresia in 12 of 48 (25%) cases and that it was commonly associated with a single mid–small-bowel atresia.[73] Intussusception was not detected as a cause of atresia in instances of high-jejunal, apple-peel, or multiple atresias. Similar to intussusception after birth, the cause of intrauterine intussusception is unknown.[62,151] Most of these infants are full term without associated malformations and have a cord or gap type of atresia unassociated with cystic fibrosis.[52,103,113,131,140] Postnatal intussusception as a cause of jejunal atresia in a premature infant has also been described.[109] In the 194 patients with jejunoileal atresia or stenosis treated at Riley Children's Hospital, volvulus was detected in 64, malrotation in 32, intussusception in 5, internal hernia in 2, gastroschisis in 28, and evidence of meconium peritonitis in 24. The late occurrence of such events accounts for the relatively low incidence (7%) of associated extraintestinal anomalies.[32] In rare instances, jejunoileal atresia has been observed to coexist with biliary atresia, duodenal atresia, colon atresia, gastric atresia, Hirschsprung's disease, and arthrogryposis and to occur in identical twins.[24,49,52,75,77,89,159] Fortunately, most infants with jejunoileal atresia have only this single abnormality and are otherwise normal. Gross and coworkers reported familial instances of combined duodenal and jejunal atresia.[53] Guttman and colleagues,[54] Aigrain and associates,[2] Kimble and coworkers,[69] Puri and Fujimoto,[108] and Fourcade and colleagues[42] described hereditary instances of multiple intestinal atresias without evidence of vascular insults or bile pigment, lanugo hairs, or squames distal to the atresia, indicating a malformed process possibly due to an autosomal recessive transmission. Kilani and associates described a familial pattern of jejunal atresia with renal dysplasia that was most likely inherited as an autosomal dominant trait.[66] Walker and associates[150] described a case of multiple atresias of the bowel associated with graft-versus-host disease and immunosuppression, and Rothenberg and coworkers noted an instance of multiple atresias associated with severe immunodeficiency characterized by agammaglobulinemia, B-cell deficiency, and impaired T-cell function.[119]

DIAGNOSIS

Clinical Presentation

The pertinent signs of jejunoileal atresia include maternal polyhydramnios, bilious vomiting, abdominal distention, jaundice, and failure to pass meconium on the first day of life (Table 80-1).[32,48,79,95,114,148] Polyhydramnios is observed in 24% of cases and is more commonly noted in instances of proximal jejunal atresia (38%).[32] Bilious vomiting is slightly more common in jejunal atresia (84%), whereas abdominal distention is more frequently noted in cases of ileal atresia (98%).[48] Jaundice occurs in 32% of infants with jejunal atresia and 20% of those with ileal atresia.[32] Jaundice in these cases of small-bowel obstruction is characteristically associated with an elevation of indirect bilirubin.[17,100] Although most infants fail to pass meconium in the first 24 hours of life, occasionally meconium and necrotic tissue may be passed per rectum.[48,51,99,114,140] Abdominal distention is a frequent clinical feature in instances of jejunoileal atresia. Proximal jejunal atresia may be associated with upper abdominal distention. More generalized distention usually denotes a low obstruction (e.g., distal small bowel or colon) in which many loops of bowel are filled with air proximal to the level of obstruction. Severe distention may be associated with respiratory distress as a result of elevation of the diaphragm, easily visible veins, and *intestinal patterning* characterized by visible loops of bowel (occasionally with peristaltic waves) noted on the abdominal wall during physical examination. Although distention usually develops 12 to 24 hours after birth, abdominal distention noted immediately at birth suggests the presence of giant cystic meconium peritonitis.[19,48]

Prenatal Ultrasound Findings

Prenatal ultrasonography in mothers with polyhydramnios has identified small-bowel obstruction associated with atresia, volvulus, and meconium peritonitis.[3,4,78,83] Prenatal ultrasonography is more reliable in detection of duodenal atresia than more distal lesions. Antenatal diagnosis of small-bowel atresia is suspected by the appearance of multiple distended loops of bowel with vigorous peristalsis.[116] Intestinal atresia is also suspected in fetuses with gastroschisis with intestinal dilatation on prenatal ultrasound examination.[3,91] Phelps and coworkers[105] reported that only 42% of prenatally diagnosed gastrointestinal malformations were confirmed postnatally and only 35 of 220 (16%) gastrointestinal malformations observed at birth were detected by prenatal ultrasound studies. Although the appearance of echogenic bowel on prenatal ultrasonography is frequently associated with a gastrointestinal malformation, only 12 of 44 (27%) were confirmed after delivery.[105] Basu and Burge reported that 31% of patients with small-bowel atresias were diagnosed on prenatal ultrasonography.[4] They noted that gastrointestinal abnormalities are more frequently detected when ultrasound scanning is performed later in pregnancy and may be missed if the pregnant mother receives only one scan in the 16th week of gestation. Dalla Vecchia and colleagues and Tam and Nicholls similarly noted that antenatal diagnosis of intestinal atresia was relatively infrequent with less than a third of the cases recognized on ultrasound study.[30,136] When recognized, the atresia was more often in a proximal location and the infants required prolonged postnatal treatment. These observations suggest that prenatal ultrasonography has a relatively poor predictive value for bowel abnormalities and remains a somewhat unreliable method of either detecting or excluding a fetal gastrointestinal malformation. Early studies concerning fetal magnetic resonance imaging (MRI) indicate that this modality can identify gastrointestinal abnormalities and suggest that this modality may be more accurate than ultrasound in the prenatal diagnosis of bowel atresia.[120,147]

TABLE 80-1 Jejunoileal Atresia: Clinical Presentation

Finding	Jejunal Atresia (%)	Ileal Atresia (%)
Polyhydramnios	38	15
Bilious vomiting	84	81
Abdominal distention	78	98
Failure to pass meconium	65	71
Jaundice	32	20

Radiographic Findings

The diagnosis of jejunoileal atresia usually is confirmed by radiographic examination of the abdomen. Erect and recumbent abdominal radiographs are obtained in each case. Thumb-sized intestinal loops *(rule-of-thumb)* and air-fluid levels are highly suggestive of intestinal obstruction in the newborn.[50] High jejunal atresia may present with a few air-fluid levels and no further gas beyond that point (Fig. 80-1). The more distal the atresia, the more apparent the clinical distention and the greater the number of distended intestinal loops and air-fluid levels observed on the abdominal radiograph. The site of atresia may appear as a larger loop with a significant air-fluid level (Fig. 80-2). Peritoneal calcification is seen in 12% of cases on plain abdominal radiographs and signifies the presence of meconium peritonitis, a sign of intrauterine intestinal perforation (Fig. 80-3). In addition, instances of intraluminal calcification *(mummification)* may be observed, indicating an antenatal volvulus.[9,60] In instances of giant cystic meconium peritonitis, plain radiographs of the abdomen may demonstrate a large air-fluid level in a meconium pseudocyst.[19] This type of occurrence is related to a late intrauterine perforation, resulting in an encapsulated mass (pseudocyst) of perforated bowel and contained meconium.[48,114]

The newborn rarely demonstrates colonic haustral markings on a plain abdominal radiograph, which may simply show dilated loops of intestine without actually differentiating between the small and large bowel. A barium enema should be performed in each instance of suspected neonatal intestinal obstruction. The first enema

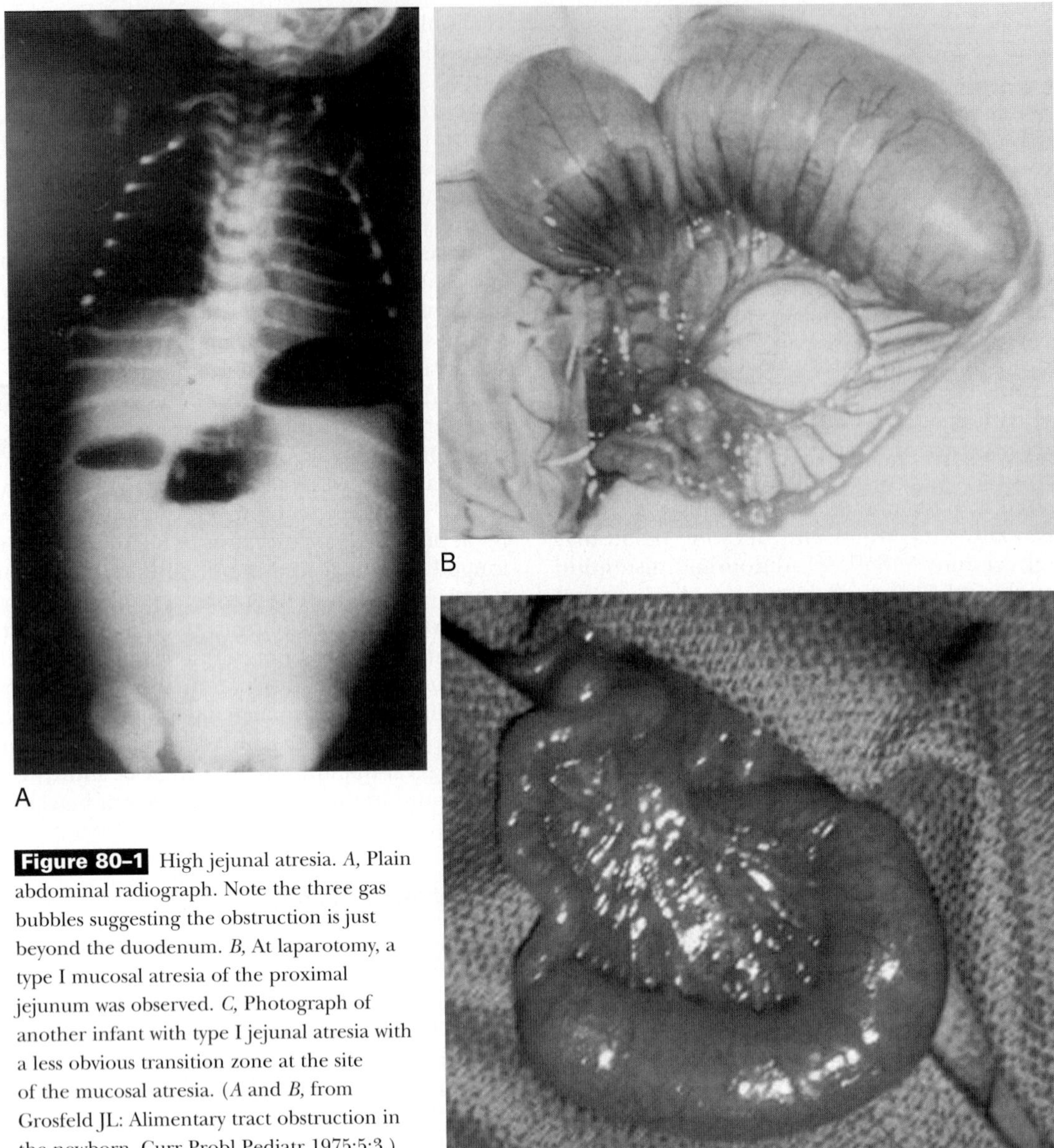

Figure 80–1 High jejunal atresia. *A*, Plain abdominal radiograph. Note the three gas bubbles suggesting the obstruction is just beyond the duodenum. *B*, At laparotomy, a type I mucosal atresia of the proximal jejunum was observed. *C*, Photograph of another infant with type I jejunal atresia with a less obvious transition zone at the site of the mucosal atresia. (*A* and *B*, from Grosfeld JL: Alimentary tract obstruction in the newborn. Curr Probl Pediatr 1975;5:3.)

the infant receives should be the contrast enema, which, when performed by trained radiologists with experience in obstructive cases in neonates and infants, usually involves minimal risk. The contrast enema serves three purposes: (1) to distinguish between small- and large-bowel distention, (2) to determine if the colon is used or unused *(microcolon)*, and (3) to locate the position of the cecum in regard to the possible presence of anomalies of intestinal rotation and fixation.[48] The great majority of infants with jejunoileal atresia demonstrate a microcolon, an observation that usually limits the obstruction to the distal small intestine (see Fig. 80-3). Microcolon is directly related to the fact that little succus entericus has passed the area of obstruction in the distal fetal small intestine, and the unused colon does not distend.[8] Rarely, however, the colon may appear of normal caliber if the intrauterine vascular catastrophe leading to atresia occurred extremely late in gestation. This is particularly true in instances of atresia related to intrauterine intussusception (Fig. 80-4).[51,111,140] Malrotation has been observed in approximately 10% of patients with jejunoileal atresia[32,99] and was noted in 32 of the 194 patients (16.5%) with jejunoileal atresia at our children's hospital.

There is usually no indication to perform upper gastrointestinal contrast studies in instances of complete obstruction. In cases of intestinal stenosis, however, with an incomplete obstruction this study may prove quite useful. A small-bowel contrast enteroclysis study has a higher diagnostic yield than a routine small-bowel series.

Differential Diagnosis

Newborns with intestinal obstruction from other causes may present with a clinical picture quite similar to that of infants with jejunoileal atresia. These causes include

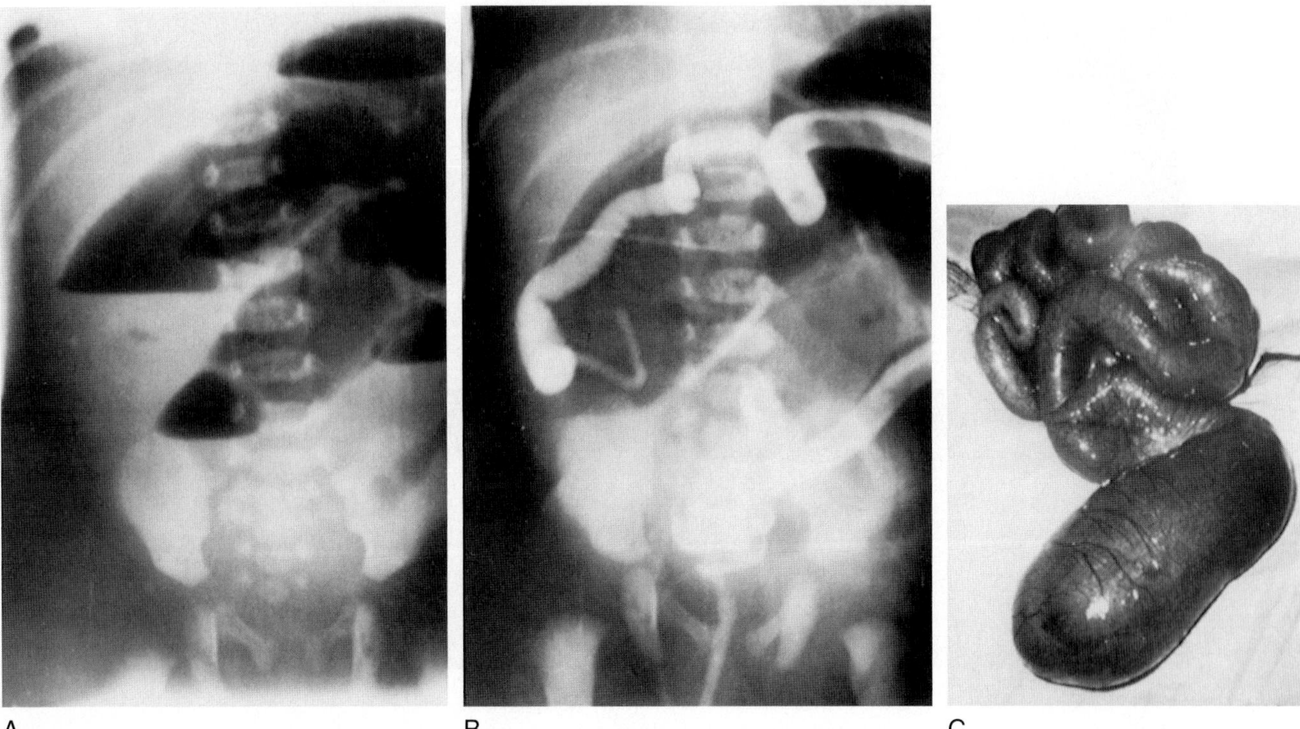

Figure 80–2 Ileal atresia. *A*, Erect abdominal radiograph showing distended intestinal loops with air-fluid levels. *B*, Contrast enema demonstrates a microcolon (unused) suggestive of small bowel obstruction. *C*, Atresia of the ileum (type IIIa) at laparotomy. (From Grosfeld JL: Alimentary tract obstruction in the newborn. Curr Probl Pediatr 1975;5:3.)

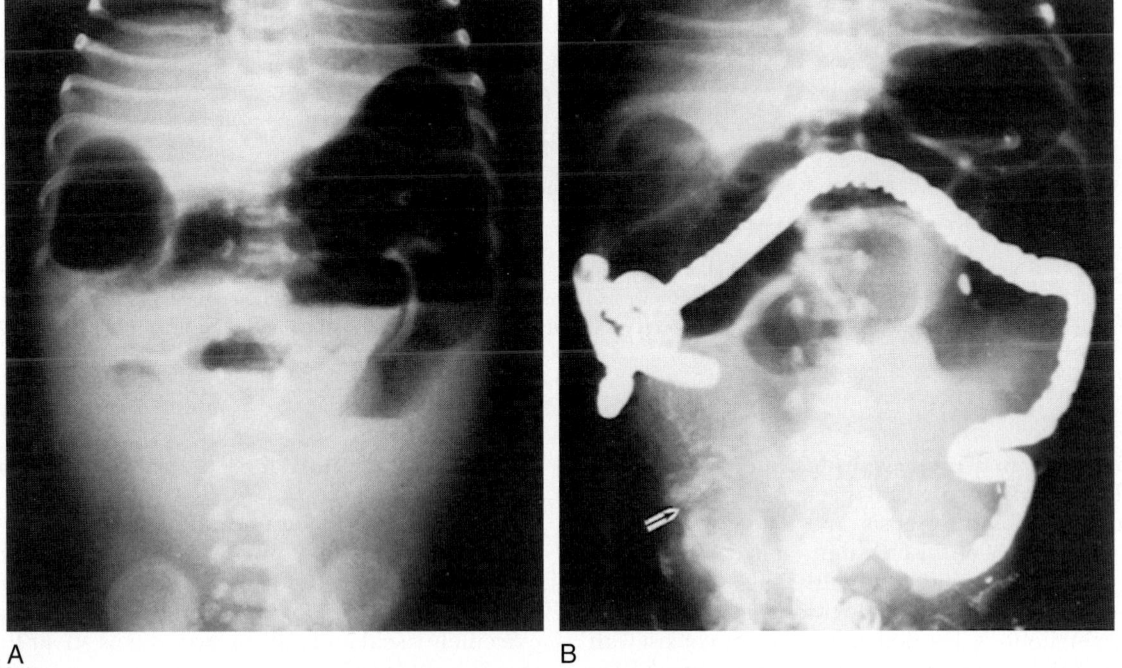

Figure 80–3 Meconium peritonitis. *A*, Erect radiograph of the abdomen demonstrates greater than thumb-sized loops of intestine with multiple air-fluid levels. *B*, Barium enema demonstrates an unused colon (microcolon) with incomplete rotation (cecum in right upper quadrant) and calcification in the right lower quadrant *(arrow)* indicative of meconium peritonitis. (From Grosfeld JL: Alimentary tract obstruction in the newborn. Curr Probl Pediatr 1975;5:3.)

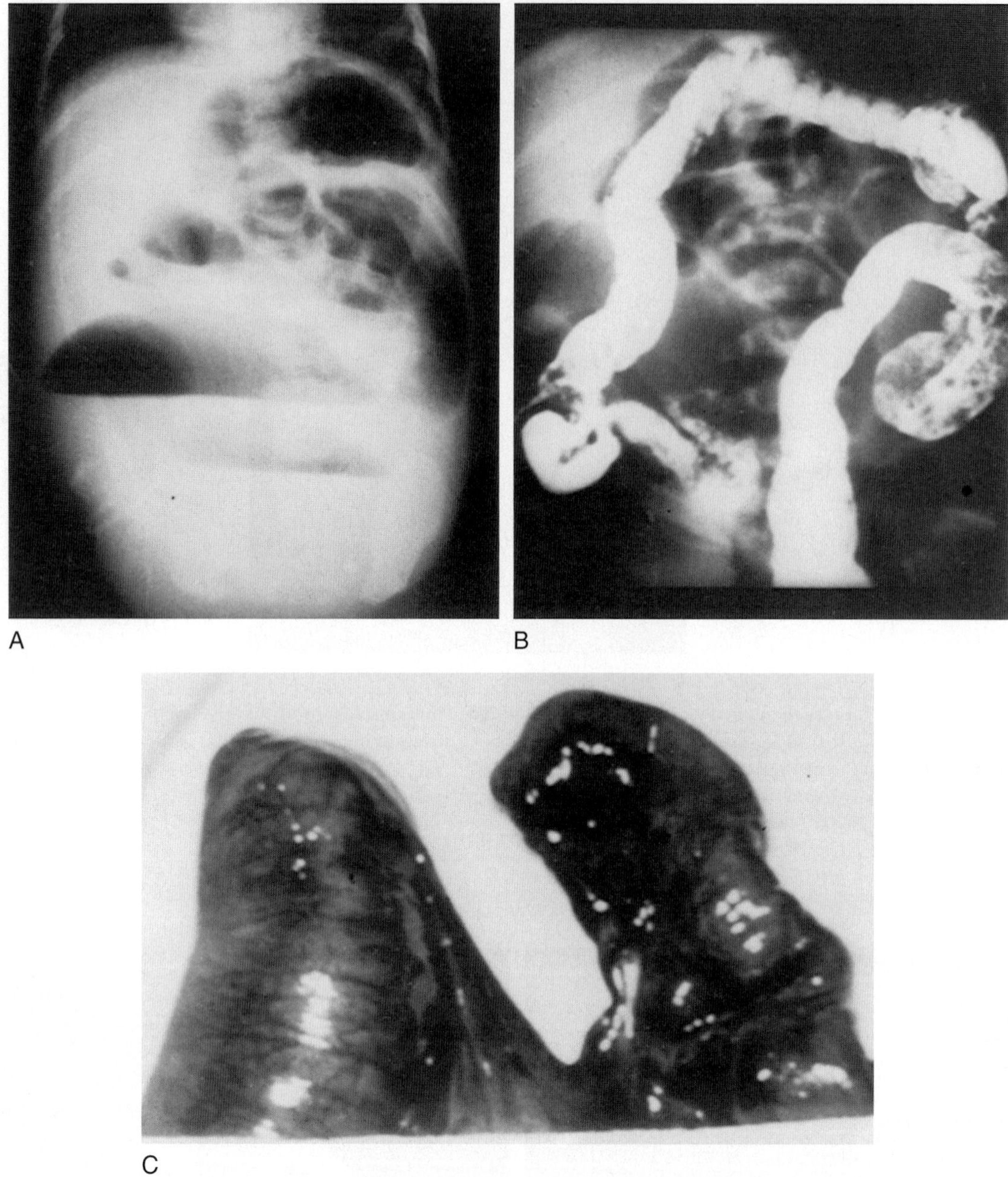

Figure 80–4 Ileal atresia. *A,* Upright radiograph of abdomen, showing distended loops of intestine with air-fluid levels. *B,* Contrast enema showing normal-caliber colon filled with debris. *C,* At laparotomy, ileal atresia with a V-shaped defect in the mesentery (type IIIa) and evidence of an intrauterine intussusception were found. (From Grosfeld JL: Alimentary tract obstruction in the newborn. Curr Probl Pediatr 1975;5:3.)

malrotation with or without volvulus, meconium ileus, intestinal duplication, internal hernia, colonic atresia, adynamic ileus related to sepsis, and total colonic aganglionosis.[20,75,80] The contrast barium enema often yields valuable information that frequently rules out certain causes of obstruction, particularly colonic atresia and low segment aganglionosis. Jejunoileal atresia may coexist with malrotation (10% to 18%), meconium peritonitis (12%), meconium ileus (9% to 12%), total colonic aganglionosis, and, rarely, intestinal neuronal dysplasia, so that a clear differentiation is not always possible.[13,48,63,75,80,86,99,102] A careful family history regarding cystic fibrosis may permit preoperative identification of infants with meconium ileus.[30,48,49,114]

Infants with uncomplicated meconium ileus often have significant dilation of bowel loops of similar size and few, if any, air-fluid levels. This latter observation is related to the fact that meconium in these patients is extremely viscid and fails to layer out as an air-fluid interface.[48] A *ground-glass appearance* (Neuhauser's sign)[96] or the *soap-bubble sign* of Singleton[127] may be observed in the right lower quadrant and represents viscid meconium mixed with air. Careful evaluation of these patients may avoid an unnecessary operation because at least half of

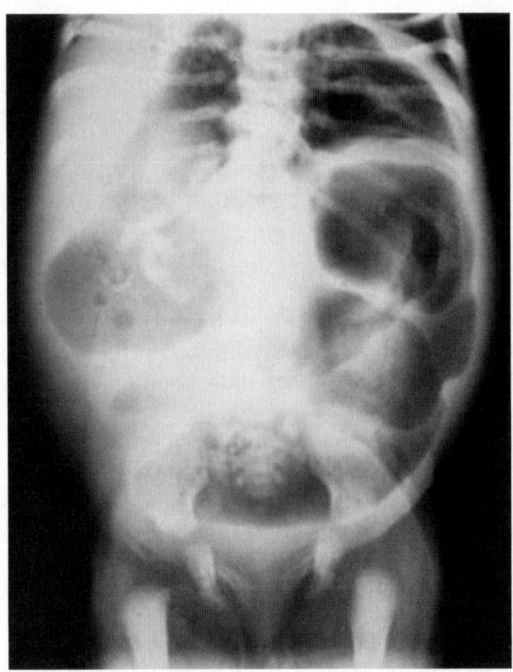

B

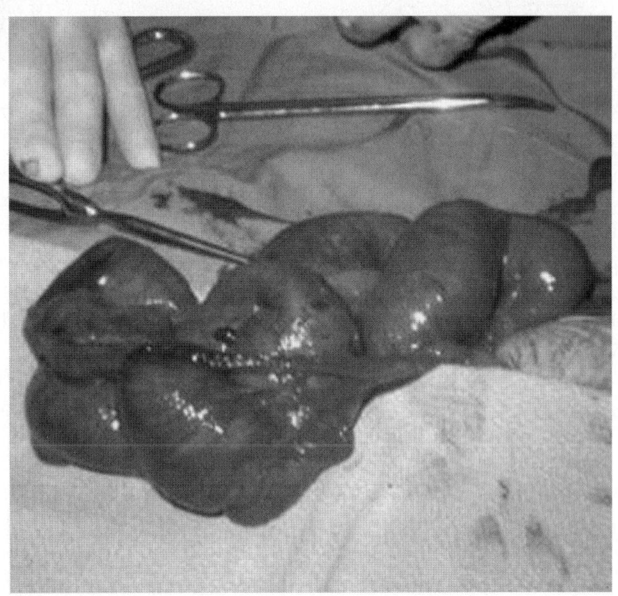

Figure 80–5 *A,* Abdominal radiograph in a neonate with numerous dilated intestinal loops. *B,* Barium enema shows an unused microcolon indicating the dilated intestine is small bowel. *C,* At laparotomy a volvulus was observed with multiple intestinal atresias due to complicated meconium ileus. *(See color plate.)* The infant had cystic fibrosis.

the uncomplicated cases of meconium ileus respond to nonoperative therapy in the form of a diatrizoate (Gastrografin) enema (see Chapter 81). Instances of meconium ileus complicated by atresia, volvulus, or gangrenous bowel require operative intervention, and the appropriate diagnosis in such obstructed patients is made at the time of laparotomy (Fig. 80-5). Occasionally, instances of colonic atresia may also present as a soap-bubble appearance in the atretic segment on plain abdominal radiography.[30]

Pathologic Findings

Atresias of the small intestine are equally distributed between jejunum (51%) and the ileum (49%). The proximal jejunum is the site of atresia in 31% of cases; distal jejunum, 20%; proximal ileum, 13%; and distal ileum, 36%.[27] The atresia is usually single (>90%) but may be multiple in 6% to 20% of cases.[31,32,49] Multiple atresias more often involve the proximal jejunum.[5,57,107,108]

The classification of jejunoileal atresia has changed only slightly since the early observations of Bland-Sutton[15] and Spriggs.[132] Louw[81] recognized three types of jejunoileal atresia. Type I referred to a mucosal (septal) atresia with an intact bowel wall and mesentery. Type II has two atretic blind ends connected by a band of fibrous tissue (cord) and an intact mesentery, and type III has the two ends of atretic bowel separated by a gap (V-shaped defect) in the mesentery (Fig. 80-6). This was the classification used most extensively throughout the early literature on the subject, particularly in the large reviews.[32,99,141,142] In evaluating 559 cases of jejunoileal atresia, de Lorimier and coworkers[32] noted 19% were type I, 31% were type II,

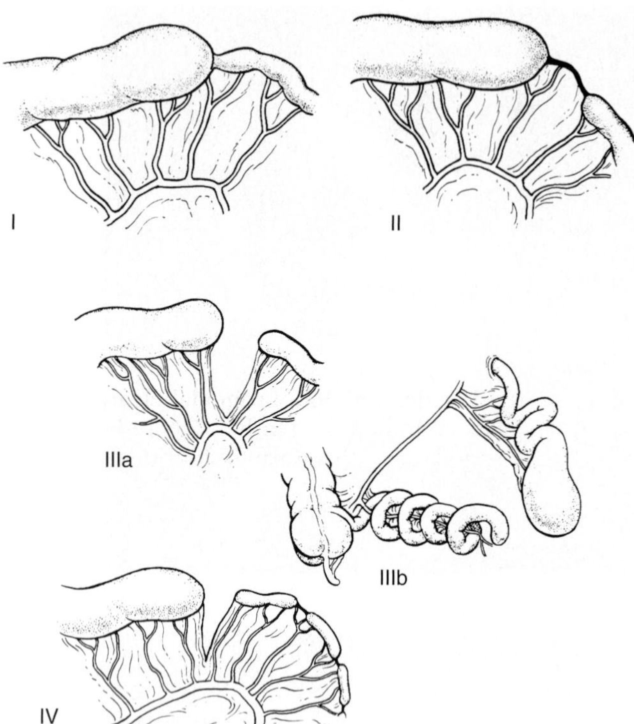

Figure 80–6 Classification of intestinal atresia. Type I, mucosal (membranous) atresia with intact bowel wall and mesentery. Type II, blind ends are separated by a fibrous cord. Type IIIa, blind ends are separated by a V-shaped (gap) mesenteric defect. Type IIIb, apple-peel atresia. Type IV, multiple atresias (string of sausages). (From Grosfeld JL, Ballantine TVN, Shoemaker R: Operative management of intestinal atresia and stenosis based on pathologic findings. J Pediatr Surg 1979;14:368.)

and 46% were type III. Nixon and Tawes[99] similarly found type III cases to be the most common variant. Although many type III cases are associated with shorter bowel length owing to intrauterine resorption of fetal gut subjected to a vascular insult, most type I and II cases have reasonably normal length of remaining intestine. Foglia and colleagues[40] reported an unusual type I case in which a 40-cm segment of intestine had an occluded lumen.

Until relatively recently, little attention has focused on cases of multiple atresias and foreshortened intestine associated with prematurity and a high mortality. At operation, there is a *string-of-beads* or *string-of sausages* appearance (see Fig. 80-6). Rittenhouse and colleagues[115] reported that multiple atresias occurred in 14% of cases and noted one infant with 25 separate atresias. Intrauterine inflammation was considered a possible cause. Small-bowel diverticulosis has been observed in association with multiple atresias.[126] Guttman and colleagues[54] reported a family pattern of multiple atresias affecting the stomach, duodenum, small bowel, and colon occurring in French-Canadians near the St. John River in Quebec. Because of the high degree of consanguinity observed in this group, these authors, as well as Teja and colleagues,[138] proposed that extensive multiple atresias occur most likely as an expression of a rare autosomal recessive gene. Mishalany and Najjar[90] reported three cases of jejunal atresia in one family. More cases concerning multiple atresias have been reported subsequently.[2,24,69,107,108,150] Familial jejunal atresia associated with renal dysplasia has been observed and is likely due to an autosomal dominant trait.[58,66] Bilodeau and associates[11] described an autosomal recessive mode of inheritance in 16 cases of multiple intestinal atresias associated with IgM deficiency (patients who were originally described by Guttman[54] in 1974) followed over 30 years. All the patients have died. The etiology remains unclear. A reliable method of prenatal diagnosis or an effective surgical therapy was not found. The authors considered this to be an invariably lethal condition due to a specific gene mutation not yet elucidated.[11]

Another unusual group of patients are those with *apple-peel* atresia or *Christmas-tree* deformity. These patients present with jejunal atresia near the ligament of Treitz, foreshortened bowel, and a large mesenteric gap, and the blood supply to the bowel distal to the atresia is precariously supplied in a retrograde fashion by anastomotic arcades from the ileocolic, right colic, or inferior mesenteric arteries.[36,47,124,155,160,161] Ros Mar and colleagues[118] observed 12 cases of apple-peel deformity among 37 cases of jejunoileal atresia (32.4%). Zerella and Martin,[160] however, observed the apple-peel variant of atresia in only 7 of 59 cases (11%) of jejunoileal atresia. Patients with this distinct variation of atresia often have a familial pattern, are often of low birth weight (70%), are premature (70%), have malrotation (54%), and have an increased number of associated anomalies.[16,129] Apple-peel atresia has also been observed in siblings with ocular anomalies and microcephaly.[133]

In 1976, Martin and Zerella[85] proposed a new classification to include instances of multiple atresia and apple-peel atresia. I modified this classification in 1979 to retain the previous nomenclature of Louw[80] and to add apple-peel atresia as a special form of type III (IIIb) and to consider multiple atresias as type IV (see Fig. 80-6).[49] This latter classification has generally been accepted to describe bowel atresias for the past 25 years.[49]

TREATMENT

During initial evaluation, the infant is maintained in a warm humidified environment (either in an Isolette or under an overhead warmer) to avoid hypothermia. An orogastric tube (10 French) is passed. The stomach contents are aspirated and presence of bile noted. The tube is placed on drainage to decompress the stomach and to prevent vomiting and further gaseous distention of the obstructed intestine from swallowed air. This is a key prerequisite if the infant is to be transferred from a community or general hospital to a tertiary neonatal intensive care facility. These precautions also should be in effect before the infant is evaluated in the radiology department because aspiration during transportation is a significant complication and should be carefully avoided. During transport, the infant should always be attended by experienced personnel.

The infant's weight is determined, and blood samples for baseline laboratory data (i.e., complete blood cell and platelet counts, blood urea nitrogen, serum bilirubin, glucose, calcium, pH, blood gas tensions, serum electrolytes) and for type and crossmatch are obtained by microtechniques. Urinary volume, specific gravity, and osmolality are also measured. The extent of the preoperative preparation depends primarily on the delay in diagnosis, the degree of fluid and electrolyte imbalance, severe associated anomalies, and the presence of peritonitis. An adequate intravenous route is established by percutaneous insertion of a short 22- or 24-gauge silicone catheter in the dorsum of the foot or hand. I avoid cutdowns because they are rarely necessary. Peripherally inserted central catheter lines and traditional central venous subclavian catheters used for total parenteral nutrition (TPN) can be inserted percutaneously. Routine catheterization of the umbilical vein is also avoided because of the increased risk of sepsis; it is used occasionally, however, for short-term exchange transfusion in the patient with a very high level of indirect hyperbilirubinemia. If the infant has associated respiratory distress related to aspiration of vomitus or severe abdominal distention, a percutaneous arterial catheter is inserted into the right radial artery for more accurate PaO_2 monitoring above the level of neonatal right-to-left shunts through the patent ductus and foramen ovale. Pulse oximetry may be sufficient to monitor oxygen saturation levels in stable patients.

The infant's fluid deficits are evaluated, and replacement therapy is initiated. Bilious drainage from the orogastric tube is replaced with equal amounts of lactated Ringer's solution. In instances of peritonitis or severe distention (or both), lactated Ringer's solution is administered at a rate of 20 mL/kg over a 30-minute period, and in instances of obstruction without perforation an empirical infusion of 10 mL/kg is employed to correct hypovolemia related to third-space losses sequestered in the peritoneal cavity or the obstructed proximal intestine. Additional fluids (salt-poor serum albumin or lactated Ringer's solution) may be necessary to maintain the infant's blood pressure above 50 mm Hg and establish appropriate urine flow (1 to 2 mL/kg/hr). A 10% dextrose in 0.25% or 0.33% normal saline solution is employed for maintenance.

Vitamin K_1 oxide (phytonadione [AquaMEPHYTON], 1 mg intramuscularly) is routinely given. Intravenous antibiotics are usually employed (ampicillin, 125 mg/kg/day, and gentamicin, 5 mg/kg/day). Preoperative preparation may take from 1 to 4 hours, according to the severity of the infant's condition and the degree of hypovolemia.

Operating Room Care

After appropriate preparation, the infant is taken to the operating room and similar precautions concerning transportation and preservation of an appropriate thermal environment are observed. The operating room temperature is kept between 75°F and 80°F. The patient is placed under a heat lamp on a protected warming blanket, and the limbs are wrapped with soft cotton roll. A small cloth- or aluminum-lined cap is placed on the baby's head to reduce radiant heat loss. The umbilicus is prepared with a warm iodophor solution and suture ligated after resection of the clamped cord. The obstructed patient should be intubated while awake to avoid aspiration, and the location of the endotracheal tube should be evaluated by careful auscultation. A pulse oximeter is useful to monitor oxygen saturation. Monitoring of blood pressure (Doppler), electrocardiogram, pulse, and temperature (skin or axillary probe) is routine in each case. Arterial pH and blood gas tensions are acquired as necessary. The anesthetic gases are warmed and humidified to prevent heat loss and drying of the tracheobronchial tree. Dry anesthetic gases may cause destruction of cilia, desquamation of cells into the lumen, and a decrease in mucus production.[22,84] These changes result in an increased incidence of postoperative pulmonary complications related to delayed endobronchial clearance and plugging. The abdomen is gently prepared (painted rather than scrubbed) with a warm iodophor (povidone-iodine [Betadine]) solution. Towels are used to drape the abdomen and are held in place with a sterile transparent adhesive iodophor plastic drape, which is applied over the operative field. This drape is then covered by a pediatric laparotomy sheet with an aperture through which the procedure is carried out. The large plastic covering helps maintain body heat.

A right supraumbilical transverse incision allows excellent access to all areas of the neonate's peritoneal cavity. I routinely employ a fine-tipped infant electrocoagulator with a pencil-like fingertip control to achieve hemostasis. This approach avoids blood loss and obviates the need for time-consuming clamping and tying techniques during entry. Fluid administration during operation usually consists of an infusion of 5 to 10 mL/kg/hr of 5% dextrose in lactated Ringer's solution to replace sequestered tissue fluid losses related to dissection. Equal volumes of lactated Ringer's solution are administered to replace intraoperative losses from the orogastric tube and any bowel content aspirated during the procedure. Warmed packed red blood cells are transfused if losses are greater than 10% to 15% of the estimated blood volume (80 mL/kg). Small-volume aspiration collecting systems and close monitoring of sponge weights facilitate these estimates. Blood loss up to 10% to 15% of the estimated blood volume is corrected with infusion of 5% dextrose in lactated Ringer's solution.

Operative Techniques

The operation of choice in jejunoileal atresia and stenosis is related to the pathologic findings and the specific set of circumstances encountered in each individual case.[48] The actual decision as to the most appropriate procedure depends on the pathologic type of obstruction (e.g., stenosis or atresias types I, II, IIIa, IIIb, or IV); the presence of malrotation, volvulus, meconium ileus, or variants of meconium peritonitis; and the infant's general condition (Fig. 80-7). An additional set of complicated circumstances occurs in infants with atresia or stenosis associated with gastroschisis or omphalocele, when primary closure of the abdominal wall may present a problem.[45,91,114,125,129,145]

Retention and use of the dilated blind proximal atretic segment of intestine in any type of anastomosis usually

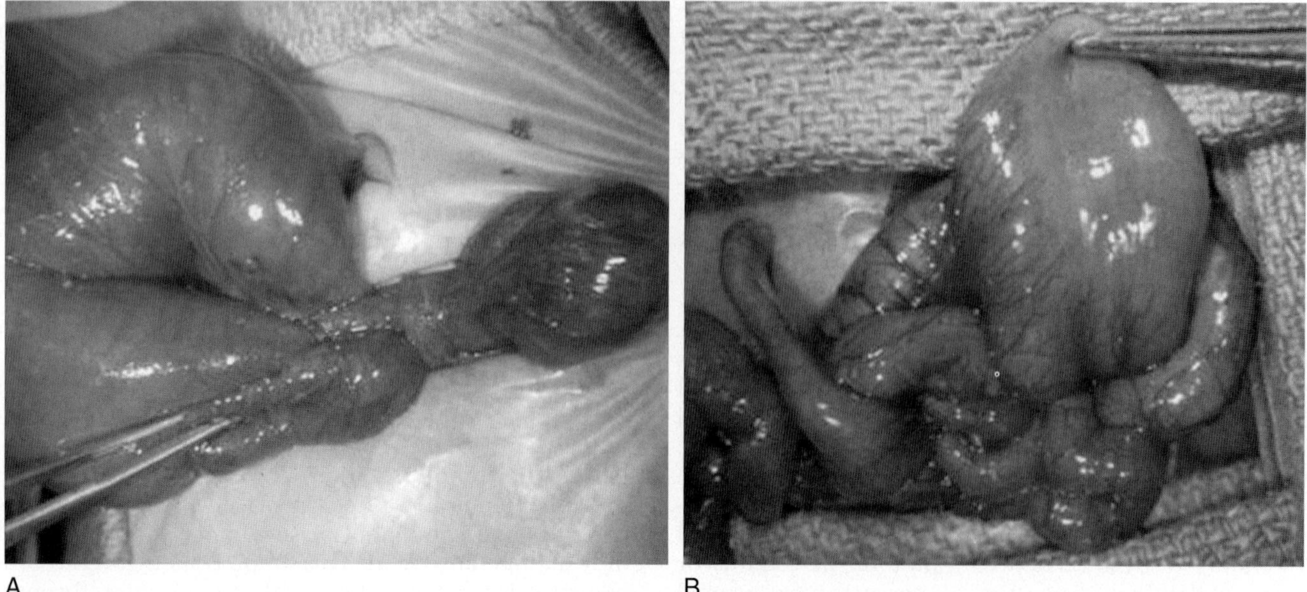

Figure 80–7 *A*, Photograph shows an ileal atresia resulting from intrauterine volvulus around a peritoneal band. *B*, Jejunal atresia resulting from intrauterine midgut volvulus due to malrotation. Note the appendix in the mid upper abdomen at the site of the twist.

results in a functional obstruction. Although a side-to-side anastomosis was commonly used in early attempts at surgical correction of jejunoileal atresia, functional anastomotic obstruction and subsequent development of the blind loop syndrome frequently complicated this operation.[8,80,98,99] Nixon[98,99] noted that the change in the dilated proximal atretic segment consisted of smooth muscle hypertrophy and enlargement of the bowel diameter. He suggested this segment of intestine had ineffective peristalsis and failed to function at lower pressures after operation. de Lorimier and associates[34] and Cloutier[23] suggested that hyperplasia is the main change occurring in intestinal smooth muscle above a chronic obstruction. In instances of chronic complete obstruction, such as jejunal atresia, hyperplasia may be so extreme that a state of decompensation is reached in which even strong contractions never close the intestinal lumen sufficiently to increase pressure or to allow efficient propulsion at the normal inlet pressure.[23] Schoenberg and Kluth[123] described structural changes in the enteric nervous system in chicks with experimentally induced small-bowel atresia and attributed these abnormalities to proximal bowel dilatation. Masumoto and associates described hypoplasia of enteric intramural nerves and C-*kit* positive pacemaker cells in the proximal segments of atretic bowel excised from neonates.[87]

In the clinical setting, experience has shown that in most cases of proximal jejunal atresia (with adequate length of intestine) resection of the dilated atretic segment at the ligament of Treitz followed by an end-to-oblique anastomosis usually obviates these complications and results in a successful outcome. When there is a limited length of remaining intestine (e.g., short gut), an antimesenteric tapering jejunoplasty, as suggested by Thomas,[139] has proved useful. Reports by Howard and Othersen,[61] Weber and associates,[154] and others[65,104,152] confirm the applicability of tapering enteroplasty in selected cases. de Lorimier and Harrison[33] reported that intestinal imbrication effectively reduces the caliber of distended intestine and restores function. Although the imbrication technique preserves mucosal surface area, it has a tendency to break down, with recurrent dilation occurring. Kimura and coworkers[70] modified this approach by performing an elliptical seromuscular resection to taper the dilated proximal bowel while preserving the mucosal layer. Kling and colleagues described the use of lateral duodenectomy and duodenojejunostomy for cases of jejunal atresia occurring at the ligament of Treitz that did not respond favorably to a tapering procedure.[71]

Wide proximal resection and anastomosis is also used for instances of single or multiple atresias of the middle small intestine or distal ileum in the presence of adequate bowel length. An end-to-side ileoascending colonic anastomosis is a reasonable alternative in instances of distal ileal atresia.[8] The major disadvantage of this procedure is bypassing the ileocecal valve.

At operation, the intestine is carefully inspected, and the proximal and distal ends of the atresia are identified. Gentle evisceration often facilitates this inspection. Malrotation, volvulus, or segments of partially resorbed fetal intestine that may be involved in an intrauterine volvulus may be seen. The twisted bowel is carefully reduced so that a complete evaluation of the pathologic anatomy is possible. A pursestring suture is placed in the distal atretic end of the intestine, and saline (or air) is injected through a 24-gauge venous catheter to rule out an unsuspected distal atretic mucosal membrane or web. If bowel length is adequate, the proximal dilated atretic segment is resected back to the level where the intestine diameter approaches 1.0 to 1.5 cm (in instances of ileal atresia) or near the

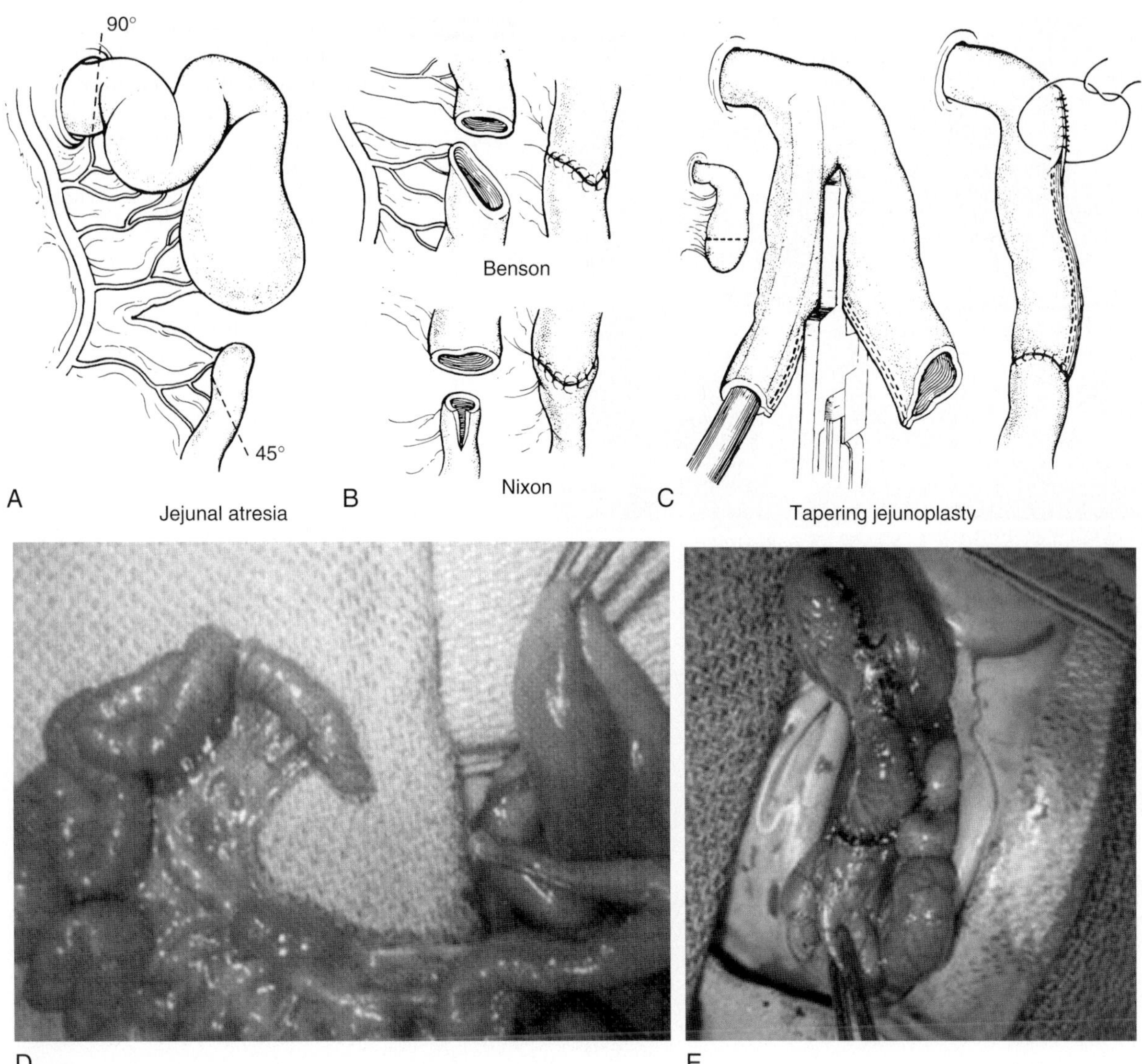

Figure 80–8 Jejunal atresia: Techniques of anastomosis. *A,* The proximal jejunal atretic segment is resected at the ligament of Treitz at a 90-degree angle and the distal segment at a 45-degree angle. *B,* End-to-oblique anastomosis is carried out by the techniques of Benson (one-layer) or Nixon (two-layer) with fine interrupted silk sutures. *C,* Tapering proximal jejunoplasty: The bulbous distal portion of the atresia is resected, and a tube is placed in the mesenteric side of the lumen; antimesenteric resection with an autostapler device is carried out up to the ligament of Treitz. End-to-end anastomosis completes the procedure. Note that the staple line is also oversewn with interrupted 5-0 silk sutures. *D,* Photograph of proximal jejunal atresia with a type IIIb gap and apple-peel distal atresia. *E,* The tapering jejunoplasty and anastomosis have been completed.

ligament of Treitz in instances of proximal jejunal atresia. A Bainbridge infant bowel clamp is applied at a 90-degree angle on the proximal bowel. A short segment of the distal atretic segment is resected at a 45-degree angle more distal on the antimesenteric side, and an additional Bainbridge clamp is applied (Fig. 80-8A). If there is still a discrepancy in the size of the two lumina, a short antimesenteric incision in the distal atretic intestine alleviates this difference. A two-layer interrupted 5-0 silk end-to-oblique anastomosis is then performed (see Fig. 80-8B). All of the posterior outer layer seromuscular sutures are inserted (usually no more than five) before being tied. The clamps are removed, and the crushed tissue is trimmed. The posterior inner layer sutures are inserted and brought around anteriorly as an interrupted inverting Connell suture (in-out, out-in) with the knots on the inside. The anastomosis is completed with an outer anterior seromuscular interrupted 5-0 silk Lembert closure. As an alternative, 5-0 Vicryl or PDS suture for the inner layer and PDS for the outer layer can be used. Some pediatric surgeons prefer a single-layered anastomosis. We have observed a slightly higher leak rate with the single-layered technique and stenosis after an interrupted two-layered repair is uncommon. The mesenteric defect is carefully approximated, tucking the longer proximal mesentery to prevent a kink at the anastomosis.[99] In instances of multiple atresias especially when the bowel length is a problem, an effort is made to preserve as much

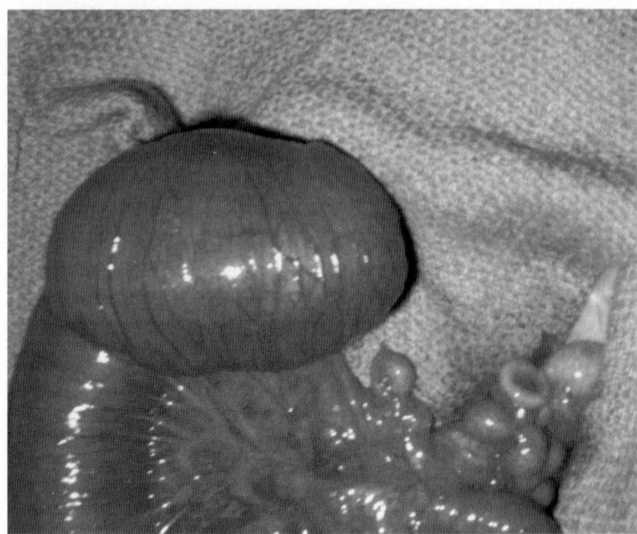

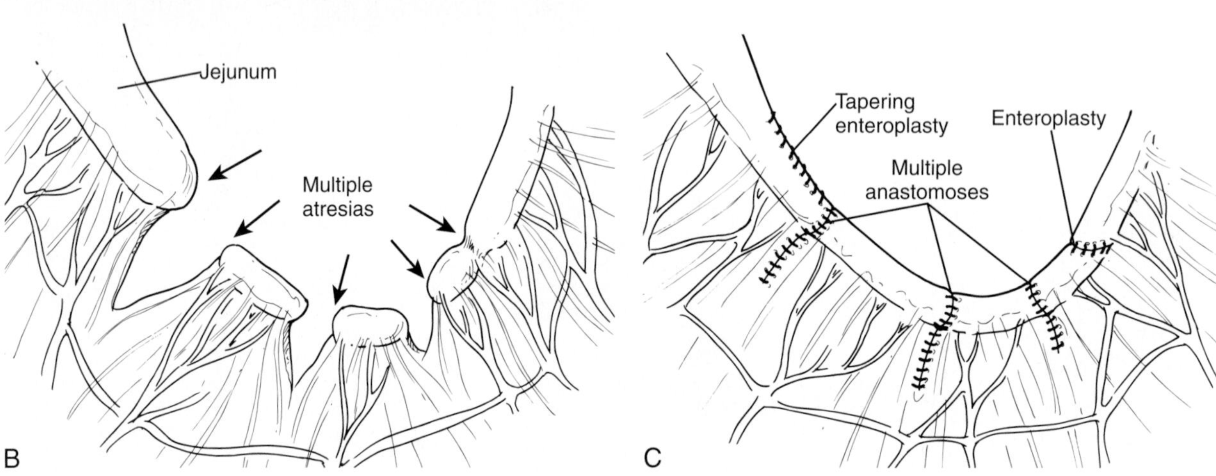

Figure 80-9 *A,* Operative photograph of an infant with dilated proximal jejunal atresia and numerous distal atresias of various types (types I, II, and IIIa). *B,* Illustration documents multiple atresias. The distal atresias are not dilated. *C,* A proximal tapering jejunoplasty and multiple anastomoses for types II and IIIa atresias and a transverse enteroplasty for type I atresia were performed to preserve bowel length.

intestine as possible. Multiple anastomoses may be necessary to accomplish this goal.[56,122] The decompressed distal atretic segments are usually not dilated and if the lumen is completely patent, resection is unnecessary and a direct anastomosis to the next segment can be performed for type II or III atresias or a transverse enteroplasty for type I mucosal atresias (Fig. 80-9). Dinsmore and colleagues[35] and Chaet and coworkers[21] described intraluminal stenting as a method to manage multiple atresias or perforations, but I have no experience with this technique.

In cases of jejunal atresia with significantly foreshortened bowel, a tapering antimesenteric jejunoplasty is accomplished with an autostapling device (U.S. Surgical Corporation, Norwalk, CT) (see Fig. 80-8C). The most bulbous distal portion of the proximal atretic segment is resected, and a 24 to 26 French catheter is inserted into the lumen along the mesenteric side. The antimesenteric border of the bowel is then resected between two rows of autostaples up to the ligament of Treitz. The remaining staple line is oversewn with interrupted 5-0 silk or PDS sutures and the procedure completed by an end-to-oblique anastomosis, as previously described (see Fig. 80-8D and E). The dissection and anastomosis are presently performed with the aid of magnifying loupes of 2.5× to 3× power. These loupes allow a much more precise placement of the anastomotic sutures and greatly facilitate the operative procedure especially in premature infants. Although a primary anastomosis is preferred (Fig. 80-10A and B), it may not be advisable in instances of ileal atresia associated with volvulus when the vascular integrity of the intestine is in question, in severe cases of meconium peritonitis, or in some instances of complicated meconium ileus. In these cases, resection of the atretic ileal segments and exteriorization is performed. The most expeditious procedure is a side-by-side (modified Mikulicz)[6,12,112,117] double-barrel enterostomy brought out through the wound and fixed to the abdominal wall layers with a few 5-0 interrupted silk sutures (see Fig. 80-10C). The Bishop-Koop (distal stoma),[13] Santulli (proximal stoma),[121] and Rehbein (tube)[113] anastomotic enterostomies are probably equally acceptable procedures in this regard. I prefer to use the double-barrel enterostomy because it is rapidly performed, avoids an initial intraperitoneal anastomosis, and allows the stomas to be easily evaluated for intestinal viability in the postoperative period. Although this does create an end-ileostomy stoma, appropriate stomal

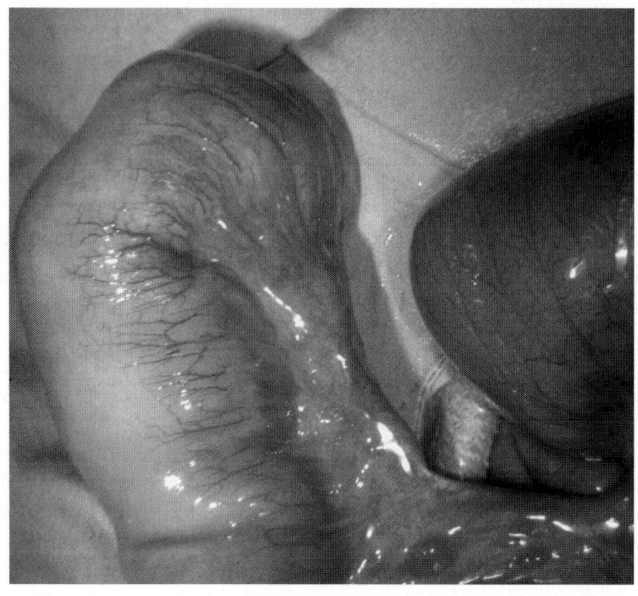

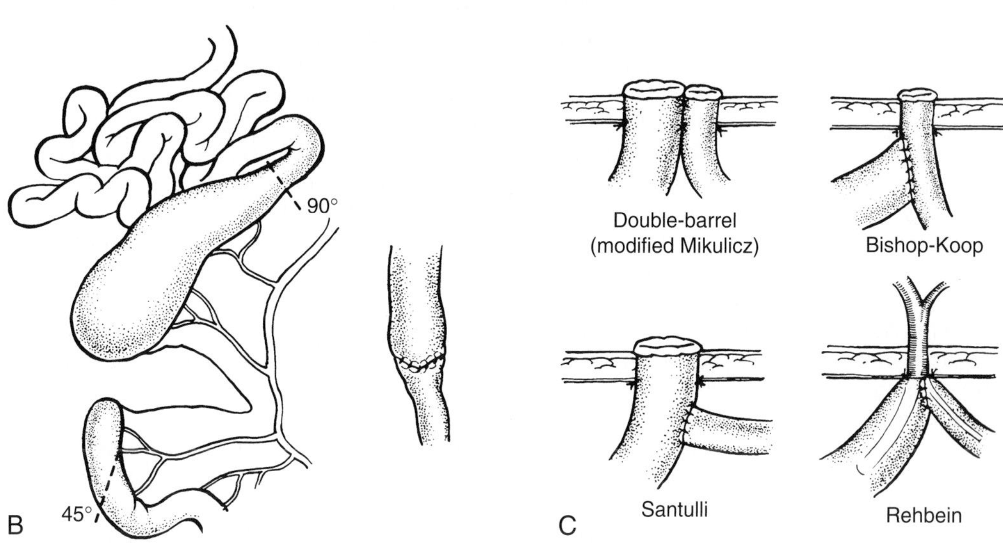

Figure 80-10 Ileal atresia: Techniques of operation. *A,* Dilated proximal ileal atresia (type IIIa). *B,* Resection of proximal ileal atresia back to a segment of bowel 1.0 to 1.5 cm in diameter. An end-to-oblique anastomosis is performed. *C,* Types of exteriorization procedures used in instances of severe peritonitis, questionable bowel viability, and meconium ileus. The double-barrel side-by-side (modified Mikulicz) enterostomy is preferred.

and skin care and use of parenteral nutrition by either a central or peripheral route usually obviate any problems. Reoperation at a later date requires a limited *target* laparotomy to restore intestinal continuity by end-to-end anastomosis. I have neither employed transanastomotic Silastic decompression catheters through a proximal jejunal anastomosis[60] nor used an appendicostomy catheter (as suggested by Suruga and coworkers[134]) in cases in which a distal ileal anastomosis is constructed. The abdominal wall is closed in layers, using continuous 4-0 polyglactin 910 (Vicryl) or polyglyconate (Maxon) on the peritoneum and interrupted inverting 4-0 Vicryl or Maxon sutures on the fascial layers. Use of PDS suture is a reasonable alternative. Scarpa's fascia is approximated with a continuous 5-0 Vicryl suture, and the skin edges are approximated with a 5-0 subcuticular suture and Steri-Strips. A dry sterile dressing is then applied under Op-Site adhesive.

At the Riley Children's Hospital, operative treatment in 194 infants with jejunoileal atresia and stenosis included resection of the atretic segment with primary anastomosis in 38%, resection with tapering enteroplasty and anastomosis in 18%, resection with a temporary enterostomy in 23%, creation of an ostomy without resection in 19%, and enterostomy with web excision in four infants (2%). Six patients with gastroschisis had the atretic bowel initially replaced in the abdomen at the time of closure with a delayed anastomosis at 3 weeks. Of the other 22 cases of gastroschisis, 2 patients were treated by resection and primary anastomosis and 20 had a temporary enterostomy. These cases are included in the aforementioned data. Six patients in the resection and anastomosis group had previously undergone a jejunal anastomosis using the atretic segment elsewhere before transfer to our facility. In each instance, a functional obstruction resulted, necessitating eventual resection of the atretic segment and a new anastomosis or tapering. Gastrostomy tubes were placed in 5 patients with a short bowel length but are otherwise not used routinely.

POSTOPERATIVE CARE

After a brief period of close observation in the recovery room, the infant is returned to the newborn intensive care unit and placed in a warm, humid, well-monitored thermoneutral environment. The head of the Isolette is elevated at 30 degrees. Maintenance fluids are administered at 80 to 100 mL/kg/day; a solution containing 10% dextrose in 0.25% or 0.33% normal saline is used. Potassium chloride (2 to 3 mEq/kg/day) is also infused, not in excess of 40 mEq/L. Losses related to orogastric tube drainage are replaced equally with 0.45% normal saline in 5% dextrose and water if the drainage fluid is clear (gastric juice) and by 5% dextrose and water in lactated Ringer's solution if it is green (intestinal drainage). Intravenous infusions should contain vitamins B and C, which are required for wound healing. Occasionally, an additional fluid bolus to counteract excessive third-space losses may be required. A urine output of 40 to 50 mL/kg/day, specific gravity of 1.005 to 1.015, and weight stability usually indicate appropriate hydration. The infant's glucose levels, acid-base balance, and serum bilirubin levels are closely monitored to avoid hypoglycemia, acidosis, and kernicterus. Serum electrolyte values are obtained daily for the first few postoperative days.

When the infant has spontaneous bowel motions and the gastric drainage fluid is clear and of minimal volume, the orogastric tube is elevated as a *burp tube.* If no excessive gastric or intestinal reflux occurs, the tube is removed and clear liquids are initiated (Pedialyte) at 0.5 oz every 3 hours and advanced in volume, and then a half-strength and finally a full-strength low osmolar small-curd formula (Isomil) is given. The newborn requires 120 calories/kg/day to grow. Lactose intolerance is a frequent problem after major bowel resection, and milk-curd obstruction of the small intestinal anastomosis may occur if a large-curd formula (Similac or Enfamil) is used initially.[25] Malabsorption and diarrhea may be significant in infants with short bowel length, those in whom the ileocecal valve has been resected, and those with multiple atresias or apple-peel atresia.[48,49,85,114,124] Formulas that contain long-chain fats should be avoided in these patients. Instead, a medium-chain triglyceride or casein hydrolysate diet (Pregestimil) is offered. Occasionally a carbohydrate-free or an easily absorbable elemental diet such as infant Vivonex may also be useful.

If the aforementioned formulas are not tolerated, TPN with a high-calorie (18% glucose, 2.5% amino-acid) infusion is delivered via a centrally placed Silastic (Broviac) catheter tunneled from the chest wall to a venotomy in the external or internal jugular vein or cephalic vein and advanced to the superior vena cava. This solution delivers 1 calorie/mL of infusate. In addition, a 10% intravenous fat solution (Intralipid) should be given. This material is isosmolar, supplies free fatty acids, and delivers an additional 1.1 calories/mL. These vital adjunctive measures of therapy prevent inanition relating to protein-calorie malnutrition in cases of prolonged gastrointestinal tract malfunctions and allow time for bowel adaptation to occur. Ninety-four of 194 (49%) infants with jejunoileal atresia at Riley Children's Hospital received TPN. During the postoperative period, all infants with jejunoileal atresia undergo a sweat chloride test and cytogenetic testing for the *DF508* gene mutation to rule out cystic fibrosis, which occurred in 24 of 194 cases (12.5%) (see Chapter 81).

MORBIDITY AND MORTALITY

The most common cause of early death in infants with jejunoileal atresia is infection related to pneumonia, peritonitis, or sepsis.[32] The most significant postoperative complications include functional intestinal obstruction at the site of anastomosis and anastomotic leak.[32,99] Other contributing factors affecting morbidity and mortality include associated anomalies, respiratory distress, prematurity, short-bowel syndrome, and postoperative bowel obstruction owing to volvulus with bowel infarction.[32] Nixon and Tawes[99] found that the most common primary cause of death was anastomotic leak or dysfunction, which occurred in 15% of cases.

In the past, a relatively lower survival rate (58%) was observed in instances of jejunal atresia.[32] The prognosis improved with more distal obstructions, with a 75% survival rate noted in instances of ileal atresia. At the time, an increased mortality was observed in instances of multiple atresias (57%) and apple-peel atresias (71%) and when atresia was associated with meconium ileus (65%), meconium peritonitis (50%), and gastroschisis (66%).[32,48,85,108,114,124,128,145]

In 1971, Nixon and Tawes[99] suggested the use of *risk* and *treatment* groups for critical evaluation of survival in infants with intestinal atresia. Infants were placed into three risk groups: group A patients were infants weighing more than 5.5 lb with no other significant abnormalities; group B infants weighed 4.0 to 5.5 lb or had a moderately severe associated abnormality; and group C infants weighed less than 4.0 lb or had associated severe abnormalities. Infants in group C had the worst survival data (32%), whereas infants in group A or B had an 81% survival rate. Treatment groups were divided into groups with high-jejunal, mid–small-bowel, and terminal ileal atresias. Patients with high-jejunal atresia in group A or B had a 60% survival, whereas all eight patients in group C died. Survival occurred in 82% of mid–small-bowel atresias in group A or B, whereas survival was only 32% in group C. Survival for atresias involving the terminal ileum in infants in group A or B was 100% but dropped to 50% for infants in group C.

de Lorimier and associates[32] evaluated the effect of wide proximal resection and end-to-end anastomosis on survival. Resection improved survival in jejunal atresia from 39% to 66% but had little effect on the overall survival in instances of ileal atresia. Louw[80] reported a 94% survival rate after wide proximal resection and end-to-oblique one-layer anastomosis in 33 infants with jejunoileal atresia. There were two anastomotic leaks. The only two deaths in this series occurred in infants categorized as group C patients. Martin and Zerella[85] reported a 100% survival rate in 23 patients with jejunoileal atresia treated since 1968.

In recent years, most reports concerning jejunoileal atresia describe overall survival rates ranging from 80%

TABLE 80-2 Percent Survival of Jejunoileal Atresia

Author/Year	% of Cases
de Lorimier et al., 1969[32]	68
Nixon and Tawes, 1971[99]	62
Louw, 1967[81]	94
Martin and Zerella, 1976[85]	100
Rescorla and Grosfeld, 1983[114]	90
Smith and Glasson, 1989[128]	78
Touloukian, 1993[142]	91
Dalla Vecchia et al., 1998[30]	84
Hou and Zhang 1999[59]	82
Sweeney et al., 2001[135]	80
Grosfeld, 2004 (current data)	87

to 90% or greater (Table 80-2).[30,114,135,143] With the advent of sophisticated care in neonatal intensive care units, prematurity is much less of an adverse factor than in previous decades. The predictive risk group outcome classification based on birth weight as described by Nixon in 1971 is less applicable.[98,99] Smith and Glasson[128] reported a 78% survival listing malrotation, associated anomalies, and use of stomas as adverse factors. Operative mortality (at 30 days) was 1.5% with three deaths in 194 cases at the Riley Children's Hospital. Death was related to sepsis and multiple organ failure in two infants with meconium peritonitis and to sepsis and respiratory failure in a premature infant. However, there were 21 late deaths from 3 months to 8 years after initial treatment (overall mortality of 12.5%). Deaths were due to sepsis and multiple organ system failure in 10 patients, including 5 with short-bowel syndrome and 3 with atresia associated with gastroschisis. Three patients with short-bowel syndrome developed liver failure related to long-term administration of TPN. An additional patient with gastroschisis and bronchopulmonary dysplasia died of progressive respiratory failure. One infant with apple-peel atresia succumbed after a septic episode. One anastomotic leak occurred in an infant with ileal atresia and volvulus. All but 1 infant with multiple atresias, 9 of 11 infants with apple-peel atresia, and 24 of 28 infants associated with gastroschisis survived. In regard to infants with gastroschisis, initial stomas should be avoided if a synthetic prosthetic device (silo) is required to achieve closure of the abdominal wall defect.[91,129] Returning the atretic bowel segment to the abdomen and performing a delayed primary anastomosis is well tolerated. A higher mortality persists in subsets of patients with familial instances of multiple atresias associated with ill-defined immunodeficiency syndromes.[11]

Improved survival in patients with jejunoileal atresia is related to appropriate resection or tapering enteroplasty and end-to-oblique anastomosis or exteriorization with a late anastomosis in selected cases. The aggressive use of TPN as an adjunctive method of therapy has significantly improved the overall outlook for these infants.[110] In a review of 449 cases of intestinal atresia at the Beijing Children's Hospital, the mortality diminished from 64.7% to 18.6% in the recent era, with the use of TPN and longitudinal oblique anastomoses.[59] Excellent long-term outcomes (80% survival) have been observed even in patients with apple-peel atresias.[30,38,149] TPN avoids protein-calorie malnutrition, establishes positive nitrogen balance, and allows for a relatively safe waiting period in instances of jejunoileal atresia associated with anastomotic dysfunction or gastroschisis. It has also been extremely useful in instances of short-bowel syndrome and in infants with temporary exteriorization procedures who have enterostomy dysfunction. In infants with small-bowel atresia complicating gastroschisis, Molik and coworkers noted 7 of 27 developed short-bowel syndrome and required an extended period of hospital stay and long-term TPN support.[91] After massive bowel resection, TPN maintains the nutritional needs of the infants while allowing appropriate healing and time for adaptation to occur.[110] Intestinal adaptation is characterized by villus hypertrophy, mucosal cell hyperplasia, and increased bowel wall thickness and circumference. Short-bowel syndrome is a topic covered extensively elsewhere in this textbook (see Chapter 86). Unfortunately, TPN may be associated with severe cholestasis, occasionally resulting in progressive liver disease and subsequent hepatic failure. Two deaths at our institution were related to liver failure associated with TPN.

Infants with mid–small-bowel resection have a better prognosis than those in whom the ileocecal valve has been resected. Wilmore's review[158] of 50 infants with significant small-bowel resection suggests that most infants with more than 35 cm of intestine after mid–small-bowel resection and with an intact ileocecal valve survive. Survival drops to 50% if only 15 to 25 cm of the bowel remains and decreases to 0% in infants with less than 15 cm of remaining small bowel and an intact ileocecal valve or less than 40 cm of proximal bowel if the ileocecal valve has been resected. I believe that TPN and special elemental diets have changed these observations somewhat because I have treated two infants with 20 cm and 30 cm of remaining small bowel with excision of the ileocecal valve who have adapted and survived. There is good evidence to suggest that the premature infant's bowel may lengthen in the first year of life, which may play a role in these observations.[143,157] The administration of growth hormone, glutamine, and other growth factors may be beneficial in selected cases.[74,88,158] The Bianchi longitudinal lengthening procedure and serial transverse enteroplasty (STEP) procedure devised by Kim and associates are methods that attempt to increase the bowel length in instances of extreme short-bowel syndrome (for details see Chapter 86).[10,67,68] For patients who fail to adapt, an isolated intestinal transplantation procedure may be an alternative treatment pathway (see Chapter 46).[18] In those infants who remain unadapted and develop TPN-related liver failure in addition to their short-bowel syndrome, a multivisceral organ transplantation procedure may be lifesaving (see Chapter 46). Infants who have severe liver dysfunction at the time of bowel-lengthening procedures rarely benefit from that procedure and usually proceed to transplantation.[18]

Although most infants with a 50% mid–small-bowel resection have normal growth and development, others with more extensive resections may not. Infants with more distal resections, particularly those in whom the ileocecal valve is excised, are more subject to malabsorption (fat, bile salts, vitamin B_{12}, calcium, magnesium), diarrhea (steatorrhea), and increased bacterial proliferation in the small bowel.[7,157,158] Although many infants with short-bowel syndrome survive, they may continue to have problems that must be closely monitored, including renal stones, gallstones, and malabsorption. One patient at my institution developed iron-deficiency anemia and had evidence of blood in the stool. An anastomotic ulcer was detected on endoscopy at age 11 years and was resected. Similar observations regarding bleeding due to late anastomotic ulcers have been reported by Sondheimer and colleagues[130] and Couper[26] and associates. Long-term follow-up of infants treated for jejunoileal atresia in the neonatal period is strongly recommended.

REFERENCES

1. Abrams JS: Experimental intestinal atresia. Surgery 1968; 64:185-191.
2. Aigrain Y, Enezian G, Sonsino E, et al: Multiple intestinal atresias: Report of 2 cases. Chir Pediatr 1989;30:61-64.
3. Alyulymon OM, Monteiro H, Ouzounian JG, et al: Clinical significance of prenatal ultrasonographic intestinal dilatation in fetuses with gastroschisis. Am J Ostet Gynecol 1996; 175:982-984.
4. Basu R, Burge DM: The effect of antenatal diagnosis on the management of small bowel atresia. Pediatr Surg Int 2004;20:177-179.
5. Baxi LV, Yeh MN, Blanc WA, Schullinger JN: Antepartum diagnosis and management of in-utero intestinal volvulus with perforation. N Engl J Med 1983;308:1519-1521.
6. Bell RH, Johnson FE, Lilly JR: Intestinal anastomosis in neonatal surgery. Ann Surg 1976;83:276-281.
7. Benson CD, Lloyd JR: Surgical lesions of the small intestine in the newborn. Dis Colon Rectum 1962:5:89-104.
8. Benson CD, Lloyd JR, Smith JD: Resection and primary anastomosis in the management of stenosis and atresia of the jejunum and ileum. Pediatrics 1960;26:265-272.
9. Berdon WE, Baker DH, Santulli TV, et al: Microcolon in newborn infants with intestinal obstruction: Its correlation with the level and time of onset of obstruction. Radiology 1968;90:878-885.
10. Bianchi A: Experience with intestinal lengthening and tailoring. Eur J Pediatr Surg 1999;9:256-259.
11. Bilodeau A, Prasil O, Cloutier R, et al: Hereditary multiple intestinal atresia: 30 years later. J Pediatr Surg 2004;39: 726-730.
12. Birtch AG, Coran AG, Gross RE: Neonatal peritonitis. Surgery 1967;61:305-313.
13. Bishop HC, Koop CE: Management of meconium ileus: Resection, Roux-en-Y anastomosis and ileostomy irrigation with pancreatic enzymes. Ann Surg 1957;145:410-414.
14. Black PR, Meuller D, Chow J, et al: Mesenteric defect as a cause of intestinal volvulus after malrotation and as the possible primary etiology of intestinal atresia. J Pediatr Surg 1994;29:1339-1343.
15. Bland-Sutton J: Imperforate ileum. Ann J Med Sci 1889; 98:457.
16. Blyth H, Dickson JAS: Apple-peel syndrome (congenital intestinal atresia): A family study of 7 index patients. J Med Genet 1969;6:275-277.
17. Boggs TR Jr, Bishop H: Neonatal hyperbilirubinemia associated with high obstruction of the small bowel. J Pediatr 1965;66:349-356.
18. Bueno J, Guiterrez J, Mazariegos GV, et al: Analysis of patients with longitudinal lengthening procedure referred for intestinal transplantation. J Pediatr Surg 2001;36:178-183.
19. Careskey JM, Grosfeld JL, Weber TR, Malangoni MA: Giant cystic meconium peritonitis (GCMP): Improved survival based on clinical and laboratory observations. J Pediatr Surg 1982;17:482-489.
20. Careskey JM, Weber TR, Grosfeld JL: Total colonic aganglionosis: Analysis of 16 cases. Am J Surg 1982;143:160-168.
21. Chaet MS, Warner BW, Sheldon CA: Management of multiple jejunoileal atresias with an intraluminal Silastic stent. J Pediatr Surg 1994;29:1604-1606.
22. Chalon J, Loew DA, Malebranche J: Effects of dry anesthetic gases on tracheobronchial ciliated epithelium. Anesthesiology 1972;37:338-343.
23. Cloutier R: Intestinal smooth muscle response to chronic obstruction: Possible application in jejunal atresia. J Pediatr Surg 1975;10:3-8.
24. Collins DL, Kimura K, Morgan A: Multiple intestinal atresia and amyoplasia congenita in four unrelated infants. J Pediatr Surg 1986;21:331-333.
25. Cook RCM, Rickham PP: Neonatal intestinal obstruction due to milk curds. J Pediatr Surg 1969;4:599-605.
26. Couper RT, Durie PR, Stafford SE, et al: Late gastrointestinal bleeding and protein loss after distal small-bowel resection in infancy. J Pediatr Gastroenterol Nutr 1989;9:454-460.
27. Courtois B: Des origines foetales des occlusions congenitales due grele dites par atresia. J Chir 1959;78:405.
28. Cragan JD, Martin ML, Moore CA, Khoury MJ: Descriptive epidemiology of small intestinal atresia, Atlanta, Georgia. Teratology 1993;48:441-450.
29. Cragan JD, Martin ML, Waters GD, Khoury MJ: Increased risk of small intestinal atresia among twins in the United States. Arch Pediatr Adolesc Med 1994;148:733-739.
30. Dalla Vecchia L, Grosfeld JL, West KW, et al: Intestinal atresia and stenosis: A 25 year experience with 277 cases. Arch Surg 1998;133:490-496.
31. Davis DL, Poynter CWM: Congenital occlusions of intestine with report of a case of multiple atresias of jejunum. Surg Gynecol Obstet 1922;34:35.
32. de Lorimier AA, Fonkalsrud EW, Hays DM: Congenital atresia and stenosis of the jejunum and ileum. Surgery 1969;65:819-827.
33. de Lorimier AA, Harrison MR: Intestinal imbrication in the treatment of atresia. J Pediatr Surg 1983;18:734-737.
34. de Lorimier AA, Norman DA, Goodling CA, Preger L: A model for the cinefluoroscopic and manometric study of chronic intestinal obstruction. J Pediatr Surg 1973;8: 785-791.
35. Dinsmore JE, Jackson RJ, Wagner CW: Management of multiple atresias and perforation with intraluminal stenting. Pediatr Surg Int 1998;13:226-228.
36. Dickson JA: Apple-peel small bowel: An uncommon variant of duodenal and jejunal atresia. J Pediatr Surg 1970;5: 595-600.
37. Evans CH: Atresias of the gastrointestinal tract. Surg Gynecol Obstet 1951;92:1-8.
38. Festen S, Brevoord JC, Goldhoorn GA, et al: Excellent long-term outcome for survivors of apple peel atresia. J Pediatr Surg 2002;37:61-65.
39. Fockens P: Ein operativ geheilter Fall von Kongenitaler Duenndarm Atresie. Zentrlbl Chir 1911;38:532.
40. Foglia RP, Jobst S, Fonkalsrud EW, Ament ME: An unusual variant of a jejuno-ileal atresia. J Pediatr Surg 1983;18: 182-184.

41. Forrester MB, Merz RD: Population-based study of small intestinal atresia and stenosis, Hawaii, 1986-2000. Public Health 2004;118:434-438.
42. Fourcade L, Shima H, Miyazaki E, Puri P: Multiple gastrointestinal atresias result from disturbed morphogenesis. Pediatr Surg Int 2001;17:361-364.
43. Gillick J, Giles S, Bannigan S, Puri P: Midgut atresias result from abnormal development of the notochord in an Adriamycin rat model. J Pediatr Surg 2002;37:719-722.
44. Gluer S: Intestinal atresia following intraamniotic use of dyes. Eur J Pediatr Surg 1995;5:240-242.
45. Gornall P: Management of intestinal atresia complicated by gastroschisis. J Pediatr Surg 1989;24:522-524.
46. Graham JN, Marin-Padilla M, Hoefnagel D: Jejunal atresia associated with Cafergot ingestion during pregnancy. Clin Pediatr 1983;22:226.
47. Gray SW, Skandalakis JE: Embryology for Surgeons. Philadelphia, WB Saunders, 1994.
48. Grosfeld JL: Alimentary tract obstruction in the newborn. Curr Probl Pediatr 1975;5:3-47.
49. Grosfeld JL, Ballantine TVN, Shoemaker R: Operative management of intestinal atresia and stenosis based on pathologic findings. J Pediatr Surg 1979;14:368-375.
50. Grosfeld JL, Clatworthy HW Jr: Intrauterine midgut strangulation in a gastroschisis defect. Surgery 1970;67:519-520.
51. Grosfeld JL, Clatworthy HW Jr: The nature of ileal atresia due to intrauterine intussusception. Arch Surg 1970;100:714-717.
52. Grosfeld JL, Dawes L, Weber TR: Current management of abdominal wall defects: Gastroschisis and omphalocele. Surg Clin North Am 1981;61:1037-1049.
53. Gross E, Armon Y, Abu-Dalu K, et al: Familial combined duodenal and jejunal atresia. J Pediatr Surg 1996;31:1573.
54. Guttman FN, Braun P, Garance PH, et al: Multiple atresias and a new syndrome of hereditary multiple atresias involving the gastrointestinal tract from stomach to rectum. J Pediatr Surg 1973;8:633-640.
55. Harris J, Kallen B, Robert E: Descriptive epidemiology of alimentary tract atresia. Teratology 1995;52:15-29.
56. Hasegawa T, Sumimura J, Nose K, et al: Congenital multiple intestinal atresia successfully treated with multiple anastomoses in a premature infant: Report of a case. Surg Today 1996;26:849-851.
57. Heij HA, Moorman-Voestermans CG, Vos A: Atresia of the jejunum and ileum: Is it the same disease? J Pediatr Surg 1990;25:635-637.
58. Herman TE, McAlister WH: Familial type I jejunal atresia and renal dysplasia. Pediatr Radiol 1995;25:272-274.
59. Hou D, Zhang J: 40 years' review of intestinal atresia. China Med J (Engl) 1999;112:583-585.
60. Houston CS, Wittenborg MH: Roentgen evaluation of anomalies of rotation and fixation of the bowel in children. Radiology 1965;84:1-18.
61. Howard ER, Othersen HB: Proximal jejunoplasty in the treatment of jejunal atresia. J Pediatr Surg 1973;8:685-690.
62. Imai Y, Nishijima E, Muraji T, et al: Fusion of intussusceptum and intussuscipiens in intrauterine intussusception: A rare type of intestinal atresia. Pathol Int 1999;9:962-967.
63. Janik JP, Wayne ER, Janik JS, Price MR: Ileal atresia with total colonic aganglionosis. J Pediatr Surg 1997;32: 1502-1503.
64. Johnson FP: The development of the mucous membrane of the esophagus, stomach, and small intestine in the human embryo. Am J Anat 1910;10:521.
65. Kazandjian V, Aigrain Y, Enezian G, et al: Upper jejunal atresia: Treatment using jejunal resection, duodenal modeling, and duodenal jejunal or ileal anastomosis. Chir Pediatr 1989;30:191-195.
66. Kilani RA, Hmiel P, Garver MK, et al: Familial jejunal atresia with renal dysplasia. J Pediatr Surg 1996;31:1427-1429.
67. Kim HB, Fauza D, Garza J, et al: Serial transverse enteroplasty (STEP): A novel bowel lengthening procedure. J Pediatr Surg 2003;38:425-429.
68. Kim HB, Lee PW, Garza J, et al: Serial transverse enteroplasty for short bowel syndrome: A case report. J Pediatr Surg 2003;38:881-885.
69. Kimble RM, Harding JE, Kolbe A: Jejuno-ileal atresia, an inherited condition? Pediatr Surg Int 1995;10:5.
70. Kimura K, Perdzynski W, Soper RT: Elliptical seromuscular resection for tapering the proximal dilated bowel in duodenal or jejunal atresia. J Pediatr Surg 1996;31:1405-1406.
71. Kling K, Applebaum H, Dunn J, et al: A novel technique for correction of intestinal atresia at the ligament of Treitz. J Pediatr Surg 2001;36:353-355.
72. Koga Y, Hayashida Y, Ikeda K, et al: Intestinal atresia in fetal dogs produced by localized ligation of mesenteric vessels. J Pediatr Surg 1975;10:949-953.
73. Komuro H, Hori T, Amagai T, et al: The etiologic role of intrauterine volvulus and intussusception in jejunoileal atresia. J Pediatr Surg 2004;39:1812-1814.
74. Ladd AP, Grosfeld JL, Pescovitz OH, Johnson NB: The effect of growth hormone supplementation on late nutritional independence in pediatric patients with short bowel syndrome. J Pediatr Surg 2005;40:442-445.
75. Lally KP, Chwals WJ, Weitzman JJ, et al: Hirschsprung's disease: A possible cause of anastomotic failure following repair of intestinal atresia. J Pediatr Surg 1992;27:469-470.
76. Landor JH, Armstrong JH, Dickerson OB, Westerfeld RA: Neonatal obstruction of bowel caused by accidental clamping of small omphalocele: Report of two cases. South Med J 1963;56:1236-1238.
77. LeCoultre C, et al: An unusual association of small bowel atresia and biliary atresia: A case report. J Pediatr Surg 1983;18:136.
78. Lituania M, Cordone MS: Prenatal diagnosis of jejunal atresia by ultrasound (apple-peel syndrome). Gaslini 1980;12:197.
79. Lloyd JR, Clatworthy HW Jr: Hydramnios as an aid to the early diagnosis of congenital obstruction of the alimentary tract: A study of maternal and fetal factor. Pediatrics 1958;21:903-909.
80. Louw JH, Barnard CN: Congenital intestinal atresia: Observations on its origin. Lancet 1955;2:1065-1067.
81. Louw JH: Resection and end-to-end anastomosis in the management of atresia and stenosis of the small bowel. Surgery 1967;62:940-950.
82. Lynn HB, Espinas EE: Intestinal atresia: An attempt to relate location to embryologic processes. Arch Surg 1959; 79:357-361.
83. Mogliner BM, Appelman Z, Lancet M, Casif R: Antenatal diagnosis of fetal intestinal obstruction by ultrasonography. Harefuah 1981;101:5.
84. Marfatia S, Donahoe PK, Hendren WH: Effect of dry and humidified gases on the respiratory epithelium in rabbits. J Pediatr Surg 1975;10:583-592.
85. Martin LW, Zerella JT: Jejunoileal atresia: Proposed classification. J Pediatr Surg 1976;11:399-404.
86. Martucciello G, Torre M, Pini Prato A, et al: Associated anomalies. I: intestinal neuronal dysplasia. J Pediatr Surg 2002;37:219-223.
87. Masumoto K, Suita S, Nada O, et al: Abnormalities of enteric neurons, intestinal pacemaker cells, and smooth muscle in human intestinal atresia. J Pediatr Surg 1999; 34:1463-1468.
88. Matarese LE, Seidner DL, Steiger E: Growth hormone, glutamine and modified diet for intestinal adaptation. Am J Diet Assoc 2004;104:1265-1272.

89. Matsumoto Y, Komatsu K, Tabata T: Jejuno-ileal atresia in identical twins: Report of a case. Surg Today 2000;30:438-440.
90. Mishalany HG, Najjar FB: Familial jejunal atresia: Three cases in one family. J Pediatr Surg 1968;73:753-755.
91. Molik KA, Gingalewski CA, West KW, et al: Gastroschisis: A plea for risk categorization. J Pediatr Surg 2001;36:51-55.
92. Moorman-Voestermans CG, Heij HA, Vos A: Jejunal atresia in twins. J Pediatr Surg 1990;25:638-639.
93. Moreno LA, Gottrand F, Tvack D, et al: Severe combined immunodeficiency syndrome associated with autosomal recessive familial multiple gastrointestinal atresia: Study of a family. Am J Med Genet 1990;37:143-146.
94. Moya F, Apgar V, James LS, Berrien C: Hydramnios and congenital anomalies: Study of a series of 74 patients. JAMA 1960;173:1552-1556.
95. Murphy DA: Internal hernias in infancy and childhood. Surgery 1964;55:311-316.
96. Neuhauser EB: Roentgen changes associated with pancreatic insufficiency in early life. Radiology 1946;46:319.
97. Nixon HH: Intestinal obstruction in the newborn. Arch Dis Child 1955;30:13-22.
98. Nixon HH: An experimental study of propulsion in isolated small intestine and applications to surgery in the newborn. Ann R Coll Surg Engl 1960;24:105-124.
99. Nixon HH, Tawes R: Etiology and treatment of small intestinal atresia: Analysis of a series of 127 jejunoileal atresias and comparison with 62 duodenal atresias. Surgery 1971;69:41-51.
100. Odell GB: Physiologic hyperbilirubinemia in the neonatal period. N Engl J Med 1967;277:193-195.
101. Okmian LG, Kovamees A: Jejunal atresia with intestinal aplasia: Strangulation of the intestine in the extraembryonic coelom of the belly stalk. Acta Paediatr Scand 1964; 53:65-69.
102. Olsen MM, Luck SR, Lloyd-Still J, Raffensperger JG: The spectrum of meconium disease in infancy. J Pediatr Surg 1982;17:479-481.
103. Parkkulainen KV: Intrauterine intussusception as a cause of intestinal atresia: A contribution to the etiology of intestinal atresia. Surgery 1958;44:1106-1111.
104 Paterson-Brown S, Stalewski H, Brereton RJ: Neonatal small bowel atresia, stenosis and segmental dilatation. Br J Surg 1991;78:83-86.
105. Phelps S, Fisher R, Partington A, Dykes E: Prenatal ultrasound diagnosis of gastrointestinal malformations. J Pediatr Surg 1997;32:438-440.
106. Pokorny WJ, Harberg FJ, McGill CW: Gastroschisis complicated by intestinal atresia. J Pediatr Surg 1981;16:261-263.
107. Prasad SR, Mitra DK, Bhatnagar V, Mathur M: Multiple atresias of the bowel with reference to Tandler's theory of embryogenesis. Ind Pediatr 1993;30:1036-1039.
108. Puri P, Fujimoto T: New observations in the pathogenesis of multiple intestinal atresias. J Pediatr Surg 1988;23: 221-225.
109. Puvabandisin S, Garrow E, Sanransamraujkit R, Lopez LA: Postnatal intussusception in a premature infant causing intestinal atresia. J Pediatr Surg 1996;31:711-712.
110. Quiros-Tejeira RE, Ament ME, Reyen L, et al: Long-term parenteral nutritional support and intestinal adaptation in children with short bowel syndrome: A 25-year experience. J Pediatr 2004:145:157-163.
111. Rachelson MH, Jernigan JR, Jackson WF: Intussusceptum in the newborn infant with spontaneous expulsion of the intussusception: Case report and review of the literature. J Pediatr 1955;47:87-94.
112. Randolph JG, Zollinger RM Jr, Gros RE: Mikulicz resection in infants and children: A 20-year survey of 196 patients. Ann Surg 1963;158:481-491.
113. Rehbein F, Halsband H: A double tube technique for the treatment of meconium ileus and small bowel atresia. J Pediatr Surg 1968;3:723.
114. Rescorla FJ, Grosfeld JL: Intestinal atresia and stenosis: Analysis of survival in 120 cases. Surgery 1983;98:668-676.
115. Rittenhouse EA, Beckwith JB, Chappell JS, Bill AH: Multiple septa of the small bowel: Description of an unusual case with review of the literature and consideration of etiology. Surgery 1972;71:371-379.
116. Romero R, Shidini A, et al: Gastrointestinal tract and abdominal wall defects. In Brock DJH, Rodeck CH, Ferguson-Smith MA (eds): Prenatal Diagnosis and Screening. Edinburgh, Churchill Livingstone, 1992, p 237.
117. Rosenman JE, Kosloske AM: A reappraisal of the Mikulicz enterostomy in infants and children. Surgery 1982;91:34-37.
118. Ros Mar Z, Diez Pardo JA, Ros Miquel M, Benavent I: Apple-peel small bowel: A review of 12 cases. Z Kinderchir Grenzgeb 1980;29:313-317.
119. Rothenberg ME, White FV, Chilmonczyk B, Chatila T: A syndrome involving immunodeficiency and multiple intestinal atresias. Immunodeficiency 1995;5:171-178.
120. Saguintaah M, Couture A, Veyrac C, Baud C: MRI of the fetal intestinal tract. Pediatr Radiol 2002;32:395-404.
121. Santulli TV, Blanc WA: Congenital atresia of the intestine: Pathogenesis and treatment. Ann Surg 1961;154:939-948.
122. Sapin E, Carricaburu E, De Boissieu D, et al: Conservative intestinal surgery to avoid short-bowel syndrome in multiple intestinal atresias and necrotizing enterocolitis: 6 cases treated by multiple anastomoses and Santulli-type enterostomy. Eur J Pediatr Surg 1999;9:24-28.
123. Schoenberg RA, Kluth D: Experimental small bowel obstruction in chick embryos: Effects on the developing enteric nervous system. J Pediatr Surg 2002;37:735-740.
124. Seashore JH, Collins FS, Markowitz RI, Seashore MR: Familial apple-peel atresia: Surgical, genetic and radiographic aspects. Pediatrics 1987;80:540-544.
125. Shah R, Wooley MM: Gastroschisis and intestinal atresia. J Pediatr Surg 1991;26:788-790.
126. Shenoy MU, Robson K, Broderick N, Kapila L: Congenital small bowel diverticulosis and intestinal atresia: A rare association. J Pediatr Surg 2000;35:636-637.
127. Singleton EB: Congenital abnormalities of the small bowel: Meconium ileus. In Singleton EB (ed): X-Ray Diagnosis of the Alimentary Tract in Infants and Children. Chicago, Year Book , 1959, pp 199-205.
128. Smith GH, Glasson M: Intestinal atresia: Factors affecting survival. Aust N Z J Surg 1989;59:151-156.
129. Snyder CL, Miller KA, Sharp RJ, et al: Management of intestinal atresia in patients with gastroschisis. J Pediatr Surg 2001;36:1542-1544.
130. Sondheimer JM, Sokol RJ, Narkewicz MR, Tyson RW: Anastomotic ulceration: A late complication of ileocolonic anastomosis. J Pediatr 1995;127:225-230.
131. Spencer R: The various patterns of intestinal atresia. Surgery 1968;64:661-668.
132. Spriggs NL: Congenital intestinal occlusion. Guys Hosp Rep 1912;66:143.
133. Stromme P, Dahl E, Flage T, Sten-Johansen H: Apple peel intestinal atresia in siblings with ocular anomalies and microcephaly. Clin Genet 1993;44:208-210.
134. Suruga K, Hirai Y, Nagashima K, et al: Congenital intestinal atresia. Shujutsu 1968:22:726-733.
135. Sweeney B, Surana R, Puri P: Jejunoileal atresia and associated malformations: Correlation with timing of in-utero insult. J Pediatr Surg 2001;36:774-776.
136. Tam PK, Nicholls G: Implications of antenatal diagnosis of small-intestinal atresia in the 1990s. Pediatr Surg Int 1999;15:486-487.

137. Tandler J: Zur Entwicklungsgeschichte des menschlichen Duodenum in fruhen Embryonalstadien. Morphol Jahrb 1900;29:187.
138. Teja K, Schnatterly P, Shaw A: Multiple intestinal atresia: Pathology and pathogenesis. J Pediatr Surg 1981;16:194-199.
139. Thomas CG Jr: Jejunoplasty for correction of jejunal atresia. Surg Gynecol Obstet 1969;129:545-546.
140. Todani T, Tabuchi K, Tanaka S: Intestinal atresia due to intrauterine intussusception: Analysis of 24 cases in Japan. J Pediatr Surg 1975;10:445-451.
141. Touloukian RJ: Intestinal atresia and stenosis. In Holder TM, Ashcraft KW (eds): Pediatric Surgery. Philadelphia, WB Saunders, 1980.
142. Touloukian RJ: Diagnosis and treatment of jejunoileal atresia. World J Surg 1993;17:310-317.
143. Touloukian RJ, Smith GJ: Normal intestinal length in preterm infants: An autopsy study. J Pediatr Surg 1983; 18:720-723.
144. Tovar JA, Sunol M, Lopez de Torre B, et al: Mucosal morphology in experimental intestinal atresia: Studies in the chick embryo. J Pediatr Surg 1991;26:184-189.
145. Van Hoorn WA, Hazebrook FW, Molenaar JC: Gastroschisis with atresia—a plea for delay in resection. Z Kinderchir 1985;40:368-370.
146. Vassy LE, Boles ET: Iatrogenic ileal atresia secondary to clamping of an occult omphalocele. J Pediatr Surg 1975; 10:797-800.
147. Veyrac C, Coutre A, Saguintaah M, Baud C: MRI of fetal GI tract abnormalities. Abdom Imaging 2004;29:411-420.
148. Wagner ML, Rudolph AJ, Singleton EB: Neonatal defects associated with abnormalities of the amnion and amniotic fluid. Radiol Clin North Am 1968;6:279-294.
149. Waldhausen JH, Sawin RS: Improved long-term outcomes for patients with jejunoileal apple peel atresia. J Pediatr Surg 1997;32:1307-1309.
150. Walker MW, Lovell MA, Kelly TC, et al: Multiple areas of intestinal atresia associated with immunodeficiency and post-transfusion graft-versus-host disease. J Pediatr 1993;123:93-95.
151. Wang NL, Yeh ML, Chang PY, et al: Prenatal and neonatal intussusception. Pediatr Surg Int 1998;13:232-236.
152. Ward HC, Leake J, Milla PJ, Spitz L: Brown bowel syndrome: A late complication of intestinal atresia. J Pediatr Surg 1992;27:1593-1595.
153. Webb CH, Wangensteen OH: Congenital intestinal atresia. Am J Dis Child 1931;41:262.
154. Weber TR, Vane DW, Grosfeld JL: Tapering enteroplasty in infants with bowel atresia and short gut. Arch Surg 1982;117:684-688.
155. Weitzman JJ, Vanderhoof RS: Jejunal atresia with agenesis of the dorsal mesentery with "Christmas tree" deformity of the small intestine. Am J Surg 1966;111:443-449.
156. Werler MM, Sheehan JE, Mitchell AA: Maternal medication use and risks of gastroschisis and small intestinal atresia. Am J Epidemiol 2002;155:26-31.
157. Wilkinson AW: Some effects of extensive intestinal resection in childhood: Symposium on resection in the newborn infant. Bibl Pediatr 1968;87:191-207.
158. Wilmore DW: Factors correlating with a successful outcome following extensive intestinal resection, intestinal absorption and malabsorption, Zurich 1967. Mod Probl Paediatr 1968;11:191.
159. Yanagihara J, Nakamura K, Shimotake D, et al: An association of multiple intestinal atresia and biliary atresia. Eur J Pediatr Surg 1995;5:372-374.
160. Zerella JT, Martin LW: Jejunal atresia with absent mesentery and a helical ileum. Surgery 1976;80:550-553.
161. Zwiren GT, Andrews HG, Ahmann P: Jejunal atresia with agenesis of the dorsal mesentery ("apple-peel small bowel"). J Pediatr Surg 1972;7:414-419.

Chapter 81

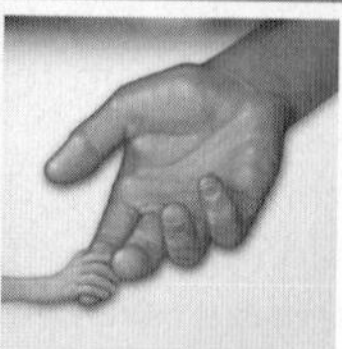

Meconium Ileus

Moritz M. Ziegler

HISTORY

Meconium ileus was first described in 1905 when Landsteiner linked the observation of meconium obstructing the small bowel with pathologic changes in the pancreas that he attributed to a putative enzyme deficiency. Subsequent authors recognized a similar association of a thickened and tenacious meconium with a mechanical pancreatic duct obstruction or stenosis.[4,31,54,64] The term *cystic fibrosis of the pancreas* was first coined in 1936 by Fanconi to describe the association of chronic pulmonary disease of infancy with pancreatic insufficiency.[124] However, it was Anderson who described, in 1938, the relationship of the histologic likeness of pancreatic abnormalities in both meconium ileus and cystic fibrosis (CF) and described meconium ileus as an early and more severe manifestation of the overall lung and pancreatic insufficiency.[2,3] Subsequent authors defined the inspissated nature of meconium, linking the finding to both pancreatic insufficiency as well as to abnormal mucus secreted by the intestine of patients with CF.[38,94,102,103,104,125]

With improved genetics, it became recognized that CF was the most common potentially lethal autosomal recessive disease in the white population. Meconium ileus itself carried an almost uniformly fatal prognosis into the late 1940s,[39,48,125] when a series of interventions were devised that by design either eliminated or bypassed the obstructing inspissated intraluminal meconium, minimizing the operative intestinal manipulation and even the need for a general anesthetic to minimize the physiologic insult to the infant. In 1969, a novel therapy applied a transrectal irrigation and solubilization of the desiccated and tenacious meconium with the use of the hyperosmolar diatrizoate (Gastrografin) enema, permitting treatment of uncomplicated meconium ileus without the need for any operative intervention, a success that has been sustained for more than two thirds of patients.[81] By the early 1970s these advances along with an improved management of the electrolyte, nutritional, and pulmonary abnormalities of CF had improved patient survival to almost 75%.[20,99]

In the past 2 decades we have seen continued progress. First, the genetic lesion of a mutation in the CF transmembrane regulator *(CFTR)* gene was defined as the causal lesion of CF,[60,61] and it is now recognized that patients with meconium ileus likely represent a distinct phenotype with earlier presentation and worse pulmonary function.[69,78] Second, the diagnostic criteria remain largely the same clinically, with definitive diagnosis achieved by a combination of biochemical and now genetic testing. Interestingly, when enema irrigation is not successful in managing meconium ileus and relieving its bowel obstruction, the preferred operative intervention is that described originally in 1948, namely, enterotomy followed by irrigation, typically using meconium-solubilizing agents. These strategies, coupled with aggressive attention to the pulmonary and nutritional status of the patient, have seen a continued improvement of patient survival now approaching 95% to 100%.[20,52,57]

PATHOPHYSIOLOGY

Genetics

Cystic fibrosis is an autosomal recessive disease that occurs among whites with a heterozygote frequency of 1 in 29 births. It is rare in blacks (1/17,000 live births), and it is almost unheard of in Asians (1/90,000 live births) and Africans. The 5% to 6% carrier rate of the abnormal gene in whites results in a CF incidence of 1 per 1150 to 2500 live births. An offspring of two heterozygous parents has a 1 in 4 chance of developing the disease.[1] Meconium ileus, potentially unique to CF, represents a disorder of neonates characterized by intestinal obstruction secondary to the intraluminal accumulation of inspissated and desiccated meconium. Meconium ileus is the earliest clinical manifestation of CF, because such patients are typically diagnosed and treated in the immediate neonatal period.[23] Meconium ileus has been reported to be the presenting feature of 20.8% of the CF population in the United States. Importantly for in utero diagnosis, a family history of CF has been found in 10% to 40% of new patients with meconium ileus. In the presence of an index case of meconium ileus complicating CF, reports have suggested that an incidence of subsequent meconium ileus in the presence of CF varies from 30% to 40%.

In 1989 the genetic mutation that codes for the cell membrane protein termed the CF transmembrane regulator was identified by Francis Collins as that locus associated with the diagnosis of CF.[91,92] This locus was identified on the long arm of chromosome 7, band q31.[63] The protein was identified as a cyclic adenosine monophosphate–induced chloride channel that regulates ion flow across the apical surface of epithelial cells.[113] A mutation of the *CFTR*, and more than 400 mutations have been identified, produces abnormal electrolyte content along the external apical environment of epithelial membranes. Tubular structures lined by such affected epithelia will be characterized by desiccation and reduced clearance of their secretions, and the affected systems include epithelial cells of respiratory, gastrointestinal, biliary, pancreatic, and reproductive systems. The clinical correlate of this pathophysiology has included pancreatic insufficiency (90%), meconium ileus (10% to 20%), diabetes mellitus (20%), obstructive biliary disease (15% to 20%), and azoospermia (nearly 100%). The exact mechanism of the epithelial glandular abnormality and the elaboration of a hyperviscous mucin remain unsolved. Certainly, the tenacious meconium protein and water content and its increased viscosity have all been described.

The *ΔF508* mutation is the most common of many *CFTR* gene locations, occurring as a homozygous pair in almost 50% of CF patients, whereas another 25% to 30% of patients will have one copy of this mutation. Such homozygous individuals nearly always phenotypically express pancreatic exocrine insufficiency, and they also present with a higher incidence of meconium ileus. A similar higher frequency of meconium ileus is also seen in *ΔF508* expressing patients who also express *G542X*. However, the disease etiology is less clear when it is recognized that not all such genotypic patients will have meconium ileus. The association of obstructive lung disease with meconium ileus suggests other *CFTR* modifier genes or even environmental factors that may play a role in this disorder. Furthermore, large patient consortia have failed to identify predictors of the complications of CF, including an incidence for meconium ileus.

Pathogenesis

The defect of CF is an exocrine-eccrine gland dysfunction, particularly of the mucus-secreting and sweat glands.[15] Pancreatic achylia was thought to be the mechanism responsible for meconium ileus because of early reports of meconium-induced bowel obstruction in patients with congenital stenosis of the pancreatic ducts. However, data began to accumulate in the 1940s that suggested that lesions in the pancreas of patients with CF were variable and were most profound in children older than 1 year of age. In contrast, the preponderance of intestinal mucosal gland abnormalities in the subset of patients with CF and meconium ileus was more striking, suggesting that these glandular lesions were the more likely origin of the tenacious material that causes the intraluminal obstruction in patients with meconium ileus.[30] Additional pathologic data have been interpreted to suggest that intestinal glandular disease plays the dominant role and pancreatic disease a secondary role in the pathogenesis of meconium ileus.[50,111]

The glandular abnormality accounting for or producing these changes is less certain. Various explanations include the glandular secretion of hyperpermeable mucus mediated by calcium that influences the physicochemical properties of mucus to be viscid and permeable to the loss of water, further concentrating intraductal secretions. This glandular-obstructing mucus would lead to the pathologic lesions noted earlier. A second hypothesis is that an impairment of fluid movement to and from the extravascular space through secretory cells exists that may prevent the normal dilution of the cellular lumen.[23,24] The highly concentrated material then becomes toxic to those cells laden with the product.

Soon after the *CFTR* gene was located on chromosome 7 by restriction fragment length polymorphism analysis, it was recognized that *CFTR* was itself a membrane chloride channel and that it further regulated chloride conductance through other channels.[27] This may be the mechanism that forms the basis for the increased levels of sodium and chloride in the eccrine sweat gland secretions that characterize patients with CF. Here a defect in electrolyte resorption of sodium and water by ductular cells and the impermeability of these cells to chloride ions result in an excretory product high in both sodium and chloride. This theory may be supported by the known characteristics of the CFTR membrane protein, which as a chloride channel, functions to regulate salt and water transport onto epithelial surfaces. Thus, a disturbed function alters exocrine secretion electrolyte content and may lead to desiccation and reduced clearance of such secretions.

Meconium itself has a variable composition, as seen from samples from varying intestinal locations of normal infants at varying gestational ages that are contrasted to meconium isolated from patients with CF with and without meconium ileus.[65] The meconium concentrations of sodium, potassium, and magnesium are almost twice as high in samples from normal children or well siblings than in samples from children with CF with or without meconium ileus. Similarly, the enzyme-catalyzing heavy metals are also at higher levels in meconium from control and well siblings than from children with CF with or without meconium ileus. Samples from patients with meconium ileus also differ from normal meconium by containing greater amounts of protein nitrogen and lesser amounts of carbohydrate. Analysis of the protein content of abnormal meconium results in a further identification of abnormal mucoproteins. These products are two-thirds protein and one-third carbohydrate, a composition similar to duodenal fluid from patients with CF. The origin of these proteins is uncertain, but they may arise either from glandular secretions or from swallowed amniotic fluid in utero. Because most of this protein is albumin, it is speculated that the intraluminal proteins are of plasma origin. They react with mucopolysaccharides, and, in the absence of degrading enzymes, they impart a highly viscid rubbery character to the involved secretions. The viscosity of these mucoproteins could be further influenced by the surrounding electrolyte environment.

Finally, this increased albumin content of meconium from patients with CF has led to the development of a meconium screening test for the diagnosis of the disease.

In summary, two simultaneous pathogenetic events in meconium ileus appear to begin in utero and result in an intraluminal accumulation of a highly viscid and tenacious meconium: the developments of pancreatic exocrine enzyme deficiency and the secretion of hyperviscous mucus by pathologically abnormal intestinal glands. The thickened meconium accumulates and begins in utero to obstruct the intestine intraluminally. This accumulation accounts for the mechanism of the complications of meconium ileus (i.e., twist of a heavy loop with perforation, peritonitis, and cyst or atresia) and the pattern of abdominal distention and obstruction seen in the neonate. The proximal ileum dilates, and its wall thickens as it becomes filled with the tenacious and tarry meconium. Concomitantly, the narrowed distal small bowel, and at times the colon, contains beaded or "boxcar" concretions of gray-white, putty-like inspissated meconium. The more distal colon is small or unused, a microcolon.

CLINICAL FEATURES

Spectrum of the Disorder

Meconium ileus presents in the neonate as *uncomplicated* or *simple* or as *complicated.* In the older child or young adult the presentation is as a *meconium ileus equivalent* or *distal ileal obstruction syndrome.*

Uncomplicated meconium ileus typically presents immediately at birth with the recognition of abdominal distention, a unique feature of inspissated meconium filling and obstructing the distal small bowel. This problem may first have been heralded by an in utero genetic diagnosis of CF and an ultrasound suggestive of intestinal obstruction with echogenic bowel. In addition to the distention, intestinal obstruction is heralded by bilious vomiting and failure to stool.

In contrast, *complicated meconium ileus* will present either in utero or postnatally with evidence of bowel obstruction complicated by evidence of previous intestinal perforation and/or necrosis: crescents or speckles of intra-abdominal calcification may be present, or on clinical assessment there may be evidence of peritonitis, including an erythematous or edematous abdominal wall and/or demonstrable abdominal tenderness.[21]

Clinical History

A family history of CF is present in 10% to 33% of patients with meconium ileus.[25] This history, coupled with in utero amniocentesis with restriction fragment length polymorphism analysis, permits the accurate diagnosis of the fetus afflicted with CF. Coupling this information with the results of serial in utero sonography permits the accurate predication of which infants are at risk for the development of the intestinal obstruction of meconium ileus (about 20% of the CF population) with or without a complicating meconium cyst. Maternal polyhydramnios may be a feature of in utero meconium ileus, a finding putatively resulting from the high-grade intestinal obstruction. Such excess maternal fluid accumulation occurs in the mothers of almost 20% of newborns with meconium ileus and at a frequency still higher for the patient with a complicated meconium ileus. Although in utero growth retardation is common, prematurity and other associated anomalies are rare.

Physical Examination

Neonates with meconium ileus often are born with abdominal distention (Fig. 81-1). In fact, meconium ileus is the only variety of neonatal intestinal obstruction that produces abdominal distention at birth before the neonate swallows air. Visible peristaltic waves and palpable, doughy bowel loops are often present. Finger pressure over a firm loop of bowel may hold the indentation, the so-called putty sign. In simple or uncomplicated meconium ileus, no findings of peritoneal irritation are present. The findings of a rectal examination are unremarkable, but characteristically on withdrawal of the examining finger a spontaneous expulsion of meconium does not follow. In the presence of an in utero perforation with meconium peritonitis and "cyst" formation, a palpable abdominal mass, discoloration of the abdominal wall, and signs of peritoneal irritation are often observed. Physical evidence of hypovolemia may rapidly develop in infants with peritonitis. On passage of a nasogastric tube a quantity of bile-stained gastric fluid usually exceeds 20 mL.

Radiologic Study

In utero, meconium ileus bowel not only may be distended but an echogenic bowel wall in the third trimester

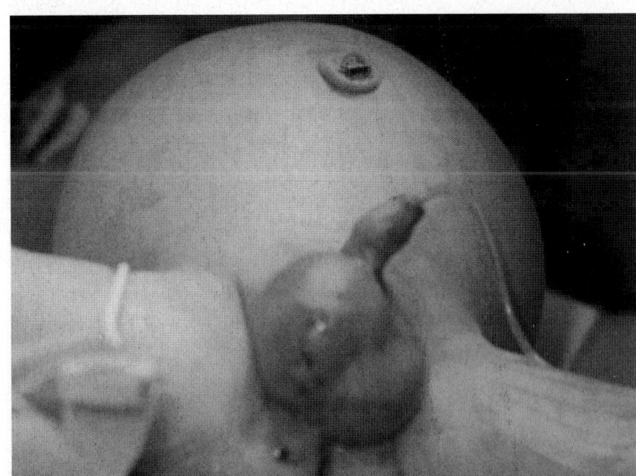

Figure 81-1 Newborn with abdominal distention at birth. There was a family history of cystic fibrosis, and this newborn had a cytogenic diagnosis of cystic fibrosis in utero. On fetal ultrasound examination there was evidence of a hyperechoic bowel wall compatible with a diagnosis of meconium ileus.

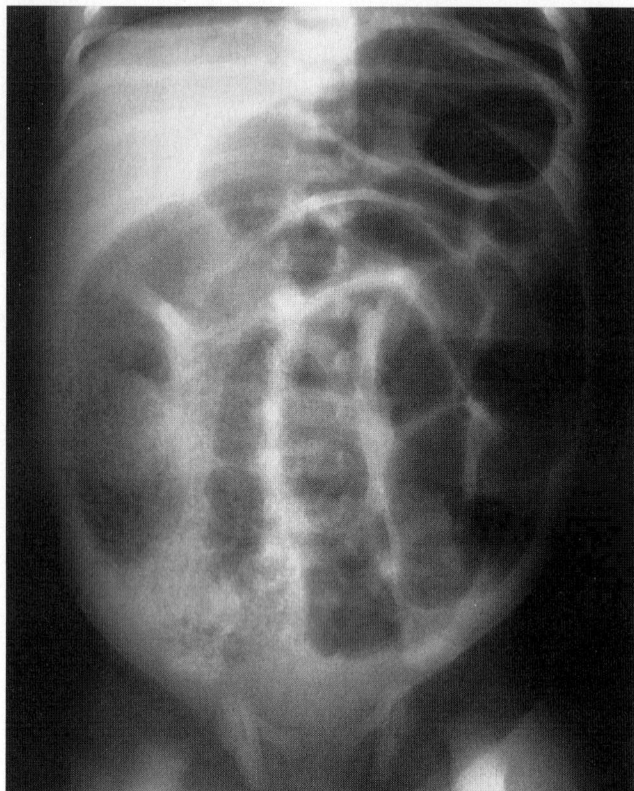

Figure 81–2 An abdominal plain upright radiograph is compatible with the diagnosis of meconium ileus. There are dilated small bowel loops of disparate size, few air-fluid levels, and a "ground-glass" or "soap-bubble" appearance in the right lower quadrant. (From Rescorla FJ, Grosfeld JL: Contemporary management of meconium ileus. World J Surg 1993;17:381.)

may be diagnostic.[5,56,79] After delivery, uncomplicated meconium ileus is characterized by a typical plain obstruction radiographic series of the abdomen (Fig. 81-2).[47,59] In addition to the supine and erect films appearing remarkably similar, the characteristic findings include the following: (1) great disparity in the size of the intestinal loops because of the configuration of different segments of the bowel; (2) no or few air-fluid levels on the erect film because swallowed air cannot layer above the thickened inspissated meconium; and (3) a granular, "soap bubble," or "ground-glass" appearance seen frequently in the right half of the abdomen, a finding that requires swallowed air bubbles to intermix within the sticky meconium (Fig. 81-3).[121] Each of these features alone is not exclusively diagnostic of meconium ileus and may be seen with other causes of intestinal obstruction. Collectively, however, they strongly suggest meconium ileus. Plain radiography done for differential diagnosis will include any cause of a distal small bowel obstruction, including ileal atresia, Hirschsprung's disease, or the meconium plug syndrome. A confirming study that may support the plain radiographic diagnosis of meconium ileus is the contrast enema. A contrast enema (whether with barium, Gastrografin, or any water-soluble contrast agent) will outline a normally positioned colon of appropriate length but of small caliber (see Fig. 81-3).[70] It will be empty or will contain pellets of inspissated meconium. The colon will be the typical "unused" colon or "microcolon." If reflux of contrast agent into the terminal ileum occurs, it will outline pellets of inspissated meconium.[12,59] If the contrast agent refluxes more proximally into the ileum, the transition into dilated loops of small bowel will be encountered. Failure to reflux contrast medium into the proximal dilated small bowel will neither prove the diagnosis of meconium ileus nor determine the exact level of the intestinal obstruction; and with this failure of the contrast medium to reflux into the dilated segment, operative intervention for diagnosis and treatment becomes necessary.

Laboratory Testing

The definitive study to confirm the diagnosis of CF is the sweat test. With the use of the pilocarpine iontophoresis method, sweat is collected from the infant's forearm, leg, or back; the amount is quantified, and the concentration of sodium and chloride in the sample is measured.[36,87] The minimum amount of sweat to be collected is 100 mg, and a measured concentration of sweat chloride in excess of 60 mEq/L is diagnostic of CF. The adequacy of the size of the sweat sample is the factor that usually precludes application of this test to the newborn, despite reports to the contrary. A few individuals have been identified with elevated sweat chloride levels but with no other features of CF. These problems, plus a potentially elevated sweat sodium and chloride level in normal newborns, may make it necessary to defer application of the sweat chloride test until the neonate reaches several weeks of age.

Genetic testing for CF can be done by analyzing cellular DNA for *CFTR*, thus establishing the carrier status of parents of a putative child with CF presenting with features of meconium ileus. However, because of the minimum number of mutations tested by these commercial analyses, negative results become less meaningful. If a family has known *CFTR* mutations, then amniocentesis with fetal DNA restriction fragment length polymorphism analysis may predict a fetal CF diagnosis.

The pathophysiologic alteration of an increased albumin concentration in meconium may prove useful as a diagnostic screening tool for meconium ileus.[43,44] This test, which uses a tetrabromophenolethylester blue indicator, detects meconium albumin concentrations in excess of 20 mg/g of stool; however, a persisting incidence of false-positive results was seen from such factors as prematurity, melena, gastroschisis, and intrauterine infection. A false-negative rate has been reported as well. This simple and relatively inexpensive tool is straightforward and rapid, and the colorimetric indicator is easy to interpret.[52,107] Meconium from normal neonates has an albumin concentration of less than 5.0 mg/g of stool, whereas meconium from neonates with CF has values at times in excess of 80 mg/g.[9,10]

Stool trypsin and chymotrypsin analysis has historically been a popular screening test for meconium ileus.[9,10,46] A trypsin level less than 80 mg/g of stool, coupled with

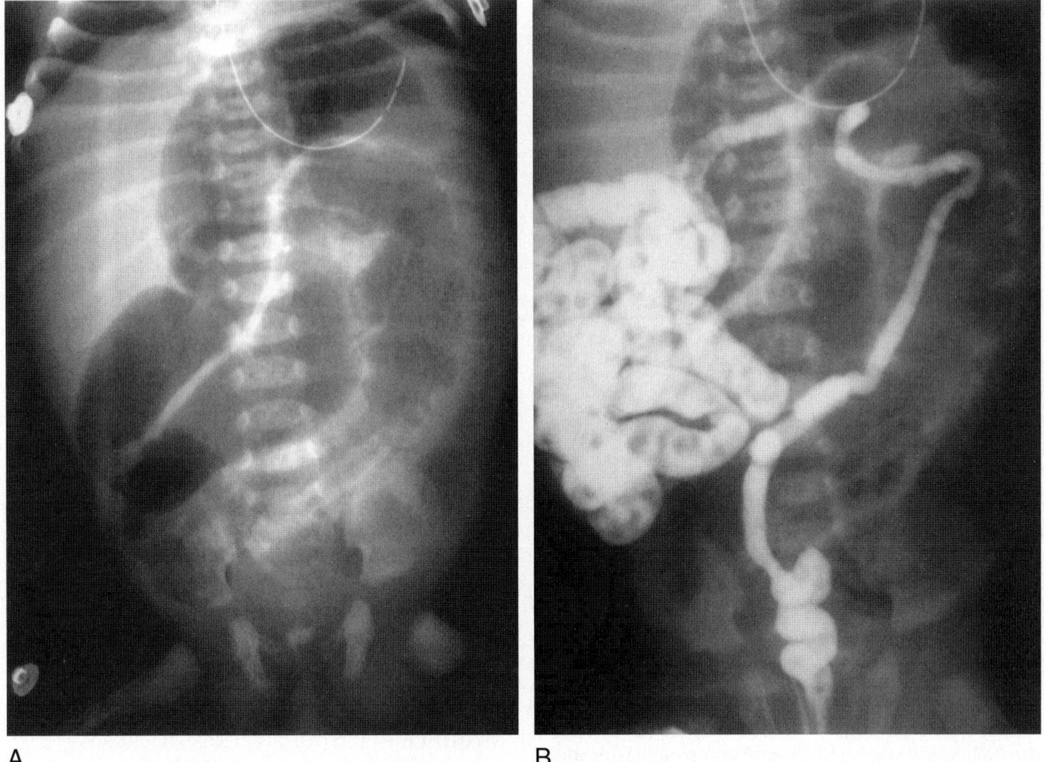

Figure 81-3 *A,* Abdominal plain radiograph is compatible with the diagnosis of meconium ileus. There are distended bowel loops of disparate size, few air-fluid levels, and a "soap bubble" right lower quadrant appearance. *B,* Same patient as in *A* is studied further with a contrast enema. A microcolon or unused colon is demonstrated, and contrast agent refluxes into dilated more proximal small bowel where inspissated intraluminal pellets of meconium are seen. These findings strongly suggest the diagnosis of meconium ileus.

operative findings, supports the diagnosis of meconium ileus. Some centers have advocated for population CF screening using a measurement of immunoreactive trypsinogen in blood.

Operative tissue specimens that aid in the diagnosis of CF include intestinal (rectal) or appendiceal pathognomonic changes that include goblet cell hyperplasia and the accumulation of secretions within the crypts or within the lumen.[84] If operation is done for putative meconium ileus and an appendicostomy is used as a bowel intraluminal irrigation site, appendectomy may be warranted to obtain such a diagnostic pathologic specimen.

Differential Diagnosis

The combination of family history, physical examination, and radiologic evaluation in the neonate are the three criteria of high sensitivity that permit an accurate clinical diagnosis of meconium ileus. The addition of linkage analysis on maternal amniocentesis samples or a sweat test confirms the diagnosis of CF. A definitive diagnosis depends on the confirmation of the cause of intestinal obstruction. Meconium ileus accounts for 10% to 25% of cases in large series of patients with neonatal intestinal obstruction. Therefore, the major differential diagnosis lies with the variety of causes of neonatal intestinal obstruction, including ileal atresia, Hirschsprung's disease, neonatal small left colon, and the meconium plug syndrome.[73]

Ileal atresia is usually suggested by a distal bowel obstruction pattern on plain radiographs with the associated presence of air-fluid levels.[19,97] If a microcolon is demonstrated on contrast enema, the contrast agent will not reflux into the proximal dilated "atretic" bowel as it might in both meconium ileus and Hirschsprung's disease (Fig. 81-4). Once ileal atresia is suspected, the final confirmation of the diagnosis requires operative exploration. Meconium ileus can be associated with ileal atresia, and at operation the findings characteristic of the sticky meconium of meconium ileus should raise this possibility (Fig. 81-5). Hirschsprung's disease, especially total colonic aganglionosis, as well as extended small bowel aganglionosis, may also mimic meconium ileus.[62,109,122] In fact, nearly all cases of total intestinal aganglionosis were initially misdiagnosed as meconium ileus.[55] A definitive diagnosis of Hirschsprung's disease may be suggested both radiographically and by anorectal manometrics, but ultimately it depends on the histochemical findings of increased acetylcholinesterase content or the histopathologic findings of aganglionosis seen on rectal biopsy. The radiographic features of colonic Hirschsprung's disease likely will include a transition zone; in patients with total colonic Hirschsprung's disease, a reflux of contrast medium into the terminal

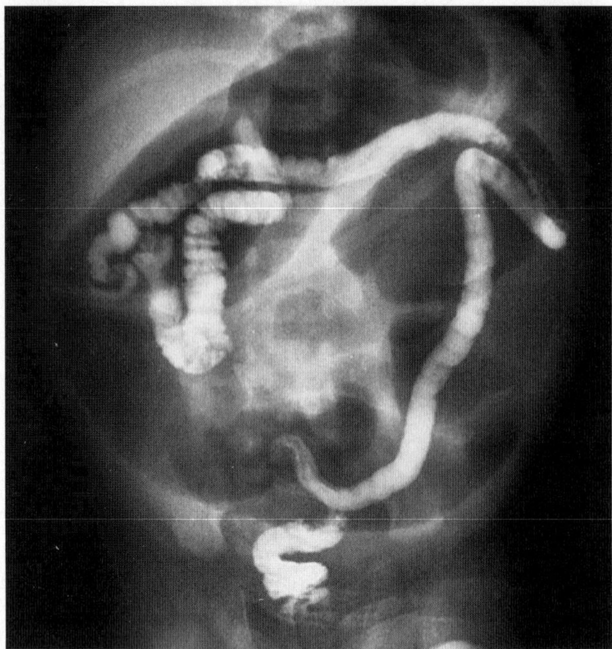

Figure 81-4 A contrast enema is done in a newborn with a distal bowel obstruction evident on plain radiography. A microcolon is found leading to a small-caliber distal ileum, and contrast agent does not reflux into the dilated intestine. This is most compatible with the diagnosis of a distal intestinal atresia. (From Rescorla FJ, Grosfeld JL: Contemporary management of meconium ileus. World J Surg 1993;17:381.)

ileum will typically not demonstrate the filling defects of meconium ileus but, rather, will show air-fluid levels and a proximally dilated bowel.

Neonatal small left colon syndrome may also require the differentiation from meconium ileus.[18,86,108] This abnormality is confined to the left colon, appears as a funnel-shaped tapering on contrast enema, and is often

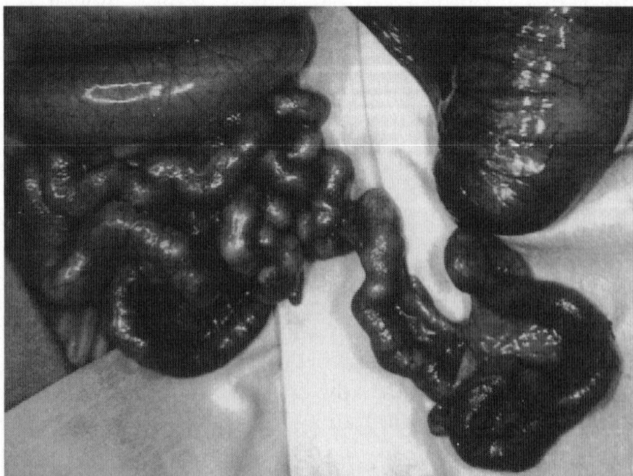

Figure 81-5 Operative findings of a case of meconium ileus complicated by an acquired ileal atresia. The small bowel is distended proximal to the atresia, and there are inspissated pellets of meconium in the distal ileum and colon.

associated with a diagnosis of maternal diabetes, hyperthyroidism, drug abuse, or eclampsia (Fig. 81-6). Rectal biopsy is required to exclude Hirschsprung's disease. Other features of meconium ileus are usually not present.

Meconium plug syndrome is usually confirmed by a contrast enema radiograph with finding of "plugs" or "casts" of meconium in the sigmoid or descending colon (see Fig. 81-6).[14,29,93,110] Such plugs will often spontaneously pass after withdrawal of the enema catheter and expulsion of the enema. There is a significant association of meconium plug syndrome with other gastrointestinal anomalies, and as many as 14% of neonates with CF will be seen to have meconium plug syndrome.[112] The pathogenesis of the meconium plug is poorly understood but may relate to a bowel hypomotility. Meconium plug syndrome has also been associated with prematurity, hypotonia, hypermagnesemia, respiratory distress, sepsis, hypothyroidism, diabetes, and Hirschsprung's disease.[16,106] These associations suggest that patients with meconium plug syndrome should be studied with both a sweat test to exclude CF and a rectal biopsy to exclude Hirschsprung's disease after symptoms of obstruction have been relieved.[37,115]

Meconium ileus may occur in the absence of CF in term or preterm infants with pancreatic or intestinal insufficiency from a variety of causes.[25,89,101] These intraluminal obstructions result from the accumulation of an inspissated sticky meconium in the terminal ileum or right colon, but the meconium is neither tar-like nor resistant to conventional enema irrigation that usually proves to be therapeutic. Whether intestinal secretion insufficiency or a pancreatic achylia is etiologic is variable, but rarely has pancreatic insufficiency been documented. Definitive exclusion of CF clinically requires a sweat chloride analysis, DNA analysis, or both.

NONOPERATIVE MANAGEMENT

Nonoperative management of meconium ileus depends on the dissolution of the inspissated intraluminal meconium in an otherwise patent and uncompromised ileocolon.[8,11,82] Although various solubilizing agents historically had been administered by mouth, intraoperatively, or by rectum, the mainstay of meconium ileus treatment remained an operative procedure.[82] In 1969, several additional reports suggested that solvents were effective and the value of nonoperative application of such solvents was suggested both clinically and experimentally.[98] Noblett reported the successful use of a hypertonic contrast enema in four neonates with uncomplicated meconium ileus. She described the need to fulfill the flowing criteria before applying such therapy: (1) an initial diagnostic contrast enema should exclude other causes of distal intestinal obstruction; (2) the complications of volvulus, atresia, perforation, or peritonitis must be excluded; (3) the enema must be performed with careful fluoroscopic control; (4) intravenous antibiotics should be administered; (5) the patient should be attended by a pediatric surgeon during the procedure; (6) the patient should have a full fluid resuscitation with fluids given aggressively (one to three times

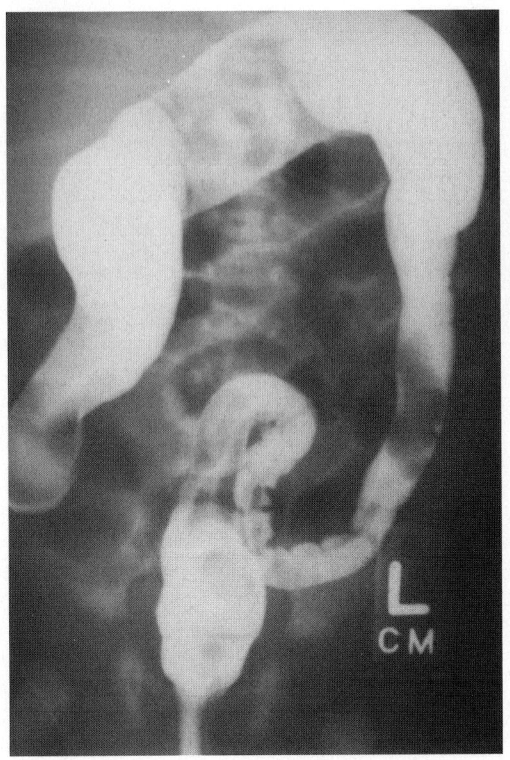

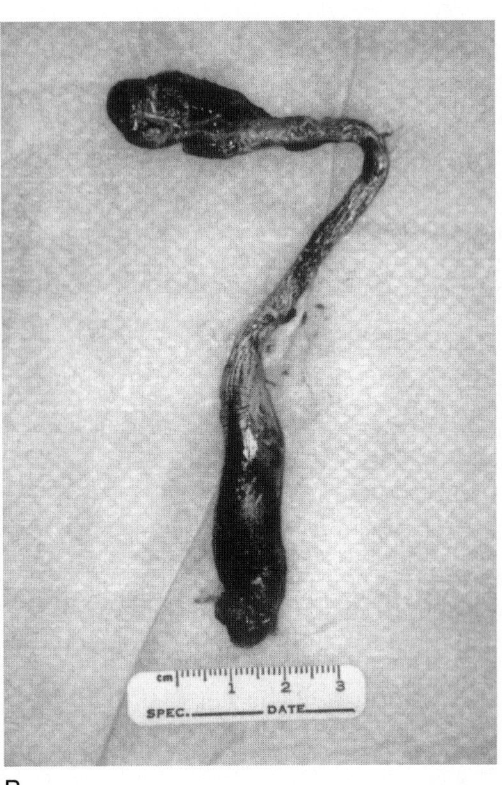

A B

Figure 81–6 The differential diagnosis of meconium ileus includes several entities characterized by left colon pathology. *A,* A contrast enema in a newborn presenting with a plain radiographic pattern of a distal bowel obstruction depicts tapering of the colon below the splenic flexure and an intraluminal filling defect in the rectosigmoid colon. These findings would suggest Hirschsprung's disease, neonatal small left colon syndrome, or meconium plug syndrome. *B,* After the removal of the enema catheter, the patient spontaneously passed a "plug" of meconium and the obstruction was relieved. A sweat test and a rectal biopsy may be indicated to exclude the diagnoses of cystic fibrosis and Hirschsprung's disease, respectively.

maintenance) during the procedure; and (7) the patient should be prepared for imminent operation should complications develop.[95,96] Since that report, a Gastrografin enema has been the standard of nonoperative treatment. Meglumine diatrizoate is a hyperosmolar, water-soluble, radiopaque solution containing 0.1% polysorbate 80 (Tween 80), a solubilizing or wetting agent, and 37% organically bound iodine. The meglumine is a 76% aqueous solution of sodium-methyl-glucamine salt of n1n1-diacetyl-3,5-diamino-2,4,6-triiodobenzoic acid, and this hypertonic solution has an osmolality of 1900 mOsm/L, a property that draws fluid into the intestinal lumen and aids in the release of the inspissated meconium. After administration, both a transient osmotic diarrhea and a putative osmotic diuresis occur, factors that emphasize the importance of aggressive fluid resuscitation. In addition, the product is radiopaque, which enables a safe fluoroscopically monitored administration. Polysorbate 80 (Tween 80) is a nonionic surface-active emulsifier that not only may better define radiographically the bowel mucosal pattern but may also facilitate the passage of the hypertonic Gastrografin between the mucosa and the adherent meconium at the site of obstruction. Polysorbate 80 as a 10% solution has been administered intraoperatively by way of an enterostomy to liquefy meconium. Other hypertonic water-soluble agents (e.g., 40% sodium diatrizoate [40% Hypaque]) not containing polysorbate 80 are also effective in relieving the obstruction, and they may prevent the adverse influence of Gastrografin on colonic mucosa.[11,34]

The technique of solubilizing enema treatment of meconium ileus continues to use the aforementioned guidelines of Noblett. After fluid resuscitation and nasogastric decompression have been performed, and after physical examination assessment and plain abdominal radiographs have excluded the diagnosis of peritonitis or perforation, the diagnostic contrast enema with barium or water-soluble agent is administered. When the preliminary diagnostic study has been completed, an enema-tip non-balloon catheter is inserted into the anorectum and the buttocks are taped together around the catheter. With fluoroscopic guidance and an initial solution of 50% Gastrografin in water, the contrast agent is slowly injected by a catheter-tipped syringe. When contrast medium traverses the colon and reaches the dilated meconium-impacted ileum, the study is terminated and the infant is returned to a bed for monitoring, fluid administration (two times maintenance), and normalization of body temperature. Spontaneous passage of the inspissated meconium per rectum should follow. An abdominal radiograph should be repeated in 8 to 12 hours to determine whether the obstruction has been relieved.

If instead the evacuation is incomplete and obstruction persists, the enema may be repeated with the same concentration of Gastrografin. If either no evacuation occurs after a successfully refluxing enema or if contrast medium cannot be refluxed into dilated bowel, then this technique should be abandoned and operative intervention planned. Similarly, signs of worsening obstruction, clinical distention, greater distention of loops on radiograph, or signs of peritonitis resulting from a possible perforation are also indications for operative intervention. Noblett suggests that after a successful enema, 5 mL of a 10% *N*-acetylcysteine solution should be administered every 6 hours through a nasogastric tube to liquefy upper gastrointestinal secretions.[76] Furthermore, when formula feedings are begun, supplemental pancreatic enzymes must be administered with each feeding.[85,105]

The success of nonoperative treatment is variable.[58,118] The initial report of Noblett suggested that as many as two thirds of patients were successfully treated by this technique. Advantages of the nonoperative therapy include a reduction in pulmonary morbidity and a reduced length of hospital stay. Disadvantages of therapy include a delay in operative intervention for those unsuccessfully treated by the enema, the risk of immediate and delayed intestinal injury or perforation, and the induction of hypovolemia. Bowel injury leading to a potential perforation may be a product of repeated enemas, injudicious inflation of an enema catheter balloon, or a direct mucosal injury induced by the enema agent.[33,42,68,71,123] The mechanism of such an injury may be related to bowel distention or to the polysorbate 80 content. The latter injury may be prevented by using a solubilizing enema agent containing 1% to 2% polysorbate 80 with isotonic Gastrografin diluted with water to a final osmolality of 320 to 340 mOsm/L or by using an alternate isotonic contrast agent.

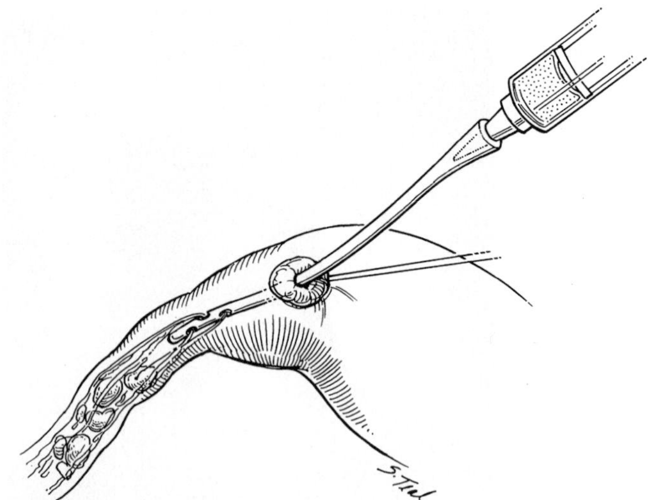

Figure 81-7 The most commonly preferred contemporary operative management of meconium ileus is shown. An enterotomy is made in the dilated small bowel segment just proximal to the site of inspissated distal meconium, and an irrigating catheter is inserted. After instillation of solubilizing agent, the catheter may be removed and the enterotomy closed; instead, the catheter may be left in place or replaced with a T-tube for continued postoperative solubilizing agent instillation. (From Rescorla FJ, Grosfeld JL: Contemporary management of meconium ileus. World J Surg 1993;17:381.)

OPERATIVE MANAGEMENT

Multiple indications for operative intervention in the management of meconium ileus exist.[22,26,41] One third to one half of patients undergoing operation represent cases of simple or uncomplicated meconium ileus that have failed to respond to nonoperative treatment with enema solubilizing agents. The remaining one half to two thirds of patients have complications of meconium ileus, which include intestinal atresia, volvulus, perforation, meconium cyst formation with peritonitis, intestinal gangrene, or combinations of these events. In the management of simple meconium ileus, the goal of operation is the relief of intraluminal ileocolonic obstruction by either the evacuation of the adherent intraluminal meconium or by resection of the portion of bowel filled with inspissated material.[83]

Simple Meconium Ileus

A variety of operative procedures are available for the management of patients with meconium ileus (Figs. 81-7 and 81-8).[83] The initial patient survivors underwent enterotomies with irrigation coupled with a limited resection. This operative technique is the one most commonly in use today. Irrigating solutions may include warmed saline, a 50% diatrizoate solution, a 1% solution of pancreatic enzymes (Viokase; A.H. Robbins Co., Richmond, VA), hydrogen peroxide, and, most commonly, either a 2% or a 4% solution of *N*-acetylcysteine (Mucomyst; Apothecon, Princeton, NJ).[76,100] More concentrated solutions of *N*-acetylcysteine or Gastrografin or the use of hydrogen peroxide and its attendant risk of air embolism may produce greater risk than benefit. After solubilization by the irrigant, injected through an enterotomy catheter, the meconium is gently milked distally into the colon or evacuated through the enterotomy (see Fig. 81-7). The enterotomy and the abdomen may then either be closed, an enterostomy may be created, or the site can be controlled by insertion of a T-tube.[45,74,80,116] This last treatment has been designed to be located at the junction of proximal distended ileum with distal (more collapsed) ileum where intraluminal balls of inspissated meconium are found. Leaving this tube in place and attaching the enterotomy site against the anterior abdominal wall ensures a controlled fistula as well as a route of gastrointestinal access for the instillation of pancreatic enzyme solutions beginning on the first postoperative day. By the 7th to 14th postoperative day, the irrigant should pass freely into the colon, the obstruction should be relieved, and thereafter the catheter can be removed. This avoids the need for reoperation and enterostomy closure. An alternative technique is appendectomy with appendicostomy, with meconium evacuation or irrigation through this route.[32] A temporary indwelling

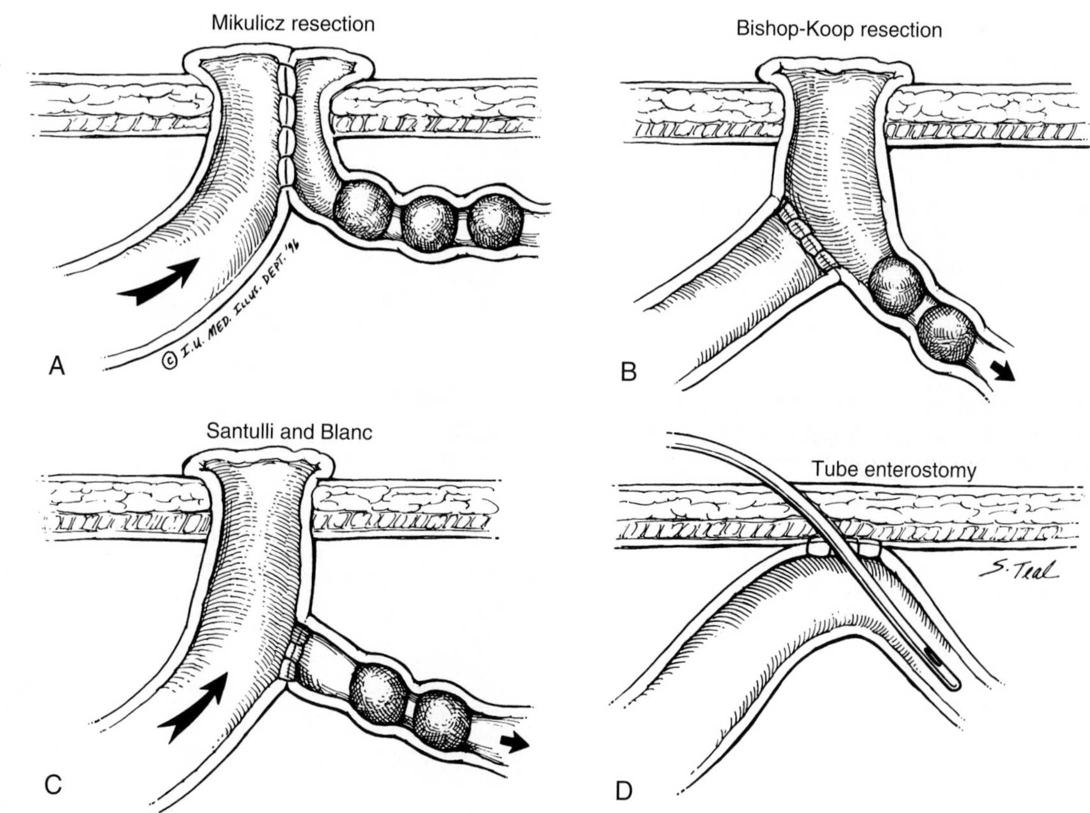

Figure 81–8 The operative options for simple meconium ileus. *A,* The Mikulicz resection and enterostomy. *B,* The Bishop-Koop resection and enterostomy. *C,* The Santulli enterostomy. *D,* Tube enterostomy. (From Rescorla FJ, Grosfeld JL: Contemporary management of meconium ileus. World J Surg 1993;17:381.)

tube cecostomy may alternatively be left in place. For such an irrigant technique to be successful, the bowel must be handled gently, not overdistended, and not excessively massaged or "milked" in an effort to evacuate the inspissated meconium.

An alternative operation to enterotomy-irrigation is placement of a temporary obstruction-relieving stoma with or without an associated partial resection. Gross initially advocated placement of the Mikulicz double-barreled enterostomy, which could be performed quickly and which did not require intraoperative meconium evacuation (see Fig. 81-8). The exteriorized bowel loop could be opened after the abdominal incision has been closed, thereby minimizing intraperitoneal contamination. After the obstruction is relieved and the infant has recovered, a spur-crushing Mikulicz clamp can be applied externally at the stoma to complete a side-to-side anastomosis. It may not be necessary to return to the operating room to close the stoma because after the clamp-induced anastomosis, the residual enterocutaneous fistula may spontaneously close. An alternate to such an "extra-abdominal resection" and delayed stomal closure was the primary resection and anastomosis recommended a decade later by Swenson and Noblett. After meconium had been evacuated, a primary intraperitoneal anastomosis could be performed, or the infant could be allowed to recover more fully, after which the stoma could be closed in delayed fashion by an end-to-end anastomosis.

An alternative operation is resection coupled with a distal chimney enterostomy, the so-called Bishop-Koop procedure (see Fig. 81-8).[67] This technique was developed with the following criteria: (1) limit intraoperative bowel trauma in the neonatal period; (2) resect the disparately enlarged ileal loop filled with inspissated thickened meconium; (3) create an appropriately sized end of proximal to side of distal ileum anastomosis close to the abdominal wall exiting the distal ileum, to serve as a functionally decompressing "proximal stoma" while distal obstruction persisted; (4) provide access for insertion of a catheter into the distal bowel containing inspissated meconium pellets so that solubilizing pancreatic enzymes could be instilled postoperatively; and (5) permit an eventual enterostomy closure by bedside ligation of the "chimney stoma," putatively avoiding the risks of an additional anesthetic in a child with known CF. Intraoperatively, a No. 8 French rubber catheter is passed through the ostomy chimney into the distal ileum. Within 12 to 24 hours after the operation, catheter irrigations are begun with a pancreatic enzyme solution (1 teaspoon Viokase per 1 oz water) repeated every 4 to 6 hours until the distal intraluminal obstruction is relieved, at which time the catheter is removed. After an initial large volume of enterostomy output, the ostomy drainage will diminish as the more distal obstruction is relieved. The transcolonic passage of stool will follow. Thereafter, the output from the stoma may cease altogether. Eventually the chimney may be treated by one of two techniques. At the bedside the "stoma" may be ligated. If the result of this noninvasive technique is a persistent enterocutaneous fistula, then a formal intraperitoneal or extraperitoneal stomal closure can be performed with the patient under a general anesthetic. This latter procedure is necessary in approximately 75% of patients treated by this technique.[20]

Santulli described a proximal chimney enterostomy, an operation that in essence is the reverse of the resection coupled with a distal chimney enterostomy (see Fig. 81-8). The distal ileal end is anastomosed end-to-side to the proximal ileum at a level corresponding to an immediate subfascial plane, and the proximal ileum is exited as an end enterostomy. With this stoma arrangement, irrigation and decompression of the proximal ileum is enhanced. As with the Bishop-Koop procedure, an intraoperative catheter passed through the stoma is positioned into the distal ileum for the postoperative instillation of solubilizing agent. Because a high-output functional end enterostomy has been created, it is necessary to close such a stoma early to avoid the complications induced by excessive fluid and electrolyte losses.

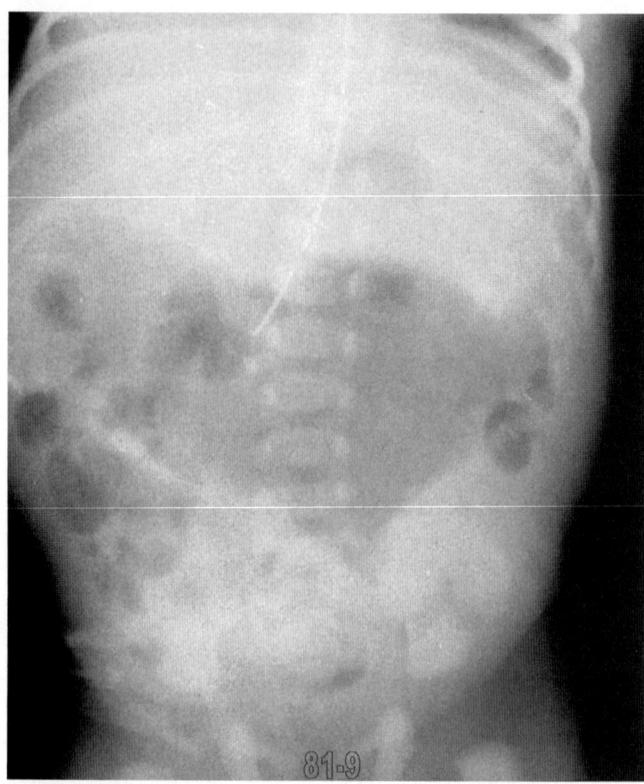

Figure 81-9 A plain abdominal radiograph compatible with the diagnosis of complicated meconium ileus. The large central air-filled mass suggests intestinal perforation and giant meconium cyst formation. If the perforation had been of longer standing, intraperitoneal calcification may also be present. (From Rescorla FJ, Grosfeld JL: Contemporary management of meconium ileus. World J Surg 1993;17:381.)

Complicated Meconium Ileus

The treatment of complicated meconium ileus almost always requires an operation,[49] an exception being the rare in utero perforation that has left a telltale remnant of extraluminal intraperitoneal calcified meconium, a spontaneously sealed perforation, and no interruption in intestinal continuity.[67] Another finding for the latter process is calcified meconium seen in a patent processus vaginalis during a hernia operation or by abdominal radiograph later in life. In contrast, operative indications include persisting intestinal obstruction, an enlarging abdominal mass, and signs of peritonitis, which may include abdominal wall edema and discoloration, tenderness on physical examination, and clinical and laboratory signs of ongoing sepsis (Fig. 81-9).

Meconium peritonitis may be seen as one of several varieties. A meconium pseudocyst is a result of meconium accumulating in the peritoneal cavity for weeks to months. A calcified "pseudocyst" fibrous wall forms around an accumulation of meconium, and spared bowel loops are peripheral to this cyst (see Fig. 81-9). Adhesive meconium peritonitis follows meconium contamination of the peritoneal cavity for days to weeks before delivery. Dense and vascular adhesions make operative relief of the adhesive intestinal obstruction difficult. Scattered calcifications may be present. When intestinal perforation occurs only a few days before delivery, an abdomen filled with meconium ascites results and calcification is absent. The fourth variant of meconium peritonitis is bacterially infected ascites, which occurs when colonized intestinal organisms penetrate from the perforated intestine into the peritoneal cavity.

At operation, it is mandatory to assess residual intestinal length, and it is critical to use conservative resection. An effective armamentarium of operative options is needed to optimize treatment of meconium peritonitis, volvulus, atresia, or the ischemic intestine that may be encountered. Only the presence of a diffuse bacterial peritonitis precludes a primary anastomosis. The Bishop-Koop, Mikulicz, and Santulli procedures each have application in the management of patients with complicated meconium ileus.

POSTOPERATIVE MANAGEMENT

After the operative management of meconium ileus, care must be centered on support of the infant's general physiology, as well as on the evacuation of any residual proximal or distal gastrointestinal inspissated intraluminal meconium. Generally, the latter can be treated by instillation of 2% or 4% acetylcysteine (Mucomyst) delivered through a nasogastric tube, which will solubilize the residual meconium. When gut patency is verified clinically or by plain film radiograph, enteral nutrition may begin with an elemental formula such as Pregestimil (Mead-Johnson, Evansville, IN). When enteral feedings begin, supplemental pancreatic enzymes must also be started (Viokase, Pancrease [McNeil Pharmaceuticals, Spring Hill, PA], and Cotazym-S [Organon Inc., West Orange, NJ] are alternatives). If postoperative ileus is prolonged, or if short-bowel syndrome is a product of the operative treatment, then total parenteral nutrition becomes an important early and potentially prolonged form of postoperative nutritive therapy. Early enteral or parenteral nutrition therapy must include maintenance of salt and mineral balance; appropriate vitamin supplementation, including vitamin K; and aggressive management of any associated short-bowel syndrome deficiencies. The association of the inherent malabsorption of CF coupled with the potential of an extreme short-bowel syndrome resulting from complicated meconium ileus makes for an extremely difficult management combination.[114,120]

Short-term postoperative parenteral antibiotics are used for the care of either simple or complicated meconium ileus, but directed and more prolonged antibiotics may be continued to minimize potential pulmonary complications. Vigorous pulmonary physiotherapy is initiated early after operation and is continued indefinitely. Teaching parents to perform such pulmonary physiotherapy that includes postural drainage is a mandatory component of predischarge planning. In those patients with an enterostomy, teaching parents appropriate stomal care is also important. Only in those circumstances in which a Bishop-Koop ileostomy or a Mikulicz ileostomy was created would bedside ligation of the chimney or application of a Mikulicz clamp, respectively, be considered before hospital discharge.

Perhaps the most important feature of postoperative care is to secure the diagnosis of CF as the cause of the patient's meconium ileus. A series of reports exist in which neonatal intraluminal inspissated meconium is the cause of small bowel obstruction and the same management scheme as outlined earlier is applied. However, postoperatively these patients are not found to have abnormal sweat electrolytes. Such cases have been carefully distinguished from the colonic meconium plug syndrome because the plugging has been confined to the small bowel. This condition has been reported in premature infants, in siblings without CF, in patients with partial pancreatic aplasia, and in patients with pancreatic ductal stenosis.[117] These findings remain an important distinction if the alternative diagnosis is meconium ileus associated with CF.

COMPLICATIONS

Gastrointestinal

Many gastrointestinal complications of meconium ileus exist and include an increased incidence of intussusception and rectal prolapse. However, in the child and adolescent with CF, the most common gastrointestinal problem is distal intestinal obstruction termed *meconium ileus equivalent* or *distal intestinal obstruction syndrome.*[40] A partial bowel obstruction by intraluminal material may be a product of steatorrhea or noncompliance with oral enzyme therapy. Signs and symptoms are heralded by crampy abdominal pain, distention, and a palpable right lower quadrant mass; and a high-grade obstruction is associated with obstipation, distention, and vomiting. It is important to consider a broad differential diagnosis that may include constipation, intussusception, and even appendicitis; and the plain abdominal radiograph supplemented with contrast body imaging should prove diagnostic. Once the diagnosis is established, the preferred treatment is solubilizing agents, such as acetylcysteine and Gastrografin, given both orally and per rectum. Operative intervention is rarely required. Adjustment of oral enzyme therapy supplemented with better hydration and the use of stool softeners may be used to prevent recurrence. Both histamine H_2 blockers and proton pump inhibitors may prove efficacious by increasing intestinal pH, and prokinetic agents have also been utilized.

Appendiceal luminal obstruction that produces signs and symptoms compatible with both *acute* and *"chronic appendicitis"* may also occur.[17] The diagnosis of appendiceal pathology depends on both clinical assessment and the potential use of contrast medium–enhanced computed tomography. These complications, and the most common gastrointestinal complication, *malabsorption,* are improved with appropriate enzyme replacement therapy. Malabsorption of carbohydrates, protein, and fat may all occur, a problem worsened both by the extent of peritoneal inflammation and the magnitude of the short-bowel syndrome. The latter may be functional or anatomic, an anatomy foreshortened because of atresia or a resection. The malabsorption is worsened by a disaccharidase deficiency and by inspissated biliary secretions that produce both jaundice and impaired fat absorption. This same pathophysiology may account for the occurrence of gallstones in about one fourth of patients with CF as well as the incidence of symptomatic *chronic calculous cholecystitis* or *biliary dyskinesia,* which also characterizes this population. The nutrient malabsorption takes on greater significance if a concomitant increased energy need occurs in the presence of recurrent and chronic pulmonary infection. The application of total parenteral nutrition may prove beneficial to supplement enteral nutrients and to provide gut rest as well as appropriate calories during periods of prolonged postoperative ileus, especially if anastomotic healing or closure of enterocutaneous fistulas is required. Furthermore, evidence suggests that the malnutrition of meconium ileus is significantly different, or even worse, than that seen in age-matched peers who have CF without meconium ileus.

Intussusception occurs in approximately 1% of older CF patients, likely secondary to inspissated intraluminal stool serving as the lead point. The site of pathology is typically ileocolic, but small bowel and large bowel intussusception may also occur. Typically, the diagnosis is difficult to establish and distinguish from other right lower quadrant CF pathology, and operation with reduction and/or resection becomes the usual therapeutic outcome.

Rectal prolapse may be the first clinical presentation of a child subsequently proven by sweat test to have CF. As many as one third to one fifth of children with CF develop prolapse typically between the ages of 1 and 3 years of age. The preferred treatment after the diagnosis of CF is established is oral enzyme therapy, and rarely will more aggressive transanal rectal submucosal sclerotherapy or operative rectopexy be indicated.

Colonic strictures[33,85,105,123] presumptively secondary to large-dose oral enzyme therapy have been reported in CF children, half of whom previously have had meconium ileus. Most commonly such disease is localized to the right colon, but segmental colitis and even pancolonic disease has been reported. The local signs of obstruction and pain must be distinguished from the meconium ileus equivalent patient, and a contrast enema is typically diagnostic. Regulation of enzyme therapy may be tried, but most commonly resection is indicated for intractable strictures.

Pulmonary

The early morbidity and mortality of meconium ileus predominantly has a pulmonary origin, the products of which include *bacterial sepsis* and *bronchopneumonia.* Some authors suggest that beyond 6 months after the treatment of meconium ileus, the prognosis and morbidity assumes that of a patient with CF without meconium ileus. However, other studies suggest that children with meconium ileus have worse lung function and more *obstructive lung disease* between ages 8 and 12 years than those with CF but without meconium ileus. These changes occur with relatively reduced lung volumes. When *Pseudomonas,* coliforms, or other specific colonizing or pathogenic organisms are identified, the early and aggressive use of aminoglycosides and semisynthetic penicillins has been shown to improve survival and outcome, even if used in a prophylactic manner. Finally, the use of aggressive physical therapy and postural drainage may further minimize pulmonary complications.

Inguinoscrotal Disease

Children with CF have been reported to have an increased incidence of *inguinal hernias* and *hydroceles* as well as an increased incidence of *cryptorchidism.*[53,119] Two operative findings at the time of inguinal hernia repair may suggest the underlying diagnosis of CF, namely, the presence of calcified meconium in the hernia sac and the *absence of a vas deferens.*[90] Both findings in the absence of a previous diagnosis of CF suggest the need for a diagnostic sweat test. In addition, infertile males without a vas deferens may actually be asymptomatic heterozygotes carrying the CF gene.

RESULTS OF TREATMENT

The outcome of the treatment of patients with meconium ileus, whether the condition is complicated or simple, has steadily improved during the past 3 decades, the most recently reported survival rates approaching 100% (Fig. 81-10).[13,20] In a series of patients treated both nonoperatively and operatively, survival rates at 5 and 10 years for the two categories improved steadily from the 1960s (30% and 10%, respectively) through the 1970s (80% and 70%, respectively) and the 1980s (100% at 5-year follow-up).[35,57,75,77] In the past, nonoperative

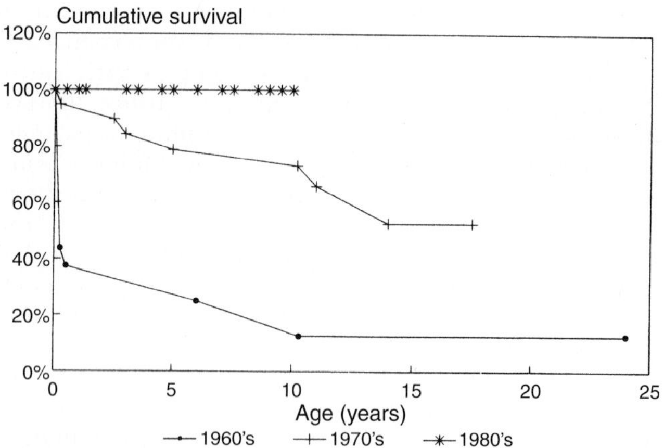

Figure 81-10 Long-term survival rates of patients with meconium ileus depicted by decade. A statistically significant improvement in survival is seen when 1960s, 1970s, and 1980s survival data are compared ($P < 0.0001$). (From Del Pin CA, Czyrko C, Ziegler MM, et al: Management and survival of meconium ileus: A 30-year review. Ann Surg 1992;215:179-185.)

treatment had contributed to an improved survival rate, but in the past decade the survival rate for both operative and nonoperative treatment was 100%. The significant improvement in operative survival has come since the 1960s when the 6-month survival rate was only 33%.[72] The operative 6-month survival rate had improved to 60% before 1979 and to 100% between 1979 and 1989.[88] No significant overall differences in outcome were observed with regard to patient gender, whether complication of meconium ileus was present, or with regard to the type of operation performed (ileostomy, resection with primary anastomosis, resection and Mikulicz ileostomy, and Bishop-Koop enterostomy). Additionally, the long-term survival rates (measured at 6 years) of patients treated with the Bishop-Koop procedure (62% survival) did not differ from those of patients with alternate operations. Furthermore, all deaths in patients older than 6 months of age were cardiopulmonary or pneumonitic deaths related to the underlying CF and not to complications of operation. Interestingly, both simple and complicated cases of meconium ileus had 72% 10-year survival rates.

Death occurs from multiple causes, which include intraperitoneal sepsis from unrecognized leakage, pulmonary sepsis and bronchopneumonia, or short-bowel syndrome with complicating liver failure.

REFERENCES

1. Allan DL, Robbie M, Phelan PD, et al: Familial occurrence of meconium ileus. Eur J Pediatr 1981;135:291-292.
2. Anderson DH: Cystic fibrosis of the pancreas and its relation to celiac disease. Am J Dis Child 1938;56:344-399.
3. Anderson DH: Cystic fibrosis of the pancreas. J Chron Dis 1958;7:58-90.
4. Auburn RP, Feldman SA, Gadacz TR, et al: Meconium ileus secondary to partial aplasia of the pancreas: Report of a case. Surgery 1969;65:689-693.

5. Benacerraf BR, Chaudhury AK: Echogenic fetal bowel in the third trimester associated with meconium ileus secondary to cystic fibrosis: A case report. J Reprod Med 2001; 46:697-698.
6. Bishop HC, Koop CE: Management of meconium ileus: Resection, Roux-en-Y anastomosis and ileostomy irrigation with pancreatic enzymes. Ann Surg 1957;145:410.
7. Bishop HC, Ziegler MM: Meconium ileus. In Spitz L, Nixon HH (eds): Rob and Smith's Operative Surgery, 4th ed. Boston, Butterworth, 1988, vol 10, pp 300-310.
8. Bowring AC, Jones RFC, Kern IB: The use of solvents in the intestinal manifestations of mucoviscidosis. J Pediatr Surg 1970;5:338-343.
9. Bruns WT, Connell TR, Lacey JA, et al: Test strip meconium screening for cystic fibrosis. Am J Dis Child 1977;131:71-73.
10. Buchanan DJ, Rapoport S: Chemical comparison of normal meconium and meconium from a patient with meconium ileus. Pediatrics 1952;9:304-310.
11. Burke MS, Rag JM, Karamanoukian HL, et al: New strategies in nonoperative management of meconium ileus. J Pediatr Surg 2002;37:760-764.
12. Byrk D: Meconium ileus: Demonstration of the meconium mass on barium enema study. AJR Am J Roentgenol 1965;95:214-216.
13. Caniano DA, Beaver BL: Meconium ileus: A fifteen year experience with forty-two neonates. Surgery 1987;102: 699-703.
14. Clatworthy HW Jr, Howard WHR, Lloyd J: The meconium plug syndrome. Surgery 1956;39:131-142.
15. Colin AA, Wohl MEB: Cystic fibrosis. Pediatr Rev 1994; 15:192-200.
16. Cooney DR, Rosevear W, Grosfeld JL: Maternal and postnatal hypermagnesemia and the meconium plug syndrome. J Pediatr Surg 1976;11:167-172.
17. Coughlin JP, Gauderer MWI, Stern RC, et al: The spectrum of appendiceal disease in cystic fibrosis. J Pediatr Surg 1990;25:835-839.
18. Davis WS, Allen RP, Favara BE, et al: Neonatal small left colon syndrome. AJR Am J Roentgenol 1974;120:322-329.
19. Delorimier AA, Fonkalsrud EW, Hays DM: Congenital atresia and stenosis of the jejunum and ileum. Surgery 1969;65:819-827.
20. Del Pin CA, Czyrko C, Ziegler MM, et al: Management and survival of meconium ileus, a 30 year review. Ann Surg 1992;215:179-185.
21. Dirkes K, Crombleholme TM, Craigo SD, et al: The natural history of meconium peritonitis diagnosed in utero. J Pediatr Surg 1995;30:979-982.
22. Dey DL: The surgical treatment of meconium ileus. Med J Aust 1963;50:179-180.
23. di Sant'Agnese PA, Davis PB: Research in cystic fibrosis. N Engl J Med 1976;295:481-485.
24. di Sant'Agnese PA, Dische Z, Danilczenko A: Physiochemical differences of mucoproteins in duodenal fluid of patients with cystic fibrosis of the pancreas and controls. Pediatrics 1957;19:252-260.
25. Dolan TF Jr, Touloukian RJ: Familial meconium ileus not associated with cystic fibrosis. J Pediatr Surg 1974;9: 821-824.
26. Donnison AB, Shwachman H, Gross RE: A review of 164 children with meconium ileus seen at the Children's Hospital Medical Center, Boston. Pediatrics 1966;37:1-18.
27. Egan M, Flotte T, Alfone S, et al: Defective regulation of outwardly rectifying Cl channels by protein kinase A corrected by insertion of CFTR. Nature 1992;358:581-584.
28. Ein S, Shandling B, Reilly B, et al: Bowel perforation with nonoperative treatment of meconium ileus. J Pediatr Surg 1987;22:146-147.
29. Ellis DG, Clatworthy HW Jr: The meconium plug syndrome revisited. J Pediatr Surg 1966;1:54-61.
30. Emery JL: Laboratory observations of the viscidity of meconium. Arch Dis Child 1954;29:34-37.
31. Farber SJ: The relation of pancreatic achylia to meconium ileus. J Pediatr 1944;24:387-392.
32. Fitzgerald R, Conlan K: Use of the appendix stump in the treatment of meconium ileus. J Pediatr Surg 1989;24: 899-900.
33. Fitzsimmons SC, Burkhart GA, Borowitz D, et al: High dose pancreatic enzyme supplements and fibrosing colonopathy in children with cystic fibrosis. N Engl J Med 1997;336: 1283-1289.
34. French RS, McAlister WH, Ternberg J, et al: Meconium ileus relieved by 40% water-soluble contrast enemas. Radiology 1970;94:341-342.
35. George L, Norman AP: Life tables for cystic fibrosis. Arch Dis Child 1971;46:139-143.
36. Gibson LE, Cooke RE: A test for concentration of electrolytes in sweat in cystic fibrosis of the pancreas utilizing pilocarpine by iontophoresis. Pediatrics 1959;23:545-549.
37. Gilis DA, Grantmyre EB: The meconium plug syndrome and Hirschsprung's disease. Can Med Assoc J 1965;92: 225-227.
38. Glanzmann E: Dysporia entero-broncho-pancreatica congenita familiaris. Ann Paediat 1946;166:289.
39. Glanzmann E, Berger H: Uber mekoniumileus. Ann Pediatr 1950;175:33.
40. Goldschmidt Z, Cohen H, Issacsohn M, et al: Meconium ileus equivalent in an infant, aggravated by soybean formula. Clin Pediatr 1977;16:284-286.
41. Graham WP, Halden A, Jaffe BF: Surgical treatment of patients with cystic fibrosis. Surg Gynecol Obstet 1966;122:373.
42. Grantmyre EB, Butler GJ, Gillis DA: Necrotizing enterocolitis after Renografin-76 treatment of meconium ileus. Am J Radiol 1981;136:990.
43. Green MN, Clarke JT, Shwachman H: Studies in cystic fibrosis of the pancreas: Protein pattern in meconium ileus. Pediatrics 1958;21:635-641.
44. Green MA, Shwachman H: Presumptive tests for cystic fibrosis based on serum protein in meconium. Pediatrics 1968;41:989-992.
45. Harberg FJ, Senekjian EK, Pokorny WJ: Treatment of uncomplicated meconium ileus via T-tube ileostomy. J Pediatr Surg 1981;16:61-63.
46. Hauerback BJ, Dyce BJ, Gutentag PJ, et al: Measurement of trypsin and chymotrypsin in stool. Gastroenterology 1963;44:588-597.
47. Henson RE: Meconium ileus. Radiology 1957;68:568-571.
48. Hiatt RB, Wilson PE: Celiac syndrome: Therapy of meconium ileus: Report of eight eases with a review of the literature. Surg Gynecol Obstet 1948;87:317-327.
49. Hill JT, Snyder WH, Pollock WF: Management of complicated meconium ileus. Am J Surg 1964;108:233-238.
50. Hinden E: Meconium ileus with no pancreatic abnormality. Arch Dis Child 1950;25:99-100.
51. Holsclaw DS, Eckstein HB, Nixon HH: Meconium ileus: A 20 year review of 109 cases. Am J Dis Child 1965;109: 101-113.
52. Holsclaw DS Jr, Keith HH, Palmer J: Meconium screening for cystic fibrosis. Pediatr Ann 1978;7:29-40.
53. Holsclaw DS, Schwachman H: Increased incidence of hydrocele and undescended testicles in males with cystic fibrosis. Pediatrics 1971;3:442.
54. Hurwill ES, Arnheim EE: Meconium ileus associated with stenosis of the pancreatic ducts. Am J Dis Child 1942;64:443-454.

55. Ikeda K, Goto S: Total colonic aganglionosis with or without small bowel involvement: An analysis of 137 patients. J Pediatr Surg 1986;21:319-322.
56. Irish MS, Ragi JM, Karamanoukian H, et al: Prenatal diagnosis of the fetus with cystic fibrosis and meconium ileus. Pediatr Surg Int 1997;12:434-436.
57. Kalayoglu M, Sieber WK, Rodnan JB, et al: Meconium ileus: A critical review of treatment and eventual prognosis. J Pediatr Surg 1971;6:290-300.
58. Kao SCS, Franken EA Jr: Non-operative treatment of simple meconium ileus: A survey of the Society for Pediatric Radiology. Pediatr Radiol 1995;25:97-100.
59. Keats TE, Smith TH: Meconium ileus: A demonstration of the ileal meconium mass by barium enema examination. Radiology 1967;89:1073-1074.
60. Kerem BS, Rommens JM, Buchanan JA, et al: Identification of the cystic fibrosis gene: Genetic analysis. Science 1989;245:1073-1080.
61. Kerem E, Corey M, Kerem B, et al: Clinical and genetic comparisons of patients with cystic fibrosis, with or without meconium ileus. J Pediatr 1989;114:767-773.
62. Kleinhaus S, Boley SJ, Sheran M, et al: Hirschsprung's disease: A survey of the members of the surgical section of the American Academy of Pediatrics. J Pediatr Surg 1979;14:588-597.
63. Knowlton RG, Cohen-Haguenauer O, VanCong N, et al: A polymorphic DNA marker linked to cystic fibrosis is located on chromosome 7. Nature 1985;318:380-382.
64. Kornblith BA, Otani S: Meconium ileus with congenital stenosis of the main pancreatic duct. Am J Pathol 1929;5:249-262.
65. Kopito L, Shwachman H: Mineral composition of meconium. J Pediatr 1966;68:313-314.
66. Lansteiner K: Darmverschlus durch eingedictes meconium pankreatitis. Zentralbl Allg Pathol 1905;16:903-907.
67. Leonidas JC, Berdon WE, Baker DH, et al: Meconium ileus and its complications: A reappraisal of plain film roentgen diagnostic criteria. AJR Am J Roentgenol 1970;108:598.
68. Leonidas JC, Burry VF, Fellows RA, et al: Possible adverse effect of methylglucamine diatrizoate compounds on the bowel of newborn infants with meconium ileus. Radiology 1976;121:693-696.
69. Li Z, Lai HC, Kosorok MR, et al: Longitudinal pulmonary status of cystic fibrosis children with meconium ileus. Pediatr Pulmonol 2004;38:277-284.
70. Lillie JG, Chrispin AR: Investigation and management of neonatal obstruction by Gastrografin enema. Ann Radiol 1972;15:237.
71. Lutzger LG, Factor SM: Effects of some water-soluble contrast media on the colonic mucosa. Radiology 1976; 118:545-548.
72. MacDonald JA, Trusler GA: Meconium ileus: An eleven-year review at the Hospital for Sick Children, Toronto. Can Med Assoc J 1960;83:881-885.
73. Manchaurin C: Functional ileus of the newborn. Aust NZ J Surg 1964;34:196.
74. Mak GZ, Harberg FJ, Hiatt P, et al: T-tube ileostomy for meconium ileus: Four decades of experience. J Pediatr Surg 2000;35:349-352.
75. McPartlin JF, Dickson JAS, Swain VAJ: Meconium ileus immediate and long-term survival. Arch Dis Child 1972;47:207-210.
76. Meeker IA, Kincannon WN: Acetylcysteine used to liquefy inspissated meconium causing intestinal obstruction in the newborn. Surgery 1964;56:419-425.
77. Mabogunje OA, Wang CI, Mahour GH: Improved survival of neonates with meconium ileus. Arch Surg 1982;117: 37-40.
78. Mornet E, Serre JL, Farrell M, et al: Genetic differences between cystic fibrosis with or without meconium ileus. Lancet 1988;1:376-378.
79. Neuhauser EBD: Roentgen changes associated with pancreatic insufficiency in early life. Radiology 1946;46: 319-328.
80. Nguyen LT, Youssef S, Guttman FM, et al: Meconium ileus: Is a stoma necessary? J Pediatr Surg 1986;21:766-768.
81. Noblett HR: Treatment of uncomplicated meconium ileus by Gastrografin enema: A preliminary report. J Pediatr Surg 1969;4:190-197.
82. Olim CB, Ciuti A: Meconium ileus: A new method of relieving obstruction. Ann Surg 1954;140:736-740.
83. O'Neill JA, Grosfeld JL, Boles ET Jr, et al: Surgical treatment of meconium ileus. Am J Surg 1970;119:99-105.
84. Oppenheimer EH, Easterly JR: Pathological evidence of cystic fibrosis patients with meconium ileus. Pediatr Res 1973;7:339.
85. Pettei MJ, Leonidas JC, Levine JJ, Garvoy JD: Pancolonic disease in cystic fibrosis and high dose pancreatic enzyme therapy. J Pediatr 1994;125:587-589.
86. Philipart AI, Reed JO, Georgenson KE: Neonatal small left colon syndrome: Intramural not intraluminal obstruction. J Pediatr Surg 1975;10:733-740.
87. Quinton PM, Bijman J: Higher bioelectric potentials due to decreased chloride absorption in the sweat glands of patients with cystic fibrosis. N Engl J Med 1983;308: 1185-1189.
88. Rescorla FJ, Grosfeld J, West KJ, et al: Changing patterns of treatment and survival in neonates with meconium ileus. Arch Surg 1989;124:837-840.
89. Rickham DP, Boeckman CR: Neonatal meconium obstruction in the absence of mucoviscidosis. Am J Surg 1965;109:173-177.
90. Rigot JM, Lafitte JJ, Dumur V, et al: Cystic fibrosis and congenital absence of the vas deferens. N Engl J Med 1991; 325:64-65.
91. Riordan JR, Rommens JM, Kerem BS, et al: Identification of the cystic fibrosis gene: Cloning and characterization of complementary DNA. Science 1989;245:1066-1073.
92. Rommens JM, Iannazzi MC, Kerem B, et al: Identification of cystic fibrosis gene: Chromosome walking and jumping. Science 1989;245:1059-1065.
93. Rosenstein BJ: Cystic fibrosis presenting with the meconium plug syndrome. Am J Dis Child 1978;132:167-169.
94. Rosenstein BJ, Langbaum TS: Incidence of meconium abnormalities in newborn infants with cystic fibrosis. Am J Dis Child 1980;134:72-73.
95. Rowe MI, Furst AJ, Altman DH, et al: The neonatal response to Gastrografin enema. Pediatrics 1971;48:28-35.
96. Rowe MI, Seagram G, Weinberger M: Gastrografin-induced hypertonicity. Am J Surg 1973;125:185-188.
97. Santulli TV, Blanc WA: Congenital atresia of the intestine: Pathogenesis and treatment. Ann Surg 1961;154: 939-948.
98. Schiller M, Grosfeld JL, Morse TS: Nonoperative treatment of meconium ileus: An experimental study in rats. Am J Surg 1971;122:22-26.
99. Shariatzadeh AN, Enderle FJ, Fitzgerald JF, et al: Meconium ileus. Surg Gynecol Obstet 1973;136:234-236.
100. Shaw A: Safety of *N*-acetylcysteine in treatment of meconium obstruction of the newborn. J Pediatr Surg 1969;4:119-125.
101. Shigemoto H, Endo S, Isomoto T, et al: Neonatal meconium obstruction in the ileum without mucoviscidosis. J Pediatr Surg 1978;13:475-479.
102. Shwachman H: Gastrointestinal manifestations of cystic fibrosis. Pediatr Clin North Am 1975;22:787-805.

103. Shwachman H, Dooley RR, Guilmette R, et al: Cystic fibrosis of the pancreas with varying degrees of pancreatic insufficiency. Am J Dis Child 1956;92:347-368.
104. Shwachman H, Lebenthal E, Khaw KT: Recurrent acute pancreatitis in patients with cystic fibrosis with normal pancreatic enzymes. Pediatrics 1975;55:86-95.
105. Smyth RH, Van Velzen D, Smyth AR, et al: Stricture of ascending colon in cystic fibrosis and high-strength pancreatic enzymes. Lancet 1994;343:85-86.
106. Sokol MM, Koenigsberger MR, Rose JS, et al: Neonatal hypermagnesemia and the meconium plug syndrome. N Engl J Med 1972;286:823-825.
107. Stephan U, Busch EW, Kollberg H, et al: Cystic fibrosis detection by means of a test strip. Pediatrics 1975;55:35-38.
108. Stewart DR, Nixon GW, Johnson DG, et al: Neonatal small left colon syndrome. Ann Surg 1977;186:741-745.
109. Stringer MD, Brereton RJ, Drake DP, et al: Meconium ileus due to extensive intestinal aganglionosis. J Pediatr Surg 1994;29:501-503.
110. Swischuk LE: Meconium plug syndrome: a cause of neonatal intestinal obstruction. Am J Roentgenol Radiat Ther Nucl Med 1968;103:339-346.
111. Thomaidis TS, Arey JB: The intestinal lesions in cystic fibrosis of the pancreas. J Pediatr 1963;63:444-453.
112. Townes PL, Kopelman AE: Meconium plug syndrome, cystic fibrosis, and exocrine pancreatic deficiency. Am J Dis Child 1978;132:1043-1044.
113. Tsui LC, Buchwald M: Biochemical and molecular genetics of cystic fibrosis. Adv Human Genet 1991;202:153.
114. Vaisman N, Pencharz P, Corey M, et al: Energy expenditure of patients with cystic fibrosis. J Pediatr 1987;111: 496-500.
115. VanLeeuwen G, Riley WC, Glenn L, et al: Meconium plug syndrome with aganglionosis. Pediatrics 1967;40: 665-666.
116. Venugopal S, Shandling B: Meconium ileus: Laparotomy without resection, anastomosis or enterostomy. J Pediatr Surg 1979;14:715-718.
117. Vinograd I, Mogle P, Peleg O, et al: Meconium disease in premature infants with very low birth weight. J Pediatr 1983;103:963-966.
118. Wagget J, Bishop HC, Koop CE: Experience with Gastrografin enema in the treatment of meconium ileus. J Pediatr Surg 1970;5:649-654.
119. Wang CI, Kwok S, Edelbrock H: Inguinal hernia, hydrocele, and other genitourinary abnormalities in boys with cystic fibrosis and their male siblings. Am J Dis Child 1970;119:236-237.
120. Warner BW, Ziegler MM: Management of the short bowel syndrome in the pediatric population. Pediatr Clin North Am 1993;40:1335-1350.
121. White H: Meconium ileus: A new roentgen sign. Radiology 1956;66:567.
122. Wildhaben J, Seelentag WKF, Spiegel R, Schoni MH: Cystic fibrosis associated with neuronal intestinal dysplasia type B: A case report. J Pediatr Surg 1996;31:951-954.
123. Wood BP, Katzberg RW, Ryan DH, et al: Diatrizoate enemas: Facts and fallacies of colonic toxicity. Radiology 1978;126:441-444.
124. Ziegler MM: Meconium ileus. Curr Probl Surg 1994;31:736-777.
125. Zuelzer WW, Newton WA: Pathogenesis of fibrocystic disease of the pancreas. Pediatrics 1949;4:53-69.

Chapter 82

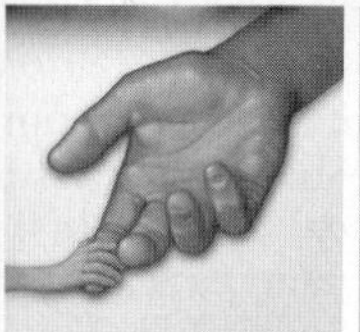

Meckel's Diverticulum

Charles L. Snyder

HISTORY

The first known description of Meckel's diverticulum was in 1598 by Hildanus.[23,32] Lavater described the lesion in 1672, as did the Dutch anatomist Ruysch in 1701.[50] In the same era, Littre reported the presence of the diverticulum in a hernia.[33] In 1809 anatomist and physician Meckel (known as Meckel the Younger) identified the origin of the diverticulum as the omphalomesenteric duct[38,39] and suggested it as a potential cause of disease. Heterotopic pancreatic mucosa in the diverticulum was identified in 1861 by Zenker,[67] and gastric mucosa was identified in 1904 by Salzer.[51] At the turn of the 19th century, inflammatory and obstructive complications of the diverticulum were first described.[17,30,56,63]

EMBRYOLOGY AND ANATOMY

During early fetal development, the embryonic disk is in contact with the yolk sac. As the embryo grows, it folds inward, and the yolk sac narrows and lengthens. The intracoelomic yolk sac forms the gut. The fetal midgut is attached to the yolk sac via the omphalomesenteric duct (also known as the vitelline duct or yolk stalk; Fig. 82-1). Ductal regression usually occurs at 5 to 7 weeks' gestation, as the functioning placenta replaces the yolk sac as the primary source of nourishment for the developing fetus.[59] Meckel's diverticulum results from failure of the proximal duct to obliterate. Abnormal regression of the vitelline duct can also result in other abnormalities—cysts, fibrous bands linking the intestine to the abdominal wall, umbilical sinuses, and complete persistence (patent vitelline duct) as an omphaloileal fistula.[42] These abnormalities are illustrated in Figure 82-2. The right and left vitelline arteries originate from the aorta within the yolk stalk: the left involutes, and the right persists as the superior mesenteric artery and terminally supplies the diverticulum. Distal vitelline artery remnants may persist as mesodiverticular bands, extending out to the tip of the diverticulum and occasionally attaching to the abdominal wall.

Meckel's diverticulum is the most common vitelline duct abnormality. Located on the antimesenteric border of the small bowel, it is a true intestinal diverticulum (containing all normal layers of the intestinal wall).[56] An abdominal wall attachment is found in about 25% of patients.[59] The precise site of a Meckel's diverticulum is variable, although most are within 90 cm (about 3 feet) of the ileocecal valve, and as many as one third are proximal. At least 5 feet of small bowel should be examined in older children to adequately document the absence of a Meckel's diverticulum.[26,59] The frequency with which heterotopic mucosa (normal tissue in an abnormal location) is found depends on the clinical presentation. About 15% of incidentally removed diverticula have abnormal mucosa. However, approximately 67% of symptomatic patients have heterotopic tissue.[65,66] Gastric tissue and pancreatic tissue predominate, with reported incidences of 60% to 85% and 5% to 16%, respectively.[12,35,62,64] Other types of mucosa (colonic, endometrial, pancreatic islets) are quite rare.

The "rule of 2s" is often used as a mnemonic for Meckel's diverticulum. The diverticulum is within 2 feet of the end of the small intestine, is 2 inches in length, occurs in about 2% of the population, is twice as common in males as in females, is often symptomatic by 2 years of age, and contains two types of heterotopic mucosa—gastric and pancreatic.

INCIDENCE

Meckel's diverticulum is the most common congenital anomaly of the gastrointestinal tract, found in approximately 1% to 2% of the population in large autopsy and surgical series.[2,20,21,36,60] The underlying genetic defects that cause Meckel's diverticulum have not yet been identified. The male-female ratio is nearly equal in asymptomatic patients; among symptomatic patients, however, the condition occurs more frequently in males (3:1 to 4:1).[4] Many individuals with a Meckel's diverticulum remain asymptomatic, but more than three quarters of symptomatic patients present in the first 2 decades of life, and often in the first 2 years.[59]

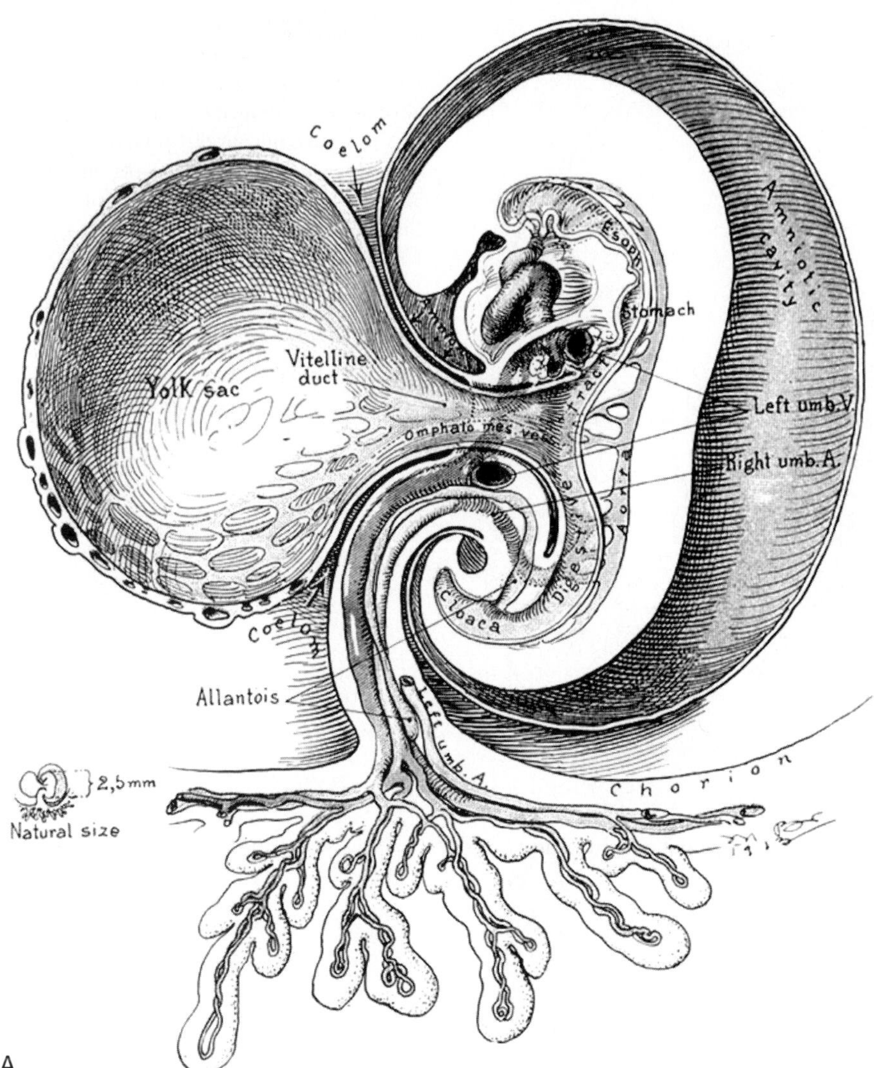

Figure 82–1 The embryo before complete involution of the omphalomesenteric structures. *A,* In an earlier stage, the large yolk sac empties, via the vitelline or omphalomesenteric duct, into the fetal midgut. The body stalk and umbilical vessels going to the placenta are seen adjacent to the vitelline duct.

Continued

ASSOCIATIONS

Although most cases are sporadic, an increased incidence of Meckel's diverticulum has been reported in association with many other congenital anomalies, including esophageal atresia, duodenal atresia, imperforate anus, omphalocele, malrotation, Hirschsprung's disease, Down syndrome, congenital diaphragmatic hernia, and various congenital neurologic and cardiovascular malformations.[44,58,60,62] The incidence of associated anomalies is much higher in autopsy-based series than in those derived from clinical data.[10,59] In one large autopsy series, the incidence of Meckel's diverticulum was greater than 10% in those with esophageal atresia or imperforate anus,[58] and approximately 5% of infants with neurologic or cardiovascular abnormalities had a diverticulum. The presence of a Meckel's diverticulum does not generally mandate a search for other anomalies, because less than 5% of patients have any associated anomalies.[58] Interestingly, concomitant urachal and omphalomesenteric abnormalities are rare.

Meckel's diverticulum was found in nearly 6% of 294 consecutive patients undergoing right hemicolectomy for Crohn's disease—much higher than would be anticipated based on the incidence in the general population.[3] None of the patients had heterotopic mucosa, a finding reported in another smaller series of patients with Crohn's disease.[14]

EPIDEMIOLOGY

Accurately assessing the lifetime probability of complications from an incidentally discovered Meckel's diverticulum is difficult. Two large studies estimated the probability to be 4.2% and 6.4%.[11,61] The incidence of complications may decrease with advancing age,[35,61] although contradictory results have been reported.[5,11,65] Factors reportedly associated with an increased likelihood of complications from Meckel's diverticulum include age younger than 40 years, male sex, presence of heterotopic mucosa, and diverticular length greater than 2 cm.[6,18,34-36]

Elective resection of incidentally discovered diverticula is indicated in uncomplicated patients with palpable thickening suggestive of heterotopic mucosa, in those with

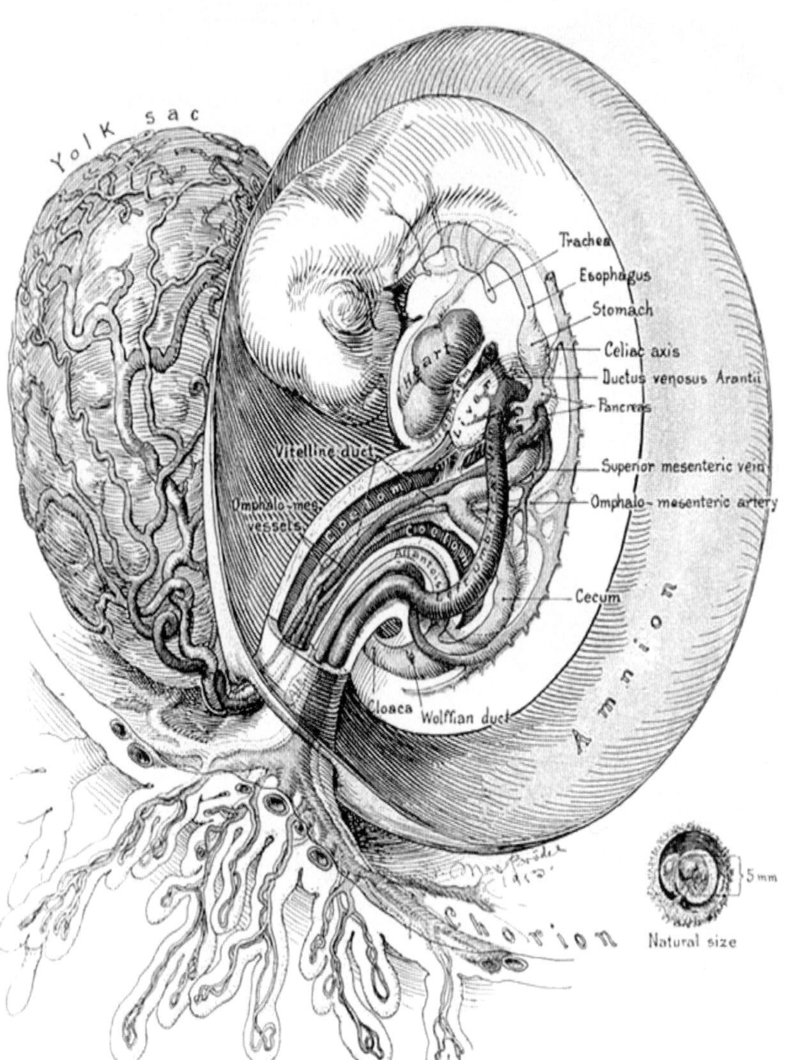

Figure 82-1 *Continued B,* At a slightly later stage, the vitelline duct fuses with the body stalk to form the umbilical cord. Note the vitelline vessels draped over the yolk sac. The yolk sac is initially the primary source of nourishment for the fetus; the placenta eventually assumes this function. (From Cullen TS: Embryology, Anatomy and Diseases of the Urachus. Philadelphia, WB Saunders, 1916. Drawings by Max Brödel.)

a history of unexplained abdominal pain, and in patients with abdominal wall attachments. Elective resection of an incidental diverticulum is generally contraindicated in immunocompromised patients, in patients undergoing insertion of prosthetic material, and in babies with gastroschisis (owing to the presence of a thickened serosal peel or prosthetic patch).

The most common complication developing after elective removal of a Meckel's diverticulum is adhesive bowel obstruction, occurring in as many as 5% to 10% of patients.[31] The mortality rate of elective resection for asymptomatic patients should approach zero.[36,64] The reported mortality rate for complications of Meckel's diverticulum ranges from 0% to 10%.[5,11,13,34,35,40,66] It has been suggested that improved surgical care and technique (particularly stapled laparoscopic resection), reflected by the minimal morbidity and mortality in recent reports on elective diverticulectomy, tilt the balance toward elective resection of incidentally discovered diverticula.[65] However, long-term data are not yet available.

CLINICAL MANIFESTATIONS

The most common signs and symptoms of a Meckel's diverticulum are bleeding, obstruction, and inflammation. Meckel's diverticulum has been called the "great imitator" because of its relative infrequency and varied manifestations. Most symptomatic patients are children younger than 10 years.[59] The type of presentation also correlates with age (Fig. 82-3).

Bleeding

Bleeding is the most common symptom of Meckel's diverticulum. An ulcer is often found at the junction between the ileal and heterotopic gastric mucosa in the diverticulum, but it may be within the heterotopic mucosa or in adjacent normal ileum on the mesenteric side opposite the diverticulum. These ulcers are often small and can be identified only by histopathologic examination.

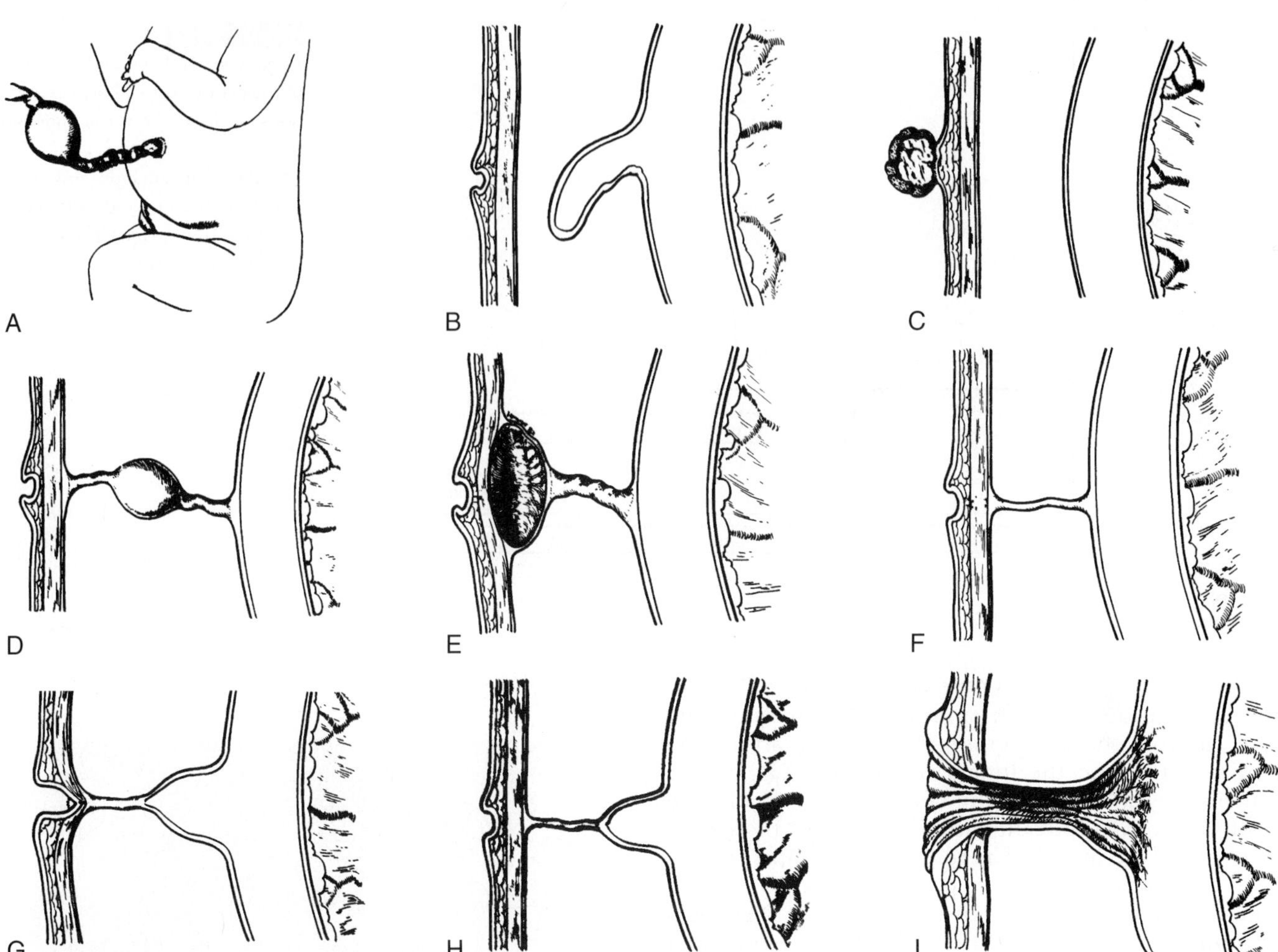

Figure 82–2 Meckel's diverticulum and umbilical abnormalities. *A,* Mucosa-lined cyst in the umbilical cord distant from the umbilicus. This is clinically insignificant and is removed when the cord is divided at birth. *B,* Meckel's diverticulum. Approximately three fourths are not attached to the abdominal wall. *C,* Umbilical polyp appears as a pouting tuft of reddish intestinal mucosa in the umbilical dimple. Although they are usually independent anomalies, these polyps may penetrate the abdominal wall and connect with deeper structures. Mucosal polyps can be mistaken for the more common umbilical granuloma. *D,* Vitelline cyst with mucosal lining and muscular coat, which persists after the proximal and distal duct obliterates. *E,* Mucosa-lined cyst with a muscular wall within the preperitoneum, beneath the umbilicus and sometimes extending through the umbilicus to the skin. *F,* Vitelline (omphalomesenteric) vessels persist as a fibrous cord attached to the abdominal wall after complete involution of the diverticulum. *G,* Persistent umbilical sinus represents an external vestige of the vitelline duct. It can be a source of infection with purulent drainage. The sinus shown here can be connected to a Meckel's diverticulum by an obliterated internal portion of the vitelline duct or by a patent continuation of the duct. Rarely, the tract attaches directly to the vitelline duct without an intervening Meckel's diverticulum. *H,* Meckel's diverticulum attached to the abdominal wall by a fibrous cord resulting from involution of the distal vitelline duct. Volvulus can occur around the band. *I,* Omphaloileal (umbilical-intestinal) fistula resulting from persistent patency of the vitelline duct with the fetal intestine. Note the intestinal folds extending from the ileal lumen to the skin. In some cases, this lining contains gastric mucosa. Treatment involves circumscribing the umbilical opening and tracing the duct to the ileum, where it is amputated and the ileum is closed.

Meckel's diverticulum accounts for nearly 50% of all instances of lower gastrointestinal bleeding in children, usually occurring in infants and toddlers. Adult patients with symptomatic Meckel's diverticula are more likely to have inflammatory or obstructive symptoms (see Fig. 82-3).[13,35] Bleeding is generally painless, frequently episodic, and sometimes massive. Stools may be bright red, brick red, or maroon.[37,49] Tarry stools are uncommon. A significant decrease in the hemoglobin level is often observed. Occult bleeding with anemia is rare.

The differential diagnosis of lower gastrointestinal bleeding in a child includes inflammatory bowel disease, intestinal polyps, intestinal duplications, and hemangiomas or arteriovenous malformations. Peptic ulcer disease and variceal bleeding may present in a similar fashion but can be distinguished by bloody nasogastric aspirates or with upper endoscopy. *Helicobacter pylori* is rarely identified in the heterotopic gastric mucosa of a bleeding Meckel's diverticulum, even when sought.[1,8,16,24,28,41] This organism plays a major role in ulcer pathogenesis elsewhere but is not a significant factor in inflammatory or bleeding complications from the heterotopic gastric mucosa in Meckel's diverticula. Bile salt toxicity affecting this microorganism may be responsible for its absence.

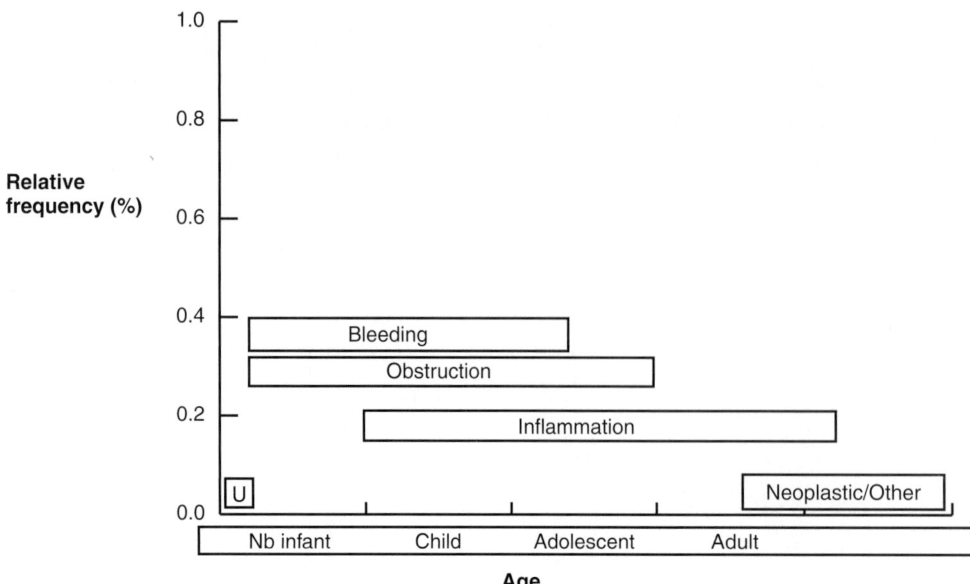

Figure 82-3 Approximate frequencies (relative and absolute) of the various clinical presentations of Meckel's diverticulum and the typical ages of presentation. Umbilical abnormalities present in the newborn period, and neoplasms present primarily in adults. Bleeding, obstruction, and inflammation can occur in a broad range of ages.

Technetium 99m scans have been used since 1970 to detect heterotopic gastric mucosa.[27] Pertechnetate ions carrying the technetium 99m isotope are stored and secreted into the lumen of the bowel by gastric mucosal cells.[55] A small number of identical cells are scattered throughout the entire bowel, but the excretory rate of the intestinal mucosa is low compared with that of gastric mucosa. A positive Meckel's scan is shown in Figure 82-4. A 10-year review of 954 technetium 99m scans of Meckel's diverticula found that 1.7% were false-negative and 0.05% were false-positive. The sensitivity was 85%, the specificity was 95%, and the accuracy was 90%.[54] Scintigraphy is significantly less accurate in adults.[13,53]

Pentagastrin, histamine blockers, and glucagon may enhance the accuracy of scanning.[55] Pentagastrin stimulates the gastric uptake of pertechnetate, and histamine blockers inhibit the secretion of pertechnetate once it is taken up. Glucagon inhibits peristalsis, decreasing the "wash-out" of pertechnetate into the small intestine from the stomach, and increasing its retention in the diverticulum. Fasting, nasogastric suction, and bladder catheterization may increase the yield of scanning. Scintigraphy must sometimes be repeated if the diagnosis is still suspected after a negative initial study. Bleeding from an intestinal duplication witih ectopic gastric mucosa may result in a positive technetium scan. Other conditions in the differential diagnosis (e.g., juvenile or hamartomatous polyps, inflammatory bowel disease, ulcers, intestinal vascular malformations) yield negative results on a Meckel's scan. Angiography is invasive but can sometimes detect a Meckel's diverticulum, even in the absence of bleeding.[46] However, if the diagnosis is strongly suspected after negative scintigraphy and endoscopy, laparoscopy (or laparotomy) is a reasonable option.[15,25,52] Severe life-threatening bleeding is uncommon but may mandate operative exploration without a definitive preoperative diagnosis.

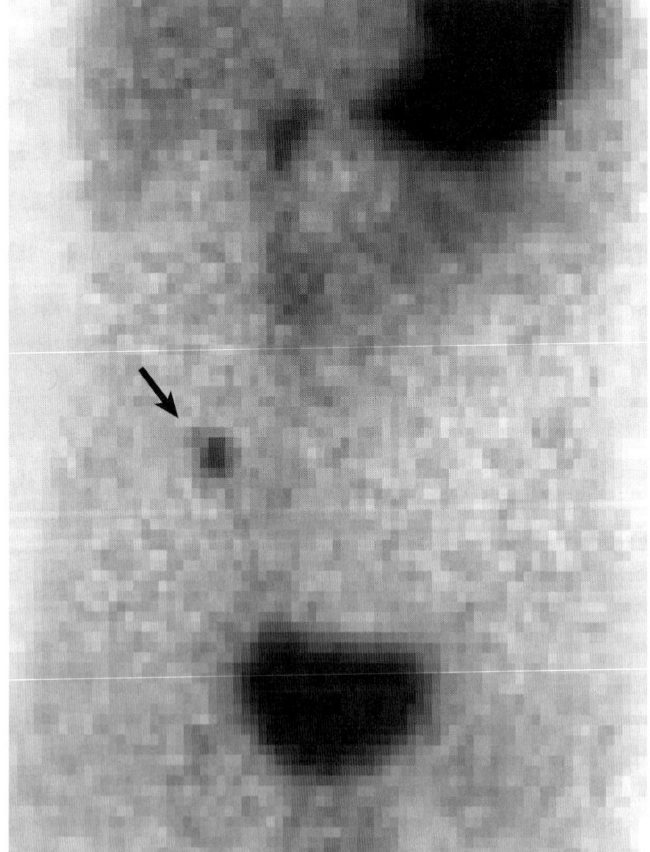

Figure 82-4 Meckel's scan. Technetium 99m pertechnetate selectively concentrates in gastric mucosa, whether in the stomach or in a Meckel's diverticulum. It is excreted from the stomach into the duodenum and proximal small bowel. Isotope excreted in the urine collects in the bladder. Sites of isotope accumulation appear as dark areas on the scan. In this case, isotope outlines the stomach, proximal intestine, Meckel's diverticulum *(arrow)*, and urinary bladder.

An elective operation can usually be deferred until the patient is stabilized, because bleeding from Meckel's

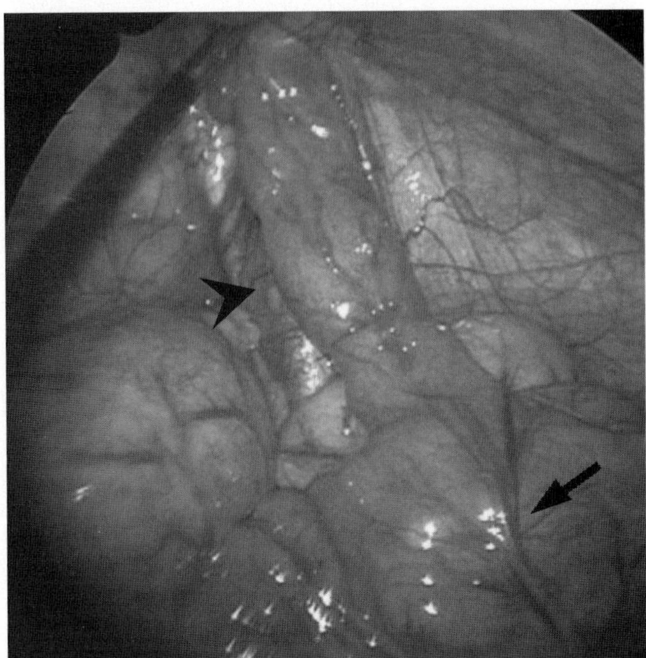

Figure 82-5 This bleeding Meckel's diverticulum was resected laparoscopically. The discoloration in the stalk of the diverticulum *(arrowhead)* is due to intraluminal blood. The arterial supply is from a persistent right vitelline artery *(arrow)*, which can usually be identified and ligated. The ulcer may not be visualized and is often located either at the junction of the heterotopic gastric and ileal mucosa or in normal ileum at the base of the diverticulum.

diverticulum tends to be episodic and frequently stops spontaneously. Blood transfusion and rehydration are often necessary. Laparoscopic or open techniques can be used (Fig. 82-5).

A Meckel's diverticulum can be removed either by simple resection of the diverticulum and transverse closure across the base or by resection of a short segment of ileum containing the diverticulum and reanastomosis. Ulceration may be present on the mesenteric border opposite the diverticulum, and resection of the ileal segment with the diverticulum is the safest option. The feeding (diverticular) artery on the surface of the ileum should be clearly identified and ligated (see Fig. 82-5). Concomitant incidental appendectomy is often performed. Overall, the results of diverticulectomy for bleeding are excellent.

Obstruction

Meckel's diverticulum can cause intestinal obstruction by one of several mechanisms: intussusception (most common), volvulus, internal hernia, an inflammatory process (see later), and prolapse through a patent vitelline duct (rare). In a combined series of more than 1000 patients, intussusception accounted for 46% of obstructions, and volvulus accounted for 24%.[21,29,35,40,49,62,64]

Intussusception occurs when the Meckel's diverticulum inverts and acts as a pathologic lead point. Intussusception in children older than 5 years is more likely to be associated with underlying pathology, making a diverticulum more likely. Overall, less than 3% of intussusceptions result from a Meckel's diverticulum (Fig. 82-6A).[21] In a classic review of 160 cases of Meckel's diverticulum with intussusception, nearly half the patients were younger than 10 years.[21]

In children, the clinical presentation of intussusception includes vomiting, intermittent abdominal pain, bloody stools, a palpable lower abdominal mass, and eventual progression to dehydration and lethargy. Either ultrasonography or pneumatic enema usually confirms the diagnosis of intussusception but rarely identifies the underlying cause. If complete reduction is obtained with pneumatic or contrast enema, elective diverticulectomy can be performed. However, complete reduction is usually unsuccessful, and the diverticulum is often discovered unexpectedly during an operation or when the resected specimen is examined. Surgical management consists of resection of the obstructed bowel with end-to-end anastomosis.

Volvulus related to Meckel's diverticulum can occur through several mechanisms. Persistent vascular or vitelline remnants from the bowel or diverticulum attached to the abdominal wall may allow twisting, kinking, or herniation (see Figs. 82-2D to I, 82-6B and C). A long diverticulum can even knot on itself, causing obstruction (Fig. 82-6E). Mesodiverticular bands from the tip of the diverticulum to the mesentery may allow loops of intestine to herniate underneath, causing obstruction, ischemia, and gangrene. These bands are embryologic remnants of the fetal vitelline circulation and supply the diverticulum (Fig. 82-6F). Giant Meckel's diverticula or vitelline cysts may result in volvulus in newborns.[7,19]

Preoperative preparation consists of intravenous hydration, correction of electrolyte abnormalities, nasogastric decompression, and antibiotics (especially if strangulation is suspected). After resuscitation, resection of the diverticulum and involved bowel (if irreversibly injured) is the treatment of choice. An end-to-end anastomosis is usually possible.

Inflammation

Inflammatory signs of a Meckel's diverticulum usually present at a later age and are often mistaken for appendicitis. The finding of a normal appendix at operation for suspected appendicitis should always prompt a search for a Meckel's diverticulum (Fig. 82-7). In a series of more than 8000 cases of suspected appendicitis, Meckel's diverticulitis was found in 0.76% of patients.[2] Heterotopic mucosa (usually gastric, but occasionally pancreatic) is almost always present, although severe inflammation may obscure it in the resected specimen. Meckel's diverticulum can mimic peptic ulcer disease, gastroenteritis, biliary colic, inflammatory bowel disease, and other conditions. Intestinal perforation may result in localized or diffuse contamination. Inflammatory complications are treated by resection of either the diverticulum alone or the diverticulum and the involved bowel. Primary anastomosis of the bowel is usually possible. On rare occasions, the child is so ill that exteriorization or a temporary stoma may be necessary.

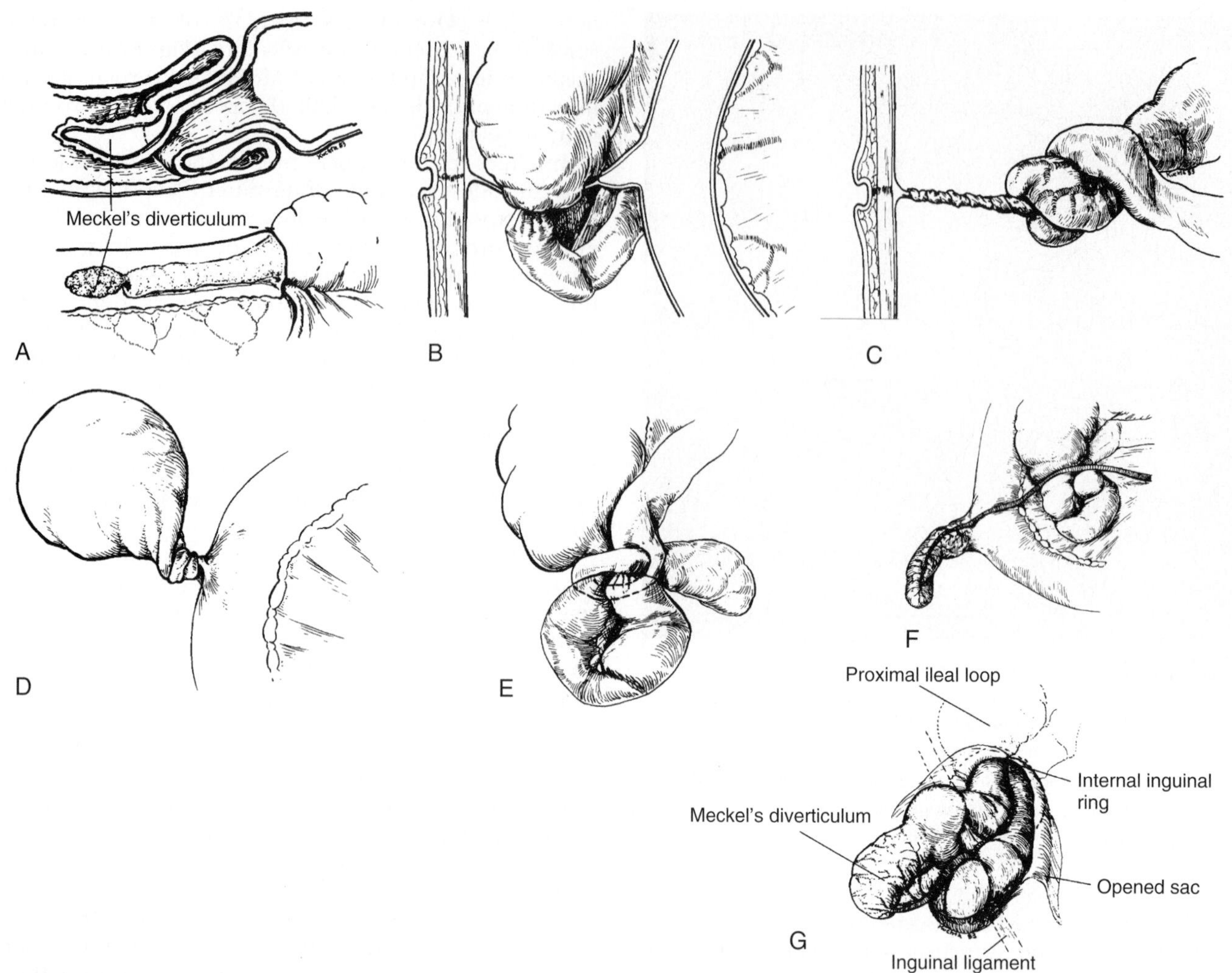

Figure 82-6 Meckel's diverticulum and possible mechanisms of intestinal obstruction. Intussusception *(A)* and obstruction related to cordlike remnants of the vitelline duct (*B* and *C*) are the most common mechanisms. The other mechanisms *(D–G)* are seldom encountered. *A*, Intussusception. *Top,* Meckel's diverticulum is inverted into the ileum as the lead point in an ileoileal intussusception. The diverticulum itself may not be turned inside out. *Bottom,* Diverticulum has intussuscepted further and can progress into the ascending colon as an ileoileal-ileocolic intussusception. *B,* Kinking of a loop of small bowel on a cordlike vitelline duct remnant between Meckel's diverticulum and the umbilicus. *C,* Volvulus caused by torsion of loops of small intestine around the fixed point of a fibrous cord remnant of the vitelline duct. *D,* Twisting of Meckel's diverticulum at its base, causing diverticular obstruction with possible infarction. *E,* Obstruction of ileum by a long Meckel's diverticulum that has formed a knot by looping around itself. It can obstruct both the ileum and itself. *F,* Mesodiverticular band containing the vitelline vessels passes across the ileum to the diverticulum. It is separated from the mesentery and forms a band under which a loop of small intestine has herniated and become obstructed. *G,* Littre's hernia consists of a loop of ileum with a Meckel's diverticulum in an inguinal hernia sac. Shown here is an indirect hernia that contains intestine and diverticulum. The hernia sac has been opened before reduction and inguinal herniorrhaphy. The proximal limb of intestine is dilated because of obstruction by the constricting internal inguinal ring, and the distal limb has emptied beyond the obstruction.

Other

Approximately 5% of patients with symptomatic Meckel's diverticulum present with umbilical abnormalities (see Fig. 82-2C, G, and I).[60-62] External, mucosa-lined cysts of the umbilical cord are rare lesions that can be seen at birth. These are typically isolated anomalies with no connection to bowel (see Fig. 82-2A).

Persistent polypoid tissue or granulation tissue in the umbilicus is a common problem in newborns. Most umbilical polyps are not associated with intraperitoneal abnormalities, and local treatment (ligature or silver nitrate application for umbilical granulomas) suffices. If the polyp fails to resolve after ligation, if the umbilical granuloma persists after one or two treatments, or if the patient has a history of umbilical drainage or an identifiable tract, further intervention is necessary. The "polyp" or tract may contain intestinal mucosa (see Fig. 82-2C). A fistulous tract from the umbilicus can sometimes be identified by careful passage of a small-caliber catheter. Alternatively, a sinogram may demonstrate the fistula.

The umbilicus may have the appearance of an ileostomy because the mucosa of the persistent vitelline duct prolapses outward (see Fig. 82-2I; Fig. 82-8). Severe prolapse may cause intestinal obstruction and may even

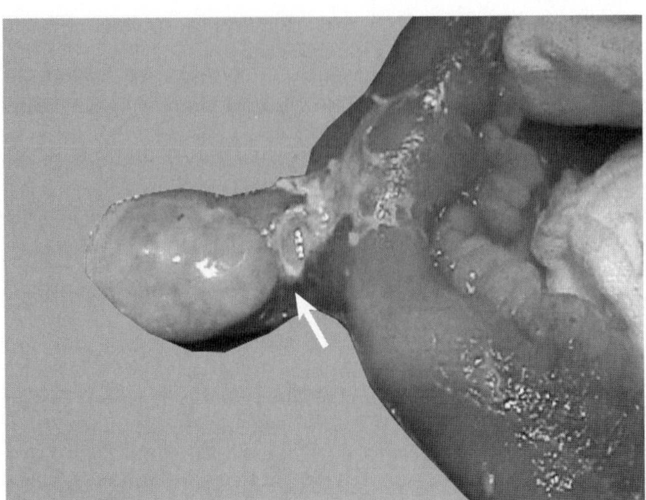

Figure 82-7 Meckel's diverticulum with inflammation and perforation at the base *(arrow)*. The tip of the diverticulum is markedly thickened from heterotopic gastric mucosa and inflammatory changes. Segmental intestinal resection or simple diverticulectomy with transverse bowel closure can be performed, depending on the clinical scenario and the character of the adjacent bowel, as well as the severity of the inflammatory reaction.

compromise the blood supply to the bowel. Umbilical sinus or fistula anomalies are best approached through infraumbilical or transumbilical incisions. Placing a catheter in the tract may facilitate dissection. The umbilical end of the tract is transected or circumscribed, detached, and removed in continuity with any persistent abnormal structures. The intestinal attachment can usually be excised and the bowel closed transversely.

Foreign bodies or stones have been reported within Meckel's diverticulum, as have parasitic infections such as schistosomiasis or ascariasis.[22,47,48,65]

Primary gastrointestinal cancer (carcinoid, sarcoma, lymphoma, adenocarcinoma, leiomyoma) has been reported rarely in patients with Meckel's diverticulum.[9,43,57] These tumors are generally found in adults; carcinoid tumors are the most common. In a literature review of 104 cases of carcinoid tumors, the mean age was 57 years, with men affected 2.5 times more commonly than women.[45] These were relatively aggressive tumors (three quarters had metastases at diagnosis); immunophenotypically and biologically, they resembled jejunoileal carcinoids rather than appendiceal carcinoids.[43] Tumors larger than 5 mm were associated with a significantly increased risk for metastasis. Carcinoid syndrome can also occur. Resection of the ileal segment that contains the diverticulum and its associated mesentery is the treatment of choice. Second primary malignancies have been reported in patients with carcinoid tumors and Meckel's diverticulum.[57]

REFERENCES

1. Ackerman Z, et al: Role of *Helicobacter pylori* infection in complications from Meckel's diverticulum. Dig Dis Sci 2003;48:1068.
2. Albu I, et al: The ileal diverticulum: Morpho-clinical and epidemiological study. Rom J Morphol Embryol 1993; 39:37.
3. Andreyev HJ, et al: Association between Meckel's diverticulum and Crohn's disease: A retrospective review. Gut 1994;35:788.
4. Androulakis JA, et al: The sex ratio of Meckel's diverticulum. Am Surg 1969;35:455.
5. Arnold JF, Pellicane JV: Meckel's diverticulum: A ten-year experience. Am Surg 1997;63:354.
6. Artigas V, et al: Meckel's diverticulum: Value of ectopic tissue. Am J Surg 1986;151:631.
7. Bell MJ, et al: Ileal dysgenesis in infants and children. J Pediatr Surg 1982;17:395.
8. Bemelman WA, et al: Role of *Helicobacter pylori* in the pathogenesis of complications of Meckel's diverticula. Eur J Surg 1993;159:171.
9. Chatterjee CR: Sarcomas of Meckel's diverticulum. Can J Surg 1970;13:163.
10. Christie A: Meckel's diverticulum: A pathologic study of 63 cases. Am J Dis Child 1931;42:544.

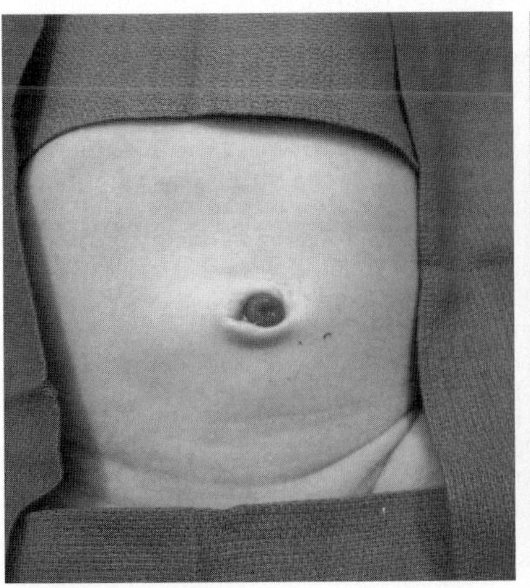

A

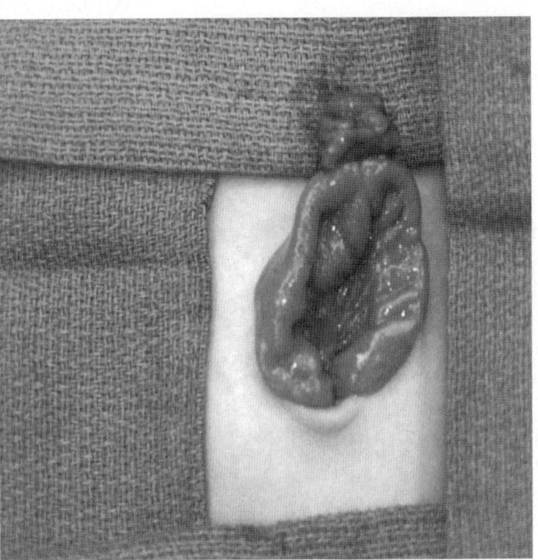

B

Figure 82-8 Omphaloileal fistula. *A,* The umbilicus has the appearance of an ileostomy. *B,* The fistula tract is broad and short. The skin and abdominal wall attachments to the fistula were taken down, and the ileum was delivered through the umbilical defect and transversely closed. These defects are relatively rare.

11. Cullen JJ, et al: Surgical management of Meckel's diverticulum: An epidemiologic, population-based study. Ann Surg 1994;220:564.
12. DeBartolo HM Jr, van Heerden JA: Meckel's diverticulum. Ann Surg 1976;183:30.
13. Diamond T, Russell CF: Meckel's diverticulum in the adult. Br J Surg 1985;72:480.
14. Eckman CN: Regional enteritis associated with Meckel's diverticulum: A report of five cases. Gastroenterology 1958;34:130.
15. Fansler RF: Laparoscopy in the management of Meckel's diverticulum. Surg Laparosc Endosc 1996;6:231.
16. Fich A, et al: Does *Helicobacter pylori* colonize the gastric mucosa of Meckel's diverticulum? Mayo Clin Proc 1990;65:187.
17. Gramen K: Chronischen ulcus in einem Meckelshen Divertikel mit perforation and diffuser peritonitis. Nord Med Ark Kirkurgi 1915;48:1.
18. Groebli Y, et al: Meckel's diverticulum in adults: Retrospective analysis of 119 cases and historical review. Eur J Surg 2001;167:518.
19. Grosfeld JL, Franken EA: Intestinal obstruction in the neonate due to vitelline duct cysts. Surg Gynecol Obstet 1974;138:527.
20. Haber J: Meckel's diverticulum. Am J Surg 1947;73:468.
21. Harkins H: Intussusception due to invaginated Meckel's diverticulum. Ann Surg 1933;98:1070.
22. Haynes S, Reid HA: Meckel's diverticulitis due to *Schistosomiasis mansoni*. Am J Gastroenterol 1976;66:559.
23. Hildanus F: Opera observationum et curationum medico—chururgicarum, quae extant omnia, etc. Francof, J Beyeri, 1646.
24. Hill P, Rode J: *Helicobacter pylori* in ectopic gastric mucosa in Meckel's diverticulum. Pathology 1998;30:7.
25. Huang CS, Lin LH: Laparoscopic Meckel's diverticulectomy in infants: Report of three cases. J Pediatr Surg 1993;28:1486.
26. Jay GD III, et al: Meckel's diverticulum: A survey of one hundred and three cases. Arch Surg 1950;61:158.
27. Jewett TC, et al: The visualization of Meckel's diverticulum with 99m Tc-pertechnetate. Surgery 1970;68:567.
28. Kumar S, et al: *Helicobacter pylori* and Meckel's diverticulum. J R Coll Surg Edinb 1991;36:225.
29. Kusumoto H, et al: Complications and diagnosis of Meckel's diverticulum in 776 patients. Am J Surg 1992;164:382.
30. Kuttner H: Ileus durch intussusception eines Meckelschen divertikel. Beitr Klin Chir 1898;21:289.
31. Leijonmarck CE, et al: Meckel's diverticulum in the adult. Br J Surg 1986;73:146.
32. Lichtenstein ME: Meckel's diverticulum. Q Bull Northwest Univ Med 1941;15:296.
33. Littre A: Observation sur une nouvelle espece de hernia. Hist Acad Roy Sci 1719;300.
34. Ludtke FE, et al: Incidence and frequency of complications and management of Meckel's diverticulum. Surg Gynecol Obstet 1989;169:537.
35. Mackey WC, Dineen P: A fifty year experience with Meckel's diverticulum. Surg Gynecol Obstet 1983;156:56.
36. Matsagas MI, et al: Incidence, complications, and management of Meckel's diverticulum. Arch Surg 1995;130:143.
37. Mayo CW: Meckel's diverticulum. Proc Mayo Clin 1933;8:230.
38. Meckel J: Uber die Divertikel am Darmkanal. Arch Physiol 1809;9:421.
39. Meckel J: Handbuch der pathologischen Anatomie. Leipzig, CH Reclam, 1812, p 533.
40. Meguid M, et al: Complications of Meckel's diverticulum in infants. Surg Gynecol Obstet 1974;139:541.
41. Morris A, et al: *Campylobacter pylori* infection in Meckel's diverticula containing gastric mucosa. Gut 1989;30:1233.
42. Moses WR: Meckel's diverticulum: A report of two unusual cases. N Engl J Med 1947;237:118.
43. Moyana TN: Carcinoid tumors arising from Meckel's diverticulum: A clinical, morphologic, and immunohistochemical study. Am J Clin Pathol 1989;91:52.
44. Nicol JW, MacKinlay GA: Meckel's diverticulum in exomphalos minor. J R Coll Surg Edinb 1994;39:6.
45. Nies C, et al: Carcinoid tumors of Meckel's diverticula. Dis Colon Rectum 1992;35:589.
46. Okazaki M, et al: Angiographic findings of Meckel's diverticulum: The characteristic appearance of the vitelline artery. Abdom Imaging 1993;18:15.
47. Pujari BD, Deodhare SG: Ascarideal penetration of Meckel's diverticulum. Int Surg 1978;63:113.
48. Roessel CW: Perforation of Meckel's diverticulum by foreign body: Case report and review of the literature. Ann Surg 1962;156:972.
49. Rutherford RB, Akers DR: Meckel's diverticulum: A review of 148 pediatric patients, with special reference to the pattern of bleeding and to mesodiverticular vascular bands. Surgery 1966;59:618.
50. Ruysch F: Thesaurus Anatomicus. 2nd ed. Amsterdam, 1701.
51. Salzer H: Uber das Offerene Meckelesche Divertikel. Wien Klin Wochenschr 1904;17:614.
52. Schier F, et al: Laparoscopic removal of Meckel's diverticula in children. Eur J Pediatr Surg 1996;6:38.
53. Schwartz MJ, Lewis JH: Meckel's diverticulum: Pitfalls in scintigraphic detection in the adult. Am J Gastroenterol 1984;79:611.
54. Sfakianakis GN, Conway JJ: Detection of ectopic gastric mucosa in Meckel's diverticulum and in other aberrations by scintigraphy. I. Pathophysiology and 10-year clinical experience. J Nucl Med 1981;22:647.
55. Sfakianakis GN, Conway JJ: Detection of ectopic gastric mucosa in Meckel's diverticulum and in other aberrations by scintigraphy. II. Indications and methods—a 10-year experience. J Nucl Med 1981;22:732.
56. Sibley WL: Meckel's diverticulum: Dyspepsia meckeli from heterotopic gastric mucosa. Arch Surg 1944; 49:156.
57. Silk YN, et al: Carcinoid tumor in Meckel's diverticulum. Am Surg 1988;54:664.
58. Simms MH, Corkery JJ: Meckel's diverticulum: Its association with congenital malformation and the significance of atypical morphology. Br J Surg 1980;67:216.
59. Skandalakis JE, et al: The small intestines. In Skandalakis JE, Gray SW (eds): Embryology for Surgeons, 2nd ed. Baltimore, Williams & Wilkins, 1994, p 184.
60. Soderlund S: Meckel's diverticulum, a clinical and histologic study. Acta Chir Scand Suppl 1959;248:213.
61. Soltero MJ, Bill AH: The natural history of Meckel's diverticulum and its relation to incidental removal: A study of 202 cases of diseased Meckel's diverticulum found in King County, Washington, over a fifteen year period. Am J Surg 1976;132:168.
62. St-Vil D, et al: Meckel's diverticulum in children: A 20-year review. J Pediatr Surg 1991;26:1289.
63. Thompson JE: Perforated peptic ulcer in Meckel's diverticulum. Ann Surg 1937;105:44.
64. Vane DW, et al: Vitelline duct anomalies: Experience with 217 childhood cases. Arch Surg 1987;122:542.
65. Yahchouchy EK, et al: Meckel's diverticulum. J Am Coll Surg 2001;192:658.
66. Yamaguchi M, et al: Meckel's diverticulum: Investigation of 600 patients in Japanese literature. Am J Surg 1978; 136:247.
67. Zenker FA: Nebenpancreas in des Darmwand. Virchow Arch Pathol Anat 1861;21:369.

Chapter 83

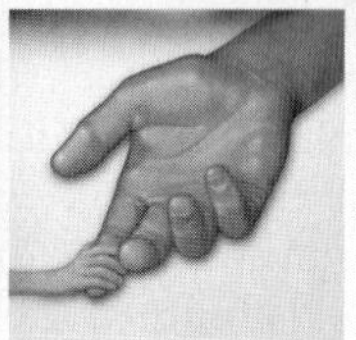

Intussusception

Sigmund H. Ein and Alan Daneman

HISTORY

We can learn from the past, and this certainly applies to the history of intussusception.[111,144,145,183] Intussusception was recognized as far back as the late 1600s (Barbette, Peyer), but was first described in detail by Hunter in 1793.[93,167] Raffensperger[142] has written that as far back as Hippocrates' time, there were allusions to reduction of intussusception by the injection of air or fluid into the rectum. However, Ravitch[144] reported that in the Littré translation, Hippocrates was talking only of ileus; therefore, there exists some doubt in historical recording and reporting, as one might expect. The suggested treatments of intussusception at that time were bleeding and quicksilver, to which Hunter added emetics followed by purgatives if the former failed. Subsequently, Hunter's principles of reduction were improved by using a hand bellows applied to the anus and blowing vigorously in an attempt to reduce the intussuscepting bowel back into its original position. Apparently, such treatments were tried in Hippocrates' time[110]; however, it was not until the early 1800s that the first descriptions of pneumatic reduction appeared in the medical literature (Blacklock, 1818; Mitchell, 1836; Gorham, 1838).[111] These cases were not well documented, some involved adults, and many were doubted (as with Hippocrates) as true intussusception. In 1864 a surgeon named Greig[68,111] was the first to lay down strict criteria for the clinical diagnosis of intussusception. He tried to persuade others that his use of hand bellows successfully reduced four of five actual pediatric intussusceptions: "Contrary to our expectations the air passed readily into the bowel and seemed to give the child great relief." This technique, however, was only one of many competing methods (effervescent powder, cold water, hypertonic saline, long bougies per rectum, electricity, belladonna, opium), which, as expected, were not very successful, and therefore the condition remained fatal in most infants and children.

Wilson (1831)[183] operatively reduced an intussusception in an adult, but it was not until 40 years later that Hutchinson (1871)[94,183] performed the first successful operative reduction of intussusception in an infant. Operative intervention at that time, however, was quite hazardous. Treves (1885)[167,171] suggested a plan of management that remains little changed up to the present day, but with this he also reported a 73% mortality rate for his first 33 cases of intussusception treated operatively. In 1876, Hirschsprung[84] published the first of a series of reports on hydrostatic reduction with results (23% mortality) that were superior to operative treatment until the mid 1900s. By the late 1800s, it was understood that successful reduction of intussusception by hydrostatic and pneumatic means depended on the pressure exerted, and various devices were developed to capitalize on the growing popularity of this form of treatment. Some authors (Forest, 1886[61]) even questioned whether liquid, gas, or both was the best agent to use; he later calculated that 6 lb of pressure per square inch was an acceptable pressure to use in attempting to reduce an intussusception. Mortimer (1891)[123] was also concerned about the danger of these new methods.

Wide acceptance of hydrostatic reduction was in vogue at the turn of the 20th century. However, that did not prevent enterprising and daring surgeons from still trying the operative route. Around 1900, Clubbe[22] and Peterson[145] both for the first time successfully resected a pediatric intussusception. The drift toward surgical treatment had begun, and as surgical techniques slowly improved, so did surgical results, particularly in the United States, Britain, and Australia, even in the face of a much lower (23%) mortality rate (in 84 patients) for hydrostatic reduction reported by Hirschsprung in 1905.[85,111]

Probably the most important advancement in the diagnosis and treatment of intussusception occurred in 1913, when Ladd[144] first reported the use of diagnostic imaging via bismuth enemas. His report contained the first published photographs of roentgenologic pictures of intussusception. Although Lehman[144] had made the same observation 3 years earlier, he did not report the same findings as Ladd until 1914. Ladd was convinced that this was a good diagnostic technique without any therapeutic value.[144] It took another 14 years (1927) before hydrostatic reduction of an intussusception via barium guided by fluoroscopy was accomplished by Olsson and Pallin,[131] Poulquien,[137] and Retan.[147] By this time Australia was quite involved in the nonoperative treatment of pediatric intussusception. Hipsley (1926)[83] published a series of 100 cases, 62 of which were treated by hydrostatic saline enema, with only 1 death. At the same time, hydrostatic enema with barium became popular in Scandinavia and South America.[111] Despite the newly described ability of the radiologist to diagnose and reduce an intussusception, surgery had become the primary mode of treatment in the United States, yet this choice of therapy was not evidence based.

It was not until Ravitch and McCune (1948)[146] reported a surgical mortality rate of 32% that attention focused on nonoperative reduction. After this revelation, reduction via hydrostatic barium enema (BE) and fluoroscopy was gradually reintroduced, spearheaded by both laboratory research and clinical confirmation from Ravitch and McCune[146] in 1948, 1952, 1954, and 1958, in which reduction rates of up to 75% were achieved with a zero mortality rate. Even so, in 1953 Gross[69] (much like his predecessor Ladd[144]) acknowledged that this nonoperative method could be effective but strongly opposed it in the belief that the definitive treatment of intussusception was operative. However, the hydrostatic method persisted and became the primary, safest, and most successful means of treating intussusception.

Since then, radiologists have been at the clinical forefront and have made further advances in the nonoperative treatment of intussusception, with air (pneumatic reduction) used as the contrast medium (Fiorito et al.,[59] 1959; Guo et al.,[73] 1986); ultrasonography (US) used for screening, diagnosis, and monitoring reduction (Burke and Clarke,[16] 1977); and delayed repeat enema reduction attempts (Guo et al., 1986). Surgery is now the accepted backup for radiologic-guided reduction of intussusception.

INTRODUCTION

Intussusception is derived from the Latin words "*intus*" (within) and "*suscipere*" (to receive).[74] Intussusception is the invagination of one part of the intestine into another (Fig. 83-1). Swenson[169] described it quite clearly: three cylinders of intestinal wall are involved; the inner and middle cylinders are the invaginated bowel (intussusceptum) and the outer cylinder is the recipient of the

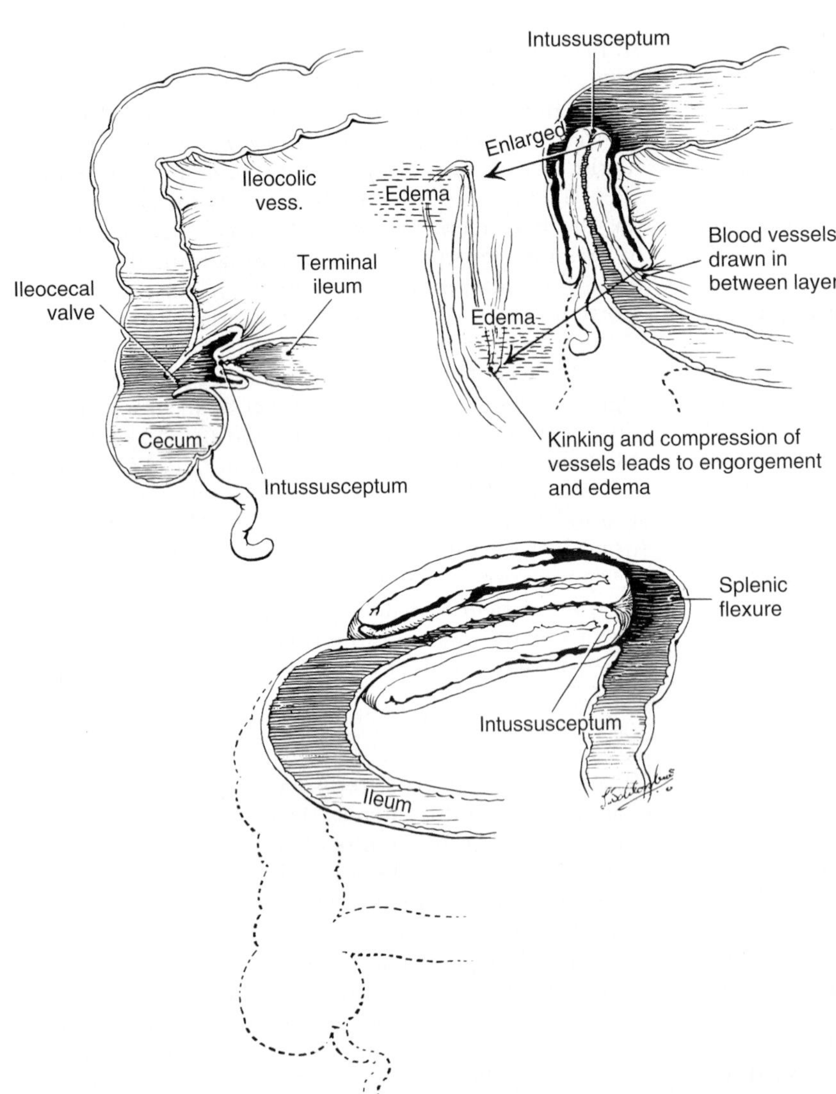

Figure 83–1 Diagram of the most common (idiopathic, ileocolic) types of intussusception. As it develops in the terminal ileum with its prograde bowel peristalsis, the proximal invaginated bowel (intussusceptum) carries its mesentery into the recipient bowel (intussuscipiens) and the mesenteric vessels are angulated, squeezed, and compressed between the layers of the intussusceptum. This causes intense local edema of the intussusceptum, which produces venous compression, stasis, and congestion leading to an outpouring of mucus and blood from the engorged intussusceptum, often producing stool with the appearance of currant jelly. If this vicious cycle continues, the bowel congestion and pressure increase and produce ischemic changes resulting in bowel necrosis (gangrene). The outermost layer of the intussusceptum becomes devitalized first, the innermost layer of the intussusceptum becomes gangrenous much later, and the outermost layer of bowel (intussuscipiens) loses its viability last.[144] However, a review of perforations during attempted hydrostatic enema reduction showed the perforations to be in the colon (intussuscipiens) near the intussusceptum.[48,92,113]

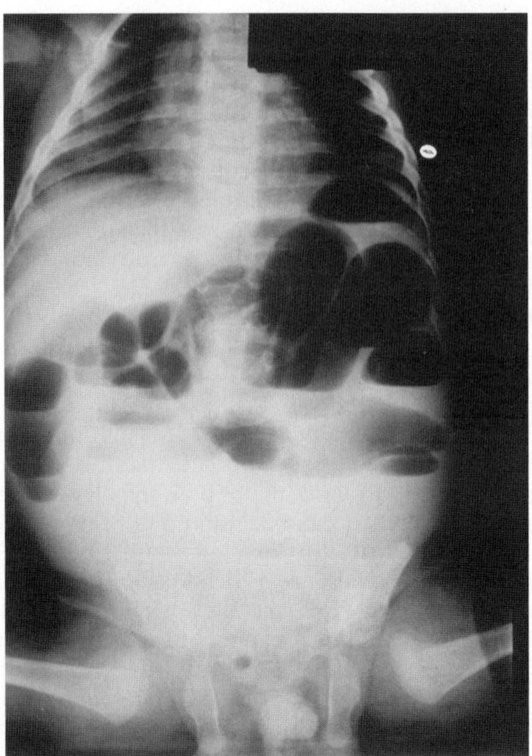

Figure 83-2 Radiologic picture of small bowel obstruction. It can occur in an infant or preschool child and is most often caused by idiopathic intussusception (usually ileoileocolic) or postoperative intussusception.

invaginated bowel (intussuscipiens). Intussusception is probably the second most common cause of acute abdominal pain in infants and preschool children after constipation. Furthermore, intussusception is often a cause of acute small bowel obstruction (SBO) in the same age groups (Fig. 83-2). Therefore, it is essential for all medical personnel who treat infants and children to know about intussusception, especially its diagnosis in all of its parameters and variations. Some authors have stated that intussusception can be difficult to diagnose, but this difficulty can be eliminated if people treating the pediatric population know about it, think of it, and also realize that a small number (15%) do not have the classic colicky pain as the telltale symptom.[52] Fifty years ago, Gross[69] correctly stated: "There are few illnesses in which the clinical history and physical findings are more suggestive of the correct diagnosis."

Many improvements and innovations in the diagnosis and treatment of intussusception by pediatric radiologists have often escaped the attention, interest, or expertise of regional and nonspecialist pediatric centers,[8] including the use of US, the change from hydrostatic to pneumatic reduction techniques, and the introduction of delayed repeat enemas. The small number of cases of intussusception that these latter institutions see and treat results in a relative lack of familiarity and experience with this common pediatric condition and, consequently, a reluctance to try anything new.[14] This scenario, as expected, promotes an unchanging and unacceptable higher surgical rate than there should be. This problem can be overcome if pediatric (tertiary and quaternary care) centers provide a network of continuing support, communication, education, and cooperation to raise the level of the playing field, so to speak, and allow all infants and children with intussusception to achieve similar outcomes.[18]

Throughout this chapter, facts and figures are quoted from the vast intussusception experience from The Hospital for Sick Children (HSC) Toronto, from which more than 40 reports have been published since 1952. During the first 53 years (1915 to 1968), there were more than 1000 intussusceptions (25 per year), and since 1968,[51] another 1300 (35 per year) have been diagnosed and treated. These patients are all included in their many publications.

Much of this chapter results from the wisdom and experience found in the classic writings of Ravitch[146] and Young,[183] the authors of the previous chapters on intussusception in this two-volume textbook. To this have been added other facts, figures, and opinions, as well as the latest in clinical research (Tables 83-1 and 83-2) (more than 500 abstracts and publications) since the last (fifth) edition was published in 1998.

At present, diagnosis and especially treatment represent a combined effort between the pediatric radiologist and pediatric surgeon, with most of the current treatment successfully completed by the former group. Nonetheless, one must never lose sight of the sage words of Zachary, who, at the First Annual Congress of the British Association of Paediatric Surgeons in London in 1954 said, "... the procedure (treatment) should be in responsible hands and the child must be under the direct care of the surgeon who may have to operate."[40,179,184]

TABLE 83-1 Pathologic Lead Points in Case Reports, 1998–2004

Appendix—28	Cystic fibrosis—2
Lipoma—22	Hamartoma—2
Polyp—17	Leukemia—2
Peutz-Jeghers syndrome—13	Lymphoid hyperplasia—2
Duodenogastric intussusception—11	Meckel's diverticulum—2
Adenoma—10	Myofibroma—2
Lymphoma—7	Osteosarcoma—2
Tube—6	Angioneurotic edema—1
Carcinoma—5	Carcinoid—1
Enterocolitis—5	Choriocarcinoma—1
Celiac disease—4	Ectopic gastric mucosa—1
Crohn's disease—4	Ectopic pancreas—1
Henoch-Schönlein purpura—4	Foreign body—1
Pneumatosis—4	Internal hernia—1
Trauma—4	Lymphangioma—1
Duplication—3	Lymphoproliferative—1
Endometriosis—3	Nerve sheath tumor—1
Histiocytoma—3	Renal cell carcinoma—1
Melanoma—3	Sarcoid—1
Angioma—2	Splenosis—1
Bezoar—2	Worm—1

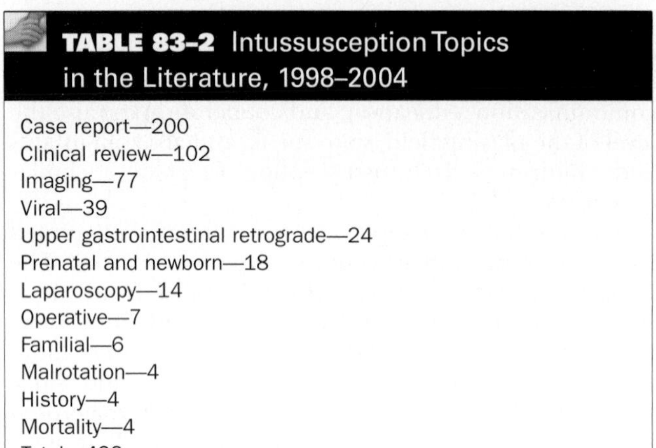

TABLE 83-2 Intussusception Topics in the Literature, 1998–2004

Case report—200
Clinical review—102
Imaging—77
Viral—39
Upper gastrointestinal retrograde—24
Prenatal and newborn—18
Laparoscopy—14
Operative—7
Familial—6
Malrotation—4
History—4
Mortality—4
Total—499

INCIDENCE AND DEMOGRAPHICS

Intussusception occurs throughout the world wherever children are treated, but there are quite noticeable variations in the numbers reported from many pediatric centers.[51,144,145,183] Reviewing reports concerning intussusception gives one the immediate impression that China[73] has by far the highest incidence of intussusception in the world (500 per year), but this may simply be a population factor. Scandinavia is next (50 to 60), followed by Toronto, Glasgow, and Melbourne (35); England (Birmingham, Newcastle-on-Tyne) and Boston are next with 20 to 30 cases per year. Other children's hospitals in the United States (Baltimore, Chicago, Cincinnati, Denver, Los Angeles, Milwaukee, New Orleans, New York, St. Louis) have reported treating 5 to 14 cases a year.

Young[183] drew several conclusions from his literature review. He noted that Australia, Canada, and New Zealand reported intussusception rates similar to those of Europe and the United States and that the frequency of intussusception in Egypt, Rhodesia, and South Africa is said to be similar to that of Scotland. Strangely, though, in Nigeria intussusception is more common in children older than 5 years and tends to be subacute or chronic; Ravitch[145] stated that the same is true for mainland China and Taiwan.

Intussusception occurs in approximately 1 in 2000 infants and children. Two English and two Scottish studies reported the incidence of intussusception to be 1.5 to 4 per 1000 live births.[145,183] For comparison's sake, 1 of every 50 pediatric patients will have an inguinal hernia, and 6 of every 100 will have appendicitis.

Most series report more males than females with intussusception, usually at a 2:1 or 3:2 ratio (Fig. 83-3). Ravitch[145] claimed that no satisfactory explanation has been offered for this male preponderance, which MacMahon[183] said was much more evident (78% males) after 9 months of age than before (55%). Intussusception is reported to occur in greater numbers in white infants and children, the proportion depending on what part of the globe is being studied.

Although intussusception has been found in all pediatric ages from prenatal[120] to the late teens (and in adults and animals as well), 75% occur within the first 2 years of life, and more than 40% are seen between 3 and 9 months of age in Toronto.[51] Most series tend to support these Toronto results, with mild variations. Intussusception has been observed in utero[136] and may result in intestinal atresia (usually ileal atresia)[54,154,170]; in some cases the end of the intussusceptum can be found in the distal part of the bowel.[141,183] Why this happens is

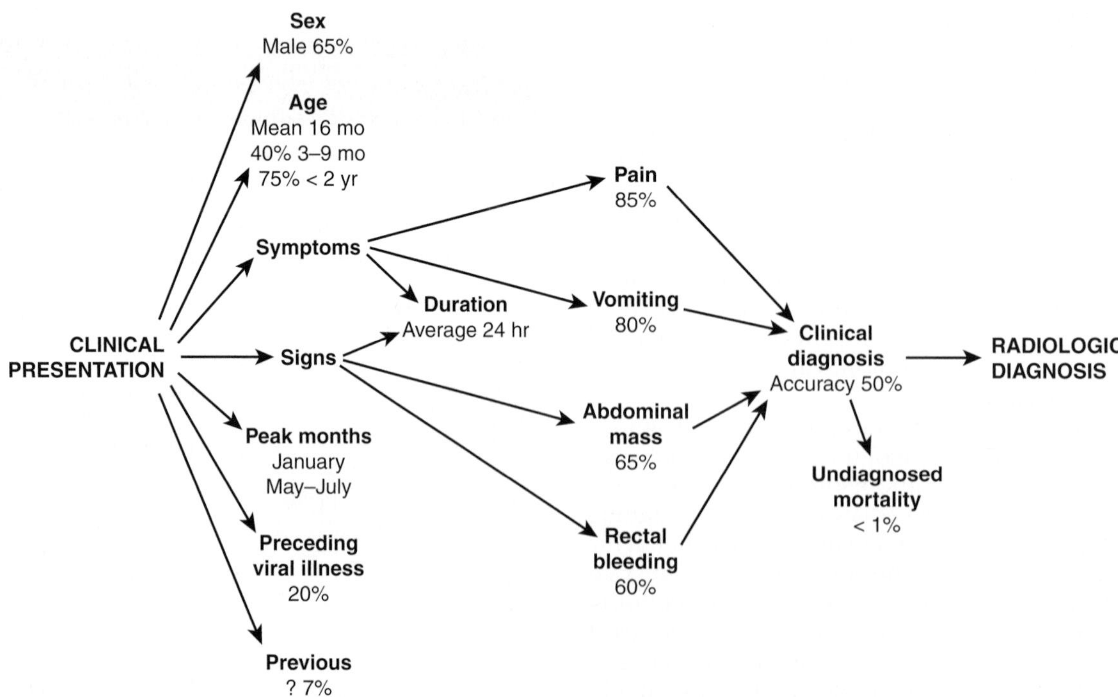

Figure 83-3 Algorithm detailing the clinical features and diagnosis of intussusception. (Note that this algorithm can be joined in sequence to all the other algorithms.)

as yet unexplained. Intussusception also occurs in newborns (within the first 30 days),[120] but like older patients with intussusception, there is a greater chance that a pathologic lead point (PLP) can be identified as the cause.[174] Most of these babies (0.3% of all intussusceptions) are otherwise quite normal.[183]

Intussusception has also been reported in families[165] and relatives (identical twins, sibling cases, as well as in fathers and sons from four different areas of the world: Tel-Aviv, Tenerife [Canary Islands], Adelaide, United States), but their histories all seem to indicate a viral cause more than a genetic cause.[144,145] There is no evidence of any increased likelihood that intussusception will occur in a sibling once one child of the family has been affected, as happens with pyloric stenosis.

The incidence of intussusception tends to vary by season from one study to another, and even within the same institution in different eras.[46,51] Most, but not all writers have indeed noticed a seasonal variation that usually correlates with viral infections (respiratory or gastrointestinal, or both).[145,183] The only thing that really changed significantly (when Toronto reviewed its cases of intussusception 25 years later) was the seasonal peak months, which changed from one peak (May and June in 1959 to 1968[51]) to two peaks (January and July in 1985 to 1990[46]). The incidence of a preceding viral infection was about 20% in both series, yet there was no apparent reason for this monthly split other than that viral illnesses are more commonly seen in the colder months in Toronto. In most series, the busiest time of the year for intussusception seems to be May, June, and July.[144,145,183]

In 1905, Hirschsprung[85] stated that he never saw a malnourished child with an intussusception. Since that time, affected infants and children have been described as being healthy, sturdy, well developed, well nourished, and in a good state of nutrition.[95] The exact meaning of what Hirschsprung tried to convey in his classic statement will never be known. Despite this view, both Ravitch[144,145] and Mayell,[109a] in their respective series, showed that this observation was not necessarily correct. Janik and Firor[97] said that children from Chicago with intussusception exhibited lower weight percentiles irrespective of socioeconomic status. Hirschsprung's assumption that "well nourished" means that a majority of the children with intussusception will have a higher weight percentile or weight-for-length percentile was similarly not verified by a Toronto study.[95]

Though seemingly hard to prove, Ravitch[145] reported that 7% of his patients had a previous similar attack of abdominal pain from 6 months to 10 days before the proven manifestation of intussusception; he believed that this event may indicate a PLP. The implication is that spontaneous reduction of the intussusception had occurred, which may well be open to speculation.

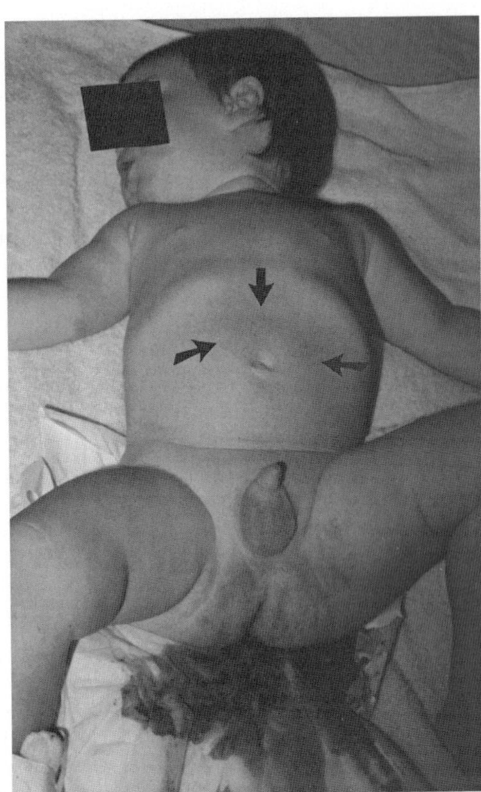

Figure 83-4 Pale, lethargic infant with intussusception and the classic currant jelly stool. Note the epigastric mass (*arrows*). (*See color plate.*)

PATHOGENESIS

Pathologic Anatomy

Each intussusception has the following pathologic anatomy (see Fig. 83-1): as the intussusception develops with its prograde bowel peristalsis, the proximal invaginated bowel (intussusceptum) carries its mesentery into the distal recipient bowel (intussuscipiens), and the mesenteric vessels are angulated, squeezed, and compressed between the layers of the intussusceptum. This causes intense local edema of the intussusceptum, which in turn produces venous compression, congestion, and stasis leading to an outpouring of mucus and blood from the engorged intussusceptum, often (but not always) with the classic red currant jelly stool (Fig. 83-4). If and when this process continues unabated, bowel congestion and pressure increase and ultimately produce ischemic changes leading to bowel necrosis (gangrene) in the intussusceptum. This anatomic observation was also demonstrated experimentally by Ravitch[144]; he noted that the outermost layer of bowel containing the intussusceptum becomes devitalized first, the innermost layer of the intussusceptum becomes gangrenous much later, and the outermost layer of the intussuscipiens rarely, if ever, loses its viability. However, a combined Toronto/Ottawa 1981[48,92,113] review of seven perforations during attempted hydrostatic enema reduction over a 25-year period showed the perforations to occur in the colon (intussuscipiens) near the intussusceptum. The pathologic specimens had one or several perforations from pinpoint to 2-cm tears through an area or areas of necrotic colon, often inches apart; three colons had multiple perforations.[48] There was one area of ischemia in the terminal ileum (intussusceptum). Microscopic examination revealed full-thickness ischemia at the areas of perforation. In each of the seven cases, the intussusceptum was edematous and some were necrotic. All the intussusceptions were ileocolic and none had a PLP. In a 1995 Toronto series of seven more enema perforations (this time with air), the perforations were again located in the intussuscipiens (colon).[33] Karnak et al.[98] (1999) recognized a pathologically weakened longitudinal linear area in five patients who had resected intussusception bowel segments. The bowel wall was grossly very thin and effaced on palpation along the taenia; it appeared as a whitish line and microscopically showed mucosal necrosis, disruption of the muscularis mucosa, and loss of some of its muscular tissue. This line is said to result from compression of the inner layers of the intussuscipiens wall between the intussusceptum and the noncompliant outer layer taenia. This location on the antimesenteric border and under the taenia libera can be explained by local vascular compromise as a result of the distribution of the terminal arteries of the colon. Thus, the antimesenteric border (as well as the mesenteric side) should be checked carefully for a longitudinal weakened pressure line. Recognition of such a potentially dangerous weak line on the bowel wall is an indication for resection. The HSC/Ottawa[48] study further calculated that when ischemic necrosis is present, the intussuscipiens (almost always the colon) had contained the swollen intussusceptum for longer than 72 hours. Moreover, the completeness of the SBO suggested that the tightness of the intussusceptum within the intussuscipiens contributed to the aforementioned findings.

Two events, which Ravitch[145] considered "evidences of neglect," will occur if the ischemic process goes undiagnosed. Ravitch estimated that this event would be fatal (if untreated) between 2 and 5 days. Just as rare, it has been known from the earliest days of our knowledge about intussusception that it can become gangrenous and slough, with the bowel fusing and the separated necrotic intussusceptum passing out the rectum, provided that the patient does not die of intestinal obstruction or sepsis. This latter occurrence was at a much earlier date in intussusception history and represented almost the only hope for survival. Earlier publications[145] claimed that bowel slough took 10 to 20 days to develop and occurred mostly in older children. These two very serious complications of pediatric intussusception are at present seldom, if ever seen.

Types

Intussusception can be categorized into four types (general, specific, anatomic, and other) based on different features: (1) the two general types are permanent (fixed, 80%) and transient (spontaneous reduction, 20%); (2) the specific types can be described as idiopathic (no PLP, 95%), PLP (4%), and postoperative (1%); (3) when classified by anatomic types, their actual occurrence is ileocolic (85%); ileoileocolic (10%); appendicocolic, cecocolic, or colocolic (2.5%); jejunojejunal, ileoileal (2.5%); and around tubes; and (4) the fourth type is "other," and under this category is recurrent (5%). These types will be discussed as listed and in order of appearance on the pathogenesis algorithm (Fig. 83-5).

General

Permanent (Fixed)

The vast majority (80%) of intussusceptions are permanent (fixed), mostly symptomatic (85%), and all require treatment.

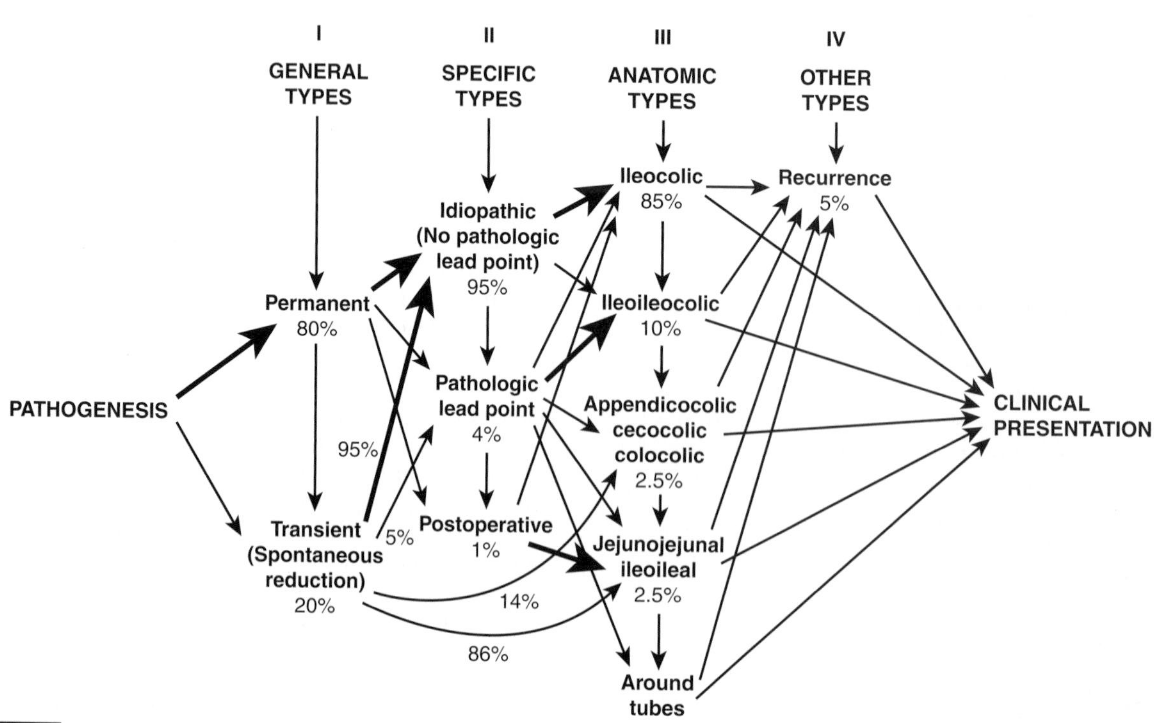

Figure 83-5 Algorithm of the pathogenesis of intussusception.

Transient (Spontaneous Reduction)

Spontaneous reduction of an intussusception is not an uncommon event and has been reported to occur in almost 20% of intussusceptions (transient) (see Fig. 83-5).[126] It can range from the pre-intussusception story, where 7% of parents claim that their infant or child had a similar attack (? unproven intussusception), and if so it must have undergone spontaneous complete reduction.[145] This remains open to speculation. In the 1968 Toronto series,[51] when the rate of reduction was not as successful as it is now, 10% of intussusceptions that were not reduced by hydrostatic BE were found at subsequent laparotomy to have spontaneously reduced as denoted by bruising and edema of the lead point area. Furthermore, it has always been a recognized phenomenon in laparotomy (in which retroperitoneal dissection or resection and a lot of bowel handling and retraction have taken place) that there are occasional (sometimes multiple) small bowel intussusceptions of a few (<2) centimeters at different sites that also spontaneously reduce. Currently, the larger number of infants and children reported with spontaneously reduced intussusceptions may be related to the more frequent use of abdominal US[121] and a better appreciation of the imaging appearance of an intussusception documented while performing small bowel barium studies, as well as on many computed tomography studies.[126] Eighty-six percent of these transient intussusceptions involve only the small bowel[168] and are noted in the central and left abdominal regions.[126] More than half of these children are asymptomatic, and intussusception is an incidental finding on the aforementioned studies performed for other diseases and abnormalities, some of which may predispose to the occurrence of transient intussusception because of bowel wall thickness and abnormal motility. Transient intussusception may also be seen with the clinical symptoms of gastroenteritis, probably because of hyperactivity of the inflamed bowel. One interesting aspect of these intussusceptions is that the small bowel intussusception does not always correlate with the presence of colicky abdominal pain. Moreover, Kornecki et al.[104] and Siaplaouras et al.[158] reported that only 5% to 6% of the patients who were symptomatic had some kind of gastrointestinal pathology that may have served as a PLP.[126] Other reports claim a larger percentage of cases with a PLP.[126] The smaller number of these transient, spontaneously reduced intussusceptions may indicate a sampling difference because some pediatric radiologists do not routinely evaluate the bowel on abdominal US in asymptomatic patients.[126] In an otherwise normal asymptomatic child, it can be assumed that an asymptomatic small bowel intussusception (and those found in an infant or child with acute gastroenteritis) will spontaneously reduce and require no more than clinical observation, with no additional imaging necessary as long as the intussusception remains asymptomatic.

Specific

Idiopathic (No Pathologic Lead Point)

Most (95%) idiopathic intussusceptions occur in the ileocolic area (ileocolic, 85%; ileoileocolic, 10%) and are said to have no PLP (see Fig. 83-5). Actually, all intussusceptions have a lead point of some kind, but in the vast majority (more than 90%) the lead point is thickened bowel wall lymphoid tissue (Peyer's patches).[129,144,145,183] Infants and children have considerable masses of lymphoid tissue (tonsils, adenoids, lymph nodes), and when viral infections (respiratory, gastrointestinal) involve the lymphoid tissues, there may be enlargement (hypertrophy) of the distal ileal wall lymphoid tissues (lymphoid hyperplasia). Usually, Peyer's patches are located in the antimesenteric area of the bowel wall, but as one approaches the distal ileum, the Peyer patches begin to involve the entire circumference of the bowel and narrow the lumen for the oncoming peristaltic wave, thereby setting up the impending obstructing ileocolic intussusception. Furthermore, the nearby mesenteric lymph nodes may also be enlarged as a result of the viral disease or because of the actual intussusception, or both. This association of viral illness preceding or contributing to pediatric intussusception definitely occurs in about 20% of series (Dennison,[41] Strang,[163] Toronto[51]). Both adenovirus[119,176] and rotavirus[124,185] infections (and their vaccines) give rise to lymphoid hyperplasia and have been associated with childhood intussusception. As a matter of fact, this prompted the U.S. Food and Drug Administration to suspend the tetravalent rotavirus vaccine in July 1999 because of a possible link with 20 cases of intussusception. This issue remains hotly debated in the literature,[159] and much research continues in this area (see Table 83-2). There is no question that intussusception tends to occur most often during certain times of the year when there is a peak (outbreak) of viral infections.[46,51]

Pathologic Lead Point

In a review of the literature, Blakelock and Beasley[11] found that the incidence of a PLP causing intussusception in an infant or child ranged from 1.5% to 12% (see Fig. 83-5). The average seems to be 8%; the Toronto experience is 4%.[34,36,44-46,50,51,53,126,128] The incidence of PLP also increases with age: from 5% in the first year to 60% in the 5- to 14-year-old group. Turner[183] reported a 22% incidence in children older than 2 years, and Navarro and Daneman[126] showed that 44% occurred within the first 5 years of life. They are also present in 4% of infants and children who have one recurrent intussusception and in up to 14% of those with multiple recurrences.

Two types of PLP may occur: focal (single) lesions or diffuse abnormalities of the gastrointestinal tract. Virtually all papers on this topic confirm that the most common cause of a PLP is an inverted Meckel diverticulum,[36,134] followed by polyps[6] (mostly ileal) (Fig. 83-6) and duplications (mostly ileal and cecal).[1,7,45] Other less common focal PLPs that have been reported are periappendicitis, appendiceal stump, appendiceal mucocele, local suture line, massive local lymphoid hyperplasia, ectopic pancreas, abdominal trauma, benign tumors (adenoma, leiomyoma, carcinoid, neurofibroma, hemangioma), and malignant tumors (lymphoma, sarcoma, leukemia).[126] Diseases that involve the bowel more diffusely by causing bowel wall thickening or affecting bowel motility (or both) and have caused intussusception[126] include

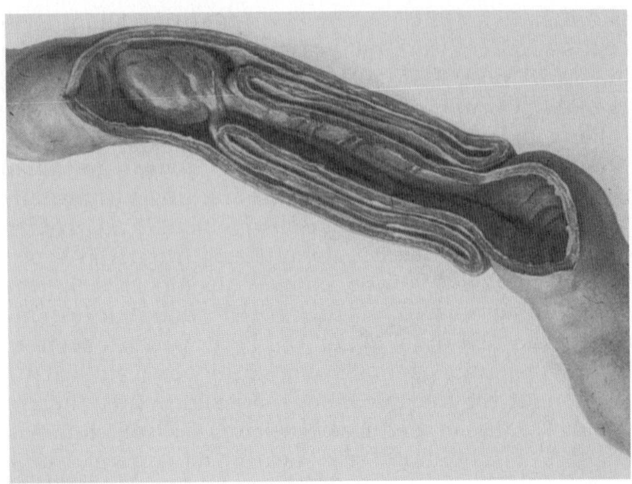

Figure 83–6 Small bowel intussusception caused by the second most common focal (single) pathologic lead point (polyp, mostly in the distal ileum).

Henoch-Schönlein purpura,[89] cystic fibrosis,[87] celiac disease, disordered coagulation, hemophilia, neutropenic colitis, Hirschsprung's enterocolitis, Peutz-Jeghers syndrome, and familial polyposis. A more extensive list of the less common PLPs is found in a 1992 report by Stringer et al.,[166] and this list has been updated in case reports from 1998 to 2004 (see Table 83-1).

Intussusception originating from a PLP remains a diagnostic challenge[32,37] because of the varied and often nonspecific manifestations and the wide spectrum of types of lesions and diffuse bowel abnormalities.[126,128] Differentiation of an intussusception secondary to a PLP from the more common ileocolic intussusception (idiopathic because it does not have a PLP) is relevant in that management may be different in each group. Because the focal lesions causing an intussusception usually have no specific initial symptoms or signs, the most significant clinical clue to an intussusception caused by a PLP is the presence of an underlying disease that may predispose to the development of an intussusception.[126] The intussusception is due to thickening of the bowel wall, abnormal bowel motility, impaction of secretions, or the presence of multiple polyps. These diseases result in diffuse abnormalities that involve the bowel wall, as well as other parts of the body. Navarro and Daneman[126] reported that 35% of their PLP patients had one of these predisposing conditions (underlying disease). Four other important factors that may be associated with the presence of a PLP include an ileoileocolic intussusception, an older child, the association of a long duration of symptoms with weight loss, and recurrent intussusception.

Most PLPs are anatomically manifested as ileoileocolic intussusceptions, with a smaller percentage being jejunojejunal, ileoileal, ileocolic, appendicocolic, cecocolic, and colocolic intussusceptions. Although ileoileocolic intussusception does occur without a PLP, 40% are caused by a definite PLP.[45]

Even though PLP-associated intussusceptions do occur in older children (or older children tend to have intussusceptions caused by a PLP), Ong and Beasley[132] documented that the greatest number of episodes of PLP-associated intussusception still occurs in the first year of life. Blakelock and Beasley[11] showed that the percentage of intussusceptions secondary to a PLP increases with age: from 5% in children younger than 1 year to 60% in those between 5 and 14 years of age. Therefore, although the age of the patient may be considered a predictor of the possible presence of a PLP (particularly when the intussusception occurs in a neonate or a child older than 5 years), it is important to be aware that a PLP can and does occur often even in infants and children who are in the most common age range for ileocolic (idiopathic) intussusception.

Most of these PLP-related intussusceptions also have the same symptoms and signs seen in the more common idiopathic ileocolic type. The concern about missing a malignant small bowel tumor (lymphoma) is quite overstated in the literature.[114,174] A study of over 1200 infants and children in Toronto[53] over a 40-year period revealed 11 lymphomas manifested as an intussusception caused by a PLP. Most patients were older than 4½ years, were chronically ill, sometimes for several months, and had weight loss and an abdominal mass, all of which pointed to a malignant process. Ten of the 11 ileocolic lymphoma intussusceptions were reduced with barium, but all 10 left a residual filling defect. On US, a lymphoma appears as a lobulated, hypoechoic mass in the intussusceptum[126]; however, there have been rare cases reported in which benign reactive lymphoid hyperplasia was so prominent that it mimicked the appearance of a lymphoma and required resection for histologic clarification.[128] Therefore, all things considered, it is really quite difficult to miss the rare lymphoma that causes a pediatric intussusception.

The overall incidence of PLP reported in infants and children varies widely and ranges up to 12%, but the Toronto[126] experience indicates that the incidence of PLP may be higher in patients with recurrent intussusception, up to 33%.[34] Navarro et al.[127] noted that there was no pattern of recurrence or clinical indicators that was predictive of a PLP. Therefore, imaging plays a major role in documentation of the presence or absence of a PLP.[117] They did show that a PLP was present in 4% to 5% of those who had just one recurrence, as opposed to 14% to 19% (in several series) of their patients who had more than one recurrent intussusception. Although multiple recurrences do suggest the presence of a PLP, most pediatric patients with a PLP will have only a single episode of recurrence because the PLP will be diagnosed on imaging findings (during evaluation of the first episode of intussusception) or at surgery because of its irreducibility. It must be remembered that the majority of infants and children who do have recurrences will not have a PLP. In the Toronto series,[126] long-term follow-up of patients (with as many as eight successfully reduced recurrences) revealed no further clinical problems or documentation of a PLP after their last intussusception, thus suggesting that these recurrences were unlikely to be due to a PLP.

Irreducibility of an intussusception (after one or several enema attempts) does not necessarily predict a PLP, but it is a moot point because such irreducibility is an absolute indication for surgery. In an earlier publication[45] it was stated that all intussusceptions caused by a PLP were irreducible by hydrostatic enema and, of necessity, required operative intervention. That has since been shown to be incorrect (Toronto, 1986),[50] and in a later series (Toronto, 2000),[128] the BE reduction rate of intussusceptions caused by a PLP was 50% and the air enema (AE) reduction rate was as high as 60%.[42] In PLP-associated intussusceptions that are reduced by BE, a persistent filling defect is often (40%) noted in the barium column in the ileocolic area or colon (Fig. 83-7); however, such is frequently not the case in those reduced by AE (11%). US proved to be the cornerstone modality in this series because it diagnosed two thirds of the PLPs.[35]

US skill is very operator dependent. The Toronto group diagnosed 64% of all PLPs—74% of focal PLPs, 40% of diffuse PLPs—and provided a specific diagnosis of the exact type of PLP in 32%.[126] They concluded that US was extremely useful in the diagnosis of a duplication cyst and lymphoma as a PLP, but less so for a Meckel diverticulum[35] and a polyp, and US was not expected to be specific with a PLP that affects the bowel diffusely.

If US is used routinely for the diagnosis of intussusception, the radiologist has an opportunity to look for the presence of a PLP. No scientific data are available on what to do in patients in whom the US findings are negative but the index of suspicion for the presence of a PLP is high.[126] There is little information in the literature regarding the use of other imaging modalities to look for a PLP not identified by US; computed tomography[28] was of limited value. Contrast studies of the small and large bowel[39] and colonoscopy may be of some value if a polyp is suspected despite negative US results. An initially negative US study should never exclude repeat US in suspicious cases.

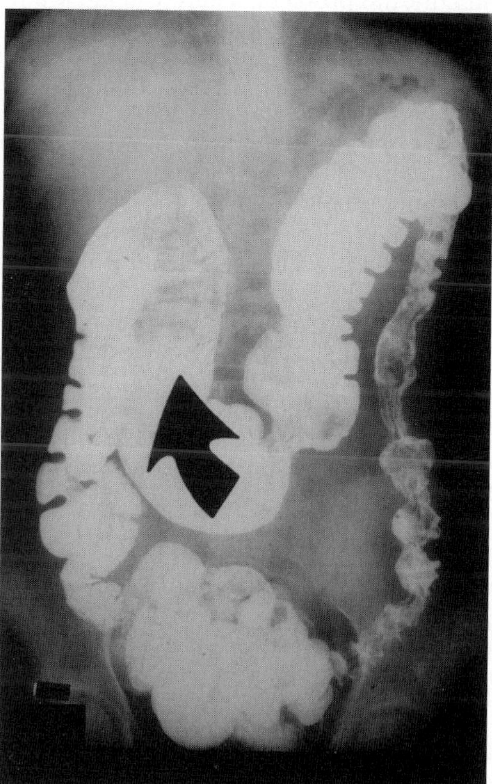

Figure 83-7 Rare hydrostatic contrast enema reduction of colocolic intussusception caused by a large Peutz-Jeghers polyp in the right transverse colon. The pathogenic lead point remains as a filling defect after successful reduction.

Postoperative

The third most common category of intussusception is postoperative[3,10,47,86,118,177] (1%) (see Fig. 83-5), and it is manifested as SBO (see Fig. 83-2). It is usually found after a prolonged laparotomy with significant bowel retraction and handling, almost always involves only the small bowel, but is occasionally ileocolic. Small bowel intussusceptions (the first component of an ileoileocolic intussusception) often (40%) have a PLP as the cause,[51] although the typical postoperative small bowel intussusception does not (Fig. 83-8).[20] Given that the risk for adhesive bowel obstruction after pediatric laparotomy performed for any reason is 5% (with 80% occurring within the first 2 years after laparotomy), it is estimated that this type of intussusception accounts for 5% to 10% of all postoperative SBO in pediatric patients.[96] The majority of SBOs seem to occur after retroperitoneal dissection (Wilms' tumor, neuroblastoma) or an extensive bowel procedure (abdominoperineal pull-through, the Ladd procedure).[126] During many laparotomies it is not unusual to see one or several small (<2 cm) intussusceptions involving the small bowel that spontaneously reduce as they are observed; they generally signify nothing pathologic and seldom if ever become of any clinical significance. They are not predictive of later postoperative intussusception.

On the other hand, a number of authors[11,100,177] have reported cases of intussusception occurring after surgery performed on structures *outside* the abdomen. Abnormal peristalsis from many causes—abnormal

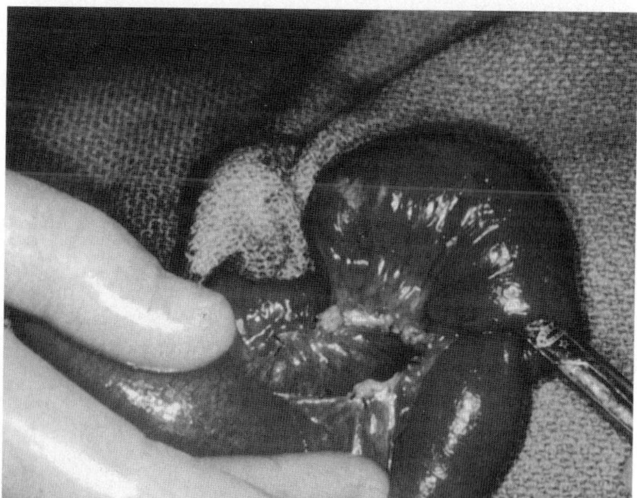

Figure 83-8 Small bowel intussusception most often caused by a pathologic lead point (PLP). It is the most common type of postoperative intussusception, but in the latter case it is almost never associated with a PLP.

serum electrolytes, chemotherapy, radiotherapy, anesthesia, drugs, and neurogenic factors—have been implicated. This seems rather coincidental, probably speculative, and about as common as acute appendicitis developing in someone in the hospital while recovering from another surgical procedure. The key to the diagnosis of a "true" postoperative intussusception is to remember that it can and does occur, especially after a major laparotomy. It is manifested early in the postoperative course as an SBO and may be imperceptible from immediate postoperative adynamic ileus. US is diagnostic, and if it is thought to be a rare ileocolic intussusception, an attempt at enema reduction is warranted; otherwise, an operation is required to reduce the intussusception and is curative. Further postoperative recurrence is exceedingly rare.[55]

Anatomic

Ileocolic

Ileocolic is the most common type and was discussed earlier in the section "Idiopathic (No Pathologic Lead Point)" (see Fig. 83-5).

Ileoileocolic

The second most common (4%) type of intussusception, ileoileocolic[51] (see Fig. 83-5), has two anatomic components: the first is the ileoileal portion, which then invaginates into the cecum and colon and becomes ileoileocolic (Fig. 83-9). The incidence of this type has been reported to be as high as 5% to 12% in other series.[69,169] These intussusceptions are often characterized by a more complete SBO and, as such, are more difficult to reduce (25% success with BE,[48] probably higher with AE). Although an ileoileocolic intussusception can occur in the idiopathic group with no PLP, 40% will have a PLP as its underlying cause.[51]

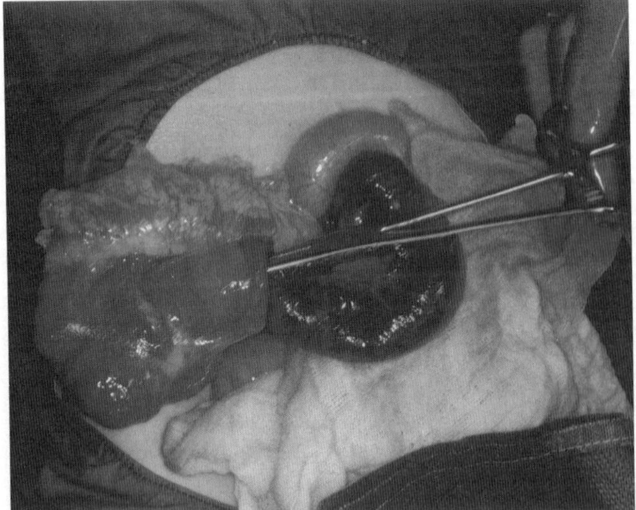

Figure 83-9 Ileoileocolic intussusception showing reduction of the ileocolic component (note the cecum and ascending colon congested but empty) and partial reduction of the ileoileal component with obvious necrotic terminal ileum.

Appendicocolic, Cecocolic, and Colocolic

These types of intussusception are much less common (2.5%) and are usually associated with PLPs (see Fig. 83-5).

Jejunojejunal and Ileoileal

Jejunojejunal and ileoileal intussusceptions occur infrequently (2.5%) and usually have a PLP (see Fig. 83-5), except when they occur as a postoperative intussusception (see Fig. 83-8).

Around Tubes

Intussusception around tubes in the intestinal tract has become an increasing problem noted over the last decade, during which time tubes have become much more commonly used either for decompression or for feeding (see Fig. 83-5). It has been reported (Hughes and Connolly[90]) that an intussusception develops with 16% of gastrojejunostomy tubes.[91] This complication does occur with all different types of catheters and tubes placed into the jejunum (regardless of the route), with the pigtail variety being the most frequent culprit. These intussusceptions are antegrade (prograde), usually occur in the jejunum either along or at the end of the gastrojejunostomy[25] or nasojejunal tube,[90] and cause a high SBO with bilious vomiting but without cramps or pain. The diagnosis is easily made by US, and removing, replacing, pulling back, or converting the tube to a gastrostomy or nasogastric tube will cure the problem. There is seldom a need for surgical reduction of the intussusception, but they can be recurrent. Many of these intussusceptions are also transient and undergo spontaneous reduction, which suggests that their actual prevalence is probably underestimated. It is not unusual for such a tube-induced intussusception to be found both incidentally and asymptomatically, for which the only treatment may be conservative clinical monitoring. Retrograde jejunoduodenogastric intussusceptions[60,63,175] occur when gastrostomy tubes migrate by gastric peristalsis through the pylorus and into the duodenum or jejunum (or both). Once again, they develop painlessly in a child with a functioning feeding tube (with the feedings going in distally) and a high SBO accompanied by bile vomiting without any evidence of the feeding. The causative factor here is attempted pull-back of the migrated gastrostomy tube with the balloon (if present) still inflated. Although US again can make the diagnosis, an operation may be required. An even more unusual intussusception that has occasionally been reported is antegrade or retrograde jejunogastric intussusception through a gastroenterostomy, which is usually manifested as a gastric outlet obstruction. This intussusception almost always requires operative reduction.

Other

Recurrent

In the 1968 Toronto series,[51] the overall recurrence rate was 5%: 11% after BE reduction, 3% after operative manual reduction, and of more than interest, 0% after

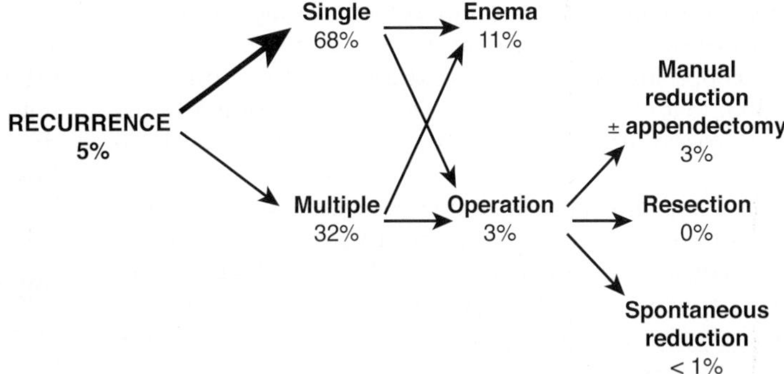

Figure 83-10 Algorithm for recurrent intussusception.

operative resection of an intussusception (see Fig. 83-5). Other series have reported total recurrence rates of 8% to 15%.[38] In 1998, a 17-year review from Toronto[34] (compared with the 1968 review[51]) showed that the demographics of all patients with recurrences were similar regardless of management of the previous intussusception with BE or AE. Previous reports have documented recurrence rates mainly related to management with BE because there is less information in series using AE.

The pattern of recurrences showed that 68% of children with a recurrence had only one such recurrence and most occurred within the first few days after the initial intussusception (Fig. 83-10).[34] Some recurred within hours after a successful complete reduction; one was even documented by US before the patient had been taken off the radiology table. The closer the recurrence (in time) to the initial reduction, the more it should be suspected that the initial reduction was incomplete and not recurrent. The remaining 32% of patients had multiple recurrences that occurred as isolated episodes over a period of days, weeks, months, or years or in clusters of up to eight during the initial hospitalization.[34] In 2000, Lin et al.[107] used intramuscular dexamethasone as a premedication before AE in an attempt to decrease the rate of early recurrence by minimizing the lymphoid hyperplasia. There was only one recurrence in 122 patients who received the steroid over a 6-month follow-up, which was statistically better than controls. Though seemingly beneficial, further validation has not been forthcoming.

Several series[34,44,57] have shown a very high reducibility rate of both the initial and recurrent intussusceptions in patients with recurrence (90% and 95%, respectively), with no perforations occurring in one series.[34] This high rate is due to several factors: (1) the time between the onset of recurrent symptoms and signs and arrival at the hospital is shorter (average of 8 hours) in children who have had a previous intussusception because of the awareness of the parents.[44] The earlier the diagnosis, the greater the chance for successful reduction. (2) It has been suggested that recurrent intussusceptions are looser (may have better perfusion) and therefore easier to reduce, but they also have a greater chance of recurring.[34] The reduction rate is higher (95%) in the more recent series,[34] which probably reflects more persistent (but controlled) techniques.

It has been shown that a PLP was present in 4% of the children who had one recurrence and 14% of those with multiple recurrences.[126] It is therefore essential to consider the presence of a PLP in all infants and children with a recurrence, particularly in those with multiple recurrences. Despite these facts, it must be remembered that most pediatric intussusceptions that are recurrent are not associated with a PLP. Aside from some diffuse bowel problems that suggest a PLP as the cause of the recurrent intussusception, there is usually no clinical indication that a PLP may be present, nor is there any pattern of recurrence that is suggestive of a PLP. There is no absolute rule regarding how many recurrences a child has to have before one looks for a PLP; US should be used early and often, possibly supplemented by bowel contrast studies. Management depends on one's comfort level with this approach and, of course, the proximity to experienced radiologic and surgical care before considering surgery. Previous reports[57] have recommended that operative reduction is warranted in infants and children with one or two recurrences. The reasons given include the search for a PLP (especially a lymphoma in the distal ileum) and an attempt to diminish the possibility of future recurrences. However, most of these infants and children with a recurrence (even multiple) do not have a PLP, and furthermore, operative reduction does not guarantee against recurrence, although it lowers the risk from 11% to 3%.[51] Therefore, because of the high reduction rate (95%) of these recurrences, a low perforation rate (<1%), and favorable long-term follow-up, it is generally recommended that image-guided reduction (preferably AE) be undertaken for any and all recurrent intussusceptions. Surgery should be used only for irreducible recurrences after delayed repeat attempts are unsuccessful, if there is a perforation from the enema, or if the presence of a PLP is documented by an imaging procedure.

CLINICAL FINDINGS AND DIAGNOSIS

The presence of two classic symptoms (abdominal pain, vomiting) and two classic signs (abdominal mass, rectal bleeding) helps make the diagnosis of intussusception in an infant or child (see Fig. 83-3).[51] The average length of time before any combination of these four symptoms and signs leads to a diagnosis is about 24 hours (42% in 12 hours and 70% in 24 hours).[51] Strangely, for no explicable reason the average time until diagnosis increased to 36 hours when the group in Toronto looked at almost 300 more intussusceptions from 1985 to 1990,[46] 25 years after its previous series of more than 300 cases from 1959 to 1968.[51] Not unexpectedly, however, it took only 8 hours for recurrent intussusception to be diagnosed, thanks to astute parents.[44]

The symptoms and signs needed to make the clinical diagnosis of intussusception should not be difficult to recognize, as long as one is aware of them.[69,145] However, all that is needed is a history of crampy abdominal pain, especially in an infant. Usually, one, two, or three of the other classic symptoms or signs (vomiting, rectal bleeding, abdominal mass) are present to help confirm the diagnosis. If one waits for all four classic symptoms and signs to be present (in only 30% of cases!) before making the diagnosis, it will be delayed.[51] Similarly, three of four symptoms and signs are present in only 40% of cases, two of four in 20%, and one of four in 10%.[52] Moreover, in about 20% of pediatric intussusception patients, (viral) diarrhea[51] precedes the intussusception symptoms and signs and is also a cause for delay in diagnosis. Not infrequently, these infants and children with diarrhea[51] are either sent home or admitted to the infectious disease unit with the incorrect diagnosis of gastroenteritis. This delay may have potentially serious consequences.[145] Temperature and laboratory investigations generally correlate with the clinical picture, with shock and hypovolemia being later events in the intussusception spectrum.

Symptoms

The most common (85%) classic symptom of pediatric intussusception is a sudden onset of severe, colicky, intermittent abdominal pain that brings the legs up (in infants) and lasts only a few minutes.[51] After the episode of pain the infant is often quiet, pale, and sweaty and then returns to normal activity for a while. An older child can frequently complain about the pain and indicate where it is located. Of major importance is the fact that 15% of these infants and children have no obvious pain. This was described in a report from Toronto in 1976,[52] and one of the authors (the late Clint Stephens) insisted on its publication. As a matter of fact, the first editor of the *Journal of Pediatric Surgery* (C. Everett Koop) wrote the authors questioning the authenticity of the painless history of the intussusception. Patients who have no pain with their intussusception (for reasons that are as yet unexplained) when first seen (later than usual), are pale and listless and appear quite ill. Indeed, the absence of pain (even with vomiting, an abdominal mass, and rectal bleeding all present) doubles the duration of time to 51 hours before diagnosis.[52] Ravitch[145] noted that pain, when present, was more common in a child older than 2 years. Needless to say, the absence of pain does not rule out intussusception.

Both Ravitch[145] and Young[183] wrote that not only did most countries have similar clinical pictures of intussusception, but surprisingly, they also found that vomiting was the most common initial symptom (44%), ahead of the classic abdominal pain. Both Toronto series 25 years apart found that vomiting was the second most common symptom after pain, 80% in 1959 to 1968[51] and 48% in 1985 to 1990.[46] This vomiting tends to occur more in infants than in older children, and bilious vomiting secondary to SBO tends to occur in children with later-diagnosed intussusception.[48] The absence of vomiting, however, does not rule out intussusception.

Signs

Of the two classic signs (abdominal mass and rectal bleeding), both occur with about the same frequency.[51]

The abdominal mass, which has been called sausage-like, is most often palpated in the right upper part of the abdomen and extends to the left (epigastrium) along the transverse colon. It is present in most series 65% of the time, but in the 1997 Toronto series,[46] it decreased to 22% for no obvious reason. The mass may be slightly tender and may be appreciated only when the infant or child is lying quietly between attacks of pain. It is therefore understandable that a pediatric patient with a painless intussusception is recognized at a much later time; many of these patients are first seen in shock and are pale, listless, and quite ill. An abdominal mass is usually first appreciated at this time, sometimes visually before palpation (see Fig. 83-4). Of less interest is the so-called absence of palpable bowel in the right lower quadrant, the "signe de Dance."[69] Occasionally, the intussusception passes quite far distally, and 5% were palpated on rectal examination; in two instances the intussusception prolapsed out the rectum, where it was mistakenly diagnosed as a rectal prolapse.[51] Ravitch reported that this so-called rectal prolapse happened 3% of the time.[145] These observations suggest that the absence of a palpable abdominal mass does not rule out an intussusception.

The second sign of note is rectal bleeding, which is more frequently present than an abdominal mass according to Ravitch[145] (95% of infants, 65% of older children). Rectal bleeding occurred in 60% in the 1968 Toronto series[51] and then, for some unexplained reason, in only 43% in the 1997 Toronto series.[46] After the intussusception has occurred and the colon has cleared itself of stool, the blood per rectum is considerable and has a mucus-like texture and, classically, a currant jelly appearance (see Fig. 83-4). It is most alarming to parents, and if there has been a delay in seeking medical care before this event, it usually gets the patient to hospital quickly. Although it was impossible to elicit the one specific symptom or sign that prompted parents to seek medical attention for their infant or child, it was our impression that next to the pain, blood from the rectum was certainly high on the list.[46,51] Most doctors who know about intussusception are aware of the colicky pain and the currant jelly stools, but the delay in diagnosis is often due to the fact that the latter has not occurred. Because the first evidence of blood is frequently seen only when a rectal examination is done or because the bleeding may be occult, a test for blood in the stool must not be omitted if an intussusception is suspected. Rectal bleeding is usually the last sign to occur.[51] Clearly, the absence of rectal bleeding does not rule out intussusception.

The five principles of diagnosis stated by Wansbrough (Toronto, 1953,[51] from a 35-year review of almost 600 cases from 1915 to 1950) still apply: "It is the physicians' duty to exclude intussusception in any infant who refuses to eat or vomits over a period of several hours; rectal blood, or a mass in the abdomen in such an infant should be sought for; the presence of diarrhea does not exclude intussusception; older children with signs of intestinal obstruction may have an intussusception; intussusception should be considered in any infant who passes blood per rectum." To which must be added: Do not forget the colicky abdominal pain!

RADIOLOGIC DIAGNOSIS

Plain Radiograph of the Abdomen

The clinical history and examination may suggest the diagnosis of an intussusception without too much doubt. It is, however, estimated that clinical diagnostic accuracy is about 50%.[9] Therefore, it is our reliance on pediatric radiologists and their imaging that will either confirm or make the correct diagnosis (Fig. 83-11),[75] which is the initial aspect of their involvement, followed by their therapeutic participation (see later).

The role of abdominal radiographs in pediatric patients with suspected intussusception remains controversial.[32] In a 1999 survey of members of the European Society of Pediatric Radiology,[153] the abdominal radiograph was routinely used by 73% of the radiologists. This probably reflects customary practice in all children with symptoms and signs suggestive of any abdominal problem. Usually, two abdominal radiographic findings can confidently exclude the classic idiopathic ileocolic intussusception: (1) an abdominal radiograph filled with gas throughout and (2) a colon completely outlined with stool. Although it may be interesting to know the amount and distribution of bowel gas and fluid before attempting reduction, these features can easily be defined by US or fluoroscopy at the start of the enema. The data available in the literature show that these films (supine, upright, or cross-table lateral) are often not helpful in such patients because false negatives occur (much more frequently than false positives) and their interpretation is variable.[143] Nonetheless, some signs of intussusception are characteristic on a plain radiograph (meniscus sign and target sign).[37] Probably easier to notice are the nonspecific radiographic findings suggestive of a right-sided soft tissue mass combined with an absence of cecal gas (Fig. 83-12).

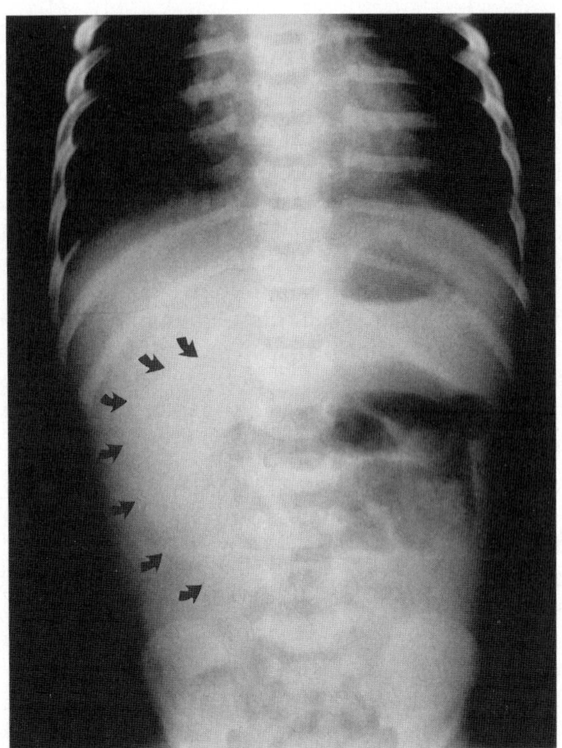

Figure 83-12 Plain radiograph of the abdomen with nonspecific findings suggestive of a right-sided soft tissue mass (*arrows*) combined with an absence of cecal gas.

However, in 45% of children 5 years or younger, the sigmoid colon (filled with gas and stool) often occupies the right lower quadrant and may be misinterpreted as the cecum.[58] Some institutions still rely on plain radiographs for the diagnosis or exclusion of intussusception, but few published studies have evaluated the accuracy of this modality in this clinical setting. Two series have shown that intussusception was correctly identified on plain radiographs in only 45% (Sargent et al.[151]) and 50% (Bolin[12]) of cases. Therefore, these authors concluded that the abdominal radiograph was often unhelpful and, furthermore, agreement on interpretation of the radiographic findings was limited.[178] Eklöf and Hartelius[56] found that even three views of the abdomen enabled intussusception to be excluded in only about 25% of their patients. These extra views are primarily used to identify air-fluid levels and free intraperitoneal air. Air-fluid levels are present almost as frequently in those without intussusception as in those with it. There has yet

Figure 83-11 Algorithm for the radiologic diagnosis of intussusception.

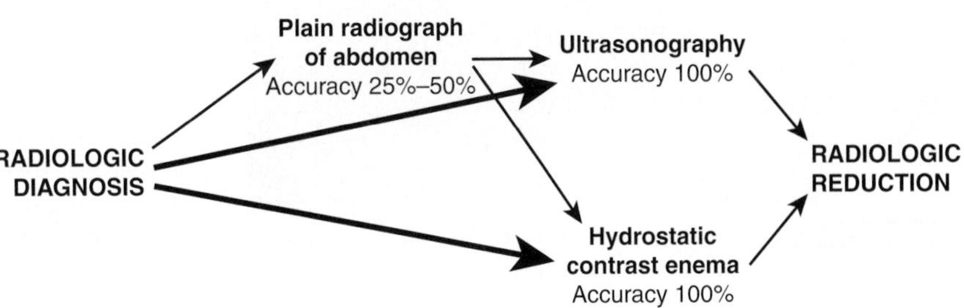

to be found a patient documented in the literature who has had an untreated intussusception and perforation in which free air was present on the abdominal radiographs before attempted enema reduction.[32]

It is now widely believed that if US is used diagnostically (see later), the abdominal film may be safely omitted in the vast majority of infants and children suspected of having an intussusception. This applies to conditions in the developed world, where patients are usually brought for medical attention in a more timely manner. There is probably a greater need for abdominal radiographs, because of the higher probability of peritonitis and perforation, in the developing world, where the delay in diagnosis is longer and patients consequently have an increased incidence of nonviable bowel.[112,172]

Sonography

In 1987, Pracros et al.[140] reported 100% accuracy of US for the diagnosis of intussusception, and since then this high accuracy rate has been verified by several other authors (see Fig. 83-11).[37,75]

Intussusception has a characteristic US appearance that makes diagnosis extremely easy: a 3- to 5-cm (diameter) mass (donut or target sign) usually found just deep to the anterior abdominal wall, mostly on the right side (Fig. 83-13).[37] Without question, the quality, accuracy, and interpretation of the study are operator dependent, thus causing some concern about its use by radiologists who may lack experience and confidence with this technique. With the appropriate training in US and with the use of high-frequency, high-resolution transducers, the diagnosis of intussusception and differentiation of it from other conditions can be achieved. Furthermore, a major advantage is that it is a noninvasive modality. Nonetheless, the use of US for the diagnosis of intussusception, as expected, varies in different parts of the world for the following reasons: lack of expertise, cost, and availability of equipment.[37,153]

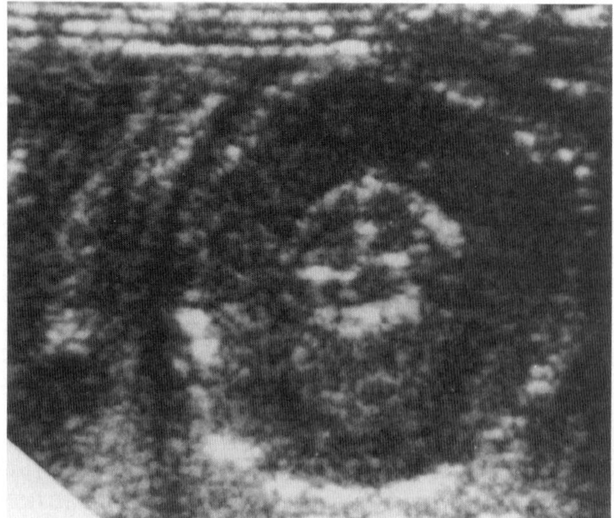

Figure 83-13 Ultrasonogram showing intussusception on cross section in the right lower quadrant just deep to the anterior abdominal wall. This has been referred to as the donut or target sign.

In a patient suspected of having an intussusception, the role of US is not simply limited to the diagnosis or exclusion of this entity. It can also be extremely effective for documenting the presence or absence of a PLP. The series of Navarro et al.[128] found a PLP by US in 66% of patients, 26% more than was found by BE and 55% more than by AE. Pracros et al.[140] reported a 4% detection rate of other intra-abdominal diseases (urinary tract pathology, ovarian cyst torsion, small bowel volvulus) in children suspected of having an intussusception when no intussusception was found.

Sonographic features have also been evaluated in an attempt to predict the reducibility of the intussusception by enema and the presence of bowel necrosis.[36] These signs include a thick peripheral hypoechoic rim of the intussusception, free intraperitoneal fluid, fluid trapped within the intussusceptum, enlarged lymph nodes dragged with the mesentery into the intussusception, a PLP, and of most importance, absence of blood flow in the intussusception on Doppler interrogation. Many studies have shown that none of these US signs are 100% predictive of a successful reduction or not.[36] Therefore, in practice, it is extremely difficult to predict which intussusception will be irreducible or may have necrosis on the basis of US features alone. However, observation of any of the aforementioned features may alert one to the possibility of irreducibility or necrosis, or both, but should not preclude attempting reduction by enema.

Contrast Enema

Barium study of the colon (BE) was considered the gold standard for the diagnosis or exclusion of an intussusception in many parts of the world until the mid-1980s, when the value of US was recognized.[36] However, some institutions still consider contrast enema (with barium) to be the quickest and most cost-effective method.[181] The 1999 European survey of pediatric radiologists[153] showed that contrast enema was used for the diagnosis of an intussusception by 34% of the respondents (Fig. 83-14). The main reasons given for its use included the following: one is less likely to miss an intussusception, it is well known to all radiologists, and the diagnostic procedure (if positive) becomes a therapeutic one. There is no question that this modality is the preferred choice for diagnosis in many parts of the world, and its accuracy in this respect is 100% (see Fig. 83-11).[139,181]

The disadvantages of contrast enema include the fact that it is an invasive procedure that also requires a small dose of radiation.[36] These facts should be considered when deciding to use contrast enema instead of US just for diagnosis since several authors have shown that more than 50% of diagnostic contrast enemas in infants and children suspected of having an intussusception turn out to be negative.[36] This means that the clinical findings with other acute abdominal problems often mimic an intussusception. Finally, contrast enemas (barium, 40%) may not depict as well as US (66%) the presence of other

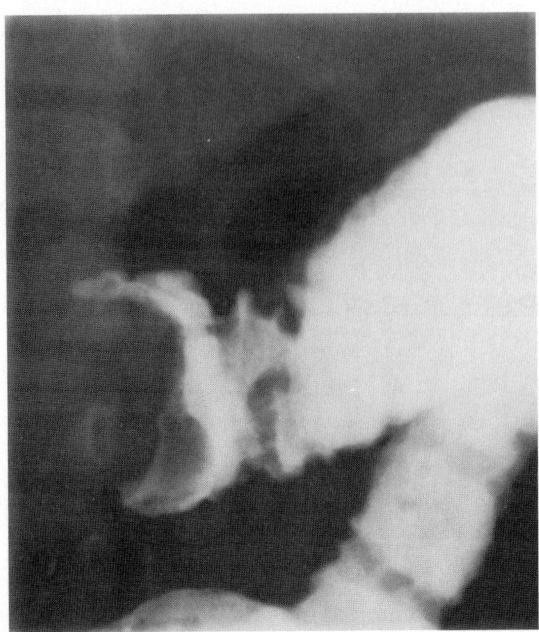

Figure 83-14 Hydrostatic contrast enema with barium showing intussusception in the left transverse colon. Note the concave meniscus the barium makes around the head of the intussusception (intussusceptum).

intra-abdominal pathology (if there is no intussusception), nor the presence of a PLP (if there is an intussusception).[128]

Although other diagnostic modalities (small bowel follow-through,[39] computed tomography,[28] magnetic resonance imaging[173]) can depict an intussusception, their use in the clinical situation of the most common ileocolic and ileoileocolic intussusception is rare. They should be reserved for closer evaluation of selected patients with more complex findings or an atypical US appearance of the intussusception or for better delineation of a suspected PLP.[36,128]

TREATMENT

Treatment of an infant or child with an intussusception must start in the emergency department when they are first seen, and the surgeon must be involved right from the beginning.[179] It is of utmost importance that the patient be properly fluid-resuscitated and, if vomiting, have a nasogastric tube placed on suction. The latter can be omitted if there is a short history and no vomiting. Antibiotics (with anaerobic coverage) should be given as for any other situation in which the vascular supply of the bowel may be jeopardized and bowel surgery is a possibility. The patient's blood should be crossmatched in case a transfusion is needed. While all of this is being done, preparations should be made for radiologic confirmation of the diagnosis (see Fig. 83-11), followed by the necessary treatment. The operating room should be notified so that if the nonoperative management is unsuccessful, the patient can go from the radiology suite directly to the operating room.

The treatment options are really quite simple: medical (under very occasional and specific situations); radiologic reduction (Fig. 83-15) (hydrostatic = fluid, pneumatic = air); or operative reduction, resection, closure of an enema perforation, or excision of a PLP by laparotomy or laparoscopy (Fig. 83-16). Without question, the major change (improvement) in the treatment of intussusception in the past 25 years has been the increased use of attempts at radiologic reduction.[102] Previously in the 1968 Toronto series,[51] only 75% of intussusception patients received a trial of hydrostatic reduction via BE. Currently, virtually all the infants and children receive an attempt at hydrostatic reduction with barium or water-soluble contrast or with pneumatic reduction with air, regardless of the length of the history.

Medical

Under very specific conditions a few intussusceptions, caused by PLPs of the diffuse thickened bowel wall variety, can be treated with steroids before, along with, and/or after radiologic reduction attempts (successful or otherwise). Treatment of at least two such entities (lymphoid hyperplasia, Henoch-Schönlein purpura [HSP]) in this manner has been reported with some degree of success (lymphoid hyperplasia, two cases, 100%[157]; HSP, seven cases, 50%[161]).

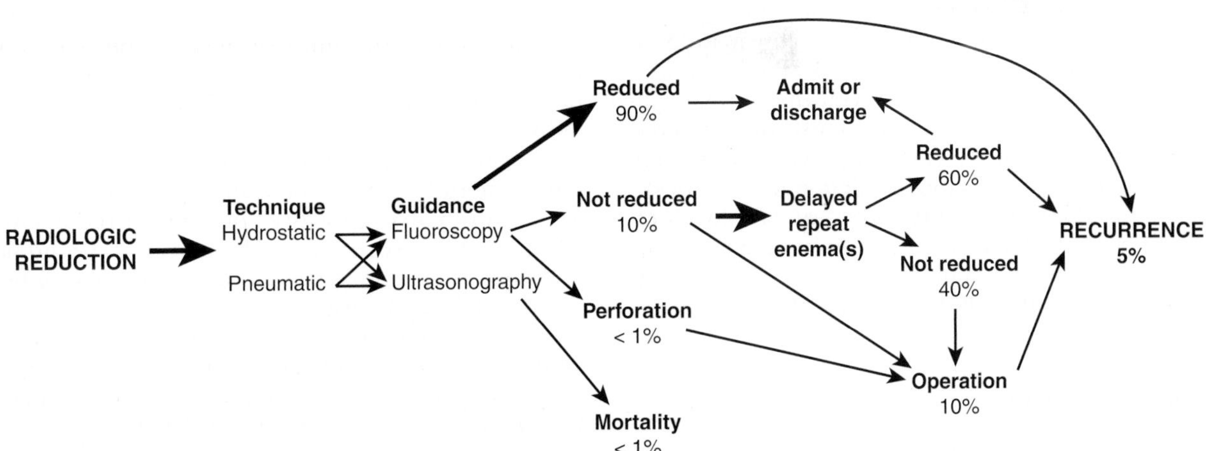

Figure 83-15 Algorithm for radiologic reduction of intussusception.

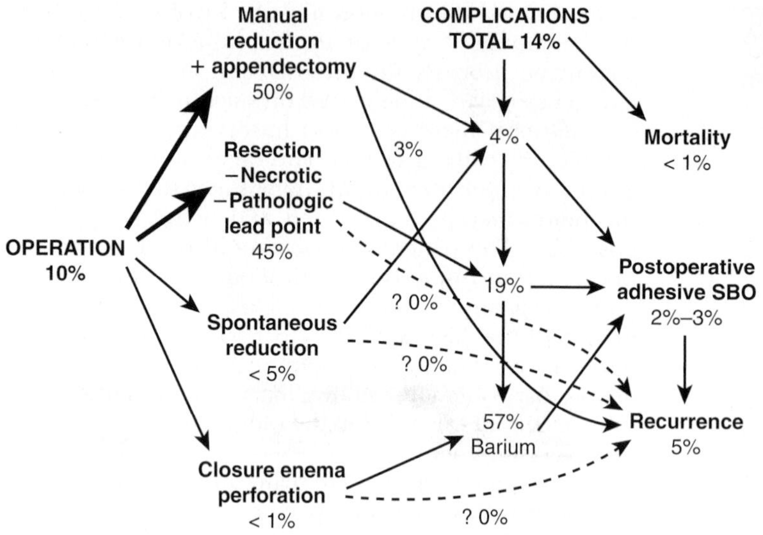

Figure 83-16 Algorithm for surgical intervention for intussusception. SBO, small bowel obstruction.

The mechanism by which steroid treatment affects lymphoid hyperplasia remains unclear. Kokkonen and Karttunen[103] speculated that this entity "can represent a long-standing upregulation of intestinal immunologic activity as a response to luminal food antigens. If this is true, a lymphopenic effect of steroid therapy may be the reason for decrease in lymphoid hyperplasia."

Most patients with HSP have gastrointestinal symptoms,[64] which are initially treated conservatively[26,27]; however, rates of laparotomy performed because of life-threatening complications range from 5% to 22%.[30,76,161] The most frequent of these complications is intussusception, which occurs in 3% of HSP patients.[21] Although these intussusceptions have been reported to occur equally as ileoileal or ileocolic types, six of seven in the aforementioned series were ileoileal. Only the ileocolic intussusceptions are amenable to enema reduction attempts.

The use of steroids in the treatment of HSP patients in general is controversial.[161] A study (comparing patients who received steroids with those who did not) revealed that morbidity such as gastrointestinal pain resolved in a shorter time (usually 24 to 48 hours) in the steroid group. One can deduce from the literature that steroids are beneficial for relieving the symptoms caused by HSP, but not for curing them. This effect of steroids on gastrointestinal symptoms has been attributed to their ability to resolve the edema of the intestinal wall. Whether steroids are effective in preventing intussusception during the course of HSP is unknown.

If steroid treatment is initiated with the intussusception still unreduced, the patient must be observed closely. As Sönmez et al.[161] stated: "Conservative therapy is feasible for HSP patients with small bowel intussusception as long as the time of onset is known, an ultrasonographic and x-ray diagnosis is confirmed, emergency operating facilities are available, and an experienced pediatric surgical team follows up the patients."

Radiologic Reduction

It is important to carefully select infants and children who are suitable candidates for attempted image-guided hydrostatic or pneumatic enema reduction, as opposed to the rare patients who need immediate surgery (see Fig. 83-15). This selection should be delayed until fluid resuscitation is under way and the patient is stable enough for any kind of investigation or treatment. Some investigators have suggested that a contraindication to enema reduction is evidence of peritonitis or free intra-abdominal air. The former is highly unusual and the latter has not occurred in the Toronto experience, nor has a case of intussusception been reported initially with a perforation.[32,37] Several factors are indicative of a possible BE perforation: age younger than 6 months, symptoms present for 72 hours, and complete SBO. These symptoms and signs may even preclude obtaining a diagnostic enema.[48] In general, there is seldom, if ever any reason to not attempt an enema reduction.[38,130] This opinion will vary from one treatment center to another and in different parts of the world. In the developed world, intussusception is diagnosed in the vast majority of pediatric patients and medical care provided in timely fashion. In contrast, operative management remains the usual, primary, and necessary treatment in much of the developing world, as has been described in recent reports from Nigeria[112] and Indonesia.[172] In these areas of the world, infants and children have a significantly longer duration of symptoms and signs, an increased incidence of nonviable bowel, and a mortality rate of 18% to 20%.[38] In such cases, Meier et al.[112] suggested that the use of nonoperative BE reduction would not have significantly improved the high mortality rate.

Four techniques of nonoperative radiologic reduction are commonly used at present[38]: pneumatic reduction with fluoroscopic guidance, pneumatic reduction with US guidance, hydrostatic reduction with US guidance, and hydrostatic reduction with fluoroscopic guidance (see Fig. 83-15). In evaluating these four reduction techniques, one has to be cautious when making comparisons among the various series, even when some radiologists use apparently similar techniques.[116] Two surveys of pediatric radiology departments in North America[115] and members of the European Society of Pediatric Radiology[153] showed that their management of intussusception varied even more than in previous years, but there was a trend toward a change from hydrostatic to pneumatic reduction techniques with greater use of US.[150] The clear advantage of US is that it avoids radiation exposure, provides more information than fluoroscopic techniques do, has high accuracy and reliability for monitoring the reduction process, visualizes all components of the intussusception, including the post-reduction edematous ileocecal valve, and can more easily recognize PLPs.[38] The main disadvantage is the need for a radiologist who is comfortable using US for reduction guidance. There is less experience with pneumatic reduction under US guidance, especially recognizing a perforation when using either hydrostatic or pneumatic reduction techniques.[38]

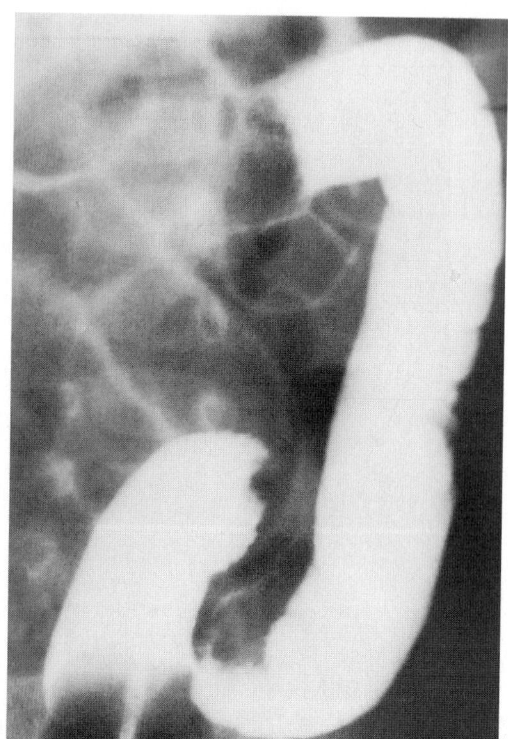

Figure 83–17 Hydrostatic contrast enema showing that when the intussusception is displaced, the meniscus (in Figure 83-14) flattens out.

Hydrostatic Barium Enema

The major advantage of the hydrostatic BE reduction technique is the vast experience and familiarity with this contrast agent and the use of fluoroscopy by most (if not all) radiologists.[18,19,38,133] It is simple, safe, and efficacious. The disadvantages of barium (and any liquid medium) are that they are messy to use and, if a perforation occurs, there are larger colonic tears, increased peritoneal contamination, especially with barium (permanent), and rapid fluid shifts with hypertonic water-soluble agents.[33,48,92]

In the past, the hydrostatic BE technique used in Toronto was a modification of that used by Ravitch.[145] The barium column is started from a height of 3 ft, but it is slowly raised to a higher level if necessary. They did not abandon the BE if the barium column was unchanged for 10 minutes, but would probably not persist for 45 minutes, as suggested by Ravitch.[145] There is great variation in the speed with which the reduction is achieved; it may occur quite rapidly or it may be stubbornly slow. There is usually a pause when the barium column meets the intussusception. Typically, the rounded barium column suddenly becomes concave and forms a meniscus around the head of the intussusception (see Fig. 83-14). When the intussusception is displaced, the meniscus flattens out (Fig. 83-17). Because the intussusceptum fits more loosely in the larger-caliber intussuscipiens, barium seeps between the two and produces the characteristic radiologic appearance of a coiled spring (Fig. 83-18). Filling of the cecum is often slow, and it may become quite distended for a while (Fig. 83-19) before the sudden rush of barium into the distal ileum indicative of reduction. If the ileum does not fill freely for several feet (not inches), one cannot (must not) assume that the reduction is complete (Fig. 83-20). This process may have to be repeated if barium leaks out of the rectum or if the tube becomes dislodged, plugged, or both. Once the reduction is successful, the infant or child is relieved of the pain and usually falls asleep.

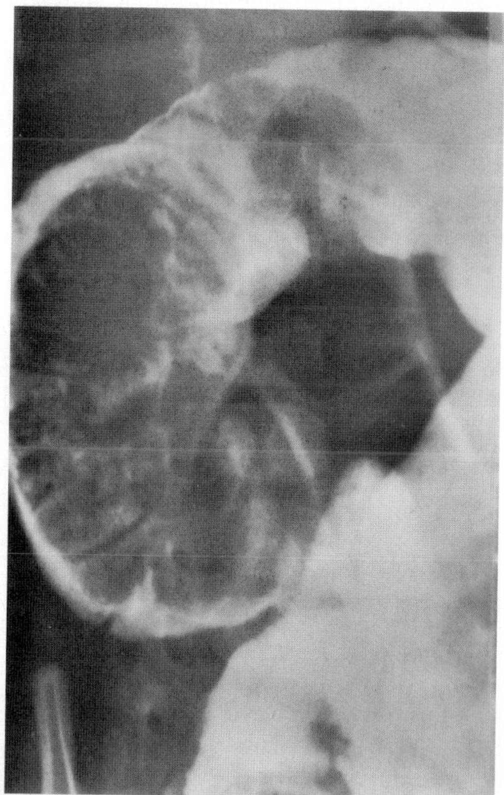

Figure 83–18 Hydrostatic contrast enema showing that when the intussusceptum fits more loosely in the larger-caliber intussuscipiens, contrast seeps between the two and produces the characteristic radiologic appearance of a coiled spring.

Pneumatic Air Enema

The pneumatic reduction technique under fluoroscopy has gained wide acceptance because of several advantages: it is easy to perform, can be done quickly, is less

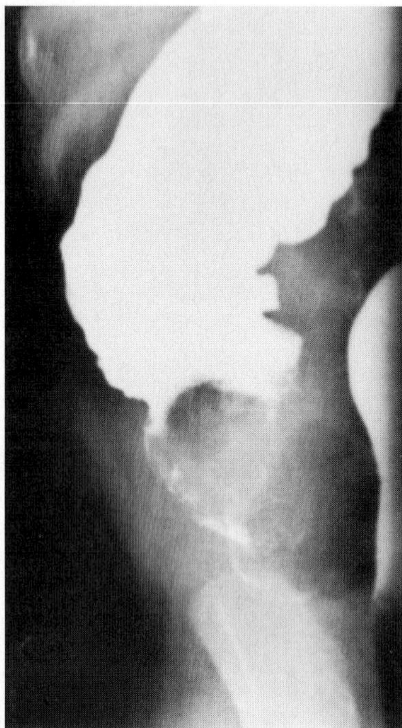

Figure 83-19 Hydrostatic contrast enema showing that filling of the cecum is often slow and it becomes quite distended for a period before the sudden rush of contrast into the distal ileum denotes reduction of the intussusception.

messy, delivers less radiation exposure, is more comfortable, and results in smaller perforations and less peritoneal contamination (Fig. 83-21).[164] Disadvantages of this technique are the passage of air into the terminal ileum without complete reduction of the ileocolic intussusception[79,125] and a possible tension pneumoperitoneum should a rare perforation occur.[164] The Toronto pediatric radiologists[32,35-38,46,133] have written frequently about this technique since it was introduced to them by Gu et al.[70] They start with a low (but often successful) pneumatic pressure of 50 mm Hg and slowly increase the pressure as necessary, never exceeding 110 to 120 mm Hg.[156]

Methods to Improve Reduction Rates

Some authors have advocated practices that they believe may improve the rate of enema reduction.

Medications

For the use of steroids, see the earlier section "Medical." Smooth muscle relaxants (especially glucagon[62,88]) and sedation have been used to help in attempts to reduce an intussusception, with indefinite and variable results.[2,62,108,122] Until the more recent cautious, persistent attempts by pediatric radiologists to increase the reduction rate of irreducible intussusceptions that required surgery, 10% were found in the operating room to already be reduced. Either they reduced spontaneously, or more likely, reduction was induced by the sedation and muscle relaxation from general anesthesia. In a 1992 survey by Meyer,[115] it was found that glucagon and sedation were not being used in most North American pediatric radiology departments. Similarly, in a 1999 survey of European pediatric radiologists, sedation was routinely used by only 35%.[153] Overall, little clinical evidence either supports or condemns the use of sedation in reducing an intussusception. These results are similar to those reported by Ravitch[145] when he reviewed publications concerning this topic from 1977 to 1986.

Transabdominal Manipulation

Despite Ravitch's opposition[145] to transabdominal manipulation by manual pressure, Grasso et al.[67] found that such manipulation improved their AE reduction rate from 58% to 76%. Although some believe that this

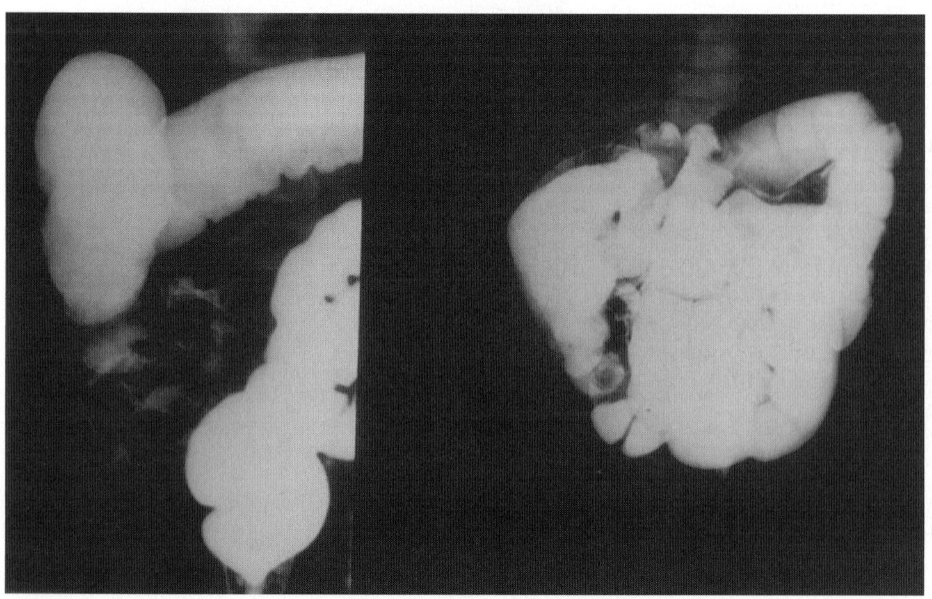

Figure 83-20 Hydrostatic contrast enema showing incomplete reduction of intussusception with only a trickle of contrast into the terminal ileum on the left. Note the complete reduction with flooding of the terminal ileum with contrast on the right.

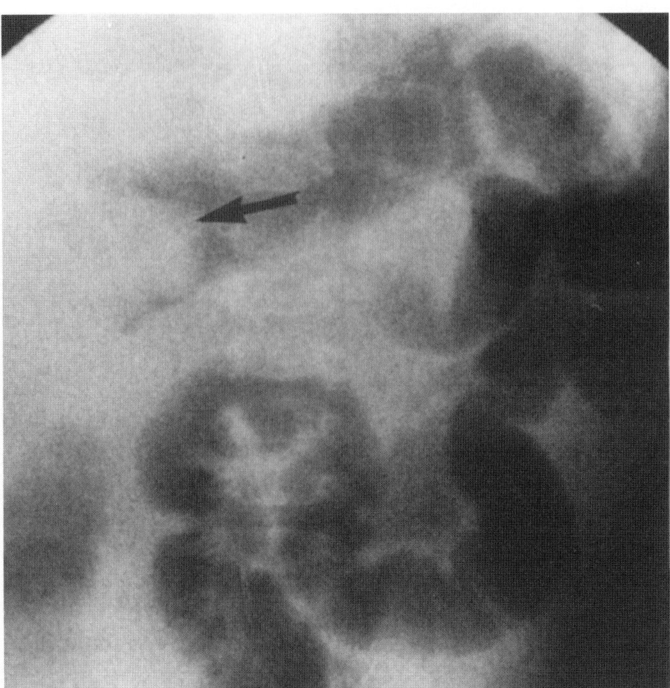
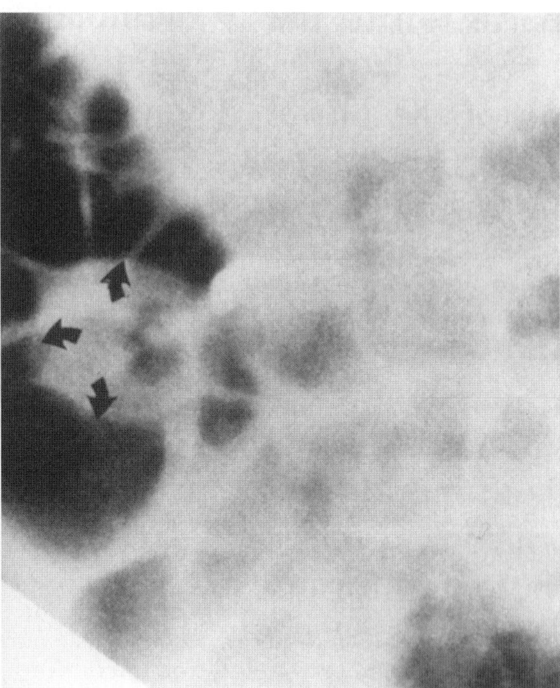

Figure 83-21 Pneumatic air enema showing the intussusception meniscus (*arrow*) in the right transverse colon on the *left*. The picture on the *right* shows successful reduction of intussusception with reflux of air into the terminal ileum. Note the residual edema of the ileocecal valve (*arrows*).

technique may be more widely used than reported, its true benefit is difficult to evaluate.[38] Moreover, even higher rates of reduction have been achieved at other institutions that used AE without the use of assisted manual manipulation.

Delayed Repeat Enema

In the past it was considered standard practice that immediate operative intervention was required if an intussusception was irreducible by enema techniques.[145] However, at surgery 10% were found to already be reduced and another 40% were easily reduced manually.[51] It was therefore speculated that surgical intervention may possibly have been avoided in half the cases if a different approach to their enema technique were attempted by radiologists. With this rationale, an operation would then be required only for cases that are difficult to reduce manually or have necrotic intussusceptions, enema perforations, or PLPs. Earlier reports by Guo et al.[73] and Collins et al.[23] described the use of delayed repeat enema before proceeding to the operating room. However, these and other reports[65,66,152] did not clearly define the time interval between attempts. Although delayed repeat enema without anesthesia has only recently received more attention in the literature, it had been used successfully in Toronto and at other institutions for many years.[24,32,38,49,127,149,152] Given the initial 90% success rate of current radiologic enema techniques, the need to rely on delayed repeat enema is only applicable (necessary) in a minority (Toronto, 12%)[127] of pediatric intussusceptions (see Fig. 83-15). It has been suggested that partial reduction and the time interval between delayed repeat enema allow the venous congestion and edema of the bowel wall to decrease, thereby facilitating reduction of the residual, less congested intussusception during the repeat attempts. The guidelines for delayed repeat enema set forth by a Toronto study[149] on the basis of their experience were as follows: (1) the duration of symptoms and signs is less than 36 hours, (2) the patient's temperature is less than 38° C, (3) the pulse rate is less than 150/min, (4) the intussusception moves (the closer to the ileocecal valve, the better), (5) the patient becomes asymptomatic, and (6) an interval of 2 to 4 hours between attempts seems appropriate and safe (although longer intervals may be tried if the patient is stable). The success rate was 60% and reduction was achieved in 9 of 10 patients on the first repeat attempt. Collins et al.[23] were successful in 84% of second repeat enema attempts, but the second enema was performed in the operating room under general anesthesia.

This approach requires close cooperation between experienced pediatric radiologists and pediatric surgeons. The risks may outweigh the benefits, unless these infants and children are carefully monitored between delayed repeat enema reduction attempts with strict adherence to the suggestions just outlined.

Post-reduction Care

After attempted enema reduction, the infant or child should be observed closely for at least a few hours, depending on the general condition of the patient and the success of the enema reduction. Occasionally, if the intussusception was recognized early, the child is not vomiting, the enema reduction was successful and easy, the parents are reliable, and the child lives within a reasonable distance from the hospital, the patient can be discharged home without admission if asymptomatic and tolerating fluids for a short period after the reduction.[106] Most patients (even those with a successful enema reduction) are admitted to a pediatric general surgical unit for observation and further treatment.

If the enema reduction is successful, the child can be started on clear fluids and progressed to a regular diet as tolerated. Intravenous fluids can be decreased and discontinued accordingly. If the patient initially had SBO and required insertion of a nasogastric tube (even though the SBO was relieved by reduction of the intussusception), it may take a number of hours for the obstructed small bowel to decompress. Therefore, it may be wise to leave the nasogastric tube in place overnight (or if no nasogastric tube has been used, kept fasted) and maintain an intravenous infusion. The preoperative gram-negative and anaerobic bacterial coverage need not be continued unless the patient was febrile before or after reduction and the reduction was difficult (tight intussusception). The presence of fever usually indicates bacteremia, endotoxemia, cytokine (tumor necrosis factor, interleukin) and lysozyme release, and even the production of reactive lymphocytes, in which case antibiotics should be continued for at least 48 hours.[145,160,176,180,182] Animal studies have shown that even when viable intussusceptions are reduced operatively under sterile conditions and tissue for culture is taken from the apparently intact serosal surface, pathogenic bacteria are frequently recovered.[144] Bacterial translocation (the old theory of transmural migration of bacteria)[138] may in part account for the common high fever that accompanies reduction, as well as the aforementioned factors. Somekh et al.[160] performed serial blood cultures before attempted AE reduction, immediately after, and 1 hour later to assess the risk for bacteremia related to attempted AE reduction. Their results showed that although fever may develop after AE reduction attempts, the risk for clinically significant bacteremia and sepsis was extremely low.

Although Ravitch insisted on giving patients charcoal by mouth or in the nasogastric tube to prove that the SBO has been relieved (by passage of a charcoal stool),[145] most pediatric surgeons are satisfied if the child is afebrile and pain free and the gastrointestinal tract is functioning normally. There is usually no need for a follow-up appointment, but the parents should be aware of the 10% recurrence rate after an enema reduction (higher with barium [10%] than with air [4%]).[108,133]

If any doubt remains concerning the success of the enema reduction or the pain recurs, or both, a repeat US study is valuable.[43] If the intussusception recurs, the enema process can be repeated. After any successful enema reduction, the ileocecal valve often remains edematous and thickened for a day or more (see Fig. 83-21).[38] This appearance can easily be differentiated from a recurrence because it lacks the typical concentric rings and the invaginated mesentery, is smaller than the typical target sign of a true intussusception, and will disappear with time.[78,148] The ileocecal thickening can also be appreciated as a filling defect or narrowing if a contrast enema is performed (Fig. 83-22). Recognition of these signs is

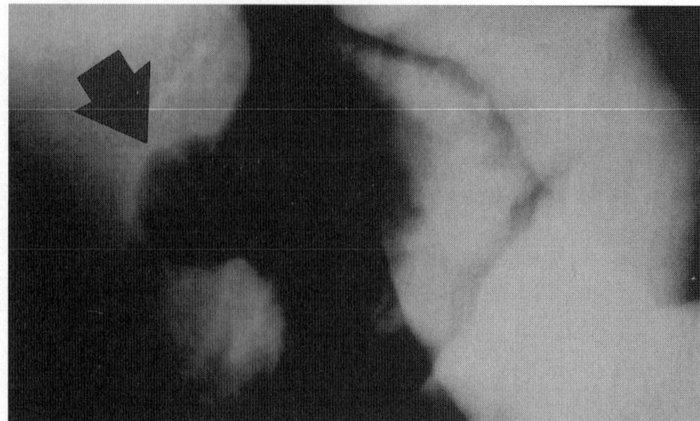

Figure 83-22 Edematous ileocecal valve (*arrow*) after successful hydrostatic contrast enema reduction of an ileocolic intussusception.

important when attempting to confirm complete reduction and also to differentiate post-reduction edema from PLP or recurrent intussusception. Post-reduction US[43] is essential in the following difficult situations: to confirm the reduction by AE when the intussusception disappears but there is minimal or no passage of air into the distal end of the small bowel, to delineate an unreduced ileocolic or ileoileal component of an ileoileocolic intussusception when there is a large amount of air in the large and small bowel,[125] and to rule out a PLP. If US shows only enlarged mesenteric lymph nodes, marked bowel wall thickening, and hyperemia (on Doppler evaluation), there may be an ongoing inflammatory process (*Clostridium difficile, Yersinia enterocolitica*) that originally caused the intussusception.[15,82] Sonography is also important in the re-evaluation of a previous partial reduction of an intussusception to exclude spontaneous reduction before attempting delayed repeat enema reduction.

Operative Management

Laparotomy

If all of the aforementioned attempts at reduction have failed (10%), an operation is necessary (see Fig. 83-16). By this time, the patient has an intravenous catheter and a nasogastric tube in place. Fluid resuscitation is in progress, and the patient has received intravenous triple antibiotics and is crossmatched for a possible blood transfusion. After general endotracheal anesthesia is initiated, the abdomen is prepared and draped for laparotomy. The incision of choice is usually a fairly small right-sided transverse incision (either above or below the umbilicus). Under anesthesia, the intussusception mass can generally be palpated, and this may influence the surgeon regarding the incision desired. An alternative option is an upper midline incision, with the flexibility (depending on what is found and what has to be done) to extend the incision down through (or around) the umbilicus in the midline and below. The size and position of the incision must allow access to the intussusception, which is usually on the right side, sometimes centrally located in the epigastrium, and less commonly on the left side of the colon. The more distal the intussusception, the more difficult it is to reduce. The cecum in an infant is usually poorly fixed, and therefore most intussusceptions on the right side can easily be delivered through any of the incisions just noted. This seems to be wiser than to reduce it inside the abdomen, as initially suggested by Ravitch[144] and Gross.[69] Most lower right-sided transverse incisions (because they resemble appendectomy incisions) require that the appendix be removed. On the other hand, many (but not all surgeons) remove the appendix after manual reduction of the intussusception, claiming that division of a prominent peritoneal attachment (Jackson's veil) and local operative adhesions will diminish the chance of a recurrence; this has yet to be proved, however.[183]

On entering the abdomen, one can usually diagnose necrotic bowel by the presence of serosanguineous (red as opposed to clear yellow) peritoneal fluid. Once all the fluid has been aspirated, most of which is a transudate, the intussusception is usually able to be delivered out of the wound en masse without much difficulty. The key to successful manual reduction is slow, constant pinching, squeezing (like a tube of toothpaste), or milking backward (proximally) in retrograde fashion of the most distal part of the intussusceptum through the wall of the intussuscipiens (Fig. 83-23). This can be aided by the assistant gently and slowly pulling the intussusceptum out of the intussuscipiens. Ravitch suggested that such pulling should not be done, whereas Gross said it could be done with the "utmost delicacy."[69,145] This combined maneuver (primarily the pinching, squeezing, or milking proximally) is the absolutely essential part of the manual reduction and must be done slowly and steadily without interruption. In effect, this technique increases intraluminal pressure just as an enema does. Ravitch[145] suggested that gentle injection of sterile mineral oil between the intussusceptum and intussuscipiens might enhance the reduction. On the other hand, he objected to gently placing a finger in this space or spreading a Kelly clamp to evacuate some of the edema fluid (Fig. 83-24). In similar fashion, the index finger can be gently inserted between the intussuscipiens and intussusceptum to create a wider space between the two (modified Hutchinson's maneuver).[77] Gross[69] said that "only through experience can an operator know how long to persist in attempts at reduction. Sometimes it is better to spend twenty minutes... than it is to resort too soon to resection.... On the other hand, long-continued unsuccessful attempts at reduction may so exhaust the child." Some surgeons suggest that the occurrence of a serosal tear during attempted manual reduction is an indication that the irreducible bowel is gangrenous (necrotic) and of necessity will require resection. However, such is not always the case. Gross[69] wrote: "Small tears in the peritoneal coats of the gut are in themselves not particularly dangerous, but they serve as a warning to the operator that the muscularis or mucosa will soon give way if subjected to undue pressure. If peritoneal tears are long or deep (extending into the musculature), a few quickly placed sutures will suffice to repair them." Therefore, if the reduction continues to progress, regardless of the serosal (peritoneal) tears, one should cautiously "press on." If there are serosal (peritoneal) tears and no progress in the reduction, however, resection of the irreducible intussusception should be performed (usually a right hemicolectomy). If an ileoileocolic intussusception is present, it is always reduced in two increments: the ileocolic component first and, once it is through the ileocecal valve, the ileoileal component (see Fig. 83-9). Once reduced, the bowel (especially the leading area of the intussusceptum) may be quite blue, congested, bruised, and possibly worrisome with regard to its viability (see Fig. 83-24). However, with time (5 to 10 minutes) and patience, the bowel will almost

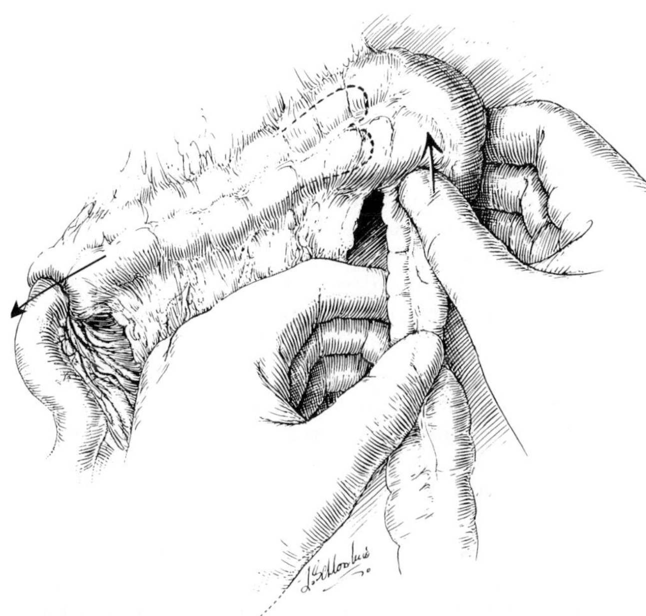

Figure 83-23 The key to successful manual reduction of an intussusception is slow constant pinching, squeezing (like a tube of toothpaste), or milking backward (proximally) in retrograde fashion of the most distal intussusceptum through the wall of the intussuscipiens. This can be aided by the assistant gently and slowly pulling the intussusceptum out of the intussuscipiens.

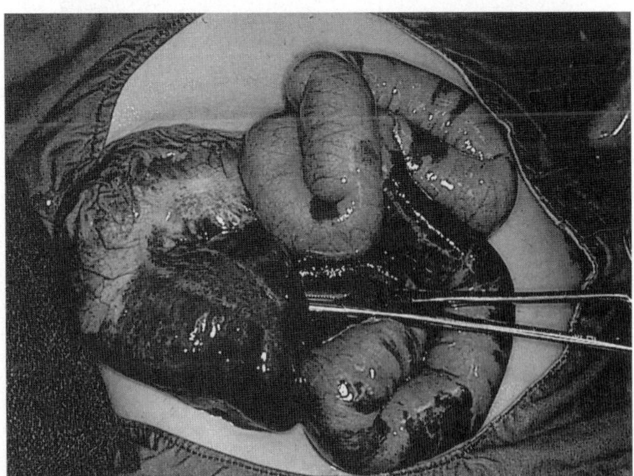

Figure 83-24 Ileocolic intussusception incompletely reduced. The cecum and ascending colon are congested and full. Note the partially reduced, congested, but viable terminal ileum. *(See color plate.)*

always become pink with warm saline packs. The concept that it is impossible to reduce necrotic bowel anywhere in a pediatric patient is not always true. Ein and Stephens claimed that 50% of nonviable intussusceptions could be manually reduced before resection (see Fig. 83-9).[51] During attempted reduction one must weigh the benefits of the procedure and the risk for perforation (with subsequent contamination) against a successful reduction requiring a smaller resection of only the necrotic bowel, which is less than a larger en masse ileocolic resection or right hemicolectomy of the irreducible intussusception.

If the viability of the bowel in the reduced intussusception (usually the distal ileum) is at all in doubt, it should be resected. Rarely, if there is a small area suspicious for necrosis, it can likewise be resected or inverted with a layer of nonabsorbable sutures.

Operations for perforations during attempted enema reduction (<1%[38]) have their own problems.[33,48,92] Usually, the perforation occurs before the intussusception is reduced and often sooner than expected. Although most (but not all) of these intussusceptions have necrotic bowel, 50% can still be manually reduced (after closing the perforation with a bowel clamp), thereby decreasing the length of bowel that may need resection.[51] If this is not possible, the entire intussusception and nearby colon perforation can be resected en masse. The perforations caused by hydrostatic enema fluid usually result in large colon tears, and if barium is used, an irremovable mixture of barium and stool will remain in the peritoneal cavity (Fig. 83-25) and leave a permanent radiologic picture that looks like a snowstorm (Fig. 83-26). Daneman et al. showed that patients perforated with barium had longer anesthetic times, more often required bowel resection, and had increased morbidity and a longer hospital stay than did those perforated with air.[33] Apart from these significant and worrisome clinical observations, there have been experimental studies in a guinea pig model that assessed the deleterious effects of fecal soiling with various contrast agents in the peritoneal cavity.[80] Hernanz-Schulman et al.[81] showed that fecal spill with barium caused the most deleterious effects when compared with fecal soiling with water-soluble contrast media, saline, and air. Barium is a significant activator of phagocytic cells, which leads to blunting of the subsequent response to phagocyte challenge and adversely affects the response to all bacteria tested. This explains the enhanced and prolonged adverse clinical effect of the barium fecal contamination just described.

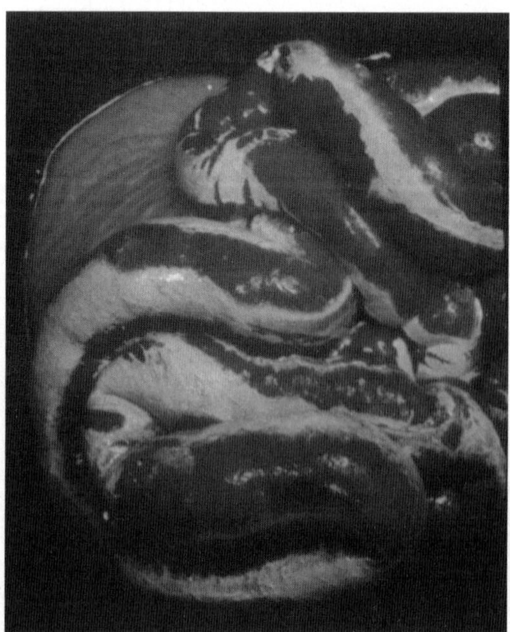

Figure 83-25 Peritoneal cavity after a perforation caused by hydrostatic barium enema. Note the gross soiling with an admixture of barium and stool, which is very difficult to remove.

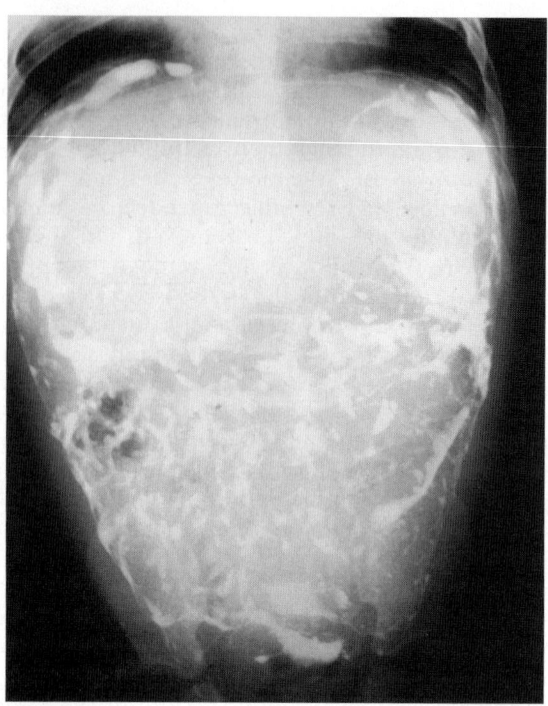

Figure 83-26 Postoperative radiograph after a perforation caused by hydrostatic barium enema. Note the contamination throughout the abdomen. This snowstorm picture lasts for life.

Water-soluble contrast (if not isotonic) rapidly sequesters a lot of fluid into the peritoneal cavity and thereby increases the fecal contamination. In contrast, when a pneumatic AE perforation occurs, the colonic hole is smaller and the peritoneal contamination is much less and easier to evacuate.[33,71] Free air can easily be recognized with modern fluoroscopic equipment.

Rarely, immediately after the perforation occurs and while still on the radiology table, there may be a tension pneumoperitoneum that is quite symptomatic and requires urgent needle aspiration (best done in the midline above the umbilicus with an 18-gauge needle).[70] It may, however, be avoided by immediately discontinuing the enema as soon as the free air is recognized and opening the rectal enema tube to decompress the colon. If no resection is necessary, the hole can usually be closed primarily without resection and at most with some local trimming of the wound edges.

If a resection for irreducible or necrotic bowel is required (see Fig. 83-9), it should be done in the manner preferred by the operating surgeon. A primary end-to-end anastomosis can be accomplished in most cases. If the infant (more likely) or the child is desperately ill, after the resection (hastily done without tying the vessels on the specimen side), the two ends of the bowel should be exteriorized as temporary stomas.[69,144,145] In the current era this is quite unusual.

If manual reduction has been successfully completed, especially if it was an ileoileocolic intussusception (see Fig. 83-9), one must check for a PLP,[128] most commonly an inverted Meckel diverticulum[101] or distal ileal polyp (see Fig. 83-6),[127,128] and if found, it should be resected. An ileoileocolic intussusception is often manifested as a complete (tight) SBO (see Fig. 83-2), frequently (40%[51]) caused by a PLP and not very often (25%[48]) reduced by enema; the success rate with BE is 50% and with AE it is as high as 60%.[48,51,128] If reduction does occur, there will be an obvious residual filling defect in the terminal ileum, cecum, or colon (see Fig. 83-7) (regardless of whether the reduction was done with barium or air), other than the very common edematous ileocecal valve, which always disappears in a few days on subsequent enema (Fig. 83-22) or US studies (see Fig. 83-21). If the filling defect remains, the PLP should be resected. The location of the lesion will often dictate the choice of incision since the operation is elective. Unfortunately, an unnecessary resection is occasionally performed for a so-called PLP that is usually a small area of puckering on the antimesenteric border of the terminal ileum, often mistaken as a PLP lymphosarcoma but is really an indurated Peyer patch—the most common non-PLP. Most distal ileal lymphosarcomas are much larger tumor masses than the serosal puckering (dimpling) just mentioned.[126]

Laparoscopy

Laparoscopy has recently been applied to the aforementioned surgical endeavors with equally good results. Since the last (fifth) edition of this two-volume textbook in 1998 (in which no mention was made of laparoscopy),[183] there have been six published papers concerning laparoscopy in pediatric intussusception, with one report[78] devoted only to confirmation (instead of laparotomy) of the radiologic reduction. If US is unavailable or inadequate, laparoscopy may be warranted to prove the adequacy of the reduction.[29] The other publications concerned the successful reduction of a failed enema reduction with fairly good results (50% to 65%).[40] Though a moot point, the incision needed for the laparotomy is often no larger than that used by surgeons preferring a laparoscopic-assisted bowel resection.[105] It may also assist in removal of a PLP.[31] The most recent series (from Ann Arbor, Michigan[99]) shows that laparoscopy uniformly improves only the length of hospital stay by a few days. It remains to be seen whether laparoscopy will allow technically acceptable manipulation of a difficult irreducible intussusception equal to that of open manual reduction. One may surmise that with questionably less bowel handling and retraction with laparoscopy, there may well be less postoperative intussusception, adhesions, and obstruction. Davis et al.[40] suggested in 2003 that the role of laparoscopy in the forum of intussusception is still not clearly defined and its future use will depend on local laparoscopic skills and zeal.

Postoperative management depends on the extent of the procedures performed. Attention must still be directed to the presence of fever and administration of antibiotics for 48 hours if the patient is febrile and a minimum of 5 days if a bowel resection (without bowel preparation) or closure of a perforation (with or without fecal spillage) was required.

COMPLICATIONS

Radiologic

The major complication from attempted enema reduction is perforation of the bowel (see Fig. 83-15).[38] Perforation rates with the various enema techniques are extremely low in experienced hands (less than 1%), with only a few series having rates higher than 1%.[33,48,92,155] Perforation should be recognizable with any technique. In a review from 40 pediatric hospitals in North America in 1989, Campbell[19] found that only 55 perforations occurred during hydrostatic enema reduction in more than 14,000 patients (0.39% = 1 in 250). However, in 1992 Stein et al.[162] reported a relatively higher perforation rate (2.8%) with AE. This fueled the controversy regarding the safety of the pneumatic technique. In contrast, Guo et al.[73] in 1986 reported an AE perforation rate of 0.14% in more than 6000 intussusceptions, and in 1993 Gu et al.[71] reported a 0.16% rate in 9000 patients. Furthermore, Gu et al.[72] reported no perforations in almost 3000 AEs since 1988 when they began using a new pump that limits the pressure delivered. Lower perforation rates could also be expected in institutions where some patients are considered to be at a higher risk for perforation and thus no enema is attempted and they go immediately to the operating theater.

Bramson and Blickman[13] suggested that perforation is solely related to bowel wall necrosis and could therefore be expected to occur in the inner intussusceptum. However, of 14 perforations described by Daneman et al., all occurred in the outer intussuscipiens.[33] Moreover, 8 of these 14 perforated in the absence of necrosis, thus suggesting that technical factors play a role in some patients. Such factors might include the overly persistent use of pressure that was either too high or changed too quickly during the enema. There certainly is a learning curve with a new technique. It should be emphasized that perforation has indeed occurred with pressure as low as 60 mm Hg.[33,71] The latter suggests that the perforation may possibly have been present before the attempted enema reduction. Apposition of the intussusceptum (with the questionable perforation) against the intussuscipiens may prevent intraluminal air from escaping into the peritoneal cavity.[13] This may explain the absence of free intraperitoneal air on plain abdominal radiographs before enema reduction in many of these patients. Partial reduction by enema may then uncover the existing perforation and allow the passage of contrast or air into the peritoneal cavity. Daneman et al. compared the clinical status of seven pediatric patients whose bowel was perforated after BE with another seven who sustained a perforation after AE.[33] The clinical situation was similar in both groups: perforation occurred in infants younger than 6 months with a longer duration of symptoms and signs (>36 hours). This was confirmed in other series involving patients with perforations (Bramson and Blickman,[13] Maoate and Beasley[109]). It is prudent that independent of what technique is used, special care regarding attempted enema reduction be taken in younger infants with a longer duration of symptoms and signs.[48] No specific guidelines on how to deal differently with this specific clinical situation have been established; performing the enema more slowly and keeping the pressure as low as possible may diminish the risk for perforation in some of these patients.[156]

Surgical

The usual surgical complications after laparotomy and laparoscopy can be expected (see Fig. 83-16). Preoperative antibiotics are administered and continued postoperatively if the patient is febrile or septic or if a bowel resection was performed (without bowel preparation) or a perforation was closed. In a series of 354 intussusceptions in 336 infants and children, Ein and Stephens reported an overall 14% postoperative complication rate in 251 operated cases, 4% in those who required only manual reduction with or without appendectomy and 19% in those who underwent an enterotomy or bowel resection.[51] Twenty-six percent had a wound infection, and 8% had wound dehiscence and evisceration if bowel surgery was performed, as opposed to 2% and 0% if no bowel procedure took place. Both groups had an equal amount of postoperative adhesive SBO (2% to 3%). Although others have reported SBO after a postoperative intussusception operation, a large review of SBO from Toronto[96] showed that postoperative intussusception was tied for the third most common procedure on the list (7%). There was a 5% risk for adhesive SBO after any pediatric laparotomy (especially appendectomy and subtotal colectomy), with 80% of cases of SBO occurring within 2 years of the initial operation and the same recurrence rate after any number of SBO events.[96] The complication rate after surgery for a BE perforation in the 1981 Toronto series[48] was 57%.

RESULTS AND OUTCOME

Clinical

At this point in time (mid-2004), the overall results of documenting the diagnosis of a pediatric intussusception are excellent. The clinical diagnosis of pediatric intussusception is accurate 50% of the time (see Fig. 83-3),[9] whereas US and hydrostatic or pneumatic enemas both have an accuracy rate of 100% (see Fig. 83-11).[37] The results of treatment of pediatric intussusception continue to be equally good. The major improvement over the last 25 years (based on two large Toronto series, 1968[51] and 1997[46]) has been in the effectiveness of nonoperative treatment, with a success rate close to 90% with hydrostatic or pneumatic reduction, or with both. With a more persistent radiologic approach, including the cautious use of delayed repeat attempts at enema reduction (with a 60% success rate) (see Fig. 83-12),[127] the only pediatric patients with intussusception who reach the operating room (10%) are those who require prolonged and difficult manual reduction (50%), resection for necrotic bowel or removal of a PLP (45%), spontaneous reduction (<5%), or closure of enema perforation (<1%) (see Fig. 83-16).[149] Recurrent intussusception occurs in 8% to 15% of cases.[37] Approximately 10% of cases occur after hydrostatic or pneumatic enema reduction, 3% after operative manual reduction (with or without appendectomy), and virtually none after bowel resection (see Fig. 83-10). This rate of recurrence has not changed in 25 years.[46] Of all the infants and children with recurrent intussusception, 68% have only one recurrence (most often within the first few days after the initial intussusception), and 32% have multiple recurrences that may occur as isolated episodes over a period of days, weeks, months, or years or in a cluster (up to eight) during the initial hospitalization.[38] The reduction rate for recurrent intussusceptions is higher (95%), possibly because the intussusceptions are diagnosed earlier by the parents and they are said to be looser (better perfusion) and therefore more likely to recur, but also easier to reduce.[34] The long-term outcome of infants and children who have had an intussusception, once recovered, is otherwise normal.

Mortality

This century has seen a steady decline in the mortality rate associated with pediatric intussusception.[183] Gross[69] reported that the mortality rate in Boston fell from 59% in 1922 to 2.7% in 1947. Other reports showed similar trends. An observation made by Gross[69] in 1948 remains true to this day: "The interval between onset of symptoms and institution of treatment is of paramount importance and the mortality rates will more nearly approach zero the more frequently treatment is instituted within 24 hours of onset." However, occasional deaths continue to be reported. Stringer et al.[166] noted that 61% of the deaths in their series could potentially have been avoided. Avoidable factors included delay in diagnosis, inadequate intravenous fluid resuscitation and antibiotic therapy, delay in recognizing recurrent or residual intussusception after nonsurgical reduction, and surgical complications. Since the last (fifth) edition of this text in 1998, there have been four publications specifically related to mortality associated with pediatric intussusception (United States, 2000; Australia, 2001; and two from Nigeria, 2002). Parashar et al.[135] (Centers for Disease Control and Prevention, United States) reported that intussusception-associated infant mortality rates declined from 6.4 per 1 million live births in 1979 to 1981 to 2.3 during 1985 to 1997. These authors concluded from their review that infants whose mothers were younger than 20 years, nonwhite, and unmarried and had an education level below grade 12 were at risk for intussusception-associated death. Byard and Simpson[17] in Australia reported two deaths from intussusception between 1961 and 1995, both in infants (5 and 6 months of age) who had only nonspecific and apparent minor manifestations of illness until rapid deterioration occurred. It was concluded that although unexpected death is more likely to occur in older children with purely small bowel intussusception, these two infants demonstrate that unexpected death may occur at any time with intussusception at any level. The two publications from Ameh[4,5] (Nigeria) showed an 8% mortality rate after operative manual reduction and a 67% rate after resection of the intussusception. The current overall mortality rate in the pediatric population in developed countries is very low (<1%). The mortality rate is less than 1% for an undiagnosed intussusception (see Fig. 83-3), less than 1% for radiologic reduction (see Fig. 83-15), and less than 1% for surgical intervention (see Fig. 83-16).[32,46,51,183] An American study[135] published in 2000 best sums up the mortality risk as follows: "Although intussusception-associated infant deaths in the United States have declined substantially over the past 2 decades, some deaths seem to be related to reduced access to, or delays in seeking, health care and are potentially preventable."

RESEARCH UPDATE AND THE FUTURE

Since the last edition of this text, there have been more than 500 publications concerning intussusception in the pediatric age group.[183] During this time span the authors have also been asked to review more than 40 papers specifically related to intussusception for pediatric surgery, pediatric radiology, and pediatric journals. All of these submitted and published papers have been tallied for the reader's interest. Nearly half (200) of the papers involved case reports describing more than 40 specific lesions (PLPs) that caused intussusception (see Table 83-1). The most common PLPs are appendix, lipoma, polyp, Peutz-Jeghers hamartomatous polyp, and duodenogastric intussusception. After these case reports, the six most common intussusception topics were clinical reviews, imaging, viral (especially rotavirus), duodenogastric retrograde intussusception, prenatal and newborn intussusception, and laparoscopy (see Table 83-2).

As we enter the 21st century, pediatric intussusception will continue to occur unless viral illnesses are eliminated, as well as all of the PLPs listed in Table 83-1. Realistically, the best we can expect is that the enema reduction rate will increase past 90% with pneumatic AE reduction and that only 10% or less will require surgery (see Fig. 83-16).[149] Ideally, of this 10%, there should be none that are found to have spontaneously reduced; the intussusceptions that are found should require a difficult manual reduction; resection for ischemic, gangrenous, and necrotic bowel; repair of a perforation from the AE; or resection of a PLP.

SUMMARY

Intussusception is a relatively common cause of abdominal pain and gastrointestinal obstruction in 1 in 2000 infants and children. A careful history is the mainstay of diagnosis and is typical in 85% of cases. A high index of suspicion must be maintained for atypical cases, such as the 15% whose intussusception is painless.[52] Abdominal radiographs and especially US are the primary adjuncts to clinical diagnosis. Patients with intussusception (usually ileocolic, 95%) are optimally managed by hydrostatic or pneumatic enema reduction. If these nonoperative methods fail, operative repair (manual reduction and/or resection) is performed. Delay in diagnosis is the primary avoidable factor that contributes to morbidity and mortality.[51] The mortality rate has steadily declined during the past century to less than 1% in industrialized (developed) countries.[183]

REFERENCES

1. Adamsbaum C, Sellier N, Helardot P: Ileocolic intussusception with enterogenous cyst: Ultrasonic diagnosis. Pediatr Radiol 1989;19:325.
2. Allan RA, Heenan S, Given-Wilson R, Adam EJ: Re: K. Rosenfeld, K. McHugh. Survey of intussusception reduction in England, Scotland and Wales: How and why we could be better. Clin Radiol 2000;55:895.
3. Allbery SM, Swischuk LE, John SD, et al: Post-operative intussusception: Often an elusive diagnosis. Pediatr Radiol 1998;28:271.
4. Ameh EA: The morbidity and mortality of laparotomy for uncomplicated intussusception in children. West Afr J Med 2002;21:115.
5. Ameh EA: The morbidity and mortality of right hemicolectomy for complicated intussusception in infants. Niger Postgrad Med J 2002;9:123.
6. Baldisserotto M, Spolidoro JVN, Bahu MGS: Graded compression sonography of the colon in the diagnosis of polyps in pediatric patients. AJR Am J Roentgenol 2002; 179:201.
7. Barr LL, Hayden CK Jr, Stansberry SD, et al: Enteric duplication cysts in children: Are their ultrasonographic wall characteristics diagnostic? Pediatr Radiol 1990;20:326.
8. Beasley S: Intussusception. Pediatr Radiol 2004;34:302.
9. Beasley SW, Auldist AW, Stokes KB: The diagnostically difficult intussusception: Its characteristics and consequences. Pediatr Surg Int 1988;3:135.
10. Beek FJ, Rövekamp MH, Bax NM, et al: Ultrasound findings in post-operative jejunojejunal intussusception. Pediatr Radiol 1990;20:601.
11. Blakelock RT, Beasley SW: The clinical implications of non-idiopathic intussusception. Pediatr Surg Int 1998;14:163.
12. Bolin H: Conventional roentgenography in diagnosis of intussusception in children. Acta Radiol Diagn 1964;2:32.
13. Bramson RT, Blickman JG: Perforation during hydrostatic reduction of intussusception: Proposed mechanism and review of the literature. J Pediatr Surg 1992;27:589.
14. Bratton SL, Haberkern CM, Waldhausen JH, et al: Intussusception: Hospital size and risk of surgery. Pediatrics 2001;107:299.
15. Burchfield DJ, Rawlings D, Hamrick HJ: Intussusception associated with *Yersinia enterocolitica* gastroenteritis. Am J Dis Child 1983;137:803.
16. Burke LF, Clarke E: Ileocolic intussusception—a case report. J Clin Ultrasound 1977;5:346.
17. Byard RW, Simpson A: Sudden death and intussusception in infancy and childhood—autopsy considerations. Med Sci Law 2001;41:41.

18. Calder FR, Tan S, Kitteringham L, et al: Patterns of management of intussusception outside tertiary centres. J Pediatr Surg 2001;36:312.
19. Campbell J: Contrast media in intussusception. Pediatr Radiol 1989;19:293.
20. Carnevale E, Graziani M, Fasanelli S: Post-operative ileo-ileal intussusception: Sonographic approach. Pediatr Radiol 1994;24:161.
21. Choong CK, Kimble RM, Pease P, et al: Colo-colic intussusception in Henoch-Schönlein purpura. Pediatr Surg Int 1988; 14:173.
22. Clubbe CPB: The Diagnosis and Treatment of Intussusception, 2nd ed. London, Hodder & Stoughton, 1921.
23. Collins DL, Pinckney LE, Miller KE, et al: Hydrostatic reduction of ileocolic intussusception: A second attempt in the operating room with general anesthesia. J Pediatr 1989;115:204.
24. Connolly BL, Alton DJ, Ein SH, et al: Partially reduced intussusception: When are repeated delayed reduction attempts appropriate? Pediatr Radiol 1995;25:104.
25. Connolly BL, Chait PG, Siva-Nandan R, et al: Recognition of intussusception around gastrojejunostomy tubes in children. AJR Am J Roentgenol 1998;170:467.
26. Connolly BL, O'Halpin D: Sonographic evaluation of the abdomen in Henoch-Schönlein purpura. Clin Radiol 1994; 49:320.
27. Courture A, Veyrac C, Baud C, et al: Evaluation of abdominal pain in Henoch-Schönlein syndrome by high frequency ultrasound. Pediatr Radiol 1992;22:12.
28. Cox TD, Winters WD, Weinberger E: CT of intussusception in the pediatric patient: Diagnosis and pitfalls. Pediatr Radiol 1996;26:26.
29. Cuckow PM, Slater RD, Najmaldin AS: Intussusception treated laparoscopically after failed air enema reduction. Surg Endosc 1996;10:671.
30. Cull DL, Rosario V, Lally K, et al: Surgical implications of Henoch-Schönlein purpura. J Pediatr Surg 1990;23:741.
31. Cunningham JD, Vine AJ, Karch L, et al: The role of laparoscopy in the management of intussusception in the Peutz-Jeghers syndrome: Case report and review of the literature. Laparosc Endosc Percutan Techn 1998;8:17.
32. Daneman A, Alton DJ: Intussusception: Issues & controversies related to diagnosis and reduction. Radiol Clin North Am 1996;34:743.
33. Daneman A, Alton DJ, Ein S, et al: Perforation during attempted intussusception reduction in children—a comparison of perforation with barium and air. Pediatr Radiol 1995;25:81.
34. Daneman A, Alton DJ, Lobo E, et al: Patterns of recurrence of intussusception in children: A 17-year review. Pediatr Radiol 1998;28:913.
35. Daneman A, Lobo E, Alton DJ, et al: The value of sonography, CT and air enema for detection of complicated Meckel diverticulum in children with nonspecific clinical presentation. Pediatr Radiol 1998;28:928.
36. Daneman A, Myers M, Shuckett B, et al: Sonographic appearances of inverted Meckel diverticulum with intussusception. Pediatr Radiol 1997;27:295.
37. Daneman A, Navarro O: Intussusception Part 1: A review of diagnostic approaches. Pediatr Radiol 2003;33:79.
38. Daneman A, Navarro O: Intussusception Part 2: An update on the evolution of management. Pediatr Radiol 2004;34:97.
39. Daneman A, Reilly BJ, De Silva M, et al: Intussusception on small bowel examination in children. AJR Am J Roentgenol 1982;139:299.
40. Davis CF, McCabe AJ, Raine PAM: The ins and outs of intussusception: History and management over the past fifty years. J Pediatr Surg 2003;38:60.
41. Dennison WM: Acute intussusception in infancy and childhood. Glasgow Med J 1948;29:71.
42. Don S, Cohen MD, Wells LJ, et al: Air reduction of an intussusception caused by a pathologic lead point in an infant. Pediatr Radiol 1992;22:326.
43. Dugougeat F, Navarro O, Daneman A: The role of sonography in children with abdominal pain after recent successful reduction of intussusception. Pediatr Radiol 2000;30:654.
44. Ein SH: Recurrent intussusception in children. J Pediatr Surg 1975;10:751.
45. Ein SH: Leading points in childhood intussusception. J Pediatr Surg 1976;11:209.
46. Ein SH, Alton D, Palder SB, et al: Intussusception in the 1990s: Has 25 years made a difference? Pediatr Surg Int 1997;12:374.
47. Ein SH, Ferguson JM: Intussusception—the forgotten postoperative obstruction. Arch Dis Child 1982;57:788.
48. Ein SH, Mercer S, Humphry A, et al: Colon perforation during attempted barium enema reduction of intussusception. J Pediatr Surg 1981;16:313.
49. Ein SH, Palder SB, Alton DJ, et al: Intussusception: Toward less surgery? J Pediatr Surg 1994;29:433.
50. Ein SH, Shandling B, Reilly BJ, et al: Hydrostatic reduction of intussusceptions caused by lead points. J Pediatr Surg 1986;21:883.
51. Ein SH, Stephens CA: Intussusception: 354 cases in 10 years. J Pediatr Surg 1971;6:16.
52. Ein SH, Stephens CA, Minor A: The painless intussusception. J Pediatr Surg 1976;11:563.
53. Ein SH, Stephens CA, Shandling B, et al: Intussusception due to lymphoma. J Pediatr Surg 1986;21:786.
54. Ein SH, Venogopal S, Mancer K: Ileocaecal atresia. J Pediatr Surg 1985;20:525.
55. Eke N, Adotey JM: Postoperative intussusception, causal or casual relationships? Int Surg 2000;85:303.
56. Eklöf O, Hartelius H: Reliability of the abdominal plain film diagnosis in pediatric patient with suspected intussusception. Pediatr Radiol 1980;9:199.
57. Fecteau A, Flageole H, Nguyen LT, et al: Recurrent intussusception: Safe use of hydrostatic enema. J Pediatr Surg 1996; 31:859.
58. Fiorella DJ, Donnelly LF: Frequency of right lower quadrant position of the sigmoid colon in infants and young children. Radiology 2001;219:91.
59. Fiorito ES, Recalde Cuestas LA: Diagnosis and treatment of acute intestinal intussusception with controlled insufflation of air. Pediatrics 1959;24:241.
60. Fisher D, Hadas-Halpern I: Jejunoduodenogastric intussusception—A rare complication of gastrostomy tube migration. Pediatr Radiol 2001;31:455.
61. Forest WE: Intussusception in children. Am J Obstet 1886; 19:673.
62. Franken EA Jr, Smith WL, Chernish SM, et al: The use of glucagon in hydrostatic reduction of intussusception: A double-blind study of 30 patients. Radiology 1983; 146:687.
63. Gasparri MG, Pipinos II, Kralovich KA: Retrograde jejunogastric intussusception. South Med J 2000;93:499.
64. Glasier CM, Siegel MJ, McAlister WH, et al: Henoch-Schönlein syndrome in children: Gastrointestinal manifestations. AJR Am J Roentgenol 1998;136:1081.
65. González-Spínola J, Del Pozo G, Tejedor D, et al: Intussusception: The accuracy of ultrasound-guided saline enema and the usefulness of a delayed attempt at reduction. J Pediatr Surg 1999;34:1016.
66. Gorenstein A, Raucher A, Serour F, et al: Intussusception in children: Reduction with repeated, delayed air enema. Radiology 1998;206:721.

67. Grasso SN, Katz ME, Presberg HJ, et al: Transabdominal manually assisted reduction of pediatric intussusception: Reappraisal of this historical technique. Radiology 1994; 191:777.
68. Greig D: On insufflation as a remedy in intussusception. Edinb Med J 1864;10:306.
69. Gross RE: Intussusception. In The Surgery of Infancy and Childhood. Philadelphia, WB Saunders, 1953, p 281.
70. Gu L, Alton DJ, Daneman A, et al: Intussusception reduction in children by rectal insufflation of air. AJR Am J Roentgenol 1988;150:1345.
71. Gu L, Wong S, Gu A: Perforations during attempted intussusception reduction: 14 patients from 9,028 examinations over a 20 year period. J Intervent Radiol (China) 1993;2:36.
72. Gu L, Zhu HY, Wang S, et al: Sonographic guidance of air enema for intussusception reduction in children. Pediatr Radiol 2000;30:339.
73. Guo JZ, Ma XY, Zhou QH: Results of air pressure enema reduction of intussusception: 6396 cases in 13 years. J Pediatr Surg 1986;21:1201.
74. Hamby LS, Fowler CL, Pokorny WJ: Intussusception. In Donnellan WL (ed): Abdominal Surgery of Infancy and Childhood. Australia, Harwood, 1996, p 1.
75. Harrington L, Connolly BL, Hu X, et al: Ultrasonographic and clinical predictors of intussusception. J Pediatr 1998; 132:836.
76. Harvey JG, Colditz PB: Henoch-Schönlein purpura—A surgical review. Aust Pediatr J 1994;20:13.
77. Hase T, Kodama M, Mizukuro T, et al: Manual reduction with the index finger for infantile intussusception. A modification of Hutchinson's maneuver. Pediatr Surg Int 1998;13:223.
78. Hay SA, Kabesh AA, Soliman HA, et al: Idiopathic intussusception: The role of laparoscopy. J Pediatr Surg 1999; 34:577.
79. Hedlund GL, Johnson JF, Strife JL: Ileocolic intussusception: Extensive reflux of air preceding pneumatic reduction. Radiology 1990;174:187.
80. Hernanz-Schulman M, Foster C, Maxa R, et al: Experimental study of mortality and morbidity of contrast media and standardized fecal dose in the peritoneal cavity. Pediatr Radiol 2000;30:369.
81. Hernanz-Schulman M, Vanholder R, Waterloos MA, et al: Effect of radiographic contrast agents on leukocyte metabolic response. Pediatr Radiol 2000;30:361.
82. Hervás JA, Alberti P, Bregante JI, et al: Chronic intussusception associates with *Yersinia enterocolitica* mesenteric adenitis. J Pediatr Surg 1992;27:1591.
83. Hipsley PL: Intussusception and its treatment by hydrostatic pressure: Based on an analysis of one hundred consecutive cases so treated. Med J Aust 1926;2:201.
84. Hirschsprung H: Tilfaelde af subakut tarminvagination. Hospitals-Tilende 1876;3:321.
85. Hirschsprung H: 107 Falle von Darminvagination bei Kindern, behandelt in Konigen Louis-en-Kinderhospital in Kopenhagen vahrend der Jahre 1871-1904. Mitt Grenzgeb Med Chir 1905;14:555.
86. Holcomb GW 3rd, Ross AJ 3rd, O'Neill JA Jr: Postoperative intussusception: Increasing frequency or increasing awareness? South Med J 1991;84:1334.
87. Holsclaw DS, Rocmans C, Shwachman H: Intussusception in patients with cystic fibrosis. Pediatrics 1971;48:51.
88. Hsiao JY, Kao HA, Shih SL: Intravenous glucagon in hydrostatic reduction of intussusception: A controlled study of 63 patients. Acta Paediatr Sinensis 1988;29:242.
89. Hu SC, Feeney M, McNicholas M, et al: Ultrasonography to diagnose and exclude intussusception in Henoch-Schönlein purpura. Arch Dis Child 1991;66:1065.
90. Hughes UM, Connolly BL: Small-bowel intussusceptions occurring around nasojejunal enteral tubes—Three cases occurring in children. Pediatr Radiol 2001;31:456.
91. Hughes UM, Connolly BL, Chait PG, et al: Further report of small-bowel intussusceptions related to gastrojejunostomy tubes. Pediatr Radiol 2000;30:614.
92. Humphry A, Ein SH, Mok PM: Perforation of the intussuscepted colon. AJR Am J Roentgenol 1981;137:1135.
93. Hunter J: On introsusception. Trans Soc Improv Med Surg Knowledge 1793;1:103.
94. Hutchinson J: A successful case of abdominal section for intussusception. Proc R Med Chir Soc 1873;7:195.
95. Janik JS, Cranford J, Ein SH: The well-nourished infant with intussusception. Am J Dis Child 1981;135:600.
96. Janik JS, Ein SH, Mancer K: An assessment of the surgical treatment of adhesive small bowel obstruction in infants and children. J Pediatr Surg 1981;16:225.
97. Janik JS, Firor HV: Intussusception and nutritional status. J Pediatr 1976;99:358.
98. Karnak I, Senocak ME, Kale G, et al: A previously unmentioned surgical observation in the treatment of intussusception. Surg Today 1999;29:979.
99. Kia K, Mony V, Eustace S, et al: Laparoscopic versus open surgical approach for intussusception requiring operative intervention. Paper presented at a meeting of the American Pediatric Surgical Association, May 2004, Ponte Vedra Beach, Florida.
100. Kidd J, Jackson R, Wagner CW, et al: Intussusception following the Ladd procedure. Arch Surg 2000;135:713.
101. Kim G, Daneman A, Alton DJ, et al: The appearance of inverted Meckel diverticulum with intussusception on air enema. Pediatr Radiol 1997;27:647.
102. Kirks DR: Diagnosis and treatment of pediatric intussusception: How far should we push our radiologic techniques? Radiology 1994;191:622.
103. Kokkonen J, Karttunen JK: Lymphonodular hyperplasia on the mucosa of the lower gastrointestinal tract in children: An indication of enhanced immune response? J Pediatr Gastroenteral Nutr 2002;34:42.
104. Kornecki A, Daneman A, Navarro O, et al: Spontaneous reduction of intussusception: Clinical spectrum, management and outcome. Pediatr Radiol 2000;30:58.
105. Lai IR, Huang MT, Lee WJ: Mini-laparoscopic reduction of intussusception for children. J Formos Med Assoc 2000;99:510.
106. Le Masne A, Lortat-Jacob S, Sayegh N, et al: Intussusception in infants and children: Feasibility of ambulatory management. Eur J Pediatr 1999;158:707.
107. Lin SL, Kong MS, Houng DS: Decreasing early recurrence rate of acute intussusception by the use of dexamethasone. Eur J Pediatr 2000;159:551.
108. Liu KW, MacCarthy J, Guiney EJ, et al: Intussusception—current trends in management. Arch Dis Child 1986;61:75.
109. Maoate KM, Beasley SW: Perforation during gas reduction of intussusception. Pediatr Surg Int 1998;14:168.
109a. Mayell MJ: Intussusception in infancy and childhood in South Africa. Arch Dis Child 1972;47:20.
110. McAlister WH: Intussusception: Even Hippocrates did not standardize his technique of enema reduction. Radiology 1998;206:595.
111. McDermott VG: Childhood intussusception and approaches to treatment: A historical review. Pediatr Radiol 1994; 24:153.
112. Meier DE, Coln CD, Rescorla FJ, et al: Intussusception in children: International perspective. World J Surg 1996; 20:1035.
113. Mercer S, Carpenter B: Mechanism of perforation occurring in the intussusception. Can J Surg 1982;25:481.

114. Mestel AL: Lymphosarcoma of the small intestine in infancy and childhood. Ann Surg 1959;149:87.
115. Meyer JS: The current radiologic management of intussusception: A survey and review. Pediatr Radiol 1992;22:323.
116. Meyer JS, Dangman BC, Buonomo C, et al: Air and liquid contrast agents in the management of intussusception: A controlled, randomized trial. Radiology 1993;188:507.
117. Miller SF, Landes AB, Dautenhahn LW, et al: Intussusception: Ability of fluoroscopic images obtained during air enemas to depict lead points and other abnormalities. Radiology 1995;197:493.
118. Mollitt DL, Ballantine TVN, Grosfeld JL: Postoperative intussusception in infancy and childhood: Analysis of 119 cases. Surgery 1979;86:402.
119. Montgomery EA, Pokek EJ: Intussusception, adenovirus, and children: A brief reaffirmation. Hum Pathol 1994; 25:169.
120. Mooney DP, Steinthorsson G, Shorter NA: Perinatal intussusception in premature infants. J Pediatr Surg 1996;31:695.
121. Morrison SC, Stork E: Documentation of spontaneous reduction of childhood intussusception by ultrasound. Pediatr Radiol 1990;20:358.
122. Mortensson W, Eklöf O, Laurin S: Hydrostatic reduction of childhood intussusception: The role of adjuvant glucagon medication. Acta Radiol Diagn 1984;25:261.
123. Mortimer JD: On the treatment of intussusception by injection or inflation and its dangers. Lancet 1891;1:1144.
124. Mulcahy DL, Kamath KR, deSilva LM, et al: A two part study of the aetiological role of rotavirus in intussusception. J Med Virol 1982;9:51.
125. Murakami JW, Winters WD, Weinberger E, et al: Extensive reflux of air during enema for intussusception without reduction: Case report. Can Assoc Radiol J 1998;49:334.
126. Navarro O, Daneman A: Intussusception Part 3: Diagnosis and management of those with an identifiable or predisposing cause and those that reduce spontaneously. Pediatr Radiol 2004;34:305.
127. Navarro O, Daneman A, Chae A: Intussusception: The use of delayed repeat reduction attempts and the management of intussusceptions due to pathologic lead points in pediatric patients. AJR Am J Roentgenol 2004;182:1169.
128. Navarro O, Dugougeat F, Kornecki A, et al: The impact of imaging in the management of intussusceptions owing to pathologic lead points in children: A review of 43 cases. Pediatr Radiol 2000;30:594.
129. Nissan S, Levy E: Intussusception in infancy caused by hypertrophic Peyer's patches. Surgery 1966;59:1108.
130. Okuyama H, Nakai H, Okada A: Is barium enema reduction safe and effective in patients with a long duration of intussusception? Pediatr Surg Int 1999;15:105.
131. Olsson G, Pallin G: Uber das Bild der akuten Darminvagination mit Hilfe von Kontrastlavements. Acta Chir Scand 1927;61:371.
132. Ong NT, Beasley SW: The leadpoint in intussusception. J Pediatr Surg 1990;25:640.
133. Palder SB, Ein SH, Stringer DA, et al: Intussusception: Barium or air? J Pediatr Surg 1991;26:271.
134. Pantongrag-Brown L, Levine MS, Elsayed AM, et al: Inverted Meckel diverticulum: Clinical, radiologic, and pathologic findings. Radiology 1996;199:693.
135. Parashar UD, Holman RC, Cummings KC, et al: Trends in intussusception-associated hospitalizations and deaths among US infants. Pediatrics 2000;106:1413.
136. Parkkulainen KV: Intrauterine intussusception as a cause of intestinal atresia. Surgery 1958;44:1106.
137. Poulquien M: Indication du lavement bismuthe dans certaines formes d'invaginations intestinales. Bull Mem Soc Nat Chir 1927;53:1016.
138. Power D: The Hunterian lectures on the pathology and surgery of intussusception. BMJ 1897;1:381-388, 453-456, 514-516.
139. Poznanski AK: Why I still use barium for intussusception. Pediatr Radiol 1995;25:92.
140. Pracros JP, Tran-Minh VA, Morin DE, et al: Acute intestinal intussusception in children: Contribution of ultrasonography (145 cases). Ann Radiol 1987;30: 525-530.
141. Rachelson MH, Jernigan JP, Jackson WF: Intussusception in the newborn infant with spontaneous expulsion of the intussusception: A case report and review of the literature. J Pediatr 1955;47:87.
142. Raffensperger JG: The Acute Abdomen in Infancy and Childhood. Philadelphia, JB Lippincott, 1970, p 52.
143. Ratcliffe JF, Fong S, Cheong I, et al: The plain abdominal film in intussusception: The accuracy and incidence of radiographic signs. Pediatr Radiol 1984;22:110.
144. Ravitch MM: Intussusception in Infants and Children. Springfield, IL, Charles C Thomas, 1959.
145. Ravitch MM: Intussusception. In Welch KJ, Randolph JG, Ravitch MM, et al (eds): Pediatric Surgery, 4th ed. Chicago, Year Book, 1986, p 868.
146. Ravitch MM, McCune RM Jr: Reduction of intussusception by hydrostatic pressure: An experimental study. Bull Johns Hopkins Hosp 1948;82:550.
147. Retan GM: Nonoperative treatment of intussusception. Am J Dis Child 1927;33:765.
148. Rohrschneider W, Tröger J, Betsch B: The post reduction donut sign. Pediatr Radiol 1994;24:156.
149. Sandler AD, Ein SH, Connolly BL, et al: Unsuccessful air-enema reduction of intussusception: Is a second attempt worthwhile? Pediatr Surg Int 1999;15:214.
150. Sanz N, Sánchez M, García Aroca J, et al: Intussusception: Barium vs. pneumatic reduction. Cir Pediatr 1996;9:21.
151. Sargent MA, Babyn P, Alton DJ: Plain abdominal radiography in suspected intussusception: A reassessment. Pediatr Radiol 1994;24:17.
152. Saxton V, Katz M, Phelan E, et al: Intussusception: A repeat delayed gas enema increases the nonoperative reduction rate. J Pediatr Surg 1994;29:588.
153. Schmit P, Rohrschneider WK, Christmann D: Intestinal intussusception survey about diagnostic and nonsurgical therapeutic procedures. Pediatr Radiol 1999;29:752.
154. Senocak ME, Büyükpamakcu N, Hicsönmez A: Ileal atresia due to intrauterine intussusception caused by Meckel's diverticulum. Pediatr Surg Int 1990;5:64.
155. Shiels WE 2nd, Kirks DR, Keller GL, et al: Colonic perforation by air and liquid enemas: Comparison study in young pigs. AJR Am J Roentgenol 1993;160:931.
156. Shiels WE 2nd, Maves CK, Hedlund GL, et al: Air enema for diagnosis and reduction of intussusception: Clinical experiences and pressure correlates. Radiology 1991; 181:169.
157. Shteyer E, Koplewitz BZ, Gross E, et al: Medical treatment of recurrent intussusception associated with intestinal lymphoid hyperplasia. Pediatrics 2003;111:682.
158. Siaplaouras J, Moritz JD, Gortner L, et al: Dünndarminvaginationen im Kindesalter: Diagnostik und Bedeutung (Small bowel intussusception in childhood). Klin Padiatr 2003;215:53.
159. Simonsen L, Morens D, Elixhauser A, et al: Effect of rotavirus vaccination programme on trends in admission of infants to hospital for intussusception. Lancet 2001; 358:1224.
160. Somekh E, Serour F, Gonçalves D, et al: Air enema reduction of intussusception in children: Risk of bacteremia. Radiology 1996;200:217.

161. Sönmez K, Turkyilmaz Z, Demirogullari B, et al: Conservative treatment for small intestinal intussusception associated with Henoch-Schönlein's purpura. Surg Today 2002;32:1031.
162. Stein M, Alton DJ, Daneman A: Pneumatic reduction of intussusception: 5-year experience. Radiology 1992;183:681.
163. Strang RP: Intussusception in infancy and childhood: A review of 400 cases. Br J Surg 1959;46:484.
164. Stringer DA, Ein SH: Pneumatic reduction: Advantages, risks and indications. Pediatr Radiol 1990;20:475.
165. Stringer MD, Homes SJK: Familial intussusception. J Pediatr Surg 1992;27:1436.
166. Stringer MD, Pablot SM, Brereton RJ: Paediatric intussusception. Br J Surg 1992;79:867.
167. Stringer MD, Willetts IE: John Hunter, Frederick Treves and intussusception. Ann R Coll Surg Engl 2000;82:18.
168. Strouse PJ, DiPietro MA, Sáez F: Transient small bowel intussusception in children on CT. Pediatr Radiol 2003; 33:316.
169. Swenson O: Pediatric Surgery, 2nd ed. New York, Appleton-Century-Crofts, 1962, p 328.
170. Todani T, Tabuchi K, Tanake S: Intestinal atresia due to intrauterine intussusception: Analysis of 24 cases in Japan. J Pediatr Surg 1975;10:445.
171. Treves F: The treatment of intussusception. Proc Med Soc London 1885;8:83.
172. van Heek NT, Aronson DC, Halimun EM, et al: Intussusception in a tropical country: Comparison among patient populations in Jakarta, Jogyakarta, and Amsterdam. J Pediatr Gastroenterol Nutr 1999;29:402.
173. Warshauer DM, Lee JKT: Adult intussusception detected at CT or MR imaging: Clinical-imaging correlation. Radiology 1999;212:853.
174. Wayne ER, Campbell JB, Kosloske AM, et al: Intussusception in the older child—suspect lymphosarcoma. J Pediatr Surg 1976;11:789.
175. Weber A, Nadel S: CT appearance of retrograde jejunoduodenogastric intussusception: A rare complication of gastrostomy tubes. AJR Am J Roentgenol 1991; 156:957.
176. West KW, Grosfeld JL: Intussusception in infants and children. In Wyllie R, Hyams JS (eds): Pediatric Gastrointestinal Disease. Philadelphia, WB Saunders, 1993, p 472.
177. West KW, Stephens B, Rescorla FJ, et al: Postoperative intussusception: Experience with 36 cases in children. Surgery 1988;104:781.
178. White SJ, Blane CE: Intussusception: Additional observations on the plain radiograph. AJR Am J Roentgenol 1982; 139:511.
179. Wilson-Storey D, MacKinlay GA, Prescott S, et al: Intussusception: A surgical condition. J R Coll Surg Edinb 1988;33:270.
180. Willetts IE, Kite P, Barclay GR, et al: Endotoxin, cytokines and lipid peroxides in children with intussusception. Br J Surg 2001;88:878.
181. Winstanley JHR, Doig CM, Brydon H: Intussusception: The case for barium reduction. J R Coll Surg Edinb 1987; 32:285.
182. Yeung CP, Ip SM, Lee KH, et al: The significance of bacteraemia, endotoxaemia and cytokine release in the production of fever in childhood intussusception. Paper presented at the 42nd Meeting of the British Association of Paediatric Surgeons, 1995, Sheffield, England.
183. Young DG: Intussusception. In O'Neill JA Jr, Rowe MI, Grosfeld JL, et al (eds): Pediatric Surgery, 3rd ed. Chicago, Year Book, 1998, p 1185.
184. Zachary RB: Acute intussusception in children. Arch Dis Child 1955;30:32.
185. Zanardi LR, Haber P, Mootrey GT, et al: Intussusception among recipients of rotavirus vaccine: Reports to the vaccine adverse event reporting system. Pediatrics 2001; 107:E97.

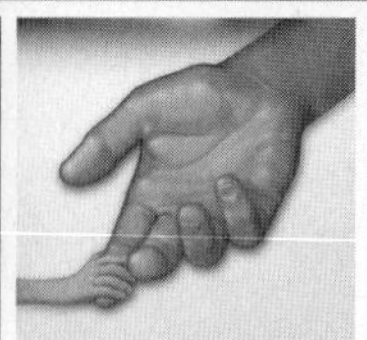

Chapter 84

Disorders of Intestinal Rotation and Fixation

Samuel D. Smith

HISTORY

Information on the failure of rotation and fixation of the intestinal tract has accumulated slowly. Before 1900, only individual cases found at surgery or autopsy were described; these reports could not be placed in context until the embryology was understood.

The first meaningful description of the embryology was written in 1898 by Mall,[36] professor of anatomy at Johns Hopkins, who had studied in Germany with His, the celebrated embryologist. On the basis of his own studies of reconstructed embryos, as well as those of His, Mall described the process of rotation and then fixation of the bowel. Fraser and Robbins[19] expanded Mall's observations with their own studies of a large group of embryos.

In 1923 Dott[15] published his classic paper on the embryology and surgical aspects of anomalies of intestinal rotation. This was the first clear correlation between clinical and embryologic observations. Dott correlated the findings in 2 of his own cases and 40 collected from the literature with various failures of development. Most subsequent articles described clinical cases in relation to Dott's analysis of the stage of embryologic failure. In 1928 Waugh[55] described two cases of volvulus due to nonrotation. In 1931 Haymond and Dragstedt[24] described the clinical findings and embryology of one type of internal hernia. In the 1930s Gardner and Hart[21] reported 2 cases of their own and classified 104 additional reported cases, Wakefield and Mayo[53] described 13 cases, and McIntosh and Donovan[39] described 20 cases. In 1932 Ladd[32] described 10 cases of malrotation with volvulus and recommended treatment by counterclockwise detorsion. In 1936 Ladd[33] wrote the classic article on the treatment of this condition and described 21 cases. He emphasized the importance of dividing the bands over the duodenum and then placing the cecum in the left upper quadrant. Actually, this article shows that Ladd focused his attention on the rarely found bands that go to the right of the duodenum. He did not identify the more frequently encountered bands that enclose the duodenum and cecum. Ladd's procedure of releasing the duodenum and placing the cecum in the left upper quadrant remains the cornerstone of surgical treatment for nonrotation with midgut volvulus. Fixation by sutures has been reported but is no longer advocated because it is not effective.[9,10] In 1953 Gross[23] reported 156 cases in the first comprehensive review of the subject. The Boston Children's Hospital's experience has been updated.[24,51]

In 1954 Snyder and Chaffin[48] published a clear and insightful description of anomalies of rotation. In this report, the embryology of malrotation was compared to the twisting of a loop of rope around a central band that represented the superior mesenteric vessels.

NORMAL ROTATION AND FIXATION

Rotation may be described according to how it affects the two ends of the intestinal tract, that is, the proximal duodenojejunal loop and the distal cecocolic loop and the simultaneous rotation of these two components. Most authorities refer to the process as involving the midgut, but it is best to include the entire intestinal tract.[23,34]

Duodenojejunal Loop

The normal adult position of the stomach, duodenum, and first part of the jejunum is well known. Starting at the upper end of the adult intestinal tube and observing its fixed relation to the superior mesenteric artery, it is clear that the stomach is above or anterior to the artery, the second portion of the duodenum is to the right of the artery, the third portion of the duodenum lies beneath the artery, and the fourth portion (the distal duodenum and first part of the jejunum) is to the left of the artery. The duodenojejunal loop starts in the embryo in the same position as that of the stomach in the adult (Fig. 84-1). If the other components of the loop eventually take the position as previously described, the duodenojejunal

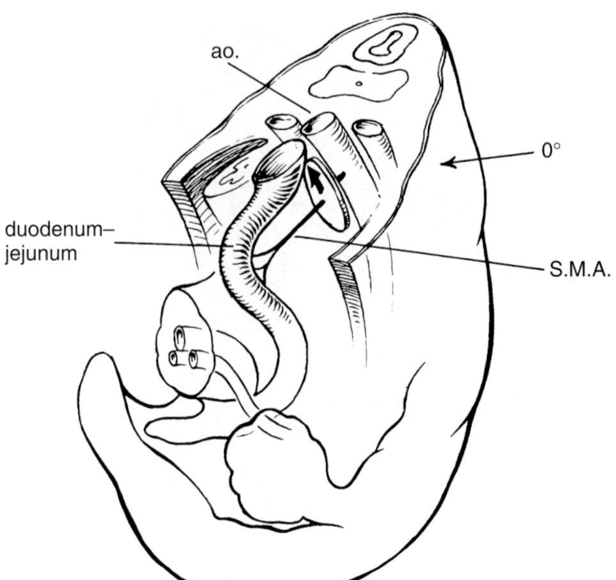

Figure 84–1 Schematic ventrolateral view of a 5-mm embryo. The intestinal tract forms a slight curve forward. The superior mesenteric artery (SMA) passes at right angles from the aorta (ao) to the curve of the intestine. A disk has been drawn around the SMA at its base; the *arrow* points superiorly to the starting position, or 0 degrees rotation, of the duodenojejunal loop. Rotation proceeds around the artery as an axis.

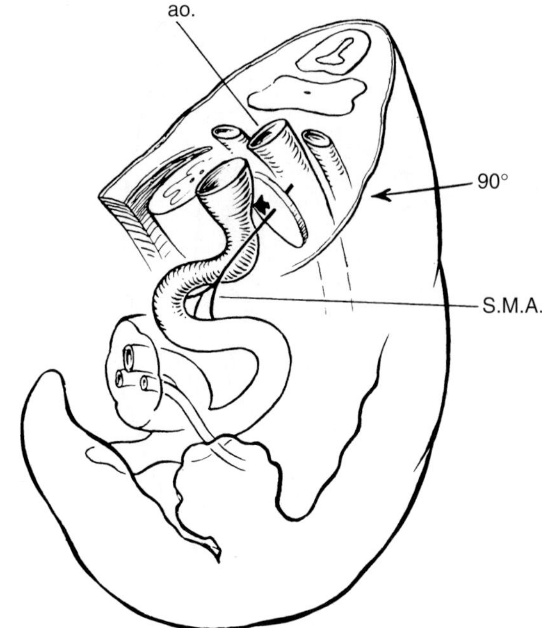

Figure 84–2 Schematic ventrolateral view of a 10-mm embryo. The duodenojejunal loop has passed from a position above the superior mesenteric artery (SMA) to the right of the artery and thus has rotated through an arc of 90 degrees from its starting position, as indicated by the *arrow* in the disk. aorta (ao, aorta.).

loop has rotated around the superior mesenteric artery from above (see Fig. 84-1), to the right 90 degrees (Fig. 84-2), and to the bottom another 90 degrees, for a total thus far of 180 degrees (Fig. 84-3), then to its final place to the left of the artery for an additional swing of another 90 degrees, or a total arc of 270 degrees (Fig. 84-4). The direction of the swing is determined by the normal final position of the stomach and all four portions of the duodenum.

Orientation for Side and Direction of Rotation

In the preceding description, the right side is the patient's right, not the right side of the observer facing the patient. However, when the usual direction of rotation is described according to the hands of a clock, the direction noted is from the viewpoint of the observer. If an imaginary clock is placed face up on the posterior wall of the embryo or baby, the pivot point of the hands (i.e., the axis of their rotation) is the superior mesenteric artery. The duodenojejunal loop moves counterclockwise.

Cecocolic Loop

In the adult, the terminal ileum, cecum, and right colon reside on the right side of the abdomen to the right of the superior mesenteric artery. In the embryo, they lie beneath the artery. This cecocolic loop, like the duodenojejunal loop, passes counterclockwise from its starting point beneath the artery (Fig. 84-5), to the left of the artery 90 degrees (Fig. 84-6), above to 180 degrees (Fig. 84-7), and to the right of the artery, through a total arc of 270 degrees (Fig. 84-8). In this manner, the cecocolic loop normally achieves its adult position.

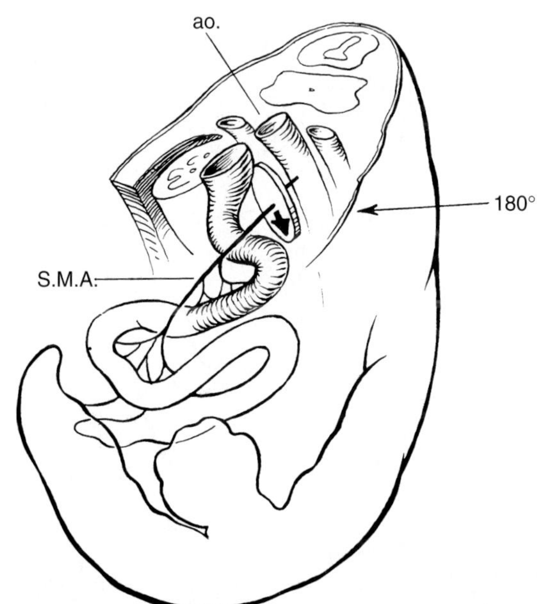

Figure 84–3 Schematic ventrolateral view of a 25-mm embryo, indicating further rotation of the duodenojejunal loop to a position below the superior mesenteric artery (SMA), through an arc of 180 degrees. Extension of the remainder of the intestines into the cord is not shown. aorta (ao, aorta.).

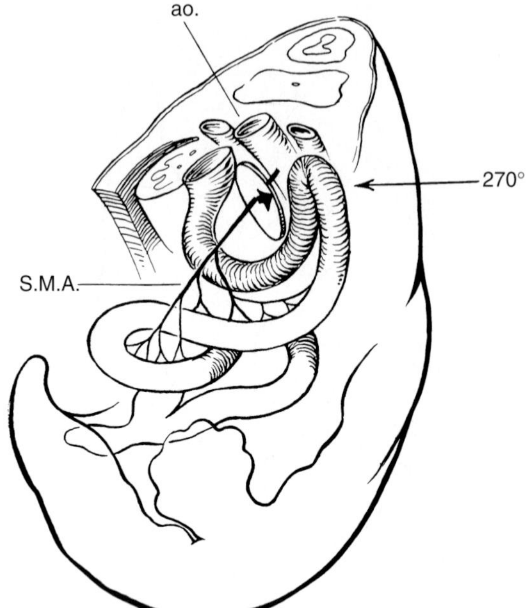

Figure 84–4 Schematic ventrolateral view of a 40-mm embryo, indicating final rotation of the duodenojejunal loop to a position immediately to the left of the superior mesenteric artery (SMA). This loop has passed from a position superior, to the right beneath, and to the left, or through an arc of 270 degrees in a counterclockwise direction. This final rotation of the duodenojejunal loop takes place as the intestines return from the cord. aorta (ao, aorta.).

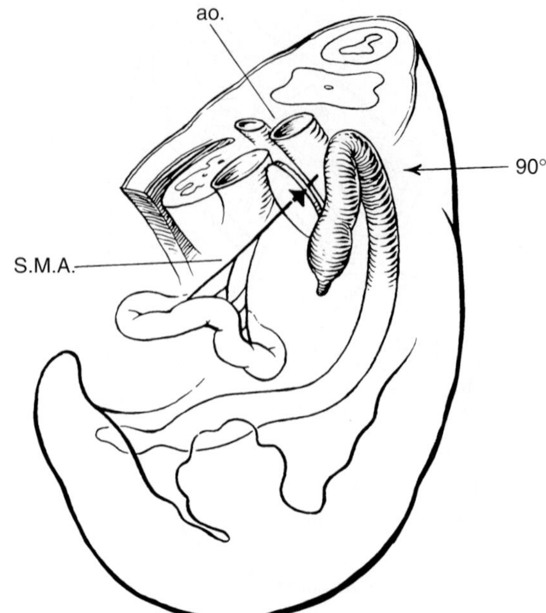

Figure 84–6 Schematic ventrolateral view of a 40-mm embryo, showing the position of the cecocolic loop at the left of the superior mesenteric artery (SMA). The loop has rotated through an arc of 90 degrees from its starting position inferior to the artery (see the disk at the base of the SMA). This phase of rotation is maintained while the intestines are in the cord and at the moment they drop back into the abdomen. aorta (ao, aorta.).

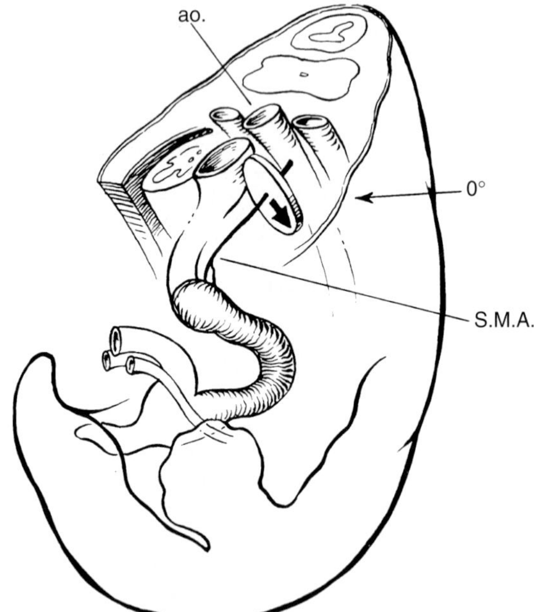

Figure 84–5 Schematic ventrolateral view of a 5-mm embryo, indicating the forward bend of the intestinal tract. The cecocolic loop is emphasized as it lies inferior to the superior mesenteric artery (SMA), or in a position of 0 degrees rotation, indicated on the disk around the base of the SMA. The 0-degree rotation position for this loop is inferior to the SMA, whereas that for the duodenojejunal loop is superior. aorta (ao, aorta.).

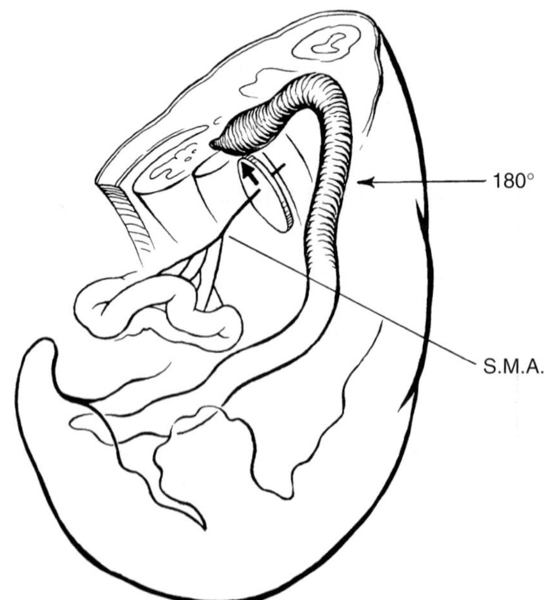

Figure 84–7 Schematic ventrolateral view of a 40-mm embryo, indicating rotation of the cecocolic loop to a position superior to the superior mesenteric artery (SMA), or rotation through an arc of 180 degrees from the starting position inferior to the SMA. This phase takes place immediately after return of the intestines from the cord into the abdomen.

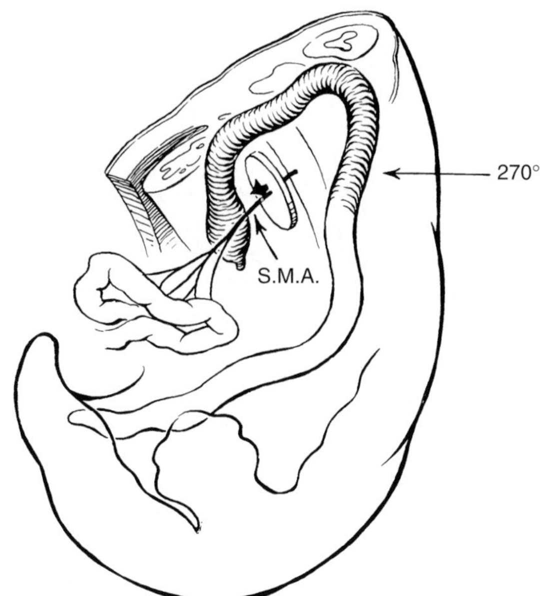

Figure 84–8 Schematic ventrolateral view of a 40-mm embryo, showing the final position of the cecocolic loop to the right of the superior mesenteric artery (SMA). This loop has passed from a position beneath, to the left, superior, and finally to the right of the SMA, or through an arc of 270 degrees in a counterclockwise direction.

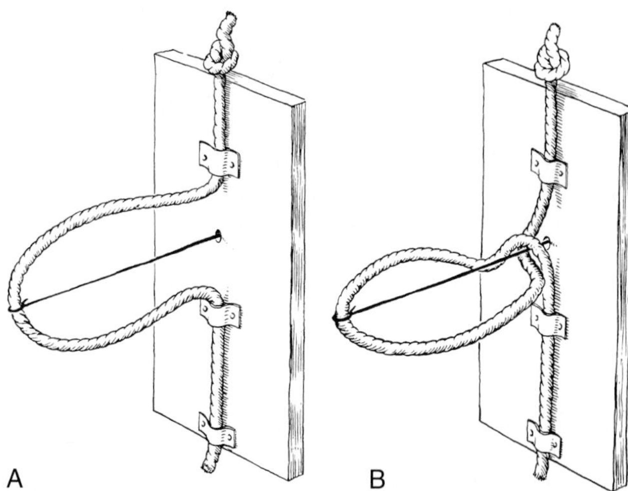

Figure 84–9 Mechanical demonstration of intestinal rotation. A rope is attached to a board at both ends, with a wire extending at right angles from the board to the base of the loop. *A,* The top limb of the rope corresponds to the duodenojejunal loop, the wire corresponds to the superior mesenteric artery, and the bottom limb corresponds to the cecocolic segment. *B,* The rope loop has been grasped by the hand and rotated through an arc of 270 degrees, or three quarters of a complete turn around the wire as the axis, in a counterclockwise direction. Thus, the top limb has become the bottom one, and the bottom limb the top. By following the movements of the two limbs around the wire close to the board, one can visualize the process of rotation of the intestine in the embryo.

Simultaneous Rotation of Both Ends and of the Entire Intestinal Tract

Rotation is best visualized by attaching a loop of rope above and below a metal spoke (wire) on a piece of wood (Fig. 84-9). The loop is grasped in the left hand and turned through three quarters of a turn to the left. The proximal portion of the upper limb of the rope should be watched. This portion turns from its initial position above the wire, to the right of it, beneath it, and to the left of it. At the same time, the lower limb of the rope lies beneath the wire at the start of the turn, then goes to the left, above, and finally to the right of the wire. If the upper limb of the rope represents the duodenojejunal loop, the wire represents the superior mesenteric artery, and the lower limb represents the cecocolic loop, the position of these structures in the process of rotation should be clear. The entire process can be studied in minute detail with a dissecting microscope and a large series of embryos ranging in age from 4 to 12 weeks. In the fourth week of fetal life, or when the embryo has reached the 5-mm stage, the intestinal tract is almost a straight tube, with a slight anterior bulge in the central portion. The superior mesenteric artery comes forward from the posterior wall to the center of the bulge (see Figs. 84-1 to 84-5). Changes occur rapidly as the intestine forms within an extension of the abdominal wall into the umbilical cord. The stomach remains in its original position anterior and above the superior mesenteric artery. The duodenum then begins to curve downward and to the right of the artery. The jejunum and small intestine extend into the umbilical cord, along with the cecum, right colon, and part of the transverse colon. Both loops have thus passed from a position in front of the artery to the side of the artery (see Figs. 84-2 and 84-6).

It was previously thought that both loops remained in this position until the intestines returned from the cord into the abdomen.[15,19] However, it was demonstrated by Mall[36] and verified by Snyder and Chaffin[48] that the duodenojejunum continues to rotate during the extracoelomic phase of intestinal development, and at about the eighth week, the third portion of the duodenum comes to lie beneath the artery (see Fig. 84-3). This increases the rotation of this segment to 180 degrees. Finally, at about 10 weeks (or when the embryo is about 40 mm long), the intestines return to the abdomen. This must be a rapid process, because few specimens of this stage of development have been described. The small bowel is the first segment of the intestines to return to the abdominal cavity, and it pushes the fourth portion of the duodenum and jejunum to the left of the superior mesenteric artery. This completes the rotation of this segment of the bowel (see Fig. 84-4). The cecum and right colon return to the abdomen last, on the left side (see Fig. 84-6). This loop then passes anterior or above the artery (see Fig. 84-7) and finally to its adult position on the right side of the artery (see Fig. 84-8).

To use another analogy, placing a hand on top of an imaginary automobile steering wheel and making a three-quarter turn to the left executes the process of rotating the duodenojejunal loop around the steering post (superior mesenteric artery). With a hand on the bottom of the steering wheel, a three-quarter turn to the left executes the rotation of the cecocolic loop.

This is the process of normal rotation; the sequence of events has been postulated from bits of evidence contributed by many observers. It does not lend itself to a breakdown into stages I, II, and III, as previously described, because it is a continuing process and is better understood by comparing it with the swing of a twisted rope or the turn of a steering wheel.[19] That description may be an oversimplification, but it is easy to remember in the operating room.

Kluth and Lambrecht[31] proposed a slightly different explanation for intestinal malrotation, based on rat embryo studies. They emphasized that rapid growth and lengthening of the duodenum force the tip of the duodenojejunal loop to grow under the mesenteric root. The distal midgut also rapidly lengthens and forces the cecum from a caudal to a cranial position; this may appear to be rotation, but the rest of the colorectum is not involved in the process. These authors view fixation and position of the intestine to be a process of differential growth rather than rotation because they did not find gross changes in the straight midgut in their embryo studies. They postulate that maldevelopment of the embryonic duodenal loop is the major problem involved in the pathogenesis of midgut malformations. Reduced growth of the duodenal loop or abnormal insertion of the mesenteric root, functioning as a barrier to growth of the duodenal loop, may explain the abnormal location of the duodenum and the ligament of Treitz. They believe that cecal and colonic movement plays a more passive or minor role in causing abnormalities of intestinal position and fixation.

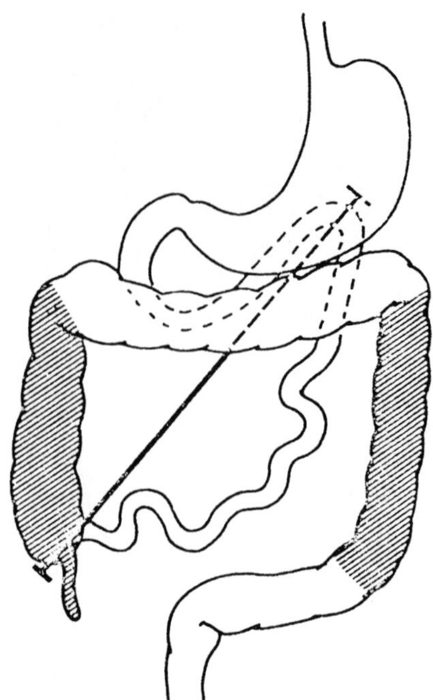

Figure 84–10 Normal fixation of the mesentery of the midgut. The normal broad base extends from the ligament of Treitz to the ileocecal junction and prevents twisting of the intestine. Both the ascending and descending colon are fixed retroperitoneally. (From Filston HC, Kirks DR: Malrotation—the ubiquitous anomaly. J Pediatr Surg 1981;16:614.)

CLASSIFICATION OF ABNORMALITIES OF INTESTINAL ROTATION

Normal fixation of the duodenum and colon is illustrated in Figure 84-10. The normal mesenteric attachment extends from the ligament of Treitz, located at the level of the gastric outlet, to the cecum. Both the ascending and descending colon are fixed retroperitoneally. The abnormalities of intestinal rotation represent a spectrum with many variations. The surgical problems resulting from these abnormalities of rotation are best classified by understanding the errors in growth, rotation, and position of the duodenum and ligament of Treitz. Any defined stages are arbitrary, but referring to Figure 84-11, which shows the stages of normal rotation, may be helpful in determining the maldevelopment that may have occurred in an individual case.[4]

The term *malrotation* refers to all abnormalities of intestinal position and attachment[16] and includes the more recent concept of atypical malrotation or malrotation variant. Atypical malrotation results when the ligament of Treitz is to the left of midline, defined by the vertebral body, or below the gastric outlet on upper gastrointestinal (GI) contrast studies. The term *nonrotation* is used for the first stage (see Fig. 84-10), and the terms *incomplete rotation* and *mixed rotation* are used for abnormalities of the second stage.

Reverse rotation is a rare anomaly in which the duodenum and colon rotate clockwise in relation to the superior mesenteric artery and vein. The transverse colon eventually lies behind the vessels, which may result in acute or chronic colonic obstruction.

Rotation and fixation abnormalities are also known to coexist with heterotaxia, but rarely with situs inversus.[11] Heterotaxia, previously known as situs ambiguus, is defined as an abnormal arrangement of body organs or complete situs inversus. Major cardiac anomalies are commonly associated with heterotaxia. GI anomalies include midline liver, malposition of the stomach, anomalies of intestinal rotation and fixation, intraperitoneal pancreas, and either asplenia or polysplenia.[11]

Malrotation is an integral part of congenital diaphragmatic hernia and abdominal wall defects. In gastroschisis, the midgut is nonrotated and may be suspended and stretched outside the fetal abdominal cavity; this leads to ischemic injury without volvulus. Infants with omphalocele or diaphragmatic hernia have varying degrees of normal rotation and fixation, depending on the extent of intestinal displacement.

Associated anomalies are found in 30% to 60% of patients with malrotation.[17,30,41,53] Duodenal atresia has been found in conjunction with malrotation and perinatal volvulus. Intrinsic duodenal obstruction from a partially obstructing web must not be overlooked in cases of malrotation. Filston and Kirks[17] found midgut malrotation as an associated malformation in half of jejunal and one third of duodenal atresia cases. Malrotation is rarely associated with Hirschsprung's disease and anorectal malformations.[36] Mesenteric cysts have been observed in association with malrotation, but whether this is a primary

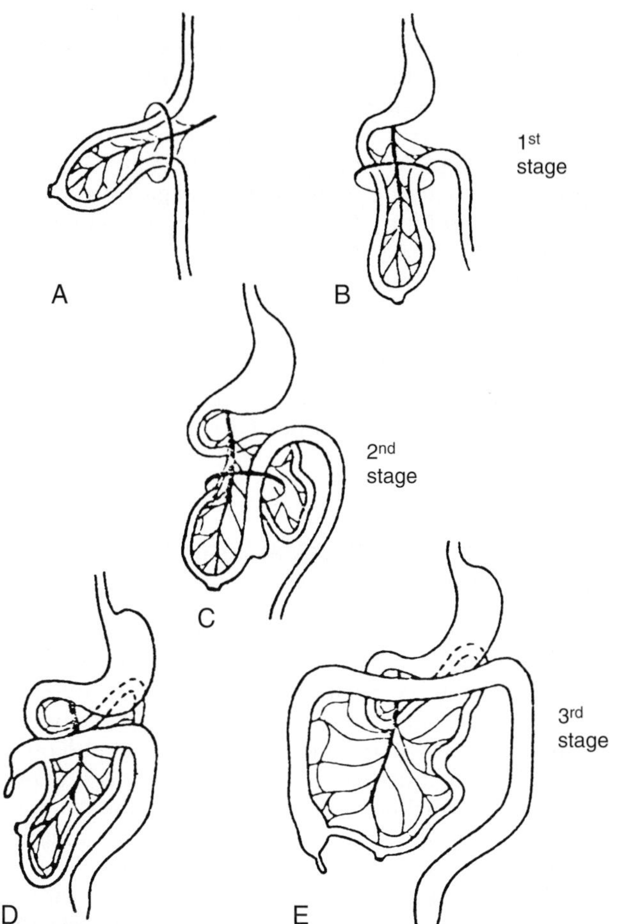

Figure 84–11 Normal intestinal rotation. *A,* Six weeks' gestational age: nonrotation. *B,* Eight weeks' gestational age: incomplete rotation. *C,* Nine weeks' gestational age: incomplete rotation. *D,* Eleven weeks' gestational age. *E,* Twelve weeks' gestational age. (From Filston HC, Kirks DR: Malrotation—the ubiquitous anomaly. J Pediatr Surg 1981;16:614.)

anomaly or results from lymphatic obstruction due to chronic volvulus is not clear.[7]

CLINICAL MANIFESTATIONS

Various clinical presentations, ranging from chronic abdominal pain to acute midgut volvulus with ischemic bowel injury, may result from failure of normal intestinal rotation and fixation. In general, it is possible to correlate the various clinical syndromes with the observed anatomic findings, but there are many variables and exceptions.

Acute Midgut Volvulus

The narrow pedicle formed by the base of the mesentery in malrotation predisposes the midgut to clockwise twisting from the duodenum to the transverse colon (Fig. 84-12). Excessive length of the mesentery or a point of adhesion at the convexity of the loop may act as an axis for a twist.[15] The actual inciting mechanism is

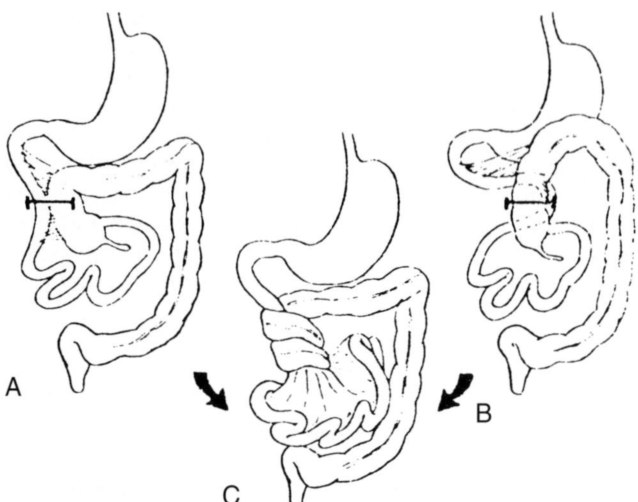

Figure 84–12 Pathophysiology of midgut volvulus with malrotation. *A,* The narrow mesenteric attachment in nonrotation *(B)* or incomplete rotation *(C)* predisposes the patient to midgut volvulus. (From Filston HC, Kirks DR: Malrotation—the ubiquitous anomaly. J Pediatr Surg 1981;16:614.)

unknown, but various possibilities have been suggested, including unusual movement of the torso, abnormal intestinal peristalsis, or segmental bowel distention.[13]

Most patients with midgut volvulus present in the first month of life.[46] In a group of 74 patients, 23 were seen in the first 7 days of life; 16 from 7 to 30 days of life, and 24 from 1 to 12 months; only 11 were older than 1 year.[3] Fourteen of 22 patients described by Torres and Ziegler[52] presented during the first month of life.

The primary presenting sign of malrotation is the sudden onset of bilious vomiting in a previously healthy, growing infant.[43] With the onset of proximal intestinal obstruction, the distal colon empties; soon after the onset of vomiting, the lower abdomen may appear scaphoid. As vascular compromise progresses, intraluminal bleeding may occur, and blood is often passed per rectum. Crampy abdominal pain is common. Innocent "colic" or hypertrophic pyloric stenosis may be ruled out on the basis of bilious vomiting.

Infants with complete obstruction rapidly develop intestinal ischemia with a firm, distended abdomen, hypovolemia, and shock. Abdominal tenderness varies with the degree of vascular compromise, but signs of peritonitis are invariably present.

A high index of suspicion for midgut volvulus is based on the history, physical examination findings, and presence of metabolic acidosis. The decision whether to confirm the diagnosis by either Doppler ultrasonography or upper GI contrast radiography or to proceed directly to laparotomy or laparoscopy must be based on the condition of the patient and the risk of vascular compromise if there is any delay.

Chronic Midgut Volvulus

Intermittent or partial midgut volvulus results in lymphatic and venous obstruction, with enlargement of the mesenteric lymph nodes. This situation is more commonly encountered in children older than 2 years.[18,26,27,43,49] Based on our review of malrotation in children older than 2 years, the most frequent presenting complaints are chronic vomiting (68%), intermittent colicky abdominal pain (55%), diarrhea (9%), hematemesis (5%), and constipation (5%).[37] The average duration of symptoms before an operation was performed was 28 months. Absorption and nutrient transport can be impaired by venous and lymphatic stasis, leading eventually to protein-calorie malnutrition in severe cases of long-standing incomplete rotation with partial obstruction.[26,49] An increased predisposition to infection has also been observed.[26]

Failure to suspect this diagnosis has resulted in dietary manipulation and even psychiatric evaluation in some patients. Bilious vomiting in conjunction with abdominal pain should be considered a surgical problem until proved otherwise.[14] Nonbilious vomiting may also occur as a neurogenic response to gastroduodenal distention.

Typical Malrotation in Asymptomatic or Minimally Symptomatic Patients

The incidental finding of malrotation on radiography or at the time of an operation raises the question of the eventual risk of complications in an asymptomatic patient. In a study of 50 adults with malrotation, Wang and Welch[54] found that 26 actually had symptoms referable to the abnormality. The general consensus is that a corrective surgical procedure is indicated at any age.[17,20,46]

The issue of asymptomatic patients with malrotation was brought into focus by Chang et al.,[11] who reported on 34 patients with heterotaxia and complex heart disease. Four of 28 developed acute or chronic signs of midgut volvulus requiring an emergency Ladd procedure. A subsequent group of six patients with heterotaxia had upper GI radiography that detected anomalies of intestinal fixation and rotation in all of them. Each patient underwent an uncomplicated elective Ladd procedure once the cardiac condition stabilized.

The first indication of malrotation may be noted during surgical exploration for an acute abdomen. Locating an acutely inflamed appendix in a patient with malrotation may be anticipated by radiographic absence of a cecal shadow in the right lower quadrant. In Collins's[12] study of 71,000 human appendix specimens, 2849 were in an abnormal position because of incomplete rotation of the large bowel. Further evaluation of such patients by upper GI radiography is indicated after their recovery from emergency surgery.

Acute Duodenal Obstruction Secondary to Congenital Bands

Acute duodenal obstruction results from peritoneal bands (Ladd's bands) extending across the third portion of the duodenum, causing extrinsic compression of the lumen or kinking of the bowel at the site of fixation. Duodenal obstruction is more common in neonates and infants but can occur later in life as well. Volvulus is not a principal finding in these patients.

An infant or newborn usually presents with forceful, bilious vomiting. Abdominal distention may or may not be present, depending on the degree of gastric emptying achieved by vomiting. Gastric peristaltic waves may occasionally be observed.[40] The obstruction may be complete or incomplete, so that meconium or stool may have been passed. Jaundice may be seen.[42] In a newborn, symptomatic malrotation with bands is often associated with intrinsic duodenal obstruction. A "double bubble" due to duodenal obstruction is usually seen on plain abdominal radiographs, but an upper GI contrast study of the duodenum is diagnostic.

Chronic Duodenal Obstruction Secondary to Congenital Bands

Chronic, recurrent, or subacute obstruction of the duodenum results when the prearterial limb does not complete its normal rotation and is fixed by adhesions and peritoneal bands that may twist, angulate, or kink the duodenum.[35] Some degree of volvulus may pull on the bands and contribute to the kinking. The obstruction is usually in the third portion of the duodenum.

Bilious vomiting is the main finding at presentation. Failure to gain weight and intermittent colicky abdominal pain are commonly observed. The age at diagnosis ranges from infancy to preschool age. Transient dilatation of the duodenum without reflux can, by reflex, stimulate gastric regurgitation. Contrast studies, although diagnostic, must be performed carefully because the degree of enlargement may be subtle.

Reverse Rotation with Colonic Obstruction

In this rare abnormality (Fig. 84-13), the duodenum and jejunum lie anterior to the superior mesenteric vessels and obstruct the posteriorly lying transverse colon. The transverse colon must pass through a tunnel beneath the mesentery, and this produces a chronic incomplete or complete obstruction of the colon. This condition is usually seen in adults and is rarely reported in children.[54]

Internal Hernia

Lack of fixation of the mesentery of the right or left colon, or of the duodenum, may result in the formation of potential spaces for hernias. Internal hernias are associated with recurrent entrapment of bowel with partial obstruction, which may eventually progress to complete obstruction and strangulation. The most commonly seen internal hernias are the right and left mesocolic hernias described by Willwerth et al.[56] The term *mesocolic* is preferred to the alternative term *paraduodenal*. A right mesocolic hernia is produced when the prearterial limb fails to rotate around the superior mesenteric artery and the bowel loops are entrapped by the mesentery of the cecum and colon (Fig. 84-14A). A left mesocolic hernia is produced when the unsupported area of the descending mesocolon between the inferior mesenteric vein and the posterior parietal colonic attachment is ballooned out by the small intestine as it migrates to the left superior portion of the abdominal cavity. Usually, the cecum has completely rotated and lies in a normal position in the right lower quadrant. The ileum exits from the sac, but at a variable distance from the ileocecal valve (Fig. 84-14B and C).

Signs and symptoms of an internal hernia are related to recurrent, intermittent bouts of intestinal obstruction characterized by recurrent colic. The latter may lead to constant abdominal pain, vomiting, and, sometimes, constipation. The symptoms are often mild and are occasionally thought to be psychological. Radiographs obtained during an attack of colic may suggest obstruction of the small intestine.

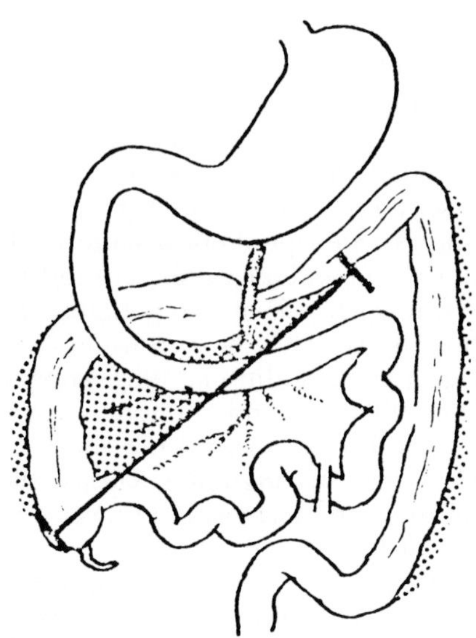

Figure 84-13 Reverse rotation of the duodenum and colon. When the colon rotates beneath the superior mesenteric artery, the midtransverse colon may become partially obstructed. This is caused by pressure of the vessels and by bands from the mesentery to the small bowel.

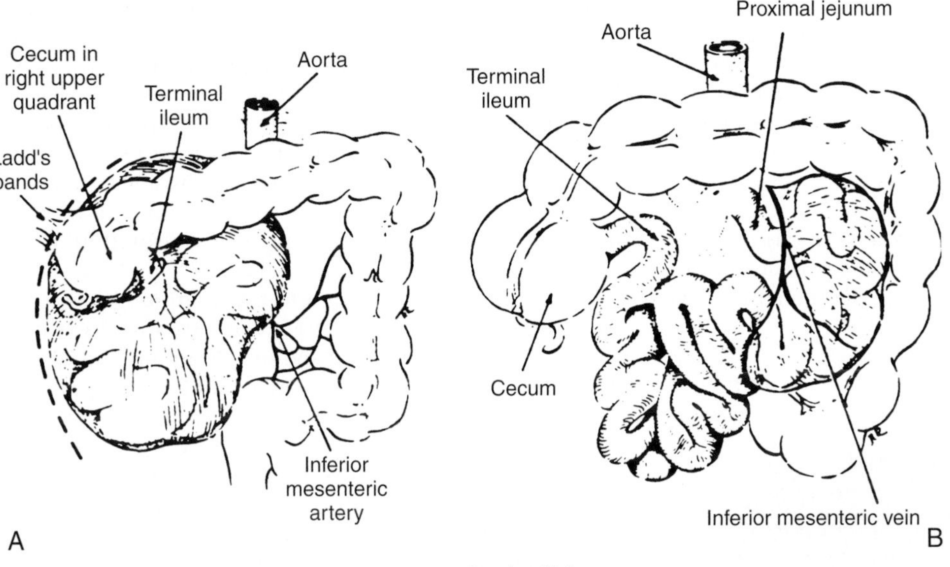

Figure 84-14 Mesocolic hernias. *A*, Right mesocolic hernia. The prearterial segment of the midgut has failed to rotate. The postarterial segment does not rotate and traps most of the small bowel behind the right mesocolon. The *hatched line* indicates the surgical incision used to reduce the hernia. *B*, Left mesocolic hernia. Initial rotation of the small intestine is normal. During migration to the left superior portion of the abdomen, the bowel invaginates an avascular portion of the left mesocolon posterior to the inferior mesenteric vein. *C*, Left mesocolic hernia. The small intestine, except for portions of the distal ileum, is trapped beneath the left mesocolon. Note that the inferior mesenteric vein delineates the right margin of the sac and is an integral part of the neck of the sac. (From Willwerth BM, Zollinger RM, Izant RJ: Congenital mesocolic [paraduodenal] hernia: Embryologic basis of repair. Am J Surg 1974;128:358, 1974. *B* and *C*, Based on Callander CL, et al: Surg Gynecol Obstet 1935;60:1052.)

Volvulus of the Cecum

Cecal volvulus, seen most often in patients older than 60 years, is caused by lack of fixation of the cecum, terminal ileum, and proximal ascending colon. The main symptoms are acute, severe abdominal pain and nausea associated with right-sided abdominal distention. Complete obstruction frequently develops. The characteristic abdominal radiograph shows a large air-filled loop of colon occupying the left upper quadrant (the convex surface faces the left lower quadrant), associated with small bowel obstruction.[2]

RADIOLOGIC DIAGNOSIS OF ABNORMALITIES OF ROTATION AND FIXATION

Contrast radiography is essential for the clinical evaluation and diagnosis of disorders of intestinal rotation and fixation. The normal relations of the stomach, duodenum, ligament of Treitz, and ileocecal area are shown schematically in Figure 84-11 and radiographically in Figure 84-15. The extent of normal mesenteric attachment is largely predictive of the radiographic findings.[4,8,25,45]

Plain abdominal radiography is often nondiagnostic because differentiation between gas-filled small intestine and large intestine may be difficult in neonates and small infants.[28] However, some useful signs are occasionally seen, including the "double bubble" of acute duodenal obstruction (Fig. 84-16A) or the absence of a normal colonic gas pattern in an older patient with a displaced cecum. Volvulus of the midgut is often characterized by a "gasless" abdomen, but distal intestinal obstruction may also be found.[28] In these instances, the intestine may be thickened and edematous (Fig. 84-16B).

Figure 84–15 Normal duodenal rotation and duodenojejunal fixation. The duodenum descends to the right of midline, courses transversely to the left, and ascends to the left of midline to the level of the duodenal bulb before becoming intraperitoneal beyond the duodenojejunal junction. (Courtesy of Marc S. Keller, MD, Yale University School of Medicine.)

Ultrasonography has become a useful study for the detection of many intra-abdominal conditions. It is a good screening device for infants suspected of having midgut volvulus because it can define vascular flow through the superior mesenteric vessels. Pracros et al.[44] reported an ultrasonographic "whirlpool" flow pattern of the superior mesenteric vein and mesentery around the superior mesenteric artery in 15 of 18 patients with midgut volvulus; this pattern was best seen using color Doppler imaging (Fig. 84-17). Additional ultrasonographic findings are a fluid-filled, distended duodenum and dilated, thick-walled bowel loops located mainly to the right of the spine. Computed tomography may also demonstrate a "whirlpool" flow pattern with intravenous and oral contrast (Fig. 84-18).

An upper GI contrast study with careful delineation of the duodenojejunal course is now the preferred study for evaluating a patient with a possible abnormality of intestinal rotation. The position of the ligament of Treitz is assessed relative to the midline or center of the vertebral body and the level of gastric outlet. A normal finding is defined as the ligament of Treitz to the left of the vertebral body and at the level of the gastric outlet (Fig. 84-19). Malrotation is described by many pediatric radiologists as "typical" if the ligament is to the right of midline or absent, and "atypical" if the ligament of Treitz is midline or to the left and below the gastric outlet (Fig. 84-20). Cecal position is classified as either right lower quadrant (normal) or somewhere other than right lower quadrant (abnormal). The surgical dilemma of managing patients with atypical malrotation is discussed later.

The radiographic distinction between midgut volvulus and obstruction from peritoneal bands may be subtle. Ablow et al.[1] described a Z-shaped duodenojejunal loop in older children with intermittent abdominal pain and vomiting. Upper GI contrast radiography reveals a sharply angulated, to-and-fro course of the distal duodenum and jejunum, which may cross to the left of the midline, rather than the usual smooth duodenojejunal loop at the ligament of Treitz (Fig. 84-21B). The Z sign is diagnostic of incomplete rotation and broad peritoneal bands extending across and fixing the involved small intestine without an accompanying volvulus. These Z-band findings can be distinguished from the corkscrew appearance of midgut volvulus.

Radiographic examination of an infant with heterotaxia is particularly challenging because of the ambiguous location of the stomach, liver, and spleen. In our experience,[11] most patients have a fixation abnormality of the duodenum and jejunum that is recognized by contrast radiography regardless of whether the stomach is right or left sided (Fig. 84-22).

Thickening of the mucous membrane of the small intestine, often seen in malabsorption syndromes, is an additional sign of chronic obstruction and volvulus.[16] With a right mesocolic hernia, the relation of the ascending and transverse colon may be abnormal, and contrast studies may show entrapment of the small intestine.

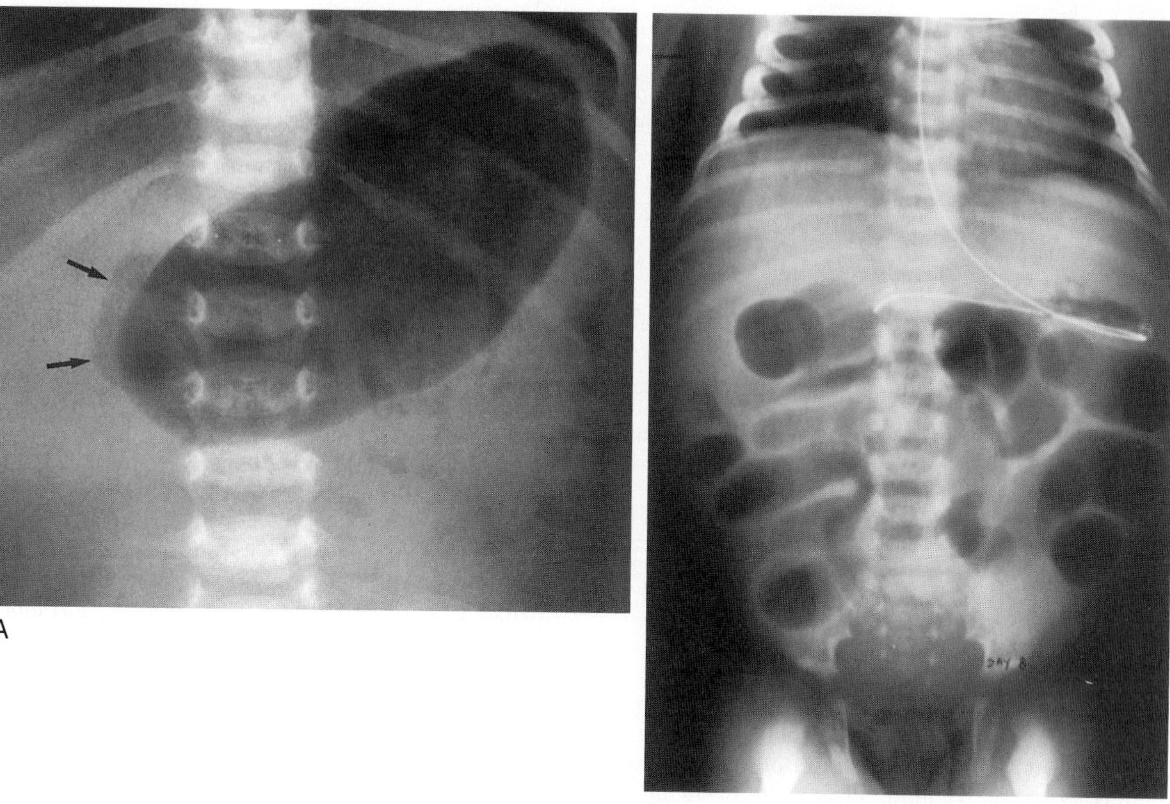

Figure 84–16 *A*, Plain radiograph of an infant with midgut volvulus. Obstruction of the descending duodenum may result in the pattern of gaseous distention of the stomach and duodenum *(arrows)* seen here, with a paucity of gas noted distally. *B*, Eight-day-old infant with midgut volvulus. This pattern of distal intestinal obstruction with thickened walls is much less common than that of proximal duodenal obstruction, but it is associated with more severe vascular compromise and clinical illness. (*A*, Courtesy of Marc S. Keller, MD, Yale University School of Medicine.)

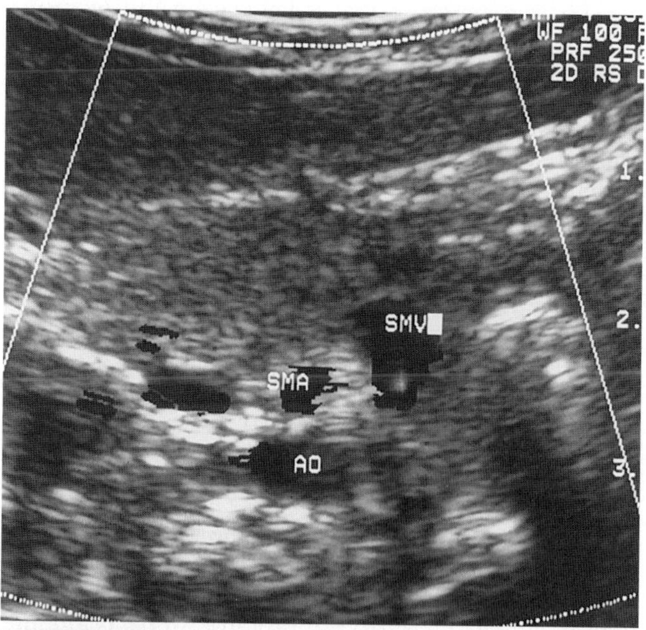

Figure 84–17 Color Doppler image of malrotation of a transverse upper abdomen. The abnormal position of the superior mesenteric vein (SMV) to the left of the superior mesenteric artery (SMA) can be seen just anterior to the abdominal aorta (AO). (Courtesy of Marc S. Keller, MD, Yale University School of Medicine.)

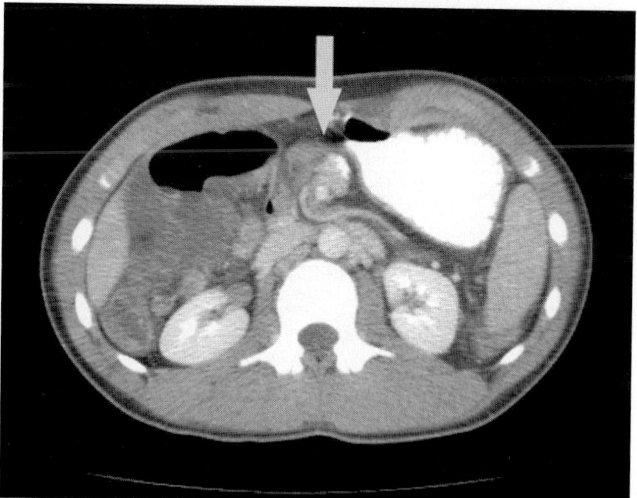

Figure 84–18 Computed tomography scan of malrotation with volvulus (note the spiral configuration of the mesenteric vessels *[arrow]*).

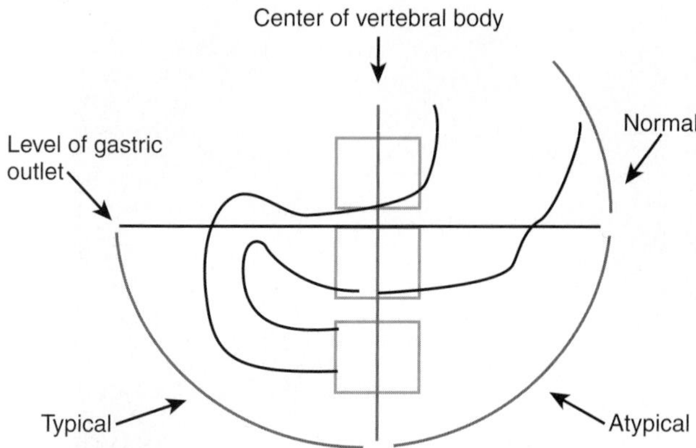

Figure 84–19 Classification of malrotation based on the location of the ligament of Treitz in comparison to the midline of the vertebral body and the level of gastric outlet.

TREATMENT

Preoperative Management

Infants with suspected midgut volvulus and vomiting may be dehydrated and show signs of hypovolemia and hypochloremia and require rapid intravenous resuscitation with a physiologic salt solution. Prolonged resuscitation efforts are not warranted, however, because expeditious laparotomy is essential for survival. Additional measures, including placement of a nasogastric tube, satisfactory intravenous access, and administration of parenteral antibiotics, should be accomplished as quickly as possible.

Operative Technique

The Ladd procedure corrects the fundamental abnormalities associated with malrotation with or without midgut volvulus. This procedure consists of the following important steps, which must be carried out in the proper sequence: (1) evisceration of the bowel and inspection of the mesenteric root; (2) counterclockwise derotation of the midgut volvulus; (3) lysis of Ladd's peritoneal bands, with straightening of the duodenum along the right abdominal gutter; (4) appendectomy; and (5) placement of the cecum in the left lower quadrant.

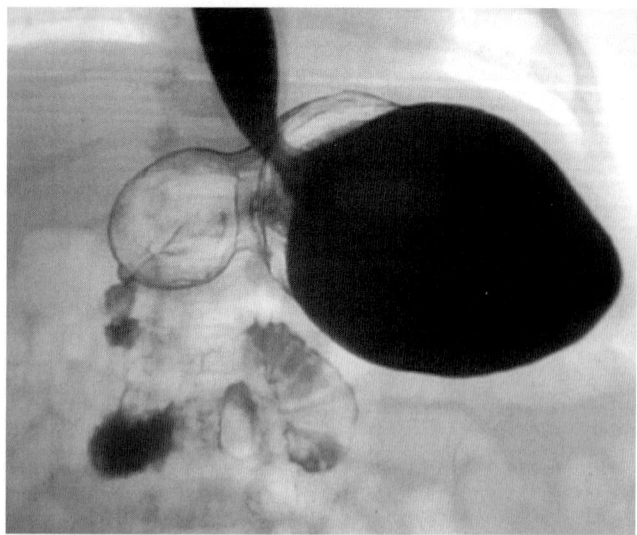

Figure 84–20 Contrast study of atypical malrotation or malrotation variant. The ligament of Treitz fails to reach its normal position left of midline and at the level of gastric outlet.

Recognition of Abnormalities of Rotation and Fixation

The peritoneal cavity should be entered through a supraumbilical right transverse incision extending from the midline laterally. The incision must be long enough to permit adequate inspection of the entire midgut. The entire bowel should be removed from the abdomen so that its orientation and fixation can be examined completely.

The two most constant anatomic points in the abdomen are the pylorus and the splenic flexure; their positions are not altered in patients with malrotation. A seemingly normal position of the cecum in the right middle or lower abdomen and a partial leftward course of the duodenum neither prove normal rotation nor rule out malrotation.

Several signs suggest a rotational anomaly: (1) abnormal peritoneal bands extending from the ileum or right colon to the parietal peritoneum over or to the duodenum; (2) fixation of the duodenum or upper jejunum to the cecum or right colon; (3) visualization of the entire duodenum, particularly the third and fourth portions at the base of the transverse colon mesentery; and (4) abnormal position and mobility of the cecum or of the duodenum along the right gutter.

It is helpful to locate the ileocecal region and orient the ileal mesentery so that it lies flat on the surgeon's palm. If normal, the cecum lies to the right of the ileum. In many cases, the location of the mesentery is uncertain, but a narrow mesenteric attachment is usually apparent. Sometimes, only after the cecum and right colon separate at the duodenocolic isthmus is a malrotation clearly evident.

Reduction of Volvulus

With midgut volvulus, the colon is not evident as the abdomen is opened because it lies posteriorly. In addition, the small bowel may appear congested and blue, with dilated mesenteric veins (Fig. 84-23A).

The entire mass of small and large intestine should be delivered from the peritoneal cavity, avoiding traction on the mesentery. With this maneuver, the twist at the base of the mesentery may be visualized (Fig. 84-23B). The bowel should then be cradled between the surgeon's hands and the volvulus derotated in a counterclockwise fashion (Fig. 84-23C). I prefer to reduce the bowel in steps of 180-degree turns until the transverse colon and cecum are brought into view anterior to the mesenteric pedicle (Fig. 84-23D). Improvement in the color of the intestine usually accompanies the reduction unless the bowel is already severely compromised or necrotic. Generally, two to three full rotations of the bowel are required to completely reduce the volvulus.

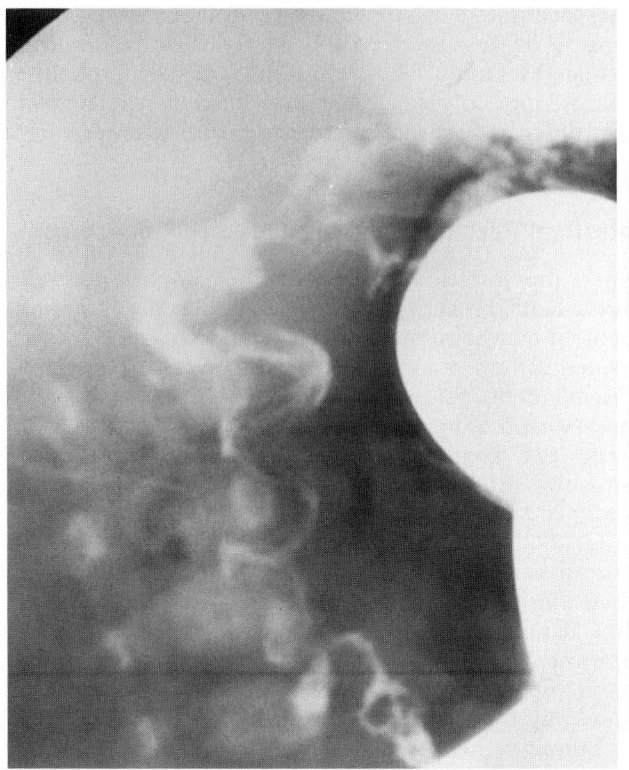

A

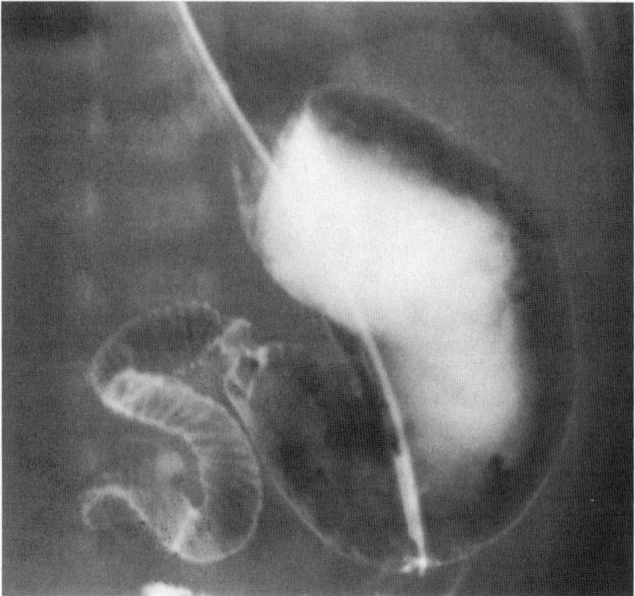

B

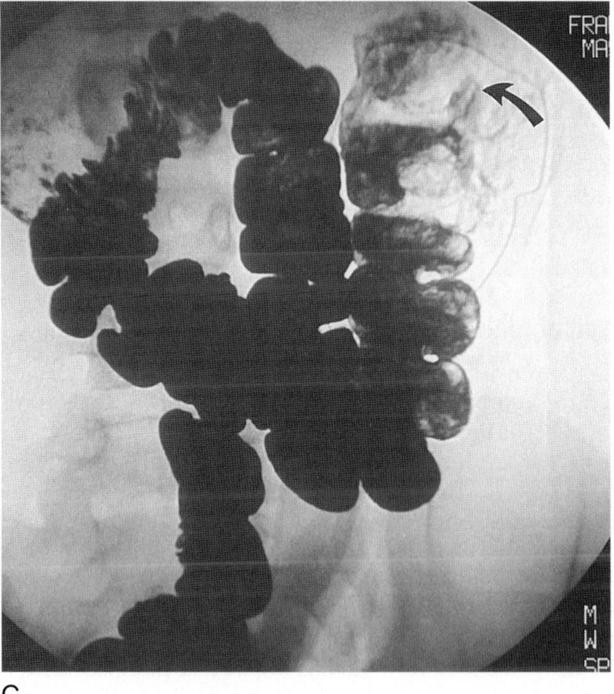

C

Figure 84–21 *A*, Malrotation with midgut volvulus. The entire duodenum and proximal jejunum lie unfixed to the left of midline and spiral inferiorly in a corkscrew configuration. *B*, Z-band configuration of the duodenum in malrotation. The abnormal duodenal course is fixed by congenital bands in this infant with malrotation. *C*, Colon malposition in malrotation. Delayed radiograph obtained after an upper gastrointestinal series shows an unfixed colon with the cecum *(arrow)* in the left upper quadrant. (Courtesy of Marc S. Keller, MD, Yale University School of Medicine.)

Relief of Duodenal Obstruction and Division of Ladd's Bands

After reduction of the volvulus, any duodenal bands causing obstruction should be identified; division is then begun at either the pyloric or the duodenojejunal end (see Fig. 84-23D). The bands usually attach the duodenum to the cecum or the right colon near the superior mesenteric vessels, the so-called duodenocolic isthmus. Dissection is carried out close to the serosa of the duodenum (with careful attention to the superior mesenteric vessels) and to the hepatoduodenal ligament superiorly and medially. Obstructing bands may also involve the ileum or progress down onto the jejunum. Houston and Wittenborg[25] pointed out that these bands may also

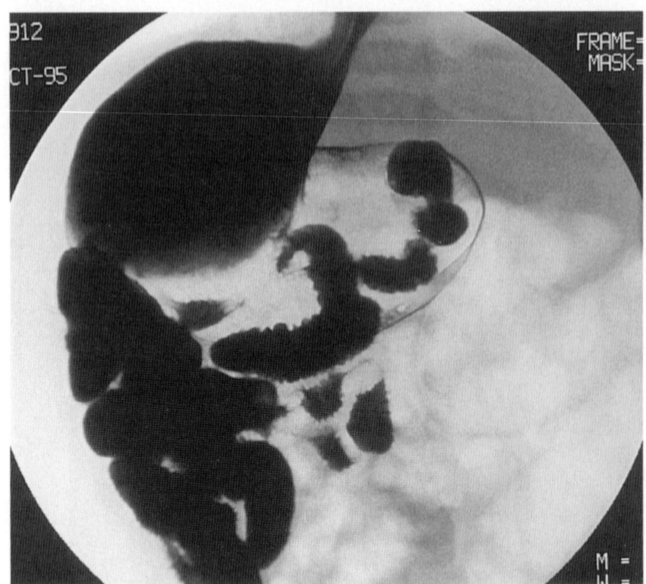

Figure 84-22 Malrotation with heterotaxy. Note the horizontal liver margin and the right upper quadrant stomach in this neonate with congenital heart disease. The duodenum descends left of midline and courses transversely to the right but does not ascend to a point of duodenojejunal junction fixation. (Courtesy of Marc S. Keller, MD, Yale University School of Medicine.)

extend superiorly to the gallbladder and the liver. Sharp dissection is used in most cases. Fairly vascular attachments can be anticipated in older children with chronic duodenal obstruction.

In all cases, it is imperative to prove that no associated intrinsic obstruction exists. This can be tested by passing a nasogastric tube of adequate size or, alternatively, a catheter through a gastrotomy, through the duodenum, into the jejunum (Fig. 84-23E). Demonstrating that air passes through the duodenum is not sufficient to rule out a duodenal diaphragm or "windsock" web, a condition that may be totally unsuspected in a neonate.

Once Ladd's bands have been dissected, the duodenum should have a relatively straight downward course along the right abdominal gutter (see Fig. 84-23E). Failure to lyse all the bands may cause recurring duodenal obstruction or midgut volvulus. Any temptation to "stabilize" the mesentery by fixation of the duodenum or colon should be resisted, because this procedure may actually increase the risk for recurrent obstruction from adhesions or internal hernia.[3,30,50,51]

The Ladd procedure is completed by performing an appendectomy. Some authors[52] have advised an inversion-ligation appendectomy to avoid the unlikely possibility of fecal contamination in an otherwise clean case. The cecum is then placed into the left lower quadrant to maximally widen the mesentery.

Laparoscopic Versus Open Reduction

There have been a number of small series or case reports describing the use of laparoscopy to diagnose or correct malrotation.[5,6,38] All the studies reported 12 or fewer cases diagnosed or treated successfully by laparoscopy. Because of the absence of large series or randomized, prospective trials comparing the open approach to laparoscopy, no clear recommendations can be made regarding the best method for surgical treatment.

Intestinal Resection and Second-Look Procedures

When the intestine appears viable, simple enterolysis and a Ladd procedure suffice. A localized gangrenous segment may be resected and a primary anastomosis performed if there is ample remaining bowel that is viable. The incidence of ischemic injury requiring resection varies with the duration of symptoms. Thirty percent of Torres and Ziegler's patients had intestinal necrosis,[52] but only 3 of 40 patients (7.5%) required resection in Seashore and Touloukian's series.[46]

Second-look laparotomy is usually performed when there are multiple areas of bowel of questionable viability, when the entire midgut appears nonviable, or when clinical signs and symptoms suggest progressive loss of intestine. At 12 to 24 hours, recovery of questionable bowel or demarcation of the areas of frankly necrotic bowel requiring resection is usually obvious.

Although the management of patients with frankly necrotic or marginally viable intestine must be individualized, three principles should be considered: (1) preserving the minimum length of intestine required for survival has the highest priority, and one should err on the side of preserving intestine, particularly the terminal ileum and ileocecal valve, for a second-look procedure; (2) anastomoses between ends of intestine of questionable viability should be avoided; and (3) resection of the entire midgut will necessitate lifelong parenteral nutrition or small intestinal transplantation.

Atypical Malrotation or Malrotation Variant

The diagnosis of malrotation variant is increasingly made by radiologists on upper GI contrast studies.[47] Patients with this finding are frequently referred to pediatric surgeons for evaluation and possible surgical treatment. These patients present a dilemma for surgeons, because the risks of operation versus nonoperative treatment are not clear in this subgroup of patients, many of whom were diagnosed during a workup for presumed gastroesophageal reflux. My colleagues and I reviewed our experience with the surgical treatment of malrotation variant over a 5-year period,[40] during which 201 patients underwent operation for malrotation (excluding infants with diaphragmatic hernia and abdominal wall defects). Typical malrotation was present in 75 patients, and malrotation variant in 101. Volvulus and internal hernia were more common in typical malrotation (16% versus 2% and 21% versus 7%, respectively). Persistent symptoms and complications such as postoperative obstruction were more common in the malrotation variant group (21% versus 12% and 12% versus 0%, respectively). The only patients who presented with ischemic volvulus were those with typical malrotation. These data reaffirm the

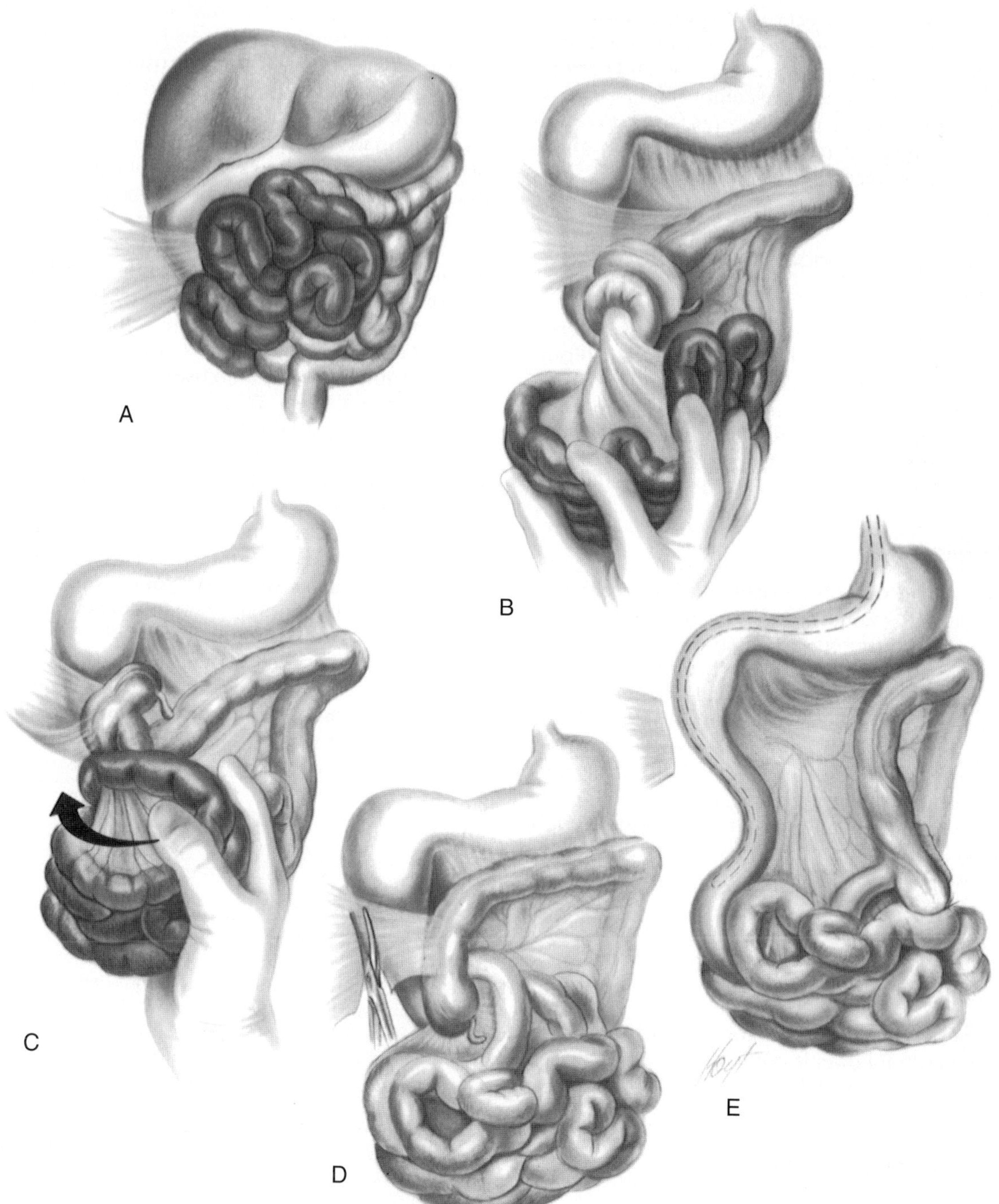

Figure 84–23 Malrotation of the intestine. *A,* Appearance of viscera as the abdominal cavity is opened. The small intestine is seen at once and seems to hide the colon. Vascular compromise of the intestine may be obvious. *B,* The entire intestinal mass is delivered out of the wound and drawn downward, showing the base of the mesentery. Coils of intestine or ascending colon are wrapped around the root of an incompletely anchored mesentery. The volvulus has taken place in a clockwise direction. The descending duodenum is dilated because of extrinsic pressure from Ladd's bands or peritoneal folds that cross it. *C,* The volvulus is reduced by taking the entire intestinal mass in the hand and rotating it counterclockwise (in most cases). *D,* With reduction of the volvulus, the cecum lies in the right paravertebral gutter. The peritoneal folds from the cecum obstruct the duodenum. The folds are incised close to the lateral serosal border of the duodenum. The underlying superior mesenteric pedicle is identified and carefully preserved. *E,* Appearance of the intestines and ascending colon at the end of surgery. The duodenum descends along the right gutter. The small intestine lies on the right side of the abdomen, and the cecum and ascending colon are in the midline or on the left side of the abdomen. The superior mesenteric artery and its branches are left exposed, as shown. A nasogastric tube has been passed into the jejunum to rule out intrinsic obstruction. (Modified from Ladd WE, Gross RE: Abdominal Surgery of Infancy and Childhood. Philadelphia, WB Saunders, 1941.)

importance of operative correction of typical malrotation. However, because patients with malrotation variant were less likely to have volvulus or internal hernias, and because of the higher rate of postoperative complications in those patients, we questioned the need for operative correction in asymptomatic atypical malrotation patients or those with only gastroesophageal reflux symptoms.

Colonic Obstruction Secondary to Reversed Rotation

In the past, division of the colon with anastomosis anterior to the duodenum was recommended for treating colonic obstruction secondary to reversed rotation. It is now recognized that this form of obstruction can be relieved by freeing the duodenum and the underlying mesenteric vessels anteriorly and laterally off the transverse colon.[54]

Mesocolic Hernia

Right mesocolic hernia is best treated by incising the lateral peritoneal reflection of the right colon and rotating the colon to the left, thereby freeing the small intestine.[56] Treatment of left mesocolic hernia is more technically challenging. The small intestine can sometimes be reduced through the neck of the sac. The key to repair and reduction is mobilization of the inferior mesenteric vein; this vein, which runs along the anterior margin of the neck of the sac, should be spared (see Fig. 84-14B and C). The bowel can be reduced if an incision is made to the right of the vein. The peritoneum adjacent to the vein is sutured to the posterior peritoneum to close the neck of the sac.

Cecal Volvulus

Reduction of cecal volvulus is followed by fixation or by cecostomy when the bowel is viable. Resection is advised if the bowel is compromised.

POSTOPERATIVE MANAGEMENT AND COMPLICATIONS

Return of intestinal function depends on the duration of obstruction and the extent of bowel compromise. In an uncomplicated extrinsic obstruction caused by duodenal bands, peristalsis returns in 1 to 5 days, at which point feedings may be initiated.[30] In patients without evidence of volvulus or obstruction, I no longer routinely decompress the stomach with a nasogastric tube. Older patients with chronic malrotation or those with evidence of chronic obstruction frequently have a prolonged ileus that requires nasogastric drainage and parenteral support.

Patients who have marginally viable bowel with mucosal injury and short-bowel syndrome pose special problems. Total parenteral nutrition is essential to sustain infants with massive loss of intestine until adaptation and compensatory growth of the residual bowel can occur.[22] Small amounts of enteral nutrition are recommended to encourage adaptation and provide nutrition for the intestinal mucosa. The need for gastrostomy tube insertion to assist in nutrition must be assessed individually.

Coombs et al.[13] described a group of children with malrotation who were older than 1 year and had recurrent and often long-standing symptoms suggestive of intestinal dysmotility. Such children did not seem to benefit from a Ladd procedure. These findings of pseudo-obstruction may be an incidental finding or may be related to a neurogenic bowel injury from long-standing partial obstruction.

Complications encountered (aside from those related to malnutrition, diarrhea, and dehydration in short-bowel syndrome) are similar to those associated with any type of abdominal operation. Postoperative intussusception was noted in 3.1% of all patients who underwent a Ladd procedure, compared with 0.05% of other laparotomies.[29] The typical presentation was distention and bilious emesis between 5 and 8 days after the procedure. The incidence of postoperative adhesive bowel obstruction was 4%.

The incidence of recurrent volvulus is low. In the Boston series of 441 patients, only 2 had recurrent obstruction; in the Los Angeles series, no patients had recurrence.[3] Only 2 of our 159 patients who underwent a Ladd procedure had recurrent midgut volvulus.[40]

Death is associated primarily with peritonitis from extensive intestinal necrosis in midgut volvulus, late nutritional complications, or catheter sepsis, particularly in infants younger than 1 year. The mortality rate is at least 65% when more than 75% of the bowel is necrotic.[40]

REFERENCES

1. Ablow RC, et al: Z-shaped duodenojejunal loop: Sign of mesenteric fixation anomaly and congenital bands. Am J Radiol 1983;141:461.
2. Anderson A, Bergdahl L, Van der Linden W: Volvulus of the cecum. Ann Surg 1975;181:876.
3. Andrassy RJ, Mahour GH: Malrotation of the midgut in infants and children. Arch Surg 1981;116:158.
4. Balthazar EJ: Intestinal malrotation in adults: Roentgenographic assessment with emphasis on isolated complete and partial nonrotations. AJR Am J Roentgenol 1976;126:358.
5. Bass KD, Rothenberg SS, Chang JH: Laparoscopic Ladd's procedure in infants with malrotation. J Pediatr Surg 1998; 33:279.
6. Bax NM, ven der Zee DC: Laparoscopic treatment of intestinal malrotation in children. Surg Endosc 1988;12:1314.
7. Bentley JFR: Mesenteric cysts with malrotated intestine. BMJ 1959;2:223.
8. Berdon WE, et al: Midgut malrotation and volvulus. Radiology 1970;96:365.
9. Bill AH, Grauman D: Rationale and technic for stabilization of the mesentery in cases of nonrotation of the midgut. J Pediatr Surg 1966;1:127.
10. Brennom WS, Bill AH: Prophylactic fixation of the intestine for midgut nonrotation. Surg Gynecol Obstet 1974;138:181.
11. Chang J, Brueckner M, Touloukian RJ: Intestinal rotation and fixation abnormalities in heterotaxia: Early detection and management. J Pediatr Surg 1993;28:1281.
12. Collins DC: 71,000 Human appendix specimens: A final report, summarizing forty years' study. Am J Proctol 1963; 14:365.

13. Coombs RC, Burch RG, Gornall PG: Intestinal malrotation: The role of small intestinal dysmotility in the cause of persistent symptoms. J Pediatr Surg 1991;26:553.
14. Devlin HB: Midgut malrotation causing intestinal obstruction in adult patients. Ann R Coll Surg Engl 1971;48:227.
15. Dott NM: Anomalies of intestinal rotation: Their embryology and surgical aspects with report of five cases. Br J Surg 1923;11:251.
16. Estrada RL: Anomalies of Intestinal Rotation and Fixation. Springfield, Ill, Charles C Thomas, 1958.
17. Filston HC, Kirks DR: Malrotation—the ubiquitous anomaly. J Pediatr Surg 1981;16:614.
18. Firor HV, Steiger E: Morbidity of rotational abnormalities of the gut beyond infancy. Cleve Clin Q 1983;50:303.
19. Fraser JE, Robbins RH: On the factors concerned in causing rotation of the intestine in man. J Anat Physiol 1915;50:75.
20. Fukuya T, Brown BP, Lu CC: Midgut volvulus as a complication of intestinal malrotation in adults. Dig Dis Sci 1993; 38:438.
21. Gardner CE, Hart D: Anomalies of intestinal rotation as a cause of intestinal obstruction. Arch Surg 1934;29:942.
22. Georgeson KE, Breaux CW Jr: Outcome and intestinal adaptation in neonatal short-bowel syndrome. J Pediatr Surg 1992;27:344.
23. Gross RE: The Surgery of Infancy and Childhood. Philadelphia, WB Saunders, 1953.
24. Haymond HE, Dragstedt LR: Anomalies of intestinal rotation. Surg Gynecol Obstet 1931;53:316.
25. Houston CS, Wittenborg MH: Roentgen evaluation of anomalies of rotation and fixation of the bowel in children. Radiology 1965;84:1.
26. Howell CG, et al: Malrotation, malnutrition and ischemic bowel disease. J Pediatr Surg 1982;17:469.
27. Janik JS, Ein SH: Normal intestinal rotation with nonfixation: A cause of chronic abdominal pain. J Pediatr Surg 1979;14:670.
28. Kassner EG, Kottmeier PK: Absence and retention of small bowel gas in infants with midgut volvulus: Mechanisms and significance. Pediatr Radiol 1975;4:28.
29. Kidd J, Jackson R, Wagner C, Smith S: Intussusception following the Ladd's procedure. Arch Surg 2000;135:713.
30. Kiesewetter WB, Smith JW: Malrotation of the midgut in infancy and childhood. Arch Surg 1958;77:483.
31. Kluth D, Lambrecht W: Disorders of intestinal rotation. In Freeman NV, Burge DM, Griffiths DM, Malone PSJ (eds): Surgery of the Newborn. New York, Churchill Livingstone, 1994.
32. Ladd WE: Congenital obstruction of the duodenum in children. N Engl J Med 1932;206:277.
33. Ladd WE: Surgical diseases of the alimentary tract in infants. N Engl J Med 1936;215:705.
34. Ladd WE, Gross RE: Abdominal Surgery of Infancy and Childhood. Philadelphia, WB Saunders, 1941.
35. Lewis JE Jr: Partial duodenal obstruction with incomplete duodenal rotation. J Pediatr Surg 1966;1:47.
36. Mall FP: Development of the human intestine and its position in the adult. Bull Johns Hopkins Hosp 1898;9:197.
37. Maxson RT, Franklin PA, Wagner CW: Malrotation in the older child: Surgical management, treatment, and outcome. Am Surg 1995;61:135.
38. Mazziotti MV, Strasberg SM, Langer JC: Intestinal rotational anomalies without volvulus: The role of laparoscopy. J Am Coll Surg 1997;185:172.
39. McIntosh R, Donovan EJ: Disturbances of rotation of the intestinal tract. Am J Dis Child 1939;57:116.
40. Mehall JR, et al: Management of typical and atypical intestinal malrotation. J Pediatr Surg 2002;37:1169.
41. Messineo A, et al: Clinical factors affecting mortality in children with malrotation of the intestine. J Pediatr Surg 1992;27:1343.
42. Porto SO: Jaundice in congenital malrotation of the intestine. Am J Dis Child 1969;117:684.
43. Powell DM, Othersen HB, Smith CD: Malrotation of the intestines in children: The effect of age on presentation and therapy. J Pediatr Surg 1989;24:777.
44. Pracros JP, et al: Ultrasound diagnosis of midgut volvulus: The "whirlpool" sign. Pediatr Radiol 1992;22:18.
45. Schey WL, Donaldson JS, Sty JR: Malrotation of bowel: Variable patterns with different surgical considerations. J Pediatr Surg 1993;28:96.
46. Seashore JH, Touloukian RJ: Midgut volvulus: An ever present threat. Arch Pediatr Adolesc Med 1994;148:43.
47. Simpson AJ, et al: Roentgen diagnosis of midgut malrotation: Value of upper gastrointestinal radiographic study. J Pediatr Surg 1972;7:243.
48. Snyder WH, Chaffin L: Embryology and pathology of the intestinal tract: Presentation of 48 cases of malrotation. Ann Surg 1954;140:368.
49. Spigland N, Brandt ML, Yazbeck S: Malrotation presenting beyond the neonatal period. J Pediatr Surg 1990;25:1139.
50. Stauffer UG, Herrmann P: Comparison of late results in patients with corrected intestinal malrotation with and without fixation of the mesentery. J Pediatr Surg 1980;15:9.
51. Stewart DR, Colodny AL, Daggett WC: Malrotation of the bowel in infants and children: A 15-year review. Surgery 1976;79:716.
52. Torres AM, Ziegler MM: Malrotation of the intestine. World J Surg 1993;17:326.
53. Wakefield EG, Mayo CW: Intestinal obstruction produced by mesenteric bands. Arch Surg 1936;33:47.
54. Wang CA, Welch CE: Anomalies of intestinal rotation in adolescents and adults. Surgery 1963;54:839.
55. Waugh GE: Congenital malformation of the mesentery: A clinical entity. Br J Surg 1928;15:438.
56. Willwerth BM, Zollinger RM, Izant RJ: Congenital mesocolic (paraduodenal) hernia: Embryologic basis of repair. Am J Surg 1974;128:358.

Chapter 85

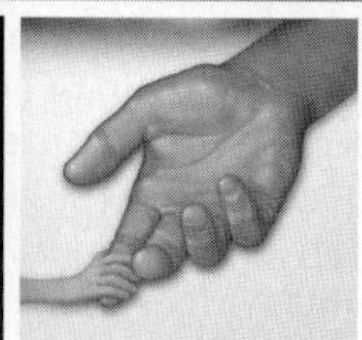

Other Causes of Intestinal Obstruction

Cynthia A. Gingalewski

Intestinal obstruction can occur at any age from newborn infants to adults. The etiology of the obstruction varies greatly, depending on the age that it occurs and the past surgical history. Common congenital causes include atresia/stenosis, malrotation, Hirschsprung's disease, imperforate anus, and meconium diseases of the newborn. These topics are discussed in detail in other chapters of this text. In this chapter, other common and uncommon causes of intestinal obstruction of both the small and large intestine are reviewed.

Early diagnosis depends on recognition of symptoms of obstruction (bilious vomiting, abdominal distention, and tenderness) and proper radiographic interpretation. In most circumstances, management of intestinal obstruction in infants and children involves a pediatric surgeon.

EMBRYOLOGY

With a few exceptions, the etiology of bowel obstruction in infants and children is embryologic in origin, especially in the group younger than 1 year. These entities are discussed in detail in other chapters. Where relevant, the embryologic basis of obstruction is discussed in this chapter.

SPECTRUM OF DISORDERS

Small bowel obstruction in infants and children is more common than large bowel obstruction. There are many causes, both congenital and acquired, including adhesive small bowel obstruction; hernias, which may be congenital or acquired; and intramural and extramural intestinal lesions. By far the most common of these is adhesive small bowel obstruction, which accounts for up to 60% of small bowel obstructions. Adhesions are followed by tumors (20%), hernias (10%), inflammatory bowel disease (5%), volvulus (3%), and various miscellaneous causes of intestinal obstruction.[4]

POSTOPERATIVE ADHESIONS

Differentiating a prolonged postoperative ileus from postoperative bowel obstruction can be difficult. Radiographic demonstration of dilated bowel loops may not distinguish between the two entities. Adhesive small bowel obstruction most commonly develops after pelvic surgery, including appendectomy, gynecologic procedures, and colorectal surgery. The obstruction is thought to be secondary to adhesive band formation in the pelvis, where the bowel is more mobile and likely to twist and obstruct around the adhesions.

The incidence of postoperative small bowel obstruction in children ranges from 2% to 30% and is greater in neonates. Festen[22] documented a 2.2% incidence of adhesive small bowel obstruction in 1476 abdominal operations. Eighty percent of obstructions occurred within 3 months of the initial operation, and 70% were secondary to a single adhesive band. The incidence was 57% greater in neonates than in infants and children and was more common after procedures for gastroschisis and atresias. In children, the most common inciting operation was appendectomy, and there was no difference in occurrence after perforated, nonperforated, or negative appendectomies. Similarly, at the Hospital for Sick Children in Toronto, operations for adhesive small bowel obstruction ranked seventh as a cause of pediatric bowel obstruction.[28] Obstruction occurred most often after appendectomy (16%) and within 2 years of the initial operation (82%).

Diagnosis

The key to the diagnosis of adhesive bowel obstruction is abdominal distention and bilious emesis in a patient with previous abdominal surgery. In the early stages of intestinal obstruction, it may be difficult to discern obstruction from infectious gastroenteritis. Initially, the emesis may be nonbilious, but with time it progresses to bilious or "feculent" emesis. The child complains of crampy abdominal pain and has anorexia. With a partial obstruction there continues to be passage of flatus or small stools. In children with complete obstruction, both cease. As the obstruction progresses, the child becomes increasingly lethargic. The presence of a fever should make one suspect bowel compromise.

Physical findings may not be initially obvious, but abdominal distention with either high-pitched or hypoactive bowel sounds evolves over time. Eventual progression of the obstruction leads to continuous, localized pain that is not relieved by nasogastric decompression. This ominous sign is indicative of compromised intestine. Persistent localized abdominal pain is the only reliable predictor of ischemic intestine. In a series of 131 obstructions reported by Janik et al.,[28] persistent pain after nasogastric decompression was a 100% predictor of intestinal gangrene.

Radiographs can help differentiate obstruction from infectious causes. All children should have plain abdominal films, including at least two views of the abdomen (Fig. 85-1). Obstruction is manifested by dilated bowel loops with air-fluid levels. The presence of air in the colon and rectum may signify a partial bowel obstruction. Free intraperitoneal air is indicative of bowel perforation and requires urgent operative treatment. The diagnosis of intestinal obstruction can be confirmed with computed tomography (CT) or a contrast-enhanced upper gastrointestinal series with small bowel follow-through (UGISBFT) (Fig. 85-2). The advantage of a CT scan is that it can rule out other diagnoses, can identify the transition zone of the obstruction, and uses water-soluble contrast that does not become diluted as rapidly as the water-soluble contrast with UGISBFT in the presence of obstruction.

Treatment

There continues to be debate whether immediate surgery is warranted in all cases of small bowel obstruction as opposed to conservative, decompressive management. All children with suspected obstruction should receive aggressive intravenous fluid and electrolyte replacement and placement of a nasogastric tube to decompress the stomach. A complete blood count should be obtained, and the presence of leukocytosis with a left shift in the differential count should raise suspicion of compromised intestine. The decision to proceed to the operating room should be based on the child's physical condition. If there is complete obstruction with no passage of flatus or stool, the child needs immediate laparotomy. Observation is warranted, however, if there is a partial bowel obstruction in the absence of fever, leukocytosis, and localized abdominal pain. Observation should include frequent abdominal examinations, serial abdominal radiographs, and frequent measurement of serum electrolytes. Conservative treatment was successful in 74% of patients in a retrospective review of 230 adhesive obstructions.[1] However, patients treated conservatively had a 36% incidence of recurrent episodes of obstruction as compared with a 19% incidence in those treated by lysis of adhesions. The frequency of recurrent episodes of obstruction after lysis of adhesion ranges from 5% to 19%.

Laparoscopic lysis of adhesions can be performed in instances of obstruction despite the presence of dilated intestinal loops. The more proximal the obstruction, the easier it is to accomplish adhesiolysis with laparoscopic techniques. The reported rate of bowel injury during open laparotomy for adhesive obstruction is 11%.[28] In a retrospective review of adult bowel obstructions treated

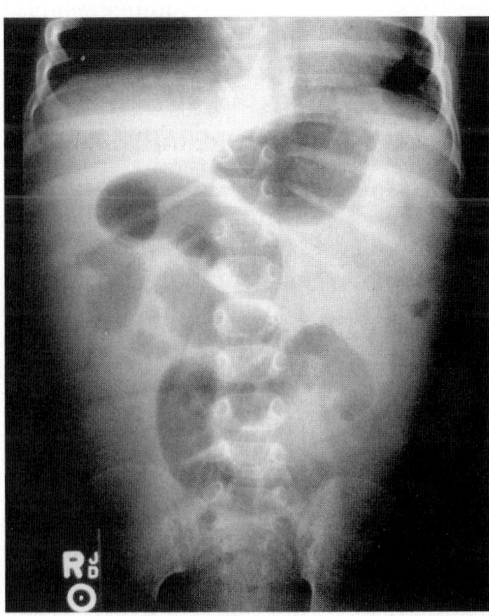

A

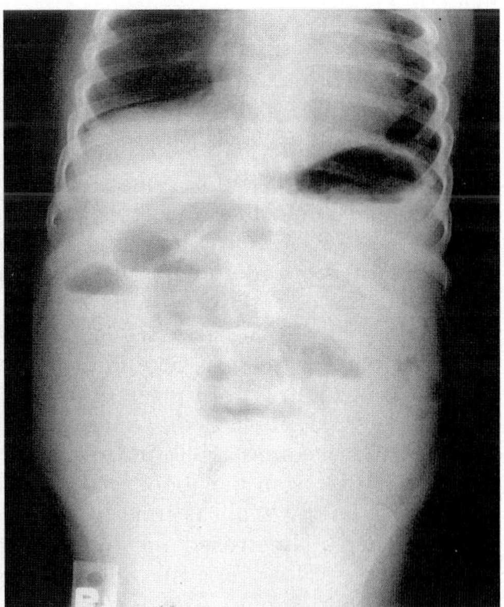

B

Figure 85–1 Complete intestinal obstruction. *A*, Supine plain abdominal radiograph demonstrating dilated small bowel loops and absence of air in the colon in a child who had previously undergone a Ladd procedure for malrotation. *B*, Upright abdominal radiograph from the same patient illustrating air-fluid levels in the dilated small bowel loops and absence of gas in the large intestine.

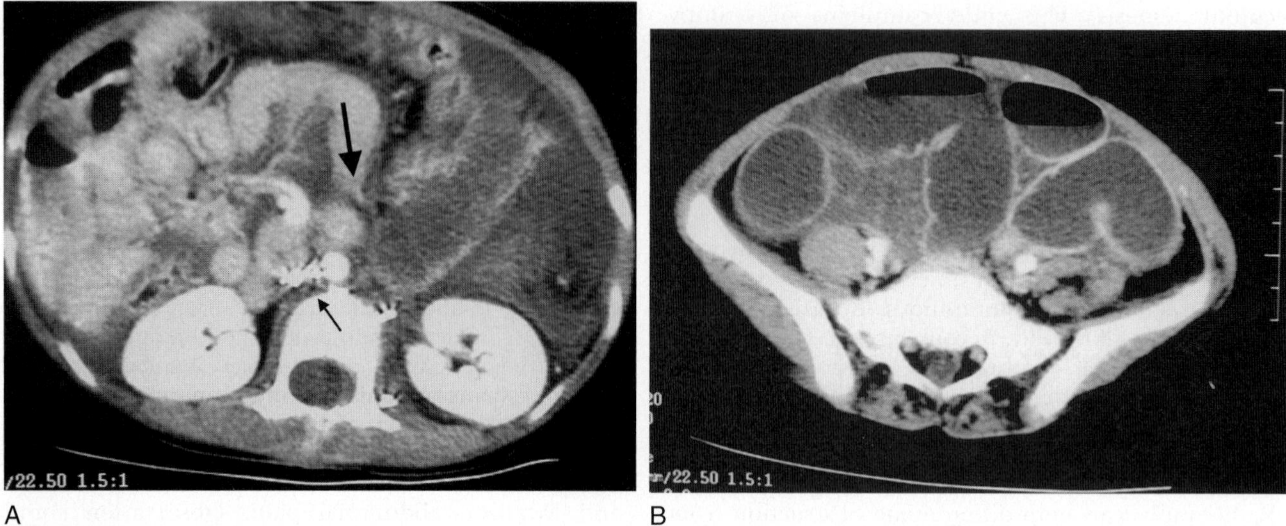

Figure 85–2 Incomplete small bowel obstruction. *A*, Contrast computed tomography (CT) scan of child with a partial small bowel obstruction after resection of a ganglioneuroma. The *small arrowhead* points to surgical clips from the previous resection. The *large arrowhead* demonstrates the transition zone of the obstruction. Note the dilution effect of the contrast in the dilated bowel. Partial obstruction is noted with passage of contrast past the transition point. *B*, Contrast CT scan from the same patient demonstrating proximal dilated fluid-filled bowel loops in the pelvis with air-fluid levels present.

by open or laparoscopic surgery, there was a 32% conversion rate from laparoscopic to open technique because of an inability to find the transition point, inability to achieve pneumoperitoneum, dense adhesions, and gangrenous intestine.[16] Intraoperative bowel injury occurred four times more frequently in the open group. Morbidity was higher in the open group and included pneumonia, prolonged ileus, and wound infection. However, the only death and unresolved obstruction occurred in the laparoscopically treated group. A conversion rate of greater than 50% was found in another retrospective study in adults.[52] A higher incidence of complications was observed in the laparoscopically treated group, including bowel injury and anastomotic leak. No such comparisons have been made in children.

Prevention

A multitude of reports have described the prevention of intra-abdominal adhesions; however, a "magic bullet" to prevent adhesion formation has yet to be found. General principles of gentle bowel handling, careful hemostasis, irrigation of the abdominal cavity, and prevention of prolonged bowel exposure to air have not eliminated the occurrence of adhesions. Commercially available adhesion barriers such as Seprafilm, a hyaluronic acid and carboxymethylcellulose membrane, have been widely used and publicized. The Seprafilm membrane hydrates and becomes a gel within 24 hours and is then slowly absorbed from the abdominal cavity over a period of 7 days. Several clinical trials using Seprafilm have demonstrated a decreased incidence of postoperative adhesions.[7,8,50] However, one should avoid wrapping Seprafilm around an anastomosis because it may lead to an increased risk for anastomotic leaks. The difficulty with Seprafilm is that it is sticky and difficult to handle and cannot be used laparoscopically. A second iteration of Seprafilm, Seprafilm II, is due out on the market soon and may be easier to handle. Other substances that have been used in the peritoneal cavity in an attempt to reduce adhesion formation include high-molecular-weight dextran, oxidized regenerated cellulose (Interceed), fibrin sealant, and hydrogel. The only substance that has shown a consistent reduction in adhesions in clinical trials has been Interceed.[6]

In an animal model of adhesion formation, Springhall and Spitz demonstrated almost a 50% reduction in adhesions with the postoperative use of oral cisapride in the rat.[48] Because this drug has been removed from the market, no human clinical trials have been conducted to substantiate this effect.

POSTOPERATIVE ILEUS

Differentiating postoperative ileus from obstruction can at times be difficult. Radiographic evidence of dilated bowel loops may not distinguish between the two entities, and thus a contrast-enhanced gastrointestinal series may be necessary. In the majority of patients, postoperative ileus resolves within 5 to 7 days. Passage of flatus signifies the return of colonic function and usually indicates that the ileus has resolved. The duration of postoperative ileus is prolonged by use of narcotics in a dose-dependent manner. Anesthetic agents, excessive trauma to the bowel, intra-abdominal bleeding, and preoperative gastric obstruction also prolong the return of normal bowel function.

Opiates have an inhibitory effect on gastric motility, increase tone in the antrum and the first portion of the duodenum, and have a biphasic effect on the small intestine.[11]

Morphine is initially stimulatory to phase II of the migrating motor complex (MMC), but this stimulation is followed by atony and slowing of gastrointestinal transit time.[24] Treatment with morphine antagonists such as naloxone have not proved beneficial in shortening the duration of postoperative ileus.[24,33]

Anesthetic agents exert their greatest antimotility effect on the large intestine because of the lack of intercellular gap junctions.[33] The anesthetic agents halothane and enflurane also cause decreased gastric emptying. Thoracic epidural anesthesia with local anesthetics increases splanchnic blood flow, impedes afferent and efferent inhibitory reflexes, and when administered in the thoracic region, has demonstrated a significant reduction in the duration of postoperative ileus.[12,29] Interestingly, lumbar epidural administration failed to have a similar effect on postoperative ileus.[32,41]

Laparoscopic surgery, early enteral feeding, and various pharmacologic agents have been used in an attempt to shorten postoperative ileus. Early feeding has not shortened the duration of postoperative ileus.[35] On the other hand, both animal and human studies have demonstrated a reduction in ileus duration when the surgical procedure was performed laparoscopically.[10,30] Of the numerous pharmacologic agents tested, the only benefit in humans was achieved with cisapride (now unavailable except for compassionate use). The somatostatin analogue Octreotide, known to inhibit several gastrointestinal hormones, shortened the duration of postoperative ileus in dogs.[13,18,31] Nonsteroidal anti-inflammatory drugs (NSAIDs) help lessen the duration of ileus by reducing the dose of narcotic analgesia required. Metoclopramide hydrochloride (Reglan), a prokinetic agent that is a cholinergic agonist and a dopamine antagonist, stimulates phase II of the MMC. Repeated studies, however, have failed to demonstrate any benefit from postoperative administration. Erythromycin, a motilin receptor agonist, also failed to shorten the duration of postoperative ileus in prospective, randomized trials.[47]

POSTOPERATIVE INTUSSUSCEPTION

Children are more prone to the development of postoperative intussusception, especially after operative procedures for retroperitoneal tumors, Hirschsprung's disease, and other neurocrestopathies. The sudden occurrence of bilious emesis after a normal postoperative return of bowel function should make one suspect small bowel intussusception. The diagnosis can be made by a contrast-enhanced upper gastrointestinal series. Because the majority of postoperative intussusceptions occur in the small bowel, they require surgical exploration for correction.

INFLAMMATORY ADHESIONS

Episodes of intra-abdominal inflammation, including, but not limited to ovarian torsion, ventriculoperitoneal shunt infection, Crohn's disease, acquired immunodeficiency syndrome, and pelvic inflammatory disease, can lead to adhesion formation and subsequent intestinal obstruction in the absence of previous surgical procedures.

HERNIAS

Although hernias account for only 10% of small bowel obstructions, they are more likely to be associated with strangulation of the bowel. Such hernias include inguinal, ventral, and internal hernias. Internal hernias, caused by internal bands or defects in the mesentery after bowel resection, are likely to cause a "closed-loop" bowel obstruction. This condition can rapidly progress to bowel ischemia and is characterized by pain often out of proportion to an unimpressive abdominal examination.

Congenital hernias include paraduodenal hernias, inguinal hernias, internal hernias secondary to omphalomesenteric duct remnants, congenital bands of nonembryonic origin, and nonfixation of the falciform ligament. Postsurgical causes of hernia include incomplete closure of the mesentery and parastomal hernias.

Paraduodenal Hernias

Paraduodenal (mesocolic) hernias are rare congenital lesions that result from abnormal rotation of the gut. The name "paraduodenal" is a misnomer but implies herniation of the small intestine posterior to the mesocolon. A right mesocolic hernia occurs when the prearterial limb of the midgut fails to properly rotate around the superior mesenteric artery. The majority of the small bowel then remains to the right of this artery (Fig. 85-3A). The etiology of a left mesocolic hernia is less clear. The rotation of the intestine is normal, and the intestine is introduced into an avascular area between the ligament of Treitz and the transverse colon, below the inferior mesenteric vein (Fig. 85-3B). Fusion of the mesocolon and the mesentery of the duodenum is incomplete, thus resulting in a defect.[15] It may lead to incarceration of the jejunum and varying lengths of ileum in the left upper quadrant. Despite their congenital origin, mesocolic hernias are most frequently diagnosed in adults. Left mesocolic hernias are three times more common than those on the right. They are the most frequent cause of internal hernias and account for 50% of cases.

A high index of suspicion is necessary to make the diagnosis of a paraduodenal hernia. These internal hernias cause vague symptoms, including recurrent bouts of abdominal pain, vomiting, abdominal distention, and melena.[39] Imaging techniques, including an upper gastrointestinal series or CT scan, are the only means of accurate preoperative diagnosis.

Surgical treatment of both right and left paraduodenal hernia consists of opening the sac, reduction of the small intestine, and repair of the defect. Sac removal should not be attempted. Laparoscopic repair of a paraduodenal hernia has also been reported.[49]

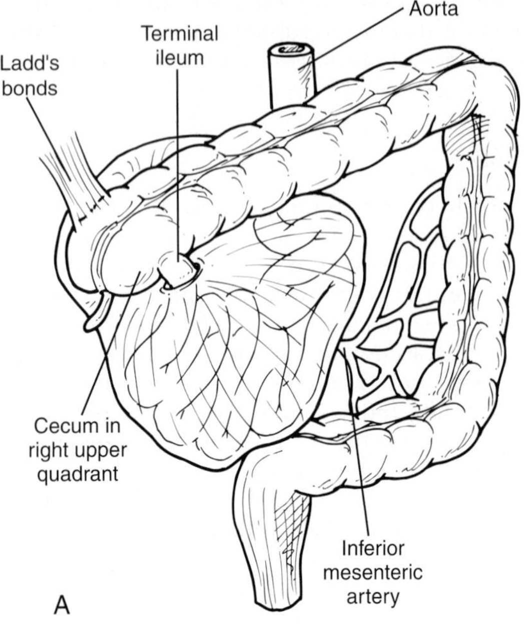

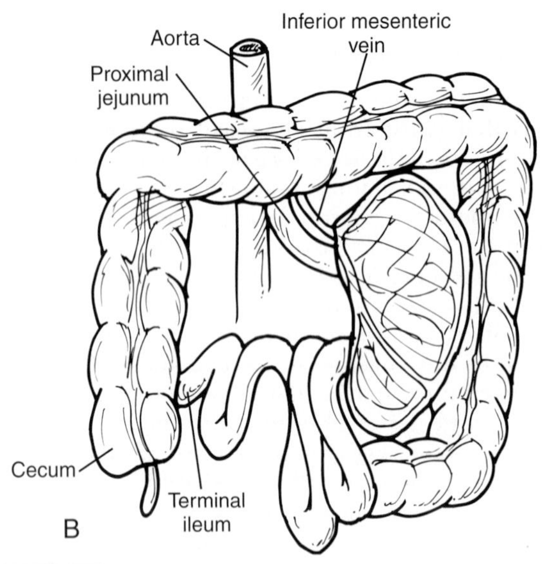

Figure 85-3 Paraduodenal (mesocolic) hernias. *A*, Right paraduodenal hernia. Note the abnormal bowel rotation with the cecum in the right upper quadrant and the presence of Ladd's bands. The majority of the small bowel is trapped behind the right mesocolon. *B*, Left paraduodenal hernia. The bowel rotation is normal in a left paraduodenal hernia. The small bowel becomes trapped behind the left mesocolon, posterior to the inferior mesenteric vein. (Adapted from Willwerth BM, Zollinger RM Jr, Izant RJ Jr, et al: Congenital mesocolic (paraduodenal) hernia. Embryologic basis of repair. Am J Surg 1974;128:358-361.)

Omphalomesenteric Duct Remnants

The omphalomesenteric (vitelline) duct is a normal component of fetal development. It connects the fetal intestine to the yolk sac. When these structures persist in a newborn, they are called omphalomesenteric duct remnants. They vary in appearance from a fistula to the umbilicus, a fibrous band between the ileum and umbilicus, and a Meckel diverticulum. Though one of the most common congenital anomalies (2% prevalence in the population), they are least likely (2%) to cause symptoms. In a review of 46 cases, 28% of symptomatic omphalomesenteric remnants were associated with intestinal obstruction (intussusception, internal hernia, volvulus).[38] Treatment is surgical, and there have been reported cases of laparoscopic excision.[14] This topic is covered in depth in Chapter 82.

Congenital Bands of Nonembryonic or Inflammatory Origin

The presence of intestinal obstruction as a result of congenital bands has been described sparingly in the literature. The etiology of these bands is unknown, but they are not secondary to known embryologic remnants such as omphalomesenteric duct or vitelline vessel remnants. A review of eight patients with anomalous bands demonstrated them to occur between the ascending colon and the terminal ileum (50%), the ligament of Treitz and the terminal ileum (25%), the right lobe of the liver and the terminal ileum (12.5%), and the right lobe of the liver and the ascending colon (12.5%).[2]

Patients may have chronic abdominal pain or an acute bowel obstruction. A high index of suspicion is required to make the diagnosis. Division of the band is therapeutic.

Nonfixation of the Falciform Ligament

The falciform ligament normally consists of two closely applied layers of peritoneum and attaches the liver to the anterior abdominal wall. It has three borders: the diaphragm, the anterior abdominal wall to the level of the umbilicus, and the free inferior edge of the liver, in which runs the obliterated umbilical vein. Failure of the peritoneum to fuse around the umbilical vein would lead to this unusual "nonfixation" of the falciform ligament and allow the small bowel to herniate around it like a congenital band (Fig. 85-4). The defect appears to be of congenital origin inasmuch as internal hernias around the falciform ligament have been reported in newborn infants.[9,19,45]

Since the first report of this entity in 1937, fewer than 10 cases of internal hernias involving the falciform ligament have been reported in the world literature. Of these, only two have been in neonates, and there have been no reports of this entity in a child. The remaining cases have involved adults. Defects in the falciform ligament have ranged from a "free-floating falciform" to an aperture within the peritoneal leaves of the ligament. Such hernias commonly contain small intestine, but they can contain omentum or large intestine.[27]

The diagnosis is usually made in the operating room during exploration for an acute small bowel obstruction in the absence of external hernias or previous surgery. A preoperative CT scan showing intestine above the liver that is centered around the falciform ligament can be

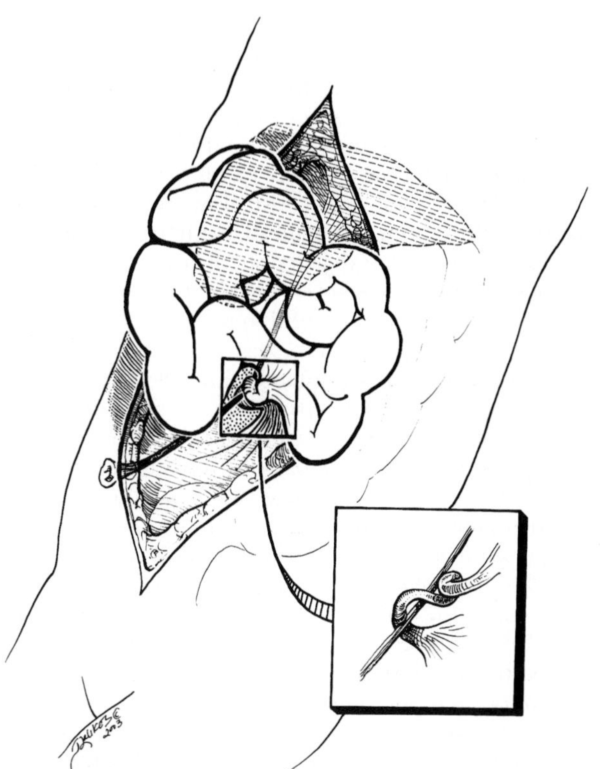

Figure 85-4 Internal hernia secondary to nonperitonealization of the falciform ligament. The falciform ligament acts like a congenital band when it is not fixed to the anterior abdominal wall by the double layer of peritoneum. This allows the small bowel to herniate around the falciform ligament, thereby causing an internal hernia.

suggestive (Fig. 85-5). The presence of ascites is an ominous sign indicative of compromised bowel. Release of the obstruction by dividing the falciform ligament is therapeutic.

Mesenteric Defects

During any surgical procedure involving bowel resection, great care must be taken to close all defects created in the mesentery. Closure can be performed with absorbable or nonabsorbable suture and in running or interrupted fashion. The advantage of interrupted suture is that unraveling of a single stitch is unlikely to make a large enough defect in the mesentery for an internal hernia to occur.

Parastomal Hernias

Parastomal hernias are a common problem after a colostomy. The incidence of parastomal hernia ranges from 2% to 35%. Most hernias appear within 2 years after creation of an ostomy and are more common in patients who are obese or malnourished. The use of steroids and postoperative wound infection also increase the risk. To minimize the risk for development of a parastomal hernia, the colon should be brought through the rectus muscle, the subcutaneous fat should be left in place, and the fascial defect created should not be excessive. Suture fixation of the bowel serosa to the stomal defect may reduce the risk for hernia in infants.

For repair, the colostomy should be taken down, if possible. In cases in which the colostomy is permanent, a small, asymptomatic parastomal hernia can be observed. Surgical repair should be offered when the hernia is large, interferes with appliance fitting, causes pain, or becomes incarcerated. Options include relocation, fascial closure, and mesh repair. The results of surgical repair in adults are dismal, with a recurrence rate of 33% to 50% after relocation, 50% to 100% after fascial repair, and 50% after mesh repair. A second recurrence of a parastomal hernia after initial attempts at repair is associated with even more dismal surgical outcomes approaching a 90% to 100% recurrence rate.

LARGE BOWEL OBSTRUCTION

Volvulus

Though not an uncommon etiology of large bowel obstruction in adults, colonic volvulus is a rare entity in children. There have been several case reports, however, that describe cecal, sigmoid, and transverse colon volvulus in children.[5,36,43,46] Associated medical problems include mental retardation, Hirschsprung's disease, intestinal dysmotility, and chronic constipation. Children have an acute onset of abdominal pain and obstruction.

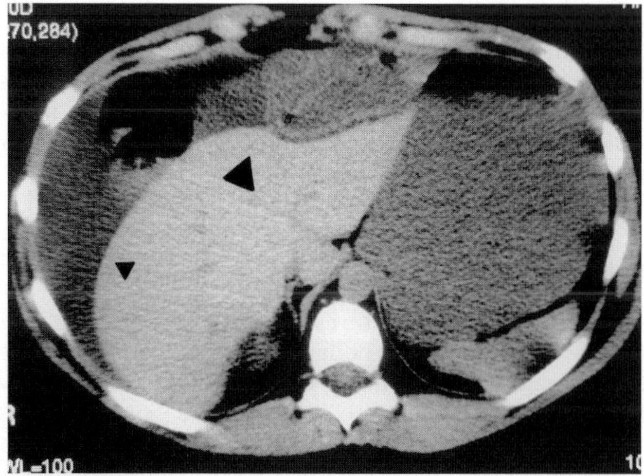

Figure 85-5 Preoperative contrast-enhanced computed tomography scan of a patient with an internal hernia around the falciform ligament. The patient had feculent emesis and no past surgical history. The *large arrowhead* demonstrates small bowel loops around the falciform ligament, above the liver edge. The right colon is also noted to be above the liver in the right upper quadrant. The *small arrowhead* demonstrates the presence of ascites. The patient was found to have gangrenous small bowel loops present. The falciform ligament was divided, the gangrenous bowel resected, and primary anastomosis performed.

Abdominal radiographs demonstrate dilated loops proximal to the obstruction, and barium enema is diagnostic by demonstrating the characteristic "bird's beak" appearance in the involved bowel segment.

Treatment includes nonoperative reduction with colonoscopy followed by laparotomy or primary laparotomy with detorsion. Cecal volvulus should be managed by primary resection and anastomosis or cecopexy.[25] Volvulus of the transverse colon is the only bowel reported to twist in a counterclockwise direction. Resection plus end-to-end anastomosis is the treatment of choice for volvulus occurring in the transverse colon, splenic flexure, and sigmoid colon. In all cases, nonoperative reduction alone is not recommended because of the high risk of recurrence.

Cancer

Carcinoma of the colon is one of the most frequent types of cancer; however, only 1% of all colonic malignancies occur in patients younger than 30 years. Very few cases have been reported in children younger than 10 years. There is a slight male predilection. The location of colonic tumors is equally distributed throughout the colon, and 48% of all tumors are of the mucinous adenocarcinoma, signet-ring variety. In children, colon cancer is associated with rapid progression of disease and a poor prognosis. The overall 5-year survival rate is 2.5%.[3]

The signs and symptoms are similar to those of adults, but the diagnosis is rarely entertained. Pain, anemia, abdominal distention, changes in bowel habits, and rectal bleeding are most commonly observed. In addition, children can have symptoms of an acute or insidious bowel obstruction.

Diagnosis and staging procedures include colonoscopy with biopsy and CT scan of the abdomen and pelvis. The value of obtaining carcinoembryonic antigen levels is uncertain in the pediatric population. Treatment consists of surgical resection for cure or palliation. Unlike adult patients, chemotherapeutic regimens and radiotherapy provide little palliative or curative value.[42]

Colonic Stricture

Acquired colonic strictures can cause partial bowel obstruction, which may be high grade. Strictures may be the sequelae of necrotizing enterocolitis, inflammatory bowel disease, trauma, or cystic fibrosis (cystic fibrosis colonopathy). Treatment is similar for all and includes segmental resection and anastomosis.

MISCELLANEOUS CAUSES OF SMALL AND LARGE INTESTINAL OBSTRUCTION

Intramural and Extramural Lesions

Numerous causes of intramural and extramural lesions throughout the gastrointestinal tract can lead to intestinal obstruction. The obstruction can be a consequence of the lesion itself, secondary to intussusception with the lesion as a lead point, or due to volvulus around the lesion.

Various cancerous lesions occur both intramurally and extramurally, including lymphoma (in particular Burkitt's) and leiomyosarcoma. Any child older than 3 years with intussusception should have these diagnoses entertained as the culprit lead point. A detailed small bowel follow-through with specific attention paid to the right lower quadrant by a pediatric radiologist is helpful in identifying intraluminal lead points in this population.

Noncancerous causes include juvenile polyps of the colon, inflammatory polyps, submucosal hemorrhage, hemangiomas, and foreign body ingestion. Juvenile polyps are the most frequent type of polyp encountered in pediatric patients and are seen in 1% to 2% of children.[26] Their peak incidence is between 2 and 5 years. They are manifested as painless rectal bleeding. Initial complaints may also include a prolapsing rectal mass, mucopurulent stools, abdominal pain, and colocolonic intussusception. These polyps are hamartomas, and the etiology is unknown. Colonoscopy can be diagnostic and therapeutic with endoscopic removal at the time of diagnosis.

Inflammatory polyps, composed of chronic inflammatory cells such as eosinophils, are frequently found in the stomach and small bowel, rarely in the colon, and are non-neoplastic. They can cause intussusception and obstruction at the level of the small bowel. They are frequently manifested as abdominal pain, and surgical excision is the treatment of choice. Because of their location in the small bowel, the diagnosis can be difficult to make. Endoscopy with a wireless capsule endoscope, as well as intraoperative endoscopy, may be helpful in locating the polyp.[37]

Submucosal hemorrhage can occur throughout the gastrointestinal tract. Causes include Henoch-Schönlein purpura, platelet disorders, anticoagulant therapy, and a complication of chemotherapy. They can also serve as a lead point for small bowel intussusception.

Ingestion of various foreign bodies, including peanuts, phytobezoars, trichobezoars, and pica in the mentally disabled, can cause partial or complete bowel obstruction in children. Common locations of intestinal obstruction include the gastric outlet and terminal ileum. Gastric outlet obstructions can be relieved endoscopically. Ileal obstructions require operative exploration and removal.

Inflammatory Pseudotumor

Inflammatory pseudotumor (IPT) is synonymous with inflammatory myofibroblastic tumor (IMT) and plasma cell granuloma. IPTs represent a group of tumors that have been found throughout the gastrointestinal tract, thorax, head, and neck. The etiology of these lesions remains obscure. Histologically, these tumors consist of plasma cells, histiocytes, and lymphocytes in a matrix of myofibroblasts. Although they can be locally invasive, as a whole these tumors are benign.

Alimentary tract IMTs can cause obstructive symptoms, weight loss, and abdominal pain. Laboratory evaluation reveals anemia and elevation in the erythrocyte sedimentation rate. Typical abdominal locations include the appendix and stomach, but lesions have been reported to arise from the small intestine, colon, and Meckel's diverticulum.

Treatment is complete surgical excision. The recurrence rate of this tumor ranges from 18% to 40%.[44] The risk of recurrence is greater with incomplete resection, and malignant degeneration has been associated with multiple recurrences of these tumors. There has been variable success with preoperative and postoperative treatment with NSAIDs in these patients.

Milk Curd Syndrome

Neonatal small bowel obstruction by milk curds was initially described in 1969 by Cook and Richman.[17] This entity consists of distal small bowel obstruction within the first 6 weeks of life by inspissated formula containing aggregates of fatty acids and calcium. The exact incidence is unknown, but it appears to have a male preponderance and a predilection for extremely-low-birth-weight infants, although it has occurred in term infants as well.

The syndrome is manifested as distal small bowel obstruction (bilious vomiting, abdominal distention) in an infant who has passed meconium. If suspected, it can be diagnosed and treated nonoperatively. The diagnosis is based on characteristic radiographic findings. Because the milk plug does not stick to the mucosal wall, an abdominal radiograph will show an intraluminal mass surrounded by a halo of air or air within the fecal mass itself. All affected infants have been fed formula, either entirely or in conjunction with breast milk.

Treatment is similar to that of meconium ileus, with attempts at nonoperative management by administration of a diatrizoate meglumine (Gastrografin) enema. Enemas should be reserved for infants in whom the diagnosis of necrotizing enterocolitis has been ruled out. In the event that conservative therapy fails, operative intervention is required. The most common location of the milk plug is the terminal ileum. It is typically 2 to 3 cm in length and can be milked through the ileocecal valve. If this technique is unsuccessful, an enterotomy is required with saline or *N*-acetylcysteine irrigation.

The etiology of the inspissation is not clear. Rectal biopsies, when performed, show normal ganglion cells. The obstruction is probably related to a combination of high-fat and high-calcium intake in an increasing population of extremely-low-birth-weight infants.

Abdominal Cocoon

An abdominal cocoon is a rare cause of intestinal obstruction. It is found primarily in adolescent girls from tropical/subtropical countries.[23] An abdominal cocoon is characterized by a thick, fibrous sac covering the small bowel, the etiology of which is unknown. Clinically, these patients have symptoms of chronic intestinal obstruction and weight loss or acute small bowel obstruction with pain and a palpable abdominal mass. Although the diagnosis is usually made at laparotomy, preoperative assessment by CT with contrast demonstrates a "cauliflower sign" in which coiling of the small bowel in a serpentine fashion is seen.[40] The degree of small bowel encasement varies from several feet to the entire length. Surgery remains the cornerstone of therapy, with careful dissection and excision of the thick sac and small bowel release.

Ascariasis

A common tropical infection is infestation with the nematode *Ascaris lumbricoides.* The estimated worldwide prevalence of *Ascaris* infection is over 1 billion cases, and death primarily results from intestinal obstruction. Human transmission is hand to mouth. The infection is generally asymptomatic; however, heavy infestation (>60 worms) can cause partial or complete obstruction of the gastrointestinal tract or biliary tree.[20] The diagnosis is made by ultrasonographic demonstration of worms in the biliary tree, pancreas, or intestine. Treatment consists of antihelmintic chemotherapy with mebendazole, albendazole, levamisole, or pyrantel. If medical treatment fails, endoscopic retrograde cholangiopancreatography can be used to extract worms from the biliary tree, and surgical enterotomy can accomplish worm removal from the intestinal tract.

Post-traumatic Intestinal Stricture

Acute perforations of the gastrointestinal tract are the most common intestinal injury after automobile accidents.[34] They are secondary to seat-belt trauma and are usually detected shortly after injury has occurred. A late sequela of a seat-belt injury is an intestinal stricture manifested as intestinal obstruction.

Abdominal pain and bilious vomiting 10 days to 3 weeks after blunt traumatic injury should lead one to suspect post-traumatic intestinal stricture. Abdominal radiographs are consistent with partial small bowel obstruction, and contrast series demonstrate dilated proximal intestine, focal narrowing, or delayed passage of contrast material, or any combination of these signs.

The etiology of post-traumatic intestinal stricture appears to be a direct crush of the intestine when trapped between the seat belt and spinal column. When severe enough, it causes focal ischemia, hematoma, and subsequent fibrosis and luminal narrowing. More than one segment of intestine can be involved. It is a progressive process leading to a delay in symptoms 1 to 3 weeks after injury.

Lymphatic Malformation

Cystic lymphatic malformations are rare causes of abdominal masses in infants and children. They are also known as mesenteric or omental cysts and can be manifested as an asymptomatic abdominal mass, with or without abdominal pain, intestinal obstruction, and volvulus. These are true cysts in that they are lined with endothelium, and it is postulated that they are secondary to ectopic proliferation of lymphatic structures that lack communication with the normal lymphatic system.[21] Mesenteric cysts may be found throughout the gastrointestinal tract and are most common in the ileum. They are best diagnosed by ultrasonography and appear as a well-circumscribed cystic structure with thin walls and septae. The diagnosis can be complemented by CT scan, which shows the extent of disease and rules out pancreatic, renal, and ovarian cysts. Treatment is complete surgical excision, which may require simultaneous bowel resection. The cyst can be marsupialized if complete enucleation is not possible. There has been a recent report of laparoscopic cyst excision in a young adult.[51]

Duplication Cysts

Duplications of the gastrointestinal tract are uncommon congenital anomalies. They lie within the wall of a segment of intestine or within the mesentery. Duplications are diagnosed pathologically by the presence of smooth muscle in the wall of the cyst. They can exist anywhere in the gastrointestinal tract and are usually symptomatic early in life. Symptoms include an abdominal mass, pain, intestinal obstruction as a result of volvulus or intussusception, and free air secondary to perforation. The diagnosis can be made preoperatively with ultrasound and CT. Surgical excision is the treatment of choice.

Pseudo-obstruction

Intestinal pseudo-obstruction is a syndrome in which there are signs or symptoms of intestinal obstruction without a mechanical lesion obstructing the intestinal lumen. Though typically associated with an older patient, pseudo-obstruction can occur as a primary phenomenon in neonates, as well as be due to secondary causes in an adolescent patient (Table 85-1). The disorder is not confined to the small intestine. It is generally agreed that motility of the intestine is abnormal, the etiology of which is either myopathic or neuropathic.

Patients have recurrent attacks of variable length and frequency consisting of nausea, vomiting, abdominal distention, and diarrhea or constipation. They frequently have steatorrhea secondary to slow transit time and bacterial overgrowth in the small intestine. Radiographic studies demonstrate the slow gastrointestinal transit time with dilation of both small and large bowel loops.

Satisfactory treatment of this group of patients is difficult to achieve. After mechanical lesions are ruled out with a barium contrast study, the mainstay of therapy is medical. Erythromycin (50 to 100 mg) stimulates motilin receptors and enhances gastric emptying. At low doses it stimulates intestinal contractions, yet more is not better. At high doses it inhibits intestinal motility. Octreotide (50 µg, parenterally) has been used to stimulate rhythmic contractions of the small intestine. New treatment regimens aimed at serotonin receptors in the intestinal tract are now available (alosetron, 1 mg orally) or are currently in clinical trials. Surgical therapy is limited to patients who have a short segment of dysmotile intestine. Surgery should be avoided in patients with diffuse dysmotility because recurrent symptoms and radiographic abnormalities are practically impossible to distinguish from adhesive small bowel obstruction in a previously operated patient.

TABLE 85-1 Secondary Causes of Intestinal Pseudo-obstruction

Endocrine disorders
Diabetes mellitus
Pheochromocytoma
Hypoparathyroidism
Hypothyroidism
Neurologic disorders
Hirschsprung's disease
Chagas' disease
Familial autonomic dysfunction
Neurofibromatosis
Diseases involving intestinal smooth muscle
Muscular dystrophy
Nontropical sprue
Systemic lupus erythematosus
Pharmacologic causes
Narcotics
Tricyclic antidepressants
Phenothiazines
Clonidine
Amanita (mushroom) poisoning

REFERENCES

1. Akgur FM, Tanyel FC, Buyukpamukcu N, et al: Adhesive small bowel obstruction in children: The place and predictors of success for conservative treatment. J Pediatr Surg 1991;26:37-41.
2. Akgur FM, Tanyel FC, Buyukpamukcu N, et al: Anomalous congenital bands causing intestinal obstruction in children. J Pediatr Surg 1992;27:471-473.
3. Andersson A, Bergdahl L: Carcinoma of the colon in children: A report of six new cases and a review of the literature. J Pediatr Surg 1976;11:967-971.
4. Angood PB, Gingalewski CA, Andersen DK: Surgical complications. In Townsend C (ed): Sabiston's Textbook of Surgery, 16th ed. Philadelphia, WB Saunders, 2001, pp 189-225.
5. Asabe K, Ushijima H, Bepu R, et al: A case of transverse colon volvulus in a child and a review of the literature in Japan. J Pediatr Surg 2002;37:1626-1628.
6. Azziz R: The INTERCEED (TC7) adhesion barrier study group II. Microsurgery alone or with Interceed absorbable

adhesion barrier for pelvic sidewall adhesion re-formation. Surg Gynecol Obstet 1993;77:135-139.

7. Beck DE, Cohen Z, Fleshman JW, et al: Prospective, randomized, multicenter, controlled study of the safety of Seprafilm adhesion barrier in abdominopelvic surgery of the intestine. Dis Colon Rectum 2003;46:1305-1309.
8. Belluco C, Meggiolaro F, Pressato D, et al: Prevention of postsurgical adhesions with an autocrosslinked hyaluronan derivative gel. J Surg Res 2001;100:217-221.
9. Blunt A, Rich GF: Intestinal strangulation through an aperture in the falciform ligament. Aust N Z J Surg 1968; 37:310.
10. Bohm B, Milsom JW, Fazio VW: Postoperative intestinal motility following conventional and laparoscopic intestinal surgery. Arch Surg 1995;130:415-419.
11. Borody TJ, Quigley EM, Phillips SF, et al: Effects of morphine and atropine on motility and transit in the human ileum. Gastroenterology 1985;89:790-796.
12. Bredtmann RD, Herden HN, Teichmann W, et al: Epidural analgesia in colonic surgery: Results of a randomized prospective study. Br J Surg 1990;77:638-642.
13. Brown TA, McDonald J, Williard W: A prospective randomized, double-blinded, placebo controlled trial of cisapride after colorectal surgery. Am J Surg 1999;177: 399-401.
14. Bueno LJ, Serralta SA, Planeeis RM, et al: Intestinal obstruction caused by omphalomesenteric duct remnant: Usefulness of laparoscopy. Rev Esp Enferm Dig 2003;95: 736-738.
15. Callander CL, Rusk GH, Nemir A: Mechanism, symptoms and treatment of hernia into the descending mesocolon (left duodenal hernia). A plea for a change in nomenclature. Surg Gynecol Obstet 1935;60:1052-1064.
16. Chopra R, McVay C, Phillips E, et al: Laparoscopic lysis of adhesions. Am Surg 2003;69:966-968.
17. Cook RC, Richman PP: Neonatal intestinal obstruction due to milk curds. J Pediatr Surg 1969;4:599-605.
18. Cullen JJ, Eagon JC, Kelly KA: Gastrointestinal peptide hormones during postoperative ileus: Effect of octreotide. Dig Dis Sci 1994;39:1179-1184.
19. Davies CJ, Franks RE: Herniation through a defect in the falciform ligament. Guys Hosp Rep 1974;123:171-175.
20. De Silva NR, Guyatt HL, Bundy DA: Worm burden in intestinal obstruction caused by *Ascaris lumbricoides.* Trop Med Int Health 1997;2:189-190.
21. Egozi EI, Ricketts RR: Mesenteric and omental cysts in children. Am Surg 1997;63:287-290.
22. Festen C: Postoperative small bowel obstruction in infants and children. Ann Surg 1982;196:580-583.
23. Foo KY, Ng KC, Rauff A, et al: Unusual small intestinal obstruction in adolescent girls: The abdominal cocoon. Br J Surg 1978;65:427-430.
24. Foss JF: A review of the potential role of methylnaltrexone in opioid bowel dysfunction. Am J Surg 2001;182(Suppl 5A): 19S-26S.
25. Gupta S, Gupta SK: Acute caecal volvulus: Report of 22 cases and review of the literature. Ital J Gastroenterol 1993;25: 380-384.
26. Horrileno EG, Eckert C, Ackerman LV: Polyps of the rectum and colon in children. Cancer 1957;10: 1210-1220.
27. Jamieson NV: The 'falciform ligament window': An unusual site for an internal hernia causing small bowel obstruction. J R Coll Surg Edinb 1987;32:374-375.
28. Janik JS, Ein SH, Filler RM, et al: An assessment of the surgical treatment of adhesive small bowel obstruction in infants and children. J Pediatr Surg 1981;16:225-229.
29. Jorgensen H, Fomsgaard JS, Dirks J, et al: Effect of epidural bupivacaine vs. combined bupivacaine and morphine on gastrointestinal function and pain after major gynaecological surgery. Br J Anaesth 2001;87: 727-732.
30. Lacy AM, Garcia-Valdecasas JC, Pique JM, et al: Short-term outcome analysis of a randomized study comparing laparoscopic vs. open colectomy for colon cancer. Surg Endosc 1995;9:1101-1105.
31. Lander, B, Redkar R, Nicholls G, et al: Cisapride reduces neonatal postoperative ileus: Randomized placebo controlled trial. Arch Dis Child Fetal Neonatal Ed 1997;77: F119-F122.
32. Liu SS, Carpenter RL, Mackey DC, et al: Effects of perioperative analgesic technique on rate of recovery after colon surgery. Anesthesiology 1995;83:757-765.
33. Livingston EH, Passaro EP: Postoperative ileus. Dig Dis Sci 1990;35:121-131.
34. Lynch JM, Albanese CT, Meza MP, et al: Intestinal stricture following seat belt injury in children. J Pediatr Surg 1996; 31:1354-1357.
35. Macmillan SLM, Kammer-Doak D, Rogers RG, et al: Early feeding and the incidence of gastrointestinal symptoms after major gynecologic surgery. Obstet Gynecol 2000; 96:604-608.
36. Mercado-Deane MG, Burton EM, Howell CG: Transverse colon volvulus in pediatric patients. Pediatr Radiol 1995;25: 111-112.
37. Miyata T, Yamamoto H, Kita H, et al: A case of inflammatory fibroid polyp causing small bowel intussusception in which retrograde double-balloon enteroscopy was useful for the preoperative diagnosis. Endoscopy 2004;36: 344-347.
38. Moore TC: Omphalomesenteric duct anomalies. Surg Gynecol Obstet 1956;103:569-580.
39. Moran JM, Salas J, Sanjuan S, et al: Paramesocolic hernias: Consequences of delayed diagnosis. Report of three new cases. J Pediatr Surg 2004;39:112-116.
40. Navani S, Shah P, Pandya S, Doctor N: Abdominal cocoon—the cauliflower sign of barium small bowel series. Indian J Gastroenterol 14:19, 1995.
41. Neudecker J, Schwenk W, Junghans T, et al: Randomized controlled trial to examine the influence of thoracic epidural analgesia on postoperative ileus after laparoscopic sigmoid resection. Br J Surg 1999;98:1292-1295.
42. Pratt CB, Rivera G, Shanks E, et al: Colorectal carcinoma in adolescents: Implications regarding etiology. Cancer 1977; 40(5 Suppl):2464-2472.
43. Salas S, Angel CA, Salas N, et al: Sigmoid volvulus in children and adolescents. J Am Coll Surg 2000;190: 717-723.
44. Sanders BM, West KW, Gingalewski C, et al: Inflammatory pseudotumor of the alimentary tract: Clinical and surgical experience. J Pediatr Surg 2001;36:169-173.
45. Schutz RB, Zeigler AM: Persistent fetal tachycardia and neonatal intestinal obstruction due to internal hernia beneath the umbilical vein. Am J Obstet Gynecol 1937;33: 692-694.
46. Shah SS, Louie JP, Fein JA: Cecal volvulus in childhood. Pediatr Emerg Care 2002;18:300-302.
47. Smith AJ, Nissan A, Lanouette NM, et al: Prokinetic effect of erythromycin after colorectal surgery: Randomized, placebo-controlled, double-blind study. Dis Colon Rectum 2000;43:333-337.
48. Springhall RG, Spitz L: The prevention of post-operative adhesions using a gastrointestinal prokinetic agent. J Pediatr Surg 1989;24:530-533.

49. Uematsu T, Kitamura H, Iwase M, et al: Laparoscopic repair of a paraduodenal hernia. Surg Endosc 1998;12:50-52.
50. Vrijland WW, Tseng LNL, Eijkman HJM, et al: Fewer intraperitoneal adhesions with the use of hyaluronic acid–carboxymethylcellulose membrane: A randomized clinical trial. Ann Surg 2002;235:193-199.
51. Vu JH, Thomas EL, Spencer DD: Laparoscopic management of a mesenteric cyst. Am Surg 1999;65:264-265.
52. Wullstein C, Gross E: Laparoscopic compared with conventional treatment of acute adhesive small bowel obstruction. Br J Surg 2003;90:1147-1151.

Chapter 86

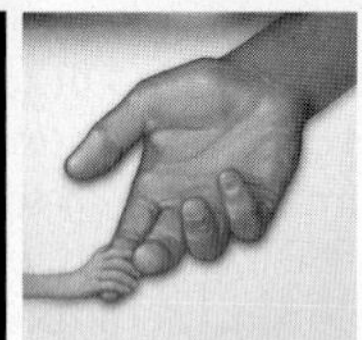

Short-Bowel Syndrome

Brad W. Warner

Short-bowel syndrome (SBS) encompasses a spectrum of pathophysiologic disorders that occur as a consequence of insufficient absorptive and digestive small intestinal mucosal surface area. The clinical features of SBS generally include progressive malnutrition, weight loss, and diarrhea. Although this problem most commonly results from an anatomic deficiency of intestinal mucosa, it may also occur in the context of normal surface area from perturbed intestinal absorption, motility, or both. Because most cases of SBS in the pediatric population arise from surgical removal of diseased intestine as well as congenitally shortened bowel, the focus of the majority of this discussion is on the consequences of reduced intestinal length.

ETIOLOGY

The specific causes of SBS in the pediatric population have evolved over the years. In earlier reports, the most common causes were midgut volvulus and intestinal atresia.[87] In more recent reports, the most common cause of SBS has emerged to be neonatal necrotizing enterocolitis (Fig. 86-1).[80,81] Additional frequent causes of SBS in children include intestinal atresia and bowel necrosis secondary to midgut volvulus. Other less frequent causes include mesenteric vascular occlusion due to invasive aortic monitoring devices, neonatal aortic thrombosis, or cardiogenic emboli. Reduced perfusion states secondary to cardiogenic, hypovolemic, or septic shock, as well as the use of vasoconstrictive inotropic agents, may also result in ischemic or necrotic bowel. Meconium ileus or plugging may promote the development of a volvulus with intestinal necrosis.

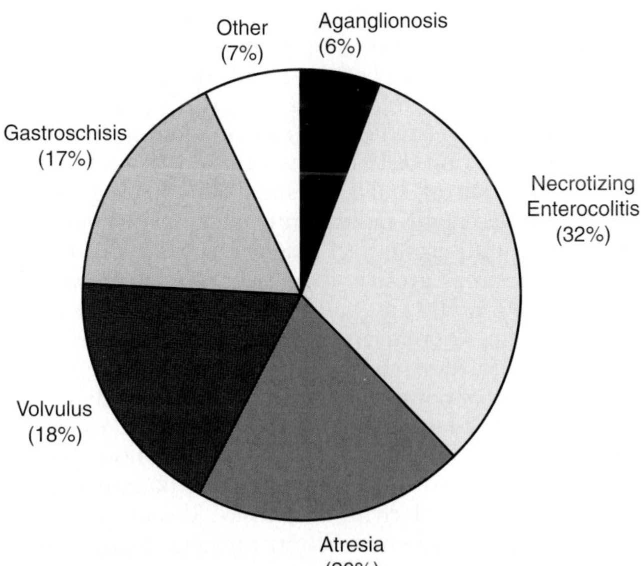

Figure 86-1 Etiology of short-bowel syndrome compiled from 466 pediatric patients. (Data from references 3, 13, 40, 78, and 81.)

Functional disorders in which the actual bowel length is normal but motility and the ability to provide enteral nutrition are impaired include long-segment aganglionosis and the syndrome of idiopathic intestinal pseudo-obstruction. Gastroschisis is associated with SBS owing to a combination of foreshortened intestinal length as well as dysfunctional peristalsis of the thickened bowel loops. Crohn's disease may be associated with SBS because of multiple, extensive resections, bypassed absorptive mucosa due to fistulas, or impaired mucosal absorptive capacity.

INTESTINAL ADAPTATION

After massive intestinal resection there is a compensatory response within the remnant bowel termed *adaptation*. Resection-induced adaptation provokes alterations that affect intestinal morphology, kinetics of cell turnover, as well as overall function.[51] In terms of morphologic changes, the bowel increases in its length and caliber as hyperplasia and hypertrophy of all intestinal layers are noted. Mucosal surface area is augmented as villi become taller and crypts are deeper, with increased bowel caliber and longitudinal growth. In addition to the morphologic changes, the rates of enterocyte turnover are enhanced, as demonstrated by increased proliferation as well as rates of programmed cell death (apoptosis) within enterocytes.[29] Functional adaptation, as gauged by digestive and absorptive enzyme activity per unit area, is augmented as well.

The significance of the adaptation response is best illustrated by the clinical observation that many patients who were previously unable to tolerate full enteral feeding are ultimately able to wean completely from supplemental parenteral nutrition over time. On the other hand, if adaptation is incomplete, then the patient is committed to a lifetime of supplemental parenteral nutrition and its allied morbidity. A thorough understanding of the pathophysiology of adaptation and ability to enhance this process is therefore an area of intense and promising research.

Multiple mechanisms and mediators have been proposed for the initiation and maintenance of the post-resection adaptation response. Three main mechanisms involve humoral factors, enteral nutrient, and pancreaticobiliary secretions. Serum levels of multiple peptides, hormones, as well as growth factors have been found to be elevated after massive intestinal resection. Indeed, administration of these factors individually after intestinal resection has variably resulted in an enhanced adaptation response. One of the more compelling experiments to substantiate the contribution of hormones to adaptation is the parabiosis model. In animals sharing a common circulation, intestinal resection in one animal has been demonstrated to initiate adaptive changes in the intestine of the unoperated animal.[86] In addition, serum harvested from animals that have undergone massive intestinal resection is capable of stimulating the growth of a prototype intestinal epithelial cell line.[37] No single factor in the serum has been identified that sufficiently accounts for all adaptive changes in intestinal morphology and function.

Enteral nutrients appear to stimulate intestinal adaptation via several mechanisms, including direct contact with epithelial cells as well as stimulation of trophic gastrointestinal hormones and pancreatic and biliary secretions.[84] The contributions of luminal nutrients to the adaptive response of the intestine is underscored by the observations that gut mucosal atrophy is associated with starvation and is reversed by refeeding. Furthermore, surgical transposition of a segment of the ileum into the more proximal intestinal stream results in structural and functional "jejunalization" of the transposed ileum.[2,22] Not only is the presence of luminal nutrition important for adaptation, but so is the composition of the nutrition. Luminal administration of non-nutrient substrates has little effect on adaptation. More complex nutrients requiring more metabolic energy to absorb and digest appear to induce the greatest adaptation response, by virtue of a so-called functional workload hypothesis.[80] Enteral fats appear to be the most trophic of the macronutrients in inducing adaptation.[11] More specifically, longer-chain and more unsaturated fats may provide an even greater adaptive stimulus.[76]

Multiple experimental observations contribute to the notion that endogenous gastrointestinal secretions are important for adaptation. Experimental models of surgical transposition of the ampulla of Vater to areas more distal in the gastrointestinal tract show villous hyperplasia beyond the transposed segment.[1,85] Bile alone has been demonstrated to stimulate intestinal RNA and DNA content when directly delivered to the mid small bowel, but the effect seems to be more profound when combined with the pancreatic secretions.[1] In other studies, pancreatic secretions seem to be more trophic to the intestinal mucosa when compared with bile.[85] Further evidence that pancreaticobiliary secretions are important for post-resection adaptation is the observation that somatostatin, an agent that dramatically diminishes the output of endogenous gastrointestinal secretions, is also associated with an inhibited adaptation response.[5]

Other factors that likely contribute toward the genesis of adaptation include the nutritional status of the host. Restriction of caloric intake after intestinal resection is associated with a blunted adaptation response.[20] It is unclear whether this occurs because of reduced enteral nutrient content or the effect of lack of calories. Other considerations in the genesis and maintenance of intestinal adaptation include mechanical factors. Experimental creation of a partial intestinal obstruction in pigs has been demonstrated to induce adaptive changes in the proximal intestine.[18] This observation has been extended clinically by the same group to facilitate bowel distention before a subsequent intestinal lengthening procedure.[25] Along these lines, gut motility may also be important. Multiple motility abnormalities have been observed after massive intestinal resection.[56,57] It is presently unclear whether this response is primary to the generation of adaptation or secondary to several of the previously mentioned factors. The effect of pharmacologic blockade of the perturbed motility on the adaptation response is unknown.

FACTORS INFLUENCING SHORT-BOWEL SYNDROME

The clinical response to massive intestinal loss is dependent on several key features, including the length and site of intestinal resection as well as the presence of an ileocecal valve. Probably the most fundamentally important factor is the length of intestine removed. The normal small intestine length for a full-term infant is 200 to 250 cm. In the fetus, the overall rate of growth of the gastrointestinal tract increases with age, with the period of most rapid growth occurring during the last trimester. In fact, the small bowel can be expected to double in length between the period of 19 to 27 weeks' and 35 weeks' gestation.[73] The rate of small intestinal lengthening due to growth alone remains rapid during infancy with continued elongation until crown-heel length reaches about 60 cm. Slower intestinal growth then occurs at a crown-heel length of 60 to 100 cm, and there is little change above 100 to 140 cm. Therefore, after massive enterectomy in the neonatal population, consideration should be given to the expected rate of bowel lengthening due to growth alone.

The ability to predict long-term need for total parenteral nutrition (TPN) is difficult because most series of SBS are composed of a heterogeneous patient population with varied underlying diagnoses. As such, a neonate requiring a massive enterectomy for necrotizing enterocolitis would likely demonstrate an adaptation response that is very different from a neonate born with the same intestinal length but with gastroschisis. Despite these limitations, Sondheimer and associates found in a series of infants that intestinal length at the time of initial resection and percentage of enteral calories tolerated by 12 weeks of age were independently predictive of long-term TPN dependency.[62] In this report, a Cox proportional hazard equation permitted plotting of these two parameters to predict TPN dependence. For example, it could be predicted that roughly 20% of infants would be permanently TPN dependent if they had 25 cm of remaining intestine at the time of initial resection but tolerating 50% of their calories by the enteral route by 3 months of age. If they had 75 cm, nearly all would be predicted to be TPN free even if they were tolerating the same amount of enteral nutrition at this same age. On the other hand, if they were tolerating only 25% of their total calories after 3 months with 25 cm of intestine remaining, nearly 40% would be predicted to be permanently TPN dependent.

In an important study from France, Messing and colleagues were able to calculate survival probabilities in a series of adults based primarily on initial intestinal length.[48] This series comprised 124 consecutive patients, and cutoff values for small bowel length distinguishing transient from permanent TPN dependence were 100 cm for patients with an end enterostomy, 65 cm with a jejunocolic anastomosis, and 30 cm in which a jejunoileocolic anastomosis was possible. Variables affecting probability of TPN dependency are shown in Figure 86-2.

Despite the significance of intestinal length as a major prognostic factor, the actual measurement of intestinal length is quite subjective and highly variable. Furthermore, taking time to measure remnant intestinal length is not infrequently overlooked in the midst of performing an extensive enterectomy, particularly in a physiologically tenuous patient. Efforts have therefore been directed toward identification of other, more objective and reproducible markers of intestinal failure that may be predictive of the need for long-term TPN. Besides the clinical ability to advance enteral nutrition, Crenn and coworkers reported a strong correlation between plasma citrulline levels and TPN dependency in a series of adult patients with SBS.[19] Low levels of this amino acid, which is almost exclusively produced within the intestinal mucosa, may become a useful marker in the future to predict TPN dependency in the pediatric population.

The use of TPN has resulted in a remarkable improvement in survival for patients with SBS. Unfortunately, the most common cause of death in these patients is TPN-induced hepatic dysfunction.[67] Despite this problem, survival for patients with less than 40 cm of residual small bowel length is routine, and long-term survival of infants with as little as 20 to 30 cm of small bowel can be expected. Indeed, an infant was reported who survived off TPN with only 11 cm of small bowel and without an ileocecal valve.[34] Overall, at least 70% of patients with SBS leave the hospital and nearly all are alive at the end of 1 year.

The site of enterectomy is also an important variable influencing the clinical response to intestinal resection. Removal of the jejunum produces minimal permanent defect in the absorption of macronutrients and electrolytes because the ileum has the greatest capacity to adapt and take over these absorptive functions. Several of the intestinal hormones responsible for inhibiting gastric secretion are distributed mainly in the jejunum, and therefore jejunectomy is more likely to result in gastric hypersecretion.[61]

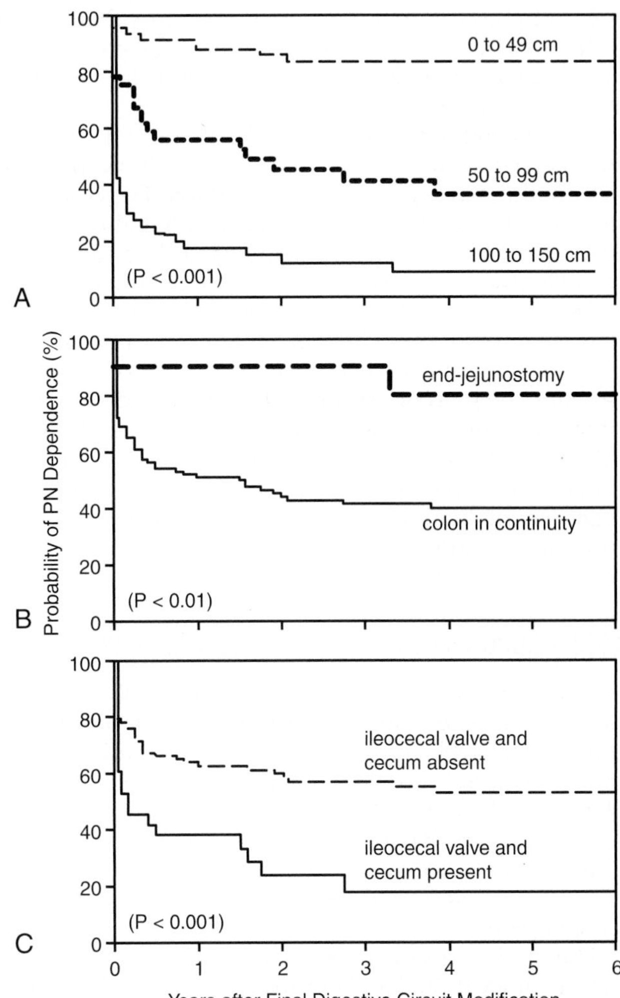

Figure 86–2 Predicted parenteral nutrition (PN) dependence derived from 124 adult patients with short-bowel syndrome. Three main factors predictive of PN dependency included (*A*) length of remnant intestine, (*B*) presence or absence of colon in continuity, and (*C*) presence or absence of an ileocecal valve. (From Messing B, Crenn P, Beau P, et al: Long-term survival and parenteral nutrition dependence in adult patients with the short bowel syndrome. Gastroenterology 1999;117:1043.)

In contrast, the ileum has a pronounced effect in slowing intestinal transit. Thus, ileal resection generally results in increased intestinal transit. The ileum is also an essential site for the absorption and recycling of bile salts. As such, extensive ileal resection is associated with depletion of the bile salt pool, leading to a higher incidence of cholelithiasis and fat malabsorption. It is for this reason that prophylactic cholecystectomy may be beneficial.[68] The malabsorption of fat leads to the deficiency of fat-soluble vitamins A, D, E, and K. Malabsorption of vitamin B_{12} occurs after the resection of more than 60 cm of ileum. The intestine appears to be largely unable to adaptively recruit new vitamin B_{12} receptors into residual ileum or jejunum.

Preservation of the colon in cases of major small intestinal resection should be done as much as possible because this may lessen the severity of SBS. The colon not only provides an absorptive surface area but also exerts a braking effect on early gastric emptying. It is capable of passively absorbing carbohydrate, protein, and fat.

The ileocecal valve slows intestinal transit, thereby increasing contact time between luminal nutrient and the small intestinal mucosal surface. In studies of neonates with SBS, the presence of an ileocecal valve did not significantly correlate with successful weaning from TPN, but it did reduce the duration of TPN dependency.[16,26] In addition, the ileocecal valve serves as a barrier preventing the migration of luminal colonic microorganisms into the distal small bowel.

HOST RESPONSE TO MASSIVE ENTERECTOMY

The clinical course of patients with SBS involves several stages. There is an initial perioperative period of extreme fluid and electrolyte loss. This is followed by initiation of enteral feeding and the period of dynamic intestinal adaptation. Finally, a chronic or plateau stage is reached after 1 to 2 years. It is in this final phase whereby the problems of malabsorption, diarrhea, parenteral nutrition, and chronic nutritional deficiencies occur if adaptation is incomplete.

The initial postoperative management is therefore directed toward fluid and electrolyte replacement. Large volumes of fluid may be lost from an ostomy, and replacement with a solution containing comparable electrolyte concentrations may be required to avoid fluid and electrolyte imbalance. The early postoperative care may be further complicated by the need for re-exploration because of intra-abdominal infections and/or fistulas.

Diarrhea is inevitable after extensive enterectomy and is due to multiple factors: reduced absorptive surface area; increased intestinal transit; gastric, small intestinal, and colonic hypersecretion; increased osmolality of colonic contents; and bacterial overgrowth in the small intestine. In addition, colonic hypersecretion results from increased spillage of bile acids and fat into the colon, where they are converted into secretory stimulants by luminal bacteria.

Post-resection hypergastrinemia and gastric hypersecretion occur almost immediately after intestinal resection and can result in massive fluid and electrolyte losses, the potential for the development of peptic ulcers, and compromised intestinal absorption. Pancreatic lipase activity is reduced in the setting of a more acidic duodenal lumen, which leads to impaired micelle formation and reduced fat absorption. Gastric hypersecretion responds well to histamine receptor antagonists or proton pump inhibitors and usually resolves spontaneously.

Unabsorbed carbohydrates entering the colon are metabolized by bacteria into short-chain fatty acids and contribute further to diarrhea by a direct osmotic effect as well as directly stimulating the colon to secrete fluid and electrolytes. Rarely, children with extensive resections may develop D-lactic acidosis. This occurs secondary to alterations in colonic pH and growth inhibition of *Bacteroides* species, thereby fostering the growth of acid-resistant anaerobes capable of producing D-lactate.[10] Owing to a greater content of luminal free fatty acids that bind and prevent calcium absorption, the bioavailability of dietary oxalate is increased, leading to hyperoxaluria and nephrolithiasis.

Mineral deficiencies are common, and aggressive supplementation is necessary. Sodium and potassium losses may be substantial and require prompt replacement. Malabsorbed fatty acids form luminal soap complexes with calcium and magnesium. Although vitamin D and calcium supplements are usually helpful in preventing calcium deficiency, magnesium deficiency is more complicated to treat because enteral administration of most magnesium salts usually is associated with diarrhea.

MEDICAL AND NUTRITIONAL MANAGEMENT

The most important therapeutic objective in the management of SBS is to maintain the patient's nutritional status and to support continued growth. TPN should begin early to prevent significant weight loss and to establish a positive nitrogen balance. It is essential to start enteral nutrition as soon as possible, with the ultimate aim for the patient to eat as normal a diet as possible.[81] The first decision that needs to be made is the type of feeding to use. In infants younger than 1 year of age, increased permeability to food antigens may occur, resulting in the development of a protein allergy to the formula. Hypoallergenic formulas therefore have a theoretical advantage and include Nutramigen, Pregestimil (Mead Johnson Laboratories, Evansville, IN), and Alimentum (Ross Laboratories, Columbus, OH). To reduce the allergic risk even further in highly susceptible patients, an amino acid formula such as Neocate (SHS, Liverpool, England) can be used. Another advantage of these formulas is that a high percentage of their calories are in the form of fat, which is better tolerated than carbohydrates. Breast milk, when available, is probably the best source of nutrition for neonates. It is known that human milk can have a very positive influence on cell proliferation and on the adaptive transformation of the residual intestine. The probable explanation for these benefits is the presence of a plethora of trophic growth factors that are yet to be completely understood. Older children tolerate more complex and less costly enteral feedings. Rarely is protein absorption a problem in older children.

Gastrostomy tubes are an important adjunct in the management of these patients because this will allow access for continuous enteral feeding. Continuous feeding is preferred over bolus feeding because the total percentage of calories absorbed is greater owing to continuous saturation of absorptive transporter proteins in the small intestine. The enteral infusion should be maintained isotonic and advanced at an extremely slow rate. Ultimately, the volume of enteral feedings can be gradually increased as the volume of parenteral feedings is decreased based on the patient's tolerance. Stool losses increasing by more than 50% in a 24-hour period are usually a contraindication to advancing fluids. Stool losses greater than 40 to 50 mL/kg/day, which are strongly positive for reducing substances, suggest that enteral feedings should not be advanced. Under these circumstances, the rate of feeding has reached the limit of the patient's absorptive capacity.[74]

Once the patient's condition has been stabilized with a combination of parenteral and enteral nutrition, the TPN should be transitioned from an around-the-clock continuous infusion to a cyclical night-time infusion. This infusion schedule is safe and permits fewer limitations in daytime activities for the patient and parent.

Feeding behavior is an important component in the management of patients with SBS. Young infants should be encouraged to continue sucking and swallowing, and intermittent bottle feedings of small amounts of formula should be encouraged. Because it is difficult to completely withhold food from older children, they should be allowed to experiment with foods that are both palatable and not associated with a large stool output.

Pharmacologic agents that reduce gastric hypersecretion and include histamine H_2 receptor antagonists and proton pump inhibitors are indicated in the early management of patients with SBS. Because gastric hypersecretion usually decreases after 6 to 12 months after extensive enterectomy, treatment beyond this time is seldom necessary.

Pharmacologic agents can also be used to slow intestinal transit, thus improving nutritional absorption and potentially allowing the patient to wean from parenteral nutrition. The mainstay of pharmacologic therapy to slow intestinal transit has been the use of opioid substances. Opioid agents most commonly used to treat diarrhea include codeine, diphenoxylate, and loperamide. Loperamide was more effective than diphenoxylate in the control of diarrhea in several clinical trials.[23,52] Codeine, although quite effective for the control of diarrhea, has significant central nervous system side effects and a clear abuse potential.

Somatostatin and its long-acting analogue octreotide have been investigated in the management of severe refractory diarrhea in SBS, with mixed outcomes. Octreotide inhibits essentially all exocrine and endocrine gastrointestinal and pancreatic secretions. In some clinical trials of adult patients with SBS, the need for supplemental electrolytes and nutrition was decreased, secretory fluid and electrolyte losses were reduced, and quality of life was improved.[50,55] In a more recent trial, octreotide resulted in a slowed intestinal transit but was without significant beneficial effects on macronutrient absorption or weight gain.[49] In an animal model of SBS, administration of octreotide resulted in a reduction in mucosal active transport of nutrients.[59] In some studies, octreotide has also been shown to inhibit intestinal adaptation, perhaps by decreasing the significant adaptive enhancing effects of exocrine gastrointestinal secretions.[5,65] On the other hand, the inhibitory effect of octreotide on adaptation has not been universally observed.[75] The experience with octreotide in the pediatric population has been somewhat limited. One theoretical concern is the potential long-term effect of this agent on growth. For all these reasons, octreotide cannot be endorsed for routine use in pediatric patients with SBS.

Cholestyramine may be beneficial in the management of diarrhea in patients with SBS. It is effective only when the diarrhea is related to the cathartic effect of unabsorbed bile salts reaching the colon. It should be considered in patients with diarrhea who have had an extensive ileal resection.[69] Alternatively, fat malabsorption in SBS in part may be caused by decreased bile secretion. Exogenous administration of a synthetic conjugated bile acid (cholylsarcosine) that is resistant to bacterial degradation with no cathartic activity may be beneficial by promoting fat absorption in patients with SBS.[31]

In addition to the myriad of fluid, electrolyte, and nutritional obstacles that the patient with SBS faces, several other complications must be anticipated. These include central venous catheter complications, TPN-induced liver disease, and intestinal bacterial overgrowth. TPN-induced liver disease is frequent in infants with SBS and along with sepsis is the leading cause of death in these patients. It appears to be a multifactorial process that is often reversible but may lead to severe steatosis, cholestasis, and eventually cirrhosis. It occurs more frequently in children than adults and accounts for one third of deaths of patients receiving long-term TPN. TPN-induced liver disease remains one of the main indications for liver/small bowel transplant.

Avoidance of parenteral overfeeding and provision of as many calories as possible via the enteral route may help to prevent this complication.[69] Exogenous cholecystokinin may lead to improved hepatic function when administered to patients with SBS and TPN-induced liver disease.[66] In addition, administration of the bile salt ursodeoxycholic acid may attenuate liver dysfunction in these patients by stimulating bile flow.[6] More recently, it was found that a related bile salt, tauroursodeoxycholic acid, had no significant effect.[30] This might have been because this bile salt is given orally and absorption was limited in this SBS population. Avoidance of central venous line sepsis and aggressively managing small bowel bacterial overgrowth may also help to decrease the progression of TPN-related cholestasis.

Detection of bacterial overgrowth in dysfunctional intestinal segments requires a high degree of suspicion. Colonization of the small intestine leads to decreased luminal concentration of conjugated bile acids with resultant fat malabsorption. Secretory diarrhea then develops as a consequence of malabsorbed fatty acids, increased formation of short-chain fatty acids with increased osmotic load and gas, and impaired vitamin B_{12} absorption.[45] In addition, bacterial overgrowth causes mucosal inflammation, thereby exacerbating malabsorption of all nutrients. Patients without an ileocecal valve may be at increased risk for this complication owing to the potential for reflux of bacteria from the colon. Colonization should be suspected when the patient's absorptive capacity and diarrhea acutely change and dilated bowel loops are radiographically evident. Treatment is often empirical with antibiotics targeted to anaerobic and both gram-positive and gram-negative aerobic organisms. Typical regimens include combinations of cephalexin-metronidazole or monotherapy with metronidazole, trimethoprim-sulfamethoxazole, or oral gentamicin. Further studies need to confirm whether probiotics may play a role in prevention and treatment by inhibiting the growth of pathogenic bacteria.[33]

PHARMACOLOGIC ENHANCEMENT OF INTESTINAL FUNCTION

As mentioned earlier, several growth factors, peptides, and hormones have been administered in various animal models of SBS with resultant enhanced adaptation. In the clinical setting, most information has been accrued with the use of the combination of growth hormone (GH) and glutamine (GLN), as well as with glucagon-like peptide-2 (GLP-2). Although several of the clinical studies outlined here show only modest improvement in response to these factors, the results are encouraging. Unfortunately, many of the studies are composed of SBS patients with mixed diagnoses and often several years beyond the post-resection adaptation phase. There is experimental evidence to suggest that the post-resection time, route of administration, and dosage are critical variables that must be considered to maximally encourage adaptation and intestinal function.[63]

In the first major study, Byrne and coworkers reported on a series of 47 adult patients with mostly TPN-dependent SBS who received GLN (preferred enterocyte fuel), GH, and a defined diet (high carbohydrate, low fat).[14] After 28 days of treatment, 57% of these patients no longer required TPN, whereas another 30% reduced the amount of daily TPN required. After the study period, they were discharged to home on diet and GLN alone and the GH was discontinued. At follow-up ranging from 5 months to 5 years, TPN independence had reduced to 40% while the TPN-reduced subset of patients had increased to 40%.

In contrast to this report, Scalopio and colleagues performed a randomized, 6-week, double-blind, placebo-controlled, crossover study of GLN/GH/defined diet (high carbohydrate, low fat) in eight adult patients with SBS.[58] Minimal benefit to this combination therapy was observed. Using this same study design, a more recent report by Seguy and associates found that GLN/GH in the context of a hyperphagic Western diet resulted in significantly greater absorption of luminal nutrients, along with improved weight gain and lean body mass.[60] The experience with GH and GLN in the pediatric population is extremely limited. At the present time, the use of this hormone and specific enterocyte nutrient in combination with a select diet as therapy for patients with SBS remains controversial.

The proglucagon-derived peptide GLP-2 is intestinotrophic[15] and secreted from L cells in the distal intestine after nutrient ingestion. It is therefore not surprising that serum levels of GLP-2 in patients who have had extensive resections of the distal bowel are markedly decreased.[35] In balance studies performed on a small subset of patients with SBS and ileocolic resections, GLP-2 administration resulted in improved weight gain and intestinal absorption of energy.[36] At the present time, GLP-2 is not commercially available; however, studies using specific analogues of this peptide in the treatment of SBS are ongoing.

SURGICAL OPTIONS TO ENHANCE INTESTINAL FUNCTION

Prevention of SBS is the earliest and best approach. Timely surgical intervention in patients with necrotizing enterocolitis and/or volvulus and a conservative approach to intestinal resection are crucial to avoid SBS. Once the patient is beyond the initial operation, the ultimate goal is to provide all calories by means of the enteral route and to discontinue TPN altogether. Patients often develop complications related to TPN or reach a point at which stool output and/or electrolyte losses limit the ability to advance enteral feeding. In addition, the conditions of some patients may actually worsen and require increasing, rather than decreasing, amounts of parenteral nutrition. Those who fall into these groups (complications of TPN, failure to advance enteral nutrition, worsening tolerance of enteral feeding) are those in whom operative intervention should be considered.

The optimal timing for consideration of operative intervention is important. If surgery is performed too early, it might be unnecessary, because normal post-resection adaptation or intestinal lengthening due to normal growth may prevent the need for long-term TPN. If surgery is offered too late, the patient may suffer complications as well as the added cost of prolonged TPN support. A period of at least 1 year is a reasonable minimal interval of time to allow for adaptation to complete. Even after this period, if the patient is making progress with regard to tolerance of enteral feeding and there are minimal problems with the provision of TPN, operative intervention should be postponed. However, this policy may need to be reconsidered in the context of significant TPN complications.

One major goal of surgical intervention is to increase intestinal absorptive and digestive capacity. Along these lines, as part of the early management program, patients with diverting stomas should have intestinal continuity restored if feasible. Most surgical procedures have been created to address the specific anatomic and physiologic abnormalities of the intestine in patients with SBS. These abnormalities include rapid intestinal transit, decreased mucosal surface area, ineffective peristalsis, and reduced intestinal length. The various surgical procedures may therefore be categorized based on the abnormality they primarily address.

Determining the indications for each procedure requires a careful preoperative workup and a meticulous operative plan. As a first step, a thorough understanding of the patient's intestinal anatomy and function should be obtained. This is gleaned through plain abdominal radiographs and a contrast upper gastrointestinal series with small bowel follow-through. Areas of partial obstruction and efficiency of transit should be sought. Simple interventions to relieve areas of partial intestinal obstruction such as lysis of adhesions or resection of a focal stricture may be all that is necessary for the patient to significantly improve. Surgical procedures designed to slow intestinal transit would obviously not be indicated for a patient with obvious delayed transit. Although not entirely accurate, an idea of small intestinal length and caliber may also be deduced from the upper gastrointestinal series. In patients with a proximal stoma, it is also prudent to obtain a contrast enema, which will provide information as to how much distal bowel is available for subsequent reanastomosis as well as to identify potential areas of stricture.

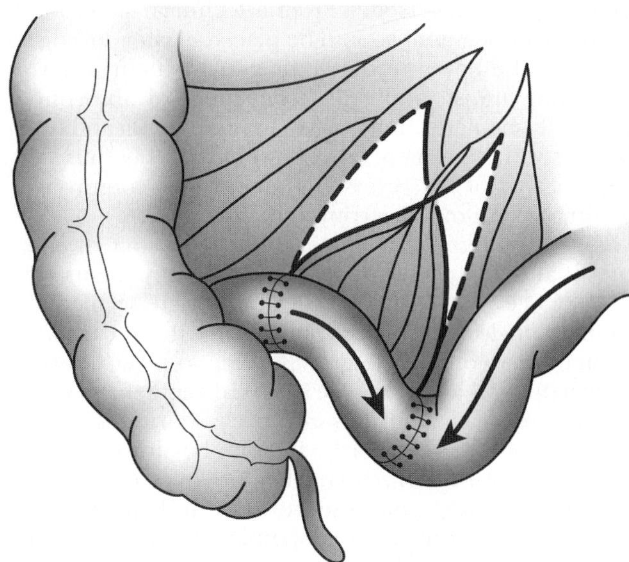

Figure 86-4 Reversed intestinal segment designed to slow intestinal transit. A small segment of distal intestine is excised with the mesenteric blood supply intact. It is then flipped 180 degrees and reanastomosed in continuity with the remaining gastrointestinal tract. In theory, the direction of peristalsis in the reversed segment will contract against the wave of peristalsis in the native intestine to act as a physiologic valve, thus slowing transit.

Intestinal Valves

The importance of the ileocecal valve has been well appreciated by those caring for patients with SBS. In 1972, Wilmore documented that survival in infants with an ileocecal valve required a minimal bowel length of 15 cm.[87] However, in those infants without this valve, the minimal bowel length required for survival was significantly longer (40 cm). More recently, it has been reported that up to 89% of patients without an ileocecal valve and with less than 40 cm of small bowel will survive.[16] In this same report, it was also noted that an absent valve was associated with a significantly longer duration of TPN. Preservation of the ileocecal valve should therefore be a major goal during any operative intervention.

Based on the observed importance of the ileocecal valve, multiple techniques for the construction of similar valves have been described. The simplest techniques include the placement of sutures or an external Teflon collar around the circumference of the bowel.[64] A more technically involved procedure involves everting a segment of bowel to create a small intussusceptum and thus slow transit (Fig. 86-3). The more variable and less well understood aspects of these procedures center around the optimum length of bowel to be everted, as well as the direction of the intussusception. If too large a segment of bowel is intussuscepted, a functional bowel obstruction will result.

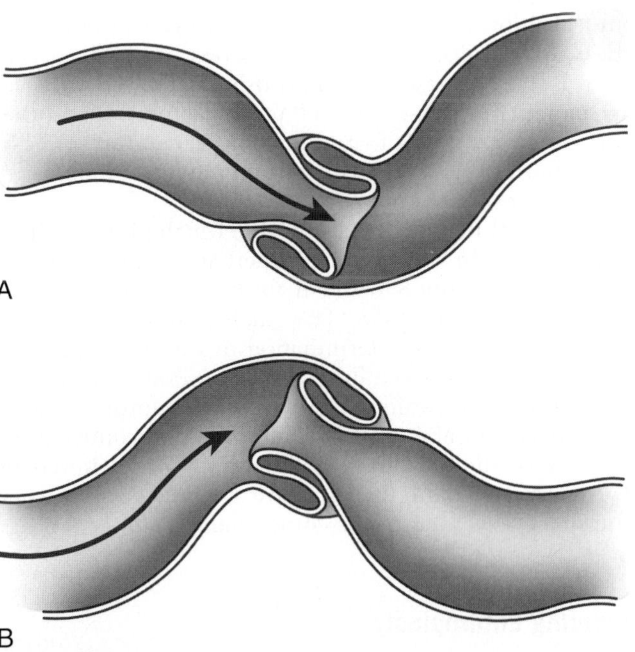

Figure 86-3 Intestinal valves constructed to slow intestinal transit. A valve may be constructed in either an iso- (*A*) or anti- (*B*) peristaltic limb and is then intussuscepted into the other limb.

The clinical experience with intestinal valves is sparse and limited to small series or case reports. Creation of a partially obstructing valve has been shown to induce intestinal dilatation and mucosal adaptation.[18] Taking advantage of this observation, Georgeson and associates reported a series of pediatric patients with SBS in whom an intussuscepting valve was initially constructed and followed by an intestinal lengthening procedure at a later date.[25] Several of these patients improved as a result of the ability to lengthen the previously nondilated bowel.

Reversed Intestinal Segments

Most experience has accumulated with the use of reversed segments of intestine to slow peristalsis in patients with postvagotomy diarrhea or dumping syndrome. A "physiologic" valve is thought to be created by the interposition of a segment of bowel in which peristalsis is in the opposite direction (Fig. 86-4). The exact length of bowel to be reversed is critical, because a segment that is too short may be ineffective in slowing peristalsis whereas too long of a segment may create a functional bowel obstruction. Various lengths of reversed bowel probably contribute to the disparate results obtained in many experimental and clinical series. Although 10 cm seems to be the most common length utilized in adult patients, beneficial effects have been described in infants when as little as

3 cm has been reversed.[79] From a technical standpoint, the reversed segment should be placed in the most distal aspect of the bowel to derive maximal benefit in terms of slowing transit and enhancing mucosal absorption. Reversed segments may have limited applicability in patients with extremely short bowel lengths because the construction of the reversed segment may compromise an already tenuous absorptive mucosal mass.

Favorable results have been reported using reversed intestinal segments in more than 30 adult patients with SBS.[4,53] The long-term success of reversed segments is presently unclear. In children, it is possible that the reversed segment may continue to grow, leading to possible bowel obstruction. In addition, the reversed segment may not function normally and thus effectively shorten the intestinal remnant, particularly if complications such as obstruction or ischemia occur. The use of a reversed segment has also been proposed to provide benefit over a short period while adaptation occurs.[61] Most of the reports of reversed intestinal segments remain anecdotal and infrequent compared with some of the other surgical options. There may be a role for this procedure as well as for intestinal valves when the bowel caliber is normal and transit is rapid.

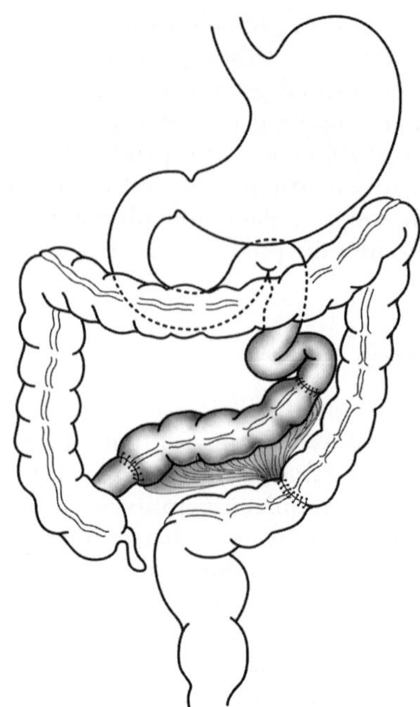

Figure 86-5 Colon interposition. A section of sigmoid colon with its intact blood supply is interposed between the segments of small intestine to act as a physiologic brake, thus slowing transit.

Recirculating Loops

Theoretically, if a loop of intestine was created such that luminal nutrient recirculated several times before proceeding distally, then the exposure time of the nutrients and mucosa would be prolonged. Furthermore, overall intestinal transit would be slowed. Unfortunately, these theoretical advantages are seldom realized. Several experimental studies have failed to show any benefit of these procedures. Morbidity and mortality are generally increased in direct relationship to the complexity of the loop. Another interesting observation is that although enteral contents have been radiographically demonstrated to recirculate, absorption was not improved.

Recirculating loops have been performed in a few patients with discouraging results. At the present time, the clinical utility of recirculating loops in the management of SBS is fairly limited. Morbidity is prohibitive while efficacy is unproved. Recirculating intestinal loops should probably not be performed and are mentioned only for completeness.

Colon Interposition

The interposition of a segment of colon between two limbs of small bowel in patients with rapid intestinal transit has been studied experimentally and applied clinically (Fig. 86-5). Although the exact mechanism by which this procedure is effective is not well understood, the interposed colon segment is generally placed proximally and probably slows intestinal transit by virtue of its slow, segmental peristaltic contractions, thereby slowing the rate at which nutrients are delivered to the distal bowel. The interposed colon is also capable of absorbing nutrients, water, and electrolytes. There appears to be adaptive changes within the transposed colon segment involving the mucosa[47] as well as the longitudinal smooth muscle layer.[46]

Isoperistaltic colon interposition in the management of SBS was first reported in beagle puppies following 90% small bowel resection.[32] When compared with animals undergoing resection alone, the dogs with the interposition had a prolonged intestinal transit, better weight gain, less stool output, and reduced fecal fat excretion. Colon interposition has been clinically beneficial in both children and adults. In the largest series of children with SBS, isoperistaltic colon interposition allowed three of six patients to wean from TPN completely.[27] The other three patients died of complications secondary to TPN. No reported morbidity or mortality was associated with the interposition procedure.

The ideal length of colon to use for the interposition is unknown. In the just-mentioned series the length of colon ranged from 8 to 15 cm. Others have reported segments as long as 24 cm. The small number of patients reported precludes determination of the most appropriate length of colon to utilize in interposition. This appears to be a useful technique for increasing intestinal transit, with success in about 50%, while not compromising the viability of the small bowel. This procedure should be considered in patients who have an intact colon when the small bowel has not become dilated.

Tapering Enteroplasty

Dilated segments of intestine are an accepted cause of functional bowel obstruction. The mechanism is ineffective peristalsis due to failure of bowel wall apposition

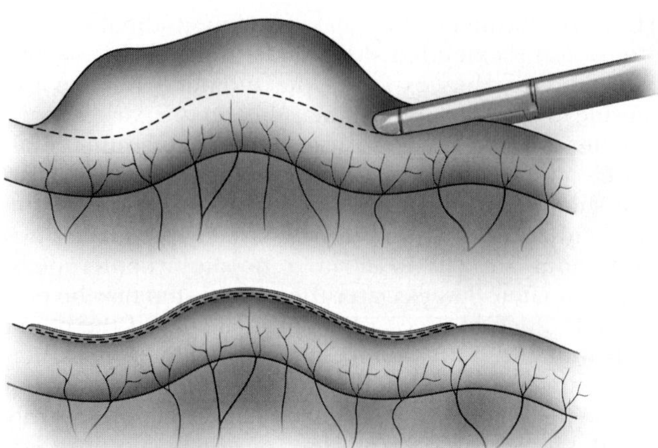

Figure 86–6 Tapering enteroplasty. A stapling devise is used to longitudinally excise the dilated antimesenteric portion of the intestine. The remaining bowel is therefore smaller in caliber and demonstrates improved motility.

during contraction. The dilated bowel has low contraction pressures, resulting in a to-and-fro motion of the enteric contents. This situation sets the stage for stasis, bacterial overgrowth with associated toxin production, and malabsorption. In patients with a short segment of affected bowel and a sufficient length of remaining intestine, resection of the dilated bowel would be considered optimal management. Unfortunately, in the patient with SBS, the majority of the bowel is typically dilated and the overall length is short. Resection is therefore not usually a viable option.

Tapering enteroplasty reduces the caliber of the bowel while preserving intestinal length. This is accomplished by excising an antimesenteric portion of the bowel, leaving the mesenteric tube of bowel intact (Fig. 86-6). The tapered intestine has a significantly smaller caliber and therefore peristalsis becomes more effective.[82]

A variation of this technique consists of antimesenteric plication of the bowel. Instead of resecting the antimesenteric portion of intestine, the bowel is folded into the lumen and plicated. This theoretically results in preservation of the mucosa for better absorption while at the same time decreasing the overall caliber of the bowel.[21] Unfortunately over time, the suture lines tend to break down and bowel dilation and functional obstruction recur.

In a large series of 160 adult and pediatric patients with SBS,[70] 11 children ranging in age from 6 months to 9 years had dilated intestinal segments and remnant lengths longer than 30 cm. All of these children had associated bacterial overgrowth and malabsorption. Enteroplasty was performed on the duodenum (n = 3), jejunum (n = 3), or ileum (n = 5) with the length of the tapered segment longer than 15 cm in 7 of the 11 patients. Nine of the 11 patients were weaned completely from parenteral nutrition, and the other 2 required decreased amounts of TPN. Two patients subsequently underwent intestinal lengthening because of recurrent malabsorption. Tapering has much less morbidity than a lengthening procedure and is usually the procedure of choice as long as the patient has reasonable length of small intestine.

Intestinal Lengthening Procedures

An important procedure to actually increase the length of the intestine was first described by Bianchi in 1980.[7] This procedure, like other post-resection surgical options, appears to be most successful for patients who have undergone a period of normal bowel adaptation after initial bowel resection.[8] This method takes advantage of the anatomic features of the mesenteric blood supply to the bowel. Just before reaching the edge of the bowel wall, the blood vessels within the mesentery bifurcate to supply one half of the bowel circumference. This segmental blood supply pattern permits the bowel to be safely divided along its longitudinal axis into two tubes that measure one half of the circumference of the original bowel. This is facilitated with a gastrointestinal anastomosis (GIA) stapling device but can be sutured by hand. Once the bowel has been divided along its longitudinal axis, the two newly constructed tubes of bowel are sewn together in an isoperistaltic fashion (Fig. 86-7). The overall

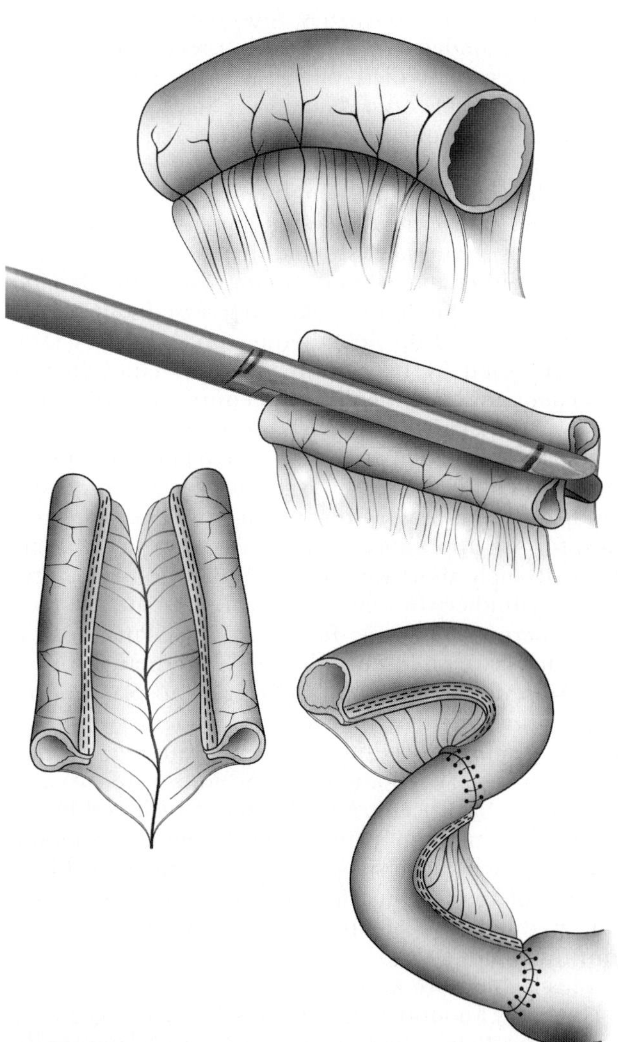

Figure 86–7 The Bianchi intestinal lengthening procedure. The bowel is divided in a longitudinal plane to create two tubes, which when reanastomosed results in doubling of the intestinal length at the expense of halving the bowel wall circumference.

result is a segment of bowel in which the length is doubled and overall circumference has been halved. Thus, this procedure not only lengthens the bowel to increase absorption but also improves peristalsis by decreasing bowel caliber. A variation of this technique involves entering one side of the bowel limb at the initiation of the lengthening and exiting the other side once the lengthening has completed.[17] This permits the need for only a single anastomosis and is a very useful technical modification.

Dilated bowel is generally easier to lengthen, since the GIA stapler may be used. Extensive intraperitoneal adhesions from prior surgery are often encountered in patients subjected to the lengthening procedure, and care must always be taken to avoid injury to the mesenteric blood supply. In addition, variability in blood supply to the bowel wall may be present, possibly contributing to technical failures.[72] In patients without the significant spontaneous dilation of the bowel that makes the Bianchi procedure technically feasible, a staged sequential lengthening procedure as described by Georgeson and associates may be undertaken.[25]

Thompson and colleagues reported a series of six patients who underwent the Bianchi procedure.[71] In this series, one patient died of sepsis, four patients were weaned completely off TPN, and the final patient had a decreased TPN requirement. In another series, Figueroa-Colon and coworkers reported a series of seven patients who underwent intestinal lengthening and showed that the tolerance of enteral calories increased significantly by 9 months.[24] They also showed that all growth parameters were either maintained or improved and that the number of hospitalization days decreased during the second year after the lengthening procedure. A large series reported by Bianchi included 20 children who underwent this lengthening procedure over 16 years.[9] The long-term survival was 45%. Survivors generally had an intestinal length greater than 40 cm and no evidence for significant liver disease (as gauged by the absence of jaundice) at the time of reconstruction. The same concerns for the application of this procedure for patients with extremely short intestinal length (< 50 cm), presence of jaundice, or when performed in the neonatal period were outlined by the group from Pittsburgh in their analysis of children with failed lengthening procedures who were referred for intestinal transplantation.[12] Finally, the persistent morbidity of patients who have undergone this procedure was well illustrated by Waag and associates.[77] The long-term morbidity of 18 survivors of the Bianchi procedure in this series included hyperphagia, hyponatremia and hypochloremia, metabolic acidosis, D-lactic acidosis, cholelithiasis and urolithiasis, gastroesophageal reflux, and symptoms caused by secondary dilatation of the lengthened bowel loops. Continued long-term follow-up of these complex patients is therefore warranted.

The Iowa (Kimura) procedure was described as a means of treating SBS in patients who are not candidates for the Bianchi procedure or have limited mesentery associated with very short bowel.[44] The procedure is a two-stage process. The first step is initial coaptation of the antimesenteric surface of the bowel to a host blood supply. This is performed by first making a longitudinal seromyotomy that is extended along the antimesenteric border of the bowel, thus exposing the submucosa. Then the capsule of the anterior liver margin and the parietal peritoneum on the undersurface of the abdominal wall muscles are removed to create a denuded tissue surface. The submucosa and the denuded tissue surface of the liver and abdominal wall muscles are coapted using two continuous sutures to form a hepatomyoenteropexy. Approximately 8 weeks later the second step may be performed, which involves a longitudinal split of the bowel to provide two bowel loops. These bowel loops may then be arranged in series by end-to-end anastomosis to double the bowel length (Fig. 86-8). So far, there are only anecdotal reports of the use of this procedure.[25,44]

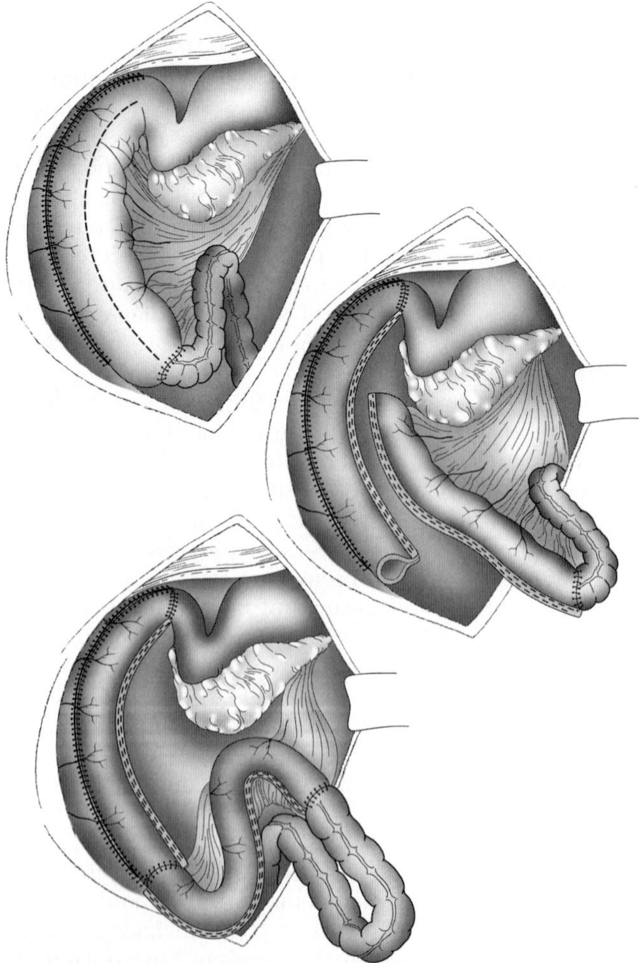

Figure 86–8 The Iowa (Kimura) intestinal lengthening procedure. The antimesenteric bowel wall is pexed to the undersurface of the abdominal wall. A seromyotomy along the bowel wall and mechanical abrasion of the abdominal wall before pexing promotes neovascularization of the antimesenteric bowel, based on the systemic-derived abdominal wall. Several months later, the bowel may be longitudinally divided into two limbs. The first is based on the systemic blood supply to the antimesenteric limb, whereas the other is based on the mesenteric blood supply. These two limbs are then reapproximated to double the intestinal length.

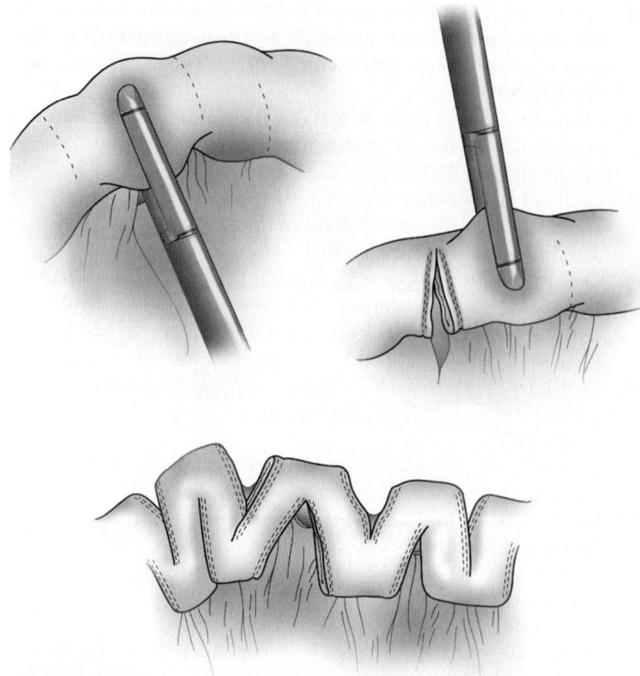

Figure 86-9 The serial transverse enteroplasty (STEP) procedure. Multiple fires of an anastomotic stapling device to alternating sides of the bowel wall result in decreased bowel caliber with an increased length of enteral nutrient transit.

It appears to be specifically useful in children in whom the remaining bowel is limited to the duodenum, thus limiting the applicability of the Bianchi procedure. A similar procedure has also been proposed using the omentum as a source of parasitized blood supply. In a preliminary study using dogs, it was demonstrated that the neovascularization improved both absorption and adaptation.[77]

Recently, a novel bowel lengthening operation termed the *serial transverse enteroplasty* procedure has been described.[41] A pig model was used in which dilated small bowel was lengthened by serial transverse applications of a GIA stapler, from opposite directions, to create a zigzag channel (Fig. 86-9). Near doubling of bowel length resulted. This procedure has subsequently been applied clinically with encouraging outcome.[42] Further studies are required, and careful clinical evaluation in relation to the traditional Bianchi lengthening technique is needed.

A proposed algorithm for management of patients with SBS taking into account the presence or absence of intestinal caliber is presented in Figure 86-10.

Tissue Engineering

Tissue engineering represents an exciting new frontier that is presently in the early stages of investigation. These models utilize tubular microporous biodegradable polymers that are seeded with intestinal epithelial organoid units. The blood supply is derived from the mesentery. It is noted that there is formation of neointestinal cysts, which can then be anastomosed to the native intestine.[38,39,43] The use of neointestine in humans has not yet been reported, but the field of tissue engineering will likely play a significant role in the future treatment of patients with SBS.[28]

INTESTINAL TRANSPLANTATION

Transplantation of the small bowel is an important final option for management of SBS and is covered elsewhere in this book. Intestinal transplantation is promising definitive therapy but associated with significant morbidity and mortality. Current results demonstrate 1-year patient and graft survival rates of 70% and 65%, respectively.[54] However, at 3 years after transplantation, the patient and graft survival rates are reduced to the range of 40% to 55% and of 50%, respectively.[42,56] The complex immunosuppression as well as the myriad of infectious complications continues to provide difficult hurdles in the management of these complex patients.

Figure 86-10 Proposed algorithm for management of patients with short-bowel syndrome, taking into account the presence or absence of intestinal caliber.

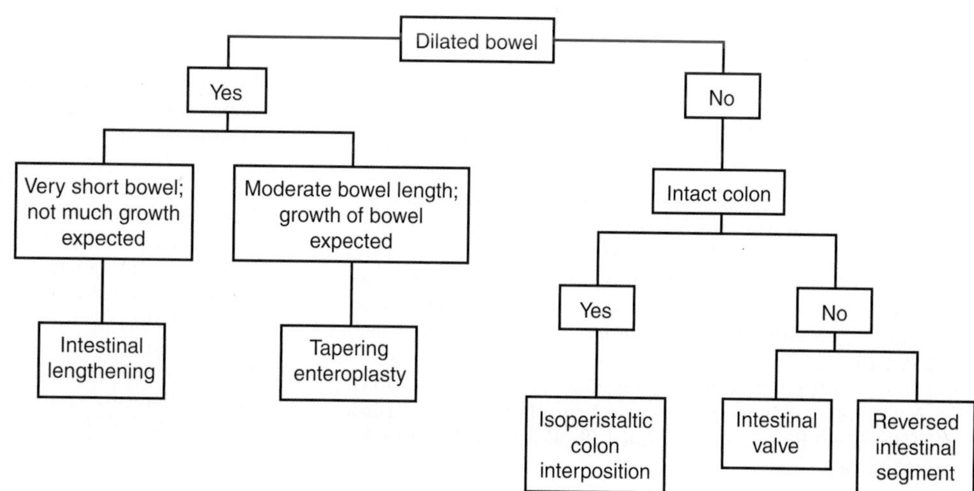

CONCLUSION

Overall, the care of the patient with SBS has advanced significantly. Whereas multiple surgical procedures have been devised to address the intestinal abnormalities that develop after massive SBS, they have not been tried in sufficient numbers of patients to permit valid outcome comparisons. The ultimate goal of all procedures should be to allow the patient to advance to enteral feeding so that the complications of TPN are avoided and the patient may return to as normal a lifestyle as possible. Perhaps as important in the management of patients with SBS is an understanding of endogenous regulation of mucosal growth and the genetic regulation of post-resection adaptation responses.

REFERENCES

1. Altmann GG: Influence of bile and pancreatic secretions on the size of the intestinal villi in the rat. Am J Anat 1971; 132:167.
2. Altmann GG, Leblond CP: Factors influencing villus size in the small intestine of adult rats as revealed by transposition of intestinal segments. Am J Anat 1970;127:15.
3. Andorsky DJ, Lund DP, Lillehei CW, et al: Nutritional and other postoperative management of neonates with short bowel syndrome correlates with clinical outcomes. J Pediatr 2001;139:27.
4. Barros D'sa AB: An experimental evaluation of segmental reversal after massive small bowel resection. Br J Surg 1979; 66:493.
5. Bass BL, Fischer BA, Richardson C, et al: Somatostatin analogue treatment inhibits post-resectional adaptation of the small bowel in rats. Am J Surg 1991;161:107.
6. Beau P, Labat-Labourdette J, Ingrand P, et al: Is ursodeoxycholic acid an effective therapy for total parenteral nutritrion related liver disease? J Hepatol 1994;20:240.
7. Bianchi A: Intestinal loop lengthening—a technique for increasing small intestinal length. J Pediatr Surg 1980; 15:145.
8. Bianchi A: Autologous gastrointestinal reconstruction. Semin Pediatr Surg 1995;4:54.
9. Bianchi A: Experience with longitudinal intestinal lengthening and tailoring. Eur J Pediatr Surg 1999;9:256.
10. Bongaerts G, Bakkeren J, Severijnen R, et al: Lactobacilli and acidosis in children with short small bowel. J Pediatr Gastroenterol Nutr 2000;30:288.
11. Booth IW: Enteral nutrition as primary therapy in short bowel syndrome. Gut 1994;35(Suppl):S69-S72.
12. Bueno J, Guiterrez J, Mazariegos GV, et al: Analysis of patients with longitudinal intestinal lengthening procedure referred for intestinal transplantation. J Pediatr Surg 2001;36:178.
13. Bueno J, Ohwada S, Kocoshis S, et al: Factors impacting the survival of children with intestinal failure referred for intestinal transplantation. J Pediatr Surg 1999;34:27.
14. Byrne TA, Persinger RL, Young LS, et al: A new treatment for patients with short-bowel syndrome: Growth hormone, glutamine, and a modified diet. Ann Surg 1995; 222:243.
15. Chance WT, Foley-Nelson T, Thomas I, et al: Prevention of parenteral nutrition-induced gut hypoplasia by co-infusion of glucagon-like peptide-2. Am J Physiol 1997;273(2 pt 1): G559-G563.
16. Chaet MS, Farrell MK, Ziegler MM, et al: Intensive nutritional support and remedial surgical intervention for extreme short bowel syndrome. J Pediatr Gastroenterol Nutr 1994;19:295.
17. Chahine AA, Ricketts RR: A modification of the Bianchi intestinal lengthening procedure with a single anastomosis. J Pediatr Surg 1998;33:1292.
18. Collins J III, Vicente Y, Georgeson K, et al: Partial intestinal obstruction induces substantial mucosal proliferation in the pig. J Pediatr Surg 1996;31:415.
19. Crenn P, Coudray-Lucas C, Thuillier F, et al: Postabsorptive plasma citrulline concentration is a marker of absorptive enterocyte mass and intestinal failure in humans. Gastroenterology 2000;119:1496.
20. Cronk DR, Ferguson DC, Thompson JS: Malnutrition impairs postresection intestinal adaptation. J Parenter Enteral Nutr 2000;24:76.
21. de Lorimier AA, Harrison MR: Intestinal plication in the treatment of atresia. J Pediatr Surg 1983;18:734.
22. Dowling RH, Booth CC: Structural and functional changes following small intestinal resection in the rat. Clin Sci 1967; 32:139.
23. Ericsson CD, Johnson PC: Safety and efficacy of loperamide. Am J Med 1990;88(Suppl):10S.
24. Figueroa-Colon R, Harris PR, Birdsong E, et al: Impact of intestinal lengthening on the nutritional outcome for children with short bowel syndrome. J Pediatr Surg 1996; 31:912.
25. Georgeson K, Halpin D, Figueroa R, et al: Sequential intestinal lengthening procedures for refractory short bowel syndrome. J Pediatr Surg 1994;29:316.
26. Georgeson KE, Breaux CW Jr: Outcome and intestinal adaptation in neonatal short-bowel syndrome. J Pediatr Surg 1992;27:344.
27. Glick PL, de Lorimier AA, Adzick NS, et al: Colon interposition for the short bowel syndrome. J Pediatr Surg 1984; 19:719.
28. Grikscheit TC: Tissue engineering of the gastrointestinal tract for surgical replacement: A nutrition tool of the future? Proc Nutr Soc 2003;62:739.
29. Helmrath MA, Erwin CR, Shin CE, et al: Enterocyte apoptosis is increased following small bowel resection. J Gastrointest Surg 1998;2:44.
30. Heubi JE, Wiechmann DA, Creutzinger V, et al: Tauroursodeoxycholic acid (TUDCA) in the prevention of total parenteral nutrition-associated liver disease. J Pediatr 2002;141:237.
31. Heydorn S, Jeppesen PB, Mortensen PB: Bile acid replacement therapy with cholylsarcosine for short-bowel syndrome. Scand J Gastroenterol 1999;34:818.
32. Hutcher NE, Mendez-Picon G, Salzberg AM: Prejejunal transposition of colon to prevent the development of short bowel syndrome in puppies with 90 per cent small intestine resection. J Pediatr Surg 1973;8:771.
33. Hwang ST, Shulman RJ: Update on management and treatment of short gut. Clin Perinatol 2002;29:181.
34. Iacono G, Carroccio A, Montalto G, et al: Extreme short bowel syndrome: A case for reviewing the guidelines for predicting survival. J Pediatr Gastroenterol Nutr 1993;16:216.
35. Jeppesen PB, Hartmann B, Hansen BS, et al: Impaired meal stimulated glucagon-like peptide 2 response in ileal resected short bowel patients with intestinal failure. Gut 1999;45:559.
36. Jeppesen PB, Hartmann B, Thulesen J, et al: Glucagon-like peptide 2 improves nutrient absorption and nutritional status in short-bowel patients with no colon. Gastroenterology 2001;120:806.

37. Juno RJ, Knott AW, Erwin CR, et al: A serum factor(s) after small bowel resection induces intestinal epithelial cell proliferation: Effects of timing, site, and extent of resection. J Pediatr Surg 2003;38:868.
38. Kaihara S, Kim SS, Benvenuto M, et al: Successful anastomosis between tissue-engineered intestine and native small bowel. Transplantation 1999;67:241.
39. Kaihara S, Kim SS, Kim BS, et al: Long-term follow-up of tissue-engineered intestine after anastomosis to native small bowel. Transplantation 2000;69:1927.
40. Kato T, Mittal N, Nishida S, et al: The role of intestinal transplantation in the management of babies with extensive gut resections. J Pediatr Surg 2003;38:145.
41. Kim HB, Fauza D, Garza J, et al: Serial transverse enteroplasty (STEP): A novel bowel lengthening procedure. J Pediatr Surg 2003;38:425.
42. Kim HB, Lee PW, Garza J, et al: Serial transverse enteroplasty for short bowel syndrome: A case report. J Pediatr Surg 2003;38:881.
43. Kim SS, Kaihara S, Benvenuto MS, et al: Effects of anastomosis of tissue-engineered neointestine to native small bowel. J Surg Res 1999;87:6.
44. Kimura K, Soper RT: A new bowel elongation technique for the short-bowel syndrome using the isolated bowel segment Iowa models. J Pediatr Surg 1993;28:792.
45. King CE, Toskes PP: Small intestine bacterial overgrowth. Gastroenterology 1979;76:1035.
46. King DR, Anvari M, Jamieson GG, et al: Does the colon adopt small bowel features in a small bowel environment? Aust NZ J Surg 1996;66:543.
47. Kono K, Sekikawa T, Iizuka H, et al: Interposed colon between remnants of the small intestine exhibits small bowel features in a patient with short bowel syndrome. Dig Surg 2001;18:237.
48. Messing B, Crenn P, Beau P, et al: Long-term survival and parenteral nutrition dependence in adult patients with the short bowel syndrome. Gastroenterology 1999;117:1043.
49. Nehra V, Camilleri M, Burton D, et al: An open trial of octreotide long-acting release in the management of short bowel syndrome. Am J Gastroenterol 2001;96:1494.
50. Nightingale JMD, Walker ER, Burnham WR: Octreotide (a somatostatin analogue) improves the quality of life in some patients with a short intestine. Aliment Pharmacol Ther 1989;3:367.
51. O'Brien DP, Nelson LA, Huang FS, et al: Intestinal adaptation: Structure, function, and regulation. Semin Pediatr Surg 2001;10:56.
52. O'Brien JD, Thompson DG, McIntyre A: Effect of codeine and loperamide on upper intestinal transit and absorption in normal subjects and patients with postvagotomy diarrhoea. Gut 1988;29:312.
53. Panis Y, Messing B, Rivet P, et al: Segmental reversal of the small bowel as an alternative to intestinal transplantation in patients with short bowel syndrome. Ann Surg 1997; 225:401.
54. Reyes J: Intestinal transplantation for children with short bowel syndrome. Semin Pediatr Surg 2001;10:99.
55. Rodrigues CA, Lennard-Jones JE, Thompson DG: The effects of octreotide, soy polysaccharide, codeine and loperamide on nutrient, fluid and electrolyte absorption in the short-bowel syndrome. Aliment Pharmacol Ther 1989;3:159.
56. Schmidt T, Pfeiffer A, Hackelsberger N, et al: Effect of intestinal resection on human small bowel motility. Gut 1996;38:859.
57. Scolapio JS, Camilleri M, Fleming CR: Gastrointestinal motility considerations in patients with short-bowel syndrome. Dig Dis 1997;15:253.
58. Scolapio JS, Camilleri M, Fleming CR, et al: Effect of growth hormone, glutamine, and diet on adaptation in short-bowel syndrome: A randomized, controlled study. Gastroenterology 1997;113:1074.
59. Seydel AS, Miller JH, Sarac TP, et al: Octreotide diminishes luminal nutrient transport activity, which is reversed by epidermal growth factor. Am J Surg 1996;172:267.
60. Seguy D, Vahedi K, Kapel N, et al: Low-dose growth hormone in adult home parenteral nutrition-dependent short bowel syndrome patients: A positive study. Gastroenterology 2003;124:293.
61. Shanbhogue LKR, Molenaar JC: Short bowel syndrome: Metabolic and surgical management. Br J Surg 1994; 81:486.
62. Sondheimer JM, Cadnapaphornchai M, Sontag M, et al: Predicting the duration of dependence on parenteral nutrition after neonatal intestinal resection. J Pediatr 1998; 132:80.
63. Shin CE, Helmrath MA, Falcone R Jr, et al: Epidermal growth factor augments adaptation following small bowel resection: Optimal dosage, route, and timing of administration. J Surg Res 1998;77:11.
64. Stahlgren LH, Roy RH, Umana G: A mechanical impediment to intestinal flow: Physiological effects on intestinal absorption. JAMA 1964;187:41.
65. Sukhotnik I, Khateeb K, Krausz MM, et al: Sandostatin impairs postresection intestinal adaptation in a rat model of short bowel syndrome. Dig Dis Sci 2002;47:2095.
66. Teitelbaum DH, Han-Markey T, Drongowski RA, et al: Use of cholecystokinin to prevent the development of parenteral nutrition-associated cholestasis. J Parenter Enteral Nutr 1997;21:100.
67. Teitelbaum DH, Tracy T: Parenteral nutrition-associated cholestasis. Semin Pediatr Surg 2001;10:72.
68. Thompson JS: The role of prophylactic cholecystectomy in the short-bowel syndrome. Arch Surg 1996;131:556.
69. Thompson JS: Management of the short bowel syndrome. Gastroenterol Clin North Am 1994;23:403.
70. Thompson JS, Langnas AN, Pinch LW, et al: Surgical approach to short-bowel syndrome: Experience in a population of 160 patients. Ann Surg 1995;222:600.
71. Thompson JS, Pinch LW, Murray N, et al: Experience with intestinal lengthening for the short-bowel syndrome. J Pediatr Surg 1991;26:721.
72. Thompson JS, Vanderhoof JA, Antonson DL: Intestinal tapering and lengthening for short bowel syndrome. J Pediatr Gastroenterol Nutr 1985;4:495.
73. Touloukian RJ, Walker Smith GJ: Normal intestinal length in preterm infants. J Pediatr Surg 1983;18:720.
74. Vanderhoof JA: Short bowel syndrome. Clin Perinatol 1996; 23:377.
75. Vanderhoof JA, Kollman KA: Lack of inhibitory effect of octreotide on intestinal adaptation in short bowel syndrome in the rat. J Pediatr Gastroenterol Nutr 1998; 26:241.
76. Vanderhoof JA, Park JH, Herrington MK, et al: Effects of dietary menhaden oil on mucosal adaptation after small bowel resection in rats. Gastroenterology 1994;106:94.
77. Waag KL, Hosie S, Wessel L: What do children look like after longitudinal intestinal lengthening. Eur J Pediatr Surg 1999;9:260.
78. Wales PW, de Silva N, Kim J, et al: Neonatal short bowel syndrome: Population-based estimates of incidence and mortality rates. J Pediatr Surg 2004;39:690.
79. Warden MJ, Wesley JR: Small bowel reversal procedure for treatment of the "short gut" baby. J Pediatr Surg 1978; 13:321.

80. Warner BW, Vanderhoof JA, Reyes JD: What's new in the management of short gut syndrome in children? J Am Coll Surg 2000;190:725.
81. Warner BW, Ziegler MM: Management of the short bowel syndrome in the pediatric population. Pediatr Clin North Am 1993;40:1335.
82. Warner BW, Chaet MS: Nontransplant surgical options for management of the short bowel syndrome. J Pediatr Gastroenterol Nutr 1993;17:1.
83. Williams JK, Carlson GW, Austin GE, et al: Short gut syndrome: Treatment by neovascularization of the small intestine. Ann Plast Surg 1996;37:84.
84. Williamson RC: Intestinal adaptation. Structural, functional and cytokinetic changes. N Engl J Med 1978; 298:1393.
85. Williamson RC, Bauer FL, Ross JS, et al: Proximal enterectomy stimulates distal hyperplasia more than bypass or pancreaticobiliary diversion. Gastroenterology 1978;74:16.
86. Williamson RC, Buchholtz TW, Malt RA: Humoral stimulation of cell proliferation in small bowel after transection and resection in rats. Gastroenterology 1978;75:249.
87. Wilmore DW: Factors correlating with a successful outcome following extensive intestinal resection in newborn infants. J Pediatr 1972;80:88.

Chapter 87

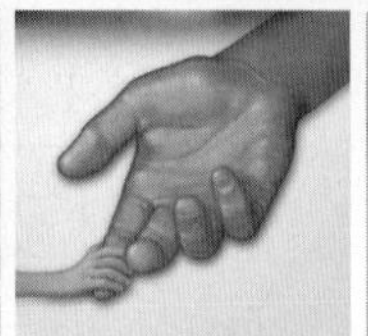

Gastrointestinal Bleeding

Robert M. Arensman, Marybeth Browne, and Mary Beth Madonna

Gastrointestinal (GI) bleeding accounts for 10% to 15% of referrals to pediatric gastroenterologists.[1] Even a small amount of blood appears large when mixed with stool or vomitus, and it can be alarming for both the parents and the physician. In the pediatric population, such bleeding is usually self-limited, and its cause can often be determined with a careful history and physical examination (Figs. 87-1 and 87-2).

Experience has demonstrated that most children stop bleeding spontaneously or early in the hospital course; however, because the blood volume in children is small, it is important to begin resuscitation as early as possible. In children, age-appropriate tachycardia is the most sensitive indicator of critical blood loss, and any patient with greater than 10% blood loss should be monitored in a critical care setting.[7] It is important to remember that

Presents with hematemesis, heme (+) gastric secretions, or melena

Irrigate through nasogastric tube to verify upper GI bleed (bilious aspirate with no blood = lower GI bleed, Fig. 87-2)

Blood (+)

Blood clears with irrigation

Observe, PPIs, H_2 blockers, or antacids

Neonate

Infant

Child

- Swallowed blood?
- Coagulopathy?
- Gastritis?

- Gastritis?
- Esophagitis?
- PUD?
- Hypertrophic pyloric stenosis?

- Esophagitis?
- Gastritis?
- PUD?
- Varies?

Apt test, coagulopathy

(+)

(–)

Observe, Vitamin K

Gastritis?

Ultrasound (projectile emesis)

Endoscopy

Nondiagnostic

Diagnostic (biopsy, sclerotherapy, ligation)

Bleeding (–)

Bleeding (+)

Observe, PPIs, H_2 blockers

Angiography, laparotomy

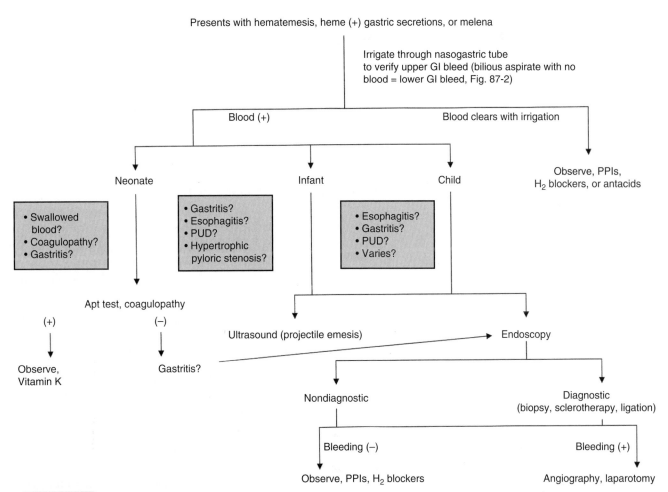

Figure 87-1 Diagnostic algorithm for upper gastrointestinal (GI) hemorrhage. PPI, proton pump inhibitor; PUD, peptic ulcer disease.

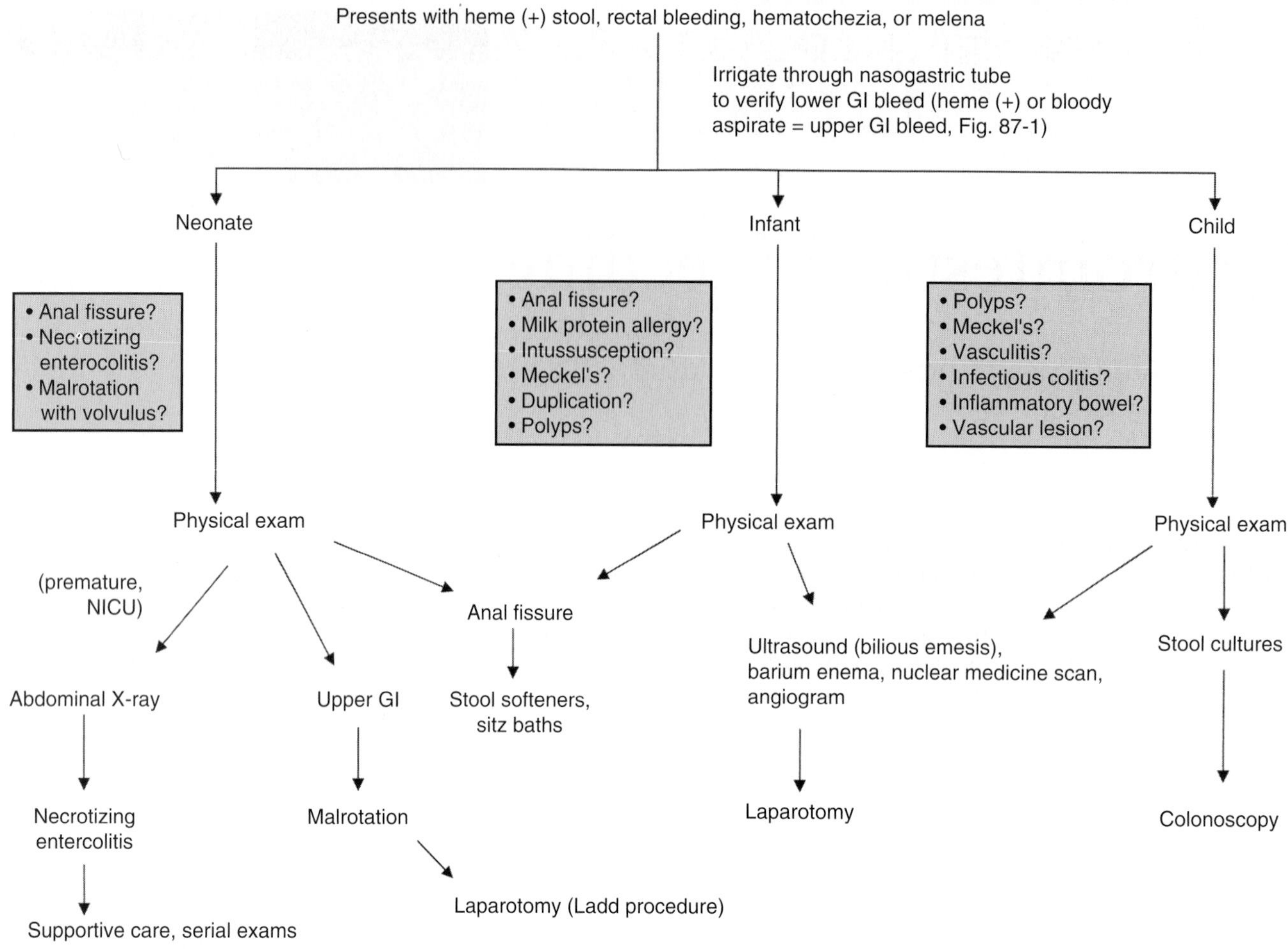

Figure 87-2 Diagnostic algorithm for lower gastrointestinal (GI) hemorrhage. NICU, neonatal intensive care unit.

most children can sustain their blood pressure despite massive blood loss.[1,10] The magnitude of the bleeding determines the extent of the resuscitation. While the medical history is obtained, a nasogastric tube is placed to evaluate for upper GI bleeding, and intravenous fluids are started. To begin fluid resuscitation, an initial bolus of 20 mL/kg of normal saline or lactated Ringer's solution is given. Blood products are considered only when the patient has no response to crystalloid, has ongoing bleeding, or has a preexisting heart or lung condition.

In the pediatric population, GI bleeding occurs in all age groups, each with its own age-related diagnoses (Table 87-1). This chapter discusses the evaluation and treatment of the most common causes of bleeding in individual age groups, while keeping in mind some of the more remote causes.

COMMON CAUSES OF BLEEDING IN NEONATES

The most common causes of upper GI tract bleeding in neonates are:

Hemorrhagic disease of the newborn
Swallowed maternal blood
Stress gastritis

The most common causes of lower GI tract bleeding in neonates are:

Anal fissure
Necrotizing enterocolitis
Malrotation with volvulus

Most GI bleeding in a healthy neonate is benign and self-limited. Infants who are born prematurely or experience physiologic distress often have "coffee grounds" gastric aspirate or melena. Even if the bleeding is minor, vitamin K deficiency should be considered, and coagulation studies should be obtained. Hemorrhagic disease of the newborn is a self-limited bleeding disorder caused by a deficiency in vitamin K-dependent coagulation factors. Vitamin K-dependent clotting factors decline rapidly after birth, reaching their lowest point 48 to 72 hours postnatally. Since the introduction of routine vitamin K administration shortly after birth, this disorder has nearly disappeared. Risk of occurrence is increased, however, with failure to treat with vitamin K, altered bowel flora due to antibiotic treatment, fat malabsorption due to cystic fibrosis, viral or bacterial newborn sepsis, and breast-feeding.[7]

Hematemesis or a large amount of blood in the gastric aspirate may result from swallowed maternal blood

TABLE 87-1 Causes of Gastrointestinal Tract Hemorrhage

Age	Upper Gastrointestinal Bleeding	Lower Gastrointestinal Bleeding
Neonate	Hemorrhagic disease of the newborn Swallowed maternal blood Stress gastritis Coagulopathy Septicemia Vascular malformations	Anal fissure Necrotizing enterocolitis Malrotation with volvulus Hirschsprung's disease with enterocolitis
Infant (1 mo to 2 yr)	Gastritis Esophagitis Hypertrophic pyloric stenosis Trauma secondary to gastrostomy tube Foreign body NSAIDs	Anal fissure Milk protein allergy (allergic proctocolitis) Intussusception Lymphonodular hyperplasia Intestinal duplication Gangrenous bowel Infectious diarrhea Eosinophilic gastroenteropathy Acquired thrombocytopenia
Child (>2 yr)	Peptic ulcer Esophageal varices Gastric varices Gastritis Esophagitis Mallory-Weiss tear Trauma secondary to gastrostomy tube Eosinophilic gastroenteropathy Munchausen syndrome by proxy NSAIDS Foreign body Chemotherapy	Polyps Lymphonodular hyperplasia Meckel's diverticulum Hemolytic uremic syndrome Henoch-Schönlein purpura Infectious colitis Anal fissure Eosinophilic gastroenteropathy Inflammatory bowel disease Vascular lesions

NSAIDs, nonsteroidal anti-inflammatory drugs.

during delivery.[4] This diagnosis can be confirmed by using the Apt test, which is performed by placing bright red blood from the stomach of the neonate onto filter paper with 1% sodium hydroxide. Maternal blood is reduced and appears rusty brown, whereas fetal blood is resistant to reduction and remains pink or red.

"Coffee grounds" gastric aspirate in neonates who experienced a stressful delivery, required resuscitation, are premature, or are undergoing mechanical ventilation is most likely due to stress gastritis. This occurs in up to 20% of patients in the neonatal intensive care unit. With a negative Apt test and coagulopathy excluded, these neonates should be treated with passage of an oral gastric tube, gastric irrigation, and intravenous H_2 blockers. Further evaluation may be delayed unless bleeding persists or worsens.

When bright red blood is noted on the outside of the infant's stool or there are small drops in the diaper, the most common diagnosis in a healthy-appearing infant is an anal fissure, or tear in the anal mucosa, most often due to trauma from hard stool. A simple anal examination with careful evaluation of the posterior midline usually confirms the diagnosis.[12] Treatment is administration of stool softeners and warm sitz baths; excision is rarely necessary. If a fissure is noted in an older child or on the anterior anal mucosa, inflammatory bowel disease should be considered.

Premature infants who pass blood per rectum should be evaluated for necrotizing enterocolitis. Mortality from this condition can be as high as 40%, and 1% to 7.7% of babies cared for in the neonatal intensive care unit are diagnosed with this problem.[12] These babies may present with an adynamic ileus, abdominal distention, bilious vomiting, abdominal wall erythema or mass, and GI bleeding. Plain abdominal radiographs may demonstrate bowel wall thickening, pneumatosis intestinalis, portal venous gas, or pneumoperitoneum.[13] Contrast studies are neither recommended nor indicated. These patients are managed with a nasogastric tube, broad-spectrum antibiotics, intravenous fluid resuscitation, bowel rest, total parenteral nutrition, and serial examinations. Operative management is considered in cases of clinical deterioration or evidence of gangrenous or perforated bowel; this may consist of a laparotomy, drainage, resection, or decompression. Recurrent bleeding after initial treatment may indicate a second episode of necrotizing enterocolitis or a post–necrotizing enterocolitis stricture (see Chapter 92).

Malrotation with midgut volvulus is the most critical surgical emergency in the newborn period. It presents with the sudden onset of melena and bilious vomiting in a previously health infant. Early in its course, the baby has a benign clinical examination, followed by progressive distention and tenderness. An emergent upper GI contrast study is warranted. This demonstrates an abnormally positioned duodenojejunal junction and possibly a "corkscrew" appearance of the proximal small bowel or a "bird's beak" cutoff if the obstruction is complete.[13] Immediate laparotomy is performed for bowel derotation, assessment of bowel viability, lysis of Ladd's bands, and appendectomy (Ladd procedure) (see Chapter 84).

COMMON CAUSES OF BLEEDING IN INFANTS AGED 1 MONTH TO 2 YEARS

The most common causes of upper GI tract bleeding in infants are:

Esophagitis
Gastritis
Hypertrophic pyloric stenosis
Peptic ulcer disease

The most common causes of lower GI tract bleeding in infants are:

Anal fissures
Milk protein allergy (allergic proctocolitis)
Intussusception
Intestinal duplication
Meckel's diverticulum

The two most common causes of upper GI bleeding in infants between 1 month and 2 years of age is esophagitis and gastritis. Peptic esophagitis is due to gastroesophageal reflux, and children present with regurgitation, pain on swallowing (odynophagia), dysphagia leading to food aversion, or failure to thrive.[1] Viral esophagitis caused by herpes simplex virus, cytomegalovirus, or herpes zoster is found more commonly in immunocompromised children but has similar presenting symptoms. An esophagogram, intraluminal pH probe, esophagoscopy with biopsies, manometry, and technetium 99m milk scanning can help differentiate between viral and peptic causes and assess the extent of the reflux. For peptic esophagitis, proton pump inhibitors (PPIs) and propulsive agents are first-line therapy.[8] Treatment with acyclovir and ganciclovir is used for herpes simplex virus and cytomegalovirus, respectively. An antireflux procedure is rarely performed to control bleeding but is considered in children who are unresponsive to medical management, are at risk for stricture formation, or have pulmonary complications due to aspiration.

The most common causes of gastritis in children are primary gastritis and peptic ulcer disease (PUD), both of which are associated with *Helicobacter pylori* infection.[1] The infection is most likely antral but may involve the entire stomach.[6] Secondary gastritis and PUD occur in association with severe systemic illnesses such as burns, head trauma, and Crohn's disease; mechanical trauma from a foreign body or gastrostomy tube; or the use of nonsteroidal anti-inflammatory drugs. Gastritis is a histologic diagnosis and requires upper GI endoscopy with biopsies. *H. pylori* infection is treated with a combination of PPI, antibiotics, and bismuth. With the advent of PPIs, an operation for PUD or gastritis is necessary only for unremitting bleeding, chronic ulcers, or perforation (see Chapter 77).[12]

Hypertrophic pyloric stenosis occasionally presents with blood-tinged or "coffee grounds" emesis due to gastritis.[14] The diagnosis is suspected in children of the appropriate age and sex with a history of nonbilious projectile vomiting. A pyloromyotomy corrects the problem and stops the bleeding (see Chapter 76).

The most common cause of rectal bleeding in infants is milk protein allergy or allergic colitis.[15] This allergy can produce either occult blood loss or even gross bleeding and is associated with irritability, poor feeding, diarrhea, vomiting, and failure to thrive.[1] The diagnosis is usually made clinically, but eosinophils noted in the blood and stool and colonic biopsies support the diagnosis. Soy intolerance is found in only about 14% of patients, but soy protein or peptide sensitivity must be considered if symptoms persist despite a formula change.[16] Additionally, if the symptoms are severe, breast-feeding mothers are instructed to avoid drinking milk.

Intussusception is a common cause of hematochezia in babies between the ages of 6 and 18 months. Ninety percent of intussusceptions are ileocolic, likely due to the rich lymphoid tissue in the Peyer's patches of the terminal ileum of the infant. The clinical presentation in 60% of cases is intermittent crampy abdominal pain, bilious or nonbilious vomiting, and bloody mucoid or "currant jelly" stools.[2] Ultrasonography has a 97% to 100% diagnostic accuracy rate and a 100% negative predictive value; however, many radiologists still favor a barium enema because it can be both diagnostic and therapeutic.[5] Pneumatic (air) reduction with ultrasound or fluoroscopic guidance is also effective. Although the standard of care remains immediate surgery if contrast reduction is unsuccessful, several reports have emphasized that repeated enemas increase the success rate from 71% to 90%.[9] During operative reduction, the bowel is carefully milked from distal to proximal. Resection is performed if serosal tears are noted or if the bowel appears ischemic. Many surgeons also perform an appendectomy to avoid future confusion because of the presence of a right lower quadrant wound. It must be remembered that intussusception recurs in 5% to 10% of children after nonoperative reduction and in 1% to 4% after operative reduction (see Chapter 83).[5]

Two possible causes of massive blood loss in children from 1 month to 2 years of age are intestinal duplication and Meckel's diverticulum. Meckel's diverticulum is the most common form of serious rectal bleeding in children.[3] Ectopic gastric mucosa found within the diverticulum causes peptic ulceration in the neighboring ileal mucosa, which leads to painless, intermittent, or massive rectal bleeding.[3] If there is a high index of suspicion for bleeding secondary to a Meckel's diverticulum, a technetium 99m pertechnetate scan is the initial test of choice. This study is 85% sensitive and 95% specific in localizing the ectopic gastric mucosa. If the bleeding is severe and the scan is negative, an angiogram should be performed to attempt localization and embolization. With symptoms of bleeding and a diagnosis of a Meckel's diverticulum, diverticulectomy or resection is performed, along with an appendectomy (see Chapter 82).

Intestinal duplication, like Meckel's diverticulum, may cause rectal bleeding due to the presence of ectopic gastric mucosa. Duplications can occur anywhere along the GI tract, and these patients usually present with rectal bleeding or a painful, enlarging abdominal mass. The technetium 99m pertechnetate scan can be useful if gastric mucosa is present; however, intestinal duplication is often not diagnosed preoperatively, and resection is required when the lesion is noted at laparotomy (see Chapter 88).

COMMON CAUSES OF BLEEDING IN CHILDREN OLDER THAN 2 YEARS

The most common causes of upper GI tract bleeding in children older than 2 years are:

Esophageal varices
Peptic ulcer disease
Gastritis
Esophagitis

The most common causes of lower GI tract bleeding in children older than 2 years are:

Polyps
Meckel's diverticulum
Inflammatory bowel disease
Trauma
Vascular lesions
Infectious colitis

Esophageal varices develop as a result of portal hypertension caused by prehepatic, intrahepatic, or suprahepatic obstruction. Patients usually present with sudden massive hematemesis. With prehepatic obstruction, bleeding usually stops spontaneously or with minimal intervention due to normal liver function. In these patients, therapy is focused on long-term elimination of the portal hypertension. The treatment for intra- and suprahepatic obstruction associated with liver cirrhosis is a temporizing measure until a liver transplant becomes available.[10] Resuscitation for bleeding esophageal varices is started immediately, although volume overload and excessive transfusions may increase portal pressure and lead to continued blood loss.[10] Once the patient is stable, upper esophagogastroduodenoscopy is performed to confirm the diagnosis of esophageal varices and evaluate the stomach and duodenum. Sclerotherapy and variceal ligation can also be performed during this examination. Vasopressin, somatostatin, and octreotide are all vasoconstrictors that have been successful in controlling variceal bleeding in children and can be initiated after confirming the diagnosis. Transjugular intrahepatic portosystemic shunt can be considered in cirrhotic patients in whom endoscopy is not successful. As a last resort, an emergent surgical shunt can be considered (see Chapter 106).

Low-volume intermittent or continuous rectal bleeding may be caused by GI polyps. Juvenile inflammatory polyps are the most common cause of rectal bleeding in children older than 2 years. The bleeding is usually temporally related to a recent bowel movement and is rarely massive. These polyps are diagnosed with a contrast barium enema or at colonoscopy and can be managed conservatively with a simple endoscopic polypectomy. Often, these polyps slough and are passed spontaneously. In children disposed to form juvenile polyps, the tendency usually regresses by adolescence (see Chapter 91).

Fifteen percent to 20% of cases of inflammatory bowel disease are diagnosed during childhood.[11] Both ulcerative colitis and Crohn's disease can present with bloody diarrhea. Although the cause can be inferred by the characteristic results of a barium enema, colonoscopy with biopsies is required for a definitive diagnosis. Bleeding usually stops spontaneously with medical management of the disease (see Chapters 93 and 94).

A child presenting with diarrhea and lower GI bleeding should be evaluated for infectious colitis. Symptoms may be indistinguishable from those of inflammatory bowel disease but can easily be excluded with stool cultures. *Clostridium difficile* should be considered in any child with a history of prior antibiotic therapy; however, this diagnosis is unlikely in a neonate or an infant owing to the absence of the toxin receptor in the intestinal epithelium at this age.[1] Oral metronidazole (Flagyl) or vancomycin for 10 days is effective in about 95% of patients. Other bacteria such as *Escherichia coli* (0157:H7), *Salmonella, Shigella,* and *Campylobacter* are invasive and can cause bloody diarrhea. These infections are usually self-limited and require only supportive care, except for those who are severely ill.

Vascular lesions affecting the GI tract are relatively rare in the pediatric population but can cause acute or chronic blood loss. These lesions include hemangiomas, venous malformations, arteriovenous malformations, and vasculitis. Upper or lower GI endoscopy is usually the first-line therapy if the volume of blood loss is low. This intervention often provides both diagnosis and treatment. If endoscopy is nondiagnostic or the bleeding is too profuse for visualization, a nuclear scan or angiogram is considered. An operation is considered only to permit accurate localization or in cases of continued bleeding despite the previously mentioned measures.

REFERENCES

1. Arain Z, Rossi TM: Gastrointestinal bleeding in children: An overview of conditions requiring nonoperative management. Semin Pediatr Surg 1999;8:172-180.
2. Bisset GS III, Kirks DR: Intussception in infants and children: Diagnosis and therapy. Radiology 1988;168:141-145.
3. Brown RL, Azizkhan RG: Gastrointesinal bleeding in infants and children: Meckel's diverticulum and intestinal duplication. Semin Pediatr Surg 1999;8:202-209.
4. Bulstrode NW, Cuckow PM, Spitz LS: Neonatal gastrointestinal pseudohaemorrhage. J R Coll Surg Edinb 1998;43:355-356.
5. DiFiore JW: Intussusception. Semin Pediatr Surg 1999;8: 214-220.
6. Drumm B: *Helicobacter pylori* in the pediatric patient. Gastroenterol Clin North Am 1993;22:169.
7. Fox VL: Gastrointestinal bleeding in infancy and childhood. Gastroenterol Clin North Am 2000;29:37-66.

8. Glassman M, George D, Grill B: Gastrointestinal reflux in children. Gastroenterol Clin North Am 1995;24:71-98.
9. Gorenstein A, Raucher A, Serour F: Intussusception in children: Reduction with repeated delayed air enema. Radiology 1998;206:721-724.
10. Karrer FM, Narkewicz MR: Esophageal varices: Current management in children. Semin Pediatr Surg 1999;8:193-201.
11. O'Hara SM: Acute gastrointestinal bleeding. Radiol Clin North Am 1997;35:879-895.
12. Pearl RH, Irish MS, Caty MG, Glick PL: The approach to common abdominal diagnoses in infants and children: Part II. Pediatr Clin North Am 1998;45:1287-1326.
13. Racadio JM, Agha A, Johnson ND, Warner BW: Imaging and radiological interventional techniques for gastrointestinal bleeding in children. Semin Pediatr Surg 1999;8:181-192.
14. Spitz L, Batcup G: Haematemesis in infantile hypertrophic pyloric stenosis: The source of the bleeding. Br J Surg 1979;66:827.
15. Teach SJ, Fleicher GR: Rectal bleeding in pediatric emergency department. Ann Emerg Med 1994;23:1252-1258.
16. Zeiger RS, Sampson HA, Bock SA, et al: Soy allergy in IgE-associated cow's milk allergy. J Pediatr 1999;134:614-622.

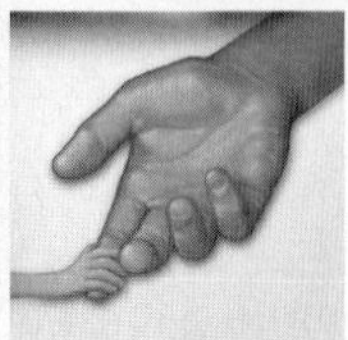

Chapter 88

Alimentary Tract Duplications

Dennis P. Lund

The term *duplications of the alimentary tract* encompasses a wide variety of mass lesions throughout the course of the gastrointestinal tract that are either tubular or cystic. The first report was by Calder in 1733,[6] and these lesions have been referred to by a large number of descriptive names depending on their location and associated structures. What are now commonly referred to as alimentary tract, or enteric, duplications have been variously referred to as giant diverticula, enterogenous cysts, ileum or jejunal duplex, giant thoracic cysts, duplications and reduplications, and unusual Meckel diverticula. No single classification system exists that adequately explains the embryology, location, and clinical manifestations of all of these lesions.

In 1937, William E. Ladd tried to simplify the nomenclature by suggesting the use of the term *duplications of the alimentary tract*,[26] and we owe the widespread use of the term to his influence. Ladd applied the term to congenital lesions having three characteristics: (1) the presence of a well-developed coat of smooth muscle, (2) an epithelial lining representing some portion of intestinal tract mucosa, and (3) intimate anatomic association with some portion of the gastrointestinal tract. Ladd and Gross reported 18 such cases in their 1941 text *Abdominal Surgery of Infancy and Childhood*,[27] and Gross reported 68 cases in his 1953 text *Surgery of Infancy and Childhood*.[16] Swenson devoted a chapter to the topic in his 1958 text *Pediatric Surgery*,[50] but Potts made no reference to duplications in his shorter book *The Surgeon and the Child*, in 1959.[39]

Alimentary tract duplications have a reported incidence of 1 in 4500 by autopsy series[38] and can occur anywhere from the oropharynx to the anus. There seems to be a slight predominance in males.[20] A meta-analysis by Heiss of 12 large series of enteric duplications encompassing 580 patients is shown in Table 88-1 and demonstrated that about 20% of these lesions occurred in the chest and the remainder were located in the abdomen, with a small percentage being thoracoabdominal.[17] Although the embryologic site of origin is not certain, it is common to refer to duplications as foregut, midgut, or hindgut derived, depending on their location. Enteric duplications frequently contain mucosa similar to that of their adjacent gastrointestinal location, but this is not always the case. For example, some duplications contain gastric mucosa and may cause peptic ulceration or bleeding as the presenting symptom regardless of location, and the presence of rectal mucosa has even been reported in cervical duplications. In 10% to 20% of patients enteric duplication are multiple and the presence of one such lesion should warrant a search for others.[20]

Finally, children with enteric duplications seem to have a high incidence of other associated anomalies. Spinal malformations have been noted in a number of cases, particularly with thoracic or thoracoabdominal lesions, and intestinal malrotation or atresias have been noted with abdominal duplications. Urinary tract anomalies have been reported with midgut and hindgut malformations; and in one series all patients with multiple duplications also had a skeletal or urinary tract anomaly.[20]

EMBRYOLOGY

Ladd's motivation for use of the term *alimentary tract duplications* derived from his belief that they shared

TABLE 88-1 Location of 580 Enteric Duplications

Location	No.	%
Cervical	6	1
Mediastinal	95	18
Thoracoabdominal	13	2
Gastric	35	7
Duodenal	30	6
Jejunal and ileal	282	53
Colonic	68	13
Rectal	19	4
Other	3	0.5
Total	580	100

Meta-analysis from Heiss K: Intestinal duplications. In Oldham KT, Colombani PM, Foglia RP (eds): Surgery of Infants and Children: Scientific Principles and Practice. Philadelphia, Lippincott-Raven, 1997.

a similar embryologic mechanism. As the science of embryology has advanced, multiple theories have arisen to explain the occurrence of enteric duplications but no single theory can account for all the known variants. Four major theories have been implicated and are able to account for most of the variants seen.

Partial or Abortive Twinning

The first possibility is that duplications may arise as a function of partial or abortive twinning. Doubling anomalies of the head, mouth, upper alimentary tract, hindgut, as well as lower genitourinary tract have been reported, and this mechanism seems most likely to account for them. Multiple cases have been reported that describe complete doubling of the colon, bladder, urethra, and external genitalia.[2] Some of these children had severe skeletal anomalies as well. The timing of these twinning anomalies may explain the extent of the twinning; for example, a split in the primitive streak earlier in gestation followed by subsequent caudal growth may result in complete twinning of the caudal end of the fetus, whereas a split at a later date may result only in colonic duplication.

Split Notochord Theory and Anomalous Adhesion

In 1960, Bentley and Smith postulated the theory of split notochord syndrome to describe the many anomalies involving the spine, gastrointestinal tract, and skin in the thoracic region.[3] According to this theory, in the third week of gestation (stage 8), the notochord appears growing cephalad. The notochord, starting in close association with the endoderm, normally separates from the endodermal cells. During this separation, a gap sometimes appears in the notochord through which a diverticulum from the foregut (endoderm) can herniate by incomplete detachment. These endodermal cells from the developing foregut then attach to ectoderm and can form a cyst, or, if they remain attached to the notochord, may act as a barrier to the later anterior fusion of the vertebral mesoderm, resulting in anterior spina bifida of the type seen with neuroenteric cysts. Thus, this mechanism may account for the dorsal location of most alimentary tract duplications in the chest and would explain those instances of spinal column anomalies associated with them. Whether it accounts for all foregut duplications is not known. A similar mechanism of anomalous adhesions may also explain the rare long duplications arising in the abdomen but seemingly tethered to the spinal column high in the chest. Such adhesions would have to occur early, possibly even before the appearance of the notochord, to account for the long distances such duplications sometimes traverse.[48]

Diverticula and Canalization Defects

The fetal gastrointestinal tract goes through what some embryologists referred to as a "solid stage" after which progressive growth of the luminal side of the intestine generally from the cranial to caudal direction leads to the formation of a lumen. For years, it has been known that many diverticula exist in mammalian embryos.[30] These diverticula are most frequently located in the ileum, the site of most enteric duplications. Thus, it seems reasonable to postulate that this mechanism may contribute to the formation of enteric duplications. However, this theory fails to explain the instances of heterotopic mucosa, particularly that of stomach, or the dorsal location of the majority of duplications, whereas most diverticula are located on the antimesenteric side of the bowel. Bremer postulated that some enteric duplications result from errors in the canalization of the intestine.[5] Moutsouris, who examined many embryos, thought this might also play a role in the formation of atretic segments.[35] What is clear is that the lumen is normally completely restored by the 18-mm stage. Bremer suggested that duplications arise as a result of incomplete or defective vacuolization of the intestine. This theory explains the presence of duplications without associated anomalies but suffers from many of the same shortcomings of the diverticula theory, particularly failing to explain the predominantly mesenteric location of duplications or mucosal heterotopia.

Environmental Factors

Finally, it is known that there are significant environmental stresses on the fetus at different times. Mellish and Koop postulated that trauma and hypoxia could induce duplications and attempts at twinning.[34] This theory is supported by data that suggest that other anomalies, particularly intestinal atresias, may be induced by intrauterine vascular accidents.[32] It is not known what role any or all of these embryologic theories may play in the development of enteric duplications. Clearly, during embryologic development, there is much tissue growth, differentiation, migration, preprogrammed cell death, and tissue adherence. Disorders of any of these mechanisms of development may be involved in the formation of enteric duplications. Most likely, just as there are many forms of malformations known as enteric duplications, there are also many factors that may lead to their development.

CLINICAL MANIFESTATIONS

Enteric duplications are generally cystic or tubular masses. They present in a variety of ways depending on their size, location, adjacencies, and whether they contain heterotopic gastric mucosa. The majority of duplications are diagnosed in the first 2 years of life. Frequently, the presenting symptoms of an enteric duplication can be confused with other gastrointestinal pathology, such as acute appendicitis. Many duplications will have few or no symptoms and are found incidentally in the pursuit of symptoms such as cough, abdominal pain, or gastroesophageal reflux. The diagnosis of enteric duplication may be made by prenatal ultrasonography. Cystic masses appear as black holes on ultrasonography and are therefore easily seen if they are of sufficient size.[11]

If the mass is in the chest, it may present as wheezing, pneumonia, or dysphagia that may prompt a chest radiograph. Other potential symptoms include failure to thrive, respiratory distress, and vomiting. Chest pain is a rare symptom unless the mass acutely enlarges from hemorrhage or infection.

Abdominal pain, vomiting, and an abdominal mass are the most common symptoms and signs attributable to enteric duplications located in the abdomen.[21] Because a duplication is a cystic mass, acute distention with secretions or infection of the mass may cause severe abdominal pain. If the duplication contains heterotopic gastric mucosa, ulceration and bleeding or even perforation may result. An acutely enlarging cystic mass may cause obstruction of the adjacent bowel and result in nausea, vomiting, and cramping. A large duplication may even cause localized volvulus of the adjacent intestine. A mobile mass may be palpable in up to 50% of patients.[14] Gastric and duodenal duplications may cause vomiting, abdominal distention, melena, and perforation. Gastric duplications in particular may be quite large. Duplications in the stomach have also been reported to present similar to hypertrophic pyloric stenosis with gastric outlet obstruction.[15] Duodenal duplications may be a cause of recurrent pancreatitis and may result in significant morbidity.[54]

Duplications of the midgut or hindgut are more likely to cause abdominal pain, distention, melena, or perforation. Those arising in the ileum may be confused with acute appendicitis and may be difficult to diagnose preoperatively. Small bowel duplications may also present as intussusception by acting as a lead point.

Colon and hindgut duplications may simply present as a second opening on the perineum. In females, this opening may be in the back wall of the vagina, suggesting the possibility of a rectovaginal fistula.[43] Hindgut duplications may also cause symptoms by mass effect, obstructing the urinary tract or causing severe constipation, particularly if they are intrapelvic. Presacral duplications can mimic sacrococcygeal tumors such as teratoma or dermoid cyst.

DIAGNOSIS

Antenatal diagnosis of duplications of the alimentary tract is becoming much more common because of the availability of prenatal ultrasonography. Experience with antenatal diagnosis began to appear in the literature as early as 1984,[51] but reports were rare. As more experience was acquired over the ensuing decades, the majority of cases were identified in the chest or the upper abdomen, where they were more easily visualized by ultrasound. Chest lesions may occasionally cause hydrops fetalis as a result of mediastinal shift and are managed with in utero thoracoamniotic shunting.[10] By the year 2000, 14 abdominal cases of duplication were diagnosed antenatally.[7]

The experience in prenatal ultrasound detection has increased rapidly: by 2003, the group in Montreal reported their 22-year experience with enteric duplications and described 18 patients who had a prenatal diagnosis.[40] Interestingly, in their cohort of neonates with the diagnosis of the enteric duplication, the incidence of volvulus was 23.8%, arguing for either early surgical intervention or very close postnatal follow-up when the prenatal diagnosis of enteric duplication is made.

The history and physical examination are extremely important in establishing a diagnosis, and this is no different in the case of an enteric duplication. The history may include the symptoms just mentioned, and on physical examination an abdominal mass may be palpable. The mass is typically boggy and mobile and may or may not be tender depending on the child's symptoms. Chest masses may be accompanied by locally diminished breath sounds if the mass is large. Laboratory evaluation is of little help except that the child may be anemic if the lesion has caused bleeding because of heterotopic gastric mucosa. The patient with a duplication cyst in the head of the pancreas may have elevated serum amylase and lipase levels along with the other manifestations of pancreatitis.

Postnatal diagnosis can also be aided by ultrasound examination, because these lesions are usually quite visible. The cysts are typically anechoic on ultrasonography unless there had been ulceration and bleeding. The wall is typically 2 to 3 mm thick because it is composed of smooth muscle and mucosa, as opposed to other types of cysts such as mesenteric, omental, or ovarian cysts, which are typically larger and have a simpler wall. The mucosal lining of an enteric duplication cyst produces a characteristic echogenic signal on the inside of the cyst (Fig. 88-1).[51] Other forms of ultrasound, such as in endoscopic ultrasonography,[12] have been used to accurately diagnose enteric duplications, particularly in the foregut.

Other radiologic studies such as plain radiographs, gastrointestinal contrast studies, and computed tomography (CT) or magnetic resonance imaging (MRI) may assist in the diagnosis and localization of the mass (Fig. 88-2). Gastrointestinal imaging often will not image the lesion per se because cystic duplications do not communicate with the intestine. However, gastrointestinal imaging may show an impression from the mass on the intestine and

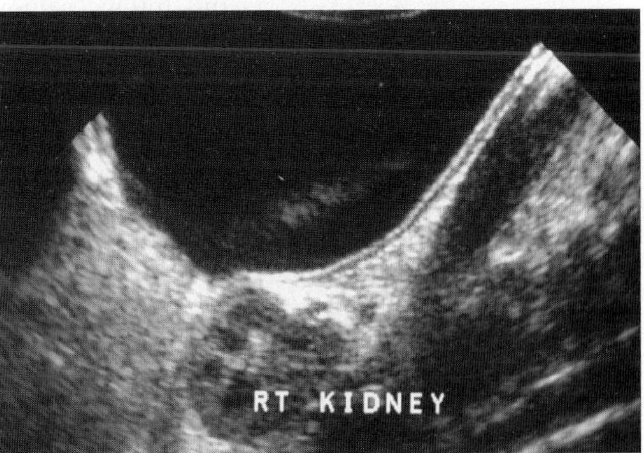

Figure 88–1 Ultrasound study of an ileal duplication shows the characteristic echogenic signal of the mucosal lining.

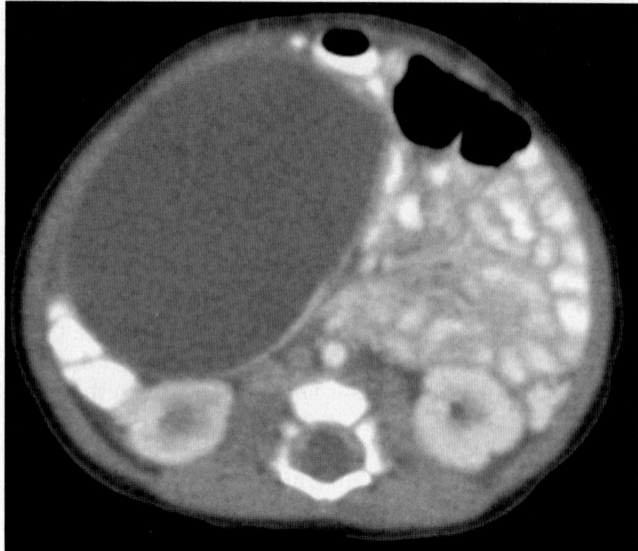

Figure 88-2 CT scan demonstrates a large cystic mass in the region of the head of the pancreas that turned out to be a duodenal duplication. (Courtesy of Dr. Aimen Shaaban.)

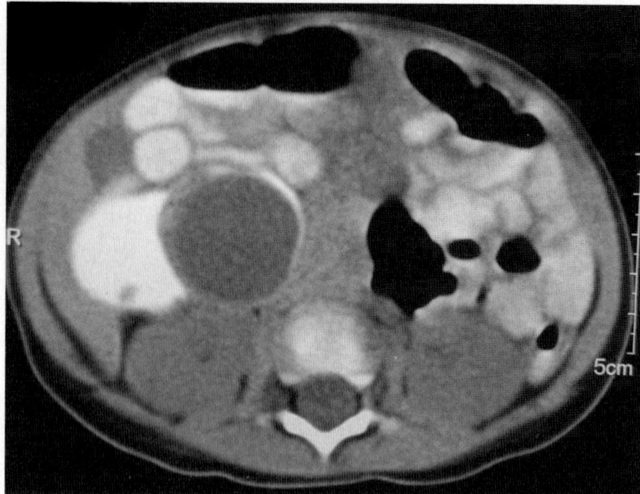

Figure 88-4 CT scan from an infant showing a cystic duplication of the ileum with an enhancing rim.

can be very helpful in the diagnosis (Fig. 88-3). On CT, enteric duplications typically appear as cystic masses with an enhancing rim and can therefore be confused with an abscess (Fig. 88-4). However, in the absence of a clinical picture of sepsis (e.g., fever and elevated white blood cell count), such an image on CT should suggest an enteric duplication rather than an abscess. Preoperative investigation of other structures, including the urinary tract, may be necessary to delineate the extent and the impact of the duplication on surrounding structures and may influence the safe treatment of the lesion.

Midgut and hindgut duplications may be more difficult to diagnose, and their diagnosis is often made at operation. These lesions may present as volvulus or intussusception and are discovered only at the time of operation. As was previously mentioned, many duplications contain heterotopic gastric mucosa. In the proper clinical setting, for example, in a child with anemia and abdominal pain, it may be helpful to evaluate the child with a technetium-99m pertechnetate scan just as one would use to diagnose Meckel's diverticulum.[52] In fact, enteric duplications are often confused with Meckel's diverticulum because many of them are located in the ileum. Therefore, the wary surgeon should always include both conditions in the differential diagnosis when evaluating a patient for either.

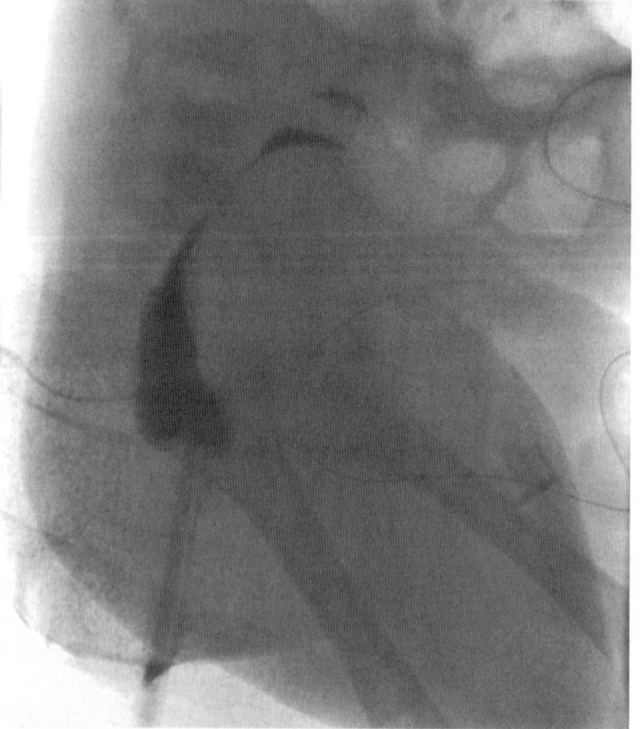

Figure 88-3 A barium enema study shows anterior compression of the rectum from a rare anterior rectal duplication.

CERVICAL ESOPHAGEAL DUPLICATIONS

Duplication cysts of the cervical esophagus are exceedingly rare. In the last edition of this text, it was stated that fewer than 10 cases had been reported in the literature. Since then, only one other single case report has appeared.[55] Almost all such cases present early in life with respiratory distress that can be life threatening. Symptoms often appear before a mass is apparent. Intubation, rapid diagnosis, and intervention are often necessary. The mass may be appreciated on physical examination, but CT is the best diagnostic modality. The differential diagnosis includes other cystic masses of the neck, such as lymphatic malformations and cysts of the airway or branchial apparatus, or thyroglossal cysts. Treatment consists of excision if possible. If complete excision is not possible, the mucosa should be removed from the duplication to allow for obliteration of the cyst cavity.

THORACIC AND THORACOABDOMINAL DUPLICATIONS

Approximately 20% of alimentary tract duplications arise in the thorax or are thoracoabdominal in location. In the differential diagnosis of mediastinal masses in infants and young children, enteric duplications are second only to neurogenic tumors.[42] The majority of lesions are located in the lower half of the posterior mediastinum and may protrude into either hemithorax. Many of these fall into the class of lesions also referred to as *neuroenteric cysts,* because they are associated with connections from the enteric duplication to the spinal canal with associated vertebral anomalies. There is also a class of very rare cystic lesions existing in the central nervous system, such as in the cerebellum or the optic nerve, without connection to the gastrointestinal tract but containing heterotopic gastrointestinal mucosa that cause symptoms by local pressure on the nervous structure.[33,44] Although neuroenteric cysts are most common in the thoracic region, they may occur in other locations where they make up a much smaller percentage of the enteric duplications seen below the diaphragm.[1] Lesions in the thorax should be suspected when vertebral anomalies are noted. Almost all patients with neuroenteric cysts have vertebral anomalies, but not all enteric duplications in the thorax are neuroenteric. In the series reported by Holcomb and associates, 5 of 21 patients with thoracic duplications had vertebral anomalies.[19]

As previously mentioned, thoracic lesions have been identified on prenatal ultrasonography, and attempts at in utero therapy have been made in the setting of fetal distress.[10] The most common symptom of a thoracic enteric cyst is respiratory distress, although often they are asymptomatic and may be noted on routine radiographs taken for other reasons.[19,20] Occasionally, enteric duplications may be noted in association with other anomalies, such as esophageal atresia or diaphragmatic hernia. The combination of a thoracic enteric duplication with other anomalies, including spinal anomalies, should prompt a search for multiple duplications, because these may occur in as many as a third of cases. Once a cystic mass is suspected in the chest, the best technique for evaluation of the lesion is CT, which should include the abdomen because one fourth of thoracic enteric duplications are associated with a second duplication in the abdomen.[19,37] A barium swallow study may be helpful to delineate the relationship of the duplication to the esophagus and to help with operative planning (Fig. 88-5). An echocardiogram may also be helpful if a pericardial cyst is suspected; although the vast majority of enteric cysts will occur in the posterior mediastinum, pericardial cysts are more likely to be located in the anterior or middle mediastinum. Finally, if the cyst is neuroenteric, MRI of the spine will be helpful to detail the intimate nature of the cyst with the spinal column and spinal canal. MRI has largely replaced the use of myelography for this purpose.

Treatment of thoracic and thoracoabdominal alimentary tract duplications consists primarily of excision, and this should be performed whenever possible. Removal may be accomplished thoracosopically, although this is not always possible. Decompression of the cyst may assist in removal, but often the dissection is aided by leaving the

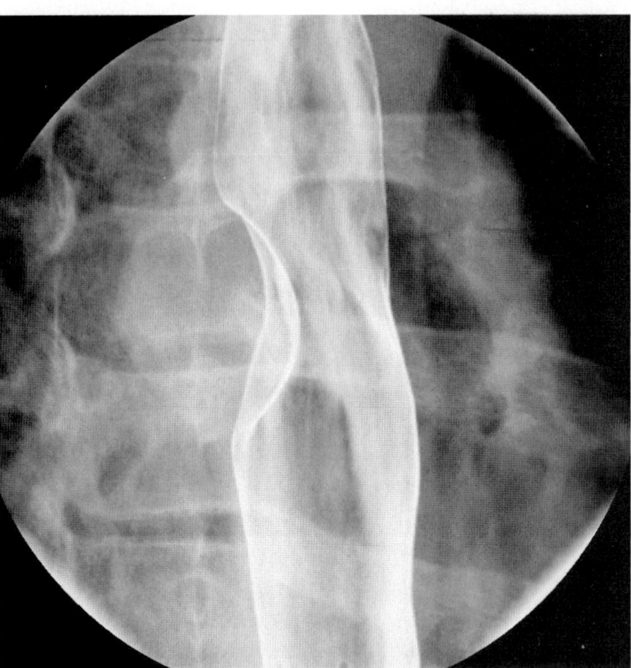

Figure 88–5 Barium swallow study shows compression of the mid-esophagus from an esophageal duplication. This teenage boy presented with chest pain, and the duplication was resected thoracoscopically.

cyst intact as long as possible if the cyst is small. Cysts in the wall of the esophagus can be removed by opening the esophageal muscle and performing an extramucosal excision of the cyst, leaving the esophageal mucosa intact. After cyst removal, particularly if the removal was performed through the thoracoscope, the surgeon must be sure that the esophageal lumen was not entered by instilling fluid or air in the lumen. An unrecognized esophageal leak will lead to mediastinitis and severe morbidity.

If there is an intraspinal component to a neuroenteric cyst, collaboration should be sought with a neurosurgeon and the intraspinous portion of the cyst should probably be removed first. This will lead to less morbidity from the potential for meningitis and will reduce postoperative swelling when the cyst is removed.

Large thoracoabdominal cysts may be removed in a staged manner to avoid the morbidity of a large thoracoabdominal incision. When undertaking a staged approach, the remaining portion of the duplication must have a mechanism for decompression (e.g., drainage into the intestine), avoiding postoperative sepsis due to leakage from an obstructed cyst. In cases in which the entire cyst cannot be removed, it is important to remove all of the mucosa so that the cyst cavity does not recur and potential ectopic gastric mucosa is removed. Curettage and gauze packing of the cyst cavity to promote sclerosis are discouraged because these forms of treatment have higher complication rates than complete removal or formal mucosal stripping.

ABDOMINAL FOREGUT DUPLICATIONS

Gastric and duodenal duplications can often be quite large (Fig. 88-6) and are frequently symptomatic. Most such

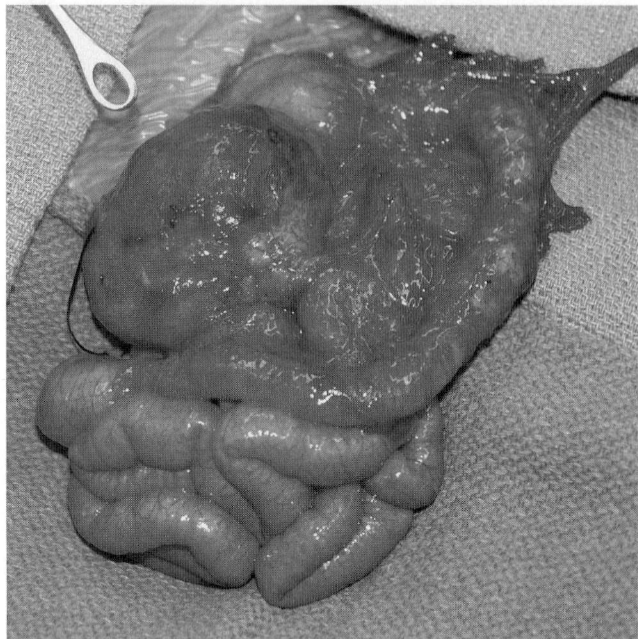

Figure 88–6 This cystic mass occurred in an infant with vomiting and gastric outlet obstruction and was completely resected. The CT scan of this giant duodenal duplication is shown in Figure 88-2. (Courtesy of Dr. Aimen Shaaban.)

duplications are cystic. They cause symptoms due to mass effect and pressure on surrounding structures, resulting in gastric outlet obstruction, pancreatitis,[54] or ulcer-type symptoms from unbuffered hyperacidity with poor feeding and abdominal pain, or in infants they may mimic hypertrophic pyloric stenosis.[41]

The term *gastric duplication* can be somewhat confusing because it is sometimes used to refer to lesions in association with the stomach, and some may use this term to refer to lesions containing ectopic gastric mucosa, regardless of their location. For purposes of this discussion, the term *gastric duplication* refers to those lesions associated with the stomach, which most often occur on the greater curvature. Patients typically present at a young age, and a palpable mass is frequently present. These lesions may be seen on antenatal ultrasonography.[13] Signs and symptoms may include failure to thrive, vomiting, anemia, gastroesophageal reflux, and abdominal pain. Such lesions may lead to perforation with pneumoperitoneum[24] or spontaneous hemoperitoneum.[22] Ultrasound evaluation is typically diagnostic of a large cystic mass in the upper abdomen and differentiates this lesion from hypertrophic pyloric stenosis. If the mass is in the right upper quadrant, it can be confused with a choledochal cyst, but foregut duplications are not usually associated with jaundice unless they obstruct the common bile duct. Upper gastrointestinal contrast studies may help delineate the extent of the lesion and its relationship to the stomach, duodenum, and pancreas.

The treatment of a gastric duplication is resection. Frequently, these lesions are very large or may be intimately involved with either the gastroesophageal junction or the pylorus. Resection without violating the lumen of the stomach is ideal but often is not possible. Segmental gastric resection or even partial cyst resection with mucosal stripping might be necessary. A gastrostomy or even a feeding jejunostomy may be beneficial if gastric emptying is likely to be prolonged after resection. Finally, the surgeon should be aware of the rare instance of communication of a gastric duplication cyst with the pancreatic ductal system, although this is more likely to occur with duplications arising in the duodenum.[18]

Duodenal duplications may present as biliary or pancreatic symptoms such as jaundice or pancreatitis. Symptoms are typically vague, consisting of upper abdominal pain, early satiety, or failure to thrive. The lesions are most commonly located in the medial and posterior portions of the second and third portions of the duodenum. These cysts may be confused with choledochal cysts, especially if the major symptom is jaundice. Recurrent bouts of pancreatitis have also been reported. These lesions most commonly contain duodenal or small intestinal mucosa and may occasionally communicate with the lumen of the duodenum. A mass compressing the duodenum may be noted on upper gastrointestinal series or ultrasonography during an investigation of vague abdominal symptoms. It is especially important to have good imaging preoperatively with duodenal duplications. CT, endoscopic retrograde cholangiopancreatography, and MR cholangiography may all be helpful to determine the relationships of the cystic mass with the pancreas and the biliary tree.

Although endoscopic or percutaneous drainage of a duodenal duplication may be possible, the preferred treatment is resection. In certain cases in which resection would have the potential for significant morbidity, internal drainage may also be safe and efficacious. The treating surgeon must have command of a variety of techniques to perform such procedures, because these cases can be very challenging. For example, localized duodenal resection and reconstruction may suffice[47] but marsupialization of the cyst to the duodenum or to a Roux-en-Y loop of intestine may be preferable depending on the anatomy of the lesion. Finally, a pancreaticoduodenectomy (Whipple procedure) may rarely be necessary to adequately deal with the cyst.[54] Whatever procedure is chosen, it is safest to use intraoperative cholangiography to ensure that the biliary tree is intact and unobstructed after the cyst is treated. In cases in which the cyst contains gastric mucosa, it is wisest to remove all such ectopic gastric mucosa either by cyst excision or mucosal stripping.

DUPLICATIONS OF THE SMALL INTESTINE

Duplications found in proximity to the small intestine are the most common enteric duplications encountered, and the majority of these occur in the ileum. They may be either cystic or tubular, and most are located on the mesenteric side of the intestine. This is in contradistinction to Meckel's diverticula, which occur on the antimesenteric side of the intestine. Frequently, the duplication shares its muscular wall and blood supply with the adjacent intestine such that the duplication resides in the leaves of the mesentery. This has implications for treatment of the duplication in that resection of the duplication may necessitate resection of the adjacent bowel. Communication with the lumen of the intestine may be variable. Increasingly, intestinal duplications are diagnosed as an intestinal anomaly on prenatal ultrasonography.

Signs and symptoms due to small intestinal duplications may vary as well, but abdominal pain and/or a mass are the most common. Small cystic duplications can act as a lead point for small bowel intussusception or result in localized volvulus. If the duplication enlarges or swells, it can lead to compression of the adjacent intestine and cause obstructive symptoms. This is more likely if the duplication is tubular and has a proximal communication with the bowel. Duplications that have a distal communication are less likely to become engorged or cause obstructive-type symptoms. Some duplications contain ectopic gastric mucosa that can cause peptic ulceration, bleeding, or perforation. Those with ectopic gastric mucosa can be diagnosed by technetium-99m pertechnetate scanning (Meckel's scan), and patients who pass blood per rectum should be evaluated with this test. Frequently, the correct diagnosis of a duplication is not made until an operation is undertaken.

In a report from Beijing Children's Hospital published in 1998, Li and colleagues studied the blood supply of small intestinal duplications in 80 cases.[31] They characterized two types of duplications based on their blood supply. In type I lesions (parallel type), the duplication seemed to be more to one side of the mesentery with an artery supplying the duplication while the opposite vessel went directly to the native bowel. In type II lesions (intramesenteric type), the duplication was truly centered in the mesentery and vessels from both sides of the mesentery traversed the duplication to get to the native bowel. Interestingly, Li and colleagues found that type II lesions represented the minority of lesions (24.6%) but over 90% of these lesions were associated with thoracic vertebral anomalies whereas only 5% of type I lesions had spinal anomalies. Li and colleagues used these findings to argue that these two types of intestinal duplications must have different embryologic causes. They also suggested that knowledge of the vascular anatomy of intestinal duplications allows for resection of these lesions without the need for resection of the adjacent bowel.[31]

Optimal treatment for small intestinal duplications is removal. In the case of cystic duplications, this is usually accomplished by excising the duplication with its adjacent bowel with primary reanastomosis (Fig. 88-7). This can be done either by open or by laparoscopic technique.[29,45,46] Laparoscopy may also be a useful adjunct to open operation to diagnose these lesions and to allow for decompression of large lesions to do an open resection through a much smaller incision. Limited resection should have no deleterious effect on the patient. If resection is not possible, one may drain the lesion into a Roux-en-Y loop of small intestine or create a large window to adjacent intestine. At the time of operation, it is wise to thoroughly inspect the length of the intestine because of the high incidence of multiple lesions in these patients. There have also been reports of duplications in association with intestinal atresia, which would

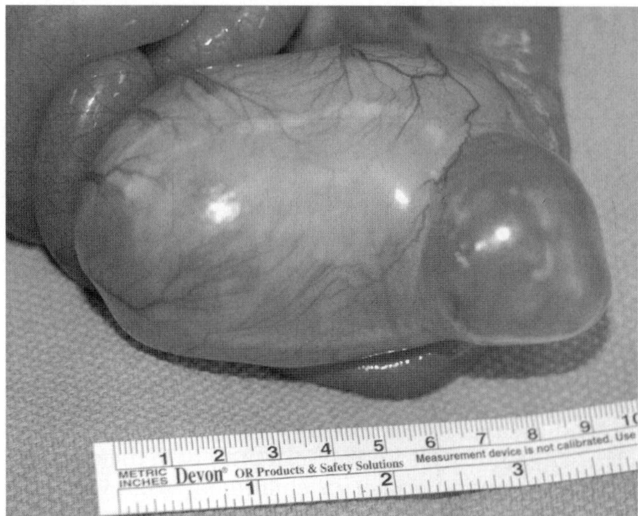

Figure 88-7 This cystic duplication of the ileum with the adjacent 5.0 cm of bowel was resected from a 2-month-old girl. Intestinal continuity was reestablished with a primary anastomosis. This mass was diagnosed on prenatal ultrasonography.

present in the newborn period.[19] Infants who have duplications diagnosed on prenatal ultrasonography do not need to undergo resection in the neonatal period unless they present with bowel obstruction. However, resection should be undertaken within a few months to avoid complications such as obstruction or volvulus. At least six cases of adenocarcinoma arising in small intestinal duplications, mainly later in life, have been reported, so these lesions should not be left indefinitely if they can be resected without much morbidity.[25]

Long tubular duplications of the small intestine represent a greater surgical challenge, particularly if resection of the adjacent intestine would lead to short-bowel syndrome. Ectopic gastric mucosa, if present, should be removed, either by limited resection or by mucosal stripping, because this can lead to bleeding or perforation. The duplication should be carefully inspected and the mesentery opened to ascertain if it is possible to resect only the duplication while leaving the adjacent intestine intact. The technique pioneered by Bianchi for longitudinal intestinal lengthening can be used for the mesenteric dissection.[4] Finally, creation of large windows (marsupialization) between the duplication and the adjacent intestine both proximally and distally may suffice so that the duplication is well drained. This can easily be accomplished with a linear gastrointestinal stapler. If marsupialization is chosen for treatment, these patients must be followed in case they later develop symptoms that may be secondary to retained gastric mucosa.

HINDGUT DUPLICATIONS

Duplications of the colon and rectum constitute about 17% of all enteric duplications. They can be simple cystic lesions in the wall or mesentery of the colon or quite extensive, running the entire length of the colon and emerging on the perineum as a separate opening, sometimes in the back wall of the vagina They also may be associated with abortive twinning anomalies and have been reported in conjoined twins[36] and with duplication or other anomalies of the urinary tract and the genitalia,[49] in which case these complex anomalies may also be associated with lower spinal anomalies. Colonic duplications usually contain colonic mucosa and rarely contain ectopic gastric mucosa. Kottra and Dodds[23] described a classification system of hindgut duplications with various types of short (type I) duplications and long, tubular (type II) duplications. However, this classification is of little use clinically. Rectal duplications typically are cystic masses of variable size that present in the presacral space behind the rectum, although occasional anterior masses are seen (see Fig. 88-3). They can present in the newborn period or any time later in childhood, and even occasionally in teenagers (Fig. 88-8).

There seem to be three general classes of hindgut duplications. The first are the cystic or short tubular masses that reside in the mesentery of the colon and are analogous to many midgut duplications. These tend to be quite rare. The second are the masses that reside in the midline, usually in front of the sacrum or coccyx and behind the rectum. These sometimes will be intimately involved in the blood supply of the rectum, especially if they extend upward into the abdomen, and may require extensive resection and reconstruction. Other times, they are much more like cystic masses that can be excised without interfering with the blood supply of the rectum. Finally, there are side-to-side duplications of the colon and rectum that can vary in length and location. These tend to occur more frequently in females and may be associated with other lower abdominal and caudal anomalies such as genitourinary anomalies or spina bifida. Treatment of these lesions can be quite complex and frequently involves partial resection and/or fenestration of the extra lumen.

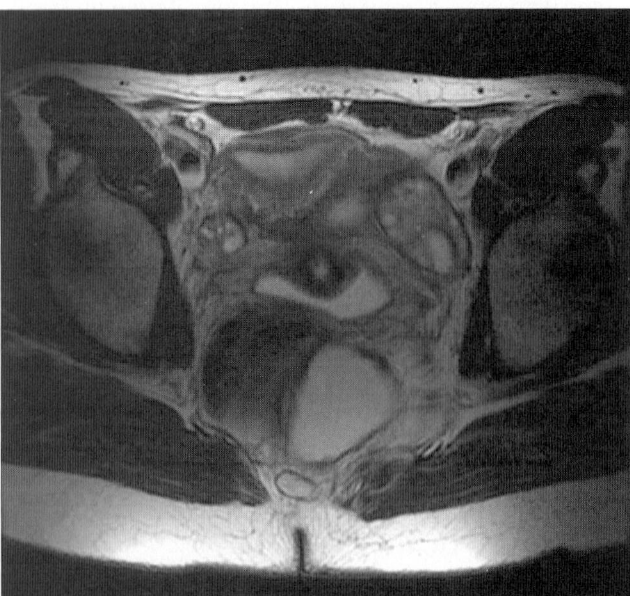

Figure 88–8 MR image in a 17-year-old girl with a rectal duplication that became infected. It was initially treated with percutaneous external drainage followed by subsequent resection using a posterior sagittal approach.

Given the myriad of duplications that occur in the hindgut, it is not surprising that there may be a wide variety of symptoms associated with them. A cystic mass may be present, or there may be distention and obstructive symptoms. Many are minimally symptomatic or may be associated with vague abdominal pain, constipation, or failure to thrive. Duplications that open into the vagina can present with signs and symptoms of rectovaginal fistula (Fig. 88-9), such as passing gas or stool through the vagina. Rectal duplications can present as pain or rectal obstruction. Rare cases can also be associated with urinary obstruction or retention. They can be confused with perirectal abscesses or fistulas if they become infected. Other presentations include rectal bleeding or prolapse.[28]

The diagnosis of hindgut duplications may be difficult. Accurate imaging and preoperative evaluation with CT, MRI, and sometimes a barium enema are essential to determine proper treatment. Second openings on the perineum may by studied by retrograde injection of contrast media. Rectal duplications should be evaluated by CT or MRI, which will show the extent of the lesion as well as the relationship to the rectum, spine, and urinary tract. A triad of findings—presacral mass, rectal stenosis, and sacral bony anomalies—known as the Currarino triad is inherited in an autosomal dominant condition.[8] Just as with some small intestinal duplications, short or cystic hindgut duplications may sometimes only be diagnosed at the time of operation. Technetium scanning is rarely helpful because hindgut duplications rarely contain gastric mucosa.

As with most enteric duplications, surgical removal (when possible) is the optimal treatment. With short cystic duplications of the colon, this may be done with only a limited colon resection or simply by "shelling out" the lesion from the mesentery.

If a presacral duplication presents as an abscess, it is wise to drain it externally rather than through the rectum. Transrectal drainage leads to contamination of the lesion with fecal flora and recurrent abscess formation. Midline presacral rectal duplications can frequently be removed using a posterior sagittal approach,[9] sometimes with an associated limited rectal wall resection but often without. A nerve stimulator may be helpful to delineate the pelvic and sphincteric muscle during the dissection and during the reconstruction. It is always wise to have the bowel prepared preoperatively if possible in case bowel resection is required. It is also wise to "prep" the patient in the operating room in such a way that a combined abdominal and perineal approach is available if needed. Midline duplications in front of the rectum are fortunately rare but represent a formidable surgical challenge. Resection is difficult and dangerous because it may be necessary to move the rectum out of the way to resect the lesion and there is risk to the bladder neck and sphincter. In some cases, these procedures may be approached from above with removal of the mucosa from the lesion while leaving the muscular wall in place. To avoid the risk of pelvic sepsis, the surgeon should always be prepared to utilize a temporary diverting colostomy when the resection and reconstruction become tenuous or complicated. The most common complication of resection of a rectal duplication

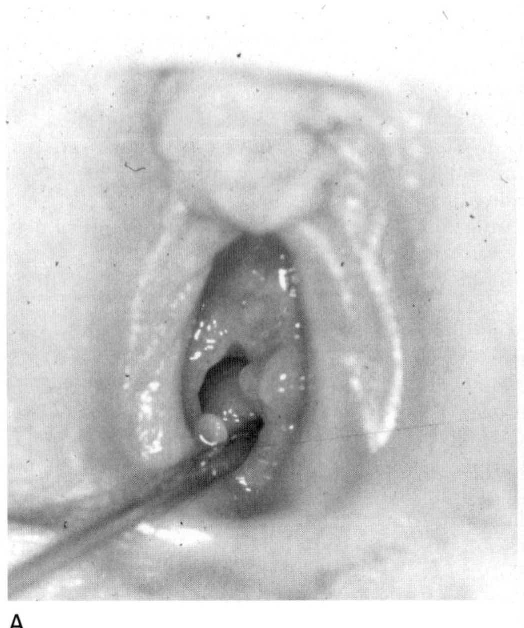

A

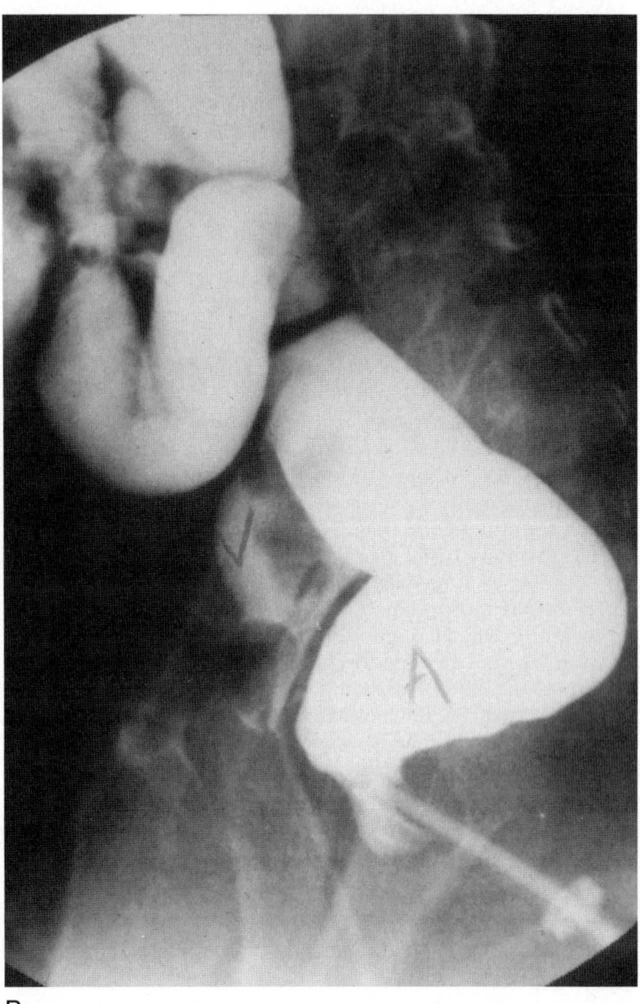

B

Figure 88-9 *A*, This infant girl's parents noted that she passed stool through the vagina. Here a probe demonstrates a second orifice in the back wall of the vagina. *B*, This is a contrast enema study demonstrating the two distal lumina of what turned out to be a total colonic duplication.

is recurrence if all the mucosa of the duplication is not removed.

Long tubular duplications of the hindgut require a creative surgical approach. Resection often would require total or significant subtotal colectomy due to the shared blood supply of the native bowel and the duplication. This is not usually a desirable option in a small child. Also, there are frequently variations of the duplication in the region of the ileocecal valve; for example, there may be a cystic component in the distal ileum with a long tubular component adjacent to the colon.[43] Finally, if there is a portion of the duplication opening onto the perineum or into the genitourinary tract, that communication also must be treated. Cases of long side-by-side duplication of the colon may be treated by fenestrating the two lumina extensively both proximally and distally. This can be done through a colotomy at either end using a linear stapling device or a hand-sewn side-to-side anastomosis. If there is an opening to the perineum, the distal portion of the duplication that does not pass through the sphincter mechanism (e.g., a pathway that opens into the back wall of the vagina) should ideally be resected and the mucosa should be removed or at the very least be left so that it is well drained and separated from the fecal stream. To adequately treat such duplications, the surgeon may have to move the rectum or reconstruct the sphincter complex after resection.

CONCLUSION

Intestinal duplications may present in diverse ways and encompass a wide variety of lesions from the neck to the anus. They can be simple and cystic, complex, multiple, or tubular. They can have other anomalies associated with them, including spinal and genitourinary anomalies. Optimal treatment is resection, but in complex cases a variety of approaches may be required, including fenestration or mucosal stripping. With proper treatment, children born with enteric duplications should do well and have excellent long-term outcomes and quality of life.

REFERENCES

1. Alrabeeah A, Gillis DA, Giacomantonio M, Lau H: Neurenteric cysts—a spectrum. J Pediatr Surg 1988;23:752.

2. Beach PD, Brascho DJ, Hein WR, et al: Duplication of the primitive hindgut of the human with double colon, anus, bladder, uterus, vagina and vulva. Surgery 1961;49:794.
3. Bentley JFR, Smith JR: Developmental posterior enteric remnants and spinal malformations. Arch Dis Child 1960;35:76.
4. Bianchi A: Intestinal loop lengthening—a technique for increasing small intestine length. J Pediatr Surg 1980;15:145.
5. Bremer JL: Diverticula and duplications of the intestinal tract. Arch Pathol 1952;38:132.
6. Calder J: Medical Essays Obser 1733;1:205.
7. Correia-Pinto J, Tavares ML, Monteiro J, et al: Prenatal diagnosis of abdominal enteric duplications. Prenat Diagn 2000;20:163.
8. Currarino G, Coln D, Votteler T: Triad of anorectal, sacral, and presacral anomalies. AJR Am J Roentgenol 1981;137:395.
9. deVries PA, Pena A: Posterior sagittal anorectoplasty. J Pediatr Surg 1982;17:638.
10. Martinez-Ferro MM, Milner R, Voto L, et al: Intrathoracic alimentary tract duplication cysts treated in utero by thoracoamniotic shunting. Fetal Diagn Ther 1998;13:343.
11. Foley PT, Sithasanan N, McEwing R, et al: Enteric duplications presenting as antenatally detected abdominal cysts: Is delayed resection appropriate? J Pediatr Surg 2003;38:1810.
12. Geller A, Wang KK, DiMagno EP: Diagnosis of foregut duplication cysts by endoscopic ultrasonography. Gastroenterology 1996;109:838.
13. Granata C, Dell'Acqua A, Lituania M, et al: Gastric duplication cyst: Appearance on prenatal US and MRI. Pediatr Radiol 2003;33:148.
14. Grosfeld JL, Boles ET, Reiner C: Duplication of the pylorus in the newborn: A rare cause of gastric outlet obstruction. J Pediatr Surg 1970;5:365.
15. Grosfeld JL, O'Neill JA, Clatworth HW: Enteric duplications in infancy and childhood: An 18-year review. Ann Surg 1970;172:83.
16. Gross RE: Surgery of Infancy and Childhood. Philadelphia, WB Saunders, 1953.
17. Heiss K: Intestinal duplications. In Oldham KT, Colombani PM, Foglia RP (eds): Surgery of Infants and Children: Scientific Principles and Practice. Philadelphia, Lippincott-Raven, 1997.
18. Hoffman M, Sugerman HJ, Herman D: Gastric duplication cyst communicating with aberrant pancreatic duct: A rare cause of recurrent acute pancreatitis. Surgery 1987; 101:369.
19. Holcomb GW 3rd, Gheissari A, O'Neill JA Jr, et al: Surgical management of alimentary tract duplications. Ann Surg 1989;209:167.
20. Ildstad ST, Tollerud DJ, Weiss RG, et al: Duplications of the alimentary tract: Clinical characteristics, preferred treatment, and associated malformations. Ann Surg 1988;208:184.
21. Iyer CP, Mahour GH: Duplications of the alimentary tract in infants and children. J Pediatr Surg 1995;30:1267.
22. Kleinhaus S, Boley SJ, Winslow P: Occult bleeding from a perforated gastric duplication in an infant. Arch Surg 1981; 116:122.
23. Kottra JJ, Dodds WJ: Duplication of the large bowel. AJR Am J Roentgenol 1971;113:310.
24. Kremer RM, Kepoff RB, Izant RJ Jr: Duplication of the stomach. J Pediatr Surg 1970;5:360.
25. Kusunoki N, Shimada Y, Fukumoto S, et al: Adenocarcinoma arising in a tubular duplication of the jejunum. J Gastroenterol 2003;38:781.
26. Ladd WE: Duplications of the alimentary tract. South Med J 1937;30:363.
27. Ladd WE, Gross RE: Abdominal Surgery of Infancy and Childhood. Philadelphia, WB Saunders, 1941.
28. LaQuaglia MP, Feins N, Eraklis A, et al: Rectal duplications. J Pediatr Surg 1990;25:980.
29. Lee KH, Tam YH, Yeung CK: Laparoscopy in the management of intestinal duplication in childhood. Aust N Z J Surg 2000;70:542.
30. Lewis FT, Thyng FW: Regular occurrence of intestinal diverticula in embryos of pig, rabbit and man. Am J Anat 1908;7:505.
31. Li L, Zhang JZ, Wang YX: Vascular classification for small intestinal duplications: Experience with 80 cases. J Pediatr Surg 1998;33:1243.
32. Louw JH: Congenital intestinal atresia and stenosis in the newborn. Ann R Coll Surg Engl 1959;25:209.
33. Mehta VS, Chowdhury C, Bhatia R: Neuroenteric cyst of the cerebellum. Postgrad Med J 1984;60:287.
34. Mellish RWP, Koop CE: Clinical manifestations of duplication of the bowel. Pediatrics 1961;27:397.
35. Moutsouris C: The "solid stage" and congenital intestinal atresia. J Pediatr Surg 1966;1:446.
36. O'Neill JA Jr, Holcomb GW 3rd, Schnaufer L, et al: Surgical experience with thirteen conjoined twins. Am Surg 1988;208:299.
37. Pokorny WJ, Golstein IR: Enteric thoracoabdominal duplications in children. J Thorac Cardiovasc Surg 1984;87:821.
38. Potter EL: Pathology of the Fetus and Newborn. Chicago, Year Book Medical Publishers, 1961.
39. Potts W: The Surgeon and the Child. Philadelphia, WB Saunders, 1959.
40. Puligandla PS, Nguyen LT, St-Vil D, et al: Gastrointestinal duplications. J Pediatr Surg 2003;38:740.
41. Ramsey GS: Enterogenous cyst of the stomach simulating hypertrophic pyloric stenosis. Br J Surg 1957;44:632.
42. Ravitch MM: Duplications of the alimentary tract. In Ravitch MM, et al (eds): Pediatric Surgery, 3rd ed. Chicago, Year Book Medical Publishers, 1982.
43. Sarpel U, Le MN, Morotti RA, Dolgin SE: Complete colorectal duplication. J Am Coll Surg 2005;200:304.
44. Scaravilli F, Lidov H, Spalton DJ, Symon L: Neuroenteric cyst of the optic nerve: Case report with immunohistochemical study. J Neurol Neurosurg Psychiatry 1992;55:1197.
45. Schalamon J, Schleef J, Hollwarth ME: Experience with gastro-intestinal duplications in childhood. Langenbeck Arch Surg 2000;385:402.
46. Schleef J, Schalamon J: The role of laparoscopy in the diagnosis and treatment of intestinal duplication: A report of two cases. Surg Endosc 2000;14:865.
47. Siddiqui AM, Shamberger RC, Filler RM, et al: Enteric duplications of the pancreatic head: Definitive management by local resection. J Pediatr Surg 1998;33:1117.
48. Skandalakis JE, Gray SW (eds): Embryology for Surgeons: The Embryologic Basis for the Treatment of Congenital Anomalies, 2nd ed. Baltimore, Williams & Wilkins, 1994.
49. Smith ED, Stephens FD: Duplication and vesicointestinal fissure. Birth Defects Orig Article Series 1988;24:551.
50. Swenson O: Pediatric Surgery. New York, Appleton-Century-Crofts, 1958.
51. Teele RL, Share JC: Ultrasonography of Infants and Children. Philadelphia, WB Saunders, 1991.
52. Torgerson CL, Young DW, Vaid YN, et al: Intestinal duplication: Imaging with Tc-99m sodium pertechnetate. Clin Nucl Med 1996;21:968.
53. Van Dam LJ, de Groot CJ, Hazebroek FW, Wladimiroff JW: Case report: Intrauterine demonstration of bowel duplication by ultrasound. Eur J Obstet Gynecol Reprod Biol 1984;18:229.
54. Williams WH, Hendren WH: Intrapancreatic duodenal duplication causing pancreatitis in a child. Surgery 1971; 69:708.
55. Wootton-Gorges SL, Eckel GM, Poulos ND, et al: Duplication of the cervical esophagus: A case report and review of the literature. Pediatr Radiol 2002;32:533.

Chapter 89

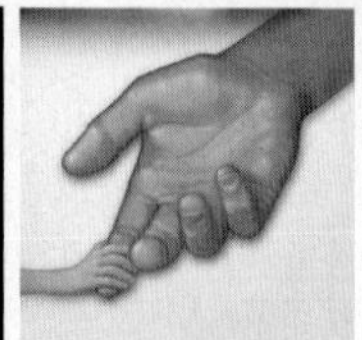

Mesenteric and Omental Cysts

Richard R. Ricketts

HISTORY

A mesenteric cyst was first recorded in an autopsy of an 8-year-old boy by the Florentine anatomist Benevieni in 1507.[2] In 1842 vonRokitansky[41] first described a chylous mesenteric cyst; Gairdner[12] reported an omental cyst in 1852. The first successful surgery for a cystic mass in the mesentery was performed by the French surgeon Tillaux[38] in 1880. Pean performed the first successful marsupialization of a mesenteric cyst in 1883.[40] In 1890 Carson presented the first U.S. report of a chylous cyst of the mesentery.[2] An estimated 600 cases of mesenteric cysts were recorded in the literature by 1950.[40] By 1994 that number had grown to around 820 patients.[9,22] Beahrs et al.[2] classified cystic disease of the mesentery into four categories: embryonic and developmental cysts, traumatic or acquired cysts, neoplastic cysts, and infective or degenerative cysts. This chapter discusses only the first category.

INTRODUCTION

Mesenteric and omental cysts are rare; the incidence is approximately 1 per 105,000 admissions to general hospitals and 1 per 20,000 admissions to pediatric hospitals.[7,20,40] The experience reported in this chapter is with 16 children admitted to Children's Healthcare of Atlanta at Egleston over 30 years. Modern series show that nearly one third of mesenteric cysts occur in children younger than 15 years and that one fourth occur in patients younger than 10 years.[3,5,27] These cysts are reportedly more common in females than in males and in white persons than in nonwhite persons.[4,5,34,39,40,42] In pediatric series, however, the age range is from birth to 18 years (mean, 4.35 years), and the cysts occur slightly more often in males (60%). The age and sex distribution of the 16 patients in Atlanta is shown in Table 89-1; note that in one patient the cyst was diagnosed in utero, and all but two patients were younger than 10 years.

Some authors differentiate between cystic lymphangiomas and mesenteric-omental cysts.[3,18,24,37] Cystic lymphangiomas are simple cysts with an endothelial cell lining, foam cells, and thin walls that contain small lymphatic spaces, lymphoid tissue, and smooth muscle. The wall of a mesenteric cyst lacks smooth muscle and lymphatic spaces, and the lining cells are cuboidal or columnar.[37] Lymphangiomas occur in the mesentery or retroperitoneum and tend to present early in life with acute abdominal symptoms, whereas mesenteric cysts are limited to the mesentery and present in adulthood as asymptomatic masses.[18,37] Because the evaluation and therapeutic objectives for mesenteric, omental, and retroperitoneal cysts are the same, and because they are all anterior extensions of what were retroperitoneal structures during the embryo stage,[14] they share common characteristics. In this chapter, a mesenteric cyst is defined as any cyst located in the mesentery; it may or may not extend into the retroperitoneum, which has a recognizable lining of endothelial or mesothelial cells.[3] An omental cyst has the same histologic characteristics but is confined to the greater or lesser omentum.

EMBRYOLOGY

Several mechanisms have been suggested to account for the development of mesenteric and omental cysts, including failure of the embryonic lymphatic spaces to join with the venous system, deficiency of the normal

TABLE 89-1 Age and Sex Distribution of Patients with Mesenteric Cysts

Age	No. Male	No. Female	Total
0-1 mo	1	1	2*
1 mo-1 yr	2	1	3
1-5 yr	4	3	7
5-10 yr	1	1	2
>10 yr	2	0	2
Total	10 (62.5%)	6 (37.5%)	16

*In one patient, the cyst was diagnosed in utero.

lymphaticovenous shunts in perinodal tissue, failure of the leaves of the mesentery to fuse, occult trauma, neoplasia, and localized degeneration of lymph nodes.[2,37] The most commonly accepted theory, proposed by Gross,[13] is benign proliferation of ectopic lymphatics in the mesentery that lack communication with the remainder of the lymphatic system. These cysts are thought to arise from lymphatic spaces associated with the embryonic retroperitoneal lymph sac, analogous to cystic hygromas of the neck arising in association with the jugular lymph sac.[36] The role of lymphatic obstruction is questionable, because experimental occlusion of lymph channels in animals fails to produce these cysts owing to the rich collaterals in the lymphatic system.[2,36,37] In addition, obstructed lymphatics have not been demonstrated with lymphangiography.[40]

SPECTRUM OF DISORDERS AND DIFFERENTIAL DIAGNOSIS

Mesenteric cysts can occur in the mesentery anywhere along the gastrointestinal tract from the duodenum to the rectum[2]; they may extend from the base of the mesentery into the retroperitoneum. Omental cysts are located in the lesser or greater omentum. Mesenteric cysts are 4.5 times more common than omental cysts.[42] In a thorough review of 162 cases reported between 1950 and 1985, Kurtz et al.[20] found that 60% were located in the small bowel mesentery, 24% in the large bowel mesentery, and 14.5% in the retroperitoneum. The most common location is in the ileal mesentery. In the colonic mesentery, cysts occur most commonly in the sigmoid mesocolon.[5,40] Cyst location in several pediatric series is shown in Table 89-2.

The differential diagnosis of mesenteric and omental cysts is shown in Table 89-3. Modern imaging studies can usually determine the organ where cystic lesions within the abdominal cavity originate. The differentiation between intestinal duplication cysts and mesenteric cysts may be problematic, because both are often intimately associated with the bowel wall. The former share a common blood supply and muscular layer with the adjacent bowel and have a well-defined mucosal layer that mesenteric cysts lack.[3,6,7,26,27] At the time of surgery, duplication cysts require resection of the involved bowel, whereas mesenteric cysts can often be enucleated from between the leaves of the mesentery.[11]

TABLE 89-3 Differential Diagnosis of Mesenteric and Omental Cysts

Intestinal duplication cyst
Ovarian cyst
Choledochal cyst
Pancreatic, splenic, or renal cyst
Hydronephrosis
Cystic teratoma, dermoid
Hydatid cyst
Ascites

The pathologic features of these cysts can vary considerably. They can be single or multiple, unilocular or multilocular; they can have serous, chylous, hemorrhagic, or mixed fluid contents; and their lining can vary from a flattened endothelial monolayer to a cuboidal or columnar epithelium to patchy fibrosis.[5,8,14,24,42] Rarely, the cyst wall contains calcium.[4,8,40] Unlike duplication cysts, mesenteric and omental cysts contain no mucus-producing cells.[5] Mesenteric cysts are most commonly single and multiloculated; the fluid is generally serous when the cyst involves the distal small bowel or colonic mesentery and chylous when it is located in the proximal small bowel mesentery.[27,40] Omental cysts almost always contain serous fluid.[8] The pathologic features of the cysts in this series are shown in Table 89-4.

CLINICAL PRESENTATION

The clinical presentation of mesenteric and omental cysts can vary from an incidental finding during laparotomy performed for another reason to an acute, life-threatening intra-abdominal catastrophe. In adults, these cysts are found incidentally in approximately 40% of patients[34,40,42] and present as acute abdominal emer-

TABLE 89-2 Location of Mesenteric and Omental Cysts

Author	Date	No. of Patients	Mesentery	Omentum	Retroperitoneum
Mollitt[27]	1978	11	8	0	3
Molander[26]	1982	6	3	3	0
Radhakrishma[31]	1989	8	5	3	0
Adejuyigbe[1]	1990	5	3	2	0
Kosir[18]	1991	13	9	0	4
Chung[7]	1991	15	9	2	4
Hebra[14]	1993	22	13	6	3
Bliss[3]	1994	10	10	0	0
Senocak[35]	1994	19	14	5	0
Okur[29]	1997	10	7	1	2
Egozi[10]	1997	14	10	2	2
Total		133	91 (68%)	24 (18%)	18 (14%)

TABLE 89-4 Pathologic Features of Mesenteric and Omental Cysts

Feature	Number (%)
Number	
Single	11 (69)
Multiple	5 (31)
Type	
Multilocular	14 (88)
Unilocular	2 (12)
Fluid content	
Hemorrhagic	7 (44)
Serous	3 (19)
Chylous	2 (12)
Infected	1 (6)
Not specified	3 (19)
Size (cm)	
Smallest: 4 × 4.5 × 1.7	
Largest: 30 × 40 × 10	

Data from references 2, 6, 7, 11, 12, 15, 16.

TABLE 89-5 Symptoms and Signs of Mesenteric and Omental Cysts ($N = 16$)

Symptoms	Number	Signs	Number
Pain	8	Distention	10
Vomiting	7	Mass	8
Anorexia	6	Fever	3
Diarrhea	3	Fluid wave	3
Constipation	1	Tenderness	1
Abdominal erythema	1		
None	4		

Data from references 2, 6, 7, 11, 13, 15, 16.

gencies in up to 60% of patients. The classic presentation is that of a low-grade, partial intestinal obstruction combined with a palpable, freely movable abdominal mass.[4] The most common mode of acute presentation in children is a small bowel obstruction, sometimes associated with volvulus and intestinal infarction.[8,18,27] Small bowel obstruction can also develop from acute enlargement of the cyst secondary to hemorrhage or from extrinsic compression of the bowel as it is stretched over an enlarging cyst (Fig. 89-1).

The signs and symptoms of the 16 children in this series are shown in Table 89-5, and the general mode of presentation is shown in Table 89-6. In no patient was the cyst found incidentally, although four patients were asymptomatic. In one of these four, a cystic intra-abdominal mass was identified by prenatal ultrasonography. In this series, 75% of the patients had abdominal symptoms, and all patients had findings on abdominal examination. In only two patients (12.5%) did the condition present as an acute abdominal emergency.

The following case summaries of five patients illustrate the varying presentations of mesenteric and omental cysts:

1. A 7-day-old female infant presented with a 48-hour history of vomiting and diarrhea and was found to have fever, abdominal distention, and erythema of the abdominal wall. *Escherichia coli* sepsis was documented. The patient had multiple infected omental and mesenteric cysts involving the greater omentum and transverse mesocolon, all of which were excised. The patient recovered.

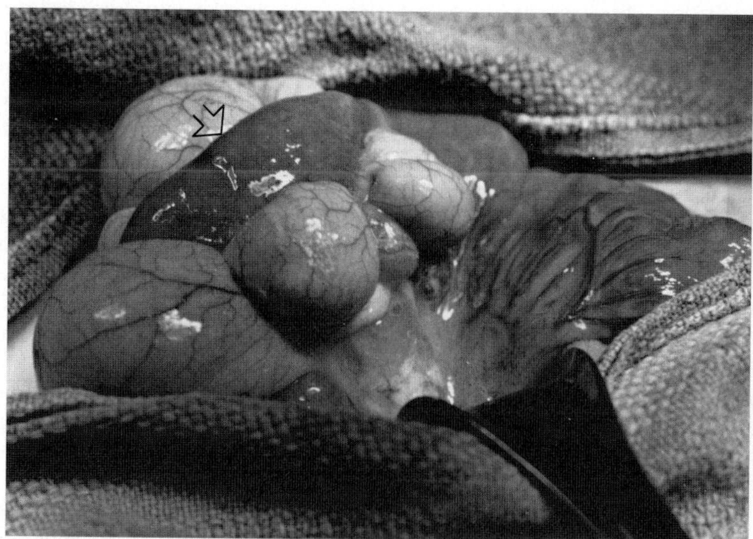
A

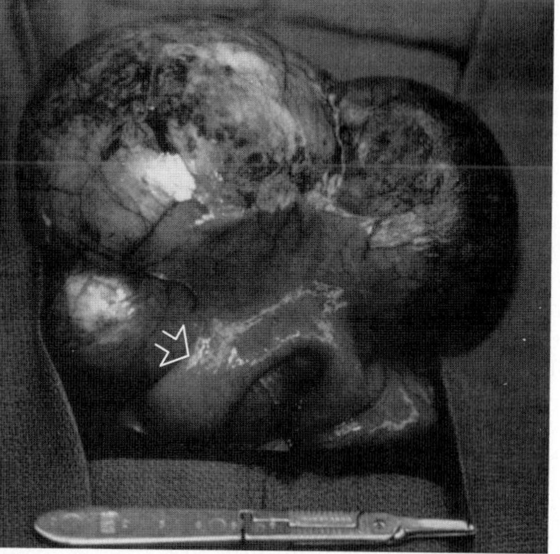
B

Figure 89-1 *A*, Multiple mesenteric cysts filled with chylous fluid surrounding the proximal small bowel *(arrow)*. *B*, Large multilocular mesenteric cyst compressing the overlying bowel *(arrow)* and causing a chronic partial intestinal obstruction. Both patients required bowel resection for complete cyst excision.

TABLE 89-6 Mode of Presentation of Mesenteric and Omental Cysts ($N = 16$)

Presentation	Number
Chronic (<2 mo) abdominal symptoms	5
Subacute (<2 mo) abdominal symptoms	5
Pain, vomiting, increased girth	3
Pain, vomiting, anorexia	1
Pain, anorexia	1
Asymptomatic abdominal mass, distention	4
Acute (<48 hr) abdominal symptoms	2
Vomiting, distention	1
Vomiting	1

Data from references 2, 6, 7, 11, 12, 15.

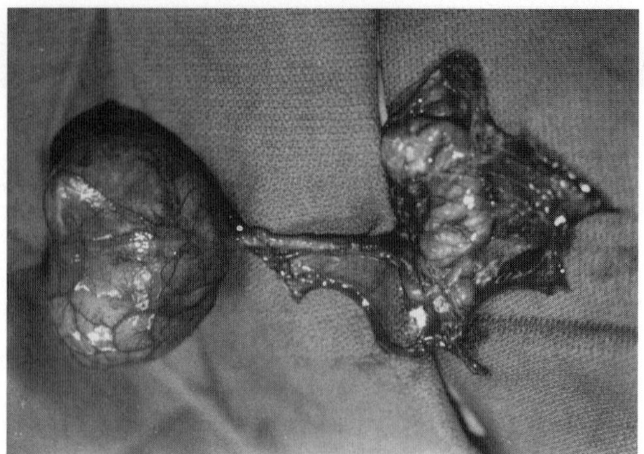

Figure 89-2 Asymptomatic but palpable, freely movable omental cyst first seen on prenatal ultrasonography and excised electively at age 6 months.

2. A 3-day-old male infant presented with signs and symptoms consistent with a small bowel obstruction. He was found to have one ileal multiloculated mesenteric cyst with volvulus that required small bowel resection with primary anastomosis.
3. A 2-year-old boy had an asymptomatic abdominal mass that was found to be a multilocular mesenteric cyst involving the transverse mesocolon and pancreas. Excision of the cyst and distal pancreatectomy were performed for cure.
4. A 2-year-old girl presented with a 2-week history of asymptomatic abdominal distention. She was found to have a single 30- by 40- by 10-cm multilocular mesenteric cyst that extended along the base of the mesentery from the ligament of Treitz to the transverse mesocolon. Near-total excision of the cyst with marsupialization of the residual cyst into the peritoneal cavity and sclerosis of the wall with tincture of iodine resulted in long-term cure.
5. A female fetus was found to have an intra-abdominal cystic mass on routine prenatal ultrasonography. After birth, the infant was jaundiced, which suggested a choledochal cyst; this was excluded by normal radionuclide scanning. After phototherapy, the patient remained asymptomatic but had a palpable, freely movable, nontender abdominal mass. She underwent elective resection of an omental cyst at the age of 6 months (Fig. 89-2).

Various complications have been associated with mesenteric and omental cysts. These include intestinal obstruction (most common), volvulus, hemorrhage into the cyst, infection,[16] rupture, torsion of the cyst,[42] obstruction of the urinary or biliary tract,[21] and malignancy.[2,20,27,39,40] The reported incidence of malignant conditions (sarcoma, lymphangioendothelioma, or, rarely, adenocarcinoma) is 3%[20]; no malignant mesenteric or omental cysts have been reported in children.

DIAGNOSIS

On physical examination, a majority of children with mesenteric and omental cysts have abdominal distention with or without a palpable mass. A definite mass may be difficult to palpate because of its large size, soft and fluid consistency, and great mobility. The mass may be huge, filling the abdominal cavity and simulating ascites.[15-17,32,33,35] It is dull to percussion. Omental cysts can sometimes be distinguished from ascites by the relative sparing of the flanks; ascites causes the flanks to bulge out, whereas omental cysts do not. If there is no other reason for ascites (e.g., liver or renal disease), a mesenteric or omental cyst should be considered.[11] If a definite mass is palpable, mesenteric cysts are generally movable in the transverse plane, whereas omental cysts are movable in the transverse and craniocaudal planes.[3,40]

Modern imaging studies can usually establish (or at least strongly suggest) the diagnosis of a mesenteric or omental cyst. A plain abdominal radiograph shows a gasless, homogeneous, water-dense mass that displaces bowel loops around it.[8] Omental cysts may compress bowel loops posteriorly, whereas mesenteric cysts may be surrounded by bowel loops (Fig. 89-3).[6] Fine calcifications can sometimes be seen.[4,8] Abdominal ultrasonography and computed tomography (CT) have almost eliminated the need for contrast studies such as upper gastrointestinal series, barium enema, and intravenous pyelography. Abdominal ultrasonography is currently the imaging procedure of choice.[6,18,26] This test reveals a well-circumscribed, thin-walled, fluid-filled cystic structure that usually contains thin internal septi and sometimes contains internal echoes from hemorrhage, infection, or debris (Fig. 89-4).[3,6,26] Enteric duplication cysts are thick-walled structures that share a common muscular wall with the adjacent bowel.[6] They also have a clearly visible mucosal lining on ultrasonography. CT adds little additional information; with the administration of a gastrointestinal contrast agent, however, it can show the relation of the bowel to the cystic mass (Fig. 89-5) and demonstrate that the cyst does not arise from any other organ such as the kidney, pancreas, or ovary.[40] A normal radionuclide scan of the biliary tract excludes choledochal cysts from diagnostic consideration.

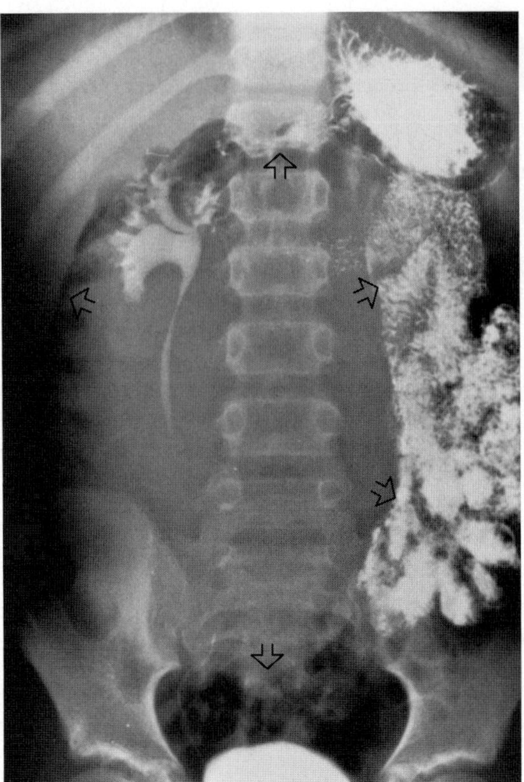

Figure 89–3 Abdominal radiograph obtained after the administration of gastrointestinal and intravenous contrast material demonstrating a large mass *(arrows)* surrounded by bowel loops; the mass is not displacing retroperitoneal structures. These features are characteristic of a mesenteric cyst.

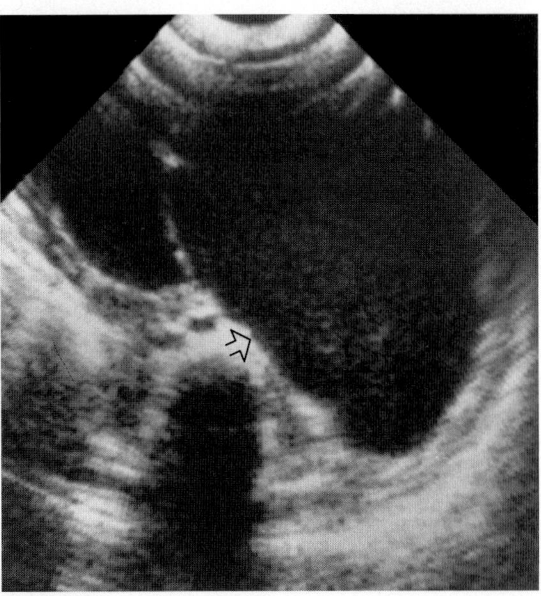

Figure 89–4 Ultrasonogram showing a large, multilocular cystic mass in the anterior abdomen, consistent with the diagnosis of a mesenteric cyst. Fine internal echoes represent hemorrhage within the cyst *(arrow)*.

TREATMENT

The goal of surgery is complete excision of the mass. Omental cysts are easily removed and almost never require bowel resection.[8,14] Omental cysts can be excised using laparoscopic techniques.[15,19,44] Partial drainage of the cyst may be necessary to confirm the site of origin of the cyst and allow its removal through the umbilical port.[28] The preferred treatment of mesenteric cysts is enucleation.[11,14,20,40] In adults, the cyst can often be "shelled out" from between the leaves of the mesentery[11]; in children, however, bowel resection is frequently required to totally eradicate the mass and ensure that the blood supply to the bowel is not compromised. A bowel resection is necessary in only about 33% of adults but 50% to 60% of children with mesenteric cysts.[3,8,18,20,23,27,29] For this reason, a mechanical bowel preparation is recommended before surgery, if time permits.[7] If bowel

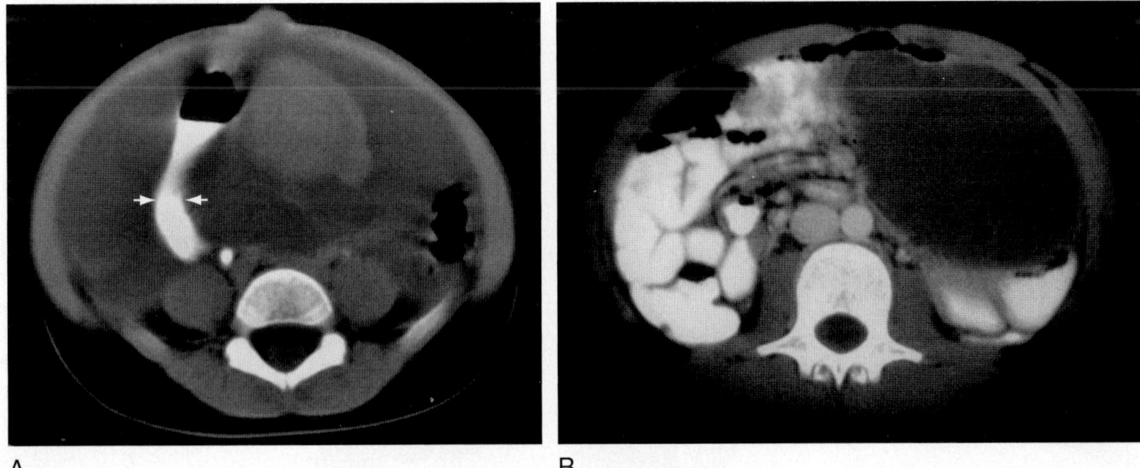

Figure 89–5 *A,* Computed tomography scan with gastrointestinal contrast showing a large cystic mass surrounding a loop of small bowel *(arrows)*. *B,* Computed tomography scan demonstrating a large unilocular cyst that is displacing bowel loops laterally and posteriorly.

resection is required, intestinal continuity can usually be reestablished primarily. The laparoscopic approach to resection of mesenteric cysts has been described.[9,25,28,30] For those cases requiring a concomitant bowel resection, either an intracorporeal technique or a laparoscopic-assisted extracorporeal technique can be used.

If enucleation or resection is not possible, the third option is partial excision with marsupialization of the remaining cyst into the abdominal cavity. Approximately 10% of patients require this form of treatment.[20] If this procedure is done, the cyst lining should be sclerosed with 10% glucose solution,[5] electrocautery, or tincture of iodine in an attempt to minimize recurrence. Percutaneous injection of the lyophilized incubation mixture of group A *Streptococcus pyogenes* OK432 has been successful in the treatment of large, nonresectable lymphangiomas in children.[24] The mechanism of action of OK432 seems to be related to activation of the white cells (an increased number of natural killer cells and T cells) and an increase in cytokine-mediated endothelial permeability (increased activity of tumor necrosis factor and interleukin-6), resulting in shrinkage of the cystic spaces.[24] This agent may be useful to complement the surgical treatment of mesenteric cysts extending into the retroperitoneum. Partial excision and drainage are not indicated because of the high recurrence rate associated with these procedures.[20]

Recently, a simple and universal pathologic classification system that considers the different varieties of mesenteric cysts has been proposed (Fig. 89-6).[24] Types 1 and 2 are easily cured with resection or enucleation, with or without concomitant bowel resection. Types 3 and 4, extending into the retroperitoneum, require complex surgical procedures and often sclerotherapy as well. Recurrence in types 3 and 4 is more common than in types 1 and 2.

The surgical treatment used for the current series is shown in Table 89-7. All 3 omental cysts were totally excised. Eleven of the 13 (85%) mesenteric cysts were completely excised; 2 (15%) were marsupialized into the peritoneal cavity and had the cyst lining sclerosed with electrocautery (1) or tincture of iodine (1). Of the completely excised cysts, 5 (45%) required concomitant bowel resection, and 1 required distal pancreatectomy. None of the cysts was simply drained. No major short- or long-term complications, deaths, or recurrences occurred in this series.

TABLE 89-7 Surgical Treatment of Mesenteric and Omental Cysts

Treatment	Mesenteric Cyst (N = 13), No. (%)	Omental Cyst (N = 3), No. (%)
Enucleation, excision	5 (38.5)	3 (100)
Intestinal resection*	5 (38.5)	0
Excision, distal pancreatectomy	1 (8)	0
Marsupialization, cautery	2 (15)	0
Drainage	0	0

*One patient with volvulus.

Data from references 2, 4, 6, 11, 12, 24; there were no deaths or recurrences.

OUTCOME

The overall results of treatment in patients, particularly children, with mesenteric and omental cysts are very favorable. The reported recurrence rate ranges from 0% to 13.6%, averaging about 6.1% in a series of 162 adults and children.[20] Most recurrences occur in patients with retroperitoneal cysts or those who had a partial excision.[14,18,20,42] The overall mortality rate in adults and children is 2%.[20] Only one child's death has been reported since 1950. That patient was a 26-month-old girl who presented with small bowel infarction from a volvulus associated with a mesenteric cyst.[43]

SUMMARY

Mesenteric and omental cysts are rare, but they are more commonly encountered in children's hospitals than in

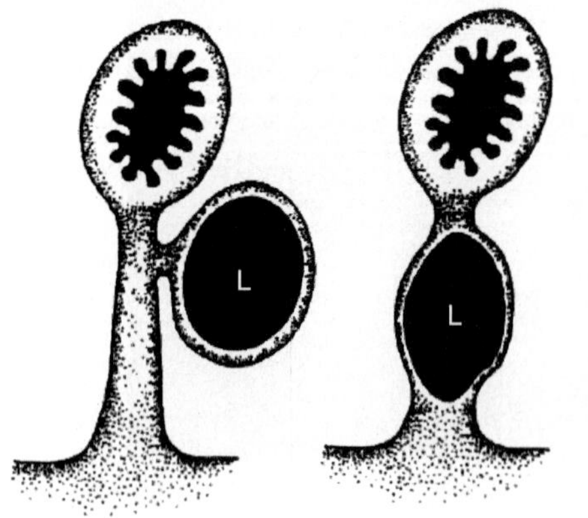

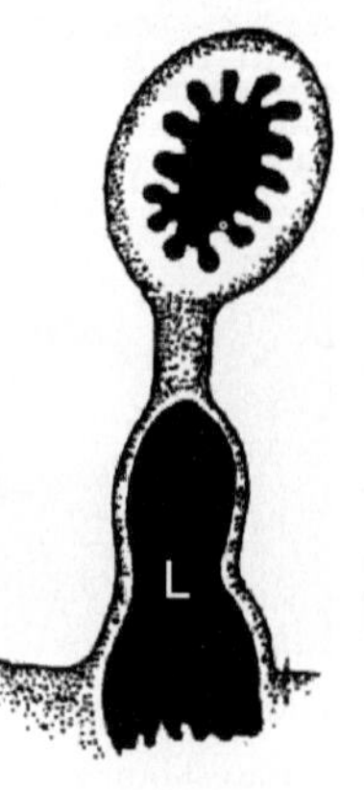

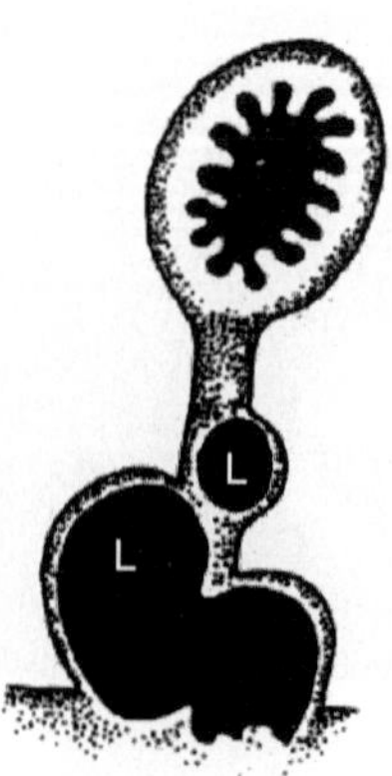

Figure 89-6 Classification of mesenteric cysts. Type 1—pedicled; easily resected. Type 2—sessile in leaves of mesentery; requires bowel resection. Type 3—extending into retroperitoneum; often incompletely resected. Type 4—multicentric; may require complex operations, sclerotherapy, or both. (From Losanoff JE, Richman BW, El-Sherif A, et al: Mesenteric cystic lymphangioma. J Am Coll Surg 2003;196:598.)

adult general hospitals. Most cysts are developmental in origin and are related to a congenital abnormality of the lymphatic system. This abnormality leads to altered production and flow of lymph in ectopic lymphatic tissue, which lacks communication with central channels. The cysts can be located in the mesentery or omentum of any part of the gastrointestinal tract and may extend into the retroperitoneum. With modern imaging studies, these cysts can usually be differentiated from cystic lesions of other organs within the abdominal cavity. They may present incidentally, insidiously, or as an acute life-threatening emergency. In children, acute presentations from intestinal obstruction with or without volvulus are relatively common. In adults, less acute modes of presentation are the rule. The goal of treatment is complete removal of the cyst by either resection or enucleation. In children, concomitant bowel resection is often required. At times, a portion of the cyst wall must be left in situ and marsupialized into the peritoneal cavity and sclerosed. The short- and long-term prognosis of children with mesenteric and omental cysts is excellent, with a low recurrence rate, few complications related to treatment, and essentially no mortality.

REFERENCES

1. Adejuyigbe O, Lawal OO, Akinula DO, et al: Omental and mesenteric cysts in Nigerian children. J R Coll Surg Edinb 1990;35:181.
2. Beahrs OH, Judd ES, Docherty MB: Chylous cysts of the abdomen. Surg Clin North Am 1950;30:1081.
3. Bliss DP Jr, Coffin CM, Bower RJ, et al: Mesenteric cysts in children. Surgery 1994;115:571.
4. Burnett WE, Rosemand GP, Bucher RM: Mesenteric cysts: Report of three cases, in one of which a calcified cyst was present. Arch Surg 1950;60:699.
5. Chirathivat S, Shermeta D: Recurrent retroperitoneal mesenteric cyst. Gastroenterol Radiol 1979;4:191.
6. Chou YH, Tiu CM, Lui WY, et al: Mesenteric and omental cysts: An ultrasonographic and clinical study in 15 patients. Gastrointest Radiol 1991;16:311.
7. Chung MA, Brandt ML, St-Vil D, et al: Mesenteric cysts in children. J Pediatr Surg 1991;26:1306.
8. Colodny A: Mesenteric and omental cysts. In Welch KJ (ed): Pediatric Surgery, 4th ed. Chicago, Year Book Medical Publishers, 1986.
9. Dequanter D, Lefebvre JC, Belva P, et al: Mesenteric cysts: A case treated by laparoscopy and a review of the literature. Surg Endosc 2002;16:1493.
10. Egozi EI, Ricketts RR: Mesenteric and omental cysts in children. Am Surg 1997;63:287.
11. Feins NR, Raffensperger JG: Cystic hygroma, lymphangioma, and lymphedema. In Raffensperger JG (ed): Swenson's Pediatric Surgery, 5th ed. Norwalk, Conn, Appleton & Lange, 1990.
12. Gairdner WT: A remarkable cyst in the omentum. Trans Pathol Soc Lond 1852;3:1851.
13. Gross RE: Omental cysts and mesenteric cysts. In Gross RE (ed): The Surgery of Infancy and Childhood. Philadelphia, WB Saunders, 1953.
14. Hebra A, Brown MF, McGeehin KM, et al: Mesenteric, omental, and retroperitoneal cysts in children: A clinical study of 22 cases. South Med J 1993;86:173.
15. Horiuchi T, Shimomatsuya T: Laparoscopic excision of an omental cyst. J Laparoendosc Adv Surg Tech A 1999; 9:411.
16. Iuchtman M, Soimu U, Amar M: Peritonitis caused by a ruptured infected mesenteric cyst. J Clin Gastroenterol 2001; 32:452.
17. Klin B, Lotan G, Efrati Y, et al: Giant omental cyst in children presenting as pseudoascites. Surg Laparosc Endosc 1997;7:291.
18. Kosir MA, Sonnino RE, Gauderer MWL: Pediatric abdominal lymphangiomas: A plea for early recognition. J Pediatr Surg 1991;26:1309.
19. Kuriansky J, Bar-Dayan A, Shabtai M, et al: Laparoscopic resection of huge omental cyst. J Laparoendosc Adv Surg Tech A 2000;10:283.
20. Kurtz RJ, Heimann TM, Beck AR, et al: Mesenteric and retroperitoneal cysts. Ann Surg 1986;203:109.
21. Lawrence RA, Putnam TC, Webb SR: Omental cyst: Presentation in an infant with jaundice and increasing abdominal girth. J Pediatr Gastroenterol Nutr 1992;15:97.
22. Liew SCC, Glenn DC, Storey DW: Mesenteric cyst. Aust N Z J Surg 1994;64:741.
23. Lin JI, Fisher J, Caty MG: Newborn intraabdominal cystic lymphatic malformations. Semin Pediatr Surg 2000;9:141.
24. Losanoff JE, Richman BW, El-Sherif A, et al: Mesenteric cystic lymphangioma. J Am Coll Surg 2003;196:598.
25. Mason JE, Soper NJ, Brunt LM: Laparoscopic excision of mesenteric cysts: A report of two cases. Surg Laparosc Endosc Percutan Tech 2001;11:382.
26. Molander ML, Mortenssen W, Uden R: Omental and mesenteric cysts in children, Acta Pediatr Scand 1982; 71:227.
27. Mollitt DL, Ballantine TVN, Grosfeld JL: Mesenteric cysts in infancy and childhood. Surg Gynecol Obstet 1978; 147:182.
28. Morrison CP, Wemyss-Holden SA, Maddern GJ: A novel technique for laparoscopic resection of mesenteric cysts. Surg Endosc 2002;16:219.
29. Okur H, Kucukaydin M, Ozokutan BH, et al: Mesenteric, omental, and retroperitoneal cysts in children. Eur J Surg 1997;163:673.
30. Polat C, Ozacmak ID, Yucel T, et al: Laparoscopic resection of giant mesenteric cyst. J Laparoendosc Adv Surg Tech A 2000;10:337.
31. Radhakrishma K, Rao PLNG: Intraabdominal lymphatic cysts in children. Indian Pediatr 1989;26:1214.
32. Rahman GA, Johnson AW: Giant omental cyst simulating ascites in a Nigerian child: Case report and critique of clinical parameters and investigative modalities. Ann Trop Paediatr 2001;21:81.
33. Rattan KN, Budhiraja S, Pandit SK, et al: Huge omental cyst mimicking ascites. Indian J Pediatr 1996;63:707.
34. Sardi A, Parikh KJ, Singer JA, et al: Mesenteric cysts. Am Surg 1987;53:58.
35. Senocak ME, Gundogdu H, Buyukpamukcu N, et al: Mesenteric and omental cysts in children: Analysis of nineteen cases. Turk J Pediatr 1994;36:295.
36. Skandalakis JE, Gray SW, Ricketts RR: The lymphatic system. In Skandalakis JE, Gray SW (eds): Embryology for Surgeons, 2nd ed. Baltimore, Williams & Wilkins, 1994.
37. Takiff H, Calabria R, Yin L, et al: Mesenteric cysts and intraabdominal cystic lymphangiomas. Arch Surg 1985;120:1266.
38. Tillaux PJ: Cyste du mesentere un homme: Ablation par la gastromie: Quersion. Rev Ther Med Chir Paris 1880; 47:479.
39. Tykka H, Koivuniemi A: Carcinoma arising in a mesenteric cyst. Am J Surg 1975;129:709.

40. Vanek VW, Phillips AK: Retroperitoneal, mesenteric, and omental cysts. Arch Surg 1984;119:838.
41. vonRokitansky CF: Handbuch der pathologischen anatomie, bd2. Handbuch der Speciellen Pathologischen Anatomie. Wien, Braumuller & Seidel, 1842.
42. Walker AR, Putnam TC: Omental, mesenteric, and retroperitoneal cysts. Ann Surg 1973;178:13.
43. Wong SW, Gardner V: Sudden death in children due to mesenteric defect and mesenteric cyst. Am J Forensic Med Pathol 1992;13:214.
44. Yao CC, Wu TL, Wong HH, et al: Laparoscopic resection of an omental cyst with pedicle torsion. Surg Laparosc Endosc Percutan Tech 1999;9:372.

Chapter 90

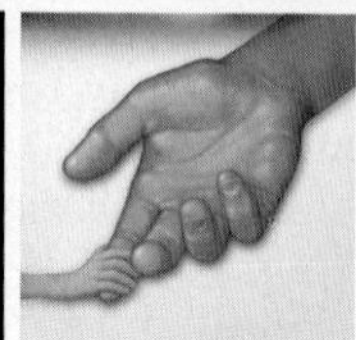

Ascites

Eugene D. McGahren III

Ascites is the pathologic accumulation of excess fluid in the peritoneal cavity. The word "ascites" is derived from the Greek *askos* and *askites*, meaning "bag," "bladder," or "belly."[18] Ascites has been recognized since the time of Hippocrates (400 BC), whereas modern descriptions of ascites in fetuses and infants date to the 17th century.[9,14,17,67] A wide variety of conditions, both congenital and acquired, cause ascites in infants and children (Table 90-1). The more common causes of ascites are addressed in this chapter.

ANATOMY AND PATHOPHYSIOLOGY

There are two major sources of abdominal lymph fluid. One is the flow of blood through the liver. Blood flow from the hepatic artery and portal vein perfuses the hepatic sinusoids and then exits via the hepatic veins. Pressure in the sinusoids is typically low because precapillary resistance is greater than postcapillary resistance. The space of Disse is defined by hepatocytes on one side and sinusoidal lining cells on the other side. Hepatic lymph is formed by the filtration of sinusoidal plasma into the space of Disse. It then drains from the liver via transdiaphragmatic lymphatics to the thoracic duct, which then empties into the subclavian vein. The sinusoidal endothelium is highly permeable to albumin, and the concentration of protein in hepatic lymph is close to that of plasma. Thus, there is normally no significant osmotic gradient across the sinusoidal membrane.[18]

The second major source of abdominal lymph fluid is via the mesenteric venous system. Blood from the mesenteric capillaries flows through the mesenteric veins into the portal vein. The mean pressure of the mesenteric capillary is about 20 mm Hg. Intestinal lymph drains from regional lymphatics into the thoracic duct. The mesenteric capillary membrane is relatively impermeable to albumin. Because the concentration of protein in mesenteric lymph is only about 20% that of plasma, there is a significant osmotic gradient that promotes the return of lymph fluid into the capillary under normal conditions. In an adult-sized patient, there is normally less than 150 mL of free fluid in the abdomen, and normal flow of lymph into the thoracic duct is about 800 to 1000 mL/day.[18]

Ascites occurs when there is an alteration in the normal hydrostatic, osmotic, and electrochemical forces that determine fluid balance. The hydrostatic and osmotic pressure of the hepatic and mesenteric capillaries causes a net transfer of fluid from blood vessels to lymph vessels that exceeds the drainage capacity of the

TABLE 90-1 Causes of Ascites

Hepatocellular
Glycogen storage disorders, lysosomal storage disorders, galactosemia, alpha$_1$-antitrypsin deficiency, viral hepatitis, neonatal hepatitis, congenital hepatic fibrosis, cirrhosis, hepatic or portal vein thrombosis, Budd-Chiari syndrome, malignancy, veno-occlusive disease, biliary atresia

Biliary
Bile duct perforation, injury to bile ducts

Chromosomal
Trisomy 21, Turner's syndrome

Cardiac
Congestive heart failure, arrhythmias

Infection
Appendicitis, tuberculosis and atypical acid-fast bacilli, cytomegalovirus, parvovirus, syphilis, varicella zoster, enterovirus, listeriosis, toxoplasmosis, hepatitis A, *Chlamydia*, fungus

Renal/Urinary
Posterior urethral valves, ureteroceles, ureteral stenosis, urethral stenosis or atresia, neurogenic bladder, bladder perforation, nephrotic syndrome, urogenital sinus, cloacal malformation

Gastrointestinal
Atresia, malrotation, volvulus, intestinal perforation, enteropathy, meconium peritonitis, lymphangiectasia, trauma (including child abuse), congenital obstruction from a peritoneal band, gastroschisis, cardiac surgery, abdominal surgery for tumor, other abdominal surgery, lymphangioma, intussusception

Pancreatic
Pancreatitis from any cause, pseudocysts, trauma

Gynecologic
Ruptured ovarian cyst, hydrometrocolpos

Miscellaneous
Ventriculoperitoneal shunt, peritoneal dialysis, pseudomyxoma peritonei, granulomatous peritonitis, myxedema, neoplasms (e.g., lymphoma, neuroblastoma, ovarian), metabolic storage diseases

lymph system. More specifically, alterations in hydrostatic pressure may result from cardiac insufficiency or compromise of blood flow through the caval or portal venous systems. Changes in colloid pressure may result from hypoproteinemia secondary to liver compromise or from disturbances in capillary membrane permeability from a variety of inflammatory, metabolic, genetic, or neoplastic causes. Abnormalities in lymphatic drainage may result from trauma, including surgery and child abuse, or from congenital or other anomalies that result in obstruction of the lymphatic system. Finally, ascites may be caused by direct communication between the urinary tract and the abdominal cavity.[18,65,69]

CLINICAL FEATURES

Abdominal distention is the most common physical finding associated with ascites.[66,67] Other physical signs may include bulging flanks, prominent abdominal wall vasculature, an everted umbilicus if there is an umbilical hernia or an inverted umbilicus if there is no hernia, inguinal hernias, scrotal or labial edema, a fluid wave, total-body edema, and shifting dullness to percussion.[1,59,65,66,69] Other physical findings related to the cause of the ascites may also be present, such as a cardiac murmur; enlarged liver, spleen, or kidney; or an abdominal mass. Urinary output may be diminished because of intravascular depletion, increased intra-abdominal pressure, or urinary leak.[6] Signs of peritoneal irritation suggest a primary inflammatory or infectious cause of the ascites or a secondary infection of ascitic fluid. Nausea and vomiting may occur.[67] Respiratory compromise may be present, depending on the degree of fluid accumulation and resulting diaphragmatic elevation.[5,14]

DIAGNOSIS

Plain radiographs of the abdomen typically show medial displacement of bowel, as well as diffuse abdominal opacification with a ground-glass appearance (Fig. 90-1). Separation of the properitoneal fat stripe from the colon and separation of air-filled bowel loops are two other nonspecific findings. The liver may appear to be rounded and pushed to the center. Calcifications may be present if the ascites is associated with bowel perforation and peritonitis.[20,65,69]

Ultrasonography (US) is sensitive in detecting free fluid in the peritoneal cavity. Free fluid in the abdomen appears as shifting echo-free zones in dependent locations. Small amounts of fluid can be detected in the hepatorenal or splenorenal fossa, as well as in the pelvis. As little as 50 to 100 mL may be visible in the abdomen on US (see Fig. 90-1).[65] Repositioning the patient can help differentiate free from loculated fluid collections. US may also be helpful in identifying inciting causes of ascites and is particularly useful in diagnosing urinary tract anomalies that are associated with ascites, such as posterior urethral valves.[66] US cannot distinguish between types of ascitic fluid, however. Prenatal US routinely detects fetal ascites and allows consideration of prenatal and postnatal strategies to aid the infant.[20,24] Computed tomography (CT) may be helpful in determining the cause of ascites, but it does not usually add any information about the fluid beyond that provided by US.

Ascitic fluid should be obtained by paracentesis and analyzed according to the clinical suspicion (Table 90-2). US may be very helpful in locating a site to be aspirated, especially if there are scars from previous surgery.[18] An aspirate of 10 to 20 mL should be sufficient for complete analysis. Macroscopic appearance is assessed, and the fluid

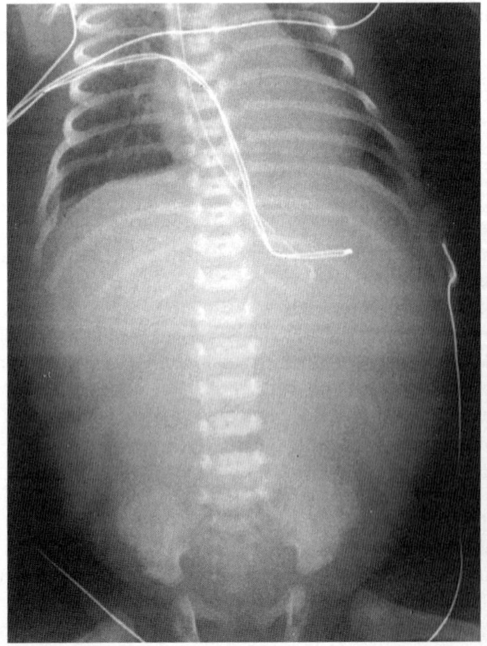

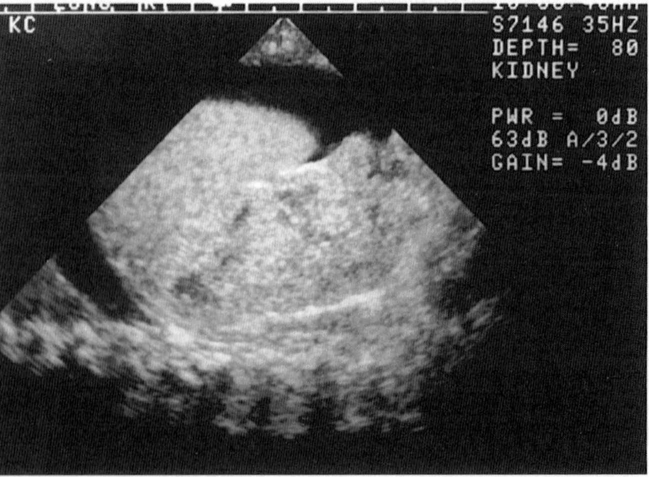

Figure 90–1 A newborn with hepatocellular ascites. The plain radiograph shows diffuse opacification with minimal bowel gas; the ultrasonogram shows fluid in the hepatorenal fossa.

TABLE 90-2 Laboratory Analysis of Ascites

Type of Ascites	Albumin Level	Bilirubin Level	Triglyceride Level	pH	Creatinine Level
Hepatocellular	2-3 g/dL	≈ Serum level	<50 mg/dL	7.35	<1 mg/dL
Biliary	≈3 g/dL	2-3 times serum level	<50 mg/dL	>7.4	<1 mg/dL
Chylous	<3 g/dL	<1 mg/dL	1000-1500 mg/dL	7.5	<1 mg/dL
Urinary	<1 g/dL	<1 mg/dL	<50 mg/dL	<7.0	<5-10 mg/dL

may be straw colored, turbid, bloody, or chylous. Laboratory evaluation of ascitic fluid should include a cell count with differential, Gram stain and culture, cytologic assessment if indicated, and chemical analysis, including pH, lactate dehydrogenase, albumin, protein, amylase, bilirubin, creatinine, and triglyceride levels.[60,65,69]

HEPATOCELLULAR ASCITES

Neonatal hepatitis, biliary atresia, inborn errors of metabolism, congenital hepatic fibrosis, and alpha$_1$-antitrypsin deficiency commonly lead to cirrhosis, portal hypertension, and subsequently, ascites in children. Ascitic fluid is a transudate that results from increased portal venous pressure, increased intraluminal pressure in the mesenteric capillaries, and loss of fluid into the peritoneal cavity. Loss of albumin potentiates these losses and triggers renal absorption of sodium and water.[60] Diagnosis of each of these conditions is based on the results of various tests, including specific biochemical assays for inborn errors, viral cultures, tests for viral antibody titers, and liver histologic testing. Analysis of ascitic fluid should include a serum-ascites albumin gradient. A gradient greater than 1.1 g/dL is 97% accurate in predicting portal hypertension.[55] The cell count should be low, and no bacteria should be visualized, although primary peritonitis can complicate preexisting ascites.

Initial therapy for ascites of hepatic cause consists of salt and fluid restriction. Sodium intake should be limited to 1 to 2 mEq/kg/day, and water intake should be no more than 75% of daily maintenance, although severe water restriction is not needed unless significant hyponatremia is present (<125 mg/dL).[60,66] Gentle diuresis is commonly established along with salt and fluid restriction. The goal of diuresis is to attain excretion of extracellular water and sodium. Spironolactone is a favored initial agent because of its potassium-sparing characteristic.[60,69] Repeated large-volume paracentesis is required in patients for whom salt and fluid restriction fails, particularly if there are symptoms of respiratory insufficiency. Paracentesis with replacement of the ascitic fluid removed with salt-poor albumin or dextran has been shown to be safe and effective, especially when combined with diuretic therapy and sodium restriction.[6,35,62,64]

Peritoneovenous shunt procedures for intractable ascites of hepatic and other causes has been described in a few infants and children with good results.[27,52,56] Limitations attributable to the large size of the pump mechanism and venous tubing have made the use of such devices less common in pediatric patients. Modifications have been made by manufacturers to help customize the Denver-type shunt for newborns.[52] An intraperitoneal vascular port has been successfully used for palliative relief of tense malignant ascites caused by hepatocellular carcinoma.[12] A newborn peritoneal dialysis catheter is also effective in draining ascitic fluid in a controlled manner. Transjugular intrahepatic portosystemic shunt (TIPS) therapy has been successful in managing ascites in a teenager and may have a role in therapy for selected children.[36]

BILIARY ASCITES

Biliary ascites usually results from a spontaneous perforation of the common bile duct, most commonly at its junction with the cystic duct.[25,37,38,40,61] Rare instances of cystic duct perforation have been reported.[29] Spontaneous biliary duct perforation is a relatively rare condition, with about 150 cases reported in the literature as of 2003.[20] Although many theories have been proposed, the cause of bile duct perforation is speculative. Distal duct obstruction, pancreatic fluid reflux up the common bile duct, congenital weakness of the common bile duct, a localized mural malformation of the wall of the common duct, and pancreaticobiliary maljunction have been proposed as possible causes.[22,30,38,48] It has been suggested that the proposed bile duct wall defects that may predispose to perforation may be part of a larger spectrum of defects that includes malformations such as choledochal cysts.[70] It should be mentioned that perforation of the biliary tree may also result from trauma.[49,61]

Biliary ascites from spontaneous bile duct perforation typically occurs in infants and toddlers from birth up to about 2 years of age, but it may occur in older children as well.[7,15,28,30,32,61] Biliary ascites may also occur prenatally.[15] Most patients are otherwise healthy and have no predisposing conditions associated with the disorder. A typical scenario is the development of progressive painless abdominal distention with jaundice over a 1- to 4-week period. Vomiting, abdominal pain, and clay-colored stools may also be present. The condition is usually indolent in its manifestation, although if biliary peritonitis is the initial finding, a toxic-appearing state may be seen. However, most patients can tolerate large amounts of bile in the peritoneal cavity without evidence of infection or peritonitis.[61] Physical examination is notable for abdominal distention, the presence of fluid within the abdomen, and possibly inguinal hernias and bile-stained hydroceles.[7,15,28,30,32,61,70]

Biliary ascites should be suspected when the findings just noted occur in the absence of any liver disease.

US can confirm the presence of fluid within the abdomen, and nuclear scintigraphy can aid in identification and localization of a biliary leak.[23,32,70] The diagnosis can be definitively established by paracentesis. The fluid is bile stained with bilirubin levels of 100 to 400 mg/mL, although the level may be lower in patients with more chronic manifestations.[7]

The primary goal in the treatment of biliary ascites is external drainage.[7,15,31,32,61,70] The approach may involve open exploration of the right upper quadrant with cholecystostomy and cholecystography to document the size and location of the perforation. If there is evidence of distal obstruction, some advocate a biliary-intestinal anastomosis; otherwise, this is rarely needed.[7,31] Moreover, additional internal drainage procedures, such as cholecystojejunostomy or duodenotomy with sphincteroplasty, are generally unnecessary and fraught with difficulty because no intrinsic obstruction usually exists and inflammation tends to distort the anatomy.[38,53] The region is frequently heavily scarred, and a sac filled with thick bile can be mistaken for a choledochal cyst.[70] External drainage can be accomplished by placing a Penrose or closed suction drain in the porta hepatis. A cholecystostomy tube may be useful to help with decompression and to further assess the biliary tree in the future.[7] External drainage has also been successfully accomplished by a percutaneous technique, thus avoiding open laparotomy.[32] Alternatively, laparoscopy offers an option to allow localization of the leak and precise drain placement.[7] Bile duct stenosis is the most common complication after external drainage. Portal vein thrombosis, bile leak, and cholangitis have also been reported.[32,70]

With adequate external drainage, the vast majority of patients survive and need no additional surgical intervention. Eighty percent of perforations heal within 3 weeks.[7,25,32,38,40,53,61] Antibiotics and complete bowel rest with total parenteral nutrition (TPN) are important adjuncts in these patients. Fat-free enteral infant formulas are also used, but no studies have compared these two nutrition options in patients with biliary ascites. The cholecystostomy and peritoneal drains should remain in place until normal ductal anatomy has been shown through cholecystography.

CHYLOUS ASCITES

Chylous ascites is the excessive collection of lymph fluid in the peritoneal cavity. The most common cause (in 45% to 60% of cases) in infants and children is idiopathic and presumed to be congenital malformation of the lymphatic channels.[17,41,57,66,67] Known congenital lymphatic abnormalities that lead to chylous ascites include atresia or stenosis of the major lacteals at the base of the mesentery or the cisterna chyli, mesenteric cysts, generalized lymphangiomatosis, and lymphangioma.[13,19,34,66,67] The next most common cause of chylous ascites is thought to be obstruction of lymphatic channels by conditions such as intussusception, malrotation, incarcerated hernia, primary or metastatic cancer, tuberculosis, gastroschisis, and inflammatory lesions causing lymph node enlargement.[13,19,39,41,59,66,67] Finally, injury to the lymphatics is responsible for an additional 15% to 20% of cases of chylous ascites. This category may include injury from trauma, injury after surgery for a variety of conditions, and child abuse. Ascites may not be noticed until days or weeks after the inciting event.[8,9,17,23,39,68]

Chylous ascites can occur in children of all age groups, although most are infants and toddlers.[41,66,67] Abdominal distention is the most common initial sign. It may develop gradually or acutely and may be accompanied by abdominal pain and respiratory compromise.[4,9,17,39,41,46,66,67] Other signs and symptoms may include vomiting, diarrhea, inguinal hernia, and edema.[43,67]

The main confirmatory diagnostic study is abdominal paracentesis, which reveals a milky white fluid if the patient is receiving a fat-containing enteral diet. The fluid is characterized by an elevated triglyceride concentration (often greater than 1000 mg/dL), a cell differential that is predominantly lymphocytes (70% to 90%), and elevated total protein and cholesterol concentrations.[17,41,55,65-67]

Determining the cause of chylous ascites can be challenging, especially if the child has no obvious condition that commonly predisposes to a lymph leak. Studies such as US, CT, and gastrointestinal contrast studies may be helpful in identifying predisposing conditions such as malrotation, lymphangioma, tumor, or mesenteric cysts. In newborns in whom ascites has no readily recognizable explanation, a congenital lymph channel malformation is the most likely diagnosis. Lymphangiography is described in older series, but it is difficult to perform in children, it is not always possible to demonstrate the mesenteric lymphatics via pedal access, and it has helped direct treatment in only a minority of the children in whom it was used.[55,66] Moreover, in an era when nonsurgical intervention is a preferred therapy in the absence of known inciting causes, lymphangiography arguably adds little to the treatment strategy.

Surgically correctable lesions such as malrotation, mesenteric cysts, intussusception, or incarcerated hernias should be corrected. For patients without a surgically correctable lesion, the initial treatment is aimed at reducing lymph flow through the damaged or obstructed lymph channels. This is accomplished by suspending enteral intake and initiating TPN. Some patients respond quickly to this intervention, with resolution of the ascites within 2 weeks. If the patient's nutritional and hydration status can be maintained, courses of TPN for up to 10 weeks can be considered.[4,68] Because medium-chain triglycerides (MCTs) are absorbed directly into the portal system and therefore do not stimulate lymph flow, they have traditionally been advocated for the treatment of chylous ascites. Hard data confirming the benefit of an MCT formula have been lacking. Nonetheless, the use of a low-fat, MCT-enhanced formula such as Portagen has been reported in multiple successful nonoperative treatment courses and should be considered as an adjunct to TPN or as the initial enteral formula in patients who respond to TPN.[4,8,23,59,68] Prolonged use of low-fat infant formulas has been associated with poor neurologic development, possibly from fatty acid deficiency.[57] Treatment with low-fat formula should therefore be limited to 3 to 6 months. Paracentesis in addition to bowel rest should be reserved for patients with respiratory compromise.

Surgical intervention is warranted if nonoperative therapy is not successful after 6 to 10 weeks or if the patient becomes otherwise symptomatic.[41,57,66,68] As noted earlier, the role of preoperative lymphangiography is not clear because such studies often poorly highlight the mesenteric and portal lymphatics. More commonly, a successful strategy is to feed the patient a high-fat diet (usually milk) up to 6 hours before surgical exploration. Copious creamy lymph flow affords a better chance of identifying the leak. Addition of Sudan dye to the milk may further aid in identifying the leak.[46,51] The most common location of the lymph leak is at the base of the superior mesenteric vessels, although various retroperitoneal and mesenteric lymphatics may be involved.[5,41,46,51,57,66] Complete mobilization of the duodenum and the head of the pancreas and thorough exploration of the entire retroperitoneum should be performed.[13] Ligation of an identified leaking lymphatic is curative in 85% of patients.[46,66] Recent reports also describe the potential usefulness of laparoscopy in localizing lymph leaks and the use of fibrin glue for the control of lymph leaks.[5,46] Peritoneovenous shunting may be a useful treatment strategy as a primary surgical intervention or as an intervention in children in whom surgical exploration has failed to resolve the ascites.[43,56,68] In some older series, mortality from chylous ascites was significant and ranged from 24% to 30%.[66,67] However, with current nutritional support and surgical intervention capabilities, a successful outcome can now usually be expected.

URINARY ASCITES

Urinary ascites is a rare condition, though a common cause of ascites in newborns, and accounts for up to a third of cases of isolated ascites.[14,65] Males outnumber females by a ratio of 7:1.[21] Obstruction of the lower urinary tract, particularly from posterior urethral valves, accounts for approximately 70% of cases of urinary ascites. Other obstructive causes of urinary ascites include ureteroceles, ureteral stenosis, neurogenic bladder, and urethral stenosis or atresia.[14,21,26,44,65] Urinary extravasation from a discrete perforation is noted in approximately 65% of patients with an obstructive cause. The posterior fornix is the weakest part of the urinary system. Thus, the site of perforation is most commonly located in the renal pelvis, although bladder perforation is also common.[14,44] Other causes of urinary ascites that are not obstructive in nature include trauma to the urachal remnant, often as a result of attempted umbilical arterial catheterization, spontaneous rupture of the bladder in infants with connective tissue disorders, and in females with a persistent urogenital sinus or cloacal malformation, leakage of urine directly into the peritoneal cavity through the uterus and fallopian tubes.*

Most patients with urinary ascites are recognized soon after birth. However, prenatal ultrasound may also detect ascites.[3,10,11,32,42] On physical examination, abdominal distention, frequently with palpable flank masses, is the most common finding. Respiratory distress and acidosis (absorption of urine from the peritoneal cavity) may be present. Potter's syndrome (maternal oligohydramnios and renal, pulmonary, and chest wall hypoplasia) may be detected. Prune-belly syndrome may likewise be a physical finding.[14,42,50] Hyponatremia, hyperkalemia, and an elevated serum blood urea nitrogen level and creatinine level are also common.[14,16,21]

The workup should begin with abdominal ultrasonography, which will demonstrate the ascitic fluid. It will also identify most common urinary tract abnormalities that are associated with urinary ascites, such as hydronephrosis, dilated ureters, and a dilated or thickened bladder.[65] Voiding cystourethrography (VCUG) demonstrates any obstructing lesions and may show the point of extravasation.[26,44,63] Intravenous pyelography (IVP) or renal scanning with diethylenetriamine pentaacetic acid (DTPA) or mercaptoacetyltriglycerine (MAG 3) may provide information about the degree of renal parenchymal damage caused by the long-standing obstruction and may show the point of extravasation.[22]

Treatment is focused on the underlying urinary tract obstruction. Fluid resuscitation, antibiotics, and distal urinary tract drainage constitute the initial treatment in these patients.[26,44,63] Prenatal intervention for significant urinary obstruction may also be considered.[47] Urinary tract decompression may be accomplished by Foley catheterization, particularly in the case of posterior urethral valves. Cystoscopy with valve ablation is then performed electively if Foley catheter drainage is successful. Other decompression strategies may include percutaneous nephrostomy or surgical vesicostomy or pyelostomy, depending on the offending lesion and the condition of the patient.[26,44] Although some advocate routine drainage of ascites, drainage of the ascites or repair of the perforation usually is not necessary because the urinary ascites is reabsorbed once urinary drainage has been achieved and the perforation heals quickly.[14,21,44] Drainage of ascites is necessary in the presence of respiratory compromise or infection.[14] Once the aforementioned measures have been successfully completed, definitive surgery can be undertaken to address the offending lesion. There is a risk of compromised long-term renal function because of the chronic obstruction. However, spontaneous decompression of an obstruction that results in urinary ascites is thought to be protective of renal function. Thus, a significant number of patients retain good renal function, although it must be monitored on a long-term basis.[3,14,21,33,65] With improvements in neonatal care and early recognition of these conditions, the mortality rate from urinary ascites has decreased from 70% to 0%.[44]

*References 2, 14, 21, 26, 44, 45, 54, 58, 63, 65.

REFERENCES

1. Ackerman Z: Ascites in nephrotic syndrome: Incidence, patients' characteristics, and complications. J Clin Gastroenterol 1996;22:31.
2. Adams MC, Ludlow J, Brock JW 3rd, Rink RC: Prenatal urinary ascites and persistent cloaca: Risk factors for poor drainage of urine or meconium. J Urol 1998;160:2179.

3. Adzick NS, Harrison MR, Flake AW, deLorimier AA: Urinary extravasation in the fetus with obstructive uropathy. J Pediatr Surg 1985;20:608.
4. Alliet P, Young C, Lebenthal E: Chylous ascites: Total parenteral nutrition as primary therapeutic modality. Eur J Pediatr 1992;151:213.
5. Antao B, Croaker D, Squire R: Successful management of congenital chyloperitoneum with fibrin glue. J Pediatr Surg 2003;38:7.
6. Baden HB, Morray JP: Drainage of tense ascites in children after cardiac surgery. J Cardiothorac Vasc Anesth 1995; 9:720.
7. Banani SA, Bahador A, Nezakatgoo N: Idiopathic perforation of the extrahepatic bile duct in infancy: Pathogenesis, diagnosis, and management. J Pediatr Surg 1993;28:950.
8. Beshay VE, Beshay JE, Rosenberg AJ: Chylous ascites: A case of child abuse and an overview of a rare condition. J Pediatr Gastroenterol Nutr 2001;32:487.
9. Besson R, Gottrand F, Saulnier P, et al: Traumatic chylous ascites: Conservative management. J Pediatr Surg 1992; 27:1543.
10. Bettelheim D, Pumberger W, Deutinger J, Bernaschek G: Prenatal diagnosis of fetal urinary ascites. Ultrasound Obstet Gynecol 2000;16:473.
11. Blessed WB, Sepulveda W, Romero R, et al: Prenatal diagnosis of spontaneous rupture of the fetal bladder with color Doppler ultrasonography. Am J Obstet Gynecol 1993; 169:1629.
12. Borger JA, Pitel P, Crump G: Management of malignant ascites with a vascular port. J Pediatr Surg 1993;28:1606.
13. Chang JHT, Newkirk J, Carlton G, et al: Generalized lymphangiomatosis with chylous ascites—treatment by peritoneo-venous shunting. J Pediatr Surg 1980;15:748.
14. Checkley AM, Sabharwal AJ, MacKinlay GA, et al: Urinary ascites in infancy: Varied etiologies. Pediatr Surg Int 2003; 19:443.
15. Chilukuri S, Bonet V, Cobb M: Antenatal spontaneous perforation of the extrahepatic biliary tree. Am J Obstet Gynecol 1990;163:1201.
16. Clarke HS, Mills ME, Parres JA, Kropp KA: The hyponatremia of neonatal urinary ascites: Clinical observations, experimental confirmation and proposed mechanisms. J Urol 1993;150:778.
17. Cochran WJ, Klish WJ, Brown MR, et al: Chylous ascites in infants and children: A case report and literature review. J Pediatr Gastroenterol Nutr 1985;4:668.
18. Colletti RB, Krawitt EL: Ascites. In Wyllie R, Hyams JS (eds): Pediatric Gastrointestinal Disease, 2nd ed. Philadelphia, WB Saunders, 1999.
19. Craven CE, Goldman AS, Larson DL, et al: Congenital chylous ascites: Lymphangiographic demonstration of obstruction of the cisterna chyli and chylous reflux into the peritoneal space and small intestine. J Pediatr 1967;70:340.
20. DeRusso PA, Benson J, Lau H: Intestinal malrotation and omental cyst presenting as fetal ascites. J Pediatr Gastroenterol Nutr 2003;36:283.
21. De Vries SH, Klijn AJ, Lilien MR, De Jong TP: Development of renal function after neonatal urinary ascites due to obstructive uropathy. J Urol 2002;168:675.
22. Donahoe PK, Hendren WH: Bile duct perforation in a newborn with stenosis of the ampulla of Vater. J Pediatr Surg 1976;11:823.
23. Drinnen D, Filston HC: An unusual case of gastroschisis with gallbladder evisceration and late postrepair chylous ascites. J Pediatr Surg 1997;12:1804.
24. Favre R, Dreux S, Dommergues M, et al: Nonimmune fetal ascites: A series of 79 cases. Am J Obstet Gynecol 2004; 190:407.
25. Fitzgerald RJ, Parbhoo I, Guiney EJ: Spontaneous perforation of bile ducts in neonates. Surgery 1978;83:303.
26. Greenfield SP, Hensle TW, Berdon WE, Geringer AM: Urinary extravasation in the newborn male with posterior urethral valves. J Pediatr Surg 1982;17:751.
27. Guttman FM, Montupet P, Bloss RS: Experience with peritoneovenous shunting for congenital chylous ascites in infants and children. J Pediatr Surg 1982;17:368.
28. Haller JO, Condon VR, Berdon WE, et al: Spontaneous perforation of the common bile duct in children. Radiology 1989;172:621.
29. Hammar B, Sanders E: Spontaneous biliary peritonitis in infancy. J Pediatr Surg 1968;3:84.
30. Hasegawa T, Udatsu Y, Kamiyama M, et al: Does pancreaticobiliary maljunction play a role in spontaneous perforation of the bile duct in children? Pediatr Surg Int 2000; 16:550.
31. Ibanez DV, Vila JJ, Fernandez MS, et al: Spontaneous biliary perforation and necrotizing enterocolitis. Pediatr Surg Int 1999;15:401.
32. Kasat LS, Borwankar SS, Jain M, Naregal A: Spontaneous perforation of the extrahepatic bile duct in an infant. Pediatr Surg Int 2001;17:463.
33. Kobata R, Isukahara H, Takeuchi M, et al: Early detection of prune belly syndrome in utero by ultrasonography. Acta Paediatr Jpn 1997;39:705.
34. Konen O, Rathous V, Dlugy E, et al: Childhood abdominal cystic lymphangioma. Pediatr Radiol 2002;32:88.
35. Kramer RE, Sokol RJ, Yerushalmi B, et al: Large-volume paracentesis in the management of ascites in children. J Pediatr Gastroenterol Nutr 2001;33:245.
36. Lee WS, McKiernan PJ, de Ville de Goyet JV, et al: Successful treatment of refractory ascites in a child with transjugular intrahepatic portosystemic shunt. Acta Paediatr 2001;90:1352.
37. Lees W, Mitchell JE: Bile peritonitis in infancy. Arch Dis Child 1966;48:188.
38. Lilly JR, Weintraub WH, Altman RP: Spontaneous perforation of the extrahepatic bile ducts and bile peritonitis in infancy. Surgery 1974;75:664.
39. Lloyd D: Gastroschisis, malrotation, and chylous ascites. J Pediatr Surg 1991;26:106.
40. Lloyd DA, Mickel RE: Spontaneous perforation of the extra-hepatic bile ducts in neonates and infants. Br J Surg 1980;67:621.
41. Loiterman DL, Bleicher MA: Chylous ascites: An etiology of peritonitis in infancy. J Pediatr Surg 1985;5:538.
42. Lowenstein L, Solt I, Talmon R, et al: In utero diagnosis of bladder perforation with urinary ascites. A case report. Fetal Diagn Ther 2003;18:179.
43. Man DWK, Spitz L: The management of chylous ascites in children. J Pediatr Surg 1985;20:72.
44. Mann CM, Leape LL, Holder TM: Neonatal urinary ascites: A report of 2 cases of unusual etiology and a review of the literature. J Urol 1974;111:124.
45. Mata JA, Livne PM, Gibbons MD: Urinary ascites: Complication of umbilical artery catheterization. Urology 1987;30:375.
46. Mitsunaga T, Yoshida H, Iwai J, et al: Successful surgical treatment of two cases of congenital chylous ascites. J Pediatr Surg 2001;36:1717.
47. Nakayama DK, Harrison MR, de Lorimier AA: Prognosis of posterior urethral valves presenting at birth. J Pediatr Surg 1986;21:43.
48. Ohkawa H, Takahashi H, Maie M: A malformation of the pancreaticobiliary system as a cause of perforation of the biliary tract in childhood. J Pediatr Surg 1977; 12:541.

49. Pandit SK, Budhiraja S, Rattan KN: Post traumatic bile ascites. Indian J Pediatr 2000;67:72.
50. Patil KK, Wilcox DT, Samuel M, et al: Management of urinary extravasation in 18 boys with posterior urethral valves. J Urol 2003;169:1508, discussion 1511.
51. Pearl J, Joyner J, Collins DL: Chylous ascites: The first reported surgical cure by direct ligation. J Pediatr Surg 1977;12:687.
52. Pettitt BJ: Use of a modified Denver peritoneovenous shunt in a newborn with intractable ascites. J Pediatr Surg 1992;27:108.
53. Prevot J, Babist M: Spontaneous perforation of the biliary tract. In Rickham PP, Hecker WC, Prevot J (eds): Progress in Pediatric Surgery. Baltimore, University Park Press, 1971.
54. Redman JF, Seibert JJ, Arnold W: Urinary ascites in children owing to extravasation of urine from the bladder. J Urol 1979;122:411.
55. Runyon BA, Montano AA, Akriviadis EA, et al: The serum-ascites albumin gradient in the differential diagnosis of ascites is superior to the exudate/transexudate concept. Ann Intern Med 1992;117:215.
56. Ryan JA, Smith MD, Page CP: Treatment of chylous ascites with peritoneovenous shunt. Am Surg 1981;47:384.
57. Sanchez RE, Mahour GH, Brennan LP, Woolley MM: Chylous ascites in children. Surgery 1971;69:183.
58. Sayan A, Demircan M, Erikci VS, et al: Neonatal bladder rupture and unusual complication of umbilical catheterization. Eur J Pediatr Surg 1996;6:378.
59. Solans CV, Sockolow RE: Chylous ascites associated with gastroschisis. Clin Pediatr (Phila) 1996;35:415.
60. Squires R: Complications of end-stage liver disease. In Rudolph CD, Rudolph AM (eds): Rudolph's Pediatrics, 21st ed. New York, McGraw-Hill, 2003.
61. Stringel G, Mercer S: Idiopathic perforation of the biliary tract in infancy. J Pediatr Surg 1983;18:546.
62. Terg R, Berreta J, Abecasis R, et al: Dextran administration avoids hemodynamic changes following paracentesis in cirrhotic patients: A safe and inexpensive option. Dig Dis Sci 1992;37:79.
63. Thompson IM, Bruns TNC: Neonatal ascites: A reflection of obstructive disease. J Urol 1972;107:509.
64. Tito L, Gines P, Arroyo V, et al: Total paracentesis associated with intravenous albumin management of patients with cirrhosis and ascites. Gastroenterology 1990;98:146.
65. Towers H: Neonatal ascites. In Burg FD (ed): Gellis & Kagan's Current Pediatric Therapy 17. Philadelphia, WB Saunders, 2002.
66. Unger SW, Chandler JG: Chylous ascites in infants and children. Surgery 1983;93:455.
67. Vasko JS, Tapper RI: The surgical significance of chylous ascites. Arch Surg 1967;95:355.
68. Weiser AC, Lindgren BW, Ritchey ML, Franco I: Chylous ascites following surgical treatment for Wilms tumor. J Urol 2003;170:1667, discussion 1669.
69. Wyllie R, Arasu TS, Fitzgerald JF: Ascites: Pathophysiology and management. J Pediatr 1980;97:167.
70. Xanthakos SA, Yazigi NA, Rychman FC, Arkovitz MS: Spontaneous perforation of the bile duct in infancy: A rare but important cause of irritability and abdominal distension. J Pediatr Gastroenterol Nutr 2003;36:28.

Chapter 91

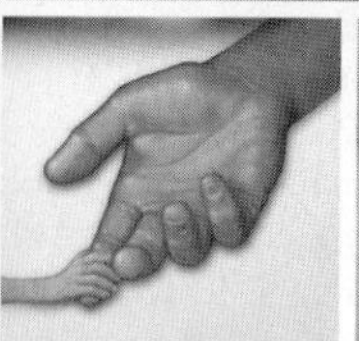

Polypoid Diseases of the Gastrointestinal Tract

Joseph L. Lelli, Jr.

Polypoid diseases of the gastrointestinal tract include lesions isolated to the intestine (juvenile, lymphoid, and adenomatous polyps), uncommon syndromes of the gastrointestinal tract that involve polyps, and disorders in other areas of the body (Peutz-Jeghers' syndrome, Gardner's syndrome, and Turcot's syndrome). Most polyps of the gastrointestinal tract are benign and result from hamartomas of the mucosa or lymphoid hyperplasia of the submucosa. Adenomatous polyps, however, represent a disturbing alteration in the mucosa that has substantial malignant potential.

Polyps are common during childhood, occurring in approximately 1% of preschool- and school-aged children.[113] Because of their high incidence, polyps of the gastrointestinal tract represent the most frequent cause of rectal bleeding in toddlers and preschoolers 2 to 5 years of age. Juvenile polyps are most common (80%) and are followed by lymphoid polyps (15%).[106] Adenomatous polyps occur in less than 3% of all children with polyps.

JUVENILE POLYPS

History

Juvenile polyps were first described by Verse in 1908.[177] For many years, all polyps in children were considered adenomas[66] and were often treated with radical procedures. Horrileno[75] first used the term *juvenile polyp* in 1957 to describe a histologically distinctive colorectal polyp that occurred predominately during childhood. In 1962, Morson[116] made an important contribution when he demonstrated that juvenile polyps were benign hamartomas, thereby distinguishing them from potentially malignant adenomas. Less radical treatments of these polyps, however, were slow to follow. The distinction between isolated juvenile polyps and juvenile polyposis was first made by McColl and colleagues in 1964,[109] and three distinct forms of juvenile polyposis were further defined by Sachatello in 1972.[146] Kaschula, in 1971,[89] followed by Enterline, in 1976,[39] reported cases of children with both juvenile and adenomatous polyps. Billingham and coworkers[12] reported the presence of solitary adenomas in children with juvenile polyps in 1980. These early reports of the coexistence of juvenile and adenomatous polyps led to the identification of adenomatous and malignant changes in juvenile polyps.[60,114,131] However, only polyps associated with juvenile polyposis have malignant potential in children.[25,55,147] The distinction between the commonly occurring isolated juvenile polyps, which are benign, and the rare juvenile polyposis syndromes, which may be malignant, has become increasingly important.[25,55,83,119]

Jass[81] has proposed the following criteria for increased risk for cancer in children with polyps: (1) more than five juvenile polyps in the colon, (2) polyps throughout the gastrointestinal tract, and (3) any number of polyps associated with a family history of juvenile polyposis. Jass' criteria clarify the three distinct juvenile polyposis syndromes originally described by Sachatello in 1972.[146] Based on Jass' and Sachatello's studies, the following classification of juvenile polyps is most commonly used:

I. *Isolated Juvenile Polyps* (nonmalignant): fewer than five polyps confined to the colon without a family history of juvenile polyposis
II. *Juvenile Polyposis Syndromes* (malignant potential):
   A. *Diffuse juvenile polyposis of infancy:* widespread polyposis of entire gastrointestinal tract in patients younger than 6 months of age.
   B. *Diffuse juvenile polyposis:* multiple polyps throughout the gastrointestinal tract but mostly in the stomach, distal colon, and rectum, usually occurring in patients 6 months to 5 years of age.
   C. *Juvenile polyposis coli:* multiple juvenile polyps confined to the distal colon and rectum in patients 5 to 15 years of age.

Isolated Juvenile Polyps

Pathology

Juvenile polyps, which are also known as retention, inflammatory, or cystic polyps, are the most common type of polyp found in the gastrointestinal tract and account for 80% of polyps in children. Such polyps are generally considered hamartomas[116] or a malformation in which normal colonic tissue has become arranged in a haphazard manner.[81]

Grossly, the typical polyp has a glistening, smooth, spherical, reddish head and ranges from 2 mm to several centimeters in diameter (Fig. 91-1). Polyps will often have an ulcerated surface, which accounts for the rectal bleeding. A cross section shows cystic spaces filled with mucus (Fig. 91-2). Juvenile polyps are typically attached by a long, narrow stalk covered by colonic mucosa. This stalk predisposes the polyp to torsion, which results in venous congestion, surface ulceration, bleeding, and autoamputation.

Microscopically, the surface of the polyp has a single layer of colonic epithelium. This epithelial layer is often ulcerated or replaced with granulation tissue. When inflammation occurs, the epithelium may show a reactive hyperplasia that can mimic dysplasia or adenomatous changes.[10] The main body of the polyp consists of dilated or cystic epithelial tubules that are lined by normal colonic epithelium. These tubules and cystic lakes are embedded in a lamina propria and an abundant, loose, vascular, and fibrous stroma (Fig. 91-3). The stroma is usually heavily infiltrated with neutrophils, eosinophils, lymphocytes, and monocytes. Mitotic figures are rarely seen. Only two descriptions of malignant changes in a solitary juvenile polyp are present in the literature,[103,149] and, according to Jass,[81] only one of these may be a true malignant condition. In a longitudinal study of patients with solitary polyps, no increased risk for developing colorectal cancer could be found.[130]

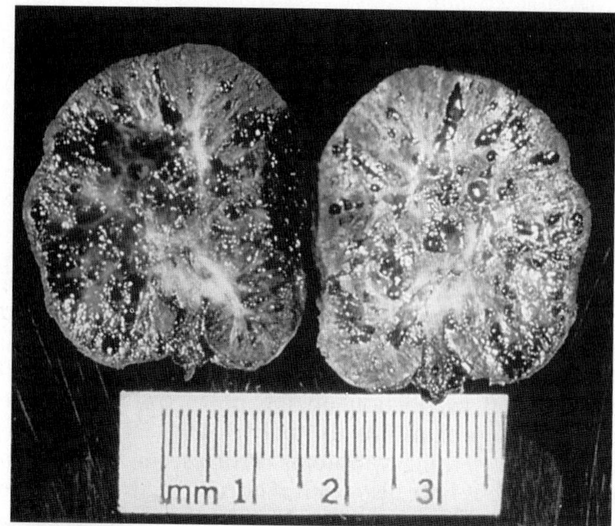

Figure 91-2 Gross cross section of juvenile polyp with typical cystic "lakes" that are filled with mucus.

Etiology

The etiology of juvenile polyps is unknown but several authors have suggested hereditary,[58] genetic,[90] hamartomatous malformation,[116] and inflammatory causes.[143] Recent data suggest that juvenile polyps are the result of a structural rearrangement of the mucosa secondary to an inflammatory process.[49] The initial event is probably ulceration and subsequent inflammation of the mucosa, leading to obstruction of regional, small colonic glands of the mucosa. The obstructed glands proliferate, branch, and dilate, forming a cystic structure. The cystic structure pushes up the mucosa, leading to further ulceration, inflammation, and formation of granulation tissue. As the cycle continues, an increasingly larger and larger mass pushes into the lumen. The fecal stream and peristalsis push the mass down the lumen, causing the stalk to elongate and resulting in the typical pedunculated appearance of the juvenile polyp.

Incidence

Although the incidence of juvenile polyps is unknown, they are believed to occur in approximately 1% of all preschool-aged children.[113] Most juvenile polyps appear in the first decade of life, with the peak incidence between 3 and 5 years of age.[113] The polyps are solitary in 50% of cases, with the remainder of patients having 2 to 10 polyps. The location of these polyps has changed over

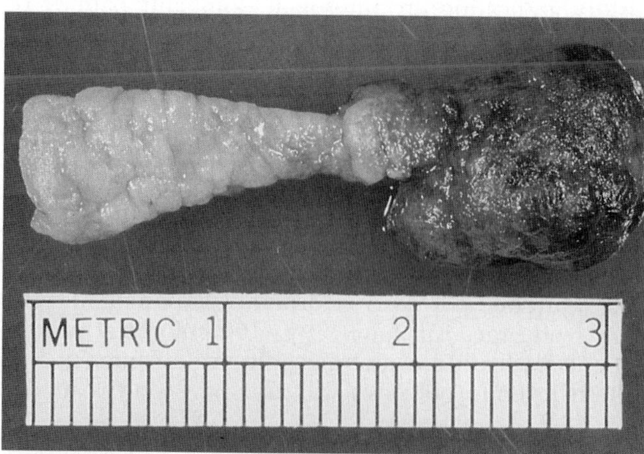

Figure 91-1 Typical juvenile polyp with its stalk attached.

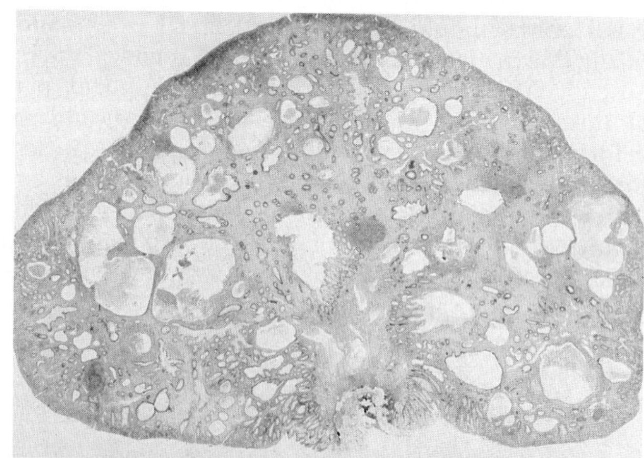
Figure 91-3 Photomicrograph of typical juvenile polyp. The surface shows a smooth, flattened, colonic epithelium. Large tubular and cystic lakes are present, embedded in an abundant, loose stoma.

the past 10 years. Historically, 70% of the polyps were found in the rectum. Today, only 40% are found in the rectum or sigmoid colon whereas 60% are found evenly distributed throughout the proximal colon.[113] Juvenile polyps are rarely seen after adolescence.

Clinical Presentation

The most common presenting symptom of a juvenile polyp is bleeding (93%) that results from ulceration of the polyp surface. Blood loss is usually minimal and appears as bright red streaks of blood over the surface of the stool. Abdominal pain (10%), which is believed to be caused by traction on the polyp from peristaltic activity, and prolapse of the polyp (4%) are other less common presenting symptoms. Prolapse of the rectum and encopresis have also been reported.[113] Many juvenile polyps will autoamputate, resulting in spontaneous cessation of rectal bleeding.[122]

The differential diagnosis of juvenile polyps encompasses all of the causes of rectal bleeding in toddlers and children up to 6 years of age. Anal fissures and rectal prolapse cause rectal bleeding but are easily distinguished from polyps on physical examination. Bleeding from a Meckel diverticulum or duplication of the intestine usually causes more substantial blood loss than that from a polyp, and the blood usually coming less with the stool rather than coating it. Bleeding from an intussusception is accompanied by abdominal pain that is substantially worse than that seen with polyps. Inflammatory bowel disease is usually accompanied by diarrhea, which is not seen with polyps. Blood dyscrasias, bowel hemangioma, and autoimmune phenomena such as Henoch-Schönlein purpura should also be considered in the differential diagnosis.

Treatment

The diagnosis and treatment of juvenile polyps requires a combination of obtaining an accurate history, digital rectal examination, and colonoscopy. The shift of juvenile polyps to the more proximal colon[122] and the concern for the presence of juvenile polyposis (more than five polyps), with its increased risk of malignancy, mandates that the entire colon be surveyed. Children with suspected polyps should have a digital rectal examination initially. Polyps in the rectum can be easily removed during anoscopy. After removal of a rectal juvenile polyp, pancolonoscopy, in a well-prepared bowel, should be performed to determine if additional polyps are present more proximally.[64] Children with juvenile polyposis and adenomatous changes are more likely to have right-sided colonic polyps[73]; therefore, all polyps should be removed and undergo histologic evaluation. Complications after endoscopic removal of polyps are rare.

Juvenile Polyposis Syndromes

Juvenile polyposis syndromes are uncommon. These syndromes can be separated into three distinct clinical entities: diffuse juvenile polyposis of infancy, diffuse juvenile polyposis, and juvenile polyposis coli.[146]

Types

Diffuse Juvenile Polyposis of Infancy

Diffuse juvenile polyposis of infancy presents within the first few months of life,[25] usually without any family history.[81] Presenting signs include diarrhea, rectal bleeding, intussusception, protein-losing enteropathy, macrocephaly, clubbing of fingers and toes, and hypotonia.[62,140,145,148,158] The extent of diarrhea, rectal bleeding, and protein-losing enteropathy is directly related to the number of polyps present. The entire gastrointestinal tract is frequently involved. Treatment for this syndrome is usually aggressive, starting with total parenteral nutrition and intestinal rest. The latter measure reduces the protein and blood loss and decreases the incidence of intussusception.[157] When the nutritional status of the patient has been stabilized, portions of the intestine with the most polyps are removed. Despite appropriate treatment this disease is almost universally fatal, only 2 of 12 patients are reported as surviving beyond 2 years of age.*

Diffuse Juvenile Polyposis

Children with diffuse juvenile polyposis are usually 6 months to 5 years of age and present with mild rectal bleeding and prolapse but may also have a protein-losing enteropathy, intussusception, and malnutrition.[25] In this age group it is important to distinguish juvenile polyposis from familial adenomatous polyposis. Polyps associated with diffuse polyposis are found throughout the bowel, most often in the stomach, distal colon, and rectum.[25] Endoscopic polypectomy and segmental bowel resection are used in the treatment of this disease. These children usually do well, although the need for recurrent therapy is common.

Juvenile Polyposis Coli

Juvenile polyposis coli occurs in children between the ages of 5 and 15 years of age. This disorder is usually characterized by bleeding of bright red blood from the rectum, anemia, rectal prolapse, or all of these disorders. Polyps are usually limited to the distal colon and rectum.[25] Approximately 50% of the patients will have a family history, indicating an autosomal dominant pattern of inheritance.[147] Associated congenital defects including cleft palate, malrotation, polydactyly, and abnormalities of the heart and cranium have been described.[81]

Pathology

Any child with five or more polyps, polyps throughout the gastrointestinal tract, or even one polyp if the child has a family history of juvenile polyposis is considered to have a juvenile polyposis syndrome.[81] Most patients with such syndromes will have 50 to 100 colorectal polyps. Patients with diffuse juvenile polyposis of infancy and diffuse juvenile polyposis will also have polyps in the

*See references 3, 18, 62, 98, 109, 140, 145, 147, 148, 158, and 175.

Figure 91-4 Gross specimen of colon in a patient with juvenile polyposis syndrome. Note small adenomas as well as the multilobular clusters of polyps attached to stalks.

stomach and small intestine or both. The importance of identifying children with a polyposis syndrome lies in the need for long-term surveillance owing to the high risk of carcinoma (17%) occurring at an early age (mean age at diagnosis of carcinoma is 35.5 years).[25]

The gross appearance of a polyp in juvenile polyposis is the same as one in isolated juvenile polyps. Approximately 20% of the polyps in juvenile polyposis, however, present grossly as a multilobular mass resembling a cluster of polyps attached to a stalk (Fig. 91-4).[83] Histologically, these polyps demonstrate more epithelium with a villous or papillary configuration. Epithelial dysplasia can occur in juvenile polyps* and in coexisting adenomas found in conjunction with juvenile polyps.† Severe dysplasia that could be considered carcinoma in situ has been found in patients with juvenile polyps associated with juvenile polyposis syndrome.[87] Lobular polyps have a higher propensity for more severe dysplasia (47%) than the nonlobular polyps (10%).[83] Several reports of infiltrating adenocarcinoma of the colon and rectum in association with juvenile polyposis exist.[57,60,79,142,146,156,162] According to the St. Mark's Polyposis Registry in London the cumulative risk for cancer in patients with a juvenile polyposis syndrome by age 60 is 68%.[65,119]

Treatment

The autosomal dominant pattern of inheritance and the 68% cumulative risk for cancer by age 60 means that treatment must include long-term follow-up of patients with polyposis and their family members. Some advocate prophylactic colectomy and rectal mucosectomy with endorectal ileoanal pull-through as a primary treatment.[79] Others recommend regular screening (every 2 years) with colonoscopy and random biopsy[77] and subsequent colectomy if severe dysplasia, rapid polyp formation, or bleeding occurs.[55] One patient had a colectomy and ileosigmoidostomy at 4 years of age only to develop inoperable cancer of the sigmoid colon at 27 years of age.[83] First-degree relatives should be screened because of the familial nature of the disease. The approach to patients with juvenile polyposis should be similar to that taken for patients with familial adenomatous polyposis.

*See references 55, 58, 60, 63, 65, 79, 83, 89, 102, 114, 131, 142, and 176.
†See references 5, 6, 23, 55, 83, 89, 131, 139, 142, and 176.

PEUTZ-JEGHERS SYNDROME

History

The association of intestinal polyps with mucocutaneous pigmentation spots of the mouth, hands, and feet was first reported by Peutz in 1921.[135] In 1944,[84] Jeghers reported two cases; and in 1949,[85] he and his colleagues added 8 more to 12 other cases he had collected from personal communications. Jeghers and colleagues[85] subsequently defined the two main features of the syndrome: (1) melanin spots on the buccal mucosa and lips, with variable melanin pigmentation on the face and digits, and (2) polyposis of the intestinal tract. In 1954, Bruwer and associates[15] were the first to use the term *Peutz-Jeghers syndrome.* In recent years, reports of intestinal and extraintestinal cancers have led to a reassessment of the management of these patients.[136]

Pathology

Peutz-Jeghers syndrome is characterized by melanotic spots, ranging in color from brown to black, occurring on the lips, around the mouth, and on the buccal mucosa. These spots can also be found on the hands, feet, nasal mucosa, and conjunctiva and in the rectum.[136] The pigmented spots are usually present at infancy and often fade at puberty.

Although the polyps associated with Peutz-Jeghers syndrome can be found anywhere from the stomach to the rectum, they occur most commonly in the small intestine (55%). Approximately 30% of these polyps are found in the stomach and duodenum, and 15% are found in the colon and rectum.[169] Grossly, the polyps range from a few millimeters to several centimeters and present as smooth, firm, pedunculated lesions that are lobulated in contrast to juvenile polyps that are not lobulated. Peutz-Jeghers polyps are classified histologically as hamartomas of the muscularis mucosa[136] and demonstrate strands of smooth muscle fibers that divide the polyp into sectors (Fig. 91-5).[82,117,118] Adenomas can occur concurrently with Peutz-Jeghers polyps.

Etiology and Incidence

Peutz-Jeghers syndrome is rare and has an equal sex distribution; it has been described in all ethnic groups. Most cases of Peutz-Jeghers syndrome are inherited in an autosomal dominant pattern but some develop de novo, most likely representing new, spontaneous mutations. Recently two groups of investigators have defined the genetic mutation associated with Peutz-Jeghers syndrome. In individuals affected with Peutz-Jeghers syndrome, many (but not all) have a mutation of a novel serine/threonine

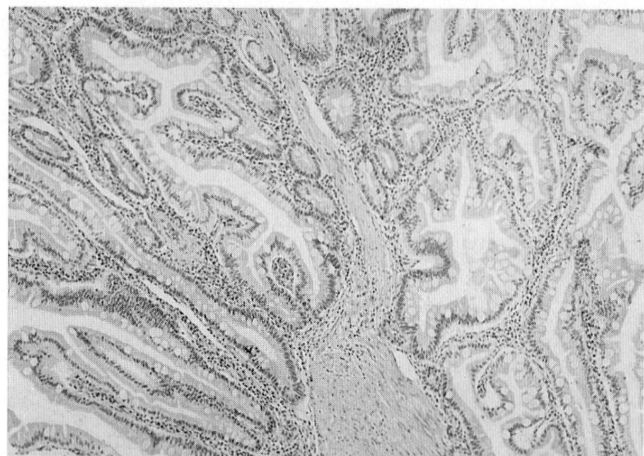

Figure 91-5 Photomicrograph of a Peutz-Jeghers polyp demonstrating a hamartomatous alteration of the muscularis mucosa. Smooth muscle fibers divide the polyp into sectors.

kinase (LKB1 or STK11) with loss of kinase activity.[67,86] Routine genetic testing and gene therapy for this disease are under investigation but currently not available.[110]

Clinical Presentation

Because of the familial association of Peutz-Jeghers syndrome, the syndrome is often revealed in patients through screening programs. If there is no family history, patients usually present with crampy abdominal pain related to transient intussusception of a polyp. Abdominal radiographs will often demonstrate dilated or partially obstructed small intestine but rarely complete obstruction. Anemia resulting from occult blood loss and malignant conditions are other presenting signs. Thirty percent of patients present with signs and symptoms in the first 10 years of life, with 50% presenting by 20 years of age.[35,169]

Several reports of intestinal tumors in association with Peutz-Jeghers syndrome have been published.[16,45,56,74,159,171] Malignant changes in hamartomatous polyps of Peutz-Jeghers syndrome have been commonly reported.[26,76,94,108,126,134,152,154,159] Separate adenomatous and carcinomatous changes in hamartomas have also been reported, which suggests that the adenoma-carcinoma sequence occurs in the small intestine of patients with Peutz-Jeghers syndrome.[26] A review of 72 patients with the syndrome[159] showed that 22% developed cancer, nine cases were gastrointestinal or pancreatic in origin, and seven cases were extraintestinal. Compared with an age-matched general population, patients with Peutz-Jeghers syndrome had a relative risk for death from gastrointestinal cancer alone that is 13 times greater, and the risk for death from all cancers is 9 times greater. The chance of dying of cancer by the age of 60 is approximately 50% in patients with Peutz-Jeghers syndrome.[136]

Extraintestinal tumors associated with Peutz-Jeghers syndrome include ovarian, cervical, and testicular neoplasms. Reported ovarian tumors include cystadenomas,[35,78,107] granulosa cell tumors,[23] and sex-cord tumors.[9,70,150,190] Adenocarcinoma of the cervix can occur and is usually associated with an ovarian tumor.[189] Sertoli cell tumors of the testis have been found and cause gynecomastia in 50% of cases. These tumors are usually benign but have malignant potential[101,138,153]; thus an orchiectomy is recommended. Cancer of the breast, thyroid, bile duct, pancreas, and gallbladder have all been described in association with Peutz-Jeghers syndrome.[136]

Treatment

Peutz-Jeghers syndrome should be suspected in any child who presents with colicky abdominal pain or occult anemia and melanotic pigmented spots. Recommendations for treatment have changed over the past decade because of the increasing concern of malignancy. The management protocol proposed by Phillips and Spigelman[136] includes the following annual evaluations: (1) symptoms related to polyps, (2) blood cell count to detect anemia caused by blood loss, (3) breast and pelvic examinations with cervical smears and pelvic ultrasonography in girls, (4) testicular examination with ultrasonography in boys, and (5) pancreatic ultrasonography. In addition, esophagogastroduodenoscopy and colonoscopy are recommended on a biennial basis, along with small intestine contrast studies. Recently, magnetic resonance imaging (MRI) has shown promise as a surveillance modality for small intestinal screening.[95] Mammography is recommended at 25, 30, 35, and 38 years of age, biennially until 50 years of age, and then annually.

All polyps larger than 0.5 mm found at endoscopy should be removed. Laparotomy with intraoperative enteroscopy is recommended for removal of all small bowel polyps greater than 15 mm in diameter. The previous practice of radical intestinal resections should be avoided because of the recurrent nature of the polyps and the ensuing short-bowel syndrome that can occur. Any intestinal or extraintestinal tumors should be treated aggressively. Historical data indicate that the chance of patients with Peutz-Jeghers syndrome dying by the age of 60 is close to 60% compared with 25% in an age-matched general population.[136]

LYMPHOID POLYPS

History

The first case of lymphoid hyperplasia of the terminal ileum was described by Marina-Fiol and Rof-Carballo in 1941, as reported by Patel and Awen.[133] Fieber and Schaefer[43] reviewed 8 cases previously described in the literature and added 4 of their own in 1966. Byrne and colleagues[20] reported only 44 cases in the world literature; however, lymphoid polyps were identified in 60% of children studied by Franken for remote abdominal complaints.[48] Thus, the incidence of lymphoid polyps is probably higher than reported, but clearly most of them are asymptomatic and, therefore, never identified.

Pathology

Lymphoid polyps vary in size from a few millimeters to 3.0 cm in diameter and are usually sessile. The polyps are caused by elevation of hyperplastic submucosal lymphoid aggregates. The overlying mucosa often becomes ulcerated, which gives the polyp the volcano-like appearance. Ulceration of the mucosa leads to occult blood loss. Hyperplasia of the submucosal lymphoid tissue is believed to be caused by nonspecific infections of childhood.[1,2,4,106]

Incidence

Lymphoid polyps tend to develop in young children within the first few years of life as a result of exposure to new bacteria and viruses.[157] The peak incidence is at 4 years of age and significantly diminishes by 5 years of age.

Clinical Presentation

Anemia resulting from blood loss and occasionally substantial rectal bleeding are the usual presenting signs of lymphoid polyps. Colonoscopy, air-contrast barium enema, or both are the diagnostic methods of choice for diagnosing lymphoid polyps of the colon. An air-contrast barium enema will show small, uniform, umbilicated, polypoid filling defects that are distinct from juvenile or adenomatous polyps (Figs. 91-6 and 91-7).[20,48] Small elevations of otherwise-normal mucosa are seen on endoscopy and biopsy will confirm the diagnosis.

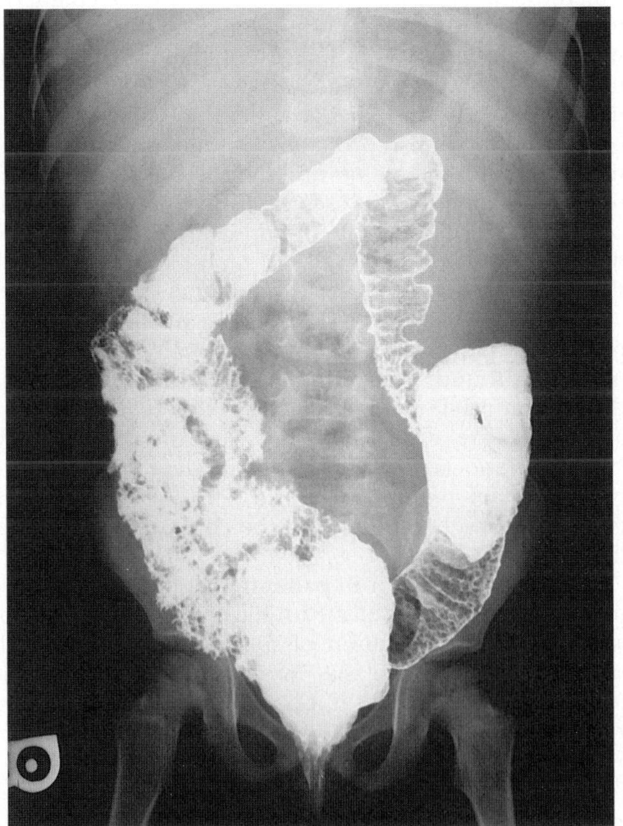

Figure 91-6 Barium enema showing multiple, small 1- to 2-mm mucosal nodules throughout the entire colon and terminal ileum. The central umbilication within these nodules seen on this postevacuation film is diagnostic of diffuse lymphoid hyperplasia.

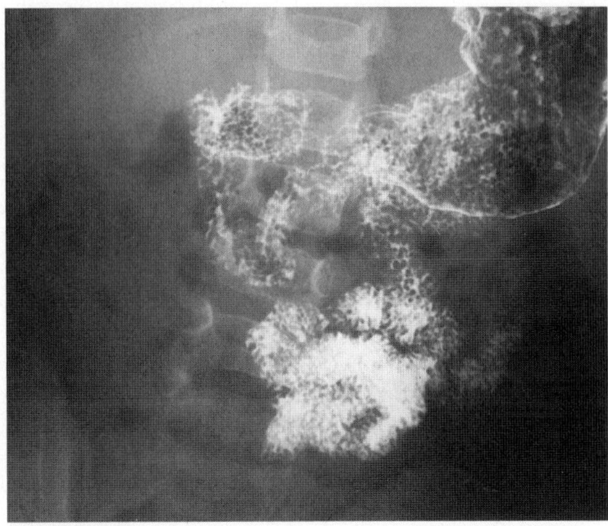

Figure 91-7 An upper gastrointestinal series showing diffuse lymphoid hyperplasia throughout the stomach and small intestine.

Histologic evaluation reveals lymphoid aggregates with large germinal follicles.[157]

Treatment

Lymphoid polyps are benign, self-limiting, and tend to regress spontaneously.[21,106] Once a histologic diagnosis is made, expectant measures will usually be rewarded by regression of the lesions. Substantial uncontrolled bleeding and intussusception may require a more aggressive surgical approach.

FAMILIAL ADENOMATOUS POLYPOSIS

History

The first case of adenomatous polyposis was recorded by Covisart in 1847,[28] but it was Chargelaigue[22] who 12 years later gave the first definitive account of the disease in a 16-year-old girl and a 21-year-old man. The first pathologic description of these colonic polyps was reported by Virchow in 1867,[178] with Woodward in 1881[188] being the first to distinguish between neoplastic and inflammatory polyps. The first familial association of these polyps was described by Cripps in 1882[32] between a 9-year-old boy and his 17-year-old sister. However, the malignant potential of these polyps was not recognized until 1890 by Handford.[66]

The first recorded operations for polyposis are credited to Lilienthal[10] in North America and subsequently to Lockhart-Mummery at St. Mark's Hospital in London, as reported by Thomson and Watne.[168,183] Lockhart-Mummery, in 1925,[104] concluded that (1) multiple adenomatous polyps develop in succeeding generations, (2) afflicted individuals develop cancer at an early age, and (3) the adenomas are an antecedent to cancer. In 1927, Cockayne[27] described the mode of inheritance as mendelian dominant, which was later confirmed by Dukes in 1930[37] and Lockhart-Mummery and Dukes in 1939.[105]

Figure 91-8 Gross specimen of the total colon in a patient with familial adenomatous polyposis demonstrating thousands of adenomatous polyps. Note the large adenoma in the ascending portion of the colon.

Figure 91-9 Close-up view of colonic mucosa demonstrating a "carpet" of small 1- to 2-mm adenomas in a patient with familial adenomatous polyposis.

Since that time, familial adenomatous polyposis (FAP) has become a model for understanding the adenoma-carcinoma sequence.[36]

The detection of a deletion in chromosome 5q[69] in a patient with Gardner's syndrome has led to characterization of the gene responsible for FAP, the *APC* gene.* The 5q deletion or alteration in the *APC* gene results in a gene product with a truncated protein, which subsequently causes the *APC* gene to act as a tumor suppressor gene.[29,137] Mouse models for FAP have been developed,[164] and these will facilitate research in gene therapy.

Pathology

Familial adenomatous polyposis is defined as the presence of at least 100 visible adenomatous polyps in the large intestine.[17] However, patients with fewer polyps have been diagnosed as having FAP, and one patient who had early onset of colorectal cancer and had a 5q gene deletion had only one endoscopically detectable polyp.[99]

Colorectal polyps are the hallmark of FAP. Although 100 polyps is the usual threshold for diagnosing this disorder, patients coming to colectomy in their teenage years typically have thousands of polyps (Fig. 91-8). Two types of FAP seem to exist: the sparse type, which is characterized by hundreds of polyps, and the profuse type, which is characterized by thousands of polyps. Utsunomiya and associates[174] have shown that the history of the two types is different—patients with the profuse type tend to develop adenocarcinoma at an earlier age.

In FAP, the polyps are typically scattered throughout the colon, which allows diagnosis by sigmoidoscopy. The polyps vary in size from 1.0 to 2.0 mm in diameter; when present, pedunculated polyps can be 1 cm in diameter or larger (Fig. 91-9). During duodenoscopy, biopsy of normal-appearing duodenal mucosa may reveal microscopic adenomas too small to be seen macroscopically. These microadenomas may consist of only three or four dysplastic crypts that usually have a tubular adenomatous structure.[185]

Adenomatous polyps result from a neoplastic transformation of at least one epithelial cell that is in the proliferative portion of a crypt.[121] The transformed clone then populates the upper part of the crypt that divides by budding.[121] Crypt fusion is then responsible for further growth of the adenoma. This neoplastic transformation, called dysplasia, implies atypical morphologic characteristics, with nuclear enlargement and stratification. Adenomas seem to pass through gradations of dysplasia until invasive adenocarcinoma develops.[120] Extension of neoplastic cells into the basement membrane of the colonic epithelium represents carcinoma in situ. As the neoplastic cells extend beyond the basement membrane, the tumor becomes microscopically invasive. Because the colonic mucosa does not contain lymphatics, metastasis does not usually occur until the tumor invades through the muscularis mucosa into the submucosa.

Small intestinal mucosa can also be involved with adenomatous polyps. Polyps of the small intestine are frequently found in the duodenum around the orifice of the common bile duct.[160] Polyps in this region are variable in size, are often microscopic, and involve only a few crypts. Adenocarcinoma of the duodenal papilla and periampullary regions occurs in 2.9% of patients with FAP[160] and has been found in the common bile duct of these patients.[161]

Gastric polyps occur in patients with FAP, but they are usually benign polyps of the fundic gland.[34] These polyps result from cystic dilation of specialized gastric glands rather than from dysplasia. No evidence that neoplastic transformation occurs in polyps of the fundic gland exists.[165]

Etiology

The incidence of FAP ranges from 1 in 6000 to 1 in 12,000 births.[80,141,184] FAP is inherited as an autosomal

*See references 13, 61, 71, 88, 92, 93, 100, 111, 115, and 127.

dominant trait with a moderate incidence (10%) of new mutations.[72] The manifestations of FAP differ greatly, probably as a result of variation in the mutation of the *APC* gene. Although the occurrence of polyps is strongly related to genetics, the phenomena of regression of rectal polyps after colectomy and ileorectal anastomosis was recognized 1988[42,125] and points to the fact that the luminal environment also plays a role in the development of polyps.

FAP is caused by a mutation in the *APC* gene on the long arm of chromosome 5, where a variable deletion or alteration of the gene is associated with the disease. The *APC* gene codes for a protein product that acts as a tumor suppressor.[72] Because of this gene deletion, the probability of cancer (as diagnosed by biopsy during sigmoidoscopy) by 25 years of age is 90%.[66] In colorectal cancer cell lines that have an intact chromosome 5 introduced into the cells, the ability of the cells to induce tumor growth in mice is considerably reduced.[59,166] Similar results have been found for other tumor suppressor genes, namely, the *TP53* gene on chromosome 17p and the deleted colorectal cancer gene *(DCC)* on chromosome 18q.[72] It has become apparent there is genetic heterogeneity in FAP. Certain germline mutations of the *APC* gene predispose to attenuated disease expression.[31,112] Further evidence indicates that additional modifier genes influence the severity of FAP.[30]

Clinical Presentation

Although FAP has been recognized in infancy and early childhood, it is most frequently identified in early adolescence. Most patients are asymptomatic, but some present with increased frequency of defecation, rectal bleeding, anemia, and abdominal pain. Most (90%) are identified by routine surveillance because of a familial history of adenomatous polyposis.

Diagnosis is established by sigmoidoscopy and occasionally by air contrast barium enema. Sigmoidoscopy usually reveals a fine carpet of polyps that cover the entire surface of the colon. Biopsy of at least 10 polyps will confirm the diagnosis. In some patients with FAP, most of the polyps will be located in the proximal colon. If the diagnosis of FAP is made in a patient who represents a new mutation (no other family members known to have the disease), a careful examination of all family members is required.

Polyps are found in the stomach in up to 50% of patients with FAP, but only 6% of the polyps are adenomatous,[34] with the rest being fundic gland polyps (hamartomas). Polyps occur in the duodenum less often than in the stomach; however, duodenal polyps are much more likely to be adenomatous. Several series have demonstrated that up to 98% of FAP patients have visible duodenal polyps or at least a histologic abnormality with dysplasia, unicrypt adenomas, or hyperplasia in the duodenal mucosa.[34,160,173] Adenocarcinoma of the duodenal papilla or periampullary region eventually develops in 2.9% of patients with FAP.[160] For these reasons, upper endoscopy is necessary in all patients with this disorder.

Treatment

Malignant conditions of the colon will occur in all patients with FAP if left untreated. The average age for developing cancer is 39 years, with 7% developing cancer by age 20 and 15% by age 25.[128] Surgical removal of the entire colonic mucosa will prevent colorectal carcinoma. Most patients who present with symptomatic polyps already have a malignant condition.[128] Therefore, colectomy is recommended at any age, if the child is symptomatic.

A wide range of surgical options exists. Total proctocolectomy with a permanent ileostomy prevents cancer but leaves a young patient with a permanent abdominal wall stoma. The physiologic and psychological impact of a permanent ileostomy is substantial in adolescence. This operation can cause substantial sequelae because of the extensive pelvic dissection, namely, damage to the nervi erigentes with resultant bladder atony and, in males, impotence. For these reasons, total proctocolectomy is not the treatment of choice for FAP in a pediatric patient.

Total abdominal colectomy with an ileorectal anastomosis and continued surveillance of the retained rectum has probably been the most common operation for FAP performed in the past. St. Mark's Hospital in London reported its results with 215 patients undergoing this procedure.[168] Immediate postoperative complications included prolonged ileus (7%), anastomotic breakdown (2%), and bleeding (<1%), for a total complication rate of 10%. Frequency of defecation at late follow up (6.5 years) was three stools per day, and fewer than 10% reported night-time soiling. Continence was considered completely normal in 72%. Forty-four percent of the patients, however, required subsequent treatment for their rectal polyps. Depending on the density of the rectal polyps, the patients were evaluated every 3 to 6 months, with sigmoidoscopy and fulguration of any polyps greater than 5.0 mm in diameter. Ten percent developed carcinoma in their rectal stump. The cumulative risk for rectal cancer was 10% at 50 years of age and 29% by 60 years of age.[128] The risk is considerably less if the rectum was completely free of polyps at the time of the initial procedure.

In more recent years, total colectomy with a rectal mucosectomy and an ileoanal pouch procedure has become the preferred operation for children with FAP.[155] The J-pouch is the preferred technique because of simplicity of construction and few complications.[47] Geiger and coworkers[54] reported a novel technique of a double-stapled, ileoanal, J-pouch anastomosis with excellent outcomes. An inverse relationship exists between the size of the reservoir and the frequency of defecation.[11,68,97,124] Other factors that influence frequency of defecation include inflammation, sphincter function, and small intestinal motility. Larger reservoirs allow less frequent defecation but tend to cause more frequent bouts of inflammation of the reservoir ("pouchitis"), which probably results from stool stasis. In several recent series that studied 450 patients with reservoirs, the frequency of defecation ranged from 3.3 to 7.2 with an average of 5.8 stools per day.[7,44,46,123,132,172] Large series of patients with reservoirs, however, report an average rate of pouchitis of 23% and a pelvic sepsis rate of 8%. The incidence of pouchitis in patients with FAP is much less than those receiving this operation for ulcerative colitis.

Follow-Up

Endoscopy of the upper gastrointestinal tract and sigmoidoscopy should be performed annually in all patients. Removal of polyps in the duodenum can be done by endoscopic snaring or by open duodenotomy. Size larger than 1.0 cm in diameter, rapid growth, polyp induration, severe dysplasia, or villous change suggests the need for a more aggressive intervention. Recent data have shown that 42% of adenomas of the ampulla of Vater that are larger than 1.0 cm in diameter contain a foci of cancer compared with only 13% of those smaller than 1.0 cm.[151] Sigmoidoscopy can be done easily in patients with an ileoanal pull-through. The anal canal and any short segment of rectal mucosa left behind must be carefully evaluated.

Other Treatments

Drugs and several dietary supplements have been used to treat polyps. These include vitamin C,[19,179] sulindac,[179] dietary fiber,[33] and calcium.[163,167] In a randomized, double-blind study of the use of sulindac, inhibition of both rectal and duodenal polyp growth was observed,[129] and other studies have confirmed this finding.[96,187] In a randomized double-blind, placebo-controlled study, however, standard doses of sulindac did not prevent the development of adenomas in subjects with FAP.

Gardner's Syndrome

Between 1951 and 1955, Gardner and colleagues[50-53] established the association of colonic FAP and the extracolonic findings of multiple osteomas, fibromas, and epidermoid cysts. They also demonstrated that the syndrome was inherited in an autosomal dominant pattern.[50,52] The natural history and treatment of the colonic polyps is the same as in patients with FAP. The osteomas are most frequently found in the skull and facial bones, and abnormal dentition with impaction and early tooth decay and supernumerary teeth are observed.[40] Sebaceous cysts are most commonly found on the legs, followed in frequency by the face, scalp, and arms. Lipomas and fibromas are also noted.

Periampullary cancer was thought to be more prevalent in Gardner's syndrome than in FAP, but surveillance of the duodenum in patients with FAP has shown a high incidence of duodenal abnormalities in all patients. Because detailed surveillance of all patients with familial polyposis has revealed many subtle extracolonic manifestations, the distinction between Gardner's syndrome and FAP is becoming less clear. FAP is probably an all-encompassing syndrome, in which patients manifest different signs as the condition evolves.[14]

Desmoid tumors of the abdominal wall and mesentery of the small intestine occur in approximately 20% of patients with Gardner's syndrome. These tumors also occur in patients who only have the colonic manifestations of FAP and are the leading cause of death in those who have undergone a prophylactic colectomy. Desmoid tumors are a dense, fibroplastic proliferation that may remain localized or may become widespread throughout the mesentery, the abdominal wall, and occasionally the retroperitoneum. All stages of fibrous dysplasia have been seen, including fibrosarcoma. Most desmoid tumors appear after a surgical procedure, usually within 6 to 30 months.[41] Desmoid tumors of the body wall may be observed initially, because many of them remain static or even regress over several years.[41] For those that continue to grow or reach 10 cm in diameter, complete local excision is advised when possible and is accompanied by a recurrence rate of less than 10%, which is considered satisfactory. Most intra-abdominal desmoid tumors do not become evident until they have reached a nonresectable size. Because of the difficulty in resecting intra-abdominal desmoid tumors, several drugs have been tried with varied rates of success. Such drugs include corticosteroids, antiestrogen agents (progesterone, tamoxifen, and toremifene), and nonsteroidal anti-inflammatory agents.[8,38,91,180-182,186]

Turcot's Syndrome

Turcot and colleagues[170] described two siblings who initially presented with colonic familial adenomatous polyposis and eventually died of intracranial brain tumors (glioblastoma and medulloblastoma). Turcot believed that the brain tumors were extracolonic manifestations of FAP. Ependymomas and carcinoma of the thyroid (which is usually papillary in origin)[14] have also been described in Turcot's syndrome.

REFERENCES

1. Ackerman LV: Malignant potential of polypoid lesions of the large intestine. S Afr Cancer Bull 1965;9:5.
2. Alvear DT: Localized lymphoid hyperplasia: An unusual cause of rectal bleeding. Contemp Surg 1984;25:29-33.
3. Arbeter AM, Courtney RA, Gaymor AF: Diffuse gastrointestinal polyposis associated with chronic blood loss, hypoproteinemia, and anasarca in an infant. J Pediatr 1970;76:609-611.
4. Atwell JD, Burge D, Wright D: Nodular lymphoid hyperplasia of the intestinal tract in infancy and childhood. J Pediatr Surg 1985;20:25-29.
5. Baptist SJ, Sabatini MT: Coexisting juvenile polyps and tubulovillous adenoma of colon with carcinoma in-situ: Report of a case. Hum Pathol 1985;16:1061-1063.
6. Barge J, Desvignes G, Maillard J-N, et al: Polypose colique associant des aspects juveniles et adenomataux. Gastroenterol Clin Biol 1977;1:159-164.
7. Beart RW, Metcalf AM, Dozois RR, et al: The J ileal pouch-anal anastomosis: The Mayo Clinic experience. In Dozois RR (ed): Alternatives to Conventional Ileostomy. Chicago, Year Book Medical Publishers, 1985.
8. Belliveau P, Graham AM: Mesenteric desmoid tumor in Gardner's syndrome treated by sulindac. Dis Colon Rectum 1984;27:53-54.

9. Benagiano G, Bigotti G, Buzzi M, et al: Endocrine and morphological study of a case of ovarian sex-cord tumor with annular tubules in a woman with Peutz-Jeghers syndrome. Int J Gynaecol Obstet 1988;26:441-452.
10. Berg HK, Herrera L, Petrelli NG, et al: Mixed juvenile-adenomatous polyp of the rectum in an elderly patient. J Surg Oncol 1985;29:40-42.
11. Berger A, Tiret E, Parc R, et al: Excision of the rectum with colonic J pouch anal anastomosis for adenocarcinoma of the low and mid-rectum. World J Surg 1992;16:470-477.
12. Billingham RP, Bowman HE, MacKeigan J: Solitary adenomas in juvenile patients. Dis Colon Rectum 1980;23:26-30.
13. Bodmer WF, Bailey CJ, Bodmer J, et al: Localization of the gene for familial adenomatous polyposis on chromosome 5. Nature 1987;328:614-616.
14. Brett MCA, Hershman MJ, Glazer G: Other manifestations of familial adenomatous polyposis. In Phillips RKS, Spigelman AD, Thomson JPS, et al (eds): Familial Adenomatous Polyposis and Other Polyposis Syndromes. Boston, Little, Brown, 1994.
15. Bruwer A, Bargen JA, Kierland RR: Surface pigmentation and generalized intestinal polyposis (Peutz-Jeghers syndrome). Mayo Clin Proc 1954;29:168-171.
16. Burdick D, Prior JT, Scanlon GT: Peutz-Jeghers syndrome: A clinical-pathological study of a large family with a 10-year follow-up. Cancer 1963;16:854-867.
17. Bussey HJ: Familial Polyposis Coli Family Studies: Histopathology, Differential Diagnosis, and Results of Treatment. Baltimore, Johns Hopkins University Press, 1975.
18. Bussey HJ: Gastrointestinal polyposis. Gut 1970;11:970-978.
19. Bussey HJ, DeCosse JJ, Deschner EE, et al: A randomized trial of ascorbic acid in polyposis coli. Cancer 1982;50:1434-1439.
20. Byrne WJ, Jimenez JF, Euler AR, Golladay ES: Lymphoid polyps (focal lymphoid hyperplasia) of the colon in children. Pediatrics 1982;69:598-600.
21. Capitanio MA, Kirkpatrick JA: Lymphoid hyperplasia of the colon in children: Roentgen observations. Radiology 1970;94:323-327.
22. Chargelaigue A: Des polypes du rectum. Thesis. Paris, 1859.
23. Chevrel JP, Amouroux J, Guerad JP: La polypose juvenile—apropos des 3 familial cases. Med Chir Dig 1976;5:47-54.
24. Christian CD, McCloughlin TG, Cathcart CR, Eisenberg MM: Peutz-Jeghers syndrome associated with functioning ovarian tumor. JAMA 1964;190:935-938.
25. Cobum MC, Pricolo VE, DeLuca FG, Bland KI: Malignant potential in intestinal juvenile polyposis syndromes. Ann Surg Oncol 1995;2:386-391.
26. Cochet B, Carrel J, Desbaillets L, Widgren S: Peutz-Jeghers syndrome associated with gastrointestinal carcinoma: Report of two cases in a family. Gut 1979;20:169-175.
27. Cockayne EA: Heredity in relation to cancer. Cancer Rev 1927;2:337.
28. Covisart L: Hypertrophie partielle de la muquese intestinale. Bull Soc Anat 1847;22:400.
29. Cottrell S, Bicknell D, Kaklamanis L, Bodmer WF: Molecular analysis of APC mutations in familial adenomatous polyposis and sporadic colon carcinomas. Lancet 1992;340:626-630.
30. Crabtree MD, Tomlinson IP, Hodgson SV, et al: Explaining variation in familial adenomatous polyposis: Relationships between genotype and phenotypes and evidence for modifier genes. Gut 2002;51:420-423.
31. Crabtree MD, Tomlinson IP, Talbot IC et al: Variability in the severity of colonic disease in familial adenomatous polyposis results from differences in tumor initiation rather than progression and depends relatively little on patient age. Gut 2001;49:540-543.
32. Cripps WH: Two cases of disseminated polypus of the rectum. Trans Pathol Soc Lond 1882;33:165.
33. DeCosse JJ, Miller HH, Lesser ML: Effect of wheat fiber and vitamins C and E on rectal polyps in patients with familial adenomatous polyposis. J Natl Cancer Inst 1989;81:1290-1297.
34. Domizio P, Talbot IC, Spigelman AD, et al: Upper gastrointestinal pathology in familial adenomatous polyposis: Results from a prospective study of 102 patients. J Clin Pathol 1990; 43:738-743.
35. Dorrnandy TL: Gastrointestinal polyps with mucocutaneous pigmentation (Peutz-Jeghers syndrome). N Engl J Med 1957; 236:1093, 1141-1186.
36. Dukes C: Simple tumors of the large intestine and their relation to cancer. Br J Surg 1925;13:720.
37. Dukes CE: The hereditary factor in polyposis intestine or multiple adenomata. Cancer Rev 1930;5:241.
38. Eagel BA, Zentler-Munro P, Smith IE: Mesenteric desmoid tumors in Gardner's syndrome—review of medical treatments. Postgrad Med J 1989;65:497-501.
39. Enterline HT: Polyps and cancer of the large bowel. In Morson C (ed): Current Topics in Pathology, Vol 63, Pathology of the Gastro-intestinal Tract. Berlin, Springer Verlag, 1976.
40. Fader M, Kline SM, Spatz SS, Zobrow HG: Gardner's syndrome (intestinal polyposis, osteomas, sebaceous cysts) and a new dental discovery. Oral Surg 1962;15:153-172.
41. Farmer KCR, Hawley PR, Phillips RKS: Desmoid disease. In Phillips RKS, Spigelman AD, Thomson JPS, et al (eds): Familial Adenomatous Polyposis and Other Polyposis Syndromes. Boston, Little, Brown, 1994.
42. Feinberg SM, Jagelman DG, Sarre RG, et al: Spontaneous resolution of rectal polyps in patients with familial polyposis following abdominal colectomy and ileorectal anastomosis. Dis Colon Rectum 1988;31:169-175.
43. Fieber SS, Schaefer HJ: Lymphoid hyperplasia of terminal ileum—clinical entity. Gastroenterology 1966;50:83-98.
44. Fleshman JW, Cohen Z, McLeod RS, et al: The ileal reservoir and ileoanal anastomosis procedure: Factors affecting technical and functional outcomes. Dis Colon Rectum 1988;31:10-16.
45. Foley TR, McGarrity TJ, Abt AB: Peutz-Jeghers syndrome: A clinicopathologic survey of the Harrisburg family with a 49-year follow-up. Gastroenterology 1988;95:1535-1540.
46. Fonkalsrud EW, Stelzner M, McDonald N: Experience with the endorectal ileal pull-through with lateral reservoir for ulcerative colitis and polyposis. Arch Surg 1988;123: 1053-1058.
47. Fonkalsrud EW, Thakur A, Beanes S: Ileoanal pouch procedures in children. J Pediatr Surg 2001;36:1689-1692.
48. Franken EA: Lymphoid hyperplasia of the colon. Radiology 1970;94:323-334.
49. Franzin G, Zamboni G, Dina R, et al: Juvenile and inflammatory polyps of the colon: A histological and histochemical study. Histopathology 1983;7:719-728.
50. Gardner EJ: A genetic and clinical study of intestinal polyposis: A predisposing factor for carcinoma of the colon and rectum. Am J Hum Genet 1951;3:167-176.
51. Gardner EJ: Mendelian pattern of dominant inheritance for a syndrome including intestinal polyposis, osteomas, fibromas, and sebaceous cysts in a human family group. In Gedda L (ed): Novant'anni delle Leggi Mendelione, Milan, Italy, 1995, pp 321-329.
52. Gardner EJ, Plenk HP: Hereditary pattern for multiple osteomas in a family group. Am J Hum Genet 1952;4:31-36.
53. Gardner EJ, Richards RC: Multiple cutaneous and subcutaneous lesions occurring simultaneously with hereditary polyposis and osteomatosis. Am J Hum Genet 1953;5:139-147.
54. Geiger JD, Teitelbaum DH, Hirschl RB, et al: A new operative technique for restorative proctocolectomy: The endorectal pull-thru combined with a double-stapled ileo-anal anastomosis. Surgery 2003;134:492-495.

55. Giardiello FM, Hamilton SR, Kern SE, et al: Colorectal neoplasia in juvenile polyposis or juvenile polyps. Arch Dis Child 1991;66:971-975.
56. Giardiello FM, Welsh FB, Hamilton SR, et al: Increased risk of cancer in Peutz-Jeghers syndrome. N Engl J Med 1987;316:1511-1514.
57. Goodman ZD, Yardley JH, Milligan FD: Pathogenesis of colonic polyps in multiple juvenile polyposis: Report of a case associated with gastric polyps and carcinoma of the rectum. Cancer 1979;43:1906-1913.
58. Gowin TS: Polyps of colon and rectum in children. South Med J 1961;54:526-529.
59. Goyette MC, Cho K, Fasching CL, et al: Progression of colorectal cancer is associated with multiple tumor suppressor gene defects but inhibition of tumorigenicity is accomplished by correction of any single defect via chromosome transfer. Mol Cell Biol 1992;12:1387-1395.
60. Grigioni WF, Alampi G, Martinelli G, Piccaluga A: Atypical juvenile polyposis. Histopathology 1981;5:361-376.
61. Groden J, Thliveris A, Samowitz W, et al: Identification and characterization of the familial adenomatous polyposis coli gene. Cell 1991;66:589-600.
62. Grosfeld JL, West KW: Generalized juvenile polyposis coli: Clinical management based on long-term observations. Arch Surg 1986;121:530-534.
63. Grotsky HW, Rickert RR, Smith WD, Newsome JF: Familial juvenile polyposis coli. Gastroenterology 1982;82:494-501.
64. Gupta SK, Fitzgerald JF, Croffie JM, et al: Experience with juvenile polyps in North American children: The need for pancolonoscopy. Am J Gastroenterol 2001;96: 1695-1697.
65. Haggitt RC, Pitcock JA: Familial juvenile polyposis of the colon. Cancer 1970;26:1232-1238.
66. Handford H: Disseminated polypi of the large intestine becoming malignant; strictures (malignant adenoma) of the rectum and of the splenic flexure of the colon; secondary growths of the liver. Trans Pathol Soc Lond 1890;41: 133-137.
67. Hemminki A, Markie D, Tomlinson I, et al: A serine/threonine kinase gene defective in Peutz-Jeghers syndrome. Nature 1998;391:184-187.
68. Heppell J, Kelly KA, Phillips SF: Physiologic aspects of continence after colectomy, mucosal proctocolectomy, and endorectal ileoanal anastomosis. Ann Surg 1982;195: 435-443.
69. Herrera L, Kakati S, Gibas L, et al: A brief clinical report: Gardner syndrome in a man with an interstitial deletion of 5q. Am J Med Genet 1986;25:473-476.
70. Herruzo AJ, Redondo E, Perez de Avila I, et al: Ovarian sex-cord tumour with annular tubules and Peutz-Jeghers syndrome. Eur J Gynaecol Oncol 1990;11:141-144.
71. Hockey KA, Mulcahy MT, Montgomery P, Levitt S: Deletion of chromosome 5q and familial adenomatous polyposis. J Med Genet 1989;26:61-62.
72. Hodgson SV, Spigelman AD: Genetics. In Phillips RKS, Thomson JPS, et al (eds): Familial Adenomatous Polyposis and Other Polyposis Syndromes. Boston, Little, Brown, 1994.
73. Hoffenberg EJ, Sauaia A, Maltzanos T, et al: Symptomatic colonic polyps in childhood: Not so benign. J Pediatr Gastroenterol Nutr 1999;28:175-181.
74. Hood AB, Krush AJ: Clinical and dermatologic aspects of the hereditary intestinal polyposes. Dis Colon Rectum 1983;26:546-548.
75. Horrileno E, Eckert C, Ackerman L: Polyps of the rectum and colon in children. Cancer 1957;10:1210-1220.
76. Hsu SD, Zaharopoulos M, May JT, Costanzi JJ: Peutz-Jeghers syndrome with intestinal carcinoma: Report of the association in one family. Cancer 1979;44:1527-1532.
77. Huer W, Beveridge I, Domizio P, et al: Clinical management and genetics of gastrointestinal polyps in children. J Pediatr Gastroenterol Nutr 2000;31:469-479.
78. Humphries AL, Shepherd MH, Peters HJ: Peutz-Jeghers syndrome with colonic adenocarcinoma and ovarian tumor. JAMA 1966;197:138-140.
79. Jarvinen H, Fransilla KO: Familial juvenile polyposis coli: Increased risk of colorectal cancer. Gut 1984;25:792-800.
80. Jarvinen HJ, Peltokallio P, Landtman M, Wolf J: Gardner's stigma in patients with familial adenomatosis coli. Br J Surg 1982;69:718.
81. Jass JR: Juvenile polyposis. In Phillips RKS, et al (eds): Familial Adenomatous Polyposis and Other Polyposis Syndromes. Boston, Little, Brown, 1994.
82. Jass JR: The large intestine: Epithelial polyps. In Morson BC (ed): Systemic Pathology, Vol 3, Alimentary Tract. London, Churchill Livingstone, 1987.
83. Jass JR, Williams CB, Bussey HJ, Morson BC: Juvenile polyposis: A precancerous condition. Histopathology 1988;13: 619-630.
84. Jeghers H: Pigmentation of the skin. N Engl J Med 1944; 231:122.
85. Jeghers H, McCusick VA, Katz KH: Generalized intestinal polyposis and melanin spots of the oral mucosa, lips, and digits: A syndrome of diagnostic significance. N Engl J Med 1949;241:1031-1036.
86. Jenne DE, Reimann H, Nezu J, et al: Peutz-Jeghers syndrome is caused by mutations in a novel serine threonine kinase. Nat Genet 1998;18:38-43.
87. Jones MA, Herbert JC, Trainer TD: Juvenile polyp with intramucosal carcinoma. Arch Pathol Lab Med 1987; 111:200-201.
88. Joslyn G, Carlson M, Thliveris A, et al: Identification of genetic mutations and three new genes at the familial polyposis locus. Cell 1991;66:601-613.
89. Kaschula ROC: Mixed juvenile, adenomatous and intermediate polyposis coli: Report of a case. Dis Colon Rectum 1971;14:368-374.
90. Kennedy RLJ: Polyps of rectum and colon in infants and in children. Am J Dis Child 1941;62:481.
91. Kinzbrunner B, Ritter S, Domingo J, Rosenthal CJ: Remission of rapidly growing desmoid tumors after tamoxifen therapy. Cancer 1983;52:2201-2204.
92. Kinzler KW, Nilbert NC, Su LK, et al: Identification of FAP locus gene from chromosome 5q 21. Science 1991;253: 661-665.
93. Kinzler KW, Nilbert NC, Vogelstein B, et al: Identification of a gene located at chromosome 5q 21 that is mutated in colorectal cancers. Science 1991;251:1366-1370.
94. Konishi F, Wyse NE, Muto T, et al: Peutz-Jeghers polyposis associated with carcinoma of the digestive organs: Report of three cases and review of the literature. Dis Colon Rectum 1987;30:790-799.
95. Kurugoglu S, Aksoy H, Kantarci F, et al: Radiological work-up in Peutz-Jeghers syndrome. Pediatr Radiol 2003;33:766-771.
96. Labayle D, Fischer D, Vielh P, et al: Sulindac causes regression of rectal polyps in familial adenomatous polyposis. Gastroenterology 1991;101:635-639.
97. Lazorthes F, Fages P, Chiotassol P, et al: Resection of the rectum with construction of colonic reservoir and coloanal anastomosis for carcinoma of the rectum. Br J Surg 1986; 73:136-138.
98. LeFevre HWJ, Jacques TF: Multiple polyposis in an infant of four months. Am J Surg 1951;81:90.
99. Leppert M, Burt R, Hughes JP, et al: Genetic analysis of an inherited predisposition to colon cancer in a family with a variable number of adenomatous polyps. N Engl J Med 1990;332:904-908.

100. Leppert M, Dobbs M, Scambler P, et al: The gene for familial polyposis maps to the long arm of chromosome 5. Science 1987;238:1411-1413.
101. Lindegaard-Madsen E, Morck-Hultberg B: Metastasizing Sertoli cell tumors of the testis: A report of two cases and a review of the literature [letter]. Acta Oncol 1990;129: 946-949.
102. Lipper S, Kahn LB, Sandler RS, Varma V: Multiple juvenile polyposis: A study of the pathogenesis of juvenile polyps and their relationship to colonic adenomas. Hum Pathol 1981;12:804-813.
103. Liu T-H, Chen MC, Tseng HC, et al: Malignant change of juvenile polyp of colon: A case report. Chin Med J 1978; 4:434-439.
104. Lockhart-Mummery JP: Cancer and heredity. Lancet 1925; 1:427-429.
105. Lockhart-Mummery JP, Dukes CE: Familial adenomatosis of the colon and rectum: Its relationship to cancer. Lancet 1939;2:586-589.
106. Louw JH: Polypoid lesions of the large bowel in children with particular reference to benign lymphoid polyposis. J Pediatr Surg 1968;3:195-209.
107. Lucidarme P, Dribda M, elKhoury S, et al: Ovarian tumour and Peutz-Jeghers syndrome: A case report. Gastroenterol Clin Biol 1990;14:1015-1018.
108. Matuchansky C, Babin P, Coutrot S, et al: Peutz-Jeghers syndrome with metastasizing carcinoma arising from a jejunal hamartoma. Gastroenterology 1979;77:1311-1315.
109. McColl I, Bussey HJ, Veale AM, Morson BC: Juvenile polyposis coli. Proc R Soc Med 1964;57:896-897.
110. McGarrity TJ, Kulin HE, Zaino RJ: Peutz-Jeghers syndrome. Am J Gastroenterol 2000;95:596-604.
111. Meera Khan P, Tops CM, vd Broek M, et al: Close linkage of a polymorphic marker (DSS37) to familial polyposis (FAP) and confirmation of FAP localization on chromosome 5q21-q22. Hum Genet 1988;79:183-185.
112. Meldrum RJ, Croaks R, Spigelmen AD, et al: Familial adenomatous polyposis: More evidence for disease diversity and genetic heterogeneity. Gut 2001;48:508-514.
113. Mestre JR: The changing pattern of juvenile polyps. Am J Gastroenterol 1986;81:312-314.
114. Mills SE, Fechner RE: Unusual adenomatous polyps in juvenile polyposis coli. Am J Surg Pathol 1982;6:177-183.
115. Miyoshi Y, Ando H, Nagase H, et al: Germ-line mutations of the *APC* gene in 53 familial adenomatous polyposis patients. Proc Natl Acad Sci U S A 1992;89:4452-4456.
116. Morson BC: Some peculiarities in the histology of intestinal polyps. Dis Colon Rectum 1962;5:337-344.
117. Morson BC, Dawson IMP: Developmental abnormalities. In Gastrointestinal Pathology, 2nd ed. Oxford, Blackwell, 1979.
118. Morson BC, Jass JR: Histological classification of precancerous lesions of the gastrointestinal tract. In Gastrointestinal Pathology, 2nd ed. Oxford, Blackwell, 1979.
119. Murday V, Slack J: Inherited disorders associated with colorectal cancer. Cancer Surveys 1989;8:138-157.
120. Muto T, Bussey HJR, Morson BCM: The evolution of cancer of the colon and rectum. Cancer 1975;36:2251-2270.
121. Nakamura S, Kino I: Morphogenesis of minute adenomas in familial polyposis coli. J Natl Cancer Inst 1984;3:41-49.
122. Nelson EW, Rodgers BM, Zawatsky L: Endoscopic appearance of auto amputated polyps in juvenile polyposis coli. J Pediatr Surg 1977;12:773-776.
123. Nicholls RJ, Lubowski DZ: Restorative proctocolectomy: The four loop (W) reservoir. Br J Surg 1987;74:564-566.
124. Nicholls RJ, Pezim ME: Restorative proctocolectomy with ileal reservoir for ulcerative colitis and familial adenomatous polyposis: A comparison of three reservoir designs. Br J Surg 1985;72:470-474.
125. Nicholls RJ, Springall RG, Gallagher P: Regression of rectal adenomas after colectomy and ileorectal anastomosis for familial adenomatous polyposis. BMJ 1988;296: 1707-1708.
126. Niimi K, Tomoda H, Furusawa M, et al: Peutz-Jeghers syndrome associated with adenocarcinoma of the cecum and focal carcinomas in hamartomatous polyps of the colon: A case report. Jpn J Surg 1991;21:220-223.
127. Nishisho I, Nakamura Y, Miyoshi Y, et al: Mutations of chromosome 5q21 genes in FAP and colorectal cancer patients. Science 1991;253:665-669.
128. Nugent KP, Northover J: Total colectomy and ileorectal anastomosis. In Phillips RKS, Spigelman AD, Thomson JPS, et al (eds): Familial Adenomatous Polyposis and Other Polypoid Syndromes. Boston, Little, Brown, 1994.
129. Nugent KP, Farmer KC, Spigelman AD, et al: Randomized controlled trial of the effect of sulindac on duodenal and rectal polyposis and cell proliferation in familial adenomatous polyposis. Br J Surg 1993;80:1618-1619.
130. Nugent KP, Talbot IC, Hodgson SV, Phillips RK: Solitary juvenile polyps: Not a marker for subsequent malignancy. Gastroenterology 1993;105:698-700.
131. O'Riordain DS, O'Dwyer PJ, Cullen AF, et al: Familial juvenile polyposis coli and colorectal cancer. Cancer 1991;68:889-892.
132. Oresland T, Fasth S, Nordgren S, Hulten L: The clinical and functional outcome after restorative proctocolectomy: A prospective study in 100 patients. Int J Colorect Dis 1989;4:50-56.
133. Patel VK, Awen CF: Benign lymphoid polyposis of ileum: Three cases and a review of the literature. Can J Surg 1971;14:402-405.
134. Pesta J, Orlowska J: Small intestine carcinoma in the Peutz-Jeghers syndrome. Materia Med Polona 1989;21:43-47.
135. Peutz JLA: On a very remarkable case of familial polyposis of the mucous membrane of the intestinal tract and nasopharynx accompanied by peculiar pigmentations of the skin and mucous membrane. Ned Tijdschr Geneesk 1921;10:136-146.
136. Phillips RKS, Spigelman AD: Peutz-Jeghers syndrome. In Phillips RKS, Spigelman AD, Thomson JPS, et al (eds): Familial Adenomatous Polyposis and Other Polypoid Syndromes. Boston, Little, Brown, 1994.
137. Powell SM, Zilz SN, Beazer-Barclay Y, et al: APC mutations occur early during colorectal carcinogenesis. Nature 1992;359:235-237.
138. Proppe KH, Scully RE: Large-cell calcifying Sertoli cell tumor of the testis. Am J Clin Pathol 1980;74:607-619.
139. Rabin ER, Patel T, Chen FH, et al: Juvenile colonic polyposis coli with villous adenoma and retroperitoneal fibrosis: Report of a case. Dis Colon Rectum 1979;22:63-67.
140. Ravitch MM: Polypoid adenomatosis of the entire gastrointestinal tract. Ann Surg 1948;128:283.
141. Reed TE, Neal JV: A genetic study of multiple polyposis of the colon. Am J Hum Genet 1955;7:236-263.
142. Restrepo C, Moreno J, Duque E, et al: Juvenile colonic polyposis in Colombia. Dis Colon Rectum 1978;21: 600-612.
143. Roth SI, Helwig EB: Juvenile polyps of the colon and rectum. Cancer 1963;16:468-479.
144. Rozen P, Baratz M: Familial juvenile polyposis with associated colon cancer. Cancer 1982;49:1500-1503.
145. Ruymann FB: Juvenile polyps with cachexia. Gastroenterology 1969;57:431-438.
146. Sachatello CR: Gastrointestinal polypoid diseases. J Ky Med Assoc 1972;70:540-544.
147. Sachatello CR, Hahn IS, Carrington CB: Juvenile gastrointestinal polyposis in a female infant: Report of a case and

review of the literature of a recently recognized syndrome. Surgery 1974;75:107-113.
148. Scharf GM, Becker JHR, Laage NJ: Juvenile gastrointestinal polyposis or the infantile Cronkite-Canada syndrome. J Pediatr Surg 1986;21:953-954.
149. Schilla FW: Carcinoma in a rectal polyp. Am J Surg Pathol 1954;4:434-439.
150. Scully RE: Sex-cord tumor with annular tubules: A distinctive ovarian tumor of the Peutz- Jeghers syndrome. Cancer 1970;25:1107-1121.
151. Sellner F: Investigations on the significance of the adenoma-carcinoma sequence in the small bowel. Cancer 1990; 66:702-715.
152. Settaf A, Mansori F, Bargach C, et al: Peutz-Jeghers syndrome with carcinomatous degeneration of a duodenal hamartomatous polyp. Ann Gastroenterol Hepatol 1990;26:285-288.
153. Sharma S, Seam RK, Kapoor HL: Malignant Sertoli cell tumor of the testis in a child. J Surg Oncol 1990;44:129-131.
154. Shibata HR, Phillips MJ: Peutz-Jeghers syndrome with jejunal and colonic adenocarcinomas. Can Med Assoc 1970;103:285-287.
155. Shilyansky J, Lelli JL, Drongowski RA, Coran AG: The efficacy of the straight endorectal pull-through in the management of familial adenomatous polyposis: A 16 year experience. J Pediatr Surg 1997;32:1139-1143.
156. Smilow PC, Pryor CA, Swinton NW: Juvenile polyposis coli: A report of three patients in three generations. Dis Colon Rectum 1966;9:248-254.
157. Soper RT: Gastrointestinal neoplasms. In Ashcraft KW, Holder TM (eds): Pediatric Surgery. Philadelphia, WB Saunders, 1993.
158. Soper RT: Intestinal polyps. In Holder T, Ashcraft K (eds): Pediatric Surgery, 2nd ed, Philadelphia, WB Saunders, 1980.
159. Spigelman AD, Murday V, Phillips RKS: Cancer and the Peutz-Jeghers syndrome. Gut 1989;30:1588-1590.
160. Spigelman AD, Williams CB, Talbot IC, et al: Upper gastrointestinal cancer in patients with familial adenomatous polyposis. Lancet 1989;2:783-785.
161. Spigelman AD, Farmer KC, James M, et al: Tumors of the liver, bile ducts, pancreas, and duodenum in a single patient with familial adenomatous polyposis. Br J Surg 1991;78:979-980.
162. Stemper TJ, Kent TH, Summers RW: Juvenile polyposis and gastrointestinal carcinoma. Ann Intern Med 1975;83: 639-646.
163. Stern HS, Gregoire RC, Kashtan H, et al: Long-term effects of dietary calcium on risk markers for colon cancer in patients with familial polyposis. Gut 1990;108:528-533.
164. Su LK, Kinzler KW, Vogelstein B, et al: Multiple intestinal neoplasia caused by a mutation in the murine homolog of the *APC* gene. Science 1992;256:668-670.
165. Talbot IC: Pathology. In Phillips RKS, Spigelman AD, Thomson JPS, et al (eds): Familial Adenomatous Polyposis and other Polypoid Syndromes. Boston, Little, Brown, 1994.
166. Tanaka K, Oshimura M, Kikuchi R, et al: Suppression of tumorigenicity in human colon carcinoma cells by introduction of normal chromosome 5 or 18. Nature 1991;349: 340-342.
167. Thomas MG, Thomson IPS, Williamson RCN: Oral calcium inhibits rectal epithelial proliferation in familial adenomatous polyposis. Br J Surg 1993;80:499-501.
168. Thomson JPS: Familial adenomatous polyposis: The large bowel. Ann R Coll Surg Engl 1990;72:177-180.
169. Tovar JA, Eizaguirre AA, Jimenez J: Peutz-Jeghers syndrome in children: Report of two cases and review of the literature. J Pediatr Surg 1983;18:1-6.
170. Turcot J, Despres J-P, St. Pierre F: Malignant tumors of the central nervous system associated with familial polyposis of the colon: Report of two cases. Dis Colon Rectum 1959;2:465-468.
171. Utsunomiya J, Gocho H, Miyanaga T, et al: Peutz-Jeghers syndrome: Its natural course and management. Johns Hopkins Med J 1975;136:71-82.
172. Utsunomiya J, Iwama T: The J ileal pouch-anal anastomosis: The Japanese experience. In Dozois RR (ed): Alternatives to Conventional Ileostomy. Chicago, Year Book Medical Publishers, 1985.
173. Utsunomiya J, Maki T, Iwama T, et al: Gastric lesion of familial polyposis coli. Cancer 1974;34:745-754.
174. Utsunomiya J, et al: Phenotypic expressions of Japanese patients with familial adenomatous polyposis. In Herrera L (ed): Familial Adenomatous Polyposis. New York, Alan R. Liss, 1990.
175. Veale AM, McColl I, Bussey HJ, Morson BC: Juvenile polyposis coli. J Med Genet 1966;3:5-16.
176. Velcek FT, Coopersmith IS, Chen CK, et al: Familial juvenile adenomatous polyposis. J Pediatr Surg 1976;11:781-787.
177. Verse M: Ueber die Histogenese der Schleirnhautcarcinome. Verh Dtsch Ges Pathol 1908;2:95.
178. Virchow RL: Die Frankhaften Geschwulste. Berlin, A. Hirshwald, 1863, p 243.
179. Waddell WR, Ganser GF, Cerise EJ, Loughry RW: Sulindac for polyposis of the colon. Am J Surg 1989;57:175-179.
180. Waddell WR, Gerner RE: Indomethacin and ascorbic acid inhibit desmoid tumors. J Surg Oncol 1980;5:85-90.
181. Waddell WR, Gerner RE, Reich MP: Nonsteroidal anti-inflammatory drugs and tamoxifen for desmoid tumors and carcinoma of the stomach. J Surg Oncol 1983;2:197-211.
182. Waddell WR, Kirsch WM: Testolactone, sulindac, warfarin, and vitamin K for unresectable desmoid tumors. Am J Surg 1991;61:416-421.
183. Watne AL: The syndromes of intestinal polyposis. Curr Probl Surg 1987;24:269-340.
184. Watne AL: In Syndromes of Polyposis Coli and Cancer. Chicago, Year Book Medical Publishers, 1982.
185. Williams CB: Imaging: Endoscopy. In Phillips RKS, Spigelman AD, Thomson JPS, et al (eds): Familial Adenomatous Polyposis and Other Polypoid Syndromes. Boston, Little, Brown, 1994.
186. Wilson AJ, Baum M, Singh L, Kangas L: Anti-estrogen therapy of pure mesenchymal tumor. Lancet 1987;1:508.
187. Winde G, Gumbinger HG, Osswald H, et al: The NSAID sulindac reverses rectal adenomas in colectomized patients with familial adenomatous polyposis: Clinical results of a dose-finding study on rectal sulindac administration. Int J Colorect Dis 1993;8:13-17.
188. Woodward JJ: Pseudo-polypi of the colon: An anomalous result of follicular ulceration. Am J Med Sci 1881;81:142-155.
189. Young RH, Scul ly RE: Mucinous ovarian tumors associated with mucinous adenocarcinomas of the cervix: A clinicopathological analysis of 16 cases. Int J Gynecol Pathol 1988;7:99-111.
190. Young RH, Welch WR, Dickersin GR, Scully RE: Ovarian sex-cord tumor with annular tubules: Review of 74 cases including 27 with Peutz-Jeghers syndrome and four with adenoma malignum of the cervix. Cancer 1982;50: 1384-1402.

Chapter 92

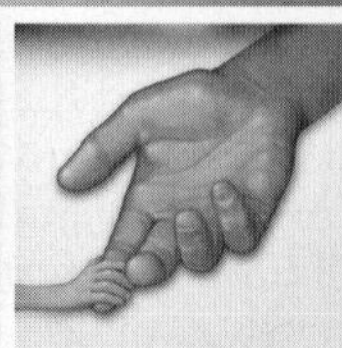

Necrotizing Enterocolitis

Stephen S. Kim and Craig T. Albanese

Necrotizing enterocolitis (NEC) is a leading cause of morbidity and mortality in neonatal intensive care units (NICUs) around the world. Advances in perinatal and neonatal care have contributed to a growing population of premature infants at risk for NEC. It is now the most common newborn surgical emergency, with a mortality rate that far exceeds that of any other gastrointestinal (GI) condition requiring surgical intervention. Despite extensive research, the precise cause and pathogenesis remain elusive.

HISTORY

In 1888, Paltauf[223] described five patients who died of overwhelming peritonitis, the cause being suggestive of NEC in three of them. Despite this report, many credit Generisch[88] with publishing the first report of NEC in 1891, but on careful review of his description of the findings, it almost certainly was a case of meconium peritonitis rather than NEC.

In 1939, Thelander[289] reported 16 cases of perforation of the stomach, 30 of the duodenum, and 39 of the small and large intestines. Many of the patients who had intestinal perforations probably had NEC. The first report of a successfully treated infant with a localized ileal perforation as a result of NEC is attributed to Agerty et al.[2] in 1943. In 1953, Schmid and Quaiser[264] first used the term *necrotizing enterocolitis.* In 1959, Rossier and colleagues[249] described 15 infants, 14 of whom died of "ulcerative-necrotic enterocolitis of the premature."

In 1964, Berdon et al.[22] reported the clinical and radiographic findings of 21 patients with NEC. A year later, Mizrahi et al.[195] reported 18 cases of NEC in premature infants. The incidence of NEC in the New York Babies' Hospital nursery between 1953 and 1963 was 0.9%, but the disease caused 2.3% of all nursery deaths. In 1975, Santulli et al.[257] hypothesized that development of the disease had three essential components: injury to the intestinal mucosa, the presence of bacteria, and the availability of a metabolic substrate.

During the 1960s, treatment of NEC was early surgery. By 1970 it was recognized that with early diagnosis, most patients could be managed without surgery. In 1978, Bell et al.[21] published a severity-based classification scheme that was helpful in selecting therapy and allowing comparison of outcomes. In 1979, the International Classification of Diseases established a code for death from NEC, thereby allowing more precise epidemiologic and outcome analyses.

INCIDENCE

The true incidence of NEC is unknown. It varies significantly within the United States and worldwide. NEC accounts for 1% to 7% of all NICU admissions in the United States, or 1 to 3 cases per 1000 live births.[100,102,131,152] In infants born with very low birth weight (VLBW, <1500 g), the disease occurs in approximately 10% to 12%, but ranges between 2% and 22%, depending on the center of inquiry.[44,51,131,174,291] Worldwide, the incidence of NEC in VLBW infants varies from 1% to 2% in Japan, 7% in Austria, 10% in Greece, 14% in Argentina, and 28% in Hong Kong.[44,76,101,131,271]

Several confounding factors may account for this variability, including the number and survival of low-birth-weight infants, the source of patient referrals (in- or outborn), and the diagnostic criteria used. A relatively large multicenter survey of VLBW infants noted an incidence of 10.1% for definite NEC and 17.2% for suspected NEC, although there was considerable intercenter variability.[291] In another study, the incidence of definite NEC versus suspected NEC was 8.6% and 18.6%, respectively.[152] In a report by Pokorny et al.[234] of more than 18,000 in-born neonates, including 1735 low-birth-weight infants, the incidence of NEC was 3 per 1000 live births. This and many other series may be underestimating the frequency of NEC because the incidence is often defined as the total number of cases of NEC divided by the total number of patients admitted to the NICU. Thus, these figures may include many premature infants who die within the first 3 days of life of cardiorespiratory disease and do not live long enough for NEC to develop. One study that excluded early neonatal deaths and included only infants who had been fed reported an incidence of 15%.[146]

Most recent reports demonstrate a strong association between NEC and prematurity, with preterm babies of low gestational age and birth weight being at particular risk. It is estimated that only 7% to 13% of all NEC cases occur in full-term infants.[27,221,311] The advent of early surfactant therapy and improved methods of mechanical ventilation has resulted in significant improvement in the survival of low- and extremely low-birth-weight infants.[51,113] As a result, an increasing population of tiny infants is now at risk for the development of NEC. In the future, NEC may surpass respiratory distress syndrome as the principal cause of death in premature infants.[141]

EPIDEMIOLOGY AND PATHOGENESIS

Epidemiology

Age and Maturity

NEC is predominantly a disease of premature low-birth-weight infants rather than those who are small for gestational age. Kliegman and Fanaroff[142] reported that the mean gestational age of 123 patients with NEC was 31 weeks (average birth weight, 1460 g). Only 7.3% of the patients were full-term and 10.5% were small for gestational age. Infants with extremely low birth weight (<1000 g) and those 28 weeks' gestational age or less are at greatest risk.[115,254] In a large multicenter prospective study involving 4438 infants weighing between 501 and 1500 g, Lemons et al.[174] demonstrated an inverse relationship between the incidence of NEC and birth weight. The incidence of NEC was highest in infants weighing between 501 and 750 g (14%) and declined with increasing weight: 751 to 1000 g (9%), 1001 to 1250 g (5%), 1251 to 1500 g (3%).

Tesdale et al.[288] reported an inverse relationship between the age at onset of NEC and gestational age. Infants in whom NEC developed in the first week of life were more mature (average gestational age, 36.1 weeks) than those in whom NEC developed after 1 week of age (average gestational age, 33.4 weeks). Complications were more common and the mortality rate was higher in patients with early-onset disease. Ostlie et al.[221] demonstrated a similar inverse relationship between gestational age and the onset of NEC. Full-term (≥38 weeks) infants had a significantly earlier onset of NEC (4.9 days) than did preterm (<38 weeks) infants (13 days). Similarly, Martinez-Tallo et al.[187] also demonstrated an earlier onset of NEC (3.3 days) in infants with a birth weight greater than 2000 g.

Wilson et al.[310] calculated the birth weight–specific, weekly attack rate in patients with NEC. The risk period for NEC decreased as birth weight increased. They found a consistent pattern of sharply declining risk with attainment of age equivalent to 35 to 36 weeks' gestation. It was suggested that functional maturation of the GI tract may play a principal role in determining the risk for NEC. The preterm GI tract has decreased gastric acid production and lower levels of protective mucus,[19,213] increased mucosal permeability,[292] and an absence of normal coordinated peristaltic activity until around 34 to 35 weeks' gestation.[19,213]

Feedings

NEC develops in approximately 90% of infants after being fed, whereas it develops in only 10% or less before feedings are initiated.[144,147,157,185,281] In 1978, Brown and Sweet[33] proposed that aggressive feeding protocols contributed to the pathogenesis of NEC. They found that before they changed to a slowly progressive feeding regimen in July 1974, 14 cases of NEC occurred in 1745 low-birth-weight infants. From July 1974 to June 1978, when a cautious approach to feeding was practiced, only 1 case developed in 932 low-birth-weight infants and 2557 total patients admitted to the NICU. In a longitudinal cohort study reviewing the incidence of NEC for a 3-year period before and after implementing a "standardized feeding schedule" for infants weighing between 1250 and 2500 g and less than 35 weeks' gestation, Kamitsuka et al.[132] reported an 84% reduction in the risk for NEC. Other studies have also suggested an association between an increase in the incidence of NEC and advancement of formula feedings at rates greater than 20 kcal/kg/day.[9,165,291,313] Despite these reports, however, randomized trials have failed to demonstrate any difference in the incidence of NEC related to fast versus slow, early versus delayed, or continuous versus intermittent bolus feedings.[136,137,238,243] In a randomized trial involving 185 VLBW infants in which slow (15-mL/kg/day increments; 10-day schedule to full feeding) and fast (35-mL/kg/day increments; 5-day schedule to full feeding) feeding advancements were compared, Rayyis et al.[243] demonstrated no significant difference in the incidence of NEC (13% versus 9%), perforation (4% versus 2%), and mortality (2% versus 3%) in both groups. In a review of randomized trials comparing continuous versus intermittent bolus tube feeding for premature infants weighing less than 1500 g, Premji and Chessell[238] could find no significant differences in the incidence of NEC between the two groups.

In a recent randomized trial investigating the incidence of NEC in VLBW infants assigned to receive either minimal-volume feeding (20 mL/kg/day) for 10 days before advancing to full-volume feeding or a standard feeding advancement protocol (starting at 20 mL/kg and increasing by 20 mL/kg/day to full-volume feeding), Berseth et al.[24] reported a significantly lower incidence of NEC in the minimal-volume group than in the standard group (1.4% versus 10%). The difference in the risk for NEC was so great that the study was closed early. The prolonged use of "trophic feeding" volumes is thought to trigger maturation of GI function. This study reinforces previous studies that gut stimulation protocols are beneficial to VLBW infants[71] and that initiation of a minimal-volume feeding protocol for 7 to 10 days followed by modest advancement of feeding may greatly reduce the incidence of NEC.[258]

Hyperosmolar Formulas and Medications

The osmolarity and composition of enteral feedings have also been associated with an increase in the incidence of NEC. Formulas with high osmolarity have been shown to increase the incidence of NEC in infants and cause intestinal mucosal injury in animal models. De Lemos et al.[65] demonstrated intestinal lesions resembling NEC in newborn goats that were fed a hyperosmolar formula. Book et al.[29] prospectively studied 16 preterm infants fed either an elemental (650 mOsm/kg of body weight) or a milk (350 mOsm/kg) formula and found that NEC developed in 85% of the infants fed the elemental diet and 25% of the infants fed the milk formula. Grantmyre and associates[96] described one patient in whom fatal NEC developed after a Renografin-76 (osmolality, 1900 mOsm/kg) enema was administered for the treatment of meconium ileus.

Many oral medications, such as vitamin preparations, use hyperosmolar vehicles that could potentially lead to mucosal injury in the bowel. Willis et al.[309] reported a significantly higher incidence of NEC in infants fed undiluted calcium lactate (osmolality, 1700 mOsm/kg) than in infants fed no calcium or those fed calcium lactate diluted with water or formula. White and Harkavy[306] reported that many oral medications commonly used in the intensive care nursery have very high osmolality, even when mixed with formula, and that it is usually the vehicle rather than the medication itself that is responsible for the high osmolality. Finer et al.[82] reported a 13.4% incidence of NEC in preterm infants receiving an oral hyperosmolar vitamin E preparation as compared with a 5.7% incidence in infants who were given a parenteral preparation of vitamin E. The proposed mechanism of injury from the introduction of hyperosmolar solution into the GI tract, though not proved clinically, has been a reduction in intestinal mucosal blood flow secondary to rapid fluid shifts from the intravascular space into the bowel lumen.[108,252,255] How relevant this mechanism of intestinal injury in the development of NEC is in the clinical setting is unknown.

Pharmacologic Agents

Xanthine derivatives (e.g., theophylline, aminophylline), which are known to slow intestinal motility and produce oxygen free radicals during their metabolism to uric acid, have been reported to be associated with NEC. In 1980, Williams[307] and Robinson et al.[248] described three patients in whom NEC developed after receiving oral and intravenous xanthines for apnea of prematurity. In animal experiments, Cronin et al.[59] demonstrated alterations in GI blood flow and oxygen delivery after aminophylline administration in newborn lambs that may result in depletion of the GI oxygen reserve and mucosal injury. Despite these earlier reports, subsequent results in large patient studies have failed to confirm this association.[63,112]

Administration of large doses of vitamin E to premature infants has been linked to an increase in NEC.[124] Vitamin E is given to reduce the incidence of adverse sequelae of retinopathy in premature infants and has been shown to interfere with intracellular killing of bacteria by leukocytes. The increased incidence of NEC, however, has been noted only after oral administration of hyperosmolar preparations and not after intramuscular administration.[82]

Indomethacin blocks prostaglandin synthetase and causes vasoconstriction. This effect has been exploited to close the patent ductus arteriosus (PDA) in premature infants with congestive heart failure. GI perforation and NEC have been noted in low-birth-weight infants treated with high-dose indomethacin.[7,98,162] It has been postulated that indomethacin increases mesenteric vascular resistance and reduces mesenteric blood flow by 16% to 20%.[99] Norton et al.[215] demonstrated that the use of indomethacin as a tocolytic agent was associated with an increased incidence of NEC in babies delivered before 30 weeks' gestational age (mean age at delivery, 27.6 weeks); however, indomethacin did not increase the incidence of NEC in babies born after 32 weeks' gestation. In a retrospective study involving 252 premature infants with symptomatic PDA treated with intravenous indomethacin, Grosfeld et al.[97] found a 35% incidence of NEC. In contrast, two randomized controlled trials involving more than 500 low-birth-weight premature infants receiving early low-dose indomethacin versus placebo for closure of PDA demonstrated no difference in the subsequent incidence of NEC.[89,183] Indomethacin by itself may not be enough to cause NEC; however, in the setting of hypoxia, heart failure, or sepsis, its adverse GI effects contribute to the development of NEC in VLBW infants.[156]

Cocaine

Cocaine has very potent vasoconstrictive properties, and with the dramatic increase in its abuse since the 1980s, it has been implicated as a risk factor for NEC.[235,265,286] In addition to its vasoconstrictive effects, cocaine has also been shown to block the reuptake of catecholamines at nerve terminals, thereby resulting in increased circulating levels of catecholamines in pregnant women.[312] Prenatal cocaine exposure has been associated with many adverse perinatal events, including stillbirths, abruptio placentae, intrauterine growth retardation, preterm delivery, sudden infant death syndrome, and maternal hypertension.[16,70,125] The proposed mechanism involves increased uterine vascular resistance, decreased uterine blood flow, and chronic placental insufficiency with accompanying fetal hypoxemia, hypertension, and tachycardia.[37,110,202]

Despite these concerns, there have been few studies investigating the vascular and inflammatory effects of cocaine on the neonatal GI tract. Studies in pregnant rats exposed to cocaine demonstrated severe inflammatory changes in the uterus, placenta, and GI tract of the embryos.[37] Newborn piglets receiving high doses of cocaine had a prolonged increase in mesenteric vascular resistance and a decrease in mesenteric blood flow by Doppler evaluation.[110] In a study using radiolabeling techniques in which pregnant and nonpregnant rats were compared, exposure to cocaine resulted in a significant dose-dependent decrease in perfusion of the uterus, placenta, and fetus in the pregnant group but no change in perfusion of the uterus in the nonpregnant animals.[138]

In retrospective studies involving infants with confirmed NEC, several differences have been reported between infants with and without prenatal exposure to cocaine. Czyrko et al.[61] noted a significantly greater need for surgical intervention (72.7% versus 38%), higher incidence of massive intestinal gangrene (54% versus 12%), and higher mortality (54.5% versus 18%) in infants with prenatal cocaine exposure than in those without exposure. Case-controlled analysis matching for race, sex, and birth weight demonstrated a 2.5-fold increased risk for the development of NEC in the cocaine-exposed group versus the nonexposed group. Lopez et al.[178] reported a 12% incidence of NEC in infants exposed to cocaine as compared with 3% in nonexposed babies. In addition, NEC developed in a significantly greater number of infants within the first 7 days of life in the cocaine-exposed group. In a retrospective cohort study of infants with a birth weight between 750 and 1500 g, Hand et al.[106] compared 48 infants prenatally exposed to only cocaine with 101 infants who had no drug exposure. There was no significant difference in the incidence of NEC between the two groups.

Despite the well-known adverse effects of cocaine, it is difficult to establish a definite causal relationship with NEC. Mothers who abuse cocaine during pregnancy report an ill-defined duration and extent of use, may have used it at a remote time before delivery, and may not have had adequate prenatal care. In addition, maternal cocaine use may be associated with the use of other recreational drugs, alcohol, and tobacco, and thus these mothers are at higher risk for having a baby who is premature or small for gestational age, or both.

Cytokines and Growth Factors

Cytokines and growth factors play a critical role in mediating the proliferation, maturation, chemotaxis, and activation of hematopoietic and immune-related cells. It is recognized that cytokines and growth factors have important effects on a number of cells from various tissues, including those in the GI tract (Table 92-1). Intestinal cells are exposed to cytokines secreted by intestinal endothelial cells, by mucosal fibroblasts, and by enterocytes themselves.[172,214,224,226,316]

Epidermal growth factor (EGF) is known to be an important trophic factor for the developing GI tract. EGF receptors have been demonstrated throughout the fetal and neonatal intestine.[50,57,126,184] EGF is secreted into the gut lumen primarily by the salivary glands and Brunner glands of the duodenum and has been shown to be present in high concentration in human breast milk.[233,244] Significantly reduced levels of salivary and serum EGF have been demonstrated in premature infants in whom NEC developed versus age-matched controls.[111,267] Inactivation of the EGF receptor in knockout mice has been shown to result in a hemorrhagic enteritis that is histologically similar to NEC.[191] In studies using a neonatal rat model of NEC that involved exposure to asphyxia and cold stress, enterally administered supplements of EGF have been shown to significantly decrease the incidence and severity of NEC in rat pups,[72] thus suggesting that this protective effect may be mediated by down-regulation of the proinflammatory cytokine interleukin-18 (IL-18) and increased production of the anti-inflammatory cytokine IL-10.[103] Fagbemi et al.[80] investigated the association of NEC with EGF receptors in the intestinal mucosa of preterm infants undergoing resection for severe NEC and confirmed the presence of intact EGF receptors located on the basolateral membrane of enterocytes.

Erythropoietin (Epo) is a growth factor produced by the kidneys that regulates red blood cell production in response to anemia. Since development of the recombinant protein, rEpo has become widely used in the NICU.[127,218] Epo has been found in human breast milk, and functional Epo receptors have been demonstrated in fetal and neonatal small intestine, thus suggesting a possible role in GI development.[128,130,149] In a retrospective study comparing 260 VLBW infants who received rEpo with 233 matched controls, Ledbetter and Juul[171] demonstrated a significantly lower incidence of NEC in

TABLE 92-1 Cytokines and Growth Factors with Important Effects in the Gastrointestinal Tract

Cytokine	Hematopoietic Effects	Proinflammatory	Anti-inflammatory	Protective Effects in the Gut	Trophic Effects in Enterocytes
EGF		No	Yes	Yes	Yes
Epo	RBC proliferation	No	No	Yes	Yes
IL-1	Acute phase response	Yes	No	Unknown	Yes
IL-2	T-, B-, and NK-cell growth and activation	Yes	No	Yes	Unknown
IL-3	Proliferation and differentiation of early heme cells	Yes	No	Unknown	Yes
IL-4	T- and B-cell and macrophage regulation	Yes	Yes	Yes	Unknown
IL-10	Decreases macrophage activation	No	Yes	Yes	Unknown
IL-11	Increases megakaryocyte and macrophage production	No	Yes	Yes	Yes
IL-15	T-, B-, and NK-cell activation	Yes	Unknown	Unknown	Yes
NO	Regulates platelet aggregation and adhesion, regulates leukocyte-endothelial interactions	Yes	Yes	Yes	No

EGF, epidermal growth factor; Epo, erythropoietin; IL, interleukin; NK, natural killer; NO, nitric oxide.
Data modified from Ledbetter DJ, Juul SE: Necrotizing enterocolitis and hematopoietic cytokines. Clin Perinatol 2000;27:697.

the rEpo group (4.6%) than in the control group (10.8%). Studies in neonatal rats given rEpo enterally have demonstrated a dose-dependent increase in intestinal mucosal villus surface area and increased cellular proliferation, thus suggesting a role of rEpo as a trophic factor in the developing small intestine.[129] In a neonatal rat model of NEC involving exposure to hypoxia and reoxygenation, pretreatment with intraperitoneal injections of rEpo resulted in significantly decreased mucosal inflammation and necrosis, which was thought to be mediated by decreased production of nitric oxide (NO).[163]

Cytokines are endogenous mediators of the inflammatory cascade. Proinflammatory and anti-inflammatory cytokine production is tightly regulated by complex feedback mechanisms to maintain homeostasis.[285,297] Overproduction of either may have significant untoward effects. Overproduction of proinflammatory cytokines (IL-1, IL-2, IL-6, IL-8, IL-12, tumor necrosis factor-α [TNF-α], interferon-γ, platelet-activating factor [PAF]) may lead to shock, multiorgan failure, and death.[188,232] Overproduction of anti-inflammatory cytokines (IL-4, IL-10, IL-11) may result in excessive suppression of immune function.[28,83] A number of different inflammatory mediators have been implicated in the pathogenesis of NEC.[47,107] In vitro studies comparing the response of mature human intestinal cell lines and fetal intestinal cell lines to inflammatory stimulation by TNF-α, IL-1β, or lipopolysaccharide (LPS) demonstrated an exaggerated secretion of IL-8 by the fetal cells.[56,210] Pretreatment of cells with Epo inhibited TNF-α–induced IL-8 secretion to control levels. In a study evaluating serial serum levels of two proinflammatory cytokines (IL-1β, IL-8) and two anti-inflammatory cytokines (IL-1 receptor antagonist [IL-ra], IL-10) in infants with NEC, Edelson et al.[73] demonstrated significantly higher levels of IL-8 and IL-10 in infants with severe NEC from the onset of disease through 24 hours than in infants with less severe NEC. They noted that counter-regulatory mediators in premature infants are secreted in appropriate concentrations, are released later after the onset of disease, and may be useful as a marker of more severe disease. Nadler et al.[209] investigated the pattern of cytokine expression in infants undergoing resection for severe NEC and infants undergoing intestinal resection for other inflammatory conditions. Significant up-regulation of IL-8 mRNA was seen in the specimens from infants with NEC as compared with controls. In addition, they noted significant up-regulation of IL-11 mRNA in infants with NEC and found an inverse correlation between IL-11 expression and the likelihood of pan-necrosis, thus suggesting that IL-11 secretion may be an adaptive response to limit the extent of intestinal damage. Several of the interleukins (IL-4, IL-10, IL-11) have been shown to have a protective or trophic role in the GI tract. IL-4 has been demonstrated to possess cytoprotective effects in human intestinal epithelial cells by reducing bacterial translocation, increasing leukocyte superoxide production, and inducing decay-accelerating factor, which protects the host from the attack of autologous complement activation.[10,268] IL-10 is known to be a potent anti-inflammatory cytokine that inhibits the production of proinflammatory cytokines.[168] In a neonatal rat hypoxia-reoxygenation model of NEC, recombinant IL-10 administered subcutaneously was found to significantly attenuate the extent of intestinal injury when compared with control animals, thus suggesting a protective effect of its anti-inflammatory properties.[222] IL-11 has been shown to be a pleiotropic cytokine that promotes epithelial regeneration and enhances adaptation after bowel resection.[177] Subcutaneous administration of recombinant IL-11 in rats undergoing placement of a defunctionalized (Thiry-Vella) loop of intestine or massive small bowel resection has resulted in prevention of mucosal atrophy in the defunctionalized loop and enhanced mucosal adaptation and absorptive function in the remaining intestine after resection.[4,68]

A tremendous amount of investigation has been performed to define the role of NO in the pathogenesis of a number of different inflammatory processes. There is evidence to support a possible dichotomous function of NO as both a beneficial and a detrimental molecule, especially with regard to the GI tract.[159,161] NO is produced from arginine by three isoforms of nitric oxide synthase (NOS). NOS-1 (neuronal, nNOS) and NOS-3 (endothelial, eNOS) are constitutively present at low levels in the small intestine. NOS-2 (inducible, iNOS) is a form that can be induced in response to inflammatory cytokines.[5,211] The constitutive forms of NOS and constitutive levels of NO have been demonstrated to modulate a number of important functions in the GI tract, including maintenance of mucosal integrity, regulation of mucosal permeability and blood flow, regulation of motility, and inhibition of leukocyte adhesion and activation.[6,18,90,198,279]

Inhibition of NO synthesis in a variety of animal models of intestinal injury induced by ischemia-reperfusion, LPS, or PAF has resulted in marked exacerbation of mucosal injury.[41,117,158,181,193,239] Administration of exogenous sources of NO, including L-arginine, sodium nitroprusside, and nitroglycerin, greatly attenuates these detrimental effects.[3,69,95,228] In a prospective study of 53 premature infants, Zamora et al.[317] demonstrated a significantly lower plasma arginine level at the time of diagnosis in infants in whom NEC developed than in controls. In a randomized prospective placebo-controlled study of VLBW infants assigned to receive either daily oral or parenteral L-arginine supplements (261 mg/kg) or placebo for the first 28 days of life, Amin et al.[8] found a significantly lower incidence of NEC in the supplement group (6.7%) than in the control group (27.3%). Throughout the study, the group that received arginine supplementation had significantly higher mean plasma arginine levels than the control group did. Interestingly, in both groups the infants in whom NEC developed had significantly lower plasma arginine levels at the time of diagnosis than their respective peers did. It is not known whether the decreased arginine levels represent increased utilization for NO production, consumption for the synthesis of other proteins, or decreased enteral absorption. This study suggests the possible benefits of arginine supplementation and potentially other NO donors in the prevention of NEC.

The inducible form of NO synthase (NOS-2, iNOS) is known to be up-regulated in response to inflammatory cytokines. Within several hours of stimulation, NOS-2 expression and activity within the intestinal epithelium increase up to 15-fold and result in the production of large amounts of NO.[287] Although the low levels of NO produced by the constitutive isoforms of NOS may play a homeostatic role in the GI tract, sustained release of NO as a result of up-regulation of NOS-2 has been suggested to have deleterious effects by inducing cellular injury and failure of the mucosal barrier.[53,60,287] This is thought to occur by the reaction of excess NO with superoxide (O_2^-) to produce peroxynitrite ($ONOO^-$), which is a potent reactive nitrogen intermediate that may trigger cytotoxic processes, including lipid peroxidation and DNA damage.[60,242,256] In a prospective study investigating NOS-2 expression in the intestine of infants undergoing resection for NEC, Ford et al.[84] demonstrated marked up-regulation of NOS-2 gene expression in the intestinal epithelium and increased apoptosis of enterocytes in the apical villi. In addition, increased levels of nitrotyrosine residues were detected in the apical villi, thus suggesting that the mucosal injury and increased apoptosis were mediated through the formation of NO and peroxynitrite. In a neonatal rat hypoxia model of NEC in which breast milk-fed animals were compared with formula-fed animals, Nadler et al.[208] demonstrated a significantly higher incidence of NEC, NOS-2 expression, and enterocyte apoptosis and decreased IL-12 mRNA in the formula-fed group than in the breast milk-fed group. The decreased IL-12 expression is thought to be mediated by NO and theorized to contribute to intestinal injury by attenuating bacterial clearance.

PAF, an endogenous phospholipid inflammatory mediator, has been shown to play an important role in the pathophysiology of intestinal injury in animal and human studies.[44] PAF has diverse biologic effects, including mesenteric vasoconstriction, capillary leakage, increased intestinal mucosal permeability, and neutrophil and platelet activation.[105,160,274] Clinically, increased PAF levels have been demonstrated in formula-fed premature infants, as well as those in whom NEC developed.[107,182] In a neonatal rat model of NEC, Caplan et al.[39] have shown that intestinal PAF concentrations, intestinal phospholipase A_2 (PAF-synthesizing enzyme) mRNA expression, and intestinal PAF receptor mRNA expression are elevated. In other animal experiments, exogenous PAF administration results in severe bowel necrosis[94]; endogenous intestinal production of PAF is up-regulated in response to various stimuli, including LPS, hypoxia, and TNF-α[48,79,116,284]; and administration of PAF receptor antagonist, or PAF acetylhydrolase (PAF-degrading enzyme), reduces the risk for NEC.[40,45,79] In human studies, PAF acetylhydrolase activity has been demonstrated to be present in human breast milk; it has been shown to be decreased in neonates, with levels approaching adult enzyme activity at around 6 weeks of life, and has been found to be deficient in infants with NEC.[42,47,206] In a prospective study of 164 infants at risk for NEC, Rabinowitz et al.[241] monitored serial plasma levels of PAF and PAF-related lipids (PAF-LL) to investigate the changes that occur with NEC. There was a significantly higher peak in PAF-LL levels in infants in whom NEC developed than in controls. In addition, rising PAF-LL levels were positively correlated with progression of the severity of NEC; these levels returned to baseline levels during recovery.

TNF-α has many proinflammatory effects, including neutrophil activation, induction of leukocyte and endothelial adhesion molecules, and induction of other cytokines, such as PAF.[121,300] TNF-α has been demonstrated to produce profound hypotension and severe intestinal necrosis similar to NEC in animals. This effect has been shown to be mediated by PAF and attenuated by PAF receptor antagonists.[284]

LPS (endotoxin) is a bacterial product that has the capacity to produce potent inflammatory responses through the induction of various proinflammatory cytokines such as PAF and TNF. Systemic injection of LPS has been shown to produce hypotension, shock, and severe intestinal necrosis.[115] It has been used in animal models of NEC to reliably generate intestinal injury that resembles NEC. LPS-induced intestinal injury has been demonstrated to be mediated by PAF and TNF-α and can be prevented with PAF antagonists.[116]

Cyclooxygenase (COX) catalyzes the rate-limiting step of arachidonic acid metabolism into prostaglandins, leukotrienes, and thromboxanes.[212] Two isoforms of the COX enzyme have been identified. COX-1 is constitutively expressed in many tissues, including the GI tract.[308] COX-2 is the inducible form that is expressed in inflammatory conditions of the GI tract such as inflammatory bowel disease.[11,270] Proinflammatory cytokines (IL-1, IL-6, TNF-α), as well as the proinflammatory transcription factor nuclear factor-κB (NF-κB), have been shown to increase COX-2 expression.[266] NF-κB is an important protein in the activation of a number of inflammatory mediators and cytokines.[189] A marked increase in COX-2 expression has been demonstrated in intestine resected from infants with severe NEC.[55] To elucidate the mechanisms involved in COX-2 expression in NEC, Chung et al.,[55] in a neonatal rat model of NEC, demonstrated a coordinated induction of NF-κB activation and COX-2 expression during the early phase of the injurious event.

Pathogenesis

Despite many years of extensive investigation and identification of several risk factors, the pathogenesis of NEC remains elusive. The etiology is probably multifactorial and involves some combination of mucosal compromise, pathogenic bacteria, and feedings that in a susceptible host result in bowel injury and an inflammatory cascade. Of the risk factors, prematurity is the most consistent and important. Another important risk factor involves enteral feeding of formula. Commercially available formulas lack many of the beneficial properties present in breast milk. These protective agents include gut trophic hormones, factors that induce intestinal maturation, factors that enhance colonization by nonvirulent bacteria, anti-inflammatory mediators, vitamins and other antioxidants, and components that provide cellular and humoral immunity.[34,38,92,104]

Evidence for an Impaired Gut Barrier

The preterm GI tract is characterized by an immaturity of cellular and humoral immunity,[32,278] increased permeability,[294] reduced gastric acid secretion,[12] reduced concentration of proteolytic enzymes,[293] incomplete innervation and decreased motility,[19,23] and immaturity of the intestinal epithelium and microvilli.[225] Decreased barrier function is evident in otherwise healthy preterm infants by their ability to systemically absorb and deliver undigested macromolecules, whole bacteria, and LPS.[91,247,303] Compromise of the intestinal epithelial mucosal barrier appears to be the first event leading to activation of the inflammatory cascade.

Reduced mucosal blood flow leading to cellular hypoxia and injury is one of the most frequently cited etiologic factors for NEC. Touloukian[290] emphasized the high incidence of perinatal physiologic stressors that may primarily or secondarily cause intestinal ischemia. Chief among these factors are hypoxic and hypotensive episodes, exchange transfusions through the umbilical vein, umbilical artery catheters, cardiovascular lesions, and serum hyperviscosity. An atavistic "diving reflex" in which blood is preferentially diverted away from the splanchnic circulation in order to maintain adequate perfusion of the heart and brain has been hypothesized to occur during these episodes.[216] During periods of low blood flow and subsequent reperfusion, Parks et al.[227] found that a reaction between xanthine oxidase, hypoxanthine, and molecular oxygen results in a burst of superoxide radical production. These free radicals may cause damage to cellular and mitochondrial membranes and alter the permeability of the intestinal mucosal barrier. Although animal studies provide support for this theory, clinical correlation has been lacking, and prospective clinical trials have not been able to consistently establish an association between a hypoxic event and the development of NEC.[145]

Extensive investigation into the critical role of various inflammatory mediators in the pathogenesis of NEC has been conducted. Studies in animal models and human specimens have identified PAF, LPS, NO, and TNF-α as potential mediators of the disease.[48,84,94] The effects of LPS and TNF-α have been shown to be mediated by PAF. Increased mucosal permeability and susceptibility allowing translocation of bacteria or bacterial toxin and activation of the inflammatory cascade are thought to be the critical steps leading to the final collapse of intestinal epithelial integrity.[654,167]

Very little is known about the early chain of events that occur at the onset of tissue damage. Recent studies have suggested that the disruption in the intestinal mucosal barrier results from accelerated apoptosis. All of the key mediators identified in NEC (PAF, NO, LPS, TNF-α) have been shown to cause apoptosis of intestinal epithelial cells.[58,84,119,314] In a neonatal rat model of NEC involving formula-fed animals exposed to hypoxia and cold stress and mother-fed controls, Jilling et al.[123] demonstrated a marked increase in apoptosis in the epithelial layer of the NEC group in comparison to controls, although the mechanism was undetermined. The accelerated apoptosis was shown to precede gross morphologic changes in the intestinal epithelium. Administration of a pan-caspase inhibitor to inhibit intestinal apoptosis resulted in a significantly reduced rate of epithelial apoptosis, as well as a decreased incidence of NEC, thus suggesting that apoptosis was the underlying cause of the subsequent mucosal damage ultimately leading to NEC.

Sustained overproduction of NO because of up-regulation of NOS-2 in the GI tract in response to an inflammatory stimulus has been suggested to induce cellular injury and disruption of the intestinal epithelial barrier by production of the potent oxidant peroxynitrite.[53] Ford et al.[84] demonstrated up-regulation of NOS-2 and NO in the intestinal wall of infants with NEC and increased apoptosis of enterocytes mediated by the peroxynitrite. This accelerated apoptosis is thought to result in a "bare area" at the villus tip representing a break in the intestinal mucosal barrier where bacteria may attach, translocate, and initiate an inflammatory cascade.[236] In addition, peroxynitrite has also been shown to inhibit the proliferation of intestinal epithelial cells in rat models of NEC.[237] The data suggest that in conditions associated with sustained overproduction of NO or peroxynitrite (e.g., NEC), intestinal epithelial barrier dysfunction may result from an imbalance caused by accelerated epithelial injury and blunted tissue repair mechanisms.

Role of Infectious Agents

The type of feeding and pattern of intestinal colonization may determine the risk for development of NEC. Breast-feeding infants become colonized predominantly with bifidobacteria (gram-positive bacteria), which help control the growth of gram-negative bacteria.[139,315] In contrast, formula-fed infants become colonized predominantly by coliforms, enterococci, and *Bacteroides* species.[140]

The importance of bacteria in the pathogenesis of NEC is supported by the following evidence: (1) NEC occurs in episodic, epidemic waves, affected patients were related in place and time or had the same infectious agent, and the initiation of infection control measures has been shown to stop epidemics[26,31]; (2) during clustered occurrences, the identical microorganisms can be isolated from both afflicted babies and their caretakers[109]; (3) NEC can occur in infants with no known risk factors; (4) NEC can develop several weeks or months after a perinatal insult, when the GI tract is fully colonized and has had sufficient time to recover from any perinatal insult[148,154]; (5) administration of large doses of vitamin E (interferes with intracellular killing of bacteria by leukocytes) to premature infants has been linked with an increase in the incidence of NEC[124]; (6) an NEC-like disease occurs in vulnerable hosts after the ingestion of *Clostridium* species[169]; (7) lesions resembling NEC can be reproduced experimentally with the administration of LPS[47]; (8) endotoxemia is demonstrated in 80% of those with NEC and positive blood cultures for gram-negative bacteria[263]; and (9) pneumatosis intestinalis is a common radiographic finding and represents submucosal gas collections produced by bacterial fermentation.[33,78]

UNIFYING HYPOTHESIS FOR NECROTIZING ENTEROCOLITIS

The following common clinical scenario supports a unified hypothesis for the pathogenesis of NEC. A premature infant is admitted to the NICU, usually for treatment of respiratory distress, and is exposed to the potentially pathogenic nosocomial flora. The infant may experience intermittent episodes of apnea and bradycardia. The broad-spectrum antibiotics that are routinely administered eliminate the infant's anaerobic flora, which normally functions as a barrier to colonization and overgrowth of potentially pathogenic gram-negative organisms. Instead of breast milk, formula feedings are usually administered. Formula provides substrate for bacterial growth and contains none of the protective factors present in breast milk. Poor peristalsis of the GI tract permits overgrowth by pathogenic bacteria. Depending on the quantity and virulence of the microorganisms and the presence or absence of mucosal damage, bacteria may breach the mucosal barrier. Because of deficiencies in both specific and nonspecific immune defenses, bacterial killing is ineffective. Either through episodes of decreased perfusion and reperfusion or through mild infection, the mucosal barrier is damaged. Proinflammatory cytokines are induced and result in initiation of the inflammatory cascade. This cascade leads to increased mucosal permeability, which in turn causes further damage to the mucosa and bowel wall. More bacteria and bacterial by-products invade through the mucosal breaks, and progressive bowel damage results in full-thickness necrosis and perforation.

PATHOLOGY

NEC may involve single (50%) or multiple (discontinuous) segments of intestine, most commonly in the terminal ileum, followed by the colon.[15] Involvement of both the large and small intestine occurs in 44% of cases. Pan-involvement (pan-necrosis, NEC totalis) is a fulminant form of NEC characterized by necrosis of at least 75% of the gut, and it accounts for 19% of all cases of surgically treated NEC and most of the deaths.[254]

At surgery, the gross appearance of NEC is fairly constant. The bowel is markedly distended with patchy areas of thinning. The serosal surfaces are typically red to gray and may be covered by a fibrinous exudate. With frank gangrene, the serosal surface is black. Subserosal gas collections are frequently encountered. The mucosal surface may be ulcerated with wide areas of epithelial sloughing. Bloody peritoneal fluid is seen when bowel necrosis is present, and brown and turbid fluid is seen when perforation has occurred.

Bowel inflammation is nearly ubiquitous in NEC (Fig. 92-1A). The degree and nature, however, vary from one area to another. Acute and chronic inflammatory changes coexist in 60% of cases. The most common microscopic lesion is bland or coagulation necrosis of the superficial mucosa (89%).[133] Edema and hemorrhage of the submucosa follow complete mucosal necrosis (Fig. 92-1B). Pneumatosis intestinalis is initially seen in the submucosa and later in the muscularis and subserosa. Bacteria in the bowel lumen and wall are present in up to 40% of cases and are occasionally found in gas cysts. Transmural necrosis, characterized by hyaline eosinophilia and loss of nuclear detail in the muscular layers, is present in advanced disease. Epithelial regeneration, formation of granulation tissue, and early fibrosis are often present.

A

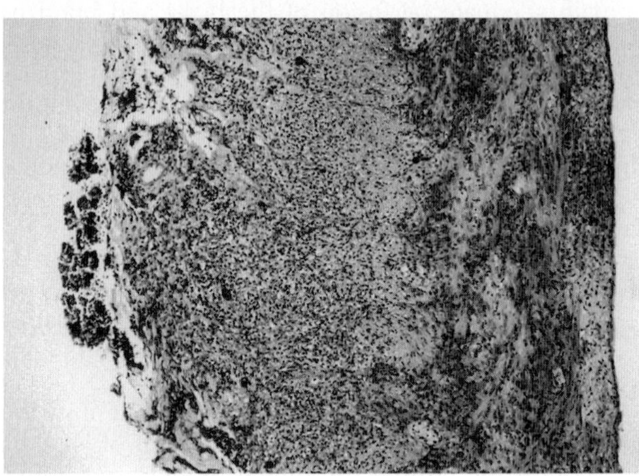

B

Figure 92-1 *A,* Histologic section demonstrating early necrotizing enterocolitis with inflammation and pneumatosis intestinalis in the submucosa (hematoxylin-eosin stain, ×150). *B,* Histologic section demonstrating advanced necrotizing enterocolitis with transmural necrosis and loss of villus and crypt architecture (hematoxylin-eosin stain, ×150). (*See color plate.*)

This suggests a suppurative process lasting at least a few days. Granulation tissue with mucosal and submucosal fibrosis may be seen adjacent to areas of active mucosal and submucosal necrosis and may account, in part, for late stricture formation. Thrombi are sometimes noted in small mesenteric vessels and in small arterioles of the submucosa. Small-vessel thrombosis within necrotic tissue is considered a secondary change. Large-vessel thrombosis is a relatively rare finding at autopsy.

DIAGNOSIS

Clinical Features

NEC is commonly heralded by nonspecific clinical findings that simply represent physiologic instability.[52,133]

These findings include lethargy, temperature instability, recurrent apnea, bradycardia, hypoglycemia, and shock. More specific symptoms related to the GI tract include abdominal distention (70% to 98%), blood per rectum (79% to 86%), high gastric residuals after feeding (>70%), vomiting (>70%), and diarrhea (4% to 26%). Gross blood in the stool is present in 25% to 63% of cases and occult blood in 22% to 59%. Rectal bleeding is seldom massive.

Because the spectrum of disease severity varies, physical examination may initially demonstrate only subtle abdominal distention and minimal tenderness. As the disease progresses, abdominal palpation may elicit tenderness and demonstrate palpable bowel loops, a fixed or mobile mass, or abdominal wall crepitus. Edema and erythema of the abdominal wall as a result of the underlying peritonitis are present initially in approximately 4% of cases, but are more common later in the course of the disease. In males, there may be discoloration of the scrotum, indicative of perforation. In a small subset of patients, the disease is rapidly progressive and the initial manifestation is heralded by florid clinical findings and death within 24 hours.

Laboratory Findings

Infants with NEC usually have neutropenia, thrombocytopenia, and metabolic acidosis. The total leukocyte count may be elevated, but it is generally low. In one study, 37% of infants had absolute neutrophil counts less than 1500 cells/mm^3.[118] The infants with the lowest counts in this study had the worst prognosis. Neutrophil counts less than 6000 cells/mm^3 are most commonly associated with concomitant gram-negative septicemia.

Thrombocytopenia is nearly universally present and seems to be associated with gram-negative sepsis and platelet binding by endotoxin. The incidence of thrombocytopenia in NEC is 65% to 90%, essentially unchanged from the earliest reports from the 1970s.[118,275] O'Neill[219] demonstrated that in a cohort of 40 infants who underwent surgery for NEC, 95% had platelet counts less than 150,000 cells/mm^3. Rowe et al.[251,253] found that platelet counts less than 150,000 cells/mm^3 were present in patients who had positive cultures for gram-negative organisms. The nadir platelet count during the course of the disease was noted to be lower in patients with more severe disease and in those who died.[299] A platelet count less than 10^9/L or a rapid fall is a poor prognostic indicator.

Metabolic acidosis is very common (40% to 85% of patients with NEC) and is believed to result from hypovolemia and sepsis. It is not a specific indicator of intestinal necrosis. Stool samples are commonly positive for occult blood and reducing substances. Book et al.[30] reasoned that intestinal mucosal damage from NEC leads to carbohydrate malabsorption. Poorly digested carbohydrates pass into the colon where they are fermented and excreted in stool. The authors tested the stool of formula-fed infants for reducing substances with Clinitest tablets and found that 71% of formula-fed infants in whom NEC developed had greater than 2+ reducing substances in their stool. Colonic bacterial fermentation increases the local production of D-lactate, which is absorbed and excreted by the kidneys. Garcia et al.[86] could show elevated urinary D-lactate levels in infants with NEC but not in control infants. With recovery from NEC or administration of enteral antibiotics, D-lactate excretion decreased. Similarly, hydrogen excretion in the breath is elevated when fermentation is increased. This test is helpful in ruling out NEC. A negative result on a breath hydrogen test is 99% accurate in ruling out NEC.[54]

C-reactive protein (CRP), an acute phase reactant, has been measured in an attempt to correlate its level with the presence, absence, or resolution of the disease.[120] CRP may serve as an early indicator of NEC when its level rises more than 10 mg/L within 48 hours of the suspected diagnosis (reported sensitivity, 92%; specificity, 81%). Failure of CRP to return to normal within 10 days was an indicator of abscess, stricture, or septicemia.

MICROBIOLOGY

It has proved extremely difficult to identify common offending infectious agents. Organisms recovered from the blood and stool of patients with NEC vary depending on the GI tract flora, the nosocomial flora, the site cultured, and the duration of previous antibiotic therapy. It is unclear whether the bacteria cultured represent pathogens causing NEC or, instead, secondary opportunistic invaders selected by the antibiotic regimen. Furthermore, lack of sufficiently matched controls and complete bacteriology data on other patients in similar environments makes study of the microbiology of NEC difficult.

Bacteriology

Bacteriologic data for NEC have primarily been based on cultures obtained from the blood, stool, and peritoneal cavity. Blood cultures are positive in 30% to 35% of patients.[140] Cultures commonly grow *Escherichia coli*, *Klebsiella pneumoniae*, *Proteus mirabilis*, *Staphylococcus aureus*, *Staphylococcus epidermidis*, enterococci, *Clostridium perfringens*, and *Pseudomonas aeruginosa*. *K. pneumoniae* and *E. coli* cause the majority of positive blood cultures. The organisms most frequently cultured from stool specimens are *E. coli*, *K. pneumoniae*, *Enterococcus cloacae*, *P. aeruginosa*, *Salmonella* species, coagulase-negative staphylococci (*S. epidermidis*), *C. perfringens*, *Clostridium difficile*, and *Clostridium butyricum*.[25,304] Peritoneal cultures most commonly grow *Klebsiella* species, *E. coli*, coagulase-negative staphylococci, *Enterobacter* species, and yeast.[197]

Fungal Cultures

In contrast to bacteria, no data implicate a fungus as an initiating organism in the pathogenesis of NEC. Fungi are believed to be secondary invaders. In 1991, the National Institute of Child Health and Human Development Neonatal Research Network study of NEC reported that 5% to 17% of blood cultures were positive for fungus.[293]

In 1993, Karlowicz[135] reported an increase in fungal peritonitis from 7% in 1980 to 1989 to 35% in 1989 to 1991 at the same institution. Fungal septicemia with *Candida* species has been implicated in many late NEC deaths.[272] In a retrospective premortem and postmortem examination of body fluid and tissue cultures from 30 patients who died of NEC by Smith et al., 47% of patients had evidence of fungus.[272] Colonization was found in 20%; the first positive culture was obtained a mean of 22 ± 8.9 days after surgery. Eight patients (27%) had fungal sepsis: seven with *Candida* species and one with *Torulopsis* species. The first positive fungal culture was obtained 16.5 ± 7.0 days after surgery. Fungal sepsis was diagnosed before death in only four of the eight patients.

Bacterial Toxins

Mucosal injury may be mediated by toxin in some cases of NEC.[259] Toxins produced by *C. difficile*, *C. butyricum*, and *E. coli* have been isolated from stool samples during epidemics. Studies by Scheifele et al.[260,261] have demonstrated that a delta toxin is elaborated from coagulase-negative staphylococci and is present in the stool of 56% of coagulase-negative staphylococcal cases of NEC. This toxin is rarely found in patients colonized with coagulase-negative staphylococci without NEC.

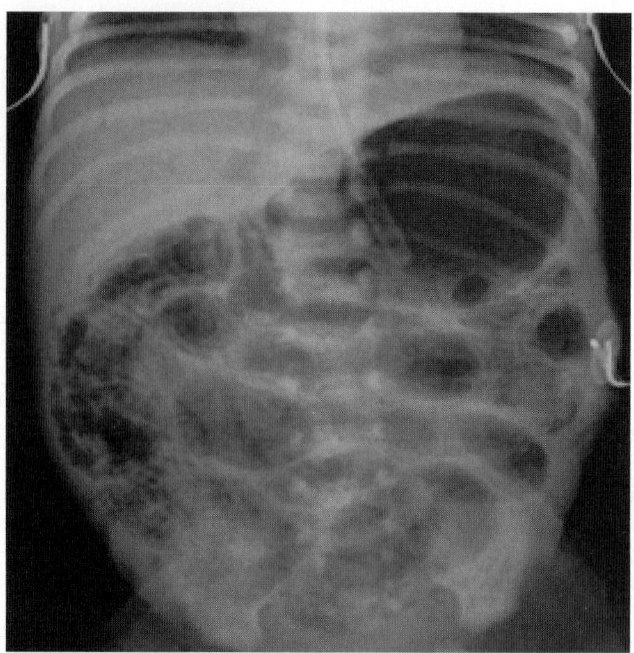

Figure 92–2 Plain abdominal radiograph demonstrating extensive pneumatosis intestinalis (cystic and linear) and an arborizing pattern of air over the liver shadow representing gas dispersed within the radicles of the portal venous system.

Clustered Epidemics

In most large series, sporadic cases have been followed by the sudden appearance of a cluster of a relatively large number of cases. In many of the epidemics, no specific pathogen has been identified. Book et al.,[31] as part of an ongoing nosocomial infection surveillance program, prospectively studied 74 infants in whom NEC developed between 1972 and 1977. Six temporally and geographically related clusters of cases of NEC occurred, and no specific organisms were isolated. During these episodes, nursery personnel experienced concomitant acute GI illnesses. Implementation of infection control measures was associated with a significant decrease in the rate of NEC. Similar epidemics without specific pathogens were noted at Rainbow Babies and Children's Hospital in 1972, 1973, 1974, 1975, and 1978.[140] At the Children's Hospital of Philadelphia,[199] 11 sporadic cases of NEC occurred, but no pathogen was identified in the stools of infants in the nursery. Van Acker et al.[295] reported an outbreak of NEC in 12 infants over a 2-month period associated with *Enterobacter sakazakii*. This pathogen was found to be a contaminant of the powdered milk formula that was used in the NICU. Other epidemic outbreaks have identified *E. coli*, *Salmonella* species, *C. difficile*, rotavirus, and a coronavirus-like organism.[26,259]

IMAGING

The cornerstone of the diagnosis of NEC is plain anteroposterior and left lateral decubitus radiographs. Any or all of the following findings are associated with NEC: ileus pattern (nonspecific bowel distention), pneumatosis intestinalis (linear or cystic) (Fig. 92-2), portal vein gas, pneumoperitoneum, intraperitoneal fluid, and persistently dilated, fixed loops.[204] Both pneumatosis and portal vein gas are often fleeting signs.

Bowel Distention

Multiple gas-filled loops of intestine are the earliest and most common radiologic finding in patients with NEC (55% to 100% of cases).[62] As fluid and air accumulate, air-fluid levels are visible on the decubitus view. The degree of dilatation and the distribution of bowel loops are related to the clinical severity and progression of the disease. In some cases, nonspecific intestinal dilatation precedes clinical symptoms suggestive of NEC by several hours.

Pneumatosis Intestinalis

Demonstration of pneumatosis intestinalis (intramural gas) in the appropriate clinical setting is diagnostic of NEC. The air mainly comprises hydrogen, a by-product of bacterial metabolism. The frequency of pneumatosis intestinalis ranges from 19% to 98%, although it may be absent in up to 14% of patients with NEC (even severe disease).[143] Conversely, extensive pneumatosis may be present with minimal signs; it often responds promptly to medical management.

Pneumatosis is fleeting, may appear before the onset of clinical symptoms, and is commonly an early rather than a late finding. It is most frequently noted when infants have been fed (84%), in contrast to unfed babies (14%).[185] Pneumatosis intestinalis is not specific for NEC and has been noted in infants with enterocolitis of Hirschsprung's disease, inspissated milk syndrome, pyloric stenosis, severe diarrhea, carbohydrate intolerance, and other disorders.

Two forms of pneumatosis intestinalis are recognized radiographically: cystic and linear. The cystic form has a granular or foamy appearance and represents gas in the submucosa. It is often confused with fecal material in the large intestine. Linear pneumatosis consists of small bubbles collected within the muscularis and subserosa to form a thin linear or curvilinear gas pattern outlining the wall of a segment of the intestine.

Portal Vein Gas

Portal vein gas appears as linear branching radiolucencies overlying the liver and often extending to its periphery. It represents gas dispersed through the fine radicles of the portal venous system. The presence of portal vein gas is fleeting, which perhaps accounts for the low reported incidence of 10% to 30%.[35] In most series, the presence of portal vein gas is associated with a poor prognosis.[143] In cases with pan-involvement, the gas is present in 61% of patients. The genesis of portal vein gas may involve accumulation of gas in the bowel wall as a result of bacterial invasion, dissection into the venous system, and migration to the radicles of the portal vein. Alternatively, it may represent the action of gas-forming bacteria within the portal venous system.

Pneumoperitoneum

Free air in the peritoneal cavity associated with perforation of the intestine can be demonstrated in 12% to 30% of patients. It is best noted on the left lateral decubitus or cross-table lateral view. Upright radiography is unnecessary. A supine view of the abdomen can demonstrate free air by outlining the falciform ligament ("football sign"), the umbilical artery, or urachal remnants or by revealing the "double wall" sign. This sign refers to visualization of air on both sides of the wall (lumen and peritoneal cavity). In patients who have intestinal perforation proved by surgery, radiographic evidence shows free air in only 63%, thus demonstrating that perforation can occur in a surprisingly high number of patients without evidence of free air.

One must keep in mind that pneumoperitoneum may occur without intestinal perforation from mechanical ventilation for severe lung disease. In this clinical situation, barotrauma may produce alveolar rupture with air dissection into the abdomen through the mediastinum. The patient's signs, symptoms, and laboratory findings will often differentiate the cause of the air. If one is unsure, abdominal paracentesis may be performed and any aspirated fluid analyzed. If there is no ascites, a water-soluble contrast study via the gastric tube may be performed to rule out gastric perforation.

Intraperitoneal Fluid

Several plain radiographic findings suggest free fluid in the peritoneal cavity that is amenable to paracentesis: (1) a grossly distended abdomen devoid of gas, (2) gas-filled loops of bowel in the center of the abdomen surrounded by opacity out to the flanks, (3) increased haziness within the abdomen, and (4) separation of bowel loops. These findings have been reported in 11% of cases. Both ascites and portal vein gas are radiographic findings associated with high mortality rates. Twenty-one percent of patients with surgically proven intestinal perforation have ascites. However, 16% of all patients with proven intestinal perforation have neither ascites nor free air on plain radiographs.

Persistent Dilated Loops

The "persistent dilated loop sign" is a plain radiographic finding that was described by Wexler[305] in a study of five babies with NEC in whom a single loop or several loops of dilated bowel remained unchanged in position and configuration for 24 to 36 hours. Full-thickness necrosis subsequently developed in these patients. This finding, however, does not always indicate bowel necrosis. Leonard et al.[175] found a persistent loop in 33% of 21 patients with proven NEC. Fifty-seven percent of infants with a persistent loop had necrotic intestine at surgery or autopsy, but necrosis never developed in 43% and they recovered with nonoperative treatment.

Contrast Studies

Radiopaque contrast studies of the upper GI tract may occasionally be useful to improve diagnostic accuracy in patients with equivocal clinical and radiologic signs of NEC. However, overdiagnosis by contrast radiography is possible and may lead to unwarranted treatment. Careful attention to the type of contrast agent used for the study is critical.[305] Barium should never be used because extravasation of a barium and stool mixture through a perforation may intensify the peritonitis. Unlike barium, water-soluble contrast agents are absorbed by both the bowel and the peritoneal cavity. The practical implication of this absorption is a transient (6 to 12 hours) increase in urinary specific gravity. Historically, water-soluble agents were hyperosmolar and caused dangerously large intraluminal fluid shifts, especially in premature patients. Current water-soluble agents are nonionic, have much lower osmolarity, and produce excellent opacification of the GI tract. NEC is suspected when intestinal contrast enhancement demonstrates bowel wall loops separated by edematous walls, an irregular mucosa with ill-defined margins, mucosal ulceration, bowel wall spiculation, or pneumatosis intestinalis. The examination may be performed at the bedside.

Though advocated by some,[134] contrast enemas should not be performed because of the risk for rectosigmoid perforation. Unless there is colonic disease or reflux of contrast into a diseased distal ileum, the contrast enema will not be diagnostic of NEC. It may, in fact, overdiagnose NEC because contrast enemas have been shown to produce pneumatosis and transient portal venous air. Unlike the bedside upper GI series, contrast enema must be performed with simultaneous fluoroscopy, which necessitates transfer of the critically ill neonate to the radiology suite. In an infant who has recently completed a course of therapy for NEC but signs of partial small bowel obstruction or blood-tinged stools develop, contrast enemas are very useful in identifying strictures.

Ultrasonography

Ultrasonography (US) has been used to identify necrotic bowel, intraperitoneal fluid, and portal venous air. Theoretically, US may have significant value if it can identify patients who require surgery in a more sensitive and timely manner than is possible with conventional clinical and radiographic methods.

Abnormal bowel loops on US are characterized by a hypoechoic rim with a central echogenic focus ("target sign").[150] Pericholecystic hyperechogenicity, believed to represent either pericholecystic venous gas or extension of the foamy inflammatory infiltrate of NEC into the pericholecystic space, was described by Avni et al.[13]

The use of US for the diagnosis of NEC is most applicable to patients with questionable clinical and radiologic findings or to localize intra-abdominal fluid for paracentesis.

Magnetic Resonance Imaging

Magnetic resonance imaging (MRI) is a noninvasive modality that has recently been used to identify infants with ischemic bowel secondary to NEC. Although MRI is capable of demonstrating the cardinal findings of NEC, the need to use this study is limited at most.[180]

CLASSIFICATION

To select the appropriate treatment (nonoperative versus operative) and to determine the impact of therapy on survival and late outcome, it is essential that investigators use comparable criteria for classifying the stages of NEC. Several classification schemes have been proposed. In 1978, Bell et al.[21] introduced the now most commonly used classification, a three-stage system (suspected, definite, and advanced) that categorizes patients by historical factors, GI manifestations, radiologic findings, and systemic signs (Table 92-2). The Bell staging criteria have been modified[148]; the three stages are still used, but subsets are included in an effort to identify specific prognostic factors. Infants with stage I disease have features suggestive of NEC, patients with stage II disease have definitive NEC without an indication for surgical intervention, and patients with stage III disease have advanced NEC with evidence of bowel necrosis or perforation.

TABLE 92-2 Necrotizing Enterocolitis Staging System

Stage I (Suspected)
Any one or more historical factors producing perinatal stress
Systemic manifestations—temperature instability, lethargy, apnea, bradycardia
Gastrointestinal manifestations—poor feeding, increasing pregavage residuals, emesis (may be bilious or test positive for occult blood), mild abdominal distention, occult blood in stool (no fissure)
Abdominal radiographs showing distention with mild ileus
Stage II (Definite)
Any one or more historical factors
Above signs and symptoms plus persistent occult or gross gastrointestinal bleeding, marked abdominal distention
Abdominal radiographs showing significant intestinal distention with ileus, small bowel separation (edema in bowel wall or peritoneal fluid), unchanging or persistent "rigid" bowel loops, pneumatosis intestinalis, portal venous gas
Stage III (Advanced)
Any one or more historical factors
Above signs and symptoms plus deterioration of vital signs, evidence of septic shock, or marked gastrointestinal hemorrhage
Abdominal radiographs showing pneumoperitoneum in addition to the findings listed for stage II

From Bell MJ, Temberg JL, Feigin RD, et al: Neonatal necrotizing enterocolitis: Therapeutic decisions based upon clinical staging. Ann Surg 1978;187:1.

MANAGEMENT

Nonoperative

In the absence of intestinal necrosis or perforation, the mainstay of treatment for patients with NEC is supportive. Feedings are stopped, the GI tract is decompressed through a sump gastric tube, and intravenous fluid resuscitation is initiated. A complete blood count, platelet count, blood gas analysis, and CRP and serum electrolyte levels are obtained. Blood and urine samples are sent for culture, and broad-spectrum intravenous antibiotic therapy is initiated. Until recently, most antibiotic regimens included a penicillin, an aminoglycoside, and an agent effective against anaerobic organisms. It seems logical that coverage for anaerobic organisms be included because these infants are usually 1 to 2 weeks old, but in carefully performed studies, anaerobes are sparse. To date, no controlled study has shown the efficacy of this therapy. The antibiotic regimen is best tailored not only to the most common organisms found with NEC but also to the nosocomial nursery flora. Because of recent reports of patients with stool and blood cultures positive for coagulase-negative staphylococci, some groups now empirically treat patients with a combination of vancomycin and gentamicin or vancomycin and a third-generation cephalosporin.[262] The incidence of fungal sepsis in infants who die of NEC is high, so a strong index of suspicion must be maintained and empirical antifungal therapy should be considered if the patient continues to be symptomatic without an obvious bacterial cause.

Close clinical observation consists of frequent physical examination, two-view abdominal radiography performed every 6 to 8 hours, serum platelet and leukocyte counts, and blood gas analysis.

Once feedings resume, stools are tested for reducing substances and occult blood. Feedings are discontinued if the result of either test becomes positive. Patients with definite disease of moderate severity (Bell stage II) are treated by bowel rest, decompression, and antibiotic therapy for at least 7 to 14 days. A central venous catheter may be placed for total parenteral nutrition. If the patient is clinically well, small amounts of diluted formula may be restarted. The infant is constantly and carefully monitored for abdominal distention, vomiting, or nonspecific signs or symptoms of NEC. Feedings are progressed slowly to goal volumes while avoiding the use of concentrated formulas or large-volume feeding. Infants who have undergone surgery receive 1 to 2 weeks of postoperative intravenous antibiotics. Feedings are initiated when the patient is clinically well and return of bowel function has been established.

Indications for Surgery

The principal goals of surgical intervention in the setting of NEC are to remove gangrenous bowel and preserve intestinal length.[81,229] Ideally, surgery should not be undertaken until gangrene is present but be performed before perforation occurs. Unfortunately, no combination of clinical examination or adjunct testing has been shown to have high sensitivity for intestinal gangrene.[153,155] Thus, there remains controversy regarding the indications for surgery, the most appropriate timing of intervention, and the optimal surgical treatment strategy. The most widely accepted indication for surgery is the presence of pneumoperitoneum. In an attempt to identify characteristics that may serve as predictors of intestinal gangrene, Kosloske[153] reviewed 12 criteria used as indications for surgery in 147 patients with NEC and stratified these criteria according to sensitivity, specificity, positive/negative predictive value, and prevalence. The "best" indicators (specificity and positive predictive value [PPV] approaching 100%, prevalence >10%) were pneumoperitoneum, positive paracentesis (aspiration of >0.5 mL brown or yellow fluid containing bacteria on Gram stain), and portal venous gas. "Good" indicators (specificity and PPV approaching 100%, prevalence <10%) were a fixed intestinal loop, erythema of the abdominal wall, and a palpable abdominal mass. A "fair" indicator (specificity of 91%, PPV of 94%, prevalence of 20%) was "severe" pneumatosis intestinalis as graded by a radiographic system. "Poorer" indicators were clinical deterioration (PPV of 78%), platelet count lower than 100,000/mm^3 (PPV of 50%), abdominal tenderness (PPV of 58%), severe GI hemorrhage (PPV of 50%), and gasless abdomen with ascites (0%). Unfortunately, none of the indicators had sensitivity greater than 48%. Currently, the only absolute indication for surgery is pneumoperitoneum. Relative indications include a positive paracentesis, palpable abdominal mass, abdominal wall erythema, portal venous gas, fixed intestinal loop, and clinical deterioration despite maximal medical therapy.

Pneumoperitoneum

Infants in whom pneumoperitoneum develops during nonoperative treatment should undergo either laparotomy or peritoneal drain placement. Unfortunately, pneumoperitoneum is not always demonstrable in neonates with gut perforation, with one study reporting that only 63% of infants with perforation demonstrated free air.[85]

Paracentesis

A positive result on paracentesis, defined as free-flowing aspiration of more than 0.5 mL of brown or yellow-brown fluid that contains bacteria on gram stain,[53] is highly specific for intestinal necrosis. A negative result on paracentesis is rare with intestinal necrosis but can occur when a localized, walled-off perforation is present or a segment of bowel is injured but not perforated.[246] There is no absolute indication for paracentesis. Kosloske[153] recommends abdominal paracentesis for patients with extensive pneumatosis intestinalis or for those who do not improve with nonoperative management. If no peritoneal fluid is aspirated, peritoneal lavage is performed by instilling up to 30 mL/kg of normal saline solution into the peritoneal cavity, turning the patient from side to side, and then withdrawing the fluid. Ricketts and Jerles[246] reported a greater than 70% survival rate when a positive result on abdominal paracentesis was used as the indication for surgery in 51% of their patients; three false negatives occurred. They performed paracentesis when there was erythema and edema of the abdominal wall, portal vein gas, a fixed and dilated loop on sequential abdominal radiography, a fixed and tender abdominal mass, or persistent clinical deterioration. The indications used for paracentesis in this report are considered indications for surgery by many surgeons.

Portal Venous Gas

To determine the significance of portal vein gas in relation to the presence and extent of bowel necrosis and mortality, Kurkchubasche et al.[164] reviewed the experience of Children's Hospital of Pittsburgh, as well as the world literature. Of the 616 patients collected, 118 (19%) had portal vein gas on plain radiography. Of these 118 patients, 102 underwent surgery, usually 24 hours after the radiographic appearance of portal vein gas. All 102 patients had full-thickness bowel necrosis, and 52% had necrosis of more than 75% of the length of the entire small intestine. The overall surgical mortality rate for patients with portal vein gas was 52%, and more than 90% of those with pan-involvement died. Of the 15 patients who had portal vein gas and did not undergo surgery, bowel necrosis requiring surgery developed in 6 (40%), and 5 of the 6 died. In a separate study, Rowe et al.[254] suggested that intestinal necrosis will develop in more than 90% of infants with portal venous gas, with pan-involvement developing in 52%. More recently, in a review of 40 infants with NEC and portal venous gas, Molik et al.[196] reported a 54% overall operative mortality and pan-involvement in 25%.

Fixed Persistent Intestinal Loop

A fixed dilated intestinal loop is defined by persistent location and configuration for more than 24 hours. Approximately half the patients recover without an operation.[230] Laparoscopy has been used to assess two patients with dilated intestinal loops.[231] NEC was confirmed in one case and ruled out in the other.

Clinical Deterioration

There are many criteria for operating on children who show continued clinical deterioration despite adequate supportive therapy,[245] but none by themselves are absolute indications. These criteria include abdominal wall erythema, peritonitis on physical examination, persistent/increasing acidosis, and persistent/progressive thrombocytopenia.

Ascites

As mentioned, pneumoperitoneum may not always be evident with intestinal perforation. A gasless abdomen, suggestive of a fluid-filled abdominal cavity, may be the only indication of perforation. Frey et al.[85] reported that in 21% of infants with intestinal perforation, the only radiographic evidence was ascites. They noted that radiographs are imprecise and that evidence of ascites in the appropriate clinical setting of NEC mandates paracentesis for further evaluation.

Operative Management

Advanced disease requiring surgical intervention develops in up to 50% of infants with NEC.[36,151] Because of the lack of quality prospective randomized trials, the optimal surgical treatment strategy for NEC remains controversial. The goals of surgery are to remove gangrenous bowel and preserve intestinal length. Within this context, a number of different options exist, but most agree that the surgical approach should be determined by the extent of intestinal involvement.

The patient's general condition should be optimized before surgery with aggressive ventilatory support, treatment of shock, administration of broad-spectrum antibiotics, and correction of anemia and coagulopathy. Ideally, a minimum urine output of 1 mL/kg/hr and an age-appropriate mean arterial pressure should be achieved. Operative procedures may be performed in the NICU under appropriate conditions without an increase in complications.[87]

Primary Peritoneal Drainage

Treatment of intestinal perforation in VLBW infants remains controversial. In 1977, Ein et al.[77] reported the use of peritoneal drainage (PD) as a means of stabilizing and improving the systemic status of premature infants with perforation before laparotomy. Since then, primary treatment with PD has been used in a variety of settings, and some investigators have suggested that it may serve as definitive therapy.[14,66,93,176,203] In a prospective study involving 44 infants treated with PD as primary management for advanced NEC, Demestre et al.[66] reported 28 patients (63.6%) treated with PD only and 16 patients (36.4%) who required laparotomy after PD. The survival rate after PD only was 64%, although 86% demonstrated improvement after drainage. After PD, 54% of infants required delayed surgery. Morgan et al.[203] used PD as primary treatment of NEC and perforation for infants weighing less than 1500 g and for unstable babies heavier than 1500 g. They reported a 79% survival rate after PD, with 17 of 23 (73.9%) survivors requiring no other operative intervention. Moss et al.[205] recently performed a meta-analysis of PD versus laparotomy for perforated NEC and reviewed 10 published studies on this topic. Because of the marked bias in treatment assignment, with a greater proportion of smaller babies undergoing PD versus laparotomy, the authors were unable to determine the relative merits of PD. Currently, most surgeons propose PD as the initial treatment in VLBW infants with perforated NEC to allow resuscitation and stabilization before definitive laparotomy. In an attempt to address this issue, two multicenter prospective randomized controlled trials are currently in progress to compare PD with primary laparotomy in premature infants less than 1000 g (A. Pierro: NET trial) or less than 1500 g (R.L. Moss: NECSTEPS trial).

Laparotomy

At laparotomy, the extent of NEC may be classified as focal, multifocal, or pan-intestinal (<25% viable bowel). Depending on the disease and patient characteristics at the time of surgery, a number of different surgical options may be undertaken, including resection with enterostomy, resection with anastomosis, proximal enterostomy, the "clip and drop" technique, and the "patch, drain, and wait" technique. The abdomen is entered via a right transverse supraumbilical incision with precautions taken to not injure the liver. Samples of peritoneal fluid may be harvested for culture of aerobic, anaerobic, and fungal organisms. The entire GI tract is systematically examined to assess the extent of disease and viability of the bowel. At the conclusion of the procedure, one should record the length of viable intestine remaining and note the presence or absence of the ileocecal valve.

A rarely cited complication of laparotomy for NEC is spontaneous intraoperative liver hemorrhage from injury caused by retractors or finger dissection. VanderKolk et al.[296] reported this complication in 11.8% of operations for NEC over a 5-year period. The mean gestational age of those with liver hemorrhage was 28 weeks (mean weight, 1262 g). Only one of these patients survived. The authors identified low mean preoperative arterial pressure and high preoperative fluid administration over the preceding 24 hours as significant predisposing factors. This complication occurred shortly after the abdomen was opened and the intestine was eviscerated. Liver congestion was followed by subcapsular hematoma and then free rupture.

Focal Disease

When a single area of bowel is necrotic or perforated, only limited resection is necessary. Creation of a proximal enterostomy and distal mucus fistula has been the standard of care. We prefer to exteriorize the stomas through the wound (either juxtaposed or separated) because (1) the mesentery is often thick and foreshortened, thus making passage of the stoma and its blood supply through the abdominal wall difficult, (2) stoma closure is facilitated, and (3) the incidence of wound complications is not increased in comparison to stomas at remote locations. The enterostomy is created by suturing the intestine to the fascia with interrupted sutures. About 2 cm of bowel is left protruding from the abdominal wall, and no attempt is made to use sutures to "mature" the end of the intestine. If stoma viability is in question after surgery, a small portion of the full thickness of the intestine is excised at the bedside and the cut ends are observed for bleeding.

Resection with primary anastomosis for isolated disease may be performed in carefully selected patients. Proponents of primary anastomosis cite the high morbidity associated with enterostomies in infants and no need for a second operation.[1] To safely perform this technique, the following criteria must be met: (1) a sharply localized, usually proximal segment of disease, (2) undamaged appearance of the remaining intestine, and (3) good overall patient condition without evidence of rapidly progressive sepsis or coagulopathy.

Multisegmental Disease (>50% Viable)

If the patient has multiple areas of necrosis separated by viable bowel, several options are available. Historically, the surgeon excises each diseased segment individually and creates multiple stomas rather than performing a massive resection. Conversely, a single high stoma (proximal jejunum) may be created and the distal bowel "spliced" together, thereby avoiding multiple stomas. A proximal jejunostomy can cause significant fluid and electrolyte loss and peristomal skin complications, although aggressive skin care with measurement and replacement of the stoma losses can avoid these potential complications. Anastomotic strictures are not uncommon and are addressed at the time of jejunostomy closure. Resection plus anastomosis has also gained increased acceptance as a valid treatment option for severe NEC and for multifocal disease.[229] In a study involving 46 infants with multifocal NEC, Fasoli et al.[81] reported a higher survival rate after resection and primary anastomosis (85%) versus enterostomy (50%).

Moore[200] described a controversial approach termed the "patch, drain, and wait" procedure in 1989. The principles of this potentially bowel length–preserving method are transverse single-layer suture approximation of perforations (patch), insertion of two Penrose drains that exit in the lower quadrants (drain), and a commitment to long-term parenteral nutrition (wait). The Penrose drains capture fecal fistulas and function as de facto enterostomies as the peritoneal cavity is rapidly obliterated by adhesions.[201] This procedure does not address the issue of ongoing sepsis because necrotic bowel is not resected, the general peritoneal cavity is difficult to drain, and the thin-walled perforated bowel often cannot handle suture.

Vaughan et al.[298] described a promising novel technique aimed at avoiding multiple enterostomies, circumventing the complications of a high jejunostomy, and preserving bowel length. The authors performed the "clip and drop back" technique in three patients with NEC. In this procedure, the obviously necrotic bowel is removed, and the cut ends are closed with titanium clips or staples. Re-exploration is performed 48 to 72 hours later, the clips are removed, and all segments are reanastomosed without any stomas. In one of the three patients, re-resection was required during the second-look operation, the bowel ends were clipped again, and a successful primary anastomosis was performed during a third operation. Follow-up for this very small series was 6 months to 7 years with no anastomotic complications or delayed reoperations.

Pan-involvement (NEC Totalis, <25% Viable)

Pan-involvement develops in 19% of patients[164]; it poses an enormous treatment problem and is a highly controversial management issue. The overriding consideration is to spare as much intestine as possible. Treatment options include resection of all necrotic bowel with placement of proximal or multiple stomas or proximal diversion without bowel resection, with plans for a second-look procedure. The decision to forego any treatment is supported by studies that demonstrate a 42% to 100% mortality rate in patients with pan-involvement, with almost all survivors left with short-bowel syndrome. The mortality rate is nearly 100% for infants who weigh less than 1000 g.

Diverting the intestinal stream by high proximal jejunostomy (without bowel resection) may facilitate healing of injured bowel through distal intestinal decompression, a reduction in its metabolic demands, and a decrease in the number of bacteria and possibly their by-products. This technique was initially reported by Martin and Neblett[186] and involves performing a high jejunostomy without resection, with plans for a second-look operation after 6 to 8 weeks. In a series of 10 patients with pan-involvement, Sugarman and Kiely[283] reported 8 infants surviving to undergo a second procedure. Resection of necrotic segments plus anastomosis was performed successfully, but the long-term survival rate was only 50%.

Stoma Closure and Complications

There is neither an ideal weight and age nor a universally agreed upon time at which intestinal continuity should be restored. The principal determinants are time since surgery, weight gain, and stoma output. In general, the enterostomy may be safely closed anytime after 4 weeks since the last operation, the risk period for strictures; attempted closure at less than 4 weeks after surgery may be met with a peritoneal cavity that is obliterated by vascular adhesions and resolving inflammation. Before enterostomy closure, patency of the distal end of the bowel should be confirmed by either a retrograde or antegrade contrast study. A study by Musemeche et al.[207] examined the complication rate after stomas were closed less than 3 months after surgery, 3 to 5 months after surgery, and more than 5 months after surgery; no differences were found. They also noted no difference in complications between patients who underwent closure at a body weight less than 2.5 kg, 2.5 to 5.0 kg, or greater than 5.0 kg.

Although enterostomy in neonates may be lifesaving, it is also a major cause of morbidity. In recent studies, enterostomies in newborns had an associated complication rate ranging from 34% to 68%.[217,302] Complications included wound infections, wound dehiscence, stoma stenosis requiring revision, incisional hernia, parastomal hernia, prolapse or intussusception, and small bowel obstruction.

SURVIVAL

Over the past decades, the survival of infants with NEC has progressively improved (Table 92-3).[250] This improvement has been attributed to earlier diagnosis and more effective supportive treatment for premature infants. Effective supportive treatment includes improved ventilatory strategies, surfactant therapy, total parenteral nutrition, improved understanding of the pathophysiology and management of critically ill newborns, and advancements in pediatric anesthesia. The increased survival has been most noticeable in infants who weigh less than 1000 g and are less than 28 weeks' gestational age. In a recent review of 754 premature infants born between 22 and 25 weeks' gestation, the overall survival rate was 63%, with a range of 14% at 22 weeks' gestation to 76% at 25 weeks' gestation.[51] Mortality was still significantly higher in VLBW infants than larger patients. This is highlighted by studies that examined the outcome of VLBW infants in comparison to "standard" premature infants (>1000 g) with pan-involvement NEC. Snyder et al.[273] found that infants weighing less than 1000 g are more likely to require surgery (51% versus 34%) and to eventually have pan-involvement (10% versus 4%) than infants greater than 1000 g. Pan-involvement was associated with 100% mortality in both groups. In a retrospective study of 70 infants weighing less than 1000 g with perforated NEC, Erhlich et al.[75] demonstrated that infant survival was independent of the type of surgical treatment (PD versus laparotomy), but instead was inversely related to the number of comorbid conditions associated with the patient.

We do not believe that the differences in mortality rates between series are attributable to differences in the effectiveness of the treatment programs used. In different groups of patients, the disease varies from predominantly localized disease to extensive necrosis. The patient population differs between the various series. The mortality rate can vary considerably, depending on birth weight, coexisting disease, virulence of the disease process, and whether the patient is in-born locally versus transferred. The precarious state of patients at risk for NEC is emphasized by the fact that in one series that compared patients who had NEC with matched controls, the mortality rate in the controls was 33%.[280]

COMPLICATIONS

Gastrointestinal

Intestinal Strictures

The first clinical and radiologic description of intestinal stricture after recovery from acute NEC was reported in 1968 by Rabinowitz et al.[240] The reported overall incidence varies from 9% to 36%,[114,269] and stricture formation is more frequent after nonoperative treatment. The incidence of strictures after NEC is increasing as the mortality rate from the disease decreases. Strictures result from fibrotic healing of an area of severe ischemic injury. Regardless of whether the stricture follows operative or nonoperative therapy, the most common site of

TABLE 92-3 Survival after Medical and Surgical Treatment of Necrotizing Enterocolitis

			Survival (%)	
Authors	**Years of Review**	**Patients (*N*)**	**Medically Treated**	**Surgically Treated**
Touloukian[290]	1955-1966	25	20	27
Wilson et al.[310]	1958-1968	16	14	13
Dudgeon et al.[250]	1970-1972	63	59	26
O'Neill[219]	1970-1974	52	69	60
Philippart and Rector[250]	1974-1976	73	73	81
Grosfeld et al.[98]	1972-1982	176	68	51
Ricketts and Jerles[246]	1980-1988	100	—	70
Grosfeld et al.[98]	1983-1990	126	95	75
Lemelle et al.[173]	1985-1990	331	82	65
Snyder et al.[273]	1971-1996	266	—	68
Ehrlich et al.[75]	1991-1998	70	—	75
Guthrie et al.[100]	1998-2000	390	95	77

Adapted from Rowe MI: Necrotizing enterocolitis. In Welch KJ, Randolph JG, Ravitch MM, et al (eds): Pediatric Surgery, 4th ed. Chicago, Year Book, 1986.

involvement has been the colon (80%). The next most common site is the terminal ileum (15%). Sixty percent of colonic strictures involve the left colon, and the most common colonic site is the splenic flexure (21%). Most patients have single strictures, but multiple strictures can occur (15%).[122] An intestinal stricture should be suspected after nonoperative management of NEC in an infant with failure to thrive, rectal bleeding, or bowel obstruction. These signs and symptoms occur in 50% of patients with strictures and should be evaluated with a contrast enema. If the study demonstrates a stricture in a symptomatic patient, elective resection with anastomosis is usually indicated.

Intestinal Malabsorption and Short-Bowel Syndrome

Malabsorption may result from a variety of factors, including decreased bowel length, decreased mucosal absorptive area, enzyme depletion, gut hypermotility, hypersecretion of gastric acid, bacterial overgrowth, decreased intestinal transit time, vitamin B_{12} deficiency, and bile salt deficiency. Short-bowel syndrome (see Chapter 86) is the most serious long-term GI complication associated with surgically treated NEC. It occurs in up to 23% of NEC survivors who undergo surgical resection.[245]

Cholestatic Liver Disease

Cholestatic liver disease results from a number of factors, but primarily from prolonged administration of total parenteral nutrition. It is characterized by direct hyperbilirubinemia, hepatomegaly, and elevated aminotransferase levels. Although the condition is multifactorial, the most important contributing factor is probably prolonged fasting. It has been shown that the most effective treatment is establishment of early, small-volume enteral feeding, concomitant with the administration of total parenteral nutrition, which aids in bowel adaptation by conferring a trophic effect on the intestinal mucosa and by stimulating bile flow.

Recurrent Necrotizing Enterocolitis

NEC can recur after operative and nonoperative management. The incidence is 4% to 6%.[246,282] No consistent association has been noted between recurrent NEC and the type or timing of enteral feeding, the anatomic site, or the method of initial management. More than 70% of patients were successfully treated nonoperatively for recurrence by Stringer et al.[282]

Anastomotic Ulceration

A late complication that may occur many years after resection for NEC is the development of anastomotic ulceration. Sondheimer et al.[276] reported six children who underwent ileocolonic resection and anastomosis in the neonatal period in whom lower GI bleeding developed at 5 to 13 years of age. Anastomotic ulceration was diagnosed by colonoscopy, and treatment entailed ulcer resection in five of six patients. Recurrence of marginal ulcers developed in four of five patients who underwent resection. Histologic examination revealed shallow ulcers penetrating only to the muscularis. The cause of the ulcers is unknown.

Neurodevelopmental Complications

The length of hospitalization of infants has been strongly associated with developmental progress at 1 to 2 years of age.[269] This probably reflects the adverse effects of medical and social factors on the developing brain. It is recommended that developmental screening be performed every 4 months during the first year and every 6 months during the second year because long-term follow-up data suggest that normal premature infants and survivors of severe NEC remain at high risk for neurologic developmental morbidity.

Approximately 50% of infants surviving NEC are neurodevelopmentally normal.[246,280] Historically, it was believed that any adverse neurodevelopmental outcome in a patient treated for NEC was due to underlying prematurity and comorbid conditions rather than the NEC itself, but recent evaluations of surviving infants contest this assumption. Vohr et al.[301] studied the neurodevelopmental, neurosensory, and functional outcomes of 1151 extremely low-birth-weight (401 to 1000 g) survivors at 18 to 22 months' corrected age and reported significant deficits in neurologic development (25%), a Bayley II Mental Developmental Index less than 70 (37%), a Psychomotor Development Index less than 70 (29%), vision impairment (9%), and hearing impairment (11%). NEC was specifically associated as a risk factor for both an abnormal neurologic examination and a low Bayley Psychomotor Development Index. In a study assessing the effect of NEC on neurodevelopment, Sonntag et al.[277] compared VLBW infants with NEC with matched infants without NEC at 12 and 20 months' corrected age. Despite normal somatic growth in infants with NEC not complicated by short-bowel syndrome, the authors demonstrated significant neurodevelopmental delay at both 12 and 20 months of age. Fifty-five percent of infants with NEC were noted to be severely retarded versus only 22.5% of infants without NEC.

PREVENTION

Attempts to reduce the incidence of or prevent NEC must consider the probable pathogenesis of the disease and some of the putative perinatal risk factors. Investigations into preventive measures for NEC, including limiting the nosocomial spread of microorganisms, augmenting host defense, decreasing bacterial colonization and overgrowth in the GI tract, providing factors that enhance intestinal maturation, and attenuating the inflammatory cascade, may be useful. Infection control measures, breastfeeding, cautious feeding of sick premature babies, immunoglobulin supplementation of feedings, corticosteroid therapy, administration of growth factors, and use of inflammatory mediator antagonists are some of the preventive strategies that have been studied.

Infection Control Measures

Adoption of infection control measures in the nursery may limit the incidence and restrict the spread of infections, thereby potentially eliminating the epidemic waves of NEC. The traditional prophylaxis for nosocomial epidemics includes strict hand washing with a germicidal agent, long-sleeved gown and gloves, separate diaper and laundry bags for each patient, cohorting and isolation of confirmed cases, and separate rooms and nurses for confirmed cases (without cross-covering). It has been demonstrated that the initiation of infection control measures stops epidemics of NEC.[31,109] During clustered occurrences, identical microorganisms can be isolated from both the afflicted neonates and their caretakers.

Augmentation of Host Defense

Oral Immunoglobulin Preparations

The protective immunoglobulins, principally IgA, are deficient in the premature gut. In the absence of breastfeeding, there are only trace amounts of secretory IgA and gut-associated IgG and IgM. Secretory IgA acts as an "antiseptic paint" by binding bacteria and preventing their attachment to the intestinal mucosa. Eibl et al.[76] demonstrated that enteral administration of an IgG-IgA preparation decreases the incidence of NEC. Their randomized trial involved feeding 179 high-risk infants weighing 800 to 2000 g a human preparation of IgG and IgA with their formula, whereas controls received formula alone. Neither group received breast milk. No cases of NEC developed in the immunoglobulin group, but 6 cases developed in the 91 controls. In a recent study in rabbits, Dickinson et al.[67] demonstrated that IgA supplementation in feedings prevented bacterial translocation by enhancing gut mucosal barrier functions. This effect was not seen with IgG or lactoferrin. In a randomized double-blind controlled trial, enteral IgG supplementation in infants failed to reduce the incidence of NEC.[170]

Maternal Glucocorticoid Administration

Glucocorticoids have been shown to accelerate mucosal cell maturation and improve gut barrier function. The action is mediated by glycosylation on the intestinal surface, which impairs bacterial attachment. Glucocorticoids have also been shown to down-regulate the inflammatory response by stimulating the enzymatic degradation of PAF.[274] These observations have been made experimentally and clinically.[76,101] Bauer et al.[20] retrospectively noted a significant reduction in the incidence of NEC in babies born to mothers who received antenatal glucocorticoids for fetal pulmonary maturation as compared with controls (2% versus 7%). This large, multicenter, placebo-controlled trial was well controlled for many potentially confounding variables. Halac et al.[101] conducted a randomized, controlled trial of prenatal glucocorticoid administration to mothers in preterm labor. The control mothers received placebo, but their infants received an immediate postnatal course of high-dose dexamethasone for 7 days. The rate of NEC within and between groups significantly decreased after prenatal and postnatal steroid treatment. Although postnatal therapy did not decrease the incidence as effectively as prenatal therapy did, it improved the clinical outcome of NEC; however, many potentially confounding factors were not assessed in this study. Confirmatory prospective data and assessment of potential postnatal toxicity are needed.

Breast Milk

Breast milk decreases the risk for a number of neonatal infections, including lower respiratory tract illness, otitis media, bacteremia, meningitis, and NEC.[34] Human milk provides an array of humoral and cellular anti-infectious factors, growth factors, and probiotics, as well as essential vitamins and nutrients. Milk factors include IgA, macrophages, lymphocytes, components of the complement system, lactoferrin, lysozyme, transferrin, interferon, EGF, alpha fetoprotein, erythropoietin, the probiotics *Bifidobacterium infantis* and *Lactobacillus acidophilus*, PAF acetylhydrolase, and several inflammatory mediators. Strong evidence exists for the protective role of secretory IgA, the main immune component of the enteromammary axis. Breast milk also inhibits the growth of *E. coli* by providing an acidic environment, promoting competitive growth of *Lactobacillus bifidus*, and binding iron (an element essential for the growth of *E. coli*).[17]

Because invasion by infectious agents seems to be a prime factor in the pathogenesis of NEC, breast milk appears to be ideally suited to protect the infant against the disease. Administration of breast milk prevents experimental NEC.[17,65] Formula-fed babies have four to six times the incidence of NEC as breast-fed infants do.[179]

Feeding Practices

There is little disagreement that NEC is more common in fed infants and that bacterial overgrowth is facilitated by the substrate provided by formula. Although the potential benefit of careful regulation of feeding to prevent NEC is widely accepted, randomized trials have failed to demonstrate any difference in the incidence of NEC related to fast versus slow, early versus delayed, or continuous versus intermittent bolus feeding.[136,137,166,220,238,243]

Low-birth-weight infants and infants with illnesses or prenatal problems are not fed for 7 to 10 days. Nutrition is provided parenterally. If no symptoms suggestive of NEC develop, feedings are cautiously begun. The type, concentration, and rate of increase are not universally accepted, although most clinicians begin with a hypocaloric formula at a slow rate. Feedings are withheld and the infant is evaluated if gastric residuals increase or any clinical findings potentially associated with NEC develop.

Methods to Decrease Intestinal Bacterial Colonization and Overgrowth

Administration of Probiotics

Probiotic bacteria are defined as "live microbial supplements that colonize the intestine to provide benefit to the host."[43,192] The use of anaerobic bacterial supplementation in the treatment or prevention of GI disease has been well described. There has been increasing interest in using probiotics for the prevention of NEC. Bifidobacteria are gram-positive anaerobic bacteria that predominantly colonize the gut in healthy breast-feeding neonates but are much less prevalent in the intestinal tract of premature infants at highest risk for NEC. Preliminary investigations in a neonatal rat model of NEC using probiotic supplementation have demonstrated a significant reduction in the incidence of NEC.[43,46] Future human clinical trials are needed.

Enteral Antibiotics

Nonabsorbable broad-spectrum antibiotics that inhibit bacterial growth have been administered in an effort to prevent NEC. The use of an enteral aminoglycoside (e.g., kanamycin or gentamicin) has been proposed as a means to decrease the incidence of perforation during nonoperative treatment. However, randomized, controlled studies found no difference in the clinical course, complications, or mortality rate between infants who received the antibiotic and those who did not.[74,194] In addition, oral aminoglycosides may be absorbed across the damaged gut, which can lead to increased serum levels and thereby potentially contribute to drug toxicity. Resistant strains of bacteria emerged after treatment with enteral kanamycin,[74] and there is the omnipresent risk for promotion of the growth of fungal species. In a recent randomized placebo-controlled study of oral vancomycin in preventing NEC in preterm infants, Siu et al.[271] reported a 50% reduction in the incidence of NEC in the vancomycin group in comparison to controls.

The available studies do not support the routine administration of enteral antibiotics to all high-risk premature infants, many of whom have poor intestinal motility. Effectiveness has not been proved, and resistant organisms may develop. Administering specific antibiotics to infants may be indicated in nurseries in which an outbreak of NEC is associated with a specific organism.

Acidification of Formula

Carrion and Egan[49] conducted a small prospective double-blinded study in which feedings given to premature infants were acidified with HCl to a pH of 2.5 to 5.5. Acidification of feedings significantly decreased the rate of gastric bacterial colonization in infants with a gastric pH less than 4.0. They also found a significantly lower incidence of NEC in infants given acidified feedings than in controls.

Inflammatory Mediator Antagonists

The effects of PAF are mediated by receptors, and many compounds that function as receptor antagonists or enzymes that degrade these proteins have been described. Animal experiments using PAF antagonists (WEB 2086, WEB 2170, SRI 63-441) or PAF-degrading enzyme (PAF acetylhydrolase) have demonstrated the capacity to prevent bowel injury produced by the administration of endotoxin or hypoxia in rats.[47,115] PAF acetylhydrolase is also known to be present in breast milk. Despite promising results in animal models, no human trials using PAF antagonists or degrading enzyme in the treatment of NEC have been reported.

REFERENCES

1. Ade-Ajayi N, Kiely E, Drake D, et al: Resection and primary anastomosis in necrotizing enterocolitis. J R Soc Med 1996; 89:385.
2. Agerty HA, Ziserman AJ, Shollenberger CL: A case of perforation of the ileum in a newborn infant with operation and recovery. J Pediatr 1943;22:233.
3. Akisu M, Ozmen D, Baka M, et al: Protective effect of dietary supplementation with L-arginine and L-carnitine on hypoxia/reoxygenation-induced necrotizing enterocolitis in young mice. Biol Neonate 2002;81:260.
4. Alavi K, Prasad R, Lundgren K, et al: Interleukin-11 enhances small intestine absorptive function and mucosal mass after intestinal adaptation. J Pediatr Surg 2000; 35:371.
5. Alderton WK, Cooper CE, Knowles RG: Nitric oxide synthases: Structure, function and inhibition. Biochem J 2001; 357:593.
6. Alican I, Kubes P: A critical role for nitric oxide in intestinal barrier function and dysfunction. Am J Physiol 1996; 33:G225.
7. Alpan G, Eyal F, Vinograd I, et al: Localized intestinal perforation after enteral administration of indomethacin in premature infants. J Pediatr 1985;106:277.
8. Amin HJ, Zamora SA, McMillan DD, et al: Arginine supplementation prevents necrotizing enterocolitis in premature infants. J Pediatr 2002;140:425.
9. Anderson DM, Kliegman RM: The relationship of neonatal alimentation practices to the occurrence of endemic necrotizing enterocolitis. Am J Perinatol 1991;8:62.
10. Andoh A, Fujiyama Y, Sumiyoshi K, et al: Interleukin-4 acts as an inducer of decay-accelerating factor gene expression in human intestinal epithelial cells. Gastroenterology 1996;111:911.
11. Appleby SB, Ristimaki A, Neilson K, et al: Structure of the human cyclooxygenase-2 gene. Biochem J 1994;302: 723.
12. Auricchio S, Rabino A, Murset G: Intestinal glycosidase activities in the human embryo, fetus, and newborn. J Pediatr 1965;35:944.
13. Avni EF, Rypens F, Cohen E, Pardou A: Peri-cholecystic hyper-echogenicity in necrotizing enterocolitis: A specific sonographic sign? Pediatr Radiol 1991;21:179.
14. Azarow KS, Ein SH, Shandling B, et al: Laparotomy or drain for perforated necrotizing enterocolitis: Who gets what and why. Pediatr Surg Int 1997;12:137.
15. Ballance WA, Dahms BB, Shenker N, et al: Pathology of neonatal necrotizing enterocolitis: A ten-year experience, J Pediatr 1990;117:56.
16. Bandstra ES, Bukett G: Maternal-fetal and neonatal effects of in utero cocaine exposure. Semin Perinatol 1991;15:288.
17. Barlow B, Santulli TV, Heird WC, et al: An experimental study of neonatal enterocolitis—the importance of breast milk. J Pediatr Surg 1984;9:587.
18. Barry MK, Aloisi JD, Pickering SP, et al: Nitric oxide modulates water and electrolyte transport in the ileum. Ann Surg 1994;219:382.
19. Bates MD: Development of the enteric nervous system. Clin Perinatol 2002;29:97.

20. Bauer CR, Morrison JC, Poole WK, et al: A decreased incidence of necrotizing enterocolitis after prenatal glucocorticoid therapy. Pediatrics 1984;73:682.
21. Bell MJ, Temberg JL, Feigin RD, et al: Neonatal necrotizing enterocolitis: Therapeutic decisions based upon clinical staging. Ann Surg 1978;187:1.
22. Berdon WE, Grossman H, Baker DH, et al: Necrotizing enterocolitis in the premature infant. Radiology 1964;83:879.
23. Berseth CL: Gestational evolution of small intestine motility in preterm and term infants. J Pediatr 1989;115:646.
24. Berseth CL, Bisquera JA, Paje VU: Prolonging small feeding volumes early in life decreases the incidence of necrotizing enterocolitis in very low birth weight infants. Pediatrics 2003;111:529.
25. Blakey JL, Lubitz L, Campbell NT, et al: Enteric colonization in sporadic neonatal necrotizing enterocolitis. J Pediatr Gastroenterol Nutr 1985;4:591.
26. Boccia D, Stolfi I, Lana S, et al: Nosocomial necrotising enterocolitis outbreaks: Epidemiology and control measures. Eur J Pediatr 2001;160:385.
27. Bolisetty S, Lui K: Necrotizing enterocolitis in full-term neonates. J Paediatr Child Health 2001;37:413.
28. Bone RC: Immunologic dissonance: A continuing evolution in our understanding of the systemic inflammatory response syndrome and the multiple organ dysfunction syndrome. Ann Intern Med 1996;125:690.
29. Book LS, Herbst JJ, Atherton SO, et al: Necrotizing enterocolitis in low birth weight infants fed elemental formula. J Pediatr 1975;87:602.
30. Book LS, Herbst JJ, Jung AL: Carbohydrate malabsorption in necrotizing enterocolitis. Pediatrics 1976;57:201.
31. Book LS, Overall JC, Herbst JJ: Clustering of necrotizing enterocolitis: Interruption by infection-control methods. N Engl J Med 1977;297:984.
32. Bousvaros A, Walker WA: Development and function of the intestinal mucosal barrier. In McDonald TT (ed): Ontogeny of the Immune System of the Gut. Boca Raton, FL, CRC Press, 1990, p 2.
33. Brown EG, Sweet AY: Preventing necrotizing enterocolitis in neonates. JAMA 1978;240:2452.
34. Buescher ES: Host defense mechanisms of human milk and their relations to enteric infections and necrotizing enterocolitis. Clin Perinatol 1994;21:247.
35. Buonomo C: Neonatal imaging: The radiology of necrotizing enterocolitis. Radiol Clin North Am 1999;37:1187.
36. Butter A, Glageole H, Laberge J: The changing face of surgical indications for necrotizing enterocolitis. J Pediatr Surg 2002;37:496.
37. Buyukunal C, Kilic N, Dervisoglu S, et al: Maternal cocaine abuse resulting in necrotizing enterocolitis—an experimental study in a rat model. Acta Paediatr Suppl 1994; 396:91.
38. Caplan MS, Amer M, Jilling T: The role of human milk in necrotizing enterocolitis. Adv Exp Med Biol 2002;503:83.
39. Caplan MS, Hedlund E, Adler L, et al: Role of asphyxia and feeding in a neonatal rat model of necrotizing enterocolitis. Pediatr Pathol 1994;14:1017.
40. Caplan MS, Hedlund E, Adler L, et al: The platelet-activating factor receptor antagonist WEB 2170 prevents necrotizing enterocolitis in rats. J Pediatr Gastroenterol Nutr 1997;24:296.
41. Caplan MS, Hedlund E, Hill N, et al: The role of endogenous nitric oxide and platelet-activating factor in hypoxia-induced intestinal injury in rats. Gastroenterology 1994; 106:346.
42. Caplan MS, Hsueh W, Kelly A, et al: Serum PAF acetylhydrolase increases during neonatal maturation. Prostaglandins 1990;39:705.
43. Caplan MS, Jilling T: Neonatal necrotizing enterocolitis: Possible role of probiotic supplementation. J Pediatr Gastroenterol Nutr 2000;30:S18.
44. Caplan MS, Jilling T: New concepts in necrotizing enterocolitis. Curr Opin Pediatr 2001;13:111.
45. Caplan MS, Lickerman M, Adler L, et al: The role of recombinant platelet-activating factor acetylhydrolase in a neonatal rat model of necrotizing enterocolitis. Pediatr Res 1997;42:779.
46. Caplan MS, Miller-Catchpole, R, Kaup S, et al: Bifidobacterial supplementation reduces the incidence of necrotizing enterocolitis in a neonatal rat model. Gastroenterology 1999;117:577.
47. Caplan MS, Sun XM, Hsueh W, et al: Role of platelet activating factor and tumor necrosis factor-alpha in neonatal necrotizing enterocolitis. J Pediatr 1990;116:960.
48. Caplan MS, Sun XM, Hsueh W: Hypoxia causes ischemic bowel necrosis in rats: The role of platelet-activating factor. Gastroenterology 1990;99:979.
49. Carrion V, Egan E: Prevention of neonatal necrotizing enterocolitis. J Pediatr Gastroenterol Nutr 1990;11:317.
50. Chailler P, Menard D: Ontogeny of EGF receptors in the human gut. Font Biosci 1999;4:D87.
51. Chan K, Ohlsson A, Synnes A, et al: Survival, morbidity, and resource use in infants of 25 weeks' gestational age or less. Am J Obstet Gynecol 2001;185:220.
52. Chandler JC, Hebra A: Necrotizing enterocolitis in infants with very low birth weight. Semin Pediatr Surg 2000;9:63.
53. Chen K, Inoue M, Okada A: Expression of inducible nitric oxide synthase mRNA in rat digestive tissues after endotoxin and its role in intestinal mucosal injury. Biochem Biophys Res Commun 1996;224:703.
54. Cheu HW, Brown DR, Rowe MI: Breath hydrogen excretion as a screening for the early diagnosis of necrotizing enterocolitis. Am J Dis Child 1989;143:156.
55. Chung DH, Ethridge RT, Kim S, et al: Molecular mechanisms contributing to necrotizing enterocolitis. Ann Surg 2001;233:835.
56. Claud EC, Savidge T, Walker WA: Modulation of human intestinal epithelial cell IL-8 secretion by human milk factors. Pediatr Res 2003;53:419.
57. Cohen S: The epidermal growth factor (EGF). Cancer 1983;51:1787.
58. Coopersmith CM, O'Donnell D, Gordon JI: Bcl-2 inhibits ischemia-reperfusion–induced apoptosis in the intestinal epithelium of transgenic mice. Am J Physiol 1999; 276:G677.
59. Cronin CM, Canose J, Buchanan D, et al: The effect of aminophylline on gastrointestinal blood flow and oxygen metabolism in the conscious newborn lamb. J Pediatr Gastroenterol Nutr 1989;8:371.
60. Crow JP, Beckman JS: Reactions between nitric oxide, superoxide, and peroxynitrite: Footprints of peroxynitrite in vivo. Adv Pharmacol 1995;34:17.
61. Czyrko C, Del Pin CA, O'Neill JA Jr, et al: Maternal cocaine abuse and necrotizing enterocolitis: Outcome and survival. J Pediatr Surg 1991;26:414.
62. Daneman A, Woodward S, deSilva M: The radiology of neonatal necrotizing enterocolitis: A review of 47 cases and the literature. Pediatr Radiol 1978;7:70.
63. Davis JM, Abbasi S, Spitzer AR, et al: Role of theophylline in pathogenesis of necrotizing enterocolitis. J Pediatr 1986;109:344.
64. Deitch EA: Role of bacterial translocation in necrotizing enterocolitis. Acta Paediatr Suppl 1994;396:33.
65. de Lemos RA, Rogers JR Jr, McLaughlin GW: Experimental production of necrotizing enterocolitis in newborn goats [abstract]. Pediatr Res 1974;8:830.

66. Demestre X, Ginovart G, Figueras-Aloy J, et al: Peritoneal drainage as primary management in necrotizing enterocolitis: A prospective study. J Pediatr Surg 2002;37:1534.
67. Dickinson EC, Gorga JC, Garrett M, et al: Immunoglobulin A supplementation abrogates bacterial translocation and preserves the architecture of the intestinal epithelium. Surgery 1998;124:284.
68. Dickinson EC, Tuncer R, Nadler EP, et al: Recombinant human interleukin-11 prevents mucosal atrophy and bowel shortening in the defunctionalized intestine. J Pediatr Surg 2000;35:1079.
69. Di Lorenzo M, Bass J, Krantis A: Use of L-arginine in the treatment of experimental necrotizing enterocolitis. J Pediatr Surg 1995;30:235.
70. Downing GJ, Horner SR, Kilbride HW: Characteristics of perinatal cocaine exposed infants with necrotizing enterocolitis. Am J Dis Child 1991;145:26.
71. Dunn L, Hulman S, Weiner J, et al: Beneficial effects of early hypocaloric enteral feeding on neonatal gastrointestinal function: Preliminary report of a randomized trial. J Pediatr 1988;112:622.
72. Dvorak B, Hallpern MD, Holubec H, et al: Epidermal growth factor reduces the development of necrotizing enterocolitis in a neonatal rat model. Am J Physiol Gastrointest Liver Physiol 2002;282:G156.
73. Edelson MB, Bagwell CE, Rozycki HJ: Circulating pro- and counterinflammatory cytokine levels and severity in necrotizing enterocolitis. Pediatrics 1999;103:766.
74. Egan EA, Nelson RM, Mantilla G, Eitzman DV: Additional experience with routine use of oral kanamycin prophylaxis for necrotizing enterocolitis in infants under 1,500 grams. J Pediatr 1977;90:331.
75. Ehrlich PF, Sato TT, Short BL, et al: Outcome of perforated necrotizing enterocolitis in the very low birth weight neonate may be independent of the type of surgical treatment. Am Surg 2001;67:752.
76. Eibl MM, Wolf HM, Furnkranz H, et al: Prevention of necrotizing enterocolitis in low-birth-weight infants by IgA-IgG feeding. N Engl J Med 1988;319:1.
77. Ein SH, Marshall DG, Girvan D: Peritoneal drainage under local anesthesia for necrotizing enterocolitis. J Pediatr Surg 1977;12:963.
78. Engel RR, Virning NL, Hunt CE, et al: Origin of mural gas in necrotizing enterocolitis. Pediatr Res 1973;7:292.
79. Ewer AK, Al-Salti W, Coney AM, et al: The role of platelet-activating factor in a neonatal piglet model of necrotising enterocolitis. Gut 2004;53:207.
80. Fagbemi AO, Wright N, Lakhoo K, et al: Immunoreactive epidermal growth factor receptors are present in gastrointestinal epithelial cells of preterm infants with necrotising enterocolitis. Early Hum Dev 2001;65:1.
81. Fasoli L, Turi RA, Spitz L, et al: Necrotizing enterocolitis: Extent of disease and surgical treatment. J Pediatr Surg 1999;34:1096.
82. Finer NN, Peters KL, Hayek Z, et al: Vitamin E and necrotizing enterocolitis. Pediatrics 1984;73:387.
83. Fisher CJ, Agosti JM, Opal SM, et al: Treatment of septic shock with the tumour necrosis factor: Fc fusion protein. N Engl J Med 1996;334:1697.
84. Ford H, Watkins S, Reblock K, et al: The role of inflammatory cytokine and nitric oxide in the pathogenesis of necrotizing enterocolitis. J Pediatr Surg 1997;32:275.
85. Frey EE, Smith W, Franken EA, et al: Analysis of bowel perforation in necrotizing enterocolitis. Pediatr Radiol 1987; 17:380.
86. Garcia J, Smith FR, Cucinell SA: Urinary D-lactate excretion in infants with necrotizing enterocolitis. J Pediatr 1984; 104:268.
87. Gavilanes A, Heineman E, Herpers M, et al: Use of neonatal intensive care unit as a safe place for neonatal surgery. Arch Dis Child 1997;76:F51.
88. Generisch A: Bauchfellentzündung beim Neugeborenen in folge von Perforation des Ileums. Virchows Arch Pathol Anat 1891;126:485.
89. Gersony WM, Peckham GJ, Ellison RC, et al: Effects of indomethacin in premature infants with patent ductus arteriosus: Results of a national collaborative study. J Pediatr 1983;102:895.
90. Gianotti L, Alexander JW, Pyles T, et al: Arginine-supplemented diets improve survival in gut-derived sepsis and peritonitis by modulating bacterial clearance. The role of nitric oxide. Ann Surg 1993;217:644.
91. Glode MP, Sutton A, Moxon ER, et al: Pathogenesis of neonatal *Escherichia coli* meningitis: Induction of bacteremia and meningitis in infant rats fed *E coli* K1. Infect Immunol 1977;16:75.
92. Goldman AS, Thorpe LW, Goldblum RM, et al: Anti-inflammatory properties of human milk. Acta Paediatr Scand 1986;75:689.
93. Gollin G, Abarbanell A, Baerg J: Peritoneal drainage as definitive management of intestinal perforation in extremely low-birth-weight infants. J Pediatr Surg 2003; 38:1814.
94. Gonzalez-Crussi F, Hsueh W: Experimental model of ischemic bowel necrosis: The role of platelet-activating factor and endotoxin. Am J Pathol 1983;112:127.
95. Graf JL, Vanderwall KJ, Adzick NS, et al: Nitroglycerin attenuates the bowel damage of necrotizing enterocolitis in a rabbit model. J Pediatr Surg 1997;32:283.
96. Grantmyre EB, Butler GJ, Gillis DA: Necrotizing enterocolitis after Renografin-76 treatments of meconium ileus. AJR Am J Roentgenol 1981;136:990.
97. Grosfeld JL, Chaet M, Molinari F, et al: Increased risk of necrotizing enterocolitis in premature infants with patent ductus arteriosus treated with indomethacin. Ann Surg 1996;224:350.
98. Grosfeld JL, Cheu H, Schlatter M: Changing trends in necrotizing enterocolitis: Experience with 302 cases in two decades. Ann Surg 1991;214:300.
99. Grosfeld JL, Kamman K, Gross K, et al: Comparative effects of indomethacin, prostaglandin E, and ibuprofen on bowel ischemia. J Pediatr Surg 1983;18:738.
100. Guthrie SO, Gordon PV, Thomas V, et al: Necrotizing enterocolitis among neonates in the United States. J Perinatol 2003;23:278.
101. Halac E, Halac J, Begue EF, et al: Prenatal and postnatal corticosteroid therapy to prevent neonatal necrotizing enterocolitis: A controlled trial. J Pediatr 1990;117:132.
102. Hallstrom M, Koivisto AM, Janas M, et al: Frequency of and risk factors for necrotizing enterocolitis in infants born before 33 weeks of gestation. Acta Paediatr 2003; 92:111.
103. Halpern MD, Dominguiz JA, Dvorakova K, et al: Ileal cytokine dysregulation in experimental necrotizing enterocolitis is reduced by epidermal growth factor. J Pediatr Gastroenterol Nutr 2003;36:126.
104. Hamosh M: Bioactive factors in human milk. Pediatr Clin North Am 2001;48:69.
105. Hanahan DJ: Platelet activating factor: A biologically active phosphoglyceride. Annu Rev Biochem 1986;55:483.
106. Hand IL, Noble L, McVeigh, et al: The effects of intrauterine cocaine exposure on the respiratory status of the very low birth weight infant. J Perinatol 2001;21:372.
107. Harris MC, Costarino AT Jr, Sullivan JS, et al: Cytokine elevations in critically ill infants with sepsis and necrotizing enterocolitis. J Pediatr 1994;124:105.

108. Harris PD, Neuhauser EBD, Gerth R: The osmotic effect of water soluble contrast media on circulating plasma volume. Am J Roentgenol Radium Ther Nucl Med 1964;91:694.
109. Healthy People 2000: National Health Promotion and Disease Prevention Objective (DHHS Publication [PHS] No. 21-59212:365). Washington, DC, Department of Health and Human Services, 1991.
110. Hebra A, Brown MF, McGeehin K, et al: Systemic and mesenteric vascular effects of platelet-activating factor and cocaine. In vivo effects on a neonatal swine model. Am Surg 1993;59:50.
111. Helmrath MA, Shin CE, Fox JW, et al: Epidermal growth factor in saliva and serum of infants with necrotising enterocolitis. Lancet 1998;351:266.
112. Henderson-Smart DJ, Subramaniam P, Davis P: Continuous positive airway pressure versus theophylline for apnea in preterm infants. Cochrane Database Syst Rev 2001;4: CD001072.
113. Horbar JD, Wright EC, Onstad L: NICHD Neonatal Research Network: Decreasing mortality associated with the introduction of surfactant therapy: An observational study of neonates weighing 601 to 1300 grams at birth. Pediatrics 1993;92:191.
114. Horwitz JR, Lally KP, Cheu HW, et al: Complications after surgical intervention for necrotizing enterocolitis: A multicenter review. J Pediatr Surg 1995;30:994.
115. Hsueh W, Caplan MS, Qu XW, et al: Neonatal necrotizing enterocolitis: Clinical considerations and pathogenetic concepts. Pediatr Dev Pathol 2002;6:6.
116. Hsueh W, Gonzalez-Crussi F, Arroyave JL: Platelet activating factor is an endogenous mediator for bowel necrosis in endotoxemia. FASEB J 1987;1:403.
117. Hutcheson IR, Whittle BJR, Boughton-Smith NK: Role of nitric oxide in maintaining vascular integrity in endotoxin-induced acute intestinal damage in the rat. Br J Pharmacol 1990;101:815.
118. Hutter JJ, Hathaway WE, Wayne ER: Hematologic abnormalities in severe neonatal necrotizing enterocolitis. J Pediatr 1976;88:1026.
119. Inagaki-Ohara K, Yada S, Takamura N, et al: P53-dependent radiation-induced crypt intestinal epithelial cell apoptosis is mediated in part through TNF-TNFR1 system. Oncogene 2001;20:812.
120. Isaacs D, North J, Lindsell D, Wilkinson AR: Serum acute phase reactants in necrotizing enterocolitis. Acta Paediatr Scand 1987;76:923.
121. Jaattela M: Biologic activities and mechanisms of action of tumor necrosis factor-alpha/cachectin. Lab Invest 1991; 64:724.
122. Janik JS, Ein SH, Mancer K: Intestinal strictures after necrotizing enterocolitis. J Pediatr Surg 1981;16:438.
123. Jilling T, Lu J, Jackson M, et al: Intestinal epithelial apoptosis initiates gross bowel necrosis in an experimental rat model of neonatal necrotizing enterocolitis. Pediatr Res 2004;55:622.
124. Johnson L, Bowen FW Jr, Abbasi S, et al: Relationship of prolonged pharmacologic serum levels of vitamin E to incidence of sepsis and necrotizing enterocolitis in infants with birth weight 1500 grams or less. Pediatrics 1985; 75:619.
125. Jones KL: Developmental pathogenesis of defects associated with prenatal cocaine exposure: Fetal vascular disruption. Clin Perinatol 1991;18:139.
126. Jones MK, Tomikawa M, Mohajer B, et al: Gastrointestinal mucosal regeneration: Role of growth factors. Front Biosci 1999;4:D303.
127. Juul SE: Erythropoietin in the neonate. Curr Probl Pediatr 1999;29:129.
128. Juul SE, Joyce AE, Zhao Y, et al: Why is erythropoietin present in human milk? Studies of erythropoietin receptors on enterocytes of human and rat neonates. Pediatr Res 1999;46:263.
129. Juul SE, Ledbetter DJ, Joyce AE, et al: Erythropoietin acts as a trophic factor in neonatal rat intestine. Gut 2001;49:182.
130. Juul SE, Yachnis AT, Christensen RD: Tissue distribution of erythropoietin and erythropoietin receptor in the developing human fetus. Early Hum Dev 1998;52:235.
131. Kafetzis DA, Skevaki C, Costalos C: Neonatal necrotizing enterocolitis: An overview. Curr Opin Infect Dis 2003; 16:349.
132. Kamitsuka MD, Horton MK, Williams MA: The incidence of necrotizing enterocolitis after introducing standardized feeding schedules for infants between 1250 and 2500 grams and less than 35 weeks of gestation. Pediatrics 2000;105:379.
133. Kanto WP Jr, Hunter JE, Stoll BJ: Recognition and medical management of necrotizing enterocolitis. Clin Perinatol 1994;21:335.
134. Kao SCS, Smith KWL, Franklin EA Jr, et al: Contrast enema diagnosis of necrotizing enterocolitis. Pediatr Radiol 1992; 22:115.
135. Karlowicz MG: Risk factors associated with fungal peritonitis in very low birth weight neonates with severe necrotizing enterocolitis: A case-control study. Pediatr Infect Dis J 1993;12:574.
136. Kennedy KA, Tyson JE, Chamnanvanakij S: Rapid versus slow rate of advancement of feedings for promoting growth and preventing necrotizing enterocolitis in parenterally fed low-birth-weight infants. Cochrane Database Syst Rev 2000;(2):CD001241.
137. Kennedy KA, Tyson JE, Chamnanvanakij S: Early versus delayed initiation of progressive enteral feedings for parenterally fed low birth weight or preterm infants. Cochrane Database Syst Rev 2000;(2):CD001970.
138. Kilic N, Buyukunal C, Dervisoglu S, et al: Maternal cocaine abuse resulting in necrotizing enterocolitis. An experimental study in a rat model. II. Results of perfusion studies. Pediatr Surg Int 2000;16:176.
139. Kleessen B, Bunke H, Tovar K, et al: Influence of two infant formulas and human milk on the development of faecal flora in newborn infants. Acta Paediatr 1995;84: 1347.
140. Kliegman RM: Neonatal necrotizing enterocolitis: Implications for an infectious disease. Paediatr Clin North Am 1979;26:327.
141. Kliegman RM: Neonatal necrotizing enterocolitis: Bridging the basic science with the clinical disease. J Pediatr 1990;117:833.
142. Kliegman RM, Fanaroff AA: Neonatal necrotizing enterocolitis: A nine-year experience. Am J Dis Child 1981; 135:608.
143. Kliegman RM, Fanaroff AA: Neonatal necrotizing enterocolitis in the absence of pneumatosis. Am J Dis Child 1982;136:608.
144. Kliegman RM, Fanaroff AA: Neonatal necrotizing enterocolitis. N Engl J Med 1984;310:1093.
145. Kliegman RM, Hack M, Jones P, et al: Epidemiologic study of necrotizing enterocolitis among low-birth-weight infants. J Pediatr 1982;100:440.
146. Kliegman RM, Pittard WB, Fanaroff AA: Necrotizing enterocolitis in neonates fed human milk. J Pediatr 1979; 95:450.
147. Kliegman RM, Walker WA, Yolken RH: Necrotizing enterocolitis: Research agenda for a disease of unknown etiology and pathogenesis. Pediatr Res 1993;34:701.

148. Kliegman RM, Walsh MC: Neonatal necrotizing enterocolitis: Pathogenesis, classification, and spectrum of illness. Cur Probl Pediatr 1987;17:213.
149. Kling PJ, Sullivan TM, Roberts RA, et al: Human milk as a potential enteral source of erythropoietin. Pediatr Res 1998;43:216.
150. Kodroff MB, Hartenberg MA, Goldschmidt RA: Ultrasonographic diagnosis of gangrenous bowel in neonatal necrotizing enterocolitis. Pediatr Radiol 1984; 14:168.
151. Kosloske AM: Surgery for necrotizing enterocolitis. World J Surg 1985;9:277.
152. Kosloske AM: Epidemiology of necrotizing enterocolitis. Acta Paediatr Suppl 1994;396:2.
153. Kosloske AM: Indications for operation in necrotizing enterocolitis revisited. J Pediatr Surg 1994;29:663.
154. Kosloske AM, Musemeche CA: Necrotizing enterocolitis of the neonate. Clin Perinatol 1989;16:97.
155. Kosloske AM, Papile LA, Burstein J: Indications for operation in acute necrotizing enterocolitis of the neonate. Surgery 1980;87:502.
156. Krasna IH, Kim H: Indomethacin administration after temporary ischemia causes bowel necrosis in mice. J Pediatr Surg 1992;27:805.
157. Krouskop RW, Brown EG, Sweet AY: The relationship of feeding to necrotizing enterocolitis. Pediatr Res 1974; 8:383.
158. Kubes P: Ischemia-reperfusion in feline small intestine: A role for nitric oxide. Am J Physiol 1993;264:G143.
159. Kubes P: Inducible nitric oxide synthase: A little bit of good in all of us. Gut 2000;47:6.
160. Kubes P, Arfors KE, Granger DE: Platelet-activating factor–induced mucosal dysfunction: Role of oxidants and granulocytes. Am J Physiol 1991;260:G965.
161. Kubes P, McCafferty DM: Nitric oxide and intestinal inflammation. Am J Med 2000;109:150.
162. Kuhl G, Wille L, Bolkenius M, et al: Intestinal perforation associated with indomethacin treatment in premature infants. Eur J Pediatr 1985;143:213.
163. Kumral A, Baskin H, Duman N, et al: Erythropoietin protects against necrotizing enterocolitis of newborn rats by the inhibiting nitric oxide formation. Biol Neonate 2003;84:325.
164. Kurkchubasche AG, Smith SD, Rowe MI: Portal venous air—an old sign and new operative indication for necrotizing enterocolitis [abstract]. Paper presented at the 38th BAPS Annual International Congress, July 1991, Budapest.
165. La Gamma EF, Browne LE: Feeding practices for infants weighing less than 1500 g at birth and the pathogenesis of necrotizing enterocolitis. Clin Perinatol 1994;21:271.
166. La Gamma EF, Ostertag SG, Birenbaum H: Failure of delayed oral feedings to prevent necrotizing enterocolitis. Results of study in very-low-birth-weight neonates. Am J Dis Child 1985;139:385.
167. Langer JC, Sohal SS, Mumford DA: Mucosal permeability in the immature rat intestine: Effects of ischemia-reperfusion, cold stress, hypoxia, and drugs. J Pediatr Surg 1993;28:1380.
168. Lauw FN, Pajkrt D, Hack CE, et al: Proinflammatory effects of IL-10 during human endotoxemia. J Immunol 2000;165:2783.
169. Lawrence G, Bates J, Gaul A: Pathogenesis of neonatal necrotizing enterocolitis. Lancet 1982;72:317.
170. Lawrence G, Tudehope D, Baumann K, et al: Enteral human IgG for prevention of necrotising enterocolitis: A placebo-controlled, randomized trial. Lancet 2001;357: 2090.
171. Ledbetter DJ, Juul SE: Erythropoietin and the incidence of necrotizing enterocolitis in infants with very low birth weights. J Pediatr Surg 2000;35:178.
172. Ledbetter DJ, Juul SE: Necrotizing enterocolitis and hematopoietic cytokines. Clin Perinatol 2000;27:697.
173. Lemelle JL, Schmitt M, de Miscault G, et al: Neonatal necrotizing enterocolitis: A retrospective and multicentric review of 331 cases. Acta Paediatr Suppl 1994;396:70.
174. Lemons JA, Bauer CR, Oh W, et al: Very low birth weight outcomes of the National Institute of Child Health and Human Development Neonatal Research Network, January 1995 through December 1996. Pediatrics 2001; 107:e1.
175. Leonard T Jr, Johnson F, Pettett PG: Critical evaluation of the persistent loop sign in necrotizing enterocolitis. Radiology 1982;142:385.
176. Lessin MS, Luks FI, Wesselhoeft CW Jr, et al: Peritoneal drainage as definitive treatment for intestinal perforation in infants with extremely low birth weight (less than 750 grams). J Pediatr Surg 1998;33:370.
177. Liu Q, Du XX, Schindel DT, et al: Trophic effects of interleukin-11 in rats with experimental short bowel syndrome. J Pediatr Surg 1996;31:1047.
178. Lopez SL, Taeusch HW, Findlay RD, et al: Time of onset of necrotizing enterocolitis in newborn infants with known prenatal cocaine exposure. Clin Pediatr (Phila) 1995;34:424.
179. Lucas A, Cole TJ: Breast milk and neonatal necrotizing enterocolitis. Lancet 1990;336:1519.
180. Maalouf EF, Fagbemi A, Duggan PJ, et al: Magnetic resonance imaging of intestinal necrosis in preterm infants. Pediatrics 2000;105:510.
181. MacKendrick W, Caplan M, Hsueh W: Endogenous nitric oxide protects against platelet-activating factor–induced bowel injury in the rat. Pediatr Res 1993;34:222.
182. MacKendrick W, Hill N, Hsueh W, et al: Increase in plasma platelet-activating factor levels in enterally fed preterm infants. Biol Neonate 1993;64:89.
183. Mahony L, Caldwell RL, Girod DA, et al: Indomethacin therapy on the first day of life in infants with very low birth weight. J Pediatr 1985;106:801.
184. Malo C, Menard D: Influence of epidermal growth factor on the development of sucking mouse intestinal mucosa. Gastroenterology 1982;83:28.
185. Marchildon MB, Buck BE, Abdenour G: Necrotizing enterocolitis in the unfed infant. J Pediatr Surg 1982;17:620.
186. Martin LW, Neblett WW: Early operation with intestinal diversion for necrotizing enterocolitis. J Pediatr Surg 1981; 16:252.
187. Martinez-Tallo E, Claure N, Bancalari E: Necrotizing enterocolitis in full-term or near-term infants: Risk factors. Biol Neonate 1997;71:292.
188. Marty C, Misset B, Tamian F, et al: Circulating interleukin-8 concentrations in patients with multiple organ failure of septic and nonseptic origin. Crit Care Med 1994;22:673.
189. Mercurio F, Manning AM: NF-κB as a primary regulator of the stress response. Oncogene 1999;42:477.
190. Merritt CRB, Goldsmith JP, Sharp MJ: Sonographic detection of portal venous gas in infants with necrotizing enterocolitis. AJR Am J Roentgenol 1984;143:1059.
191. Miettinen PJ, Berger JE, Meneses J, et al: Epithelial immaturity and multiorgan failure in mice lacking epidermal growth factor receptor. Nature 1995;376:337.
192. Millar M, Wilks M, Costeloe K: Probiotics for preterm infants? Arch Dis Child 2003;88:F354.
193. Miller MJS, Zhang XJ, Sadowska-Krowicka H, et al: Nitric oxide release in response to gut injury. Scand J Gastroenterol 1993;28:149.

194. Miranda JC, Schimmel MS, Mimms GM, et al: Gentamicin absorption during prophylactic use for necrotizing enterocolitis. Dev Pharmacol Ther 1984;7:303.
195. Mizrahi A, Barlow O, Berdon W, et al: Necrotizing enterocolitis in premature infants. J Pediatr 1965;66:697.
196. Molik KA, West KW, Rescorla FJ, et al: Portal venous air: The poor prognosis persists. J Pediatr Surg 2001;36:1143.
197. Mollit DL, Tepas JJ, String DL, et al: Does patient age or intestinal pathology influence the bacteria found in cases of necrotizing enterocolitis? South Med J 1990;84:879.
198. Moncada S, Palmer RM, Higgs EA: Nitric oxide: Physiology, pathophysiology, and pharmacology. Pharmacol Rev 1991; 43:109.
199. Moomjian AS, Sokal MM, Vijayan S: Necrotizing enterocolitis—endemic vs epidemic form. Pediatr Res 1978; 12:530.
200. Moore TC: Management of necrotizing enterocolitis by "patch, drain, and wait." Pediatr Surg Int 1989;4:110.
201. Moore TC: Successful use of the "patch, drain, and wait" laparotomy approach to perforated necrotizing enterocolitis: Is hypoxia-triggered "good angiogenesis" involved? Pediatr Surg Int 2000;16:356.
202. Moore TR, Sorg J, Miller L, et al: Hemodynamic effects of intravenous cocaine on the pregnant ewe and fetus. Am J Obstet Gynecol 1986;157:686.
203. Morgan JL, Shochat SJ, Hartman GE: Peritoneal drainage as primary management of perforated NEC in the very low birth weight infant. J Pediatr Surg 1994;29:310.
204. Morrison SC, Jacobson JM: The radiology of necrotizing enterocolitis. Clin Perinatol 1994;21:347.
205. Moss RL, Dimmitt RA, Henry MCW, et al: A meta-analysis of peritoneal drainage versus laparotomy for perforated necrotizing enterocolitis. J Pediatr Surg 2001;36:1210.
206. Moya FR, Eguchi H, Zhao B, et al: Platelet-activating factor acetylhydrolase in term and preterm human milk: A preliminary report. J Pediatr Gastroenterol Nutr 1994; 19:236.
207. Musemeche CA, Kosloske AM, Ricketts RR: Enterostomy in necrotizing enterocolitis: An analysis of techniques and timing of closure. J Pediatr Surg 1987;22:479.
208. Nadler EP, Dickinson E, Knisely A, et al: Expression of inducible nitric oxide synthase and interleukin-12 in experimental necrotizing enterocolitis. J Surg Res 2000; 92:71.
209. Nadler EP, Stanford A, Zhang XR, et al: Intestinal cytokine gene expression in infants with acute necrotizing enterocolitis: Interleukin-11 mRNA expression inversely correlates with extent of disease. J Pediatr Surg 2001;36:1122.
210. Nanthakumar NN, Fusunyan RD, Sanderson I, et al: Inflammation in the developing human intestine: A possible pathophysiologic contribution to necrotizing enterocolitis. Proc Natl Acad Sci U S A 2000;97:6043.
211. Nathan C, Xie Q: Nitric oxide synthases: Roles, tolls, and controls. Cell 1994;78:915.
212. Needleman P, Turk J, Jakschik BA, et al: Arachidonic acid metabolism. Annu Rev Biochem 1986;55:69.
213. Neu J, Bernstein H: Update on host defense and immunonutrients. Clin Perinatol 2002;29:41.
214. Nilsen EM, Johansen FE, Jahnsen FL, et al: Cytokine profiles of cultured microvascular endothelial cells from the human intestine. Gut 1998;42:635.
215. Norton ME, Merrill J, Cooper BA, et al: Neonatal complications after administration of indomethacin for preterm labor. N Engl J Med 1993;329:1602.
216. Nowicki P: Intestinal ischemia and necrotizing enterocolitis. J Pediatr 1990;117:S14.
217. O'Connor A, Sawin RS: High morbidity of enterostomy and its closure in premature infants with necrotizing enterocolitis. Arch Surg 1998;133:875.
218. Ohls RK: Erythropoietin to prevent and treat the anemia of prematurity. Curr Opin Pediatr 1999;11:108.
219. O'Neill JA Jr: Neonatal necrotizing enterocolitis. Surg Clin North Am 1981;61:1013.
220. Ostertag SG, LaGamma EF, Reisen CE, Ferrentino FL: Early enteral feeding does not affect the incidence of necrotizing enterocolitis. Pediatrics 1986;77:275.
221. Ostlie DJ, Spilde TL, St Peter SD, et al: Necrotizing enterocolitis in full-term infants. J Pediatr Surg 2003;38:1039.
222. Ozturk H, Dokucu A, Ogun C, et al: Protective effects of recombinant human interleukin-10 on intestines of hypoxia-induced necrotizing enterocolitis in immature rats. J Pediatr Surg 2002;37:1330.
223. Paltauf A: Die spontane dickdarm Rupture der Neugeborenen. Virchows Arch Pathol Anat 1888;111:461.
224. Pang G, Couch L, Batey R, et al: GM-CSF, IL-1 alpha, IL-1 beta, IL-6, IL-8, IL-10, ICAM-1, and VCAM-1 gene expression and cytokine production in human duodenal fibroblasts stimulated with lipopolysaccharide, IL-1 alpha and TNF-alpha. Clin Exp Immunol 1994;96:437.
225. Pang KY, Bresson JL, Walker WA: Development of the gastrointestinal mucosal barrier. III. Evidence for structural differences in microvillus membranes from newborn and adult rabbits. Biochem Biophys Acta 1983;727:201.
226. Parikh AA, Salzman AL, Kane CD, et al: IL-6 production in human intestinal epithelial cells following stimulation with IL-1 beta is associated with activation of the transcription factor NF-kappa B. J Surg Res 1997;69:139.
227. Parks DA, Bulkley GB, Granger DN: Role of oxygen-derived free radicals in digestive tract diseases. Surgery 1983;94:415.
228. Payne D, Kubes P: Nitric oxide donors reduce the rise in reperfusion-induced intestinal mucosal permeability. Am J Physiol 1993;265:G189.
229. Pierro A: Necrotizing enterocolitis: Pathogenesis and treatment. Br J Hosp Med 1997;58:126.
230. Pierro A, Hall N: Surgical treatment of infants with necrotizing enterocolitis. Semin Neonatol 2003;8:223.
231. Pierro A, Hall N, Ade-Ajayi A, et al: Laparoscopy assists surgical decision making in infants with necrotizing enterocolitis. J Pediatr Surg 2004;39:902.
232. Pinsky MR, Vincent JL, Deviere J, et al: Serum cytokine levels in human septic shock: Relation to multiple-system organ failure and mortality. Chest 1993;103:565.
233. Playford RJ, Wright NA: Why is epidermal growth factor present in the gut lumen? Gut 1996;38:303.
234. Pokorny WJ, Garcia-Prats JA, Barry YN: Necrotizing enterocolitis: Incidence, operative care, and outcome. J Pediatr Surg 1986;21:1149.
235. Porat R, Brodsky N: Cocaine: A risk factor for necrotizing enterocolitis. J Perinatol 1991;11:30.
236. Potoka DA, Nadler EP, Upperman JS, et al: Role of nitric oxide and peroxynitrite in gut barrier failure. World J Surg 2002;26:806.
237. Potoka DA, Upperman JS, Zhang XR, et al: Peroxynitrite inhibits enterocytes' proliferation and modulates Src kinase activity in vitro. Am J Physiol Gastrointest Liver Physiol 2003;285:G861.
238. Premji S, Chessell L: Continuous nasogastric milk feeding versus intermittent bolus milk feeding for premature infants less than 1500 grams. Cochrane Database Syst Rev 2003;(1):CD001819.
239. Qu XW, Rozenfeld RA, Huang W, et al: Roles of nitric oxide synthases in platelet-activating factor–induced intestinal necrosis in rats. Crit Care Med 1999;27:356.
240. Rabinowitz JG, Wolf BS, Feller MR, et al: Colonic changes following necrotizing enterocolitis in the newborn. Am J Roentgenol Radium Ther Nucl Med 1968;103:359.

241. Rabinowitz SS, Dzakpasu P, Piecuch S, et al: Platelet-activating factor in infants at risk for necrotizing enterocolitis. J Pediatr 2001;138:81.
242. Radi R, Beckman JS, Bush KM, et al: Peroxynitrite-induced membrane lipid peroxidation: The cytotoxic potential of superoxide and nitric oxide. Arch Biochem Biophys 1991;288:481.
243. Rayyis SF, Ambalavanan N, Wright L, et al: Randomized trial of "slow" versus "fast" feed advancements on the incidence of necrotizing enterocolitis in very low birth weight infants. J Pediatr 1999;134:293.
244. Read LC, Francis GL, Wallace JC, et al: Growth factor concentrations and growth-promoting activity in human milk following premature birth. J Dev Physiol 1985;7:135.
245. Ricketts RR: Surgical treatment of necrotizing enterocolitis and the short bowel syndrome. Clin Perinatol 1994;21:365.
246. Ricketts RR, Jerles ML: Neonatal necrotizing enterocolitis: Experience with 100 consecutive surgical patients. World J Surg 1990;14:600.
247. Robertson DM, Paganilli R, Dinwiddie R, et al: Milk antigen absorption in the preterm and term neonate. Arch Dis Child 1982;57:369.
248. Robinson MJ, Clayden GS, Smith MF: Xanthines and necrotizing enterocolitis. Arch Dis Child 1980;55:494.
249. Rossier A, Sarrot S, Deplanque J: L'entcolite ulceronecrotique du premature. Semin Hop Paris 1959;35:1428.
250. Rowe MI: Necrotizing enterocolitis. In Welch KJ, Randolph JG, Ravitch MM, et al (eds): Pediatric Surgery, 4th ed. Chicago, Year Book, 1986.
251. Rowe MI, Buckner DM, Newmark S: The early diagnosis of gram negative septicemia in the pediatric surgical patient. Ann Surg 1975;182:280.
252. Rowe MI, Furst AJ, Poole CA: The neonatal response to Gastrografin enema. Pediatrics 1971;48:29.
253. Rowe MI, Marchildon MB, Arango A, et al: The mechanisms of thrombocytopenia in experimental gram-negative septicemia. Surgery 1978;84:87.
254. Rowe MI, Reblock KK, Kurkchubasche AG, et al: Necrotizing enterocolitis in the extremely low birthweight infant. J Pediatr Surg 1994;29:987.
255. Rowe MI, Seagram G, Weinberger M: Gastrografin-induced hypertonicity. Am J Surg 1973;125:185.
256. Rubbo H, Radi R, Trujillo M, et al: Nitric oxide regulation of superoxide and peroxynitrite-dependent lipid peroxidation. Formation of novel nitrogen-containing oxidized lipid derivatives. J Biol Chem 1994;269:26066.
257. Santulli TV, Schullinger JN, Heird WC, et al: Acute necrotizing enterocolitis in infancy: A review of 64 cases. Pediatrics 1975;55:376.
258. Schanler RJ, Shulman RJ, Lau C, et al: Feeding strategies for premature infants: Randomized trial of gastrointestinal priming and tube-feeding method. Pediatrics 1999; 103:434.
259. Scheifele DW: Role of bacterial toxins in neonatal necrotizing enterocolitis. J Pediatr 1990;117:S44.
260. Scheifele DW, Bjornson GL: Delta toxin activity in coagulase-negative staphylococci from the bowels of neonates. J Clin Microbiol 1988;26:279.
261. Scheifele DW, Bjornson GL, Dyer RA, Dimmick JE: Delta-like toxin produced by coagulase-negative staphylococci is associated with necrotizing enterocolitis. Infect Immun 1983;55:2268.
262. Scheifele DW, Ginter GL, Olsen E, et al: Comparison of two antibiotic regimens for neonatal necrotizing enterocolitis. J Antimicrobial Chemother 1987;30:421.
263. Scheifele DW, Melton PW: Endotoxinemia in neonates with necrotizing enterocolitis [abstract]. Clin Res 1981; 29:127.
264. Schmid O, Quaiser K: Uer eine besondere schwere Verlaufende form von Enteritis beim Saugling. Oesterr Z Kinderh 1953;8:114.
265. Sehgal S, Ewing C, Waring P, et al: Morbidity of low-birth-weight infants with intrauterine cocaine exposure. J Natl Med Assoc 1993;85:20.
266. Serou MJ, DeCoster MA, Bazan NG: Interleukin-1 beta activates expression of cyclooxygenase-2 and inducible nitric oxide synthase in primary hippocampal neuronal culture: Platelet-activating factor as a preferential mediator of cyclooxygenase-2 expression. J Neurosci Res 1999;58:593.
267. Shin CE, Falcone RA Jr, Stuart L, et al: Diminished epidermal growth factor levels in infants with necrotizing enterocolitis. J Pediatr Surg 2000;35:173.
268. Shou J, Motyka LE, Daly JM: Intestinal microbial translocation: Immunologic consequences and effects of interleukin-4. Surgery 1994;116:868.
269. Simon NP: Follow-up for infants with necrotizing enterocolitis. Clin Perinatol 1994;21:411.
270. Singer II, Kawka DW, Schloemann S, et al: Cyclooxygenase 2 is induced in colonic epithelial cells in inflammatory bowel disease. Gastroenterology 1998;115:297.
271. Siu YK, Ng PC, Jung SC, et al: Double blind, randomized, placebo controlled study of oral vancomycin in prevention of necrotizing enterocolitis in preterm, very low birth weight infants. Arch Dis Child Fetal Neonatal Ed 1998; 79:F105.
272. Smith SD, Tagge ED, Miller J, et al: The hidden mortality in surgically-treated necrotizing enterocolitis: Fungal sepsis. J Pediatr Surg 1990;25:1030.
273. Snyder CL, Gittes GK, Murphy JP, et al: Survival after necrotizing enterocolitis in infants weighing less than 1,000 grams: 25 years' experience at a single institution. J Pediatr Surg 1997;32:434.
274. Snyder F: Platelet-activating factor and related acetylated lipids as potent biologically active cellular mediators. Am J Physiol 1990;259:C697.
275. Sola M, Vecchio A, Rimsza L: Evaluation and treatment of thrombocytopenia in the neonatal intensive care unit. Neonatal Hematol 2000;27:655.
276. Sondheimer JM, Sokol RJ, Narkewicz MR, et al: Anastomotic ulceration: A late complication of ileocolonic anastomosis. J Pediatr 1995;127:225.
277. Sonntag J, Grimmer I, Scholz T, et al: Growth and neurodevelopmental outcome of very low birthweight infants with necrotizing enterocolitis. Acta Paediatr 2000;89:528.
278. Spencer T, McDonald TT: The ontogeny of human mucosal barrier immunity. In McDonald TT (ed): Ontogeny of the Immune System of the Gut. Boca Raton, FL, CRC Press, 1990, p 23.
279. Stark ME, Szurszeski JH: Role of nitric oxide in gastrointestinal and hepatic function and diseases. Gastroenterology 1992;103:1928.
280. Stevenson DK, Kerner JA, Malachowski N, et al: Late morbidity among survivors of necrotizing enterocolitis. Pediatrics 1980;66:925.
281. Stoll BJ: Epidemiology of necrotizing enterocolitis. Clin Perinatol 1994;21:205.
282. Stringer MD, Brereton RJ, Drake DP, et al: Recurrent necrotizing enterocolitis. J Pediatr Surg 1993;28:979.
283. Sugarman ID, Kiely EM: Is there a role for high jejunostomy in the management of severe necrotising enterocolitis? Pediatr Surg Int 2001;17:122.
284. Sun XM, Hsueh W: Bowel necrosis induced by tumor necrosis factor in rats is mediated by platelet-activating factor. J Clin Invest 1988;81:1328.
285. Taniguchi T, Koido Y, Aiboshi J, et al: Change in the ratio of interleukin-6 to interleukin-10 predicts a poor outcome

in patients with systemic inflammatory response syndrome. Crit Care Med 1999;27:1262.
286. Telsey AM, Merrit TA, Dixon SD: Cocaine exposure in a term neonate. Necrotizing enterocolitis as a complication. Clin Pediatr (Phila) 1988;27:547.
287. Tepperman BL, Brown JF, Whittle BJR, et al: Nitric oxide synthase induction and intestinal cell viability in rats. Am J Physiol 1993;265:G214.
288. Tesdale F, Le Guennec JC, Bard H, et al: Neonatal necrotizing enterocolitis: The relationship of age at the time of onset and prognosis. Can Med Assoc J 1980;123:387.
289. Thelander HE: Perforation of the gastro-intestinal tract of the newborn infant. Am J Dis Child 1939;58:371.
290. Touloukian RJ: Neonatal necrotizing enterocolitis: An update on etiology, diagnosis and treatment. Surg Clin North Am 1976;56:281.
291. Uauy RD, Fanaroff AA, Korones SB, et al: Necrotizing enterocolitis in very low birth weight infants: Biodemographic and clinical correlates. J Pediatr 1991; 119:630.
292. Udall JN Jr: Gastrointestinal host defense and necrotizing enterocolitis. J Pediatr 1990;117:S33.
293. Uauy RD, Fanaroff AA, Korones SB, et al: Necrotizing enterocolitis in very low birth weight infants: Biodemographic and clinical correlates. National Institute of Child Health and Human Development Neonatal Research Network. J Pediatr 1991;119:630.
294. Udall JN, Pang K, Fritze L, et al: Development of gastrointestinal mucosal barrier. I. The effect of age of intestinal permeability to macromolecules. Pediatr Res 1981; 15:241.
295. Van Acker J, De Smet F, Muyldermans G, et al: Outbreak of necrotizing enterocolitis associated with *Enterobacter sakazakii* in powdered milk formula. J Clin Microbiol 2001;39:293.
296. VanderKolk WE, Kurz P, Daniels J, et al: Liver hemorrhage during laparotomy in patients with necrotizing enterocolitis. J Pediatr Surg 1996;31:1063.
297. van Dissel JT, van Langevelde P, Westendorp RGJ, et al: Anti-inflammatory cytokine profile and mortality in febrile patients. Lancet 1998;351:950.
298. Vaughan WG, Grosfeld JL, West K, et al: Avoidance of stomas and delayed anastomosis for bowel necrosis: The 'clip and drop-back' technique. J Pediatr Surg 1996; 31:542.
299. Ververidis M, Kiely EM, Spitz L, et al: The clinical significance of thrombocytopenia in neonates with necrotizing enterocolitis. J Pediatr Surg 2001;36:799.
300. Vilcek J, Lee TH: Tumor necrosis factor. New insights into the molecular mechanisms of its multiple actions. J Biol Chem 1991;266:7313.
301. Vohr BR, Wright LL, Dusick AM, et al: Neurodevelopmental and functional outcomes of extremely low-birth-weight infants in the National Institute of Child Health and Human Development Neonatal Research Network, 1993-1994. Pediatrics 2000;105:1216.
302. Weber TR, Tracy TF Jr, Silen ML, et al: Enterostomy and its closure in newborns. Arch Surg 1995;130:534.
303. Wells CL, Maddaus MA, Simmons RL: Proposed mechanism for the translocation of intestinal bacteria. Rev Infect Dis 1988;10:958.
304. Westra-Meijer CMM, Degener JE, Dzoljic-Danilovic G, et al: Quantitative study of the aerobic and anaerobic fecal flora in neonatal enterocolitis. Arch Dis Child 1983; 58:523.
305. Wexler HA: The persistent loop sign in neonatal necrotizing enterocolitis: A new indication for surgical intervention? Radiology 1978;126:201.
306. White KC, Harkavy KL: Hypertonic formula resulting from added oral medications. Am J Dis Child 1982; 136:931.
307. Williams AJ: Xanthines and necrotizing enterocolitis. Arch Dis Child 1980;55:973.
308. Williams CS, Dubois RN: Prostaglandin endoperoxide synthase: Why two isoforms? Am J Physiol 1996;270:G393.
309. Willis DM, Chabot J, Radde IC, et al: Unsuspected hyperosmolarity of oral solutions contributing to necrotizing enterocolitis in very low birth weight infants. Pediatrics 1977;60:535.
310. Wilson R, Kanto WP Jr, McCarthy BJ, et al: Age at onset of necrotizing enterocolitis: An epidemiologic analysis. Pediatr Res 1982;16:82.
311. Wiswell TE, Robertson CF, Jones TA, et al: Necrotizing enterocolitis in full-term infants. A case-control study. Am J Dis Child 1988;142:532.
312. Woods JR, Plessinger MA, Clark KE: Effect of cocaine on uterine blood flow and fetal oxygenation. JAMA 1987;257:957.
313. Wright LL, Uauy RD, Younes N, et al: Rapid advances in feeding increase the risk of necrotizing enterocolitis in very low birth weight infants [abstract]. Pediatr Res 1993; 33:313.
314. Xu DZ, Lu Q, Swank GM, et al: Effect of heat shock and endotoxin stress on enterocytes viability apoptosis and function varies based on whether the cells are exposed to heat shock or endotoxin first. Arch Surg 1996;131:1222.
315. Yoshioka H, Iseki K, Fujita K: Development and differences of intestinal flora in the neonatal period in breast-fed and bottle-fed infants. Pediatrics 1983;72:317.
316. Yu Y, Chadee K: *Entamoeba histolytica* stimulates interleukin-8 from human colonic epithelial cells without parasite-enterocyte contact. Gastroenterology 1997;112:1536.
317. Zamora SA, Amin HJ, McMillan DD, et al: Plasma L-arginine concentrations in premature infants with necrotizing enterocolitis. J Pediatr 1997;131:226.

Chapter 93

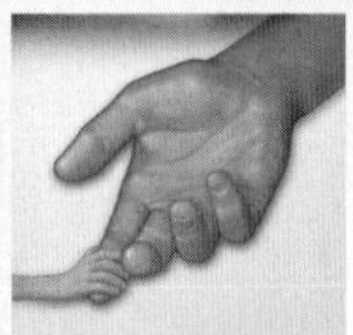

Crohn's Disease

Fred Alexander

Crohn's disease is a chronic inflammatory condition of the gastrointestinal tract that has emerged as one of the most costly and debilitating chronic diseases affecting young people today. Although there were scattered reports of "chronic intestinal enteritis" in the late 19th and early 20th centuries,[11,25] the first report of Crohn's disease as a clinical entity was provided by Crohn, Oppenheimer, and Ginsberg in 1932,[10] who described a disease of the terminal ileum characterized by subacute or chronic necrotizing inflammation leading to intestinal stenosis and fistulas.

The etiology of Crohn's disease is unknown; however, there are a number of significant contributing factors, including genetic, infectious, and immunologic. Equally significant is the observation that the disease is virtually unknown in the Third World. Typically, the inflammation in Crohn's disease is panenteric, full thickness, and characterized by aphthous ulceration and cobblestoning with rectal sparing. In the colon, Crohn's disease may be confused with ulcerative colitis, for which clinical and histologic differences are sometimes difficult to distinguish. In fact, the histology may be indeterminate in as many as 10% of young people with chronic colitis. Both Crohn's disease and ulcerative colitis are associated with similar extraintestinal manifestations, and both have a higher than predicted risk for colorectal cancer. Despite these apparent similarities, the surgical treatment and outcomes of these two diseases are vastly different. For this reason, it is imperative that each patient receive a complete evaluation and that all treatment options be fully weighed and discussed by a multidisciplinary team consisting of pediatric gastroenterologists, surgeons, and pathologists.

EPIDEMIOLOGY

Crohn's disease is more common than ulcerative colitis; it occurs in 11 cases per 100,000 population per year versus 2.3 cases of ulcerative colitis per 100,000 population per year in the pediatric age group.[17] The incidence of Crohn's disease is age specific, with 2.5 cases per 100,000 population per year occurring in persons younger than 15 years as compared with 16 cases per 100,000 population per year in persons 15 to 19 years of age.[36] Males and females are equally affected, and Crohn's disease occurs more commonly in the white and Jewish populations than in other ethnic groups. Finally, the incidence of juvenile Crohn's disease appears to be rising in Western cultures as evidenced by a threefold rise in Scotland between 1968 and 1983.[16]

ETIOLOGY

The etiology of Crohn's disease is unknown; however, a number of risk factors appear to be operative. For example, there appears to be a genetic predisposition in that patients with Crohn's disease have a 5% to 25% chance of having a first-degree relative with inflammatory bowel disease.[35] The likelihood of Crohn's disease developing in a sibling is 7%, whereas in an offspring it is 9%. In addition, there is a high concordance between monozygotic twins. Moreover, certain infectious agents have been implicated, such as *Mycobacterium paratuberculosis* and measles virus, both of which may cause granulomatous inflammation, sepsis, and fistulas.

Tissue destruction in patients with Crohn's disease occurs in areas heavily infiltrated by lymphocytes, which appear to lose the usual self-limited response to antigenic stimulation with poorly controlled release of cytokines, arachidonic acid metabolites, and reactive oxygen intermediates. Recent studies[29] have shown that cytokines, including interleukin-1 (IL-1), IL-4, IL-8, IL-12, tumor necrosis factor (TNF), and interferon-γ, work together to recruit inflammatory cells, promote collagen deposition, and induce eosinophil degranulation, thereby stimulating chloride secretion and causing diarrhea. The sequence of steps involved in the progression from immune activation to tissue injury is not well understood but probably involves abnormal helper T-cell response or release of oxygen metabolites that are potent cytotoxins (or both).[30] Finally, although there is no direct evidence that Crohn's disease may be stimulated by dietary allergens, it is known that serum antibodies to cow's milk protein are elevated in many patients with Crohn's disease.

PATHOLOGY

In a series of 361 patients treated for Crohn's disease at the Cleveland Clinic Foundation, the disease involved the terminal ileum and colon in 60% of patients, the small bowel in only 30%, and the large bowel in only 10%.[31] The involved bowel and mesentery is thickened from collagen deposition and edema along with fat migration over the serosal surfaces (fat wrapping). Histologically, there is extensive aphthous ulceration of mucosa that grossly has a cobblestone appearance because of adjacent areas of mucosal ulceration and regeneration, a finding sometimes referred to as a bear claw deformity (Fig. 93-1). Often, the inflammation is interspersed with normal-appearing bowel that gives the appearance of skip areas. The inflammation is usually transmural and tends to erode into adjacent structures, with resultant fistulas from the bowel to other structures, including the bowel, bladder, abdominal wall, vagina, or perineum. Fistulas may also end blindly and form localized areas of inflammation or phlegmon. Histologic evidence of granulomas is found in 40% of affected small bowel, 60% to 80% of endoscopic biopsy samples taken from the stomach, and 25% of endoscopic specimens taken from the colon.[38]

CLINICAL FEATURES

Crohn's disease occurs with increasing frequency in older age groups, with 4% of new cases occurring at 6 to 10 years, 31% at 11 to 15 years, and 65% at 15 to 20 years.[11] Most young people have been symptomatic for 2 years when the diagnosis of Crohn's disease is made. The diagnosis is suggested by a history of chronic, intermittent, crampy abdominal pain associated with diarrhea, weight loss, rectal bleeding, and a family history of inflammatory bowel disease. Clinical findings include abdominal tenderness or a mass with perianal disease, clubbing, stomatitis, or rash. Serial measurements of height and weight may demonstrate weight loss or growth failure.

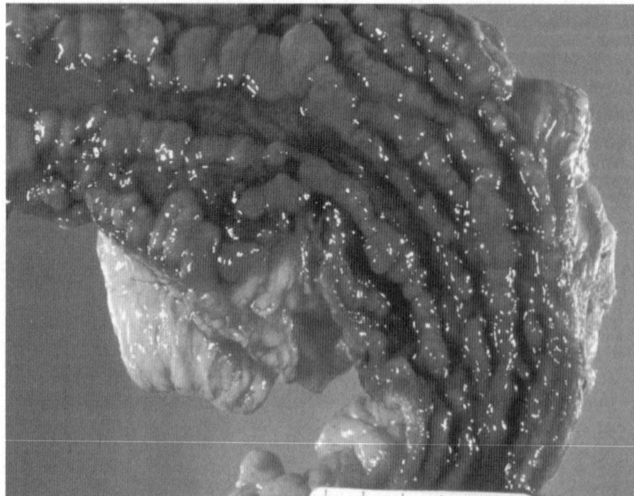

Figure 93-1 Bear claw deformity in Crohn's colitis.

Growth failure manifested by a delayed onset of puberty, sexual infantilism, and short stature occurs as a result of anorexia, malnutrition, diarrhea, and corticosteroid inhibition of insulin-like growth factor type I and collagen metabolism. Of these, the most important contributing factor is anorexia leading to suboptimal protein and calorie ingestion. Linear growth impairment, weight loss, or both often occur before any other signs or symptoms of disease and may be seen in up to 40% of children with this condition. All of the following may be observed separately or in conjunction: poor weight gain below the 5th percentile of weight for age defined by the National Center for Health Statistics, subnormal growth velocity below 5.0 cm per year, and growth less than 2.0 cm below the preceding year according to Tanner's growth velocity curves. Overall, growth failure or weight loss (or both) may occur in as many as 85% of patients with Crohn's disease.

Additionally, extraintestinal manifestations occur in many children with Crohn's disease. Arthralgia and arthritis develop in approximately 10% of children and may become apparent several years before the bowel disease. Skin manifestations such as erythema nodosum and pyoderma gangrenosum occur in 1% to 4% of patients, and eye manifestations such as iritis and uveitis occur in less than 10% of patients (Table 93-1).[23] Renal stones composed of calcium oxalate and uric acid develop in up to 5% of patients with Crohn's disease, and likewise, gallstones are seen in 2% to 5% of patients.[30]

DIAGNOSIS

Laboratory studies for patients with Crohn's disease are nonspecific but often contributory. Seventy percent of patients are anemic, 60% have thrombocytosis, and 80% have an elevated erythrocyte sedimentation rate. Nutritional markers, including albumin and prealbumin, transferrin, and retinol binding protein, are abnormally low in more than half of all patients with Crohn's disease. Measurements of the C-terminal propeptide of type I collagen or the N-terminal propeptide of type III collagen correlate with growth velocity. Stool guaiac is positive in a third of patients, and all stools should be thoroughly evaluated for enteric pathogens such as *Clostridium difficile*, rotavirus, and *Campylobacter*.

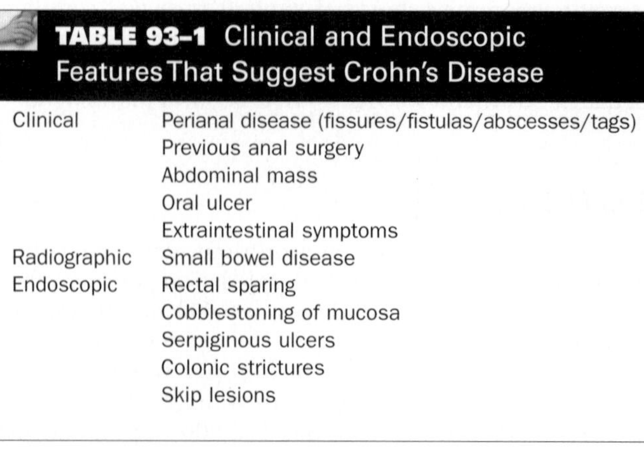

TABLE 93-1 Clinical and Endoscopic Features That Suggest Crohn's Disease

Clinical	Perianal disease (fissures/fistulas/abscesses/tags)
	Previous anal surgery
	Abdominal mass
	Oral ulcer
	Extraintestinal symptoms
Radiographic	Small bowel disease
Endoscopic	Rectal sparing
	Cobblestoning of mucosa
	Serpiginous ulcers
	Colonic strictures
	Skip lesions

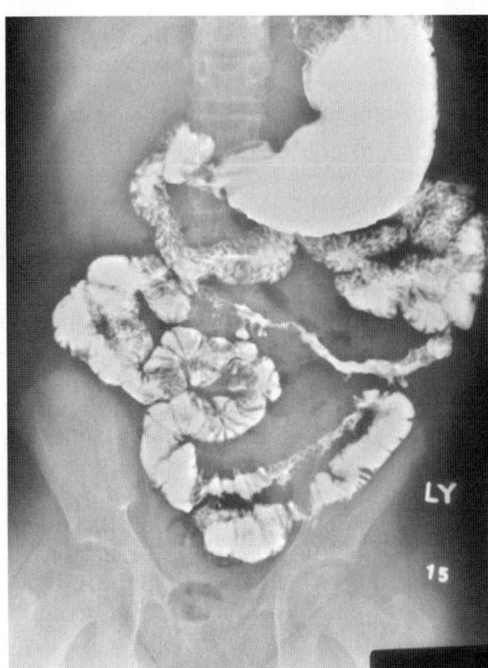

Figure 93–2 Panenteric Crohn's disease.

Radiographic studies are a useful screening tool in patients with Crohn's disease. More than 80% of patients have small bowel involvement, and thus upper gastrointestinal series and small bowel follow-through should be performed in most cases. Positive findings include terminal ileal nodularity and narrowing, as well as separation of bowel loops (Fig. 93-2). Computed tomography with intravenous gastrointestinal contrast may show thickened bowel loops and is helpful in identifying phlegmon or abscess formation.

Finally, upper and lower endoscopy allows direct observation and histologic sampling. The finding of rectal sparing by colonoscopy eliminates the possibility of ulcerative colitis, and documentation of ileal involvement or granulomas is adequate to establish the diagnosis of Crohn's disease.

MEDICAL THERAPY

Current medical treatment of Crohn's disease is complicated by the proliferation of pharmaceutical agents, including corticosteroids, 5-aminosalicylic acid (ASA) preparations, metronidazole, 6-mercaptopurine or azathioprine, methotrexate, cyclosporine, monoclonal antibodies (e.g., infliximab [Remicade]), and enteral nutrition supplements. Corticosteroids remain first-line induction therapy for both small and large bowel disease. Prednisone is given orally in a dose of 1 to 2 mg/kg/day (maximum of 40 to 60 mg) until remission is achieved, and the dose is then lowered by 5 mg every 1 to 2 weeks. Alternatively, the equivalent dose of prednisolone (Solu-Medrol) may be given intravenously to hospitalized patients. Corticosteroids exert their anti-inflammatory effects primarily by blocking expression of IL-1, which stimulates helper T cells to attract and activate natural killer cells and macrophages. Discontinuation of steroids may result in a relapse rate as high as 70% within 1 year. On the other hand, repetitive or continuous use of corticosteroids may result in serious adverse effects, including Cushing's syndrome, growth suppression, cataracts, glaucoma, and vertebral collapse as a result of osteoporosis, muscle weakness, and depression. Alternative strategies for maintenance therapy include alternate-day corticosteroids to minimize systemic exposure or the use of corticosteroid analogues with enhanced receptor binding properties and more rapid metabolism. Budesonide has more than 100 times the receptor binding affinity than cortisone does[23] and is inactivated with first pass through the liver. Extensive clinical trials[18,46] have shown that budesonide is slightly less effective than prednisolone in achieving remission of Crohn's disease but has significantly fewer side effects.

Another strategy for maintaining remission is the use of oral 5-ASA agents.[47] Sulfasalazine (Azulfidine) is metabolized in the colon to form sulfapyridine, a sulfonamide antibiotic that serves as carrier agent, and mesalamine (5-ASA), which is the active anti-inflammatory component. Clinical trials have shown that sulfasalazine is effective in treating mild disease and maintaining remission in patients with ileocolic Crohn's disease and Crohn's colitis.[34,50] Side effects of sulfasalazine are dose dependent and related to the sulfapyridine moiety; they include headache, nausea, fatigue, azotemia, and hypersensitivity reactions such as rash, fever, hepatitis, hemolytic anemia, and bone marrow suppression. Mesalamine is available in a coated acrylic resin (Asacol) or in encapsulated ethylcellulose microspheres (Pentasa), which maximize its release at sites of inflammation and minimize absorption.[20] Both Pentasa and Asacol are effective in maintaining remission in Crohn's disease after induction therapy with corticosteroids and surgery. Mesalamine has also been formulated as a suppository and enema for rectal administration in patients with perianal Crohn's disease.

Immunomodulatory drugs such as azathioprine and 6-mercaptopurine may be used in conjunction with 5-ASA agents to allow tapering of corticosteroids and prevent relapse in patients with Crohn's disease. Azathioprine is converted to mercaptopurine in red cells, which in turn is converted to active metabolites in the liver that inhibit DNA synthesis.[22] Both drugs are well tolerated and effective in up to two thirds of patients with steroid-dependent or refractory Crohn's disease.[27] The mechanism of action appears to be inhibition of lymphocytes, primarily T cells, and natural killer cells. These drugs have a prolonged onset of action (usually 3 to 6 months) and side effects that include pancreatitis, marrow suppression, and liver disease.[43] The drugs also cause a dose-related neutropenia that must be monitored closely; however, their carcinogenic potential appears to be low in children.[9] Methotrexate is another immunomodulatory drug that is extremely beneficial in Crohn's disease, especially in patients with arthritis and arthralgia. Methotrexate has significant corticosteroid-sparing effects when given in weekly injections of 25 mg.[15] Clinical studies[33] in children have shown a response rate of 64% within 3 to 4 weeks. Similar to other immunomodulatory drugs, methotrexate causes bone marrow suppression and liver disease. Cyclosporine is less commonly used to induce remission in patients with severe, refractory Crohn's disease before other therapies have taken effect or in whom surgery is deemed inappropriate. Cyclosporine selectively blocks activation of helper and cytotoxic lymphocytes and has a shorter onset of action than other immunomodulatory drugs do. It is most effective when given by constant intravenous infusion and is not effective in maintaining remission when given in a lower-dose oral regimen.[6,48] Cyclosporine is a potent immunosuppressive agent that may cause renal dysfunction, neurotoxicity, and seizures, as well as opportunistic infections. Finally, a newer immunomodulatory agent has shown great promise in treating Crohn's disease, especially in patients with colonic or perianal involvement (or both). Infliximab is a monoclonal antibody to TNF. When given intravenously, it binds to TNF and produces a high response rate within days to weeks.[24] Many patients with Crohn's colitis have shown dramatic resolution of disease, but multiple infusions are often required because the relapse rate is high.

Antibiotics—especially ciprofloxacin (Cipro) and metronidazole (Flagyl)—have a supportive role in the treatment of Crohn's disease. In high doses, these antibiotics are effective in treating perianal disease, and metronidazole has been shown to be as effective as sulfasalazine in treating patients with mild or moderately active disease.[52] Metronidazole may also delay anastomotic recurrence after surgery,[45] but it must be administered on a long-term basis to avoid recurrence. Prolonged treatment with metronidazole may cause nausea, a metallic taste, and peripheral neuropathy, especially in doses exceeding 40 mg/kg/day.

Finally, nutritional therapy in the form of elemental diets and total parenteral nutrition has been successfully used not only to reverse growth retardation but also to improve symptoms and reduce corticosteroid requirements.[4,44] In addition, enteric-coated fish oil has been shown to be effective in maintaining remission in Crohn's disease.[5] It is speculated that mucosal suffusion of omega-3 fatty acids may divert the arachidonic acid metabolism away from proinflammatory leukotriene B_4 toward less active by-products in the leukotriene C or D classes.[21] Most clinical trials that demonstrate renewed growth and remission of symptoms in response to enteral supplementation require the use of continuous nasogastric or gastrostomy tube feeding.[4,39,42,44] Many teenagers find this type of therapy objectionable. Moreover, others dislike taking the large doses of fish oil required and the fishy breath that ensues. Furthermore, recurrence of symptoms develops rapidly once the enteral therapy is discontinued. It is currently unclear whether liquid polymeric diets that are less expensive and more palatable are as effective as elemental diets in promoting growth and remission of symptoms. Finally, for patients with severe Crohn's disease who are unable to tolerate enteral feedings of any kind, total parenteral nutrition with bowel rest will improve symptoms and serve as a bridge to surgical therapy. All other patients for whom medical therapy fails to restore an acceptable quality of life or causes harmful side effects should be considered candidates for surgical therapy.

OPERATIVE INDICATIONS AND SURGICAL THERAPY

Surgery does not cure Crohn's disease and should be reserved for complications of the disease or failure of medical therapy, or both. Furthermore, because recurrence of Crohn's disease is inevitable, a conservative surgical strategy is generally warranted. The specific surgical procedure indicated in each case depends on the site of involvement and the type of complications (Table 93-2). The most common complications of Crohn's disease include bowel obstruction, perforation, intra-abdominal and perirectal abscess, fistula, and megacolon. In many cases these complications give rise to fulminate signs and symptoms that resolve completely with surgical treatment.

Fifty percent to 60% of children and adolescents with Crohn's disease have right lower quadrant pain because of localized disease in the terminal ileum and cecum. Disease in this region of the intestine is frequently complicated by mechanical bowel obstruction, abscess, phlegmon, fistula formation, or any combination of these problems. Many patients with these complications and associated symptoms may be successfully treated with intravenous antibiotics and steroids. If the symptoms do not completely resolve with medical therapy or become associated with growth failure (or both), surgery will generally become necessary. The recommended procedure in this situation is ileocecectomy and primary anastomosis with resection of phlegmon and fistulas. The resection margin of the involved small intestine should encompass gross disease only because resection of microscopic disease offers no protection against recurrence.[28] Fistulas may be safely resected without the need for wide resection of the wall of the end-organ, whether it is small intestine, large intestine, bladder, or vagina. In these patients, the fistulas may be transected flush with the end-organ and the defect closed with two layers of sutures.

Approximately 20% to 30% of children and adolescents with Crohn's disease have acute or chronic small bowel obstruction (or both) as a result of multiple small bowel strictures. Once again, these patients may respond initially to anti-inflammatory medications and immunotherapy. However, chronic bowel obstruction with prolonged intermittent abdominal pain and growth failure will develop in most patients. In the past, surgical treatment was limited to small bowel resection of each stricture, sometimes leading to short-gut syndrome as a result of multiple bowel resections. Currently, small bowel resection

TABLE 93-2 Principles of Conservative Surgery for Crohn's Disease (Birmingham, United Kingdom)

Crohn's disease is panintestinal
Surgery does not cure the disease
Surgery should be as safe as possible
The surgeon is required to treat only the complications
Recurrence is (almost) inevitable, so bowel conservation should be practiced
Stenotic complications may be safely treated without excising bowel

is indicated in patients with small bowel perforation, fistula formation, or extreme bowel wall thickening that precludes strictureplasty. In addition, patients with strictures, contiguous involvement of greater than 30 cm, or ileocecal disease should preferentially undergo bowel resection. In virtually all other situations, strictureplasty is the surgical treatment of choice (Fig. 93-3). Short strictures up to 7 to 10 cm in length may be treated by Heineke-Mikulicz strictureplasty. This procedure is performed by making a longitudinal incision across the stricture and 1 to 2 cm into "normal" bowel on either side of the stricture. The bowel is then closed transversely with a single layer of closely spaced interrupted full-thickness dissolvable (usually chromic) sutures. Longer strictures up to 25 to 30 cm may be treated by a Finney side-to-side anastomosis performed with a back wall of seromuscular sutures and then full-thickness dissolvable sutures on the back and front wall of the bowel. Strictureplasty is recommended for all strictures with a linear diameter of 2 cm or less measured by a Foley catheter balloon. However, because of the progressive nature of the disease, it may be advisable to treat all strictures except in cases in which the caliber is not compromised. Strictureplasty provides relief of obstructive symptoms and allows discontinuation of corticosteroid use in 85% of patients while preserving small intestinal length.[40] Complications of strictureplasty include anastomotic leak and hemorrhage, which occur in 5% to 10% of patients, comparable to bowel resection. The overall frequency of recurrent disease at the site of previous strictureplasty does not differ from that after resection. Moreover, anecdotal reports have described complete healing of bowel that had undergone previous strictureplasty. Thus, preservation of the diseased bowel does not appear to predispose to early recurrence of disease at the strictureplasty site.

In 10% to 20% of children with Crohn's disease, inflammation is limited to the colon and rectum. Crohn's colitis may be patchy or diffuse and is often associated with rectal sparing, which never occurs in patients with ulcerative colitis. Crohn's colitis may be associated with perianal disease; however, perianal disease does not necessarily signal the presence of Crohn's colitis. Complications such as perforation, abscess, and fistula formation are rare with this form of disease, although strictures may occasionally develop in the descending and sigmoid colon. Most patients with Crohn's colitis require surgery for intractable abdominal pain and diarrhea. When Crohn's colitis is unresponsive to medical therapy, surgical options include partial colectomy, total colectomy with ileostomy or ileorectal anastomosis, and total proctocolectomy with end ileostomy. Partial colectomy should be avoided because it is associated with a high recurrence rate approaching 60% in 5 years.[51] Total colectomy is an excellent alternative procedure that preserves the possibility of reconstituting the normal fecal stream. When the rectum is severely diseased or there is severe perianal Crohn's disease, total colectomy should be performed with end ileostomy and Hartmann's pouch as a first-stage procedure. When the rectum is spared as judged by normal sphincter and rectal distensibility with insufflation, primary ileorectal anastomosis may be safely performed. Ileorectal anastomosis may also be performed as a second-stage procedure after resolution of the rectal disease (Fig. 93-4). Total proctocolectomy with a permanent ileostomy is the treatment of choice for patients with severe unrelenting rectal or perianal disease, failed ileorectal anastomosis because of recurrent Crohn's disease, or biopsy-proven carcinoma in situ. It is important when performing this procedure to preserve all tissue extrinsic to the muscular wall of the rectum, including the sphincter muscles, in order to avoid the problem of postoperative perineal sinus tracts.

Although ileal pouch–anal anastomosis (IPAA) has become the procedure of choice for ulcerative colitis, it is not appropriate for patients with Crohn's colitis, in whom a high risk of recurrent disease within the pouch may require excision of the pouch and loss of precious small bowel. Indeterminate colitis does not appear to be a contraindication to IPAA.[1] However, if Crohn's disease is suspected because of rectal-sparing or perianal disease, total colectomy with end ileostomy and Hartmann's

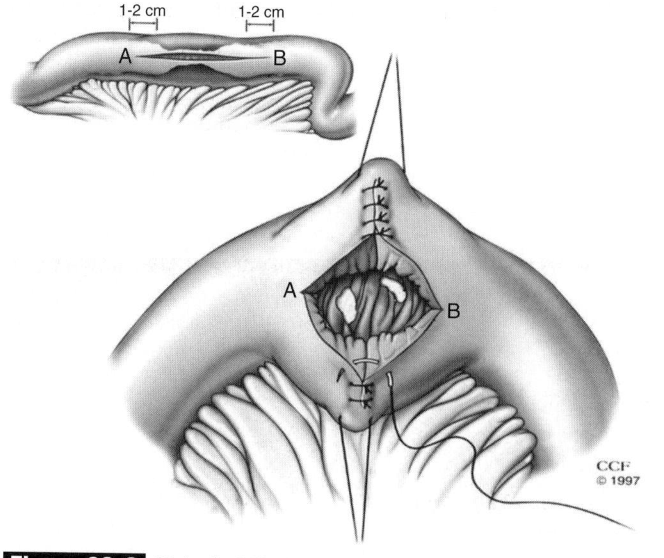

Figure 93-3 Heineke-Mikulicz strictureplasty. (Courtesy of Cleveland Clinic Foundation, 1997.)

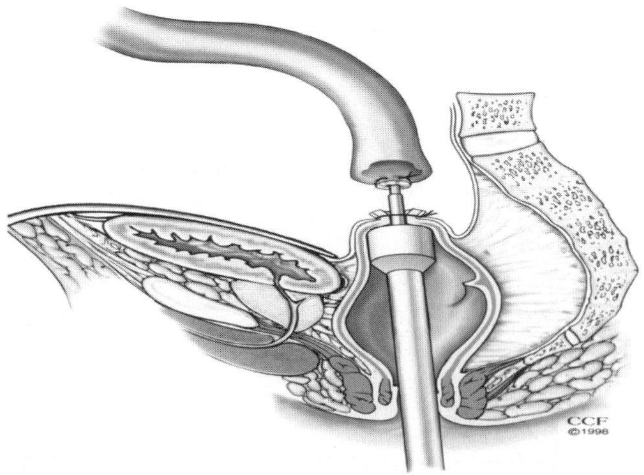

Figure 93-4 Ileorectal anastomosis for severe Crohn's colitis. (Courtesy of Cleveland Clinic Foundation, 1998.)

pouch is indicated. Subsequently, the decision to perform an ileorectal anastomosis with IPAA can be based on specimen pathology.

Severe perianal disease occurs in 5% to 10% of children with adolescent Crohn's disease, often in association with ileal or distal colonic disease. Perianal disease is very uncommon in patients with ulcerative colitis. Similar to intra-abdominal Crohn's disease, perianal Crohn's disease typically responds to medical therapy, and surgery is reserved for complications. The most common indication for surgery is a perianal abscess requiring incision, drainage, and debridement. Small abscesses may then be loosely packed with gauze, which is removed in 24 to 48 hours. Larger abscesses involving the ischiorectal space should be intubated with mushroom drains, depending on the extent of involvement. To accomplish this, water-soluble contrast studies are performed in the operating room with fluoroscopy to identify horseshoe abscesses that may require secondary drains. Drains should be left in place for 4 to 8 weeks to create a controlled fistula. Patients are then treated with either metronidazole or ciprofloxacin and frequent daily baths until the abscess cavity resolves completely as documented by follow-up contrast studies. At this point, the drains may be removed and the drain tract or tracts treated with silver nitrate and injection of fibrin glue.[7] Fistulas in ano are another complication of perianal Crohn's disease that may respond to antibiotics (metronidazole or ciprofloxacin) and immunosuppressive therapy (corticosteroids and infliximab). Infrasphincteric fistulas in ano respond quite well to fistulotomy/fistulectomy, as long as the intestinal component of the disease is well controlled medically. Suprasphincteric fistulas in ano are more difficult to treat and carry the risk of fecal incontinence when fistulotomy/fistulectomy is performed. They are best treated by placement of a Seton stitch or by debridement and instillation of silver nitrate and fibrin glue.[40] Proximal diversion (i.e., end colostomy) is indicated for patients who fail to respond to the aforementioned medical or surgical therapy. This operation may be done in conjunction with limited bowel resection or partial versus subtotal colectomy, depending on the site and extent of disease. In many cases, the fistula will resolve within 6 to 12 months after diversion, at which time patients may be considered for a second-stage undiversion with a colostomy or ileorectal anastomosis. Fissures in patients with Crohn's disease are best treated with medical therapy. Fissurectomy is not recommended in patients with Crohn's disease because poor wound healing and recurrence are extremely common. Severe fissures may be treated with similar efficacy by dietary restriction and total parenteral nutrition or by proximal diversion, depending on the circumstances of the case.

SURGICAL OUTCOMES

The cumulative risk of recurrence requiring reoperation after resection for Crohn's disease approaches 20% at 5 years, 35% at 10 years, and nearly 45% by 15 years (Fig. 93-5).[35] Moreover, it appears that this progressive risk of recurrence is not diminished after a second operative procedure for Crohn's disease.[49] Several studies, including one at the Cleveland Clinic Foundation, have shown that the risk of recurrence after surgery is not dependent on the clinical features of the case (Table 93-3).[31] For example, recurrence is not affected by sex, age at onset, time from symptoms to resection, or indications for surgery, including obstruction, mass, fistula, or intractability. Furthermore, it appears that the risk of recurrence after intestinal resection is equivalent in patients with combined terminal ileal and large bowel disease, small bowel disease, and large bowel disease.[35] Finally, histologic studies have shown that the margin of resection does not affect recurrence, and thus a resection margin greater than 3 to 5 cm in length is not necessary to prevent recurrence. The only surgical procedure that appears to decrease recurrence is creation of a permanent stoma. This procedure is eventually required for salvage in nearly 25% of patients with a juvenile onset of Crohn's disease by 10 years after the onset of disease.[1]

Given its panintestinal nature and high risk of recurrence, Crohn's disease confers a significant risk of short-bowel syndrome. In several large adult series reviewed by

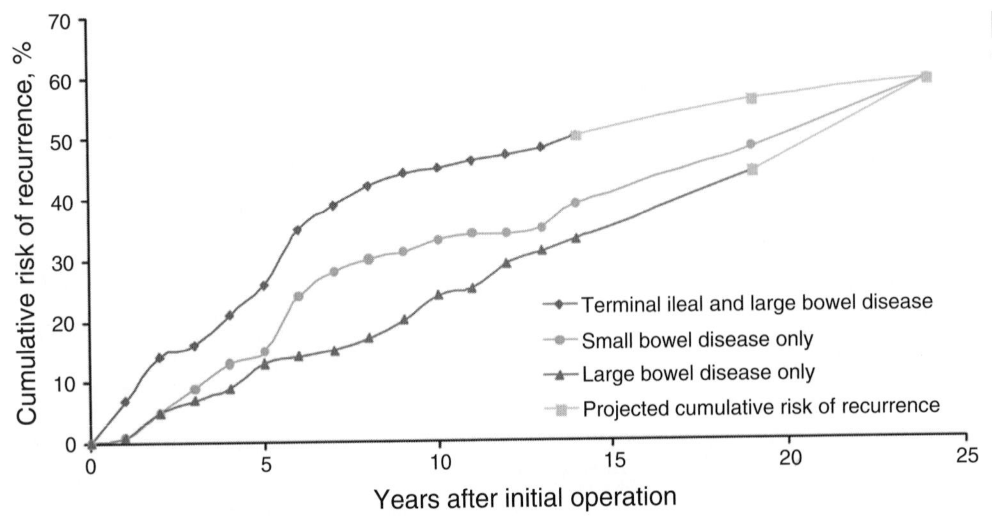

Figure 93-5 Effect of initial site of disease on cumulative risk of recurrence. (From Lock MR, Farmer RG, Fazio VW, et al: Recurrence and reoperation for Crohn's disease: The role of disease location in prognosis. N Engl J Med 1981;304:1586-1588.)

TABLE 93–3 Crohn's Disease: Recurrence by Clinical Feature

Clinical Feature	No. of Patients without Recurrence	No. of Patients with Recurrence	*P* Value
Site of Crohn's disease			
Jejunum-ileum	5	2	NS
Terminal ileum	20	23	NS
Colon and ileum	25	25	NS
Indications for surgery			
Obstruction	20	20	NS
Mass	1	18	NS
Fistula	14	16	NS
Intractability	8	9	NS

Dr. Douglas Wilmore,[53] patients with Crohn's disease accounted for 24% of those with less than 200 cm of jejunum-ileum and 90% of patients with less than 50 cm of jejunum-ileum with colon in continuity. To reduce the risk for short-gut syndrome in patients with Crohn's disease, a consensus group at the University of Birmingham recommended routine use of strictureplasty for the treatment of small intestinal stenosis without excision of bowel.[14] Strictureplasty is safe and effective and is complicated by hemorrhage or recurrent stenosis of the strictureplasty site in less than 5% of patients and fistula/leak/abscess in less than 10% of patients.[3] Strictureplasty successfully relieves obstruction in nearly 100% of patients and has been shown to increase growth and weight gain in nearly 75% of young patients with Crohn's disease.[38] Postoperative recurrence of Crohn's disease after strictureplasty follows the same pattern as it does after intestinal resection, with the rate approaching 50% at 10 years (Fig. 93-6).[49] However, in many cases the strictureplasty site was found to be free of active disease at the time of re-exploration.

Crohn's colitis differs from small bowel disease in that the major indications for surgery in adolescents are intractable disease and poor response to therapy rather than intestinal obstruction. Surgical strategies may include partial colectomy, total colectomy with ileorectal anastomosis or ileostomy and Hartman's pouch, and total proctocolectomy with ileostomy. Most clinical studies have shown that proctocolectomy is associated with the lowest recurrence rate, approximately 15% at 5 years and 20% at 10 years.[13] Recurrence after total colectomy approximates 30% at 5 years and 50% at 10 years. Finally, partial colectomy has the highest recurrence rates, approximately 50% at 5 years and 65% at 10 years.[49]

Total colectomy and ileorectal anastomosis are currently the most commonly performed procedures in one or two stages and are associated with an overall complication rate of 15%, including anastomotic leak in 3%, sepsis in 4%, bowel obstruction in 2%, and other complications in 6%.[32] Ileorectal anastomosis functions at least as well as an ileopouch, with complete daytime and nighttime continence and approximately four bowel movements per day. In a report of 131 patients who underwent ileorectal anastomosis, 72 had a functioning and 36 had a nonfunctioning anastomosis at a mean follow-up of 7.5 years.[53] Indications for proctectomy or fecal diversion in the 36 patients included poor function, excessive steroid requirement, and bleeding. In these patients, perineal proctectomy provides excellent salvage therapy.

Severe perianal Crohn's disease is exceedingly difficult to treat. In approximately 20% to 30% of patients, the perianal disease resolves when treated by either resection of the proximal small or large bowel or intestinal diversion.[41] If these surgical procedures fail to palliate perianal disease, proctectomy or proctocolectomy may be used for salvage, with a 10% risk of further surgery at 5 years and a 30% risk at 10 years.[40]

CANCER

The most important factor in assessing the risk for cancer in patients with Crohn's disease or ulcerative colitis is the duration of disease. It is estimated that the risk for cancer in patients with ulcerative colitis increases at a

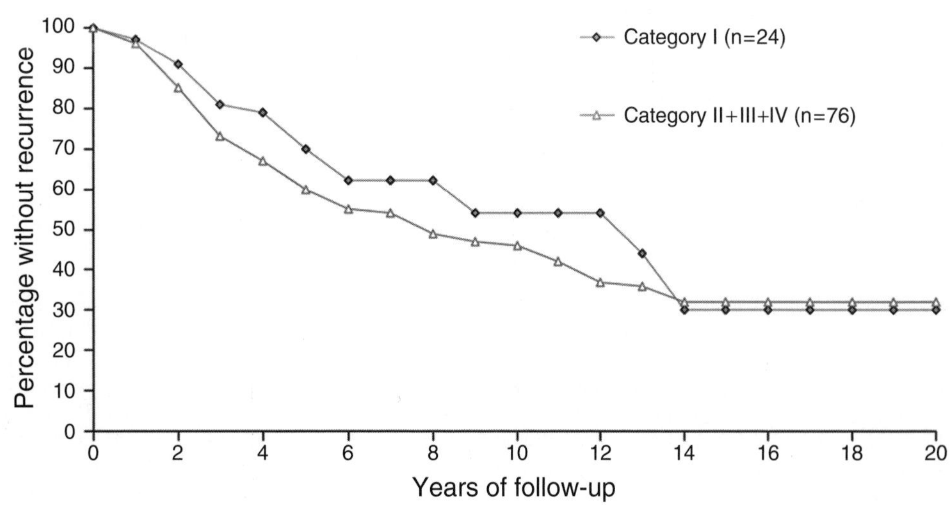

Figure 93–6 Cumulative recurrence-free rates for a normal histologic margin of resection versus any histologic abnormality at the margins. There is no significant difference between the curves. (From Kotanagi H, Kramer K, Fazio VW, Petras RE: Do microscopic abnormalities at resection margins correlate with increased anastomotic recurrence in Crohn's disease? Dis Colon Rectum 1991;34:909-916.)

rate of 1% per year after the first 10 years of disease.[12] Patients with total colonic disease are at highest risk, but those with partial ulcerative colonic disease have a higher risk for cancer than the normal population does.[3,8] Additionally, patients with Crohn's disease have a higher risk.[19] In a 20-year retrospective study conducted at the Cleveland Clinic Foundation, colorectal cancer developed in 10 of 454 adolescents with ulcerative colitis and 2 of 834 adolescents with Crohn's disease.[37] Thus, yearly surveillance should be performed in all patients with ulcerative colitis 8 to 10 years after diagnosis regardless of whether they are symptomatic.[26] Furthermore, patients with severe perianal or rectal Crohn's disease should be periodically examined and biopsy promptly performed on any suspicious anorectal mass.

REFERENCES

1. Alexander F, Sarigol S, DiFiore J, et al: Fate of the pouch in 151 pediatric patients after ileal pouch anal anastomosis. J Pediatr Surg 2003;38:78-82.
2. Alexander-Williams J, Haynes IG: Conservative operations for Crohn's disease of the small bowel. World J Surg 1985; 9:945-951.
3. Bansai P, Sonnenberg A: Risk factors of colorectal cancer in inflammatory bowel disease. Am J Gastroenterol 1996; 91:44-48.
4. Belli DC, Seidman E, Bouthillier L, et al: Chronic intermittent elemental diet improves growth failure in children with Crohn's disease. Gastroenterology 1988;94:503-510.
5. Belluzzi A, Brignola C, Campieri M, et al: Effect of an enteric-coated fish-oil preparation on relapses in Crohn's disease. N Engl J Med 1996;334:1551-1560.
6. Benkov KJ, Rosh JR, Schwersenz A, et al: Cyclosporine as an alternative to surgery in children with inflammatory bowel disease. J Pediatr Gastroenterol Nutr 1994;19:290-294.
7. Cintron JR, Park JJ, Orsay CP, et al: Repair of fistulas-in-ano using fibrin adhesive. Dis Colon Rectum 2000;43:944-950.
8. Collins RH, Feldman M, Fordtran JS: Colon cancer, dysplasia, and surveillance in patients with ulcerative colitis. A critical review. N Engl J Med 1987;316:1654-1658.
9. Connell WR, Kamm MA, Dickson M, et al: Long-term neoplasia risk after azathioprine treatment in inflammatory bowel disease. Lancet 1994;343:1249-1252.
10. Crohn BB, Ginsberg L, Oppenheimer GD: Regional enteritis: A pathologic and clinical entity. JAMA 1932;99:1323-1329.
11. Dalziel TK: Chronic intestinal enteritis. BMJ 1913;2: 1068-1069.
12. Devroede GJ, Taylor WT, Sauer WG, et al: Cancer risk and life expectancy of children with ulcerative colitis. N Engl J Med 1971;285:17-21.
13. Dietz DW, Lauret S, Strong SA, et al: Safety and long term efficacy of strictureplasty in 314 patients with obstructing small bowel Crohn's disease. J Am Coll Surg 2001;192:333-337.
14. Fazio VW, Galandiuk S, Jagelman DG, Lavery IC: Strictureplasty in Crohn's disease. Ann Surg 1989;210: 621-625.
15. Feagan BG, Rochon J, Fedorak RN, et al: Methotrexate for the treatment of Crohn's disease. N Engl J Med 1995;332: 292-297.
16. Gilat T: Incidence of inflammatory bowel disease: Going up or down? Gastroenterology 1983;85:196-197.
17. Grand RJ, Ramakrishna J, Calenda KA: Inflammatory bowel disease in the pediatric patient. Gastoenterol Clin North Am 1995;24:613-632.
18. Greenberg GR, Feagan BG, Martin F, et al: Oral budesonide for active Crohn's disease. N Engl J Med 1994;331:36-41.
19. Greenstern AJ, Sachar DB, Smith H, et al: A comparison of cancer risk in Crohn's disease and ulcerative colitis. Cancer 1981;12:2742-2745.
20. Hanauer SB: Drug therapy: Inflammatory bowel disease. N Engl J Med 1996;334:841-848.
21. Hawthorne AB, Daneshmend TK, Hawkeg CJ, et al: Treatment of ulcerative colitis with fish oil supplementation: A prospective 12 month randomized controlled trial. Gut 1992;33:922-928.
22. Hawthorne AB, Hawkey CJ: Immunosuppressive drugs in inflammatory bowel disease: A review of efficacy and place in therapy. Drugs 1989;38:267-288.
23. Hyams JS: Extraintestinal manifestations of inflammatory bowel disease. J Pediatr Gastroenterol Nutr 1994;19:7-21.
24. Hyams JS, Markowitz J, Wyllie R: Use of infliximab in the treatment of Crohn's disease in children and adolescents. J Pediatr 2000;137:192-196.
25. Janowitz HD: Inflammatory Bowel Disease, New York, Field, Rich & Associates, 1985.
26. Jonsson B, Ahsgren L, Anderson LO, et al: Colorectal cancer surveillance in patients with ulcerative colitis. Br J Surg 1994;81:689-691.
27. Kirschner BS: Safety of azathioprine and 6-mercaptopurine in pediatric patients with inflammatory bowel disease. Gastroenterology 1998;115:813-821.
28. Kotanagi H, Kramer K, Fazio VW, Petras RE: Do microscopic abnormalities at resection margins correlate with increased anastomotic recurrence in Crohn's disease? Dis Colon Rectum 1991;34:909-916.
29. Lawrance IC, Wu F, Leite AZ, et al: A murine model of chronic inflammation-induced intestinal fibrosis down-regulated by antisense NF-Kappa B. Gastroenterology 2003;125:1750-1761.
30. Levin KE, Pemberton JH, Phillips SF, et al: Role of oxygen free radicals in the etiology of pouchitis. Dis Colon Rectum 1992;35:452-456.
31. Lock MR, Farmer RG, Fazio VW, et al: Recurrence and reoperation for Crohn's disease: The role of disease location in prognosis. N Engl J Med 1981;304:1586-1588.
32. Longo WE, Oakley JR, Lavery K, et al: Outcome of ileorectal anastomosis for Crohn's colitis. Dis Colon Rectum 1992; 35:1066-1070.
33. Mack DR, Young R, Kaufman SS, et al: Methotrexate in patients with Crohn's disease after 6-mercaptopurine. J Pediatr 1998;132:830-835.
34. Malchaw H, Ewe K, Brandes JW, et al: European Cooperative Crohn's Disease Study (ECCDS): Results of drug treatment. Gastroenterology 1984;86:249-266.
35. Michener WM, Caufield M, Farmer RG, et al: Genetic counseling and family history in IBD: 30 years experience at The Cleveland Clinic. Can J Gastroenterol 1990;4:350-354.
36. Michener WM, Caulfield M, Wyllie R, Farmer RG: Management of inflammatory bowel disease: 30 years of observation. Cleve Clin J Med 1990;57:685-691.
37. Michener WM, Farmer RG, Mortimer EA: Long-term prognosis of ulcerative colitis with onset in childhood or adolescence. J Clin Gastroenterol 1979;1:301-305.
38. Michener WM, Wyllie R: Management of children and adolescents with inflammatory bowel disease. Med Clin North Am 1990;74:103-117.
39. Morin CL, Roulet M, Roy CC, Weber A: Continuous elemental enteral alimentation in children with Crohn's disease and growth failure. Gastroenterology 1980;79:1205-1210.
40. Oliva RT, Wyllie R, Alexander F, et al: The results of strictureplasty in pediatric patients with multifocal Crohn disease. J Pediatr Gastroenterol Nutr 1994;18:307-311.

41. Orkin BA, Telander RL: The effect of intra-abdominal resection or fecal diversion on perianal disease in pediatric Crohn's disease. J Pediatr Surg 1985;20:343-347.
42. Polk DB, Hattner JA, Kerner JA Jr: Improved growth and disease activity after intermittent administration of a defined formula diet in children with Crohn's disease. J Parenter Enteral Nutr 1992;16:499-504.
43. Present DH, Korelitz BL, Wisch N, et al: Treatment of Crohn's disease with 6-mercaptopurine: A long-term randomized double-blind study. N Engl J Med 1981;302:981-987.
44. Russka T, Vaajalahti P, Arajarvi P, Maki M: Prospective evaluation of upper gastrointestinal mucosal lesions in children with ulcerative colitis and Crohn's disease. J Pediatr Gastroenterol Nutr 1994;19:181-186.
45. Rutgeerts P, Hiele M, Geboes K, et al: Controlled trial of metronidazole treatment for prevention of Crohn's recurrence after ileal resection. Gastroenterology 1995;108: 1617-1621.
46. Rutgeerts P, Lofgerg R, Malchaw H, et al: A comparison of budesonide with prednisolone for active Crohn's disease. N Engl J Med 1994;331:842-845.
47. Sachar DB: Maintenance therapy in ulcerative colitis and Crohn's disease. J Clin Gastroenterol 1995;20:117-122.
48. Sandborn WJ: A critical review of cyclosporin therapy in inflammatory bowel disease. Inflamm Bowel Dis 1995;1: 48-63.
49. Sedgwick DM, Barton JR, Hamer-Hodges DW, et al: Population-based study of surgery in juvenile onset Crohn's disease. Br J Surg 1991;78:171-175.
50. Summer RW, Switz DM, Sessions JT Jr, et al: National Cooperative Crohn's Disease Study: Results of drug treatment. Gastroenterology 1979;77:847-869.
51. Tjandra JJ, Fazio VW: Surgery for Crohn's colitis. Int Surg 1992;77:9-14.
52. Ursing B, Alm T, Barany F, et al: A comparison study of metronidazole and sulfasalazine for Crohn's disease: The Cooperative Crohn's Disease Study in Sweden II. Gastroenterology 1982;83:550-562.
53. Wilmore D: Short bowel syndrome. World J Surg 2000;24: 1487-1493.

Chapter  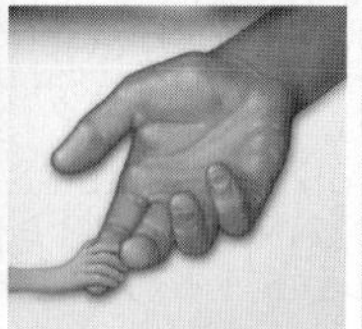

Ulcerative Colitis

Eric W. Fonkalsrud

It is believed that Wilks and Moxon[91] were the first to describe ulcerative colitis (UC) in 1859. By the end of the 19th century, fecal diversion was standard practice for severe cases, although improvement was rarely more than transient. In the early 20th century, tube appendicostomy and frequent colonic lavage with bicarbonate solution were recommended.[89] Total fecal diversion by ileostomy, as advocated by Browne[8] in 1913, became widely practiced, despite significant morbidity and mortality. Until the mid-1940s, ileostomy appliances were primitive and were routinely associated with soiling and skin irritation. Surgical intervention was usually delayed until patients were critically ill; subsequent closure of the ileostomy commonly resulted in reactivation of the disease.

It was not until 1944 that Strauss and Strauss[81] introduced proctocolectomy with ileostomy for treatment of severe UC. A three-stage operation—(1) ileostomy, (2) subtotal colectomy and sigmoid colostomy, and (3) abdominoperineal rectal resection—was recommended by Cattell[9] in 1948. Shortly thereafter, a two-stage operation evolved consisting of initial ileostomy and simultaneous subtotal colectomy; by 1951, this procedure was associated with a mortality of only 4.4%.[35] Ripstein[67] in 1952 and Goligher[38] in 1954 recommended ileostomy with one-stage proctocolectomy, which until 2 decades ago was considered the standard elective operation for patients with UC.

Although total proctocolectomy with ileostomy provided a cure for UC, many patients were unwilling to accept a permanent ileostomy; as a result, the operation was often delayed until the patients had advanced disease, were malnourished, and had complications from the extended medical therapy. Factors that were instrumental in improving the quality of life of patients with ileostomies include the eversion technique ("maturing") of ileostomy construction recommended by Brooke[7] in 1952 and the development of adhesive ileostomy appliances. Subsequent improvements in peristomal skin care by Turnbull[86] and others, along with special training in stomal care for nurses, have made it possible for most patients to leave the appliance attached to the skin for 4 to 6 days. With the goal of developing a continent ileostomy that requires no stoma appliance and can be irrigated at a convenient place and time, Kock[48] created an intra-abdominal reservoir with a nipple valve in the ileostomy stoma in 1969.

The search for a sphincter-saving operation for patients with UC began more than 60 years ago when Devine[15] of Melbourne recommended a staged ileosigmoidostomy. Aylett[3] of London became the leading proponent of colectomy with ileoproctostomy, and in 1966 he reported excellent results with 300 patients and a mortality rate of only 5.7%. Parc et al.[59] reviewed 17 studies totaling 1206 patients with colectomy and ileorectal anastomosis for UC and found that patients averaged 4.5 bowel movements per day, and the majority were continent. Proctectomy was eventually required in more than 15% of patients because of persistent rectal disease. The risk of developing cancer in the retained rectum ranged from 2% to 20%. Ileoproctostomy is rarely used today, and only in patients with minimal rectal disease.

In 1947 Ravitch and Sabiston[65] modified the previously unsuccessful procedure of ileoanal anastomosis and added the technique of rectal mucosectomy. Most patients who had this procedure had an unacceptable degree of defecation frequency and urgency, and the operation was rarely used over the next 3 decades.[64] In 1964 Soave[74] described an endorectal colonic pull-through procedure after distal rectal mucosectomy for Hirschsprung's disease and reported good clinical results. Application of distal rectal mucosal stripping was combined with total colectomy and a straight endorectal ileoanal anastomosis by Safaie and Soper[70] in 1973 in four young patients with familial polyposis coli. In 1977 Martin et al.[54] reported satisfactory results using this technique in young patients with UC.

The ileoanal pull-through procedure has undergone many modifications over the years. The most important of these was the addition of a pouch constructed from the distal ileum and placed immediately proximal to the anal anastomosis to reduce stool frequency and urgency. The development of the ileal reservoir was based on canine studies by Valente and Bacon[88] in 1955, using a triple-limb ileal pouch; by Karlan et al.,[44] using a double-barrel isoperistaltic pouch; and by Ferrari and Fonkalsrud,[23] using an S-shaped pouch and ileoanal anastomosis. In 1978 Parks and Nicholls[60] combined an S-shaped ileal reservoir with rectal mucosectomy and a pouch-anal anastomosis and reported acceptable results in adult patients. Total colectomy with the ileoanal pouch procedure (IAPP) is now widely accepted as the best option for the surgical treatment of UC in patients of all ages.[14,19,29,58,66]

CAUSE

The cause of UC remains undetermined. Various investigators have incriminated transmissible bacteria or viruses; however, pathogenic organisms have been implicated inconsistently.[39] Others believe that bacteria or viruses are secondary invaders rather than primary agents and that dietary factors may have an important role.[4] Currently, an immunologic response to an autologous bacterial or chemical antigen is the most attractive theory of the origin of UC. Approximately 15% of patients with UC have one or more family members with inflammatory bowel disease. Studies of patients with idiopathic ankylosing spondylitis, uveitis, and UC by HLA-W27 testing suggest a genetic predisposition; however, no definite predictable relationship has been determined. Although a specific gene locus has not been identified in patients with UC, linkages with genes on chromosomes 3, 5, 7, and 12 have been found in some studies. Although psychological factors have often been cited as contributing to UC, it is not currently believed that a "premorbid personality" exists. Psychological factors and stress may provoke relapses and contribute to the chronic nature of the disease but do not necessarily initiate the condition.

PATHOLOGY

Ulcerative colitis is a chronic inflammatory disease of the rectal and colonic mucosa and submucosa. The rectum is involved in more than 95% of cases, and the inflammation extends proximally in a contiguous manner.[73] If the distal ileum is involved, one must consider that the patient may have Crohn's disease rather than UC. The term *backwash ileitis* may be a misnomer, because there is no scientific evidence that refluxing of luminal contents from the cecum induces ileal mucosal inflammation any more than normal isoperistaltic flow does. When the entire colon is involved (pancolitis), the most severe changes usually occur in the rectum and sigmoid colon. Children are more likely to develop pancolitis than are adults.

The characteristic microscopic appearance of UC consists of crypt abscesses that lead to mucosal ulceration, with undermining of adjacent mucosa. Mucosal bridging with pseudopolyp formation often develops in a circumferential pattern; in contrast, the ulcerations of granulomatous colitis are usually linear and located on the mesenteric side of the colonic lumen (Fig. 94-1). As the disease progresses in the acute phase, the colon distends, peristalsis decreases, and the muscularis becomes thin and diffusely hemorrhagic. If inadequately treated, the disease may progress to acute dilatation, bacteremia, peritonitis, and, rarely, perforation from toxic megacolon. With chronic UC, however, the muscularis becomes thickened and fibrotic, with flattening of haustral folds and reduction of meaningful peristaltic contractions.

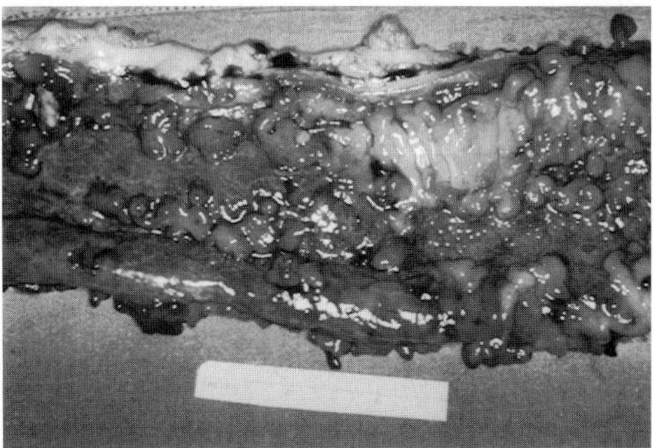

Figure 94–1 Open segment of the left colon from a 16-year-old with chronic ulcerative colitis. Note the presence of large pseudopolyps and the absence of normal mucosal folds.

The mucosa becomes atrophic and may become dysplastic in long-standing disease. The colonic mesentery becomes shortened, and the serosal surface often develops increased superficial vascularity and an overabundance of adipose tissue. In remission, the mucosa may return to a nearly normal appearance on microscopic examination. Mucosal biopsy is helpful to confirm the diagnosis of UC and assess disease activity.

From the immune perspective, the mucosa in UC consists of a dominant $CD4^+$ population of T lymphocytes.[43] These T cells have an atypical phenotype with an increased production of transforming growth factor-ß and interleukin (IL)-5. These cells seem to be activated by antigen presentation from adjacent epithelial cells. Additional mediators of inflammation are derived from activated macrophages, which express many inflammatory cytokines, including tumor necrosis factor, IL-1, and IL-6. These inflammatory factors form the basis of some of the newer medical therapies for UC.

CLINICAL MANIFESTATIONS

Less than 4% of patients with UC experience the onset of symptoms before 10 years of age. In approximately 18%, symptoms begin between 10 and 20 years of age. The onset of UC most commonly occurs in persons in their late 20s, and males and females are equally affected. The disease is four times more prevalent in whites than in blacks, Latinos, or Asians; it is three times more common in Jews than in non-Jews. Symptoms typically begin insidiously with persistent diarrhea, followed by the appearance of blood, mucus, and pus in the stools. Intermittent, cramping lower abdominal pain; tenesmus; and anemia are common. Anorexia, weight loss, and growth retardation from chronic inflammation, poor appetite, and prolonged use of corticosteroids often occur when the disease becomes chronic. As a result, many children often feel tired and lack the desire to participate in social and physical activities. Most children develop unremitting colitis with periodic relapses that are often precipitated by emotional stress or intercurrent infections. Patients occasionally achieve permanent remission; however, many progress to chronic colitis with shorter and less frequent remissions. A single attack with complete remission occurs in less than 10% of children.

In approximately 15% of children, the onset of UC is fulminating, with profuse bloody diarrhea, severe abdominal cramps, fever, and occasionally sepsis, necessitating prompt treatment.[29] Most of these patients improve with medical therapy, although some patients (5%) develop toxic megacolon that requires emergency surgery.[1] In my experience, more than 50% of all children with UC eventually require colectomy.

Carcinoma of the colon or rectum has been reported in 3% of patients during the first 10 years of the disease and increases by approximately 10% to 15% in each subsequent decade.[16] Malignancy may develop even in patients with apparent remission of colitis. Cancer is more common in patients who have pancolitis, those whose symptoms began before age 17 years, those with primary sclerosing cholangitis, and those who have frequent flare-ups.[17,76] Evidence of dysplasia of the colonic mucosa on biopsy indicates a high risk for subsequent carcinoma.

Extracolonic manifestations of UC include growth retardation, arthralgias, delay of sexual maturation, skin lesions, anemia, osteoporosis, primary sclerosing cholangitis, nephrolithiasis, uveitis, and stomatitis (Fig. 94-2). Growth retardation with delay in bone development frequently accompanies chronic UC in adolescence. Delayed sexual maturation may be caused in part by abnormally low levels of urinary gonadotropins.[55] Growth hormone levels are usually in the normal range for the patient's age.

Arthralgias occur in approximately 25% of children with UC, often dependent on the duration and severity of the disease, and commonly involve the knees, ankles, wrists, fingers, and hips. Joint symptoms, which occasionally precede the onset of intestinal symptoms, may be confused with juvenile rheumatoid arthritis. Ankylosing spondylitis may be seen in 1% to 6%, and sacroileitis may occur in 4% to 18% of patients. Symptoms often regress when patients receive corticosteroids; however, they may recur when steroids are withdrawn, regardless of the UC status, and may become permanently disabling.

The most common skin lesions are erythema nodosum of the trunk and occasionally the limbs. Pyoderma gangrenosum (chronic ulcerations of the skin) occurs in less than 5% of children with UC, usually on the lower limbs. These lesions are often resistant to local or systemic therapy and may not heal until the patient goes into remission or the disease is surgically corrected.

Abnormal liver function tests are found in approximately 15% of patients and may stem from a variety of hepatic disorders. Almost 80% of UC patients have some abnormality of the liver on biopsy, with more than 50% having some degree of fatty infiltration. Sclerosing cholangitis is uncommon in children, although it may occur in as many as 15% of adult patients with chronic UC.[45] Anemia is common and usually results from overt or occult blood loss in the stools.

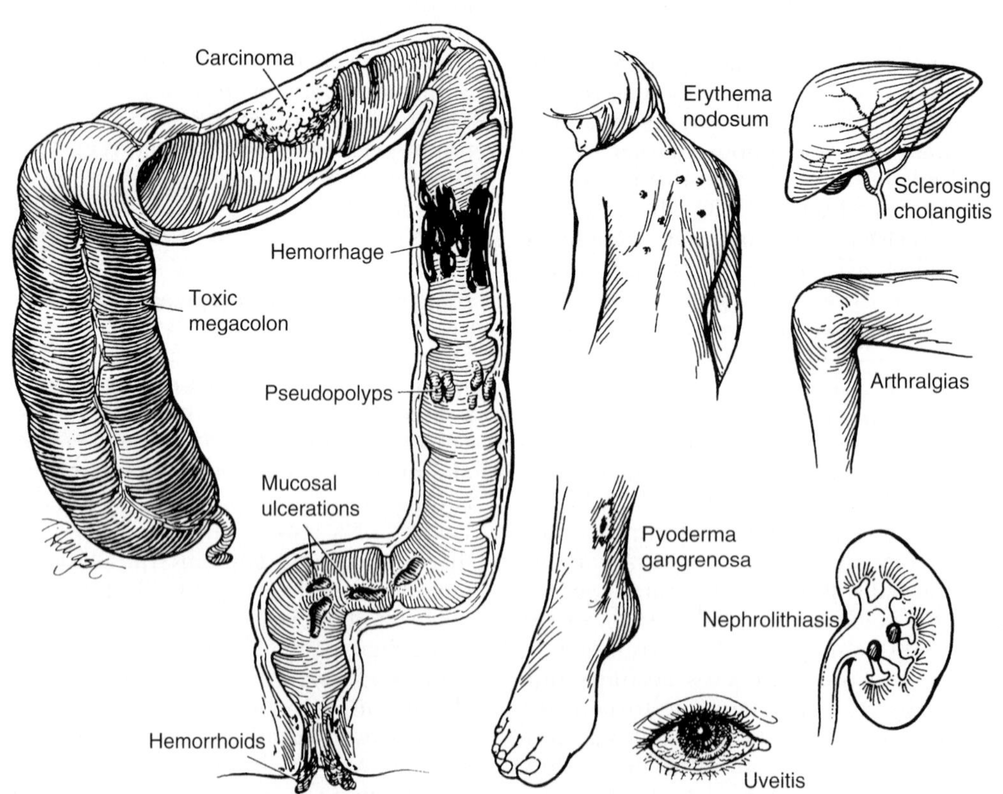

Figure 94-2 Manifestations of ulcerative colitis in the colon and rectum. Extracolonic disorders occur in more than 60% of children with ulcerative colitis.

Osteoporosis and osteomalacia may occur from decreased calcium absorption associated with diminished uptake of fat-soluble vitamins and increased urinary losses of calcium resulting from steroid therapy. Nephrolithiasis occurs in approximately 8% of patients with UC, largely because of inadequate fluid intake to compensate for fluid loss through diarrhea.[80] Uveitis (inflammation of the iris) occurs in less than 2% of patients. Aphthous stomatitis is common in patients with UC, particularly during flare-ups.

CLINICAL EXAMINATION

Children with mild UC or those in remission may manifest few positive findings on physical examination, although endoscopy may demonstrate friable and edematous colonic mucosa with a thin, purulent exudate. Children with chronic UC often show delayed growth in height, delayed sexual maturation, anemia, pallor, and cushingoid features from long-term steroid therapy. With acute disease, fever, dehydration, and systemic toxicity are common. Pain is often elicited by palpation over the sigmoid colon. External hemorrhoids commonly develop from diarrhea and frequency of defecation; however, anal fistulas, fissures, and abscesses are rare and, if present, suggest Crohn's disease. Sigmoidoscopy or colonscopy often shows an edematous and hemorrhagic mucosa that contains superficial ulcers and is covered with a purulent, bloody exudate (Fig. 94-3).

Anemia from blood loss occurs in approximately two thirds of patients. The erythrocyte sedimentation rate is typically elevated, the prothrombin time is prolonged, and the serum albumin level is usually low. Hyponatremia and hypokalemia often occur with protracted diarrhea. Stool cultures are consistently negative for pathogenic bacteria and parasites.

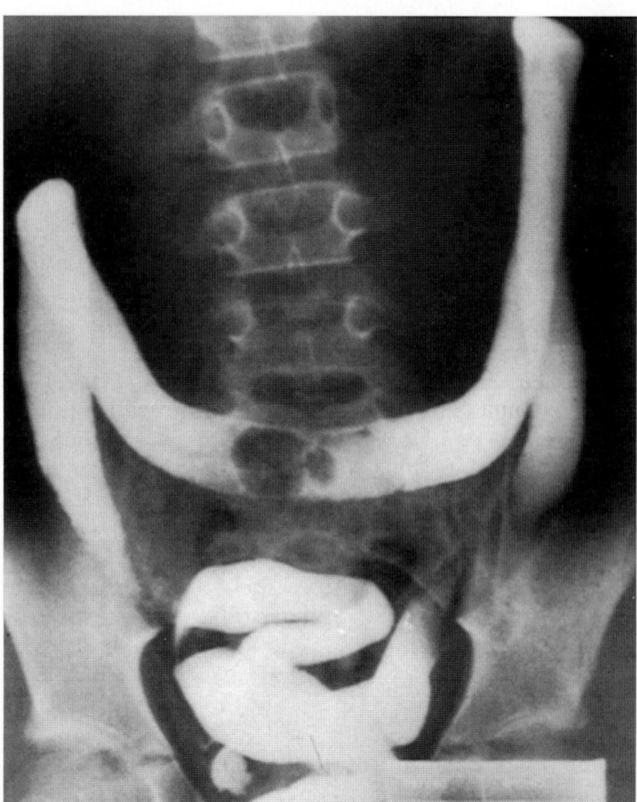

Figure 94–4 Barium enema radiograph from a 17-year-old girl with chronic ulcerative colitis. Note the shortening of the colon and loss of haustral markings, which give the colon a characteristic "lead-pipe" appearance.

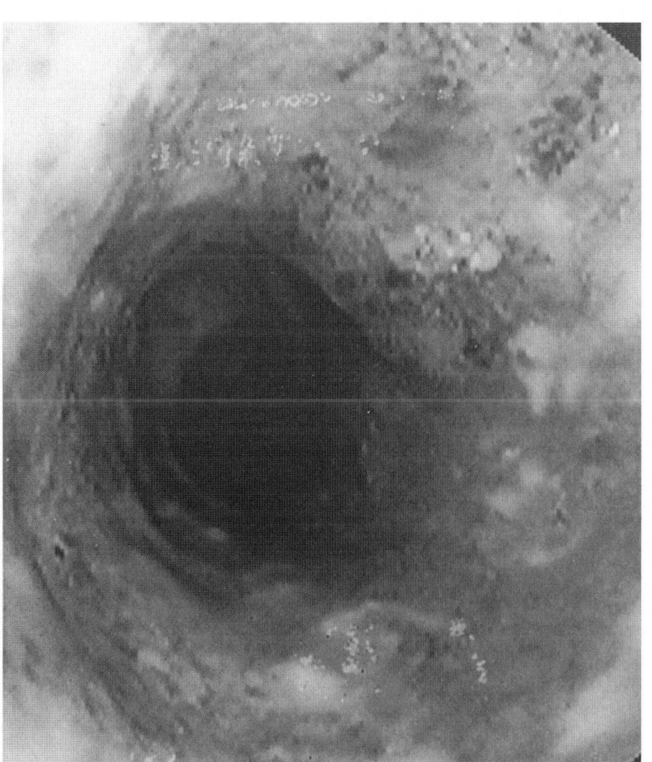

Figure 94–3 Appearance of the transverse colon from an 18-year-old boy with severe ulcerative colitis as viewed through a colonoscope. Note the mucosal ulceration and loss of mucosal folds.

Barium enema radiographs in a patient with chronic UC may show a shortened, narrow, and rigid colon with loss of haustral folds ("lead-pipe" appearance) and extensive formation of pseudopolyps (Fig. 94-4). In acute colitis, the intestinal contour may have an irregular, serrated border from mucosal ulcerations. The edematous mucosa between areas of ulceration appear as pseudopolyps. Because a contrast barium enema can stimulate acute manifestations of colitis, and because more meaningful information can be obtained from colonscopy, contrast enemas are now used infrequently.

MEDICAL MANAGEMENT

Medical therapy for severe UC is nonspecific and is based on providing symptomatic relief. It is unlikely, however, that the ultimate course of the disease will be altered or that a cure can be achieved by nonsurgical treatment. Many children with mild UC that is localized to the rectum and sigmoid colon and those in remission may improve for long periods with the administration of 5-aminosalicylate-based compounds such as sulfasalazine or mesalamine.[62] These anti-inflammatory compounds are believed to block the production of prostaglandins and leukotrienes. They also block bacterial peptide-induced secretion and scavenging of reactive oxygen metabolites. For patients with chronic disease who develop acute flare-ups, a course of corticosteroids (prednisone) for 2 to 3 months may induce remission. Steroid doses are rapidly tapered, and alternate-day therapy is initiated as soon as possible. Prolonged use of steroids in young patients is often associated with side effects, including growth failure, osteoporosis, hypertension, hyperglycemia, and cushingoid features, as well as striae on the trunk and thighs in females. Rectal steroids (hydrocortisone) or mesalamine compounds such as Pentasa, Asacol, or Rowasa enemas may be helpful in treating colitis confined to the rectum and lower left colon. Steroids should be accompanied by H_2-blocking drugs and oral antacids to reduce the incidence of peptic ulcer or gastritis. Patients receiving steroids often benefit from taking calcium, vitamin D, and bisphosphonates.

Antidiarrheal medications such as diphenoxylate hydrochloride with atropine sulfate (Lomotil) or loperamide hydrochloride (Imodium) may reduce the number of bowel movements and decrease rectal spasm, but they should be used cautiously; these drugs, as well as opiates, may occasionally induce toxic megacolon.[36] Other beneficial medications include tranquilizers and antibiotics such as metronidazole. Dietary modification is encouraged to minimize intestinal stimulants such as chocolate, vinegar, spicy foods, fresh vegetables, and nuts. Severe anemia and hypoalbuminemia may require infusions of blood, albumin, or both.

Immunosuppressive drugs, including azathioprine, 6-mercaptopurine (6-MP), and cyclosporine, are frequently given to patients with chronic UC; however, their efficacy is not universally acknowledged, and the side effects may be appreciable.[34] Azathioprine and 6-MP affect subgroups of T cells and require lengthy administration before becoming effective. These drugs have some toxicity and may cause pancreatitis or hepatitis. They are helpful in allowing steroid therapy to be tapered and are useful in maintaining remission. Cyclosporine has a faster action than azathioprine and may be almost as effective as corticosteroids in treating patients with severe UC. Cyclosporine is highly immunosuppressive and prevents T-cell activation and inhibits IL-2 and IL-2 receptor expression. The use of a monoclonal antibody to the proinflammatory cytokine tumor necrosis factor-α (infliximab) for the treatment of UC is controversial.[18]

Psychotherapy may help patients with chronic UC adjust to the disease, its complications, and its side effects. Even more important is the ready availability of a sympathetic and interested physician and an understanding family on whom the patient can rely.

During acute flare-ups of UC, most patients require hospitalization with intravenous fluids, intestinal rest, increased doses of steroids, and parenteral nutrition. These measures commonly correct metabolic deficits and reduce clinical symptoms but do not alter the course of the colitis. The primary benefit of parenteral nutrition is to reduce the surgical risk by improving the patient's nitrogen balance. Progression of the colitis or failure to respond to therapy is an indication for urgent operation.

Complications following surgical resection of UC in children increase with the duration of the disease and the length and dosage of medications.[24,58] My experience with the surgical treatment of children receiving high doses of corticosteroids and immunosuppressive drugs shows that the complication rate is considerably higher in children who have received longer courses of therapy.[29] Although reports indicate that intravenous cyclosporine therapy is rapidly effective in patients with severe corticosteroid-resistant UC, the need for colectomy in more than 60% of patients within 6 months after discontinuation of cyclosporine therapy suggests that the drug merely delays colectomy.[51]

Steroids have been demonstrated to have an adverse effect on the healing of colonic anastomoses.[23] Further, aggressive medical therapy for UC may increase the incidence of emergency staged colectomy, with a resultant increase in morbidity, hospital stay, and cost and a less than optimal functional result.[24] Restorative proctocolectomy, however, may be safely carried out in selected patients requiring emergency surgery for severe, acute UC. In many cases, medical management should be abbreviated if prompt control of colitis cannot be achieved.[40]

Reports suggest that cigarette smoking may reduce the incidence of UC and that appendectomy is a protective factor against UC.[69] Preliminary studies suggest that the addition of transdermal nicotine to conventional maintenance therapy may improve the symptoms of UC.[63]

SURGICAL MANAGEMENT

Although medical therapy often induces remission for varying periods, UC can rarely be cured without removing the diseased colon and rectum. Because the IAPP provides excellent long-term results, surgery should be seriously considered for any patient with UC before severe disability and major complications develop. Elective surgery is done for patients with persistent symptoms of UC despite medical therapy, growth retardation, severe limitation of activities, and an unacceptable quality of life. It is often distressing for both the patient and the family when the child misses many days of school and must limit participation in physical and social activities because of severe symptoms. Emergency surgery is indicated for patients (approximately 20%) with fulminant disease that is refractory to medical therapy, extensive rectal bleeding, or toxic megacolon. Children with UC are more likely than adults to have an acute onset and more severe symptoms. In children, the severely diseased colon should be removed while the epiphyses are still open to allow for optimal growth and development. The child's condition should be evaluated periodically during the course of therapy by a surgeon and a gastroenterologist to consider alternatives to long-term medical therapy. In approximately 8% of children with chronic colitis, the distinction between UC and Crohn's disease cannot be clearly made despite sophisticated diagnostic tests and pathologic evaluation of tissue specimens, in which case the term *indeterminate colitis* is applied.[2] I favor treating these patients as if they had UC, although approximately one fourth will require eventual pouch removal.[13] Patients undergoing IAPP for indeterminate colitis should be apprised that a risk exists for late pouch failure due to emerging Crohn's disease and that permanent ileostomy may be necessary.

Surgical options should be discussed in detail with the patient and the parents. It is often helpful for the patient to speak to another child who has had surgery to alleviate fear and concern about an ileostomy and to support the decision for surgery. A preoperative discussion with an enterostomal therapist helps prepare the child and the parents for the temporary ileostomy. Although ileostomy care is usually easily mastered by children, the presence of a stoma appliance often creates embarrassment during physical and social activities. Impotence and bladder dysfunction after proctocolectomy are uncommon in children; however, these major concerns have caused many children, parents, and physicians to defer surgery until the colitis becomes debilitating and the steroid and immunosuppressive therapy causes systemic complications.

Anemia, hypoalbuminemia, and electrolyte abnormalities should be corrected before surgery, but it is rarely necessary to give more than a short course of parenteral hyperalimentation. Corticosteroid therapy is maintained until surgery to avoid an acute flare-up. Oral intake is restricted to clear liquids for 48 hours before surgery; cathartics and hyperosmolar solutions such as GoLYTELY are not used. Cleansing enemas are avoided because they may stimulate an acute flare-up of colitis. Oral antibiotics (erythromycin and neomycin) are given the day before surgery, and intravenous antibiotics (gentamicin and clindamycin) are started 2 hours before surgery.

For more than 60 years, total proctectomy with permanent ileostomy has been the standard surgical treatment of UC that is refractory to medical therapy. This procedure cures the disease, is associated with a relatively low rate of complications, and has good long-term results. Nevertheless, patients of all ages find the need to wear an ileostomy appliance for life very disturbing. Approximately 30% of patients with ileostomies experience appliance-related problems, including skin discomfort, skin irritation, leakage, and odor. In the United States it is estimated that ileostomy maintenance costs more than $1500 per year. Currently, few patients select proctocolectomy with permanent ileostomy when presented with good surgical alternatives.

The Kock continent ileal reservoir with a nipple valve obviates the need to wear an ileostomy drainage bag—a Silastic catheter is inserted into the reservoir several times a day for drainage—and was initially reported to be a good alternative to permanent ileostomy.[49] However, many patients required repeat surgery and pouch removal owing to complications related to the nipple valve and stagnant loop syndrome with pouchitis.[5] Modifications of the Kock pouch are currently used primarily for unusual situations, such as when sphincter injury or perirectal abscesses or sinuses preclude use of the IAPP.

Subtotal colectomy with ileorectal anastomosis is currently used only in patients with an unclear diagnosis and in those rare patients with UC and relative rectal sparing. Active colitis continues in the rectum in almost all these patients and eventually requires total surgical removal.

Ileoanal Pouch Procedure

Because UC is primarily a disease of the mucosa, colectomy with rectal mucosectomy and the IAPP has become the most frequent operation for patients whose disease is refractory to medical therapy. Removal of the entire rectal mucosa down to the dentate line does not appreciably interfere with function of the anal sphincter or the ability to discriminate among gaseous, liquid, and solid contents.[61] This procedure avoids a permanent ileostomy stoma, does not require repeated catheterizations (as is necessary with a Kock pouch), and permits a near-normal pattern of defecation.[41]

The early operations used a straight endorectal ileal pull-through technique, and most patients experienced persistent defecation frequency, urgency, and varying degrees of incontinence; an occasional report indicated somewhat better results in children.[11,56] The straight endorectal ileal pull-through retains peristaltic contractions and generates spike waves down to the anal anastomosis. More recently, however, surgeons have occasionally reported better results when the straight pull-through technique is done in conjunction with multiple vertical linear myotomies on the distal 12 to 15 cm proximal to the anal anastomosis.[26] Almost all surgeons currently performing the pull-through operation construct an ileal pouch or reservoir above the ileoanal anastomosis to reduce peristalsis in the distal ileum and to allow storage of fecal matter.[19] Regardless of the type of reservoir used, as long as the lower 4 cm of the rectal muscle is not damaged, the resting and squeezing pressures of the anal sphincter will approach normal values within 3 months.[77] Long-term quality of life with an IAPP is usually equated with the effectiveness of bowel function.[47]

Although it may be appealing to perform a one-stage IAPP in children, experience has shown that a diverting ileostomy for approximately 3 months minimizes the risk of pouch leak or pelvic infection.[27] Attention to the many technical details of the operation is necessary to minimize the many potential complications. Leaks occur more than twice as frequently, and recovery is often protracted, when an ileostomy is not used.[10] To be considered for a one-stage IAPP, a patient should have good nutrition, be taking minimal immunosuppressive medications or steroids, have minimal rectal inflammation, and not be obese.[20] In addition, there should be no adverse intraoperative events, and the anastomoses should be constructed optimally and without tension. Although I favor the use of a temporary ileostomy in almost all patients with UC, no complications occurred in any of the few carefully selected children who underwent a one-stage IAPP. The patient should be advised that recovery is protracted when the ileostomy is omitted.

Four pouch configurations have been used clinically: lateral, S-, J-, and W-shaped pouches (Fig. 94-5). Both the S- and W-shaped pouches are hand-sutured and require a longer operating time than the stapled J-shaped and lateral pouches. Stasis is more common in large pouches, and catheter irrigations are occasionally required for adequate emptying.[78] After several months, many pouches with an ileal spout develop stasis and enlarge.

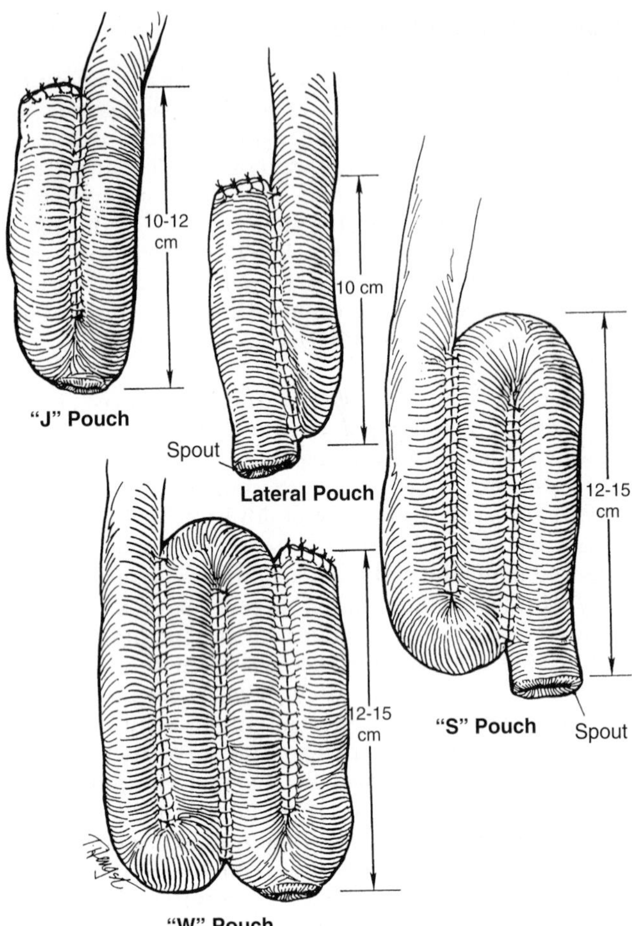

Figure 94–5 Four ileoanal pouch configurations have been used clinically. The lateral and S-shaped pouches have a short "spout." The J-shaped pouch is used most frequently.

The J-shaped pouch configuration, which was first described by Utsunomiya et al.,[87] has been used most widely, is the simplest to construct, and produces the fewest long-term complications in children and adults. The lateral ileal reservoir was used in the past for children and achieves good long-term results, provided that the ileal spout between the lower end of the pouch and the anus is short.[29] The lateral pouch is currently reserved only for patients with a short ileal mesentery in whom it is difficult to obtain sufficient length for a J-shaped pouch (i.e., it cannot reach the anus without tension). Reservoir configuration is relatively unimportant as long as the pouch is kept short (<12 cm), which allows for most efficient function, and a spout is avoided, if possible. If a spout is present, it should not be longer than 1.5 cm. Laparoscopic-assisted colectomy and IAPP have been used with increasing frequency. The operative time is considerably longer, pouch construction is more complex, and the hospital stay is not shortened compared with the open technique.

Two-Stage Ileoanal Pouch Construction

For most patients, the IAPP is performed in two stages. During the first operation, the patient is given general anesthesia and placed on the operating table in the lithotomy position. A nasogastric tube and bladder catheter are placed. Through a midline incision that extends from the pubis to slightly above the umbilicus, the entire colon and omentum are removed. If there is any inflammation present in the distal ileum, the possibility of Crohn's disease should be considered, which would preclude performing the IAPP until the diagnosis is clarified. Recent studies indicate that resection of more than 15 cm of distal ileum may accelerate gastric emptying and increase stool frequency in patients undergoing an IAPP.[84] The rectum is thoroughly irrigated with antibiotic solution from below. The peritoneal reflection is incised circumferentially, and the rectum is mobilized with cautery dissection downward to within 4 cm of the dentate line, where it is divided (Fig. 94-6). The specimen is examined by the pathologist to rule out the possibility of Crohn's disease. The anus is dilated, and the rectal mucosa is mobilized from the rectal muscles below, using scissors and cautery dissection. Dilute epinephrine solution is injected between the mucosa and muscularis to facilitate the plane of dissection. All mucosa is removed down to the dentate line, and meticulous hemostasis is achieved. Some surgeons perform the endorectal dissection from the pelvis rather than the perineum.

The ileal mesentery is mobilized adjacent to the superior mesenteric vessels into the upper abdomen to provide sufficient length for the distal ileum to reach the anus without tension. The distal 10 to 12 cm of ileum is doubled back on itself, which places the antimesenteric surfaces adjacent to each other (Fig. 94-7A). A small incision is made at the apex of the loop, and a GIA stapling device is inserted through the incision to construct the pouch (Fig. 94-7B). The upper end of the pouch is closed with inverting sutures. A second layer of absorbable suture is placed around the pouch staple and suture lines. The pouch is brought through the pelvis and rectal muscle canal; the open apex is sutured to the anoderm and rectal muscularis at the level of the dentate line with interrupted absorbable sutures (Fig. 94-8). Tension on the anastomosis should be avoided by adequate mobilization of the ileal mesentery. The ileum is transected approximately 15 cm proximal to the upper end of the ileal reservoir, and the proximal end of the divided ileum is constructed into an end ileostomy stoma (Fig. 94-9). In children, construction of an everting stoma is not necessary, because suturing the ileal muscularis to the adjacent dermis will result in an everting stoma within 2 weeks and is not likely to cause stomal edema or obstruction. The distal ileum is stapled, closed, and loosely attached to the internal abdominal wall adjacent to the stoma, to enhance easy access when closure is performed. Loop ileostomies are not recommended in children because of the increased tension on the superior mesenteric vessels, extending to the pouch in the pelvis, and the difficulty of having a well-functioning ileostomy appliance.[32] The pelvis is drained transabdominally for approximately 4 days.

Intravenous steroids are tapered rapidly after operation; oral prednisone can usually be discontinued within 3 weeks. Most children are discharged from the hospital by the sixth day after surgery. A meglumine diatrizoate (Gastrografin) contrast enema is done within 2 months

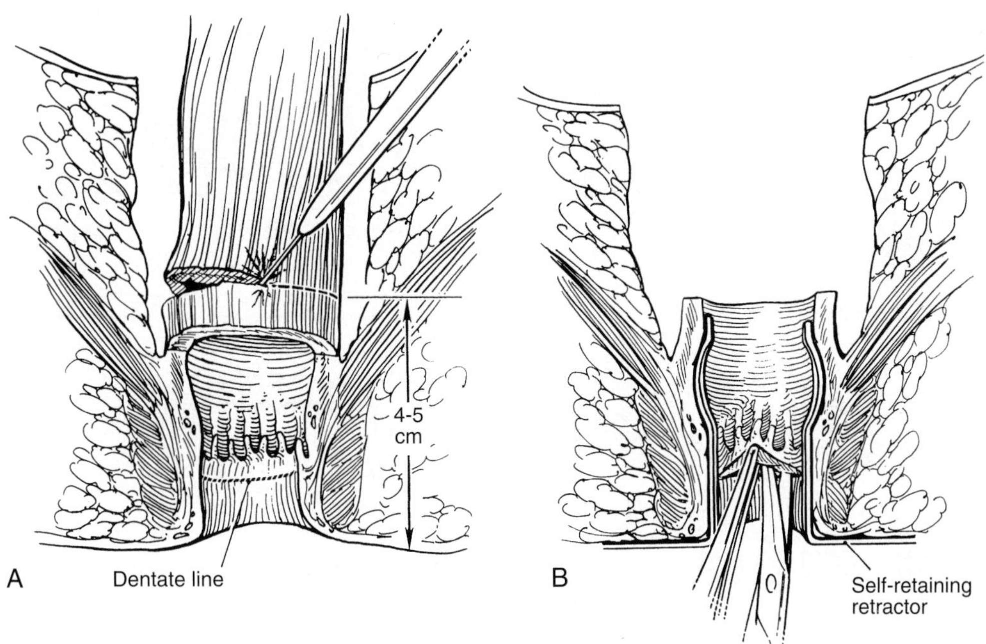

Figure 94–6 *A,* The rectum is mobilized with cautery dissection to within 4 cm of the dentate line, where it is divided. *B,* A circumferential incision is made through the rectal mucosa at the level of the dentate line with electrocautery. The mucosa is elevated from the muscularis with scissors or cautery dissection.

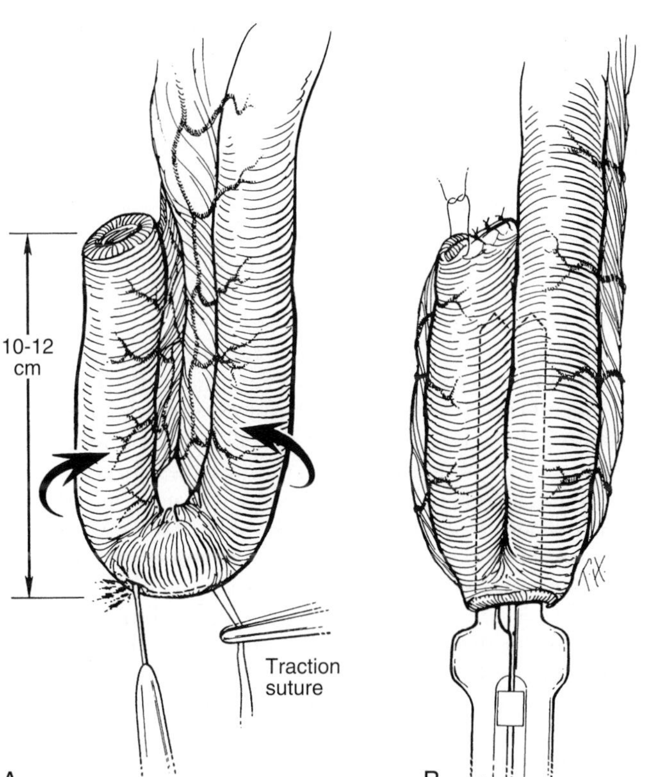

Figure 94–7 *A,* The distal 10 to 12 cm of ileum is doubled back on itself, and the antimesenteric sides are placed adjacent to each other. A small incision is made at the apex of the loop for placement of the GIA stapler. *B,* A GIA stapler is fired after being inserted through an incision in the apex of the J-loop; two firings are usually necessary to construct a pouch. The open upper end of the pouch is closed with inverting sutures.

to ensure that the ileal reservoir has no leaks or sinus tracts (Fig. 94-10). Most children resume full physical activities within 3 weeks.

Approximately 3 months after the first operation, the patient is rehospitalized for laparotomy with ileostomy closure and sigmoidoscopy. The ileoanal anastomosis is dilated under anesthesia. When oral feedings are resumed, spicy foods, chocolate, and vinegar salad dressings are avoided to minimize diarrhea. Low-dose metronidazole is given for approximately 6 weeks to reduce inflammation of the ileal mucosa caused by storage of fecal matter in the reservoir. Medications to reduce peristalsis (e.g., Lomotil, Imodium) counteract the normal stimulus for pouch contraction and promote stasis. These medications are rarely necessary, however, except to control frequent nocturnal defecation during the first few weeks after surgery. Bulking agents are rarely helpful. Daily dilatation of the ileoanal anastomosis with a large Hegar dilator is initiated for those patients with ileoanal anastomotic stenosis by the fourth day after surgery and is continued at least twice weekly during the ensuing 3 to 6 months to prevent long-term rectal stricture, with resultant pouch distention and stasis.

CLINICAL EXPERIENCE

During the past 20 years, 184 children younger than 19 years (141 with UC, 29 with polyposis, 12 with Hirschsprung's disease, and 2 with idiopathic colonic inertia) have undergone colectomy, mucosal proctectomy, and endorectal ileal pull-through operations at UCLA Medical Center. Nineteen patients were younger than 10 years. During the same period, an additional 604 patients aged

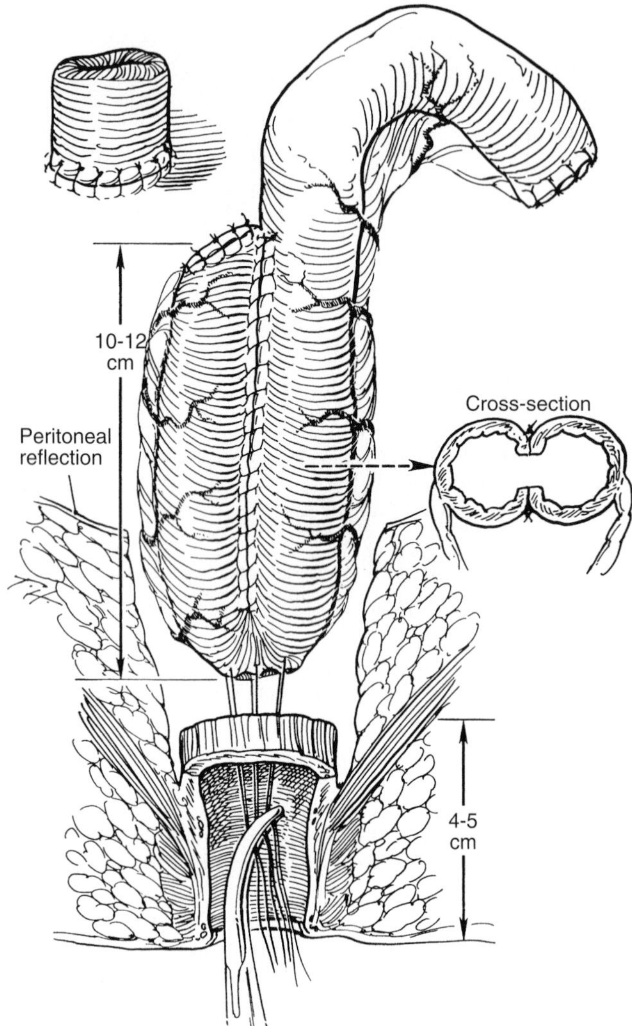

Figure 94–8 The completed pouch is drawn through the pelvis and rectal muscle canal with traction stitches. The open apex of the ileal pouch is sutured to the anoderm and rectal muscularis at the level of the dentate line with interrupted absorbable sutures.

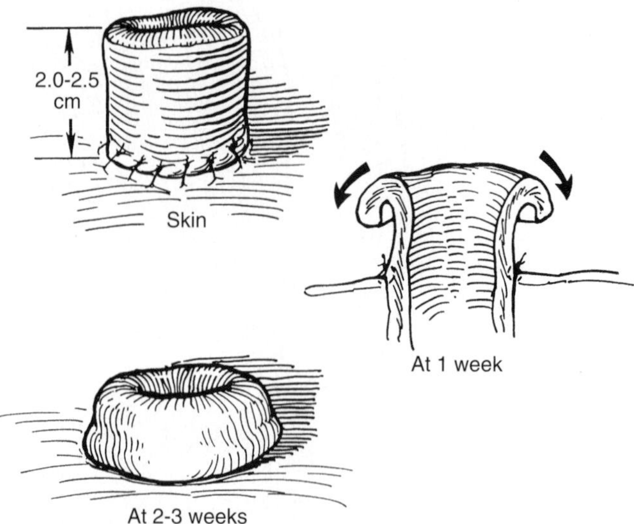

Figure 94–9 Technique for construction of an end ileostomy in children. The mesentery is mobilized from the distal 3 cm of the ileum. Approximately 2.0 to 2.5 cm of ileum is advanced beyond the skin level. The ileal muscularis is sutured to the dermis with interrupted, fine monofilament, absorbable sutures. No deeper stitches are placed. Within 2 to 3 weeks, the end of the ileum folds over and attaches to the skin for complete maturation.

19 years and older with UC or colonic polyposis underwent IAPP.

Long-term follow-up with J-shaped and lateral pouches in children has shown that the average number of bowel movements per day at 3 months is 6.1; at 6 months, it decreases to 4.2.[26] Nocturnal staining or soiling more than twice weekly was present in 17% at 3 months, particularly in young patients with UC. By 6 months, the incidence had decreased to only 6% of patients. In another large collected series of adult patients, 90% were continent at night.[6] Nineteen of the 68 female patients have delivered normal babies following IAPP, 10 by the vaginal route. Ovarian cysts are more common in females who have undergone IAPP for UC and may slightly lower the likelihood of fecundity.[57,82] None of the patients has experienced bladder dysfunction, and none of the 73 males is impotent, although one has retrograde ejaculation. Many of the patients participate in vigorous athletic activities, including football, competitive swimming, and marathon racing.

Measurements of fecal bile salts and serum B_{12} levels were within the normal range in the 19 children in whom those parameters were evaluated.[46] Within several months, the mucosa of the ileal pouch begins to function in a manner similar to that of the normal colon.[79] A detailed review of the last 85 consecutive children shows that all but 2 are currently functioning well, indicating a decreased number of complications as clinical experience has increased. Functional results and quality of life are considered good to excellent in 95% of the patients, similar to that in other large series of older patients.[14,21,75]

Measurement of residual fecal volume after defecation closely correlates with the patient's clinical function, similar to that observed with residual urine volume and bladder function. In a review of the last 150 pediatric and adult patients examined more than 6 months after surgery, when the residual fecal volume was less than 10 mL, the number of stools per day was 4.6 and the number of soiling episodes per week was 0.4, compared with 9.4 stools per day and 4.8 soiling episodes per week when the residual fecal volume was greater than 30 mL. When the residual fecal volume was less than 10 mL, the average time a patient could withhold defecation after an initial urge was more than 2 hours. Seventy-eight percent of patients with a low residual fecal volume were able to pass flatus without stool, and 82% could urinate without having a bowel movement.

Complications following the IAPP are reported to occur in 35% to 65% of patients[21,22,25-27,33,72,75,90] (41% in our series of 141 children with UC).[28] The mortality rate is less than 1%. Pouchitis is the most frequent complication of pelvic pouch surgery and occurs in 10% to 50% of patients, as determined during long-term follow-up. Obstruction of the small intestine occurs in 10% to 25% of patients; pelvic abscess, fistula, or sepsis in 3% to 10%;

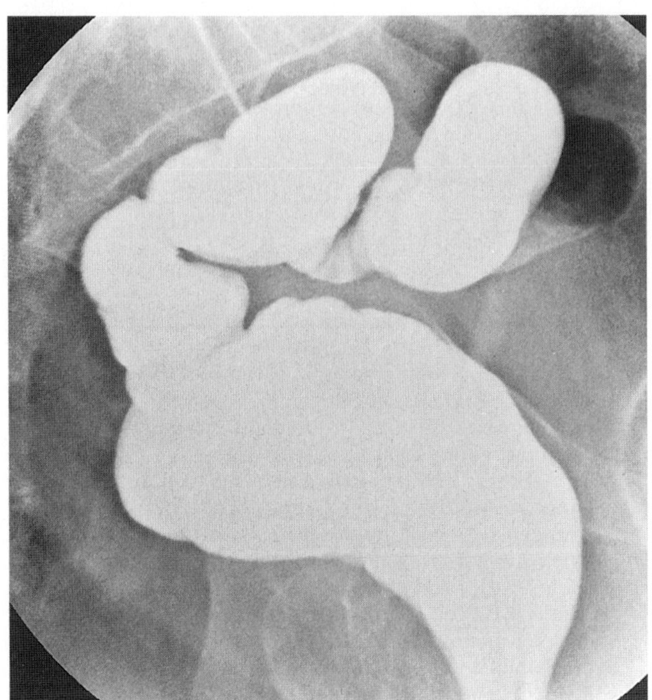

Figure 94–10 Lateral view of a meglumine diatrizoate enema performed 8 weeks after colectomy and ileoanal pouch procedure with a J-shaped pouch in a 16-year-old boy with ulcerative colitis.

ileostomy obstruction or dysfunction in 1% to 6%; wound infection in 5% to 15%; incisional hernia in 3% to 8%; anal stricture in 2% to 15%; rectovaginal fistula in 1% to 6%; pouch hemorrhage in 1% to 5%; and severe incontinence in 2% to 6%. Approximately 15% to 45% of patents require a repeat operation.[42,85] Three percent to 15% require removal of the pouch and construction of a permanent ileostomy.[6] For approximately one fourth of patients who require pouch removal, the diagnosis is found to be Crohn's disease instead of UC.

Pouchitis is a clinical syndrome of persistent pouch inflammation with watery diarrhea, fever, malaise, occasional arthralgias, and other extraintestinal symptoms.[53,71] Pouchitis is most common in the first 2 years after IAPP; episodes are more frequent and severe in children.[68] The cause of pouchitis is unclear; however, intramural aerobic facultative bacteria counts are often elevated. Patients with a positive pANCA serologic marker have the greatest risk of developing pouchitis. Patients with pancolitis, especially those with "backwash ileitis," have an increased frequency of pouchitis. With construction of an ileal pouch, the primary function of the distal ileum changes from absorption to storage. Prolonged storage of fecal matter in the pouch often causes bacterial overgrowth, which may cause mucosal inflammation.[6,50] Effective pouch emptying with minimal residual fecal volume is associated with a low frequency of pouchitis.[26] Routine rectal dilatation after an IAPP and aggressive surgical correction of outflow obstruction have resulted in a less than 10% incidence of pouchitis in patients with UC. Routine sigmoidoscopy during the first few years after IAPP often identifies early evidence of pouchitis, which may respond to therapy. Patients who have IAPP for polyposis or Hirschsprung's disease rarely develop pouchitis. Treatment for pouchitis with antibiotics (metronidazole or ciprofloxacin) is usually successful. Daily pouch washouts with tap water or use of mesalamine (Rowasa suppositories) may also be helpful. For persistent cases, oral mesalamine and hydrocortisone acetate retention enemas (Cortifoam) may be added. Treatment of pouchitis should be continued until it is completely cleared, even if symptoms resolve. For a patient with recalcitrant pouchitis, mucosal biopsy and evaluation for Crohn's disease should be undertaken. A diverting ileostomy may be considered for the rare child with UC in whom chronic pouchitis may cause delayed growth and development. Recent studies indicate that a probiotic preparation with living microorganisms (e.g., lactobacillus, streptococci) may alter the pouch flora and reduce the frequency of pouchitis.[37]

Although many complications associated with IAPP occur during the first several months after ileostomy closure, pouch dysfunction may become progressively more severe 1 or more years later. Meaningful contractions of the pouch may be reduced by distention, large size, or chronic inflammation. Complete pouch emptying is also adversely affected by increased outlet resistance from any cause, including stricture, elongated spout, or sphincter spasm caused by skin irritation or perianal fistulas or fissures. Prolonged storage of fecal matter in the pouch with incomplete emptying commonly leads to stasis with pouchitis and resultant diarrhea, increased short-chain fatty acids, urgency and frequency, decreased oral intake, and, on occasion, incontinence and systemic symptoms such as arthralgias. Routine rectal dilatation after ileostomy closure for patients with ileoanal stenosis greatly reduces the frequency of symptoms from reservoir outlet obstruction.

For a 24-hour period, the usual adult stool output is rarely more than 750 mL after IAPP; however, this is almost three times more than that from a normal colon. Near-complete emptying of the pouch with each bowel movement produces approximately three to five stools of 150 to 200 mL each per day. Incomplete pouch emptying may lead to frequent stools with low volume. Over the past 20 years, ileoanal pouches have gradually been shortened by most surgeons to approximately 10 to 15 cm, with a resultant improvement in clinical results and a lower incidence of complications.

For symptomatic pediatric and adult patients who developed pouch dysfunction resulting from mechanical causes, we have performed reconstructive operations on most, with good success.[30,33] Seventeen patients with straight endorectal ileal pull-through procedures were so symptomatic that they requested reoperation; each underwent successful mobilization of the ileum from the pelvis with construction of a J-pouch.[31] An occasional patient without a pouch has an acceptable result, although it is difficult to identify these patients preoperatively; I therefore use a pouch in all children. Eighty-three patients underwent abdominoperineal pouch reconstruction, and 95% achieved good results. Fifty-eight patients with lateral pouches underwent spout shortening, with 97% obtaining good results. Seven patients underwent pouch removal with construction of a new pouch. A temporary ileostomy was used for only 5% of patients who had a secondary reconstruction procedure.

Controversy still surrounds the benefits of a hand-sewn ileal pouch–anal anastomosis versus anal transitional zone preservation and stapled anastomosis.[52,83] On the one hand, the stapled anastomosis is technically less demanding, and the procedure minimizes trauma to the rectal muscle complex. Additionally, the ileal anastomosis to the rectum can be constructed without tension. On the other hand, patients with UC often have severe disease in the rectum, which can interfere with healing of the ileoanal or rectal anastomosis and cause fistulas or obstruction to pouch outflow. Coull et al.,[12] in a study of 105 patients, showed reactive atypia and severe acute and chronic inflammation on mucosal biopsies of the columnar cuff a mean of 5.5 years after stapled pouch-anal anastomosis. Anal transitional zone preservation and stapled anastomosis may be best suited for patients in whom tension is necessary to bring the ileal pouch down to the anus. Severe rectal UC, synchronous colon cancer, or mucosal dysplasia contraindicates rectal mucosal preservation. Children with an onset of UC before age 16 years are at much higher risk of developing carcinoma of the colon or rectum than are older patients, and those with the stapled anastomosis require a lifetime of annual surveillance with sigmoidoscopy.

CONCLUSION

UC is a more severe disease associated with more acute symptoms in children compared with adults. A child's growth may be markedly delayed by the debilitating effects of UC. In addition, there may be serious consequences from the long-term administration of steroids and immunosuppressive medications. If surgery to cure the disease is not performed until late adolescence, the child may never have an opportunity to experience "catch-up" growth and may bear the consequences of childhood medical therapy for life. Because most children with severe UC continue to have symptoms into adulthood and eventually require proctocolectomy, serious consideration should be given to removing the colon and curing the disease during childhood before the epiphyses have closed.

It is now generally accepted that endorectal IAPP is a safe and desirable alternative to proctocolectomy with permanent ileostomy for patients with UC and familial polyposis coli. Virtually all patients prefer this procedure over permanent ileostomy. The majority of postsurgical complications are correctable. Pouch reconstruction for many types of malfunction reduces the need for pouch removal and permanent ileostomy. The J-shaped pouch has been used most widely, with approximately 95% of children and 96% of adults functioning well more than 5 years after surgery.

REFERENCES

1. Adams JT: Toxic dilatation of the colon: A surgical disease. Arch Surg 1973;106:678.
2. Atkinson KG, et al: Restorative proctocolectomy and indeterminate colitis. Am J Surg 1994;167:516.
3. Aylett SO: Three hundred cases of diffuse ulcerative colitis treated by total colectomy and ileo-rectal anastomosis. BMJ 1966;1:1001.
4. Bacon HE: Ulcerative Colitis. Philadelphia, JB Lippincott, 1958.
5. Beahrs OH: Use of ileal reservoir following proctocolectomy. Surg Gynecol Obstet 1975;141:363.
6. Becker JM: Surgical management of inflammatory bowel disease. Curr Opin Gastroenterol 1993;9:600.
7. Brooke BN: The management of an ileostomy including its complications. Lancet 1952;2:102.
8. Browne JY: Value of complete physiological rest of large bowel in ulcerative and obstructive lesions. Surg Gynecol Obstet 1913;16:610.
9. Cattell RB: The surgical treatment of ulcerative colitis. Gastroenterology 1948;10:63.
10. Cohen Z, et al: Continuing evolution of the pelvic pouch procedure. Ann Surg 1992;216:506.
11. Coran A: A personal experience with 100 consecutive total colectomies and straight ileoanal endorectal pull-throughs for benign disease of the colon and rectum in children and adults. Ann Surg 1990;212:242.
12. Coull DB, et al: Risk of dysplasia in the columnar cuff after stapled restorative proctocolectomy. Br J Surg 2003;90:72.
13. Delaney CP, et al: Equivalent function, quality of life and pouch survival rates after ileal pouch-anal anastomosis for indeterminate and ulcerative colitis. Ann Surg 2002;236:43.
14. Delaney CP, et al: Prospective age-related analysis of surgical results, functional outcome, and quality of life after ileal pouch-anal anastomosis. Ann Surg 2003;238:221.
15. Devine H: Method of colectomy for desperate cases of ulcerative colitis. Surg Gynecol Obstet 1943;76:136.
16. Devroede GJ, et al: Cancer risk and life expectancy of children with ulcerative colitis. N Engl J Med 1971;185:17.
17. Ekborn A, et al: Ulcerative colitis and colorectal cancer, a population-based study. N Engl J Med 1990;323:1228.
18. Escher JC, et al: Treatment of inflammatory bowel disease in childhood: Best available evidence. Inflam Bowel Dis 2003;9:34.
19. Farouk F, et al: Functional outcomes after ileal pouch-anal anastomosis for chronic ulcerative colitis. Ann Surg 2000;231:919.
20. Fazio VW: Surgery of the colon and rectum. Am J Gastroenterol 1994;89:S106.
21. Fazio VW, et al: Ileal pouch-anal anastomoses complications and function in 1005 patients. Ann Surg 1995;222:120.
22. Fazio VW, et al: Quantification of risk for pouch failure after ileal pouch anal anastomosis surgery. Ann Surg 2003; 238:605.
23. Ferrari BT, Fonkalsrud EW: Endorectal ileal pullthrough operation with ileal reservoir after total colectomy. Am J Surg 1978;136:113.
24. Ferzoco SJ, Becker JM: Does aggressive medical therapy for acute ulcerative colitis result in a higher incidence of staged colectomy? Arch Surg 1994;129:420.
25. Fleshman JW, et al: The ileal reservoir and ileoanal anastomosis procedure: Factors affecting technical and functional outcome. Dis Colon Rectum 1988;31:10.
26. Fonkalsrud EW: Clinical and physiologic studies with restorative proctocolectomy. In Deutsche Gesellsch: Langenbeck's archiv chirurg suppl kongressbericht. Berlin, Springer Verlag, 1994.
27. Fonkalsrud EW: Long-term results after colectomy and ileoanal pullthrough procedure in children. Arch Surg 1996;131:881.
28. Fonkalsrud EW: In Bayless TM, Hanauer SB (eds): Ileoanal pouch surgery in childhood. Advanced Therapy of Inflammatory Bowel Disease. Hamilton, Ontario, BC Decker, 2001, p 215.
29. Fonkalsrud EW, Loar N: Long-term results after colectomy and endorectal ileal pullthrough procedure in children. Ann Surg 1992;215:57.

30. Fonkalsrud EW, Phillips JD: Reconstruction of malfunctioning ileoanal pouch procedures as an alternative to permanent ileostomy. Am J Surg 1990;160:245.
31. Fonkalsrud EW, Stelzner M, McDonald N: Construction of an ileal reservoir in patients with a previous straight endorectal ileal pullthrough. Ann Surg 1988;208:50.
32. Fonkalsrud EW, Thakur A, Roof L: Comparison of loop versus end ileostomy for fecal diversion after restorative proctocolectomy for ulcerative colitis. J Am Coll Surg 2000; 190:418.
33. Fonkalsrud EW, et al: Reconstruction for chronic dysfunction of ileoanal pouches. Ann Surg 1999;229:1.
34. Furst MB, et al: Colonic anastomoses: Bursting strength after corticosteroid treatment. Dis Colon Rectum 1994; 37:12.
35. Gardner C, Miller CG: Total colectomy for ulcerative colitis. Arch Surg 1951;63:370.
36. Garrett JM, Sauer WG, Moertel CG: Colonic motility in ulcerative colitis after opiate administration. Gastroenterology 1967;53:93.
37. Gionchetti P, et al: Prophylaxis of pouchitis onset with probiotic therapy: A double-blind, placebo-controlled trial. Gastroenterology 2003;124:1202.
38. Goligher JC: Primary excisional surgery in the treatment of ulcerative colitis. Ann R Coll Surg Engl 1954;15:316.
39. Hanauer SB: Medical therapy of ulcerative colitis. Lancet 1993;342:412.
40. Harms BA, et al: Management of fulminant ulcerative colitis by primary restorative proctocolectomy. Dis Colon Rectum 1994;39:971.
41. Heppell J, et al: Physiologic aspects of continence after colectomy, mucosal proctectomy, and endorectal ileoanal anastomosis. Ann Surg 1982;195:435.
42. Heuschen UA, et al: Risk factors for ileoanal J pouch-related septic complications in ulcerative colitis and familial adenomatous polyposis. Ann Surg 2002;235:207.
43. Joossens S, et al: The value of serologic markers in indeterminate colitis: A prospective follow-up study. Gastroenterology 2002;122:1240.
44. Karlan M, McPherson RC, Watman RN: An experimental evaluation of fecal continence, sphincter and reservoir in the dog. Surg Gynecol Obstet 1959;108:469.
45. Kartheuser AH, et al: Complications and risk factors after ileal pouch-anal anastomosis for ulcerative colitis associated with primary sclerosing cholangitis. Ann Surg 1993;217:314.
46. Kelly RE Jr, et al: Early and long-term effects of colectomy and endorectal ileal pullthrough on bile salt profile. Ann Surg 1993;217:321.
47. Ko CY, et al: Long-term outcomes of the ileal pouch anal anastomosis: The association of bowel function and quality of life 5 years after surgery. J Surg Res 2001;98:102.
48. Kock NG: Intra-abdominal reservoir in patients with permanent ileostomy: Preliminary observations on a procedure resulting in fecal continence in five ileostomy patients. Arch Surg 1969;99:223.
49. Kock NG, et al: The quality of life after proctocolectomy and ileostomy: A study of patients with conventional ileostomies converted to continent ileostomies. Dis Colon Rectum 1974;17:287.
50. Levitt MD, Kuan M: The physiology of ileo-anal pouch function. Am J Surg 1998;176:384.
51. Lichtiger S, et al: Cyclosporine in severe ulcerative colitis refractory to steroid therapy. N Engl J Med 1994;330:1841.
52. Luukkonen P, Jarvinen H: Stapled vs hand-sutured ileoanal anastomosis in restorative proctocolectomy: A prospective randomized study. Arch Surg 1994;128:437.
53. Mahadevan U, Sanborn WJ: Diagnosis and management of pouchitis. Gastroenterology 2003;124:1636.
54. Martin LW, Le Coultre C, Schubert WK: Total colectomy and mucosal proctectomy with preservation of continence in ulcerative colitis. Ann Surg 1977;186:477.
55. McCaffery TD, et al: Severe growth retardation in children with inflammatory bowel disease. Pediatrics 1970;45:386.
56. Morgan RA, Manning PB, Coran AG: Experience with the straight endorectal pullthrough for management of ulcerative colitis and familial polyposis in children and adults. Ann Surg 1987;206:595.
57. Olsen KO, et al: Female fecundity before and after operation for familial adenomatous polyposis. Br J Surg 2003; 90:227.
58. Orkin BA, et al: The surgical management of children with ulcerative colitis: The old vs the new. Dis Colon Rectum 1990;33:947.
59. Parc R, et al: Current results: Ileorectal anastomosis after total abdominal colectomy for ulcerative colitis. In Dozois RR (ed): Alternatives to Conventional Ileostomy. Chicago, Year Book Medical Publishers, 1985.
60. Parks AG, Nicholls RJ: Proctocolectomy without ileostomy for ulcerative colitis. BMJ 1978;2:85.
61. Pescatori M, Parks AG: The sphincteric and sensory components of preserved continence after ileoanal reservoir. Surg Gynecol Obstet 1984;158:517.
62. Podolsky DK: Inflammatory bowel disease. N Engl J Med 2002;347:417.
63. Pullan RD, et al: Transdermal nicotine for active ulcerative colitis. N Engl J Med 1994;330:811.
64. Ravitch MM: Anal ileostomy with sphincter preservation in patients requiring total colectomy for benign conditions. Surgery 1948;24:170.
65. Ravitch MM, Sabiston DC: Anal ileostomy with preservation of the sphincter: A proposed operation in patients requiring total colectomy for benign lesions. Surg Gynecol Obstet 1947;84:1095.
66. Rintala RJ, Lindahl HG: Proctocolectomy and J-pouch ileoanal anastomosis in children. J Pediatr Surg 2002;37:66.
67. Ripstein CB: Results of the surgical treatment of ulcerative colitis. Ann Surg 1952;135:14.
68. Robb BW, et al: Restorative proctocolectomy with ileal pouch-anal anastomosis in very young patients with refractory ulcerative colitis. J Pediatr Surg 2003;38:863.
69. Rutgeerts P, et al: Appendectomy protects against ulcerative colitis. Gastroenterology 1994;106:1251.
70. Safaie S, Soper RT: Endorectal pullthrough procedure in the surgical treatment of familial polyposis coli. J Pediatr Surg 1973;8:711.
71. Sanborn WJ: Pouchitis following ileal pouch-anal anastomosis: Definition, pathogenesis, and treatment. Gastroenterology 1994;107:1856.
72. Sarigol S, et al: Ileal pouch-anal anastomosis in children with ulcerative colitis. Inflam Bowel Dis 1996;2:82.
73. Sloan WP, Bargen JA, Gage RP: Life histories of patients with chronic ulcerative colitis: A review of 2000 cases. Gastroenterology 1950;16:25.
74. Soave F: A new surgical technique for treatment of Hirschsprung's disease. Surgery 1964;56:1007.
75. Stavio P, et al: Pediatric pouch-anal anastomosis: Functional outcomes and quality of life. J Pediatr Surg 2003;28:935.
76. Stelzner M, Fonkalsrud EW: The endorectal ileal pullthrough procedure in patients with ulcerative colitis and familial polyposis with carcinoma. Surg Gynecol Obstet 1989;169:187.
77. Stelzner M, Fonkalsrud EW: Assessment of anorectal function after mucosal proctectomy and endorectal ileal pullthrough for ulcerative colitis. Surgery 1990;107:201.

78. Stelzner M, et al: Significance of the reservoir length in the endorectal ileal pullthrough with ileal reservoir. Arch Surg 1988;123:1265.
79. Stelzner M, et al: Adaptive changes in ileal mucosal nutrient transport following colectomy and endorectal ileal pullthrough with ileal reservoir. Arch Surg 1990; 125:586.
80. Stelzner M, et al: Nephrolithiasis and urine ion composition in ulcerative colitis patients undergoing colectomy and endorectal ileal pullthrough. J Surg Res 1990; 48:552.
81. Strauss AA, Strauss SF: Surgical treatment of ulcerative colitis. Surg Clin North Am 1994;24:211.
82. Thakur A, et al: Management of ovarian cysts in women undergoing restorative proctocolectomy for ulcerative colitis. Am Surg 2003;69:339.
83. Thompson-Fawcett MW, et al: "Cuffitis" and inflammatory changes in the columnar cuff, anal transition zone, and ileal reservoir after stapled pouch-anal anastomosis. Dis Colon Rectum 1999;42:348.
84. Tomita R, et al: Gastric emptying function after ileal J-pouch anal anastomosis for ulcerative colitis. Surgery 2004;135:81.
85. Tulchinsky J, et al: Long-term failure after restorative proctocolectomy for ulcerative colitis. Ann Surg 2003;238:229.
86. Turnbull RP: Management of an ileostomy. Am J Surg 1953;86:617.
87. Utsunomiya AJ, et al: Total colectomy, mucosal proctectomy and ileoanal anastomosis. Dis Colon Rectum 1980; 23:459.
88. Valente MA, Bacon HE: Construction of pouch using "pantaloon" technique for pull-through following total colectomy. Am J Surg 1955;90:6621.
89. Weir RF (1902): Quoted by Corbet RS: A review of the surgical treatment of chronic ulcerative colitis. Proc R Soc Med Lond 1945;38:277.
90. Wexner SD, et al: Long-term functional analysis of the ileoanal reservoir. Dis Colon Rectum 1989;32:275.
91. Wilks S, Moxon DW: Lectures on Pathologic Anatomy. London, Longmans, Green, 1875.

Chapter 95

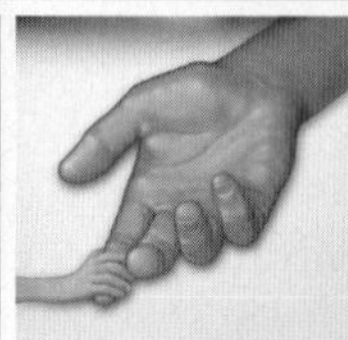

Primary Peritonitis

Karen W. West

Primary peritonitis (PP) (also referred to as idiopathic or spontaneous peritonitis) has been defined as an infectious process involving the peritoneal cavity that has no intra-abdominal source.[7,10,11] The infection may reach the abdomen through hematogenous or lymphatic routes or by direct extension from the vagina. With the exception of the ends of the fallopian tubes, the peritoneal cavity is a completely closed space that can be penetrated by foreign bodies such as ventriculoperitoneal shunts and peritoneal dialysis catheters. In prepubertal and adolescent girls, retrograde spread of fluid out through the fallopian tubes may account for the presence of an ascending vulvovaginitis or "swimming pool peritonitis."[5,13,23,51]

The first reported case of fatal spontaneous bacterial peritonitis (SBP) may have been in 1581 in a girl who expired after an episode of painless diarrhea.[21] By the early 1900s, as many as 10% of abdominal operations in children fell into the category of PP and carried an associated mortality of up to 50%.[10] Today, this condition represents less than 1% of all pediatric laparotomies because the diagnosis is made and treatment initiated without the need for an operation.[11] Most cases of PP in the pediatric age group are associated with nephrotic syndrome (NS) or chronic hepatic states in which ascites or cirrhosis is present. This group includes infants and children with biliary atresia, cystic fibrosis, hepatic fibrosis, and lupus erythematosus (Table 95-1).[9,24,26] Organisms isolated from the peritoneal cavity will vary according to the various associated conditions (Table 95-2). For instance, gram-positive organisms, including *Streptococcus pneumoniae* and group A streptococci, and a variety of gram-negative species are most commonly found in patients with NS.[1,17,22] The same gram-positive groups are cultured in patients with underlying liver disease, whereas the spectrum of gram-negative isolates includes *Esherichia coli, Klebsiella pneumoniae,* and *Pseudomonas* species.

In earlier reported series, most of the patients were girls and the vagina was often implicated as the source of the infections. However, vaginitis was uncommon, and the ultimate source of the infection remained obscure.[21] The prepubertal cervix lacks the endocervical glands that may harbor bacteria, so ascending infections in this age group would more likely be associated with some traumatic force that pushes the bacteria up through the vagina, as in sexual abuse cases or by jumping feet first into swimming pool or lake water.[13] In more recent series the incidence of PP is equally distributed between boys and girls.[31,35,50] In some cases the same bacteria causing the peritoneal infection have also been cultured from the respiratory and urinary tract, as well as from the oral cavity.[7]

CLINICAL HISTORY, LABORATORY DATA, AND DIAGNOSTIC STUDIES

Children with PP have acute abdominal pain associated with a febrile illness, nausea, vomiting, diarrhea, or other viral-like prodromes. The time course may be more

TABLE 95–1 Conditions Associated with Primary Peritonitis in Childhood

Nephrotic syndrome
Hepatic dysfunction
Adrenogenital syndrome
Cystic fibrosis
Chronic renal failure with the need for chronic ambulatory peritoneal dialysis
Complications after splenectomy
Diseases requiring long-term steroid administration (systemic lupus erythematosus, dermatomyositis)

TABLE 95–2 Microorganisms Associated with Primary Peritonitis

Streptococcus species (*S. pneumoniae*; group A streptococci)
Escherichia coli
Gonococcus
Haemophilus influenzae
Klebsiella pneumoniae
Listeria monocytogenes
Parainfluenza
Salmonella typhi
Serratia marcescens
Yersinia enterocolitica

protracted than that for secondary peritonitis, and diffuse rebound tenderness is often present. The absence of localized pain may result from irritation of visceral organ surfaces.[31,37]

Diagnostic paracentesis may be helpful in the presence of ascites, as is sampling of the dialysate in children with renal failure on ambulatory peritoneal dialysis programs. The diagnosis of PP is made when the peritoneal fluid leukocyte count is higher than 500/mm^3 and granulocytes predominate (lymphocytes are usually present in higher numbers in normal peritoneal fluid). The fluid has a pH of less than 7.35 and an elevated lactate level (>25 mg/dL). Sending a minimum of 10 mL of fluid for Gram stain and culture analysis will increase the number of positive isolates, yet cultures may be negative in as many as 60% of reported cases.[15] If more than one organism is present on Gram stain, a perforated viscus should be suspected. The isolation of specific bacteria decreases the spectrum of antibiotics required and potentially eliminates the use of nephrotoxic drugs in patients with compromised renal function.[17] Samples of blood and urine are sent for culture, and radiographs of the chest and abdomen are obtained. This will help eliminate a perforated viscus or a pneumonic process as the cause of the abdominal pathology. Low serum protein levels and concomitant decreased opsonins may contribute to the development of PP.[36]

Ultrasound studies and computed tomography (CT) of the abdomen have been used to differentiate primary from secondary peritonitis (caused by such common pediatric processes as appendicitis) when the clinical picture is confusing. Double-contrasted CT scan findings in SBP include the presence of a patent appendiceal lumen, diffusely distributed peritoneal fluid, and secondary enhancement of the bowel wall.[8]

NEPHROTIC SYNDROME

PP may affect up to 17% of children with NS, and the incidence has not varied over the past 3 decades.[1,3,19,39,48,49] Before the availability of antibiotic therapy, PP was the leading cause of death in this group of patients. An increased susceptibility to infection in these patients may be influenced by impaired cellular immunity and chemotaxis, decreased opsonization, and reduced levels of circulating immunoglobulins. Complement proteins I and B are reduced in the serum, but increased in the urine of patients with peritonitis and NS.[29] The episodes of peritonitis are recurrent in 26% of cases and have been associated with decreased levels of circulating IgG.[19]

Large reported series in children indicate that gram-negative organisms are isolated in 6% to 30% of patients with NS and peritonitis, whereas *S. pneumoniae* was cultured in 4% to 38%.[1,19,47] Even when the peritoneal fluid shows no bacterial isolates, children symptomatically responded to the systemic administration of intravenous penicillin.[24] In almost 80% of children with NS in whom SBP developed, either steroids were being used as treatment of the condition or a relapse of NS had occurred.[1,19,49]

The most common symptoms at the time of diagnosis are diffuse abdominal pain, fever, rebound tenderness, nausea, and vomiting. In up to 29% of cases chest radiographs may show an infiltrate, and 15% to 27% of children may experience more than one episode of peritonitis. Pneumococcal vaccination (Pneumovax) has been recommended in this group of patients, yet peritonitis has occurred despite protective immunization.[33,47] Additional reports indicate that resistant organisms can develop in children treated with oral penicillin prophylaxis.[33] Initial treatment of PP should include the administration of antibiotics to cover both gram-positive and gram-negative bacteria. In cases in which clinical improvement does not occur in 24 hours after the initiation of therapy, further diagnostic studies such as abdominal CT or diagnostic laparoscopy have been suggested to eliminate other causes of peritonitis. Laparoscopy and abdominal irrigation have been successfully used with medical management when the clinical course was not improving, but abdominal CT scans were not helpful in differentiating primary from secondary peritonitis.

HEPATIC DYSFUNCTION

In a child with impaired hepatic function, cirrhosis, and ascites, the SBP that develops is often associated with the gram-negative organisms that normally populate the intestinal tract, such as *E. coli* and *K. pneumoniae*, whereas the gram-positive isolates include *S. pneumoniae* and *Staphylococcus aureus*.[32,35] The liver with its rich reticuloendothelial tissue normally filters the bacteria found in the portal circulation. As cirrhosis develops, portal venous flow is partially shunted away from the liver, thereby decreasing the clearance of bacteria and fungi from both the blood and lymphatic systems. This decreased clearance may allow for the persistence of bacteria in ascitic fluid.[26,40,41–43] Children will have fever and abdominal pain in 50% of SBP cases. Paracentesis fluid that has greater than 500 leukocytes/mm^3, bacteria on Gram stain, and a pH of less than 7.35 had 100% sensitivity and 96% specificity for active SBP.[17] Patients with cystic fibrosis and hepatic dysfunction as a result of cirrhosis or impaired synthetic function are also at risk for episodic PP.[9]

ASSOCIATION OF PRIMARY PERITONITIS WITH PERITONEAL DIALYSIS

Peritonitis (either bacterial or fungal) in patients maintained on continuous ambulatory peritoneal dialysis (CAPD) occurred at a rate of one episode per 11.1 to 13.2 patient-months in two separate multi-institutional studies.[14,22,34,38] Gram-positive organisms were isolated in 48.7% of cases, gram-negative bacteria in 21.6%, and fungi in 1.8%, and 21.6% of the symptomatic patients did not have positive cultures.[14] Risk factors for the development of peritonitis in this group of children include contamination of the connectors during dialysate fluid exchange, exit site or tunnel infections, local trauma to the tunnel site, and nasal colonization with staphylococcal organisms.[14] Because peritonitis was twice as likely to develop in patients who had a local site or tunnel infection, elimination of this problem could decrease the

TABLE 95-3 Organisms Involved in Peritonitis in Children Maintained on Chronic Ambulatory Peritoneal Dialysis (CAPD)*

Organism	%
Staphylococcus aureus	38.9
Staphylococcus epidermidis	13.2
Group A streptococci	9.7
Pseudomonas species	9.0
Other bacteria or fungi	13.9
No organisms found on culture	13.9

*Data from 144 episodes of peritonitis in 66 children at J.W. Riley Hospital for Children, Indianapolis, IN.

number of episodes of infection. Clinical findings include abdominal pain, fever, and an elevated neutrophil count in the cloudy dialysate. The fluid is cultured, and both intravenous and intraperitoneal antibiotics are instituted, with close monitoring of antibiotic levels. Current treatment guidelines include a combination of first- and third-generation cephalosporins for uncomplicated situations and simultaneous glycopeptide and third-generation cephalosporins in young children with recurring infections and a history of recent methicillin-resistant peritonitis.[46] Symptoms should begin to improve within 24 to 36 hours after initiation of therapy.[44] Normal skin flora, including *S. aureus* and *Staphylococcus epidermidis* remain the most common organisms isolated from the fluid, but a variety of organisms have been cultured (Table 95-3). Gonococcal peritonitis has been reported in a sexually active adolescent undergoing peritoneal dialysis.[51] Long-term multi-institutional longitudinal studies suggest that the peritoneal dialysis catheter must be removed to eradicate the infection when *Pseudomonas*, *Candida*, or atypical mycobacterial species are involved.[2,14,22,25] There is also a risk of peritoneal membrane failure when these organisms are involved, thus precluding the continued use of peritoneal dialysis. Peritonitis rates are decreased when a two-cuff system is used and when the exit site is directed downward.[14,50] Additional risk factors for the development of CAPD-related peritonitis include the duration of CAPD (longer than a year), chronologic age younger than 2 years, and decreased serum IgG levels.[25]

SPONTANEOUS BACTERIAL PERITONITIS IN HEALTHY CHILDREN

Gross reported 58 cases of PP in 1950 in a group of previously healthy infants and toddlers (mean age, 2 years) who had a preceding upper respiratory infection. The complex of initial symptoms included vomiting, fever, irritability, abdominal distention, and tenderness, and *S. pneumoniae* was the predominant organism isolated. A later series from the same facility recorded 33 patients (mean age, 5 years) treated for SBP over the next 30 years.[21,28] The decrease in the number of affected children was considered the result of increased availability and use of oral antibiotics. Although multiple potential sources of infection have been implicated, including hematogenous (dental procedures, bacteremia), lymphatic, gut translocation, and ascending gynecologic processes, the etiology remains unclear in most cases. In 1985, two previously healthy children with dehydration, abdominal distention, and group A streptococcal peritonitis were reported. At the time of laparotomy no source of the infection was identified, although one of the children had a concomitant right-sided diaphragmatic hernia.[45] The literature has since identified a group of healthy children with idiopathic peritonitis and simultaneously positive cultures for group A streptococci from the trachea, pharynx, or tonsils.[4,12,18,20] In prepubertal girls with gonococcal vaginitis, 6% may have evidence of peritonitis. Treatment with parenteral cephalosporins is indicated, and the presence of other associated simultaneous sexually transmitted bacteria should be investigated.[23] *Haemophilus parainfluenzae* has recently been isolated during an abdominal exploration when no intestinal pathology was identified.[30]

When the clinical picture is not improving despite intravenous antibiotics, diagnostic laparoscopy or laparotomy is indicated. An appendectomy can be done safely even in the presence of cloudy exudate, and the bowel surface can be inspected for secondary causes of the infection. After the surgical intervention, antibiotics are continued until the leukocytosis normalizes and the ileus resolves.[10,37]

UNUSUAL CONDITIONS ASSOCIATED WITH PRIMARY PERITONITIS

Familial Mediterranean fever (recurrent serositis, periodic disease) is inherited as an autosomal recessive trait and primarily affects Armenians, Turks, and Jews originating from the Mediterranean area. There are frequent episodes of inflammation of the peritoneum (85%), joints (50%), and pleura (33%) associated with high fever and abdominal tenderness. The abdominal symptoms begin to abate within 12 hours of onset, with resolution within 24 to 48 hours. If surgical intervention is undertaken, the bowel is characteristically seen at surgery to be coated with a sterile exudate containing fibrin. Long-term complications include the development of adhesive small bowel obstruction in 3% of pediatric cases. The use of colchicine may decrease the severity of painful episodes and reduce the incidence of long-term adhesive small bowel disease.[6,27]

SBP also has been described in children with indwelling ventriculoperitoneal shunts without evidence of cerebrospinal fluid infection. Cultures from these patients have resulted in a variety of gram-positive organisms, and improvement in peritoneal irritation occurs with exteriorization of the shunt tubing.[16]

REFERENCES

1. Alwadhi RK, Mathew JL, Roth B: Clinical profile of children with nephrotic syndrome not on glucocorticoid therapy but presenting with infection. J Pediatr Child Health 2004;40:28.

2. Andreoli SP, Langefield CD, Stadler S: Risks of peritoneal membrane failure in children undergoing long-term peritoneal dialysis. Pediatr Nephrol 1993;7:543.
3. Barness LA, Moll GH, Janeway CA: Nephrotic syndrome I. Natural history of the disease. Pediatrics 1950;5:486.
4. Brase R, Kuckelt W, Manhold C, et al: Spontaneous bacterial peritonitis without ascites. Anasthesiol Intensivmed Notfallmed Schmerzther 1992;27:325.
5. Burry VF: Gonococcal vulvovaginitis and possible peritonitis in prepubertal girls. Am J Dis Child 1971;121:536.
6. Ciftci AO, Tanyel FC, Buyukpamukcu N, et al: Adhesive small bowel obstruction caused by familial Mediterranean fever: The incidence and outcome. J Pediatr Surg 1995;30:1319.
7. Clark JH, Fitzgerald JF, Kleiman MB: Spontaneous bacterial peritonitis. J Pediatr 1984;104:495.
8. Dann PH, Amodio JB, Rivera R, et al: Primary bacterial peritonitis in otherwise healthy children: Imaging findings. Pediatr Radiol 2005;35:198.
9. Doershuk CF, Stern RC: Spontaneous bacterial peritonitis in cystic fibrosis. Gut 1994;35:709.
10. Ein SH: Primary peritonitis. In Welch KJ, Randolph JG (eds): Pediatric Surgery, 4th ed. Chicago, Year Book, 1986, p 976.
11. Fowler R: Primary peritonitis: Changing aspects 1956-1970. Aust Paediatr J 1971;7:73.
12. Freij BJ, Votteler TP, McCracken GH: Primary peritonitis in previously healthy children. Am J Dis Child 1984;138:1058.
13. Fuld GL: Gonococcal peritonitis in a prepubertal child. Am J Dis Child 1968;115:621.
14. Furth SL, Donaldson LA, Sullivan EK, et al: Peritoneal dialysis catheter infections and peritonitis in children: A report of the North American Pediatric Renal Transplant Cooperative Study. Pediatr Nephrol 2000;15:179.
15. Garcia-Tsao G, Conn HO, Lerner E: The diagnosis of bacterial peritonitis: Comparison of pH lactate concentration and leukocyte count. Hepatology 1985;5:91.
16. Gaskill SJ, Marlin AE: Spontaneous bacterial peritonitis in patients with ventriculoperitoneal shunts. Pediatr Neurosurg 1997;36:115.
17. Gilbert JA, Karnath PS: Spontaneous bacterial peritonitis, an update. Mayo Clin Proc 1995;70:365.
18. Gillespie RS, Hauger SB, Holt RM: Primary group A streptococcal peritonitis in a previously healthy child. Scand J Infect Dis 2002;34:847.
19. Gorensek MJ, Lebel MH, Nelson JD: Peritonitis in children with nephrotic syndrome. Pediatrics 1988;81:849.
20. Graham JC, Moss PJ, McKendrick MW: Primary group A streptococcal peritonitis. Scand J Infect Dis 1995;27:171.
21. Harken AH, Shochat SJ: Gram-positive peritonitis in children. Am J Surg 1973;125:769.
22. Holitta TM, Ronnholm KA, Jalanko J, et al: Peritoneal dialysis in children under 5 years of age. Perit Dial Int 1997;17:573.
23. Ingram DL: *Neisseria gonorrhoeae* in children. Pediatr Ann 1994;23:341.
24. Krensky AM, Ingelfinger JR, Grupe WE: Peritonitis in childhood nephrotic syndrome. Am J Dis Child 1982;136:732.
25. Kuizon B, Melocoton TL, Holloway M, et al: Infections and catheter related complications in pediatric patients treated with peritoneal dialysis at a single institution. Pediatr Nephrol 1995;9(Suppl):S12.
26. Larcher VF, Manolaki N, Vegnente A, et al: Spontaneous bacterial peritonitis in children with chronic liver disease: Clinical features and etiologic factors. J Pediatr 1985;106:907.
27. Majeed HA, Barakat M: Familial Mediterranean fever (recurrent hereditary polyserositis) in children: Analysis of 88 cases. Eur J Pediatr 1989;148:636.
28. Marshall R, Teele DW, Klein JO: Unsuspected bacteremia due to *Haemophilus influenzae*: Outcome in children not initially admitted to hospital. J Pediatr 1979;95:690.
29. Matsell DG, Wyatt RJ: The role of I and B in peritonitis associated with the nephrotic syndrome of childhood. Pediatr Res 1993;34:84.
30. Mayer MP, Schweizer P: Primary peritonitis in a child caused by *Haemophilus parainfluenzae*. Pediatr Surg Int 2002;18:728.
31. McDougal WS, Izant RJ Jr, Zollinger RM Jr: Primary peritonitis in infancy and childhood. Ann Surg 1974; 181:310.
32. Mihas AA, Toussaint J, Hsu HS, et al: Spontaneous bacterial peritonitis in cirrhosis: Clinical and laboratory features, survival and prognostic indicators. Hepatogastroenterology 1992;39:520.
33. Milner LS, Berkowitz FE, Ngwenya E, et al: Penicillin resistant pneumococcal peritonitis in nephrotic syndrome. Arch Dis Child 1987;62:964.
34. Mocan H, Murphy AV, Beattie TJ, et al: Peritonitis in children on continuous ambulatory peritoneal dialysis. J Infect 1988;16:243.
35. Moskovitz M, Ehrenberg E, Grieco R, et al: Primary peritonitis due to group A streptococcus. J Clin Gastroenterol 2000;30:332.
36. Nguyen MH, Yu VL: *Listeria monocytogenes* peritonitis in cirrhotic patients: Value of ascitic fluid gram stain and a review of the literature. Dig Dis Sci 1994;39:215.
37. Nohr CW, Marshall DA: Primary peritonitis in children. Can J Surg 1984;27:179.
38. Orkin BA, Fonkalsrud EW, Saluksy IB, et al: Continuous ambulatory peritoneal dialysis catheters in children. Arch Surg 1983;118:1398.
39. Pahmer M: *Pneumococcus* peritonitis in nephrotic and nonnephrotic children. J Pediatr 1940;17:90.
40. Rimola A, Soto R, Bory F, et al: Reticuloendothelial system phagocytic activity in cirrhosis and its relation to bacterial infections and prognosis. Hepatology 1984;4:53.
41. Runyon BA: Patients with deficient ascitic fluid opsonic activity are predisposed to spontaneous bacterial peritonitis. Hepatology 1980;8:632.
42. Runyon BA: Low-protein-concentration ascitic fluid is predisposed to spontaneous bacterial peritonitis. Gastroenterology 1986;91:1343.
43. Runyon BA, Umland ET, Merlin T: Inoculation of blood culture bottles with ascitic fluid: Improved detection of spontaneous bacterial peritonitis. Arch Intern Med 1987; 147:73.
44. Schaefer F: Management of peritonitis in children receiving chronic peritoneal dialysis. Paediatr Drugs 2003;5:315.
45. Serlo W, Heikkinen E, Kouvalainen K: Group A streptococcal peritonitis in infancy. Ann Chir Gynaecol 1985; 74:183.
46. Silva MM, Pecoits-Filho R, Rocha CS, et al: The recommendations from the International Society for Peritoneal Dialysis for Peritonitis Treatment: A single-center historical comparison. Adv Perit Dial 2004;20:74.
47. Speck WT, Dresdal SS, McMillan RW: Primary peritonitis and the nephrotic syndrome. Am J Surg 1974;127:267.
48. Tapaneya-Olarn C, Tapaneya-Olarn W: Primary peritonitis in childhood nephrotic syndrome: A changing trend in causative organisms. J Med Assoc Thailand 1991;74:502.
49. Tsau YK, Cxhen CH, Tsai WS, et al: Complications of nephrotic syndrome in children. J Formosan Med Assoc 1991;90:555.
50. Warady BA, Sullivan EK, Alexander SR: Lesson from the peritoneal dialysis patient database: A report of the North American Pediatric Renal Transplant Cooperative Study. Kidney Int Suppl 1996;53:568.
51. Wolfson AB, Naehamkin I, Singer I, et al: Gonococcal peritonitis in a patient treated with CAPD. Am J Kidney Dis 1985;6:257.

Chapter 96

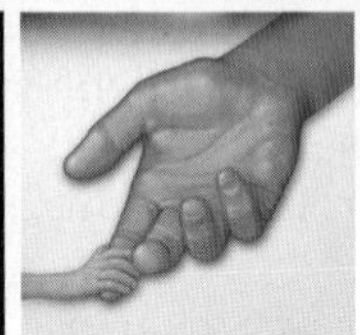

Stomas of the Small and Large Intestine

Michael W. L. Gauderer

HISTORICAL NOTE

Intestinal stomas, considered basic surgical procedures, have a long and colorful history. As a method of treating intestinal obstruction, colostomies date back to the latter part of the 18th century, and some of the first survivors of this procedure were children with imperforate anus.[52,77,90,95,97] Despite sporadic early successes, the use of stomas in the large intestine and later the small intestine in children evolved slowly. Surgeons were understandably reluctant and even strongly opposed to performing these drastic procedures, which were associated with major complications.[77,95] However, as the experience of surgeons increased toward the end of the 19th century and beginning of the 20th century, colostomies and occasionally jejunostomies were used to manage a few pediatric conditions. With the advent of modern pediatric surgical practice and survival of children with conditions that were formerly likely to be fatal, the need for stomas increased. Enterostomal construction techniques, originally developed for adults,[10,54,55,98] were modified and adapted for use in children, particularly newborns with congenital intestinal obstruction.[5,6,11,53,63,69,76] New techniques that combined proximal decompression and distal feeding for neonates with atresia of the duodenum or high jejunum were introduced next.[16,35,71] Procedures designed to provide postpyloric feeding access in children with foregut dysmotility continue to be developed and evaluated,[3,20,62,74,80,88] and the ongoing advances in minimally invasive surgery provide new and exciting opportunities for the creation of feeding as well as venting, decompressing, irrigating, and special purpose stomas.[34,36,37,57,62,81]

In the past few decades, enterostomal therapy has evolved into a specialty in its own right[7,91,97] and great strides have been made in pediatric stomal care, including child-specific appliances, better-tolerated biomaterials, and the creation of nonmedical support systems.[19,46,60] Additionally, there is now greater awareness and acceptance of ostomates, as well as the recognition of their needs and rights among the population.[7,9,60,97] Understanding of stomal physiology and of specialized enteral and parenteral nutrition have further improved care and outcome.[44,74,97] The creation, management, and closure of enterostomas now occupies a substantial portion of modern pediatric surgical practice.[56]

STOMAS IN CHILDREN

An enterostoma in a child is a major disruption of normality and frequently leads to substantial psychological trauma for the child and parents. However, most intestinal stomas in the pediatric age group are temporary, and correction of the underlying problem very often leads to closure of the diverting opening. Although pediatric surgeons continuously search for alternatives to intestinal exteriorization,[84,89] an appropriately indicated, properly constructed temporary stoma is frequently unavoidable and lifesaving. Moreover, in several instances of noncorrectable and crippling pathologic conditions of the lower large intestine, a permanent, well-functioning stoma contributes to an improved quality of life.[9,93,99] Although often considered simple mechanisms, enterostomas encompass a wide spectrum of basic types, techniques, and methods of care and are associated with a surprisingly high rate of both early and late complications. These facts present the surgeon, the enterostomal therapist, the nurses, the parents, and the child with major challenges.* Therefore, when the need for a stoma arises, the best results are achieved by carefully evaluating the child's pathologic condition and health status, weighing the pros and cons of diversion, planning ahead whenever possible, and considering both construction and takedown as major interventions. In addition to the well-defined guidelines for stomal placement established for adult patients, such factors as anatomic and physiologic differences, delicate structures, growth, and physical and

*See references 2, 4, 6, 8, 11, 13-15, 17, 23, 27, 30, 32, 33, 38, 40, 49, 50, 53, 56, 58, 64-66, 68, 70, 72, 78, 82, 83, 87, 96, and 97.

emotional maturity need to be considered. The surgeon and members of the surgical team must always keep in mind that the quality of life of a patient with a stoma is largely related to the quality of that stoma.

TYPES OF ENTEROSTOMAS

The four basic types of enterostomas, primary purposes, and technique options are listed in Table 96-1. Examples of these methods are illustrated in Figures 96-1 to 96-3. Options for bringing the proximal stoma through the abdominal wall and handling the distal stoma are listed in Table 96-2. Examples are found in Figures 96-3 to 96-5.

INDICATIONS FOR ENTEROSTOMAS IN CHILDREN

Temporary and occasionally permanent stomas of the small and large intestine are used in the management of a wide variety of surgical and nonsurgical pathologic conditions in neonates, infants, and children. With the exception of feeding access, more than one half of stomas are placed in the neonatal period and another one fourth in infants younger than 1 year of age.[56]

Jejunostomies are used primarily for enteral feedings in neurologically impaired children with complex problems related to foregut dysmotility[20,21,62,74,100]; in patients with acute surgical problems benefiting from early enteral feedings, such as major trauma[3,74]; and in individuals needing long-term supplemental feedings, such as

TABLE 96-1 Applications and Considerations for Enterostomas

Administration of Feedings, Medication, or Both
- Without entering the jejunal wall: nasojejunal tube, gastrostomy-jejunostomy tube[34,74]
- Direct access through the jejunal wall: tunneled catheter,[98] needle catheter,[3] T-tube,[41] button,[88] other
- Isolated jejunal loop brought directly to abdominal wall: Roux-en-Y[20,100]

Proximal Decompression and Distal Feedings
- Gastrostomy and distal feeding tube, same stoma or separately[16,34]
- Double-lumen tube in dilated proximal jejunum with feeding end across an anastomosis[71]; or two single-lumen tubes inserted separately into divided, closed loops of small intestines[35]
- Divided intestinal segments brought directly to skin level, with pouch applied to proximal stoma and feeding catheter inserted into distal one

Access for Antegrade Irrigation
- Appendix or other intestinal conduit brought to abdominal wall for intermittent catheterization[5,52,85]
- Catheter, T-tube, skin level device placed in intestinal lumen[37,41,81,88]

Decompression, Diversion, or Evacuation
- End stoma, single opening[10]
- Double-barrel stoma[55,69,73]
- End stoma with an anastomosis below the abdominal wall[5,76]
- Loop over a small rod or skin bridge[6,54,63]
- Closed loop with catheter[35] or open loop with occluding valve-type device[28,67] allowing controlled egress
- Special stomas, such as a catheterizable pouch[36,47]

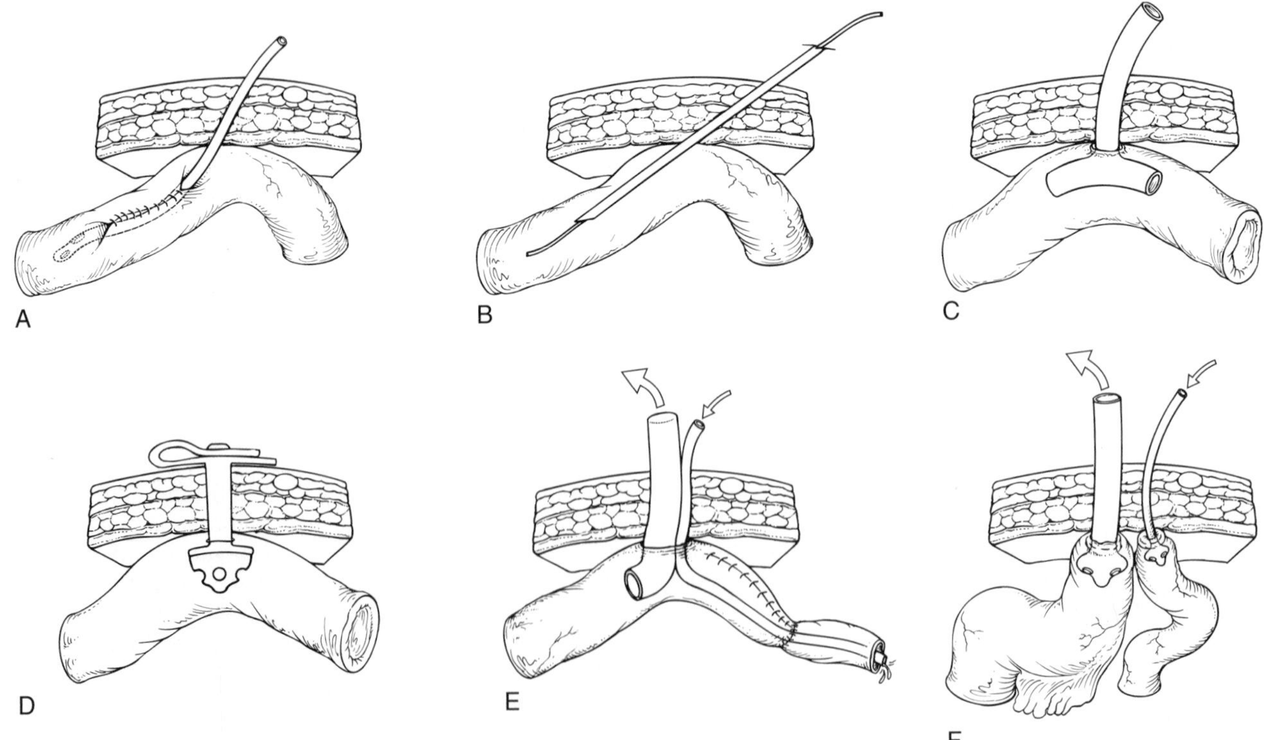

Figure 96-1 Diagrams of select-feeding and decompressing-feeding jejunostomies. *A*, Tunneled catheter.[98] *B*, Needle catheter.[3] *C*, T-tube.[41] *D*, Button.[88] *E*, Proximal decompression and distal feeding across an anastomosis.[71] *F*, Temporary decompression feeding using catheters when primary anastomosis is unsafe and intestinal exteriorization is undesirable.[35]

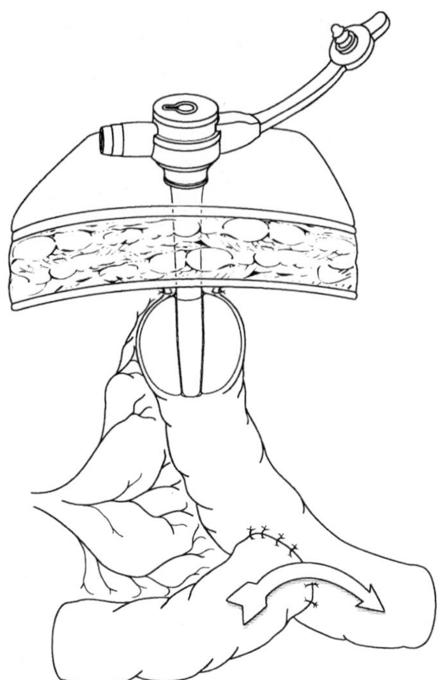

Figure 96–2 Roux-en-Y feeding jejunostomy with a balloon-type skin-level access device.[20]

TABLE 96–2 Enterostoma Exit

Proximal Stoma
- Through celiotomy incision
- Through separate opening
- With proximal and distal limbs close to each other
- With proximal and distal openings apart
- Multiple stomas
- Variations of the above

Distal Stoma
- Exteriorization as mucus fistula adjacent to or separate from proximal intestine
- Partial closure and placement next to the proximal stoma[92]
- Closure and replacement into abdominal cavity
- Closure after placement of a catheter for subsequent access for irrigation or contrast studies

patients with cystic fibrosis (Fig. 96-6).[82] Combined gastric decompression and transanastomotic jejunal feeding is a time-honored and helpful approach in selected patients with atresia of the duodenum or high jejunum.[16,34] Various types of exteriorized jejunal segments have been used in the management of children with biliary atresia.[42] However, enthusiasm for this practice has decreased, in

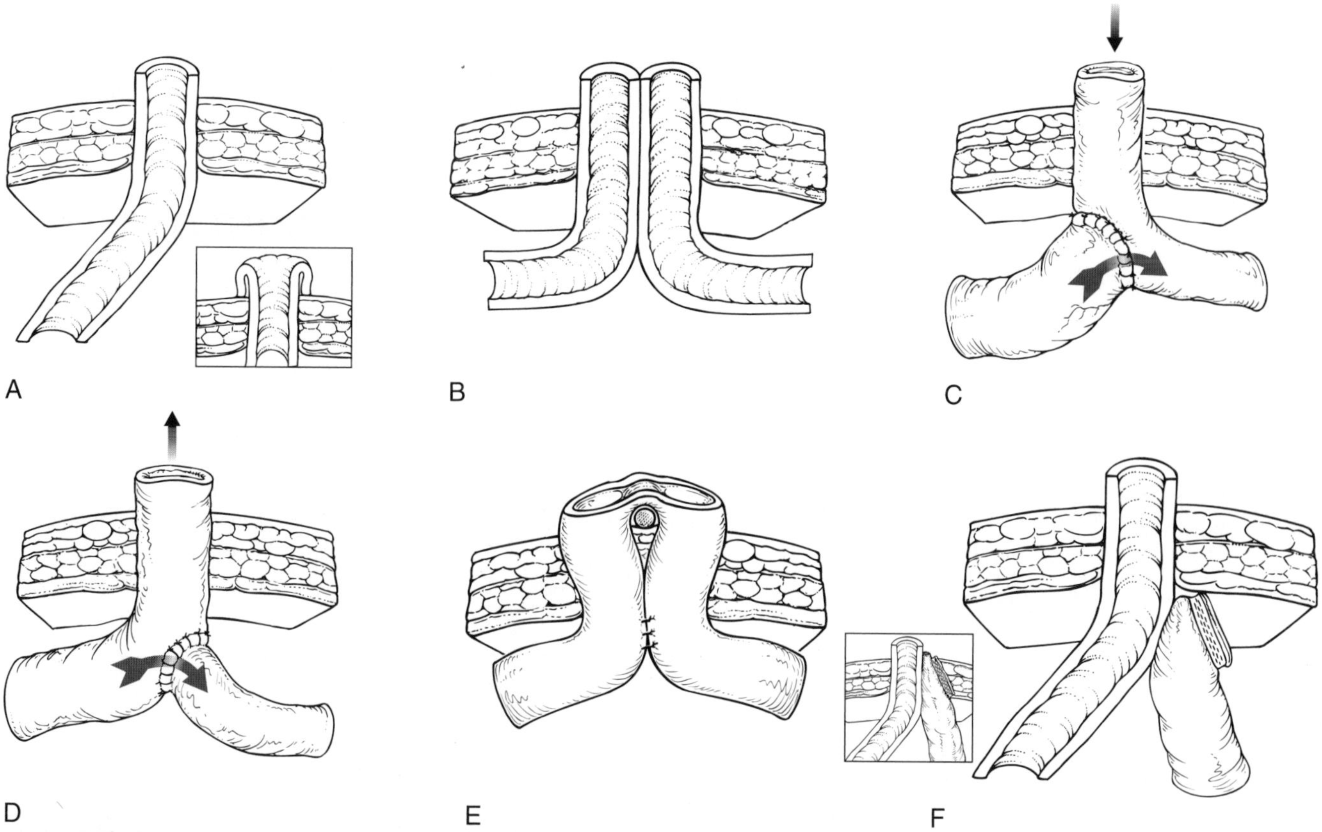

Figure 96–3 Examples of decompressing, diverting, or evacuating stomas. *A,* End stoma (*inset* shows typical maturation).[10] *B,* Double-barrel stoma.[55] *C,* End-to-side anastomosis with distal vent for irrigation.[5] *D,* Side-to-end anastomosis with proximal vent.[76] *E,* Loop stoma.[54] *F,* End stoma with closed subfascial distal of the end of the intestine (*inset* shows rodless end-loop stoma[92]).

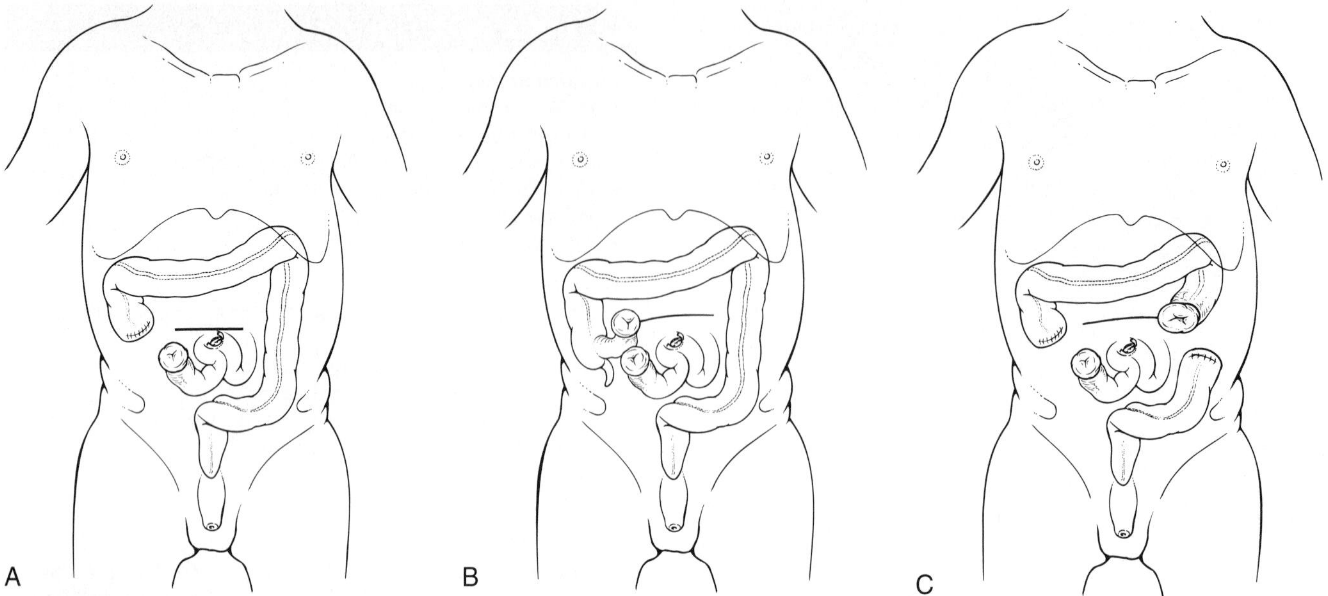

Figure 96–4 Examples of options for the management of infants after intestinal resection. *A,* Exteriorization of proximal intestine through a counterincision and closure of distal intestine beneath the abdominal wall. *B,* Same procedures as in *A* with exteriorization of proximal end of distal intestine through the wound edge. *C,* Arrangement after resection of two intestinal segments.

part because of such secondary problems as bleeding from stomal varices associated with portal hypertension.[83] On the other hand, the use of a segment of intestine interposed between the gallbladder and the abdominal wall for partial external drainage of bile in children with certain cholestatic syndromes is promising.[24,36] Exteriorization or tube decompression is clearly indicated after jejunal resection when peritonitis or intestinal ischemia is present.[1,40,61,73]

Ileostomies are widely used when primary anastomosis is impossible or unsafe. Typical indications include neonatal necrotizing enterocolitis (Figs. 96-7 and 96-8) or other adverse intra-abdominal events.[1,40,52,56,61,73] Stomas of the distal small intestine are essential in the management of neonates with certain types of obstruction, such as long-segment Hirschsprung's disease, complex meconium ileus, and gastroschisis with atresia.[5,41,56,69] Ileostomies are used extensively in the management of ulcerative

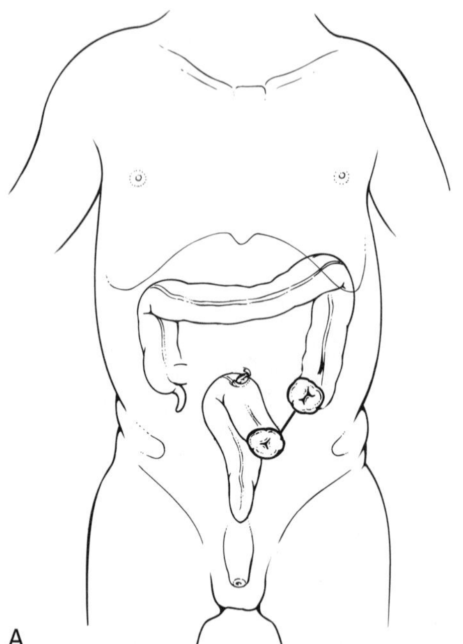

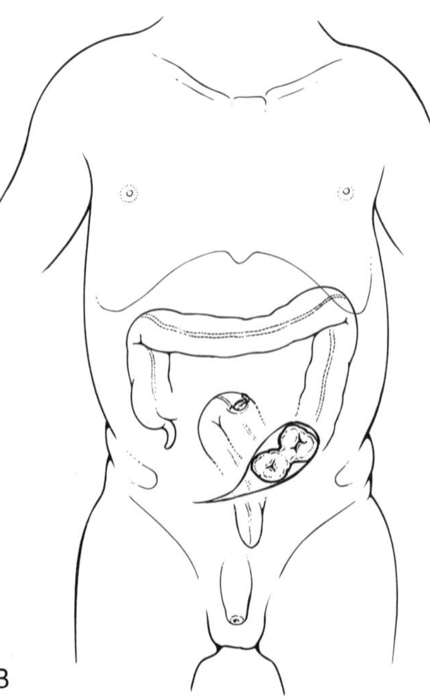

Figure 96–5 Sigmoid colostomies. *A,* Separated stomas. The proximal intestine is at the upper end of the incision, and the mucus fistula is at the lower one. *B,* Loop colostomy. The intestine is exteriorized over a rod or skin bridge or with the help of sutures. The circumscribing comma-shaped incision is used for takedown and pull-through procedures.

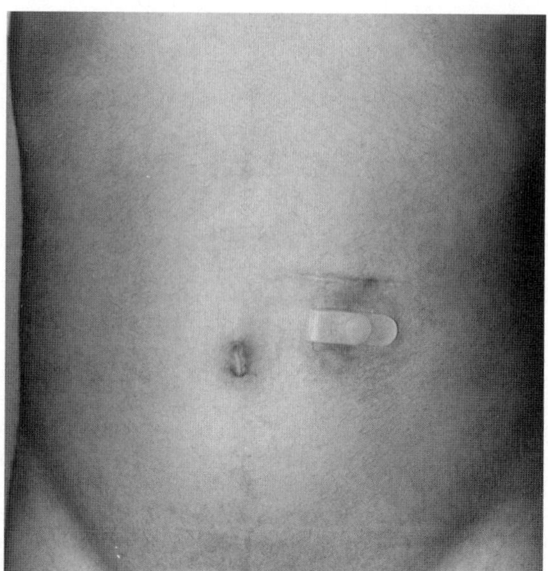

Figure 96-6 Jejunostomy button for supplemental nocturnal feedings in a child with cystic fibrosis. The skin-level device was brought out through a counterincision.[88]

colitis and familial polyposis as temporary, protective, or permanent stomas.[10,30,31,47,52,67,91,97]

Cecostomies, appendicostomies, and sigmoidostomies (Fig. 96-9) are used as access sites for antegrade intestinal irrigation in children with complex anal sphincter and hindgut problems or with myelodysplasia.[22,37,81,85]

Colostomies have the longest history,[77] and extensive experience with these stomas has accrued in the management of multiple conditions, including high forms

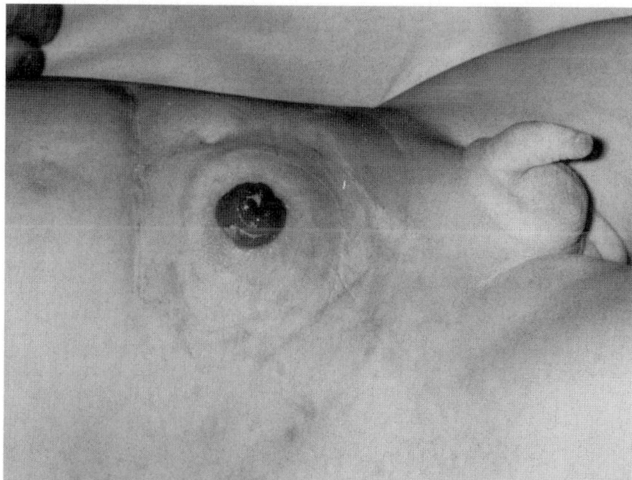

Figure 96-7 One-year-old boy with severe necrotizing enterocolitis with loss of distal ileum and colon down to the peritoneal reflection before reanastomosis. Liquid stools precluded earlier reestablishment of intestinal continuity. Notice the appliance mark and the appropriate distance from the incision, the umbilicus, the inguinoabdominal fold, and the right anterior superior iliac spine.

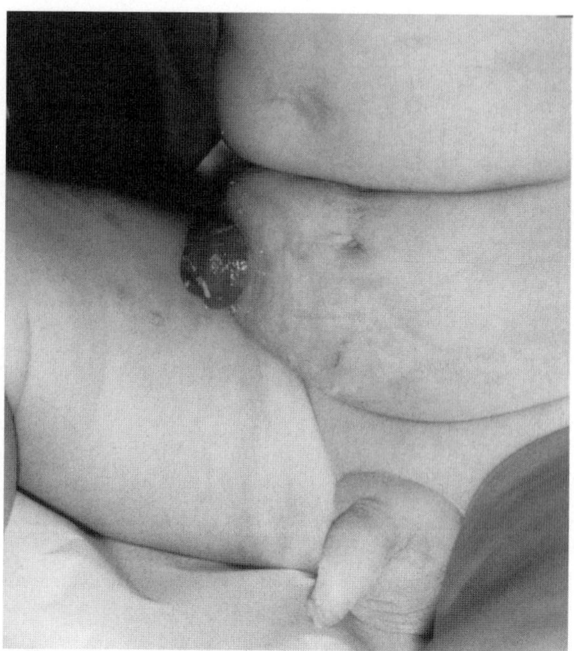

Figure 96-8 Same child as in Figure 96-7 in a sitting position. Notice the deep crease produced by the transverse supraumbilical incision. A stoma brought out through such an incision would have precluded proper use of the pouch, and a revision would have become necessary.

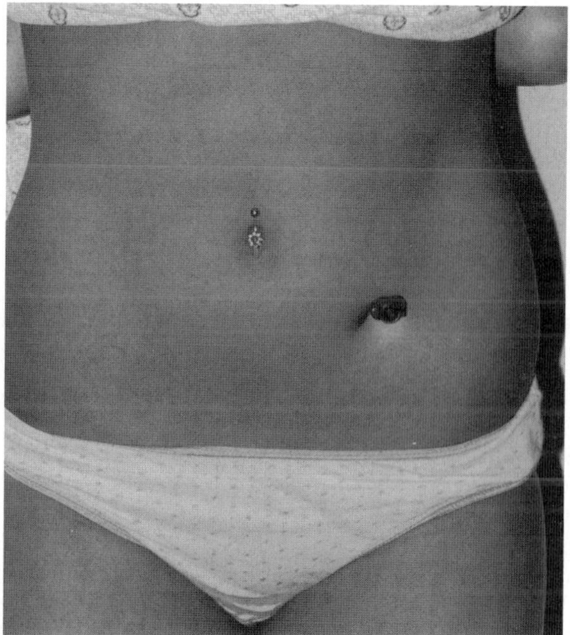

Figure 96-9 Sixteen-year-old patient, 7 years after placement of a sigmoid irrigation tube.[37] She had been unable to evacuate without enemas since early infancy. Rectal biopsies were normal. Colonic transit of radiopaque markers and anal manometry confirmed the diagnosis of pelvic floor dysfunction with complications of acquired megarectum and increased rectal sensitivity threshold. She had failed to respond to laxative, prokinetic, and biofeedback therapy. She irrigates herself every 2 to 3 days with 600 to 900 mL of tap water and has no stooling-related difficulties. The skin-level device was changed twice.

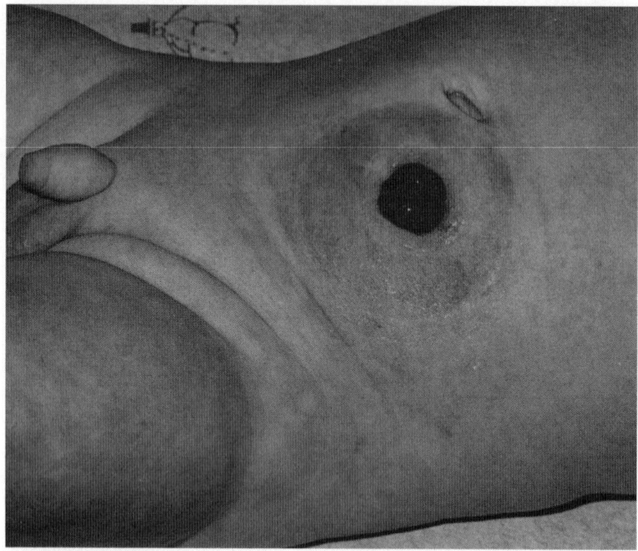

Figure 96–10 Five-month-old child with high imperforate anus. The high sigmoid loop colostomy is equidistant from the umbilicus, the anterior superior iliac spine, and the inguinal fold. The original incision is only slightly longer than the stoma. Notice the raised "spur" between the two lumina, essential for proper diversion of stool.

of imperforate anus (Fig. 96-10) and complex pelvic malformations, Hirschsprung's disease, colonic atresias, colonic or anorectal trauma, and malignant conditions.* Exteriorized segments of the ileum or colon have been previously used as urinary conduits. However, with modern urinary tract reconstruction techniques, this approach is now rarely, if ever, used in children.[43] On the other hand, the appendix has been mobilized to serve as a catheterizable conduit to the bladder.[57,86]

CHOICE OF ENTEROSTOMA

Feeding Jejunostomy

Nasojejunal and gastrojejunal tubes are only appropriate for brief or intermediate use (days to weeks) because they are prone to occlusion, dislodgment, and intestinal perforation.[34,74] Because conventional tunneled straight, long catheters[98] (see Fig. 96-1A and B) can be difficult to immobilize and replace, my preference for long-term access to the jejunum is a T-tube for infants and small children (see Fig. 96-1C) and a button[88] for older pediatric patients (see Figs. 96-1D and 96-6). In these jejunostomies the wall of the intestine is approximated directly to the abdominal wall as in a gastrostomy, using a conventional celiotomy, a percutaneous endoscopic approach, or a laparoscopic technique.[12,62,74] The T-tube and the button are both replaceable as an office procedure. An alternative is the use of a string-guided replaceable straight tube.[80] Because of the possibility of stomal leakage, some surgeons prefer a Roux-en-Y jejunostomy, either in its original form as a catheterizable mucosa-lined conduit or the modified approach in which a catheter or a skin-level device accesses the loop attached to the parietal peritoneum (see Fig. 96-2).[20,100]

*See references 2, 6, 11, 14, 15, 17, 18, 25, 29, 32, 52, 54, 56, 58, 63, 64, 68, 70, 72, 75, 78, 87, 93, 96, and 99.

Ileostomy

The child's pathologic condition, age, and estimated length of use of the stoma help determine the choice of ileostomy. In neonatal necrotizing enterocolitis or other major intra-abdominal events requiring intestinal resection, I prefer to bring a single end stoma (see Fig. 96-3A) out through a counterincision (see Figs. 96-4A to C and 96-7). A more expedient alternative is to bring the proximal intestine through the end of the incision. However, in my experience with this approach, wound complications tend to be more common; and if the stoma must remain for a prolonged period and the child gains weight, the fold created by the celiotomy incision may interfere with fitting of the stomal appliance (see Figs. 96-7 and 96-8). With a healthy distal intestine and anticipated downstream patency, I close the distal limb and place it intra-abdominally adjacent to the proximal stoma (Fig. 96-11). Otherwise, exteriorization as a mucus fistula is prudent (see Fig. 96-4B). The use of a loop instead of an end stoma is an alternative in which the intact mesentery provides maximal perfusion.[1] A double-barrel stoma is another option (see Fig. 96-3B).[61,69,73] To save as much intestine as possible, the placement of multiple stomas may be necessary (see Fig. 96-4C). In children with ulcerative colitis or familial polyposis, the enterostomal principles are similar to those established for adult patients

Figure 96–11 Four-month-old child with gastroschisis and small bowel atresia during reestablishment of bowel continuity. The dilated and edematous ileus was brought out as an end stoma through the umbilical site. The proximal closed end of the colon was attached to the side of the ileum underneath the abdominal wall. This maneuver allows prompt identification of the distal bowel, minimizing dissection and incision size.

(see Figs. 96-3A, 96-12B, and 96-13).[10,30,47,52,90,97] Choices for a temporary protective diverting ileostomy include a simple loop (see Fig. 96-3E),[31,54] an end loop (see Fig. 96-3F, inset),[92] and an end stoma with the closed end under the fascia (see Fig. 96-3F).

Appendicostomy, Tube Cecostomy, Tube Sigmoidostomy

Several approaches, accessing either the right or the left colon, are available for antegrade enemas. If the appendix is present, it is exteriorized with or without interposition of a valve by an open[22,85] or laparoscopically assisted technique. If there is no appendix, the wall of the cecum may be fashioned into a catheterizable conduit that is then brought to the skin. Additionally, a catheter[81] or a skin-level device, such as the button,[88] can be placed using closed or open techniques. In patients with normal colonic motility, direct access to the sigmoid may be physiologically advantageous (see Fig. 96-9).[37]

Colostomy

Most colostomies fall into three categories: right transverse, left transverse, and sigmoid. The main differences between the stomas used for fecal diversion in children with imperforate anus are outlined in Table 96-3. My preference is for a high sigmoid loop colostomy (see Figs. 96-5B and 96-10). However, separating the ends of the colon, particularly in boys (see Fig. 96-5A),[32] has been a strongly encouraged alternative.[14,96] Advantages of separation are less contamination of the urinary tract and lower rate of prolapse, most notably in the distal limb. Disadvantages include a longer incision, greater potential for wound problems, and greater difficulty applying a stoma device in small neonates or when weight gain creates creases.

In children with Hirschsprung's disease the best site for a colostomy is the dilated segment that contains normal ganglion cells found immediately proximal to the transition zone. A loop colostomy is usually chosen because of its simplicity in construction and takedown. Because most transition zones are in the sigmoid colon, this lower left quadrant stoma is taken down at the time of the definitive corrective operation (see Fig. 96-5B). However, at times an end stoma is preferable because of massive bowel dilatation, making the loop more difficult to construct and manage postoperatively. If separation of the stomas is chosen, the distal intestine should only be oversewn if the distal segment is short. In all other cases this should not be done because mucus cannot be appropriately evacuated or washed out. Although similar data are not available in children, loop colostomies are fully diverting in adults.[59]

TECHNICAL ASPECTS

For placement of a tube-feeding enterostoma, using an "open" technique, the proximal jejunum is approached through a small, upper left quadrant incision (see Fig. 96-6). The ligament of Treitz is identified, and the catheter or skin-level device is inserted in the antemesenteric portion of the intestine, 10 to 20 cm distal to the ligament. A pursestring suture of fine multifilament synthetic absorbable material is placed around the enterotomy and tied. The catheter is then brought out

TABLE 96-3 Colostomies for Imperforate Anus

Sigmoid Colostomies	
Advantages	**Disadvantages**
Rectosigmoid pelvic reflection permits precise identification of loop.	If low or midsigmoid colon is used, length for pull-through may be jeopardized.
Stools are firmer; pouches are not always needed; there is less tendency for skin excoriation or dehydration.	Interference with blood supply is possible.
With firmer stools, less overflow occurs into distal stoma when a loop is used.	With distal obstruction, sigmoid may be larger than the transverse colon.
There is less tendency to prolapse.	
There is less surface for urine absorption.	
Distal colon is easier to clean.	
Colostogram is easier to perform.	
There is no scarring of epigastrium.	
Transverse Colon Colostomies	
Advantages	**Disadvantages**
Bowel length is adequate.	Stools are looser, particularly in the right transverse colon; pouches are always necessary; skin maceration and dehydration are more common.
Mobilization is easy.	There is a higher rate of prolapse.
Diameter is smaller and there is less meconium.	Absorptive surface for urine is greater in distal limb.
	Cleaning of distal limb is difficult or impossible.
	Epigastric scars are more visible.

through a counterincision. A second pursestring suture, made of monofilament synthetic absorbable suture is applied, with the stitches being alternated between the intestine and the exit site of the catheter in the abdominal wall. When tied, this second suture approximates the intestinal serosa to the parietal peritoneum in a watertight manner.[34,88] Alternatives to this approach are the direct percutaneous endoscopic jejunostomy and the laparoscopically assisted jejunostomy.[74]

Decompressing ileostomies are usually placed in the lower right quadrant (see Figs. 96-4 and 96-7). Figure 96-12A illustrates both appropriate and undesirable stoma exit sites in neonates, infants, and small children (e.g., those with necrotizing enterocolitis). Figure 96-12B demonstrates ideal exit sites in older children or adolescents (e.g., those with ulcerative colitis or familial polyposis). Incisions in the lower quadrants should be avoided in patients who may eventually have long-standing or permanent stomas because such incisions can create an uneven surface that interferes with appliance adherence. The umbilicus is a possible site for a stoma[29] and is an excellent choice for the distended proximal intestine in newborns who have gastroschisis with atresia (see Fig. 96-11). In children, it is most helpful when the position of the stoma, as well as possible alternatives, is marked on the abdominal wall before the incision is made. This planning is desirable in both elective and emergency settings. For elective, long-standing stomas, the best location is marked the day before the operation (Fig. 96-13). The exit site should be located over the convex midportion of the rectus muscle, away from the incision, umbilicus, bony prominences, and skin folds. Special attention must be paid in overweight children because of the deep creases of the abdominal wall. When using a counterincision for a small intestinal stoma in infants, I have at times used an ophthalmic trephine because this circular cutting device, which is available in several diameters, makes sharp, perfectly round openings in the skin and the anterior rectus sheet. The rectus muscle is cut transversely with a cautery or simply split. The posterior rectus sheet is cut transversely or in a cruciate fashion. In older children, I prefer to make the opening for planned ileostomies before making the vertical midline celiotomy incision to achieve a straight course and avoid distortion of the layers by traction on the edge of the incision. The openings should be just big enough to allow comfortable passage of the ileum without interfering with the blood supply. Depending on the size of the child, ileostomies must be at least 1 cm to a couple of centimeters above the skin level to allow proper pouch immobilization.

Stomas in neonates, particularly those established for necrotizing enterocolitis, should not be matured because it will interfere with the already tenuous blood supply. The exteriorized end of the stoma is simply anchored to the skin with four delicate sutures of a synthetic absorbable material. An antibacterial ointment is applied and dressings are avoided; a pouch is applied with the onset of defecation. In infants, the mucosa grows rapidly over the exteriorized serosal surface. Stomas in older children are sutured to the layers of the abdominal wall and matured initially (see Fig. 96-2A). Deep, full-thickness sutures should be avoided because they may cause a fistula from the lumen to the peristomal tissue. Some surgeons do not mature stomas, regardless of the age of the children because the projecting intestinal edge everts spontaneously without the addition of sutures. In older patients, I secure the ileal loop intraperitoneally to the abdominal wall to prevent torsion and internal hernia and to decrease the possibility of prolapse. At the end of the procedure, a stoma pouch is applied.

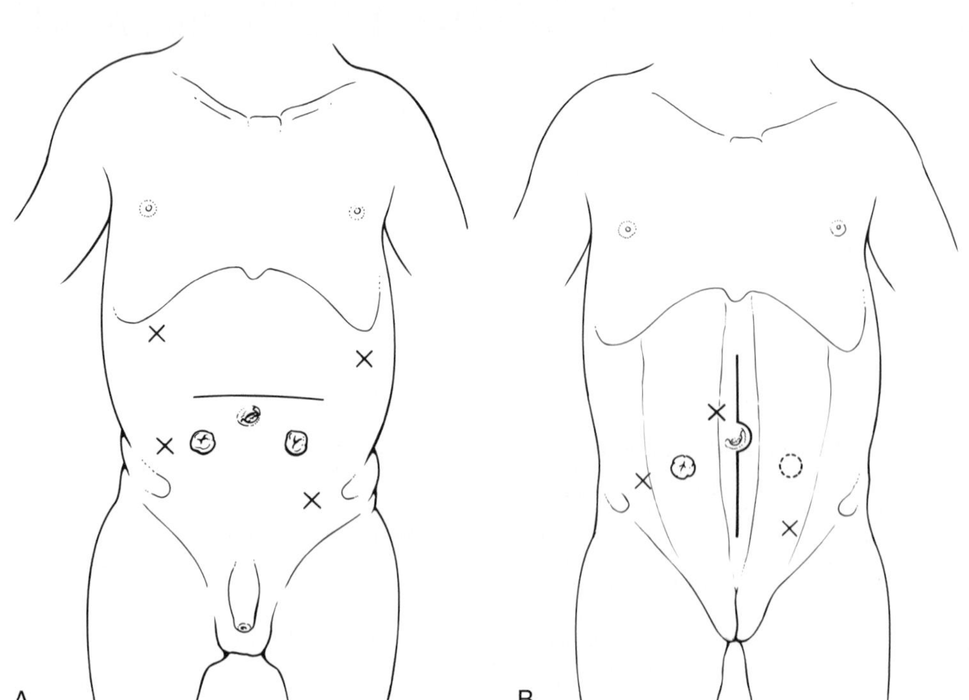

Figure 96-12 Ideal sites for stomas. *A*, Infant. The end stoma can be brought out through a counterincision in the lower right or left quadrants. The sites marked with an "X" are unsuitable because they are too close to the rib cage, the anterior superior iliac spine, the flank, or the groin. *B*, Older child or adolescent. The best site for the stoma is in the mid rectus abdominis muscle in the right lower quadrant. The opposite side is an alternative. Areas marked with an "X" are unsuitable.

A

B

C

D

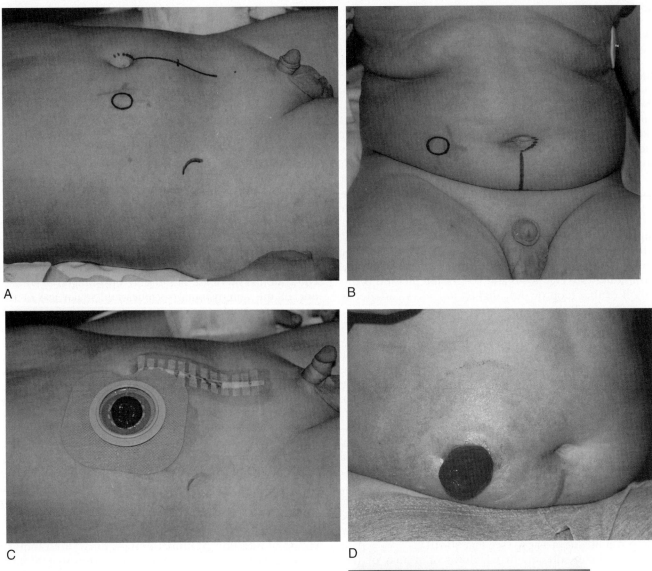

Figure 96–13 Eight-year-old boy with intractable ulcerative colitis that failed to respond to aggressive medical management including corticosteroids, azathioprine, and infliximab. He underwent a total abdominal colectomy and ileostomy as a preliminary stage to an ileoanal anastomosis. *A,* The patient in a supine position. The stoma site had been determined several days before the procedure. The boy was asked to wear a two-piece pouch using the selected site as a guide. *B,* Bringing the already anesthetized patient into a sitting position confirmed the adequacy of the stoma site away from major abdominal folds. *C,* Skin barrier with flange (two-piece system) applied to the ileostoma at the completion of the colectomy. *D,* Six weeks later the stoma was well healed with very mild residual edema. *E,* Same boy wearing a two-piece system with an opaque pouch. He empties the pouch three to four times during the day and two to three times evening and nights. He enjoys full physical activities, including basketball. He does not use an ostomy belt and changes the skin barrier and the pouch every 3 days.

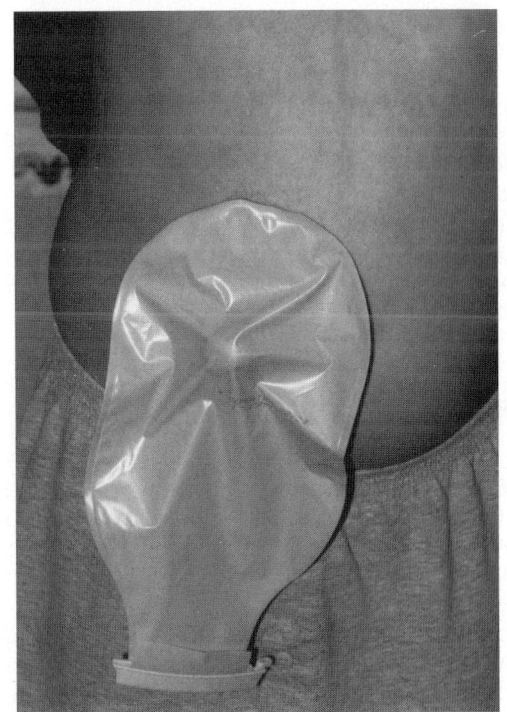

E

The preferred colostomy site is the lower left quadrant. In children with imperforate anus, the meconium-filled sigmoid colon and the pelvic peritoneal reflection are identified once the abdominal cavity is opened. A suitable portion of the uppermost sigmoid colon is selected, and the bowel is exteriorized. When the dividing technique is used (see Fig. 96-5A), the stomas are placed at each end of the incision and the intestine is secured with fine, synthetic, absorbable suture to all layers of the abdominal wall. There should be enough space between the two openings to permit a good fit for a pouch over the proximal stoma (or the distal stoma must be flush with the skin). To avoid excessive narrowing of the stoma, an appropriately sized Hegar dilator or catheter is inserted into the intestinal lumen at the time of wound closure. End colostomies should only protrude slightly. With a loop stoma (see Fig. 96-5B and 96-10), the incision is the length of that loop or only slightly longer. A catheter is placed through the mesentery of the selected segment, which is then lifted above the level of the skin. Triangulating sutures approximate the two limbs to each other and to the peritoneum on both sides to prevent internal hernias. The full circumference of the intestine is then attached to the peritoneum and fascia. Sutures lift the posterior bowel wall above the skin level. I have abandoned the use of rods or catheters because these interfere with appliance fitting.[79] The intestine is opened longitudinally and the edges everted. In all children with imperforate anus, the distal, meconium-filled segment of intestine is flushed out at the time of colostomy placement. This is important to avoid formation of a fecaloma. In patients with Hirschsprung's disease, the construction of the loop stoma must also be meticulous and may include tightening of the distended intestine to decrease the possibility of prolapse (see Fig. 96-10).

To facilitate subsequent takedown of stomas of the small or large intestine, the two ends of intestine should be kept in proximity; however, interference with the stoma appliance must be avoided. If the distal limb is placed underneath the abdominal wall, it is tagged with a nonabsorbable suture or a metallic clip (or both) and placed as close as possible to the exiting stoma to simplify identification and reanastomosis. Placing a metallic clip helps with radiographic identification of the proximal end of the distal bowel. This is particularly useful when a barium enema is performed before reestablishment of bowel continuity in children with necrotizing enterocolitis.

STOMA CARE

Proper care of an enterostoma is essential. Parents, as well as older children, must be carefully taught and reassured before leaving the hospital and on subsequent follow-up visits. Ileostomies and proximal colon colostomies always require pouches. With the well-formed stools that result from sigmoid stomas, some parents have used a skin barrier, tissue, and diapers instead. A large variety of stoma appliances are commercially available, including disposable and reusable pouches for all ages and sizes, even the smallest premature infants. Skin barriers, adhesives, powders, vented pouches, and odor control solutions are among the products that facilitate the care of today's ostomate.[7,17,19,52,60,91,97]

Properly fitted appliances should remain in situ for several days. Three days is a reasonable expectation. There are two basic types of pediatric appliances: the one-piece pouching system in which the adhesive skin barrier is already attached to the pouch and the two-piece system in which the adhesive skin barrier is separate from the pouch. In the latter, the pieces snap together with a flange (see Fig. 96-13C and E). Because of the holding power of contemporary adhesive skin barriers, additional fixation with tape or belts is usually not needed. The skin barrier is cut to the proper stoma size with the help of a template provided with the pouches. In addition to instructions provided by the surgeon, nurses, and the enterostomal therapist, parents are encouraged to contact one of the enterostomal societies and make use of the extensive available educational material.[46,52,60,97] Although "continent stomas" using special intra-abdominal intestinal pouches,[26,47] magnetic caps,[28] short balloon catheters,[67] and other forms of intraluminal occlusion[52,97] have been attempted, there is limited experience with such operations or devices in children.[26]

Candidiasis remains a common problem in the parastomal skin, and local antifungal medication should be used at the earliest sign of irritation. With skin excoriation, the area is exposed to air and a synthetic barrier is applied; a hair dryer can be very useful. Mild stomal bleeding is usually self-limiting. The application of silver nitrate may be needed to control granulation tissue around the mucosa-skin interface in the early stages. Remaining sutures may be the cause and should be removed. I do not routinely dilate stomas and only occasionally irrigate the distal intestine. Malfunctioning stomas often require early takedown or revision before more serious complications occur. Dietary and select pharmacologic manipulations are helpful in producing firmer stools. Children with high ileostomies must be carefully monitored to prevent electrolyte imbalance and insufficient nutrient absorption.[8,27,38,44]

REESTABLISHING INTESTINAL CONTINUITY

Timing of enterostoma closure varies widely depending on the underlying condition, health status of the child, and presence or absence of stoma-related complications.[45,61,94] Unnecessary delays in the reestablishment of bowel continuity tend to increase morbidity and should be avoided.[4,14] The more proximal the stoma, the earlier it should be closed to decrease complications.[14,27,38] Children who undergo stoma placement with resection of ischemic intestine must have a preoperative contrast study of the distal segment to rule out strictures or complete luminal obstruction. Reestablishment of small intestinal continuity generally does not require intestinal preparation. Takedown of a colostomy is preceded by antegrade intestinal irrigation, supplemented by conventional enemas. Although I routinely administer perioperative intravenous antibiotics, I do not use intraluminal antibiotic solutions. When reestablishing continuity involves the left colon or sigmoid colon, I insert a soft catheter into the rectum to facilitate with intraoperative identification of that loop. Good exposure with full mobilization of the intestinal ends is very important. Although extraperitoneal closure has been used in children, it is not recommended for routine use.[18] For the intestinal anastomoses I employ a single layer technique using fine synthetic absorbable suture material.

COMPLICATIONS OF ENTEROSTOMAS

Problems related to construction, care, and closure of stomas in the small and large intestines are numerous and common and can lead to significant morbidity and occasional mortality (Table 96-4). Analysis of pediatric series reveals complication rates that often reach and sometimes exceed 50%.* In addition, stoma revision or early take-down is frequently necessary.[45,56,58,94] Complications of enterostomas used for feeding are often accentuated by the patient's underlying disease, particularly in malnourished, neurologically impaired children.[12,82,100] Stomas used for evacuation of the small intestine are associated with a higher morbidity than are colostomies because these stomas are compounded by fluid, electrolyte, and absorption losses.[8,27,38] Transverse colostomies are more prone to complications than are sigmoid stomas[2,14,15,32,58]; in several series, divided colostomies have been preferred over loop colostomies.[14,32,96]

Among the more common serious complications are prolapse (Fig. 96-14), stricture, and retraction.† The incidence of prolapse in children is as high as 21.7%[11] and is more common if the distal loop is exteriorized.‡

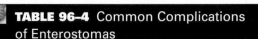

TABLE 96-4 Common Complications of Enterostomas
Prolapse
Stricture
Retraction
Wound separation, dehiscence
Wound infection, postoperative sepsis
Parastomal hernia
Intestinal wall separation or perforation with catheter change
Exteriorization of wrong intestinal segment or end
Intestinal obstruction (adhesion, internal hernia)
Intestinal torsion with ischemia
Fistula formation
Perforation by feeding or irrigating catheter
Poor appliance fitting and leakage
Psychological trauma
Skin excoriation, candidiasis, dermatitis
Mucosal excoriation and bleeding
Granulation tissue of mucosa-skin interface
Variceal bleeding with portal hypertension
Electrolyte imbalance
Acidosis (caused by urine absorption in the distal loop of intestine)
Fecal impaction (in the distal loop of intestine)

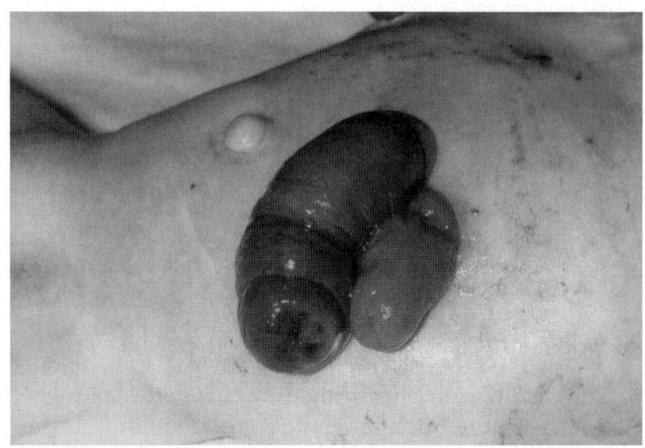

Figure 96–14 Six-month-old child with Down syndrome and Hirschsprung's disease. Proximal and distal colon prolapse have occurred through a left transverse colon loop colostomy. Notice the three openings at the end of the larger everted loop that correspond to the lumen of the cecum, the ileocecal valve opening, and the lumen of the appendix.

Major prolapse requires prompt attention, and general anesthesia is often needed for intestinal reduction. Temporizing measures for control of prolapse include a modified pursestring suture technique[39,49,50] or placement of a U-shaped stitch from the lumen of the reduced intestine through the abdominal wall over an internal and external pledget.[33,48] The pledgets hold the intestine against the abdominal wall and prevent the suture from cutting through. Stricture, if mild, may respond to dilatation.[11,58] However, if evacuation is decreased and the proximal intestine begins to dilate, revision is advisable. This procedure is usually possible by incising all layers around the strictured stoma and bringing out healthy, at times dilated, bowel. The opening should not be excessive, however, because this might lead to prolapse. If the problem is more complex or a parastomal hernia is present, the pathologic process is addressed through a counterincision. Retraction of an end stoma results in poor fitting of the appliance and may lead to skin-level stricture and obstruction, whereas retraction of a loop stoma interferes with proper evacuation and leads to filling of the distal intestinal loop with stool. Intestinal reanastomosis is also associated with a high rate of complications, most notably wound infection, dehiscence, fistula formation, and intestinal obstruction.[14,45,58,64,94] Among the various factors contributing to this morbidity are poor timing, inadequate bowel preparation, technical errors, and shortcuts such as improper choice of suture material and the excessive use of the electrocautery. Malnourished, debilitated, anemic patients and those on corticosteroids are at greatest risk for complications. These contributing factors should be corrected before reestablishment of intestinal continuity is contemplated.

*See references 2, 11, 14, 23, 40, 53, 56, 58, 64-66, 70, 72, 78, 82, 87, and 94.
†See references 2, 4, 11, 14, 40, 56, 58, 64-66, and 78.
‡See references 2, 5, 11, 14, 15, 32, 56, 58, 70, and 78.

Placement and takedown of any stoma should be carefully planned and considered a major procedure. Requirements include ideal operating conditions and, in a teaching setting, appropriate supervision. Pediatric stomas are quite different from adult stomas, and the importance of meticulous attention to detail cannot be overemphasized.

REFERENCES

1. Alaish SM, Krummel TM, Bagwell CE, et al: Loop enterostomy in newborns with necrotizing enterocolitis. J Am Coll Surg 1996;182:457-458.
2. Al-Salem AH, Grant C, Khawaja S: Colostomy complications in infants and children. Int Surg 1992;77:164-166.
3. Andrassy RJ, Page CP, Feldtman RW, et al: Continual catheter administration of an elemental diet in infants and children. Surgery 1977;82:205-210.
4. Bakx R, Busch OR, Benelman WA, et al: Morbidity of temporary loop ileostomies. Dig Surg 2004;21:277-281.
5. Bishop HC, Koop CE: Management of meconium ileus: Resection, Roux-en-Y anastomosis and ileostomy irrigation with pancreatic enzymes. Ann Surg 1957;145:410-414.
6. Bishop HC: Colostomy in the newborn: Indications, techniques, complications and care. Am J Surg 1961;101: 642-648.
7. Borkowski S: Pediatric stomas, tubes, and appliances. Pediatr Clin North Am 1998;45:1419-1435.
8. Bower TR, Pringle KC, Soper RT: Sodium deficit causing decreased weight gain and metabolic acidosis in infants with ileostomy. J Pediatr Surg 1988;23:567-572.
9. Branagan G, Tromans A, Finnis D: Effect of stoma formation on bowel care and quality of life in patients with spinal cord injury. Spinal Cord 2003;41:680-683.
10. Brooke BN: Historical perspectives. In Dozois RR (ed): Alternatives to Conventional Ileostomy. Chicago, Year Book Medical Publishers, 1985, pp 19-28.
11. Cain WS, Kieswetter WB: Infant colostomy. Arch Surg 1965;91:314-320.
12. Campos AC, Marchesini JB: Recent advances in the placement of tubes for enteral nutrition. Curr Opin Clin Nutr Metab Care 1999;2:265-269.
13. Caldamone AA, Emmens RW, Rabinowitz R: Hyperchloremic acidosis and imperforate anus. J Urol 1979;122: 817-818.
14. Chandramouli B, Srinivasan K, Jagdish S, et al: Morbidity and mortality of colostomy and its closure in children. J Pediatr Surg 2004;39:596-599.
15. Chowdhary SK, Chalapathi G, Narasimhan KL, et al: An audit of neonatal colostomy for high anorectal malformations: The developing world perspective. Pediatr Surg Int 2004;20:111-113.
16. Coln D, Cywes S: Simultaneous drainage gastrostomy and feeding jejunostomy in the newborn. Surg Gynecol Obstet 1977;145:594-595.
17. Cooney DE, Grosfeld JL: Care of the child with a colostomy. Pediatrics 1977;59:469-472.
18. Das S: Extraperitoneal closure of colostomy in children. J Indian Med Assoc 1991;89:253-255.
19. Davies A: Children with ostomies: Parents helping parents. JET Nurs 1992;19:207-212.
20. DeCou JM, Shorter NA, Karl SR: Feeding Roux-en-Y jejunostomy in the management of severely neurologically impaired children. J Pediatr Surg 1993;28:1276-1279.
21. Di Lorenzo C, Flores AF, Buie T, et al: Intestinal motility and jejunal feeding in children with chronic intestinal pseudo-obstruction. Gastroenterology 1995;108:1379-1385.
22. Driver CP, Barrow C, Fishwick J, et al: The Malone antegrade colonic enema procedure: Outcome and lessons of six years' experience. Pediatr Surg Int 1998;13:370-372.
23. Duchesne JC, Wang YZ, Weintraub SL, et al: Stoma complications: A multivariated analysis. Am Surg 2002;68:961-966.
24. Emond JC, Whitington PF: Selective surgical management of progressive familial intrahepatic cholestasis (Byler's disease). J Pediatr Surg 1995;30:1635-1641.
25. Ein SH: Divided loop colostomy that does not prolapse. Am J Surg 1984;147:250-252.
26. Ein SH: A ten-year experience with the pediatric Kock pouch. J Pediatr Surg 1987;22:764-766.
27. Festen C, Severijnen RSVM, vd Staak FHJ: Early closure of enterostomy after exteriorization of the small intestine for abdominal catastrophes. J Pediatr Surg 1987;22:144-145.
28. Feustel H, Henning G: Kontinente Kolostomie durch Magnetverschluss. Dtsch Med Wochenschr 1975;100: 1063-1064.
29. Fitzgerald PG, Lau GY, Cameron GJ: Use of the umbilical site for temporary ostomy: Review of 47 cases. J Pediatr Surg 1989;24:973.
30. Fonkalsrud EW: Special aspects of ostomies in infancy and childhood. In Barker WF, et al (eds): The Creation and Care of Enterocutaneous Stomas. Curr Probl Surg 1975; 12:54-62.
31. Fonkalsrud EW, Thakur A, Roof L: Comparison of loop versus end ileostomy for fecal diversion after restorative proctocolectomy for ulcerative colitis. J Am Coll Surg 2000; 190:418-422.
32. Gauderer MWL: Colostomy for anorectal malformations—problems related to technique and management. In Hofmann V, Kap-herr S (eds): Anorektale Fehlbildungen. Stuttgart, Gustav Fisher, 1983, pp 99-104.
33. Gauderer MWL, Izant RJ Jr: A technique for temporary control of colostomy prolapse in children. J Pediatr Surg 1985;20:653-655.
34. Gauderer MWL, Stellato TA: Gastrostomies: Evolution, techniques, indications and complications. Curr Probl Surg 1986;23:657-719.
35. Gauderer MWL: Double-tube enterostomy for temporary small bowel decompression. Pediatr Surg Int 1986;1:60-62.
36. Gauderer MWL, Boyle JT: Cholecystoappendicostomy in a child with Alagille syndrome. J Pediatr Surg 1997;32: 166-167.
37. Gauderer MWL, DeCou JM, Boyle JT: Sigmoid irrigation tube for the management of chronic evacuation disorders. J Pediatr Surg 2002;37:348-351.
38. Gertler JP, Seashore JH, Touloukian RJ: Early ileostomy closure in necrotizing enterocolitis. J Pediatr Surg 1987;22: 140-143.
39. Golladay ES, Bernay F, Wagner CW: Prevention of prolapse in pediatric enterostomies with purse string technique. J Pediatr Surg 1990;25:990-991.
40. Haberlik A, Hollworth ME, Windhager U, Schober PH: Problems of ileostomy in necrotizing enterocolitis. Acta Paediatr Suppl 1994;396:74-76.
41. Harberg FJ, Senekjian EK, Pokorny WJ: Treatment of uncomplicated meconium ileus via T-tube ileostomy. J Pediatr Surg 1981;16:61-63.
42. Hays DM, Kimura K: Biliary atresia: New concepts of management. Curr Probl Surg 1981;18:541-608.
43. Hendren WH: Diversion and undiversion. In O'Neill JA Jr, et al (eds): Pediatric Surgery, 5th ed. St. Louis, Mosby, 1998, pp 1653-1670.

44. Hill GL: Physiology of conventional ileostomy. In Dozois RR (ed): Alternatives to Conventional Ileostomy. Chicago, Year Book Medical Publishers, 1985, pp 129-139.
45. Kiely EM, Sparnon AL: Stoma closure in infants and children. Pediatr Surg Int 1987;2:95-97.
46. Kirkland S: Ostomy dolls for pediatric patients. J Enterostomal Ther 1985;12:104-105.
47. Kock NG, Dare N, Hulten L, et al: Ileostomy. Curr Probl Surg 1977;14:6-52.
48. Koga H, Yamataka A, Yoshida, et al: Laparoscopic-assisted repair for prolapsed colostomy in an infant. Pediatr Endosurg Innov Tech 2004;8:275-278.
49. Krasna IH: A simple pursestring suture technique for treatment of colostomy prolapse and intussusception. J Pediatr Surg 1979;14:801-802.
50. Lau JTK, Saing H, Ong GB: Double pursestring suture technique for loop colostomy prolapse in infants. Aust Paediatr J 1982;18:58-59.
51. Lyerly HK, Mault JR: Laparoscopic ileostomy and colostomy. Ann Surg 1994;219:317-322.
52. MacKiegan JM, Cataldo PA: Intestinal Stomas: Principles, Techniques and Management. St. Louis, Quality Medical Publishing, 1993.
53. MacMahon RA, Cohen SJ, Eckstein HB: Colostomies in infancy and childhood. Arch Dis Child 1963;38:114-117.
54. Maydl K: Zur Technik der Kolostomie. Zentalbl Chir 1888; 15:433-436.
55. Mikulicz J: Chirurgische Erfahrungen über das Darmkarzinom. Arch Klin Chir 1903;69:28-47.
56. Millar AJ, Lakhoo K, Rode M, et al: Bowel stomas in infants and children: A five-year audit of 203 patients. S Afr J Surg 1993;31:110-113.
57. Mitrofanoff P: Cystostomie continente trans-appendiculaire dans le traitement des vessies neurologiques. Chir Pediatr 1980;21:297-305.
58. Mollitt DL, Malangoni MA, Ballantine TV, et al: Colostomy complications in children: An analysis of 146 cases. Arch Surg 1980;115:455-458.
59. Morris DM, Rayburn D: Loop colostomies are totally diverting in adults. Am J Surg 1991;161:668-671.
60. Mullen BD, McGinn KA: The ostomy book: Living comfortably with colostomies, ileostomies and urostomies. Palo Alto, CA, Bull Publishing, 1992.
61. Musemeche CA, Kosloske AM, Ricketts RR: Enterostomy in necrotizing enterocolitis: An analysis of techniques and timing of closure. J Pediatr Surg 1987;22:479-483.
62. Nagle AP, Murayama KM: Laparoscopic gastrostomy and jejunostomy. J Long Term Eff Med Implants 2004; 14:1-11.
63. Nixon HH: Colostomy: A simple technique, and observations on indications. Z Kinderchir 1966;3:98-103.
64. Nour S, Beck J, Stringer MD: Colostomy complications in infants and children. Ann R Coll Surg Engl 1996;78: 526-530.
65. Park JJ, Del Pindo A, Orsay CP, et al: Stoma complications: The Cook County Hospital experience. Dis Colon Rectum 1999;42:1575-1580.
66. Pearl RK, Prasad ML, Orsay CP, et al: Early local complications from intestinal stomas. Arch Surg 1985;120: 1145-1147.
67. Pemberton JH, Kelly KA, Phillips SA: The continent ostomy valve: Concept and experience. In Dozois RR (ed): Alternatives to Conventional Ileostomies. Chicago, Year Book Medical Publishers, 1985, pp 211-225.
68. Quarmby CJ, Millar AJ, Rode H: The use of diverting colostomies in paediatric peri-anal burns. Burns 1999;25: 645-650.
69. Randolph JG, Zolinger RM Jr, Gross RE: Mikulicz resection in infants and children: A 20 year survey of 196 patients. Ann Surg 1963;158:481-485.
70. Rees BI, Thomas DF, Negam M: Colostomies in infancy and childhood. Z Kinderchir 1982;36:100-102.
71. Rehbein F, Halsband M: A double-tube technique for the treatment of meconium ileus and small bowel atresia. J Pediatr Surg 1968;3:723-726.
72. Rokhsar S, Harrison EA, Shaul DB, et al: Intestinal stoma complications in immunocompromised children. J Pediatr Surg 1999;34:1757-1761.
73. Rosenman JE, Kosloske AM: A reappraisal of the Mikulicz enterostomy in infants and children. Surgery 1982;91:34-37.
74. Ryan JA Jr, Page CP: Intrajejunal feedings: Development and current status. J Parenter Enteral Nutr 1984;8:187-198.
75. Sangkhathat S, Patrapinyokul S, Tadyathikom K: Early enteral feeding after closure of colostomy in pediatric patients. J Pediatr Surg 2003;38:1516-1519.
76. Santulli TV, Blanc WA: Congenital atresia of the intestine, pathogenesis and treatment. Ann Surg 1961;154:939-948.
77. Schärli WF: The history of colostomy in childhood. Prog Pediatr Surg 1986;20:188-198.
78. Schier F, Antoniu D, Waldschhmidt J: Komplikationen der Kolostomie im Kindesalter. Zentralbl Chir 1990;115: 1435-1440.
79. Simson JNL, Brereton RJ: Temporary antimesenteric stomas without a skin bridge in infants. Ann R Coll Surg Engl 1985;67:363-365.
80. Schimpl G, Mayr J, Gauderer MWL: Jejunostomy with replaceable feeding tube: A new technique. J Am Coll Surg 1997;184:652-654.
81. Shandling B, Chait PG, Richards HF: Percutaneous cecostomy: A new technique in the management of fecal incontinence. J Pediatr Surg 1996;31;534-537.
82. Smith D, Soucy P: Complications of long-term jejunostomy in children. J Pediatr Surg 1996;31:787-790.
83. Smith S, Wiener ES, Starzl TE, et al: Stoma-related variceal bleeding: An under-recognized complication of biliary atresia. J Pediatr Surg 1988;23:243-245.
84. So HB, Becker JM, Schwartz DL, et al: Eighteen years' experience with neonatal Hirschsprung's disease treated by endorectal pull through without colostomy. J Pediatr Surg 1998;33:673-675.
85. Squire R, Kiely EM, Carr B, et al: The clinical application of the Malone antegrade colonic enema. J Pediatr Surg 1993;28:1012-1015.
86. Stein JP, Daneshmand S, Dunn M, et al: Continent right colon reservoir using a cutaneous appendicostomy. Urology 2004;63:577-580.
87. Steinau G, Ruhl KM, Hornchen H, et al: Enterostomy complications in infancy and childhood. Langenbecks Arch Surg 2001;386:346-349.
88. Stellato TA, Gauderer MWL: Jejunostomy button as a new method for long-term jejunostomy feedings. Surg Gynecol Obstet 1989;168:552-554.
89. Teitelbaum DH, Cilley RE, Sherman NJ, et al: A decade of experience with the primary pull-through for Hirschsprung's disease in the newborn period: A multicenter analysis of outcomes. Ann Surg 2000;232:372-380.
90. Turnbull RB Jr, Weakley FL: Atlas of Intestinal Stomas. St. Louis, CV Mosby, 1967.
91. Turnbull RW, Turnbull GB: The history and current status of paramedical support for the ostomy patient. J ET Nurs 1993;20:102-104.
92. Unti JA, Abcarian H, Pearl RK, et al: Rodless end-loop stomas: A seven-year experience. Dis Colon Rectum 1991; 34:999-1004.

93. Villarreal J, Sood M, Zangen T, et al: Colonic diversion for intractable constipation in children: Colonic manometry helps guide clinical decision. J Pediatr Gastroenterol Nutr 2001;33:588-591.
94. Weber TR, Tracy TF Jr, Silen ML, Powell MA: Enterostomy and its closure in newborns. Arch Surg 1995;130:534-537.
95. Webster R: Historical review. In Stephens FD, Smith ED (eds): Ano-rectal Malformations in Children. Chicago, Year Book Medical Publishers, 1971, pp 1-13.
96. Wilkins S, Peña A: The role of colostomy in the management of anorectal malformations. Pediatr Surg Int 1988; 3:105-109.
97. Winkler R: Stoma Therapy: An Atlas and Guide for Intestinal Stomas. New York, Thieme, 1986, pp 2-104.
98. Witzel O: Zur Technik der Magenfistelanlegung. Zentralbl Chir 1891;18:601-618.
99. Woodward MN, Foley P, Cusick EL: Colostomy for treatment of functional constipation in children: A preliminary report. J Pediatr Gastroenterol Nutr 2004;38:75-78.
100. Yoshida NR, Webber EM, Gillis DA, et al: Roux-en-Y jejunostomy in the pediatric population. J Pediatr Surg 1966;31:791-793.

Chapter 97

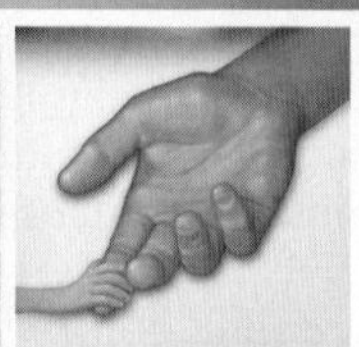

Atresia, Stenosis, and Other Obstructions of the Colon

Keith T. Oldham and Marjorie J. Arca

ATRESIA AND CONGENITAL STENOSIS OF THE COLON

History

Binninger first described colonic atresia in 1673.[22] The first survivor of the disease was not reported until 1922, when Gaub[27] treated a child with atresia of the sigmoid colon with a proximal diverting colostomy. In 1947 Potts[48] performed a primary anastomosis of the transverse colon in a newborn, with subsequent survival. Congenital colonic stenosis has been reported infrequently—only eight cases since 1966.[1,9,21,55,56] Most cases were managed with resection of the involved colonic segment and end-to-end anastomosis, but a staged approach using a decompressive colostomy in the proximal dilated segment was judged necessary in several patients. All the reported infants with congenital colonic stenosis have survived.

Introduction

Colonic atresia is a rare cause of intestinal obstruction in neonates. The reported incidence varies widely, from 1 in 1498 live births[22] to 1 in 40,000.[25] The figure of 1 in approximately 20,000 births is widely referenced[9,69] and appears to be realistic, with one or two cases of isolated colonic atresia seen annually at most major children's hospitals in the United States. Approximately 1.8%[26] to 15% of intestinal atresias occur in the colon[9,49,56]; these estimates exclude related malformations of the rectum, which are traditionally considered within the spectrum of imperforate anus. There is no known gender or racial predilection of colonic atresia or stenosis. Although a similar abnormality is commonly inherited in an autosomal recessive pattern in Holstein cattle,[64] no familial association is known in humans.

Colonic atresia is associated with several important anomalies of the musculoskeletal system (e.g., syndactyly, polydactyly, clubfoot, absent radius),[46] eye,[49] heart,[49] gastrointestinal tract,[46] and abdominal wall (e.g., gastroschisis, omphalocele, bladder or cloacal exstrophy).[12,58] Facial hemiaplasia and anophthalmia have been reported with cloacal exstrophy as well.[65] In the largest relevant report, 22 of 36 infants with colonic atresia had no associated anomalies.[46] Of the remaining 14 infants in that report, 9 had midline abdominal wall defects and 5 had jejunal atresia.

Approximately 15% to 20% of infants with colonic atresia have proximal small intestinal atresia,[46,49] so neonates with mid to distal small intestinal atresia should routinely have the patency of the colon evaluated in the operating room or with preoperative contrast enema.

Hirschsprung's disease has been recognized in at least 2% of patients with colonic atresia.[3,23,33,35,70] Some authors have hypothesized that when a vascular insult occurs before retroperitoneal fixation of the colon at 11 weeks' gestation, caudal migration of the enteric nerves is interrupted.[23] Therefore, it is imperative to rule out Hirschsprung's disease before reestablishing intestinal continuity in every patient with colonic atresia.

Embryology

Most contemporary analyses suggest that in utero vascular insufficiency after organogenesis is responsible for colonic atresia.[37,44,54] Possible causes of vascular insult include colonic volvulus, intussusception, embolic or thrombotic events, and incarceration or strangulation secondary to hernias or abdominal wall defects. Focal resorption of the compromised gut occurs after ischemic necrosis. The spectrum of observed abnormalities is similar to that of small intestinal atresia, in which experimental work by Louw[37] and Barnard and Louw[6] has confirmed the pathogenic role of in utero vascular occlusion. The classification system of Bland-Sutton[11] and Louw[37] for small intestinal atresia is also applied to the colon. Briefly, type I lesions are intraluminal obstructive webs; type II lesions are blind proximal and distal segments connected by a fibrous cord; and type III lesions are completely separated segments of intestine, with an intervening V-shaped mesenteric defect. Type III abnormalities are the most common.[12,49] Complex mesenteric defects and multiple atresias have been described. This classification system has limited clinical value because surgical principles and outcome are not dictated by the type of lesion.

Congenital colonic stenosis is much less common than colonic atresia. Seven of the eight reported cases of congenital colonic stenosis demonstrated a segmental stricture of the colon, with lengths ranging from 3 to 16.5 cm.[1,9,21,55,56] The cause of these stenoses has also been attributed to interference in the blood supply of the developing colon. Recently, a partially obstructing intraluminal membrane was described as the cause of colonic stenosis.[42]

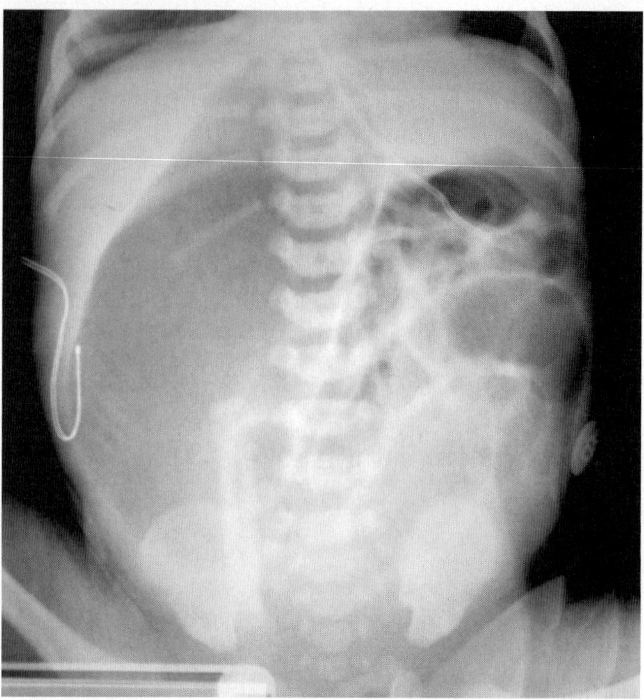

Figure 97–1 Colonic atresia. This plain radiograph of a patient 24 hours old shows marked proximal intestinal distention and no air-filled spaces in the rectum or lower left quadrant. On exploration, the atresia was at the level of the hepatic flexure. (Courtesy of J. Sty, MD.)

Clinical Presentation

Prenatal diagnosis of distal intestinal atresia is possible with contemporary ultrasonographic techniques; it may show an enlarged loop of intestine or colon that is larger than expected for gestational age.[5,25] Polyhydramnios is usually not seen because amniotic fluid is absorbed in the small intestine proximal to the point of obstruction.

An infant with colonic atresia or stenosis usually has no evident problem at birth but develops a distended abdomen with 24 to 48 hours. Because the obstruction is distal and usually complete, abdominal distention is predictably marked and progressive, usually becoming profound by the second or third day of life if untreated. Mechanical ventilatory support may be necessary due to massive intestinal dilatation and abdominal distention. Vomiting may be delayed in onset or relatively minor because of the distal site of the obstruction. Feculent vomiting is a late manifestation. Infants with colonic atresia typically pass little or no fecal matter. Rectal examination yields white mucus rather than meconium. In neonates, musculoskeletal or abdominal wall abnormalities may be apparent on inspection.

Diagnosis

Any neonate with suspected intestinal obstruction should have a plain abdominal radiograph. Radiographs of infants with colonic atresia show multiple distended intestinal loops with air-fluid levels. A distal cutoff may be present (Fig. 97-1). Although the small intestine and colon are not distinguishable in the neonatal period, the degree of distention immediately proximal to the obstruction is often more marked in the colon than in similarly obstructed small intestine (see Fig. 97-1). Pneumoperitoneum is a sign of proximal colon perforation and is present in approximately 10% of infants with this disorder at the time of diagnosis.[46] A competent ileocecal valve creates a segment of colon obstructed in both proximal and distal directions, theoretically increasing the risk for perforation.

Contrast enema radiography with isotonic contrast agent is the standard test to establish the diagnosis of colonic atresia or stenosis. Complete obstruction is characterized by a distal "microcolon," which is diminutive from disuse but is intrinsically normal in most circumstances. The contrast medium typically fills the lumen of the distal colon, terminating at the point of obstruction immediately adjacent to the segment that is most distended with luminal air (the cutoff point). Congenital stenosis is characterized by narrowing of the intestine and limited proximal filling with contrast medium; proximal intestinal dilatation is often seen.

A contrast enema is important in the evaluation of any neonate with suspected distal intestinal atresia because the surgeon must identify any distal obstruction before repair. In addition, this study is crucial in the evaluation for other causes of distal obstruction, such as meconium plug syndrome, Hirschsprung's disease, or neonatal small left colon syndrome.[5] In patients with colonic atresia or stenosis, no other imaging is needed to define the intestinal anatomy. Screening for cardiac disease may be needed if the patient has associated anomalies.

Treatment

An infant with intestinal obstruction should have decompression with a nasogastric tube and resuscitation with intravenous fluids. Broad-spectrum antibiotics should be administered before operation. The most common finding in colonic atresia is two blind ends of colon with no intervening mesentery (type III). Operative management should not be delayed because of the risks of perforation and segmental volvulus. In the past, emphasis was placed on the relevance of the site of atresia in surgical decision making.[49] Right colon lesions were believed best managed with primary anastomosis; those in the left or sigmoid colon were treated with proximal colostomy and staged reconstruction in an effort to decrease the risk of infection or anastomotic complications. In contemporary practice, primary anastomosis is preferred regardless of the site of obstruction, provided the infant is medically stable. Enthusiasm for primary anastomosis should be tempered, however, if there is possible vascular compromise, significant size mismatch of luminal diameter, or excessive fecal soilage.

Surgical principles include the following: Laparotomy is undertaken through a generous incision, usually in a transverse, supraumbilical position. Compromised or excessively dilated proximal intestine (usually right colon) and the obstructing lesion are resected to facilitate functional recovery. Preservation of intestinal length and the ileocecal valve is desirable. Patency of the distal segment should be demonstrated either preoperatively or intraoperatively. Intestinal continuity is reestablished with a single-layer end-oblique anastomosis.

Because of the association with Hirschsprung's disease, a suction rectal biopsy to evaluate for ganglion cells should be performed in the operating room if primary anastomosis is planned. Similarly, if a colostomy is deemed appropriate, the myenteric plexus at the colostomy site should be examined at operation, and a rectal suction biopsy should be performed before reanastomosis.

The experience with local coloplasty techniques is limited, and coloplasty is not recommended, given the excellent outcome of resection and anastomosis. Complex colonic atresias and those associated with midline abdominal wall defects may require other approaches, such as proximal stoma formation and staged repair of the colon.

Results

Complications of colonic atresia and stenosis repair are generally the same as for other types of colonic surgery. The most common complications are anastomotic stricture, leak, and proximal segment dysfunction. Adhesive small intestinal obstruction, wound infection, and stoma-related problems have been reported as well.[4,46,49] In a report by Powell and Raffensperger,[49] 15 complications occurred in 19 patients treated between 1946 and 1978; a mortality rate of 10.5% was associated with colonic atresia. DellaVecchia et al.[19] reported 21 patients with colonic atresia and stenosis presenting from 1972 to 1997; 12 of these patients had complications, including wound infection (1), stoma prolapse (1), prolonged ileus (2), and late adhesive bowel obstruction (8). There was no operative mortality in that series, and the long-term survival rate was 100%.

ACQUIRED COLONIC STENOSIS

Various inflammatory, infectious, traumatic, and neoplastic processes may lead to acquired colonic stenosis in infants and children.[59] Of these, neonatal necrotizing enterocolitis is the most common. As many as 10% to 25% of infants with this disorder develop late colonic strictures.[7,8,51] Excessive local production of tumor necrosis factor has been implicated as a pathologic cause.[66] Gobet et al.[29] reported that of 47 infants who required surgical treatment for necrotizing enterocolitis, 22 (47%) developed colonic strictures that required resection. Stenosis usually occurs within 3 months after the initial illness. The sigmoid colon is the most common site of narrowing, but the entire intraperitoneal colon and small intestine are at risk. Several lesions may be present and are usually partially obstructing (Fig. 97-2). Feeding intolerance, bilious vomiting, and abdominal distention are typical. The diagnosis is established by contrast enema radiography. Treatment consists of segmental surgical resection. Resection with proximal diversion and staged reconstruction is an alternative in high-risk patients. Successful balloon catheter dilatation of focal colonic strictures has been reported, but the experience is quite limited; this technique is rarely used in contemporary practice.[45]

Other infectious and inflammatory disease states have been associated with colonic strictures. They have been reported as sequelae of hemolytic uremic syndrome[67] and methicillin-resistant *Staphylococcus aureus* enterocolitis.[39] In children with human immunodeficiency virus, angioinvasive *Candida* species have been reported to cause acute colonic obstruction and death.[38] Chronic nonsteroidal anti-inflammatory drug use has been implicated in colonic

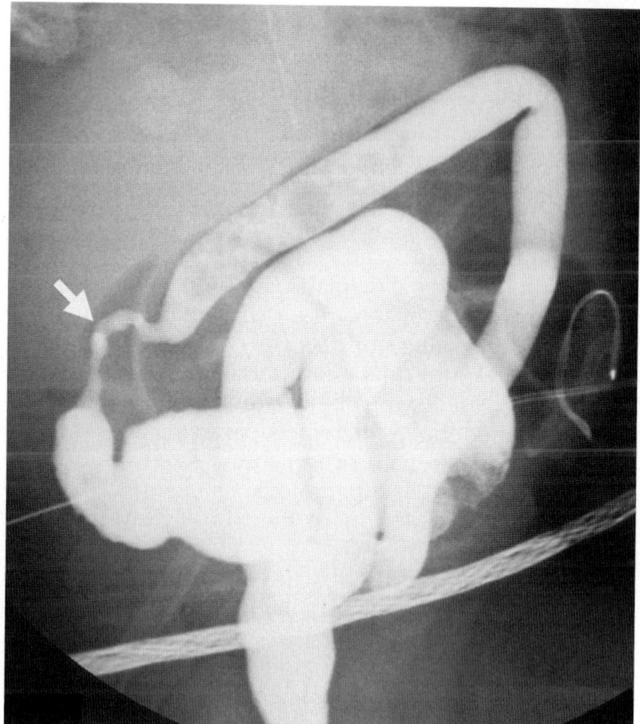

Figure 97-2 Contrast enema radiograph in a 3-month-old infant with a history of necrotizing enterocolitis, treated without surgical intervention. He developed feeding intolerance, vomiting, and abdominal distention. A stricture is seen in the ascending colon *(arrow)*. Segmental resection and primary anastomosis were curative. (Courtesy of J. Sty, MD.)

stenosis in adults,[34] but thus far, there are no reports of this problem in the pediatric population.

Neoplastic processes can cause colonic obstruction by intraluminal growth (polyps, neurofibromas,[31,53] adenocarcinoma[13,16,22]), extrinsic compression (lymphoma, retroperitoneal sarcomas or teratomas), or intramural infiltration (tuberous sclerosois, neurofibromatosis).[61] None of these is common. In all cases, the underlying disease should be controlled, if possible. In general, focal benign lesions are resected, with primary reanastomosis of the colon. Malignant and complex lesions may require fecal diversion, staged procedures, or more complex reconstruction of the colon.

Adenocarcinoma of the colon occurs rarely in young patients. Obstructive pain is the presenting complaint in 97% of patients younger than 21 years with adenocarcinoma.[29] Overall survival in children is approximately 25%; in adults, survival approaches 50%.[62] Delay in diagnosis,[52,68] advanced disease at presentation,[67] and unfavorable histopathologic characteristics[40] all contribute to the lower survival rate in children. LaQuaglia et al.[36] reviewed 29 pediatric patients with adenocarcinoma and concluded that children are more likely to have poor-prognosis lesions, such as "signet ring" or undifferentiated lesions (69%), compared with the moderately differentiated or in situ carcinoma (31%) found in adults. Histopathologic characteristics and lymph node involvement were the most important predictors of mortality in patients who had resection. Patients with high-grade lesions or involved regional nodes should be considered for adjuvant therapy in addition to resection.[36]

FUNCTIONAL COLONIC OBSTRUCTION

Various disease processes are associated with functional colonic obstruction. These forms of colonic obstruction are discussed in detail in Chapters 99 and 100 but are noted here as part of the differential diagnosis of colonic obstruction in infants and children.

Intestinal neuronal dysplasia is a disorder of the myenteric nervous system that has a presentation similar to that of Hirschsprung's disease (see also Chapters 99 and 100).[41] Type A intestinal neuronal dysplasia is characterized by decreased sympathetic innervation of the intestine, with moderately increased parasympathetic nerve fibers. Type B has giant or immature ganglia and thickened nerve fibers. Histopathologic changes may be seen in a segment of colon or in the whole gastrointestinal tract.

Ogilvie's syndrome is an acute distention of the colon in the absence of an identifiable mechanical cause. It is usually seen in adults but may also occur in children and adolescents. The cecum and the right colon are frequently involved. Risk factors for developing Ogilvie's syndrome include electrolyte abnormalities and the use of certain medications, particularly narcotics, that impair intestinal motility. Distention of the cecum impedes the natural propulsive activity of the colon. Cecal distention may cause ischemic necrosis. Nasogastric suction, discontinuation of relevant medications, and colonoscopic decompression are the mainstays of therapy. Recently, the use of neostigmine (0.007 to 0.75 mg/kg), an acetylcholinesterase inhibitor, has been reported in the pediatric literature.[28] The precise mechanism by which neostigmine functions in this setting is unclear. Speculation is that its cholinomimetic effect corrects an acquired dysfunction of the colonic autonomic nervous system.

Chronic idiopathic intestinal pseudo-obstruction occurs in children and adults.[15,57] Abnormalities of the intestinal smooth muscle (myopathy), myenteric plexus (neuropathy), or a combination of both may occur.

In neonates, a visceral myopathy known as the megacystis-microcolon-intestinal hypoperistalsis syndrome is characterized by an anatomically patent intestinal tract with normal ganglion cells, but clinical evidence of obstruction secondary to ineffective peristalsis. This syndrome is often fatal because definitive medical or surgical therapy is not available.[4,10,50,59]

The meconium plug syndrome and the small left colon syndrome seem to be specific but related entities in the spectrum of functional neonatal colonic obstruction. For clarity, they are considered separately.

Meconium Plug Syndrome

Meconium plug syndrome is a relatively common cause of functional colonic obstruction in neonates (see also Chapter 99).[17,20] Affected infants may be premature but are generally normal otherwise. It has been suggested that the syndrome results from an immature myenteric nervous system causing ineffective peristalsis[14] and excessive water absorption, thereby producing meconium plugs that obstruct the colon. The pathogenesis is unproved but is thought to be related to temporary dysmotility. The clinical presentation is the same as that for distal intestinal obstruction. The diagnosis may be established by a rectal examination, which delivers inspissated meconium and relieves symptoms. A water-soluble contrast enema is usually both diagnostic and therapeutic, but repeated enemas may be needed for resolution (Fig. 97-3). Surgical management is rarely indicated. Suction rectal biopsy is appropriate to identify the rare child with Hirschsprung's disease, although some reserve this procedure for children who remain constipated after evacuation of the plug. Likewise, this syndrome may be indistinguishable from meconium ileus of the colon. Therefore, a diagnostic sweat test may be appropriate to rule out cystic fibrosis.

Small Left Colon Syndrome

Small left colon syndrome refers to a dysfunctional, diminutive left colon that causes transient obstructive symptoms and is occasionally subject to perforation.[18,47] Approximately 40% to 50% of infants with this disorder have diabetic mothers, almost all of whom are insulin dependent. Davis and Campbell[18] reported that 50% of asymptomatic infants of diabetic mothers also have radiographic evidence of a small left colon. The obstruction is typically partial and involves the descending colon distal to the splenic flexure (Fig. 97-4). The degree of

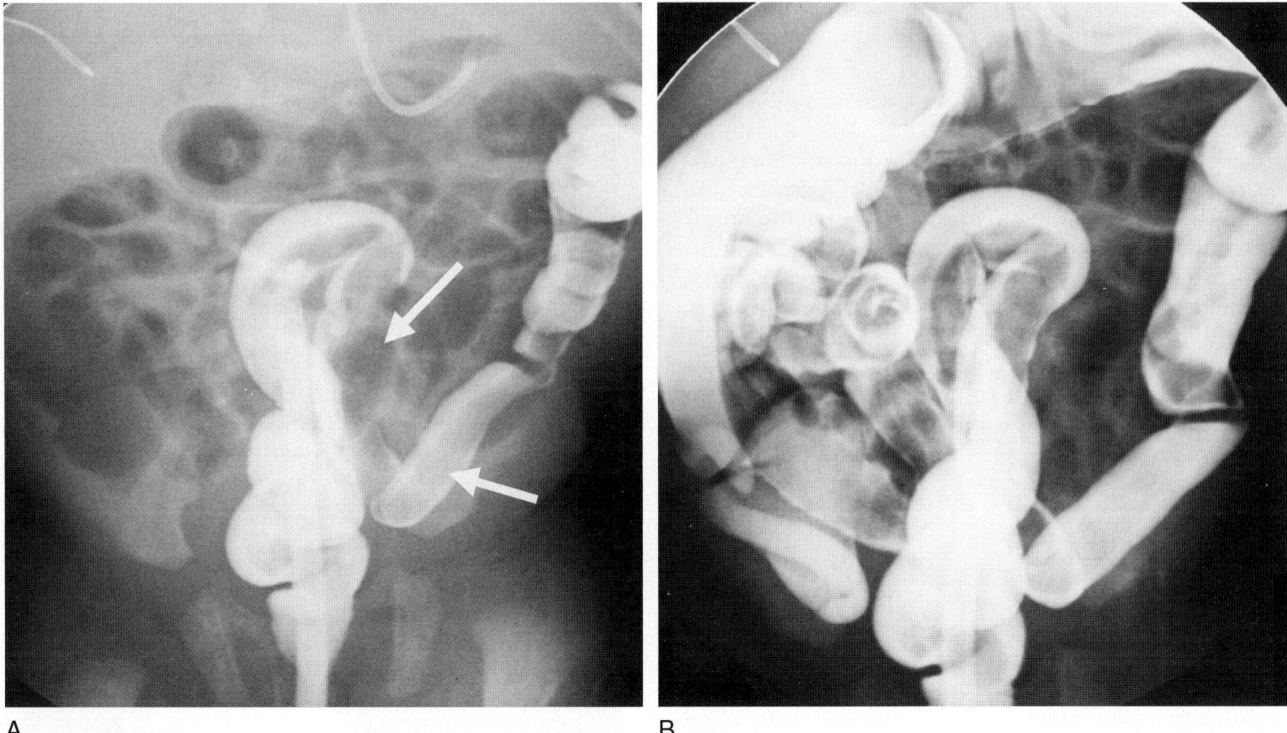

Figure 97-3 Radiographs of a normal but premature infant with the meconium plug syndrome. *A*, The initial contrast enema radiograph confirms the diagnosis by demonstrating many intraluminal filling defects (meconium plugs) throughout the colon *(arrows)*. *B*, The final contrast radiograph in this patient shows complete luminal filling of the colon. (Courtesy of J. Sty, MD.)

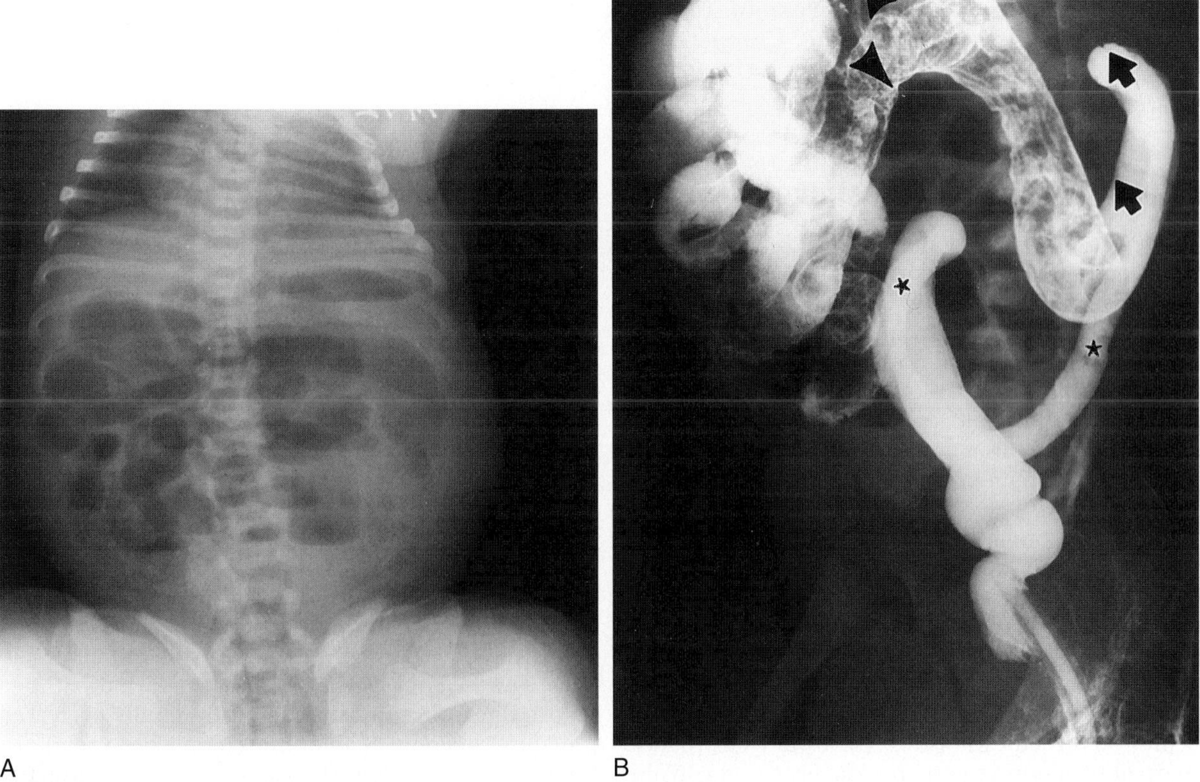

Figure 97-4 A, Plain radiograph of an infant born to a diabetic mother illustrating a distal intestinal obstruction. B, Barium enema radiograph shows typical findings of the small left colon syndrome. Note the distal microcolon *(asterisks)*, the splenic flexure transition *(arrows)*, and the dilated transverse colon proximal to the point of obstruction *(arrowheads)*. (Courtesy of D. Frush, MD.)

obstruction varies. Proximal perforation, especially of the cecum, is well described.[43] The pathogenesis is thought to be related to hypoglycemia-induced release of glucagon in the infant. For reasons that are unclear, the neonatal left colon seems to be particularly sensitive to the smooth muscle constrictive effects of glucagon and other agents.[47] The problem is transient and resolves 24 to 48 hours after birth, corresponding to normalization of the infant's endogenous insulin output. A contrast enema is diagnostic and may be therapeutic by hastening resolution of the functional obstruction. The radiographic appearance of small left colon syndrome is quite similar to that of Hirschsprung's disease because of the splenic flexure transition zone, so suction rectal biopsy is routinely performed to eliminate this possibility. It is prudent to also rule out cystic fibrosis.

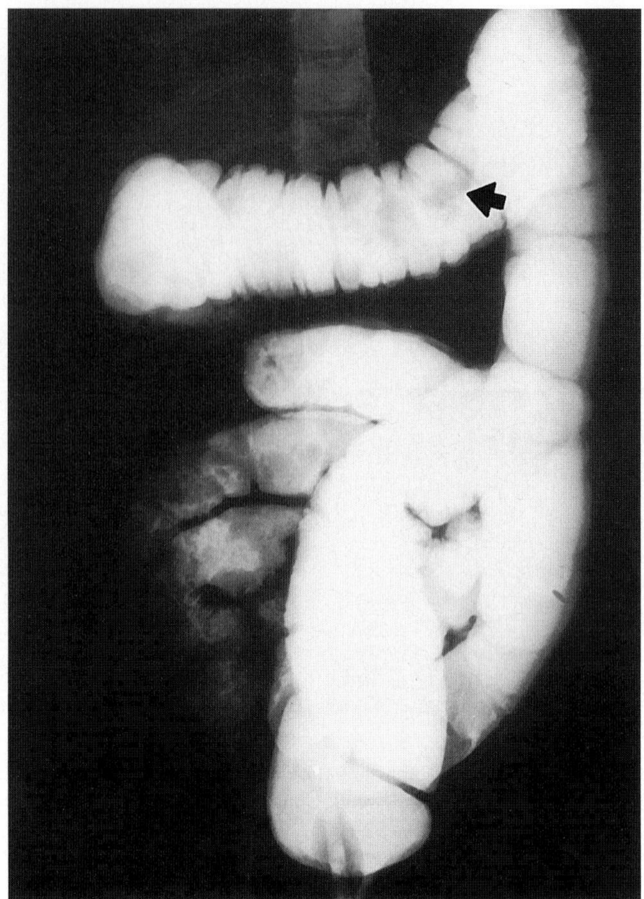

Figure 97–5 Barium enema radiograph illustrates inspissated stool in the transverse colon *(arrow)*. The patient was an adolescent patient with cystic fibrosis who had recurrent obstructive episodes that were consistent with meconium ileus.

MECONIUM ILEUS

Meconium ileus is the intestinal obstructive entity associated with cystic fibrosis and is discussed in Chapter 81. Exocrine pancreatic insufficiency and water-deficient intestinal secretions are features of cystic fibrosis that combine to create thick, viscid stools that can impact and obstruct the small intestine or colon. This is classically seen in newborns but may also be a problem in adolescents with cystic fibrosis, whose compliance with exocrine enzyme replacement therapy may be erratic. The diagnosis is often revealed by the history and plain radiography but can be confirmed by contrast enema (Fig. 97-5). The preferred treatment is colonic irrigation in an antegrade or retrograde direction and the resumption of pancreatic enzyme replacement. Chronic problems may require gastrostomy or cecal access for formal, periodic irrigation of the intestine.

MISCELLANEOUS CAUSES OF OBSTRUCTION

Several rare causes of colonic obstruction merit brief mention. Among these are cecal or sigmoid volvulus, a wide variety of rare neoplastic lesions, anomalous congenital peritoneal bands,[2] hindgut duplication,[62] and congenital segmental dilatation (ectasia) of the colon.[30] Segmental dilatation of the colon is an idiopathic problem of infants and children and presents as partial colonic obstruction. It is a focal, functional defect in which the involved segment of colon lacks peristalsis and has no taeniae coli. Because both the proximal and distal colon are functionally and anatomically normal, surgical resection is curative.[24]

Segmental volvulus of the colon may present in the sigmoid colon or the cecum (Fig. 97-6). The typical patient is a child or adolescent with a long-standing history of constipation or pseudo-obstruction. The clinical presentation is abdominal distention, nausea, and vomiting. It may be difficult to distinguish from exacerbation of pseudo-obstruction in certain patients. Cecal volvulus has been reported in two children with Cornelia de Lange's syndrome.[32] The diagnosis is established with a contrast enema. Operative intervention, usually to resect the involved segment, is typically required.

In the mid-1990s, long-segment colonic fibrosis was described in patients with cystic fibrosis. Colonic injury was determined to be caused by the ingestion of high doses of pancreatic enzymes (>19,000 units/kg per day).[24] Resection of involved bowel was required in many of these patients. Alteration of the dosage of pancreatic enzymes has decreased the occurrence of this complication in recent years.

SUMMARY

The causes of colonic obstruction in infants and children are diverse. Generally, anatomic obstruction is easily addressed by surgical resection with primary anastomosis. Functional obstructions have a varied pathogenesis, and a nonsurgical approach is generally preferred. The clinical outcome of anatomic colonic obstruction is excellent in contemporary pediatric surgical practice; the exceptions are children with concurrent illness or peritonitis with sepsis at presentation.

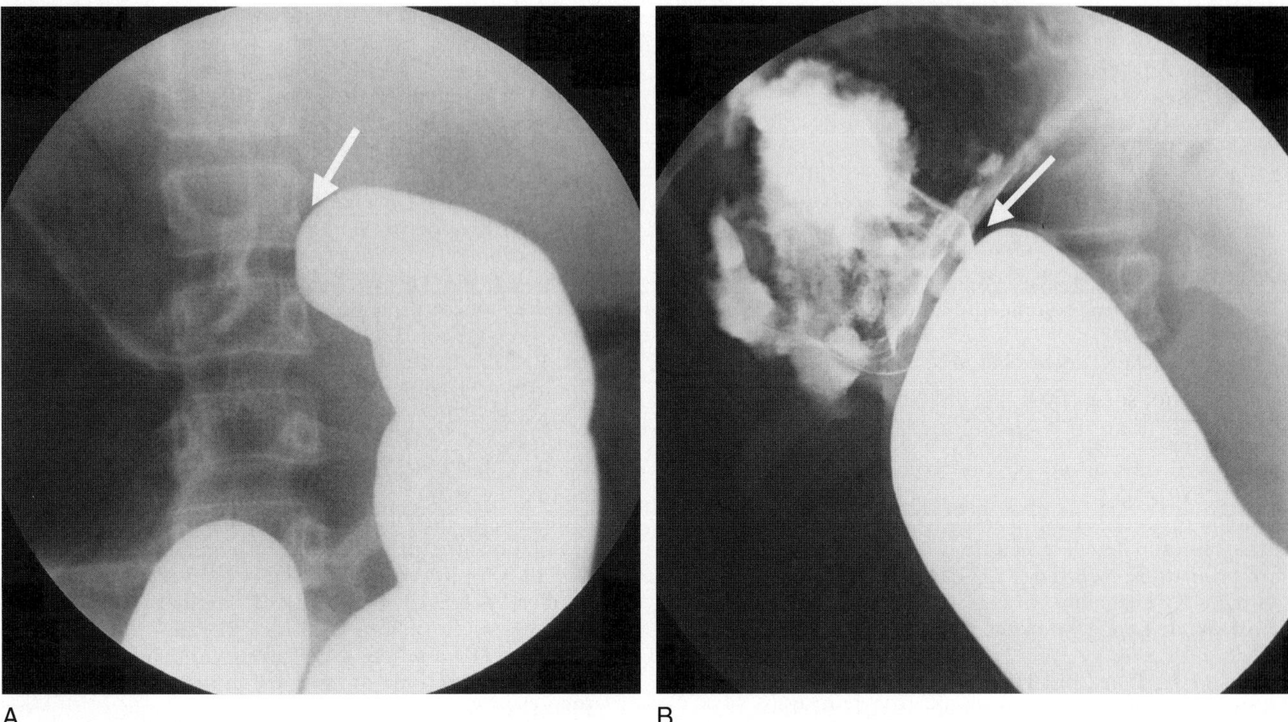

Figure 97-6 A, Contrast enema in a child with sigmoid volvulus. The *arrow* depicts the point of obstruction. B, Further administration of contrast minimally fills the colon proximal to the obstruction. (Courtesy of J. Sty, MD.)

REFERENCES

1. Abu-Jedeh HH, Methratta S, Ybasco A, et al: Congenital colonic stenosis. South Med J 2001;94:344-346.
2. Akgur FM, Tanyel FC, Buyukpamukcu N, et al: Anomalous congenital bands causing intestinal obstruction in children. J Pediatr Surg 1992;27:471-473.
3. Akgur FM, Tanyel FC, Buyukpamukcu N, et al: Colonic atresia and Hirschsprung's disease association shows further evidence for migration of enteric neurons. J Pediatr Surg 1993;28:635-636.
4. Al-Rayess M, Ambler MW: Axonal dystrophy presenting as the megacystis-microcolon-intestinal hypoperistalsis syndrome. Pediatr Pathol 1992;12:743-750.
5. Anderson N, Malpas T, Robertson R: Prenatal diagnosis of colon atresia. Pediatr Radiol 1993;23:63-64.
6. Barnard CN, Louw JF: The genesis of intestinal atresia. Minn Med 1956;39:745-753.
7. Beardmore HE, Rodgers BM, Outerbridge E: Necrotizing enterocolitis (ischemic enteropathy with the sequel of colonic atresia). Gastroenterology 1978;74:914-917.
8. Bell MJ, Ternberg JL, Askin FB, et al: Intestinal stricture in necrotizing enterocolitis. J Pediatr Surg 1976;11:319-327.
9. Benson CD, Lotfi MW, Brough AJ: Congenital atresia and stenosis of the colon. J Pediatr Surg 1968;3:253-257.
10. Berdon WE, Baker DH, Blanc WA, et al: Megacystis-microcolon-intestinal hypoperistalsis syndrome: A new cause of intestinal obstruction in the newborn. Report of radiologic findings in five newborn girls. AJR Am J Roentgenol 1976;126:957-964.
11. Bland-Sutton JD: Imperforate ileum. Am J Med Sci 1889;98:457-462.
12. Boles ET Jr, Vassy LE, Ralston M: Atresia of the colon. J Pediatr Surg 1976;11:69-75.
13. Brown RA, Rode H, Millar AJ, et al: Colorectal carcinoma in children. J Pediatr Surg 1992;27:919-921.
14. Bughaighis AG, Emery JL: Functional obstruction of the intestine due to neurological immaturity. Prog Pediatr Surg 1971;3:37-52.
15. Byrne WJ, Cipel L, Euler AR, et al: Chronic idiopathic intestinal pseudo-obstruction syndrome in children—clinical characteristics and prognosis. J Pediatr Surg 1977;90:585-589.
16. Chabalko JJ, Fraumeni JF Jr: Colorectal cancer in children: Epidemiologic aspects. Dis Colon Rectum 1975;18:1-3.
17. Clatworthy HW Jr, Howard WHR, Lloyd JR: The meconium plug syndrome. Surgery 1956;39:131-142.
18. Davis WS, Campbell JB: Neonatal small left colon syndrome: Occurrence in asymptomatic infants of diabetic mothers. Am J Dis Child 1975;129:1024-1027.
19. DellaVecchia LK, Grosfeld JL, West KW, et al: Intestinal atresia and stenosis: A 25-year experience with 277 cases. Arch Surg 1998;133:490-496.
20. Ellis DG, Clatworthy HW Jr: The meconium plug syndrome revisited. J Pediatr Surg 1966;1:54-61.
21. Erskine JM: Colonic stenosis in the newborn: The possible thromboembolic etiology of intestinal stenosis and atresia. J Pediatr Surg 1970;5:321-333.
22. Evans CW: Atresias of the gastrointestinal tract. Surg Gynecol Obstet 1951;92:1-8.
23. Fishman SJ, Islam S, Buonoma C, et al: Nonfixation of an atretic colon predicts Hirschsprung's disease. J Pediatr Surg 2003;36:202-204.
24. FitzSimmons SC, Burkhart GA, Borowitz D, et al: High-dose pancreatic-enzyme supplements and fibrosing

colonopathy in children with cystic fibrosis. N Engl J Med 1997;336:1283-1289.
25. Franken EA Jr (ed): Gastrointestinal Imaging in Pediatrics, 2nd ed. New York, Harper & Row, 1982.
26. Freeman NV: Congenital atresia and stenosis of the colon. Br J Surg 1966;53:595-599.
27. Gaub OC: Congenital stenosis and atresia of the intestinal tract above the rectum, with a report of an operated case of atresia of the sigmoid in an infant. Trans Am Surg Assoc 1922;40:582.
28. Gmora S, Poenau, D, Tsai E: Neostigmine for the treatment of pediatric acute colonic pseudoobstruction. J Pediatr Surg 2002;37:E28.
29. Gobet R, Sacher P, Schwobel MG: Surgical procedures in colonic strictures after necrotizing enterocolitis. Acta Paediatr Suppl 1994;396:77-79.
30. Helikson MA, Shapiro MB, Garfinkel DJ, et al: Congenital segmental dilatation of the colon. J Pediatr Surg 1982;17:201-202.
31. Hochberg FH, Dasilva AB, Galdabini J, et al: Gastrointestinal involvement in von Recklinghausen's neurofibromatosis. Neurology 1974;24:1144-1151.
32. Husain K, Fitzgerald P, Lau G: Cecal volvulus in the Cornelia de Lange syndrome. J Pediatr Surg 1994;29:1245-1247.
33. Johnson JF, Dean BL: Hirschsprung's disease coexisting with colonic atresia. Pediatr Radiol 1981;11:97-98.
34. Khan AZ, George K, Defriend DJ: Non-steroidal anti-inflammatory drug-induced colonic stenosis: An unusual cause of a right-sided colonic mass: Report of a case. Dis Colon Rectum 2003;46:403-405.
35. Kim PCW, Superina RA, Ein S: Colonic atresia combined with Hirschsprung's disease: A diagnostic and therapeutic challenge. J Pediatr Surg 1995;30:1216-1217.
36. LaQuaglia MP, Heller G, Filippa DA, et al: Prognostic factors and outcome in patients 21 years and under with colorectal carcinoma. J Pediatr Surg 1992;27:1085-1089.
37. Louw JH: Jejunoileal atresia and stenosis. J Pediatr Surg 1966;1:8-23.
38. Loveland J, Bowley DMG, Beavon IR, et al: Bowel obstruction in an infant with AIDS. Arch Dis Child 2003;88: 825-826.
39. Masunaga K, Masaki R, Endo A, et al: Colonic stenosis after severe methicillin-resistant *Staphylococcus aureus* enterocolitis in a newborn. Pediatr Infect Dis J 1999;18:169-171.
40. Mayo CW, Pagtalunan RJG: Malignancy of the colon and rectum in patients under 30 years of age. Surgery 1963;53:711-718.
41. Meier-Ruge WA, Schmidt PC, Stoss F: Intestinal neuronal dysplasia and its morphometric evidences. Pediatr Surg Int 1995;10:447-450.
42. Mizuno M, Kato T, Hebiguchi T, et al: Congenital membranous colonic stenosis—case report of an extremely rare anomaly. J Pediatr Surg 2003;38:E13-E15.
43. Nixon GW, Condon VR, Stewart DR: Intestinal perforation as a complication of the neonatal small left colon syndrome. Am J Roentgenol Rad Ther Nuclear Med 1975;125:75-80.
44. Peck DA, Lynn HB, Harris LE: Congenital atresia and stenosis of the colon. Arch Surg 1963;87:428-439.
45. Peer A, Klin B, Vinograd I: Balloon catheter dilatation of focal colonic strictures following necrotizing enterocolitis. Cardiovasc Intervent Radiol 1993;16:248-250.
46. Philippart AI: Atresia, stenosis, and other obstructions of the colon. In Welch KJ, et al (eds): Pediatric Surgery, 4th ed. Chicago, Year Book Medical Publishers, 1986.
47. Philippart AI, Reed JO, Georgeson KE: Neonatal small left colon syndrome: Intramural not intraluminal obstruction. J Pediatr Surg 1975;10:733-740.
48. Potts WJ: Congenital atresia of intestine and colon. Surg Gynecol Obstet 1947;85:14-18.
49. Powell RW, Raffensperger JG: Congenital colonic atresia. J Pediatr Surg 1982;17:166-170.
50. Puri P, Lake BD, Gorman F, et al: Megacystis-microcolon-intestinal hypoperistalsis syndrome: A visceral myopathy. J Pediatr Surg 1983;8:64-69.
51. Rabinowitz JG, Wolf BS, Feller MR, et al: Colonic changes following necrotizing enterocolitis in the newborn. AJR Am J Roentgenol 1968;103:359-364.
52. Rao BN, Pratt CB, Fleming ID, et al: Colon carcinoma in children and adolescents: A review of 30 cases. Cancer 1985;55:1322-1326.
53. Riccardi VM: Von Recklinghausen neurofibromatosis. N Engl J Med 1981;305:1617-1627.
54. Santulli TV, Blanc WA: Congenital atresia of the intestine: Pathogenesis and treatment. Ann Surg 1961;154:939-948.
55. Sax EJ: Pediatric case of the day: Congenital colonic stenosis. AJR Am J Roentgenol 1991;156:1315-1317.
56. Schiller M, Aviad I, Freund H: Congenital colonic atresia and stenosis. Am J Surg 1979;138:721-724.
57. Schuffler MD, Deitch EA: Chronic idiopathic intestinal pseudo-obstruction: A surgical approach. Ann Surg 1980;192:752-761.
58. Shah R, Woolley M: Gastroschisis and intestinal atresia. J Pediatr Surg 1991;26:788-790.
59. Shono T, Suita S, Taguchi T, Nagasaki A: Manometric evaluation of gastrointestinal motility in a case of megacystis-microcolon-intestinal hypoperistalsis syndrome (MMIHS). Eur J Pediatr Surg 1992;1:52-54.
60. Srikanth MS, Ford EG, Isaacs H Jr, et al: Megacystis microcolon intestinal hypoperistalsis syndrome: Late sequelae and possible pathogenesis. J Pediatr Surg 1993;28:957-959.
61. Staple TW, McAlister WH, Anderson MS: Plexiform neurofibromatosis of the colon simulating Hirschsprung's disease. Am J Roentgenol Rad Ther Nuclear Med 1964; 91:840-845.
62. Stringer MD, Spitz L, Abel R, et al: Management of alimentary tract duplication in children. Br J Surg 1995;82:74-78.
63. Sugarbaker PH, Gunderson LL, Wittes RE: Colorectal cancer. In DeVita VT Jr, Hellman S, Rosenberg S (eds): Cancer: Principles and Practice of Oncology. Philadelphia, JB Lippincott, 1985.
64. Syed M, Shanks RD: Atresia coli inherited in Holstein cattle. J Dairy Sci 1992;75:1105-1111.
65. Szavay PO, Schiephake H, Hubert O, Gluer S: Colon atresia, facial hemiaplasia and anophthalmia: A case report. J Pediatr Surg 2002;37:1498-1500.
66. Tan X, Hsueh W, Gonzalez-Crussi F: Cellular localization of tumor necrosis factor (TNF)-α transcripts in normal bowel and in necrotizing enterocolitis. Am J Pathol 1993;142:1858-1865.
67. Tapper D, Tarr P, Avener E, et al: Lessons learned in the management of hemolytic uremic syndrome in children. J Pediatr Surg 1995;30:158-163.
68. Umpleby HC, Williamson RCN: Carcinoma of the large bowel in the first four decades. Br J Surg 1984;71:272-277.
69. Webb CH, Wangensteen OH: Congenital intestinal atresia. Am J Dis Child 1932;14:262-284.
70. Williams MD, Burrington JD: Hirschsprung's disease complicating colon atresia. J Pediatr Surg 1993;28:637-639.

Chapter 98

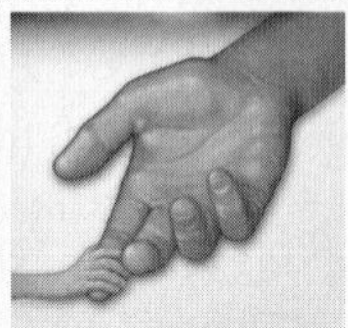

Appendicitis

James C. Y. Dunn

Appendicitis remains the most common acute surgical condition of the abdomen and is the most commonly misdiagnosed. Many aspects of its treatment remain controversial, giving rise to a voluminous literature and an enduring interest on the part of pediatric surgeons. The geographic variation in the incidence of appendicitis is widespread. In the United States, more than 70,000 children are diagnosed with appendicitis annually, or approximately 1 per 1000 children per year. This accounted for an estimated 254,000 hospital days and 680 million dollars of charges in 1997.[65] Appendicitis occurs less frequently in Third World countries.[96] Over the past few decades, the worldwide incidence has steadily decreased.[9,75,96,160]

HISTORY

The first medical references to a disease similar to appendicitis appeared approximately 500 years ago.[99] Perityphlitis was used to describe this pathologic process. The cecum was believed to be the source of this disease until Melier proposed the inflammation of the appendix to be the cause of the disease in 1827. In 1886, Fitz[54] conclusively demonstrated that perityphlitis began with inflammation of the appendix and coined the term *appendicitis.*

The first successful appendectomy was credited to Amyand, who drained a scrotal abscess and removed a perforated appendix through a scrotal incision in 1735. Morton is credited with performing the first deliberate appendectomy for a perforated appendix in the United States in 1887.[99,132] In 1889, McBurney[95] reported his treatment of appendicitis with appendectomy before rupture and in so doing described "the seat of greatest pain…has been very exactly between an inch and a half and two inches from the anterior spinous process of the ilium on a straight line drawn from the process to the umbilicus." From then on, this location was known as McBurney's point. Modern surgical care and antibiotic therapy have made this once frequently fatal disease rarely so today. Appendicitis remains, however, a continuing source of morbidity in children and adolescents.[122]

EMBRYOLOGY AND ANATOMY

During embryogenesis, the appendix first becomes visible during the eighth week of gestation as a continuation of the inferior tip of the cecum.[28,148] The appendix rotates to its final position on the posteromedial aspect of the cecum, about 2 cm below the ileocecal valve, during late childhood. The variability in this rotation leads to multiple possible final positions of the appendix. The appendix is intraperitoneal in 95% of cases, but the exact location varies widely.[172] In 30% of cases, the tip of the appendix is in the pelvis, in 65% it is behind the cecum, and in 5% it is truly extraperitoneal in the retrocolic or retrocecal position. In cases of malrotation or situs inversus, the malpositioned appendix may give rise to signs of inflammation in unusual locations.

The appendix averages 8 cm in length but can vary from 0.3 to 33 cm. The diameter of the appendix ranges from 5 to 10 mm. Its blood supply is the appendiceal branch of the ileocolic artery, which passes behind the terminal ileum. The base of the appendix arises at the junction of the three taeniae coli, a useful landmark in locating an elusive appendix. Its colonic epithelium and circular and longitudinal muscle layers are contiguous with the cecal layers. A few submucosal lymph follicles are present at birth. These increase to approximately 200 by age 12 and reduce abruptly after the age of 30, with only a trace remaining after age 60.

Suppression of cecal development results in appendicular hypoplasia or agenesis. Appendiceal duplication has a reported incidence of 4 in 100,000.[20,33] The duplicated appendix may be partial (bifid appendix) or full, and they may have separate or common orifices in the cecum, which may also be duplicated.

The function of the appendix is unknown. Primates have an appendix but most mammals do not. Curiously rabbits do have an appendix, and it is believed to be an important site for the immunologic development of B cells.[153]

SPECTRUM OF DISEASE

The lifetime risk for appendicitis is 9% for men and 7% for women.[1] About one third of patients with appendicitis are younger than 18 years of age. Appendicitis occurs more commonly in whites and during the summer in the United States. The peak incidence occurs between ages 11 and 12. Although the disorder is uncommon in infants, this group has a disproportionate number of complications because of delays in diagnosis. Perforation may also be the end result of another disease process, as is seen in neonates with Hirschsprung's disease.[90] Regardless of where and with what frequency it occurs, appendicitis remains an enigma—a simple disease that, despite our best efforts, remains the most commonly misdiagnosed surgical emergency. Although the diagnosis and treatment have improved, appendicitis continues to cause significant morbidity and still remains, although rarely, a cause of death.[111,125]

Many terms have been used to describe the varying stages of appendicitis, including *acute appendicitis, suppurative appendicitis, gangrenous appendicitis,* and *perforated appendicitis.* These distinctions are vague, and only the clinically relevant distinction of simple and complicated appendicitis should be made. Because gangrenous appendicitis represents dead intestine that functionally acts as a perforation, we will use complicated appendicitis to describe both gangrenous and perforated appendicitis.

The existence of chronic or recurrent cases of appendicitis has been debated for decades. Recent literature contends that they do exist and should be considered in the differential diagnosis of recurrent lower abdominal pain.[93,150] Inflammation of the appendix does not inevitably lead to perforation, because spontaneous resolution does occur.[36,68] Recognition of this may contribute to the decreasing number of appendectomies.[75,160]

PRESENTATION

Traditional teaching is that appendicitis evolves as a continuum from simple inflammation to perforation, typically occurring after 24 to 36 hours of symptoms with subsequent abscess formation occurring over a period of 2 to 3 days.[24,143] Nevertheless the variability of the clinical presentation of appendicitis leads to laparotomies that do not reveal an inflamed appendix. Clinical experience and advances in imaging methods have improved the diagnostic accuracy but are not foolproof. The clinical presentation of appendicitis can be understood in terms of its pathophysiology.

Appendicitis results from luminal obstruction followed by infection. This process was first described by van Zwalenberg[169] in 1905 and experimentally confirmed by Wangensteen[173] in 1939. Wangensteen showed that the human appendix continues to secrete mucus even when intraluminal pressures exceed 93 mm Hg. Although it is clear that luminal obstruction causes appendicitis, the cause of the obstruction is not always clear. Inspissated and sometimes calcified fecal matter, known as a fecalith, often plays a role.[114] Fecaliths can be surgically found in approximately 20% of children with acute appendicitis and are reported in 30% to 40% of children with perforated appendicitis.[40,159] The presence of fecaliths can often be documented radiographically. Hyperplasia of appendiceal lymphoid follicles frequently causes luminal obstruction, and the incidence of appendicitis closely parallels the amount of lymphoid tissue present.[27] Causes of local or generalized reaction of lymphatic tissue, such as *Yersinia, Salmonella,* and *Shigella,*[11,129,136,139] can lead to luminal obstruction of the appendix, as can parasitic infestations by *Entamoeba, Strongyloides, Enterobius vermicularis, Schistosoma,* or *Ascaris* species.[2,108,146] Enteric and systemic viral infections, such as measles, chickenpox, and cytomegalovirus, may also cause appendicitis.[81,167] Patients with cystic fibrosis have an increased incidence of appendicitis, which presumably results from alterations in the mucus-secreting glands.[38,115] Carcinoid tumors can obstruct the appendix, especially when they are located in the proximal third. Foreign bodies, such as pins, vegetable seeds, and cherry stones, have been implicated as causes of appendicitis for more than 200 years. Trauma also has been reported as a cause,[69] as has psychological stress[39] and heredity.[8]

Initially the patient may describe mild gastrointestinal symptoms before the onset of pain, such as decreased appetite, indigestion, or subtle changes in bowel habits. Anorexia is a helpful sign, particularly in children, because a hungry child rarely has appendicitis. Any severe gastrointestinal symptoms before the onset of pain, however, should suggest an alternative diagnosis. Distention of the appendix results in activation of its visceral pain fibers. Typical early visceral pain is nonspecific in the periumbilical region. This initial pain is poorly localized as a deep, dull pain in the T10 dermatome. The continued distention of the appendiceal wall elicits nausea and vomiting, which typically follows the onset of pain within a few hours. Nausea is common, but vomiting is typically not severe. The appearance of these symptoms before the onset of pain casts doubt on the diagnosis.

The obstructed appendix is a perfect breeding ground for trapped bacteria. As intraluminal pressure increases, lymphatic drainage is inhibited, leading to further edema and swelling. Finally, the increase in pressure causes venous obstruction, which leads to tissue ischemia, infarction, and gangrene. Bacterial invasion of the wall of the appendix then occurs. Fever, tachycardia, and leukocytosis develop as a consequence of mediators released by ischemic tissues, white blood cells, and bacteria. When the inflammatory exudate from the appendiceal wall contacts the parietal peritoneum, somatic pain fibers are triggered and the pain localizes near the appendiceal site, most typically at McBurney's point. Pain occasionally occurs only in the right lower quadrant without the early visceral component. With a retrocecal or pelvic appendix, this somatic pain is often delayed in onset because the inflammatory exudate does not contact the parietal peritoneum until rupture occurs and infection spreads. Pain of a retrocecal appendix may be in the flank or back. A pelvic appendix resting near the ureter or testicular vessels can cause urinary frequency, testicular pain, or both. Inflammation of the ureter or bladder by an inflamed appendix can also lead to pain on micturition or the deceptive pain of a distended bladder secondary to urinary retention.

Further breakdown of the appendiceal wall leads to perforation with spillage of infected intraluminal contents with localized abscess formation or generalized peritonitis. This process depends on the rapidity of progression to perforation and on the patient's ability to mount a response and contain the spilled contents of the appendix. Signs of perforated appendicitis include a temperature higher than 38.6°C (101.5°F), leukocyte count greater than 14,000/mm^3,[137] and the presence of more generalized peritoneal signs. Other reported risk factors include the male sex, extremes of age, and such anatomic factors as a retrocecal position of the appendix.[119,143] However, perforated and nonperforated appendicitis may be entirely separate entities.[9] Spontaneous resolution of appendicitis does occur. Patients may be asymptomatic before perforation, and symptoms may be present for longer than 48 hours without perforation. In general, however, the longer duration of symptoms is associated with a greater risk for perforation. Constipation is unusual, but the sensation of rectal fullness or tenesmus is common. Diarrhea occurs more frequently in children than in adults and can result in a misdiagnosis of gastroenteritis. Diarrhea is typically of short duration and often results from irritation of the terminal ileum or cecum; however, it may indicate a pelvic abscess.

Younger children typically present with complicated appendicitis due to their inability to give an accurate history and physicians' low index of suspicion that leads to misdiagnosis.[64,67,84] The most frequent presenting symptom in preschool-aged children is vomiting, followed by fever and abdominal pain.[5] Perforation is almost always the finding at laparotomy, and the patient may have associated small bowel obstruction secondary to extensive inflammation in the terminal ileum and cecum.

DIAGNOSIS

Physical Examination

As with most disease processes, much can be learned before the patient is touched. Children with appendicitis usually lie in bed with minimal movement. A squirming, screaming child rarely has appendicitis. An exception to this is the child with retrocecal appendicitis and subsequent irritation of the ureter presenting with pain similar to renal colic. Older children may limp or flex the trunk, whereas infants may flex the right leg over the abdomen. A recall of localized pain elicited by bumps in the road on the ride to the hospital is helpful.

After obtaining the clinical history, I usually begin by asking the child to point with one finger to the location of the abdominal pain. With the knees bent to relax the abdominal muscles, gentle palpation of the abdomen should begin at a point away from the location of perceived pain. Palpating the abdomen in an area remote from the site of pain may elicit tenderness in the right lower quadrant (Rovsing's sign of referred pain), indicating peritoneal irritation. Younger children may be more cooperative if their hand or the stethoscope is used for palpation. The stethoscope can have several roles in the evaluation of a patient who potentially has appendicitis, the least important of which is auscultation. Although patients often have diminished or absent bowel sounds, this is not uniform and auscultation of the abdomen is of little benefit. However, auscultation of the chest to examine for lower respiratory infection is useful, because right lower lobe pneumonia can mimic appendicitis. Cutaneous hyperesthesia, a sensation derived from the T10 to L1 nerve roots, is often an early although inconsistent sign of appendicitis. Lightly touching the patient with the stethoscope creates this uncomfortable sensation.

Localized tenderness is essential for diagnosis and is noted either on palpation or percussion. Tenderness can be mild and even masked by more generalized abdominal pain, especially during initial stages. McBurney's point is the most common location. Retrocecal appendicitis may be detected by tenderness midway between the 12th rib and the posterior superior iliac spine. Pelvic appendicitis produces rectal tenderness. A child with malrotation will have localized tenderness that corresponds to the position of the exudative drainage from the inflamed appendix.

As the disease progresses to perforation, peritonitis ensues. Again, the pattern of pain depends on the location of the appendix. Perforation may result in temporary relief of symptoms as the pain of the distended viscus is relieved. Initially, peritonitis is reflected as local muscular rigidity. This progresses from simple involuntary guarding to generalized rigidity of the abdomen. Other signs include rigidity of the psoas muscle (demonstrated by right hip extension or raising the straight leg against resistance) or of the obturator muscle (demonstrated by passive internal rotation of the right thigh), both of which indicate irritation of these muscles due to retrocecal appendicitis. Other tests of peritoneal inflammation, such as rebound tenderness, are seldom needed for diagnosis and cause unnecessary discomfort.

The routine use of rectal examination in the diagnosis of appendicitis has been questioned.[23,43,47] Pain during this examination is nonspecific for appendicitis. If other signs point to appendicitis, the rectal examination is unnecessary. However, it may be a helpful diagnostic maneuver in questionable cases, such as when a pelvic appendix or abscess is suspected or when uterine or adnexal pathologic conditions are being considered.

If appendicitis is allowed to progress, either diffuse peritonitis and shock will occur or the infection will become isolated and an abscess will be created. Diffuse peritonitis is more common in infants, probably because of the absence of omental fat. Older children and teenagers are more likely to have an organized abscess. The physical examination in cases of an organized abscess reveals a boggy, tender mass over the abscess.

A frequently unreported but critical aspect of the evaluation is serial examinations done by the same person. The safety and efficacy of serial observation was first reported by White and associates in 1975[176] and has since been reinforced by other studies. Surana and colleagues[161] reported a prospective study showing no increase in morbidity with appendectomy after active observation in a hospital compared with urgent appendectomy. When the diagnosis is unclear, serial abdominal examinations permit the physician to decrease the number of unnecessary laparotomies without increased risk to the patient.

Laboratory Studies

Much has been discussed concerning the laboratory findings of appendicitis. Total leukocyte and neutrophil counts have been extensively investigated.[21,45,72] The sensitivity of an elevated leukocyte count ranges from 52% to 96% and that of a left-shifted neutrophil count from 39% to 96%. The latter is of better diagnostic value, but misinterpretation of the values is still very common. Normal leukocyte count occurs in 5% of patients with appendicitis. Greater specificity and sensitivity have been reported using a neutrophil-lymphocyte ratio greater than 3.5.[61]

Positive values for C-reactive protein and the erythrocyte sedimentation rate are useful,[123] but negative values do not necessarily rule out the disorder, thereby making measurement of these values of limited clinical value. Combinations of all these tests may be the most helpful. Dueholm[46] found that a normal total leukocyte count, neutrophil percentage, and C-reactive protein level correctly ruled out appendicitis with 100% accuracy. However, abnormal values are not necessarily diagnostic of the disorder.

In the majority of children with suspected appendicitis, the combination of clinical history, physical findings, and laboratory studies should provide sufficient data for making the diagnosis. Nevertheless, misdiagnosis leading to negative appendectomy ranging from 10% to 30% has been reported.[138] An appendicitis score based on weighing eight clinical factors (localized right lower quadrant tenderness, leukocytosis, pain migration, left shift, fever, nausea/vomiting, anorexia, peritoneal irritation) was proposed to improve the diagnostic accuracy.[6,76] In prospective evaluations of children with acute abdominal pain, the sensitivity of the scoring system ranged from 76% to 100%, and its specificity ranged from 79% to 87%.[88,138] In cases where the diagnosis is equivocal, serial observation followed by imaging would be warranted.

Radiologic Studies

Radiographic and radiopharmaceutical studies have variable success in improving diagnostic accuracy. Plain radiography can be helpful. Fecaliths are present in 10% to 20% of patients and are an indication for surgery even when symptoms are mild. An abnormal gas pattern in the right lower quadrant, lumbar scoliosis away from the right lower quadrant, and obliteration of the psoas shadow or fat stripe on the right are also helpful. A chest radiograph to rule out pneumonia may be indicated.

A barium enema contrast radiograph may show absent or incomplete filling of the appendix, irregularities of the appendiceal lumen, and an extrinsic mass effect on the cecum or terminal ileum. The sensitivity and specificity of this technique are low,[140] and it is best used in the diagnosis of nonspecific abdominal pain.

Tagged leukocyte scans have been used with 87% sensitivity and 92% specificity, but they take 3 to 5 hours to perform.[51] A study restricted to the pediatric population showed that technetium-99m hexamethylpropylene amine oxime leukocyte scintigraphy was not accurate or reliable as a diagnostic tool in children with an initial clinical presentation that suggests appendicitis.[74]

In skilled hands, ultrasonography has proved to be an effective diagnostic aid. A prospective study showed that ultrasonography was more accurate than the surgeon's initial clinical impression.[171] Most studies demonstrate a sensitivity greater than 85% and a specificity greater than 90%.[178] Demonstration of a noncompressible appendix that is 7 mm or larger in anteroposterior diameter is the primary criterion for the diagnosis. The presence of an appendicolith is helpful. Such techniques as graded compression, self-localization,[32] and transvaginal, or transrectal ultrasound approaches[103] have also improved results.

In the past decade, computed tomography (CT) has become more widely used in the diagnosis of appendicitis.[19,29,89,157] The findings of an enlarged appendix (>6 mm), appendiceal wall thickening (>1 mm), periappendiceal fat stranding, and appendiceal wall enhancement are useful diagnostic criteria.[34,66] The sensitivity of CT scans is over 90%, and its specificity is over 80%.[14] Comparisons of ultrasonography and CT have shown that the latter is more sensitive whereas the former is more specific.[19,73,178] These two imaging modalities, however, should be employed only if the diagnosis is uncertain. In a protocol that evaluated children with equivocal clinical findings for appendicitis, the combination of pelvic ultrasound followed by limited CT with rectal contrast, if necessary, yielded a sensitivity of 94% and a specificity of 94%.[59] The same protocol reduced the negative appendectomy rate from 12% to 6% at the same institution during the study period but performed imaging in almost 80% of children with suspected appendicitis. The perceived improved diagnostic accuracy led to a dramatic increase in the number of CT scans performed in the pediatric population,[25,60,124] even though there is no good evidence that supports the routine use of CT in the diagnosis of appendicitis.[91] In addition to the hospital resource utilization and the delay in surgical care, the potential cancer risk associated with ionizing radiation from CT should be considered.[25]

These diagnostic methods are only necessary if the diagnosis is unclear. The routine use of barium enema contrast radiography, CT, or ultrasonography does not substantially affect the diagnosis or clinical course of patients with acute appendicitis.[140] Furthermore, although some studies report superior results compared with a single surgical physical examination, serial examination by the same examiner is the safest and most accurate diagnostic tool.[12] In a recent retrospective report, a pediatric surgical evaluation combined with the selective use of body imaging (<40% of children with suspected appendicitis) was highly sensitive (99%) and specific (92%) and was associated with a low negative appendectomy rate (5%).[79]

Differential Diagnoses

Acute appendicitis can mimic virtually any intra-abdominal process.[37] The differential diagnosis of appendicitis is listed in Table 98-1. Consideration of these other disease processes before surgery is as important as it is to examine for them carefully when the patient is under anesthesia and during surgery in the case of a normal appendix.

The clinical diagnosis of appendicitis is challenging because many symptoms of appendicitis are nonspecific and the presentations can be variable. Acute gastroenteritis is a common cause of abdominal pain in children. It is usually due to a viral illness and is self-limited. The symptoms include watery diarrhea, crampy abdominal pain, fever, nausea, and vomiting. Constipation is another common pediatric problem and may cause abdominal pain, nausea, and vomiting. Pain is usually persistent but is not progressive. History and a plain radiograph will suggest the diagnosis. Urinary tract infection will also cause fever, nausea, and vomiting. A urinalysis should be obtained if urinary symptoms are present.

Despite advances in diagnostic imaging, laparotomy done for appendicitis does not always reveal an inflamed appendix. Formerly accepted rates of laparotomy that did not reveal appendicitis range from 15% to 40%.[143] These rates are not supported by the recent literature that report negative appendectomy rates to be less than 10%.[22,49,110,128] When a normal appendix is encountered, most surgeons recommend that it be removed to allow for pathologic examination and to avoid potential confusion if the patient experiences right lower quadrant pain in the future. An exploration of the right lower quadrant should be performed to look for other causes of the symptoms. The terminal ileum may demonstrate mesenteric adenitis—enlarged lymph nodes in the ileal mesentery that may be secondary to an upper respiratory infection. These patients may have abdominal pain, fever, and nausea, but their tenderness is not as well localized as that in appendicitis. Lymphocytosis may be noted on the blood cell count differential. A search for Meckel's diverticulum should be done, but it rarely causes pain. Painless bleeding and obstruction are the more common presenting symptoms. If the patient has Crohn's disease, the appendix should not be removed if it or the cecum is involved in the disease process because removal is associated with a high incidence of subsequent fistula formation.[177]

The diagnostic accuracy for appendicitis is lowest among young women because of the variety of gynecologic conditions that can cause low abdominal pain. Ectopic pregnancy should be considered in teenage girls with low abdominal pain. They may present with vaginal bleeding, amenorrhea, dizziness, nausea and vomiting. Rupture of ovarian cysts and ovarian torsion may also present as low abdominal pain. Sexually active girls with pelvic inflammatory disease may present with low abdominal pain, vaginal discharge, and adnexal enlargement. Most will have cervical motion tenderness and will respond to antibiotics. Operative intervention may be indicated for those who do not respond or have persistent abscess.

Carcinoid tumors are present in less than 1% of patients undergoing appendectomy.[63] Most appendiceal carcinoid tumors lack the serotonin-containing cells that are typical of midgut carcinoid tumors so they are rarely symptomatic and typically present incidentally at appendectomy.[135] Most are benign, and simple appendectomy is curative.[102,121] Controversy surrounds the proper surgical management of potentially malignant carcinoid tumors. The consensus is that carcinoid tumors larger than 2 cm in diameter, those that have obviously metastasized, and those located at the base of the appendix require right hemicolectomy,[118,135] whereas those that are smaller than 1 cm in diameter and have not metastasized at the time of diagnosis are treated by appendectomy alone. Treatment of tumors that are 1 to 2 cm in diameter remains controversial. Moertel and coworkers[102] believe that a conservative surgical procedure is all that is required regardless of tumor size or location as long as it has not metastasized.

TABLE 98-1 Differential Diagnosis of Acute Appendicitis

Appendix	**Urinary Tract**
Appendiceal tumor, carcinoid tumor	Hydronephrosis
Appendiceal mucocele	Pyelonephritis
Crohn's disease	Ureteral or renal calculus
	Wilms' tumor
Cecum and Colon	**Uterus, Ovary**
Cecal carcinoma	Ectopic pregnancy
Diverticulitis	Ovarian torsion
Crohn's disease	Ruptured ovarian cyst
Intestinal obstruction	Salpingitis
Stercoral ulcer	Tubo-ovarian abscess
Typhlitis (leukemic, amebic)	
	Other
Hepatobiliary	Cytomegalovirus infection
Cholecystitis	Diabetic ketoacidosis
Hepatitis	Henoch-Schönlein purpura
Cholangitis	Kawasaki disease
	Burkitt's lymphoma
	Omental torsion
Small Intestine	Rectus sheath hematoma
Adenitis	Pancreatitis
Duodenal ulcer	Parasitic infection
Gastroenteritis	Pleuritis
Intestinal obstruction	Pneumonia
Intussusception	Porphyria
Meckel's diverticulitis	Psoas abscess
Tuberculosis	Sickle cell disease
Typhoid (ulcer perforation)	Torsion of appendix epiploica

TREATMENT

Although all surgeons would agree that the treatment for appendicitis is appendectomy, the details of the perioperative management vary considerably.[107] The optimal care in many areas is unknown. For example, surgical techniques such as the use of drains, the necessity of peritoneal irrigation, the handling of the appendiceal stump, and the closure of the incision continued to be debated. The use of ultrasonography and CT for diagnosis and guided drainage for management of abscesses are affecting the need for early surgery. The need for interval appendectomy after initial nonoperative management of an appendiceal phlegmon has been questioned. The choice of antibiotics and the length of its use vary considerably from surgeon to surgeon.

Antibiotics

The use of antibiotics for the treatment of appendicitis is clearly beneficial.[7] Intraoperative cultures have not been shown to alter the treatment outcome.[97,104] The best regimen and duration of antibiotics use is a subject of continued controversy. In a recent survey among pediatric surgeons, the use of antibiotics is widely divergent.[107] A 10-day course of intravenous ampicillin, gentamicin, and clindamycin or metronidazole is the gold standard for the treatment of complicated appendicitis,[149] and the effectiveness of other antibiotic combinations is usually measured against this empirical regimen. This combination is selected because of the frequency of bacterial involvement, including *Escherichia coli, Enterococcus, Klebsiella,* and *Bacteroides.* As new generations of antibiotics become available, other combinations may be equally effective, including cefotaxime and clindamycin,[147] cefoxitin alone,[101] clindamycin and amikacin,[15] clindamycin and aztreonam,[15] cefepime and metronidazole,[18] ticarcillin and clavulanate,[126,154] and piperacillin and tazobactam.[109]

There is a trend toward decreasing the duration of antibiotic therapy.[142] Only perioperative antibiotics are required for early appendicitis. The recommended duration is from a single dose to 48 hours.[16,83] A prospective double-blind study has shown that single-dose cefoxitin (which has a half-life of 0.8 hour) is not as effective as single-dose cefotetan (half-life, 3.5 hours) or 24-hour coverage with cefoxitin.[83] The duration of treatment, therefore, depends on the choice of drug. For complicated appendicitis, recent studies have suggested that as little as 48 hours of coverage is adequate.[103] Others suggest that treatment be continued as long as 5 days with time added as clinically indicated using the leukocyte count and presence of fever as guides.[18,35,154] There is also a trend to use oral antibiotics instead of intravenous antibiotics when gastrointestinal function returns. A prospective, randomized study demonstrates equivalency between a 10-day course of intravenous antibiotics and a 10-day course of intravenous antibiotics followed by oral antibiotics for complicated appendicitis.[133] Standard antibiotic therapy at my institution is preoperative treatment with cefoxitin for suspected acute appendicitis and ampicillin, gentamicin, and clindamycin for complicated appendicitis. Coverage is continued if clinically indicated by fever or an elevated leukocyte count.

Appendectomy

The most generally accepted treatment of acute appendicitis is prompt surgery. There is evidence that some cases of acute appendicitis can resolve spontaneously,[36] but no studies delineate the future risk for developing complicated appendicitis if no initial operation is performed. There is no recognized radiographic study, laboratory value, or clinical sign that helps determine which acute inflammatory processes will resolve and which will lead to complications, and this nonoperative approach to acute appendicitis has few followers. There is a trend away from performing immediate operation, including procedures done in the middle of the night.[162,179] According to a survey of members of the American Pediatric Surgical Association, only half of the surgeons will perform appendectomy in the middle of the night.[107] There was no increased rate of perforation or incidence of complications noted between a group of patients diagnosed with acute appendicitis and having surgery within 6 hours of admission and those having surgery between 6 and 18 hours of admission.[161,176] Nevertheless, most patients with the diagnosis of acute appendicitis still have prompt surgery. The majority of pediatric surgeons will perform appendectomy within 8 hours.[107]

In the open technique, a transverse or oblique right lower quadrant incision is made through McBurney's point (Fig. 98-1). The muscles of the abdominal wall are usually split. After the abdomen is entered, the cecum and appendix are mobilized and the appendix is brought out through the incision. The mesoappendix is then divided, and the base of the appendix is ligated. A short base is left to avoid inflammation in the stump.[52] The stump is managed by simple ligation, ligation with inversion using a pursestring or Z-stitch suture, or inversion without ligature. Simple ligation can be done quickly and is claimed to reduce adhesions.[158] Inversion theoretically leads to better hemorrhage control, a doubly secure closure, and less chance of contamination; however, it can create artifacts on future contrast examinations and can cause intussusception.[70] A review comparing simple ligation with ligation and inversion concluded that simple ligation seems to be at least as effective as ligation with inversion and is associated with less adhesion formation.[158] For simple appendicitis, irrigating the wound is unnecessary. The wound is closed in layers, and no drains are placed. A normal diet can be given soon after surgery, and the patient can be discharged 1 to 2 days after surgery. If a normal appendix is found, the peritoneal cavity should be inspected for inflammatory bowel disease, mesenteric adenitis, Meckel's diverticulitis, or, in females, pathologic conditions of the ovary.

"Endoscopic" appendectomy was first described in 1983.[151] Laparoscopic appendectomy can be done by a laparoscopic-assisted technique in which the appendix is mobilized laparoscopically using one or two ports and is drawn through a small abdominal opening and removed by standard open technique.[50,168] Alternatively, the appendix can be removed entirely laparoscopically. Three trocars

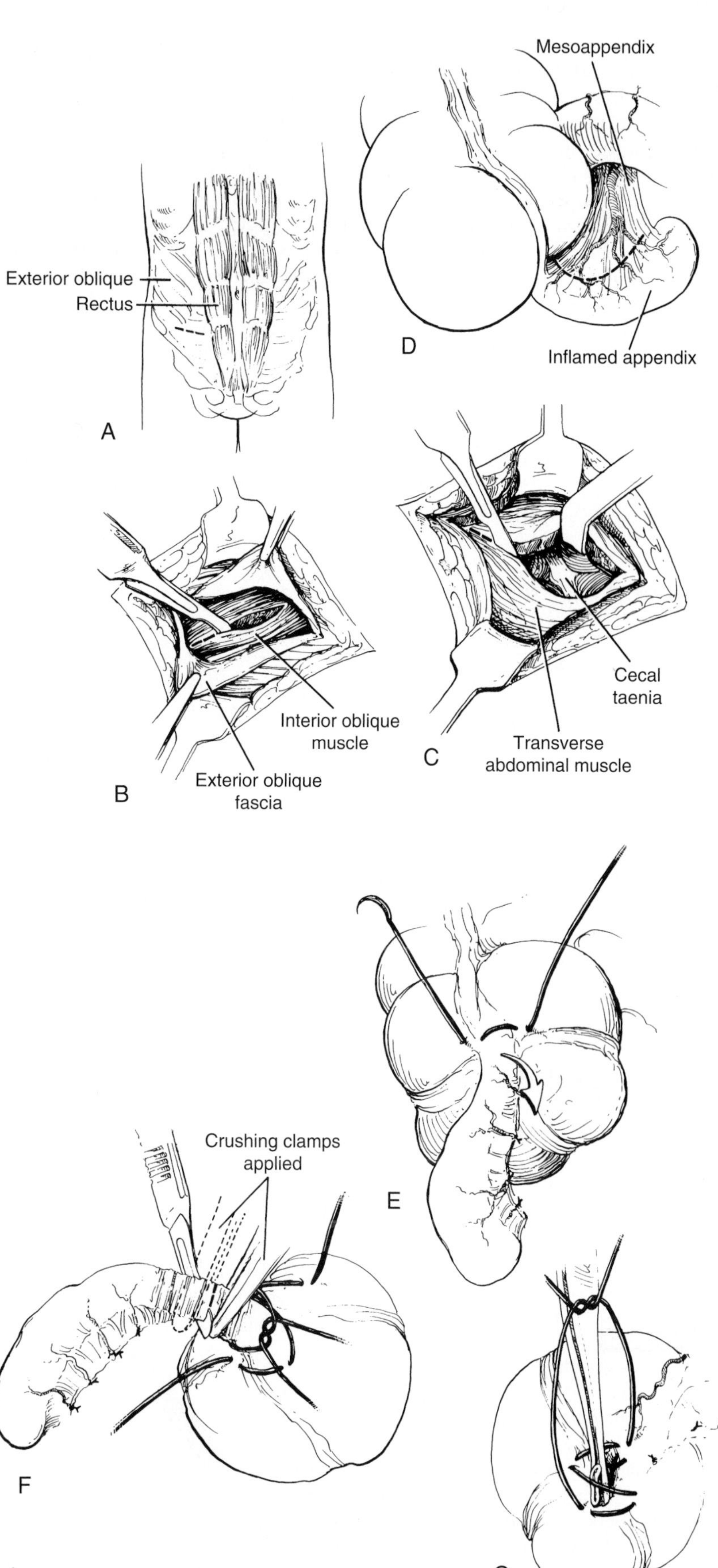

Figure 98–1 *A,* A transverse incision is made in the right lower quadrant over the lateral musculature. *B,* The external oblique fascia is incised, exposing the internal oblique fascia and muscle. *C,* The transverse abdominal muscle and peritoneum are opened, and the cecum is identified. *D,* An inflamed appendix is identified; and the mesoappendix is isolated, clamped, divided, and tied. *E,* A pursestring suture is placed in the cecal wall. *F,* The base of the appendix is crushed and tied, and the appendix is excised. *G,* The appendiceal stump is inverted into the cecal wall, and the pursestring suture is tied. (From Rowe M, O'Neill J, Grosfeld J, et al: Essentials of Pediatric Surgery. Philadelphia, CV Mosby, 1995.)

are usually employed: one at the umbilicus for the scope, one in the right upper quadrant, and one in the left lower quadrant for retraction and dissection (Fig. 98-2). The appendix is found by following the cecum, and the mesoappendix is grasped near the tip to lift the appendix toward the abdominal wall. A window is made in the mesoappendix near the base to allow its division by applying clips, staples, or the harmonic scalpel. Many variations of ligating and removing the appendix have been described.[49,152] The simplest technique applies an endoscopic stapler to the base of the appendix, and the appendix is delivered through the umbilical trocar site.

Despite prospective, randomized trials that compared open and laparoscopic appendectomy, the advantages and disadvantages of laparoscopic appendectomy continue to be debated.* Advantages claimed include shorter hospitalizations, decreased postoperative pain, decreased wound complications, increased ability to diagnose uncertain cases, surgical ease in an obese patient, and faster postoperative recovery.[22,42,49,57,58,80,87] Disadvantages are a higher cost because of equipment needs and longer time for surgery, increased training and experience required for surgeons and ancillary support staff, increased incidence of finding a normal appendix, and an increased incidence of intra-abdominal infection.[10,22,97,144,165] Although the conclusions regarding the advantages of this technique over the open technique vary widely, especially in children, laparoscopic appendectomy seems to be a safe and effective means of performing an appendectomy and prospective, randomized trials generally support this method.

Treatment of patients with complicated appendicitis is more controversial than that of patients with simple appendicitis. Owing to social, cultural, economic, and medical influences on the diagnosis and treatment of this disease process, perforation rates vary from 16% to 57% in different institutions. There is no consensus on the optimal treatment of patients with complicated appendicitis. Opinions range from nonoperative treatment to aggressive surgical resection with antibiotic irrigation, drainage of the peritoneal cavity, and delayed wound closure.[17,31,53,94,101]

*See references 30, 82, 85, 86, 92, 116, 120, 130, 134, and 141.

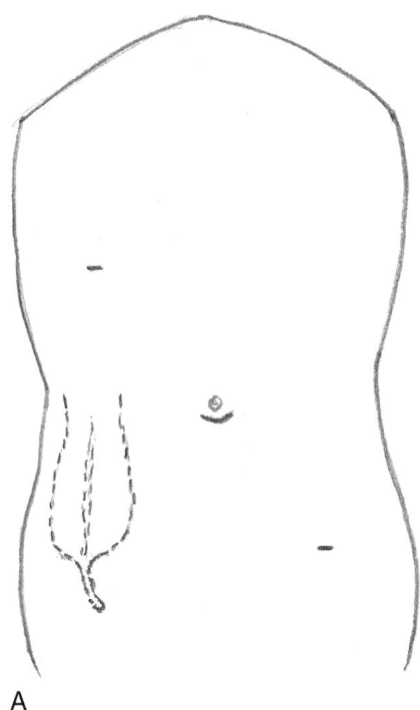

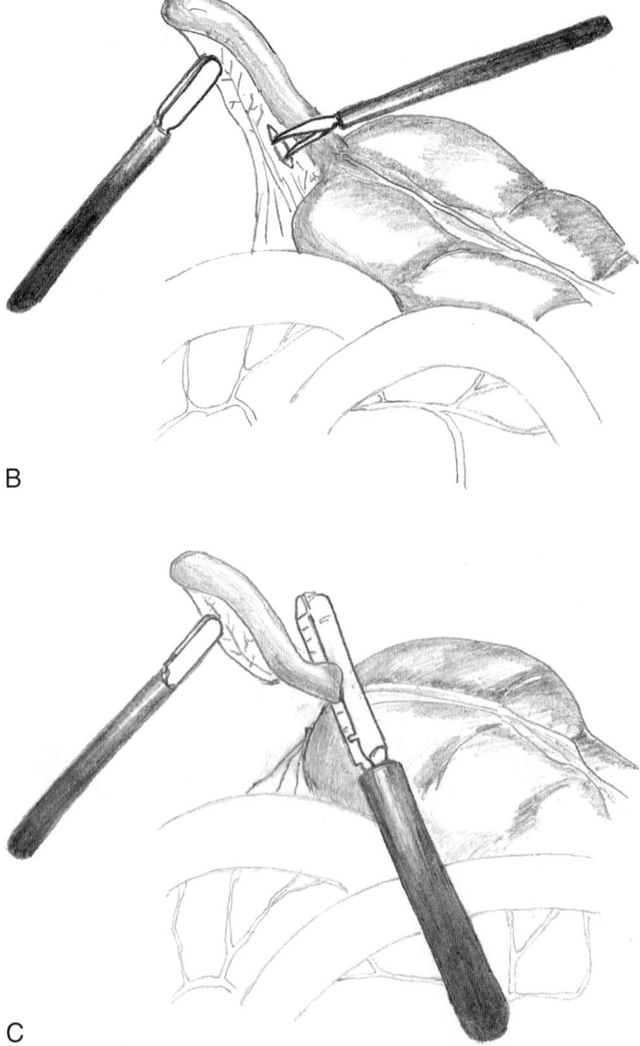

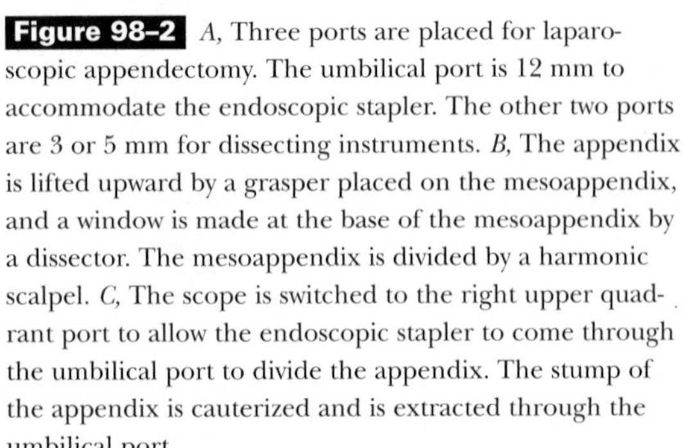

Figure 98–2 *A,* Three ports are placed for laparoscopic appendectomy. The umbilical port is 12 mm to accommodate the endoscopic stapler. The other two ports are 3 or 5 mm for dissecting instruments. *B,* The appendix is lifted upward by a grasper placed on the mesoappendix, and a window is made at the base of the mesoappendix by a dissector. The mesoappendix is divided by a harmonic scalpel. *C,* The scope is switched to the right upper quadrant port to allow the endoscopic stapler to come through the umbilical port to divide the appendix. The stump of the appendix is cauterized and is extracted through the umbilical port.

Weiner and colleagues[175] reported no significant differences in the number of hospital days, cost of treatment, or overall complication rates using initial nonoperative treatment of complicated appendicitis followed by interval appendectomy in 8 weeks. In another study that examined initial nonoperative therapy for complicated appendicitis confirmed by imaging, 22% of the patients were converted to appendectomy because of small bowel obstruction.[77] Bandemia over 15% correlated with failure of the initial nonoperative strategy. Operative treatment remains the standard approach because of the difficulty in determining before surgery whether perforation has occurred.

The operative procedure for complicated appendicitis is appendectomy. There is continued controversy regarding the details of the procedure: whether to drain the peritoneal cavity, whether to close the wound or leave it open with delayed closure, whether to irrigate the peritoneal cavity and, if so, whether to use antibiotic solutions. Drains have been described as increasing infectious complications as well as preventing them.[40,41,137,145,159,164] Most studies do not support the use of drains, with the possible exception of retrocecal abscesses that cannot be properly débrided. Delayed wound closure is not supported by the literature[49,110,128,137,149] and does not seem to be warranted, because the wound infection rate associated with appendectomy is less than 3%. Irrigation remains controversial. Putnam and associates[128] suggest that irrigation prolongs ileus and may cause small intestinal obstruction and report excellent results without irrigation. Other recent studies support saline irrigation of the peritoneal cavity with or without antibiotics.[40,49,110,137,149] My standard treatment of children with complicated appendicitis is appendectomy, evacuation of purulent fluid, saline irrigation, no drains, and primary wound closure.

Management of patients with a palpable abdominal mass is another controversial topic. It occurs in a small but significant fraction of patients with complicated appendicitis, especially in young children after perforation. Some advocate immediate appendectomy,[166] and others perform the procedure only if a mass is confirmed with the patient under anesthesia. If an operation is done, care should be taken to avoid damage to adjacent structures subject to inflammatory processes, such as the small intestine, the fallopian tubes and ovaries, and the ureter. Surana[163] and Nitecki[113] recommend treatment with intravenous antibiotics until the leukocyte count is normal and the patient remains afebrile for 24 hours. If the patient's condition worsens or the mass enlarges on serial ultrasonography, the mass is drained percutaneously, followed by interval appendectomy. Interval appendectomy prevents repeated episodes of appendicitis and affords the surgeon the opportunity to evaluate the patient for other conditions that can masquerade as an appendiceal mass. Whether an interval appendectomy is needed is also debated.[13,26,48,71,105,113,131] Nitecki and coworkers[113] have suggested that interval appendectomy is unnecessary because only 14% of patients have recurrent symptoms and recurrence within 2 years after initial diagnosis is uncommon. The current standard of treatment is conservative management with interval appendectomy after 8 to 12 weeks.

COMPLICATIONS

The incidence of complications increases with the degree of severity of the appendicitis, but all complications have shown a steady decline in recent years. Complications include wound infection, intra-abdominal abscess formation, postoperative intestinal obstruction, prolonged ileus, and, rarely, enterocutaneous fistula. Wound infection is the most common complication, but the rate has fallen from 50% to less than 5%, even in complicated appendicitis.[40,49,110,119,128,159] Intra-abdominal abscess formation is also more common in complicated appendicitis but is still less than 2%. The abscess can be drained percutaneously under CT guidance or transrectally in the operating room, although others have advocated more conservative management.[44,62,117] Postoperative intestinal obstruction occurs in 1% of patients with complicated appendicitis, which often requires operative adhesiolysis.[3] Enterocutaneous fistula is a rare complication and will usually respond to nonoperative management. Suppurative pylephlebitis is a particularly serious, although rare, complication.[170] Sepsis and multisystem organ failure can occur in young children who had prolonged illness before diagnosis. Major complications, including postoperative intestinal obstruction and intra-abdominal abscess formation, have also fallen to an incidence of less than 5%.

An unresolved issue is the effect of complicated appendicitis on fertility in females. Available studies contradict each other. Puri and associates[127] report that complicated appendicitis before puberty plays little if any role in the cause of tubal infertility, whereas Mueller and coworkers[106] report that the condition is associated with a fourfold risk for tubal infertility. The consequences of complicated appendicitis may be mitigated through both public and medical education that ensures prompt, early treatment before perforation.

OUTCOMES

The mortality rate for complicated appendicitis has dropped to nearly zero. Antibiotics have markedly decreased the incidence of infectious complications. Although the length of hospitalization and the morbidity of patients with complicated appendicitis still far exceed those with simple appendicitis, the overall morbidity in children with complicated appendicitis is less than 10%.

The widely varied postoperative management of appendicitis is beginning to be addressed by implementing evidence-based clinical pathways.[156,174] Prompted primarily by economic pressures, there is increasing scrutiny of patient treatment and outcome.[55,56,112] Early outcome research has shown that hospitals that perform less than one appendectomy per week are associated with higher likelihood of misdiagnosis.[155] There are also reports that suggest better outcome in younger children with appendicitis when they are cared for by pediatric surgeons.[4,78] The combination of surgical evaluation, prompt operation when the diagnosis is clear, a period of observation if the diagnosis is equivocal followed by imaging if necessary, and care provided by experienced clinicians and institutions will lead to the best outcome for children with appendicitis.

REFERENCES

1. Addiss DG, Shaffer J, Fowler BS, Tauxe RV: The epidemiology of appendicitis and appendectomy in the United States. Am J Epidemiol 1990;132:910.
2. Adebamowo CA, Akang EE, Ladipo JK, Ajao OG: Schistosomiasis of the appendix. Br J Surg 1991;78:1219.
3. Ahlberg G, Bergdahl S, Rutqvist J, et al: Mechanical small-bowel obstruction after conventional appendectomy in children. Eur J Pediatr Surg 1997;7:13.
4. Alexander F, Magnuson D, DiFiore J, et al: Specialty versus generalist care of children with appendicitis: An outcome comparison. J Pediatr Surg 2001;36:1510.
5. Alloo J, Gerstle T, Shilyansky J, Ein SH: Appendicitis in children less than 3 years of age: A 28-year review. Pediatr Surg Int 2004;19:777.
6. Alvarado A: A practical score for the early diagnosis of acute appendicitis. Ann Emerg Med 1986;15:557.
7. Andersen BR, Kallehave FL, Andersen HK: Antibiotics versus placebo for prevention of postoperative infection after appendicectomy. Cochrane Database Syst Rev 2003; CD001439.
8. Andersson N, Griffiths H, Murphy J, et al: Is appendicitis familial? BMJ 1979;2:697.
9. Andersson R, Hugander A, Thulin A, et al: Indications for operation in suspected appendicitis and incidence of perforation. BMJ 1994;308:107.
10. Apelgren KN, Molnar RG, Kisala JM: Laparoscopic is not better than open appendectomy. Am Surg 1995;61:240.
11. Attwood SE, Mealy K, Cafferkey MT, et al: *Yersinia* infection and acute abdominal pain. Lancet 1987;1:529.
12. Bachoo P, Mahomed AA, Ninan GK, Youngson GG: Acute appendicitis: The continuing role for active observation. Pediatr Surg Int 2001;17:125.
13. Bagi P, Dueholm S: Nonoperative management of the ultrasonically evaluated appendiceal mass. Surgery 1987; 101:602.
14. Balthazar EJ, Megibow AJ, Siegel SE, Birnbaum BA: Appendicitis: Prospective evaluation with high-resolution CT. Radiology 1991;180:21.
15. Barboza E, del Castillo M, Yi A, Gotuzzo E: Clindamycin plus amikacin versus clindamycin plus aztreonam in established intraabdominal infections. Surgery 1994;116:28.
16. Bauer T, Vennits B, Holm B, et al: Antibiotic prophylaxis in acute non-perforated appendicitis. Ann Surg 1989;209:307.
17. Bennion RS, Thompson JE: Early appendectomy for perforated appendicitis in children should not be abandoned. Surg Gynecol Obstet 1987;165:95.
18. Berne TV, Yellin AE, Appleman MD, et al: A clinical comparison of cefepime and metronidazole versus gentamicin and clindamycin in the antibiotic management of surgically treated advanced appendicitis. Surg Gynecol Obstet 1993;177(Suppl):18.
19. Birnbaum BA, Balthazar EJ: CT of appendicitis and diverticulitis. Radiol Clin North Am 1994;32:885.
20. Bluett MK, Halter SA, Salhany KE, O'Leary JP: Duplication of the appendix mimicking adenocarcinoma of the colon. Arch Surg 1987;122:817.
21. Bolton JP, Craven ER, Croft RJ, Menzies-Gow N: An assessment of the value of the white-cell count in the management of suspected acute appendicitis. Br J Surg 1975;62:906.
22. Bonanni F, Reed J 3rd, Hartzell G, et al: Laparoscopic versus conventional appendectomy. J Am Coll Surg 1994;179:273.
23. Bonello JC, Abrams JS: The significance of "positive" rectal examination in acute appendicitis. Dis Colon Rectum 1979; 22:97.
24. Brender JD, Marcuse EK, Keopsell TD, Hatch EI: Childhood appendicitis: Factors associated with perforation. Pediatrics 1985;76:301.
25. Brenner DJ: Estimating cancer risks from pediatric CT: Going from the qualitative to the quantitative. Pediatr Radiol 2002;32:228.
26. Bufo AJ, Shah RS, Li MH, et al: Interval appendectomy for perforated appendicitis in children. J Laparoendosc Adv Surg Tech A 1998;8:209.
27. Burkitt DP: The aetiology of appendicitis. Br J Surg 1971; 58:695.
28. Buschard K, Kjaeldgaard A: Investigation and analysis of the position, fixation, length and embryology of the vermiform appendix. Acta Chir Scand 1973;139:293.
29. Callahan MJ, Rodriguez DP, Taylor GA: CT of appendicitis in children. Radiology 2002;224:325.
30. Canty TG Sr, Collins D, Losasso B, et al: Laparoscopic appendectomy for simple and perforated appendicitis in children: The procedure of choice? J Pediatr Surg 2000; 35:1582-1585.
31. Chen C, Botelho C, Cooper A, et al: Current practice patterns in the treatment of perforated appendicitis in children. J Am Coll Surg 2003;196:212.
32. Chesbrough RM, Burkhard TK, Balsara ZN, et al: Self-localization in US of appendicitis: An addition to graded compression. Radiology 1993;187:349.
33. Chew DK, Borromeo JR, Gabriel YA, Holgersen LO: Duplication of the vermiform appendix. J Pediatr Surg 2000; 35:617.
34. Choi D, Park H, Lee YR, et al: The most useful findings for diagnosing acute appendicitis on contrast-enhanced helical CT. Acta Radiol 2003;44:574.
35. Ciftci AO, Tanyel FC, Buyukpamukcu N, Hicsonmez A: Comparative trial of four antibiotic combinations for perforated appendicitis in children. Eur J Surg 1997; 163:591.
36. Cobben LP, de Van Otterloo AM, Puylaert JB: Spontaneously resolving appendicitis: Frequency and natural history in 60 patients. Radiology 2000;215:349.
37. Cope Z: Appendicitis and the differential diagnosis of acute appendicitis. In Silen W (ed): Cope's Early Diagnosis of the Acute Abdomen. New York, Oxford University Press, 1991.
38. Coughlin JP, Gauderer MW, Stern RC, et al: The spectrum of appendiceal disease in cystic fibrosis. J Pediatr Surg 1990;25:835.
39. Creed F: Life events and appendectomy. Lancet 1981; 1:1381.
40. Curran TJ, Meunchow SK: The treatment of complicated appendicitis in children using peritoneal drainage: Results from a public hospital. J Pediatr Surg 1993;28:404.
41. David IB, Buck JR, Filler RM: Rational use of antibiotics for perforated appendicitis in childhood. J Pediatr Surg 1982; 17:494.
42. DeWilde RL: Goodbye to late bowel obstruction after appendicectomy [Letter]. Lancet 1991;338:1012.
43. Dixon JM, Elton RA, Rainey JB, Macleod DA: Rectal examination in patients with pain in the right lower quadrant of the abdomen. BMJ 1991;302:368.
44. Dobremez E, Lavrand F, Lefevre Y, et al: Treatment of post-appendectomy intra-abdominal deep abscesses. Eur J Pediatr Surg 2003;13:393.
45. Doraiswany NV: Leucocyte counts in the diagnosis and prognosis of acute appendicitis in children. Br J Surg 1979;66:72.
46. Dueholm S, Bagi P, Bud M: Laboratory aid in the diagnosis of acute appendicitis: A blinded, prospective trial concerning diagnostic value of leukocyte count, neutrophil differential

count and C-reactive protein. Dis Colon Rectum 1989; 32:855.
47. Dunning PG, Goldman MD: The incidence and value of rectal examination in children with suspected appendicitis. Ann R Coll Surg Engl 1991;73:233.
48. Ein SH, Shandling B: Is interval appendectomy necessary after rupture of an appendiceal mass? J Pediatr Surg 1996; 31:849.
49. El Ghoneimi A, Valla JS, Limonne B, et al: Laparoscopic appendectomy in children: Report of 1379 cases. J Pediatr Surg 1994;29:786.
50. Esposito C: One-trocar appendectomy in pediatric surgery. Surg Endosc 1998;12:177.
51. Evetts BK, Foley CR, Latimer RG, Rimkus DS: Tc-99 hexamethylpropyleneamineoxide scanning for the detection of acute appendicitis. J Am Coll Surg 1994;179:197.
52. Feigin E, Carmon M, Szold A, Seror D: Acute stump appendicitis. Lancet 1993;341:757.
53. Fishman SJ, Pelosi L, Klavon SL, O'Rourke EJ: Perforated appendicitis: Prospective outcome analysis for 150 children. J Pediatr Surg 2000;35:923.
54. Fitz RH: Perforating inflammation of the vermiform appendix, with special reference to its early diagnosis and treatment. Trans Assoc Am Phys 1886;1:107.
55. Flum DR, Morris A, Koepsell T, Dellinger EP: Has misdiagnosis of appendicitis decreased over time? A population-based analysis. JAMA 2001;286:1748.
56. Flum DR, Koepsell T: The clinical and economic correlates of misdiagnosed appendicitis: Nationwide analysis. Arch Surg 2002;137:799.
57. Frazee RC, Roberts JW, Symmonds RE, et al: A prospective randomized trial comparing open versus laparoscopic appendectomy. Ann Surg 1994;219:725.
58. Fritts LL, Orlando R: Laparoscopic appendectomy. Arch Surg 1993;128:521.
59. Garcia Pena BM, Mandl KD, Kraus SJ, et al: Ultrasonography and limited computed tomography in the diagnosis and management of appendicitis in children. JAMA 1999;282:1041.
60. Garcia Pena BM, Cook EF, Mandl KD: Selective imaging strategies for the diagnosis of appendicitis in children. Pediatrics 2004;113:24.
61. Goodman DA, Goodman CB, Monk JS: Use of the neutrophil: Lymphocyte ratio in the diagnosis of appendicitis. Am Surg 1995;61:257.
62. Gorenstein A, Gewurtz G, Serour F, Somekh E: Postappendectomy intra-abdominal abscess: A therapeutic approach. Arch Dis Child 1994;70:400.
63. Gouzi JL, Laigneau P, Delalande JP, et al: Indications for right hemicolectomy in carcinoid tumors of the appendix. Surg Gynecol Obstet 1993;176:543.
64. Grosfeld JL, Weinberger M, Clatworthy HW Jr, et al: Acute appendicitis in the first two years of life. J Pediatr Surg 1973;8:285.
65. Guthery SL, Hutchings C, Dean JM, Hoff C: National estimates of hospital utilization by children with gastrointestinal disorders: Analysis of the 1997 kids' inpatient database. J Pediatr 2004;144:589.
66. Gwynn LK: Appendiceal enlargement as a criterion for clinical diagnosis of acute appendicitis: Is it reliable and valid? J Emerg Med 2002;23:9.
67. Huang CB, Yu HR, Hung GC, et al: Clinical features and outcome of appendicitis in children younger than three years of age. Chang Gung Med J 2001;24:27.
68. Heller MB, Skolnick LM: Ultrasound documentation of spontaneously resolving appendicitis. Am J Emerg Med 1993;11:51.
69. Hennington MH, Tinsley EA Jr, Proctor HJ, Baker CC: Acute appendicitis following blunt abdominal trauma: Incidence or coincidence? Ann Surg 1991;214:61.
70. Hoehner JC, Kimura K, Soper RT: Intussusception as a complication of inversion appendectomy. Pediatr Surg Int 1995;10:51.
71. Hoffman J, Lindhard A, Jensen HE: Appendix mass: Conservative management without interval appendectomy. Am J Surg 1984;148:379.
72. Hoffman J, Rasmussen OO: Aids in the diagnosis of acute appendicitis. Br J Surg 1989;76:774.
73. Kaiser S, Frenckner B, Jorulf HK: Suspected appendicitis in children: US and CT—a prospective randomized study. Radiology 2002;223:633.
74. Kanegaye JT, Vance CW, Parisi M, et al: Failure of technetium-99m hexamethylpropylene amine oxime leukocyte scintigraphy in the evaluation of children with suspected appendicitis. Pediatr Emerg Care 1995;11:285.
75. Kang JY, Hoare J, Majeed A, et al: Decline in admission rates for acute appendicitis in England. Br J Surg 2003;90:1586.
76. Klein MD, Rabbani AB, Rood KD, et al: Three quantitative approaches to the diagnosis of abdominal pain in children: Practical applications of decision theory. J Pediatr Surg 2001;36:1375.
77. Kogut KA, Blakely ML, Schropp KP, et al: The association of elevated percent bands on admission with failure and complications of interval appendectomy. J Pediatr Surg 2001;36:165.
78. Kokoska ER, Minkes RK, Silen ML, et al: Effect of pediatric surgical practice on the treatment of children with appendicitis. Pediatrics 2001;107:1298.
79. Kosloske AM, Love CL, Rohrer JE, et al: The diagnosis of appendicitis in children: Outcomes of a strategy based on pediatric surgical evaluation. Pediatrics 2004;113:29.
80. Kum CK, Ngoi SS, Goi PM, et al: Randomized controlled trial comparing laparoscopic and open appendectomy. Br J Surg 1993;80:1599.
81. Kwong MS, Dinner M: Neonatal appendicitis masquerading as necrotizing enterocolitis. J Pediatr 1980;96:918.
82. Lavonius MI, Liesjarvi S, Ovaska J, et al: Laparoscopic versus open appendectomy in children: A prospective randomised study. Eur J Pediatr Surg 2001;11:235.
83. Liberman MA, Greason KL, Frame S, Ragland JJ: Single-dose cefotetan or cefoxitin versus multiple-dose cefoxitin as prophylaxis in patients undergoing appendectomy for acute appendicitis. J Am Coll Surg 1995;180:77.
84. Lin YL, Lee CH: Appendicitis in infancy. Pediatr Surg Int 2003;19:1.
85. Lintula H, Kokki H, Vanamo K: Single-blind randomized clinical trial of laparoscopic versus open appendicectomy in children. Br J Surg 2001;88:510.
86. Little DC, Custer MD, May BH, et al: Laparoscopic appendectomy: An unnecessary and expensive procedure in children? J Pediatr Surg 2002;37:310.
87. Lujan Mompean JA, Robles Campos R, Parrilla Paricio P, et al: Laparoscopic versus open appendectomy: A prospective assessment. Br J Surg 1994;81:133.
88. Macklin CP, Radcliffe GS, Merei JM, Stringer MD: A prospective evaluation of the modified Alvarado score for acute appendicitis in children. Ann R Coll Surg Engl 1997; 79:203.
89. Malone AJ Jr, Wolf CR, Malmed AS, Melliere BF: Diagnosis of acute appendicitis: Value of unenhanced CT. AJR Am J Roentgenol 1993;160:763.
90. Martin LW, Perrin EV: Neonatal perforation of the appendix in association with Hirschsprung's disease. Ann Surg 1967;166:799.

91. Martin AE, Vollman D, Adler B, Caniano DA: CT scans may not reduce the negative appendectomy rate in children. J Pediatr Surg 2004;39:886.
92. Marzouk M, Khater M, Elsadek M, Abdelmoghny A: Laparoscopic versus open appendectomy: A prospective comparative study of 227 patients. Surg Endosc 2003; 17:721.
93. Mattei P, Sola JE, Yeo CJ, et al: Chronic and recurrent appendicitis are uncommon entities often misdiagnosed. J Am Coll Surg 1994;178:385.
94. Mazziotti MV, Marley EF, Winthrop AL, et al: Histopathologic analysis of interval appendectomy specimens: Support for the role of interval appendectomy. J Pediatr Surg 1997;32:806.
95. McBurney C: Experience with early operative interference in cases of disease of the vermiform appendix. NY Med J 1889;50:676.
96. McCahy P: Continuing fall in the incidence of acute appendicitis. Ann R Coll Surg Engl 1994;76:282.
97. McKinlay R, Neeleman S, Klein R, et al: Intraabdominal abscess following open and laparoscopic appendectomy in the pediatric population. Surg Endosc 2003;17:730.
98. McNamara MJ, Pasquale MD, Evans SRT: Acute appendicitis and the use of intraperitoneal cultures. Surg Gynecol Obstet 1993;177:393.
99. Meade RH: The evolution of surgery for appendicitis. Surgery 1964;55:741.
100. Meier DE, Guzzetta PC, Barber RG, et al: Perforated appendicitis in children: Is there a best treatment? J Pediatr Surg 2003;38:1520.
101. Meller JL. Reyes HM, Loeff DS, et al: One-drug versus two-drug antibiotic therapy in pediatric perforated appendicitis: A prospective randomized study. Surgery 1991;110:764.
102. Moertel CL, Weiland LH, Telander RL: Carcinoid tumor of the appendix in the first two decades of life. J Pediatr Surg 1990;25:1073.
103. Moore L, Wilson SR: Ultrasonography in obstetric and gynecologic emergencies. Radiol Clin North Am 1994; 32:1005.
104. Mosdell DM, Morris DM, Fry DE: Peritoneal cultures and antibiotic therapy in pediatric perforated appendicitis. Am J Surg 1994;167:313.
105. Mosegaard A, Nielson OS: Interval appendectomy. Acta Chir Scand 1979;145:109.
106. Mueller BA, Daling JR, Moore DE, et al: Appendectomy and the risk of tubal infertility. N Engl J Med 1986; 315:1506.
107. Muehlstedt SG, Pham TQ, Schmeling DJ: The management of pediatric appendicitis: A survey of North American Pediatric Surgeons. J Pediatr Surg 2004;39:875.
108. Nadler S, Coppell MS, Bhatt B, et al: Appendiceal infection by *Entamoeba histolytica* and *Strongyloides stercoralis* presenting like acute appendicitis. Dig Dis Sci 1990; 35:603.
109. Nadler EP, Reblock KK, Ford HR, Gaines BA: Monotherapy versus multi-drug therapy for the treatment of perforated appendicitis in children. Surg Infect 2003; 4:327.
110. Neilson IR, Laberge JM, Nguyen LT, et al: Appendicitis in children: Current therapeutic recommendations. J Pediatr Surg 1990;25:1113.
111. Neuspiel DR, Kuller LH: Fatalities from undetected appendicitis in early childhood. Clin Pediatr 1987;26:573.
112. Newman K, Ponsky T, Kittle K, et al: Appendicitis 2000: Variability in practice, outcomes, and resource utilization at thirty pediatric hospitals. J Pediatr Surg 2003;38:372.
113. Nitecki S, Assalia A, Schein M: Contemporary management of the appendiceal mass. Br J Surg 1993;80:18.
114. Nitecki S, Karmeli R, Sarr MG: Appendiceal calculi and fecaliths as indications for appendectomy. Surg Gynecol Obstet 1990;171:185.
115. Oestreich AE, Adelstein EH: Appendicitis as the presenting complaint in cystic fibrosis. J Pediatr Surg 1982; 17:191.
116. Oka T, Kurkchubasche AG, Bussey JG, et al: Open and laparoscopic appendectomy are equally safe and acceptable in children. Surg Endosc 2004;18:242.
117. Okoye BO, Rampersad B, Marantos A, et al: Abscess after appendicectomy in children: The role of conservative management. Br J Surg 1998;85:1111.
118. Parkes SE et al: Carcinoid tumours of the appendix in children 1957-1986: Incidence, treatment and outcome. Br J Surg 1993;80:502.
119. Pearl RH, Hale DA, Molloy M, et al: Pediatric appendectomy. J Pediatr Surg 1995;30:173.
120. Pedersen AG, Petersen OB, Wara P, et al: Randomized clinical trial of laparoscopic versus open appendicectomy. Br J Surg 2001;88:200.
121. Pelizzo G, La Riccia A, Bouvier R, et al: Carcinoid tumors of the appendix in children. Pediatr Surg Int 2001;17:399.
122. Peltokallio P, Tykka H: Evolution of the age distribution and mortality of acute appendicitis. Arch Surg 1981; 116:153.
123. Peltola H, Ahlqvist J, Rapola J, et al: C-reactive protein compared with white blood cell count and erythrocyte sedimentation rate in the diagnosis of acute appendicitis in children. Acta Chir Scand 1986;152:55.
124. Pena BM, Taylor GA, Fishman SJ, Mandl KD: Effect of an imaging protocol on clinical outcomes among pediatric patients with appendicitis. Pediatrics 2002;110:1088.
125. Pledger HG, Fahy LT: Deaths in children with a diagnosis of acute appendicitis. BMJ Clin Res 1987;295:1233.
126. Pokorny WJ, Kaplan SL, Mason EO: A preliminary report of ticarcillin and clavulanate versus triple antibiotic therapy in children with ruptured appendicitis. Surg Gynecol Obstet 1991;172(Suppl):54.
127. Puri P, McGuinness EPJ, Guiney EJ: Fertility following perforated appendicitis in girls. J Pediatr Surg 1989;24:547.
128. Putnam TC, Gagliano NG, Emmons RW: Appendicitis in children. Surg Gynecol Obstet 1990;170:527.
129. Rabau MY, Avigad I, Wolfstein I: Rubella in acute appendicitis. Pediatrics 1980;66:813.
130. Rangel SJ, Henry MC, Brindle M, Moss RL: Small evidence for small incisions: Pediatric laparoscopy and the need for more rigorous evaluation of novel surgical therapies. J Pediatr Surg 2003;38:1429.
131. Ranson JHC: Nonoperative treatment of the appendiceal mass: Progress of regression? Gastroenterology 1987; 93:1439.
132. Ravitch MM: Appendicitis. In Welch KJ, et al (eds): Pediatric Surgery. Chicago, Year Book Medical Publishers, 1986.
133. Rice HE, Brown RL, Gollin G, et al: Results of a pilot trial comparing prolonged intravenous antibiotics with sequential intravenous/oral antibiotics for children with perforated appendicitis. Arch Surg 2001;136:1391.
134. Richards W, Watson D, Lynch G, et al: A review of the results of laparoscopic versus open appendectomy. Surg Gynecol Obstet 1993;177:473.
135. Roggo A, Wood WC, Ottinger LW: Carcinoid tumors of the appendix. Ann Surg 1993;217:385.
136. Rodgers B, Karn G: *Yersinia* enterocolitis. J Pediatr Surg 1975;10:497.

137. Samelson SL, Reyes HM: Management of perforated appendicitis in children revisited. Arch Surg 1987;122:691.
138. Samuel M: Pediatric appendicitis score. J Pediatr Surg 2002;37:877.
139. Sanders DY, Cort CR, Stubbs AJ, et al: Shigellosis associated with appendicitis. J Pediatr Surg 1972;7:315.
140. Sarfati MR, Hunter GC, Witzke DB, et al: Impact of adjunctive testing on the diagnosis and clinical course of patients with acute appendicitis. Am J Surg 1993; 166:660.
141. Sauerland S, Lefering R, Neugebauer EA: Laparoscopic versus open surgery for suspected appendicitis. Cochrane Database Syst Rev 2002;CD001546.
142. Schein M, Assalia A, Bachus H: Minimal antibiotic therapy after emergency abdominal surgery: A prospective study. Br J Surg 1994;81:989.
143. Scher KS, Coil JA Jr: Appendicitis: Factors that influence the frequency of perforation, South Med J 1980;73:1561.
144. Schirmer BD, Schmieg RE Jr, Dix J, et al: Laparoscopic versus traditional appendectomy for suspected appendicitis. Am J Surg 1993;165:670.
145. Schmit PJ, Hiyama DT, Swisher SG, et al: Analysis of risk factors of postappendectomy intraabdominal abscess. Surg Gynecol Obstet 1994;179:721.
146. Schnell VL, Yandell R, Van Zandt S, Dinh TV: *Enterobius vermicularis* salpingitis: A distant episode from precipitating appendicitis. Obstet Gynecol 1992;80:553.
147. Schropp KP, Kaplan S, Golladay ES, et al: A randomized clinical trial of ampicillin, gentamicin and clindamycin versus cefotaxime and clindamycin in children with ruptured appendicitis. Surg Gynecol Obstet 1991;172:351.
148. Schumpelick V, Dreuw B, Ophoff K, Prescher A: Appendix and cecum: Embryology, anatomy, and surgical applications. Surg Clin North Am 2000;80:295.
149. Schwartz MZ, Tapper D, Solenberger RI: Management of perforated appendicitis in children. Ann Surg 1983;197:407.
150. Seidman JD, Andersen DK, Ulrich S, et al: Recurrent abdominal pain due to chronic appendiceal disease. South Med J 1991;84:913.
151. Semm K: Endoscopic appendectomy. Endoscopy 1983; 15:5.
152. Shalaby R, Arnos A, Desoky A, Samaha AH: Laparoscopic appendectomy in children: Evaluation of different techniques. Surg Laparosc Endosc Percutan Tech 2001; 11:22.
153. Sinha RK, Mage RG: Developing neonatal rabbit appendix, a primary lymphoid organ, is seeded by immature blood-borne B cells: Evidence for roles for CD62L/PNAd, CCR7/CCL21, alpha4beta1 and LFA-1. Dev Comp Immunol 2004;28:829.
154. Sirinek KR, Levine BA: A randomized trial of ticarcillin and clavulanate versus gentamicin and clindamycin in patients with complicated appendicitis. Surg Gynecol Obstet 1991;172(Suppl):30.
155. Smink DS, Finkelstein JA, Kleinman K, Fishman SJ: The effect of hospital volume of pediatric appendectomies on the misdiagnosis of appendicitis in children. Pediatrics 2004;113:18.
156. Smink DS, Finkelstein JA, Garcia Pena BM, et al: Diagnosis of acute appendicitis in children using a clinical practice guideline. J Pediatr Surg 2004;39:458.
157. Stephen AE, Segev DL, Ryan DP, et al: The diagnosis of acute appendicitis in a pediatric population: To CT or not to CT. J Pediatr Surg 2003;38:367.
158. Street D, Bodai BI, Owens LJ, et al: Simple ligation vs stump inversion in appendectomy. Arch Surg 1988;123:689.
159. Stringel G: Appendicitis in children: A systematic approach for a low incidence of complications. Am J Surg 1987;154:631.
160. Stringer MD, Pledger G: Childhood appendicitis in the United Kingdom: Fifty years of progress. J Pediatr Surg 2003;38(7 Suppl):65.
161. Surana R, O'Donnell B, Puri P: Appendicitis diagnosed following active observation does not increase morbidity in children. Pediatr Surg Int 1995;10:76.
162. Surana R, Quinn F, Puri P: Is it necessary to perform appendicectomy in the middle of the night in children? BMJ 1993;306:1168.
163. Surana R, Puri P: Appendiceal mass in children. Pediatr Surg Int 1995;10:79.
164. Tander B, Pektas O, Bulut M: The utility of peritoneal drains in children with uncomplicated perforated appendicitis. Pediatr Surg Int 2003;19:548.
165. Tate JJ, Dawson JW, Chung SC, et al: Laparoscopic versus open appendectomy: Prospective randomised trial. Lancet 1993;342:633.
166. Vakili C: Operative treatment of appendix mass. Am J Surg 1976;131:312.
167. Valerdiz-Casasola S, Pardo-Mindan FJ: Cytomegalovirus infection of the appendix in patient with the acquired immunodeficiency syndrome. Gastroenterology 1991; 101:247.
168. Valioulis I, Hameury F, Dahmani L, Levard G: Laparoscope-assisted appendectomy in children: The two-trocar technique. Eur J Pediatr Surg 2001;11:391.
169. van Zwalenburg C: The relation of mechanical distention to the etiology of appendicitis. Ann Surg 1905;41:437.
170. Vanamo K, Kiekara O: Pylephlebitis after appendicitis in a child. J Pediatr Surg 2001;36:1574.
171. Wade DS, Marrow SE, Balsara ZN, et al: Accuracy of ultrasound in the diagnosis of acute appendicitis compared with the surgeon's clinical impression. Arch Surg 1993; 128:1039.
172. Wakeley CPG: Position of vermiform appendix as ascertained by analysis of 10,000 cases. J Anat 1933;67:277.
173. Wangensteen OH, Dennis C: Experimental proof of obstructive origin of appendicitis. Ann Surg 1939;110:629.
174. Warner BW, Rich KA, Atherton H, et al: The sustained impact of an evidenced-based clinical pathway for acute appendicitis. Semin Pediatr Surg 2002;11:29.
175. Weiner DJ, Katz A, Hirschl RB, et al: Interval appendectomy in perforated appendicitis. Pediatr Surg Int 1995;10:82.
176. White JJ, Santillana M, Haller JA: Intensive in-hospital observation. a safe way to decrease unnecessary appendectomy. Am Surg 1975;41:793.
177. Wolff BG: Current status of incidental surgery. Dis Colon Rectum 1995;38:435.
178. Yacoe ME, Jeffrey RB: Sonography of appendicitis and diverticulitis. Radiol Clin North Am 1994;32:899.
179. Yardeni D, Hirschl RB, Drongowski RA, et al: Delayed versus immediate surgery in acute appendicitis: Do we need to operate during the night? J Pediatr Surg 2004;39:464.

Chapter 99

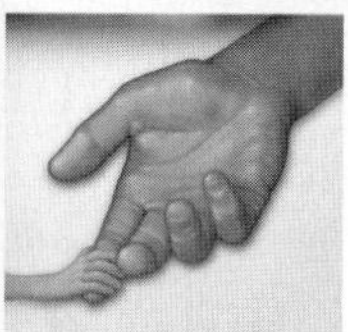

Hirschsprung's Disease and Related Neuromuscular Disorders of the Intestine

Daniel H. Teitelbaum and Arnold G. Coran

HISTORICAL REVIEW

Harald Hirschsprung, senior pediatrician at the Queen Louise Children's Hospital in Copenhagen, presented the classic description of the disease that now carries his name to the Pediatric Congress in Berlin in 1886.[131,213] He described two children with the classic clinical and anatomic characteristics of the disease. The children died at 7 and 11 months of age from what appeared to be repeated bouts of enterocolitis. Previous descriptions of children with megacolons date back to the 17th century, when Frederick Ruysch (1691), a Dutch anatomist, described a 5-year-old girl who died of an intestinal obstruction. A number of authors reported similar cases consistent with Hirschsprung's disease; however, a true appreciation of this disease did not occur until after Hirschsprung's report. Subsequently, several case reports were presented, including 10 additional children by Hirschsprung in 1904; he called the disease congenital dilatation of the colon.

An understanding of the pathogenesis of Hirschsprung's disease took several more decades. Three basic theories were advanced. The first was the "malfunction theory," which stated that the hypertrophied colon was the primary congenital defect.[233] The second was the "obstructive theory," which attributed the dilated colon to a mechanical blockage caused by redundancies of the colon or rectal valves.[339] The "spastic theory," which posited that the distal colon was in spastic contraction, causing a functional obstruction, was initially put forward by Fenwick in 1900.[339] An appreciation that the distal colon was the actual abnormality was initially advanced by Tittel[333] in 1901, who identified an absence of ganglion cells in the distal colon of a child with Hirschsprung's disease. Because some children with primary constipation were included in the diagnosis of Hirschsprung's disease, confusion about the cause continued until the late 1940s. Ehrenpreis[75] in 1946 was the first to appreciate that the colon became secondarily dilated due to the more distal obstruction. In 1948 both Whitehouse and Kernohan[361] and Zuelzer and Wilson[383] definitively documented the absence of ganglion cells of the myenteric plexus in patients with Hirschsprung's disease. The first corrective surgery for Hirschsprung's disease was performed by Swenson and Bill[311] in 1948, and a historical perspective of the cause and treatment of this disease was recently published by Swenson.[309,310] These landmark advances led to the basic principles guiding the clinical management of Hirschsprung's disease. Recent advances in molecular genetics and the pathophysiology of the enteric nervous system have led to an explosion in the understanding of Hirschsprung's disease. Half of all articles written on the subject have been published in the past 10 years.

INCIDENCE

The incidence of Hirschsprung's disease ranges from 1 in 4400 to 1 in 7000 live births.[245,304] The male-female ratio in patients with classic Hirschsprung's disease is generally reported as 4:1 in favor of males.[278,296] In long-segment disease, the ratio approaches 1:1 and may actually become reversed, favoring females.[245] The racial distribution is similar to that of the general population in most series. Among the families of children with Hirschsprung's disease, the incidence increases to approximately 6%, with a range of 2% to 18%.[250,305] Badner et al.,[21] in a study of the genetics of Hirschsprung's disease, found that brothers of patients with short-segment Hirschsprung's disease had a higher risk (4%) than sisters (1%) of having the disease. In long-segment Hirschsprung's disease, brothers and sons of affected females had the greatest risk of being affected (24% and 29%, respectively).

DIAGNOSIS

Clinical Presentation

The diagnosis of Hirschsprung's disease can present quite a clinical challenge. Hirschsprung's disease should be considered in any child who has a history of constipation dating back to the newborn period. The median age at which children are diagnosed with Hirschsprung's disease has progressively decreased over the decades, from 2 to 3 years during the 1920s and 1930s to a mean age of 3 to 6 months during the 1950s to 1970s.[314] More recent series have noted that Hirschsprung's disease is diagnosed in the newborn period in more than 90% of patients.[127,183,260] The usual presentation of Hirschsprung's disease in newborns consists of a history of delayed passage of fecal matter within the first 48 hours of life. Ninety-five percent of full-term infants defecate within the first 24 hours of life, and the remainder pass their first stool by 48 hours.[57] Importantly, this history may be absent in 6% to 42% of patients.[162,314] Other presenting signs and symptoms include constipation, abdominal distention, poor feeding, and emesis. Clinical signs beyond the newborn period include constipation, abdominal distention, and failure to thrive.[37,86,325] Differentiation of Hirschsprung's disease from other forms of chronic constipation or encopresis can be difficult in older children (discussed later). Patients with Hirschsprung's disease may also present with a history of constipation followed by explosive diarrhea, often indicating the development of enterocolitis. A family history should be sought in all cases. As one moves from the newborn period to older children, the diagnosis of Hirschsprung's disease is much less frequently encountered, and a rational plan to approach such patients is important.[155,269]

Physical examination often demonstrates abdominal distention that was absent at birth. Assessment of the anal position on the perineum is important. A subtle, low-lying imperforate anus with an opening that is displaced in an anterior direction may also be a cause of constipation. Rectal examination of patients with Hirschsprung's disease reveals a tight anus that may be incorrectly diagnosed as anal stenosis.

Radiographic Studies

Imaging begins with supine and positional (cross-table lateral, upright, or decubitus) abdominal radiographs. These images commonly reveal distended loops of intestine and may show a paucity of air in the location of the rectum. Radiographic findings are similar with other causes of distal intestinal obstruction in a newborn. Rarely, a transition point is outlined by gas within bowel. Although it is extremely rare, free intraperitoneal air on an abdominal radiograph in a newborn may be the initial presenting sign of perforation of the proximal intestine due to Hirschsprung's disease.[15,238] In this setting, it is important for the surgeon to consider and rule out Hirschsprung's disease as a potential cause. A missed or delayed diagnosis of Hirschsprung's disease may also lead to spontaneous perforation of the small or large intestine during the neonatal period, which is associated with high morbidity and mortality.[205] Perforation is most common in infants with long-segment involvement.[296]

A contrast enema often facilitates the diagnosis of Hirschsprung's disease. In neonates, the enema can differentiate other causes of distal intestinal obstruction from Hirschsprung's disease. Several technical points are relevant when performing an enema for suspected Hirschsprung's disease. First, in newborns, the enema should contain water-soluble contrast material rather than barium, in the unlikely event of an occult perforation (to avoid barium peritonitis) and because it is more effective than barium in relieving obstructing meconium. Water-soluble contrast material is just as accurate as barium in making the diagnosis of Hirschsprung's disease in neonates.[241] Hyperosmolar solutions should be avoided because of their potential to cause fluid and electrolyte imbalances. Beyond the neonatal period, when occult perforation is of little concern, barium is preferred for suspected Hirschsprung's disease because it provides greater definition. Contrast enema is not recommended during active enterocolitis.

Rectal examinations and washouts before the enema should be avoided because they may distort or obliterate the transition zone. The catheter is inserted just inside the anus, and the catheter balloon is *not* inflated. Careful attention to early filling is necessary. Initial contrast is instilled slowly in a controlled manner. It is best to start with the patient in a decubitus position so that the initial bolus of barium in the rectum is visualized in the lateral projection. Occasionally, a transition point is seen only on the early filling images and is obscured with further filling and greater distention. Contrast is instilled retrograde until a transition point is documented or the entire colon is opacified. The catheter is then removed, and the child is allowed to evacuate the colon. A postevacuation image is obtained.

Classic radiographic findings of Hirschsprung's disease are a narrow, spastic distal intestinal segment with a dilated proximal segment. The point of caliber change, or transition zone, is the key radiographic finding when diagnosing Hirschsprung's disease by contrast enema (Fig. 99-1). Most commonly, the transition point is in the rectosigmoid region; however, it can occur anywhere within the colon. Poor evacuation of contrast is corroborating evidence of an abnormality.[277] Twenty-four-hour delayed films are no longer routine but may be obtained to assess for prolonged retention of contrast. Poor evacuation of contrast, even without demonstration of a transition point, should prompt a further workup in children in whom Hirschsprung's disease is suspected.

Unfortunately, contrast enema does not diagnose all cases of Hirschsprung's disease. Some investigators have reported good diagnostic accuracies: 76% by Swenson et al.,[314] 87% by Lister,[193] and 92% by Klein et al.[162,163] Others have found that contrast enema is only marginally helpful. Taxman et al.[322] noted a 29% rate of false-positive results and a 20% false-negative rate, with lack of barium evacuation being a poor indicator of Hirschsprung's disease. Contrast enema is also of limited diagnostic utility in patients with poorly defined transition points. Transition points may be less well defined in neonates and in patients with short-segment disease and total colonic aganglionosis.

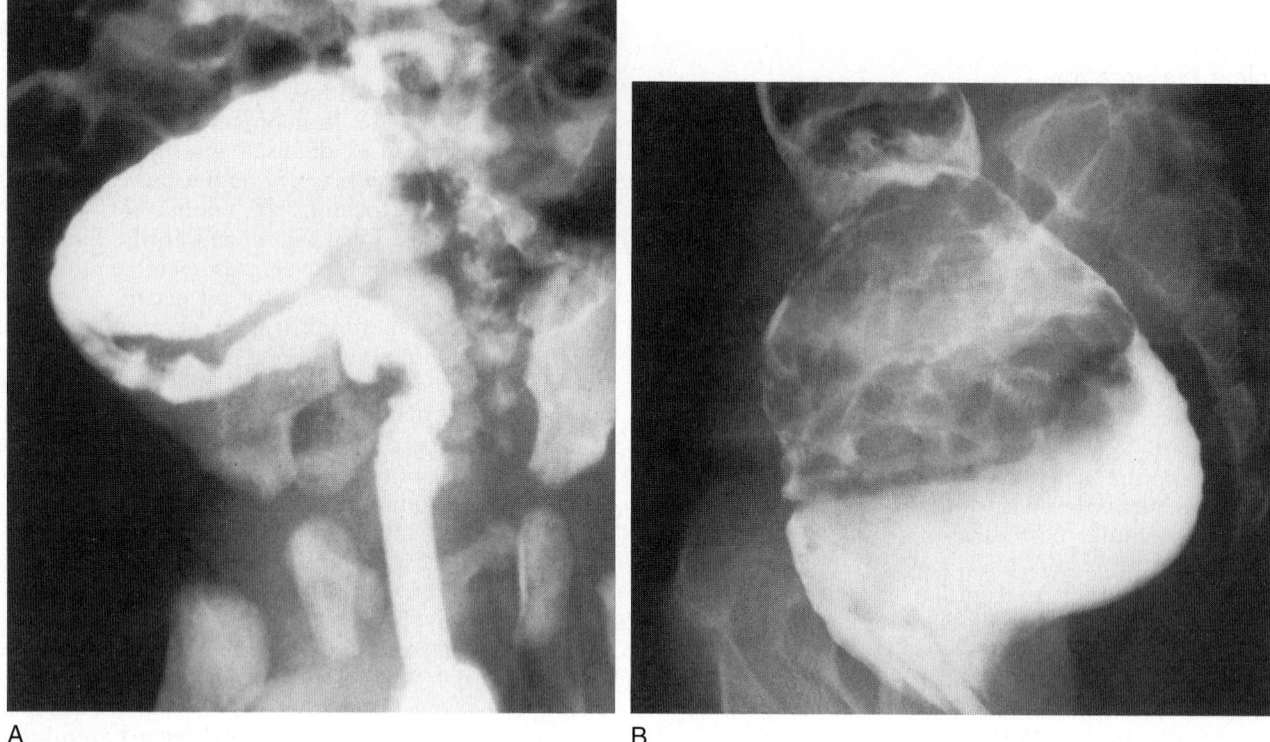

Figure 99–1 Contrast enemas in a patient with Hirschsprung's disease *(A)* and in a patient with constipation *(B)*. Note the narrowed segment in the patient with Hirschsprung's disease and the patulous rectal vault in the constipated patient.

An advantage of performing the enema is that delineation of the transition point may facilitate surgical planning and approach. One group of investigators, however, noted that as many as 53% of contrast studies erred in determining the transition zone.[299] Although there was radiologist agreement on the site of the transition zone in 90% of the contrast enema studies, the concordance between the radiographic transition zone and the pathologic extent of aganglionic bowel was only 62.5%. In a subgroup of patients with long-segment Hirschsprung's disease, a concordance of only 25% was found.[147] Therefore, caution is required when using contrast enemas to delineate transition points for surgical planning.

The contrast enema may occasionally show findings consistent with occult enterocolitis, demonstrating edema, spasm, and even ulceration of the intestinal mucosa (Fig. 99-2). Sawtooth contractions within the spastic distal aganglionic segment are frequently seen and are not indicative of colitis. It should be noted that if a patient is clinically suspected of having enterocolitis, an enema is contraindicated because there is an increased risk of perforation and sepsis.

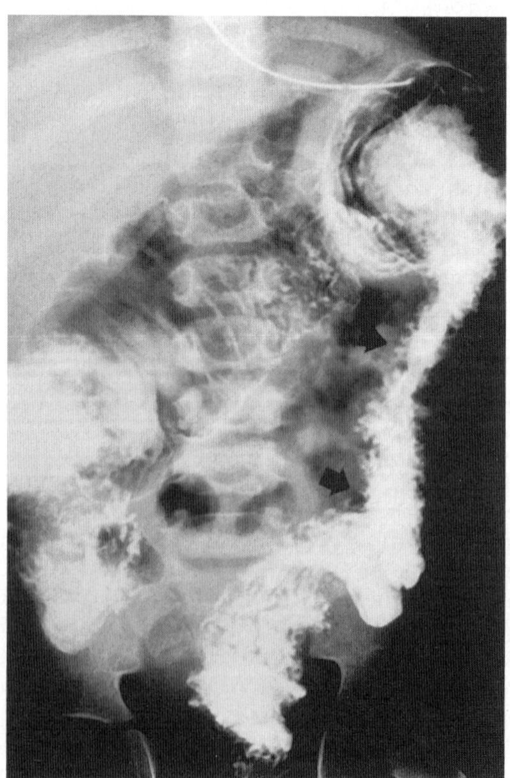

Figure 99–2 Barium enema in a child with enterocolitis demonstrating a markedly irrregular mucosal lining extending down into the aganglionic rectum.

Anorectal Manometry

Anorectal manometry is another method of diagnosing Hirschsprung's disease. The physiologic basis of this technique is discussed later in the section on pathophysiology. Three parameters are assessed in this study. First, the

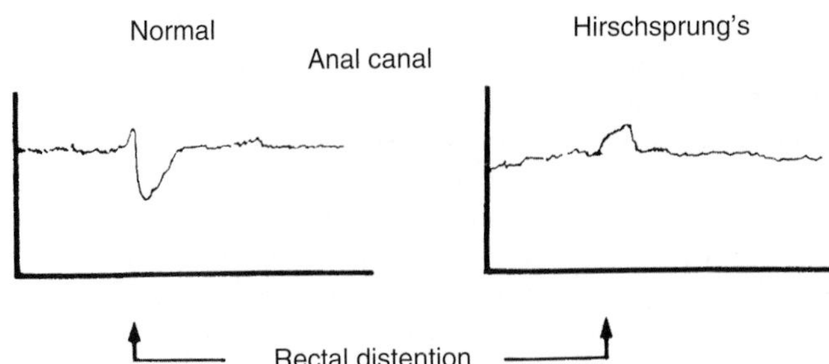

Figure 99-3 Anorectal manometry in a normal patient (left) and in a patient with Hirschsprung's disease (right). Note the abnormally increased contraction *(arrow)* of the upper anal canal with rectal distention and the absence of the relaxation reflex in the patient with Hirschsprung's disease. Appropriate relaxation reflex *(arrow)* is seen in the normal patient. (From Walker AW, et al: Pediatric Gastrointestinal Disease: Pathophysiology, Diagnosis, Management. Philadelphia, BC Decker, 1990.)

technique classically measures the absence of a relaxation reflex after a distending bolus is created in the rectal lumen (Fig. 99-3). Additional information obtained from the study is the resting anal sphincter pressure (elevated with Hirschsprung's) and, in older children, an assessment of a full sensation with balloon distention. This study can be done at the bedside or as an outpatient procedure and is associated with virtually no complications. This technique was initially advocated by Swenson[308,311,313] as a first approach to children with this disorder; it was further refined by Callaghan and Nixon[47] in 1964. Limitations of anorectal manometry relate to the test being contingent on the presence of a normal physiologic state. If patients are examined during an abnormal physiologic state (e.g., sepsis, hypothyroidism), an inaccurate test result is possible.[377] Other limitations include the need to sedate young children to avoid numerous artifacts created by movement or crying.

The accuracy rates of anorectal manometry vary widely among reported series. Some authors consider this examination to be quite diagnostic[319,377]; others report numerous inaccurate results.[64] The rate of false-negative results (i.e., a normal study in a child who is subsequently found to have Hirschsprung's disease) varies from 0%[319] to 24%.[217] The reported rate of false-positive results (i.e., inability to induce an anorectal inhibitory reflex in a patient who is subsequently found not to have Hirschsprung's disease) ranges from 0%[195,319] to 62%.[222,223] Holschneider et al.[135] suggested that the anorectal reflex is not completely developed in premature or full-term infants younger than 12 days old. Ito et al.[143] suggested that the test is unreliable when the subject's postconceptional age (gestational age plus age after birth) is less than 39 weeks and the weight is less than 2.7 kg. Loening-Baucke et al.[196] reported that anorectal manometry is more difficult in newborns because of the limitations of equipment sensitivity. The results seem to be most accurate when the test is done by an operator with considerable experience.

The technique can also be used to follow children after a definitive pull-through procedure to assess for abnormal stooling.[218,344,380] Total colonic manometry may yield useful information in patients with persistent problems.[206] Interestingly, post–pull-through infants typically do not regain the rectosphincteric reflex; however, this does not appear to influence their overall control of stool.[344,380]

Rectal Biopsy

The rectal biopsy is the gold standard for the diagnosis of Hirschsprung's disease (Fig. 99-4). Swenson et al.[312] first described the method of full-thickness rectal biopsy in 1959; disadvantages included bleeding, scarring, and the need for general anesthesia. The method of suction rectal biopsy was developed through a series of advances in

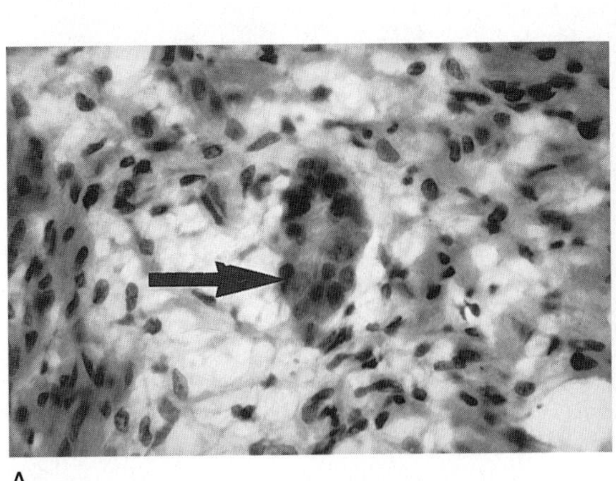

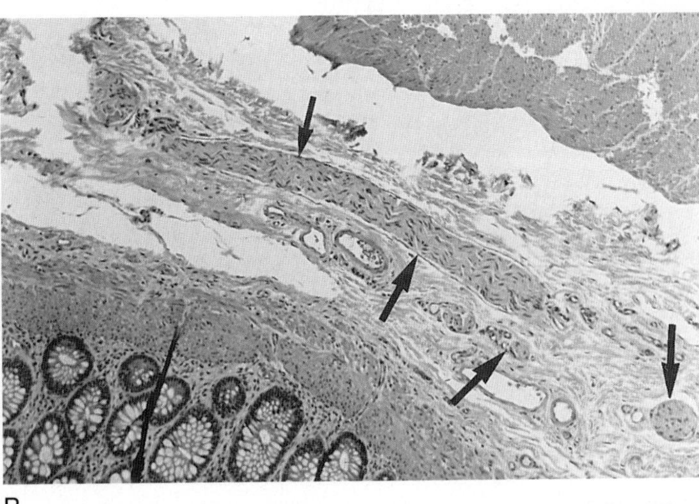

Figure 99-4 Histopathology of Hirschsprung's disease. *A,* Typical ganglion cell complex *(arrow)* in the proximal (ganglionated) segment. *B,* Aganglionic section has an absence of ganglion cells and markedly hypertrophied nerves *(arrows).*

the understanding of distal rectal pathology. Shandling[293] reported that a more superficial punch biopsy was adequate for the diagnosis of Hirschsprung's disease. In 1960 Gherardi[106] demonstrated that the level of aganglionosis was identical in the submucosa and myenteric plexis. This observation led to the first submucosal biopsy by Bodian[34] that same year. Refinement of the technique and development of a suction biopsy instrument[43] led to the development of the suction rectal biopsy by Dobbins and Bill[69] in 1965, which has greatly facilitated the diagnosis of Hirschsprung's disease.

Biopsies may be performed at the bedside or in a clinic. Although the diagnostic accuracy is reportedly as high as 99.7%, errors can occur. The most common problem is an inadequate specimen with an insufficient amount of submucosa, thus precluding an evaluation for ganglion cells. Another problem is performance of the biopsy too close to the anal sphincter. The normal anus has a paucity or absence of ganglion cells at the level of the internal sphincter. A detailed analysis of autopsies of premature infants, term infants, and children by Aldridge and Campbell[6] showed that the level of normal hypoganglionosis is generally longer in the submucosal plexus than in the myenteric plexus in the anal canal. Further, a similar length of normal hypoganglionosis is seen in all age groups, averaging 9 to 10 mm above the dentate line (range, 3 to 17 mm). This led to the accepted practice of obtaining the suction rectal biopsy at 2 cm above the anal valves. The average length of normal hypoganglionosis in the myenteric plexus is 2 to 6 mm above the dentate line; thus, a more distal location may be selected when performing a full-thickness biopsy.

The technique of suction rectal biopsy is quite safe, although complications have been described. In a review of 1340 consecutive biopsies at one institute, three clinical perforations (0.2%) and three rectal hemorrhages requiring transfusion occurred.[267] One of the children with perforation developed gangrene of the buttocks and died. The accuracy of the test has been well demonstrated. In one of the largest reviews on the use of suction rectal biopsy, Andrassy et al.[11] found only one false-negative result among 444 patients.

The pathologic evaluation of a suction rectal biopsy for the diagnosis of Hirschsprung's disease is considerably more difficult than that of a full-thickness biopsy. A recent multicenter analysis of methodologies used to diagnose Hirschsprung's disease showed a wide variation in strategies and emphasized the need for a highly skilled pathologist.[266] The use of acetylcholinesterase staining has facilitated the task. The technique was initially introduced for the diagnosis of Hirschsprung's disease by Meier-Ruge et al.,[215] based on the staining technique of Karnovsky and Roots. The method has since been improved to yield a darker stain.[179] In Hirschsprung's disease, intense staining of the hypertrophied nerve fibers is noted throughout the lamina propria and muscularis propria (Fig. 99-5). The diagnostic accuracy of this stain has been examined by several investigators, who reported excellent results.[137,178] In a review of 497 rectal suction biopsies by Schofield et al.,[288] eight children who had Hirschsprung's disease and nine who did not needed acetylcholinesterase staining because a definitive diagnosis could not be made by hematoxylin-eosin staining alone. Another review, however, showed that 5 of 96 cases of Hirschsprung's disease lacked classic findings on acetylcholinesterase staining and required standard hematoxylin-eosin staining for a definitive diagnosis.[55] False-negative results are unusual but have been reported.[18]

When the diagnosis cannot be made by suction rectal biopsy, a full-thickness posterior rectal wall biopsy should be performed in the operating room. A full-thickness biopsy is also useful in older children in whom a suction biopsy may

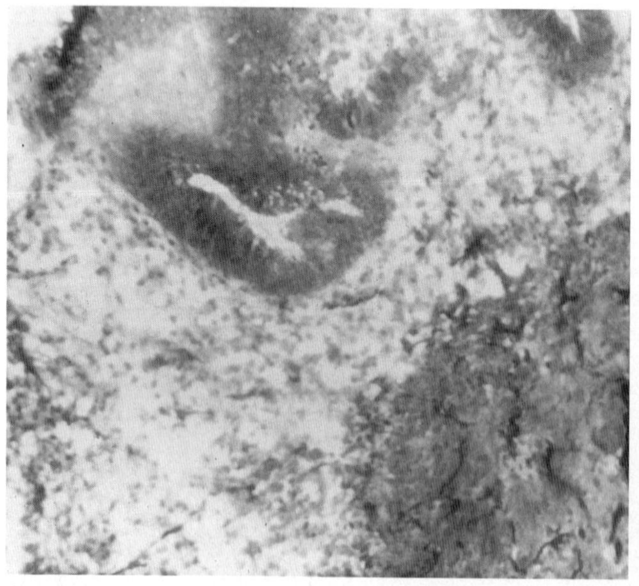
A

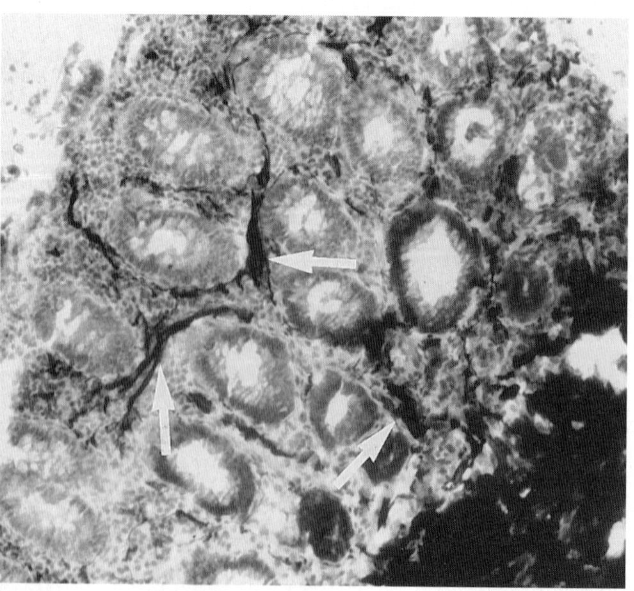
B

Figure 99-5 Acetylcholinesterase staining of ganglionic *(A)* and aganglionic *(B)* bowel. Note the markedly increased staining reaction in the aganglionic bowel (black nerve fibers, *white arrows*) extending into the mucosal lamina propria and muscularis propria (lower right). (Courtesty of Stephen Qualman, MD.)

not obtain a sufficient amount of submucosal tissue. In this latter case it is often not necessary to biopsy completely through the muscularis propria.

DIFFERENTIAL DIAGNOSIS

Various diseases must be considered when a child is being evaluated for Hirschsprung's disease. Table 99-1 lists the more common differential diagnoses. Children with meconium ileus often present in a manner similar to those with Hirschsprung's disease in the first few days of life. Abdominal radiographs may show a ground-glass appearance in the abdomen, particularly in the lower right quadrant, and a contrast enema demonstrates a microcolon. Patients with complete atresia of the colon or distal small intestine also present with a low intestinal obstruction, which may initially mimic Hirschsprung's disease. A complete obstruction, such as an atresia, also results in a microcolon on contrast enema studies. In meconium plug syndrome, a contrast enema can be both diagnostic and curative.[81] The child often passes a meconium plug after the study and is relieved of the obstructive symptoms. In patients with the small left colon syndrome, barium enema contrast studies demonstrate the classic finding of a constricted left colon, and the infant may have a diabetic mother. However, this contrast enema may look quite similar to that of a child with Hirschsprung's disease. In infants with either meconium plug syndrome or small left colon syndrome, suction rectal biopsy is essential to rule out Hirschsprung's disease because the latter may be associated with either of these two syndromes.[253,268] Functional ileus may be caused by various diseases of both systemic and gastrointestinal origin. The large intestine of premature infants functions poorly, and many such infants do not defecate in the first several days of life. Children with functional ileus or a dysfunctional large intestine may present with a microcolon.[9] Sepsis, electrolyte imbalance, and hypothyroidism may also mimic a gastrointestinal obstruction in infancy. Finally, older children with benign functional constipation may have symptoms that resemble those of Hirschsprung's disease. Factors that help differentiate these two entites are discussed in the section "Idiopathic Constipation and Encopresis."

TABLE 99–1 Differential Diagnosis of Hirschsprung's Disease

Other mechanical obstructions
Meconium ileus
Distal ileal or colonic atresia
Small intestinal stenosis
Low imperforate anus
Functional obstructions of the intestinal tract
Prematurity
Small left colon syndrome
Meconium plug syndrome
Sepsis and electrolyte imbalance
Cretinism and myxedema
Functional constipation
Intestinal neuronal dysplasia

CAUSE

An understanding of the pathophysiology of Hirschsprung's disease allowed a rational approach to its diagnosis and treatment, but the precise cause of Hirschsprung's disease is still being sought. This section summarizes the current understanding of this process by first presenting the known genetic mutations associated with Hirschsprung's disease and then correlating these changes with the pathophysiologic disturbances found in the process.

Genetics and Molecular Basis of Hirschsprung's Disease

G. Martucciello, A. Baban, N. Jibri, and V. Jasonni

Sporadic occurrence accounts for 80% to 90% of cases of Hirschsprung's disease. Variable expressivity (different length of aganglionic segments between patients) and incomplete sex-dependent penetrance (whether the individual shows a phenotype of his or her genotype) are observed. For years, all these features of Hirschsprung's disease were suggestive of a more complex pattern of inheritance (multifactorial) and the involvement of many genes (genetic heterogeneity). An effort to identify the major genes involved in Hirschsprung's disease initially took place at Gaslini Institute in Genoa, Italy. This was performed in a girl with total colonic aganglionosis and interstitial deletion in the long arm of chromosome 10 (46XX, del.10q11.21-q21.2) (Fig. 99-6).[207] Through deletion mapping, the region was further reduced to a

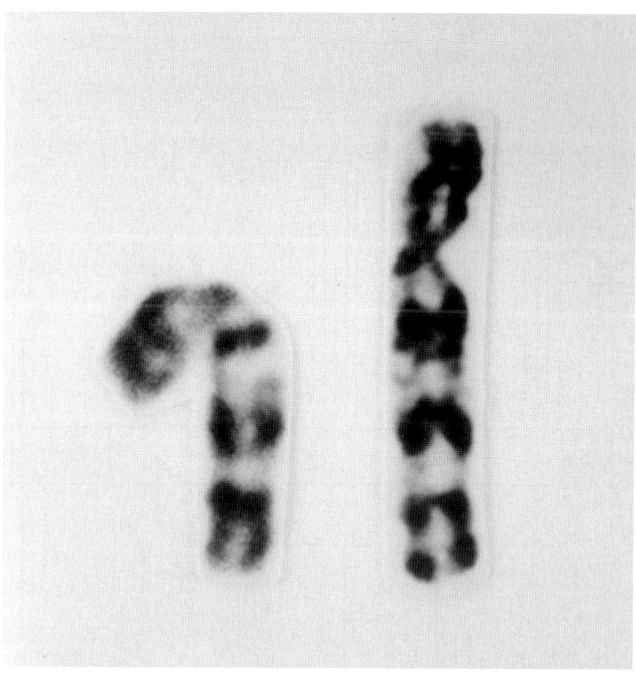

Figure 99–6 Interstitial deletion in the long arm of chromosome 10 (10q11-21) in a case of total colonic aganglionosis.

small 200-kB interval where the *RET* proto-oncogene is located.[53] This discovery led to further studies of peculiar aspects of this gene and additional genetic defects associated with Hirschsprung's disease. Much of the genetic information was initially obtained through animal models affected with colonic aganglionosis, which helped direct investigators to human aganglionic genetic defects. Segregation analysis of different sets of patients and their families suggested that there were different forms of inheritance, depending on the length of the aganglionic segment. The genetic mutations associated with Hirschsprung's disease can best be understood by examaining how they relate to the family of neurocristopathies, many of which have similar genetic patterns. Using the Bolande classification, neurocristopathies can be divided into two basic types. The simple type involves a single pathologic process that is unifocal and localized. It can be further subdivided into a dysgenetic, non-neoplastic form (e.g., Hirschsprung's disease) and a neoplastic form (e.g., medullary thyroid carcinoma and others). The second type of neurocristopathy involves more complex and even syndromic forms that correspond to multifocal disease and associations of simple neurocristopathies (Table 99-2).[35]

TABLE 99-2 Classification of Neurocristopathies

Simple Neurocristopathies
Non-neoplastic dysgenetic
Hirschsprung's disease
Albinism
Mandibulofacial dysostosis
Otocephaly
Congenital central hypoventilation syndrome (CCHS)
Neoplastic
Neuroblastoma
Pheochromocytoma
Medullary thyroid carcinoma
Nonchromaffin paraganglioma
Carcinoid tumors
Complex Neurocristopathies (Neoplastic and Non-neoplastic)
Neurofibromatosis (von Recklinghausen's disease)
Multiple endocrine neoplasia (MEN) type 1
MEN2A
MEN2B
Neurocutaneous melanosis
Familial neuroblastoma with Hirschsprung's disease
Haddad syndrome (CCHS + Hirschsprung's disease)
Shah-Waardenburg syndrome (Waardenburg's syndrome + Hirschsprung's disease)

RET Protein Expression

RET is a proto-oncogene that is expressed primarily during embryonic life in the neural crest, urogenital precursors, adrenal medulla, and thyroid and throughout postnatal life in the central and peripheral nervous systems and the endocrine system.[216] The *RET* gene was found to be mutated in approximately 35% of sporadic cases and 49% of familial cases of Hirschsprung's disease and in a higher percentage of long-segment (76%) versus short-segment (32%) disease.[54,231] *RET* mutations that lead to Hirschsprung's disease can occur throughout the 21 exons of the gene,[216] and at least 89 mutations have been identified, including nonsense mutations, missense mutations, small deletions, and insertions (Fig. 99-7).[54] In contrast, mutations that lead to multiple endocrine

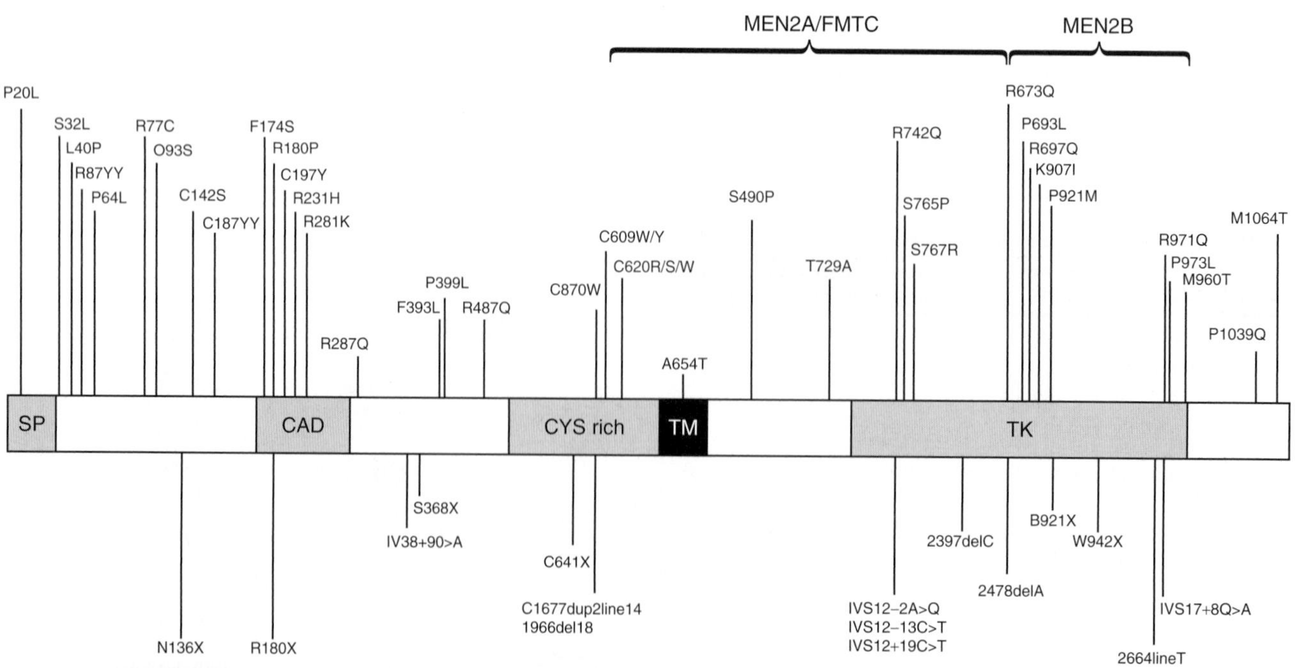

Figure 99-7 *RET* gene mutations that lead to Hirschsprung's disease can occur throughout the 21 exons of the gene.

neoplasia type 2A (MEN2A) or familial medullary thyroid carcinoma (FMTC) are point mutations localized in one of five cysteines of the extracellular domains; they are activating mutations, unlike those that cause Hirschsprung's disease.[41,89,143] Hirschsprung's mutations in the *RET* gene lead to a loss of functional alleles and are heterozygous in nature, which suggests haploinsufficiency. Although Hirschsprung's disease and MEN2 are usually observed in isolated cases and probably result from different molecular and cellular mechanisms owing to the different mutation types, the identification of *RET* mutations (C618 and C620) in families that have both Hirschsprung's disease and MEN2 (FMTC and MEN2A) was surprising. The underlying mechanism that leads to both diseases is unknown,[231] and a number of families have Hirschsprung's disease but carry the mutation that leads to MEN2.[143] This association may yield a clue to the peculiar molecular mechanisms underlying each disease. To explain how the same mutations can produce such diverse phenotypes, we can hypothesize that they are the result of mutations occurring in different periods of embryonic and postnatal life.

Another explanation for the complex inheritance pattern of Hirschsprung's disease and the low detection rate of *RET* mutations is the presence of several common polymorphisms of the *RET* gene that are associated with a variable risk of causing Hirschsprung's disease. Specific *RET* haplotypes act as either protective or predisposing factors or serve to modulate disease severity.[40,41,52,88,89,111,112] A specific haplotype of a rare allele of a single nucleotide polymorphism (SNP) of exon 2 (A45A) has been strongly associated with Hirschsprung's disease, whereas the haplotype of an allele in exon 14 SNP (S836s) seems to be a low-penetrant protective factor against the disease.[88,111]

RET proto-oncogene expression was initially found in a number of neurocristopathy-related tumors. This association was noted in neuroblastoma cell lines, pheochromocytoma, and medullary thyroid carcinoma.[286] These findings in human tumors suggest that the RET protein may be involved in the differentiation of neural crest cells and that its overexpression and activation may lead to their malignant transformation. These studies suggest that the RET receptor might normally function in particular stages or lineages of differentiation but not in a wide variety of cell types, and that its expression is localized to only restricted tissues.[340] Concerning immunohistochemical studies, the first localization of RET protein in the enteric nervous system occurred in 1995,[208] and ganglion cells stained strongly positively. In the case of Hirschsprung's disease, with complete deletion or codon mutations[276] of the *RET* gene, markedly reduced staining (Fig. 99-8) was clearly observed. This finding may support the hypothesis of loss of function due to reduced amounts of RET protein.

Many investigators have tried to explain the absence of *RET* mutations, especially in familial cases with no regular mendelian inheritance. A study of families with more than three affected individuals in multiple generations revealed a susceptibility locus on human chromosome 9q31 in the absence of a coding sequence of *RET* mutations.[38] In addition, a linkage analysis study performed in families with short-length Hirschsprung's disease showed two other loci (3p21 and 19q12) in addition to *RET* alleles.[19]

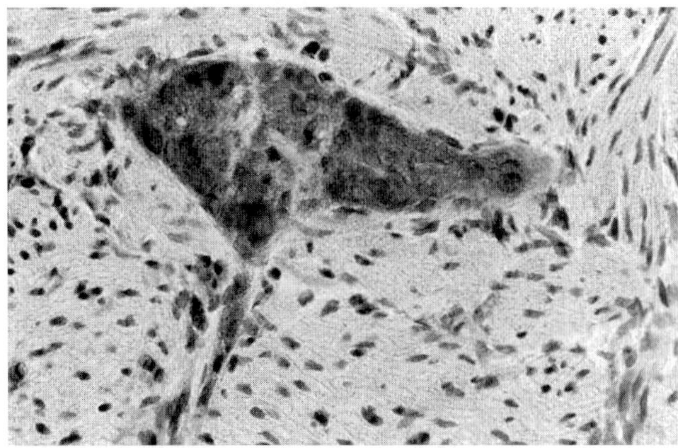
A

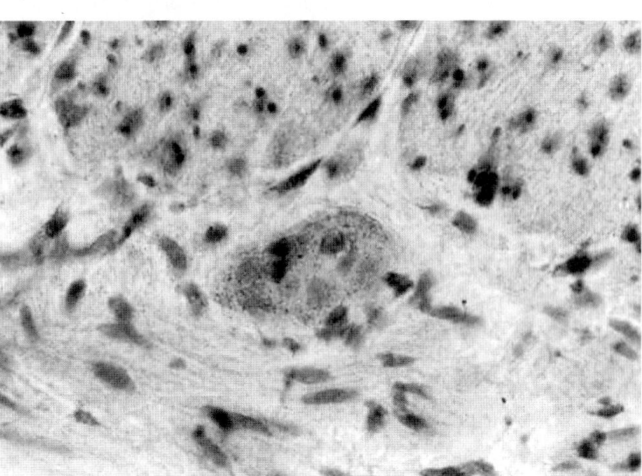
B

Figure 99-8 *A*, RET protein immunostaining in normal ganglion. *B*, Reduced RET protein immunoreactivity in a case of Hirschsprung's disease with a stop codon mutation.

Other Genes Involved in Hirschsprung's Disease

About 5% to 10% of patients show mutations in other genes, such as glial cell line–derived neurotrophic factor (GDNF), neurturin (NTN), endothelin-3 (EDN3), endothelin-B receptor (EDNRB), endothelin converting enzyme-1 (ECE1), the transcriptional factor SOX10, Smad interacting protein-1 (SIP1), and paired like homeobox 2B (PHOX2B).[8,21,38,54,100] The small percentage of patients with known mutations (less than half) raises suspicion about the involvement of other modifier genes or additional risk factors, some of which are already being mapped.[38,52,100] The research in this field is continuous, and based on our present knowledge, the following gene mutations can be associated with the Hirschsprung's phenotype.

Glial Cell–Line Derived Neurotrophic Factor

GDNF (chromosome 5p13) is one of the ligands of the RET receptor (Fig. 99-9). In the complex glycosyl phosphatidyl inositol–linked protein there is GDNFR-α, which

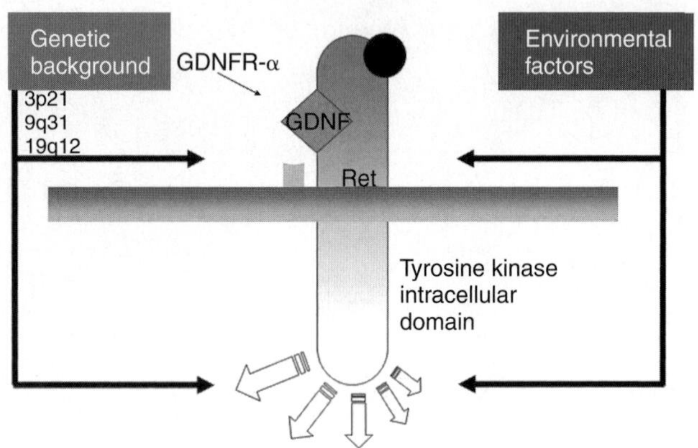

Figure 99–9 GDNF-RET receptor signaling system.

provides the ligand binding between RET protein and GDNF. The absence of either GDNF or GDNFR-α leads to decreased or absent RET signaling (see Fig. 99-9). Two heterozygous mutations in exon 2 of *GDNF* have been identified. These mutations were detected in about 0.9% to 5.5 % of Hirschsprung's cases[13,145] and were found predominantly in patients with *RET* mutations, suggesting that *GDNF* mutations alone are not enough to cause Hirschsprung's disease.[13,145] Even without a genetic mutation, GDNF protein expression may actually be decreased in a number of patients with Hirschsprung's disease compared with normal controls.[209] A GDNF expression deficit in the aganglionic segment may be an important cofactor in Hirschsprung's disease pathogenesis and could lead to missing or reduced activation of the RET receptor in the absence of *RET* proto-oncogene mutations, causing enteric neuroblast migration arrest and Hirschsprung's disease.

Neurturin

In addition to GDNF, RET has another ligand, NTN (located on chromosome 19p13.3), and it has a coreceptor (NTNR-α). This multi-subunit ligand works on the activation of RET.[23,285] Additional coreceptors have been identified, including GDNFR-β, GDNFR-α2, GDNFR-α3, and others (see Fig. 99-7).[150,371] Doray et al.[70] reported the first heterozygous *NTN* missense mutation in a large nonconsanguineous family, including four children affected by long-segment Hirschsprung's disease. They also identified *RET* missense mutations in the same family, inherited from the apparently unaffected father. In addition, there were two unaffected children with isolated heterozygous *NTN* mutations and another one with an isolated *RET* mutation. In conclusion, *NTN* can play a role in the development of Hirschsprung's disesase, but *NTN* mutations alone are not sufficient to cause Hirschsprung's disease; the interaction of *RET* mutations is required, and there may be other susceptible loci not yet identified.[70] This suggests that *RET* could be a single common transducer for multiple pathways for the migration or differentiation of neural crest cells.

Endothelin-3 and Endothelin-B Receptor

Endothelins are a family of 21-amino-acid vasoactive isopeptides: EDN1, EDN2, and EDN3. These three isopeptides vary by no more than six amino acids. Each one is produced as an inactive polypeptide known as "big endothelin." EDN3 is a ligand of the endothelin-B receptor (EDNRB); this ligand-receptor system plays an important role in the development of the enteric nervous system.

During the early developmental stage, EDN3 and EDNRB play a role in neural crest migration and differentiation. In the absence of EDNRB, activation of two neural crest subpopulations are affected—the early melanoblasts (pigmentary cells) and the neuroblast precursors of the enteric nervous system. Because both the melanocytes and the enteric nervous system have common signaling pathways, abnormalities in skin, hair, or eye pigmentations result, collectively called Waardenburg's syndrome. This is a complex neurocristopathy syndrome that includes pigmentary abnormalities (white forelock of hair, usually in the midline, and hypopigmented patches of skin), sensorineural deafness, heterochromia or pale blue irides (sapphire blue color) with hypopigmented fundi, and an absent enteric nervous system in a variable length of the distal gut. The association of Hirschsprung's disease and Waardenburg's syndrome is called the Shah-Waardenburg syndrome or Waardenburg type 4,[70] which has a complex genetic background because it can be caused by *EDN3* and *EDNRB* mutations as well as *SOX10* mutations. Patients who are homozygous for *EDNRB* or *EDN3* express the full picture of the disease plus Hirschsprung's disease,[173,347] whereas heterozygous patients show features of Waardenburg's syndrome, Hirschsprung's disease, or both. Patients who carry

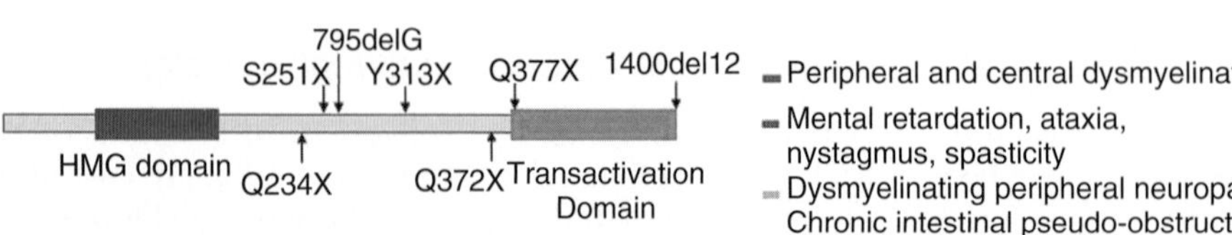

Figure 99–10 *SOX10* gene structure. Different mutations along *SOX10* can lead to diverse phenotypes (Gossens et al., personal communication, 2004).

mutations of *EDNRB* or *EDN3* usually have asymptomatic parents, reflecting autosomal recessive inheritance, with a 25% occurrence rate; *SOX10* has autosomal dominant inheritance, with a 50% occurrence risk in the siblings of affected subjects.[347] Isolated Hirschsprung's disease with *EDNRB* mutation represents a rare cause of sporadic cases of Hirschsprung's disease.[8,20,133,142,176,281,307,320]

Transcriptional Factor SOX10

Human *SOX10* (chromosome 22q12-q13) is a member of the *SOX* gene family of transcriptional regulators. It is selectively expressed in neural crest cells during early stages of development and in glial cells of the peripheral and central nervous systems in both embryonic and adult life.[174] As previously mentioned, *SOX10* mutations can cause a neurocristopathy (Shah-Waardenburg syndrome) that is also caused by *EDN3* and *EDNRB* mutations.[271] The length of aganglionic segment in Shah-Waardenburg syndrome is variable, but unlike isolated Hirschsprung's disease, most patients with Shah-Waardenburg have long-segment or even total colonic aganglionosis.

Recent data have shown that unlike *EDN3* and *EDNRB, SOX10* mutations also cause a wide range of syndromes that can affect the central nervous system, peripheral nervous system, enteric nervous system, and melanocytes through the interaction of other known or unknown factors. Included are (1) Waardenburg's syndrome, peripheral demyelinating neuropathy, and central dysmyelinating leukodystrophy;[234,255] (2) chronic intestinal pseudo-obstruction, which may occur in the presence of normal ganglion cells, indicating that aganglionosis is not the only underlying mechanism for intestinal dysfunction in patients with *SOX10* mutations;[256] and (3) Yemenite deaf-blind hypopigmentation syndrome, in which affected patients suffer from cutaneous hypo- or hyperpigmentation, microcornea, coloboma, deafness, and other features, but not Hirschsprung's disease.[39] Different mutations scattered along the *SOX10* gene can lead to different phenotypes, as illustrated in Figure 99-10.

Other Involved Loci

A number of other mutations have been identified (Table 99-3), but a discussion of these is beyond the scope of this chapter. These include PHOX2B, associated with Ondine's curse,[152] or central hypoventilation syndrome; SIP1, associated with Mowat-Wilson syndrome; and ECE1, associated with a number of congenital anomalies.

TABLE 99-3 Genetic Mutations Associated with Hirschsprung's Disease

Human Gene	Map Location	Percentage
RET	10q11	Sporadic 35% Familial 49% Long-segment 76%
GDNF	5p13	0.9–5.5%
NTN	1qp13.3	Rare (1 known mutation)
EDNRB	13q22	Rare (15 known mutations)
EDN3	20q13	Rare (2 known mutations)
ECE1	1p36	Rare (1 known mutation)
SOX10	22q12–13	Rare
ZFHX1B (SIP1)	2q22–23	Rare
PHOX2B	4p12	Rare

Genetic Counseling

Hirschsprung's disease is a part of many multigenic or multifactorial conditions, raising the issue of genetic counseling. Hirschsprung's disease can be defined as a sex-modified multifactorial disorder with an overall risk of 4% for siblings and first-degree relatives of the proband. It is more difficult to estimate the risk in isolated cases, but it can be done by taking into account certain data such as the sex of the proband and other family members and the length of the aganglionic segment.[21] Counseling is easier in familial cases with known *RET* mutations, in which case the pattern of inheritance is autosomal dominant; there is a 50% risk of offspring having the mutation, but the penetrance and expressivity of the trait cannot be predicted. A study of 17 Hirschsprung's families showed that *RET* penetrance is sex dependent (72% in males and 51% in females).[19] So we can assume that Hirschsprung's disease exhibits marked sex differences that depend on the length of aganglionic segment and gender; penetrance is almost two- to fourfold higher in males than in females.[54] All these factors make genetic counseling difficult and make the prenatal diagnosis of Hirschsprung's disease infeasible. In addition, genetic counseling must take into account the great improvements in the surgical management of Hirschsprung's disease in recent decades. Special attention should be paid to those patients who carry mutations in one of the critical cysteine residues of exons 10 and 11 of the extracellular domain of *RET*, which may predispose to MEN2A.[12,230,292] These patients and other susceptible family members should be followed carefully with proper surveillance and biochemical testing because they are at risk of developing neuroendocrine tumors.

Embryology

Normal Embryologic Formation of the Enteric Nervous System

An understanding of the normal embryologic development of the enteric nervous system is necessary to appreciate the development of Hirschsprung's disease. Normal ganglion cell development consists of several unique phases. The first is the induction phase, which is subject to spatial and timing requirements that depend on multiple factors and different molecular signals.[186] The second step is neural crest cell migration to distant locations throughout the embryo.[185,186] The third step is differentiation of the neural crest cell precursors into multiple cell types. The mechanism of this differentiation remains largely unknown, with many unanswered questions (Fig. 99-11). In normal embryologic development,

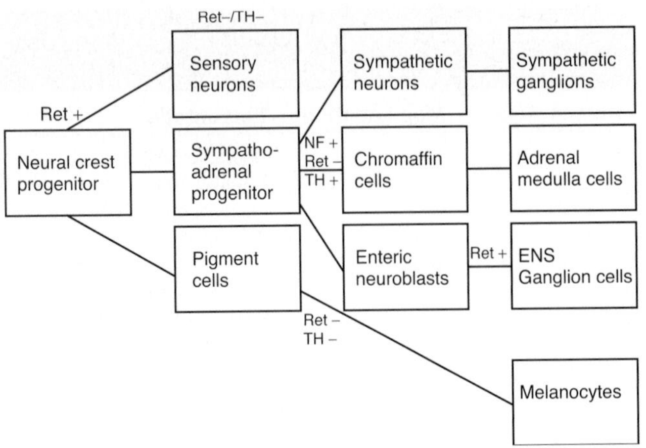

Figure 99–11 Neural crest cell development. Neural crest precursors can differentiate into different types. ENS, enteric nervous system.

neuroenteric cells migrate from the neural crest to the upper end of the alimentary tract and then proceed down in an aboral direction.[187] The first nerve cells arrive in the esophagus by the 5th week of gestation.[242] By the 7th week, nerve cells are at the midgut, and migration to the distal colon is achieved by the 12th week (Fig. 99-12). Migration occurs first into Auerbach's (myenteric) plexus; subsequently these cells move into the submucosal plexus. Neural crest cells are guided in this migration by glycoproteins such as fibronectin and hyaluronic acid (laminar protein),[95] as well as by a number of neural growth factors.

Two basic theories exist regarding the embryologic defect in Hirschsprung's disease: the "failure of migration" theory and the "hostile environment" theory. Clearly, as additional genetic mutations associated with Hirschsprung's disease are identified, we can better appreciate the number of critical proteins that must be expressed in an appropriate spatial and temporal setting to allow the achievement of normal ganglion cell development.[146] Based on the findings of RET interactions with other signaling proteins (GDNF and NTN), it appears that a combination of factors may be necessary to develop the full aganglionic phenotype. Figure 99-13 gives a schematic overview of the various mechanisms that may contribute to the development of Hirschsprung's disease.

Aberrancy in the Migration of Enteric Neurons

All the neurons and glial cells that constitute the enteric nervous system are derived from the neural crest.[186] Normal migration is complex and is dependent on a

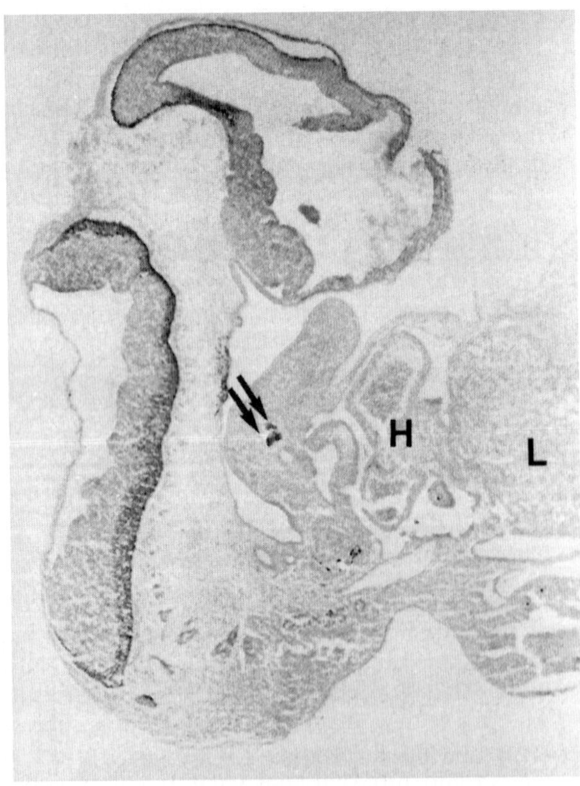

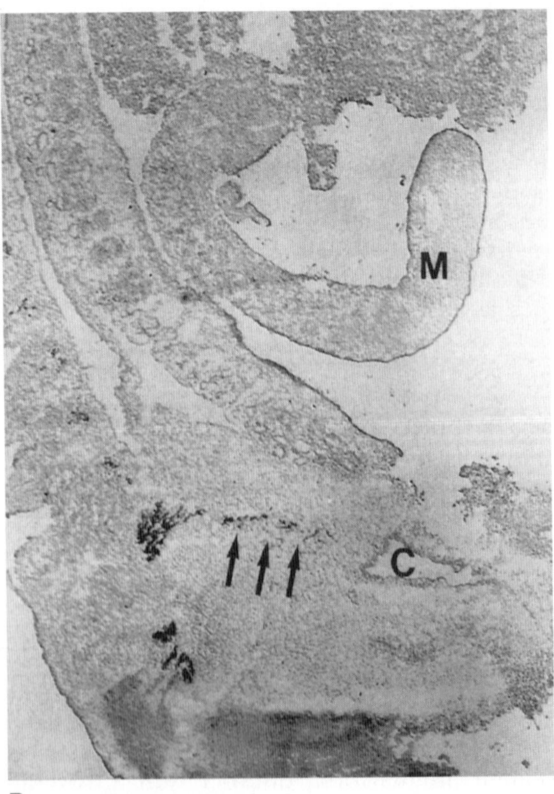

Figure 99–12 Neurofilament protein in a 4-week human fetus. *A*, Neural crest–derived cells first appear in the upper esophagus *(double arrows)*. *B*, At the same time, immunoreactive strands (filaments) are moving toward the cloaca, thus preceding the presence of neural crest cells (*arrows*). C, cloaca; H, heart; L, lung; M, mouth. (From Fujimoto T, Hata J, Yokoyama S, Mitomi T: A study of the extracellular matrix protein as the migration pathway of neural crest cells in the gut: Analysis in human embryos with special reference to the pathogenesis of Hirschsprung's disease. J Pediatr Surg 1989;24:550-556.)

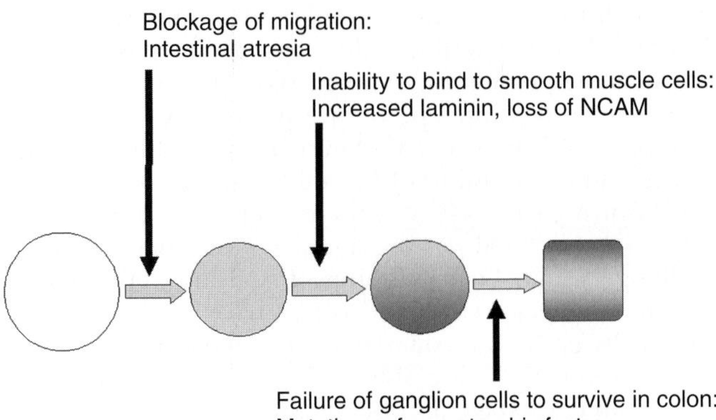

Figure 99-13 Potential mechanisms for the pathogenesis of Hirschsprung's disease.

number of factors. It was originally thought that the bowel receives neural crest cells from both a vagal and a sacral origin. It is now appreciated that the vagal neural crest cells are the main source of ganglion cells, and they clearly migrate to the gut before cells from other sources do.[46] The sacral neural crest cells make up a smaller component of the enteric nervous system and contribute primarily to the hindgut. Several investigators have hypothesized that an aberration of neural crest migration occurs in Hirschsprung's disease and that the neuroblasts' failure to achieve the most distal migration is the cause of the disease. Okamoto and Ueda[242] were the first to hypothesize that the absence of ganglion cells was due to a failure of normal neural crest migration. Experiments performed to obtain total ablation of vagal neural crest cells resulted in total aganglionosis from the anus to the midgut; ablation adjacent to somites 3 to 5 resulted in aganglionosis of the hindgut only, and ablation other than in this segment had no effect on the enteric nervous system's development.[251,252] Investigators have demonstrated that the development of distal colonic aganglionosis may occur with the transection of a chick embryo at the hindgut level. With implantation of pigeon ganglion cells distal to the level of transection, normal incorporation into the distal bowel wall occurs. This suggests that one cause of Hirschsprung's disease is a blockage of normal neural crest cell migration.

Alterations in the Extracellular Matrix

One mechanism by which neural crest cells are guided in their migration is through a variety of neural glycoproteins or fibers whose development precedes neural crest migration.[95,248,249] These glycoproteins include fibronectin and hyaluronic acid, which appear to create a pathway through which neural cells migrate. These supporting fibers progress down the gastrointestinal tract and then move through the bowel, starting at the basement membrane and ending up in the muscular layer. Neural crest cells subsequently use these structures to migrate into the intestinal wall. It is possible that after migration into the intestinal wall these neuroblasts are placed in a "hostile" or nonsupportive environment, which leads to a failure of ganglion cell development. A number of investigators have demonstrated an abnormal distribution of fibronectin and laminin in the aganglionic intestinal wall.[101,247-249,330] These investigators have shown abnormally large amounts of laminin accumulating in the extracellular spaces and speculate that this buildup may prevent the migration of ganglion cells into their new environment.

Loss of Neurotrophic Factors

Exactly what prevents normal migration or incorporation of the neural crest cells is unknown. One critical factor, and one that may have the greatest influence in the pathogenesis of Hirschsprung's disease, is the expression of neurotrophic factors. The RET signaling pathway is one such factor. RET and its coreceptor GFR-α1 are expressed in migrating vagal neural crest cells and are essential for enteric nervous system development.[46] The ligand for the RET–GFR-α1 complex is GDNFR. GDNF is expressed in the gastrointestinal wall and acts as a chemoattractant for enteric neurons. Maximal GDNF-responsiveness is found in areas just preceding those where neural crest cells are about to migrate to, thus acting as a guide to direct normal migration and appears to be counter-regulated by endothelin-3 (EDN3).[123] As pointed out earlier, all these factors may have genetic mutations in Hirschsprung's patients, which may preclude normal migration. Other factors that are important in guiding neural crest cell migration include NTN and EDN3.[144] Once neural crest cells have successfully migrated into the gastrointestinal wall, a series of maturational steps occurs. Defects in the function of neural crest cells may have an essential role in the development of Hirschsprung's disease.[146] Embryologically, the first expressable factor to be detected by neural crest cells is nitric oxide, followed by a number of other neurotransmitters. A loss of nitric oxide expression has also been identified in aganglionic areas of the intestine (see later). Two additional neurotrophic factors that have been identified as contributing to neural crest maturation are transcriptional factors Mash1 and SOX10; *SOX10* mutations have been identified in some cases of Hirschsprung's disease (see earlier).[246]

Loss of Cellular Adhesion Molecular Expression

In support of the hostile environment theory, Langer et al.[181] demonstrated that ganglion cells cultured with smooth muscle tissue from aganglionic colon showed a significantly decreased ability to adhere to smooth muscle cells, suggesting a lack of cell-to-cell adherence. This finding was substantiated by showing that there is a loss of neural cell adhesion molecule (NCAM) activity in Hirschsprung's disease. Kobayashi et al.[167] studied NCAM reactivity in colonic specimens of Hirschsprung's disease patients and compared them with age- and sex-matched controls. Bowel containing ganglion cells (both in control patients and in those with Hirschsprung's disease) had strong NCAM reactivity, whereas there was an absence of NCAM-positive nerve fibers in the myenteric plexus of aganglionic segments. NCAM is believed to be important in neurocyte migration and localization of neurocytes to specific sites during embryogenesis. Other adhesion molecules that show decreased expression in areas of aganglionosis include L1CAM and N-cadhedrin.[378] Possibly to compensate for this loss of nerve migration, intercellular adhesion molecule 1 (ICAM-1) is markedly increased in areas of aganglionosis.[166]

Immunologic Factors

Major histocompatibility complex class II antigens were shown to be markedly elevated in areas of aganglionosis.[175] This observation has been confirmed by other investigators,[130,166] which suggests that one mechanism for the loss of ganglion cells may be a heightened immune response against self-antigens on the ganglion cell. An increase in ICAM-1 expression, as noted earlier, also suggests an inflammatory response to a perceived foreign tissue.[166] Another potential mechanism of ganglion cell loss is via an increase in apoptosis. Although this area of investigation is still quite new, there is evidence that areas of aganglionosis have a loss of Bcl-2, a critical factor that blocks apoptosis, thus potentially allowing for greater levels of ganglion cell loss.[302]

Future Applications of Genetic and Pathophysiologic Information

Through genetic manipulation, both mouse and rat models of aganglionosis have been developed. Among these models are two strains of mice consisting of the piebald-lethal strain (S^LS^L-homozygote) and a lethal spotting strain (L^S-heterozygote). These mice develop megacolon and generally die of diarrhea and presumed enterocolitis within the first few months of life.[50,94] Although not precisely like the human version of the disease, these models and others have helped identify other potential genetic mutations and have led to the study of new modalities to treat Hirschsprung's disease. As stem cell research advances, therapeutic options may be developed that involve the implantation of ganglion cells into the aganglionic portion of the intestine. Recent work has shown that ganglion cell stem cells can be isolated in rodents.[172,297] Recently, rats with a targeted disruption of EDNRB or with the S^L mutation (spotting lethal) have been successfully treated by embryonic transfection with the *EDNRB* gene.[102] This resulted in the complete expression of EDNRB as well as colonic ganglion cells in these rats, with the prevention of megacolon. This exciting new area of investigation opens the question whether such therapeutic maneuvers could ever be applied in humans. A better understanding of the mutations associated with Hirschsprung's disease and the detection of these disorders in a prenatal setting may be essential. Another challenge would be the timing of such an approach. It appears that such therapy would have to be applied during the embryonic stage to effect adequate expression of ganglion cells. Being able to detect a genetic disorder at such an early stage and being able to transfect genetic material to an embryo will be difficult challenges.

PATHOLOGY

The gross features of Hirschsprung's disease vary with the duration of the untreated disease. In the early neonatal period, the intestine may appear fairly normal. As the infant ages, the proximal ganglionic bowel hypertrophies and is thicker and longer than normal. Well-defined taeniae are lost, and a hypertrophied longitudinal muscle layer appears to completely surround the colon. The transition zone from ganglionic to aganglionic intestine may be funnel-like and vary in length. The distal bowel appears normal or contracted.

Histologically, the absence of ganglion cells in the distal intestine is the hallmark of the disease. Ganglion cells are absent in both the submucosal (Meissner's) plexus and the intermuscular (Auerbach's) plexus (see Fig. 99-4A). Associated with this finding is a marked increase in nerve fibers that extend into the submucosa (see Fig. 99-4B). These fibers may be seen on routine hematoxylin-eosin stained slides but are more easily seen using an acetylcholinesterase stain (see "Diagnosis," earlier; see Fig. 99-5A and B). The classic extent of the aganglionosis is the rectosigmoid region in approximately 80% of cases.[195,222,223,238] The distribution of the level of aganglionosis in several large series is shown in Table 99-4. The process of aganglionosis is almost always continuous in nature, with no interruptions until the proximal ganglionic segment is reached. Exceptions have been documented, but these cases are so rare that the finding of ganglion cells proximal to an aganglionic segment almost always indicates that one has reached the transition zone. Although many surgeons identify the transition zone using frozen sections

TABLE 99-4 Extent of Aganglionosis in Hirschsprung's Disease

	Location in Selected Series (%)					
Transition Zone	Polley[260]	Kleinhaus[164]	Klein[163]	Teitelbaum[327]	Ikeda[140]	Swenson[314]
Rectosigmoid	74	74	58	71	79	73
Long segment	11	18	26	13	13	24
Total colonic	12	8	12	10	5	3
Small bowel	3	*	0	0	3	0.4

*Small bowel included in total colonic cases.

at the time of pull-through, inaccuracies can occur. In a review of 80 patients with Hirschsprung's disease who had frozen sections, concurrence between the permanent specimen findings and frozen section findings was only 80%. Further, two patients had suboptimal procedures owing to an inaccurate reading of the frozen section.[200] These findings underscore the need for an experienced pathologist to assist the pediatric surgeon. New techniques to rapidly perform acetylcholinesterase or NADPH-diaphorase staining may help avoid such errors.[168,237]

The length of the transition zone varies and may extend for several centimeters. Although ganglion cells may be present in the transition zone, colonic motility may not be normal. The presence of hypertrophied nerve fibers in this area indicates that transitional elements are still present. The presence of these hypertrophied nerves, and possibly the finding of intestinal neuronal dysplasia at the transition zone, may be the cause of bowel dysfunction after the definitive pull-through.[217] Additionally, despite the presence of ganglion cells on one side of the bowel wall, the transition zone may be present elsewhere along the circumference, supporting the concept of selecting a pull-through level a few centimeters higher than the frozen section would suggest.[107]

A variety of neuronal and peptide markers have been developed to help identify alterations in the innervation and ganglionic distribution in Hirschsprung's disease. Decreased staining of vasoactive intestinal polypeptide, substance P, gastrin-releasing peptide, and met-enkephalin has been shown in aganglionic segments.[114,341,342] Other intrinsic nerve fibers are either unchanged (galanin or calcitonin gene-related peptide) or increased (neuropeptide Y) in aganglionic segments.[184] The pathophysiologic significance of these changes has not yet been elucidated.

A number of other histologic markers have been identified that have distinct patterns within the gastrointestinal tracts of children with Hirschsprung's disease. These include reduced amounts of neuron-specific enolase, neurofilament, and S-100 protein.[165,316,353,373] A monoclonal antibody to Schwann cells, D_7, has been shown to be completely absent in aganglionic tissue and may be one of the best markers of aganglionosis.[96] Additionally, the absence of NADPH-diaphorase staining may be a useful indicator of Hirschsprung's disease.[225] Finally, alterations in the interstitial cells of Cajal have been seen in patients with Hirschsprung's disease, including an absence of these cells in the anal sphincter[258] and a complete absence of staining in the aganglionic segments of the colon in children with Hirschsprung's disease.[346] Although none of these markers has been used on a widespread basis, some may eventually become useful adjuncts in the diagnosis of Hirschsprung's disease.

PATHOPHYSIOLOGY

The intestine contains three neuronal plexuses: the submucosal or Meissner's plexus, the intermuscular myenteric or Auerbach's plexus, and a much smaller mucosal plexus.[291,370] Each contains a finely integrated neuronal network that acts to control many functions of the gut (absorption, secretion, blood flow, motility) with relatively little control from the body's central nervous system. In fact, the intestine contains the same number of neurons as the spinal cord.[370] Normal intestinal motility is controlled primarily by these intrinsic neurons in each ganglion. Loss of extrinsic control still allows for adequate function of the intestine.[326] These ganglia can cause contraction or relaxation of the smooth muscle; however, relaxation predominates under normal circumstances. Extrinsic control of the intestine is through both preganglionic cholinergic fibers and postganglionic adrenergic fibers. The cholinergic fibers result in contraction through the neurotransmitter acetylcholine. The adrenergic fibers are predominantly inhibitory but also contain some excitatory pathways, and they use norepinephrine to mediate their function. The intestine also contains an intrinsic nervous system with a neurotransmitter that is predominantly inhibitory in nature; this system was previously referred to as the noncholinergic, nonadrenergic nervous system. The neurotransmitter responsible for this class of nerves was not identified until 1990, when Bult et al.[45] showed that nitric oxide (NO) was the mediator of this inhibitory action. In the normal intestine, a fine balance of contractile and relaxation forces keeps the smooth muscle finely controlled (Fig. 99-14).

In addition to abnormal migration of ganglion cells, the pacemaker cells of the intestine—the interstitial cells of Cajal (ICCs)—have been hypothesized to be diminished in involved areas of Hirschsprung's disease. Studies demonstrating both normal and diminished ICC distribution in Hirschsprung's disease have been published.[239,301] Of interest is that ICCs use carbon monoxide as a neurotransmitter. Potentially, a loss of ICCs may contribute significantly to the pathophysiology of Hirschsprung's disease.[257]

A normal motility reflex is present in the distal rectum. This mechanism was initially described by Gowers[110] in 1877. A mildly distending bolus in the distal rectum initiates a contraction above the bolus and relaxation below the bolus. Such a reflex is purely intrinsic to the intestine itself. The absence of this reflex denotes an abnormality or absence of the intramural ganglion cells (see the earlier section on anorectal manometry).

With the absence of ganglion cells, the extrinsic nervous system develops a markedly increased innervation

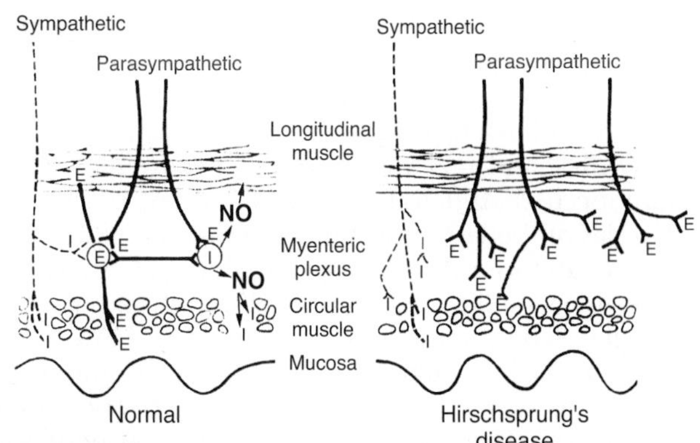

Figure 99-14 Schematic representation of the neuroinnervation of ganglionated bowel (left) and aganglionic bowel (right). E, excitatory fibers; I, inhibitory fibers; NO, nitric oxide.

of the intestine. The adrenergic and cholinergic systems show a two- to threefold increase in innervation in the aganglionic intestine.[26,138,335,337] It is speculated that the adrenergic excitatory system predominates over the inhibitory function in the aganglionic segment, thus creating increased smooth muscle tone. Cholinergic innervation is markedly increased in the aganglionic tissue and is predominantly excitatory. Another component that explains the mechanism of the contracted aganglionic segment is the loss of NO, which is normally expressed by ganglion cells.[317] Several investigators have demonstrated a loss of NO synthase (the enzyme required for NO production) in the myenteric plexus of aganglionic intestine,[27,167,243] whereas normal amounts of NO synthase are found in ganglionic sections.[317] It seems that this loss of NO, along with an increase in adrenergic and excitatory cholinergic fibers, leads to the overly contractile smooth muscle. What is difficult to resolve in these studies is that NO synthase shows strong reactivity in the submucosal plexus of aganglionic regions but is absent in the myenteric plexus. It is possible that the source of NO in these locations is from an ingrowth of extrinsic nerves, and the absence of NO synthase in the myenteric plexus is enough to account for the spastic nature of the colon.

ASSOCIATED ANOMALIES

Hirschsprung's disease is usually an isolated disorder of full-term, otherwise healthy infants. However, several associated congenital anomalies have been recognized. One of the best described associations is with trisomy 21 (Down syndrome), which has been reported to occur in 4.5% to 16% of children with Hirschsprung's disease.[49,109] In a study by Quinn et al.,[267] 13% of their patients with Hirschsprung's disease had trisomy 21. The prognosis for these patients was poor. Although a definitive pull-through procedure was performed in 13 of 17 patients, only one achieved normal intestinal function. Others have reported better clinical results. In the series by Caniano et al.,[49] 6 of 13 patients with trisomy 21 were considered to be candidates for a definitive pull-through procedure. Each of these children had a good result with daytime continence, although nighttime incontinence did occur. Similar results have been reported more recently and suggest that the treatment of high-functioning patients with trisomy 21 should be similar to that used in other patients with Hirschsprung's disease.[116] Importantly, a higher incidence of enterocolitis has been noted in patients with Hirschsprung's disease in conjunction with trisomy 21[323] and may be caused by a combined T- and B-lymphocyte dysfunction in these children.[189]

Atresias of the large and small intestine have also been noted in patients with Hirschsprung's disease. An association between colonic atresia and Hirschsprung's disease has been noted in several cases reports.[3,136,368] The cause of this occurrence is unknown, but it may be the result of a late vascular accident.[3] Although rare, one should always suspect Hirschsprung's disease in a patient with colonic atresia. The pediatric surgeon should insist on a careful pathologic inspection of the distal colon for aganglionosis[3] and should consider a suction rectal biopsy. The diagnosis of Hirschsprung's disease is often missed until after intestinal continuity is established and an obstructive pattern develops.[227,365] The occurrence of Hirschsprung's disease with small intestinal atresias is somewhat more common than with colonic atresia, with an incidence of 0.25% to 0.8% in all patients with Hirschsprung's disease.[140,227] Gauderer et al.[103] recommended that the distal intestine always be examined for Hirschsprung's disease in cases of small intestinal atresia. Anorectal atresias have also been described in association with Hirschsprung's disease. Kiesewetter et al.[156] reported an incidence of 3.4% among 296 patients with Hirschsprung's disease, and Watanatittan et al.[354] found 9 cases among 321 patients (2.8%). Some of the reported cases of ultrashort Hirschsprung's disease may merely represent the fact that the fistula in patients with imperforate anus lacks ganglion cells.

Other anomalies associated with Hirschsprung's disease are trisomy 18, Ondine's curse,[77] and a variety of neurocristopathologic disorders discussed earlier.[58,157,244] Currarino's triad has also been associated with Hirschsprung's disease,[24] as has Smith-Lemli-Opitz syndrome. Other anomalies previously believed to be associated with Hirschsprung's disease (e.g., urinary tract anomalies) have since been rejected.

ENTEROCOLITIS

Enterocolitis of Hirschsprung's disease remains the major cause of significant morbidity and mortality. This entity is manifested clinically as explosive diarrhea, abdominal distention, and fever.[32,77] The pathophysiology of the enterocolitis of Hirschsprung's disease has not been fully elucidated; however, based on experimental and clinical studies, several contributory factors have been identified that may help explain its development. Figure 99-15 demonstrates the theory surrounding the development of enterocolitis associated with Hirschsprung's disease. Because of aganglionosis, a persistent state of colonic and small intestinal stasis occurs. It seems that when this type of stasis is left untreated, a greater incidence of enterocolitis is observed.[48,108] Many investigators believe that stasis leads to bacterial overgrowth and altered states of blood flow to the mucosa. Bacteria that have enteroadhesive and enteroinvasive properties may then enter the intestinal epithelium through defects in the intestinal defense mechanism.[323] At least two defects in intestinal defense mechanisms have been identified in Hirschsprung's disease. First, there are significant alterations in the mucin composition.[4,16,17,212] Changes in mucin gene expression and the post-translational character of mucin may interfere with the normal protective function of mucins. In particular, infants with enterocolitis virtually lack MUC2, which is the major form of mucin in human colons.[212] Second, infants with Hirschsprung's disease have localized immunologic aberrancies, including defects in the amount of immunoglobulin A present in the intestine.[50,94,366,367] Additional defects in T-lymphocyte function have been identified in mouse models as well as in humans with enterocolitis.[50,97,366,367] This latter point is supported by an increased incidence of enterocolitis in

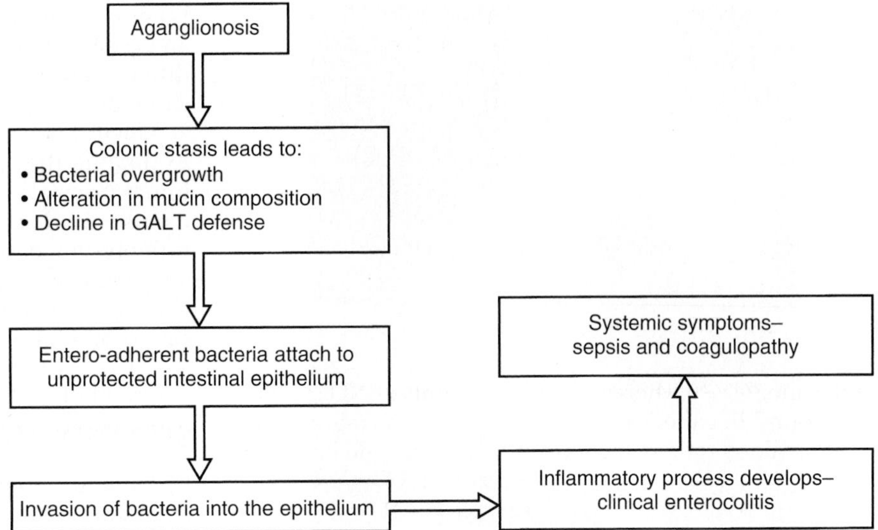

Figure 99–15 Possible pathophysiologic basis for the development of Hirschsprung's-associated enterocolitis. GALT, gut-associated lymphoid tissue.

patients with both Hirschsprung's disease and trisomy 21.[325] Patients with trisomy 21 are known to have defects in both the humoral and the cellular immunologic systems.[189] Once bacteria are able to gain access to the intestinal epithelium, bacteria that have enteroadhesive properties can adhere to and then invade the wall of the intestine, leading to clinical enterocolitis.[323]

Pathologically, enterocolitis is defined as an acute inflammatory infiltrate into the crypts and mucosa of the colonic or small intestinal epithelium (Fig. 99-16). Histologically, a progression of changes may be seen. Early stages show large amounts of inspissated mucins within the colonic crypts, a finding unique to only two diagnoses—Hirschsprung's disease and cystic fibrosis.[80,323] Subsequent changes include the formation of crypt abscesses, mucosal ulceration, and, finally, complete perforation of the intestinal wall. A pseudomembranous colitis may develop, which can be lethal.[61,323] The process may be seen in ganglionic as well as aganglionic intestine.[80,323] Some have suggested that children who initially present with Hirschsprung's disease and enterocolitis may have an increased risk for recurrent enterocolitis after a pull-through procedure.[192,232] Although others disagree,[115] it is clear that the finding of enterocolitis on histopathologic biopsies early in life places the child at risk for clinical recurrences of enterocolitis after the pull-through procedure.[80] It has been suggested that severe post–pull-through enterocolitis may be associated with local intestinal neuronal dysplasia in the neorectum.[169] Some patients with severe enterocolitis may develop changes in the small intestine associated with malabsorption.[44]

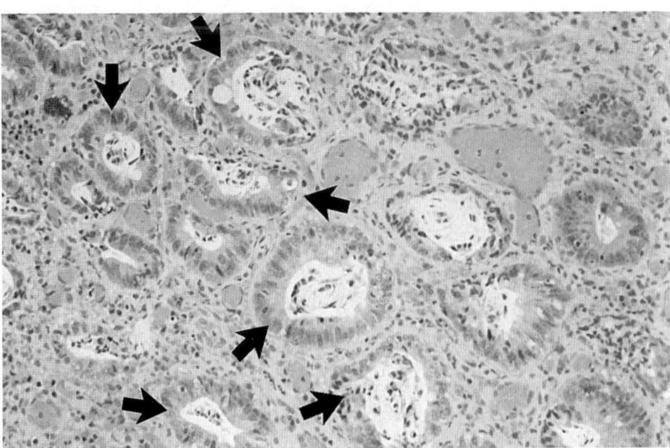

Figure 99–16 Histopathology of a patient with enterocolitis. Note the numerous crypt abscesses *(arrows)*.

The incidence of enterocolitis as the initial presentation of Hirschsprung's disease has decreased substantially over the past 50 years because Hirschsprung's disease is now being diagnosed at earlier ages. Enterocolitis most commonly presents after the definitive pull-through procedure. The overall incidence of post–pull-through enterocolitis ranges from 5% to 46% but is typically between 20% and 30%, depending on how the diagnosis is defined.[48,80,85,115,183,226,262,323,327] Post–pull-through enterocolitis may be caused by an excessively tight pull- through or may be related to spasm of the internal anal sphincter.[120,327] An anatomic stricture or narrowing of the anastomosis has been closely associated with enterocolitis.[115,323,327] One risk factor associated with an increased incidence of enterocolitis is long-segment disease,[48,272,325] although this has not been uniformly observed by all investigators.

The diagnosis of enterocolitis is made on the basis of a clinical history of diarrhea (69%), vomiting (51%), fever (34%), and lethargy (27%).[78] On physical examination, the child often has a distended abdomen and explosive diarrhea after a rectal examination.[32,48] Along with the history and physical examination, the finding of an intestinal "cut-off sign" on abdominal radiographs has a high degree of sensitivity (74%) and specificity (86%) for enterocolitis (Fig. 99-17).[78] Contrast enemas should be avoided because there is a risk of perforation; however, such a study would typically show an irregular mucosal pattern with a "sawtooth" appearance (see Fig. 99-2). The mortality rate associated with Hirschsprung's enterocolitis ranges from 0% to 30%.[32,115,140,164,325]

The treatment of Hirschsprung's-associated enterocolitis begins with a series of aggressive washouts using a rectal

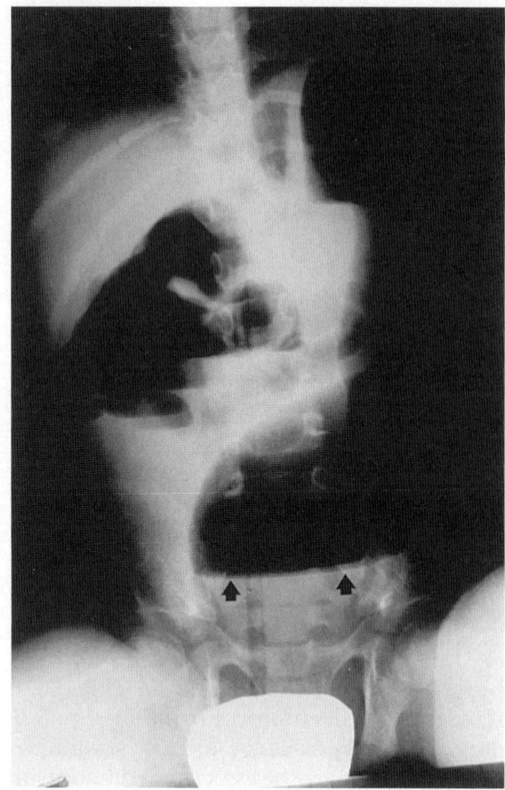

Figure 99–17 Abdominal radiograph in a child with enterocolitis. Note the abrupt "cut-off sign" *(arrows)* at the pelvic brim.

tube to decompress the colon above the anal sphincter. Enemas alone are ineffective because they do not allow adequate decompression of the colon. These serial washouts should be accompanied by intravenous antibiotics or oral metronidazole, depending on the severity of the clinical presentation. Washouts are often not effective in long-segment disease, and a decompressive ostomy may be required. Some patients may benefit from rectal dilatations or relaxation of the internal sphincter with botulinum toxin injection.[220] Use of sodium cromoglycate (a nonabsorbable mast cell stabilizing agent used to treat inflammatory bowel disease) may also be beneficial in preventing recurrent enterocolitis.[275] The majority of patients with enterocolitis outgrow the process. However, patients with repetitive episodes of enterocolitis after an adequate pull-through procedure may benefit from a posterior myotomy or myomyectomy.[364] The use of post–pull-through washouts has been advocated and is associated with a significantly decreased rate of enterocolitis.[211]

THE APPENDIX

Hirschsprung's disease may present initially as perforated appendicitis, commonly in the newborn period.[15,201,287] Serial biopsies of the colon are required in infants who present with such a clinical picture. In general, these perforations often denote longer lengths of aganglionosis. A great deal of controversy surrounds the use of the appendix to diagnose total colonic Hirschsprung's disease; however, histologic evaluation of the appendix is generally an excellent diagnostic tool.[10] Innervation of the appendix differs slightly from that of the rest of the intestine; in cases of total colonic aganglionosis, the appendix has a paucity of nerve fibers and neuroendocrine cells.[295] Evaluating the appendix at a relatively early stage in the initial surgical exploration of a child with Hirschsprung's disease often expedites the diagnosis. In one case, a child with presumed total colonic aganglionosis and aganglionosis of the appendix was subsequently found to have normal ganglion cells in the transverse colon.[10] This extremely rare case represents segmental Hirschsprung's disease.

SEGMENTAL AND ACQUIRED DISEASE

Segmental aganglionosis, whereby an isolated segment is aganglionic but the distal colon possesses ganglion cells, is exceedingly rare. The case of a skip lesion is one such example. A few additional cases of zonal aganglionosis have been reported,[69,153,379] and the process has also been described in an adult.[93] The embryology of these conditions is unknown; however, Okamoto and Ueda[242] suggested that zonal aganglionosis is caused by interference in the orderly process of the craniocaudal migration of neuroblasts. Similarly, Kapur et al.[153] presented evidence from lethal spotted mice that skip areas are secondary to an extramural phase of neuroblast migration that is unique to the colon. Because of the rarity of this condition, it should be suspected only when the clinical course differs considerably from the histopathologic description.

Acquired Hirschsprung's disease refers to a condition in which a child with Hirschsprung's disease initially has ganglion cells at a particular level of the intestine but later is found to have an absence of ganglion cells at that level. This condition is seen infrequently but can be quite challenging clinically.[67,336,338] The cause of acquired disease is unknown, but it may be the result of a selective ischemic event, because histologic evidence of ischemic changes has been found in some cases.[59,336] An experimental correlate involves the injection of a mercuric chloride agent into the mesenteric vessels of the rectum; this results in an aganglionic segment that mimics Hirschsprung's disease in many ways.[242] A variant of acquired Hirschsprung's disease is seen in infants who, after a leveling colostomy, develop ostomy dysfunction caused by a loss of ganglion cells from a postoperative ischemic event. Similarly, acquired aganglionosis has been documented after pull-through for imperforate anus. Another potential cause of acquired Hirschsprung's disease is lengthening of the small residual aganglionic segment in the distal rectum following a pull-through procedure.

DISEASE IN ADOLESCENTS AND ADULTS

Hirschsprung's disease may have an atypical presentation in adolescents and adults. Over a 10-year period, two adolescents and three adults were diagnosed with Hirschsprung's disease at our institute (3% of all patients).[260] A review of the literature reveals approximately 200 cases of adults with Hirschsprung's disease.[359] In general, these patients adapt to their disease by compensatory dilatation of the proximal intestine and through regular use of cathartics and enemas.[14] Swenson et al.[313] reported the largest experience of adults with Hirschsprung's disease; of 282 patients treated by the Swenson pull-through procedure, 71 (25%) were adults. However, the outcome of these adult patients was not compared with that of the pediatric patients.[315] In general, the complication rate of most procedures in adults and adolescents is higher than that in children. Thus, a more conservative approach should be taken with adolescents and adults. Often, a primary pull-through procedure without colostomy cannot be done because of the markedly dilated nature of the colon. Posterior anorectal myectomy may be considered, provided the length of aganglionosis is extremely short (<5 cm).[199] However, in a report of five adult cases by Wu et al.,[372] the two patients who underwent myectomy alone had persistent stooling problems. Better results have been achieved in adult patients with retained aganglionic tissue when a low anterior resection accompanied the myectomy.[87]

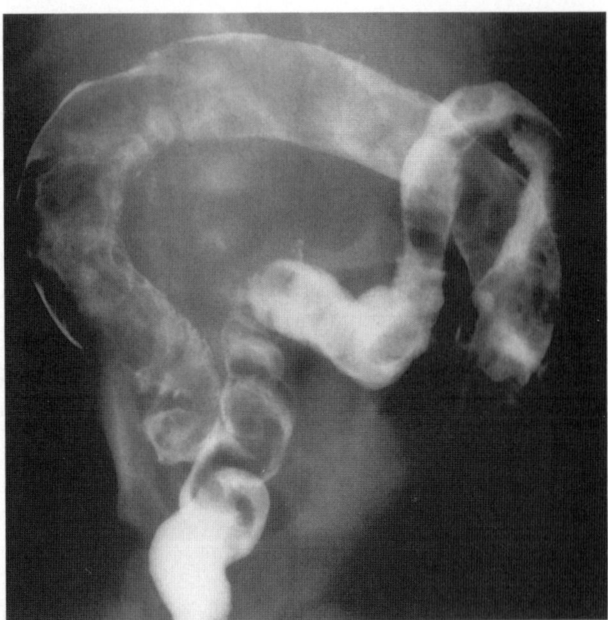

Figure 99–18 Contrast enema in an infant with total colonic aganglionosis. Note the "question mark" shape of the colon, with rounded hepatic and splenic flexures.

ULTRASHORT DISEASE

Ultrashort Hirschsprung's disease (or anorectal achalasia) has caused a great deal of confusion regarding its diagnosis and treatment, and even regarding the occurrence of the disease itself. The major problem with ultrashort Hirschsprung's disease is that the gold standard for diagnosing standard Hirschsprung's disease—namely, the rectal biopsy—may show ganglion cells if the specimen is obtained too proximal from the anal verge. Further, many children with ultrashort Hirschsprung's disease have chronic constipation, often for many years, in conjunction with fecal soiling, which makes its differentiation from encopresis difficult.[236,290] Detailed reviews of this disorder identify some common characteristics, including a history of chronic constipation, the presence of ganglion cells on suction rectal biopsy at 3 and 5 cm, and a contrast enema without a transition zone. Manometry may be quite useful to demonstrate failure of anorectal reflex relaxation with rectal distention.[236] It is possible that children with this form of the disease may be overlooked, because many centers do not routinely perform anorectal manometry. Similarly, it is possible to misdiagnose ultrashort Hirschsprung's disease in a child who has idiopathic constipation if the rectal biopsy is obtained too low, where aganglionosis is normally observed in the anal canal. The preferred treatment for a patient with definitive ultrashort Hirschsprung's disease is anorectal myectomy.[199]

TOTAL COLONIC AGANGLIONOSIS

Total colonic aganglionosis accounts for approximately 3% to 12% of infants with Hirschsprung's disease (see Table 99-4). These patients are a challenging subset because of the associated increase in morbidity and mortality. Total colonic aganglionosis can be very difficult to diagnose. Radiographic studies may show dilated loops of intestine, and a contrast enema study may show an unused colon or a question mark–shaped colon, which results from the rounded edges of the splenic and hepatic flexures (Fig. 99-18). Radiographic studies, however, are diagnostic in only 20% to 30% of all patients with total colonic aganglionosis.[30] The diagnosis is generally made at the time of laparotomy for suspected intestinal obstruction or perforation or while a leveling colostomy for Hirschsprung's disease is being performed. As mentioned previously, a frozen section of the appendix is almost always diagnostic and substantially reduces operative time.[10,240] A family history of Hirschsprung's disease can be found in a significantly higher number of children with total colonic versus sigmoid aganglionosis, ranging from 12.4% to 33%.[10,240] Additionally, the male-female ratio is lower, at 1.3:1[261]; in cases of extensive aganglionosis (i.e., extensive small intestinal involvement), this ratio is reduced to 0.8:1.[141] The proximal extent of aganglionosis is the terminal ileum in approximately 75% of cases, the mid-ileum in 20%, and the jejunum in 5%.[148,240] Complications associated with total colonic aganglionosis are numerous and are considerably more common than in standard-length Hirschsprung's disease. Many patients with total colonic Hirschsprung's disease require parenteral nutrition owing to excessive fluid losses, making catheter sepsis, failure to thrive, stomal dysfunction, electrolyte imbalance, and dehydration commonly encountered complications. Mortality rates range from 0%[151] to 44%,[141,363] emphasizing the severity of this variant of Hirschsprung's disease.

Treatment for total colonic aganglionosis begins with the creation of a properly formed enterostomy. Intake of fluids and electrolytes is monitored closely. Nutrition is usually initiated parenterally and then slowly converted to the enteral route. Failure to thrive is common, but attention to sodium and bicarbonate replacement may prevent this complication.[280,290] Although successful experiences with primary endorectal pull-through have been reported in the newborn period,[80] the pull-through procedure is ideally performed when the child is older, because excoriation of the perineum can be severe when no colon is present. Long-term outcome in patients with total colonic aganglionosis is similar to that in patients with standard-length aganglionosis, based on psychosocial evaluation and endosonographic examination of the anal sphincters.[198] The ideal pull-through procedure for a child with total colonic aganglionosis is hotly debated. A detailed surgical approach to the condition is provided later in the chapter.

HIRSCHSPRUNG'S DISEASE IN PREMATURE INFANTS

Hirschsprung's disease characteristically occurs in full-term infants; however, the disease has been reported in several premature infants. In a review of 172 patients treated at our hospital, the gestational age was identified in 142. Of these, 14 (9.5%) had a gestational age of 36 weeks or less. A review of other series shows a distribution between 4% and 8%. This incidence closely parallels the incidence of prematurity in the United States, which is reported to range from 6.5% to 10%.[161] Hirschsprung's disease is rare in very premature infants but has been described.[288]

SURGICAL TECHNIQUES

Therapeutic options for Hirschsprung's disease have gradually become refined through trial and error. The first treatment consisted of a diverting colostomy, which relieved the child's symptoms; however, symptoms returned after closure of the ostomy.[213] Attempts at bypass or removal of the redundant portions of the colon were uniformly unsuccessful. One of the more intriguing approaches was a lumbar sympathectomy, or spinal anesthesia.[2,122,349] Theoretically, removal of the sympathetic input to the distal rectum would result in a predominance of parasympathetic or relaxation impulses. Several patients had an improvement in symptoms with this approach, but the procedure was eventually condemned by Ladd. Figure 99-19 summarizes some of the most common procedures performed throughout the historical development of the surgical treatment of Hirschsprung's disease. Swenson and Bill[311] are credited with the first successful surgical approach. This technique consisted of a rectosigmoidectomy and circumferential anastomosis near or including the internal sphincter. These authors reported good results, but others found a high rate of incontinence and stricture formation. Subsequent modifications of this operation by Swenson involved a more oblique anastomosis, with sparing of the internal sphincter.

Following is a discussion of some of the currently popular operations for the treatment of Hirschsprung's disease. Although an endorectal dissection via a transrectal approach has become the predominant approach over the past decade, it is important for pediatric surgeons to be familiar with other methods. These approaches may prove useful if an endorectal dissection cannot be performed or a redo procedure is required.

Full-Thickness Rectal Biopsy

Suction rectal biopsy, because of its relative ease and low morbidity, has become the preferred method for

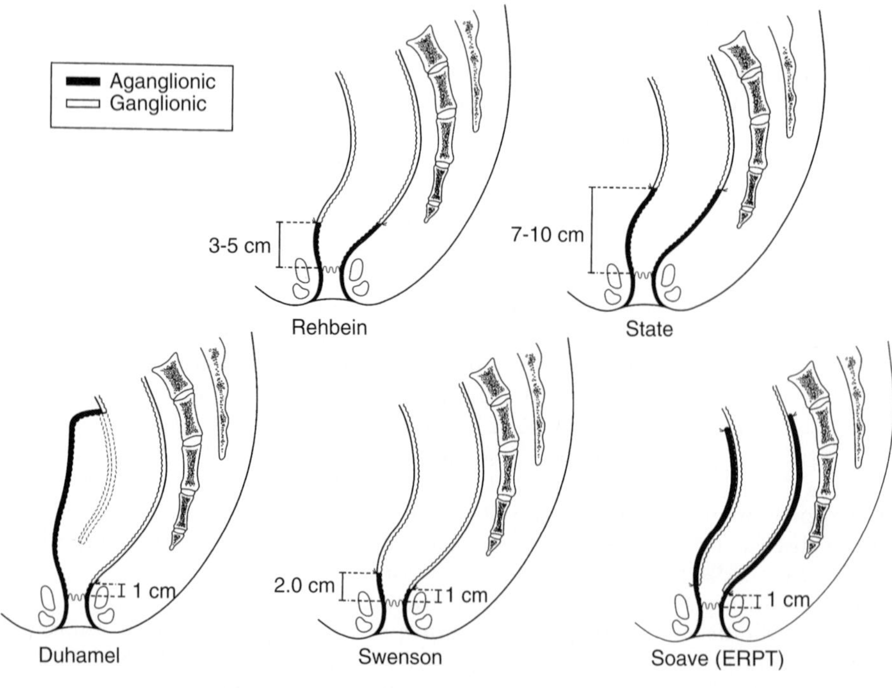

Figure 99-19 Commonly performed surgical procedures for Hirschsprung's disease during the last half century. The State procedure is shown for historical purposes only. ERPT, endorectal pull-through. (From Spitz L, Coran A [eds]: Rob & Smith's Operative Surgery: Pediatric Surgery. London, Chapman Hall Medical, 1995.)

the diagnosis of Hirschsprung's disease. Nevertheless, full-thickness rectal biopsies are occasionally required. Full-thickness biopsy is most commonly indicated in children who have had more than one nondiagnostic suction rectal biopsy.

Preoperative Preparation

No formal intestinal preparation is required. The child's rectum is irrigated with saline at the time of surgery. A sponge is placed into the proximal rectal vault to prevent stool from entering the surgical field.

Positioning, Incision, and Specimen Collection

The patient is placed in the lithotomy position. The buttocks are positioned at the end of the table and supported with a folded towel. The feet are placed together (plantar surfaces adjoined) with a cotton roll, and both legs are suspended on an ether screen and flexed at the hips.

Digital dilatation is followed by the placement of two narrow anal retractors. The posterior aspect of the dentate line is identified, and a Vicryl (polyglycolic acid) suture (3-0) is placed just above this and used for traction. Two additional sutures are placed on the posterior wall of the rectum, at 1 and 2 cm proximal to the dentate line (Fig. 99-20A). The surgeon's nondominant hand holds the middle suture. Using sharp, curved scissors, a full-thickness incision is made along the lower half of the rectal wall between the dentate line and the middle suture. Once this is done, the scissors can be placed in the presacral space and gently spread. Bleeding may obstruct the view at this point; however, by maintaining traction on the middle suture, the upper half of the rectum can be incised with two smooth cuts of the scissors. Each cut should sweep approximately half the tissue suspended by the middle suture. The specimen is inspected and, if satisfactory, submitted for histologic study (Fig. 99-20B). The rectal defect is closed with a single running or interrupted layer of absorbable suture. Hemostasis is achieved fairly quickly once the sutures have been placed.

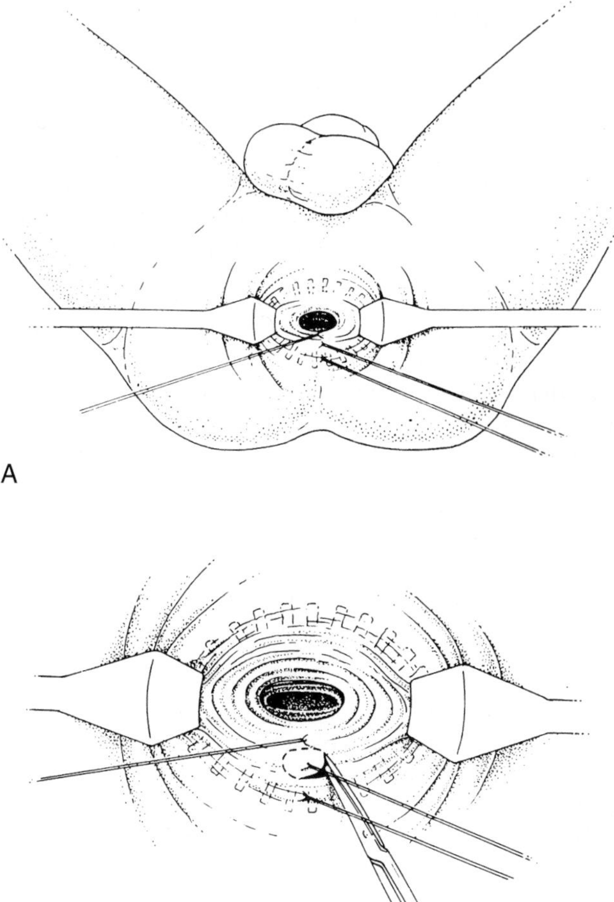

Figure 99–20 Full-thickness rectal biopsy. *A,* Sutures are placed to facilitate traction during the biopsy. *B,* The specimen is taken between the distal and proximal sutures with traction on the middle one. (From Spitz L, Coran A [eds]: Rob & Smith's Operative Surgery: Pediatric Surgery. London, Chapman Hall Medical, 1995.)

Leveling Colostomy

Although a primary pull-through procedure is the preferred approach to children with Hirschsprung's disease, some children benefit from an initial leveling colostomy. A colostomy is indicated in infants who suffer from severe enterocolitis or who have a markedly dilated proximal colon that might preclude performance of a primary pull-through.

In general, a left lower quadrant oblique incision is made, and a gross transition zone is sought. The proximal ganglionated bowel usually has a hypertrophied longitudinal muscular layer that is lacking distinguishable taeniae. A biopsy of the muscularis is made by incising the smooth muscle of the bowel wall with a fine, sharp scissors on the antimesenteric border; this layer is bluntly dissected off the underlying submucosa. Importantly, the transition zone may extend for several centimeters. Along this zone, it is not uncommon for ganglion cells to be present on one portion of the circumference of the bowel but not on the other; thus, it is safest to place the ostomy more proximally.[360] The muscle layer is fairly thick in Hirschsprung's disease, which facilitates the dissection. A 0.5-cm segment is sent for frozen section, and the muscularis is reapproximated with interrupted absorbable suture. Selecting a proper site in the proximal colon above the transition zone is important. The portion of colon used in a colostomy should contain many ganglion cells and lack hypertrophied nerves. A loop colostomy is created just proximal to this point. Because of the initially large caliber of the bowel, stomal prolapse is a common problem. Thus, the colon is sutured to the fascia in multiple places to secure its position. To further secure the bowel, a stitch is placed by carrying a fascial suture through a small rent in the mesentery, incorporating a seromuscular bite of the proximal and distal segments of colon.

Endorectal Pull-Through

History

Although Soave described an endorectal approach in 1964, this approach was first used by Yancey in 1952 to treat two adult Hirschsprung's patients.[374] The technique is quite similar to the current open endorectal pull-through method, but initially, the pediatric surgical community did not fully appreciate this method. The operation involves removing the mucosa and submucosa of the rectum and pulling ganglionic intestine through the aganglionic muscular cuff. The procedure was modified by Boley,[36] who performed a primary anastomosis at the anus, and further modified by Coran and Weintraub,[60] who everted the submucosal-mucosal tube onto the perineum to facilitate performance of the anastomosis. By remaining within the muscular cuff of the aganglionic segment, important sensory fibers and the integrity of the internal sphincter are preserved. Although leaving aganglionic muscle surrounding normal intestine would theoretically lead to a high incidence of constipation, this has not been the experience clinically.

The procedure is commonly performed as a primary pull-through procedure in neonates without the need for an initial leveling colostomy (single stage).[51,56,300] Comprehensive comparisons have shown that the complication rate observed with the single-stage repair is identical to that seen with the standard two-stage approach.[117,254,327] Endorectal dissection is technically easier to perform in newborns than in older subjects.

Over the past decade, the endorectal pull-through has evolved from a transabdominal dissection to a transanal approach. This striking transition has been prompted by a number of innovative surgical approaches. The transanal approach to children with Hirschsprung's disease was initially reported by Rintala and Lindahl[274] and was combined with an open laparotomy to complete the mobilization of the aganglionic intestine. Subsequently, Georgeson et al.[105] described laparoscopic-assisted mobilization of the aganglionic colon, along with a transanal dissection of the mucosa and submucosa. In cases in which the length of the aganglionic segment is confined to the rectum, de la Torre-Mondragon and Ortega-Salgado[66] performed the entire dissection and mobilization via the transanal route. Several reports have shown that early results with the transanal approach are similar to those obtained with the transabdominal approach.[5,79,118,134,183] Because many of these series are recent, long-term studies evaluating stooling patterns are not yet available. However, postoperative anal sphincter pressures, as detected by manometric studies, are similar in patients undergoing either a transabdominal or a transanal pull-through.[344]

Preoperative Preparation

Even in the newborn period, serial rectal washouts (10 mL/kg) and digital dilatations of the rectum are performed before the pull-through is begun. One percent neomycin should be added to the final rectal irrigation. Intravenous antibiotics are given within 1 hour preoperatively and continued for two additional doses after the operation.

Surgical Technique

Open Approach

A number of approaches for the endorectal pull-through exist, and a detailed description is beyond the scope of this chapter. Figure 99-21 demonstrates the main elements of the open approach to the endorectal pull-through. A key element to a successful pull-through is careful positioning of the child, such that an abdominal and perineal approach can be easily achieved. Typically, the child's buttocks are brought to the end of the operating table, and the legs are padded and positioned on wooden skis or leg supports. A left lower quadrant oblique incision is made, and (if not done previously) the extent of aganglionosis is determined by visual inspection and a series of carefully marked seromuscular frozen section biopsies. Because pull-through procedures performed close to the transition zone may be associated with poorer outcomes, it is wise to try to be at least 5 cm proximal to the first area of normal ganglion cells. The endorectal dissection is started approximately 2 cm below the peritoneal reflection by incising the seromuscular layer with either sharp dissection or cautery. The dissection is carried down to within 0.5 cm of the dentate line in newborns, all via the abdominal approach (see Fig. 99-21A and B). An easy way to determine whether there is adequate length is to ensure that the ganglionic bowel can be stretched over the pubis and to the level of the anal verge. Proximal mobilization to and across the lienocolic ligament may be needed. When more length is needed, it is often beneficial to ligate the inferior mesenteric artery near its origin and preserve the marginal blood vessel arcade closer to the bowel wall.

Attention is then directed to the perineum. The operating surgeon everts the mucosal-submucosal tube (see Fig. 99-21C), and the tube is incised on the anterior half, 0.5 cm above the dentate line. A Kelly clamp is inserted into this opening, and the normal ganglionic intestine is brought down to this point by grasping the two previously placed traction sutures (see Fig. 99-21D). Great care is taken not to twist the intestine as it is brought through the muscular cuff. Different-colored sutures (dyed and undyed) on each side of the intestine are quite helpful for maintaining orientation. The anastomosis is then completed with interrupted absorbable sutures (see Fig. 99-21E and F).

Recognition that the internal sphincter may cause persistent obstructive symptoms[334] has led many surgeons to pursue a more distal incision posteriorly into the internal sphincter during the definitive pull-through.[224,350] This may be beneficial and does not appear to compromise continence.

Laparoscopic Approach

The basic operative principles are virtually the same with the laparoscopic approach. Trocar placement is shown in Figure 99-22A, with the initial trocar in the

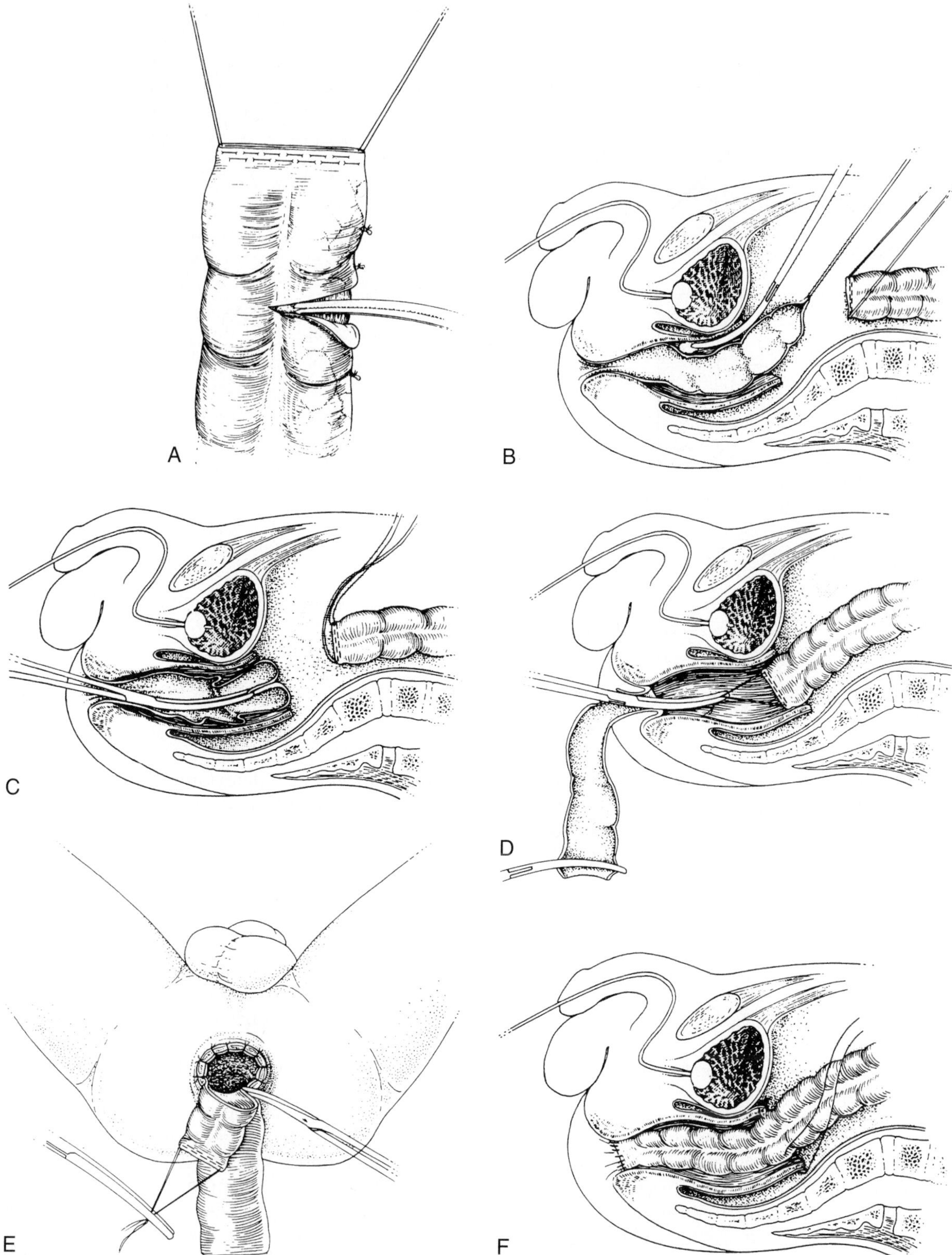

Figure 99–21 Open approach. *A*, Initiation of the endorectal dissection begins with a circumferential release of the muscular layer from the submucosa. *B*, Subsequent dissection proceeds to within 1.5 cm of the anal opening. *C*, The submucosal-mucosal tube is everted out onto the perineum. *D*, Ganglionic bowel is pulled through the muscular cuff after the everted submucosal-mucosal tube is incised anteriorly 1 cm proximal to the dentate line. *E*, Anastomosis of the submucosal-mucosal tube to the ganglionic bowel. *F*, Final appearance of the anastomosis. (From Spitz L, Coran A [eds]: Rob & Smith's Operative Surgery: Pediatric Surgery. London, Chapman Hall Medical, 1995.)

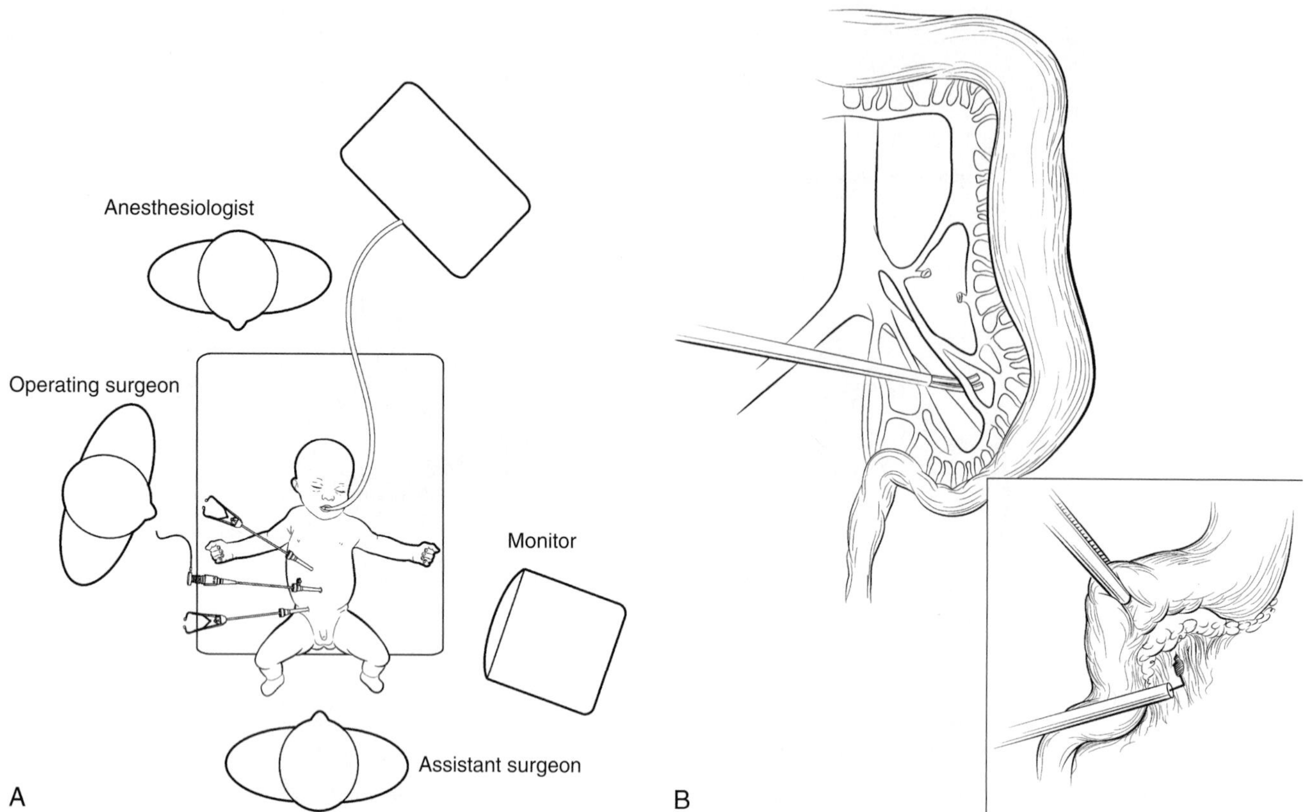

Figure 99-22 Laparoscopic approach. *A,* Trocar placement for laparoscopic-assisted pull-through. *B,* Laparoscopic-assisted pull-through. Dissection of the colic vessels is shown.

right upper quadrant and the remaining ones placed in the upper abdomen, left upper quadrant, and suprapubic area. Dissection and leveling of the aganglionic segment are performed as in the open technique. Blood vessels may be ligated with surgical clips or cautery for smaller vessels (Fig. 99-22B). Once mobilization is complete, the surgeon moves to the perineum, where a transanal dissection and anastomosis are performed (see later).

Transanal Approach

The key element when beginning the case is to place either a self-supporting retractor (e.g., Lone Star Medical Products, Houston, Tex.) or a series of sutures that retract the anal verge (Fig. 99-23A). An incision 0.5 cm above the dentate line is begun with cautery in a circumferential fashion (Fig. 99-23B). Traction sutures are placed on the mucosal-submucosal tube, and dissection is carried out proximally, primarily with blunt technique. Once the dissection is extended proximal to the peritoneal reflection, the muscular layer is entered, and the dissection becomes full thickness (Fig. 99-23C). A key point is to split the muscular tube down to the internal sphincter in the posterior midline; this splitting avoids retraction of the muscular cuff, causing a relative obstruction (Fig. 99-23D and E). Although dissection of the mesenteric vessels is easier with the laparoscopic approach, for rectal Hirschsprung's disease, many of these vessels can be dissected via the transanal route. Biopsies are sent to determine the level of ganglionic bowel, and the anastomosis is completed.

Duhamel Operation

History

Duhamel first described his operation for Hirschsprung's disease in 1956.[71,72] The procedure consisted of a retrorectal dissection, whereby a significant portion of the aganglionic rectum was preserved and anastomosed to ganglionated proximal colon. The advantages of this procedure included ease of performance, reduction of anastomotic leaks and strictures, retention of anal sensory receptors, and preservation of the nervi erigentes. The initial operative approach actually avoided an anastomosis, using instead a crush-clamping of ganglionated to aganglionic intestine.[73,74] Duhamel devised his operation as a simplified variation of the Swenson rectosigmoidectomy and intended to apply it earlier in infancy.[73,74] In his early series, he reported decreases in mortality, functional incontinence, constipation or diarrhea, anastomotic leaks, and intestinal obstruction compared with contemporary reports of the Swenson operation.[73,74]

Modifications of the Duhamel procedure have been numerous, including placement of the anastomosis above the internal sphincter to avoid incontinence.[113] Additional modifications have involved the creation of the anastomosis with the use of mechanical stapling devices.[139,303,318]

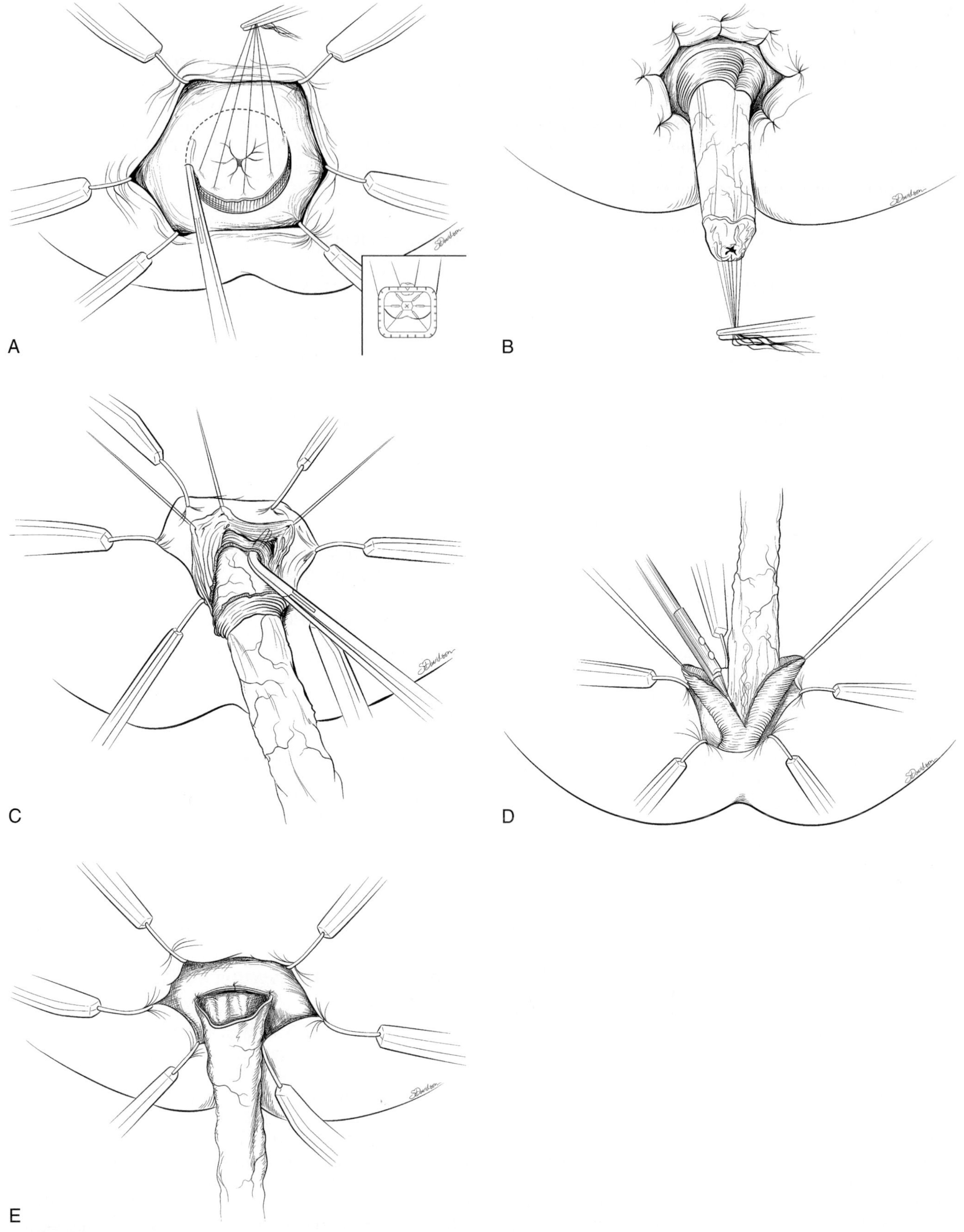

Figure 99–23 Transanal approach. *A,* Performance of the endorectal dissection via the transanal approach. A self-supporting retractor (Lone Star Medical Products, Houston, Tex.) is used (inset). *B,* The endorectal dissection is begun using a fine electrocautery tip. Here, retraction of the anal opening is performed using multiple sutures. *C,* Once the dissection is carried close to the level of the peritoneum, the full thickness of the rectum is entered. *D,* Before pulling down the more proximal colon, the muscular cuff of the rectum is split posteriorly using cautery. *E,* The anastomosis is performed with interrupted absorbable sutures.

An additional modification has centered around eliminating the proximal rectal pouch "spur" in the aganglionic rectum, which can trap large accumulations of stool. Martin and Altemeier[203] and Martin and Caudill[204] described careful clamp placement to entirely eliminate the rectal pouch. Use of stapling devices for the colorectal anastomosis facilitates division of the common rectal wall. More recently, the Duhamel procedure has been performed using laparoscopic techniques, with excellent results.[62]

Definitive Pull-Through

The procedure is conventionally used in infants between 9 and 12 months of age, although several groups have reported primary Duhamel pull-throughs in younger patients.[194,221,343] For these latter procedures, an endo-GIA stapler, which is smaller, is used for the anastomosis.

The bowel is irrigated to ensure that it is clean. The colostomy (if present) is mobilized, and the peritoneum is entered using an extension from the left-sided colostomy in an oblique fashion to the midline. Frozen sections are obtained to determine the level of normally ganglionated bowel if there was no previous leveling colostomy. The proximal colon is then mobilized to ensure a tension-free pull-through.

The aganglionic distal bowel is mobilized below the peritoneal reflection, carefully protecting the ureters. The colon is stapled across at the level of the peritoneal reflection, and traction sutures are applied along this staple line. Gentle, blunt dissection of the presacral retrorectal space is then begun. Typically, this is done with the surgeon's finger or a small dissection sponge (Fig. 99-24A). The proximal ganglionated colon has sutures placed on the right and left sides (different colors for each side) to prevent torsion of the bowel during the pull-through.

The surgeon then moves to the perineum. The anal sphincter is gently dilated, and narrow retractors are introduced. The posterior 180 degrees of rectal wall is exposed from three to nine o'clock, and the landmarks of the dentate line and columns of Morgagni are identified. Using electrocautery, a full-thickness curvilinear incision, directed on the posterior wall, is made from three to nine o'clock at a level 1 cm above the dentate line (Fig. 99-24B). This maneuver connects the lumen of the aganglionic rectum with the retrorectal space developed above. Full-thickness traction sutures are placed on both edges of this incision using absorbable suture. After the presacral tunnel is adequately enlarged, the ganglionated rectum is pulled into position, with careful orientation and guidance from above, and its lumen is opened (Fig. 99-24C). The proximal colon is opened, and an anastomosis is created with absorbable sutures. A surgical stapler is then used—typically, a GIA 80-mm stapler, or an endo-GIA stapler in smaller infants. Importantly, 4.8-mm staples are required because of the increased thickness of the anastomosis. Before firing the device, one ensures a correct orientation from both the perineum and the abdomen (Fig. 99-24D). Along the superior staple line of the native rectum, a colotomy incision is made. A lateral absorbable retracting suture is placed to approximate these two walls. A reloaded GIA stapler is then directed distally into each lumen and guided by the surgeon's finger inserted in the rectum (Fig. 99-24E). After the stapler has been fired, complete elimination of the common rectal wall is confirmed by digital examination. The redundant intrapelvic proximal native rectum is resected, and the colocolonic anastomosis is completed by a two-layer technique.

Swenson Procedure

Figure 99-25 shows a schematic approach to the Swenson procedure. Although still used, the Swenson procedure has become less popular in recent years. In excellent hands, the outcome of this procedure is comparable to or better than that of the Duhamel procedure and endorectal pull-through; however, the technique is demanding, and injury to adjacent neurovascular structures is possible. Thus, details of the Swenson procedure are not given here. Readers are referred to other descriptions of this technique.[324,357,358]

Operative Approach to Unusual Problems in Hirschsprung's Disease

Right-Sided Disease

When pull-through operations are performed in patients with extended colonic disease (to the right of the middle colic vessels), it is often difficult to maintain the colon in the correct orientation, and there is a greater risk of torsion of the pulled-through intestine. This problem was recognized by Duhamel early on and can best be approached by rotating the right colon in a counterclockwise fashion, as shown in Figure 99-26A. Because the small bowel then exits the colon from the patient's left side, it is sometimes necessary to perform a complete release of the ligament of Treitz (i.e., create a malrotation; Fig. 99-26B). Alternatively, the colon can be flipped anteriorly, with reasonably good results (Fig. 99-26C).

Total Colonic Hirschsprung's Disease

Several surgical approaches have been proposed for total colonic disease. In 1953 Sandegard[282] was the first to report a successful pull-through procedure for total colonic disease. The next advance came with a modification of the Duhamel pull-through technique by Martin,[202] which consisted of a longer segment of retained aganglionic rectum and left colon to facilitate the absorption of electrolytes and water. This technique is still used by several surgeons.[76] However, many others have found that the longer length of retained colon adversely affects these children's ability to defecate and increases the incidence of postprocedural enterocolitis.[63,132] A technique advocated by Kimura et al.[160] uses a cecal patch with a parasitized blood supply to the ganglionic small bowel. This cecal patch achieves an absorptive function similar to that of the aganglionic rectum, with good clinical results.[160,164,190] Most surgeons, however, have had reasonably good results

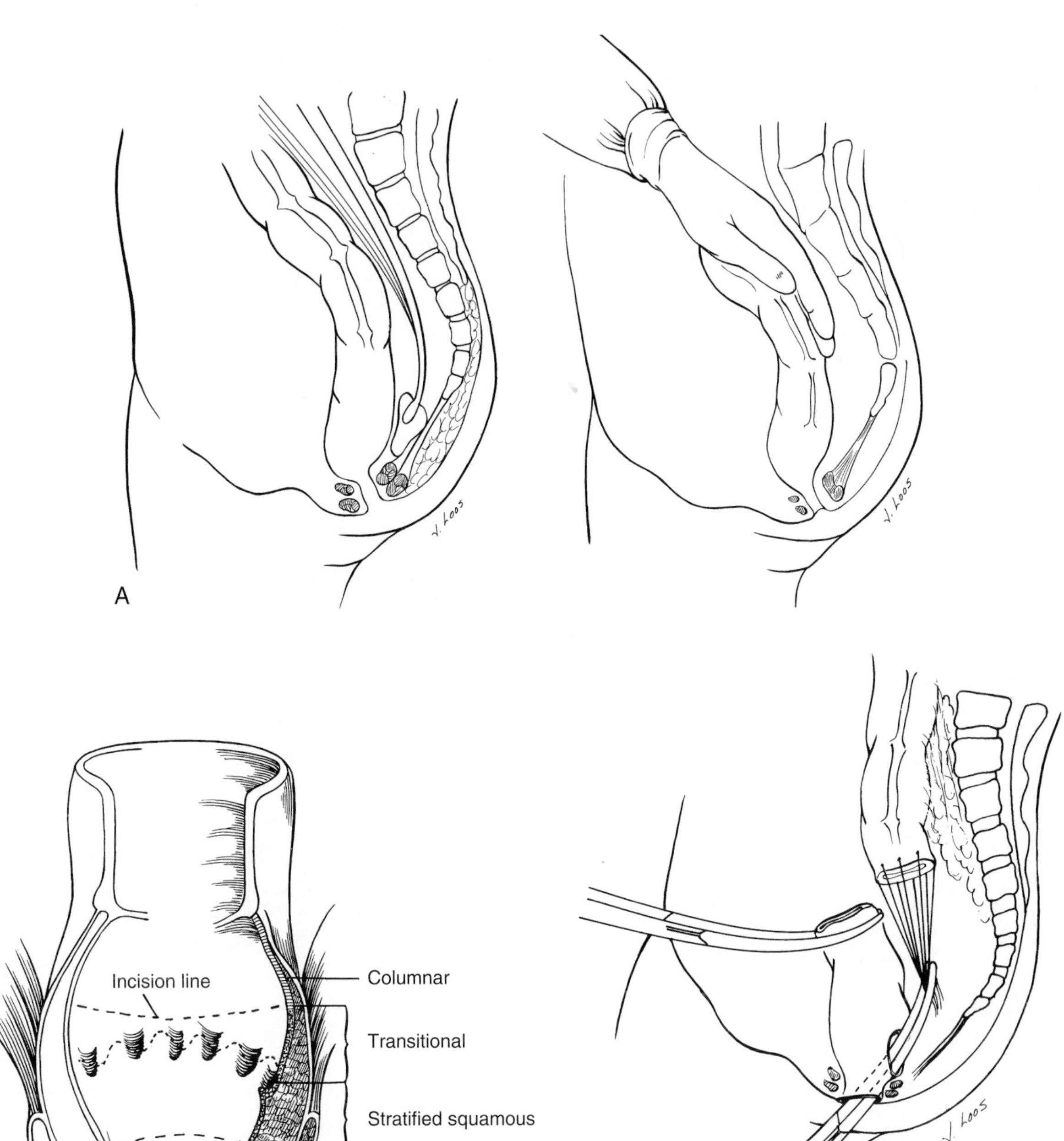

Figure 99–24 *A,* Creation of a retrorectal presacral tunnel by blunt dissection. *B,* Posterior full-thickness rectal wall incision from three to nine o'clock, 1 to 2 cm proximal to the dentate line. *C,* Proximal ganglionated bowel, with its mesentery oriented posteriorly, is guided through the retrorectal space to the level of the incision in the posterior wall of "old" rectum.

Continued

using a standard-length endorectal pull-through or a Duhamel procedure for this process.[30,151] Outcomes of endorectal pull-through versus a Duhamel procedure are quite similar,[132,363] whereas patients undergoing a Martin modification of the Duhamel procedure (extended anastomosis of aganglionic colon and ganglionic ileum) have had uniformly poor results.[132] Long-term outcomes are reasonably good for most patients,[129,198] although overall, these patients perceive themselves as being less satisfied with their quality of life than their peers are.[129]

Extended Small Intestinal Disease

Patients with extended small intestinal disease have extreme morbidity. All these children require long-term parenteral nutrition support, and the mortality rate is exceedingly high (some approaching 50%).[159,160] The surgical alternatives for more extensive small intestinal Hirschsprung's disease tend to be complex because the length and function of the residual ganglionated small intestine must be taken into account, and the surgeon

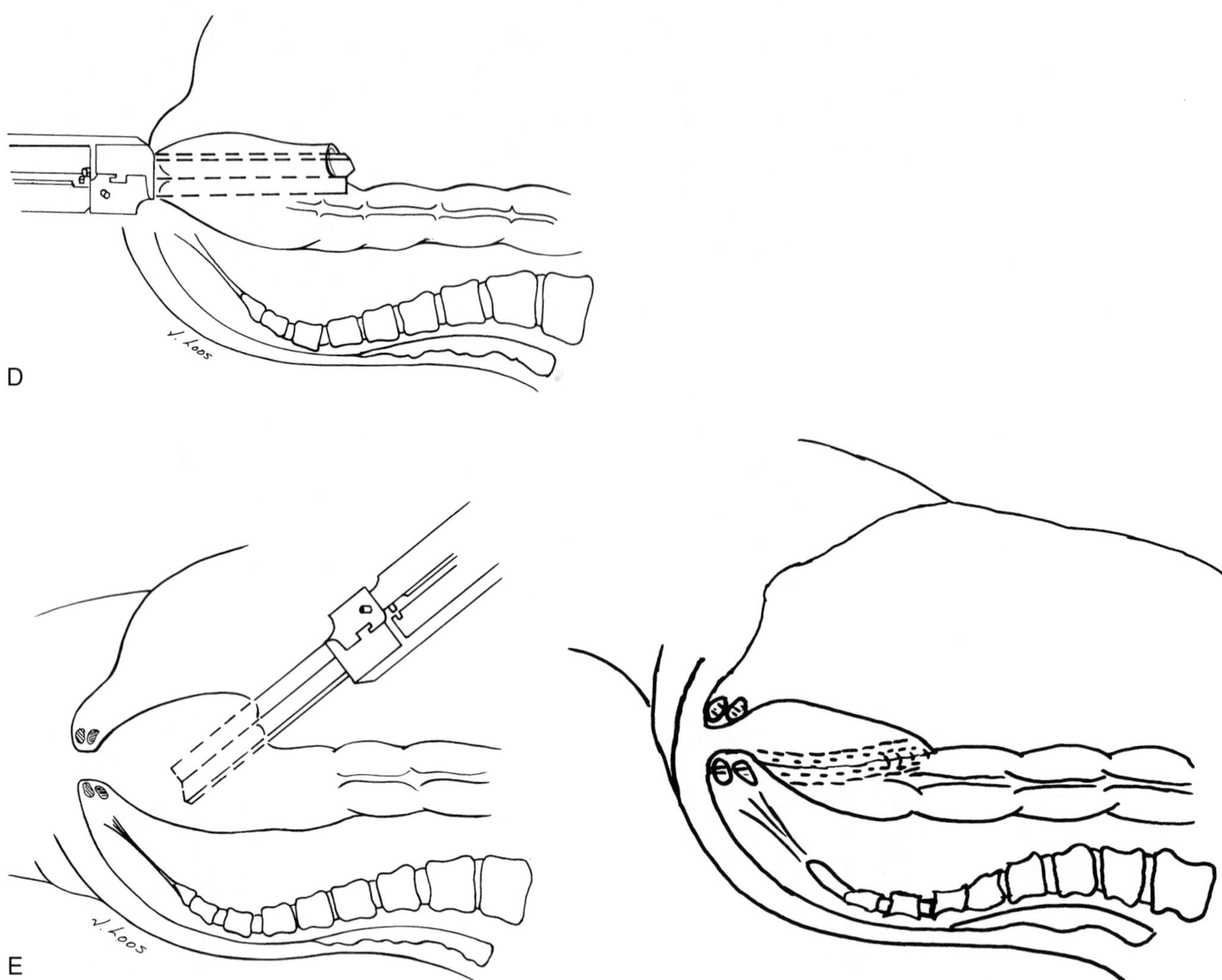

Figure 99–24 Cont'd *D,* After tying the sutures from the anocutaneous junction to the posterior wall of "new" rectum from three to nine o'clock, one arm of the GIA stapler is inserted into the lumen of the old rectum and one arm into the lumen of the new rectum. After confirmation of the stapler position by palpation from within the pelvis, the stapler is closed and fired, and the end-to-side anastomosis is completed. *E,* After returning to the abdominopelvic field, the GIA stapler is reinserted from proximal to distal in the rectum, and any residual common wall is eliminated. The colotomy is then closed.

must gauge the degree of short-bowel syndrome. For jejunoileal disease, a number of individuals have used a patch of ileum[170] or, more commonly, right colon.[159,306] In this case, a staged approach with an initial leveling ostomy is used. The right colon is anastomosed to the functional proximal stoma (Kimura-Stringel procedure). After several weeks, a pull-through of this joined side-to-side bowel is performed, with preservation of the blood supply to both portions of the intestine, using either a Soave or a Swenson-type pull-through (Fig. 99-27). The bulk of the aganglionic bowel is generally excised, because this is often viewed as a potential source of sepsis.

For infants with less than 40 cm of ganglionated small intestine, an extended myotomy or myectomy may be the best approach (Fig. 99-28). As described by Ziegler et al.,[381,382] the myectomy is begun at the level of transition between ganglionated and aganglionic small bowel. Two antimesenteric border incisions are made parallel along the longitudinal axis of the intestine. The depth of the incision is stopped superficial to the submucosa to allow a 1-cm-wide strip of seromuscular layer (with the underlying submucosal tube left intact) to be excised for an extended length. The extension onto normally ganglionated bowel should be limited so that peristalsis in the proximal ganglionated bowel cannot push intraluminal contents distally. At the end of this segment, which is optimally about 50 to 70 cm below the ligament of Treitz, the intestine is exited as an end stoma. If any aganglionic distal intestine remains, it must be vented.

Finally, when attempts at intestinal salvage fail, small intestine transplantation or liver-intestine transplantation may be performed. Two groups have reported the successful management of patients with total intestinal aganglionosis with intestinal transplantation.[294,376]

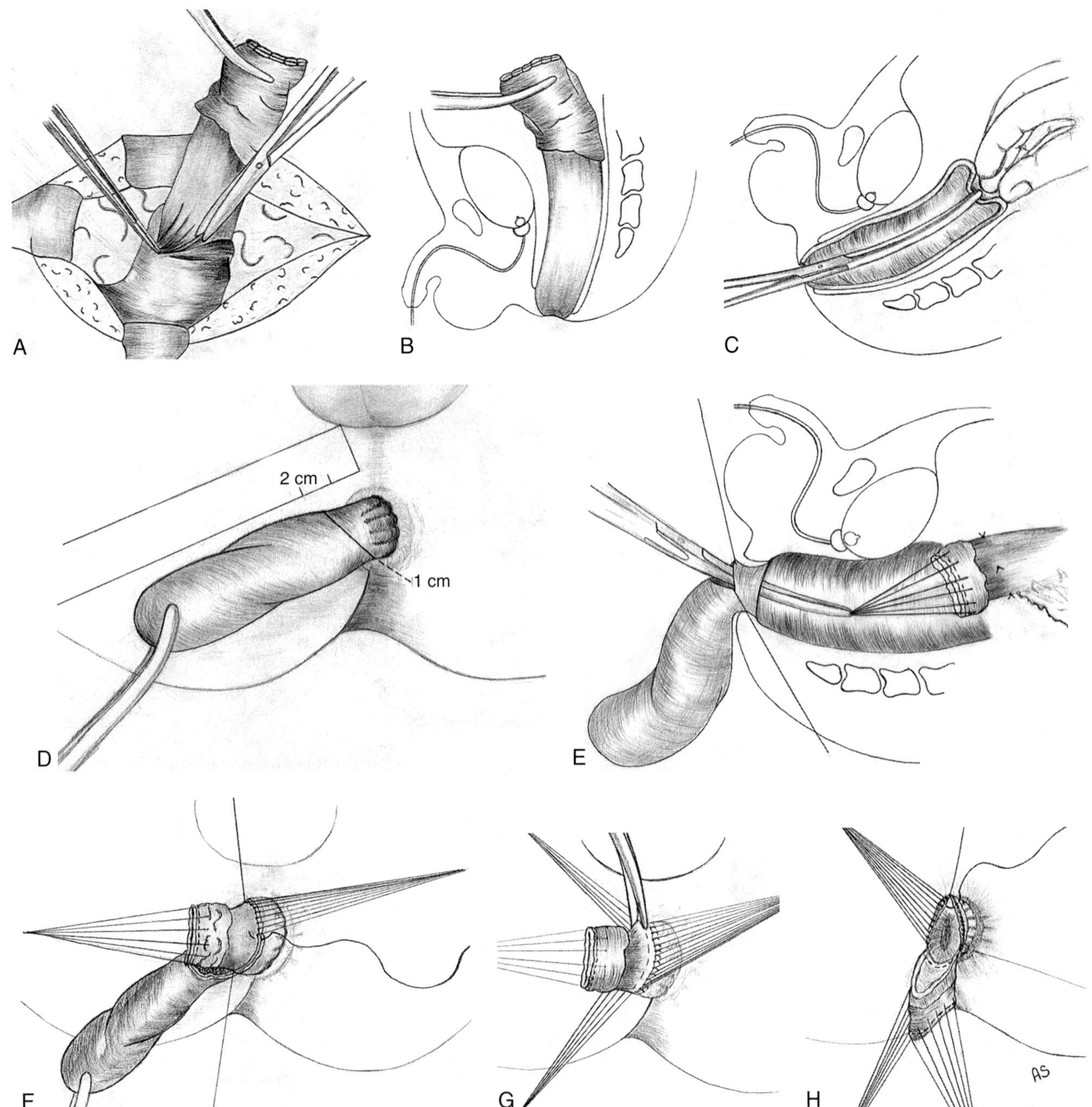

Figure 99-25 Sequential steps of the Swenson procedure. *A,* Placing traction on the rectosigmoid colon and tissue adherent to the rectum, the rectal wall is dissected directly. *B,* The rectum is dissected out to the level of the internal sphincter. Dissection is done in a slightly less anterior direction. *C,* Following dilatation of the anal sphincter, a long clamp is inserted into the rectum, and the stapled end of the rectum is inserted into the clamp. *D,* The rectum is everted onto the perineum, and after the dissection is complete, the diagonal level where the rectum will be incised is determined. *E,* The everted rectum is incised at the predetermined level. A clamp is passed through this incision, and the normal colon is pulled through the pelvis and out through the incision in the everted rectum. *F,* The anterior muscular anastomosis is complete. With traction on the three o'clock and six o'clock sutures, the left posterior quadrant of the muscular anastomosis is done. In a similar manner, the right posterior quadrant of the anastomosis is completed. *G,* After the muscular anastomosis is completed, the end of the pulled-through colon is incised a few millimeters from the muscular suture line. *H,* The mucosa of the cuff of the everted rectum is anastomosed to the mucosa of the pulled-through colon. (Courtesy of Adriana Smith, RN.)

Persistent Difficulty in Stooling

The evaluation of a child with constipation or recurrent enterocolitis after an apparently successful pull-through procedure requires a thorough history, physical examination, and diagnostic workup. Stooling difficulty may be due to aberrancies in the remaining ganglionated nervous system, and these may not be amenable to surgery.[284] Symptoms are often short in duration and improve with time. Physical examination can rule out the

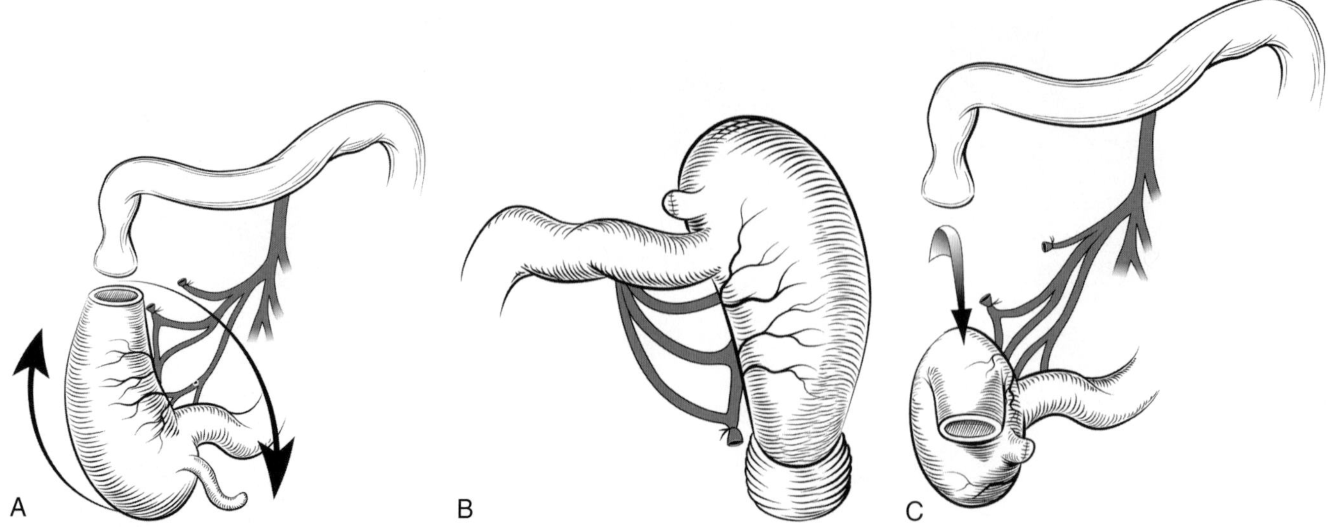

Figure 99-26 Approaches in a child with colonic aganglionosis proximal to the middle colic vessels. *A,* Rotation of the bowel in a clockwise direction. *B,* As a result, the ileum enters the cecum on the patient's right side; this may require a release of the ligament of Treitz. *C,* An alternative approach is to rotate the colon anteriorly.

development of a postoperative stricture (see later). Endoscopy or a contrast enema can demonstrate a twisted pull-through or the formation of a spur in an improperly performed Duhamel procedure. In the absence of a mechanical obstruction, a complete diagnostic evaluation is required. A review of this problem showed that the most informative workup was obtained by performing a rectal biopsy.[229] In that series, the authors identified 16 of 178 children with Hirschsprung's disease who still had constipative or obstructive symptoms at 4 years of age or older. An extensive workup showed that 13 of the 16 patients had abnormal findings, including 4 with a retained aganglionic segment and 9 with evidence of intestinal neuronal dysplasia (see Chapter 100). A manometric workup was not predictive of a poor outcome and did not help in the overall assessment of patients. Anal manometry, however, may provide useful information about persistent spasticity of the internal sphincter and may help predict the cause of either constipation or incontinence.[154] Based on two recent reviews of patients with persistent stooling problems, a detailed protocol for the appropriate workup has been developed (Fig. 99-29).[180,364]

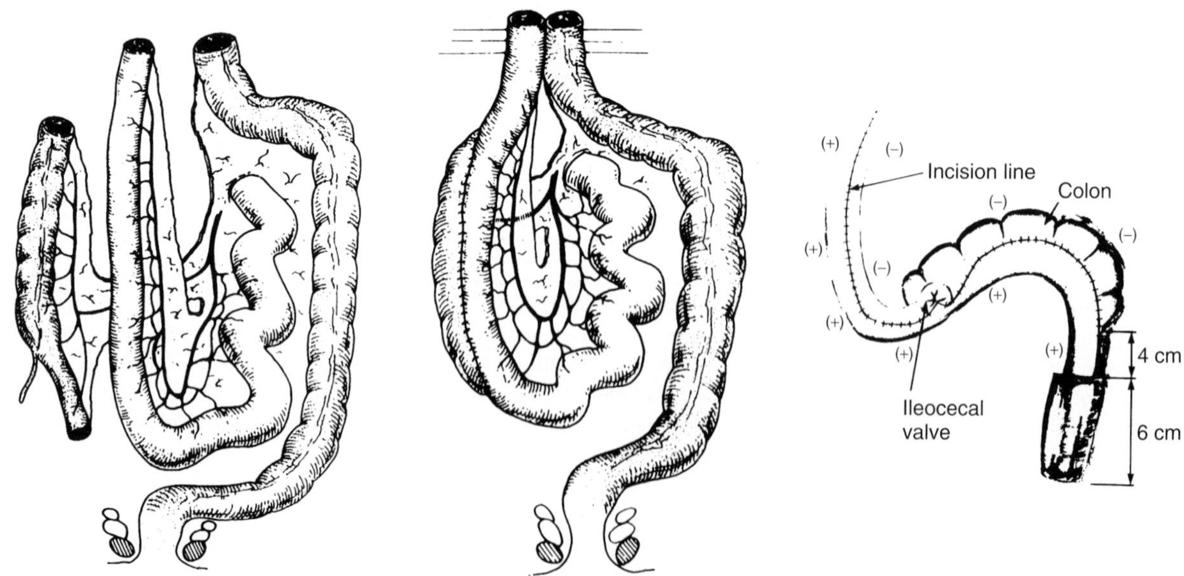

Figure 99-27 Staged Kimura-Stringel operation in which the ganglionated small intestine is patched onto the aganglionic terminal ileum and right colon. In the second stage, the right colon mesentery is divided, and the composite intestine that is vascularized by the small intestine mesentery is prepared for pull-through.

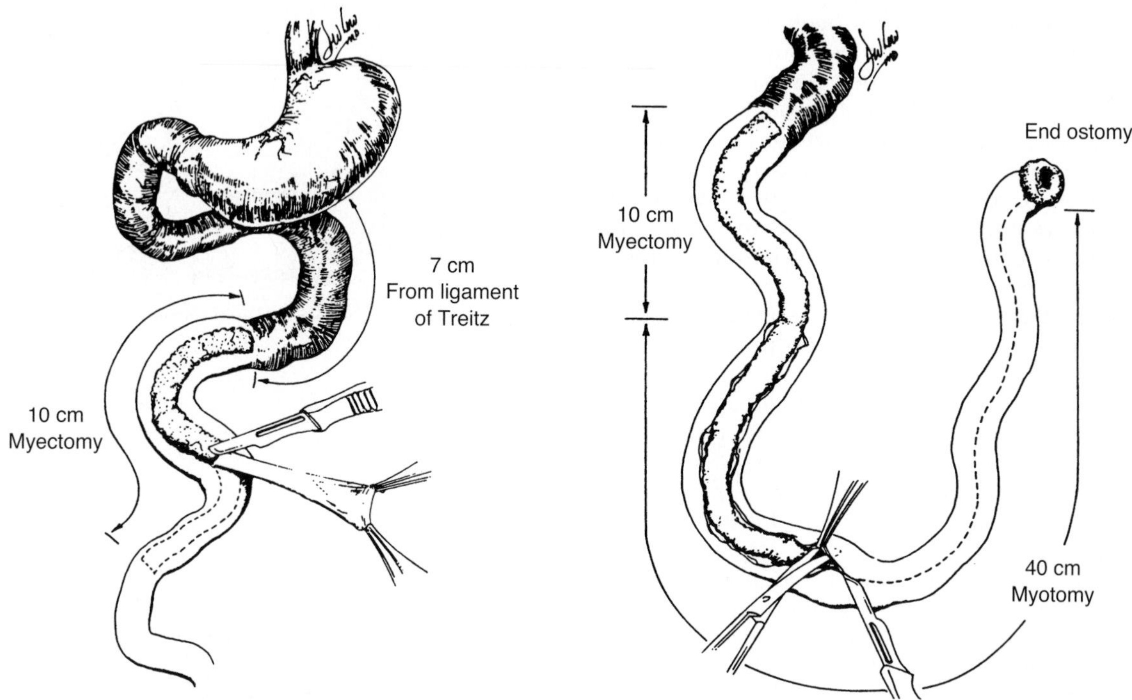

Figure 99–28 An extended myotomy-myectomy begins in a proximal direction to the transition zone and extends for a length that will leave the patient with enough small intestine compatible with survival.

Anorectal Myectomy

Anorectal myectomy is the standard operation used to treat patients with short-segment Hirschsprung's disease. The operation can be done through either a transanal[199] or a posterior sacral approach.[331,332] The advantage of this procedure is that it avoids abdominal surgery. The procedure must be confined to patients with very short-segment Hirschsprung's disease (in general, ≤5 cm). The surgeon must be certain that the myectomy has been extended proximal to the level of normal ganglionated bowel. Inadequate myectomy may adversely affect the

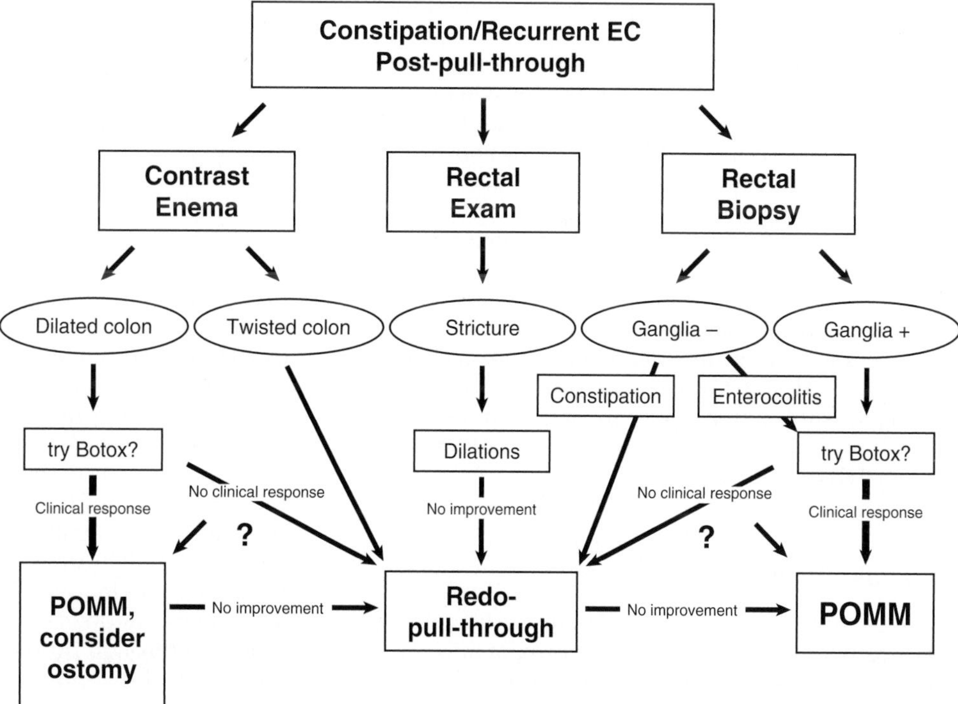

Figure 99–29 Flow chart for the workup and treatment of patients with chronic constipation or recurrent enterocolitis (EC) after a pull-through operation for Hirschsprung's disease. Note that a botulinum toxin (Botox) injection may be used before proceeding to myectomy. If the patient derives long-term benefit from Botox, no further treatment is needed. If the patient develops transient improvement with Botox, a myectomy should be considered. POMM, posterior myotomy or myectomy.

outcome of a subsequent pull-through procedure. We believe that if there is any uncertainty about the level of disease, myectomy should be avoided. Preparation of the patient is similar to that for other pull-through procedures.

Myectomy is more commonly used to treat patients with postoperative stooling problems (see Fig. 99-29). Several groups have demonstrated good results in patients who have either persistent difficulty stooling or recurrent enterocolitis after a pull-through procedure.[25,33,158] Presumably, the efficacy of the myectomy is due to incision of a persistently spastic internal sphincter, despite a normal pull-through procedure.[224] Patients who undergo a posterior myotomy or myectomy generally have markedly improved results.[158] Wildhaber et al.[364] recently reported the largest series of these procedures and showed that the outcome is excellent in patients with recurrent enterocolitis; however, in those with a persistent aganglionic segment, a myectomy is almost uniformly unsuccessful, and a redo pull-through is required.

The child is placed in the same position as for a full-thickness rectal biopsy. Digital dilatation is performed, and two narrow anal retractors are inserted and held by assistants. The posterior aspect of the dentate line is identified. A 2-cm transverse incision is made through the mucosa and submucosa, starting 1 cm above the dentate line. Next, a submucosal dissection is carried upward for several centimeters. The mucosal flap is held up with silk sutures and can be extended proximally with vertical incisions on either side (Fig. 99-30A).

Myectomy is done by sharply incising the full thickness of the muscle layer, followed by Bovie cautery to excise a 0.5- to 1-cm-wide muscle strip in the midline. The initial strip removed should be at least 5 cm long (Fig. 99-30B). Before transecting the muscle strip, two sutures are placed proximal to the point of transection. This is done to prevent the proximal muscle from being retracted beyond the view of the surgeon in the event that further dissection is necessary. The strip should be mounted on a tongue depressor with pins or suture; proximal and distal orientation must be clearly depicted . A frozen section that confirms ganglion cells at the proximal margin must be obtained before the procedure can be finished. Dissection can be done in this manner for approximately 7 to 8 cm. Once a sufficient length of muscle has been removed, hemostasis is achieved with cautery. The wound is irrigated and closed with fine interrupted absorbable sutures that approximate the mucosa and submucosa.

For patients who have had several procedures, obtaining a submucosal plane may be quite difficult, and it is simpler to perform a vertically oriented elliptic full-thickness excision (Fig. 99-31A). Closure is performed with a running absorbable suture that approximates only the mucosa and submucosa, leaving a defect in the muscular layer (Fig. 99-31B).

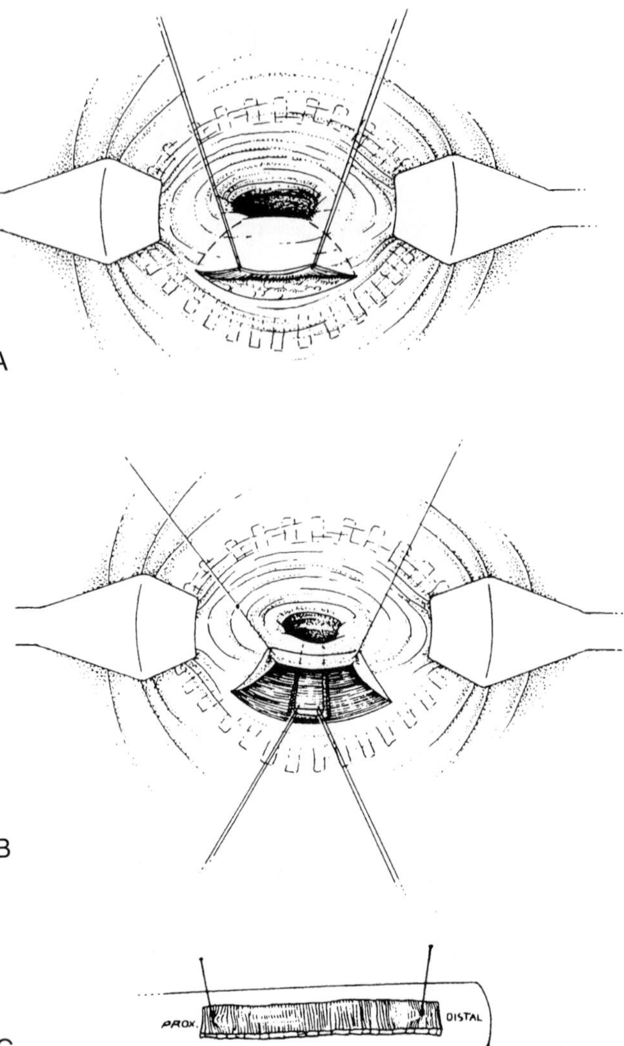

Figure 99-30 Transanal myectomy. *A*, A submucosal-mucosal flap is dissected to expose the muscularis propria. The myectomy is performed with traction sutures, facilitating the upward dissection. *B* and *C*, Note the importance of orienting the specimen for the pathologist. (From Spitz L, Coran A [eds]: Rob & Smith's Operative Surgery: Pediatric Surgery. London, Chapman Hall Medical, 1995.)

Redo Pull-Through

Although the vast majority of children who undergo a pull-through procedure do well, approximately 5% have poor results, and a small portion of these may benefit from reoperation. Indications for a redo pull-through include retained or acquired aganglionosis, severe strictures, dysfunctional bowel, and intestinal neuronal dysplasia. Additionally, there are patients with marked dilatation of the rectosigmoid colon secondary to years of constipation, and this bowel segment is unable to regain its muscular tone. A schematic diagram outlining the surgical approach to such patients is shown in Figure 99-32. Overall outcomes for patients who require a redo pull-through are generally not as good as those undergoing an initial pull-through. However, several authors have reported series in which 70% to 80% of patients can expect a reasonable improvement in stooling function following a redo pull-through procedure.[182,345,356,362] Nevertheless, the incidence of incontinence is considerably higher in this group of patients.

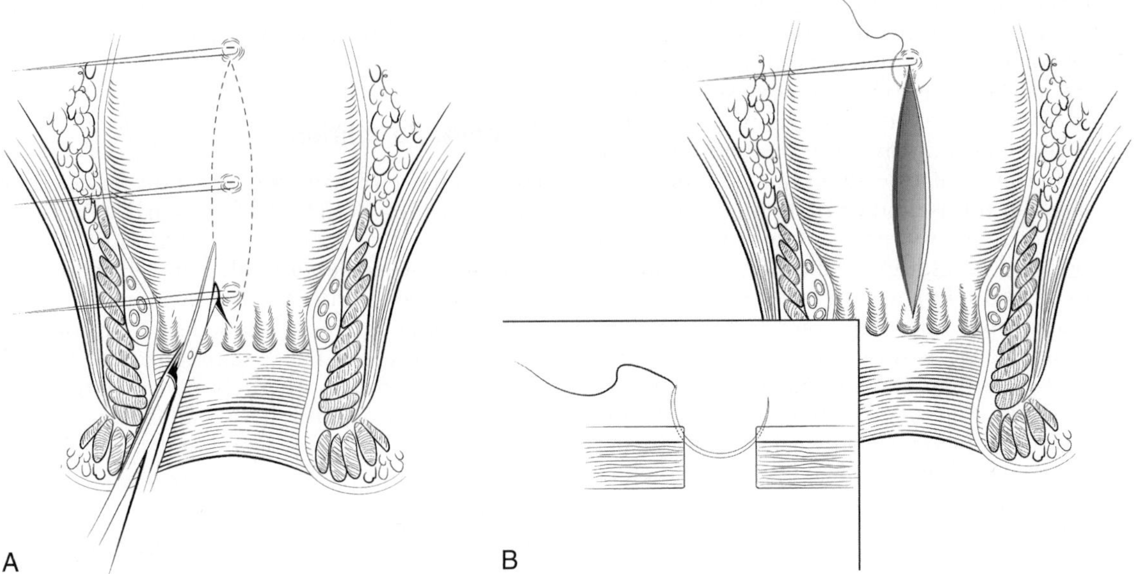

Figure 99-31 Alternative transanal myectomy approach. *A,* A series of traction sutures is placed in a vertical fashion. A full-thickness incision is made initially with scissors. The most cephalad suture is retained for traction. Visualization is hampered by bleeding, and hemostasis is achieved with cauterization of the edges. *B,* Closure is performed with a running suture starting at the cephalic edge, grasping only the mucosal and submucosal layers.

COMPLICATIONS AND OUTCOME

An assessment of the outcome of most infants and children with Hirschsprung's disease can generally be broken down into early and late findings, as well as the overall quality of life. Over the past half century, the outcome of patients with Hirschsprung's disease has improved significantly; however, morbidity is common, and many series have noted an occasional death.[327,357]

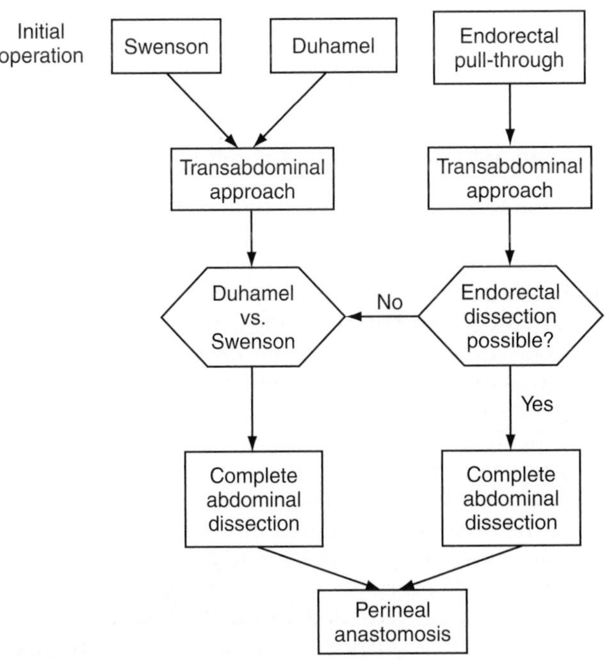

Figure 99-32 Algorithm for a redo pull-through procedure after various initial pull-throughs for Hirschsprung's disease.

Early Post–Pull-Through Complications

Early post–pull-through complications include intestinal obstruction requiring laparotomy, which occurs in approximately 8% to 13% of cases. The incidence of wound infection is similar to that in most colorectal procedures, approximately 10% to 15%. Early anorectal stenosis is reported in 10% to 20% of cases, and most of these can be managed by office or home anal dilatations. Anastomotic disruption or leak occurs in roughly 2% of cases. One interesting approach for dealing with a large disruption is to advance the pull-through segment farther out, thus preventing soilage of the pelvis. The anastomosis occurs in a secondary fashion, similar to the original approach used by Soave.[177]

Late Post–Pull-Through Complications

The late follow-up of children with Hirschsprung's disease offers the best opportunity to critically evaluate the efficacy and results of any particular surgical procedure. In general, the most commonly encountered problems are incontinence, constipation, and enterocolitis, along with the disease's overall impact on lifestyle. Other complications such as fistula, obstruction, and impotence are rare.

Incontinence

Probably no other complication has a greater impact on the overall quality of life than incontinence. One problem with many series is that incontinence rates are not reported. Overall, a few generalities can be made regarding continence rates. First, several authors have noted higher rates of incontinence in patients with trisomy 21 or other syndromes related to mental retardation.[49,117,267]

The typical incidence of incontinence ranges from 3% to 8%, but several series noted higher percentages.[22,68,228,375] When only neurologically normal patients are examined far beyond the newborn period, however, excellent outcomes are recorded, with continence rates no different from those of age-matched controls.[125,329] There is some question whether transanal dissection leads to higher rates of incontinence, but this is doubtful. Although follow-up times are short in many reports, several series suggest reasonably good outcomes.[105,118,183] Further, manometric measurements of anal sphincter tone are similar to those of patients undergoing open laparotomy dissection.[344] However, sphincter tone is diminished compared with age-matched controls.[126] In general, incontinence issues improve as the patient ages.[126,273] These results strongly suggest that pediatric surgeons treating patients with incontinence should use aggressive medical treatment, dietary modification, and constipating agents before considering any form of surgical therapy.

Stooling Frequency and Constipation

Stooling frequency is rarely documented in large reports of Hirschsprung's disease, but the majority of patients have normal stooling frequency.[191,321] Stooling frequency is fairly high in the first 3 months after a pull-through procedure but then decreases to normal levels (two to three per day) by 6 months.[329,352]

Constipation is a frequent complaint of children after a pull-through procedure for Hirschsprung's disease. Most forms of constipation have no histopathologic correlate and can be readily managed without an extensive evaluation. Rates of constipation range from 6% to 30% in most series. Puri and Nixon[264] found that 34.5% of children were constipated after a Swenson procedure. Rescorla et al.[273] reported that 27% of their patients undergoing a Duhamel procedure had some complaints of constipation that required medication, but this rate progressively decreased with age.

Enterocolitis

The pathophysiology of enterocolitis has already been discussed. Rates of post–pull-through enterocolitis vary widely among series, ranging from 2% to 40%; this is probably related to the authors' definition of enterocolitis versus spasm of the internal sphincter. Postoperative enterocolitis has been associated with a moderate rate of morbidity and occasional mortality.[48,328] When examining deaths attributable to Hirschsprung's disease, several series noted that approximately 50% were caused by complications directly related to an episode of enterocolitis.[48,328] Virtually all such episodes occurred within the first 2 years after the pull-through. Appropriate management of these patients may circumvent many of these episodes. It is the practice of many groups to discharge patients on a 1- to 2-month course of oral metronidazole. Marty et al.[211] advocated prophylactic rectal irrigations in all infants discharged after a pull-through; this resulted in a significant improvement in overall clinical outcome. An occasional child needs a posterior myectomy if enterocolitis episodes are persistent.[364] However, a significant period of conservative therapy should be tried first, because most patients with post–pull-through enterocolitis improve over time.

Stricture Formation

The incidence of stricture formation varies widely among reported series, from 0%[84,191] to as high as 20%,[321] depending on the definition of stricture. Most strictures respond to conservative treatment with rectal dilatations. Heikkinen et al.[125] stated that the highest incidence of strictures was in those patients who developed early postoperative leaks. However, Swenson et al.[315] stated that only 3 of 23 patients who developed late strictures had a history of an early postoperative leak, and they could find no obvious predisposing factor. The rate of post–pull-through enterocolitis is higher in patients with early strictures.[183,327]

Impotence and Urinary Dysfunction

The performance of any operative procedure in the pelvis can result in nerve injury. Many of the operations for Hirschsprung's disease have been designed specifically to avoid these structures. Overall, the incidence of impotence and urinary dysfunction is quite low. Intuitively, the Swenson procedure, because of its design, would be expected to have the highest risk of nerve injury. However, in a review of 282 patients, 101 men had gone through puberty, and none had developed impotence; 80 were married and had a total of 146 children.[314] Puri and Nixon[264] found that 2 of 84 patients had an absence of ejaculation, despite a normal erection, after the Swenson procedure. Late urologic disturbances are a very rare complication. It is thought that procedures with the least amount of pelvic dissection are associated with the lowest incidence of urination problems. In Puri and Nixon's 1977 review,[264] 7of 52 patients undergoing a Duhamel procedure had nocturnal enuresis, and 2 had daytime urinary dribbling. More recent series report no incidence of impotence or urinary problems.[105,183,327]

Outcome with Total Colonic Aganglionosis

The long-term outcome of patients with total colonic aganglionosis needs to be examined separately because the overall results in this particular group of patients are significantly worse than those who have standard or even long-segment Hirschsprung's disease. Nevertheless, the overall quality of life is generally good.[121]

Analysis of outcome is hampered, however, by the lack of separation of this group of patients in many series, as well as by the small number of patients with total colonic aganglionosis that one particular institution may see. In Ikeda and Goto's series,[140] there were 67 patients (4%) with total colonic aganglionosis. In that report, the Duhamel procedure was the predominant pull-through, with an overall mortality of 13%. In a review for the American Academy of Pediatrics, the majority of surgeons performed either a Duhamel or a Swenson procedure, with an associated morbidity of 62% and 70%, respectively, and mortality rates of 25% and 30%.[164]

In both of the aforementioned series, good results were obtained with the endorectal pull-through procedure, with no morbidity or mortality; however, a combined total of only nine patients underwent this procedure. Overall stooling frequency was not mentioned in either of these series, but stooling frequency and incontinence appeared to be quite high in the series of Marty et al.,[210] who noted that 40% of their patients with total colonic aganglionosis had severe soiling. Heij et al.[124] noted that six of their seven patients with total colonic aganglionosis were incontinent. The majority of patients in these latter series underwent a Duhamel or a Martin procedure. This is in contrast to the series by Endo et al.,[83] who noted that despite a history of loose stools in all nine of their patients (one to five loose stools per day), the frequency of bowel movements improved steadily over time and often decreased to two to five times a day by 2 to 3 years of age. All their patients with total colonic aganglionosis underwent a Kimura patch procedure just proximal to the ileoanal anastomosis. The authors noted a significantly higher frequency of stooling in patients with more proximal and extensive aganglionosis.

Quality of Life

Relatively few reports have studied the overall quality of life in patients with Hirschsprung's disease. A few generalities can be made, however. First, overall quality of life is reasonably good[125] and is significantly better than in patients with other anorectal malformations.[121] Bai et al.[22] measured quality of life in 45 children with Hirschsprung's disease versus 44 normal age-matched controls. They found that quality-of-life scores were good or fair in 87% of Hirschsprung's patients; however, their scores were significantly lower than those of controls. Further, patients with any degree of fecal soiling had significantly lower scores; a similar trend was noted by other investigators.[121,125,228,375] With time, most quality-of-life issues improve, particularly as patients approach adolescence.[375] With newer tools to study quality-of-life issues in these patients, additional information should be forthcoming.[119]

OTHER DYSMOTILITY DISORDERS

With increasing knowledge of the physiology of gastrointestinal motility, it became apparent that other motility disorders of the gastrointestinal tract existed in addition to Hirschsprung's disease. Gastrointestinal motility is controlled by various mechanisms, including the intrinsic nervous system and the central nervous system, and is modulated by various gastrointestinal peptides.[98,99,219] Several disorders have been described and are generally referred to as chronic (idiopathic) intestinal pseudo-obstructions. Although several classifications have been proposed,[171] dysmotility disorders can be divided into primary disorders of the gastrointestinal tract and systemic disorders that involve two or more sites. Finally, these processes may be either familial or, more commonly, sporadic in nature. Most patients present with abdominal distention accompanied by intermittent attacks of abdominal pain, obstructive or constipative symptoms, and malnutrition. Intestinal bacterial overgrowth is frequent.

Intestinal Neuronal Dysplasia

Intestinal neuronal dysplasia was initially described by Meier-Ruge in 1971.[214] This disorder was classified as a colonic dysplasia, although the disease can involve any portion of the gastrointestinal tract. This disorder is discussed in depth in Chapter 100.

Chronic Intestinal Pseudo-obstruction Syndrome

Chronic intestinal pseudo-obstruction (CIP) is a clinical and pathologic syndrome characterized by an abnormal peristaltic condition of the intestine.[128] The syndrome can be divided into three basic disorders: disorders secondary to abnormalities of the smooth muscle (myopathies), disorders of the myenteric plexus (neuropathies), and mesenchymopathies, or changes in the interstital cells of Cajal (ICC) network. CIP may be due to a primary disorder (idiopathic) or secondary to a wide array of pathologic conditions.[65] Most patients with this disorder have massive abdominal distention (Fig. 99-33) and an inability to ingest enteral nutrition.

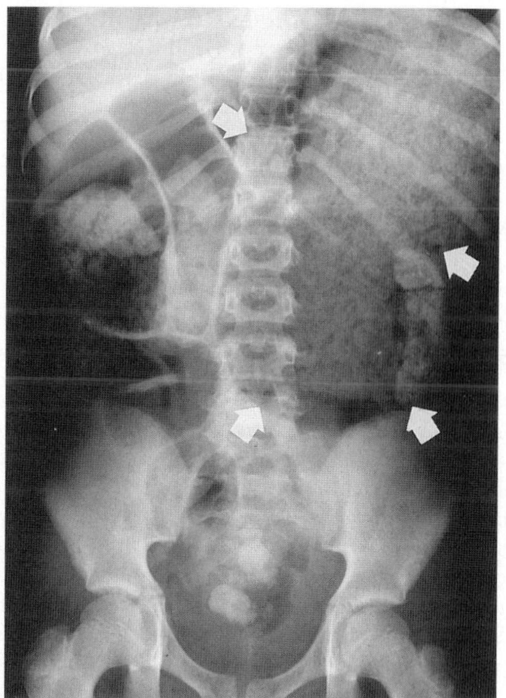

Figure 99-33 Abdominal radiographs of a patient with a visceral myopathy. The child has massive distention of her stomach ("soap bubble" appearance; *arrows*) and other loops of bowel. She has a history of bladder and colonic dysfunction as an infant. (Courtesy of Robert Murray, MD.)

Familial cases have been described, particularly in children with neuropathies[128]; however, most cases are sporadic in nature. The typical clinical features of this disorder include recurrent episodes of abdominal pain, bloating, nausea, and vomiting. Weight loss is common, and the vast majority of patients require prolonged courses of total parenteral nutrition.[128] In some patients, associated urinary symptoms may exist.

The diagnosis is most commonly suspected in the first few months of life (three quarters of cases manifest within the first year of life), and some cases have been detected prenatally.[128] Evidence of excessive drug use, urinary tract involvement, or a family history is particularly important. Laboratory tests are not diagnostic. The workup should include suction rectal biopsy to exclude an atypical or late presentation of Hirschsprung's disease and to evaluate for intestinal neuronal dysplasia. Although contrast radiologic studies are not always helpful, they can rule out a mechanical obstruction. Additionally, malrotation, short-bowel syndrome, and spastic left colon or microcolon have all been observed in a significant number of patients.[128] In some neuropathic disorders, however, normal emptying of the stomach and proximal intestine may be seen on upper gastrointestinal series, but emptying of enteral contents may be markedly abnormal. In general, myopathic disorders demonstrate weak contractility and an increased intestinal diameter, whereas disorders of the myenteric plexus show stronger but uncoordinated contractions and a smaller intestinal lumen. Evaluation of the genitourinary system is also important because, in some series, as many as one third of patients with CIP have dilatation of the bladder or ureters.[92]

Electrogastrography has been used to make the diagnosis in some cases, although this is not a uniformly available study.[42] Several reports have advocated serial full-thickness biopsies; unfortunately, pathologists who are unfamiliar with these disorders may miss the diagnosis.[65] Further, surgical manipulation of the gastrointestinal tract may worsen the motility disorder. Krishnamurthy and Schuffler[171] described a comprehensive review of the pathologic classification of CIP.

In addition to this general overview of CIP, there are some specific qualities of each classification.

Visceral Myopathies

Visceral myopathies are rare disorders characterized by degeneration of the smooth muscle of the gastrointestinal tract, with subsequent replacement of the muscle with fibrous tissue. Visceral myopathies are characterized as familial and sporadic. There are three basic types of familial visceral myopathies.[171] Type 1 is inherited as an autosomal dominant trait and is associated with a dilated esophagus, duodenum, and colon and with megacystis. Type 2 has an autosomal recessive pattern and is associated with ptosis and ophthalmoplegia; the proximal intestine is usually dilated. Type 3 has a possible autosomal recessive inheritance and is not associated with extraintestinal manifestations. The sporadic type of primary visceral myopathy involves the entire gastrointestinal tract and occasionally the bladder. Megacystis-microcolon-intestinal hypoperistalsis, which is related to these disorders, is discussed later.

Visceral Neuropathies

There are at least two types of familial visceral neuropathies.[279,289] In one type, systemic neurologic abnormalities and gastrointestinal motility disturbances are present, and the syndrome may be an autosomal recessive trait. Autopsy results have shown degeneration of the myenteric plexus. In the second type, the disease is an autosomal dominant trait and is confined to the gastrointestinal tract. Neuropathies may also be classified as inflammatory or degenerative. The inflammatory variant has a lymphocytic and plasma cell infiltrate around the two major ganglionated plexuses and axons of the enteric nervous system. These diseases may be associated with a number of extrinsic processes, including Chagas' disease (caused by the parasite *Trypanosoma cruzi*), carcinoid, neuroblastoma, thymoma, and connective tissue disease. Tissues are typically reactive to antinuclear neuronal and anti-Hu antibodies. The degenerative variant may be due to endogenous or exogenous injury to the neurons. Other patients have had CIP associated with MEN2.[235]

Mesenchymopathies

These disorders involve alterations in the ICCs. A quantitative decrease in ICCs is noted by immunohistochemial staining with cKIT antibody. Additionally, other structural abnormalities, including loss of neuronal architecture, are identified.[283]

Megacystis-Microcolon-Intestinal Hypoperistalsis Syndrome

Berdon et al.[29] first described the megacystis-microcolon-intestinal hypoperistalsis syndrome in 1976. Although quite distinct from other pseudo-obstructions, this disorder is one of the most severe forms of functional obstruction and should be classified as a visceral myopathy. This disorder often presents in the newborn period and has been called the neonatal hollow visceral myopathy syndrome by Puri.[262] In a review by Puri and Tsuji,[265] females were affected more than males by a 4:1 ratio. An autosomal recessive pattern of inheritance was suggested. Small intestinal motility is severely compromised in this disorder, resulting in an absence of stool in the colon. Megacystis and associated hydronephrosis are related to the gastrointestinal problems and usually respond to drainage procedures. In addition, these patients have lax abdominal wall musculature, incomplete intestinal rotation, and microcolon. Surgical bypass procedures are usually not effective. Pathologically, this syndrome is characterized by an increased number of ganglion cells; however, the number of ganglion cells can decrease as the disease progresses. Electron microscopy shows a thinning of the longitudinal muscle coat, with abundant amounts of connective tissue.[263] The long-term outlook for these patients is grave. The mortality rate is

87%, and long-term survivors are dependent on total parenteral nutrition.

Treatment

Promotility drugs have been tried in a number of studies, but the response is generally transient or lacking.[65] Cisapride is the most effective drug, although the response is often incomplete.[128,298] Currently, use of this drug is severely restricted owing to its association with cardiac arrhythmias. In one series, 6 of 15 adult patients responded to moderately high doses of erythromycin.[82] Decompressing stomas may have the greatest benefit in patients who are unresponsive to medications. In general, a feeding enterostomy (typically a jejunostomy) along with a "decompressing" ostomy is useful. Colostomy is effective in only half of patients; end-ileostomy appears to have a slightly greater benefit.[128] Stomal complications, including prolapse, are common, with at least one revision of the ostomy required in almost half the infants. Intestinal transplantation is a viable option for patients who fail to respond to more conservative measures. Recent publications concerning bowel transplantation for CIP show good results, although in patients with abnormal urinary bladders, problems will persist.[197]

Because of prolonged stasis in the gastrointestinal tract, evaluation for bacterial overgrowth and vitamin B_{12} deficiencies should be performed periodically. The diagnosis of bacterial overgrowth can be made by a hydrogen breath test and quantitative small bowel cultures ($>10^5$ organisms/mm^3). A stool pH of 5.0 or less is also suggestive of bacterial overgrowth.[91]

IDIOPATHIC CONSTIPATION AND ENCOPRESIS

Constipation is a common problem in the pediatric population. Chronic constipation with soiling has been reported in up to 3% of patients referred to teaching hospitals and clinics.[188] Despite the frequency of this problem, the definition of constipation is vague. Infants that are breast-fed or fed cow's milk have an average of 2.7 bowel movements per day in the first month of life; this declines to 1.7 bowel movements by 1 year of age[369] and then to approximately 1.2 bowel movements per day at 4 years of age.[355] To help develop a uniform manner in which to diagnose infants, the Rome II Multinational Consensus Document on Functional Gastrointestinal Disorders was developed.[270] Although some diagnoses do not fall under these criteria,[348] the consensus divides stooling abnormalities into four main categories: infant dyschezia, functional constipation, functional fecal retention, and nonretentive fecal soiling (Table 99-5).

The causes of constipation are multifactorial, including anatomic, physiologic, and genetic. The most common form of constipation is idiopathic in origin. A genetic predisposition to this type of constipation may exist, because up to 65% of constipated children demonstrate a tendency for this disorder by 6 months of age.[322] In addition, a family history of constipation is commonly found in such children. Constipation may become evident or be exacerbated as the child becomes aware of his or her voluntary control of defecation (i.e., during toilet training). As constipation progresses, the anorectal vault progressively dilates and accommodates a larger amount of stool. As the stool increases in firmness, pain during defecation causes the formation of anal fissures, which exacerbate symptoms. If the symptoms of constipation continue, the rectum will reach a maximal size beyond which it can accommodate no more stool. Liquid stool then leaks around the obstructing fecal mass and causes soiling (i.e., encopresis).

TABLE 99-5 Rome II Classification of Functional Disorders of Defecation

Infant dyschezia: at least 10 min of straining and crying before successful passage of soft stools in an otherwise healthy infant younger than 6 mo
Functional constipation: in infants and preschool children, at least 2 wk of:
Scybalous, pebble-like, hard stools for a majority of stools; or
Firm stools ≤2 times/wk; and
No evidence of structural, endocrine, or metabolic disease
Functional fecal retention: from infancy to age 16 yr, a history of at least 12 wk of:
Passage of large-diameter stools at intervals <2 times/wk; and
Retentive posturing, avoidance of defecation by purposefully contracting the pelvic floor; as pelvic floor muscles fatigue, the child uses the gluteal muscles, squeezing the buttocks together
Nonretentive fecal soiling: in children older than 4 yr, a history of the following ≥1 time/wk for the preceding 12 wk:
Defecation into places and at times inappropriate to the social context;
No structural or inflammatory disease; and
No signs of fecal retention

Functional, nonretentive fecal soiling or encopresis is defined as fecal soiling that has no obvious organic basis.[90] Although encopresis has been associated with psychological and emotional problems, a more detailed analysis demonstrates that only 20% of children with encopresis have significant psychological problems, and many of those problems started after the onset of encopresis.[1] Encopresis usually begins after 3 years of age. Levin[188] found a mean age of 7 years in his study. Urinary tract infections may often be associated with this disorder.

Differentiating patients with Hirschsprung's disease from those with chronic constipation is a common problem for pediatric surgeons. There are several signs, symptoms, and studies that can help differentiate the two processes. Patients with idiopathic constipation classically have soiling (often from overflow of liquid stool) and a dilated ampulla filled with stool. Both these findings are unusual in patients with typical Hirschsprung's disease. In fact, the ampulla is usually narrow in Hirschsprung's disease and may be empty on digital examination. Barium enema contrast studies also show a dilated ampulla down to the anal verge in chronic constipation, whereas contrast enema radiography in Hirschsprung's disease shows a narrowed and constricted rectum or rectosigmoid area (see Fig. 99-1).

TABLE 99-6 Clinical Comparison between Idiopathic Constipation and Hirschsprung's Disease

Signs, Symptoms, and Diagnostic Studies	Idiopathic Constipation	Hirschsprung's Disease
Soiling	Common	Unusual
Stool in ampulla	Common	Unusual
Obstructive symptoms	Rare	Common
Stool retentive behavior	Common	Rare
Enterocolitis	Never	Possible
Anorectal examination	Dilated ampulla	Narrow
Contrast enema	Dilated ampulla	Narrowed distal segment

Table 99-6 compares and contrasts some of these signs and symptoms.

The treatment for constipation includes dietary manipulation, medication, enema treatments, and behavioral conditioning in younger children. In infants, simple dietary manipulations with laxative-type fruits (e.g., apricots, prunes) may be sufficient to treat constipation. The addition of medications may be helpful. Although a variety of medications have been recommended, only polyethylene glycol 3350 has been shown to be safe for long-term use in the pediatric population.[28] Before the diagnosis of functional, idiopathic constipation is made, other anatomic and physiologic reasons for the disorder must be ruled out; suction rectal biopsy is often necessary. Often, an anus that is displaced anteriorly (which may be subtle) mimics benign constipation and may be amenable to surgical therapy. For children with severe, chronic constipation or encopresis, a series of maneuvers is necessary to break the cycle of a chronically impacted state and to modify and increase the frequency of defecation. Figure 99-34 shows a suggested treatment protocol for this type of child. It is important to note that the treatment of each child must be individualized, depending on the duration and severity of symptoms as well as the compliance of the parents and child.

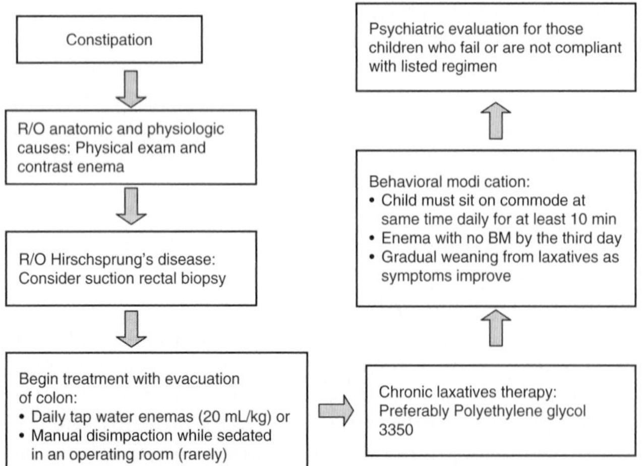

Figure 99-34 Treatment protocol for a child with idiopathic constipation. Before treatment, anatomic and physiologic causes need to be ruled out (R/O) by physical examination, contrast studies, and a suction rectal biopsy. Because most patients have fecal impaction associated with constipation, colonic evacuation is required to break the cycle of a dilated colon that retains huge amounts of stool. This can be done with a daily enema (tap water or phosphate) for at least 1 to 2 weeks. The enemas must be continued if the child fails to have a bowel movement (BM) at least every 3 days. Should a child be noncompliant or fail this regimen, a psychiatric evaluation should be obtained.

REFERENCES

1. Abrahamian F, Lloyd-Still J: Chronic constipation in childhood: A longitudinal study of 186 patients. J Pediatr Gastroenterol Nutr 1984;3:460-467.
2. Adson A: Hirschsprung's disease: Indications for and results obtained by sympathectomy. Surgery 1937;1:859.
3. Akgur F, Tanyel F, Buyukpamukcu N, Hicsonmez A: Colonic atresia and Hirschsprung's disease association shows further evidence for migration of enteric neurons. J Pediatr Surg 1993;28:635-636.
4. Akkary S, Sahwy E, Kandil W, Hamdy M: A histochemical study of the mucosubstances of the colon in cases of Hirschsprung's disease with and without enterocolitis. J Pediatr Surg 1981;16:664-668.
5. Albanese CT, Jennings RW, Smith B, et al: Perineal one-stage pull-through for Hirschsprung's disease. J Pediatr Surg 1999; 34:377-380.
6. Aldridge R, Campbell P: Ganglion cell distribution in the normal rectum and anal canal: A basis for the diagnosis of Hirschsprung's disease by anorectal biopsy. J Pediatr Surg 1968;3:475-490.
7. Amiel J, Attie T, Jan D, et al: Heterozygous endothelin receptor B (EDNRB) mutations in isolated Hirschsprung disease. Hum Mol Genet 1996;5:355-357.
8. Amiel J, Lyonnet S: Hirschsprung disease, associated syndromes, and genetics: A review. J Med Genet 2001;38: 729-739.
9. Amodio J, Berdon W, Abramson S, Stolar C: Microcolon of prematurity: A form of functional obstruction. AJR Am J Roentgenol 1986;146:239-244.
10. Anderson K, Chandra R: Segmental aganglionosis of the appendix. J Pediatr Surg 1986;21:852-854.
11. Andrassy R, Isaacs H, Weitzman J: Rectal suction biopsy for the diagnosis of Hirschsprung's disease. Ann Surg 1981; 193:419-424.
12. Angrist M, Bolk S, Halushka M, et al: Germline mutations in glial cell line-derived neurotrophic factor (GDNF) and RET in a Hirschsprung disease patient. Nat Genet 1996; 14:341-344.
13. Angrist M, Bolk S, Thiel B, et al: Mutation analysis of the RET receptor tyrosine kinase in Hirschsprung disease. Hum Mol Genet 1995;4:821-830.
14. Anuras S, Hade J, Soffer E, et al: Natural history of adult Hirschsprung's disease. J Clin Gastroenterol 1984;6:205-210.
15. Arliss J, Holgersen L: Neonatal appendiceal perforation and Hirschsprung's disease. J Pediatr Surg 1990;25:694-695.
16. Aslam A, Spicer RD, Corfield AP: Turnover of radioactive mucin precursors in the colon of patients with Hirschsprung's disease correlates with the development of enterocolitis. J Pediatr Surg 1998;33:103-105.
17. Aslam A, Spicer RD, Corfield AP: Histochemical and genetic analysis of colonic mucin glycoproteins in Hirschsprung's disease. J Pediatr Surg 1999;34:330-333.

18. Athow A, Filipe M, Drake D: Problems and advantages of acetylcholinesterase histochemistry of rectal suction biopsies in the diagnosis of Hirschsprung's disease. J Pediatr Surg 1990;25:520-526.
19. Attie T, Pelet A, Edery P, et al: Diversity of RET proto-oncogene mutations in familial and sporadic Hirschsprung disease. Hum Mol Genet 1995;4:1381-1386.
20. Auricchio A, Casari G, Staiano A, Ballabio A: Endothelin-B receptor mutations in patients with isolated Hirschsprung disease from a non-inbred population. Hum Mol Genet 1996;5:351-354.
21. Badner J, Sieber W, Garver K, Chakravarti A: A genetic study of Hirschsprung disease. Am J Hum Genet 1990;46: 568-580.
22. Bai Y, Chen H, Hao J, et al: Long-term outcome and quality of life after the Swenson procedure for Hirschsprung's disease. J Pediatr Surg 2002;37:639-642.
23. Baloh R, Tansey M, Golden J, et al: TrnR2, a novel receptor that mediates neurturin and GDNF signaling through RET. Neuron 1997;18:793-802.
24. Baltogiannis N, Mavridis G, Soutis M, Keramidas D: Currarino triad associated with Hirschsprung's disease. J Pediatr Surg 2003;38:1086-1089.
25. Banani SA, Forootan H: Role of anorectal myectomy after failed endorectal pull-through in Hirschsprung's disease. J Pediatr Surg 1994;29:1307-1309.
26. Baumgarten H, Holstein A, Stelzner F: Nervous elements in the human colon of Hirschsprung's disease (with comparative remarks on neuronal profiles in the normal human and monkey colon and sphincter ani internus). Virchows Arch A Pathol Anat 1973;358:113-136.
27. Bealer J, Natuzzi E, Flake A, et al: Effect of nitric oxide on the colonic smooth muscle of patients with Hirschsprung's disease. J Pediatr Surg 1994;29:1025-1029.
28. Bell E, Wall G: Pediatric constipation therapy using guidelines and polyethylene glycol 3350. Ann Pharmacother 2004;38:686-693.
29. Berdon W, Baker D, Bland W: Megacystis-microcolon intestinal hypoperistalsis syndrome: A new cause of intestinal obstruction in the newborn. Report of radiologic findings in five newborn girls. Ann Roentgenol 1976;126:957-964.
30. Bickler S, Harrison M, Campbell T, Campbell J: Long-segment Hirschsprung's disease. Arch Surg 1992;127: 1047-1050.
31. Bielschowsky M, Scholfield G: Studies on the inheritance and neurohistology of megacolon in mice. Proc Univ Otago Med Sch 1960;38:14-15.
32. Bill AH Jr, Chapman N: The enterocolitis of Hirschsprung's disease: Its natural history and treatment. Am J Surg 1962; 103:70-74.
33. Blair GK, Murphy JJ, Fraser GC: Internal sphincterotomy in post-pull-through Hirschsprung's disease. J Pediatr Surg 1996;31:843-845.
34. Bodian M: Pathological aids in the diagnosis and management of Hirschsprung's disease. In Recent Advances in Clinical Pathology. London, Churchill, 1960.
35. Bolande R: The neurocristopathies: A unifying concept of disease arising in neural crest maldevelopment. Hum Pathol 1974;5:409-429.
36. Boley S: An endorectal pull-through operation with primary anastomosis for Hirschsprung's disease. Surg Gynecol Obstet 1968;127:353-357.
37. Boley S, Dinari G, Cohen M: Hirschsprung's disease in the newborn. Clin Perinatol 1978;5:45-60.
38. Bolk S, Pelet A, Hofstra R, et al: A human model for multigenic inheritance: Phenotypic expression in Hirschsprung disease requires both the RET gene and a new 9q31 locus. Proc Natl Acad Sci U S A 2000;97:268-273.
39. Bondurand N, Kuhlbrodt K, Pingault V, et al: A molecular analysis of the Yemenite deaf-blind hypopigmentation syndrome: SOX10 dysfunction causes different neurocristopathies. Hum Mol Genet 1999;8:1785-1789.
40. Borrego S, Ruiz A, Saez M, et al: RET genotypes comprising specific haplotypes of polymorphic variants predispose to isolated Hirschsprung disease. J Med Genet 2000;37:572-578.
41. Borrego S, Saez M, Ruiz A, et al: Specific polymorphisms in the RET proto-oncogene are over-represented in patients with Hirschsprung disease and may represent loci modifying phenotypic expression. J Med Genet 1999;36:771-774.
42. Bracci F, Iacobelli B, Papadatou B, et al: Role of electrogastrography in detecting motility disorders in children affected by chronic intestinal pseudo-obstruction and Crohn's disease. Eur J Pediatr Surg 2003;13:31-34.
43. Brandborg L, Rubin G, Quinton W: Multipurpose instrument for suction biopsy of esophagus, stomach, small bowel and colon. Gastroenterology 1959;37:1-16.
44. Branski D, Lebenthal E: Small intestinal changes in enterocolitis complicating Hirschsprung's disease. J Clin Gastroenterol 1979;1:237-240.
45. Bult H, Boeckxstaens G, Pelckmans P: Nitric oxide as an inhibitory non-adrenergic non-cholinergic neurotransmitter. Nature 1990;345:346-347.
46. Burns A, Pasricha P, Young H: Enteric neural crest-derived cells and neural stem cells: Biology and therapeutic potential. Neurogastroenterol Motil Suppl 2004;1:3-7.
47. Callaghan R, Nixon H: Megarectum: Physiological observation. Arch Dis Child 1964;39:153.
48. Caneiro P, Brereton R, Drake D, et al: Enterocolitis in Hirschsprung's disease. Pediatr Surg Int 1992;7:356-360.
49. Caniano D, Teitelbaum D, Qualman S: Management of Hirschsprung's disease in children with trisomy 21. Am J Surg 1990;159:402-404.
50. Caniano D, Teitelbaum D, Qualman S, Shannon B: The piebald-lethal murine strain: Investigation of the cause of early death. J Pediatr Surg 1989;24:906-910.
51. Carcassonne M, Morisson-Lacombe G, Letourneau JN: Primary corrective operation without decompression in infants less than three months of age with Hirschsprung's disease. J Pediatr Surg 1982;17:241-243.
52. Carrasquillo M, McCallion A, Puffenberger E, et al: Genome-wide association study and mouse model identify interaction between RET and EDNRB pathways in Hirschsprung disease. Nat Genet 2002;32:237-244.
53. Ceccheini I, Yin L, Pasini B, et al: Close linkage with RET protooncogene and deletion mutation in autosomal dominant Hirschsprung disease. Hum Mol Genet 1993;2:1803-1808.
54. Chakravarti A, Lyonnet S: Hirschsprung disease. In Scriver C, Beaudet A, Valle D, Sly W (eds): The Metabolic and Molecular Bases of Inherited Disease, 8th ed. New York, McGraw-Hill, 2000.
55. Challa V, Moran J, Turner C, Lyerly A: Histologic diagnosis of Hirschsprung's disease: The value of concurrent hematoxylin and eosin and cholinesterase staining of rectal biopsies. Am J Clin Pathol 1987;88:324-328.
56. Cilley R, Statter M, Hirschl R, Coran A: Definitive treatment of Hirschsprung's disease in the newborn with a one-stage procedure. Surgery 1994;115:551-556.
57. Clark D: Times of first void and first stool in 500 newborns. Pediatrics 1977;60:457-459.
58. Clausen N, Andersson P, Tommerup N: Familial occurrence of neuroblastoma, von Recklinghausen's neurofibromatosis, Hirschsprung's aganglionosis and jaw-winking syndrome. Acta Paediatr Scand 1989;78:736-741.
59. Cohen MC, Moore SW, Neveling U, Kaschula RO: Acquired aganglionosis following surgery for Hirschsprung's disease: A report of five cases during a 33-year experience

with pull-through procedures. Histopathology 1993;22: 163-168.
60. Coran A, Weintraub W: Modification of the endorectal procedure for Hirschsprung's disease. Surg Gynecol Obstet 1976;143:277-282.
61. Corkery JJ: Hirschsprung's disease. Clin Gastroenterol 1975;4:531-544.
62. Curran TJ, Raffensperger JG: Laparoscopic Swenson pull-through: A comparison with the open procedure. J Pediatr Surg 1996;31:1155-1156.
63. Davies M, Cywes S: Inadequate pouch emptying following Martin's pull-through procedure for intestinal aganglionosis. J Pediatr Surg 1983;18:14-20.
64. Davies M, Cywes S, Rode H: The manometric evaluation of the rectosphincteric reflex in total colonic aganglionosis. J Pediatr Surg 1981;16:300-303.
65. De Giorgio R, Sarnelli G, Corinaldesi R, Stanghellini V: Advances in our understanding of the pathology of chronic intestinal pseudo-obstruction. Gut 2004;53:1549-1552.
66. de la Torre-Mondragon L, Ortega-Salgado JA: Transanal endorectal pull-through for Hirschsprung's disease. J Pediatr Surg 1998;33:1283-1286.
67. Dimler M: "Acquired" Hirschsprung's disease. J Pediatr Surg 1981;16:844-845.
68. Diseth TH, Bjornland K, Novik TS, Emblem R: Bowel function, mental health, and psychosocial function in adolescents with Hirschsprung's disease. Arch Dis Child 1997;76:100-106.
69. Dobbins W, Bill A: Diagnosis of Hirschsprung's disease excluded by rectal suction biopsy. N Engl J Med 1965;272:990.
70. Doray B, Salomon R, Amiel J, et al: Mutation of the RET ligand, neurturin, supports multigenic inheritance in Hirschsprung disease. Hum Mol Genet 1998;7:1449-1452.
71. Duhamel B: Une nouvelle operation pour le megacolon congenital: L'abaissement retrorectal et trans-anal du colon, et son application possible au traitement de quelques autres malformations. Presse Med 1956;64:2249.
72. Duhamel B: Therapies Chirurgicale Infantile. Paris, 1957.
73. Duhamel B: A new operation for the treatment of Hirschsprung's disease. Arch Dis Child 1960;35:38-40.
74. Duhamel B: Retrorectal and transanal pull-through procedure for the treatment of Hirschsprung's disease. Dis Colon Rectum 1964;7:455.
75. Ehrenpreis T: Megacolon in the newborn. Acta Chir Scand Suppl 1946;94:7-113.
76. Ein SH, Shandling B, So H: A new look at an old operation for aganglionosis. J Pediatr Surg 1994;29:1228-1230.
77. Elhalaby E, Coran A: Hirschsprung's disease associated with Ondine's curse: Report of three cases and review of the literature. J Pediatr Surg 1994;29:530-535.
78. Elhalaby E, Coran A, Blane C, et al: Enterocolitis associated with Hirschsprung's disease: A clinical-radiological characterization based on 168 patients. J Pediatr Surg 1995;30:76-83.
79. Elhalaby EA, Hashish A, Elbarbary MM, et al: Transanal one-stage endorectal pull-through for Hirschsprung's disease: A multicenter study. J Pediatr Surg 2004;39:345-351.
80. Elhalaby EA, Teitelbaum DH, Coran AG, Heidelberger KP: Enterocolitis associated with Hirschsprung's disease: A clinical histopathological correlative study. J Pediatr Surg 1995;30:1023-1026.
81. Ellis D, Clatworth H: The meconium plug revisited. J Pediatr Surg 1966;1:54-61.
82. Emmanuel A, Shand A, Kamm M: Erythromycin for the treatment of chronic intestinal pseudo-obstruction: Description of six cases with a positive response. Aliment Pharmacol Ther 2004;19:687-694.
83. Endo M, Watanabe K, Fuchimoto Y, et al: Long-term results of surgical treatment in infants with total colonic aganglionosis. J Pediatr Surg 1994;29:1310-1314.
84. Erdek M, Wilt E: Hirschsprung's disease: One institution's ten year experience and long-term follow-up. Am Surg 1994;60:625-628.
85. Estevao-Costa J, Carvalho JL, Soares-Oliveira M: Risk factors for the development of enterocolitis after pull-through for Hirschsprung's disease. J Pediatr Surg 1999;34: 1581-1582.
86. Felman A, Talbert J: Failure to thrive. How about Hirschsprung's disease? Clin Pediatr 1971;10:125-126.
87. Fishbein R, Handelsman J, Schuster M: Surgical treatment of Hirschsprung's disease in adults. Surg Gynecol Obstet 1986;163:458-464.
88. Fitze G, Cramer J, Ziegler A, et al: Association between c135G/A genotype and RET protooncogene germline mutations and phenotype of Hirschsprung's disease. Lancet 2002;359:1200-1205.
89. Fitze G, Schreiber M, Kuhlisch E, et al: Association of RET protooncogene codon 45 polymorphism with Hirschsprung disease. Am J Hum Genet 1999;65:1469-1473.
90. Fitzgerald J: Encopresis, soiling, constipation. What's to be done? Pediatrics 1975;56:348-349.
91. Forstner G, Sherman P, Lichtman S: Bacterial overgrowth. In Walker W, Durie P, Hamilton J, et al (eds): Pediatric Gastrointestinal Disease, vol 1. Philadelphia, BC Decker, 1991, pp 689-700.
92. Framken E, Smith W, Frey E, et al: Intestinal motility disorders of infants and children: Classification, clinical manifestations, and roentgenology. CRC Crit Rev Diagn Imaging 1987;27:203-237.
93. Fu CG, Muto T, Masaki T, Nagawa H: Zonal adult Hirschsprung's disease. Gut 1996;39:765-767.
94. Fujimoto T, Reen DJ, Puri P: Inflammatory response in enterocolitis in the piebald lethal mouse model of Hirschsprung's disease. Pediatr Res 1988;24:152-155.
95. Fujimoto T, Hata J, Yokoyama S, Mitomi T: A study of the extracellular matrix protein as the migration pathway of neural crest cells in the gut: Analysis in human embryos with special reference to the pathogenesis of Hirschsprung's disease. J Pediatr Surg 1989;24:550-556.
96. Fujimoto T, Reen D, Puri P: Immunohistochemical characterization of abnormal innervation of colon in Hirschsprung's disease using D7 monoclonal antibody. J Pediatr Surg 1987;22:246-251.
97. Fujimoto T, Reen DJ, Puri P: Inflammatory response in enterocolitis in the piebald lethal mouse model of Hirschsprung's disease. Pediatr Res 1988;24:152-155.
98. Furness J, Costa M: The adrenergic innervation of the gastrointestinal tract. Erg Physiol 1974;69:1.
99. Furness J, Costa M: Types of nerves in the enteric nervous system. Neuroscience 1980;5:1-20.
100. Gabriel S, Salomon R, Pelet A, et al: Segregation at three loci explains familial and population risk in Hirschsprung disease. Nat Genet 2002;31:89-93.
101. Gaillard D, Birembaut P, Ploton D, et al: Colonic nerve network demonstrated by quinacrine. Bull Assoc Anat 1982;66:63-70.
102. Gariepy CE, Williams SC, Richardson JA, et al: Transgenic expression of the endothelin-B receptor prevents congenital intestinal aganglionosis in a rat model of Hirschsprung disease. J Clin Invest 1998;102:1092-1101.
103. Gauderer M, Rothstein F, Izant R Jr: Ileal atresia with long-segment Hirschsprung's disease in a neonate. J Pediatr Surg 1984;19:15-17.
104. Georgeson K, Fuefner M, Hardin W: Primary laparoscopic pull-through for Hirschsprung's disease in infants and children. J Pediatr Surg 1995;30:1017-1022.
105. Georgeson KE, Cohen RD, Hebra A, et al: Primary laparoscopic-assisted endorectal colon pull-through for

Hirschsprung's disease: A new gold standard. Ann Surg 1999;229:678-682.

106. Gherardi G: Pathology of the ganglionic-aganglionic junction in congenital megacolon. Arch Pathol (Chicago) 1960;69:520.
107. Ghose SI, Squire BR, Stringer MD, et al: Hirschsprung's disease: Problems with transition-zone pull-through. J Pediatr Surg 2000;35:1805-1809.
108. Glotzer D, Gpihl B: Experimental obstructive colitis. Arch Surg 1966;92:1-8.
109. Goldberg E: An epidemiological study of Hirschsprung's disease. Int J Epidemiol 1984;13:479-485.
110. Gowers W: The automatic action of the sphincter ani. Proc R Soc Med 1877;26:77.
111. Griseri P, Pesce B, Patrone G, et al: A rare haplotype of the RET proto-oncogene is a risk-modifying allele in Hirschsprung disease. Am J Hum Genet 2002;71:969-974.
112. Griseri P, Sancandi M, Patrone G, et al: A single-nucleotide polymorphic variant of the RET proto-oncogene is underrepresented in sporadic Hirschsprung disease. Eur J Hum Genet 2000;8:721-724.
113. Grob M: Intestinal obstruction in the new born infant. Arch Dis Child 1960;35:40.
114. Guo R, Nada O, Suita S, et al: The distribution and co-localization of nitric oxide synthase and vasoactive intestinal polypeptide in nerves of the colon with Hirschsprung's disease. Virchows Arch 1997;430:53-61.
115. Hackam DJ, Filler RM, Pearl RH: Enterocolitis after the surgical treatment of Hirschsprung's disease: Risk factors and financial impact. J Pediatr Surg 1998;33:830-833.
116. Hackam DJ, Reblock K, Barksdale EM, et al: The influence of Down's syndrome on the management and outcome of children with Hirschsprung's disease. J Pediatr Surg 2003;38:946-949.
117. Hackam DJ, Superina RA, Pearl RH: Single-stage repair of Hirschsprung's disease: A comparison of 109 patients over 5 years. J Pediatr Surg 1997;32:1028-1031.
118. Hadidi A: Transanal endorectal pull-through for Hirschsprung's disease: Experience with 68 patients. J Pediatr Surg 2003;38:1337-1340.
119. Hanneman MJ, Sprangers MA, De Mik EL, et al: Quality of life in patients with anorectal malformation or Hirschsprung's disease: Development of a disease-specific questionnaire. Dis Colon Rectum 2001;44:1650-1660.
120. Harrison M, Deitz D, Campbell J, Campbell T: Diagnosis and management of Hirschsprung's disease: A 25 year perspective. Am J Surg 1986;152:49-56.
121. Hartman EE, Oort FJ, Aronson DC, et al: Critical factors affecting quality of life of adult patients with anorectal malformations or Hirschsprung's disease. Am J Gastroenterol 2004;99:907-913.
122. Hawksley M: Spinal anaesthsia in the treatment of Hirschsprung's disease. Br J Surg 1943-1944;31:245-252.
123. Hearn C, Murphy M, Newgreen D: GDNF and ET-3 differentially modulate the numbers of avian enteric neural crest cells and enteric neurons in vitro. Dev Biol 1998; 197:93-105.
124. Heij HA, de Vries X, Bremer I, et al: Long-term anorectal function after Duhamel operation for Hirschsprung's disease. J Pediatr Surg 1995;30:430-432.
125. Heikkinen M, Rintala R, Louhimo I: Bowel function and quality of life in adult patients with operated Hirschsprung's disease. Pediatr Surg Int 1995;10:342-344.
126. Heikkinen M, Rintala R, Luukkonen P: Long-term anal sphincter performance after surgery for Hirschsprung's disease. J Pediatr Surg 1997;32:1443-1446.
127. Helbig D: Hirschsprung's disease in infancy and childhood. In Holschneider A (ed): Hirschsprung's Disease. New York and Stuttgart, Hippokarates Verlag, Thieme-Stratton, 1982, pp 93-102.
128. Heneyke S, Smith V, Spitz L, Milla P: Chronic intestinal pseudo-obstruction: Treatment and long term follow up of 44 patients. Arch Dis Child 1999;81:21-27.
129. Hengster P, Pernthaler H, Gassner I, Menardi G: Twenty-three years of follow-up in patients with total colonic aganglionosis. Klin Padiatr 1996;208:3-7.
130. Hirobe S, Doody DP, Ryan DP, et al: Ectopic class II major histocompatibility antigens in Hirschsprung's disease and neuronal intestinal dysplasia. J Pediatr Surg 1992;27: 357-362.
131. Hirschsprung H: Stuhltragheit neugeborner in folge von dilatation and hypertrophie des colons. Jaharb Kinderch 1887;27:1-7.
132. Hoehner JC, Ein SH, Shandling B, Kim PC: Long-term morbidity in total colonic aganglionosis. J Pediatr Surg 1998;33:961-965.
133. Hofstra R, Osinga J, Tan-Sindhunata G, et al: A homozygous mutation in the endothelin-3 gene associated with a combined Waardenburg type 2 and Hirschsprung phenotype (Shah-Waardenburg syndrome). Nat Genet 1996; 12:445-447.
134. Hollwarth ME, Rivosecchi M, Schleef J, et al: The role of transanal endorectal pull-through in the treatment of Hirschsprung's disease: A multicenter experience. Pediatr Surg Int 2002;18:344-348.
135. Holschneider A, Kellner E, Streibl P, Sippell W: The development of anorectal continence and its significance in the diagnosis of Hirschsprung's disease. J Pediatr Surg 1976;11:151-156.
136. Hyde G Jr, De Lorimier A: Colon atresia and Hirschsprung's disease. Surgery 1968;64:976-978.
137. Ikawa H, Kim S, Hendren W, Donahoe P: Acetylcholinesterase and manometry in the diagnosis of the constipated child. Arch Surg 1986;121:435-438.
138. Ikawa H, Yokoyama J, Morikawa Y, et al: A quantitative study of acetylcholine in Hirschsprung's disease. J Pediatr Surg 1980;15:48-52.
139. Ikeda K: New techniques in the surgical treatment of Hirschsprung's disease. Surgery 1967;61:503-508.
140. Ikeda K, Goto S: Diagnosis and treatment of Hirschsprung's disease in Japan: An analysis of 1628 patients. Ann Surg 1984;199:400-405.
141. Ikeda K, Goto S: Total colonic aganglionosis with or without small bowel involvement: An analysis of 137 patients. J Pediatr Surg 1986;21:319-322.
142. Inoue M, Hosoda K, Imura K, et al: Mutational analysis of the endothelin-B receptor gene in Japanese Hirschsprung's disease. J Pediatr Surg 1998;33:1206-1208.
143. Ito S, Iwashita T, Asai N, et al: Biological properties of RET with cysteine mutations correlate with multiple endocrine neoplasia type 2A, familial medullary thyroid carcinoma, and Hirschsprung's disease phenotype. Cancer Res 1997; 57:2870-2872.
144. Ito Y, Donahoe P, Hendren W: Maturation of the rectoanal response in premature and perinatal infants. J Pediatr Surg 1977;12:477-481.
145. Ivanchuk SM, Myers SM, Eng C, Mulligan LM: De novo mutation of GDNF, ligand for the RET/GDNFR-alpha receptor complex, in Hirschsprung disease. Hum Mol Genet 1996;5:2023-2026.
146. Iwashita T, Kruger G, Pardal R, et al: Hirschsprung disease is linked to defects in neural crest stem cell function. Science 2003;301:972-976.
147. Jamieson D, Dundas S, Belushi S, et al: Does the transition zone reliably delineate aganglionic bowel in Hirschsprung's disease? Pediatr Radiol 2004;34:811-815.

148. Jasonni V, Martucciello G: Total colonic aganglionosis. Semin Pediatr Surg 1998;7:174-180.
149. Jiang Y, Liu M, Gershon M: Netrins and DCC in the guidance of migrating neural crest-derived cells in the developing bowel and pancreas. Dev Biol 2003;258: 364-384.
150. Jing S, Yu Y, Fang M, et al: GFRalpha-2 and GFRalpha-3 are two new receptors for ligands of the GDNF family. J Biol Chem 1997;272:33111-33117.
151. Jordan F, Coran A, Weintraub W, Wesley J: An evaluation of the modified endorectal procedure for Hirschsprung's disease. J Pediatr Surg 1979;14:681-685.
152. Kanai M, Numakura C, Sasaki A, et al: Congenital central hypoventilation syndrome: A novel mutation of the RET gene in an isolated case. Tohoku J Exp Med 2002;196: 241-246.
153. Kapur RP, deSa DJ, Luquette M, Jaffe R: Hypothesis: Pathogenesis of skip areas in long-segment Hirschsprung's disease. Pediatr Pathol Lab Med 1995;15:23-37.
154. Keshtgar AS, Ward HC, Clayden GS, de Sousa NM: Investigations for incontinence and constipation after surgery for Hirschsprung's disease in children. Pediatr Surg Int 2003;19:4-8.
155. Khan AR, Vujanic GM, Huddart S: The constipated child: How likely is Hirschsprung's disease? Pediatr Surg Int 2003;19:439-442.
156. Kiesewetter W, Sukarochana K, Sieber W: The frequency of aganglionosis associated with imperforate anus. Surgery 1965;58:877-880.
157. Kim E, Boutwell W: Smith-Lemli-Opitz syndrome associated with Hirschsprung disease, 46,XY female karyotype, and total anomalous pulmonary venous drainage [letter]. J Pediatr 1985;106:861.
158. Kimura K, Inomata Y, Soper RT: Posterior sagittal rectal myectomy for persistent rectal achalasia after the Soave procedure for Hirschsprung's disease. J Pediatr Surg 1993;28:1200-1201.
159. Kimura K, Nishijima E, Muraji T: A new surgical approach to extensive aganglionosis. J Pediatr Surg 1981;16: 840-843.
160. Kimura K, Nishijima E, Muraji T, et al: Extensive aganglionosis: Further experience with the colonic patch graft procedure and long-term results. J Pediatr Surg 1988;23: 52-56.
161. Klaus M, Fanaroff A: Care of the High-Risk Neonate, 4th ed. Philadelphia, WB Saunders, 1993.
162. Klein M, Coran A, Wesley J, Drongowski R: Hirschsprung's disease in the newborn. J Pediatr Surg 1984;19: 370-374.
163. Klein M, Philippart A: Hirschsprung's disease: Three decades' experience at a single institution. J Pediatr Surg 1993;28:1291-1293.
164. Kleinhaus S, Boley S, Sheran M, Sieber W: Hirschsprung's disease—a survey of the members of the Surgical Section of the American Academy of Pediatrics. J Pediatr Surg 1979;14:588-597.
165. Kluck P, van Muijen G, van der Kamp A, et al: Hirschsprung's disease studied with monoclonal antineurofilament antibodies on tissue sections. Lancet 1984;1:652-654.
166. Kobayashi H, Hirakawa H, Puri P: Overexpression of intercellular adhesion molecule-1 (ICAM-1) and MHC class II antigen on hypertrophic nerve trunks suggests an immunopathologic response in Hirschsprung's disease. J Pediatr Surg 1995;30:1680-1683.
167. Kobayashi H, O'Briain D, Puri P: Lack of expression of NADPH-diaphorase and neural cell adhesion molecule (NCAM) in colonic muscle of patients with Hirschsprung's disease. J Pediatr Surg 1994;29:301-304.
168. Kobayashi H, O'Briain DS, Hirakawa H, et al: A rapid technique of acetylcholinesterase staining. Arch Pathol Lab Med 1994;118:1127-1129.
169. Kobayashi H, Yamataka A, Lane GJ, Miyano T: Inflammatory changes secondary to postoperative complications of Hirschsprung's disease as a cause of histopathologic changes typical of intestinal neuronal dysplasia. J Pediatr Surg 2004;39:152-156.
170. Kottmeier P, Jongco B, Velcek F: Absorptive function of the aganglionic ileum. J Pediatr Surg 1981;16:275-278.
171. Krishnamurthy S, Schuffler M: Pathology of neuromuscular disorders of the small intestine. Gastroenterology 1987; 93:610-639.
172. Kruger G, Mosher J, Bixby S, et al: Neural crest stem cells persist in the adult gut but undergo changes in self-renewal, neuronal subtype potential, and factor responsiveness. Neuron 2002;35:657-669.
173. Kruger GM, Mosher JT, Tsai YH, et al: Temporally distinct requirements for endothelin receptor B in the generation and migration of gut neural crest stem cells. Neuron 2003;40:917-929.
174. Kuhlbrodt K, Herbarth B, Sock E, et al: SOX10, a novel transcriptional modulator in glial cells. J Neurosci 1998; 18:237-250.
175. Kuroda T, Doody D, Donahoe P: Aberrant colonic expression of MHC class II antigens in Hirschsprung's disease. Aust N Z J Surg 1991;61:373-379.
176. Kusafuka T, Wang Y, Puri P: Novel mutations of the endothelin-B receptor gene in isolated patients with Hirschsprung's disease. Hum Mol Genet 1996;5:347-349.
177. Laberge JM, Adolph VR, Flageole H, Guttman FM: Salvage of Soave-Boley endorectal pull-through by conversion to a classical Soave procedure. Eur J Pediatr Surg 1996;6: 362-363.
178. Lake B, Malone M, Risdon R: The use of acetylcholinesterase (AChE) in the diagnosis of Hirschsprung's disease and intestinal neuronal dysplasia. Pediatr Pathol 1989;9:351-354.
179. Lake B, Puri P, Nixon H, Claireaux A: Hirschsprung's disease: An appraisal of histochemically demonstrated acetylcholinesterase activity in suction rectal biopsy specimens as an aid to diagnosis. Arch Pathol Lab Med 1978;102:244-247.
180. Langer J: Persistent obstructive symptoms after surgery for Hirschsprung's disease: Development of a diagnostic and therapeutic algorithm. J Pediat Surg 2004;39:1458-1462.
181. Langer J, Betti P, Blennerhassett M: Smooth muscle from aganglionic bowel in Hirschsprung's disease impairs neuronal development in vitro. Cell Tissue Res 1994;276: 181-186.
182. Langer JC: Repeat pull-through surgery for complicated Hirschsprung's disease: Indications, techniques, and results. J Pediatr Surg 1999;34:1136-1141.
183. Langer JC, Durrant AC, de la Torre ML, et al: One-stage transanal Soave pullthrough for Hirschsprung disease: A multicenter experience with 141 children. Ann Surg 2003;238:569-576.
184. Larsson L, Malmfors G, Sundler F: Neuropeptide Y, calcitonin gene-related peptide, and galanin in Hirschsprung's disease: An immunocytochemical study. J Pediatr Surg 1988;23:342-345.
185. Le Douarin N: Cell migrations in embryos. Cell 1984;38: 353-360.
186. Le Douarin N, Kalcheim C: The Neural Crest. Cambridge, UK, Cambridge University Press, 1999.
187. Le Dourin F, Teillet M: The migration of neural crest cells to the wall of the digestive tract in avian embryo. J Embryol Exp Morphol 1973;30:31-48.

188. Levin M: Children with encopresis: A descriptive analysis. Pediatrics 1975;56:412-416.
189. Levin S: The immune system and susceptibility to infections in Down's syndrome. In McCoy E, Epstein C (eds): Oncology and Immunology in Down's Syndrome. New York, Alan R Liss, 1987, pp 143-162.
190. Levy M, Reynolds M: Morbidity associated with total colon Hirschsprung's disease. J Pediatr Surg 1992;27:364-366.
191. Liem NT, Hau BD, Thu NX: The long-term follow-up result of Swenson's operation in the treatment of Hirschsprung's disease in Vietnamese children. Eur J Pediatr Surg 1995; 5:110-112.
192. Lifschitz C, Bloss R: Persistence of colitis in Hirschsprung's disease. J Pediatr Gastroenterol Nutr 1985;4:291-293.
193. Lister J: Hirschsprung: The man and the disease. J R Coll Surg Edinb 1977;22:378-384.
194. Liu CS, Chin TW, Wei CF: Neonatal Duhamel's pull-through for Hirschsprung's disease. Chung Hua I Hsueh Tsa Chih 2002;65:398-402.
195. Loening-Baucke V: Anorectal manometry: Experience with strain gauge pressure transducers for the diagnosis of Hirschsprung's disease. J Pediatr Surg 1983;18:595-600.
196. Loening-Baucke V, Pringle K, Ekwo E: Anorectal manometry for the exclusion of Hirschsprung's disease in neonates. J Pediatr Gastroenterol Nutr 1985;4:596-603.
197. Loinaz C, Mittal N, Kato T, et al: Multivisceral transplantation for pediatric intestinal pseudo-obstruction: Single center's experience of 16 cases. Transplant Proc 2004;36: 312-313.
198. Ludman L, Spitz L, Tsuji H, Pierro A: Hirschsprung's disease: Functional and psychological follow up comparing total colonic and rectosigmoid aganglionosis. Arch Dis Child 2002;86:348-351.
199. Lynn H, van Heerden J: Rectal myectomy in Hirschsprung disease: A decade of experience. Arch Surg 1975;110: 991-994.
200. Maia DM: The reliability of frozen-section diagnosis in the pathologic evaluation of Hirschsprung's disease. Am J Surg Pathol 2000;24:1675-1677.
201. Managoli S, Chaturvedi P, Vilhekar KY, et al: Perforated acute appendicitis in a term neonate. Indian J Pediatr 2004;71:357-358.
202. Martin L: Surgical management of Hirschsprung's disease involving the small intestine. Arch Surg 1968;97:183-189.
203. Martin L, Altemeier W: Clinical experience with a new operation (modified Duhamel procedure) for Hirschsprung's disease. Ann Surg 1962;156:678.
204. Martin L, Caudill D: A method for elimination of the blind rectal pouch in the Duhamel operation for Hirschsprung's disease. Surgery 1967;62:951-953.
205. Martin L, Perrin E: Neonatal perforation of the appendix in association with Hirschsprung's disease. Ann Surg 1967; 166:799-802.
206. Martin MJ, Steele SR, Mullenix PS, et al: A pilot study using total colonic manometry in the surgical evaluation of pediatric functional colonic obstruction. J Pediatr Surg 2004;39:352-359.
207. Martucciello G, Biocchi M, Dodero P, et al: Total colonic aganglionosis associated with interstitial deletion of the long arm of chromosome 10. Pediatr Surg Int 1992;7: 308-310.
208. Martucciello G, Favre A, Takahashi M, et al: Immunohistochemical localization of RET protein in Hirschsprung's disease. J Pediatr Surg 1995;30:433-436.
209. Martucciello G, Thompson H, Mazzola C, et al: GDNF deficit in Hirschsprung's disease. J Pediatr Surg 1998;33:99-102.
210. Marty T, Seo T, Matlak M, et al: Gastrointestinal function after surgical correction of Hirschsprung's disease: Long-term follow-up in 135 patients. J Pediatr Surg 1995;30:655-658.
211. Marty TL, Seo T, Sullivan JJ, et al: Rectal irrigations for the prevention of postoperative enterocolitis in Hirschsprung's disease. J Pediatr Surg 1995;30:652-654.
212. Mattar A, Drongowski R, Coran AG, Teitelbaum DH: MUC-2 mucin production in Hirschsprung's disease: Possible association with enterocolitis development. J Pediatr Surg 2003;38:417-421.
213. McCready R, Beart R Jr: Classic articles in colonic and rectal surgery: Constipation in the newborn as a result of dilation and hypertrophy of the colon: Harald Hirschsprung, Jahrbuch fur Kinderheilkunde, 1888 adult Hirschsprung's disease: Results of surgical treatment at Mayo Clinic. Dis Colon Rectum 1981;24:408-410.
214. Meier-Ruge W: [Casuistic of colon disorder with symptoms of Hirschsprung's disease.] Verh Dtsch Ges Pathol 1971;55:506-510.
215. Meier-Ruge W, Lutterbeck P, Herzog B, et al: Acetylcholinesterase activity in suction biopsies of the rectum in the diagnosis of Hirschsprung's disease. J Pediatr Surg 1972;7:11-17.
216. Meijers JH, van der Sanden MP, Tibboel D, et al: Colonization characteristics of enteric neural crest cells: Embryological aspects of Hirschsprung's disease. J Pediatr Surg 1992;27:811-814.
217. Meunier P, Marechal J, Mollard P: Accuracy of the manometric diagnosis of Hirschsprung's disease. J Pediatr Surg 1978;13:411-415.
218. Miele E, Tozzi A, Staiano A, et al: Persistence of abnormal gastrointestinal motility after operation for Hirschsprung's disease. Am J Gastroenterol 2000;95:1226-1230.
219. Milla P, Cucchiara S, DiLorenzo C, et al: Motility disorders in childhood: Working group report of the First World Congress of Pediatric Gastroenterology, Hepatology, and Nutrition. J Pediatr Gastroenterol Nutr 2002;35 (Suppl 2):S187-S195.
220. Minkes RK, Langer JC: A prospective study of botulinum toxin for internal anal sphincter hypertonicity in children with Hirschsprung's disease. J Pediatr Surg 2000;35: 1733-1736.
221. Mir E, Karaca I, Gunsar C, et al: Primary Duhamel-Martin operations in neonates and infants. Pediatr Int 2001;43: 405-408.
222. Mishalany H, Woolley M: Chronic constipation: Manometric patterns and surgical considerations. Arch Surg 1984;119: 1257-1259.
223. Mishalany H, Woolley M: Postoperative functional and manometric evaluation of patients with Hirschsprung's disease. J Pediatr Surg 1987;22:443-446.
224. Miyano T, Yamataka A, Urao M, et al: Modified Soave pull-through for Hirschsprung's disease: Intraoperative internal sphincterotomy. J Pediatr Surg 1999;34:1599-1602.
225. Miyazaki E, Ohshiro K, Puri P: NADPH-diaphorase histochemical staining of suction rectal biopsies in the diagnosis of Hirschsprung's disease and allied disorders. Pediatr Surg Int 1998;13:464-467.
226. Moore S, Albertyn R, Cywes S: Clinical outcome and long-term quality of life after surgical correction of Hirschsprung's disease. J Pediatr Surg 1996;31:1496-1502.
227. Moore S, Rode H, Miller A, et al: Intestinal atresia and Hirschsprung's disease. Pediatr Surg Int 1990;5:182-184.
228. Moore SW, Albertyn R, Cywes S: Clinical outcome and long-term quality of life after surgical correction of Hirschsprung's disease. J Pediatr Surg 1996;31: 1496-1502.
229. Moore SW, Millar AJ, Cywes S: Long-term clinical, manometric, and histological evaluation of obstructive symptoms in

the postoperative Hirschsprung's patient. J Pediatr Surg 1994;29:106-111.

230. Mulligan L, Eng C, Attie T, et al: Diverse phenotypes associated with exon 10 mutations of the RET proto-oncogene. Hum Mol Genet 1994;3:2163-2167.
231. Mulligan L, Ponder B: Genetic basis of endocrine disease: Multiple endocrine neoplasia type 2. J Clin Endocrinol Metab 1995;80:1989-1995.
232. Murthi GV, Raine PA: Preoperative enterocolitis is associated with poorer long-term bowel function after Soave-Boley endorectal pull-through for Hirschsprung's disease. J Pediatr Surg 2003;38:69-72.
233. Mya G: Due asservazioni di dilatazione ed impertrofia congenita del colon. Sperimentale 1894;48:215.
234. Nakagawa M, Takashima H: Molecular mechanisms of hereditary neuropathy: Genotype-phenotype correlation. Rinsho Byori 2003;51:536-543.
235. Navarro J, Sonsino E, Boige N, et al: Visceral neuropathies responsible for chronic intestinal pseudo-obstruction syndrome in pediatric practice: Analysis of 26 cases. J Pediatr Gastroenterol Nutr 1990;11:179-195.
236. Neilson I, Yazbeck S: Ultrashort Hirschsprung's disease: Myth or reality. J Pediatr Surg 1990;25:1135-1138.
237. Nemeth L, O'Briain S, Puri P: Whole-mount NADPH-diaphorase histochemistry is a reliable technique for the intraoperative evaluation of extent of aganglionosis. Pediatr Surg Int 1999;15:195-197.
238. Newman B, Nussbaum A, Kirkpatrick J Jr, Colodny A: Appendiceal perforation, pneumoperitoneum, and Hirschsprung's disease. J Pediatr Surg 1988;23: 854-856.
239. Newman C, Laurini R, Lesbros Y, et al: Interstitial cells of Cajal are normally distributed in both ganglionated and aganglionic bowel in Hirschsprung's disease. Pediatr Surg Int 2003;19:662-668.
240. N-Fekete C, Ricour C, Martelli H, et al: Total colonic aganglionosis (with or without ileal involvement): A review of 27 cases. J Pediatr Surg 1986;21:251-254.
241. O'Donovan A, Habra G, Somers S, et al: Diagnosis of Hirschsprung's disease. AJR Am J Roentgenol 1996;167: 517-520.
242. Okamoto E, Ueda T: Embryogenesis of intramural ganglia of the gut and its relation to Hirschsprung's disease. J Pediatr Surg 1967;2:437-443.
243. O'Kelly T, Davies J, Tam P, et al: Abnormalities of nitric-oxide-producing neurons in Hirschsprung's disease: Morphology and implications. J Pediatr Surg 1994;29: 294-299.
244. Omenn G, McKusick V: The association of Waardenburg syndrome and Hirschsprung megacolon. Am J Med Genet 1979;3:217-223.
245. Orr J, Scobie W: Presentation and incidence of Hirschsprung's disease. BMJ 1983;287:1671.
246. Paratore C, Goerich D, Suter U, et al: Survival and glial fate acquisition of neural crest cells are regulated by an interplay between the transcription factor SOX10 and extrinsic combinatorial signaling. Development 2001;128: 3949-3961.
247. Parikh DH, Tam PK, Lloyd DA, et al: Quantitative and qualitative analysis of the extracellular matrix protein, laminin, in Hirschsprung's disease. J Pediatr Surg 1992; 27:991-995.
248. Parikh DH, Tam PK, Van Velzen D, Edgar D: Abnormalities in the distribution of laminin and collagen type IV in Hirschsprung's disease. Gastroenterology 1992;102: 1236-1241.
249. Parikh DH, Tam PK, Van Velzen D, Edgar D: The extracellular matrix components, tenascin and fibronectin, in Hirschsprung's disease: An immunohistochemical study. J Pediatr Surg 1994;29:1302-1306.
250. Passarge E: The genetics of Hirschsprung's disease: Evidence for heterogeneous etiology and a study of sixty-three families. N Engl J Med 1967;276:138-143.
251. Peters van der Sanden M: The Hindbrain Neural Crest and the Development of the Enteric Nervous System. Rotterdam, Erasmus University, 1994.
252. Peters van der Sanden M, Kirby M, Gittenberger-de Groot A, et al: Ablation of various regions within the avian vagal crest has differential effects on ganglion formation in the fore, mid and hindgut. Dev Dyn 1993;196:183-194.
253. Philippart A, Reed J, Georgeson K: Neonatal small left colon syndrome: Intramural not intraluminal obstruction. J Pediatr Surg 1975;10:733-740.
254. Pierro A, Fasoli L, Kiely EM, et al: Staged pull-through for rectosigmoid Hirschsprung's disease is not safer than primary pull-through. J Pediatr Surg 1997;32:505-509.
255. Pingault V, Bondurand N, Le Caignec C, et al: The SOX10 transcription factor: Evaluation as a candidate gene for central and peripheral hereditary myelin disorders. J Neurol 2001;248:496-499.
256. Pingault V, Girard M, Bondurand N, et al: SOX10 mutations in chronic intestinal pseudo-obstruction suggest a complex physiopathological mechanism. Hum Genet 2002;111: 198-206.
257. Piotrowska A, Solari V, de Caluwe D, Puri P: Immunocolocalization of the heme oxygenase-2 and interstitial cells of Cajal in normal and aganglionic colon. J Pediatr Surg 2003;38:73-77.
258. Piotrowska AP, Solari V, Puri P: Distribution of interstitial cells of Cajal in the internal anal sphincter of patients with internal anal sphincter achalasia and Hirschsprung disease. Arch Pathol Lab Med 2003;127:1192-1195.
259. Polley T, Coran A: Hirschsprung's disease in the newborn. Pediatr Surg Int 1986;1:80-83.
260. Polley T Jr, Coran A, Wesley J: A ten-year experience with ninety-two cases of Hirschsprung's disease: Including sixty-seven consecutive endorectal pull-through procedures. Ann Surg 1985;202:349-355.
261. Prevot J, Bodart N, Babut J, Mourot M: Hirschsprung's disease with total colonic involvement: Therapeutic problems. Prog Pediatr Surg 1972;4:63-89.
262. Puri P: Hirschsprung's disease: Clinical and experimental observations. World J Surg 1993;17:374-384.
263. Puri P, Lake D, Gorman F, et al: Megacystis-microcolon-intestinal hypoperistalsis syndrome: A visceral myopathy. J Pediatr Surg 1983;18:64-69.
264. Puri P, Nixon HH: Long-term results of Swenson's operation for Hirschsprung's disease. Prog Pediatr Surg 1977;10:87-96.
265. Puri P, Tsuji M: Megacystis-microcolon-intestinal hypoperistalsis syndrome (neonatal hollow visceral myopathy). Pediatr Surg Int 1992;7:18-22.
266. Qualman SJ, Jaffe R, Bove KE, Monforte-Munoz H: Diagnosis of Hirschsprung disease using the rectal biopsy: Multi-institutional survey. Pediatr Dev Pathol 1999;2: 588-596.
267. Quinn F, Surana R, Puri P: The influence of trisomy 21 on outcome in children with Hirschsprung's disease. J Pediatr Surg 1994;29:781-783.
268. Rangecroft L: Neonatal small left colon syndrome. Arch Dis Child 1979;54:635-637.
269. Rantis PC Jr, Vernava AM 3rd, Daniel GL, Longo WE: Chronic constipation—is the work-up worth the cost? Dis Colon Rectum 1997;40:280-286.
270. Rasquin-Weber A, Hyman P, Cucchiara S, et al: Childhood functional gastrointestinal disorders. Gut 1999;45: II60-II68.

271. Read A, Newton V: Waardenburg syndrome. J Med Genet 1997;34:656-665.
272. Reding R, de Ville de Goyet J, Gosseye S, et al: Hirschsprung's disease: A 20-year experience. J Pediatr Surg 1997;32:1221-1225.
273. Rescorla F, Morrison A, Engles D, et al: Hirschsprung's disease: Evaluation of mortality and long-term function in 260 cases. Arch Surg 1992;127:934-941.
274. Rintala R, Lindahl H: Transanal endorectal coloanal anastomosis for Hirschsprung's disease. Pediatr Surg Int 1993;8:128-131.
275. Rintala RJ, Lindahl H: Sodium cromoglycate in the management of chronic or recurrent enterocolitis in patients with Hirschsprung's disease. J Pediatr Surg 2001;36:1032-1035.
276. Romeo G, Ronchetto P, Luo Y, et al: Point mutations affecting the tyrosine kinase domain of the RET proto-oncogene in Hirschsprung's disease. Nature 1994;367:377-378.
277. Rosenfield N, Ablow R, Markowitz R, et al: Hirschsprung disease: Accuracy of the barium enema examination. Radiology 1984;150:393-400.
278. Ross M, Chang J, Burrington J, et al: Complications of the Martin procedure for total colonic aganglionosis. J Pediatr Surg 1988;23:725-727.
279. Roy A, Bharucha H, Nevin N, et al: Idiopathic intestinal pseudo-obstruction: A familial visceral neuropathy. Clin Genet 1980;18:290-297.
280. Sacher P, Hirsig J, Gresser J, Spitz L: The importance of oral sodium replacement in ileostomy patients. Prog Pediatr Surg 1989;24:226-231.
281. Sakai T, Nirasawa Y, Itoh Y, et al: Japanese patients with sporadic Hirschsprung: Mutation analysis of the receptor tyrosine kinase proto-oncogene, endothelin-B receptor, endothelin-3, glial cell line-derived neurotrophic factor and neurturin genes: A comparison with similar studies. Eur J Pediatr 2000;159:160-167.
282. Sandegard E: Hirschsprung's disease with ganglion cell aplasia of the colon and terminal ileum: Report of a case treated with total colectomy and ileo-anostomy. Acta Chir Scand 1953;106:367-376.
283. Sanders K, Ordog T, Ward S: Physiology and pathophysiology of the interstitial cells of Cajal: From bench to bedside. IV. Genetic and animal models of GI motility disorders caused by loss of interstitial cells of Cajal. Am J Physiol Gastrointest Liver Physiol 2002;282: G747-G756.
284. Sandgren K, Larsson L, Ekblad E: Widespread changes in neurotransmitter expression and number of enteric neurons and interstitial cells of Cajal in lethal spotted mice: An explanation for persisting dysmotility after operation for Hirschsprung's disease? Dig Dis Sci 2002;47:1049-1064.
285. Sanicola M, Hession C, Worley D, et al: Glial cell line-derived neurotrophic factor-dependent RET activation can be mediated by two different cell-surface accessory proteins. Proc Natl Acad Sci U S A 1997;94:6238-6243.
286. Santoro M, Rosati R, Greco M, et al: The RET proto-oncogene is consistently expressed in human pheochromocytoma and medullary thyroid carcinoma. Oncogene 1990;5:1595-1598.
287. Sarioglu A, Tanyel FC, Buyukpamukcu N, Hicsonmez A: Appendiceal perforation: A potentially lethal initial mode of presentation of Hirschsprung's disease. J Pediatr Surg 1997;32:123-124.
288. Schofield D, Devine W, Yunis E: Acetylcholinesterase-stained suction rectal biopsies in the diagnosis of Hirschsprung's disease. J Pediatr Gastroenterol Nutr 1990;11:221-228.
289. Schuffler M, Bird T, Sumi S, Cook A: A familial neuronal disease presenting as intestinal pseudo-obstruction. Gastroenterology 1978;75:889-898.
290. Schwarz K, Ternberg J, Bell M, Keating J: Sodium needs of infants and children with ileostomy. J Pediatr 1983;102: 509-513.
291. Scott B: Motility disorders. In Walker W, Durie P, Hamilton J, et al (eds): Pediatric Gastrointestinal Disease, vol 1. Philadelphia, BC Decker, 1991, pp 784-799.
292. Seri M, Yin L, Barone V, et al: Detection of RET mutation is higher among long segment than short segment Hirschsprung patients. Hum Mutat 1996;9:243-249.
293. Shandling B: New technique in diagnosis of Hirschsprung's disease. Can J Surg 1961;4:298-305.
294. Sharif K, Beath SV, Kelly DA, et al: New perspective for the management of near-total or total intestinal aganglionosis in infants. J Pediatr Surg 2003;38:25-28.
295. Shaw P: The innervation and neuroendocrine cell population of the appendix in total colonic aganglionosis. Histopathology 1990;17:117-121.
296. Sherman J, Snyder M, Weitzman J, et al: A 40-year multinational retrospective study of 880 Swenson procedures. J Pediatr Surg 1989;24:833-838.
297. Sidebotham EL, Kenny SE, Lloyd DA, et al: Location of stem cells for the enteric nervous system. Pediatr Surg Int 2002;18:581-585.
298. Sinha SK, Kochhar R, Rana S, et al: Intestinal pseudo-obstruction due to neurofibromatosis responding to cisapride. Indian J Gastroenterol 2000;19:83-84.
299. Smith G, Cass D: Infantile Hirschsprung disease: Is a barium enema useful? Pediatr Surg Int 1991;6:318-321.
300. So HB, Schwartz DL, Becker JM, et al: Endorectal "pull-through" without preliminary colostomy in neonates with Hirschsprung's disease. J Pediatr Surg 1980;15:470-471.
301. Solari V, Piotrowska A, Puri P: Histopathological differences between recto-sigmoid Hirschsprung's disease and total colonic aganglionosis. Pediatr Surg Int 2003;19:349-354.
302. Song Y, Li J, Li M: Bcl-2 expression in enteric neurons of Hirschsprung's disease and its significance. Shi Yan Sheng Wu Xue Bao 2002;35:155-158.
303. Soper R: Surgery for Hirschsprung's disease. AORN J 1968;8:69-81.
304. Spouge D, Baird P: Hirschsprung disease in a large birth cohort. Teratology 1985;32:171-177.
305. Stannard V, Fowler C, Robinson L, et al: Familial Hirschsprung's disease: Report of autosomal dominant and probable recessive X-linked kindreds. J Pediatr Surg 1991;26:591-594.
306. Stringel G: Extensive intestinal aganglionosis including the ileum: A new surgical technique. J Pediatr Surg 1986; 21:667-670.
307. Svensson PJ, Tapper-Persson M, Anvret M, et al: Mutations in the endothelin-receptor B gene in Hirschsprung disease in Sweden [letter]. Clin Genet 1999;55:215-217.
308. Swenson O: My early experience with Hirschsprung's disease. J Pediatr Surg 1989;24:839-844.
309. Swenson O: How the cause and cure of Hirschsprung's disease were discovered. J Pediatr Surg 1999;34:1580-1581.
310. Swenson O: Hirschsprung's disease: A review. Pediatrics 2002;109:914-918.
311. Swenson O, Bill A: Resection of rectum and rectosigmoid with preservation of the sphincter for benign spastic lesions producing megacolon. Surgery 1948;24:212-220.
312. Swenson O, Fisher J, Gherardi G: Rectal biopsy in the diagnosis of Hirschsprung's disease. Surgery 1959;45:690-695.
313. Swenson O, Rheinlander H, Diamond I: Hirschsprung's disease: A new concept of the etiology—operative results in thirty-four patients. N Engl J Med 1949;241:551-556.
314. Swenson O, Sherman J, Fisher J: Diagnosis of congenital megacolon: An analysis of 501 patients. J Pediatr Surg 1973;8:587-594.

315. Swenson O, Sherman J, Fisher J, Cohen E: The treatment and postoperative complications of congenital megacolon: A 25 year follow-up. Ann Surg 1975;182:266-273.
316. Taguchi T, Tanaka K, Ikeda K: Immunohistochemical study of neuron specific enolase and S-100 protein in Hirschsprung's disease. Virchows Arch A Pathol Anat Histopathol 1985;405:399-409.
317. Takahashi T: Pathophysiological significance of neuronal nitric oxide synthase in the gastrointestinal tract. J Gastroenterol 2003;38:421-430.
318. Talbert J, Seashore J, Ravitch M: Evaluation of a modified Duhamel operation for correction of Hirschsprung's disease. Ann Surg 1974;179:671-675.
319. Tamate S, Shiokawa C, Yamada C, et al: Manometric diagnosis of Hirschsprung's disease in the neonatal period. J Pediatr Surg 1984;19:285-288.
320. Tanaka H, Moroi K, Iwai J, et al: Novel mutations in the endothelin-B receptor gene in patients with Hirschsprung's disease and their characterization. J Biol Chem 1998; 273:11378-11383.
321. Tariq GM, Brereton RJ, Wright VM: Complications of endorectal pull-through for Hirschsprung's disease. J Pediatr Surg 1991;26:1202-1206.
322. Taxman T, Yulish B, Rothstein F: How useful is the barium enema in the diagnosis of infantile Hirschsprung's disease? Am J Dis Child 1986;140:881-884.
323. Teitelbaum D, Caniano D, Qualman S: The pathophysiology of Hirschsprung's-associated enterocolitis: Importance of histologic correlates. J Pediatr Surg 1989;24:1271-1277.
324. Teitelbaum D, Langer J: Hirschsprung's disease. In Ziegler M, Weber TR, Azizkhan RG (eds): Operative Pediatric Surgery. New York, McGraw-Hill, 2002.
325. Teitelbaum D, Qualman S, Caniano D: Hirschsprung's disease: Identification of risk factors for enterocolitis. Ann Surg 1988;207:240-244.
326. Teitelbaum D, Sonnino R, Dunaway D, et al: Rat jejunal absorptive function after intestinal transplantation: Effects of extrinsic denervation. Dig Dis Sci 1993;38: 1099-1104.
327. Teitelbaum DH, Cilley RE, Sherman NJ, et al: A decade of experience with the primary pull-through for Hirschsprung disease in the newborn period: A multicenter analysis of outcomes. Ann Surg 2000;232:372-380.
328. Teitelbaum DH, Coran AG: Enterocolitis. Semin Pediatr Surg 1998;7:162-169.
329. Teitelbaum DH, Drongowski RA, Chamberlain JN, Coran AG: Long-term stooling patterns in infants undergoing primary endorectal pull-through for Hirschsprung's disease. J Pediatr Surg 1997;32:1049-1052.
330. Tennyson V, Pham T, Toth T, Gershon M: Abnormalities of smooth muscle, basal laminae, and nerves in the aganglionic segments of the bowel of the lethal spotted mutant mouse. Anat Rec 1986;215:267-281.
331. Thomas C Jr: Posterior sphincterotomy in Hirschsprung's disease. Surg Gynecol Obstet 1967;124:365-366.
332. Thomas C Jr, Bream CA, DeConnick P: Posterior sphincterotomy and rectal myotomy in the management of Hirschsprung's disease. Ann Surg 1970;171:796-810.
333. Tittel K: Uber eine angeborene Missbildung des Dickdrmes. Wien Klin Wochenschr 1901;14:903.
334. Tomita R: Regulation of the enteric nervous system in the internal anal sphincter in Hirschsprung's disease. Hepatogastroenterology 1999;46:215-219.
335. Touloukian R, Aghajanian G, Roth R: Adrenergic hyperactivity of the aganglionic colon. J Pediatr Surg 1973;8:191-195.
336. Touloukian R, Duncan R: Acquired aganglionic megacolon in a premature infant: Report of a case. Pediatrics 1975;56:459-462.
337. Touloukian R, Morgenroth V, Roth R: Sympathetic neurotransmitter metabolism in Hirschsprung's disease. J Pediatr Surg 1975;10:593-598.
338. Towne G, Stocker J, Thompson H: Acquired aganglionosis. J Pediatr Surg 1979;14:688-690.
339. Treeves F: Idiopathic dilatation of the colon. Lancet 1898;1:276.
340. Trupp M, Arenas E, Fainzilber M, et al: Functional receptor for GDNF encoded by the c-ret proto-oncogene. Nature 1996;381:785-789.
341. Tsuto T, Obata-Tsuto HL, Iwai N, et al: Fine structure of neurons synthesizing vasoactive intestinal peptide in the human colon from patients with Hirschsprung's disease. Histochemistry 1989;93:1-8.
342. Tsuto T, Okamura H, Fukui K, et al: An immunohistochemical investigation of vasoactive intestinal polypeptide in the colon of patients with Hirschsprung's disease. Neurosci Lett 1982;34:57-62.
343. van der Zee DC, Bax KN: One-stage Duhamel-Martin procedure for Hirschsprung's disease: A 5-year follow-up study. J Pediatr Surg 2000;35:1434-1436.
344. van Leeuwen K, Geiger JD, Barnett JL, et al: Stooling and manometric findings after primary pull-throughs in Hirschsprung's disease: Perineal versus abdominal approaches. J Pediatr Surg 2002;37:1321-1325.
345. van Leeuwen K, Teitelbaum DH, Elhalaby EA, Coran AG: The long-term follow-up of redo-pullthrough procedures for Hirschsprung's disease. J Pediatr Surg 2000;35: 829-834.
346. Vanderwinden JM, Rumessen JJ, Liu H, et al: Interstitial cells of Cajal in human colon and in Hirschsprung's disease. Gastroenterology 1996;111:901-910.
347. Verheij J, Hofstra R: EDNRB, EDN3 and SOX10 and the Shah-Waardenburg syndrome. In Epstein C, Erickson R, Wynshaw-Boris A (eds): Inborn Errors of Development. New York, Oxford University Press, 2004.
348. Voskuijl W, Heijmans J, Heijmans H, et al: Use of Rome II criteria in childhood defecation disorders: Applicability in clinical and research practice. J Pediatr 2004;145:213-217.
349. Wade R, Royle N: The operative treatment of Hirschsprung's disease: A new method. Med J Aust 1927;14:137.
350. Wang G, Sun X, Wei M, Weng Y: Heart-shaped anastomosis for Hirschsprung's disease: Operative technique and long-term follow-up. World J Gastroenterol 2005;11:296-298.
351. Wang J, Lee JC, Huang F, et al: Unexpected mortality in pediatric patients with postoperative Hirschsprung's disease. Pediatr Surg Int 2004;20:525-528.
352. Wang NL, Lee HC, Yeh ML, et al: Experience with primary laparoscopy-assisted endorectal pull-through for Hirschsprung's disease. Pediatr Surg Int 2004;20: 118-122.
353. Watanabe Y, Ito F, Ando H, et al: Morphological investigation of the enteric nervous system in Hirschsprung's disease and hypoganglionosis using whole-mount colon preparation. J Pediatr Surg 1999;34:445-449.
354. Watanatittan S, Suwatanaviroj A, Limprutithum T, Rattanasuwan T: Association of Hirschsprung's disease and anorectal malformation. J Pediatr Surg 1991;26: 192-195.
355. Weaver L, Steiner H: The bowel habits of young children. Arch Dis Child 1984;59:649-652.
356. Weber TR, Fortuna RS, Silen ML, Dillon PA: Reoperation for Hirschsprung's disease. J Pediatr Surg 1999;34: 153-156.

357. Weitzman J: Management of Hirschsprung's disease with the Swenson procedure with emphasis on long-term follow-up. Pediatr Surg Int 1986;1:100-104.
358. Weitzman J, Hanson B, Brennan L: Management of Hirschsprung's disease with the Swenson procedure. J Pediatr Surg 1972;7:157-162.
359. Wheatley M, Wesley J, Coran A, Polley T Jr: Hirschsprung's disease in adolescents and adults. Dis Colon Rectum 1990; 33:622-629.
360. White F, Langer J: Circumferential distribution of ganglion cells in the transition zone of children with Hirschsprung disease. Pediatr Dev Pathol 2000;3:216-222.
361. Whitehouse E, Kernohan J: Myenteric plexus in congenital megacolon. Arch Intern Med 1948;82:75-111.
362. Wilcox DT, Kiely EM: Repeat pull-through for Hirschsprung's disease. J Pediatr Surg 1998;33:1507-1509.
363. Wildhaber B, Coran A, Teitelbaum D: Total colonic Hirschsprung's disease: A 28-year experience. J Pediatr Surg 2005;40:203-206.
364. Wildhaber B, Pakarinen M, Rintala R, et al: Posterior myotomy/myectomy for persistent stooling problems in Hirschsprung's disease. J Pediatr Surg 2004;39:920-926.
365. Williams M, Burrington J: Hirschsprung's disease complicating colon atresia. J Pediatr Surg 1993;28:637-639.
366. Wilson-Storey D, Scobie W: Impaired gastrointestinal mucosal defense in Hirschsprung's disease: A clue to the pathogenesis of enterocolitis? J Pediatr Surg 1989; 24:462-464.
367. Wilson-Storey D, Scobie W, Raeburn J: Defective white blood cell function in Hirschsprung's disease: A possible predisposing factor to enterocolitis. J R Coll Surg Edinb 1988;33:185-188.
368. Wolloch Y, Dintsman M: Colonic atresia associated with Hirschsprung's disease. Isr J Med Sci 1976;12: 202-207.
369. Wolman I: Intestinal motility in infancy and childhood. In Wolman I (ed): Laboratory Applications in Clinical Pediatrics. New York, McGraw-Hill, 1957, p 696.
370. Wood J: Physiology of the enteric nervous system. In Johnson L (ed): Physiology of the Gastrointestinal Tract, 2nd ed. New York, Raven Press, 1987, p 67.
371. Worby C, Vega Q, Chao H, et al: Identification and characterization of GFRalpha-3, a novel co-receptor belonging to the glial cell line-derived neurotrophic receptor family. J Biol Chem 1998;273:3502-3508.
372. Wu JS, Schoetz DJ Jr, Coller JA, Veidenheimer MC: Treatment of Hirschsprung's disease in the adult: Report of five cases. Dis Colon Rectum 1995;38:655-659.
373. Yamataka A, Nagaoka I, Miyano T, et al: Quantitative analysis of neuronal innervation in the aganglionic bowel of patients with Hirschsprung's disease. J Pediatr Surg 1995;30:260-263.
374. Yancey AG, Cromartie JE, Ford JR, et al: A modification of the Swenson technique for congenital megacolon. J Nat Med Assoc 1952;44:356-363.
375. Yanchar NL, Soucy P: Long-term outcome after Hirschsprung's disease: Patients' perspectives. J Pediatr Surg 1999;34:1152-1160.
376. Yann R, Yves A, Dominique J, et al: Improved quality of life by combined transplantation in Hirschsprung's disease with a very long aganglionic segment. J Pediatr Surg 2003;38:422-424.
377. Yokoyama J, Namba S, Ihara N, et al: Studies on the rectoanal reflex in children and in experimental animals: An evaluation of neuronal control of the rectoanal reflex. Prog Pediatr Surg 1989;24:5-20.
378. Yoneda A, Wang Y, O'Briain DS, Puri P: Cell-adhesion molecules and fibroblast growth factor signalling in Hirschsprung's disease. Pediatr Surg Int 2001; 17:299-303.
379. Yunis E, Sieber W, Akers D: Does zonal aganglionosis really exist? Report of a rare variety of Hirschsprung's disease and review of the literature. Pediatr Pathol 1983;1:33-49.
380. Zaslavsky C, Loening-Baucke V: Anorectal manometric evaluation of children and adolescents postsurgery for Hirschsprung's disease. J Pediatr Surg 2003;38:191-195.
381. Ziegler H, Heitz P, Kasper M, et al: Aganglionosis of the colon: Morphologic investigations in 524 patients. Pathol Res Pract 1984;178:543-547.
382. Ziegler M, Ross AI, Bishop H: Total intestinal aganglionosis: A new technique for prolonged survival. J Pediatr Surg 1987;22:82-83.
383. Zuelzer W, Wilson J: Functional intestinal obstruction on a congenital neurogenic basis in infancy. Am J Dis Child 1948;75:40-64.

Chapter 100

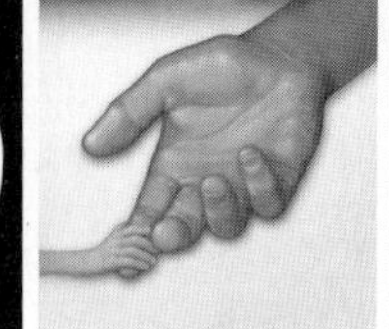

Intestinal Neuronal Dysplasia

Prem Puri

HISTORY

Intestinal neuronal dysplasia (IND) was first described by Meier-Ruge[21] in 1971 as a malformation of enteric plexus. The first association between IND and Hirschsprung's disease (HD) was reported by my colleagues and me[33] in a 5-year-old Arab boy who had rectosigmoid aganglionosis and IND of descending and transverse colon. In 1983, Fadda and associates[4] classified IND into two clinically and histologically distinguished subtypes: type A, which occurs in less than 5% of cases, is characterized by congenital aplasia or hypoplasia of the sympathetic innervation, and presents acutely in the neonatal period with episodes of intestinal obstruction, diarrhea, and bloody stools; and type B, which is clinically indistinguishable from HD, is characterized by a malformation of the parasympathetic submucous and myenteric plexuses, and accounts for more than 95% of cases of IND.[41,15] IND occurring in association with HD is of type B. Since its original description, little has been written about IND type A. IND has become synonymous with IND type B.

PATHOGENESIS

The enteric nervous system is the largest and the most complex division of the peripheral nervous system.[31,32] It contains more neurons than the spinal cord and is responsible for the coordination of normal bowel motility and secretory activities.[5] As our understanding of the enteric nervous system improves, it becomes clear that it is no longer sufficient to simply determine whether enteric ganglion cells are present. We are learning the importance of determining whether the correct number and types of ganglion cells are present. This is further complicated by the fact that the morphology of the myenteric plexus varies with the age as well as the location of the gastrointestinal tract.[48] For many years, the problem of neural crest development was addressed primarily at the cellular level, using avian embryos as an experimental system. The past few years have seen an explosion of information about genes that control the development of neural crest cells.[36] Recently, several genes have been identified that control morphogenesis and differentiation of the enteric nervous system. These genes, when mutated or deleted, interfere with development of this system.[5,31,32,36,48]

Many investigators have raised doubts about the existence of IND as a distinct histopathologic entity.[16,40] It has been suggested that the pathologic changes seen in IND may be part of normal development or may be a secondary phenomenon induced by congenital obstruction and inflammatory disease.[16,26] On the other hand, the literature contains several familial cases of IND suggesting that genetic factors may be involved in this condition. Martuccielo and coworkers[19] observed three families with multiple IND cases, and Moore and associates[29] and Kobayashi and colleagues[13] reported IND in monozygotic twins. The strongest evidence that IND is a real entity stems from the animal models. *Hox11L1* is a homeobox gene involved in peripheral nervous system development and is reported to play a role in the proliferation or differentiation of neural crest cell lines. Two different *Hox11L1* knockout mouse models have been generated. In both cases, homozygous mutant mice were viable but developed megacolon at the age of 3 to 5 weeks. Histologic and immunohistochemical analysis showed hyperplasia of myenteric ganglia, a phenotype similar to that observed in human IND type B.[8,44] However, the mutation screening of this gene in 48 patients with IND did not show any sequence variant, either causative missense mutation or neutral substitution.[3]

In 2002 Von Boyen and colleagues[47] reported abnormalities of the enteric nervous system in heterozygous *EDNRB*-deficient rats resembling IND in humans. They showed that a heterozygous 301-base-pair deletion of the *EDNRB* gene led to abnormalities of the enteric nervous system. Malformations of the enteric nervous system observed in +/sl rats included hyperganglionosis, giant ganglia, and hypertrophied nerve fibers in the submucous plexus resembling the histopathologic features of IND type B in humans. These findings support the concept that IND may be linked to a genetic defect. However, no mutations of the *EDNRB* gene were detected in a small series of IND patients.[6]

INCIDENCE

Intestinal neuronal dysplasia is the most commonly encountered variant of HD.[6,10,37,42] The incidence of isolated IND has varied from 0.3% to 40% of all suction rectal biopsies in different centers.[2,18,22,34] The incidence varies considerably among different countries. IND immediately proximal to a segment of aganglionosis is not uncommon and often presents as persistent obstructive symptoms after a pull-through operation for HD.[12] Some investigators have reported that 25% to 35% of patients with HD have associated IND.[4,41] However, others have rarely encountered IND in association with HD. The uncertainty regarding the incidence of IND has resulted from the considerable confusion regarding the essential diagnostic criteria.[23,24,35] The diagnostic difficulty is centered on a wide variability encountered in the literature, not only in terms of age of the patient, the type of specimen examined, and the stains performed but also in the diagnostic criteria used.[35]

CLINICAL PRESENTATION

The characteristic clinical pattern of IND can be found in infants younger than 1 year old with a history of constipation and abdominal distention, thus mimicking HD. Montedonico and associates[28] classified IND according to the severity of histochemical changes in rectal biopsies. The criteria used for the diagnosis of severe IND included hyperplasia of submucous plexus, giant ganglia, ectopic ganglia, and increased acetylcholinesterase (AChE) activity in the lamina propria or around submucosal blood vessels. Any biopsy that showed giant ganglia of the submucous plexus with only one of the other criteria was considered mild. Montedonico and associates reported that the patients with severe IND begin their symptoms at an earlier age than those with mild IND (5.2 ± 112 months versus 17.5 ± 23 months). In Meier-Ruge and coworkers' series,[23] half of all isolated cases were diagnosed in patients older than 2 years of age, and the mean age for the remaining patients was 18 months.

The incidence of associated anomalies in IND has been reported to be between 25% and 30%.[19,28] The common associated anomalies include anorectal malformations, intestinal malrotation, megacystis, microcolon, intestinal hypoperistalsis syndrome, congenital short bowel, hypertrophic pyloric stenosis, necrotizing enterocolitis, and Down syndrome.

DIAGNOSTIC CRITERIA

Since the first description in 1971, most controversy surrounding IND has been regarding which histologic diagnostic criteria are required for definitive diagnosis. The presently recognized diagnostic criteria, previously reported by our group and supported by others, are hyperganglionosis and giant ganglia, in addition to the presence of at least one of the following on suction rectal biopsy: ectopic ganglia in the lamina propria and increased AChE-positive nerve fibers around submucosal blood vessels and in the lamina propria.[1,2,11,15,34,36,41] However, Lumb and Moore[17] believe that giant ganglia can be a normal feature in normal bowel, having identified them in segments of adult bowel removed during surgery for colorectal carcinoma. To overcome the confusion in diagnostic criteria, Borchard and coworkers[1] produced guidelines for identifying IND in mucosal rectal biopsies. These comprised two obligatory criteria (hyperplasia of the submucous plexus and an increase in AChE-positive nerve fibers around submucosal blood vessels) and two additional criteria (neuronal heterotopia and increased AChE activity in the lamina propria). In our experience, hyperganglionosis and giant ganglia are the most important features for the diagnosis of IND in suction rectal biopsies, except in the newborn, when hyperganglionosis is a normal finding.[36]

Another controversial area surrounding IND is whether the histologic findings are age related. The recent description of hyperganglionosis, considered to be one of the most important criteria of IND, as an age-dependent finding has caused further confusion. Recent studies have found that the enteric nervous system continues to develop in the postnatal period. Wester and coworkers[48] investigated the number of ganglion cells per ganglion and ganglion cell density in whole-mount preparations of the submucous plexus of normal distal colon and found a marked decrease of ganglion cell density with increasing age, but the number of ganglion cells per ganglion remained constant. Knowledge of the ganglion cell density of the normal human enteric nervous system is scanty, because of the huge variation among reports of the normal neuron density in the myenteric plexus. The reported density varies more than 200 times among the different studies.[9,20,46] This results in difficulties defining conditions such as hyperganglionosis. Schofield and Yunis[43] reported that 8.3% of 456 investigated cases had features of IND, using increased AChE activity in the lamina propria and hyperganglionosis (defined as more than five ganglia per high-power field in the submucosa) as diagnostic criteria. These patients had a high incidence of prematurity, indicating that some histologic features of IND may be related to age and development. Age-related alterations of the enteric ganglia were discussed further by Smith,[45] who described a significantly higher number of submucous ganglia in children younger than 4 weeks of age compared with older children. It would be desirable with better knowledge of the enteric nervous system and also with quantitative diagnostic criteria of IND to distinguish normal variation from pathologic conditions. Moore and associates[30] introduced a morphologic scoring system based on the findings of hyperganglionosis, giant ganglia, maturity of neurons, heterotopic neuronal cells, and AChE activity in the lamina propria, muscularis mucosa, or adventitia of submucosal blood vessels. Hyperganglionosis and increased AChE activity of nerve fibers in the lamina propria were of major importance in this scoring system.

DIAGNOSIS

Suction rectal biopsy is the principal method for the diagnosis of disorders of intestinal innervation. It is necessary to include a sufficient amount of submucosa in

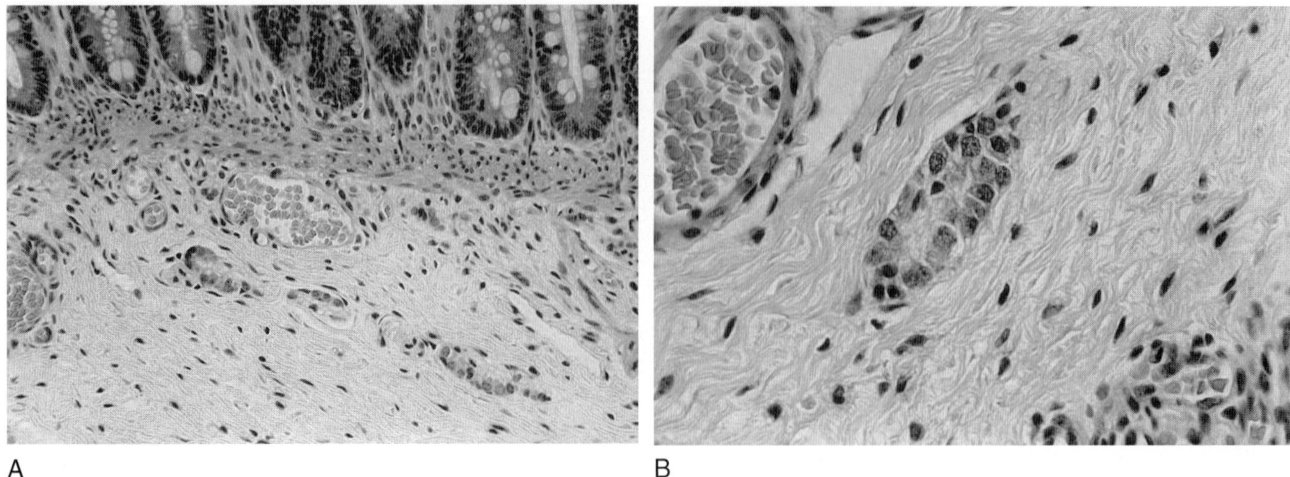

Figure 100–1 Hematoxylin and eosin staining of suction rectal biopsy from a patient with intestinal neuronal dysplasia. *A,* Hyperganglionosis. *B,* Giant ganglia.

the suction biopsy specimens. Traditionally, hematoxylin and eosin and AChE histochemical staining (Figs. 100-1 and 100-2) in suction rectal biopsy specimens have provided the basis for the diagnostic evaluation of IND. However, there has been discussion about whether AChE histochemistry is sufficient for the accurate diagnosis of IND and other additional staining techniques have been proposed. Meier-Ruge and coworkers suggest lactate dehydrogenase histochemistry.[23-25] In my laboratory, newer neuronal markers currently are being used, such as reduced nicotinamide-adenine dinucleotide phosphate (NADPH) diaphorase histochemistry and immunohistochemistry using antibodies raised against neural cell adhesion molecule, Protein Gene Product 9.5 (PGP9.5), S-100, Peripherin, and Synaptophysin.[27,36,38,39] Ganglion-cell counting can be difficult. Standard immunohistochemical techniques, using antibodies raised against neuron-specific enolase or PGP9.5, which are commonly used to display the enteric nervous system, are less suitable for cell counting because they stain not only the cell bodies but also the axonal processes. Recently, cuprolinic blue staining has been proposed as the method that stains the largest number of ganglion cells.[48] Furthermore, this method stains only the cell bodies and not the axons, which makes it relatively easy to distinguish the individual cells.

Barium enema in IND does not show any specific radiologic features other than rectosigmoid distention. Similarly, anorectal manometry may show the rectosphincteric reflex to be present, absent, or atypical.

CORRELATION BETWEEN HISTOLOGIC FINDINGS AND CLINICAL SYMPTOMS

Several investigators have raised doubts about the existence of IND as a distinct histopathologic entity.[16,40] One reason for this has been the weak correlation found between the severity of clinical symptoms and the histologic findings.[14] It has been suggested that the histologic findings of IND can be a part of normal development or secondary to prolonged constipation. Recently, Montedonico and coworkers[28] correlated specific clinical, radiologic, and manometric findings with the severity of histopathologic findings in 44 patients with IND treated at their institution over 20 years. They classified IND according to the severity of histochemical alteration into two groups: mild IND and severe IND. The criteria used for the diagnosis of severe IND included hyperplasia of the submucous plexus, giant ganglia with more than seven ganglion cells, increased AChE activity in the lamina propria or surrounding submucosal blood vessels, and heterotopic neuronal cells in the lamina propria. Any biopsy specimen that showed giant ganglia of the submucous plexus with only one of the other elements was considered mild IND. According to their results, the characteristic clinical pattern of severe IND can be found in infants younger than 1 year old with a history of constipation and abdominal distention, thus mimicking HD, with absence of internal sphincter relaxation in anorectal manometry but who have a normal barium enema. The median age at presentation of severe IND was 5 months, and similar results have been reported in other series.[4] These authors found a correlation between the histologic severity of IND and the clinical symptoms, suggesting that IND is a distinct entity. Although many cases of IND are clinically indistinguishable from HD, barium enema findings in IND often are equivocal or show slight to moderate rectosigmoid distention but lack the typical narrow segment of aganglionosis.

MANAGEMENT

Current treatment of IND type B is in the first instance conservative, consisting of laxatives and enemas. In the majority of patients the clinical problem resolves or is

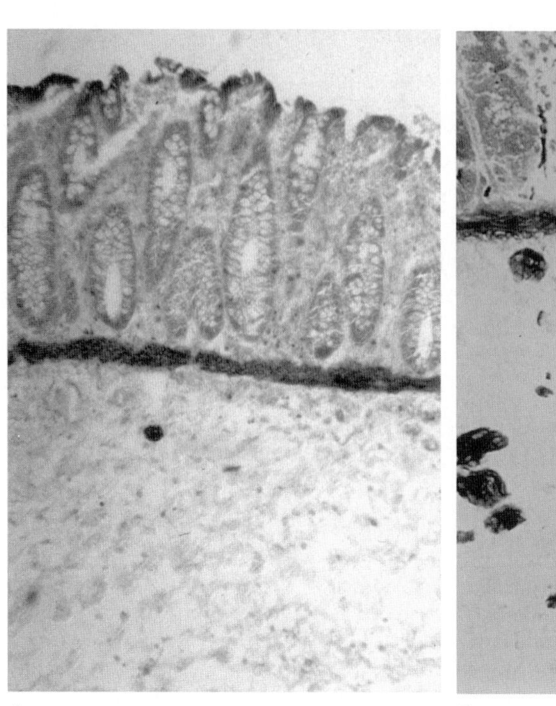
A

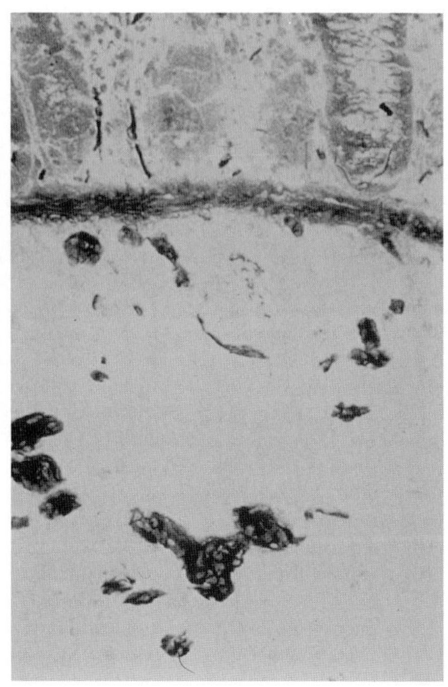
B

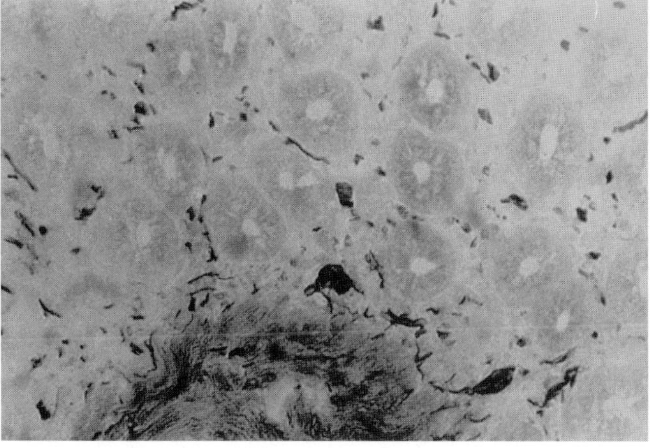
C

Figure 100–2 Acetylcholinesterase staining of suction rectal biopsy. *A*, Normal biopsy showing a submucosal ganglion. *B*, Biopsy from a patient with intestinal neuronal dysplasia showing hyperganglionosis and giant ganglia. *C*, Ectopic ganglia in the lamina propria and increased AChE activity in the lamina propria in a biopsy specimen from a patient with intestinal neuronal dysplasia.

manageable in this way. If bowel symptoms persist after at least 6 months of treatment, internal sphincter myectomy should be considered. Resection and a pull-through operation are rarely indicated in IND. The indication for surgery should not be determined on the basis of histopathologic findings alone; rather, the decision must be based on the individual patient's clinical symptoms.

OUTCOME

Recently Gillick and colleagues[7] reported results of treatment in 33 patients with IND observed for periods ranging from 1 to 8 years (mean 2.4 years). Twenty-one (64%) patients had a good response to conservative management and currently have normal bowel habits. Twelve patients (36%) underwent internal sphincter myectomy after failed conservative management. Seven of these patients now have normal bowel habits. Two patients were able to stay clean with regular enemas. Three patients who continued to have persistent constipation after myectomy and underwent resection of redundant and dilated sigmoid colon now had normal bowel habits. Scharli and coworkers[41] reported that 13 of their 22 cases required internal sphincter myectomy, which resulted in satisfactory results in 90% of the patients within 3 months.

REFERENCES

1. Borchard F, Meier-Ruge W, Wiebecke B, et al: [Disorders of the innervation of the large intestines—classification and diagnosis.] Pathologe 1991;12:171-174. German.
2. Cord-Udy CL, Smith VV, Ahmed S, et al: An evaluation of the role of suction rectal biopsy in the diagnosis of intestinal neuronal dysplasia. J Pediatr Gastroenterol Nutr 1997: 24:1-6.
3. Costa M, Fava M, Seri M, et al: Evaluation of the *HOX11L1* gene as a candidate for congenital disorders of intestinal innervation. J Med Genet 2000;37:Eq (Electronic letters).
4. Fadda B, Maier WA, Meier-Ruge W, et al: [Neuronal intestinal dysplasia: Critical 10-years' analysis of clinical and biopsy diagnosis.] Z Kinderchir 1983;38:302-312. German.
5. Gariepy CE: Intestinal motility disorders and development of the enteric nervous system. Pediatr Res 2000;49: 605-613.
6. Gath R, Goessling A, Keller KM, et al: Analysis of the *RET, GDNF, EDN3* and *EDNRB* genes in patients with intestinal neuronal dysplasia and Hirschsprung's disease. Gut 2001; 48:671-675.
7. Gillick J, Tazawa H, Puri P: Intestinal neuronal dysplasia: Results of treatment in 33 patients. J Pediatr Surg 2001: 36:777-779.
8. Hatano M, Aoki T, Dezawa M, et al: A novel pathogenesis of megacolon in *Ncx/Hox11L1* deficient mice. J Clin Invest 1997;100:795-801.
9. Ikeda K, Goto S, Nagasaki A, Taguchi T: Hypogenesis of intestinal ganglion cells: A rare cause of intestinal obstruction simulating aganglionosis. Z Kinderchir 1988;43: 52-53.
10. Kapur RP: Neuronal dysplasia: A controversial pathological correlate of intestinal pseudo-obstruction. Am J Med Genet 2003;122:287-293.
11. Kobayashi H, Hirakawa H, Puri P: What are the diagnostic criteria for intestinal neuronal dysplasia? Pediatr Surg Int 1995;10:459-464.
12. Kobayashi H, Hirakawa H, Surana R, et al: Intestinal neuronal dysplasia is a possible cause of persistent bowel symptoms after pull-through operation for Hirschsprung's disease. J Pediatr Surg 1995;30:253-259.
13. Kobayashi H, Mohamed A, Puri P: Intestinal neuronal dysplasia in twins. J Pediatr Gastroenterol Nutr 1996;22: 398-401.
14. Koletzko S, Ballauff A, Hadziselimovic F, Enck P: Is histological diagnosis of neuronal intestinal dysplasia related to clinical and manometric findings in constipated children? Results of a pilot study. J Pediatr Gastroenterol Nutr 1993; 17:59-65.
15. Koletzko S, Jesch I, Faus-Kebetaler T, et al: Rectal biopsy for diagnosis of intestinal dysplasia in children: A prospective multicentre study on inter-observer variation and clinical outcome. Gut 1999;44:853-861.
16. Lake BD: Intestinal neuronal dysplasia: Why does it only occur in parts of Europe? Virchows Arch 1995;426:537-539.
17. Lumb PD, Moore L: Are giant ganglia a reliable marker of intestinal neuronal dysplasia type B (IND B). Virchow's Arch 1998;432:103-106.
18. Martucciello G, Caffarena PE, Lerone M, et al: Neuronal intestinal dysplasia: Clinical experience in Italian patients. Eur J Pediatr Surg 1994;4:287-292.
19. Martucciello G, Torre M, Pini Prato A, et al: Associated anomalies in intestinal neuronal dysplasia. J Pediatr Surg 2002;37:219-223.
20. Meier-Ruge W, Morger R, Rehbein F: Das hypoganglionare Megakolon als Begleitkrankheit bei Morbus Hirschsprung. Z Kinderchir 1970;8:254-264.
21. Meier-Ruge W: Uber ein Ekrankungsbild des colon mit Hirschsprung-Symptomatik. Vehr Dtsch Ges Pathol 1971; 55:506-510.
22. Meier-Ruge W: Epidemiology of congenital innervation defects of the distal colon. Virchows Arch A Pathol Anat 1992;420:171-177.
23. Meier-Ruge W, Gambazzi F, Kaufeler RE, et al: The neuropathological diagnosis of neuronal intestinal dysplasia (NID B). Eur J Pediatr Surg 1994;4:267-273.
24. Meier-Ruge W, Bronnimann PB, Gambazzi F, et al: Histopathological criteria for intestinal neuronal dysplasia of the submucous plexus (type B). Virchows Arch 1995; 426:549-556.
25. Meier-Ruge W: Is intestinal neuronal dysplasia really a myth or an invented disease? Pediatr Surg Int 1995;10:439.
26. Milla PJ, Smith VV: Intestinal neuronal dysplasia. J Pediatr Gastroenterol Nutr 1993;17:356-357.
27. Miyazaki E, Ohshiro K, Puri P: NADPH-diaphorase histochemical staining of suction rectal biopsies in the diagnosis of Hirschsprung's disease and allied disorders. Pediatr Surg Int 1998;13:464-467.
28. Montedonico S, Acevedo S, Fadda B: Clinical aspects of intestinal neuronal dysplasia. J Pediatr Surg 2002;37:1772-1774.
29. Moore SW, Kaschula ROC, Cywes S: Familial and genetic aspects of intestinal neuronal dysplasia and Hirschsprung's disease. Pediatr Surg Int 1993;8:406-409.
30. Moore SW, Laing D, Kaschula RD, Cywes S: A histological grading system for the evaluation of co-existing NID with Hirschsprung's disease. Eur J Pediatr Surg 1994;4: 293-297.
31. Newgreen D, Young HM: Enteric nervous system: Development and developmental disturbances: I. Pediatr Dev Pathol 2002;5:224-247.
32. Newgreen D, Young HM: Enteric nervous system: Development and developmental disturbances: II. Pediatr Dev Pathol 2002;5:329-349.
33. Puri P, Lake BD, Nixon HH, et al: Neuronal colonic dysplasia: An unusual association of Hirschsprung's disease. J Pediatr Surg 1977;12:681-685.
34. Puri P: Variant Hirschsprung's disease. J Pediatr Surg 1997; 32:149-157.
35. Puri P, Wester T: Intestinal neuronal dysplasia. Semin Pediatr Surg 1998;7:181-186.
36. Puri P, Shinkai T: Pathogenesis of Hirschsprung's disease and variants: Recent progress. Semin Pediatr Surg 2004; 13:18-24.
37. Puri P, Rolle U: Variant Hirschsprung's disease. Semin Pediatr Surg 2004;13:293-299.
38. Rolle U, Nemeth L, Puri P: Nitrergic innervation of the normal gut and in motility disorders of childhood. J Pediatr Surg 2002;37:551-567.
39. Rolle U, Piotrowska AP, Puri P: Abnormal vasculature in intestinal neuronal dysplasia. Pediatr Surg Int 2003;19: 345-348.
40. Sacher P, Briner J, Hanimann B: Is neuronal intestinal dysplasia (NID) a primary disease or a secondary phenomenon? Eur J Pediatr Surg 1993;3:228-230.
41. Scharli AF: Neuronal intestinal dysplasia. Pediatr Surg Int 1992;7:2-7.
42. Schimpl G, Uray E, Ratschek M, et al: Constipation and intestinal neuronal dysplasia type B: A clinical follow-up study. J Pediatr Gastroenterol Nutr 2004;38:308-311.
43. Schofield DE, Yunis EJ: Intestinal neuronal dysplasia. J Pediatr Gastroenterol Nutr 1991;12:182-189.
44. Shirasawa S, Yunker AM, Roth KA, et al: *Enx (Hox11L1)*-deficient mice develop myenteric neuronal hyperplasia and megacolon. Nat Med 1997;3:646-650.

45. Smith VV: Isolated intestinal neuronal dysplasia: A descriptive pattern or a distinct clinicopathological entity. In Hadziselimovic F, Herzog B (eds): Inflammatory bowel disease and morbus Hirschsprung. Dordrecht, The Netherlands, Kluwer Academic, 1992, pp 203-214.
46. Smith VV: Intestinal neuronal density in childhood: A baseline for the objective assessment of hypo- and hyperganglionosis. Pediatr Pathol 1993;13:225-237.
47. Von Boyen GBT, et al: Abnormalities of the enteric nervous system in heterozygous endothelin B receptor deficient (spotting lethal) rats resembling intestinal neuronal dysplasia. Gut 2002;51:414-419.
48. Wester T, O'Briain DS, Puri P: Notable postnatal alterations in the myenteric plexus of normal human bowel. Gut 1999; 44:666-674.

Chapter 101  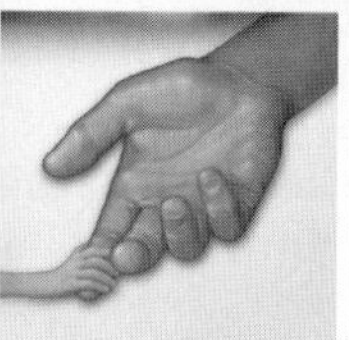

Anorectal Malformations

Alberto Peña and Marc A. Levitt

HISTORY

Throughout history, surgeons have attempted to treat infants and children with anorectal malformations. The written accounts describe very few patients, so it is likely that most patients died without treatment.[45,58] Successful maneuvers involved rupturing an obstructing membrane with a finger or the point of a knife[17] and evolved to making an incision to find the bowel in the perineum[4] or in the hollow of the sacrum. The first inguinal colostomy was performed in 1783,[21,36] but most infants died, and colostomy was thought of as a method of last resort. Amussat in 1835 mobilized the bowel through a perineal incision, sutured it to the skin,[3] and thus was able to avoid the strictures that were common with the earlier procedures. In the 1700s and 1800s, several authors suggested that the peritoneum be opened if the bowel was not encountered from below.[26,31,38,62] In the mid-1900s, single-stage abdominoperineal procedures became popular[42,54] and usually involved resection of the rectosigmoid. Shortly after these reports, Stephens described a procedure that emphasized passage of the rectum within the puborectalis sling.[60] Until the early 1980s, this surgery plus its modifications was the standard approach, but it involved blind dissection near the posterior urethra. A progressive increase in the length of the perineal incision to gain exposure eventually led to posterior sagittal anorectoplasty,[20] which was rapidly adopted because it allowed full visualization of the sphincteric complex and more clearly showed the relationship of the rectum to the urologic system and the surrounding vital structures.

INCIDENCE

The cause of anorectal malformation is unknown. Most authors have written that the average incidence worldwide is 1 in 5000 live births,[11] although the condition is more common in certain areas. Some families have a genetic predisposition, with anorectal malformations being diagnosed in succeeding generations. In addition, imperforate anus occurs in association with several syndromes.[51,66] A slight male preponderance exists.[60]

The most common defect in females is rectovestibular fistula, whereas the most common defect in males is rectourethral fistula. Cloacal malformations are more common than formerly thought, most likely because they were previously misdiagnosed as rectovaginal fistulas.[53] Imperforate anus without fistula occurs in 5% of patients, but interestingly, half of them also have Down's syndrome. Patient with Down's syndrome and anorectal malformations have this type of defect 95% of the time.[66]

CLASSIFICATION

The classification system shown in Table 101-1 is purely descriptive and has therapeutic and prognostic implications.

EMBRYOLOGY

The cloaca in the embryo is a cavity into which open the hindgut, tailgut, allantois, and later, the mesonephric ducts. The cloaca is first formed at around 21 days' gestation; it is U shaped, with the allantois lying anteriorly and the hindgut posteriorly. The septum in the middle grows downward and fuses with lateral folds (Rathke's plicae) until it joins the cloacal membrane. In this 6-week process, a urogenital cavity anteriorly and an anorectal cavity

TABLE 101-1 Classification of Anorectal Malformations

Males	Females
Perineal fistula	Perineal fistula
Rectourethral fistula	Vestibular fistula
Bulbar	Persistent cloaca
Prostatic	<3-cm common channel
Rectovesical fistula (bladder neck)	>3-cm common channel
Imperforate anus without fistula	Imperforate anus without fistula
Rectal atresia	Rectal atresia
Complex defects	Complex defects

posteriorly are created. Rapid growth of the genital tubercle changes the shape of the cloaca and the orientation of the cloacal membrane, which is displaced posteriorly. The cloacal membrane breaks down at 7 weeks' gestation, thereby creating two openings: the urogenital and anal openings.[19,61,68] The muscles that surround the rectum develop at the same time and are seen in the sixth and seventh weeks of gestation,[32] and by the ninth week, all relevant structures are in place. At this stage, differentiation into male or female external genitalia has not yet occurred.

ASSOCIATED MALFORMATIONS

Most babies with imperforate anus have one or more abnormalities that affect other systems.[9,57] The incidence varies from 50% to 60%. Higher abnormalities are associated with more malformations. Many are incidental findings, but others, such as cardiovascular defects, may be life threatening.

Cardiovascular Anomalies

Cardiovascular anomalies are present in approximately a third of patients with imperforate anus,[9,24,64,65] but only 10% require treatment. The most common lesions are atrial septal defect and patent ductus arteriosus, followed by the tetralogy of Fallot and ventricular septal defect. Transposition of the great arteries and hypoplastic left heart syndrome are rare.

Gastrointestinal Anomalies

A wide spectrum of gastrointestinal anomalies have been described. Tracheoesophageal abnormalities occur in about 10% of cases.[24,57] Duodenal obstruction caused by atresia or malrotation has been reported to have an incidence of 1% to 2%.[24,44] Hirschsprung's disease has been found in 3 patients in our series of 1710. Overdiagnosis of this association is probably due to the high incidence of constipation seen in patients with anorectal malformations.

Spinal and Vertebral Anomalies

Lumbosacral anomalies such as hemivertebrae, scoliosis, butterfly vertebrae, and hemisacrum are common. The most frequent spinal problem is tethered cord,[30,35] but spinal lipomas, syringomyelia, and myelomeningocele are also commonly seen. The more complex the anorectal anomaly, the more likely the presence of an associated spinal and vertebral anomaly. These problems are found (by ultrasound or magnetic resonance imaging) in a third to a half of patients with anorectal malformations.[4,12,55,63] It is still unclear how many of these lesions are clinically significant and which lesions require prophylaxis.[33,67] A sacral defect, particularly hemisacrum, in association with imperforate anus and a presacral mass is known as Currarino's triad[18] and has a strong familial tendency.[1,5,15] The sacral ratio is a valuable prognostic tool (Fig. 101-1) because it quantifies the degree of sacral hypodevelopment. Patients with ratios less than 0.3 are universally incontinent. Ratios that approach 1.0 usually predict a good prognosis.

Genitourinary Anomalies

Urologic abnormalities predominate. Improved imaging has shown an increasing range of upper and lower urinary tract anomalies. The incidence ranges from a third to a half of patients in several series and increases with increasing complexity of anorectal defect.[39,44] Vesicoureteric reflux is the most common anomaly found, and renal agenesis and dysplasia are the next most frequent findings.[16,39] Cryptorchidism is reported in 3% to 19% of males with imperforate anus,[16,28] and hypospadias occurs in approximately 5%.[28]

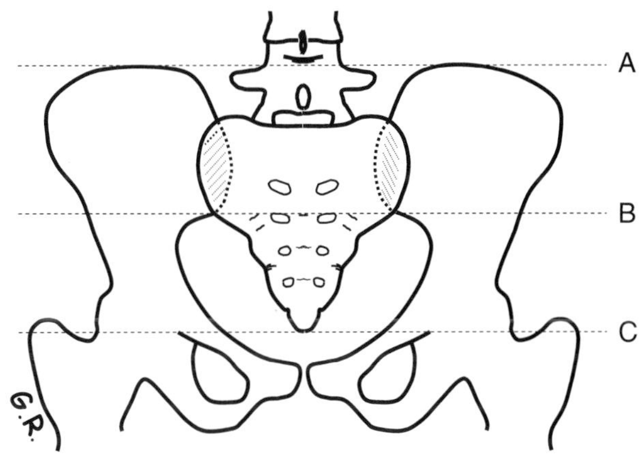

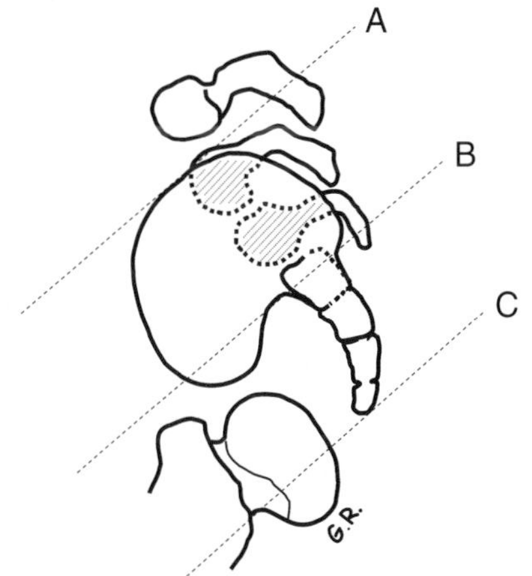

Figure 101-1 Anterior-posterior (*A*) and lateral (*B*) sacral ratios.

Gynecologic Anomalies

Associated gynecologic anomalies have emerged as a significant concern in patients with anorectal malformations. In the newborn period, hydrocolpos can lead to urinary obstruction or can cause pyocolpos. Müllerian anomalies may be manifested later when teenagers have obstruction of menstrual flow. Large intra-abdominal collections and peritonitis can develop, or patients may have amenorrhea because of absence of the müllerian structures. Asymmetric obstruction to menstrual flow can occur as a result of an anatomic abnormality at any level, such as an obstruction of the tube, atresia of the cervix, or a blind hemivagina.[35,69] Uterine malformations (predominantly bicornuate uterus and uterus didelphys) and vaginal abnormalities (particularly a vaginal septum[35]) occur in approximately a third of patients. Investigation of the gynecologic anatomy for hydrocolpos needs to be performed in the newborn period and then during definitive repair or at the time of colostomy closure to prevent immediate and long-term sequelae. The full obstetric impact of these anomalies is not yet known.

ANORECTAL ANATOMY AND PATHOPHYSIOLOGY

Bowel control implies the ability to detect and retain flatus and stool until the appropriate time for evacuation. It is the result of a complex interplay among sphincter function, anorectal sensation, and colonic motility. All these factors are affected in children with anorectal malformations.

Sphincter Mechanism

The muscle groups of the sphincter mechanism are traditionally described as including the voluntary striated muscles of the external sphincter, the levator musculature, and the involuntary, smooth muscle (internal sphincter). These muscles are innervated by the pudendal nerve, both motor to the external sphincter and sensory to the skin around the anus and derived from the sacral plexus roots S2 to S4, as well as the autonomic nervous system via the nervi erigentes, also derived from segments S2 to S4 of the spinal cord. The posterior sagittal approach has demonstrated that the external sphincter runs in a paramedian direction. In addition, the muscular boundaries of the external sphincter are fused, and thus the components of the external sphincter are indistinguishable. During posterior sagittal dissection, the junction of the levator musculature with the external sphincter is defined by a vertical group of striated muscle fibers called the muscle complex. Electrical stimulation of the upper end of the levator group pulls the rectum forward. Stimulation of the muscle complex (vertical fibers) elevates the anus, and stimulation of the paramedian fibers of the external sphincter closes the anus. Children with anorectal malformations have varying degrees of striated muscle development from almost normal-appearing muscle to virtually no muscle at all. In very high defects, the rectum may rest at the upper part of the funnel-shaped muscle structure, and in lower defects, the rectum may traverse the base of the muscular funnel.

The characteristics and precise limits of the internal sphincter have not been accurately described in normal individuals. In patients with anorectal malformations, this structure has been a matter of speculation, and few attempts at scientific evaluation have been made.[27]

Sensation and Proprioception

Under normal circumstances, the anal canal is an exquisitely sensitive area. It allows the individual to discriminate solids from liquids and even from gas. The overwhelming majority of children with anorectal malformations are born without an anal canal and therefore cannot discriminate like a normal individual can. There is, however, another kind of sensation called proprioception. This is described as a vague feeling that is perceived when the rectum is distended, supposedly simultaneous with stretching of the voluntary muscle that surrounds the rectum. Proprioception seems to be present in different degrees in most patients with anorectal malformations. The clinical implications are obvious. These patients lose control when they suffer an episode of diarrhea. They have the ability to be toilet-trained when they can form solid stool and can learn to perceive it.

Colonic and Rectosigmoid Motility

Normally, it takes between 3 and 6 hours for the gastric contents to transit the small bowel. The intestinal contents reach the cecum in a liquid state. It then takes about 20 to 24 hours for that fecal material to reach the rectum and become formed (solid). The rectosigmoid acts as a reservoir and keeps the fecal material for a variable time. The anal canal (below the pectinate line) is usually empty because of the action of the surrounding sphincteric mechanism. Occasionally, however, there are peristaltic waves that push the fecal material toward the anus. The rectal contents move distally and touch the exquisitely sensitive tissue of the anal canal, thereby providing the individual with valuable information related to the nature of the rectal contents (gas, solid, liquid). Depending on the surrounding social circumstances, the individual may let the rectal contents escape or may contract the sphincteric mechanism to push stool or gas back into the rectum. The distention of the rectum produces a vague sensation of fullness or even colicky pain (proprioception) but does not provide specific information concerning the physical characteristic of the contents. Very little is known about the mechanism that triggers peristalsis of the rectosigmoid to defecate, but it is clear that the degree of rectal fullness has an important role. Thus, when the time comes, the rectosigmoid generates waves of peristalsis aimed at emptying the lumen. Individuals can restrain this process temporarily by using the voluntary sphincter. With a voluntary decision to allow the stool to come out, the sphincter is relaxed and the individual waits for the next peristaltic wave. Normal defecation allows massive emptying of the rectosigmoid, followed by another resting period of about 24 hours, during which the rectosigmoid again acts as a reservoir. The importance of rectosigmoid motility and its relevance for bowel control have largely been underestimated.

Children with anorectal malformations have a spectrum of rectosigmoid motility disorders. Children subjected to surgical techniques that preserve the rectosigmoid suffer from constipation. Constipation, one of the most important functional sequelae, is probably the result of hypomotility of the rectosigmoid. The hypomotility is self-perpetuating and self-aggravating to the point that if left untreated, megasigmoid develops. In extreme cases, fecal impaction and encopresis or overflow pseudoincontinence may develop. It seems that constipation is worse with lower defects. Knowing this and the fact that hypomotility can begin a vicious cycle leading to megasigmoid, it is incumbent on the pediatric surgeon to avoid the cycle of hypomotility, constipation, and megasigmoid. Aggressive patient follow-up plus dietary, mechanical, and pharmacologic treatment prevents this cycle.

Children with anorectal malformations who, for whatever reason, have lost their rectosigmoid suffer from the exact opposite (i.e., tendency for diarrhea). These children have no reservoir capacity, are highly sensitive to fruits and vegetables, and worst of all, suffer from incontinence.

CLINICAL FINDINGS AND INITIAL MANAGEMENT

Figure 101-2 shows the decision-making algorithm for the initial management of male patients.

A clinician called to see a newborn male with an anorectal malformation must perform a thorough perineal inspection, which usually provides the most important clues about the type of malformation that the patient has (Fig. 101-3). It is important to not make a decision about colostomy or primary surgery before 24 hours of age. The reason for this delay is that significant intraluminal pressure is required for meconium to be forced through a fistula orifice. Passing of meconium through a fistula is the most valuable sign of the location of the fistula in these babies. If meconium is seen on the perineum, it is evidence of a rectoperineal fistula. If there is meconium in the urine, the diagnosis of a rectourinary fistula is obvious (see Fig. 101-3).

Radiologic evaluations do not show the real anatomy before 24 hours because the rectum is collapsed. It takes a significant amount of intraluminal pressure to overcome the muscle tone of the sphincters that surround the lower part of the rectum. Therefore, radiologic evaluations done too early (before 24 hours) will most likely reveal the presence of a "very high rectum" and yield a false diagnosis.

During the first 24 hours, the baby should receive intravenous fluids, antibiotics, and nasogastric decompression to prevent aspiration. The clinician should use these hours to rule out the presence of associated defects such as cardiac malformations, esophageal atresia, and urologic problems. An echocardiogram can be performed, and the baby should be checked for the presence of esophageal atresia. A plain radiograph of the lumbar spine and sacrum should be taken to evaluate for hemivertebrae and sacral anomalies. Spinal ultrasound helps screen for tethered cord and other spinal problems. Ultrasonography of the abdomen evaluates for the presence of hydronephrosis.

If the baby has signs of a perineal fistula, anoplasty can be performed without a protective colostomy during the first 48 hours of life.

After 24 hours, if no meconium is seen on the perineum or in the urine, we recommend obtaining a cross-table lateral x-ray film with the baby in prone position.[40] If the gas in the rectum is located below the coccyx and the baby is in good condition with no significant associated defects, depending on the surgeon's experience, a posterior sagittal operation without a protective colostomy can be considered. A more conservative alternative would be to perform a colostomy, with the definitive repair planned for a second stage.

If rectal gas is seen above the coccyx and the patient has meconium in the urine, significant associated defects, and an abnormal sacrum or a flat bottom, a colostomy is recommended with postponement of the main repair for

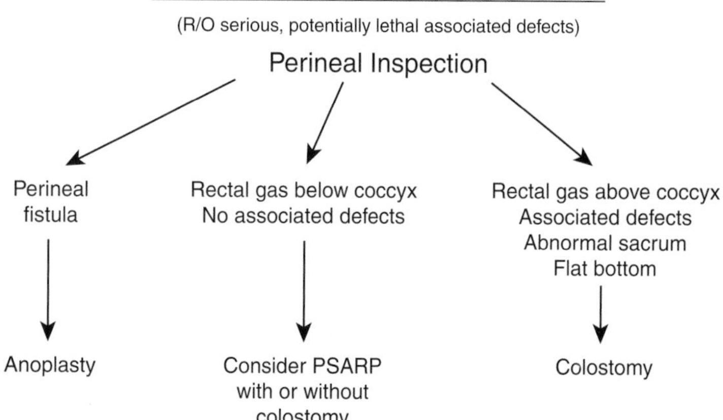

Figure 101-2 Algorithm for the treatment of a male newborn with an anorectal malformation. PSARP, posterior sagittal anorectoplasty; R/O, rule out.

Figure 101–3 External appearance of the perineum of male patients with anorectal malformations. *A*, Perineal fistula. *B*, Rectum–urethral bulb fistula. *C*, Rectoprostatic fistula. *D*, Rectum–bladder neck fistula.

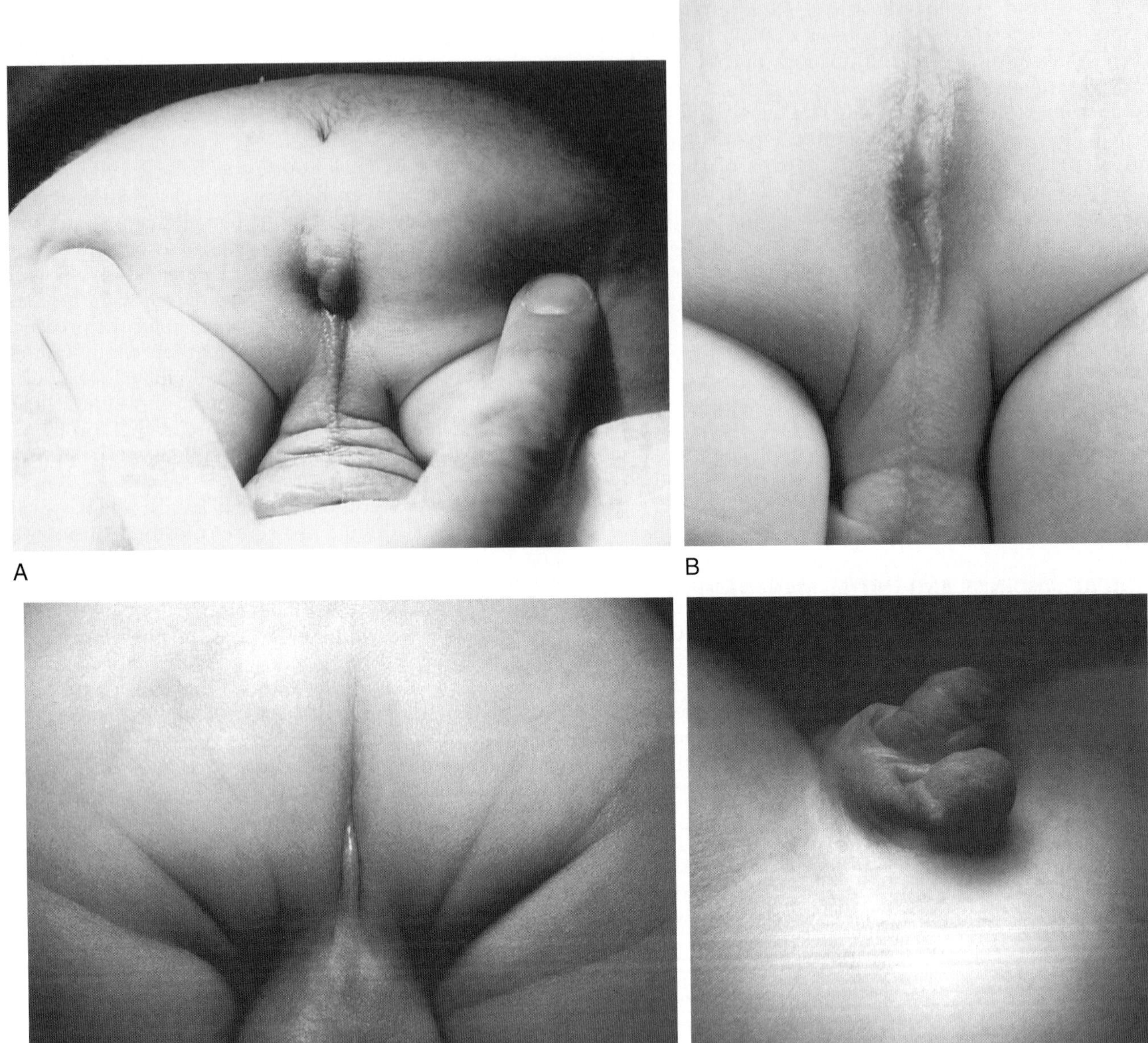

a subsequent operation, which can be performed 4 weeks later, provided that the baby is gaining weight normally.

Performing the definitive repair at 1 month of age has important advantages for the patient, including less time with an abdominal stoma, less size discrepancy between the proximal and distal bowel at the time of colostomy closure, easier anal dilation, and no recognizable psychological sequelae from painful perineal maneuvers. In addition, at least theoretically, placing the rectum in the right location early in life may provide an advantage in terms of the potential for acquired local sensation.

The potential advantages of an early operation must be weighed against the possible disadvantages of an inexperienced surgeon unfamiliar with the minute anatomic structures of the pelvis of a young infant.

A trend to repair these defects without a protective colostomy exists.[2,23,37] The concern about such a repair without a colostomy is that there is no precise anatomic information about the specific type of anorectal defect that the surgeon is dealing with. The most catastrophic complications seen in patients operated on at other institutions without a colostomy occurred in patients in

Figure 101–4 Algorithm for the treatment of a female newborn with an anorectal malformation. R/O, rule out.

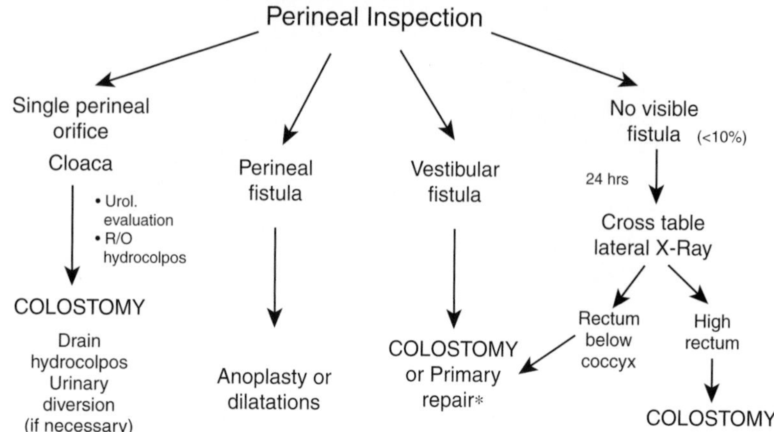

whom the surgeon did not have a preoperative distal colostogram. While looking for the rectum the surgeon might inadvertently find and injure the urethra, an ectopic ureter, the bladder neck, the vas deferens, or the seminal vesicles.[29]

Figure 101-4 shows a decision-making algorithm for the initial management of female patients. As in male babies, the most important step in diagnosis and decision making is perineal inspection (Fig. 101-5). The first 24 hours should also be used to rule out important serious, potentially lethal associated defects. Perineal inspection may disclose the presence of a solitary perineal orifice. This single finding establishes the diagnosis of a cloaca. The clinician should know that such a patient has a high likelihood of suffering from a urologic defect. The patient needs a urologic evaluation, and the presence of hydrocolpos should be ruled out by ultrasound.

Such a baby needs a colostomy. It is important to perform the colostomy proximally enough to allow repair of the malformation without interference from the colostomy. In other words, the surgeon must leave enough redundant, distal rectosigmoid to allow a pull-through maneuver to be performed. During opening of the colostomy, it is mandatory that the hydrocolpos be drained when present. If the hydrocolpos is not large enough to reach the abdominal wall above the bladder, it can be drained with a rubber tube. Because a significant number of these patients have two hemivaginas, the surgeon must be certain that the tube inserted into the hydrocolpos is really draining both hemivaginas. Occasionally, the surgeon has to open a window in the vaginal septum to drain both with a single tube. At times the hydrocolpos is so large that it may even produce respiratory distress; these giant vaginas may be drained by connecting the vaginal wall to the abdominal wall as a tubeless vaginostomy. Rarely, some patients with cloaca are not able to empty their bladder because the common channel is almost atretic. In such circumstances, the baby may require a vesicostomy or suprapubic cystotomy. Endoscopy is recommended in babies with cloaca to determine the anatomy and particularly the length of the common channel, which helps with surgical planning.

Perineal inspection may show the presence of a perineal fistula, and primary anoplasty can be performed without a colostomy with this type of defect. Occasionally, the surgeon may face the problem of a premature or very sick baby with severe associated defects and a perineal fistula. In this case, fistula dilatations can be performed to facilitate emptying of the colon while delaying the definitive repair.

The presence of a vestibular fistula is the most common finding in female patients. This malformation may be repaired during the neonatal period without a protective colostomy. These operations unfortunately represent the most common source of complications in such patients. The decision to repair this malformation primarily or to open a colostomy should be based on the experience of the particular surgeon who is going to perform the procedure. Colostomy is still the most effective way to protect these patients.

Occasionally (less than 10% of cases), no fistula is visible and there is no meconium apparent even after 24 hours of observation. This small group of patients requires a cross-table lateral radiograph. If the radiograph shows gas in the rectum located very near the skin, the patient probably suffers from an imperforate anus with no fistula. If the patient is in good condition, one can perform a primary operation without a colostomy, depending on the surgeon's experience. Many of these patients with no fistula also have Down's syndrome.[66]

The occasional patient with a perineal or vestibular fistula who is very sick for other medical reasons may undergo only dilatation of the fistula to allow decompression of the colon. Such patients can be repaired later in life. The repair can be done with a protective colostomy or in primary fashion, again depending on the surgeon's experience. When patients are subjected to primary repair of a vestibular fistula or perineal fistula later in life, strict preoperative bowel irrigation 24 hours in advance should be performed. During the operation a central venous line is inserted, and for 7 days the patient is kept

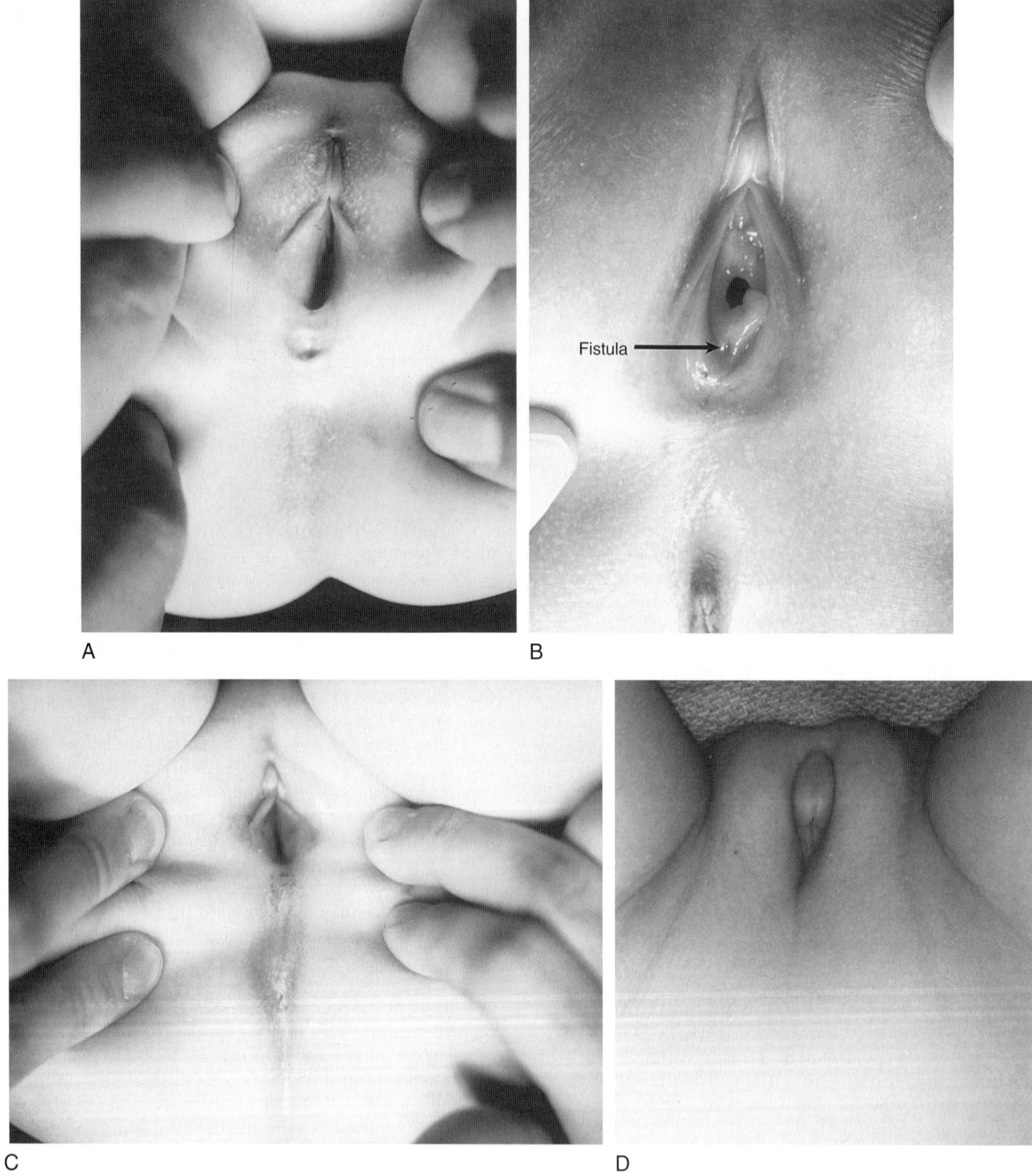

Figure 101-5 External appearance of the perineum of female patients with anorectal malformations. *A*, Perineal fistula. *B*, Vestibular fistula. *C*, Cloaca. *D*, Very high cloaca, flat bottom.

with nothing by mouth and receives parenteral nutrition. In our series, no infections have occurred with this type of regimen.

With emerging advancements in perinatology and prenatal ultrasound techniques, anorectal malformations are more commonly being suspected. Sonographic findings such as a dilated rectum or hydrocolpos or demonstration of an associated anomaly such as an absent kidney, a vertebral anomaly such as a hemisacrum, or an orthopedic problem such as a missing radius can make the perinatologist suspicious that the fetus may in fact have an anorectal malformation. With improving technology, it is likely that this area of diagnosis and even fetal intervention will continue to advance.[13,56]

In either sex, abdominal ultrasonography to evaluate for associated urologic problems and echocardiography should be performed during the initial admission. It is also convenient at this time to perform a spinal ultrasound to evaluate for associated spinal anomalies such as meningomyelocele or a tethered cord. Such an ultrasound is an excellent screening examination for these anomalies, but it must be performed before sacral ossification, which occurs at 3 months of age. If screening is done later, magnetic resonance imaging is required. From a plain anteroposterior and lateral radiograph of the sacrum, a sacral ratio can be calculated, which can be helpful in predicting the prognosis for fecal continence (see Fig. 101-1).

During the evaluation conducted before performance of either anoplasty or colostomy, the baby is maintained on an intravenous infusion, with a nasogastric tube in place to decompress the stomach. No oral feeding is allowed. Antibiotics are given at the time of surgery.

Limited Posterior Sagittal Anorectoplasty

When a low anomaly (perineal fistula) is diagnosed, the surgeon must decide which procedure is appropriate. In the presence of a fistulous track to the perineum, in which the anus is always located anterior to the sphincter mechanism, a limited posterior sagittal anorectoplasty can be performed in the newborn period. In babies who cannot undergo such a procedure in the newborn period because they are ill and have significant associated anomalies, dilatation of the fistulous tract is appropriate with a plan for repair in the future. Occasionally, such babies escape detection in the newborn period, and delayed primary repair is then appropriate. It is advantageous to perform this operation in the first 48 hours of life because the meconium is sterile. When such an operation is delayed and performed at several months of life, a complete bowel preparation, including a postoperative period of parenteral nutrition without oral intake, is recommended to avoid a perineal infection.

For a limited posterior sagittal anorectoplasty, the baby is placed prone. In males, a urinary catheter is inserted. The distal end of the rectum is intimately attached to the posterior urethra, and urethral injury must be avoided. Multiple 6-0 silk sutures are placed at the mucocutaneous junction around the fistula orifice. An incision divides the posterior sphincter in half and is continued circumferentially around the fistula. While traction is maintained on the bowel, a circumferential dissection is performed to mobilize the bowel and reposition it within the limits of the external sphincter. Mucosa is sutured to skin with fine, absorbable sutures under slight tension. The perineal body is reconstructed.

Colostomy

Colostomy is usually performed as a first stage in a newborn with a high anomaly. A descending colostomy is a relatively trouble-free stoma. It also leaves the sigmoid colon entirely free for reconstruction. It is fashioned by making an oblique left lower quadrant incision. The stoma is divided, with the bowel openings at opposite ends of the wound. The proximal part of the stoma is placed at the start of the sigmoid colon, just after the colon comes off its left retroperitoneal attachment. Stomas placed in mobile portions of the colon are prone to prolapse. The distal part of the stoma, in the upper sigmoid, is made intentionally small in an attempt to prevent prolapse. The distal segment should be copiously irrigated to remove all meconium.

A colostomy can result in significant morbidity, so it is vital to construct it meticulously. Transverse colostomies often lead to prolapse, make cleaning the distal segment difficult, make delineation of the downstream rectourinary anatomy during the distal augmented-pressure colostogram challenging, and can result in perforation of the colonic segment.[25] Such colostomies also lead to megarectosigmoid and a left microcolon in the defunctionalized segment, particularly when the colostomy is left in place for many months. A colostomy that is placed too low in the sigmoid can limit pull-through maneuvers. A loop colostomy leads to distal contamination of the urinary stream if there is a fistula and to a dilated megarectosigmoid from stool spillage.

Later Management after Colostomy

Before reconstruction, the anatomy of the anorectal malformation is delineated by high-pressure distal colostography (loopography).[25] In patients who have not already undergone cystourethrography, the necessary information may be gained during the distal colostogram (Figs. 101-6 and 101-7). Patience is required when performing

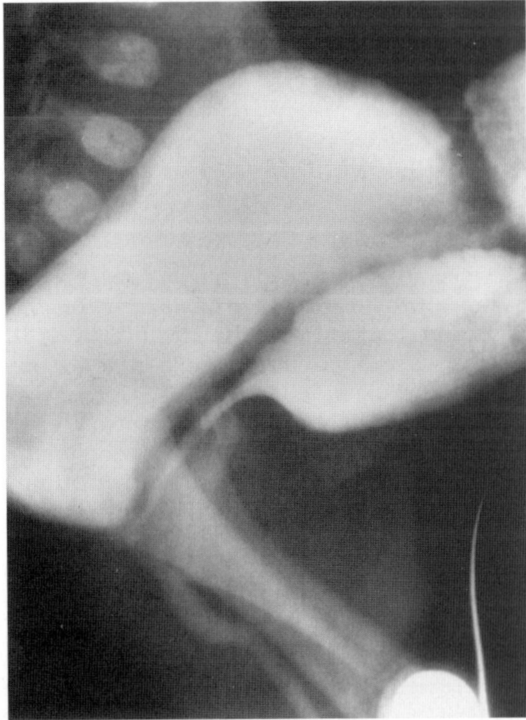

Figure 101-6 Distal colostogram showing a rectum–urethral bulbar fistula.

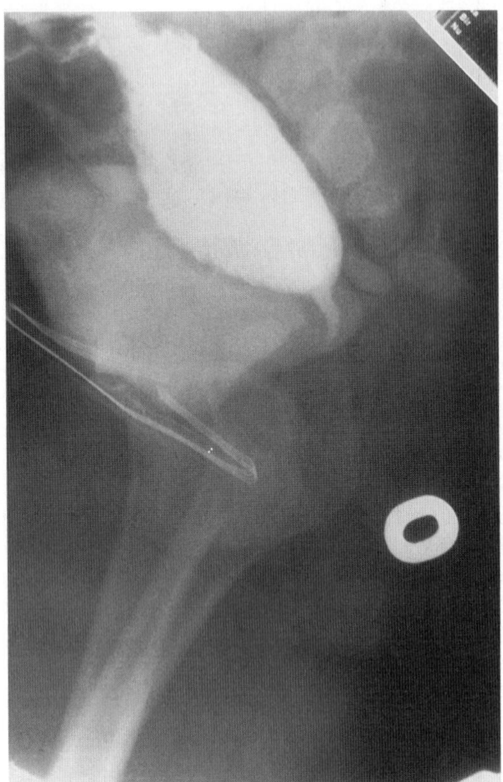

Figure 101-7 Distal colostogram showing a rectum–bladder neck fistula.

loopography with slow distention of the distal rectum. The muscles of the pelvis are normally contracted, and thus the distal rectum is compressed and can at first appear flat at the pubococcygeal line. With gentle pressure, this flat line begins to bulge, and it is at this point that the examiner can visualize the true extent of the rectum and the presence of a rectourinary fistula.

ANORECTAL RECONSTRUCTION

Basic Principles

All defects can be repaired through a posterior sagittal approach. Approximately 10% of male patients (those with a rectum–bladder neck fistula) and about 40% of female patients with a cloaca may in addition require an abdominal approach, either via laparoscopy or via laparotomy, for mobilization of a high rectum or vagina. Because a spectrum of defects exist, the surgeon must be prepared to explore the anatomic area and introduce technical variants according to the specific anatomic findings.

The patient is placed in a prone position with the pelvis elevated. Special care must be taken to cushion all the pressure areas of the baby's body. Two small bolsters must be used in front of each deltopectoral groove to avoid hyperextension of the neck and shoulders. A Foley catheter is inserted into the bladder before the patient is positioned. The catheter sometimes goes into the rectum through the fistula rather than into the bladder. To avoid misplacement, the surgeon can direct the catheter with a lacrimal probe inserted in the tip of the Foley catheter to function as a guide. Occasionally, the catheter must be positioned intraoperatively once the fistula is exposed. Electrical stimulation of the perineum allows evaluation of the strength of the sphincter contraction. A midline incision is created, and the sphincteric mechanism is divided exactly in the midline, with equal amounts of muscle left on each side. The rationale for this approach is based on the fact that important nerves or vessels do not cross the midline. Everything seems to be terminal in the midline, and there is even a midline raphe that helps the surgeon know that the opening is exactly in the midline. Sharp Weitlaner retractors are used to achieve good exposure. The retractors should be placed superficially to avoid pressure damage to the nerves that run close to the wound.

Posterior Sagittal Anorectoplasty for Anomalies in Males

Rectourethral Fistula (Bulbar and Prostatic)

The size of the incision must be adapted to the specific anatomy of the patient (Fig. 101-8). No deleterious effects are caused by extending the incision, provided that it remains in the midline. The incision usually extends from the lower portion of the sacrum through the center of the anal dimple; it is sometimes extended to the perineal body, particularly in boys with a rectum–urethral bulbar fistula. Below the skin and running parallel to the midline are the parasagittal muscle fibers. Medial to these muscle structures and located within the limits of the anal dimple are other muscle structures that run perpendicular to the previous ones. These structures extend from the skin to the levator muscle and are called the muscle complex. Deeper to the parasagittal fibers, the ischiorectal fat becomes evident; at this point the midline raphe becomes extremely thin and thus is easily violated. The levator muscle is located deeper to the ischiorectal fat. This muscle is also divided in the midline. Electrical stimulation of the levator muscle pushes the rectum forward. Stimulation of the muscle complex makes the anal dimple more prominent and elevates the skin toward the upper part of the pelvis. The crossing of the muscle complex fibers with the parasagittal muscle structures defines the anterior and posterior limits of the new anus. These limits can be determined most clearly with use of the electrical stimulator.

In boys with a rectum–urethral bulbar fistula, the bowel is very evident and prominent and extends toward the lower part of the incision. In boys with a rectoprostatic fistula, the rectum is much smaller and located much higher in the incision. The distal colostogram provides information that is valuable at this point for determining where the location of the rectum can be expected. In the case of a rectum–bladder neck fistula, the rectum is not visible through a posterior sagittal approach and should not be searched for.

Temporary silk sutures are placed in the posterior rectal wall for traction, and the rectum is opened exactly in the midline. The incision in the rectal wall is extended distally. As the rectum is being opened, more sutures are placed to hold the edge of the rectal wall and improve exposure

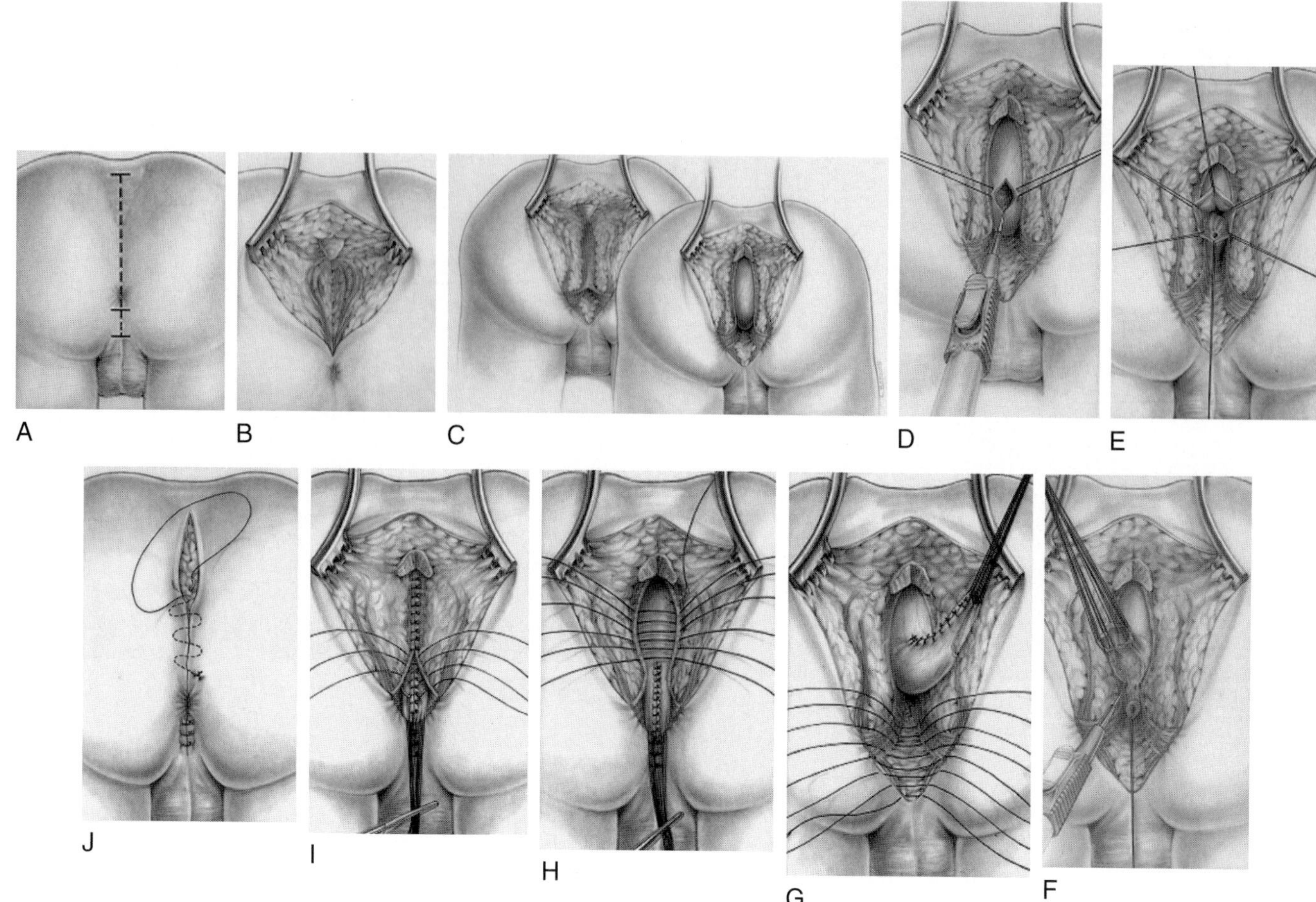

Figure 101–8 Essential steps for posterior sagittal anorectoplasty in male patients. *A*, Planned posterior sagittal incision. *B*, Posterior sagittal approach with the parasagittal fibers and ischiorectal fat split in the midline. *C*, Posterior rectal wall exposed. *D*, Posterior rectal wall opened in the midline. *E*, Posterior rectal wall opened until the rectourethral fistula is identified. *F*, Separation of the rectum from the posterior urethra with dissection above the fistula. *G*, The rectum fully mobilized and tapered. Sutures are placed anteriorly to close the perineal body. *H*, The rectum pulled through and placed within the limits of the sphincter mechanism. *I*, Closure of the levator and tacking of the posterior edge of muscle complex to the posterior rectal wall. *J*, Closure of the posterior sagittal incision and completed anoplasty.

of the rectal lumen. The incision must be extended distally until the fistula site is found (Fig. 101-9).

Because there is no plane of separation between the rectum and urethra, the surgeon must be extremely careful while separating the rectum from the urinary tract. Multiple 6-0 silk sutures are placed above the fistula site in a semicircular fashion (Fig. 101-10). These sutures allow the surgeon to exert uniform traction on the rectum while dissecting and separating it from the urethra. The dissection proceeds in the submucosal plane, particularly in the midline, for approximately 5 to 7 mm; both structures, the rectum and urethra, gradually separate and become independent. A single suture is placed at the fistula site so that it can easily be identified and closed later. Once the rectum is fully separated from the urinary tract, circumferential perirectal dissection is performed to gain enough rectal length to reach the perineum. To achieve this objective, the fascia that surrounds the rectum must be divided, including blood vessels and nerves attached to the rectum. While the surgeon is applying traction to the rectum with the sutures previously placed, the dissection continues in a circumferential manner. The vessels that hold the rectum are coagulated and divided until enough rectal length has been achieved. The rectum has an excellent intramural blood supply; even with a very high prostatic fistula, sufficient length can be obtained without making the rectum ischemic. When the rectal wall is injured, however, this blood supply is damaged and ischemia may occur. Therefore, every effort must be made to perform this dissection as close as possible to the rectal wall but without interfering with the intramural blood supply. Once enough length has been achieved to perform a tension-free bowel-to-skin anastomosis, the size of the rectum must be evaluated and compared with the available space. If necessary, the rectum can be tapered by removing part of its posterior wall. The rectum is then reconstructed by closing the posterior incision with two layers of long-term absorbable interrupted sutures. The anterior rectal wall in the portion that used to be attached to the posterior urethra may require a few stitches to reinforce the wall by bringing the seromuscular layer together. The urethral fistula is closed with interrupted sutures of absorbable material.

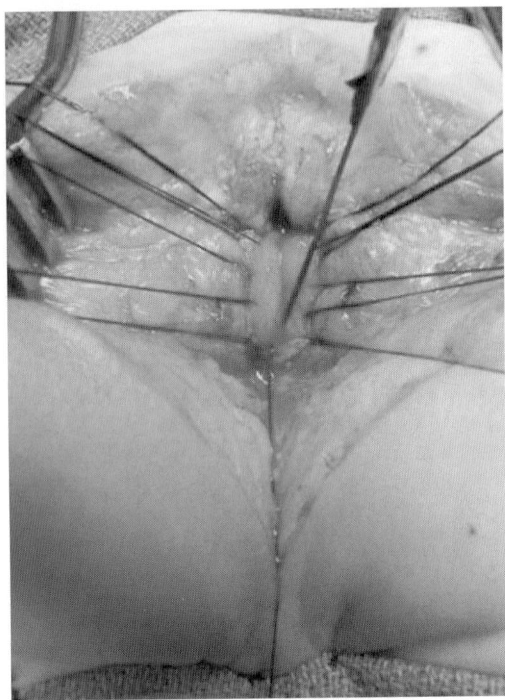

Figure 101-9 Operative view. A rectourethral fistula is seen; a metallic probe is passing through it.

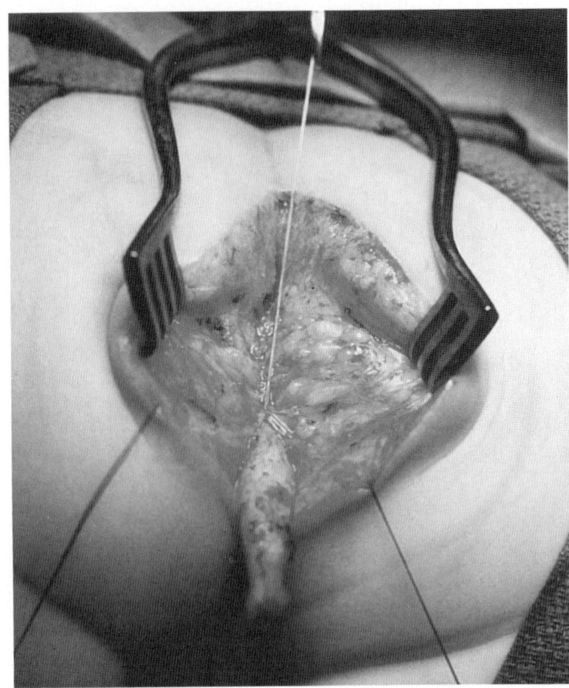

Figure 101-11 Levator muscle sutured behind the rectum.

The perineal body is reconstructed by bringing together the anterior limits of the external sphincter, which was previously marked with temporary silk sutures. The levator muscle must be sutured behind the rectum (Fig. 101-11; see also Fig. 101-8), and the posterior edge of the muscle complex must be sutured together in the midline while taking, with the same stitches, part of the posterior rectal wall to anchor the rectum and prevent prolapse (Fig. 101-12). The ischiorectal fossa fat and the subcutaneous tissue must be reapproximated so that no dead space is left. The skin is usually closed with a

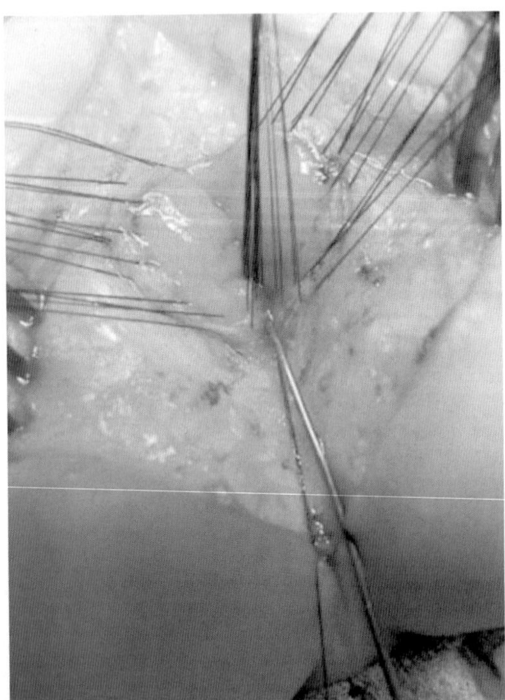

Figure 101-10 Operative view. Fine silk sutures are placed through the mucosa of the cephalad hemicircumference of the fistula.

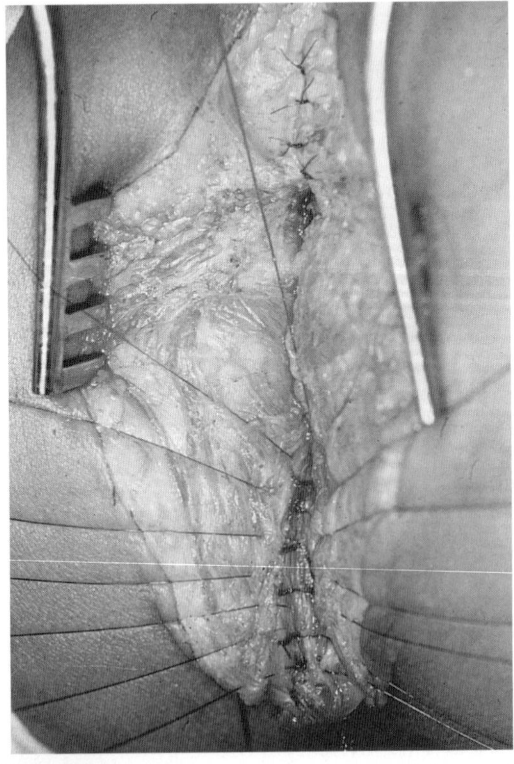

Figure 101-12 Sutures on the posterior edge of the muscle complex anchor the rectum.

subcuticular stitch. Anoplasty is performed by placing the rectum within the limits of the external sphincter with the use of interrupted long-term absorbable sutures.

Rectum–Bladder Neck Fistula

In patients with a rectum–bladder neck fistula, an abdominal approach via either laparoscopy or laparotomy, in addition to the posterior sagittal approach, is necessary to mobilize the rectum. The fistula is separated from the back of the bladder neck. Laparoscopy is applicable and well suited for this stage. The challenge is often mobilization of adequate rectal length to reach the perineum. Such mobilization, plus the fact that the rectum in this malformation frequently requires tapering, makes the laparoscopic stage technically demanding. For other lesions such as a rectourethral fistula, a laparoscopic approach has also been advocated with a technique that involves the use of a very minimal perineal incision.[22] This approach may have value, particularly with a high rectoprostatic fistula, which is often a challenge to mobilize through the posterior sagittal incision. Lower lesions, such as a rectum–urethral bulbar fistula, can be safely repaired with a posterior sagittal incision in a minimally invasive fashion without laparoscopic assistance.

Before beginning such an operation, the entire body surface from chest to toes is prepared so that the surgeon can work simultaneously in the abdomen and the perineum by flipping the patient from prone to supine without difficulty. The sphincteric mechanism is divided in the midline. A rubber tube is placed in front of the levator muscle behind the urinary tract in the presacral space. This tube is placed within the limits of the muscle complex and in front of the sacrum to simulate the presence of the rectum. The entire sphincteric mechanism is reconstructed around the rubber tube. The patient is turned face up and the abdomen is entered via either laparoscopy or laparotomy (Fig. 101-13B). The sigmoid is identified and dissected down to the bladder neck (Fig. 101-13A). The neck is usually located approximately 2 cm below the peritoneal floor and therefore requires minimal pelvic dissection. No endorectal type of dissection is needed. It is very important to remember that the vas deferens and ureters run very close to the rectum; thus, the dissection must be carried out as close as possible to the rectal wall. The rectum narrows very rapidly and opens into the bladder neck in a T-shaped manner. It is very easy to separate the rectum from the urinary tract because the fistula forms less of a common wall the higher the malformation. The rectum is divided at its most distal part, and the fistula is closed with absorbable suture. The rubber tube is situated in the retroperitoneum, and the size of the rectum can be compared with the size of the tube to determine whether rectal tapering is necessary. The bowel is then anchored to the rubber tube and pulled down, along with the rectum, to reach the perineum.

In this type of very high defect, mobilization of the rectum is sometimes limited by branches of the inferior mesenteric vessels. Surgeons have traditionally been advised to divide the inferior mesenteric vessels at their origin from the aorta. This technique is contraindicated in these patients since this is often the only blood supply

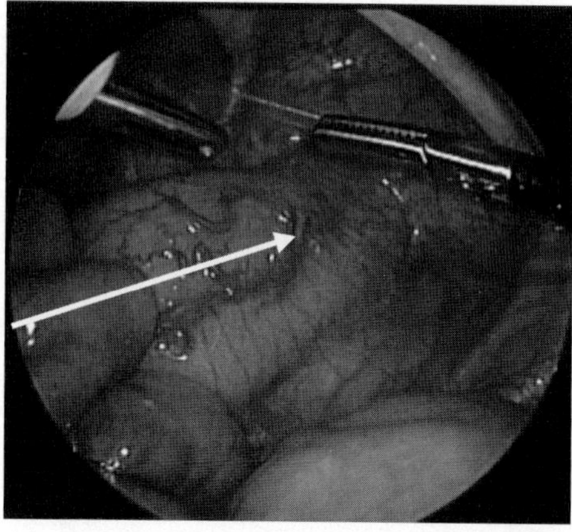

A

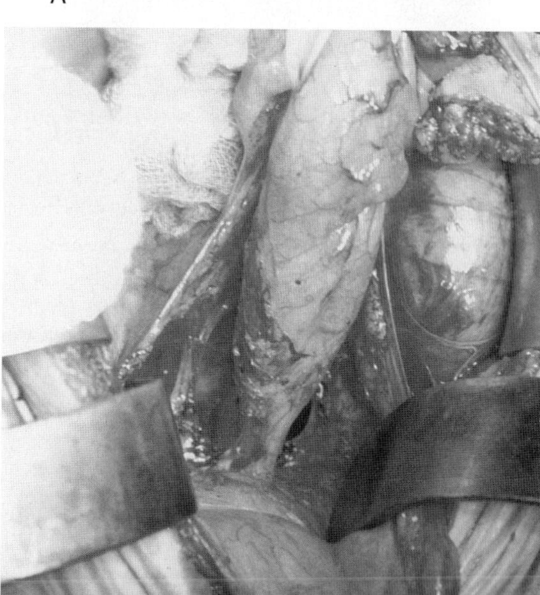

B

Figure 101–13 Operative aspects showing the rectosigmoid ending at the bladder neck. *A*, Laparoscopic view. *B*, View from laparotomy.

of the rectosigmoid because the opening of the colostomy frequently interferes with the continuity of the arcade that connects the middle colic vessels with the inferior mesenteric vessels. Therefore, the blood supply of the distal part of the rectum may depend solely on the patency of the inferior mesenteric vessels. Preservation of the main trunks is crucial to preserve the intramural blood supply of the rectum (Fig. 101-14). In extremely high defects, the rectum can be elongated by rectoplasty. Anoplasty should be performed as previously described. Tacking of the rectum to the muscle complex is particularly important because these patients have poor pelvic musculature and are particularly prone to prolapse.

Imperforate Anus without a Fistula

In patients with an imperforate anus and no fistula, the blind end of the rectum is located at the same level as in a patient with a bulbar urethral fistula. However, because the rectum is still intimately attached to the posterior

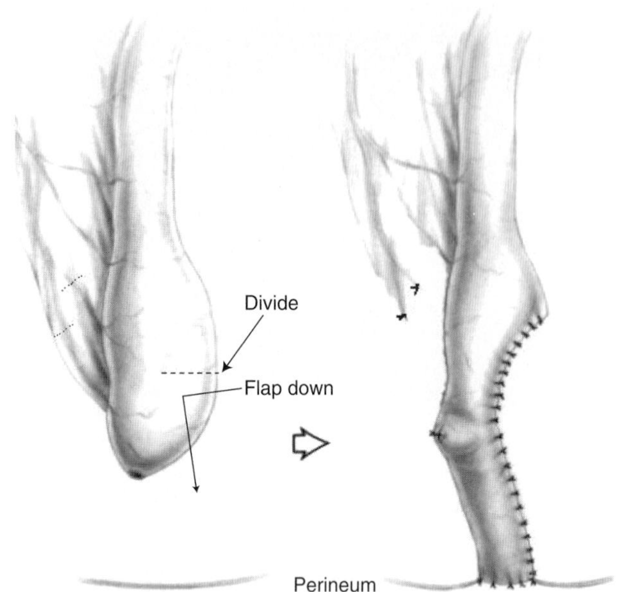

Figure 101–14 Ligation of the peripheral branches of the inferior mesenteric vessels with preservation of the main trunks. Rectoplasty is performed to gain extra length.

urethra, separation from the urethra requires careful dissection. The rest of the repair is performed as described for rectourethral fistulas.

Rectal Atresia and Stenosis

Repair of rectal atresia and stenosis is straightforward. The goal of this procedure is to connect the blind dilated end of the rectum proximally with the anal canal distally. Both structures are usually separated by a few millimeters of fibrous tissue. The rectum must be sufficiently mobilized to allow the performance of an end-to-end anastomosis to the anal canal. The wound is then closed by reconstructing all the muscle structures, as previously described.

Posterior Sagittal Anorectoplasty for Anomalies in Females

Vestibular Fistula

The complexity of this defect is frequently underestimated. Patients with a vestibular fistula are born with the potential for bowel control. Thus, every effort should be made to give these patients the best opportunity to undergo successful reconstruction with a single operation. Wound dehiscence and infection may compromise the final functional result. A protective colostomy minimizes these complications.

If the surgeon has adequate experience with this malformation, a primary repair can be performed in the newborn period. Occasionally, such patients escape detection in the newborn period and undergo surgery several months later in life. A primary repair without colostomy under these circumstances can also be performed. However, to avoid a perineal infection, meticulous technique, excellent bowel preparation, 1 week without oral intake, and parenteral nutrition postoperatively are vital.

With the patient in the prone position, a midline incision is performed, but it is not usually necessary to extend the incision as high as the middle portion of the sacrum. The midline incision continues around the fistula into the vestibule; multiple 5-0 sutures are placed circumferentially at the fistula site. While traction is placed on these sutures, the rectum is dissected in a circumferential manner. The posterior rectal wall can easily be identified, and the dissection must start from the posterior aspect and be extended laterally. The last step, separation of the rectum from the vagina, is the most delicate part of the dissection. The common wall between the rectum and vagina in this kind of defect is long and extremely thin. Branches of the hemorrhoidal vessels are usually found on the lateral aspects of the rectum, and by taking these vessels, the rectum is mobilized as previously described to gain enough length to perform a tension-free bowel-to-skin anastomosis. The limits of the sphincteric mechanism are electrically determined and marked with temporary silk sutures. The perineal body is then reconstructed by bringing together the anterior limit of the external sphincter. The anterior edge of the muscle complex is reapproximated as described previously for males. The levator muscle is not usually exposed and thus does not need to be reconstructed. The muscle complex must, however, be reconstructed posterior to the rectum by taking bites of the posterior rectal wall. The anoplasty and wound closure are performed as described for males.

For the extremely unusual case of a vaginal fistula, the technique is the same except that the rectum requires more mobilization to reach the perineum.

Persistent Cloaca

This female malformation is managed by a variation of posterior sagittal anorectoplasty. It is considered separately because of its complexity. Repair of a persistent cloaca presents a serious challenge. It requires a very delicate, meticulous technique, as well as creativity, imagination, and a resourceful, experienced surgeon. Repair of this defect has three main goals: achievement of bowel control, urinary control, and sexual function. Because a spectrum of defects exist, these goals are achieved in some cases; in others, however, the defect is repaired anatomically but the patients are left with functional sequelae that require extensive medical assistance to provide a good quality of life. During surgical exploration, the surgeon must be prepared to find bizarre anatomic arrangements of the rectum, vagina, and urinary tract (Fig. 101-15A to C). A long midsagittal incision is made that extends from the middle portion of the sacrum through the external sphincter and down into the single perineal opening.

Before undertaking repair of a cloaca, the surgeon should perform an endoscopic study with the specific purpose of determining the length of the common channel. There are two well-characterized groups of patients with a cloaca.[50] These two groups represent different technical challenges and must be recognized preoperatively. The first consists of patients with a common channel shorter than 3 cm. Fortunately, this group represents the majority of those with cloacas. These patients can usually be repaired via a posterior sagittal approach alone, without laparotomy.

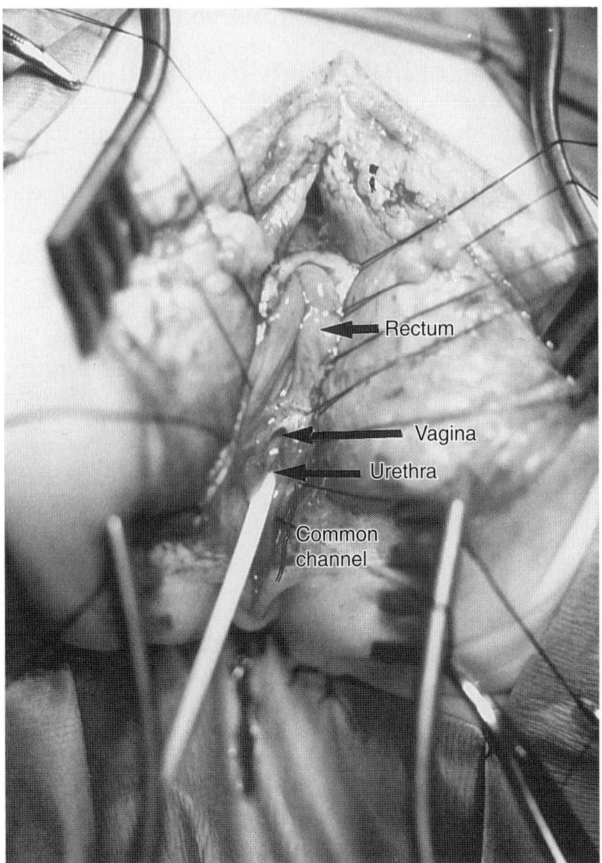

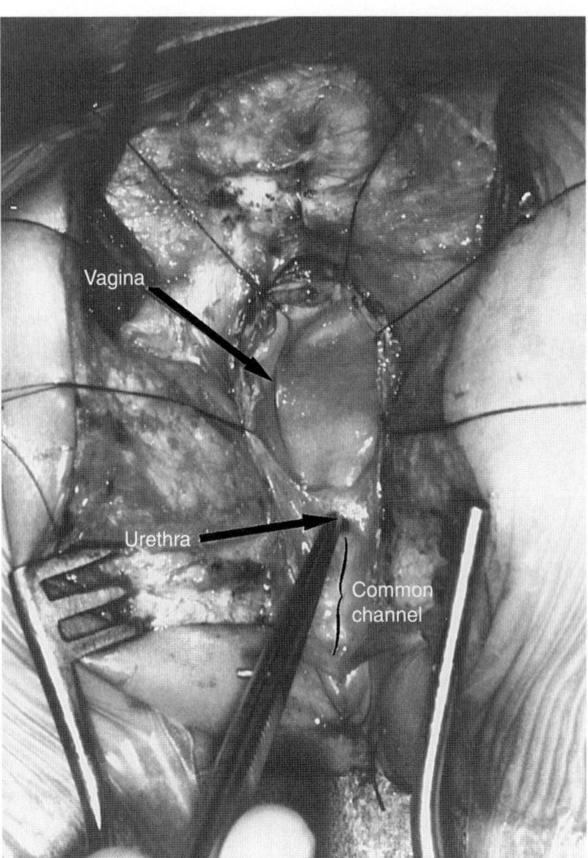

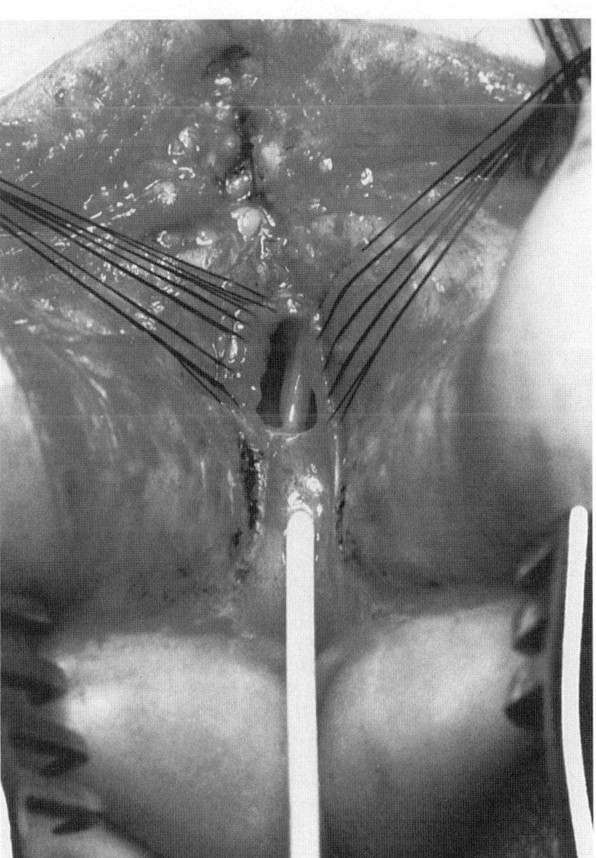

Figure 101–15 *A,* A typical cloaca with a common channel of about 2.5 cm. *B,* A cloaca with a very large vagina (hydrocolpos). The rectum opens higher in the vagina and therefore is not seen here. *C,* Cloaca with a vaginal septum. The rectal opening is located in the posterior aspect of the vaginal septum.

The second group consists of patients with longer common channels. These patients usually need laparotomy, followed by a decision-making process that requires experience and special training in urology; this group should be cared for at centers with special dedication to the repair of these defects.

Cloacas with a Common Channel Shorter than 3 cm

The incision extends from the middle portion of the sacrum down to the single perineal orifice. All of the sphincter mechanism is divided in the midline. The first structure that the surgeon will find after division of the sphincter mechanism is the rectum. The rectum is opened in the midline and silk stitches are placed along the edges of the posterior rectal wall. The incision is extended distally through the posterior wall of the common channel. The entire common channel is exposed to allow confirmation of the length of the common channel under direct vision (Fig. 101-16A). The rectum is then separated from the vagina (Fig. 101-16B). This is performed in the same way as for repair of a rectovestibular fistula because the rectum and vagina share the same common wall already described. In patients with a vaginal septum, the rectum must be searched for at the posterior aspect of this septum.

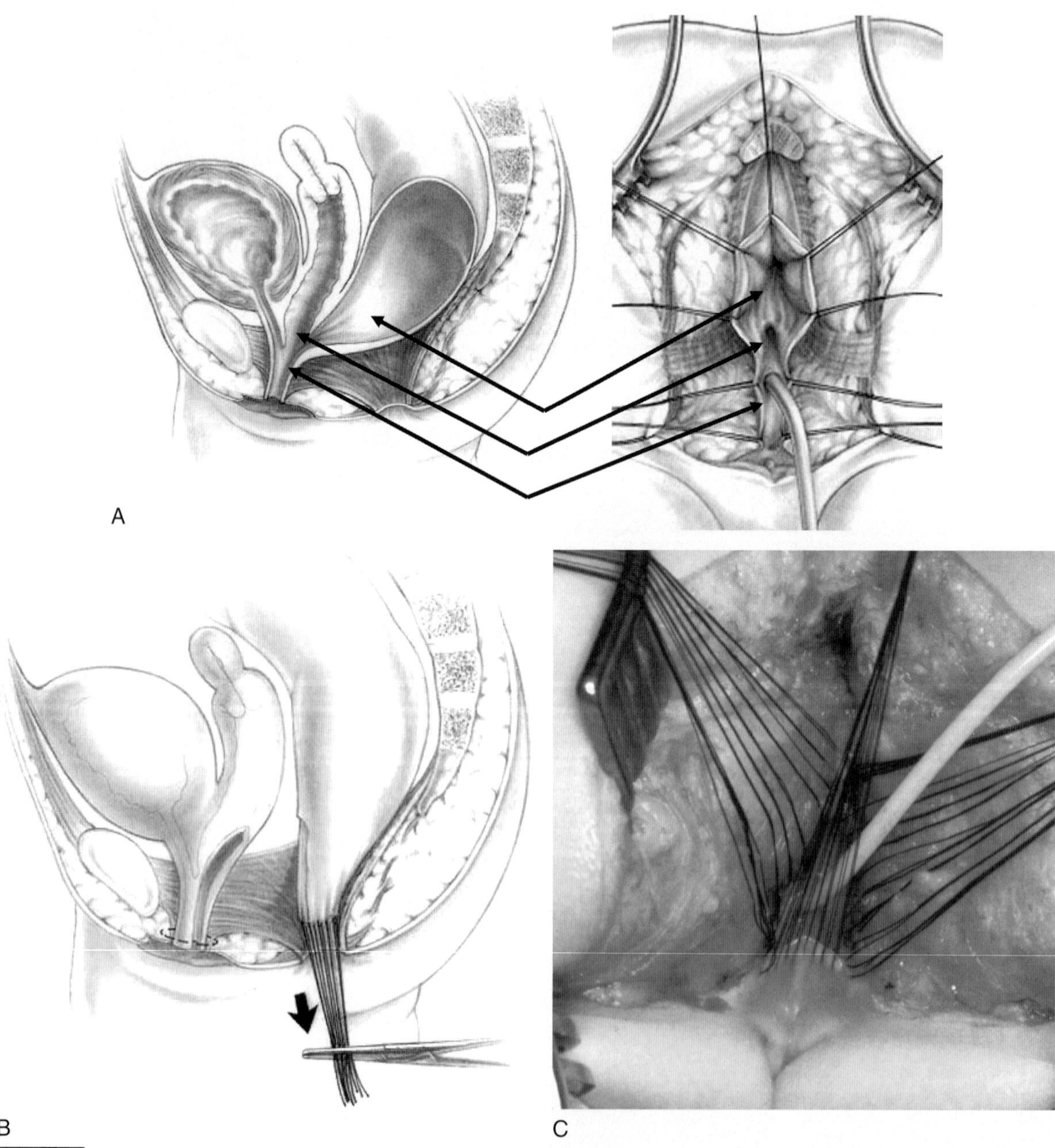

Figure 101–16 Total urogenital mobilization (cloaca with a short common channel, <3 cm). *A*, The incision extends down to the single perineal orifice. *B*, The rectum is separated from the urogenital sinus. *C*, Sutures are placed around the urogenital sinus for uniform traction.

Continued

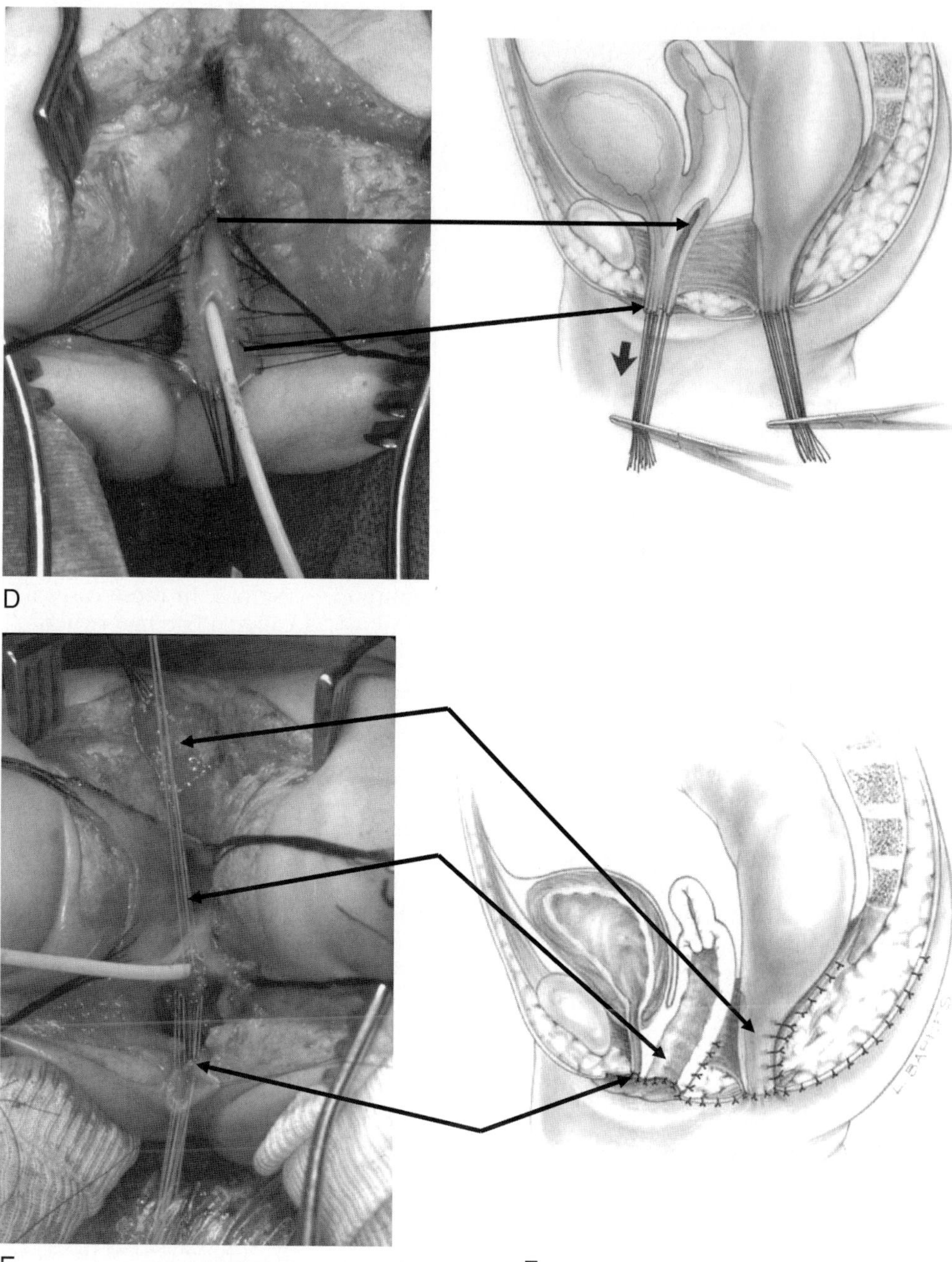

Figure 101–16 *Continued*
D, The urogenital sinus is mobilized. *E*, The urogenital sinus is sutured adjacent to the clitoris. *F*, Completion of the procedure.

Once the rectum has been completely separated from the vagina, a maneuver called total urogenital mobilization is used.[47] In the past, the vagina was separated from the urinary tract, which was a technically challenging maneuver associated with significant morbidity. Total urogenital mobilization consists of mobilization of both the vagina and urethra as a unit without separating them. After the rectum has been separated, multiple silk stitches are placed through the edges of the vagina and the common channel to apply uniform traction on the urogenital sinus (Fig. 101-16C). Another series of fine stitches are placed across the urogenital sinus approximately 5 mm proximal to the clitoris. The urogenital sinus is transected between the last row of silk stitches and the clitoris. The dissection takes advantage of the fact that there is a natural plane between it and the pubis. Very rapidly and in a bloodless field, one can reach the upper edge of the pubis. There, a fibrous, avascular structure that gives support to the vagina and bladder is identified. This structure is called the suspensory ligament of the urethra and bladder. This ligament is divided, which immediately provides significant mobilization (between 2 and 3 cm) of the urogenital complex (Fig. 101-16D). One can then dissect the lateral and dorsal walls of the vagina to gain an extra 5 to 10 mm. This dissection is enough to repair about 60% of all cloacas and is a reproducible maneuver. It has the additional advantage of preserving an excellent blood supply to both the urethra and vagina and places the urethral opening in a visible location to facilitate intermittent catheterization when necessary.

It also provides a smooth urethra that can easily be catheterized. What used to be the common channel is divided in the midline to form two lateral flaps that are sutured to the skin to create the new labia (Fig. 101-16E). The vaginal edges are then mobilized to reach the skin to create an excellent introitus. The limits of the sphincter are electrically determined. The perineal body is reconstructed by bringing together the anterior limit of the sphincter. The rectum is placed within the limits of the sphincter in the manner previously described (Fig. 101-16F). Patients can eat the same day, and the pain is usually easily controlled. Patients are discharged 48 hours after surgery.

Cloacas with a Common Channel Longer than 3 cm

When endoscopy shows that the patient has a long common channel, the surgeon must be prepared to face a very significant technical challenge. Surgeons who have limited experience or lack specialized urologic training should ask for help from someone with that kind of experience. Being a pediatric urologist does not necessarily imply familiarity with the technical challenges of cloacas; special training is necessary to be familiar with this problem.

Patients with a long common channel should receive a total-body preparation because it is likely that laparotomy will be required. The rectum is separated from the vagina and urethra via a posterior sagittal incision or via laparotomy when it is located very high. The presence of a very long common channel (more than 5 cm) indicates that there is no way that total urogenital mobilization will be sufficient to repair the malformation, and therefore it is advisable to leave the common channel in place, which can be used as urethra for intermittent catheterization. In this situation, the vagina should be partially separated from the urinary tract by placing multiple 6-0 silk sutures through the vaginal wall to try to create a plane of dissection between the vagina and the urinary tract. This is a very delicate, meticulous, and tedious maneuver. With this dissection one can achieve separation of the vagina from the urinary tract for approximately 2.0 cm. The rest of the separation must be completed through the abdomen.

A midline laparotomy is recommended, the bladder is opened in the midline, and feeding tubes are placed into the ureters to protect them. In these types of malformations there is an extensive common wall between vagina and bladder. Both ureters run through that common wall, and therefore during separation of the vagina from the urinary tract, the ureters must sometimes be skeletonized and thus need to be protected. The surgeon must be familiar with the different techniques of ureteral reimplantation because these patients frequently require that operation during the same procedure.

Once in the abdomen, the patency of the müllerian structures are investigated by passing a No. 3 feeding tube through the fimbriae of the fallopian tubes and injecting saline. If one of the systems is not patent, the atretic müllerian structure should be excised, with great care taken to avoid damage to the blood supply of the ovary. When both müllerian structures are atretic, we advise that they be left in place. The patient must be monitored closely and further investigated with ultrasound when she nears puberty.

Separation of the vagina or vaginas from the urinary tract is the most tedious and technically demanding step of the procedure; usually, both structures share a very long common wall located in an area that is not easily accessible. The dissection is performed with the bladder opened and with catheters inserted in the ureters. Once the separation has been completed, the surgeon has to make decisions based on the specific anatomic findings.

Vaginal Switch Maneuver

A specific group of patients are born with hydrocolpos and two hemivaginas. The hemivaginas are very large and the two hemiuteri are very separated, the distance between them being longer than the vertical length of both hemivaginas. In these cases it is ideal to perform a maneuver called a "vaginal switch" (Fig. 101-17).

One of the hemiuteri and the ipsilateral fallopian tube is resected with particular care taken to preserve the blood supply of the ovary. The blood supply of the hemivagina of that particular side is sacrificed. The blood supply of the contralateral hemivagina is preserved and most of the time provides good blood supply for both hemivaginas. The vaginal septum is resected, and both hemivaginas are tubularized into a single vagina by taking advantage of the long lateral dimension of both hemivaginas together. Then what used to be the dome of the hemivagina where the hemiuterus was resected is turned down to the perineum. This is a useful maneuver that can be performed only when the anatomic characteristics fulfill the requirements described here.

Vaginal Replacement

In a patient with a small vagina or vaginas or in the rare case of an absent vagina, it must be replaced. In such cases the choices are rectum, colon, or small bowel. When the patient has internal genitalia or a cuff of vagina or cervix, the upper part of the bowel used for replacement must be sutured to the small vaginal cuff. When the patient has no internal genitalia (no vagina and no uterus), a vagina is created and left with its upper portion blind; it is used only for sexual purposes, not for reproduction.

Rectum: This form of vaginal replacement is feasible only in patients who have a megarectum that is large enough to be able to divide it longitudinally into a portion with its own blood supply that will represent a new vagina and another portion with enough circumference to reconstruct an adequately sized rectum (Fig. 101-18). The blood supply of the rectum will be provided transmurally from branches of the inferior mesenteric vessels. It can also be done in patients with a rectosigmoid long enough to allow the distal portion to be used as a new vagina with its own blood supply and the upper portion to be pulled down as a new rectum.

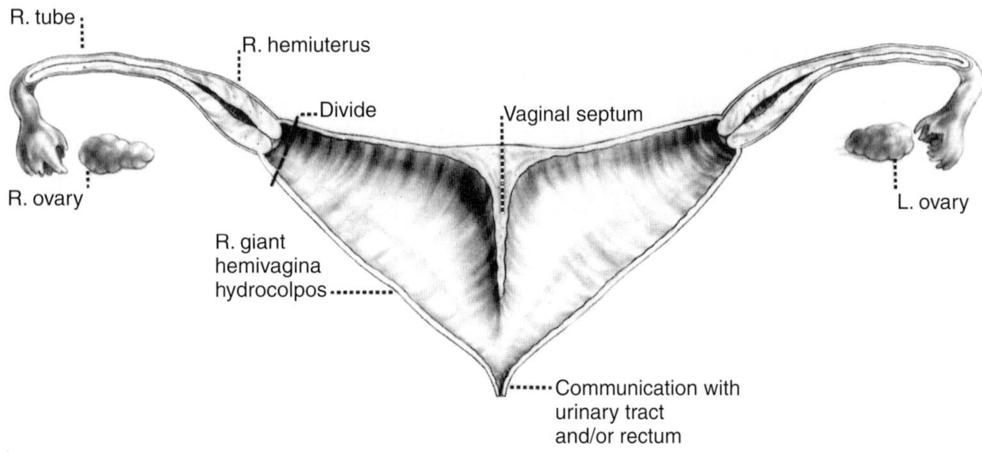

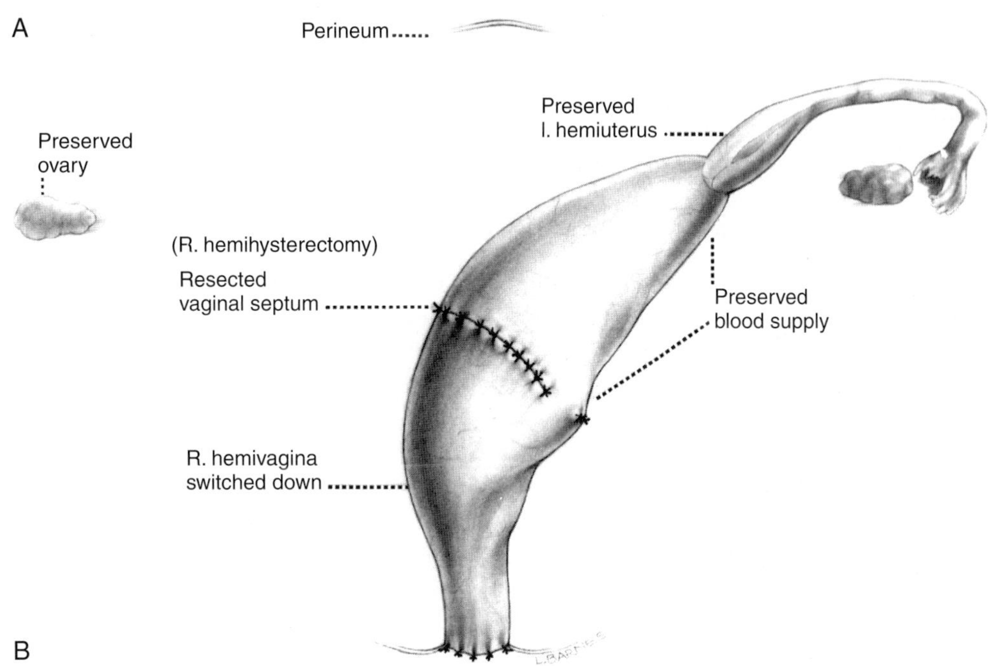

Figure 101–17 *A*, Very large hemivaginas with a vaginal septum and long common channel. *B*, Vaginal switch maneuver.

Colon: The colon seems to be the ideal substitute to replace the vagina. However, sometimes the location of the colostomy interferes with this type of reconstruction. When available, the sigmoid colon is preferable. One must take the most mobile portion of the sigmoid colon in order to have a substitute with a long mesentery (Fig. 101-19).

Small Bowel: When the colon is not available, the most mobile portion of the small bowel is used for vaginal reconstruction. The mesentery of the small bowel is longer in an area located approximately 15 cm proximal to the ileocecal valve. This is the best portion of the small bowel for vaginal replacement. A portion of this ileum is isolated and pulled down while preserving its blood supply (Fig. 101-20).

In the highest type of cloaca one may find two little hemivaginas attached to the bladder neck or even to the trigone of the bladder. In these cases, the rectum also opens in the trigone (Fig. 101-21). Separation of these structures is done abdominally. Unfortunately, when the separation is completed, the patient is frequently left with no bladder neck or a very severely damaged one. At that point the surgeon must have enough experience to make a decision whether to reconstruct the bladder neck or close it permanently. In the first situation, most patients will require intermittent catheterization to empty the bladder, and there is no guarantee that the bladder neck reconstruction will work. In the second situation (permanent closure of the bladder neck), a vesicostomy is created, and the patient will require a continent diversion type of procedure and sometimes bladder augmentation,

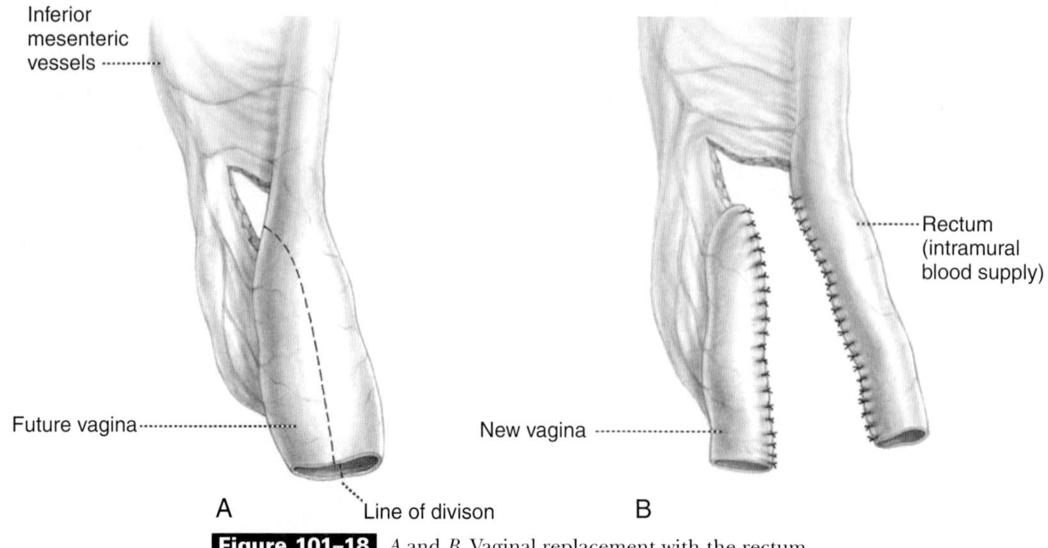

Figure 101-18 *A* and *B*, Vaginal replacement with the rectum.

done at the age of urinary continence (3 to 4 years old). In this particular type of malformation, the patient usually also needs a vaginal replacement, which should be performed in one of the ways previously described.

At the time of colostomy closure, endoscopy should be performed to be sure that the repair is intact. If the cloaca repair did not require laparotomy, the time of colostomy closure is the opportunity to investigate the patency of the müllerian structures.

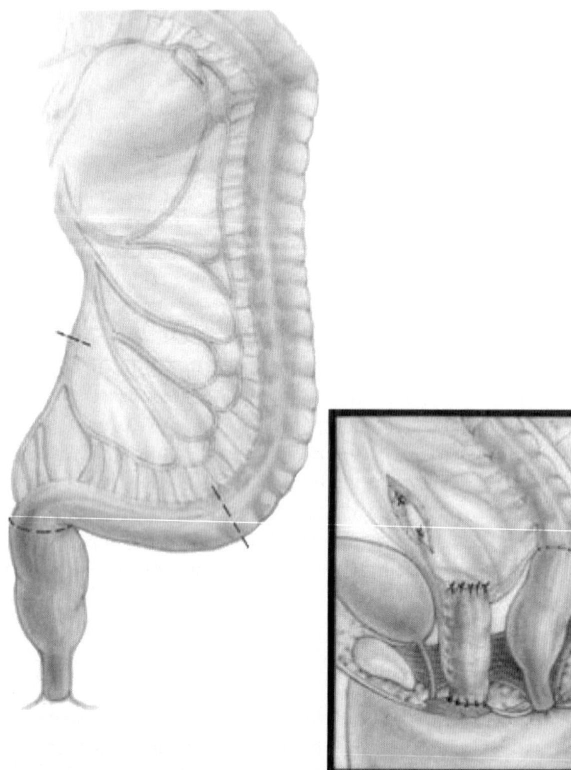

Figure 101-19 Vaginal replacement with the sigmoid colon.

General Principles of Postoperative Care

In the absence of a laparotomy, oral feedings may begin in a matter of hours. Antibiotics are given for 48 hours. In males who had a rectourethral fistula, the urinary catheter should be left in place for 7 days. In patients who have undergone cloaca repair, the urethral catheter is left in place for at least 3 weeks. If a laparotomy was required for the repair, a suprapubic cystostomy is sometimes used, and in certain cases a vesicostomy is created.

A dilatation program is begun 2 weeks after surgery. The anus is calibrated and a dilator that fits snugly is initially used to dilate the anus twice a day. Every week, the size of the dilator is increased by one unit until the desired size is reached. The optimal size of dilator is shown in Table 101-2. Once the correct size is reached, the colostomy is closed. Dilatations must continue after closure. Once the dilator can be inserted easily, the schedule is reduced to once a day for 1 month, twice a week for 1 month, once a week for 1 month, and then once a week for 3 months.

After the colostomy is closed, the patient may have multiple bowel movements and perineal excoriation may develop. A constipating diet may be helpful in the treatment of this problem. After several weeks the number of bowel movements decreases, and most patients will suffer from constipation. After 6 months, a more regular

TABLE 101-2 Anal Dilatation Program

Patient Age	Hegar Dilator
1-4 mo	Size No. 12
4-8 mo	Size No. 13
8-12 mo	Size No. 14
1-3 yr	Size No. 15
3-12 yr	Size No. 16
>12 yr	Size No. 17

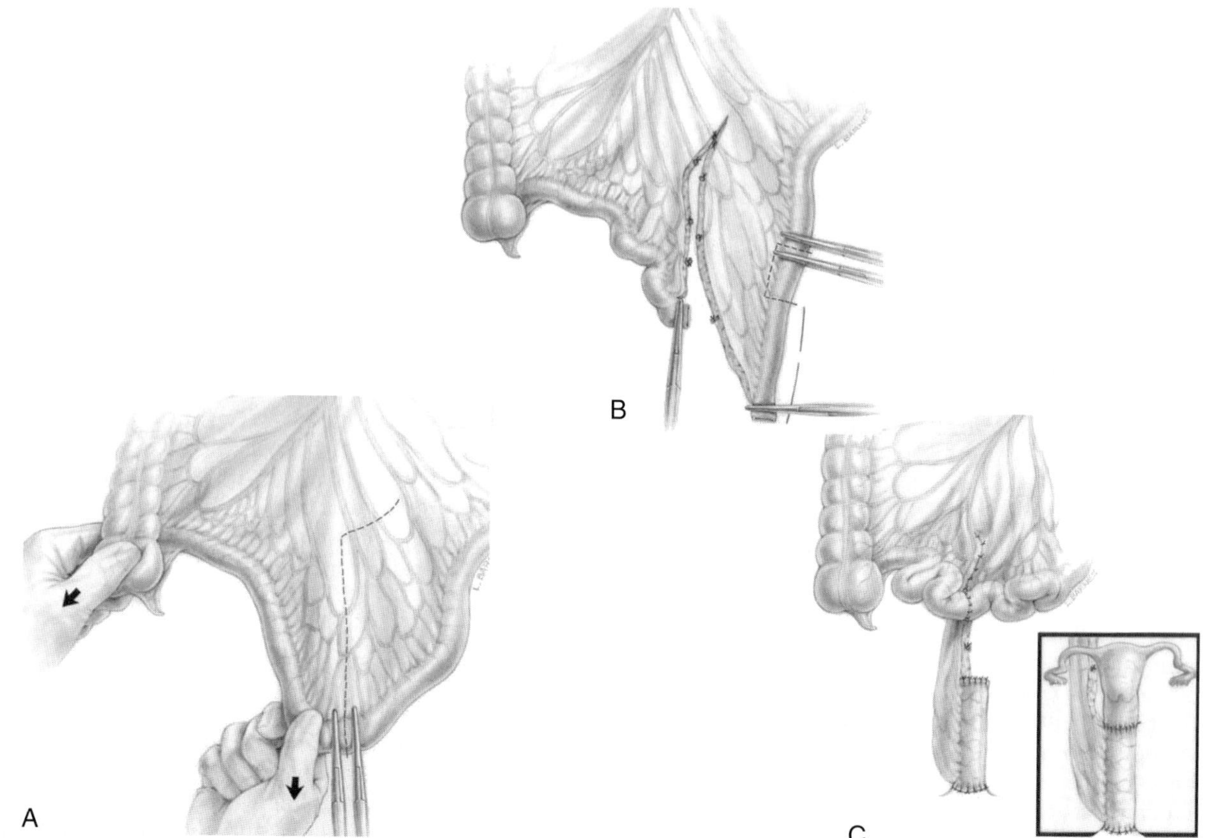

Figure 101-20 Vaginal replacement with small bowel. *A* and *B*, Using the portion of ileum with the longest mesentery. *C*, Pulling the small bowel down as a neovagina (the *insert* shows an anastomosis to the upper part of the vagina).

bowel movement pattern develops. A patient who has one to three bowel movements per day, remains clean between bowel movements, and shows evidence of a feeling of pushing during bowel movements has a good bowel movement pattern and generally has a good prognosis.

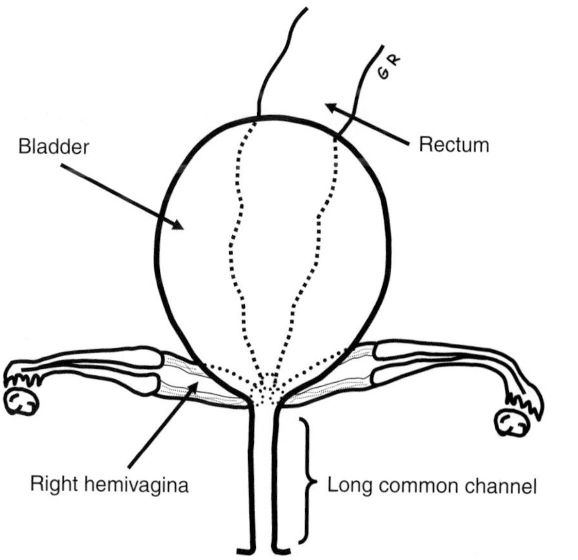

Figure 101-21 Extremely long common channel—hemivaginas and rectum connected to the bladder neck.

This type of patient is trainable. A patient with multiple bowel movements or one who is passing stool constantly without showing any signs of sensation or pushing typically has a poor functional prognosis.

Patients after cloaca repair usually keep the Foley catheter in place for 2 to 3 weeks. If the urethral meatus is not perfectly visible because of swelling, we prefer to retain the Foley catheter. Once we are able to see the urethral orifice, the Foley catheter can be removed. The baby is watched to see whether she is capable of emptying her bladder. If she cannot pass urine, we can teach the caregiver to pass the catheter intermittently. In patients with a very long common channel, a suprapubic tube is left in place, and 1 month after surgery a suprapubic cystogram is performed; patients then start with clamping of the tube and measuring residual urine, which is an indicator of the efficiency of bladder function. The suprapubic tube remains in place until there is evidence of good bladder function or the caregiver learns to catheterize the bladder when indicated.

OUTCOMES

Complications

All the usual postoperative complications may occur after surgery of this nature. In addition, some specific problems develop both early in the postoperative course and later on.

Wound infection and retraction are known to occur. When the infection affects only the superficial layers of the wound, is not accompanied by dehiscence of the structures pulled through, and is promptly treated, it is likely that no functional sequelae will result. On the other hand, infection accompanied by dehiscence may reach catastrophic proportions and leave sequelae that include incontinence (with a predictably good prognosis), strictures, acquired atresias, recurrent fistulas, and severe pelvic fibrosis. At our institution we have reoperated on more than 200 patients who suffered these kinds of complications and were referred to us for a secondary procedure. In our series, minor infections with no sequelae developed in 23 patients, retraction of the rectum occurred in 6 patients, and retraction of the vagina occurred in 8.

Catastrophic infections and dehiscence have occurred mainly in patients operated on primarily, without a colostomy. Therefore, although we recognize the benefit of the trend to operate earlier, primarily, and without a colostomy, we also insist that a colostomy is a very valuable adjunct in the management of these defects. Every surgeon must make a decision regarding this issue based on personal experience.

It is very difficult to determine the precise causes of these complications; however, we know that the main contributing factors are obvious fecal contamination, ischemia, and suture line tension.

Rectal or vaginal strictures (or both) are usually due to the previously mentioned complications, although they may occur independently. An anal dilatation program is recommended to avoid strictures; however, these maneuvers prevent only minor, ring-like strictures. Difficult anal dilatations usually reflect a major problem related to ischemia that will result in a long narrow stricture or even acquired atresia. We still recommend the use of anal dilatations, particularly in patients with good sphincters that maintain the anus closed postoperatively.

Rectal mucosal prolapse is not uncommon after reconstruction. The rate of prolapse after posterior sagittal anorectoplasty in the authors' series was 3.8%.[6] Mucosal prolapse is uncommon after posterior sagittal anorectoplasty, probably because of several key technical steps: (1) tacking of the posterior rectal wall to the posterior edge of the muscle complex, (2) tapering a dilated rectum if necessary, and (3) performing the anoplasty under tension so that after the sutures of the anoplasty are cut, the rectum retracts slightly with no mucosa being visible. Mucosal prolapse is managed by trimming and is performed when prolapse causes excess mucus production or ulceration or interferes with anal sensation.

A review of patients operated on at other institutions has revealed significant urologic injuries in male patients who underwent attempted repair of anorectal malformations. The posterior sagittal approach, when performed without a good preoperative distal colostogram, was the most important source of these complications. Urethral, ureteral, vas deferens, and seminal vesicle injuries can occur. Postoperative neurogenic bladder in male patients who undergo a technically correct operation for the treatment of anorectal malformations must be extremely unusual because it happens only in patients with a very abnormal sacrum.[8] Otherwise, it may reflect a poor surgical technique with denervation of the bladder and bladder neck during the repair.[29]

Constipation is the most common partially preventable sequela after surgical repair of anorectal malformations. The lower the malformation, the more likely the development of constipation. Megarectosigmoid leads to constipation, and constipation that is not properly managed can lead to megarectosigmoid. A vicious cycle can thus result and lead to overflow pseudoincontinence. Patients appear to be incontinent, but if their constipation is managed appropriately, they become continent. Occasionally, such patients benefit from sigmoid resection to reduce their laxative requirement.[14,48,52]

We have evidence indicating that a dilated rectosigmoid preoperatively will result in severe constipation. Therefore, every effort must be made to maintain a collapsed and clean bowel from the moment the baby is born. Transverse colostomies left for a long period lead to severe megarectosigmoid. Loop colostomies may also contribute to distal fecal impaction, dilation, and subsequent constipation.

Continence

It is not clear how many patients born with an imperforate anus have the capacity for normal bowel control. The results of the various types of surgery are difficult to assess if the child's original potential is unknown.[41] Long-term studies suggest that good bowel control is usually achieved in about 75% of patients.

The results obtained by the authors according to the type of abnormality are shown in Tables 101-3 through 101-6. Patients with low anomalies and rectal atresia have done well; those with high lesions have done less well.

Future continence may be predicted within months of stoma closure. The presence of one to three bowel movements per day with no soiling in between is associated with a favorable outcome and is considered a good bowel movement pattern. Infant behavior indicating that defecation is imminent, coupled with straining, suggests

TABLE 101-3 Constipation and Type of Defect

Defect	No. of Patients with Defect	Patients with Constipation *n*	%
Vestibular fistula	101	64	60.3
Bulbar fistula	91	53	58.3
Perineal fistula	53	30	56.6
Imperforate anus without fistula	40	22	55
Atresia or stenosis	8	4	50
Prostatic fistula	94	42	44.7
Cloaca common channel <3 cm	87	33	37.9
Cloaca common channel >3 cm	45	17	37.7
Bladder neck fistula	45	7	15.5
Vaginal fistula	45	0	
Total	568	269	47.4

TABLE 101-4 Voluntary Bowel Movement and Type of Defect

Defect	No. of Patients with Defect	Patients with Voluntary Bowel Movement	
		n	%
Atresia or stenosis	8	8	100
Perineal fistula	41	41	100
Vestibular fistula	98	90	91.8
Imperforate anus without fistula	35	30	86.7
Bulbar fistula	83	68	81.9
Vaginal fistula	4	3	75
Prostatic fistula	72	53	73.6
Cloaca common channel <3 cm	73	53	72.6
Cloaca common channel >3 cm	41	17	41.5
Bladder neck fistula	29	9	31.0
Total	484	372	76.9

that the sensory side of continence is intact, which is associated with a better outcome. Establishing the prognosis as early as possible is vital to avoid parents' false expectations.

All patients with anorectal malformations, regardless of the complexity of the defect, can and must be kept completely dry of urine and clean of stool after the age of 3, either because they achieve bowel and urinary control or because we implement a program to keep them artificially dry and clean.

The bowel management program uses enemas to ensure adequate emptying for a 24-hour period of cleanliness. With the rational administration of bowel irrigation, diet, and drugs, most patients, including those with severe fecal incontinence, are able to remain clean for 24 hours.[49] Only patients with severe diarrhea secondary to an absent or a short colon have been candidates for a permanent colostomy.

Patients suffering from fecal incontinence are evaluated and classified into those with constipation and those with increased motility (tendency to have diarrhea). In the first group, bowel irrigation must be aggressive. A rubber tube is usually introduced high into the sigmoid to clean the bowel. This program takes advantage of the decreased bowel motility in constipated patients; they remain clean for the next 24 hours. No laxatives or diets are given as part of this protocol. The second group (patients who suffer from increased bowel motility because of loss of the rectal reservoir) require a constipating diet, medication to decrease bowel motility, and a program of colonic irrigation.

The treatment is adjusted by trial and error over a period of 1 week, with 95% of patients remaining clean and having an acceptable social life. Bowel management is started when the patient has to go to school and all classmates are already wearing regular underwear. Most patients and parents are very happy with the implementation of this program. However, when the patient reaches the age of 7 to 12 years or sometimes younger, more independence is generally needed.

At that point, creation of a continent appendicostomy (Malone procedure) is recommended.[34,59] This operation creates a communication between the abdominal wall and the cecum through the appendix of the patient; the valve mechanism created allows catheterization of the cecum but prevents leakage of stool. Patients are able to administer their own enema while sitting on the toilet. The operation consists of plicating the cecum around the native appendix of the patient and exteriorizing the appendix in the deepest part of the umbilicus to make it inconspicuous. A significant number of patients do not have an appendix. In such cases we make an appendix with a tubularized flap of the cecum and then plicate the cecum around it. The stoma is also exteriorized through the umbilicus. Most patients who have undergone this operation express a great deal of satisfaction.

Our experience with biofeedback has not been as encouraging as has been reported by others.[43]

TABLE 101-5 Soiling and Type of Defect

Defect	No. of Patients with Defect	Soiling and Type of Defect	
		n	%
Perineal fistula	45	4	8.9
Atresia or stenosis	8	2	25
Vestibular fistula	101	37	36.6
Imperforate anus without fistula	37	18	48.6
Bulbar fistula	89	48	53.9
Cloaca common channel <3 cm	77	47	61.0
Prostatic fistula	88	68	77.3
Vaginal fistula	5	4	80
Cloaca common channel >3 cm	40	35	87.5
Bladder neck fistula	41	36	87.8
Total	531	299	56.3

TABLE 101-6 Totally Continent* Patients and Type of Defect

Defect	No. of Patients with Defect	Totally Continent	
		n	%
Perineal fistula	41	36	87.8
Atresia or stenosis	8	6	75
Vestibular fistula	98	63	64.3
Imperforate anus without fistula	35	18	51.4
Bulbar fistula	83	34	41.0
Cloaca common channel <3 cm	73	28	38.4
Vaginal fistula	4	1	25
Prostatic fistula	72	16	22.2
Cloaca common channel >3 cm	41	4	9.8
Bladder neck fistula	29	2	6.9
Total	484	208	43.0

*Voluntary bowel movement and no soiling.

TABLE 101-7 Urinary Continence in Patients with Cloacas

	Common Channel <3 cm		Common Channel >3 cm		Total	
	n	%	*n*	%	*N*	%
Normal	59	72.0	11	20.4	70	51.5
Dry with intermittent catheterization	16	19.5	20	37.0	36	26.5
Dry with continent diversion	7	8.5	23	42.6	30	22.0
Total	82		54		136	

Certain patients in whom the rectum was mislocated during the original operation may be candidates for reoperation. This is recommended only in patients who were born with a good sacrum, good sphincters, and a malformation with a good prognosis. The results of this procedure vary, with worthwhile continence achieved in 15% to 46% of patients.[10,46]

Urologic problems in male patients and in female patients without cloacas are rare.[8] In patients with a cloaca, the 28% with a common channel shorter than 3 cm require intermittent catheterization or a continent diversion to empty their bladder. Patients with common channels longer than 3 cm require intermittent catheterization or a continent diversion 70% to 80% of the time (Table 101-7).

REFERENCES

1. Aaronson I: Anterior sacral meningocele, anal canal duplication and covered anus occurring in one family. J Pediatr Surg 1970;5:559-563.
2. Albanese CT, Jennings RW, Lopoo JB, et al: One-stage correction of high imperforate anus in the male neonate. J Pediatr Surg 1999;34:834-836.
3. Amussat JZ: Histoire d'une operation d'anus artificial practique avec success par un nouveau procede. Gaz Med Paris 1835;3:753.
4. Appignani BA, Jaramillo D, Barnes PD, Poussaint TY: Dysraphic myelodysplasias associated with urogenital and anorectal anomalies: Prevalence and types seen with MR imaging. AJR Am J Roentgenol 1994;163:1199-1203.
5. Ashcraft KW, Holder TM: Hereditary presacral teratoma. J Pediatr Surg 1974;9:691-697.
6. Belizon A, Levitt MA, Shoshany G, et al: Rectal prolapse following posterior sagittal anorectoplasty for anorectal malformations. J Pediatr Surg 2005;40:192-196, discussion 196.
7. Bell B: A System of Surgery, vol 2, 3rd ed. Edinburgh, 1787.
8. Boemers TM, van Gool JD, de Jong TP, Bax KM: Urodynamic evaluation of children with caudal regression syndrome (caudal dysplasia sequence). J Urol 1994;151: 1038-1040.
9. Boocock GR, Donnai D: Anorectal malformation: Familial aspects and associated anomalies. Arch Dis Child 1987;62:576-579.
10. Brain AJL, Kiley EM: Posterior sagittal anorectoplasty for reoperation in children with anorectal malformations. Br J Surg 1989;76:57-59.
11. Brenner EC: Congenital defects of the anus and rectum. Surg Gynecol Obstet 1975;20:579-588.
12. Carson JA, Barnes PD, Tunell WP, et al: Imperforate anus: The neurological implication of sacral abnormalities. J Pediatr Surg 1984;19:838-842.
13. Cilento BG Jr, Benacerraef BR, Mandell J: Prenatal diagnosis of cloacal malformation. Urology 1994;43:386-388.
14. Cloutier R, Archambault H, D'Amours C, et al: Focal ectasia of the terminal bowel accompanying low anal deformities. J Pediatr Surg 1987;22:758-760.
15. Cohn J, Bay-Nielsen E: Hereditary defect of the sacrum and coccyx with anterior sacral meningocele. Acta Paediatr Scand 1969;58:268-274.
16. Cortes D, Thorup JM, Nielsen OH, Beck BL: Cryptorchidism in boys with imperforate anus. J Pediatr Surg 1995;30:631-635.
17. Cule JH: John Pugh, 1814-1874. A scholar surgeon's operation on the imperforate anus in 1854. Ann R Coll Surg Engl 1965;37:247-257.
18. Currarino G, Coln D, Votteler T: Triad of anorectal, sacral and presacral anomalies. AJR Am J Roentgenol 1981;137: 395-398.
19. de Vries PA, Friedland GW: The staged sequential development of the anus and rectum in human embryos and fetuses. J Pediatr Surg 1974;9:755-769.
20. de Vries PA, Pena A: Posterior sagittal anorectoplasty. J Pediatr Surg 1982;17:638-643.
21. Dubois A: Recueil Periodique de la Societe de Medecine de Paris 1783;3:125.
22. Georgeson KE, Inge TH, Albanese CT: Laparoscopically assisted anorectal pullthrough for high imperforate anus: A new technique. J Pediatr Surg 2000;35:927-931.
23. Goon HK: Repair of anorectal anomalies in the neonatal period. Pediatr Surg Int 1990;5:246-249.
24. Greenwood RD, Rosenthal A, Nadas AS: Cardiovascular malformations associated with imperforate anus. J Pediatr 1975;86:576-579.
25. Gross GW, Wolfson PJ, Peña A: Augmented-pressure colostogram in imperforate anus with fistula. Radiology 1991;21:560-562.
26. Hadra R: Demonstration zweier Fälle von Atresie ani vulvalis. Berlin Klin Wochenschr 1885;22:340.
27. Hedlund H, Peña A: Does the distal rectal muscle in anorectal malformations have the functional properties of a sphincter. J Pediatr Surg 1990;25:985-989.
28. Hoekstra WJ, Scholtmeijer RJ, Molenoar JC, et al: Urogenital tract abnormalities associated with congenital anorectal anomalies. J Urol 1983;130:962-963.
29. Hong AR, Rosen N, Acuña MF, et al: Urological injuries associated with the repair of anorectal malformations in male patients. J Pediatr Surg 2002;37:339-344.
30. Karrer FM, Flannery AM, Nelson MD Jr, et al: Anorectal malformations: Evaluation of associated spinal dysraphic syndromes. J Pediatr Surg 1988;23:45-48.
31. Leisrink H: Atresia Ani, Fehlen des Rectum: Operation nach der Methode von Stromeyer. Dtsch Z Chir 1872;1:494.

32. Levi AC, Borghi F, Garavoglia M: Development of the anal canal muscles. Dis Colon Rectum 1991;34:262-266.
33. Levitt MA, Patel M, Rodriguez G, et al: The tethered spinal cord in patients with anorectal malformations. J Pediatr Surg 1997;32:462-468.
34. Levitt MA, Soffer SZ, Peña A: Continent appendicostomy in the bowel management of fecal incontinent children. J Pediatr Surg 1997;32:1630-1633.
35. Levitt MA, Stein DM, Peña A: Gynecological concerns in the treatment of teenagers with cloaca. J Pediatr Surg 1998;33:188-193.
36. Littre A: Diverses observations anatomiques, histoire de l'a-cadamemie royale de Science. Paris, 1710.
37. Moore TC: Advantages of performing the sagittal anoplasty operation for imperforate anus at birth. J Pediatr Surg 1990;25:276-277.
38. McLeod N: Case of imperforate rectum, with a suggestion for a new method of treatment. BMJ 1880;2:657.
39. McLorie GA, Sheldon CA, Fleisher M, Churchill BM: The genitourinary system in patients with imperforate anus. J Pediatr Surg 1987;22:1100-1104.
40. Narasimharao KL, Prasad GR, Katariya S, et al: Prone cross-table lateral view: An alternative to the invertogram in imperforate anus. AJR Am J Roentgenol 1983;140:227-229.
41. Nixon HH, Puri P: The results of treatment of anorectal anomalies: A thirteen to twenty year follow up. J Pediatr Surg 1977;12:27-37.
42. Norris WJ, Brophy TW III, Brayton D: Imperforate anus: A case series and preliminary report of one-stage abdomino-perineal operation. Surg Gynecol Obstet 1949;88:623-625.
43. Olness K, McParland FA, Piper J: Biofeedback: A new modality in the management of children with fecal soiling. J Pediatr 1980;96:505-509.
44. Partridge JP, Gough MH: Congenital abnormalities of the anus and rectum. Br J Surg 1961;49:37-50.
45. Paulus A: On the imperforate anus. In The Seven Books, Book VI, Section LXXXI; translated by Adams F for the Sydenham Society, London, 1844.
46. Peña A: Advances in the management of fecal incontinence secondary to anorectal malformations. Surg Annu 1990; 22:143-167.
47. Peña A: Total urogenital mobilization—an easier way to repair cloacas. J Pediatr Surg 1997;32:263-268.
48. Peña A, El-Behery M: Megasigmoid—a source of pseudo-incontinence in children with repaired anorectal malformations. J Pediatr Surg 1993;28:1-5.
49. Peña A, Guardino K, Tovilla JM, et al: Bowel management for fecal incontinence in patients with anorectal malformations. J Pediatr Surg 1998;33:133-137.
50. Peña A, Levitt MA, Hong AR, Midulla PS: Surgical management of cloacal malformations: A review of 339 patients. J Pediatr Surg 2004;39:470-479.
51. Pinsky L: The syndromology of anorectal malformation (atresia, stenosis, ectopia). Am J Med Genet 1978;1:461-474.
52. Powell RW, Sherman JO, Raffensperger JG: Megarectum: A rare complication of imperforate anus repair and its surgical correction by endorectal pullthrough. J Pediatr Surg 1982;17:786-795.
53. Rosen NG, Hong AR, Soffer SZ, et al: Recto-vaginal fistula: A common diagnostic error with significant consequences in female patients with anorectal malformations. J Pediatr Surg 2002;37:961-965.
54. Rhoads JE, Pipes RL, Randall JP: A simultaneous abdominal and perineal approach in operations for imperforate anus with atresia of the rectum and rectosigmoid. Ann Surg 1948;127:552.
55. Rivosecchi M, Lucchetti MC, Zaccara A, et al: Spinal dysraphism detected by magnetic resonance imaging in patients with anorectal anomalies: Incidence and clinical significance. J Pediatr Surg 1995;30:488-490.
56. Shimada K, Hosokawa S, Matsumoto F, et al: Urological management of cloacal anomalies. Int J Urol 2001;8:282-289.
57. Smith ED, Saeki M: Associated anomalies in anorectal malformations in children: Update 1988. Birth Defects 1988; 24:501.
58. Soranus E: On the care of the newborn. In Soranus' Gynecology Book II; translated by Temkin O. Baltimore, Johns Hopkins University Press, 1956.
59. Squire R, Kiely EM, Carr B, et al: The clinical application of the Malone antegrade colonic enema. J Pediatr Surg 1993;28:1012-1015.
60. Stephens FD: Malformations of the anus. Aust N Z J Surg 1953;23:9-24.
61. Stephens FD: Embryology of the cloaca and embryogenesis of anorectal malformations. Birth Defects Orig Artic Ser 1988;24:177-209.
62. Stromeyer H: Handbuch der Chirurgie, vols 1 and 2. Freiburg, Germany, 1844-1848.
63. Tasakyannis DE, Shamberger RC: Association of imperforate anus with occult spinal dysraphism. J Pediatr Surg 1995; 30:1010-1012.
64. Teixera OHP, Malhotra K, Sellers J, Mercer S: Cardiovascular anomalies with imperforate anus. Arch Dis Child 1983;58:747-749.
65. Templeton JM, Ditesheim JA: High imperforate anus—quantitive results of long-term fecal continence. J Pediatr Surg 1985;20:645-652.
66. Torres P, Levitt MA, Tovilla JM, et al: Anorectal malformations and Down's syndrome. J Pediatr Surg 1998;33:1-5.
67. Tuuha SE, Aziz D, Drake J, et al: Is surgery necessary for asymptomatic tethered cord in anorectal malformation patients? J Pediatr Surg 2004;39:773-777.
68. von de Putte SCJ, Neeteson FA: The pathogenesis of hereditary congenital malformations of the anorectum in the pig. Acta Morphol Neerl Scand 1984;22:17-40.
69. Warne SA, Wilcox DT, Creighton S, Ransley PG: Long-term gynecologic outcome of patients with persistent cloaca. J Urol 2003;170:1493-1496.

Chapter 102

Other Disorders of the Anus and Rectum, Anorectal Function

Risto J. Rintala and Mikko Pakarinen

ANATOMY (Fig. 102-1)

The anal canal measures 2.5 to 4.0 cm in length.[107] It is the area between the anal verge and the junction of the stratified cuboidal and columnar epithelium (dentate line).[61] It is lined by squamous epithelium in the lower anal canal below which sebaceous glands and hair follicles arise, but changes to stratified cuboidal and, finally, columnar epithelium of the rectum. Sensitive sensory receptors in this epithelium and in the more proximal anal mucosa respond to a variety of stimuli, permitting discrimination of solid, liquid, and gas. The mucosa of the rectum meets the epithelial lining of the anal canal at the dentate or pectinate line, marking the oral extension of the anal columns and valves. High in the anal canal the mucosa forms four to six longitudinal folds.

The smooth muscle of the internal anal sphincter (IAS) is continuous with the inner circular muscle of the rectum. It becomes more prominent low in the anal canal. It is approximately 3 cm long and 5 mm thick.[45] The IAS is bound to the voluntary external sphincter and perianal skin by muscular strands. It is involuntarily in a tonic state of contraction, providing at least 85% of the resting anal canal pressure that keeps the anal canal closed.[23] The IAS can increase contraction only slightly, but it relaxes completely by reflex in response to rectal distention.[105] This reflex, mediated by the myenteric plexus, is intrinsic and thus remains independent from extrinsic innervation.

Both sympathetic and parasympathetic nerves innervate the internal sphincter.[36] Sympathetic innervation is primarily excitatory, contracting the IAS, and is supplied by the lumbar splanchnic nerves from L2 to L4 ganglia and by the hypogastric nerves from the inferior mesenteric ganglion. α-Adrenergic stimulation is excitatory, but β-adrenergic stimulation is inhibitory. The continuous tonic state of IAS appears to be mediated by excitatory fibers of both adrenergic and cholinergic innervation.

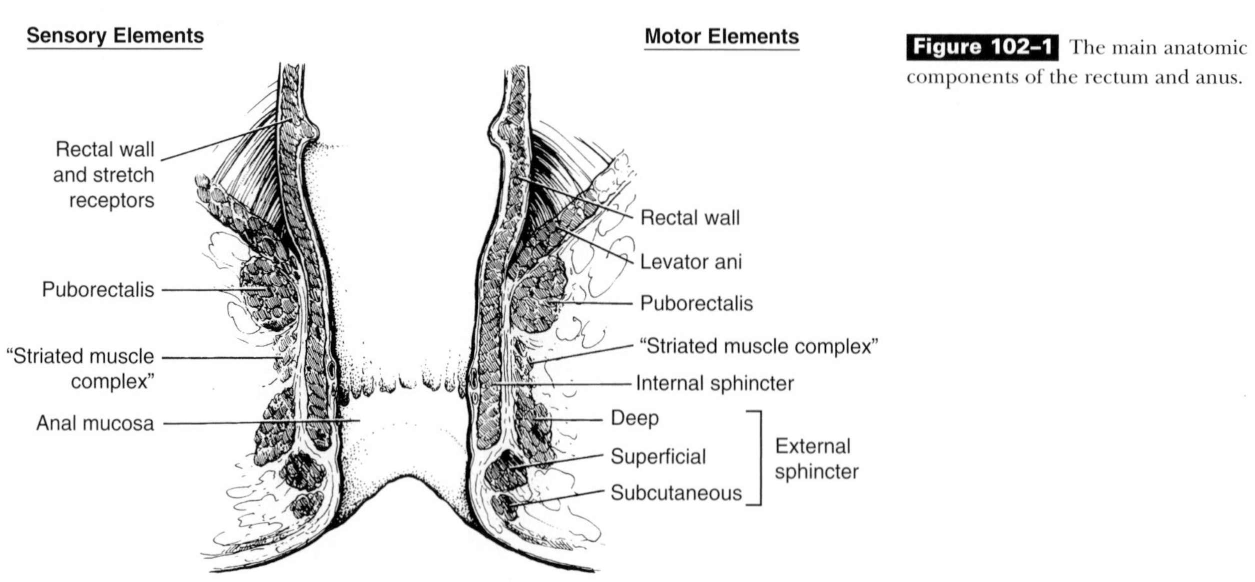

Figure 102-1 The main anatomic components of the rectum and anus.

Parasympathetic innervation comes from the S2 to S4 ganglia through the pelvic nerves and is generally inhibitory, causing the IAS to relax.[3,12]

The IAS also has an important intrinsic innervation, which is responsible for reflex relaxation in response to rectal distention. These intrinsic nerves lie in intramural plexuses and in the myenteric (Auerbach's), deep submucosal (Henke's), and submucosal (Meissner's) plexuses and are nonadrenergic and noncholinergic in origin.[3,36]

The external anal sphincter is a striated muscle that is partially under voluntary control. The muscle surrounds the anus below the dentate line and is attached anteriorly to the perineal body and posteriorly to the anococcygeal raphe. The external anal sphincter has traditionally been divided into three anatomic components: subcutaneous, superficial, and deep. It is innervated by rami of the pudendal and perineal nerves, which originate from sacral roots 2 to 4.[64]

Although capable of phasic contraction, the external anal sphincter may also have tonic contraction.[17] Unlike the IAS, the tonic contraction of the external sphincter depends on extrinsic efferent innervation. The phasic contractions are both voluntary and involuntary; thus, the external anal sphincter provides part (10% to 15%) of the resting anal sphincter tone.[77]

The pelvic floor muscles consist of the levator ani muscle group, one part of which, the puborectal muscle, forms a sling around the anorectal junction. Although a striated muscle, the puborectalis remains in tonic contraction.[48] This creates an angle between the anus and the rectum, the anorectal angle, which is 80 to 90 degrees at rest and during defecation more obtuse, at 100 to 105 degrees.[42] With coughing, straining, or other sudden increases in intra-abdominal pressure, the puborectalis automatically increases its tonic contraction, thereby maintaining the sharp anorectal angle that plays a significant role in fecal continence.[48] The levator ani muscle complex is shaped like a funnel that surrounds the rectum and tapers down to the anal canal, where its fibers merge with the voluntary anal sphincter. Anteriorly, the levator is firmly fixed and its fibers blend into the vaginal and urethral sphincters. The levator complex, except the puborectalis, is attached posteriorly and contracts in a vertical plane.

PHYSIOLOGY OF ANAL CONTINENCE

The adaptive compliance of the colon and the retentive mechanism of the anorectum are required for fecal continence. The simple anatomic impedance to the descending fecal mass occurs because the distal end of the gastrointestinal tract is not a straight tube. The angulations in the sigmoid colon and the valves of Houston in the rectum impede the caudal movement of fecal contents. The 80-degree anorectal angle also assists in fecal continence.[91] Apart from merely causing circuiting of the stool masses, these angulations help in maintaining continence during sudden rises in intra-abdominal pressure such as sneezing, laughing, and postural change. The longitudinal mucosal folds in the anus also contribute to continence of semisolid or fluid feces by the way they fold together, even when the internal sphincter partially relaxes.

The anal sphincters play an important role in maintaining continence, and both the voluntary external sphincter and the involuntary internal sphincter have a resting tone. Fecal continence requires a normally functioning IAS, external sphincter complex, and levator funnel, as well as intact sensory input from the rectum and anal canal.[10,38] The rectum has stretch receptors, which have an increasing sensitivity the more distal they are sited. The anal canal is richly endowed with sensory receptors for most modalities of sensation.[88] These receptors allow us to distinguish between flatus, fluid, and feces.

Gross continence—the ability to hold large volumes of solid or liquid feces—is a function of the intact anorectal angle and tonic contraction of both external and internal sphincter systems. Fine continence—the control of small volumes of feces or flatus—is the function of the coordinated action of the sphincters. The distal 2 cm of the anal canal above and at the dentate line is the critical site of fine continence.[113] This is the site where the "sampling reflex," the discrimination between solid stool, liquid, or gas, is initiated.[30]

PHYSIOLOGY OF DEFECATION

The defecation sequence is a complex combination of involuntary actions and voluntary accomplishments that are controlled by higher cerebral centers. The rectum fills gradually by colonic action. The distention of the rectum stimulates stretch receptors in the rectal wall and levator and induces an initial contraction of the voluntary sphincter complex, retrograde emptying of the distal rectum, and relaxation of the IAS. This causes a sensation of a desire to defecate that increases in intensity as the rectum fills. Stool is temporarily allowed to contact the sensitive mucosa of the anal canal and is sampled by the exquisitely sensitive sensory receptors in the anal mucosa, which allow evaluation of stool consistency and recognition of flatus. The need to defecate is appreciated, but this urge can be voluntarily inhibited. The external anal sphincter and puborectalis can be contracted voluntarily to abort the fecal expulsion. The rectum and colon stretch compliantly, decreasing the intrarectal pressure and the urge to stool.

As more stool is delivered to the rectum, the sensation increases and rectal waves intensify. The urge to defecate is increased, and the reflex inhibition of the sphincters becomes greater. The reflex suppression of the tonic contraction of the external anal sphincter and puborectalis begins; if time and place are appropriate, voluntary defecation can occur.

The individual adopts a sitting or squatting position and performs a Valsalva maneuver against a closed glottis, increasing intra-abdominal pressure. In the flexed squatting position, the anorectal angle is straightened and the levator ani muscles contract; these movements prevent downward descent of the pelvic floor. Mass nonperistaltic contractions in the colon are initiated, and long segments of the colon are emptied in an antegrade fashion.[98]

After fecal expulsion, the external sphincter system contracts, the internal sphincter exhibits closing activity of the anal canal, and the anorectal angle is reestablished.

Fecal continence is defined as the ability to control bowel contents that reach the terminal bowel with unconscious or conscious retention and voluntary defecation. The major components of this continence mechanism are a reservoir, an appropriate consistency of stool, and a functional sphincter system.[125]

Young children have shorter intestinal transit time than older children, and this correlates with the more frequent bowel movements in infants.[27] Infants who are fed by breast milk or cow's milk–based formula have one to seven bowel movements per day.[127] In children between 1 and 4 years of age, 85% pass stool once or twice per day.[128] Normal English schoolchildren have mean transit times of 26 hours and in constipated children the transit time is 80 hours.[15] Healthy young adults have transit times of 30 to 48 hours.[117]

CONSTIPATION

Constipation in children is a common condition especially in the Western World. Unresolved constipation can lead to fecal retention and impaction and finally to overflow incontinence. In the overwhelming majority of patients the exact cause of constipation remains obscure; in this case the condition is called *functional constipation.*

Definitions

Functional constipation in children is defined as constipation not associated with congenital abnormalities, acquired diseases, or medication. Constipation is defined as a stool frequency of less than three per week and associated symptoms such as pain or overflow soiling or as stool retention with or without soiling even when the stool frequency is three per week or more.[66,121] Constipation and soiling are seen mostly in children younger than the age of 7 years. Both constipation and soiling are common. Soiling has been reported in approximately 3% of children older than 4 years of age, and constipation accounts for at least 3% of all medical and 25% of pediatric gastroenterology referrals.[29,35,62,67] More than 50% of constipated children have a familial incidence, and most studies suggest a male predominance, with the reported ratios ranging between 1.5:1 and 3:1.[1,63]

The following classification of functional defecation disorders has been suggested by Clayden[19]:

Constipation: difficulty or delay in the passage of stools
Soiling: frequent passage of loose or semisolid stools in clothing
Encopresis: passage of normal stools in an abnormal place

Because constipation during the neonatal period, usually associated with distention and vomiting, is never functional, anatomic or mechanical obstruction must be suspected. Most (94% to 98%) full-term and most (76%) preterm normal infants pass meconium during the first 24 hours after birth. All normal infants (100% full-term and 99% preterm) have a first stool within the first 48 hours of life.[18] During the first year of life, symptomatic constipation warrants an evaluation and organic causes for constipation should be ruled out.

During infancy, constipation often begins after dietary manipulations, such as with the change from breast- to bottle-feeding or the introduction of solid foods.[109] Specifically in children, anal fissure or perianal dermatitis with group A *Streptococcus* causes painful defecation and a vicious cycle of stool withholding, painful defecation, and chronic constipation may develop. A suggested alternative etiology is cow's milk protein intolerance.[50] Dietary fiber is poorly correlated with constipation except in older children.[99] Constipated parents are more likely to have constipated children.[55] Slow transit constipation is a major problem in adults and is probably important in a subset of children with constipation.[11,49] Psychological problems are common in constipated children, but they are secondary to constipation in the majority of cases.[1,68]

Acute Constipation

Acute constipation may be secondary to inactivity, changes of environment or diet, or an anal fissure. Presentation as acute abdominal pain is common. Acute constipation presenting as abdominal pain is usually relieved by one single enema. The management of acute constipation is usually straightforward, especially in infants and toddlers. Adding more water to the diet and restriction of cow's milk intake usually relieve the symptoms. Older children and those who have an acute anal fissure require bulk laxatives for a variable period of time.

Chronic Constipation

Persistent constipation that does not rapidly respond to dietary manipulation or simple laxative treatment can be defined as chronic. A child with chronic constipation can present with fecal soiling. Encopresis, which is the passage of normal stools in abnormal places and at abnormal times, is more likely to be related to psychological disturbance.[20] Organic causes that should be taken into account in the diagnostic workup for chronic constipation are summarized in Table 102-1.

Studies of children with constipation and overflow soiling show that 40% were never completely toilet trained and that enuresis is an associated problem in more than 30%.[62] Chronic constipation and soiling usually develop between ages 2 and 4 years.[24] One fourth of the patients, however, have the onset of chronic constipation during the first year of life. The incidence of both constipation and soiling increases markedly when the toddler is beginning to gain control over defecation.

The diagnosis of chronic constipation relies on history and clinical examination. A detailed bowel history should focus on the age at which constipation first occurs; the frequency and description of stools; and therapeutic interventions previously attempted, including any

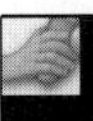

TABLE 102-1 Differential Diagnosis of Chronic Constipation: Organic and Acquired Causes

Hirschsprung's Disease and Allied Disorders
Internal sphincter achalasia
Intestinal neuronal dysplasia (hyperganglionosis)
Hypoganglionosis

Congenital Anomalies
Anal stenosis
Anterior perineal anus

Acquired Diseases
Chronic anal fissure
Chronic anal fistula
Crohn's disease

Associated with Systemic Disease
Hypothyroidism
Hypercalcemia
Cerebral palsy and neurological impairment
Uremia

Psychiatric Disease
Depression
Anorexia nervosa
Primary encopresis

Medication
Anticonvulsive drugs
Psychiatric drugs
Anticholinergic drugs

medications taken. Anticonvulsants, diuretics, antacids, and supplemental iron preparations are frequently associated with constipation. Family history can be important, particularly a history of Hirschsprung's disease, cystic fibrosis, or familial constipation. The incidence of clinical findings in patients with chronic constipation is summarized in Table 102-2.

TABLE 102-2 Clinical Features of Severe Functional Constipation

Age at onset	
0-1 yr	20-25%
1-5 yr	70%
> 5 yr	10-15%
Boys:girls	1-3:1
Previous attempts to treat	80-90%
Soiling	70-75%
Unsuccessful toilet training	70-80%
Pain at defecation	70-80%
Abdominal pain	50-60%
Occasional blood in stool	25-30%
Poor appetite	20-30%
Enuresis	20-30%
Primary psychopathology	15-20%
Rectal prolapse	3%

Data from references 1, 19, 20, 55, 62, 66, 68, and 70.

On clinical examination the child's abdomen is usually nontender and rarely distended. Stool masses are frequently palpable above the pubic symphysis and in the lower left abdomen. The perineum must be inspected carefully for the position and condition of the anus and the perianal skin and for soiling marks. The normal position of the anus must be defined because malpositioning is a well-recognized cause of constipation.[8,119] Reisner and colleagues[95] defined normal values by using a ratio of the midanal to fourchette distance and the fourchette to coccyx distance in the female and a ratio of the midanal to posterior scrotum distance and the posterior scrotum to coccyx distance in the male. If the ratio is less than 0.34 in the female (usual values: newborn, 0.44; age 4 to 18 months, 0.40) and less than 0.46 in the male (usual values: newborn, 0.58; age 4 to 18 months, 0.56) the child should be investigated carefully, especially if constipation is present. To differentiate between anterior anus and perineal ectopic anus is often difficult, especially if the anterior position of the anus is associated with stenosis. Final diagnosis may require muscle stimulation under general anesthesia.

Perianal sensation can be evaluated by stroking the perianal tissue gently with a cotton-tipped applicator, watching for the anal puckering, and ascent of the perineum. The child's underwear should also be examined for soiling.

Digital rectal examination may reveal a shortened anal canal. The sphincter tone may appear diminished, especially if the rectal ampulla is full of stool. The fecal mass that fills the rectum may have developed to a fecaloma that can be stone hard. Overflow soiling is associated with fecaloma formation. The external sphincter is usually intact, and the child can volitionally contract on the examining finger. The retrorectal space must be examined to feel masses within the hollow of the sacrum. The closing reflex should be seen when the finger is withdrawn. The absence of either the perineal cutaneous or closing reflexes suggests an underlying neurologic disorder.

If the clinical history and physical examination do not suggest organic etiology, a trial of medical treatment can be initiated. A small infant with a history of neonatal symptoms and early onset constipation should undergo barium enema without bowel preparation. An abnormal barium enema should be followed by rectal biopsy and possibly anorectal manometry to rule out Hirschsprung's disease and allied disorders. In an older child without any history of significant neonatal or infantile constipation a primary barium enema or biopsies are not necessary[39,56] before the onset of medical management. Barium enema and other imaging such as plain abdominal radiography, transit time studies, or magnetic resonance imaging (MRI) are indicated in patients who have poor response to appropriate medical treatment or abnormal clinical findings such as neurologic symptoms. Patients who have a poor response to optimal medical therapy should also undergo rectal biopsy and anorectal manometry to rule out rare forms of dysganglionoses such as hypoganglionosis, intestinal neuronal dysplasia, and internal sphincter achalasia (see Chapters 99 and 100).

Barium enema usually shows dilatation of the rectosigmoid that extends to the anal canal. This rules out classic Hirschsprung's disease but not internal sphincter-achalasia.[76,94] Plain abdominal radiography may reveal spinal vertebral anomalies in patients who have clinical findings suggesting a neurologic disorder. In the case of vertebral anomalies, MRI should be performed to rule out intraspinal pathology such as tethering and intraspinal lipomas.[100] Transit time studies by radiopaque markers[11,96] or radioisotopes[49] have been used to assess colonic motility in patients with poor response to standard medical management. These studies have revealed that slow-transit constipation occurs in a significant proportion of patients with recalcitrant constipation. The main methodologic problem with transit studies in children is the lack of standardized methods and normal values in healthy children.

Anorectal manometry is useful only for the diagnosis of Hirschsprung's disease and internal sphincter achalasia. In both these conditions the rectoanal relaxation reflex is missing. In patients suffering from functional constipation, anorectal manometry does not improve diagnostic or therapeutic accuracy.[121] In other dysganglionoses such as hypoganglionosis and intestinal neuronal dysplasia, anorectal manometry shows variable findings and is usually not diagnostic.[58] On the other hand, in intestinal neuronal dysplasia and hypoganglionosis, anorectal manometry may guide management decisions. According to our experience, the patients with very high resting anal pressure (>100 cm H_2O) often benefit from internal sphincter myotomy or myectomy. Some constipated children with normal histology also have manometric evidence of anal outlet obstruction and paradoxically contract the sphincter complex with straining, so-called rectoanal dyssynergy.[5,54,69,76]

Management

The general approach to the management of a child with chronic constipation includes providing parental counseling and education, determining whether a fecal impaction is present, disimpacting the fecaloma if it is present, and beginning oral medications.[20,68]

The counseling and education of the family is the first step in the management. The pathogenesis of constipation needs to be explained to the parents. If the patient has fecal soiling the involuntary nature of overflow incontinence needs to be clarified to the parents. Parents are encouraged to maintain a consistent supportive attitude during the long period of treatment. Education of the child and parents, emotional support, and a commitment to continue to see the family until normal stooling is established are all important elements of the program.[20,51,54] The patient and the parents need to be aware that it may take 6 to 12 months or even years before a normal stooling pattern is achieved.

If the patient has fecal impaction or a fecaloma, disimpaction is necessary before initiation of oral maintenance therapy. A fecaloma can be identified by physical examination as a hard mass in the lower abdomen, by rectal examination, or by radiographic methods. A typical symptom of fecal impaction is overflow incontinence. Disimpaction has been traditionally accomplished with bowel washouts, but oral medication is effective, too.[32,116]

Oral disimpaction can be accomplished by high doses of stimulant laxatives, docusate, mineral oil, and polyethylene glycol-electrolyte solutions.[51,116] Osmotic laxatives such as lactulose or sorbitol can be used in combination with other medication. Oral disimpaction is often associated with abdominal pain and colic and also initial increase in fecal soiling.

Rectal washout works usually faster than oral medication in disimpaction. It is, however, invasive and painful, especially in patients who have associated anal pathology. Therefore, rectal disimpaction is contraindicated in children with anal fissure. Saline, docusate, mineral oil, or phosphate enemas are recommended by different investigators.[20,85,103] When rectal disimpaction is used, it is essential that the number of enemas is kept to a minimum. Usually one to three washouts are all that is required for complete disimpaction. In recalcitrant cases manual evacuation under general anesthesia may be considered.

The goal of maintenance therapy is to produce one to two soft stools per day and prevent recurrent fecal impaction. This ensures that the vicious cycle of hard stools and painful defecation will be abolished.

The treatment consist of dietary interventions, laxatives, and behavioral modification. Dietary changes are universally advised, particularly increased intake of fluids and fiber. The role of fiber may not be significant in children.[99] Too much milk is discouraged.[87] There is no evidence that any particular drug treatment regimen is superior. Good compliance with the selected treatment is more essential. In the early phases of management after the disimpaction more effective medication is often required. Stimulant laxatives (senna, sodium picosulfate) should be used for as short periods as possible and should be replaced by less harmful therapies. Osmotic laxatives (lactulose, docusate, PEG) can be safely used for months and years. Having achieved a regular pattern of bowel movements, the medication needs to be continued as long as necessary. This usually means months and sometimes years. A good thumb rule is that the treatment continues as long as the patient has had symptoms before the management. The dosage of the medication needs to be tapered regularly; the goal is to use a minimal effective dose.

Behavioral therapy varies with the age of the patient. In infants and toddlers, behavioral therapy has no role; too early and too aggressive toilet training is discouraged. In children younger than 2 to 3 years of age, the toilet should be avoided and diapers reinstituted until the child is ready to go back to the toilet.[20] Older children may benefit from regular toilet routines after a major meal during the day. Praise, rewards, and a diary may contribute to a successful outcome.[32]

Long-Term Outcome

There are few studies on the long-term results of the management of chronic idiopathic constipation.[55,73,110] The reported final cure rates after 5 years of follow-up are only about 50%. A positive family history is predictive of a poor outcome. A reassuring fact, however, is that symptomatic constipation and especially overflow incontinence are very uncommon in puberty.[1,9] Patients with early-onset disease and with a family history may continue to have abnormal bowel habits beyond childhood.[116]

Surgical Options

The vast majority of children with chronic constipation improve with appropriate medical therapy or with time. Most patients also comply even with aggressive medical therapy. However, there remain a few children who despite optimal and maximal medical management have persistent constipation, abdominal symptoms, and soiling throughout and beyond childhood. There are no controlled studies in children that are devoted to the surgery of pediatric idiopathic constipation.

For pediatric patients who are refractory to all medical therapy there are some viable surgical options. It is essential that organic causes of constipation are ruled out. The MACE procedure[75] that had been originally used for neuropathic incontinence or incontinence after management of anorectal anomalies has been successfully used also for idiopathic constipation.[57,130] The MACE procedure can be easily reversed, which makes it an attractive alternative to enemas and laxatives especially for pubertal and adolescent patients. Colostomy has been used in selected patients with significant patient and parent satisfaction.[129] Colonic manometry has been used to guide surgery in some recent series, but these studies are still very preliminary.[49,131]

FUNCTIONAL FECAL SOILING WITHOUT CONSTIPATION

There is a small subset of patients who present with fecal soiling and do not have associated constipation or an organic or psychiatric disorder.[28,41,122] A typical age at presentation is between 4 and 8 years. The main symptom is involuntary passage of variable amounts of stool on the underwear one to several times a day. Most commonly soiling occurs daily. At least one third of these patients suffer from day-time or night-time enuresis. We have encountered approximately 20 such patients during the past decade.

This form of soiling has been considered a manifestation of psychiatric disturbance. However, no serious psychological disorders have been observed in these children and treatment with psychotherapy alone is usually disappointing.[14] We have performed comprehensive investigations in these 20 patients and have not found any evidence of psychiatric disorders and no signs of myelopathy on MRI, and results of barium enemas and spinal radiographs were normal. The incidence of day- or night-time enuresis was 40%. The only measurable abnormality was an isolated impairment of rectal sensibility at anorectal manometry; sphincter function was comparable to that of healthy individuals. Treatment consisted of counseling, toilet training, and dietary modification. Most patients improved with decreased frequency of soiling. All the patients who have reached adolescence have experienced complete disappearance of soiling.

RECTAL PROLAPSE

Rectal prolapse is a relatively common, usually self-limited condition in children. The peak incidence is between 1 and 3 years of age. Prolapse can be either partial or complete. In partial prolapse the rectal mucosa protrudes only 1 to 3 cm from the anal verge, with characteristic radiating folds from the center of the anal aperture. In complete prolapse, the full thickness of the rectum is involved: 5 cm or more of the rectum protrudes, and the prolapse is distinguished by the circular folds of the mucosa (Fig. 102-2). There is significant controversy as to whether rectal prolapse in children is partial or complete.

Pathogenesis and Diagnosis

The following anatomic features are thought to be important in the etiology of rectal prolapse in children[65,83,93,132]:

- The vertical course of the rectum
- Less prominent lateral and anterior/posterior curves to the rectum
- A flatter surface anterior/posterior to the coccyx and sacrum
- The relatively low position of the rectum and other pelvic organs
- Lack of support by the levator ani muscle

The vast majority of patients suffering from rectal prolapse do not have any predisposing factors. The children suffering from idiopathic rectal prolapse are usually otherwise healthy. The role of constipation as an etiologic factor is controversial; only 3% of patients suffering from severe chronic constipation have rectal prolapse.[1]

There are several organic conditions that predispose to rectal prolapse. Cystic fibrosis is associated with

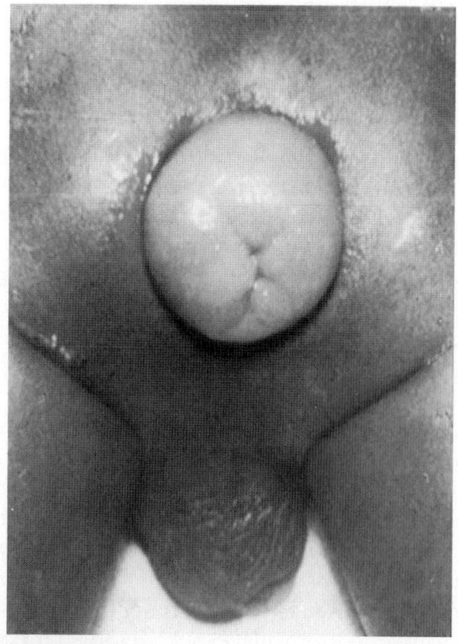

Figure 102-2 Rectal prolapse in a 2-year-old boy.

rectal prolapse.[132] More than one fifth of the patients with cystic fibrosis develop rectal prolapse.[59,108] The neuropathic causes of complete rectal prolapse, such as myelomeningocele, are rare. Nevertheless, paralysis of the levator ani with raised intra-abdominal pressure leads to procidentia and prolapse. In ectopia vesicae there is wide separation of the symphysis pubis and the puborectalis muscle; this wide hiatus predisposes to prolapse of the pelvic organs, including the rectum.

Iatrogenic full-thickness rectal prolapse may occur after pull-through operations for high anorectal anomalies. Much more common is mucosal prolapse that is usually not circumferential.[97] Rectal prolapse or mucosal ectopia were much more common before the era of the posterior sagittal approach procedure.[90] Rectal polyps may be a leading point for a prolapse. Severe malnutrition also predisposes to rectal prolapse.

The diagnosis of rectal prolapse is usually based on history. Most commonly a rosette of rectal mucosa is noted after defecation. The child complains that something comes out of the anus. Usually the prolapse reduces spontaneously, but sometimes it must be reduced manually. In mild forms the prolapse comes out occasionally after major straining or during diarrheal illness. The problem is more annoying and worrying for the patient and parents if the prolapse occurs after every defecation.

Usually the prolapse cannot be provoked when the child is brought to consultation. Rectal examination is indicated to rule out rectal polyps. If there is a history of rectal bleeding, colonoscopy may infrequently be needed to look for higher polyps or other lead points. No other diagnostic studies are usually required.

Treatment

In acute prolapse, reduction may occur spontaneously on standing up. If not, the prolapse must be reduced as soon as possible. The parents often rush the child to hospital when the prolapse appears for the first time. The tip of the herniated bowel can usually be gently pushed into the anus. If edema has formed, a gentle squeezing pressure may be required. Reduction technique must be taught to the parents.

There is spontaneous cure in most cases of recurrent prolapse.[2] In many cases the prolapse reduces spontaneously. In cases without spontaneous reduction the parents can reduce the prolapse gently if appropriately instructed. There is no evidence that conservative treatment methods such as strapping of the buttocks, altering the position of defecation when using a toilet, or trying to get the child to defecate while lying on his or her side are helpful. A stool softening program often cures the problem. Local transanal treatments such as injections of the prolapse, multiple linear thermocauterization to the mucosa, excision of redundant mucosa, or insertion of a subcutaneous suture around the anus (Thiersch wire) have not been tested in controlled trials. Our experience is that these methods are successful in cases that would resolve spontaneously. However, many pediatric surgeons advocate for these methods, especially the Thiersch wire, because they are often successful in many children.

Surgery is indicated in rare cases with intractable prolapse and may be considered in patients who are not spontaneously cured in 12 to 18 months of follow-up. Patients older than 4 years of age require surgery much more often than younger children. There are several surgical methods that have been used with success for recurrent prolapse. The posterior sagittal approach with muscle repair and suspension of the rectum to the sacrum,[6,7,89,104] posterior rectal plication,[118] and Ekehorn's rectosacropexy[102] are reported to be associated with a high cure rate. We prefer laparoscopic suspension of the rectum to anterior sacrum. This approach has been successful in several patients who have required surgery. The procedure is associated with minimal postoperative pain and short hospital stay.

Secondary surgery is indicated for iatrogenic prolapse after a pull-through operation in symptomatic patients. Typical symptoms include bleeding and leak of mucus. In patients with mucosal prolapse, treatment involves excision of the mucosal ectopia and reconstruction of a skin-lined anal canal with a local skin flap. Patients with a complete prolapse require a repeat posterior reconstruction of the levator funnel and external sphincter complex and rectal suspension.

ANAL FISSURE

Anal fissure is a longitudinal tear or ulcer in the distal anal canal epithelium extending to the anal verge. Most acute fissures heal spontaneously within few weeks but a proportion become chronic. Anal fissure is the most common cause of hematochezia in childhood, and it is one of the most common lesions to consider in the differential diagnosis of anal pain. Anal fissures are common, although their exact incidence in children is unknown.

Pathogenesis

The pathogenesis of idiopathic anal fissure is still incompletely understood, and it may differ between adults and children.[80] Anal fissures in childhood are often associated with secondary constipation due to painful passage of stools. The classic concept of mechanical tear caused by hard stools as a primary causative factor may be too simple and outdated. However, deliberate avoiding of defecation does cause rectal distention and leads to decreased rectal sensation, which in turn, results in infrequent, bulky, and hard stools that prevent healing of a fissure. Fear of painful defecation may lead to fecal retention and gives rise to a vicious circle.

There is a widely accepted theory on the pathogenesis of anal fissure in adults.[80,120] According to this theory increased internal sphincter pressure and muscle spasm lead to impaired tissue perfusion and finally epithelial ulceration. Spasm of the internal anal sphincter is so severe that ischemia results and causes a fissure. The most common site of idiopathic anal fissure is the posterior midline, which is less vascularized than other areas of the anal canal. Anal canal resting pressure is increased in patients with anal fissure. Decrease of anal canal pressure after surgical or pharmacologic sphincter relaxation is accompanied by improved perfusion of the anoderm and healing of chronic fissures. Currently, it is unknown whether this theory also applies to pediatric patients. In children, a vast majority of idiopathic anal fissures heal without any specific therapy. This may be due to relatively better tissue perfusion of the anal canal, greater regenerative capacity or a different pathogenesis in children than in adults. An unhealed fissure may become inflamed owing to bacterial infection and chemical and mechanical irritation. As a result of long-standing inflammation chronic anal fissures may have hypertrophied anal papillae proximally and a sentinel skin tag distally. This kind of chronic anal fissure is only rarely seen in children, and it should raise suspicion of underlying Crohn's disease.[112]

Diagnosis

Anal fissure may occur at any age. Typical age at presentation is around 2 years. Most often anal fissures present with bright red rectal bleeding that may be associated with painful defecation. The child may cry with bowel movements and have stools streaked with bright-red blood. Anal fissure is often associated with constipation, which is caused by fecal retention from fear of painful defecation.

The diagnosis is made by direct inspection. The typical longitudinal tear distal to the dentate line can be visualized by retracting the perianal skin gently away. No further diagnostic modalities are needed. The most common location of idiopathic anal fissure is the posterior midline but, especially in infants, may be found anywhere in the anal circumference. In female infants a common site of anal fissure is the anterior midline. A sentinel pile or skin tag at the area of the fissure is associated with chronic or subchronic fissure. Atypical fissures may be multiple and often off the midline and are commonly large and irregular. An atypical appearance of a fissure should initiate further investigations, including biopsy, cultures, and colonoscopy to rule out Crohn's disease, immunodeficiency states, tuberculosis, venereal infection, and malignancies.

Treatment

Most idiopathic anal fissures in children heal without any specific treatment in a few months.[53,115] Only symptomatic fissures require treatment. If a fissure is associated with constipation and/or painful defecation, stool softening with dietary modification and bulk laxatives is indicated. Lubricants ease painful passage of stools. The goal is to interrupt the vicious circle of painful defecation, fecal retention, hard stools, and prevention of healing of the fissure. As expected, most fissures respond promptly to stool softening and heal in several weeks.[53] Hematochezia stops when the fissure heals. Occasionally, a child presents with a typical history after the symptoms have disappeared and the fissure has healed. Initially, these patients may be treated expectantly unless no abnormal clinical signs are present and hematochezia has not recurred.

After encouraging results in adults, several recent randomized placebo-controlled trials have assessed efficiency of topical glyceryl trinitrate in anal fissures in children.[53,81,114,115] Two studies have reported faster healing of fissures and relief of symptoms in children treated with glyceryl trinitrate,[114,115] whereas no benefit was found in one.[53] One of the studies documented significant decrease in maximum anal resting pressure after application of glyceryl trinitrate.[115] Few children experienced temporary incontinence, and none reported headache during glyceryl trinitrate treatment.[53,114,115] A recent meta-analysis including adult and pediatric patients concluded that glyceryl trinitrate for anal fissures is marginally better than placebo.[81] Topical glyceryl trinitrate may be indicated in selected cases in children, when laxative treatment has been unsuccessful. Daily application of the ointment should be continued for at least 6 to 8 weeks to be effective.[114,115]

Surgical therapies reported for treatment of anal fissure in children include fissurectomy, anal dilatation under general anesthesia, and lateral internal sphincterotomy.[22,60] Fissure cure rates (80%) after fissurectomy combined with laxatives are comparable to simple laxative therapy alone.[53,60] Lateral subcutaneous sphincterotomy also appears to be an effective procedure in children.[22] Anal dilatation causes unpredictable degrees of sphincter damage and should be avoided. In adult patients, lateral sphincterotomy is associated with an incontinence rate of 10%.[82] Anal stretch has a significantly higher risk of minor incontinence than sphincterotomy.[82] The effects of different surgical therapies for fissure on fecal continence are poorly characterized in children. Thus, lateral internal sphincterotomy should be reserved for those very rare cases in which the anal fissure has progressed to a real chronic fissure after topical treatment with glyceryl trinitrate has failed. In these cases a biopsy should be obtained to rule out possible Crohn's disease.

PERIANAL ABSCESS AND FISTULA IN ANO

Perianal sepsis is not uncommon in small infants. The vast majority of patients are male.[86] A congenital etiology has been suggested for infant anal fistulas.[34,106] A proposed relationship to androgens resulting in congenital deep, epithelialized crypts may explain the predominant occurrence in male infants.[4,106] A typical presentation is a perianal abscess in a child younger than 12 months (Fig. 102-3); the majority occur before the age of 6 months. After initial incision the condition may progress to or recur as an anal fistula. The incidence of fistula formation in patients with perianal abscess may be as low as 10% to 20%.[73,84] The fistula may present alone without a preceding perianal abscess. The fistula is typically subcutaneous and straight. It usually traverses from the affected crypt through the subcutaneous external sphincter to the perianal skin. The fistulas are usually distributed evenly around the anal circumference. Multiple lesions occur in 15% to 20% of cases (Fig. 102-4).[84,126]

The traditional management of perianal abscess is incision and drainage. This is associated with a significant recurrence rate.[79,126] However, most abscesses are

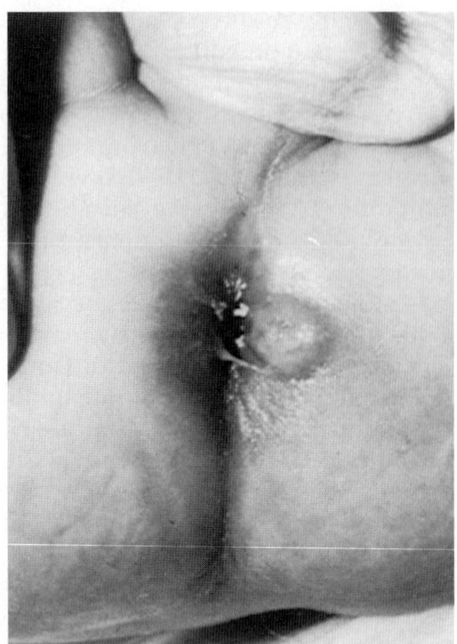

Figure 102-3 Typical perianal abscess in a male infant.

eventually cured by expectant treatment only.[101,126] Fistula-in-ano has been considered an indication for surgical treatment. The traditional method has been identification of the affected anal crypt and fistulotomy by deroofing of the fistula tract. Recurrent fistulas occur in 10% to 20% of cases. Recent reports have advocated expectant treatment for asymptomatic fistula-in-ano; most fistulas heal within 12 to 24 months without further sequelae.[101,126]

Fistulas in older children or adolescents are cryptoglandular or associated with inflammatory bowel disease, mainly Crohn's disease. Crohn's disease should be ruled out in all children who present outside the typical age groups. Treatment of adolescent fistula-in-ano should be

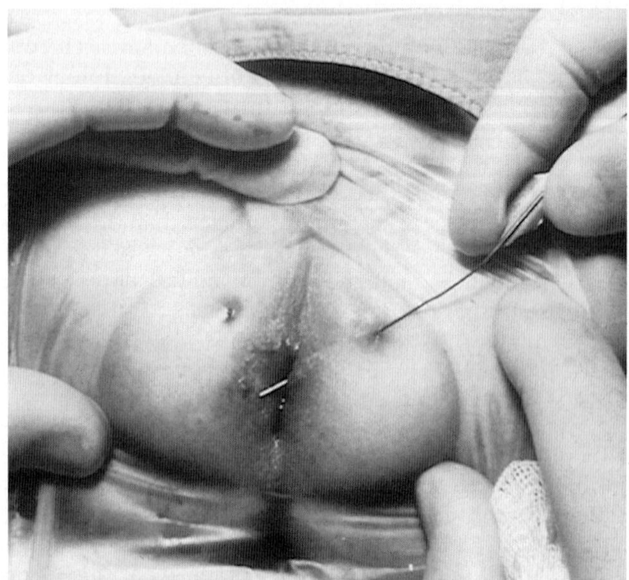

Figure 102-4 Bilateral fistula-in-ano. The probe passes straight from the skin opening to the corresponding anal crypt.

the same as in adults. The fistulous tract, once identified, is either incised and left open to granulate or excised with primary closure of the defect.

VASCULAR MALFORMATIONS

The classifications of intestinal vascular malformations has been confusing as different labels are put on similar lesions without knowledge of their clinical and biologic properties. The classification of vascular malformations by Mulliken and Glowacki[78] is based on biologic properties of the lesion. The classification distinguishes between hemangiomas, which are true neoplasms and usually regress spontaneously, and vascular malformations, which are nonproliferative lesions that do not regress. Intestinal bleeding from vascular malformations in children is rare. The most common sites are distal colon and rectum.[26] In the minority of cases the vascular lesion is a part of a systemic disease such as Klippel-Trenaunay (congenital varicose veins, cutaneous hemangiomas, and ectatic hypertrophy of the lower limbs) and Osler-Rendu-Weber (multiple telangiectasia) syndromes.

The diagnosis of vascular anomalies may be difficult. In the distal bowel, endoscopy may show findings that suggest localized inflammation; dilated vessels are rarely visible. More proximal and especially small bowel lesions may be best visualized by wireless capsule endoscopy.[123] MRI and angiography are still the best methods to diagnose and localize intestinal vascular lesions. Nonoperative methods may be used to control bleeding, but permanent cure is best achieved by complete resection of the lesion. Lesions that extend to the low rectum and anal canal are best treated by endorectal pull-through and coloanal anastomosis.[33,71] This sphincter-saving operation eradicates bleeding episodes for long periods of time if not permanently.

HEMORRHOIDS

Hemorrhoids are uncommon in children except in those with portal hypertension. One third of the children with portal hypertension have hemorrhoids. Hemorrhoids are more common in patients with extrahepatic portal hypertension than in those with intrahepatic disease.[43] Symptomatic hemorrhoids, however, are uncommon.

Hemorrhoids also occur in otherwise healthy children but are rare (Fig. 102-5). We have seen approximately one healthy child with hemorrhoids per year during the past 15 years. Usually there are no symptoms but the child or parents have noticed something protruding from the anal opening. A more common finding, especially in constipated children, is a prominent venous plexus around the anal opening. This is a common source of rectal bleeding in constipated children. Adult-type hemorrhoids begin to occur in adolescents and may be complicated by thrombosis of the external part of the hemorrhoids.

In otherwise healthy children, hemorrhoids do not require surgical therapy. Major bleeding does not occur. Symptomatic patients with portal hypertension may

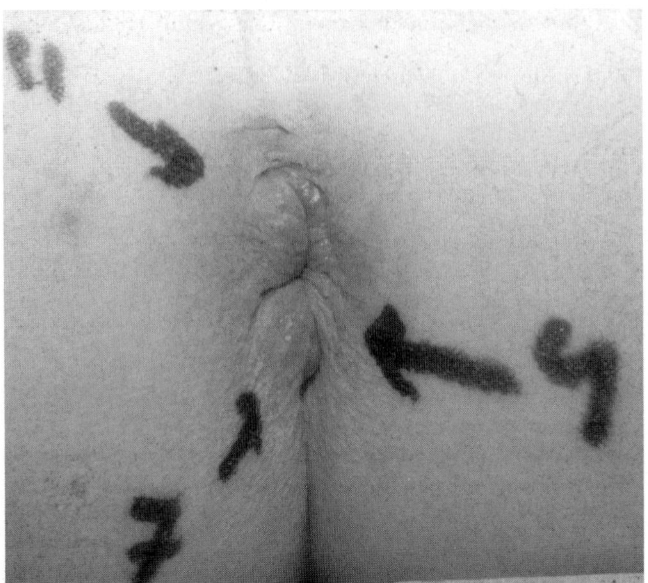

Figure 102-5 Hemorrhoids in a 5-year-old boy, without any underlying conditions. Note the typical adult type piles at 4, 7, and 11 o'clock.

require treatment. Banding or sclerotherapy control the symptoms in the majority of cases.[44]

SOLITARY RECTAL ULCER

Solitary rectal ulcer syndrome is a chronic, benign disorder characterized by hematochezia, mucous discharge, tenesmus, and local perianal pain. It is rare in children but should be kept in mind in patients with local anal symptoms.[31] In children, the macroscopic finding at endoscopy is a thickened and edematous lesion that may have an ulcerative or polypoid appearance in the anterior rectal wall 2 to 5 cm above the anal verge. We have encountered six cases in the past 10 years. Some patients have a feeling of incomplete evacuation with frequent visits to the toilet associated with chronic straining at stool. Rectal prolapse has been reported to occur in a significant percentage of cases.[40] According to our experience, conservative management with stool softeners and local corticosteroid suppositories is successful in most children. Open or laparoscopic rectopexy[13,31] has been suggested to correct the external or internal rectal prolapse that is often associated with solitary rectal ulcer syndrome.

INFANTILE PROCTOCOLITIS

Apart from anal fissure the most common cause of hematochezia in infants younger than 3 months of age is eosinophilic proctocolitis. The infantile proctocolitis typically presents at the age of 3 to 4 weeks with fresh blood streaks mixed in the stools. The stools often contain mucus. Usually there are no other symptoms and the growth and development of the infant is normal.[59a] Colonoscopy shows colitis that is often patchy and rarely extends beyond the left colon. Histology reveals marked eosinophilic infiltration. Some patients may also have an elevated eosinophilic count in the peripheral blood. An allergic etiology has been suggested because of these findings.[74] The condition is self-limiting, and symptoms usually subside within a few weeks. Diet change also has been reported to be helpful in reversing the symptoms.[16]

SEXUAL ABUSE

Child sexual abuse is a common and worldwide problem. In Europe the incidence appears to occur in 6% to 36% of girls and in 1% to 15% of boys younger than 16 years of age.[52] Sexual abuse rarely causes death but its consequences can be serious and persist through adulthood. In child sexual abuse, the significance of findings in the vagina and hymen are well recognized. In the context of anal abuse, the findings are more controversial and difficult to verify.

Hobbs and Wynne[46] stated that "dilatation and reflex anal dilatation" are not seen in normal children and are signs of abuse. Reflex anal dilatation (even gross) was found on routine examination in 28 of 200 children (14%) examined consecutively in community health clinics, a pediatric outpatient clinic, a district hospital, and a rectal clinic.[111] Constipation or feces in the rectum, without associated sexual abuse, may often produce gaping of the anus on separation of the buttocks.[21] Hobbs and Wynne[47] also suggested that an anal fissure was a sign of abuse in 53% of 143 cases quoted. Pierce[92] found that the majority of children with a strong or definite history of anal abuse had anal fissures or scars. However, an anal fissure is far too common a finding in routine clinical practice to be regarded as a cause for suspicion of sexual abuse.[37]

Obvious laceration, bruising around the anus or inner thighs, and scratches, especially with a suspicious or definitive history of abuse, are more conclusive. This sort of forensic evidence is rarely found in children because there is usually a significant time lapse between the abuse and medical examination.

If a child displays total passiveness and indifference to physical examination, or to inspection and examination of the anus, with no attempt to withdraw or tighten the striated muscle complex when a rectal examination is attempted, the clinician should be alert to the possibility of sexual abuse.

Perianal warts caused by the human papillomavirus should always raise the possibility of sexual abuse, because this is the most likely mode of transmission.[25,72] Although many studies suggest a high association with sexual abuse (60% to 90% of cases), recent studies have questioned this association, particularly in infants. Parents of children with condylomata often have warts on nongenital skin, and vertical transmission between mother and child has been well documented. The presence of condyloma acuminata in infants younger than 1 year of age may represent vertical transmission from the mother; older children must be treated with a very high index of suspicion for child abuse.

REFERENCES

1. Abrahamian FP, Lloyd-Still JD: Chronic constipation in children: A longitudinal study of 186 patients. J Pediatr Gastroenterol Nutr 1984;3:460.
2. Adeyemi SD: Childhood rectal prolapse: A prospective clinical study including trial of a rationalized conservative treatment modality. Int J Pediatr Surg 1991;5:21.
3. Aldridge RT, Campbell PE: Ganglion cell distribution in the normal rectum and anal canal. J Pediatr Surg 1968;3:475.
4. Al-Salem AH, Laing W, Talwalker V: Fistula-in-ano in infancy and childhood. J Pediatr Surg 1994;29:436.
5. Arhan P, Devroede G, Jehannin B, et al: Idiopathic disorders of fecal continence in children. Pediatrics 1983;71:774.
6. Ashcraft KW, Amoury RA, Holder TM: Levator repair and posterior suspension for rectal prolapse. J Pediatr Surg 1977;12:241.
7. Ashcraft KW, Garred JL, Holder TM: Rectal prolapse—17-year experience with the posterior repair and suspension. J Pediatr Surg 1990;25:992.
8. Bar-Maor JA, Eitan A: Determination of the normal position of the anus. J Pediatr Gastroenterol Nutr 1987;6:559.
9. Bellman M: Studies on encopresis. Acta Paediatr Scand 1966;1(Suppl):170.
10. Bennett DL, Duthie HL: The functional importance of the internal anal sphincter. Br J Surg 1964;51:355.
11. Benninga MA, Buller HA, Tytgat GN, et al: Colonic transit time in constipated children: Does pediatric slow-transit constipation exist? J Pediatr Gastroenterol Nutr 1996; 23:241.
12. Bitar KN, Makhlour GM: Purinergic receptors on isolated smooth muscle cells. Gastroenterology 1982;82:1018.
13. Bonnard A, Mougenot JP, Ferkdadji L, et al: Laparoscopic rectopexy for solitary ulcer of the rectum syndrome in a child. Surg Endosc 2003;17:1156.
14. Brazzelli M, Griffiths P: Behavioural and cognitive interventions with or without other treatments for defaecation disorders in children. Cochrane Database Syst Rev 2001;4: CD002240.
15. Burkitt D, Morley D, Walker A: Dietary fibre in under- and overnutrition in childhood. Arch Dis Child 1980; 55:803.
16. Chang JW, Wu TC, Wang KS, et al: Colon mucosal pathology in infants under three months of age with diarrhea disorders. J Pediatr Gastroenterol Nutr 2002;35:387.
17. Christensen J: Motility of the colon. In Johnson LR (ed): Physiology of the Gastrointestinal Tract, 2nd ed. New York, Raven Press, 1987.
18. Clark DA: Times of first void and first stool in 500 newborns. Pediatrics 1977;60:457.
19. Clayden GS: Constipation and soiling in childhood. BMJ 1976;1:515.
20. Clayden G, Agnarsson U: Constipation in Childhood. Oxford, Oxford Medical Publications, 1991.
21. Clayden GS: Reflex anal dilatation associated with severe chronic constipation in children. Arch Dis Child 1988;63:832.
22. Cohen A, Dehn TCB: Lateral subcutaneous sphincterotomy for treatment of anal fissure in children. Br J Surg 1995;82:1341.
23. Culver PS, Rattan S: Genesis of anal canal pressures in the opossum. Am J Physiol 1986;251:765.
24. Davidson M, Kugler MM, Bauer CH: Diagnosis and management in children with severe and protracted constipation and obstipation. J Pediatr 1964;62:261.
25. de Jesus LE, Cirne Neto OL, Monteiro do Nascimento LM, et al: Anogenital warts in children: Sexual abuse or unintentional contamination? Cad Saude Publica 2001; 17:1383.
26. de la Torre L, Carrasco D, Mora MA, et al: Vascular malformations of the colon in children. J Pediatr Surg 2002; 37:1754.
27. Di Lorenzo C, Flores AF, Hyman PE: Age-related changes in colon motility. J Pediatr 1995;127:593.
28. Di Lorenzo C, Benninga MA: Pathophysiology of pediatric fecal incontinence. Gastroenterology 2004;126:S33.
29. Doyles DM: Enuresis and encopresis. In Ollendick TH, Hersen M (eds): Handbook of Child Psychopathology. New York, Plenum Press, 1983.
30. Duthie HL: Dynamics of the rectum and anus. Clin Gastroenterol 1975;4:467.
31. Ertem D, Acar Y, Karaa EK, et al: A rare and often unrecognized cause of hematochezia and tenesmus in childhood: Solitary rectal ulcer syndrome. Pediatrics 2002; 110:E79.
32. Felt B, Wise CG, Olson A, et al: Guideline for the management of pediatric idiopathic constipation and soiling. Multidisciplinary team from the University of Michigan Medical Center in Ann Arbor. Arch Pediatr Adolesc Med 1999;153:380.
33. Fishman SJ, Shamberger RC, Fox VL, et al: Endorectal pull-through abates gastrointestinal hemorrhage from colorectal venous malformations. J Pediatr Surg 2000; 35:982.
34. Fitzgerald R, Harding B, Ryan W: Fistula-in-ano in childhood, a congenital etiology. J Pediatr Surg 1985; 20:80.
35. Fleisher DR: Diagnosis and treatment of disorders of defecation in children. Pediatr Ann 1986;5:71.
36. Freckner B, Ihre T: Influence of autonomic nerves on the internal anal sphincter in man. Gut 1976;17:306.
37. Freeman NV: Anorectal problems in childhood. In Taylor I (ed): Progress in Surgery. Edinburgh, Churchill Livingstone, 1989, p 92.
38. Gaston EA: The physiology of fecal continence. Surg Gynecol Obstet 1948;87:280.
39. Ghosh A, Griffiths DM: Rectal biopsy in the investigation of constipation. Arch Dis Child 1998;79:266.
40. Godbole P, Botterill I, Newell S, et al: Solitary rectal ulcer syndrome in children. J R Coll Surg Edinb 2000; 45:411.
41. Griffiths DM: The physiology of fecal continence: Idiopathic fecal constipation and soiling. Semin Pediatr Surg 2002;11:67.
42. Hardcastle JD, Parks AG: A study of anal incontinence and some principles of surgical treatment. Proc R Soc Med 1970;63:116.
43. Heaton ND, Davenport M, Howard ER: Incidence of haemorrhoids and anorectal varices in children with portal hypertension. Br J Surg 1993;80:616.
44. Heaton ND, Davenport M, Howard ER: Symptomatic hemorrhoids and anorectal varices in children with portal hypertension. J Pediatr Surg 1992;27:833.
45. Henry MM: Anorectal neuromuscular physiology. In Decosse JJ, Todd IP (eds): Anorectal Surgery. Edinburgh, Churchill Livingstone, 1988.
46. Hobbs CJ, Wynne JM: Buggery in childhood: A common syndrome of child abuse. Lancet 1986;2:792.
47. Hobbs CJ, Wynne JM: Child sexual abuse: An increasing rate of diagnosis. Lancet 1987;2:837.
48. Holschneider AM: The problem of anorectal continence. Prog Pediatr Surg 1976;9:85.
49. Hutson JM, Catto-Smith T, Gibb S, et al: Chronic constipation: No longer stuck! Characterization of colonic dysmotility as a new disorder in children. J Pediatr Surg 2004;39:795.

50. Iacono G, Cavataio F, Montalto G, et al: Intolerance of cow's milk and chronic constipation in children. N Engl J Med 1998;339:1100.
51. Ingebo KB, Heyman MB: Polyethylene glycol-electrolyte solution for intestinal clearance in children with refractory encopresis. Am J Dis Child 1988;142:340.
52. Johnson CF: Child sexual abuse. Lancet 2004;364:462.
53. Kenny SE, Irvine T, Driver CP, et al: Double blind randomized controlled trial of topical glyceryl trinitrate in anal fissure. Arch Dis Child 2001;85:404.
54. Keren S, Wagner Y, Heldenberg D, Golan M: Studies of manometric abnormalities of the rectoanal region during defecation in constipated and soiling children: Modification through biofeedback therapy. Am J Gastroenterol 1988;83:827.
55. Keuzenkamp-Jansen CW, Fijnvandraat CJ, Kneepkens CM, Douwes AC: Diagnostic dilemmas and results of treatment for chronic constipation. Arch Dis Child 1996; 75:36.
56. Khan AR, Vujanic GM, Huddart S: The constipated child: How likely is Hirschsprung's disease? Pediatr Surg Int 2003; 19:439.
57. Kokoska ER, Keller MS, Weber TR: Outcome of the antegrade colonic enema procedure in children with chronic constipation. Am J Surg 2001;182:625.
58. Koletzko S, Ballauff A, Hadziselimovic F, Enck P: Is histological diagnosis of neuronal intestinal dysplasia related to clinical and manometric findings in constipated children? Results of a pilot study. Pediatr Gastroenterol Nutr 1993;17:59.
59. Kopel FB: Gastrointestinal manifestations of cystic fibrosis. Gastroenterology 1972;62:483.
59a. Lake AM: Food-induced eosinophilic proctocolitis. J Pediatr Gastroenterol Nutr 2000;30(Suppl):S58.
60. Lambe GF, Driver CP, Morton S, Turnock RR: Fissurectomy as a treatment for anal fissures in children. Ann R Coll Surg Engl 2000;82:254.
61. Lawson JO: Pelvic anatomy II: Anal canal and associated sphincters. Ann R Coll Surg Engl 1974;54:288.
62. Levine MD: The school child with encopresis. Pediatr Rev 1981;2:285.
63. Levine MD: Children with encopresis: A descriptive analysis. Pediatrics 1975;56:412.
64. Lockhart RD, Hamilton GF, Fyfe FW: Anatomy of the Human Body. London, Faber and Faber, 1969.
65. Lockhart-Mummery JP: Surgical procedures in general practice: Rectal prolapse. BMJ 1939;1:345.
66. Loening-Baucke V: Encopresis. Curr Opin Pediatr 2002; 14:570.
67. Loening-Baucke VA: Sensitivity of the sigmoid colon and rectum in children treated for chronic constipation. J Pediatr Gastroenterol Nutr 1984;3:454.
68. Loening-Baucke V: Encopresis and soiling. Pediatr Clin North Am 1996;43:279.
69. Loening-Baucke V: Persistence of chronic constipation in children after biofeedback treatment. Dig Dis Sci 1991; 36:153.
70. Loening-Baucke V: Constipation in early childhood: Patient characteristics, treatment, and long-term follow up. Gut 1993;34:1400.
71. Luukkonen P, Jarvinen HJ, Rintala R: Colo-anal sleeve resection for rectal hemangioma: Case report. Acta Chir Scand 1989;155:613.
72. McCoy CR, Appelbaum H, Besser AS: Condylomata acuminata: An unusual presentation of child abuse. J Pediatr Surg 1982;17:505.
73. Macdonald A, Wilson-Storey D, Munro F: Treatment of perianal abscess and fistula-in-ano in children. Br J Surg 2003;90:220.
74. Machida HM, Catto Smith AG, Gall DG, et al: Allergic colitis in infancy: Clinical and pathologic aspects. J Pediatr Gastroenterol Nutr 1994;19:22.
75. Malone PS, Ransley PG, Kiely EM: Preliminary report: The antegrade continence enema. Lancet 1990;336: 1217.
76. Meunier P, Louis D, Jaubert de Beaujeu M: Physiologic investigation of primary chronic constipation in children: Comparison with the barium enema study. Gastroenterology 1984;87:1351.
77. Monges H, Salducci V, Nardy F, et al: Electrical activity of internal anal sphincter. In Christensen J (ed): Gastrointestinal Motility. New York, Raven Press, 1980 p 495.
78. Mulliken JB, Glowacki J: Classification of pediatric vascular lesions. Plast Reconstr Surg 1982;70:120.
79. Murthi GV, Okoye BO, Spicer RD, et al: Perianal abscess in childhood. Pediatr Surg Int 2002;18:689.
80. Nelson R: Nonsurgical therapy for anal fissure (Cochrane review). In The Cochrane Library, Issue 2. Chichester, UK, John Wiley & Sons, 2004.
81. Nelson R: A systematic review of medical therapy for anal fissure. Dis Colon Rectum 2004;47:422.
82. Nelson R: Operative procedures for fissure in ano (Cochrane review). In The Cochrane Library, Issue 2. Chichester, UK, John Wiley & Sons, 2004.
83. Nigro ND: Restoration of the levator sling in the treatment of rectal procidentia. Dis Colon Rectum 1958;1:123.
84. Nix P, Stringer MD: Perianal sepsis in children. Br J Surg 1997;84:819.
85. Nurko S, Garcia-Aranda JA, Guerrero VY, Worona LB: Treatment of intractable constipation in children: Experience with cisapride. J Pediatr Gastroenterol Nutr 1996;22:38.
86. Oh JT, Han A, Han SJ, et al: Fistula-in-ano in infants: Is nonoperative management effective? J Pediatr Surg 2001;36:1367.
87. Olness K, Tobin J: Chronic constipation in children: Can it be managed by diet alone? Postgrad Med J 1982; 72:149.
88. Ottaviani G: Histologische-anatomische untersuchungen uber die innervation des mesdarmes. A Microscop-Anat Forsch 1940;47:151.
89. Pearl RH, Ein SH, Churchill B: Posterior sagittal anorectoplasty for paediatric recurrent rectal prolapse. J Pediatr Surg 1989;24:1100.
90. Peña A: Anorectal malformations: Experience with the posterior sagittal approach. In Stringer MD, Oldham KT, Mouriquand PDE, Howard ER (eds): Pediatric Surgery and Urology: Long Term Outcomes. Philadelphia, WB Saunders, 1998, p 375.
91. Phillips SE, Edwards DAW: Some aspects of anal continence and defaecation. Gut 1965;6:396.
92. Pierce AM: Anal fissures and anal scars in anal abuse—are they significant? Pediatr Surg Int 2004;20:334.
93. Potter NH: A physiological study of the pelvic floor in rectal prolapse. Ann R Coll Surg Engl 1962;31:379.
94. Puri P: Variant Hirschsprung's disease. J Pediatr Surg 1997;32:149.
95. Reisner SH, Sivan Y, Nitzan M, Merlob P: Determination of anterior displacement of the 1 anus in newborn infants and children. Pediatrics 1984;73:216.
96. Rintala RJ, Marttinen E, Virkola K, et al: Segmental colonic motility in patients with anorectal malformations. J Pediatr Surg 1997;32:453.
97. Rintala R, Lindahl H, Louhimo I: Anorectal malformations: Results of treatment and long-term follow-up in 208 patients. Pediatr Surg Int 1991;6:36.
98. Ritchie JA: Mass peristalsis in the human colon after contact with oxyphenisatin. Gut 1972;13:211.

99. Roma E, Adamidis D, Nikolara R, et al: Diet and chronic constipation in children: The role of fiber. J Pediatr Gastroenterol Nutr 1999;28:169.
100. Rosen R, Buonomo C, Andrade R, Nurko S: Incidence of spinal cord lesions in patients with intractable constipation. J Pediatr 2004;145:409.
101. Rosen NG, Gibbs DL, Soffer SZ, et al: The nonoperative management of fistula-in-ano. J Pediatr Surg 2000;35:938.
102. Sander S, Vural O, Unal M: Management of rectal prolapse in children: Ekehorn's rectosacropexy. Pediatr Surg Int 1999;15:111.
103. Sarahan T, Weintraub WH, Coran AG, Wesley JR: The successful management of chronic constipation in infants and children. J Pediatr Surg 1982;17:171.
104. Sarin YK, Sharma AK: Posterior sagittal rectoplasty for rectal prolapse. Indian Pediatr 1993;30:541.
105. Schuster MM, Hendrix TR, Mendeloff AI: The internal anal sphincter response: Manometric studies on its normal physiology, neural pathways and alteration in bowel disorders. J Clin Invest 1963;42:196.
106. Shafer AD, McGlone TP, Flanagan RA: Abnormal crypts of Morgagni: The cause of perianal abscess and fistula-in-ano. J Pediatr Surg 1987;22:203.
107. Shapiro O: Applied anatomy of infants and children: Proctology. Rev Gastroenterol 1948;15:307.
108. Shwachman H, Redmond A, Khaw K-T: Studies in cystic fibrosis: Report of 130 patients diagnosed under 3 months of age over a 20-year period. Pediatrics 1970;46:335.
109. Silverberg M: Constipation in infants and children. Pract Gastroenterol 1987;11:43.
110. Staiano A, Andreotti MR, Greco L, et al: Long-term follow-up of children with chronic idiopathic constipation. Dig Dis Sci 1994;39:561.
111. Stanton A, Sutherland R: Prevalence of reflex anal dilatation in 200 children. BMJ 1989;298:802.
112. Sweeney JL, Ritchie JK, Nichols RJ: Anal fissure in Crohn's disease. Br J Surg 1988;75:57.
113. Swenson O, Bill AH: Resection of the rectum and rectosigmoid with preservation of the sphincter. Surgery 1948;24:212.
114. Sönmez K, Demirogullari B, Ekingen G, et al: Randomized, placebo-controlled treatment of anal fissure by lidocaine, EMLA, and GTN in children. J Pediatr Surg 2002;37:1313.
115. Tander B, Güven A, Demirbag S, et al: A prospective, randomized, double-blind, placebo-controlled trial of glyceryl-trinitrate ointment in the treatment of children with anal fissure. J Pediatr Surg 1999;34:1810.
116. Tolia V, Lin CH, Elitsur Y: A prospective randomized study with mineral oil and oral lavage solution for treatment of faecal impaction in children. Aliment Pharmacol Ther 1993;7:523.
117. Triboulet H: Durée de la traverse chez l'enfant modale épreuve du carmin. Bull Soc Pediatr Paris 1909; 11:512.
118. Tsugawa C, Matsumoto E, Muraji T, et al: Posterior plication of the rectum for rectal prolapse in children. J Pediatr Surg 1995;30:692.
119. Upadhyaya P: Mid-anal sphincteric malformation, cause of constipation in anterior perianal anus. J Pediatr Surg 1984;19:183.
120. Utzig MJ, Kroesen AJ, Buhr HJ: Concepts in pathogenesis and treatment of chronic anal fissure—a review of the literature. Am J Gastroenterol 2003;98:968.
121. van Ginkel R, Buller HA, Boeckxstaens GE, et al: The effect of anorectal manometry on the outcome of treatment in severe childhood constipation: A randomized, controlled trial. Pediatrics 2001;108:E9.
122. van Ginkel R, Benninga MA, Blommaart PJ, et al: Lack of benefit of laxatives as adjunctive therapy for functional nonretentive fecal soiling in children. J Pediatr 2000; 137:808.
123. Van Gossum A, Hittelet A, Schmit A, et al: A prospective comparative study of push and wireless-capsule enteroscopy in patients with obscure digestive bleeding. Acta Gastroenterol Belg 2003;66:199.
124. Wald A: Diagnosis of constipation in primary and secondary care. Rev Gastroenterol Disord 2004;4:S28.
125. Wald A: Disorders of defecation and fecal continence. Cleve Clin J Med 1989;56:491.
126. Watanabe Y, Todani T, Yamamoto S: Conservative management of fistula in ano in infants. Pediatr Surg Int 1998; 13:274.
127. Weaver LT, Ewing G, Taylor LC: The bowel habits of milkfed infants. J Pediatr Gastroenterol Nutr 1988;7:568.
128. Weaver LT, Steiner H: The bowel habit of young children. Arch Dis Child 1984;59:649.
129. Woodward MN, Foley P, Cusick EL: Colostomy for treatment of functional constipation in children: A preliminary report. J Pediatr Gastroenterol Nutr 2004;38:75.
130. Youssef NN, Barksdale E Jr, Griffiths JM, et al: Management of intractable constipation with antegrade enemas in neurologically intact children. J Pediatr Gastroenterol Nutr 2002;34:402.
131. Youssef NN, Pensabene L, Barksdale E Jr, Di Lorenzo C: Is there a role for surgery beyond colonic aganglionosis and anorectal malformations in children with intractable constipation? J Pediatr Surg 2004;39:73.
132. Zempsky WT, Rosenstein BJ: Cause of prolapse in children. Am J Dis Child 1988;142:338.

Chapter 103

The Jaundiced Infant: Biliary Atresia

R. Peter Altman and Terry L. Buchmiller

HISTORY

In 1892, Thomson[177] designated biliary atresia as a specific disease entity in the *Edinburgh Medical Journal*. Holmes[76] reviewed all reported cases and introduced the concept of "correctable" and "noncorrectable" forms of disease in 1916, terms that have little relevance today. Ladd[108] reported the first successful surgery for correctable biliary atresia in 1928. In 1953, Gross[63] noted that biliary atresia was the most common cause of neonatal obstructive jaundice, but with most infants having noncorrectable disease. Bill et al.[24] subsequently reported only 52 successful operations between 1927 and 1970. Several novel but unsuccessful surgical trials were attempted in the 1950s and early 1960s, including partial hepatectomy with intrahepatic cholangiojejunostomy,[119] artificial bile duct placement,[166] and establishment of lymphatic drainage through both the liver hilum[55] and thoracic duct.[2,141]

During the 1960s, early surgery for persisting jaundice was controversial because most cases of biliary atresia could not be differentiated from "neonatal hepatitis" or cholestatic syndromes. In 1968, Thaler and Gellis[176] contended that neonatal hepatitis was worsened by surgical intervention, thus recommending that surgery be postponed until 4 months of age. Descriptions of "spontaneous" cure of biliary atresia[93,106] further confounded the stance on early surgery. Second-look surgery was occasionally recommended with the optimistic opinion that the fibrotic extrahepatic ducts may eventually become patent.[34,50] Outcomes in patients with proven noncorrectable biliary atresia were fatal.

In 1957, Kasai et al.[96,99] ushered in the contemporary era for the treatment of infants traditionally considered to have noncorrectable biliary atresia with the introduction of hepatic portoenterostomy. Though originally meeting skepticism,[32,105] gradual confirmation of Kasai's results was reported by both Japanese and American pediatric surgeons, including Bill et al.[24] and Lilly and Altman.[115] Kasai's hepatic portoenterostomy involving Roux-en-Y reconstruction, with the current modification that omits stoma placement, remains the standard surgical treatment of biliary atresia. Primary biliary drainage is achieved in over two thirds of patients, although nearly half ultimately have progressive liver failure.

Liver transplantation was originally introduced by Starzl in 1963[165] and is the cornerstone of salvage therapy for the initial failed hepatic portoenterostomy and for those in whom end-stage liver disease later develops. With the availability of reduced-size and living related organs, the outlook for patients with biliary atresia is increasingly optimistic.

INTRODUCTORY ISSUES

Neonatal hyperbilirubinemia is usually physiologic, unconjugated, and self-limited. Only 2% to 15% of neonates remain jaundiced past 2 weeks of life, and just 0.2% to 0.4% have cholestatic jaundice from either intrahepatic cholestasis or structural abnormalities that cause biliary obstruction.[41] Intrahepatic cholestasis may result from numerous infectious or inflammatory causes, as well as from inherited metabolic defects. The major structural diseases include biliary atresia and choledochal cyst (Chapter 104). A variable element of hepatocellular dysfunction is common to all, thus rendering initial discrimination between medical and surgical cholestatic disease challenging.

The incidence of biliary atresia ranges from 1 in 10,000 to 1 in 16,700 live births, with a stable incidence over the past several decades.[95,126,139,143] There is a female preponderance of 1.4 to 1.7:1. The extrahepatic ducts are not entirely absent in biliary atresia. They remain, rather, as combinations of obliterated fibrous cords. Multiple classification systems have been developed that are based on the anatomy of these fibrous biliary remnants.

The common variations seen in biliary atresia are depicted in Figure 103-1. Most frequently, the entire extrahepatic ductal system is obliterated, with the next most common variant, occurring in nearly 20%, characterized by distal patency of the gallbladder and the cystic and common ducts.

The Japanese Association of Pediatric Surgeons has proposed an additional classification system that divides biliary atresia into three main types: type I, atresia at the site of the common bile duct (relative frequency of 11.9%); type II, atresia at the site of the hepatic duct

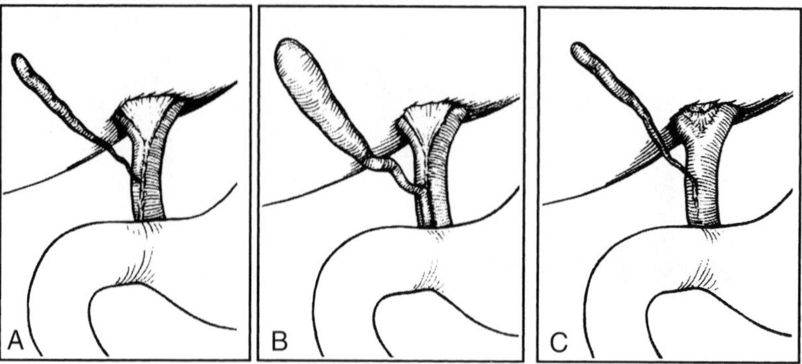

Figure 103–1 The pattern of fibrous obliteration of the extrahepatic ducts varies at exploration. *A*, The most common pattern with fibrotic extrahepatic ducts in continuity. *B*, The gallbladder, cystic, and common ducts are patent with fibrous obliteration at the porta. *C*, Fibrous cord representing the gallbladder; the remaining biliary tree is scanty to absent. (From Altman RP, Lilly JR, Greenfeld J, et al: A multivariable risk factor analysis of the portoenterostomy [Kasai] procedure for biliary atresia: Twenty-five years of experience from two centers. Ann Surg 1997;226:348, discussion 353. Courtesy of Lippincott Williams & Wilkins.)

(2.5%); and type III, atresia at the porta hepatis (84.1%).[139] Subtypes are also delineated, but a full review is beyond the scope of this chapter.

No racial differences or genetic factors appear to be related to disease occurrence. Associated congenital malformations occur in 11% to 20%.[139] Polysplenia is the most common associated anomaly and occurs in 7.5% overall. "Polysplenia syndrome" is defined as polysplenia with variable associations that may include a preduodenal portal vein, malrotation, and abdominal situs inversus. Polysplenia syndrome occurs in conjunction with maternal diabetes and may be associated with poorer outcomes.[44] Other congenital findings, such as asplenia, heart disease, inferior vena cava anomalies, annular pancreas, bowel atresia, and genitourinary anomalies, have occasionally been reported in association with biliary atresia.[35,49,126]

An expeditious diagnostic evaluation is essential and combines serology, ultrasonography, radionuclide scanning, and liver biopsy in the majority of cases. It is emphasized that an efficient diagnostic workup and early surgical treatment are essential to achieve higher success rates in the treatment of this disease.

EMBRYOLOGY AND ETIOLOGY

The biliary system originates from the hepatic diverticulum of the foregut at 4 weeks of embryonic life and differentiates into cranial and caudal components. The cranial component gives rise to the proximal extrahepatic ducts and the majority of the intrahepatic biliary system, whereas the caudal component gives rise to the gallbladder, cystic duct, and common bile duct.

Genetic, immune-mediated, and infectious causes have all been implicated in the pathogenesis of biliary atresia, but remain unproven. A congenital origin of biliary atresia is theorized to result from failure of recanalization of the extrahepatic biliary system during ductal embryogenesis. However, embryonic duct occlusion and subsequent vacuolization have not yet been confirmed[171] to definitively support this recanalization failure theory. It has also been suggested that failure of the extrahepatic and intrahepatic biliary ducts to meet during development may underlie certain types of biliary atresia with partial patency of the ductal system.

The ductal plate malformation theory was initially proposed by Desmet.[46] Tan et al.[171] suggested a failure of bile duct remodeling at the hepatic hilum. They hypothesized that these abnormal fetal bile ducts are poorly supported by mesenchyme and subsequently leak as perinatal bile flow increases. This leakage of bile triggers an intense local inflammatory reaction with subsequent obliteration of the biliary tree.

In many, biliary atresia is considered to be an acquired rather than a congenital anomaly.[26] This premise is supported by clinical observations that approximately 40% of patients pass normal meconium at birth and up to 60% pass cholic stools initially and for a short period after birth.[38]

Although biliary atresia occurs in twins sporadically,[81,135] a genetic etiology is unproven. Additional speculative factors underlying biliary atresia include a loss of blood supply,[104] abnormal bile acid metabolism,[92] pancreaticobiliary maljunction,[131] and Landing's concept of "infantile obstructive cholangiopathy."[109] Viral etiologies, including both rotavirus[156] and reovirus type 3,[180] have been proposed, but causation remain unproven.[30] An animal model of biliary atresia has been developed by reovirus infection in mice.[150]

Active investigation of biliary atresia in laboratory models is ongoing and includes the induction of neonatal viral infection. Despite all the aforementioned theories, the cause of biliary atresia remains unknown. It may prove to be a combination of factors, such as an immune event triggered by an infectious agent in a genetically susceptible host.

PATHOLOGIC CHARACTERISTICS

Histopathologic examination of the fibrous biliary remnants shows various stages of inflammation believed to underlie the progressive destruction of the ductal system.[36,56,101,116] Specimens occasionally contain lumina that correspond to altered biliary ducts. The varying appearances suggest that loss of the gross patency of the biliary system is a gradual process. Finally, completely obliterated ductal remnants have cicatricial granulation tissue with chronic inflammation (Fig. 103-2). The type and size of ductal remnants present in the resected portal plate have prognostic significance (see later).

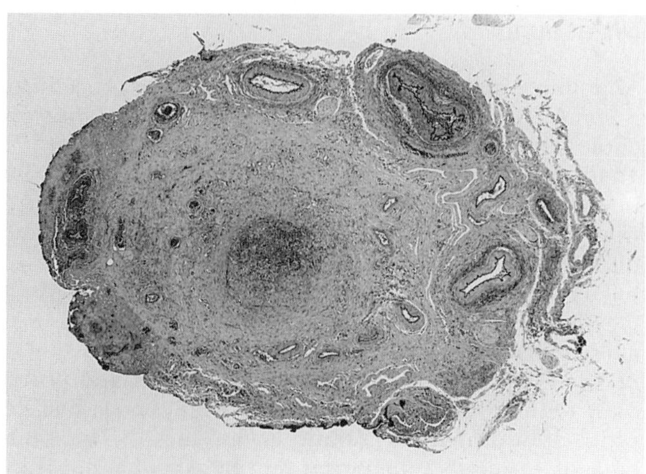

Figure 103-2 Histopathology of a completely obliterated common bile duct in biliary atresia reveals cicatricial granulation tissue with a chronic inflammatory reaction (hematoxylin-eosin stain, 40×).

Three specific types of biliary structures are seen microscopically in the transected surface of the fibrous remnant at the porta hepatis: preexisting bile ducts, collecting ductules, and biliary glands.[147] Only the bile ductules communicate with the intrahepatic biliary system and are potential conduits for drainage of bile after hepatic portoenterostomy. If bile flow is sustained, these ductules become internal biliary fistulas at the porta hepatis within several months (Fig. 103-3).

Histologic examination of the liver in biliary atresia reveals the hallmark finding of ductular proliferation. Additional features of diagnostic importance are bile stasis, distortion of the liver cell cords, giant cell transformation, focal necrosis, and intralobular portal fibrosis.[26,97,134,144] Widening of the portal area occurs, and hepatic fibrosis, periportal edema, cell infiltration, and various degrees of bile stasis are seen in the interlobular spaces. Both hyperplasia and hypertrophy of the hepatic arterial branches in the portal area are characteristic, although the significance is unclear.[75] Percutaneous liver biopsy is reliable for the diagnosis of biliary atresia when the biopsy specimens represent an adequate sample of portal areas.

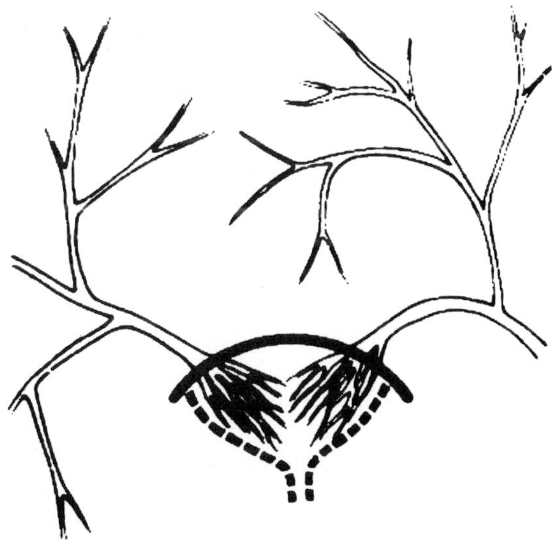

Figure 103-3 Schematic showing patent proliferating biliary ductules invested by the fibrous cone. Bile drainage is through these internal biliary fistulas at the porta hepatis after a successful Kasai procedure. (Courtesy of M. Kasai, MD.)

It is generally accepted that the pathologic changes in the biliary system[64,87,153] primarily affect both the intrahepatic and the extrahepatic biliary structures. The intrahepatic bile ducts are narrowed, distorted in configuration, and irregular in shape.[115] Some authors, however, believe that the intrahepatic biliary system is secondarily damaged from obliteration of the extrahepatic bile ducts during liver development.[144] The latter theory is supported by the clinical observation that the earlier corrective surgery is performed, the better the outcome. The intrahepatic bile duct involvement is important both pathologically and clinically because the degree of intrahepatic biliary damage is responsible for much of the morbidity after hepatic portoenterostomy. The fate of intrahepatic biliary involvement after portoenterostomy remains controversial.

CLINICAL FINDINGS

Signs and Symptoms

When jaundiced infants have acholic stools, dark urine, and an enlarged, firm liver, biliary atresia should be strongly suspected. The pathologic jaundice seen with biliary atresia typically appears within weeks after birth, but it may follow benign neonatal jaundice in some. The first meconium is usually normal in most, with a period of variably cholic stools in more than 50%.[38] As jaundice persists, the stools become acholic. Patients are initially active, and their growth appears normal during the first few weeks to months after birth.

As biliary obstruction persists, the liver gradually increases in size and develops a firm consistency. Cirrhosis will ultimately develop, and splenomegaly may follow. Malabsorption of fat-soluble vitamins can lead to anemia, malnutrition, and growth failure. If untreated, most children will die of hepatic decompensation, esophageal variceal bleeding, or infection within 19 months. Karrer et al.[95] report a less than 10% 3-year survival rate in children who do not undergo a definitive biliary drainage procedure.

Diagnosis

Pathologic jaundice is suspected when the conjugated fraction of bilirubin accounts for more than 20% of the total serum bilirubin, and this finding necessitates prompt evaluation.[20] Because the etiology may be diverse, serologic evaluation can help distinguish between infection, hematologic problems, metabolic diseases, and genetic disorders (e.g., α_1-antitrypsin deficiency). Neonatal hepatitis and biliary hypoplasia (paucity of the interlobular bile ducts) are most likely to be confused with biliary atresia. Because no individual test is absolutely reliable,

TABLE 103-1 Diagnosis of Biliary Atresia

Physical examination with an emphasis on
- Stool color
- Liver consistency

Liver function tests
Ultrasonography
Hepatobiliary scintigraphy (diisopropyliminodiacetic acid [DISIDA]) with phenobarbital preconditioning
Percutaneous liver biopsy

a combination of serologic evaluation, ultrasonography, hepatobiliary scintigraphy, and percutaneous liver biopsy is included in an expeditious evaluation of an infant with suspected biliary atresia (Table 103-1). By judiciously combining these data, greater than 90% accuracy in preoperatively predicting biliary atresia is expected. An absolute definitive diagnosis of biliary atresia requires surgical exploration.

Serologic Evaluation

Conventional serologic liver function tests are often nonspecific, but discrimination between parenchymal and extrahepatic ductal disease is usually possible. Hyperbilirubinemia secondary to intrahepatic cholestasis or biliary obstruction is characterized by elevations in both the direct and indirect fractions. Slight fluctuations in serum bilirubin are typical in biliary atresia. The transaminases are similarly elevated in both cholestatic and obstructive conditions unless there is overwhelming hepatocellular disease. Synthetic function of the liver, as assessed by the prothrombin time, partial thromboplastin time, total protein, and serum albumin, is seldom impaired early in the course of biliary atresia.

Because intrauterine infection can be manifested as postnatal jaundice, TORCH (toxoplasmosis, other viruses, rubella, cytomegalovirus, and herpes simplex virus) antibody titers should be determined routinely. Likewise, because infants with the metabolic abnormality α_1-antitrypsin deficiency may be jaundiced at birth, screening is recommended. Affected infants are homozygous at the protease inhibitor locus (Pi), which codes for α_1-antitrypsin, and have the PiZZ genotype.[152] Current treatment of α_1-antitrypsin deficiency is limited to organ transplantation for hepatic failure.[186]

Additional investigative serologic tests warrant mention but are not currently recommended in routine evaluation. Serum bile acids are increased in infants with cholestatic jaundice. A newborn mass screening program in Japan[124] found differentiation of biliary atresia from other cholestatic diseases by either the total bile acid level or the ratio of chenodeoxycholic acid to cholic acid[91] to be challenging.

Serum lipoprotein X (Lp-X) is positive in all patients with biliary atresia,[151,174] and the absence of Lp-X excludes biliary atresia. However, a significant overlap in up to 40% of patients with neonatal hepatitis limits its specificity.

γ-Glutamyl transpeptidase (γ-GTP) levels are also elevated in patients with biliary atresia.[192] Profiles combining Lp-X and γ-GTP are under investigation.[175]

Ultrasound

Abdominal ultrasound, a simple, noninvasive procedure, is sometimes useful in the evaluation of an infant with cholestatic jaundice and suspected biliary atresia.[1,161] To identify a normal gallbladder (>1.5 cm in length), the infant must be fasting for 4 hours before the examination.[11] The finding of a choledochal cyst or intrahepatic ductal dilatation effectively excludes the diagnosis of biliary atresia.[11] If the gallbladder is shrunken or not visualized, biliary atresia is suspected. A contraction in gallbladder size after feeding eliminates the possibility of biliary atresia. The fibrous cord remnant and portal plate found in biliary atresia can sometimes be visualized with sophisticated ultrasound techniques.[39] The presence of a preduodenal portal vein or asplenia/polysplenia is further supportive of biliary atresia.[1] Care must be taken to not misinterpret the parallel hepatic artery channel as a patent ductal structure. The use of Doppler improves diagnostic accuracy.[11]

Hepatobiliary Scintigraphy

Hepatobiliary scintigraphy commonly uses isotopes of technetium 99m (e.g., Tc-labeled diisopropyliminodiacetic acid [DISIDA]). DISIDA scans are widely used to confirm ductal patency and help differentiate biliary atresia from other causes of infantile cholestasis.[47,120,145] Severe intrahepatic cholestasis can affect tracer uptake because of liver dysfunction. Pretreatment with phenobarbital (5 mg/kg/day) for 3 to 5 days before imaging will enhance excretion and thus increase discrimination between biliary atresia and nonobstructive causes of intrahepatic cholestasis[120] and is therefore always recommended. Visualization of the radionuclide in the intestine confirms ductal patency and excludes biliary atresia. Isotope excretion may be delayed because of hepatic dysfunction, so it is essential to obtain images 24 hours after injection if earlier images fail to confirm radionuclide in the intestine. Failure of the isotope to appear in the intestine after 24 hours, particularly after pretreatment with phenobarbital, is highly suggestive of ductal obstruction as a result of biliary atresia.

Liver Biopsy

Percutaneous liver biopsy interpreted by an experienced hepatopathologist is highly accurate in assessing a jaundiced infant. The authors consider liver histology to be the most reliable study for the diagnosis of biliary atresia.[20,113] Several portal tracts should be examined for the greatest accuracy. The predominant discriminatory finding commonly seen in biliary atresia is ductular proliferation, which is not encountered in nonobstructive syndromes. Additional supportive findings include bile duct plugs within the portal triad ducts; canalicular and cellular bile stasis; portal tract edema and fibrosis; swelling, vacuolization, and sloughing of the biliary epithelium into the duct lumen; inflammatory cell infiltration; and giant cell transformation of hepatocytes. The differentiation between biliary atresia and paucity syndromes is typically readily apparent.[113]

Adjunctive Tests

Aspiration of duodenal fluid by nasoduodenal intubation has been recommended as an inexpensive, noninvasive, and rapid test.[54,60] The diagnosis of biliary atresia is excluded if the typical yellow bilirubin pigment is detected either by 24-hour collection or in serial duodenal intubations. However, subjectivity limits widespread usefulness. Assessment of fecal pigment by near-infrared reflectance spectroscopy has been introduced for the differentiation of infant cholestatic jaundice.[4]

The use of endoscopic retrograde cholangiopancreatography (ERCP) in infants has progressed with the development of small side-viewing endoscopes for use even in young infants.[111,169] However, ERCP has a limited role in the evaluation of infantile jaundice and is not routinely performed.

Some advocate ultrasound-guided percutaneous cholangiography when standard diagnostic tests have been inconclusive. The presence of a dilated gallbladder is necessary for percutaneous access, thus limiting widespread use in the most common types of biliary atresia. Meyers and colleagues[128] suggest that this may serve as an alternative to ERCP and contend that surgical exploration may be precluded when alternative diagnoses are confirmed.

Magnetic resonance cholangiopancreatography has shown 100% diagnostic accuracy in the evaluation of biliary and pancreatic disease in a small series of patients with biliary atresia.[132] Further evaluation is warranted, however, before universal application can be recommended.

Laparoscopic exploration with cholangiography for the evaluation of neonatal cholestatic jaundice has not yet found wide acceptance.

No single diagnostic test, nor combination thereof, is absolutely reliable. In infants in whom biliary atresia is highly suspected or in those with an unclear etiology after thorough diagnostic evaluation, expeditious surgical exploration is recommended.

TREATMENT

Preoperative Management

In addition to the routine preoperative care for abdominal surgery in infants and children, a dose of vitamin K (1 to 2 mg/kg intramuscularly) is administered several days before surgery. We do not perform a routine bowel preparation. Infants can usually be admitted the morning of surgery. Broad-spectrum antibiotics are administered in the operating room just before the incision.

SURGICAL TECHNIQUE

Hepatic portoenterostomy (the Kasai procedure) is the standard operation for the treatment of biliary atresia and has been the cornerstone of therapy for nearly 30 years. The extrahepatic biliary structures are totally excised en bloc, and the fibrous cone transected at the liver hilus is anastomosed to a Roux-en-Y jejunal limb.[96] The microscopic biliary structures contained within the transected fibrous tissue drain bile into the intestinal conduit. Over time, autoanastomosis occurs between the intestinal and ductal epithelial elements and provides biliary drainage (see Fig. 103-3). The details of Kasai portoenterostomy are provided in the following text.

The infant is positioned supine to ensure a nonobstructed view should cholangiography, which is not routine, be required. Surgical exploration commences through an upper abdominal transverse incision centered to the right. This incision can be extended across the midline if biliary reconstruction is required. The authors first examine the left upper quadrant to determine splenic anatomy. Polysplenia alerts one to the possibility of a preduodenal portal vein and situs inversus.

Next, liver consistency is noted and the porta hepatis inspected. Some surgeons reflect the liver from the abdominal cavity after dividing both triangular ligaments.[13,45] This maneuver is neither necessary, nor advised, for routine cases. In biliary atresia the liver texture is coarse and fibrotic with a green discoloration. In cases of neonatal hepatitis and Alagille's syndrome (see later), the liver appears smooth and chocolate brown.

Most infants undergoing exploration with a presumptive diagnosis of biliary atresia will have a fibrotic rudimentary gallbladder. When the gallbladder persists only as a fibrous remnant, the diagnosis of biliary atresia is established and portal dissection proceeds. If the gallbladder is indeterminate, an absorbable purse-string suture is placed and the fundus aspirated. The presence of "white bile" usually confirms the clinical suspicion of biliary atresia. We would proceed with portal dissection, without cholangiography, in this situation. In some infants, however, the gallbladder may be of nearly normal size or appear to contain bile. Cholangiography has a distinct role in this patient subset.

If the gallbladder has a lumen, diluted contrast material (diatrizoate [Hypaque]) is injected to determine the continuity of the biliary tree between the liver and duodenum. Complete extrahepatic duct patency is confirmed when contrast appears distally in the duodenum and proximally in the liver radicles. The size of the ducts is assessed by cholangiography to determine whether biliary hypoplasia or obstruction to bile flow from inspissation is present. If the contrast material moves only distally into the duodenum and not into the liver, gently occluding the distal common bile duct while reinjecting the gallbladder may encourage proximal ductal filling, although this maneuver rarely succeeds. If extrahepatic biliary patency is demonstrated, regardless of whether the ducts are of normal caliber or diminutive (Fig. 103-4), a liver biopsy is performed and the incision closed. We have not found it helpful to leave a cholecystostomy catheter in place; instead, the catheter is removed, the purse-string suture tied, and the gallbladder left in situ. If ductal patency is not confirmed, portal dissection and biliary reconstruction are performed (the Kasai procedure).

Although it is anatomically feasible to perform portocholecystostomy in the 20% with distal patency, such treatment was historically associated with a high rate of anastomotic complications. Many patients later required revision to a portoenterostomy.[9] Therefore, contemporary

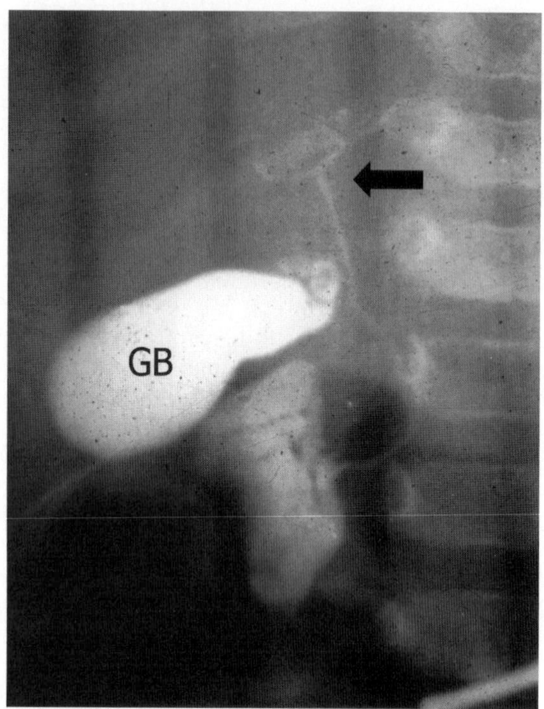

Figure 103–4 Biliary hypoplasia: operative cholangiogram demonstrating patent, but markedly diminutive extrahepatic biliary structures (*arrow*). GB, gallbladder.

reconstruction entails primary portoenterostomy even in the setting of a patent gallbladder, cystic duct, and common bile duct.

Portal exploration commences with early mobilization of the remnant gallbladder to facilitate identification of the fibrous hepatic ducts. The superficial peritoneum over the hepatoduodenal ligament is incised. The use of electrocautery reduces postoperative lymphatic leakage. Ductal and hepatic arterial anatomy are assessed.

The fibrous common duct is ligated distally with nonabsorbable suture and transected. Gentle traction applied to the remnant facilitates dissection toward the porta, where a cone of fibrous tissue anterior to the bifurcating portal vein is encountered. Occasionally, it is necessary to gently retract the right hepatic artery by carefully encircling it with a vessel loop.

It is emphasized that the bifurcation of the portal vein into right and left branches is the only reliable landmark for transection of the fibrous cone.[15,103] Several small, but constant "middle" branches of the portal vein entering the fibrous tissue must be identified to avoid troublesome bleeding. The authors prefer cautery with avulsion of these smaller branches, although careful ligation may also be performed. The absence of a cone at the portal plate is exceedingly unusual, and if the cone is not initially apparent, further meticulous exploration is encouraged.

When there is discontinuity of the biliary tree, exploration of the tissue overlying the portal vein bifurcation will almost invariably reveal the fibrous cone. Placing a suture in this fibrous tissue will facilitate establishing the plane above the portal vein.

Once dissection is complete, fine stay sutures are placed at the lateral margins of the fibrous cone. While maintaining moderate tension, the fibrous cone is sharply transected, thereby removing the extrahepatic biliary structures. It is neither necessary nor desirable to cut into the liver parenchyma because scarring of Glisson's capsule could hinder potential biliary drainage. Operative success depends on the microscopically patent biliary channels found in this cone of tissue. After irrigation, a warm saline pad is placed at the porta hepatis, thus completing the portal phase of the operation.

The resected biliary structures with attached gallbladder remnant are sent for permanent section with a request to measure the size of the biliary ductules for later prognostic evaluation. Although some authors[12,115] confirm the presence of microscopically patent ducts at the level of the anastomosis by frozen section, we have not found it useful because the precise level of transection is not optional. Finally, some Japanese pediatric surgeons recommend much wider transection and wide suturing that extends over the vessels in the hepatic hilus. Readers are referred to these publications for greater technical details.[52,88,148,178]

A Roux-en-Y limb is prepared by transecting the proximal jejunum approximately 10 cm from the ligament of Treitz. The distal jejunal margin is closed with inverting sutures. Intestinal continuity is restored by an end-to-side jejunojejunostomy 40 cm beyond the transected jejunum. A long 50-cm limb is preferred by Japanese surgeons.[90] The Roux-en-Y limb is brought into proximity to the previously transected fibrous tissue by passing the limb through an avascular aperture created in the mesentery of the transverse colon. The conduit is opened on its antimesenteric border several centimeters distal to the closed jejunal end.

Portoenterostomy commences by placing a posterior row of six or so double-armed fine sutures along the inferior cut margin of the fibrous tissue with the preplaced corner sutures used as a guide. Placement is meticulous to ensure complete incorporation of the potential biliary channels into the intestinal lumen when the bowel is subsequently apposed. Often, the portal vein must be gently retracted inferiorly to fully expose the portal plate.

The second needle of each stitch is placed into the back wall of the open jejunum. The sutures are tied so that the jejunum is in apposition to the cut fibrous surface. The anterior row of interrupted sutures is now placed. At completion, the entire cut surface of fibrous tissue is contained in the jejunal lumen. This single-layer reconstruction is essentially the only way in which our reconstruction differs from the original report of Kasai.

Finally, care is taken to repair the mesenteric defect of the Roux limb, as well as tack the Roux limb to the mesenteric window to prevent tension or an internal hernia. A drain is placed near the portoenteric anastomosis and brought through a right lower quadrant stab incision. The abdominal wound is closed in layers. A schematic of the completed operation is presented in Figure 103-5.

An initial experience with laparoscopic Kasai portoenterostomy has been described by Lee and colleagues.[112] In the exceedingly rare case of an infant with end-stage liver failure (Child's C classification) from undiagnosed biliary atresia, proceeding to primary transplantation can be cautiously considered.

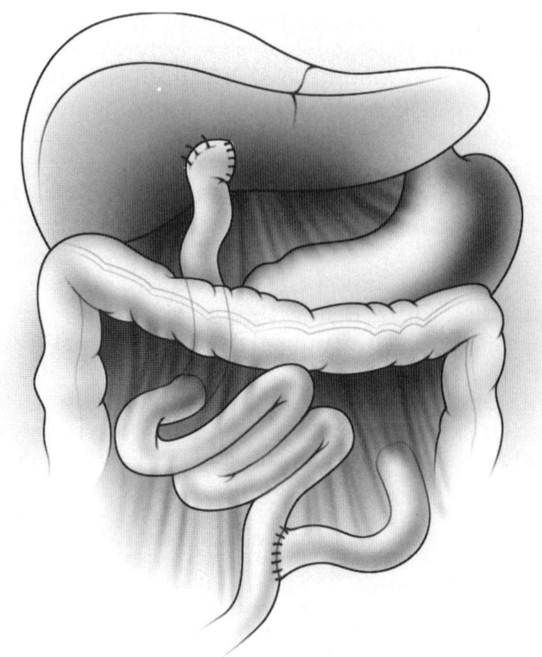

Figure 103–5 Kasai procedure: schematic of the completed hepatic portoenterostomy. The Roux-en-Y limb is 40 cm and passes through the transverse mesocolon.

Operative Modifications

Many innovative modifications have been devised, primarily by Japanese pediatric surgeons, in an effort to reduce postoperative cholangitis.[38] Historically, the biliary conduit was initially externalized as a stoma to provide monitoring of bile drainage and theoretically minimize postoperative cholangitis by the disassociation of enteric contents.[10,117] Once biliary drainage was established, the stoma was closed 3 to 6 months later to restore continuity of the conduit. Although stoma formation may decrease the initial severity of cholangitis,[38] experience has shown that externalization does not decrease the incidence of cholangitis, may worsen liver function,[17] invites stoma complications,[121] and complicates potential liver transplantation.[147] The use of a stoma is currently not recommended.

Similarly, the use of an intussusception valve for the theoretical prevention of enteric reflux was proposed,[38,52,138,172] but is not currently recommended.[110,121] Only one prospective nonrandomized study has compared the inclusion of an intussusception antireflux valve, with no benefit on either the incidence or duration of cholangitis.[142]

Use of the appendix as a biliary conduit by the creation of a portoappendiceal duodenostomy has been reported with mixed results. In a recent review by Tsao and colleagues,[179] patients with a primary appendiceal conduit had similar overall survival rates, but successful biliary drainage in only 31% and eventual liver transplantation in 88%. This use of technique cannot currently be supported.

Few have advocated transplantation as the initial therapy for an infant with biliary atresia.[158] This would subject the third of patients who are apparently "cured" by portoenterostomy to the long-term risks involved in transplantation. Others propose a selective approach and offer primary transplantation to infants in whom biliary atresia is diagnosed at more than 120 days of age or to those with unfavorable histology.[19,98,191] We view portoenterostomy and transplantation as sequential, complementary procedures to treat biliary atresia.[16]

Postoperative Management

Nasogastric drainage is continued until intestinal function returns, usually within 48 hours. Intravenous antibiotics are continued until a diet commences, at which time long-term oral antibiotics are initiated. The drain is typically removed before discharge. Length of stay averages 5 days. Virtually all agree that prolonged use of antibiotics and choleretic agents is warranted as prophylaxis to prevent postoperative cholangitis. The use of steroids has been controversial and is discussed in the next section. Our current postoperative medical regimen is shown in Table 103-2 and includes the use of steroids.

Steroid Use

Steroids have pronounced anti-inflammatory and immunosuppressive effects and are observed to decrease edema and collagen deposition, arrest the migration of monocytes and lymphocytes, and inhibit scarring. They have been postulated to have a choleretic effect by stimulation of bile flow through the bile salt–independent fraction induced by Na^+,K^+-ATPase activity. However, attempts to document increased biliary drainage by measuring bile output through an external conduit were unsuccessful.[14] The salutary effect of steroid use in the management of biliary atresia has been difficult to prove because many potential confounding variables exist. Additionally, many studies have been underpowered to draw significant statistical conclusions.[136]

However, many authors have reported improved outcomes with the use of steroid therapy in the postoperative period. In 1985, Karrer and Lilly[94] reported successful "blast" steroid therapy (high dose/short duration) when used for approximately 1 week for the treatment of cholangitis or for diminution of bile flow after a Kasai procedure. Dillon et al.[48] were the first to advocate long-term steroid use (6 weeks minimum) and reported 76% to be jaundice-free with their native liver at 4-year follow-up. Muraji et al.[137] reported on the use of steroids

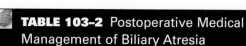

TABLE 103–2 Postoperative Medical Management of Biliary Atresia

Ursodiol (Actigall), 10-15 mg/kg/day
Trimethoprim-sulfamethoxazole suspension; trimethoprim component, 2 mg/kg/day
Vitamin ADEKs drops, 1 mL/day
Prednisone, 2 mg/kg/day divided twice daily; taper over a 2- to 3-week period

commencing 1 week after portoenterostomy with subsequent tapering. If stools became acholic, the regimen was repeated. Meyers and colleagues[127] compared an intravenous methylprednisolone (Solu-Medrol) taper followed by 8 to 12 weeks of oral prednisone combined with ursodeoxycholic acid versus no steroid use. Patients receiving steroids had significantly lower conjugated bilirubin by 3 to 4 months after surgery, and fewer required liver transplantation or died during the first year.[127]

Insignificant adverse sequelae associated with steroid use include fluid retention and appetite stimulation. No increase in infections, hernias, or ascites has been reported. Although the optimal dose, route of administration, and length of course are still debated, steroid use appears to be justified by accumulating data. Over the past year, we have incorporated a tapering 2- to 3-week course of steroids into our postoperative management regimen.

OUTCOMES

The Kasai portoenterostomy has dramatically improved survival for what had been a uniformly fatal diagnosis 40 years ago. The mortality rate within the first 30 days is extremely low and ranges from 0% to 0.5%.[16,137,179] The initial establishment of bile drainage is heralded by the appearance of cholic stools and improvement in jaundice, usually within 10 to 14 days. Biliary drainage typically occurs in more than two thirds of patients (range, 25% to 86%[16,121,179]) but is not a guarantee of cure. Of those who achieve initial bile drainage, half (25% to 35% of the total) will be "cured," with sustained bile flow and clearing of jaundice, and remain free of long-term sequelae. These children grow and develop according to normal standards. Liver transplantation is not required.

In the other half of those achieving initial bile drainage (≈35% of the total), progressive liver insufficiency will insidiously develop, with the return of jaundice in 21% accompanied by portal hypertension and its sequelae. In those with diminished bile flow, jaundice decreases postoperatively in 14%, but not to normal levels. These children may have failure to thrive. Though achieving significant initial palliation, liver transplantation may be required at a mean of 5.4 years.[16]

The remaining 15% to 30% who never drain bile after primary portoenterostomy experience unchanged jaundice, and progressive liver failure develops that can be salvaged only by transplantation. The donor pool for infants, once critically limited by the deceased donor liver shortage, has dramatically increased with the use of both living related and deceased donor reduced-size liver transplantation. This permits salvage for patients with a failed portoenterostomy, ideally before being compromised by end-stage hepatic failure.[27]

The 10-year survival rate after hepatic portoenterostomy has steadily increased and currently ranges from 40% to 67%. The Biliary Atresia Registry of the United States and Canada[95] initially reported that 5- and 10-year actuarial survival rates in 670 children were approximately 48% and 30% from 1976 to 1989. The U.K. experience shows that 64% were alive with their native liver 3.6 years after initial portoenterostomy.[126] The University of Hong Kong reported that 68% were transplant-free at 10 years.[184] However, only 20% to 30% survive past the age of 20 years without liver transplantation, despite the initial encouraging outcome.[140,162] Tsao and colleagues reported that 50% will ultimately require liver transplantation.[179] We have reported a median survival without a liver transplant of 15 years and a 49% 20-year survival rate.[16]

The Japanese Biliary Atresia Registry has provided robust follow-up of nearly 1400 patients since 1989.[139] The 5-year survival rate ranged from 53% to 64% without liver transplantation and increased to 78% with the addition of transplantation.[138] Their reported 10-year survival rate was 67% with the native liver and 53% without it.[139] Overall 5- and 10-year survival rates were 75% and 67%, respectively.[139]

Predicting Outcome

We[16] and others[74,185,187] have attempted to elucidate predictors of clinical outcome after hepatic portoenterostomy (a third cured, a third with progressive liver dysfunction, a third nonresponders). The relative percentage of patients in each category is dependent on many factors, such as age at surgery, precise dissection and transection of the porta hepatis, the severity of liver disease, the initial postoperative course, and the occurrence of postoperative complications, particularly cholangitis.

Significant independent variables include the age at surgery, as determined by multivariate analysis.[16] Patients were stratified into three groups (0 to 49 days, 50 to 70 days, and >70 days). No difference in outcome was demonstrated in the two younger groups. However, infants older than 70 days had a higher risk for failure than did both younger cohorts. The long-term survival rate also steadily decreases with increasing age of the patient at surgery. The 10-year survival rate for patients undergoing surgery before 60 days of age was 68%; 61 to 70 days old, 39%; 71 to 90 days old, 33%; and older than 91 days of age, only 15%.

Many other reports[33,62,74,129,159] corroborate this improved outcome when infants were operated on within the first 8 to 12 weeks of life. The Japanese Biliary Atresia Registry[139] now reports equivalent success rates up to 90 days of age, but worsening bile flow thereafter. Although age older than 70 days at surgery is widely accepted as a risk factor, some recent reports are at variance.[42,121,127,184]

Davenport et al. recently examined the outcome of older (>100 days) infants undergoing portoenterostomy.[43] Despite 37% having evidence of a "cirrhotic" liver, 5- and 10-year actuarial survival rates were 45% and 40% with their native liver. One third have their native liver, and 28% have undergone transplantation. No discriminatory factors were identified. With these reasonable intermediate survival results, use of the Kasai operation, even as the primary surgical therapy in an older infant, is supported.

The next independent variable relates to both the gross and microscopic appearance of the remnant ducts. When the three types of biliary anatomy were examined (see Fig. 103-1), patients with a patent gallbladder (type B) had improved outcomes when compared with those with complete fibrous obliteration (type A) or absence of the fibrous cone (the rare type C).[105]

Microscopic ductal pathology at the portal plate was also relevant to prognosis. Many studies have examined the correlation between the number and size of biliary ductal structures at the porta hepatis and the success rate of portoenterostomy. We have determined the histologic characteristics of the ductal remnants at the portal plate to be a highly significant predictor of clinical outcome.[16] Three distinct type of ducts have been identified and classified on the basis of luminal size: type I, ductular lumen greater than 150 μm; type II, ductular lumen smaller than 150 μm and invested by abundant connective tissue; and type III, concentric fibrous tissue without a biliary lumen.[36] Bile drainage was achieved in all patients with type I ducts, 86% of those with type II ducts, but only 12% of those with type III ducts. We conclude that ductal size is a highly significant independent predictor of outcome.[16] Other investigators[16,64,87,101,147,153,168] also support this strong positive correlation, but others do not.[56,111,127,171]

Liver histology[160,170] at the time of the definitive operation has been proposed as a prognostic determinant. Though counterintuitive, we[16] and others[8] have found that the extent of hepatic fibrosis does not correlate with patient age, type of ductal histology, or clinical outcome.

Finally, surgery performed in earlier decades (1970s) had a higher risk for failure than those performed more recently. This difference may well reflect the "learning curve" of the operation, as well as maturation of strategies in the management of complications such as cholangitis, portal hypertension, and nutritional deficiencies.

Additional markers of liver function and clinical outcome are under investigation, although prognostic significance remains speculative. Several of the more promising studies are discussed in the following text. ^{99m}Tc-diethylenetriaminepentaacetic acid (DTPA)-galactosyl–labeled human serum albumin directly binds to hepatocyte receptors and allows scintigraphy to directly measure functional hepatic reserve, thereby showing correlation with outcome.[85] Serial assessments estimate the prognosis of the liver and may have a role in predicting unrecognized deterioration or the need for future liver transplantation.

Insulin-like growth factor type I (IGF-I) has been investigated as a serum marker of hepatic reserve.[194] Levels of IGF-I are low in patients with biliary atresia, even in the absence of growth retardation and normal levels of growth hormone.

Serum aspartate transaminase (AST) at 1 year was an independent predictor that significantly correlated with quality of life and liver dysfunction[182] in 35 long-term (>5 year) survivors who were jaundice-free (bilirubin <1.0 mg/dL). The serum level of hyaluronic acid is a sensitive marker of liver fibrosis in biliary atresia.[70] Soluble intercellular adhesion molecule-1 (ICAM-1) has shown promise as a marker of disease activity in biliary atresia.[130] Doppler ultrasonography of the hepatic artery has been used to calculate a "resistive index" that has prognostic value in predicting rapid deterioration after the Kasai procedure.[28]

Mathematical models have been used for 30 years in an attempt to predict outcome after portoenterostomy.[74] A biliary atresia prognostic index using a multivariate linear regression model to predict outcome after primary surgery has been formulated.[53] Variables include both serologic and physical parameters stratified by age (<1 year). The risk for morbidity from progressive liver cirrhosis was quantified and allowed earlier consideration for transplantation.

The Pediatric End-Stage Liver Disease (PELD) risk scoring system[189] has been evaluated as a severity index for biliary atresia,[163] with significant correlation in distinguishing survivors without transplantation from nonsurvivors. However, use in children younger than 1 year and in older patients with severe complications is cautioned, thus probably limiting its overall applicability.[163]

COMPLICATIONS

Nutritional Complications

Weight gain after surgery may be retarded if hepatic dysfunction persists. Additionally, because the enterohepatic circulation has been impaired for several months, various metabolic perturbations involving fat and protein metabolism and vitamin and trace mineral absorption may occur.[18,61] Essential fatty acid deficiency and rickets may develop in up to 32%.[22] Careful long-term monitoring of clinical status and nutritional supplementation are required. The use of medium-chain triglyceride–containing formulas is recommended when bile flow is absent or scanty.

Cholangitis

Cholangitis is the most frequent and serious complication after hepatic portoenterostomy, with an incidence ranging from 33% to 60%.[77,90,143,184] Cholangitis is more common in the first few years after surgery and contributes to progressive liver dysfunction and the development of cirrhosis. Prevention of cholangitis is paramount in sustaining bile drainage after portoenterostomy.

The cause and pathogenesis of cholangitis remain incompletely understood. Theories include direct contamination via reflux of intestinal contents through the Roux limb, portal venous infection,[40] impaired lymphatic drainage at the porta hepatis,[73] and systemic bacterial translocation. Predisposing factors may include biliary stasis caused by partial obstruction of the intrahepatic bile ducts and bacterial overgrowth of the intestinal conduit.

Cholangitis is heralded by fever, decreased bile flow, and progressive jaundice. Children are lethargic and irritable and may appear septic. Serologic evaluation is confirmatory by the demonstration of increased serum bilirubin levels, leukocytosis with a left shift, and an elevation in C-reactive protein. Alkaline phosphatase, the transaminases, and γ–GGT are elevated over baseline. Liver biopsy is not routinely recommended but, if obtained, will demonstrate acute inflammatory infiltrates in the portal and periportal areas, including the biliary duct epithelium. In more severe cases, microabscess formation is seen. Enteric gram-negative and anaerobic organisms[29] have been most frequently isolated.

Early postoperative cholangitis (within 3 months) is frequently followed by the temporary cessation of bile flow, with repeated episodes causing progressive deterioration of hepatic function. Six to 9 months after surgery, as the biliary stasis resolves and bile flow is brisk, the incidence of cholangitis decreases.

Treatment of cholangitis includes fluid therapy, broad-spectrum intravenous antibiotics (including anaerobic coverage), and choleretic agents. Steroid use is empirical in an attempt to diminish edema and inflammation. Short courses of high-dose steroids have been successful and are recommended.[94] Laboratory investigation in rat models of biliary atresia and cholangitis are beginning to determine modulators of the anti-inflammatory effects of steroids.[80]

Attempts to prevent recurrent cholangitis are warranted. The efficacy of prophylactic oral antibiotics remains encouraging, but controversial.[51,133] Use of either trimethoprim-sulfamethoxazole (TMP-SMZ) or neomycin in patients after the first attack of cholangitis has shown promise in both delaying and reducing the number of future attacks versus historic controls (4 mg/kg/day TMP and 20 mg/kg/day SMZ divided in two doses or neomycin, 25 mg/kg/day divided four times daily 4 days per week).[31] The use of postoperative steroids has also resulted in a lower incidence of cholangitis (28% versus 43%).[127] Novel therapies, including the use of herbal medications,[84] have shown promise in limited trials.

Attempts to reestablish biliary drainage by operative revision of the hepatic portoenterostomy have been proposed when patients with an initially successful Kasai operation have either cessation of bile flow[9] or intractable cholangitis.[12] However, a second operation significantly complicates potential future liver transplantation. Despite initial enthusiasm, mounting experience suggests extreme caution when contemplating remedial surgery.

Hasegawa et al. reviewed 25 patients who underwent redo hepatic portoenterostomy for insufficient bile drainage in biliary atresia.[69] Only 20% achieved disappearance of jaundice within 3 months, and survival was 6 months to 11 years. Of the remaining 20, 8 died and 10 underwent transplantation. Additionally, if liver histology showed advanced fibrosis or cirrhosis at re-exploration, the results were poor. We have also confirmed similar results, with only two of seven achieving sustained drainage.[9] Favorable late results are expected only for patients with active bile excretion after the initial operation.[83]

Muraji and colleagues[137] reported on the reoperative treatment of 11 patients with severe, intractable cholangitis. A 3-cm antireflux intussusception valve was created in the Roux limb and the limb lengthened if less than 50 cm. Cholangitis resolved after a few brief postoperative episodes. Two ultimately required liver transplantation, but had an improved quality of life in the interim. The Japanese Biliary Atresia Registry reported no difference with or without the creation of a valve.[139]

A novel technique in the management of late-onset liver failure has recently been described in two patients[86]: intrahepatic biliary dilatation in one and creation of an intrahepatic bile lake in the other. By combining percutaneous decompression and stenting, the dilated ducts were ultimately surgically connected to the Roux conduit. Jaundice resolved in short-term follow-up (<2 years).

Notwithstanding the occasional successes achieved by reoperation, with the results of liver transplantation in the current era, we discourage reoperation to rescue a failed Kasai procedure.

Portal Hypertension

A degree of hepatic fibrosis is invariably present in patients with biliary atresia at the initial surgery and can be graded histologically. Intrahepatic disease may progress despite successful hepatic portoenterostomy.[8] Portal hypertension, which occurs in 34% to 76% and is the most serious late complication, may develop in even initially jaundice-free patients.[3,118,167] Postoperative cholangitis is a significant predictor associated with the development of portal hypertension.[146] Spontaneous alleviation of portal hypertension, though rare, correlates with a reduction in portal pressure and improved liver histology.[102,141]

Portal hypertension is manifested as ascites in 63%. Esophageal varices occur in 49% of long-term survivors (>3 years), with bleeding complications in 20% to 60%. Patients at risk should be monitored carefully by upper endoscopic surveillance, as frequently as one to two times per year.[53] In a randomized, controlled trial, prophylactic sclerotherapy significantly reduced the incidence of hemorrhage from esophageal varices.[58]

Severe esophageal varices or variceal bleeding is primarily treated by endoscopic injection sclerotherapy. Multiple sessions are typically required (6.3 per patient).[84] Pharmacologic treatment with octreotide or beta blockade and variceal ligation have also been used.[66,78,79] Variceal hemorrhage is not an absolute indication for transplantation, nor necessarily a prognostic indicator of end-stage liver failure.[184]

Hypersplenism occurs in 16% to 35% of long-term survivors after hepatic portoenterostomy. Severe thrombocytopenia increases the risk for gastrointestinal tract bleeding.[157] Treatment of symptomatic hypersplenism associated with marked thrombocytopenia (platelet count <5000 cells/mm^3) should be considered. Earlier surgical interventions for portal hypertension and hypersplenism included splenectomy and splenorenal shunt procedures. Partial splenic embolization has also been described with reasonable success.[71] However, in the contemporary era of liver transplantation, the authors recommend against interventional procedures such as portosystemic shunts, esophageal transection, and splenic embolization. Instead, referral for liver transplantation should be expedited.

Psychosocial follow-up has been evaluated in long-term survivors. Growth and development are retarded in 65%.[22] Kuroda and colleagues[107] reported on 44 patients with a follow-up of longer than 15 years. The majority (93%) are employed or highly educated, or both. Psychological problems occurred in 18%.[107]

Long-term follow-up is now available in adults previously treated for biliary atresia. Menstrual disorders such as delayed menarche and amenorrhea correlate significantly with liver function at puberty. Pubertal disorders are considered to be predictive signs of progressive liver dysfunction and a harbinger for transplantation. Menstrual disorders normalize after successful liver transplantation.[107]

Reports are emerging on the effect of pregnancy in expectant women. Maternal portal hypertension is uniformly accelerated during pregnancy, and esophageal varices developed in all with their native livers.[107] Newborns have been small for gestational age, but have had good postnatal growth without congenital anomalies. Problems after delivery included deterioration of liver function in 37.5%, ascending cholangitis in 25%, and severe fatigue with liver dysfunction from nursing, all leading to liver transplantation.[162]

Even if one's initial postoperative course is favorable, unexpected complications can occur during pregnancy. Meticulous monitoring is essential during pregnancy, including increased endoscopic surveillance for varices. Prophylactic sclerotherapy for women wishing to conceive may be advisable.

Liver Transplantation

Liver transplantation is discussed in detail in Chapter 45 and is the treatment of end-stage liver disease. Biliary atresia accounts for nearly half of all pediatric liver transplants. Liver transplantation is considered for patients with biliary atresia when (1) bile drainage cannot be established after the initial portoenterostomy, (2) inadequate bile drainage leads to chronic liver failure with the onset of developmental retardation, and (3) the sequelae of chronic liver disease become uncontrollable.

A 4% mortality rate has been observed while awaiting transplantation.[126] To address the problems of an insufficient donor pool for infants and children, two additional transplant techniques are now available. The first uses a reduced-size or split-liver deceased donor liver transplant as introduced by Bismuth and Houssin in 1984.[25] The second involves living related liver transplantation.[27] Transplantation programs have adopted these techniques across the world for pediatric recipients.[59,173] A comprehensive review is outside the scope of this chapter, but readers are referred to several multicenter reviews for further detail.[57,59,154,155]

The dramatic improvement in survival after liver transplantation with advances in immunosuppression has raised the question of primary transplantation for biliary atresia.[89,164] Though debated,[191] the consensus among pediatric surgeons is that the Kasai portoenterostomy is preferred as the initial therapy for biliary atresia. The rationale includes the fact that nearly half can achieve adequate liver function and hepatic portoenterostomy delays the need for liver transplantation in many patients.[183] Donor shortage is a significant problem in the pediatric age group, and liver transplantation is associated with attendant morbidity (including serious infections and oncogenesis) and mortality. However, liver transplantation remains an integral part of the rescue therapy for biliary atresia,[183] with recent 5-year survival rates nearing 85%.[125]

OTHER SURGICAL LESIONS RESPONSIBLE FOR JAUNDICE IN INFANCY

Surgical lesions other than biliary atresia that may cause jaundice in infancy and childhood include choledochal cysts (Chapter 104), interlobular biliary hypoplasia, inspissated bile syndrome, cholelithiasis, spontaneous perforation of the bile ducts, sclerosing cholangitis, pyogenic cholangitis, traumatic stricture, cholecystitis, benign or malignant tumors of the extrahepatic bile ducts, and extramural compression. Three of the more common entities are described in the following sections.

Biliary Hypoplasia

Biliary hypoplasia is a unique classification within the cholestatic spectrum, but it is often erroneously labeled "intrahepatic biliary atresia." The liver histology is characterized by a paucity of intrahepatic ducts, unlike the ductal proliferation seen in biliary atresia. The paucity of interlobular bile ducts is defined as a reduction in the number of interlobular bile ducts (i.e., a significantly decreased ratio of the number of interlobular bile ducts to the number of portal tracts).[65] Biliary hypoplasia is best regarded as a condition secondary to decreased bile flow from the liver rather than a primary structural abnormality of the ducts.[72]

Two types of biliary hypoplasia are observed in infants and children[7] and are classified as either syndromic (Alagille's) or nonsyndromic. Nonsyndromic patients may initially be confused with those who have biliary atresia. Differentiation is crucial because transplantation is the only appropriate therapy for the end-stage liver disease in biliary hypoplasia.

Percutaneous liver biopsy samples from affected infants lack the hepatic fibrosis and ductal proliferation characteristic of biliary atresia. If diagnostic exploration is required, the liver is smooth and often "chocolate brown." Cholangiography demonstrates a diminutive biliary tree, which precludes the need for biliary reconstruction (see Fig. 103-4). Extensive portal exploration may jeopardize the integrity of these delicate ducts and is not advised.[114] Instead, a generous liver biopsy specimen is obtained. We do not recommend leaving the cholecystostomy catheter in place for postoperative study. Outcomes range from clinical improvement with resolution of cholestasis to end-stage liver disease with progressive cirrhosis.

Syndromic Paucity of the Interlobular Bile Ducts (Alagille's Syndrome)

Alagille and colleagues originally described a syndromic population of infants who had biliary ductal paucity with five main clinical features: characteristic facies, jaundice from chronic cholestasis, posterior embryotoxon, butterfly-like vertebral arch defects, and branch pulmonary artery hypoplasia or stenosis.[5,6] Less frequent features include growth retardation, mental retardation, renal disturbances, bone abnormalities, high-pitched voice, and pubertal delay.[6] This well-defined syndromic type of disease occurs more frequently than the nonsyndromic type.

Infants with Alagille's syndrome manifest cholestasis and pruritus before 1 year of age. All have hepatomegaly, but cirrhosis and portal hypertension develop in only 25%. Serology confirms cholestasis with very high total bile acid, cholesterol, and triglyceride levels. The diagnosis of Alagille's syndrome is based on the association of a histologic paucity of interlobular bile ducts and the characteristic clinical features. Alagille's syndrome has a familial incidence with an autosomal dominant pattern of inheritance. As more patients with Alagille's syndrome reach adulthood, this syndrome may be accompanied by long-term manifestations of chronic liver disease.

Nonsyndromic Paucity of the Interlobular Bile Ducts

In the nonsyndromic type of biliary hypoplasia, incomplete obstruction from cholestasis begins during the first month of life and pruritus ensues. Laboratory test results are identical to those seen with the syndromic type and are nonspecific. The diagnosis is confirmed only by cholangiography and liver biopsy showing a decrease or absence of the interlobular bile ducts with a variable degree of portal fibrosis.

The nonsyndromic type of biliary hypoplasia may result from either active destruction or atrophy of formed ducts. It may occur in other clinical settings, including concomitant liver disorders such as cytomegalovirus infection, rubella virus infection, α_1-antitrypsin deficiency, cystic fibrosis, graft-versus-host disease, Down's syndrome, and hypopituitarism. An increase in trihydroxycoprostanic acid levels is observed. Patients with the nonsyndromic type of biliary hypoplasia have a worse prognosis than those with the syndromic type. Cirrhosis with portal hypertension will develop in half, and they may die of liver failure within the first year of life. A solitary case of complete clinical and histopathologic resolution has been described.[23]

Treatment

Biliary hypoplasia cannot be cured by any surgical maneuver except liver transplantation. Medical therapy is supportive and consists of medium-chain triglyceride feeding, supplementation of fat-soluble vitamins, and the administration of phenobarbital and cholestyramine for symptomatic, severe pruritus. Liver transplantation is warranted for end-stage liver disease or severe pruritic complications.[181]

Inspissated Bile Syndrome

Inspissated bile syndrome is defined as partial or complete obstruction of the extrahepatic biliary system by impaction of thick bile or sludge in the distal common bile duct during the neonatal period. A predisposition is postulated in disorders that either increase the viscosity or decrease the solubility of bile. Inspissated bile syndrome can occur in infants with dehydration, hemolysis, impaired hepatic bile secretion, and cystic fibrosis and in those receiving diuretic therapy[188] or total parenteral nutrition.[123] It may be initially difficult to differentiate inspissated bile syndrome from biliary atresia because both are characterized by jaundice and acholic stools. Inspissation of bile may precede cholelithiasis.

Abdominal ultrasound demonstrates mild to moderate proximal biliary dilatation and sludge or stones in the distal common bile duct. Radionuclide scans show a hepatic concentration of isotope without excretion into the intestine.

Inspissated bile syndrome usually resolves spontaneously[100] as the underlying disease or predisposing factors are treated. Persistent obstruction is evaluated and treated at surgical exploration by intraoperative cholangiography performed through the gallbladder fundus, which will confirm the diagnosis and exclude biliary atresia (Fig. 103-6). Cholangiography is often curative and may be augmented by intraoperative saline irrigation. Duodenotomy or choledochotomy is rarely required.

Idiopathic Perforation of the Common Bile Duct

Spontaneous perforation of the extrahepatic biliary system is a rare, but important clinical entity in infants that necessitates prompt recognition and surgical correction. In most patients, the perforation occurs at the union of the cystic and common bile ducts. The etiology of spontaneous perforation remains speculative. Popular theories hypothesize a congenital weakness of the bile duct,[37,149] but additional causes include inspissated bile, viral infection, pancreatitis, and stenosis of the ampulla of Vater associated with elevated ductal pressure. Some authors[149,193] have identified the presence of pancreaticobiliary

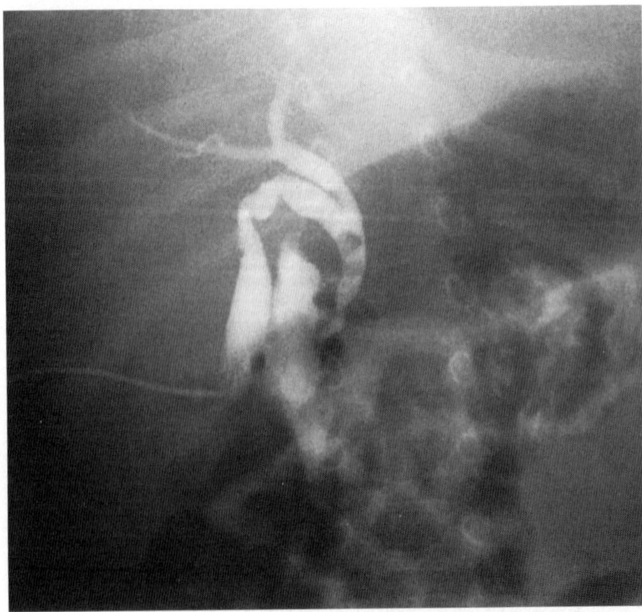

Figure 103-6 Operative cholangiogram in a 2-month-old infant showing inspissated bile in the distal common bile duct. Irrigation through the gallbladder was curative.

maljunction in many patients and have suggested that idiopathic perforation of the bile duct and choledochal cysts may be differing manifestations of a spectrum of congenital biliary ductal defects.[11]

Clinical Features and Diagnosis

Most infants have jaundice, painless abdominal distention with ascites, clay-colored stools, and failure to thrive.[21] The increased intra-abdominal pressure from the ascites may unmask inguinal and umbilical hernias. The bile duct perforation is usually tiny and allows slow egress of bile. Occasionally, the leak may become encapsulated by the formation of a pseudocyst.[111] Less commonly, the infant has an acute onset of fulminating biliary peritonitis.[82]

Serum bilirubin levels are typically less than 8 mg/dL, with minimal elevation of serum transaminases. Abdominal ultrasonography shows either generalized ascites or a loculated fluid collection in the right upper quadrant in the absence of biliary dilatation.[67] Radionuclide scanning (DISIDA) demonstrates isotope in the ascitic fluid or contained by the occasional pseudocyst.[122]

Treatment and Outcome

Patients with idiopathic perforation of the common bile duct may be malnourished and dehydrated, thus making aggressive preoperative resuscitation paramount. Definitive treatment is provided by surgical exploration. Operative cholangiography through the gallbladder excludes pancreaticobiliary maljunction, distal obstruction, or other pathologic lesions. When bile duct perforation is confirmed, most favor leaving the cholecystostomy catheter in situ, thereby providing both biliary decompression and the ability to perform postoperative cholangiography to assess healing.[68] Suture repair of the tiny perforation is not recommended. Instead, simple drainage of the porta in the region of the perforation, without suture repair, is advised. The outlook for complete recovery in most, without long-term hepatobiliary sequelae, is excellent.

REFERENCES

1. Abramson SJ, Berdon WE, Altman RP, et al: Biliary atresia and noncardiac polysplenic syndrome: US and surgical considerations. Radiology 1987;1632:377.
2. Absolon KB, Rikkers H, Aust JB: Thoracic duct lymph drainage in congenital biliary atresia. Surg Gynecol Obstet 1965:120:123.
3. Akiyama H, Saeki M, Ogata T: Portal hypertension after successful surgery for biliary atresia. In Kasai M (ed): Biliary Atresia and Its Related Disorders. Amsterdam, Excerpta Medica, 1983.
4. Akiyama T, Yamauchi Y: Use of near infrared reflectance spectroscopy in the screening for biliary atresia. J Pediatr Surg 1994:29:645.
5. Alagille D: Cholestasis in the first three months of life. Prog Liver Dis 1979:6:471.
6. Alagille D, Estrada A, Hadchouel M, et al: Syndromic paucity of interlobular bile ducts (Alagille syndrome or arteriohepatic dysplasia): Review of 80 cases. J Pediatr 1987;110:195.
7. Alagille D, Odievre M, Gautier M, Dommergues JP: Hepatic ductular hypoplasia associated with characteristic facies, vertebral malformations, retarded physical, mental, and sexual development, and cardiac murmur. J Pediatr 1975;86:63.
8. Altman RP: The portoenterostomy procedure for biliary atresia: A five year experience. Ann Surg 1978;188:351.
9. Altman RP: Results of re-operations for correction of extrahepatic biliary atresia. J Pediatr Surg 1979;14:305.
10. Altman RP: Long term results after the Kasai procedure. In Daum F (ed): Extrahepatic Biliary Atresia. New York, Marcel Dekker, 1983.
11. Altman RP, Abramson S: Potential errors in the diagnosis and surgical management of neonatal jaundice. J Pediatr Surg 1985;20:529.
12. Altman RP, Anderson KD: Surgical management of intractable cholangitis following successful Kasai procedure. J Pediatr Surg 1982;176:894.
13. Altman RP, Chandra R, Lilly JR: Ongoing cirrhosis after successful porticoenterostomy in infants with biliary atresia. J Pediatr Surg 1975;10:685.
14. Altman RP, Levy J: Biliary atresia. Pediatr Ann 1985;14:481.
15. Altman RP, Lilly JR: Technical details in the surgical correction of extrahepatic biliary atresia. Surg Gynecol Obstet 1975;140:952.
16. Altman RP, Lilly JR, Greenfeld J, et al: A multivariable risk factor analysis of the portoenterostomy (Kasai) procedure for biliary atresia: Twenty-five years of experience from two centers. Ann Surg 1997;226:348, discussion 353.
17. Ando H, Ito T, Nagaya M: Use of external conduit impairs liver function in patients with biliary atresia. J Pediatr Surg 1996;311:1509.
18. Andrews WS, Pau CM, Chase HP, et al: Fat soluble vitamin deficiency in biliary atresia. J Pediatr Surg 1981;16:284.
19. Azarow KS, Phillips MJ, Sandler AD, et al: Biliary atresia: Should all patients undergo a portoenterostomy? J Pediatr Surg 1997;32:168, discussion 172.
20. Balistreri WF: Neonatal cholestasis. J Pediatr 1985;106:171.
21. Banani SA, Bahador A, Nezakatgoo N: Idiopathic perforation of the extrahepatic bile duct in infancy: Pathogenesis, diagnosis, and management. J Pediatr Surg 1993;28:950.
22. Barkin RM, Lilly JR: Biliary atresia and the Kasai operation: Continuing care. J Pediatr 1980;96:1015.
23. Berezin S, Beneck D, Altman RP, Schwarz SM: Resolution of nonsyndromic paucity of intrahepatic bile ducts in infancy. Dig Dis Sci 1995;40:82.
24. Bill AH, Brennom WS, Huseby TL: Biliary atresia. New concepts of pathology, diagnosis, and management. Arch Surg 1974;109:367.
25. Bismuth H, Houssin D: Reduced-sized orthotopic liver graft in hepatic transplantation in children. Surgery 1984;95:367.
26. Brent RL: Persistent jaundice in infancy. J Pediatr 1962;61:111.
27. Broelsch CE, Whitington PF, Emond JC, et al: Liver transplantation in children from living related donors. Surgical techniques and results. Ann Surg 1991;214:428, discussion 437.
28. Broide E, Farrant P, Reid F, et al: Hepatic artery resistance index can predict early death in children with biliary atresia. Liver Transpl Surg 1997;36:604.
29. Brook I, Altman RP: The significance of anaerobic bacteria in biliary tract infection after hepatic portoenterostomy for biliary atresia. Surgery 1984;95:281.
30. Brown WR, Sokol RJ, Levin MJ, et al: Lack of correlation between infection with reovirus 3 and extrahepatic biliary atresia or neonatal hepatitis. J Pediatr 1988;113:670.
31. Bu LN, Chen HL, Chang CJ, et al: Prophylactic oral antibiotics in prevention of recurrent cholangitis after the Kasai portoenterostomy. J Pediatr Surg 2003;38:590.

32. Campbell DP, Poley JR, Alaupovic P, Smith EI: The differential diagnosis of neonatal hepatitis and biliary atresia. J Pediatr Surg 1974;9:699.
33. Canty TG Sr: Encouraging results with a modified Sawaguchi hepatoportoenterostomy for biliary atresia. Am J Surg 1987;154:19.
34. Carlson E: Salvage of the "noncorrectable" case of congenital extrahepatic biliary atresia. Arch Surg 1960;81:893.
35. Chandra RS: Biliary atresia and other structural anomalies in the congenital polysplenia syndrome. J Pediatr 1974; 85:649.
36. Chandra RS, Altman RP: Ductal remnants in extrahepatic biliary atresia: A histopathologic study with clinical correlation. J Pediatr 1978;93:196.
37. Chen W, Chang C, Hung W: Congenital choledochal cyst: With observations on rupture of the cyst and intrahepatic ductal dilatation. J Pediatr Surg 1973;8:529.
38. Chiba T: Japanese Biliary Atresia Registry. In Ohi R (ed): Biliary Atresia. Tokyo, Icom Associates, 1991.
39. Choi SO, Park WH, Lee HJ, Woo SK: 'Triangular cord': A sonographic finding applicable in the diagnosis of biliary atresia. J Pediatr Surg 1996;31:363.
40. Danks DM, Campbell PE, Clarke AM, et al: Extrahepatic biliary atresia: The frequency of potentially operable cases. Am J Dis Child 1974;128:684.
41. Davenport M, Betalli P, D'Antiga L, et al: The spectrum of surgical jaundice in infancy. J Pediatr Surg 2003;38:1471.
42. Davenport M, Kerkar N, Mieli-Vergani G, et al: Biliary atresia: The King's College Hospital experience (1974-1995). J Pediatr Surg 1997;32:479.
43. Davenport M, Puricelli V, Farrant P, et al: The outcome of the older (> or =100 days) infant with biliary atresia. J Pediatr Surg 2004;39:575.
44. Davenport M, Savage M, Mowat AP, Howard ER: Biliary atresia splenic malformation syndrome: An etiologic and prognostic subgroup. Surgery 1993;113:662.
45. Davies MR: Facilitating the operative exposure of the portal plate in cases of biliary atresia by dislocating the whole liver onto the abdominal wall. J Pediatr Surg 1992;27:1391.
46. Desmet VJ: Intrahepatic bile ducts under the lens. J Hepatol 1985;15:545.
47. Dick MC, Mowat AP: Biliary scintigraphy with DISIDA. A simpler way of showing bile duct patency in suspected biliary atresia. Arch Dis Child 1986;61:191.
48. Dillon PW, Owings E, Cilley R, et al: Immunosuppression as adjuvant therapy for biliary atresia. J Pediatr Surg 2001;361:80.
49. Dimmick JE, Bove KE, McAdams AJ: Extrahepatic biliary atresia and the polysplenia syndrome [letter]. J Pediatr 1975;86:644.
50. Donovan EJ: Congenital atresia of the bile ducts. Ann Surg 1937;106:737.
51. Ecoffey C, Rothman E, Bernard O, et al: Bacterial cholangitis after surgery for biliary atresia. J Pediatr 1987;111:824.
52. Endo M, Katsumata K, Yokoyama J, et al: Extended dissection of the portahepatis and creation of an intussuscepted ileocolic conduit for biliary atresia. J Pediatr Surg 1983;18:784.
53. Endo M, Masuyama H, Watanabe K, et al: Calculation of biliary atresia prognostic index using a multivariate linear model. J Pediatr Surg 1995;30:1575.
54. Faweya AG, Akinyinka OO, Sodeinde O: Duodenal intubation and aspiration test: Utility in the differential diagnosis of infantile cholestasis. J Pediatr Gastroenterol Nutr 1991;13:290.
55. Fonkalsrud EW, Kitagawa S, Longmire WP Jr: Hepatic lymphatic drainage to the jejunum for congenital biliary atresia. Am J Surg 1966;112:188.
56. Gautier M, Jehan P, Odievre M: Histologic study of biliary fibrous remnants in 48 cases of extrahepatic biliary atresia: Correlation with postoperative bile flow restoration. J Pediatr 1976;89:704.
57. Goldstein MJ, Salame E, Kapur S, et al: Analysis of failure in living donor liver transplantation: Differential outcomes in children and adults. World J Surg 2003;27:356.
58. Goncalves ME, Cardoso SR, Maksoud JG: Prophylactic sclerotherapy in children with esophageal varices: Long-term results of a controlled prospective randomized trial. J Pediatr Surg 2000;35:401.
59. Goss JA, Shackleton CR, Swenson K, et al: Orthotopic liver transplantation for congenital biliary atresia. An 11-year, single-center experience. Ann Surg 1996;224:276, discussion 284.
60. Greene H: Nutritional aspects in the management of biliary atresia. In Daum F (ed): Extrahepatic Biliary Atresia. New York, Marcel Dekker, 1983.
61. Greene HL, Helinek GL, Moran R, O'Neill J: A diagnostic approach to prolonged obstructive jaundice by 24-hour collection of duodenal fluid. J Pediatr 1979;95:412.
62. Grosfeld JL, Fitzgerald JF, Predaina R, et al: The efficacy of hepatoportoenterostomy in biliary atresia. Surgery 1989;106:692, discussion 700.
63. Gross R: Obstructive jaundice in infancy. In Gross R (ed): The Surgery of Infancy and Childhood. Philadelphia, WB Saunders, 1953.
64. Haas JE: Bile duct and liver pathology in biliary atresia. World J Surg 1978;2:561.
65. Hadchouel M, Hugon RN, Gautier M: Reduced ratio of portal tracts to paucity of intrahepatic bile ducts. Arch Pathol Lab Med 1978;102:402.
66. Hall RJ, Lilly JR, Stiegmann GV: Endoscopic esophageal varix ligation: Technique and preliminary results in children. J Pediatr Surg 1988;23:1222.
67. Haller JO, Condon VR, Berdon WE, et al: Spontaneous perforation of the common bile duct in children. Radiology 1989;172:621.
68. Hammoudi SM, Alauddin A: Idiopathic perforation of the biliary tract in infancy and childhood. J Pediatr Surg 1988;23:185.
69. Hasegawa T, Kimura T, Sasaki T, et al: Indication for redo hepatic portoenterostomy for insufficient bile drainage in biliary atresia: Re-evaluation in the era of liver transplantation. Pediatr Surg Int 2003;19:256.
70. Hasegawa T, Sasaki T, Kimura T, et al: Measurement of serum hyaluronic acid as a sensitive marker of liver fibrosis in biliary atresia. J Pediatr Surg 2000;35:1643.
71. Hayashi Y: Effect of partial splenic embolization on hypersplenism in patients with biliary atresia. In Ohi R (ed): Biliary Atresia. Tokyo, Professional Postgraduate Services, 1987.
72. Hays DM, Woolley MM, Snyder WH Jr, et al: Diagnosis of biliary atresia: Relative accuracy of percutaneous liver biopsy, open liver biopsy, and operative cholangiography. J Pediatr 1967;71:598.
73. Hirsig J, Kara O, Rickham PP: Experimental investigations into the etiology of cholangitis following operation for biliary atresia. J Pediatr Surg 1978;13:55.
74. Hitch DC, Shikes RH, Lilly JR: Determinants of survival after Kasai's operation for biliary atresia using actuarial analysis. J Pediatr Surg 1979;14:310.
75. Ho CW, Shioda K, Shirasaki K, et al: The pathogenesis of biliary atresia: A morphological study of the hepatobiliary system and the hepatic artery. J Pediatr Gastroenterol Nutr 1993;16:53.
76. Holmes JB: Congenital obliteration of the bile ducts: Diagnosis and suggestions for treatment. Am J Dis Child 1916;11:405.

77. Howard ER: Extrahepatic biliary atresia: A review of current management. Br J Surg 1983;70:193.
78. Howard ER, Stamatakis JD, Mowat AP: Management of esophageal varices in children by injection sclerotherapy. J Pediatr Surg 1984;19:2.
79. Howard ER, Stringer MD, Mowat AP: Assessment of injection sclerotherapy in the management of 152 children with oesophageal varices. Br J Surg 1988;75:404.
80. Hsieh CS, Huang CC, Huang LT, et al: Glucocorticoid treatment down-regulates chemokine expression of bacterial cholangitis in cholestatic rats. J Pediatr Surg 2004;39:10.
81. Hyams JS, Glaser JH, Leichtner AM, Morecki R: Discordance for biliary atresia in two sets of monozygotic twins. J Pediatr 1985;1073:420.
82. Hyde GA Jr: Spontaneous perforation of bile ducts in early infancy. Pediatrics 1965;35:453.
83. Ibrahim M: Indications and results of reoperation for biliary atresia. In Ohi R (ed): Biliary Atresia. Tokyo, Icom Associates, 1991.
84. Iinuma Y, Kubota M, Yagi M, et al: Effects of the herbal medicine Inchinko-to on liver function in postoperative patients with biliary atresia—a pilot study. J Pediatr Surg 2003;38:1607.
85. Ishii T, Nio M, Shimaoka S, et al: Clinical significance of 99mTc-DTPA-galactosyl human serum albumin liver scintigraphy in follow-up patients with biliary atresia. J Pediatr Surg 2003;38:1486.
86. Islam S, Dasika N, Hirschl RB, Coran AG: A novel approach to the management of late-onset liver failure in biliary atresia. J Pediatr Surg 2004;39:371.
87. Ito T, Horisawa M, Ando H: Intrahepatic bile ducts in biliary atresia—a possible factor determining the prognosis. J Pediatr Surg 1983;18:124.
88. Ito T, Nagaya M, Ando H, et al: Modified hepatic portal enterostomy for biliary atresia. Z Kinderchir 1984;39:242.
89. Iwatsuki S, Shaw BW Jr, Starzl TE: Liver transplantation for biliary atresia. World J Surg 1984;8:51.
90. Japanese Biliary Atresia Society: Nationwide Registry of Biliary Atresia, 1998. Jpn J Pediatr Surg 2000;36:311.
91. Javitt NB, Keating JP, Grand RJ, Harris RC: Serum bile acid patterns in neonatal hepatitis and extrahepatic biliary atresia. J Pediatr 1977;90:736.
92. Jenner RE, Howard ER: Unsaturated monohydroxy bile acids as a cause of idiopathic obstructive cholangiopathy. Lancet 1975;2:1073.
93. Kanof A, Donovan EJ, Berner H: Congenital atresia of the biliary system;delayed development of correctibility. Am J Dis Child 1953;86:780.
94. Karrer FM, Lilly JR: Corticosteroid therapy in biliary atresia. J Pediatr Surg 1985;20:693.
95. Karrer FM, Lilly JR, Stewart BA, Hall RJ: Biliary atresia registry, 1976 to 1989. J Pediatr Surg 1990;25:1076, discussion 1081.
96. Kasai M: Treatment of biliary atresia with special reference to hepatic porto-enterostomy and its modifications. Prog Pediatr Surg 1974;6:5.
97. Kasai M, Kimura S, Asakura Y, et al: Surgical treatment of biliary atresia. J Pediatr Surg 1968;3:665.
98. Kasai M, Mochizuki I, Ohkochi N, et al: Surgical limitation for biliary atresia: Indication for liver transplantation. J Pediatr Surg 1989;24:851.
99. Kasai M, Okamoto A, Ohi R, et al: Changes of portal vein pressure and intrahepatic blood vessels after surgery for biliary atresia. J Pediatr Surg 1981;16:152.
100. Kasai M, Suzuki S: A new operation for "non-correctable" biliary atresia: Hepatic portoenterostomy. Shujyutsu 1959;13:733.
101. Kasai M, Yakovac WC, Koop CE: Liver in congenital biliary atresia and neonatal hepatitis. A histopathologic study. Arch Pathol 1962;74:152.
102. Keller MS, Markle BM, Laffey PA, et al: Spontaneous resolution of cholelithiasis in infants. Radiology 1985;157:345.
103. Kimura K, Tsugawa C, Kubo M, et al: Technical aspects of hepatic portal dissection in biliary atresia. J Pediatr Surg 1979;14:27.
104. Klippel CH: A new theory of biliary atresia. J Pediatr Surg 1972;7:651.
105. Koop CE: Biliary atresia and the Kasai operation. Pediatrics 1975;55:9.
106. Krovetz LJ: Congenital biliary atresia. Surgery 1960;47:453.
107. Kuroda T, Saeki M, Nakano M, Morikawa N: Biliary atresia, the next generation: A review of liver function, social activity, and sexual development in the late postoperative period. J Pediatr Surg 2002;37:1709.
108. Ladd WE: Congenital atresia and stenosis of the bile ducts. JAMA 1928;91:1082.
109. Landing BH: Considerations of the pathogenesis of neonatal hepatitis, biliary atresia and choledochal cyst—the concept of infantile obstructive cholangiopathy. Prog Pediatr Surg 1974;6:113.
110. Lazar EL, Altman RP: Surgical disease of the biliary tract. In Oxford Textbook of Surgery. Oxford, Oxford University Press, 1999.
111. Lebwohl O, Waye JD: Endoscopic retrograde cholangiopancreatography in the diagnosis of extrahepatic biliary atresia. Am J Dis Child 1979;133:647.
112. Lee H, Hirose S, Bratton B, Farmer D: Initial experience with complex laparoscopic biliary surgery in children: Biliary atresia and choledochal cyst. J Pediatr Surg 2004;39:804, discussion 807.
113. Lefkowitch JH: Biliary atresia. Mayo Clin Proc 1998;73:90.
114. Lilly JR: The surgery of biliary hypoplasia. J Pediatr Surg 1976;11:815.
115. Lilly JR, Altman RP: Hepatic portoenterostomy (the Kasai operation) for biliary atresia. Surgery 1975;78:76.
116. Lilly JR, Hitch DC: Postoperative ascending cholangitis following portoenterostomy for biliary atresia: Measures for control. World J Surg 1978;2:581.
117. Lilly JR, Stellin G: Variceal hemorrhage in biliary atresia. J Pediatr Surg 1984;19:476.
118. Lilly JR, Weintraub WH, Altman RP: Spontaneous perforation of the extrahepatic bile ducts and bile peritonitis in infancy. Surgery 1974;75:664.
119. Longmire WP Jr, Sanford MC: Intrahepatic-cholangiojejunostomy with partial hepatectomy for biliary obstruction. Surgery 1948;24:264.
120. Majd M, Reba RC, Altman RP: Hepatobiliary scintigraphy with ^{99m}Tc-PIPIDA in the evaluation of neonatal jaundice. Pediatrics 1981;67:140.
121. Maksoud JG, Fauza DO, Silva MM, et al: Management of biliary atresia in the liver transplantation era: A 15-year, single-center experience. J Pediatr Surg 1998;33:115.
122. Marshall DG, Brabyn DG, Vezina WC: Spontaneous perforation of the common bile duct in infancy detected by ^{99m}Tc HIDA scanning. Can J Surg 1984;27:590.
123. Matos C, Avni EF, Van Gansbeke D, et al: Total parenteral nutrition (TPN) and gallbladder diseases in neonates. Sonographic assessment. J Ultrasound Med 1987;6:243.
124. Matsui A, Ishikawa T: Identification of infants with biliary atresia in Japan. Lancet 1994;343:925.
125. McDiarmid SV: Current status of liver transplantation in children. Pediatr Clin North Am 2003;50:1335.

126. McKiernan PJ, Baker AJ, Kelly DA: The frequency and outcome of biliary atresia in the UK and Ireland. Lancet 2000;355:25.
127. Meyers RL, Book LS, O'Gorman MA, et al: High-dose steroids, ursodeoxycholic acid, and chronic intravenous antibiotics improve bile flow after Kasai procedure in infants with biliary atresia. J Pediatr Surg 2003;38:406.
128. Meyers RL, Book LS, O'Gorman MA, et al: Percutaneous cholecysto-cholangiography in the diagnosis of obstructive jaundice in infants. J Pediatr Surg 2004;39:16.
129. Middlesworth W, Altman RP: Biliary atresia. Curr Opin Pediatr 1997;9:265.
130. Minnick KE, Kreisberg R, Dillon PW: Soluble ICAM-1 (sICAM-1) in biliary atresia and its relationship to disease activity. J Surg Res 1998;76:53.
131. Miyano T, Suruga K, Suda K: Abnormal choledocho-pancreatico ductal junction related to the etiology of infantile obstructive jaundice diseases. J Pediatr Surg 1979;14:16.
132. Miyazaki T, Yamshita Y, Tang Y, et al: Single-shot MR cholangiopancreatography of neonates, infants, and young children. AJR Am J Roentgenol 1998;170:33.
133. Mones RL, DeFelice AR, Preud'Homme D: Use of neomycin as the prophylaxis against recurrent cholangitis after Kasai portoenterostomy. J Pediatr Surg 1994; 29:422.
134. Moore TC: Congenital atresia of the extrahepatic bile ducts; report of 31 proved cases. Surg Gynecol Obstet 1953;96:215.
135. Moore TC, Hyman PE: Extrahepatic biliary atresia in one human leukocyte antigen identical twin. Pediatrics 1985; 76:604.
136. Muraji T, Higashimoto Y: The improved outlook for biliary atresia with corticosteroid therapy. J Pediatr Surg 1997;32:1103, discussion 1106.
137. Muraji T, Tsugawa C, Nishijima E, et al: Surgical management for intractable cholangitis in biliary atresia. J Pediatr Surg 2002;37:1713.
138. Nakajo T, Hashizume K, Saeki M, Tsuchida Y: Intussusception-type antireflux valve in the Roux-en-Y loop to prevent ascending cholangitis after hepatic portojejunostomy. J Pediatr Surg 1990;25:311.
139. Nio M, Ohi R, Miyano T, et al: Five- and 10-year survival rates after surgery for biliary atresia: A report from the Japanese Biliary Atresia Registry. J Pediatr Surg 2003;38:997.
140. Nio M, Ohi R, Shimaoka S, et al: [Long-term outcome of surgery for biliary atresia.] Nippon Geka Gakkai Zasshi 1996;97:637.
141. Odièvre M: Long-term results of surgical treatment of biliary atresia. World J Surg 1978;2:589.
142. Ogasawara Y, Yamataka A, Tsukamoto K, et al: The intussusception antireflux valve is ineffective for preventing cholangitis in biliary atresia: A prospective study. J Pediatr Surg 2003;38:1826.
143. Ohi R: The present status of surgical treatment for biliary atresia: Report of the questionnaire for the main institutions in Japan. In Ohi R (ed): Biliary Atresia. Tokyo, Professional Postgraduate Services, 1987.
144. Ohi R, Chiba T, Endo N: Morphologic studies of the liver and bile ducts in biliary atresia. Acta Paediatr Jpn 1987;29:584.
145. Ohi R, Klingensmith WC 3rd, Lilly JR: Diagnosis of hepatobiliary disease in infants and children with Tc-99m-diethyl-IDA imaging. Clin Nucl Med 1981;6:297.
146. Ohi R, Mochizuki I, Komatsu K, Kasai M: Portal hypertension after successful hepatic portoenterostomy in biliary atresia. J Pediatr Surg 1986;21:271.
147. Ohi R, Shikes RH, Stellin GP, Lilly JR: In biliary atresia duct histology correlates with bile flow. J Pediatr Surg 1984;19:467.
148. Ohi R, Takahashi T, Kasai M: Intrahepatic biliary obstruction in congenital bile duct atresia. Tohoku J Exp Med 1969;99:129.
149. Ohkawa H, Takahashi H, Maie M: A malformation of the pancreatico-biliary system as a cause of perforation of the biliary tract in childhood. J Pediatr Surg 1977;12:541.
150. Petersen C, Biermanns D, Kuske M, et al: New aspects in a murine model for extrahepatic biliary atresia. J Pediatr Surg 1997;32:1190.
151. Poley JR, Smith EI, Boon DJ, et al: Lipoprotein-X and the double 131 I-rose bengal test in the diagnosis of prolonged infantile jaundice. J Pediatr Surg 1972;7:660.
152. Povey S: Genetics of alpha 1-antitrypsin deficiency in relation to neonatal liver disease. Mol Biol Med 1990;7:161.
153. Raweily EA, Gibson AA, Burt AD: Abnormalities of intrahepatic bile ducts in extrahepatic biliary atresia. Histopathology 1990;17:521.
154. Renz JF, Emond JC, Yersiz H, et al: Split-liver transplantation in the United States: Outcomes of a national survey. Ann Surg 2004;239:172.
155. Renz JF, Yersiz H, Reichert PR, et al: Split-liver transplantation: A review. Am J Transplant 2003;3:1323.
156. Riepenhoff-Talty M, Gouvea V, Evans MJ, et al: Detection of group C rotavirus in infants with extrahepatic biliary atresia. J Infect Dis 1996;174:8.
157. Saeki M, Ogata T, Nakano M: Problems in long-term survivors of biliary atresia. In Ohi R (ed): Biliary Atresia. Tokyo, Professional Postgraduate Services, 1987.
158. Sandler AD, Azarow KS, Superina RA: The impact of a previous Kasai procedure on liver transplantation for biliary atresia. J Pediatr Surg 1997;323:416.
159. Schweizer P: Treatment of extrahepatic bile duct atresia: Results and long-term prognosis after hepatic portoenterostomy. Pediatr Surg Int 1986;1:30.
160. Segawa O, Miyano T, Fujimoto T, et al: Actin and myosin deposition around bile canaliculi: A predictor of clinical outcome in biliary atresia. J Pediatr Surg 1993;28:851.
161. Sera Y, Ikeda S, Akagi M: Ultrasonographic studies for the diagnosis of infantile cholestatic disease. In Ohi R (ed): Biliary Atresia. Tokyo, Professional Postgraduate Services, 1987.
162. Shimaoka S, Ohi R, Saeki M, et al: Problems during and after pregnancy of former biliary atresia patients treated successfully by the Kasai procedure. J Pediatr Surg 2001;36:349.
163. Shinkai M, Ohhama Y, Take H, et al: Evaluation of the PELD risk score as a severity index of biliary atresia. J Pediatr Surg 2003;38:1001.
164. Starzl TE, Iwatsuki S, Van Thiel DH, et al: Evolution of liver transplantation. Hepatology 1982;2:614.
165. Starzl TE, Marchioro TL, VonKaulla KN, et al: Homotransplantation of the liver in humans. Surg Gynecol Obstet 1963;117:659.
166. Sterling JA: Artificial bile ducts in the management of congenital biliary atresia: A clinical report. J Int Coll Surg 1961;36:293.
167. Stringer MD, Howard ER, Mowat AP: Endoscopic sclerotherapy in the management of esophageal varices in 61 children with biliary atresia. J Pediatr Surg 1989;24:438.
168. Suruga K, Miyano T, Kitahara T, et al: Treatment of biliary atresia: A study of our operative results. J Pediatr Surg 1981;16(4 Suppl 1):621.
169. Takahashi H: ERCP in jaundiced infants. In Ohi R (ed): Biliary Atresia. Tokyo, Professional Postgraduate Services, 1987.

170. Tan CE, Davenport M, Driver M, Howard ER: Does the morphology of the extrahepatic biliary remnants in biliary atresia influence survival? A review of 205 cases. J Pediatr Surg 1994;29:1459.
171. Tan CE, Driver M, Howard ER, Moscoso GJ: Extrahepatic biliary atresia: A first-trimester event? Clues from light microscopy and immunohistochemistry. J Pediatr Surg 1994;29:808.
172. Tanaka K, Shirahase I, Utsunomiya H, et al: A valved hepatic portoduodenal intestinal conduit for biliary atresia. Ann Surg 1991;213:230.
173. Tanaka K, Uemoto S, Tokunaga Y, et al: Surgical techniques and innovations in living related liver transplantation. Ann Surg 1993;217:82.
174. Tazawa Y, Konno T: Semiquantitative assay of serum lipoprotein-X in differential diagnosis of neonatal hepatitis and congenital biliary atresia. Tohoku J Exp Med 1980;130:209.
175. Tazawa Y, Yamada M, Nakagawa M, et al: Significance of serum lipoprotein-X and gammaglutamyltranspeptidase in the diagnosis of biliary atresia. A preliminary study in 27 cholestatic young infants. Eur J Pediatr 1986;145:54.
176. Thaler MM, Gellis SS: Studies in neonatal hepatitis and biliary atresia. I. Long-term prognosis of neonatal hepatitis. Am J Dis Child 1968;1163:257.
177. Thomson J: On congenital obliteration of the bile ducts. Edinb Med J 1892;37:724.
178. Toyosaka A, Okamoto E, Okasora T, et al: Extensive dissection at the porta hepatis for biliary atresia. J Pediatr Surg 1994;29:896.
179. Tsao K, Rosenthal P, Dhawan K, et al: Comparison of drainage techniques for biliary atresia. J Pediatr Surg 2003;38:1005.
180. Tyler KL, Sokol RJ, Oberhaus SM, et al: Detection of reovirus RNA in hepatobiliary tissues from patients with extrahepatic biliary atresia and choledochal cysts. Hepatology 1998;27:1475.
181. Tzakis AG, Reyes J, Tepetes K, et al: Liver transplantation for Alagille's syndrome. Arch Surg 1993;128:337.
182. Uchida K, Urata H, Suzuki H, et al: Predicting factor of quality of life in long-term jaundice-free survivors after the Kasai operation. J Pediatr Surg 2004;39:1040.
183. Vacanti JP, Shamberger RC, Eraklis A, Lillehei CW: The therapy of biliary atresia combining the Kasai portoenterostomy with liver transplantation: A single center experience. J Pediatr Surg 1990;25:149.
184. van Heurn LW, Saing H, Tam PK: Portoenterostomy for biliary atresia: Long-term survival and prognosis after esophageal variceal bleeding. J Pediatr Surg 2004;39:6.
185. Vazquez-Estevez J, Stewart B, Shikes RH, et al: Biliary atresia: Early determination of prognosis. J Pediatr Surg 1989;24:48, discussion 50.
186. Vennarecci G, Gunson BK, Ismail T, et al: Transplantation for end stage liver disease related to alpha 1 antitrypsin. Transplantation 1996;61:1488.
187. Weber TR, Grosfeld JL, Fitzgerald JF: Prognostic determinants after hepatoportoenterostomy for biliary atresia. Am J Surg 1981;141:57.
188. Whitington PF, Black DD: Cholelithiasis in premature infants treated with parenteral nutrition and furosemide. J Pediatr 1980;97:647.
189. Wiesner RH, McDiarmid SV, Kamath PS, et al: MELD and PELD: Application of survival models to liver allocation. Liver Transpl 2001;7:567.
190. Williams LF, Dooling JA: Thoracic duct–esophagus anastomosis for relief of congenital biliary atresia. Surg Forum 1963;14:189.
191. Wood RP, Langnas AN, Stratta RJ, et al: Optimal therapy for patients with biliary atresia: Portoenterostomy ("Kasai" procedures) versus primary transplantation. J Pediatr Surg 1990;25:153, discussion 160.
192. Wright K, Christie DL: Use of gamma-glutamyl transpeptidase in the diagnosis of biliary atresia. Am J Dis Child 1981;135:134.
193. Yano H, Matsumoto H: Choledochal cyst following operation for idiopathic perforation of the biliary tract in childhood. Jpn J Surg 1983;13:441.
194. Yoshida S, Nio M, Hayashi Y, et al: Serum insulinlike growth factor-I in biliary atresia. J Pediatr Surg 2003;38:211.

Chapter 104

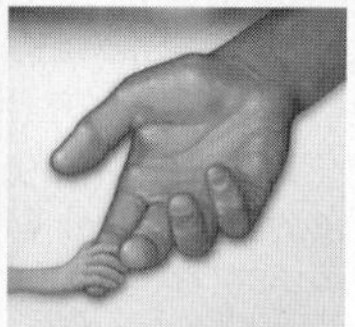

Choledochal Cyst

James A. O'Neill, Jr.

A monograph published by Vater in 1723 presented a series of studies describing normal and abnormal anatomy of the biliary tree, including the first description of a fusiform dilatation of the common bile duct.[91] In 1852, Douglas published the first clinical description of a patient with dilatation of the common bile duct, which he suggested was probably congenital in origin.[14] Other than occasional reports of choledochal cyst that were published after that, it was not until 1959 that Alonso-Lej and colleagues published the first series of patients with choledochal cysts, reporting 2 of their own cases and reviewing 94 others previously published in the literature.[1] This landmark paper was the first to describe a classification including the three common forms of choledochal cyst for which different approaches to treatment were suggested. This paper subsequently led to a better understanding of the pathophysiology of this anomaly, which in turn has led to new approaches to treatment.

ANATOMIC CLASSIFICATION

Types I, II, and III forms of choledochal cyst were originally described by Alonso-Lej and colleagues.[1] Subsequently, Todani and associates and others have further classified this anomaly into five main types and additional subtypes, based on analyses of cholangiograms.[83,85] The common varieties are as follows (Fig. 104-1):

Type I—saccular or diffuse fusiform dilatation of the extrahepatic bile duct
Type II—diverticulum of the extrahepatic bile duct
Type III—choledochocele
Type IV—multiple cysts of the intra- or extrahepatic ducts (or both)
Type V—single or multiple intrahepatic cysts.

We and others have found types III and IV to sometimes coexist. Also, unusual variants of type I (see Fig. 104-1b and c) have been seen such as isolated dilatation of the cystic duct or only one hepatic duct and entry of the cystic duct into either the choledochal cyst or a normal common hepatic duct above the level of an extrahepatic choledochal cyst. For example, White and Becker[93] reported an isolated left hepatic choledochal cyst in an adult, and my colleagues and I have encountered an isolated right hepatic choledochal cyst in a child. Single or multiple intrahepatic biliary cysts that are classified as type V have been referred to as Caroli's disease when they are associated with hepatic fibrosis, and sometimes these cysts are seen to occur in a sequential fashion over a number of years.[7] Ninety to 95 percent of choledochal cysts are of the type I variety, being either fusiform or saccular, with the fusiform type being more common.[57] In the most common form of this anomaly, the gallbladder enters the choledochal cyst and the right and left hepatic ducts as well as the intrahepatic ducts are normal in size. In the diverticular type II form, the entire intrahepatic and extrahepatic biliary tree is otherwise normal. Type III choledochocele is usually intraduodenal, but occasionally it occurs in the intrapancreatic portion of the biliary tree. Otherwise, the ductal system is normal and the common bile duct usually enters the choledochocele in the wall of the duodenum. In cases of choledochocele, the common bile duct and main pancreatic duct enter the choledochocele either together or separately, but the openings are often stenotic because of chronic inflammation. The choledochocele itself empties into the main duodenal lumen through a narrow opening (Fig. 104-2). Manning and associates reviewed 40 cases of choledochocele and described two main anatomic variations.[47] In the more frequent form, the common bile duct and pancreatic duct enter the intraduodenal choledochocele separately. In the second type, the choledochocele is a diverticulum off the common bile duct at the level of the ampulla of Vater, with the pancreatic duct entering the end of the common bile duct in the usual location. I have reviewed other variants of choledochal cysts extensively.[55]

PATHOLOGY

Histologic sections of the wall of extrahepatic choledochal cysts in my patients have demonstrated a thick-walled structure of dense connective tissue interlaced with strands of smooth muscle. In most instances, some degree

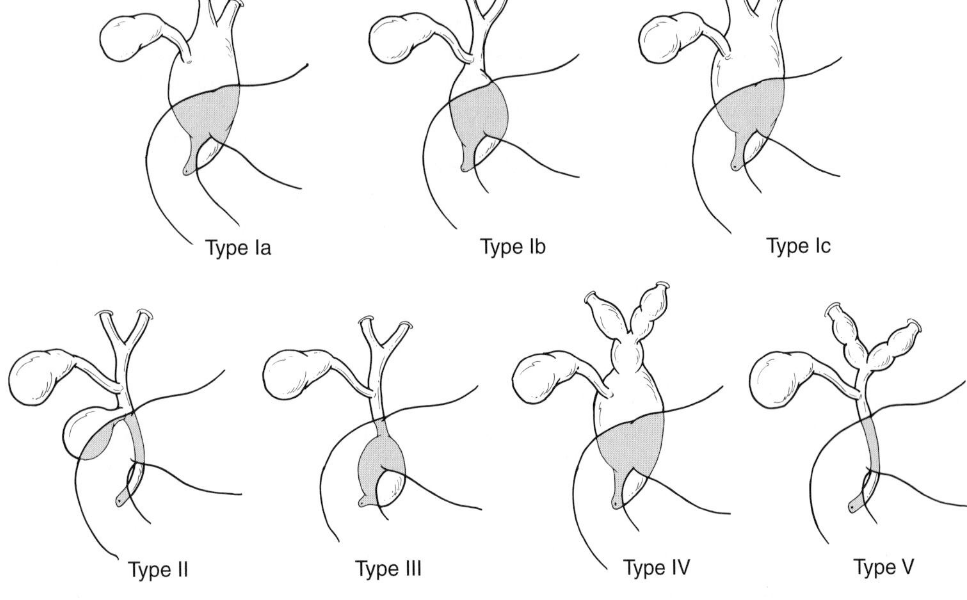

Figure 104–1 The five major forms of choledochal cyst malformations as shown by cholangiography. Careful delineation of anatomy by operative cholangiography dictates the approach to surgical management. See text for description of anatomic subtypes.

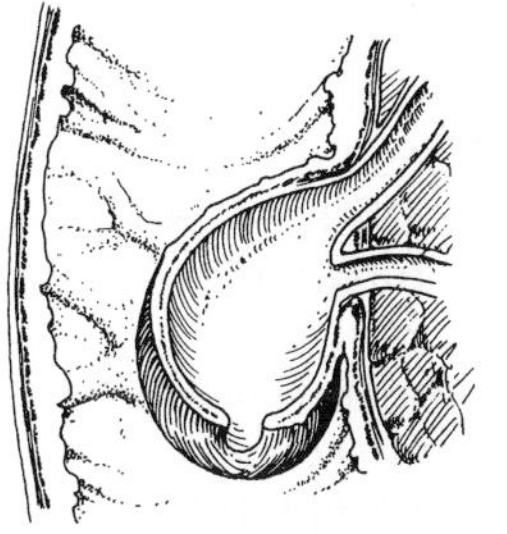
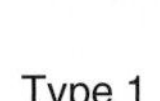
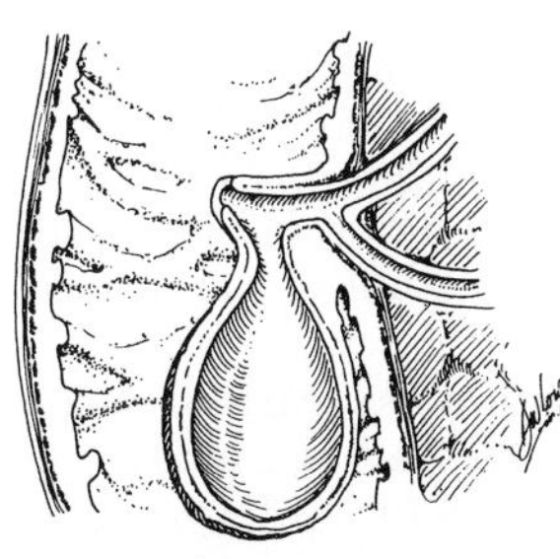

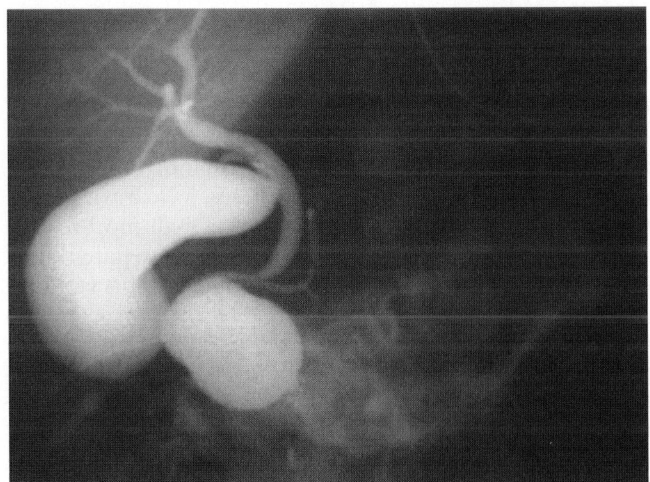

Figure 104–2 *A,* The two generally encountered forms of choledochocele: type I is the more common. These malformations occur most frequently in the duodenum but on rare occasions are found in the head of the pancreas. *B,* This operative cholangiogram in a 6-year-old boy performed via the gallbladder defines an intraduodenal choledochocele that is partially obstructed, an anomalous pancreaticobiliary junction, and a normal bile duct system. (*A* from O'Neill JA: Choledochal cyst. Curr Probl Surg 1992;29:374. Used with permission.)

of inflammatory reaction is noted, although it is minimal in infants and gradually becomes more marked as patients get older. Additionally, the degree of pericystic inflammation becomes more severe beyond the age of 10 years or so, and adherence to surrounding structures is evident; only a relatively acellular cyst lining is typically noted, not typical biliary mucosa. In young patients, occasional islands of columnar epithelium as well as microscopic bile ducts in the wall of the cyst may be seen. Intramural glands and duct-like structures, when seen, include mucin-secreting cells and immunoreactive gastrin and somatostatin-containing cells, which are suggestive of gastrointestinal mucosa that has undergone destruction and regrowth.[63] The older the subject, the more likely that no remnant of mucosal lining will be seen in the cyst. Inflammatory changes are usually most marked in instances of intrahepatic cysts.

The histologic appearance of other forms of choledochal cysts is similar, with the exception of choledochocele. In these cysts, the lining is most commonly duodenal mucosa and only occasionally resembles lining of the bile duct. Although the bile duct is usually normal in appearance on histologic section, inflammation may be present and stones and sludge may be seen in the common bile duct and occasionally in the intrahepatic ducts of older patients.

With regard to the distal common duct, two general findings may be seen. Most affected infants have complete obstruction at the level of the duodenum suggestive of a form of biliary atresia. Older patients usually have a patent distal common duct, and Suda and coworkers have suggested that these narrow segments are derived from the ventral pancreatic duct.[77] In the next section on etiology, reference will be made to the anomalous junction of the common bile duct and the pancreatic duct, which represents a common channel, extra-ampullary form of malformation. Most patients with choledochal cysts have such an anomalous pancreaticobiliary junction.

The findings on liver biopsy also vary with the age of the patient. In a newborn, the histologic appearance of the liver is usually interpreted as normal or having mild bile duct proliferation consistent with chronic biliary obstruction. Occasionally, in older patients, mild periportal fibrosis is noted. Although none of my patients has had cirrhosis at the time of initial presentation, Ramirez and associates,[65] and others, have reported the coexistence of congenital hepatic fibrosis with choledochal cyst. Landing has presented the concept of a neonatal obstructive cholangiopathy linking choledochal cyst, neonatal hepatitis, and biliary atresia; he reported occasional giant cell transformation of the liver in patients later shown to have choledochal cysts.[38] Additionally, he and others have shown that choledochal cysts can occur in the presence of biliary atresia in infants.[56] Portal hypertension has not been a significant accompanying feature in our patients with choledochal cyst with the exception of patients who later develop biliary cirrhosis on the basis of long-standing postoperative cholangitis, and such patients are rare. Carcinomas arising in the wall of choledochal cysts are well recognized and are believed to be the result of chronic inflammation. Biliary carcinoma has been noted in patients with anomalous pancreaticobiliary junction without choledochal cyst.[2,35,63] Carcinoma in the wall of a choledochal cyst has rarely been reported in childhood and is primarily a problem in adults. The typical form of malignancy is adenosquamous carcinoma as well as occasional small cell carcinoma. Although the majority of these malignancies occur in the wall of the choledochal cysts, other sites have included the gallbladder and the head of the pancreas in the region of the pancreaticobiliary junction. Because of the long interval over which these lesions seem to develop, it is presumed that they are the result of chronic inflammation from cholangitis. Inflammation is not a prominent feature in patients who have choledochoceles, although mild inflammation may lead to stenosis of the common bile duct and the pancreatic duct.

ETIOLOGY AND EMBRYOLOGY

Theories regarding the etiology of choledochal cysts have changed through the years as additional information has come to light. The recent development of accurate diagnostic imaging techniques has permitted additional thoughts regarding etiology. In 1852, Douglas speculated that the common fusiform type of the anomaly might be some sort of congenital weakness of the common bile duct.[14] In 1936, Yotsuyanagi reported an analysis of three patients with choledochal cyst, and, using known experimental embryologic information of the time, he suggested that the defect might be related to improper formation of the bile ducts during the primitive stages of development.[96] He suggested that an overproduction of epithelial cells during the solid stage of development in the region of the common duct might produce an abnormally dilated structure following canalization. Whereas similar theories have been offered to explain isolated ectasia in selected areas of the intestinal tract, most researchers do not accept Yotsuyanagi's hypothesis. Alonso-Lej and colleagues ascribed to the congenital duct weakness theory proposed by Douglas, and in a 1973 review of etiology of choledochal cyst by Glenn and McSherry it was concluded that the cause was congenital.[1,14,18] They speculated that the congenital lesion was either a primary weakness or a combination of ductal obstruction and an intrinsic structural defect of the common bile duct. Since that time, distal obstruction has been indicted as at least one factor involved in the etiology of choledochal cyst. In 1984, Todani and coworkers, in an analysis of endoscopic retrograde cholangiopancreatography (ERCP) and other cholangiographic imaging studies, suggested that most patients had an anomalous arrangement of the pancreaticobiliary ductal system in which the pancreatic duct entered the common bile duct in a proximal location well outside the circular muscle of the ampulla of Vater, which would permit reflux of pancreatic enzymes containing trypsin upward into the common bile duct during fetal development, resulting in damage to the ductal wall with subsequent dilatation.[81] I have also noted this abnormal arrangement in virtually all of our patients who have had cholangiographic studies available for analysis (Fig. 104-3).[55] This "common channel" theory related to the etiology of choledochal cyst was originally suggested by Babbitt in 1969.[5] Ito, Miyano, Spitz, and others have suggested that obstruction at the level of the duodenum is an additive factor in this process, which tends to produce saccular dilatation of the common bile duct, as shown in various experimental preparations.[28,50,51,75] Taking all of the available studies into account, there is sufficient evidence to support the concept that distal obstruction combined with pancreaticobiliary reflux in utero is responsible for degenerative dilatation of the extrahepatic ductal system. Ito and coworkers,[28] and others, have suggested that distal ductal stenosis is possibly related to abnormal insertion of the duct into the duodenum, congenital stenosis of the distal common bile duct, persistence of an epithelial membrane, abnormality of the valve itself, or neuromuscular incoordination of the sphincter. Ando and associates, who reviewed a series of 124 patients, noted that ductal malunion resulting in a common channel arrangement of the pancreatic and biliary ducts was occasionally seen in patients without choledochal cyst.[2] In their series, 117 had choledochal cysts and 7 had pancreaticobiliary maljunction without dilatation of the common bile duct. This is probably not a benign condition because such malunion has been noted in adults to have a high association with carcinoma of the biliary tree, presumably on the basis of chronic reflux and inflammation. It is also of interest that in Ando and associates' series all patients were symptomatic related to intermittent obstruction from mucus plugs.[3] Rustad and Lilly[69] proposed that ductal malunion was simply an associated malformation with choledochal cyst, but the preponderance of evidence in my experience suggests that there is a correlation between the two.

It is clear that this commonly demonstrated anomalous bile duct arrangement is congenital in origin, and this is supported by the fact that choledochal cyst has a

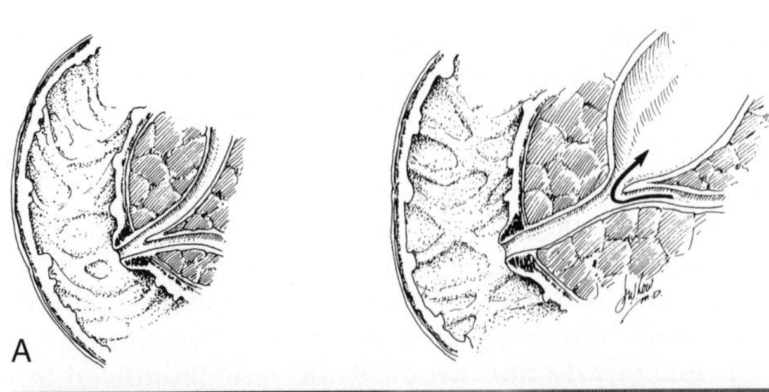

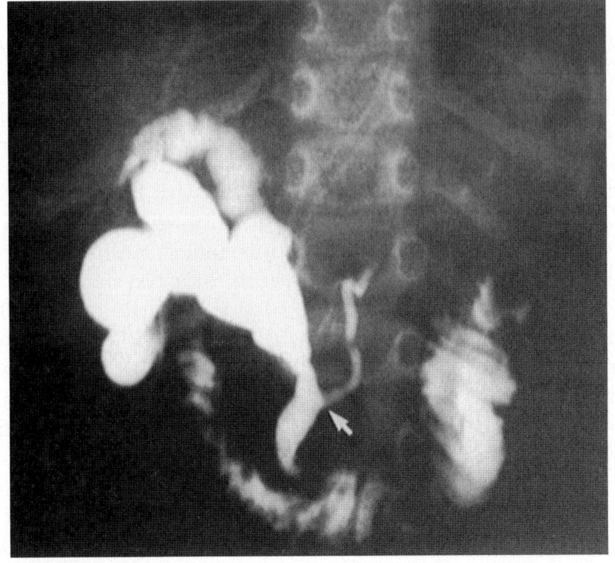

Figure 104-3 *A,* Normal anatomy (*left*) contrasted to the anomalous common channel anatomy (*right, arrow*) believed to be responsible for reflux of pancreatic enzymes presumably resulting in cyst formation in utero. *B,* Operative cholangiogram of a 3-year-old girl demonstrates the typical finding in patients with type I fusiform choledochal cyst. Note the high junction point of the pancreatic duct with the common bile duct (*arrow*), which constitutes a long common channel outside the sphincter and permits reflux of pancreatic enzymes into the biliary tree. (From O'Neill JA: Choledochal cyst. Curr Probl Surg 1992;29:279. Used with permission.)

predominance in females, suggesting a sex-linked defect, as well as a much higher incidence in Asian populations than in others. Jaunin-Stalder and coworkers reported a pair of monozygotic twins with anomalous pancreaticobiliary junction, although it has also been reported in only one of such a twin pair.[30,54] Wong and Lister have suggested that the anomalous junction is caused by arrested migration of the biliary-pancreatic junction into the duodenal wall before the eighth week of gestation.[95] In a nice review of the embryology, Li and colleagues have noted a high incidence of ectopic distal location of the ampulla of Vater as an obstructive factor in the etiology of congenital biliary dilatation.[40]

With regard to other forms of choledochal cyst such as choledochocele and Caroli's disease, it is not evident that they share a common cause with the common type I form. Additionally, the type II diverticular form may represent the end stage of a healed prenatal rupture of the common duct. Suggested causes of choledochocele indicate that it may represent a simple diverticulum occurring between the ampullary and common duct components of the sphincter resulting from low insertion and obstruction of the ampulla or that it represents a congenital duodenal duplication that arises in that region. In summary, the two most commonly accepted causes are (1) reflux of trypsin and other pancreatic enzymes into the proximal biliary ductal system because of a congenitally abnormal insertion of the pancreatic duct into the common duct, which is supported by the studies of Davenport and associates and by my colleagues and me in studies showing high levels of biliary amylase and other pancreatic enzymes in patients with congenital choledochal cysts; and (2) obstruction of the distal duct, either complete or incomplete.[13,55,57] Any degree of distal obstruction would be expected to increase the opportunity for reflux of pancreatic enzymes into the proximal biliary tree.

PRENATAL DIAGNOSIS

Prenatal ultrasonography of fetal choledochal cyst has been reported by a number of investigators.[25,44,45,48,57] In one of my patients, pregnancy was followed by ultrasonography at 17, 18, and 27 weeks' gestation. No fetal abnormalities were seen on any of these studies, but at 31.5 weeks of gestation, maternal ultrasound demonstrated a cystic mass inferior to the liver, and at 37.5 weeks the mass was noted to have contiguity with minimally dilated intrahepatic ducts (Fig. 104-4). In reports by other authors, prenatal diagnosis of choledochal cyst by maternal ultrasound was made at 15, 19, 20, 25, and

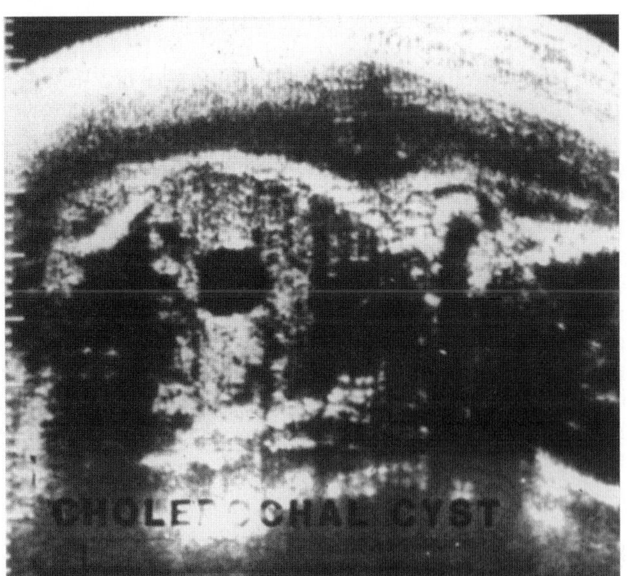

Figure 104-4 This prenatal maternal ultrasound study performed at 31 weeks' gestation shows a suspected choledochal cyst that was later confirmed. However, prenatal ultrasound should be considered to be a screening study because it is frequently unreliable. This patient had cyst excision and internal drainage at 2 weeks of age.

37 weeks.[25,44,45,48,55] In at least 20 observations, the findings indicate that choledochal cysts develop in mid-gestation, which may correspond to the prolonged period necessary for pancreatic enzymes to damage the biliary tree, although not every fetus may be susceptible to pancreaticobiliary reflux.

A key question that has been raised after prenatal diagnosis relates to appropriate timing of surgical correction when a choledochal cyst has been noted in utero. First of all, it is important to note that maternal ultrasound is not necessarily reliable as anything more than a screening study. The reports by Redkar and colleagues[66] and MacKenzie and coworkers[45] indicate that maternal ultrasound, although useful, is inaccurate and not necessarily capable of differentiating choledochal cysts from other biliary tract malformations in the fetus. However, it is clear that whenever a choledochal cyst is suspected, postnatal ultrasound should always be performed. Once the presence of a suspected choledochal cyst has been confirmed postnatally, a decision regarding treatment is in order.

Redkar and associates suggest that asymptomatic patients are best operated on at around 3 months of age.[66] Suita and coworkers have noted that patients operated on within a month of life have a lower incidence of hepatic fibrosis than those operated on later than that, indicating that earlier than 3 months may be desirable.[79] My colleagues and I have noted in our series of patients diagnosed prenatally that it takes 2 weeks or so for sludge to appear in a neonate with a choledochal cyst on ultrasound, which also corresponds to the time jaundice appears unless there is total obstruction of the biliary tree. Therefore, we have favored early correction within 2 weeks of life or thereabouts. Burnweit and colleagues reported a series of six children diagnosed before birth and who were asymptomatic and who had surgery at an average of 6 weeks of age, and all of these patients did well.[6] Ohama and coworkers reported four cases of perforated choledochal cysts and suggested that early correction might have prevented the problem.[58] Lugo-Vicenti has suggested that asymptomatic anicteric patients be followed with serial ultrasound and biochemical studies and that elective excision at approximately 6 weeks of age is appropriate.[44] Others agree.[60] As mentioned earlier, I disagree with the approach to delay operation in prenatally diagnosed patients because of the frequency of hepatic fibrosis, sometimes even noted at birth, which is known to be reversible with surgical repair, as well as the potential complications of cyst enlargement and inflammation, formation of proximal hepatic duct stenosis, hepatic dysfunction, and perforation. Thus my colleagues and I prefer to repair the defect at 2 weeks or so of age, at which time infants are usually stable.

CLINICAL PRESENTATION

Patients with choledochal cysts usually present in one of two ways, which has led to them being classified as infantile or adult in nature. With the exception of patients who are suspected to have choledochal cysts on antenatal studies, in the infantile form patients ranging from 1 to 3 months of age present with obstructive jaundice, acholic stools, and hepatomegaly with a clinical picture indistinguishable from that of biliary atresia.[12] Occasionally, signs of hepatic fibrosis are present even in young patients, which is a strong argument for early treatment. Patients with the infantile form of this anomaly do not tend to have abdominal pain or a palpable mass. Low-grade fever may be present as in patients with biliary atresia, but not with a pattern that suggests cholangitis. Infants who have been diagnosed to have a choledochal cyst prenatally do not ordinarily become jaundiced until 1 to 3 weeks after birth. Both saccular and fusiform types of choledochal cyst may cause jaundice in infancy, although jaundice may be transient in fusiform malformations. Although some advocate conservative treatment of infants if excretion appears to be normal on studies, with a policy to only operate if persistent or intermittent jaundice becomes a problem, we disagree with this approach because of the strong possibility of progressive hepatic fibrosis occurring in patients approached in this fashion. Also, on rare occasions, perforation of a cyst may occur.[4] Until recently, the incidence of the infantile and adult forms of choledochal cyst was thought to be equal. The era of laparoscopic cholecystectomy has provided new information in this regard.

In the so-called adult form of choledochal cyst, clinical manifestations do not generally become evident until after the patient is 2 years of age; and most of these patients have fusiform deformities of the common duct without high grade or complete obstruction. It is in this group of patients that the classic triad of abdominal pain, a palpable abdominal mass, and jaundice originally described by Alonso-Lej and colleagues may occasionally be noted.[1] Because only partial obstruction is the case in the adult form, symptoms are intermittent. The formation of mucus plugs and biliary sludge are associated with intermittent jaundice and vague abdominal pain in the right upper quadrant and occasionally the back. Although hepatomegaly may be seen in the adult form, it is less prominent than in the infantile form in which biliary obstruction is usually complete. The pattern of pain has been described as being similar to that of recurrent pancreatitis and is often evidenced by elevations in serum amylase levels, although most consider these episodes not to be pancreatitis but abnormal amylase clearance. In a number of instances where patients with choledochal cyst have gone unnoticed until adulthood, biliary symptoms and cholelithiasis may be present. This has led to a significant number of these patients having laparoscopic cholecystectomy, and when a cholangiogram is done at that time, a choledochal cyst may be found (Fig. 104-5). Thus, it would appear that the incidence of the adult form may actually be higher than the infantile type. We have now seen a large number of patients with choledochal cysts referred for treatment after laparoscopic cholecystectomy and cholangiography. Recurrent cholangitis may also be a feature of the clinical course in older patients. However, it is important to emphasize that symptoms in older patients tend to be very subtle and intermittent, so that the diagnosis frequently goes unrecognized; liver damage is progressive, so sometimes these patients present initially with cirrhosis and manifestations of portal hypertension. It has been noted by a number of

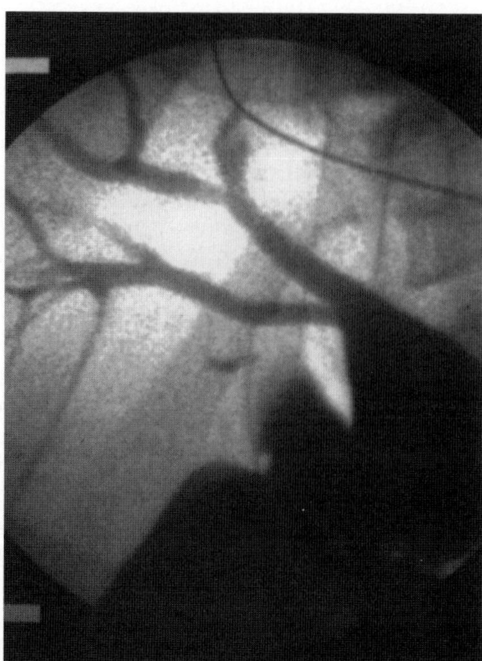

Figure 104–5 This photograph shows an unsuspected choledochal cyst on operative cholangiogram performed at the time of laparoscopic cholecystectomy for cholelithiasis in a 30-year-old woman. Many more such cysts have been discovered since the introduction of laparoscopic cholecystectomy.

individuals interested in this subject that the clinical symptoms seen in older patients with choledochal cyst are almost identical to those of biliary stone disease.

The problem with pancreatitis associated with choledochal cyst deserves special mention. As mentioned earlier, it is likely that the majority of patients with elevations in serum amylase concentration have diminished clearance rather than clinical pancreatitis. On the other hand, there is a small subset of patients who present with true pancreatitis, most likely on the basis of protein plugs accumulating in an anomalous pancreaticobiliary system as described by Narasimhan and associates,[53] Ando and colleagues,[3] and Sugiyama and coworkers.[78] The anomalous pancreaticobiliary junction in these patients would appear to be the primary predisposing factor. Also, pancreas divisum is occasionally noted in some patients with choledochal cyst anomalies. Only a few of these are pathologic and associated with areas of obstruction that might be related to pancreatitis.

DIAGNOSIS

Laboratory Studies

Laboratory studies are not capable of either making or confirming the diagnosis of choledochal cyst, but they do indicate the clinical condition of the patient. Because the most common presenting sign of choledochal cyst is jaundice, the main laboratory findings are conjugated hyperbilirubinemia, an increased serum level of alkaline phosphatase, and other serum markers of obstructive jaundice. Although the pattern of jaundice in older patients may be intermittent and mild, significant conjugated hyperbilirubinemia is the rule in infants. If biliary obstruction has been present for a substantial period, patients may even have an abnormal coagulation profile.

Imaging Studies

Regardless of the form of anatomic abnormality, some form of imaging technique is key to making the diagnosis. Upper gastrointestinal contrast radiography is capable of demonstrating an intraduodenal choledochocele, but it is not useful otherwise. Computed tomography (CT) cholangiography, once useful in making the diagnosis of choledochal cyst, has been replaced by more accurate imaging techniques. As is the case with most pancreaticobiliary abnormalities, ultrasonography (US) is the best screening study, and it may be all that is required in infants. If a choledochal cyst is suspected on US screening, 99Tc-di-isopropylphenylcarbamoyl-methylimidodiacetic acid (DISIDA) scintigraphy can confirm the diagnosis and also provide information about drainage, obstruction, and hepatic function. Of all the IDA-derivative scans available, DISIDA is probably best because the agent is lipophilic and less bound to bilirubin than other forms of the isotope. It can easily be performed in newborns as well.[94] Other advantages of US as a screening study are that it is capable of demonstrating changes in the caliber of the bile and pancreatic ducts and it can also provide information about the status of the liver in terms of density and possible fibrosis.

Invasive imaging studies, such as percutaneous transhepatic cholangiography, are best reserved for older individuals with a suspected choledochal cyst or those with intrahepatic biliary cysts. Another technique occasionally useful in older patients with a suspected ductal anomaly is ERCP, which is the technique that has provided information on the frequency of pancreaticobiliary ductal malunion.[55,94] This technique has also provided data that have led to the development of criteria for defining what constitutes malunion of the pancreatic and bile ducts.[80] ERCP is also capable of making the diagnosis of pancreas divisum. In recent years, magnetic resonance cholangiopancreatography (MRCP) has become popular as a replacement for ERCP because it is noninvasive.[34,53] Now that it is possible to perform MRCP without breath holding, the technique is being applied to infants as well.[9] Other techniques on the horizon include CT with detailed reconstruction and virtual endoscopy, a technique that may be useful in older patients who do not have complete biliary obstruction.[70] I have found that MRCP without breath holding has great promise as a diagnostic technique in patients with biliary and pancreatic ductal anomalies. Regardless of the technique used for preoperative diagnosis, operative cholangiography should be done, because it provides the most accurate anatomic information. Operative cholangiography may be performed either through the gallbladder or directly into the dilated bile duct itself, but it is important to reflux the contrast material into the intrahepatic ductal system to determine the possible presence of anomalous ducts or if associated proximal ductal obstruction or intrahepatic cysts coexist.

In the follow-up period, abdominal US, DISIDA scanning, and MRCP are helpful in that they are capable of demonstrating duct size compared with preoperative status, the rate of bile excretion, any degree of stasis present, and whether stones or sludge are present.

Although liver biopsy lacks utility as a preoperative tool, an operative liver biopsy is useful to determine whether cirrhosis is present and to what extent, so that appropriate follow-up can be carried out.

In older patients suspected to have a choledochal cyst, the differential diagnosis includes congenital hepatic fibrosis, Caroli's disease with hepatic fibrosis, primary sclerosing cholangitis, congenital cirrhosis, and congenital stricture of the common hepatic or common bile duct, but all of these can be differentiated by combinations of the previously mentioned imaging studies.[39]

SURGICAL MANAGEMENT

A variety of approaches have been used through the years for the surgical management of choledochal cyst types I, II, and IV. In the past, many patients were quite ill at the time they presented, so only limited procedures were done under those circumstances such as aspiration, marsupialization, and external drainage. Alonso-Lej and colleagues analyzed the various approaches used at the time of their 1959 report, and these authors pointed out that simple external drainage techniques were unsuccessful because already-ill patients were not able to survive a long-standing external biliary fistula.[1] In addition, other forms of external drainage of the biliary tree, such as cholecystostomy, tube drainage of the cyst, or hepatic duct drainage after excision of the cyst were tried, but the mortality rate was prohibitive. Thus more definitive approaches were proposed.

In 1924, McWhorter published the first report of excision of a choledochal cyst with anastomosis of the common hepatic duct to the duodenum.[46] At that time, this procedure was considered to be technically difficult, and, indeed, before 1960, reported series of cyst excisions had an associated mortality rate of 30%. In 1933, Gross published a review of the literature and added two cases of his own, and he concluded that choledochocystoduodenostomy was a safe and effective operation associated with a low mortality, and he continued to advocate the procedure for many years (Fig. 104-6). Fonkalsrud and Boles confirmed the low mortality rate and technical advantage of cyst duodenostomy in 1965, and so internal drainage without cyst excision became the preferred approach then.[16] Unfortunately, as patients treated by cyst duodenostomy were followed over a long period of years, it became evident that the morbidity rate during a 15-year follow-up period was 30% to 50%, and this was associated with late mortality.[1,56] The longer patients who had cyst duodenostomy were followed, the greater the number of complications that were noted.[56] Of particular importance was the observation that chronic recurrent cholangitis, probably related to reflux into the biliary tree from the duodenum, resulting in chronic inflammation and anastomotic stenosis, was characteristically associated with such mild symptoms that the diagnosis was not evident and that this led to the insidious development of severe biliary cirrhosis and portal hypertension. In most of these instances, clinical symptoms of cirrhosis did not become evident until more than 5 years after cyst duodenostomy.

As a result of the latter, Roux-en-Y cyst jejunostomy was developed as an alternative to cyst duodenostomy to avoid reflux of duodenal contents into the biliary tree (see Fig. 104-6). A number of reports in the 1970s express preference for Roux-en-Y cyst jejunostomy.[72] Although to a much lesser degree, patients with cyst jejunostomy occasionally developed cholangitis and problems similar to those of patients who had cyst duodenostomy. Reports by Spitz and O'Neill have noted good long-term results with cyst jejunostomy in more than two thirds of patients who have had this procedure.[57,74] However, the long-term risk for cancer in patients with a retained choledochal cyst is a major drawback of this procedure. Although it was appreciated that total cyst excision was the ideal surgical procedure, the mortality associated was simply too high, and the aforementioned drainage procedures were preferred because early morbidity and mortality was low.

Cyst excision began to be reconsidered as preoperative and postoperative care improved beginning in the early 1970s. In 1970, Kasai and colleagues[32] and Ishida and coworkers[27] reported favorable results with cyst excision and Roux-en-Y jejunostomy, which stimulated reintroduction of this procedure in other centers around the world. In my experience, all patients with the infantile form and almost all patients with the adult form are capable of having total cyst excision (Fig. 104-7). For many patients, particularly older ones who have had recurrent bouts of cholangitis and who have a substantial amount of pericystic inflammation and adherence to adjacent vascular structures, the technique originally reported by Lilly is useful.[41,42] In this procedure, cyst excision is accomplished using a plane of dissection between the inner and outer layers of the cyst beginning with the confluence of the cystic and common ducts with the cystic duct used as a guide to the correct layer for dissection (Fig. 104-8). Alternately, the cyst may be opened in its midportion in an anterolateral dissection with the plane determined under direct vision. The portion of the cyst wall that is adherent to the portal vein and hepatic artery are left undisturbed, as shown in Figure 104-8D. After excision of the cyst, the intrahepatic ducts should be probed and lavaged with saline to rid the ductal system of sludge and possible stones. Additionally, on occasion, obstruction may be found in the proximal biliary system, which can be dilated. I have even encountered complete obstructions of a membranous type of one of the main hepatic ducts. Following this, I prefer to use Roux-en-Y hepaticojejunostomy with a 40-cm Roux limb in older patients and a 30-cm limb in infants because their intestinal tract is expected to lengthen over time. These lengths appear to be effective in preventing reflux. Todani and coworkers have preferred to use hepaticoduodenostomy after cyst excision.[82] Gonzalez and

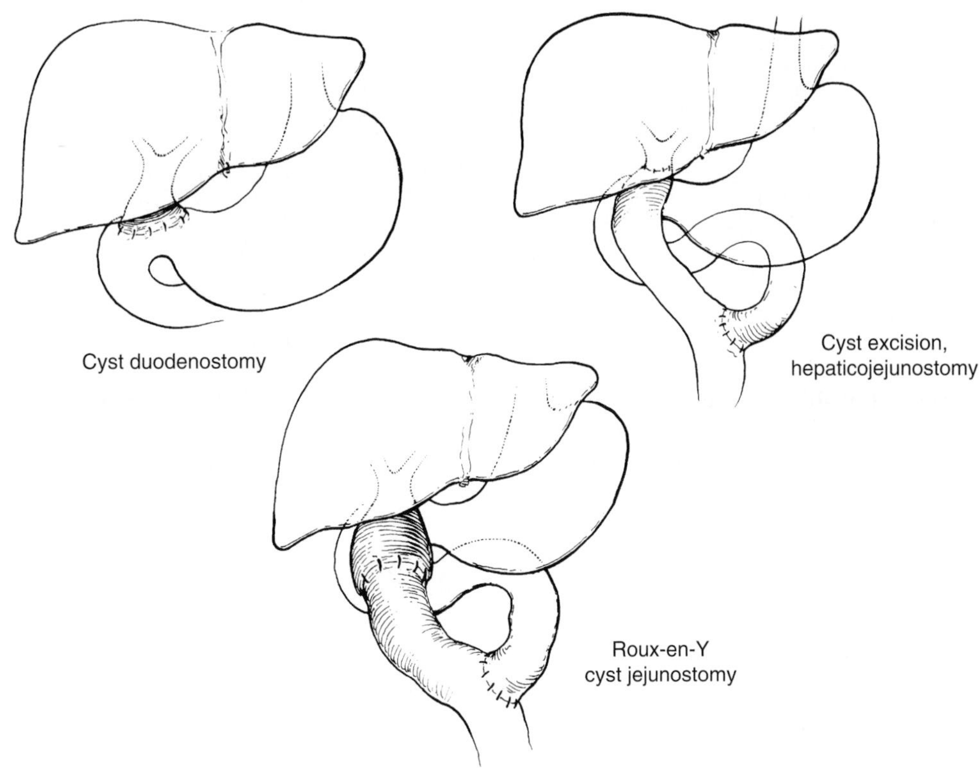

Figure 104–6 The various options available for the operative management of choledochal cyst. Cyst excision with Roux-en-Y hepaticojejunostomy is preferred.

associates[19] have proposed using a 30-cm isolated conduit of proximal jejunum interposed between the confluence of the hepatic duct and the second portion of the duodenum, and Raffensperger[64] has promoted the use of a valved jejunal interposition hepaticoduodenostomy. Follow-up studies indicate that Roux-en-Y hepaticojejunostomy is the preferred procedure, but there are not sufficient follow-up studies of the other techniques. There is some evidence to suggest that the nipple valve procedure proposed by Raffensperger and others does not remain competent over time.[51] I and others believe that the construction of a nipple valve complicates the operation, and it has not been shown to provide better results than the standard Roux-en-Y hepaticojejunostomy for patients with type I, II, or IV choledochal cysts.[51,55]

Patients with type I and IV choledochal cysts treated by cyst incision and Roux-en-Y jejunostomy will occasionally be found to have accessory ducts on cholangiography performed at the time of operation. Narasimhan and associates have reported the unfavorable results associated

Figure 104–7 Details of total cyst excision. *A*, Total cyst excision with Roux-en-Y reconstruction (*B*). Either the end or the side of the Roux limb can be used as the anatomy dictates.

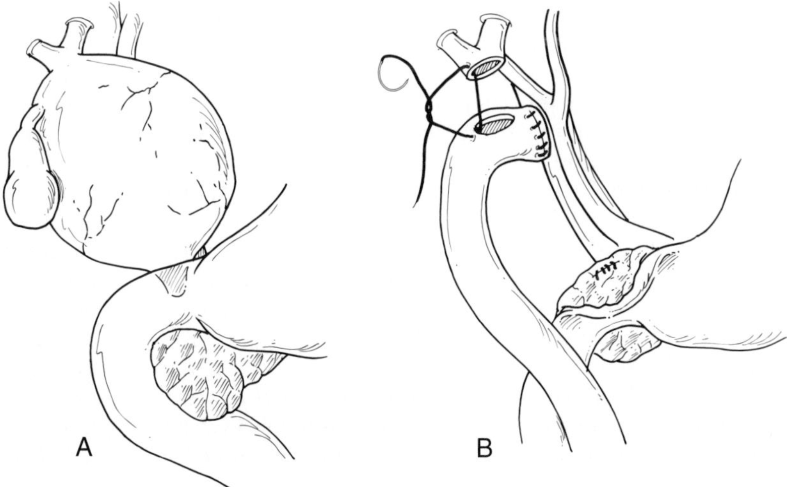

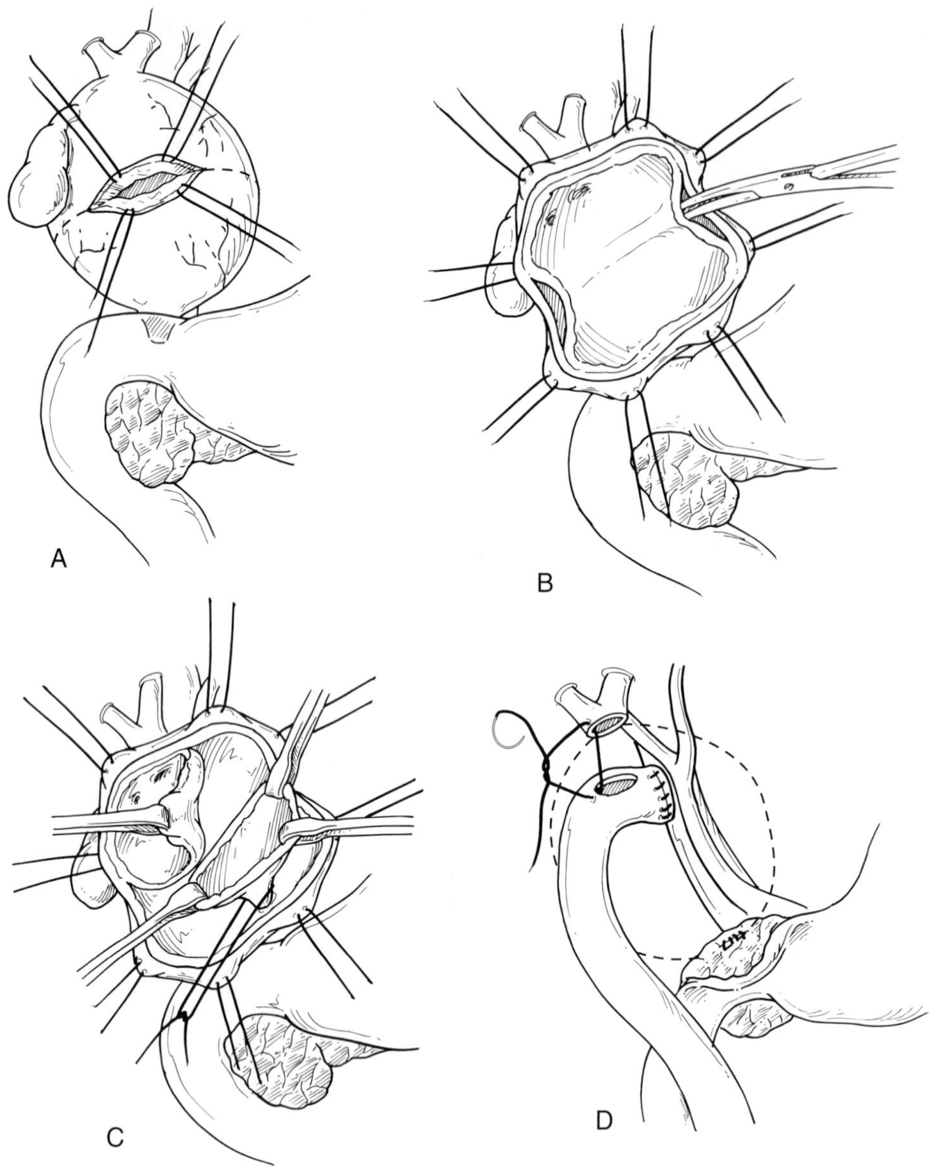

Figure 104–8 The steps in Lilly's method of intramural resection of a choledochal cyst. *A,* Transverse incision is made and continued across the entire anterior medial and lateral wall of the cyst. *B,* The posteroinferior wall of the cyst is left intact. At one corner of the incision, a plan of dissection is arbitrarily selected in the remaining posterior part of the cystic wall, which separates it into a thin outer and thick inner layer. With a small curved hemostat, dissection is carried out in this plane until the outer corner of the incision is reached. After completing the separation, the inner wall is divided to complete a circumferential transverse incision. *C,* The choledochal cyst is mobilized by blunt dissection. Mobilization is continued in a proximal and distal direction through the normal common hepatic wall that adheres to the portal vein and hepatic artery. *D,* The operation is completed by end-to-side Roux-en-Y choledochojejunostomy. The distal common duct is dissected as far as possible under the duodenum to the level of the pancreas and then closed with suture ligatures. The *dashed lines* illustrate the former location of the choledochal cyst. (Modified from O'Neill JA: Choledochal cyst. Curr Probl Surg 1992;29:398. Used with permission.)

with simple ligation of these accessory ducts, so they promote their incorporation into the anastomosis.[53] Ming and coworkers reported a series 234 patients treated by cyst excision with a short jejunal interposition into the side of the descending duodenum with a slit-like spur valve and a variation in which the appendix is used as an interposition.[49] They reported a high rate of stricture and complexity problems for both these procedures, which is undesirable. Hay and coworkers,[23] Li et al,[40] and Liu and colleagues[43] have reported and discussed the role of laparoscopic techniques in the management of patients with jaundice and choledochal cyst. Liu and colleagues' report described a case of type II diverticular cyst managed by laparoscopic excision and duct closure. However, it remains to be seen whether minimally invasive techniques will be applicable to the broad range of anomalies encountered in the management of patients with choledochal cyst malformations. For the present at least, standard open techniques are preferred. On the other hand, there is good reason to believe that robotic techniques, which provide an additional dimension in minimally invasive surgery, may be useful.

Patients with choledochoceles are not usually diagnosed until they are at least 5 years of age because the characteristic clinical symptom is abdominal pain of an intermittent nature that is not specific. A standard approach to the biliary tree through a transverse upper abdominal incision is useful for choledochoceles as well. I prefer to use a longitudinal duodenostomy once the duodenum has been "Kocherized." This permits complete exposure of an intraduodenal choledochocele. Once the choledochocele is exposed, the small aperture that drains bile on the surface of the deformity is easy to visualize. An operative cholangiogram should then be done either through the gallbladder or via a small catheter passed through the opening on the surface of the choledochocele (see Fig. 104-2B). The cystic space should be unroofed beginning at this aperture, and then the mucosa is reapproximated with multiple interrupted absorbable sutures. It is important to identify and calibrate the entry points of the common bile duct and the pancreatic duct to determine whether a sphincteroplasty of these ducts will be needed. Sphincteroplasty of the duct openings is necessary in many cases, usually because the duct openings are narrow owing to chronic inflammation of a mild nature. On rare occasions, patients will have choledochoceles located in the head of the pancreas, sometimes associated with pancreatitis, and some of these are not amenable to internal drainage into the duodenum. If no alternate internal drainage procedure can be accomplished, then pancreaticoduodenectomy may be required in those rare instances.

Patients with intrahepatic cysts or Caroli's disease are difficult to manage because they tend to develop severe recurrent bouts of cholangitis, subsequent biliary cirrhosis, and progressive segmental ductal ectasia. For this reason, these patients require frequent follow-up with US over a period of many years. A variety of techniques may be needed for management of intrahepatic cysts. Partial hepatic lobectomy may be done when the disease is localized and amenable to resection, but unroofing with drainage into a Roux limb of jejunum may be needed when proximal ductal obstruction is encountered.[52]

Patients who have had cyst excision with internal drainage have a lower incidence of postoperative cholangitis than patients with biliary atresia who have had a similar type of drainage procedure. Although patients with biliary atresia are generally placed on suppressive doses of antibiotics for indefinite periods, it is probably unnecessary in patients who have been treated for choledochal cyst. It has been my practice to continue low doses of ampicillin or trimethoprim-sulfamethoxazole for approximately 6 weeks to protect against cholangitis, after which the potential for this complication appears to diminish.

Postoperative follow-up should be every 3 months for the first year and then annually thereafter in asymptomatic patients. At each visit, liver function studies and serum amylase levels should be determined. US of the liver and pancreas is done annually or when necessary if patients become symptomatic. US of the liver is particularly important in patients who are found to have intrahepatic ductal dilatation preoperatively. US is also helpful for long-term evaluation of the Roux-en-Y ductal anastomosis because occasional patients will develop late anastomotic strictures or stones.

SURGICAL RESULTS, FOLLOW-UP, AND COMPLICATIONS

My colleagues and my series consists of 46 patients who have follow-up data, 37 of whom were female. Approximately half of the patients presented between the ages of newborn to 9 months of age, and the other half presented between 2 and 32 years of age. The patients with the infantile form had characteristic findings of complete or near-complete biliary obstruction, whereas patients with the adult form had variable presentations with combinations of abdominal pain, a palpable abdominal mass, and jaundice. Two patients had cyst duodenostomy, and both were revised to cyst excision with Roux-en-Y hepaticojejunostomy and are now doing well with an average follow-up of 18 years. Six patients had cyst jejunostomy with three revisions, one because of stenosis and cholangitis and two because of the long-term concern about the development of malignancy. All six patients, even those who have not had revision, are currently doing well, with an average follow-up of 15 years, and we are currently advising secondary cyst excision for all of these patients. Thirty-three patients had primary cyst excision in addition to the 5 patients who had secondary cyst excision. All of these patients are doing well, with an average follow-up of 10 years. Three of the patients who had simple cyst enterostomy have some degree of biliary cirrhosis and mild portal hypertension that must be watched carefully, but neither is currently a candidate for liver transplantation. One patient had a left hepatic lobectomy for an intrahepatic cyst related to Caroli's disease 15 years ago and is doing well, and another patient treated 12 years ago had internal drainage of a right hepatic cyst into a Roux limb of jejunum. Both of these patients are being followed for the potential of recurrent intrahepatic cysts, which is expected. Three patients have had treatment for choledochoceles: two had intraduodenal excision of the choledochocele associated with sphincteroplasty, and one had internal drainage of an intrapancreatic choledochocele into the duodenum. All three patients are doing well after an average of 8 years of follow-up. Thus far, one of our patients who had cyst excision and internal drainage has had to be treated for intrahepatic stones associated with stenosis of the hepaticojejunostomy. Since revision of the anastomosis, the patient has done well. None of our patients has developed malignant degeneration of either the retained cyst wall or of the small remnants remaining after excision, but the potential exists long-term, particularly for those patients who have retained cysts. The evidence in the literature would support not only primary cyst excision but also secondary cyst excision for patients who have had previous cyst-enterostomy alone.[76,84,89] The type of internal drainage probably does not have a substantial effect on outcome, but simple Roux-en-Y hepaticojejunostomy would appear to be as effective as any of the more complicated procedures, questioning why they should be undertaken in the first place.

A number of other long-term follow up studies have been published. Saing and coworkers reported long-term results in their large series of patients followed for over 20 years and stressed the importance of long-term follow-up because of occasional late complications, even after 17 years.[71] The primary problems in their experience were anastomotic stricture, cholangitis, and intrahepatic stone formation. They also acknowledged the risk of cancer but that it was markedly diminished by cyst excision. Additionally, they mentioned the possible presence of membranous stenoses presenting at the initial operation, indicating the importance of cholangiography and of probing the ducts with washout of debris, especially if intrahepatic dilatation is noted. My colleagues and I have made the same observation and believe that even if stones occurred in the future they would likely pass if no stenosis of the ducts or of the hepaticojejunostomy anastomosis were present. Tsuchida and coworkers reported a mean follow-up of 12.5 years in 103 patients and noted that stones developed postoperatively anywhere from 3 to 22 years after operation.[88] They made the following interesting observations: (1) in 50 patients with no initial dilatation of the intrahepatic ducts, only 1 patient developed intrahepatic stones later; (2) in 43 patients who were determined to have dilatation of the intrahepatic ducts but no downstream stenosis, 1 patient later developed intrahepatic stones; and (3) in 10 patients who were found to have dilatation of the intrahepatic ducts with some degree of downstream stenosis, 4 later developed intrahepatic stones. No stones were noted initially in any patient. The phenomenon of postoperative stone formation was first mentioned by Tsuchida et al. Uno and coworkers, in a study of the development of intrahepatic stones long after primary excision of a choledochal cyst, noted that in every case of late stone formation there was always a preexisting stricture; they also noted stones in patients with Caroli's disease, which usually has some degree of associated ductal obstruction.[90] Cetta presented data to indicate the same thing, that bile stasis due to bile duct stricture precedes, not follows, the formation of intrahepatic stones and that it plays a role in their pathogenesis.[8] Miyano and his group reported a 30-year experience with 180 cases of choledochal cyst, and their data led to the same conclusions.[51] Hasegawa of Okada's group measured serum total bile acid levels in long-term postoperative follow-up of patients treated for choledochal cyst and noted that elevations of serum total bile acids, indicative of some degree of cholestasis, persisted in more than one half of their patients and that they were particularly prone to occur in patients of young age who had severe cholestasis or liver fibrosis to begin with.[22] They concluded that these findings, when present, predisposed to the formation of intrahepatic stones. Okada made the additional observation that he preferred Roux-en-Y hepaticojejunostomy to jejunal interposition hepaticoduodenostomy, because even though the latter procedure is theoretically appealing, it was shown in his series of patients to often lead to bile reflux gastritis, leading him to abandon the latter procedure.[62] Chijiiwa and Tanaka reviewed their long-term results in 28 patients who had excision of choledochal cyst with Roux-en-Y hepaticojejunostomy followed for 1 to 18 years.[11] All their patients survived, and malignant degeneration was not seen. Three of their 28 patients developed intrahepatic calculi, which was believed to be associated with cholangitis but not anastomotic stricture. Long-term follow-up was recommended to avoid complications. In terms of patients with retained cysts, Rush and associates, Katyal and Lees, and Chijiiwa and Koga each reported over a 90% complication rate including cholangitis, choledocholithiasis, and hepatolithiasis.[10,33,68] Most patients required a revisionary procedure, whereas the patients in their various experiences who had cyst excision with internal drainage had uniformly favorable long-term results. The long-term potential for the formation of intrahepatic stones is now well established, and the preponderance of evidence suggests that stones occur on the basis of stasis resulting from stenosis at the level of the hepaticojejunostomy or in the proximal ductal system. In a 25-year review of patients with choledochal cysts treated by excision, Todani and colleagues reported that repeated procedures were indicated in 10 of their patients because of recurrent cholangitis with intrahepatic stones.[86] Demonstrable biliary strictures were responsible for the problem in 9 of the 10 patients who had an anastomosis at the level of the common hepatic duct and in 1 with the anastomosis at the level of the bifurcation. This study suggested that biliary complications may develop in patients treated with excision because of anastomotic stricture or primary ductal stricture, so they proposed creation of a wide anastomosis at the level of the hepatic hilum.

In Miyano and associates' 30-year experience with 180 cases of hepaticoenterostomy after excision of choledochal cyst, the data provide information about the incidence of complications.[51] In 171 of their patients observed for a mean of 11 years who had conventional hepaticoenterostomy, 4 patients developed cholangitis and intrahepatic stones. These complications did not occur in patients younger than 5 years of age at the time of operation. Because some of these patients had intrahepatic stenoses, they also advocated intraoperative cyst endoscopy at the time of cyst excision. They believe that most patients can be treated by conventional drainage of the common hepatic duct and that patients will only occasionally require higher level anastomoses. However, Todani and his group disagree and believe that a wide anastomotic stoma at the level of the bifurcation of the right and left hepatic ducts, which yields free drainage of bile after cyst excision, is essential.[86]

Okada and colleagues have made recommendations regarding technical details for management of choledochal cyst based on their broad experience.[61,62] They stress that anastomosis to the common hepatic duct is sufficient provided that a stricture of the right or left hepatic duct is not left in place, and I agree. I also agree that careful exploration and cholangiography to avoid leaving a stricture in place is sufficient. Okada and colleagues have also emphasized excision of the distal end of the choledochal cyst well under the duodenum into the head of the pancreas, but I have not found that extensive dissection into the head of the pancreas is necessary.

By now, numerous reported cases of malignant degeneration in a retained cyst wall have been reported.[11,15,35,67,83] Theoretically, total or intramural cyst excision should be capable of preventing malignant degeneration of the cyst wall, provided that chronic inflammation is alleviated.[92] Otherwise, malignant degeneration could potentially occur because small remnants of the cyst remain at either extent of the resection, even with extensive cyst excision. Kobayashi and colleagues discussed the risk of bile duct carcinogenesis after excision of extrahepatic ducts in pancreaticobiliary maljunction, including choledochal cyst patients, and they noted that if there is any degree of chronic inflammation and stasis that there is a distinctly higher risk of carcinoma of the gallbladder and proximal biliary ducts and that it occurs at an earlier age than in the normal population. However, there is no question that the greatest risk is in patients who previously had cyst-enteric anastomosis with a retained cyst. In Tsuchiya and coworkers' series of 13 patients who previously had cyst-enteric anastomosis, 3 patients developed adenocarcinoma in the cyst and another patient developed adenocarcinoma of the gallbladder.[89] This 20% incidence of malignancy was the same as in Rossi and colleagues' series.[67] These series raise a management question for patients who previously had a cyst internal drainage procedure regarding whether they should have elective excision of their cysts. I have taken the practical approach that if patients who have had such procedures can be proved to have no chronic recurrent cholangitis or other signs of chronic inflammation they may continue to be observed without intervention. I have previously advised elective cyst excision only for patients with recurrent cholangitis, and the intramural resection technique has been used under those circumstances. With the accumulation of reports of late occurrence of carcinoma in retained cysts[31] and with a better understanding of etiology, I have begun to take a more aggressive position in this respect to excise asymptomatic retained cysts. However, secondary cyst excision may be complicated. Although I have encountered only a single patient with recurrent cholangitis after total cyst excision, long-term follow-up indicates that a careful search should be made for stenosis of the hepaticojejunostomy or infection in intrahepatic cysts, as suggested by Ohi and colleagues.[59] Thus far, none of our patients has developed malignant degeneration but they may not be old enough yet.

It has been assumed that chronic inflammation is the basic cause of the development of carcinoma in the wall of a choledochal cyst or in the biliary tree otherwise in patients who have total excision. Imazu and coworkers recently reported on factors related to carcinogenesis in choledochal cyst.[26] They reported that patients with fusiform cysts had gallbladder mucosal hyperplasia, higher levels of biliary amylase, and higher pressure differentials between the sphincter of Oddi and the duodenum than patients with low amylase levels. They reported a case of adenocarcinoma in a 12-year-old child with a cystic form of choledochal cyst associated with high biliary amylase levels and suggested that the anomalous pancreaticobiliary junction with chronic reflux of pancreatic secretions into the biliary tree was the basic cause. Iwai and coworkers[29] reported that reflux of pancreatic juice because of lack of sphincter of Oddi function causes a variety of histologic damage to the bile duct wall and potentially leads to the development of bile duct malignancy, much as Todani and colleagues suggested. Tokiwa and Iwai also reported early mucosal changes in the gallbladder of patients with anomalous arrangement of the pancreaticobiliary duct.[87] Shimotake and associates presented data to suggest that carcinogenesis in anomalous pancreaticobiliary junction is related to DNA change from chronic inflammation accompanied by multistep genetic mutational events.[73] They studied gene mutations in biliary tract epithelium in children with anomalous ductal junction and found that *KRAS* gene mutation occurs early in epithelial hyperplasia or metaplasia, whereas inactivation of the *DPC4* gene occurs late in the progression of biliary tract adenocarcinoma. Similar studies were performed by Pushparani and Redkar and their associates.[63,66] Hahn and coworkers also reported mutations of the *DPC4/SMAD4* gene in biliary tract adenocarcinoma.[21] Fumino and colleagues[17] and Hayashi and associates[24] reported that enhanced expression of cyclooxygenase-2 is related to mucosal hyperplasia of the gallbladder in patients with anomalous ductal drainage and that cyclooxygenase-2 was upregulated when comparing normal human bile duct epithelial cells and bile duct neoplasms. Thus there is the suggestion that cyclooxygenase-2 inhibition might be a potential way to prevent the late occurrence of bile duct carcinoma in susceptible subjects.

Finally, rare patients may develop pancreatitis after cyst excision and Roux-en-Y jejunostomy, although I have not encountered this complication. Komuro and coworkers presented a series of 62 patients with choledochal cyst observed for a number of years, and the patients included all age groups.[36] Acute pancreatitis due to protein plug formation was observed in over 20% of their patients followed long term. Their study suggested that their patients who had pancreatic problems preoperatively did not have resolution of pancreatic complications postoperatively and that sphincteroplasty was ineffective in preventing the recurrence of protein plugs in the residual duct. However, they believe that early diagnosis and complete excision lower the incidence of recurrent pancreatitis. Koshinaga and Fukuzawa have suggested that the morphology of the pancreatic duct and ductal dilatation, possibly caused by long-standing stagnation of pancreatic juice, may be associated with postoperative pancreatitis in choledochal cyst patients.[37] Overall, however, pancreatitis is an uncommon event after excision and internal drainage of a choledochal cyst.

REFERENCES

1. Alonso-Lej F, Revor WB, Pessagno DJ: Congenital choledochal cyst, with a report of 2, and an analysis of 94 cases. Surg Gynecol Obstet Int Abstr Surg 1959;108:1-30.
2. Ando H, Ito T, Nagaya M, et al: Pancreaticobiliary maljunction without choledochal cyst in infants and children: Clinical features and surgical therapy. J Pediatr Surg 1995;30:1658-1662.
3. Ando H, Kaneko K, Ito F, et al: Surgical removal of protein plugs complicating choledochal cysts: Primary repair after adequate opening of the pancreatic duct. J Pediatr Surg 1998;33:1265-1267.
4. Ando K, Miyano T, Kohno S, et al: Spontaneous perforation of choledochal cyst: A study of thirteen cases. Eur J Pediatr Surg 1998;8:23-25.

5. Babbitt DP: Congenital choledochal cyst: New etiological concept based on anomalous relationships of common bile duct and pancreatic bulb. Ann Radiol 1969;12: 231-240.
6. Burnweit CA, Birken JA, Heiss K: The management of choledochal cyst in the newborn. Pediatr Surg Int 1996; 11:130-133.
7. Caroli J, Soupalt R, Kossakowski J, et al: La dilatation polykystique congenitale des voies biliaires intrahepatiques: Essai de classification. Semin Hop Paris 1958;34:488-495.
8. Cetta F: Biostasis due to bile duct stricture precedes, not follows, the formation of primary intrahepatic stones and plays a basic role in their pathogenesis. Am J Gastroenterol 1996;91:2451-2452.
9. Chen JH, Chai JW, Chu WC, et al: Free breathing cholangiopancreatography (MRCP) at end expiration: A new technique to expand clinical application. Hepatogastroenterology 2002;49:593-596.
10. Chijiiwa K, Koga A: Surgical management and long-term follow-up of patients with choledochal cyst. Am J Surg 1993:165:238-242.
11. Chijiiwa K, Tanaka M: Late complications after excisional operation in patients with choledochal cyst. J Am Coll Surg 1994;179:139-144.
12. Davenport M, Betalli P, D'Antiga L, et al: The spectrum of surgical jaundice in infancy. J Pediatr Surg 2003;38: 1471-1479.
13. Davenport M, Stringer MD, Howard ER: Biliary amylase and congenital choledochal dilatation. J Pediatr Surg 1995;30:474-477.
14. Douglas AH: Case of dilatation of the common bile duct. Monthly J Med Sci (Lond) 1852;14:97.
15. Fieber SS, Nance FC: Choledochal cyst and neoplasm: A comprehensive review of 106 cases and presentation of two original cases. Am Surg 1997;63:982-987.
16. Fonkalsrud EW, Boles ET: Choledochal cysts in infancy and childhood. Surg Gynecol Obstet 1965;121:733-742.
17. Fumino S, Takewa K, Ono S, Iwai N: Cyclooxygenase-2 expression in the gallbladder of patients with anomalous arrangement of the pancreaticobiliary duct. J Pediatr Surg 2003;38:585-589.
18. Glenn F, McSherry CK: Congenital segmental cystic dilatation of the biliary ductal system. Ann Surg 1973;177:705-713.
19. Gonzalez EM, Garcia IG, Pascual H, et al: Choledochal cyst resection and reconstruction by biliary-jejuno-duodenal diversion. World J Surg 1989;13:232-237.
20. Gross RE: Idiopathic dilatation of the common bile duct in children. J Pediatr 1933;3:370-375.
21. Hahn SA, Bartsch D, Schroers A, et al: Mutations of the *DPC-4/Smad-4* gene in biliary tract carcinoma. Cancer Res 1998;58:1124-1126.
22. Hasegawa T, Shukri N, Sasaki T, et al: Measurement of serum total bile acid levels in long-term postoperative follow-up of patients with congenital bile-duct dilatation. Pediatr Surg Int 2002;18:227-230.
23. Hay SA, Soliman HE, Sherif HM, et al: Neonatal jaundice: The role of laparoscopy. J Pediatr Surg 2000;35:1706-1709.
24. Hayashi N, Yawamoto H, Hiraoka N: Differential expression of cyclooxygenase-2 (COX-2) in human bile duct epithelial cell and bile duct neoplasm. Hepatology 2001;34:638-650.
25. Howell CG, Templeton JM, Weiner S, et al: Antenatal diagnosis and early surgery for choledochal cyst. J Pediatr Surg 1983;18:387-393.
26. Imazu M, Iwai N, Tokiwa K, et al: Factors of biliary carcinogenesis in choledochal cyst. Eur J Pediatr Surg 2001;11:24-27.
27. Ishida M, Tsuchida Y, Saito S, et al: Primary excision of choledochal cysts. Surgery 1970;68:884-888.
28. Ito T, Ando H, Nagaya M, et al: Congenital dilatation of the common bile duct in children—the etiologic significance of the narrow segment distal to the dilated common bile duct. Z Kinderchir 1984;39:40-45.
29. Iwai N, Yanagihira J, Tokiwa K, et al: Congenital choledochal dilatation with emphasis on pathophysiology of the biliary tract. Ann Surg 1992;215:27-30.
30. Jaunin-Stalder N, Stahelin-Massik J, Knuchel J, Gnehm HE: A pair of monozygotic twins with anomalous pancreaticobiliary junction and pancreatitis. J Pediatr Surg 2002;37: 1485-1487.
31. Kaneko K, Ando H, Watanabe Y, et al: Secondary excision of choledochal cyst after previous cyst-enterostomies. Hepatogastroenterology 1999;46:2772-2775.
32. Kasai M, Asakura Y, Taira Y: Surgical treatment of choledochal cyst. Ann Surg 1970;172:844-851.
33. Katyal D, Lees GM: Choledochal cyst: A retrospective review of 28 patients and a review of the literature. Can J Surg 1992;35:584-588.
34. Kim MJ, Han SJ, Yoon CS, et al: Using MR cholangiopancreatography to reveal anomalous pancreaticobiliary ductal union in infants and children with choledochal cysts. AJR Am J Roentgenol 2002;179:209-214.
35. Kobayashi S, Asano T, Yamasaki M, et al: Risk of bile duct carcinogenesis after excision of extrahepatic ducts in pancreaticobiliary maljunction. Surgery 1999;126:939-944.
36. Komuro H, Makino SI, Yasuda Y, et al: Pancreatic complications in choledochal cyst and their surgical outcomes. World J Surg 2001;25:1519-1523.
37. Koshinaga T, Fukuzawa M: Pancreatic ductal morphological pattern and dilatation in postoperative abdominal pain in patients with congenital choledochal cyst: An analysis of postoperative pancreatograms. Scand J Gastroenterol 2000;35:1324-1329.
38. Landing BH: Considerations of the pathogenesis of neonatal hepatitis, biliary atresia and choledochal cyst—the concept of infantile obstructive cholangiopathy. Prog Pediatr Surg 1974;6:113-139.
39. Levy AD, Rohrmann CA, Murakata LA, Lonergan GJ: Caroli's disease: Radiologic spectrum with pathologic correlation. AJR Am J Roentgenol 2002;179:1053-1057.
40. Li L, Yamataka A, Wang Y-X, et al: Ectopic distal location of the papilla of Vater in congenital biliary dilatation: Implications for pathogenesis. J Pediatr Surg 2001;36: 1617-1622.
41. Lilly JR: The surgical treatment of choledochal cyst. Surg Gynecol Obstet 1979;149:36-42.
42. Lilly JR: Total excision of choledochal cyst. Surg Gynecol Obstet 1978;146:254-258.
43. Liu DC, Rodriguez JA, Merick F, Geiger JO: Laparoscopic excision of a rare type II choledochal cyst: Case report and review of the literature. J Pediatr Surg 2000;35:1117-1119.
44. Lugo-Vicente HL: Prenatally diagnosed choledochal cysts: Observation or early surgery? J Pediatr Surg 1995;30: 1288-1290.
45. MacKenzie TC, Howell LJ, Flake AW, Adzick NS: The management of prenatally diagnosed choledochal cysts. J Pediatr Surg 2001;36:1241-1243.
46. McWhorter GL: Congenital cystic dilatation of the common bile duct: Report of a case with cure. Arch Surg 1924; 8:604-626.
47. Manning PB, Polley TZ, Oldham KT: Choledochocele: An unusual form of choledochal cyst. Pediatr Surg Int 1990;5:22-26.

48. Marchildon MB: Antenatal diagnosis of choledochal cyst: The first four cases. Pediatr Surg Int 1988;3:431-436.
49. Ming F, Wang Y-X, Zhang J-Z: Evolution in the treatment of choledochus cyst. J Pediatr Surg 2000;35:1344-1347.
50. Miyano T, Suruga K, Suda K: Anomalous pancreatocholedochal ductal junction syndrome: A proposal of a new classification. J Jpn Soc Pediatr Surg 1985;21:75-81.
51. Miyano T, Yamataka A, Kato Y, et al: Hepaticoenterostomy after excision of choledochal cyst in children: A thirty-year experience with 180 cases. J Pediatr Surg 1996;31:1417-1421.
52. Nakayama H, Masuda H, Ugajin W, et al: Left hepatic lobectomy for type IV-A choledochal cyst. Am Surg 2000; 66:1020-1022.
53. Narasimhan KL, Chowdhry SK, Rao KLN: Management of accessory hepatic ducts in choledochal cysts. J Pediatr Surg 2001;36:1092-1093.
54. Narita H, Tsuruga N, Hashimoto T, et al: Congenital choledochal dilatation in one of monozygotic twins. J Jpn Soc Pediatr Surg 1990;26:89-95.
55. O'Neill JA: Choledochal cyst. Curr Probl Surg 1992;29:365.
56. O'Neill JA, Clatworthy HW: Management of choledochal cysts: A 14-year followup. Am Surg 1971;37:230-237.
57. O'Neill JA, Templeton JM, Schnaufer L, et al: Recent experience with choledochal cyst. Ann Surg 1987;205:533-540.
58. Ohama K, Tsuchida K, Yazaki U, et al: Perforated choledochal cyst in childhood: Four cases and a review of Japanese literature. J Jpn Soc Pediatr Surg 1996:32:776-780.
59. Ohi R, Yaoita S, Kamiyama T, et al: Surgical treatment of congenital dilatation of the bile duct with special reference to late complications after total excisional operation. J Pediatr Surg 1990;25:613-617.
60. Ohtsuka Y, Yoshida H, Matsunaga T, et al: Strategy of management for congenital biliary dilatation in early infancy. J Pediatr Surg 2002;37:1173-1176.
61. Okada A, Hasegawa T, Oguchi Y, Nakamura T: Recent advances in pathophysiology and surgical treatment of congenital dilatation of the bile duct. J Hepatobiliary Pancreat Surg 2002;9:342-351.
62. Okada A, Nakamura T, Okumura K, et al: Surgical treatment of congenital dilatation of bile duct (choledochal cyst) with technical considerations. Surgery 1987;101: 238-243.
63. Pushparani P, Redkar RG, Howard ER: Progressive biliary pathology associated with common pancreatico-biliary channel. J Pediatr Surg 2000;35:649-651.
64. Raffensperger J (ed): Choledochal cyst. In Swenson's Pediatric Surgery. New York, Appleton-Century-Crofts, 1980, pp 614-619.
65. Ramirez MJ, Nieto J, Valencia P: Fibrosis hepatica congenita asociada a quiste de coledoco. Bol Med Hosp Infant Mex 1989;46:803-807.
66. Redkar R, Davenport M, Howard ER: Antenatal diagnosis of congenital anomalies of the biliary tract. J Pediatr Surg 1998;33:700-704.
67. Rossi RL, Silverman ML, Braasch JW, et al: Carcinomas arising in cystic conditions of the bile ducts: A clinical and pathologic study. Ann Surg 1987;205:377-384.
68. Rush E, Podesta L, Norris M, et al: Late surgical complications of choledochal cystoenterostomy. J Am Surg 1994;60: 620-624.
69. Rustad DG, Lilly JR: Letter to the editor. Surgery 1987; 101:240-251.
70. Saing T, Chan JKF, Lam WWM, Chan K-L: Virtual intraluminal endoscopy: A new method for evaluation and management of choledochal cyst. J Pediatr Surg 1998;33: 1686-1689.
71. Saing T, Han H, Chan KL, et al: Early and late results of excision of choledochal cyst. J Pediatr Surg 1997;32:1563-1566.
72. Scharli A, Bettex M: Congenital choledochal cyst: Reconstruction of the normal anatomy. J Pediatr Surg 1968;3:604-607.
73. Shimotake T, Aoi S, Tomiyama H, Iwai N: *DPC-4 (Smad-4)* and *K-ras* gene mutations in biliary tract epithelium in children with anomalous pancreaticobiliary ductal union. J Pediatr Surg 2003;38:694-697.
74. Spitz L: Choledochal cyst. Surg Gynecol Obstet 1978; 146:444-452.
75. Spitz L: Experimental production of cystic dilatation of the common bile duct in neonatal lambs. J Pediatr Surg 1977; 12:39-42.
76. Stringer MD, Dhawan A, Davenport M, et al: Choledochal cyst: Lessons learned from twenty year experience. Arch Dis Child 1995;73:528-531.
77. Suda K, Matsumoto Y, Miyano T: Narrow duct segment distal to choledochal cyst. Am J Gastroenterol 1991;86:1259-1263.
78. Sugiyama M, Atomi Y, Kuroda A: Pancreatic disorders associated with anomalous pancreaticobiliary junction. Surgery 1999;126:492-497.
79. Suita S, Shono K, Kinugasa Y, et al: Influence of age in the presentation and outcome of choledochal cyst. J Pediatr Surg 1999;34:1765-1768.
80. Todani T, Akita E, Ito T: (The Japanese Study Group on Pancreaticobiliary Maljunction) Diagnostic criteria of pancreaticobiliary maljunction. J Hep Bil Pancr Surg 1994; 1:219-221.
81. Todani T, Watanabe Y, Fujii T, et al: Anomalous arrangement of the pancreaticobiliary ductal system in patients with a choledochal cyst. Am J Surg 1984;147:672-676.
82. Todani T, Watanabe Y, Mizuguchi T, et al: Hepaticoduodenostomy at the hepatic hilum after excision of choledochal cyst. Am J Surg 1981;142:584-587.
83. Todani T, Watanabe Y, Narusue M, et al: Congenital bile duct cyst: Classification, operative procedures, and review of 37 cases including cancer arising from choledochal cyst. Am J Surg 1977;134:263-269.
84. Todani T, Watanabe Y, Toki A, et al: Carcinoma related to choledochal cyst with internal drainage operations. Surg Gynecol Obstet 1987;164:61-64.
85. Todani T, Watanabe Y, Toki A, et al: Co-existing biliary anomalies and anatomical variants in choledochal cyst. Br J Surg 1998;85:760-763.
86. Todani T, Watanabe Y, Urushishra N, et al: Biliary complications after excision procedure for choledochal cyst. J Pediatr Surg 1995;30:478-481.
87. Tokiwa K, Iwai N: Early mucosal changes of the gallbladder in patients with anomalous arrangement of the pancreaticobiliary duct. Gastroenterology 1996;110:614-618.
88. Tsuchida Y, Takahashi A, Suzuki N, et al: Development of intrahepatic biliary stones after excision of choledochal cyst. J Pediatr Surg 2002;37:165-167.
89. Tsuchiya R, Harada N, Ito T, et al: Malignant tumors in choledochal cyst. Ann Surg 1977;186:22-28.
90. Uno K, Isuchida Y, Kawarasaki H, et al: Development of intrahepatic cholelithiasis long after primary excision of choledochal cyst. J Am Coll Surg 1996;183:583-588.
91. Vater A: Dissertation in Auguralis Medica, Poes Diss.qua Scirris Biscerum Dissert, c.c. Ezlerus, vol 70. Edinburgh, University Library, 1723, p 19.
92. Watanabe Y, Toki A, Todani T: Bile duct cancer developed after cyst excision for choledochal cyst. J Hepatobiliarypancreat Surg 1999;6:207-212.

93. White JB, Becker JM: Left hepatic choledochal cyst. Surgery 1996;125:567-569.
94. Wilkinson M: The art of diagnostic imaging: The biliary tree. J Hepatol 1996;25(Suppl 1):5-19.
95. Wong KC, Lister J: Human foetal development of the hepato-pancreatic duct junction—a possible explanation of congenital dilatation of the biliary tract. J Pediatr Surg 1981;16:139-145.
96. Yotsuyanagi S: Contribution to aetiology and pathology of idiopathic cystic dilatation of the common bile duct with report of three cases. Gann 1936;30:601-752.

Chapter 105

Gallbladder Disease and Hepatic Infections

George W. Holcomb III and Walter S. Andrews

GALLBLADDER DISEASE

Cholelithiasis has been increasingly diagnosed in children during the past 3 decades. Whether the incidence is actually escalating or the diagnostic accuracy is improving because of the increasing use of ultrasonography (US) remains unclear. Moreover, hemolytic disease is no longer a prerequisite for the development of this disorder.[48,49,61] In addition, the entity of biliary dyskinesia and acalculous cholecystitis is being diagnosed much more frequently in pediatric patients.

Nonhemolytic Cholelithiasis

Several factors that seem to cause cholelithiasis in children are known. By far the most commonly reported condition associated with the development of nonhemolytic cholelithiasis, particularly in neonates and infants, is the use of total.parenteral nutrition (TPN).[60,78,98] Up to 43% of children receiving long-term TPN develop gallstones.[63] The mechanism of gallstone formation related to TPN remains unclear but may be associated with changes in bile composition caused by the amino acid infusion or the lack of enteral feeding. The lack of enteral feeding leads to ineffective gallbladder contraction and results in reduced enterohepatic circulation of bile. The administration of fat along with the TPN is believed to ameliorate the deleterious effects of the amino acids in the TPN.

Because many infants receive TPN and only very few develop gallstones, other factors are probably necessary for the development of cholelithiasis in this patient population. Septicemia, dehydration, chronic furosemide therapy, cystic fibrosis, short-bowel syndrome, and ileal resection for necrotizing enterocolitis also may be important contributing factors.[34,74,93,98] The cause of gallstone formation is probably multifactorial. Stasis, sepsis, a lack of enteral feedings, and some alteration of the enterohepatic pathway for the recirculation of bile are all important for stone development. Moreover, neonates and, particularly, premature infants are particularly susceptible to the cholestatic effects of TPN because of the immaturity of their enterohepatic circulation of bile salts. Finally, the composition of gallstones in children may be different than that found in adults. Whereas stones in adults are primarily cholesterol in composition, calcium carbonate and black pigment stones are often found in pediatric patients, especially those younger than 10 years of age.[115]

Causes associated with gallstones in older children include the use of oral contraceptives, cystic fibrosis, pregnancy, obesity, and ileal resection.[67,108,112] Cholelithiasis also has been reported in children undergoing cardiac transplantation and receiving cyclosporine and in patients who have previously undergone extracorporeal membrane oxygenation as a newborn.[3,47,82,127]

Hemolytic Cholelithiasis

Although the incidence of nonhemolytic cholelithiasis is increasing at many centers, hemolytic cholelithiasis (usually secondary to sickle cell disease) remains the most common cause of gallstones in children at many academic institutions, especially in urban areas where an active sickle cell program exists. The prevalence of pigment gallstones associated with sickle cell disease appears to be age dependent. Fifty percent of patients with sickle cell anemia develop gallstones by 20 years of age.[30,65,102] Interestingly, in one study, patients with sickle cell disease and gallstones had rates of bilirubin production, bilirubin clearance, and plasma levels of unconjugated bilirubin similar to those of patients with sickle cell hemoglobin and no gallstones.[36] Thus, the researchers suggested that excessive unconjugated hyperbilirubinemia alone is not sufficient to produce pigment gallstones. In that study, enlarged fasting and postprandial gallbladder volumes were found in patients who developed stones. It was hypothesized that stasis occurs as a result of incomplete emptying and leads to sludge and later to gallstone formation. Because gallbladder sludge is frequently documented in patients with sickle cell anemia, elective cholecystectomy has been recommended when evidence suggests the presence of sludge, with or without stones.[129] In one study of

35 patients with sickle cell disease and biliary sludge, 23 (65.7%) went on to develop gallstones.[4]

Patients with sickle cell disease represent the largest group of patients at risk for postoperative complications after cholecystectomy. In a report of 364 cases from a national sickle cell disease study group, the total complication rate was 39%, with sickle cell events representing 19%; intraoperative or recovery room problems, 11%; transfusion complications, 10%; postoperative surgical events, 4%; and death, 1%.[43] The open operation was performed in 58% of the patients and the laparoscopic route was used in 42%. The complication rates were similar between the two groups. As a result of that study it was believed that the incidence of sickle cell events may be higher in patients who were not preoperatively transfused. Moreover, the laparoscopic approach was recommended for this patient population. The acute chest syndrome can be seen in up to 20% of sickle cell patients undergoing abdominal surgery. Additionally, in one study, the laparoscopic approach did not decrease the incidence of this complication.[124] Meticulous attention to perioperative management, transfusion guidelines, and pulmonary care may reduce the incidence of acute chest syndrome.

Two other hemolytic conditions commonly associated with gallstones are hereditary spherocytosis and thalassemia. The incidence of cholelithiasis in hereditary spherocytosis patients ranges from 43% to 63% and is slightly more common in girls than boys.[6,68] Because of this association, US is recommended before elective splenectomy to determine whether concomitant cholecystectomy should be performed at the time of the splenectomy. Previously, patients with thalassemia major comprised a group of children at risk for cholelithiasis.[25] However, the incidence of cholelithiasis has markedly decreased in this patient population. This reduction has been attributed to a hypertransfusion regimen that blocks the bone marrow so that the fragile cells of thalassemia major are not produced.[13] Currently, patients with this disorder are rarely seen with cholelithiasis.

Clinical Presentation

Gallbladder disease in infants usually occurs during a systemic illness and the use of TPN. Some infants also will have undergone ileal resection because of acquired diseases such as necrotizing enterocolitis or congenital anomalies. Jaundice may occur before gallstones are detected with US. Most of these stones are composed of calcium bilirubinate.

Gallstones that develop between 2 and 12 years of age are primarily composed of mixtures of calcium bilirubinate, with varying amounts of calcium carbonate and cholesterol. Opaque gallstones are sometimes detected on plain radiographs, but the diagnosis is more frequently determined with US. Unfortunately, the diagnosis may be delayed in this young group despite abdominal pain, nausea, emesis, and, occasionally, fever. Abdominal pain may vary from the typical right upper abdominal location to vague and poorly localized pain, especially in younger children. Older patients are usually more specific in localizing the pain to the right subcostal region.

The symptoms and physical findings in teenagers are similar to those found in adults. The pain is usually described as right subcostal with some radiation to the subscapular area. Nausea and vomiting commonly occur, and intolerance to fatty foods is often mentioned.

Hydrops of the gallbladder, acalculous cholecystitis, biliary dyskinesia, and gallbladder polyps are being seen more frequently. Hydrops is characterized by massive distention of the gallbladder in the absence of stones, infection, or congenital anomalies. It has been most frequently reported in association with Kawasaki's disease and is usually due to a transient obstruction of the cystic duct or to increased mucus secretion by the gallbladder resulting in poor emptying.[10,22,26,33] With additional gallbladder distention, further angulation of the cystic duct may increase the obstruction.[105] Conservative treatment is initially recommended in this setting. Appropriate antibiotics for septic patients and early initiation of enteral feedings to stimulate gallbladder emptying often lead to resolution of this condition. If serial US examinations show progressive gallbladder distention with increasing pain, or if the gallbladder appears gangrenous, cholecystectomy is recommended.

Acalculous cholecystitis commonly occurs in association with severe illness such as sepsis, burns, or trauma that results in dehydration, hypotension, and ileus. In this setting, TPN is often used and, if prolonged, may be followed by decreased gallbladder contractility with progressive distention, stasis, and possible infection. In a recent report of 12 patients, the investigators used daily US criteria for clues for the need for cholecystectomy. In the three patients who underwent operation there was progressively increasing gallbladder wall thickness and distention along with pericholecystic fluid. In contrast, in the other patients, the daily US examinations found progressive improvement in the previous day's findings. These patients all recovered uneventfully.[53]

Biliary dyskinesia is also being increasingly diagnosed in children.[2,20,21,41,44,70,81,130] Laparoscopic cholecystectomy has been reported to be an effective treatment for this disorder, with expected resolution of symptoms in over 80% of the patients.[2,20,21,41,70,81] This disorder is characterized by poor gallbladder contractility and the presence of cholesterol crystals within the bile. This disease should be considered when patients present with typical biliary pain but no evidence of gallstones on US. Gallbladder contractility can be assessed with radionuclide scanning during cholecystokinin (CCK) injection. Recently, Lipomul has been shown to provide similar findings.[44] The ejection fraction in these patients is usually less than 35%.[16] Chronic cholecystitis is often documented on histologic examination of the gallbladder specimen.[83] In a review of 51 patients who underwent laparoscopic cholecystectomy for symptoms consistent with biliary dyskinesia, it was found that nausea, pain, and a decreased gallbladder ejection fraction of less than 15% most reliably predicted which children will benefit from cholecystectomy for this condition. In that report, children with an ejection fraction greater than 15% did not have predictable resolution of symptoms.[20]

Finally, gallbladder polyps are being found more frequently in children. Cholecystectomy is advisable if there are biliary symptoms or if the polyp is greater than or equal to 1 cm.[113,114]

The primary reason for elective cholecystectomy in patients with cholelithiasis is to prevent associated complications. Four major complications can occur: cholecystitis, jaundice, cholangitis, and biliary pancreatitis. The incidence of acute cholecystitis seems to be increasing. In one report of 100 patients undergoing laparoscopic cholecystectomy, 22% presented initially with complications related to gallstones.[47] Seven presented with acute cholecystitis, six presented with jaundice and pain, five developed gallstone pancreatitis, and four had acute biliary colic without evidence of cholecystitis. Others have reported a large number of patients presenting with symptomatic choledochal obstruction.[64,123] In such patients, management should be initially directed at trying to reduce the inflammation in the region, followed by laparoscopic cholecystectomy several days later.

Radiographic Evaluation

Although a plain abdominal radiograph is often the initial imaging study used to evaluate abdominal pain in children, it is rarely helpful with gallbladder disease unless the gallstones are calcified. The incidence of radiopaque stones has been reported to be as high as 50% in patients with hemolytic disorders compared with approximately 15% in adolescents with cholesterol stones.[111] Oral cholecystography is rarely used today because of the superior accuracy of US. Real-time US has an accuracy of approximately 96% for gallbladder disease and is effective in determining hepatic and common bile duct involvement, the presence of thickening of the gallbladder wall, and any abnormalities in the liver or head of the pancreas.[29] The most useful procedure for diagnosing acute cholecystitis is cholescintigraphy that uses technetium-99m–labeled iminodiacetic acid analogues. With this study, the gallbladder is not visualized in patients with acute cholecystitis. In critically ill patients, especially infants who are fasting, have severe associated illnesses, or are receiving TPN, there may be a false-positive result. Intravenous morphine may be useful in this setting because it causes spasm at the sphincter of Oddi, resulting in increased bile duct pressure. The latter, in turn, enhances visualization of the gallbladder and helps reduce the rate of false-positive studies.[38] Cholecystokinin-assisted or Lipomul-challenged cholescintigraphy is an accurate predictor of chronic acalculous gallbladder disease and also suggests the likelihood of symptomatic relief with cholecystectomy.[2,20,41,44,71,94]

Nonsurgical Treatment

Nonsurgical treatment for gallstones in children or adults is of historical interest only. Previously, attempts at oral dissolution therapy or extracorporal shockwave lithotripsy were attempted in adults with minimal success.[99,103,104] In one study with lithotripsy, the duration of treatment, the high cost, and the 50% risk of recurrent gallstones within 5 years were significant disadvantages.[99] In these studies, children were not included for a variety of reasons, including the fact that pigmented stones would not be amenable to these therapies. Currently, observation is not recommended for children older than age 2 or 3 years with gallstones. In some reports, gallstones that developed in infants secondary to prolonged TPN have been found to dissolve spontaneously.[17,50,54,116] Thus, a 6- to 12-month period of observation in this age group is not unreasonable after cessation of the TPN and initiation of enteral alimentation.

Surgical Treatment

Surgical treatment for symptomatic cholelithiasis consists of either cholecystectomy or cholecystolithotomy. In a preliminary report, one group reserves laparoscopic cholecystolithotomy for symptomatic cholelithiasis in patients before the onset of puberty.[121] However, long-term outcome data from this approach are lacking. In another report, of 10 patients undergoing cholecystolithotomy over 25 years with a mean follow-up of 5 years, 30% of the patients undergoing cholecystolithotomy were reported as having recurrent right upper abdominal pain and recurrent stones.[31] Because of the high recurrence rate, these authors believe that cholecystectomy is preferred in children.

The laparoscopic approach has become the standard method for cholecystectomy in children over the past decade. The major advantages of this approach include decreased discomfort and reduced length of hospitalization, an improved cosmetic result, and faster return to routine activities such as work, school, play, or participation in athletic activities. These advantages result from less muscle disruption from the small incisions and reduced trauma to the tissue, leading to less discomfort and ileus than with the open approach. In most reports, noncomplicated patients undergoing laparoscopic cholecystectomy are ready for discharge on either the first or the second postoperative day.[35,47,71,95,117]

Although most children can be discharged within 48 hours, patients with sickle cell disease require special preoperative care to prevent postoperative complications. Several authors have reported favorable results with cholecystectomy in this patient population and have emphasized the need for preoperative transfusion.[7,43,101,124,126] From recent reports, the laparoscopic approach does not appear to be more hazardous for these patients and may be preferred.[43,47,101,124]

Several special circumstances merit attention. The first is the child with hereditary spherocytosis who is undergoing splenectomy. In such patients, a gallbladder US should be performed before the splenectomy. If gallstones are present, then cholecystectomy should be performed at the time of splenectomy, regardless of whether the laparoscopic or open approach is used. Whether splenectomy protects these patients from the future development of cholelithiasis is unclear. However, in a study of 17 patients undergoing splenectomy alone in which cholelithiasis was not seen at the time of the splenectomy, none of the patients subsequently developed symptoms of cholelithiasis with a mean follow-up of 15 years.[100] Thus, prophylactic cholecystectomy at the time of splenectomy is probably not indicated in patients with hereditary spherocytosis who do not have gallstones.

The second situation is that of the patient who presents with known or suspected choledocholithiasis in addition to cholelithiasis. A number of management strategies for such patients are available.[73,86,106,131] Options include preoperative endoscopic retrograde cholangiopancreatography (ERCP) with sphincterotomy and stone extraction, laparoscopic or open common duct exploration at the time of laparoscopic cholecystectomy, or postoperative endoscopic sphincterotomy with stone extraction, which is the approach commonly used in adults. This decision analysis appears to be related to two factors: the surgeon's experience with laparoscopic common duct exploration and the availability of ERCP and sphincterotomy in children and adolescents at the treating institution. For those pediatric surgeons who are facile with laparoscopic common duct exploration, this may be an attractive approach with postoperative endoscopic sphincterotomy reserved for the unsuccessful cases. However, for most pediatric surgeons, this is probably not the best option because postoperative endoscopic sphincterotomy is a rarely performed procedure in most pediatric surgical centers. Thus, in this setting, it would appear best to perform preoperative ERCP with sphincterotomy and stone extraction if stones are found. If successful, the surgeon can then proceed with uncomplicated laparoscopic cholecystectomy in the next few days. However, if the endoscopic sphincterotomy and stone extraction are not successful, then the surgeon will know at the time of the operative procedure whether a laparoscopic or open common duct exploration is needed. This latter approach is preferred at our institution (Fig. 105-1).

A final preoperative concern is whether to perform an intraoperative cholangiogram. In the early to mid 1990s, when there was not much experience with laparoscopic cholecystectomy in children, it was suggested that most, if not all, children undergo a cholangiogram for surgeon-training purposes as well as to ensure that the correct anatomy has been visualized. A third reason was to evaluate for the presence of common duct stones, although this is often known preoperatively either from symptoms, US, or laboratory studies. As pediatric surgeons have gained more familiarity with the technique of laparoscopic cholecystectomy, routine intraoperative cholangiography for surgeon-training purposes does not appear necessary once the surgeon has become familiar with the technique.

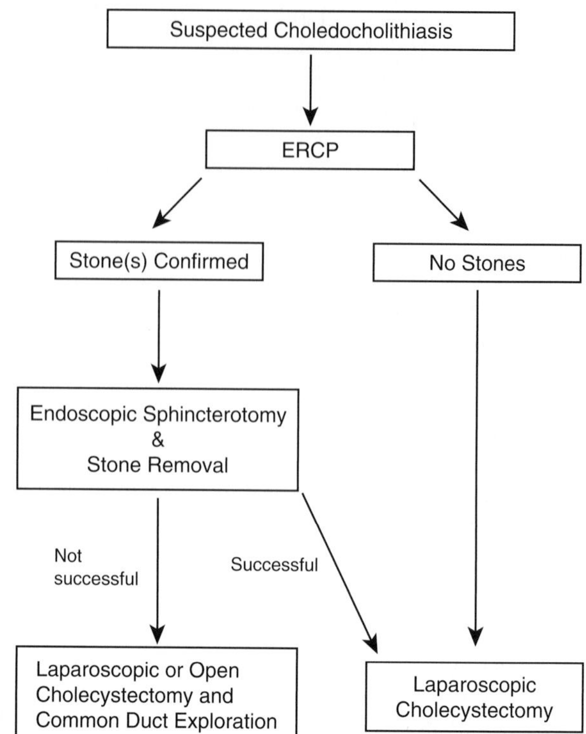

Figure 105-1 This algorithm depicts the authors' preferred strategy for managing patients with suspected choledocholithiasis. Preoperative ERCP is favored with stone extraction and sphincterotomy, if necessary, before the laparoscopic cholecystectomy. If the ERCP does not show evidence of choledocholithiasis, then laparoscopic cholecystectomy is performed. The reason this approach is favored is that, at the time of the laparoscopic cholecystectomy, the surgeon knows whether a laparoscopic or open choledochal exploration is needed.

Thus, in our minds, intraoperative cholangiography is useful primarily to ensure that the correct anatomy is visualized and to evaluate for choledocholithiasis. We routinely order an US evaluation to be performed a few days before the laparoscopic cholecystectomy to confirm the presence of gallstones and to evaluate for common duct obstruction. This approach reduces the operative time and is cost effective (Table 105-1). By using this clinical pathway, an unsuspected common duct stone has not been missed at our institution. Thus, at the time of the

TABLE 105-1 Financial Analysis of Preoperative Ultrasonography versus Intraoperative Cholangiography for Detection of Choledocholithiasis at Children's Mercy Hospital, Kansas City, MO

Immediate Preoperative Evaluation with Ultrasound	Charges	Intraoperative Cholangiography	Charges
Ultrasound study (including radiologist's fee)	$307.67	15 minutes operating room time	$734.25
		C-arm with radiologist's fee	$365.41
		Sterile drape for C-arm	$20.00
		Cholangiocatheter	$83.50
		Contrast agent for cholangiogram	$40.00
Total	$307.67	Total	$1,243.16

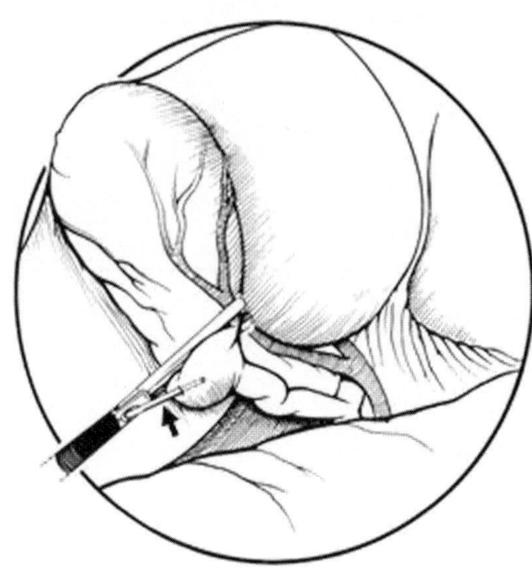

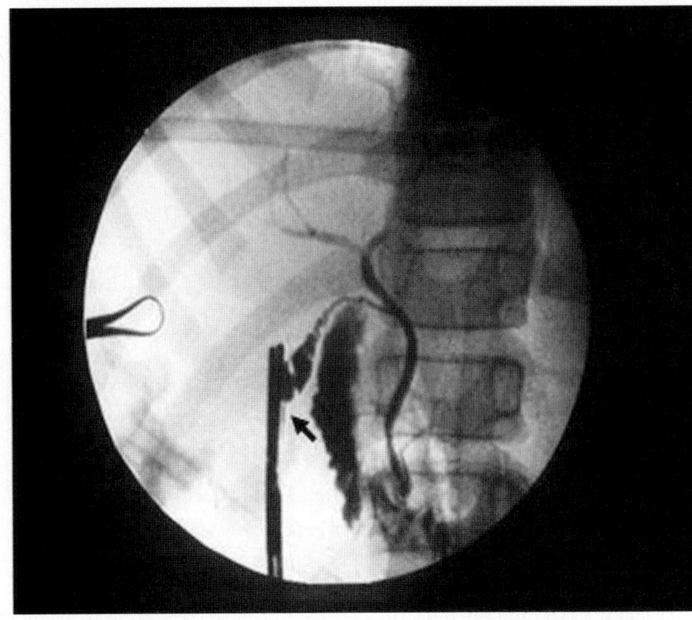

Figure 105-2 The Kumar clamp technique for cholangiography in infants and small children is depicted. Note the clamp across the infundibulum and the sclerotherapy needle (*arrow*) which exits the side arm of the clamp and is introduced into the proximal infundibulum. The advantage of this technique is that lateral incision and cannulation of the small cystic duct is not necessary.

operation, the only need for cholangiography is to ensure the correct anatomy. If the anatomy appears clear at the time of the laparoscopic operation, routine cholangiography is not performed. If cholangiography is to be performed, we still prefer the Kumar clamp technique, although a number of other techniques in which a catheter is introduced into the cystic duct through a transcystic incision are certainly appropriate.[48,51] Fluoroscopy is also used because it is more time efficient than static radiography and allows dynamic assessment of the biliary tree (Fig. 105-2).

Another modification in the authors' technique over the past several years merits mention. For many laparoscopic operations including cholecystectomy, we have adopted a "stab incision" technique for instruments that are not continually exteriorized and reinserted into the abdominal cavity during the operation. In a study of 511 patients undergoing a variety of laparoscopic procedures in which only one or two Innerdyne (U.S. Surgical, Norwalk, CT) cannulas were utilized, a reduction of $187,180 was noted in the patient charges.[88] If the Ethicon (Ethicon Endosurgery, Cincinnati, OH) cannula system was utilized, patient savings of about $123,000 would have been realized. For cholecystectomy, the instruments placed through the two right-sided incisions are not routinely changed. Thus, these two sites are optimal for the stab incision technique (Fig. 105-3). The telescope is introduced through the umbilical cannula and the main working port is in the left upper abdomen so two Innerdyne cannulas are still used in these sites.

The robotic telescope holder, Aesop, is used for laparoscopic cholecystectomy as well.[107] Advantages of this device center on a steady field of vision. Moreover, the operating surgeon is able to move the telescope and camera through voice activation. We have found that it is best to place Aesop on the right side of the operating table at the level of the patient's right femoral head. Aesop is not tilted and the robotic arm is sometimes placed in the −1 position and sometimes in the 0 (neutral) position, depending on the patient's size (Fig. 105-4).[107]

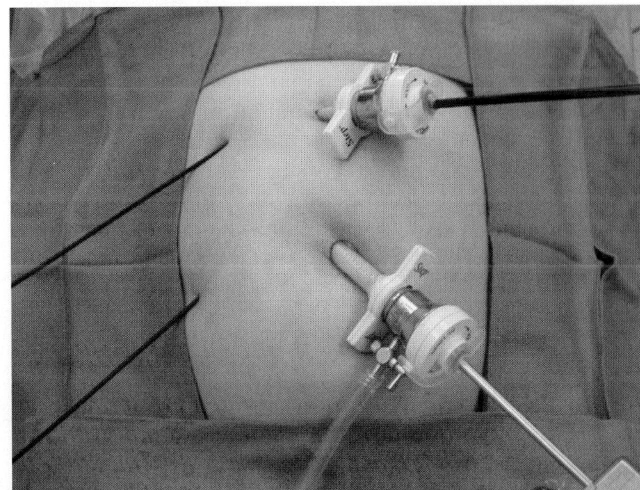

Figure 105-3 This operative photograph depicts the stab incision technique in a 5-year old undergoing laparoscopic cholecystectomy. On the patient's right side, the two 3-mm instruments were introduced through the stab incision technique without the use of cannulas. A 5-mm cannula has been placed in the epigastric region, and a 10-mm cannula is introduced into the umbilicus. This is the site of extraction of the gallbladder. One advantage of the stab incision technique is cost savings because two additional cannulas are not needed.

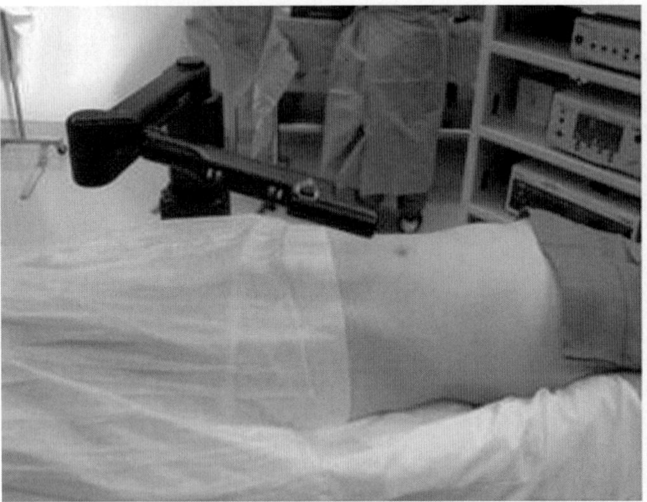

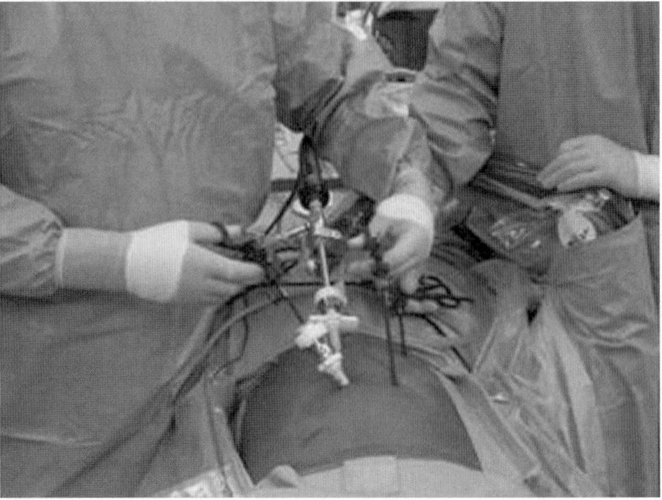

Figure 105-4 The authors utilize Aesop primarily for laparoscopic fundoplication and laparoscopic cholecystectomy. For laparoscopic cholecystectomy, Aesop is placed along the operating table's right side rail at the level of the patient's right femoral head. Aesop is not tilted, and the arm is usually adjusted to −1 degree of angulation (*left*). To operate efficiently with Aesop, the surgeon usually works over the arm (*right*). Note that the two right-sided instruments have been introduced in this patient without cannulas.

Laparoscopic Cholecystectomy

The patient is placed supine on the operating table with two video monitors situated at the head of the table. After induction of anesthesia, an orogastric tube is inserted for gastric decompression and the urinary bladder is evacuated using a Credé maneuver. A two-cannula and two "stab incision" technique is used, but the location of the incisions and the cannulas depends on the patient's age and size (Fig. 105-5). For infants and small children, the right lower abdominal incision can be positioned in the inguinal crease region and the epigastric cannula should be situated more on the patient's left to allow adequate working space between the instruments.

A 10-mm incision is made within the depth of the umbilicus, through which a 10-mm cannula is inserted into the abdominal cavity and abdominal insufflation is initiated. After creation of an adequate pneumoperitoneum, a 0- or 45-degree telescope is inserted through the umbilical cannula and connected to the camera. The image is then displayed on the video monitors. The right lower abdominal stab incision is created with a No. 11 blade and a locking, grasping forceps is inserted for retraction of the gallbladder superiorly over the liver by the assistant. Usually this is a 5-mm instrument, but a 3-mm instrument can be used in very small children. Through the right upper abdominal stab incision, a nonlocking, grasping forceps is inserted for lateral retraction of the infundibulum of the gallbladder by the operating surgeon. The epigastric port is usually 5 mm in diameter and is the main working site. In larger adolescents, a 10-mm port may be needed if a 10-mm endoscopic clip is required to completely occlude the cystic duct. Once the location of the cannulas is individualized according to the patient's size, the remaining principles of the procedure are similar to those used in adults. At this time, the telescope is attached to Aesop.

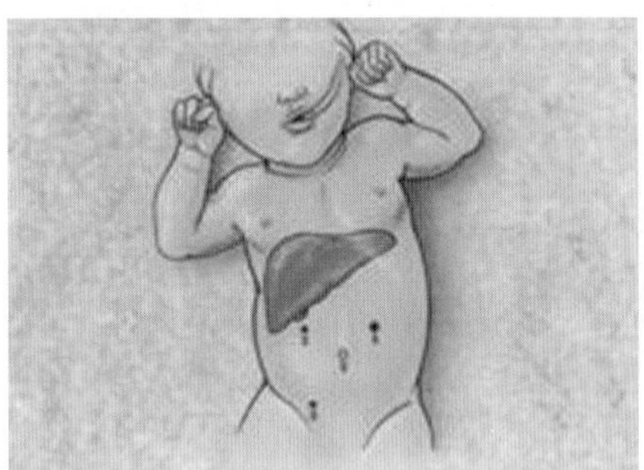

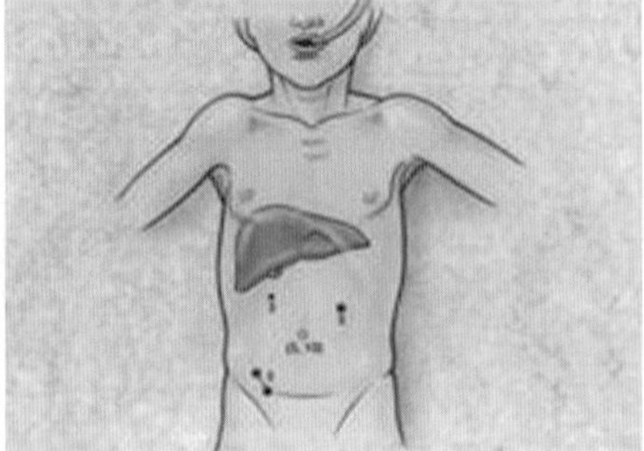

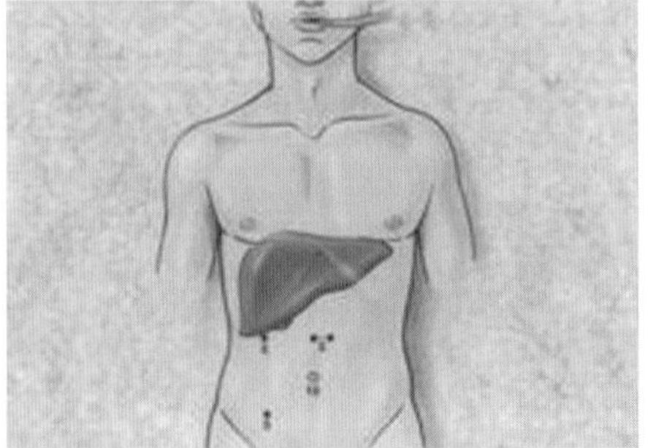

Figure 105-5 Placement of the cannulas and instruments in patients undergoing laparoscopic cholecystectomy depends on the patient's age and size. In an infant, 3- and 5-mm ports/instruments can be utilized. Also, the ports/instruments should be separated as much as possible to create an adequate working space for the operation (*left*). In a prepubertal child, the port/instruments should be widely spaced as well. A 3-mm instrument can often be used in the surgeon's left hand. In younger patients in this age range, a 5-mm umbilical cannula may be possible. However, for most patients, a 10-mm umbilical cannula is necessary to extract the gallbladder through this incision (*middle*). In a teenager, the port placement more closely resembles that seen in adults (*right*). (*See color plate.*)

For improved exposure, the patient and table are usually rotated into reverse Trendelenburg and left-dependent positions, which helps the adjacent viscera fall away from the surgical area. In addition, lateral retraction of the infundibulum is important because the cystic duct is then positioned at more of a 90-degree orientation to the common duct rather than an oblique or even parallel orientation, which occurs without such retraction (Fig. 105-6). This latter configuration may lead to misidentification of the cystic and common bile ducts resulting in injury to the common duct.

The initial surgical maneuver is to expose the cystic duct and identify the cystic artery. Adhesions between the duodenum and stomach often require lysis for access to the infundibulum and triangle of Calot. Once the cystic duct is identified, two options are present. One is to proceed with cholangiography as previously discussed. If the anatomy is clear and there is no evidence of choledochal obstruction on a preoperative US, we proceed with ligation and division of the cystic duct. Usually 5-mm clips are adequate, although a 10-mm clip may be required in larger patients. Two clips are placed on the cystic duct approximately 5 mm from its insertion into the common bile duct (Fig. 105-7). Another one or two clips are placed on the cystic duct near the infundibulum to prevent spillage of stones from the gallbladder. The cystic duct is then divided, and the cystic artery is similarly ligated and transected. Once these two structures are divided, the gallbladder is detached in a retrograde manner using one of several instruments: the hook cautery, spatula cautery, or endoscopic scissors attached to the cautery.

Before the gallbladder is completely separated from the liver bed, the triangle of Calot should be carefully inspected to ensure that all clips are secure and that there is no evidence of bleeding. After complete detachment of the gallbladder, the telescope is rotated from the umbilical port to the epigastric port. If the epigastric port is 5 mm, then a 5-mm telescope is utilized to visualize the gallbladder and a locking, grasping instrument is introduced through the umbilical cannula to secure the gallbladder. The gallbladder is then extracted through the umbilical port. In older patients, the gallbladder may be too large for removal without further incising the umbilical fascia. This opening should be enlarged in patients with large gallbladders to prevent rupture with spillage of stones and bile during removal of the gallbladder. These gallstones, if spilled, should be removed because complications from retained stones have been reported in adults.[9,19,108] After the gallbladder is extracted, the area of dissection is again carefully inspected to ensure adequate hemostasis. All irrigant is evacuated, and bupivacaine is injected into the incisions for postoperative analgesia. In smaller patients, the fascia surrounding the 5-mm cannula sites should be closed. In larger patients, fascial closure for the 5-mm ports or stab incisions is usually unnecessary, but the fascia surrounding the 10-mm cannula sites should be approximated carefully to prevent herniation. For the stab incisions, skin closure is usually all that is needed. The patients are usually hospitalized after the procedure and discharged the next morning. However, outpatient laparoscopic cholecystectomy is increasingly being performed in adults.

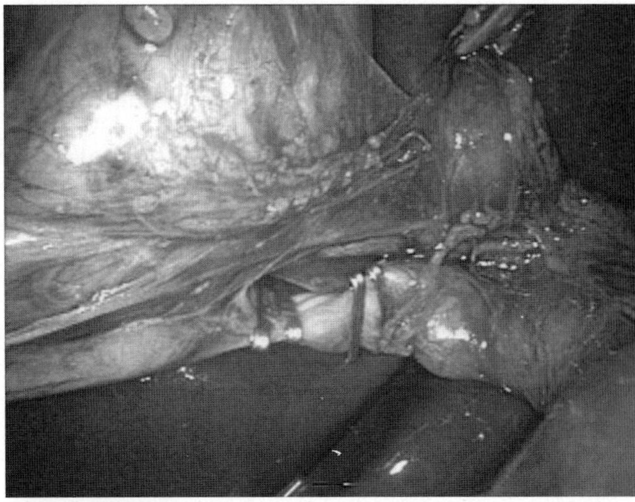

Figure 105-7 After identification and isolation of the cystic duct, the duct is doubly ligated with two clips proximal and two clips distal. The duct will be divided between the two middle endoscopic clips.

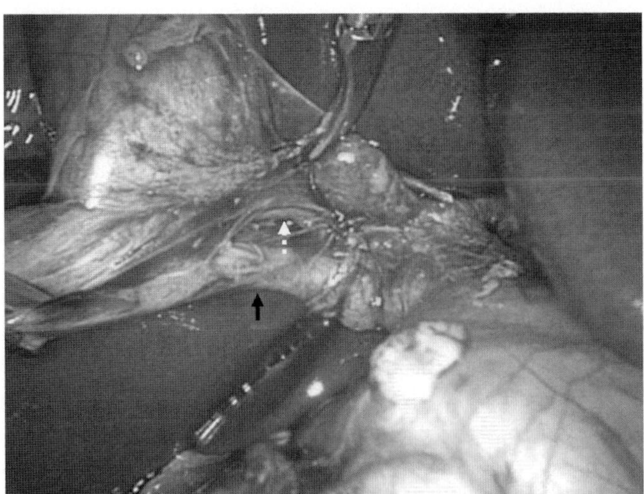

Figure 105-6 During the initial stages of the laparoscopic cholecystectomy, it is vitally important to retract the infundibulum directly lateral so as to create a 90-degree angle between the cystic duct (*solid arrow*) and common duct. Note the cystic artery (*dotted arrow*) cephalad to the cystic duct. *(See color plate.)*

Children's Mercy Hospital Experience

Despite the widespread use of laparoscopic cholecystectomy today in children, there have been very few reports in the literature, with only three reports describing a series as large as 100 patients.[47,73,123] In a 1999 review of 100 patients undergoing laparoscopic cholecystectomy at Vanderbilt University Medical Center, one of the authors (GWH) described 78 children who underwent an elective operation and 22 who required an urgent operation for acute complications of cholelithiasis.[47] In that series, 19 patients had hemolytic disease and 2 patients had biliary dyskinesia. The 6 patients who presented with jaundice underwent ERCP before the laparoscopic cholecystectomy. Stones were extracted in two patients, and the other studies were normal. In that report, 2 patients required laparoscopic choledochal exploration. The operating time and postoperative hospitalization were significantly longer for the complicated group when compared with the elective patients. No significant complications occurred such as the need for reoperation, injury to the choledochus or other viscera, bile leak, or retained choledocholithiasis.

Between 2000 and 2003, 93 children underwent laparoscopic cholecystectomy at Children's Mercy Hospital (Table 105-2). One additional child underwent laparoscopic cholecystectomy at the time of laparoscopic splenectomy for hereditary spherocytosis. Sixty-two patients were females. The mean age was 12.3 years, and the mean weight was 55.3 kg. Only 17% of the patients had evidence of a hematologic condition as the cause for their symptoms. Two children had previously undergone bone marrow transplantation for leukemia, and another patient had required chemotherapy for retinoblastoma. Three patients were diagnosed with biliary dyskinesia, two of whom appeared improved after the cholecystectomy.

Within this 4-year period, six patients were admitted through the emergency department with acute biliary colic; two patients developed gallstone pancreatitis; and one patient was admitted with marked jaundice. Two patients underwent preoperative ERCP for suspected choledocholithiasis. However, there was no evidence of common duct stones, and both patients underwent uneventful laparoscopic cholecystectomy shortly thereafter. Also, two patients were suspected to have possible choledocholithiasis, which was confirmed on intraoperative cholangiography performed at the time of laparoscopic cholecystectomy. It was elected to complete the laparoscopic cholecystectomy and have the ERCP performed postoperatively. The ERCP and sphincterotomy were performed on postoperative days 5 and 11 in these two patients. Common duct stones were removed, and both patients were discharged the following day.

Eleven patients underwent intraoperative cholangiography, and 82 patients did not. There was no evidence of injury to the common bile duct or any adjacent structures during the operation and no patient has required a second operation (other than the previously mentioned ERCP). The average operative time for the entire series was 108 minutes.

Other than the two patients mentioned above who underwent postoperative ERCP, only three patients required a postoperative hospitalization greater than 2 days. One patient with neurologic impairment and one patient with sickle cell disease were slow to recover. Another patient with spherocytosis developed an ileus postoperatively. All three patients were discharged on their third postoperative day.

Over the past 10 years, laparoscopic cholecystectomy has become the accepted standard for removal of the gallbladder in children and adolescents. Reported complications have been very few, and there are no reports of choledochal injury in children, although some have undoubtedly occurred. As additional experience is gained, pediatric surgeons may utilize intraoperative US rather than cholangiography to assess the correct anatomy and the presence of choledocholithiasis.

HEPATIC INFECTIONS

Various hepatic infections occur in infancy and childhood (Table 105-3). The focus in this section is on hepatic infections that often require surgical consultation for either diagnosis or treatment. This group includes hepatic abscess and nonviral causes of liver infection. Historically, the most frequent cause of hepatic abscess in children was secondary to perforated appendicitis. The development of hepatic infection in this setting was presumed to

TABLE 105-2 Patients Requiring Laparoscopic Cholecystectomy at Children's Mercy Hospital, Kansas City, MO, 2000-2003

Total Patients	93
Male	31
Female	62
Mean age (yr)	12.3 (2-20)
Mean weight (kg)	55.3 (11-126)
Hematologic disease	
Sickle cell	9
Hereditary spherocytosis	6
Pyruvate kinase deficiency	1
Biliary dyskinesia	3
Acute symptomatic conditions	
Acute biliary colic	6
Gallbladder pancreatitis	2
Jaundice	1

TABLE 105-3 Hepatic Infections in Children

Bacterial	**Parasitic**
Pyogenic hepatic abscess	*Entamoeba histolytica*
Cholangitis	Echinococcosis
Cat-scratch disease	Liver flukes
Perihepatitis	
Brucellosis	**Fungal**
Tuberculosis	Candidiasis
Actinomycosis	Aspergillosis
Typhoid hepatitis	Histoplasmosis
Tularemia	Cryptococcosis
Syphilis	Coccidioidomycosis
Lyme disease	Actinomycosis
Leptospirosis	
	Rickettsial
Viral	Rocky Mountain spotted fever
Hepatitis	Q fever
Cytomegalovirus infection	
Herpes	
Mononucleosis	

be due to pylephlebitis of the mesenteric and portal veins with ascending migration of bacteria into the liver. Liver abscesses are now seen most often in children with major debilitating diseases, granulocyte dysfunction, sickle cell disease, and congenital or acquired immunosuppression. In most pediatric series, more than half of liver abscesses are found in patients younger than 5 years of age. More than 25% occur during the first year of life. Multiple abscesses are found more commonly than solitary ones.[5,14,56]

Pathophysiology

Bacteria and other organisms may enter the liver through various routes, the most common being the biliary tract, the portal vein, and the hepatic artery. Also, organisms may directly invade the liver during penetrating trauma. In one report, a liver abscess occurred in 4 of 16 patients with unruptured post-traumatic intrahepatic hematomas.[40] In addition to the recognized causes of hepatic abscess, a small group of cryptogenic abscesses remains.

The clinical signs and symptoms of liver abscess are usually nonspecific. The most common signs and symptoms are fever, abdominal pain, and hepatomegaly. Abnormalities in leukocyte count, liver enzyme levels, or bilirubin levels vary in degree. Symptoms may last from days to months. The diagnosis of hepatic abscess by using imaging techniques has improved markedly with the availability of US and computed tomography (CT) (Figs. 105-8 and 105-9).[5,14]

Pyogenic Liver Abscess

Pyogenic liver abscess is uncommon in children, with a reported incidence varying between 3 to 25 per 100,000 pediatric hospital admissions.[92] Its incidence has decreased

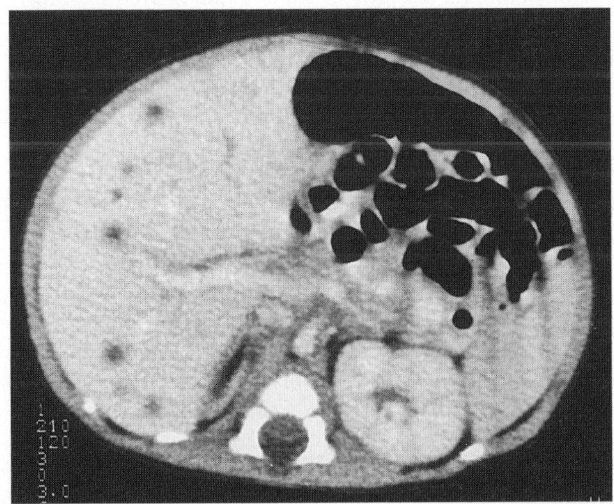

Figure 105-8 CT scan demonstrating several hepatic abscesses (defects) in a child with staphylococcal infection related to chronic granulomatous disease.

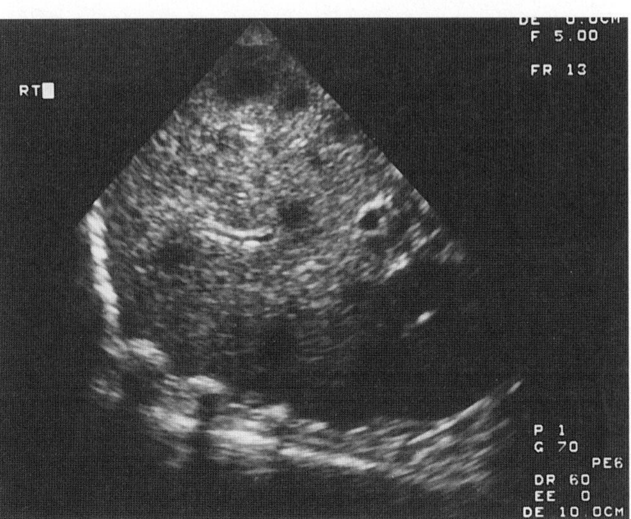

Figure 105-9 Sonogram demonstrating several hepatic abscesses (echolucent areas) in the same patient as in Figure 105-6.

since the introduction of antibiotics. In contrast to adults, in whom biliary tract disease is the primary cause of hepatic abscess, pyogenic liver abscess in children is most often seen in patients with an underlying immune deficiency. Chronic granulomatous disease (CGD) of childhood is one of the most common of these deficiencies. Acquired impairment in host resistance as a result of chemotherapy or transplantation immunosuppression also predisposes patients to hepatic abscess formation. Liver abscess secondary to biliary tract disease is most often seen after surgery for biliary atresia, choledochal cyst, or liver transplantation. Abdominal trauma, either penetrating or blunt, with liver injury is also associated with an increased incidence of hepatic abscess.[37,66] Abscesses in such cases are presumed to be secondary to bacterial seeding of the devitalized liver parenchyma and its associated hematoma. It must be remembered, however, that liver abscesses do occur in otherwise normal children who often present with a fever of unknown origin.[8,45]

In immunocompetant children, other causes for pyogenic liver abscess include intestinal infection (appendicitis), chronic cholangitis with intrahepatic abscess formation in patients with biliary atresia, umbilical vein catheterization (neonates), and systemic bacteremia of any cause.[59] In addition, in 20% of the patients the infectious source of the hepatic abscess is never found.[27]

The diagnosis of a pyogenic hepatic abscess is often dependent on its being considered as part of the differential diagnosis. The low incidence of liver abscess in childhood leads to a low index of suspicion and sometimes delays the diagnosis for weeks to months. In patients with fever, abdominal pain, jaundice, and liver enlargement, the diagnosis is less likely to be missed. However, these symptoms often develop slowly and may be associated with weight loss, thus leading to a suspicion of cancer. Usually the presenting symptoms are nonspecific, with the major symptom being abdominal pain.[8,92] The duration of symptoms is highly variable but usually the patients present between 1 week and 1 month after they become ill. Most patients are febrile, but an enlarged liver is found in only about two thirds of the patients. Right upper quadrant tenderness was found only in 40% of the patients in one report.[59] Hematologic studies are usually not helpful, as often only occasional mild leukocytosis is seen. Elevated liver function studies are found in only one half of the patients.

When the bacteriology of pyogenic abscesses is examined in children, *Staphylococcus aureus* was the primary infecting agent in between 37% to 50% of the children.[8,15,27,92] Most hepatic abscesses, however, tend to be polymicrobial with not only gram-positive cocci but also gram-negative rods, including *Escherichia coli, Klebsiella, Enterobacter,* and *Pseudomonas.* Recently, anaerobes have also been cultured from these abscesses in at least 20% of the cases.[15,23,39] Blood cultures are positive in about 50% of the patients. However, the blood cultures often will grow fewer bacterial types than are subsequently recovered from direct cultures of the abscess. As a cautionary note, in a third of the blood cultures, the organisms that were recovered from the blood were *not* subsequently recovered from the cultures of the liver abscess. Unfortunately, whereas Gram stains of a direct aspirate from a liver abscess are highly accurate for gram-positive cocci, they have only a 50% sensitivity for gram-negative organisms.[24] Fungal abscesses have been found with an increasing incidence in children who are febrile and neutropenic while being treated for acute leukemia.[79] One prospective series reported a 29% incidence of fungal hepatic and/or splenic abscesses in this population.[42] A specific ultrasonographic appearance for hepatic and splenic candidiasis has been described.[90]

Neonates comprise another special subpopulation of patients. In the perinatal period, direct transplacental bacterial seeding of the liver can occur. This seeding may be associated with premature rupture of membranes. Omphalitis, with or without catheterization of the umbilical vein, has been rarely associated with bacterial hepatitis or abscess. Most of these abscesses are miliary. There is a disproportionately high representation of gram-negative organisms in the neonatal hepatic abscess. Because they are usually miliary, they are not amenable to percutaneous drainage. Therefore, high-dose, long-term antibiotic treatment is needed.

In those neonates who presented with a solitary hepatic abscess, the offending organism is usually *S. aureus.* These patients present with an enlarging right upper quadrant mass that is often confused with a tumor. Treatment of these solitary abscesses has been resection because of the difficulty in distinguishing between an abscess and a solid tumor.[118]

Radiologic Evaluation

The best radiologic studies to establish the diagnosis of a hepatic cyst or abscess are abdominal US and CT. Ultrasound is usually preferred as the initial screening tool because of the lack of need for sedation and the absence of ionizing radiation. CT, however, is more sensitive and can discover lesions that are missed by US. In addition, CT is usually the preferred radiologic modality for localization of the abscess for percutaneous drainage.[92]

Treatment

The initial treatment of a pyogenic liver abscess should be with broad-spectrum antibiotics with coverage for gram-positive, gram-negative, and anerobic organisms. As part of the gram-negative spectrum, *Pseudomonas* coverage must be included. Percutaneous drainage should then be performed under either CT or US guidance. After the abscess has been drained and specific bacteria have been recovered, antibiotic therapy then can be tailored to cover these organisms. The recommended duration of intravenous antibiotic therapy is 4 to 6 weeks, followed by oral antibiotics for an additional 4 to 8 weeks.[56]

The percutaneous technique for drainage of hepatic abscesses has become the preferred approach in recent years. The complication rate of percutaneous drainage has been reported to be 4%, with a failure rate of 15%.[122] However, if the patient does not respond to percutaneous drainage or if percutaneous drainage is not possible, then an operative approach is warranted.[8,62] Recently there has been a study reporting the laparoscopic approach for drainage of a pyogenic liver abscess.[125] That study noted a reduced operative time, decreased blood loss, and decreased analgesic use in those patients who underwent the laparoscopic approach. With an aggressive approach to treatment of pyogenic liver abscess, the mortality of this disorder has dropped from 36% in the 1970s to 15% in the late 1980s and 10% now.

One complication of pyogenic liver abscess that has been reported in the adult population is endophthalmitis. In one series there was a 3.5% incidence of this complication, which can lead to a variety of devastating visual problems, ranging from decreased visual acuity to complete loss of eyesight.[119] The best results for recovery were associated with initiation of treatment within 24 hours of any visual symptoms. Therefore, any child who appears to be having any visual difficulties with a pyogenic abscess should undergo an ophthalmologic evaluation.

Cat-Scratch Disease

Cat-scratch disease is a subacute illness preceded by exposure to an infected cat. It is characterized by regional lymphadenitis but may involve other organ systems, including the liver, brain, and bone. This disorder was first described as oculoglandular syndrome in 1889, and the association with a scratch by a cat was reported in 1950 by Debre.[18] Since then, various infectious organisms have been postulated as the etiologic agent. Currently, cat-scratch disease is thought to be caused by *Bartonella henselae.* The disease primarily affects children and adolescents (75% to 80% of cases). A primary lesion develops at the site of inoculation in most cases, usually within 1 to 2 weeks of inoculation. This lesion is typically a single papule 2 to 5 mm in diameter. Regional lymphadenopathy develops approximately 3 weeks later and frequently involves axillary, inguinal, and cervical nodes. The primary skin lesion has often resolved by the time the adenopathy occurs. Other associated symptoms are fever, anorexia, malaise, fatigue, and headache.

It is estimated that 5% to 10% of patients present with more systemic symptoms or atypical manifestations of the disease. In these patients, the typical regional adenopathy may be absent.[77] Liver involvement is usually diagnosed by CT, which is performed as part of the evaluation for fever of unknown origin. This test typically shows multiple lesions in both lobes of the liver and, sometimes, associated splenic involvement.[18,97] The diagnosis is confirmed by liver biopsy, either open or guided by laparoscopy. The histologic features consist of a granulomatous reaction with necrosis. Cultures are negative for bacteria and fungi. Polymerase chain reaction of pus or tissue from a patient with cat-scratch disease has recently been found to be both sensitive and specific for *B. henselae.* Efforts at developing a serologic enzyme-linked immunosorbent assay are ongoing. Treatment of cat-scratch disease remains controversial because most untreated cases resolve without sequelae. Patients with marked symptoms or visceral involvement are usually treated with antibiotics (e.g., gentamicin, ciprofloxacin, rifampin, or trimethoprim- sulfamethoxazole).[76]

Perihepatitis

In the pediatric population, bacterial liver infection with either *Neisseria gonorrhoeae* or *Chlamydia trachomatis* tends to occur most frequently in teenage girls. The initial pelvic infection travels cephalad in the abdomen, resulting in a perihepatitis. If the perihepatitis is untreated, then the classic "violin string" adhesions develop between the liver and the peritoneal cavity that are associated with the Fitz-Hugh–Curtis syndrome.

In addition to the typical symptoms of pelvic inflammatory disease, including dysmenorrhea, vaginal discharge, and lower abdominal pain, these patients also present with severe pleuritic right upper quadrant abdominal pain that often radiates to the right shoulder. It is not unusual for the patient to complain of left upper quadrant pain as well. In these patients, the liver is often tender to palpation and a rub may be audible near the costal margin. Pelvic findings of acute salpingitis are usually present. Laboratory findings include leukocytosis, elevated aminotransferase levels, and occasional hyperbilirubinemia.

Perihepatitis can mimic a variety of other conditions in the upper abdomen, including cholelithiasis, hepatitis, a perforated peptic ulcer, appendicitis, or pancreatitis. In female adolescents with a history of pelvic inflammatory disease, perihepatitis must be part of the differential diagnosis when these patients present with right upper quadrant pain.

The diagnosis of perihepatitis cannot be made with certainty unless it is seen directly. In patients in whom the diagnosis is uncertain or in patients who have persistent symptoms, diagnostic laparoscopy can allow direct visualization of the perihepatic space and, if found, the classic adhesions can be lysed laparoscopically, which often results in a significant improvement in pain.[89]

Recent reports have also implicated *C. trachomatis* as well as *N. gonorrhoeae* as a cause of this syndrome.[96] Therefore, a treatment regimen that is effective against both chlamydial infection and gonococcus is necessary. This would include tetracycline, or doxycycline, or erythromycin for patients in whom tetracycline is contraindicated.[96]

Amebic Abscess

The incidence of amebic liver abscess in the United States seems to have gradually increased. Hepatic involvement by *Entamoeba histolytica* is primarily a disease of adults but does occur in younger patients, most commonly in early childhood.[84] Poor sanitation and crowded conditions are conducive to the development and spread of amebiasis. In patients with amebic colitis, trophozoites from colon ulcers travel to the liver through the portal vein, where they initiate a necrotizing process with subsequent abscess formation. In the adult population, liver involvement with an amebic abscess occurs in 10% to 50% of adults with a 90% male predominance, whereas in children liver involvement occurs in only 1% to 7% of the patients with an equal distribution between males and females.[52,91,120] Corticosteroids and immunosuppression seems to predispose patients to abscess formation.

More than 80% of amebic liver abscesses occur in the right lobe of the liver. Symptoms include fever, chills, nausea, weight loss, and abdominal distention. On physical examination, the children tend to have hepatomegaly but abdominal pain and liver tenderness are relatively infrequent. Breath sounds are often decreased in the lower right chest, and right-sided pleural effusions are common. Clinical jaundice is uncommon. A history of exposure or travel to endemic areas (Mexico, South America, or Southeast Asia) is often a better indicator of amebiasis than are the imaging studies.[28]

Laboratory findings include leukocytosis without eosinophilia, mild anemia, and normal or mildly abnormal liver function studies. Abdominal US and CT are useful for defining the location and number of lesions. The characteristic US appearance is a hypoechoic, thin-walled abscess that sometimes contains air. CT shows a nonspecific picture of a well-circumscribed, low-density lesion that is usually solitary and has predominance for the right lobe of the liver. Also, with modern imaging techniques, it is now clear that multiple amebic abscesses can be present within the liver.[110]

The diagnosis of an amebic liver abscess relies on the identification of a space-occupying lesion in the liver and the presence of positive amebic serology. Amebic serology (indirect hemoglobin assay or agargel immunodiffusion precipitant) has been found to be highly sensitive (>94%) and highly specific (>95%) for the diagnosis of amebic liver abscess.[58] If it is not possible to distinguish clinically between a pyogenic versus an amebic liver abscess, or if the abscess does not respond to appropriate medical treatment, or if serologic tests for ameba are inconclusive, then aspiration of the abscess is indicated for culture.

The current treatment for an amebic abscess is oral metronidazole (30 to 50 mg/kg/day for 7 to 10 days).

Most patients will respond to this therapy with resolution of the fever and abdominal pain. Currently there is no indication for aspiration of an uncomplicated amebic abscess because the majority of these will resolve with medical management alone.[1,12,55,110] If the patient does not respond to medical management within 4 days, if the liver abscess is greater than 10 cm in diameter, if it is located in the left lobe of the liver, or if it is believed to be in danger of rupture, then aspiration and percutaneous drainage is advisable. In addition, percutaneous catheter drainage is also indicated in patients who have had rupture of an amebic abscess into the right pleural space. Total resolution of the abscess may take months to years and can be followed by US.

The most common complication of an amebic liver abscess is erosion through the diaphragm and rupture into the right chest. Spontaneous rupture occurs in approximately 10% of patients with clinically recognized amebic hepatic abscess. Erosion into the pericardial sac is less frequent but may cause cardiac tamponade. Intraperitoneal rupture results in a clinical picture of peritonitis and shock. If this develops, fluid resuscitation, antibiotics, antiamebic drugs, and surgical exploration are necessary.

There have been attempts at developing a vaccine for *E. histolytica* in an attempt to eradicate amebiasis. However, an unfortunate problem is that natural infections with *E. histolytica* do not seem to result in long-term immunity. In fact, recurrent amebic liver abscesses are a well-known problem in areas where *E. histolytica* is endemic.[11,85,87]

Echinococcal Cyst

Hydatid disease is generally caused by infection with the larval stage of the dog tapeworm *Echinococcus granulosis*. The ingested ova burrow through the intestinal mucosa and travel to the liver through the mesenteric veins. A few ova may bypass the liver and be trapped in the lung. The reported peak incidence of echinococcal infection in children is between 5 and 15 years of age.[69,128] The usual presenting symptoms include right upper quadrant pain or a mass and right lower pleuritic type chest pain in about one half of the patients. Interestingly, about a fourth of the patients are asymptomatic at presentation. Untreated cysts tend to grow until they reach the surface of the liver, where they can then spontaneously rupture, resulting in dissemination of the parasite into the peritoneal cavity and possible anaphylaxis.[32] In one fourth of the cases, the cyst can become secondarily infected with bacteria.[110] Echinococcal liver abscess is best diagnosed by serologic testing. The indirect hemagglutination assay is the most specific test, but it lacks sensitivity for echinococcal disease. Results are considered positive for tissue invasion at a titer of 1:512, suspicious at a titer of 1:128, and negative at a titer of 1:32. By comparison, the complement fixation test yields positive results in 80% of patients with echinococcal disease. Assay by immunoelectrophoresis is even more sensitive and is quite specific. The combination of at least two serologic tests provides a positive laboratory diagnosis in more than 94% of patients with echinococcal disease.[66] Diagnostic aspiration is indicated if there is concern that the cyst could be a pyogenic or amebic abscess, but it is not indicated in echinococcal disease. Plain radiography or CT of the abdomen may show calcification of the rim of an echinococcal cyst or daughter cysts, a finding not found in amebic liver abscess (Fig. 105-10).

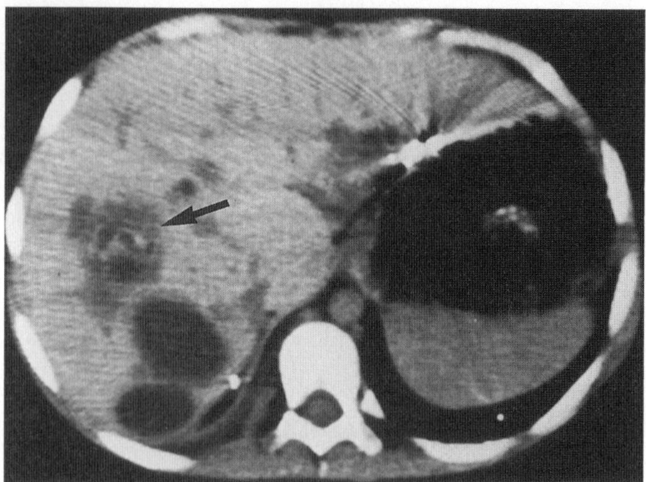

Figure 105-10 CT scan demonstrating several hepatic abscesses with one (*arrow*) containing daughter cysts characteristic of hydatid disease.

Medical treatment of hydatid cyst includes the second-generation antihelminthic albendazole. Although there are some data that suggest that albendazole does not decrease the escolex viability in liver hydatid cysts preoperatively, there is a suggestion that albendazole may decrease the recurrence rate after surgical treatment.[57,75]

Successful surgical treatment is dependent on isolation of the liver, usually with sponges soaked in hypertonic saline or a povidone-iodine (Betadine) solution, to prevent spillage of the cyst material. The cyst is then aspirated, and hypertonic saline (20%) or betadine is used to irrigate the cyst in an attempt to kill any daughter cysts. However, the effectiveness of this step has been questioned.[72] The cyst is then unroofed, and all daughter cysts are removed. Several authors have recommended the removal of not only the laminated membrane of the cyst but also the entire pericyst wall.[72,75] The recurrence rate with standard excision of the pericyst is between 10% and 20%. With radical removal of the pericyst wall, the recurrence rate has been reported to decrease to less than 2%.[72,75]

REFERENCES

1. Ahsan T, Jehangir MU, Mahmood T, et al: Amoebic versus pyogenic liver abscess. J Pak Med Assoc 2002;52:497-501.
2. Al-Homaidhi HS, Sukerek H, Klein M, et al: Biliary dyskinesia in children. Pediatr Surg Int 2002;18:357-360.
3. Almond PS, Adolph VR, Steiner R, et al: Calculous disease of the biliary tract in infants after neonatal extracorporeal membrane oxygenation. J Perinatol 1992;12:18-20.
4. Al-Salem AH, Qaisruddin S: The significance of biliary sludge in children with sickle cell disease. Pediatr Surg Int 1998;13:14-16.

5. Baetz-Greenwalt B, Goske M: Intra-abdominal infection. In Wylie R, Hyams JS (eds): Pediatric Gastrointestinal Disease: Pathophysiology, Diagnosis, Management. Philadelphia, WB Saunders, 1993.
6. Bates GC, Brown CH: Incidence of gallbladder disease in chronic hemolytic anemia (spherocytosis). Gastroenterology 1952;21:104-109.
7. Bhattacharyya N, Wayne AS, Kevy SV, Shamberger RC: Perioperative management for cholecystectomy in sickle cell disease. J Pediatr Surg 1993;28:72-75.
8. Bilfinger TV, Hayden CK, Oldham KT, et al: Pyogenic liver abscesses in nonimmunocompromised children. South Med J 1986;79:37-40.
9. Birkett DH: Spilled cells, spilled clips, spilled stones. Surg Endosc 1995;9:269-271.
10. Bishop WP, Kao SCS: Prolonged postprandial abdominal pain following Kawasaki syndrome with acute gallbladder hydrops: Association with impaired gallbladder emptying. J Pediatr Gastroenterol Nutr 1991;13:307-311.
11. Blessmann J, Pham L Van, Nu Pat, et al: Epidemiology of amebiasis in a region of high incidence of amebic liver abscess in Central Vietnam. Am J Trop Med Hyg 2002; 66:578-583.
12. Blessmann J, Binh HD, Hung DM, et al: Treatment of amoebic liver abscess with metronidazole alone or in combination with ultrasound-guided needle aspiration: A comparative, prospective and randomized study. Trop Med Int Health 2003;8:1030-1034.
13. Borgna-Pignatti C, DeStefano P, Pajno D, et al: Cholelithiasis in children with thalassemia major: An ultrasonographic study. J Pediatr 1981;99:243-244.
14. Branum GD, Tyson GS, Branum MA, et al: Hepatic abscess: Changes in etiology, diagnosis and management. Ann Surg 1990;212:655-662.
15. Brook I, Fraizer EH: Role of anaerobic bacteria in liver abscesses in children. Pediatr Infect Dis J 1993;12:743-747.
16. Brugge WR, Brand DL, Atkins HL, et al: Gallbladder dyskinesia in chronic acalculous cholecystitis. Dig Dis Sci 1986;31:461-467.
17. Carbajo Ferreira AJ, Urbaez Romero M, Medina Benitez W, et al: Biliary lithiasis in childhood. An Esp Pediatr 1992; 36:281-284.
18. Carithers HA: Cat-scratch disease: Notes on its history. Am J Dis Child 1990;119:200-203.
19. Carlin CB, Kent RB Jr, Laws HL: Spilled gallstones—complications of abdominal-wall abscesses. Surg Endosc 1995;9:341-343.
20. Carney DE, Evan R, Kokoska ER, et al: Predictors of successful outcome after cholecystectomy for biliary dyskinesia. J Pediatr Surg 2004;39:813-816.
21. Cay A, Imamoglu M, Kosucu P, et al: Gallbladder dyskinesia: A cause of chronic abdominal pain in children. Eur J Pediatr Surg 2003;13:302-306.
22. Chamberlain JW, Hight DW: Acute hydrops of the gallbladder in childhood. Surgery 1970;68:899-905.
23. Charara AI, Rockey DC: Pyogenic liver abscess. Curr Treat Op Gastroenterol 2002;5:437.
24. Chemaly RF, Hall GS, Keys TF, et al: Microbiology of liver abscesses and the predictive value of abscess Gram stain and associated blood cultures. Diagn Microbiol Infect Dis 2003;46:245-248.
25. Chittmittrapap S, Buachum V, Dharmklong-at A: Cholelithiasis in thalassemic children. Pediatr Surg Int 1990;5:114-117.
26. Choi YS, Sharma B: Gallbladder hydrops in mucocutaneous lymph node syndrome. South Med J 1989;82:397-398.
27. Chusid MJ: Pyogenic hepatic abscesses in infancy and childhood. Pediatrics 1978;62:554-555.
28. Conter RL, Tomkins RK, Longmire WP Jr, et al: Differentiation of pyogenic from amebic hepatic abscesses. Surg Gynecol Obstet 1986;162:114-120.
29. Cooperberg PL, Burhenne HJ: Real-time ultrasonography: Diagnostic treatment of choice in calculous gallbladder disease. N Engl J Med 1980;302:1277-1279.
30. Cunningham JJ, Houlihan SM, Altay C: Cholecystosonography in children with sickle cell disease: Technical approach and clinical results. J Clin Ultrasound 1981;9: 231-235.
31. DeCaluwe D, Akl U, Corbally M: Cholecystectomy versus cholecystolithotomy for cholelithiasis in childhood: Long-term outcome. J Pediatr Surg 2001;36:1518-1521.
32. deRosa F, Teggi A: Treatment of *Echinococcus granulosus* hydatid disease with albendazole. Ann Trop Med Parasital 1990;84:467-472.
33. Edwards KM, Glick AD, Greene HL: Intrahepatic cholangitis associated with mucocutaneous lymph node syndrome. J Pediatr Gastroenterol Nutr 1985;4:140-142.
34. El-Shafie M, Mah CL: Transient gallbladder distention in sick premature infants: The value of ultrasonography and radionuclide scintigraphy. Pediatr Radiol 1986;16:468-471.
35. Esposito C, Gonzalez Sabin MA, Corcione F, et al: Results and complications of laparoscopic cholecystectomy in childhood. Surg Endosc 2001;15:890-892.
36. Everson GT, Nemeth A, Kourourian S, et al: Gallbladder function is altered in sickle hemoglobinopathy. Gastroenterology 1989;96:1307-1316.
37. Fabian TC, Croce, MA, Stanford GG, et al: Factors affecting morbidity following hepatic trauma: A prospective analysis of 482 injuries. Ann Surg 1991;213:540-547.
38. Flancbaum L, Alden SM: Morphine cholescintigraphy. Surg Gynecol Obstet 1990;171:227-232.
39. Garrison RN, Polk HC: Liver abscess and subphrenic abscess. In Blumgart LH (ed): Surgery of the Liver and Biliary Tract. New York, Churchill Livingstone, 1998.
40. Geis WP, Schultz KA, Giacchino JL, et al: The fate of unruptured intrahepatic hematomas. Surgery 1981;90: 689-697.
41. Gollin G, Raschbaum GR, Moorthy C, et al: Cholecystectomy for suspected biliary dyskinesia in children with chronic abdominal pain. J Pediatr Surg 1999;34:854-857.
42. Grois N, Mostbeck G, Scherrer R, et al: Hepatic and splenic abscesses—a common complication of intensive chemotherapy of acute myeloid leukemia (AML): A prospective study. Ann Hematol 1991;63:33-38.
43. Haberkern CM, Neumayr LD, Orringer EP, et al: Cholecystectomy in sickle cell anemia patients: perioperative outcome of 364 cases from the National Preoperative Transfusion Study. Preoperative Transfusion in Sickle Cell Disease Study Group. Blood 1997;89:1533-1542.
44. Hadigan C, Fishman SJ, Connolly LP, et al: Stimulation with fatty meal (Lipomul) to assess gallbladder emptying in children with chronic acalculous cholecystitis. J Pediatr Gastroenterol Nutr 2003;37:178-182.
45. Harrington E, Bleicher MA: Cryptogenic hepatic abscess in two uncompromised children. J Pediatr Surg 1980;15: 660-662.
46. Holcomb GW III: Pediatric laparoscopic cholecystectomy: An initial five-year experience. Pediatr Ann 1993;22: 657-662.
47. Holcomb GW III, Morgan WM III, Neblett WW III, et al: Laparoscopic cholecystectomy in children: Lessons learned from the first 100 patients. J Pediatr Surg 1999;34:1236-1240.
48. Holcomb GW III, Sharp KW, Neblett WW III, et al: Laparoscopic cholecystectomy in infants and children: Modifications and cost analysis. J Pediatr Surg 1994;29: 900-904.

49. Holcomb GW Jr, O'Neill JA Jr, Holcomb GW III: Cholecystitis, cholelithiasis and common duct stenosis in children and adolescents. Ann Surg 1980;191:626-635.
50. Holgersen LO, Stolar C, Berdon WE, et al: Therapeutic and diagnostic implications of acquired choledochal obstruction in infancy; spontaneous resolution in three infants. J Pediatr Surg 1990;25:1027-1029.
51. Holzman MD, Sharp K, Holcomb GW III: An alternative technique for laparoscopic cholangiography. Surg Endosc 1994;8:927-930.
52. Hotez PJ, Strickland AD: Amebiasis. In Feigin RD, Cherry JD (eds): Textbook of Pediatric Infectious Diseases, 4th ed. Philadelphia, WB Saunders 1998;2389.
53. Imamoglu M, Sarihan H, Sari A, et al: Acute acalculous cholecystitis in children: Diagnosis and treatment. J Pediatr Surg 2002;37:36-39.
54. Jacir NN, Anderson KD, Eichelberger M, et al: Cholelithiasis in infancy: Resolution of gallstones in three or four infants. J Pediatr Surg 1986;21:567-569.
55. Jamil B, Hamid SS: Abscesses in the liver: Amoebic or pyogenic? J Pak Med Assoc 2002;52:495-496.
56. Kaplan SL: Pyogenic liver abscess. In Feigin RD, Cherry JD (eds): Textbook of Pediatric Infectious Disease. Philadelphia, WB Saunders, 1987.
57. Karpathios T, Syriopoulou V, Nicolaidou P, et al: Mebendazole and the treatment of hydatid cysts. Am J Dis Child 1984;59:894-896.
58. Katzenstein D, Rickerson V, Braude A: New concepts of amebic liver abscess derived from hepatic imaging, serodiagnosis, and hepatic enzymes in 67 consecutive cases in San Diego. Medicine (Baltimore) 1982;61:237-246.
59. Kays DW: Pediatric liver cysts and abscesses. Semin Pediatr Surg 1992;1:107-114.
60. King DR, Ginn-Pease ME, Lloyd TV, et al: Parenteral nutrition with associated cholelithiasis: Another iatrogenic disease of infants and children. J Pediatr Surg 1987;22: 593-596.
61. Kirtley JA Jr, Holcomb GW Jr: Surgical management of diseases of the gallbladder and common duct in children and adolescents. Am J Surg 1966;111:39-46.
62. Klatchko BA, Schwartz SI: Diagnostic and therapeutic approaches to pyogenic abscess of the liver. Surg Gynecol Obstet 1989;168:332-336.
63. Komura J, Yano H, Tanaka Y, et al: Increased incidence of cholestasis during total parenteral nutrition in children—factors affecting stone formation. Kurume Med J 1993; 40:7-11.
64. Kumar R, Nguyen K, Shun A: Gallstones and common bile duct calculi in infancy and childhood. Aust N Z J Surg 2000; 70:188-191.
65. Lachman BS, Lazerson J, Starshak RJ, et al: The prevalence of cholelithiasis in sickle cell disease as diagnosed by ultrasound and cholecystography. Pediatrics 1979;64:601-603.
66. Lewis RT, Barkun J: Infection in the upper abdomen: Biliary tract, pancreas, liver, and spleen. In Meakins JL (ed): Surgical Infections. New York, Scientific American, 1994.
67. Lindberg MC: Hepatobiliary complications of oral contraceptives. J Gen Intern Med 1992;7:199-209.
68. Lobe TE: Cholelithiasis and cholecystitis in children. Semin Pediatr Surg 2000;9:170.
69. Lofi M, Hashemian H: Hydatid disease of the liver and its treatment. Int Surg 1973;3:166-168.
70. Lugo-Vicente HL: Gallbladder dyskinesia in children. JSLS 1997;1:61-64.
71. Lugo-Vicente HL: Trends in management of gallbladder disorders in children. Pediatr Surg Int 1997;12:348-352
72. Magistrelli P, Masetti R, Coppola R, et al: Surgical treatment of hydatid disease of the liver. Arch Surg 1991;126:518-522.
73. Mah D, Wales P, Njere I, et al: Management of suspected common bile duct stones in children: Role of selective intraoperative cholangiogram and endoscopic retrograde cholangiopancreatography. J Pediatr Surg 2004;39: 808-812.
74. Manji N, Bistrian BR, Mascioli EA, et al: Gallstone disease in patients with severe short bowel syndrome dependent on parenteral nutrition. J Parent Enter Nutr 1989;13:461-464.
75. Manterola C, Barroso M, Vial M, et al: Liver abscess of hydatid origin: Clinical features and results of aggressive treatment. ANZ J Surg 2003;73:220-224.
76. Marglieth AM: Antibiotic therapy for cat scratch disease: Clinical study of therapeutic outcome in 268 patients and a review of the literature. Pediatr Infect Dis 1992;11:474-478.
77. Matalack JJ, Jaffe R: Granulomatous hepatitis in three children due to cat-scratch disease without peripheral adenopathy: An unrecognized cause of fever of unknown origin. Am J Dis Child 1993;147:949-953.
78. Matos C, Avni EF, VanGansbeke D, et al: Total parenteral nutrition (TPN) and gallbladder diseases in neonates. J Ultrasound Med 1987;6:243-248.
79. Maxwell AJ, Mamtora A: Fungal liver abscesses in acute leukemia: A report of two cases. Clin Radiol 1988;39:197-202.
80. McDermott EWM, Alkhalifa K, Murphy JJ: Laparoscopic cholecystectomy without exchange transfusion in sickle cell disease. Lancet 1993;342:1181.
81. Michail S, Preud'Homme D, Christian J, et al: Laparoscopic cholecystectomy: Effective treatment for chronic abdominal pain in children with acalculous biliary pain. J Pediatr Surg 2001;36:1394-1396.
82. Milas M, Ricketts RR, Amerson JR, et al: Management of biliary tract stones in heart transplant patients. Ann Surg 1996;223:747-753.
83. Misra DC, Blossom GB, Fink-Bennett D, et al: Results of surgical therapy for biliary dyskinesia. Arch Surg 1991; 126:957-960.
84. Mount AP: Liver Disorders in Childhood, 3rd ed. Oxford, Butterworth-Heinemann, 1994.
85. Nazir Z, Moazam F: Amebic liver abscess in children. Pediatr Infect Dis J 1993;12:929-932.
86. Newman KD, Powell DM, Holcomb GW III: The management of choledocholithiasis in children in the era of laparoscopic cholecystectomy. J Pediatr Surg 1997;32: 1116-1119.
87. Nordestgaard AG, Stapelford L, Worthen N: Contemporary management of amebic liver abscess. Am Surg 1992;58: 315-320.
88. Ostlie DJ, Holcomb GW III: The use of stab incisions for instrument access in laparoscopic operations. J Pediatr Surg 2003;38:1837-1840.
89. Owens S, Yeko TR, Bloy R, et al: Laparoscopic treatment of painful perihepatic adhesions in Fitz-Hugh-Curtis syndrome. Obstet Gynecol 1991;78:542-543.
90. Pastakia B, Shawker TH, Thaler M, et al: Hepatosplenic candidiasis: Wheels within wheels. Radiology 1988;166: 417-421.
91. Petri WA Jr, Sing U: Diagnosis and management of amebiasis. Clin Infect Dis 1999;29:1117-1125.
92. Pineiro-Carrerro VM, Andres JM: Morbidity and mortality in children with pyogenic liver abscess. Am J Dis Child 1989; 143:1424-1427.
93. Quigley EM, Marsh MN, Shaffer JL, et al: Hepatobiliary complications of total parenteral nutrition. Gastroenterology 1993;104:286-301.
94. Reed DN Jr, Fernandez M, Hicks RD: Kinevac-assisted cholescintigraphy as an accurate predictor of chronic acalculous gallbladder disease and the likelihood of symptom relief with cholecystectomy. Am Surg 1993;59:273-277.

95. Rescorla FJ: Cholelithiasis, cholecystitis, and common bile duct stones. Curr Opin Pediatr 1997;9:276-282.
96. Ris HW: Perihepatitis (Fitz-Hugh–Curtis syndrome): A review and case presentation. J Adolesc Health Care 1984;5:272-276.
97. Rizkallah MF, Meyer L, Nayoub EM: Hepatic and splenic abscesses in cat-scratch disease. Pediatr Infect Dis J 1988; 7:191-195.
98. Roy CC, Belli DC: Hepatobiliary complications associated with TPN: An enigma. J Am Coll Nutr 1985;4:651-660.
99. Sackmann M, Delius M, Sauerbruch T, et al: Shock-wave lithotripsy of gallbladder stones: The first 175 patients. N Engl J Med 1988;318:393-397.
100. Sandler A, Winkel G, Kimura K, et al: The role of prophylactic cholecystectomy during splenectomy in children with hereditary spherocytosis. J Pediatr Surg 1999;34: 1077-1078.
101. Sandoval C, Stringel G, Ozkaynak MF, et al: Perioperative management of children with sickle cell disease undergoing laparoscopic surgery. JSLS 2002;6:29-33.
102. Sarnaik S, Slovis TL, Corbett DP, et al: Incidence of cholelithiasis in sickle cell anemia using the ultrasonic gray-scale technique. J Pediatr 1980;96:1005-1008.
103. Schoenfield LJ, Berci G, Carnovale RL, et al: The effect of ursodiol on the efficacy and safety of extracorporeal shock-wave lithotripsy of gallstones: The Dornier National Biliary Lithotripsy study. N Engl J Med 1990;323:1239-1245.
104. Schoenfield LJ, Lachin JM, Steering Committee, National Cooperative Gallstone Study Group: Chenodiol (chenodeoxycholic acid) for dissolution of gallstones; The National Cooperative Gallstone Study: A controlled trial of efficacy and safety. Ann Intern Med 1981;95:257-282.
105. Scobie WB, Bentley JF: Hydrops of the gallbladder in a newborn infant. J Pediatr Surg 1969;4:457-459.
106. Shah RS, Blakely ML, Lobe TE: The role of laparoscopy in the management of common bile duct obstruction in children. Surg Endosc 2001;15:1353-1355.
107. Shew SB, Ostlie DJ, Holcomb GW III: Robotic telescopic assistance in pediatric laparoscopic surgery. Pediatr Endosurg Innovative Tech 2003;7:371-376.
108. Shocket E: Abdominal abscess from gallstones spilled at laparoscopic cholecystectomy. Surg Endosc 1995;9: 344-347.
109. Snyder CL, Ferrell KL, Saltzman DA, et al: Operative therapy of gallbladder disease in patients with cystic fibrosis. Am J Surg 1989;157:557-561.
110. Stanley SL Jr: Amoebiasis. Lancet 2003;361:1025-1034.
111. Stephens CG, Scott RB: Cholelithiasis in sickle cell anemia. Arch Intern Med 1980;140:648-651.
112. Stern RC, Rothstein FC, Doershuk CF: Treatment and prognosis of symptomatic gallbladder disease in patients with cystic fibrosis. J Pediatr Gastroenterol Nutr 1986;5: 35-40.
113. Stringel G, Beneck D, Bostwick HE: Polypoid lesions of the gallbladder in children. JSLS 1997;1:247-249.
114. Stringer MD, Ceylan H, Ward K, et al: Gallbladder polyps in children—classification and management. J Pediatr Surg 2003;38:1680-1684.
115. Stringer MD, Taylor DR, Soloway RD: Gallstone composition: Are children different? J Pediatr 2003;142: 435-440.
116. St-Vil D, Yazbeck S, Luks FL, et al: Cholelithiasis in newborns and infants. J Pediatr Surg 1992;27:1305-1307.
117. Tagge EP, Hebra A, Goldberg A, et al: Pediatric laparoscopic biliary tract surgery. Semin Pediatr Surg 1998;7: 202-206.
118. Tai YT, Shieh CC, Wang SM, et al: Neonatal solitary liver abscess: Report of one case. Acta Paediatr Taiwan 2002;43: 50-52.
119. Tan YM, Chee SP, Soo KC, et al: Ocular manifestations and complications of pyogenic liver abscess. World J Surg 2004;28:38-42.
120. The American Academy of Pediatrics: Amebiasis. In Pickering LK (ed): 2000 Redbook: Report of the Committee on Infectious Diseases, 25th ed. Elk Grove Village, IL, American Academy of Pediatrics, 2000.
121 Ure BM, deJong MM, Bax KN, et al: Outcome after laparoscopic cholecystectomy and cholecystectomy in children with symptomatic cholecystolithiasis: A preliminary report. Pediatr Surg 2001;17:396-398.
122. Vachon L, Diament MJ, Stanley P: Percutaneous drainage of hepatic abscesses in children. J Pediatr Surg 1986;21: 366-368.
123. Waldhausen JHT, Graham DD, Tapper D: Routine intraoperative cholangiography during laparoscopic cholecystectomy minimizes unnecessary endoscopic retrograde cholangiopancreatography in children. J Pediatr Surg 2001;36:881-884.
124. Wales PW, Carver E, Crawford MW, et al: Acute chest syndrome after abdominal surgery in children with sickle cell disease: Is a laparoscopic approach better? J Pediatr Surg 2001;36:718-721.
125. Wang W, Lee WJ, Wei PL, et al: Laparoscopic drainage of pyogenic liver abscesses. Surg Today 2004;34:323-325.
126. Ware R, Filston HC, Schultz WH, et al: Elective cholecystectomy in children with sickle hemoglobinopathies. Ann Surg 1988;208:17-22.
127. Weinstein S, Lipsitz EC, Addonizio L, Stolar CJ: Cholelithiasis in pediatric cardiac transplant patients on cyclosporine. J Pediatr Surg 1995;30:61-64.
128. Weirich W: Hydatid disease of the liver. Am J Surg 1979; 138:805-808.
129. Winter SS, Kinney TR, Ware RE: Gallbladder sludge in children with sickle cell disease. J Pediatr 1994;125: 747-749.
130. Wood J, Holland AJ, Shun A, et al: Biliary dyskinesia: Is the problem with Oddi? Pediatr Surg 2004;20:83-86.
131. Zargar SA, Javod G, Khan BA, et al: Endoscopic sphincterotomy in the management of bile duct stones in children. Am J Gastroenterol 2003;98:586-589.

Chapter 106

Portal Hypertension

Riccardo Superina

> A man who thinks that a science can perform what is outside its province, or that nature can accomplish unnatural things, is guilty of ignorance more akin to madness than to lack of learning. Our practice is limited by the instruments made available by Nature or by Art. When a man is attacked by a disease more powerful than the instruments of medicine, it must not be expected that medicine should prove victorious. —**Hippocrates**

The treatment of portal hypertension has changed dramatically in the last decade, and this change is particularly significant in children. New imaging techniques, coupled with improved medical and pharmacologic management, have permitted the application of both established and new surgical techniques in a precise manner that addresses the underlying disease processes resulting in raised portal venous pressures.

HISTORICAL BACKGROUND

The Italian physician and pathologist Guido Banti first described the relationship among splenic enlargement, anemia, and cirrhosis of the liver. The first splenectomy done for hypersplenism was done in Florence in 1903 on his advice. The constellation of symptoms later became known as Banti's syndrome.[168]

Earlier, Nikolai Eck, a German anatomist, had produced a connection between the portal vein and the inferior vena cava in a dog. Later studies described the association between the direct communication of portal and systemic venous blood and the onset of encephalopathy associated with hyperammonemia.[71,125]

The first applications of portosystemic shunting in patients were reported in the 1950s and 1960s.[30,31,106,168] More selective shunting procedures were devised when it was discovered that diversion of mesenteric blood flow into the systemic circulation could precipitate severe encephalopathy.[77,127,228,229] Nonshunt procedures aimed at interrupting the blood flow to gastric and esophageal varices were also described.[206]

Finally, with the advent of liver transplantation, portal hypertension caused by advanced and incurable liver disease was treated by replacement of the diseased organ, rather than palliative procedures that produced significant morbidity and improved symptoms for only a short time.[26,78,137,202]

EMBRYOLOGY AND ANATOMY

The portal vein develops through a complex system involving the formation and involution of primitive vessels, followed by circulatory changes at birth that affect the flow of blood in the mature portal circulation.

The left and right omphalomesenteric veins drain the developing gut as it is formed from the yolk sac during the fourth to sixth weeks of embryonic life. At the same time, the umbilical veins transport blood from the placenta to the embryo. Blood from both the umbilical and the omphalomesenteric veins drain through the nascent hepatic sinusoids in the developing liver and into the hepatic veins back to the developing heart. Some of the blood from the umbilical veins bypasses the liver and drains into the sinus venosus through the ductus venosus. Although the omphalomesenteric veins communicate by a series of intermediary vessels early in embryonic life, the right one involutes and disappears by the sixth week of gestation. The left one develops into the permanent portal vein, which drains the mesenteric venous bed through the superior mesenteric vein and its branches. The right umbilical vein also involutes, and the left remains patent until shortly after birth, when it thromboses and becomes the ligamentum teres.

The portal vein is formed by the confluence of the splenic and superior mesenteric veins posterior to the head of the pancreas. The coronary vein draining the gastric venous bed inserts into the portal vein at or just distal to the splenomesenteric confluence, and the inferior mesenteric vein drains into the splenic vein anywhere along its length, also behind the pancreas.

Despite the relative variability in the anatomy of the liver's arterial supply, the portal vein anatomy varies little. The principal extrahepatic vein divides into a left and a right branch. The left branch supplies the left lobe as it courses under the surface of segment IV of the liver, turns anteriorly in the recessus of Rex between segments II, III, and IV, and ends by dividing into the branches that supply those segments. The right branch divides into the posterior and anterior sectoral branches at or just before the liver plate at the capsule.

It is easy to imagine how the complex interaction that leads to a single portal vein from the original pair of omphalomesenteric veins in the embryo, interconnected by a series of crossing branches, can go wrong. A cavernous venous malformation may be the result of a disordered sequence of biologic steps. Thrombus in the postnatal umbilical vein may also propagate into the hepatic portal vein and occlude flow in the extrahepatic portion of the vein. Both processes may lead to the syndrome of extra- or prehepatic portal hypertension.

DEFINITION

Portal hypertension occurs whenever the free flow of blood from the mesenteric vascular bed, which includes the large and small bowel, stomach, spleen, and pancreas, is impaired. The causes of portal hypertension are most commonly obstructive in nature.[210] That is, there is an impediment to the forward flow of blood from the omphalomesenteric vascular bed through the liver and toward the heart. However, portal hypertension can also be caused by an increase in the volume of blood going to the liver or by a direct communication between the arterial and venous supplies to the liver that exposes the venous bed to abnormally high pressures.

Portal hypertension may be defined as pressure in the portal venous bed that exceeds 5 to 8 cm H_2O, or a pressure gradient of more than 5 cm H_2O between the hepatic veins and the portal circulation. When the pressure in the portal circulation exceeds those values, a series of physiologic changes leads to the symptoms common to all forms of portal hypertension, regardless of the cause.

COLLATERAL CIRCULATION

As a consequence of increased pressure in the portal vein, blood that normally goes to the liver from the superior mesenteric vein and its tributaries must find alternative routes back to the heart. The three most permissive routes for the formation of collaterals between the portal and systemic venous networks are in the rectum, the periumbilical area, and the gastroesophageal area. In the rectum, the rich network between the hemorrhoidal plexus of the superior hemorrhoidal vein and the branches of the inferior and middle hemorrhoidal vein is one possible route. In the course of the ligamentum teres of the liver and the middle umbilical ligament, small veins (paraumbilical) can establish an anastomosis between the veins of the anterior abdominal wall and the portal, hypogastric, and iliac veins. Last, the gastric veins communicate with the esophageal veins through submucosal plexuses that empty in a direction away from the liver into the hemiazygos venous system.

Other frequent locations of spontaneous shunts as a consequence of portal hypertension are between the veins of the colon and duodenum and the left renal vein; the accessory portal system of Sappey, branches of which pass in the round and falciform ligaments (particularly the latter) to unite with the epigastric and internal mammary veins and through the diaphragmatic veins to unite with the azygos vein; a single large paraumbilical vein that passes from the hilum of the liver by the round ligament to the umbilicus, producing a bunch of prominent varicose veins known as the caput medusa; the veins of Retzius, which connect the intestinal veins with the inferior vena cava and its retroperitoneal branches; the inferior mesenteric veins and the hemorrhoidal veins that open into the hypogastrics; and, rarely, the patent ductus venosus, affording a direct connection between the portal vein and the inferior vena cava.

CAUSES: A SPECTRUM OF DISORDERS

Portal hypertension can be divided into two categories: (1) portal hypertension from hepatocellular injury and liver fibrosis, and (2) portal hypertension from primary vascular causes (Table 106-1).

Hepatocellular Injury

Table 106-2 illustrates some of the common liver disorders in children that can lead to portal hypertension. Hepatocellular injury from a variety of toxins leads to cell death, initiation and progression of fibrosis, and ultimately cirrhosis. Progressive injury to hepatic tissue and replacement of normal liver with fibrous tissue lead to increased resistance to blood flow through the liver. The process of deposition of collagen in response to hepatocyte injury appears to be a complex process mediated through the transcription of proinflammatory cytokines such as osteopontin and through stellate cells.[140] The stellate cell, a normal constituent of hepatic sinusoids, is the primary source of excess extracellular matrix proteins in liver fibrosis.[44,75] It can change its phenotype from one that is fairly quiescent during normal liver homeostasis to one that undergoes myofibroblastic differentiation

TABLE 106-1 Classification of Portal Hypertension

Type	Description
Hepatocellular	Intrinsic liver disease with increased liver fibrosis (see Table 106-2)
Vascular	
Prehepatic	Extrahepatic portal vein thrombosis
	Cavernous transformation of portal vein
	Extrinsic compression of portal vein
Posthepatic	Budd-Chiari syndrome
	Intrinsic web
	Stenosis of hepatic vein orifice
High flow (hyperkinetic)	Arteriovenous communication—intra- or extrahepatic
	Congenital
	Acquired

TABLE 106-2 Hepatocellular Diseases Leading to Portal Hypertension

Biliary atresia
Postinfectious cirrhosis
Congenital hepatic fibrosis
Congenital disorders of bile acid metabolism
Sclerosing cholangitis
Autoimmune hepatitis
Drug toxicity
Metabolic diseases (e.g., alpha$_1$-antitrypsin deficiency)

or activation during episodes of hepatocyte injury. Dysregulation in the activity and number of stellate cells through faulty apoptosis or perpetuation of the insult that led to hepatocyte injury leads to ongoing deposition of proteins in the extracellular compartment of the liver. Ultimately, excess deposition of collagen in sinusoids results in portal hypertension.

Vascular Causes

Prehepatic Portal Hypertension

Prehepatic portal hypertension is caused by obstruction at the level of the extrahepatic portal vein. Extrahepatic portal vein thrombosis has been recognized and treated in both adults and children; it may be a congenital lesion or acquired at a later time. Even though the symptoms may be dramatic, patients tolerate the bleeding from varices fairly well because of the relatively intact hepatic function.[11,84] Occlusion of the main trunk of the portal vein may lead to recanalization of the vein and its transformation into a series of smaller collateral veins that assume the appearance of a venous cavernoma on ultrasonography (Fig. 106-1). In most instances the intrahepatic architecture of the portal vein is preserved. Thrombosis of the portal vein is associated with omphalitis, instrumentation and cannulation of the umbilical vein at birth, sepsis and dehydration in infancy, and mass lesions that exert extrinsic compression on the vein. These lesions may be inflammatory or malignant; examples include reactive enlargement of the lymph nodes in the hilum of the liver from histoplasmosis or compression from non-Hodgkin's lymphoma involving the hilum of the liver.

Unlike children with preexisting liver disease, children with extrahepatic portal vein thrombosis are usually completely well before the sudden onset of symptoms. In my experience, more than 50% of children present with unheralded hematemesis or hematochezia from gastroesophageal varices. Others are diagnosed with splenomegaly of unknown cause and may be referred to an oncologist for suspected hematologic malignancy.

Hypersplenism is often remarkable. Platelet counts of less than 50,000 and leukocyte counts of less than 1000 are not uncommon. Some children require hematopoietic growth factors to decrease the likelihood of spontaneous bleeding from thrombocytopenia or bacterial infections from dangerously low neutropenia.[160]

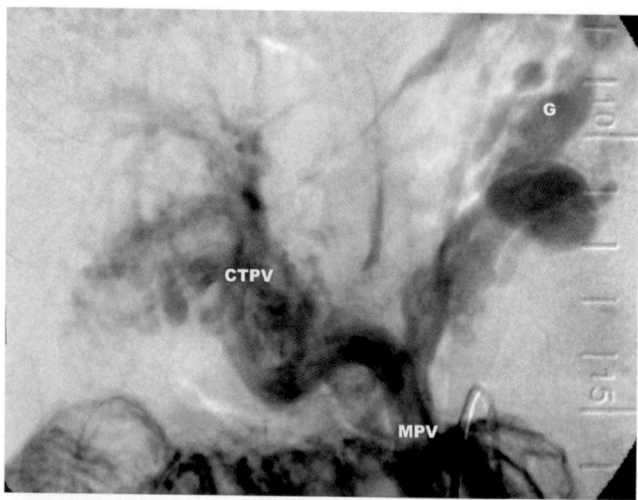

Figure 106-1 Digital angiogram in a child with extrahepatic portal vein obstruction and bleeding esophageal varices. This is the venous phase of a superior mesenteric arterial injection. Contrast outlines the proximal main portal vein (MPV); the cavernous transformation of the portal vein (CTPV), with absence of normal intrahepatic portal vein anatomy; and the large coronary vein (G) that shunts blood away from the liver and to the gastroesophageal junction and esophageal varices.

In the past, treatment was guided by two principles: children tolerated bleeding well, and surgical treatment was difficult and often unsuccessful. Therefore, the lives of these children were often characterized by frequent hospital admissions, numerous blood transfusions, and repeated endoscopic procedures for the sclerosis or banding of esophageal varices. It was not until the advent of more reliable and effective surgical options that more expeditious operative treatment became common in children. Surgical options include selective and nonselective portosystemic shunts to decompress the mesenteric circulation. Selective shunts, such as the Warren, are favored in children with hemorrhagic complications of portal hypertension because of the potential for postshunt encephalopathy when nonselective shunts are used. One of the first large surgical series reported excellent results and no deaths in more than 50 children with extrahepatic portal vein thrombosis.[25] Others reported equally good results as the surgical expertise in treating small children with liver disease grew and as experience doing vascular anastomoses in small vessels increased with the advent of pediatric liver transplantation.[69,137,159,194,195] More recently, a procedure to divert mesenteric blood back into the liver was described in children with portal vein thrombosis after transplantation; it has also been used successfully in children with idiopathic portal vein thrombosis.[19,59,61,62]

Posthepatic Portal Hypertension

Posthepatic portal hypertension is caused by occlusion of large or small veins draining blood from the liver into the inferior vena cava. Obstruction at this level leads to passive congestion of the liver and necrosis of the hepatocytes in

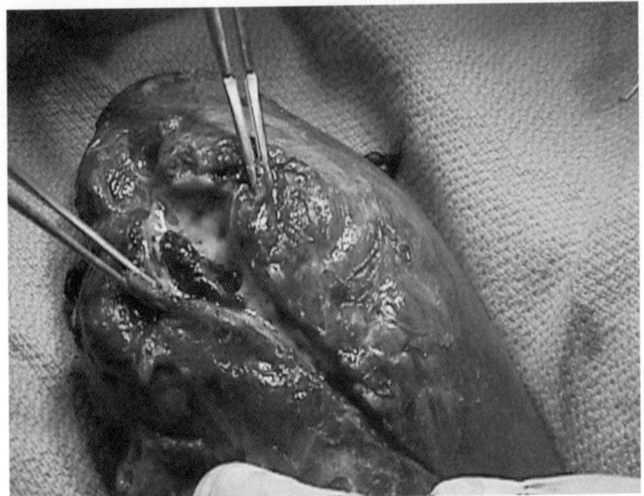

Figure 106-2 Acute hepatic venous obstruction after split liver transplantation, caused by a blood clot in the left hepatic vein of a segment II-III transplant. The child was retransplanted.

the central areas of the hepatic lobule. Acute venous obstruction may lead to massive hepatic necrosis and cell death unless it is relieved in an urgent fashion. The Budd-Chiari syndrome, sometimes referred to as Chiari's disease, was first described in 1845.[40,50] It is uncommon in children.[9] Outflow occlusion is caused by congenital venous webs in the hepatic veins,[219] hydatid disease,[110] myeloproliferative diseases,[17,47] hypercoagulable states,[22,49,102,107,111,153,174] and increased estrogen levels, most commonly from oral contraceptives.[118,124,133] It can also occur after liver transplantation (Fig. 106-2).

Microvascular nonthrombotic occlusion of hepatic venules is termed veno-occlusive disease, and it is being seen with increasing frequency in patients following bone marrow transplantation.[126,170,226,230] Cytoreductive regimens involving busulfan and cyclophosphamide are thought to induce obliterative phlebitis in the small veins of the liver, and damage to the endothelial cells is induced through the depletion of endogenous glutathione S transferase stores in the cells.[199] Other causes of veno-occlusive disease have been described, such as ingestion of herbal teas containing pyrrolizidine alkaloids.[117,156,197] Other diverse agents, including contrast media, estrogen, and thioguanine, have also been associated with the development of veno-occlusive disease.[4,15,16,38,148,155,169,205,220] This disease has a very high mortality rate, and treatment is limited to withdrawal of the offending agents, if possible, coupled with implementation of thrombolytic therapy and transjugular intrahepatic portosystemic shunting if feasible.[16,18,134]

High-Flow States

A congenital or acquired communication between an artery and vein in the mesenteric circulation is a rare but known cause of portal hypertension. Portal hypertension from such abnormal communications between arteries and veins in the portal circulation is termed hyperkinetic,[94] because of the hyperdynamic circulation responsible for the increased portal pressure. Patients have well-preserved liver function and present with bleeding from gastrointestinal (GI) varices, ascites, or splenomegaly. The site of the communication between the artery and vein is quite varied. The splenic and gastric arteries have been reported as sites of these fistulas, as well as the more common site of the hepatic artery within the parenchyma of the liver. Arteriovenous fistulas causing portal hypertension have been reported in all age groups.[6,23,73,93] Most often they are congenital, but some are thought to be acquired through a pathologic process or iatrogenically.[87,99,109,113,157,167,204,233,237] Patients may present with varied symptoms that depend on the site of the arteriovenous communication. Bleeding from varices may be severe, and because of the exposure to arterial pressures, the usual therapeutic maneuvers may be inadequate to control it.[68]

Treatment of high-output fistulas requires interruption of the abnormal communication between the artery and vein. Although surgery, including hemihepatectomy[23] and surgical ligation of extrahepatic fistulas,[20,68] has been described as a means of removing the fistula, access by radiologic means and the use of selective transcatheter embolization to interrupt flow is the treatment of choice for this condition.[6,46]

CLINICAL PRESENTATION

Gastrointestinal Hemorrhage

Bleeding from the GI tract is one of the most common, dramatic, and dangerous signs of portal hypertension. Bleeding most commonly occurs from varices in the distal esophagus and gastric cardia. Although the incidence of bleeding in adults with portal hypertension from nonvariceal sites may be as high as 25%,[39] there is no evidence that the same holds true in children. In one study of children presenting with upper GI bleeding, the vast majority of unselected patients had bleeding from varices secondary to portal hypertension, with no other source.[232] The importance of portal hypertension as a cause of upper GI bleeding in children may vary in different parts of the world. Peptic ulcer disease is still a frequent finding at endoscopy in children in the Western Hemisphere.[203] In children with portal hypertension of any cause, upper GI bleeding is almost universally caused by variceal hemorrhage, although portal hypertensive gastropathy may cause less acute bleeding.[114] Therefore, variceal hemorrhage is usually the only source of bleeding in children with portal hypertension, and it is the most common cause of bleeding from the upper GI tract in nonhospitalized children older than 2 years.

Variceal hemorrhage may take the form of hematemesis, hematochezia, melena, or chronic anemia. Bleeding most commonly originates from the lower esophagus and the cardia of the stomach. Thin-walled varices that contain blood under raised venous pressure are eroded from gastric acid or medications such as aspirin or nonsteroidal anti-inflammatory drugs, and blood fills the stomach. In the absence of advanced liver disease, the blood clots and gathers in the stomach, producing gastric distention and eventually hematemesis. The bleeding may be sudden and dramatic and is usually not accompanied by abdominal pain. A previously well child can vomit large quantities of altered or fresh blood. Although this can be extremely frightening to both the child and the parents, the bleeding usually stops spontaneously. Varices may be present in the lower GI tract as well. Rectal bleeding is less common and occurs from rectal and sigmoid varices. Melena or the passage of gross blood through the rectum or accompanying a bowel movement may occur in the absence of hematemesis.

Although most patients with portal hypertension have varices, not all varices bleed. Predicting the risk of bleeding from varices is based on Laplace's law, which states that the transmural tension in the wall of a vessel is directly related to the pressure inside the vessel and inversely related to the thickness of the vessel.[161] Unfortunately, intravariceal pressure cannot be easily measured; therefore, the risk of bleeding in adults has been linked to the size of the varix, the severity of liver disease, and the appearance of red wale markings on the vessel wall, which may indicate epithelial thickness.[196]

Predicting which patient is likely to bleed from varices is important in determining treatment options, particularly for those who may be candidates for prophylactic therapy of any kind. It is estimated that 30% to 50% of patients bleed from varices once they are diagnosed,[32] and that 10% to 50% of patients with liver disease die every year after the first hemorrhage.[234] Therefore, aggressive therapy is indicated after the first bleed in patients who have any kind of liver disease. This varies from portosystemic shunting in Child's class A patients to liver transplantation in those with more advanced disease. There may be a role for noninvasive or even invasive surgical therapy in those who are at high risk for bleeding but have not yet bled, provided the morbidity and mortality associated with bleeding can be reduced with an acceptably low risk of complications.

In children with portal hypertension from extrahepatic portal vein thrombosis, mortality from bleeding is much less than in those with liver disease, and bleeding is generally well tolerated. However, the same principles apply: early intervention and implementation of a long-term plan to reduce hospital admissions and invasive procedures. Because these children have a vascular problem rather than hepatic disease, they are more amenable to surgical intervention and generally obtain excellent long-term results.

Hypersplenism

Silent splenomegaly without any other history suggestive of portal hypertension is often the first sign of a serious underlying disorder (Fig. 106-3). Splenomegaly may be detected in infancy or early childhood and can easily be misinterpreted as a sign of hematologic malignancy, particularly in children with extrahepatic portal vein thrombosis and no other stigmata of liver disease. With the advent of Doppler ultrasound examinations of the abdomen, portal vein thrombosis is more readily diagnosed and can be appropriately monitored. In addition to splenic enlargement, patients may present with severe thrombocytopenia and leukopenia from splenic sequestration of platelets and white blood cells. Children are often prevented from engaging in sporting activities for fear that even slight trauma to the abdomen may result in splenic rupture and catastrophic intra-abdominal bleeding, exacerbated by raised venous pressure and low platelet counts.

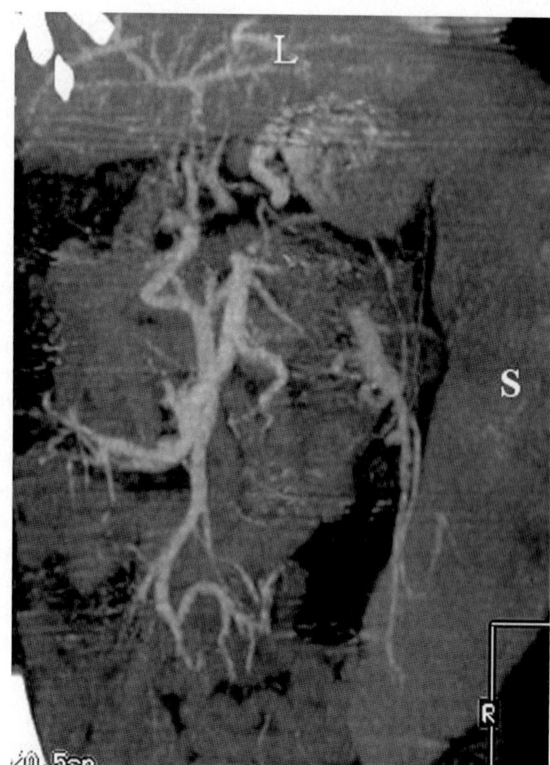

Figure 106–3 This 3-year-old girl presented with massive splenomegaly, severe thrombocytopenia, and leukopenia. The computed tomography angiogram demonstrates a spleen (S) that extends into the pelvis and dwarfs the liver (L) in size. The angiogram clearly demonstrates extrahepatic portal vein thrombosis and a patent intrahepatic portal venous tree.

Encephalopathy

Encephalopathy is extremely unusual in the absence of signs of advanced liver disease, such as jaundice and low levels of liver-dependent coagulation factors or low albumin levels. Learning disabilities and behavioral abnormalities are manifestations of encephalopathy in children, in contrast to the traditional signs of disorientation, memory loss, and drowsiness commonly seen in adults. Children may also have accompanying hyperammonemia.[3]

Bleeding from Nongut Sites

Severe thrombocytopenia can lead to hematuria, menorrhagia in adolescent girls, epistaxis, and hematochezia. In severe cases, spontaneous intracranial bleeding can also occur, with serious neurologic consequences.

Liver-dependent coagulation factor deficiencies also lead to bleeding, typically from the genitourinary tract or from the nose. In cases of advanced liver disease, hemorrhagic complications in the lungs may cause severe respiratory compromise

Ascites

Children with ascites may have advanced liver disease with synthetic failure. Ascites may be accompanied by a low serum albumin level and decreased plasma oncotic pressure. Dilated lymphatics in the abdomen from increased hydrostatic pressure in all portal tributaries can lead to transudation of fluid across capillary membranes and accumulation of fluid in the abdominal cavity. Additional mechanisms include increased nitric oxide production in capillaries, causing vasodilatation, and an increase in renal tubular absorption of sodium in patients with decompensated cirrhosis.[120,146,200] Ascites can also occur in the setting of Budd-Chiari syndrome and outflow obstruction. Ascites is an alarming symptom that may herald the onset of liver decompensation on a wider scale.

Pulmonary Disorders

Pulmonary hypertension can occur in children with both cirrhotic and noncirrhotic forms of portal hypertension.[123,152] Pulmonary hypertension may be secondary to an increase in vasoactive substances that exert a vasoconstrictive or direct toxic effect on pulmonary vessels.[214] An increase in blood levels of prostaglandin $F_{2\alpha}$, thromboxane, and angiotensin I in patients with portal and pulmonary hypertension suggests that these agents play a role in mediating pulmonary hypertension by reaching the pulmonary circulation in blood shunted around the liver. In experimental studies, portal hypertension induced by portal vein ligation was associated with increased amounts of inducible nitric oxide synthetase and heme oxygenase-1 messenger RNA and protein in the lungs, compared with animals in the control group.[186] This suggests that the pulmonary pathology seen with portal hypertension is associated with the production of nitric oxide and carbon monoxide in the lung.

Patients with both pulmonary and portal hypertension may develop pulmonary symptoms before there is any evidence of bleeding from portal hypertension. Symptoms may include exertional dyspnea or chest pain, or there may be no symptoms other than unheralded syncope or sudden death.[189,214] Treatment of portal hypertension may be problematic in children with advanced pulmonary hypertension, and medical treatment for both conditions may be limited in scope and duration.[64,173]

The hepatopulmonary syndrome includes persistent hypoxemia from arteriovenous shunting in the lungs. Cirrhosis may be required, in addition to portal hypertension, for hepatopulmonary syndrome to become clinically apparent. It is associated with increased production of endothelin-1 by the liver, increased levels of circulating endothelin-1, and increased production of endothelial nitric oxide in the lungs.[88,131]

Whereas pulmonary hypertension from prehepatic portal hypertension may be reversed after eliminating portosystemic shunting,[76] hepatopulmonary syndrome may require liver transplantation.[88] Both conditions may be aggravated by surgically creating a portosystemic shunt.[88,189]

DIAGNOSIS

The diagnosis of the underlying cause of portal hypertension depends on the synthesis of the clinical information gathered from the parents and the child and the results of imaging tests and laboratory investigations.

Clinical Information

Hepatomegaly

An enlarged liver is usually a sign of hepatocellular disease, although patients with cirrhosis may present with impalpable shrunken livers. If the liver is hard or nodular to palpation, this is further evidence that the cause of the portal hypertension is a diseased liver. Children with congenital hepatic fibrosis often present with very enlarged livers that may extend as far as the iliac crest on palpation. Children with venous outflow obstruction may also present with easily palpable liver enlargement.

Splenomegaly

Enlargement of the spleen is a common finding in children with portal hypertension and is often the first abnormality found on a routine physical examination before the onset of bleeding. Splenomegaly occurs in all forms of portal hypertension and is not helpful in diagnosing the cause.

Jaundice

Jaundice and portal hypertension usually do not occur together unless there is advanced liver disease. Children with extrahepatic portal vein obstruction may have mild elevation of the total bilirubin level, but jaundice is not a clinical feature. If jaundice is a prominent symptom in a child with portal hypertension, it may indicate that liver failure is imminent.

Encephalopathy

Clinically evident encephalopathy is a sign of advanced liver disease. Signs of encephalopathy may be hard to discern or quantify in young children. Although encephalopathy may be exacerbated by acute bleeding because of the increased protein load in the gut, it usually signifies advanced hepatocellular disease that may require the patient to be evaluated for liver transplantation.

Laboratory Investigations

A full set of laboratory tests is usually required to arrive at a correct determination of the cause of portal hypertension. In the acute setting, a complete blood count and electrolyte levels are necessary to treat a patient who is bleeding.

Children with long-standing portal hypertension may have nothing more than thrombocytopenia and leukopenia, particularly those with extrahepatic portal vein thrombosis. An increase in the direct bilirubin fraction, a low albumin level, and a prolonged prothrombin time all indicate significant hepatocellular disease and possible cirrhosis as the underlying cause of the portal hypertension. A raised serum ammonia level indicates significant portosystemic shunting and may occur with all forms of portal hypertension.

Children with extrahepatic portal vein thrombosis may have laboratory evidence of disordered synthesis of liver-dependent coagulation factors in both the procoagulant and plasminolytic pathways, but this is generally not evident clinically without detailed testing.[132]

Endoscopy

After stabilization in the intensive care unit, upper GI endoscopy provides direct confirmation of the bleeding source. Varices, if present, will be most prominent in the distal third of the esophagus and in the cardia of the stomach. Endoscopy should be done only by those who are well trained in the procedure and familiar with the equipment. Endoscopy provides an opportunity to intervene therapeutically as well as to rule out other sources of bleeding, such as peptic ulcers, Mallory-Weiss tears of the esophagus, or hemorrhagic gastritis.

If endoscopy is done before the onset of bleeding because of suspected portal hypertension, the appearance of the varices provides valuable clues about the likelihood of future bleeding.[92] Variceal diameter greater than 5 mm, the appearance of red wale markings, and more advanced liver disease based on Child-Pugh class indicate a greater chance for future bleeding and may justify the institution of prophylactic treatment.

Imaging

The first imaging study in any child who presents with hematemesis should be abdominal ultrasonography.[116] The status of the portal vein is one of the most important considerations in arriving at a diagnosis. Cavernous transformation of the portal vein and portal vein thrombosis are best diagnosed by ultrasonography with Doppler interrogation of the vessels of the liver. A complete evaluation of the intra-abdominal vasculature, including the hepatic veins, the patency of the splenic and superior mesenteric veins, and the inferior vena cava, is possible. In addition, information about the size of the spleen can be obtained to confirm the clinical examination. Liver parenchymal abnormalities such as nodularity, inhomogeneity, or the presence of cysts can be seen. The appearance of the kidneys can yield useful diagnostic clues, because children with congenital hepatic fibrosis may also have autosomal dominant polycystic kidney disease and other renal abnormalities.[149,217]

Computed tomography (CT) and magnetic resonance (MR) angiography are excellent diagnostic tools and have supplanted conventional digital angiography for most purposes. Both modalities provide excellent information about all the intra-abdominal vessels and detailed information about the liver anatomy, including the bile ducts. CT-angiography has several advantages; it can be done more quickly and is less prone to image degradation from motion artifact than is MR angiography, unless the MR study is done under general anesthesia with ventilatory arrest for the duration of the study.

Conventional angiography is an invasive modality that has few indications as a diagnostic tool in children with portal hypertension. The exceptions are rare cases of unusual vascular malformations, such as arteriovenous communications in the abdomen or liver, that may best be delineated by angiography. Also, angiographic visualization is essential as a prelude to angiographic embolization or stenting of a vascular abnormality.

Splenoportography is a technique that was written about extensively in the past but is almost never used for diagnostic purposes today.[150,151]

Transjugular hepatic venography is a useful test to measure pressures in the hepatic veins, and it provides definitive imaging of the hepatic veins and their junction with the vena cava.[231] This modality can also be used therapeutically, for the placement of a transjugular intrahepatic portosystemic shunt (TIPS) or the dilatation of congenital or acquired strictures causing venous outflow obstruction.

Liver Biopsy

Almost all children who present with portal hypertension undergo a liver biopsy. This can be done percutaneously in most cases. In children with mild coagulopathies that can be corrected with vitamin K, fresh frozen plasma, and platelets, the procedure can be performed safely in an intensive care setting, where any bleeding from the biopsy site can be treated promptly. Children with more profound coagulopathies, as manifested by a prothrombin time in excess of 20 seconds, should have a transjugular biopsy in the interventional radiology suite or an open biopsy in the operating room. In general, the limiting factor in the radiologist's ability to do a transjugular biopsy is the patient's size. The difficulty and technical limitations are greatest in infants and babies. The liver biopsy results range from subtle diagnostic abnormalities in cases of extrahepatic portal vein thrombosis to advanced fibrosis and cirrhosis in children with chronic liver disease.

TREATMENT

The treatment of a child with portal hypertension is predicated first on the underlying pathophysiology of the disease and then on the severity of the symptoms.

Children with liver disease and portal hypertension do not tolerate bleeding as well as those with essentially normal livers whose portal hypertension is caused by primary vascular malformations. Acute hemorrhage adversely affects liver function, which may already be abnormal. The prognosis of a child with liver disease and portal hypertension depends entirely on the hepatic reserve. Children with relatively stable cirrhosis and preserved synthetic function require a completely different therapeutic approach from those with hypoalbuminemia, growth failure, and coagulopathy. The Child-Pugh[51] score was devised in an attempt to categorize patients according to degree of hepatic reserve and thus arrive at a prognosis for survival if left untreated or with surgery.[10,135,192,193] More recently, a pediatric-specific score (pediatric end-stage liver disease [PELD]) has been developed to stratify children on liver transplant waiting lists in a way that accurately reflects the severity of the underlying liver disease.[57,144] Children with age-appropriate growth, normal coagulation, and no jaundice have low PELD scores; their treatment for the complications of portal hypertension is very different from that of children with high scores, who would be better served by liver transplantation.

In children with Child-Pugh scores of 5 or 6 or PELD scores lower than 10 who have a predicted 1-year survival of more than 90%, it is justified to consider complex surgical therapy to alleviate the symptoms of portal hypertension. The expectation is that these children will survive the surgery and have a good long-term prognosis without the need for liver transplantation in the short term. For children with bleeding from varices in addition to ascites or advanced coagulopathy and with high PELD scores, aggressive medical therapy of portal hypertension is indicated as they await transplantation. Surgery is not indicated in children with advanced hepatic disease because it would be poorly tolerated and not address the underlying issue of poor hepatic reserve.

Pediatricians and pediatric gastroenterologists closely follow all patients with portal hypertension and liver disease. When portal hypertension becomes symptomatic, it is rarely a surprise, and the parents are usually well versed in the medical issues. Under ideal circumstances, surgery can be considered for the control of symptoms when bleeding is imminent or likely to recur. Selective shunting is generally the procedure of choice, as discussed later.

In contrast, patients with noncirrhotic forms of portal hypertension can develop symptoms quite unexpectedly and as the first manifestation of a serious underlying condition.

Medical Management of Bleeding Varices

Patients admitted with acute variceal hemorrhage require intense resuscitation with blood and crystalloids, replacement of coagulation factor deficiencies with fresh frozen plasma, and control of the bleeding. Bleeding from varices may be exacerbated by disseminated intravascular coagulation, fibrinolysis, and a decrease in circulating platelet counts. The availability of exogenous recombinant factor VII to treat those with compromised liver synthetic function has enhanced the care of these patients. Factor VII replacement decreases the amount of sodium and fluid necessary to correct the liver-dependent factor deficiencies, although its use is limited to some extent by its cost.[7,41] Patient care is best delivered in the intensive care unit where vital signs can be monitored, including central venous and arterial pressures, hourly urine output, and oxygen saturation. Monitoring of mental status is also essential in those with cirrhosis, because bleeding into the GI tract may exacerbate or unmask encephalopathy.

Cessation of bleeding is the most important therapeutic goal, along with the replacement of extracellular fluid and blood. In the past, Sengstaken-Blakemore tube tamponade of varices was the most effective method of short-term control of blood loss.[70] Pharmacologic therapy has proved to be just as effective in adults,[14,103] rendering the balloon method almost obsolete. Pharmacologic control of variceal bleeding has improved greatly with the use of intravenous octreotide, the octapeptide analogue of somatostatin. It has a longer half-life than somatostatin and fewer side effects. Octreotide has largely replaced vasopressin in the management of acute variceal bleeding because of the severe vascular side effects of the latter drug.

Octreotide and other somatostatin analogues, such as vapreotide, reduce hepatic blood flow and wedged hepatic vein pressure and constrict splanchnic arterioles by a direct effect on arteriolar smooth muscle. Somatostatin analogues are very effective in reducing and temporarily stopping the bleeding from portal hypertension and can be used in the initial 24 to 72 hours while awaiting direct endoscopic management of varices.[1,2,42,82,172] Octreotide is started as a continuous infusion at 1.0 to 2.0 μg/kg per hour, up to a maximum of 100 μg/hour, and continued for as long as symptoms of bleeding persist.

The long-term medical management of children with portal hypertension includes the use of nonselective beta blockers such as propranolol or nadolol, either alone or in combination with nitrate vasodilators such as isosorbide-5-mononitrate. Some authors, however, have shown that local control of varices with banding is equivalent to long-term pharmacologic management. In a majority of patients, surveillance endoscopy and intermittent banding may be sufficient,[32] with equivalent survival and rebleeding rates in endoscopically managed and pharmacologically managed groups. The role of beta blockers in reducing splanchnic blood flow and wedge hepatic vein pressure is well documented; their use may decrease the incidence of recurrent bleeding by as much as 50% and lessen the need for liver transplantation in patients with liver disease.[224,225] Assessment of wedge hepatic vein pressure reduction has been promoted as the best way to determine the impact of medications on portal pressure and to guide and refine pharmacologic management,[2,212] but these studies are all adult based and may represent a less practical approach in children.

Prophylactic Treatment of Varices

Intervention of any kind before the onset of bleeding is controversial. However, the benefit to the patient of preventing a first bleed may be considerable and may justify early prophylactic management. Studies in both adults and children have demonstrated that prophylactic treatment of varices by pharmacologic means[86,130] and with endoscopic ligation[48] reduces the frequency of bleeding. Surgery for the prevention of an initial bleed is more controversial if there is no other primary goal, such as the treatment of severe hypersplenism.

Endoscopic Sclerosis or Banding of Varices

Surgeons were involved in the earliest attempts to control variceal bleeding by injecting sclerosing solutions into the tissue around a varix or directly into a varix to obliterate the vessel lumen.[104,105,211] This method has proved to be effective and safe in children in the acute phase of bleeding.[29,97,138,158,180,181] Sclerosing solutions include sodium morrhuate, ethanolamine, sodium tetradecyl sulfate, and polidocanol. Long-term follow-up in children after sclerotherapy for the control of initial bleeding has demonstrated success in almost 90% of patients. Initial sclerotherapy should be followed by repeat endoscopy at regular intervals until all the varices are obliterated or too small to inject and then at longer (yearly) intervals for at least 4 years to check for reappearance of varices.[236] Generally, two to three injections at 1 mL per injection are required for each varix, up to a maximum of 10 to 15 mL per session. The endoscopist should proceed circumferentially from the distal esophagus at the gastroesophageal junction to the more proximal esophagus.

Sclerotherapy is associated with a fairly high incidence of complications, both major and minor, in at least one third of patients. Acute complications include chest pain, esophageal ulceration, and mediastinitis; chronic ones include esophageal strictures from fibrosis after multiple injection sessions.

Esophageal banding has become an increasingly popular method of treating varices. In one prospective trial in children with portal hypertension from extrahepatic portal vein thrombosis, banding was found to be a more effective, more rapid, and safer method of reducing the chance of bleeding from varices.[235] The incidence of complications and of long-term rebleeding was lower with banding. Others reporting smaller series have shown equal efficacy and safety, including among children with portal hypertension from intrinsic liver disease.[108,166] New technology, such as the multiband ligator scope, has made it possible to apply bands to multiple varices; this method was first used in adults but has recently been extended to children.[145] This technique increases the speed and safety with which esophageal varices can be ligated in children as young as 3 months old; obliteration of varices was accomplished in almost 100% of children after only two sessions.

Esophageal banding in concert with pharmacologic control has become the procedure of choice in the early therapy of bleeding esophageal varices. Subsequent sessions are aimed at ligating residual varices or varices that arise after the larger ones are tied off. Ligation is effective in most children and is not associated with many of the adverse side effects of sclerotherapy.

Injection Therapy for Gastric Varices

With the advent of more effective means of controlling esophageal varices, bleeding from varices lower in the GI tract has become more problematic. Injection with *N*-butyl-2-cyanoacrylate has had modest success in adults with bleeding from gastric varices,[181] but results in children have not been reported. Gastric varices may coexist with esophageal varices in as many as 15% to 20% of patients, or they may be isolated.[182-184] Gastric varices may emerge after the obliteration of esophageal varices, or they may persist after esophageal varices have been ligated. Experience in adults suggests that in patients with gastric varices, cirrhosis, and advanced liver disease, bleeding can be controlled with minimal morbidity, but there is a high incidence of rebleeding at 1 year after treatment.[8] In adults, injection of gastric varices results in relatively poorer control of bleeding in patients with extrahepatic portal vein thrombosis (35%) than in those with liver disease (75%).[112] Given the fact that extrahepatic portal vein thrombosis is a more important cause of bleeding varices in children than in adults, injection therapy for gastric varices in pediatric patients is not justified, except in the setting of a formal study to determine its safety and efficacy compared with surgery or other medical therapies.

Transjugular Intrahepatic Portosystemic Shunts

The percutaneous insertion of vascular stents to create channels between the portal vein and hepatic veins within the parenchyma of the liver heralded a new way of treating patients with advanced liver disease and portal hypertension.[55] The main indication for TIPS is variceal hemorrhage recalcitrant to more conservative therapy with endoscopy or octreotide. It is usually reserved for patients with advanced liver disease and serves as a bridge to transplantation.[91,143] Other indications include refractory ascites, hepatic venous outflow obstruction in both transplant and nontransplant patients, and hepatorenal syndrome.

In children, the experience is limited. TIPS may act as a bridge to transplantation in children with portal hypertensive gastropathy or in those whose variceal bleeding is difficult to control by other means. The TIPS method has been used in children with cystic fibrosis (Fig. 106-4),[163] biliary atresia,[98] and congenital hepatic fibrosis[21] with apparent success, and in infants as young as 1 year.[45]

Its primary limitation is the high rate of shunt thrombosis. Vigilance is required to monitor shunt patency and to declot the shunt when it is thrombosed. The other limitation is the aggravation of preexisting encephalopathy in approximately 20% of patients and the hastening of liver failure in patients whose livers are already borderline; TIPS facilitates the shunting of blood without the benefit of hepatic clearance in these extremely debilitated patients.[201]

Hepatic encephalopathy is less common after TIPS in children than in adults, but the incidence of shunt occlusion is higher because of the smaller shunt diameter.

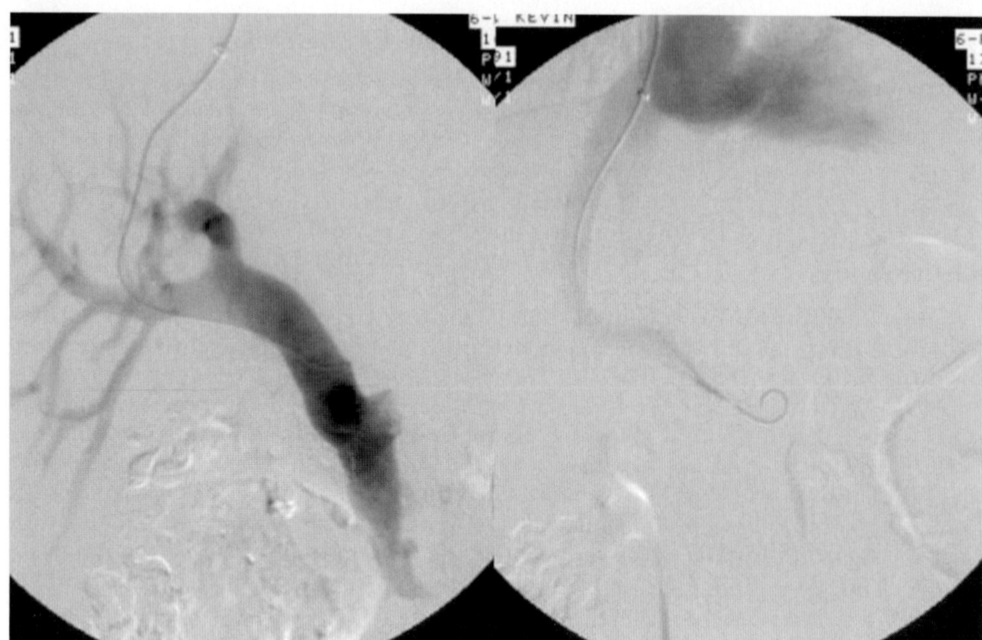

Figure 106–4 This boy with cystic fibrosis was bleeding from esophageal and gastric varices. To stabilize him while he awaited a liver transplant, a transjugular intrahepatic portosystemic shunt (TIPS) procedure was performed. A percutaneous catheter is inserted through the jugular vein into the right hepatic vein. The catheter is advanced into the right portal vein *(left image)*. The stent is then deployed so that the proximal end is in the main trunk of the portal vein and the distal end is in the distal hepatic vein.

Shunt Surgery

Early shunt surgery diverted all the mesenteric blood flow into the systemic circulation, as first described by Eck.[65] Later authors reported the application of portacaval shunting in the setting of severe bleeding from portal hypertension in adults with advanced liver disease,[27,28,118,119,141,162,165] as well as in children with prehepatic and intrahepatic causes of portal hypertension.[24,25,52-54]

Shunts can be described as nonselective or selective. Selective shunts preserve the majority of portal or mesenteric blood flow to the liver while shunting blood from high-pressure gastroesophageal varices into the low-pressure systemic venous circulation. In essence, selective shunts divide the portal circulation into two separate entities, although it is impossible to fully divide all communications. In contrast, nonselective shunts divert a large proportion of mesenteric blood flow away from the liver so that the entire GI tract, including the spleen and pancreas, is decompressed. Nonselective shunts can be further subdivided into total or partial portal diversions.

Nonselective Shunts

Total Diversion

The end-to-side portacaval shunt as first described by Eck[65] is the classic example of a total portal diversion. Portal blood is completely redirected into the inferior vena cava below the liver, and the hepatic end of the portal vein is oversewn.

The proximal splenorenal shunt is another example of a total diversion shunt. The splenic vein is divided close to the spleen, and the mesenteric end is sewn to the side of the left renal vein so that all the blood from the superior and inferior mesenteric veins is shunted into the systemic venous circulation through the left renal vein.[35,67,95,147,187,209] This procedure almost invariably includes splenectomy and sometimes a direct attempt to ligate the varices of the esophagus and stomach.

Wide-diameter mesocaval shunts also completely divert mesenteric blood away from the liver. This procedure can be done directly as a side-to-side anastomosis between the two veins or with the interposition of a short autologous vein graft or prosthetic graft.[63,80,175] Use of an interposition graft is the more common method. Exposure of both the superior mesenteric vein at the root of the bowel mesentery and the inferior vena cava below the duodenum is required.

Mesocaval shunting has been used in children in a wide variety of settings and diseases, with uniformly acceptable results.[12,24,85,142] Some prefer this method because it allows an anastomosis between two large-diameter vessels and because the length of the anastomosis can be increased to some extent to facilitate the creation of a large venous fistula, which is technically easier to perform than a splenorenal shunt. In addition, in contrast to the proximal splenorenal shunt, the spleen is preserved, which is thought to be important in preventing postsplenectomy sepsis.[92,213]

The side-to-side portacaval shunt allows blood from the intestine and spleen to flow easily into the vena cava. In addition, and unlike with the end-to-side portacaval shunt, the hepatic end of the portal vein is changed into an outflow tract. In cases of Budd-Chiari posthepatic portal hypertension, the liver is decompressed by this operation; this may result in long-term palliation of the disease, with arrest or delay in the progression of hepatic fibrosis and ultimate failure.[5,9,43,118] Other effective operations for Budd-Chiari syndrome are mesocaval and central splenorenal shunts, which allow portal blood in the liver to empty in a retrograde fashion through the patent portal vein.

Partial Diversion

Partially diverting shunts depend on a fixed, narrow communication between a vessel in the portal circulation and one in the systemic venous circulation.[177] The Sarfeh shunt is able to divert enough blood from the portal circulation to drop mesenteric pressure below 12 cm H_2O and thus decompress the varices and reduce the chance of bleeding while maintaining enough pressure in the portal bed to allow hepatopetal flow and hepatic blood flow preservation.[179] Although there may be less encephalopathy with the Sarfeh shunt because of sustained hepatic portal flow, it is associated with a higher incidence of thrombosis and recurrence of hemorrhage.[56]

The relationship between deprivation of portal blood to the liver and encephalopathy has long been noted following portacaval shunt surgery.[71,122] Sarfeh[179] was able to determine the diameter shunt that would preserve forward flow in the portal vein, decompress the portal circulation so that bleeding from varices decreased, and minimize the incidence of encephalopathy.

Selective Shunts

To diminish the encephalopathy that followed portacaval shunting, Warren et al.[228] described a shunt between the portal end of the splenic vein and the side of the renal vein (Fig. 106-5). The splenic confluence with the portal vein was ligated, and the coronary vein was also interrupted. In this manner, the gastroesophageal varices were decompressed across the short gastric vessels and the spleen into the renal vein. Long-term studies have shown that the disconnection between the lower-pressure splenic circulation and the higher-pressure hepatic one is not always maintained, and the connection may re-form over time. Hepatopetal flow may decrease and be redirected to the coronary circulation around the stomach; as a result, the hepatic flow decreases, just as in more central shunts.[90,185,198] In this case, there would be both angiographic and endoscopic evidence of gradual conversion of a selective shunt to a less selective shunt over time. A more complete pancreaticosplenic disconnection may avoid the reestablishment of communication between the splenic and hepatic circulations. Long-term mortality and rebleeding rates in adults are equivalent with selective and nonselective shunts,[83] but the rate of encephalopathy is reduced with selective shunts.[36,77]

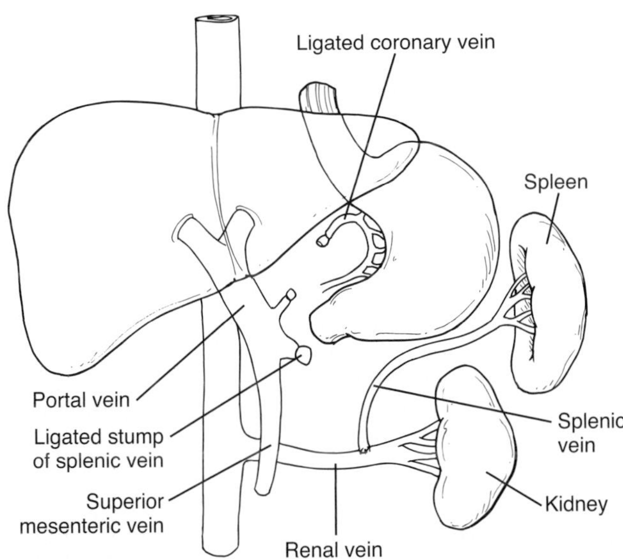

Figure 106-5 Distal splenorenal shunt. The lesser sac is entered, and the splenic vein is dissected off the inferior border of the pancreas, ligating and dividing small pancreatic branches. The left renal vein is then found and mobilized, preserving the gonadal and adrenal branches. The splenic vein is divided close to the confluence with the superior mesenteric vein and anastomosed end to side with the left renal vein. The vein should lie in a smooth curve to avoid kinking. The coronary vein and gastroepiploic veins are ligated and divided. Blood flows from the gastric and esophageal varices via the short gastric veins, across the spleen, and into the splenic vein. The spleen is also decompressed in this fashion while portal flow to the liver is preserved.

In children, the selective shunt as described by Warren[228] or with minor modifications has been used successfully for the treatment of bleeding varices,* as well as for the treatment of hypersplenism.[194] Long-term patency rates exceeding 90% have been reported in most series, with resolution of bleeding in all children whose shunts remain patent.

Distal splenorenal shunting is used primarily in children with extrahepatic portal vein thrombosis,[194] stable Child's class A or B cirrhosis,[34,137,171] or less common forms of intrahepatic portal hypertension, such as congenital hepatic fibrosis with well-preserved liver function but symptomatic variceal bleeding.

The preservation of neurocognitive function is particularly important in children; thus, all forms of nonselective shunting should be avoided. Encephalopathy in children may manifest as learning disorders or behavioral abnormalities that are not usually attributed to portosystemic shunting.[227] Although no study has reported careful neurocognitive testing in the follow-up of children after distal splenorenal shunting, no series has reported clinically evident encephalopathy in patients with stable cirrhosis or extrahepatic portal hypertension.

Hypersplenism may be particularly problematic in children and has led to splenectomy or splenic embolization in some children.[101,178,190,215,223] The distal splenorenal shunt has been beneficial in children with advanced hypersplenism. Spleen size regresses, and the platelet and leukocyte counts return toward normal. Following splenic decompression by shunting, hematologic indices may continue to improve for years after the procedure.

Splenectomy and splenic embolization were advocated in the past for hypersplenism. However, these procedures are not without complications and may, in the long run, exacerbate bleeding from gastroesophageal varices and leave the child prone to postsplenectomy sepsis.[89] In addition, splenectomy removes the possibility of later distal splenorenal shunting if the child continues to suffer from variceal bleeding. Pediatric surgeons should preserve the

*See references 25, 34, 66, 69, 90, 121, 137-139, 142, 194, 218, 222.

spleen whenever possible, leaving splenectomy as the last resort in children who have no other options.

Mesenteric-to-Left Portal Vein Bypass

The treatment of extrahepatic portal vein thrombosis has been evolving since the advent of mesenteric vein–to–left portal vein bypass in 1992 (Fig. 106-6). The operation was originally described as a way to revascularize liver transplant grafts after post-transplant portal vein thrombosis,[58,61] but the indications were later expanded to treat children with idiopathic portal vein thrombosis. Approximately 30 to 50 children have been reported in the literature from a small group of institutions worldwide.[13,19,59,60,62,76]

Essentially, the operation relieves portal hypertension by redirecting blood from the obstructed mesenteric system to the still patent intrahepatic portal vein. The prerequisites for a successful bypass operation are threefold: (1) no intrinsic liver disease, (2) a patent intrahepatic portal tree, and (3) a suitable vein in the mesenteric circulation to function as a suitable inflow tract for mesenteric blood.

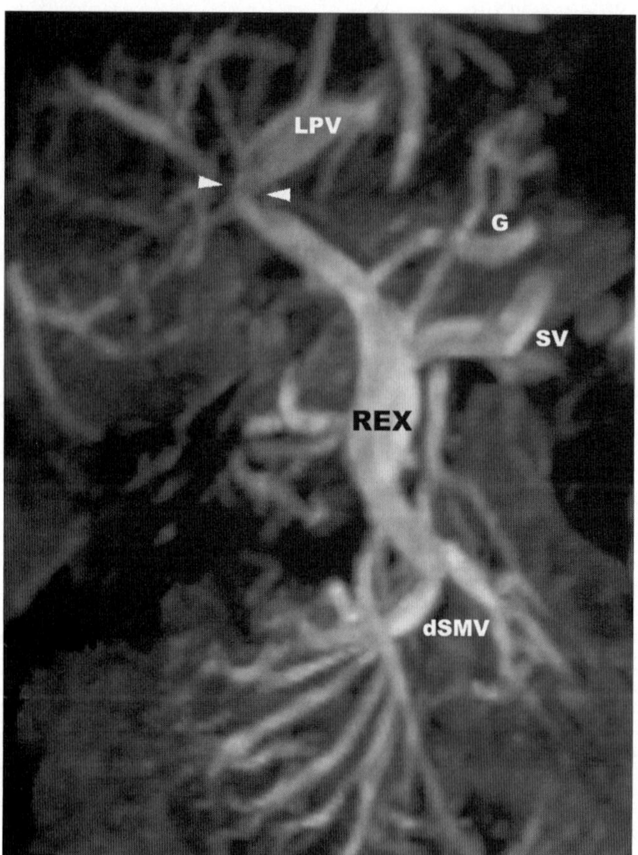

Figure 106-6 Computed tomography angiogram illustrates the appearance of a mesenteric–to–left portal vein bypass graft for extrahepatic portal vein thrombosis 1 week after a successful procedure. Contrast flows from the superior mesenteric vein (dSMV), through the vein graft (REX), and ultimately to the intrahepatic portal vein (LPV). Blood from the splenic vein (SV) and coronary vein (G) flows into the vein graft and to the liver.

In portal vein thrombosis, the extrahepatic portal vein is replaced by a network of small collaterals that supply the liver with a small amount of mesenteric blood and keep the intrahepatic portal circulation patent. The intrahepatic portal tree in these children is patent but hypoplastic.

The preoperative workup includes CT-angiography to assess the caliber and patency of the intrahepatic portal vein, a liver biopsy to rule out intrinsic liver disease, and a coagulation workup to rule out a hereditary hypercoagulable state. It was once thought that a hereditary hypercoagulable state caused the thrombosis of the portal vein.[96,128,136,154] However, it has been reported that deficiencies in the plasminolytic pathway may be secondary to the hepatic deprivation of portal blood and are reversible after the successful restoration of portal flow.[132]

The operation starts by dissecting out the intrahepatic portal vein in the recessus of Rex where the round ligament inserts between segments III and IV of the liver. Portions of segments III and IV are removed. All the branches to segments II, III, and IV are controlled. If it is suitable, the superior mesenteric vein is dissected out at the root of the mesentery. Alternative sources of blood for the bypass have been described, including the inferior mesenteric vein and the coronary vein.

Once the inflow vein has been isolated, the jugular vein (either right or left) is removed and sewn first to the intrahepatic portal vein and then to the superior mesenteric vein. The vein graft usually goes through the mesocolon and the lesser sac, up behind the stomach, through the lesser omentum, and up to the liver. In children with malrotation or other congenital disorders, the route of the graft may vary, depending on the child's individual anatomy.

Unlike portosystemic shunting, the mesenteric–to–left portal vein bypass, or Rex shunt, is restorative rather than palliative. It restores portal flow to the liver and relieves the symptoms of portal hypertension. With proper patient selection, patency rates have been in excess of 90%. Patency depends primarily on the quality of the intrahepatic portal vein and the number of branches that allow for sufficient runoff to permit blood flow to be sustained. The intrahepatic portal vein may be difficult to visualize by preoperative imaging, and a final assessment may be possible only at the time of surgery.

Nonshunt Operations

Nonshunt operations for portal hypertension are generally limited to a direct attack on the varices by operative interruption and ligation, and esophageal transection to interrupt the intramural varices within the esophagus.[121,191,216] Esophageal transection and resuturing or stapling have limited utility because of their high morbidity and high recurrence rate.

Sugiura et al.[206,207]described an operation in which all perigastric and periesophageal vessels were separated from the incisura of the stomach to the midesophagus at the level of the inferior pulmonary vein. In addition, the esophagus was divided and reattached. This radical approach to portal hypertension presented an alternative to shunting procedures, but it may have additional morbidity. A modified Sugiura operation in which the esophagus is transected and reanastomosed by a stapling device and in which the spleen is preserved has been described in children.[208] As experience with shunting and other vascular surgery in children has increased, the use of these effective but palliative and unphysiologic operations has decreased.

COMPLICATIONS OF SURGERY

Shunt Thrombosis

Any vascular operation has the potential for thrombosis. Prophylaxis against thrombosis may be instituted in the immediate postoperative period with low-dose heparin and antiplatelet agents such as aspirin or dipyridamole and continued for 3 to 6 months. Once a shunt is thrombosed, it may not be salvageable, and other solutions, such as devascularization, must be sought if bleeding recurs. Fortunately, in expert hands, the reported rate of thrombosis is less than 5%.

Ascites

Ascites is common after shunt operations because of disruption of the retroperitoneal lymphatic channels. In most cases, this resolves spontaneously. Oral diuretics may be necessary for a short time. A reduced-fat diet may also be helpful, because all the ascites is chylous in nature. Rarely, paracentesis may be necessary if the ascites is tense and persistent. If so, parenteral nutrition may be used to eliminate any chylous flow for a short time until the lymphatic leak seals. If ascites does not resolve with these measures, it may indicate that the hepatic reserve is small, and transplantation may be necessary.

Esophageal Strictures

After devascularization procedures accompanied by esophageal transection, it is not uncommon for the esophagus to narrow at the site of transection. Overt leaks are an uncommon but serious complication that requires thoracostomy drainage, prolonged antibiotics, and possibly reoperation. Fortunately, most strictures are manageable by esophageal dilatation, although some may require repeated sessions to achieve satisfactory patency.

OUTCOME

The outcome of treatment in a child with portal hypertension depends on the cause of the hypertension and the underlying state of the liver. In the last decade, the care of these patients has improved considerably because of better medical and surgical options and the availability of liver transplantation in children with poor hepatic reserve.

Emergency Bleeding from Varices

Medical control of portal hypertension has improved to the point that emergency shunts in children are the exception rather than the rule. Endoscopic control of esophageal varices by ligation is excellent. Emergency shunts, when necessary, are very effective in controlling hemorrhage, with good long-term patency rates reported.[69] However, the patency rate of emergency shunts is lower than the 90% or greater patency rate reported for elective operations. Emergency mesocaval shunting is seldom reported today, owing to the availability of medical and endoscopic means of controlling acute variceal hemorrhage.

Intermittent Bleeding from Esophageal or Gastric Varices

Today, because of the effectiveness of endoscopy and medications, few patients with extrahepatic portal vein thrombosis present with acute variceal bleeding requiring surgery. Patients are presenting with greater frequency with advanced hypersplenism and well-controlled varices. Controlling variceal bleeding does, however, require numerous endoscopies, occasional transfusions, and treatment with beta blockers and vasodilators.

As surgical options have become more effective and the results more predictable, definitive surgery for extrahepatic portal hypertension should be offered at an earlier point in the disease process rather than waiting until all other therapy has failed. This is especially relevant with the advent of the Rex shunt, because this operation restores normal portal pressure and relieves hypersplenism by redirecting mesenteric blood back to the liver. The effects of restoring portal blood to the liver are not yet apparent and may have far-reaching metabolic consequences during the child's early development. The correction of coagulation parameters back to normal after portal flow restoration[132] may be only one of many ameliorations in hepatic function that take place. The common belief that a child with portal vein thrombosis and portal hypertension has "normal" hepatic function may not be correct.

Selective shunting, through either a distal splenorenal shunt or a coronary–to–vena cava graft, to correct portal hypertension from portal vein thrombosis has been established as a procedure with minimal morbidity and no mortality when done by experienced surgeons. Patency rates exceed 95%, and hospital stays of less than a week are common. In the long run, selective shunting may be better for children than repeated hospital admissions for banding and long-term medication use to control bleeding. In addition, advanced hypersplenism occurs in many of these children when definitive surgical therapy is delayed. Even when variceal banding is instituted prophylactically, bleeding may shift away from the esophagus and into the stomach in many children over time. Surgical therapy (Rex shunt or distal splenorenal shunt) controls bleeding, reduces hospital admissions, decreases the need for medications, and relieves hypersplenism in a physiologic way that does not expose the child to the lifelong risk of overwhelming sepsis after splenectomy.

Shunting for portal hypertension caused by intrinsic liver disease is a more complex proposition, because it has to take into account the health of the liver. Selective shunting is excellent at decompressing the child's portal tree, with minimal morbidity in patients with low Child-Pugh or PELD scores. Although the theory behind the distal splenorenal shunt is that it separates the splenic and gastric venous drainage from the intestinal and mesenteric venous flow, careful studies have shown that separation between the two systems is not always complete and may disappear over time as the body forms collateral veins to replace the ones that were interrupted.[79,198] Nevertheless, selective shunts that attempt to preserve hepatopetal flow result in less encephalopathy and better hepatic function than do nonselective shunts in both children and adults.[81]

If a child with well-preserved liver function and portal hypertension cannot have a selective shunt because of a previous failed shunt or because of unfavorable anatomy, it may be better to consider a devascularization procedure to minimize the potential for encephalopathy.[115,188] The only role for nonselective shunts in children may be the rare child with well-preserved liver function and obstructive venopathy that cannot be stented or opened by an interventional radiologic approach.[176]

Hypersplenism

As the treatment for esophageal variceal bleeding has improved, more children are presenting with bleeding from gastric varices, portal hypertensive gastropathy,[81] or complications of advanced and debilitating hypersplenism.[194] There is no medical therapy for hypersplenism other than stimulating the bone marrow with granulocyte colony-stimulating factor.[100] Surgery is the only alternative.

Almost all shunts have been shown to decrease the severity of hypersplenism when done primarily for the indication of bleeding from symptomatic varices. The same two principles should govern the choice of surgery

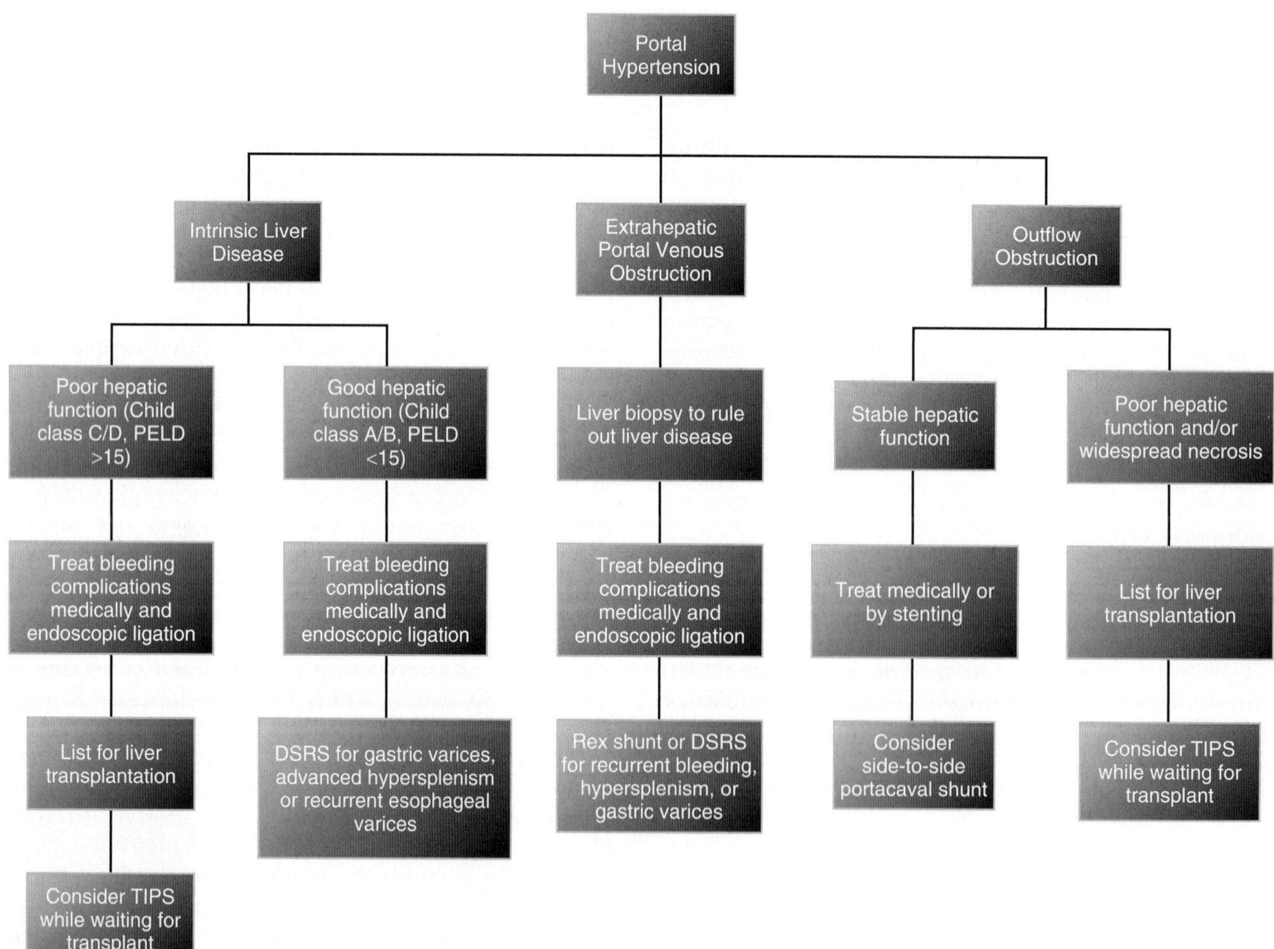

Figure 106-7 Treatment algorithm according to the underlying cause of portal hypertension. Portal hypertension accompanied by advanced liver dysfunction from either venous outflow obstruction or intrinsic liver disease is ultimately treated by transplantation, with or without a transjugular intrahepatic portosystemic shunt (TIPS) procedure. If the liver dysfunction is acceptable and not rapidly progressive, an appropriate shunt may be a good long-term solution. For symptomatic portal hypertension from extrahepatic portal hypertension, mesenteric–to–left portal vein bypass is the procedure of choice, followed by distal splenorenal shunt (DSRS). PELD, pediatric end-stage liver disease.

done primarily for hypersplenism: splenic preservation and the avoidance of encephalopathy. The distal splenorenal shunt has been shown to ameliorate hypersplenism in children. In children with extrahepatic portal vein thrombosis, the Rex shunt has had excellent results in terms of resolving hypersplenism.[19]

SUMMARY

A child with portal hypertension presents a unique challenge to the surgeon. The number of treatment options has increased over the last decade, including a wider variety of effective medications that reduce the pressure in the mesenteric tree and diminish the blood flow in the portal circulation. These options have greatly decreased the need for emergency surgery in children with portal hypertension. Figure 106-7 summarizes the treatment options discussed in this chapter, based on the underlying cause of portal hypertension.

Ancillary interventions such as endoscopic ligation of varices and radiologically guided placement of intrahepatic stents have also reduced the reliance on surgery to control bleeding in patients with advanced liver disease. Such interventions increase the chance that these patients will survive to receive a liver transplant.

Although the need for surgery has been reduced, the results of surgery have improved so that both shunt and nonshunt procedures offer a more permanent solution to bleeding and hypersplenism in patients with pre- and posthepatic portal hypertension and in those with well-compensated cirrhosis. With the decreased morbidity associated with portal hypertension surgery, the excellent long-term patency rates reported even in infants and small children after shunt surgery, and the increased number of surgical options available for children, surgery for portal hypertension offers a good alternative to medical treatment, even early in the course of treatment.

REFERENCES

1. Abraldes JG, Bosch J: Somatostatin and analogues in portal hypertension. Hepatology 2002;35:1305-1312.
2. Abraldes JG, et al: Hemodynamic response to pharmacological treatment of portal hypertension and long-term prognosis of cirrhosis. Hepatology 2003;37:902-908.
3. Abramowsky C, Romero R, Heffron T: Pathology of noncirrhotic portal hypertension: Clinicopathologic study in pediatric patients. Pediatr Dev Pathol 2003;6:421-426.
4. Adler M, et al: Hepatic vascular disease after kidney transplantation: Report of two cases and review of the literature. Nephrol Dial Transplant 1987;2:183-188.
5. Ahn SS, et al: Selective surgical therapy of the Budd-Chiari syndrome provides superior survivor rates than conservative medical management. J Vasc Surg 1987;5:28-37.
6. Aithal GP, et al: Portal hypertension secondary to arterioportal fistulae: Two unusual cases. Liver 1999;19:343-347.
7. Aitken MG: Recombinant factor VIIa. Emerg Med Australas 2004;16:446-455.
8. Akahoshi T, et al: Long-term results of endoscopic Histoacryl injection sclerotherapy for gastric variceal bleeding: A 10-year experience. Surgery 2002;131(1 Suppl):S176-S181.
9. Alagille D, Le Tan V, Odievre M: [Budd-Chiari syndrome and veno-occlusive disease in children (apropos of 3 cases)]. Arch Fr Pediatr 1968;25:1039-1058.
10. Albers I, et al: Superiority of the Child-Pugh classification to quantitative liver function tests for assessing prognosis of liver cirrhosis. Scand J Gastroenterol 1989;24:269-276.
11. Aldrete JS, Slaughter RL, Han SY: Portal vein thrombosis resulting in portal hypertension in adults. Am J Gastroenterol 1976;65:236-243.
12. Altman RP: Portal decompression by interposition mesocaval shunt in patients with biliary atresia. J Pediatr Surg 1976;11:809-814.
13. Ates O, et al: Extrahepatic portal hypertension treated by anastomosing inferior mesenteric vein to left portal vein at Rex recessus. J Pediatr Surg 2003;38:E10-E11.
14. Avgerinos A, et al: A prospective randomized trial comparing somatostatin, balloon tamponade and the combination of both methods in the management of acute variceal haemorrhage. J Hepatol 1991;13:78-83.
15. Avner ED, Ellis D, Jaffe R: Veno-occlusive disease of the liver associated with cysteamine treatment of nephropathic cystinosis. J Pediatr 1983;102:793-796.
16. Azoulay D, et al: Successful treatment of severe azathioprine-induced hepatic veno-occlusive disease in a kidney-transplanted patient with transjugular intrahepatic portosystemic shunt. Clin Nephrol 1998;50:118-122.
17. Bachleitner-Hofmann T, Grumbeck E, Gisslinger H: Oral anticoagulants as secondary prophylaxis of thrombosis in patients with polycythemia vera: A retrospective analysis of 15 patients. Thromb Res 2003;112:229-232.
18. Bajwa RP, et al: Recombinant tissue plasminogen activator for treatment of hepatic veno-occlusive disease following bone marrow transplantation in children: Effectiveness and a scoring system for initiating treatment. Bone Marrow Transplant 2003;31:591-597.
19. Bambini DA, et al: Experience with the Rex shunt (mesenterico-left portal bypass) in children with extrahepatic portal hypertension. J Pediatr Surg 2000;35:13-18.
20. Baranda J, et al: Mesenteric arteriovenous fistula causing portal hypertension and bleeding duodenal varices. Eur J Gastroenterol Hepatol 1996;8:1223-1225.
21. Benador N, et al: Transjugular intrahepatic portosystemic shunt prior to renal transplantation in a child with autosomal-recessive polycystic kidney disease and portal hypertension: A case report. Pediatr Transplant 2001;5:210-214.
22. Bhattacharyya M, et al: Inherited prothrombotic defects in Budd-Chiari syndrome and portal vein thrombosis: A study from north India. Am J Clin Pathol 2004;121:844-847.
23. Billing JS, Jamieson NV: Hepatic arterioportal fistula: A curable cause of portal hypertension in infancy. HPB Surg 1997;10:311-314.
24. Bismuth H, Franco D: Portal diversion for portal hypertension in early childhood. Ann Surg 1976;183:439-446.
25. Bismuth H, Franco D, Alagille D: Portal diversion for portal hypertension in children: The first ninety patients. Ann Surg 1980;192:18-24.
26. Bismuth H, Houssin D: Reduced-sized orthotopic liver graft in hepatic transplantation in children. Surgery 1984;95:367-370.
27. Blakemore AH: Portacaval shunt for portal hypertension: Follow-up results in cases of cirrhosis of the liver. JAMA 1951;145:1335-1339.
28. Blakemore AH: The portacaval shunt for portal hypertension with special reference to cirrhosis of the liver. Bull N Y Acad Med 1951;27:477-494.
29. Blanchard H, et al: [Portal hypertension of extra-hepatic origin in children]. Chir Pediatr 1982;23:221-225.

30. Bolton GC: Portal vena caval shunt surgery Eck fistula. Med Arts Sci 1951;5:131-134.
31. Bono RF, et al: Studies on portal hypertension. V. A comparison between the experimentally induced state of portal hypertension and that observed in human beings. Surgery 1960;48:119-141.
32. Bosch J, Garcia-Pagan JC: Complications of cirrhosis. I. Portal hypertension. J Hepatol 2000;32(1 Suppl):141-156.
33. Bosch J, Garcia-Pagan JC: Prevention of variceal rebleeding. Lancet 2003;361:952-954.
34. Botha JF, et al: Portosystemic shunts in children: A 15-year experience. J Am Coll Surg 2004;199:179-185.
35. Boyd DP: Portal hypertension following stricture of the common duct: A report of 2 cases in which splenectomy and splenorenal shunt were carried out. Lahey Clin Bull 1954;8:217-220.
36. Britton RC: The clinical effectiveness of selective portal shunts. Am J Surg 1977;133:506-511.
37. Broelsch CE, et al: Liver transplantation in children from living related donors: Surgical techniques and results. Ann Surg 1991;214:428-437.
38. Broxson EH, et al: Portal hypertension develops in a subset of children with standard risk acute lymphoblastic leukemia treated with oral 6-thioguanine during maintenance therapy. Pediatr Blood Cancer 2005;44:226-231.
39. Buccino RV, et al: Endoscopic approach to patients with portal hypertension: A complex diagnosis. A retrospective study based on 10 years' experience. Surg Endosc 1990;4:76-79.
40. Budd G: On Diseases of the Liver. London, John Churchill, 1845, p 146.
41. Caldwell SH, Chang C, Macik BG: Recombinant activated factor VII (rFVIIa) as a hemostatic agent in liver disease: A break from convention in need of controlled trials. Hepatology 2004;39:592-598.
42. Cales P, et al: Early administration of vapreotide for variceal bleeding in patients with cirrhosis. French Club for the Study of Portal Hypertension. N Engl J Med 2001;344:23-28.
43. Cameron JL, et al: The Budd-Chiari syndrome: Treatment by mesenteric-systemic venous shunts. Ann Surg 1983;198: 335-346.
44. Canbay A, Friedman S, Gores GJ: Apoptosis: The nexus of liver injury and fibrosis. Hepatology 2004;39:273-278.
45. Cao S, et al: Emergency transjugular intrahepatic portosystemic shunt (TIPS) in an infant: A case report. J Pediatr Surg 1997;32:125-127.
46. Capron JP, et al: Inferior mesenteric arteriovenous fistula associated with portal hypertension and acute ischemic colitis: Successful occlusion by intraarterial embolization with steel coils. Gastroenterology 1984;86:351-355.
47. Cario H, et al: Familial polycythemia vera with Budd-Chiari syndrome in childhood. Br J Haematol 2003;123:346-352.
48. Celinska-Cedro D, et al: Endoscopic ligation of esophageal varices for prophylaxis of first bleeding in children and adolescents with portal hypertension: Preliminary results of a prospective study. J Pediatr Surg 2003;38:1008-1011.
49. Chen LH, et al: Antiphospholipid syndrome: A survey of clinical characters in ten cases. J Zhejiang Univ Sci 2003;4: 616-619.
50. Chiari H: Über die selbstandige phlebitis obliterans der hauptstamme der venae hepaticae als todesursache. Beitr Z Pathol Anat 1899;26:1-18.
51. Child CG, Turcotte JG: Surgery and portal hypertension. In Child CG (ed): Major Problems in Clinical Surgery, vol 1, The Liver and Portal Hypertension. Philadelphia: WB Saunders, 1964.
52. Clatworthy HW Jr, Boles ET Jr: Extrahepatic portal bed block in children: Pathogenesis and treatment. Ann Surg 1959;150:371-383.
53. Clatworthy HW Jr, Delorimer AA: Portal decompression procedures in children. Am J Surg 1964;107:447-451.
54. Clatworthy HW Jr, Nahmad M, Hollabaugh RS: Presinusoidal extrahepatic portal hypertension: A review of thirty-five cases variously treated. Prog Pediatr Surg 1978;11:125-139.
55. Colapinto RF, et al: Formation of intrahepatic portosystemic shunts using a balloon dilatation catheter: Preliminary clinical experience. AJR Am J Roentgenol 1983;140:709-714.
56. Collins JC, Rypins EB, Sarfeh IJ: Narrow-diameter portacaval shunts for management of variceal bleeding. World J Surg 1994;18:211-215.
57. Davies DB: The impact of PELD on OPTN liver allocation: Preliminary results. Clin Transpl 2003:13-20.
58. de Ville de Goyet J, Clapuyt P, Otte JB: Extrahilar mesenterico-left portal shunt to relieve extrahepatic portal hypertension after partial liver transplant. Transplantation 1992;53:231-232.
59. de Ville de Goyet J, et al: Original extrahilar approach for hepatic portal revascularization and relief of extrahepatic portal hypertension related to later portal vein thrombosis after pediatric liver transplantation: Long term results. Transplantation 1996;62:71-75.
60. de Ville de Goyet J, et al: Direct bypassing of extrahepatic portal venous obstruction in children: A new technique for combined hepatic portal revascularization and treatment of extrahepatic portal hypertension. J Pediatr Surg 1998; 33:597-601.
61. de Ville de Goyet J, et al: Mesenterico-left intrahepatic portal vein shunt: Original technique to treat symptomatic extrahepatic portal hypertension. Acta Gastroenterol Belg 1998;61:13-16.
62. de Ville de Goyet J, et al: Treatment of extrahepatic portal hypertension in children by mesenteric-to-left portal vein bypass: A new physiological procedure. Eur J Surg 1999; 165:777-781.
63. Drapanas T: Interposition mesocaval shunt for treatment of portal hypertension. Ann Surg 1972;176:435-448.
64. D'Souza R, et al: Lessons to be learned: A case study of the temporal onset of pulmonary hypertension with preexistent cirrhotic portal hypertension. J R Soc Health 2001; 121:257-261.
65. Eck N: On the question of ligature of the portal vein. Voyenno Med 1973;130:1.
66. Eizaguirre I, et al: [Warren's shunt in the treatment of portal hypertension in children]. Cir Pediatr 1991;4:134-139.
67. Ellis EE, Holman E: Portal hypertension accompanying cholangitis due to stricture of the common bile duct: Correction by splenorenal shunt; a case report. Surgery 1955;37:463-468.
68. Estrada O, et al: Posttraumatic intrapancreatic aortosplenic fistula causing portal hypertension. Asian Cardiovasc Thorac Ann 2003;11:272-274.
69. Evans S, et al: Selective distal splenorenal shunts for intractable variceal bleeding in pediatric portal hypertension. J Pediatr Surg 1995;30:1115-1118.
70. Feneyrou B, et al: Initial control of bleeding from esophageal varices with the Sengstaken-Blakemore tube: Experience in 82 patients. Am J Surg 1988;155:509-11.
71. Fischer JE: Hepatic coma in cirrhosis, portal hypertension, and following portacaval shunt: Its etiologies and the current status of its treatment. Arch Surg 1974;108:325-336.
72. Fonkalsrud EW, Longmire WP Jr: Reassessment of operative procedures for portal hypertension in infants and children. Am J Surg 1969;118:148-157.
73. Foster JH, Sandblom P: Portal hypertension secondary to an hepato-portal arteriovenous fistula. Ann Surg 1961;154: 300-304.

74. Freeman RB Jr: MELD/PELD: One year later. Transplant Proc 2003;35:2425-2427.
75. Friedman SL: Seminars in medicine of the Beth Israel Hospital, Boston. The cellular basis of hepatic fibrosis: Mechanisms and treatment strategies. N Engl J Med 1993;328:1828-1835.
76. Fuchs J, et al: Mesenterico-left portal vein bypass in children with congenital extrahepatic portal vein thrombosis: A unique curative approach. J Pediatr Gastroenterol Nutr 2003;36:213-216.
77. Galambos JT, et al: Selective and total shunts in the treatment of bleeding varices: A randomized controlled trial. N Engl J Med 1976;295:1089-1095.
78. Gartner JCJ, et al: Orthotopic liver transplantation in children: Two-year experience with 47 patients. Pediatrics 1984;74:140-145.
79. Gawish Y, et al: Devascularization procedure and DSRS: A controlled randomized trial on selected haemodynamic portal flow pattern in schistosomal portal hypertension with variceal bleeding. Int Surg 2000;85:325-330.
80. Gliedman ML: The mesocaval shunt for portal hypertension. Am J Gastroenterol 1971;56:323-333.
81. Goncalves ME, Cardoso SR, Maksoud JG: Prophylactic sclerotherapy in children with esophageal varices: Long-term results of a controlled prospective randomized trial. J Pediatr Surg 2000;35:401-405.
82. Gonzalez-Abraldes J, Bosch J, Garcia-Pagan JC: Pharmacological treatment of portal hypertension. Curr Opin Investig Drugs 2001;2:1407-1413.
83. Grace ND, et al: Distal splenorenal vs portal-systemic shunts after hemorrhage from varices: A randomized controlled trial. Hepatology 1988;8:1475-1481.
84. Grauer SE, Schwartz SI: Extrahepatic portal hypertension: A retrospective analysis. Ann Surg 1979;189:566-574.
85. Grosfeld JL, et al: Portal hypertension in infants and children with histiocytosis X. Am J Surg 1976;131:108-113.
86. Groszmann RJ, et al: Hemodynamic events in a prospective randomized trial of propranolol versus placebo in the prevention of a first variceal hemorrhage. Gastroenterology 1990;99:1401-1407.
87. Handa M, et al: [Portosystemic A-V fistula and portal hypertension associated with islet-cell tumor of the pancreas]. Nippon Geka Gakkai Zasshi 1985;86:953-958.
88. Hannam PD, et al: Post-surgical shunt hepatopulmonary syndrome in a case of non-cirrhotic portal hypertension: Lack of efficacy of shunt reversal. Eur J Gastroenterol Hepatol 1999;11:1425-1427.
89. Hansen K, Singer DB: Asplenic-hyposplenic overwhelming sepsis: Postsplenectomy sepsis revisited. Pediatr Dev Pathol 2001;4:105-121.
90. Hasegawa T, et al: Distal splenorenal shunt with splenopancreatic disconnection for portal hypertension in biliary atresia. Pediatr Surg Int 1999;15:92-96.
91. Hassoun Z, Pomier-Layrargues G: The transjugular intrahepatic portosystemic shunt in the treatment of portal hypertension. Eur J Gastroenterol Hepatol 2004;16:1-4.
92. Hay JM, Valayer J, Maillard JN: [Experience with mesocaval shunt with jugular vein interposition for treatment of portal hypertension in children]. Chir Pediatr 1982;23:211-213.
93. Helikson MA, Shapiro DL, Seashore JH: Hepatoportal arteriovenous fistula and portal hypertension in an infant. Pediatrics 1977;60:920-924.
94. Hirner A, et al: [Hyperkinetic portal hypertension. Arterioportal fistula: problems—case reports—review of the literature]. Chirurg 1978;49:303-310.
95. Holliday RW: Splenorenal shunt combined with ligation of esophageal varices through left thoracotomy. N Y State J Med 1961;61:4088-4090.
96. Horing E, et al: [Portal hypertension due to thromboses of the portal, splenic and mesenteric veins in congenital protein C deficiency]. Dtsch Med Wochenschr 1988; 113:1847-1849.
97. Howard ER, Stringer MD, Mowat AP: Assessment of injection sclerotherapy in the management of 152 children with oesophageal varices. Br J Surg 1988;75:404-408.
98. Huppert PE, et al: Transjugular intrahepatic portosystemic shunts in children with biliary atresia. Cardiovasc Intervent Radiol 2002;25:484-493.
99. Hyde GL: Postsplenectomy arteriovenous fistula causing portal hypertension. J Ky Med Assoc 1979;77:113-115.
100. Ishizone S, et al: Effect of granulocyte colony-stimulating factor on neutropenia in liver transplant recipients with hypersplenism. J Pediatr Surg 1994;29:510-513.
101. Israel DM, et al: Partial splenic embolization in children with hypersplenism. J Pediatr 1994;124:95-100.
102. Jagtap A, Shanbag P, Vaidya M: Budd-Chiari syndrome due to antithrombin III deficiency. Indian J Pediatr 2003;70:1003-1005.
103. Jaramillo JL, et al: Somatostatin versus Sengstaken balloon tamponade for primary haemostasia of bleeding esophageal varices: A randomized pilot study. J Hepatol 1991;12: 100-105.
104. Johnston GW: Bleeding oesophageal varices in the absence of intrahepatic or extrahepatic obstruction of the portal system and without portal hypertension. Ulster Med J 1965;34:23-26.
105. Johnston GW, Rodgers HW: Management of bleeding oesophageal varices when portal systemic shunt is inadvisable, with particular reference to the use of balloon tamponade and sclerosing injections. Ulster Med J 1964; 33:110-115.
106. Jones JD: The results of treatment of portal hypertension. Br J Surg 1961;49:168-173.
107. Karasu Z, et al: Liver transplantation in a patient with Budd-Chiari syndrome secondary to factor V Leiden mutation. Transplant Proc 2003;35:3008-3010.
108. Karrer FM, et al: Portal vein thrombosis: Treatment of variceal hemorrhage by endoscopic variceal ligation. J Pediatr Surg 1994;29:1149-1151.
109. Kayser S, et al: Rapidly progressive portal hypertension 23 years after post-traumatic arterioportal fistula of the liver. Am J Gastroenterol 1996;91:1442-1446.
110. Khaldi F, et al: [Hepatic hydatidosis and portal hypertension in children: Is it the Budd-Chiari syndrome?]. Ann Pediatr (Paris) 1993;40:631-634.
111. Khubchandani RP, D'Souza S: Antiphospholipid antibody syndrome as a cause of Budd-Chiari syndrome. Indian Pediatr 2003;40:907-908.
112. Kind R, et al: Bucrylate treatment of bleeding gastric varices: 12 years' experience. Endoscopy 2000;32:512-519.
113. Kirchgatterer A, et al: Portal hypertension due to traumatic hepatic arterioportal fistula: Report of successful embolization. Eur J Gastroenterol Hepatol 1998;10:1057-1059.
114. Kitano S, Dolgor B: Does portal hypertension contribute to the pathogenesis of gastric ulcer associated with liver cirrhosis? J Gastroenterol 2000;35:79-86.
115. Klempnaue J, Schrem H: Review: Surgical shunts and encephalopathy. Metab Brain Dis 2001;16:21-25.
116. Koslin DB, Mulligan SA, Berland LL: Duplex assessment of the portal venous system. Semin Ultrasound CT MR 1992;13:22-33.
117. Kumana CR, et al: Hepatic veno-occlusive disease due to toxic alkaloid herbal tea. Lancet 1983;2:1360-1361.
118. Lang H, et al: The Budd-Chiari syndrome: Clinical presentation and diagnostic findings in 45 patients treated by surgery. Bildgebung 1994;61:173-181.

119. Large A, Johnston CG, Preshaw DE: The portacaval venous shunt, with special reference to side-to-side portacaval anastomosis. Ann Surg 1952;135:22-33.
120. Lauler DP: An overview of the pathophysiology and management of portal hypertension and ascites. J Hepatol 1993;17(Suppl 2):S1-S3.
121. Le Tourneau JN, Carcassonne M: [Portal hypertension: Choice of therapy for children under 10 years: Shunt or palliative surgery?]. Chir Pediatr 1983;24:34-36.
122. Leffman H, Payne JT: Episodic coma due to meat intoxication as a fatal complication of portacaval shunt in the human being. Am Surg 1955;21:488-498.
123. Levine OR, et al: Progressive pulmonary hypertension in children with portal hypertension. J Pediatr 1973;83: 964-972.
124. Lewis JH, Tice HL, Zimmerman HJ: Budd-Chiari syndrome associated with oral contraceptive steroids: Review of treatment of 47 cases. Dig Dis Sci 1983;28:673-683.
125. Lichtenheld FR: [Eck fistula coma and hepatic coma: An experimental study]. Z Gesamte Exp Med 1959;132:42-50.
126. Litzow MR, et al: Veno-occlusive disease of the liver after blood and marrow transplantation: Analysis of pre- and post-transplant risk factors associated with severity and results of therapy with tissue plasminogen activator. Leuk Lymphoma 2002;43:2099-2107.
127. Longmire WP Jr: Personal reflections on the surgical treatment of portal hypertension. Jpn J Surg 1985;15:243-248.
128. Lopez Serrano P, et al: [Extrahepatic portal hypertension: Spleno-portal thrombosis secondary to protein C deficiency]. An Med Interna 2003;20:473-476.
129. Lowe RC, Grace ND: Pharmacologic therapy for portal hypertension. Curr Gastroenterol Rep 2001;3:24-29.
130. Lui HF, et al: Primary prophylaxis of variceal hemorrhage: A randomized controlled trial comparing band ligation, propranolol, and isosorbide mononitrate. Gastroenterology 2002;123:735-744.
131. Luo B, et al: ET-1 and TNF-alpha in HPS: Analysis in prehepatic portal hypertension and biliary and nonbiliary cirrhosis in rats. Am J Physiol Gastrointest Liver Physiol 2004;286:G294-G303.
132. Mack CL, Superina RA, Whitington PF: Surgical restoration of portal flow corrects procoagulant and anticoagulant deficiencies associated with extrahepatic portal vein thrombosis. J Pediatr 2003;142:197-199.
133. Maddrey WC: Hepatic vein thrombosis (Budd Chiari syndrome): Possible association with the use of oral contraceptives. Semin Liver Dis 1987;7:32-39.
134. Maedler U, et al: Restoration of liver function and portosystemic pressure gradient after TIPSS and late TIPSS occlusion. Cardiovasc Intervent Radiol 2002;25:148-151.
135. Maggi U, et al: Child-Pugh score and liver transplantation. Transplant Proc 1993;25:1769-1770.
136. Majluf-Cruz A, et al: The incidence of protein C deficiency in thrombosis-related portal hypertension. Am J Gastroenterol 1996;91:976-980.
137. Maksoud JG, Goncalves ME: Treatment of portal hypertension in children. World J Surg 1994;18:251-258.
138. Maksoud JG, et al: The endoscopic and surgical management of portal hypertension in children: Analysis of 123 cases. J Pediatr Surg 1991;26:178-181.
139. Malec Z: [Two cases of Warren's distal splenorenal anastomosis in children with portal hypertension]. Wiad Lek 1984;37:677-683.
140. Mann DA, Smart DE: Transcriptional regulation of hepatic stellate cell activation. Gut 2002;50:891-896.
141. Mantz FA Jr, Craige E: Portal axis thrombosis with spontaneous portacaval shunt and resultant cor pulmonale. AMA Arch Pathol 1951;52:91-97.
142. Martelli H, et al: [Surgical treatment of portal hypertension in children: Retrospective study of 157 cases]. Chir Pediatr 1982;23:171-178.
143. McCashland TM: Current use of transjugular intrahepatic portosystemic shunts. Curr Gastroenterol Rep 2003;5: 31-38.
144. McDiarmid SV, et al: Selection of pediatric candidates under the PELD system. Liver Transpl 2004;10(10 Suppl 2):S23-S30.
145. McKiernan PJ, Beath SV, Davison SM: A prospective study of endoscopic esophageal variceal ligation using a multiband ligator. J Pediatr Gastroenterol Nutr 2002;34: 207-211.
146. Michielsen PP: Physiopathology of ascites in portal hypertension. Acta Gastroenterol Belg 1996;59:191-197.
147. Mino RA, Murphy AI Jr, Livingstone RG: Sarcoidosis producing portal hypertension: Treatment by splenectomy and splenorenal shunt. Ann Surg 1949;130:951-957.
148. Mion F, et al: Azathioprine induced liver disease: Nodular regenerative hyperplasia of the liver and perivenous fibrosis in a patient treated for multiple sclerosis. Gut 1991;32:715-717.
149. Misra A, Loyalka P, Alva F: Portal hypertension due to extensive hepatic cysts in autosomal dominant polycystic kidney disease. South Med J 1999;92:626-627.
150. Misra S, et al: Splenoportovenography: Safety, success rate and hemodynamic changes, and incidence and natural history of splenic hematoma. Indian J Gastroenterol 1991;10:49-50.
151. Nagabhusan G, et al: Ultrasonography in portal hypertension: A sensitive noninvasive test to demonstrate portal-vascular anatomy. Gastroenterol Jpn 1989;24:442-445.
152. Nakatani Y, et al: Pulmonary hypertension associated with portal hypertension in childhood: Case report of a 6-year-old child and review of the literature. Acta Pathol Jpn 1988;38:897-907.
153. Nezakatgoo N, et al: Liver transplantation for acute Budd-Chiari syndrome in identical twin sisters with factor V Leiden mutation. Transplantation 2003;76:195-198.
154. Okuda K: Idiopathic portal hypertension and protein C deficiency. Hepatology 1989;10:903.
155. Olsen TS, Fjeldborg O, Hansen HE: Portal hypertension without liver cirrhosis in renal transplant recipients. APMIS Suppl 1991;23:13-20.
156. Ortiz Cansado A, et al: [Veno-occlusive liver disease due to intake of *Senecio vulgaris* tea]. Gastroenterol Hepatol 1995;18:413-416.
157. Osborne DR: Porto-biliary fistula and portal hypertension due to gallstones: A case report. Acta Chir Scand 1980;146:363-365.
158. Pasqualini M, et al: [Role of sclerotherapy in bleeding esophageal varices in children with portal hypertension]. Minerva Chir 1988;43:1027-1030.
159. Paulus H, et al: [Diagnosis and therapy of portal hypertension caused by portal vein thrombosis]. Med Klin (Munich) 1987;82:860-864.
160. Peck-Radosavljevic M: Hypersplenism. Eur J Gastroenterol Hepatol 2001;13:317-323.
161. Polio J, Groszmann RJ: Hemodynamic factors involved in the development and rupture of esophageal varices: A pathophysiologic approach to treatment. Semin Liver Dis 1986;6:318-331.
162. Postlethwait RW, Moseley V: Esophageal varices: The treatment of portal hypertension by portacaval shunt. J S C Med Assoc 1950;46:305-308.
163. Pozler O, et al: Transjugular intrahepatic portosystemic shunt in five children with cystic fibrosis: Long-term results. Hepatogastroenterology 2003;50:1111-1114.

164. Prediction of the first variceal hemorrhage in patients with cirrhosis of the liver and esophageal varices: A prospective multicenter study. The North Italian Endoscopic Club for the Study and Treatment of Esophageal Varices. N Engl J Med 1988;319:983-989.
165. Preshaw DE, Large A, Johnson AF: Effect of portacaval venous shunt on sulfobromophthalein (bromsulphalein) retention. AMA Arch Surg 1951;62:801-805.
166. Price MR, et al: Management of esophageal varices in children by endoscopic variceal ligation. J Pediatr Surg 1996;31:1056-1059.
167. Rajiv M, et al: Splenic artery aneurysm with arteriovenous fistula as a cause of portal hypertension. Indian J Gastroenterol 2004;23:36-37.
168. Ratnoff OD, Conley CL, Berthrong M: The differentiation between extrahepatic and intrahepatic obstruction of the portal circulation: A clinical study of the Banti syndrome. Bull Johns Hopkins Hosp 1950;87:305-327.
169. Read AE, et al: Hepatic veno-occlusive disease associated with renal transplantation and azathioprine therapy. Ann Intern Med 1986;104:651-655.
170. Reiss U, et al: Hepatic venoocclusive disease in blood and bone marrow transplantation in children and young adults: Incidence, risk factors, and outcome in a cohort of 241 patients. J Pediatr Hematol Oncol 2002;24:746-750.
171. Renard TH, et al: Use of distal splenorenal shunt in children referred for liver transplant evaluation. J Pediatr Surg 1994;29:403-406.
172. Reynaert H, Geerts A: Pharmacological rationale for the use of somatostatin and analogues in portal hypertension. Aliment Pharmacol Ther 2003;18:375-386.
173. Ribas J, et al: Isosorbide-5-mononitrate in the treatment of pulmonary hypertension associated with portal hypertension. Eur Respir J 1999;13:210-212.
174. Rizzati R, et al: Budd-Chiari syndrome associated with systemic lupus erythematosus: Diagnostic imaging and percutaneous treatment. Radiol Med (Torino) 2003;105: 519-523.
175. Rosenberg N, Konigsberg SF, Noronha J: Mesocaval and portacaval shunts using panelled bovine arterial H grafts. Arch Surg 1974;109:754-758.
176. Rossle M, et al: The Budd-Chiari syndrome: Outcome after treatment with the transjugular intrahepatic portosystemic shunt. Surgery 2004;135:394-403.
177. Rypins EB, Sarfeh IJ: Partial portal decompression: Two approaches to the management of portal hypertension. Hepatology 1990;12:370-372.
178. Santambrogio R, et al: [Role of splenectomy in the therapy of hypersplenism associated with intrahepatic portal hypertension]. Minerva Chir 1984;39:953-956.
179. Sarfeh IJ, et al: Portacaval H-graft: Relationships of shunt diameter, portal flow patterns and encephalopathy. Ann Surg 1983;197:422-426.
180. Sarin SK, et al: Endoscopic sclerotherapy for varices in children. J Pediatr Gastroenterol Nutr 1988;7:662-666.
181. Sarin SK, et al: Endoscopic sclerotherapy in the treatment of gastric varices. Br J Surg 1988;75:747-750.
182. Sarin SK, et al: The natural history of portal hypertensive gastropathy: Influence of variceal eradication. Am J Gastroenterol 2000;95:2888-2893.
183. Sarin SK, et al: A randomized controlled trial of cyanoacrylate versus alcohol injection in patients with isolated fundic varices. Am J Gastroenterol 2002;97:1010-1015.
184. Sarin SK, et al: Isolated gastric varices: Prevalence, clinical relevance and natural history. Dig Surg 2003;20:42-47.
185. Saubier EC, et al: [Warren's operation for portal hypertension: Evaluation of results by early angiography in 23 cases]. J Chir (Paris) 1980;117:147-153.
186. Schroeder RA, et al: Pulmonary expression of iNOS and HO-1 protein is upregulated in a rat model of prehepatic portal hypertension. Dig Dis Sci 2000;45:2405-2410.
187. Sedgwick CE, Poulantzas JK, Kune GA: Management of portal hypertension secondary to bile duct strictures: Review of 18 cases with splenorenal shunt. Ann Surg 1966;163:949-953.
188. Selzner M, et al: Current indication of a modified Sugiura procedure in the management of variceal bleeding. J Am Coll Surg 2001;193:166-173.
189. Shah HA, Piris J, Finlayson ND: Primary pulmonary hypertension developing 11 years after a splenorenal shunt for portal hypertension in hepatic cirrhosis. Eur J Gastroenterol Hepatol 1995;7:283-286.
190. Shah R, et al: Partial splenic embolization: An effective alternative to splenectomy for hypersplenism. Am Surg 1990;56:774-777.
191. Sharma D, et al: A modified technique of devascularization for surgical management of portal hypertension in children. Trop Doct 2001;31:93-95.
192. Shetty K, Rybicki L, Carey WD: The Child-Pugh classification as a prognostic indicator for survival in primary sclerosing cholangitis. Hepatology 1997;25:1049-1053.
193. Shibata M: [Clinical course and prognostic value of Child-Turcotte criteria and Child-Pugh score in medically treated cirrhosis positive for HCV antibody—in comparison with cirrhosis positive for HBs Ag]. Nippon Rinsho 1995;53(Suppl):711-719.
194. Shilyansky J, Roberts EA, Superina RA: Distal splenorenal shunts for the treatment of severe thrombocytopenia from portal hypertension in children. J Gastrointest Surg 1999;3:167-172.
195. Shun A, et al: Portosystemic shunting for paediatric portal hypertension. J Pediatr Surg 1997;32:489-493.
196. Snady H, Feinman L: Prediction of variceal hemorrhage: A prospective study. Am J Gastroenterol 1988;83: 519-525.
197. Sperl W, et al: Reversible hepatic veno-occlusive disease in an infant after consumption of pyrrolizidine-containing herbal tea. Eur J Pediatr 1995;154:112-116.
198. Spina GP, et al: Early hemodynamic changes following selective distal splenorenal shunt for portal hypertension: Comparison of surgical techniques. World J Surg 1990;14:115-121.
199. Srivastava A, et al: Glutathione S-transferase M1 polymorphism: A risk factor for hepatic venoocclusive disease in bone marrow transplantation. Blood 2004;104: 1574-1577.
200. Stanley AJ, Bouchier IA, Hayes PC: Pathophysiology and management of portal hypertension. 2. Cirrhotic ascites. Br J Hosp Med 1997;58:74-78.
201. Stanley AJ, et al: Longterm follow up of transjugular intrahepatic portosystemic stent shunt (TIPSS) for the treatment of portal hypertension: Results in 130 patients. Gut 1996;39:479-485.
202. Starzl TE, et al: Extended survival in 3 cases of orthotopic homotransplantation of the human liver. Surgery 1968;63: 549-563.
203. Stav K, Reif S: [Gastrointestinal bleeding in children—etiology and diagnosis: Survey of patients in a Tel Aviv medical center, in the years 1990 to 1997]. Harefuah 2000;138: 534-538, 615.
204. Steffani KD, et al: [Recurrent intestinal bleeding in a patient with arterio-venous fistulas in the small bowel, limited mesenteric varicosis without portal hypertension and malrotation type I]. Z Gastroenterol 2003;41:587-590.
205. Stickel F, Seitz HK: The efficacy and safety of comfrey. Public Health Nutr 2000;3:501-508.

206. Sugiura M, Futagawa S: A new technique for treating esophageal varices. J Thorac Cardiovasc Surg 1973;66: 677-685.
207. Sugiura M, Futagawa S, Hidai K: A new technique for the treatment of esophageal varices. Bull Soc Int Chir 1975; 34:175-177.
208. Superina RA, Weber JL, Shandling B: A modified Sugiura operation for bleeding varices in children. J Pediatr Surg 1983;18:794-799.
209. Szecseny A: [Results of splenectomy and splenorenal shunt in a case of splenomegalic cirrhosis]. Orv Hetil 1954;95:218-219.
210. Tahan V, et al: Adrenomedullin in cirrhotic and non-cirrhotic portal hypertension. World J Gastroenterol 2003; 9:2325-2327.
211. Terblanche J, et al: A prospective controlled trial of sclerotherapy in the long term management of patients after esophageal variceal bleeding. Surg Gynecol Obstet 1979;148:323-333.
212. Thalheimer U, et al: Monitoring target reduction in hepatic venous pressure gradient during pharmacological therapy of portal hypertension: A close look at the evidence. Gut 2004;53:143-148.
213. Tocornal J, Cruz F: Portosystemic shunts for extrahepatic portal hypertension in children. Surg Gynecol Obstet 1981;153:53-56.
214. Tokiwa K, et al: Pulmonary hypertension as a fatal complication of extrahepatic portal hypertension. Eur J Pediatr Surg 1993;3:373-375.
215. Trobs RB, Bennek J: Partial splenectomy, transposition of the spleen to the abdominal wall or splenohepatoplasty in portal hypertensive rats: Effects on portal venous pressure and homeostasis—microscopical appearance of the transposed spleen. Eur J Pediatr Surg 1998;8:155-162.
216. Uchiyama M, et al: Long-term results after nonshunt operations for esophageal varices in children. J Pediatr Surg 1994;29:1429-1433.
217. Uno A, et al: Portal hypertension in children and young adults: Sonographic and color Doppler findings. Abdom Imaging 1997;22:72-78.
218. Valayer J: [The choice of an operation for correction of portal hypertension in children]. Chir Pediatr 1982;23:214-217.
219. Vallat G, et al: [Portal hypertension by membranous occlusion of the inferior vena cava at its termination. Budd-Chiari-type syndrome]. Med Chir Dig 1980;9: 717-719.
220. van Erpecum KJ, et al: Generalized peliosis hepatis and cirrhosis after long-term use of oral contraceptives. Am J Gastroenterol 1988;83:572-575.
221. van Hoek B: The spectrum of liver disease in systemic lupus erythematosus. Neth J Med 1996;48:244-253.
222. van Vroonhoven TJ, Molenaar JC: Distal splenorenal shunt for decompression of portal hypertension in children with cystic fibrosis. Surg Gynecol Obstet 1979; 149:559-560.
223. Vazquez-Estevez J, et al: [Partial splenic embolization in hypersplenism]. An Esp Pediatr 1984;21:798-802.
224. Villanueva C, et al: Nadolol plus isosorbide mononitrate compared with sclerotherapy for the prevention of variceal rebleeding. N Engl J Med 1996;334:1624-1629.
225. Villanueva C, et al: Maintenance of hemodynamic response to treatment for portal hypertension and influence on complications of cirrhosis. J Hepatol 2004;40: 757-765.
226. Vogelsang GB, Dalal J: Hepatic venoocclusive disease in blood and bone marrow transplantation in children: Incidence, risk factors, and outcome. J Pediatr Hematol Oncol 2002;24:706-709.
227. Voorhees AB Jr, et al: Portal-systemic encephalopathy in the noncirrhotic patient: Effect of portal-systemic shunting. Arch Surg 1973;107:659-663.
228. Warren WD, Zeppa R, Fomon JJ: Selective trans-splenic decompression of gastroesophageal varices by distal splenorenal shunt. Ann Surg 1967;166:437-455.
229. Warren WD, et al: Preoperative assessment of portal hypertension. Ann Surg 1967;165:999-1012.
230. Willner IR: Veno-occlusive disease. Curr Treat Options Gastroenterol 2002;5:465-469.
231. Wilson MW, et al: Percutaneous transhepatic hepatic venography in the delineation and treatment of Budd-Chiari syndrome. J Vasc Interv Radiol 1996;7:133-138.
232. Yachha SK, et al: Gastrointestinal bleeding in children. J Gastroenterol Hepatol 1996;11:903-907.
233. Yamamoto S, et al: Case report of a pancreatic pseudocyst ruptured into the splenic vein causing extrahepatic portal hypertension. Jpn J Surg 1982;12:387-390.
234. Zaman A: Current management of esophageal varices. Curr Treat Options Gastroenterol 2003;6:499-507.
235. Zargar SA, et al: Endoscopic ligation compared with sclerotherapy for bleeding esophageal varices in children with extrahepatic portal venous obstruction. Hepatology 2002;36:666-672.
236. Zargar SA, et al: Fifteen-year follow up of endoscopic injection sclerotherapy in children with extrahepatic portal venous obstruction. J Gastroenterol Hepatol 2004;19:139-145.
237. Zheng RQ, Chung H, Kudo M: Hepatobiliary and pancreatic arterioportal fistula causing portal hypertension. J Gastroenterol Hepatol 2003;18:873.

Chapter 107

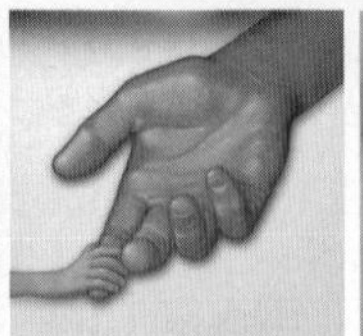

The Pancreas

Takeshi Miyano

EMBRYOLOGY

The pancreas originates from two endodermal buds that arise from the caudal part of the foregut. One is the ventral bud, which arises from the base of the hepatic diverticulum and is closely related to the bile duct; the other arises from the dorsal surface of the duodenum immediately opposite and in a slightly rostral direction to the liver diverticulum.[142] Both fuse at approximately the sixth or seventh week of gestation.

The dorsal bud appears before the ventral bud, grows faster, and becomes larger.[129,137] An axial duct is formed and opens into the gut tube by the beginning of the sixth week of gestation, and short branches appear soon thereafter.[73,128]

The ventral bud of the pancreas transiently consists of two lobules[105]; small ducts form within these lobules and open into the hepatic diverticulum close to the gallbladder. The ventral bud is carried away from the duodenum by elongation of the proximal part of the hepatic diverticulum from which it arises. This proximal part is called the common bile duct. The left ventral bud lobule later regresses completely. Because of rapid growth of the duodenum, which is limited to the left half of its circumference,[63] the right ventral bud and the developing common bile duct rotate backward and become situated close to the posterior and inferior surface of the dorsal pancreatic bud. The outcome of this rotation is to bring the opening of the common bile duct to the same side as the dorsal bud so that the duct lies ventral to and below the opening of its duct. The tip of the right ventral bud lobule eventually rests behind the superior mesenteric artery.

During the seventh week of gestation, the smaller ventral bud fuses with the proximal part of the dorsal pancreas.

Secretory acini appear during the third month as clusters of cells around the ends of the ducts from which they are derived.[109] No evidence has been found of secretory activity in the fetal acini, even though zymogen granules are present from the fifth month onward.[24] Trypsin may appear as early as 22 weeks, but lipase is present only near term.[197] Acinar cells and islet cells are both derived and differentiate from the duct cells of the pancreas. Whether this differentiation is permanent or whether acinar cells may become islet cells by subsequent differentiation is not known.[1,11,88]

Pancreatic anomalies are numerous and are listed in Table 107-1.

Annular Pancreas

During the sixth week of gestation, the common duct and the right ventral bud lobule are carried in a dorsal direction around the circumference of the duodenum. The longer duct of the dorsal pancreas anastomoses with that of the ventral pancreas to establish the main pancreatic duct. Developmental errors at this stage are believed to cause an annular pancreas. This anomaly occurs in 1 in 20,000 births and is more frequent in males than females with a ratio of 2:1.[55] The appearance of an annular pancreas in a woman and her child,[155] as well as in members of two successive generations,[74] suggests a possible hereditary link, which, however, has yet to be proved. It can be manifested as duodenal stenotic or obstructive symptoms from the first days of life.[119]

TABLE 107-1 Errors in Pancreatic Development

Errors in Pancreatic Development
Aplasia and hypoplasia
Hyperplasia and hypertrophy
Dysplasia
Ductal anomalies
Pancreas divisum
Annular pancreas
Rotational anomalies
Heterotopic pancreas
Cysts
Arterial, vascular, and lymphatic anomalies
Neoplasm
Cystic fibrosis

Pancreas Divisum

The adult pancreas is derived from ventral and dorsal pancreatic buds that fuse by the end of the eighth week of gestation. Most of the gland is derived from the dorsal bud and includes the superior anterior part of the head, body, and tail; it is drained by the duct of Santorini through the minor papilla. The ventral bud becomes the posterior and inferior part of the head. The ventral pancreatic bud is drained by the duct of Wirsung into the major papilla of Vater. With fusion of the ventral and dorsal pancreas and their duct system, the duct of Wirsung becomes the major duct, and the duct of Santorini usually regresses with the minor papilla in approximately 90% of people. Failure of the two ductal systems to unite results in the anatomic variant known as pancreas divisum. In this disorder, the duct of Wirsung is very small, and the duct of Santorini becomes the major ductal system and maintains communication with the duodenum through the minor papilla. This configuration is found in 4% to 11% of cadavers and in 3.25% of patients undergoing endoscopic retrograde cholangiopancreatography (ERCP).

Congenital Short Pancreas

Congenital shortening of the pancreas is an unusual anomaly that has been described in individuals with polysplenia syndrome,[75] as well as being an isolated anomaly.[162] It has also been seen in conjoined twins with a shared duodenum. In this condition, the pancreas appears blunted and lacks tissue in the region of the body and tail, which is believed to be caused by agenesis of the dorsal pancreatic bud.[75,162] Pancreatic function generally remains normal despite partial absence of the pancreatic parenchyma.[84]

SURGICAL ANATOMY

The pancreas is composed of a head, body, and tail, although these areas have no distinct anatomic borders. The head sits to the right on L2, the body covers L1, and the tail rises to T12 on the left. The abdominal aorta and vena cava provide some cushioning effect against the vertebrae; however, certain forces (such as seat-belt and steering wheel injuries) can cause blunt trauma to the body of the pancreas.

Virtually all of the pancreas is extraperitoneal. Anatomic continuity is established by peritoneal reflections from the transverse mesocolon, small intestinal mesentery, and the splenorenal and phrenicolic ligaments. Thus, mesenteric planes exist for the direct spread of extravasated pancreatic enzymes.[132] These anatomic relationships are important for understanding the pathophysiology of the various radiographic signs seen in patients with acute pancreatitis.

The splenic artery provides most of the blood supply to the pancreas and lies along its superior border with the splenic vein. It seems that the blood supply is generally greatest to the head of the pancreas. The head of the pancreas shares its blood supply with the duodenum through the superior and inferior pancreaticoduodenal arteries, which may complicate surgery on the head of the pancreas. Blood to the pancreas drains in a posterior direction into the superior mesenteric vein via small, delicate branches.

Several anomalies of the pancreatic (third) part of the common bile duct have been noted: (1) the bile duct may be partly covered by a tongue of the pancreas (44%), (2) the bile duct may be completely covered by the pancreas (30%), (3) the posterior surface of the bile duct may be uncovered (16.5%), and (4) the bile duct may be covered by two tongues of the pancreas (9%). Surgeons must be aware of these variants during surgery involving the head of the pancreas.[166]

PANCREATITIS

Pancreatitis is uncommon during childhood; however, it must be considered in every child with unexplained acute or recurrent abdominal pain. The prognosis in children is generally good, with the exception of pancreatitis occurring with multiorgan failure. Regardless of the cause, certain common features are found in all types of pancreatitis. However, because numerous disease entities can cause pancreatitis, patient management must be highly individualized.

Acute Pancreatitis

Clinically, acute pancreatitis is defined as a single or recurrent episodes of abdominal pain associated with elevated serum pancreatic enzyme levels. The morphologic correlate is acute focal or diffuse swelling and inflammation of the pancreas. Resolution of symptoms and normalization of blood biochemistry and anatomic abnormalities follow an acute episode. A continuum exists between acute and chronic pancreatitis; as a result, recurrent episodes of acute pancreatitis may evolve into the typical clinical and morphologic features of chronic pancreatitis.

Etiology

Although pancreatitis in adults is usually related to alcohol abuse or biliary tract disease, in children the causes are more diverse.[150,175,191,207,214] Most cases of acute pancreatitis in children result from systemic infection, trauma, choledocholithiasis, anomalies of the pancreaticobiliary duct system, and drugs (Table 107-2).[153,175] Less common causes include idiopathic disease, metabolic disorders, and miscellaneous conditions such as familial pancreatitis and Crohn's disease.[153,175]

Six percent to 33% of cases of pancreatitis are related to disorders of the biliary or pancreatic duct,[23,40,180,191,207,214] with choledochal cyst and cholelithiasis being the most common. A choledochal cyst is often associated with malunion of the pancreatic and biliary ducts (pancreaticobiliary malunion), and a long common channel may form and permit reflux of bile into the pancreatic duct.[126,17] The common channel is seen easily on ERCP; this channel is often dilated and contains protein plugs

TABLE 107-2 Causes of Acute Pancreatitis in Children

Systemic infection
Mumps
Rubella
Coxsackie B virus
Trauma
Blunt abdominal trauma
Iatrogenic (e.g., surgery, ERCP)
Anomalies of the pancreaticobiliary duct system
Pancreaticobiliary malunion
Pancreas divisum
Hypertensive sphincter of Oddi
Choledochal cyst
Choledocholithiasis
Drugs
Azathioprine
Tetracycline
L-Asparaginase
Immunosuppressants
Valproic acid
Metabolic abnormalities
Hypertriglyceridemia
Hypercalcemia
Cystic fibrosis
Liver transplantation
Miscellaneous
Idiopathic

ERCP, endoscopic retrograde cholangiopancreatography.

or stones, which may cause obstructive pancreatitis or jaundice.

Cholelithiasis in children is frequently associated with various hemolytic disorders, including spherocytosis, β-thalassemia, and sickle cell disease. It may also be caused by obesity and the use of total parenteral nutrition.[5] The role of pancreatic duct anomalies, such as pancreatic divisum and stenosis of the ampulla of Vater, has only recently been appreciated.[26,28,66,125,154,181,214] Pancreaticobiliary malunion not associated with a choledochal cyst is drawing clinical attention because it tends to be overlooked on ultrasonography (US); most patients with the disorder have recurrent abdominal pain as a result of pancreatitis.[107,125,181,202] Tagge et al.[181] found ductal anomalies in 6 of 61 (10%) patients with pancreatitis. They noted that patients with ductal abnormalities usually had recurrent episodes and that relapsing or chronic pancreatitis was also associated with ductal anomalies.

Severe abdominal trauma may cause immediate acute symptoms.[198] However, less severe trauma may result in a delayed onset and subacute manifestation. Child abuse should be considered in all children with acute pancreatitis who have a vague history.[214] Finally, trauma may also be iatrogenically induced during the course of abdominal surgery or ERCP.[163]

Drugs cause 8% to 25% of cases of pancreatitis. The use of certain immunosuppressive drugs can be associated with acute pancreatitis; however, in our experience, this type of acute pancreatitis responds well to gabexate mesylate, but it must be used in large doses and be administered early. Drugs that cause pancreatitis most frequently include didanosine, azathioprine, mercaptopurine, L-asparaginase, and valproic acid.[62,118,180,190,206,207] Recently, liver transplantation has been reported as a possible cause of acute pancreatitis. The incidence of this complication and the mortality rate in children were 1.9% and 43%, respectively.[186] A strong association between the development of acute pancreatitis after liver transplantation and several risk factors, such as the diagnosis of fulminant hepatic failure, retransplantation, extensive dissection at the time of liver transplantation, and the use of infrarenal arterial grafts, has been reported.[41]

Certain variants of the trypsinogen gene and cystic fibrosis transmembrane regulation (*CFTR*) gene may cause acute recurrent pancreatitis. Many patients with the diagnosis of idiopathic pancreatitis have compound heterozygote genotypes in which both alleles of the *CFTR* gene are abnormal, thus constituting a variant of cystic fibrosis. There are also numerous reports of an association between chronic pancreatitis and a number of *CFTR* mutations both in patients with cystic fibrosis and in carriers with a single mutation.[22,117,215]

In certain conditions, destruction of the pancreas begins antenatally. Infants with Shwachman-Diamond syndrome, an autosomal recessive disorder recently mapped to the centromeric region of chromosome 7,[58] have pancreatic insufficiency at birth, generally with very low serum trypsinogen levels, indicative of nearly total exocrine pancreatic atrophy by birth.[38]

Diagnosis

The diagnosis of acute pancreatitis is based on the clinical history, physical examination, results of laboratory tests, and the findings of diagnostic imaging investigations. Determination of amylase isoenzymes has also been used to increase diagnostic accuracy by identifying the tissue from which the amylase originates. Serum lipase levels may also complement pancreatitis testing and increase the yield of positive diagnoses.[68] A new scoring system for acute pancreatitis has been proposed that has better sensitivity than the Ranson and Glasgow scores do.[31] The parameters are age (<7 years), weight (<23 kg), admission white blood cell count (>18,500), admission lactate dehydrogenase level (>2000), 48-hour trough Ca^{2+} level (<8.3 mg/dL), 48-hour trough albumin level (<2.6 g/dL), 48-hour fluid sequestration (>75 ml/kg/48 hr), and 48-hour rise in blood urea nitrogen (>5 mg/dL).

Plain radiographs of the chest and abdomen are obtained to exclude intestinal perforation.[150,153] Occasionally, radiopaque gallstones, a gas-filled right colon, or a distended loop of small intestine (sentinel loop) may be seen. Left basal pleural effusion is relatively common, and mottling of the lung field is a sign of systemic cytokine release. Radiographic studies enhanced by water-soluble contrast of the upper gastrointestinal tract are occasionally useful, particularly in cases of trauma when injury to the duodenum or small intestine is strongly suspected.

US and computed tomography (CT) are useful for detecting pancreatic abnormalities.[59,91] Trauma-induced injuries to abdominal organs, particularly the pancreas, are readily detected on CT.

ERCP is rarely indicated for acute pancreatitis; however, it eventually becomes essential in any child who has pancreatitis with an unclear cause.[28,66,125,181] This technique is very useful in cases of relapsing pancreatitis associated with pancreaticobiliary malunion.[28,66,99,125,181]

ERCP is, however, an invasive method that can aggravate the pancreatitis and is often not an option during the acute phase of pancreatitis. Magnetic resonance cholangiopancreatography (MRCP) is a noninvasive method of obtaining images of the pancreaticobiliary tract. MRCP images the common bile duct in more than 96% of patients and detects common bile duct stones with a sensitivity of 71% to 100%, thus exceeding the sensitivity of US (20% to 65%) and CT (45% to 85%). Visualization of the smaller pancreatic duct is successful in more than 80% of patients.[83] We previously evaluated the efficacy of MRCP in pediatric patients with acute pancreatitis.[164] Patients were divided into two groups: group 1 consisted of seven patients in whom choledochal cysts were sonographically diagnosed, and group 2 consisted of nine patients with no obvious cause of acute pancreatitis. Pancreaticobiliary malunion was detected in six of seven in group 1 and in one of nine in group 2. Pancreatic divisum was detected in one patient in group 1 but could not be confirmed in any of group 2. Dilatation of the main pancreatic duct was detected in one in group 1 and in three in group 2. These findings indicate that MRCP is a potentially useful method for identifying and ruling out structural abnormalities of the pancreaticobiliary tract in children.

Treatment

Treatment of acute pancreatitis has two primary goals: (1) to minimize any causative factors and (2) to provide meticulous supportive care, including liberal use of analgesics, administration of parenteral fluids, maintenance of nutrition, prevention of infection, and inhibition of endocrine and exocrine activity.

Parenteral analgesia with narcotics or nonsteroidal anti-inflammatory agents is generally required, even in mild cases of pancreatitis, because the pain can be extreme. It is traditional to administer meperidine rather than morphine because the latter produces ampullary spasm.

Nasogastric suction is usually initiated to reduce vomiting and abdominal distention; however, unless the patient is vomiting, the value of nasogastric decompression is questionable.[48] Aspiration of gastric acid also may reduce pancreatic exocrine secretion by limiting the release of secretin.

Oral feeding must be withheld to reduce pancreatic stimulation. Total parenteral nutrition should be initiated early to avoid malnutrition.[165] In addition, early placement of a central venous catheter in patients with severe disease will provide access for aggressive intravascular volume support and nutrition.

The hematocrit and serum levels of glucose and calcium should be measured, and hourly urine output should be monitored carefully.

Although the advantages of prophylactic antibiotics have not been proved, patients with necrotizing pancreatitis may benefit.[44] Other treatment strategies involving somatostatin, glucagon, anticholinergics, histamine blockers, and protease inhibitors have been recommended,[19] but to date they have not shown conclusive benefit.

Standard medical treatment must be used in patients with acute pancreatitis in an attempt to control the disorder before surgical intervention, which is rarely required in children but is occasionally performed if the diagnosis is uncertain or a complication develops after an acute episode, such as a pseudocyst or an abscess. Patients with acute pancreatitis associated with underlying pancreaticobiliary disease generally require surgical correction of the underlying condition before cure can be expected.[153]

In the management of severe acute pancreatitis, a major decision is whether and when surgery for pancreatic necrosis or infection is necessary. Infection of necrotic pancreatic tissue is the major risk factor for mortality in severe acute pancreatitis and is an indication for surgery. On the other hand, there is support for nonsurgical conservative management of sterile pancreatic necrosis, including antibiotic treatment. The reported death rate is 1.8% with sterile pancreatic necrosis and 24% with infected necrosis.[20] Early surgery has been associated with increased mortality and should be delayed, if not avoided.[146]

Chronic Relapsing Pancreatitis

Chronic relapsing pancreatitis is characterized by recurrent episodes of upper abdominal pain associated with varying degrees of pancreatic exocrine and endocrine dysfunction. Relatively few reports of chronic relapsing pancreatitis in childhood exist, although it is more frequently being suspected in children with recurrent episodes of abdominal pain.[30,43,54,92,138] The disease produces a wide variation of progressive and irreversible structural changes in the pancreas.[54] At present, the most controversial aspect of treatment of this disorder is the choice of an appropriate surgical procedure.

Causes and Pathophysiology

In children, the most common causes of chronic relapsing pancreatitis are trauma,[60,179] heredity,[13,161] systemic disease,[50] and malformations of the pancreaticobiliary duct such as pancreas divisum,[2] annular pancreas,[34] and choledocholithiasis.[72] In addition, various unusual conditions, including metabolic disease, endocrine disorders, and inflammatory bowel disease,[13] may cause the disorder. Causes of chronic relapsing pancreatitis are listed in Table 107-3.

Certain congenital anomalies affect the pancreas and surrounding tissue,[2,26,28,34,66,72,125] several of which are associated with chronic relapsing pancreatitis. Obstruction of pancreatic flow caused by a stenotic papilla of Vater and bile reflux resulting from a common channel are believed to be responsible for the resultant inflammation, which may be reversible if the obstruction is relieved. A relatively common cause of relapsing pancreatitis is pancreas divisum,[2] in which most of the pancreatic fluid flows through the minor duct of Santorini, with the possibility

TABLE 107-3 Causes of Chronic Relapsing Pancreatitis in Children

- Congenital anomalies of the pancreatic duct
  - Pancreaticobiliary malunion
  - Pancreas divisum
  - Annular pancreas
- Biliary tract disorders
  - Choledocholithiasis
  - Cholelithiasis
- Trauma
- Systemic infection
- Hereditary pancreatitis
- Hyperlipoproteinemia
- Hyperparathyroidism and hypercalcemia
- Cystic fibrosis
- Inborn errors of metabolism
- Chronic inflammatory conditions
  - Crohn's disease
  - Ulcerative colitis
  - Systemic lupus erythematosus
- Chronic fibrosing pancreatitis
- Juvenile tropical pancreatitis
- Idiopathic chronic pancreatitis

of reactive obstruction to flow because of anatomy and flow dynamics. Some series have reported an increased incidence of pancreas divisum in patients with idiopathic chronic pancreatitis.[2,28] Annular pancreas, which results from an error of rotation or fixation of the embryologic pancreatic primordium, has also been associated with chronic pancreatitis (Fig. 107-1).[34] Pancreaticobiliary malunion with or without choledocholithiasis may likewise result in relapsing chronic pancreatitis.[107,125,181]

In the last few years, several genes have been identified as being associated with hereditary and idiopathic chronic pancreatitis: *PRSS1*, *CFTR*, and *SPINK1*. *SPINK1* mutations were found predominantly in patients without a family history. These mutations were most common in those with idiopathic chronic pancreatitis, whereas patients with hereditary chronic pancreatitis predominantly had *PRSS1* mutations.[211]

Diagnosis

Blood Biochemistry: The degree of permanent damage to the pancreas may be assessed by blood tests (pancreatic enzymes), stool tests (pancreatic enzymes, fecal fat), and noninvasive tests of pancreatic function, such as the pancreatic stimulation (secretin) test.

Diagnostic Imaging: In 30% to 50% of adolescents and adults with chronic pancreatitis, plain radiographs of the abdomen reveal pancreatic calcification. Calcification is diagnostic of chronic pancreatitis, even if clinical evidence of pancreatic disease is absent. However, the incidence of calcification in children with chronic relapsing pancreatitis is low, except in younger children with hereditary pancreatitis, in whom the incidence is high.[13]

US is ideal for examining the pancreas in children. Dilatation of the pancreatic or biliary tracts may be noted, and calcification and complications such as pseudocysts, abscesses, calculi, and ascites can be seen. CT is useful for visualizing the size of the pancreas and its ducts (Fig. 107-2) and for detecting small calculi that may be missed on plain radiographs and US. ERCP is an important tool in the diagnosis and management of chronic relapsing pancreatitis in adults and children.[26,28,30,66] Pancreaticobiliary malunion with or without dilatation of the bile duct may be detected.[66,70,181] ERCP is up to 90% accurate in diagnosing ductal abnormalities. However, as described earlier, MRCP has been greatly refined in the past decade. MRCP is considered to be equivalent to ERCP for the diagnosis of many pancreatic and biliary conditions and is preferable because it is noninvasive and safer.[83,164]

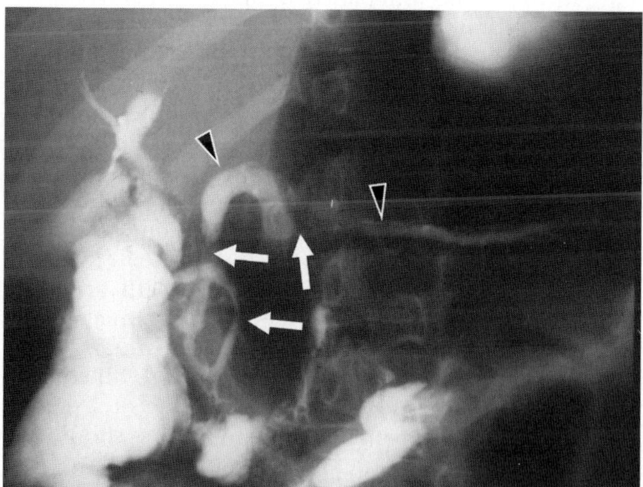

Figure 107-1 Preoperative endoscopic retrograde cholangiopancreatography in a patient with an annular pancreas. A complex anomaly of the pancreatic duct with dilatation (*arrowheads*) and stenosis (*arrows*) is shown. The patient underwent a longitudinal pancreaticojejunostomy (Puestow) procedure.

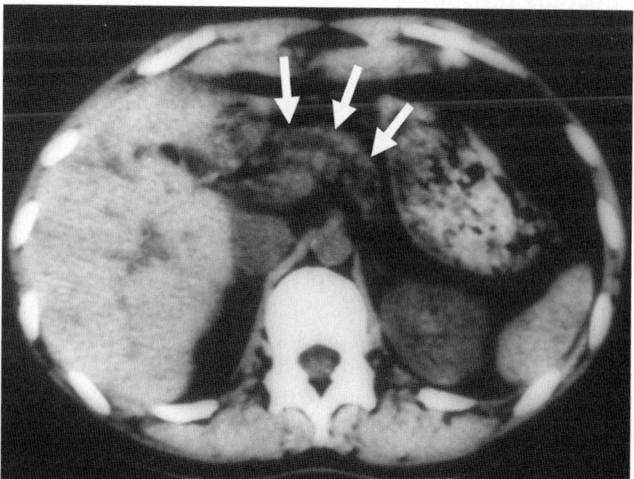

Figure 107-2 Computed tomographic scan of a patient with an irregularly dilated pancreatic duct (*arrows*). The patient underwent a longitudinal pancreaticojejunostomy (Puestow) procedure.

Surgical Treatment

Surgery for chronic relapsing pancreatitis is done to relieve pain, treat complications, or both. Surgery on the pancreas is generally of three types: (1) sphincteroplasty,[89,133,154] (2) pancreatic drainage via longitudinal pancreaticojejunostomy (Puestow)[148] or end-to-end pancreaticojejunostomy (Duval),[39] or (3) pancreatogastrostomy (Smith)[167] and pancreatectomy.[49]

Several groups of investigators have attested to the success of sphincteroplasty in controlling the symptoms of chronic pancreatitis in carefully selected patients.[52,133] Correct use of this procedure, however, demands that intrapancreatic ductal obstruction be ruled out by pancreatography. O'Neill and colleagues[138] reported good results in six of seven children who underwent sphincteroplasty for chronic pancreatitis.

The general indication for the use of a direct ductal decompression procedure is evidence of pancreatic ductal ectasia with multiple intrapancreatic duct strictures. An important secondary feature of drainage procedures is preservation of existing endocrine function by avoiding major pancreatic resection. Longitudinal pancreaticojejunostomy (Puestow technique) in adults has been successful in eliminating or ameliorating pain from chronic pancreatitis in 70% to 97% of patients.[147,167,204,208,209] In children, some authors maintain that the Puestow procedure improves pancreatic function, decreases hospitalization, and increases body weight toward ideal.[35] Others have reported that distal pancreatectomy and pancreaticojejunostomy are effective whereas longitudinal pancreaticojejunostomy is ineffective.[205] Regarding appropriate operative procedures, further consideration is warranted in pediatric cases.

Subtotal or total pancreatectomy is associated with considerable morbidity and mortality and is reserved for patients with intractable pain who have diffuse parenchymal damage without duct dilatation.[67] The procedure is not generally indicated in children.

Pancreas Divisum

The embryology of this entity was described in the first section of this chapter. Pancreas divisum is suspected on MRCP or ERCP when the duct of Wirsung fails to be visualized after injection of the major papilla or when it is attenuated and rudimentary. MRCP is a useful and noninvasive diagnostic tool for pancreas divisum (Fig. 107-3),[164] but ERCP can provide detailed information on the pancreatic duct. If pancreas divisum is suspected after injection of the papilla of Vater, an attempt should be made to find and cannulate the minor papilla, but this is possible in less than half the cases because of its small size and the angle at which it meets the duodenum. If the minor papilla can be entered, ERCP will demonstrate that the duct of Santorini is the dominant duct and that it extends the entire length of the body and tail of the pancreas. Imaging of the duct of Santorini occasionally demonstrates dilatation, irregularity, or stricture suggestive of chronic pancreatitis.

Autopsy studies have suggested that pancreas divisum, which is found in 4% to 11% of patients, is the most

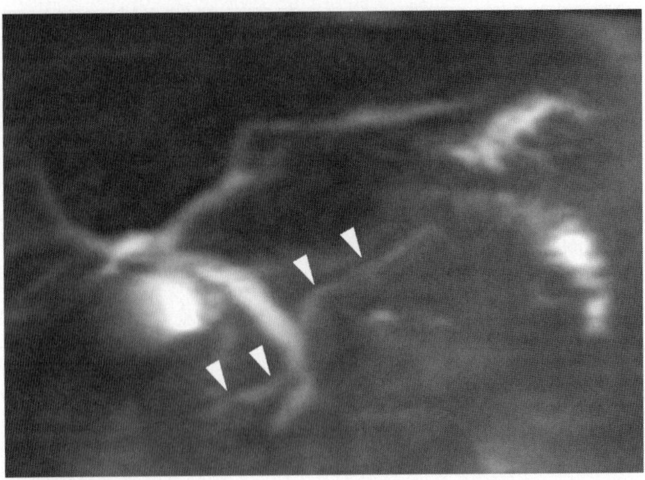

Figure 107-3 Magnetic resonance cholangiopancreatography in a patient with recurrent pancreatitis. The duct of Santorini is the dominant duct, and it extends the entire length of the body and tail of the pancreas (*arrowheads*).

common congenital anomaly of the pancreas. When absence of the duct of Wirsung is associated with pancreas divisum, approximately 10% of affected patients have anomalous anatomy resulting in most or all of the pancreatic secretions draining by means of the accessory papilla.[200]

Pancreas divisum should not be regarded as a disease. However, if the orifice of the accessory papilla is stenotic, pancreatitis can result. Stenosis of the minor papilla is probably developmental because the orifice is usually very small with no evidence of inflammation. The incidence of pancreas divisum may be significantly higher in patients with unexplained recurrent pancreatitis, and it was detected in up to 25% of patients in one series.[28] Neblett and O'Neill recently reported that pancreas divisum was identified in 7.4% of all children with pancreatitis and 19.2% of children with relapsing or chronic pancreatitis. In 10 patients with pancreas divisum, 8 had complete pancreas divisum and 2 had incomplete variants.[134]

The primary goal of treatment of pancreas divisum associated with pancreatitis is to establish adequate drainage of the duct of Santorini. The progression of disease to pancreatic insufficiency can be arrested when the obstruction is relieved early. Correction may not only preserve pancreatic function but may also help ensure that normal growth and development occur.

Several reports have shown that adequate drainage of the duct of Santorini can be achieved with accessory papilla sphincteroplasty.[2,115,167,196,201] Endoscopic sphincterotomy has been performed, but restenosis and recurrence of symptoms have been reported.[93] If chronic pancreatitis has developed in the presence of a dilated duct, longitudinal pancreaticojejunostomy should be performed.[138,148] Neblett and O'Neill[134] reported that 8 of 10 patients with pancreas divisum underwent surgery: 7 underwent transduodenal sphincteroplasty of the accessory papilla, along with sphincteroplasty of the major papilla in 2 (plus septoplasty in 1). Three patients underwent longitudinal pancreaticojejunostomy, as a primary procedure in one patient with mid-ductal stenosis and in two because of recurring pancreatitis after sphincteroplasty without endocrine and exocrine pancreatic insufficiency. Surgical intervention is directed toward relief of ductal obstruction and may involve accessory duct sphincteroplasty alone or in conjunction with major sphincteroplasty and septoplasty. Patients with more distal ductal obstruction or ductal ectasia may benefit from pancreaticojejunostomy. In an extremely rare case, we treated a patient with coexistence of pancreas divisum, choledochal cyst, and pancreaticobiliary malunion. Figure 107-4 shows the preoperative ERCP and intraoperative cholangiogram. This patient underwent complete excision of the choledochal cyst with a Roux-en-Y hepaticojejunostomy, followed by transduodenal papilloplasty to allow complete drainage of the common channel.[106]

CYSTS AND PSEUDOCYSTS

Pancreatic cysts are relatively unusual in children. The causes of these cysts tend to be diverse and include both congenital and acquired conditions.[199] Pancreatic cysts can be classified as congenital and developmental, retention, enteric duplication, and pseudocysts.

Congenital and Developmental Forms

Congenital and developmental cysts of the pancreas are very rare and may be encountered in a fetus, infant, child, or adult.[3] Only 22 cases have been reported in the pediatric literature to date.[7,8,124,143] These cysts have a female preponderance. They are most common in the body and tail of the pancreas, are more often unilocular than multilocular, and are lined with epithelium. The cysts are usually filled with a cloudy, yellow sterile fluid that has no enzyme activity, and they are remarkably free of adhesions and infection. They have been reported to occur simultaneously in other organs; for example, von Hippel-Lindau disease is characterized by hereditary cerebellar cysts, retinal hemangiomas, and cysts of the pancreas and other organs.[79] The cysts that occur with cystic fibrosis are not considered pancreatic pseudocysts and are not discussed in this chapter.

Clinically, congenital and developmental cysts are detected as an incidental finding or as polyhydramnios in the prenatal period. After birth, they may be manifested as asymptomatic abdominal distention, as vomiting or jaundice caused by extrinsic pressure on neighboring organs, or as an asymptomatic mass. Surgical treatment consists of total excision of cysts located in the pancreatic body or tail and internal drainage of those in the head of the pancreas.

Retention Cysts

Retention cysts of the pancreas are rare and believed to result from chronic obstruction of the gland.[111] They contain cloudy fluid composed of pancreatic exocrine secretions and a high concentration of pancreatic enzymes. Such cysts are lined with ductal epithelium

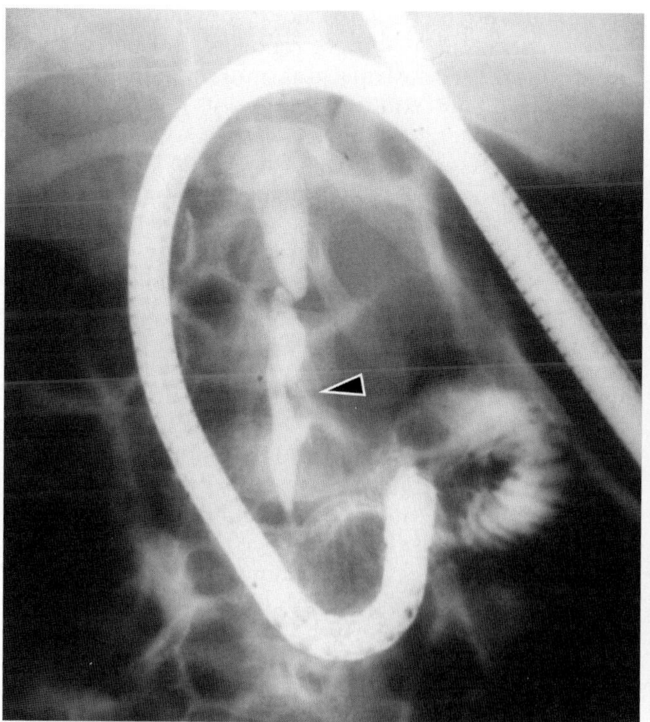

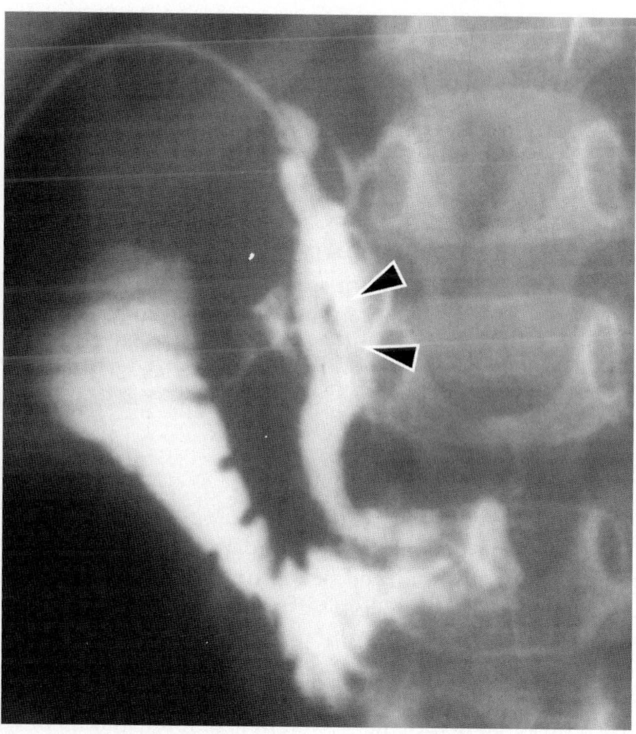

Figure 107-4 (*A*) Preoperative endoscopic retrograde cholangiopancreatography and (*B*) intraoperative cholangiogram in a patient with a choledochal cyst associated with pancreas divisum. The septum (*arrowheads*) in the intrapancreatic bile duct is also seen.

unless it has been destroyed by chronic dilatation or inflammation from enzyme exposure.[140]

Enteric Duplications

Enteric duplication involving the pancreas is rare and usually associated with gastric duplication.[136] This duplication is most likely to result from failure of regression of an enteric diverticulum formed from the pancreatic duct.[5] Many of the reported cases of enteric duplication involving the pancreas communicate with the pancreatic duct, are lined with gastric-type epithelium, and contain ectopic pancreatic tissue in their walls.

The most common symptom in these patients is recurrent abdominal pain, often postprandial. Pancreatitis associated with enteric duplication cysts is believed to be caused by obstruction of the pancreatic ducts by viscous secretions from the cyst or by blood and debris from peptic ulceration within the cyst.[112,187] In patients without pancreatitis, pain may be caused by tension on the wall of the cyst as a result of accumulation of secretions and muscular contraction.[121]

Pancreatic cysts have also been noted on fetal US.[101]

To date, all duplication cysts in the literature have been treated by extirpation, and some have required pancreaticoduodenectomy and internal drainage.[112]

Pseudocysts

Clinical Features

Pancreatic pseudocysts are localized collections of pancreatic secretions that do not have an epithelial lining and develop after pancreatic injury, inflammation, or duct obstruction.[79] The most common causes of pseudocysts in children are trauma and infection.[123] Drug-induced acute pancreatitis, such as with valproic acid, is also a rare cause of pancreatic pseudocyst.[149]

These cysts typically lie in the lesser sac behind the stomach and are composed of a fibrous capsule surrounded by inflamed connective tissue.[15] The capsule of the cyst may also be formed by neighboring tissue, such as the stomach, duodenum, colon, small intestine, or omentum. Cyst fluid is clear or straw colored in most cases and may contain toothpaste-like debris. The amylase level of cyst fluid is typically higher than 50,000 Somogyi U/mL.[145]

Diagnosis

The presence of a pancreatic pseudocyst is suggested by a history of blunt abdominal trauma, an illness resembling pancreatitis, followed by a symptom-free interval of weeks to months, or palpation of a mass in the epigastrium or left upper quadrant.

Abdominal pain is the most common symptom, with jaundice, chest pain, signs of gastric obstruction, vomiting, gastrointestinal hemorrhage, weight loss, fever, and ascites also being features.

US, CT, and magnetic resonance imaging are helpful and accurate in diagnosis. These studies are also invaluable for evaluating the thickness of the cyst wall and for observing changes in the cyst during the ensuing period of treatment (Fig. 107-5).[14,48,59,97] ERCP is often useful because it can definitively determine the status of the pancreatic duct and thus guide surgical interventions.[97,151,152,192]

Treatment

Optimal management of a pancreatic pseudocyst remains controversial. Treatment options range from conservative medical management to surgical drainage.[114,158,198] Conventional management involves supportive therapy over a 6-week waiting period, during which time either the cyst resolves spontaneously or the cyst wall undergoes fibrous maturation, thereby permitting internal surgical drainage to the stomach or jejunum.[156,195] This 6-week interval is what has traditionally been accepted, but CT may demonstrate thickening of the cyst wall sufficient to hold sutures as early as 3 to 4 weeks. Surgical drainage is usually performed in adults when necessary but is controversial in children because most pancreatic pseudocysts in this group resolve without surgical intervention and have a low risk for recurrence.[14,144]

Octreotide acetate, a long-acting analogue of somatostatin, has been shown to be successful in reducing exocrine function after pancreatic surgery and more recently in the management of pancreatic pseudocysts.[131]

A significant risk for complications, such as infection or major hemorrhage in untreated pseudocysts or persistence of severe symptoms, may be an indication for earlier intervention. If the patent cannot withstand major surgery, external surgical drainage is preferred.[139] There is significant evidence indicating that internal drainage, especially transgastric cystogastrostomy, is effective in the treatment of pancreatic pseudocyst.[90] In contrast to this approach, others[45,85,94] have reported that percutaneous drainage and endoscopic transmural drainage are safe and efficient procedures. However, it is generally recognized that external drainage carries a higher risk for complications such as fistula formation and a higher recurrence rate than internal drainage does.[25,42] Transgastric cystogastrostomy cannot be accomplished until the wall of the pseudocyst has matured.[96] Recent studies have shown that drainage should be performed in patients with pseudocysts that are more than 6 weeks old and have a diameter larger than 5 cm because a large proportion of pseudocysts regress during the first 6 weeks after diagnosis and the risks associated with managing the pseudocyst are reduced.[96]

Though less commonly used than other operative procedures, cystoduodenostomy seems to be indicated and may be effective when a cyst is closely adherent to the duodenum.[71,157,212] Roux-en-Y cystojejunostomy is the most widely used internal drainage procedure for this problem and is associated with the lowest rate of complications and recurrence.[159]

Either pancreaticoduodenectomy or distal pancreatectomy, as indicated, is effective in treating patients with pseudocysts under ideal circumstances.[145] Distal pancreatic resection is indicated in patients with a pseudocyst in the body or tail of the pancreas associated with multiple small cysts.[212]

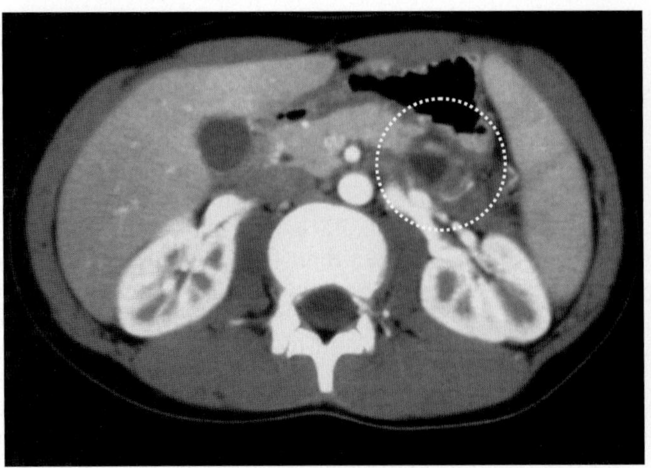

A

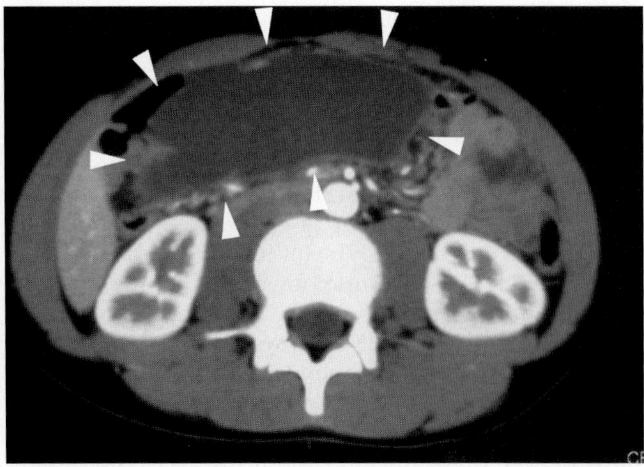

B

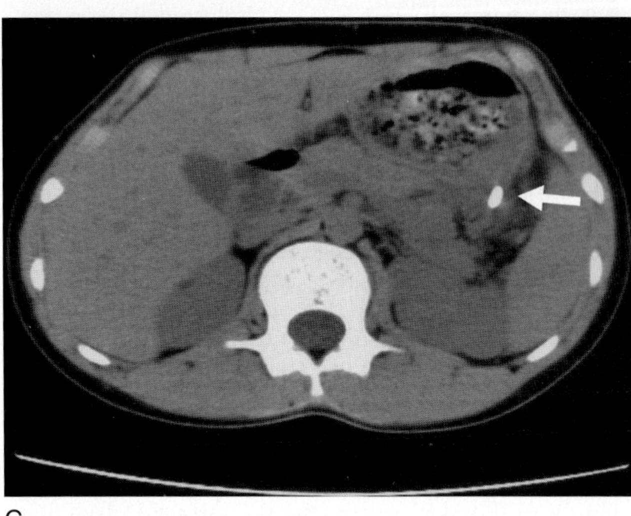

C

Figure 107-5 Computed tomographic scans of a post-traumatic pseudocyst in the abdomen of a 12-year-old boy. *A*, The pancreas body is interrupted (*dotted circle*). *B*, A large cyst (*arrowheads*) developed 2 weeks after injury. *C*, Percutaneous external drainage (*arrow*) was performed.

Cysts involving the head and uncinate process of the pancreas that are not amenable to internal drainage are rare and may require proximal pancreatic resection, but such resection should be done only as a last resort.[48,129,151,152]

HYPERINSULINISM

Hypoglycemia in infants and children has many causes. In newborns, prompt evaluation and treatment are essential because persistent hypoglycemia may result in permanent brain damage. The role of the pancreas in hypoglycemia has been postulated since 1921, when Banting and Best[9] isolated insulin as the active hormone. When blood glucose falls to hypoglycemic levels in normal individuals, simultaneous serum insulin levels are low; however, insulin levels are inappropriately elevated in these individuals in the presence of hypoglycemia. In less than 5 years, this disorder, formerly termed nesidioblastosis or persistent hyperinsulinemic hypoglycemia of infancy (PHHI), has been defined at the molecular, genetic, and clinical level, thereby permitting a rational approach to classification, diagnosis, treatment, and prognosis (Table 107-4).[168]

Pathophysiology

Pancreatic insulin secretion is a complex, highly integrated process regulated by nutrients, hormones, and the autonomic nervous system. These signals target the pancreatic beta cell, where insulin secretion is ultimately

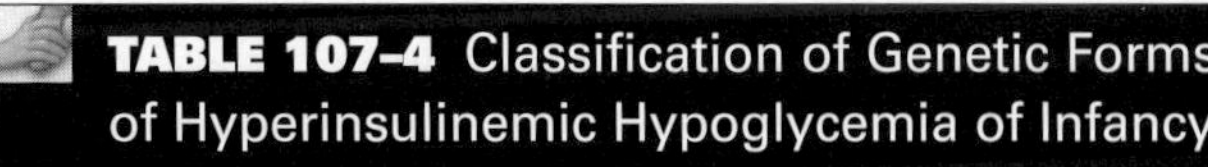

TABLE 107-4 Classification of Genetic Forms of Hyperinsulinemic Hypoglycemia of Infancy

K_{ATP} channel defects
SUR1 mutations
Kir6.2 mutations
Loss of heterozygosity
Glucokinase-activating mutation
Glutamate dehydrogenase–activating mutation
Undefined
Autosomal dominant
Autosomal recessive
Sporadic
Beckwith-Wiedemann syndrome
Beta-cell adenoma—multiple endocrine neoplasia type I

regulated by an adenosine triphosphate (ATP)–sensitive potassium channel (K_{ATP}) that controls the polarity of the beta cell membrane. The molar ratio of ATP to adenosine diphosphate (ADP) maintains patency of the K_{ATP} channel and permits efflux of potassium from its normally high intracellular concentration to the extracellular environment so that the cell membrane remains polarized. The pancreatic K_{ATP} channel consists of two protein subunits—the sulfonylurea receptor 1 (SUR1) and the inward rectifying potassium channel Kir6.2, whose distinct genes are located at adjacent loci on chromosome 11 (11p15.1).[4,141] Glucose transported into the beta cell by the insulin-independent glucose transporter GLUT2 undergoes phosphorylation by glucokinase and is then metabolized, which results in an increase in the ATP/ADP ratio. An increase in the ATP/ADP ratio closes the K_{ATP} channel and initiates the cascade of events characterized by an increase in intracellular potassium concentration, membrane depolarization, calcium influx, and release of insulin from storage granules. Mutations of these genes are responsible for familial forms of PHHI. Activating mutations in glucokinase and glutamate dehydrogenase stimulate insulin secretion at inappropriately low glucose concentrations, thereby producing hypoglycemia with inappropriate hyperinsulinemia.[57,173] The gene for glucokinase has been localized to chromosome 7.

Most cases of autosomal recessive PHHI are caused by mutations in the *SUR1/Kir6.2* genes,[135,183,184] whereas the autosomal dominant form of PHHI is not caused by such mutations. Currently, there are two known causes of autosomal dominant PHHI. One form is ascribed to a gain-of-function mutation in the glucokinase gene.[57] Another cause of autosomal dominant PHHI is an activating mutation in the gene coding for the mitochondrial glutamate dehydrogenase enzyme.[173]

The majority of cases of PHHI, that is, probably more than 95% in the general population, are sporadic PHHI. Focal PHHI represents 30% to 40% of reported cases, with the remaining 60% to 70% having a diffuse phenotype.[32,194] Focal PHHI is characterized by focal adenomatous hyperplasia of islet-like cells, with small beta cell nuclei packed closely together. In contrast, in diffuse PHHI, the islets of Langerhans throughout the pancreas are irregular in size, with hypertrophied insulin-secreting cells containing large abnormal beta nuclei. A recent study showed loss of the maternal alleles in the p15 region of chromosome 11 and mutation in the K_{ATP} channel, which results in hyperinsulinism.[32] On the other hand, the etiology of the many cases of sporadic PHHI with the diffuse phenotype remains unclear.

Beckwith-Wiedemann syndrome is caused by a mutation in the chromosome 11p15.5 region, with duplications of this region implicated in its pathogenesis. It is generally thought that insulin-like growth factor type II (IGF-II) overexpression has an important role in somatic overgrowth and the development of embryonal tumors. To date, there have been no reports of mutations in the SUR1/Kir6.2 components of the K_{ATP} channel to explain the hyperinsulinemia and hypoglycemia associated with this syndrome.

Diagnosis

Diagnosis of hyperinsulinism is based on the following criteria: (1) inappropriately raised plasma insulin levels in relation to blood glucose levels measured at various times postprandially and during periods of fasting (e.g., insulin level greater than 10 μU/mL associated with a simultaneous glucose level less than 50 mg/dL), (2) a glucose infusion rate greater than 10 mg/kg/min required to maintain a blood glucose concentration above 35 mg/dL in the absence of glucosuria, (3) low plasma concentrations of free fatty acids and blood ketone bodies during hypoglycemia because insulin inhibits lipolysis and hence the production of ketone bodies, and (4) a glycemic response to glucagon despite hypoglycemia.

Hyperinsulinism associated with a functional defect in the K_{ATP} channel should be suspected in a macrosomic infant who does not possess the stigmata of Beckwith-Wiedemann syndrome and who was not born of a diabetic mother. In such infants, hypoglycemia may develop within hours or days of birth, thus making the diagnosis even more likely.

An alternative test is the measurement of IGF binding protein 1 (IGFBP1) levels at the time of hypoglycemia.[104] Secretion of IGFBP1 is actually inhibited by insulin, and IGFBP1 concentrations in serum are more stable than those of insulin. IGFBP1 levels rise during fasting in normal children and those with various endocrine or metabolic causes of hypoglycemia other than hyperinsulinism, whereas patients with PHHI have serum IGFBP1 concentrations approximately 10% to 20% of control values. Usually, these values are less than 50 ng/mL, as opposed to approximately 300 ng/mL in control populations. Thus, an inappropriately low concentration of IGFBP1 at the time of hypoglycemia in an infant or child is an additional marker of hyperinsulinism.

Percutaneous transhepatic portal and pancreatic vein catheterization with serial measurement of insulin, which has been used in adults,[82] has recently been under investigation for use in children. Glucose, insulin, and the insulin-to–peptide C ratio in the veins that drain each portion of the pancreas are measured to localize the lesions. These studies are limited in their usefulness because of the time involved in analysis.

Differential Diagnosis

The workup of a child with suspected hypoglycemia of pancreatic origin is complex (Fig. 107-6). The three major categories of hypoglycemia are hyperinsulinism, inborn errors of metabolism, and endocrine deficiencies. Endocrine disorders, such as adrenal insufficiency, panhypopituitarism, isolated growth hormone deficiency, hypothyroidism, and congenital adrenal hyperplasia, are usually identified by physical findings and specific hormonal assays. Hepatic causes must be considered when hepatomegaly is present.

Ketotic hypoglycemia is the most common cause in children younger than 1 year. It is suggested by a history of low birth weight, early morning symptoms after an

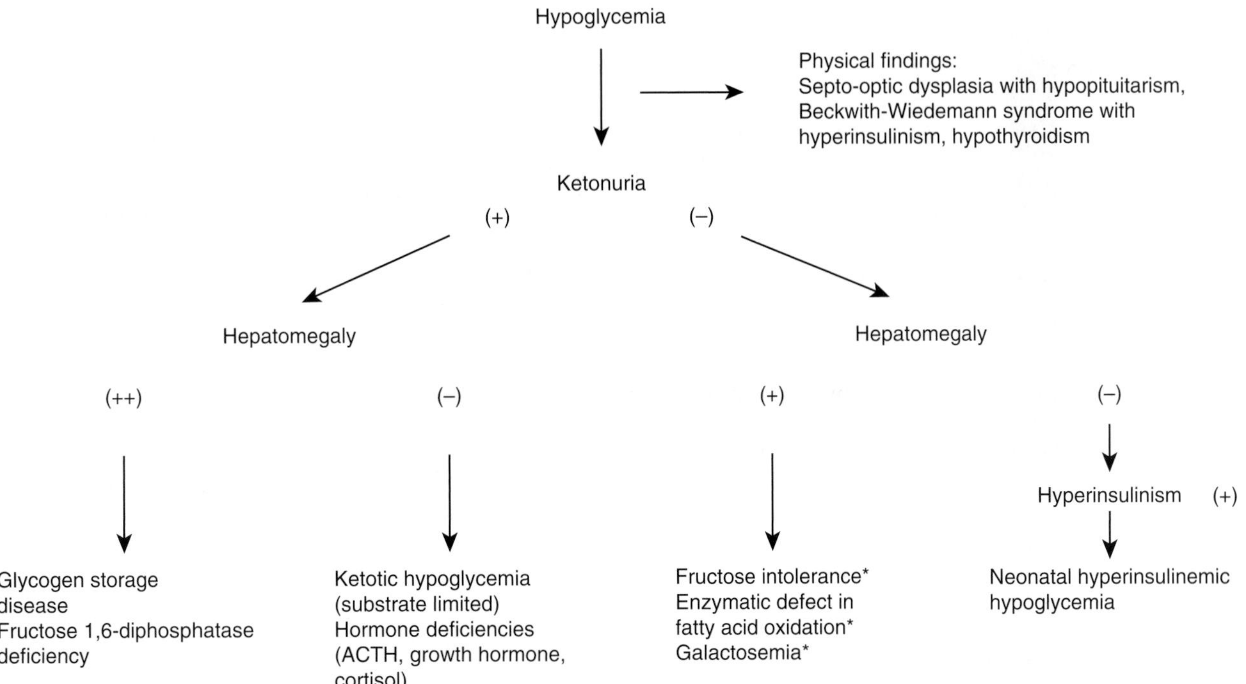

Figure 107–6 Schematic approach to the differential diagnosis of hypoglycemia. ACTH, adrenocorticotropic hormone.

overnight fast, and concomitant ketonemia and ketonuria. The specific biochemical workup of the various inborn errors of metabolism has been detailed by Stanley and Baker.[172] Hypoglycemic episodes in these children tend to resolve spontaneously with age. Beckwith-Wiedemann syndrome is often associated with hypoglycemia but resolves spontaneously with careful medical treatment.

Treatment

Medical Management

A correlation of clinical features with molecular defects in PHHI is presented in Table 107-5.[168]

Medical treatment involves providing 15% to 20% intravenous glucose to prevent hypoglycemia. The infusion should be continuous and regulated at the minimum rate required to maintain normoglycemia. Central venous catheters are frequently required.

Frequent feedings are given to provide a constant input of glucose. Several pharmacologic agents—diazoxide, octreotide, glucagon, and mesoxalyl urea—have been used.

Diazoxide is the mainstay of medical management. It acts to inhibit the SUR1 component of the K_{ATP} channel, thereby preventing closure of the potassium channel and leading to diminished insulin secretion. The usual starting dose is 8 to 10 mg/kg/day, and it is increased progressively until normoglycemia is achieved. The maximum dose is 15 to 20 mg/kg/day. The success rate has been established to range between 50% and 75%,[61,130] but in severely affected neonates, the success rate is lower than 50%. A lack of response to diazoxide may reflect the absence of functional pancreatic K_{ATP} channels, as seen in patients with mutations in the *SUR1/Kir6.2* genes. Calcium channel blockers, particularly the long-acting somatostatin analogue octreotide, may be more efficacious as medical therapy, with reports of success in as many as half of affected infants.[56,102,108,185] Failure of these methods of medical management, a common event, is a clear indication for surgical pancreatectomy in an attempt to avoid long-term neurologic sequelae.

Surgical Management

Patients unable to sustain a normal fasted blood glucose level despite optimal medical management should be offered surgery at an early stage to avoid the possibility of unrecognized hypoglycemia and resultant brain damage. The goal of the surgery is to reduce excessive insulin production, but the procedure is unphysiologic and inexact.[29,172] The current recommendation is a 95% resection with only a rim of tissue left on the duodenum and bile duct[98,103,113,170] rather than the traditional 75% resection (Fig. 107-7). Serum glucose levels are monitored closely throughout the operation. The procedure is performed through an upper abdominal transverse incision. The lesser sac is entered to expose and mobilize the entire pancreas, and a Kocher maneuver is performed on the duodenum. The pancreas is then closely inspected along its length for reddish brown nodular adenomas, which are extirpated and submitted for frozen section analysis. It is important to be

TABLE 107–5 Correlation of Clinical Features with Molecular Defects in Persistent Hyperinsulinemic Hypoglycemia in Infancy

Type	Macrosomia	Hypoglycemia/ Hyperinsulinemia	Family History	Molecular Defects	Associated Clinical, Biochemical, or Molecular Features	Response to Medical Management	Recommended Surgical Approach	Prognosis
Sporadic	Present at birth	Moderate/severe in first days to weeks of life	Negative	? SUR1/Kir6.2	Loss of heterozygosity in microadenomatous tissue	Generally poor; may respond to somatostatin better than diazoxide	Partial pancreatectomy if frozen section shows beta-cell crowding with small nuclei—microadenoma	Excellent
							Near total (>95%) pancreatectomy if frozen section shows giant nuclei in beta cells—diffuse hyperplasia	Guarded; diabetes mellitus develops in 50% of patients; hypoglycemia persists in 33%
Autosomal recessive	Present at birth	Severe in first days to weeks of life	Positive	SUR/Kir6.2	Consanguinity a feature in some populations	Poor	Subtotal pancreatectomy	Guarded
Autosomal dominant	Unusual	Moderate onset usually after 6 months of age	Positive	Glucokinase (activating)	None	Very good to excellent	Surgery usually not required/ partial pancreatectomy only if medical management fails	Excellent
Autosomal dominant	Unusual	Moderate onset usually after 6 months of age	Positive	Glutamate dehydrogenase (activating)	Modest hyperammonemia	Very good to excellent	Surgery usually not required	Excellent
Beckwith-Wiedemann syndrome	Present at birth	Moderate, spontaneously resolves after ≈6 months	Negative	Duplication/ imprinting in chromosome 11p15.1	Macroglossia, omphalocele, hemihypertrophy	Good	Not recommended	Excellent for hypoglycemia; associated with embryonal tumors (Wilms', hepatoblastoma)

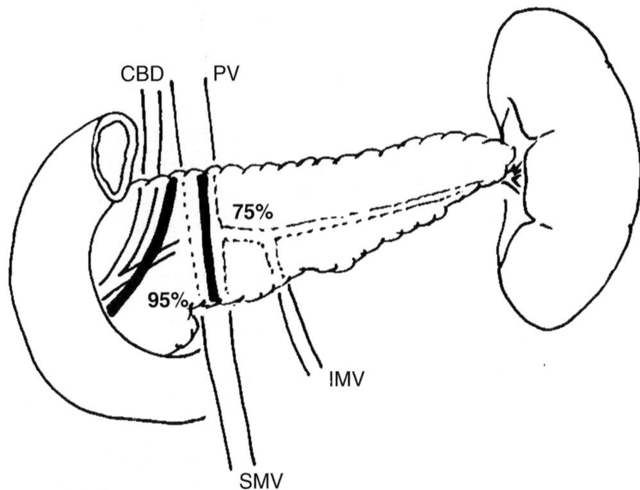

Figure 107-7 Extent of dissection of the pancreas. CBD, common bile duct; IMV, inferior mesenteric vein; PV, portal vein; SMV, superior mesenteric vein.

aware of the coexistence of adenomas and diffuse disease, particularly in infants.[169] Biopsy specimens from the head, body, and tail of the pancreas should be obtained, as indicated, for microscopic studies. If no localized lesion is found, the pancreas is mobilized from left to right. The tail of the pancreas is dissected from the hilum of the spleen and preserved. Multiple short pancreatic vessels arising from the splenic vessels are ligated and divided. Once the body of the pancreas is freed beyond the superior mesenteric artery, the portal vein can be viewed. Much care must be taken to dissect the uncinate process, which partially encircles the superior mesenteric vein. The common bile duct must be identified and protected during the 95% to 98% pancreatectomy that includes the uncinate process. Ectopic pancreatic tissue should be removed. Lesser resection is appropriate for the focal form of the disease when recognized, as shown by Cretolle et al.[29]

Blood glucose levels should be measured frequently after surgery. Hyperglycemia is usually observed initially, but it is transient and increased glucose is generally required to maintain normoglycemia until the infant can tolerate oral feedings. Pharmacologic management is occasionally required, but insulin is rarely needed.

Results

The major postoperative complications are persistence of hypoglycemia and mental retardation. However, the risk for diabetes mellitus is low. Spitz et al.[170] reported that prolonged postoperative hyperglycemia requiring insulin developed in 4 of 21 patients treated by 95% pancreatectomy, but only 1 of the 4 required it long-term. Mental retardation is probably already established before surgery.

Although the results of surgery generally correlate with the extent of pancreatectomy, they are not entirely predictable. In a review by Thomas et al.,[182] subtotal pancreatectomy (75% to 90%) was performed in 125 of 165 patients. Thirty-five of the 125 patients (28%) required a second operation, and 4 patients required a third operation for persistent hypoglycemia. Near-total pancreatectomy (95% to 98%) was performed as the initial procedure in 40 patients. Two (5%) of these patients required a second operation because of persistent hypoglycemia. The incidence of mental retardation was 12.5% in these 40 patients who underwent near-total pancreatectomy. Ten percent required diazoxide supplementation, and 7.5% required long-term insulin. The mortality rate was 2.5%. In their earlier experience with subtotal resection from 1943 to 1971, the mortality rate was 8.3% and the incidence of mental retardation was 52%. Generally, postoperative exocrine function is not impaired.[36,160] Lovvorn et al. and other recent reports describe series with no mortality and minimal complications.[113]

Islet Cell Adenoma

A functioning beta cell adenoma (insulinoma) can cause hyperinsulinism, most frequently in older children (also see the section on insulinoma). Overall, 10% of beta cell tumors are malignant, but malignancy is rare in children. Symptoms generally occur after 4 years of age, but up to a third of adenomas occur during the neonatal period.[37]

Most insulinomas are solitary, but they may be multiple or associated with nesidioblastosis. Because of their small size, they cannot be detected on US or CT; in contrast, selective celiac arteriography is diagnostic in 60% of older patients.[75] If a tumor is located in the head or central portion of the pancreas, the tumor can simply be enucleated. Most investigators, however, recommend 80% to 90% distal resection of the gland for control of nonpalpable lesions.[192] Measurement of intraoperative insulin levels is recommended to avoid missing lesions.

Multiple endocrine neoplasia type I (MEN-I) is characterized by endocrine tissues in the gut and pancreas, including insulin-secreting tumors, but expression is usually delayed beyond the first decade of life. MEN-I is rare, with a frequency not exceeding approximately 1 in 10,000. The gene for MEN-I has been localized to the long arm of chromosome 11 and functions as a tumor suppressor gene, unrelated to the functional alterations in the SUR1/Kir6.2 components of K_{ATP} on the short arm of chromosome 11.[21]

NEOPLASMS

Pancreatic neoplasms are relatively rare in infants and children. They can be cystic, solid, and benign or malignant and may or may not be hormonally active.

In 1818, Todd[27] reported the first pediatric case of pancreatic carcinoma simplex in a 14-year-old girl. In 1885, Bohn[12] published another case report of carcinoma simplex, in a 7-month-old infant. In 1990, Grosfeld et al.[65] reported 13 cases of pancreatic tumor in children, including 5 insulinomas, 2 mucinous cystadenomas, 2 rhabdomyosarcomas, and 4 carcinomas. In 1992, Jaksic et al. reported 6 cases of pediatric pancreatic tumor,[86] and by now more than 150 cases have been reported in the English literature.[99,136,173,174,175,176]

Cystic Neoplasms

Cystic neoplasms of the pancreas are relatively rare.[16,109] Howard et al.[80] classified these lesions into (1) cystadenoma and cystadenocarcinoma, which include benign (microcystic) cystadenoma, benign and malignant mucinous (macrocystic) cystadenoma and cystadenocarcinoma, papillary-cystic epithelial neoplasm, and acinar cell cystadenocarcinoma (not reported in children), and (2) teratomatous cysts.

Cystadenoma and Cystadenocarcinoma

Cystadenoma of the pancreas is rare in children and adults. Only six cases, including one in a newborn, have been reported in the pediatric population to date.[17,65,69,87] Cystadenoma and cystadenocarcinoma should be divided into two groups. Because large mucinous cystic adenomas have considerable malignant potential, these tumors should be distinguished from serous cystadenomas, which are benign; the latter tumors are glycogen-rich and contain little or no mucin.[23]

Serous Cystadenoma and Cystadenocarcinoma

Serous cystic neoplasms of the pancreas are rare in children and adults, are more often observed in females, and are found mainly in the body and tail of the pancreas. These tumors consist predominantly of small cysts (microcystic adenomas).[77] Calcification is often demonstrated on CT and US. Serous cysts do not need to be excised unless they create a mechanical obstruction because nearly all of them are benign with no malignant potential. Biopsy is required. Serous cystadenocarcinoma is virtually nonexistent in children, and only a few cases have been reported in adults.[53,213]

Mucinous Cystadenoma and Cystadenocarcinoma

Mucinous cystic neoplasms of the pancreas are usually large and often multilocular; they form papilla lined with columnar, mucin-producing epithelium, are more often observed in females, and are found mainly in the body and tail of the pancreas.[116] Other features are the association of large blood vessels within the capsule and the presence of subepithelial hemorrhage. A common differential diagnosis is pancreatitis with pseudocyst formation. Mucinous cystadenocarcinoma of the pancreas represents 1% of all malignant conditions of the pancreas, occurs at an earlier age than conventional solid pancreatic tumors do, and seems to be approximately half as common as cystadenoma. The clinical and radiologic manifestations of mucinous cystadenocarcinoma are similar to those of mucinous cystadenoma.[10] It is not always possible to differentiate mucinous cystadenoma from cystadenocarcinoma pathologically. It is also common to find apparently benign epithelium[23] in the same tumors as malignant epithelium, thus suggesting that a malignant focus may develop within a mucinous cystadenoma. A few reports have documented that more conservative treatment can lead to the development of fatal pleomorphic adenocarcinoma[110] or malignant sarcoma in the cyst wall.[64] Therefore, mucinous cystadenoma should be considered a premalignant lesion that should be completely excised after incomplete excision or marsupialization.[16,23] However, the prognosis for this form of pancreatic malignancy is significantly better than that for the common typical solid ductal adenocarcinoma because of its slow growth and lack of metastatic potential.[110]

Papillary-Cystic Epithelial Neoplasm

The first cases of papillary-cystic endothelial tumors of the pancreas were reported by Franz in 1959.[47] Since the time that these tumors were described as solid and cystic acinar cell tumors of the pancreas by Kloppel and colleagues,[95] increasing numbers have been reported in children. They occur predominantly in girls and young women and are manifested as large, encapsulated masses, usually with extensive necrosis and varying amounts of cystic change. Histologically, they are composed of solid areas of rather small cells with pseudorosette formation reminiscent of endocrine tumors and cystic areas with papillary structures.[171] Immunohistochemically, the tumor cells of solid and cystic pancreatic neoplasms contain periodic acid–Schiff–positive granules and often have progesterone receptors. Immunologic hallmarks are immunoreactivity with alpha-antitrypsin, alpha-antichymotrypsin, phospholipase A_2, and neuroendocrine markers such as neuron-specific enolase and synaptophysin. However, they are generally free of the usual markers of pancreatic carcinoma, such as carcinoembryonic antigen, CA19-9, and tissue peptide antigen.[178] These tumors seem to be associated with a much better prognosis than the usual type of pancreatic carcinoma but still have malignant potential.[100] The tumor follows a benign course after resection in most cases. We have experienced one case with metastatic disease to the liver, spleen, and lung at the time of initial clinical evaluation. Metastasis or recurrence has occurred in 5% of cases in Japan.[77] Thus, complete extirpation is necessary because of the poor prognosis associated with metastatic disease.

Other Cystic Neoplasms in Children

In 1992, Flaherty and Benjamin[46] reported a case of multicystic pancreatic hamartoma in a 20-month-old girl. In 1990, Mester et al.[122] reviewed 10 cases of cystic teratoma of the pancreas, including one of their own. Cystic teratomas were usually seen as benign extragonadal germ cell tumors in younger patients; 5 of 10 patients were younger than 11 years.

Hormonally Active Tumors

Endocrinologically active tumors are usually identified by their symptoms, and most of them originate in the islet cells. Beta cell tumors secrete insulin; alpha cell tumors, glucagon; gamma cell tumors, gastrin; delta cell tumors, somatostatin; and $delta_1$ cell tumors, vasoactive intestinal polypeptide (VIP) and possibly substance P and secretin. Glucagonomas and somatostatinomas have not been identified in children.

Insulinoma

Insulinomas are the most common tumor arising from islet cells and are usually benign (90%), solitary (80%) lesions that occur in children older than 4 years.[51,65,216] A plasma insulin-to-glucose ratio greater than 1.0 is diagnostic (<0.4 is normal),[51] and the ratio increases with fasting. Concomitant measurement of C peptide levels may be used to exclude factitious hypoglycemia. Elevated proinsulin levels may indicate malignancy.[64] CT, US, arteriography, and transhepatic portal venous sampling can be used to localize an insulinoma. The tumor is usually discrete and well encapsulated, and most can be enucleated. The introduction of intraoperative US has allowed obscure lesions to be identified. If all methods of tumor localization are unsuccessful, distal pancreatectomy with careful sectioning of the gland is advisable. Most infants and children with insulinoma can be cured.

Gastrinoma

The second most commonly reported pancreatic hormonal tumor is the gamma cell tumor. The clinical syndrome related to gastrinoma is often referred to as Zollinger-Ellison syndrome,[205] a condition characterized by hypergastrinemia with severe peptic ulcer disease. This syndrome is rare in children, with only 44 cases reported.[189] Gastrinoma is part of the MEN-I syndrome and is commonly malignant, multicentric, and metastatic at discovery.[65] The diagnosis is usually made after recurrent episodes of peptic ulceration associated with an elevated gastrin level (>500 pg/mL). Calcium infusion and secretin simulation tests are used for diagnosis. CT, percutaneous transhepatic venous sampling, and gastrin assay have been useful for localization. Although total gastrectomy was the most common method of treatment, the development of inhibitors of gastric acid secretion, such as H_2 blockers[33] and omeprazole,[120] has changed the direction of treatment of gastrinoma substantially. Children with gastrinoma generally require lifelong medical treatment, and somatostatin, although beneficial because it decreases gastric acid secretion, also inhibits growth hormone secretion, so it cannot be used long-term. Surgical treatment should thus be aggressive, especially if a solitary tumor is found with no evidence of metastasis at the time of laparotomy. However, total gastrectomy may still be required for patients in whom medical treatment has failed or those with residual tumor or metastatic disease.[33,65]

VIPoma

VIPoma in children is far more commonly related to other neurogenic neoplasms, such as neuroblastoma or ganglioneuroma, than to tumors of primary pancreatic origin. Only two cases of VIPoma in children have been reported.[189] The VIP that is produced by a pancreatic VIPoma probably originates from neural cells in the islets.[51] Patients have profuse, watery diarrhea associated with hypokalemia and hypochlorhydria (WDHA syndrome), and metabolic acidosis and prerenal azotemia secondary to dehydration are often present. Although medical therapy includes the use of streptozotocin and somatostatin, long-term use of somatostatin is undesirable. Surgical extirpation of the tumor-bearing gland is recommended whenever possible because 50% of pancreatic VIPomas are malignant.[65]

Carcinoma

Carcinoma of the pancreas is common in adults but rare in children, and the clinical features are different in that obstructive jaundice is the primary finding in adults whereas an abdominal mass is the initial feature in children.[99] Pancreatic carcinoma in children can be divided into four groups: islet cell carcinoma, adenocarcinoma, pancreatoblastoma, and miscellaneous lesions.

Islet Cell Carcinoma

Islet cell carcinoma in children may or may not be functional. Functioning beta cell and non–beta cell islet cell carcinoma occurs in infants and children with hypoglycemia in conjunction with Zollinger-Ellison syndrome, but it is not associated with a palpable mass. A beta cell carcinoma is usually discovered during laparotomy for insulinoma.[64] Four functional islet cell carcinomas have been described in children; all were treated by surgical extirpation, with good long-term survival.[81,177,188] Seven of the eight children with Zollinger-Ellison syndrome described by Wilson had non–beta cell carcinoma with metastatic disease.[210]

Nonfunctioning islet cell carcinomas are more common in children than adults. Because these tumors are usually discovered by palpation of an abdominal mass, they are often diagnosed late, and many affected infants and children have distant metastatic disease at the time of diagnosis.[64] Most nonfunctional tumors are large, solitary lesions that can appear in any location within the gland. In general, although most of these tumors grow slowly, aggressive surgical therapy is warranted because of their malignant potential.[6]

Adenocarcinoma

Adenocarcinoma of the pancreas is very rare in children. Vejcho[193] reviewed 37 cases of adenocarcinoma in 1993. The clinical manifestation differs from that of adults in that the incidence of pain with jaundice is lower.[188] Abdominal pain and a palpable epigastric mass are the primary findings in children. Classification is still controversial and is based on tumor activity and histopathologic and immunohistochemical findings. Kloppe et al. classified adenocarcinoma into three types: acinar cell carcinoma, solid and cystic tumor (papillary cystic tumor), and pancreatoblastoma.[95] Acinar cell tumors are proportionately more common in children.[100,116] It seems that children with an acinar cell tumor have a somewhat better prognosis than do those with an adenocarcinoma of the duct cell type. The prognosis for children with adenocarcinoma of the duct cell type is discouraging and similar to that for adults.[78] CT and sonography are useful for diagnosis. For localized lesions, pancreaticoduodenectomy seems to be associated with a favorable prognosis. Infants and children tolerate radical resection of the pancreas somewhat better than adults do and have a lower mortality rate and better long-term survival.[6]

Pancreatoblastoma

In 1977, Horie et al.[78] reported two cases of pancreatic carcinoma, which they termed pancreatoblastoma, an infantile type of pancreatic carcinoma. In 1984, Buchino et al.[18] reviewed eight patients with pancreatoblastoma, six of whom survived after surgical extirpation. Grosfeld et al.[65] and Jaksic et al.[86] each reported one case. Pancreatoblastomas have a better prognosis because they have an encapsulated organoid structure that does not directly interfere with the main duct system. The criteria for diagnosing pancreatoblastoma have been described by Buchino et al.[18] Although there is no agreement on the pathology of these rare lesions, terminology based on recognizable lines of differentiation seems preferable (e.g., islet cell, duct cell, acinar cell, and undifferentiated lesions).[100]

Miscellaneous Carcinomas

The following miscellaneous carcinomas in children have been reported in the literature: one case of carcinoma simplex,[12] one case of medullary carcinoma,[203] six cases of sarcoma (two lymphosarcomas[203] two with sarcomatous degeneration from cystadenoma,[64,188] and two rhabdomyosarcomas[65]), four cases of undifferentiated carcinoma,[18,188] and two cases of cylindrical cell adenocarcinoma.[12,27]

REFERENCES

1. Adams DJ, Harrison RG: The vascularization of the rat pancreas and the effect of ischemia on the islets of Langerhans. J Anat 1953;87:257.
2. Adzick NS, Shamberger RC, Winter HS, Hendren WH: Surgical treatment of pancreas divisum causing pancreatitis in children. J Pediatr Surg 1989;25:54.
3. Agha FP: Spontaneous resolution of pancreatic pseudocysts. Surg Gynecol Obstet 1984;158:22.
4. Aguilar-Bryan L, Nichols CG, Wechsler SW, et al: Cloning of the beta cell high-affinity sulfonylurea receptor: A regulator of insulin secretion. Science 1995;268:423.
5. Albu E, Buiumsohn A, Lopez R, Gerst PH: Gallstone pancreatitis in adolescents. J Pediatr Surg 1987;22:960.
6. Aszodi A, Leeming RA, Lash RH, et al: Giant nonfunctioning islet cell tumor requiring pancreaticoduodenectomy and complete liver revascularization. J Surg Oncol 1993; 53:273.
7. Auringer ST, Ulmer JL, Sumner TE, Turner CS: Congenital cyst of the pancreas. J Pediatr Surg 1993;28:1570.
8. Baker LL, Hartman GE, Northway WH: Sonographic detection of congenital pancreatic cysts in the newborn; report of a case and review of the literature. Pediatr Radiol 1990;20:488.
9. Banting FG, Best CH: The internal secretion of the pancreas. J Lab Clin Med 1922;7:251.
10. Becker WF, Welsh RA, Pratt HS: Cystadenoma and cystadenocarcinoma of the pancreas. Ann Surg 1965;261:845.
11. Bencosme SA: The histogenesis and cytology of the pancreatic islets in the rabbit. Am J Anat 1955;96:103.
12. Bohn A: [Cancer of the liver, the portal and retroperitoneal lymph glands and the pancreas in a 6 month old child.] Jahrb Kinderh 1885;23:143.
13. Bousvaros A: Acute and chronic pancreatitis. In International Seminars in Paediatric Gastroenterology and Nutrition, vol 4. Hamilton, Ontario, Canada, 1995, Decker Periodicals.
14. Bradley EL, Clements LJ: Spontaneous resolution of pancreatic pseudocysts. Implications for timing of operative intervention. Am J Surg 1975;129:23.
15. Brooks JR: Pseudocysts of the pancreas. In Brooks JR (ed): Surgery of the Pancreas. Philadelphia, WB Saunders, 1983.
16. Brugge WR, Lauwers GY, Sahani D, et al: Cystic neoplasms of the pancreas. N Engl J Med 2004;35:1218.
17. Brunschwig A: Surgery of Pancreatic Tumors, St Louis, CV Mosby, 1942.
18. Buchino JJ, Castello FM, Nagaraj HS: Pancreatoblastoma: A histochemical and ultrastructural analysis. Cancer 1984; 53:963.
19. Buchler M, Malfertheiner P, Uhl W, et al: Gabexate mesilate in human acute pancreatitis. German Pancreatitis Study Group. Gastroenterology 1993;104:1165.
20. Buchler MW, Gloor B, Muller CA, et al: Acute necrotizing pancreatitis: Treatment strategy according to the status of infection. Ann Surg 2000;232:619.
21. Chandrasekharappa SC, Guru SC, Manickam P, et al: Positional cloning of the gene for multiple endocrine neoplasia-type 1. Science 1997;276:404.
22. Cohn JA, Bornstein JD, Jowell PS: Cystic fibrosis mutations and genetic predisposition to idiopathic chronic pancreatitis. Med Clin North Am 2000;84:621.
23. Compagno J, Oertel JE: Mucinous cystic neoplasms of the pancreas with overt and latent malignancy (cystadenocarcinoma and cystadenoma): A clinicopathologic study of 41 cases. Am J Clin Pathol 1978;69:573.
24. Conklin JL: Cytogenesis of the human fetal pancreas. Am J Anat 1962;111:181.
25. Cooney DR, Grosfeld JL: Operative management of pancreatic pseudocysts in infants and children: A review of 75 cases. Ann Surg 1976;182:590.
26. Cooperman M, Ferrara JJ, Carey LC, et al: Idiopathic acute pancreatitis: The value of endoscopic retrograde cholangiopancreatography. Surgery 1981;90:666.
27. Corner BD: Primary carcinoma of the pancreas in an infant aged 7 months. Arch Dis Child 1943;18:106.
28. Cotton PB: Congenital anomaly of pancreas divisum as cause of obstructive pain and pancreatitis. Gut 1980;21:101.
29. Cretolle C, Fekete CN, Jan D, et al: Partial elective pancreatectomy is curative in focal form of permanent hyperinsulinemic hypoglycemia in infancy: A report of 45 cases from 1983-2000. J Pediatr Surg 2002;37:155.
30. Crombleholme TM, deLorimier AA, Wayu LW, et al: The modified Puestow procedure for chronic relapsing pancreatitis in children. J Pediatr Surg 1990;25:749.
31. DeBanto JR, Goday PS, Pedroso MR, et al: Acute pancreatitis in children. Am J Gastroenterol 2002;97:1726.
32. de Lonlay P, Fournet JC, Rahier J, et al: Somatic deletion of the imprinted 11015 region in sporadic persistent

hyperinsulinemic hypoglycemia of infancy is specific of focal adenomatous hyperplasia and endorses partial pancreatectomy. J Clin Invest 1997;100:802.
33. Deveney CW, Deveney KE: Zollinger-Ellison syndrome (gastrinoma): Current diagnosis and treatment. Surg Clin North Am 1987;67:411.
34. Drey NW: Symptomatic annular pancreas in the adult. Ann Intern Med 1957;46:756.
35. Dubay D, Sandler A, Kimura K, et al: The modified Puestow procedure for complicated hereditary pancreatitis in children. J Pediatr Surg 2000;35:343.
36. Dunger DB, Burns C, Ghale GK, et al: Pancreatic exocrine and endocrine function after subtotal pancreatectomy for nesidioblastosis. J Pediatr Surg 1988;23:112.
37. Dunn JS, McLetchie NGB: Experimental alloxan diabetes in the rat. Lancet 1943;2:384.
38. Durie P: Pancreatic aspects of cystic fibrosis and other inherited causes of pancreatic dysfunction. Med Clin North Am 2000;84:609.
39. Duval MK Jr: Caudal pancreaticojejunostomy for chronic relapsing pancreatitis. Ann Surg 1954;140:775.
40. Eichelberger MR, Hoelzer DJ, Koop CE: Acute pancreatitis: The difficulties of diagnosis and therapy. J Pediatr Surg 1982;17:244.
41. Eghtesad B, Reyer JD, Ashrafi M, et al: Pancreatitis after liver transplantation in children: A single-center experience. Transplantation 2003;75:190.
42. Elechi EN, Callender CO, Leffall LD Jr, Kurtz LH: The treatment of pancreatic pseudocysts by external drainage. Surg Gynecol Obstet 1979;148:707.
43. Festen C, Severijnen R, vd Staak F, Rieu P: Chronic relapsing pancreatitis in childhood. J Pediatr Surg 1991; 26:182.
44. Finch WT, Sawyers JL, Schenker S: Prospective study to determine the efficacy of antibiotics in acute pancreatitis. Ann Surg 1976;183:667.
45. Firstenberg MS, Volsko TA, Sivit C, et al: Selective management of pediatric pancreatic injuries. J Pediatr Surg 1999; 34:1142.
46. Flaherty MJ, Benjamin DR: Multicystic pancreatic hamartoma: A distinctive lesion with immunohistochemical and ultrastructural study. Hum Pathol 1992;23:1309.
47. Frantz VK: Tumor of the pancreas. In Atlas of Tumor Pathology, fascicles 27 and 28. Washington, DC, 1959, Armed Forces Institute of Pathology.
48. Frey CF: Pancreatic pseudocysts—operative strategy. Ann Surg 1978;188:652.
49. Frey CF: Role of subtotal pancreatectomy and pancreaticojejunostomy in chronic pancreatitis. J Surg Res 1981;31:36.
50. Frey C, Redo SF: Inflammatory lesions of the pancreas in infancy and childhood. Pediatrics 1978;32:143.
51. Friesen SR: An update on the diagnosis and treatment of rare neuroendocrine tumors. Surg Clin North Am 1987; 67:379.
52. Fuller RK, Loveland JP, Frankel MH: An evaluation of the efficacy of nasogastric suction treatment in alcoholic pancreatitis. Am J Gastroenterol 1981;75:349.
53. George DH, Murphy F, Michalski R, Ulmer BG: Serous cystadenocarcinoma of the pancreas: A new entity? Am J Surg Pathol 1989;13:61.
54. Ghishan FK, Greene HL, Avant G, et al: Chronic relapsing pancreatitis in childhood. J Pediatr 1983;102:514.
55. Gillette L, Lynch B: Annular pancreas. Ann Surg 1954; 139:374.
56. Glaser B, Hirch JH, Landau H: Persistent hyperinsulinism hypoglycemia of infancy: Long-term octreotide treatment without pancreatectomy. J Pediatr 1993;123:644.
57. Glaser B, Kesavan P, Heyman M, et al: Familial hyperinsulinism caused by an activating glucokinase mutation. N Engl J Med 1998;338:226.
58. Goobie S, Popovic M, Morrison J, et al: Shwachman-Diamond syndrome with exocrine pancreatic dysfunction and bone marrow failure maps to the centromeric region of chromosome 7. Am J Hum Genet 2001;68:1048.
59. Gorenstein A, O'Halpin D, Wesson DE, et al: Blunt injury to the pancreas in children: Selective management based on ultrasound. J Pediatr Surg 1987;22:1110.
60. Graham JM, Polorny WJ, Mattox KL, Jordan GL Jr: Surgical management of acute pancreatic injuries in children. J Pediatr Surg 1978;13:693.
61. Grant DB, Dunger DB, Burns EC: Long-term treatment with diazoxide in childhood hyperinsulinism, Acta Endocrinol (Copenhagen) 1986;279(Suppl):340.
62. Grauso-Eby NL, Goldfarb O, Feldman-Winter LB, McAhee GN: Acute pancreatitis in children from valproic acid: Case series and review. Pediatr Neurol 2002;28:145-148.
63. Gray SW, Skandalakis JE: The pancreas. In Embryology for Surgeons. Philadelphia, Williams & Wilkins, 1994.
64. Grosfeld JL, Clatworthy HW, Hamoudi AB: Pancreatic malignancy in children. Arch Surg 1970;101:370.
65. Grosfeld JL, Vane DW, Rescorla FJ, et al: Pancreatic tumors in childhood: Analysis of 13 cases. J Pediatr Surg 1990;25:1057.
66. Guelrud M, Mujica C, Jaen D, et al: The role of ERCP in the diagnosis and treatment of idiopathic recurrent pancreatitis in children and adolescents. Gastrointest Endosc 1994;40:428.
67. Guillemin G, Cuilleret J, Michel A, et al: Chronic relapsing pancreatitis; surgical management including 63 cases of pancreaticoduodenectomy. Am J Surg 1971;122:802.
68. Gumaste V, Dave P, Sereny G: Serum lipase: A better test to diagnose acute alcoholic pancreatitis. Am J Med 1992; 92:239.
69. Gundersen AE, Janis JF: Pancreatic cystadenoma in childhood. J Pediatr Surg 1969;4:478.
70. Gwozdz GP, Steinberg WM, Werner M, et al: Comparative evaluation of the diagnosis of acute pancreatitis based on serum and urine enzyme assays. Clin Chim Acta 1990; 187:243.
71. Hastings PR, Nance FC, Becker WF: Changing pattern in the management of pancreatic pseudocysts. Ann Surg 1975; 181:546.
72. Heikkinen ES, Salminer PM: Congenital choledochal cyst opening into the intraduodenal part of the common bile duct and complicated by cystolithiasis and acute pancreatitis. Acta Chir Scand 1954;150:183.
73. Heitz PU, Beglinger C, Gyr K: Anatomy and physiology of the exocrine pancreas. In Kloppel G, Heitz PU (eds): Pancreatic Pathology. London, Churchill Livingstone, 1984.
74. Hendricks SK, Sybert VP: Association of annular pancreas and duodenal obstruction, evidence for mendelian inheritance? Clin Genet 1991;39:383.
75. Herman TE, Siegel MJ: Polysplenia syndrome with congenital short pancreas. AJR Am J Roentgenol 1991;156:799.
76. Hermann RE: Common surgical problems. In Hermann RE (ed): Pancreatic Surgery. Chicago, Year Book, 1985.
77. Hirano T, Akoi Y, Ito T, et al: A case of solid and cystic tumor of the pancreas. J Jpn Soc Clin Surg 56:149, 1995.
78. Horie A, Yano Y, Kotoo Y, Miwa A: Morphogenesis of pancreatoblastoma, infantile carcinoma of the pancreas: Report of two cases. Cancer 1977;39:247.
79. Hough DM, Stephens DH, Johnson CD, Binkovitz LA, et al: Pancreatic lesions in von Hippel-Lindau disease: Prevalence, clinical significance, and CT findings. AJR Am J Roentgenol 1994;162:1091.

80. Howard JM, Jordan GJ Jr, Reber HA: Cysts of the pancreas. In Howard JM, Jordan GJ (eds): Surgical Diseases of the Pancreas, Philadelphia, Lea & Febiger, 1987.
81. Hurez A, Bedouelle J, Debray H, et al: Carcinoma of the islets of Langerhans with severe hypoglycemic manifestations in a nine year old child. Arch Franc Pediatr 1961;18:625.
82. Ingemansson S, Kuhl C, Larsson LI, et al: Localization of insulinomas and islet cell hyperplasias by pancreatic vein catheterization and insulin assay. Surg Gynecol Obstet 1978;146:725.
83. Jackson D: Pancreatitis: Etiology, diagnosis, and management. Curr Opin Pediatr 2001;13:447.
84. Jaffe R: The pancreas. In Stocker JT, Dehner LP (eds): Pediatric Pathology, 2nd ed. Philadelphia, Lippincott Williams & Wilkins, 2001, p 799.
85. Jaffe RB, Arata JA Jr, Matlak ME: Percutaneous drainage of traumatic pancreatic pseudocysts in children. AJR Am J Roentgenol 1989;152:591.
86. Jaksic T, Yaman M, Thorner P, et al: A 20-year-review of pediatric pancreatic tumors. J Pediatr Surg 1992;27:1315.
87. Jenkins JM, Othersen BH Jr: Cystadenoma of the pancreas in a newborn. J Pediatr Surg 1992;27:1569.
88. Johnson DD: Alloxan administration in the guinea pig: A study of the regenerative phase of the islands of Langerhans. Endocrinology 1950;47:393.
89. Jones SA, Steedman RA, Keller TB, Smith LL: Transduodenal sphincteroplasty (not sphincterotomy) for biliary and pancreatic disease. Am J Surg 1969;118:292.
90. Karaguzel G, Senocak ME, Buyukpamukcu N, Hicsonmez A: A surgical management of the pancreatic pseudocyst in children: A long-term evaluation. J Pediatr Surg 1995; 30:777.
91. Karp MP, Cooney DR, Berger PE, et al: The role of computed tomography in the evaluation of blunt abdominal trauma in children. J Pediatr Surg 1981;16:316.
92. Karp MP, Jewett TC, Cooney DR: Chronic relapsing pancreatitis in childhood caused by pancreaticobiliary ductal anomaly. J Pediatr Gastroenterol Nutr 1983;2:324.
93. Keith RG, Shapero TF, Saibil FG: Treatment of pancreatitis with pancreas divisum by dorsal duct sphincterotomy alone. Can J Surg 1982;25:622.
94. Kimble RM, Cohen R, Williams S: Successful endoscopic drainage of a posttraumatic pancreatic pseudocyst in a child. J Pediatr Surg 1999;34:1518.
95. Kloppel G, Morohoshi T, John HD, et al: Solid and cystic acinar cell tumour of the pancreas: A tumour in young women with favorable prognosis. Virchows Arch A Pathol Anat Histol 1981;392:171.
96. Kouchi K, Tenabe M, Yoshida H, et al: Nonoperative management of blunt pancreatic injury in childhood. J Pediatr Surg 1999;34:1736.
97. Kozarek RA, Christie D, Barclay G: Endoscopic therapy of pancreatitis in the pediatric population. Gastrointest Endosc 1993;39:665.
98. Kramer JL, Bell MJ, DeSchryver K, et al: Clinical and histologic indications for extensive pancreatic resection in nesidioblastosis. Am J Surg 1982;143:116.
99. Kuhn A: [Primary pancreatic carcinoma in infancy.] Klin Wochnschr 1887;24:494.
100. Lack EE, Cassady JR, Levey R, Vawter GF: Tumors of the exocrine pancreas in children and adolescents: A clinical and pathologic study of eight cases. Am J Surg Pathol 1983;7:319.
101. La Hei ER, Cohen RC: Antenatal detection of a pancreatic foregut duplication cyst. J Pediatr Surg 2001;36:501.
102. Lamberts SWJ, van der Lely AJ, de Herder WW, Holfland LJ: Octreotide. N Engl J Med 1996;334:246.
103. Langer JC, Filler RM, Wesson DE, et al: Surgical management of persistent neonatal hypoglycemia due to islet cell dysplasia. J Pediatr Surg 1984;19:786.
104. Levitt Katz LE, Satin-Smith MS, Collett-Solberg P, et al: Insulin-like growth factor binding protein-1 levels in the diagnosis of hypoglycemia caused by hyperinsulinism. J Pediatr 1997;131:193.
105. Lewis FP: The development of the liver. In Leibel F, Mall FP (eds): Human Embryology, vol 12. Philadelphia, JB Lippincott, 1912.
106. Li L, yamataka A Segawa O, Miyano T: Coexistence of pancreas divisum and septate common channel in a child with choledochal cyst. J Pediatr Gastroenterol Nutr 2001; 32:602.
107. Lilly JR, Stellin GP, Karrer FM: Forme fruste choledochal cyst. J Pediatr Surg 1985;20:449.
108. Lindley KJ, Dunne MJ, Kane C, et al: Ionic control of beta cell function in nesidioblastosis: A possible therapeutic role for calcium channel blockade. Arch Dis Child 1996; 74:373.
109. Liu HM, Potter EL: Development of the human pancreas. Arch Pathol 1962;74:439.
110. Logan SE, Voet RL, Tompkins RT: The malignant potential of mucinous cyst of the pancreas. West J Med 1982;136:157.
111. Loludice TA, Jarmolych J, Buhac I: A cause of obstructive jaundice. JAMA 1977;238:889.
112. Longmire WP 3rd, Rose AS: Hemoductal pancreatitis. Surg Gynecol Obstet 1973;136:246.
113. Lovvorn HN, Nance ML, Ferry RJ, et al: Congenital hyperinsulinism and the surgeon: Lessons learned over 35 years. J Pediatr Surg 1999;34:786.
114. Mabogunle OA: Pseudocysts of the pancreas in children: An African series. Ann Trop Paediatr 1988;8:241.
115. Madura JA: Pancreas divisum: Stenosis of the dorsally dominant pancreatic duct. Am J Surg 1986;151:742.
116. Mah PT, Loo DC, Tock EPC: Pancreatic acinar cell carcinoma in children. Am J Dis Child 1974;128:101.
117. Malats N, Casals T, Porta M, et al: Cystic fibrosis transmembrane regulator (CFTR) DeltaF508 mutation and 5T allele in patients with chronic pancreatitis and exocrine pancreatic cancer. PANKRAS II Study Group. Gut 2001;48:70.
118. Mallory A, Kern F Jr: Drug induced pancreatitis: A critical review. Gastroenterology 1980;78:813.
119. Mavridis G, Soutis M, Sakellaris D, Keramidas D: Annular pancreas, Acta Chir Hellen 1995;67:597.
120. McArthur KE, Collen MJ, Cherner JA: Omeprazole as a single dose is effective in Zollinger-Ellison syndrome. Gastroenterology 1984;86:1178.
121. Mellish RWP, Koop CE: Clinical manifestations of duplication of the bowel. Pediatrics 1961;27:397.
122. Mester M, Trajber HJ, Compton CC, et al: Cystic teratomas of the pancreas. Arch Surg 1990;125:1215.
123. Millar AJW, Rode H, Stunden RJ, Cywes S: Management of pancreatic pseudocysts in children. J Pediatr Surg 1988; 23:122.
124. Miles RM: Pancreatic cyst in the newborn. Ann Surg 1959; 149:576.
125. Miyano T, Ando KD, Yamataka A, et al: Pancreaticobiliary maljunction associated with nondilatation or minimal dilation of the common bile duct in children: Diagnosis and treatment. Eur J Pediatr Surg 1996;6:334.
126. Miyano T, Suruga K, Shimomura H, et al: Choledochopancreatic elongated common channel disorders. J Pediatr Surg 1984;19:165.
127. Miyano T, Yamataka A, Kato Y, et al: Choledochal cysts: Special emphasis on the usefulness of intraoperative endoscopy. J Pediatr Surg 1995;30:482.

128. Mizoguchi K: Anatomical studies on the opening of the ducts hepatopancreatica on the duodenal wall of Japanese. Showa Med J 1960;20:549.
129. Moor KL, Persaud TVN: Development of the pancreas. In Moor KL, Persaud TVN (eds): The Developing Human, 5th ed. Philadelphia, WB Saunders, 1993.
130. Moosa AR, Baker L, Lavelle-Jones M: Hypoglycemic syndrome in infancy and childhood. A surgeon's perspective. West J Med 1987;146:585.
131. Mulligan C, Howell C, Hatley R, et al: Conservative management of pediatric pancreatic pseudocyst using octreotide acetate. Am Surg 1995;61:206.
132. Myers MA: Intestinal effects of pancreatitis: Spread along mesenteric plan. In Dynamic Radiology of Abdomen; Normal and Pathologic Anatomy. Berlin, Springer-Verlag, 1976.
133. Nardi GL, Acosta JM: Papillitis as a cause of pancreatitis and abdominal pain: Role of evocative test, operative pancreatography and histologic evaluation. Ann Surg 1966; 164:611.
134. Neblett WW III, O'Neill JA Jr: Surgical management of recurrent pancreatitis in children with pancreas divisum. Ann Surg 2000;231:899.
135. Nestorowicz A, Glaser B, Wilson BA, et al: Genetic heterogeneity in familial hyperinsulinism. Hum Mol Genet 1998;7:1119.
136. Newman BM: Congenital abnormalities of the exocrine pancreas. In Lebenthal E (ed): Textbook of Gastroenterology and Nutrition in Infancy, 2nd ed. New York, Raven Press, 1989.
137. Odgers PNB: Some observations on the development of the ventral pancreas in man. J Anat 1930;65:1.
138. O'Neill JA Jr, Greene H, Grishan FK: Surgical implications of chronic pancreatitis. J Pediatr Surg 1982;17:920.
139. Othersen HB Jr, Moore FT, Boles ET: Traumatic pancreatitis and pseudocyst in childhood. J Trauma 1968;8:535.
140. Owor B: Chronic pancreatic disease in African children. Uganda Med J 1972;1:7.
141. Philipson LH, Steiner DF: Pas de deux or more: The sulfonylurea receptor and K^+ channels. Science 1995; 268:327.
142. Philsalix C: Etude d'un embryon humain de 10 millimetres. Arch Zool Exp Gen Hist Nat Morph Hitol Evol Animaux Ser 2 1888;6:279.
143. Pilot LM Jr, Gooselaw JG, Isaacson PJ: Obstruction of the common bile duct in the newborn by a pancreatic cyst. Lancet 1964;84:204.
144. Pokorny WJ, Rafensperger JG, Harberg FJ: Pancreatic pseudocysts in children. Surg Gynecol Obstet 1980; 151:182.
145. Pollak EW, Michas CA, Wolfman EF: Pancreatic pseudocyst. Management in fifty-four patients. Am J Surg 1978; 135:199.
146. Poves I: Results of treatment in severe acute pancreatitis. Rev Esp Enfer Diag 2000;92:586.
147. Proctor HJ, Mendes OC, Thomas CG Jr, Herbst CA: Surgery for chronic pancreatitis: Drainage versus resection. Ann Surg 1979;189:664.
148. Puestow CB, Gillesby WJ: Retrograde surgical drainage of the pancreas for chronic relapsing pancreatitis. Arch Surg 1958;76:898.
149. Queizan A, Hernandez F, Rivas S: Pancreatic pseudocyst caused by valproic acid: Case report and review of the literature. Eur J Pediatr Surg 2003;13:60.
150. Ranson JHC: Acute pancreatitis. In Schwartz SI, Ellis H (eds): Maingot's Abdominal Operations, 8th ed. Norwalk, CT, Appleton-Century-Crofts, 1985.
151. Ravelo HR, Aldete JS: Analysis of forty-five patients with pseudocysts of the pancreas treated surgically. Surg Gynecol Obstet 1979;148:735.
152. Rescorla FJ, Cory D, Vane DW, et al: Failure of percutaneous drainage in children with traumatic pancreatic pseudocysts. J Pediatr Surg 1990;25:1038.
153. Rescorla F, Grosfeld JL: Pancreatitis. In Schiller M (ed): Pediatric Surgery of the Liver, Pancreas, and Spleen. Philadelphia, WB Saunders, 1991.
154. Richter JM, Schapiro RH, Mulley AG, Warshaw AL: Association of pancreas divisum and pancreatitis, and its treatment by sphincteroplasty of the accessory ampulla. Gastroenterology 1981;81:1104.
155. Rogers JC, Harris DJ, Holder T: Annular pancreas in a mother and daughter. Am J Med Genet 1993;45:116.
156. Sanfey H, Aguilar M, Jones RS: Pseudocysts of the pancreas, a review of 97 cases. Am Surg 1994;60:661.
157. Sankaran S, Walt AJ: The natural and unnatural history of pancreatic pseudocysts. Br J Surg 1975;62:37.
158. Sawyer SM, Davidson PM, McMullin N, et al: Pancreatic pseudocysts in children. Pediatr Surg Int 1989;4:300.
159. Scharplatz D, White TT: A review of 64 patients with pancreatic cysts. Ann Surg 1972;176:638.
160. Schonau E, Deeg KH, Huemmer HP, et al: Pancreatic growth and function following surgical treatment of nesidioblastosis in infancy. Eur J Pediatr 1991;50:550.
161. Scott HW Jr, Neblett WW, O'Neill JA Jr, et al: Longitudinal pancreaticojejunostomy in chronic pancreatitis with onset in childhood. Ann Surg 1984;199:610.
162. Shah KK, DeRidder PH, Schwab RE, Alexander TJ: CT diagnosis of dorsal pancreas agenesis. J Comput Assist Tomogr 1987;11:170.
163. Sherman S, Lehman GA: ERCP- and endoscopic sphincterotomy–induced pancreatitis. Pancreas 1991;6:350.
164. Shimizu T, Suzuki R, Yamashiro Y, et al: Magnetic resonance cholangiopancreatography in assessing the cause of acute pancreatitis in children. Pancreas 2001;22:196.
165. Sitzman JV, et al: Total parenteral nutrition and alternative energy substrates in treatment of severe acute pancreatitis. Surg Gynecol Obstet 1989;168:311.
166. Smanio T: Varying relation of the common bile duct with the posterior face of the pancreas in negro and white persons. J Int Coll Surg 1954;22:150.
167. Smith R: Progress in the surgical treatment of pancreatic disease. Am J Surg 1973;125:143.
168. Sperling MA, Menon RK: Hyperinsulinemic hypoglycemia of infancy. Pediatr Endocrinol 1999;28:695.
169. Spitz L, Bhargava RK, Grant DB, Leonard JV: Surgical treatment of hyperinsulinemic hypoglycemia in infancy and childhood. Arch Dis Child 1992;67:201.
170. Spitz L, Buick DG, Grant OB, et al: Surgical treatment of nesidioblastosis. Pediatr Surg Int 1986;1:26.
171. Stamm B, Burger H, Hollinger A: Acinar cell cystadenocarcinoma of the pancreas. Cancer 1987;60:2542.
172. Stanley CA, Baker L: Hyperinsulinism in infants and children: Diagnosis and therapy. Adv Pediatr 1976;23:315.
173. Stanley CA, Lieu YK, Hsu BY, et al: Hyperinsulinism and hyperammonemia in infants with regulatory mutations of the glutamate dehydrogenase gene. N Engl J Med 1998; 338:1352.
174. Stein ML, Rossi VC, Almeida AMC: [Carcinoma of the pancreas in the infant, presentation of a case.] Pediatr Pathol 1962;33:75.
175. Steinberg W, Tenner S: Acute pancreatitis. N Engl J Med 1994;330:1198.
176. Stewart SC, Stewart LF: A case of cancer of the pancreas in a 9 year old boy. Intern Clin 1915;2:118.

177. Stokes JM, Wohltmann HJ, Hartmann AF: Pancreatectomy in children. Arch Surg 1966;93:40.
178. Stommer P, Kraus J, Stolte M, Giede J: Solid and cystic pancreatic tumors. Clinical, histochemical, and electron microscopic features in ten cases. Cancer 1991;67:1635.
179. Stone HH: Pancreatic and duodenal trauma in children. J Pediatr Surg 1972;7:670.
180. Synn AY, Mulvihill SJ, Fonkalsrud EW: Surgical management of pancreatitis in childhood. J Pediatr 1987; 22:628.
181. Tagge EP, Smith SD, Raschbaum GR, et al: Pancreatic ductal abnormalities in children. Surgery 1991;110:709.
182. Thomas CG Jr, Cuenca RE, Azizkhan RG, et al: Changing concepts of islet cell dysplasia in neonatal and infantile hyperinsulinism. World J Surg 1988;12:598.
183. Thomas PM: Molecular basis for familial hyperinsulinemic hypoglycemia of infancy. Curr Opin Endocrinol Diabetes 1997;4:272.
184. Thomas PM, Cote GJ, Wohllk N, et al: Mutations in sulfonylurea receptor gene in familial persistent hyperinsulinemic hypoglycemia of infancy. Science 1995;268:426.
185. Thornton PS, Alter CA, Katz LE, et al: Short- and long-term use of octreotide in the treatment of congenital hyperinsulinism. J Pediatr 1993;123:637.
186. Tissieres P, Simon L, Debray D, et al: Acute pancreatitis after orthotopic liver transplantation in children: Incidence, contributing factors, and outcome. J Pediatr Gastroenterol Nutr 1998;26:315.
187. Traverso LW, Longmire WP Jr: Pancreatitis of unusual origin. Surg Gynecol Obstet 1975;141:383.
188. Tsukimoto I, Watanaber K, Lin JB, Nakajima T: Pancreatic carcinoma in children in Japan. Cancer 1973;31:1203.
189. Tudor RB: Childhood Disease Registry, Bismarck, ND, 1988.
190. Tudor RB: Pancreatitis and pancreatic pseudocysts. In Childhood Gastroenterology Registry, Report No. 3. Bismarck, ND, 1989.
191. Van Camp JM, Polley TZ, Coran AG: Pancreatitis in children: Diagnosis and etiology in 57 patients. Pediatr Surg Int 1994;9:492.
192. Vane DW, Grosfeld JL, West KW, Rescorla FJ, et al: Pancreatic disorders in infancy and childhood: Experience with 92 cases. J Pediatr Surg 1989;24:771.
193. Vejcho S: Carcinoma of the pancreas in childhood: A case report of long term survival. J Med Assoc Thai 1993; 76:177.
194. Verkarre V, Fournet JC, de Lonlay P, et al: Paternal mutation of the sulfonylurea receptor (SUR1) gene and maternal loss of 11p15 imprinted genes lead to persistent hyperinsulinism in focal adenomatous hyperplasia. J Clin Invest 1998; 102:1286.
195. Wade JW: Twenty-five year experience with pancreatic pseudocysts. Are we making progress? Am J Surg 1985; 149:705.
196. Wagner CW, Golladay ES: Pancreas divisum and pancreatitis in children. Am Surg 1988;54:22.
197. Warkany J: Embryology as related to fibrocystic disease of the pancreas. 18th Report of the Ross Pediatric Research Conference. Columbus, OH, Ross Laboratories, 1956.
198. Warner RL, Othersen HB Jr, Smith CD: Traumatic pancreatitis and pseudocyst in children: Current management. J Trauma 1989;29:597.
199. Warren WD, Marsh WH, Sandusky WR: Pancreatic cysts: An appraisal of surgical procedures of pancreatic pseudocysts. Ann Surg 1958;147:903.
200. Warshaw AL: Pancreas divisum: A case for surgical treatment. Adv Surg 1987;21:93.
201. Warshaw AL, Richter J, Schapiro RH: The cause and treatment of pancreatitis associated with pancreas divisum. Ann Surg 1983;198:443.
202. Warshaw AL, Simeone J, Schapiro RH, et al: Objective evaluation of ampullary stenosis with ultrasonography and pancreatic stimulation. Am J Surg 1985;149:65.
203. Warthen RO, Sanford MD, Rice EC: Primary malignant tumor of the pancreas in a fifteen-month-old boy. Am J Dis Child 1952;83:663.
204. Way LW, Gadacz T, Goldman L: Surgical treatment of chronic pancreatitis. Am J Surg 1974;127:202.
205. Weber TR, Keller MS: Operative management of chronic pancreatitis in children. Arch Surg 2001;136:550-555.
206. Weetman RM, Baehner RL: Latent onset of clinical pancreatitis in children receiving L-asparaginase therapy. Cancer 1974;34:780.
207. Weizman Z, Durie PR: Acute pancreatitis in childhood. J Pediatr 1988;113:24.
208. White TT, Keith RG: Long term follow-up study of fifty patients with pancreaticojejunostomy. Surg Gynecol Obstet 1973;136:353.
209. White TT, Slavotinik AH: Results of surgical treatment of chronic pancreatitis. Report of 142 cases. Ann Surg 1979; 189:217.
210. Wilson SD: Zollinger-Ellison syndrome in children: A 25-year followup. Surgery 1991;110:696.
211. Witt H: Gene mutations in children with chronic pancreatitis. Pancreatology 2001;1:432.
212. Yellin AE, Vecchione TR, Donovan AJ: Distal pancreatectomy for pancreatic trauma. Am J Surg 1972;124:135.
213. Yoshimi N, Sugie S, Tanaka T, et al: A rare case of serous cystadenocarcinoma of the pancreas. Cancer 1992;69:2449.
214. Ziegler DW, Long JA, Philippart AI, Klein MD: Pancreatitis in childhood: Experience with 49 patients. Ann Surg 1988;207:257.
215. Zielenski J: Genotype and phenotype in caustic fibrosis. Respiration 2000;67:117-133.
216. Zollinger RM, Ellison EH: Primary peptic ulcerations of the jejunum associated with islet cell tumors of pancreas. Ann Surg 1955;142:709.

Chapter 108

The Spleen

Frederick J. Rescorla

Splenic physiology can be broadly categorized into red blood cell maintenance and reservoir and immunologic functions. Children frequently require splenectomy for disease processes involving abnormalities in red cell deformability or the presence of antiplatelet antibodies resulting in excessive splenic red cell destruction or platelet sequestration. The vital role of the spleen as an immunologic organ not only has led to nonoperative management of splenic trauma but also has affected the timing of elective splenectomy and renewed interest in partial splenectomy for certain disorders. The technique of splenectomy has changed significantly with the advent of advanced laparoscopy and, unfortunately, as in most laparoscopic procedures, laparoscopic splenectomy has been accepted as the standard without supporting evidence from randomized controlled studies. The technique of laparoscopic splenectomy and the available evidence comparing it with open splenectomy are discussed in the latter part of this chapter.

HISTORY

The role of the spleen has been the subject of debate for over 300 years. Billroth is credited with developing the open circulation theory of the splenic microcirculation, and the endothelial cords of the red pulp bear his name. The recognition of the spleen as a functional organ in health and disease has been well documented in the 20th century. One of the more important observations was that of King and Shumaker in 1952, who noted the susceptibility of infants to infection after splenectomy.[62] The value of the spleen in bacterial infections prompted pediatric surgeons to study the role of nonoperative management of splenic injuries,[29] a development that evolved into the preferred method for treating both childhood and adult splenic injuries. Another significant development in the surgical management of splenic disorders was the initial report of laparoscopic splenectomy in 1991 by Delaitre and Maignien.[28] This technique has quickly become the preferred technique for splenectomy in children.

EMBRYOLOGY AND ANATOMY

The splenic primordium is first recognized at the 8- to 10-mm stage as a mesenchymal bulge in the left dorsal mesogastrium between the stomach and pancreas. By the 10- to 12-mm stage a true epithelium is noted and sinusoids are present with communication to capillaries. By 4 months of fetal life, the spleen produces red and white cells; however, this function ceases later in gestation, and the spleen is rarely the site of clinically significant hematopoiesis in childhood. The anatomic arrangement of the spleen is consistent with the various functions of the spleen. Blood enters the spleen through splenic artery segmental vessels that branch into trabecular arteries; and, after further bifurcations, small arteries enter the white pulp. The white pulp consists of lymphocytes and macrophages arranged as a germinal center around the central artery. Branches off of the central artery deliver suspended particulate material into the white pulp, an arrangement that may facilitate antibody formation in response to particulate antigens.[84,87,98,99] Approximately 20% of the volume of the spleen is white pulp, whereas the remainder is the red pulp, consisting of the endothelial cords of Billroth.[108] Blood passing through the spleen traverses in either an "open" or "closed" fashion. Ten to 20 percent of blood passes through the closed system directly from capillaries into venous sinusoids. The remainder passes directly into the red pulp. These cells and other particulate material must pass through in an open fashion within the cords of Billroth and then migrate into the sinusoids, which enter into trabecular veins.

FUNCTION

The function of the spleen is closely related to the anatomic arrangements and can be divided into red cell maintenance, immune function, and reservoir. Derangements in the substrate entering the spleen often lead to excessive function of one of the splenic roles, thus leading to the need for splenectomy. The spleen destroys red cells at the end of their life span and repairs other damaged red cells. The spleen selectively removes abnormal cells such as spherocytes, and removal of the spleen increases the life span of these cells. As blood passes through the spleen, Howell-Jolly bodies (nuclear remnants), Heinz bodies (denatured hemoglobin), and Pappenheimer bodies (iron granules) are removed, and after splenectomy they are noted in red cells.

The immune function of the spleen is characterized by specific and nonspecific responses. The specific immune function of the spleen is primarily related to antigen processing. Antigens come into contact with macrophages and helper T cells in the area of the arterioles of the white pulp. T-cell populations respond with synthesis of cytokines as part of the cellular response, and activated T cells then circulate to modulate the response. A humoral response can occur as antigens come in contact with macrophages and helper T cells and are then transmitted to antibody synthesizing cells.[76]

The nonspecific function involves removal of the particulate matter from the blood primarily by macrophages. The spleen is also the principal source of nonspecific opsonins, which further activate the complement system, facilitating the destruction of organisms.

Another aspect of the immune function is simply serving as a biologic filter. If little antibody is available for opsonization of bacteria, the spleen assumes a greater role in clearance of bacteria. This may be the basis for the age-related differences in postsplenectomy infections, because young children lack adequate antibody response.[87] The spleen also serves as a reservoir, which in humans is primarily limited to platelets. The proportion of platelets in the spleen is increased in cases of splenomegaly, occasionally leading to thrombocytopenia. The spleen also serves as a reservoir for factor VIII.

ANATOMIC ABNORMALITIES

Accessory Spleens

Accessory spleens represent the most common anatomic abnormality and are present in 15% to 30% of children. They most likely originate from mesenchymal remnants that do not fuse with the main splenic mass. The majority (75%) are located near the splenic hilum, followed by the tail of the pancreas; and they occur along the splenic artery, omentum, mesentery, and retroperitoneum and have even been noted in the scrotum.[32] Of those with accessory spleens, 86% have one, 11% have two, and 3% have three or more,[51,52] with the hilum the most common site of multiple accessory spleens. Surgeons must be cognizant of these locations and routinely check for their presence because a missed accessory spleen can be a cause of recurrence of immune thrombocytopenic purpura (ITP) or hereditary spherocytosis. Recurrence with ITP is frequently early,[45,116] whereas recurrence with hereditary spherocytosis has been reported as long as 31 years later.[22]

Wandering Spleen

Wandering spleen is characterized by lack of ligamentous attachments to the diaphragm, colon, and retroperitoneum.

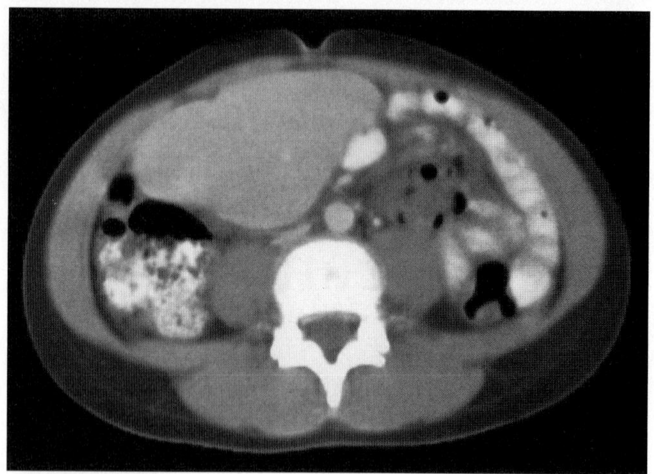

Figure 108–1 CT scan of a wandering spleen in a 7-year-old boy with intermittent abdominal pain and an abdominal mass. A laparoscopic splenopexy was used to secure a left upper quadrant fixation.

The embryologic basis of this is probably related to failure of development of the splenic ligaments from the dorsal mesentery.[109] Children with this condition often present with torsion and infarction, although they may also present with episodic pain and an abdominal mass (Fig. 108-1)[50,72,82,103,104] Although splenectomy is required for infarction, splenopexy is preferred in nonischemic and incidentally detected cases. Splenopexy has been performed with various techniques, including placement in an extraperitoneal pocket,[104] use of Dexon mesh basket,[2] suture splenopexy,[112] and colonic displacement with gastropexy.[16] Laparoscopic detorsion and splenopexy can be performed with the use of an absorbable mesh bag that is closed around the splenic hilum and then tacked to the diaphragm and posterolateral abdominal wall.

Splenic Cysts

Primary splenic cysts have an epithelial lining, frequently with a trabeculated internal appearance. They most likely originate from inclusion of the surface mesothelium into the splenic parenchyma. They may be asymptomatic or may present as pain,[121] rupture,[91] abscess,[120] or symptoms due to gastric compression. Symptomatic cysts are usually greater than 8 cm.[121] Small (<5 cm) simple cysts can be observed; however, larger, enlarging or symptomatic cysts require definitive treatment. Percutaneous aspiration and sclerosis have been utilized, but recurrence is common and partial splenectomy has been required.[78] Alcohol sclerosis of a congenital cyst has been reported with success, although the length of follow-up was not specified.[1] Marsupialization can be associated with recurrence if an adequate segment of cyst is not removed.[80,114] Laparoscopic partial cyst excision[64,100] and cyst resection with partial splenectomy[13,47,123] have been reported with good success. Partial splenectomy with excision of the cyst at the margin with the spleen can be performed with the Harmonic scalpel (Ethicon Endo-Surgery, Cincinnati, Ohio)[73,101,106] or with the use of stapling devices in an open[130] or laparoscopic fashion.[38,105] Use of cautery,[105] sutures, and omental packing of the defect may also be useful.[106] Splenic pseudocysts lack an epithelial lining and most frequently occur after trauma. Large (>8.0 cm), enlarging, and symptomatic cysts should be excised.[117]

Asplenia and Polysplenia

Asplenia and polysplenia syndromes have many similar features. Congenital asplenia is usually noted with complex congenital heart disease as well as bilateral "right-sidedness," including bilateral three-lobed lungs, right-sided stomach, and a central liver.[5] Intestinal malrotation has also been observed.[122] Howell-Jolly bodies are noted on peripheral smear and infants have the risk of overwhelming infection.

Polysplenia in which the spleen is divided into multiple splenic masses is often associated with biliary atresia. Other associated features included preduodenal portal vein, situs inversus, malrotation, and cardiac defects.[5] These children have adequate splenic immune function.

Splenic Gonadal Fusion

Splenogonadal fusion occurs as a result of early fusion between the spleen and left gonad.[90] The remnant may be continuous with a fibrous band or discontinuous with splenic tissue attached to the gonad. Another abnormality identified has been ectopic splenic tissue in the scrotum apart from a gonadal fusion.

INDICATIONS FOR SPLENECTOMY

Hereditary Spherocytosis

Hereditary spherocytosis is the most common inherited red cell disorder among northern European descendants. Approximately 75% of affected children have an autosomal dominant inheritance pattern, with the remainder being new mutations or autosomal recessive. Membrane defects in ankyrin or spectrin proteins result in poorly deformable spherocytes. The degree of splenic hemolysis can range from mild to severe. Most children are noted to have anemia, an elevated reticulocyte count, and a mild elevation of bilirubin. The presence of spherocytes along with a positive osmotic fragility test confirms the diagnosis. In affected children, an aplastic crisis can occur secondary to parvovirus B19 infection, with suppression of red cell production and a resultant low hematocrit due to ongoing destruction.[133] Splenectomy is usually required for moderate to severe anemia. Gallstones are common, increasing in frequency with the age of the child and degree of hemolysis, and thus a gallbladder ultrasound is required before splenectomy. Hereditary elliptocytosis is a similar disorder associated with spectrin defects, but most patients are asymptomatic without significant hemolysis.

Immune Thrombocytopenic Purpura

ITP occurs when antiplatelet autoantibodies, usually IgG, bind with platelets, leading to destruction in the reticuloendothelial system. Treatment options include corticosteroids, which may function by inhibiting the reticuloendothelial binding of platelet-antibody complexes; intravenous immunoglobulin (IVIG), which competitively inhibits the Fc receptor binding of platelets by macrophages; use of Rho (D) immunoglobulin in Rh-positive children, which binds to red cells that then saturate the splenic capacity and spares the antibody-coated platelets; and splenectomy. Response to corticosteroids, IVIG, or both predicts response (97%) to splenectomy, whereas failure to respond to either predicts a 70% failure rate to splenectomy.[25] Others have noted the response to IVIG to be a better predictor of response to splenectomy than corticosteroids.[57] Childhood ITP is usually a self-limited, acute disorder, and splenectomy is only required in chronic cases.

Sickle Cell Disease

Sickle cell disease occurs from a substitution of valine for glutamic acid in the β chain of normal hemoglobin A, resulting in hemoglobin S. These red cells become rigid when oxygen saturation decreases, with subsequent capillary occlusion and shortened red cell life. Children with homozygous sickle cell anemia and with hemoglobin sickle cell disease have significant rates of painful crisis and acute chest syndrome. Splenic sequestration with rapid drop in hemoglobin and platelet counts can occur and, if severe or recurrent, merit splenectomy to reduce the chance of further episodes.

Thalassemia

The thalassemias are a group of disorders characterized by abnormal production of α or β chains of hemoglobin. Thalassemia major (Cooley anemia; β-thalassemia) results in the most severe clinical anemia among this group of disorders. Some children develop significant splenomegaly with sequestration. Splenectomy has been utilized to decrease the need for transfusions in children with severe anemia and those with significant splenomegaly and platelet or white cell sequestration.

Gaucher's Disease

Gaucher's disease is a metabolic disorder characterized by deficiency of the enzyme β-glucocerebrosidase, which results in excessive glucocerebroside in macrophages of the spleen, liver, bone marrow, and lungs. It is an autosomal recessive disorder found most commonly in Ashkenazi Jews. Splenomegaly can be severe, and both partial and total splenectomy have been utilized to alleviate the hypersplenism and increase the red cell, leukocyte, and platelet counts.[40] However, recurrence has been reported after partial splenectomy.

Abscess

Splenic abscesses are rare but have been noted with increasing frequency with the increased numbers of immunocompromised children. Organisms are frequently fungal or mycobacterial.[111] Children frequently have fever, pain, and positive blood cultures. In view of the diffuse nature frequently noted by computed tomography (CT), splenectomy is often required.

SPLENECTOMY

Open Splenectomy

A left upper quadrant subcostal incision provides excellent exposure for most spleens even in cases of splenomegaly. The spleen is retracted medially, and the splenorenal, splenophrenic and splenocolic ligaments are divided. This can usually be accomplished with a relatively small incision, and the spleen is removed from the abdominal cavity by delivering the lower pole first, taking advantage of the concave medial surface of the spleen. The gastrosplenic ligament and short gastric vessels are divided, followed by the hilar vessels. If the pancreas is very close to the hilum, it may be necessary to divide the segmental vessels. A careful search is made for accessory spleens; and, if present, they are removed. An alternative open approach utilizes a lateral muscle-splitting incision,[43] and this has been associated with a 2.7-day length of stay, comparable to some laparoscopic series.[37,79,126] Complications are relatively rare after splenectomy. Thrombosis of the splenic, portal, and mesenteric veins has been reported after splenectomy and should be considered in the evaluation of abdominal pain after splenectomy.[110]

Laparoscopic Splenectomy

Technique

The laparoscopic technique for splenectomy was initially reported in 1991[28] and over the subsequent 5 years has become the preferred method at most institutions. Less pain, as reflected in lower pain medication use, shorter length of stay, and improved cosmesis are the main benefits compared with open splenectomy. The laparoscopic procedure has a steep learning curve for those unfamiliar with advanced laparoscopic techniques, can be difficult in cases of splenomegaly, and is associated with longer operative times than the open procedure. The efficacy of accessory spleen detection has been questioned in adult studies,[45,116] although comparison of open and laparoscopic pediatric series has found similar detection rates.[37,77,79,92,94,126]

The technique of laparoscopic splenectomy has evolved with the development of smaller instruments and advanced technology such as the Harmonic scalpel. Although preoperative splenic artery embolization was reported in many initial adult series,[42] complications such as pain, abscess, and retroperitoneal necrosis[85,88] have occurred; and some have noted no difference in the risk of bleeding or transfusion requirement. Embolization for spleens between 20 and 30 cm in length and open splenectomy if the organ is larger than 30 cm have been recommended, but most childhood spleens in cases of splenomegaly are smaller, so this appears unnecessary in children.[88] Hand-assisted procedures have also been described in adults[48] for large spleens, but the accessory incision prolongs the stay[46] and also appears to have no role in children.

Although some initial reports utilized an anterior approach, most surgeons currently use a lateral approach, as depicted in Figure 108-2. At my institution the patient is placed approximately 45 degrees left side up with slight elevation of the right flank to increase access on the left side. The table is rotated to the patient's left side for trocar placement and then to the right to achieve a right lateral decubitus position for the procedure. The general principle is for the assistant to use two grasping instruments through the upper abdominal midline sites (see a and b in Figure 108-2) to elevate the spleen and provide traction on surrounding tissues. In young children and older patients with small spleens, 3-mm instruments are used at those sites and placed directly into the abdominal cavity through small stab incisions without the use of trocars. If a trocar is not used, the surgeon must be cognizant of the risks associated with cautery conduction injuries. If the spleen is large, at least one of the upper

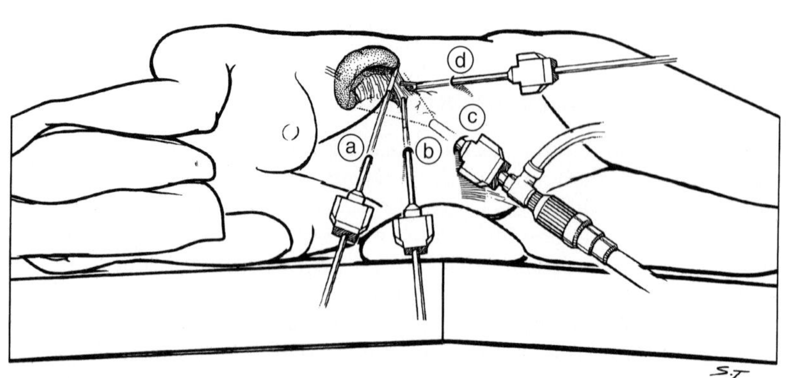

Figure 108-2 Patient position and port size and location for lateral approach: a and b, 3 or 5 mm midline; c, umbilical 12 or 15 mm; d, 5 mm left lower quadrant.

midline trocars must accommodate 5-mm instruments. For most of the procedure the lead surgeon holds the camera in the left hand (umbilical port) and the Harmonic scalpel in the right hand. The umbilical port is most commonly a 15-mm port to accommodate the 15-mm diameter Endocatch II (United States Surgical Corp, Norwalk, CT) device and the endovascular stapling devices. Use of the 5-mm 30-degree telescope allows its use through the left lower quadrant site, which is necessary when stapling and for placement of the retrieval device through the umbilical site.

The splenocolic ligament is divided with the Harmonic scalpel, allowing the splenic flexure to fall away from the spleen (Fig. 108-3A). The gastrosplenic ligament is divided, utilizing the Harmonic scalpel to divide the short gastric vessels; thus the surgeon rarely needs to remove the device (see Fig. 108-3B). The division of the most superior aspect is difficult, owing to the close proximity of the spleen and stomach, and care must also be taken to avoid injury to the diaphragm. Accessory spleens identified at the hilum can often be removed en bloc with the spleen and others from the lesser sac or omentum removed separately, usually through the umbilical trocar.

The spleen is then held up from the superior and inferior poles and the hilum approached, often dividing the inferior set of segmental vessels with either the Harmonic scalpel or with clips and the scissors. The surgeon must

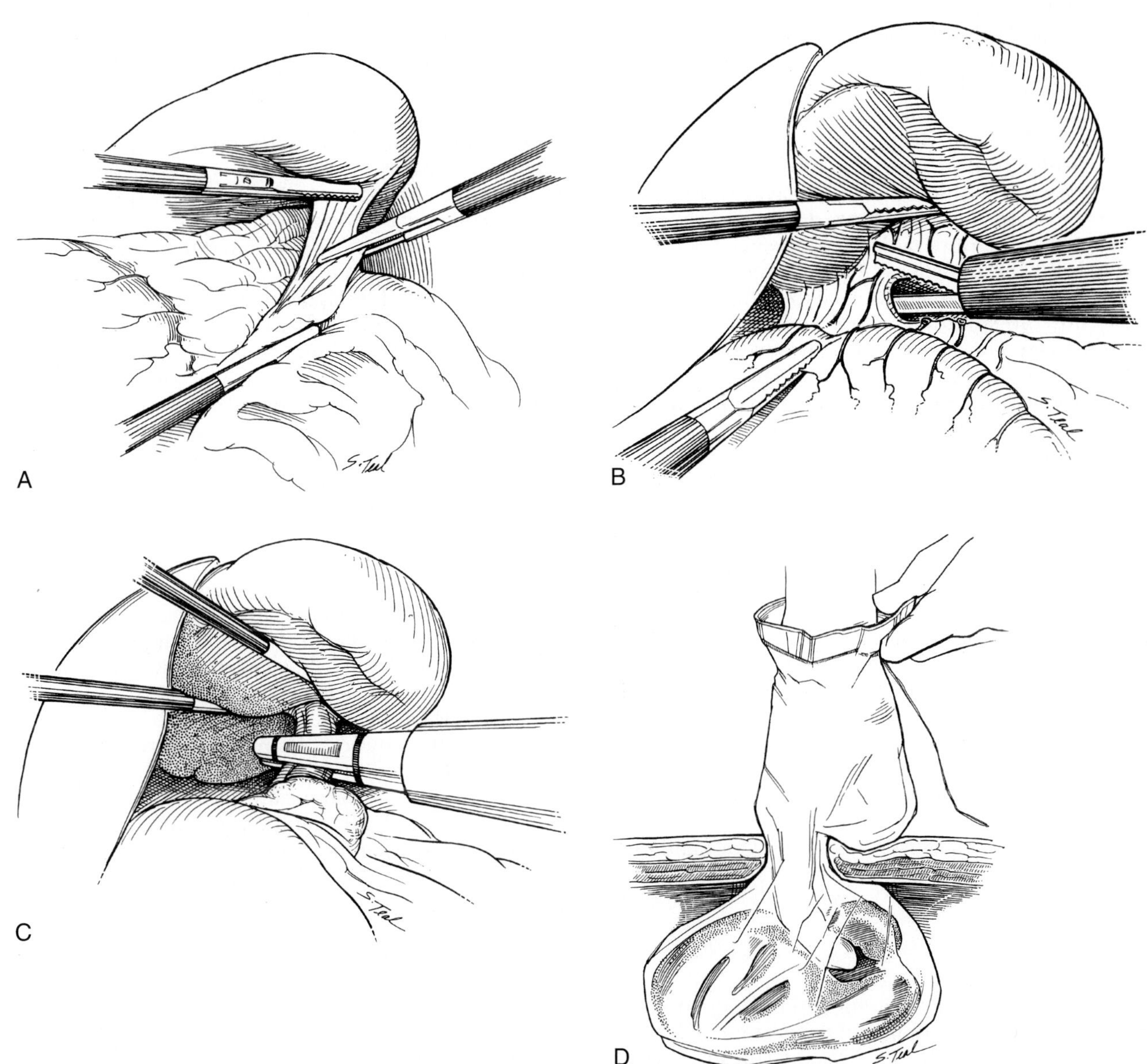

Figure 108-3 Division of the splenocolic (*A*) and gastrosplenic (*B*) ligaments with the Harmonic scalpel. The endovascular stapler is utilized to divide the splenic hilum (*C*) and, after placement in the retrieval bag, delivered out the umbilical port (*D*). Finger fracture and forceps are used to remove splenic fragments.

decide between the use of clips or an endovascular stapler for the remaining segmental or polar vessels. If the vessels are individually divided, the surgeon must be prepared, should bleeding occur, to control the vessel proximally with a grasper and either clip the vessel or staple the remainder of the hilum. If the stapler is utilized, the splenorenal ligament can be divided so that the posterior arm of the stapler can easily pass posterior to the hilum. Care must be taken at this step to avoid injury to the tail of the pancreas (see Fig. 108-3C). Other operative adjuncts at this point include use of a suction cup grasper to manipulate the spleen,[44] a wall-lifting device,[83] and placement of umbilical tape around the hilum to elevate and immobilize the spleen.[102] Another alternative to the Harmonic scalpel and stapler is use of the LigaSure vessel sealing device (United States Surgical, Norwalk, CT) which utilizes bipolar energy and pressure to achieve a seal.[97] Use of the da Vinci surgical robot has also been reported.[19]

The Endocatch II retrieval device is placed through the umbilical port. The bag when opened is 13 cm in diameter and 23 cm deep and accommodates most pediatric spleens. If the spleen is small, a 10- or 12-mm umbilical port can be used with a 10-mm bag (Endopouch, Ethicon Surgery, Inc, Cincinnati, OH). The spleen is then placed in the retrieval bag and the neck of the bag delivered out the umbilicus. A finger and ring forceps are placed through the external opening and used to fracture the splenic capsule and remove splenic fragments (see Fig. 108-3D). The use of an ultrasonic morcellator and liposucker[66] to fragment the spleen has been described, and another technique utilized transvaginal removal of the bag.[125] In some cases of splenomegaly it may be difficult to place the spleen in the bag. Hebra and colleagues[54] utilized a coring device to remove portions of the spleen before its placement in a bag. This is not recommended in cases of hereditary spherocytosis in which splenosis could potentially lead to recurrent anemia. The fascia at the umbilical site and, if convenient, the anterior fascia layers at the 5-mm sites are closed. The orogastric tube and Foley catheter utilized intraoperatively are removed at the end of the procedure. Diet is advanced as tolerated the day of surgery, and pain control is achieved with intravenous morphine and nonsteroidal anti-inflammatory agents, followed by oral pain medications when the patient is tolerating liquids. The techniques of laparoscopic splenectomy are applicable to other procedures, including partial splenectomy for disease or lesions such as cysts, splenopexy for wandering spleen, as well as treatment of traumatic splenic injuries.[15,63]

Conversion

Conversion to open splenectomy is most frequently due to splenomegaly or bleeding and is reported in 1.3% to 2.8% in several large series.[36,77,95,118,127] Giant spleens with malignancy are more difficult situations, and one author noted a 41% conversion rate in adults with malignancy compared with a 3% conversion rate for benign conditions.[9] In another adult series, Mahon and Rhodes noted that their conversion rate was 0% for spleens weighing less than 1 kg and 60% for those weighing more than 1 kg.[71] A lower conversion rate with increasing surgeon experience has been observed in some series.[85,131] A multivariate analysis in adult patients with ITP identified obesity and operator experience as factors predisposing to conversion to open procedure.[27]

Accessory Spleen Detection

Several adult studies have questioned the ability of laparoscopy to adequately detect accessory spleens. One report identified residual splenic function in 9 of 18 adults despite an original accessory spleen rate of 41%.[45] One of the three symptomatic patients had an accessory spleen identified at exploration. Parenchymal disruption was associated with a 75% residual function rate compared with 36% in those with no disruption, thus emphasizing the need to avoid spill. Three of nine failures of splenectomy in another study had residual splenic function.[116] Although some have recommended preoperative CT and/or scintigraphy,[36,81] most have abandoned this, with some studies noting higher detection rates with laparoscopy.[45,61] One report has also utilized intraoperative scintigraphy for accessory spleen localization.[21] The available data from six pediatric comparative studies do not identify a significant difference[37,77,79,92,94,126]: 20.3% accessory spleen rate in 128 open splenectomies versus 20.2% in 139 laparoscopic procedures. An evaluation of six adult or pediatric series with at least 50 laparoscopic splenectomies identified accessory spleens in 14.7% of a total of 585 patients.[36,42,46,61,85,95] Laparoscopic removal of missed accessory spleens has been reported,[4,115] one of which was a symptomatic accessory spleen identified 30 years after open splenectomy for ITP.[14] The occurrence of splenosis at the retrieval port site has also been observed.[65]

Operative Time

Comparative series have uniformly observed longer operative time with the laparoscopic technique,[37,77,79,92,94,126] and several have noted shorter times with increased surgeon experience.[24,95] In a review of 112 laparoscopic splenectomies at my institution, a longer operative time (115 versus 98 minutes) was noted in the first 50 procedures compared with the next 62 procedures but the differences were not significant.[95] The shorter times were still longer than the 83-minute procedure time reported by my colleagues and me for open splenectomy.[94]

Pain

The pediatric reports do not utilize pain scores but rely on pain medication usage as a reflection of pain. All available comparative studies report lower morphine equivalent dose usage for pain control for laparoscopic compared with open splenectomy, but the difference did not reach statistical significance in two of the five studies.[8,23,79,92,94] This is consistent with an adult study that noted equal quality of life and control of the hematologic disease with less pain in the laparoscopic group.[124]

Length of Stay

Length of stay ranges from 1.3 to 3.6 days, with the more recent studies stating 1.7 to 1.8 days.[77,92,94] All pediatric comparative studies have noted a shorter length of stay with the laparoscopic technique (laparoscopic, 1.3 to 3.6 days; open, 2.5 to 4.9 days), with the reduction ranging from 18% to 56%.[37,77,79,92,94,126] The underlying disorder can affect length of stay because infants and children with sickle cell disease have been noted to require a longer stay than those with ITP and hereditary spherocytosis (2.5 versus 1.4 days).[94] This has been due to the occurrence of postoperative acute chest syndrome. Splenomegaly alone, in children, does not appear to adversely affect length of stay because splenomegaly with hereditary spherocytosis is the most frequent indication for splenectomy and is associated with a short length of stay (1.4 days). A meta-analysis of all reports (primarily adults) from 1991 through 2002 (2940 patients; 2119 laparoscopic procedures, 821 open procedures) noted longer mean operative time (laparoscopic, 180 minutes; open, 114 minutes; $P<.0001$) but a shorter hospital stay (laparoscopic, 3.6 days; open, 7.2 days; $P<.001$) with laparoscopic splenectomy.[129] Unproven benefits of the laparoscopic approach concern the child's return to full activity and the effect of return to school on the parent's return to work. Children undergoing laparoscopic splenectomy have been observed to return to full activity 1 to 5 weeks earlier than with the open procedure.[126] In addition, parents who had themselves undergone splenectomy view the laparoscopic technique better than the open technique.

Cost

The presumption of most authors is that the shorter length of stay with laparoscopy will offset the higher operative charges related to the longer operative time and the use of disposable materials. Data from comparative studies note three studies with higher[23,59,126] and three with lower[37,92,94] hospital charges with laparoscopy. The method by which individual hospitals determine charges or cost for supplies, operating room time, and inpatient days makes comparison difficult. The available cost data do not appear to confer an advantage to either procedure.

Complications

The most significant evaluation of a new procedure is the evaluation of complications. The Clavien[20] classification system stratifies complications as follows:

Grade I: minor, resolves spontaneously or with bedside procedure (atelectasis, gastric distention requiring nasogastric tube, temperature > 38.5° C)
Grade II: potentially life threatening, usually requires intervention, iatrogenic, complication resulting in doubling of hospital stay
Grade III: residual or lasting disability, iatrogenic organ resection
Grade IV: death as a result of complication

This system was applied to a group of 344 laparoscopic and 369 open splenectomies in children performed between 1995 and 2002.* In this evaluation there was no statistical difference between the rate of grade I (laparoscopic 2.9% versus open 4.9%; $P=0.18$) or grade II (laparoscopic 6.7% versus open 4.9%; $P=0.30$), and there were no reported Grade III or IV complications in any of the series.

The largest adult single institution comparative study (63 laparoscopic, 74 open) noted equivalent grade I and II complications (5% to 9%) but higher grade III (41% versus 0%) and grade IV (3% versus 0%) complications with the open technique.[42] A meta-analysis of 26 comparison studies (adult and pediatric) performed from 1991 through 2002 noted a total complication rate of 15.5% for laparoscopic and 26.6% for open splenectomy ($P<0.0001$).[129] The laparoscopic group had fewer pulmonary, wound, and infectious complications ($P<0.0001$) but had more hemorrhagic complications when conversions for bleeding were included.

Partial Splenectomy

Total splenectomy with removal of accessory spleens eliminates splenic hemolysis and sequestration for congenital hemolytic anemias. Concerns of overwhelming postsplenectomy sepsis, particularly in children younger than 5 years of age, have led to the development of partial splenectomy. This has primarily been utilized for hemolytic anemias such as hereditary spherocytosis but has also been utilized for Gaucher's disease,[40] Hodgkin's disease staging,[55] trauma,[89] hypersplenism with cystic fibrosis,[119] as well as excision of splenic cysts,[105] hamartomas,[53] and hemangiomas.[7] When this technique is utilized for splenic volume reduction, 85% to 95% of the disease-affected splenic mass is removed to leave approximately 25% of a normal splenic remnant. Anatomic studies of the splenic blood supply indicate that 86% of spleens have two lobar vessels and 12% have three lobar arteries.[69] In addition, 77% have either four or five segmental vessels, thus allowing preservation of either an upper or lower pole segmental vessel supplying 20% to 25% of the spleen. The spleen is divided with either a stapling device, cautery, or the Harmonic scalpel; and hemostasis is achieved with cautery, argon beam coagulation, or topical agents as needed. If the spleen is totally mobilized, the remnant can be fixed to the retroperitoneum to prevent torsion. This procedure can be performed laparoscopically utilizing the Harmonic scalpel to both divide the spleen and provide hemostasis. (Fig. 108-4).

Long-term follow-up has noted increased red blood cell half-life, higher hemoglobin level, and lower reticulocyte count and bilirubin levels.[6,96] Preservation of splenic phagocytic function has been demonstrated by elimination of Howell-Jolly bodies on peripheral smear and decreased numbers of pitted red cells.[96] Other parameters have included normal IgM and IgG levels of specific antibody titers to *Streptococcus pneumoniae*. Splenic regrowth occurs in all patients with hemolytic

*See references 3, 8, 23, 35, 37, 39, 43, 59, 68, 77, 79, 86, 92-95, 102, 126, and 132.

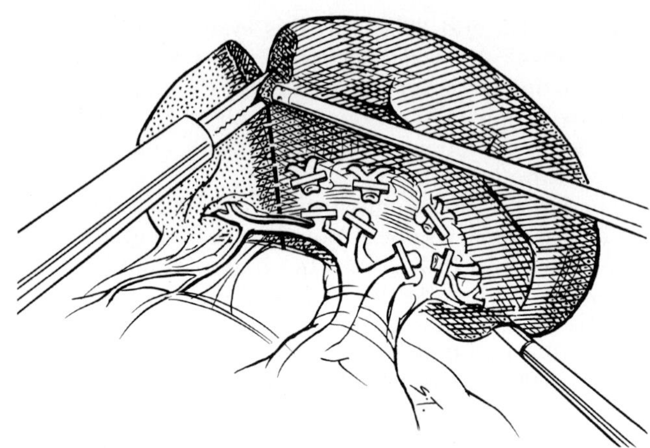

Figure 108-4 Laparoscopic partial splenectomy utilizing the ultrasonic dissector.

anemias, although the degree of regrowth does not correlate with hemolysis. Complications of post–partial splenectomy hemolysis can include ongoing development of cholelithiasis (7% to 22%), recurrent anemia with need for transfusion, or subsequent total splenectomy.[26,96] Caution must be exercised in the assumption of normal splenic function because one patient with evidence of residual splenic function by scan after partial splenectomy for trauma died of an *S. pneumoniae* infection 13 years later.[135] This patient had not received pneumococcal vaccine. Preoperative immunization is recommended, and postoperative antibiotics are administered at least until splenic immunologic competence is noted.

Postsplenectomy Sepsis

The occurrence of overwhelming postsplenectomy infection (OPSI) was first reported by King and Shumacker in 1951 in a series of five infants younger than 6 months of age undergoing splenectomy for hereditary spherocytosis.[62] All five developed serious infections, and two died. Since then numerous reports have documented this risk as well as the increased risk (60-100 fold) in children younger than 5 years of age as well as during the first few years after splenectomy. The etiology is probably related to decreased clearance of encapsulated bacteria[12] as well as decreased immunoglobulin levels.[17] The spleen is particularly important in infancy and childhood because the phagocytic function in infection occurs almost exclusively in the spleen.[67]

A cumulative review of the literature reported in the 1970s[31] identified the incidence of OPSI at 3.75%, with a mortality of 1.7%. The rate in pediatric cases was 4.1% compared with 1.9% in adults and a mortality rate of 1.8% in children compared with 1.1% identified in adults. Other studies in the 1980s and 1990s had a wide range of OPSI; and as of the mid 1990s the overall incidence of OPSI ranged from 0.13% to 8.1% in children younger than 15 years of age compared with 0.28% to 1.9% in adults.[70] *S. pneumoniae* is causative in 50% to 90% of all infections and is responsible for 60% of all fatal infections.[31,41,107,113] *Haemophilus influenzae* accounts for 32% of mortality,[56] and the meningococcus and group A *Streptococcus* are also significant pathogens.

The risk of late infectious mortality also varied with the disease state with a rate of 0.51% for spherocytosis and 2.67% for ITP.[33] Others also noted a higher mortality in children younger than 4 years of age (mortality: 8.1% in those younger than 4 years of age, 3.3% in older patients) with most deaths within 4 years of splenectomy.[34,58] In view of this, penicillin prophylaxis was advocated. The increased risk in children relative to adults was documented with an incidence of fatal OPSI of 3.77% in children compared with 0.39% in adults.[18] Many of these early reports were performed before widespread vaccination and use of prophylactic antibiotics, and more recent studies have somewhat lower rates of OPSI of 3.5% to 3.8%.[60,75] Vaccination has been shown to decrease the risk of bacteremia.[30]

A comparison study of an early era of splenectomy with no immunizations or prophylactic antibiotics compared with a later era with a 70% immunization and a 100% prophylaxis rate noted a decrease in the infection rate (6% to 3.8%) and mortality (3.9% to 0.9%).[60] Even in this more recent study the rate of infection was related to age at splenectomy (birth to 5 years, 13.8%; >5 years, 0.5%). The historical mortality associated with OPSI has been 50% to 70%,[10,49,70,113] but more recently a mortality of around 10% has been observed.[11,60]

From the previous studies it appears that the risk of postsplenectomy sepsis can be reduced with the use of immunizations to *S. pneumoniae,* meningococcus, and *H. influenzae* as well as use of prophylactic antibiotics. With the availability of vaccinations, standard recommendations have included preoperative immunization, with many children currently receiving routine childhood immunizations against pneumococci and *H. influenzae.* Lifelong prophylactic penicillin has been recommended by some,[74] whereas others recommend it for 10 years[134] or less. The highest rate for OPSI is in children and within 2 years of splenectomy, leaving long-term recommendations unclear.[128]

LAPAROSCOPIC SPLENIC PROCEDURES AT THE J. W. RILEY HOSPITAL FOR CHILDREN

At my institution laparoscopic splenectomy was introduced in August 1995, and within 4 months this was the predominant technique. A total of 190 children underwent laparoscopic splenic procedures; 178 had splenectomy, 5 had partial splenectomy, 5 had laparoscopic splenic cystectomy for epithelial or traumatic cyst, and 2 had splenopexy for wandering spleen. Hereditary spherocytosis is the most common indication for splenectomy, followed by ITP and sickle cell disease with splenic sequestration. Four (2.2%) required conversion to an open procedure: 2 for splenomegaly, 1 for bleeding, and 1 due to adhesions from prior surgery. The average length of stay was 1.51 days; 1.23 days for hereditary spherocytosis, 1.15 days for ITP, and 2.24 days for sickle cell disease. One child with hemolytic anemia required an open accessory splenectomy for a missed accessory spleen, and one child who was not taking prophylactic antibiotics died of postsplenectomy sepsis.

REFERENCES

1. Akhan O, Baykan Z, Oguzkurt L, et al: Percutaneous treatment of a congenital splenic cyst with alcohol: a new therapeutic approach. Eur Radiol 1997;7:1067.
2. Allen KB, Andrews G: Pediatric wandering spleen—the case for splenopexy: review of 35 reported cases in the literature. J Pediatr Surg 1989;24:432.
3. Al-Salem AH: Is splenectomy for massive splenomegaly safe in children? Am J Surg 1999;178:42.
4. Amaral JF, Meltzer RC, Crowley JP: Laparoscopic accessory splenectomy for recurrent idiopathic thrombocytopenic purpura. Surg Laparosc Endosc 1997;7:340.
5. Anderson C, Devine WA, Anderson RH, et al: Abnormalities of the spleen in relation to congenital malformations of the heart: A survey of necropsy findings in children. Br Heart J 1990;63:122.
6. Bader-Meunier B, Gauthier F, Archambaud F, et al: Long-term evaluation of the beneficial effect of subtotal splenectomy for management of hereditary spherocytosis. Blood 2001;97:399.
7. Bailez MM, Elmo G: Laparoscopic partial splenectomy for a hemangioma of the spleen. Pediatr Endosurg Innov Tech 2004;8:147.
8. Beanes S, Emil S, Kosi M, et al: A comparison of laparoscopic versus open splenectomy in children. Am Surg 1995;61:908.
9. Berman RS, Yahanda A, Mansfield PF, et al: Laparoscopic splenectomy in patients with hematologic malignancies. Am J Surg 1999;178:530.
10. Brigden ML: Overwhelming post-splenectomy infection—still a problem. West J Med 1992;157:440.
11. Brigden ML, Pattullo AL: Prevention and management of overwhelming postsplenectomy infection—an update. Crit Care Med 1999;27:836.
12. Brown EJ, Hosea SW, Frank MM: The role of the spleen in experimental pneumococcal bacteremia. J Clin Invest 1981;67:975.
13. Brown MF, Ross III, AJ, Bishop HC, et al: Partial splenectomy: The preferred alternative for the treatment of splenic cysts. J Pediatr Surg 1989;24:694.
14. Budzynski A, Bobrzynski A, Sacha T, et al: Laparoscopic removal of retroperitoneal accessory spleen in patient with relapsing idiopathic thrombocytopenic purpura 30 years after classical splenectomy. Surg Endosc 2002;16:1636.
15. Carbon RT, Baar S, Waldschmidt J, et al: Innovative minimally invasive pediatric surgery is of therapeutic value for splenic injury. J Pediatr Surg 2002;37:1146.
16. Caracicolo F, Bonatti PC, Castruci G, et al: Wandering spleen: Treatment with colonic displacement. J R Coll Surg Edinb 1986;31:242.
17. Chaimoff C, Douer D, Pick IA, et al: Serum immunoglobulin changes after accidental splenectomy in adults. Am J Surg 1978;136:332.
18. Chalkof EL, McCabe CJ: Fatal overwhelming postsplenectomy infection. Am J Surg 1985;49:534.
19. Chapman WH, Albrecht RJ, Kim VB, et al: Computer-assisted laparoscopic splenectomy with the da Vinci surgical robot. J Laparoendosc Adv Surg Tech A 2002; 12:155.
20. Clavien PA, Sanabria JR, Strasberg SM: Proposed classification of complications of surgery with examples of utility in cholecystectomy. Surgery 1992;111:518.
21. Coventry BJ, Watson DI, Tucker K, et al: Intraoperative scintigraphic localization and laparoscopic excision of accessory splenic tissue. Surg Endosc 1998;12:159.
22. Crawford DL, Pickens PV, Moore JT: Hypertrophied splenic remnants in hereditary spherocytosis. Contemp Surg 1998;53:103.
23. Curran TJ, Foley MI, Swanstrom LL, et al: Laparoscopy improves outcomes for pediatric splenectomy. J Pediatr Surg 1998;33:1498.
24. Cusick RA, Waldhausen JH: The learning curve associated with pediatric laparoscopic splenectomy. Am J Surg 2201; 181:393.
25. Davis PW, Williams DA, Shamberger RC: Immune thrombocytopenia: Surgical therapy and predictors of response. J Pediatr Surg 1991;26:407.
26. de Buys Roessingh AS, de Lagausie P, Rohrlich P, et al: Follow-up of partial splenectomy in children with hereditary spherocytosis. J Pediatr Surg 2002;37:1459.
27. Delaitre B, Blezel E, Samama G, et al: Laparoscopic splenectomy for idiopathic thrombocytopenic purpura. 2002;12:412.
28. Delaitre B, Maignien B: Splenectomy by the coelioscopic approach: Report of a case. Presse Med 1991;20:2263.
29. Douglas GJ, Simpson JS: The conservative management of splenic trauma. J Pediatr Surg 1971;6:565.
30. Ejstrud P, Kristensen B, Hansen JB, et al: Risk and patterns of bacteraemia after splenectomy: A population-based study. Scand J Infect Dis 2000;32:521.
31. Ellison EC, Fabri PJ: Complications of splenectomy. Surg Clin North Am 1983;63:1313.
32. Emmett JM, Dreyfuss ML: Accessory spleen in the scrotum: Review of literature on ectopic spleens and their associated surgical significance. Ann Surg 1943;117:754.
33. Eraklis AJ, Filler RM: Splenectomy in childhood: A review of 1413 cases. J Pediatr Surg 1972;7:382.
34. Eraklis AJ, Kewy SV, Diamond LK: Hazard of overwhelming infection after splenectomy in childhood. N Engl J Med 1967;276:1225.
35. Esposito C, Corcione F, Garipoli V, et al: Pediatric laparoscopic splenectomy: Are there real advantages in comparison with the traditional open approach? Pediatr Surg Int 1997;12:509.
36. Esposito C, Schaarschmidt K, Settimi A, et al: Experience with laparoscopic splenectomy. J Pediatr Surg 2001;36:309.
37. Farah RA, Rogers ZR, Thompson RW, et al: Comparison of laparoscopic and open splenectomy in children with hematologic disorders. J Pediatr 1997;131:41.
38. Feliciotti F, Sottili M, Guerrieri M, et al: Conservative ultrasound-guided laparoscopic treatment of posttraumatic splenic cysts: Report of two cases. Surg Laparosc Endosc 1996;6:322.
39. Fitzgerald PG, Langer JC, Cameron BH, et al: Pediatric laparoscopy splenectomy using the lateral approach. Surg Endosc 1996;10:859.
40. Fonkalsrud EW, Philippart M, Feig S: Ninety-five percent splenectomy for massive splenomegaly: A new surgical approach. J Pediatr Surg 1990;25:267.
41. Francke EL, Neu HA: Postsplenectomy infection. Surg Clin North Am 1981;61:135.
42. Friedman RL, Hiatt JR, Korman JL, et al: Laparoscopic or open splenectomy for hematologic disease: Which approach is superior? J Am Coll Surg 1997;185:49.
43. Geiger JD, Dinh VV, Teitelbaum DH, et al: The lateral approach for open splenectomy. J Pediatr Surg 1998;33:1153.

44. Gentilli S, Velardocchia M, Ferrero A, et al: Laparoscopic splenectomy. How to make it easier using an innovative atraumatic suction grasper. Surg Endosc 1998;12:1345.
45. Gigot JF, Jamar F, Ferrant A, et al: Inadequate detection of accessory spleens and splenosis with laparoscopic splenectomy: A shortcoming of the laparoscopic approach in hematologic diseases. Surg Endosc 1998;12:101.
46. Gigot JF, Legrand M, Cadiere GB, et al: Is laparoscopic splenectomy a justified approach in hematologic disorders? Primary results of a prospective multicenter study. Int Surg 1995;80:299.
47. Golinski D, Freud E, Steinberg R, et al: Vertical partial splenectomy for epidermoid cyst. J Pediatr Surg 1995; 30:1704.
48. Gossot D, Fritsch S, Celerier M: Laparoscopic splenectomy: Optimal vascular control using the lateral approach and ultrasonic dissection. Surg Endosc 1999;13:21.
49. Green JB, Shackford SR, Sise MJ, et al: Late septic complications in adults following from trauma: a prospective analysis in 144 patients. J Trauma 1986;26:999.
50. Greig JD, Sweet EM, Drainer IK: Splenic torsion in a wandering spleen, presenting as an acute abdominal mass. J Pediatr Surg 1994;29:571.
51. Halpert B, Alden ZA: Accessory spleens in or at the tail of the pancreas. Arch Pathol 1964;77:652.
52. Halpert B, Gyorkey F: Lesions observed in accessory spleens of 311 patients. Am J Clin Pathol 1959;32:165.
53. Havlik RJ, Touloukian RJ, Markowitz RI, et al: Partial splenectomy for symptomatic splenic hamartoma. J Pediatr Surg 1990;25:1273.
54. Hebra A, Walker JD, Tagge EP, et al: A new technique for laparoscopic splenectomy with massively enlarged spleens. Am Surg 1998;64:1161.
55. Hoekstra HJ, Tamminga RYJ, Timens W: Partial splenectomy in children: An alternative for splenectomy in the pathological stage of Hodgkin's disease. Ann Surg Oncol 1994;1:480.
56. Holdsworth RJ, Irving AD, Cuschieri A: Postsplenectomy sepsis and its mortality rate: Actual versus perceived risks. Br J Surg 1991;78:1031.
57. Holt D, Brown J, Terrill K, et al: Response to intravenous immunoglobulin predicts splenectomy response in children with immune thrombocytopenic purpura. Pediatrics 2003;111:87.
58. Horan M, Colebatch JH: Relation between splenectomy and subsequent infection. Arch Dis Child 1962;37:398.
59. Janu PG, Rogers DA, Lobe TE: A comparison of laparoscopic and traditional open splenectomy in childhood. J Pediatr Surg 1996;31:109.
60. Jugenburg M, Haddock G, Freedman MH, et al: The morbidity and mortality of pediatric splenectomy: Does prophylaxis make a difference? J Pediatr Surg 1999; 34:1064.
61. Katkhouda N, Hurwitz MB, Rivera RT, et al: Laparoscopic splenectomy: Outcome and efficacy in 103 consecutive patients. Ann Surg 1998;228:568.
62. King H, Shumaker HB Jr: Splenic studies: I. Susceptibility to infection after splenectomy performed in infancy. Ann Surg 1953;136:239.
63. Koehler RH, Smith S, Fry WR: Successful laparoscopic splenorrhaphy using absorbable mesh for grade III splenic injury: Report of a case. Surg Laparosc Endosc 1994;4:311.
64. Kum CK, Ngoi SS, Goh P, et al: A rare wandering splenic cyst removed with laparoscopic assistance. Singapore Med J 1993;34:179.
65. Kumar RJ, Borzi PA: Splenosis in a port site after laparoscopic splenectomy. Surg Endosc 2001;15:413.
66. Lai PB, Leung KL, Ho WS, et al: The use of liposucker for spleen retrieval after laparoscopic splenectomy. Surg Laparosc Endosc Percutan Tech 2000;10:39.
67. Lane PA: The spleen and children. Curr Opin Pediatr 1995;7:36.
68. Liu DC, Meyers MO, Hill CB, et al: Laparoscopic splenectomy in children with hematologic disorders: Preliminary experience at the Children's Hospital of New Orleans. Am Surg 2000;66:1168.
69. Liu DL, Xia S, Xu W, et al: Anatomy of vasculature of 850 spleen specimens and its applications in partial splenectomy. Surgery 1996;119;27.
70. Lynch AM, Kapila R: Overwhelming postsplenectomy infection. Infect Dis Clin North Am 1996;4:693.
71. Mahon D, Rhodes M: Laparoscopic splenectomy: Size matters. 2003;85:248.
72. Maxwell-Armstrong CA, Clarke EDV, Tsang TM, et al: The wandering spleen. Arch Dis Child 1996;74:247.
73. McLean AL, Broussard E, McCarter MD, et al: Laparoscopic marsupialization of nonparasitic splenic cysts. Contemp Surg 2000;56:541.
74. McMullen M, Johnston G: Long-term management of patients after splenectomy. BMJ 1993;307:1372.
75. Meekes I, van der Staak, van Oostrom C: Results of splenectomy performed on a group of 91 children. Eur J Pediatr Surg 1995;5:19.
76. Meyer AA: Spleen. In Greenfield LJ, Mulholland MW, Oldham KT, et al (eds): Surgery, 2nd ed. Philadelphia, Lippincott-Raven, 1997, p 262.
77. Minkes RK, Lagzdins M, Langer JC: Laparoscopic versus open splenectomy in children. J Pediatr Surg 2000;35:699.
78. Moir C, Guttman F, Jequier S, et al: Splenic cysts: Aspiration, sclerosis, or resection. J Pediatr Surg 1989; 24:646.
79. Moores, DC, McKee MA, Wang H, et al: Pediatric laparoscopic splenectomy. J Pediatr Surg 1995;30:1201.
80. Morgenstern L: Nonparasitic splenic cysts: Pathogenesis, classification, and treatment. J Am Coll Surg 2002;194:306.
81. Morris KT, Horvath KD, Jobe BA, et al: Laparoscopic management of accessory spleens in immune thrombocytopenic purpura. Surg Endosc 1999;13:520.
82. Muckmel E, Zer M, Dintsman M: Wandering spleen with torsion of pedicle in a child presenting as an intermittently-appearing abdominal mass. J Pediatr Surg 1978;13:127.
83. Nishizaki T, Takahashi I, Onohara T, et al: Laparoscopic splenectomy using wall-lifting procedure. Surg Endosc 1999; 13:1055.
84. Nossal GJV, Austin CM, Pye J, et al: Antigens in immunity: XII. Antigen trapping in the spleen. Int Arch Allergy 1966; 29:368.
85. Park AE, Birgisson G, Mastrangelo MJ, et al: Laparoscopic splenectomy: Outcomes and lessons learned from over 200 cases. Surgery 2000;128:660.
86. Park A, Heniford BT, Hebra A, et al: Pediatric laparoscopic splenectomy. Surg Endosc 2000;14:527.
87. Pearson HA: The spleen and disturbances of splenic function. In Nathan DG, Orkin SH (eds): Hematology of Infancy and Childhood, 5th ed. Philadelphia, WB Saunders, 1998, vol II, p 1051.
88. Poulin EC, Mamazza J, Schlachta CM: Splenic artery embolization before laparoscopic splenectomy. Surg Laparosc Endosc 1995;5:463.
89. Poulin EC, Thibault C, DesCoteaux JG, Cote G: Partial laparoscopic splenectomy for trauma: Technique and case report. Surg Laparosc Endosc 1995;5:306.
90. Putschar WGJ, Manion WC: Splenic-gonadal fusion. Am J Pathol 1986;32:15.

91. Rathaus V, Zissin R, Goldberg E: Spontaneous rupture of an epidermoid cyst of the spleen: Preoperative ultrasonographic diagnosis. J Clin Ultrasound 1991;19:235.
92. Reddy VS, Phan HH, O'Neill JA, et al: Laparoscopic versus open splenectomy in the pediatric population: A contemporary single-center experience. Am Surg 2001;67: 859.
93. Rescorla FJ: Laparoscopic splenectomy. In Langer JC, Albanese CT (eds): Pediatric Minimal Access Surgery: A Principle and Evidence Based Approach. New York, Marcel Dekker, in press.
94. Rescorla FJ, Breitfeld PP, West KW, et al: A case-controlled comparison of open and laparoscopic splenectomy in children. Surgery 1996;124:670.
95. Rescorla FJ, Engum SA, West KW, et al: Laparoscopic splenectomy has become the gold standard in children. Am Surg 2002;68:297.
96. Rice HE, Oldham KT, Hillery CA, et al: Clinical and hematologic benefits of partial splenectomy for congenital hemolytic anemias in children. Ann Surg 2003;237:281.
97. Romano F, Caprotti R, Franciosi C, et al: The use of LigaSure during pediatric laparoscopic splenectomy: A preliminary report. Pediatr Surg Int 2003;19:721.
98. Rowley DA: The effect of splenectomy on the formation of circulating antibody in the adult male albino rat. J Immunol 1950;64:289.
99. Rowley DA: The formation of circulating antibody in the splenectomized human being following intravenous injection of heterologous erythrocytes. J Immunol 1950; 65:515.
100. Salky B, Zimmerman M, Bauer J, et al: Splenic cyst—definitive treatment by laparoscopy. Gastrointest Endosc 1985;31:213.
101. Sardi A, Ojeda HF, King D: Laparoscopic resection of a benign true cyst of the spleen with the Harmonic scalpel producing high levels of CA 19-9 and carcinoembryonic antigen. Am Surg 1998;64:1149.
102. Schleef J, Morcate JJ, Steinau G, et al: Technical aspects of laparoscopic splenectomy in children. J Pediatr Surg 1997;32:615.
103. Schmidt SP, Andrews HG, White JJ: The splenic snood: An improved approach for the management of the wandering spleen. J Pediatr Surg 1992;27:1043.
104. Seashore JH, McIntosh S: Elective splenopexy for wandering spleen. J Pediatr Surg 1990;25:270.
105. Seshadri PA, Poenaru D, Park A: Laparoscopic splenic cystectomy: A case report. J Pediatr Surg 1998;33:1439.
106. Sierra R, Brunner WC, Murphy JT, et al: Laparoscopic marsupialization of a giant post-traumatic splenic cyst. JSLS 2004;8:384.
107. Singer DB: Postsplenectomy sepsis. In Rosenberg HS, Bolander RP (eds): Perspectives in Pediatric Pathology. Chicago, Year Book Medical Publishers, 1973, p 285.
108. Skandalakis PN, Colborn GL, Skandalakis LJ, et al: The surgical anatomy of the spleen. Surg Clin North Am 1993; 73:747.
109. Skandalakis LJ, Gray SW, Ricketts R, et al: The spleen. In Skandalakis JE, Gray SW (eds): Embryology for Surgeons, 2nd ed. Baltimore, Williams & Wilkins, 1994, p 334.
110. Skarsgard E, Doski J, Jaksic T, et al: Thrombosis of the portal venous system after splenectomy for pediatric hematologic disease. J Pediatr Surg 1993;28:1109.
111. Smith MD, Nio M, Carmel JE, et al: Management of splenic abscess in immunocompromised children. J Pediatr Surg 1993;28:823.
112. Stringel G, Soucy P, Mercer S: Torsion of the wandering spleen: Splenectomy or splenopexy? J Pediatr Surg 1982;17:373.
113. Styrt B: Infection associated with asplenia: risks, mechanisms, and prevention. Am J Med 1990;88:33.
114. Sullivan CA, Konefal SH: Epidermoid cyst of the spleen successfully treated by marsupialization. Clin Pediatr 1987;26:203.
115. Szold A, Schwartz J, Abu-Abeid S, et al: Laparoscopic splenectomies for idiopathic thrombocytopenic purpura: Experience of sixty cases. Am J Hematol 2000;63:7.
116. Targarona EM, Espert JJ, Balagué C, et al: Residual splenic function after laparoscopic splenectomy: A clinical concern. Arch Surg 1998;133:56.
117. Targarona EM, Martínez J, Ramos C, et al: Conservative laparoscopic treatment of posttraumatic splenic cyst. Surg Endosc 1995;9:71.
118. Terrosu G, Baccarani U, Bresadola V, et al: The impact of splenic weight on laparoscopic splenectomy for splenomegaly. Surg Endosc 2002;16:103.
119. Thalhammer GH, Eber E, Uranus S, et al: Partial splenectomy in cystic fibrosis patients with hypersplenism. Arch Dis Child 2003;88:143.
120. Thorne MT, Chwals WJ: Treatment of complicated congenital splenic cysts. J Pediatr Surg 1993;28:1635.
121. Tsakayannis DE, Mitchell K, Kozakewich HPW, et al: Splenic preservation in the management of splenic epidermoid cysts in children. J Pediatr Surg 1995;30:1468.
122. Tu ST, Wu JM, Yeh BH, et al: Intestinal obstruction in asplenia syndrome: Report of three cases. Acta Paediatr Sin 1994;35:70.
123. Uranüs S, Kronberger L, Kraft-Kine J: Partial splenic resection using the TA-stapler. Am J Surg 1194;168:49.
124. Velanovich V, Shurafa MS: Clinical and quality of life outcomes of laparoscopic and open splenectomy for haematological diseases. Eur J Surg 2001;167:23.
125. Vereczkei A, Illenyi L, Arany A, et al: Transvaginal extraction of the laparoscopically removed spleen. Surg Endosc 2003;17:157.
126. Waldhausen JHT, Tapper D: Is pediatric laparoscopic splenectomy safe and cost-effective? Arch Surg 1997;132:822.
127. Walsh RM, Heniford BT, Brody F, et al: The ascendance of laparoscopic splenectomy. Am Surg 2001;67:48.
128. West KW, Grosfeld JL: Postsplenectomy sepsis: Historical background and current concepts. World J Surg 1985;9:477.
129. Winslow ER, Brunt LM: Perioperative outcomes of laparoscopic versus open splenectomy: A meta-analysis with an emphasis on complications. Surgery 2003;134:647.
130. Yavorski CC, Greson KL, Egan MC: Splenic cysts: A new approach to partial splenectomy—case report and review of the literature. Am Surg 1998;64:795.
131. Yee LF, Carvajal SH, de Lorimier AA, et al: Laparoscopic splenectomy: The initial experience at University of California, San Francisco. Arch Surg 1995;130:874.
132. Yoshida K, Yamazaki Y, Mizuno R, et al: Laparoscopic splenectomy in children: Preliminary results and comparison with the open technique. Surg Endosc 1995;9:1279.
133. Young NS, Brown KE: Parvovirus B19. N Engl J Med 2004; 350:586.
134. Zarrabi MH, Rosner F: Serious infections in adults following splenectomy for trauma. Arch Intern Med 1984; 144:1421.
135. Ziske CG, Müller T: Partial splenectomy: Uses of error. Lancet 2002;359, 1144.

Part VIII

Genitourinary Disorders

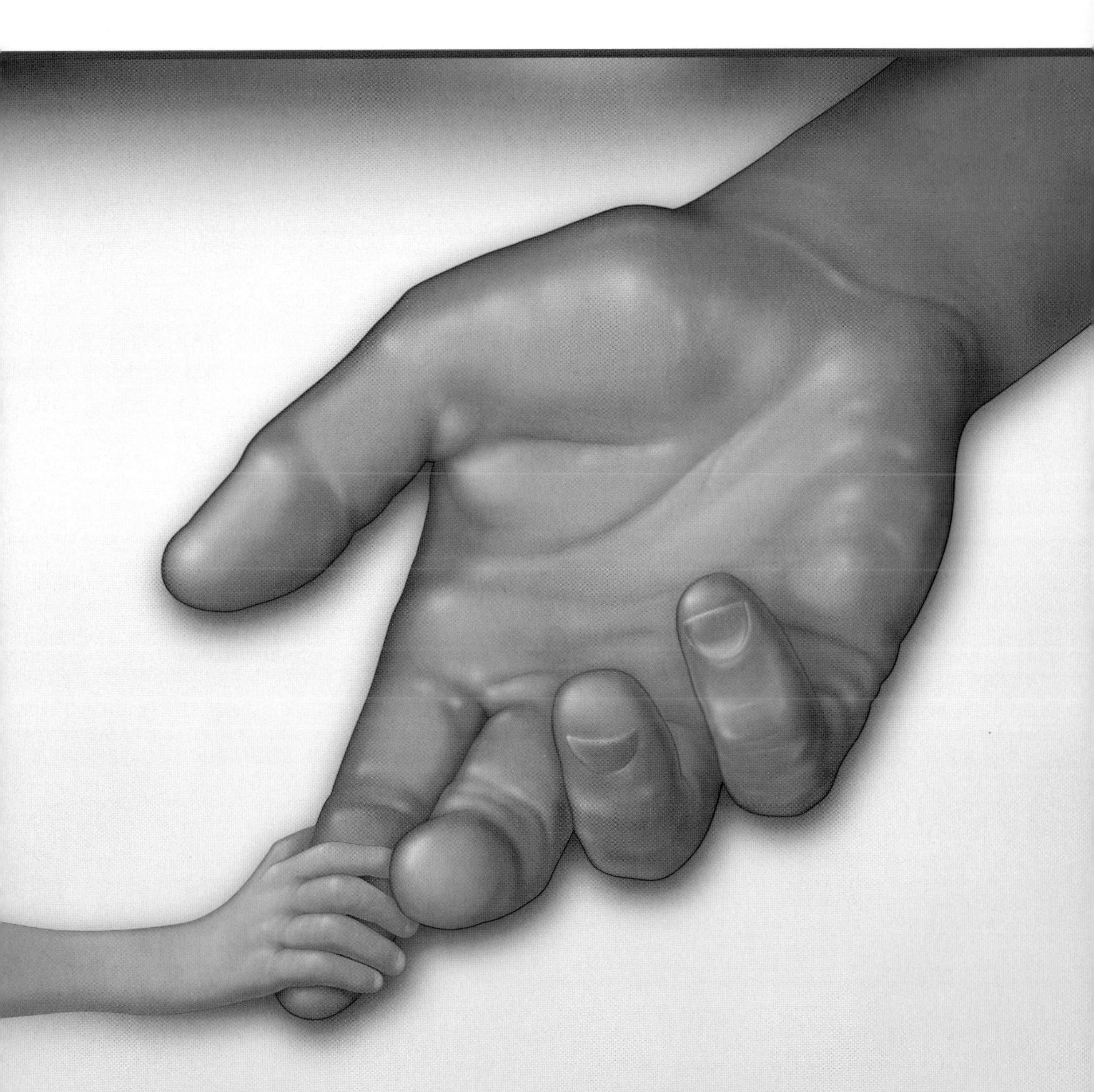

Chapter 109

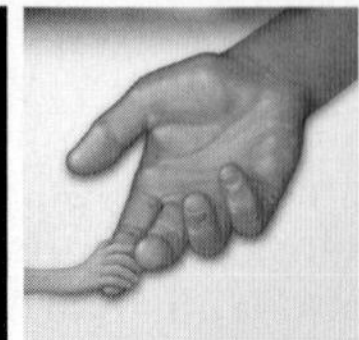

Renal Agenesis, Dysplasia, and Cystic Disease

Kenneth I. Glassberg

RENAL DEVELOPMENT

More than 400 genes have been identified as playing a role in renal development. A defect in any of the more important genes can lead to specific abnormalities of development, such as renal dysplasia, hypoplasia, or cystic disease. Many forms of cystic disease have been associated with specific mutations of genes; when these genes are normal, they play a significant role in renal development, but when they are mutated, they lead to cyst development.

The kidney develops as a result of cross-talk between the wolffian duct (later, the ureteric bud) and the future metanephric blastema; each sends messages to the other, sometimes simultaneously and sometimes in response to the message received. Each step of renal development is dependent on the expression of different genes and their protein products. For example, the mesenchymal cells of the metanephric blastema persist and proliferate in response to insulin-like growth factor-2 (IGF-2). Expression of the Wilms' tumor 1 gene *(WT1)* suppresses IGF-2 and allows a cascade of events to occur, including development of the ureteric bud from the wolffian duct and conversion of mesenchymal cells into epithelial cells. This latter conversion is initiated by the *PAX2* gene.

Ureteric bud formation from the wolffian duct occurs in response to a protein produced by the mesenchymal cells called glial cell line–derived neurotrophic factor (GDNF). This protein binds to a tyrosine kinase c-ret receptor on the caudal wolffian duct, inducing the formation of the ureteric bud. The ureteric bud elongates and penetrates the nearby mesenchymal blastema where it undergoes multiple generations of bud divisions. Mesenchymal (blastemal) cells cluster around the tip of each terminal branch and differentiate into epithelial, stromal and endothelial cells, the building blocks of the metanephric kidney. The epithelial cells first form into a hollow ball (renal vesicle) which elongates into a prenephron tubular structure that eventually attaches to the terminal branches of the ureteric bud, the future collecting ducts.[16]

Decreased ureteric bud branching will be associated with fewer clusters of mesenchymal cells and therefore fewer nephrons, i.e., hypoplasia. Poor communication between the branching bud tips and the clusters of mesenchymal cells or absence of continuity between the collecting ducts and developing nephrons can lead to persistence of immature structures, i.e., dysplasia. Overexpression or lack of expression of specific growth factors can lead to hyperproliferative renal disorders such as Wilms' tumor and renal cystic disease. For example, the aforementioned gene *IGF2* is overexpressed in most sporadic Wilms' tumor and *WT1*, a tumor suppressor gene, is mutated in many syndromal Wilms' tumors.

RENAL DYSGENESIS

Maldevelopment of the kidney that affects its size, shape, or structure is referred to as renal dysgenesis. There are three principal forms: hypoplasia, dysplasia, and cystic dysplasia (as well as various other forms of renal cystic disease). Hypoplasia refers to a kidney or a segment of a kidney with a decreased number of nephrons. Sometimes cysts appear in dysplastic kidneys or in areas of dysplasia. The cysts may be microscopic or macroscopic, focal or diffused. The hallmark of dysplasia is the presence of primitive ducts, structures thought to represent earlier stages of development and characterized by a surrounding collar of smooth muscle and collagen but lacking elastin.[10] When the entire kidney is involved with both dysplasia and cysts, it is referred to as a multicystic dysplastic kidney. Multicystic dysplastic kidneys may involute with time to become a "nubbin" of tissue; this is referred to as renal aplasia. The latter represents a tiny cluster of cells with no reniform shape. Kidneys that are severely dysplastic have either very immature or absent collecting systems.

RENAL AGENESIS

A defect of the wolffian ducts, the ureteric bud, or the metanephric blastema can lead to absence of kidney development, or renal agenesis. Renal agenesis occurs bilaterally in 1 of every 4000 births, with a predominance in males.[31] Because of the lack of urine production, oligohydramnios develops, and affected infants are born with immature lungs, pneumothorax, and Potter facies (hypertelorism, prominent inner canthal folds, and recessive chin). Unilateral renal agenesis is compatible with life; its incidence is 1 in 450 to 1000 births.[23] It is difficult to accurately determine the true incidence of unilateral renal agenesis because in some conditions, such as a multicystic kidney, the organ can regress into a nubbin of tissue that does not appear on imaging studies.

Unilateral renal agenesis is associated with other urologic abnormalities, including primary vesicoureteral reflux (28%), obstructive megaureter (11%), and ureteropelvic junction obstruction (3%).[6] Either unilateral renal agenesis or renal ectopia can be associated with ipsilateral müllerian defects and vaginal agenesis; this association is referred to as Mayer-Rokitansky-Küster-Hauser syndrome. Bilateral renal agenesis can also appear as part branchio-oto-renal syndrome.

TABLE 109-1 Classification of Cystic Disease of the Kidney

Genetic
Autosomal dominant (adult) polycystic kidney disease
Autosomal recessive (infantile) polycystic kidney disease
Juvenile nephronophthisis–medullary cystic disease complex
Juvenile nephronophthisis (autosomal recessive)
Medullary cystic disease (autosomal dominant)
Congenital nephrosis (familial nephritic syndrome; autosomal recessive)
Familial hypoplastic glomerulocystic disease (autosomal dominant)
Multiple malformation syndromes with renal cysts (e.g., tuberous sclerosis, von Hippel-Lindau disease)
Nongenetic
Multicystic kidney (multicystic dysplastic kidney)
Benign multilocular cyst (cystic nephroma)
Simple cyst
Medullary sponge kidney
Sporadic glomerulocystic kidney disease
Acquired renal cystic disease
Caliceal diverticulum (pyelogenic cyst)

HYPOPLASIA AND HYPODYSPLASIA

With hypoplasia, an entire kidney or a segment of one has a decreased number of nephrons. A hypodysplastic kidney also has a decreased number of nephrons; it may have a reniform shape but contains areas of dysplasia. Kidneys associated with ectopic orifices may be totally dysplastic, hypoplastic, or hypodysplastic. Ectopic orifices may be secondary to an abnormal ureteric bud site on the wolffian duct and are associated abnormal renal development.

RENAL CYSTIC DISEASE

Renal cysts may be congenital, sporadic, or acquired; single or multiple; unilateral or bilateral. The majority arise from nephrons and collecting ducts. Multicystic dysplastic kidneys contain cysts that form from tubular structures before the nephrons develop. Benign multilocular cysts are a form of neoplasia and must be differentiated from possible malignant tumors. The origin of simple cysts is not clear; the majority develop in kidneys that are otherwise normal.

Renal cysts vary in size from microscopic to macroscopic. All cysts are lined by epithelial cells. Some actually represent ectatic tubules or collecting ducts and remain continuous with the nephron. Others may pinch off from the nephron and become isolated structures. According to Gardner,[14] any duct that is dilated to four times the normal diameter is considered a cyst.

The classification system used in this chapter is based on that proposed by the Committee on Terminology, Nomenclature, and Classification of the Section on Urology of the American Academy of Pediatrics, which divides the various conditions into genetic and nongenetic disease.[18] Some modifications based on more recent findings have been added (Table 109-1).[16]

From the outset, it must be clarified that although the terms *multicystic* and *polycystic* both mean "many cysts," they describe different conditions. The former refers to a dysplastic entity, and the latter refers to a number of separate entities, most of which are inherited, most of which are associated at some point in life with cysts in communication with nephrons or collecting ducts, but not all of which are associated with dysplasia. The most common conditions associated with the term *polycystic kidney disease* are autosomal recessive polycystic kidney disease (ARPKD) and autosomal dominant polycystic kidney disease (ADPKD). These conditions may progress to renal failure.

The entities with more important surgical implications include the various forms of multilocular cysts and the neoplasms associated with von Hippel-Lindau disease and tuberous sclerosis. Although multicystic kidneys often present as an abdominal mass, they rarely are removed. The large cysts in ADPKD have been treated with laparoscopic unroofing, but this author is unaware of any unroofing procedures performed in children.

AUTOSOMAL DOMINANT (ADULT) POLYCYSTIC KIDNEY DISEASE

ADPKD was formerly referred to as adult polycystic kidney disease because it is seen predominantly in adults; however, it may manifest in childhood or even in utero. ADPKD is the most common cause of renal failure, accounting for 10% to 15% of patients requiring kidney dialysis and transplantation.[12] Its incidence ranges from 1 in 500 to 1 in 1000 individuals. The condition affects both kidneys, although it may present predominantly on one side before it manifests on the contralateral side.

Genetics: ADPKD has been associated with three different mutations: *PKD1* on chromosome 16 accounts for approximately 90% of cases,[30,32] *PKD2* on chromosome 4 accounts for 5% to 10% of cases,[13,29] and *PKD3* has not yet been characterized. Penetrance is thought to be 100%, and 50% of the offspring of affected individuals have the potential of developing the disease. According to Gabow,[13] ADPKD will manifest in 96% of affected individuals by age 90 years.

Clinical Features: Because 50% of them will eventually develop the disease, the offspring of patients with ADPKD are screened by ultrasonography. By age 25 years, at least 85% of individuals will have cysts, but most will be asymptomatic.[17] Family members of individuals with ADPKD are unable to obtain life insurance before age 25 years because of the possibility of developing the disease.

The majority of individuals present between 30 and 70 years of age with findings that include microscopic and gross hematuria, flank pain, hypertension, and renal colic secondary to either clots or stones. In adults, the disease is associated with colonic diverticula, hepatic cysts, and berry aneurysms. Hepatic cysts appear much more frequently in adults than in children and are more common in females.

ADPKD occasionally presents in utero or in infancy; when it does, 50% of the kidneys are large and usually contain macrocysts. Sometimes the large cysts are not apparent, and the kidneys are hyperechogenic due to the reverberation of ultrasound waves caused by the multiple interfaces between dilated ducts and tubules; the later presentation is more typical for ARPKD (Fig. 109-1). Eventually, the cysts enlarge to macroscopic size. When prenatal ultrasonography identifies a patient suspected of having ADPKD or ARPKD, genetic or ultrasound studies of the parents must be obtained. It is important to monitor these children for hypertension, because control of blood pressure delays the onset of renal failure. Those with elevated serum creatinine levels, increased urinary protein excretion, and high blood pressure at a young age tend to decline faster and go on to renal failure. Almost all patients who present in utero or in the first year of life eventually develop renal failure, but with close monitoring, the onset can be delayed.

AUTOSOMAL RECESSIVE (INFANTILE) POLYCYSTIC KIDNEY DISEASE

This entity is no longer referred to as infantile polycystic kidney disease because it is now realized that some patients can present as adolescents or in their early 20s. ARPKD is a relatively rare disease occurring in approximately 1 of every 40,000 live births.[33] All patients have some degree of congenital hepatic fibrosis. In general, younger patients with severely affected kidneys have the mildest congenital hepatic fibrosis.

Genetics: The disease is transmitted by *PKHD1,* a gene located on chromosome 6.[34] Both the severe and mild forms of ARPKD are associated with this mutation. Because it is an autosomal recessive trait, one of four offspring is affected, and neither parent shows evidence of the disease.

Clinical Features: For infants with ARPKD identifiable in utero or at birth, death in the first 2 months of life from uremia or respiratory failure is not unusual. If they survive the first month of life, their chances of living for a year with proper supportive therapy are improved. Eventually, all infants with ARPKD develop renal failure (Fig. 109-2). In children who present later in life, hypertension presents later and is more controllable, and progression to renal failure is slow.

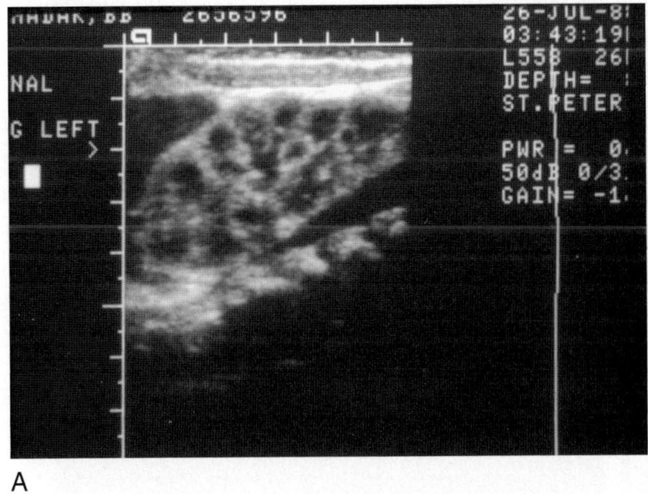

A

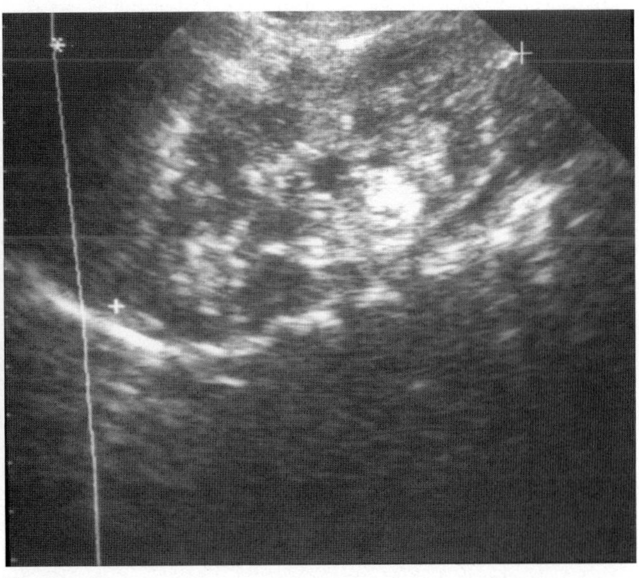

B

Figure 109–1 *A,* Multiple cysts are seen throughout the left kidney on this ultrasound study in a newborn with autosomal dominant polycystic kidney disease. *B,* Newborn with autosomal recessive polycystic kidney disease. Note the increased echogenicity and the small cysts. (Courtesy of Walter Berdon, MD.)

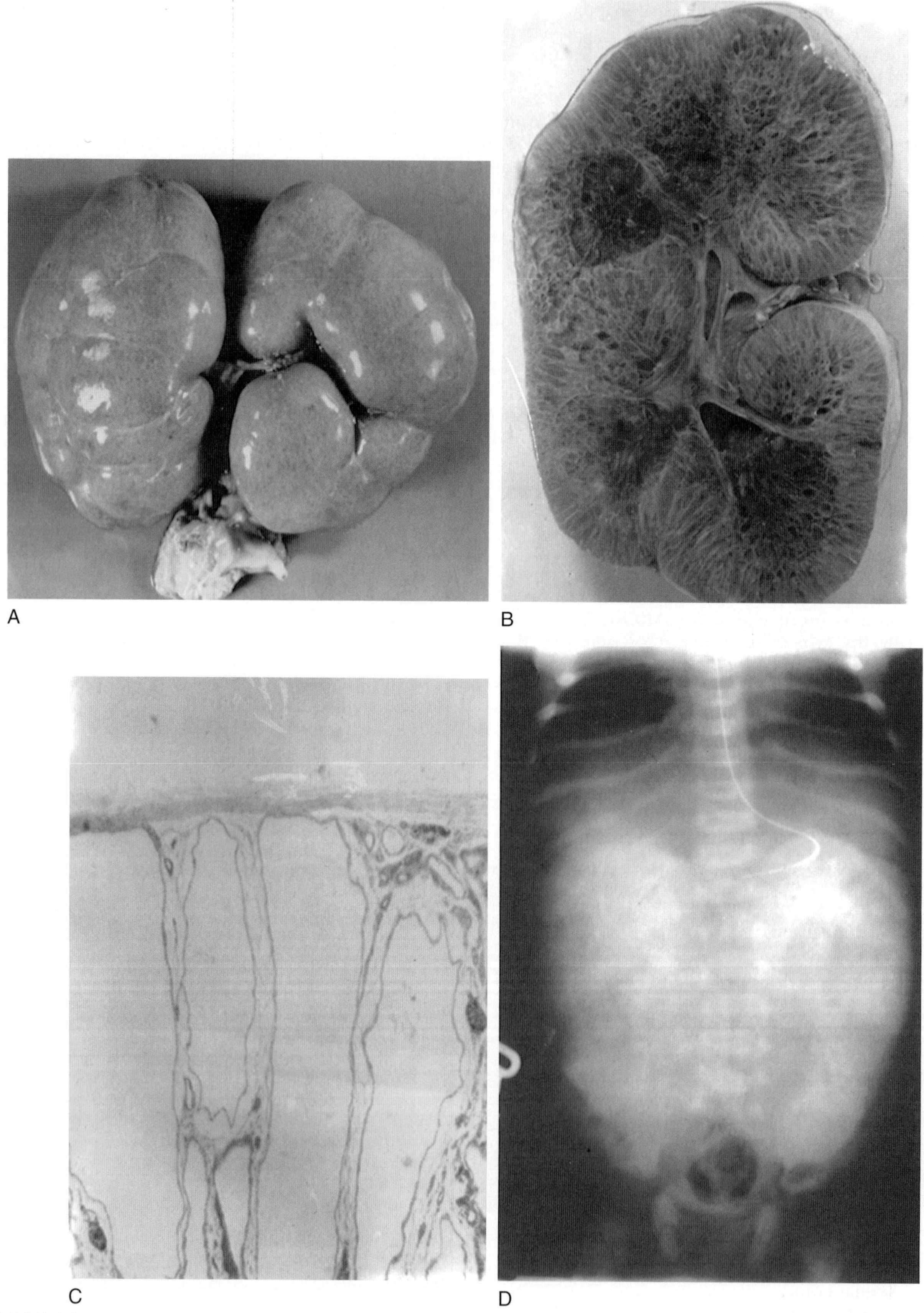

Figure 109–2 Autosomal recessive polycystic kidney disease. *A,* Gross specimen with diffuse, small subcapsular cysts. *B,* Radially arranged, elongated, "cystic," dilated collecting ducts. *C,* On low-power microscopic view, dilated collecting ducts are seen. *D,* On intravenous urography, the characteristic delayed "sunburst" pattern is identified, secondary to contrast pooling in the dilated collecting ducts.

Newborns with ARPKD may have significant nephromegaly. The kidneys can be so large that they compromise breathing or cause a difficult delivery. When severe, oligohydramnios may be present, as well as Potter facies and deformities of the limbs. Rarely, the kidneys are so enlarged that the diaphragm is significantly elevated, resulting in respiratory compromise; in these cases, nephrectomy may be required.

Those with advanced congenital hepatic fibrosis may have portal hypertension, esophageal varices, and hepatosplenomegaly. Variceal bleeding due to portal hypertension may require a splenorenal shunt. The kidneys in utero are typically very large and hyperechogenic on ultrasound examination. Hyperechogenicity is due to the presence of numerous small microscopic cysts and dilated ducts and tubules within the kidney, creating reverberations of the sound waves. With time, macrocysts develop. As these patients get older, their kidneys get smaller, contrary to the sequence of events in ADPKD. On histologic examination, the collecting ducts are elongated and very dilated. There is no cure for the condition. Respiratory care helps extend the child's life.

MULTIPLE MALFORMATION SYNDROMES WITH RENAL CYSTS

There are a number of multiple malformation syndromes characterized by renal cysts. Two that are of particular interest to surgeons are tuberous sclerosis and von Hippel-Lindau disease.

Tuberous Sclerosis

Tuberous sclerosis is associated with the classic triad of epilepsy (80% of cases), adenoma sebaceum (75% of cases), and mental retardation (60% of cases).[28] Adenoma sebaceum consists of flesh-colored papules of fibroma located on the malar area of the face. The hallmark lesion is a superficial cortical hematoma of the cerebrum, which looks like a hardened gyrus, suggesting the appearance of a tuber (root). Hematomas affect other areas of the body as well, especially the kidneys and eyes. Other kidney lesions include angiomyolipomas and cysts.

Genetics: The trait is transmitted in 25% to 60% of cases and occurs either sporadically or as a genetic condition with variable or incomplete penetrance. Two genes have been identified as being responsible for the autosomal dominant transmission of tuberous sclerosis.[5,21] *TSC1* is located on chromosome 9, and *TSC2* on chromosome 16. The latter gene defect is located at a site contiguous with *PKD1*, the mutation most commonly associated with ADPKD. The fact that both *TSC* gene mutations result in similar clinical manifestations suggests that both genes are involved in a common developmental pathway. When either gene does not produce its normal protein product, similar results occur. Both are considered tumor suppressor genes, because a mutation of either can result in tumor development.

Clinical Features: Twenty percent of patients develop renal cysts, and these usually manifest before 3 years of age. One third of children who present with cysts are younger than 1 year. The disease may be detected on prenatal ultrasonography because of the presence of cysts. When it does present in utero, there is a greater likelihood that it is secondary to a mutation of the *TSC2* gene on chromosome 16. In such cases, defects of the adjacent *PKD1* gene (responsible for ADPKD) may also be present. The renal cysts rarely cause a problem. In the past, many of these patients died early of central nervous system lesions; however, they are now living longer, and in the future, it may be discovered that renal cysts cause compromised kidney function.

Renal angiomyolipomas occur in 40% to 60% of patients.[7,19] These lesions are rarely seen before 6 years of age and are common after age 10.[4] Large angiomyolipomas have a predisposition to bleed.

On histologic examination, the cysts have a unique appearance and are lined by hypertrophic, hyperplastic eosinophilic cells. In theory, these hyperplastic cells may account for the 2% incidence of renal cell carcinoma in patients with tuberous sclerosis. Patients as young as 7 years have been reported with this tumor.

Von Hippel-Lindau Disease

This autosomal dominant condition is associated with cerebellar hemangioblastomas, retinal angiomas, cysts of the pancreas, epididymis and kidney epididymal cystadenoma, pheochromocytoma, and clear cell renal cell carcinoma. Its incidence is approximately 1 in 35,000.[26]

Genetics: The *VHL* gene (a tumor suppressor gene) is located on chromosome 3 and has a dominant transmission; 50% of offspring of affected persons can expect to develop the disease. Individuals are born heterozygous for the disease initially. When the second allele of the *VHL* gene mutates in a specific organ, the typical lesions develop in that site. Different mutations of the *VHL* gene have been found in cases or renal cell carcinoma not associated with von Hippel-Lindau disease.

Clinical Features: The mean age of presentation is 35 to 40 years; rarely, von Hippel-Lindau disease presents in childhood. Renal cysts are the most common renal lesion and are the first manifestation of the disease in 76% of patients.[25] Pheochromocytomas occur in 10% to 17% of affected individuals but seem to be more common in specific families.[20,24] Some patients present with seizures because of hemangioblastomas of the central nervous system. Because the cells lining the cysts are hyperplastic, these patients have a high risk of developing renal cell carcinoma. In adulthood, the possibility of bilateral renal cell carcinoma should be considered, even if it is not bilateral initially. Annual or biannual examinations of the kidney, usually by computed tomography, are recommended after age 30 years, particularly when small tumors, representing benign adenomas, are present.

MULTICYSTIC DYSPLASTIC KIDNEY

This condition represents an extreme form of dysplasia involving the entire kidney (Fig. 109-3). When occurring in one pole of a kidney, it is likely associated with a duplicated system. When patients have the disease bilaterally, it is incompatible with life and is therefore associated with stillbirth, oligohydramnios, and Potter facies. The condition is usually associated with atretic ureters and no renal pelvis. When a renal pelvis is present, the entity is referred to as a hydronephrotic form of multicystic kidney (Fig. 109-4). When the kidney appears solid, with fewer cysts, the disease is referred to as solid cystic dysplasia. Typically, however, the appearance is that of a bunch of grapes, and on ultrasound studies the kidney has a nonreniform shape; the cysts have a haphazard appearance, with no central or medial cyst, suggesting the presence of a renal pelvis (Fig. 109-5). This form of multicystic kidney must be differentiated from hydronephrosis, in which there is a central or medial cyst—the largest—and there is communication with peripheral cysts, representing dilated calices. In the past, it was thought that the cysts do not communicate; however, injection of contrast into one cyst invariably demonstrates communication between cysts (Fig. 109-6).[17]

Clinical Features: Multicystic dysplasia is the most common form of renal cystic disease, and it and ureteropelvic obstruction are the most common causes of a palpable abdominal mass in an infant. It is important to evaluate the contralateral system, because 3% to 12% of infants with multicystic kidney disease have a contralateral ureteropelvic junction obstruction, and 18% to 43% have contralateral vesicoureteral reflux.[1,2,11,32] Because of the latter finding, voiding cystourethrography should be obtained in all infants diagnosed with the entity.

Historically, these kidneys were detected in the first year of life by palpation. Before the use of ultrasonography, most multicystic kidneys were removed because it was hard to confidently differentiate them from renal tumors and because of rare reports of Wilms' tumors being identified in multicystic kidneys. To help differentiate a multicystic kidney from a hydronephrotic kidney, a dimercaptosuccinic acid (DMSA) scan is obtained; there is little

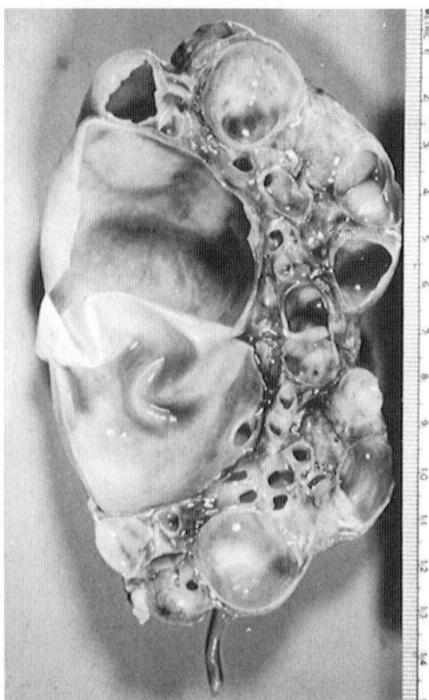

Figure 109-4 Hydronephrotic form of multicystic dysplastic kidney. The largest cyst is located centrally and medially, and the smaller cysts are at the periphery.

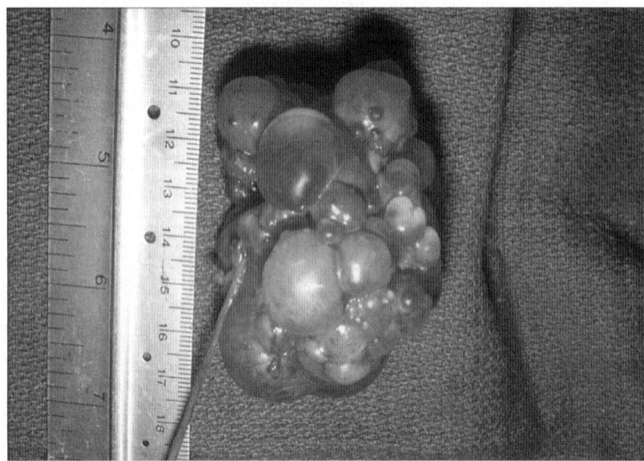

Figure 109-3 Typical multicystic kidney with atretic ureter. Note the "bunch of grapes" appearance. (From Shah SH, Glassberg KI: Multicystic dysplastic kidney disease. In Gearhart JP, Rink RC, Moriquand PDE [eds]: Pediatric Urology. Philadelphia, WB Saunders, 2001, p 279.) *(See color plate.)*

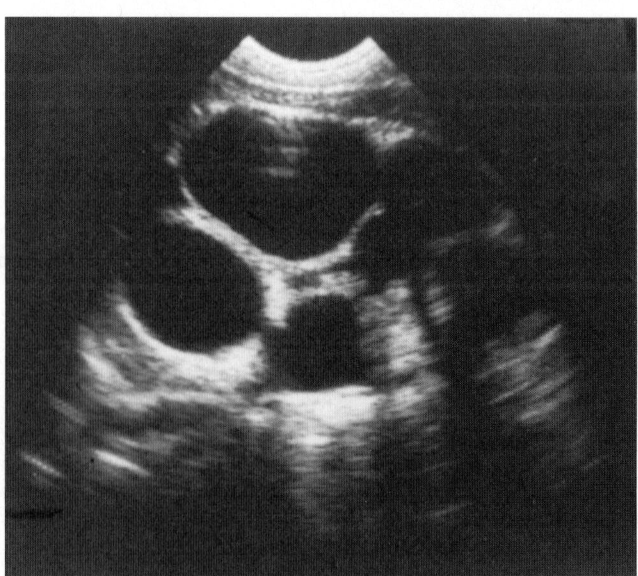

Figure 109-5 Typical ultrasound appearance of a multicystic kidney. Three large cysts are seen, with some smaller cysts in between. Little parenchyma is identified.

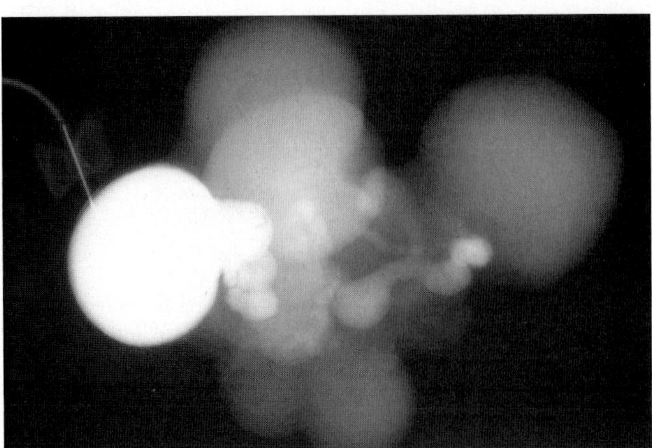

Figure 109-6 Multicystic dysplastic kidney. Contrast material injected into one cyst is identified moments later in all cysts, demonstrating a ductlike communication between them. Although the cysts do not appear to communicate on ultrasonography, they are invariably found to communicate when contrast material is injected into excised specimens.

if any function in a multicystic kidney, whereas a hydronephrotic kidney rarely has no function. The decision must be made whether a multicystic dysplastic kidney requires removal. With ultrasonography and other imaging studies providing a more definitive evaluation, the incidence of nephrectomy has fallen dramatically.

Most cases of Wilms' tumor in multicystic dysplastic kidneys have occurred in kidneys that were not previously known to be multicystic. Thus, it is unclear whether the multicystic dysplastic kidney led to the development of the Wilms' tumor. Two reports in the literature that imply that these kidneys should be removed describe a total of 120 patients, 5 of whom were found to have nephrogenic rests of nodular renal blastoma.[5,27] One had Wilms' tumorlets in the hilar region. However, renal blastomas have been reported to occur in normal kidneys as well, so it is not clear that the presence of these rarely seen tumorlets in multicystic kidneys implies a greater risk of developing Wilms' tumor. According to Beckwith,[3] only 5 of 7500 Wilms' tumor specimens in the Wilms' Tumor Registry occurred in multicystic kidneys. Beckwith calculated that multicystic kidneys have a fourfold increased risk of developing Wilms' tumor, and this low incidence does not justify prophylactic nephrectomy. He pointed out that even if Wilms' tumor did develop, the current survival rate is now greater than 90% with treatment. Zerres et al.[34] suggested conservative therapy for multicystic kidneys as long as there is follow-up ultrasound surveillance every 3 months until 8 years of age. They calculated a $2000 to $5000 cost for such surveillance, in comparison to a simple nephrectomy at $5000 to $7000.

There have been isolated case reports of hypertension developing in association with a multicystic kidney, with removal of the kidney curing the hypertension. In the National Multicystic Kidney Registry of the Section on Urology of the American Academy of Pediatrics, most neonatal cystic kidneys became smaller or stayed the same size over a 5-year period, with a very small percentage becoming larger.[33] Therefore, many kidneys that become smaller will disappear from view on ultrasonography. This does not mean that the kidney itself has disappeared; it implies that the cysts have disappeared (Fig. 109-7). The cells that lined the cysts persist, however; this amorphous group of cells forms a nubbin of kidney without any function (renal aplasia).

Although it is customary to follow multicystic kidneys with ultrasound studies every 3 to 6 months during the early years of life and at progressively longer intervals until 8 years of age, it is not clear whether it is necessary to follow a patient whose kidney disappears on imaging studies, or even when those findings persist. Because these cells remain without the cyst fluid, their presence, by itself, should not determine whether to obtain ultrasound follow-up.

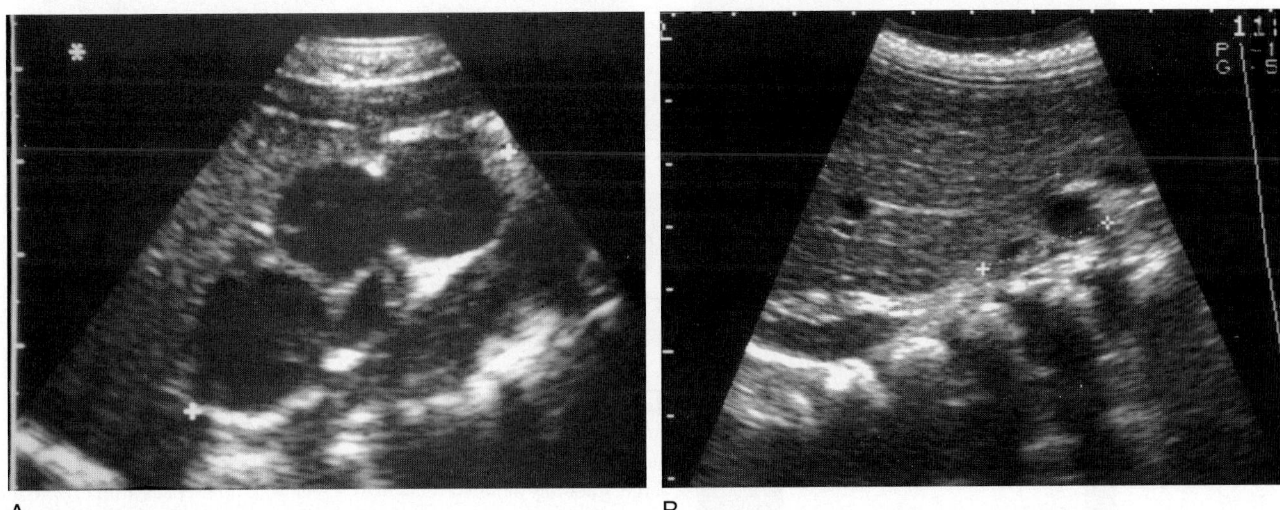

Figure 109-7 *A*, Multicystic kidney identified on ultrasonography in a newborn. *B*, At age 9 months, the cysts have shrunken, and the kidney is barely visible. (From Shah SM, Glassberg KI: Multicystic dysplastic kidney disease. In Gearhart JP, Rink RC, Moriquand PDE [eds]: Pediatric Urology. Philadelphia, WB Saunders, 2001, p 284.)

BENIGN MULTILOCULAR CYST (CYSTIC NEPHROMA)

A benign multilocular cyst is a neoplasm of the kidney that is not associated with renal dysplasia. The lesions are large and circumscribed by a thick capsule. There usually is normal renal parenchyma adjacent to the lesion. The loculi, which represent cysts within the lesion, can measure a few millimeters to a few centimeters in size and do not intercommunicate. The cysts are lined by cuboidal or low columnar epithelial cells. The septa of a benign multilocular cyst are composed of fibrous tissue, and no poorly differentiated tissues or blastema cells are present.

It is important to note that when a multilocular cystic lesion is identified on an imaging study, particularly an ultrasound study, it is impossible to determine whether it is a benign multilocular cyst, a multilocular cyst with

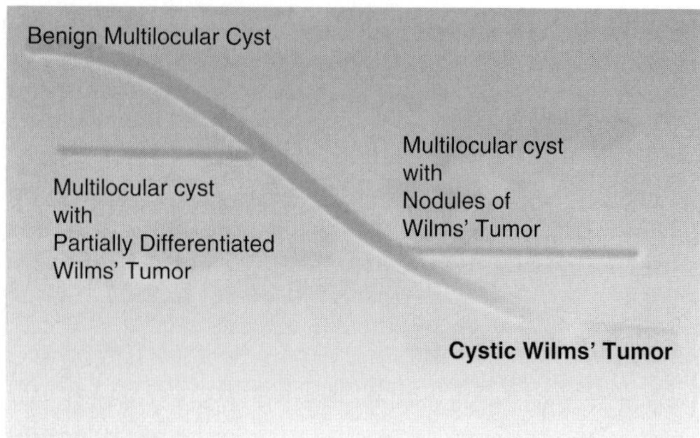

Figure 109-8 Spectrum of multilocular cystic lesions in childhood. Because imaging studies cannot differentiate one type of lesion from another, the diagnosis must be made under the microscope.

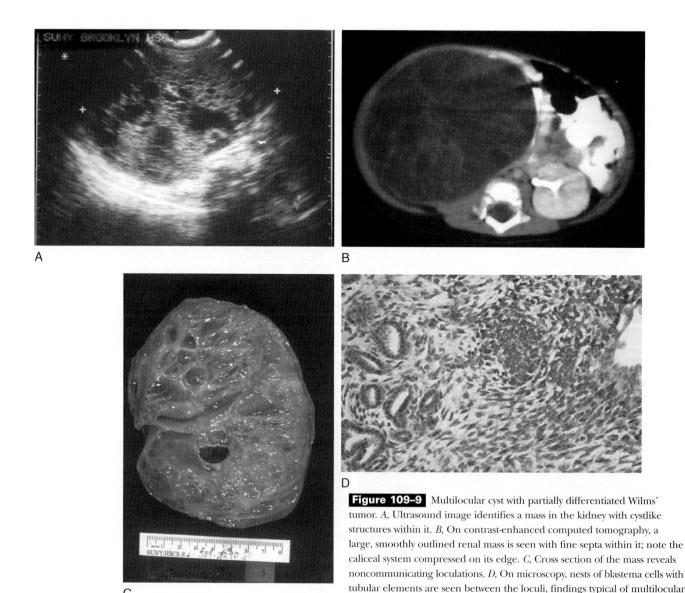

Figure 109-9 Multilocular cyst with partially differentiated Wilms' tumor. *A*, Ultrasound image identifies a mass in the kidney with cystlike structures within it. *B*, On contrast-enhanced computed tomography, a large, smoothly outlined renal mass is seen with fine septa within it; note the caliceal system compressed on its edge. *C*, Cross section of the mass reveals noncommunicating loculations. *D*, On microscopy, nests of blastema cells with tubular elements are seen between the loculi, findings typical of multilocular cyst with partially differentiated Wilms' tumor. *(C and D, see color plate.)*

partially differentiated Wilms' tumor, a benign multilocular cyst with nodules of Wilms' tumor, or a cystic Wilms' tumor. Thus, multilocular cystic lesions can be considered a spectrum of entities, and there have been no reports of one entity converting into another (Fig. 109-8). Because imaging studies cannot differentiate them, it is essential that these lesions be removed (Fig. 109-9). If they are located in one pole of the kidney and there is a large remaining portion of normal parenchyma present, a partial nephrectomy should be considered. Even when the lesion is not a typical benign multilocular cyst, there is very little chance of the disease being aggressive. None of these conditions involves expansive nodules, and metastasis rarely if ever occurs.[9] The lesion should not be confused with a Wilms' tumor that contains necrotic areas, which can simulate cysts on ultrasonography; the latter represents a more aggressive tumor.

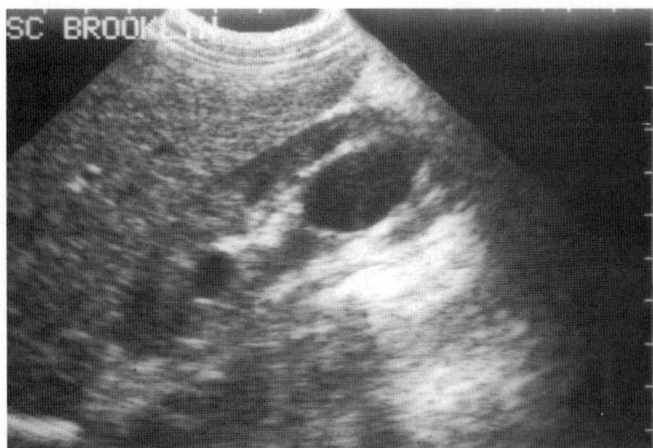

Figure 109–10 Two simple renal cysts in a 7-year-old. Note the whiteness (hyperechogenicity) just outside the kidney on ultrasonography. This is referred to as acoustic enhancement, a finding typical of simple cysts. It occurs secondary to increased sound wave reverberation through the cyst and its interfaces with the kidney. It is important not to confuse this finding with an atypical, asymmetrical presentation of autosomal dominant polycystic kidney disease.

SIMPLE CYST

Simple cysts are discrete findings within the kidney that usually appear oval to round with a smooth border. The cysts usually contain clear or straw-colored fluid, and when they manifest in utero, they usually disappear by birth. When they appear during childhood, they should be evaluated just as in adults with simple renal cysts. Because cysts were once considered such an infrequent finding in children, and because the ability to clearly define a cyst was limited, most simple renal cysts were operated on in the past. In children, renal cysts are rarely symptomatic. When more than one simple renal cyst is present in a kidney, the patient should be followed and the contralateral kidney carefully evaluated with imaging studies, because unilateral multiple cysts may represent an initial asymmetrical presentation of ADPKD.

The sonographic criteria for a classic benign simple cyst are as follows:

1. Sharply defined, thin, distinct wall with smooth and distinct margin.
2. Absence of internal echoes.
3. Good transmission of sound waves through the cyst with acoustic.
4. Spherical or slightly ovoid shape (Fig. 109-10).

If all these criteria are met, the chance of malignancy is negligible.[19] Sometimes there is a cluster of renal cysts at one pole of a kidney, and this must be differentiated from a multilocular cystic lesion. When the cysts are all simple, the condition may be referred to as unilateral renal cystic disease, a variant of simple cysts.[15] Although follow-up recommendations have not been established with evidence-based reports, it seems reasonable to follow these patients with sequential ultrasonography with decreasing frequency, mainly to ensure the stability of the simple cyst and screen for an asymmetrical presentation of ADPKD.

ACQUIRED RENAL CYSTIC DISEASE

Acquired renal cystic disease is common in dialysis patients with chronic renal failure. There are few reports on acquired renal cystic disease in children, but as in adults, the incidence increases with the length of time on dialysis. Young patients exposed to dialysis may develop the condition later in childhood. Once renal cysts develop, the kidneys should be followed regularly with imaging studies to rule out tumors. After renal transplantation, the cysts regress in size. New cysts can form in transplanted patients, but they tend to be small.

CALICEAL DIVERTICULUM

A caliceal diverticulum is an oval, smoothly outlined sac, usually located at one of the poles, most frequently the upper one. It communicates with the pelvicaliceal system by means of a narrow neck. It has also been referred to as a pyelogenic cyst; that term, however, is best used when the lesion communicates with the renal pelvis. These diverticula have the same lining as calices, with a smooth layer of transitional epithelium. Caliceal diverticula are benign lesions but may be a cause of hematuria or infection. Because of urinary stasis, small stones sometimes form.

REFERENCES

1. Al-Khaldi N, Watson AR, Zuccollo J, et al: Outcome of antenatally detected cystic dysplastic kidney disease. Arch Dis Child 1994;70:520.
2. Atiyeh B, Husmann D, Baum M: Contralateral renal abnormalities in multicystic-dysplastic kidney disease. J Pediatr 1992;121:65.
3. Beckwith JB: Editorial comment. J Urol 1997;158:2259.
4. Bernstein J, Gardner KD Jr: Cystic disease of the kidney and renal dysplasia. In Walsh PC, Gittes RF, Perlmutter AD, et al (eds): Campbell's Urology, 5th ed. Philadelphia, WB Saunders, 1986, p 1760.
5. Brook-Carter PT, Peral B, Ward CJ, et al: Deletion of the TSC2 and PKD1 genes associated with severe infantile

polycystic kidney disease—a contiguous gene syndrome. Nat Genet 1994;8:328.
6. Cascio S, Paran S, Prori P: Associated urological anomalies in children with unilateral renal agenesis. J Urol 1999;162:1081.
7. Chonko AM, Weiss JM, Stein JH, et al: Renal involvement in tuberous sclerosis. Ann J Med 1974;56:124.
8. Dimmick J, Johnson HW, Coleman GU, et al: Wilms tumorlet, nodular renal blastema and multicystic renal dysplasia. J Urol 1998;142:484.
9. Eble JN, Bonsib SM: Extensively cystic renal neoplasms: Cystic nephroma, cystic partially differentiated nephroblastoma, multilocular cystic renal cell carcinoma and cystic pelvis. Semin Diagn Pathol 1998;15:2.
10. Ericsson NO: Renal dysplasia. In Johnson JH, Goodwin WE (eds): Reviews in Pediatric Urology. Amsterdam, Excerpta Medica, 1974, p 25.
11. Flack CE, Bellinger MF: The multicystic dysplastic kidney and contralateral reflux: Protection of the solitary kidney. J Urol 1993;150:1873.
12. Gabow PA: Polycystic kidney disease: Clues to pathogenesis. Kidney Int 1991;40:989.
13. Gabow PA: Autosomal dominant polycystic kidney disease. N Engl J Med 1993;329:332.
14. Gardner KD Jr: Pathogenesis of human renal cystic disease. Annu Rev Med 1988;39:185.
15. Glassberg KI: Unilateral renal cystic disease [editorial]. Urology 1999;53:1227.
16. Glassberg KI: Normal and abnormal development of the kidney: A clinician's interpretation of current knowledge. J Urol 2002;167:2339.
17. Glassberg KI: Renal dysgenesis and cystic disease of the kidney. In Walsh PC, Retik AB, Vaughan ED Jr, Wein AJ (eds): Campbell's Urology, 8th ed. Philadelphia, WB Saunders, 2002, p 1950.
18. Glassberg KI, Stephens FD, Lebowitz RL, et al: Renal dysgenesis and cystic disease of the kidney: A report of the Committee on Terminology, Nomenclature and Classification, Section on Urology, American Academy of Pediatrics. J Urol 1987;138:1085.
19. Goldman SM., Hartman DS: The simple renal cysts. In Pollack HM (ed): Clinical Urography. Philadelphia, WB Saunders, 1990, p 1603.
20. Gomez MR: Tuberous Sclerosis. New York, Raven Press, 1979.
21. Horton WA, Wong V, Eldridge R: Von Hippel-Lindau disease: Clinical and pathological manifestations in nine families with 50 affected members. Arch Intern Med 1976; 136:769.
22. Kandt RS, Haines JL, Smith M, et al: Linkage of an important gene locus for tuberous sclerosis to a chromosome 16 member for polycystic kidney disease. Nat Genet 1992;2:37.
23. Kass EJ, Bloom D: Anomalies of the urinary tract. In Edelman CM (ed): Pediatric Kidney Disease. Boston, Little, Brown, 1992, p 2023.
24. Lagos JC, Gomez MR: Tuberous sclerosis: Reappraisal of a clinical entity. Mayo Clin Proc 1967;42:26 .
25. Levine E, Collins DL, Horton WA, et al: CT screening of the abdomen in von Hippel-Lindau disease. AJR Am J Roentgenol 1982;139:505.
26. Neuman HPH, Wiestler OD: Clustering of features of von Hippel-Lindau syndrome: Evidence for a complex genetic locus. Lancet 1991;337:1052.
27. Noe HN, Marshall JH, Edward OP: Nodular renal blastema in the multicystic kidney. J Urol 1989;127:486.
28. Pampigliana G, Moynahan EJ: The tuberous sclerosis syndrome: Clinical and EEG studies in 100 children. J Neurol Neurosurg Psychiatry 1976;39:666.
29. Peters DJM, Spiruit L, Sari JJ, et al: Chromosome 4 localization of a second gene for autosomal dominant polycystic kidney disease. Nat Genet 1993;5:359.
30. Pieke SA, Kimberling WJ, Kenyon KG, et al: Genetic heterogenicity of polycystic kidney disease: An estimate of the proportion of families unlinked to chromosome 16. Am J Hum Genet 1989;45:458.
31. Potter EL: Bilateral absence of ureters and kidneys: A report of 50 cases. Obstet Gynecol 1965;25:3.
32. Reeders ST, Bruening MH, Davies KE, et al: A highly polymorphic DNA marker linked to adult polycystic kidney disease on chromosome 16. Nature 1985;317:542.
33. Wacksman J: Multicystic dysplastic kidney. In Ball TP (ed): AUA Update Series, vol 17. Houston, American Urological Association, Office of Education, 1998, p 66.
34. Zerres K, Hansman M, Mallman R, et al: Autosomal recessive polycystic kidney disease: Problems of prenatal diagnosis. Prenat Diagn 1988;8:215.

Chapter 110

Renal Fusions and Ectopia

Pierre Mouriquand

EMBRYOLOGY

The embryology of congenital anomalies of the kidneys involves two protagonists and three events. The two protagonists are the nephrogenic material (pronephros, mesonephros, metanephros) and the ureteral buds (wolffian structures). The three events are induction of metanephric tissue (renal construction), ascent of the kidneys (cephalad migration), and positioning of the kidneys (partition and rotation). Incidents occurring during these three phases (first 8 weeks of gestation) may affect the presence, number, and location of the kidneys.

The nephrogenic cord is divided into three parts (Fig. 110-1)[1]: the most cranial segments collectively constitute the pronephros; the intermediate segments, the mesonephros; and the most caudal segments, the metanephros or kidney. This classification is purely topographic, and the nephrogenic material arises from the same source and exhibits identical properties throughout its craniocaudal extent.[26] The pronephros (eight-somite–stage embryo) degenerates completely; however, it contributes its duct to formation of the mesonephros. In an embryo with 23 somites, the mesonephros forms mesonephric vesicles and excretory tubules, which also degenerate with a few embryonic remnants left such as the paradidymis in the male and the paroöphoron in the female.[32] The metanephros develops from the portion (metanephric blastema) of the nephrogenic cord caudal to the mesonephros.

The ureteral buds arise from the mesonephric duct near its junction with the cloaca during the fourth to fifth week of gestation. The cranial end of the ureter then ascends to meet the nephrogenic cord, which begins to develop into the metanephros and continues its cephalad migration. The cranial end of the ureteral bud begins a series of branchings to form the renal pelvis, the calices, and a portion of the collecting ducts.[55] The cephalad migration of the kidneys ends at the eighth week of gestation, as well as their axial rotation of 90 degrees medially. During their ascent, the kidneys receive their blood supply from the neighboring vessels. Blood is initially supplied by the middle sacral artery, then the common and inferior mesenteric arteries, and finally the aorta. Renal development is closely related to the location of the origin of the ureteral buds.[44] The ureteral ducts (which in the first phases of development are permeable until the 35th day) subsequently undergo a process of obstruction and recanalization of their lumen until the embryo is 41 days of age.[2,60] The muscular and neurologic construction and maturation of the urinary excretory system are a slow phenomenon (Fig. 110-2) that, when impaired, may affect the entire anatomic organization of the urinary tract. Any delay or mislocation of these complex events may lead to the following renal anomalies[49]: renal agenesis, multicystic dysplastic kidney and other renal cystic diseases, small congenital kidney, supernumerary kidney, and renomegaly (discussed in Chapter 109). Anomalies related to abnormal ascent and abnormal fusion are discussed in the following sections.

ANOMALIES RELATED TO ABNORMAL ASCENT OF THE KIDNEYS (ECTOPIC KIDNEYS)

Pelvic Kidney

A pelvic location (sacral or pelvic) below the aortic bifurcation is the most common location of ectopic kidneys.[71] A pelvic kidney (Fig. 110-3) is generally unilateral with a slight predilection for the left side. It is found bilaterally in 10% of cases.[58] In addition to its abnormal location, a pelvic kidney is frequently small, with an irregular shape, variable rotation, and extrarenal calices.

Lumbar or Iliac Ectopic Kidney

These kidneys are fixed above the crest of the ileum but are below the level of L2 and L3. Such kidneys can be difficult to differentiate from an aptotic kidney, which has a normal ureteral length, is not malrotated, is mobile, and can usually be manipulated into its normal position.[58]

Thoracic Kidney

Thoracic kidneys (Fig. 110-4A and B) are rare (1 in 16,000)[5,6,13,19] and may be related to delayed mesonephric

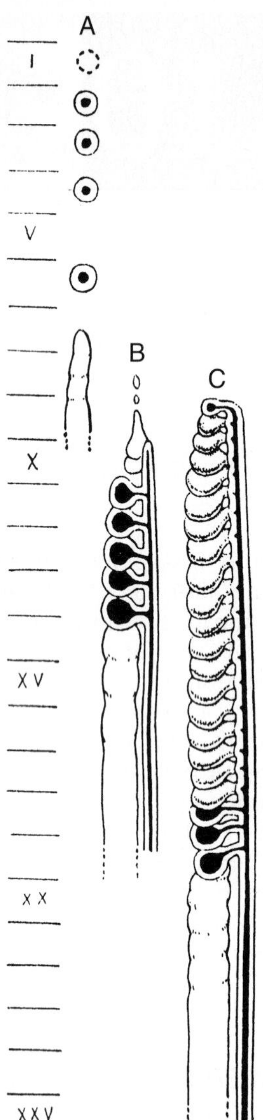

Figure 110–1 Schemes showing early development of the human nephros. *A,* Ten-somite embryo. *B,* Twenty-somite embryo. *C,* Twenty-five-somite embryo. The *Roman numerals* indicate the level in somites. The *circles* indicate nephrotomes that do not contribute to the nephros (based on Torrey[72]). (From Hamilton WJ, Boyd JD, Mossman HW [eds]: Human Embryology, 3rd ed. Cambridge, Heffer, 1962.)

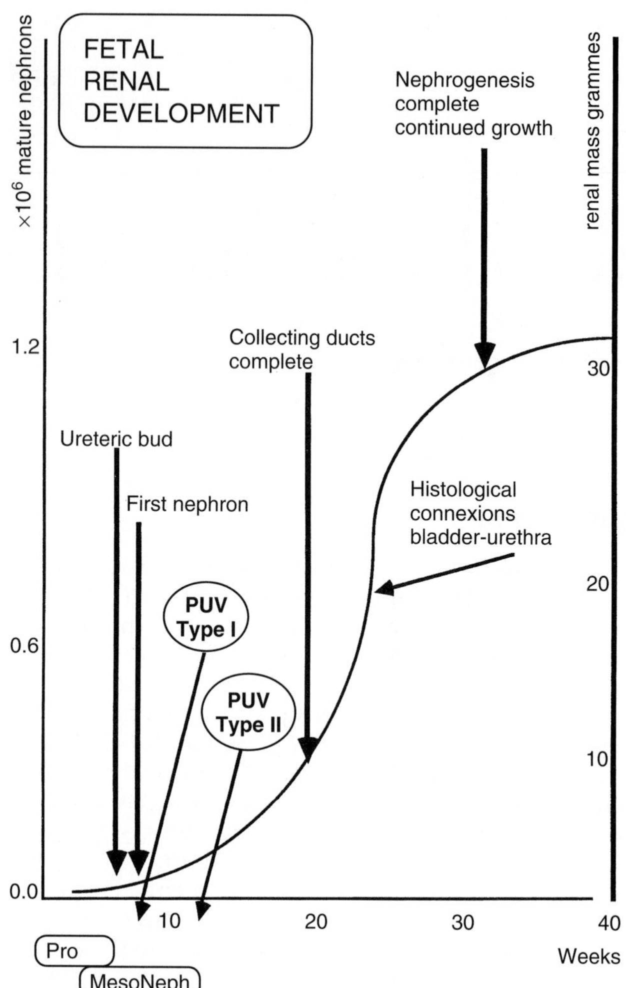

Figure 110–2 Chronology of development of the urinary tract. PUV, posterior urethral valves.

involution (i.e., persistence of the nephrogenic cord).[34] Thoracic kidneys may be associated with cardiovascular, pulmonary, and spinal anomalies.[45,51]

Associated Abnormalities

Ectopic kidneys are often associated with genital and contralateral urinary abnormalities, such as the absence of a vagina,[35] retrocaval ureter,[37] bicornuate uterus, supernumerary kidney,[24] and contralateral ectopic ureter.[11] An ectopic kidney can be a component of a more complex syndrome such as the Mayer-Rokitansky-Küster-Hauser syndrome,[7,69,70] Fanconi's anemia,[70] or conjoined twins.[68] Cephalad kidneys have also been reported in patients with omphalocele.[3]

Diagnosis of Ectopic Kidneys

Ectopic kidneys may be an incidental finding that requires no surgery or may be associated with impaired drainage or reflux that may require surgical correction. Isotopic studies, ultrasonography, magnetic resonance imaging (MRI) (Fig. 110-5), or intravenous urography usually allows identification of the ectopic renal parenchyma. These investigations can be complemented by retrograde contrast studies when required. Computed tomography (CT) has been reported as a possible method for identifying ectopic renal tissue, especially in the thoracic cavity.[6] An ectopic kidney can be suspected antenatally, especially if the abnormality is associated with some degree of dilatation.

ANOMALIES RELATED TO ABNORMAL FUSION OF THE KIDNEYS

Horseshoe Kidney

A horseshoe kidney is the most common fusion defect of the kidneys. The incidence of horseshoe kidneys

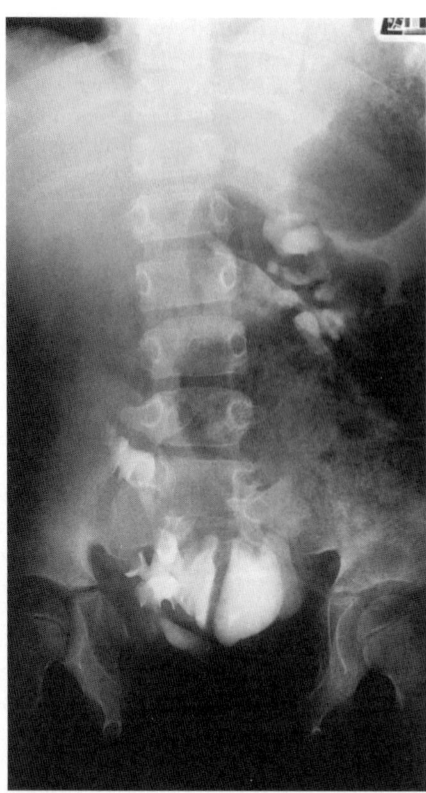

Figure 110-3 Pelvic kidney. (Courtesy of Professor I. Gordon, Department of Radiology, Great Ormond Street Hospital, London.)

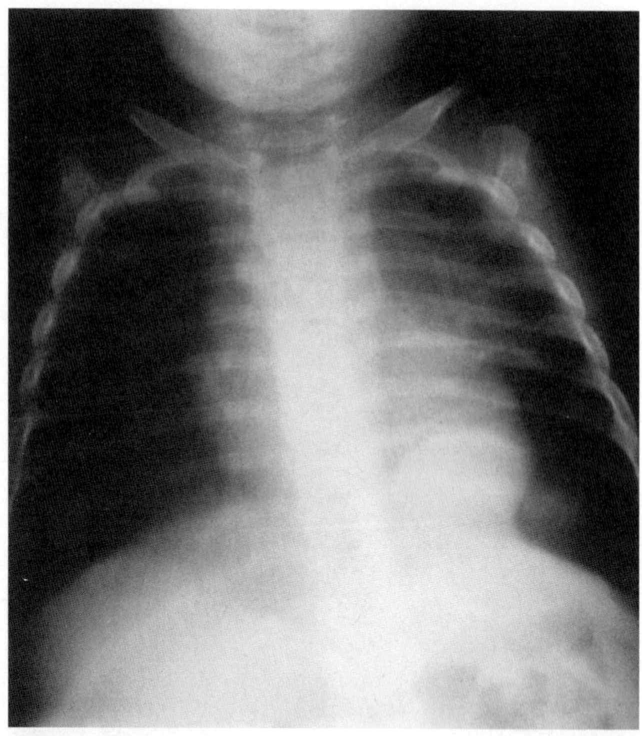

A

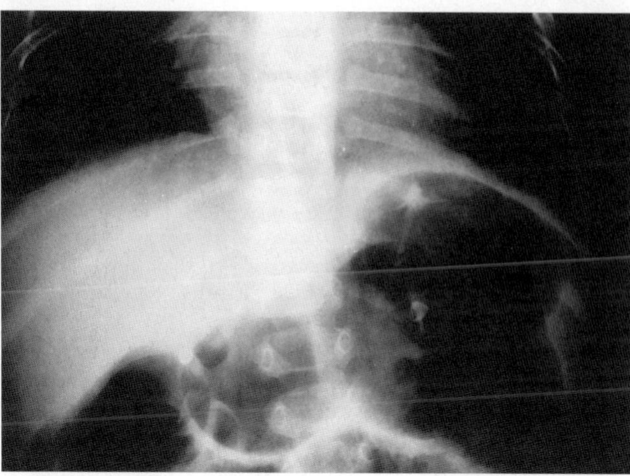

B

Figure 110-4 *A* and *B*, Thoracic kidney (intravenous urography). (Courtesy of Professor I. Gordon, Department of Radiology, Great Ormond Street Hospital, London.)

(Figs. 110-6A and B and 110-7A and B) varies from 1 in 400[28] to 1 in 1800[14] autopsies. The condition is more common in male patients. Horseshoe kidney and other renal fusion abnormalities, such as crossed ectopia, have been reported to occur in more than one member of a family, including apparently identical twins. These findings suggest a genetic influence.[17,30,40] In 95% of cases, the lower poles of the two kidneys are joined by a bridge of renal tissue that can be either normal renal tissue or dysplastic or fibrous tissue. In approximately 40% of cases, the isthmus lies at the level of L4, just beneath the origin of the inferior mesenteric artery; in 20% of cases, the isthmus is in the pelvis; and in the remaining cases, it lies at the level of the lower poles of normally placed kidneys.[35] Although the isthmus usually passes anterior to the great vessels, it may pass posterior to the aorta or inferior vena cava.[16] It is postulated that the inferior mesenteric artery obstructs the isthmus and prevents further ascent. A few horseshoe kidneys have fusion at their upper poles. Ureters arch anteriorly to pass over the isthmus.[12] The blood supply of horseshoe kidneys varies considerably, a fact that must be borne in mind at the time of surgery: 30% of patients have a renal blood supply that consists of one renal artery for each kidney. However, the supply may be asymmetric, with duplicate or even triplicate vessels. The isthmus may be supplied by the aorta or by the renal, inferior mesenteric, common or external iliac, or sacral arteries. In addition, the entire blood supply may enter through the isthmus.[56] Duplication of the horseshoe kidney and communicating renal duplication have also been mentioned in previous reports.[62,75] One part of the horseshoe kidney may be dysplastic and nonfunctioning.[10]

Associated abnormalities are common and occur in 78% of cases.[77] The most common involve the central nervous system, gastrointestinal tract, and the skeletal and cardiovascular systems. In children with trisomy 18, the incidence of fused kidneys is 20%.[8,74] More than 60% of patients with Turner's syndrome have renal abnormalities, including horseshoe kidneys[57] (7%).[36] Horseshoe kidneys can be complicated later in life by aortic aneurysms.[54]

Horseshoe kidneys are diagnosed with the same investigations mentioned earlier; isotopic studies usually give the clearest information. On intravenous urography, the

Figure 110-5 Magnetic resonance image of a pelvic kidney (*arrow*). (Courtesy of Professor J. P. Pracros, Department of Radiology, Debrousse Hospital, Lyon, France.)

diagnosis is clearly indicated by malrotation of each kidney with a projection of the calices medially to the renal pelvis, a renal axis that is more vertical or shifted outward, and the low position of the excretory cavities. The course of the ureters varies, but their upper segments seem to be laterally displaced by the parenchymal bridge. Association with a dilated renal pelvis is common and due to either anterior projection of the ureter (which can be kinked) or obstruction of the pyeloureteric junction caused by an anomaly of the junction itself or the disposition of the blood vessels around the junction. It is usual in these cases for the horseshoe kidney to be associated with some degree of impaired urine flow, and thus the diagnosis can be suspected antenatally. Vesicoureteric reflux is also commonly associated with horseshoe kidneys (10% to 80% of cases).[15,57,62]

The prognosis of patients with horseshoe kidneys depends on the associated anomalies. Most horseshoe kidneys are asymptomatic throughout life. However, associated hydronephrosis, reflux, lithiasis, or dysplastic tissue may lead to surgical intervention because of recurrent urinary tract infections, pain, or hematuria. A horseshoe kidney carries a conceivably increased risk for nephroblastoma and an approximately threefold to fourfold higher risk for cancer of the renal pelvis.[47,67] Tumors that arise (mostly in the bridge of a horseshoe kidney) can mimic the symptoms of an intra-abdominal disease process. A parenchymatous renal isthmus that is the result of an abnormal migration process may be predisposed to the development of renal cell carcinoma.[36] The risk for primary renal carcinoid tumor is even greater, and it might arise from neuroendocrine cells within foci of

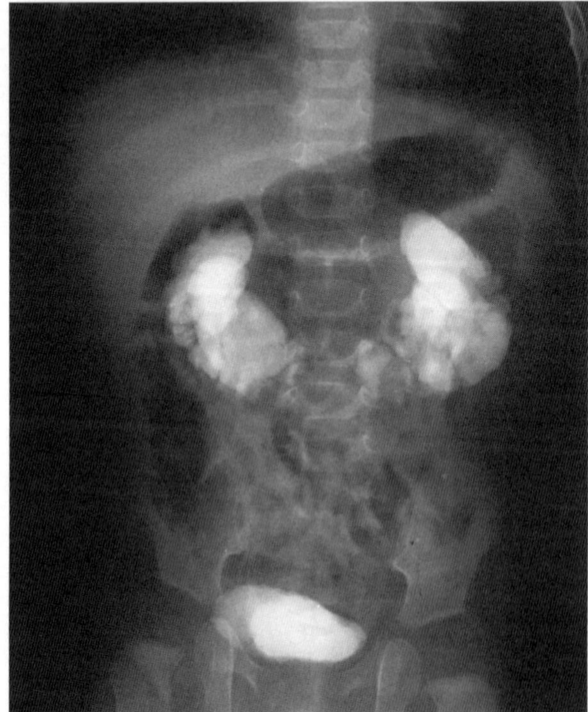

A

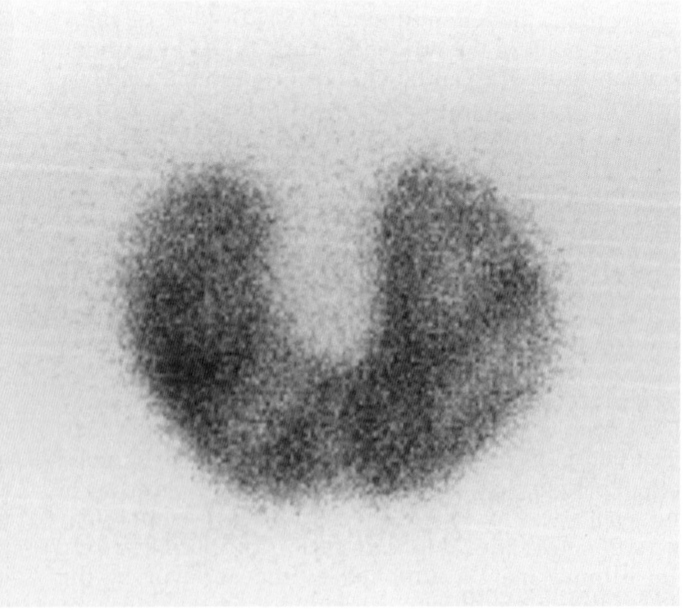

B

Figure 110-6 *A* and *B*, Horseshoe kidney (*A*, intravenous urogram; *B*, dimercaptosuccinic acid [DMSA] scan). (Courtesy of Professor. I. Gordon, Department of Radiology, Great Ormond Street Hospital, London.)

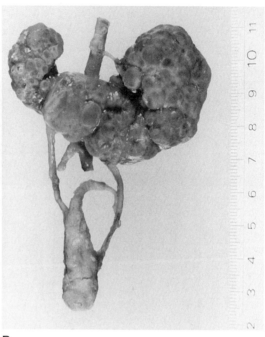

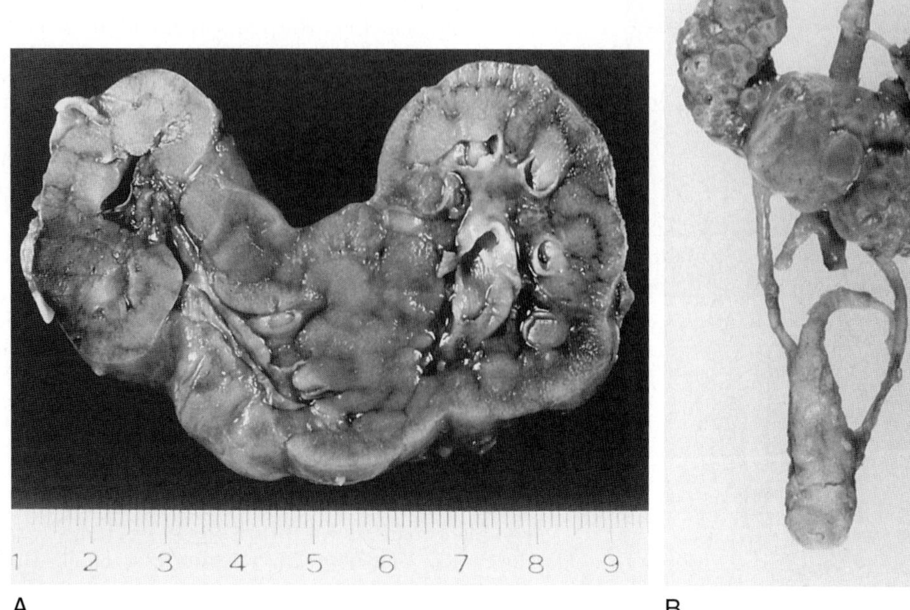

Figure 110-7 *A* and *B*, Horseshoe kidney pathology specimens. (Courtesy of Professor A. R. Risdon and Dr. G. Anderson, Department of Histopathology, Great Ormond Street Hospital, London.)

metaplastic or teratomatous epithelium within the kidney.[42] Association with ganglioneuroblastoma has also been reported.[53] An infected caliceal diverticulum can be associated with this malformation.[64] Xanthogranulomatous pyelonephritis in a horseshoe kidney is another possible, though a rare complication that represents a response of the parenchyma to chronic infection.[33]

Correction of ureteropelvic junction obstruction is the most frequent indication for surgical intervention in a patient with a horseshoe kidney. Division of the isthmus is no longer recommended in most cases because the isthmus probably does not contribute to the obstruction.[18] If the position of the kidney is within normal limits and the procedure is unilateral, the traditional anterolateral extraperitoneal approach is recommended. If the kidney has a more awkward position or if the procedure is bilateral, a transperitoneal approach is preferable. Ureterocalicostomy is an excellent alternative for achieving dependent drainage of the urinary tract.[48] Endopyelotomy is another alternative but is best reserved for older children.[50]

Urolithiasis develops in 20% of patients with a horseshoe kidney[58] and can usually be treated by extracorporeal shock wave lithotripsy or percutaneous surgery. Laparoscopic heminephrectomy for benign disease of a horseshoe kidney is an elegant option for experienced surgeons.[76]

Crossed Renal Ectopia

Crossed renal ectopia (Fig. 110-8A and B) is the second most common fusion anomaly after horseshoe kidney.[58] Its incidence is around 1 in 7000 autopsies. There are four varieties of crossed renal ectopia: (1) with renal fusion (85% of cases), (2) without fusion (<10%), (3) solitary, and (4) bilateral.[1,39,46] It has a slight male preponderance, and crossing from left to right occurs more frequently than from right to left. The fusion is usually located between the upper pole of the crossed kidney and the lower pole of the normally positioned kidney (unilateral fused type). The renal pelvises remain in their anterior position with incomplete rotation. In the sigmoid or S-shaped kidney, the fusion is the same but both kidneys have completed their rotation; thus, the two renal pelvises face in opposite directions. Various degrees of fusion have also been reported rarely (e.g., lump kidney, L-shaped kidney, and superior ectopic kidney).[58] Pseudo–crossed renal ectopia secondary to ureteropelvic obstruction has likewise been reported.[9] Intravenous urography, isotopic studies, ultrasonography, MRI, and CT allow definition of the anatomic type of ectopia. This process, however, is often difficult. The vascular supply varies and may also cross the midline.[61] Most cases of crossed renal ectopia are discovered incidentally and are asymptomatic. When surgery is indicated, laparoscopy may have some targeted indications for crossed fused renal ectopia.[4]

Associated anomalies are common, including orthopedic and skeletal abnormalities, imperforate anus, cardiovascular anomalies,[1,63] genital anomalies,[21,39] spina bifida,[20] vesicoureteric reflux, reflux nephropathy,[73] crossed ectopic ureter, multicystic dysplasia,[52] renal tumors,[27,31] incarcerated ureter,[59] and testicular tumor.[41] Renal ectopia may also be a component of more complex syndromes, such as vertebral abnormalities, anal atresia, cardiac abnormalities, tracheoesophageal fistula and/or esophageal atresia, renal agenesis and dysplasia

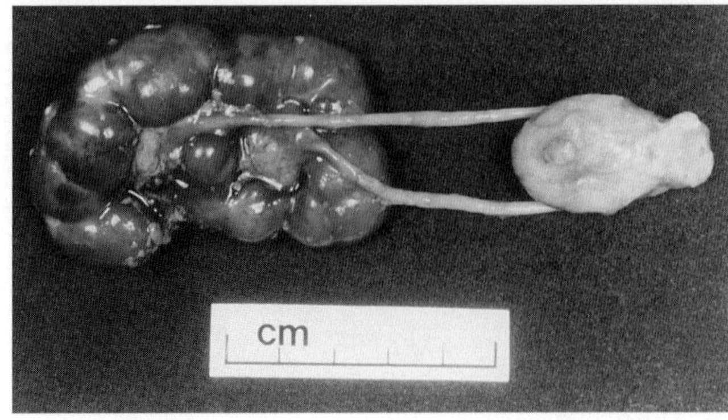

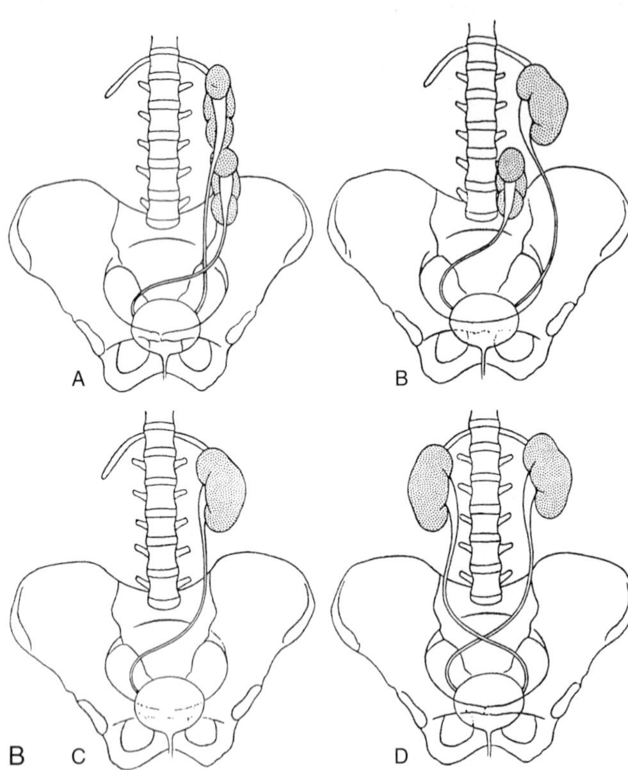

Figure 110-8 *A*, Crossed renal ectopia with renal fusion. (From Professor A. R. Risdon and Dr. G. Anderson, Department of Histopathology, Great Ormond Street Hospital, London.) *B*, The four different types of crossed renal ectopia: with fusion (*A*), without fusion (*B*), solitary (*C*), and bilateral (*D*). (From Ritchey M: Anomalies of the kidney. In Kelalis PP, King LR, Belman AB [eds]: Clinical Pediatric Urology, 3rd ed. Philadelphia, WB Saunders, 1992.)

and limb defects (VACTERL) syndrome[29] and agenesis of the corpus callosum.[25,65] The complexity of some of these anomalies can explain some of the complications reported, such as accidental ureteral ligation during repair of an inguinal hernia in a patient with crossed fused renal ectopia.[38]

REFERENCES

1. Abeshouse BS, Bhisitkul I: Crossed renal ectopia with and without fusion. Urol Int 1959;9:63.
2. Alcaraz A, Vinaixa F, Tejedo-Mateu A, et al: Obstruction and recanalization of the ureter during embryonic development. J Urol 1991;145:410.
3. Aliotta PJ, Seidel FG, Karp M, Greenfeld SP: Renal malposition in patients with omphalocele. J Urol 1987;137:942.
4. Andersen RD, Van Savage JG: Laparoscopic nephrectomy of the lower kidney for crossed fused ectopia. J Urol 2000; 163:1902.
5. Angulo JC, Lopex JI, Vilanova JR, Flores N: Intrathoracic kidney and vertebral fusion: A model of combined misdevelopment. J Urol 1992;147:1351.
6. Baillet AM, Escure MN: Apport de l'imagerie TDM au diagnostic de rein intrathoracique. J Radiol 1988;69:269.
7. Barakat AY, Seikaly MG, Der Kaloustian VM: Urogenital abnormalities in genetic disease. J Urol 1986;136:778.
8. Boatman DL, Kolln CP, Flocks RH: Congenital anomalies associated with horseshoe kidney. J Urol 1972;107:205.
9. Bolton DM, Stoller ML: Pseudo–crossed renal ectopia secondary to ureteric junction obstruction. J Urol 1995; 153:397.
10. Borer JG, Cargan FJ, Krantz R, et al: Unilateral single vaginal ectopic ureter with ipsilateral hypoplastic pelvic kidney and bicornuate uterus. J Urol 1993;149:1124.
11. Borer JG, Glassberg KI, Kassner EG, et al: Unilateral multicystic dysplasia in 1 component of a horseshoe kidney: Case reports and review of literature. J Urol 1994; 152:1568.
12. Boullier J, Chehval MJ, Purcell MH: Removal of a multicystic half of a horseshoe kidney: Significance of peroperative evaluation in identifying abnormal surgical anatomy. J Pediatr Surg 1992;27:1244.
13. Campbell MF: Renal ectopy. J Urol 1930;24:187.
14. Campbell MF: Anomalies of the kidney. In Campbell MF, Harrison JH (eds): Urology, vol 2, 3rd ed. Philadelphia, WB Saunders, 1970.
15. Cascio S, Sweeney B, Granata C, et al: Vesicoureteral reflux and ureteropelvic junction obstruction in children with horseshoe kidney: Treatment and outcome. J Urol 2002; 167:2566.
16. Dajani AM: Horseshoe kidney: A review of twenty-nine cases. Br J Urol 1966;38:388.
17. David RS: Horseshoe kidney: A report of one family. BMJ 1974;4:571.
18. Donahoe PK, Hendren WH: Pelvic kidney in infants and children: Experience of 16 children. J Pediatr Surg 1980; 15:486.
19. Donat SM, Donat PE: Intrathoracic kidney: A case report with a review of the world literature. J Urol 1988;140:131.
20. Dragun MJ, Flemming D, Knorr A, et al: Crossed fused renal ectopia in children with myelodysplasia. Urology 1994;44:562.
21. Eckford SD, Westgate J: Solitary crossed renal ectopia associated with unicornuate uterus, imperforate anus, and congenital scoliosis. J Urol 1996;156:221.
22. Evans DG, Rees HC, Spreadborough A, et al: Radial ray defects, renal ectopia, duodenal atresia and hydrocephalus: The extended spectrum for Fanconi anemia. Clin Dysmorphol 1994;3:200.
23. Fisher RM, Frank JD: Abnormal migration and fusion of the kidneys. In Gearhat JP, Rink RR, Mouriquand PDE (eds): Pediatric Urology. Philadelphia, WB Saunders, 2001, p 275.
24. Flyer MA, Haller JO, Fled M, Kantor A: Ectopic supernumerary kidney: Another cause of a pelvic mass. Abdom Imaging 1994;19:374.
25. Franco I, Rogan S, Fisher J, et al: Genitourinary malformations associated with agenesis of the corpus callosum. J Urol 1993;149:1119.

26. Fraser EA: The development of the vertebrate excretory system. Biol Rev 1950;25:159.
27. Gerber WL, Culp DA, Brown RC: Renal mass in crossed-fused ectopia. J Urol 1980;123:239.
28. Glenn JF: Analysis of 51 patients with horseshoe kidney. N Engl J Med 1959;261:684.
29. Golomb J, Ehrlich RM: Bilateral ureteral triplication with crossed ectopic fused kidneys associated with the VACTERL syndrome. J Urol 1989;141:1398.
30. Greenberg LW, Nelsen CE: Crossed fused ectopia of the kidneys in twins. Am J Dis Child 1971;122:175.
31. Gur U, Yossepowitch O, Baniel J: Transitional cell carcinoma in a fused crossed ectopic kidney. Urology 2003;62:748.
32. Hamilton WJ, Boyd JD, Mossman HW (eds): Human Embryology, 3rd ed. Cambridge, Heffer, 1962.
33. Hammadeh MY, Calder CJ, Corkery JJ: Pediatric xanthogranulomatous pyelonephritis in a horseshoe kidney. Br J Urol 1994;73:721.
34. Hawass ND, Kolawole TM, el Badawi MG, et al: Intrathoracic kidneys: Report of 6 cases and a review of the literature. Eur Urol 1988;14:83.
35. Hendren WH, Donahoe PK: Renal fusions and ectopia. In Welch KJ, Randolph JG, Ravitch MM, et al (eds): Pediatric Surgery, Chicago, Year Book, 1986.
36. Hohenfellner M, Schultz-Lampel D, Lampel A, et al: Tumor in the horseshoe kidney: Clinical implications and review of embryogenesis. J Urol 1992;147:1098.
37. Hubert J, Fournier G, Blum A, et al: Uretère rétrocave associé à une ectopie rénale pelvienne controlatérale: Apport du scanner tri-dimensionnel. Apropos d'un cas et revue de la littérature. Prog Urol 1994;4:262.
38. Hwang CM, Miller FH, Dalton DP, Hartz WH: Accidental ureteral ligation during an inguinal hernia repair of patient with crossed fused renal ectopia. Clin Imaging 2002;26:306.
39. Kakei H, Kondo H, Ogisu BI: Crossed ectopia of solitary kidney: A report of two cases and a review of literature. Urol Int 1976;31:470.
40. Kalra D, Broomhall J, Williams J: Horseshoe kidney in one of identical twin girls. J Urol 1985;134:113.
41. Key DW, Moyad R, Grossman HB: Seminoma associated with crossed fused renal ectopia. J Urol 1990;143:1015.
42. Krishnan B, Truong LD, Saleh G, et al: Horseshoe kidney is associated with an increased relative risk of primary renal carcinoid tumor. J Urol 1997;157:2059.
43. Lippe BL, Geffner ME, Dietrich RB: Renal malformation in patients with Turner's syndrome: Imaging in 141 patients. Pediatrics 1988;83:852.
44. Mackie GG, Stephens FD: Duplex kidneys: A correlation of renal dysplasia with position of the ureteral orifice. J Urol 1975;114:274.
45. Malek RS, Kelalis PP, Burke EC: Ectopic kidney in children and frequency of association with other malformations. Mayo Clin Proc 1971;46:461.
46. McDonald JH, McClellan DS: Crossed renal ectopia. Am J Surg 1957;93:995.
47. Mesrobian HGJ, Kelalis PP, Hrabovsky E, et al: Wilms tumor in horseshoe kidneys: A report from the national Wilms tumor study. J Urol 1985;133:1002.
48. Mollard P, Mouriquand P, Joubert P, Pouyau A: Urétérocalicostomie pour hydronéphrose par maladie de la jonction de l'enfant et de l'dolescent: À propos de 35 cas. Chir Pediatr 1990;31:87.
49 Mouriquand PDE, Mollard P, Ransley PG: Dilemmes soulevés par le diagnostic antenatal des uropathies obstructives et leurs traitements. Pediatrie 1989;44:357.
50. Nakamura K, Baba S, Tazaki H: Endopyelotomy in horseshoe kidney. J Endourol 1994;8:203.
51. N'Guessen G, Stephens FD, Pick J: Congenital superior ectopic (thoracic) kidney. Urology 1984;24:219.
52. Nussbaum AR, Hartman DS, Whitley N: Multicystic dysplasia and crossed renal ectopia. AJR Am J Roentgenol 1987;149:407.
53. Oguz A, Basaklar C, Gogus S, et al: Association of ganglioneuroblastoma with horseshoe kidney. Mater Med Pol 1994;26:35.
54. O'Hara PJ, Hakaim AG, Hertzer NR, et al: Surgical management of aortic aneurysm and coexistent horseshoe kidney: Review of a 31-year experience. J Vasc Surg 1993;17:940.
55. Osathanondh V, Potter EL: Development of human kidney as shown in microdissection—3 parts. Arch Pathol 1963; 76:271.
56. Perlmutter A, Retik A, Bauer S: Anomalies of the upper urinary tract. In Walsh P, Gittes PF, Perlmutter AD, et al (eds): Campbell's Urology. Philadelphia, WB Saunders, 1986.
57. Pitts WR, Muecke EC: Horseshoe kidneys: A 40 year experience. J Urol 1975;113:743.
58. Ritchey M: Anomalies of the kidney. In Kelalis PP, King LR, Belman AB (eds): Clinical Pediatric Urology, 3rd ed. Philadelphia, WB Saunders, 1992.
59. Rocklin MS, Apelgren KN, Slomski CA, Kandzari S: Scrotal incarceration of the ureter with crossed renal ectopia: Case report and literature review. J Urol 1989;142:366.
60. Ruano-Gil D, Coca-Payeras A, Tejedo-Mateu A: Obstruction and normal recanalization of the ureter in the human embryo. Its relation to congenital ureteric obstruction. Eur Urol 1975;1:287.
61. Rubinstein ZJ, Heitz M, Shanin N: Crossed renal ectopia: Angiographic findings in six cases. AJR Am J Roentgenol 1976;126:1035.
62. Segura JW, Kelalis PP, Burke EC: Horseshoe kidney in children. J Urol 1972;108:333.
63. Shaw MB, Cutress M, Papavassiliou V, et al: Duplicated inferior vena cava and crossed renal ectopia with abdominal aortic aneurysm: Preoperative anatomic studies facilitate surgery. Clin Anat 2003;16:355.
64. Shekarriz B, Upadhyay J, Bathold JS, Gonzales R: Infected caliceal diverticulum in a horseshoe kidney. J Urol 1998;160:842.
65. Shental J, Katz Z, Reich D: The persisting mesonephrotic duct syndrome in a neonate with agenesis of the corpus callosum. J Urol 1994;152:1590.
66. Smith DW: Recognizable patterns of human malformation: Genetic, embryologic and clinical aspects. In Smith DW (ed): Major Problems in Urology. Philadelphia, WB Saunders, 1970.
67. Smith-Behn J, Memo R: Malignancy associated with horseshoe kidney. South Med J 1988;81:1451.
68. Spitz L, Stringer MD, Kiely EM, et al: Separation of brachiothoraco-ischiopagus bipus conjoined twins. J Pediatr Surg 1994;29:477.
69. Strübbe EH, Willemsen WL, Lemmens JA, et al: Mayer-Rokitansky-Küster-Hauser syndrome: Distinction between two forms based on excretory urographic, sonographic, and laparoscopic findings. AJR Am J Roentgenol 1993; 160:331.
70. Tarry WF, Duckett JW, Stephens FD: The Mayer-Rokitansky syndrome: Pathogenesis, classification and management. J Urol 1986;136:648.
71. Thomson GJ, Pace JM: Ectopic kidney: A review of 97 cases. Mayo Clin Proc 1937;64:935.
72. Torrey TW: The early development of the human nephros. Contrib Embryol Carneg Instit 1954;35:175.
73. Wanatabe T: Reflux nephropathy in a patient with crossed renal ectopia with fusion. Pediatr Nephrol 2002;17:617.

74. Warkany J, Passarge E, Smith LB: Congenital malformations in autosomal trisomy syndromes. Am J Dis Child 1966; 112:502.
75. Wilson C, Azmy AF: Horseshoe kidney in children. Br J Urol 1986;58:361.
76. Yohannes P, Dinlec C, Liatsikos E, et al: Laparoscopic hemi-nephrectomy for benign disease of the horseshoe kidney. JSLS 2002;6:381.
77. Zondek LH, Zondek T: Horseshoe kidney in associated congenital malformations. Urol Int 1964;18:347.

Chapter 111

Ureteropelvic Junction Obstruction

Byron D. Joyner and Michael E. Mitchell

Hydronephrosis is defined as dilation of the renal collecting system as a result of either inadequate drainage or retrograde flow of urine. Often, it is thought to be caused by a simple mechanical impairment. More accurately, hydronephrosis is a complex syndrome resulting from interactions between glomerular hemodynamics and alterations in tubular function.[14] Hydronephrosis is typically discovered during maternal-fetal ultrasound and accounts for approximately 0.5% to 0.6% of all uropathies seen in the neonatal period. Postnatally, one in five neonates with the prenatal diagnosis of hydronephrosis will have spontaneous resolution of the hydronephrosis.[24] In neonates with persistent hydronephrosis after birth, ureteropelvic junction (UPJ) obstruction represents 44% of all postnatal causes of hydronephrosis.[110] As such, UPJ obstruction is the leading cause of postnatal hydronephrosis.

The variability in the natural history of hydronephrosis secondary to UPJ obstruction has its origin in the degree of impedance to the flow of urine from the renal pelvis. In kidneys with high-grade UPJ obstruction, inadequate drainage results in hydrostatic distention with increased intrapelvic pressure and poor outflow of urine. Chronic increases in intrapelvic pressure can result in irreversible damage to the kidney. However, in kidneys with low-grade UPJ obstruction, the kidney remains in a homeostatic state and often shows temporal growth and improvement. In between these two extremes there exists an expansive continuum and a lively debate regarding the clinical distinction of obstructed kidneys that require surgical intervention and those that do not.

ETIOLOGY/INCIDENCE

Hydronephrosis is the most common abnormality detected on maternal-fetal ultrasound and accounts for nearly 50% of all prenatally detected lesions.[69,101] The incidence of UPJ obstruction has increased from 0.02% to a screening incidence of 1% of all pregnancies, with only 1 in 500 considered significant.[88,109] UPJ obstruction is thought to be the cause of nearly 44% of all cases of congenitally significant hydronephrosis, thus placing the incidence of UPJ obstruction at 1 in 1250 births.[10,74]

UPJ obstruction is twice as common in males as females, particularly in the neonatal period, with 66% occurring on the left side,[52,105] as opposed to adults, in which there is a predilection for the right side.[16] Bilateral cases of UPJ obstruction occur in 10% to 36% of patients, with the highest percentage occurring in the younger age group.[7,105]

Koff described two types of UPJ anomalies that are discovered at the time of surgical exploration[59] (Fig. 111-1). The first is the *extrinsic* type, typically related to such mechanical factors as crossing vessels, adhesive bands, arteriovenous malformations, and fetal folds.[48,86] Extrinsic factors create an abrupt angulation by kinking or compressing the UPJ, which leads to obstruction of urine flow and progressive hydronephrosis. Similarly, Östling described pleat-like ureteral folds that occur at the level of the UPJ (Fig. 111-2).[86] Teleologically, these folds are thought to allow the dramatic increase in axial growth that children experience during the first 2 years of life and may, if persistent, represent an extrinsic type of obstruction. The second and most common UPJ anomaly is the *intrinsic* type, classically known as the "adynamic" segment. An intrinsic-type anomaly interferes with the peristaltic wave necessary for transporting a bolus of urine into the distal ureter. At surgery, these segments are of variable length and narrower than the rest of the ureter. Additionally, these segments are poorly distensible but are typically probe patent. Histologically, they are deficient

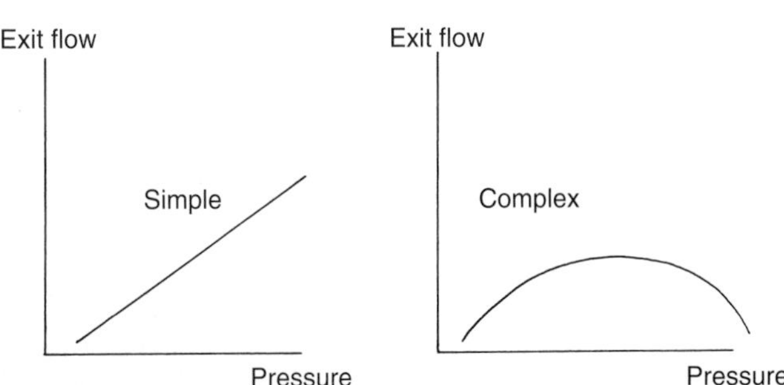

Figure 111–1 Diagrammatic representation of simple and complex pressure-flow patterns in human hydronephrosis. (From Koff SA: Pathophysiology of ureteropelvic junction obstruction: Clinical and experimental observations. Urol Clin North Am 1990;17:269.)

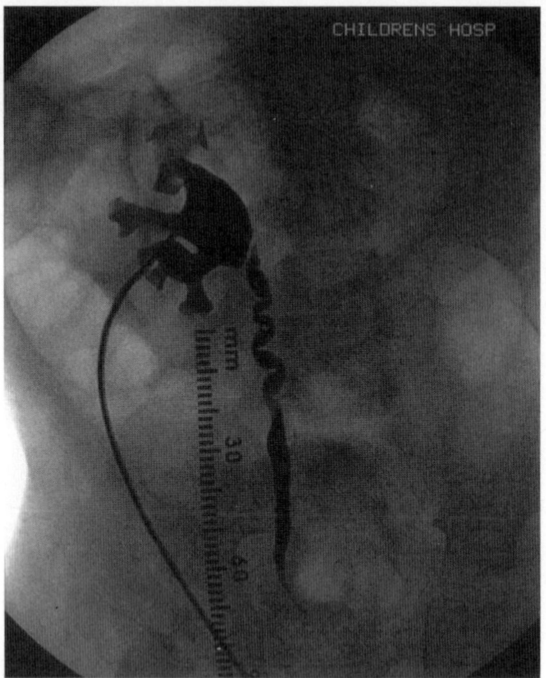

Figure 111-2 Percutaneous nephrostogram demonstrating Östling's fetal folds. (Courtesy of Children's Hospital & Regional Medical Center, Seattle.)

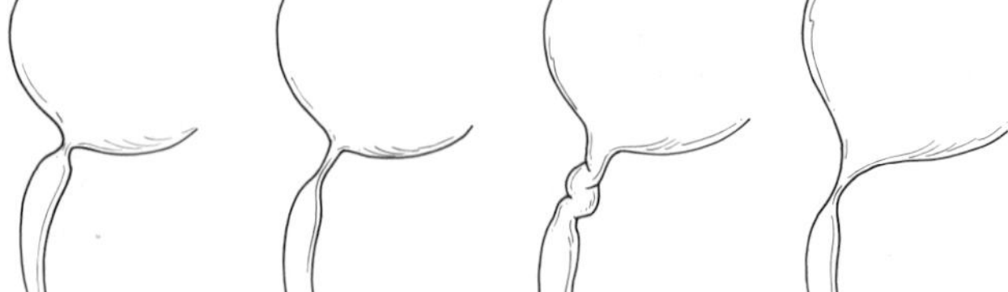

Figure 111-3 Ureteropelvic junction obstruction secondary to stenosis: simple, segmented, serpiginous, and shelving. (Courtesy of Dr. F. Douglas Stephens.) (From Fung LCT, Lakshmanan Y: Anomalies of the renal collecting system: Ureteropelvic junction obstruction [pyelocalyectasis] and infundibular stenosis. In Belman AB, King LR, Kramer SA [eds]: Clinical Pediatric Urology, 4th ed. London, Martin Dunitz, 2002, p 561.)

in circular muscle fibers, which tend to be disorganized and dysmorphic.[32,80] The combination of decreased ureteral caliber and defective muscle is thought to contribute to the intrinsic-type anomaly and poor transport of urine into the distal part of the ureter. Another way to describe these types of obstructive processes at the UPJ is by their volume-dependent (extrinsic) and pressure-dependent (intrinsic) characteristics.[59,63] Experimental and clinical observations led Koff to conclude that these parameters—or a combination thereof—may explain the many differences observed in the clinical manifestation of UPJ obstruction.[63]

A third anomaly that has been thought to cause UPJ obstruction is the *intraluminal* type of obstruction. Examples of intraluminal obstructive lesions are ureteral valves or benign fibroepithelial polyps.[1,70] These anomalies lead to partial, intermittent obstruction and typically require surgical intervention (Fig. 111-3).[35]

EMBRYOLOGY

During human embryogenesis, there are three separate and interdependent kidney systems: the pronephros, mesonephros, and metanephros—or definitive kidney. The earliest and most transient kidney is the pronephros, thought by many to be a vestigial structure found in the cervical region of the developing embryo. In the authors' opinion, the pronephros may be the essential bridge in bidirectional renal development. According to the current theory, however, the pronephros is replaced by the mesonephros by the third week of gestation. The mesonephros elongates to form a tubular structure, which eventually connects to the caudal end of the mesonephric, or wolffian, duct. At the fifth week of gestation, the dorsomedial wall of this ductal system gives rise to a diverticular outgrowth called the ureteric bud. Just as the mesonephric system regresses, the ureteric bud elongates in an ascending fashion toward the primitive metanephric anlagen. On contact, the two structures initiate a cascade of events known collectively as nephrogenesis.

During development of the urinary system, mechanical obstruction may occur at four different anatomic sites: the ureterocaliceal, ureteropelvic, ureterovesical, and vesicourethral junctions.[3] Each of these sites represents a confluence of two or more embryologic structures. These connections, which are incompletely understood at this time, may be prone to developmental error. Complex cellular "crosstalk" and induction initiated in a bidirectional manner normally culminate in precise anatomical junctions. Anatomic imprecision can result in two of the most common pathologic conditions in pediatric urology, namely, vesicoureteral reflux (VUR) and UPJ obstruction.

At one time it was thought that bidirectional recanalization of the ureter explained the frequent obstruction at the last segments to recanalize: the UPJ and ureterovesical junction (UVJ).[99] More recently, however, it has been shown that bidirectional recanalization does not occur. Recanalization occurs only at the middle portion of the ureter.[6] None of the current experimental models or theories of ureteral development explains why the UPJ is the most common site of congenital ureteral obstruction. This continues to be an active area of research. For example, a new study using an animal model of obstructive nephropathy has reported a possible genetic component of hydronephrosis.[12] Chang et al. describe a mouse model in which the gene encoding the calcineurin B type 1 isoform (*Cnb1*) has been deleted from the mesenchyme lining the urinary system. Hydronephrosis develops in these animals because of the lack of peristalsis. This study not only points to the renal pelvis as a regulator of peristalsis but may also explain congenital obstruction in which no obvious physical obstruction is identified.

Ransley previously described another theory of urinary tract obstruction at the level of the renal pelvis.[95] This explanation requires an understanding of the changes that take place in the kidney at the time of birth.

Several unique physiologic processes occur in the fetal kidney at birth. The concept of transitional nephrology that occurs during this period is essential for understanding the clinical observations with regard to transient hydronephrosis. Nephrogenesis is essentially completed by 36 weeks' gestation, but as the kidney continues to grow and develop, there is a significant increase in the glomerular filtration rate (GFR) during the last trimester and first 10 weeks of postnatal life.[103] At birth, solute and water excretion is abruptly transferred from the placenta to the neonatal kidney. Simultaneously, there is an increase in renovascular resistance, a decrease in renal blood flow, and a decrease in the GFR. This set of requisite events sets the stage for diminished excretion pressure and a tubular-caliceal gradient.[95] Perhaps in response to these events, intrarenal pelvic pressure in a neonatal kidney with UPJ obstruction generates an autoregulatory equilibrium. Disruption of this equilibrium may result in progressive hydronephrosis and rapid deterioration of renal function.

CLINICAL FEATURES

Thirty years ago, most infants with UPJ obstruction had a palpable abdominal mass at initial evaluation.[52] Today, UPJ obstruction is manifested in less than 19% of neonates in this manner.[103] With the advent of prenatal fetal ultrasonography, most infants born with UPJ obstruction are detected antenatally. The other population in which UPJ obstruction is detected consists of children with a variety of symptoms. Accordingly, there seems to be a bimodal age distribution of UPJ obstruction: asymptomatic postnatal infants and symptomatic school-aged children. Occasionally, however, some infants are discovered to have UPJ obstruction because of failure to thrive, vomiting, feeding difficulties, sepsis secondary to urinary tract infection, or rarely, hematuria related to nephrolithiasis.

Antenatal Manifestations

At the eighth week of intrauterine life, fetal urine is produced by the mesonephros. Once this transient kidney regresses, urine is made by the metanephros and continues to be made throughout gestation. The kidneys function well enough by the 12th week of gestation to reclaim sodium and concentrate urea. It is around this time that the fetal kidneys produce urine at a rate that may approach 50 mL/hr.[94] Total amniotic fluid volume is maintained by the production of fetal urine, which by the 16th week of gestation remains constant. Thus, maternal-fetal sonography should initially be performed between 16 and 20 weeks of gestation when adequate urine production has been established.[98] Most centers performing maternal-fetal ultrasound can detect normal kidneys at 17 to 19 weeks, whereas markedly dilated collecting systems can be identified as early as 12 to 14 weeks.[9]

The first report of antenatally detected urinary tract anomalies was in 1970.[38] Since that time, the American Institute for Ultrasound in Medicine's Bioeffects Committee has concluded that prenatal ultrasound screening is safe.[2] This endorsement has led to the common practice by obstetricians, as well as the expectation by the general population, that screening ultrasound be performed during the second trimester. Despite the fact that protocols for maternal-fetal ultrasonography continue to evolve in this country, they still depend in part on specific conventions and random institutional idiosyncrasies.[73]

Before the widespread use of prenatal ultrasound, most infants and school-aged children in whom congenital obstructive uropathy was diagnosed had overt clinical signs or symptoms referable to the urinary tract. Today, a prenatal diagnosis of hydronephrosis is made in the majority of neonates. Ultrasound can detect abnormal anatomy, but it is not specific for the diagnosis of particular disease processes. Sonographic features suggestive of UPJ obstruction include (1) unilateral or, less frequently, bilateral pelviectasis; (2) normal amniotic fluid volume; (3) no evidence of ipsilateral ureteral dilation; and (4) normal thickness of the bladder wall and normal cycling of the bladder. In cases in which the classic features of hydronephrosis are established, the diagnosis of UPJ is straightforward. More often, however, with early imaging, distinction between true obstructive uropathy and transient hydronephrosis of the neonate is complex. Additionally, prenatal distinction between UPJ obstruction and multicystic dysplastic kidney (MCDK) may be difficult. Sequential renal ultrasound and other complementary radiographic imaging studies are required for follow-up.

The Society of Fetal Urology (SFU) organized consensus guidelines for grading different degrees of hydronephrosis (Table 111-1) (Fig. 111-4A to D).[29,72] Once these in utero criteria are established, a prenatal diagnosis of hydronephrosis with a possibility of UPJ obstruction should be entertained by the physician and reported to the parents. In male fetuses, bilateral hydronephrosis should be excluded immediately because it might be related to a different and more urgent problem of bladder outlet obstruction, possibly caused by posterior urethral valves.

Prenatal Counseling

Parents should be advised of a presumptive diagnosis of hydronephrosis and counseled appropriately. Education

TABLE 111-1 Society of Fetal Urology Grading of Hydronephrosis

SFU Grade	Description
1	Slight splitting of the central renal complex without calyceal involvement, normal parenchyma
2	Splitting of the central renal complex with extension to nondilated calyces
3	Wide splitting of the renal pelvis, dilated outside the renal border, calyces uniformly dilated, normal parenchyma
4	Large, dilated calyces (may appear convex); thinning of the parenchyma to ≤50% of the ipsilateral (normal) kidney

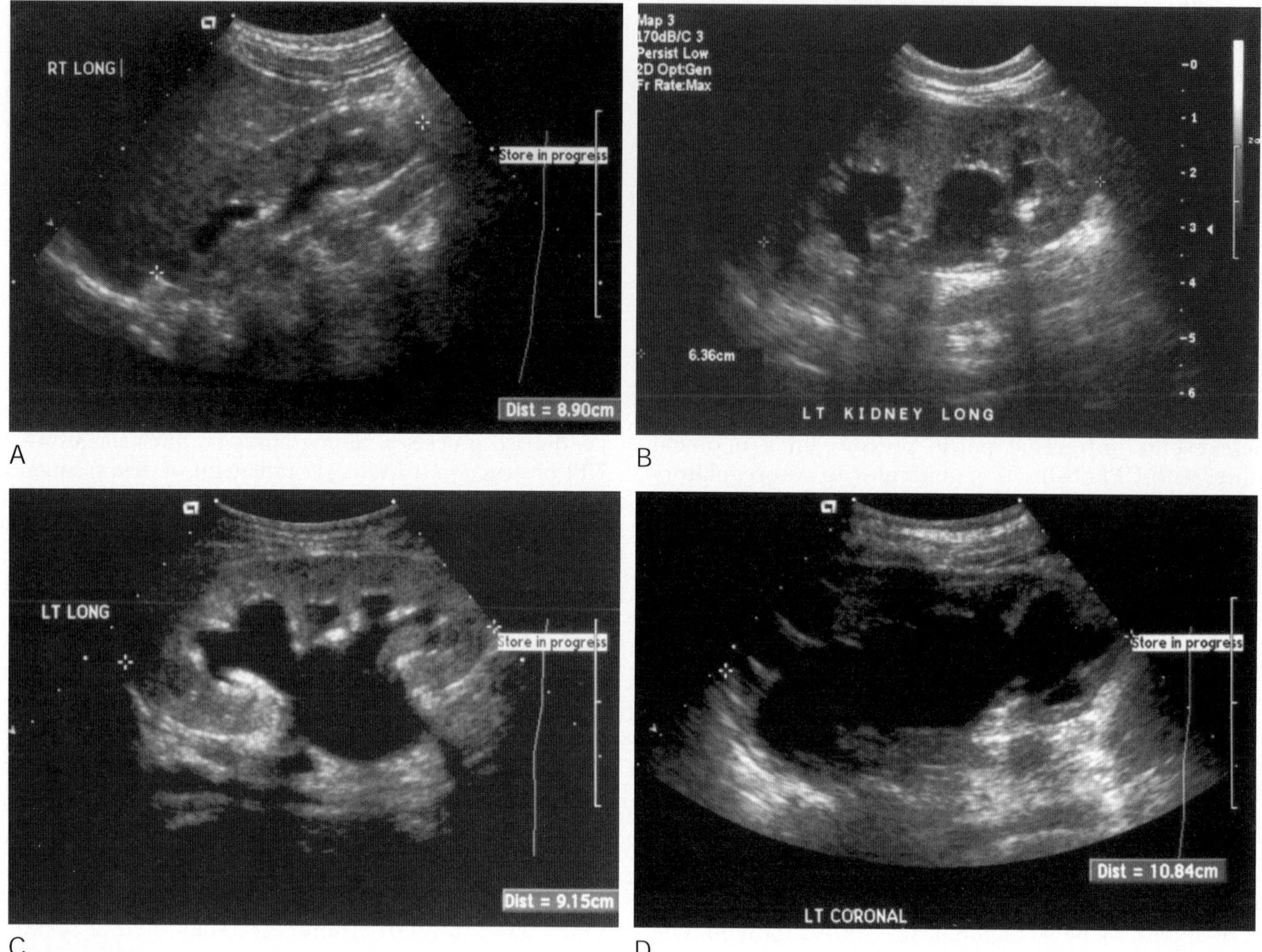

Figure 111-4 Renal ultrasound scans representing the Society for Fetal Urology (SFU) grading schema. *A*, SFU grade 1 hydronephrosis. *B*, SFU grade 2 hydronephrosis. *C*, SFU grade 3 hydronephrosis. *D*, SFU grade 4 hydronephrosis. (Courtesy of Children's Hospital & Regional Medical Center, Seattle.)

and communication are paramount in the process of prenatal counseling. The majority of antenatally detected genitourinary abnormalities are unlikely to require postnatal surgical intervention.[11,107] In fact, only 1% to 25% require surgery at 4 years of follow-up.[71,96] As such, referral to a pediatric urologist for prenatal and postnatal counseling is highly recommended. The survival rate for fetuses found to have unilateral hydronephrosis secondary to obstruction is virtually 100%. To realize this excellent prognosis for unilateral hydronephrosis, postnatal follow-up is essential to temporally track the progression of hydronephrosis, as well as establish the management principles with the family. For this reason, referral to a pediatric urologist is highly recommended.

Postnatal Manifestations

Children with UPJ obstruction have variable symptoms, such as episodic flank or abdominal pain and urinary tract infections. Cyclic abdominal pain, often associated with vomiting, is a typical finding, reminiscent of Dietl's crisis.* After a thorough evaluation for a vague gastrointestinal disorder, UPJ obstruction may be diagnosed. Stone disease may be associated with UPJ obstruction; in fact, the incidence of nephrolithiasis is 17 times higher in patients with UPJ obstruction than in asymptomatic patients who undergo intravenous urography.[67] Hematuria may also be the initial symptom in UPJ obstruction. After trivial trauma, friable mucosal vessels in the dilated collecting system presumably rupture. Some children with UPJ obstruction have insidious manifestations, with years of relative anorexia associated with difficulty gaining weight. These children are typically found to have a left UPJ obstruction. The dilated left renal pelvis creates a mass effect on the stomach that may result in early satiety, relative anorexia, and vomiting. Still other children

*Jozef Dietl (1804-1878), a Polish physician, described a syndrome characterized by violent paroxysms of colicky flank pain, nausea, chills, tachycardia, oliguria, transient hematuria or proteinuria, and a palpable enlarged tender kidney that was attributed to acute hydronephrosis caused by kinking or vascular obstruction of the ureter of a floating kidney.

with UPJ obstruction may have profound urosepsis. Snyder et al. reported that urinary tract infection is the initial sign in 30% of children with UPJ obstruction beyond the neonatal period.[105]

DIAGNOSIS

Because hydronephrosis is such a broad topic, it is practical to formulate a working differential diagnosis. One method of doing so is to develop categories of hydronephrosis, for example, obstructive and nonobstructive. Obstructive causes of hydronephrosis include UPJ obstruction (44% incidence); UVJ obstruction (21% incidence); MCDK, ureterocele, and duplicated collecting systems (12% incidence); posterior urethral valves (9% incidence); and ectopic ureter, urethral atresia, sacrococcygeal teratoma, and hydrometrocolpos. Nonobstructive causes of hydronephrosis include VUR (14% incidence), physiologic dilation, prune-belly syndrome, renal cystic diseases, and megacalicosis (Table 111-2).[77,92]

The diagnosis of unilateral UPJ obstruction by conventional testing is not difficult. It is difficult, however, to define *significant* obstruction in an infant. Even though the newer diagnostic tests assign numerical values to features of the obstructed kidney and demonstrate exceptional anatomic structure, they do not necessarily correlate with the degree of obstruction or the potential for progressive renal deterioration. In fact, none of the existing imaging modalities can accurately assess which kidneys with a suspected obstructive process are at risk for progressive loss of renal function. With this limitation in mind, several sequential radiographic studies can be used to diagnose physiologically significant UPJ obstruction that might require surgical intervention.

Intravenous Urography

Historically, intravenous urography (IVU) is the radiographic modality of choice for noninvasive assessment of the urinary tract. As an imaging study, it combines anatomic accuracy with qualitative information regarding renal function and obstruction. It may be useful in clarifying anatomic curiosities suggested by ultrasound, but in general, IVU is fairly obsolete in the assessment of a pediatric patient with obstructive uropathy. It is described here only for completeness.

Although sonography and scintigraphy have largely replaced IVU, it has characteristic features that are useful in the diagnosis of UPJ obstruction.[97] Obstruction of the kidney can be recognized as a delay in the appearance of contrast material or a negative nephrogram, a delay in drainage, a rounded renal contour, dilution of contrast medium, or uniform cortical loss. In selected patients with incongruous histories or equivocal studies, provocative IVU might be performed to simulate a "crisis" situation. In the correct situation, excellent radiographic images are obtained, and in some cases a diagnosis can be confirmed.

IVU has several pitfalls. It is not a study of choice in neonates because renal function is immature at this stage and even the normal kidney is unable to acidify or concentrate urine for the first 4 to 6 weeks of life. Therefore, the intravenous contrast used for the IVU provides poor visualization of neonatal kidneys. As with other similar functional studies of the kidney, IVU is difficult to interpret when the patient is poorly hydrated or has underlying renal insufficiency.

TABLE 111-2 Differential Diagnosis of Hydronephrosis

Obstructive	Nonobstructive
Ureteropelvic junction obstruction	Vesicoureteral reflux
Ureterovesical junction obstruction	Physiologic dilatation
Multicystic dysplastic kidney	Prune-belly syndrome
Ureterocele	Renal cystic diseases
Duplicated collecting system	Megacalycosis
Posterior urethral valves	
Ectopic ureter	
Urethral atresia	
Sacrococcygeal teratoma	
Hydrometrocolpos	

Renal Ultrasound

Renal ultrasound is a widely available, relatively inexpensive, noninvasive, safe test that provides adequate anatomic visualization without radiation exposure. Given these exceptional qualities, it is widely used both in maternal-fetal sonography and for postnatal imaging. Consequently, renal sonography has resulted in the increased diagnosis of prenatal and postnatal dilation of the upper urinary tract. In fact, renal ultrasound is the most commonly performed initial study for the postnatal evaluation of neonates who have been discovered prenatally to have hydronephrosis. It is the standard modality for postnatal evaluation of febrile urinary tract infections. Renal ultrasound is highly accurate in the diagnosis of hydronephrosis. It provides relatively good information on findings characteristic of UPJ obstruction, including pelviectasis and caliectasis, no evidence of ipsilateral ureterectasis, normal bladder filling and emptying (cycling), and normal bladder thickness. In unilateral cases of hydronephrosis, ultrasound may delineate parenchymal atrophy on the affected side in comparison to the contralateral side.

Twenty-five years ago, the general consensus among pediatric urologists had been that the amount of hydronephrosis did not correlate with the degree of obstruction. Ransley and colleagues finally established this fact.[96] In their study, progressive hydronephrosis and deterioration in renal function were uncommon in neonates and infants with a maximum anteroposterior renal pelvic diameter of less that 10 mm and no evidence of infundibular or caliceal dilation (SFU grade 1 hydronephrosis). All the patients initially in the nonoperative group who eventually required surgery had a prenatal anteroposterior renal pelvic diameter of greater than 12 mm. However, renal pelvic diameter was found

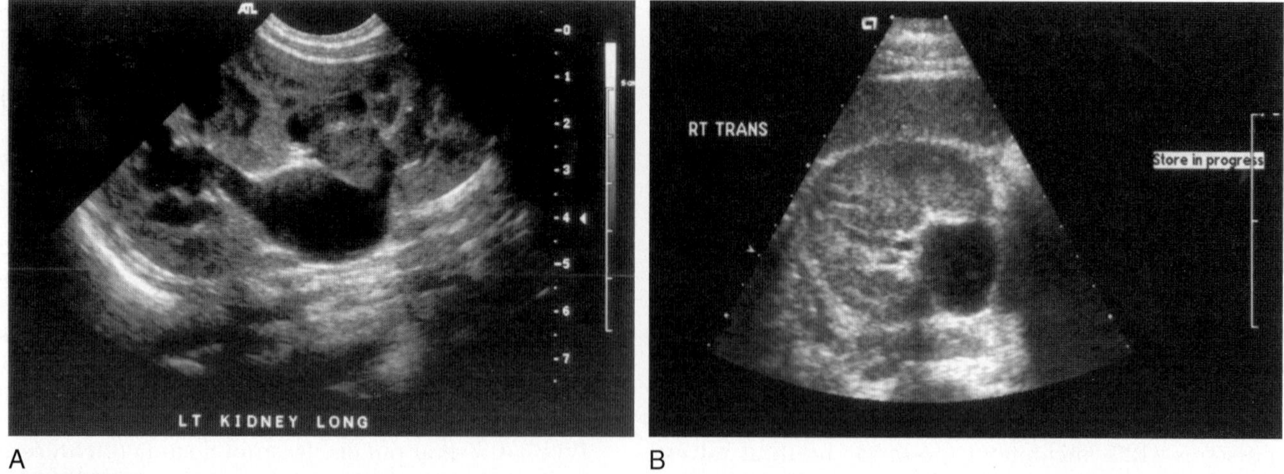

Figure 111-5 *A*, Renal ultrasound representing an obstructed ureteropelvic junction with an intrarenal pelvis. *B*, Renal ultrasound representing a nonobstructed extrarenal pelvis. (Courtesy of Children's Hospital & Regional Medical Center, Seattle.)

to be a poor positive predictor of outcome because only 34% of such patients required pyeloplasty. In some of these patients, perhaps, such mild degrees of hydronephrosis are probably physiologic, secondary to the highly compliant nature of the fetal (and neonatal) renal pelvis. Careful consideration should be given to the presence of an extrarenal pelvis, which in some cases may be mistaken for pathologic hydronephrosis (Fig. 111-5A and B). Caliceal dilatation is typically not present in patients with an extrarenal pelvis, which is thought to be a normal variant.

Koff and coworkers proposed the use of serial renal ultrasound to predict progression in unilateral cases of UPJ obstruction.[61] In addition to being able to monitor the temporal behavior of UPJ obstruction, serial renal ultrasound provides the ability to track the axial growth of the kidneys as an indicator of progression of UPJ obstruction. In cases of unilateral UPJ obstruction, the growth rate of the contralateral normal kidney can be used as an indirect expression of relative obstruction.[62] With the use of renal growth-function nomograms, compensatory hypertrophy in the contralateral "normal" kidney may be indicative of progressive obstruction in a unilaterally obstructed kidney. Conversely, a slower than normal growth rate (compensatory hypotrophy) in the contralateral normal kidney suggests that rapid recovery of function, or even supranormal function, in the unilaterally obstructed kidney would imply that obstruction is not present. Koff's data, however, have not been corroborated because of operator variability in renal length measurements.

Serial ultrasound studies are important for implementing any protocol for UPJ obstruction, but they can be problematic because they require a waiting period during which progressive renal injury can occur. For example, cortical thinning may develop. This is an important, but typically late finding. Focal cortical loss is easier to detect, though less common than global cortical thinning. Reflecting on Koff and colleagues' study,[61] it is logical to conclude that in patients with unilateral hydronephrosis, contralateral compensatory renal hypertrophy may indicate a greater risk for continued deterioration of the hydronephrotic kidney.[61] However, reliable sonographic diagnosis of renal hypertrophy requires multiple sequential measurements of renal length or volume, thus limiting its applicability for guiding early intervention.[19]

Renal ultrasound is highly accurate in the diagnosis of hydronephrosis. Like many of the tests, however, it has limitations. It cannot diagnose obstruction because the degree of hydronephrosis neither specifically indicates the presence or absence of obstruction nor predicts whether the hydronephrosis will improve or progress.[60] This is particularly apparent in a neonate, in whom hydronephrosis may be transient and is dependent on the degree of hydration and bladder fullness. Furthermore, ultrasound cannot provide any information regarding renal function.

Technetium 99m Renal Scintigraphy

Differential renal function is one of the most important parameters used in detecting a functionally significant obstruction and, as such, predicting the optimum time for surgical correction of congenital UPJ obstruction. Renal scintigraphy is the study of choice for estimation of overall and differential renal function. Three radiopharmaceuticals are primarily used in renal scintigraphy, and their characteristics are linked to their biologic activity. Technetium 99m-diethylenetriaminepentaacetic acid (^{99m}Tc-DTPA) and technetium 99m-mercaptoacetyltriglycine (^{99m}Tc-MAG-3) are preferentially concentrated by the kidney and freely filtered by the glomerulus.[54] DTPA is neither secreted nor resorbed by the renal tubules, whereas MAG-3 is secreted by the tubules. Because each is nearly completely excreted, they can be used to estimate differential renal function and urinary drainage. The third agent, technetium 99m-dimercaptosuccinic acid (^{99m}Tc-DMSA), is tightly bound to renal tubular cells and is, therefore, useful for the detection of differential renal function and clinically significant cortical lesions such as renal scars.

At least three consensus statements have been published to decrease the wide clinical variance in protocols: the Society of Nuclear Medicine's Nuclear Medicine Procedure Guidelines for Pediatric Diuretic Renography, the "Well Tempered Diuretic Renogram," and the consensus statement from the Ninth International Meeting of the Society of Radionuclides in Nephrourology, Committee on Diuretic Renography.[17,18,84] They are all very similar in methodology, as well as interpretation. Basically, a collecting system without significant obstruction will have a clearance half-time (i.e., the time for half the radiopharmaceutical to clear) after furosemide (Lasix) administration of less than 10 minutes. Longer than 20 minutes is abnormal and associated with high-grade obstruction. Clearance half-times between 10 and 20 minutes are considered indeterminate. The half-time should not be the only criterion on which to define obstruction. As in most studies, interpretation requires the use of other available data: curve analysis, differential renal function, and, of course, the clinical context (Fig. 111-6).

Currently, renal scintigraphy is the most popular modality for determining the functional significance of UPJ obstruction, mainly because several investigators have shown that most cases of severe hydronephrosis (SFU grades 3 to 4) demonstrate obstruction on diuretic renography.[72,111] As a result of these studies, the differential renal function of a hydronephrotic kidney, as determined by ^{99m}Tc-DTPA or ^{99m}Tc-MAG-3 renal scan, creates an arbitrary threshold for surgical intervention.[23] Thirty-five percent is the pivotal function around which intervention or observation is determined. If the initial ipsilateral differential renal function is greater than 35%, the neonate can be monitored conservatively by renal ultrasound every 3 months. In contrast, if the differential renal function is less than 35% on the initial study or there is a decremental change in function of 10% by repeat renal scan,[40] consideration should be given to surgical intervention.

Renal scintigraphy is the study of choice for the estimation of overall and differential renal function, except in patients with poor or immature renal function and those with capacious collecting systems. Other determinates that affect renal scintigraphy include the region of interest, time of measurement, state of hydration, bladder fullness, reservoir effect, type of protocol, renal response to Lasix, and the concept of supranormal function (Fig. 111-7).[17,18,36,81,83,108] Supranormal function is defined as greater than 55% of differential renal function in the hydronephrotic kidney in children with unilateral hydronephrosis. It has not been confirmed whether supranormal differential renal function is an artifact or a true finding, nor is there a consensus on how to manage these patients. Oh and associates examined supranormal function in human subjects and determined that supranormal function of the ipsilaterally obstructed kidney may not be true hyperfunction but merely a pathologic compensatory mechanism in response to chronic obstruction.[83] For this reason, they warned that interpretation of differential renal function should be made with this caveat in mind. Khan and associates

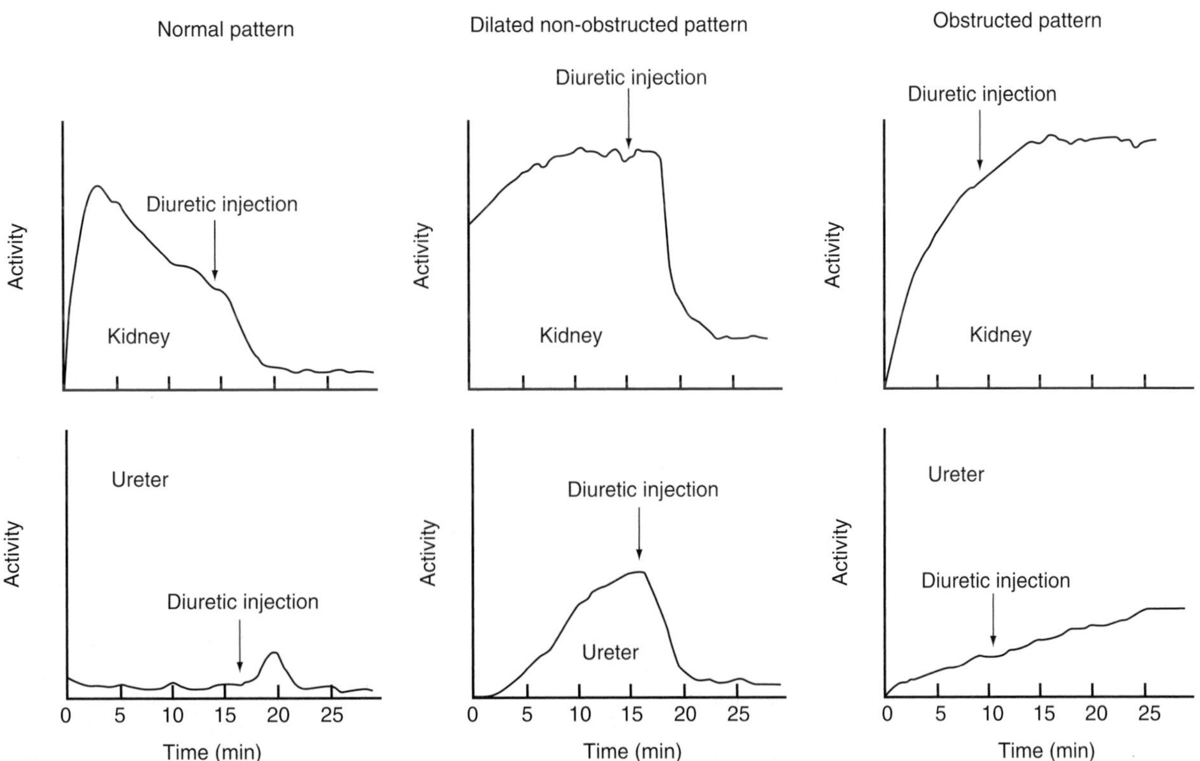

Figure 111–6 Lasix renography, classic patterns: normal, dilated nonobstructed, and obstructed.[63] (From Fung LCT, Lakshmanan Y: Anomalies of the renal collecting system: Ureteropelvic junction obstruction [pyelocalyectasis] and infundibular stenosis. In Belman AB, King LR, Kramer SA [eds]: Clinical Pediatric Urology, 4th ed. London, Martin Dunitz, 2002, p 594.)

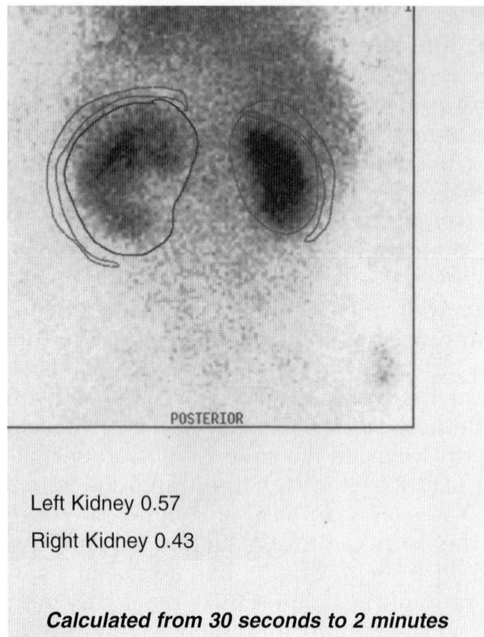

Figure 111-7 MAG-3 renal scintigraphy: supranormal renal function of a 6-month-old baby who had the prenatal diagnosis of SFU grade 4 hydronephrosis, found postnatally to have high-grade left ureteropelvic junction obstruction. (Courtesy of Children's Hospital & Regional Medical Center, Seattle.)

believe that supranormal function is an artifact that can be avoided by using MAG-3 and appropriate computer software to account for multiple algorithms.[57]

Voiding Cystourethrography

It is well known that VUR, the most common problem of the lower urinary tract in children, can coexist with UPJ obstruction, the most common pediatric problem of the upper urinary tract.[68] The exact reason for this association has not yet been established.[8] However, what is known is that approximately 9% to 14% of patients with UPJ obstruction have VUR. Conversely, 1% of patients found to have VUR are found to have UPJ obstruction. These associations, albeit low, can affect renal function and change management. Consequently, voiding cystourethrography (VCUG) is the standard of practice for the clinical evaluation of all infants with prenatal hydronephrosis, regardless of age or gender.[28,47]

Recently, several investigators have challenged this standard.[119] In a retrospective review of 106 patients who underwent pyeloplasty for UPJ obstruction, low-grade reflux coexisting with UPJ obstruction spontaneously resolved after pyeloplasty. Additionally, they found that all cases of high-grade VUR coexisting with UPJ obstruction were easily detected by renal ultrasonography. They concluded that VCUG should be limited to children with UPJ obstruction who also have a dilated ureter on ultrasonography. Caution should be practiced when evaluating children with this diagnostic dilemma because the approach to management is subtle, yet complex. Horowitz and others confirmed earlier reports that there is a racial difference with respect to detection of prenatal hydronephrosis and VUR.[4,47,66] The absence of VUR in black infants with prenatal hydronephrosis and the 17.6% incidence in nonblack infants suggest that VCUG should not be routinely performed in the black population but should continue to be the standard of care in the nonblack population.

To date, the primary diagnostic tool for VUR has been standard radiographic VCUG. It is unpleasant and invasive and may be physiologically inaccurate in some cases. More than 20 years ago, other alternatives to this test were investigated. Hofmann described real-time ultrasonography as an alternative to VCUG for the detection of VUR.[44] Despite its success in Europe, this technique has not gained popularity in the United States. Recent reports have supported the use of other modalities that diminish radiation exposure in children being evaluated for VUR, including direct radionuclide voiding cystography and echo-enhanced voiding urosonography.[55] Although each of these methods has advantages and disadvantages, they are not completely interchangeable, nor have they proved to be as efficacious as standard VCUG.

Magnetic Resonance Urography

Most recently, dynamic, gadolinium-enhanced magnetic resonance urography (Gd-MRU) has been advocated for its nonionizing radiation and its unparalleled, three-dimensional views of anatomic obstruction. Wen et al. used Gd-DTPA–enhanced MR imaging in rats and determined that it could distinguish between an obstructed and nonobstructed collecting system.[117] Using a similar technique, Kirsch recently reviewed a cohort of 200 children with hydronephrosis who underwent systematic evaluation with Gd-MRU.[58,87] When compared with sonography and renal scintigraphy, Gd-MRU provided superior anatomic images of the genitourinary system and excellent spatial resolution (Fig. 111-8). The study has been shown to be robust and reproducible with a linear regression coefficient of 0.99. The limitations of the study are that it requires general anesthesia or sedation and involves cumbersome interpretation of the images.[45] Although the technique is not yet widely available, MRU has been considered by some investigators to be a more reliable determinant of renal anatomy and function in cases of UPJ obstruction.[58]

Retrograde Pyelography

This radiographic study is rarely needed to diagnose UPJ obstruction. In a series of 108 children undergoing pyeloplasty, retrograde pyelography (RPG) did not change the surgical approach or planned procedure in any of the cases.[100] However, RPG is still commonly performed before open pyeloplasty. The reason for this is simple. During the diagnostic process, information regarding the exact anatomic location of the UPJ in relation to other anatomic structures is lacking. Therefore, to precisely identify the location of obstruction

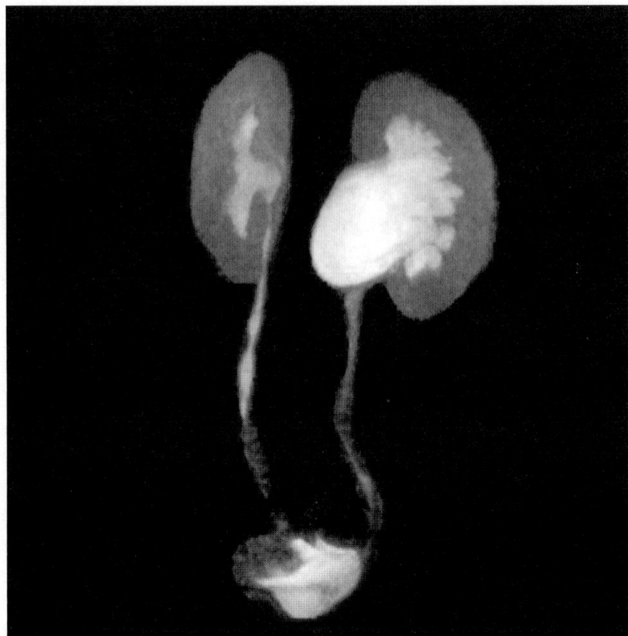

Figure 111-8 Three-dimensional maximal intensity projection reconstruction after Gd-DTPA infusion showing classic left ureteropelvic junction obstruction. (From Perez-Brayfield MR, Kirsch AJ, Jones RA, Grattan-Smith JD: A prospective study comparing ultrasound, nuclear scintigraphy and dynamic contrast-enhanced magnetic resonance imaging in the evaluation of hydronephrosis. J Urol 2003;170:1331.)

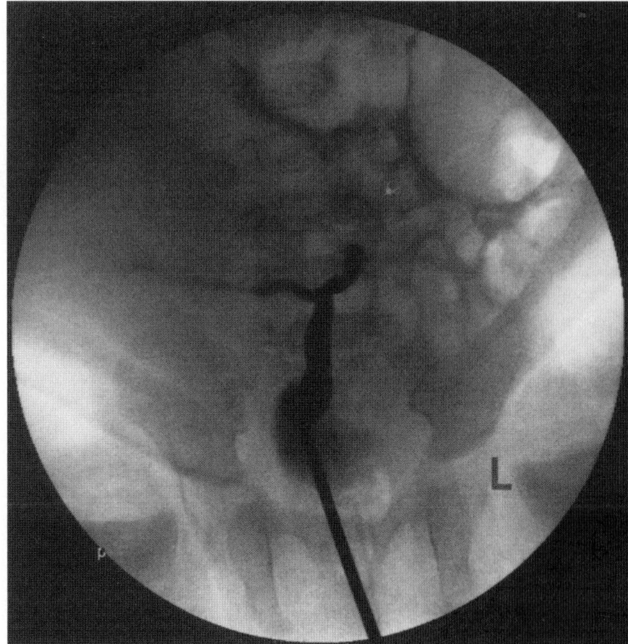

Figure 111-9 Right retrograde pyeloureterogram demonstrating right ureteropelvic junction obstruction with a wisp of contrast entering a dilated renal pelvis. Note the deviation of the proximal ureter and dilated pelvis. (Courtesy of Byron Joyner, MD, Children's Hospital & Regional Medical Center, Seattle.)

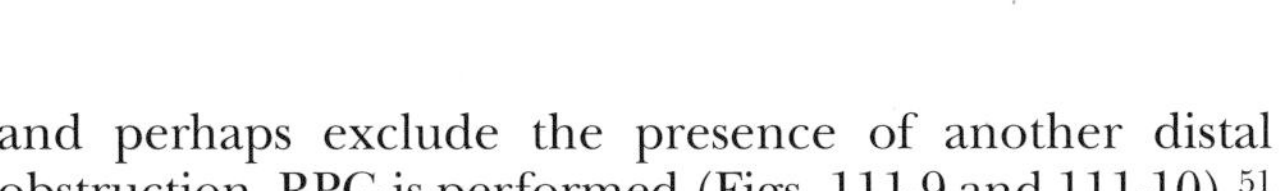

and perhaps exclude the presence of another distal obstruction, RPG is performed (Figs. 111-9 and 111-10).[51]

Pressure-Flow Study

The perfusion provocation study, introduced by Bäcklund et al. in 1965 and popularized by Whitaker in 1973, is the standard pressure-flow study and is simply referred to as the Whitaker test (Fig. 111-11).[5,118] It detects the ureter's resistance to a known flow rate by simultaneously measuring manometric pressure between the renal pelvis and bladder. The test is unaffected by the kidney's GRF, and its antegrade pyelography offers excellent anatomic location of the suspected obstructing segment. The study is most useful when there are equivocal studies regarding obstruction in a hydronephrotic kidney. It is based on the premise that obstruction produces a restriction in the outflow of urine. Therefore, with increased diuresis, renal pelvic pressure increases. Accordingly, high renal pelvic pressure relative to bladder pressure at any rate of diuresis confirms the presence of obstruction. At a flow rate of 10 mL/min, a differential pressure between the renal pelvis and the urinary bladder of less than 13 cm H_2O is considered to be normal. Arbitrary values of 14 to 20 cm H_2O indicate mild obstruction; values in excess of 35 cm H_2O indicate severe obstruction. The Whitaker test requires percutaneous access to the kidney and usually requires general anesthesia in the pediatric population. Consequently, it

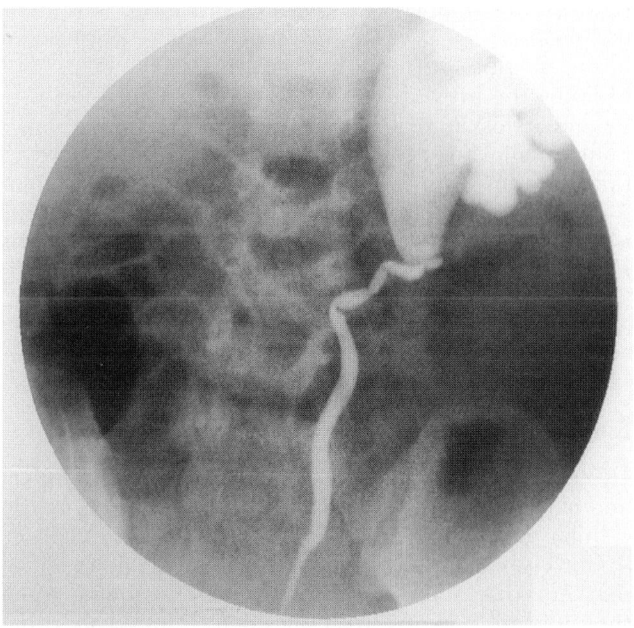

Figure 111-10 Preoperative ancillary left retrograde pyeloureterogram demonstrating a serpiginous ureteropelvic junction obstruction. The left iliac crest and spinal vertebra can be used as landmarks to plan the skin incision. (Courtesy of Richard Grady, MD, Children's Hospital & Regional Medical Center, Seattle.)

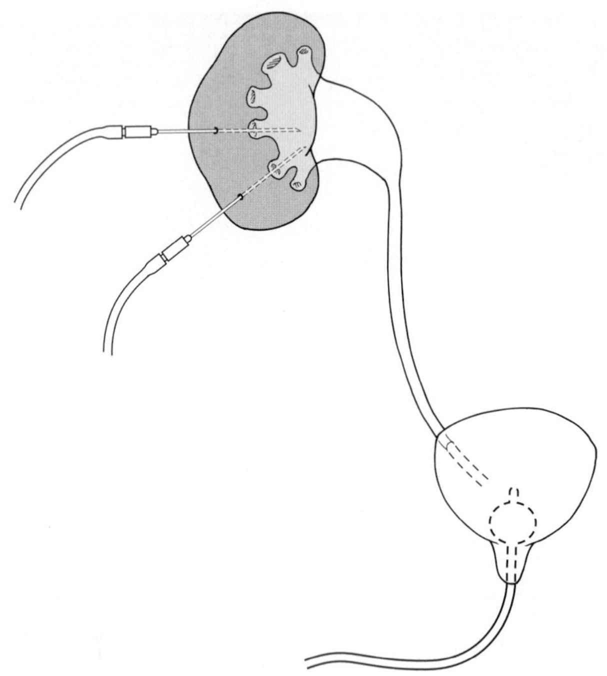

Figure 111-11 Whitaker pressure perfusion study. (From Fung LCT, Lakshmanan Y: Anomalies of the renal collecting system: Ureteropelvic junction obstruction [pyelocalyectasis] and infundibular stenosis. In Belman AB, King LR, Kramer SA [eds]: Clinical Pediatric Urology, 4th ed. London, Martin Dunitz, 2002, p 596.)

is undesirable for a routine test. It is typically indicated for equivocal cases of obstruction and is, therefore, rarely performed. In addition, the Whitaker test requires a rigid protocol and exacting measurements to avoid technical errors. Recently, investigators have proposed a more physiologic modification to the Whitaker test whereby the pressure level instead of the infusion rate was kept constant to better categorize UPJ obstruction.[116] Functionally, the pressure-flow study is less sensitive to flow variation. Normal renal pelvic pressure is less than 7 cm H_2O and may even be less than zero in patients with normal ureteral peristalsis. Therefore, if flow is not achieved at pressures of 7 cm H_2O or less, there is increased outflow resistance, a finding consistent with obstruction.

Biochemical Markers

Ureteral obstruction has been shown in both clinical and experimental studies to result in renal injury at the cellular level.[39,89] Such studies have led investigators to surmise that there might be potential biochemical markers that may be predictive of postnatal renal function in patients with elevated intrapelvic renal pressure, such as in some cases of UPJ obstruction.[82] Prospective markers include urinary sodium, calcium, and β_2-microglobulin. Other biochemical markers are being defined constantly. Recently, it has been demonstrated that persistently elevated collecting system pressure induces renal abnormalities, including an increase in tubular pressure, decrease in renal blood flow, decrease in GFR, and renal tubular dysfunction.[15,37] Fung and Atala, using a nonobstructed porcine model in which urine drained against a predetermined pressure gradient, demonstrated a progressively elevated level of urinary *N*-acetyl-β-D-glucosaminidase, an indicator of acute renal cell injury.[34] Other similar studies have demonstrated that pressure-induced renal dysfunction and pressure-induced renal cellular injury are probably interdependent processes.[15,41] Other biochemical markers in various clinical and experimental settings have been shown to be involved in the pathogenesis of obstructive uropathy and may be useful biochemical markers for the prognostication of renal disease, including urinary monocyte chemotactic peptide-1 (MCP-1) and epidermal growth factor (EGF), transforming growth factor-β (TGF-β), urinary α_1-microglobulin, and p53 and p21 (WAF-1) expression.[27,42,50,78] Biochemical markers for obstructive uropathy—and specifically for UPJ obstruction—have not been precisely defined, and their use as predictors of renal function is still unreliable. Because of the lack of standard biochemical or physiologic markers to measure renal obstruction, serial radiographic studies are necessary to evaluate the function and anatomy of a kidney with suspected UPJ obstruction.

Preoperative Vascular Imaging

Once the diagnosis of UPJ obstruction has been determined from the history and basic radiographic studies, there is often a question regarding the possibility of involvement of a crossing polar vessel in the obstructive process. This particular anatomic problem is primarily important in older children or adults with UPJ obstruction because it can influence the surgical approach.

The incidence of crossing vessels in patients with UPJ obstruction is inconsistent in the literature and ranges from 11% to 79%, mainly because of the variable definitions used to describe UPJ obstruction.[52,112] Polar vessels crossing immediately adjacent to the UPJ are designated as "crossing vessels." They are thought to exacerbate rather than initiate the obstructive process.[75] Crossing vessels have the potential to cause significant morbidity if not recognized before an endourologic procedure. Several imaging modalities can be used to search for a crossing vessel, including digital subtraction intra-arterial angiography, helical computed tomography, contrast-enhanced color Doppler imaging, endoluminal sonography, and magnetic resonance angiography. The anatomic peculiarity of polar crossing vessels makes vascular imaging important, especially when minimally invasive techniques are proposed for the management of UPJ obstruction.[56] An extensive historical review addressing crossing vessels has been published.[113]

Among pediatric urologists, the concept of preoperative vascular imaging to verify a crossing vessel is controversial, if not moot. Surgical management of most children with UPJ obstruction is open surgery, laparoscopy, or robotic surgery, but not endopyelotomy, which, if used blindly, could inadvertently disrupt an unsuspected crossing vessel.

To this date, endourologic procedures are limited in children for several reasons: (1) the available endourologic equipment is not small enough to accommodate children younger than 3 years; (2) most pediatric surgeons are trained to perform an open dismembered pyeloplasty, with the recognition that laparoscopy is an excellent choice in the proper hands; and (3) both open and laparoscopic approaches would identify an anterior crossing vessel intraoperatively.

MANAGEMENT

Despite the widespread use of prenatal ultrasound and multiple postnatal studies, the natural history of UPJ obstruction still remains unclear. Management of unilateral hydronephrosis cannot be based on either the degree of pelvic dilation on ultrasound or obstruction on diuretic renography.[64,111] Several investigators have demonstrated that nearly 50% to 80% of all cases of prenatal hydronephrosis will resolve spontaneously with postnatal follow-up.[21,43] Still others have demonstrated progressive hydronephrosis with diminution of function in follow-up 3 years post partum.[31] These different outcomes are unsettling and, as yet, unanswered. As a result of the lack of clarity of the natural history of UPJ obstruction, two schools of thought exist regarding the management of this disease entity: watchful waiting and early intervention.

The controversy regarding management of suspected unilateral UPJ obstruction does not pertain to a kidney with mild hydronephrosis (pelviectasis without caliectasis), in which long-term morbidity is relatively low and surgical intervention is unlikely. The controversy also does not involve management of a kidney with severe hydronephrosis (pelvicaliectasis with parenchymal thinning), in which surgical intervention is indicated for compromised renal function, infection, or symptoms.[98] Moreover, the controversy does not pertain to management of bilateral UPJ obstruction, which will not be addressed in this chapter. Instead, the controversy over the management of UPJ obstruction relates to three main issues. The first involves a kidney with moderate hydronephrosis (pelvicaliectasis without parenchymal thinning). Such kidneys *may* gradually improve without loss of relative renal function, but they have an unpredictable course. This leads to the second issue, which is the inherent inability to predict which kidney will deteriorate during observation. The last issue relates to the ability of surgery to reverse the adverse functional changes that often result from UPJ obstruction.

Watchful Waiting

Observational management of unilateral UPJ obstruction involves sequential radiographic studies and cautious patience. The fact that so many algorithms have been devised for the management of UPJ obstruction is a sure indication that no single algorithm is absolute. In general, however, the typical evaluation of an infant with the prenatal diagnosis of hydronephrosis begins with a directed physical examination and postnatal ultrasound. The physical examination should determine the child's vital signs, general health, and overall appearance. Respiratory distress or vomiting may be associated with a palpable abdominal mass in some cases. In most instances, however, an abdominal mass is not identified.

Postnatal ultrasound should be performed at least 2 days post partum because relative dehydration of the fetus and physiologic oliguria may result in a false-negative study after birth. The one exception to this 2-day rule is a male neonate with bilateral hydronephrosis and a thickened bladder wall, which would be suggestive of a more urgent problem such as bladder outlet obstruction secondary to posterior urethral valves. Renal sonography suggesting UPJ obstruction should be followed by additional diagnostic studies to confirm or exclude the obstruction. Further radiologic tests should be based on other possible causes of hydronephrosis, because a number of conditions can mimic or produce dilatation of the collecting system with or without urinary tract obstruction. Some of these conditions include physiologic pelviectasis, UPJ obstruction, duplication of the collecting system with an ectopic ureter (or an associated ureterocele), megaureter, MCDK, UVJ obstruction, posterior urethral valves, prune-belly syndrome, renal cystic diseases, parapelvic renal cysts, and megacalicosis. In addition, the diagnosis of hydronephrosis may be suggested by a sonolucent appearance commonly seen in the neonatal renal medullary and pyramids. This curious finding may be confused with hydronephrosis but seems to resolve with renal parenchymal maturation, which occurs within the first 3 months of life. Follow-up ultrasound reveals no apparent evidence of hydronephrosis.

Postnatal renal ultrasound can eliminate several of the aforementioned diagnoses. If a dilated ureter is demonstrated on postnatal ultrasound, for example, the diagnoses of UPJ obstruction, ectopic ureter, megaureter, UVJ obstruction, posterior urethral valves, and prune-belly syndrome are highly unlikely. Sonographic evidence of multiple, noncommunicating cysts is unusual for UPJ obstruction and is more typical of parapelvic cysts or MCDK. Parapelvic cysts are rare in the pediatric population and should not be mistaken for hydronephrosis.[20] MCDK can be confirmed by nuclear scintigraphy, typically a DMSA scan, which reveals no evidence of ipsilateral renal function.

If the postnatal sonogram confirms characteristic findings consistent with hydronephrosis, the newborn is placed on a once-daily prophylactic dose of oral antibiotics (amoxicillin, 15 mg/kg). This regimen has almost completely eliminated the development of urosepsis in infants with the prenatal diagnosis of hydronephrosis.[73] After prophylaxis has been established, VCUG is performed to rule out VUR, which can exist despite negative postnatal renal ultrasound findings.[120] In as many as 20% of cases of antenatally diagnosed hydronephrosis, postnatal ultrasound evaluations may be negative, which is the reason why all infants with this finding should be evaluated with VCUG.[21] Incidentally, the use of prophylactic antibiotics in infants with postnatal hydronephrosis in the absence of VUR continues to be controversial.[33,46,115]

Surgery

The goal of surgery for UPJ obstruction is to preserve renal function by facilitating unobstructed drainage of the renal pelvis. Two techniques are designed for this purpose. The first is the *flap technique,* which uses renal pelvic tissue to augment the narrowed UPJ segment (Fig. 111-12A to F). The second technique, *dismembered pyeloplasty,* is the most popular.[16] It involves complete removal of the narrowed (dysfunctional) segment, tailoring of the renal pelvis (if necessary), and reapproximation of the ureter to the renal pelvis in a dependent position. Neither technique sufficiently treats all the possible anatomic variations. The anatomy of the renal pelvis, in association with other intraoperative findings, dictates the technique of choice. For example, when a crossing

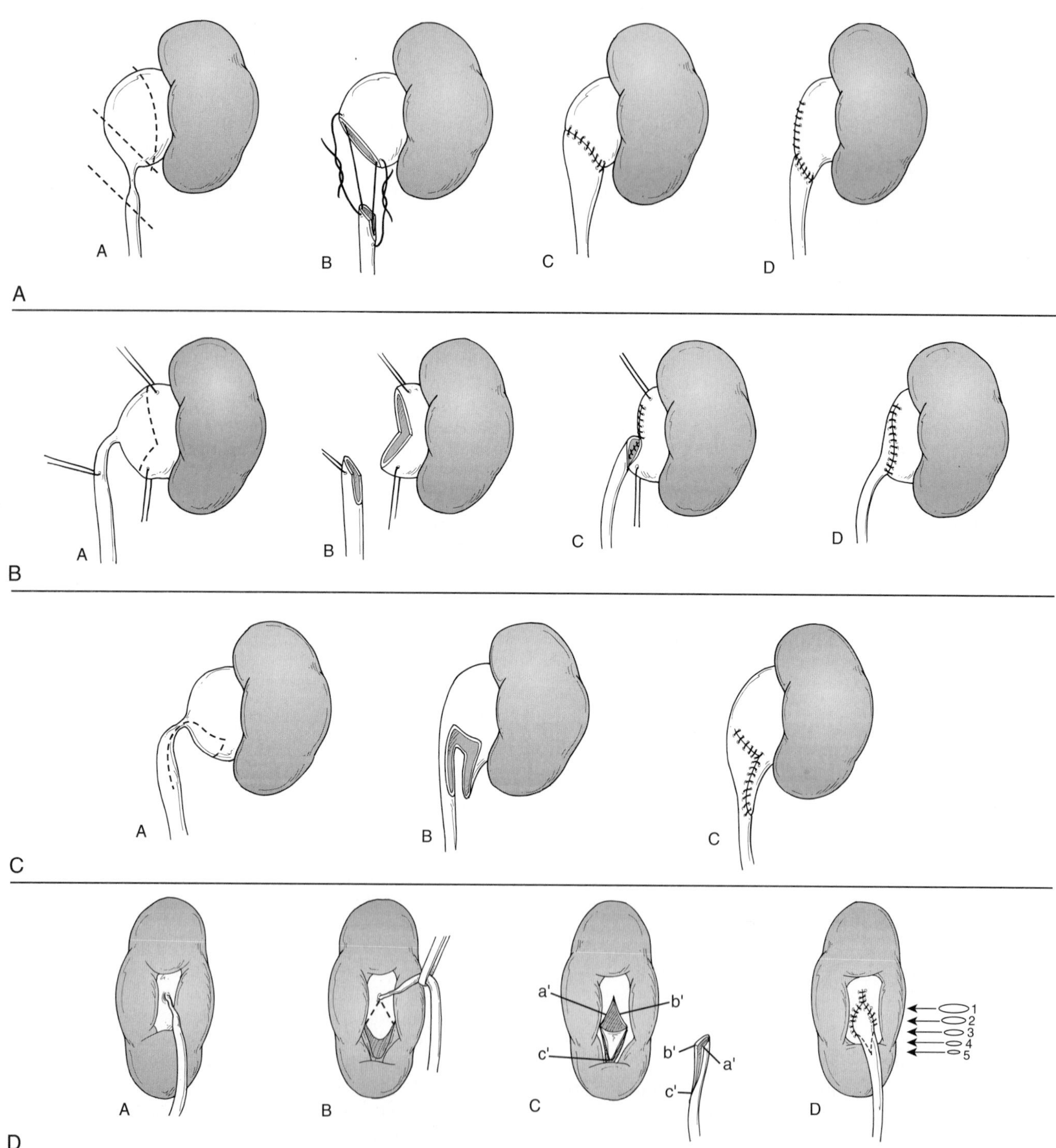

Figure 111-12 *A,* Dismembered pyeloplasty. *B,* Anderson-Hynes pyeloplasty. *C,* Foley Y-V-plasty. *D,* Variation of the Foley Y-V-plasty for proximal ureteral high insertion.

Continued

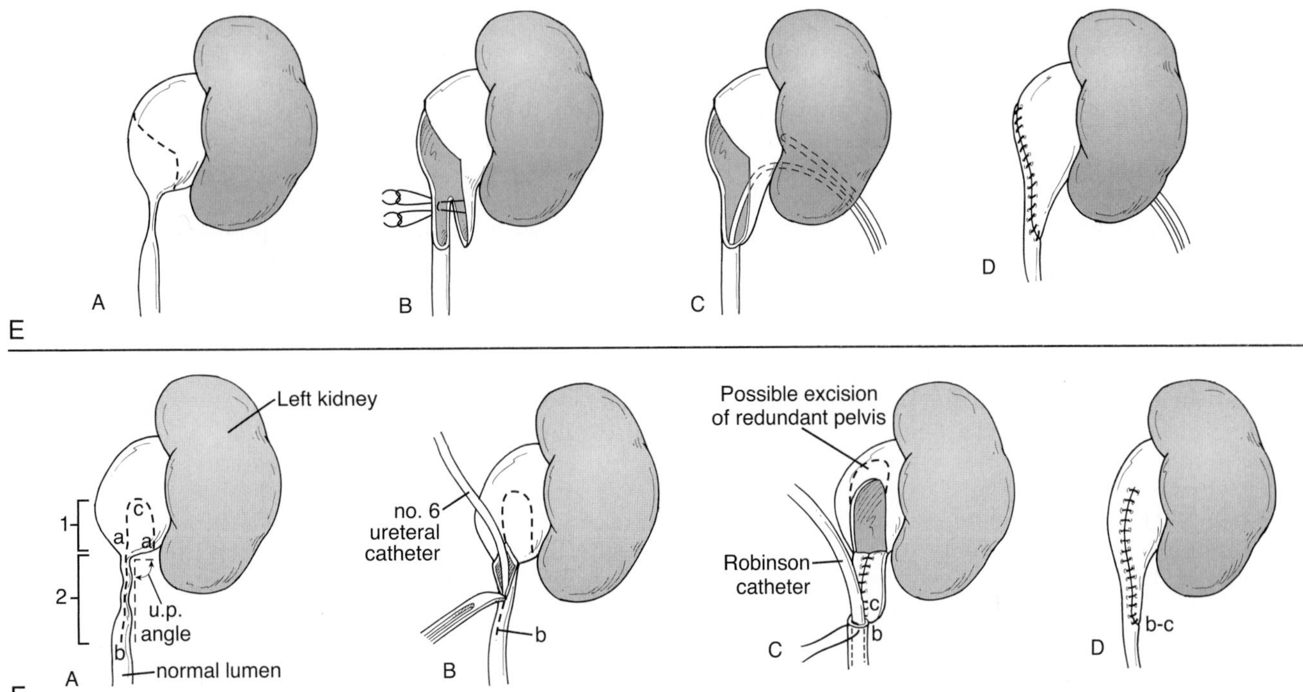

Figure 111–12—Cont'd *E*, Spiral flap. *F*, Scardino-Prince vertical flap pyeloureteroplasty for long proximal ureteral narrowing. (From Fung LCT, Lakshmanan Y: Anomalies of the renal collecting system: Ureteropelvic junction obstruction [pyelocalyectasis] and infundibular stenosis. In Belman AB, King LR, Kramer SA [eds]: Clinical Pediatric Urology, 4th ed. London, Martin Dunitz, 2002, p 612.)

vessel is identified intraoperatively, the proper surgical technique is dismembered pyeloplasty, which would involve excision of the adynamic segment and transposition of the vessel behind the UPJ. A flap technique would not be a reasonable choice in this situation. With this strategy, each technique can provide a solution to UPJ obstruction with success rates in excess of 90% to 95%.[48,76]

To perform pyeloplasty, the child is given adequate general anesthesia, with the option of using a regional block. The child is placed in the dorsal lithotomy position for intraoperative RPG. Though controversial,[51] we continue to perform this procedure to characterize the lesions and to assist in defining the appropriate site for optimum exposure. After RPG, a Foley catheter is placed in sterile manner and the child is repositioned for surgery with respect to the particular approach that is planned. A number of approaches can be used to obtain access to the retroperitoneal space to perform an open pyeloplasty, including anterior subcostal, flank, and dorsal lumbotomy. In our institution, for infants we prefer an anterior subcostal, muscle-splitting approach, which provides excellent exposure through a small incision. (In older children, use of a flank incision might be preferential given the lateral displacement of the peritoneum and the frequently thicker muscle bundles.)

The child is placed in a modified supine position with the ipsilateral side at an approximately 15- to 20-degree angle to the operating table. Small children may have both upper extremities at their side. The operating table is flexed at the level of the child's anterior superior iliac spine, which exposes the anterior abdominal area and flank. Approximately 2 fingerbreadths below the subcostal region, a 3- to 4-cm incision is made along Langer's lines. A "muscle-splitting" technique is used to separate the muscle layers without transecting them. This technique provides adequate exposure and reduces postoperative pain. The peritoneum is reflected medially. Gerota's fascia is incised in a plane vertical to the patient. A self-retaining ring retractor provides adequate exposure to the kidney and renal pelvis.

Once the kidney and renal pelvis have been exposed, careful inspection of the anatomy should allow a decision to be made regarding the best technique to use. A *dismembered pyeloplasty* is performed for most UPJ obstructions. However, there are three anatomic situations that may be treated appropriately with three different flap procedures: Foley Y-V-plasty, spiral flap, or Scardino-Prince vertical flaps. The first situation occurs when the obstructing segment is longer than 1.5 to 2 cm. The second situation occurs in a child with a small extrarenal pelvis and the renal pelvis does not need to be reduced. The last situation, in which a Foley Y-V-plasty may be the preferred technique, is when the ureter has a high insertion into the renal pelvis. In these cases, the pelvis can be funneled to construct a dependent drainage system.

When a decision is made to perform a dismembered pyeloplasty, the renal pelvis should be evaluated for possible reduction in size. Stay sutures are strategically positioned in a "diamond" pattern, and tenotomy scissors are used to excise the renal pelvis within the borders of the stay sutures. One sweeping incision is made in a superior-to-inferior manner. This maneuver provides a smooth contour for an adequate anastomosis to the ureter. The proximal, narrowed ureteral segment should be incised distally enough to provide healthy ureteral tissue of normal caliber. Before reapproximation of the ureter to the renal pelvis, distal ureteral length should be tested to ensure that the anastomosis will be tension-free. The anastomosis is begun at the inferior apex with continuous, interlocking 7-0 absorbable monofilament suture. During the anastomosis, care should be taken to include adequate adventitial tissue with less mucosal tissue to provide a watertight anastomosis. A temporary ureteral stent may be used when performing the anastomosis to reduce the risk for obstruction as a result of "back-walling." Alternatively, a double-J ureteral stent may be positioned in the distal end of the ureter and bladder with the Seldinger technique. This stent may remain in place for 4 to 6 weeks.

The dorsal lumbotomy approach provides excellent exposure, especially in the rare case of bilateral UPJ lesions (Fig. 111-13). As in the subcostal approach, a muscle-splitting technique can be used to access the retroperitoneum through a relatively short distance. The dorsal lumbotomy approach requires that the ureteral anatomy be precisely defined before embarking on the technique because it provides limited exposure to the distal part of the ureter. Therefore, RPG may be more appropriate in this situation.

Minimally Invasive Surgery for Ureteropelvic Junction Obstruction in Children

In selected children's hospitals with experience in minimally invasive surgery, laparoscopic and robotic pyeloplasty is feasible and produces good results.[90]

Indications and benefits for minimally invasive surgery in adults have been well defined.[79,106] Minimally invasive techniques to correct UPJ obstruction in adults include balloon dilation, percutaneous antegrade endopyelotomy, retrograde cutting-wire balloon endopyelotomy, ureteroscopic retrograde endopyelotomy, and laparoscopic pyeloplasty. Although technologic advancements have made minimally invasive options available for the management of pediatric patients with UPJ obstruction, open pyeloplasty continues to be the gold standard, with success rates consistently higher than 90%.[53]

In children, indications for minimally invasive surgery are less clear, and therefore endourologic procedures are less pervasive.[22] One recent study compared endopyelotomy with open pyeloplasty in children with UPJ obstruction and found the success rates to be 88% and 93%, respectively.[102] Even with these fairly comparable success rates, operative time and hospital costs were higher for endopyelotomy. Given the present situation, there is little impetus for minimally invasive surgery with respect to the management of UPJ obstruction. Open pyeloplasty has a short operative time, relatively low operative costs, and established long-term results.

Pediatric laparoscopic pyeloplasty faces the same challenges as the other minimally invasive techniques in children.[26] Much of pediatric urologic surgery is reconstructive rather than extirpative, which limits the ability of many practitioners to gain experience in basic laparoscopic skills. Given the conservative nature of most pediatric surgeons and the relatively few types of cases, operative times are long and hospital costs are high. These realities limit the utility of minimally invasive techniques, even at academic centers, where many of the

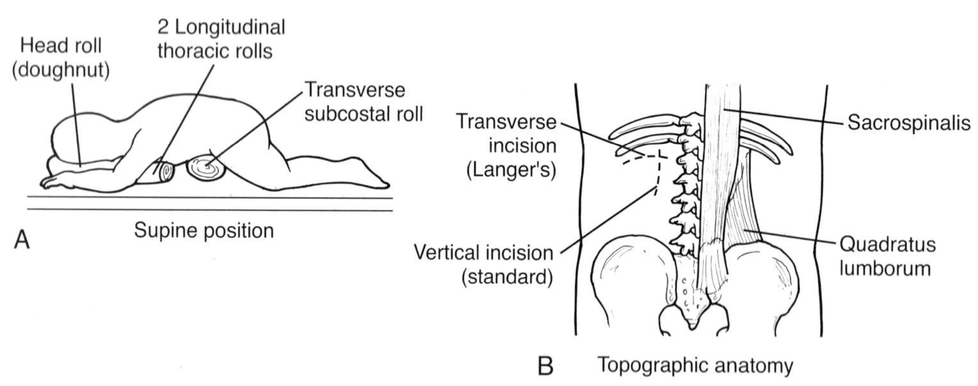

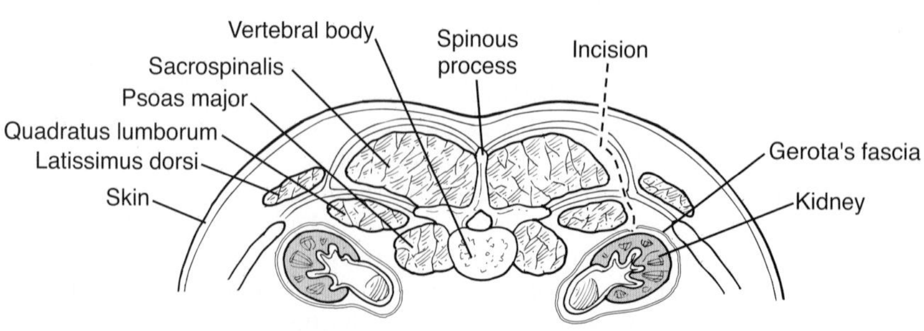

Figure 111-13 Dorsal lumbotomy approach. (From Sheldon CA, Duckett JW: Infant pyeloplasty. AUA Update Series 1988;7[Lesson 37]:293.)

pediatric surgeons have not been trained in laparoscopic techniques nor have the time to take courses. These and other problems have led to the slow expansion of pediatric laparoscopic pyeloplasty. Although laparoscopic pyeloplasty has garnered much interest during the last decade, it still remains technically challenging and requires a long learning curve. It is most successfully performed at selected tertiary medical centers by experienced surgeons with advanced laparoscopic training. Even in experienced hands, laparoscopic pyeloplasty is relatively contraindicated in patients with a small intrarenal pelvis or a history of open pyeloplasty because these situations may pose considerable technical difficulty or unnecessary risk.[65]

Robotics is another exciting and evolving area for minimally invasive surgery in children. This new technique provides excellent three-dimensional visualization, unprecedented control of endocorporeal instruments, and an ergonomic surgeon's position. Robots may advance minimally invasive surgery by allowing urologists with limited laparoscopic experience to rapidly master the endocorporeal skills necessary to treat UPJ obstruction.[49,79]

OUTCOME

A successful pyeloplasty begins preoperatively with efforts made to detect signs of renal deterioration as early as possible. According to several investigators, there is a chance to improve renal function in children whose obstruction is detected early and surgery is performed before renal impairment develops.[13,14] Meticulous attention to surgical principles contributes to intraoperative success.[30] The use of proper pediatric instruments is important, as is atraumatic tissue handling, including careful dissection and minimal disruption of adventitial and periadventitial blood vessels. The ureteropelvic anastomosis should be watertight and tension-free. The retroperitoneal space should have adequate passive drainage. Finally, the routine use of ureteral stents and percutaneous nephrostomy tubes after an open pyeloplasty remains controversial.[104] The most common reasons to leave a stent in place after pyeloplasty are to ensure proper urinary diversion, maintain ureteral caliber, and ensure anastomotic alignment. The main reasons against leaving a temporary stent in situ are that they are foreign bodies and may be nidi for infection, they may erode through the anastomotic site, and in children, internalized stents require general anesthesia for removal. At our institution, ureteral stents are used judiciously, typically only in patients with a solitary kidney, neonates with Östling's folds, or those with a failed pyeloplasty. If a double-J ureteral stent is left indwelling, it should be removed 6 to 8 weeks after the initial procedure.

The goal of pediatric pyeloplasty is to reduce hydronephrosis and preserve renal function. Postoperatively, this goal is evaluated by a variety of radiographic studies and clinical considerations. Renal ultrasound defines a successful pyeloplasty as improvement in SFU-graded hydronephrosis, temporal axial growth of the ipsilateral kidney, and a gradual increase in renal parenchyma. According to diuretic renography, successful pyeloplasty is demonstrated by improved urinary drainage and differential renal function. In older children, successful pyeloplasty is determined by the absence of symptoms.

Depending on the definition, the success rate of pyeloplasty for UPJ obstruction is as high as 98%.[48,85,91] The success rate is so high, in fact, that one investigator suggested that a satisfactory diuretic renogram 3 months after pyeloplasty eliminated the need for further urologic follow-up. Other investigators claim that ideally, follow-up should be extended to 2 years, which would include the period when initial symptoms of recurrence are most likely to take place.[93] We recommend renal ultrasound 3 months after pyeloplasty and diuretic renography 6 months later. Subsequently, renal ultrasound is performed annually for 2 years. Of course, after pyeloplasty, primary care physicians should monitor any patient with renal scars on a preoperative DMSA scan by annual blood pressure reading.

Complications of pyeloplasty can be categorized as acute and late. Acute complications have a higher incidence in infants.[105] Postoperative pyelonephritis is most commonly seen in children who had a positive intraoperative urine culture. It is treated with intravenous antibiotics. Delayed opening of the ureteropelvic anastomosis typically occurs as a result of edema and may lead to a prolonged leak around the anastomotic site. Interestingly, a transanastomotic ureteral stent does not reduce the frequency of this complication. Patients with persistent hydronephrosis or symptoms after pyeloplasty may be salvaged with placement of a percutaneous nephrostomy tube. In some of these children, a secondary procedure may be necessary, such as revision pyeloplasty or nephrectomy. Late complications can be manifested as clinical symptoms or progressively worsening radiographic studies. In either case, evaluation should determine whether optimizing drainage via a nephrostomy tube or ureteral stent improves the clinical symptoms or renal function. Typically, surgery for a failed pyeloplasty should not be considered for at least 2 months. There are five basic approaches to the treatment of secondary UPJ obstruction: revision pyeloplasty, ureterocalicostomy, endopyelotomy, laparoscopy, and nephrectomy.[25,114]

SUMMARY

UPJ obstruction is the most common congenital urinary obstruction, and management remains complex because of the variability of the lesion and the unpredictability of the manifestations. In many cases, observation alone is a viable option because the obstruction is not progressive. In other cases, radiographic studies reveal renal deterioration or progressive hydronephrosis, and surgery is required. Unfortunately, the factors that determine which kidneys require surgery have not been clearly defined at this point. However, with future developments in biochemical markers and improvements in radiographic studies, timing of surgical intervention will be defined earlier so that renal deterioration in children with suspected UPJ obstruction might be prevented.

REFERENCES

1. Adey GS, Vargas SO, Retik AB, et al: Fibroepithelial polyps causing ureteropelvic junction obstruction in children. J Urol 2003;169:1834.
2. American Institute for Ultrasound in Medicine, 1993.
3. Anderson JC, Weiss RM: Physiology and evaluation of ureteropelvic junction obstruction. J Endourol 1996;10:87.
4. Askari A, Belman B: Vesicoureteral reflux in black girls. J Urol 1982;127:747.
5. Bäcklund L, Grotte G, Reuterskiöld A: Functional stenosis as a cause of pelvi-ureteric obstruction. Arch Dis Child 1965;40:203.
6. Baker LA, Gomez RA: Embryonic development of the ureter: Acquisition of smooth muscle [abstract A1715]. J Am Soc Nephrol 1996;7:1593.
7. Bernstein GT, Mandell J, Lebowitz RL, et al: Ureteropelvic junction obstruction in the neonate. J Urol 1988;140:1216.
8. Bomalaski MD, Hirschl RB, Bloom DA: Versicoureteral reflux and ureteropelvic junction obstruction: Association, treatment options and outcome. J Urol 1997;157:969.
9. Bronstein M, Yotte JM, Brandes JM: First and early second-trimester diagnosis of fetal urinary tract abnormalities using transvaginal sonography. Prenat Diagn 1990;10:653.
10. Brown T, Mandell J, Lebowitz R: Neonatal hydronephrosis in the era of sonography. Am J Radiol 1987;148:959.
11. Callan NA, Balkemore K, Park J, et al: Fetal genitourinary tract anomalies: Evaluation, operative correction and follow-up. Obstet Gynecol 1990;75:67.
12. Chang CP, McDill BW, Neilson JR, et al: Calcineurin is required in urinary tract mesenchyme for the development of the pyeloureteral peristaltic machinery. J Clin Invest 2004;113:1051.
13. Chertin B, Fridmans A, Knizhnik M, et al: Does early detection of ureteropelvic junction obstruction improve surgical outcome in terms of renal function? J Urol 1999;162:1037.
14. Chiou YY, Chiu NT, Wang ST, et al: Factors associated with the outcomes of children with unilateral ureteropelvic junction obstruction. J Urol 2004;171:397.
15. Chisholm GD: Pathophysiology of obstructive uropathy. In Chisholm GD, Fair WR (eds): Scientific Foundations of Urology. Chicago, Year Book, 1990, p 59.
16. Clark WR, Malek RS: Ureteropelvic junction obstruction. Observations on the classic type in adults. J Urol 1987; 138:276.
17. Conway JJ: "Well-tempered" diuresis renography: Its historical development, physiological and technical pitfalls, and standardized technique protocol. Semin Nucl Med 1992;22:74.
18. Conway JJ, Maizels M: The "well-tempered" diuretic renogram: A standard method to examine the asymptomatic with hydronephrosis or hydroureteronephrosis. A report from combined meetings of The Society of Fetal Urology and members of the Pediatric Nuclear Medicine Council—The Society of Nuclear Medicine. J Nucl Med 1992;33:2047.
19. Cost GA, Merguerian PA, Cheerasarn SP, Shorliffe LMD: Sonographic renal parenchymal and pelvicaliceal areas: New quantitative parameters for renal sonographic followup. J Urol 1996;156(2S):725.
20. Cronon JJ, Amis ES, Yoder IC, et al: Peripelvic cysts: An impostor of sonographic hydronephrosis. J Ultrasound Med 1982;1:229.
21. Dejter SW, Gibbons MD: The fate of infant kidneys with fetal hydronephrosis but initially normal postnatal sonography. J Urol 1989;142:661.
22. Docimo SG: Pediatric endourology—coming into focus [editorial]. J Urol 1999;162;1731.
23. Duckett JW: When to operate on neonatal hydronephrosis. Urology 1993;42:617.
24. Ebel K: Uroradiology in the fetus and newborn: Diagnosis and follow-up of congenital obstruction of the urinary tract. Pediatr Radiol 1998;28:630.
25. Ellsworth PI, Walker RD, Elder JS: Management of the failed pyeloplasty. AUA Update Series 1997;16(Lesson 17):130.
26. Esposito C, Lima M, Mattioli G, et al: Complications of pediatric urological laparoscopy: Mistakes and risks. J Urol 2003;169:1490.
27. Everaert K, Delanghe J, Vande Wiele C, et al: Urinary alpha 1-microglobulin detects uropathy: A prospective study in 483 urological patients. Clin Chem Lab Med 1998;36:309.
28. Farhat W, McLorie G, Geary D, et al: The natural history of neonatal vesicoureteral reflux associated with antenatal hydronephrosis. J Urol 2000;164:1057.
29. Fernbach SK, Maizels M, Conway JJ: Ultrasound grading of hydronephrosis: Introduction to the system used by the Society for Fetal Urology. Pediatr Radiol 1993;23:478.
30. Flahsner SC, King LR: Ureteropelvic junction. In Kelalis PP, King LR, Belman BA (eds): Clinical Pediatric Urology, 3rd ed. Philadelphia, WB Saunders, 1992, p 693.
31. Flashner SC, Mesrobian HG, Flatt JA, et al: Non-obstructive dilation of the upper urinary tract may later convert to obstruction. Urology 1993;42:569.
32. Foote JW, Blennerhassett JB, Wiglesworth FW, MacKinnon KJ: Observations on the ureteropelvic junction. J Urol 1970;104:252.
33. Freedman ER, Rickwood AMK: Prenatally diagnosed pelviureteric junction obstruction: A benign condition? J Pediatric Surg 1994;29:769.
34. Fung LCT, Atala A: Constant elevation in renal pelvic pressure induces an increase in urinary *N*-acetyl-beta-D-glucosaminidase in a nonobstructive porcine model. J Urol 1998;159:212.
35. Fung LCT, Lakshmanan Y: Anomalies of the renal collecting system: Ureteropelvic junction obstruction (pyelocalyectasis) and infundibular stenosis. In Bellman AB, King LR, Kramer SA (eds): Clinical Pediatric Urology, 4th ed. London, Martin Dunitz, 2002, p 559.
36. Fung LC, McLorie GA, Khoury AE, et al: Contradictory supranormal nuclear renographic differential renal function: Fact or artifact? J Urol 1995;154:667.
37. Fung LCT, Stecker FE, Khoury AE, et al: Intrarenal resistive index correlates with renal pelvis pressure. J Urol 1994; 152:607.
38. Garrett WJ, Grunwald G, Robinson DE: Prenatal diagnosis of fetal polycystic kidney by ultrasound. Aust N Z J Obstet Gynaecol 1970;10:7.
39. Gillenwater JY: The pathophysiology of urinary tract obstruction. In Walsh PC, Retik AB, Stamey TA, Vaughn ED Jr (eds): Campbell's Urology, vol 1, 8th ed. Philadelphia, WB Saunders, 1992, p 499.
40. Gordon I: Antenatal diagnosis of pelvic hydronephrosis: Assessment of renal function and drainage as a guide to management. J Nucl Med 1991;32:1649.
41. Gottschalk CW, Mylle M: Micropuncture study of pressures in proximal tubules and peritubular capillaries of the rat kidney and their relation to ureteral and renal venous pressures. Am J Physiol 1956;185:430.
42. Granaliano G, Gesualdo L, Bartoli F, et al: MCP-1 and EGF renal expression and urine excretion in human congenital obstructive nephropathy. Kidney Int 2000;58:182.
43. Grignon A, Filion R, Filiatrault D, et al: Urinary tract obstruction in utero: Classification and clinical applications. Radiology 1986;160:645.

44. Hofmann V: Ultraschalldiagnostik beim vesico-ureteralen Reflux im Kindesalter. Z Urol Nephrol 1981;74:249.
45. Hollman GA, Elderbrook MK, VanDenLangenberg B: Results of a pediatric sedation program on head MRI scan success rates and procedure duration times. Clin Pediatr (Phila) 1995;34:300.
46. Holsy YL, Williot P, Danais S: Transitional neonatal hydronephrosis: Fact or fantasy? J Urol 1986;136:339.
47. Horowitz M, Gershbein AB, Glassberg KI: Vesicoureteral reflux in infants with prenatal hydronephrosis confirmed at birth: Racial differences. J Urol 1999;161:248.
48. Houben C, Wischermann A, Borner G, Slany E: Outcome analysis of pyeloplasty in infants. Pediatr Surg Int 2000;16:189.
49. Hubert J: Robotic pyeloplasty. Curr Urol Rep 2003;4:124.
50. Jabbour ME, Goldfischer ER, Anderson AE, et al: Failed endopyelotomy: Low expression of TGF beta regardless of the presence or absence of crossing vessels. J Endourol 1999;13:295.
51. Jayanthi VR, Churchill BM, Thorner PS, et al: Bilateral congenital midureteral adynamic segments. Urology 1995;45:520.
52. Johnston JH, Evans JP, Glassberg KI, Shapiro SR: Pelvic hydronephrosis in children: A review of 219 personal cases. J Urol 1977;117:97.
53. Karlin GS, Badlani GH, Smith AD: Endopyelotomy versus open pyeloplasty: Comparison in 88 patients. J Urol 1988;140:476.
54. Kass EJ, Fink-Bennett D: Contemporary techniques for the radioisotopic evaluation of the dilated urinary tract. Urol Clin North Am 1990;17:273.
55. Kenda RB: Imaging techniques for the detection of vesicoureteral reflux: What and when? Nephrol Dial Transplant 2001;16:4.
56. Khaira HS, Platt JF, Cohan RH, et al: Helical computed tomography for identification of crossing vessels in ureteropelvic junction obstruction—comparison with operative findings. Urology 2003;62:35.
57. Khan J, Charron M, Hickeson MP, et al: Supranormal renal function in unilateral hydronephrotic kidney can be avoided. Clin Nucl Med 2004;29:410.
58. Kirsch AJ: Magnetic resonance urography for the evaluation of pediatric hydronephrosis: The state of the art. Podium presentation at the 53rd Annual Meeting of the Society for Pediatric Urology, 2004, San Francisco.
59. Koff SA: Pathophysiology of ureteropelvic junction obstruction: Clinical and experimental observations. Urol Clin North Am 1990;17:263.
60. Koff SA: Neonatal management of unilateral hydronephrosis: Role for delayed intervention. Urol Clin North Am 1998;25:181.
61. Koff SA, Peller PA, Young DC, Pollifrone DL: The assessment of obstruction in the newborn with unilateral hydronephrosis by measuring the size of the opposite kidney. J Urol 1994;152:596.
62. Koff SA, Peller PA, Young DC, Pollifrone DL: Diagnostic criteria for assessing obstruction in the newborn with unilateral hydronephrosis using the renal growth–renal function chart. J Urol 1995;154:662.
63. Koff SA, Thrall JH: The diagnosis of obstruction in experimental hydroureteronephrosis: Mechanism for progressive urinary tract dilatation. Invest Urol 1981;19:85.
64. Konda R, Sakai K, Ota S, et al: Ultrasound grade of hydronephrosis and severity of renal cortical damage on ^{99m}Technetium dimercaptosuccinic acid renal scan in infants with unilateral hydronephrosis during followup and after pyeloplasty. J Urol 2002;167:2159.
65. Kumar U, Turk TM, Albala DM: The treatment of adult ureteropelvic junction obstruction: Issues and answers. AUA Update Series 2001;20(Lesson 36):282.
66. Kunin CM: A ten year study of bacteriuria in schoolgirls: Final report of bacteriologic, urologic and epidemiologic findings. J Infect Dis 1970;122:382.
67. Leary FJ, Myers RP, Greene LF: The value of excretory urography as a screening test in asymptomatic patients. J Urol 1972;107:850.
68. Lebowitz RL, Blickman JG: The coexistence of ureteropelvic junction obstruction and reflux. AJR Am J Roentgenol 1983;140:231.
69. Lettgen B, Meyer-Schwickerath M, Bedow W: [Prenatal ultrasound diagnosis of the kidneys and efferent urinary tract: Possibilities, applications and dangers.] Monatsschrift Kinderheilkunde 1993;141:462.
70. Macksood MJ, Roth DR, Chang CH, Pearlmutter AD: Benign fibro epithelial polyps as a cause of intermittent ureteropelvic junction obstruction in a child: A case report and review of the literature. J Urol 1985;134:951.
71. Madarikan BA, Hayward C, Roberts GM, Lari J: Clinical outcome of fetal uropathy. Arch Dis Child 1988;63:961.
72. Maizels M, Reisman ME, Flom LS, et al: Grading nephroureteral dilation detected in the first year of life: Correlation with obstruction. J Urol 1992;148:609.
73. Mandell J: Diagnosis and management of intrauterine urinary tract disorders. In O'Donnell B, Koff SA (eds): Pediatric Urology. Oxford, Butterworth-Heinemann, 1997, p 315.
74. Mandell J, Blyth B, Peters C, et al: Structural genitourinary defects detected in utero. Radiology 1991;178:193.
75. Martin X, Rouvière O: Radiologic evaluations affecting surgical technique in ureteropelvic junction obstruction. Curr Opin Urol 2001;11:193.
76. McAleer IM, Kaplan GW: Renal function before and after pyeloplasty: Does it improve? J Urol 1999;162:1041.
77. Merguerian P: The evaluation of prenatally detected hydronephrosis. Monogr Urol 1995;16(3):1.
78. Morrissey JJ, Ishidoya S, McCracken R, Klahr S: Control of p53 and p21 (WAF1) expression during unilateral ureteral obstruction. Kidney Int 1996;57:S84.
79. Munver R, Del Pizzo JJ, Sosa RE, Poppas DP: Minimally invasive surgical management of ureteropelvic junction obstruction: Laparoscopic and robot-assisted laparoscopic pyeloplasty. J Long-Term Effects Med Implants 2003;13:367.
80. Murnaghan G: The dynamics of the renal pelvis and ureter with reference to congenital hydronephrosis. J Urol 1958;30:321.
81. Nguyen HT, Gluckman GR, Kogan BA: Changing the technique of background subtraction alters calculated renal function on pediatric mercaptoacetyltriglycine renography. J Urol 1997;158:1252.
82. Nicolini U, Spelzini F: Invasive assessment of fetal renal abnormalities: Urinalysis, fetal blood sampling and biopsy. Prenatal Diagn 2001;21:964.
83. Oh SJ, Moon DH, Kang W, et al: Supranormal differential renal function is real but may be pathological: Assessment by 99m technetium mercaptoacetyltriglycine renal scan of congenital unilateral hydronephrosis. J Urol 2001;165:2300.
84. O'Reilly PH: Consensus Committee of the Society of Radionuclides in Nephrourology. Standardization of the renogram technique for investigating the dilated upper urinary tract and assessing the results of surgery. BJU Int 2003;91:239.
85. O'Reilly PH, Brooman PJ, Mak S, et al: The long-term results of Anderson-Hynes pyeloplasty. BJU Int 2001;87:287.
86. Östling K: The genesis of hydronephrosis particularly with regard to the changes at the ureteropelvic junction. Acta Chir Scand 1942;86(Suppl 72):1.

87. Perez-Brayfield MR, Kirsch AJ, Jones RA, Grattan-Smith JD: A prospective study comparing ultrasound, nuclear scintigraphy and dynamic contrast enhanced magnetic resonance imaging in the evaluation of hydronephrosis. J Urol 2003;170:1330.
88. Peters CA: Lower urinary tract obstruction: Clinical and experimental aspects. Br J Urol 1998;81(Suppl):22.
89. Peters CA, Carr MC, Lais A, et al: The response of the fetal kidney to obstruction. J Urol 1992;148:503.
90. Peters CA, Schlussel RN, Retik AB: Pediatric laparoscopic dismembered pyeloplasty. J Urol 1995;153:1962.
91. Pohl HG, Rushton HG, Park JS, et al: Early diuresis renogram findings predict success following pyeloplasty. J Urol 2001;165:2311.
92. Preston A, Lebowitz RL: What's new in pediatric uroradiology. Urol Radiol 1989;11:217.
93. Psooy K, Pike JG, Leonard MP: Long-term followup of pediatric dismembered pyeloplasty: How long is long enough? J Urol 2003;169:1809.
94. Rabinowitz R, Peters MT, Vyas S, et al: Measurement of fetal urine production in normal pregnancy by real-time ultrasonography. Am J Obstet Gynecol 1989;161:1264.
95. Ransley PG: Impaired renal function in the newborn: Nature of the injury (panel discussion). Society of Pediatric Urology, May 18, 1986, New York.
96. Ransley VM, Murphy JL, Mendoza SA: Postnatal management of UPJ obstruction detected antenatally. Dialogues Pediatr Urol 1985;8:6.
97. Rickard M, Whitaker RH: Pelviureteric junction obstruction in association with severe vesicoureteral reflux: A diagnostic dilemma. Urol Radiol 1984;6:1.
98. Roth JA, Diamond DA: Prenatal hydronephrosis. Currt Opin Pediatr 2001;13:138.
99. Ruano-Gil D, Coca-Payeras A, Tejedo-Maten A: Obstruction and normal recanalization of the ureter in the human embryo: Its relation to congenital ureteric obstruction. Eur Urol 1975;1:287.
100. Rushton HG, Salem Y, Belman AB, Majd M: Pediatric pyeloplasty: Is routine retrograde pyelogram necessary? J Urol 1994;152:604.
101. Saari-Keppainen A, Karjalainen O, Ylostalo P, Heinonen OP: Ultrasound screening and perinatal mortality: Controlled trial of systematic one-stage screening in pregnancy. The Helsinki Ultrasound Trial. Lancet 1990;336:387.
102. Schenkman EM, Tarry WF: Comparison of percutaneous endopyelotomy with open pyeloplasty for pediatric ureteropelvic junction obstruction. J Urol 1998;159:1013.
103. Sheldon CA, Duckett JW: Infant pyeloplasty. AUA Update Series 1988;7(Lesson 37):290.
104. Smith, KE, Holmes N, Lieb JI, et al: Stented versus nonstented pediatric pyeloplasty: A modern series and review of the literature. J Urol 2002;168:1127.
105. Snyder HM III, Lebowitz RL, Colodny AH, et al: UPJ obstruction in children. Urol Clin North Am 1980; 7:273.
106. Soper NJ, Barteau JA, Clayman RV, et al: Comparison of early postoperative results for laparoscopic versus standard open cholecystectomy. Surg Gynecol Obstet 1992;174:114.
107. Steele BT, DeMaria J, Toi A, et al: Neonatal outcome of fetuses with urinary tract abnormalities diagnosed by prenatal ultrasonography. CMAJ 1987;137:117.
108. Taylor A Jr, Thakore K, Folks R, et al: Background subtraction in technetium-99m-MAG3 renography. J Nucl Med 1997;38:74.
109. Thomas DFM: Fetal uropathy: Review. Br J Urol 1990;66:223.
110. Tripp BM, Homsy YL: Neonatal hydronephrosis—the controversy and the management. Pediatr Nephrol 1995;9:503.
111. Ulman I, Jayanthi VR, Koff SA: The long-term followup of newborns with severe unilateral hydronephrosis initially treated nonoperatively. J Urol 2000;164:1101.
112. Uson AC, Cox LA, Lattimer JK: Hydronephrosis in infants and children. II. Surgical management and results. JAMA 1968;205:327.
113. Van Cangh PJ, Nesa S, Galeon M: Vessels around the ureteropelvic junction: Significance and imaging by conventional radiology J Endourol 1996;10:111.
114. Varkorakis IM, Bhayani SB, Allaf ME, et al: Management of secondary ureteropelvic junction obstruction after failed primary laparoscopic pyeloplasty. J Urol 2004; 172:180.
115. Velicer CM, Heckbert SR, Lampe JW, et al: Antibiotic use in relation to the risk of breast cancer. JAMA 2004; 292:827.
116. Wåhlin N, Magnusson A, Persson AEG, et al: Pressure flow measurement of hydronephrosis in children: A new approach to definition and quantification of obstruction. J Urol 2001;166:1842.
117. Wen JG, Chen Y, Ringgaard S, et al: Evaluation of renal function in normal and hydronephrotic kidneys in rats using gadolinium diethylenetetramine-pentaacetic acid enhanced dynamic magnetic resonance imaging. J Urol 2000;163:1264.
118. Whitaker RH: Methods of assessing obstruction in dilated ureters. Br J Urol 1973;45:15.
119. Yerkes EB, Adams MC Pope JC IV, Brock JW III: Does every patient with prenatal hydronephrosis need voiding cystourethrography? J Urol 1999;162:1218.
120. Zerin JM, Ritchey ML, Chang AC: Incidental vesicoureteral reflux in neonates with antenatally detected hydronephrosis and other renal abnormalities. Radiology 1993;187:157.

Chapter 112  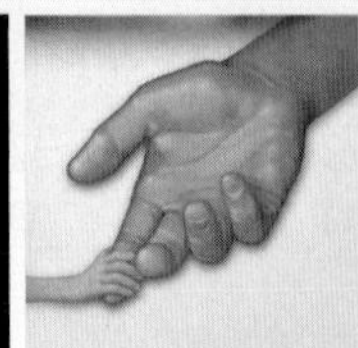

Renal Infection, Abscess, Vesicoureteral Reflux, Urinary Lithiasis, and Renal Vein Thrombosis

Leslie T. McQuiston and Anthony A. Caldamone

URINARY TRACT INFECTION, RENAL ABSCESS, AND VESICOURETERAL REFLUX

The urinary tract is the second most common site of infection in infants and children after the respiratory tract. The true incidence of urinary tract infection (UTI) in children is difficult to determine because of the challenges of diagnosis. Young children may present with only fever or failure to thrive, with no specific urinary symptoms or signs. Diagnosis and treatment of UTI are of particular importance in children, given the long-term complications, including renal scarring, hypertension, and decreased renal function. Based on several studies, the incidence of renal scarring in young children with febrile UTI may be as high as 40% to 50%.[92] Among infants between the ages of 2 months and 2 years who present with fever, approximately 5% are diagnosed with a UTI.[2,55] Age and gender are significant factors in the prevalence of UTI in the pediatric population (Table 112-1). The prevalence of UTI is greater in girls than in boys; in girls aged 1 to 5 years, the prevalence is reported to be 1% to 3%, whereas there are few UTIs reported in boys of that age.[42] Some studies have demonstrated that the incidence of UTI in uncircumcised males, particularly boys younger than 1 year, is 5 to 20 times higher than in circumcised males.[3,89] Over the past few years, there have been advances in the understanding of the pathogenesis of UTI and the identification of risk factors that predispose patients to renal damage.

Pathogenesis

There are four major pathways by which bacteria gain access to the urinary tract: ascending, hematogenous, lymphatic, and direct extension. Hematogenous access is most commonly seen in immunocompromised children or in neonates, owing to their immature immune systems. Direct extension can occur in the setting of fistulas from the vagina or the gastrointestinal tract to the genitourinary tract. The ascending route is considered the most common pathway, with bacteria entering via the urethra. Host factors, including the ability to resist infection, are important elements in the pathogenesis of UTI. There is a higher incidence of UTI in infancy, likely due to the immaturity of the neonatal immune system and the higher periurethral bacterial colonization in the first year of life.[17] Bacteria from the gastrointestinal tract colonize the periurethral mucosa and may ascend into the bladder and then the kidneys (Table 112-2).[35] Certain bacterial traits, such as the presence of fimbriae, mediate bacterial adherence to uroepithelial cells and increase bacterial virulence.

Differentiation of pyelonephritis from lower UTI is difficult because there is poor correlation between clinical symptoms and localization of bacteria to the upper versus the lower tract. In older children, however, the diagnosis of pyelonephritis may be suggested by fever, flank pain, and systemic symptoms. Persistent fever for more than 48 hours after the initiation of appropriate antibiotics may be indicative of upper tract infection. Infants with a febrile UTI should be considered to have pyelonephritis and treated accordingly.

Risk Factors

Although bacterial virulence plays an important role in the development of UTI, a variety of host characteristics may predispose to UTI, including age, gender, colonization factors, constipation, genitourinary abnormalities,

TABLE 112-1 Prevalence of Urinary Tract Infection by Age and Gender

Age (yr)	Girls (%)	Boys (%)
<1	6.5	3.3
1-2	8.1	1.9

From American Academy of Pediatrics, Committee on Quality Improvement, Subcommittee on Urinary Tract Infection: Practice parameter: The diagnosis, treatment, and evaluation of the initial urinary tract infection in febrile infants and young children. Pediatrics 1999;103:843.

sexual activity, genetic factors, and iatrogenic factors (Table 112-3).[93] The most important factors influencing prevalence are age and gender. Males are five to eight times more likely than girls to have UTIs during the first 3 months of life.[88] After that age, girls have a greater incidence of UTIs than boys. Symptomatic infections are 10 to 20 times more likely in preschool girls than boys.[89]

UTI often serves as a marker for anatomic abnormalities of the genitourinary tract. It is important to identify these abnormalities early because, if uncorrected, they may lead to recurrent infection and possible loss of renal parenchyma. Obstructive malformations, such as ureteropelvic junction obstruction, posterior urethral valves, ectopic ureters, ureteroceles, and urethral diverticula can increase the risk of UTI. Renal abnormalities, such as papillary necrosis, nonfunctioning kidneys, and unilateral medullary sponge kidney, also predispose patients to UTI.

Vesicoureteral reflux (VUR), which is the abnormal flow of urine from the bladder to the kidney, allows bacteria from the bladder to gain access to the kidney. By itself, VUR does not cause UTI; bacteriuria must be present in the setting of VUR for UTI to develop. The exception to this rule is a child with massive VUR who may have a significant postvoid residual from refluxed urine. VUR occurs in approximately 1% of the general population and is estimated to occur in 20% to 35% of children evaluated for bacteriuria.[19,36] More than 60% of children younger than 1 year are found to have VUR after their first UTI.[55] This percentage decreases to 30% in 2- to 3-year-olds and is 5% or less in adults.[55] As children grow, the submucosal tunnel elongates, and the ratio between the submucosal tunnel length and the ureteral diameter increases. In addition, filling and voiding pressures may change over time, which can improve VUR. These factors, along with changes in bladder dynamics and voiding patterns, account for the spontaneous resolution rate of VUR. VUR is graded I to V, based on the International Reflux Grading System. Grades I and II generally resolve or improve over time, whereas grades IV and V typically do not resolve spontaneously and may require intervention.

TABLE 112-2 Pathogens Associated with Infections

Organism	Comment
Escherichia coli	Accounts for 70%-90% of infections
Pseudomonas aeruginosa	Most common nonenteric gram-negative pathogen Occasionally seen in immunocompromised patients
Enterococcus	Most common gram-positive pathogen
Group B streptococci	Occasionally seen in neonates
Staphylococcus aureus	Suggests additional site (abscess, osteomyelitis, bacterial endocarditis)
Proteus mirabilis	Boys >1 yr old
Candida, coagulase-negative staphylococci	Seen after instrumentation of urinary tract
Klebsiella	Occasionally seen in immunocompromised patients

Adapted from Handel LN, Caldamone AA: Urinary tract infections in the pediatric population. Lebanese Med J 2000;52:194.

TABLE 112-3 Risk Factors for Urinary Tract Infection

- Anatomic abnormalities
  - Vesicoureteral reflux
  - Obstruction
  - Other: diverticulum, labial adhesion
- Female gender
- Uncircumcised male
- Voiding dysfunction
- Constipation
- Instrumentation
- P fimbriated bacteria
- Toilet training
- Sexual activity, pregnancy

Functional abnormalities such as a neuropathic bladder predispose to UTI as a result of increased urinary tract pressures, incomplete bladder emptying, and increased frequency of instrumentation. UTI is also more common in patients with voiding dysfunction, presumably due to incomplete bladder emptying, urinary stasis, and abnormally high urinary tract pressures. Conditions such as bladder instability, infrequent voiding, Hinman syndrome, and constipation are associated with voiding dysfunction. Periurethral colonization and preputial colonization also may increase the risk of UTI. Preputial aerobic bacterial colonization is highest during the first month after birth, decreases after 6 months, and is uncommon after 5 years of age.[56,93]

Clinical Presentation

Children with UTIs, especially those younger than 2 years, do not always present with the typical symptoms of dysuria, frequency, or pain, and the physical examination may be of limited value. Thus, it is important to maintain a high index of suspicion in infants and young children. In children younger than 2 years, parents may describe nonspecific symptoms such as fever, fussiness, vomiting, or diarrhea; patients may present with failure to thrive or difficulty feeding. In infants, often the only presenting symptom is fever. Children 2 to 5 years of age often present with fever and abdominal pain coincident with upper respiratory infection. After toilet training, children may start to demonstrate more specific symptoms such as fever, dysuria, flank pain, and urgency.

Diagnosis

Accurate diagnosis of UTI in children is critical. The method of collection can affect the accuracy of diagnosis (Table 112-4). The various methods include midstream, clean-catch void, suprapubic aspiration, transurethral bladder catheterization, and perineal bag collection. In toilet-trained children, clean-catch specimens have a contamination rate of approximately 30%.[58] The most sterile method and the gold standard for urine collection is suprapubic aspiration; this method, however, is often not favored by parents or by primary practitioners. Suprapubic aspiration may be contraindicated in patients with certain anatomic abnormalities of the genitourinary tract.

Transurethral bladder catheterization is the preferred method, with a lower false-positive rate than perineal bag collection. The sensitivity of positive urine culture is 95%, and the specificity is 99%.[2] In non-toilet-trained children, perineal bag collection is more common but has a high probability of contamination. False-positive results occur in 85% of specimens collected in this manner.[2] Perineal bag collection may be used when there is low suspicion of UTI. Current recommendations are urethral catheterization or suprapubic aspiration following a positive urinalysis or a positive urine culture from a bag specimen to eliminate the possibility of contamination.

TABLE 112-4 Criteria for the Diagnosis of Urinary Tract Infection

Method of Collection	Colony Count (Pure Culture)	Probability of Infection (%)
Suprapubic aspiration	Gram-negative bacilli: any number Gram-positive cocci: > a few thousand	>99
Transurethral catheterization	>100,000	95
	10,000-100,000	Infection likely
	1,000-10,000	Suspicious, repeat
	<1,000	Infection unlikely
Clean-voided (boy)	>10,000	Infection likely
Clean-voided (girl)	3 specimens >100,000	95
	2 specimens >100,000	90
	1 specimen >100,000	80
	50,000-100,000	Suspicious, repeat
	10,000-50,000	If symptomatic, suspicious, repeat; if asymptomatic, infection unlikely
	<10,000	Infection unlikely

Adapted from Handel LN, Caldamone AA: Urinary tract infections in the pediatric population. Lebanese Med J 2004;52:194.

On urinalysis, the combination of urine nitrite, leukocyte esterase, bacteria, and white blood cells on microscopy yields a sensitivity of 99.8% and a specificity of 70%.[2,58] However, UTI cannot be ruled out if any of these findings is absent on urinalysis or microscopy. A urine culture is the only way to accurately diagnose a UTI. Prompt treatment before final culture results are obtained is recommended owing to the increased risk of renal scarring in children younger than 5 years.

Imaging

The role of imaging after a UTI is controversial.[39] The primary goal of imaging is to identify children who are at risk for subsequent UTIs and renal damage. Imaging includes an anatomic evaluation of the kidney and bladder, as well as a functional study to identify the presence of VUR. The current American Academy of Pediatrics guidelines recommend renal and bladder ultrasonography (US) for all children younger than 2 years with a first UTI.[2] The purpose of US in these cases is to assess for the presence of any congenital structural abnormalities of the urinary tract, such as hydronephrosis (Fig. 112-1). Additionally, US allows the visualization of any renal parenchymal abnormalities, such as cysts, and identifies the presence of perinephric fluid collections. Ureteral dilatation, bladder wall thickening (Fig. 112-2), a duplicated collecting system (Fig. 112-3), ureteroceles (Fig. 112-4), bladder diverticula, and calculi are also identifiable with US. In cases of acute pyelonephritis, US may demonstrate focal or diffuse renal enlargement, as well as abnormal cortical echogenicity. Multiple studies have demonstrated obstructive lesions in 5% to 10% of patients and VUR in 20% to 50% following a UTI.[50] Thus, it is recommended that all infants and children undergo both upper and lower urinary tract imaging after a first UTI; this generally includes US of the kidneys and bladder and voiding cystourethrography (VCUG). Based on gender, the recommendation is US and VCUG for all boys with their first UTI regardless of age and for girls younger than 5 years with their first UTI.

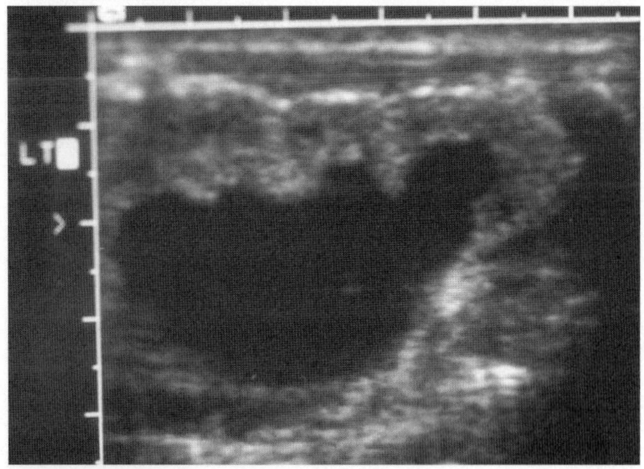

Figure 112-1 Sagittal ultrasonography of a kidney demonstrating hydronephrosis of the renal pelvis and calices.

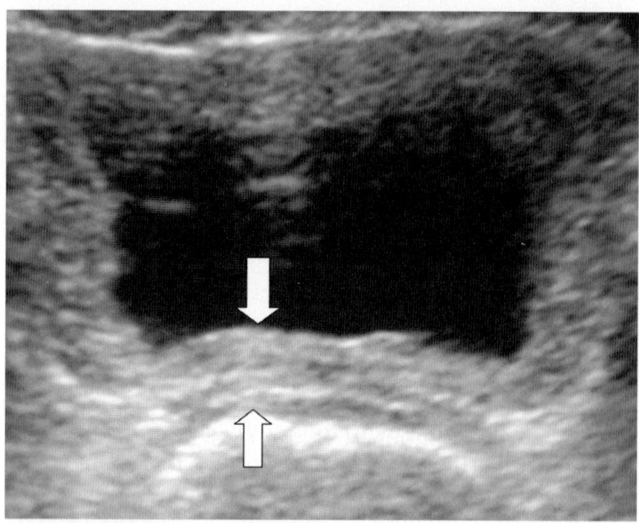

Figure 112–2 Transverse ultrasonongraphy of the bladder demonstrating posterior wall thickening *(arrows)*.

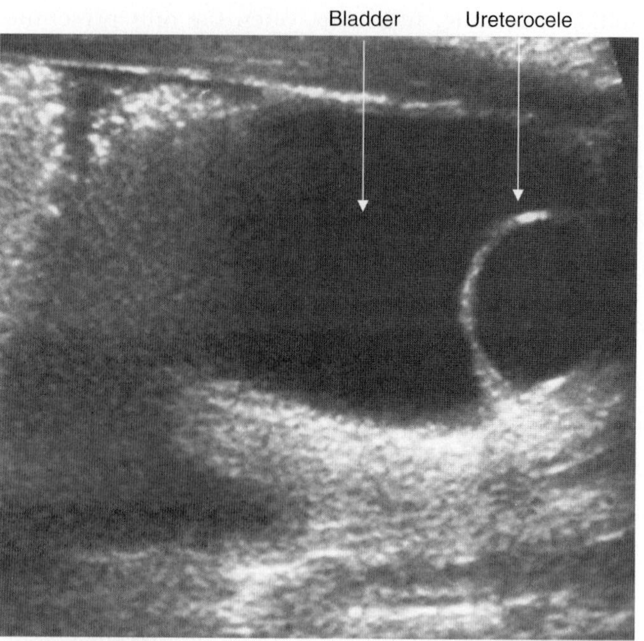

Figure 112–4 Transverse ultrasonography of the bladder demonstrating a left ureterocele.

Additionally, for girls older than 5 years, imaging should be done in those with pyelonephritis or recurrent UTIs (Table 112-5).

The most common anomaly associated with UTI in children is VUR, which is noted in about 20% to 35% of children evaluated after UTI. VCUG is used to detect the presence of VUR (Fig. 112-5). Standard VCUG is performed by instilling iodinated contrast into the bladder and then taking the image during filling and voiding. The American Academy of Pediatrics recommends VCUG as the initial study of choice in VUR, especially in male patients to rule out posterior urethral valves (Fig. 112-6).[2] Previous recommendations were that VCUG should be done 4 to 6 weeks after UTI because of possible false-positive results owing to inflammation of the bladder wall

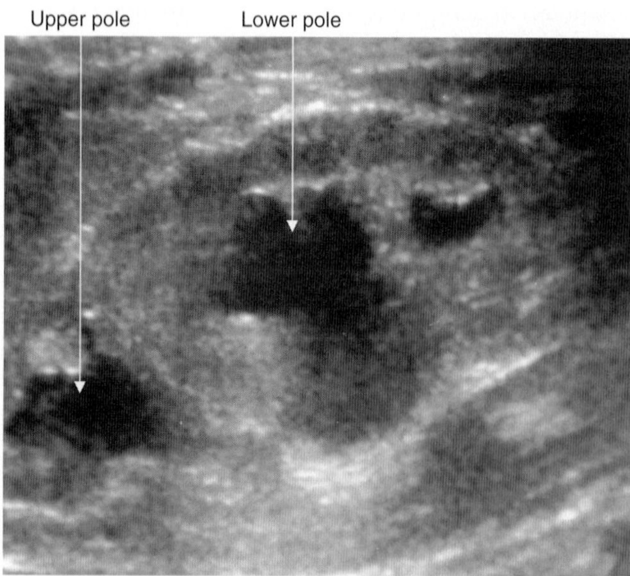

Figure 112–3 Sagittal ultrasonography of a kidney demonstrating a duplicated collecting system.

TABLE 112–5 Pediatric Genitourinary Imaging

Study	Findings	Indications
Renal/bladder US	Abscess Presence of 2 kidneys Renal size Presence of hydronephrosis (see Fig. 112-1) Bladder wall thickening (see Fig. 112-2) Postvoid residual Duplicated collecting system (see Fig. 112-3) Ureterocele (see Fig. 112-4)	All boys with first UTI
VCUG	Vesicoureteral reflux (see Fig. 112-5)	All boys with first UTI; girls <5 yr with first UTI
	Posterior urethral valves (see Fig. 112-6)	
MAG3 diuretic scan	Renal function Renal obstruction	Hydronephrosis on US, no reflux on VCUG
DMSA renal scan	Pyelonephritis	To diagnosis acute pyelonephritis To assess for renal scarring

DMSA, dimercaptosuccinic acid; MAG3, mercapto acetyltriglycine; US, ultrasonography; UTI, urinary tract infection; VCUG, voiding cystourethrography.
Adapted from Handel LN, Caldamone AA: Urinary tract infections in the pediatric population. Lebanese Med J 2004;52:194.

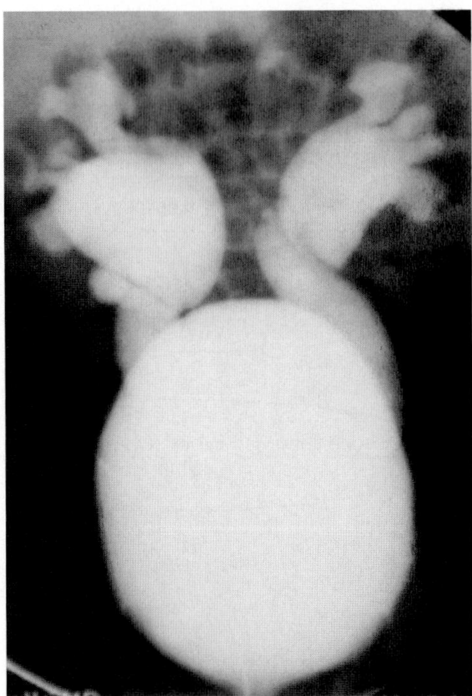

Figure 112-5 Voiding cystourethrogram demonstrating vesicoureteral reflux.

causing VUR. More recent studies have shown no difference between early (within 7 days of infection) and late VCUG.[62] VCUG can be performed once the child is afebrile and cultures are negative to prevent the risk of infected urine being forced in a retrograde fashion during the study.

Renal cortical imaging with dimercaptosuccinic acid (DMSA) is both sensitive and specific for the detection of pyelonephritis in children.[50,87] Areas with decreased uptake may represent acute pyelonephritis or renal scarring. Before the availability of DMSA, imaging techniques demonstrated that approximately 17% of children with bacteriuria had renal scarring; current studies using DMSA demonstrate that the percentage is likely twice that.[92] The use of DMSA should be limited to those patients with suspected acute UTI in whom the diagnosis is unclear but there is a high suspicion of pyelonephritis. DMSA can also be used to assess for renal scarring after UTI if the results would change the management of the patient.

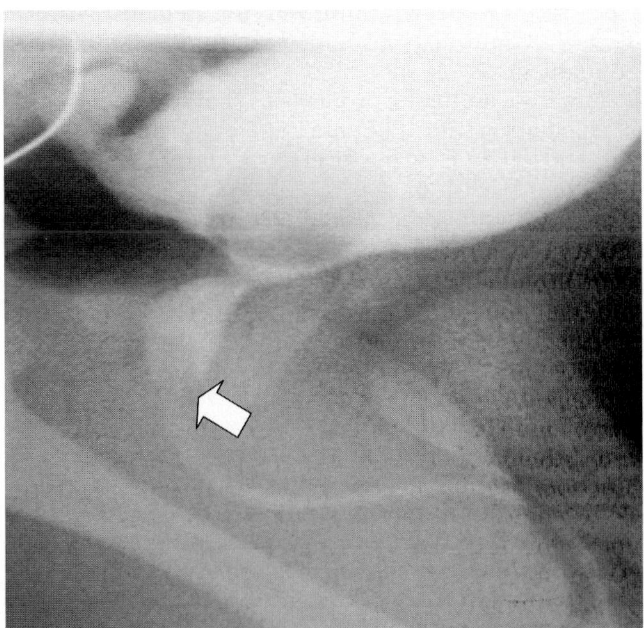

Figure 112-6 Voided cystourethrogram demonstrating posterior urethral valves *(arrow)*.

Mercapto acetyltriglycine (MAG3) or diethylenetriamine pentaacetic acid (DTPA) with a diuretic is used to assess renal function and excretion in patients with hydronephrosis without VUR and to determine the presence or absence of obstruction. Both false-positives and false-negatives are possible, so caution must be used when interpreting the study, and clinical correlation is essential.

Renal abscess is a potential complication of pyelonephritis regardless of the underlying cause. Abscess is more common in compromised patients. Gram-positive organisms such as *Staphylococcus aureus* and streptococci may be the causative agents. The diagnosis is best made by US or computerized tomography (CT). Treatment may involve long-term antibiotics, percutaneous drainage and antibiotic instillation, or open surgical drainage. Sequential follow-up with radiographic imaging is essential.

Treatment

Because of the risk of renal scarring in children, prompt diagnosis and treatment are critical (Fig. 112-7). The treatment strategy depends on various factors, particularly the child's age and the severity of illness. Children younger than 4 weeks with fever are at increased risk for bacteremia and sepsis and may require hospitalization for parenteral antibiotics. Similarly, any child younger than 5 years with a suspected UTI who appears systemically ill should be hospitalized. The American Academy of Pediatrics recommends that children who are dehydrated, are unable to tolerate oral medication, and appear toxic should receive intravenous antibiotics.[2] Additionally, children who are immunocompromised, are suspected of having urosepsis or bacteremia, or have failed oral therapy should be hospitalized. If the child is able to tolerate oral antibiotics and has reliable parents who will maintain follow-up and contact with the physician, the child may be managed as an outpatient.

Initial antibiotic treatment needs to be broad spectrum to cover the more common pathogens. Once culture results and sensitivities are complete, treatment can be tailored specifically to cover the identified organism. In patients who have had previous UTIs, the earlier culture results should be considered when selecting the initial therapy. For children who are hospitalized, parenteral treatment, such as a combination of aminoglycosides and ampicillin or cephalosporins, is continued for 48 to 72 hours until the child is afebrile and stable and sensitivities are available. Once the child is stable, oral antibiotics can be initiated based on sensitivity results. Most studies recommend treating febrile UTIs in young children for

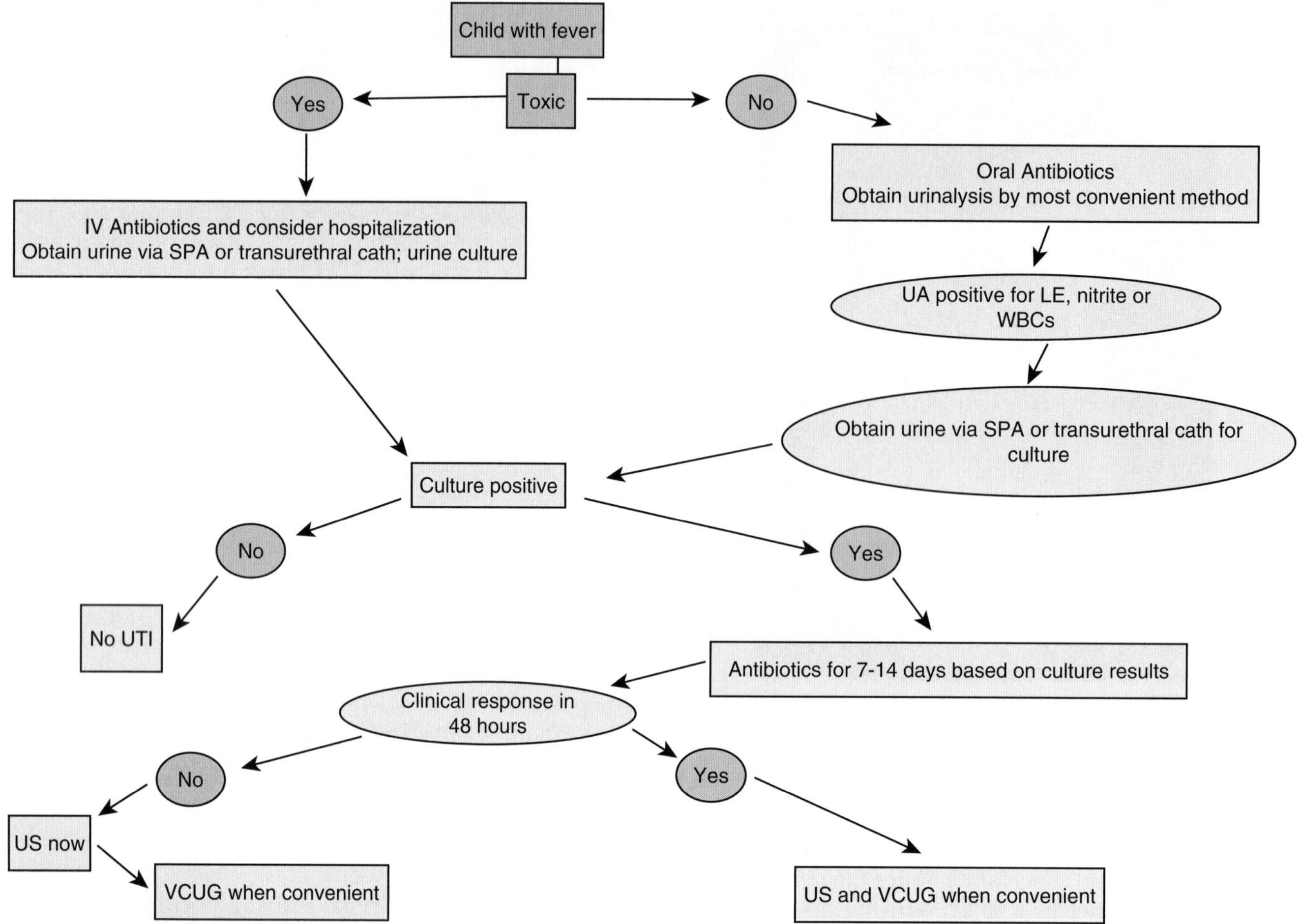

Figure 112-7 Algorithm for management of urinary tract infection (UTI). LE, leukocyte esterase; SPA, suprapubic aspiration; UA, urinalysis; US, ultrasonography; VCUG, voiding cystourethrography; WBC, white blood cell.

7 to 10 days in total.[47,108] The American Academy of Pediatrics recommends that the treatment duration be 7 to 10 days for uncomplicated UTI and 14 days for children with presumed renal involvement or who are toxic.[2] In infants younger than 6 weeks, ampicillin and gentamicin or ampicillin and a cephalosporin are good initial choices. The exception is ceftriaxone, which can increase the risk of kernicterus in young infants. For children likely to be infected with *Pseudomonas* or *Enterococcus*, ampicillin and gentamicin are the agents of choice because cephalosporins have no effect on enterococci. Gentamicin levels should be monitored closely, particularly in children with impaired renal function.

In patients who are clinically stable, a broad-spectrum oral antibiotic is recommended. In a well-appearing child, sulfisoxazole or trimethoprim-sulfamethoxazole (TMP-SMZ), a cephalosporin, or nitrofurantoin is a common choice. TMP-SMZ should not be used in children younger than 2 months because of the increased risk of kernicterus and blood dyscrasias. Nitrofurantoin, which is excreted in the urine and does not achieve therapeutic concentrations in the bloodstream, should not be used in febrile infants with UTI or in children in whom there is concern about renal involvement. The fluoroquinolones have recently been authorized for pediatric use.[30,88] Table 112-6 provides a summary of the commonly used antibiotics.

Low-dose antibiotic prophylaxis should be considered in all children with UTI until a full evaluation with renal US and VCUG is performed. Children with VUR, recurrent UTIs, or partial obstruction or who are immunocompromised should be considered for prophylactic antibiotics. The ideal prophylactic agent provides high urinary antibiotic excretion with low serum levels. Amoxicillin, nitrofurantoin, and TMP-SMZ are the most commonly prescribed agents. However, *Escherichia coli* has demonstrated increasing resistance to amoxicillin, thus limiting its use in children with symptomatic UTI. Generally, the antibiotic used for prophylaxis should be different from the antibiotic used to treat the acute infection.

In patients with normal studies and recurrent UTIs—defined as three or more infections within a 6-month period—prophylactic antibiotics may be indicated. In these cases, one must consider other factors, such as the patient's age, as well as the patient's biologic predisposition for UTIs. For children started on prophylactic antibiotics, the rate of infection usually decreases; however, the risk

TABLE 112-6 Antibiotics Used to Treat Pediatric Urinary Tract Infections

Method of Delivery	Antibiotic	Additional Information
Parenteral	Ampicillin and gentamicin	Check gentamicin levels
	Ampicillin and cephalosporin	No *Enterococcus* or *Pseudomonas* coverage
	Ceftriaxone/ cefotaxime	Contraindicated in infants <2 mo old
Oral	TMP-SMZ	Contraindicated in infants <2 mo old
	Amoxicillin	Increasing resistance by *Escherichia coli*
	Nitrofurantoin	Inadequate if renal involvement
	Cephalosporins	No *Enterococcus* or *Pseudomonas* coverage
	Ciprofloxacin	Recently approved in children

TMP-SMZ, trimethoprim and sulfamethoxazole.
Adapted from Handel LN, Caldamone AA: Urinary tract infections in the pediatric population. Lebanese Med J 2004;52:194.

of developing another UTI returns to baseline once prophylactic antibiotics are discontinued. These patients should be carefully screened for voiding dysfunction and constipation. In cases of asymptomatic bacteriuria, current recommendations include strict follow-up without antibiotic treatment.

VUR treatment depends on several factors: age at presentation, grade of reflux, presence or absence of voiding dysfunction, comorbidities, and family compliance with a treatment protocol. It is helpful to divide VUR into primary and secondary categories. Primary reflux refers to a congenital abnormality of the vesicoureteral junction resulting in a foreshortened ureteral tunnel and poor detrusor backing of the ureter. The lack of detrusor backing prevents the ureter from being collapsed as the bladder fills (Fig. 112-8). Secondary reflux refers to other

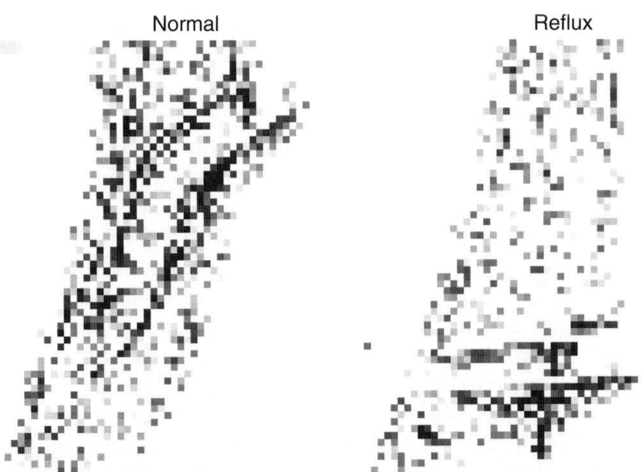

Figure 112-8 Anatomy of the normal and refluxing ureterovesical junction (UVJ). Note the lack of detrusor backing of the refluxing UVJ.

TABLE 112-7 Causes of Secondary Reflux

Anatomic
- Posterior urethral valves
- Ureterocele
- Diverticulum
- Ectopic ureter
- Prune-belly syndrome
- Bladder exstrophy

Functional
- Voiding dysfunction
- Neuropathic bladder
- Myelodysplasia
- Sacral agenesis

anatomic or functional abnormalities that may lead to reflux, such as bladder outlet obstruction or an abnormality of the vesicoureteral junction (Table 112-7).

In the majority of patients with VUR, antibiotic prophylaxis, UTI surveillance, a regular voiding pattern, constipation management, and regular follow-up US and VCUG are the mainstays of therapy.[24] Indications for surgical correction are debatable, but most would agree with the following: breakthrough upper UTIs, renal scarring developing on antibiotic prophylaxis, poor renal growth, failure to follow a treatment plan, high-grade VUR (except in young infants), a fixed anatomic defect of the ureterovesical junction, and persistence of VUR followed for 2 years or longer.

VUR in a child with a recognized voiding dysfunction requires special mention. It is clear that if the voiding dysfunction (including constipation, if present) is managed well, the incidence of breakthrough UTIs and renal scarring and the need for surgical correction of VUR are significantly reduced.[49,65,79] Voiding dysfunction is a common cause of failed ureteral reimplantation.[70]

Many surgical techniques exist using intravesical and extravesical approaches. They all require the establishment of an intramural ureter with sufficient muscular backing to provide adequate ureteral wall coaptation, with filling and contraction of the bladder such that retrograde flow of urine is prevented (Figs. 112-9 to 112-11). This approach requires an average hospital stay of 48 hours and has a complication rate of about 4%, 2% to 2.5% due to ureteral obstruction and 2% to 2.5% due to persistent VUR. The Pediatric Vesicoureteral Reflux Guidelines Panel delineated an overall surgical success rate of 95.1%.[24]

In 1981 Matouschek[64] introduced the concept of endoscopic correction of urinary incontinence and VUR by polytetrafluoroethylene (Teflon) paste injection. This method was developed and popularized by Puri and O'Donnell, initially in a piglet model in 1984 and then applied to children with VUR.[16,74] This procedure causes little postoperative discomfort and can be performed as an outpatient procedure (Figs. 112-12 and 112-13). Owing to the potential risks of particle migration and malignancy induction,[63] Teflon is not in current use.[70] Many other injectable materials have been investigated and applied to animal models and humans for VUR correction. Success rates approach 75% to 80%, depending on the grade of

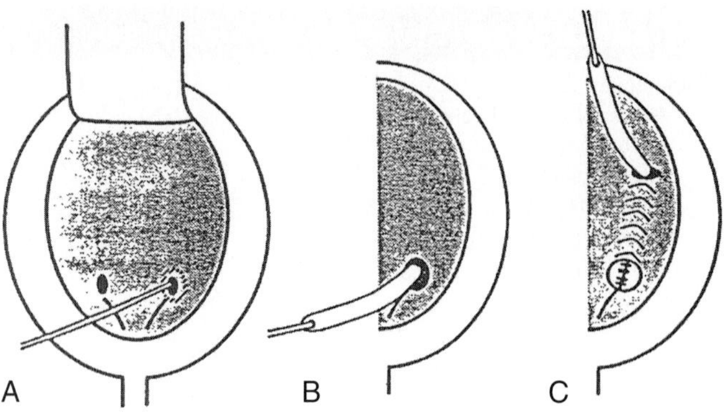

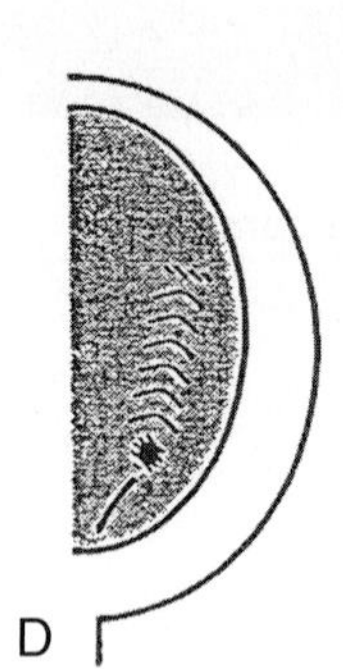

Figure 112-9 Leadbetter-Politano ureteral reimplantation. *A,* The ureter is catheterized through a midline bladder incision. *B,* The ureter is dissected from the surrounding detrusor until it is totally mobilized. *C,* A neohiatus is created by passing a right-angle clamp into the bladder. A subepithelial tunnel is created, and the detrusor defect is closed. *D,* The ureter is then passed through the tunnel, and its orifice is matured. (From Rowe M, et al: Essentials of Pediatric Surgery. St Louis, Mosby-Year Book, 1995.)

reflux and the number of injections.[48,53,82,98] Today, the most commonly used materials worldwide are dextranomer macrospheres (Deflux) and polydimethylsiloxane with polyvinylpyrroline (Macroplastique).

URINARY LITHIASIS

History and Incidence

Urinary stones, in both the bladder and the kidney, have been reported in Egyptian mummies dating from 4800 BC,[10] and urolithiasis have long been studied in an effort to understand its pathogenesis and to refine treatment strategies. Although urolithiasis has been recognized in children for centuries, the clinical picture, evaluation, and management continue to evolve.

Approximately 7% of all stones occur in children younger than 16 years.[11] Traditionally, urolithiasis was characterized by bladder calculi in children of developing countries; the incidence of upper tract calculi, occurring mainly in industrialized areas, was much lower in children than in adults. Also, in comparison to adult stone formers, children were more likely to demonstrate risk factors outside the metabolic realm, such as UTI, anatomic abnormalities, and surgical alterations in the urinary tract. Currently, the incidence of upper tract calculi in children without these predisposing factors is on the rise worldwide,[1,85] and the paradigms are changing. The importance of metabolic evaluation in children with urolithiasis has been shown, even in countries thought to have primarily endemic bladder stone disease based on diet. With the introduction of smaller endoscopic instruments and the refinement of extracorporeal shock wave lithotripsy (ESWL) technology, treatment of pediatric stone disease now closely parallels stone management in adults.

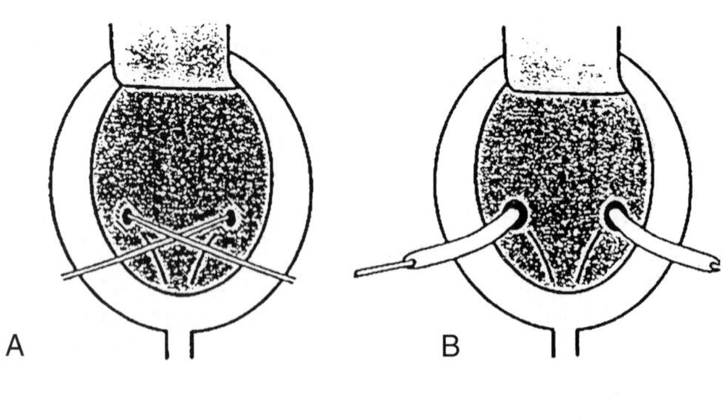

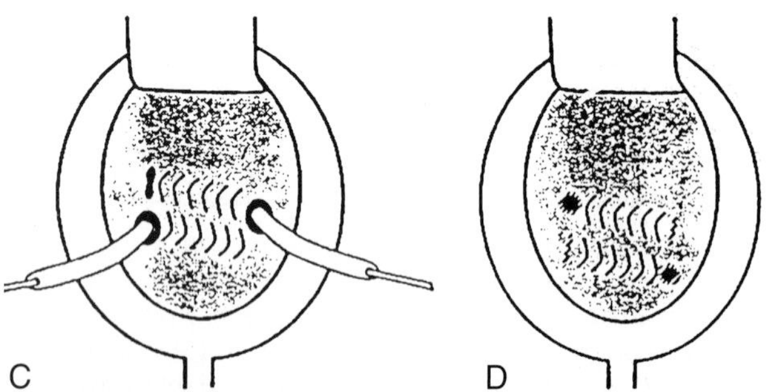

Figure 112-10 Cohen cross-trigonal ureteral reimplantation. *A,* Both ureters are catheterized. *B,* Both ureters are fully mobilized, as in the Leadbetter-Politano procedure. *C,* The detrusor is approximated around the ureter to create a normal neohiatal caliber, and two transtrigonal tunnels are created. *D,* The ureters are then passed through the respective tunnels, and the orifices of the ureters are matured. (From Rowe M, et al: Essentials of Pediatric Surgery. St Louis, Mosby-Year Book, 1995.)

Spectrum of Disorders

Although there are a number of contributing factors, the central concept in urolithiasis is urinary supersaturation. When a solute is added to a solvent, it dissolves until a certain concentration is reached, at which point the solution is saturated. Beyond this point, the solute may form crystals in the solution, and those crystals may aggregate. Supersaturation occurs when this point is surpassed and crystal precipitation occurs in the urine in the form of nucleation, the basis of urinary stones. Crystallization and aggregation must also occur for stones to form. These processes are influenced by the presence of inhibitors and promoters. Citrate, magnesium, pyrophosphate, glycosaminoglycans, nephrocalcin, and Tamm-Horsfall proteins are inhibitors of crystallization and aggregation. Bacterial infections and anatomic abnormalities such as obstruction or stasis may encourage crystal aggregation and retention, thus increasing the risk of clinically significant urolithiasis.[66,80] Multiple studies of urolithiasis in

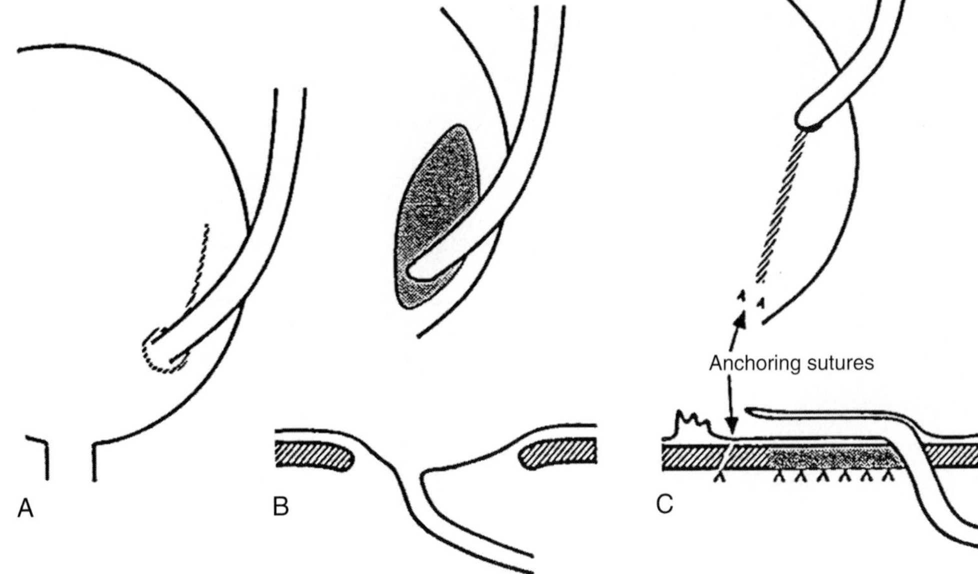

Figure 112-11 Extravesical detrusorrhaphy—a modification of the Lich-Gregoir procedure. *A,* The ureter is mobilized for several centimeters externally. The detrusor is then incised in a caudal direction and carried around the ureteral insertion. *B,* The ureter is left attached only to the underlying bladder mucosa. *C,* The distal ureter is advanced and fixed with two sutures. Then the detrusor is approximated over the ureter to re-create the tunnel, which is now longer than before. (From Rowe M, et al: Essentials of Pediatric Surgery. St Louis, Mosby-Year Book, 1995.)

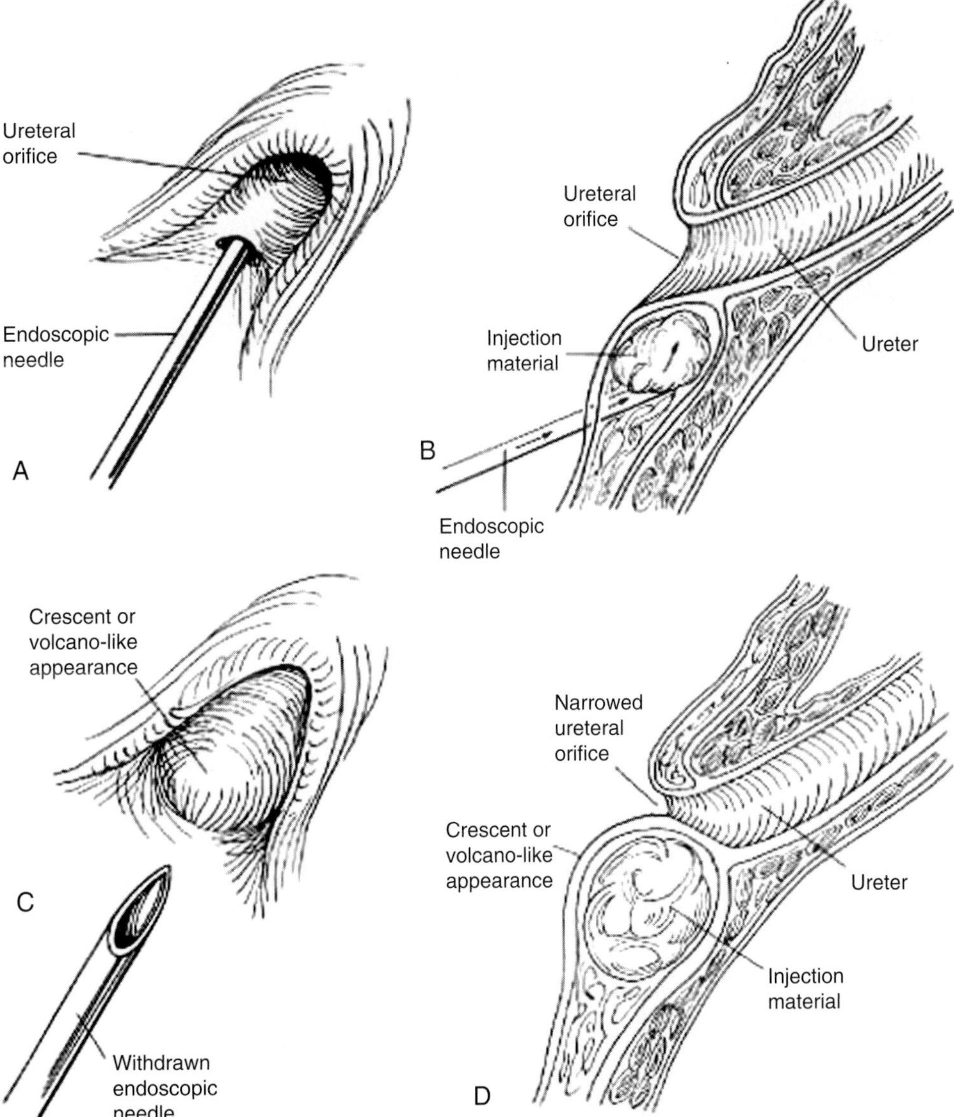

Figure 112-12 Endoscopic technique for reflux connection. *A,* The needle is placed at the 6 o'clock position, bevel up. *B,* Slow injection in subureteral space. *C,* Postinjection appearance. *D,* Appropriate position of injected material. (From Russinko PJ, Tackett LD: Endoscopic correction of reflux. In Caldamone AA [ed]: Atlas Urol Clin North Am 2004;12:55.)

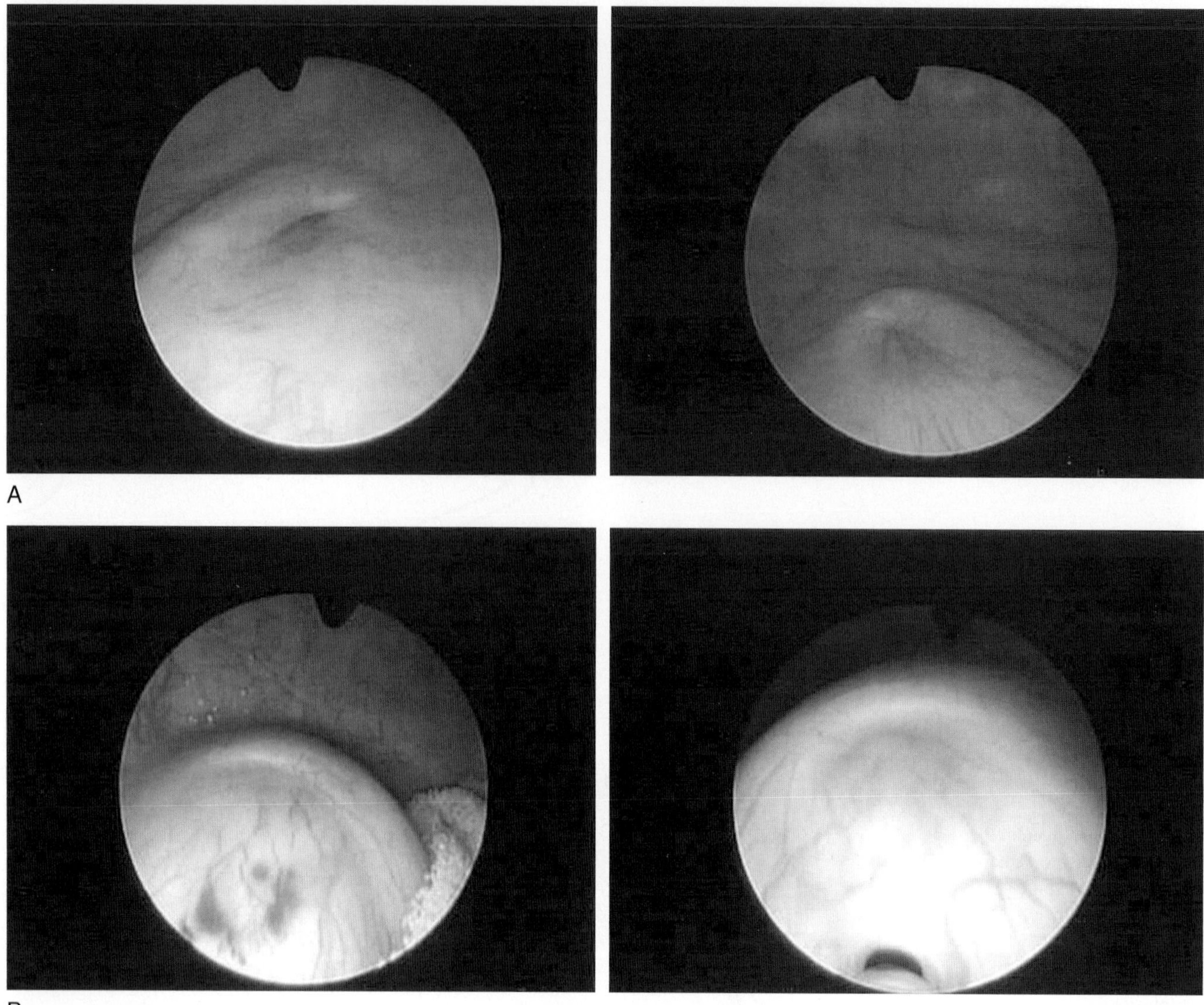

Figure 112-13 Endoscopic injection. *A,* Left and right ureteral orifices before injection. *B,* Left and right ureteral orifices demonstrating the crescent appearance after injection. *(See color plate.)*

children have shown metabolic abnormalities in up to 92% of patients, with hypercalciuria and hypocitraturia the most common.[8,71,72,80,100-102] Interestingly, even in children with urolithiasis and anatomic obstruction, the prevalence of urinary metabolic abnormalities is high.[66,72,81] The prevalence of infection-related stones is especially high in children younger than 6 years.[21] Approximately 12% of children with urolithiasis have no identifiable risk factor.[96] Urinary stone disease can therefore be classified as metabolic, anatomic, infectious, or idiopathic, based on underlying factors. The relative contribution of these factors, which may overlap in some cases, is shown in Table 112-8.

Stones can also be classified based on their location in the upper urinary tract (kidneys and ureters) or lower urinary tract (bladder and urethra), and as symptomatic or asymptomatic. These classifications may influence the decision-making process with regard to treatment options.

Clinical Presentation

In adults, upper tract calculi present in a characteristic fashion in the form of renal colic. This severe, intermittent, refractory pain, often accompanied by nausea and vomiting, is a less common presentation in children. Although classic renal colic does occur in children, more commonly, stones involving both the upper and lower tract are detected during the radiologic evaluation for UTI or hematuria. Children may also present with nonspecific abdominal pain accompanied by microscopic hematuria or, less frequently, with outlet obstruction (Fig. 112-14).

Diagnosis

History and physical examination are key components to rule out other causes of abdominal and back pain.

TABLE 112-8 Clinical Diagnoses in Children with Urolithiasis

Diagnosis	Mayo Clinic (*N* = 221) No. of Patients (%)	North America (*N* = 492)* No. of Patients (%)	Europe (*N* =481)* No. of Patients (%)
Metabolic disorder	115 (52.0)†	162 (32.9)†	59 (12.3)
Idiopathic hypercalciuria	38	39	36
Immobilization	8	39	4
Uric acid stones	8	22	2
Endemic stones (urate)	0	10	0
Cystinuria	15	15	9
Hyperoxaluria	25	12	5
Renal tubular acidosis	4	10	2
Other	38‡	25	1
Developmental anomalies of genitourinary tract	66 (29.9)†	160 (32.5)	145 (30.1)
Infection			
Primary	41 (18.6)†	21 (4.3)	209 (43.5)
All causes	—	215 (43.7)	358 (74.4)
Unknown cause	55 (24.9)	139 (28.3)	68 (14.1)

*Data from Polinsky MS, Kaiser BA, Bacuarte HJ: Urolithiasis in childhood. Pediatr Clin North Am 1987;34:683.
†Metabolic disorders often coexisted with genitourinary tract anomalies and infections.
‡More than one disorder in some patients.
From Liebermann E: Importance of metabolic contributions to urolithiasis in pediatric patients [editorial]. Mayo Clin Proc 1993;68:313.

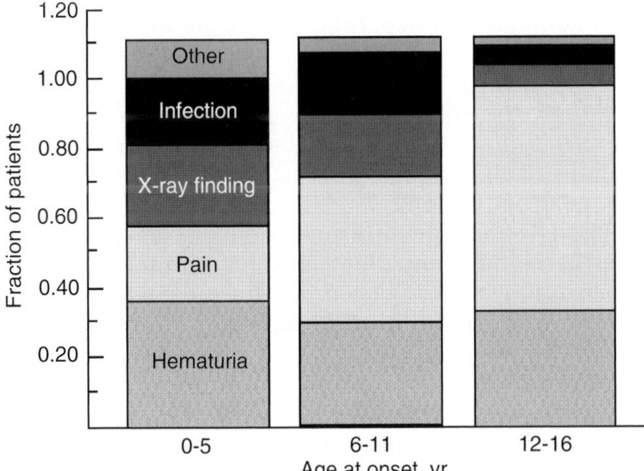

Figure 112-14 Clinical features at the time of initial assessment of 221 children and adolescents with urolithiasis who were examined at the Mayo Clinic between 1965 and 1987. (From Milliner DS, Murphy ME: Urolithiasis in pediatric patients. Mayo Clin Proc 1993;68:241.)

The history should include a dietary as well as a urologic history. One clue to the presence of urolithiasis is a positive family history for kidney stones, which may be present in up to 37% of children with stone disease.[69] Other underlying medical conditions that may predispose children to urolithiasis include hyperparathyroidism, renal tubular acidosis, inflammatory bowel disease, seizure disorders treated with a ketogenic diet,[29] cystic fibrosis, and Dent disease.[27] Urinalysis and urine culture should be obtained to assess for microscopic hematuria, urine pH, crystals in the sediment, and UTI. Baseline serum electrolytes, blood urea nitrogen, creatinine, calcium, uric acid, phosphorus, and magnesium levels should also be obtained. A 24-hour urinalysis for stone risk assessment should be obtained after treatment of the presenting stone.

Radiologic evaluation may include plain abdominal radiography, US, intravenous pyelography, and noncontrast CT. In adults, the standard imaging study is noncontrast CT because of its sensitivity and specificity. In children, however, these studies are limited, although some authors recommend CT as the first-line imaging study.[75,76] Others recommend initial abdominal US because of the varied presentation of urolithiasis in children and because of concerns about radiation exposure.[26,95] Plain abdominal radiography may not be helpful in the initial diagnosis but may assist in planning treatment, based on the ability to visualize the stone.

Treatment

Four main factors affect initial treatment decisions: the clinical scenario, stone composition, stone size, and stone location (Table 112-9). In the setting of potential urinary tract obstruction with fever or complete obstruction, urgent relief of the obstruction is warranted, either by placement of a ureteral stent or by percutaneous nephrostomy. The decision between ureteral stent placement and percutaneous nephrostomy is dependent on physician preference, available resources, and patient size and anatomy. In children, nephrostomy drainage may be performed without general anesthesia and may be the procedure of choice. After relief of the obstruction and subsequent treatment of infection, definitive therapy directed at stone clearance can be undertaken.

The most common composition of upper tract calculi is calcium oxalate. The stones are radiopaque and do not respond to dissolution therapy. Calcium oxalate monohydrate stones may be resistant to ESWL, whereas calcium oxalate dihydrate calculi, which are more common, generally respond well. Uric acid calculi are radiolucent and form at a low urinary pH. They are often identified by their characteristic Hounsfield units on noncontrast CT. Uric acid stones may be dissolved and prevented by alkalynization of the urine (pH >6.5) using sodium bicarbonate or potassium citrate. If symptoms are present, a ureteral stent or nephrostomy tube may be used for temporary relief during dissolution therapy. Struvite stones are usually associated with infection, and antibiotics should be continued throughout treatment. Because struvite stones are generally large or staghorn in shape, percutaneous

TABLE 112-9 Factors Affecting the Treatment of Stones

Factor	Treatment Consideration
Clinical scenario	
Bilateral obstruction	For all scenarios, urgent relief of obstruction via stent or nephrostomy
Obstruction of a solitary kidney	
Fever/UTI with potential obstruction	
Intractable pain	
Stone composition	
Uric acid	Consider chemodissolution
Struvite	Continue antibiotic therapy throughout treatment
Cystine	Responds poorly to ESWL
Calcium oxalate	Radiopaque; may respond well to ESWL
Stone size	
<4 mm	Approximately 90% chance of spontaneous passage
4-6 mm	Approximately 50% chance of spontaneous passage
>6 mm	Approximately 10%-20% chance of spontaneous passage
Stone location	
Renal	ESWL or PCNL
Proximal ureteral	Ureteroscopic extraction (antegrade) or ESWL
Distal ureteral	Ureteroscopic extraction (retrograde) or ESWL
Bladder	Cystolithotomy or cystolitholapaxy

ESWL, extracorporeal shock wave lithotripsy; PCNL, percutaneous nephrostolithotomy; UTI, urinary tract infection.

nephrostolithotomy (PCNL) is often the first-line treatment for these stones. Cystine stones are typically difficult to treat and frequently recur. Small renal cystine stones may be treated by ESWL, whereas larger stones will likely require PCNL or ureteroscopic extraction.[94]

Stone size can be used to predict whether the stone will pass without intervention. In adults, the likelihood of passing a stone less than 4 mm is 90%, a stone between 4 and 6 mm has an approximately 50% rate of spontaneous passage, and one greater than 6 mm has a 10% to 20% rate. Interestingly, small stones and stone fragments after ESWL have shown the same passage rate in the pediatric population, theoretically because of ureteral pliability and peristalsis.[32,80,103] Therefore, supportive care in the form of vigorous hydration (oral or intravenous, as needed) and analgesic therapy is a reasonable first step in a child with a small stone in the absence of fever or complete ureteral obstruction. Studies demonstrate that partial obstruction is well tolerated in the short term; thus, this treatment may be continued for 3 to 4 weeks on an outpatient basis to allow spontaneous passage of the stone. In the case of an obstructing stone 4 mm or greater in size, the likelihood of spontaneous passage is significantly lower, and intervention may be indicated sooner. Nonobstructing stones can be treated electively. Stones larger than 2 cm have demonstrated a poor stone-free response to ESWL, and a National Institutes of Health Consensus Conference in 1998 recommended that stones larger than 2 cm be approached by PCNL as first-line treatment. "Sandwich therapy," which is a combination of PCNL and ESWL, is an addition to the treatment armamentarium for large calculi.

Calculi are most commonly located within the renal pelvis or calices, proximal ureter, distal ureter, or bladder. Each location lends itself to different treatment approaches. For renal calculi, ESWL or PCNL is suitable. ESWL or ureteroscopic stone extraction is an appropriate choice for ureteral stones, whereas cystolitholapaxy or cystolithotomy is recommended for bladder calculi.

ESWL, first described in the early 1980s,[15] is noninvasive and well-tolerated but requires general anesthesia in many young children and special precautions in infants. Children who weigh as little as 6.8 kg have been successfully treated. This procedure may be suitable for proximal ureteral stones and even some distal ureteral stones; however, treatment of calculi more distal than the midureter is contraindicated in females because of the unknown effects of shock waves on the developing ovary. Stone-free rates after one to two treatments generally range from 70% to 97% (mean 85%).[6,18,43,54,61] Complications of ESWL therapy include incomplete fragmentation of the stone, retained fragments, Steinstrasse, perinephric hematoma, fever, renal colic, and abrasion or ecchymosis at the site of shock wave entry and exit.[31] Although the distant and long-term effects of ESWL are unknown, short-term follow-up studies suggest no demonstrable complications with regard to renal function or hypertension.[11,31,60,105]

PCNL requires nephrostomy tube placement, general anesthesia, and inpatient hospitalization. Once the nephrostomy tube is placed, the tract is dilated to a size appropriate for the nephroscope and electrohydraulic or ultrasonic lithotriptor.[91] It is a good choice for a large renal stone associated with hydronephrosis or one refractory to ESWL treatment (cystine or calcium oxalate monohydrate). PCNL and ESWL can be combined for optimal treatment in some cases, so-called sandwich therapy. PCNL can also be combined with Renacidin or hemiacidrin irrigation via the nephrostomy tube for infectious stones. Stone-free rates may approach 100%; however, multiple procedures may be required to render a child stone free.[18,52] Complications of PCNL include perforation of the collecting system, bleeding, extravasation of irrigant, pneumothorax, intestinal injury, and retained fragments.

Ureteroscopic stone extraction in children has become feasible with the development of progressively smaller ureteroscopes and working instruments. Ureteroscopic treatment of ureteral calculi may be approached in an antegrade or retrograde fashion, and the stone may be extracted intact or fragmented using a laser, ultrasound, or hydraulic lithotriptor (Swiss Lithoclast). Success rates for ureteroscopic stone extraction may exceed 95%.[14,18,38,43,84,90] An indwelling ureteral stent may be left in place for 24 to 72 hours to prevent obstruction secondary to ureteral spasm or edema. Complications include ureteral perforation, ureteral stricture, reflux, proximal migration of the stone, and loss of the stone through a perforated ureter.

Despite the success of minimally invasive treatment for pediatric stone disease, open surgical treatment is still required in up to 17% of patients,[43] which may result in decreased renal function in as many as 45%.[34] Anatomic abnormalities such as ureteropelvic junction obstruction or obstructed megaureter may be addressed concurrently with stone treatment and must be dealt with eventually to prevent recurrence and optimize renal function.[40,41]

Cystolitholapaxy, or transurethral lithopexy of bladder stones, has been the preferred approach for all but very large bladder calculi. The stone is fragmented using the electrohydraulic lithotriptor, and the fragments are irrigated from the bladder. Bladder calculi are becoming more common in children who have undergone augmentation cystoplasty, and in this population, open removal of the intact calculi may be a more prudent approach to minimize the risk of recurrence due to retained fragments, although this remains controversial.[13,20,86]

Recurrence

Children who present with urolithiasis are at risk for recurrence for a longer time than adults, thus the cumulative likelihood of recurrent stone disease is higher in children. Therefore, a thorough metabolic evaluation is strongly encouraged in children after their first presentation with urolithiasis. A 24-hour urinalysis for stone risk should be obtained, including, at a minimum, urinary volume, pH, and calcium, creatinine, uric acid, citrate, oxalate, and magnesium levels. The cornerstones for preventing stone recurrence as the child enters adulthood are the ability to render the patient stone free, elucidate and treat metabolic abnormalities, control urinary infection, and correct anatomic anomalies.

RENAL VEIN THROMBOSIS

Renal vein thrombosis is a variable clinical disorder related to the acuteness and extent of venous occlusion of the main or intrarenal veins. Rayer[83] first described renal vein thrombosis more than 150 years ago. For many decades, the condition was rarely diagnosed clinically but was discovered at operation or autopsy. Once the condition was clinically recognized, treatment initially consisted of simple nephrectomy; this procedure was advocated until the early 1960s.[46,104] In 1964 Stark[97] reported excellent recovery after conservative management, suggesting that aggressive surgical intervention was unnecessary. The use of anticoagulants or thrombolytic agents still remains controversial because of the limited number of pediatric cases and the absence of controlled trials evaluating the risks and benefits of these therapeutic interventions.

Cause

Renal vein thrombosis is a disease of infancy; approximately 80% of patients present during the first month of life.[4] It results from diminished renal blood flow, increased blood viscosity, and hypercoagulability. The neonatal kidney is particularly vulnerable because of its low renal perfusion pressure and double intrarenal capillary network. Many factors also lead to hemoconcentration, with a sluggish venous flow that predisposes patients to thrombosis. In addition, up to 50% of these patients may have prothrombotic abnormalities.[51,109] The thrombotic process may originate in the main renal vein or in the small intrarenal veins.[37] Thrombosis may be unilateral or bilateral, but thrombosis from the inferior vena cava is rare.[22]

Clinical conditions predisposing neonates to thrombosis include preterm delivery,[51] perinatal asphyxia, polycythemia, cyanotic congenital heart disease,[45] maternal diabetes,[7,77] septicemia, congenital nephrotic syndrome,[33,57] cytomegalovirus infection,[106] shock, diarrhea and dehydration,[5] activated protein C resistance,[51] factor V Leiden heterozygosity,[109] and maternal use of diuretics and corticosteroids.[9] Renal vein thrombosis has been noted in association with adrenal hemorrhage and has been recognized on prenatal US.[25,28,78]

In infants older than 1 month, renal vein thrombosis is usually associated with hypovolemia, such as with gastrointestinal fluid losses or burns,[5,23,33] or renal disease, such as nephrotic syndrome.[44,59] Renal vein thrombosis may occur secondary to prolonged inferior vena cava catheterization, with thrombus extending into the renal vasculature.[44]

Clinical Presentation

Clinical presentation varies, depending on the age, extent, and acuity of the thrombosis. Renal vein thrombosis may present prenatally or in a healthy newborn with no predisposing illness. In neonates, classic features include a palpable mass and gross hematuria; however, these signs may be found in only 13% of patients at the time of diagnosis.[106] Caval thrombosis may be suspected when the lower extremities are swollen and the superficial abdominal veins are dilated. Renal vein thrombosis may also present in infancy after a predisposing illness, or it may develop in an older child who has preexisting renal disease (nephrotic syndrome). Presentation in older children generally includes acute flank pain, hematuria, and a palpable mass.

Diagnosis

Renal vein thrombosis is frequently associated with thrombocytopenia (platelet count <75,000 cells/mm³) as a result of platelet entrapment in the renal thrombus. A consumptive coagulopathy characterized by a prolonged prothrombin time and increased fibrin degradation products may also be present. Leukocytosis is often present, and the presence of anemia varies. Serum electrolyte levels vary, depending on predisposing illness and renal function. Urinalysis usually shows blood and protein. Screening for prothrombotic abnormalities should be considered.

Imaging

An abdominal radiograph may show an enlarged renal shadow or have a lacelike pattern, similar to the renal vascular tree, but it is usually normal.[12] Renal Doppler US is the test of choice to evaluate the renal mass and image the renal vein and inferior vena cava. Diagnostic features include thrombus in the vein and renal enlargement.[67] Renal function can be monitored initially and during recovery with radionuclide scintigraphy using technetium 99m DMSA or technetium 99m MAG3. CT, magnetic resonance imaging, or inferior venacavography may be indicated to determine the extent of a thrombus (with inferior vena cava involvement) or to rule out rare causes of thrombus or thrombosis (e.g., external venous compression or thrombus from a renal tumor).

Treatment

Because of the relative infrequency of renal vein thrombosis and the lack of controlled trials, no general consensus on optimal treatment exists. Although nephrectomy and thrombectomy were previously performed during the acute phase, this was rarely needed on an emergent basis and is now limited to patients with anatomic obstruction of the inferior vena cava.[97] Initial treatment should include correction of and therapy for all predisposing conditions, aggressive fluid and electrolyte repletion, and prevention of propagation of the venous thrombus. The use of anticoagulants or thrombolytic agents is controversial because of the absence of controlled trials. In a recent retrospective study of 16 patients with renal vein thrombosis, renal function was normal in 6 of 9 patients treated with heparin or enoxaparin or both, compared with 0 of 7 patients who did not receive anticoagulation therapy.[99,109] A reasonable approach includes aggressive supportive measures in cases of unilateral renal vein thrombosis without caval extension, especially for those at increased risk of hemorrhagic complications. For unilateral renal vein thrombosis with caval extension or bilateral renal vein thrombosis, heparin therapy may be considered because of the risk of pulmonary emboli or renal failure. Thrombolytic therapy may be considered for bilateral renal vein thrombosis and renal failure. Treatment with heparin should continue for 7 to 14 days, as shown in Table 112-10.[4] Although heparin has been used successfully, hemorrhagic complications have been reported in neonates.[73,107] Low-molecular-weight heparin may be a safer alternative, with careful attention to special dosing requirements in preterm and full-term newborns.[68,109] Thrombolytic therapy with streptokinase and urokinase by systemic and regional routes has been reported.[22,33,73] Potential complications with the systemic use of streptokinase include hemorrhage and allergic reactions; these occur less often with selective regional use. Route, rate, and length of infusion of thrombolytic agents differ among various reports; thus, standardized protocols are difficult to establish.

TABLE 112-10 Protocol for Systemic Heparin Administration and Adjustment

1. Loading dose: heparin 75 U/kg IV over 10 min
2. Initial maintenance dose: 28 U/kg/hr for infants <1 yr; 20 U/kg/hr for children >1 yr
3. Adjust heparin dose to maintain APTT at 60-85 sec (assuming this reflects an antifactor Xa level of 0.35-0.70)

APTT (sec)	Bolus (U/kg)	Hold (min)	Rate Change (%)	Repeat APTT
<50	50	0	+10	4 hr
50-59	0	0	+10	4 hr
60-85	0	0	0	Next day
86-95	0	0	−10	4 hr
96-120	0	30	−10	4 hr
>120	0	60	−15	4 hr

4. Obtain blood for APTT 4 hr after administration of heparin loading dose and 4 hr after every change in infusion rate
5. When APTT values are therapeutic, perform daily CBC and APTT

APTT, activated partial thromboplastin time; CBC, complete blood count.
From Andrew M, Brooker LA: Hemostatic complications in renal disorders of the young. Pediatr Nephrol 1996;10:88.

Outcome

With improved recognition and management of renal vein thrombosis and the various predisposing conditions, the overall survival rates have improved to about 80% to 85%.[4] Most deaths are due to underlying disease rather than renal infarction. Long-term morbidity, including conditions such as hypertension, renal atrophy, and chronic UTI, has not been systematically assessed. In terms of renal function, the outcome can vary from full recovery to nonfunction. Periodic monitoring with radionuclide scintigraphy permits detailed follow-up evaluation of renal recovery. Renin-mediated hypertension in association with a small, atrophic kidney or recurrent UTIs localized to the shrunken renal unit are reasonable indications for nephrectomy.

REFERENCES

1. Al-Eisa AA, Al-Hunayyan A, Gupta R: Pediatric urolithiasis in Kuwait. Int Urol Nephrol 2002;33:3.

2. American Academy of Pediatrics, Committee on Quality Improvement, Subcommittee on Urinary Tract Infection: Practice parameter: The diagnosis, treatment, and evaluation of the initial urinary tract infection in febrile infants and young children. Pediatrics 1999;103:843.
3. American Academy of Pediatrics, Task Force on Circumcision: Circumcision policy statement. Pediatrics 1999; 103:686.
4. Andrew M, Brooker LA: Hemostatic complications in renal disorders of the young. Pediatr Nephrol 1996;10:88.
5. Arneil GC, MacDonald AM, Sweet EM: Renal vein thrombosis. Clin Nephrol 1973;1:119.
6. Ather MH, Noor MA: Does size and site matter for renal stones up to 30-mm in size in children treated by extracorporeal lithotripsy? Urology 2003;61:212.
7. Avery ME, Oppenheimer EH, Gordon HH: Renal vein thrombosis in newborn infants of diabetic mothers. N Engl J Med 1957;256:1134.
8. Battino BS, DeFoor W, Coe F, et al: Metabolic evaluation of children with urolithiasis: Are adult references for supersaturation appropriate? J Urol 2002;168:2568.
9. Belman AB: Renal vein thrombosis in infancy and childhood. Clin Pediatr 1976;15:1033.
10. Belman AB, Kaplan GW: Calculus disease. In Belman AB, Kaplan GW (eds): Genitourinary Problems in Pediatrics. Philadelphia, WB Saunders, 1981.
11. Borman V, Nagel R: Urolithiasis in childhood—a study of 181 cases. Urol Int 1982;37:178.
12. Brill PW, Mitty HA, Strauss L: Renal vein thrombosis: A cause of intrarenal calcification in the newborn. Pediatr Radiol 1977;6:172.
13. Cain MP, Casale AJ, Kaefer M, et al: Percutaneous cystolithotomy in the pediatric augmented bladder. J Urol 2002;168:1881.
14. Caione P, De Gennaro M, Capozza N, et al: Endoscopic manipulation of ureteral calculi in children by rigid operative ureteroscopy. J Urol 1990;144:484.
15. Chaussy C, Schmiedt E, Jocham D, et al: First clinical experience with extracorporeally induced destruction of kidney stones by shock waves. J Urol 1982;127:417.
16. Chertin B, Colhoun E, Velayudham M, et al: Endoscopic treatment of vesicoureteral reflux: 11 to 17 years of followup. J Urol 2002;167:1443.
17. Chon CH, Lai FC, Shortliffe LM: Pediatric urinary tract infections. Pediatr Clin North Am 2001;48:1441.
18. Choong S, Whitfield H, Duffy P, et al: The management of paediatric urolithiasis. BJU Int 2000;86:857.
19. Decter RM: Vesicoureteral reflux. Pediatr Rev 2001; 22:205.
20. DeFoor W, Minevich E, Reddy P, et al: Bladder calculi after augmentation cystoplasty: Risk factors and prevention strategies. J Urol 2004;172:1964.
21. Diamond DA, Rickwood AM, Lee PH, Johnston JH: Infection stones in children: A twenty-seven-year review. Urology 1994;43:525.
22. Duncan BW, Adzick NS, Longaker MT, et al: In utero arterial embolism from renal vein thrombosis with successful postnatal thrombolytic therapy. J Pediatr Surg 1991;26:741.
23. Duncan RE, Evans AT, Martin LW: Natural history and treatment of renal vein thrombosis in children. J Pediatr Surg 1977;12:639.
24. Elder JS, Peters CA, Arant BS, et al: Pediatric Vesicoureteral Reflux Guidelines Panel summary report on the management of primary vesicoureteral reflux in children. J Urol 1997;157:1846.
25. Errington ML, Hendry GM: The rare association of right adrenal hemorrhage and renal vein thrombosis diagnosed with duplex ultrasound. Pediatr Radiol 1995;25:157.
26. Eshed I, Witzling M: The role of unenhanced helical CT in the evaluation of suspected renal colic and atypical abdominal pain in children. Pediatr Radiol 2002;32:205.
27. Faerber GJ: Pediatric urolithiasis. Curr Opin Urol 2001; 11:385.
28. Fishman JE, Joseph RC: Renal vein thrombosis in utero: Duplex sonography in diagnosis and follow-up. Pediatr Radiol 1994;24:135.
29. Furth SL, Casey JC, Pyzik PL, et al: Risk factors for urolithiasis in children on the ketogenic diet. Pediatr Nephrol 2000;15:125.
30. Gendrel D, Chalumeau M, Moulin F, Raymond J: Fluoroquinolones in paediatrics: A risk for the patient or for the community? Lancet Infect Dis 2003;3:537.
31. Goel MC, Baserge NS, Babu RV, et al: Pediatric kidney: Functional outcome after extracorporeal shock wave lithotripsy. J Urol 1996;155:2044..
32. Gofrit ON, Pode D, Meretyk S, et al: Is the pediatric ureter as efficient as the adult ureter in transporting fragments following extracorporeal shock wave lithotripsy for renal calculi larger than 10 mm? J Urol 2001;166:1862.
33. Gonzalez R, Schwartz S, Sheldon CA, Fraley EE: Bilateral renal vein thrombosis in infancy and childhood. Urol Clin North Am 1982;9:279.
34. Gough DCS, Baillie CT: Paediatric anatrophic nephrolithotomy: Stone clearance—at what price? BJU Int 2000;85:874.
35. Handel LN, Caldamone AA: Urinary tract infections in the pediatric population. Lebanese Med J (accepted for publication).
36. Hellerstein S: Recurrent urinary tract infections in children. Pediatr Infect Dis 1982;1:271.
37. Hepler AB: Thrombosis of renal veins. J Urol 1934;31:527.
38. Hill DE, Segura JW, Patterson DE: Ureteroscopy in children. J Urol 1990;144:481.
39. Hoberman A, Charron M, Hickey RW, et al: Imaging studies after a first febrile urinary tract infection in young children. N Engl J Med 2003;348:195.
40. Husmann DA, Milliner DS, Segura JW: Ureteropelvic junction obstruction with simultaneous renal calculi: Long-term follow-up. J Urol 1995;153:1399.
41. Husmann DA, Milliner DS, Segura JW: Ureteropelvic junction obstruction with concurrent renal pelvic calculi in the pediatric patient: Long-term follow-up. J Urol 1996; 156:741.
42. Jakobsson BJ, Esbjorner E, Hansson S: Minimum incidence and diagnostic rate of first urinary tract infection. Pediatrics 1999;104:222.
43. Jayanthi VR, Arnold PM, Koff SA: Strategies for managing upper tract calculi in young children. J Urol 1999;162:1234.
44. Kaplan BS, Chesney RW, Drummond KN: The nephrotic syndrome and renal vein thrombosis. Am J Dis Child 1978; 132:367.
45. Karafin L, Stearn TM: Renal vein thrombosis in children. J Urol 1964;92:91.
46. Kaufman JH: Renal vein thrombosis. Am J Dis Child 1958; 95:377.
47. Keren R, Chan E: A meta-analysis of randomized, controlled trials comparing short- and long-course antibiotic therapy for urinary tract infections in children. Pediatrics 2002;109:E70.
48. Kirsch AJ, Perez-Brayfield MR, Scherz AC: Minimally invasive treatment of vesicoureteral reflux with endoscopic injection of dextranomer/hyaluronic acid copolymer: The Children's Hospitals of Atlanta experience. J Urol 2003;170:21.
49. Koff SA, Wagner TT, Jayanthi VR: The relationship among dysfunctional elimination syndromes, primary vesicoureteral reflux and urinary tract infections in children. J Urol 1998;160:1019.

50. Kraus SJ: Genitourinary imaging in children. Pediatr Clin North Am 2001;48:1381.
51. Kuhle S, Massicotte P, Chan A, Mitchell L: A case series of 72 neonates with renal vein thrombosis: Data from the 1-800-No-Clots Registry. Thromb Haemost 2004;92:729.
52. Kurzock EA, Huffman JL, Hardy BE, Fugelso P: Endoscopic treatment of pediatric urolithiasis. J Pediatr Surg 1996; 31:1413.
53. Lackgren G, Wahlin N, Skoldenberg E, et al: Long term followup of children treated with dextranomer/hyaluronic acid copolymer for vesicoureteral reflux. J Urol 2001;166:1887.
54. Landau EH, Gofrit ON, Shapiro A, et al: Extracorporeal shock wave lithotripsy is highly effective for ureteral calculi in children. J Urol 2001;165:23.
55. Layton KL: Diagnosis and management of pediatric urinary tract infections. Clin Fam Pract 2003;5:367.
56. Lerman SE, Liao JC: Neonatal circumcision. Pediatr Clin North Am 2001;48:1539.
57. Levy PR, Tao W: Nephrotic syndrome in association with REV1 in infancy. J Pediatr 1974;85:359.
58. Liao JC, Churchill BM: Pediatric urine testing. Pediatr Clin North Am 2001;48:1425.
59. Llach F, Pepper S, Massry SG: The clinical spectrum of renal vein thrombosis: Acute and chronic. Am J Med 1980; 9:819.
60. Lottmann HB, Archambaud F, Hellal B, et al: 99m Technetium-dimercapto-succinic acid renal scan in the evaluation of potential long-term renal parenchymal damage associated with extracorporeal shock wave lithotripsy in children. J Urol 1998;159:521.
61. Lottmann HB, Archambaud F, Traxer O, et al: The efficacy and parenchymal consequences of extracorporeal shock wave lithotripsy in infants. BJU Int 2000;85:311.
62. Mahant S, To T, Friedman J: Timing of voiding cystourethrogram in the investigation of urinary tract infections in children. J Pediatr 2001;139:568.
63. Malizia AA, Reiman HM, Myers RP, et al: Migration and granulomatous reaction after periurethral injection of Polytef (Teflon). JAMA 1984;251:3277.
64. Matouschek E: Die Behandlung des vesikorenalen refluxes durch transurethrale einspritzung von teflonpaste. Urologe A 1981;20:263.
65. McKenna PH, Herndon CD: Voiding dysfunction associated with incontinence, vesicoureteral reflux and recurrent urinary tract infections. Curr Opin Urol 2000;10:599.
66. Menon M, Resnick MI: Urinary lithiasis: Etiology, diagnosis, and medical management. In Walsh PC, et al (eds): Campbell's Urology, 8th ed. Philadelphia, WB Saunders, 2002.
67. Metreweli C, Pearson R: Echographic diagnosis of neonatal renal vein thrombosis. Pediatr Radiol 1984;14:105.
68. Michaels LA, Gurian M, Hegyi T, Drachtman RA: Low molecular weight heparin in the treatment of venous and arterial thromboses in the premature infant. Pediatrics 2004;114:703.
69. Milliner DS, Murphy ME: Urolithiasis in pediatric patients. Mayo Clin Proc 1993;68:241.
70. Noe HN: The role of dysfunctional voiding in failure or complication of ureteral reimplantation for primary reflux. J Urol 1985;134:1172.
71. Noe HN: Hypercalciuria and pediatric stone recurrences with and without structural abnormalities. J Urol 2000; 164:1094.
72. Noe HN, Stapleton FB, Jerkins GR, Roy S 3rd: Clinical experience with pediatric urolithiasis. J Urol 1983;129:1166.
73. Nuss R, Hays T, Manco-Johnson M: Efficacy and safety of heparin anticoagulation for neonatal renal vein thrombosis. Am J Pediatr Hematol Oncol 1994;16:127.
74. O'Donnell B, Puri P: Technical refinements in endoscopic correction of vesicoureteral reflux. J Urol 1998;140:1101.
75. Onen A, Jayanthi VR, Koff SA: Unenhanced spiral CT: The imaging method of choice in diagnosing renal ureteric calculi in children. BJU Int 2000;85:38.
76. Oner S, Oto A, Tekgul S, et al: Comparison of spiral CT and US in the evaluation of pediatric urolithiasis. JBR-BTR 2004;87:219.
77. Oppenheimer EH, Esterly JR: Thrombosis in the newborn: Comparison between infants of diabetic and nondiabetic mothers. J Pediatr 1965;67:549.
78. Orazi C, Fariello G, Malena S, et al: Renal vein thrombosis and adrenal hemorrhage in the newborn: Ultrasound evaluation of 4 cases. J Clin Ultrasound 1993;21:163.
79. Palmer LS, Franco I, Rotario P, et al: Biofeedback therapy expedites the resolution of reflux in older children. J Urol 2002;168:1699.
80. Pietrow PK, Pope JC 4th, Adams MC, et al: Clinical outcome of pediatric stone disease. J Urol 2002;167:670.
81. Polinsky MS, Kaiser BA, Bacuarte HJ: Urolithiasis in childhood. Pediatr Clin North Am 1987;34:683.
82. Puri P, Chertin B, Velaydham M, et al: Treatment of vesicoureteral reflux by endoscopic injection of dextranomer/hyaluronic acid copolymer: Preliminary results. J Urol 2003; 170:1541.
83. Rayer PRO: Trate des Maladies des Reins. Paris, JB Bailliere, 1841.
84. Reddy PP, Barrieras DJ, Bagli DJ, et al: Initial experience with endoscopic holmium laser lithotripsy for pediatric urolithiasis. J Urol 1999;162:1714.
85. Rizvi SA, Naqvi SA, Hussain Z, et al: Pediatric urolithiasis: Developing nation perspectives. J Urol 2002;168:1522.
86. Roberts WW, Gearhart JP, Mathews RI: Time to recurrent stone formation in patients with bladder or continent reservoir reconstruction: Fragmentation versus intact extraction. J Urol 2004;172:1706.
87. Russinko PJ, Tackett LD: Endoscopic correction of reflux. In Caldamone AA (ed): Atlas Urol Clin North Am 2004;12:55.
88. Schaad UB: Fluoroquinolone antibiotics in infants and children. Infec Dis Clin N Amer 2005;19:617.
89. Schlager TA: Urinary tract infections in infants and children. Infect Dis Clin North Am 2003;17:353.
90. Schuster TG, Russell KY, Bloom DA, et al: Ureteroscopy for the treatment of urolithiasis in children. J Urol 2002;167:1813.
91. Segura JW: Role of percutaneous procedures in the management of renal calculi. Urol Clin 1990;17:207.
92. Shortliffe LD: Urinary tract infections in infants and children. In Walsh P, Retik A, Vaughan ED, Wein A (eds): Campbell's Urology, 8th ed. Philadelphia, WB Saunders, 2002.
93. Shortliffe LM, McCue JD: Urinary tract infections at the age extremes: Pediatrics and geriatrics. Am J Med 2002; 113(Suppl 1A):55S.
94. Slavkovic A, Radovanovic M, Siric Z, et al: Extracorporeal shock wave lithotripsy for cystine urolithiasis in children: Outcome and complications. Int Urol Nephrol 2002-2003; 34:457.
95. Smith SL, Somers JM, Broderick N, Halliday K: The role of the plain radiograph and renal tract ultrasound in the management of children with renal tract calculi. Clin Radiol 2000;55:708.
96. Stapleton FB: Clinical approach to children with urolithiasis. Semin Nephrol 1996;16:389.
97. Stark H: Renal vein thrombosis in infancy. Am J Dis Child 1964;108:430.
98. Stenberg A, Lackgren G: A new bioimplant for the endoscopic treatment of vesicoureteral reflux: Experimental and short-term clinical results. J Urol 1995;154:800.

99. Streif W, Goebel G, Chan AK, Massicotte MP: Use of low molecular mass heparin (enoxaparin) in newborn infants: A prospective cohort study of 62 patients. Arch Dis Child 2003;88:365.
100. Tefekli A, Esen T, Ziylan O, et al: Metabolic risk factors in pediatric and adult calcium oxalate urinary stone formers: Is there any difference? Urol Int 2003;70:273.
101. Tekin A, Tekgul S, Atsu N, et al: A study of the etiology of idiopathic calcium urolithiasis in children: Hypocitraturia is the most important risk factor. J Urol 2000;164:162.
102. Tekin A, Tekgul S, Atsu N, et al: Ureteropelvic junction obstruction and coexisting renal calculi in children: Role of metabolic abnormalities. Urology 2001;57:542.
103. Van Savage JG, Palanca LG, Andersen RD, et al: Treatment of distal ureteral stones in children: Similarities to the American Urological Association guidelines in adults. J Urol 2000;164:1089.
104. Verhagen AD, Hamilton JP, Genel M: Renal vein thrombosis in infants. Arch Dis Child 1965;40:214.
105. Vlajkovic M, Slavkovic A, Radovanovic M, et al: Long-term functional outcome of kidneys in children with urolithiasis after ESWL treatment. Eur J Pediatr Surg 2002;12:118.
106. Vorticky LH, Balfour HH Jr: Cytomegalovirus and renal vein thrombosis in a newborn infant. Am J Dis Child 1974;1276:742.
107. Weinschenk N, Pelidis M, Fiascone J: Combination thrombolytic and anticoagulant therapy for bilateral renal vein thrombosis in a premature infant. Am J Perinatol 2001; 18:293.
108. Williams G, Lee A, Craig J: Antibiotics for the prevention of urinary tract infection in children: A systematic review of randomized controlled trials. J Pediatr 2001;138:868.
109. Zigman A, Yazbeck S, Emil S, Nguyen L: Renal vein thrombosis: A 10 year review. J Pediatr Surg 2000;35:1540.

Chapter  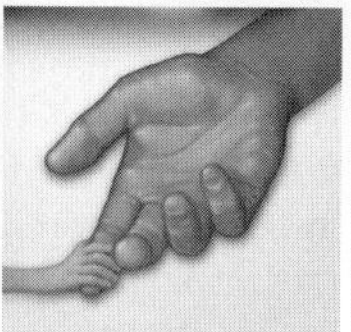

Ureteral Duplication and Ureteroceles

Victor E. Boston

The anatomy, presentation, and treatment of ureteral duplication and ureterocoeles are complex. A clear understanding of the embryology of the kidney, ureter, and bladder is imperative to comprehend the diversity and significance of these abnormalities so that appropriate treatment planning can be undertaken.

TERMINOLOGY

In the past there was confusion surrounding descriptions of the anatomy of ureteral duplication and ureteroceles. In 1984 the Urologic Section of the American Academy of Pediatrics' Committee on Terminology, Nomenclature, and Classification established the currently accepted definitions.[33]

A *duplex (duplicated) system* indicates a kidney with two pelvicaliceal systems. *Complete duplication* indicates a kidney with two ureters that drain separately into or below the bladder. *Incomplete duplication* refers to a kidney with two ureters that fuse into a single unit that drains into the bladder through a single orifice. A *bifid system* is a form of incomplete duplication.

The *upper* or *lower pole ureter* refers to the ureter draining the upper or lower pole of the kidney, respectively. The *upper* or *lower pole orifice* refers to the ureteral orifice associated with the upper or lower pole ureter, respectively. An *ectopic ureter* refers to a ureter that drains into an abnormal site.

A *ureterocele* is a cystic dilatation of the lower end of the ureter where it joins the epithelium of the lower urinary tract. An *intravesical ureterocele* lies entirely within the bladder, whereas an *ectopic ureterocele* has a portion that lies below the bladder neck. Ureteroceles are called *single system* when associated with a single ureter and *duplex system* when associated with a double ureter.

EMBRYOLOGY

There are three primitive excretory systems on either side of the developing embryo posteriorly: the pronephros, mesonephros, and metanephros. These are present from around the third week of gestation and appear sequentially in both time and space from the cranial to the caudad end of the embryo. The kidney develops from the blastema of the metanephros. The pronephros and the mesonephros disappear without a trace except for the mesonephric duct, which represents a primitive excretory duct. This communicates distally with the cloaca in the region of the developing bladder and urogenital sinus and is apparent around the fourth week of gestation.[84] In the normal embryo, toward the end of the fourth week of gestation, an outgrowth (the ureteric bud) appears from the lower end of the mesonephric duct at the point where it bends medially to enter the cloaca (Fig. 113-1A).[84] This appendage is initially a solid core of cells that subsequently canalizes.[17] It grows laterally and superiorly toward the developing kidney and, when it comes in contact with the blastema of the metanephros, induces the normal development of the glomeruli and proximal and distal tubules of the kidney (Fig. 113-1B). The ureteric bud itself forms the ureter, renal pelvis, renal calices and papillary ducts, and collecting tubules of the kidney. There appears to be a limited window of time for this interaction to take place; otherwise, renal dysplasia occurs.[54,68]

The cloaca is divided into the urogenital sinus in front and the alimentary tract behind. Around the eighth week of gestation, the distal end of the mesonephric duct plus a short segment of this duct above the ureteric bud expands and, by differential growth, is incorporated into the lower end of the posterior wall of the developing bladder and urogenital sinus (Fig. 113-1C). At this stage, the mesonephric duct lies below and medial to the ureteral orifice and is referred to as the wolffian duct. As a result of this "migration," the normal ureteral orifice is situated at the superolateral angle of the bladder trigone.[75]

In the male, the mesonephric duct becomes the epididymis, vas deferens, and seminal vesicle and enters the posterior urethra above the external urethral sphincter at the verumontanum. The associated ureteric bud must, therefore, also join the developing bladder and urethra above the external sphincter. The testis that initially arises from a region medial to the developing kidney becomes

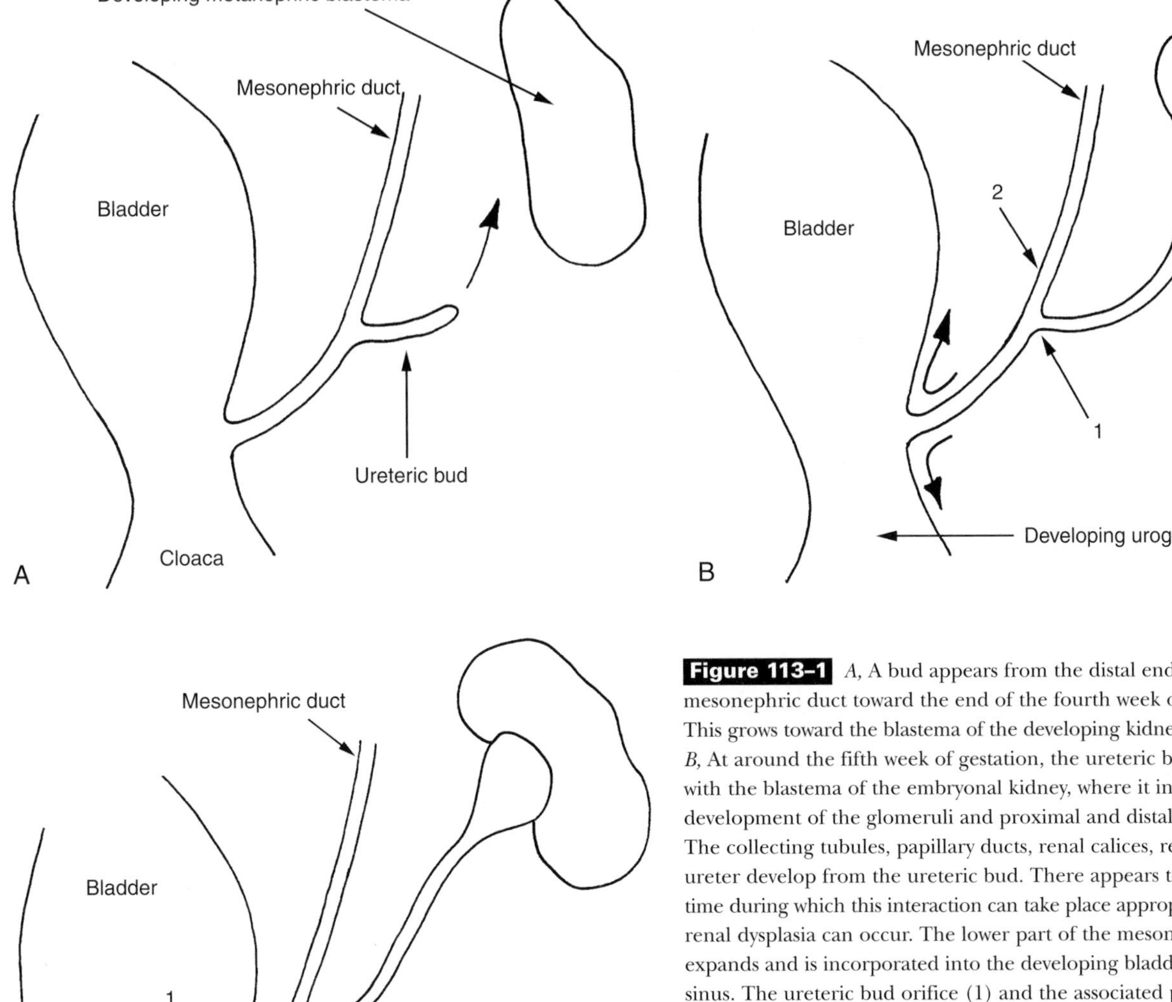

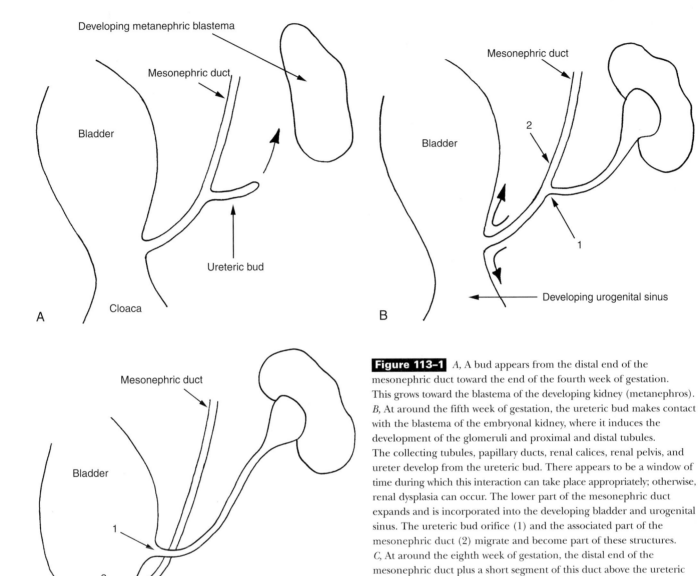

Figure 113–1 *A,* A bud appears from the distal end of the mesonephric duct toward the end of the fourth week of gestation. This grows toward the blastema of the developing kidney (metanephros). *B,* At around the fifth week of gestation, the ureteric bud makes contact with the blastema of the embryonal kidney, where it induces the development of the glomeruli and proximal and distal tubules. The collecting tubules, papillary ducts, renal calices, renal pelvis, and ureter develop from the ureteric bud. There appears to be a window of time during which this interaction can take place appropriately; otherwise, renal dysplasia can occur. The lower part of the mesonephric duct expands and is incorporated into the developing bladder and urogenital sinus. The ureteric bud orifice (1) and the associated part of the mesonephric duct (2) migrate and become part of these structures. *C,* At around the eighth week of gestation, the distal end of the mesonephric duct plus a short segment of this duct above the ureteric bud expands and, by differential growth, is incorporated into the lower end of the posterior wall of the developing bladder and urogenital sinus. At this stage, the mesonephric duct (2), which will become the vas deferens in the male, lies below and medial to the ureteral orifice (1).

attached to the mesonephric duct. As it descends to the deep inguinal ring, the vas deferens (mesonephric duct) crosses the origin of the ureter superiorly as it arches medially and inferiorly to the seminal vesicle at the level of the verumontanum.[75]

In the female, the mesonephric duct becomes Gartner's duct, which lies close to the lateral wall of the vagina. The paramesonephric ducts (müllerian ducts) develop medial to the mesonephric duct. At the caudad end of the embryo, these incorporate the distal end of the remnants of the mesonephric duct where they penetrate the cloaca near the midline. Thus, owing to differential growth, the ureteric bud may migrate with the associated paramesonephric duct structures to sites such as the vestibule, vagina, cervix, uterus, and rectum.[75]

If the single ureteric bud subsequently divides, this can lead to varying degrees of incomplete ureteral duplication. If this process occurs after the ureteric bud reaches the metanephric blastema at around the fifth week of gestation, a bifid renal pelvis results. If the division of the ureter occurs before the fifth week of gestation, two ureters result, with the bifurcation occurring anywhere along the length of the ureter, but with a single opening into the bladder.

When two ureteric buds arise from the mesonephric duct, a complete ureteral duplication occurs (Fig. 113-2A).[16] As with a single system, at around the eighth week of gestation, the distal end of the mesonephric duct plus a short segment of this duct above the ureteric bud expands and, by differential growth, is incorporated into the lower end of the posterior wall of the developing

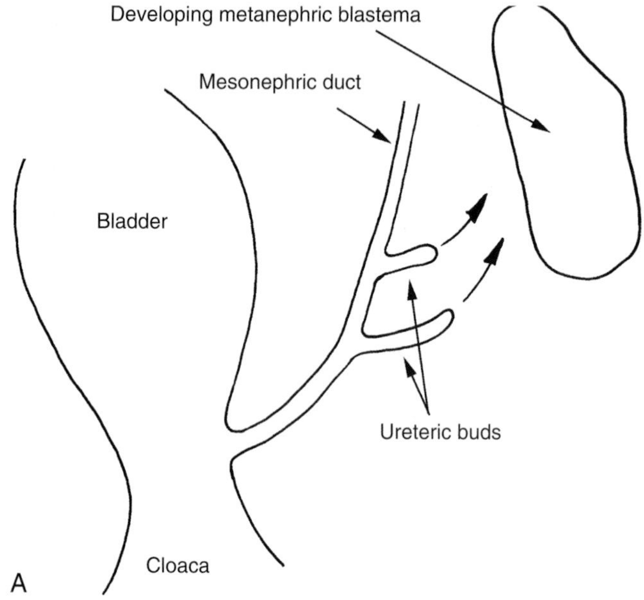

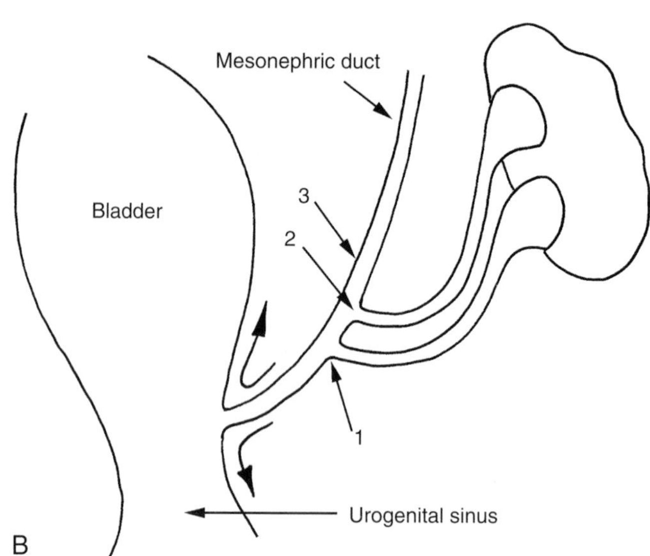

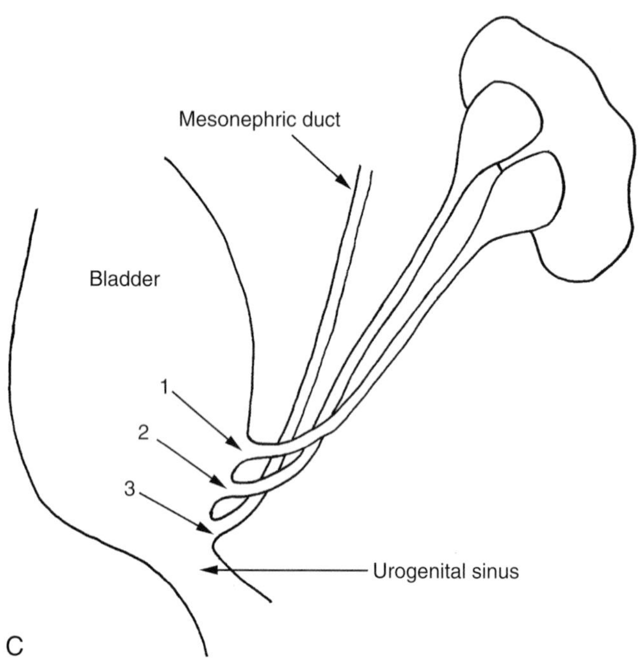

Figure 113–2 *A,* Around the fourth week of gestation, two ureteric buds arise from the distal end of the mesonephric duct. *B,* The most cranial of the two buds develops last. If this is sufficiently delayed, the upper pole ureteric bud may not appropriately induce the blastema of the developing kidney. This may cause renal dysplasia in the upper pole of the kidney. The lower part of the mesonephric duct expands and is incorporated into the developing bladder and urogenital sinus. The ureteric bud orifices (1 and 2) and the associated part of the mesonephric duct (3) migrate and become part of these structures. *C,* At around the eighth week of gestation, the distal end of the mesonephric duct plus a short segment of this duct above the ureteric buds (3) expands and, by differential growth, is incorporated into the lower end of the posterior wall of the developing bladder and urogenital sinus. Note that the lower pole ureteric bud (1) lies above the upper pole ureteric bud (2) and the distal end of the mesonephric duct (3).

bladder and urogenital sinus. What will eventually become the upper pole ureter, therefore, comes to lie inferomedially to the lower pole ureter (Fig. 113-2B and C).

It is thought that the uppermost of the two buds develops last. As a result, the more superior of the two may make contact with the blastema of the upper pole of the kidney too late to induce normal development. In clinical practice, renal dysplasia affecting the upper pole of the kidney is often encountered in duplex systems.[68]

The point of origin of the ureteric bud from the mesonephric duct is also thought to be important. If this occurs too far distally, the developing ureter is incorporated into the bladder early and “migrates” farther superiorly and laterally on the bladder wall. In this location, its eventual attachment to the detrusor vesicae may be so abnormal that vesicoureteral reflux (VUR) occurs.[7,75,77] In clinical practice, in duplex systems, VUR is more commonly observed into the lower than the upper pole ureter. If the origin of the ureteric bud is more proximal on the mesonephric duct, the ureter is incorporated late into the developing urogenital sinus and bladder. In minor variants, the upper pole ureter may be apparent in the bladder but situated more medially and inferiorly on the trigone than normal. In more extreme cases, the ureter may not enter the bladder at all. In the male in this situation, the location of the uretral orifices can be anywhere along the lower mesonephric duct or its derivatives below the bladder neck in the posterior urethra. It should be noted that in all these abnormalities in boys, the upper pole ureter enters the urinary tract above the external urethral sphincter, so urinary incontinence does not occur. In girls, however, the situation is different. During development, the mesonephric duct derivatives can open anywhere caudally from the developing bladder, commonly into the vault of the vagina.[75] Occasionally, in either complete or incomplete duplication, one of the ureters fails to meet the developing blastema of the metanephros. In this case, a blind-ending ureter occurs, with no attachment to the kidney.[56]

Rarely, an inverted Y abnormality is encountered that is presumed to be caused by double ureteric buds arising from the mesonephric duct caudally and fusing cranially before merging above with the blastema of the metanephros.[48] With regard to the site of the ureteral orifice, the same clinical problems are encountered as with complete ureteral duplication.

Even more rarely, ureteral triplication can occur.[61] Although triplication of the ureteric buds from the mesonephric duct accounts for some reported cases, most drain into the bladder through a single orifice. This implies triplication of a single ureteric bud. Quadruplication of the ureter has been reported but is very rare.[11]

The ureteric bud is initially represented by a solid core of tissue that subsequently recanalizes. It is thought that failure of this recanalization process at the junction with the mesonephric duct plays some role in the development of ureteroceles.[17] However, the embryology of this region is complex, and other factors may be important.[76] Theoretically, ureteroceles can occur in otherwise normal single-system ureters or in duplex-system ureters. In practice, they occur most often in duplex systems and are most frequently associated with the upper pole moiety ureter.[76] When a single-system ureterocele is present, it would be expected to be in the normal location within the bladder.[85] However, with an upper pole ureter, it can be in any location below the lower medial side of the trigone. In addition, in girls, this may extend beyond the urethra and present at the opening of the mesonephric duct. The most common position of a ureterocele in duplex systems in both boys and girls is at the bladder neck.[33]

INCOMPLETE URETERAL DUPLICATION

A bifid renal pelvis is a relatively common but usually asymptomatic finding, occurring in about 10% of the population. When incomplete ureteral duplications occur below the level of the renal pelvis, 50% arise in the midureter and 25% each in the proximal and distal ureter.[45] Rarely, one of the ureters ends blindly, presumably because one of the ureteric buds failed to induce the metanephric blastema.[63]

Occasionally, these abnormalities are symptomatic with urinary tract infection (UTI) or flank discomfort.[3] VUR can occur and is thought to be coincidental to the duplication. Rarely, reflux can occur from one ureter into the other, which can also lead to urinary stasis and infection. This is thought to be most likely when the bifurcation occurs in the distal ureter and is rare when the duplication arises in the intravesical portion of the ureter.[15,79] Rarely, ureteropelvic obstruction is observed, usually affecting the lower pole ureter (Fig. 113-3).[59]

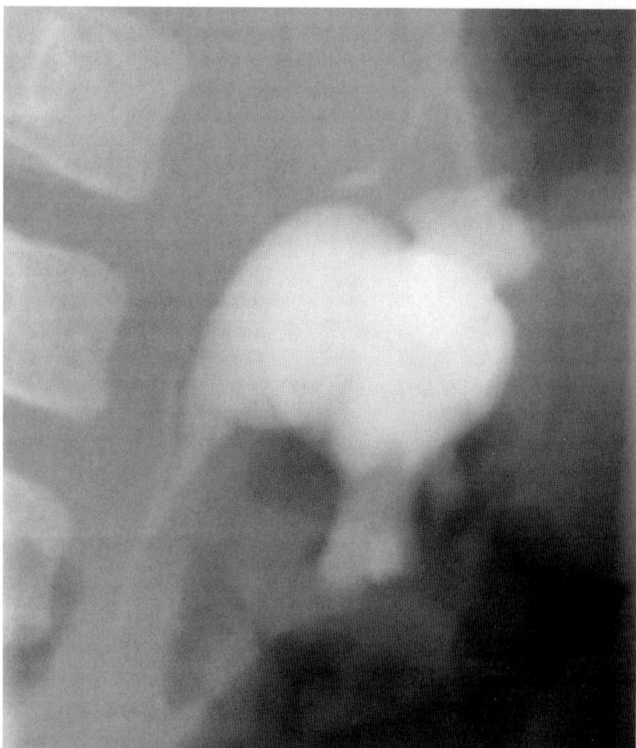

Figure 113-3 Intravenous urogram demonstrating incomplete ureteral duplication of the left kidney, with typical ureteropelvic junction obstruction affecting the lower pole ureter.

In the past, the diagnosis of incomplete ureteral duplication was usually made by intravenous pyelography (Fig. 113-4); today, this investigation is rarely undertaken. Currently, the diagnosis is most often made when investigating coincidental VUR. The two ureters are outlined during either micturating cystourethrography (MCUG)[45] or voiding indirect cystography using a mertiatide (MAG3) or diethylenetriamine pentaacetic acid (DTPA) isotope scan.

In symptomatic cases, treatment is antibiotic prophylaxis or, when medical management fails, surgical intervention. Operative options include reimplantation of both ureters if the duplication is near the bladder[4] or, for duplications arising at a higher level, ureteropyelostomy or uretero-ureterostomy, with excision of one of the ureters distally.[13]

COMPLETE URETERAL DUPLICATION AND URETEROCELE

Incidence and Presentation of Complete Ureteral Duplication

Autopsy studies indicate an incidence of complete ureteral duplication of approximately 0.8%.[16,58] The left and right ureters appear to be equally affected, and bilateral duplication occurs in about 40% of cases.[78] Females are affected twice as often as males.[64] Patients with urinary

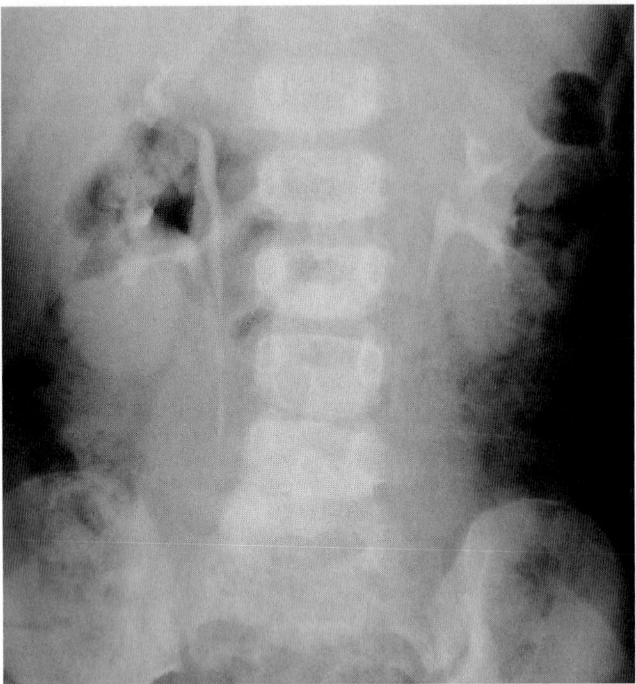

Figure 113–4 Intravenous urogram demonstrating asymptomatic, unobstructed, incomplete ureteral duplication on the right side.

symptoms, such as those associated with UTI, have about a 4% incidence of ureteral duplication.[37] Two thirds of children with duplex systems who present with UTI have VUR.[29] There is a significant familial predisposition. Between 12.5% and 30% of siblings of affected patients also have duplications.[6,8,9] It has been suggested that the mode of inheritance is autosomal dominant with incomplete penetrance.[6,82]

Some girls (but not boys) present with dribbling incontinence if the ureteral orifice is below the external urethral sphincter. This typically occurs even though the child appears to have a normal pattern of micturition.

In addition, this abnormality is often associated with either VUR or obstruction, both of which can result in UTI and renal scarring. There is also a significant predisposition to primary renal dysplasia of the upper pole of the kidney in 90% of cases because of abnormal induction of the blastema of the metanephros by the upper pole ureteric bud.[14] This is thought to be related to the delay in contact between the two structures around the fifth to sixth weeks of gestation. It is known that this dysplasia is greatest in ectopic ureters, particularly when the ureteral orifice is located at or below the external urethral sphincter.[31,54,62,68] Hypertension may result in some patients as a result of either dysplasia or scarring of the kidney.[37,49,53]

VUR typically occurs into the lower pole ureter (Fig. 113-5); this is thought to be related to the abnormal insertion into the detrusor vesicae superior to the normal location at the lateral apex of the bladder trigone.[23] However, reflux occasionally occurs into the upper pole ureter or, paradoxically, in about 10% of cases, into a ureter affected by a ureterocele.[19,69] When VUR occurs into both moieties, the ureteral orifices are usually close together and in a lateral ectopic location.

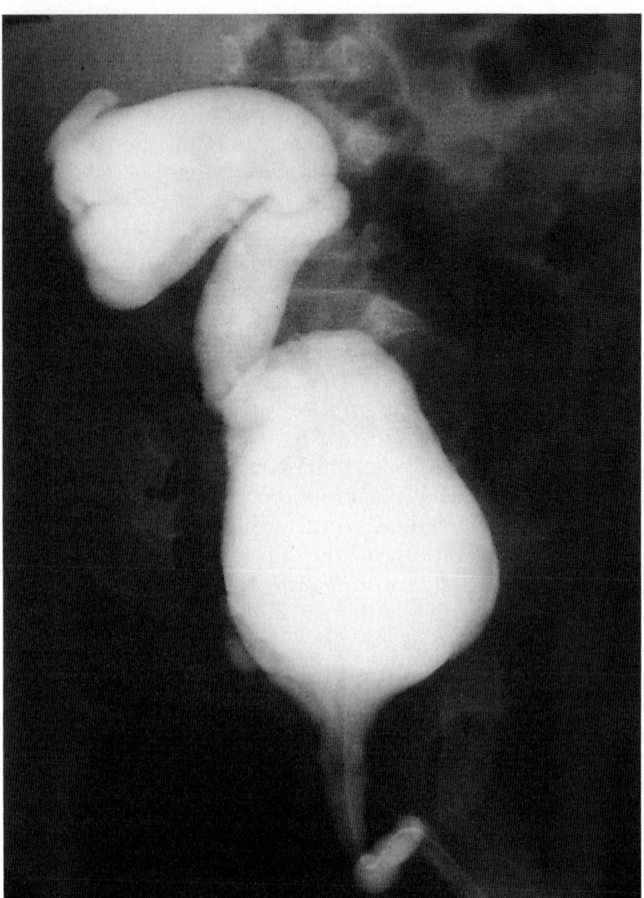

Figure 113–5 Voiding cystourethrogram in a child with a symptomatic urinary tract infection demonstrating right-sided grade 5 vesicoureteral reflux into the lower pole ureter of a complete duplex system.

Typical ureteropelvic junction obstruction also occurs, most commonly affecting the lower pole ureter and with an increased incidence compared with the normal population.[30,80]

Incidence and Presentation of Ureterocele

Autopsy studies indicate an incidence of around 1 in 4000 children.[16] Females are between four and seven times more likely to be affected than males.[27] The left side is affected slightly more frequently than the right.[67] Ten percent of ureteroceles are bilateral,[67] 60% to 80% are ectopic,[55] and 80% are associated with the upper pole ureter of a duplex system.[12] Single-system ureteroceles are uncommon, occur most often in males, and can be associated with other anomalies, including abnormalities of the kidneys such as fusion or ectopia[43] or multicystic dysplasia.[85]

This condition is commonly discovered during the investigation of asymptomatic hydronephrosis, a palpable loin mass, a UTI, or, rarely, when the ureterocele prolapses through the urethra and presents at the vulva.

Various combinations of abnormal anatomy are possible, ranging from simple single-system to complex

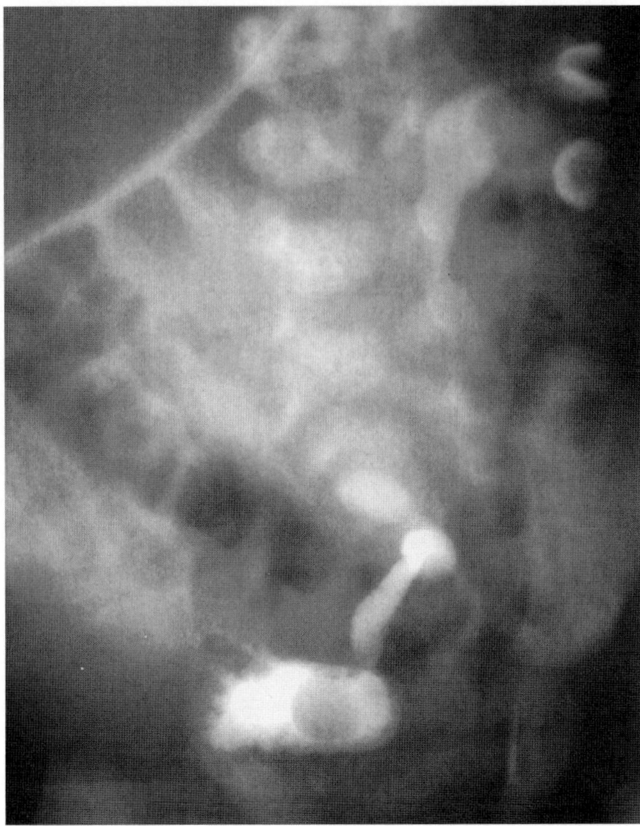

Figure 113–6 Voiding cystourethrogram demonstrating left-sided upper pole ureterocele with grade 4 vesicoureteral reflux into the ipsilateral lower pole ureter of a complete duplex system.

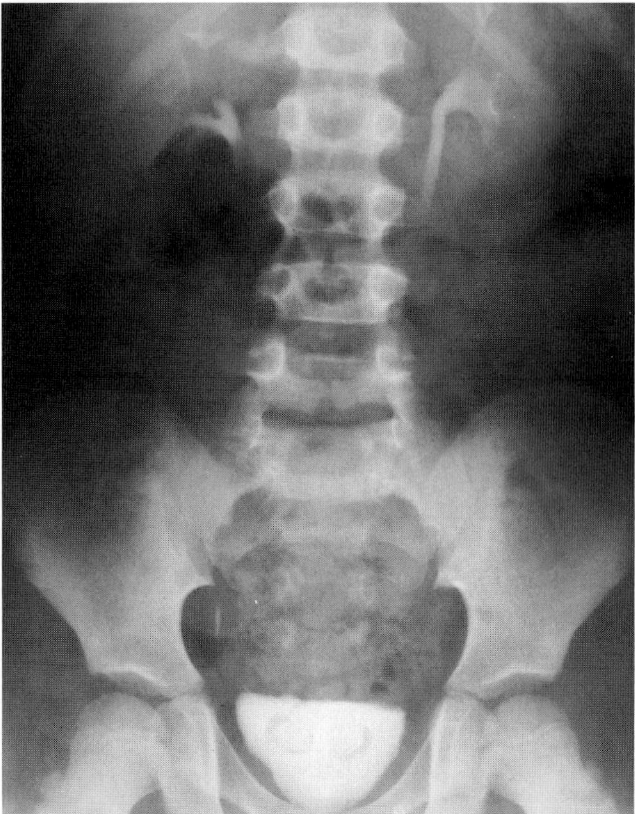

Figure 113–7 Intravenous urogram demonstrating bilateral intravesical ureteroceles associated with functioning single-system renal units.

duplex-system ureteroceles. The renal units associated with ureteroceles are usually nonfunctioning, because most are ectopic.[40] Around 10% to 15% of renal units associated with a ureterocele are situated relatively normally on the bladder trigone and have some residual function that is worth preserving.[32]

Ureteroceles most commonly obstruct the upper pole moiety ureter. This usually leads to significant impairment of the associated renal unit.[24] In extreme cases, when the ureterocele prolapses into the urethra, this can lead to obstruction of the urethra and thus affect all renal units.[26,47] Ureteroceles are the most common cause of urethral obstruction in girls.[51] When duplex ureteroceles are seen, VUR can be expected on the ipsilateral side (Fig. 113-6) in 50% of cases and on the contralateral side in 25%.[12,14,19]

Diagnosis of Complete Ureteral Duplication and Ureterocele

Most children who have not been diagnosed prenatally present with symptomatic UTIs, which in neonates may be severe and potentially life threatening.[32,36] Many of these children have either VUR or obstructed ectopic ureteroceles. As mentioned earlier, in cases of ectopic ureter, when the orifice is below the external urethral sphincter, girls present with typical continuous dribbling incontinence.[69] The clinical history in these circumstances is critical to the diagnosis. Boys with an ectopic ureter associated with either the vas or the seminal vesicle can present with epididymitis.[34,44,73] Occasionally, the diagnosis is delayed until adulthood in individuals without significant VUR or obstruction.[64]

Prenatal ultrasound screening of the kidneys often identifies some degree of hydronephrosis, which is most pronounced with ureteroceles.[83] Although there is no evidence that treatment of these prenatally diagnosed children affects the prognosis for the kidney, symptomatic UTIs can be reduced in frequency.[70,81] These children require further ultrasound assessment and MCUG, followed if necessary by intravenous pyelography or magnetic resonance imaging (MRI). Pyelography is useful for defining the anatomy and often outlines a ureterocele in a ureter associated with a functioning renal unit (Fig. 113-7).[26,40] However, when the affected moiety is nonfunctioning, the findings are more subtle, and changes on ultrasonography, dimercaptosuccinic acid (DMSA) scans, and intravenous urography (IVU) are easily missed.[26,40,60] MRI scanning is particularly useful in these circumstances (Fig. 113-8).[35] In most cases, there is some degree of hydronephrosis that is easily detectable on ultrasonography (Fig. 113-9).[22] In addition, bladder ultrasonography is usually able to demonstrate a ureterocele (Fig. 113-10) that may not be obvious on MCUG. Occasionally, a ureterocele can mimic a bladder diverticulum by prolapsing

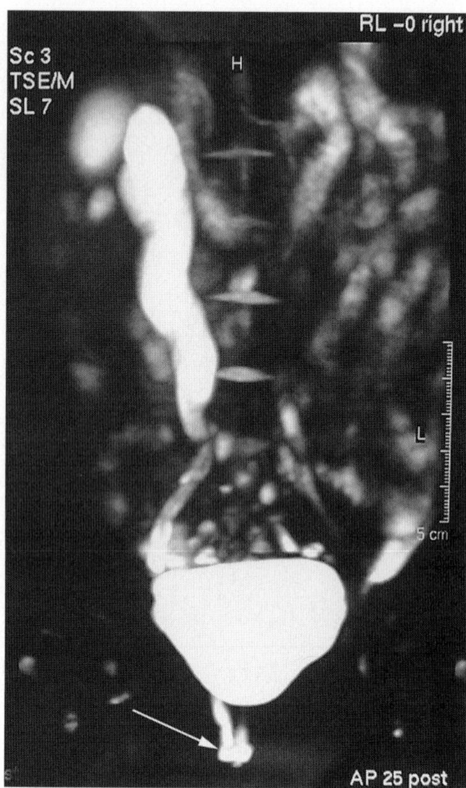

Figure 113-8 T2-weighted magnetic resonance image of a girl with dribbling incontinence. Note the hydronephrotic upper pole moiety of the right kidney, which was nonfunctioning on pyelography. The arrow denotes the insertion of the ureter into the vagina.

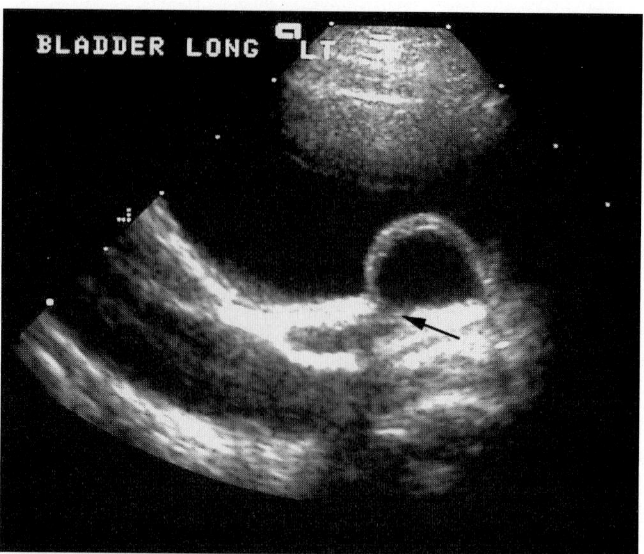

Figure 113-10 Sagittal ultrasound scan of the bladder demonstrating a ureterocele in the bladder base. Note the position of the ureter *(arrow)* as it inserts into the ureterocele.

back along the ureteral lumen at micturition (Fig. 113-11).[21] A nonfunctioning upper pole occurs in up to 90% of ectopic ureters and is apparent on DMSA scans as a negative filling defect (Fig. 113-12); on IVU, this causes the typical "drooping flower" appearance of the displaced lower pole moiety (Fig. 113-13).[40,60] In these circumstances, on IVU, the ureter is often dislocated from its usual, more lateral position and runs a spiral course around the invisible distended ureter that drains the nonfuntioning upper pole (Fig. 113-14).

Radioisotope DMSA scans to assess renal function, scarring, or dysplasia and MAG3 or DTPA renograms to assess obstruction should be deferred until around 6 to 8 weeks

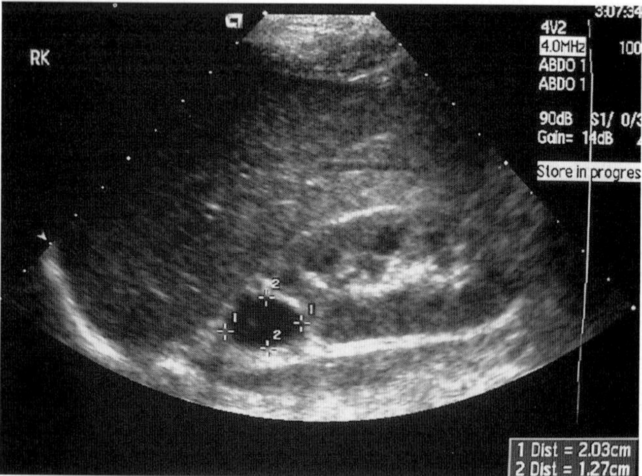

Figure 113-9 Ultrasound scan of the right kidney demonstrating a hydronephrotic upper pole moiety of a duplex system. Note that the lower pole is relatively normal and that there is a clear demarcation between the upper and lower pole moieties.

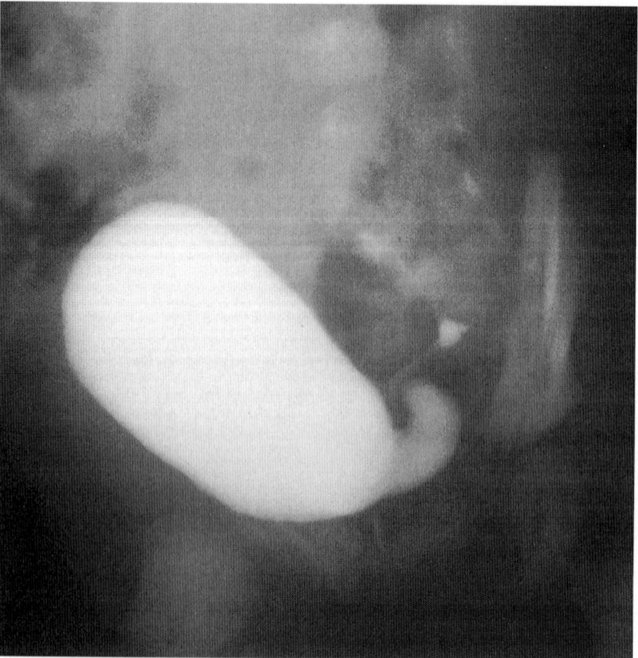

Figure 113-11 Voiding cystourethrogram demonstrating retrograde prolapse of a ureterocele into the upper pole ureter and vesicoureteral reflux into the lower pole ureter on the left side in a complete duplex system. This appearance may be confused with a bladder diverticulum.

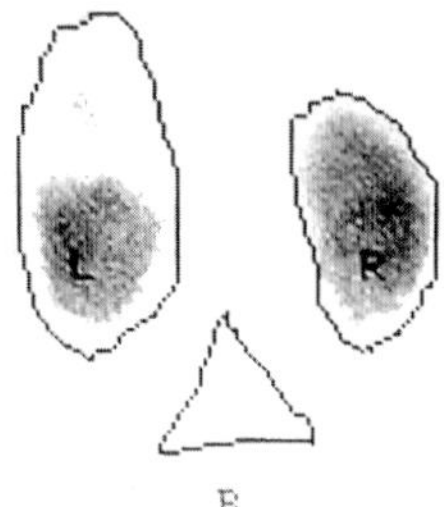

Figure 113–12 DMSA isotope scan demonstrating poorly functioning upper pole moiety in a left-sided complete duplex system. The upper pole ureter was associated with a ureterocele.

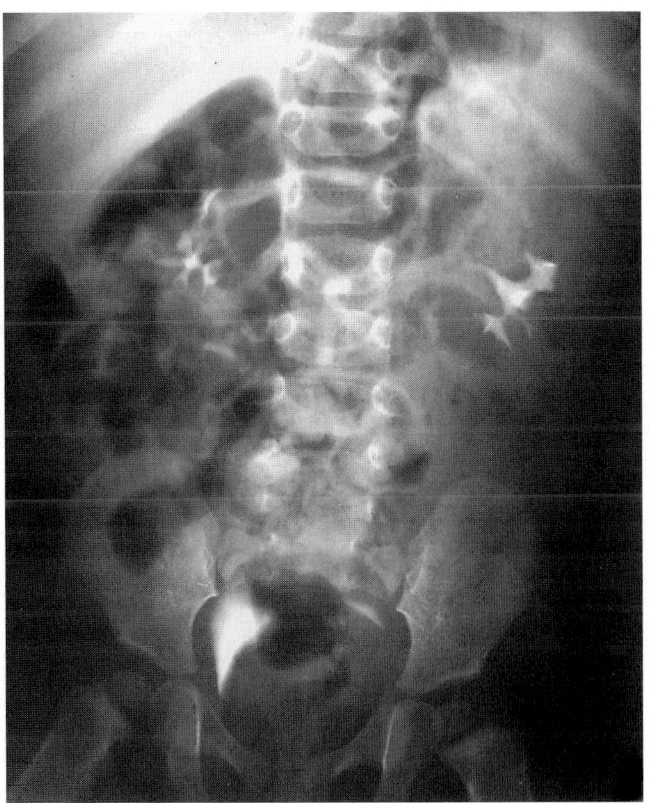

Figure 113–13 Intravenous urogram demonstrating the "drooping flower" sign on the left side. Note the ureterocele occupying most of the bladder base on the left side and the relatively normally functioning lower pole of the kidney, which is displaced downward and laterally by the nonfunctioning hydronephrotic upper pole moiety.

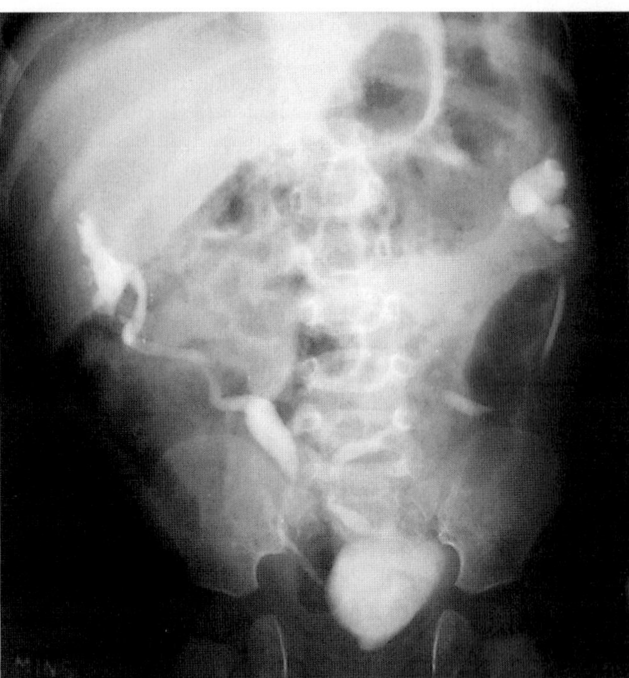

Figure 113–14 Intravenous urogram of bilateral complete duplex systems with nonfunctioning, obstructed upper pole moiety ureters. There is no demonstrable function in either upper pole moiety, and the only sign of abnormality is displacement of the functioning lower pole elements downward and laterally. Note that the lower pole ureters run a spiraling course toward the bladder, indicating the invisible presence of hydronephrotic upper pole ureters. In this case, an intravesical ureterocele is present but is not apparent.

of age because of inconsistent data in younger babies.[18] Indirect voiding radioisotope scans using MAG3 or DTPA can be used instead of MCUG to assess VUR. This is particularly useful in older children, who generally find the latter investigation unpleasant both physically and psychologically.

Treatment of Complete Ureteral Duplication and Ureterocele

Because of the spectrum of pathology in ureteral duplication and ureterocele, management should be individualized. The primary objectives are to reduce the risk of deterioration in renal function, control symptoms, and avoid surgical interventions that risk bladder function. This does not necessarily mean operative management in all cases, and there has been a recent trend toward more conservative measures. The management approaches to VUR, ureterocele, ureteropelvic obstruction, and incontinence secondary to ectopic ureters—the main complications associated with ureteral duplication and ureterocele—are discussed separately.

Vesicoureteral Reflux

Contrary to popular belief, a significant proportion of refluxing units associated with duplex systems resolve spontaneously with time. This is more likely with grade 1 and 2 VUR (up to 85%) than with higher grades.[10,39,52,60] Provided the child remains asymptomatic (as with primary VUR), antibiotic prophylaxis is justified initially. These patients must be followed carefully with sequential DMSA scans to assess the kidneys for scarring and its progression. VUR can be assessed using either indirect MAG3 or DTPA cystography or MCUG. If progressive renal scarring with deteriorating renal function is identified, or if symptomatic upper renal UTIs cannot be controlled by antibiotic prophylaxis, operative intervention is indicated.[2,57]

Endoscopic Treatment

There is much debate about the value of endoscopic treatment of VUR in duplex systems. Recent data suggest that although this technique may be less successful than its use in primary VUR, it is still very effective and should be offered as an option for correction.[39,52,60] This operation was originally described using Teflon paste that was injected under the ureteral orifice.[65] Recently, in view of concerns about migration and the long-term effects of fluorinated hydrocarbons,[46] Deflux has been introduced as a highly successful alternative to the Teflon implant. This material is a dextranomer–hyaluronic acid copolymer.[50,66] The resulting implant compresses the ureteral orifice from behind. This prevents VUR by two mechanisms. First, it alters the axis of the ureteral orifice from one that is parallel to the ureter to one that is at right angles to this plane. This has the effect of creating a "flap valve." Second, the implant itself creates a fibrous capsule that adheres to the underlying detrusor vesicae. When the bladder trigone contracts at micturition, the ureteral orifice, because of its attachment to this fibrous capsule, is drawn medially and toward the bladder outlet, thus increasing the intravesical course of the ureter. This mechanism may be equally important in reducing the risk of VUR. The injection needle is passed through the operating channel of the operating cystoscope, and the beveled tip of the needle is advanced under the ureteral orifice at the 6 o'clock position (see Chapter 112). In duplex systems in which the ureteral orifices are close together, the implant is injected under the upper pole moiety orifice (the more inferomedial). The needle is advanced below both orifices, and the injection is commenced under direct vision until both moiety orifices are compressed. It is unusual to use more than 0.3 mL of implant. When the ureteral orifices are separated by more than a few millimeters, they can be individually injected; however, caution is required when placing the injection under the lower pole orifice because the upper pole ureteral lumen may be entered in error.

Open Ureteroneocystostomy

Reimplantation of the ureters is the traditional method of treating VUR and ureteral obstruction. Because of the gross abnormality of the bladder base in duplex systems, there is a significant risk of damaging the bladder outlet in the course of mobilizing the ureters.[71] There is also a primary abnormality of bladder function in these children that is probably related to bladder outlet obstruction, comparable to that seen in posterior urethral valves.[1] Because of this, it is wise to undertake a urodynamic study before surgery. When the ureteral orifices are situated relatively normally on the trigone, both should be mobilized from the bladder base together, even if only the lower pole ureter is refluxing. This is necessary because the ureters share the same adventitial sheath and blood supply.[28] Attempts to mobilize only the affected ureter will result in ischemia of one or both ureters. Alternatively, both ureters can be mobilized to a level above the common sheath. The ureters can then be rerouted through the bladder wall using either an intravesical cross-trigonal technique or an extravesical method. The objective in both instances is to create a subepithelial tunnel for the ureters that is at least three times their diameter, thus creating a "flap valve" mechanism.

The situation is complicated by the presence of ureteroceles, their location, and whether the associated renal units are functioning (see later). If nonfunctioning renal units are present and symptomatic, they should probably be excised. Rather than risk disruption of the bladder neck and the likely functional consequences, more conservative excision of the affected part of the kidney and ureter to within 2 to 3 cm of the bladder is usually all that is required. These operations have been performed successfully by both open and endoscopic techniques. The ureteral stump that remains is rarely a problem but can be dealt with endoscopically if symptomatic VUR persists.

Open Ureteroureterostomy

In situations in which one of the ureters is refluxing and the anatomy of the bladder base is complex, a better and simpler option may be to undertake an anastomosis to the other "normal" ureter on the ipsilateral lateral side.[2,51] The distal end of the affected ureter can then be excised down to, but not into, the bladder.

Ureterocele

The method of intervention is determined by the size and location of the ureterocele and the function in the related moiety of the kidney. Surgical management varies from simple decompression to excision.

Decompression

For ureteroceles located in the urethra either primarily or by prolapse from the bladder, some form of decompression is usually indicated to avoid the long-term consequences of obstruction to the bladder outlet. Simple excision of a nonfunctioning renal unit down to, but not including, the ureterocele is often insufficient to avoid ongoing infection in the lower ureter. If this method is chosen, it should be combined with decompression or excision of the ureterocele. Decompression is the operation of choice in most cases because it is the simplest and least complicated procedure.[41]

Wide, open deroofing of the ureterocele was performed in the past. The problem with this technique is that if the ureterocele arises from the urethra, epithelial remnants that have not been completely excised may result in urethral obstruction owing to the valvelike nature of these folds.[5] In addition, with this type of operation, postoperative VUR is almost inevitable. Therefore, deroofing usually requires a subsequent antireflux procedure that is normally best undertaken as part of the initial surgery. This more aggressive approach is potentially difficult and is associated with increased morbidity.[71]

Endoscopic techniques have been used for some time to simply incise the ureterocele. This can take the form of either diathermy incision or simple puncture of the cyst.[20,72,74] During this procedure it is important not to overfill the bladder; otherwise, the ureterocele may be compressed, making it difficult to identify. If this occurs, loin compression on the affected side may assist in refilling the ureterocele. The planned decompression point on the ureterocele is important and, if possible, should not overlie the ureteral lumen where it is attached to the bladder base. This can be assessed preoperatively with ultrasonography (see Fig. 113-10). Subsequent VUR can usually be avoided. Simple decompression often reduces the size of the ureter so that secondary procedures, if required, are less difficult. In addition, associated VUR into the lower pole ureter often subsides spontaneously.[14] If VUR occurs, an endoscopic injection of either Teflon or Deflux can be attempted before more radical open surgical techniques are undertaken.[25]

Partial Nephroureterectomy

Partial nephroureterectomy is usually necessary in cases of symptomatic nonfunctioning renal units associated with an obstructive or dysplastic upper pole moiety. The ureterocele should first be decompressed from below (as described earlier); otherwise, residual stasis can lead to infection in the lower ureter, which can compromise reconstruction of the bladder base if this proves necessary in the future. The partial nephrectomy involves identifying the demarcation between the normal lower pole and the nonfunctioning upper pole and excising the ureter of the affected renal unit inferiorly, as near the bladder as possible without compromising the lower pole ureter. The potential problem of excising the lower end of the affected ureter has already been mentioned and is discussed in more detail later.

The operation may be undertaken by either open or endoscopic techniques. With the latter, the lower end of the affected ureter can be mobilized more effectively, but endoscopy is less precise in identifying the demarcation between the abnormal and normal parts of the kidney.[42] Operative time is also significantly longer with endoscopic methods. No prospective assessment of open versus endoscopic techniques has been undertaken.

At open operation, the ureter and pelvis of the affected upper pole moiety are usually distended and easily identified. After dividing the blood supply to the upper pole of the kidney, the upper end of the affected ureter is opened, and a finger is inserted into the renal pelvis. It is then possible to identify the limit of the affected upper pole, and a relatively bloodless plane can be developed between the abnormal and normal renal tissue without entering the caliceal system of the lower pole.[38] As a consequence, repair of the renal wound may be unnecessary, further avoiding compromise of the lower pole of the kidney. The ureter can then be excised down to the pelvic brim without using an additional incision.

Bladder Base Reconstruction

As mentioned earlier, bladder base reconstruction can usually be avoided. Occasionally, however, circumstances dictate that the ureterocele and the lower end of the ureter be excised. This usually produces a significant defect that necessitates a precise anatomic reconstruction; otherwise, disruption of the bladder neck and posterior urethra could lead to incontinence.[71] Fortunately, it is unusual for the ureter to open directly into the urethra; this most often occurs at a level at or just above the bladder neck. The ureterocele, however, often involves the urethra, requiring that the epithelial edges of the cyst be excised completely and then meticulously repaired. Otherwise, obstruction of the urethra may result from either the residual "valvular" remnants of the ureterocele or stricturing due to excessive scarring.[5] For the reasons mentioned earlier, it is usually necessary to mobilize the unaffected lower pole ureter with that associated with the ureterocele. If the upper pole ureter is to be excised, mobilization of both ureters should be extended above the common adventitial sheath. Alternatively, the two ureters can be separated by preferentially taking the adventitia of the affected ureter, thus preserving the blood supply to the "normal" ureter. In any case, the defect in the bladder base and outlet must be repaired without narrowing the outlet. The remaining lower pole ureter can then be reimplanted using either a cross-trigonal or an extravesical method, ensuring an adequate subepithelial course as described earlier. This operation clearly has the potential for significant postoperative voiding problems, and it is advisable to anticipate these complications and perform preoperative urodynamic studies that can be repeated postoperatively if necessary.[1,71]

Ureteropelvic Obstruction

In duplex systems, the obstruction usually affects the lower pole and is more common in boys.[30,80] The decision to operate does not have a good evidence base. Most surgeons are guided by the size and function of the renal unit involved. An increase in hydronephrosis or decreased function of the affected part of the kidney on isotope study is an indication to intervene. However, these parameters are sometimes difficult to assess objectively in a growing child. Loin pain in older children, typically preadolescents, associated with objective evidence of ureteropelvic junction obstruction on MAG3 or DTPA isotope scan, is a common indication for operation.

The surgical options are pyeloplasty or pyeloureterostomy to the unaffected upper pole ureter, with excision of the distal ureter of the affected lower pole.[30,59,80] Partial nephroureterectomy is undertaken when the function of the affected renal unit is severely impaired.

Ectopic Ureter Associated with Incontinence

The operation for renal units associated with ectopic ureters in females with incontinence is relatively simple.

Usually the bladder is unaffected and the ureter is nonobstructed. Using either an endoscopic or an open technique, a partial nephroureterectomy is undertaken to the pelvic brim, without oversewing the ureteral stump. The lower end of this ureter rarely causes problems and usually does not have to be excised.

SUMMARY

Ureteral duplications and ureteroceles represent a spectrum of often overlapping embryologic and anatomic abnormalities. Most unobstructed or nonrefluxing duplications are of no clinical significance and do not require treatment; others are associated with significant morbidity. Most incomplete duplications are of no significance. Complete duplications are often asymptomatic but can be associated with VUR or ureteroceles. Most occur in girls, have an equal incidence on both sides, and are bilateral in about 40% of cases.

VUR is the most common complication of duplications, occurring in about 65% of those with symptomatic UTIs; the reflux is usually into the lower pole ureter. VUR can often be treated expectantly, and there is a significant incidence of spontaneous resolution with low-grade VUR.

A detailed history is often useful in pointing toward the cause of incontinence. Specialized imaging techniques are often required, however, to identify the precise anatomic abnormality; these include ultrasonography, isotope scanning, MCUG, IVU, and MRI.

Based on these data, a planned approach to each case can be taken, with an emphasis on preventing deterioration in renal function, controlling symptoms, and avoiding surgical interventions that could risk bladder function. Endoscopic or open procedures can be employed in those who have deteriorating renal function or uncontrolled symptomatic UTIs. Ureteroceles can usually be treated endoscopically by simple puncture or incision. Radical reconstruction runs a significant risk of secondary bladder dysfunction and should be reserved for more complex anomalies that cannot be treated by other means.

REFERENCES

1. Abrahamsson K, Hansson E, Sillen U, et al: Bladder dysfunction: An integral part of the ectopic ureterocele complex. J Urol 1998;160:1468-1470.
2. Ahmed S, Boucaut HA: Vesicoureteral reflux in complete ureteral duplication: Surgical options. J Urol 1988;140: 1092-1094.
3. Albers DD, Geyer JR, Barnes SD: Clinical significance of the blind-ending branch of a bifid ureter: Report of 3 additional cases. J Urol 1971;105:634-637.
4. Amar AD: Treatment of reflux in bifid ureters by conversion to complete duplication. J Urol 1972;108:77-78.
5. Ashcraft KW, Hendren WH: Bladder outlet obstruction after operation for ureterocele. J Pediatr Surg 1979;14: 819-824.
6. Atwell JD, Cook PL, Howell CJ, et al: Familial incidence of bifid and double ureters. Arch Dis Child 1974;49:390-393.
7. Atwell JD, Cook PL, Strong L, Hyde I: The interrelationship between vesico-ureteric reflux, trigonal abnormalities and a bifid pelvicalyceal collecting system: A family study. Br J Urol 1977;49:97-107.
8. Aubert J, Irani J, Baumert H: Familial ureteral duplication and ureterocele: Two sisters and their father. Eur Urol 2000; 37:714-717.
9. Babcock JR Jr, Belman AB, Shkolnik A, Ignatoff J: Familial ureteral duplication and ureterocele. Urology 1977;9: 345-349.
10. Ben Ami T, Gayer G, Hertz M, et al: The natural history of reflux in the lower pole of duplicated collecting systems: A controlled study. Pediatr Radiol 1989;19:308-310.
11. Bhandarkar AD, Raju AM, Rao MS: Single unilateral ectopic bifid ureter with contralateral orthotopic quadrufid ureter—a rare combination. J Postgrad Med 1997;43:104-105.
12. Brock WA, Kaplan GW: Ectopic ureteroceles in children. J Urol 1978;119:800-803.
13. Busslinger MI, Kaiser G: Surgical significance of the duplex kidney with bifid ureter. Eur J Pediatr Surg 1992;2:150-151.
14. Caldamone AA, Snyder HM III, Duckett JW: Ureteroceles in children: Followup of management with upper tract approach. J Urol 1984;131:1130-1132.
15. Campbell JE: Ureteral peristalsis in duplex renal collecting systems. Am J Roentgenol Radium Ther Nucl Med 1967; 99:577-584.
16. Campbell MF: Anomalies of the ureter. In Campbell MF, Harrison JH (eds): Urology, 3rd ed. Philadelphia, WB Saunders, 1970, pp 1487-1670.
17. Chwalla R: The process of formation of cystic dilatations of the vesical end of the ureter and of diverticula at the ureteral ostium. Urol Cutan Rev 1927;31:499.
18. Conway JJ, Maizels M: The "well tempered" diuretic renogram: A standard method to examine the asymptomatic neonate with hydronephrosis or hydroureteronephrosis. A report from combined meetings of the Society for Fetal Urology and Members of the Pediatric Nuclear Medicine Council–the Society of Nuclear Medicine. J Nucl Med 1992;33:2047-2051.
19. Cooper CS, Passerini-Glazel G, Hutcheson JC, et al: Long-term followup of endoscopic incision of ureteroceles: Intravesical versus extravesical. J Urol 2000;164:1097-1099.
20. Coplen DE, Duckett JW: The modern approach to ureteroceles. J Urol 1995;153:166-171.
21. Cremin BJ, Funston MR, Aaronson IA: "The intraureteric diverticulum," a manifestation of ureterocoele intussusception. Pediatr Radiol 1977;6:92-96.
22. Dalla Palma L, Bazzocchi M, Cressa C, Tommasini G: Radiological anatomy of the kidney revisited. Br J Radiol 1990;63:680-690.
23. de Caluwe D, Chertin B, Puri P: Long-term outcome of the retained ureteral stump after lower pole heminephrectomy in duplex kidneys. Eur Urol 2002;42:63-66.
24. DeFoor W, Minevich E, Tackett L, et al: Ectopic ureterocele: Clinical application of classification based on renal unit jeopardy. J Urol 2003;169:1092-1094.
25. Diamond T, Boston VE: Reflux following endoscopic treatment of ureteroceles: A new approach using endoscopic subureteric Teflon injection. Br J Urol 1987;60: 279-280.
26. Diard F, Eklof O, Lebowitz R, Maurseth K: Urethral obstruction in boys caused by prolapse of simple ureterocele. Pediatr Radiol 1981;11:139-142.
27. Eklof O, Lohr G, Ringertz H, Thomasson B: Ectopic ureterocele in the male infant. Acta Radiol Diagn (Stockh) 1978; 19:145-153.
28. Ellsworth PI, Lim DJ, Walker RD, et al: Common sheath reimplantation yields excellent results in the treatment of vesicoureteral reflux in duplicated collecting systems. J Urol 1996;155:1407-1409.

29. Fehrenbaker LG, Kelalis PP, Stickler GB: Vesicoureteral reflux and ureteral duplication in children. J Urol 1972; 107:862-864.
30. Fernbach SK, Zawin JK, Lebowitz RL: Complete duplication of the ureter with ureteropelvic junction obstruction of the lower pole of the kidney: Imaging findings. AJR Am J Roentgenol 1995;164:701-704.
31. Gartell PC, MacIver AG, Atwell JD: Renal dysplasia and duplex kidneys. Eur Urol 1983;9:65-68.
32. Geringer AM, Berdon WE, Seldin DW, Hensle TW: The diagnostic approach to ectopic ureterocele and the renal duplication complex. J Urol 1983;129:539-542.
33. Glassberg KI, Braren V, Duckett JW, et al: Suggested terminology for duplex systems, ectopic ureters and ureteroceles. J Urol 1984;132:1153-1154.
34. Gravgaard E, Garsdal L, Moller SH: Double vas deferens and epididymis associated with ipsilateral renal agenesis simulating ectopic ureter opening into the seminal vesicle. Scand J Urol Nephrol 1978;12:85-87.
35. Gylys-Morin VM, Minevich E, Tackett LD, et al: Magnetic resonance imaging of the dysplastic renal moiety and ectopic ureter. J Urol 2000;164:2034-2039.
36. Hagg MJ, Mourachov PV, Snyder HM, et al: The modern endoscopic approach to ureterocele. J Urol 2000;163: 940-943.
37. Hartman GW, Hodson CJ: The duplex kidney and related abnormalities. Clin Radiol 1969;20:387-400.
38. Hurwitz RS: Easy method of upper-pole heminephroureterectomy in duplex systems in children. Urol Clin North Am 1990;17:115-119.
39. Husmann DA, Allen TD: Resolution of vesicoureteral reflux in completely duplicated systems: Fact or fiction? J Urol 1991;145:1022-1023.
40. Husmann DA, Ewalt DH, Glenski WJ, Bernier PA: Ureterocele associated with ureteral duplication and a nonfunctioning upper pole segment: Management by partial nephroureterectomy alone. J Urol 1995;154:723-726.
41. Husmann DA, Strand B, Ewalt D, et al: Management of ectopic ureterocele associated with renal duplication: A comparison of partial nephrectomy and endoscopic decompression. J Urol 1999;162:1406-1409.
42. Janetschek G, Seibold J, Radmayr C, Bartsch G: Laparoscopic heminephroureterectomy in pediatric patients. J Urol 1997; 158:1928-1930.
43. Johnson DK, Perlmutter AD: Single system ectopic ureteroceles with anomalies of the heart, testis and vas deferens. J Urol 1980;123:81-83.
44. Jonas P, Sidi A, Hertz M, Many M: A unique combination of congenital genitourinary anomalies in a child. J Urol 1977;118:349-350.
45. Kaplan N, Elkin M: Bifid renal pelves and ureters: Radiographic and cinefluorographic observations. Br J Urol 1968;40:235-244.
46. Kershen RT, Atala A: New advances in injectable therapies for the treatment of incontinence and vesicoureteral reflux. Urol Clin North Am 1999;26:81-94.
47. Klauber GT, Crawford DB: Prolapse of ectopic ureterocele and bladder trigone. Urology 1980;15:164-166.
48. Klauber GT, Reid EC: Inverted Y reduplication of the ureter. J Urol 1972;107:362-364.
49. Kumar R, Madan MS: Renal duplication with hypertension. J Pediatr Surg 1970;5:380-381.
50. Lackgren G, Wahlin N, Skoldenberg E, et al: Endoscopic treatment of vesicoureteral reflux with dextranomer/ hyaluronic acid copolymer is effective in either double ureters or a small kidney. J Urol 2003;170:1551-1555.
51. Lashley DB, McAleer IM, Kaplan GW: Ipsilateral ureteroureterostomy for the treatment of vesicoureteral reflux or obstruction associated with complete ureteral duplication. J Urol 2001;165:552-554.
52. Lee PH, Diamond DA, Duffy PG, Ransley PG: Duplex reflux: A study of 105 children. J Urol 1991;146:657-659.
53. Levy JB, Vandersteen DR, Morgenstern BZ, Husmann DA: Hypertension after surgical management of renal duplication associated with an upper pole ureterocele. J Urol 1997; 158:1241-1244.
54. Mackie GG, Stephens FD: Duplex kidneys: A correlation of renal dysplasia with position of the ureteric orifice. Birth Defects Orig Artic Ser 1977;13:313-321.
55. Mandell J, Colodny AH, Lebowitz R, et al: Ureteroceles in infants and children. J Urol 1980;123:921-926.
56. Marshall FF, McLoughlin MG: Long blind-ending ureteral duplications. J Urol 1978;120:626-628.
57. Miyakita H, Ninan GK, Puri P: Endoscopic correction of vesico-ureteric reflux in duplex systems. Eur Urol 1993; 24:111-115.
58. Nation EF: Duplication of the kidney and ureter: A statistical study of 230 new cases. J Urol 1944;51:456-465.
59. Ossandon F, Androulakakis P, Ransley PG: Surgical problems in pelviureteral junction obstruction of the lower moiety in incomplete duplex systems. J Urol 1981;125:871-872.
60. Pattaras JG, Rushton HG, Majd M: The role of 99m technetium dimercapto-succinic acid renal scans in the evaluation of occult ectopic ureters in girls with paradoxical incontinence. J Urol 1999;162:821-825.
61. Perkins PJ, Kroovand RL, Evans AT: Ureteral triplication. Radiology 1973;108:533-538.
62. Perrin EV, Persky L, Tucker A, Chrenka B: Renal duplication and dysplasia. Urology 1974;4:660-664.
63. Peterson LJ, Grimes JH, Weinerth JL, Glenn JF: Blind-ending branches of bifid ureters. Urology 1975;5:191-195.
64. Privett JT, Jeans WD, Roylance J: The incidence and importance of renal duplication. Clin Radiol 1976;27:521-530.
65. Puri P: Endoscopic correction of vesicoureteral reflux. Curr Opin Urol 2000;10:593-597.
66. Puri P, Chertin B, Velayudham M, et al: Treatment of vesicoureteral reflux by endoscopic injection of dextranomer/ hyaluronic acid copolymer: Preliminary results. J Urol 2003; 170:1541-1544.
67. Royle MG, Goodwin WE: The management of ureteroceles. J Urol 1971;106:42-47.
68. Schulman CC: [Ureter malformations and renal dysplasia—an embryological concept]. Urologe A 1978;17:273-277.
69. Sen S, Ahmed S, Borghol M: Surgical management of complete ureteric duplication abnormalities. Pediatr Surg Int 1998;13:61-64.
70. Shankar KR, Vishwanath N, Rickwood AM: Outcome of patients with prenatally detected duplex system ureterocele; natural history of those managed expectantly. J Urol 2001; 165:1226-1228.
71. Sherman ND, Stock JA, Hanna MK: Bladder dysfunction after bilateral ectopic ureterocele repair. J Urol 2003;170: 1975-1977.
72. Singh SJ, Smith G: Effectiveness of primary endoscopic incision of ureteroceles. Pediatr Surg Int 2001;17:528-531.
73. Slaughenhoupt BL, Mitcheson HD, Lee DL: Ureteral duplication with lower pole ectopia to the vas: A case report of an exception to the Weigert-Meyer law. Urology 1997;49:269-271.
74. Smith C, Gosalbez R, Parrott TS, et al: Transurethral puncture of ectopic ureteroceles in neonates and infants. J Urol 1994;152:2110-2112.
75. Tanagho EA: Embryologic basis for lower ureteral anomalies: A hypothesis. Urology 1976;7:451-464.
76. Tanagho EA: Ureteroceles: Embryogenesis, pathogenesis and management. J Contin Educ Urol 1979;7:451.

77. Tanagho EA, Hutch JA: Primary reflux. J Urol 1965;93: 158-164.
78. Timothy RP, Decter A, Perlmutter AD: Ureteral duplication: Clinical findings and therapy in 46 children. J Urol 1971;105:445-451.
79. Tresidder GC, Blandy JP, Murray RS: Pyelo-pelvic and uretero-ureteric reflux. Br J Urol 1970;42:728-735.
80. Ulchaker J, Ross J, Alexander F, Kay R: The spectrum of ureteropelvic junction obstructions occurring in duplicated collecting systems. J Pediatr Surg 1996;31:1221-1224.
81. Upadhyay J, Bolduc S, Braga L, et al: Impact of prenatal diagnosis on the morbidity associated with ureterocele management. J Urol 2002;167:2560-2565.
82. Whitaker J, Danks DM: A study of the inheritance of duplication of the kidneys and ureters. J Urol 1966;95: 176-178.
83. Whitten SM, McHoney M, Wilcox DT, et al: Accuracy of antenatal fetal ultrasound in the diagnosis of duplex kidneys. Ultrasound Obstet Gynecol 2003;21:342-346.
84. Williams PL: Embryology—urinary and reproductive systems. In Gray's Anatomy: The Anatomical Basis of Medicine and Surgery, 38th ed. London, Churchill Livingstone, 1995, pp 199-204.
85. Zerin JM, Baker DR, Casale JA: Single-system ureteroceles in infants and children: Imaging features. Pediatr Radiol 2000;30:139-146.

Chapter 114

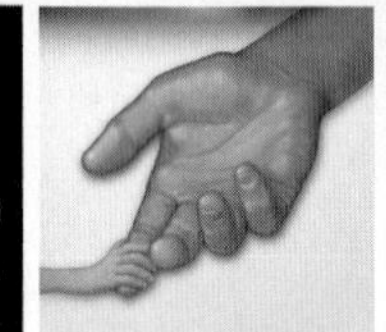

Megaureter and Prune-Belly Syndrome

Mark C. Adams and W. Hardy Hendren III

MEGAURETER

Megaureter describes a ureter that is abnormally enlarged. The ureter may be greatly elongated and tortuous as well. In general, the two principal pathologic types of megaureter are those that are obstructed and those with massive vesicoureteral reflux (Fig. 114-1). If a megaureter ends ectopically in the bladder neck or urethra, it may be obstructed during the resting state but demonstrate reflux during voiding when the bladder neck and urethra open. In some cases, the bladder is normal, and the abnormality is located in the distal ureteral segment. In other cases, megaureter may be secondary to bladder dysfunction. For example, impressive megaureters are seen in some males with high-grade urethral obstruction from posterior urethral valves. Ablating the valves can decrease intravesical voiding pressure and allow decompression of the ureters in time. Similarly, a neuropathic bladder secondary to meningomyelocele can cause physiologic obstruction of the bladder outlet with secondary megaureter. Occasionally, megaureters may represent a dysmorphic anomaly without obstruction or reflux despite the dilation. Megaureters with such pathophysiology may be classified according to an international system proposed in 1977.[69]

In addition to obstructed and refluxing megaureters, some megaureters may be both. The pathophysiology is that of a distal adynamic segment with a short intramural tunnel. This situation has the potential for increasing hydronephrosis as a result of reflux with poor drainage back into the bladder.

When the abnormality is intrinsic in the lower part of the ureter, the megaureter may be a unilateral problem, especially when it is a typical obstructive megaureter. These cases classically have a fibrous terminal ureter with a variety of histologic and ultrastructural abnormalities that cause obstruction.[35,39] Some have referred to this abnormality as an adynamic segment; it is not, however, comparable to the adynamic segment of the lower colon in Hirschsprung's disease or the lower part of the esophagus in achalasia. The ureteral orifice usually looks normal in obstructive megaureter, and true stenosis is rarely noted. Typically, a ureteral catheter can be passed through it without difficulty. The ureteral orifice of a refluxing megaureter is usually abnormally dilated. Indeed, an endoscope can readily be passed up some such megaureters. In primary reflux, there is an inadequate one-way valvular mechanism related to the diameter of the ureter and the length of submucosal ureter within the bladder wall.

Ureterocele and ectopic ureter are commonly associated with megaureter, especially in a female infant with a duplex collecting system; such cases are often accompanied by reflux into the ipsilateral lower pole ureter (see Chapter 113). Rarely, megaureter is the result of excessive urine flow, such as that seen in diabetes insipidus. The prune-belly syndrome features abnormal development of the entire urinary tract, including the ureters, which can be very elongated and tortuous. Microscopic section of such ureters may show decreased musculature and excessive connective tissue in the ureteral wall, often affecting the lower part of the ureter more than the mid or upper segments.

Megaureters are typically found in two patient populations. Newborns with the problem are usually identified in follow-up of antenatally detected hydronephrosis. The incidence of megaureter relative to other congenital upper tract anomalies is higher in this group than in older children with symptoms. The most common manifestation in older children is urinary tract infection, although some children may have intermittent pain from obstruction or hematuria. Infants may show failure to thrive. Whenever megaureters are encountered during urologic evaluation, the entire urinary tract must be examined to determine whether it is a primary or secondary problem. The kidneys and ureters are often first visualized by ultrasonography. Intravenous pyelography may also be useful; however, the diagnosis of obstruction is most often made by nuclear imaging with diuretic washout. The drainage curve after diuresis is informative, but care must be taken that the area of interest includes the entire upper system (ipsilateral kidney and ureter). Measurement of drainage

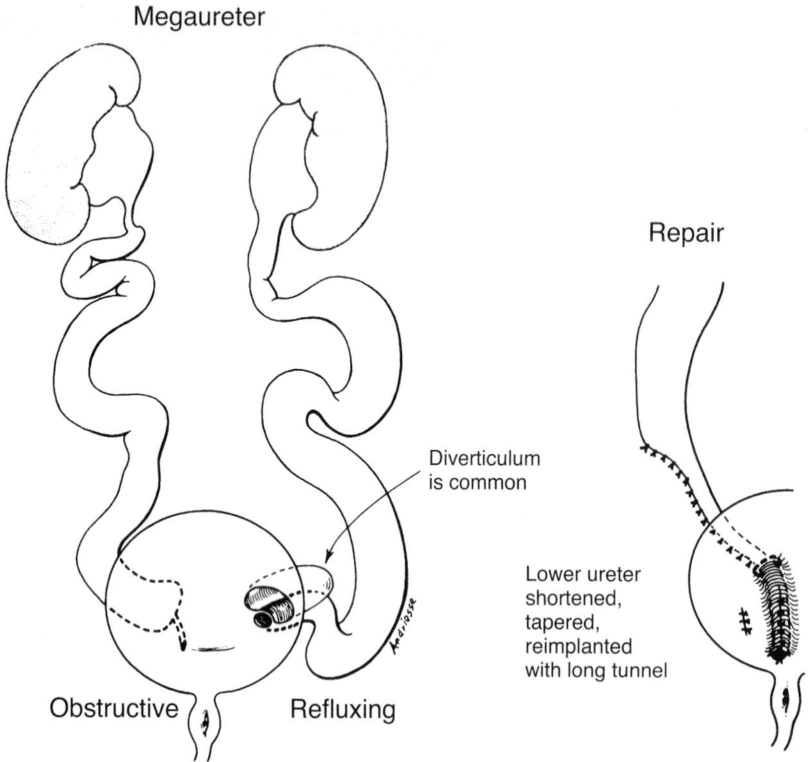

Figure 114–1 Types of megaureter and scheme of lower repair.

of radionuclide out of the kidney into the ureter and not the bladder can lead to a false-negative examination. Particularly in newborns evaluated for antenatally detected hydronephrosis, the function of the kidney must be considered when interpreting nuclear renography, and significantly decreased relative function is an indication for surgical intervention. Any decline in function on serial renography is a strong indication for immediate repair. Antegrade pyelography performed by inserting a needle into the kidney and infusing contrast medium can be helpful in selected cases to further define the anatomy and measure and record differential pressures between the upper tract and the bladder. Cystography is mandatory and shows the ureteral anatomy if reflux is present. Urodynamic study may also be a valuable adjunct in assessing these cases if any bladder abnormality is suspected. Temporary placement of an indwelling urethral catheter may likewise differentiate between primary and secondary megaureter on serial imaging. Cystoscopy should define the appearance of the lower ureteral segments but is generally performed only at the time of reconstructive surgery. As noted earlier, the orifices in obstructive megaureter usually look normal; in refluxing megaureter, they are generally widely dilated with a "gopher hole" appearance. If the primary problem is abnormal bladder dynamics, anticholinergic therapy with or without intermittent catheterization may result in improvement in ureteral dilation. If the patient has urethral valves, fulgurating the valves may suffice. Valves occur in a spectrum of severity.[22] Thus, treatment may be valve fulguration in some, valve fulguration followed by early megaureter repair in others, or occasionally, valve ablation and immediate megaureter reconstruction.[21]

The widespread use of intrauterine ultrasonography has allowed early diagnosis of many cases of megaureter. Affected babies should undergo a complete urologic investigation after birth. In those with no reflux, obstructive megaureters may improve spontaneously in the postnatal period. Thus, in some infants with mild or moderate obstructive excretory patterns and acceptable renal function, serial observation may be considered for a limited time to see whether spontaneous improvement occurs.[3,37] If improvement is not clear-cut, surgery should be performed. The retrovesical ureteral diameter is a fair predictor of the likelihood of resolution of hydronephrosis or the necessity for surgical intervention in the absence of reflux.[40]

In summary, indications for repair of megaureter vary with the etiology. In cases of primary obstructive megaureter, poor renal function (≤35% to 40% of total function by renography), a recurrent infection, scarred kidney, decreasing function on serial studies, or symptoms are clear indications for intervention. Bilateral megaureters or one involving a solitary renal unit threaten total renal function and should be treated more aggressively. Finally, failure to improve after a reasonable period of observation is an indication for surgical repair. Primary reflux into a megaureter, except in a newborn with normal renal function, is unlikely to resolve and usually will require repair. Secondary reflux may resolve with treatment of primary bladder outlet obstruction or bladder dysfunction. Intervention, when indicated, is virtually always definitive repair because the results are good even when dealing with large ureters in neonates. Diversion by cutaneous ureterostomy has occasionally been used for an infected system or when function in a neonate is so poor that it is not clear whether repair or nephrectomy is more appropriate. In such settings, temporary percutaneous nephrostomy drainage may be just as effective and less morbid. As such, cutaneous ureterostomy is rarely necessary.

Surgical Technique

In greater than 50% of cases when surgical repair is indicated, only the lower segment of the ureter requires reconstruction.[18,20,55,57,74] Although the upper part of the ureter may be tortuous, it often improves in time if the lower segment is repaired and obstruction or reflux is relieved. This type of surgery requires gentle and meticulous technique based on the principles of standard antireflux repair. The ureter should be minimally handled with forceps because they can injure its delicate wall. The ureter should be mobilized sufficiently to allow enough tapering and reimplantation into the bladder without angulation or tension. Its blood supply must be preserved. The ureter should enter into the bladder through the fixed portion of the posterior wall at a point that will prevent it from becoming obstructed or angulated when the bladder fills. The ratio of tunnel length to the diameter of the ureter must be sufficient to prevent reflux, usually 4 or 5 to 1.

Repair of Lower Megaureter

The surgical steps for lower megaureter repair are shown in Figure 114-2. The authors prefer a transverse suprapubic skin incision. A vertical fascial incision is preferable to give easy access not only to the bladder but also to the middle and lower third of the ureter. The Denis Browne universal retractor provides ideal exposure. Exposure or mobilization of the middle third of the ureter is rarely necessary in routine cases but may be accomplished by medial reflection of the colon.

As shown in Figure 114-2A, a plastic catheter is sewn into the ureteral orifice for manipulation. After the orifice is circumscribed, ureteral mobilization begins intravesically and continues until mobilization is no longer easy. Muscular and vascular attachments to the ureter within the intramural tunnel are divided and then cauterized on the bladder side but not the ureteral side. Dissection is then continued outside the bladder along the hypogastric vein. The lateral umbilical ligament is encountered and divided to allow upward and medial retraction of the peritoneum. After dissection along the anterior aspect of the ureter from below, it can be pulled through and exposed in the gutter. Paravesical dissection, which can injure the bladder's nerve supply, should be minimized. As the ureter is mobilized upward, all periureteral tissue should be reflected toward the ureter to maintain its collateral blood supply (Fig. 114-2B). During dissection of the ureter from peritoneum located medially to it, the peritoneum, not the ureter, should be skeletonized. In males, the vas deferens should be identified where it lies on the peritoneum and protected.

In cases with extreme tortuosity and in reoperative cases, the colon must be reflected medially for higher mobilization of the ureter. A vertical midline incision is preferred in such cases. Mobilization of the ureter can be facilitated if filled with saline.

After careful mobilization, the periureteral tissue is undermined on the lateral aspect of the ureter and then opened to expose the wall to be tapered (Fig. 114-2C). During our first 20 years of experience with repairing megaureters, which began in 1959, special megaureter clamps were used to exclude redundant circumference as an aid in tapering ureters. Some surgeons continue to find them very useful. In more recent years, however, we have not used the special clamps because the vascular periureteral tissue can be laid back, preserved, and then closed over the trimmed ureter more easily without clamps. The segment to be tapered is marked with a skin pencil and trimmed appropriately (Fig. 114-2D). Excision of redundant ureteral wall posteriorly places the eventual ureteral closure against the bladder muscle rather than next to mucosa. Occasionally, the dominant vessels in the ureteral adventitia are found there and should be avoided and preserved. It is important to not make the ureter too narrow, and it should be noted that 3 to 4 mm of ureteral circumference is used for closure of the ureter. Closure should be performed over a 10-French catheter, except in infants, in whom 8 French may be more appropriate. Closure should never be tight over the catheter.

The ureter is closed with a running, locking suture (Fig. 114-2E). It is helpful to interrupt the last few sutures, which allows shortening during reimplantation if necessary. The periureteral tissue that had been saved is then closed to seal the primary suture line. Both layers should be closed with fine absorbable suture. It can be helpful to retain the tip of the ureter as a handle and then trim it off after placing the first anchoring sutures during reimplantation. The adynamic segment of an obstructed megaureter should be excised in this manner.

Selection of the new hiatus through which to bring the ureter (Fig. 114-2F) is of prime importance. One mistake is to make the hiatus too lateral, which can result in angulation of the ureter and obstruction when the bladder fills. If the hiatus is located in the back wall of the bladder, this problem will not occur. The new hiatus must be large enough that it does not compress the ureter. Incising the lower rim of the new hiatus helps create a smooth course for the ureter. Care must be taken to avoid injury to the vas in males at this point in the repair.

After the ureteral hiatus has been prepared, the mucosa can be opened widely to prepare a bed in which to place the ureter (Fig. 114-2G). Opening the mucosa is more accurate than tunneling beneath intact mucosa. There is no disadvantage with this approach if the suture line in the ureter lies posteriorly against bladder muscle. In some bladders (such as with prune-belly syndrome or a neuropathic bladder), elevating mucosa is difficult and requires tedious sharp dissection. The former muscular hiatus is closed precisely. If a paraureteral diverticulum is present before surgery, the bladder mucosa must be dissected free from the original hiatus to eliminate the diverticulum.

The ureter is then sutured in its bed (Fig. 114-2H). The distal anchoring sutures at the orifice should include the detrusor and mucosa and a full thickness of ureter. The remainder of the orifice is completed with

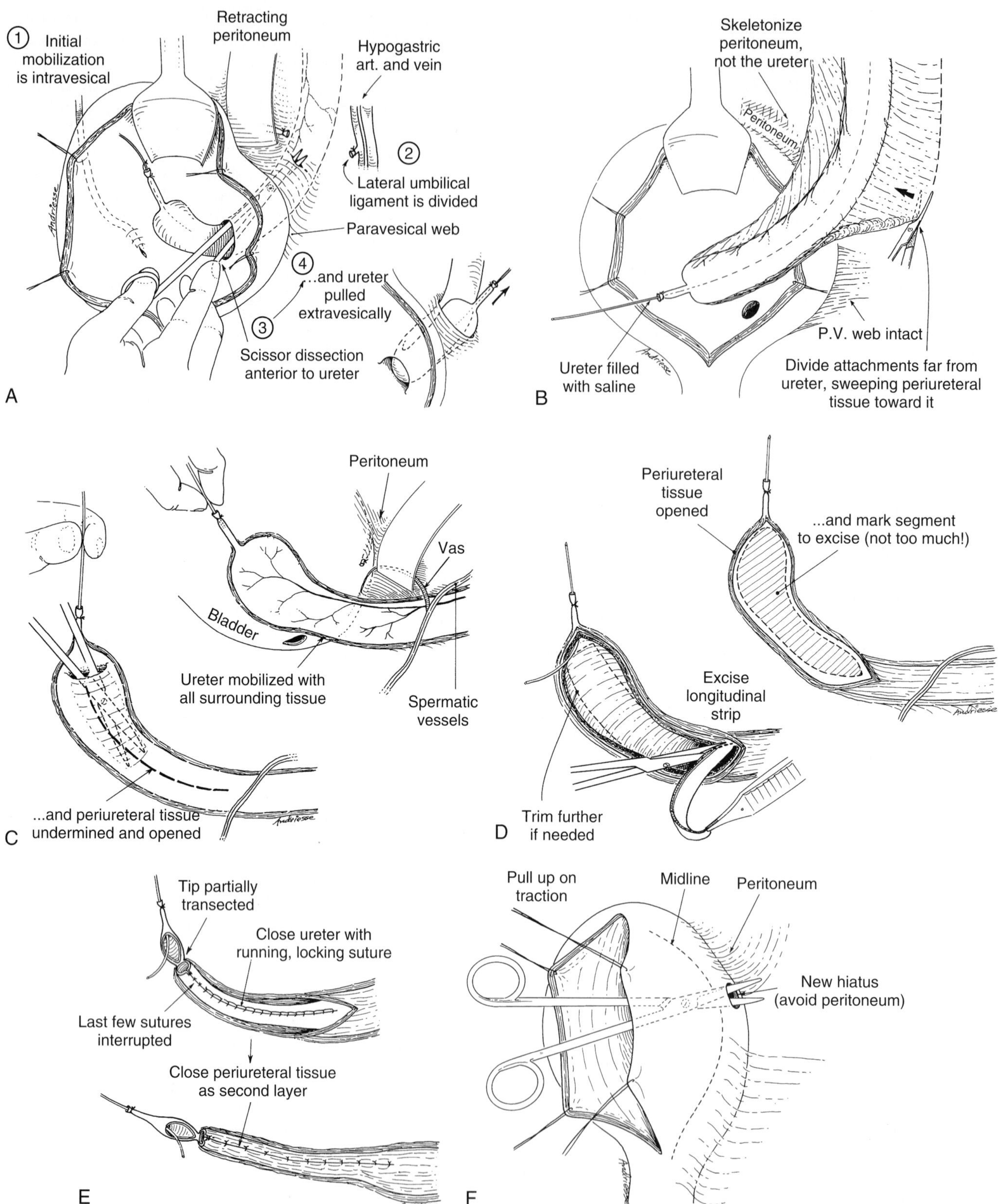

Figure 114–2 Lower ureter repair. *A*, Initial intravesical mobilization. *B*, Extravesical mobilization. P.V., paravesical. *C*, Opening the periureteral tissue. *D*, Trimming of the lower ureter. *E*, Closing the lower ureter. *F*, Preparing a new hiatus.

Continued

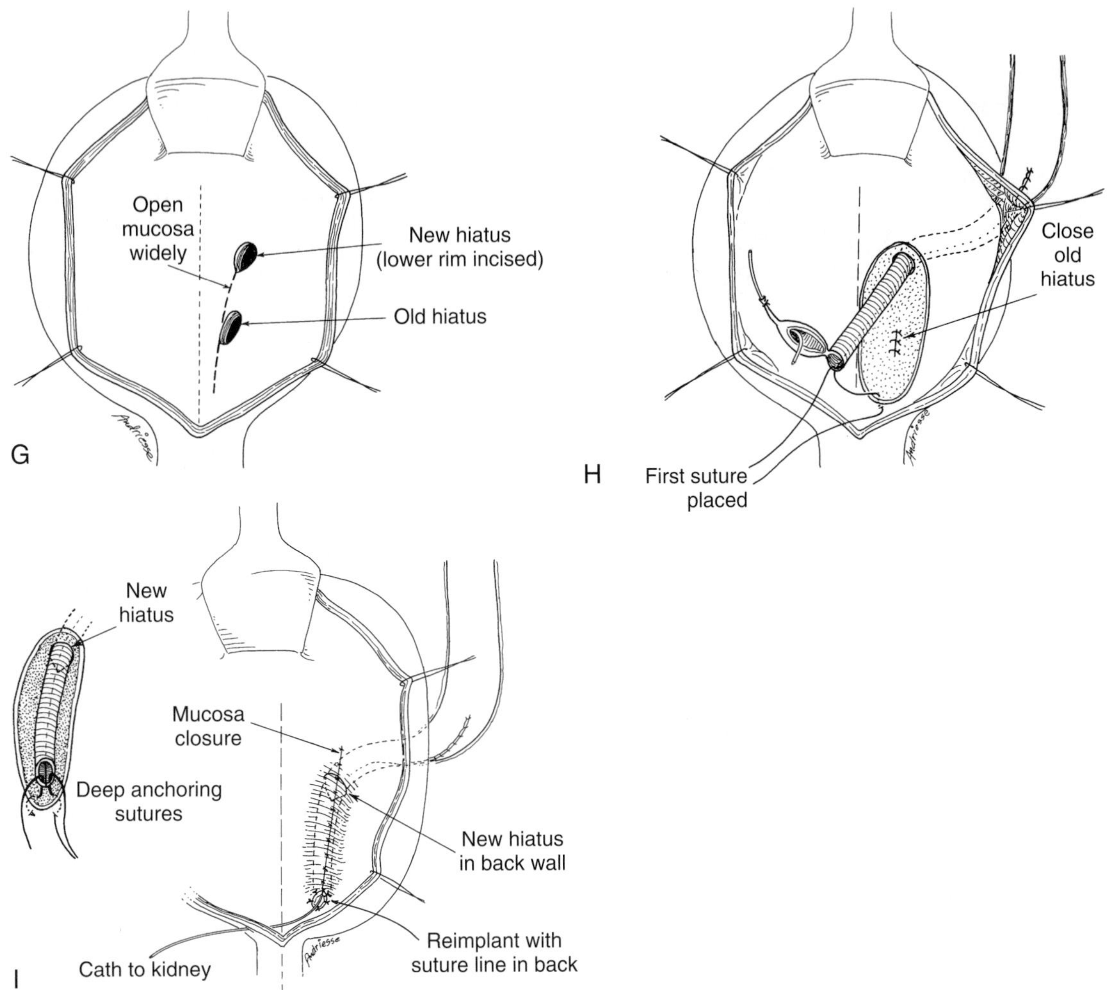

Figure 114-2—Cont'd *G*, Creating a bed for a tapered reimplant. *H*, Suturing the tapered ureter in its tunnel. *I*, Completed repair.

mucosa-to-mucosa sutures. The tapered back wall of the ureter lies against the muscle of the bladder. The tapering should begin proximally enough that it extends well outside the eventual hiatus. The taper should begin gradually to avoid the creation of an outpouching in the ureter that can behave as a diverticulum.

Figure 114-2I shows the completed repair. The mucosa is closed over the tapered ureter. A No. 5 feeding catheter is passed through the opposite bladder wall and up the ureter to the kidney to drain it for 10 to 12 days after surgery. Rarely, a double-J indwelling stent can be used. Nephrostomy drainage is seldom necessary. The technique of megaureter repair as just described is our preference for these cases. Some surgeons favor a cross-trigonal reimplantation technique, but it should be considered only if the trigone is wider than long so that a long intramural tunnel is provided. Both refluxing and nonrefluxing megaureters have been repaired extravesically.[41,54] In patients with bilateral megaureters, we routinely repair the lower segments of both ureters simultaneously.

For bladder drainage after the repair, it is best to use a straight rather than a Foley catheter through the urethra so that the balloon does not compress or irritate the ureteral repair. Only rarely is a suprapubic tube used, for example, in a patient undergoing incontinence surgery on the bladder outlet simultaneously. Ten to 12 days after surgery, contrast studies are performed by injection through the ureteral drainage catheters. Such testing rules out a leak, which is rare. The catheters are then removed, one side at a time if both sides have been repaired. Measuring urine output after each ureteral catheter is taken out indicates whether each kidney is draining appropriately.

Imbrication

The classic description of megaureter repair involves excision of part of the ureteral wall to reduce its circumference, and this is our preference. Plication or folding may be considered for a moderately dilated ureter, although such techniques may create an excessive bulky ureteral wall to reimplant when the ureter is severely dilated or thickened. This was introduced by Starr[71] and Kalicinski et al.[30] as a method to reduce the likelihood of devascularization of the ureter. We believe this is very rare if the surgery is performed as seen in Figure 114-4. In either type of plication, atraumatic clamps are briefly placed on the ureter to mark redundancy around an appropriately sized catheter. Again, the clamps should be placed so that they avoid the major blood supply in the adventitia.

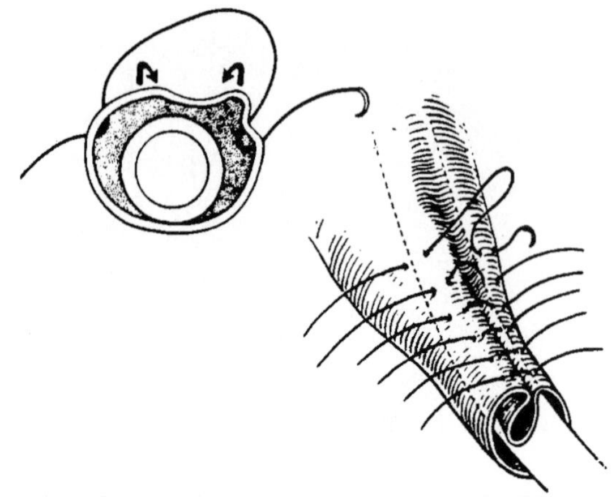

Figure 114–3 Ureteral plication performed with small interrupted absorbable sutures placed in Lembert fashion. (From Keating MA, Retik AB: Management of failures of ureteroneocystostomy. In McDougal WS [ed]: Difficult Problems in Urologic Surgery. Chicago, Year Book, 1989, p 131.)

After removal of the clamps, the ureteral wall is plicated by one of two techniques. Starr[71] described placement of Lembert sutures along the clamp marks (Fig. 114-3), which serve to imbricate the ureteral wall and reduce the size of the lumen. Kalicinski et al.[30] placed a running horizontal mattress suture to exclude the redundant portion of lumen. A second running suture is then used to fold the accessory channel against the wall of the ureter (Fig. 114-4). Histologic examination demonstrates that the folded segment undergoes progressive obliteration over months, although the second lumen remains patent.[2]

Endoscopic Injection

Since the early reports of subureteric polytetrafluoroethylene (Teflon) injection for reflux,[45] endoscopic treatment has been used for refluxing megaureters. The procedure is not indicated for obstructive megaureters. Higher grades of reflux have proved harder to eradicate endoscopically, just as they are with open surgery. The success rate with a single injection for reflux approaches 60% to 80% with a normal-sized ureter. The failure rate may increase significantly by as much as 20% more when treating a refluxing megaureter,[8] although success may increase with a second or third injection. Recurrence rates are low with long follow-up.[7] It is highly unlikely that polytetrafluoroethylene will ever be approved for use in the United States because of concern over particle migration and autoimmune reactions. Alternative biocompatible, biodegradable materials have been evaluated, with the most extensively used material being a dextranomer/hyaluronic acid copolymer (Deflux, Q-Med Scandinavia, Uppsala, Sweden).[72] The material is easier to use than Teflon and has been used with similar effect for all grades of reflux, including megaureters.[6,32,59] Ureteral hydrodistention at the time of injection and the use of an increased volume of injected material within the submucosal intraureteral space may result in more effective placement and less caudal migration of the bioimplant (Fig. 114-5).[32] Endoscopic injection has been performed in complex patients with reflux, including those with secondary reflux, duplication anomalies, and reflux after transurethral incision of a ureterocele.[33] The least effective scenario for injection appears to be reflux into ectopic ureters. Open reimplantation of a ureter previously injected with any material may be more difficult; however, the reported success rates are the same as those with primary reimplantation. In general, the ureter and bioimplant should be mobilized together initially and the distal involved segment of ureter then excised.

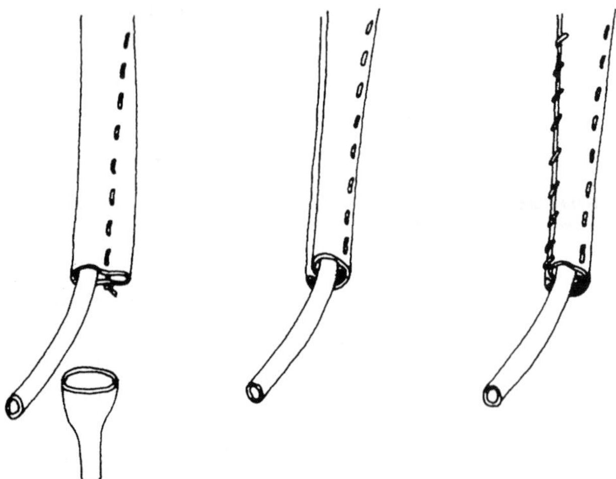

Figure 114–4 A running horizontal mattress suture isolates redundant lumen. The redundant portion is then folded and approximated to the main ureteral wall. (From Kalicinski ZH, Kansy J, Kotabinsia B, et al: Surgery of megaureters: Modification of Hendren's operation. J Pediatr Surg 1977;12:183.)

Direct repair of megaureter has worked well for 45 years in our experience, and we continue to prefer it. The small number of cases in which we have used injection therapy with a dilated ureter involved megaureters that had residual reflux despite previous surgery and a long intramural tunnel.

Upper Ureter Repair

If the primary pathophysiology was ureterovesical obstruction or severe reflux alone, upper ureteral obstruction after lower repair will most often not be needed. However, several points should be stressed regarding the upper part of the ureter. First, tortuosity can considerably improve after successful repair of a lower segment that was once obstructed or refluxing. Kinks can straighten and dilation can recede (Fig. 114-6). If the patient is doing well clinically, it is best to wait several months or longer to make any decision about proximal ureteral repair. The upper part of the ureter may be very dilated immediately after repair of the lower end because of edema surrounding the reimplantation. Imaging studies of the kidney should be repeated to rule out true obstruction. If the upper end of the ureter remains tortuous and dilated after lower repair, it should be tailored as shown in Figure 114-7. The tailoring sometimes involves merely resecting a kink that can cause poor drainage, particularly at the ureteropelvic junction. In extreme cases, tailoring includes

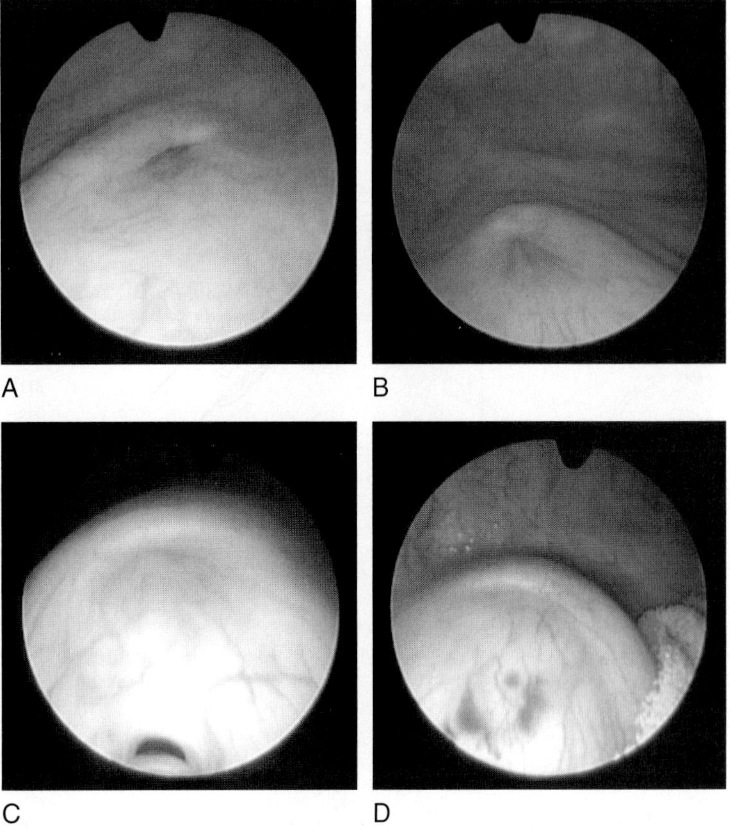

Figure 114–5 Endoscopic injection. *A* and *B*, Refluxing orifices. *C*, Needle for injection inserted in the intraureteric submucosal space. *D*, Coaptation after injection. (Courtesy of Anthony Caldamone, MD).

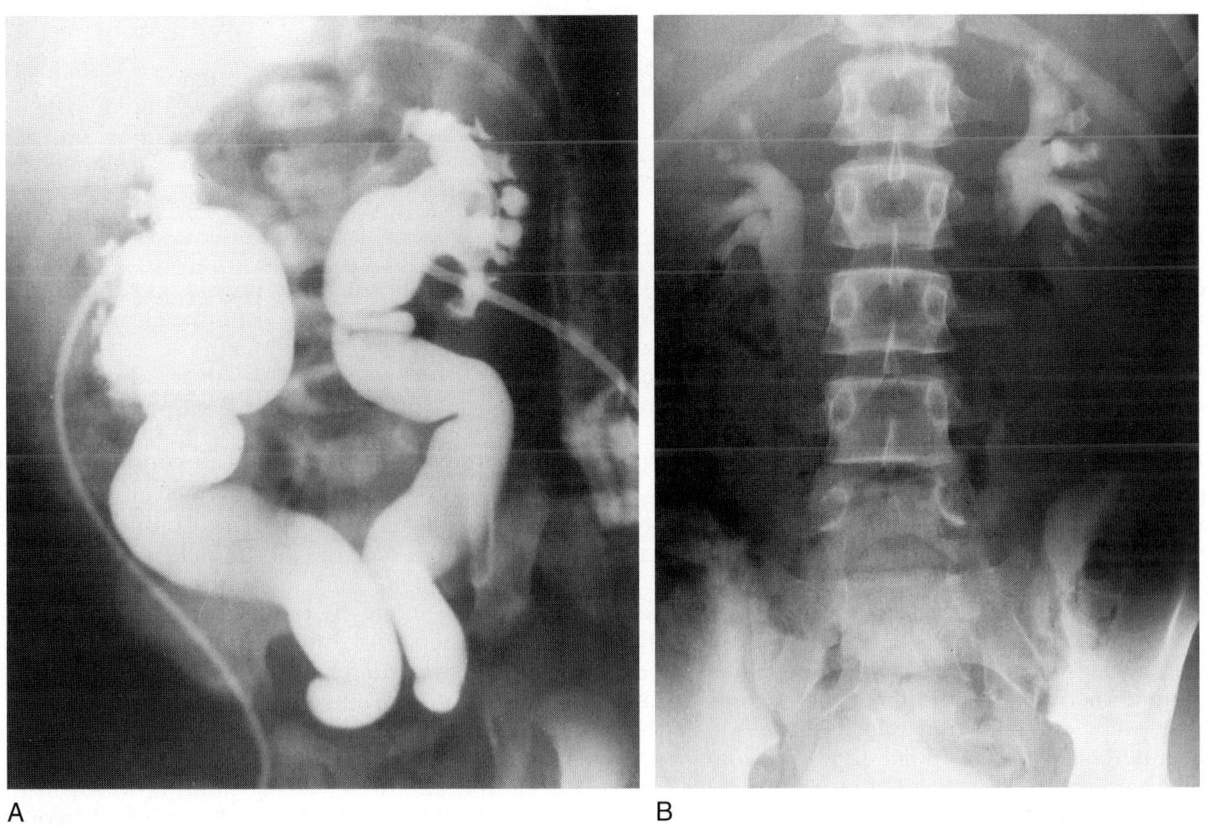

Figure 114–6 Refluxing megaureters. *A*, Massive preoperative reflux at 4 weeks of age. Previously placed nephrostomy tubes were unnecessary. *B*, Intravenous pyelogram 13 years after bilateral megaureter repair. Note the proximal improvement after distal ureteral repair alone.

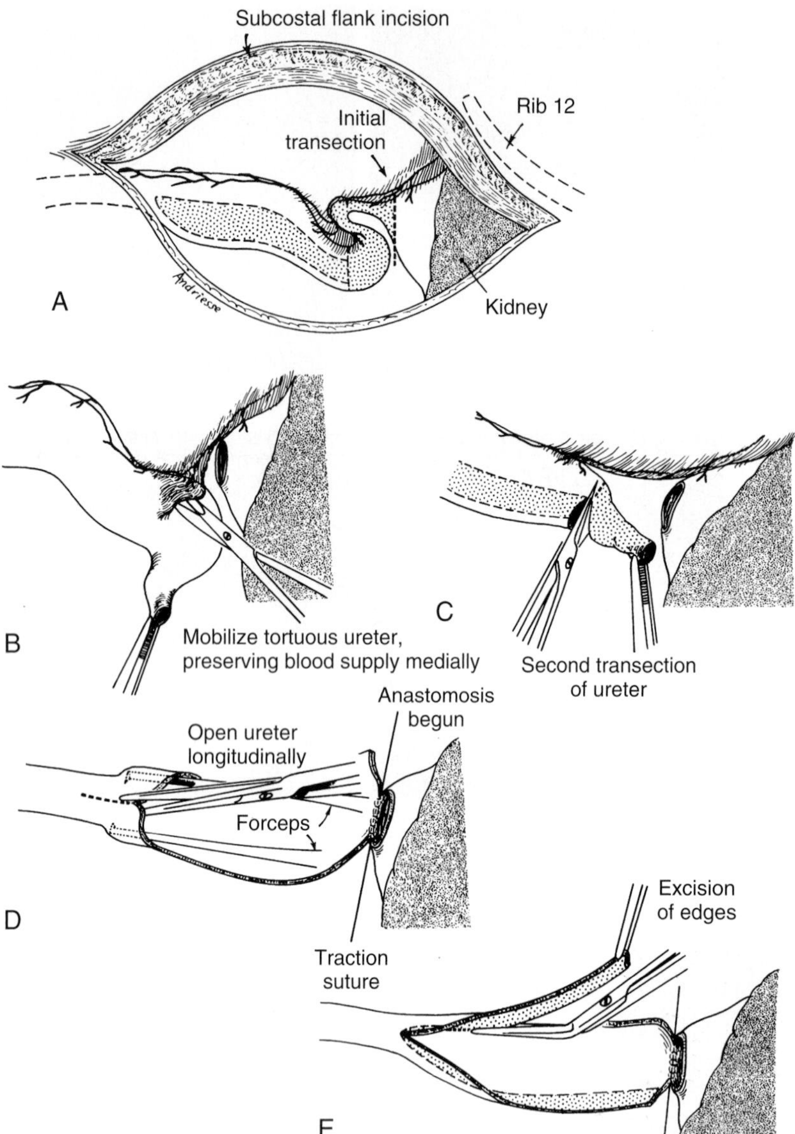

Figure 114–7 Straightening and tapering of the upper part of the ureter, which in our experience is performed in one quarter of cases, those that remain tortuous and show evidence of obstruction, especially at the ureteropelvic junction. In some, the upper end of the ureter remains dilated and does not empty well. Trimming the upper ureter can improve its emptying.

reduction of the caliber of the upper segment of ureter. The ureter is incised longitudinally, in situ, and its width is trimmed appropriately. Clamps are not necessary to taper the upper length of ureter. Temporary urinary drainage with a nephrostomy catheter or indwelling ureteral stent should be used.

It is interesting to watch a dilated ureter fluoroscopically. If the walls of the ureter cannot coapt, active peristalsis may be present but ineffective. The urine churns back and forth with ureteral peristaltic waves instead of being passed effectively into the bladder. Figure 114-8 shows a ureteral peristaltic study in a dilated ureter. Before surgery, peristaltic waves could be seen at various levels of the ureter, but they were of low amplitude and ineffective. After surgery, peristaltic waves in the tapered lower 10 cm of ureter were excellent and effective but not in the persistently dilated ureter 15 cm above the lower end. In some cases, the upper ureter was monitored for a long period before being tapered because of continued dilation and poor emptying. In one of the author's cases in which the upper end of the ureter was repaired 8 years after the lower end, the upper tract hydronephrosis improved remarkably and creatinine clearance increased substantially.

Complications

Surgical success rates by an experienced surgeon without obstruction or reflux when reimplanting a normal-sized ureter into a normal bladder should approach 98%. The success rate of megaureter repair is not quite as high. Figure 114-9 shows the principal complications that can occur with repair of a megaureter.[24] When the orifice is too lateral, the tunnel too short, or the distal end of the ureter too broad, reflux can result. A rare cause of reflux is a fistula at the top of the ureteral tunnel caused by an indwelling ureteral stent that is too stiff and can, therefore, erode the ureter at the point at which it turns to exit the bladder. A soft plastic No. 5 infant feeding tube prevents this problem. The most common cause of postoperative obstruction is compression of the ureter at its

Figure 114-8 Ureteral peristalsis study. Peristaltic waves in the lower part of the ureter were ineffective before surgery but were excellent after the lower segment was tapered. Peristalsis remained ineffective in the dilated upper ureter above the level of tapering at the time of this study.

Megaureter Pre-repair:

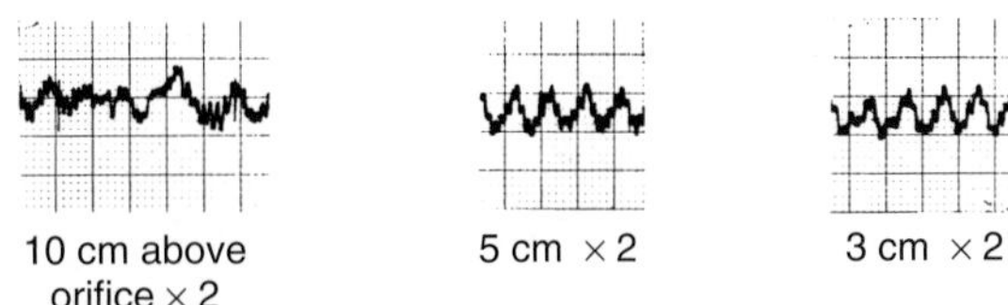

After Lower Repair (Lower 10 cm of ureter):

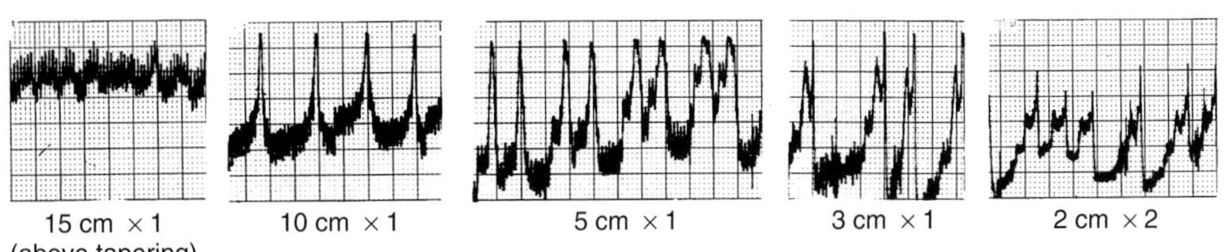

Waves of 2–3 mm Hg every 10–20 seconds in tapered segment of ureter

new hiatus through the bladder wall, which is often a result of locating the hiatus too far laterally so that the ureter angulates when the bladder fills. This complication underscores the importance of placing the new hiatus on the back wall of the bladder, not its lateral wall. In some cases, fixation of the bladder and hiatus with a psoas hitch is helpful in preventing this problem. A diverticulum is sometimes seen at the site of the new hiatus if left too large and can cause obstruction of the ureter. Fibrosis of the distal end of the ureter can be avoided by meticulously handling and preserving the blood supply of the ureter during mobilization, not making it too narrow when trimming it, and avoiding the temptation to taper so extensively that the blood supply to the lower part of the ureter is jeopardized.

In the authors' experience with tapering 404 ureters in 294 patients (217 male and 77 female), including 75 infants younger than 1 year, the success rate was 93%

Figure 114-9 The most common complications in failed surgery for megaureter.

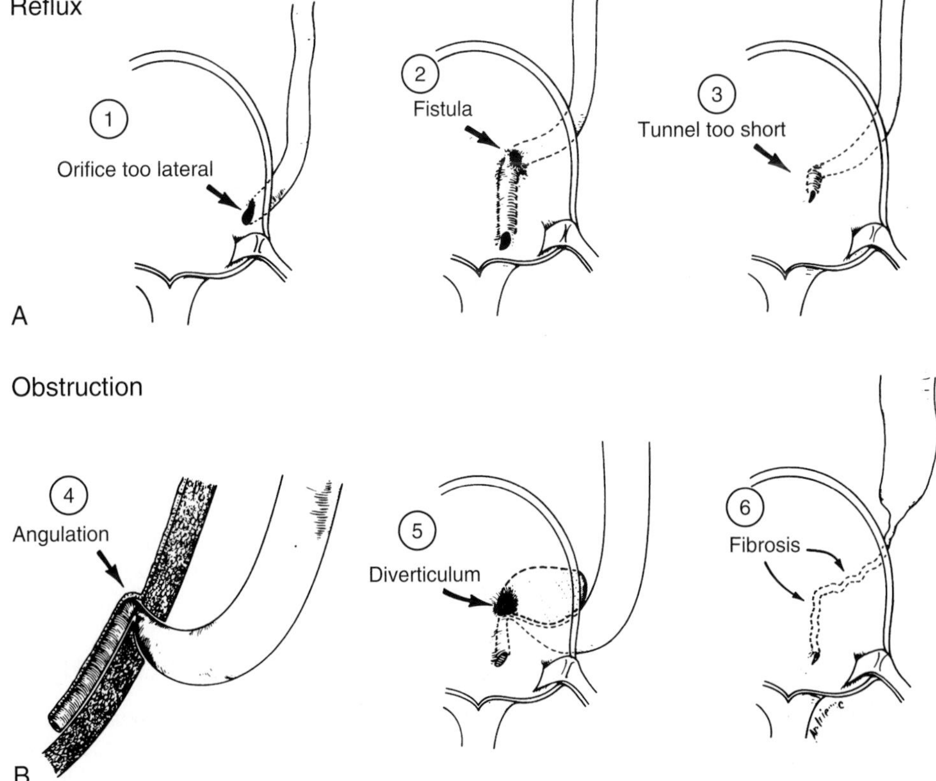

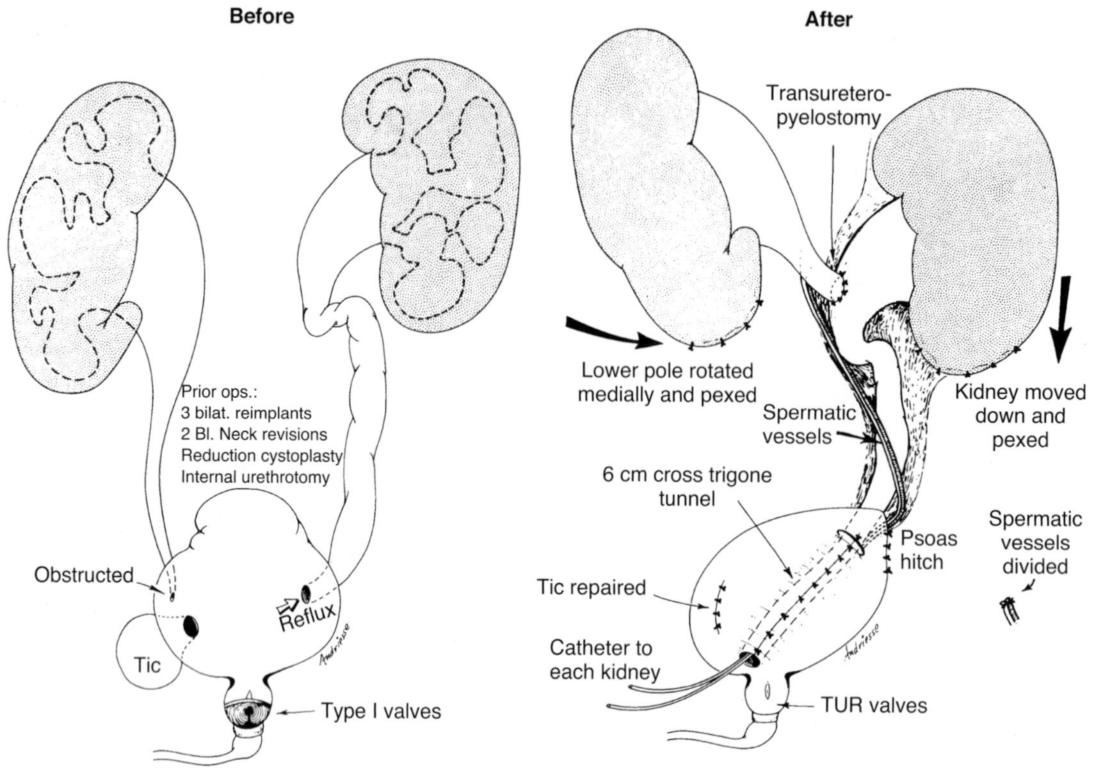

Figure 114–10 After three previous ureteral reimplantation operations, a 14-year-old boy was left with a short obstructed megaureter on the right and massive reflux on the left. The left ureter was satisfactory for tapering and a fourth reimplant, and extra length was gained by sliding the kidney down and hitching the bladder upward.[23] Blood supply to that ureter was enhanced by maintaining the spermatic vessels with it. The right side was drained by transureteropyelostomy. The diverticulum (Tic) and urethral valves (TUR valves) were removed.

for obstructive megaureter and 83% when the problem was high-grade reflux. Success was higher with a normal bladder (130 patients) than with a markedly abnormal bladder (164 patients), such as in patients with posterior urethral valves, neurogenic bladder, ureterocele, prune-belly syndrome, and exstrophy. Success was eventually achieved in most patients who underwent a second operation on the ureter (Fig. 114-10). Other methods included transureteroureterostomy, augmentation of the bladder,[28] subureteric injection of dextranomer microspheres (Deflux), and replacement of the ureter by tapered ileum in two cases. Others have reported similar results,[30,50,52,55] and problems may occur whether excision or folding techniques are used. Consistently, problems with secondary reflux and obstruction have been noted more commonly after megaureter repair for reflux variants than for obstructive ones. Increased collagen deposition and abnormal collagen-to-muscle orientation have been noted in refluxing megaureter and not seen in primary obstructive megaureter above the distal adynamic segment.[36] Such an intrinsic difference may be responsible for the difference in results for the two types.

Conclusions

The function of the ureter is to transport urine from the kidney to the bladder at low pressure. It cannot perform this task effectively when the ureter is so dilated that its walls do not coapt with peristaltic waves. When ureters store urine rather than transport it, there is little question that stasis favors bacterial growth, particularly if an inadequate ureterovesical junction allows reflux of urine. Megaureters may be repaired with a high success rate. The large ureter should be handled minimally and mobilized carefully so that its blood supply is preserved. The distal adynamic segment of ureter, when obstructing, should be completely excised. More proximal dilated ureter can then be tailored to normal size. We favor excisional tapering to achieve this, although folding techniques may be useful if the ureter is less dilated or thickened. The reconstructed ureter can then be reimplanted into the bladder by using the principles of standard antireflux surgery. Such repairs are slightly more prone to the complications of obstruction and, in particular, persistent reflux than are repairs performed for reflux into a ureter that is not dilated. These complications are more likely to occur when repair is performed for reflux than for obstruction. Longer follow-up and further experience at more centers should help define the role of endoscopic injection in the treatment of refluxing megaureters.

PRUNE-BELLY SYNDROME

Some of the most unusual and impressive megaureters are found in patients with prune-belly syndrome, a term used by William Osler in 1901 to describe the appearance of the abdominal wall in patients with congenital deficiency of the abdominal wall musculature.[46] The skin usually has an irregularly wrinkled appearance similar to that of a prune. The condition has also been called the Eagle-Barrett or triad syndrome because it has three major features: deficiency of abdominal muscles, hydroureteronephrosis, and cryptorchidism.[34,73] Its etiology is unknown, but it has been suggested that early urinary tract obstruction[47] or urinary ascites[43] might be causative or that a primary mesodermal error might lead to the abdominal wall and genitourinary findings.[67] Almost all patients are male, but the condition has been reported in females.[60] The authors have cared for 40 patients with prune-belly syndrome since 1968, only 2 of whom were female. It has been described in a pair of twins,[56] in one infant from a pair of twins, and in consecutive siblings with a mosaic chromosome abnormality.[19] Such cases suggest a genetic influence, but no clear pattern of inheritance has been identified. Like most pathologic entities, prune-belly syndrome ranges from mild to severe in the degree of both abdominal wall and urinary tract abnormality.

Abdominal Wall

The abdominal walls of four patients with the prune-belly syndrome are shown in Figure 114-11. In a typical case, the abdominal wall is lax and protuberant, and close inspection shows coarse wrinkling of the skin. The abdominal wall may be so thin that loops of dilated ureter and intestine are easily visible and peristalsis can be seen. In such severe cases, the abdominal wall has little integrity and the abdominal contents are easily palpated. A protuberant abdomen and flaring rib margins are common, and the lower part of the sternum is often depressed. As the child becomes older, the skin frequently becomes smoother; however, the lower part of the abdomen may be remarkably protuberant with a potbellied appearance. Histologic examination of the abdominal wall has revealed both absence and hypoplasia of muscle, particularly in the lower, central area.[1] The normal relationship of muscle groups may be preserved, or they may be fused as a single fibrotic layer. Innervation does appear to be intact.[44] Poor support of the lower chest wall leads to an ineffective cough mechanism in many of these children and may make them more prone to respiratory infections. The lax abdominal wall may also contribute to poor bladder and bowel function. Interestingly, wound healing does not appear to be compromised, and the appearance and function of the abdominal wall may be improved by surgical repair. The earliest and simplest techniques involved a midline incision and closure after excising redundant skin and thinned abdominal wall bilaterally. Randolph et al.[62] described a nearly transverse incision extending from the tip of the lowest rib on either side to the symphysis pubis with central excision. Techniques reported by Ehrlich[12,13] and Monfort[42,49] and their colleagues preserve a central musculofascial strip that is overlapped by better lateral muscle, fascia, and skin (Fig. 114-12). Both provide adequate exposure for orchiopexy or genitourinary reconstruction at the same time.

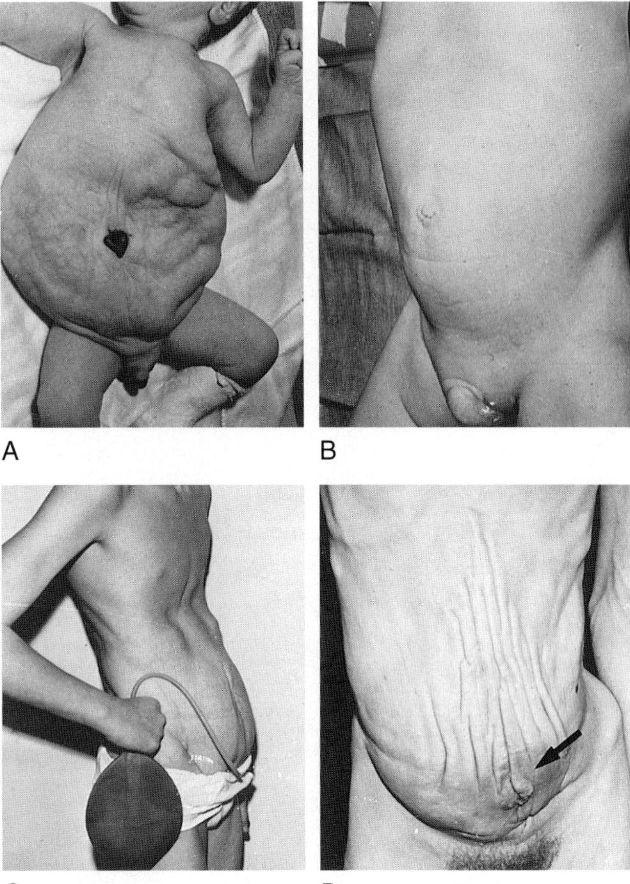

Figure 114–11 Variable appearance of the abdominal wall in the prune-belly syndrome. *A*, Neonate with the typical features of severe prune-belly syndrome. Note the sagging flanks and loops of bowel visible beneath an extremely thin abdominal wall with deficient musculature. *B*, Mild case of prune-belly syndrome in an 8-week-old boy. Note the slight wrinkling of the skin of the lower part of the abdomen and the underlying distended bladder. The abdominal wall is lax, but more developed than in the patient shown in *A*. *C*, An 18-year-old patient with the typical protuberant abdomen seen in the prune-belly syndrome. Note the inward protrusion of the lower part of the sternum, which is common in these patients. A long-standing nephrostomy and cystostomy have been present since infancy. The urinary tract was subsequently reconstructed. *D*, A 16-year-old patient with severe wrinkling of the abdominal wall. The patient had long-standing end ureterostomies (*arrow*). Marked kyphoscoliosis is present. An undiversion operation was performed subsequently.

Kidneys and Ureters

Renal architecture and function vary widely in patients with prune-belly syndrome. In some cases, the kidneys are severely dysplastic and the infants die soon after birth of pulmonary hypoplasia secondary to renal failure (Fig. 114-13).[65,66] At the other end of the spectrum of severity are patients with relatively normal kidneys. Some element of renal dysplasia is found in well over half the patients with prune-belly syndrome,[66] and its severity is a major determinant of patient prognosis. The degree of dysplasia may vary greatly from side to side in the same patient.

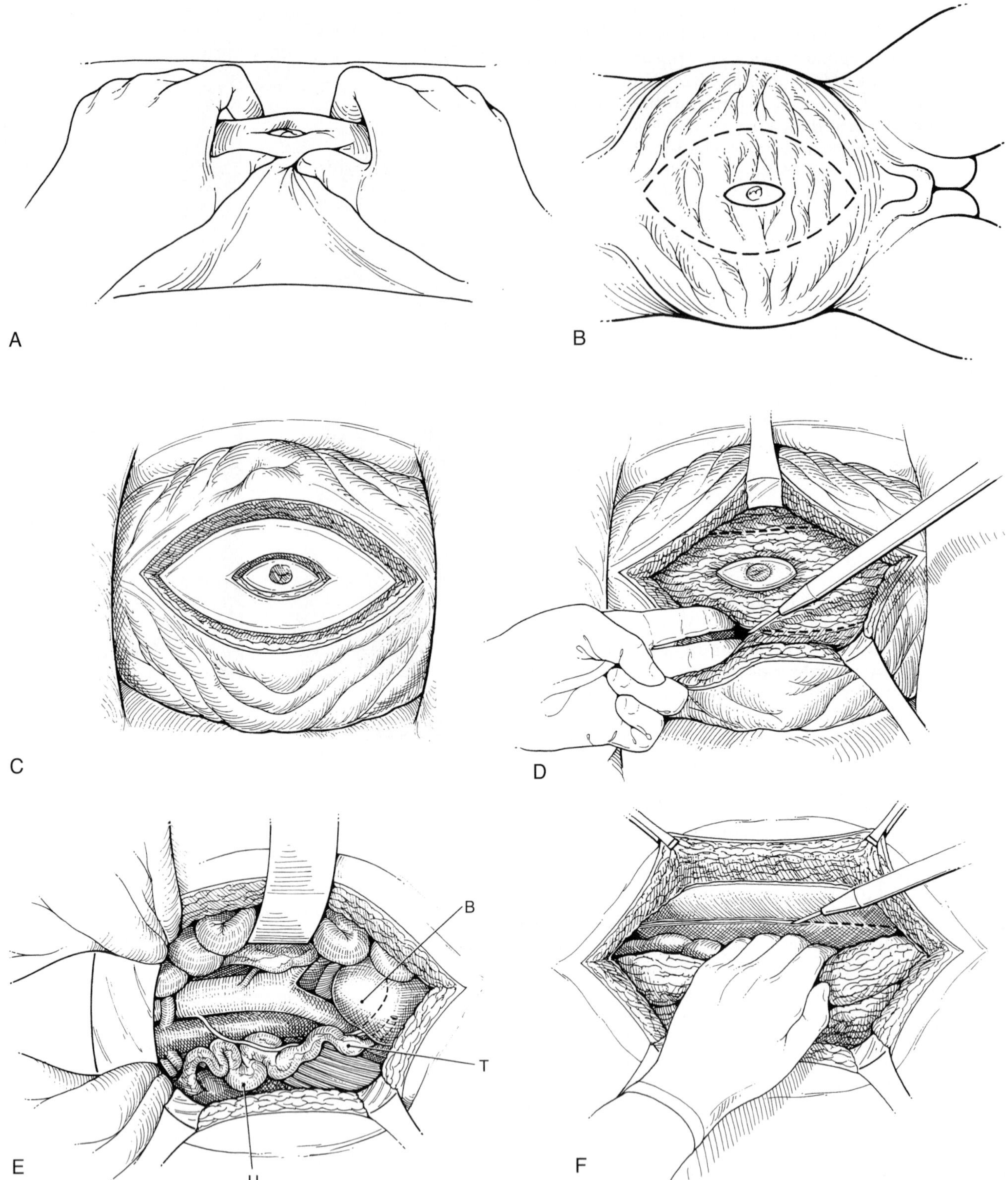

Figure 114–12 Surgical technique for a Monfort abdominoplasty. *A*, Delineation of redundancy by tenting up the abdominal wall. *B*, Skin incisions are outlined with a separate circumscribing incision to isolate the umbilicus. *C*, Skin (epidermis and dermis only) is excised with electrocautery. *D*, The abdominal wall is incised at the lateral border of the rectus muscle on either side, from the superior epigastric to the inferior epigastric vessels, to create a central musculofascial plate. *E*, Adequate exposure is provided for concomitant transperitoneal genitourinary procedures by retracting the central strip laterally. B, bladder; T, testes; U, ureter. *F*, Completion of the abdominoplasty by scoring of the parietal peritoneum underlying the lateral abdominal wall musculature with electrocautery.

Continued

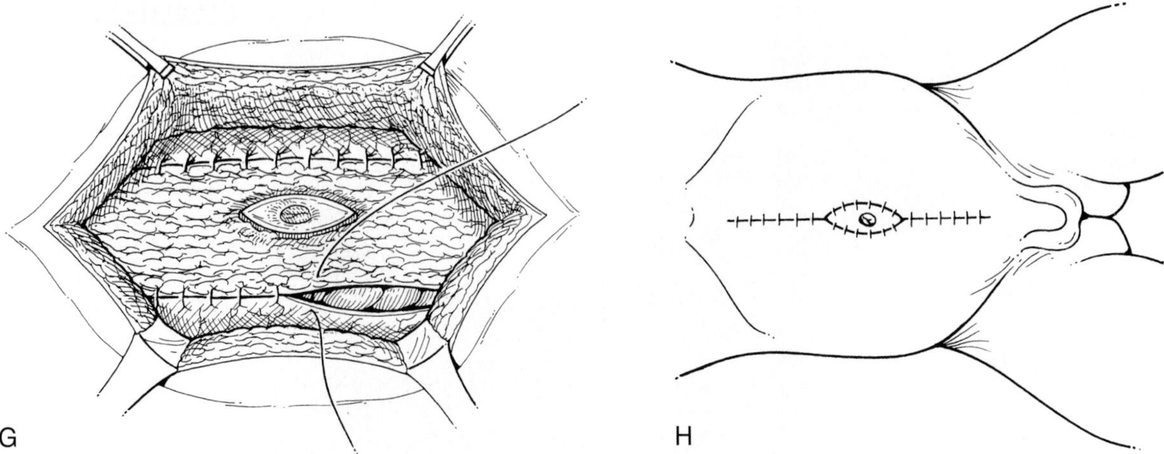

Figure 114-12—Cont'd *G*, The edges of the central plate are sutured to the lateral abdominal wall musculature along the scored line. *H*, Lateral flaps are brought together in the midline, with closed suction drains placed between the lateral flaps and the central plate. Skin is brought together in the midline to envelop the previously isolated umbilicus. (H, From Woodard JR, Perez LM: Prune-belly syndrome. In Marshall FF [ed]: Operative Urology. Philadelphia, WB Saunders, 1996.)

Renal dysplasia tends to be worse in patients with bladder outlet obstruction and an imperforate anus.[58]

This wide spectrum of severity is seen not only microscopically in the renal parenchyma but also in the collecting system of the kidney, which can be dilated and have a peculiar dysmorphic appearance (Fig. 114-14). The ureters are characteristically dilated, elongated, and tortuous to a much greater degree than seen in males with high-grade bladder outlet obstruction, such as those with urethral valves. Some patients have scant muscle in the ureteral wall; others have well-developed muscle. In general, the upper ends of the ureters have better preserved histologic architecture than the distal lower ends do.[48] Collagen is often increased and muscle mass decreased in the ureteral wall, especially when there is massive reflux.[16] In some patients, the ureteropelvic junction is extremely tortuous but not obstructed. In others, the ureteropelvic junction is obstructed. Peristalsis is poor

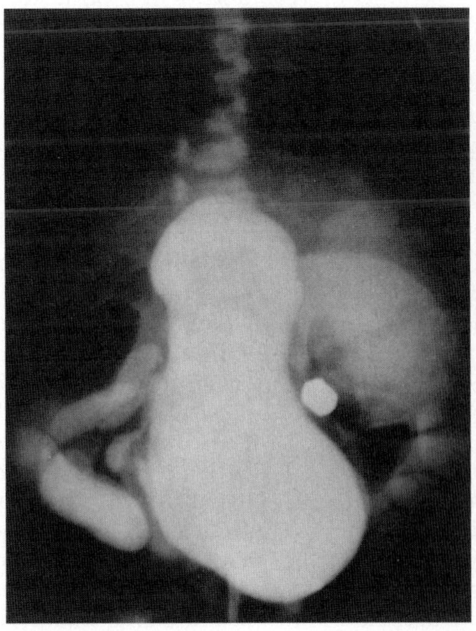

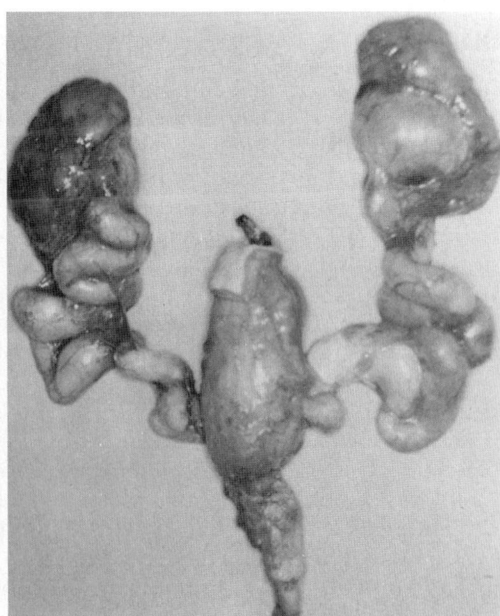

Figure 114-13 Prune-belly syndrome in a neonate who died at 1 week of age with uremia. *A*, Cystogram showing a large, elongated bladder with a diverticulum-like dome, often seen in prune-belly syndrome. Note the massive reflux into dilated, convoluted ureters. *B*, Postmortem specimen of the urinary tract. Note the attachment of the bladder to the navel and cystic, dysplastic kidneys.

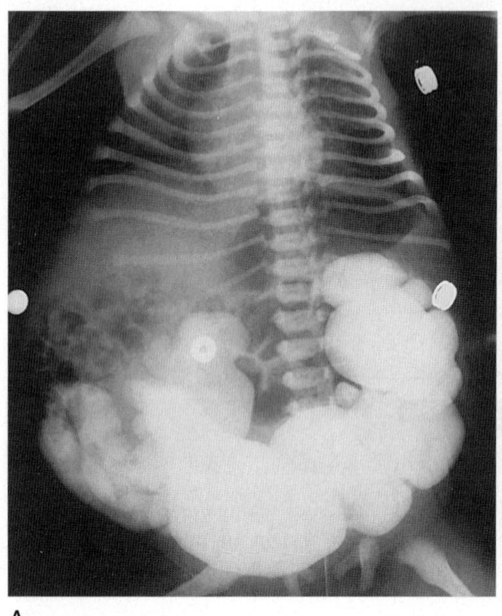

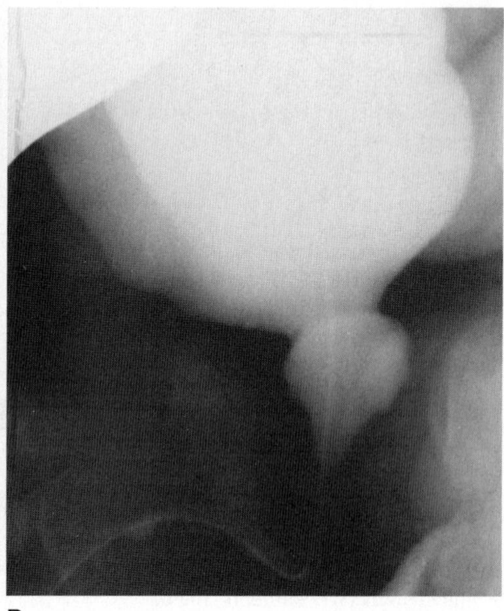

Figure 114–14 Typical severe prune-belly case. *A*, Cystogram. Note the large bladder with the appearance of an inverted light bulb and massive reflux into convoluted ureters. When straightened, the ureters were longer than the patient's legs. *B*, Cystourethrogram. Note the smooth wall of the bladder, open bladder neck, and heart-shaped urethra.

in some ureters and active, but ineffective, in others because the walls of the ureters do not coapt. Repeat urinary infection can lead to inflammation and fibrosis of the ureter, thereby aggravating an already bad situation. The hydronephrosis at the level of the kidney is often less remarkable than that at the distal end of the ureter and bladder, and the parenchyma is sometimes better preserved than might be expected from the distal dilation. Reflux occurs in most patients (85%) with prune-belly syndrome.[17] The reflux may be difficult to grade because of the dysmorphism but often involves a massive volume that may interfere with bladder dynamics and render the patient prone to urinary tract infection.

Bladder

In patients with prune-belly syndrome, the bladder usually has a large capacity. Some bladders feature a large diverticulum-like dome involving the area of the urachus (see Fig. 114-14). In patients with urethral atresia, the dome may drain through a patent urachus at the umbilicus. Endoscopy shows that the wall of the bladder is usually smooth, not trabeculated. The ureteral orifices are often very lateral and somewhat craniad from a normal position. The orifices are frequently widely dilated, consistent with the massive reflux seen in most cases. The bladder neck is abnormally wide and funnels down into a dilated, heart-shaped prostatic urethra. Grossly, the bladder wall is usually thick and quite vascular. The thickness of the bladder wall is not the result of hypertrophied muscle. Histologic examination reveals muscle and abundant collagen and fibrous tissue. The bladder will usually function as an adequate, if not enlarged, reservoir with good capacity and compliance. Massive reflux, diminished detrusor contractility, decreased sensation of fullness, poor abdominal wall support, and diverticulum-like malformations at the dome may all interfere with normal emptying. Despite these problems, about half of such patients can void spontaneously,[31] although spontaneous improvement and deterioration in the quality of voiding have been noted. Reducing the size of the bladder by excising the dome should be considered in some cases.[5,53] Domectomy can improve emptying and decrease postvoid residual urine in select cases. Some children with prune-belly syndrome can benefit from bladder emptying by intermittent catheterization.[31]

Urethra

Dilation of the posterior urethra may be secondary to congenital deficiency or hypoplasia of surrounding prostate tissue. In males with the prune-belly syndrome, the prostatic urethra appears heart shaped on voiding cystography. The external urethral sphincter is just below the apex. The narrowing of the prostatic urethra at the level of the external sphincter does not necessarily denote urethral obstruction, but some male patients have urethral atresia.[63] Congenital urethral stenosis is also sometimes present. In the 38 males we have treated, true urethral valves were seen in 5; 19 had valve-like narrowing, usually at the level of a rudimentary verumontanum. Patients with poor bladder emptying may benefit from incision of such folds (Fig. 114-15). Besides atresia, the anterior urethra may be abnormal in the form of congenital megalourethra, the fusiform variant of which may distort the development of all corpora in the phallus. Anterior urethral anomalies generally require surgical repair when present. Urethral hypoplasia may be repaired by open urethroplasty (Fig. 114-16). Megalourethra is corrected by open tailoring of the urethral mucosa, which can be covered by the investing, periurethral tissue in several overlapping layers.

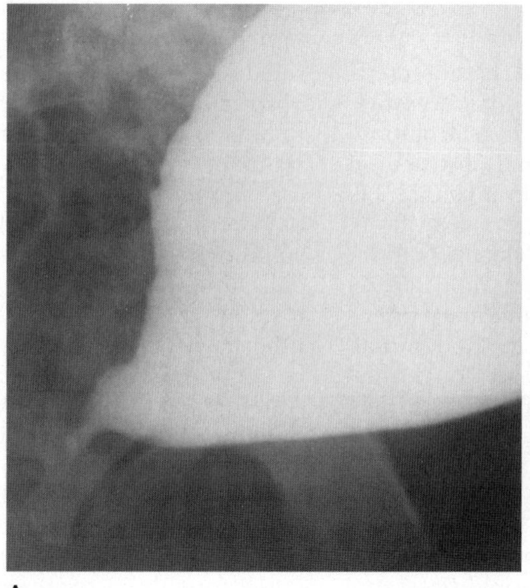
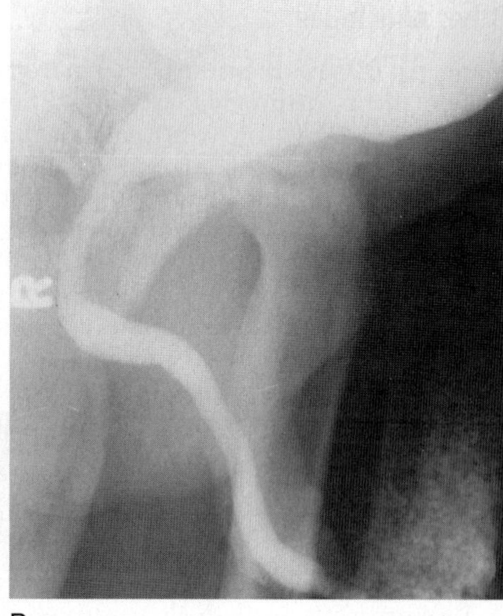

Figure 114–15 Voiding urethrograms. *A*, Preoperative study showing a typical dilated proximal urethra and wide bladder neck, with abrupt cutoff of contrast distal to the rudimentary verumontanum. There was a urethral valve. *B*, Postoperative study 7 months later showing free flow through the former valve obstruction and normal caliber of the entire urethra.

Testes

Bilateral undescended testes lie in the abdomen in most males with the prune-belly syndrome. The testes are usually smaller than normal and lie well inside the internal inguinal ring, much like ovaries in females. The spermatic vessels are shorter than normal, and the epididymis is often separate from the testis. The vasa may be tortuous, and atresia of the vas is not uncommon. The pelvic peritoneum adjacent to the vas deferens usually has an abundant blood supply, which makes the Fowler-Stephens method of orchidopexy possible.[15] This technique involves dividing the spermatic vessels in the abdomen above the testis while mobilizing the testis with a broad strip of pelvic peritoneum and collateral blood supply surrounding the vas deferens. The goal of orchidopexy is to place the testes in the scrotum, where they can be monitored for the development of malignancy and for psychological reasons. Fertility has not been reported in these patients, although Leydig cell function leading to secondary sexual development with penile growth and libido is usually normal. Most surgeons have found that bringing a high testicle into the scrotum is easier in a young infant, in whom the relative distance is shorter.[75] Laparoscopic orchidopexy has recently been used for the prune-belly syndrome[10] and may be particularly useful with a staged Fowler-Stephens technique.

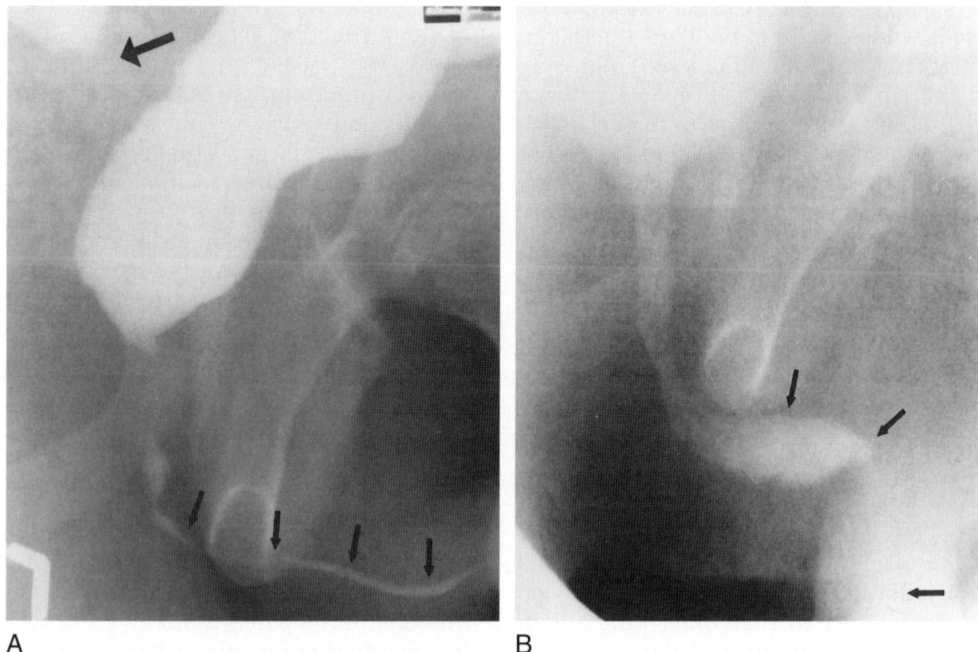

Figure 114–16 Cystourethrograms. *A*, Preoperative. Note the hypoplastic urethra (*small arrows*) and unusual obstruction of a megaureter by a ureteral valve (*large arrow*). *B*, Postoperative study after a long preputial patch graft to the urethra.

Other Anomalies

Many patients with prune-belly syndrome have musculoskeletal or orthopedic abnormalities that require treatment.[4,38] Most of these patients have malrotation and nonfixation of the colon, but intestinal obstruction with midgut volvulus is rare. Imperforate anus may be seen in the prune-belly syndrome. Both females whom we treated for prune-belly syndrome had cloacal malformations. Pulmonary hypoplasia is seen in some severe cases, and these patients are prone to pulmonary infections. Pectus excavatum is common, and the abdominal wall musculature is weak. Various types of congenital heart disease may also occur in association with prune-belly syndrome.

Clinical Management

A newborn with prune-belly syndrome should be evaluated carefully because of the potential for sepsis. Any study that involves catheterization should be performed under appropriate antibiotic coverage and with meticulous aseptic technique. The dilated urinary tract, which may contain a large volume of urine and drain poorly, does not tolerate the introduction of bacteria. In some babies with very poor renal function in association with dysplastic kidneys, early death from renal failure may be predestined. Measurement of serum creatinine levels and, in particular, creatinine clearance identifies infants who have a reasonable measure of kidney function.

The prune-belly syndrome in babies is one of the most controversial conditions in pediatric urology. At one end of the therapeutic spectrum are those who advocate watchful waiting and minimal surgical intervention.[11,70,78] On the other end are those who favor major reconstructive surgery when indicated.[9,14,21,26,27,29,61,76,77] It should be emphasized that major reconstructive surgery in an infant with the prune-belly syndrome should not be undertaken unless expert anesthesiology with complete monitoring is available and the surgeon has extensive experience performing such surgery. Furthermore, a major reconstructive operation should not be considered unless the baby's overall status is reasonable, including pulmonary function and absence of ongoing urinary tract infection. Woodard and Zucker have recommended that an aggressive approach be considered with caution because the surgery is difficult and the patients are vulnerable to pulmonary complications.[77]

Much of this controversy centers around reconstruction of the urinary tract. There is little question that the intra-abdominal testes should be brought down by orchiopexy at an early age. Likewise, many patients and families will request reconstruction of the abdominal wall, if only for psychological reasons. It is our preference to perform such repairs at the same time as urinary tract reconstruction if such is needed. If the patient will tolerate it from a pulmonary standpoint, we favor one longer reconstruction to repair everything rather than putting the patient through multiple surgeries.

When initial evaluation demonstrates clear obstruction, correction should be undertaken whether it involves the ureteropelvic junction, ureterovesical junction, or bladder outlet (Fig. 114-17). Most patients have some underlying renal dysplasia as noted, and secondary insult from obstruction should not be allowed. It is our experience that most patients with this syndrome and vesicoureteral reflux eventually undergo repair. Classic grading systems for reflux may not apply to such patients; however, reflux in patients with prune-belly syndrome is often massive in volume. Early observation while the patient is receiving daily antibiotics to prevent infection may be appropriate to allow evaluation of bladder emptying and to assess other aspects of the urinary tract. If reflux persists, correction is appropriate. When patients with reflux suffer breakthrough urinary tract infections or any deterioration in renal function, early repair of the reflux should be undertaken.

In considering the urinary system in patients with this syndrome, it may be useful to categorize them into three groups as described by Smith and Woodard.[68] The categories roughly correlate with the degree of renal dysplasia present. Group I patients usually have both severe renal dysplasia and pulmonary hypoplasia and will not survive. Urologic intervention will not rescue such patients. Group III patients generally have a mild or incomplete form of the syndrome and well-preserved renal function. Although some such patients may have impressive dilation of the urinary tract relative to patients without the syndrome, early reconstruction may be deferred if there is no infection. Group II patients have intermediate degrees of dysplasia and renal function. These patients typically have full-blown features of the syndrome and a stagnant urinary system. Clearly, some of these patients will progress to renal insufficiency with or without surgical intervention.[64,78] Many factors are at play in patients with prune-belly syndrome. It remains difficult to predict the natural history for a given patient. Careful surveillance is critical. We favor surgical intervention in group II patients if they have infection, reflux, or deterioration of renal function. The two problems often go hand in hand. We believe that correction of obstruction or reflux, optimization of bladder emptying, and avoidance of infection may prevent renal insufficiency in some patients with marginal function or at least prolong the time until they suffer insufficiency.

The authors have performed reconstructive surgery on 40 patients with prune-belly syndrome; 12 were primary cases (Figs. 114-18 and 114-19) and 28 were secondary cases that had previously been treated by surgery elsewhere. Twenty-four of the latter 28 patients had undergone urinary diversion.[25,27] This illustrates how often urosepsis occurs in patients with prune-belly syndrome and can lead to various types of surgery for diversion (Fig. 114-20). We favor reconstruction over diversion in such patients. Twelve patients had only one kidney because of previous nephrectomy. Thirty-five of the 40 patients are alive (time since surgery, 4 to 30 years). Eight patients have undergone renal transplantation. Eight more will probably require renal transplantation given their current renal function. Five patients died. One infant died in the hospital because of blood loss secondary to hemophilia and inadequate monitoring. Another infant died at home 2 months after surgery of pulmonary aspiration.

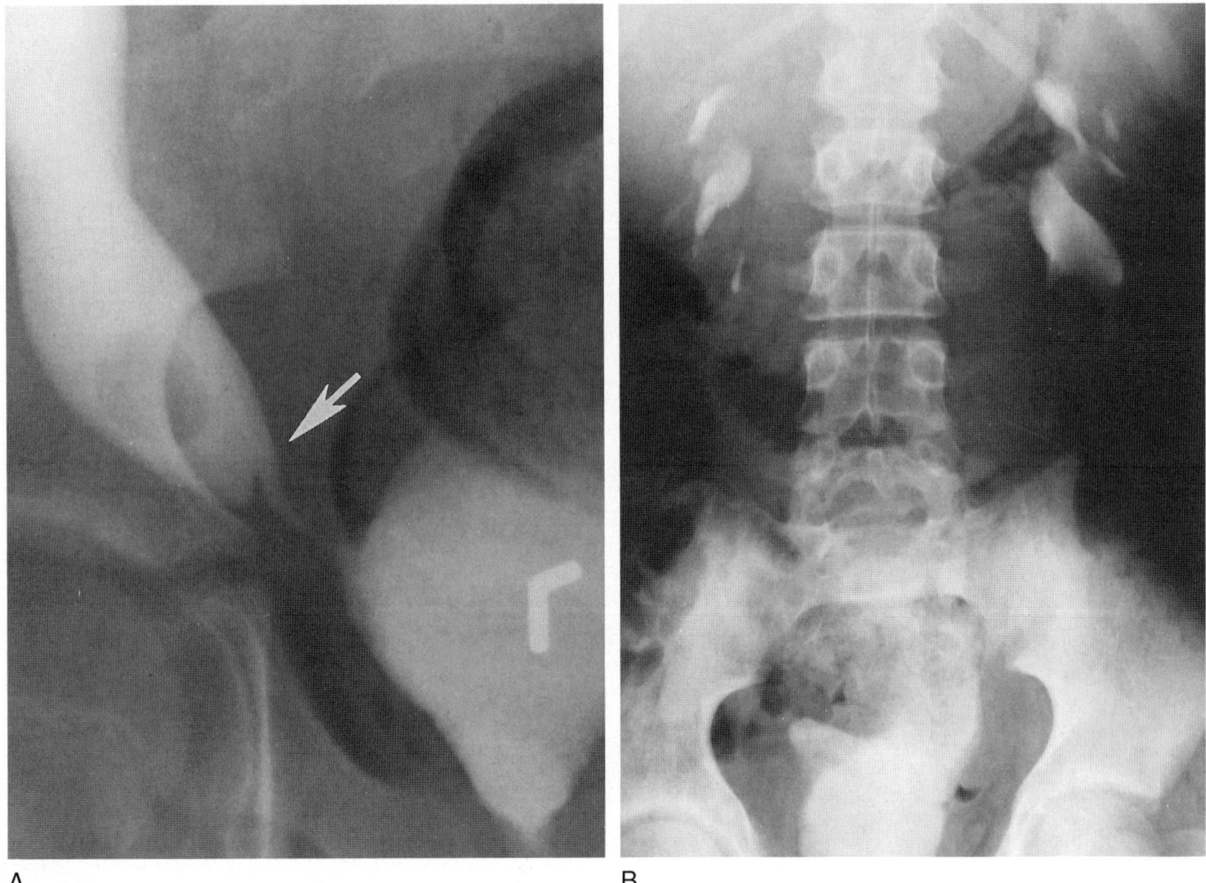

Figure 114–17 Intravenous pyelograms from same patient shown in Figures 114-16 and 114-20. *A*, Ureteral valve in the right megaureter (*arrow*). *B*, Intravenous pyelogram 3 years after extensive undiversion.

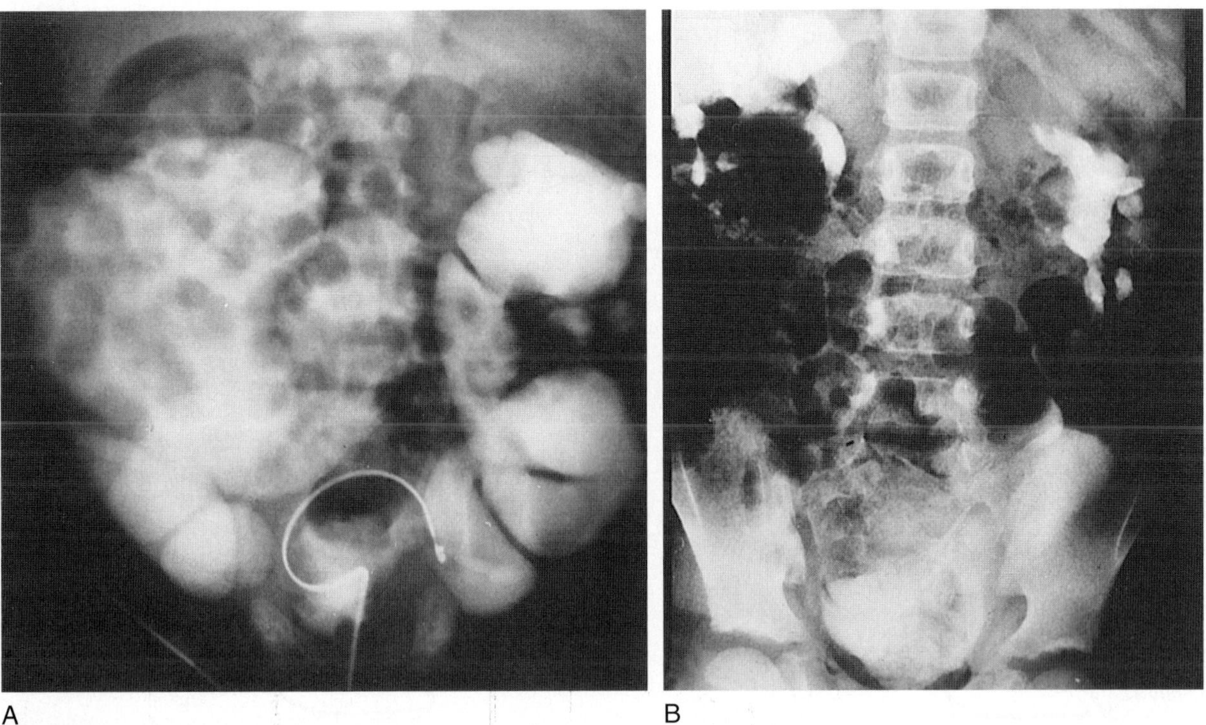

Figure 114–18 Infant with prune-belly syndrome. *A*, Preoperative cystogram. There is massive bilateral reflux outlining elongated and tortuous ureters, especially on the right side. Note the dysmorphic collecting system of the left kidney. Total reconstruction was performed. *B*, Intravenous pyelogram at 7 years of age. The patient is well with no urinary tract symptoms. Note the contrast visible in the left ureter, which is of normal caliber. It is difficult to imagine that the great improvement in appearance of the urinary tract does not equate with a longer and more healthy life. Anatomy seen in Figure 114-19.

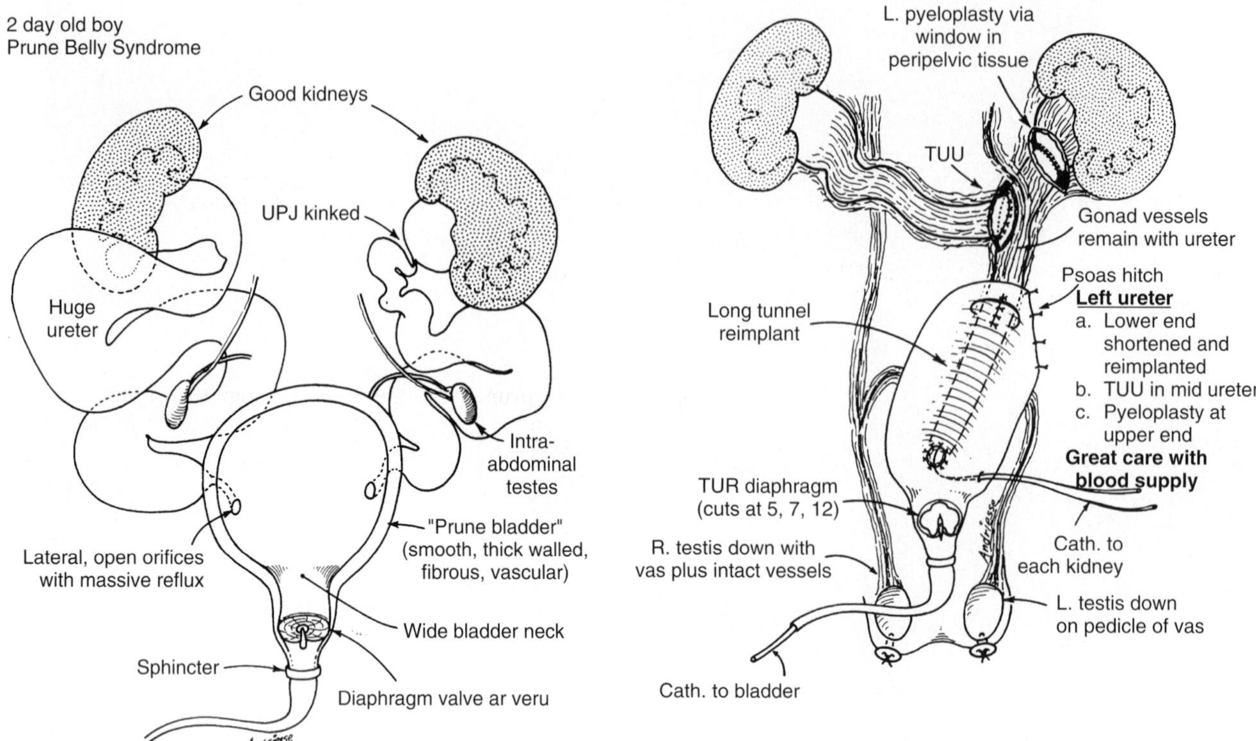

Figure 114–19 Infant with prune-belly syndrome: anatomy preoperatively and postoperatively. TUR, transurethral resection; TUU, transureteroureterostomy. For X rays see Figure 114-18.

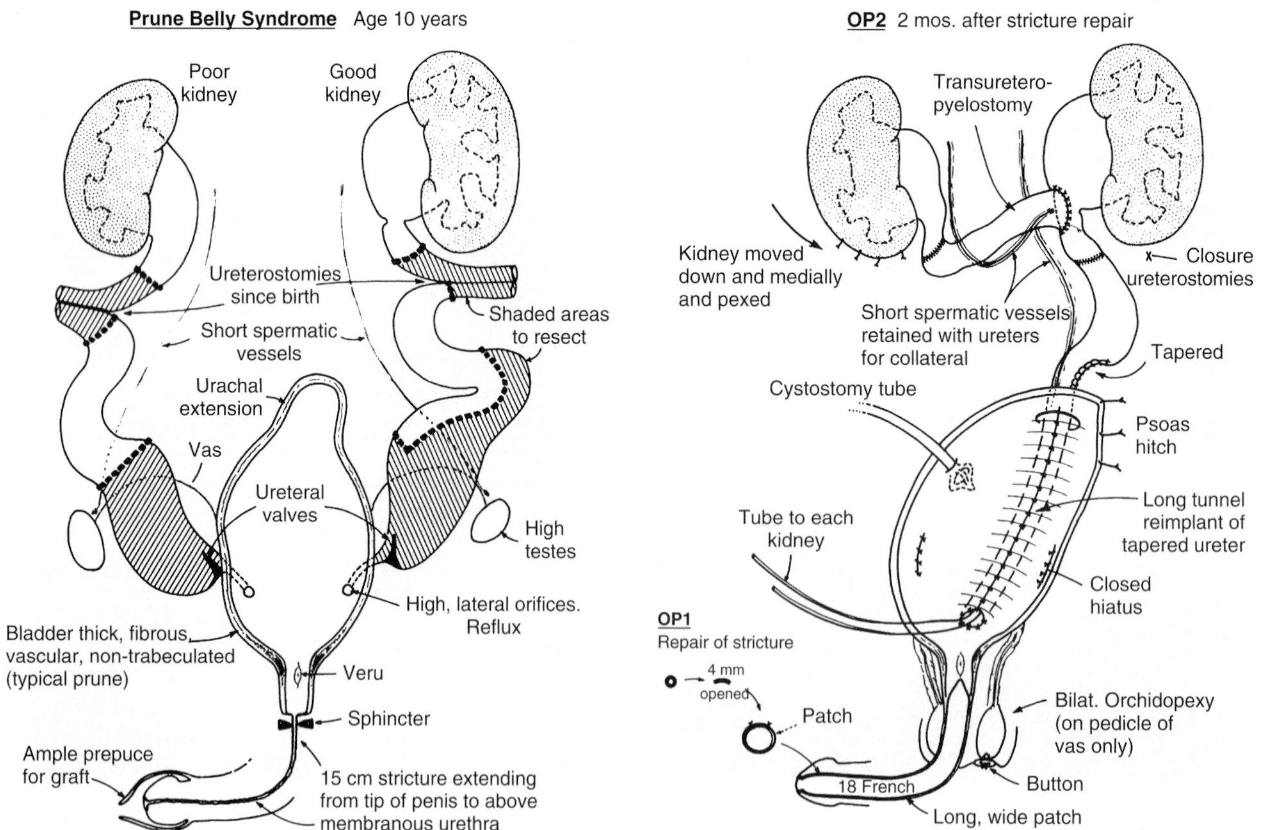

Figure 114–20 Eleven-year-old boy with prune-belly syndrome, unusual anatomic findings, and long-standing ureterostomies. In operation 1, an extensive urethroplasty was performed with a long onlay of prepuce. Two months later, undiversion with urinary reconstruction and bilateral orchiopexy was performed. The patient voids normally and is continent. Renal function has been normal (serum creatinine, 0.9 mg/dL; creatinine clearance, 106 L/m^2/day). Pyelograms are shown in Figure 114-17. He is now 35 years of age and is in excellent health.

Three late deaths occurred: one 3 years after renal transplantation, another 10 years after successful transplantation from an automobile accident, and one 11 years after reconstruction from septicemia during dialysis. It should be noted that our patients are a select group and do not reflect rates of death from renal dysplasia in an unselected group of patients with the prune-belly syndrome.

Conclusions

Some of the most impressive megaureters are found in patients with the prune-belly syndrome, and they are often then associated with other clinical problems. The philosophy of treating selective cases by aggressive surgical reconstruction is the opposite of the "watchful waiting" espoused by some. Surgical intervention is actually a conservative method in that it decreases stasis, urinary tract infection, and renal failure, the natural history of patients with the syndrome. Reconstruction is very demanding and technically difficult. It also requires extensive anesthesiology expertise to maintain metabolic homeostasis in a young child undergoing major reconstruction. This surgery should be performed in centers where surgeons concentrate on major reconstructive surgery and have access to all of the requisite backup systems.

REFERENCES

1. Afifi AK, Rebiez JM, Andonian SJ, et al: The myopathology of the prune belly syndrome. J Neurol Sci 1972; 15:153.
2. Bakker HHR, Scholtameijer RJ, Klopper PJ: Comparison of 2 different tapering techniques in megaureters. J Urol 1988; 140:1237.
3. Baskin LS, Zderic SA, Snyder HM, et al: Primary dilated megaureter: Long-term followup. J Urol 1994;152:618.
4. Brinker MR, Palutsis RS, Sarwark JF: The orthopaedic manifestations of prune-belly (Eagle-Barrett) syndrome. J Bone Joint Surg Am 1995;77:251.
5. Bukowski TP, Pearlmutter AD: Reduction cystoplasty in the prune belly syndrome: A long-term followup. J Urol 1994; 152:2113.
6. Capozza N, Caione P: Role of the endoscopic treatment of vesicoureteral reflux. A 16-years' experience. Minerva Pediatr 2003;55:607.
7. Chertin B, Colhoun E, Velayudham M, Puri P: Endoscopic treatment of vesicoureteral reflux: 11 to 17 years of followup. J Urol 2002;167:1443, discussion 1445.
8. Chertin B, De Caluwe D, Puri P: Endoscopic treatment of primary grades IV and V vesicoureteral reflux in children with subureteral injection of polytetrafluoroethylene. J Urol 2003;169:1847.
9. Cukier J: Resection of the urethra with the prune belly syndrome. Birth Defects 1977;5:95.
10. Docimo SG, Moore RG, Kavoussi LR: Laparoscopic orchidopexy in the prune belly syndrome: Case report and review of the literature. Urology 1994;45:679.
11. Duckett JW Jr: The prune-belly syndrome. In Kelalis PP, King LR, Belman AB (eds): Clinical Pediatric Urology. Philadelphia, WB Saunders, 1976.
12. Ehrlich RM, Lesavoy MA: Umbilicus preservation with total abdominal wall reconstruction in the prune-belly syndrome. Urology 1993;43:3.
13. Ehrlich RM, Lesavoy MA, Fine RN: Total abdominal wall reconstruction in the prune-belly syndrome. J Urol 1986; 136:282.
14. Fallat ME, Skoog SJ, Belman AB, et al: The prune belly syndrome: A comprehensive approach to management. J Urol 1989;142:802.
15. Fowler R, Stephens FD: The role of testicular vascular anatomy in the salvage of the high undescended testicle. Aust N Z J Surg 1959;29:92.
16. Gearhart JP, Lee BR, Partin AW, et al: A quantitative histological evaluation of the dilated ureter of childhood. II: Ectopia, posterior urethral valves and the prune belly syndrome. J Urol 1995;153:172.
17. Goulding FJ, Garrett RA: Twenty-five year experience with the prune belly syndrome. Urology 1978;7:329.
18. Hanna MK, Jeffs RD: Primary obstructive mega-ureter in children. Urology 1975;6:419.
19. Harley LM, Chen Y, Rattner WH: Prune belly syndrome. J Urol 1972;108:174.
20. Hendren WH: Operative repair of megaureter in children. J Urol 1969;101:491.
21. Hendren WH: A new approach to infants with severe obstructive uropathy: Early and complete reconstruction. J Pediatr Surg 1970;5:184.
22. Hendren WH: Posterior urethral valves in boys. A broad clinical spectrum. J Urol 1971;106:298.
23. Hendren WH: Reoperation for the failed ureteral reimplantation. J Urol 1974;111:403.
24. Hendren WH: Complications of megaureter repair. J Urol 1975;113:238.
25. Hendren WH: Complications of ureterostomy. J Urol 1978; 120:269.
26. Hendren WH: Prune-belly syndrome. In Devine CJ Jr, Stecker JF (eds): Urology in Practice. Boston, Little, Brown, 1978.
27. Hendren WH: Urinary tract refunctionalization after long-term diversion. A 20-year experience with 177 patients. Ann Surg 1990;212:478.
28. Hendren WH, Hendren RB: Bladder augmentation: Experience with 129 children and young adults. J Urol 1990;144:445.
29. Jeffs RD, Comisarow RH, Hanna MK: The early assessment for individualized treatment in the prune belly syndrome. Birth Defects 1977;13:97.
30. Kalicinski ZH, Kansy J, Kotarbinska B: Surgery of megaureters—modification of Hendren's operation. J Pediatr Surg 1977;12:183.
31. Kinahan TJ, Churchill BM, McLorie GA, et al: The efficiency of bladder emptying in the prune belly syndrome. J Urol 1992;148:600.
32. Kirsch AJ, Perez-Brayfield MR, Scherz HC: Minimally invasive treatment of vesicoureteral reflux with endoscopic injection of dextranomer/hyaluronic acid copolymer: The Children's Hospitals of Atlanta experience. J Urol 2003;170:211.
33. Perez-Brayfield M, Kirsch AJ, Hensle TW, et al: Endoscopic treatment with dextranomer/hyaluronic acid for complex cases of vesico-ureteral reflux. J Urol 2004;172:1614.
34. Kroovand RL, Al-Ansari RM, Perlmutter AD: Urethral and genital malformations in prune belly syndrome. J Urol 1982;127:94.
35. Lee BR, Partin AW, Epstein JI, et al: A quantitative histological analysis of the dilated ureter of childhood. J Urol 1992; 148:1482.
36. Lee BR, Silver RI, Partin AW, et al: A quantitative histologic analysis of collagen subtypes: The primary obstructed and refluxing megaureter of childhood. Urology 1998; 51:820.

37. Liu HY, Dhillon HK, Yeung CK, et al: Clinical outcome and management of prenatally diagnosed primary megaureters. J Urol 1994;152:614.
38. Loder RT, Guiboux JP, Bloom DA, et al: Musculoskeletal aspects of prune-belly syndrome. Description and pathogenesis. Am J Dis Child 1992;146:1224.
39. McLaughlin AP, Pfister RC, Leadbetter WF, et al: The pathophysiology of primary megaloureter. J Urol 1973;109: 805.
40. McLellan DI, Retik AB, Bauer SB, et al: Rate and predictors of spontaneous resolution of prenatally diagnosed primary nonrefluxing megaureter. J Urol 2002;168:2177.
41. McLorie GA, Jayanthi VR, Kinahan TJ, et al: A modified extravesical technique for megaureter repair. Br J Urol 1994;74:715.
42. Monfort G, Guys JM, Bocciardi A, et al: A novel technique for reconstruction of the abdominal wall in the prune belly syndrome. J Urol 1991;146:639.
43. Monie IW, Monie BJ: Prune belly syndrome and fetal ascites. Teratology 1979;7:19.
44. Nunn IN, Stephens FD: The triad system: A composite anomaly of the abdominal wall, urinary system and testes. J Urol 1961;86:782.
45. O'Donnell B, Puri P: Treatment of vesicoureteric reflux by endoscopic injection of Teflon. BMJ 1984;289:7.
46. Osler W: Congenital absence of abdominal muscles, with distended and hypertrophied urinary bladder. Bull Johns Hopkins Hosp 1901;12:331.
47. Pagon RA, Smith DW, Shepard TH: Urethral obstruction malformation complex: A cause of abdominal muscle deficiency and the "prune belly." J Pediatr 1979;94:900.
48. Palmer JM, Teluk H: Ureteral pathology in the prune belly syndrome. J Urol 1974;111:701.
49. Parrott TS, Woodard JR: The Monfort operation for abdominal wall reconstruction in the prune belly syndrome, J Urol 1992;148:688.
50. Parrot TS, Woodard JR, Wolpert JJ: Ureteral tailoring: A comparison of wedge resection with infolding. J Urol 1990; 14:328.
51. Passerini-Glazel G, Araguna F, Chiozza L, et al: The P.A.D.U.A. (Progressive augmentation by dilating the urethra anterior). J Urol 1988;140:1247.
52. Perdzynski W, Kalicinski ZH: Long-term results after megaureter folding in children. J Pediatr Surg 1996;31:1211.
53. Perlmutter AD: Reduction cystoplasty in prune belly syndrome. J Urol 1976;116:356.
54. Perovic S: Surgical treatment of megaureters using detrusor tunneling extravesical ureteroneocystostomy. J Urol 1994; 152:622.
55. Peters CA, Mandell J, Lebowitz RL, et al: Congenital obstructed megaureters in early infancy: Diagnosis and treatment. J Urol 1989;142:641.
56. Peterson DS, Fish L, Cass AA: Twins with congenital deficiency of abdominal musculature. J Urol 1972;107:670.
57. Pfister RC, Hendren WH: Primary megaureter in children and adults. Urology 1978;12:160.
58. Potter EL: Abnormal development of the kidney. In Potter EL (ed): Normal and Abnormal Development of the Kidney. Chicago, Year Book, 1972, p 154.
59. Puri P, Chertin B, Velayudham M, et al: Treatment of vesicoureteral reflux by endoscopic injection of dextranomer/hyaluronic acid copolymer: Preliminary results. J Urol 2003; 170:1541, discussion 1544.
60. Rabinowtiz R, Schillinger JF: Prune belly syndrome in the female subject. J Urol 1977;118:454.
61. Randolph J, Cavett C, Eng G: Surgical correction and rehabilitation for children with "prune-belly" syndrome. Ann Surg 1981;193:757.
62. Randolph J, Cavett C, Eng G: Abdominal wall reconstruction in the prune belly syndrome. J Pediatr Surg 1981;16:960.
63. Reinberg Y, Chelimsky G, Gonzalez R: Urethral atresia and the prune belly syndrome—report of 6 cases. Br J Urol 1993;72:112.
64. Reinberg Y, Manivel JC, Fryd D, et al: The outcome of renal transplantation in children with the prune-belly syndrome. J Urol 1989;142:1541.
65. Reinberg Y, Manivel JC, Pettinato G, et al: Development of renal failure in children with the prune belly syndrome. J Urol 1991;145:1017.
66. Rogers LW, Ostrow PT: The prune belly syndrome. Report of 20 cases and description of a lethal variant. J Pediatr 1973;83:786.
67. Smith DW: Recognizable Patterns of Human Malformation. Philadelphia, WB Saunders, 1970, p 5.
68. Smith EA, Woodard JR: Prune-belly syndrome. In Retik AB, Vaughan ED, Wein AJ (eds): Campbell's Urology, vol 3, 8th ed. Philadelphia, WB Saunders, 2002, p 2117.
69. Smith ED: Report of working party to establish an international nomenclature for the large ureter. Birth Defects Original Articles Series 1977;13(5):3.
70. Snow BW, Duckett JW: Prune belly syndrome. In Gillenwater JY, Grayhack JT, Howards SS, et al (eds): Adult and Pediatric Urology. Chicago, Year Book, 1987.
71. Starr A: Ureteral plication: A new concept in ureteral tapering for megaureter. Invest Urol 1979;17:153.
72. Stenberg A, Lackgren G: A new bioimplant for the endoscopic treatment of vesicoureteral reflux: Experimental and short-term clinical results. J Urol 1995;154:800.
73. Williams DI, Burkholder GV: The prune belly syndrome. J Urol 1967;98:244.
74. Williams DI, Hulme-Moir I: Primary obstructive megaureter. Br J Urol 1970;42:140.
75. Woodard JR, Parrott TS: Orchiopexy in the prune belly syndrome. Br J Urol 1978;50:348.
76. Woodard JR, Parrott TS: Reconstruction of the urinary tract in prune belly uropathy. J Urol 1978;119:824.
77. Woodard JR, Zucker I: Current management of the dilated urinary tract in prune belly syndrome. Urol Clin North Am 1990;17:407.
78. Woodhouse RJ, Kellett MJ, Williams DI: Minimal surgical interference in the prune belly syndrome. Br J Urol 1979; 51:475.

Chapter 115

Incontinent and Continent Urinary Diversion

Elizabeth Yerkes, Peter Metcalfe, and Richard C. Rink

Urinary diversion can be either incontinent or continent. With incontinent diversion the reservoir is external to the body (ostomy bag or diaper in children) and is emptied routinely when full. With continent urinary diversion, the urinary reservoir is routinely emptied by clean intermittent catheterization (CIC). Classically when the reservoir has been made entirely of gastrointestinal segments, that is, with no native bladder, it has been known as a continent urinary reservoir (CUR). In children, the primary diagnoses requiring urinary reconstruction are spinal dysraphism, bladder exstrophy, posterior urethral valves, or complex cloacal anomalies. In these disorders, the diseased native bladder can usually be incorporated into the reconstruction so that true CURs are rare in children. However, most will require intestinocystoplasty and a catheterizable abdominal wall channel, and, therefore, they are "continent reservoirs" and will be considered as such in this chapter. The term *undiversion* used in this chapter refers to the situation in which a child was previously treated with an incontinent urinary diversion and is converted to a continent diversion. Whereas undiversion has a great historic significance, it is quite rare in modern pediatric urologic reconstruction and, therefore, is not covered in this chapter.

Historically, permanent incontinent urinary diversion was employed to protect the kidneys from the deleterious effects of increased bladder pressure or to manage urinary incontinence. In more contemporary practice, medical management of bladder dysfunction with CIC and anticholinergic agents has limited the indications for surgical intervention.[84] Urodynamic expertise has allowed identification and aggressive management of high-risk patients.[94] The development of surgical techniques to allow storage of urine at safe pressures has virtually eliminated the use of permanent forms of incontinent urinary diversion, but this still remains an appropriate option for some patients. Temporary diversion is still required for select patients but is rarely first-line management for the bladder or the upper urinary tract.

INCONTINENT URINARY DIVERSION

Although eventual urinary continence is desirable for all children, protection of the integrity of the upper urinary tract is the primary concern. Several forms of incontinent urinary diversion are still occasionally used on either a temporary or a permanent basis to prevent upper urinary tract deterioration, prevent infection, or simplify day-to-day care of patients with very limited capability for self care.

Temporary urinary diversion is most commonly performed in infants or very young children, and the urine is easily collected in the diaper. Most permanent incontinent diversions require an ostomy appliance for hygienic collection of the urine. Compared with the alternative of continence by CIC, the incontinent stoma carries a stigma and body image issues that are better avoided in the pediatric population. For select patients and families, however, this remains a reasonable option.

Cutaneous Vesicostomy

Cutaneous vesicostomy is the most common form of incontinent urinary diversion in children today, but it is rarely utilized as first-line therapy and has limited indications. Infants with a neuropathic bladder and unsafe storage pressures may require vesicostomy if CIC and anticholinergic medications fail or if the family is unable or unwilling to execute these medical measures. Inability to incise posterior urethral valves safely owing to the small urethral caliber in some premature infants is another indication for cutaneous vesicostomy. In these patients the vesicostomy is closed when the child has grown enough for incision of the valves. Young infants with high-grade vesicoureteral reflux and multiple breakthrough urinary tract infections on antibiotic prophylaxis may also benefit from vesicostomy.[80,110] Improvement in the efficiency of both bladder and upper tract drainage reduces the incidence of urinary infection. In persistent cloaca refractory hydronephrosis, hydrocolpos or urinary infection despite intermittent catheterization of the common channel is another uncommon indication for vesicostomy.[5]

Ideally, the vesicostomy provides low-pressure drainage of bladder contents with minimal residual volume. Multiple series have confirmed the benefits of vesicostomy.[17,60,61,80,106,110] Improvement in upper urinary tract dilation and stabilization or improvement of renal function is achieved. Reflux may resolve or the degree of ureteral dilation may improve enough that ureteral tapering is not required at the time of reimplantation.[80,110] Although bacterial colonization of the open system is common, symptomatic infections and urosepsis are reduced. One concern about prolonged vesicostomy drainage in the non-neuropathic population is failure of the bladder to develop normally in the absence of cyclic filling and emptying.[32,109] However, several studies have refuted this concern.[63,69,110]

Once the urinary tract is stabilized and the long-term potential of the bladder becomes clearer, the vesicostomy is easily closed. It may be closed primarily or in combination with continent diversion. Some patients and families are not appropriate candidates for vesicostomy closure or find that vesicostomy and diaper drainage is an acceptable low-maintenance permanent option. Vesicostomy, with or without the use of an ostomy appliance, can also be performed in adult patients who are not candidates for continent diversion.[60]

Two techniques for cutaneous vesicostomy have been used for many years. Lapides described elevation of an anterior bladder wall flap with deep insertion of an abdominal skin flap to fashion the cutaneous vesicostomy.[83] The more common technique was described by Blocksom in 1957[13] and modified by Duckett[36] (Fig. 115-1).

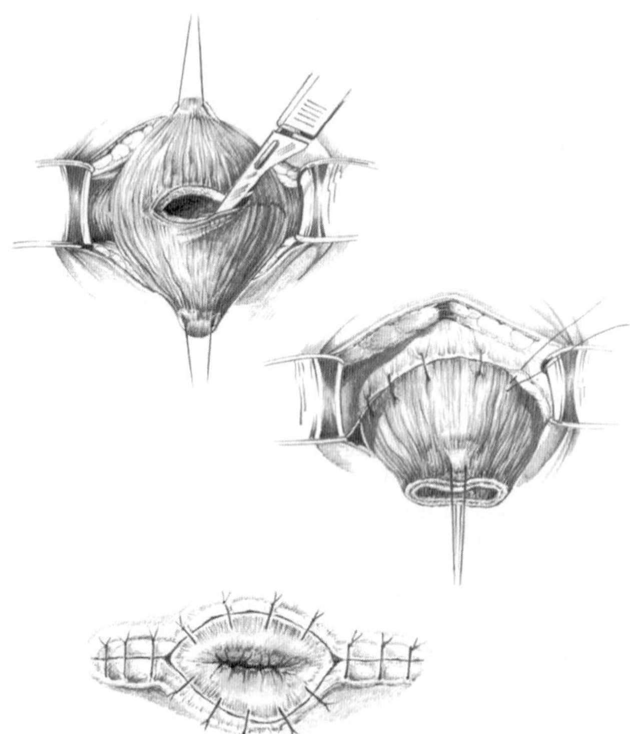

Figure 115-1 The Blocksom vesicostomy, showing the incision in the dome of the bladder, the fixation to the overlying fascia, and the everted stoma.

The Blocksom vesicostomy is fashioned through a small transverse incision halfway between the umbilicus and the pubis. The fascia is incised, and the peritoneum is pushed superiorly off the dome of the bladder. The urachal remnant is divided, and the dome of the bladder is pulled up to the skin. The fascia is secured to the bladder wall to form a No. 24 French defect, and the bladder is matured as a flush stoma.

Complications of cutaneous vesicostomy include stomal stenosis, prolapse, peristomal dermatitis, and bladder calculi. Stomal stenosis is more common with a stiff or thick bladder wall, as in posterior urethral valves. Failure to fashion the vesicostomy from the dome of the bladder may allow the posterior bladder wall to prolapse through the vesicostomy. This is one advantage of the Blocksom technique over the Lapides vesicostomy. Prolapse is managed by manual reduction with temporary catheter drainage and revision of the low vesicostomy. Dermatitis is particularly bothersome in some patients and is managed with application of a zinc oxide barrier cream or topical treatment for obvious candidiasis. Bladder calculi are unusual provided that the vesicostomy is functioning well and the upper tracts are drained.

Cutaneous Ureterostomy

Ureterostomy for temporary supravesical urinary diversion is rarely performed today. It has been used historically for drainage of a profoundly dilated upper urinary tract in the presence of urosepsis[102] or to maximize drainage of the renal units in cases of severe obstruction. Percutaneous or endourologic drainage of these systems is possible now in children, but ureteral size limits the utility of this in very small infants.[123] Low diversion can be performed as a loop or end cutaneous ureterostomy (Figs. 115-2 and 115-3), and subsequent takedown involves ureteroneocystostomy. The diversion allows the caliber of the ureter to decrease, thereby reducing the complexity of the reimplantation. Diversion at the level of the kidney is performed through a flank incision and can be performed as a loop ureterostomy, Sober ureterostomy, or end ureterostomy. A loop ureterostomy can easily be taken down and is the more appropriate choice for temporary diversion. End ureterostomy just below the ureteropelvic junction makes reconstitution of the ureter more difficult and should be reserved as a very rare permanent form of diversion in cases of severe bladder dysfunction.[123] Sober ureterostomy, with its proximal diverting limb and reanastomosis of the distal limb to the renal pelvis, is rarely used today and is technically much more involved and may therefore be less appropriate for diversion during acute illness. On the other hand it offers the advantage of diversion and continued antegrade drainage to cycle the bladder.[88] In all cases, care should be taken to preserve the medial blood supply and adventitial vessels and to create a tension-free anastomosis to the skin. Given the profoundly dilated nature of the ureter in most of these cases, stomal stenosis is rarely an issue.

Supravesical diversion may be warranted in select posterior urethral valve patients when renal function fails to improve after bladder drainage.[88] Persistent ureterovesical

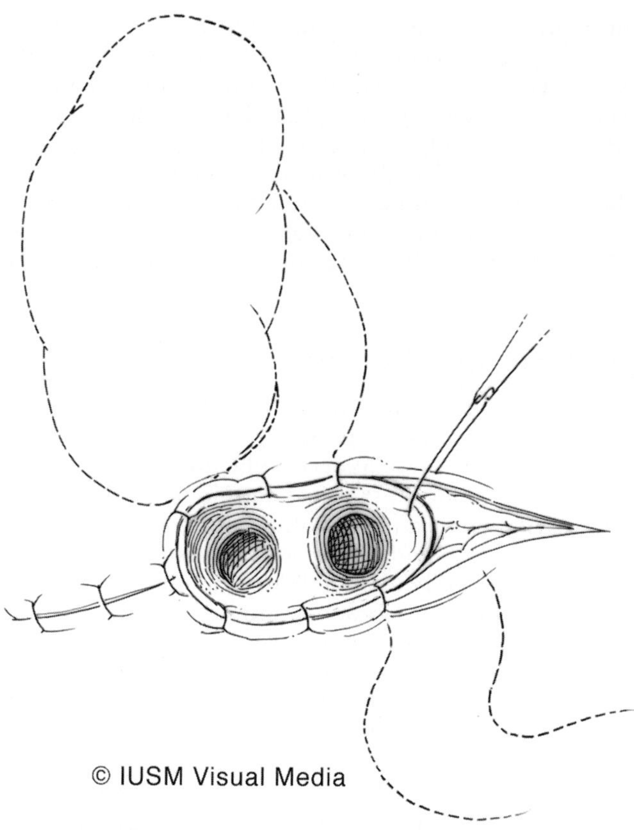

Figure 115–2 The loop ureterostomy is easily taken down and, therefore, allows for an excellent temporary diversion.

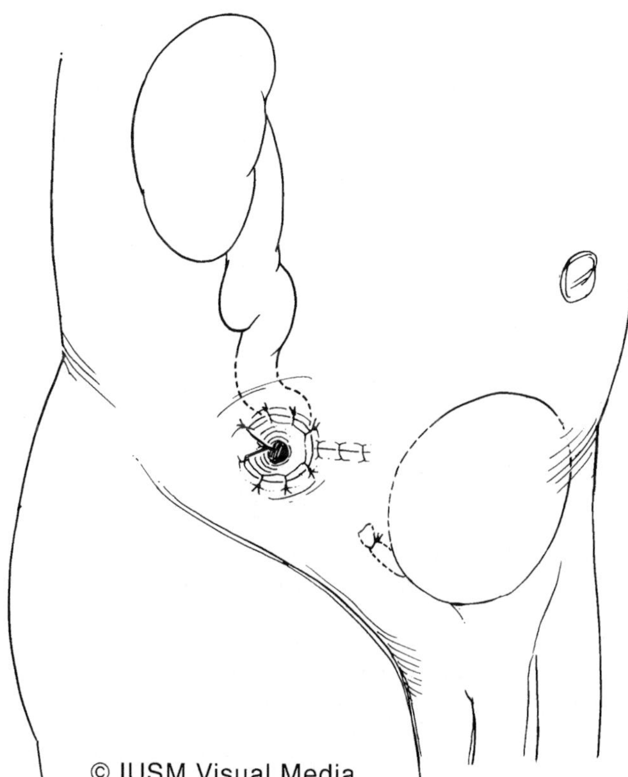

Figure 115–3 The end ureterostomy requires formal reimplantation to reverse.

junction obstruction is the concern. Ureterostomy and pyelostomy would maximize upper tract drainage, but percutaneous nephrostomy is a less invasive temporary means to assess the potential of the affected kidney.[43] Patients who demonstrate improvement in renal function after supravesical diversion may do so because of better drainage or just due to normal renal maturation.[144] As with cutaneous vesicostomy there is concern that the valve bladder will fail to develop normally if the urine is diverted. In patients with a solitary functioning kidney, a loop ureterostomy or an end ureterostomy would defunctionalize the bladder. Several studies suggest, however, that bladder dysfunction is due to bladder wall abnormalities from infravesical obstruction rather than supravesical diversion of urine.[62,69]

Cutaneous Pyelostomy

As with cutaneous ureterostomy, proximal diversion by pyelostomy has limited indications in current practice. The controversies surrounding this type of diversion are similar. With direct drainage of the renal pelvis, pyelostomy may be used for temporary diversion in select cases of obstruction at the ureteropelvic junction but could also be used as discussed earlier for posterior urethral valves. Pyelostomy requires a very dilated extrarenal pelvis to create a tension-free anastomosis to the skin. Takedown of the pyelostomy at the time of a definitive procedure is relatively simple owing to reliable blood supply to the renal pelvis.

Ileal Conduit/Colon Conduit

Permanent supravesical urinary diversion was popular many decades ago as a reliable means to manage neuropathic bladder, bladder outlet obstruction, and severe urinary incontinence. Conduit diversions have been created with most intestinal segments, although ileum (Fig. 115-4) and colon are utilized most commonly.

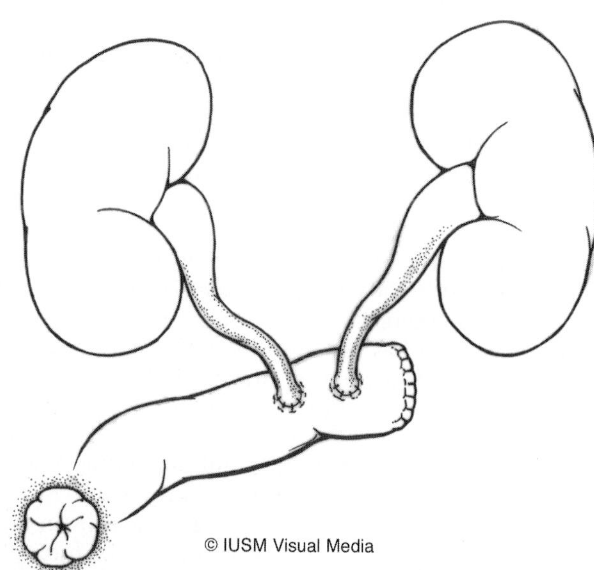

Figure 115–4 The ileal conduit is the standard permanent supravesical diversion for patients whose bladder is absent.

Both simple refluxing and tunneled nonrefluxing ureterointestinal anastomoses have been employed. The primary advantage of the colon conduit over an ileal conduit is the reliable antireflux reimplantation achievable with colon.

The risk of upper tract deterioration after ileal conduit diversion has exceeded 50% in some series.[75,128,129] Although this is not a tremendous concern in the older patient after cystectomy for bladder carcinoma, the long-term impact on the kidneys is extremely relevant in the pediatric population. The ability to create a nonrefluxing anastomosis between the ureter and colon gives colon conduits a theoretical advantage over ileal conduits. Unfortunately, deterioration of the upper tracts occurs in 26% to 48% of cases and ureteral reflux persists in 8% to 58% of colon conduits.[58] Anastomotic stricture occurs with similar frequency with ileum and colon (9% to 22%).[58,75]

Koch and associates compared a cohort of myelomeningocele patients with ileal conduit diversion to another group managed with CIC.[75] The ileal conduit group suffered renal deterioration, nephrolithiasis, and pyelonephritis significantly more than the catheterization group. Bone density was decreased in both groups, and the incidence of fractures was equal, but the diversion group had impaired linear growth, more spinal curvature, and more complications from orthopedic procedures. The metabolic alterations associated with incorporation of intestinal segments into the urinary tract do occur with incontinent diversions.

Other complications of conduit diversion included stomal stenosis, stomal prolapse, peristomal hernia, and peristomal dermatitis. Stomal stenosis occurred in 8% to 61% of cases. Stoma complications are best prevented with careful surgical technique, including preservation of intestinal perfusion, creation of a straight and adequate caliber fascial window, and fixation of the conduit to the fascia. A protuberant rosebud stoma enhances the fit of the stoma appliance and prevents stenosis.

Bacteriuria is nearly universal but does not cause upper tract damage if the ureterointestinal anastomosis and the conduit itself functions appropriately.[49,58] Stasis of colonized urine, however, may contribute to upper tract stone formation and may have other implications as well. Nitrosamines produced by the mixture of urine and bacteria appear to have some role in induction of malignancy in the isolated intestinal segment.[44,58]

Austen and Kalble reviewed the world literature and identified 81 tumors collectively in a variety of continent and incontinent diversions with incorporated bowel segments.[8] This total is exclusive of the large number of malignancies reported after ureterosigmoidostomy. Neoplasia was reported in 12 ileal conduits and 5 colon conduits, with a mean latency of 22 and 10 years, respectively. Colon conduit tumors were exclusively adenocarcinoma, but transitional cell carcinoma, squamous cell carcinoma, carcinoid, and anaplastic tumors were also found in ileal conduits. Chronic inflammation of the intestinal segment may play a role in the malignant changes. Early yearly surveillance for tumor is recommended.

Preoperative preparation for conduit diversion involves a full mechanical and antibiotic bowel preparation and parenteral antibiotic to sterilize the urine on the day before surgery. Patients with severe neuropathic bowel may actually require more than 1 day of preparation for adequate cleanout. It is critical that preoperatively an enterostomal therapist mark potential stoma sites bilaterally after examining the patient in multiple positions. The abdominal contour can change significantly in myelomeningocele patients when seated, and an ill-fitting ostomy appliance will be a lasting source of dissatisfaction.

Incontinent Ileovesicostomy

Incontinent ileovesicostomy, initially described by McGuire and associates in 1994,[127] has primarily been used in the adult population with bladder and sphincter dysfunction secondary to spinal cord injury and multiple sclerosis. Patients had failed other efforts to manage the bladder pressures and urinary incontinence and refused or were not candidates for continent diversion. Many suffered severe complications from use of a chronic indwelling urethral catheter. Several series report excellent results with regard to preservation of renal function, incidence of urinary tract infection and urolithiasis, and stomal complications.[7,41,86,104] The ileovesicostomy functions as a popoff valve to maintain safe bladder storage pressures. Stomal leak-point pressures are low, and a moderate residual urine remains.[104]

Incontinent ileovesicostomy is an option to consider in select pediatric patients with limited dexterity and social support. Although it does require a permanent stoma, preservation of renal function appears superior when compared with standard conduit diversion. In addition, the disruption of the ureterovesical junction is not required. Parents may have difficulty accepting permanent diversion even if the child has very limited potential to perform self-catheterization in the future. Some families are not ready to assume the care required for bladder augmentation or continent urinary reservoir, despite the fact that the child needs reconstruction to preserve the upper urinary tracts. In these instances, incontinent ileovesicostomy with both an efferent incontinent limb and a large open patch of ileum to augment the bladder can be considered. Consideration could be given to creation of a Mitrofanoff catheterizable channel at the time of the initial procedure. Should the family later embrace continence and the long-term care of bladder augmentation, the ileal chimney can be amputated to leave a continent diversion.[29]

Thorough preoperative bowel preparation and sterilization of the urine are required. A stoma site is carefully preplanned for the right lower quadrant to ensure optimal fit of the stoma appliance. The bladder is bivalved in the coronal plane in preparation for anastomosis to the isolated ileal segment. The proximal end of the ileum is opened widely on its antimesenteric border and anastomosed to the bladder in a running fashion. The length of the ileal segment can be tailored to account for body habitus and for the need to augment the native bladder capacity.[86] A rosebud stoma is fashioned in the right lower quadrant, and a No. 22 French catheter is left in place for 3 weeks to maintain the caliber of the ileovesical anastomosis despite bladder decompression. If significant augmentation is performed, a suprapubic catheter should be left as well to maximize perioperative drainage. A bladder neck or urethral procedure is used to create outlet resistance procedure in patients with urethral incompetence or severe preoperative urge incontinence.

CONTINENT URINARY DIVERSION

Many different types of continent urinary diversions have been developed to improve or replace the native lower urinary tract and have been generally named for the institution where they were developed or the surgeon who developed them. The chosen technique depends largely on the surgeon's experience and preference, but the primary pathology plays a large role in any given patient. Reconstruction is tailored to the specific anatomy and related functional deficits. A fundamental difference exists in pediatric lower urinary tract reconstruction versus that of adults. In adult reconstruction, a particular type of reconstruction (i.e., Koch pouch, Indiana pouch, Mainz pouch) may be chosen preoperatively because the anatomy is usually constant. In children with disorders such as cloacal exstrophy, the anatomy may be quite variable and bizarre. Therefore, the ideal storage device, a low-pressure reservoir with a means of catheterization without leakage or reflux, must be fashioned from the tissues available at the time of reconstruction. Whenever possible, enhancement of the native bladder and outlet is preferred to avoid the potential complication associated with ureteral anastomosis to a CUR. CURs are performed when the native bladder is absent or not salvageable. Patients with bladder agenesis syndromes, cloacal exstrophy, and pelvic organ destruction secondary to trauma or malignancy would be candidates for CUR.

Continent urinary diversion is now common, but one must remember that it requires a broad spectrum of surgical skills and must address the varied underlying diagnoses. By definition, a reservoir is created that must be emptied by intermittent catheterization. This may include the augmentation of an intact, but severely diseased, bladder or the creation of a reservoir completely from heterologous tissue. The surgical goals and principles are very similar: to create the ideal storage reservoir for urine that can be easily emptied with the minimum of complications. Because the gastrointestinal tract is plentiful and accessible, it is the most common source of tissue. The physiologic variability along the gastrointestinal tract allows the surgeon to tailor the reconstruction to the patient. However, these complex surgeries are not without complications, which have to be understood and anticipated.

Bladder Augmentation

Bladder augmentation is an essential component of the pediatric urologist's surgical armamentarium. It has a prominent role in the management of many lower urinary tract disorders, including neurogenic bladder, posterior urethral valves, and bladder exstrophy. The modern application often includes the use of a continent catheterizable abdominal stoma fashioned from either the appendix (a Mitrofanoff channel) or tapered ileum (a Monti channel) and may require an additional procedure to improve the continence mechanism at the bladder neck. Intermittent emptying via the native urethra remains an option, although this can be extremely challenging after bladder neck reconstruction.

As previously discussed, children with severe lower urinary tract dysfunction were historically treated with urinary diversion. The introduction of CIC by Lapides[84,85] ensured that any child could safely empty the bladder. This brought the dawning of lower urinary tract reconstruction and allowed the urinary tract to remain intact and avoid the use of external collecting devices. Advances in urodynamic monitoring improved our ability to predict who would best benefit from bladder reconstruction and, therefore, prevent renal deterioration.[94] Parallel medical advances ensured the survival of these complex patients and allowed for the shift of focus toward continence as an important aspect of their quality of life.[51,143] Recent advances with cutaneous catheterizable channels continue to simplify care and increase its popularity.[57]

The primary goal of lower urinary tract reconstruction is to store urine at safe pressures without leakage. Adequate storage requires a low-pressure, highly compliant reservoir of adequate volume, whereas continence results from limited contractility and an effective sphincter mechanism.

The vast majority of augmentations are performed with gastrointestinal segments, because bowel segments are readily available and easily configured. Ileum is currently the most popular segment,[46,115,116] but sigmoid is often used. Stomach and ileocecal segments have been used but have only a small role in contemporary management of the pediatric patient.[3,19,130,132] Their abundance ensures that adequate capacity is obtained whereas detubularization and the natural viscoelastic properties allow for the low pressure reservoir.[56,79] However, the secretive[15,120] and absorptive[72] nature of this tissue is also responsible for most of the common complications associated with this procedure.

Requirements for a successful augmentation require proper patient selection,[30] the ability and willingness to perform CIC,[82,120] proper selection of augmentation material, and recognition and treatment of complications.

Patient Evaluation and Selection

The patient, the family, and the entire health care team must be involved in the decision to pursue major surgery. The common risks of incorporating gastrointestinal segments into the urinary tract, including mucus production, urinary tract infection, bladder and renal calculi, metabolic changes, as well as life-threatening risks such as malignant degeneration and spontaneous perforation, must be explained to the family and child and *must* be understood.[15,82,120] Everyone involved in caring for the child must be committed to the appropriate postoperative care, including mandatory use of CIC and regular bladder irrigation.[82,120,121]

Clinical evaluation requires a thorough history and physical examination. Particular attention should be paid to latex allergy because this can be a fatal complication. Preoperative evaluation should include a renal-bladder ultrasound (RBUS) and a voiding cystourethrogram (VCUG). Serum chemistries are required because impaired renal function may change the gastrointestinal segment used.[82] Initially, it was suggested that a creatinine clearance of less than 60 mL/min might be a contraindication for the use of ileum as a continent urinary reservoir,[96,135] but augmentation often stabilizes renal function and reconstruction has been done before renal transplantation. Urodynamic studies are necessary to determine outlet resistance, bladder capacity, and storage pressures. Cystoscopy will confirm anatomy and ensure that no untoward findings are present that may hinder reconstruction.[120]

The net result of these investigations is a comprehensive surgical plan. The exact procedure will depend on which segment is to be used and whether the patient requires concomitant ureteric reimplantation, bladder neck procedure, and a catheterizable channel. Patients with a neurogenic bladder frequently undergo a simultaneous antegrade bowel continence procedure, usually using the appendix, to facilitate evacuation of their neurogenic bowel.[103] This must also be factored into the type of reconstruction needed, because if the appendix is used for a bowel continence procedure additional ileum may be needed for a catheterizable urinary channel.

Preoperative preparation usually involves bowel preparation, as described previously for conduit diversion. Perioperative antibiotics and a sterile urine are required and are particularly important if the patient has a ventriculoperitoneal shunt.[149]

Long-term follow-up is required with all patients. After the postoperative visit, and assuming the absence of complications, the patient should be seen annually with a history, physical examination, determination of creatinine and electrolyte levels, an ultrasound, and a cystoscopy once 5 to 10 years after surgery.[82,120]

Gastrointestinal Cystoplasty

Most children undergoing lower urinary tract reconstruction for hostile bladder dynamics can have their native bladder preserved but need to have it augmented to lower intravesical pressures, limit contractility, and improve compliance. Gastrointestinal segments are generally used, but this requires reconfiguration and detubularization to prevent their own inherent contractile properties.[3,56,79,98] Maximum storage capacity requires approximation of the spherical shape.[56] A widely bivalved bladder enables this, as well as helps to prevent the augment behaving as a diverticulum. Our preference is to offset the incision, allowing more detrusor muscle to be elevated toward the stoma. This has the advantage of providing greater access to the muscular backing of the detrusor, facilitating reimplantation of the catheterizable channel and

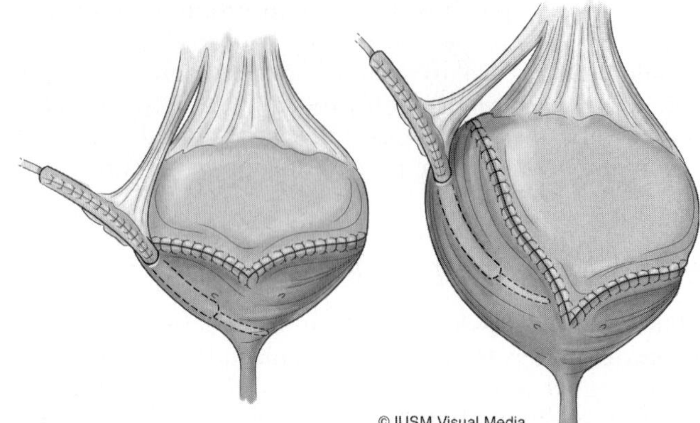

Figure 115-5 The offset cystoplasty allows for more mobility of the detrusor muscle and provides better access to the muscular backing that is essential for implantation of the catheterizable channel.

continence (Fig. 115-5). The volume of the sphere is maximized by folding the ileum into a U or S shape, which increases the potential radius and volume[82] (Fig. 115-6). This reconfiguration, as well as detubularization along the antimesenteric border, is critical to disrupting intestinal contractions because the intact intestine can create pressures of 40 to 100 cm H_2O.[40,89,90] The reconstructive surgeon should err on the side of a larger, rather than smaller, augmentation.[120] Regardless of the bowel segment selected, a watertight anastomosis using absorbable suture is done. A suprapubic tube is placed into the native bladder and secured to the abdominal wall, and a perivesical drain is placed.

Ileocystoplasty

Ileum has become the segment of choice due to its inherently low contractility, abundance, and ease of manipulation.[46,115,116] In children, 20 to 30 cm is harvested, with the distal margin located 15 to 20 cm from the ileocecal valve to prevent vitamin B_{12} and bile salt malabsorption.[79,114] Ileum is known to produce less mucus than

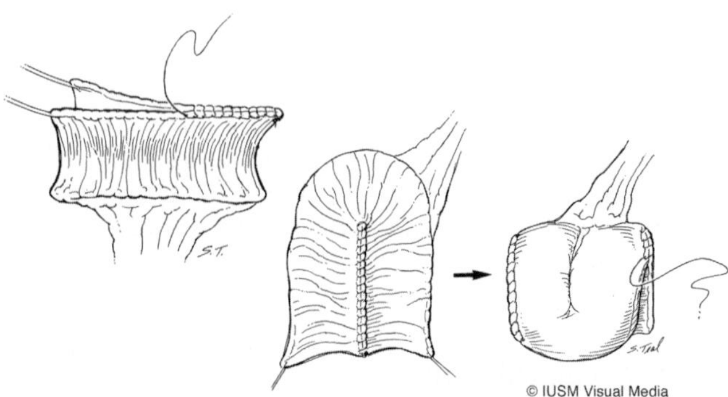

Figure 115-6 The ideal bladder augmentation will increase both capacity and compliance, which are required for continence and renal protection.

colon, and we noted a lower rate of perforation when compared with sigmoid.[35] It has the distinct disadvantage of being difficult to create submucosal tunnels for ureteral reimplantation or catheterizable channel placement.

Sigmoid Cystoplasty

Advantages of the sigmoid include its proximity to the bladder and its marked dilation in the neuropathic population. Fifteen to 20 cm is isolated and irrigated with an antibiotic solution. Owing to the extreme contractile nature of the sigmoid, complete detubularization is essential.[132] Spontaneous perforation rates have been shown to be higher with sigmoid as opposed to ileal augmentations,[117] presumably because of their increased contractile pressure.[111]

Ileocecal Cystoplasty

The main advantage of the ileocecal segment is the consistent blood supply. There are two main techniques, each with multiple variations. Either both the ileal and cecal segment are tubularized and reconfigured together or solely the cecum is tubularized and the ileum used to create a continent stoma[19] for ureteric replacement.[82] This segment is infrequently used in the neuropathic population because loss of the ileocecal valve can result in intractable diarrhea.[99]

Gastrocystoplasty

The stomach is much less absorptive than other intestinal segments, and its secretion of hydrogen ions may be beneficial in patients with chronic renal failure and metabolic acidosis.[3,108] A 10- to 15-cm wedge from the greater curvature is mobilized along the right gastroepiploic vessels and passed through the mesentery of the transverse colon to the bladder. Originally believed to be an option for all augmentation candidates, its role now is quite limited. This is primarily due to the hematuria-dysuria syndrome, which occurs in up to 70% of patients.

CONTINENT CATHETERIZABLE CHANNELS

Bladder augmentation and bladder neck surgery markedly decrease the patient's ability to empty spontaneously while increasing the consequences of incomplete emptying. Not adhering to a strict CIC schedule can result in an increased risk of urinary tract infection, bladder stones,[107] and spontaneous bladder perforation.[6,122] In 1980, Mitrofanoff introduced the principle of a continent channel by using the vermiform appendix and implanting it submucosally into the bladder.[100] What is now known as the "Mitrofanoff principle" states that any supple tube implanted submucosally with sufficient muscle backing will act as a flap valve and results in a reliable continence mechanism (Fig. 115-7).

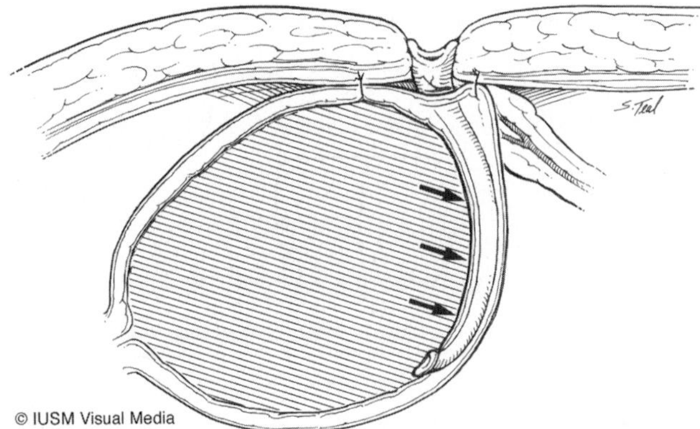

Figure 115-7 The Mitroffanof principle states that a supple tube will compress with increasing intravesical pressure and provide continence.

The Mitrofanoff principle has been widely embraced and applied to a variety of tissues, because the appendix (Fig. 115-8) is not always appropriate or available, especially if a simultaneous Malone antegrade continence enema (MACE) procedure is being performed. The use

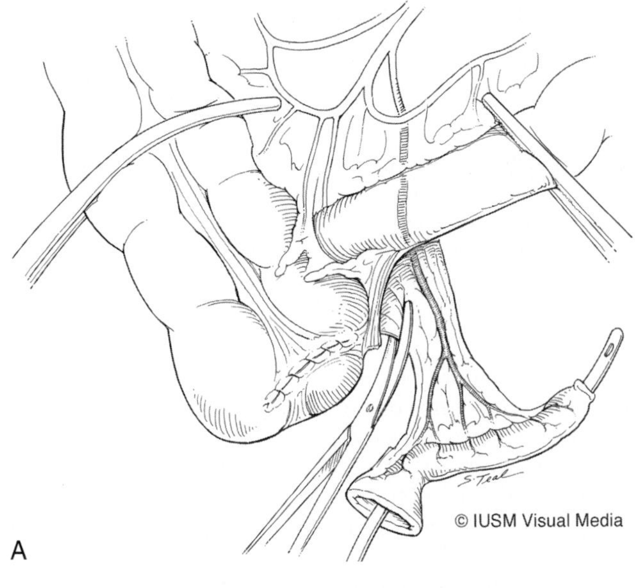

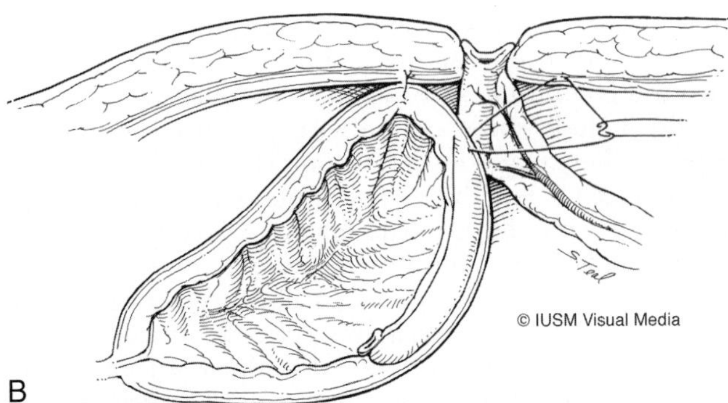

Figure 115-8 *A,* The appendix is readily accessible and mobilized with maintenance of its vasculature. *B,* It is implanted easily beneath the bladder mucosa to provide a reliable catheterizable channel.

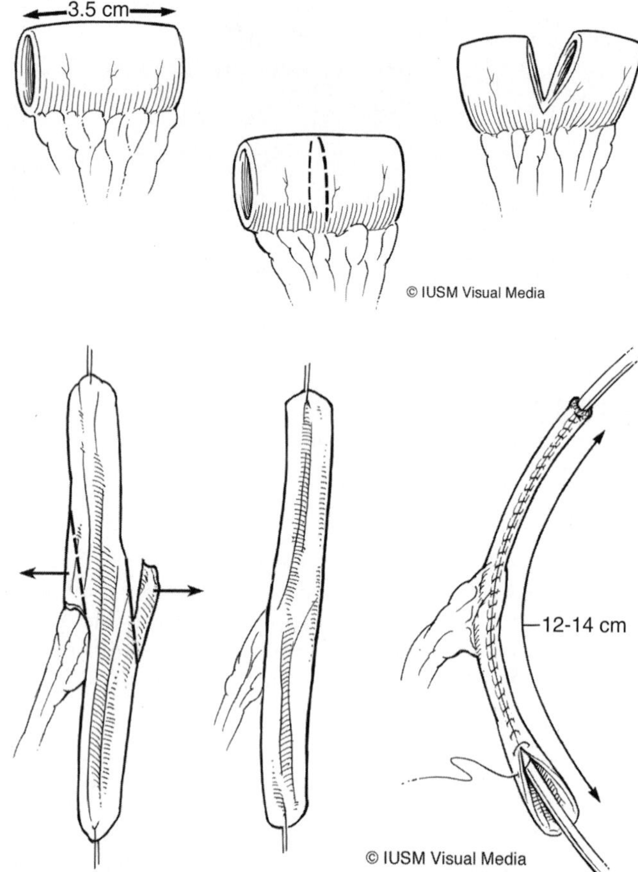

Figure 115-9 Normally, a 2-cm segment of ileum can be opened along its antimesenteric border and tubularized for an effective channel. A slightly longer piece (3.5 cm) can be partially divided, both ends tubularized, and reanastomosed for a spiral Monti, for situations demanding more channel length.

of stomach, colon, bladder, ureters, and fallopian tubes have all been reported with good success.* The reconfigured ileal channel was introduced by Yang[148] and Monti and colleagues[101] and has assumed a leading role in genitourinary reconstruction owing to its reliability, minimal loss of bowel, and ability to achieve lengths of up to 15 cm (Fig. 115-9).[21,141]

A continent catheterizable channel requires a supple tube, straight path, and short intra-abdominal segment. The appendicovesicostomy requires full mobilization of the right colon to ensure adequate mobility. Amputation should include some cecum, because this allows for a larger-caliber cutaneous stoma, or it can be tubularized to increase stomal length.[16,33] The appendix is then carefully mobilized with the mesoappendix to ensure adequate blood supply. The Monti-Yang technique requires the isolation of 2 cm of ileum, opening it along its antimesenteric border, and retubularizing it over a No. 12 French catheter. The channel is then preferentially implanted submucosally in the native bladder because its thick muscle is ideal for a continent valve; however, stomach and the tenia coli have been successfully used. Reimplantation into ileum is the most challenging and requires the creation of a seromuscular trough or a Ghoniem-type reimplantation. The stoma site can be hidden within the umbilicus or placed in the right lower quadrant, depending on surgeon preference. Regardless of location, great care is taken to ensure a catheter, usually a No. 12 French, passes easily and that the channel is as straight and tension free as possible. When satisfied, the surgeon fixes the channel and bladder to the abdominal wall with a permanent suture. Many ingenious skin flap techniques are employed to minimize the chance of stomal stenosis, all inserting into the spatulated channel. An indwelling catheter is left for 2 to 3 weeks, and the first catheterization is usually performed in the clinic setting. All family members caring for the child must learn proper catheterization technique.

Stomal continence is excellent, and rates of 90% to 99% are reported in the two largest published series.[21,64] Complications pertain primarily to difficulties with catheterization, most commonly at the skin level, but may also occur deeper within the channel itself. Stomal stenosis is reported to occur in 5% to 25%,[45,64] with a lower rate potentially seen with tubularized ileum.[21]

Several authors have described continent catheterizable tubes fashioned from native bladder. Casale's original description of the "intravesical channel"[26] was modified by Rink.[22] Although continence rates of 100% were reported, the technique is hampered by a 45% incidence of stomal stenosis. Although still a useful technique if an intraperitoneal procedure can be avoided, it has been largely replaced by the appendicovesicostomy and reconfigured ileovesicostomies.

These channels provide a more convenient and more socially acceptable means of catheterization. It is especially beneficial for those with a sensate urethra and in the obese or wheelchair-bound female. It also facilitates caregiver comfort and, most importantly, patient independence.

CONTINENT URINARY RESERVOIRS

If the entire bladder has been replaced by nonurothelial tissue (usually gastrointestinal) and requires emptying by means other than the urethra, it is referred to as continent urinary diversion. Although very popular and with many refinements over the past several decades, it is not commonly used in pediatrics today because generally the bladder can be incorporated into the reconstruction.[120]

A few diagnoses such as bladder agenesis or malignancy resulting in cystectomy will require complete bladder replacement. Patients with cloacal exstrophy may also require bladder replacement. When it is required, it allows the patient with a complex disorder to achieve continence. Patient selection for the procedure is as important as with bladder augmentation, because noncompliance will result in the same myriad of complications, despite a technically perfect operation. Preoperative evaluation is very similar to that for the bladder augmentation patient, with the acquisition of sufficient clinical, metabolic, anatomic, and functional data to develop a detailed surgical plan.

*See references 12, 20, 21, 27, 33, 38, 67, 101, 142, 145, 146, and 148.

The goals of the continent urinary diversion include the creation of a reservoir of adequate capacity and compliance, nonrefluxing ureteric implantations, a continent cutaneous stoma, and a minimum of complications.

Although the gastrointestinal tract again provides for the reservoir, several key differences exist with an augmentation. Colon and stomach have assumed a larger role, because the musculature of the tenia coli and stomach allow for more reliable nonrefluxing ureteric and catheterizable channel anastomoses. The three most common types of continent reservoir in children are a reservoir fashioned solely from ileum (Kock pouch), a gastroileal composite, and an ileocecal reservoir (Indiana pouch).[64] Each have a myriad of variations described, all attempting to decrease complications and facilitate construction. However, because published reports in children are usually limited to small numbers, each reservoir having subtle variations, and no published direct comparisons, it is impossible to determine an ideal reservoir.[64,121,147] The reconstructive surgeon, therefore, must be familiar with several techniques, because each has advantages that may require exploiting with any clinical situation.

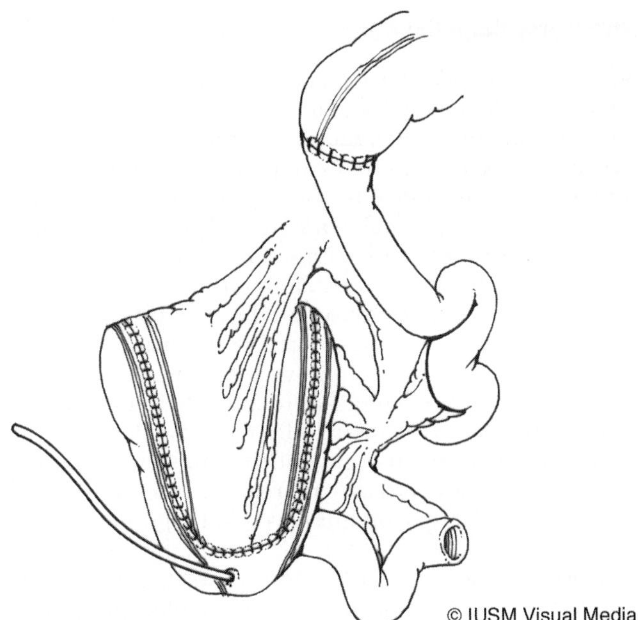

Figure 115-10 The Indiana pouch uses the ileocecal valve as a continence mechanism and the cecum for urinary storage.

Kock Pouch

Kock first described a continent ileostomy in 1971[76,77] and from this developed the Kock pouch in 1982.[78] This continent ileal reservoir was among the original nonorthotopic bladder substitutions used and maintains some popularity today.[1,2,31] It requires the construction of an efferent nipple for continence and an afferent limb for the prevention of reflux. This technically demanding aspect usually requires the use of stapling devices, and these can be the source of its most significant complications (stone formation) and long-term failure rate.[11]

Approximately 80 cm of ileum is harvested in adults, with the proximal 15 to 20 cm used in an isoperistaltic fashion to create the antireflux mechanism, and the distal 12 to 15 cm for the continent cutaneous stoma. These lengths are decreased appropriately depending on the size of the child. The bowel is intussuscepted through its full thickness, and this is secured by three rows of gastrointestinal staples, although absorbable mesh has also been described.[134] Significant modifications include removing the distal six staples from the device,[11] stripping the distal mesentery,[53] and the use of absorbable staples.[71]

Gastroileal Pouch

The advantages of both gastric and ileal segments can be maximized, while offsetting their complications, by incorporating them both into a composite reservoir. The metabolic derangements complement each other, as the acidic gastric secretion will neutralize the absorptive properties of the colon or ileum.[9,91,95] Furthermore, in patients at high risk for short gut syndrome, as in cloacal exstrophy, it allows a minimum of valuable absorptive tissue to be lost.[120] However, it is a more complex reconstruction, requiring two anastomoses and longer operating time, but is a valuable alternative for select patients.

Indiana Pouch

The ileocecal segment has been popularized owing to the potential continence or antireflux mechanism inherent to the ileocecal valve. Many surgical techniques have been described, in the attempt to maximize cutaneous continence, simplify the surgical procedure, and minimize complications. The Indiana group[124] modified the pouch described by Gilchrist and Merricks with a unique plication method that has retained its popularity. An Indiana pouch uses the detubularized cecum as its reservoir, with ureters implanted in a nonrefluxing manner into the tenia. The ileum is then plicated to the ileocecal valve, which is reinforced by Lembert sutures (Fig. 115-10). Continence has been reported in 95% to 99%,[113,124] in part owing to its very large capacity.[25] Complication rates have been acceptable, as low as 0.6%,[124] but not all surgeons have reported such success.[23] Although the Indiana pouch has achieved great popularity in the adult population, its use has been limited in children, owing to the removal of the ileocecal valve and the resultant potential for diarrhea.

COMPLICATIONS FROM THE INCORPORATION OF INTESTINE IN THE URINARY TRACT

Despite the popularity of using the gastrointestinal tract as a urinary reservoir, the potential complications are numerous and can be significant. A broad categorization would include (1) complications due to structural defects, (2) complications secondary to the loss of the intestinal segment, (3) complications due to secretions, and (4) complications from absorption.

Structural Complications

Structural complications include the requirement of a second augmentation, spontaneous perforation, and long-term malignancy potential. A secondary augmentation may be required in up to 6% of patients,[111] and most are due to high intravesical pressures from persistent bowel contractility.[52,92] The hallmark clinical signs are incontinence or hydronephrosis with screening ultrasound, and this is confirmed with urodynamic studies.

A spontaneous perforation can be a fatal complication and must not be underestimated. Early urine leaks are likely due to technical error, but late complications usually originate in the bowel, approximately 1 cm from the anastomotic line.[120] Patients often present later in the course, as their neurologic deficit impedes symptoms. Therefore, sepsis and death are realistic possibilities, and a high index of suspicion must prevail. Diagnosis is with a CT cystogram, and treatment is usually by laparotomy and primary closure,[122] but conservative treatment with catheter drainage has been successful in select patients.[136]

The development of adenocarcinoma is of concern, owing to the well-documented occurrence after ureterosigmoidostomy.[39,47,59,131,138] It arises from the ureterointestinal junction and occurs in these patients with a 7000-fold risk over the general population.[59] Although a tumor has been reported as soon as 3 years after augmentation,[24,66] the mean latency is 21.5 to 26 years.[8,59] At our institution, three malignancies have occurred in a series of over 500 augmentations. All patients died of metastatic disease, with a mean time from augmentation to diagnosis of 19 years.[137] Although most surgeons appreciate the risk, definitive guidelines for surveillance have not been established. Annual cystoscopy has been recommended to begin 5 to 10 years after augmentation.[8,120]

Loss of Intestinal Segment

Removal of an intestinal segment places the patient at risk for a bowel obstruction, and this occurs in approximately 3% of cases.[42,98,117,120] Because many of these obstructions are due to internal herniation through the pedicle of the augment, Leonard and associates have recommended early exploration to minimize the risk of augmentation ischemia.[87]

The removal of a gastrointestinal segment for CUR or augmentation is usually well tolerated; however, bowel dysfunction has been reported in 10% to 54% of patients.[55,133] Removal of the ileocecal valve can result in problematic diarrhea and rectal incontinence, especially in the neurogenic population.[48,70] Loss of the distal ileum can also result in diarrhea, in these cases owing to an interruption in the enterohepatic circulation[10]; but it can usually be prevented by leaving the distal 15 to 20 cm intact. Treatment of mild cases is usually successful with anion-exchange resins.[82]

Vitamin B_{12} deficiency can develop in up to 35% of patients after an 80-cm small bowel resection for a Kock pouch,[4] but it has not been demonstrated after ileocystoplasty,[125,140] perhaps because it is limited to a 25-cm resection in children.

Complications Due to Secretions

The acidic nature of gastric secretions can result in a hematuria-dysuria syndrome in 9% to 70% of patients.[28,87,97,120] This very troublesome complication can result in bladder spasms, suprapubic pain, dysuria, gross hematuria, and excoriation of genital skin. This is especially troublesome in sensate patients, nearly 75% of whom will have symptoms.[82,105,119] Treatment of mild cases is with histamine blockers or proton pump inhibitors[105] but may also require bicarbonate irrigations.[37,112] The net acid loss can result in a profound hypokalemic, hypochloremic, metabolic alkalosis and can be especially severe with a coexisting gastroenteritis.

Mucus production continues with all other bowel segments, although less so with ileum,[54,117,118] and can result in incomplete bladder emptying and predispose the patient to urinary tract infection and bladder stone formation.[120] Bladder stones occur in 7% to 52% of augmentations,[14,65,107] with the two largest series recording an incidence of 10% to 15%.[34,65,81] The increased risk may be due to increased levels of calcium and phosphate in mucus.[68] Their struvite composition implies a common etiology with urease-producing bacteria. The systemic acidosis common to the augmented population will decrease stone inhibitors and also promotes stone growth.[107] Prevention is aimed at regular CIC and daily bladder irrigations. Treatment is amenable to open or endoscopic means,[14,35,81,107] with open surgery reserved for the larger stones.

Bacteriuria is nearly universal in any patient performing CIC, especially when combined with an enterocystoplasty. A urinary tract infection most frequently presents as malodorous urine, but symptoms may include hematuria, incontinence exacerbation, suprapubic pain, or increased mucus production.[120] A symptomatic urinary tract infection is reported by Rink and colleagues in 22.7% of patients with an ileal augmentation but in only 8% of patients with a gastrocystoplasty.[117] Overall occurrence of a febrile urinary tract infection was reported to be 14%. Treatment of asymptomatic bacteriuria is not indicated unless culture indicates a urease-producing organism or a very virulent organism. However, treatment may decrease the risk of stone formation.

Complications Due to Absorption

The use of bowel for a urinary reservoir can be associated with profound metabolic changes owing to its absorptive nature. Colon and ileum readily absorb ammonium, hydrogen ion, and chloride, and this will result in a hyperchloremic metabolic acidosis. This is tolerated in many patients with normal renal function[74] but may require medical therapy in others. The extent of ion absorption depends primarily on intestinal contact area and length of time for contact; therefore, significant acidosis should prompt an investigation into incomplete emptying.[120] Although not all patients will be frankly acidotic, nearly all will have a rise in their serum chloride levels, albeit still in the normal range.[98] The acidosis prompts mobilization of buffers and can result in bone demineralization.

Although some believe that somatic growth impairment occurs, this remains controversial. This has been demonstrated in animal models[18,73,93] as well as in patients with bladder exstrophy, where there has been a reported 15% to 20% decrease in the patients' overall height.[50] However, in the much more prevalent myelodysplastic population the clinical correlation has been more difficult to prove. The acidosis will also result in hypocitraturia and increase the risk of both renal and bladder stone formation.[107]

Medications such as phenytoin (Dilantin) and methotrexate are readily absorbed across the bowel, and levels must be closely monitored.[126] Glucose is also absorbed, making urinary monitoring of hyperglycemia less reliable.[139]

SUMMARY

The description by Lapides of CIC revolutionized lower urinary reconstruction. It opened the door for primary reconstruction in children, allowing the urinary tract to remain intact. It virtually eliminated permanent incontinent urinary diversion with the social stigma of ostomy drainage, leaving only rare indications for temporary incontinent diversion. The Mitrofanoff principle allowed for an even more aggressive approach to achieving complete dryness in these children. Although there have been enormous gains in independence and social well-being in the affected children, the reconstructions have provided an entire new set of complications, some of which are potentially lethal. It is clear that the most important aspect is patient and family motivation. The patient and family must be willing and able to catheterize at 4 hour intervals, daily, forever. These reconstructions require a team approach, from the family, surgeon, and nursing, and they require lifelong follow-up evaluation.

REFERENCES

1. Abd-El-Gawad G, Abrahamsson K, Hanson E, et al: Early and late metabolic alterations in children and adolescents with a Kock urinary reservoir. BJU Int 1999;83:285-289.
2. Abd-el-Gawad G, Abrahamsson K, Hanson E, et al: Evaluation of Kock urinary reservoir function in children and adolescents at 3-10 years' follow-up. Scand J Urol Nephrol 1999;33:149-155.
3. Adams MC, Mitchell ME, Rink RC: Gastrocystoplasty: An alternative solution to the problem of urological reconstruction in the severely compromised patient. J Urol 1988;140:1152-1156.
4. Akerlund S: Urinary diversion via the continent ileal reservoir: Functional characteristics and long-term outcome. Scand J Urol Nephrol Suppl 1989;121:1-36.
5. Alexander F, Kay R: Cloacal anomalies: Role of vesicostomy. J Pediatr Surg 1994;29:74-76.
6. Anderson PA, Rickwood AM: Detrusor hyperreflexia as a factor in spontaneous perforation of augmentation cystoplasty for neuropathic bladder. Br J Urol 1991;67:210-212.
7. Atan A, Konety BR, Nangia A, et al: Advantages and risks of ileovesicostomy for the management of neuropathic bladder. Urology 1999;54:636-640.
8. Austen M, Kalble T: Secondary malignancies in different forms of urinary diversion using isolated gut. J Urol 2004; 172:831-838.
9. Austin PF, DeLeary G, Homsy YL, et al: Long-term metabolic advantages of a gastrointestinal composite urinary reservoir. J Urol 1997;158:1704-1707; discussion 1707-1708.
10. Barrington JW, Fern-Davies H, Adams RJ, et al: Bile acid dysfunction after clam enterocystoplasty. Br J Urol 1995; 76:169-171.
11. Benson M, Olsson C: Continent Cutaneous Urinary Diversion. Philadelphia, Elsevier Science, 2003.
12. Bihrle R, Klee LW, Adams MC, et al: Early clinical experience with the transverse colon-gastric tube continent urinary reservoir. J Urol 1991;146:751-753.
13. Blocksom BH Jr: Bladder pouch for prolonged tubeless cystostomy. J Urol 1957;78:398-401.
14. Blyth B, Ewalt DH, Duckett JW, et al: Lithogenic properties of enterocystoplasty. J Urol 1992;148:575-577; discussion 578-579.
15. Bruce AW, Reid G, Chan RC, et al: Bacterial adherence in the human ileal conduit: A morphological and bacteriological study. J Urol 1984;132:184-188.
16. Bruce RG, McRoberts JW: Cecoappendicovesicostomy: Conduit-lengthening technique for use in continent urinary reconstruction. Urology 1998;52:702-704.
17. Bruce RR, Gonzales ET Jr. Cutaneous vesicostomy: A useful form of temporary diversion in children. J Urol 1980; 123:927-928.
18. Bushinsky DA, Kittaka MK, Weisinger JR, et al: Effects of chronic metabolic alkalosis on Ca^{2+}, PTH and 1,25(OH)2D3 in the rat. Am J Physiol 1989;257:E578-E582.
19. Cain M, Hussman D: Cecal bladder augmentation with a tapered catheterizable stoma: A modification of the Indiana pouch. Presented at the meeting of the American Academy of Pediatrics, Urology Section. 1994, Dallas.
20. Cain MP, Casale AJ, Rink RC: Initial experience using a catheterizable ileovesicostomy (Monti procedure) in children. Urology 1998;52:870-873.
21. Cain MP, Casale AJ, King SJ, et al: Appendicovesicostomy and newer alternatives for the Mitrofanoff procedure: Results in the last 100 patients at Riley Children's Hospital. J Urol 1999;162:1749-1752.
22. Cain MP, Rink RC, Yerkes EB, et al: Long-term followup and outcome of continent catheterizable vesicostomy using the Rink modification. J Urol 2002;168:2583-2585.
23. Canning D: Continent Urinary Diversion. Philadelphia, WB Saunders, 1998.
24. Carr LK, Herschorn S: Early development of adenocarcinoma in a young woman following augmentation cystoplasty for undiversion. J Urol 1997;157:2255-2256.
25. Carroll PR, Presti JC Jr, McAninch JW, et al: Functional characteristics of the continent ileocecal urinary reservoir: Mechanisms of urinary continence. J Urol 1989;142:1032-1036.
26. Casale AJ: Continent vesicostomy: A new method utilizing only bladder tissue. Presented before the 60th annual meeting of the American Association of Pediatrics, New Orleans, 1991.
27. Casale AJ: A long continent ileovesicostomy using a single piece of bowel. J Urol 1999;162:1743-1745.
28. Chadwick Plaire J, Snodgrass WT, Grady RW, et al: Long-term followup of the hematuria-dysuria syndrome. J Urol 2000;164:921-923.
29. Cheng E: Personal Communication, 2005.
30. Clark T, Pope JC 4th, Adams C, et al: Factors that influence outcomes of the Mitrofanoff and Malone antegrade continence enema reconstructive procedures in children. J Urol 2002;168:1537-1540; discussion 1540.
31. Clementson Kockum C, Helin I, Malmberg L, et al: Pediatric urinary tract reconstruction using intestine. Scand J Urol Nephrol 1999;33:53-56.

32. Close CE, Carr MC, Burns MW, et al: Lower urinary tract changes after early valve ablation in neonates and infants: Is early diversion warranted? J Urol 1997;157:984-988.
33. Cromie WJ, Barada JH, Weingarten JL: Cecal tubularization: Lengthening technique for creation of catheterizable conduit. Urology 1991;37:41-42.
34. DeFoor W, Minevich E, Reddy P, et al: Bladder calculi after augmentation cystoplasty: Risk factors and prevention strategies. J Urol 2004;172:1964-1966.
35. Docimo SG, Orth CR, Schulam PG: Percutaneous cystolithotomy after augmentation cystoplasty: Comparison with open procedures. Tech Urol 1998;4:43-45.
36. Duckett JW Jr: Cutaneous vesicostomy in childhood: The Blocksom technique. Urol Clin North Am 1974;1:485-95.
37. Dykes EH, Ransley PG: Gastrocystoplasty in children. Br J Urol 1992;69:91-95.
38. Figueroa TE, Sabogal L, Helal M, et al: The tapered and reimplanted small bowel as a variation of the Mitrofanoff procedure: Preliminary results. J Urol 1994;152:73-75.
39. Filmer RB, Spencer JR: Malignancies in bladder augmentations and intestinal conduits. J Urol 1990;143:671-678.
40. Fowler JE Jr: Continent urinary reservoirs. Surg Annu 1988;20:201-225.
41. Gauthier AR Jr, Winters JC: Incontinent ileovesicostomy in the management of neurogenic bladder dysfunction. Neurourol Urodyn 2003;22:142-146.
42. Gearhart JP, Albertsen PC, Marshall FF, et al: Pediatric applications of augmentation cystoplasty: The Johns Hopkins experience. J Urol 1986;136:430-432.
43. Ghali AM, El Malki T, Sheir KZ, et al: Posterior urethral valves with persistent high serum creatinine: The value of percutaneous nephrostomy. J Urol 2000;164:1340-1344.
44. Gittes RF: Carcinogenesis in ureterosigmoidostomy. Urol Clin North Am 1986;13:201-205.
45. Glassman DT, Docimo SG: Concealed umbilical stoma: Long-term evaluation of stomal stenosis. J Urol 2001;166: 1028-1030.
46. Goldwasser B, Webster GD: Augmentation and substitution enterocystoplasty. J Urol 1986;135:215-224.
47. Golomb J, Klutke CG, Lewin KJ, et al: Bladder neoplasms associated with augmentation cystoplasty: Report of 2 cases and literature review. J Urol 1989;142:377-380.
48. Gonzalez R, Cabral B: Rectal continence after enterocystoplasty. Dial Pediatr Urol 1987;(10):3-4.
49. Gonzalez R, Reinberg Y: Localization of bacteriuria in patients with enterocystoplasty and nonrefluxing conduits. J Urol 1987;138:1104-1105.
50. Gros DA, Dodson JL, Lopatin UA, et al: Decreased linear growth associated with intestinal bladder augmentation in children with bladder exstrophy. J Urol 2000;164:917-920.
51. Hagglof B, Andren O, Bergstrom E, et al: Self-esteem before and after treatment in children with nocturnal enuresis and urinary incontinence. Scand J Urol Nephrol Suppl 1997;183:79-82.
52. Hedlund H, Lindstrom K, Mansson W: Dynamics of a continent caecal reservoir for urinary diversion. Br J Urol 1984; 56:366-372.
53. Hendren WH: Urinary diversion and undiversion in children. Surg Clin North Am 1976;56:425-449.
54. Hendren WH, Hendren RB: Bladder augmentation: Experience with 129 children and young adults. J Urol 1990;144:445-453; discussion 460.
55. Herschorn S, Hewitt RJ: Patient perspective of long-term outcome of augmentation cystoplasty for neurogenic bladder. Urology 1998;52:672-678.
56. Hinman F Jr: Selection of intestinal segments for bladder substitution: Physical and physiological characteristics. J Urol 1988;139:519-523.
57. Horowitz M, Kuhr CS, Mitchell ME: The Mitrofanoff catheterizable channel: Patient acceptance. J Urol 1995; 153:771-772.
58. Husmann DA, McLorie GA, Churchill BM: Nonrefluxing colonic conduits: A long-term life-table analysis. J Urol 1989; 142:1201-1203.
59. Husmann DA, Spence HM: Current status of tumor of the bowel following ureterosigmoidostomy: A review. J Urol 1990;144:607-610.
60. Hutcheson JC, Cooper CS, Canning DA, et al: The use of vesicostomy as permanent urinary diversion in the child with myelomeningocele. J Urol 2001;166:2351-2353.
61. Hutton KA, Thomas DF: Selective use of cutaneous vesicostomy in prenatally detected and clinically presenting uropathies. Eur Urol 1998;33:405-411.
62. Jaureguizar E, Lopez Pereira P, Martinez Urrutia MJ, et al: Does neonatal pyeloureterostomy worsen bladder function in children with posterior urethral valves? J Urol 2000; 164:1031-1033; discussion 1033-1034.
63. Jayanthi VR, McLorie GA, Khoury AE, et al: The effect of temporary cutaneous diversion on ultimate bladder function. J Urol 1995;154:889-892.
64. Kaefer M, Tobin MS, Hendren WH, et al: Continent urinary diversion: the Children's Hospital experience. J Urol 1997;157:1394-1399.
65. Kaefer M, Hendren WH, Bauer SB, et al: Reservoir calculi: A comparison of reservoirs constructed from stomach and other enteric segments. J Urol 1998;160:2187-2190.
66. Kalble T, Tricker AR, Friedl P, et al: Ureterosigmoidostomy: Long-term results, risk of carcinoma and etiological factors for carcinogenesis. J Urol 1990;144:1110-1114.
67. Keating MA, Rink RC, Adams MC: Appendicovesicostomy: A useful adjunct to continent reconstruction of the bladder. J Urol 1993;149:1091-1094.
68. Khoury AE, Salomon M, Doche R, et al: Stone formation after augmentation cystoplasty: The role of intestinal mucus. J Urol 1997;158:1133-1137.
69. Kim YH, Horowitz M, Combs A, et al: Comparative urodynamic findings after primary valve ablation, vesicostomy or proximal diversion. J Urol 1996;156:673-676.
70. King L: Protection of the Upper Tracts in Children. Chicago, Year Book Medical, 1987.
71. Kirsch AJ, Olsson CA, Hensle TW: Pediatric continent reservoirs and colocystoplasty created with absorbable staples. J Urol 1996;156:614-617.
72. Koch MO, McDougal WS: The pathophysiology of hyperchloremic metabolic acidosis after urinary diversion through intestinal segments. Surgery 1985;98: 561-570.
73. Koch MO, McDougal WS: Bone demineralization following ureterosigmoid anastomosis: An experimental study in rats. J Urol 1988;140:856-859.
74. Koch MO, McDougal WS, Reddy PK, et al: Metabolic alterations following continent urinary diversion through colonic segments. J Urol 1991;145:270-273.
75. Koch MO, McDougal WS, Hall MC, et al: Long-term metabolic effects of urinary diversion: A comparison of myelomeningocele patients managed by clean intermittent catheterization and urinary diversion. J Urol 1992;147: 1343-1347.
76. Kock NG: Ileostomy without external appliances: A survey of 25 patients provided with intra-abdominal intestinal reservoir. Ann Surg 1971;173:545-550.
77. Kock NG: Construction of a continent ileostomy. Schweiz Med Wochenschr 1971;101:729-734.
78. Kock NG, Nilson AE, Nilsson LO, et al: Urinary diversion via a continent ileal reservoir: Clinical results in 12 patients. J Urol 1982;128:469-475.

79. Koff SA: Guidelines to determine the size and shape of intestinal segments used for reconstruction. J Urol 1988; 140:1150-1151.
80. Krahn CG, Johnson HW: Cutaneous vesicostomy in the young child: Indications and results. Urology 1993;41: 558-563.
81. Kronner KM, Casale AJ, Cain MP, et al: Bladder calculi in the pediatric augmented bladder. J Urol 1998;160: 1096-1098; discussion 1103.
82. Kropp B, Cheng E: Bladder Augmentation: Current and Future Techniques, 4th ed. London, Martin Dunitz, 2002.
83. Lapides J, Ajemian EP, Lichtwardt JR: Cutaneous vesicostomy. J Urol 1960;84:609-614.
84. Lapides J, Diokno AC, Silber SJ, et al: Clean, intermittent self-catheterization in the treatment of urinary tract disease. J Urol 1972;107:458-461.
85. Lapides J, Diokno AC, Gould FR, et al: Further observations on self-catheterization. J Urol 1976;116:169-171.
86. Leng WW, Faerber G, Del Terzo M, et al: Long-term outcome of incontinent ileovesicostomy management of severe lower urinary tract dysfunction. J Urol 1999;161:1803-1806.
87. Leonard MP, Dharamsi N, Williot PE: Outcome of gastrocystoplasty in tertiary pediatric urology practice. J Urol 2000;164:947-950.
88. Liard A, Seguier-Lipszyc E, Mitrofanoff P: Temporary high diversion for posterior urethral valves. J Urol 2000;164: 145-148.
89. Light JK: Enteroplasty to ablate bowel contractions in the reconstructed bladder: A case report. J Urol 1985;134: 958-959.
90. Light JK, Engelmann UH: Reconstruction of the lower urinary tract: Observations on bowel dynamics and the artificial urinary sphincter. J Urol 1985;133:594-597.
91. Lockhart JL, Davies R, Cox C, et al: The gastroileoileal pouch: An alternative continent urinary reservoir for patients with short bowel, acidosis and/or extensive pelvic radiation. J Urol 1993;150:46-50.
92. Lytton B, Green DF: Urodynamic studies in patients undergoing bladder replacement surgery. J Urol 1989; 141:1394-1397.
93. McDougal WS, Koch MO, Shands C 3rd, et al: Bony demineralization following urinary intestinal diversion. J Urol 1988;140:853-855.
94. McGuire EJ, Woodside JR, Borden TA, et al: Prognostic value of urodynamic testing in myelodysplastic patients. J Urol 1981;126:205-209.
95. McLaughlin KP, Rink RC, Adams MC, et al: Stomach in combination with other intestinal segments in pediatric lower urinary tract reconstruction. J Urol 1995;154:1162-1168.
96. Mills RD, Studer UE: Metabolic consequences of continent urinary diversion. J Urol 1999;161:1057-1066.
97. Mingin GC, Stock JA, Hanna MK: Gastrocystoplasty: Long-term complications in 22 patients. J Urol 1999; 162:1122-1125.
98. Mitchell ME, Piser JA: Intestinocystoplasty and total bladder replacement in children and young adults: Followup in 129 cases. J Urol 1987;138:579-584.
99. Mitchell ME, Rink RC: Pediatric urinary diversion and undiversion. Pediatr Clin North Am 1987;34 1319-1332.
100. Mitrofanoff P. [Trans-appendicular continent cystostomy in the management of the neurogenic bladder]. Chir Pediatr 1980;21:297-305.
101. Monti PR, Lara RC, Dutra MA, et al: New techniques for construction of efferent conduits based on the Mitrofanoff principle. Urology 1997;49:112-115.
102. Mor Y, Ramon J, Raviv G, et al: Low loop cutaneous ureterostomy and subsequent reconstruction: 20 years of experience. J Urol 1992;147:1595-1597; discussion 1597-1598.
103. Mor Y, Quinn FM, Carr B, et al: Combined Mitrofanoff and antegrade continence enema procedures for urinary and fecal incontinence. J Urol 1997;158:192-195.
104. Mutchnik SE, Hinson JL, Nickell KG, et al: Ileovesicostomy as an alternative form of bladder management in tetraplegic patients. Urology 1997;49:353-357.
105. Nguyen DH, Bain MA, Salmonson KL, et al: The syndrome of dysuria and hematuria in pediatric urinary reconstruction with stomach. J Urol 1993;150:707-709.
106. Noe HN, Jerkins GR: Cutaneous vesicostomy experience in infants and children. J Urol 1985;134:301-303.
107. Palmer LS, Franco I, Kogan SJ, et al: Urolithiasis in children following augmentation cystoplasty. J Urol 1993;150:726-729.
108. Piser JA, Mitchell ME, Kulb TB, et al: Gastrocystoplasty and colocystoplasty in canines: The metabolic consequences of acute saline and acid loading. J Urol 1987;138:1009-1013.
109. Podesta ML, Ruarte A, Gargiulo C, et al: Urodynamic findings in boys with posterior urethral valves after treatment with primary valve ablation or vesicostomy and delayed ablation. J Urol 2000;164:139-144.
110. Podesta ML, Ruarte A, Herrera M, et al: Bladder functional outcome after delayed vesicostomy closure and antireflux surgery in young infants with 'primary' vesicoureteric reflux. BJU Int 2001;87:473-479.
111. Pope JC 4th, Keating MA, Casale AJ, et al. Augmenting the augmented bladder: Treatment of the contractile bowel segment. J Urol 1998;160:854-857.
112. Reinberg Y, Manivel JC, Froemming C, et al: Perforation of the gastric segment of an augmented bladder secondary to peptic ulcer disease. J Urol 1992;148:369-371.
113. Ring KS, Hensle TW: Urinary diversion. In Kelalis PP, King LR, Belman AB (eds): Clinical Pediatric Urology, 3rd ed. Martin Donitz, 1992, p 865-903.
114. Rink R, Mitchell M: Role of Enterocystoplasty in Reconstructing the Neurogenic Bladder. St. Louis, Mosby–Year Book, 1990.
115. Rink R, McLaughlin K: Indications for enterocystoplasty and choice of bowel segment. Prob Urol 1994:389-403.
116. Rink R: Choice of materials for bladder augmentation. Curr Opin Urol 1995:300-305.
117. Rink R, Hollensbe D, Adams M: Complications of augmentation in children and comparison of gastrointestinal segments. AUA Update Series 1995;14:122-128.
118. Rink R, Adams M: Augmentation Cystoplasty, 7th ed. Philadelphia, WB Saunders, 1998.
119. Rink R, Renschler T, Adams M, et al: Long term follow-up of the first gastrocystoplasty series. Presented before the annual meeting of the European Society of Pediatric Urology, Tours, France, 2000.
120. Rink R, Yerkes E, Adams M: Augmentation Cystoplasty. Philadelphia, WB Saunders, 2001.
121. Rink RC: Bladder augmentation: Options, outcomes, future. Urol Clin North Am 1999;26:111-23, viii-ix.
122. Rosen MA, Light JK: Spontaneous bladder rupture following augmentation enterocystoplasty. J Urol 1991;146:1232-1234.
123. Rosen MA, Roth DR, Gonzales ET Jr: Current indications for cutaneous ureterostomy. Urology 1994;43:92-96.
124. Rowland R: Present experience with the Indiana pouch. World J Urol 1995;(14):92-98.
125. Salomon L, Lugagne PM, Herve JM, et al: No evidence of metabolic disorders 10 to 22 years after Camey type I ileal enterocystoplasty. J Urol 1997;157:2104-2106.
126. Savarirayan F, Dixey GM: Syncope following ureterosigmoidostomy. J Urol 1969;101:844-845.
127. Schwartz SL, Kennelly MJ, McGuire EJ, et al: Incontinent ileo-vesicostomy urinary diversion in the treatment of lower urinary tract dysfunction. J Urol 1994;152:99-102.

128. Schwarz GR, Jeffs RD: Ileal conduit urinary diversion in children: Computer analysis of followup from 2 to 16 years. J Urol 1975;114:285-288.
129. Shapiro SR, Lebowitz R, Colodny AH: Fate of 90 children with ileal conduit urinary diversion a decade later: Analysis of complications, pyelography, renal function and bacteriology. J Urol 1975;114:289-295.
130. Sheldon CA, Gilbert A, Wacksman J, et al: Gastrocystoplasty: Technical and metabolic characteristics of the most versatile childhood bladder augmentation modality. J Pediatr Surg 1995;30:283-287; discussion 287-288.
131. Shokeir AA, Shamaa M, el-Mekresh MM, et al: Late malignancy in bowel segments exposed to urine without fecal stream. Urology 1995;46:657-661.
132. Sidi AA, Aliabadi H, Gonzalez R: Enterocystoplasty in the management and reconstruction of the pediatric neurogenic bladder. J Pediatr Surg 1987;22:153-157.
133. Singh G, Thomas DG: Bowel problems after enterocystoplasty. Br J Urol 1997;79:328-332.
134. Skinner DG, Lieskovsky G, Boyd S: Continent urinary diversion. J Urol 1989;141:1323-1327.
135. Skinner DG, Studer UE, Okada K, et al: Which patients are suitable for continent diversion or bladder substitution following cystectomy or other definitive local treatment? Int J Urol 1995;2:105-112.
136. Slaton JW, Kropp KA: Conservative management of suspected bladder rupture after augmentation enterocystoplasty. J Urol 1994;152:713-715.
137. Soergel TM, Cain MP, Misseri R, et al: Transitional cell carcinoma of the bladder following augmentation cystoplasty for the neuropathic bladder. J Urol 2004;172: 1649-1651; discussion 1651-1652.
138. Sohn M, Fuzesi L, Deutz F, et al: Signet ring cell carcinoma in adenomatous polyp at site of ureterosigmoidostomy 16 years after conversion to ileal conduit. J Urol 1990; 143:805-807.
139. Sridhar KN, Samuell CT, Woodhouse CR: Absorption of glucose from urinary conduits in diabetics and non-diabetics. BMJ (Clin Res Ed) 1983;287:1327-1329.
140. Stein R, Lotz J, Andreas J, et al: Long-term metabolic effects in patients with urinary diversion. World J Urol 1998;16:292-297.
141. Sugarman ID, Malone PS, Terry TR, et al: Transversely tubularized ileal segments for the Mitrofanoff or Malone antegrade colonic enema procedures: The Monti principle. Br J Urol 1998;81:253-256.
142. Suzer O, Vates TS, Freedman AL, et al: Results of the Mitrofanoff procedure in urinary tract reconstruction in children. Br J Urol 1997;79:279-282.
143. Thomas DF: Surgical treatment of urinary incontinence. Arch Dis Child 1997;76:377-380.
144. Tietjen DN, Gloor JM, Husmann DA: Proximal urinary diversion in the management of posterior urethral valves: Is it necessary? J Urol 1997;158:1008-1010.
145. Van Savage JG, Khoury AE, McLorie GA, et al: Outcome analysis of Mitrofanoff principle applications using appendix and ureter to umbilical and lower quadrant stomal sites. J Urol 1996;156:1794-1797.
146. Woodhouse CR, Malone PR, Cumming J, et al: The Mitrofanoff principle for continent urinary diversion. Br J Urol 1989;63:53-57.
147. Woodhouse CR, Pope AJ: Alternatives to urinary diversion with a bag: Results in 100 patients. Br J Urol 1993;72: 580-585.
148. Yang WH: Yang needle tunneling technique in creating antireflux and continent mechanisms. J Urol 1993; 150:830-834.
149. Yerkes EB, Rink RC, Cain MP, et al: Shunt infection and malfunction after augmentation cystoplasty. J Urol 2001; 165:2262-2264.

Chapter 116

Disorders of Bladder Function

Martin Kaefer

Disorders of bladder function can range from the most mundane problem of dysfunctional voiding to very complex disorders involving neuropathic bladder dysfunction. The typical symptom that underlies the initial evaluation for bladder dysfunction is wetting. Though of great concern to parents and child alike, this relatively benign-appearing outward sign of bladder dysfunction may in the extreme case reflect a far more insidious and occult problem involving injury to the lower and upper urinary tracts. This chapter begins with the physician's initial assessment of a child with voiding symptoms. Radiographic and dynamic studies relevant to bladder dysfunction are covered next. Finally, specific disorders and their treatment are discussed.

HISTORY AND PHYSICAL EXAMINATION

The evaluation of a child with bladder dysfunction should begin with establishing both day and nighttime voiding symptoms. Voiding symptoms have classically been divided into irritative and obstructive, examples of which can be found in Table 116-1. It should be noted that nearly every disorder discussed in this chapter can have a combination of these symptoms. For example, the parents of a boy with obstructing posterior urethral valves may not report that their child is suffering from urinary retention but rather that he is experiencing urinary frequency and urgency (secondary to increased bladder irritability from overdistention). It should be established whether the child has suffered from a urinary tract infection and if so whether there has been an associated fever. This later symptom will help distinguish an episode of cystitis from the more significant episode of pyelonephritis. The physician should inquire about whether the child suffers from constipation because it may reflect a form of retentive behavior (as in the case of dysfunctional elimination) or neuropathic bowel dysfunction (as in the various forms of spinal dysraphism). With regard to the later diagnosis, it is also important to record any symptoms of lower extremity weakness or change in sensation.

TABLE 116-1 Voiding Symptoms

Irritative
Dysuria
Urgency
Urge incontinence
Frequency
Obstructive
Retention
Hesitancy
Staccato voiding (starting and stopping)
Straining to void
Feeling of incomplete emptying

The physical examination of a child with bladder complaints should include evaluation of the abdomen, back, genitalia, and lower extremities. In examining the abdomen special note should be made of palpable feces and whether the bladder is palpable or percussible, or both.

Examination of the back is critical. Cutaneous findings of a hair patch or nevus overlying the lumbar spine reflect abnormal migration of the neuroectoderm, which can often signal abnormal formation of the lumbosacral spinal cord. A dimple over the lumbosacral spine may likewise signal such an abnormality (Fig. 116-1). An asymmetric gluteal crease is a further sign of potential problems of the spinal cord. This asymmetry reflects differing degrees of impaired innervation to the two groups of gluteal muscles. For example, if the right gluteal nerves are affected to a greater degree than those on the left, a greater degree of atrophy may ensue, and as a result, the crease would deviate to the right. With respect to this last outward sign of occult spinal cord dysraphism, it is critically important to note that gluteal asymmetry may be an acquired finding as the child matures and grows in axial length. Therefore, the back should be examined not only on the initial patient evaluation but during return visits of children with continued voiding complaints. Figure 116-2 demonstrates the concept of spinal cord tethering. Patients who possess any of these cutaneous findings should undergo magnetic resonance imaging (MRI) of the lumbosacral spine.

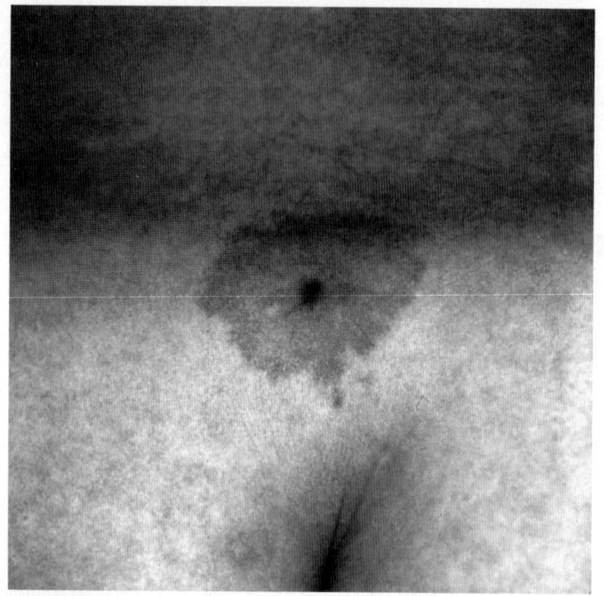

Figure 116–1 Cutaneous findings suggestive of occult spinal cord tethering. A 10-year-old child with neuropathic bladder was found on physical examination to have a cutaneous lumbar birthmark, a lumbar dimple, and asymmetry of the gluteal cleft. Magnetic resonance imaging of the lumbosacral spinal cord revealed a intraspinal lipoma responsible for cord tethering.

Examination of the male genitalia should include palpation along the entire urethra. Induration may be a sign of urethral inflammation and stricture. The position of the testicles should be noted because the incidence of cryptorchidism is increased in children with myelodysplasia.[19,49] The anus should be examined to ensure that there is good tone and proper location on the perineum. Finally, any deficits in lower extremity reflexes or motor strength should be noted because they are outward signs of neuromuscular disorders, especially disorders of the lumbosacral spinal cord.

Urinalysis should be performed in every child with voiding symptoms. The presence of red cells, white cells, glucose, and protein should be noted. A low specific gravity may reflect poor concentrating ability secondary to renal dysfunction.

RADIOGRAPHIC AND DYNAMIC ASSESSMENT OF BLADDER DYSFUNCTION

Bladder Ultrasound

Although it is the most basic of imaging modalities, bladder ultrasound can provide many clues about whether significant bladder pathology is present. In the absence of infection, a thickened bladder wall may reflect a compensatory response on the part of the bladder to either an anatomic (e.g., posterior urethral valves) or functional (e.g., detrusor-sphincter dyssynergy) form of bladder outlet obstruction (Fig. 116-3).[39] Calculation of postvoid residual urine volume is an excellent means of assessing whether the patient is able to efficiently empty the bladder.

Voiding Cystourethrography

Instillation of radiographic contrast into the bladder provides information regarding bladder, bladder neck, and urethral anatomy. Figure 116-4 demonstrates the classic radiographic findings seen in patients with neuropathic

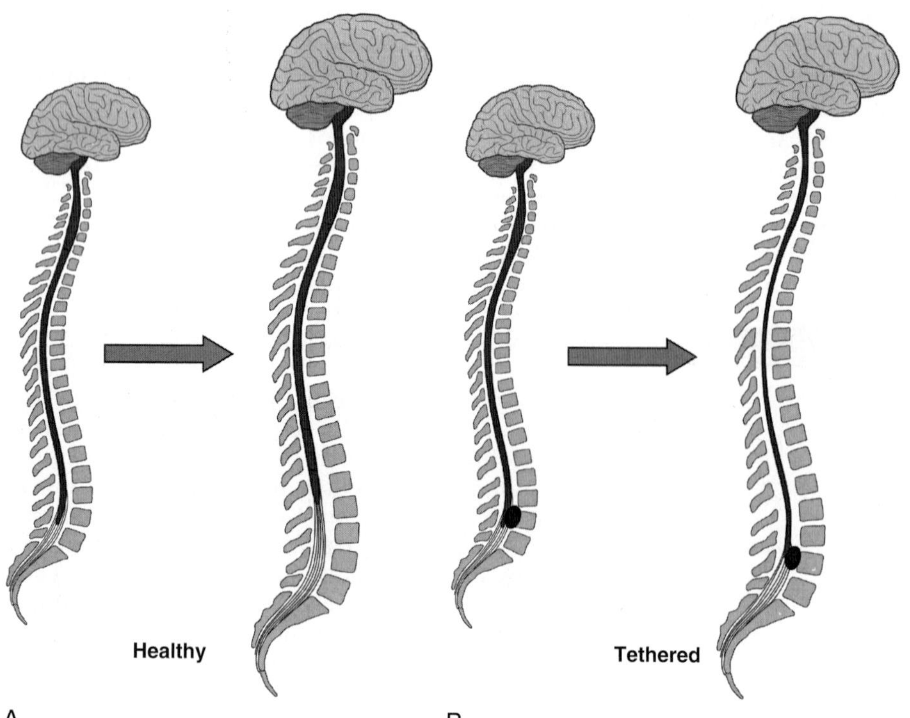

Figure 116–2 *A*, Normal spinal cord. The spinal column increases in axial length at a greater rate than the spinal cord does. As a result, the spinal cord rises to a higher position. *B*, Abnormal spinal cord anatomy with a spinal cord lipoma. As the spine grows, the spinal cord is unable to float upward and the cord is stretched. This stretching results in a relative state of hypoxia in the area of the distal cord and subsequent nerve injury to the distal spinal cord segments.

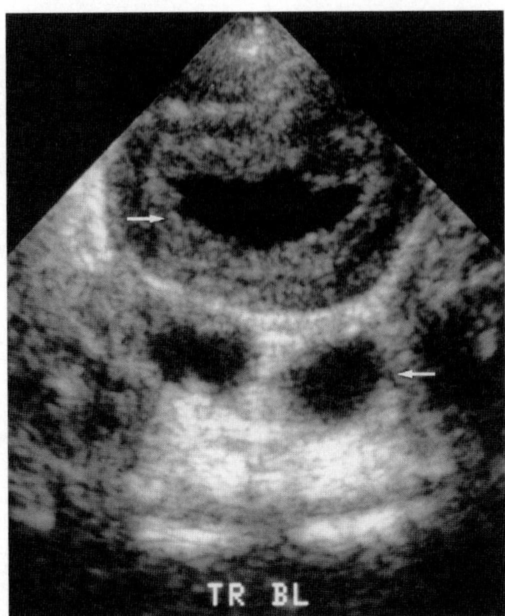

Figure 116–3 Bladder ultrasound in a child with posterior urethral valves. Note the markedly thickened bladder wall (*left arrow*) and dilatation of the distal end of the ureters (*right arrow*).

bladder dysfunction. Because of chronic high-pressure urine storage, the bladder wall becomes thick and multiple diverticula may form. In many conditions the voiding phase provides the most useful information because it is only during this time that the bladder neck and urethra can be properly evaluated. A classic example of this is a patient with posterior urethral valves. The bladder neck and urethra proximal to the site of obstruction are markedly dilated, and the bladder itself can demonstrate findings of trabeculation and diverticulum formation. Vesicoureteral reflux is a common finding in both patients with anatomic causes and those with functional causes of bladder outlet obstruction.

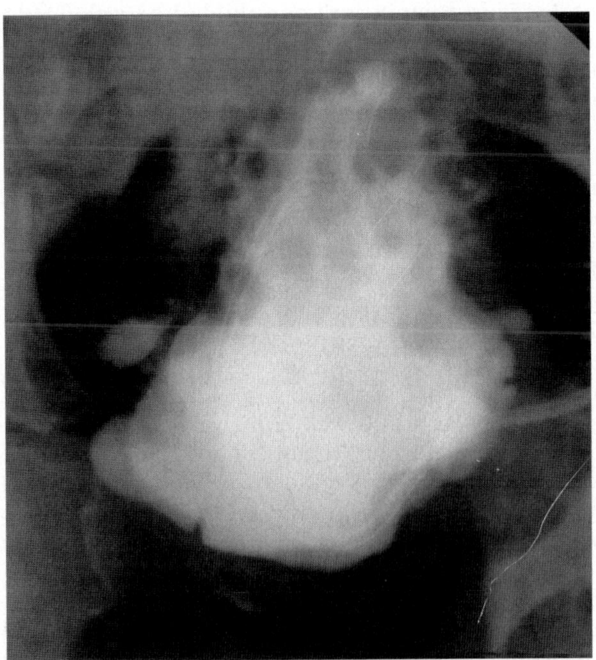

Figure 116–4 Typical voiding cystourethrogram in a child with neuropathic bladder dysfunction secondary to myelomeningocele. A "Christmas tree" appearance is a result of greater bladder wall thickening at the dome relative to the bladder base.

Urodynamic Evaluation

Urodynamic evaluation is the one test that provides in-depth functional information regarding the bladder. It establishes bladder capacity, bladder filling pressure, the patient's perception of bladder filling, and the ability of the bladder neck to open efficiently and in proper coordination with external sphincter relaxation.

Before undergoing placement of the urodynamic catheter, the child is asked to void into a toilet that measures the urinary flow rate. The catheter is then placed through the urethra (or through a suprapubic site if one is available), and intravesical pressure is measured. The bladder is subsequently emptied and residual urine measured to determine pressure at residual volume.[43] This technique may prove useful is determining whether the bladder is experiencing high resting pressure. Next, electromyographic (EMG) electrodes are placed on the perineum in the form of either patch surface sensors or needle sensors, the latter of which is placed directly into the external sphincter complex. These electrodes record the electrical activity of the muscle to determine the function of the external sphincter during bladder filling and emptying. Under normal conditions the external sphincter is active during periods of urine storage. Just before voiding there should be silencing of external sphincter activity as the bladder neck relaxes (Fig. 116-5A). Failure of the sphincter to relax before a voiding contraction is termed detrusor-sphincter dyssynergy and is commonly noted in patients with neuropathic bladder dysfunction (Figure 116-5B).

The bladder is next filled slowly with normal saline to measure bladder capacity, and the pressure-volume relationship is determined to establish bladder wall compliance. The percent expected bladder capacity is calculated by dividing the patient's actual capacity by the expected normal bladder capacity for age.[44] During the filling phase note is made of any uninhibited contractions, which are a reflection of bladder irritability. Figure 116-6 shows a comparison between pressure tracings from a compliant bladder and those of a poorly compliant, irritable bladder. During the filling phase note is also made of the leak point pressure.

NEUROPATHIC CAUSES OF BLADDER DYSFUNCTION

Neuropathic Bladder Secondary to Myelodysplasia

Myelodysplasia, defined as abnormal development of the spinal canal and spinal cord, is the most common cause of neuropathic bladder dysfunction in children. A genetic component appears to be partially responsible for

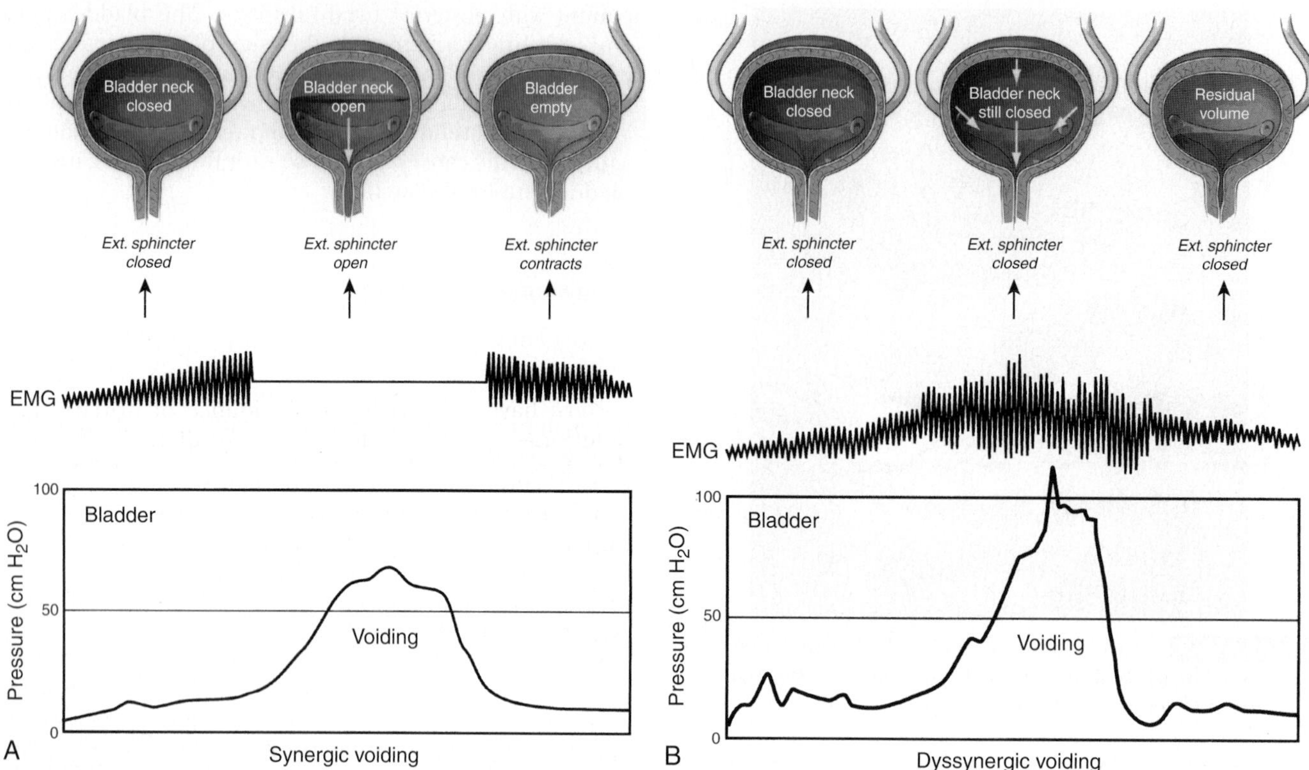

Figure 116–5 *A,* Coordinated synergic voiding. Electrical activity of the external urethral sphincter is chronically active. Just before experiencing a detrusor contraction, the activity of the external sphincter is silenced, thus providing a marked decrease in urethral resistance and thereby facilitating emptying. Intravesical pressure is shown in the *bottom panel.* EMG, electromyogram. *B,* Dyssynergic voiding, In cases of neuropathic bladder dysfunction, discoordination between bladder and sphincter activity can often be appreciated. As the bladder begins to contract, the activity of the external sphincter actually increases, thereby resulting in high outlet pressure and ineffective voiding. Intravesical pressure is shown in the *bottom panel.*

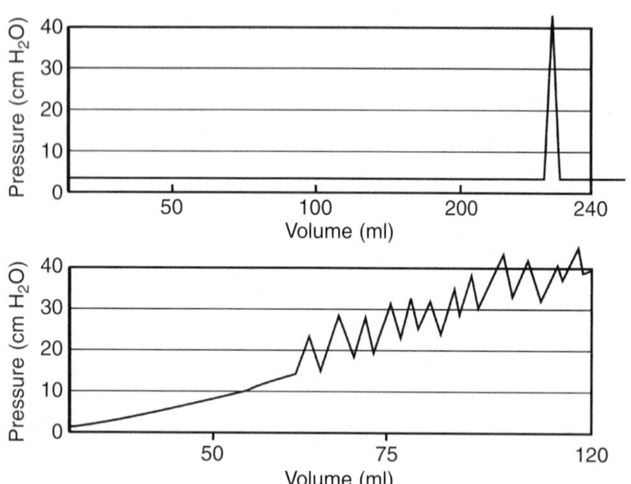

Figure 116–6 Representation of typical urodynamic tracings from a compliant bladder and a poorly compliant one. *Upper tracing,* Compliant bladder. As the bladder fills, numerous factors serve to maintain low intravesical pressure until a voiding contraction is initiated. *Lower tracing,* Poorly compliant bladder with detrusor hyperreflexia. As the bladder fills, intravesical pressure rises precipitously. Irritability of the dysfunctional detrusor muscle is reflected by numerous small pressure spikes (i.e., uninhibited contractions).

this disorder. A family with one child with myelodysplasia has a 2% to 5% chance that each subsequent sibling will suffer from the same condition. Early studies reported the incidence to be 1 in 1000 live births.[69] However, over the last 20 years there has been a steady decrease in this rate. Reasons cited for this decrease include the widespread perinatal supplementation of folic acid (a metabolite important for proper spinal cord formation) and pregnancy termination.[10,61] Dietary supplementation with folic acid can reduce the incidence of myelodysplasia by approximately 50%.

The most common forms of myelodysplasia consist of prolapse of the meninges (meningocele) and, in many cases, the presence of neural tissue (myelomeningocele) beyond the confines of the bony vertebral canal. Initial urologic evaluation of a child found to have spinal dysraphism (Fig. 116-7) should include renal ultrasound and voiding cystourethrography. In addition, random clean intermittent catheterization (CIC) is performed on multiple occasions to determine whether the child is retaining excess amounts of urine. Renal ultrasound will detect the presence of hydronephrosis. As many as 15% of newborns will be found to have an abnormal urinary tract, 3% have hydroureteronephrosis secondary to spinal shock from the closure procedure, and 10% have abnormalities that developed in utero as a result of abnormal

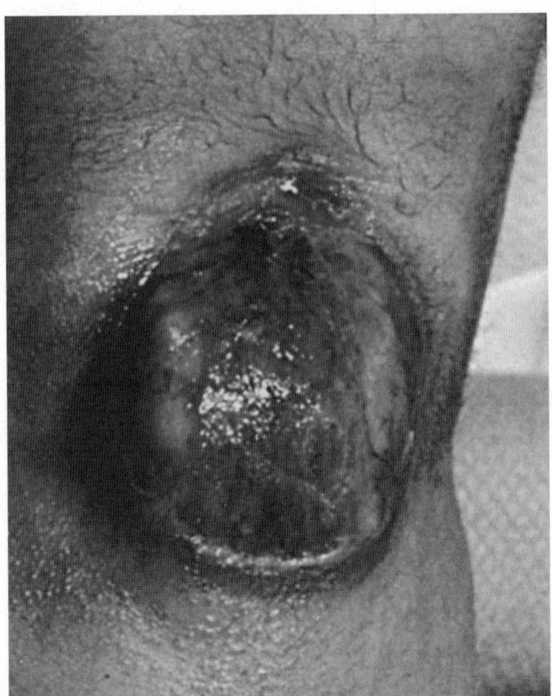

Figure 116–7 Photograph of a child with spinal dysraphism. The herniated spinal cord and associated lipoma are covered with overlying epidermis.

lower urinary tract function in the form of outlet obstruction (which may be a reflection of high bladder intravesical pressure).[2,7] Renal ultrasound serves the additional purpose of evaluating for renal fusion anomalies, which are known to be more common in patients with myelodysplasia.[38]

The voiding cystourethrogram serves the purpose of detecting vesicoureteral reflux, which is present in 3% to 5% of newborns with myelodysplasia.[20] Reflux is typically seen in children with detrusor hypertonicity or detrusor-sphincter dyssynergy. New reflux will develop in approximately 30% of children with unfavorably high-pressure bladder dynamics if proper treatment is not undertaken to lower intravesical pressure. As mentioned earlier, several random catheterizations are performed to determine the efficiency of emptying. If the volumes obtained during random catheterization are in excess of predicted capacity for age, the parents are taught CIC to be performed three times daily after discharge home.[44]

Follow-up urologic evaluation consists of urodynamic testing at 3 months of life. Performing urodynamic evaluation at an earlier time point is often discouraged because of the fact that the infant may experience a degree of spinal shock from spinal closure that may last for up to 2 months. Urodynamic testing serves two purposes. First, it serves as a baseline against which all future urodynamic evaluations can be compared. Changes in the urodynamic profile may be the first indication (often before changes in lower extremity function) that spinal cord tethering has occurred after myelomeningocele closure and that surgical intervention may be required.

The second purpose of urodynamic evaluation is to determine the overall storage characteristics of the bladder and sphincteric function. Three specific combinations of bladder contractility and external sphincter activity are seen. Bauer et al. found that 19% of patients will demonstrate synergic voiding, 45% will have dyssynergic voiding, and the remaining 36% will suffer complete denervation.[3] This system of classification is of great importance in predicting long-term renal and bladder function and thereby determining who will benefit from aggressive measures to minimize progressive urinary tract injury. Bauer et al. have shown that within the first 3 years of life, patients with a dyssynergic voiding pattern have a much higher incidence of urinary tract deterioration. They found that 71% of newborns with detrusor-sphincter dyssynergy had urinary tract deterioration on initial assessment or subsequent studies, whereas similar changes developed in only 17% of synergic children and 23% of completely denervated individuals. Notably, the small percentages of children with synergic or denervated voiding patterns who eventually demonstrated urinary tract deterioration all had subsequent conversion to high outlet resistance.

Frequent follow-up of patients with neuropathic bladder dysfunction secondary to myelomeningocele is mandatory because bladder dynamics (and thereby the effect on the upper urinary tract and continence) can change with time. Many reasons for a change in bladder dynamics exist, with the most important being spinal cord tethering.[52]

The primary goal of treatment of a neuropathic bladder is preservation of renal and bladder function. The additional goal of urinary continence is addressed once the child reaches the age at which the child's peers are achieving this developmental milestone. CIC and the use of anticholinergic medications are the cornerstones of medical therapy to provide a low-pressure storage environment for urine. Edelstein et al. demonstrated that if one aggressively and proactively treats high-risk patients—those with high outlet resistance, detrusor-sphincter dyssynergy, or bladder hypercontractility (so-called hostile bladder dynamics)—with CIC and anticholinergic medications, the rate of upper urinary tract injury could be substantially reduced.[17] Kaefer et al. subsequently showed that long-term bladder function is similarly preserved in a greater number of patients if such measures are taken (Fig. 116-8).[44] In this later study the incidence of long-term bladder deterioration requiring surgical bladder augmentation was reduced 2.5-fold. If these medical measures do not adequately reduce intravesical pressure and progressive hydronephrosis is noted in the first few years of life, surgical intervention in the form of cutaneous vesicostomy is indicated.

Urinary incontinence is likewise treated initially with conservative measures (i.e., CIC and anticholinergic medications) to decrease intravesical pressure. If such measures do not result in adequate improvement in bladder capacity and compliance, it may become necessary to enlarge the bladder by means of enterocystoplasty.[27,65] Additional surgical maneuvers may be required to provide adequate outlet resistance to achieve a state of urinary continence.[16]

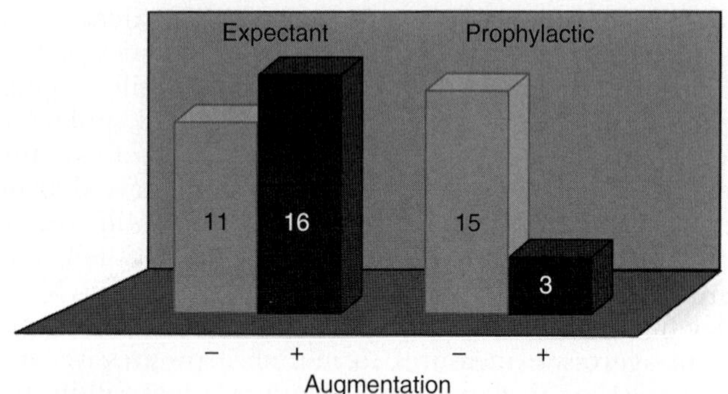

Figure 116–8 Incidence of bladder deterioration relative to the treatment regimen in patients with myelomeningocele. The expectant group consisted of patients with hostile bladder dynamics noted at birth who were started on clean intermittent catheterization and anticholinergic medications to lower bladder pressure only after signs of upper tract deterioration or worsening incontinence became evident. On average, treatment was initiated at the age of 4.1 years in this group. The prophylactic group consisted of patients with hostile bladder dynamics noted at birth who were treated with measures to lower intravesical pressure beginning in the first 3 months of life. The greater than twofold higher incidence of bladder augmentation in the expectant group is highly statistically significant (41% versus 17%). (From Kaefer M, Pabby A, Kelly M, et al: Improved bladder function after prophylactic treatment of the high risk neurogenic bladder in newborns with myelomeningocele. J Urol 1999;162:1068.)

Occult Spinal Cord Tethering

A number of congenital defects can affect development of the spinal column yet do not result in an open vertebral canal. Such defects occur in approximately 1 in every 4000 live births.[6] These lesions may result in no obvious outward neurologic signs, but many have a cutaneous abnormality overlying the lower part of the spine (see the section on physical examination). The incidence of these conditions is increased (up to 50%) in individuals with anorectal malformations, with earlier reports demonstrating that the incidence varies proportionately in relation to the height of the rectal lesion.[24,68,70] However, one recent study suggests that the incidence may not differ significantly between patients with supralevator and those with infralevator lesions.[24] All patients with a cutaneous abnormality overlying the lower part of the spine or an anorectal malformation should undergo MRI to evaluate for an intraspinal lesion.[58] In the first 6 months of life it is also possible to evaluate for spinal cord tethering with spinal ultrasound.[13]

Urologic symptoms of occult spinal cord tethering may include difficulty with toilet training, urinary incontinence after an initial period of dryness (especially during the pubertal growth spurt when the most stress is put on the tethered cord), recurrent urinary infections, or fecal soiling (or any combination of these symptoms).

Although the majority of newborns evaluated for occult spinal cord tethering have a perfectly normal physical examination, urodynamic testing will reveal abnormal lower urinary tract function in about a third of babies younger than 18 months.[45] In contrast, practically all individuals older than 3 years who have not been operated on or in whom an occult dysraphism has been belatedly diagnosed have abnormal urodynamic profiles.

Once it has been shown on MRI that signs of spinal cord tethering are present (e.g., the conus medullaris lies below the second lumbar vertebrae or there is a significant intraspinal lipoma), a judgment is made regarding the need for neurosurgical intervention. Oftentimes, the first sign of neurologic impairment is an abnormal urodynamic profile. Therefore, urodynamic testing is performed in all patients with positive MRI findings. If a decision is made to not correct spinal cord tethering, follow-up with yearly urodynamic evaluation is indicated so that any future neurologic deficits can be identified early and appropriate intervention instituted in timely fashion before irreversible nerve injury occurs.

Sacral Agenesis

Patients with sacral agenesis frequently suffer from neuropathic bladder dysfunction. The etiology of sacral agenesis is still uncertain. It is, however, known that insulin-dependent mothers have a 1% chance of giving birth to a child with this disorder and that 16% of children with sacral agenesis have a diabetic mother.[63,72] Because these children have normal sensation and little or no orthopedic deformity in the lower extremities, the underlying lesion is often overlooked. As many as 20% of children with this condition escape detection until the age of 3 or 4 years.[25] Typically, the only outward signs of this condition are flattened buttocks and a low, short gluteal cleft. The diagnosis is confirmed with a lateral film of the lower part of the spine, which reveals the missing sacral vertebrae. MRI of the lumbosacral spine, which is recommended in all patients, consistently reveals a sharp cutoff of the conus at T12.[62] Urodynamic testing shows that an almost equal number of individuals manifest a primarily upper (i.e., hypertonic, hyperreflexic) or a primarily lower (i.e., atonic) motor neuron–type lesion (35% versus 40%, respectively) whereas 25% have no sign of bladder dysfunction.[5] The number of affected vertebrae does not correlate with the type of motor neuron lesion. In contrast to the lesions noted in myelodysplasia or occult spinal cord anomalies, the injury appears to be stable. It is rare to see signs of progressive denervation such as a changing urodynamic pattern in these children as they grow. Anticholinergic agents are used to treat uninhibited contractions or relax the hypertonic detrusor, or both, whereas CIC is used in patients with impaired bladder emptying.

Cerebral Palsy

Cerebral palsy is the term used to describe a nonprogressive injury to the brain (e.g., hypoxic) occurring in the perinatal period that frequently produces a neuromuscular disability.[50] Its incidence is approximately 1 in 1000 births. However, the incidence of cerebral palsy appears to be increasing as smaller premature infants survive in intensive care units. Although a high percentage of children will be found to have uninhibited contractions on urodynamic evaluation, the majority of children with this diagnosis have the capacity to develop total urinary control.[12] Incontinence is most commonly related to the physical handicap that makes it difficult for the child to get to the bathroom in time. For this reason, continence is often achieved at a later than expected age, once the child has become adept at transferring. Properly addressing the issue of adequate access to handicapped facilities may be extremely helpful for many of these children.

As a result of the many physical issues facing a child with cerebral palsy, urodynamic evaluation is typically reserved for children who appear to be trainable, do not seem to be hampered too much by their physical impairment, and have not achieved continence by late childhood. For similar reasons, upper and lower urinary tract imaging is not recommended unless a urinary tract infection has occurred.

Treatment usually centers on abolishing the uninhibited contractions with the use of anticholinergic medications, but residual urine must be monitored closely to ensure complete evacuation with each voiding. CIC may be required for those who cannot empty their bladder. These children are also prone to severe constipation, largely because of their poor fluid intake and limited physical activity. In so far as constipation can adversely affect bladder stability and emptying, treatment to improve fecal elimination can prove beneficial in treating incontinence in these children. In a small subset of patients who do not respond to conservative measures, selective dorsal rhizotomy has improved bladder capacity, reduced the number of uninhibited contractions, and increased compliance.[35]

ANATOMIC CAUSES OF BLADDER DYSFUNCTION

Posterior Urethral Valves

The most common form of anatomic bladder outlet obstruction in the pediatric population is posterior urethral valves in boys. Other causes of bladder outlet obstruction include urethral stricture, anterior urethral diverticulum, and an obstructing ureterocele situated at the bladder outlet.[1,36,55]

The incidence of posterior urethral valves is between 1 in 5000 and 1 in 8000 male births. The condition is manifested in children in a variety of ways, depending on the degree of obstruction. Newborn children with severe outlet obstruction from posterior urethral valves typically have a palpable midline abdominal mass (a distended bladder), ascites (from urinary leak at the level of the kidney), or both. In the most extreme cases children may experience respiratory distress from pulmonary hypoplasia because of the lack of adequate amniotic fluid volume during lung development. Children who are identified later in life as having posterior urethral valves generally do not suffer from as severe an obstruction. Typically, these children are initially found to have voiding dysfunction, urinary tract infection, and on rare occasion, signs of renal failure (e.g., short stature). Today, with the widespread use of prenatal sonography, the majority of boys with bladder outlet obstruction are identified before delivery.[8]

Anatomic obstruction of the urethra results in pathologic changes at the level of both the kidney and the bladder. The bladder wall hypertrophies, diverticula can form, and the posterior urethra becomes variably dilated (Fig. 116-9). Vesicoureteral reflux is seen in 30% to 50%

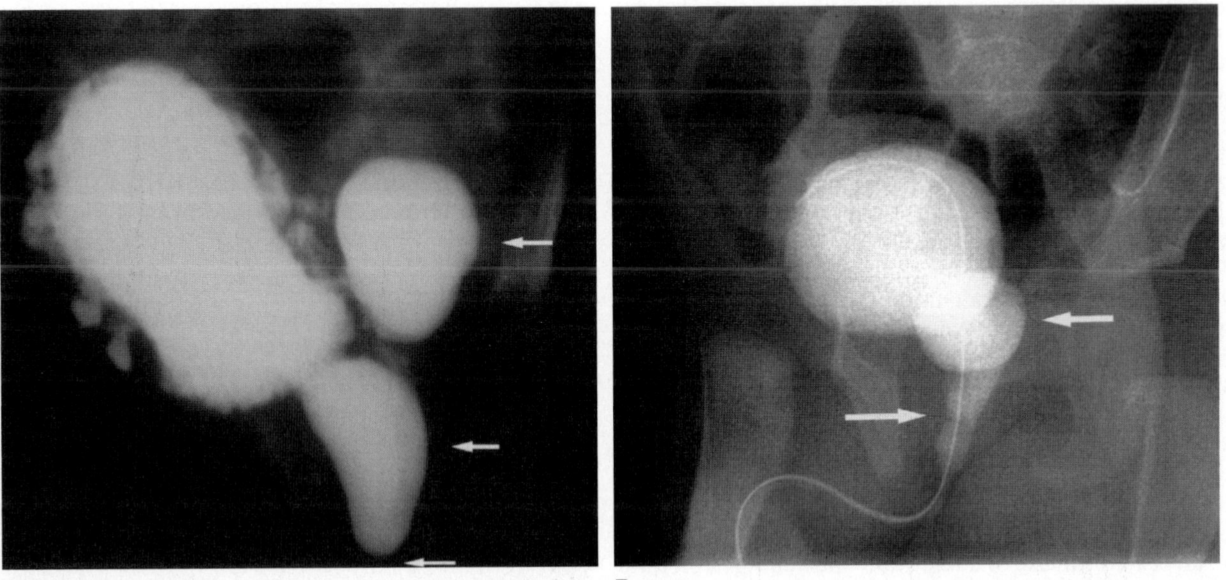

Figure 116–9 Voiding cystourethrograms in children with posterior urethral valves. *A*, Severe case in which there is dramatic bladder decompensation with multiple small and large diverticula (*uppermost arrow*) and a dilated posterior urethra (*middle arrow*). The site of valvular obstruction is shown by the *inferior arrow*. *B*, Mild case with little evidence of bladder deterioration. The *upper arrow* points to the distended posterior urethra. The *lower arrow* points to the negative impression resulting from the posterior urethral valve itself.

of patients. In approximately a third of these cases the reflux resolves once the obstruction has been relieved.[26] However, even in the absence of vesicoureteral reflux, the upper urinary tract may still suffer injury because of lower urinary tract dysfunction that arises as a result of bladder wall thickening. Both cellular hypertrophy and increased deposition of extracellular matrix are seen histologically in a bladder that is of lower capacity and decreased compliance.

Endoscopic destruction of the valve leaflets can be performed safely in nearly all term infants. An antegrade approach to valve destruction has been used in patients whose urethra is too small to accept a cystoscope.[73] Although cautery electrodes are the most frequently used device for disrupting the obstructing leaflets, cautery hooks, the neodymium:YAG laser, and antegrade withdrawal of a balloon catheter have also been used effectively for this purpose.[11,18,48]

Once the urethral obstruction has been relieved, the bladder dysfunction may persist. Most often, the bladder dysfunction is manifested as daytime urinary incontinence continuing after the child has reached school age. Initially it was thought that persistent incontinence was due to injury to the urethral sphincter during endoscopic ablation of the valves or due to abnormal bladder sphincter development as a result of the initial obstruction, or both. However, urodynamic assessment of these children has clearly shown that persistent bladder dysfunction is frequently seen well after the valves have been ablated. Several investigators have demonstrated that there are three primary abnormalities of detrusor function: bladder hypertonia, detrusor hyperreflexia, and myogenic failure.[4,22,40,64] Furthermore, some evidence suggests that urodynamic patterns can change as the child matures. A study by Holmdahl et al. has demonstrated that many children who are initially shown to have a hypercontractile, poorly compliant bladder as a newborn will later have a urodynamic pattern that is more consistent with myogenic failure.[33,34] Many children with bladder dysfunction secondary to posterior urethral valves also appear to have abnormal bladder sensation and an inability to sense when their bladder is full.[47] Adding to the problem of persistent bladder dysfunction is the common finding of renal injury and associated poor urinary concentrating ability. The large volumes of urine that result put further stress on the dysfunctional lower urinary tract.

Treatment of bladder dysfunction in children with posterior urethral valves is dependent on the severity and form of bladder dysfunction and the efficiency of bladder emptying. Patients with high-pressure voiding dynamics often benefit from the use of anticholinergic medications to improve compliance. In younger patients with an impaired ability to empty the bladder spontaneously, CIC may be required. Daytime catheterization can often be avoided in older children if they can adhere to a strict schedule of timed voiding. Recently, Koff and associates have advocated the use of a nighttime indwelling catheter to provide optimal bladder drainage. By improving nighttime drainage the authors have documented significant improvement in hydronephrosis and bladder compliance.[46,47] Although conservative measures are usually effective in modifying bladder dynamics (i.e., keeping bladder volumes sufficiently low to maintain acceptable bladder pressure), a small number of patients may still require bladder augmentation to improve bladder volume and compliance.[40] Patients with posterior urethral valves do not have altered urethral sensation, and many of these children will find catheterization through the penis painful. Creation of a continent catheterizable channel to the anterior abdominal wall can, therefore, improve the quality of life and result in improved compliance with catheterization in these children.[42]

NON-NEUROPATHIC, NONANATOMIC CAUSES OF BLADDER DYSFUNCTION

Dysfunctional Elimination Syndromes

Bladder dysfunction in the absence of anatomic bladder outlet obstruction or neurologic disease is frequently termed dysfunctional voiding. This term encompasses children who fit along a spectrum of relative urinary retention. At the most severe end of this spectrum are children who retain urine to such a great degree that they demonstrate altered bladder anatomy, upper urinary tract dilatation, and scarring, findings virtually indistinguishable from those seen in neuropathic bladder dysfunction (the so-called non-neurogenic neurogenic bladder) (Fig. 116-10).[29,30] The severity of the radiographic findings leads the physician to obtain an MRI of the lumbosacral spine, which by definition shows no abnormalities suggestive of spinal cord tethering. Urodynamic evaluation classically demonstrates a low-capacity, high-pressure bladder. Treatment of the Hinman syndrome parallels that used in true neuropathic bladder dysfunction. An attempt should be made to lower intravesical pressure with the combined use of anticholinergic medication and CIC. If conservative measures fail to adequately reduce

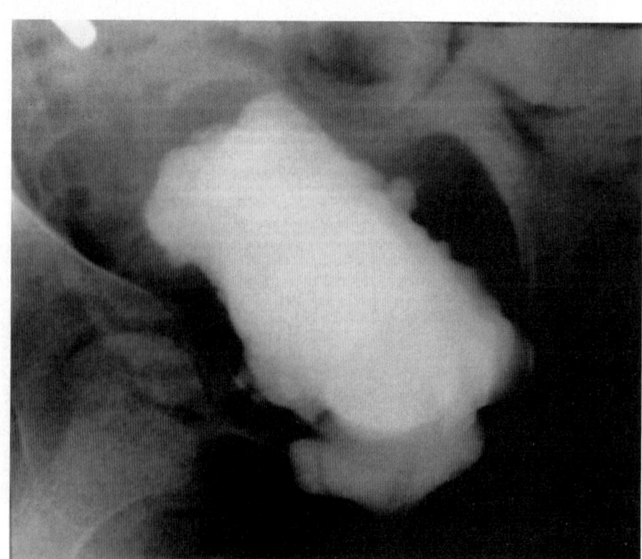

Figure 116-10 Voiding cystourethrogram from a child with the Hinman syndrome. Note the significant irregularity of the bladder outline secondary to bladder wall thickening.

storage pressure, bladder augmentation is performed. Unlike patients with true neurologic lesions, many of these children will find catheterization painful and will benefit from creation of a continent catheterizable channel to the anterior abdominal wall.

At the opposite end of the spectrum is a large population of otherwise healthy children who, as a result of relative urinary retention, experience increased irritative voiding symptoms and have a higher propensity for urinary tract infections. In the past decade it has become clear that constipation can be seen in many of these individuals and that a large fecal burden can have a significant impact on bladder function. As a result, the more encompassing term dysfunctional elimination syndrome has largely supplanted the term dysfunctional voiding.

Children affected by this condition do not empty their bowel or bladder as often or as completely as they should. As a result of poor bladder emptying, the bladder is constantly distended and as such leaves the patient prone to urge incontinence. If the child fails to empty completely, a state of fullness will be reached more often, and this may be reflected in the symptom of urinary frequency. Maintenance of a high postvoid residual leaves the patient more prone to urinary tract infections. Constipation can contribute to bladder irritability from the mass effect on the posterior aspect of the bladder and in severe cases may also inhibit bladder emptying (Fig. 116-11). Poor bladder emptying has been shown by Dohil et al. to improve after bowel treatment in constipated children, with postvoid residual urine dropping from 66% at baseline assessment to 21%.[15] Chronic constipation is associated with significant hypertrophy of the internal anal sphincter and abnormal anal sphincter EMG activity.[54] This may generate increased urethral sphincter and pelvic floor activity and explain the association with voiding dysfunction and incomplete voiding.

Radiographic findings that are highly suggestive of this diagnosis include a large stool burden on plain abdominal films, a large postvoid residual on bladder ultrasound, and a "spinning top" image of the bladder neck on voiding cystourethrography (Fig. 116-12).

Treatment of a child with dysfunctional elimination syndrome includes (1) timed voiding in which the child is asked to void every 2 hours, (2) double voiding in which the child is asked to attempt to void a second time after emptying the bladder (in an effort to minimize the chance of carrying a large postvoid residual), and (3) establishment of good bowel-emptying habits. The latter behavior can be supported by increasing dietary fiber, using stool softeners, and taking plenty of time to defecate completely. Providing adequate foot support can be very beneficial in achieving a state of balance and thereby enhancing adequate relaxation. Should these conservative measures fail to result in adequate relaxation during voiding/defecating, biofeedback may prove beneficial. Many ingenious methods for performing biofeedback have been developed, including the use of videogames.[28]

Overactive Bladder Syndrome

Although the majority of children who are evaluated by the pediatrician for wetting and urinary frequency will have retentive behavior as the cause, a smaller proportion will have these symptoms because of a state of relative detrusor overactivity in the absence of demonstrable neurologic impairment. As a result, bladder filling, even to moderate volumes, will often trigger a bladder contraction.

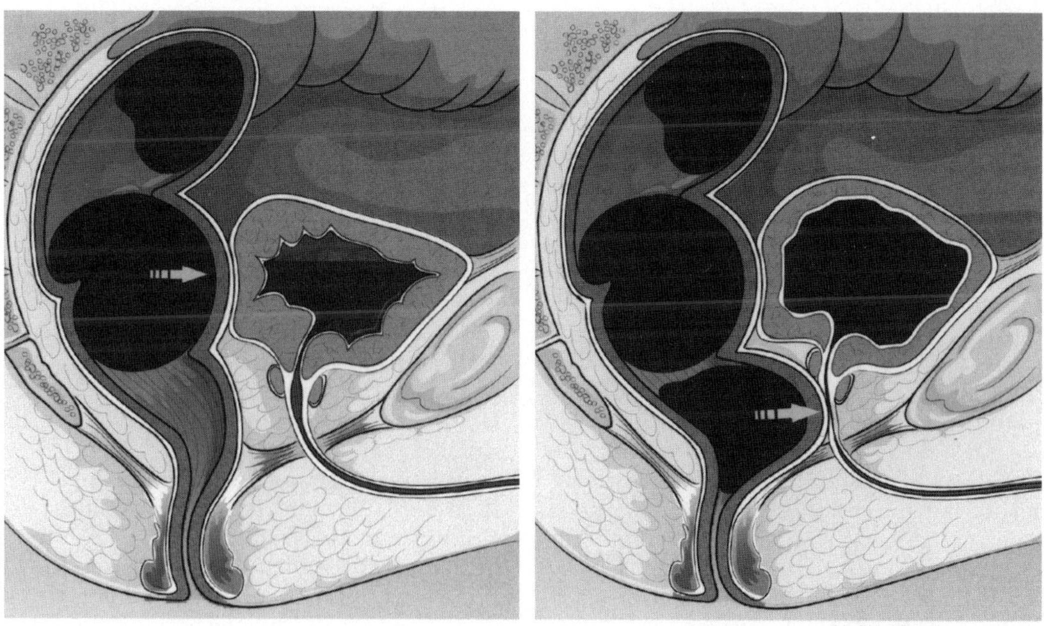

Figure 116-11 The effect of constipation on bladder function. *Left panel,* Stool in the rectum may push up on the posterior aspect of the bladder and result in bladder instability. *Right panel,* Severe forms of constipation have the potential to externally compress the bladder neck and inhibit bladder emptying.

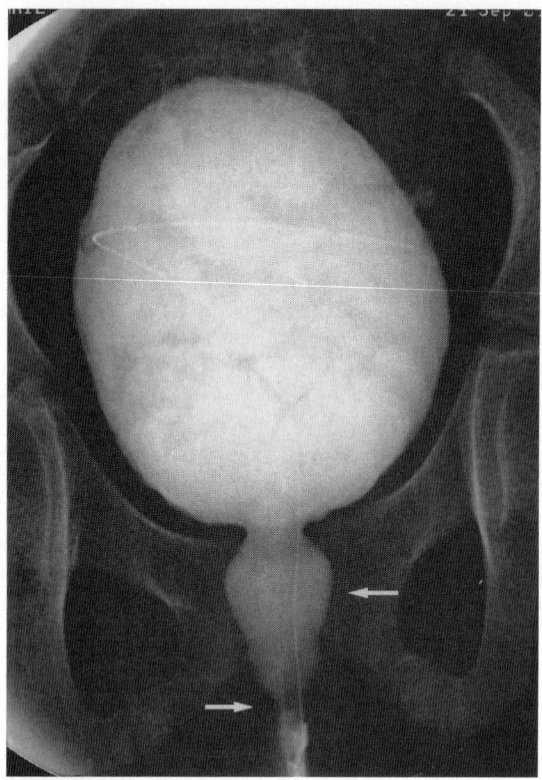

Figure 116–12 Voiding cystourethrogram from a child with dysfunctional elimination syndrome demonstrating a full bladder with a small diverticulum and a distended proximal urethra (*uppermost arrow*). The *lowermost arrow* depicts the site of the external sphincter, which because of failure to relax results in proximal urethral ballooning (so-called spinning top deformity).

This group of children does not demonstrate retentive bladder nor bowel behavior and carries minimal postvoid residual when evaluated by bladder ultrasound. A very effective treatment of this condition is the use of anticholinergic medications. These medications are competitive inhibitors of acetylcholine that block the neurotransmitter's muscarinic effects. Anticholinergic medications are typically titrated to effect. Common side effects consist of dry mouth, flushing, and constipation. Constipation especially may pose a problem because children with detrusor overactivity have a predilection for constipation, and the development of constipation may aggravate detrusor overactivity and thus counteract the beneficial effects of the drug. Oxybutynin (0.2 mg/kg two or three times daily) has been the most often used anticholinergic medication. The newer antimuscarinic drug tolterodine has, in adults, shown a more favorable therapeutic profile, with the same clinical efficacy and a lesser frequency of side effects than seen with oxybutynin.[56] Tolterodine has also been shown to be safe and effective in children.[32] A commonly used dosage for tolterodine in children is 0.01 mg/kg twice daily. Sustained-release formulations that can be taken once daily are also an option for children who can tolerate medication in pill form. Overactive bladder symptoms are typically self-limited, with even the most recalcitrant cases showing resolution within an 18-month period.[9] Failure to improve with anticholinergic medication may warrant a more thorough investigation of the patient in the form of urodynamic evaluation.

Nocturnal Enuresis

Whether a true problem of bladder function, failure of adequate nocturnal urinary concentrating ability, or an issue related to a relatively poor state of nocturnal arousal, nighttime wetting is often discussed in chapters on bladder dysfunction.[31] Various series have reported the incidence of isolated nocturnal enuresis to be between 6% and 10% in children who have reached the age of 7 years. The spontaneous cure rate in individuals between the ages of 5 and 20 is 15% annually.[21] Most children who are enuretic eventually obtain normal control.

Nocturnal enuresis is a genetically complex and heterogeneous disorder. Genetic factors play an important role in the etiology. A positive family history may be elicited in over 50% of cases. Within families, different members can have the same or different forms of wetting. Studies evaluating the incidence of nocturnal enuresis in twins have shown 46% for monozygotic pairs and 19% for dizygotic pairs.[37] The most common mode of transmission appears to be autosomal dominant.

Various pathophysiologic mechanisms appear to be at play, including nocturnal polyuria, bladder overactivity at night with a small functional bladder capacity, and a disorder of arousal.[14] Furthermore, these groupings show considerable overlap. Humans have a marked circadian rhythm of urine production, with nighttime diuresis being reduced by up to 50% of daytime levels.[51] In children, this is controlled by increased nocturnal release of arginine vasopressin, as well as angiotensin II and aldosterone.[66,67] It has long been known that some children with nocturnal enuresis have significantly larger nocturnal urine production than nonenuretic children. This group of patients has a favorable response to the arginine vasopressin analogue desmopressin (DDAVP).[59] Although it does appear that a certain subset of enuretic children have a smaller nocturnal functional bladder capacity, the incidence of functional abnormalities seems rather low in children with isolated nocturnal enuresis. Whether wetting is primarily due to a problem of urinary concentrating ability, functional bladder capacity, or other as yet unrecognized etiology, a prerequisite for wetting is failure to awaken when micturition is imminent. This has caused many to conclude that sleep disturbance per se is the major pathophysiologic factor in enuresis, and it is still a widely held belief that enuretic children are deep sleepers. However, a number of studies have been unable to convincingly show abnormalities in sleep patterns.

Treatment of nocturnal enuresis takes many forms. If present, daytime symptoms should be treated. The child should be asked to void regularly and not to delay urinating after experiencing a sense of bladder fullness. Symptoms of urgency and frequency, as well as constipation, should be addressed. A rate of enuresis cure of up to 72% has been reported after constipation has been adequately addressed.[53] To minimize the possibility of nocturnal polyuria, fluids should be limited several hours before bedtime. A low-calcium, low-sodium dietary content of the afternoon and evening meals may also be useful. The child should be instructed to void before bedtime to help minimize nocturnal bladder volume.

Enuresis that persists after the age of 6 years may be treated with medication, a bed alarm device, or both. Desmopressin is easy to administer and has an immediate effect on urinary volume. Dosing is between 0.2 and 0.6 mg orally or 20 and 40 μg intranasally at bedtime. In most trials, response to desmopressin (defined as more than a 50% reduction in the number of wet nights) was noted in 60% to 70% of patients.[23] Other options include the tricyclic antidepressant imipramine (Tofranil), which exerts a direct effect on bladder smooth muscle and has sympathomimetic effects. Unlike anticholinergic medications, which have a relatively short half-life, blood levels of imipramine build up over a period of several days. The true beneficial effect of this medication may, therefore, not become apparent for as long as 2 weeks. Approximately 50% of enuretic children improve with imipramine, yet a significant number will relapse after treatment is discontinued. It has been reported that only 17% of children who were dry during imipramine medication stay dry 6 months after cessation of the medication.[60] The major drawback to imipramine therapy is its cardiotoxic side effects, even in therapeutic doses.[71] Although anticholinergic medications should not be expected to be effective in patients with true isolated nocturnal enuresis, this medication can occasionally be of help.

Alarm therapy is the most effective method for treating nocturnal enuresis. A meta-analysis of the world literature revealed an average success rate of 68%.[31] Efficacy is reported to increase with duration of therapy to as high as 90% by 6 months.[57] Although most children will not awaken, they will stop emptying their bladder at the onset of the alarm. It therefore requires that a parent assist the child in awakening and proceeding to the toilet to finish voiding. Once the undergarments have been changed, the alarm should be reset. The exact mechanisms of alarm treatment are not known, although it is clearly an operant type of behavioral approach.

REFERENCES

1. Austin PF, Cain MP, Casale AJ, et al: Prenatal bladder outlet obstruction secondary to ureterocele. Urology 1998;52:1132.
2. Bauer S: The management of spina bifida from birth onwards. In Whitaker RH, Woodard JR (eds): Paediatric Urology. London, Butterworths, 1985, p 87.
3. Bauer S, Hallet M, Khoshbin S: The predictive value of urodynamic evaluation in the newborn with myelodysplasia. JAMA 1984;152:650.
4. Bauer SB, Dieppa RA, Labib KK, et al: The bladder in boys with posterior urethral valves: A urodynamic assessment. J Urol 1979;121:769.
5. Boemers T, Van Gool J, deJong T, et al: Urodynamic evaluation of children with caudal regression syndrome (caudal dysplasia sequence). J Urol 1994;151:1038.
6. Bruce D, Schut L: Spinal lipomas in infancy and childhood. Brain 1979;5:92.
7. Chiaramonte R, Horowitz E, Kaplan G: Implications of hydronephrosis in newborns with myelodysplasia. J Urol 1986;136:427.
8. Cromie WJ, Lee K, Houde K, et al: Implications of prenatal ultrasound screening in the incidence of major genitourinary malformations. J Urol 2001;165:1677.
9. Curran MJ, Kaefer M, Peters C, et al: The overactive bladder in childhood: Long-term results with conservative management. J Urol 2000;163:574.
10. Czeizel A, Dudas I: Prevention of the first occurrence of neural-tube defects by preconceptual vitamin supplementation. N Engl J Med 1992;321:1832.
11. Deane AM, Whitaker RH, Sherwood T: Diathermy hook ablation of posterior urethral valves in neonates and infants. Br J Urol 1988;62:593.
12. Decter RM, Bauer SB, Khoshbin S, et al: Urodynamic assessment of children with cerebral palsy. J Urol 1987; 138:1110.
13. Dick EA, Patel K, Owens CM, et al: Spinal ultrasound in infants. Br J Radiol 2002;75:384.
14. Djurhuus JC, Rittig S: Current trends, diagnosis, and treatment of enuresis. Eur Urol 1998;33(Suppl 3):30.
15. Dohil R, Roberts E, Jones KV, et al: Constipation and reversible urinary tract abnormalities. Arch Dis Child 1994;70:56.
16. Donnahoo KK, Rink RC, Cain MP, et al: The Young-Dees-Leadbetter bladder neck repair for neurogenic incontinence. J Urol 1999;161:1946.
17. Edelstein RA, Bauer SB, Kelly MD, et al: The long-term urological response of neonates with myelodysplasia treated proactively with intermittent catheterization and anticholinergic therapy. J Urol 1995;154:1500.
18. Ehrlich RM, Shanberg A, Fine RN: Neodymium:YAG laser ablation of posterior urethral valves. J Urol 1987;138:959.
19. Ferrara P, Rossodivita A, Ruggiero A, et al: Cryptorchidism associated with meningomyelocele. J Pediatr Child Health 1998;34:44.
20. Flood H, Ritchey M, Bloom D: Outcome of reflux in children with myelodysplasia managed by bladder pressure monitoring. J Urol 1994;152:1574.
21. Forsythe WI, Redmond A: Enuresis and spontaneous cure rate. Study of 1129 enuretis. Arch Dis Child 1974;49:259.
22. Glassberg KI, Schneider M, Haller JO, et al: Observations on persistently dilated ureter after posterior urethral valve ablation. Urology 1982;20:20.
23. Glazener CMA, Evans JHC: Desmopressin for nocturnal enuresis in children (Cochrane review). Cochrane Database Syst Rev 2000;(2):CD002112.
24. Golonka NR, Haga LJ, Keating RP, et al: Routine MRI evaluation of low imperforate anus reveals unexpected high incidence of tethered spinal cord. J Pediatr Surg 2002;37:966.
25. Guzman L, Bauer S, Hallet M: The evaluation and management of children with sacral agenesis. Urology 1983; 23:506.
26. Hassan JM, Pope JCT, Brock JW 3rd, et al: Vesicoureteral reflux in patients with posterior urethral valves. J Urol 2003; 170:1677.
27. Hendren WH, Hendren RB: Bladder augmentation: Experience with 129 children and young adults. J Urol 1990;144:445.
28. Herndon CD, Decambre M, McKenna PH: Interactive computer games for treatment of pelvic floor dysfunction. J Urol 2001;166:1893.
29. Hinman F: Non-neurogenic neurogenic bladder (the Hinman syndrome): 15 years later. J Urol 1986;136:769.
30. Hinman F, Baumann F: Vesical and ureteral damage from voiding dysfunction in boys without neurologic or obstructive disease. J Urol 1973;109:727.
31. Hjalmas K, Arnold T, Bower W, et al: Nocturnal enuresis: An international evidence based management strategy. J Urol 2004;171:2545.

32. Hjalmas K, Hellstrom AL, Mogren K, et al: The overactive bladder in children: A potential future indication for tolterodine. BJU Int 2001;87:569.
33. Holmdahl G, Sillen U, Bachelard M, et al: The changing urodynamic pattern in valve bladders during infancy. J Urol 1995;153:463.
34. Holmdahl G, Sillen U, Hanson E, et al: Bladder dysfunction in boys with posterior urethral valves before and after puberty. J Urol 1996;155:694.
35. Houle A, Vernot O, RJ: Bladder function before and after sacral rhizotomy in children with cerebral palsy. J Urol 1998; 160:1088.
36. Hsiao KC, Baez-Trinidad L, Lendvay T, et al: Direct vision internal urethrotomy for the treatment of pediatric urethral strictures: Analysis of 50 patients. J Urol 2003;170:952.
37. Hublin C, Kaprio J, Partinen M, et al: Nocturnal enuresis in a nationwide twin cohort. Sleep 1998;21:579.
38. Hunt GM, Whitaker RH: The pattern of congenital renal anomalies associated with neural-tube defects. Dev Med Child Neurol 1987;29:91.
39. Kaefer M, Barnewolt C, Retik AB, et al: The sonographic diagnosis of infravesical obstruction in children: Evaluation of bladder wall thickness indexed to bladder filling. J Urol 1997;157:989.
40. Kaefer M, Keating MA, Adams MC, et al: Posterior urethral valves, pressure pop-offs and bladder function. J Urol 1995; 154:708.
41. Kaefer M, Pabby A, Kelly M, et al: Improved bladder function after prophylactic treatment of the high risk neurogenic bladder in newborns with myelomeningocele. J Urol 1999; 162:1068.
42. Kaefer M, Retik AB: The Mitrofanoff principle in continent urinary reconstruction. Urol Clin North Am 1997; 24:795.
43. Kaefer M, Rosen A, Darbey M, et al: Pressure at residual volume: A useful adjunct to standard fill cystometry. J Urol 1997;158:1268.
44. Kaefer M, Zurakowski D, Bauer SB, et al: Estimating normal bladder capacity in children. J Urol 1997;158:2261.
45. Keating M, Rink R, Bauer S: Neuro-urologic implications of changing approach in management of occult spinal lesions. J Urol 1988;140:1299.
46. Koff SA, Gigax MR, Jayanthi VR: Nocturnal bladder emptying: A simple technique for reversing urinary tract deterioration in children with neurogenic bladder [abstract 60]. Presented at the 2004 Meeting of the American Academy of Pediatrics.
47. Koff SA, Mutabagani KH, Jayanthi VR: The valve bladder syndrome: Pathophysiology and treatment with nocturnal bladder emptying. J Urol 2002;167:291.
48. Kolicinski Z: Foley balloon procedure in posterior urethral valves. Dialogues Pediatr Urol 1988;11:7.
49. Kropp KA, Voeller KK: Cryptorchidism in meningomyelocele. J Pediatr 1981;99:110.
50. Kuban K, Leviton A: Cerebral palsy. N Engl J Med 1994; 330:188.
51. Lackgren G, Hjalmas K, van Gool J, et al: Nocturnal enuresis: A suggestion for a European treatment strategy. Acta Paediatr 1999;88:679.
52. Lais A, Kasabian N, Dyro F: Neurosurgical implications of continuous neuro-urological surveillance of children with myelodysplasia. J Urol 1993;150:1879.
53. Loening-Baucke V: Urinary incontinence and urinary tract infection and their resolution with treatment of chronic constipation of childhood. Pediatrics 1997;100:228.
54. Lofthouse C, Odeka EB: The problem of constipation in children: Understanding the issues. Gastroenterology 1998;8:68.
55. Merrot T, Chaumoitre K, Shojai R, et al: Fetal bladder rupture due to anterior urethral valves. Urology 2003;61:1259.
56. Millard R, Tuttle J, Moore K, et al: Clinical efficacy and safety of tolterodine compared to placebo in detrusor overactivity. J Urol 1999;161:1551.
57. Moffat MEK: Nocturnal enuresis: A review of the efficacy of treatments and practical advice for clinicians. J Dev Behav Pediatr 1997;18:49.
58. Mosiello G, Capitanucci ML, Gatti C, et al: How to investigate neurovesical dysfunction in children with anorectal malformations. J Urol 2003;170:1610.
59. Neveus T, Tuvemo T, Lackgren G, et al: Bladder capacity and renal concentrating ability in enuresis: Pathogenic implications. J Urol 2001;165:2022.
60. Nijman RJM, Butler R, van Gool J, et al: Conservative management of urinary incontinence in childhood. In Abrams P, Cardozo L, Khoury S, Wein A (eds): Incontinence, 2nd International Consultation on Incontinence, Paris, July 1-3, 2001. Plymouth, United Kingdom, Health Publication, 2002, p 515.
61. Palomaki G, Williams J, Haddow J: Prenatal screening for open neural-tube defects in Maine. N Engl J Med 1999; 340:1049.
62. Pang D: Sacral agenesis and caudal spinal cord malformations. Neurosurgery 1993;32:755.
63. Passarge E, Lenz K: Syndrome of caudal regression in infants of diabetic mothers: Observations of further cases. Pediatrics 1966;37:672.
64. Peters CA, Bolkier M, Bauer SB, et al: The urodynamic consequences of posterior urethral valves. J Urol 1990;144:122.
65. Rink RC: Bladder augmentation. Options, outcomes, future. Urol Clin North Am 1999;26:111.
66. Rittig S, Knudsen UB, Norgaard JP, et al: Abnormal diurnal rhythm of plasma vasopressin and urinary output in patients with enuresis. Am J Physiol 1989;256:F664.
67. Rittig S, Knudsen UB, Norgaard JP, et al: Diurnal variation of plasma atrial natriuretic peptide in normals and patients with enuresis nocturna. Scand J Clin Lab Invest 1991;51:209.
68. Shaul D, Harrison E: Classification of anorectal malformation: Initial approach, diagnostic test, and colostomy. Semin Pediatr Surg 1997;6:187.
69. Stein S, Feldman J, Freidlander M: Is myelomeningocele a disappearing disease? Pediatrics 1982;69:511.
70. Tsakayannis DE, Shamberger RC: Association of imperforate anus with occult spinal dysraphism. J Pediatr Surg 1995;30:1010.
71. von Gontard A, Lehmkuhl G: [Drug therapy of enuresis.] Zeitschrift Kinder Jugendpsychiatrie Psychotherapie 1996;24:18.
72. Wilmshurst J, Kelly R, Borzyskowski M: Presentation and outcome of sacral agenesis: 20 years' experience. Dev Med Child Neurol 1999;41:806.
73. Zaontz MR, Firlit CF: Percutaneous antegrade ablation of posterior urethral valves in premature or underweight term neonates: An alternative to primary vesicostomy. J Urol 1985;134:139.

Chapter 117

Structural Disorders of the Bladder, Augmentation

Eugene Minevich and Curtis A. Sheldon

Effective surgical management of an abnormal bladder requires a thorough understanding of both normal micturition and dysfunctional voiding (see Chapter 116). Urinary continence is a complex balance between intravesical pressure and bladder outlet resistance. Several variables determine intravesical pressure, only one of which is compliance, which reflects both muscular tone and interstitial elasticity. This measure is not static, but rather varies with bladder capacity. Consequently, urine output, postvoid residual volume, and frequency of bladder emptying determine the working compliance range of the bladder. Pathologic alterations (e.g., uninhibited detrusor contraction or interstitial fibrosis) may markedly alter compliance and the resultant intravesical pressure characteristics (see Chapter 116).

Bladder outlet resistance also depends on several variables and must be highly coordinated to prevent incontinence but allow voiding to occur. Reflex contraction of the sphincteric mechanism helps prevent incontinence after sudden increases in intra-abdominal pressure. Conversely, bladder outlet sphincteric mechanisms reflexively relax at the time of detrusor contraction. At this point, volitional voiding ensues. In addition, voluntary contraction of the striated muscle of the urinary sphincter adds supplementary support to prevent incontinence. In some circumstances, however, reflex contraction of the bladder sphincteric mechanism or inappropriate voluntary contraction (e.g., dysfunctional voiding) can result in dangerously high intravesical pressure. Furthermore, the bladder outlet sphincteric mechanism may fail to relax during attempts at voiding, a condition known as detrusor-sphincter dyssynergy. Structural bladder outlet resistance may be caused by congenital anatomic obstruction (e.g., posterior urethral valves) or acquired lesions (e.g., stricture).

The structural consequences of unbalanced voiding are highly variable and ominous. Bladder consequences include hypertrophy of the detrusor musculature with trabeculation. Sacculation and diverticula may develop and lead to urinary tract infection and urolithiasis. Interstitial fibrosis may also occur and cause progressive loss of bladder compliance. Of particular concern are the consequences of high bladder pressure on renal function. Even without vesicoureteral reflux, a close correlation exists between intrapelvic renal pressure and intravesical pressure.[56] Renal pelvic pressures greater than 40 cm H_2O deform the renal papillae, which may distort the orientation of the tubules draining into the papillae and result in intrarenal reflux.[124] This increases the vulnerability of the kidney to pyelonephritis.

The importance of intravesical pressure on ultimate renal function is demonstrated dramatically with posterior urethral valves (see also Chapter 120).[101] The syndrome of vesicoureteral reflux and renal dysplasia refers to congenital, unilateral, severe renal dysplasia in patients with valves. The involved kidney (usually the left) generally has little or no function. However, the contralateral kidney often has excellent function, apparently protected by a prenatal "pop-off" mechanism that results from decompression of intravesical pressure into the massively dilated refluxing system that subtends the dysplastic kidney.[42] In addition, children born with urinary ascites (usually indicating a ruptured renal fornix) have remarkably good renal function, presumably because of the same mechanisms. Similar observations have been made for patients with posterior urethral valves who have congenital diverticula.[101]

In patients with neurogenic bladder (such as those with myelodysplasia), bladder pressure and renal prognosis are closely correlated. Spontaneous urine leakage through the bladder outlet mechanism at a bladder pressure greater than 40 cm H_2O has been associated with poor prognosis for the upper urinary tract.[80] A similar correlation with maximal urethral pressure on urodynamic testing has also been demonstrated.[22] Furthermore, elevated intravesical pressure has been shown to adversely affect renal allografts.[23,99]

Otherwise healthy children with increased intravesical pressure have an increased risk for urinary tract infection and vesicoureteral reflux.[64] Oxybutynin hydrochloride, which reduces intravesical pressure, can dramatically alleviate reflux and urinary tract infection.[65,107] Failure of antireflux surgery is clearly a greater risk in patients who have high bladder pressure than in patients with normal bladder pressure.[93]

The surgeon must realize that the cause of bladder injury cannot be reliably determined from end-stage abnormalities because the ability of various primary diseases to cause bladder injury overlaps considerably. Secondary changes resulting from chronic retention, infection, stones, or surgery also confound the issue. Both primary and secondary changes may induce rather nonspecific muscular, interstitial, and urothelial changes. Therefore, one cannot predict the degree of bladder function on the basis of knowledge of such primary diseases and conditions as myelodysplasia, posterior urethral valves, prune-belly syndrome, and imperforate anus. Measurement of the physiologic properties of the bladder by formal urodynamic investigation is essential in planning any major surgical intervention.

Although it is accepted that bladder dysfunction can damage the kidney, it is less well recognized that renal disease can contribute to bladder injury. Polyuria caused by primary renal disease can substantially alter bladder function. It can result in a hypertensive bladder with extensive detrusor hypertrophy or, if decompensated, a massively dilated, flaccid, hypotensive bladder that cannot empty completely. These effects can also accompany secondary renal disease (e.g., polyuria accompanying posterior urethral valves). Such lesions injure the renal medulla and lead to loss of concentrating capacity; the resulting polyuria may further damage the bladder.

Bladder outlet obstruction is a major factor in progressive bladder and kidney injury. Structural lesions, such as urethral strictures or posterior urethral valves, are particularly problematic. Also important is detrusor-sphincter dyssynergy. This condition may be volitional or nonvolitional. With the latter, the sphincteric periurethral muscle inappropriately contracts (rather than relaxes) during detrusor contraction. In the former, the child closes the bladder outlet to prevent the incontinence that results from uninhibited detrusor activity or to delay the need for voiding when the bladder has become overfilled. Such activity may also be used to prevent painful voiding. This activity is often manifested clinically by the occurrence of Vincent's curtsy, in which the child sits on a foot, squats, or squeezes the legs together to help increase outlet resistance and prevent voiding. This symptom should always be sought by the surgeon because its consequences are particularly detrimental.

The "valve bladder" best exemplifies the interplay of these factors (Fig. 117-1). Even after valve resection, the bladder may still operate at very high pressure because of residual bladder wall changes, such as altered compliance and uninhibited detrusor contractions. The bladder may not empty completely, and substantial vesicoureteral reflux may be present. During voiding, urine is emitted through the urethra but also refluxes into the kidneys. When the patient completes voiding, urine immediately drains back into the bladder. This drainage, along with the elevated postvoid residual urine volume caused by abnormal bladder function, forces the bladder to continuously work within a range that results in high storage pressure with subsequent adverse effects on the kidneys.

Recent advances in surgical technique, the successful application of intermittent catheterization to the reconstructed urinary tract, and lessons learned from the pioneering work on urinary undiversion[48] allow even the most anatomically devastated children to be reconstructed for continence, as well as preservation of renal function. These reconstructive principles may now be applied to virtually all urinary tract anomalies with a good expectation of success. Reconstructive options are presently available even for children with end-stage renal disease for whom renal transplantation will ultimately be required. Reconstruction involves many challenges in achieving the

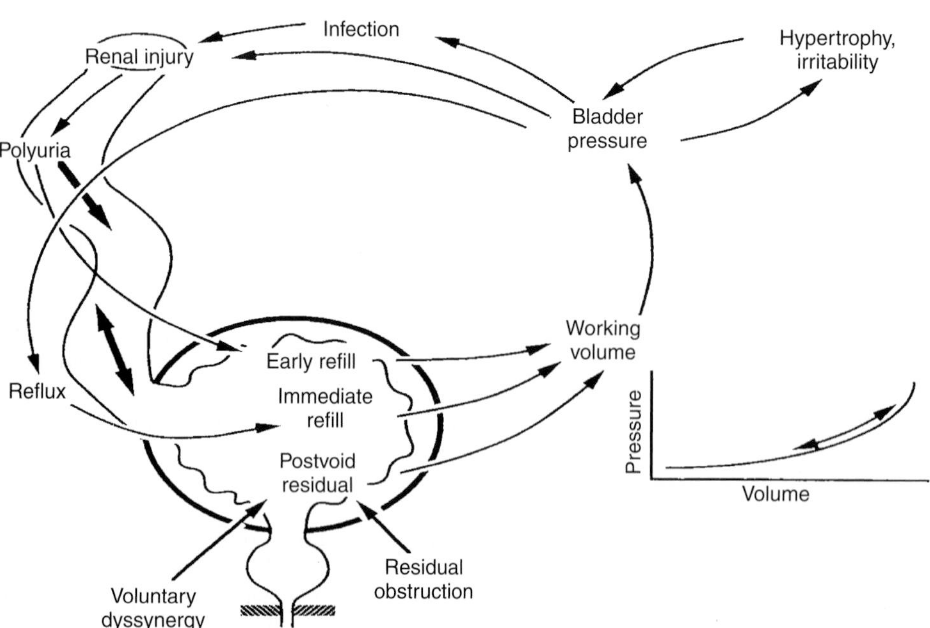

Figure 117-1 Pathophysiology of the valve bladder. (From Sheldon CA, Snyder HM: Structural disorders of the bladder, augmentation. In Grosfeld JL, et al [eds]: Pediatric Surgery. St Louis, CV Mosby, p 114.)

goals of low-pressure storage of urine and complete bladder emptying. Most frequently, such reconstruction is needed for the treatment of bladder exstrophy, posterior urethral valves, and neurogenic bladder related to myelomeningocele, other sacral dysraphisms, or the VATER complex (vertebral defects, imperforate anus, tracheo-esophageal fistula with esophageal atresia, and radial and renal dysplasia). Other disease states necessitating reconstruction include urogenital sinus and cloacal anomalies, cloacal exstrophy, and bilateral single ectopic ureters. All these conditions are commonly associated with abnormal urinary storage pressure or problems with emptying.

DISORDERS OF THE BLADDER AVD URETHRA

Anatomic Disorders of the Bladder and Urethra

Primary structural abnormalities are important and are best exemplified by posterior urethral valves (Fig. 117-2), the most common cause of structural lower urinary tract obstruction in male infants. Although these abnormalities are also discussed in Chapter 120, this section focuses on the considerations related to the bladder and upper urinary tract. Three types of posterior urethral valves have been described.[134] Type II probably does not exist. Both type I and type III involve intraluminal urethral membranes, which may be either thick or thin but are lined on each surface by transitional epithelium (Fig. 117-3). In the most common valve (type I), an obliquely oriented obstructing diaphragm originates at the verumontanum and terminates distally at a point near the membranous urethra. Type III valves represent an obstructing diaphragm that is oriented more perpendicular to the axis of the urethra and is usually more distal in the urethra than is the case with type I valves.

As a consequence of obstruction, the proximal end of the urethra is elongated and dilated, and the bladder neck is relatively narrowed because of secondary detrusor hypertrophy. The distal end of the urethra is of normal caliber, thus resulting in an abrupt transition between the dilated proximal urethra and the thin anterior urethra. The bladder exhibits detrusor hypertrophy and is irregular because of trabeculation, sacculation, and the presence of diverticula. The upper urinary tracts typically show severe hydronephrosis with or without vesicoureteral reflux. Renal impairment is frequent and often present from birth; recovery is incomplete even after valve ablation.

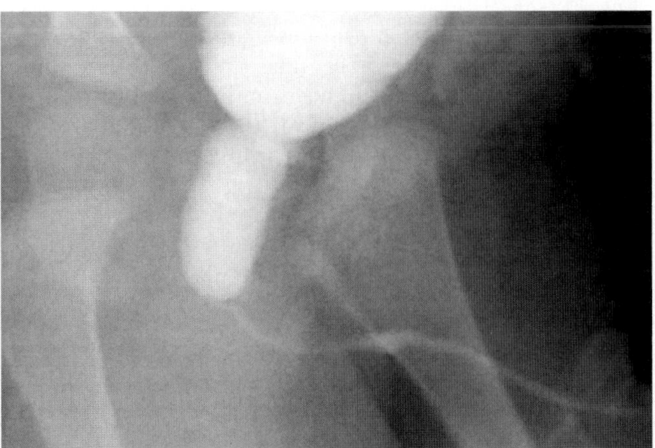

Figure 117-2 Radiographic appearance of posterior urethral valves.

Most patients are recognized during infancy: 25% to 50% of cases are detected in the neonatal period, and more than two thirds are identified within the first year of life. With the advent of perinatal ultrasonography, in utero diagnosis has become common. The ultrasonographic presence of a thick-walled bladder and hydroureteronephrosis in a male fetus is highly suggestive of the diagnosis. A newborn may have an enlarged palpable bladder or kidneys as a result of hydroureteronephrosis. An infant may have a urinary tract infection or failure to thrive because of azotemia, whereas in older children the initial manifestation may be incontinence. The urine stream is characteristically diminished in force and is sometimes described as dribbling. However, a good stream is commonly reported by the child or parents and thus should not preclude investigation.

Diagnostic evaluation includes ultrasonography of the upper urinary tract and radiographic voiding cystourethrography (VCUG). Renal function can be evaluated by renal scanning. Urodynamic investigation may later be indicated if hydronephrosis, reflux, azotemia, or incontinence persists in a child whose valves have been ablated successfully.

Infants should initially be stabilized by catheter drainage of the bladder, intravenous resuscitation, and respiratory support when needed. Urine is drained with a 5 or 8 French infant feeding tube because larger catheters or catheters with balloons may cause intense detrusor contraction, which may impede urine flow through the ureterovesical junction. Most patients are subsequently treated by valve ablation (see Fig. 117-3). In premature infants with a urethra too small for endoscopic fulguration, either antegrade ablation or vesicostomy may be performed; with current miniaturized cystoscopes, however, these procedures are rarely needed. Patients with massive reflux, particularly when accompanied by azotemia, are also candidates for vesicostomy. We have found that infants who are medically unstable and remain azotemic or septic and hydronephrotic despite adequate catheter drainage may benefit from percutaneous nephrostomy drainage until they are sufficiently stable for surgical correction.

The rare infant with profound azotemia who is unresponsive to catheter drainage may benefit from upper urinary tract diversion by way of cutaneous pyelostomy. Such low-pressure drainage may allow sufficient return of renal function that dialysis or renal transplantation can be deferred until the child is older. Both cutaneous vesicostomies and cutaneous pyelostomies are readily reversed. It is important to avoid fulguration of valves in a dry urethra (e.g., in a patient who has undergone diversion by vesicostomy or pyelostomy), which may result in urethral stricture.

In Chapter 120, the diagnosis and treatment of anterior urethral valves,[106,126] Cowper's duct cysts (Fig. 117-4),[5,74] urethral polyps, urethral duplication (Figs. 117-5 and 117-6) in both males and females, and urethral diverticula are discussed in detail. These conditions produce structural changes in the bladder that are related to obstruction.

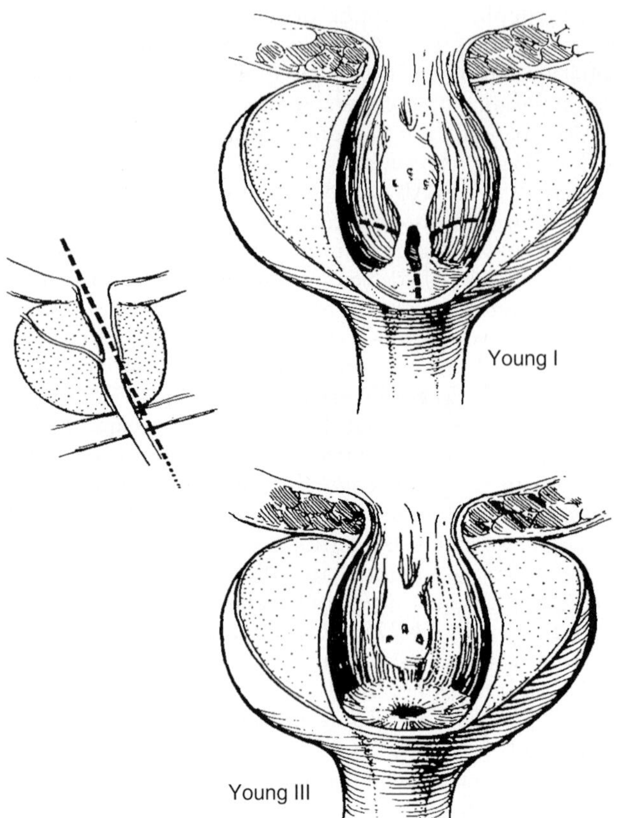

Figure 117–3 Anatomic configuration of posterior urethral valves. Transurethral fulguration is usually performed at the 5- and 7-o'clock positions, depending on the valve configuration. (Type I or III as noted.) Selected cases may be better approached by fulguration at the 12-o'clock position. (From Sheldon CA, Bukowski TP: Male external genitalia. In Rowe MI, O'Neill JA, Jr., Grosfeld JL, et al [eds]: Essentials of Pediatric Surgery. St Louis, Mosby–Year Book, 1995, p 775.)

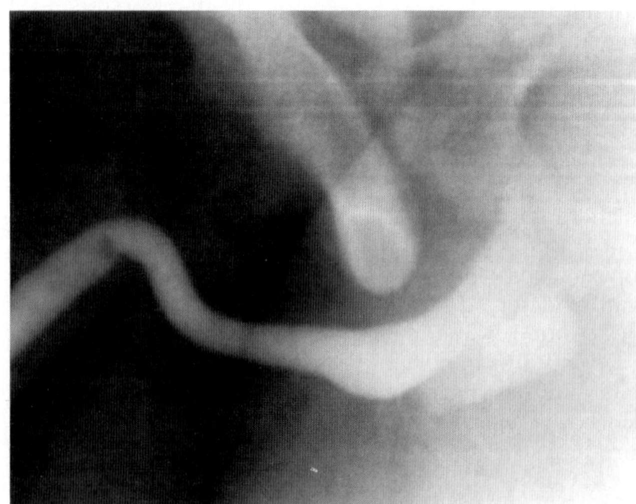

Figure 117–4 Radiographic appearance of a Cowper duct cyst and resulting diverticulum. (From Sheldon CA, Snyder HM: Structural disorders of the bladder, augmentation. In Grosfeld JL, et al [eds]: Pediatric Surgery. St Louis, CV Mosby, p 114.)

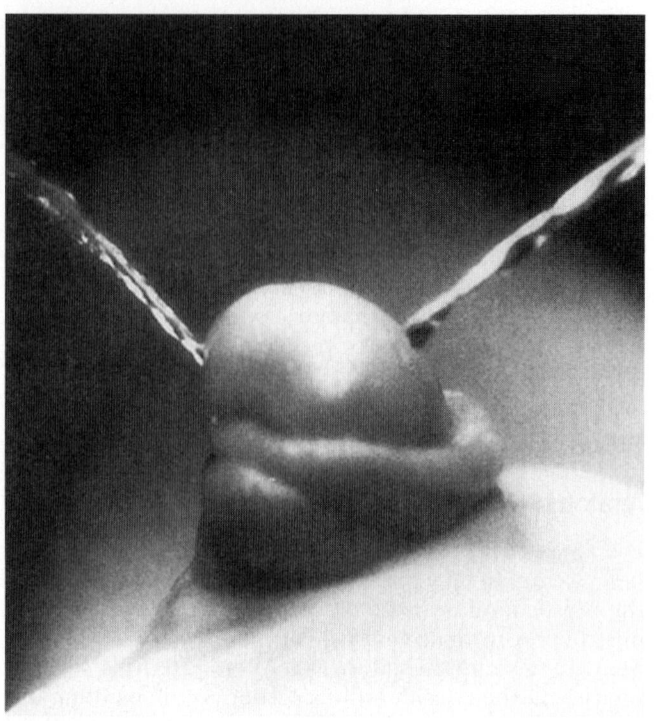

Figure 117–5 Urethral duplication. (From Sheldon CA, Bukowski TP: Male external genitalia. In Rowe MI, et al [eds]: Essentials of Pediatric Surgery. St Louis, Mosby–Year Book, 1995, p 779.)

Other congenital obstructing lesions of the urethra include utricular cysts and ectopic ureteroceles. Acquired obstructive lesions include stricture and meatal stenosis. Exstrophic bladder abnormality, epispadias, and hypospadias are other structural lesions and are discussed elsewhere (see Chapters 118 and 119).

Bladder diverticula may be a cause or a consequence of bladder outlet obstruction. These urothelial-lined pockets protrude from the urinary bladder through detrusor defects, most commonly at the ureteral hiatus. Diverticula that drain poorly may become symptomatic because of infection or calculus. Diverticula occurring at the ureteral hiatus may commonly distort the ureterovesical junction sufficiently to cause ureteral reflux or obstruction. If they protrude distally beneath the bladder outlet, they may cause bladder outlet obstruction (Fig. 117-7).[111]

Small diverticula that drain well and do not cause vesicoureteral reflux do not require surgical intervention. Most symptomatic diverticula in children require open resection. Diverticula located off the trigone are readily excised by either extravesical or transvesical procedures. However, diverticula of trigonal origin require extreme caution because of their close proximity to the ureter and vas deferens. Concomitant ureteral reimplantation is usually necessary for these diverticula.

Neurogenic Disorders of Bladder and Urethral Function

The surgeon is commonly faced with a primary abnormality of bladder innervation (a neurogenic bladder).

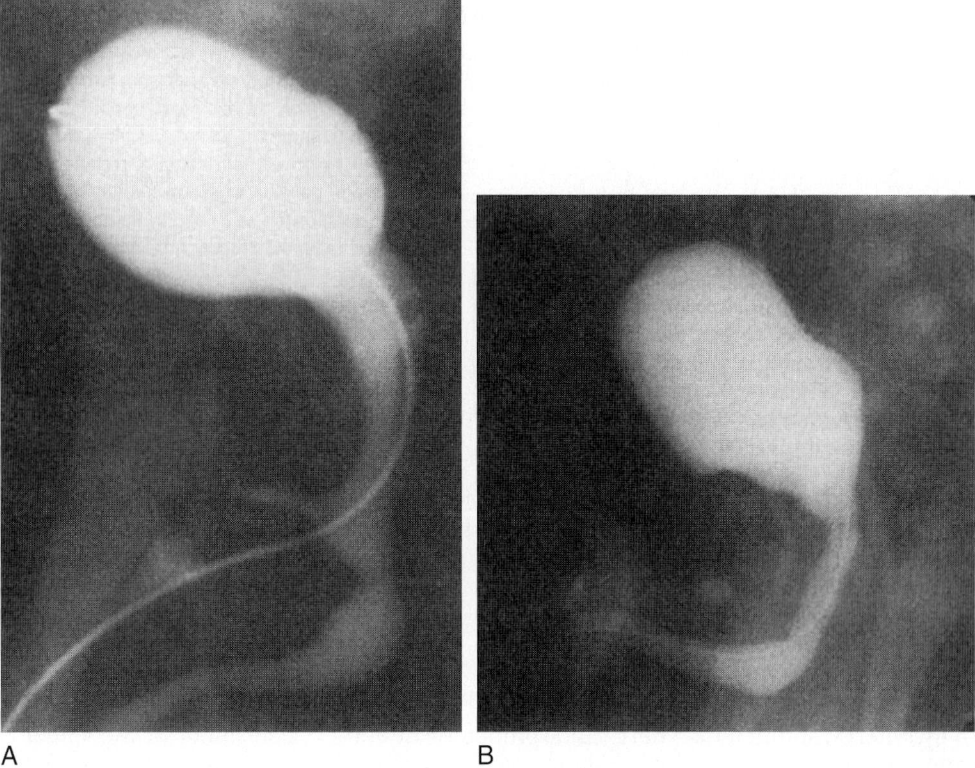

Figure 117-6 *A*, Radiographic appearance of complete urethral duplication. *B*, Radiographic appearance of incomplete urethral duplication. (From Sheldon CA, Bukowski TP: Male external genitalia. In Rowe MI, O'Neill JA, Jr., Grosfeld JL, et al [eds]: Essentials of Pediatric Surgery. St Louis, Mosby–Year Book, 1995, p 779.)

Myelodysplasia, an open dystrophic state, is particularly common. Myelomeningocele, in which neural tissue and the meninges protrude beyond the confines of the vertebral canal, is the most common defect. Whereas a meningocele involves protrusion of only the meninges, a lipomeningocele involves the presence of fatty tissue along with protruding neural tissue and meninges. The neurologic effect of these entities on the lower urinary tract varies and cannot be predicted by the observed level of the anomaly; urodynamic testing is, therefore, essential. The risk for upper urinary tract deterioration can be predicted urodynamically. Both a leak point pressure exceeding 40 cm H_2O[80] and the presence of dyssynergy[3] have been clearly shown to be associated with a poor prognosis for the upper urinary tract (Figs. 117-8 and 117-9). The risk for deterioration exceeds 70% in the presence

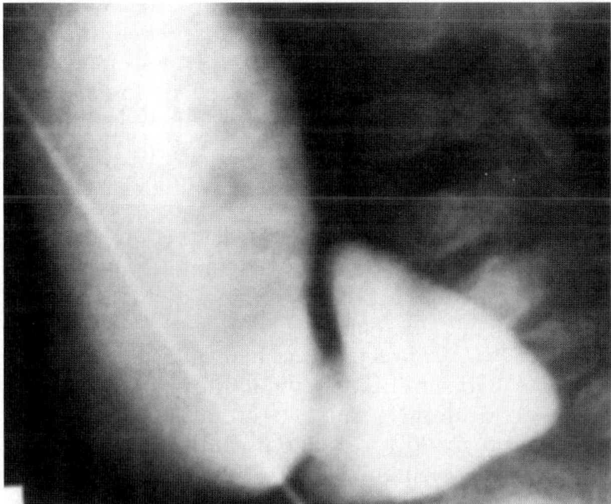

Figure 117-7 Bladder diverticulum dissecting beneath the bladder neck and resulting in bladder outlet obstruction. (From Sheldon CA, Essig KA: Congenital bladder diverticulum causing bladder outlet obstruction: Case report and review of literature. Pediatr Surg Int 1994;9:142.)

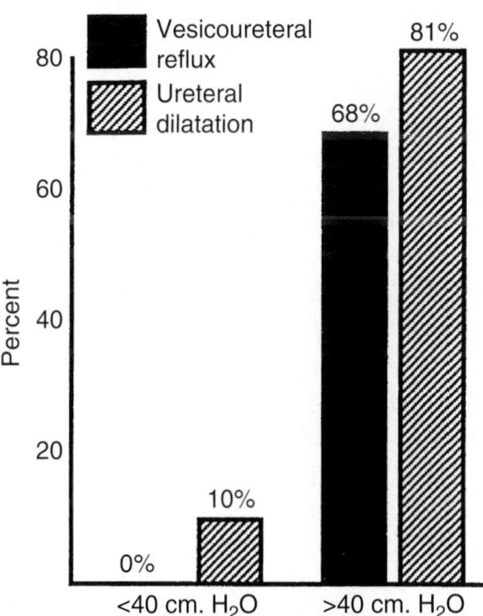

Figure 117-8 Risk for upper urinary tract injury as a function of urethral opening pressure. (From McGuire EJ, Woodside JR, Borden TA, et al: Prognostic value of urodynamic testing in myelodysplastic patients. J Urol 1981;126:208.)

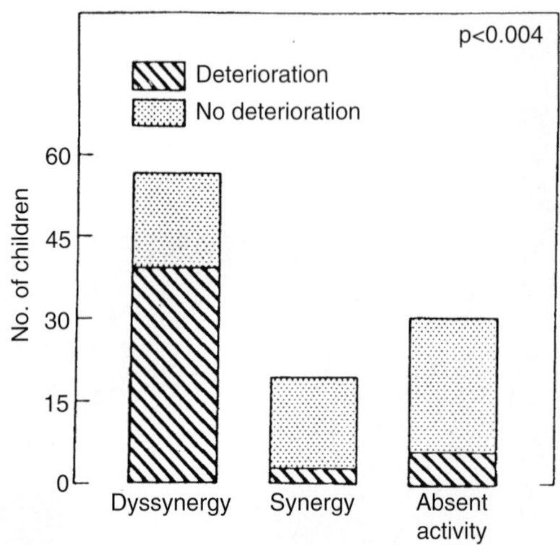

Figure 117-9 Urinary tract deterioration as a function of dyssynergia, synergy, and absent sphincteric activity. (From Bauer SB: Early evaluation and management of children with spina bifida. In King LR [ed]: Urologic Surgery in Neonates and Young Infants. Philadelphia, WB Saunders, 1988, p 256.)

of dyssynergy; sphincteric synergy and sphincteric denervation are associated with an incidence of deterioration of 15% and 25%, respectively. Unfortunately, the neurologic defect is often a dynamic one in which dyssynergy, if not present initially, may develop over time. The development of dyssynergy is often related to tethering of the spinal cord, which may result in spinal injury or spinal root injury as the child grows. The greatest risk occurs within the first 2 years of life, especially the first year, but such injury can occur throughout childhood.

Occult (closed) spinal dysraphisms include tethered cords, intradural lipomas, dermoid cysts or sinuses, diastematomyelia, and cauda equina tumors. These children commonly have urologic manifestations, including urinary tract infections and incontinence. Fortunately, however, cutaneous manifestations are obvious in most patients. Cutaneous dimpling, the presence of a skin tag, a subcutaneous lipoma or patch of hair over the bony sacrum, dermal vascular malformation, and pigmentation may indicate an underlying spinal disorder. The presence of these findings in any child with urinary incontinence or other evidence of bladder dysfunction requires exclusion of occult spinal diastrophism. These diagnoses may be confirmed by urodynamic investigation and spinal magnetic resonance imaging or, in the first 6 months of life, by ultrasonography of the spinal cord. Abnormal urinary tract function occurs in approximately 45% of patients.[14] Such lesions may be upper motor neuron, lower motor neuron, or mixed. Thus, bladder function must be measured by urodynamic study rather than just predicted.

Another important cause of neurogenic bladder is sacral agenesis, often seen in infants with an imperforate anus or in the progeny of a diabetic mother. This condition is characterized by congenital absence of all or part of two or more sacral segments. The lesion may be suggested on physical examination by the presence of an abnormal gluteal cleft or detection of an incomplete sacrum on direct palpation. The diagnosis may be confirmed by anteroposterior and lateral lumbosacral spine radiographs. Approximately 75% of such patients have abnormal urinary tract function.[7] Half of these patients have a hyperreflexive bladder, often with a hypertonic sphincter mechanism and detrusor-sphincter dyssynergy. Approximately half have an areflexive bladder, often with partial or complete denervation of the sphincteric mechanism.

Substantial functional bladder and urethral abnormalities may exist in the absence of both overt neurologic or structural disease. Examples of such abnormalities include uninhibited detrusor hyperactivity, bladder hypotonicity, and detrusor-sphincter dyssynergy. An infectious or behavioral cause can often be determined, but the cause sometimes remains elusive.

Combined Anatomic and Neurogenic Disorders

A third group of infants requiring bladder reconstruction are those with both functional and structural bladder abnormalities, such as an imperforate anus or cloaca. In these cases, a full anatomic evaluation must be done early in life, which at a minimum requires renal ultrasonography, radiographic VCUG, and ultrasonographic assessment of the spinal cord. The combination of both anatomic and functional abnormalities creates a high risk for substantial urologic morbidity. A study by McLorie et al. involving 484 consecutive patients revealed a high risk for end-stage renal disease.[81] They found that 6.4% of patients with a high imperforate anus and 1.1% of patients with a low imperforate anus died of renal failure. Non–fistula-related genitourinary anomalies were encountered in 60% of patients with high lesions and in 20% of those with low lesions. Substantial upper urinary tract abnormalities were encountered in more than a third of cases, and bilateral upper urinary tract abnormalities occurred in 14%.

Our review of 90 consecutive cases of imperforate anus showed an 18% incidence of significant neurovesical dysfunction.[110] The greatest risk was encountered in patients with a high imperforate anus. However, neurovesical dysfunction was also encountered in some patients with low lesions. In many patients, a tethered spinal cord must be addressed because of the risk for progressive injury to innervation of the bladder, urethra, anorectum, and lower extremities.

The importance of these anomalies was demonstrated in a review of 23 of our patients with imperforate anus who underwent reconstruction for either upper urinary tract preservation or achievement of continence.[113] As shown in Figure 117-10, 9% of patients had end-stage renal disease, 65% had significant renal abnormalities, and 57% had vesicoureteral reflux. Ureteral anomalies were encountered in 30% of patients and neurovesical dysfunction was present in 70%. A wide spectrum of urologic reconstructive procedures were required for these patients (Fig. 117-11). Of particular note, 43% required ureteral reimplantation, 43% required bladder augmentation, 35% required a Mitrofanoff neourethra, and 22% required bladder neck reconstruction. The urethra in boys with imperforate anus may be difficult to catheterize

Figure 117–10 Genitourinary anomalies associated with imperforate anus. ESRD, end-stage renal disease; NVD, neurovesical dysfunction; UPJ, ureteropelvic junction; VUR, vesicoureteral reflux. (From Sheldon CA, Gilbert A, Lewis AG, et al: Surgical implications of genitourinary tract anomalies in patients with imperforate anus. J Urol 1994;152:196.)

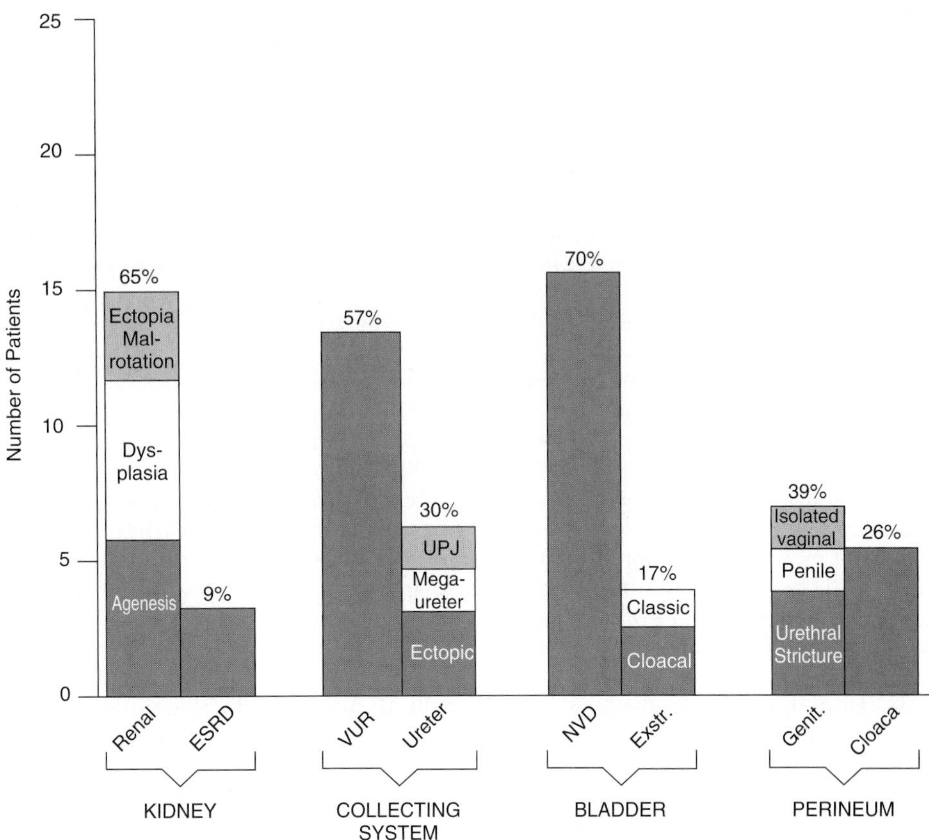

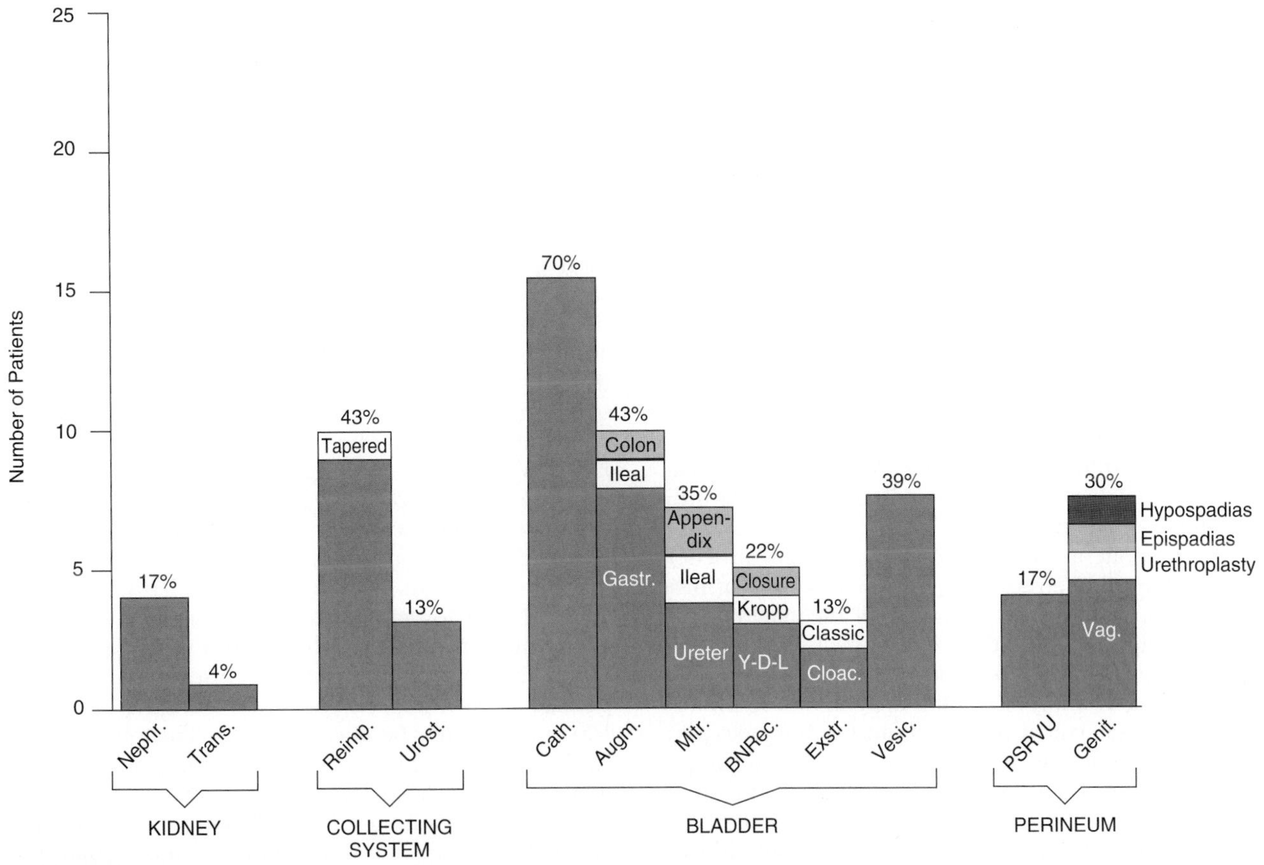

Figure 117–11 Surgical procedures performed in patients with imperforate anus. Augm., augmentation; BNRec., bladder neck reconstruction; Cath., intermittent catheterization; Exstr., exstrophy; Gastr., gastrocystoplasty; Mitr., Mitrofanoff neourethra; Nephr., nephrectomy; Reimp., reimplantation; Trans., renal transplantation; Urost., ureterostomy; Vag., vaginoplasty; Vesic., vesicostomy; Y-D-L, Young-Dees-Leadbetter procedure. (From Sheldon CA, Gilbert A, Lewis AG, et al: Surgical implications of genitourinary tract anomalies in patients with imperforate anus. J Urol 1994;152:197.)

because of urethral irregularity related to the congenital rectourethral fistula. This, along with intact urethral sensation, may necessitate the creation of a Mitrofanoff neourethra to facilitate intermittent catheterization.

Other lesions, described elsewhere in this text, may also require bladder reconstruction. Patients with urogenital sinus anomalies, in which the bladder and vagina drain through a common channel, often have associated neurovesical dysfunction. In addition to urethral and vaginal reconstruction, these patients may have an incompetent bladder outlet necessitating reconstruction. As with other conditions associated with neurovesical dysfunction, bladder augmentation may be required. Patients with exstrophy or cloacal exstrophy characteristically require complex urinary tract reconstruction. Patients with the prune-belly syndrome (Chapter 114) can usually be managed medically but sometimes require surgical intervention. These patients typically have a hypotonic bladder that operates at low pressure but empties incompletely, is highly irregular, and is prone to infection. Some patients, however, lose capacity and compliance over time. Consequently, urodynamic investigation is often needed to facilitate therapy.

RECONSTRUCTIVE PHILOSOPHY

The goals of urinary reconstruction are to preserve the upper urinary tract, attain socially acceptable continence, and maximize the child's ease of care and potential for self-care. Patients at risk for upper urinary tract injury are evaluated during the newborn period, and therapy to protect the upper urinary tracts is initiated at that time. Urinary incontinence is evaluated and treated just before school age to facilitate social integration.

In general, an attempt is made to manage the urinary tract with medical therapy before subjecting the child to surgical intervention. Therapy may include intermittent catheterization to facilitate bladder emptying, anticholinergic therapy to diminish intravesical pressure, and α-adrenergic agents to enhance bladder outlet resistance. Surgical therapy is undertaken only if medical therapy is unsuccessful. When contemplating urinary tract reconstruction, meticulous preoperative evaluation is critical, and it is essential to tailor the reconstruction to the individual needs of the patient.

Four components of balanced urinary tract function must be achieved to ensure long-term success with urinary reconstruction.[84] The first component is adequate bladder (reservoir) capacity and sufficient compliance to provide low-pressure storage. Optimal bladder capacity should allow a 4-hour catheterization or voiding interval during the day and an 8-hour interval at night without reaching excessive pressure or precipitating incontinence. The second component is adequate bladder outlet resistance to maintain urinary continence. Third, there must be a convenient, reliable mechanism for bladder (reservoir) emptying. Ideally, this should be achieved by spontaneous voiding; otherwise, intermittent catheterization is necessary.

The native urethra may be an acceptable conduit for this maneuver, although should catheterization of it prove excessively difficult or uncomfortable (preventing patient compliance), an alternative catheterizable conduit may be necessary. Finally, unobstructed and nonrefluxing sterile upper tract drainage of urine into the bladder (reservoir) is desirable to protect the upper tracts.

COMPENSATING FOR INADEQUATE BLADDER CAPACITY OR COMPLIANCE

Physiologic Considerations

Bladder capacity and compliance are increased by bladder augmentation. Indicators that augmentation is necessary include clinical symptoms, such as incontinence caused by bladder dysfunction unresponsive to medical therapy, and upper urinary tract deterioration as a result of inadequate low-pressure storage volume. Also suggestive is a measured bladder capacity that is significantly less than expected for the patient's age, according to the following formula: *capacity (ounces) = age (years) + 2*.[61] Caution must be exercised because with an incompetent bladder outlet, the bladder may drain at low pressure, thus making determination of functional bladder volume more difficult. Performing cystometrography with a Foley catheter balloon that occludes the bladder neck may provide more reliable data on functional bladder capacity. Generation of pressure exceeding 35 to 40 cm H_2O with urine volumes equal to those anticipated during 4 hours of urine production during the day or 8 hours of urine production during the night during maximal medical therapy further suggests that bladder augmentation should be considered.

Several important reconstructive concepts are pertinent to bladder augmentation. The first regards management of the recipient bladder. If bowel augmentation is performed, with the detrusor essentially left intact to generate high pressure, the former will act urodynamically as a capacious diverticulum.[125] This type of diverticular decompression instead of augmentation can occur if bowel is added to either a neurologically intact or impaired bladder. The problem can be avoided by an extended sagittal opening of the bladder from the level of the bladder neck anteriorly to the trigone posteriorly ("clam cystoplasty"). Essentially, this is a reconfiguration of the bladder from a sphere into a flat plate so that the detrusor is no longer capable of generating a contraction that produces a significant elevation in pressure.[9,10]

Just as pressure generated by the bladder detrusor is an important contributor to the pressure generated in an augmented urinary reservoir, so also is the pressure generated by the tubularized bowel segment itself. With peristaltic contractions, pressures ranging from 60 to 100 cm H_2O may be encountered.[72] This observation led Kock to develop his concept of turning the intact bowel into a reservoir incapable of effective peristalsis by creating a "pouch."[60] Opening the bowel along its antimesenteric border and closing it with disruption of the circular muscle ("detubularization") inhibits peristalsis. Once unable to undergo peristalsis, the reservoir dilates and stores urine at low pressure (Fig. 117-12).[51,62] Additionally, there is a very significant increase in the geometric capacity of the intestinal segment.[51] A third important concept is

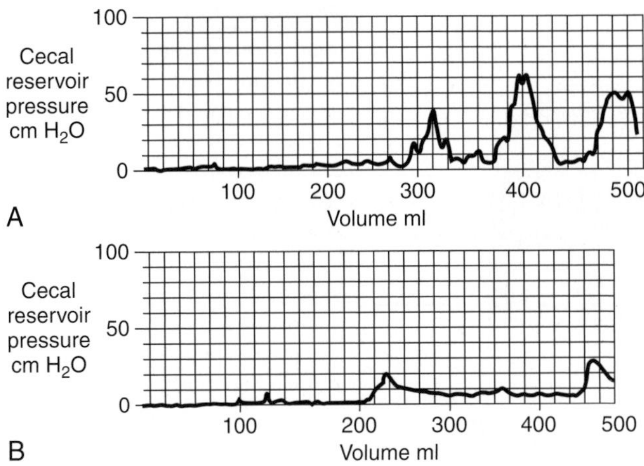

Figure 117-12 Urodynamics of the cecal reservoir. *A*, A tubular bowel produces high-pressure peristaltic waves. *B*, A cup patch bowel with disrupted peristalsis stores a large volume without a rise in pressure. (From Goldwasser HR, Webster GD: Augmentation and substitution enterocystoplasty. J Urol 1986;135:221.)

accommodation (Fig. 117-13). It is well known that a reconstructed bladder will gradually enlarge over time. At constant pressure, a structure with a larger radius will accommodate greater volume—again, an advantage of detubularized bowel segments.

Several considerations should be entertained when choosing an augmentation donor site. Anatomic considerations, such as mobility of the blood supply, favor the use of ileum, sigmoid, the ileocecal region, and the greater curvature of the stomach. The ability to implant a ureter or a Mitrofanoff neourethra may also be a consideration. Additionally, it may be important to avoid the peritoneal cavity so that the option of performing peritoneal dialysis or placement of a ventricular peritoneal shunt is preserved. Such considerations favor the use of ureteral augmentation or autoaugmentation.

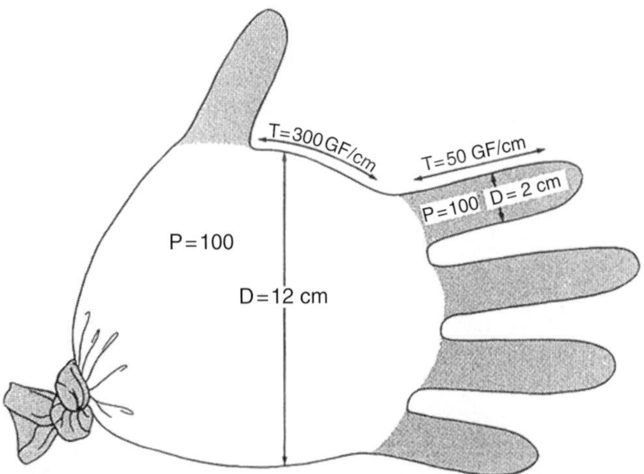

Figure 117-13 Inflated surgeon's glove illustrating the LaPlace relationship. Although pressure (P) is equal throughout, tension (T) is greater in the portion with the greater diameter (D). (From Hinman F: Selection of intestinal segments for bladder substitution: Physical and physiological characteristics. J Urol 1988;139:522.)

The choice of augmentation donor site may be limited by the patient's primary disease. Patients with a short gut may not tolerate loss of the ileocecal region or a significant length of ileum. Patients with borderline fecal continence (such as those with an imperforate anus or myelodysplasia) may not tolerate loss of the ileocecal valve or the water reabsorptive capacity of the right colon. Metabolic consequences may assume an overriding influence: the risk for absorptive acidosis and growth retardation, which may be exacerbated by chronic renal insufficiency, may favor the use of autoaugmentation, ureteral augmentation, or gastrocystoplasty techniques. Because the reconstruction must be tailored to the individual needs of the patient, the surgeon must be familiar with a wide variety of reconstructive alternatives and prepare the patient accordingly, including bowel preparation even when gastrocystoplasty, autoaugmentation, or ureteral augmentation is anticipated.

Small Bowel Procedures

Ileocystoplasty (Fig. 117-14) is one of the most commonly used bladder augmentation techniques.[52,120] The bladder is prepared by a "clam" cystoplasty incision, and a segment of ileum 20 to 40 cm in length is isolated and incised along its antimesenteric border. It is reconfigured as a "cup patch" and anastomosed to the bladder plate with running 3-0 Vicryl suture (inner layer interlocking). Bowel continuity is re-established by end-to-end anastomosis. Advantages of this procedure include its technical simplicity. However, antirefluxing implantation of the ureter or Mitrofanoff neourethra into the ileal segment is less reliable than implantation into the native bladder or other augmentation donor segments.

Other techniques of bladder augmentation or replacement using small bowel include the Camey procedure (Fig. 117-15),[13] Kock pouch (Fig. 117-16),[60] and ileal neobladder.[59,94] These procedures are less successful in achieving continence and have a significant rate of complications and reoperation in most surgeons' hands.

Ileocecal Segment Procedures

The ileocecal bowel segment has been favored by urologists for bladder reconstruction because of the natural configuration of the cecum, which gives it the appearance of an ideal substitute for the bladder.[38] This technique is technically simple to perform and also has the major advantage of allowing antirefluxing implantation of massively dilated ureters into the ileum. Reflux is prevented by the ileocecal valve, bolstered by intussusception. Unfortunately, the intussusception antireflux mechanism is inherently unstable. Consequently, various surgical modifications of the ileocecal valve have been introduced in an effort to lessen the incidence of reflux. Of greater impact is the fact that loss of the ileocecal valve from fecal continuity risks devastating fecal incontinence in patients with marginal anorectal continence (e.g., myelomeningocele or the VATER complex).

When the cecal or ileocecal segments have been used intact for bladder augmentation, nighttime incontinence

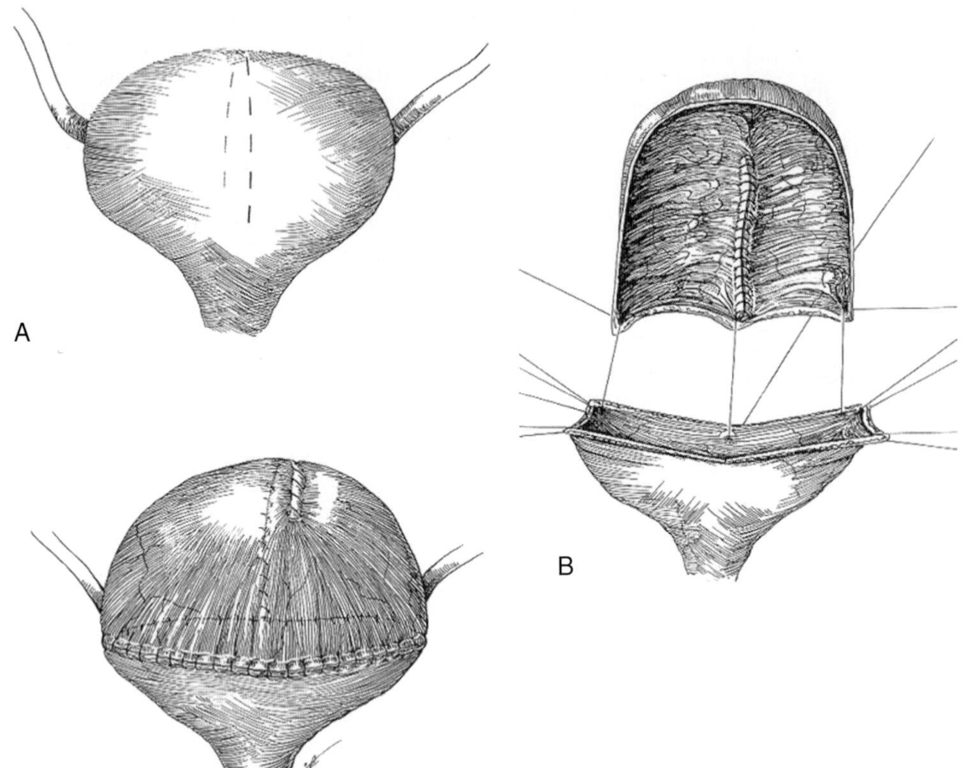

Figure 117–14 Technique of "clam" ileocystoplasty. *A*, Small, high-pressure bladder. *B*, The bladder has been prepared by a long, longitudinal incision, and a segment of ileum has been detubularized and fashioned into a cup patch. *C*, The cup patch is anastomosed to the bladder. (From Minevich E, Sheldon CA: Urinary tract reconstruction for continence and renal preservation. In Ziegler MM, Azizkhan RG, Weber TR, et al [eds]: Operative Pediatric Surgery. Norwalk, CT, Appleton & Lange, 2003, p 915.)

has been a significant problem in most series.[130] This problem most likely reflects peristaltic waves in the intact bowel segment because enuresis is rare when the cup patch technique is used. Other continent diversions using the ileocecal valve have included the Maintz pouch,[128] the Penn pouch,[31] the Indiana pouch,[103] and the Florida pouch.[97] Of these techniques, the Indiana pouch has been applied most frequently in pediatric practice but has met with variable results.[6]

Large Bowel Procedures

Mathisen reported sigmoid augmentation of the bladder performed in a manner similar to that described for ileocystoplasty earlier.[76] This procedure, too, is relatively simple to perform but allows better antirefluxing implantation of the ureter or Mitrofanoff neourethra into the taenia. This technique did not appear to differ from other bowel segments with respect to the ability to empty,

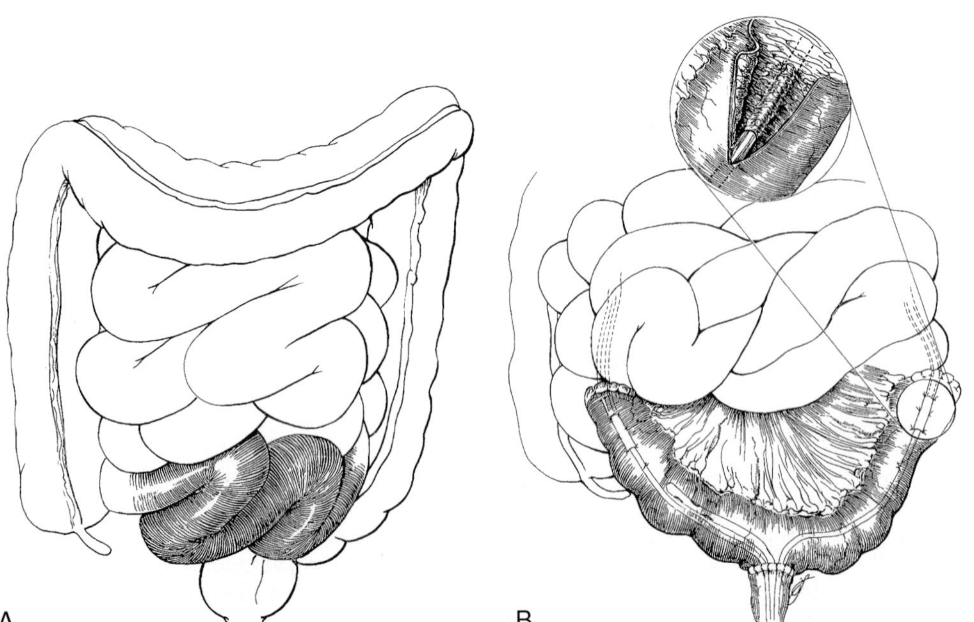

Figure 117–15 Camey enterocystoplasty. *A*, A 35- to 40-cm segment of intact ileum is anastomosed to the urethral stump to create a continent intestinal reservoir. *B*, The ureters are sutured into a 3- to 4-cm trough in the bowel mucosa in each limb of the reservoir to create effective antireflux flap valves. (From Minevich E, Sheldon CA: Urinary tract reconstruction for continence and renal preservation. In Ziegler MM, Azizkhan RG, Weber TR, et al [eds]: Operative Pediatric Surgery. Norwalk, CT, Appleton & Lange, 2003, p 916.)

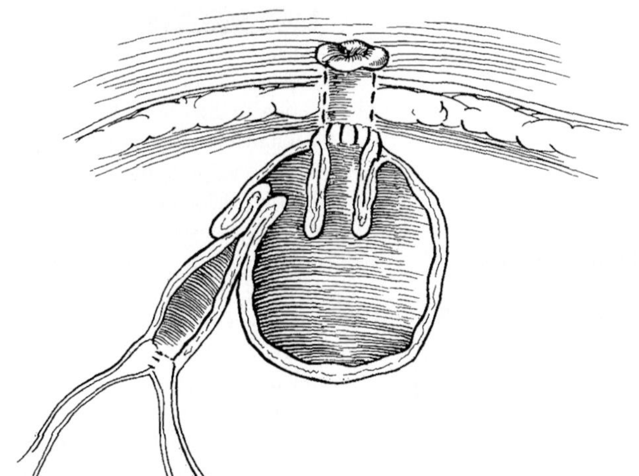

Figure 117–16 Kock pouch. A 70-cm segment of ileum is reformed into a peristaltic pouch with two nipple valves. The most recent modification involves fixation of a nipple valve to the reservoir wall to change it to a fixed flap valve. (From Minevich E, Sheldon CA: Urinary tract reconstruction for continence and renal preservation. In Ziegler MM, Azizkhan RG, Weber TR, et al [eds]: Operative Pediatric Surgery. Norwalk, CT, Appleton & Lange, 2003, p 917.)

infections, or surgical complications.[108] In patients who have previously undergone reconstruction for imperforate anus, this procedure may interrupt the blood supply to the rectum because the anorectum depends on a descending blood supply. Positive experience with construction of a colonic neobladder has been reported,[95,98] although nocturnal incontinence continues to be a problem in up to 33% of patients.[98]

Gastric Segment Procedures

The work of Mitchell and coinvestigators ushered in the modern era of use of the stomach in urinary reconstruction (Fig. 117-17).[1] They demonstrated gastrocystoplasty to be highly successful, versatile, and well tolerated even in the face of azotemia. This procedure is associated with a reduced risk for infection, mucus production, and urinary stone formation and provides excellent compliance characteristics. Implantation of a ureter or Mitrofanoff neourethra is technically easy. Our long-term follow-up of gastrocystoplasty, or gastric neobladder, reveals a continence rate of 91%, stable renal function in all patients, and upper tract deterioration in only one patient, who became noncompliant with intermittent catheterization.[28,114] Additionally, gastrocystoplasty has proved to be an excellent alternative for patients with end-stage renal disease facing subsequent kidney transplantation.[28,114] The gastric neobladder has been successfully used for reconstruction with the native urethra,[15] orthotopic ureteral neourethra,[86,114] and orthotopic appendiceal neourethra.[112] One of its limitations is the development of hematuria-dysuria syndrome.

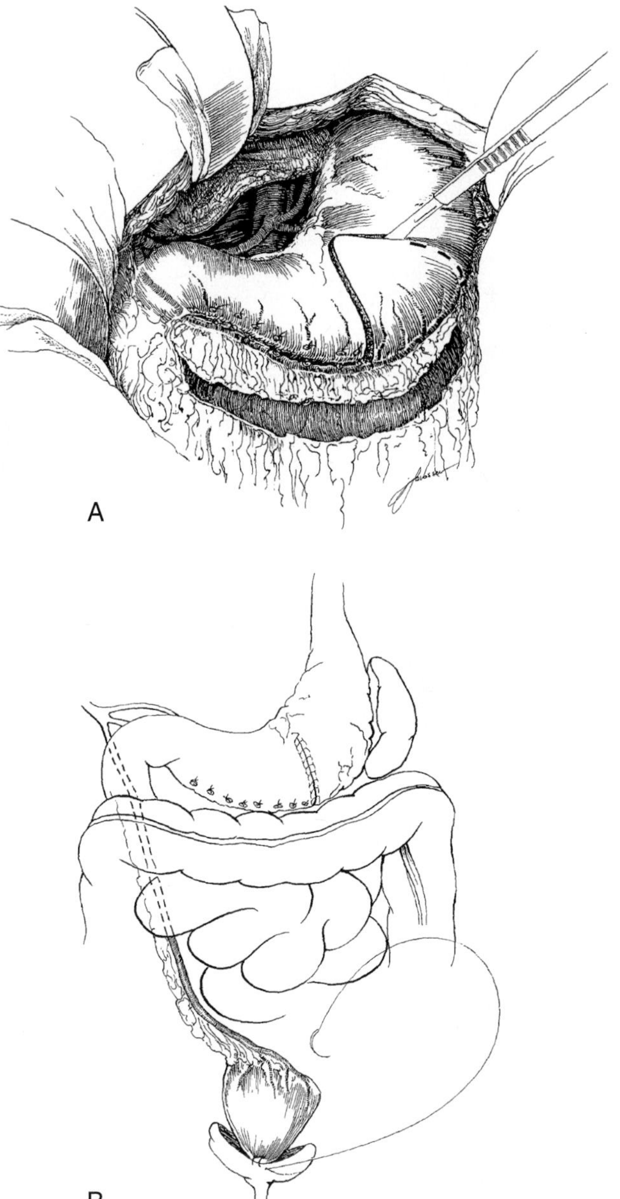

Figure 117–17 Gastrocystoplasty. *A*, Development of a right gastroepiploic pedicle and isolation of a wedge of gastric fundus. *B*, Mobilization of the right gastroepiploic pedicle through the retroperitoneal plane into the augmentation position. The stomach is closed. (From Minevich E, Sheldon CA: Urinary tract reconstruction for continence and renal preservation. In Ziegler MM, Azizkhan RG, Weber TR, et al [eds]: Operative Pediatric Surgery. Norwalk, CT, Appleton & Lange, 2003, p 918.)

Ureteral Augmentation and Autoaugmentation

Ureteral augmentation[21] (Fig. 117-18) and autoaugmentation[16] (Fig. 117-19) hold great promise because of their ability to prevent absorptive metabolic disorders and to be performed via an entirely extraperitoneal approach. However, these procedures are more likely to fail to attain adequate capacity and compliance because of an inherent restriction in the availability of surface area.[73] In the case of ureterocystoplasty, the ureter is made available either by nephrectomy or by transureteroureterostomy. Unfortunately, a sufficiently dilated ureter is rarely available for this procedure. In addition, recent reports indicate that the long-term ability of ureteral augmentation

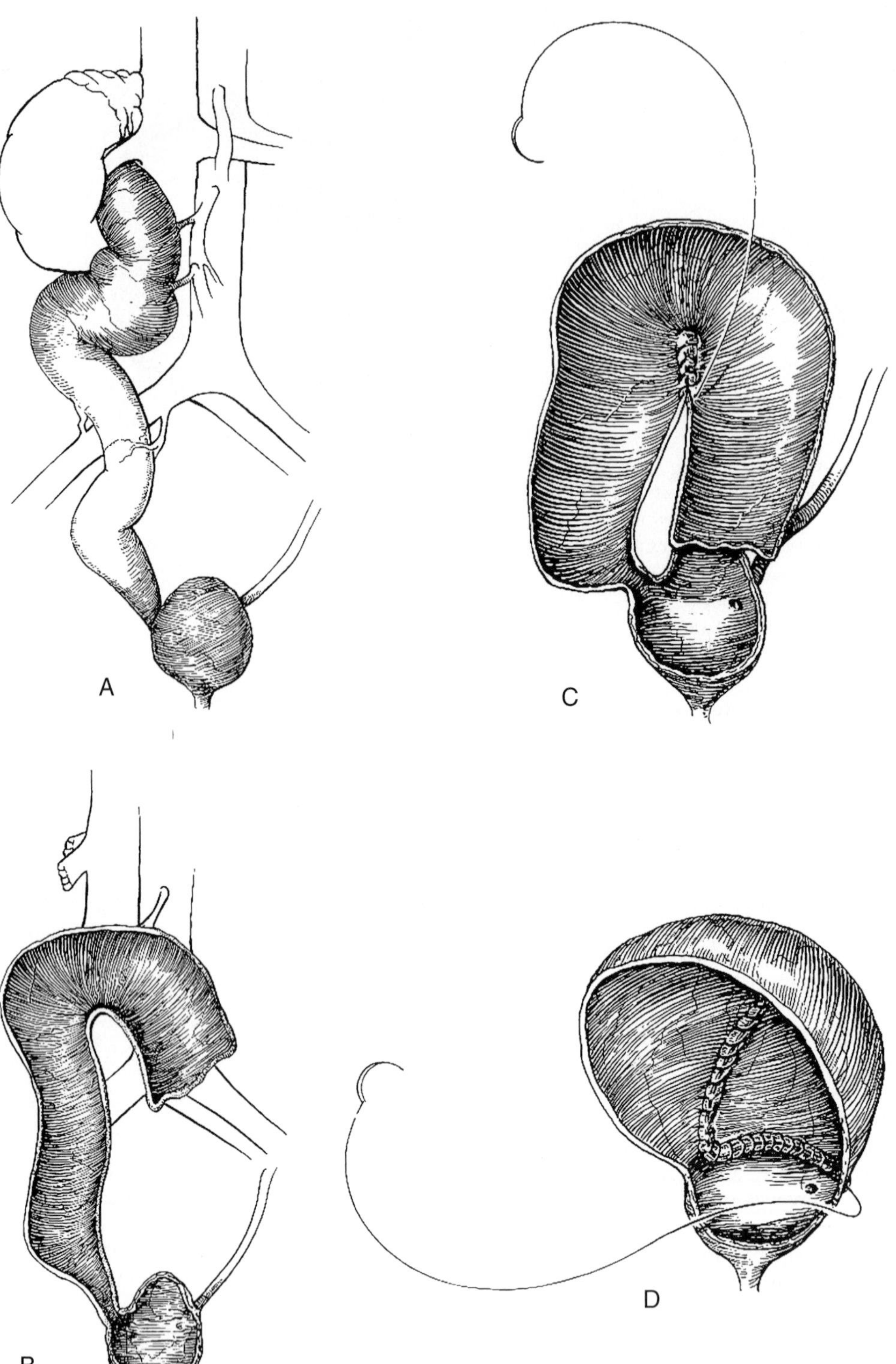

Figure 117–18 Operative stages of ureteral bladder augmentation. *A*, Normal blood supply to the ureter. *B*, Ureteral detubularization after mobilization. *C*, Reconfiguration of the ureter into a U-shaped patch. *D*, Anastomosing the ureteral patching to the native bivalved bladder. (From Minevich E, Sheldon CA: Urinary tract reconstruction for continence and renal preservation. In Ziegler MM, Azizkhan RG, Weber TR, et al [eds]: Operative Pediatric Surgery. Norwalk, CT, Appleton & Lange, 2003, p 919.)

to maintain low storage pressure and adequate capacity may be suspect.[53]

PROCEDURES TO CORRECT DEFICIENT BLADDER OUTLET RESISTANCE

Urinary continence is maintained by a complex relationship between bladder outlet resistance and pressure. To maintain dryness, bladder outlet resistance must exceed intravesical pressure not only at rest but also during changes in posture, coughing, sneezing, and straining. Bladder outlet reconstruction is necessary in patients with incontinence despite low-pressure storage of urine in the bladder. The bladder outlet in patients who have a high-pressure or low-capacity bladder is more difficult to assess because incontinence may be caused by these storage characteristics alone. The likelihood of a competent

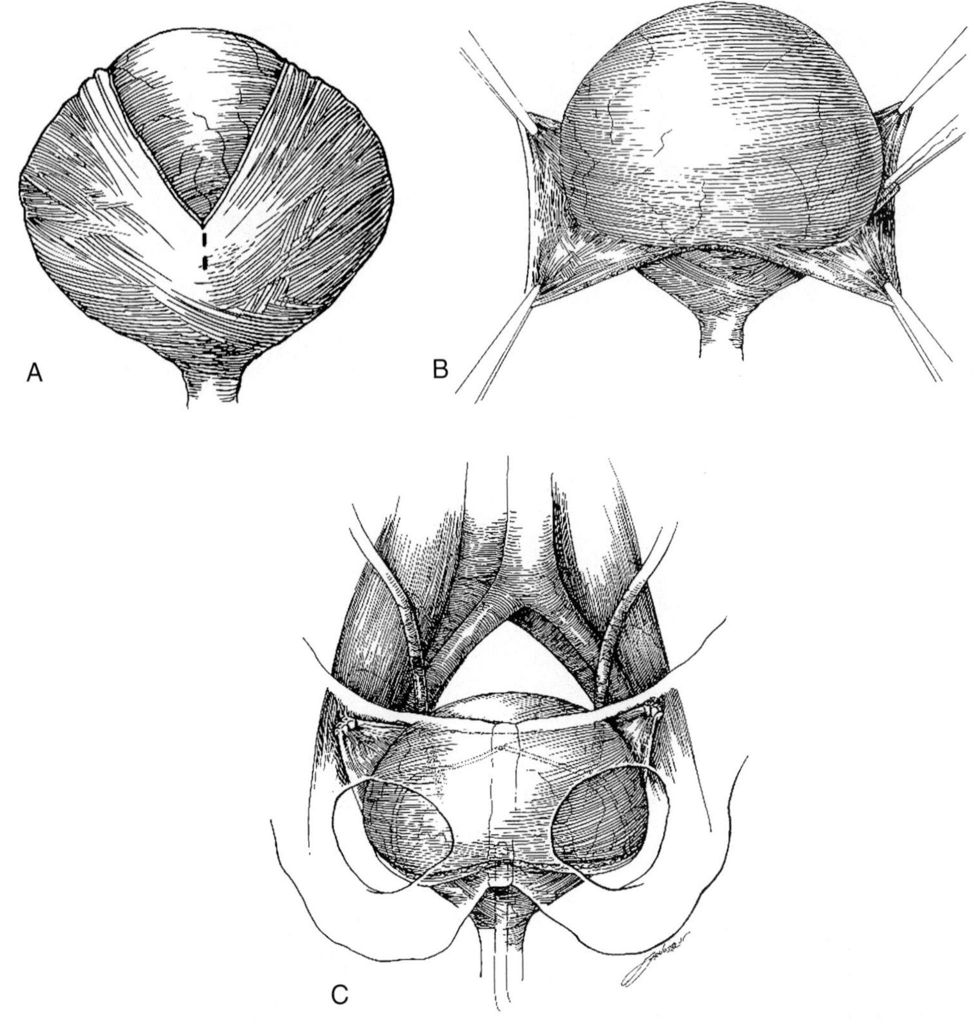

Figure 117–19 Autoaugmentation. *A*, Detrusor incised. *B*, Detrusor stripped from intact bladder epithelium. *C*, The epithelium bulges with filling of the bladder. (From Minevich E, Sheldon CA: Urinary tract reconstruction for continence and renal preservation. In Ziegler MM, Azizkhan RG, Weber TR, et al [eds]: Operative Pediatric Surgery. Norwalk, CT, Appleton & Lange, 2003, p 920.)

sphincteric mechanism in this setting is suggested by a stress leak point pressure greater than 100 cm H_2O.[129] Urethral pressure profilometry and static leak point pressure have not proved to be reliable, independent indicators of sphincteric competence. Most surgical interventions designed to achieve continence include procedures to lengthen the urethra, suspend the bladder neck, or compress or completely close the urethra.

Efforts to proximally lengthen the existing urethra through tubularization of the posterior detrusor grew out of the early work of Young.[133] In the procedure, which was later modified by Dees[26] and Leadbetter,[69] the urethra is lengthened by tubularization of a long (4 to 5 cm) segment of the posterior bladder wall. Two triangular sections of urothelium are excised, and the resultant urothelial strip is approximated over a small catheter (8 or 10 French)[37] to fashion the neourethra.[37] The adjacent detrusor is approximated to itself over this mucosal tube to add muscular support (Fig. 117-20). Anterior urethral suspension is usually achieved by suture fixation and may be supplemented by placement of a compressive fascial sling. Several variations in technique have been described.[63,70]

The specific goals of this procedure are to achieve continence and allow spontaneous voiding if the detrusor can contract. Intermittent catheterization must also be possible if the detrusor cannot effectively contract to empty the bladder. The benefits of this technique include the fact that it may allow spontaneous voiding, uses native tissue, and affords a "pop-off" mechanism. The procedure does, however, reduce bladder capacity and may make the urethra difficult to catheterize. Furthermore, catheterization may injure the continence mechanism and result in reconstructive failure.

Placement of an adjuvant Mitrofanoff neourethra in patients undergoing Young-Dees-Leadbetter bladder neck reconstruction allows a channel for intermittent catheterization, which has been useful for all such reconstructions, especially in the early postoperative period.[112] With time, as the patient learns to void through the reconstructed urethra, the Mitrofanoff neourethra can be removed in a simple outpatient surgical procedure, or because it does not leak, it can be left in situ.

The Kropp procedure (Fig. 117-21) involves the creation of an extended length of urethra by tubularization of an anterior strip of bladder wall that is left in continuity with the urethra. The tube is then implanted suburothelially into the bladder.[66] This procedure allows reliable continence and uses native tissue. It can, however, lead to

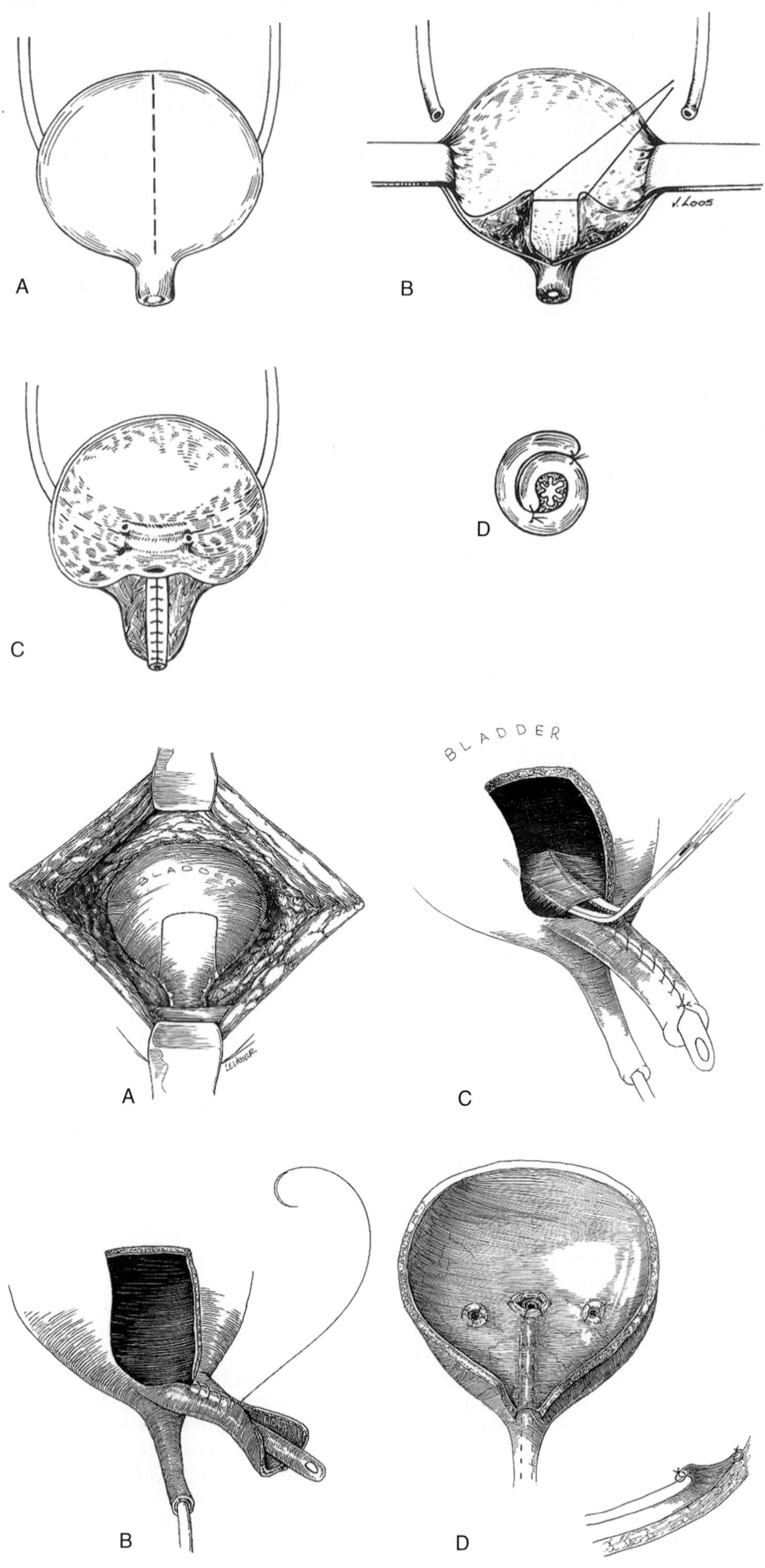

Figure 117–20 Young-Dees-Leadbetter bladder neck reconstruction. *A,* Incision in anterior bladder wall. *B,* Mucosal triangles at bladder base excised. *C,* Tubularization of mucosal strip and reimplanted ureters. *D,* Cross-section of overlapping detrosor. (From Sheldon CA, Bukowski TP: Bladder function. In Rowe MI, O'Neill JA, Jr., Grosfeld JL, et al [eds]: Essentials of Pediatric Surgery. St Louis, Mosby–Year Book, 1995, p 742.)

Figure 117–21 The Kropp procedure. A detrusor tube is created (anterior shown, posterior tube also possible) and tunneled submucosally into the bladder to create a competent flap valve. *A,* Anterior bladder flap outlined. *B,* Anterior bladder strip tubularized. *C,* Submucosal tunnel created from floor of bladder. *D,* Anterior bladder tube reimplanted into submucosal tunnel. (From Minevich E, Sheldon CA: Urinary tract reconstruction for continence and renal preservation. In Ziegler MM, Azizkhan RG, Weber TR, et al [eds]: Operative Pediatric Surgery. Norwalk, CT, Appleton & Lange, 2003, p 925.)

difficulty in catheterization. The Pippi Salle modification,[96] which involves the use of an onlay detrusor strip (with preservation of the posterior bladder strip), may permit easier catheterization. Neither the Kropp tube nor the Salle onlay allow a "pop-off" mechanism; thus, the potential for spontaneous voiding is eliminated, and bladder capacity is reduced.

Another option for the creation of bladder outlet resistance is a fascial sling. A free fascial graft is frequently used; the graft may be placed transvaginally with an endoscopically assisted technique[79] or by open retrourethral dissection.[32] Alternatively, the fascial strip may be developed in such a way that it remains attached to the ipsilateral pyramidalis (Fig. 117-22).[50] The latter approach is particularly applicable to children who have a denervated but anatomically intact sphincteric mechanism and require concomitant bladder augmentation. These procedures are technically fast and relatively simple to perform, involve native tissue, and are readily reversible. They can also be used as an adjunct to the Young-Dees-Leadbetter procedure. Spontaneous voiding is possible if the angulation is not excessive, and a "pop-off" mechanism is maintained. Excessive angulation may, however, interfere with spontaneous voiding or catheterization.

The artificial urinary sphincter (Fig. 117-23) has been shown to be effective in compressing the urethra and thus contributes to bladder outlet competence. The most popular, the current AS 800 model, consists of a cuff placed around the bladder neck or bulbar urethra, a reservoir placed intra-abdominally, and an activating pressure bulb located in the scrotum or labia. Controlled pressure is maintained in the cuff until the pump is squeezed, whereupon fluid is transferred from the cuff to the reservoir balloon and bladder emptying can take place. A delay-fill resistor in the control mechanism provides 1 to 2 minutes of lowered intraurethral pressure before the cuff is automatically refilled from the reservoir balloon. Pressure-regulating balloons of various pressure ranges are available, and a 60- to 70-cm H_2O balloon is generally selected for pediatric reconstruction.[87] Higher pressure may lead to erosion of the urethra by pressure-induced ischemia.[2]

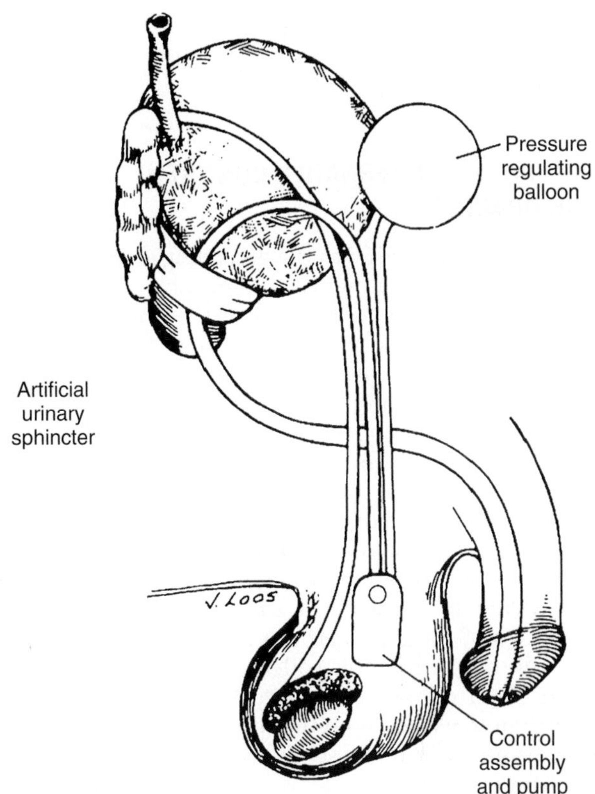

Figure 117-23 Artificial urinary sphincter. (From Sheldon CA, Bukowski TP: Bladder function. In Rowe MI, O'Neill JA, Jr., Grosfeld JL, et al [eds]: Essentials of Pediatric Surgery. St Louis, Mosby–Year Book, 1995, p 743.)

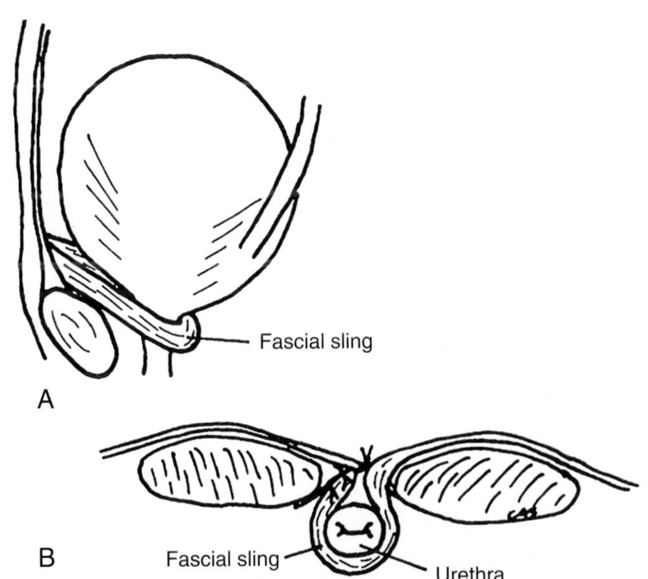

Figure 117-22 Placement of a fascial sling to enhance bladder outlet competence. *A,* Lateral sagittal view. *B,* Coronal view. (From Sheldon CA: Urinary reconstruction [rather than diversion] for continence in difficult pediatric urologic disorders. Semin Pediatr Surg 1996;5:10.)

Several series have documented the utility of the artificial urinary sphincter in patients who undergo bladder augmentation.[44,49,67,82] The advantage of this procedure is that it allows spontaneous voiding, but it also has several disadvantages. Multiple mechanical problems have occurred in patients with the artificial sphincter in place. The most common problems have been fluid leakage from the cuff or tubing kinks requiring surgical revision. The most serious complications are erosion of the sphincter into the urethra and infection around the cuff. The latter problems generally require removal of the device.

Finally, surgical urethral closure may be necessary. This is obviously a highly effective means of ensuring urethral continence, but it should be a last resort.[55,92] Simple oversewing of the mucosa at the level of the bladder neck is insufficient because recanalization occurs. Urethral division, which allows muscular approximation (proximally and distally), eliminates this risk. This procedure requires the placement of an alternative catheterizable conduit, as discussed in the next section. The advantages of this procedure are that it is definitive and technically simple. It does, however, place the patient at increased risk for bladder calculi and is difficult to reverse. In addition, the lack of a "pop-off" mechanism increases the risk for bladder rupture if the patient does not comply with regular catheterization to empty the bladder.

PROVIDING FOR ALTERNATIVE CONTINENT URINE DRAINAGE

The procedures discussed in the preceding section require the creation of a continent catheterizable conduit that connects the bladder to the skin of the abdominal wall or perineum. An alternative to catheterization of the native urethra is indicated when a urethra is difficult to catheterize because of (1) tortuosity from either previous urethral surgery or congenital irregularity or (2) physical limitations of the patient that impede access to the native urethra. Procedures directed at urethral functional replacement are based on the creation of a tubular conduit of sufficient length that is exposed to external compressive forces, thereby providing outlet resistance that cannot be overcome by intravesical (intrareservoir) pressure. The success of these procedures in terms of continence relies on attaining controlled reservoir-neourethra balance. Neourethral resistance to reservoir outflow must be sufficient to exceed both the resting and intermittently elevated intravesical pressure associated with gravity (upright posture), as well as episodic additive intra-abdominal pressure spikes (coughing, sneezing, straining, and sudden postural changes). The creation of neourethral resistance must be complemented by low intravesical (intrareservoir) pressure. This may entail bladder augmentation or replacement by bowel and should include reconfiguration by detubularization. A large capacity is imperative, as is intermittent catheter drainage before the low-compliance portion of the reservoir's pressure-volume curve is entered.

Alternative techniques include those associated with a nipple valve (procedures involving the ileal-cecal junction or ileal-ileal intussusception) and those associated with a flap valve (Fig. 117-24). The nipple valve is inherently unstable because wall tension causes distraction of the base of this continence mechanism over time, which often results in loss of effectiveness of the valve and thus incontinence. The flap valve mechanism is considerably more durable because the continence mechanism is a stable component of the reservoir wall.

The Mitrofanoff neourethra is an example of a flap valve mechanism that is particularly applicable to children.[88] In this procedure, a continent, catheterizable tubular conduit (neourethra) connecting the urinary bladder to the skin is fashioned. It provides a one-way flap valve mechanism that permits a catheter to easily be passed into the bladder. The flap valve is also a secure mechanism to prevent incontinence (Fig. 117-25). The appendix, the most common type of Mitrofanoff tube used, is removed from its cecal origin with preservation of the appendiceal mesentery. A submucosal plane is developed in the bladder by either detrusor incision or cystotomy with the creation of a long submucosal tunnel. The cecal end of the Mitrofanoff neourethra is exteriorized to the skin; a U-insertion flap technique is used to help minimize the risk for stomal stenosis. The Mitrofanoff neourethra concept has proved extremely versatile, and it has been implanted into the bladder, colon, and stomach with equal efficiency.[33,112] Multiple sites for exteriorization are possible, including the lower part of the abdomen, the umbilicus, and the perineum.[112] The versatility of this technique has been enhanced by extending the length of the appendix with tubularized cecum.[25,107,112,118] Mitrofanoff's concept and extension of these principles have permitted successful continent reconstruction of the lower urinary tract in a wide variety of situations.[11,47,57]

If the appendix is unavailable, a tapered segment of ileum (over a 12- to 14-French catheter) can be used, although currently, a transverse retubularized segment of ileum is more commonly used.[11,12,18] The length of these ileovesicostomies is limited by the circumference of the bowel segment used, which is inadequate in some cases.

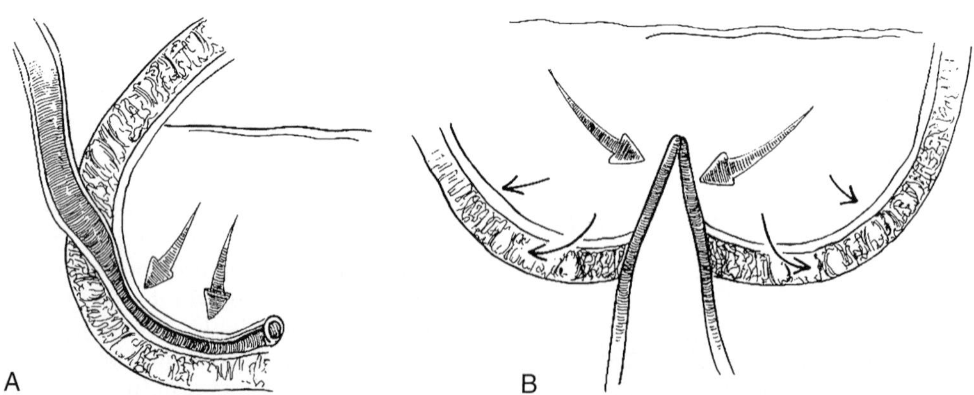

Figure 117-24 *A*, Flap valves. *B*, Nipple valves. Nipple valves are continent because the nipple is circumferentially compressed by pressure within the reservoir. Unfortunately, the intrareservoir pressure also has a lateral distraction force on the base of the nipple that is causing shortening or total effacement of the valve with loss of the continence mechanism. Flap valves are continent because the submucosal segment is compressed by filling of the reservoir (as for a reimplanted ureter with vesicoureteral reflux). Unlike nipple valves, flap valves are stable because they are fixed to the wall of the reservoir. Thus, reservoir filling does not tend to cause loss of the continence mechanism. (From Minevich E, Sheldon CA: Urinary tract reconstruction for continence and renal preservation. In Ziegler MM, Azizkhan RG, Weber TR, et al [eds]: Operative Pediatric Surgery. Norwalk, CT, Appleton & Lange, 2003, p 928.)

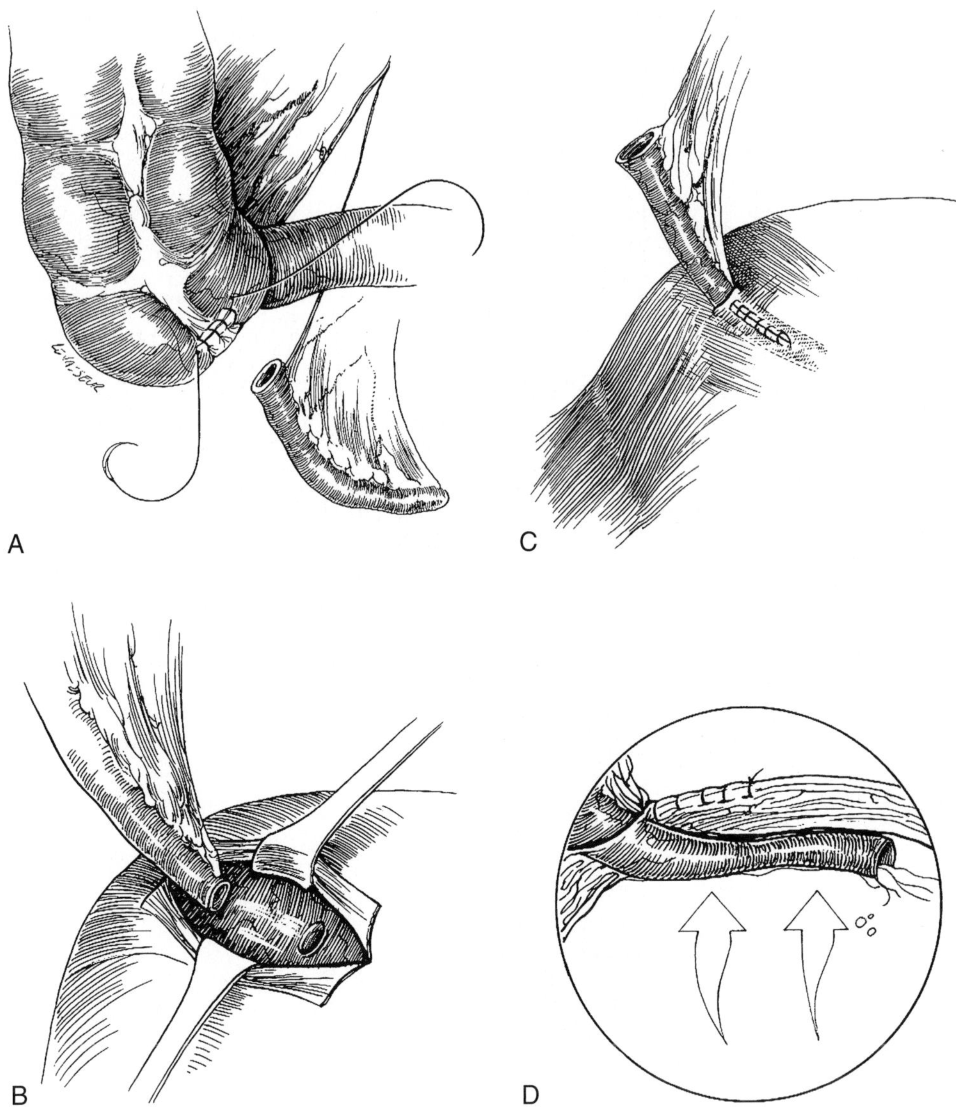

Figure 117–25 Mitrofanoff procedure. *A*, The appendix has been mobilized on its mesentery, and the cecal segment is closed. *B*, Extravesical dissection shows the mucosal orifice in which the distal end of the appendix will be implanted. *C*, The detrusor is closed over the implanted appendix, and its proximal end is then brought to the skin to serve as a catheterizable stoma. *D*, This diagram depicts the resulting continent flap valve mechanism of the Mitrofanoff procedure; a rise in intravesical pressure compresses the conduit against the detrusor, thereby occluding its lumen and achieving continence. (From Minevich E, Sheldon CA: Urinary tract reconstruction for continence and renal preservation. In Ziegler MM, Azizkhan RG, Weber TR, et al [eds]: Operative Pediatric Surgery. Norwalk, CT, Appleton & Lange, 2003, p 929.)

Casale introduced a technique that allows a doubling in length of the continent conduit.[17] The ureter also provides a source for a Mitrofanoff conduit when available if nephrectomy had been or is being done or if a transureteroureterostomy is being performed.[90] Because an ileal conduit is readily constructed, transureteroureterostomy is not recommended unless otherwise indicated. If the ureteral segment is refluxing, concomitant ureteral reimplantation may be required. Other continent, catheterizable mechanisms are available, including the Benchekroun procedure,[4] the Indiana pouch,[103] the Koch pouch,[119] and the hemi-Koch.[102] Though used less commonly in children than the Mitrofanoff flap valve, they may prove useful in selected circumstances.

The most common complication of the Mitrofanoff conduit is stomal stenosis, which requires stomal revision.[11,71] Granulation polyps can be seen occasionally.[100] We observed a case of traumatic gastrocystoplasy-Mitrofanoff fistula after a motorcycle accident.[83] Mitrofanoff neourethras that could not be negotiated or that were lost because of ischemic necrosis were only rarely encountered.

INTERFACE WITH FECAL INCONTINENCE

The urinary tract should not be reconstructed without consideration of anorectal function. Achievement of urinary continence in a patient who will still require a diaper for fecal incontinence can hardly be considered a success. Furthermore, persistent fecal soilage may potentiate the risk for urinary tract infection and progressive deterioration of the reconstructed bladder and upper urinary tracts. Therapy for urinary continence can significantly compromise gastrointestinal function. For example, anticholinergic therapy may result in severe constipation, and ileocecocystoplasty may facilitate fecal incontinence.

Management of intractable fecal incontinence may be addressed at the time of urinary reconstruction and thus should be evaluated before this undertaking. Because most patients can be managed nonsurgically by dietary restrictions, bulking agents, behavior modification, and expansion enemas, an exhaustive trial of these interventions should be undertaken before surgical reconstruction.

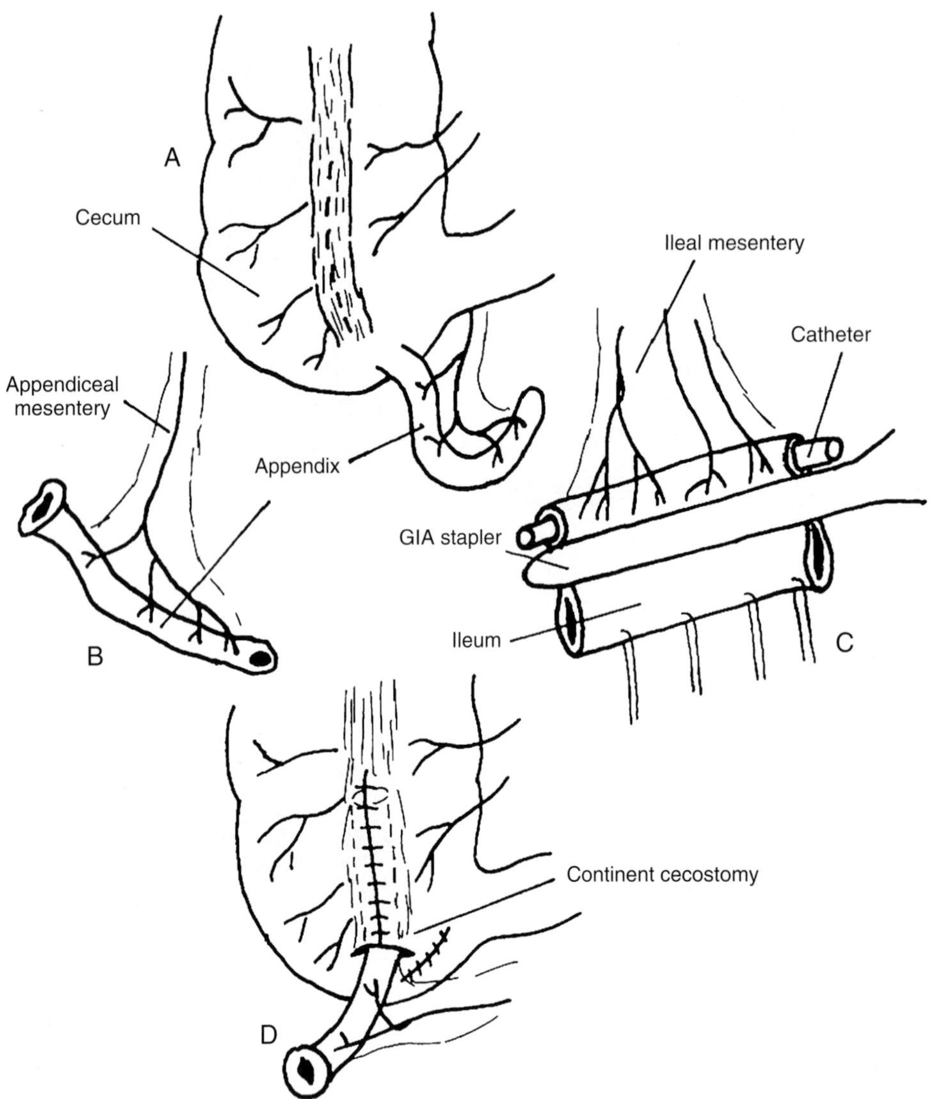

Figure 117–26 Technique for performing a continent cecostomy for an antegrade continence enema. *A*, Anatomy of the appendix and the anterior cecal tenia. *B*, The appendix is mobilized on its vascular pedicle. *C*, Alternatively, a segment of ileum is tapered and mobilized on its vascular pedicle. *D*, The final appearance of the continent cecostomy. (From Sheldon CA: Urinary reconstruction [rather than diversion] for continence in difficult pediatric urologic disorders. Semin Pediatr Surg 1996;5:14.)

In a patient who is refractory to these treatments, the antegrade continence enema (Fig. 117-26) has been shown to be an excellent alternative.[75,117,123,131] This procedure is indicated when nonoperative management is ineffective or when expansion enemas prove effective but cannot be administered by the patient.

The technique is similar to the Mitrofanoff neourethra. The appendix or a retubularized ileal segment[132] is implanted into a taenia in the cecum, and the other end is exteriorized to skin. The appendix or ileal segment is prepared in a manner identical to that described for the Mitrofanoff procedure. An incision is made along the anterior taenia of the cecum, an anastomosis is performed between it and the conduit, and a mucosal defect is created distally in the mucosal trough. The conduit is covered by muscle and the distal end exteriorized to skin. Once daily (sometimes twice daily), a catheter is inserted into the continent cecostomy while the patient sits on the commode. An antegrade enema consisting of tap water and table salt is administered by gravity flow.

URINARY RECONSTRUCTION AND END-STAGE RENAL DISEASE

Congenital urologic disease is reported to be the cause of end-stage renal disease in 20% to 30% of pediatric cases.[21,78] The adverse effect of congenital urologic disease on the success of renal transplantation is demonstrated by the increased incidence of urinary tract infection, allograft dysfunction, technical complications, and graft loss in such patients. Urinary tract infection can be particularly deleterious to both the graft and recipient in the face of immunosuppression. The risk for urinary tract infection is higher in transplant recipients with posterior urethral valves as the cause of their renal failure.[43,89] An analogous problem is seen in patients whose primary disease is vesicoureteral reflux and who continue to have reflux into the native kidneys at the time of transplantation.[8]

These data demonstrate that patients with a history of significant urologic disease must be extensively evaluated before transplantation.[109] Significant vesicoureteral reflux should be resolved by either ureteral reimplantation or nephrectomy. Whenever possible, nephrectomy is avoided to allow the production of urine output so that a functionalized bladder is maintained and dialysis therapy is still an option, either before transplantation or after, should the graft fail. Any endogenous erythropoietin production will be maintained, and this may help avoid presensitization from frequent transfusions. In addition, the ureters are preserved, which may be necessary for subsequent transplant reconstruction should a ureteral complication occur. Indications for nephrectomy include the presence of recurrent urinary tract infections, urinary tract infection–prone upper tract anatomy, refractory hypertension, severe proteinuria, and severe polyuria.

When necessary, nephrectomy is performed via lateral flank incisions or dorsal lumbotomy incisions, through which the peritoneal cavity is rarely, if ever, entered. Such procedures can be performed without interrupting peritoneal dialysis. Alternatively, a laparoscopic approach is very applicable. If bilateral nephrectomy is considered necessary and preemptive (to avoid dialysis) transplantation is desired, one may remove the worst functioning kidney first, and if the second kidney provides adequate function, dialysis can be avoided. At the time of transplantation the remaining kidney can be removed via the transplant incision.

Elevated intravesical pressure must be stabilized by either pharmacologic measures or intermittent catheterization (or both) or, when necessary, augmentation cystoplasty. When undertaking pretransplant surgery it is important to plan the surgical incision so that it minimizes interference with current or anticipated peritoneal dialysis, as well as the subsequent transplantation itself. The best means for avoiding loss of access to the peritoneal cavity for purposes of dialysis is an extraperitoneal approach to the urinary tract, which can readily be achieved for nephrectomy and ureteral reimplantation.

Surgical reconstruction of a dysfunctional bladder can be successfully performed and has been demonstrated to allow transplantation with acceptable results.[27] Such an approach allows optimal allograft preservation and appliance-free continence and is preferable to the alternative of transplantation into an intestinal conduit. Transplantation is applicable to even the most anatomically complicated child with end-stage renal failure.[30,115] The principles of transplantation into a reconstructed bladder include the following: (1) Avoid a dry reconstruction. The capacity and compliance of a reconstructed bladder can be lost if the interval until transplantation is long. This problem can be avoided by undiversion of the native kidneys (if present) or by using a living related donor allograft, for which timing can be optimized. (2) The risk of reabsorptive acidosis occurring either before transplantation, with drainage of the native kidneys into the reconstructed bladder, or after transplantation if the allograft fails over time can be minimized by avoiding the use of intestine and colon for bladder reconstruction. Specifically, gastrocystoplasty, augmentation with the ureter and pelvis, and autoaugmentation all have the potential for minimizing reabsorptive acidosis. (3) Autoaugmentation and augmentation using the ureter have the potential for being performed retroperitoneally, thereby avoiding interference with present or future peritoneal dialysis or with ventricular peritoneal shunts. (4) Whenever possible, ureteral implantation into the native bladder is preferable. If not possible, the colon, an ileocecal segment, or the stomach is the only source of augmentation tissue that will permit reliable antirefluxing anastomosis. (5) During the performance of such transplantations, the blood supply of the augmented bladder and any associated Mitrofanoff neourethra must be meticulously identified and preserved.

COMPLICATIONS

Acute Abdominal Surgical Illness

Acute abdominal surgical illness is a grave concern in a patient who has undergone urinary tract reconstruction, particularly when associated with bladder augmentation or creation of an intestinal reservoir. The most common causes of an acute surgical abdomen in this setting are perforation of the augmented bladder or intestinal reservoir and small bowel obstruction. Even though the etiology remains conjectural, the majority of perforations have been associated with augmentation of a remnant of neurogenic bladder.[29] Over two thirds of such patients have been undergoing intermittent catheterization, and total continence appears to be a common factor. Although the clinical findings are usually those of an acute abdomen, the symptoms may be quite nonspecific, and a high index of suspicion is essential. It is important to be aware of the fact that the rupture may occur many years after reconstruction. Altered sensation in patients with dysraphic states or spinal cord injury and steroid administration in renal transplant patients may confound the diagnosis. In establishing the diagnosis a cystogram is essential, but associated with a significant false-negative rate.[34,105] Computed tomography of the abdomen (with contrast in the bladder or reservoir) may be the most accurate method of making the diagnosis. However, any patient with an augmented bladder undergoing an intermittent catheterization who has abdominal pain, fever, or vomiting should be presumed to have a bladder perforation unless the symptoms can be conclusively attributed to another cause. Exploratory laparotomy may be required to make the diagnosis. Less common, but important, elements of the differential diagnosis include small bowel obstruction, pseudomembranous enterocolitis, toxic shock syndrome, and ventricular-peritoneal shunt complications.[108]

The performance of laparotomy after urinary tract reconstruction is of critical concern. Certainly, elective laparotomy should be preceded by formal bowel preparation in the face of augmentation or continent diversion. The surgeon should have access to a catheter in the bladder to allow insufflation and deflation for identification purposes, and a catheter should be placed in any catheterization conduit, such as a Mitrofanoff neourethra. Efforts must be directed at identification and preservation of the mesenteric blood supply to any gastric or intestinal segments used in reconstruction. Whenever possible, an experienced reconstructive urologist should be present.

Metabolic Complications

Metabolic alterations may be encountered when gastrointestinal segments are incorporated into the urinary tract.[46,77] These metabolic derangements are due to solute flux, both active and passive, between the urine and blood across the gastrointestinal segment wall. The character and severity of such derangements are dependent on the nature of the segment used, the absorptive surface area, the dwell time, and the metabolic reserve of the individual patient. Compensatory mechanisms for metabolic changes are provided by the kidneys, liver, and lungs. Significantly compromised function of any of these organ systems may exacerbate an underlying metabolic defect. Syndromes include alterations in acid-base status, disorders of serum electrolyte composition, hyperammonemia, and bone demineralization.

Systemic acidosis may result from the incorporation of jejunal, ileal, or colonic segments into the urinary tract. Jejunal conduits have been found to be associated with acidosis in 20% to 40% of instances.[24,58] In the jejunum, passive diffusion of solutes occurs along their concentration gradients. Passage of hypertonic urine into a jejunal segment will result in loss of sodium, chloride, and water and lead to hyponatremia, hypochloremia, and volume contraction with subsequent contraction acidosis.[20] Additionally, diminished renal blood flow results in secondary hyperaldosteronism and thus gives rise to a more hypertonic urine and hyperkalemia. The latter is further aggravated by the potassium shift as a result of acidosis.

The metabolic consequences of interposing ileal and colonic segments within the urinary tract relate to the active secretion of sodium (in exchange for hydrogen) and bicarbonate (in exchange for chloride), as well as the reabsorption of ammonium, hydrogen, and chloride. Ammonium absorption appears to quantitatively be the most important and explains many of the abnormalities encountered when ileal or colonic segments have an interface with urine. Hydrogen ion, generated from ammonium, is buffered by serum bicarbonate, and water and CO_2 are produced. The latter is readily eliminated by the lungs and results in a chronic compensatory respiratory alkalosis. The additional buffering provided by bone leads to a variable degree of demineralization and secondary hyperparathyroidism, as manifested by hypercalciuria, hyperphosphaturia, hyperoxaluria, hypocitraturia, hypocalcemia, and hypomagnesemia. Osmotic diuresis and acidosis combine to result in total-body potassium depletion.

Metabolic alkalosis is a unique complication of gastrocystoplasty. Though uncommon,[28] hypokalemic-hypochloremic metabolic alkalosis has been reported.[68,85] Excessive bicarbonate absorption is postulated to occur secondary to the combination of mineralocorticoid excess and potassium/chloride depletion.

Hypokalemia, hypocalcemia, and hypomagnesemia are significant potential sequelae of incorporating intestinal segments within the urinary tract.[77] Sufficiently severe hypokalemia to result in muscular paralysis has been reported. Although hypocalcemia is rarely severe enough to be symptomatic, it may be associated with irritability, tremors, tetany, and coma and may even prove fatal. Hypomagnesemia is also rarely severe enough to be symptomatic, but it may be manifested as altered sensorium, personality changes, delirium, psychosis, weakness, tremors, tetany, and seizures and may likewise be fatal.

Hyperammonemia complicating urinary tract reconstruction with intestine may cause altered sensoria and coma. As previously noted, ammonium ions are actively absorbed from intestinal segments and may be present in large amounts in urine because of their generation by renal tubules and production from urea by urea-splitting organisms.

Perhaps the most overriding concern of incorporating intestinal segments is the effect on childhood growth and development. Several studies have provided data strongly suggestive of defective linear growth in such cases.[35,127] This concern is particularly worrisome in patients with diminished renal function. Here, the metabolic insult is more likely and more severe because growth and development are often already significantly impaired.

Strong evidence has shown that incorporation of intestinal segments into the urinary tract has a primary effect on bone mineralization.[45] Metabolic acidosis results in defects in bone mineralization, bone disease, and linear growth failure through decreased renal tubular calcium reabsorption, depressed intestinal absorption of calcium and phosphorus, and vitamin D metabolism. Treatment with alkalinizing agents has been partially successful in preventing or reversing demineralization disease.

Hematuria-Dysuria Syndrome

Though rare in our own experience,[28] hematuria-dysuria syndrome is an important complication of bladder reconstruction with the stomach.[19] This syndrome is characterized by severe pain and urinary bleeding as a result of urothelial erosion from acid secreted in the urine after gastrocystoplasty.[91] Endoscopic evaluation of children with hematuria-dysuria syndrome suggests greater involvement of the urethra than the bladder itself. Three major factors appear to be of importance in the genesis of this complication: acid hypersecretion, profound oliguria,[114] and bladder neck incompetency. True acid hypersecretion appears to be quite rare, and presumably, the predominant mechanism for this condition would be hypergastrinemia, which has been reported in some instances.[41] H_2 receptor blockers and proton-pump inhibitors such as omeprazole have been shown to be reasonably effective in this syndrome.

Altered Gastrointestinal Function

The incorporation of intestinal segments into the urinary tract may result in significant alterations in gastrointestinal tract function. Alterations in gastric function have been reported after gastrocystoplasty.[39] Functional alterations reported include weight loss, feeding intolerance, dumping syndrome, delayed gastric emptying, and esophagitis. Our own review of gastrocystoplasty with emphasis on long-term follow-up (minimum follow-up of 5 years) failed to demonstrate any significant incidence of altered gastric function or altered acid-base status in

44 consecutive patients.[28] Technical emphasis must be placed on avoiding the vagus nerves, avoiding significant dissection in the region of the gastric pylorus, and avoiding traction distortion of the angle of His (e.g., by the gastrostomy tube), which may predispose to incompetence of the gastroesophageal junction.

Another theoretical concern is the potential for removing sufficient parietal cell mass to interfere with vitamin B_{12} absorption secondary to decreased production of intrinsic factor. Long-term follow-up will be necessary to make this determination. The ileum is also the sole site of vitamin B_{12} absorption, and ileal resection has been demonstrated to be associated with vitamin B_{12} deficiency. This deficiency is manifested as macrocytic anemia and spinocerebellar degenerative disease, but it may take many years to become apparent because of body stores of vitamin B_{12}.

Several potentially important sequelae of intestinal malabsorption may accompany intestinal resection, including diarrhea, vitamin deficiency, and fecal incontinence. Diarrhea is most frequently a result of alterations in bacterial colonization and impairment of bile acid reabsorption (with or without accompanying steatorrhea).[122] Malabsorption from ileal resection is directly related to the length of resection. Resections greater than 100 cm of ileum (adult equivalent) diminish bile acid reabsorption to a degree that cannot be compensated by increased hepatic synthesis. As a result, the bile salt pool is diminished and steatorrhea develops. Another important sequela of the diminished bile salt pool in this population is cholelithiasis which, like urolithiasis, is clinically seen at a significantly increased incidence after ileal resection. Diarrhea induced by altered bile acid reabsorption (with or without accompanying steatorrhea) is further enhanced by the rapid emptying of ileal contents into the colon, which causes a tendency for osmotic diarrhea.

Although most of the data involve adult patients, it is estimated that 10% of children undergoing resection of ileocecal valve segments will experience chronic diarrhea. This may be resolved after restoring intestinal continuity by returning the ileocecal segment to its normal position within the gastrointestinal tract.[40]

Despite these data, the use of intestinal and gastric segments appears to be extremely well tolerated in most children. It would, however, appear prudent to avoid the removal of large segments of ileum or removal of the ileocecal valve for purposes of urinary reconstruction, particularly in those already compromised. Such patients include those with preexisting malabsorption or short-gut syndromes and patients with marginal fecal continence, in whom fecal soilage may become incapacitating by loss of stool consistency. The latter patients include those with myelomeningocele and imperforate anus, who commonly require urinary tract reconstruction.

Malignancy

A majority of our understanding of urointestinal malignancy after reconstruction comes from the experience with ureterosigmoidostomy.[54,116] The incidence of malignancy developing in conduits and continent diversion has been comparably small.[36,104,121] There has been a recent report of malignancy in intestinal augmentation bladders as well.[121] In most cases, the interval between surgery and the onset of cancer is considerable. This latency interval has several important implications, and a carcinogenic effect is clearly implied. Moreover, there is a potential for early surveillance diagnosis. Clearly, long term follow-up is mandatory.

REFERENCES

1. Adams MC, Mitchell ME, Rink RC: Gastrocystoplasty: An alternative solution to the problem of urologic reconstruction in the severely compromised patient. J Urol 1988; 140:1152.
2. Barrett DM, Furlowm WL: Incontinence, intermittent self-catheterization and the artificial genitourinary sphincter. J Urol 1984;132:268.
3. Bauer SB: Early evaluation and management of children with spina bifida. In King LR (ed): Urologic Surgery in Neonates and Young Infants. Philadelphia, WB Saunders, 1988.
4. Benchekroun A, Essakalli N, Faik M, et al: Continent urostomy with hydraulic ileal valve in 136 patients: 13 years of experience. J Urol 1989;142:46.
5. Bevers RF, Abbekerk EM, Boon TA: Cowper's syringocele: Symptoms, classification and treatment of an unappreciated problem. J Urol 2000;163:782.
6. Bihrle R: The Indiana pouch continent urinary reservoir. Urol Clin North Am 1997;24:773.
7. Boemers TM, van Gool JD, de Jong TP, et al: Urodynamic evaluation of children with the caudal regression syndrome (caudal dysplasia sequence). J Urol 1994;151:1038.
8. Bouchot O, Guillonneau B, Cantarovich D, et al: Vesicoureteral reflux in the renal transplantation candidate. Eur Urol 1991;20:26.
9. Bramble FJ: The treatment of adult enuresis and urge incontinence by enterocystoplasty. Br J Urol 1982;54:693.
10. Bramble FJ: The clam cystoplasty. Br J Urol 1990;66:337.
11. Cain MP, Casale AJ, King SJ, et al: Appendicovesicostomy and newer alternatives for the Mitrofanoff procedure: Results in the last 100 patients at Riley Children's Hospital. J Urol 1999;162:1749.
12. Cain MP, Casale AJ, Rink RC: Initial experience using a catheterizable ileovesicostomy (Monti procedure) in children. Urology 1998;52:870.
13. Camey M, Richard F, Botto H: Ileal replacement of bladder. In King L, Stone AR, Webster GD (eds): Bladder Reconstruction and Continent Urinary Diversion. Chicago, Year Book, 1991, p 389.
14. Capitanucci ML, Iacobelli BD, Silveri M, et al: Long-term urological follow-up of occult spinal dysraphism in children. Eur J Pediatr Surg 1996;6(Suppl 1):25.
15. Carr MC, Mitchell ME: Gastrocystoplasty and bladder replacement with stomach. In Marshall FF (ed): Textbook of Operative Urology. Philadelphia, WB Saunders, 1996, p 500.
16. Cartwright PC, Snow BW: Bladder autoaugmentation: Early clinical experience. J Urol 1989;142:505.
17. Casale AJ: A long continent ileovesicostomy using a single piece of bowel. J Urol 1999;162:1743.
18. Castellan MA, Gosalbez R Jr, Labbie A, et al: Clinical applications of the Monti procedure as a continent catheterizable stoma. Urology 1999;54:152.
19. Chadwick Plaire J, Snodgrass WT, Grady RW, et al: Long-term followup of the hematuria-dysuria syndrome. J Urol 2000;164:921.

20. Cher ML, Roehrborn CG: Incorporation of intestinal segments into the urinary tract. In Hohenfellner A, Wammack R (eds): Continent Urinary Diversion. Edinburgh, Churchill Livingstone, 1992.
21. Churchill BM, Aliabadi H, Landon EH, et al: Ureteral bladder augmentation. J Urol 1993;150:716.
22. Churchill BM, Gilmour RF, Williot P: Urodynamics. Pediatr Clin North Am 1987;34:1133.
23. Churchill BM, Sheldon CA, McLorie GA, et al: Factors influencing patient and graft survival in 300 cadaveric pediatric renal transplants. J Urol 1988;140:1129.
24. Clark SS: Electrolyte disturbance associated with jejunal conduit. J Urol 1989;142:1201.
25. Cromie WJ, Barada JH, Weingarten J: Cecal tubularization: Lengthening technique for creation of catheterizable conduit. Urology 1991;38:41.
26. Dees JE: Congenital epispadias with incontinence. J Urol 1949;62:513.
27. DeFoor W, Minevich E, McEnery P, et al: Lower urinary tract reconstruction is safe and effective in children with end stage renal disease. J Urol 2003;170:1497, discussion 1500.
28. DeFoor W, Minevich E, Reeves D, et al: Gastrocystoplasty: Long-term followup. J Urol 2003;170:1647, discussion 1649.
29. DeFoor W, Tackett L, Minevich E, et al: Risk factors for spontaneous bladder perforation after augmentation cystoplasty. Urology 2003;62:737.
30. DeFoor W, Tackett L, Minevich E, et al: Successful renal transplantation in children with posterior urethral valves. J Urol 2003;170:2402.
31. Duckett JW, Snyder HM, Use of the Mitrofanoff principle in urinary reconstruction. World J Urol 1985;3:191.
32. Elder JS: Periurethral and puboprostatic sling repair for incontinence in patients with myelodysplasia. J Urol 1990; 144:434.
33. Elder JS: Continent appendicocolostomy: A variation of the Mitrofanoff principle in pediatric urinary tract reconstruction. J Urol 1992;148:117.
34. Elder JS, Snyder HM, Hulbert WC, et al: Perforation of the augmented bladder in patients undergoing clean intermittent catheterization. J Urol 1988;140:1159.
35. Feng AH, Kaar S, Elder JS: Influence of enterocystoplasty on linear growth in children with exstrophy. J Urol 2002; 167:2552, discussion 2555.
36. Filmer RB, Spencer JR, Malignancies in bladder augmentations and intestinal conduits. J Urol 1990;143:671.
37. Franco I, Kolligian M, Reda EF, et al: The importance of catheter size in the achievement of urinary continence in patients undergoing a Young-Dees-Leadbetter procedure. J Urol 1994;152:710.
38. Gil-Vernet JM Jr: The ileocolic segment in urologic surgery. J Urol 1965;94:418.
39. Gold BD, Bhoopalam PS, Reifen RM, et al: Gastrointestinal complications of gastrocystoplasty. Arch Dis Child 1992; 67:1272.
40. Gonzalez R, Sidi AA, Zhang G: Urinary undiversion: Indications, technique, and results in 50 cases. J Urol 1986; 136:13.
41. Gosalbez R, Woodard JR, Broecker BH, et al: Metabolic complications of the use of stomach for urinary reconstruction. J Urol 1993;150:710.
42. Greenfield SP, Hensle TW, Berdon WE, et al: Unilateral vesicoureteral reflux and unilateral nonfunctioning kidney associated with posterior urethral valves—a syndrome? J Urol 1983;130:733.
43. Groenewegen AAM, Sukhal RN, Nauta J, et al: Results of renal transplantation in boys treated for posterior urethral valves. J Urol 1993;149:1517.
44. Hafez AT, McLorie G, Bagli D, et al: A single-centre long-term outcome analysis of artificial urinary sphincter placement in children. BJU Int 2002;89:82.
45. Hafez AT, McLorie G, Gilday D, et al: Long-term evaluation of metabolic profile and bone mineral density after ileocystoplasty in children. J Urol 2003;170:1639, discussion 1641.
46. Hall MC, Koch MO, McDougal WS: Metabolic consequences of urinary diversion through intestinal segments. Urol Clin North Am 1991;18:725.
47. Harris CF, Cooper CS, Hutcheson JC, et al: Appendicovesicostomy: The Mitrofanoff procedure—a 15-year perspective. J Urol 2000;163:1922.
48. Hendren WH: Urinary tract re-functionalization after long-term diversion. A 20-year experience with 177 patients. Ann Surg 1990;212:478, discussion 494.
49. Herndon CD, Rink RC, Shaw MB, et al: The Indiana experience with artificial urinary sphincters in children and young adults. J Urol 2003;169:650, discussion 654.
50. Herschorn S, Radomski SB: Fascial slings and bladder neck tapering in the treatment of male neurogenic incontinence. J Urol 1992;147:1073.
51. Hinman F Jr: Selection of intestinal segments for bladder substitution: Physical and physiological characteristics. J Urol 1988;139:521.
52. Homsy YL, Reid EC: Ileocystoplasty. Urology 1974;4:135.
53. Husmann DA, Snodgrass WT, Koyle MA, et al: Ureterocystoplasty: Indications for a successful augmentation. J Urol 2004;171:1247.
54. Husmann DA, Spence HM: Current status of tumor of the bowel following ureterosigmoidostomy: A review. J Urol 1990;144:607.
55. Jayanthi VR, Churchill BM, McLorie GA, et al: Concomitant bladder neck closure and Mitrofanoff diversion for the management of intractable urinary incontinence. J Urol 1995;154:886.
56. Jones DA, Holden D, George NJ: Mechanism of upper tract dilatation in patients with thick walled bladders, chronic retention of urine and associated hydroureteronephrosis. J Urol 1988;140:326.
57. Kaefer M, Retik AB: The Mitrofanoff principle in continent urinary reconstruction. Urol Clin North Am 1997;24:795.
58. Klein EA, Montie JE, Montague D, et al: Jejunal conduit urinary diversion. J Urol 1986;135:244.
59. Kock NG, Ghoneim M, Lyche K: Replacement of the bladder by the urethral Kock pouch: Functional results, urodynamics, and radiological features. J Urol 1989;141:1111.
60. Kock NG, Norlen L, Philipson BM, et al: The continent ileal reservoir (Kock pouch) for urinary diversion. World J Urol 1985;3:146.
61. Koff SA: Estimating bladder capacity in children. Urology 1983;21:248.
62. Koff SA: Guidelines to determine the size and shape of intestinal segments used for reconstruction. Estimated influence of bowel length and radius on achievement of augmented bladder volume. J Urol 1988;140:1150.
63. Koff SA: A technique for bladder neck reconstruction in exstrophy; The cinch. J Urol 1990;144:549.
64. Koff SA, Lapides J, Piazza DH: Association of urinary tract infection and reflux with uninhibited bladder contractions and voluntary sphincteric obstruction. J Urol 1979;122:373.
65. Koff SA, Murtagh DS: The uninhibited bladder in children: Effect of treatment on recurrence of urinary infection and on vesicoureteral reflux resolution. J Urol 1983;130:1138.
66. Kropp KA, Angwafo FF: Urethral lengthening and reimplantation for neurogenic incontinence in children. J Urol 1986;135:533.

67. Kryger JV, Spencer Barthold J, Fleming P, et al: The outcome of artificial urinary sphincter placement after a mean 15-year follow-up in a paediatric population. BJU Int 1999;83:1026.
68. Kurzrock EA, Baskin LS, Kogan BA: Gastrocystoplasty: Long-term followup. J Urol 1998;160:2182.
69. Leadbetter GWJ: Surgical correction of total urinary incontinence. J Urol 1954;91:261.
70. Lepor H, Jeffs RD: Primary bladder closure and bladder neck reconstruction in classical bladder exstrophy. J Urol 1983;130:1142.
71. Liard A, Seguier-Lipszyc E, Mathiot A, et al: The Mitrofanoff procedure: 20 years later. J Urol 2001;165:2394.
72. Light JK, Engelmann UH: Reconstruction of the lower urinary tract: Observations on bowel dynamics and the artificial urinary sphincter. J Urol 1985;133:594.
73. MacNeily AE, Afshar K, Coleman GU, et al: Autoaugmentation by detrusor myotomy: Its lack of effectiveness in the management of congenital neuropathic bladder. J Urol 2003;170:1643, discussion 1646.
74. Maizels M, Stephens FD, King LR, et al: Cowper's syringocele: A classification of dilatations of Cowper's gland duct based upon clinical characteristics of 8 boys. J Urol 1983; 129:111.
75. Malone PS, Ransley PG, Kiely EM: Preliminary report: The antegrade continence enema. Lancet 1990;336:1217.
76. Mathisen W: Open-loop sigmoido-cystoplasty. Acta Chir Scand 1955;110:227.
77. McDougal WS: Metabolic complications of urinary intestinal diversion. J Urol 1992;147:1199.
78. McEnery PT, Stablein DM, Arbus G, et al: Renal transplantation in children. A report of the North American Pediatric Renal Transplant Cooperative Study. N Engl J Med 1992;326:1727.
79. McGuire EJ, Wang C, Usitalo H, et al: Modified pubovaginal sling in girls with myelodysplasia. J Urol 1986;135:94.
80. McGuire EJ, Woodside JR, Borden TA, et al: Prognostic value of urodynamic testing in myelodysplastic patients. J Urol 1981;126:205.
81. McLorie GA, Sheldon CA, Fleisher M, et al: The genitourinary system in patients with imperforate anus. J Pediatr Surg 1987;22:1100.
82. Miller EA, Mayo M, Kwan D, et al: Simultaneous augmentation cystoplasty and artificial urinary sphincter placement: Infection rates and voiding mechanisms. J Urol 1998;160: 750, discussion 752.
83. Minevich E, Sheldon CA: Gastrocystoplasty–ileal Mitrofanoff stoma fistula. J Urol 1999;161:271.
84. Minevich E, Sheldon CA: Urinary tract reconstruction for continence and renal preservation. In Ziegler MM, Azizkhan RG, Weber TR (eds): Operative Pediatric Surgery. Norwalk, CT, Appleton & Lange, 2003.
85. Mingin GC, Stock JA, Hanna MK: Gastrocystoplasty: Long-term complications in 22 patients. J Urol 1999;162:1122.
86. Mitchell ME, Adams MC, Rink RC: Urethral replacement with ureter. J Urol 1988;139:1282.
87. Mitchell ME, Rink RC: Experience with the artificial urinary sphincter in children and young adults. J Pediatr Surg 1983;18:700.
88. Mitrofanoff P: Cystostomie continente trans-appendiculaire dans le traitement des vessies neurologiques. Chir Pediatr 1980;21:297.
89. Mochon M, Kaiser BA, Dunn S, et al: Urinary tract infections in children with posterior urethral valves after kidney transplantation. J Urol 1992;148:1874.
90. Mor Y, Kajbafzadeh AM, German K, et al: The role of ureter in the creation of Mitrofanoff channels in children. J Urol 1997;157:635.
91. Nguyen DH, Bain M, Salmonson K, et al: The syndrome of dysuria and hematuria in pediatric urinary reconstruction with stomach. J Urol 1993;150:707.
92. Nguyen HT, Baskin LS: The outcome of bladder neck closure in children with severe urinary incontinence. J Urol 2003;169:1114, discussion 1116.
93. Noe HN: The role of dysfunctional voiding in failure or complication of ureteral reimplantation for primary reflux. J Urol 1985;134:1172.
94. Pagano F: The vesica ileale padovana. In Holenfellner P, Wammack R (eds): Continent Urinary Diversion. Edinburgh, Churchill Livingstone, 1992, p 122.
95. Parra R: A simplified technique for continent urinary diversion: An all-stapled colonic reservoir. J Urol 1991; 146:1496.
96. Pippi Salle JL, de Fraga JCS, Amarante A, et al: Urethral lengthening with anterior bladder wall flap for urinary incontinence: A new approach. J Urol 1994;152:803.
97. Pow-Sang JM, Helal M, Figueroa E, et al: Conversion from external appliance or internal urinary diversion to a continent urinary reservoir (Florida pouch I and II): Surgical technique, indications and complications. J Urol 1992; 147:356.
98. Reddy P, Lange P, Fraley E: Total bladder replacement using detubularized sigmoid colon: Technique and results. J Urol 1991;145:51.
99. Reinberg Y, Gonzalez R, Fryd D, et al: The outcome of renal transplantation in children with posterior urethral valves. J Urol 1988;140:1491.
100. Restrepo NC, Decter RM, Phillips PP, et al: Appendiceal granulation polyps: A complication of Mitrofanoff procedure. Urology 1994;43:219.
101. Rittenberg MH, Hulbert WC, Snyder HM 3rd, et al: Protective factors in posterior urethral valves. J Urol 1988; 140:993.
102. Robertson GN, King L: Bladder substitution in children. Urol Clin North Am 1986;13:333.
103. Rowland RG, Bihrle R, Mitchell ME: The Indiana continent urinary reservoir. J Urol 1987;137:1136.
104. Rowland R, Regan F: The risk of secondary malignancies in urinary reservoirs. In Hohenfellner A, Wammack R (eds): Continent Urinary Diversion. Edinburgh, Churchill Livingstone, 1992, p 299.
105. Rushton HG, Woodard JR, Parrott TS, et al: Delayed bladder rupture after augmentation enterocystoplasty. J Urol 1988;140:344.
106. Scherz HC, Kaplan GW, Packer MG: Anterior urethral valves in the fossa navicularis in children. J Urol 1987; 138:1211.
107. Scholtmeijer RJ, van Mastrigt R: The effect of oxyphenonium bromide and oxybutynin hydrochloride on detrusor contractility and reflux in children with vesicoureteral reflux and detrusor instability. J Urol 1991; 146:660.
108. Shekarriz B, Upadhyay J, Demirbilek S, et al: Surgical complications of bladder augmentation: Comparison between various enterocystoplasties in 133 patients. Urology 2000;55:123.
109. Sheldon CA, Churchill BM, McLorie GA, et al: Evaluation of factors contributing to mortality in pediatric renal transplant recipients. J Pediatr Surg 1992;27:629.
110. Sheldon C, Cormier M, Crone K, et al: Occult neurovesical dysfunction in children with imperforate anus and its variants. J Pediatr Surg 1991;26:49.
111. Sheldon CA, Essig KA: Congenital bladder diverticulum causing bladder outlet obstruction: Case report and review of literature. Pediatr Surg Int 1994;9:141.

112. Sheldon CA, Gilbert A: Use of the appendix for urethral reconstruction in children with congenital anomalies of the bladder. Surgery 1992;112:805.
113. Sheldon CA, Gilbert A, Lewis AG, et al: Surgical implications of genitourinary tract anomalies in patients with imperforate anus. J Urol 1994;152:196.
114. Sheldon CA, Gilbert A, Wacksman J, et al: Gastrocystoplasty: Technical and metabolic characteristics of the most versatile childhood bladder augmentation modality. J Pediatr Surg 1995;30:283.
115. Sheldon CA, Gonzaleas R, Burns MW, et al: Renal transplantation into dysfunctional bladder: The role of adjunctive bladder reconstruction. J Urol 1994;152:972.
116. Sheldon CA, McKinley RD, Hartig PR, et al: Carcinoma at the site of ureterosigmoidostomy. J Dis Colon Rectum 1983;26:55.
117. Sheldon CA, Minevich E, Wacksman J, et al: Role of the antegrade continence enema in the management of the most debilitating childhood recto-urogenital anomalies. J Urol 1997;158:1277, discussion 1279.
118. Sheldon CA, Minevich E, Wacksman J: Modified technique of antegrade continence enema using a stapling device. J Urol 2000;163:589.
119. Skinner DG, Lieskovsky G, Boyd SD, Continuing experience with the continent ileal reservoir (Kock pouch) as an alternative to cutaneous urinary diversion: An update after 250 cases. J Urol 1987;137:1140.
120. Smith RB, van Cangh P, Skinner DG, et al: Augmentation enterocystoplasty: A critical review. J Urol 1977;118:35.
121. Soergel MT, Cain MP, Misseri R, et al: Transitional cell carcinoma following augmentation cystoplasty for neuropathic bladder. Paper presented at a meeting of the American Academy of Pediatrics, 2003, New Orleans.
122. Steiner MS, Morton RA: Nutritional and gastrointestinal complications of the use of bowel segments in the lower urinary tract. Urol Clin North Am 1991;18:743.
123. Tackett LD, Minevich E, Benedict JF, et al: Appendiceal versus ileal segment for antegrade continence enema. J Urol 2002;167:683.
124. Thomsen H: Pyelorenal backflow. Danish Med Bull 1984;31:348.
125. Turner-Warwick R, Ashken HM: The functional results of partial subtotal and total cystoplasty. Br J Urol 1967; 39:3.
126. Van Savage JG, Khoury AE, McLorie GA, et al: An algorithm for the management of anterior urethral valves. J Urol 1997;158:1030.
127. Wagstaff KE, Woodhouse CJ, Duffy PG, et al: Delayed linear growth in children with enterocystoplasties. Br J Urol 1992;69:314.
128. Wammack R, et al: The Maintz pouch. In Holenfellner P, Wammack R (eds): Continent Urinary Diversion. Churchill Livingstone, Edinburgh, 1992, p 131.
129. Wan J, McGuire EJ, Bloom DA, et al: Stress leak point pressure: A diagnostic tool for incontinent children. J Urol 1993;150:700.
130. Whitmore WF, Gittes RF: Reconstruction of the urinary tract by cecal and ileocecal cystoplasty: Review of a 15-year experience. J Urol 1983;129:494.
131. Yerkes EB, Cain MP, King S, et al: The Malone antegrade continence enema procedure: Quality of life and family perspective. J Urol 2003;169:320.
132. Yerkes EB, Rink RC, Cain MP, et al: Use of a Monti channel for administration of antegrade continence enemas. J Urol 2002;168:1883, discussion 1885.
133. Young HH: An operation for the cure of incontinence associated with epispadias. J Urol 1922;7:1.
134. Young HH, Frontz WA, Baldwin JC: Congenital obstruction of the posterior urethra. J Urol 1919;3:289-365; J Urol 2002;167:265, discussion 268.

Chapter 118

Bladder and Cloacal Exstrophy

John W. Brock III, Romano T. DeMarco, and James A. O'Neill, Jr.

BLADDER EXSTROPHY

(John W. Brock III and Romano T. DeMarco)

The first description of bladder exstrophy was found on Assyrian tablets, circa 2000 BC, that now reside in the British Museum in London. Von Grafenberg described the medical condition of exstrophy in 1597, but it was not until 1780 that the term *exstrophie* was coined by Chausseir. Mowat was the first author to provide a complete description of bladder exstrophy in his 1748 work.[96]

Primitive treatment of bladder exstrophy included using an external urinary receptacle applied to the surface of the exposed bladder, as proposed by MacKay and Syme[80] in 1849. Syme[118] later proposed constructing a ureterosigmoid anastomosis as a means of creating a continent form of urinary diversion. This was the first such procedure performed, but the patient subsequently died of pyelonephritis. In 1869 Thiersch[119] described coverage of the exposed bladder with lateral flaps that resulted in a 100-mL capacity, but the patient was incontinent, and urosepsis was a significant problem.

In 1894 Maydl[83] used a more successful method of urinary diversion that involved transplanting the trigone that contained the ureters into the rectum. Subsequent descriptions of ureterosigmoidostomy by Coffey,[20] Nesbitt,[97] and Leadbetter and Clarke[76] refined the technique so that sigmoid-to-ureter reflux was prevented. However, the technique was still associated with infection, electrolyte abnormalities, and subsequently cancer.[8] Finally, urinary diversion was used preferentially to provide continence and control of infection, but significant problems related to anatomic reconstruction and sexual function persisted.

Paralleling efforts to develop successful urinary diversion methods were reports of bladder closure and reconstruction. Trendelenburg[121] reported bilateral sacroiliac osteotomies and application of a pelvic sling to protect the anterior bladder and abdominal wall closures. Burns[12] in 1924 and Janssen[58] in 1933 had success with procedures incorporating Trendelenburg's method, but it was not until 1942 when Young[130] reported the first female with urinary continence after closure of bladder exstrophy. Subsequently, in 1948, Michon[88] reported success in a male who had had full reconstruction.

Nonetheless, in a 1970 review of 329 cases, Marshall and Muecke[82] concluded that only 19% of patients with total reconstruction had fair to satisfactory results. This same pessimistic view of results was reported by others, supporting efforts to further refine methods of urinary diversion.[70,125] Subsequently, Lepor and Jeffs,[77] Mesrobian et al.,[86] and Hollowell and Ransley[52] reported 75% to 80% continence rates after staged reconstruction, with refinement of urethroplasty, epispadias repair, and bladder augmentation, as required. In 1999 Grady and Mitchell[46] advocated complete primary exstrophy repair (CPER) in neonates following their initial success with this procedure, which compared favorably with staged procedures. Their results prompted many centers to change their primary surgical approach to newborns with exstrophy.

INCIDENCE

On the basis of population studies, the incidence of bladder exstrophy has been estimated to be 1 in 10,000 to 1 in 50,000 live births.[73,75] The male-to-female ratio, derived from several series, is between 2.3:1 and 4:1.[109] These figures indicate that bladder exstrophy is a rare anomaly, particularly in females.

Now that patients who have had reconstruction of bladder exstrophy are living into adulthood, with the possibility of becoming parents, the risk of familial recurrence is a consideration. Ives et al. [56] characterized this risk as 1 in 100, but Shapiro et al.,[109] in a survey of 2500 indexed cases, found an incidence of only 1 in 275. Studies of identical twins have found a variation in the occurrence of exstrophy in one or both twins.[56,109] There is reason to believe that subsequent siblings of a patient with bladder exstrophy have a slight risk of occurrence, but the inheritance pattern has not been established. Nonetheless, the incidence is clearly much higher than that in the general population—estimated at 400 times greater by Shapiro et al.[109]

EMBRYOLOGY

Classic bladder exstrophy can be conceptualized by a visual analogy: one blade of a pair of scissors is passed through the urethra into the bladder of a normal person;

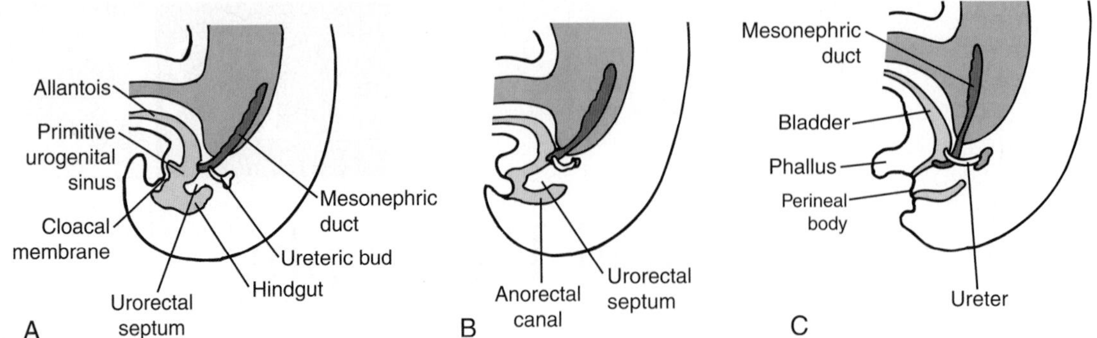

Figure 118-1 Division of the cloaca into the urogenital sinus and rectum. *A*, At the end of the fifth week. *B*, At 7 weeks. *C*, At 8 weeks. (Adapted from Sadler TW: Langman's Medical Embryology, 8th ed. Philadelphia, Lippincott Williams and Wilkins, 2000, p 316.)

the other blade is used to cut the layers of the skin, abdominal wall, anterior wall of the bladder and urethra, and symphysis pubis; and the cut edges are unfolded laterally as if opening the pages of a book. Efforts have been made to explain this phenomenon embryologically and to reproduce it experimentally.[3,89,100] Anatomic variants such as cloacal exstrophy, which is described in the addendum to this chapter, suggest that the embryogenesis of this entity involves abnormal hindgut development and that it originates somewhere between the 4th and 10th weeks of gestation.

In initial development, the common cloaca is separated from the amniotic space by the cloacal membrane, which occupies the abdominal wall below the level of the umbilicus.[89] Ingrowth of mesenchyma between the ectodermal and endodermal layers of the cloacal membrane results in formation of the muscles of the lower abdominal wall and the pubis. At the same time, the urorectal septum descends to divide the cloaca into an anterior bladder and a posterior rectum. This septum meets the posterior remnant of the cloacal membrane. The latter eventually perforates, forming anal and urogenital openings (Fig. 118-1). The paragenital tubercles migrate and fuse in the midline in front of the cloacal membrane before it perforates.

The current embryologic theory relates to the experimental studies by Muecke,[95] who demonstrated in 1964 that bladder exstrophy can be produced by inhibiting anterior cloacal membrane formation, accomplished by placing a plastic wedge above the cloacal membrane in chick embryos of 2 to 3 weeks' gestation. Research by Marshall and Muecke[81] and by Pohlman[103] strongly suggests that the basic defect results from an abnormal overdevelopment of the cloacal membrane, which prevents the migration of mesenchymal tissue and the appropriate development of the lower abdominal wall and pubis. The exact position and timing of rupture of this anterior portion of the cloacal membrane determine the form of the anomaly encountered, although classic bladder exstrophy constitutes more than half the cases.

ANATOMIC VARIANTS

Bladder exstrophy can be considered a spectrum of anatomic variants referred to as the exstrophy complex.[13] These variants include pubic diastasis, female epispadias, male epispadias, classic bladder exstrophy, superior vesical fistula, duplex exstrophy, bladder exstrophy with imperforate anus, and cloacal exstrophy (Fig. 118-2). Each represents varying degrees of abdominal wall formation related to different degrees of overdevelopment of the cloacal membrane. With extreme cases of classic bladder exstrophy and cloacal exstrophy, omphaloceles are also encountered above the level of the exposed bladder.

In classic bladder exstrophy, the size of the exposed bladder also varies. The exposed bladder plate may be large, with wide diastasis of the pubis, or one or both sides of the bladder patch may be small and hypoplastic (Fig. 118-3). Although the upper urinary tracts are usually normal at the time of birth, hydroureteronephrosis does occur. After birth, the mucosa of the exposed bladder may, over time, undergo metaplasia associated with chronic inflammation, edema, and fibrosis. This, in turn, may lead to chronic ureteral obstruction and hydroureteronephrosis. These latter considerations have implications related to the timing and performance of ultimate reconstruction.

CLINICAL PRESENTATION

In general, patients who present with variants of the exstrophy complex are born full term, without associated physiologic problems. The incidence of prematurity is increased in extreme cases of bladder exstrophy and particulalry in cloacal exstrophy. In patients with classic exstrophy of the bladder, anomalous development in other systems is unusual. However, multiple anomalies are encountered in patients with other forms of the exstrophy-epispadias complex. For example, in patients with superior vesical fissure or cloacal exstrophy, skeletal defects, myelomeningocele, and cardiovascular anomalies are common.

At birth, the typical appearance of bladder exstrophy is obvious (Fig. 118-4); there is an everted posterior bladder wall of varying size associated with separation of the symphysis pubis. Urine may be seen leaking from the inferior margin of the everted posterior bladder wall, but the ureteral orifices are not always obvious. The umbilicus is located on the immediate superior border of the bladder plate, and a small umbilical hernia or an omphalocele is ordinarily seen. The mucosa of the exposed bladder may

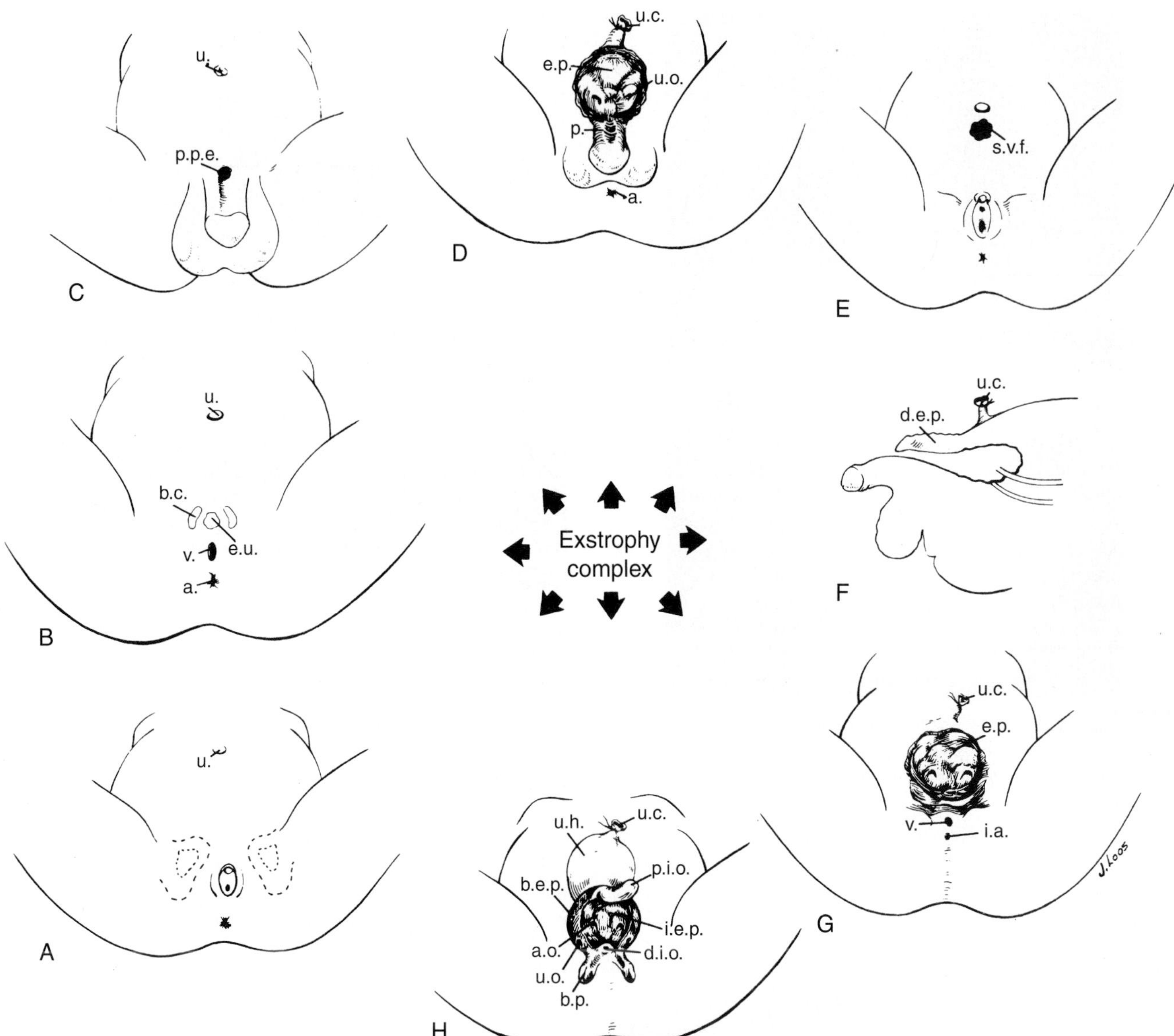

Figure 118–2 Disease spectrum of the exstrophy complex. *A,* Diastasis pubis. *B,* Female epispadias. *C,* Male epispadis. *D,* Classic bladder exstrophy. *E,* Superior vesical fistula. *F,* Duplex exstrophy. *G,* Bladder exstrophy with imperforate anus. *H,* Cloacal exstrophy. a., anus; a.o., appendiceal orifice; b.c., bifid clitoris; b.e.p., bladder exstrophic plate; b.p., bifid penis; d.e.p., duplicate exstrophic plate; d.i.o., distal intestinal orifice; e.p., exstrophic plate; e.u., epispadiac urethra; i.a., imperforate anus; i.e.p., intestinal exstrophic plate; p., penis; p.i.o., proximal intestinal orifice; p.p.e., penopubic epispadias; s.v.f., superior vesical fistula; u., umbilicus; u.c., umbilical cord; u.h., umbilical hernia; u.o., ureteral orifice; v., vagina.

look normal or have a variable number of inflammatory polyps on its surface at the time of birth; subsequently, with exposure and chronic inflammation, the mucosal surface becomes thickened and polypoid (Fig. 118-5). Although the bladder wall musculature is pliable and reasonably elastic at birth, with time, it may become fibrotic, rigid, and unyielding because of the chronic inflammation associated with prolonged exposure.

Some degree of widening of the symphysis pubis is present in all cases of bladder exstrophy. This diastasis causes an outward rotation and eversion of the pubic rami at their junctions with the ischial and iliac bones. Extreme cases have inferior and lateral separation of the innominate bones as they relate to the sacroiliac joints. Sponseller et al.,[114] using computed tomography (CT) scanning of the pelvis with three-dimensional reconstruction, noted several skeletal pelvic abnormalities in children with bladder exstrophy. These included an increased distance between the triradiate cartilages, external rotation and shortening (by 30%) of the anterior segment of the iliac bone, external rotation of the posterior segment of the ilium, and retroversion of the acetabula. Additionally, Stec et al.[117] used three-dimensional CT scanning to show that the sacroiliac joint angle was 10 degrees larger, the bony pelvis 14.7 degrees more inferior in rotation, and the sacrum 42.6% larger in volume in exstrophy patients

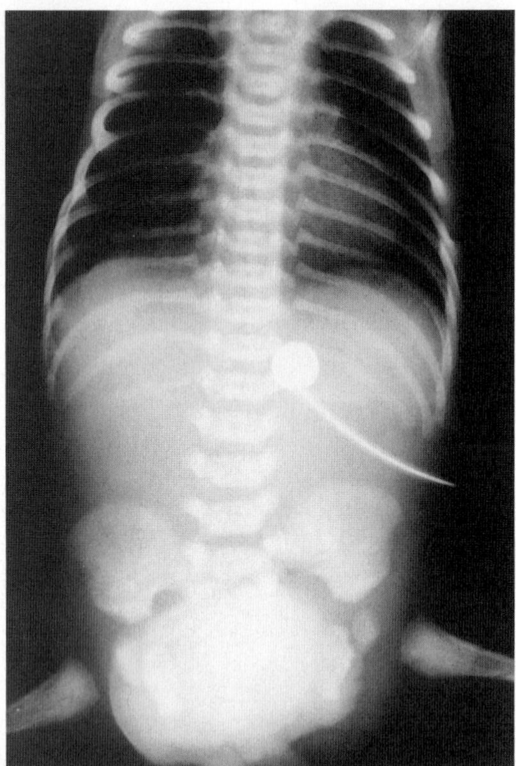

Figure 118–3 Plain radiograph of a neonate with bladder exstrophy demonstrates the soft tissue mass effect of the exposed bladder, the wide diastasis of the symphysis pubis, and the posterior rotation of the acetabula.

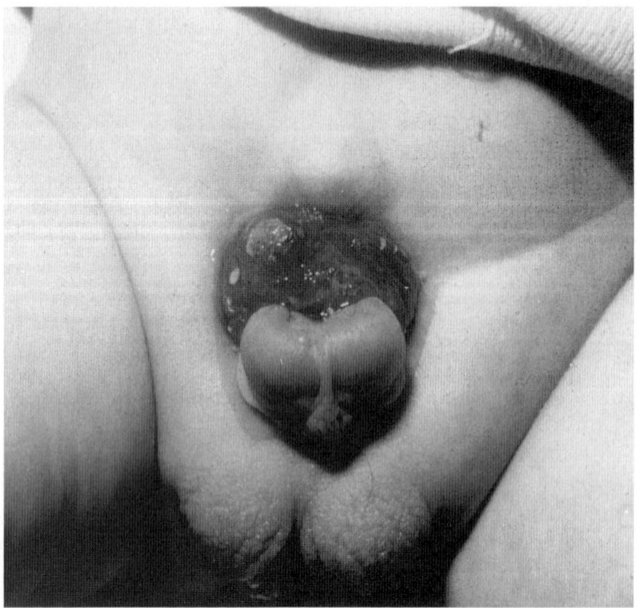

Figure 118–4 Typical findings of classic bladder exstrophy in a newborn male. The bladder plate is small, and a small hernia is evident at its superior border. The penis is foreshortened, with widely splayed corporal bodies and glanular separation. Typically, the urethral plate is short in these patients.

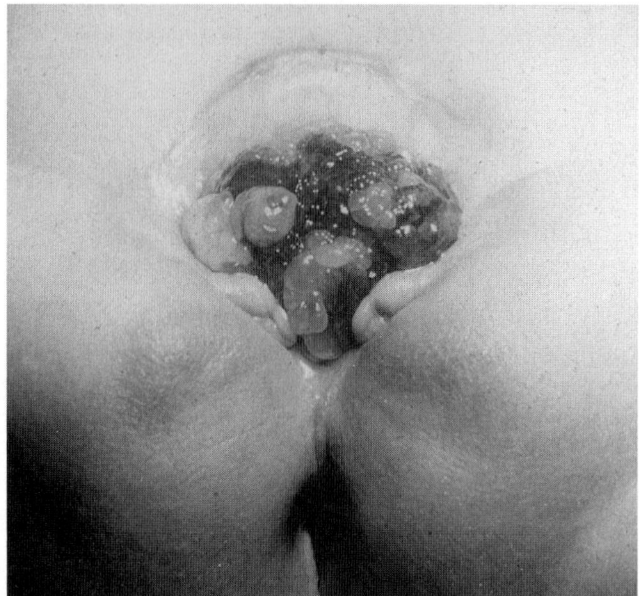

Figure 118–5 When the bladder has been exposed for at least 1 week after birth and the mucosa is subjected to exposure and inflammation, polypoid excrescences typically appear, as in this newborn female. Avoidance of this complication is a good reason to perform bladder closure as soon as possible after birth.

compared with age-matched controls. Stec et al.[116] also noted significant differences in pelvic floor musculature, particularly levator ani orientation, based on a review of three-dimensional CT scans.

It is of interest that when a child begins to walk, there is a characteristic waddling gait secondary to external rotation of the hip joints. However, internal rotation of the long bones of the lower extremities soon corrects this problem. There are few or no long-term orthopedic problems or defects in mobility, as shown by Cracchiolo and Hall[23] and Kelly.[66]

Mention has already been made of the small umbilical hernia usually associated with classic exstrophy; specific treatment is ordinarily not required unless it is large. Inguinal hernias are also commonly seen in children with bladder exstrophy. These hernias are characteristically both direct and indirect because of the large fascial deficiency involved. This fascial defect extends laterally to the divergent rectus muscles and the overlying rectus sheath and inferiorly to the open urogenital diaphragm stretched between the separated pubic bones. The indirect component of the inguinal hernia is attributable to a large, persistent processus vaginalis, large internal and external inguinal rings, and a lack of obliquity of the inguinal canal. Repair of such inguinal hernias should involve both high ligation of the hernia sac and fixation of the transversalis fascia and internal oblique by a variant of a Cooper's ligament repair for the direct component. In addition, the testes may appear to be undescended. In most case, however, the testes are retractile and eventually reside in the scrotum without the need for orchiopexy.

With bladder exstrophy, the distance between the umbilicus and the anus is foreshortened, making the perineum appear short and wide. The anus is usually situated immediately behind the urogenital diaphragm, anteriorly displaced, corresponding to the posterior limit of the large triangular fascial defect in the anterior abdominal wall. The anal canal and anus itself are usually normal but may be stenotic and require dilatation. In rare instances the anus is ectopic, presenting as a rectoperineal or rectovaginal fistula. Obviously, the anal sphincter mechanism is also displaced anteriorly, and the levator ani complex is divergent. The latter factor leads to weakness of the perineal floor and rectal prolapse in 10% to 20% of patients. Rectal prolapse may be further accentuated as a result of the abnormal straining that occurs among infants with an exposed bladder because of the stimulation caused by chronic inflammation. Infants with uncorrected exstrophy may have some degree of anal incontinence, although this ordinarily improves over time. Rectal prolapse typically resolves after bladder closure.

GENITAL DEFECTS IN THE MALE

Most patients with bladder exstrophy are male, making evaluation of the genital anatomy an important part of reconstructive planning, regardless of whether the patient is going to have functional closure or urinary diversion. Historically, it was thought that the penis had normal-caliber corporal bodies but appeared foreshortened because of the wide separation of the symphysis pubis, a prominent dorsal chordee, a shortened urethral groove, and abnormal crural attachments to the corpora cavernosa (Fig. 118-6).[127] More recently, Silver et al.[111] found that men with bladder exstrophy have a significantly shorter total and anterior corporal length, demonstrating that phallic shortening is related to both congenital corporal body and skeletal pelvic abnormalities.[111] In fact, the degree of foreshortening, especially if associated with significant dorsal chordee, may be severe enough that the penis and glans are located adjacent to the verumontanum.

In most cases, functional phallic reconstruction can be performed; however, in the rare individual with severe phallic inadequacy, sex conversion may be appropriate. A careful evaluation by an experienced physician working with a multidisciplinary team at the time of birth is critical if sex conversion is being considered.

On inspection, the glans is characteristically flattened and the halves are everted, and the prepuce is located on the ventral surface. The base of the penis and the scrotum are widely separated. The corporal bodies and the autonomic cavernous nerves that normally course along the posterolateral surface of the prostate are displaced laterally in patients with exstrophy.[107] The ejaculatory ducts and vas deferens are normal, as shown by Hanna and Williams,[49] and their entrance into the posterior urethra is usually evident on inspection (Fig. 118-7). Additional rare variants include penile duplication and unilateral hypoplasia of the glans and corpus.

GENITAL DEFECTS IN THE FEMALE

In the female, the clitoris is characteristically bifid, with divergence of the labia, mons, pubis, and clitoral halves (Fig. 118-8). The urethra and vagina are short; the vaginal orifice is almost always displaced anteriorly and is often stenotic. The uterus, fallopian tubes, and ovaries are usually normal except for the occasional case of duplicated vagina and uterus. Because the pelvic floor is deficient in all patients with bladder exstrophy, uterine prolapse is common in females until anterior closure is done.

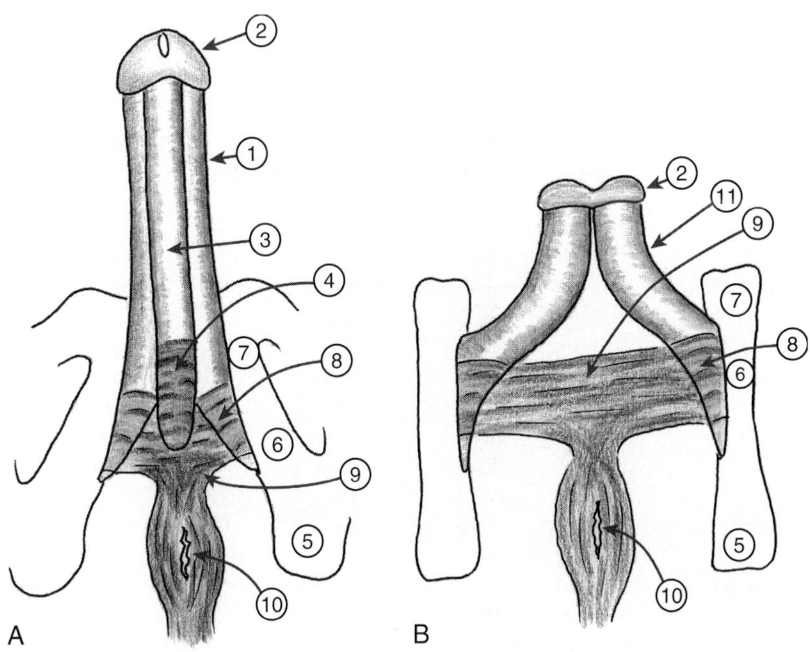

Figure 118-6 Classic exstrophy of the male bladder. Normal male perineum *(A)* and with bladder exstrophy *(B)*. Note the loss of the normal triangular shape of the perineum. 1, corpus cavernosum of the penis; 2, glans penis; 3, corpus spongiosum; 4, bulbospongiosus muscle; 5, ischium; 6, ischiopubic ramus; 7, pubis; 8, ischiocavernosus muscle and crus of penis; 9, urogenital diaphragm; 10, anus and external anal sphincter.

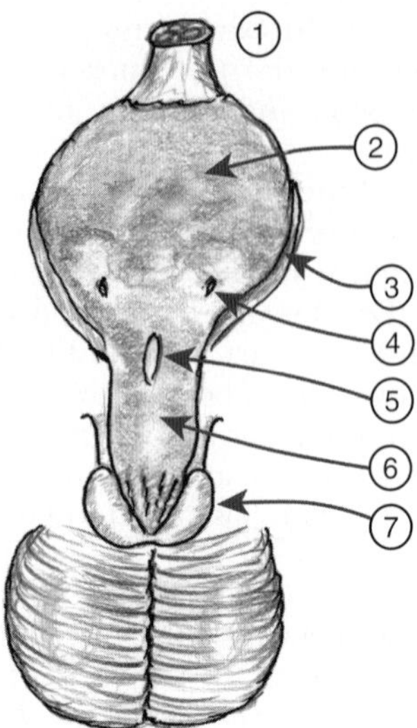

Figure 118–7 Classic exstrophy of the male bladder. The penis is drawn down to expose its dorsal aspect. 1, umbilical cord; 2, bladder mucosa; 3, paraexstrophy tissues; 4, left ureteric orifice; 5, verumontanum; 6, urethral plate; 7, glans penis.

RARE VARIANTS OF BLADDER EXSTROPHY

Covered Exstrophy

Patients with covered exstrophy present with the characteristic diastasis of the symphysis pubis and rectus abdominis muscles. The urethra is tubular and covered, but the bladder may be covered only by skin.[17] There may be a small vesicocutaneous fistula or a small patch of ectopic bladder mucosa without urinary communication. Some authors, such as Turner et al.[122] and Williams,[124] have described patients with split symphysis variants, including diastasis pubis, superior vesical fistula, and duplex exstrophy. These rare variants are more common in females and are associated with the genital anomalies referred to earlier.

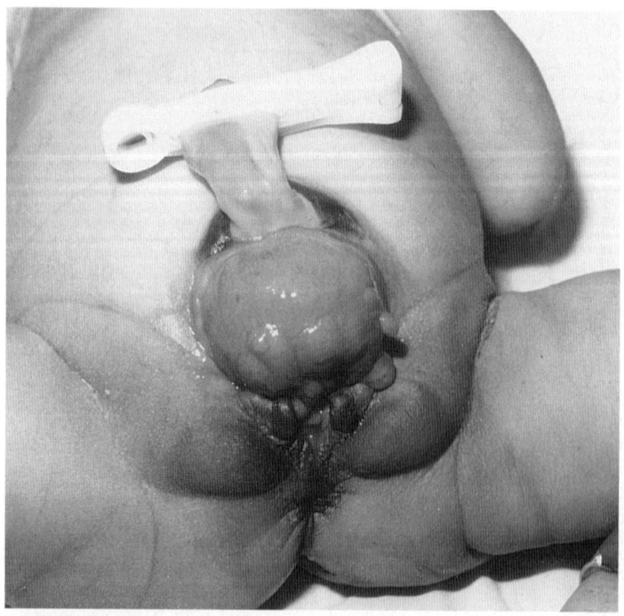

Figure 118–8 Typical appearance of classic bladder exstrophy in a female. The short distance between the anus and the genitourinary tract is the result of posterior displacement of the urogenital diaphragm.

Duplicate Exstrophy

In duplicate exstrophy, patients present with diastasis of the symphysis pubis and a patch of exstrophic bladder just below the umbilicus, with either a normal or a smaller than normal complete bladder underneath it (see Fig. 118-2F). The duplicated extroverted patch of bladder mucosa is dry. In such cases, the penis may be abnormally foreshortened, and there may be epispadiac phallic duplication.

Superior Vesical Fistula

With superior vesical fissure, the usual diastasis of the pubis and recti are present, but the only bladder eventration is below the level of the umbilicus (see Fig. 118-2E). A small opening into the bladder often permits some degree of bladder prolapse on the anterior abdominal wall. This abnormality can be differentiated from a patent urachus because of the musculoskeletal separation that is characteristic of the exstrophy complex.

Pseudoexstrophy

In pseudoexstrophy, some of the findings usually associated with classic exstrophy are present, including a low-lying umbilicus and some degree of separation of the rectus muscles attaching to modestly separated pubic bones. When full, the bladder may bulge outward between the separated lower abdominal wall structures, but the urinary tract is otherwise completely normal.

PRENATAL DIAGNOSIS

Barth et al.,[6] Jaffe et al.,[57] and Mirk et al.[90] have described the prenatal ultrasonographic findings of bladder exstrophy. The bladder is normally evident at 15 weeks' gestation, and it empties every 1 to 3 hours. Thus, if absence of the bladder is suggested in the presence of normal kidneys and amniotic fluid, and a low-set umbilicus is also present, bladder exstrophy is likely. Later in gestation, suspected diastasis of the pubic bones suggests the presence of bladder exstrophy. Gearhart et al.[35] reviewed prenatal ultrasound studies of 25 women who delivered live infants with exstrophy, and they found the following: (1) an absent bladder in 71% of the studies, (2) lower abdominal protrusion in 47%, (3) an anteriorly displaced scrotum with a small phallus in 57% of the male fetuses, (4) a low-set umbilical cord in 29%, and (5) abnormal iliac crest widening in 18%. With an accurate prenatal diagnosis, parents can be counseled, and plans for early postnatal management can be made.

Prenatal diagnosis also allows the mother to be referred to an appropriate tertiary care center before delivery and puts her and the family in touch with health care providers who have knowledge of and experience with the disorder.

DIAGNOSTIC STUDIES

After birth, physical examination usually provides most of the information necessary for planning an early repair. Physical examination allows an estimation of the size of the bladder plate and an evaluation of genital defects. Renal ultrasonography (US) is performed to determine whether hydronephrosis or other upper urinary tract abnormalities exist.

Otherwise, diagnostic evaluation beyond the routine studies (e.g., complete blood count, measurement of serum urea and glucose levels, routine radiography) is reserved for patients in whom associated anomalies of other organ systems are either evident or suspected. In low-birth-weight premature infants, evaluation of pulmonary immaturity is in order. In patients who undergo staged reconstruction of the bladder and lower urinary tract over several years, or in those being followed after primary repair, additional imaging and functional studies, including renal US, voiding cystourethrography (VCUG), and radionuclide and urodynamic studies, are performed.

TREATMENT

There are two general approaches to the management of bladder exstrophy (Fig. 118-9).[5,9,18,40,45,46] The first approach involves functional lower urinary tract reconstruction using modern techniques in a single or staged fashion. The second method involves removal of the exstrophic bladder and replacement with a form of urinary diversion, which is undertaken only when primary reconstructive options are not appropriate or when repeated efforts at functional reconstruction fail. With regard to functional reconstruction, sex conversion becomes a consideration in males who are deemed to have inadequate phallic tissue for a male orientation. Male-to-female sex conversion is now uncommon with the development of new techniques for epispadias repair. The decision to convert a patient's sex must be the result of extensive counseling involving a multidisciplinary review and should be considered only when all other options are deemed unfeasible.

Staged Functional Reconstruction

The modern staged approach to the treatment of bladder exstrophy was pioneered by Jeffs[60] in the 1970s following poor outcomes, including incontinence and renal damage, in patients who had undergone a variety of single-stage repairs.[32,33,67,82,85] Figure 118-9 provides an outline for the general timing of staged functional reconstruction. Stage I is performed at birth to protect the upper urinary tract and promote later continent reconstruction. Stage II is typically undertaken between 6 months and 1 year of age in male patients in the hope of maximizing genital structure and function and increasing outlet resistance to promote bladder growth. Finally, at approximately 4 years of age, a bladder neck repair is done, with the goal of achieving social continence and promoting self-esteem. Figure 118-10 describes the first step for initial bladder closure and urethral reconstruction in the female, and Figure 118-11 shows the complete sequence of stage I in the male.

The current status of pediatric anesthesia and postoperative intensive care has made it possible to perform major surgical procedures successfully in newborn infants. Therefore, the first reconstructive stage in patients with bladder exstrophy is performed in the immediate neonatal period; this is the best time in terms of pliability of the pelvic ring. In addition, reconstruction in the newborn period prevents damage to and scarring of the bladder plate, which inevitably occur if it is left exposed. Finally, because

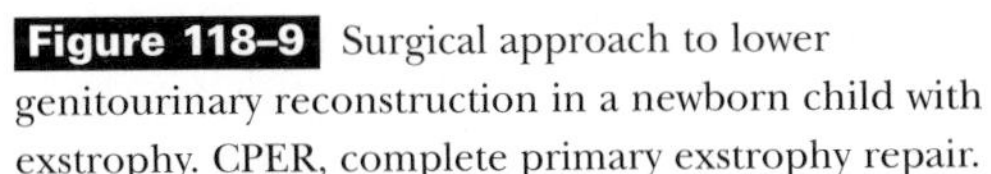

Figure 118-9 Surgical approach to lower genitourinary reconstruction in a newborn child with exstrophy. CPER, complete primary exstrophy repair.

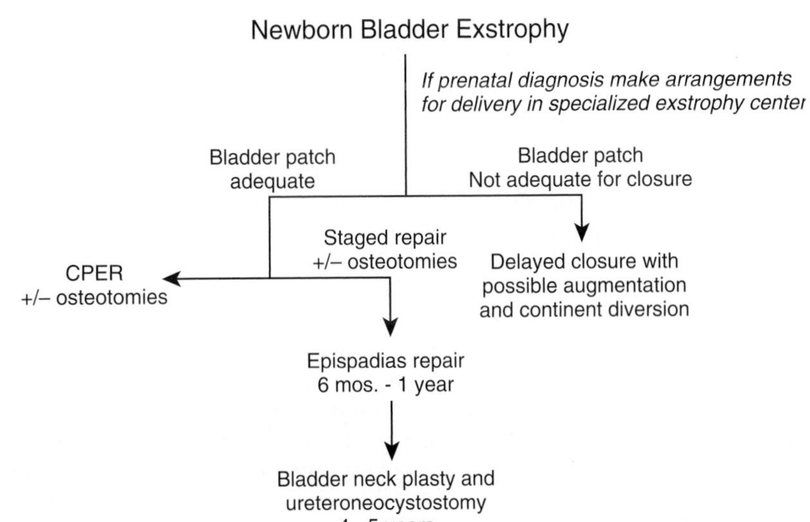

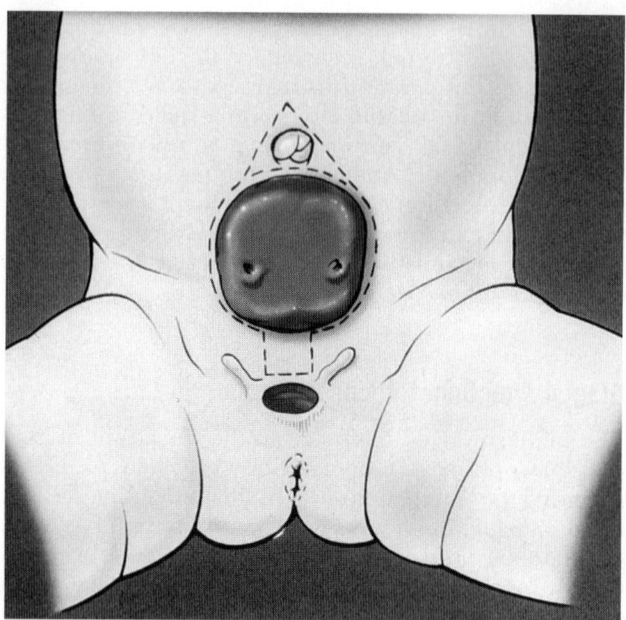

Figure 118–10 Typical findings of classic bladder exstrophy in a female and the incision used for repair.

bacterial colonization of the gastrointestinal and genitourinary tracts is minimal at birth, the potential for serious postoperative infection is lower.

Preoperative preparation involves an assessment of all organ systems to ensure that there are no associated anomalies of physiologic significance. As mentioned earlier, most infants with classic bladder exstrophy do not have such findings. Appropriate measures are taken to avoid trauma to the exposed bladder mucosa, including placement of a soft, damp dressing (preferably Teflon or Silastic sheeting) over the bladder plate to protect it from trauma, and removal of the umbilical clamp and suture of the stump to prevent mechanical damage. Antibiotics are administered preoperatively and continued after surgery. At the time of surgery, the patient should have a wide surgical preparation, including the entire body anteriorly and posteriorly below the level of the nipples so that turning is possible. Full monitoring and good intravenous access are critical, because operations of this nature are lengthy and stressful.

Figure 118-11 demonstrates the technique of initial bladder closure and urethral reconstruction in the male.[78] The most commonly used technique is based on the descriptions by Jeffs et al.[38,40,59-61] and Duckett and Caldamone.[29] This involves converting the exstrophic bladder to an incontinent epispadias.

Traction sutures of 5-0 Prolene are placed in the glans penis, and ureteral catheters are secured in each ureteral orifice (see Fig. 118-11A and G). The incision is made around the periphery of the exstrophic plate, with care taken not to include any abdominal skin. The incision is then extended distally to the verumontanum on both sides of the prostatic urethra, leaving a wide plate of bladder neck and prostatic urethra. The umbilical cord is excised to reduce the risk of wound infection, and an umbilicoplasty is usually performed during or after the initial procedure. In patients in whom urethral length is in question, paraexstrophic flaps are created, as described by Duckett[27] (see Fig. 118-11E). However, it should be mentioned that not all surgeons use such flaps. Gearhart et al.[38,42] reported a 40% complication rate in their experience with paraexstrophy flaps. Urethral stricture, the most common complication, is thought to be related to ischemia of the flaps. Duckett[27] has not reported the same incidence of such problems. One of the advantages of these flaps is that they permit bladder mobilization deep into the pelvis after division of the bladder plate from the penis by lengthening of the urethra.

The bladder must be completely mobilized, with preservation of its blood supply. The corpora cavernosa are dissected off the inferior pubic rami as far as permissible to preserve the neurovascular bundles. The corpora are then approximated carefully in the midline to promote penile elongation. The paraexstrophy flaps are mobilized, extending them along the side of the proximal urethral plate in such a fashion that ischemia is prevented. The flaps are then approximated in the midline and to the base of the bladder with absorbable suture material. The bladder and neourethra are tubularized after exteriorization of ureteral stents and placement of a Malecot suprapubic tube and a small Silastic urethral stent. There is some debate whether ureteral stents predispose patients to dehiscence; we have not found this to be the case and believe that the risk of ureteral obstruction is greater without them. After bladder closure, the pubis is approximated anteriorly to protect the bladder closure and urethral reconstruction from tension and possible disruption. Most surgeons believe that pubic closure promotes healing and subsequent continence. Closure of the pelvic ring is performed with a single nonabsorbable monofilament suture or Teflon tape, with care taken to place the suture material so that the knot and suture are anterior to the newly approximated pubis to avoid erosion into the soft tissue below.

After approximation of the pubic rami in the midline, the newly closed bladder and urethra are further covered by approximation of the rectus fascia and skin, or sometimes with fascial flaps.[99] Approximation of the pubis eliminates or minimizes the need for fascial flaps for closure of the abdominal wall. Pubic approximation without ancillary osteotomy is often possible in the newborn period. However, children older than 3 or 4 days usually require osteotomy, because flexibility of the pelvic ring is usually lost by that time (Fig. 118-12). In this situation, children are placed in Bryant's traction or external fixation for 4 to 6 weeks after surgery.

The technique for initial closure in a female with bladder exstrophy is similar. The bladder is mobilized in the same way as in the male, and similar paraexstrophy flaps are developed. Closure of the bladder and the neourethra is also performed as described earlier. With this technique, a traction suture is placed above the vagina, and the vagina is fully mobilized as a neourethra is created. The vagina is then brought downward to assume a caudal angle of entry. This technical point is important, because leaving the vaginal opening with a ventral orientation will make later reconstruction more difficult.

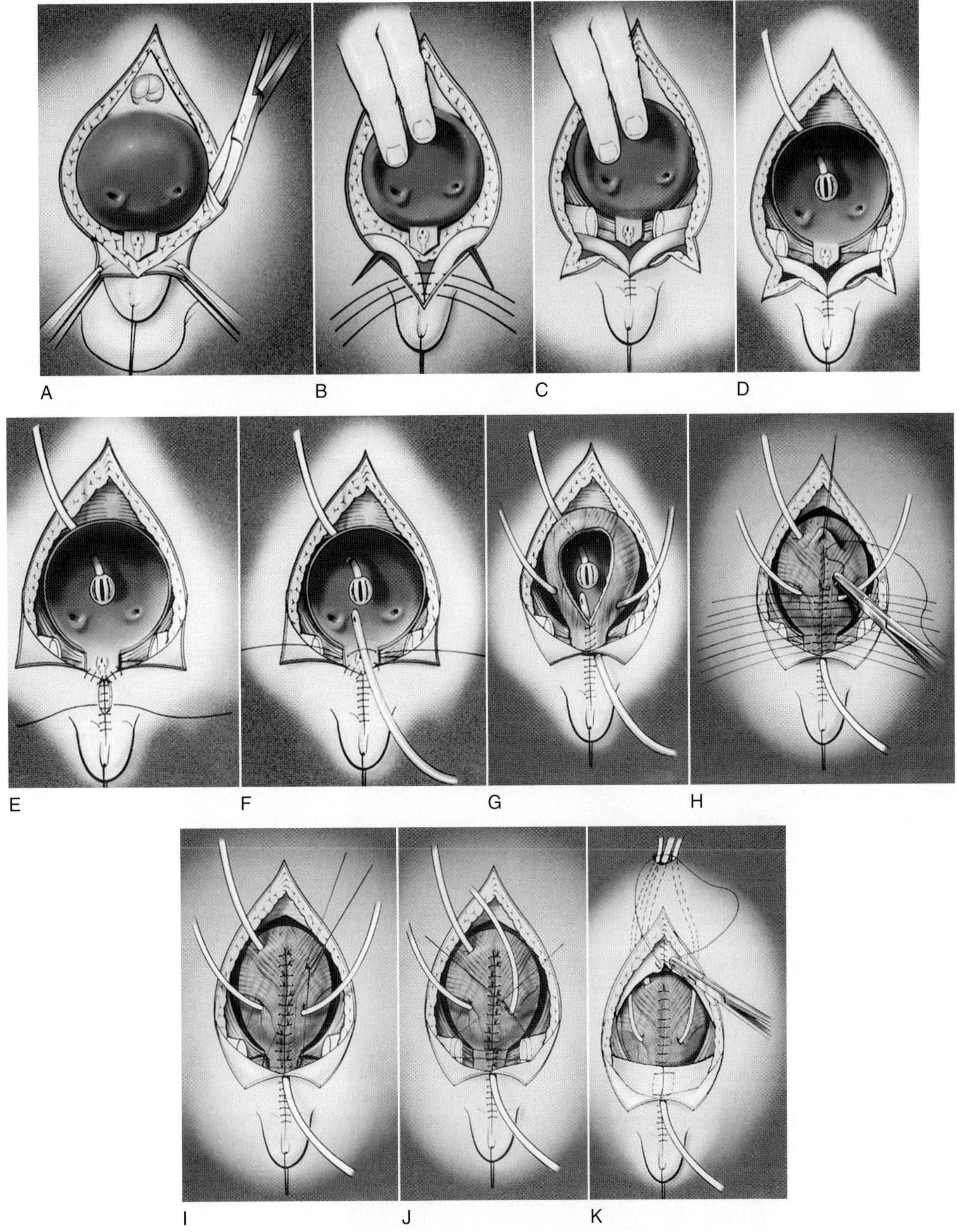

Figure 118–11 Sequence of repair of bladder exstrophy in a male. *A,* Completion of the dissection around the periphery of the bladder and the urethral plate. *B,* Inversion of the bladder plate and approximation of the corpora as a first stage in epispadias repair. Also note the inferior paraexstrophy incisions. *C,* Further closure of the skin over the corpora and their partial freeing from the pubis. *D,* Placement of a suprapubic drainage tube. *E,* Further closure of the skin inferiorly, with approximation to the urethral plate. Creation of the paraexstrophy flaps is now evident. *F,* The urethral plate is prepared for tubularization over a catheter. *G,* The urethral plate is now tubularized, and ureteral catheters are placed bilaterally and brought out on each side of the bladder. The bladder is also in the process of being tubularized. *H,* Completion of tubularization of the bladder and urethra, and location of the various drainage tubes. *I,* After two-layer closure of the bladder and urethral plate, the bladder is reduced into the pelvis and fixed with sutures. *J,* Sutures are placed to encourage approximation of the pubic halves. *K,* Drainage tubes are brought out superiorly, and fascia, subcutaneous tissue, and skin are approximated. Approximation of the pubis helps protect the bladder closure and the abdominal wall closure.

The pelvic closure is protected, and the patient is placed in Bryant's traction.

Follow-up after stage I reconstruction is similar for both males and females. Studies after discharge include determination of residual urine and renal US. Antimicrobial suppression should be continued, because vesicoureteral reflux is present in almost all cases. If the residual urine level is persistently elevated, the urethra should be calibrated to rule out stenosis.

Eventually, most patients require an antireflux procedure to correct the vesicoureteral reflux that is related, at least in part, to the abnormal orientation of the ureters. If excessive residual urine and dilatation of the upper urinary tract continue to be problematic, an antireflux procedure may be necessary in the first year of life. This is unusual, however. In most instances, the bladder gradually increases in size, and an antireflux procedure is not necessary until the child undergoes reconstruction of the bladder neck for subsequent continence. Technically, most surgeons prefer the cross-trigonal or cephalotrigonal ureteral reimplantation technique because it maximizes the potential for urethral lengthening.[14,16]

Although most surgeons believe that approximation of the pelvis anteriorly in the midline is desirable to protect the initial bladder closure, promote subsequent continence, and aid in anatomic placement of the bladder, bladder neck, and urethra in the pelvis, pelvic osteotomy is somewhat controversial (see Fig. 118-12).

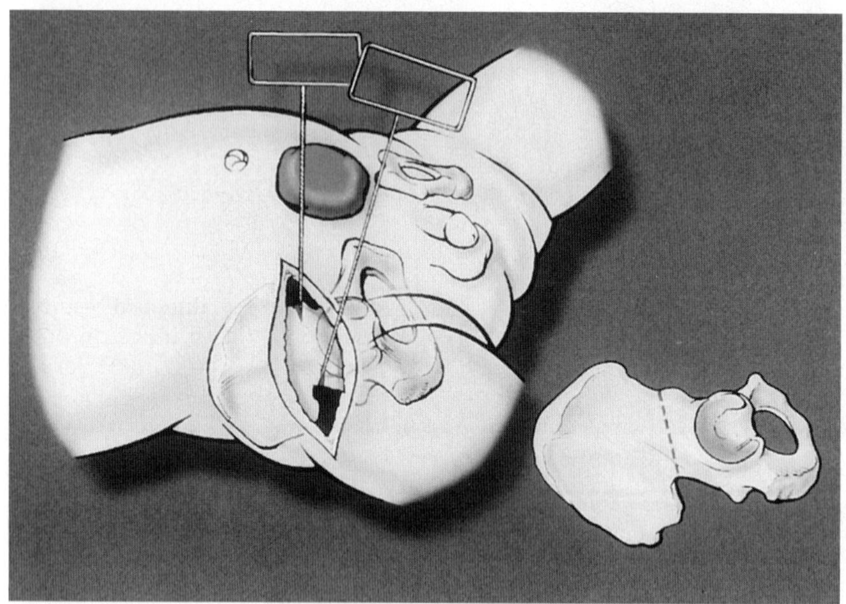

A

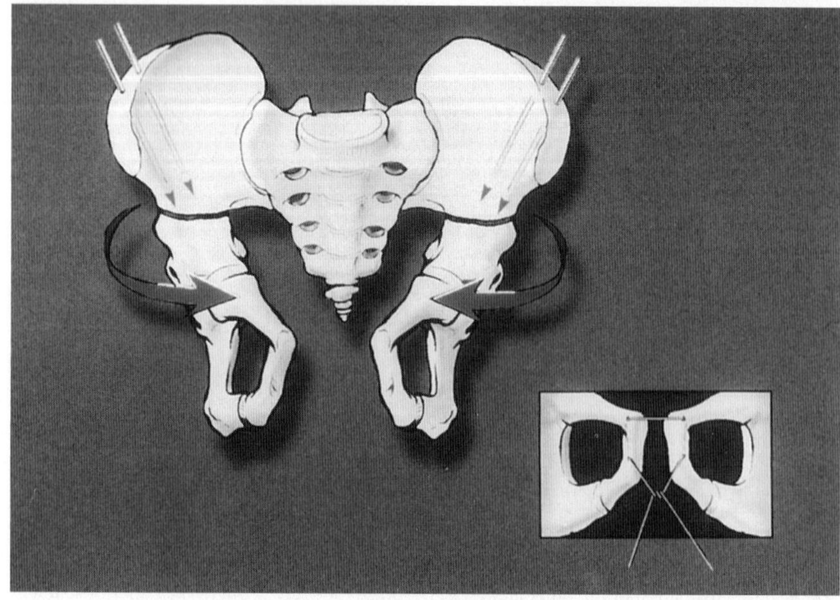

B

Figure 118–12 *A*, The pubis can often be approximated in a newborn because of the natural flexibility at that age. If the pubis cannot be approximated in a newborn or if the procedure is undertaken later, when the pelvis is less flexible, anterior or posterior osteotomies are required. The location of the anterior iliac osteotomy is shown. *B*, External fixator pins are used to hold the pelvis, and the pubic halves are brought together in the midline.

Some, including Marshall and Muecke[82] and Csontai et al.,[24] advocate approximating the pubis without the use of osteotomies. Others use anterior innominate or superior pubic ramus osteotomies, particularly because the latter procedure does not require turning of the patient. Other authors, such as Mollard,[93] favor posterior iliac osteotomy. Kelly[66] mobilizes only the inner layer of the periosteum of the pubic ramus and muscle. Gearhart[34] recommends anterior innominate and vertical iliac osteotomies in children older than 72 hours, in any patient with a nonmalleable pelvis, and in those whose pubic bones are separated 4 cm or greater.

An additional advantage to approximating the pubis in the midline is that it promotes the construction of a longer phallus. Also, it is now known that pelvic closure with or without enabling osteotomy procedures has no long-term effects on locomotion. Kelly,[66] among others, found that the ambulation of patients with uncorrected pelvic separation in childhood is not impaired and that the waddling gait seen in early childhood resolves spontaneously. The only impairment is some degree of restriction of internal rotation of the hips, but this does not appear to affect locomotion or even the ability to run.

In the male, the second stage of repair involves reconstruction of the phallus.[28] This surgery is performed between 6 and 12 months of age. Gearhart and Jeffs[37] showed that in addition to permitting maximal genital reconstruction, epispadias repair and urethroplasty also enhance bladder capacity, presumably as a result of increased outflow resistance. The goals of the various urethral lengthening procedures are to provide adequate patency and allow voiding without stricture, promote continence, and permit easy catheterization.[62,63,74,106] The first stage of the epispadias repair is performed at the initial bladder closure and proximal urethral reconstruction and includes separating the corpora from the pubic rami. This dissection is limited to avoid corporal injury or ischemia. Urethral length may be promoted with the construction of paraexstrophy flaps; at least initially, the dorsal chordee is partly released by division of the urethral plate. Isolated epispadias of the proximal type is usually associated with incontinence. In the case of bladder exstrophy, the first stage of reconstruction converts the defect to an isolated epispadias. Some degree of detachment of the corporal bodies from the pubic attachments is necessary; complete detachment is undesirable, however, because of the risk of penile devascularization. If this occurs, long-term impairment of erectile function may result.

Epispadias Repair

In the repair of epispadias, the goal is to provide adequate phallic length with appropriate dangle and release of the dorsal chordee.[30,50,51] Further, the urethra is reconstructed to allow voiding from the glans penis. Many techniques have been used, but significant advances have recently been made.[1,4,7,10,94] The Cantwell-Ransley technique, as described by Ransley et al.[105] in 1989, permits mobilization of the penile urethra to the ventrum and adequate correction of chordee with a low fistula rate (Fig. 118-13).[65,70] In this procedure, the corporal bodies are completely mobilized to the pubis; the dorsal urethral plate is left intact, having been mobilized from the dorsum and ventrally between the two corporal bodies. If the urethral plate does not tether the phallus after being mobilized, it is left intact. If it foreshortens the phallus and results in persistent chordee, it is divided, and an inner preputial or free graft may be added to the urethra.[25,26,28,123] The urethra is then rolled into a tube, the corporal bodies are incised transversely in the midphallus, and the urethra is transposed ventrally. A cavernocavernostomy is performed above the urethra. This rotates the corpora internally and provides coverage of the newly created urethra. The complication rate for this procedure has markedly decreased compared with earlier procedures, as reported by Gearhart et al.[39,41,43]

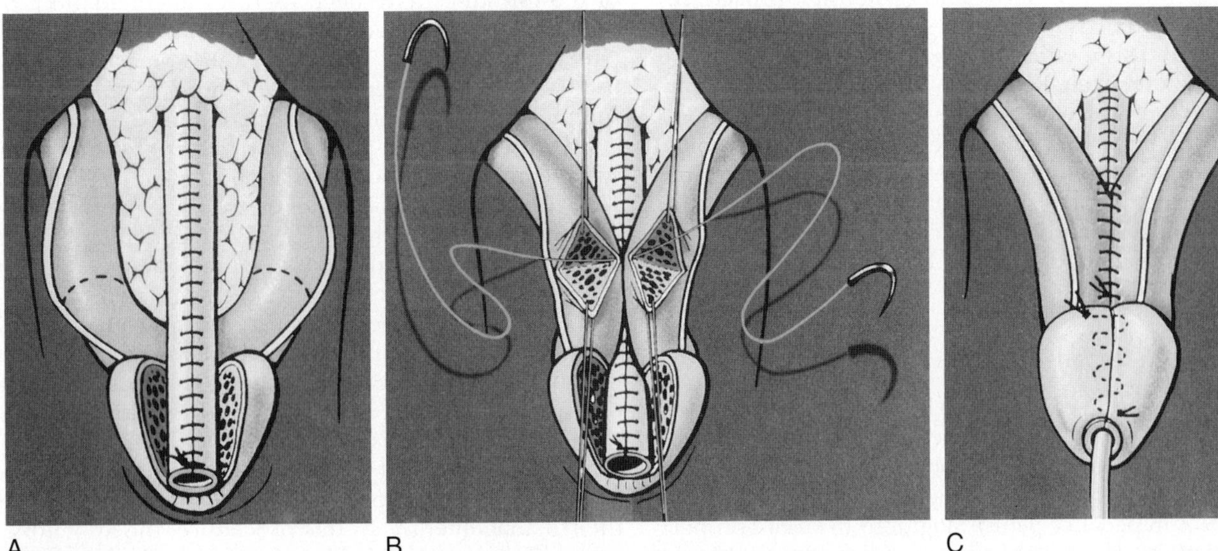

Figure 118-13 *A* to *C*, Steps in the Cantwell-Ransley epispadias repair. This procedure permits further urethral lengthening, approximation of the corpora with preservation of the blood supply, and full coverage of the urethra.

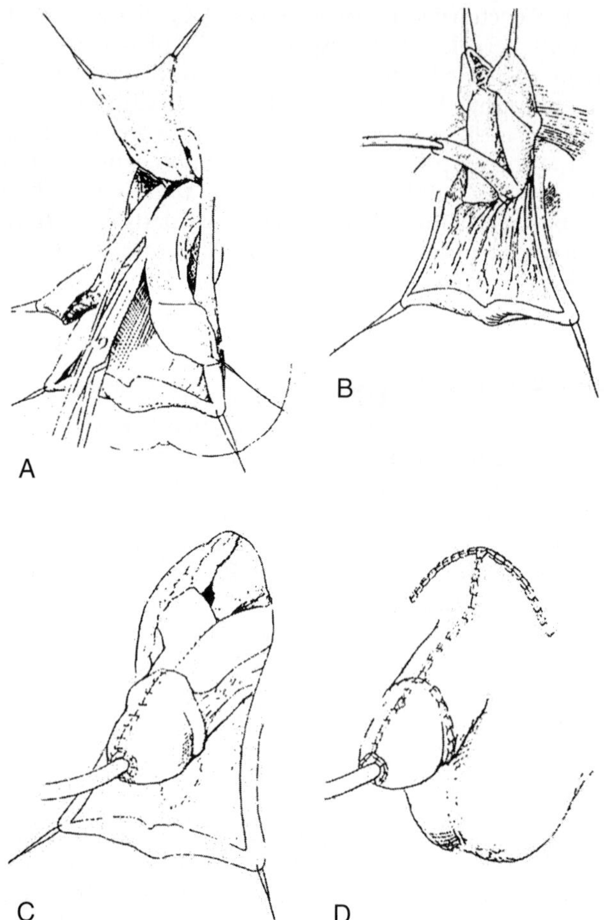

Figure 118–14 Complete penile disassembly technique. *A*, The corporal bodies and the hemiglans are separated. *B*, The urethra is tubularized and moved ventrally. *C*, The corpora are reapproximated dorsally. *D*, Glans closure is performed distally to complete the repair. (Adapted from Mitchell ME, Bagli DK: Complete penile disassembly for epispadias repair: The Mitchell technique. J Urol 1996;155:300.)

The techniques in the Cantwell-Ransley procedure have been further refined, as described by Mitchell and Bagli.[91] With this method, the penis is completely disassembled before repair. Relying on the unique blood supply of the corpora cavernosa and the glans, the three components of the penis (urethral plate, right and left corporal bodies) are separated (Fig. 118-14). This makes the glans and the urethral plate independent and separates the two corporal glanular bodies. Finally, it permits release of the rotation that contributes to dorsal chordee.

Bladder Neck Reconstruction

The final stages of reconstruction in a child with exstrophy involve the construction of a continence mechanism. This is generally undertaken around 4 years of age.[101] In the meantime, the patient is evaluated periodically with renal US or impedance plethysmography to ensure proper drainage of the upper urinary system. It is vital to avoid urinary infection and to ensure adequate urinary drainage without hydronephrosis. Bladder capacity is also measured to help determine the proper timing of reconstruction. Jeffs et al.[61] reported that the bladder capacity must be greater than 60 mL in order to have enough functional capacity after bladder neck reconstruction. Others believe that much larger capacities are necessary and rely on augmentation of the bladder to provide a capacity commensurate with the storage of urine.

Many procedures have been used to reconstruct the bladder neck, but the Young-Dees-Leadbetter technique remains the most common (Fig. 118-15). In this procedure, the ureters are mobilized and reimplanted in a cephalad position in the bladder by either a cross-trigonal or a cephalotrigonal procedure.[15,21] The posterior bladder plate is then marked to be 1.5 to 2 cm wide and 3.5 cm long. The bladder triangles lateral to the posterior bladder strip are denuded of mucosa, and the posterior strip is rolled into a tube. The triangles of the bladder muscle are then mobilized laterally at the new bladder neck and closed over the neourethra in a vest-over-pants repair. This provides a mucosal tube with muscular covering that is entirely intra-abdominal. The bladder is closed at this point if the capacity is adequate, or an intestinal augmentation is performed to improve storage.[84] Finally, the bladder neck reconstruction is enhanced by suturing the bladder neck and urethra to the pubis anteriorly.

After surgery, ureteral stents are left indwelling for approximately 1 week; a Malecot tube is left in place for 3 to 4 weeks. No urethral stent is used. Patients continue to receive antibiotics during this period, and antispasmodic agents are given to decrease bladder spasms. Voiding trials are initiated after the suprapubic tube is clamped; if residual urine levels are low, the suprapubic tube is removed. At the time of surgery, water manometry is performed to test outlet resistance. Resistances greater than 50 cm H_2O are considered necessary for continence.[13,44]

In patients who remain incontinent after bladder neck reconstruction, adequate storage capacity of the bladder must be assured.[102] Eventually, patients with a small capacity will require augmentation to decrease intravesical pressure to an acceptable level for continence. All segments of the intestines have been used for augmentation, but the ileum is preferred in cases of classic exstrophy. In patients with cloacal exstrophy, the stomach has been used successfully when bowel length is in question. Augmentation cystoplasty is discussed in Chapter 117.

In our experience, patients with exstrophy can achieve social continence following bladder neck reconstruction. However, after staged bladder exstrophy repair with bladder neck reconstruction, 72% of our patients who were socially continent and apparently had adequate voiding were found to have clinical problems related to emptying; this was confirmed objectively with urodynamics.[129] Patients with poor emptying and those with augmentation commonly require clean intermittent catheterization, but reconstruction of the urethra in children with exstrophy-epispadias complex is often associated with a markedly tortuous urethra that is difficult to catheterize. The use of the Mitrofanoff procedure has markedly changed their management.[92] In this procedure, the appendix is anastomosed to the bladder in an antirefluxing fashion and brought through the abdominal wall as a continent catheterizable stoma. This procedure markedly improves

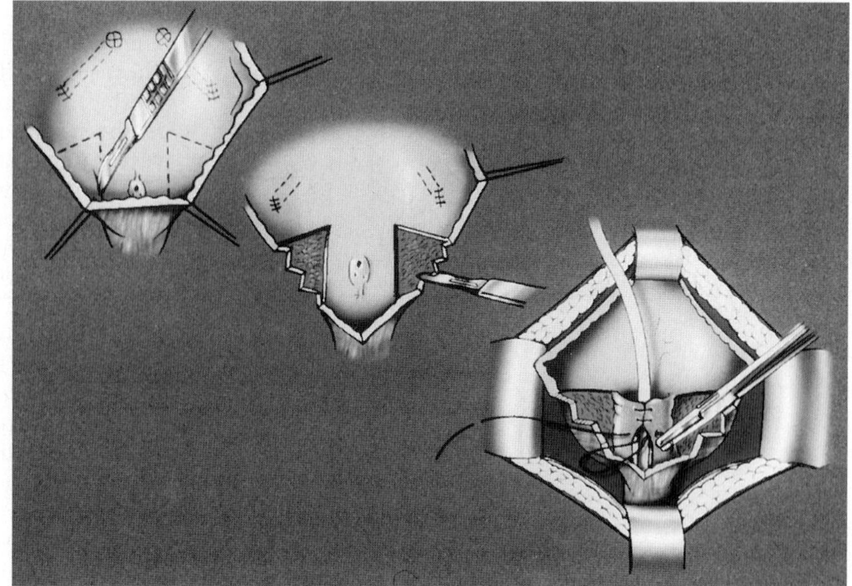

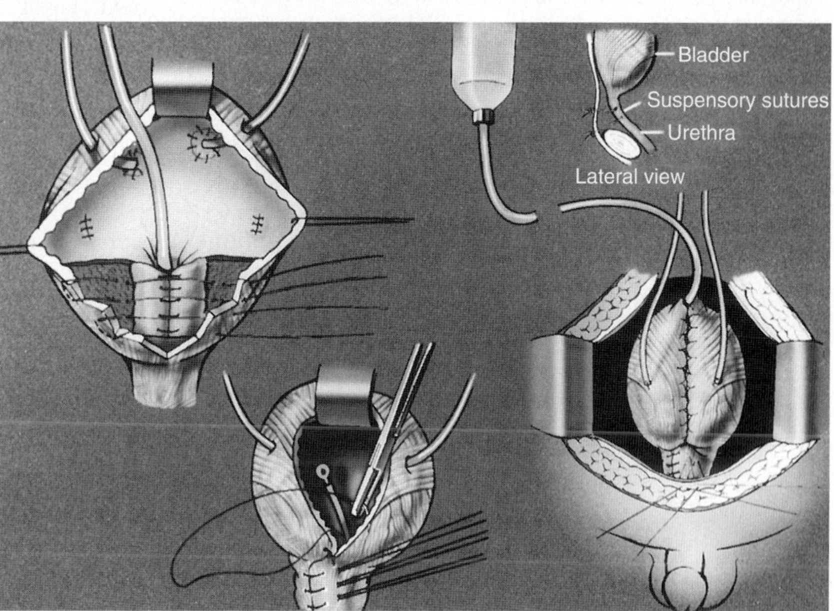

Figure 118-15 *A* and *B*, Principles of the Young-Dees-Leadbetter procedure for bladder exstrophy repair. With this procedure, the ureters are appropriately reimplanted to avoid reflux, and the base of the bladder is revised to further lengthen the urethra and strengthen the bladder neck. This provides sufficient pressure to encourage bladder enlargement without producing urethral obstruction.

the child's ability to empty by catheterization. Mitrofanoff procedures are discussed further in Chapter 117.

The adequacy of urinary control is usually known within 1 year after repair. In patients who remain incontinent, options include augmentation of outlet resistance with bulking agents,[123] repeated Young-Dees-Leadbetter surgery with or without augmentation cystoplasty, artificial urinary sphincter, closure of the bladder neck with a continent catheterizable stoma, and urinary diversion.

Most females do not require genital reconstruction until around age 4 years. At that time, if not accomplished initially, the bifid clitoris can be approximated by denuding the medial aspects of each clitoral half and joining them in the midline. If the vaginal introitus is inappropriately oriented ventrally or is stenotic, vaginoplasty is also necessary. In many females, however, these aspects of genital reconstruction can be accomplished successfully during the first stage of reconstruction. Successive stages may be required for vaginal stenosis or monsplasty.

Kelly Repair

In 1995 Kelly[66] described a variation of the staged repair for patients with bladder exstrophy. This technique involves radical soft tissue mobilization of all sphincter musculature and remodeling of the penis to achieve continence and satisfactory genital function. In males, this is accomplished in three stages; in females, only two stages are needed.

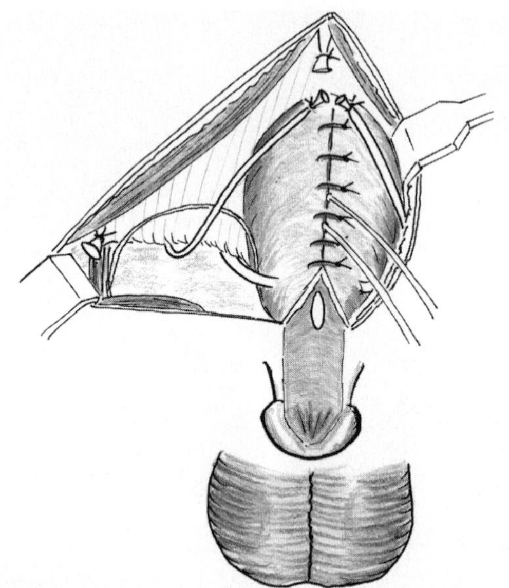

Figure 118–16 Stage I operation using the Kelly technique. The skin incision is deepened to expose the recti and peritoneum. The bladder is closed. A properitoneal right inguinal herniorrhaphy is performed. The ureters are catheterized.

In the newborn period, closure of the dome of the bladder and repair of inguinal hernias are performed (Fig. 118-16). The bladder is closed in the midline, anchored to the posterior aspect of the rectus muscles, and a temporary urinary stoma is fashioned in the midline at the level of the bladder neck. Ureteral catheters are anchored and brought through the urinary stoma, to allow several days of postoperative kidney drainage. The medial margins of the rectus muscles are approximated in the midline down to the suprapubic stoma. Anterior rectus flaps can be used to close the abdomen if there is wide separation of the muscle bellies and pubis. Vertical skin traction on the legs, lifting the buttocks off the bed, can be used for a few days to facilitate postoperative nursing.

The second stage of the Kelly repair is performed at approximately 3 to 6 months of age. The initial incision begins with dissection of the urethral plate off the dorsum of the penis. The penis is then degloved and eventually separated into the two individual corporal bodies and the urethra. The incision is carried superiorly to the abdominal wall. The lower abdominal scar is incised, and both the fascia and the bladder are opened in the midline. Transtrigonal or cephalotrigonal ureteral reimplantation surgery is then performed.

Radical mobilization of all soft tissue structures attached to the medial walls of the pelvis is undertaken next (Fig. 118-17). The periosteum of the medial surface of the anterior pelvic bones is freed, beginning on the anterior surface of the pubic bone and continuing onto the ischiopubic ramus and ischium. The levator ani is then detached from the pubis. This aggressive dissection allows mobilization of the periurethral sphincter, the levator ani muscles, and the crura of the corpora. These muscles and crura are then approximated in the midline without tension or stretching of the pudendal nerves and vessels.

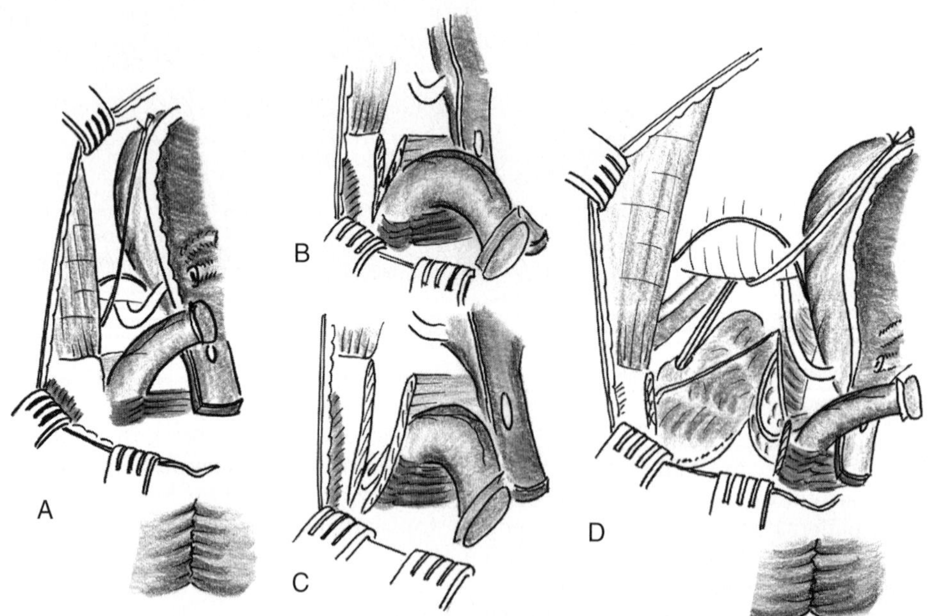

Figure 118–17 Stage II operation using the Kelly technique: soft tissue mobilization. *A,* Extraperitoneal dissection has been extended to expose the superior aspect of the levator ani muscle, and subcutaneous dissection exposes the pubis, ischiopubic ramus, and ischium. *B,* The periosteum of the pubis is incised and reflected with a slice of the underlying pubis to expose and enlarge the space beside the bladder and allow detachment of the levator ani from the lateral pelvic wall. *C,* Reflection of the periosteum and underlying bone and cartilage is continued to the ischium. The pudendal neurovascular bundle is identified on the lateral pelvic wall near the ischial spine by retracting the levator ani and the fat of the ischiorectal fossa medially. The pudendal neurovascular bundle is followed to the anterior pelvis, where it may be damaged inadvertently. *D,* The space between the lateral pelvic wall and the pelvic viscera is opened up, and the pudendal neurovascular bundle is carefully freed back to the ischial spine. Cross-trigonal ureteral reimplantation is also performed, leaving the ureteral catheters in place for 1 week.

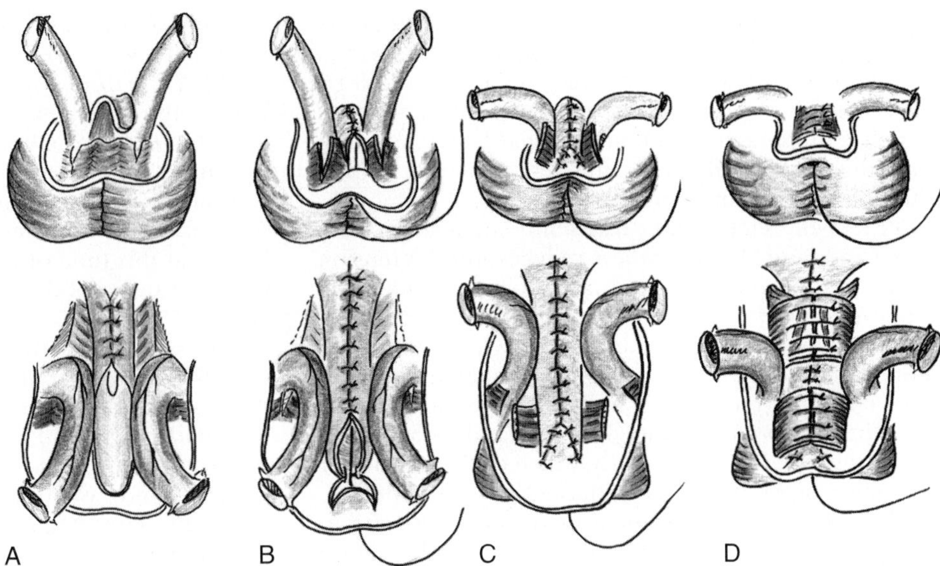

Figure 118–18 Stage II Kelly operation: creation of urethral tube and sphincters. *A,* Tubularization of the urethral plate. *B,* Production of a penoscrotal hypospadiac urethral meatus. The heavy thread passes through the hypospadiac urethral orifice, along the urethral tube, and out through the bladder wall. *C,* Urethral construction is completed. The urogenital diaphragm has been identified and freed and is now ready for incorporation as an "external sphincter" around the distal urethra. *D,* The urogenital diaphragm has been sutured as the "external sphincter." The fibrous and muscular tissue at the neck of the bladder has been mobilized and sutured to surround the bladder neck and proximal posterior urethra.

Because of the abnormal orientation of the bulbocavernosus, ischiocavernosus, transversus perinei, and sphincter urethrae muscles in children with bladder exstrophy, they lie as a continuous muscle in continuity with the external anal sphincter. These muscles are identified by a muscle stimulator and, once found at the posterior end of the corpora, dissected from the crura and wrapped with the external urethral sphincter muscles around the urethra (Fig. 118-18).

The urethra is then tubularized and positioned anterior to the corporal bodies, with a temporary urethrostomy created at the penoscrotal junction. The caudal aspect of the bladder is closed in continuity with the tubularized urethra. The internal and external sphincter muscles, together with the origins of the levator ani muscle, are wrapped around the urethra.

The corporal bodies are sutured together in the midline. Care is taken to ensure appropriate suture placement to prevent the creation of either ventral or dorsal chordee. The glans is then reconstructed distally.

At approximately 3 years of age, the third stage is performed after urinary continence is achieved. Repair of the hypospadiac urethra involves tubularization of the redundant penile shaft skin to form the neourethra. In patients with a paucity of penile shaft skin, a perineal skin flap based on the penoscrotal stoma can be used for coverage.

Female patients undergo surgical correction in a similar fashion using two stages. The first stage is similar in both sexes, but the second stage has several variations. The female urethra is tubularized caudally to the vaginal orifice. The lateral margins of the urethral mucosa are incised and rolled into a tube. The external and internal sphincter musculature, the levator ani, and the periosteum are detached from the pelvic bones and wrapped around the urethra and vagina as a unit. This unit is then placed posteriorly in the pelvis. This positioning allows the urethra and vagina to fall within the short muscle bundles of the wrap. A Y-V plasty incision is made behind the vaginal orifice, extending posteriorly in the midline for at least 1.5 cm. The two halves of the clitoral bodies are then approximated in the midline, bringing together the individual glans of the clitoral bodies.

Use of this technique resulted in a 73% continence rate in 19 patients.[66] Seven patients had normal day and nighttime continence with complete or near-complete emptying, based on direct questioning, physical examination, and VCUG. Seven patients had social continence but needed to void frequently to avoid wetting, and they had occasional urinary leakage. Five patients were incontinent following this staged repair.

Single-Stage Reconstruction

Single-stage CPER was described decades ago; however, early results were disappointing, with high rates of renal deterioration and little success in gaining continence.[85] More recently, Grady and Mitchell's work[46] led to renewed interest in this approach. Application of the total penile disassembly technique with CPER in the newborn period led to an impressive 80% urinary continence rate in their initial series.[46] This single-stage method is thought to be technically easier in newborns than in older children, and it allows earlier functionalization of the bladder by creating outlet resistance in the newborn period, which may result in better continence rates. The bony pelvis is more pliable and more malleable in neonates, and bladder fibrosis, a theoretical reason for the failure of single-stage repair in older children, is not present.[47] Grady and Mitchell postulated that CPER may have several other theoretical advantages, including early bladder cycling and the possibility of normal early postnatal development. These benefits may lead to normal lower urinary function and may obviate the need for subsequent staged procedures.[104]

CPER allows correction of the anterior positional defect in the bladder, bladder neck, and urethra in children with exstrophy. Closure of the bladder defect without positioning the bladder neck and urethra in the posterior pelvis allows this anatomic abnormality to persist. CPER moves the lower urinary tract as a unit posteriorly in the pelvis and positions the proximal urethra within the pelvic diaphragm in a more normal anatomic plane within the surrounding pelvic muscles, which may help in achieving urinary continence.

CPER involves total penile disassembly in male patients, which Grady and Mitchell believe reduces anterior tension on the urethra when it is separated from the underlying corporal bodies.[47] These attachments have the effect of pulling the urethral plate anteriorly, which limits the ability to subsequently position the proximal urethra and bladder neck in the pelvis. Combining epispadias repair with primary bladder closure allows deep division of the intersymphyseal band posteriorly, which enables posterior positioning of the bladder, bladder neck, and urethra.

CPER begins with placement of ureteral catheters in both ureteral orifices. Traction sutures are also placed into each hemiglans. These sutures are placed transversely and then rotated in a parallel vertical orientation as the corporal bodies are freed from the dorsal urethra and corpus spongiosum.

Superiorly, the bladder plate is separated from the adjacent skin in a manner similar to the first stage of a staged approach. The dissection is continued inferiorly along the ventral aspect of the penis in a circumcising manner. The plane of dissection is between Buck's fascia and the overlying tissue on the lateral and ventral aspects of the penis and continues medially over the corporal bodies. Care is taken during lateral dissection and separation of the penile shaft skin and dartos fascia from Buck's fascia to avoid injury to the neurovascular bundles, which are located in a more lateral position on the corpora.[127]

Urethral plate dissection is begun distally and continued proximally to the bladder neck. Next, the penis is disassembled into three components: the right and left corporal bodies, the individual hemiglans, and the urethral plate with the underlying corpus spongiosum. This dissection is believed to be easiest when initiated proximally and ventrally and then extended distally to separate the three structures from one another.[91] The urethra can be tubularized at this time or later in the procedure, during the ventral transfer of the urethra in relation to the corporal bodies.

Following penile disassembly, the pelvic floor is incised by making deep parallel incisions lateral and posterior to the distal posterior urethra, as described by Grady and Mitchell[46] (Fig. 118-19). Alternatively, the incision can be made in a single, midline fashion through the intersymphyseal band, as preferred by our group at Vanderbilt Children's Hospital. Adequate dissection and division of the intersymphyseal bands and release from the surrounding structures allow posterior positioning of the bladder, bladder neck, and posterior urethra in the pelvis.

Closure of the bladder and urethra is typically performed following dissection and incision of the pelvic floor (Fig. 118-20). We typically close the bladder in two layers, followed by secure placement of both a suprapubic tube and ureteral catheters. The urethra is tubularized in a two-layer fashion, if not done earlier, and a urethral stent is secured in place.

The bladder, bladder neck, and proximal urethra are then moved into the deep pelvis. The symphysis is closed without undue tension using several figure-of-eight PDS sutures placed anterior to the symphysis. Following posterior placement of the bladder and symphysis reapproximation, viability of the corporal bodies is assessed.

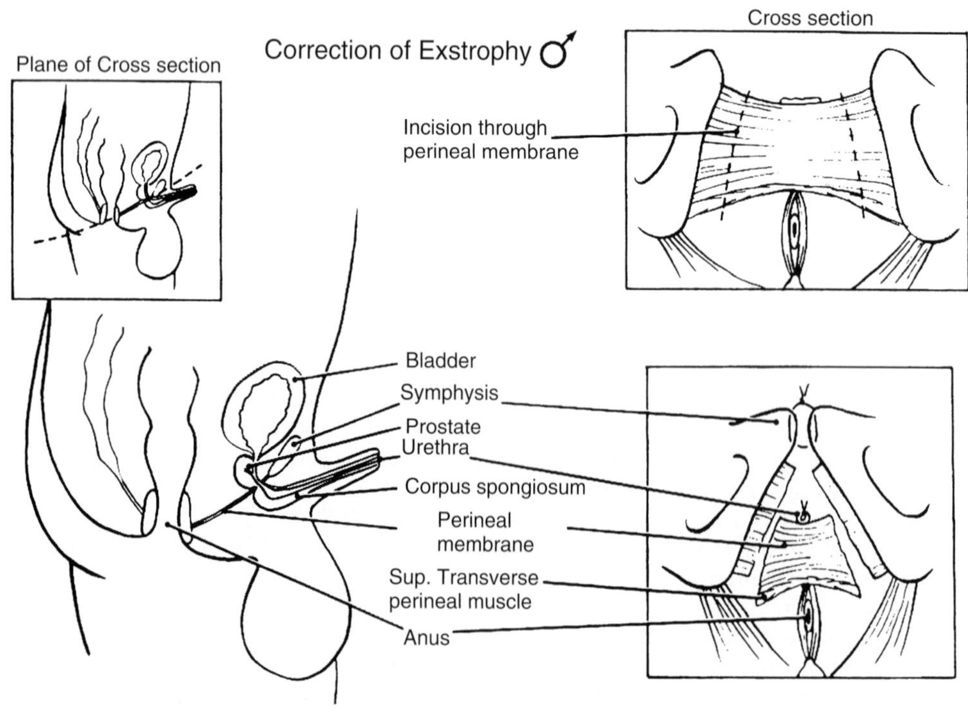

Figure 118–19 Pelvic view of male exstrophy repair. Aggressive dissection along each side of the urethra and division of the intersymphyseal band allow posterior positioning of the bladder in the pelvis. (Adapted from Grady RW, Mitchell ME: Complete primary repair of exstrophy. J Urol 1999;162:1416.)

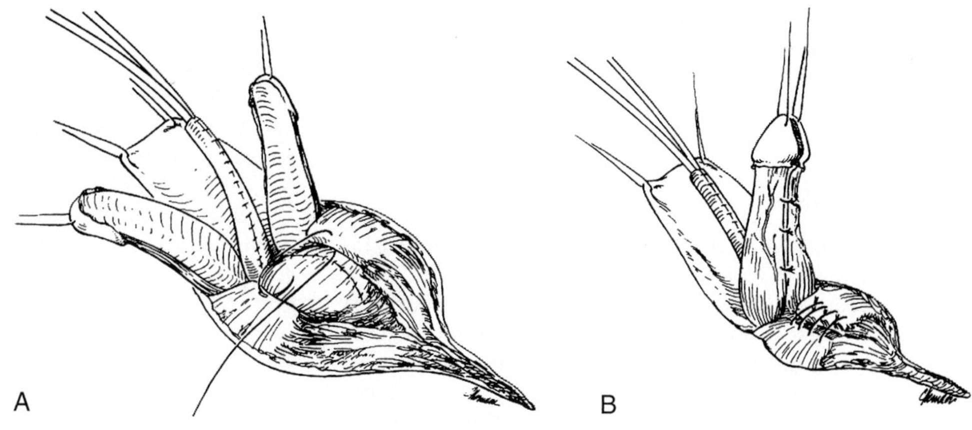

Figure 118–20 *A*, Closure of the urethral plate and bladder as a continuous unit. *B*, Placement of the urethra ventral to the corporal bodies by positioning the bladder, bladder neck, and urethra posteriorly in the pelvis. (Adapted from Grady RW, Mitchell ME: Complete primary repair of exstrophy. J Urol 1999;162:1417.)

Any hint of compromise to the vascularity of the corporal bodies necessitates takedown of the symphyseal closure and consideration of formal osteotomies.

The rectus fascia is then approximated. The urethra is transferred to the ventrum of the penis. The corporal bodies are rotated, with their stay sutures ultimately lying vertically, and reapproximated with interrupted sutures. The urethra is secured to the ventral aspect of the two corporal bodies. The glans is configured similarly to hypospadias surgery. Occasionally, the urethra lacks sufficient length to reach the glans. In this situation, the child is left with a hypospadiac urethra that will need correction in the future. Paraexstrophic flaps are not appropriate for urethral lengthening in males undergoing CPER. Penile shaft coverage is achieved using ventral rotational penile skin flaps.

Following surgery, the patient is immobilized using any of the available methods to decrease lateral stress after closure. We typically use Bryant's traction for 2 to 3 weeks. Additionally, low-dose suppressive antibiotics are administered because of the high incidence of postoperative vesicoureteral reflux.

CPER has also been used successfully in female patients with exstrophy-epispadias variants. Our group recently reported results in six patients using this technique.[2] The bladder neck and urethra were aggressively mobilized from the vagina, which allowed distal placement of the vagina and cephalad positioning of the bladder. The urethra was found to be halved on either side of the vagina in children with exstrophy variants, and paraexstrophic flaps were used for urethral lengthening in the opposite direction as classically described. The urethra was lengthened by 30 mm, and the bladder neck was then positioned with a loose pubovaginal sling. In a similar fashion, two girls with epispadias were reconstructed after mobilizing the urethra and then lengthening it with a similar flap. All children in this series had dry intervals without continuous leakage, and the one child of toilet-training age had occasional wetting but could remain dry for 2-hour intervals. The two patients with epispadias were continent day and night.

Although early continence rates following CPER were encouraging, a recent review was less optimistic. Grady et al.,[48] reporting on the long-term follow-up of their CPER patients, noted that although 77% were continent, more than 70% required a secondary bladder neck repair to achieve continence. Their group now incorporates tailoring of the bladder neck and proximal urethra at the time of primary closure in the hope of increasing urinary continence. Also, several patients in this follow-up series required intermittent catheterization through a Mitrofanoff procedure to empty efficiently. Additionally, 50% of the patients in their initial series ultimately had reflux surgery performed for breakthrough urinary tract infections.[46] Residual hypospadias following CPER was described by Grady and Mitchell[46] in their first series. More recently, El-Sherbiny et al.[31] reported a 59% incidence of hypospadias after CPER in neonates and in children after failed closures. These findings prompted several modifications to the CPER technique, including more radical posterior placement of the proximal urethra and different methods of incising the pelvic floor in the hope of achieving better continence rates.

Urinary Diversion

Urinary diversion is reserved for patients with inadequate bladder plates at primary closure or when all attempts at reconstruction fail. Advocates of urinary diversion argue that poor continence rates in some series and inadequate bladder emptying raise questions about the feasibility of bladder reconstruction. Although these questions persist, only 10% to 20% of patients who are completely incontinent after staged reconstruction require urinary diversion.[108]

Historically, the first approach to diversion was ureterosigmoidostomy, which was well accepted because it did not involve an abdominal stoma. However, intermittent pyelonephritis, hyperchloremic acidosis, ureteral obstruction, rectal incontinence, and adenocarcinoma at the ureterocolic anastomosis have been reported,[28,112,113,131] necessitating lifelong surveillance. Variations of this procedure have been devised, and both primary and staged procedures have been used, including continent diversion. Other diversionary procedures are described in Chapter 115. Impaired renal function is more common in patients who undergo diversion than in those who have staged repair.[54]

COMPLICATIONS

The initial closure of the bladder is associated with the most devastating complication, bladder dehiscence.[22,98] Wound infection has been noted in up to 42% of patients whose bladders subsequently dehisce.[79] Other factors associated with dehiscence include abdominal distention associated with untreated ileus, bladder prolapse, and loss of urethral and suprapubic catheters within 6 days of closure, leading to maceration of the perineum and subsequent infection and dehiscence.[14,55] Jeffs et al.[61] also found that dehiscence was related to catheters being left in the urethra after closure.

Management of the dehiscent bladder remains difficult. Options include (1) diversion, (2) reclosure of the bladder as a urethral tube and diversion of the urine until subsequent augmentation, and (3) leaving the bladder extruded and reclosing it in approximately 4 to 6 months. Anterior osteotomy with external fixation, as described by Sponseller et al.,[115] has been instrumental in our hands in producing successful reclosure. The external fixator immobilizes the pelvic ring during the healing phase (4 to 6 weeks) and is essential to success. We have reclosed the bladders of four patients with dehiscence, none of which has reopened.

In patients who do not gain adequate capacity even after epispadias repair, augmentation cystoplasty remains the most viable treatment option. This can be performed at the time of bladder neck reconstruction and urethral reimplantation or even after failed bladder neck reconstruction to provide adequate storage capacity. The need for bladder augmentation following functional bladder reconstruction as a means of gaining urinary continence may be significant. The group at Indiana[110] recently noted that 69% of their patients with exstrophy required bladder augmentation in addition to bladder neck repair to gain continence.

Failed bladder neck reconstruction does result in urinary incontinence. Continence is defined as having a 3-hour dry interval and is usually achieved within 1 year after reconstruction. Options for treatment have been discussed elsewhere in this chapter.

The most common complication after epispadias repair is urethrocutaneous fistula, which may occur in 35% to 50% of cases. Modern techniques, such as the Cantwell-Ransley and Mitchell techniques, have lower rates of fistula formation.[41,43] In addition, male patients continue to have problems with decreased penile length and residual chordee. Older children may benefit from further mobilization of the corpora from the pubic ramus. The use of rhomboid and other flaps, as described by Kramer and Jackson[69] and Monfort et al.,[94] allows further mobilization with better exposure.

Chordee correction may also require additional procedures.[53,71] Dermal grafts and urethral lengthening procedures may be necessary to lengthen the corpora and the urethral plate.[51,122] Koff and Eakins[68] described corporal rotation techniques to direct the phallus in a more downward direction. The newer techniques of Ransley[104,105] and Mitchell[91] have the potential to address these anatomic issues at the initial stage of epispadias repair and decrease the likelihood of later problems.

Advances in the care of patients with exstrophy have increased their longevity and brought to light additional complications unique to adult patients who have undergone staged or primary bladder reconstruction. In particular, the occurrence of adenocarcinoma is troublesome.[128] The incidence of adenocarcinoma of the bladder in patients with bladder exstrophy is approximately 250 times that in the normal population.[64] This is probably the result of chronic inflammation, infection, and metaplasia related to exteriorization of the bladder plate. Adenocarcinoma may also develop as a result of augmentation cystoplasty, in which gastrointestinal mucosa has long-term contact with urine.[36] It is uncertain whether the risk for cancer is diminished by successful bladder closure; only long-term follow-up will determine this. Other types of tumors have been encountered in patients with bladder exstrophy, including squamous cell carcinoma and rhabdomyosarcoma.

Fertility is also an issue after genital reconstruction in both male and female patients with bladder exstrophy.[72] Shapiro et al.[109] surveyed 2500 patients with exstrophy and epispadias and identified 38 men who had fathered children and 131 women who had borne offspring. This study shows that it is possible for men to father children and for women to conceive, but the success rate is much lower than normal. Undoubtedly, the diminished fertility rate in males is related to injury to the verumontanum during initial closure and retrograde ejaculation. Libido in patients with exstrophy is high, as reported by Woodhouse et al.,[126] and the erectile mechanism seems to be intact in most children after epispadias repair.[127]

Numerous cases of successful pregnancy have been reported after exstrophy closure. Clemetson's[19] 1958 review described 45 women with bladder exstrophy who successfully delivered 49 offspring. A 1986 study by Burbige et al.[11] revealed 14 pregnancies in 11 women; there were nine normal deliveries, three spontaneous abortions, and two elective abortions. Uterine prolapse was the most common complication, occurring in 7 of the 11 patients. Spontaneous vaginal deliveries have been experienced by women after previous urinary diversion, but cesarean sections were performed in women who had undergone functional bladder closure to eliminate stress on the pelvic floor and avoid traumatic injury to the sphincteric mechanism.[73]

BLADDER EXSTROPHY: SUMMARY

In most patients with bladder exstrophy, reconstruction is possible. Hollowell and Ransley,[52] Ransley et al.,[105] Lepor and Jeffs,[77] and Toguri et al.[120] reported an 80% continence rate, and Mesrobian et al.[86,87] reported a 74% long-term continence rate. Our patients have achieved an 80% continence rate following lower urinary tract reconstruction. The current trend is clearly toward augmentation in patients who do not have adequate bladder capacity or in whom continence procedures involving simple closure and bladder neck reconstruction fail. However, it must be emphasized that most patients require long-term follow-up and frequent operative intervention to achieve continence. Long-term continence outcomes can no doubt be further improved.

As with any situation that involves multiple reconstructive procedures performed over many years, especially in the formative years of life and when genital orientation is a significant factor, social and psychological adjustment is a major issue. The approach to surgical reconstruction must consider these issues. It appears that 80% of patients are well adjusted, and it is hoped that these results can be improved in the future.

CLOACAL EXSTROPHY

(James A. O'Neill, Jr.)

History of Cloacal Exstrophy

Cloacal exstrophy has been referred to in the literature as exstrophy of the cloaca, exstrophia splanchnica, and vesicointestinal fissure. Littre reported the first case in 1709, followed by Meckel in 1812; by 1900, von Recklinghausen and Schwalbe had reported series of cases.[163,173] In 1900 Steinbüchel[172] described the first partial surgical repair of cloacal exstrophy in a neonate, but the patient died at age 5 days. The first successful repair with survival was reported in 1960 by Rickham,[163] who recommended that total correction be done in stages. However, most considered surgical reconstruction of cloacal exstrophy futile because of the up to 90% mortality related to prematurity, short-bowel syndrome, sepsis, and renal and central nervous system deficits. A combination of the primitive status of reconstructive procedures for this anomaly and the deficiencies in perioperative care throughout multiple complicated surgical stages resulted in very few survivors and poor results in those who did survive. In 1979 Welch[173] reported a 50% mortality at Boston Children's Hospital. However, owing to numerous significant improvements in care and innovative approaches to reconstruction, the survival rate is now greater than 90%, and efforts are being directed toward improving the quality of life of these patients.

Incidence

Cloacal exstrophy is rare, with an incidence of approximately 1 in 200,000 to 400,000 live births, according to a number of reports. Although some studies indicate that the male-to-female ratio of occurrence is 2:1, other reviews (including this author's) suggest an approximately equal incidence. The overall incidence is probably higher than the figures just cited if one considers prenatally diagnosed cases that result in fetal loss. Of the total number of bladder exstrophy anomalies, 10% are cloacal exstrophy variants, including all the malformations associated with separation of the symphysis pubis.[161]

Embryology

The current understanding of the embryology of the bladder exstrophy complex is described in the main section of this chapter. Various studies of the many forms of exstrophy, such as those of Keppler-Noreuil[151] and Evans and Chudley,[139] provide information expressed in modern morphogenetic terms. These studies, including an extensive review by Oostra et al.,[160] indicate that cloacal exstrophy is categorized as a primary field defect midline anomaly rather than a polytopic field defect. The variable presentations of the exstrophy complex are thought to be related to differences in the timing and extent of mesenchymal ingrowth and cloacal membrane rupture. Such a developmental field defect suggests an etiologic role for homeobox genes, such as *HLXB9*, with mutations resulting in anorectal and spinal abnormalities.[151] The study by Keppler-Noreuil[151] analyzing the OEIS complex (omphalocele–exstrophy–imperforate anus–spinal defects) suggests environmental as well as genetic causes. In the same fashion, Evans and Chudley[139] postulate that the disorder is related to misexpression of one or more distal *HOX* genes, potentially 10 or 11, leading to abnormal induction and proliferation of caudal mesenchyma.

It appears that these events occur somewhere between the fourth and eighth weeks of fetal development. It is thought that when the urorectal septum descends to the level of the cloacal membrane and the membrane ruptures, classic bladder exstrophy results; if the urorectal septum has not descended sufficiently, a strip of intestine may be situated between the two bladder halves. However, Lakshmanan et al.,[152] among others, have questioned the early formation theory; using prenatal ultrasound data, they demonstrated persistence of the cloacal membrane until at least 18 weeks' gestation. Bruch et al.[135] suggested that cloacal exstrophy does not represent an arrest in development but rather abnormal embryogenesis. Both Lakshmanan and Bruch have reported cases of cloacal exstrophy in dizygotic twins, but reports of monozygotic twins indicate that both twins have cloacal exstrophy in only about half the cases. Smith et al.[167] reported cloacal exstrophy in nontwin siblings as well.

Early occurrence is supported by the fact that patients with cloacal exstrophy have many associated anomalies; the incidence of such anomalies is much higher in patients with cloacal exstrophy than in those with classic exstrophy.[136,149,156,167] Intestinal abnormalities include cecal exstrophy, imperforate anus, a blind-ending hindgut, and a foreshortened length of midgut that results in a predisposition to malabsorption and failure to thrive. Omphalocele occurs in most instances. Spinal abnormalities are very common and include sacral and other vertebral anomalies, myelomeningocele, tethered cord, and deficiencies in the pelvic floor musculature. Renal anomalies, such as renal agenesis, fusion anomalies, and ectopia, are also common. Males generally have diminutive, inadequate penile structures; females frequently have vaginal duplication, widely split clitoral halves, and, on occasion, vaginal agenesis or atresia.

Anatomic Variants

As mentioned earlier, the various forms of cloacal exstrophy are thought to be related to different levels of descent of the urorectal septum, as described by Manzoni et al.[156] The hemibladders are usually situated on either side of a centrally placed, exstrophied strip of intestine, usually the cecum. However, the hemibladders may be confluent either superior or inferior to the intestinal patch. The bladder may be covered in whole or on only one side. I have seen two cases of covered cloacal exstrophy in which the external appearance was similar to that of covered bladder exstrophy, but internally the posterior bladder was composed of ileocecal tissue. The appearance of the genitalia varies as well. The penis or clitoris may be widely split, united, or even buried within a partially covered bladder.[165] The uterus or vagina may be duplicated in as many as two thirds of affected females, and vaginal agenesis may be seen in up to one third. Inguinal hernias are the rule, as are undescended testes in males.

Skeletal anomalies, including congenital dislocation of the hips, talipes equinovarus, and various limb deficiencies, are common, occurring in up to 50% of patients. Sponseller et al.[169] described the various abnormalities of pelvic anatomy in the exstrophy complex, but the common feature is a split symphysis pubis.

The typical appearance of the exstrophied intestine is shown in Figure 118-21. There may be only a single opening with multiple apertures, or multiple apertures may be evident with a proximal orifice superiorly and a distal bowel orifice inferiorly. Either one or two appendiceal orifices, with duplication of the appendix, are present half the time. Although malabsorption related to foreshortened small bowel length has been noted, it has also been reported in patients with normal small bowel length. Associated intestinal anomalies include malrotation, duplication, intestinal atresia, and Meckel's diverticulum.

Various cardiovascular and pulmonary anomalies, including cyanotic and acyanotic forms of congenital heart disease and double aortic arch, have been reported, but these are relatively uncommon. In a series of patients reported by Howell et al.[148] and Davidoff et al.,[138] myelomeningocele occurred in 50% of patients. The majority of cases were lumbar in location, but one sacral and one thoracic myelomeningocele were encountered. Others have reported similar findings. In cases of severe spinal dysraphism, some recommend withholding treatment.

Prenatal Diagnosis

Prenatal diagnosis of cloacal exstrophy is achievable with US. In a review by Austin et al.,[132] a correct diagnosis of cloacal exstrophy was made by US alone in 19 of 22 cases studied. The absence of bladder filling, a large midline

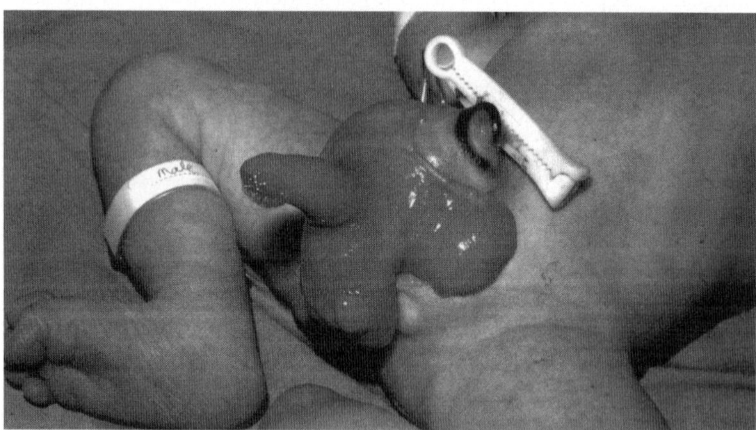

A

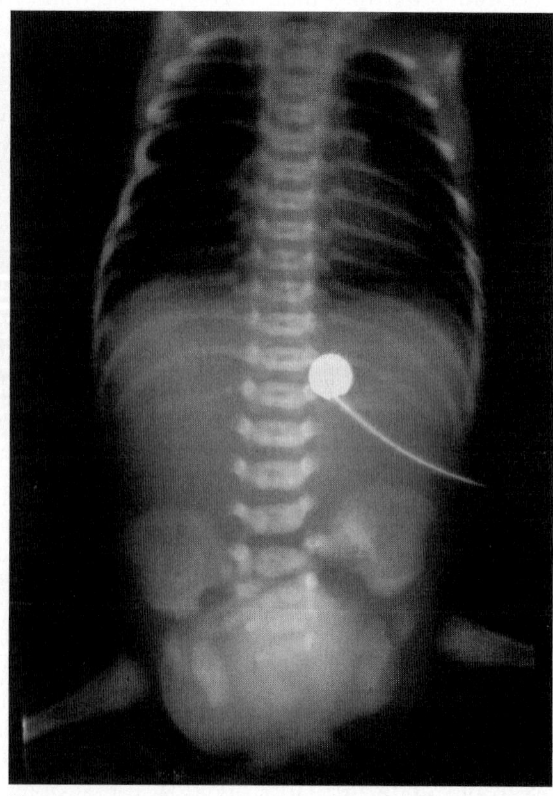

B

Figure 118–21 *A*, Classic appearance of cloacal exstrophy in a female newborn. There are split bladder halves and a centrally placed island of exstrophied cecum with two prolapsed lumens, one for the appendix and the other for the terminal ileum. The centrally placed intestine was tubularized and exteriorized on the left side of the abdomen as a colostomy, and the appendix was preserved. The two lateral bladder halves were approximated in the midline, turned in in a tubular fashion, and placed in the pelvis, approximating the pubic rami in the midline and completely closing the abdominal wall. At a second stage, a urethra was constructed at the time of epispadias repair, and the double vagina was reconstructed as one. *B*, Plain radiograph of the same patient demonstrates the soft tissue density of the exstrophied bladder and intestine, as well as the widely split pubic rami.

anterior abdominal wall defect, and associated vertebral abnormalities were considered characteristic findings. Additionally, lower extremity abnormalities, renal anomalies related to number and position, hydronephrosis, hydrocephalus, and pubic diastasis were noted. Recent improvements in prenatal maternal and fetal magnetic resonance imaging (MRI) have enhanced diagnostic accuracy. Although fetoscopy was used in the past to diagnose cloacal exstrophy, maternal and fetal MRI has obviated the need for such invasive studies. An additional advantage of accurate prenatal diagnosis is related to the definition of gender. Data obtained from prenatal US or MRI, supplemented by karyotyping by amniocentesis, allow a greater opportunity to discuss gender assignment with the parents.

It is beyond the scope of this chapter to discuss in utero surgical management of cloacal exstrophy, but it is being investigated in laboratory studies. Thus far, only the spina bifida part of the exstrophy complex has been addressed prenatally.

Treatment

Infants determined to have cloacal exstrophy prenatally are best delivered at a center that concentrates on high-risk pregnancies and sophisticated management of neonatal anomalies. At birth, few diagnostic studies are required because of the accuracy of the information provided by prenatal studies. In all instances, the physiologic condition of the newborn should be stabilized. These infants are best approached in a multidisciplinary fashion, with coordination through a single surgeon. The initial evaluation should include neonatologists, because many of these infants are either premature or small for gestational age, or both. Considerations related to respiratory distress syndrome, neonatal sepsis, necrotizing enterocolitis, and other complications of prematurity and their treatment must be integrated into the treatment plan. If delayed primary surgery is necessary, the omphalocele sac must be protected. Antibiotic prophylaxis should be administered because of the frequency of obstruction of the urinary tract. The general outline for total or staged reconstruction is provided in Figure 118-22.

In general, there are two approaches to the correction of cloacal exstrophy. The traditional approach of staged correction has been thoroughly described by Gearhart and Jeffs.[141,143] Initial total repair has been described by Howell et al.,[148] Zderic et al.,[174] Hendren,[147] and Mitchell and Plaire.[159] It has been my preference over the last 20 years to achieve initial total repair whenever possible in the first 2 to 3 days of life by joint pediatric surgery and pediatric urology teams. However, despite this preference for maximal reconstruction at birth, this is not always possible in premature infants with large omphaloceles containing liver. Any infant determined prenatally to have possible obstructive uropathy or other renal anomalies requires special attention. To the extent that sex assignment can be accomplished at birth, this should be done. This issue is discussed further in a later section.

An overall treatment plan for patients with cloacal exstrophy should be worked out in a multidisciplinary manner as soon as possible after birth, with consideration of all issues related to the genitourinary tract, gastrointestinal tract, abdominal wall, sex assignment, and management of any associated anomalies, including

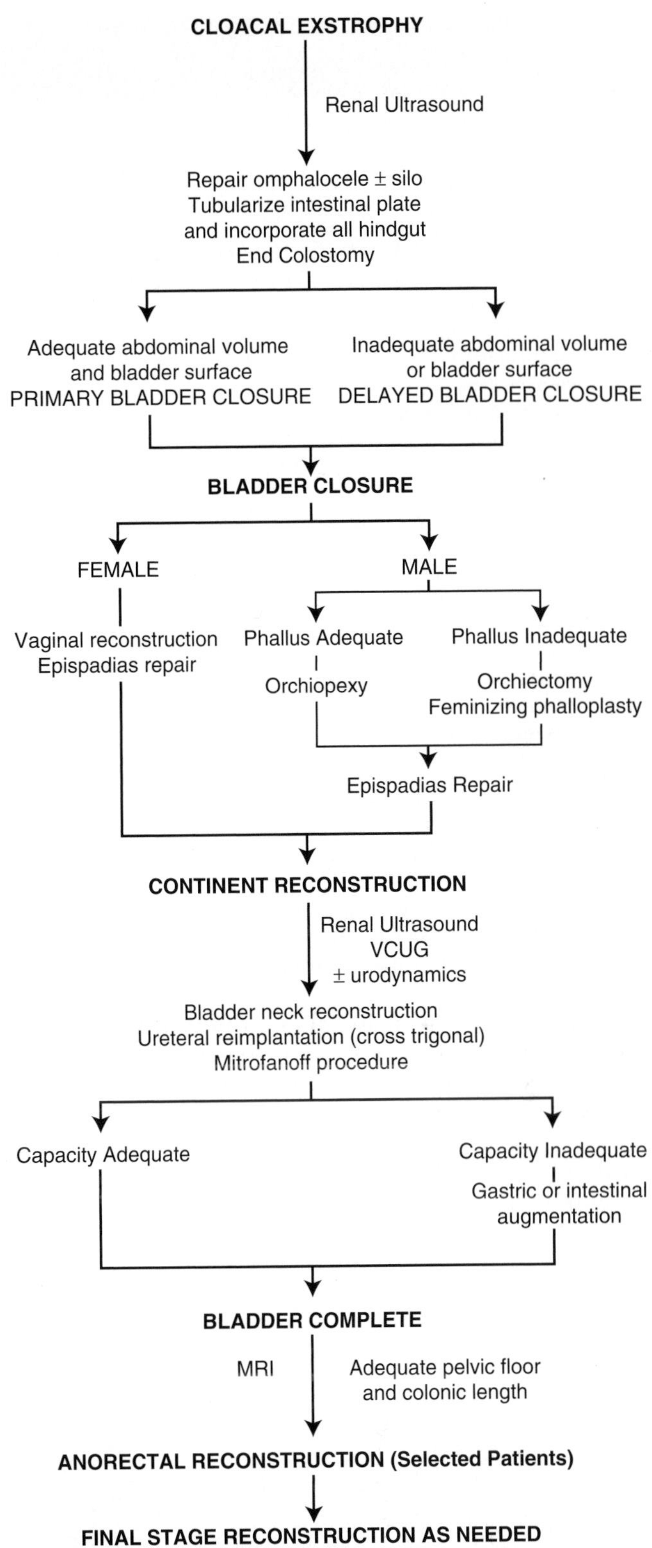

Figure 118-22 Conceptual approach to reconstruction. MRI, magnetic resonance imaging; VCUG, voiding cystourethrography.

TABLE 118-1 Spectrum of Anomalies of Cloacal Exstrophy

Omphalocele and abdominal wall deficiency
Split symphysis pubis
Bladder exstrophy with interposed midline colonic segment
Ileocecal exstrophy
Superior orifice prolapsed ileum
Single or duplicate inferior orifice short blind-ending hindgut
Duplicate appendiceal stumps in intermediate position
Imperforate anus
Bifid external genitalia
Diminutive penis
Cryptorchidism
Bifid clitoris and labia
Duplex müllerian structures
Exstrophied duplicated vaginas at base of bladder mucosa
Atretic vaginas
Myelomeningocele, myelocystocele
Other defects
Talipes equinovarus
Vertebral anomalies (scoliosis)
Dislocated hips
Renal anomalies
Agenesis or multicystic kidney
Megaureter
Hydronephrosis
Fusion anomalies, ectopia

spinal dysraphism. The spectrum of anomalies is outlined in Table 118-1. Ideally, repair is undertaken within 48 hours of birth to take advantage of the pliability of the neonatal pelvis.

Complete repair of cloacal exstrophy in the newborn includes reconstruction of the gastrointestinal tract with colostomy, bladder and posterior penile urethral closure, epispadias repair, and abdominal wall closure without bladder neck reconstruction. Bilateral innominate or vertical iliac osteotomies are occasionally required.[166,170]

Abdominal Wall Defect

The preferred approach to the usually present omphalocele is closure with complete repair of the abdominal wall. This can usually be accomplished, particularly when pubic approximation can be achieved. In premature infants in whom the omphalocele and exstrophy make up much of the abdominal wall, staged closure with a Silastic pouch or primary closure without fascial approximation may be needed. However, primary omphalocele closure is possible in at least 80% of cases.

Gastrointestinal Reconstruction

The majority of patients with cloacal exstrophy have a gastrointestinal tract sufficiently long to support normal growth and development, although true short-bowel syndrome has been reported. Regardless of whether the small bowel length is normal, every effort should be made to preserve all of the intestine, first for absorptive function and second because of the potential need to use segments of the intestinal tract for continent urinary tract reconstruction. Although Rickham[163] reported in 1960 that preservation of the exstrophied ileocecal intestine was important for survival, ileostomy was still being recommended 20 years later. In 1983 Howell et al.[148] re-emphasized the principle of maximal preservation of bowel length without discarding the colonic remnant.

At the time of repair, the mucosal junction between the bladder wall on each side and the exstrophied intestine should be incised, preserving every bit of intestinal mucosa and skin (Figs. 118-23 and 118-24) The ileocolonic plate is then folded into a tube, which restores the ileocecal junction. The edges should not be trimmed to make an end-to-end anastomosis, because mucosal surface area will be lost and the blood supply may be impaired. When duplication of the colon is present, each segment should be preserved and used. A distal segment of hindgut is often present and may be preserved separately, adjacent to the reconstructed ileocecal segment, or it may be used to augment colonic length. One or both appendixes,

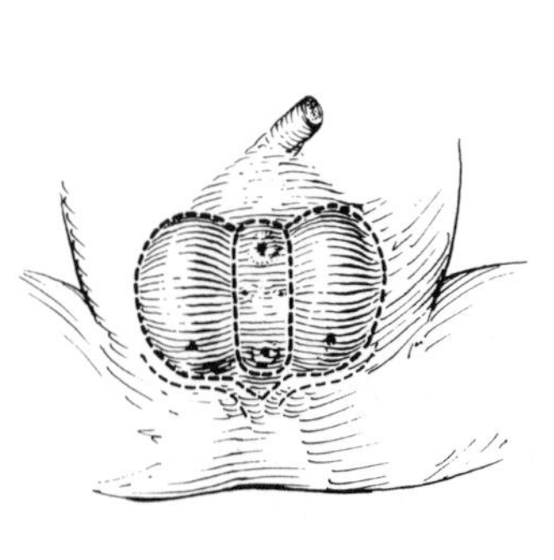

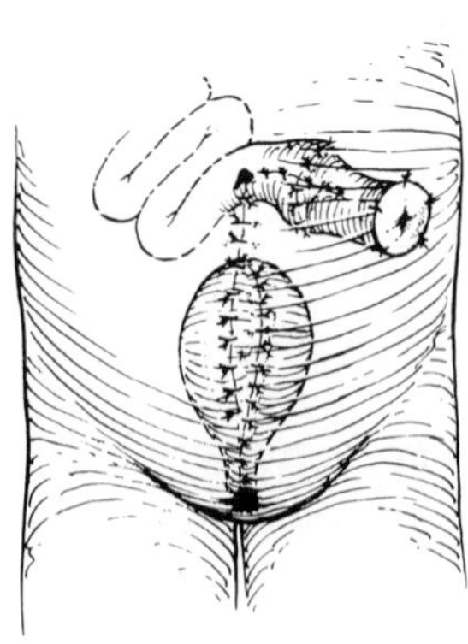

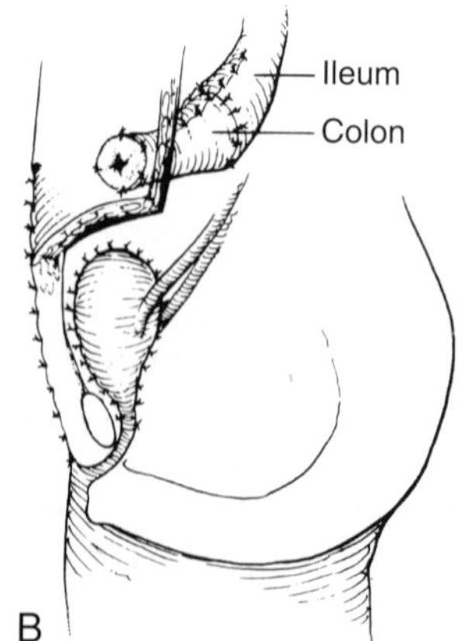

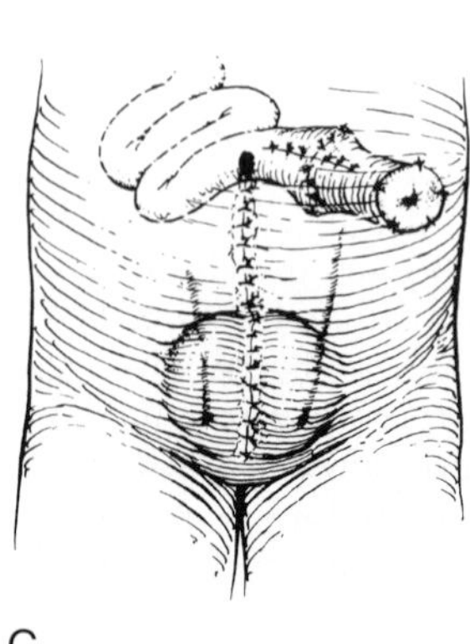

Figure 118-23 Repair of cloacal exstrophy. *A* and *B*, The bowel and bladder mucosa are separated, and the ileocecal junction is tubularized and brought out as an end colostomy. The bladder halves are turned in, as in a complete exstrophy repair, with approximation of the pubic rami. *C*, Alternatively, the bladder halves are approximated in the midline and left open for staged repair if tubularization is not possible. The omphalocele is also closed.

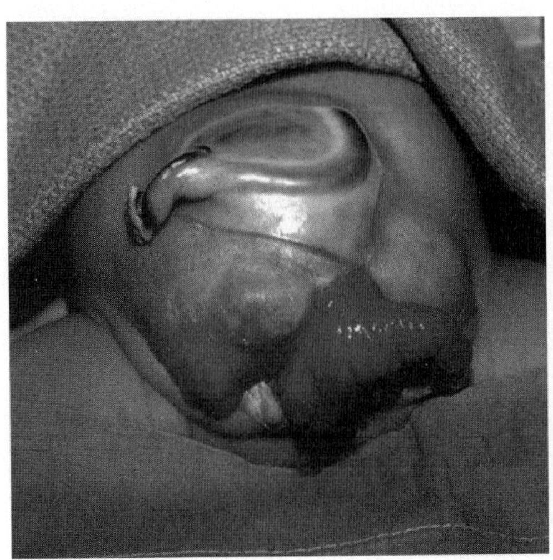
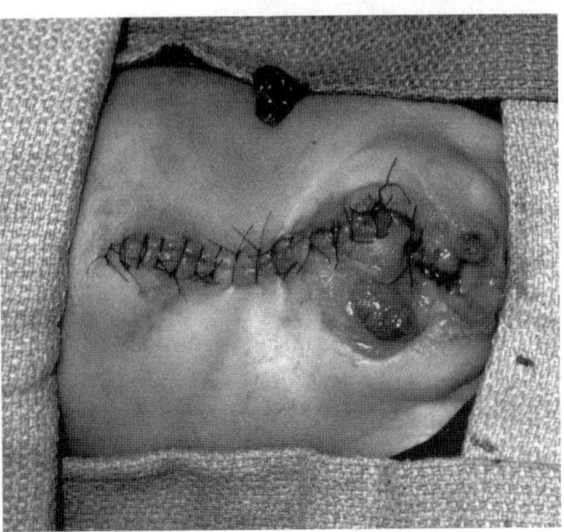

A B

Figure 118–24 *A*, Classic appearance of cloacal exstrophy in a female newborn, with an omphalocele and diminutive split bladder plates laterally. There is prolapse of the ileum from the centrally placed cecum. *B*, In this patient, the initial stage of reconstruction in the newborn period included tubularization of the centrally placed cecum and construction of a colostomy on the left side of the abdomen, as well as exteriorization of the bladder plates because they were too small for tubularization. A later stage of bladder reconstruction is planned, as well as urogenital reconstruction.

if duplicated, should be preserved for later reconstruction of the genitourinary tract. The end of the reconstructed ileocecal segment should then be exteriorized as an end colostomy well laterally to avoid contamination of the abdominal wall closure. If necessary, the end of the colonic segment can be relocated at a later stage of reconstruction. The location should take into account effective placement of an appliance. An occasional patient has an intact colon with an anteriorly placed anus, in which case anoplasty may be required. In patients with small plates of exstrophied cecum, the tubularized bowel is sometimes stenotic, but because the stenosis is so close to the ostomy, balloon dilatation is usually possible, obviating the need for revision.

I have not encountered any patients with long-term nutritional problems related to malabsorption, but prolonged adaptation is often necessary, as well as total parenteral nutrition. All early patients who had end ileostomies had nutritional problems. In the report by Davidoff et al.,[138] the average patient required total parenteral nutrition for 4 weeks, and most patients could not take enteral feedings for 2 weeks.

With regard to complete anorectal reconstruction at a later stage, patients who have spinal dysraphism or deficient pelvic musculature as assessed by CT or MRI should not have reconstruction but should be left with a permanent colostomy. Lund and Hendren[155] described 16 of 32 patients who had pull-through procedures, but only 3 of the 16 ended up being continent. In another report by Hendren,[147] results in 41 patients with cloacal exstrophy were assessed. Seven of the 41 were not operated on, 15 had colostomies, and 19 had pull-throughs of the colon, 3 of which were subsequently reversed for fecal incontinence. The majority of the patients depended on enemas to evacuate. Soffer et al.[168] described 25 patients with cloacal exstrophy managed initially by preserving all available colon and incorporating it into the fecal stream. At the end of 1 year, patients were assessed for the ability to form solid stool through their stomas. Normal colonic length, capacity to form solid stool, and success with a bowel management regimen through the stoma were considered indications for pull-through. All 25 patients underwent a pull-through procedure. Two patients with less than 10 cm of colon had ileostomies, 1 patient was incontinent, 4 were continent with occasional soiling, 11 were clean with bowel management regimens, 3 were totally continent, and 4 were too young to assess. These results are more optimistic than most experience with total anorectal reconstruction. In a series of patients from the Children's Hospital of Philadelphia, 20 of 22 with cloacal exstrophy had permanent colostomies.[174] Three patients had pull-through procedures, and two of these were converted to colostomies, leaving a single patient managed with enemas. An additional consideration in patients with fecal incontinence following pull-through procedures is a Malone or left Monti-Malone procedure for the performance of antegrade colonic washouts.[146,153]

In summary, complete anorectal reconstruction is still an open question. The majority of patients who have pull-through procedures are incontinent, and patients with associated spinal dysraphism do not achieve continence. Thus, the majority of patients, most of whom have foreshortened colons, fare best with end colostomies, but occasional patients are candidates for pull-through procedures. There is consensus, however, regarding the principle of preserving every bit of intestine in these patients.

Urinary Tract Reconstruction

The principles of urinary reconstruction in patients with cloacal exstrophy parallel those applied to patients with classic bladder exstrophy, described earlier in this chapter. The first phase of surgical management of these patients is excision of the omphalocele and careful separation of the bowel from the bladder. As outlined in Figure 118-23, it is preferable to close the bladder primarily whenever possible. When doing so, the surgeon must take into account the size and condition of the infant and the size and volume of the available bladder tissue. If complete closure of the bladder and abdominal wall would be too problematic for a premature infant with respiratory distress syndrome, or if the bladder tissue is inadequate, the two halves can simply be reapproximated and left exposed until a later staged procedure is possible, but bladder fibrosis will occur (see Fig. 118-24). An alternative approach is to perform primary bladder closure but make no attempt to tighten the bladder neck. If primary bladder closure is undertaken, it is usually best to ensure the integrity of the closure by relocating the bladder in the pelvis through pubic approximation, with or without iliac osteotomy. In term infants with adequate bladder tissue, I prefer to tighten the bladder neck with or without the use of paraurethral flaps, in addition to primary bladder closure and pubic approximation. If bladder neck reconstruction cannot be performed initially, it is done later in association with other reconstructive procedures related to continent reconstruction, ureteral reimplantation, and genital reconstruction. Continent reconstruction using segments of the intestinal tract is best deferred for approximately 4 years, when most patients have secure gastrointestinal function and all segments of the gastrointestinal tract have lengthened and increased in caliber, particularly the appendix. Details of these procedures are described in the main section of this chapter. Gearhart et al.[10-12,35] prefer a staged approach, which often avoids the disastrous complication of bladder dehiscence. Others' experience with initial total reconstruction has been favorable in terms of this potential complication.[148,159,174]

A future possibility for patients with inadequate bladder plate tissue is bladder augmentation using fetal tissue engineering.[140] However, standard techniques of bladder augmentation and continent reconstruction are the mainstays of treatment, as described earlier.

Grady and Mitchell[145] showed that the rate of urinary continence achieved with complete primary exstrophy repair compares favorably with that of staged repair. Their complication rates were significantly lower than those reported in previous series of primary closure. Overall, most patients can be rendered continent, but many will achieve this outcome only after other procedures following initial bladder neck reconstruction.[137,150,155] There is some evidence that patients who have complete urethral and bladder repair in the newborn period achieve better storage function and better eventual continence, but more data are needed to confirm this impression.[159,174] As mentioned, the focus of reconstruction has become to improve the quality of life by reducing the number of incontinent stomas, providing assistance with ambulation, and improving cosmesis.[157]

Bolduc et al.[134] observed that up to a fourth of patients with exstrophy have significant upper tract damage in the form of renal scarring or some degree of hydronephrosis. The surgical method of achieving continence was not predictive of these findings, and bladder neck closure was as safe as other forms of bladder neck reconstruction. In other words, renal damage appears to be an associated initial problem.

Schober et al.[164] recently commented on the high incidence of associated neurologic malformations affecting long-term continence, highlighting the importance of Mitrofanoff-type reconstructions with bladder neck closure and a continent catheterizable stoma. They pointed out that diminutive or absent penis has been documented in a third of males and that no documentation of paternity exists in such patients. The majority of females have a bicornuate uterus but normal fallopian tubes and ovaries. A few reports of successful conception using assisted techniques have been published.

Baker Towell and Towell[133] presented a comparative study of subjects with cloacal exstrophy and normal patients in terms of social adjustment and quality of life. The scores were comparable to those of patients with other chronic illnesses and suggested that gender assignment or reassignment does not necessarily result in psychological, emotional, or behavioral problems in childhood. They concluded that longer follow-up studies were needed. Thus, despite the complex nature of this multisystem anomaly, it is likely that aggressive management and perseverance will allow the majority of infants with cloacal exstrophy to achieve a close to normal or at least satisfactory social function and adjustment.[155,157,159,164,174]

Genital Reconstruction

The general principles of genital reconstruction have already been described. Initial reports suggested that adequate male reconstruction in patients with cloacal exstrophy was rarely possible because of the diminutive external genitalia. For this reason, many surgeons recommended that most males with this anomaly be converted to the female sex at the time of the initial operation in the newborn period. In recent years, the debate about gender management has intensified. Obviously, this is an issue only for genetic males whose anatomy is usually functionally inadequate.

Many consider the neonate to be gender neutral and believe that a child's gender identity is determined primarily by the sex of rearing. Zderic et al.[174] described the long-term results using the philosophy of early gender conversion and reported satisfactory long-term gender outcomes. However, some modification of this early gender conversion philosophy is necessary, because at least some male patients with cloacal exstrophy have sufficient phallic tissue for reconstruction using modern techniques and supplemental testosterone therapy.[159] Additionally, there is growing evidence that brain development is affected and imprinted by androgens in the fetus.[162] Although the results of gender reassignment in genetic males with cloacal exstrophy have generally been satisfactory, long-term follow-up has identified a number of patients who desired reconversion to the male gender. Thus, whenever phalloplasty is considered feasible, gender reassignment should be delayed. For males with little or no phallic remnant, sex conversion may be the only alternative.

Genetic males with cloacal exstrophy have testes with normal histology and architecture, as is the case with the ovaries in females.[158] Many females also have ovarian cysts, but not all of these require treatment.[144] Associated congenital anomalies in males, such as hypospadias, are difficult to manage, but the tubularized, incised plate urethroplasty repair appears promising.[171]

Spinal Dysraphism

Up to 50% of children with cloacal exstrophy have variants of myelomeningocele. Patients with lipomeningocele covered by skin, often associated with tethered cord, can have that anomaly repaired at a later date. Open myelomeningocele usually requires closure, and a shunt may be needed for hydrocephalus. Thus, the pediatric neurosurgeon needs to be integrated into the management team. Two general approaches are available. Priority closure of the myelomeningocele defect is usually undertaken when evidence suggests leakage of spinal fluid or impending rupture of the membrane. Alternatively, repair of the anterior abdominal wall defect is facilitated if closure of the posterior defect can be deferred for 4 to 6 weeks. The latter approach can be used safely if extreme care is taken to protect the myelomeningocele membrane. In patients with myelomeningocele and cloacal exstrophy in whom pelvic osteotomy is being considered for pubic approximation, an alternative approach to posterior iliac osteotomy, such as anterior iliac osteotomy or pubic osteotomy, must be used. I prefer not to do an osteotomy at all unless the pubic approximation is under extreme tension.

Skeletal Abnormalities

Pediatric orthopedic management of the various skeletal abnormalities in infants with cloacal malformations is best integrated into the total treatment plan. The general principles of management are the same as those for patients with isolated skeletal problems. For example, clubfeet are placed in casts immediately after birth; splinting is done and orthotics are used when indicated. Patients with skeletal malformations such as hemivertebrae, who are in jeopardy of developing significant scoliosis, should be managed aggressively and proactively. The services of physical therapists, stomal therapists, and social workers should be integrated into the management of these patients if they are to achieve a good quality of life at the earliest possible time.

In terms of hip function and gait, primary closure of the symphysis pubis with or without osteotomy provides an opportunity for an almost normal gait in these patients.[166,170]

Cloacal Exstrophy: Results

In the 1960s the reported overall survival of patients with cloacal exstrophy was around 20%; this rose to 50% in the 1970s.[163,173] By the 1980s, survival in most series had increased to 90%, where it remains today.[148,149,154,155,174,175] Currently, deaths are related to extreme prematurity, renal agenesis, or other complex associated malformations that are incompatible with life. Of interest is the fact that severe cardiovascular anomalies are unusual in patients with cloacal exstrophy.

The various complications related to the management of patients with cloacal exstrophy are similar to those of patients with classic bladder exstrophy, as described in the main section of this chapter. However, the incidence of bladder dehiscence appears to be higher in cloacal exstrophy patients than in those with classic bladder exstrophy. The nature of gastrointestinal morbidity and the methods of management were described earlier, but the majority of patients end up with satisfactory gastrointestinal function.

REFERENCES

Bladder Exstrophy

1. Abasiyanik A, Guvenc H, Koseoglu B: Penopubic flaps technique for the repair of epispadias with or without exstrophy: A preliminary report. J Pediatr Surg 1996;31:1225.
2. Adams MC, Pope JC IV, Brock JW III: Exstrophy/epispadias in the female: Complete primary repair [abstract]. Paper presented at the annual meeting of the AAP, 2002, Boston.
3. Ambrose SS, O'Brien DP III: Surgical embryology of the exstrophy-epispadias complex. Surg Clin North Am 1974; 54:1379.
4. Arap S, Giron AM, deGoes GM: Complete reconstruction of bladder exstrophy: Experimental program. Urology 1976; 7:413.
5. Arap S, Nahas WC, Giron AM, et al: Incontinent epispadias: Surgical treatment of 38 cases. J Urol 1988;140:577.
6. Barth RA, Filly RA, Sondheimer FK: Prenatal sonographic findings in bladder exstrophy. J Ultrasound Med 1990;9:359.
7. Ben-Chaim J, Peppas DS, Jeffs RD, et al: Complete male epispadias: Genital reconstruction and achieving continence. J Urol 1995;153:1665.
8. Bennett AH: Exstrophy of bladder treated by ureterosigmoidostomies: Long term evaluation. Urology 1973;2:165.
9. Boyce WH: A new concept concerning treatment of exstrophy of the bladder: 20 years later. J Urol 1972;107:476.
10. Brzezinski AE, Homsy YL, Laberge I: Orthoplasty in epispadias. J Urol 1986;136:259.
11. Burbige KA, Hensle TW, Chambers WJ, et al: Pregnancy and sexual function in women with bladder exstrophy. Urology 1986;28:12.
12. Burns JE: A new operation for exstrophy of the bladder. JAMA 1924;82:1587.
13. Caldamone AA: Anomalies of the bladder and cloaca. In Gillenwater JY, et al (eds): Adult and Pediatric Urology. St Louis, Mosby-Year Book, 1991.
14. Canning DA, et al: A computerized review of exstrophy patients managed during the past thirteen years [abstract]. Paper presented at the annual meeting of the AUA, 1989, Dallas.
15. Canning DA, Gearhart JP, Jeffs RD: Cephalotrigonal reimplant as an adjunct to bladder neck reconstruction [abstract]. Paper presented at the annual meeting of the AUA, 1990, New Orleans.
16. Cantwell FV: Operative technique of epispadias by transplantation of the urethra. Ann Surg 1895;22:689.
17. Cerniglia FR Jr, Roth DR, Gonzales ET Jr: Covered exstrophy and visceral sequestration in a male newborn: Case report. J Urol 1989;141:903.
18. Chisholm TC, McFarland FA: Exstrophy of the Urinary Bladder. Chicago, Year Book Medical Publishers, 1982.

19. Clemetson CA: Ectopia vesicae and split pelvis: An account of pregnancy in a woman with treated ectopia vesicae and split pelvis, including a review of the literature. J Obstet Gynaecol Br Emp 1958;65:973.
20. Coffey R: Transplantation of the ureter into the large intestine in the absence of a functioning bladder. Surg Gynecol Obstet 1921;32:383.
21. Cohen SJ: Ureterozystoneostomie, eine neue antirefluxtechnik. Akt Urol 1975;6:1.
22. Connor JP, Lattimer JK, Hensle TW, et al: Primary closure of bladder exstrophy: Long-term functional results in 137 patients. J Pediatr Surg 1988;23:1102.
23. Cracchiolo A 3rd, Hall CB: Bilateral iliac osteotomy: The first stage in repair of exstrophy of the bladder. Clin Orthop 1970;68:156.
24. Csontai A, Merksz M, Pirot L, et al: Results of surgical treatment in children with bladder exstrophy. Br J Urol 1992; 70:683.
25. Devine CJ, Horton CE: Hypospadias and epispadias. Clin Symp 1972;20:24.
26. Devine CJ Jr, Horton CE, Scarff JE Jr: Epispadias. Urol Clin North Am 1980;7:465.
27. Duckett JW: Use of paraexstrophy skin pedicle grafts for correction of exstrophy and epispadias repair. Birth Defects Orig Artic Ser 1977;13:175.
28. Duckett JW: The island flap technique for hypospadias repair. Urol Clin North Am 1981;8:503.
29. Duckett JW, Caldamone AA: Bladder exstrophy. AUA Update Series 1984;13:2.
30. Duckett JW Jr: Epispadias. Urol Clin North Am 1978;5:107.
31. El-Sherbiny MT, Hafez AT, Ghoneim MA: Complete repair of exstrophy: Further experience with neonates and children after failed initial closure. J Urol 2002;168:1692.
32. Engel RM: Bladder exstrophy: Vesicoplasty or urinary diversion? Urology 1973;2:20.
33. Ezell WW, Carlson HE: A realistic look at exstrophy of the bladder. Br J Urol 1970;42:197.
34. Gearhart JP: Exstrophy, Epispadias, and Other Bladder Anomalies. Philadelphia, WB Saunders, 2002, p 2136.
35. Gearhart JP, Ben-Chaim J, Jeffs RD, et al: Criteria for the prenatal diagnosis of classic bladder exstrophy. Obstet Gynecol 1995;85:961.
36. Gearhart JP, Jeffs RD: Augmentation cystoplasty in the failed exstrophy reconstruction. J Urol 1988;139:790.
37. Gearhart JP, Jeffs RD: Bladder exstrophy: Increase in capacity following epispadias repair. J Urol 1989;142:525.
38. Gearhart JP, Jeffs RD: State-of-the-art reconstructive surgery for bladder exstrophy at the Johns Hopkins Hospital. Am J Dis Child 1989;143:1475.
39. Gearhart JP, Jeffs RD: Complications of Exstrophy and Epispadias Repair, 2nd ed. Philadelphia, WB Saunders, 1990.
40. Gearhart JP, Jeffs RD: Management and Treatment of Classic Bladder Exstrophy. Philadelphia, WB Saunders, 1990.
41. Gearhart JP, Leonard MP, Burgers JK, et al: The Cantwell-Ransley technique for repair of epispadias. J Urol 1992; 148:851.
42. Gearhart JP, Peppas DS, Jeffs RD: Complications of paraexstrophy skin flaps in the reconstruction of classical bladder exstrophy. J Urol 1993;150:627.
43. Gearhart JP, Sciortino C, Ben-Chaim J, et al: The Cantwell-Ransley epispadias repair in exstrophy and epispadias: Lessons learned. Urology 1995;46:92.
44. Gearhart JP, Williams KA, Jeffs RD: Intraoperative urethral pressure profilometry as an adjunct to bladder neck reconstruction. J Urol 1986;136:1055.
45. Grady RW, Carr MC, Mitchell ME: Complete primary closure of bladder exstrophy: Epispadias and bladder exstrophy repair. Urol Clin North Am 1999;26:95.
46. Grady RW, Mitchell ME: Complete primary repair of exstrophy. J Urol 1999;162:1415.
47. Grady RW, Mitchell ME: Exstrophy and Epispadias Anomalies, 4th ed. Philadelphia, Lippincott Williams & Wilkins, 2002.
48. Grady RW, et al: The complete primary repair of exstrophy (CPRE) technique for repair of bladder exstrophy and epispadias: Long-term follow-up. Paper presented at the annual meeting of the AAP, 2003, New Orleans.
49. Hanna MK, Williams DI: Genital function in males with vesical exstrophy and epispadias. Br J Urol 1972; 44:169.
50. Hendren WH: Penile lengthening after previous repair of epispadias. J Urol 1979;121:527.
51. Hinman R: A method of lengthening and repairing the penis in exstrophy of the bladder. J Urol 1958;79:237.
52. Hollowell JG, Ransley PG: Surgical management of incontinence in bladder exstrophy. Br J Urol 1991;68:543.
53. Horton CE, Devine CJ Jr, Devine PC, et al: Aesthetic reconstructive genital surgery. Clin Plast Surg 1981;8:399.
54. Husmann DA, McLorie GA, Churchill BM: A comparison of renal function in the exstrophy patient treated with staged reconstruction versus urinary diversion. J Urol 1988; 140:1204.
55. Husmann DA, McLorie GA, Churchill BM: Closure of the exstrophic bladder: An evaluation of the factors leading to its success and its importance on urinary continence. J Urol 1989;142:522.
56. Ives E, Coffey R, Carter CO: A family study of bladder exstrophy. J Med Genet 1980;17:139.
57. Jaffe R, Schoenfeld A, Ovadia J: Sonographic findings in the prenatal diagnosis of bladder exstrophy. Am J Obstet Gynecol 1990;162:675.
58. Janssen P: Die Operation der blasenektopie ohne inanspruchnahme des Intestinums. Zentralbl Chir 1933;60:2657.
59. Jeffs RD: Exstrophy of the Urinary Bladder. Chicago, Year Book Medical Publishers, 1986.
60. Jeffs RD, Charrios R, Mnay M, et al: Primary Closure of the Exstrophied Bladder. Philadelphia, WB Saunders, 1972.
61. Jeffs RD, Guice SL, Oesch I: The factors in successful exstrophy closure. J Urol 1982;127:974.
62. Johnston JH: Lengthening of the congenital or acquired short penis. Br J Urol 1974;46:685.
63. Johnston JH: The genital aspects of exstrophy. J Urol 1975; 113:701.
64. Justrabo E, Poulard G, Arnould L, et al: [Invasive adenocarcinoma with epidermoid carcinoma on the site of bladder exstrophy: Histochemical and immunocytochemical study]. Arch Anat Cytol Pathol 1991;39:223.
65. Kajbafzadeh AM, Duffy PG, Ransley PG: The evolution of penile reconstruction in epispadias repair: A report of 180 cases. J Urol 1995;154:858.
66. Kelly JH: Vesical exstrophy: Repair using radical mobilisation of soft tissues. Pediatr Surg Int 1995;10:298.
67. King LR, Wendel EF: Primary cystectomy and permanent urinary diversion in the treatment of exstrophy of the urinary bladder. In Russell S, et al (eds): Current Controversies in Urologic Management. Philadelphia, WB Saunders, 1972.
68. Koff SA, Eakins M: The treatment of penile chordee using corporeal rotation. J Urol 1984;131:931.
69. Kramer SA, Jackson IT: Bilateral rhomboid flaps for reconstruction of the external genitalia in epispadias-exstrophy. Plast Reconstr Surg 1986;77:621.

70. Kramer SA, Kelalis PP: Assessment of urinary continence in epispadias: Review of 94 patients. J Urol 1982;128:290.
71. Kramer SA, Mesrobian HG, Kelalis PP: Long-term followup of cosmetic appearance and genital function in male epispadias: Review of 70 patients. J Urol 1986;135:543.
72. Krisiloff M, Puchner PJ, Tretter W, et al: Pregnancy in women with bladder exstrophy. J Urol 1978;119:478.
73. Lattimer JK, Beck L, Yeaw S, et al: Long-term followup after exstrophy closure: Late improvement and good quality of life. J Urol 1978;119:664.
74. Lattimer JK, Macfarlane MT: A urethral lengthening procedure for epispadias and exstrophy. J Urol 1980;123:544.
75. Lattimer JK, Smith MJ: Exstrophy closure: A followup on 70 cases. J Urol 1966;95:356.
76. Leadbetter WF, Clarke BG: Five years' experience with ureteroenterostomy by the "combined" technique. J Urol 1954;73:67.
77. Lepor H, Jeffs RD: Primary bladder closure and bladder neck reconstruction in classical bladder exstrophy. J Urol 1983;130:1142.
78. Lepor H, Shapiro E, Jeffs RD: Urethral reconstruction in boys with classical bladder exstrophy. J Urol 1984;131:512.
79. Lowe FC, Jeffs RD: Wound dehiscence in bladder exstrophy: An examination of the etiologies and factors for initial failure and subsequent success. J Urol 1983;130:312.
80. MacKay J, Syme J: Congenital exstrophy of the urinary bladder. Month J Med Sci 1849;9:934.
81. Marshall VF, Muecke EC: Variations in exstrophy of the bladder. J Urol 1962;88:766.
82. Marshall VF, Muecke EC: Functional closure of typical exstrophy of the bladder. J Urol 1970;104:205.
83. Maydl K: Uber die Radikaltherapie der Blasenectopie. Wien Med Wochenschr 1894;44:25.
84. McLaughlin KP, Rink RC, Adams MC, et al: Stomach in combination with other intestinal segments in pediatric lower urinary tract reconstruction. J Urol 1995;154:1162.
85. Megalli M, Lattimer JK: Review of the management of 140 cases of exstrophy of the bladder. J Urol 1973;109:246.
86. Mesrobian HG, Kelalis PP, Kramer SA: Long-term followup of cosmetic appearance and genital function in boys with exstrophy: Review of 53 patients. J Urol 1986;136:256.
87. Mesrobian HG, Kelalis PP, Kramer SA: Long-term followup of 103 patients with bladder exstrophy. J Urol 1988;139:719.
88. Michon L: Conservative operations for exstrophy of the bladder with particular reference to urinary incontinence. Br J Urol 1948;20:167.
89. Mildenberger H, Kluth D, Dziuba M: Embryology of bladder exstrophy. J Pediatr Surg 1988;23:166.
90. Mirk P, Calisti A, Fileni A: Prenatal sonographic diagnosis of bladder extrophy. J Ultrasound Med 1986;5:291.
91. Mitchell ME, Bagli DJ: Complete penile disassembly for epispadias repair: The Mitchell technique. J Urol 1996;155:300.
92. Mitrofanoff P: Cystomie continente trans-appendiculaire dans le traitement des vessies neurologues. Chir Ped 1980;21:297.
93. Mollard P: Bladder reconstruction in exstrophy. J Urol 1980;124:525.
94. Monfort G, Morisson-Lacombe G, Guys JM, et al: Transverse island flap and double flap procedure in the treatment of congenital epispadias in 32 patients. J Urol 1987;138:1069.
95. Muecke EC: The role of the cloacal membrane in exstrophy: The first successful experimental study. J Urol 1964;92:659.
96. Murphy LJT: The History of Urology. Springfield, Ill, Charles C Thomas, 1972.
97. Nesbitt RM: Ureterosigmoid anastomosis by direct elliptical connection: A preliminary report. J Urol 1949;61:728.
98. Oesterling JE, Jeffs RD: The importance of a successful initial bladder closure in the surgical management of classical bladder exstrophy: Analysis of 144 patients treated at the Johns Hopkins Hospital between 1975 and 1985. J Urol 1987;137:258.
99. Parkash S, Bhandari M: Rectus abdominis myocutaneous island flap for bridging defect after cystectomy for bladder exstrophy. Urology 1982;20:536.
100. Patton BM, Barry A: The genesis of exstrophy of the bladder and epispadias. Am J Anat 1952;90:35.
101. Perlmutter AD, Weinstein MD, Reitelman C: Vesical neck reconstruction in patients with epispadias-exstrophy complex. J Urol 1991;146:613.
102. Peters CA, Gearhart JP, Jeffs RD: Epispadias and incontinence: The challenge of the small bladder. J Urol 1988;140:1199.
103. Pohlman AG: The development of the cloaca in human embryos. Am J Anat 1911;21:1.
104. Ransley PG: Epispadias Repair. London, Butterworths, 1988.
105. Ransley PG, Duffy PG, Wollin M: Bladder Exstrophy Closure and Epispadias Repair, 4th ed. Edinburgh, Butterworths, 1989.
106. Schillinger JF, Wiley MJ: Bladder exstrophy: Penile lengthening procedure. Urology 1984;24:434.
107. Schlegel PN, Gearhart JP: Neuroanatomy of the pelvis in an infant with cloacal exstrophy: A detailed microdissection with histology. J Urol 1989;141:583.
108. Schwarz GR, Jeffs RD: Ileal conduit urinary diversion in children: Computer analysis of followup from 2 to 16 years. J Urol 1975;114:285.
109. Shapiro E, Lepor H, Jeffs RD: The inheritance of the exstrophy-epispadias complex. J Urol 1984;132:308.
110. Shaw MB, Rink RC, Kaefer M, et al: Continence in classic bladder exstrophy. Paper presented at the annual meeting of the AAP, 2002, Boston.
111. Silver RI, Yang A, Ben-Chaim J, et al: Penile length in adulthood after exstrophy reconstruction. J Urol 1997;157:999.
112. Spence HM, Hoffman WW, Fosmire GP: Tumour of the colon as a late complication of ureterosigmoidostomy for exstrophy of the bladder. Br J Urol 1979;51:466.
113. Spence HM, Hoffman WW, Pate VA: Exstrophy of the bladder. I. Long-term results in a series of 37 cases treated by ureterosigmoidostomy. J Urol 1975;114:133.
114. Sponseller PD, Bisson LJ, Gearhart JP, et al: The anatomy of the pelvis in the exstrophy complex. J Bone Joint Surg Am 1995;77:177.
115. Sponseller PD, Gearhart JP, Jeffs RD: Anterior innominate osteotomies for failure or late closure of bladder exstrophy. J Urol 1991;146:137.
116. Stec AA, Pannu HK, Tadros YE, et al: Pelvic floor anatomy in classic bladder exstrophy using 3-dimensional computerized tomography: Initial insights. J Urol 2001;166:1444.
117. Stec AA, Pannu HK, Tadros YE, et al: Evaluation of the bony pelvis in classic bladder exstrophy by using 3D-CT: Further insights. Urology 2001;58:1030.
118. Syme J: Ectopia vesicae. Lancet 1852;2:568.
119. Thiersch C: Ueber die entstchugsweise und operative behandlung der Epispadie. Arch Heilbundle 1869;10:20.
120. Toguri AG, Churchill BM, Schillinger JF, et al: Continence in cases of bladder exstrophy. J Urol 1978;119:538.
121. Trendelenburg F: De la cure operatoire de l'exstrophie vesicale et de l'epispadias. Arch Klin Chir 1892;43:394.
122. Turner WR Jr, Ransley PG, Bloom DA, et al: Variants of the exstrophic complex. Urol Clin North Am 1980;7:493.

123. Vyas PR, Roth DR, Perlmutter AD: Experience with free grafts in urethral reconstruction. J Urol 1987;137:471.
124. Williams DI: Split Symphysis Variants. New York, Springer-Verlag, 1947.
125. Williams DI, Keeton JE: Further progress with reconstruction of the exstrophied bladder. Br J Surg 1973;60:203.
126. Woodhouse CR, Ransley PG, Williams DI: The patient with exstrophy in adult life. Br J Urol 1983;55:632.
127. Woodhouse CR, Kellett MJ: Anatomy of the penis and its deformities in exstrophy and epispadias. J Urol 1984; 132:1122.
128. Woodhouse CR, Strachan JR: Malignancy in exstrophy patients [abstract]. Scarborough, England, British Association of Urological Surgeons, July 11, 1990.
129. Yerkes EB, Adams MC, Rink RC, et al: How well do patients with exstrophy actually void? J Urol 2000;164:1044.
130. Young HH: Exstrophy of the bladder: The first case in which a normal bladder and urinary control have been obtained by plastic operation. Surg Gynecol Obstet 1942;74:729.
131. Zabbo A, Kay R: Ureterosigmoidostomy and bladder exstrophy: A long-term followup. J Urol 1986;136:396.

Cloacal Exstrophy

132. Austin PF, Homsey YL, Gearhart JP, et al: The prenatal diagnosis of cloacal exstrophy. J Urol 1998;160:1179-1181.
133. Baker Towell DM, Towell AD: A preliminary investigation into quality of life, psychological distress and social competence in children with cloacal exstrophy. J Urol 2003;169:1850-1853.
134. Bolduc S, Capolicchio G, Upadhyay J, et al: The fate of the upper urinary tract in exstrophy. J Urol 2002;168:2579-2582.
135. Bruch SW, Adzick NS, Goldstein RB, Harrison MR: Challenging the embyrogenesis of cloacal exstrophy. J Pediatr Surg 1996;31:768-770.
136. Caldamone AA: Anomalies of the bladder and cloaca. In Gillenwater JY, et al (eds): Adult and Pediatric Urology. St Louis, Mosby-Year Book, 1991.
137. Capolicchio G, McLorie GA, Farhad W, et al: A population based analysis of continence outcomes and bladder exstrophy. J Urol 2001;165:2418-2421.
138. Davidoff AM, Hebra A, Balmer D, et al: Management of the gastrointestinal tract and nutrition in patients with cloacal exstrophy. J Pediatr Surg 1996;31:771-773.
139. Evans JA, Chudley AE: Tibial agenesis, femoral duplication, and caudal midline anomalies. Am J Med Genet 1999;85:13-19.
140. Fauza DO, Fishman SJ, Mehegan K, Atala A: Videofetoscopically assisted fetal tissue engineering: Bladder augmentation. J Pediatr Surg 1998;33:7-12.
141. Gearhart JP: Bladder exstrophy: Staged reconstruction. Curr Opin Urol 1999;9:499-506.
142. Gearhart JP: Complete repair of bladder exstrophy in the newborn: Complications and management. J Urol 2001; 165:2431-2433.
143. Gearhart JP, Jeffs RD: Techniques to create urinary continence in the cloacal exstrophy patient. J Urol 1991;146: 616-618.
144. Geiger JD, Coran AG: The association of large ovarian cysts with cloacal exstrophy. J Pediar Surg 1998;33:719-721.
145. Grady RW, Mitchell ME: Complete primary repair of exstrophy. J Urol 1999;162:1415-1420.
146. Griffiths DM, Malone PS: The Malone antegrade continence enema. J Pediatr Surg 1995;30:68-71.
147. Hendren WH: Cloaca, the most severe degree of imperforate anus: Experience with 195 cases. Ann Surg 1998;228:331-346.
148. Howell C, Caldamone AA, Snyder H, et al: Cloacal exstrophy—optimal management. J Pediatr Surg 1983;18: 365-369.
149. Hurwitz RS, Manzoni GA, Ransley PG, Stephens FD: Cloacal exstrophy: A report of 34 cases. J Urol 1987;138:1060-1064.
150. Husmann DA, Vandersteen DR, McLorie GA, Churchill BM: Urinary continence after staged bladder reconstruction for cloacal exstrophy: The effect of coexisting neurological abnormalities on urinary continence. J Urol 1999;161:1598-1602.
151. Keppler-Noreuil KM: OEIS complex (omphalocele-exstrophy-imperforate anus-spinal defects): A review of 14 cases. Am J Med Genet 2001;99:271-279.
152. Lakshmanan Y, Bellin PB, Gilroy AM, Fung LC: Antenatally diagnosed cloacal exstrophy variant with intravesical phallus in a twin pregnancy. Urology 2001;57:1178.
153. Liloku RB, Mure PY, Braga L, et al: The left Monti-Malone procedure: Preliminary results in seven cases. J Pediatr Surg 2002;37:228-231.
154. Lund DP, Hendren WH: Cloacal exstrophy: Experience with 20 cases. J Pediatr Surg 1993;28:1360-1368.
155. Lund DP, Hendren WH: Cloacal exstrophy: A 25-year experience with 50 cases. J Pediatr Surg 2001;36:68-75.
156. Manzoni GA, Ransley PG, Hurwitz RS: Cloacal exstrophy and cloacal exstrophy variants: A proposed system of classification. J Urol 1987;138:1065-1068.
157. Mathews R, Jeffs RD, Reiner WG, et al: Cloacal exstrophy—improving the quality of life: The Johns Hopkins experience. J Urol 1998;160:2452-2456.
158. Mathews RI, Perlman E, Marsh DW, Gearhart JP: Gonadal morphology in cloacal exstrophy: Implications in gender assignment. BJU Int 1999;84:99-100.
159. Mitchell ME, Plaire C: Management of cloacal exstrophy. In Zderic SA, et al (eds): Pediatric Gender Assignment: A Critical Reappraisal. New York, Kluwer Academic/Plenum Publishers, 2002.
160. Oostra RJ, Baljet B, Verbeeten BW, Hennekam RC: Congenital anomalies in the teratological collection of Museum Vrolik in Amsterdam, the Netherlands. III. Primary field defects, sequences, and other complex anomalies. Am J Med Genet 1998;80:46-59.
161. Parrott TS, Skandalakis JE, Gray SW: The bladder and urethra. In Skandalakis JE, Gray SW (eds): Embryology for Surgeons. Baltimore, Williams & Wilkins, 1994.
162. Reiner WG, Gearhart JP: Discordant sexual identity in some genetic males with cloacal exstrophy assigned to female sex at birth. N Engl J Med 2004;350:333-341.
163. Rickham PP: Vesicointestinal fissure. Arch Dis Child 1960; 35:97-100.
164. Schober JM, Carmichael PA, Hines M, Ransley PG: The ultimate challenge of cloacal exstrophy. J Urol 2002;167: 300-304.
165. Shaw MB, West K, Gitlin J, et al: Intravesical phallus in cloacal exstrophy. Urology 2003;61:644.
166. Silver RI, Sponseller PD, Gearhart JP: Staged closure of the pelvis in cloacal exstrophy: First description of a new approach. J Urol 1999;161:263-266.
167. Smith NM, Chambers HM, Furness ME, Haan EA: The OEIS complex (omphalocele-exstrophy-imperforate anus spinal defects) recurrence in sibs. J Med Genet 1992;29:730-732.
168. Soffer SZ, Rosen NG, Hong AR, et al: Cloacal exstrophy: A unified management plan. J Pediatr Surg 2000;35:932-937.

169. Sponseller PD, Bisson LJ, Gearhart JP, et al: The anatomy of the pelvis in the exstrophy complex. J Bone Joint Surg 1995;77:177-189.
170. Sponseller PD, Jani MM, Jeffs RD, Gearhart JP: Anterior innominate osteotomy in repair of bladder exstrophy. J Bone Joint Surg Am 2001;83:184-193.
171. Stein R, Thuroff JW: Hypospadias and bladder exstrophy. Curr Opin Urol 2002;12:195-200.
172. Steinbüchel W: Veter Nabelschurburch und blassen Bauchspalte mit codken Bildung von sciten des Dunndormers. Arch Gynaeckol 1900;60:465-469.
173. Welch KJ: Cloacal exstrophy. In Ravitch MM, et al (eds): Pediatric Surgery. Chicago, Yearbook Medical Publishers, 1979.
174. Zderic SA, Canning DA, Carr MC, et al: The CHOP experience with cloacal exstrophy and gender reassignment. In Zderic SA, et al (eds): Pediaric Gender Assignment: A Critical Reappraisal. New York, Kluwer Academic/Plenum Publishers, 2002.
175. Ziegler MM, Duckett JW, Howell CG: Cloacal exstrophy. In Welch KJ, et al (eds): Pediatric Surgery. Chicago, Yearbook Medical Publishers, 1986.

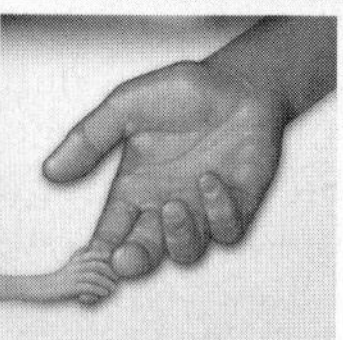

Chapter 119

Hypospadias

Laurence S. Baskin

Hypospadias is one of the most common congenital anomalies, occurring in approximately 1 in 250 newborns, or roughly 1 in 125 live male births.[118] Hypospadias can be defined as an arrest in normal development of the urethra, foreskin, and ventral aspect of the penis. This results in a wide range of abnormalities; the urethral opening can be anywhere along the shaft of the penis, within the scrotum, or even in the perineum (Fig. 119-1). Hypospadias is also associated with a downward curvature of the penis, or chordee. Left uncorrected, patients with severe hypospadias may need to sit down to void and tend to shun intimate relationships because of fears related to abnormal sexuality. Babies born with severe hypospadias and penile curvature may have "ambiguous genitalia" in the newborn period, making an immediate and accurate sex assignment difficult.

Hypospadias is classified by the location of the urethral meatus (Fig. 119-2). Anterior hypospadias may be glanular (meatus on the ventral surface of the glans penis), coronal (meatus in the balanopenile furrow), or distal (in the distal third of the penile shaft). Middle hypospadias is along the middle third of the penile shaft. Posterior hypospadias extends through the proximal third of the penile shaft to the perineum and may be described as posterior penile (at the base of the shaft), penoscrotal (at the base of the shaft in front of the scrotum), scrotal (on the scrotum or between the genital swellings), or perineal (behind the scrotum or behind the genital swellings). Classifying hypospadias into anterior, middle, and posterior is not necessarily useful in determining surgical approach, and these classifications do not take into account the associated penile curvature (Fig. 119-3). A patient with severe

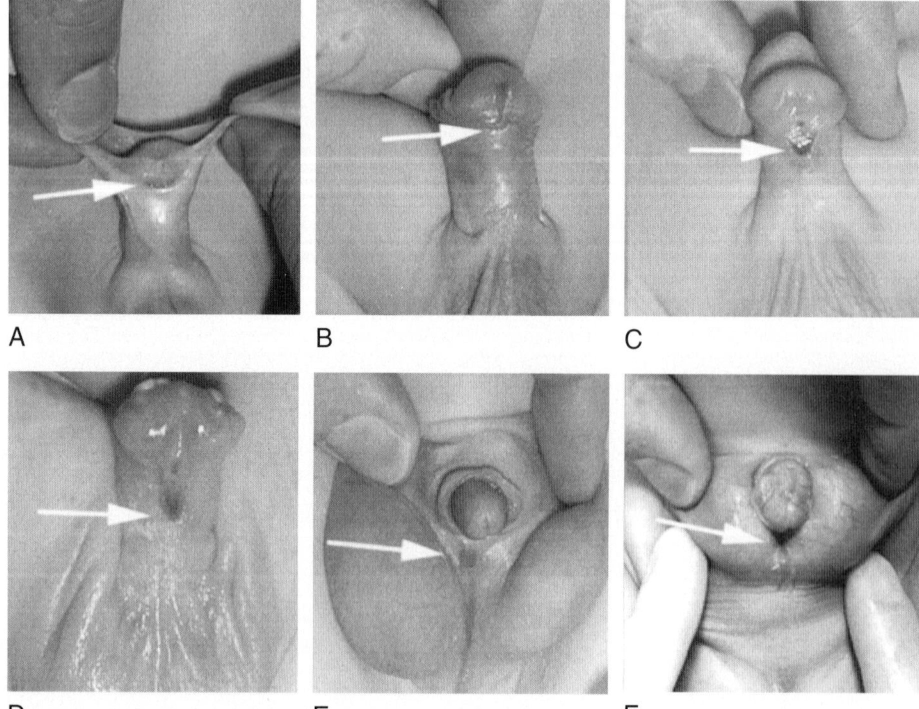

Figure 119–1 Mild to severe hypospadias. *A,* Mild hypospadias with the urethral opening on the glans. *B,* Mild hypospadias with the urethral opening at the coronal margin. *C,* Moderate hypospadias with the urethral opening on the distal penile shaft. *D,* Moderate hypospadias with the urethral opening on the midpenile shaft. *E,* Severe hypospadias with the urethral opening at the penoscrotal junction. *F,* Severe hypospadias with the urethral opening in the scrotum (the *arrows* indicate the opening of the hypospadiac urethral meatus). Note that the foreskin is absent on the ventral surface of the penis and excessive on the dorsal aspect. The more severe forms of hypospadias are associated with penile curvature. (From Baskin LS: Hypospadias and urethral development. J Urol 2000;163:951-956.)

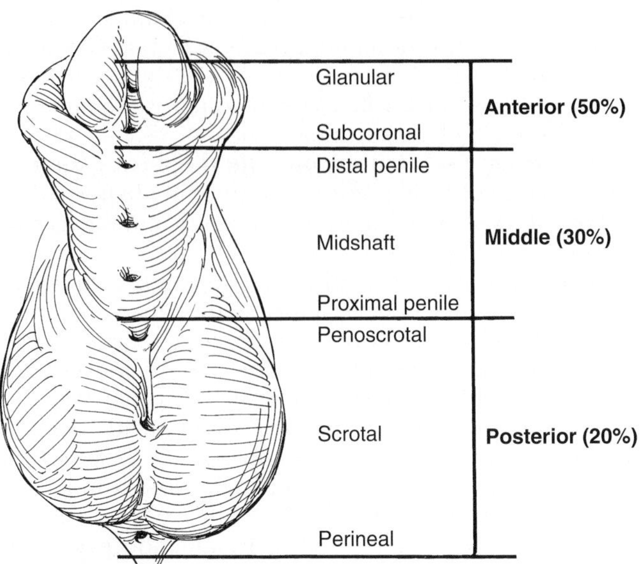

Figure 119-2 Classification and incidence of hypospadias: anterior, middle, and posterior.

curvature and an anterior urethral meatus may require more extensive surgery to correct both anomalies.

HISTORICAL NOTES

Throughout Greek culture, there was high appreciation for the goddess Hermaphrodite, who was half man and half woman. Many statues reflect hypospadiac genitalia, perhaps indicative of admiration for this condition. It is, therefore, understandable why it was not until the first and second centuries AD that the Alexandrian surgeons Heliodorus and Antyllus attempted to correct this anomaly by amputation of the distal curved portion.[132] Sexually, the dystopia of the meatus may cause *impotentia generandi*. Henry II of France was known to have hypospadias, as recorded by his physician Fernal. Henry's marriage with Catherine de Medici was infertile until Fernal "advised his patient that in such cases *coitus more ferarum* permitted him to overcome the difficulty."[155] Henry II went on to sire three kings of France, along with seven other children.

EMBRYOLOGY

Formation of the external male genitalia is a complex developmental process involving genetic programming, cell differentiation, hormonal signaling, enzyme activity, and tissue remodeling.[12] By the end of the first month of gestation, the hindgut and future urogenital system reach the ventral surface of the embryo at the cloacal membrane.[39] The cloacal membrane divides the urorectal septum into a posterior, or anal, half and an anterior half, the urogenital membrane. Three protuberances appear around the latter. The most cephalad is the genital tubercle. The other two, the genital swellings, flank the urogenital membrane on each side. Up to this point, the male and female genitalia are essentially indistinguishable. Under the influence of testosterone in response to a surge of luteinizing hormone from the pituitary, masculinization of the external genitalia takes place (Fig. 119-4). One of the first signs of masculinization is an increase in the distance between the anus and the genital structures, followed by elongation of the phallus, formation of the penile urethra from the urethral groove, and development of the prepuce.[77,87]

At 8 weeks' gestation, the external genitalia remain in the indifferent stage (see Fig. 119-4). The urethral groove on the ventral surface of the phallus is between the paired urethral folds (Fig. 119-5). The penile urethra forms as a result of fusion of the medial edges of the endodermal urethral folds. The ectodermal edges of the urethral groove fuse to form the median raphe. By 12 weeks, the coronal sulcus separates the glans from the shaft of the penis. The urethral folds have completely fused in the midline on the ventrum of the penile shaft. During the 16th week of gestation, the glanular urethra appears. The mechanism of glanular urethral formation remains controversial (see Fig. 119-5). Evidence suggests two possible explanations: (1) endodermal cellular differentiation or (2) primary intrusion of ectodermal tissue from the glans (Fig. 119-6).

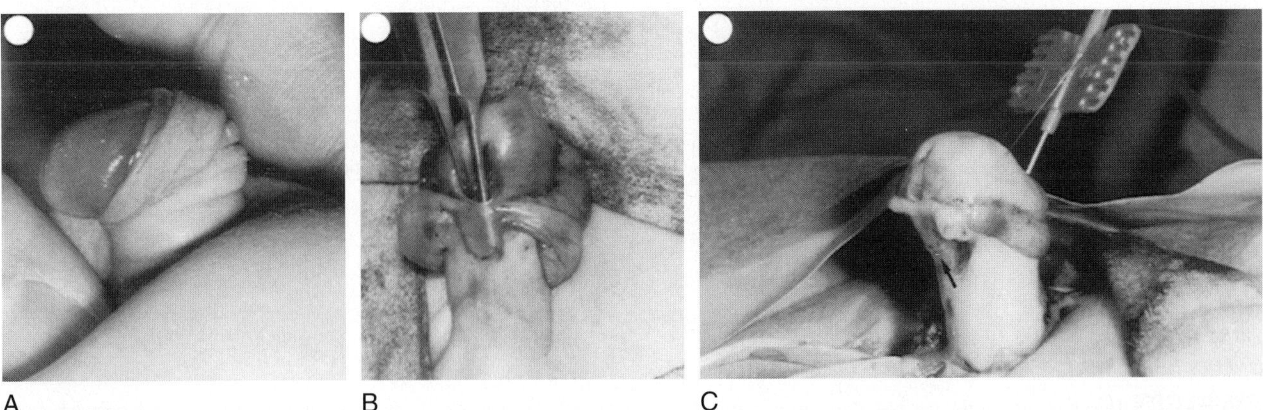

Figure 119-3 *A*, Coronal hypospadias with penile curvature. *B*, The thin ventral skin is not suitable for a parameatal-type procedure. *C*, After release of the skin and dartos fascia (straightening the penis), the meatus *(arrow)* is cut back to remove thin urethral skin in preparation for an onlay island flap urethroplasty. (From Baskin LS, Duckett JW, et al: Changing concepts of hypospadias curvature lead to more onlay island flap procedures. J Urol 1994;151:191.)

Anatomic and immunohistochemical studies advocate the theory of endodermal differentiation, based on evidence that the epithelium of the entire urethra is of urogenital sinus origin.[101] The entire male urethra, including the glanular urethra, is formed by dorsal growth of the urethral plate into the genital tubercle and ventral growth and fusion of the urethral folds. Under proper mesenchymal induction, urothelium has the ability to differentiate into a stratified squamous phenotype with characteristic keratin staining, thereby explaining the cell type of the glans penis.[100] There is no evidence of ectodermal ingrowth, as proposed under the second theory.[68]

The future prepuce is forming at the same time as the urethra and is dependent on normal urethral development. At about 8 weeks' gestation, low preputial folds appear on both sides of the penile shaft, which join dorsally to form a flat ridge at the proximal edge of the corona. The ridge does not entirely encircle the glans because it is blocked on the ventrum by incomplete development of the glanular urethra (see Fig. 119-5A). Thus, the preputial fold is transported distally by active growth of the mesenchyma between it and the glanular lamella. The process continues until the preputial fold (foreskin) covers all of the glans (see Fig. 119-5C). The fusion is usually present at birth, but subsequent desquamation of the epithelial fusion allows the prepuce to retract. If the genital folds fail to fuse, the preputial tissues do not form ventrally; consequently, in hypospadias, preputial tissue is absent on the ventrum and is excessive dorsally (see Fig. 119-1).

The chronology of penile differentiation commences when "passive," or default, female differentiation is interrupted by androgenic hormones triggered by male genes.[38] At the molecular level, testosterone must be converted to 5α-dihydrotestosterone (DHT) by the microsomal enzyme type 2 5α-reductase for complete differentiation of the penis with a male-type urethra and glans.[158] Testosterone dissociates from its carrier proteins in the plasma and enters cells via passive diffusion.[93] Once in the cell, testosterone binds to the androgen receptor (AR) and induces changes in conformation; it is protected from degradation by proteolytic enzymes.[93] This conformational change is also

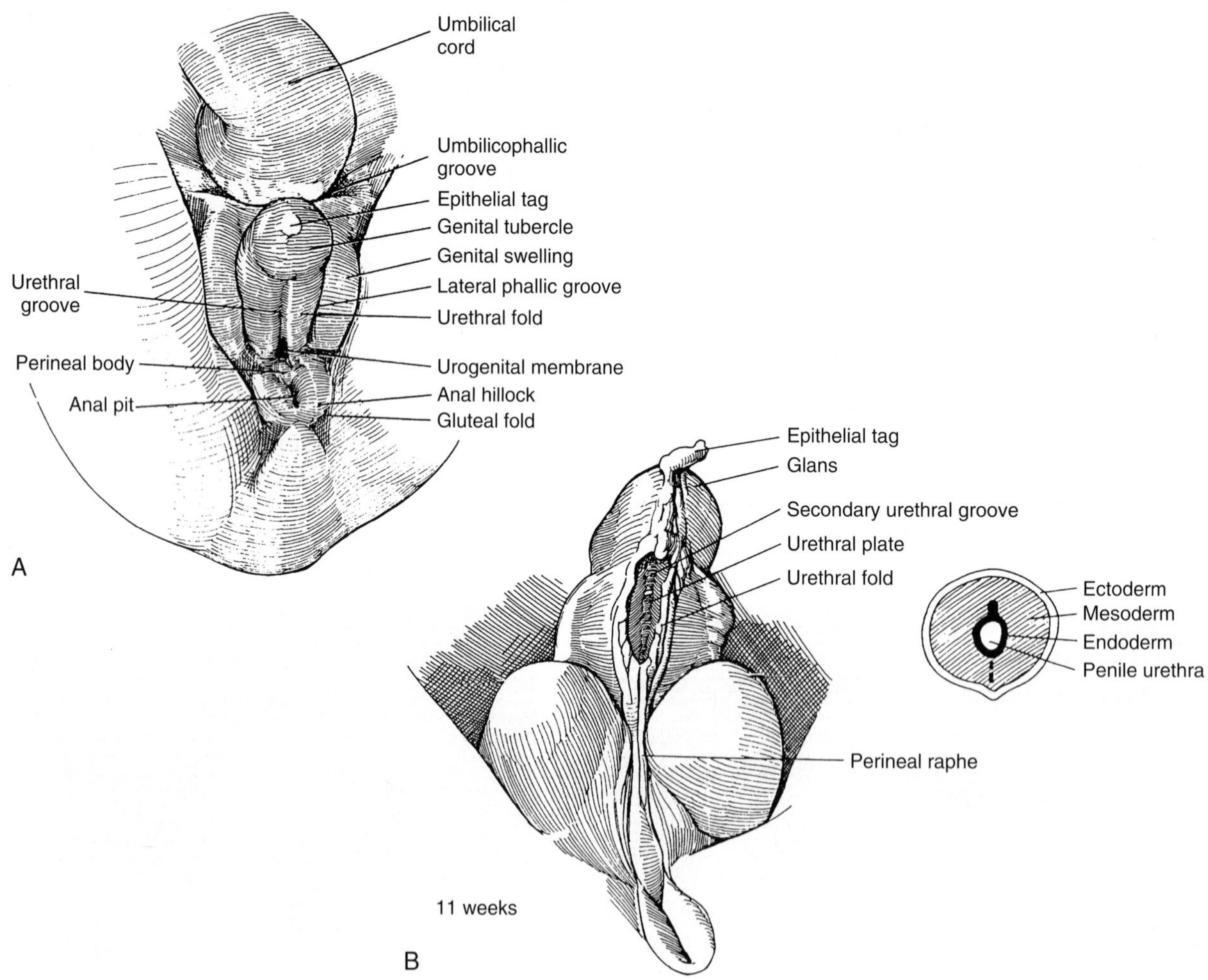

Figure 119–4 Development of the penis and urethra. *A,* Indifferent stage at about 8 weeks. Note that the primitive urethral groove forms on the caudal slope of the genital tubercle. Paired genital (labioscrotal) swellings arise on either side of the urogenital membrane above the anal pit and the perineal body. *B,* Enclosure of the urethra at 11 weeks. Beginning near the anus, the adjacent ectodermal urethral folds fuse over the urethral plate to form the penile urethra, with the distal urethra at the coronal sulcus being the last to close.

Continued

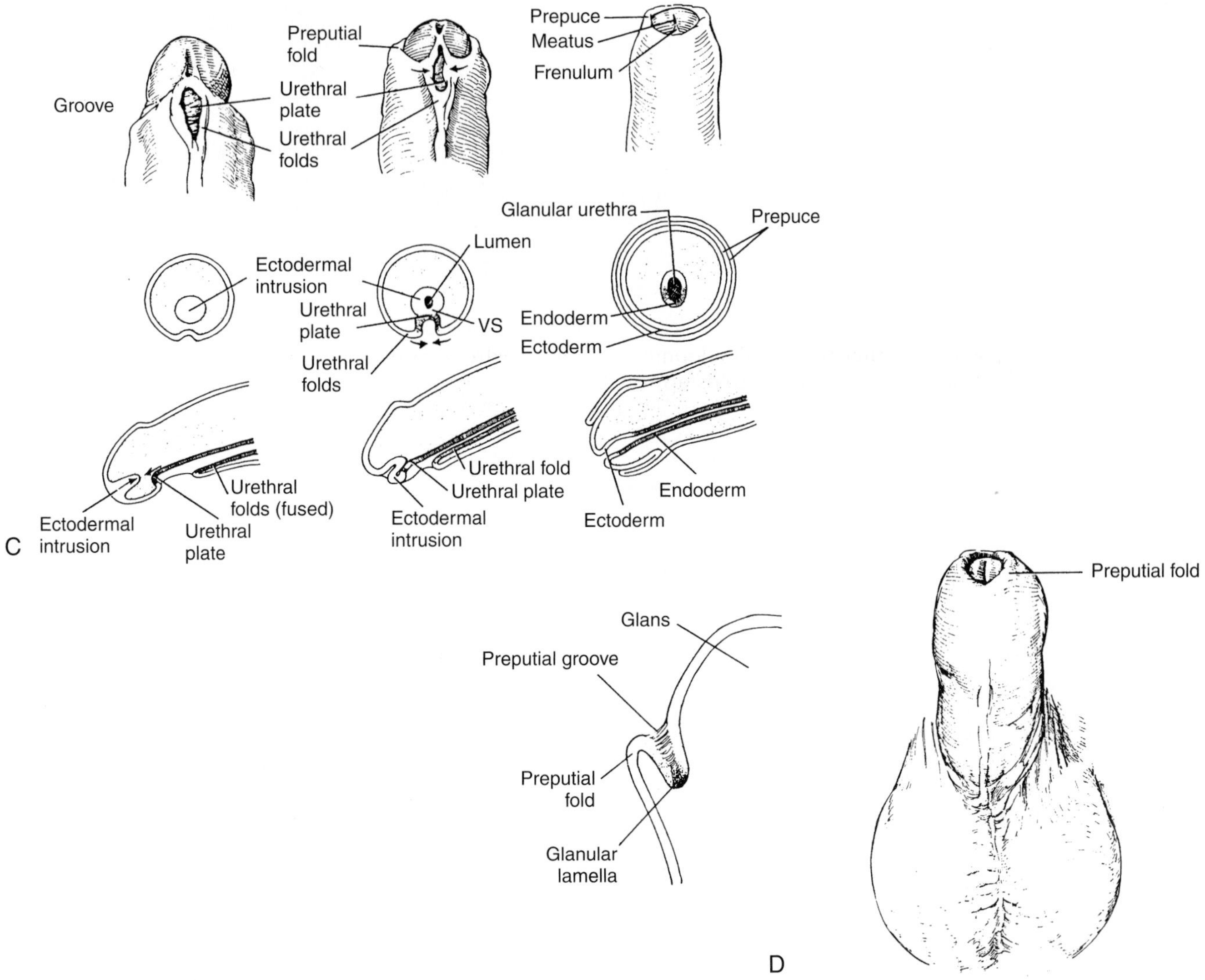

Groove
Preputial fold
Urethral plate
Urethral folds
Prepuce
Meatus
Frenulum
Glanular urethra
Prepuce
Lumen
Ectodermal intrusion
Urethral plate
VS
Endoderm
Ectoderm
Urethral folds
Urethral folds (fused)
Ectodermal intrusion
Urethral plate
Urethral fold
Urethral plate
Ectodermal intrusion
Endoderm
Ectoderm
C
Preputial fold
Glans
Preputial groove
Preputial fold
Glanular lamella
D

Figure 119-4—Cont'd *C,* Formation of the glanular urethra and fossa navicularis occurs late in gestation. A plug of ectoderm from the tip of the glans invades the mesenchyma as an ectodermal intrusion. The floor of the ectodermal intrusion makes contact with the end of the urethral plate that forms the roof of the advancing urethra, and the intervening double wall breaks down. *D,* The prepuce forms by the differentiation of the epithelial cells of the glanular lamella, which forms a groove between the preputial folds and the glans. (From Hinman F Jr: Surgical Anatomy of the Genitourinary Tract. Philadelphia, WB Saunders, 1994, pp 418-470.)

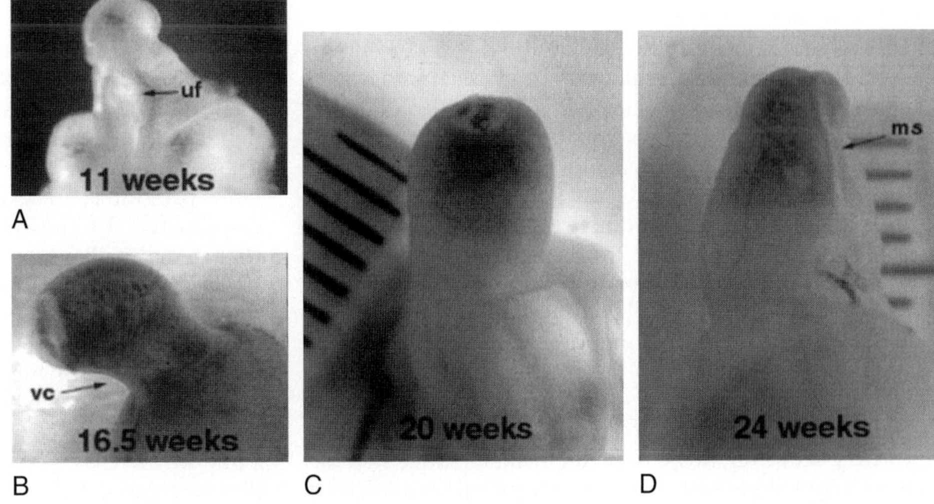

Figure 119-5 Normal human male genitalia development at 11, 16.5, 20, and 24 weeks' gestation. *A,* Note the open urethra and prominent urethral folds (uf). *B,* Note the natural phase of penile curvature that occurs during development. *C,* The foreskin is completely formed, and the curvature has resolved. *D,* Continued growth with visualization of the midline skin seam (ms).

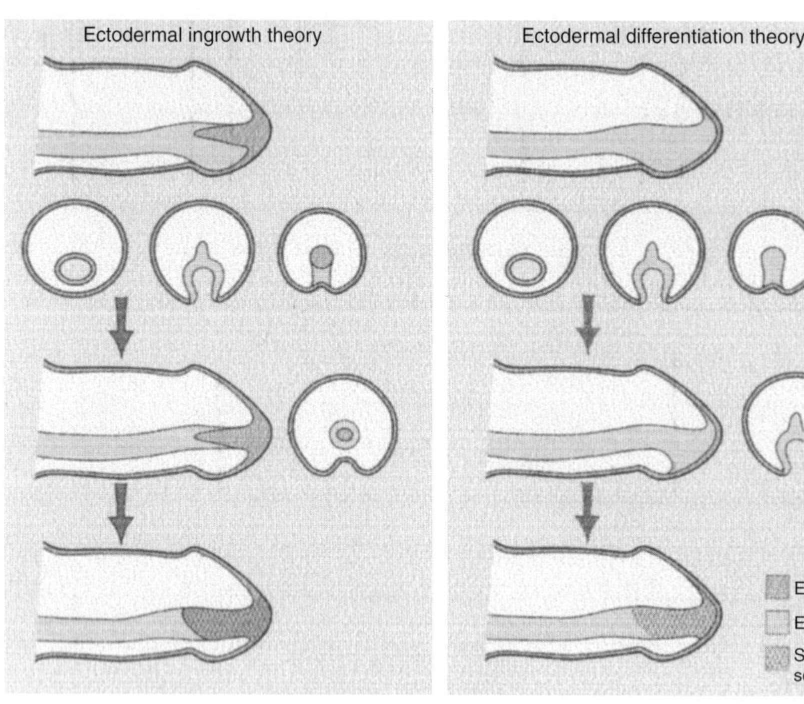

Figure 119-6 Two theories of urethral development: the older theory of ectodermal intrusion and the newer theory of endodermal differentiation. (From Kurzrock EL, Baskin LS, et al: Ontogeny of the male urethra: Theory of endodermal differentiation. Differentiation 1999;64:115-122.)

required for AR dimerization, DNA binding, and transcriptional activation, all of which are necessary for testosterone to be expressed. Androgen binding also displaces heat shock proteins, possibly relieving constraints on receptor dimerization or DNA binding. After entering the nucleus, the AR complex binds androgen response element DNA regulatory sequences within the androgen-responsive genes and activates them. DHT also binds to the AR, with enhanced androgenic activity, in part because of its slow dissociation rate from the AR.[70]

INCIDENCE

Several European countries, including Norway, Sweden, England, Wales, Hungary, Denmark, Italy, and France, as well as the United States published independent reports of increasing rates of hypospadias during the 1960s, 1970s, and 1980s.[117] More recently, data from the International Clearinghouse for Birth Defects Monitoring Systems (ICBDMS) were analyzed to determine whether these increases were worldwide and continuing and whether they had any geographic pattern. The ICBDMS data suggested that the increased incidence of hypospadias was not a worldwide trend; it was most notable in the United States, Norway, and Denmark.[117] Also, it was determined that the incidence was not increasing in the less affluent and less industrialized nations (based on gross domestic product) for which data were available. Increasing trends in England, Canada, and northern Netherlands appear to have leveled off since 1985.[117]

It is difficult to draw conclusions from the international monitoring of birth defects. Different registries have different reporting methods and diagnostic criteria, as well as varying degrees of physician compliance with reporting. However, two independent surveillance systems in the United States with consistent diagnostic criteria also reported significant increases in hypospadias. Although these surveillance programs are not flawless, the data warrant particular mention.[118]

Data from the Metropolitan Atlanta Congenital Defects Program (MACDP), a population-based registry that uses active case ascertainment in 22 hospitals and clinics in the Atlanta, Georgia, area, indicated that the total hypospadias rate almost doubled from 1968 to 1993 ($P < 10^{-6}$), with an annual rate of increase of 2.9%.[118] No one hospital in the region was responsible for the observed increase. Of particular significance is that the incidence of severe hypospadias, defined as the urethral opening on the shaft of the penis or on the scrotum or perineum, increased. Between 1968 and 1990, severe cases increased from 1.1 to 2.7 per 10,000 live births, and by 1993, there were 5.5 severe cases per 10,000 births per year ($P < 10^{-6}$).[118]

The Birth Defects Monitoring Program (BDMP), which gathers diagnoses recorded on newborn discharge summaries from hospitals nationwide, also reported an increase in hypospadias. The incidence increased from 20.2 per 10,000 live births (including both male and female births) in 1970 to 39.7 per 10,000 live births in 1993 ($P < 10^{-6}$).[118]

Both independent surveillance programs indicated a near doubling in the reported rate of hypospadias. It is unlikely that this increase is due to flaws in the surveillance programs. For example, if increased sensitivity were responsible for the observed increases, it would mean that the surveillance programs had recorded fewer than half of all defects initially. This is unlikely, because there were no major changes in case ascertainment in either the MACDP or the BDMP during the time in question. It is possible that physicians' reporting habits have changed over time, particularly an increased reporting of mild hypospadias. This is not consistent, however, with reports from the MACDP that the ratio of mild to severe hypospadias decreased from 4.2 in 1968 to 1982 to 2.6 in 1983 to 1993.[118] It is important to note, however, that as the ratio of mild to severe hypospadias decreased, the number of unclassified cases also decreased, making the data more difficult to interpret. This raises the question whether mild cases are underreported. Nonetheless, these longitudinal studies support an increasing incidence of hypospadias in the United States.

ASSOCIATED ANOMALIES

Undescended testis and inguinal hernia are the most common anomalies associated with hypospadias. In one series, 9.3% of hypospadias patients had an undescended testis; the incidence was 32% with posterior hypospadias, 6% with middle, and 5% with anterior.[95] The same investigators found the overall incidence of inguinal hernia to be 9%, with 17% of those cases associated with posterior hypospadias. Ross et al.[136] reported a similar incidence of either cryptorchidism or hernia in 16%, and Cerasaro et al.[34] found that 18% of their 301 patients had these anomalies. A utriculus masculinus (utricle) is found in a high percentage of severe cases. For example, Devine et al.[44] found that of 44 patients whose meatus was posterior, 6 (14%) had a utricle; of 7 with perineal hypospadias, 4 (57%) had a utricle; and 2 of 20 (10%) with a penoscrotal meatus had a utricle. None of the 17 patients with penile hypospadias had a utricle. Shima et al.[142] found a utricle in 1 of 29 glanular, 3 of 74 penile, 11 of 122 penoscrotal, and 10 of 29 scrotal-perineal hypospadias cases; thus, the incidence was 14% in 151 penoscrotal or perineal hypospadias cases. In both studies combined, there was an 11% incidence of a utricle in severe hypospadias. Usually, the only complications caused by the presence of a utricle are infection and difficulty passing a catheter.[130]

It is not surprising that urinary tract anomalies are infrequent, because the external genitalia are formed much later than the supravesical portion of the urinary tract. McArdle and Lebowitz[105] found only 6 genitourinary anomalies among 200 patients with hypospadias (3%). Cerasaro et al.[34] found that 1.7% of patients (4 of 233) had significant anomalies. Avellan[9] found renal anomalies in only 1% of his Swedish patients with hypospadias, whereas 7% of patients had anomalies in other systems. Based on a review of 169 patients, Shelton and Noe[141] did not recommend routine urinary tract evaluation. Khuri et al.,[95] in a review of 1076 patients, found that urinary tract anomalies considered significant included ureteropelvic junction obstruction, severe reflux, renal agenesis, Wilms' tumor, pelvic kidney, crossed renal ectopia, and horseshoe kidney. They concluded that patients with hypospadias and an associated inguinal hernia or undescended testis did not require further urinary tract evaluation; however, patients with hypospadias and other organ system anomalies should undergo upper urinary tract screening with abdominal ultrasonography.

In a study of urogenital abnormalities in 500 sons of women treated with diethylstilbestrol (DES), 2% had hypospadias, and 4.4% had abnormalities of the penile urethra.[69] Gupta and Goldman[73] implicated metabolic disturbances of the arachidonic acid cascade in midline fusion defects, such as cleft palate and hypospadias. Hypospadias occurs in association with a number of well-known syndromes as well as with Wilms' tumor.

CAUSE

Reports of the increasing incidence of hypospadias have raised questions concerning cause, treatment, and prevention. To date, there is no sound understanding of the cause of hypospadias that could result in primary prevention efforts and improve therapeutics. For example, in a recent study, 33 patients with severe (scrotal or penoscrotal) hypospadias were evaluated with a range of diagnostic techniques, including clinical assessment, ultrasonography, karyotyping, endocrine evaluation, and molecular genetic analysis of the AR gene and the 5α-reductase gene, to classify and determine the cause of hypospadias. In 12 patients (36%), diagnoses were determined. The remaining 64% of patients were classified as having hypospadias of unknown etiology.[3] Other investigators have also attempted to link abnormalities in androgen metabolism or the AR to hypospadias. For example, Gearhart et al.[65] found no deficiencies in either AR levels or 5α-reductase in their study of preputial skin from boys with hypospadias. Allera et al.[5] analyzed nine patients with severe hypospadias and found a defect in the open-reading frame of the AR in only one patient. Sutherland et al.[150] also concluded that mutations in the AR gene are rarely associated with hypospadias. Using single-strand conformational polymorphism analysis, they found a missense mutation of exon 2 of the AR gene in 1 of 40 patients with distal hypospadias. Molecular biology techniques have demonstrated that defects in the AR gene are definitely associated with isolated hypospadias. However, these genetic defects account for an extremely small subset of cases, implying that other factors are responsible for hypospadias.

Genetic Impairment

Uncertainty about the cause of hypospadias is partly a reflection of the complicated and incompletely understood molecular and cellular basis for normal phallic and urethral development.[157] It is well established that the urethral folds fuse during formation of the penile urethra in the 7th to 12th week after ovulation.[12] Fusion of the folds eventually leads to a fully formed penis that is dependent on the synthesis of testosterone by the fetal testis. Adequate virilization of the urogenital sinus and external genitalia during embryogenesis is dependent on the conversion of testosterone to DHT by 5α-reductase.

Increasingly, researchers are examining the role of cellular signals other than testosterone and DHT in the morphogenesis of the phallus and the cause of hypospadias. Normal embryogenesis of the urogenital system depends on epithelial-mesenchymal interactions, and it has been hypothesized that aberrant signaling between the epithelium and mesenchyma could lead to hypospadias.[100] For example, prostate development requires testosterone-dependent *Sonic hedgehog* (Shh) expression in the epithelium of the urogenital sinus.[120]

In mice null for Shh, penile development is inhibited, and they have cloacal defects as well.[21,164] Mice null for fibroblast growth factor 10 have a proximal urethral opening and a flattened glans, consistent with the hypospadias defect.[164] It is likely that researchers will find similar genetic signaling molecules involved in epithelial-mesenchymal interactions in the phallus that play a role in its development.

Another area of investigation with respect to the cause of hypospadias is the expression and regulation of homeobox (Hox) genes. These genes are transcriptional regulators that play an essential role in directing embryonic development. Genes of the Hox A and Hox D clusters are expressed in regionalized domains along the axis of the urogenital tract. Transgenic mice with loss of function of single *Hox A* or *Hox D* genes exhibit homeotic transformations and impaired morphogenesis of the urogenital tract.[25,48,82,121] Human males with hand-foot-genital syndrome, an autosomal dominant disorder characterized by a mutation in *Hox A13,* exhibit hypospadias of variable severity, suggesting that *Hox A13* may be important in the normal patterning of the penis.[49,63,109] Further, research has shown that the embryonic expression of certain Hox genes is regulated by hormonal factors.[103] Estrogen and the synthetic estrogen DES, for example, inhibit *Hox A9, Hox A10, Hox A11,* and *Hox A13* genes in mice. Thus, in addition to defects in Hox genes, it is possible that improper regulation or expression of hormonal factors during embryogenesis could disrupt normal expression of Hox genes and lead to reproductive tract anomalies.

Hormone Receptor Impairment

As noted earlier, studies examining the AR have yielded little insight into the cause of hypospadias. In fact, a number of studies concluded that defects in the AR or mutations in the AR coding sequence are rare in patients with hypospadias.[78,106] In addition, Bentvelsen et al.[26] measured AR expression in the foreskins of boys with hypospadias and age-matched controls and found no significant difference in mean AR content.

Enzyme Impairment

Despite the central role that testosterone plays, attempts to ascribe all hypospadias to an underlying genetic defect in this pathway have only rarely been successful. Holmes et al.[79] determined the incidence of defects in three major enzymes in the biosynthetic pathway of testosterone: 3α-hydroxysteroid dehydrogenase, 17α-hydroxylase, and 17,20-lyase. Forty-eight boys with fully descended testes and various degrees of hypospadias were compared with age-matched controls who were undergoing circumcision. Morning fasting serum samples of pregnenolone, progesterone, 11-deoxycorticosterone, 17-OH pregnenolone, 17-OH progesterone, 11-deoxycortisol, cortisol, dehydroepiandrosterone, androstenedione, androstenediol, testosterone, and dihydrotestosterone were obtained. To focus on the proximal steps in androgen biosynthesis, 12 individuals with hypospadias underwent standard adrenocorticotropic hormone (ACTH) stimulation. No significant differences in the androgen precursors and metabolites were found between the controls and the individuals with hypospadias. The response to ACTH was variable, with no significant difference between patients with different degrees of hypospadias and published controls. These data indicate that enzymatic defects in the steroidogenic steps from cholesterol to dihydrotestosterone are not a common cause of hypospadias.

Environmental Factors and Endocrine Disrupters

In the past, environmental factors were generally ruled out as causes of hypospadias.[74,149] More recently, multicausality models have included environmental contaminants to determine the risk of developing a given phenotype. For example, familial clustering of hypospadias among first-degree relatives has been perceived as being under the influence of a strong genetic and heritable component, but there have been many exceptions in which genetics was ruled out. It has thus been suggested that environmental influences should be considered as well, given that families share similar exposure. In particular, in cases in which the effects are profound, genetic predisposition exacerbated by environmental exposure should be considered.[13,62]

Attempts to determine risk factors for hypospadias have yielded a number of maternal and paternal risk factors. Among traditional studies of maternal risk factors for congenital anomalies, maternal age and primiparity are significantly associated with hypospadias, although some studies have contested the maternal age effect.[74] Paternal risk factors associated with hypospadias include abnormalities of the scrotum or testes[152] and low spermatozoa motility and abnormal sperm morphology.[62] It has been suggested that the recent increase in hypospadias reflects the improvement in fertility treatments, contributing to more subfertile men fathering children. As Fritz and Czeizel state, this "relaxed-selection hypothesis, which states that there is a redistribution in the number of children born to fertile and infertile (subfertile) couples, may account for the increasing number of other defects and cancers of male genitalia observed today and the fall in sperm counts."[62]

In addition to parental risk factors, there is strong consensus in the literature that boys with hypospadias have lower birth weights.[61] Fredell et al.[61] examined hypospadias in discordant monozygotic twins and found that the twin with hypospadias weighed 78% of the twin without hypospadias. The birth weight difference was still significant in healthy monozygotic twins. Another study found that boys with hypospadias had a lower placental weight than control boys did.[149]

A 1995 meta-analysis of first-trimester exposure to progestins and oral contraceptives did not indicate an increased risk of hypospadias.[125] Exposure to DES was excluded in that study. However, a number of other studies did list gestational exposure to progestins as a causal agent. Another recent study linked a maternal vegetarian diet during pregnancy to an increase in the incidence of hypospadias.[114] This study looked at 51 boys with hypospadias from a group of 7928 boys born to mothers taking part in the Avon Longitudinal Study of Pregnancy and Childhood. The authors hypothesized that vegetarians have a greater exposure to phytoestrogens than omnivores do. The phytoestrogens may come in the form of soy, which is high in isoflavones, or may be related to endocrine disrupters in pesticides and fertilizers.[123]

Although these risk factors may not be direct causes of hypospadias, they provide additional information that may reveal a common developmental pathway and inform future research. For example, there is growing evidence that androgens play a central role in the lower birth weight of girls compared with boys.[47] Androgens are also crucial to the development of the male reproductive tract. Thus, exposure to an agent that compromises the weight-gaining advantage of androgen during gestation could play a role in the development of hypospadias and low birth weight.

Increasing rates of hypospadias have paralleled reports of other untoward end points related to male reproductive health, including increases in testicular cancer,[29] an increased incidence of cryptorchidism, and decreased semen and sperm quality.[33] In one study, 8% of patients diagnosed with undescended testes had urogenital anomalies, and more than 50% of those had hypospadias.[36] The increasing incidence of such anomalies over the past 50 years concomitant with the increased production and use of synthetic chemicals has raised concerns that environmental factors may play a role in these problems.[13,153] It is now well documented from wildlife studies and accompanying laboratory data that a number of synthetic and natural chemicals commonly found in the environment can mimic or antagonize hormones or otherwise interfere with the development and function of the endocrine and reproductive systems.[37,133] The offspring of pregnant mice exposed in utero to both estrogen and prednisone have been shown to develop hypospadias.[96] Whether endocrine disrupters are having an impact on human male reproductive health and on hypospadias in particular is difficult to determine.[143] Regardless, public health agencies worldwide are increasingly concerned about endocrine disruption, and it remains an active area of research.[59,71,86]

NORMAL AND HYPOSPADIAC PENILE ANATOMY

Surgical repair of hypospadias requires an expert understanding of the normal anatomy of the penis, as well as an understanding of the anatomy of the hypospadiac penis. The human penis consists of paired corpora cavernosa covered by a thick, elastic tunica albuginea, with a midline septum (Fig. 119-7).[18,20,77,162,163] The urethral

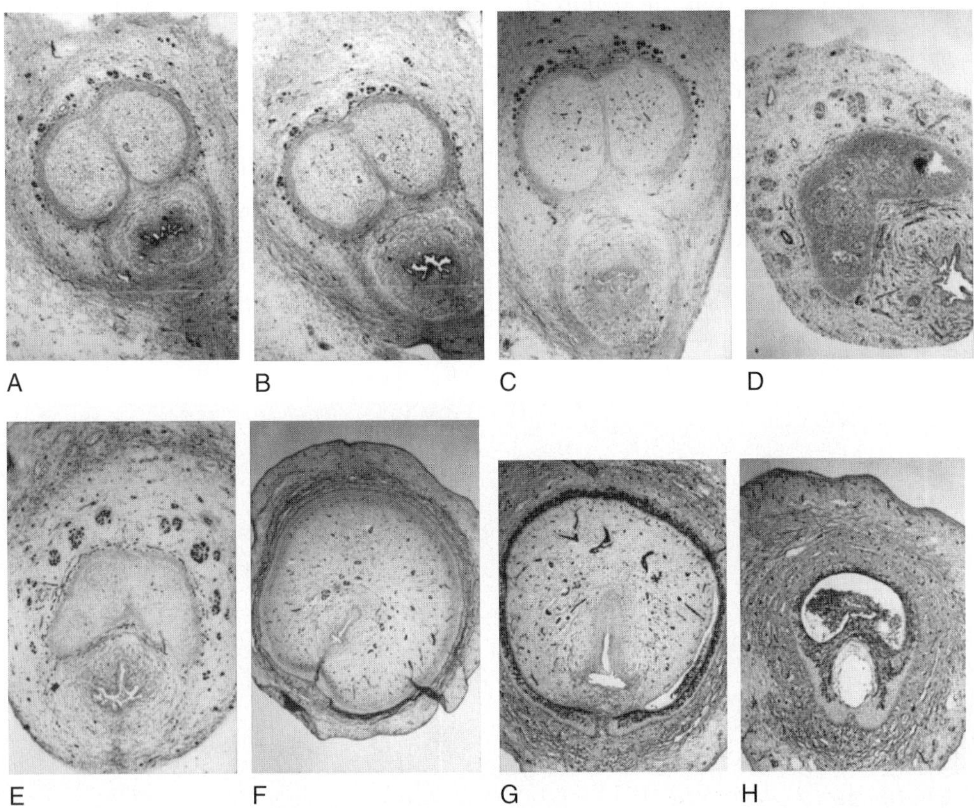

Figure 119-7 Normal human fetal penis at 25 weeks' gestation. *A* to *H*, Transverse sections, distal to proximal, immunostained with neuronal marker S-100 (25×). Note localization of the S-100 nerve marker in brown, completely surrounding the cavernous bodies up to the junction with the urethral spongiosum along the penile shaft, except at the 12 o'clock position *(A* to *D)*. On the proximal penis at the point where the corporal bodies split into two *(E)* and continue in a lateral fashion inferior and adjacent to the pubic rami, the nerves localize to an imaginary triangular area at the 11 and 1 o'clock positions. At this point *(E)*, the nerves reach their farthest vertical distance from the corporal body (about half the diameter of the corporal body) and continue *(F, G)* in a tighter formation at the 11 and 1 o'clock positions, well away from the urethra. (From Baskin LS, Erol A, et al: Anatomical studies of hypospadias. J Urol 1998;160:1108-1115.)

spongiosum lies in a ventral position, intimately engaged between the two corporal bodies. Buck's fascia surrounds the corpora cavernosa and splits to contain the corpus spongiosum in a separate compartment. Recent work has shown that the neurovascular bundle lies deep to Buck's fascia, and where the two crural bodies join to form the corporal bodies, the neurovascular bundle completely fans out around the corpora cavernosa, all the way to the junction of the corpus spongiosum (see Figs. 119-6 and 119-7).[2,162] This concept disagrees with the classic dogma that the neurovascular bundle lies in the 11 o'clock and 1 o'clock positions. Superior to Buck's fascia is the dartos fascia, which lies immediately beneath the skin. This fascia contains the blood supply to the prepuce. The prepuce is supplied by two branches of the inferior external pudendal arteries, the superficial penile arteries.[76] These arteries divide into the anterolateral and posterolateral branches. In hypospadias surgery, the island flap is typically based on the anterolateral superficial vessels. The onlay island flap, tubularized island flap, and de-epithelialized pedicle flap are dependent on careful preservation of these blood vessels. The outer skin survives from the intrinsic subcutaneous vessels.

Compared with the normal penis, the anatomy of the hypospadiac penis is no different in terms of neuronal innervation, corpora cavernosa and tunica albuginea architecture, and blood supply, except at the region of the abnormal urethral spongiosum and glans (Figs. 119-8 and 119-9).[18,19,162,163] The nerves in both the normal and the hypospadiac penis start as two well-defined bundles superior and slightly lateral to the urethra. As the two crural bodies converge into the bodies of the corpora cavernosa, the nerves diverge, spreading around the cavernosal bodies up to the junction with the urethral spongiosum, not limiting themselves to the 11 and 1 o'clock positions (see Figs. 119-7 and 119-8). The 12 o'clock position in a hypospadiac penis is spared of neuronal structures, just as in a normal penis. At the hilum of penis where the bodies of the corpora start to separate, the cavernous nerve sends nNOS-positive fibers to join the dorsal nerve of the penis, thereby changing the functional characteristics of the distal penile dorsal nerve (see Fig. 119-8). Similarly, the nNOS-negative, ventrally located perineal nerve originating from the pudendal nerve becomes nNOS reactive at the cavernosa-spongiosum junction. The redundant wiring in the penis may be important in the preservation of erectile function.[162]

The most striking difference between the normal penis and the hypospadiac penis is a difference in vascularity (see Fig. 119-9). The hypospadiac penis has huge endothelium-lined vascular channels filled with red blood cells. In contrast, the normal penis has well-defined, small capillaries around the urethra, fanning into the glans. Anatomic studies of the urethral plate show no evidence of fibrosis or scarring.[60] The urethral plate is well vascularized, has a rich nerve supply, and has an extensive muscular and connective tissue backing (Fig. 119-10). These features may explain the success of incorporating the urethral plate or abortive spongiosum into hypospadias reconstruction.[35,144]

Hypospadias repair requires attention to three major anatomic defects: (1) the abnormal urethral meatus, (2) penile curvature, and (3) the foreskin defect and, in more severe cases, scrotal anomalies.

Meatal Abnormalities

Hypospadias is characterized primarily by location and configuration abnormalities of the urethral meatus.

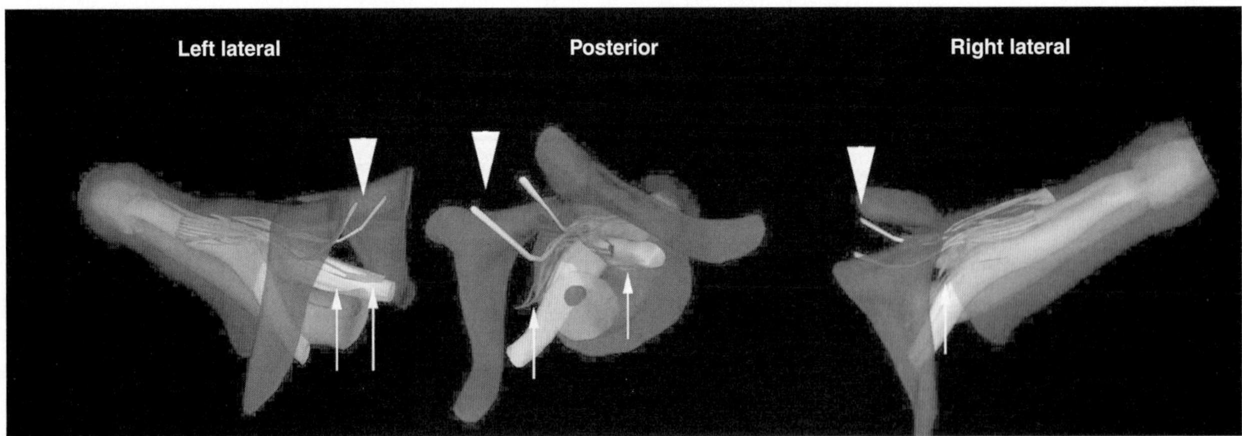

Figure 119-8 Computer-generated three-dimensional reconstruction of the normal human fetal penis at 27 weeks' gestation. Note that the pathway of the cavernosal nerves (*white arrows*) and dorsal nerves (*arrowheads*) is away from the origin of the crural bodies (*white*), which is along the ischial tuberosity. The cavernosal nerves follow a more direct pathway to reach the penile hilum, where they penetrate the corporal bodies under the pubic arch. As the cavernosal nerves travel close to the penile hilum, they send interconnecting fibers to the dorsal nerves, with subsequent positive immunostaining for nNOS. nNOS-positive dorsal nerves travel on the corporal bodies (*grey*) to the glans. As the dorsal nerves of the penis change from nNOS-negative immunostaining character into nNOS positive, the proximal nNOS-negative perineal nerves turn into nNOS-immunoreactive nerves.

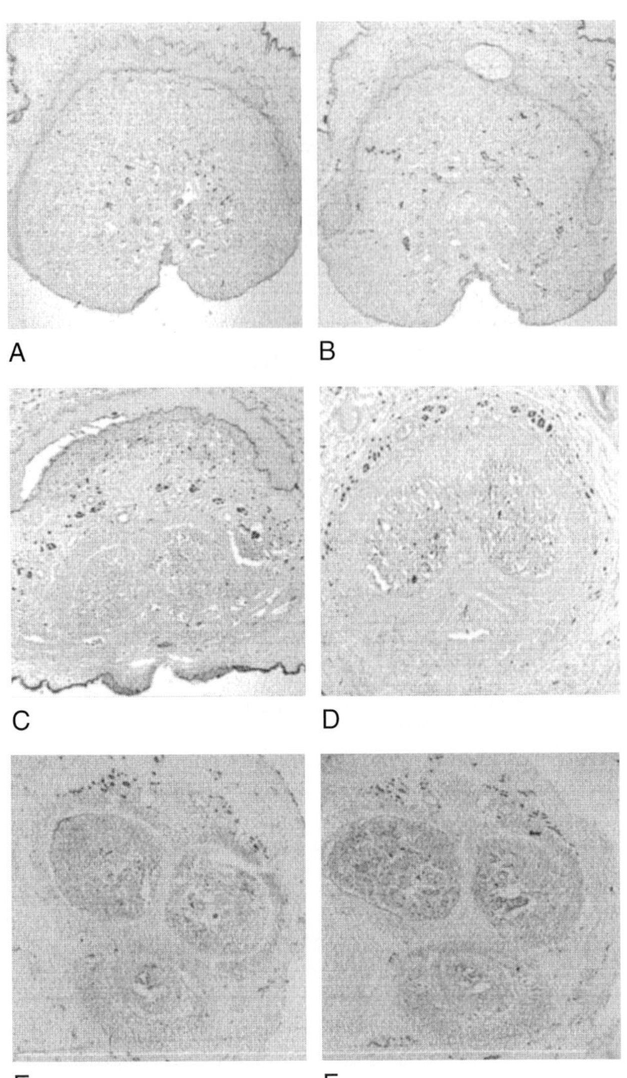

Figure 119-9 Hypospadiac penis at 33 weeks' gestation. *A* to *F,* Transverse sections, distal to proximal, immunostained with neuronal marker (dark staining) S-100 (20×). Note that the anatomy of the hypospadiac penis is the same as the normal penis, except for the abnormal formation of the distal urethra and glans *(A* to *C).* (From Baskin LS, Erol A, et al: Anatomical studies of hypospadias. J Urol 1998;160:1108-1115.)

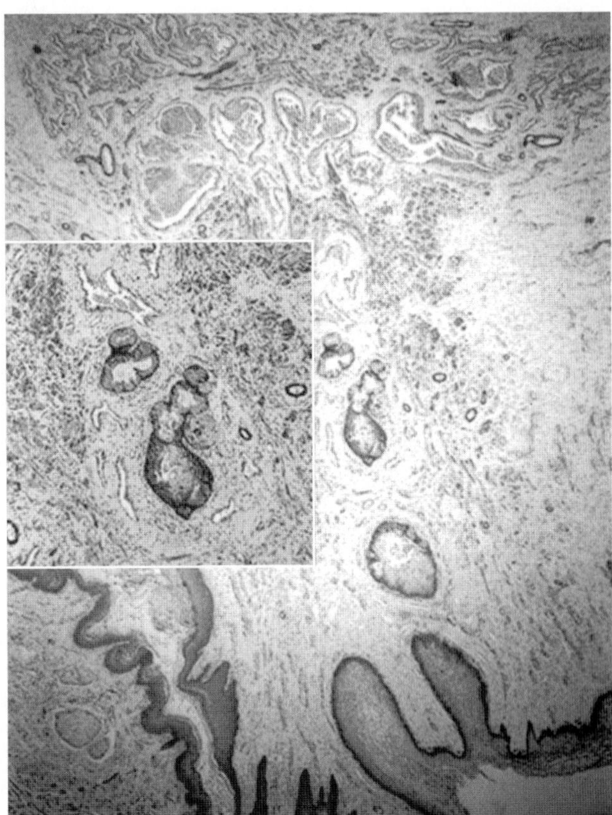

Figure 119-10 Urethral plate in a newborn human penis with proximal hypospadias (smooth muscle alpha actin immunostaining, 25×). The urethral plate is well vascularized, without any evidence of fibrosis or scarring. Epithelial nest or an abortive attempt at the formation of the urethra is seen within the plate (*inset*).

The urethral meatus may be located only slightly ventrally, just below a blind dimple at the normal meatal opening on the glans, or it may be so far back in the perineum that it appears as "vaginal hypospadias."[161] Most patients present with the meatus in one of the many transitional forms. The meatus is encountered in a variety of configurations in terms of form, diameter, elasticity, and rigidity. It can be fissured in both transverse and longitudinal directions, or it can be covered with delicate skin. In the case of the megameatus intact prepuce variant, the distal urethra is enlarged, tapering to a normal caliber in the penile shaft.[56] Often, there is an orifice of a periurethral duct located distal to the meatus that courses dorsal to the urethral channel for a short distance. It has a blind ending and does not communicate in any way with the urinary stream. The periurethral duct corresponds with Guérin's sinus or Morgagni's lacunae.[147] Unless these ducts are inadvertently closed, leading to a blind-ending epithelial pouch, they are of no clinical consequence.

Penile Curvature

The curvature of the penis is caused by a deficiency of the normal structures on the ventral side of the penis. It has been labeled chordee; however, this term implies a strand of connective tissue stretched like a cord between the meatus and the glans, giving rise to bowstringing. According to Mettauer,[107] this cord is a rudiment of the urethral corpus spongiosum. This hypothesis, however, is untenable because the corpus spongiosum is formed in the periurethral tissue only at the end of the fourth month of gestation. It can be found as a skin deficiency, a dartos fascial deficiency, a true fibrous chordee with tethering of the ventral shaft, or deficiency of the corpora cavernosa on the concave side of the penis.

There are occasional reports of other penile anomalies that represent variations of the embryologic defect causing hypospadias. They can be characterized as a defect in the course of the urethra (congenital urethral fistula) and a group of defects characterized by curvature of the penis without hypospadias.[40,131]

Skin and Scrotal Abnormalities

The skin of the penis is radically changed as a result of the disturbance in the formation of the urethra. Distal to the meatus, there is often a paucity of ventral skin, which may contribute to penile curvature. The frenulum is always absent in hypospadias. Vestiges of a frenulum are sometimes found inserting on either side of the open navicular fossa.

The skin proximal to the urethral meatus may be extremely thin, to the extent that a catheter or probe passed proximally may be readily apparent through the tissue-paper thickness of skin. When this is the case, it abrogates the use of perimeatal skin flaps in repairs (Mathieu repair).

The urethral plate extending from the meatus to the glanular groove may be well developed. Even with a meatus located quite proximal on the shaft, this normal urethral plate is elastic and typically nontethering. Artificial erection demonstrates no ventral curvature in these situations. A normal urethral plate may be incorporated into the surgical repair. However, if the urethral plate is underdeveloped, it will act as a tethering fibrous band that bends the penis ventrally during artificial erection. When this fibrous chordee tissue is divided, the penis frequently straightens out with this maneuver alone.

Normally, the genital tubercle should develop in a cranial position above the two genital swellings. The penis may be caught between the two scrotal halves and become engulfed with fusion of the penoscrotal area. The boundary between the penis and the scrotum may be formed by two oblique raphes that extend from the proximal meatus to the dorsal side of the penis.

TREATMENT

The object of therapy is to reconstruct a straight penis with a meatus as close as possible to the normal site (ventrum of the terminal aspect of the glans) to allow a forward-directed urine stream and normal coitus. There are five basic phases for a successful hypospadias outcome: (1) orthoplasty (straightening), (2) urethroplasty, (3) meatoplasty and glanuloplasty, (4) scrotoplasty, and (5) skin cover. These elements can be applied sequentially or in various combinations to achieve surgical success (Fig. 119-11). They are described in conjunction with a number of specific surgical techniques in this section.

Anterior Hypospadias

The treatment of anterior hypospadias is dependent on the cultural preference of the child's family. Many patients with anterior hypospadias do not have a functional defect, lack significant penile curvature, and will be able to stand and void with a straight stream. Therefore, the goal of placing the meatus in its normal position within the glans is essentially cosmetic. The outcome needs to be as close to perfect as possible. The present standard is outpatient surgery, typically without the need for urethral stents. The technique chosen depends on the anatomy of the hypospadiac penis. The most common procedures are the MAGPI (meatal advancement glansplasty), the GAP (glans approximation procedure), primary tubularization, the Mathieu or flip-flap, and the Snodgrass technique or tubularized incised plate urethroplasty.[51,55,104,144,145,165]

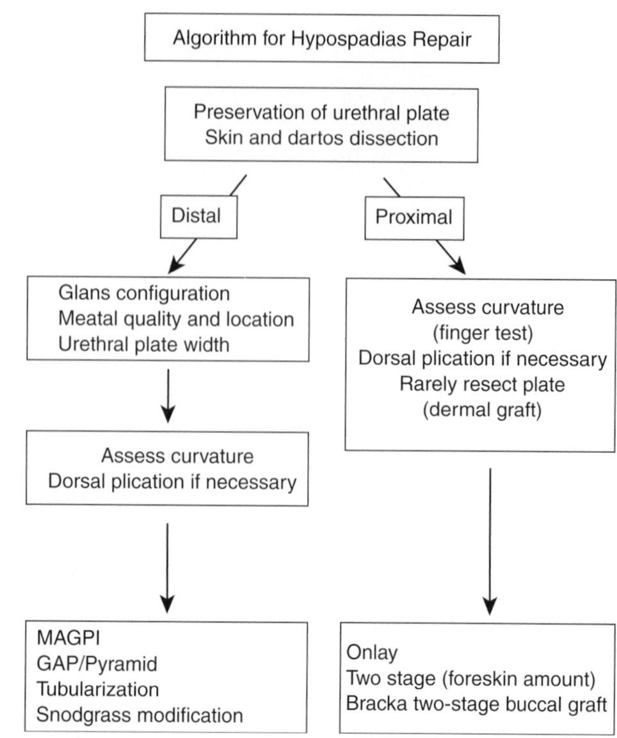

Figure 119–11 Algorithm for hypospadias repair. GAP, glans approximation procedure; MAGPI, meatal advancement glansplasty.

MAGPI Technique

The MAGPI technique was devised by Duckett[51] in 1981. This technique provides outstanding results in appropriately selected patients. The hypospadiac penis that is amenable to the MAGPI technique is characterized by a dorsal web of tissue within the glans that deflects the urine from either a coronal or a slightly subcoronal meatus. The urethra itself must have a normal ventral wall, without any thin or atretic urethral spongiosum. The urethra also must be mobile so that it can be advanced into the glans (Fig. 119-12).

A circumferential incision is made around the corona proximal to the meatus on the ventrum and 5 mm below the coronal margin to create a Firlit collar on the dorsum (see Fig. 119-12A). The penile skin is mobilized as a sleeve back to the penoscrotal junction, thus straightening the penis by freeing any tethering fibers of the skin and subdartos fascia, particularly on the ventrum. This is the most likely cause of the ventral tilt of the glans frequently seen in these cases. Penile torsion is also

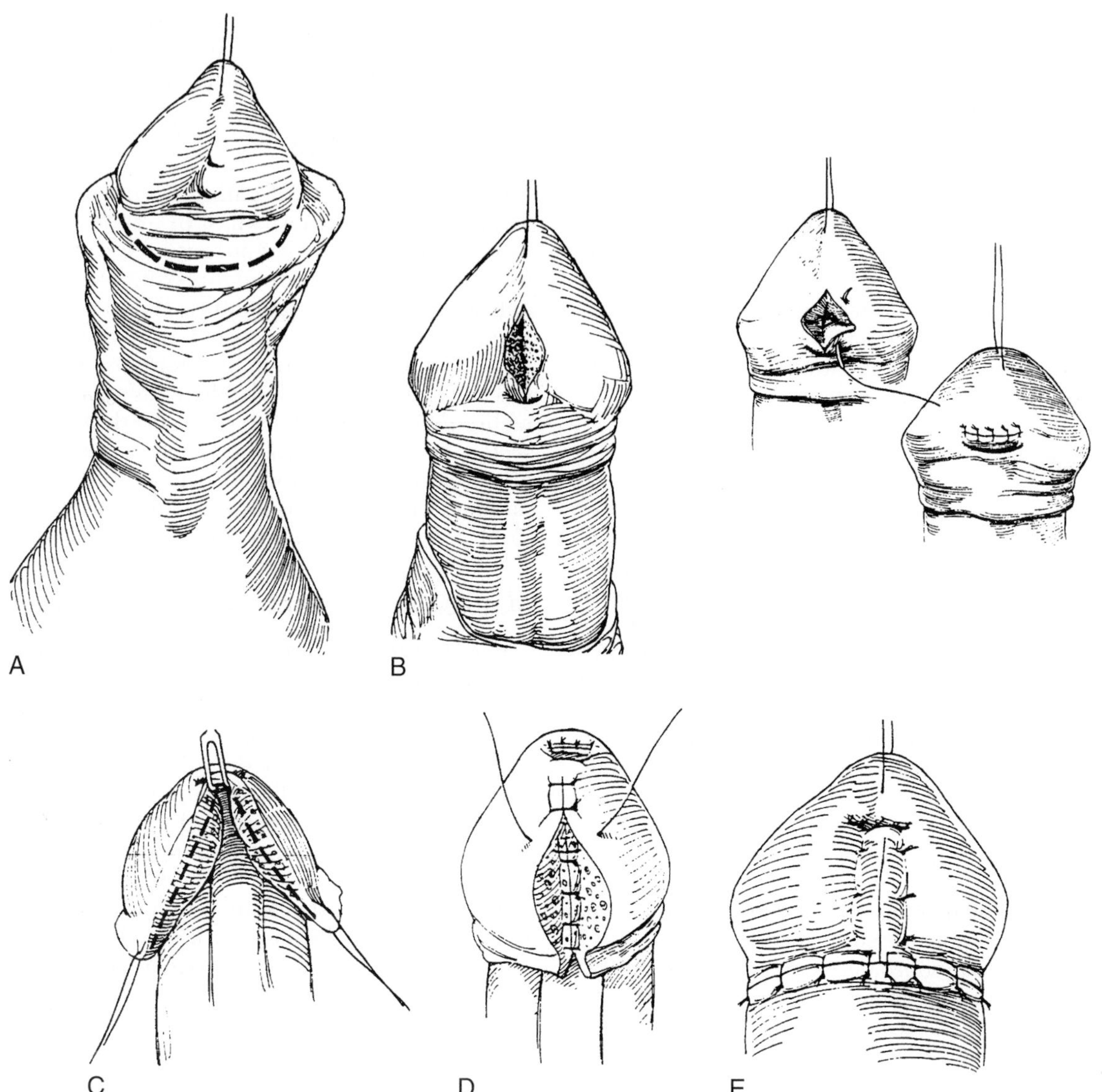

Figure 119–12 MAGPI hypospadias technique. *A,* Initial circumferential subcoronal incision. *B,* Heineke-Mikulicz closure of the dorsal meatus after excision of the dorsal web skin bridge. *C,* Exposure of the glans mesenchyme, the most critical step, is accomplished by trimming the excess skin *(dashed lines)* and advancing the mobile urethra with the use of a 6-0 chromic suture or a skin hook. *D,* Two-layer closure of the glans mesenchyme over the advanced urethra, allowing for a normal-appearing glans with excellent support of the urethra. *E,* Skin closure with a sleeve approximation of the penile shaft skin. If there is ventral skin deficiency, a Byar's flap rearrangement with a standard midline seam is appropriate. (From Hinman F Jr: Atlas of Pediatric Urologic Surgery. Philadelphia, WB Saunders, 1994, pp 575-578.)

corrected in many cases if the dissection is carried back to the base of the penis. The straightness of the penis is then checked with an artificial erection.

The meatal advancement of the dorsal urethral wall is accomplished by a Heineke-Mikulicz vertical incision and horizontal closure (see Fig. 119-12B). More commonly, a wedge of glanular tissue that includes the glanular meatal wall is removed. The horizontal closure flattens out the glanular bridge and permits the dorsal urethra to be advanced out onto the glans tissue to the apex of the glanular groove, where it is sutured with interrupted 7-0 Vicryl (see Fig. 119-12C). This flattens the deflecting ridge of glans and permits the stream to be directed forward.

The glansplasty is made by reconfiguring the flattened glans into a conical shape (see Fig. 119-12D). By rotating the lateral wings around to the midline proximal to the meatus, a proper conical glans shape can be re-created. Skin adjacent to the glanular edges must be excised in a precise angle to reapproximate the glanular wings together in the midline on the ventrum. The deep glanular tissue is brought together with interrupted 6-0 Vicryl, and the superficial epithelial edges are closed with 7-0 chromic suture (see Fig. 119-12E). In this way, mesenchymal glans tissue heals to glans tissue between the epithelial layers of the urethra and the outer epithelium of the glans; this prevents meatal retraction. The rotation of the glans wings reconfigures a nearly normal glanular appearance. A bougie à boule is used to calibrate the meatus and ensure that the glanuloplasty has not compromised the lumen of the distal glanular urethra.

A sleeve reapproximation of the penile skin is usually sufficient for skin coverage (see Fig. 119-12E). When there is ventral skin deficiency, dorsal preputial skin can be transposed in a Byar's flap fashion to the ventrum. No stents or catheters are required for diversion in children younger than 18 months. Preservation of the foreskin is possible with the MAGPI procedure as long as chordee is minimal.[46] Polus and Lotte[122] and Gilpin[66] demonstrated foreskin preservation in anterior hypospadias repair without chordee.

MAGPI procedures are done in the day surgical unit. The success of the MAGPI remains proper patient selection. A well-supported, mobile ventral urethra is necessary for the prevention of meatal regression (Fig. 119-13).

GAP Procedure

The GAP procedure is applicable in a small subset of patients with anterior hypospadias who have wide and deep glanular grooves.[165] These patients do not have a bridge of glanular tissue that typically deflects the urine stream, as seen in patients who would be more appropriately treated with the MAGPI procedure. In the GAP procedure, the wide-mouthed urethra is tubularized primarily, over a stent (Fig. 119-14). Ventral glanular tilt, meatal retraction, and splaying of the urine stream can result from the inappropriate use of the MAGPI technique in these circumstances.

Urethral Mobilization

Another method of dealing with a subcoronal meatus is urethral mobilization. Reported as far back as 1917 by Beck,[22] urethral mobilization was revived by Koff,[97] Nasrallah and Minott,[112] and de Sy and Hoebeke.[41] This technique offers little advantage over the MAGPI technique and requires a more extensive procedure to mobilize the penile urethra. The meatal stenosis rate is significant.

Pyramid Procedure

Another small subset of patients presents with a unique form of anterior hypospadias. In 6% of those with anterior hypospadias, the prepuce is intact, and a megameatus exists under the normal foreskin, with a wide glanular defect and no penile curvature (Fig. 119-15).[54,56] These anomalies may be recognized only after circumcision is performed; correction is therefore more complex. Duckett and Keating[54] designated this repair the "pyramid" technique. The enormous distal urethra is carefully dissected down the shaft of the glans and distal penis by way of a four-quadrant exposure (hence the pyramid designation). The urethra is tapered and buried in the glans, similar to an epispadias repair (see Fig. 119-15C).

Mathieu or Perimeatal-Based Flap Procedure

When the meatus is too proximal on the shaft to perform a MAGPI procedure, or when there is no deep glanular groove appropriate for a GAP or in situ tubularization technique (see later), the meatus is advanced onto the glans using the technique described in 1932 by the French surgeon Mathieu.[104] This technique involves the use of a perimeatal skin flap, based on the intrinsic blood supply. To ensure viability, the length-to-width ratio of the skin flap should not exceed 2:1. The flap has also been used essentially as a free skin graft, with no attempt made to preserve any of the subcutaneous tissue. A pedicle of foreskin is brought around, as in a vascularized flap technique, and used as a recipient bed. When designing a Mathieu

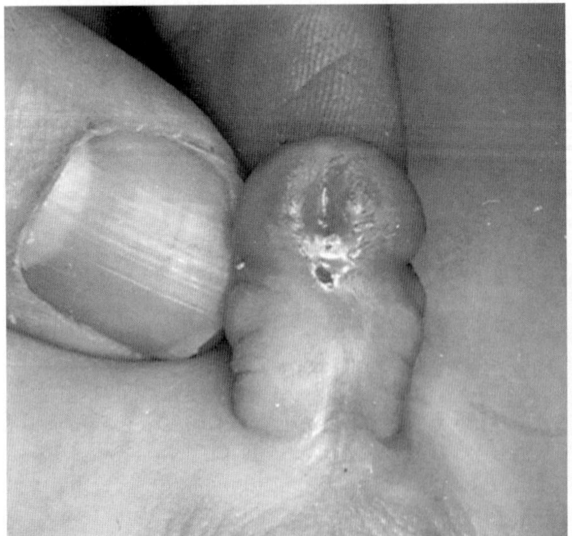

A

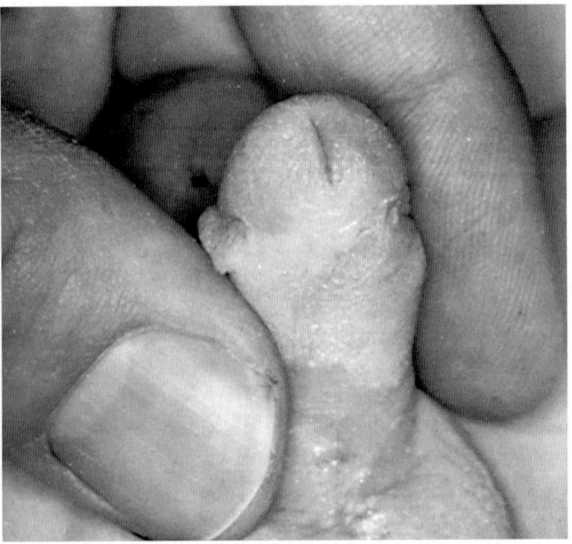

B

Figure 119–13 *A,* Preoperative patient with anterior hypospadias amenable to the MAGPI procedure. Note the dorsal web of tissue. *B,* Postoperative result of the MAGPI procedure. (From Duckett JW, Baskin LA: Hypospadias. In Gillenwater J, et al [eds]: Adult and Pediatric Urology, 3rd ed. St Louis, Mosby-Year Book, 1996.)

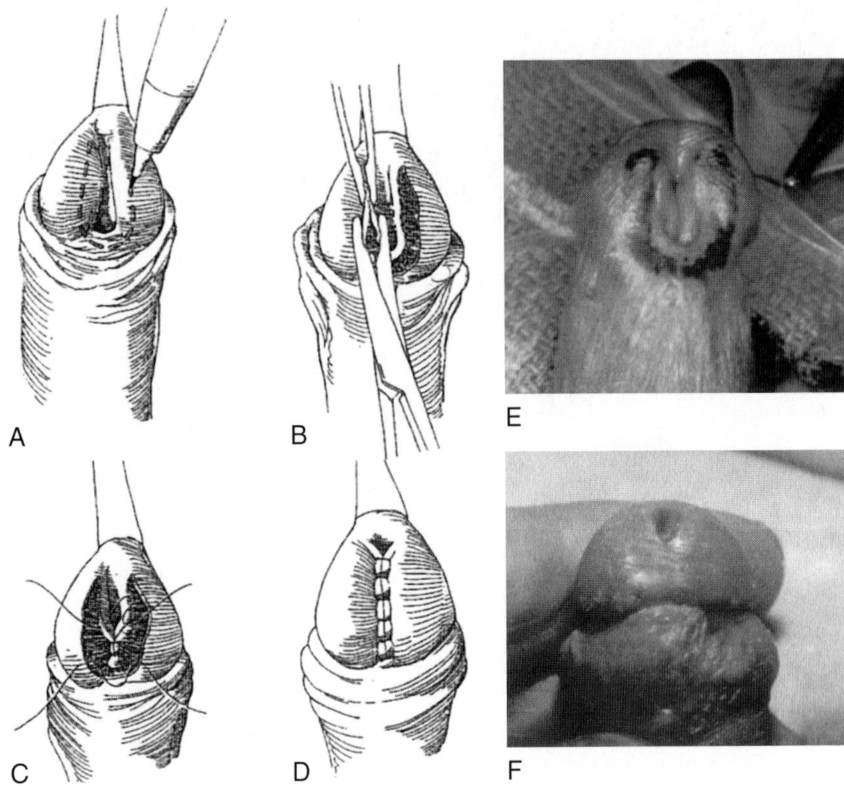

Figure 119–14 GAP hypospadias technique. *A*, Initial incision. *B*, Exposure of the glans mesenchyme by de-epithelialization of tissue. This is critical for a two-layer glans closure and provides good support of the urethroplasty. *C*, Tubularization of the neourethra, followed by glans closure. *D*, Completed repair. *E*, Anterior hypospadias with a patulous fish-mouth urethra amenable to the GAP procedure. *F*, Postoperative outcome.

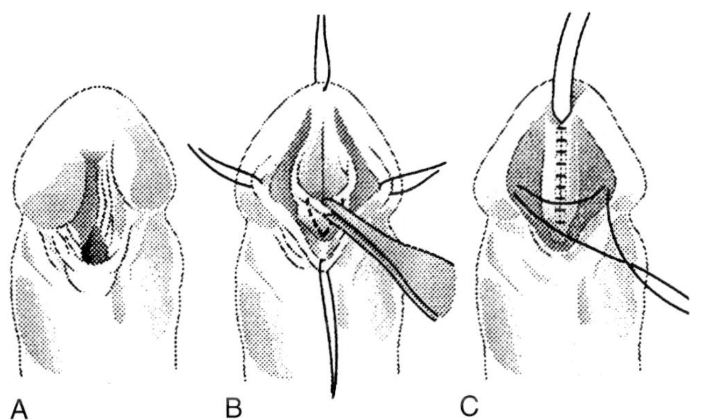

Figure 119–15 Megameatus hypospadias repaired by the pyramid procedure. *A*, Patients with a megameatus have a very wide glanular defect and no penile curvature. Calibration reveals that the meatus is 22 to 24 French in a newborn baby, compared with the normal caliber of 12 to 14 French. Often this anomaly is recognized only after circumcision. Correction, however, is the same as if the foreskin were intact. *B*, The technique involves careful periurethral dissection, exposing the urethra as well as glans tissue, and then removing a wedge of the abnormally enlarged urethra. *C*, The exposed glans tissue is closed over the newly closed neourethra. Technically, this procedure involves careful dissection down the shaft and distal penis by way of a four-quadrant exposure, hence its designation as the pyramid technique. Tapering the urethra and burying it into the glans are similar to the technique used for epispadias.

repair (Fig. 119-16), the ventral skin must be able to be advanced to its new location on the glans. Some modifications of the Mathieu procedure involve a second layer as a subcutaneous pedicle.

Redman[127] revived the Barcat[11] modification of the Mathieu procedure by mobilizing a glans flap in addition to the perimeatal-based flap and splitting the glans dorsally to bury the urethral extension further toward the apex of the glans. Koff et al.[98] have extensive experience with this technique and have reported excellent results.

Snodgrass Tubularized Incised Plate Urethroplasty

Historically, if the urethral groove was not wide enough for tubularization in situ, an alternative approach was taken, such as the Mathieu technique or, for more severe hypospadias, a vascularized pedicle flap. More recently, the concept of incising the urethral plate, with subsequent tubularization and secondary healing, was introduced by Snodgrass[144] (Fig. 119-17). Short-term results have been excellent, and this procedure is enjoying extensive popularity.[145] One appealing aspect is the slitlike meatus, which is created with a dorsal midline incision. This technique has also been applied to more posterior forms of hypospadias.[146] Theoretically, one concern is the possibility of meatal stenosis from scarring, as occurs in patients

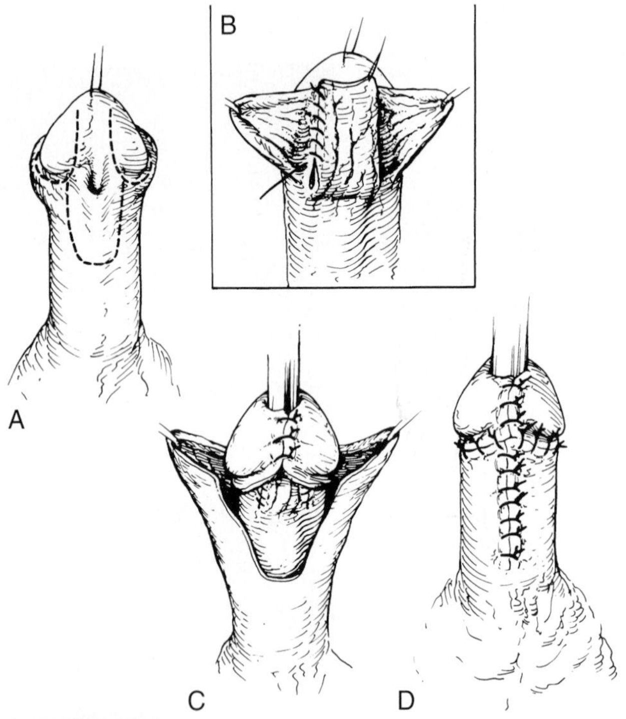

Figure 119-16 Mathieu procedure. *A, Dotted lines* outline the skin flaps. *B,* The proximal flap is rotated, and the lateral glans flaps are developed. *C,* The glans flaps cover the neourethra, and preputial skin is moved, if necessary. *D,* Completed repair. (From Duckett JW: Hypospadias. In Walsh PC, Gittes RF, Perlmutter AD, et al [eds]: Campbell's Urology, 5th ed. Philadelphia, WB Saunders, 1986, pp 1969-1999.)

with urethral stricture disease; in the latter, direct-vision internal urethrotomy often leads to recurrent stricture. However, reports of meatal stenosis have been rare.[35,84] In hypospadias, the native virgin tissue, with its excellent blood supply and large vascular sinuses, seems to respond to primary incision and secondary healing without scarring. The tubularized incised plate urethroplasty is conducive to preservation of the foreskin (Fig. 119-18). To preserve the foreskin, the incision is made only on the ventrum; therefore, patients with significant penile curvature are not candidates for this procedure. A three-layer closure of the prepuce prevents foreskin fistula. The fact that the foreskin cannot be used as a de-epithelialized flap theoretically increases the possibility of urethral fistula.

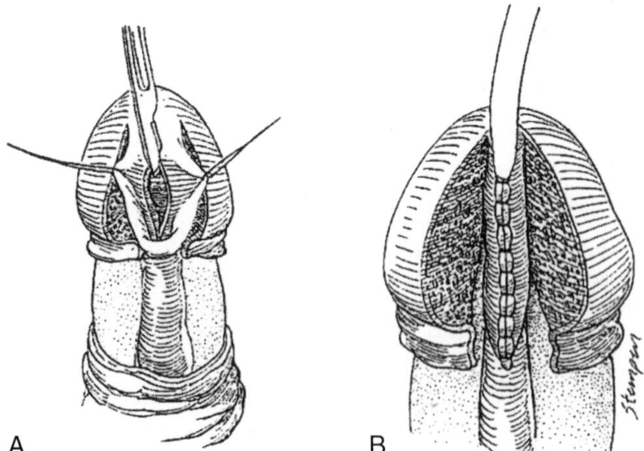

Figure 119-17 Tubularized incised plate urethroplasty. *A,* Deep incision in the urethral plate down to corporal tissue. *B,* Tubularization of the neourethra, with subsequent glansplasty.

Posterior Hypospadias

Urethral Plate Preservation

Duckett popularized the concept of preserving the urethral plate, which is now standard practice for the repair of posterior and more severe anterior hypospadias.[16,52] The urethral plate serves as the dorsal urethral wall, and the ventral urethra is created by a vascular onlay flap of tissue from the inner prepuce. Extensive experience has shown that the urethral plate is rarely the cause of penile curvature (Fig. 119-19). This knowledge was gained by repetitive resectioning of the urethral plate and subsequent artificial erection, which showed no improvement in correction of the penile curvature (see Fig. 119-19).[16] Further efforts and experience showed that the urethral plate was supple and pliable and that ancillary penile strengthening procedures, with preservation of the urethral plate, led to fewer complications, such as fistula and stenosis at the proximal anastomosis.[14,16]

The concept of preserving the urethral plate but undermining it[108,110] and exposing the corporal bodies—with the goal of releasing the chordee tissue—has not met with success. In fact, careful anatomic studies have shown the existence of an extensive network of blood vessels supplying the urethral plate in the hypospadiac penis, and lifting the urethral plate defeats the purpose of preservation by violating this intricate blood supply.[18] Thus, the technique of mobilization of the urethral plate should be abandoned.

Historically, posterior hypospadias was approached by complete resection of the abnormal urethra and all tissue down to normal corporal bodies. The urethra was replaced by a tubularized vascular preputial flap from either the inner or outer prepuce.[8,50,148] Presently, in the majority of cases of posterior hypospadias, including perineal hypospadias, the urethral plate can be preserved and a vascularized flap used in an onlay fashion. In the rare case in which the urethral plate needs to be resected, a two-stage technique can be used (see later).

Onlay Island Flap

The blood supply to the hypospadiac preputial tissue is reliable and easily delineated (see Fig. 119-18).[76,88] The abundance of cutaneous tissue on the dorsum of the penis is vascularized in a longitudinal fashion.[124] This tissue may be dissected from the penile skin, creating an island flap from the inner layer of the prepuce. The blood supply to the dorsal skin of the foreskin and the penile skin comes from its broad base and is not dependent on the subcutaneous tissues, except at the remote edges of the dorsal preputial skin. The tips of the distal portion of the penile skin flaps can be excised and not used in the repair.

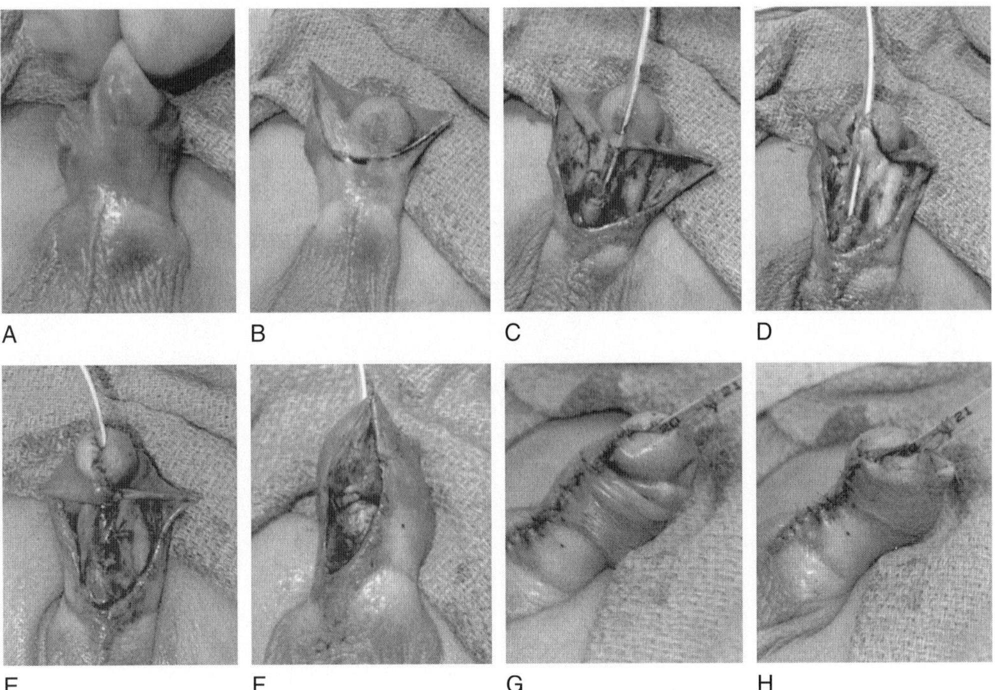

Figure 119–18 Foreskin preservation technique for distal hypospadias. *A,* Distal hypospadias. *B,* The incision is marked for foreskin preservation. *C,* Dissection of ventral skin. Note the thin spongiosum with the distal urethra exposed. *D,* Glans wings have been mobilized, and the distal urethroplasty is completed by the Snodgrass technique. *E,* Two-layer glansplasty. *F,* Three-layer foreskin reconstruction: (1) inner prepuce, (2) subcutaneous tissue to prevent foreskin fistulas, and (3) outer foreskin. *G,* Completed repair with foreskin retracted. *H,* Completed repair.

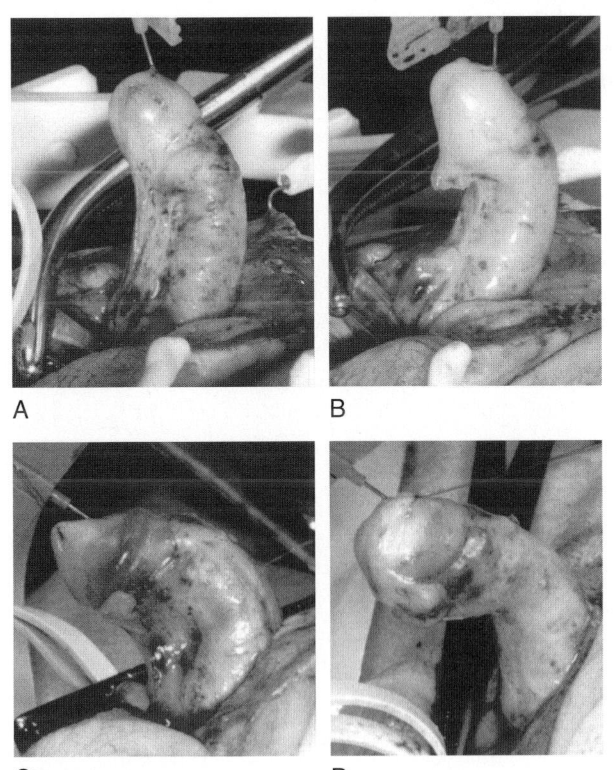

Figure 119–19 *A,* Penile curvature with preservation of the urethral plate. *B,* Resection of the urethral plate with continued severe curvature. *C,* Penile curvature with preservation of the urethral plate. *D,* Resection of the urethral plate with continued severe curvature. Extensive experience has shown that the urethral plate is rarely the cause of penile curvature.

All cases of posterior hypospadias (i.e., with or without penile curvature) are approached by initially leaving the urethral plate intact. This technique can be applied to penile shaft as well as scrotal and perineal hypospadias. The intact dorsal plate essentially avoids the complication of proximal stricture, and the excellent blood supply has decreased the fistula rate to approximately 5% to 10% for all cases of onlay island flap hypospadias repair (Fig. 119-20).[16] For shorter repairs, the flap may be dissected from half the prepuce, as described by Rushton et al.,[137] leaving the remaining half of the foreskin available for a second layer of coverage. Long-term results with the onlay island flap have been very durable.[16,58,108] For severe hypospadias, the prepuce can be designed in a horseshoe style to bridge extensive gaps (see Fig. 119-20K).

Transverse Tubularized Island Flap

The technique of using the transverse tubularized island flap was used extensively before the concept of preserving the urethral plate (Fig. 119-21). It is still successful in severe cases when the urethral plate needs to be resected, although long-term problems with diverticulum have resulted in a high reoperation rate. Technical nuances involve an oblique proximal anastomosis with interrupted sutures, to avoid stenosis; fixation of the neourethra to the corporal bodies, to prevent diverticulum and improve ease of catheterization; and a wide glans channel made underneath the glans cap, against the corporal bodies, to avoid meatal stenosis.[50] Presently, a two-stage approach is commonly employed.

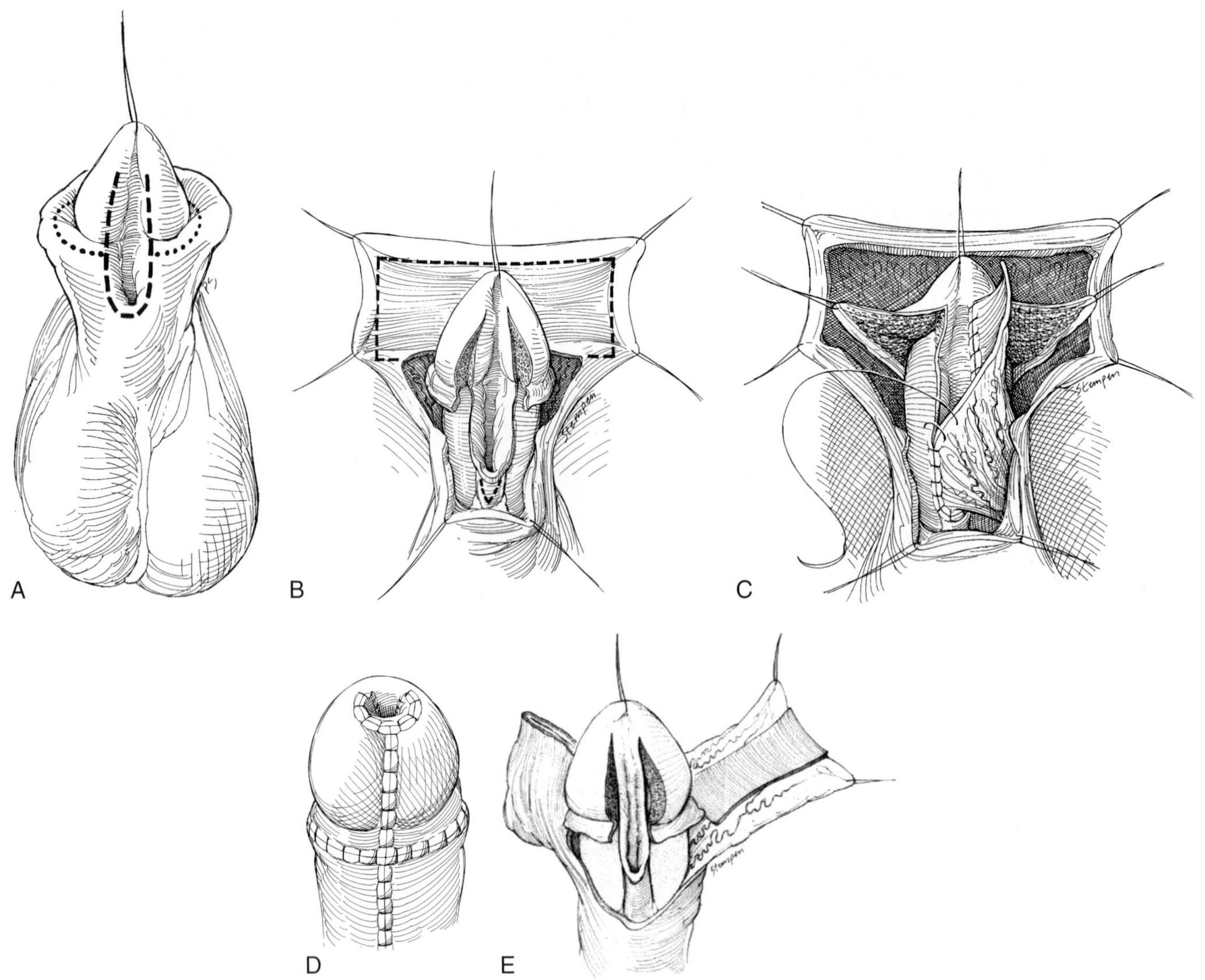

Figure 119–20 Onlay island flap hypospadias repair. *A,* A U-shaped incision is made around the urethral plate, preserving a dorsal urethral strip approximately 8 mm wide. *B,* Takedown of the skin and subcutaneous tissue, and outlining of the inner prepuce for the onlay island flap. Glans wings are mobilized along the plane of the corporal body and the glans mesenchyme. *C,* Preservation of the urethral plate with penile curvature in a case of penoscrotal hypospadias. *D,* Suturing of the onlay flap to the urethral plate with running 7-0 sutures. The flap is trimmed to obtain a 12 French bougie in a child 1 year old to prevent the complication of urethral diverticulum, which results from leaving excess tissue. The glans wings are approximated over the new urethra after maturing the meatus. The skin is then closed by a classic Byar's flap rearrangement. *E,* The split prepuce in situ technique for dissection of a short vascularized onlay island flap. This method is useful for shorter onlays, leaving the remaining half of the foreskin available for a second layer of coverage.

Continued

Two-Stage Hypospadias Repair

An alternative approach for severe hypospadias is to transfer the dorsal prepuce to the ventrum after correcting the penile curvature (Fig. 119-22). In severe cases, the urethral plate may need to be resected to correct chordee. Dermal grafting may be required, and performing a urethroplasty on top of the healing graft is not suggested. Byar's flaps can be rotated from the dorsum, setting up ventral coverage for subsequent urethroplasty.[128] Occasionally, the chordee can be corrected without resection of the urethral plate. In this case, the dorsal skin can be sutured to each side of the preserved urethral plate (see Fig. 119-22D). The second stage is performed at least 6 months after the first stage. To facilitate the urethroplasty within the glans, dorsal skin is tucked within the glans wings during the first stage. Subcutaneous secondary coverage of the reconstructed urethra is performed to prevent fistula.

Bracka Two-Stage Buccal Graft Repair

For patients with prior surgery or with severe hypospadias, Bracka described a two-stage buccal graft repair.[30] In the first stage, the penis is straightened, and the scarred urethra is discarded (Figs. 119-23 and 119-24). Buccal mucosa is harvested from either the cheek or the lip and grafted to the prepared bed.[15] Extensive quilting of the

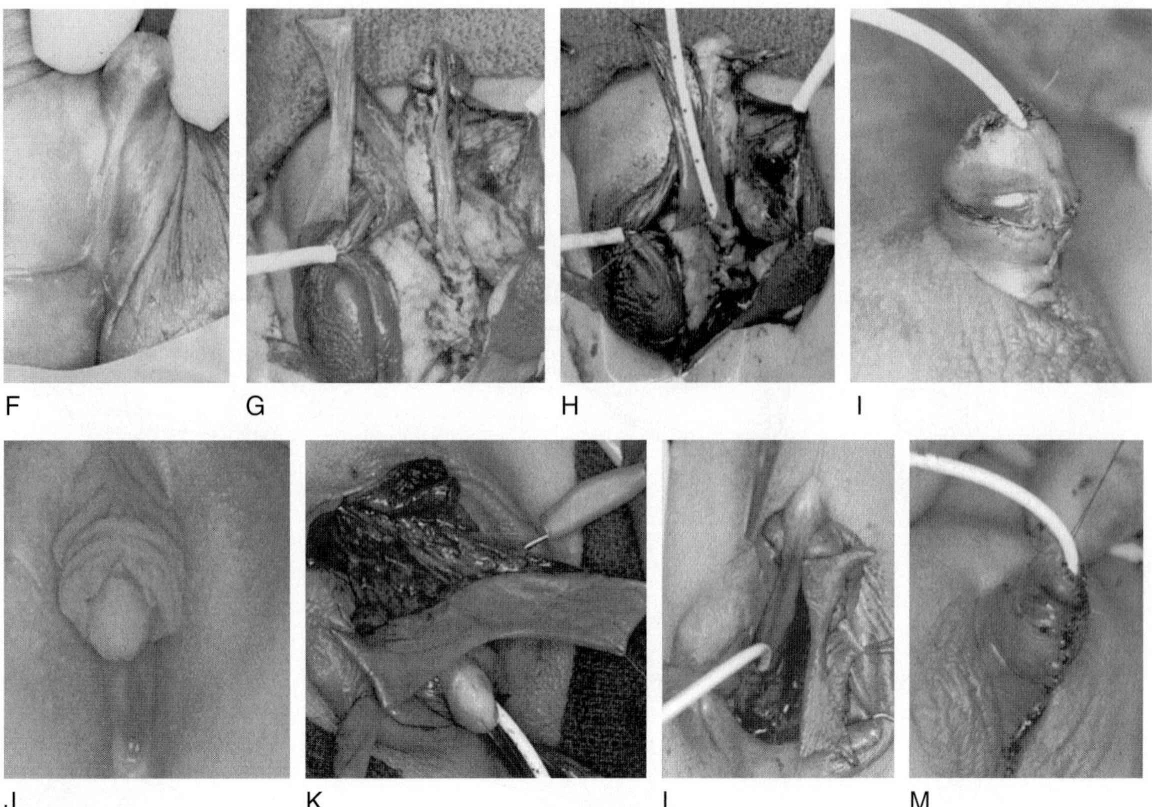

Figure 119–20—Cont'd *F,* Penoscrotal hypospadias amenable to the onlay island flap technique. *G,* Preservation of the urethral plate and flap dissection. *H,* Suturing of the onlay to the urethral plate. *I,* Completed repair. *J,* Perineal hypospadias. *K,* Horseshoe vascularized onlay island flap to bridge a long urethral deficit. *L,* Onlay flap rotated to bridge the urethral defect. *M,* Completed repair.

graft is performed to prevent hematoma from lifting off the buccal mucosa. During the first stage, glans wings are mobilized in preparation for the creation of a slitlike meatus during the second stage. The second-stage urethroplasty is undertaken at least 6 months after the first stage. In the second stage, excess buccal mucosa is trimmed off the glans, setting up a two-layer glans closure (see Figs. 119-23 and 119-24). The buccal mucosa is rolled into the new urethra, and subcutaneous tissue is used for secondary coverage.

Penile Curvature

Correction of penile curvature has evolved along with the concept of preserving the urethral plate. Artificial erection, introduced by Gittes and McLaughlin[67] in 1974, provides a mechanism to check for penile curvature and the success of correction at the time of surgery. A tourniquet is placed at the base of the penis, and a corpus cavernosum is injected with saline. Both corporal bodies fill so that it is possible to determine the extent of curvature and the success after resection of the fibrous tissue. The assurance of complete correction is essential before proceeding to urethroplasty and one-stage repair. There have been no reports of damage to the cavernous tissue with this technique, as long as care is taken to ensure that injectable saline is used.

In about 25% of hypospadias cases, the ventral curvature is attributable to a true fibrous band or fan-shaped area of fibrosis tethering the penis ventrally. When this tissue is excised, the penis straightens. This simplified explanation is not altogether applicable to the various forms of hypospadias. Certainly, the concept of a bowstring tether that requires simple excision is not true. Kaplan and Lamm[89] made a convincing case that chordee may be caused by an arrest of normal embryologic development, analogous to failure of testicular descent. In reality, all penises have chordee during development (Fig. 119-25). Thus, it is no surprise that fibrosis is conspicuously absent in some clinical cases of ventral curvature. Curvature may also result from differential growth of the dorsal and ventral aspects of the corpora,[23] which is best corrected by shortening the dorsal tunica albuginea. Some have suggested that in some cases, adherence of skin to the distal hypoplastic urethra causes chordee, and correction of the bend can be achieved by simply freeing the skin attachments, so-called skin chordee. Curvature may also be associated with a marked skin deficiency on the ventrum (see Fig. 119-25).[4] Devine and Horton[45] have offered a classification of chordee (types I to III). In their view, type III is a deficiency of dartos fascia that may contribute to penile curvature, similar to skin chordee.

For true fibrous chordee, the penis is curved ventrally, with only a short distance between the location of the meatus and the glans. An incision is made in a circumferential

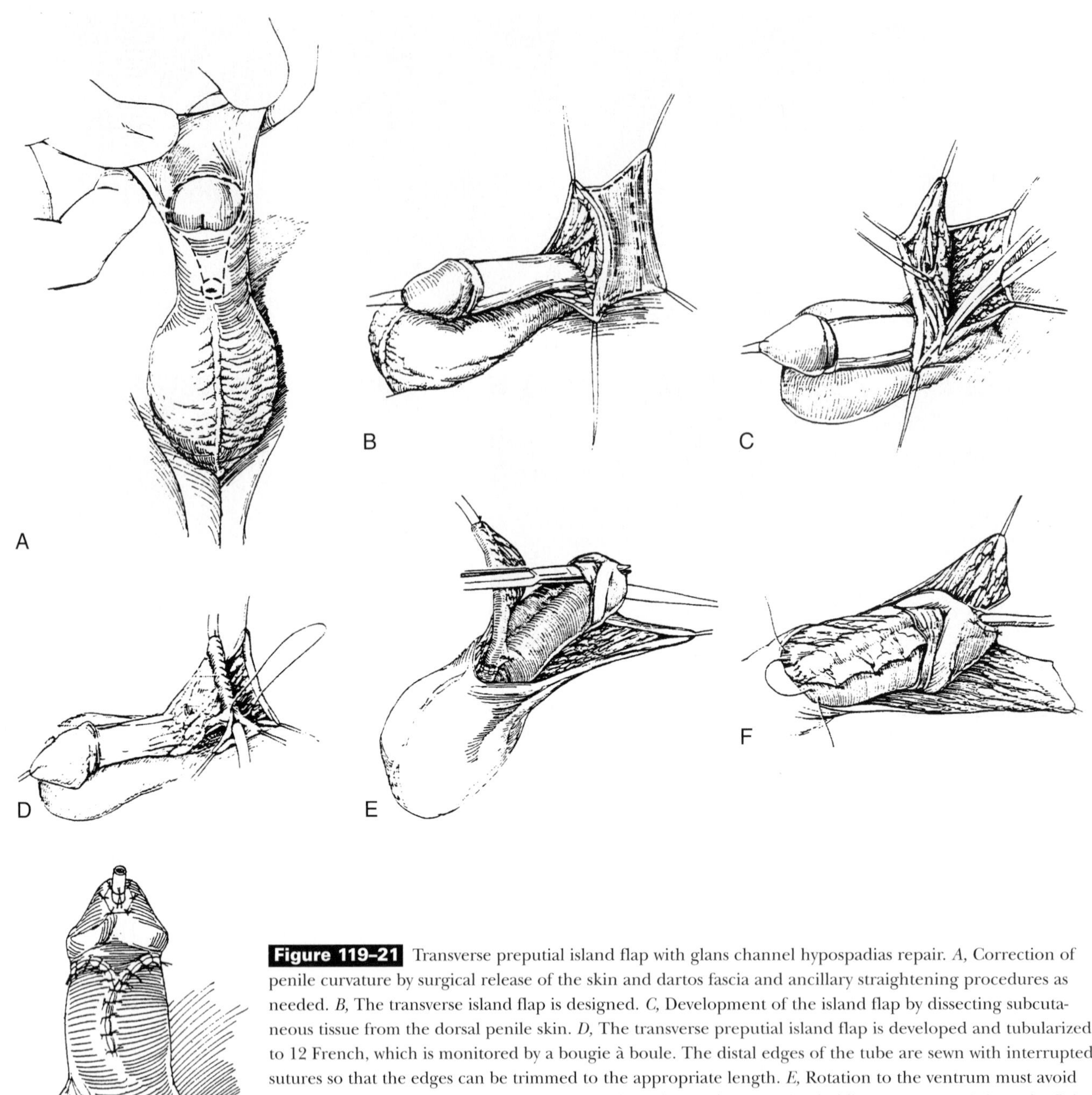

Figure 119–21 Transverse preputial island flap with glans channel hypospadias repair. *A,* Correction of penile curvature by surgical release of the skin and dartos fascia and ancillary straightening procedures as needed. *B,* The transverse island flap is designed. *C,* Development of the island flap by dissecting subcutaneous tissue from the dorsal penile skin. *D,* The transverse preputial island flap is developed and tubularized to 12 French, which is monitored by a bougie à boule. The distal edges of the tube are sewn with interrupted sutures so that the edges can be trimmed to the appropriate length. *E,* Rotation to the ventrum must avoid torsion of the shaft by freeing the base of the flap adequately. A proximal oblique anastomosis is made, fixing the urethroplasty to the tunica albuginea along its posterior anastomosis. A wide glans channel is made underneath the glans cap against the corporal bodies by removing glans tissue within the channel. *F,* The neourethra is tacked to the corporal bodies. *G,* Lateral transposition of Byar's flaps of dorsal penile skin to the midline and excision of the tips. The repair is stented with a 6 French catheter. (From Hinman F Jr: Atlas of Pediatric Urologic Surgery. Philadelphia, WB Saunders, 1994, pp 590-592.)

manner around the corona and is carried well below the glans cap, just distal to the urethral meatus and down to the tunica albuginea of the corpora cavernosa. Proximal dissection is then achieved, freeing the fibrous plaque of tissue adherent to the tunica albuginea. Sharp scissors dissection is used, moving from side to side and proximally as the ventral curvature is released. The urethra is elevated from the corpora in this en bloc dissection. In most cases, the chordee tissue surrounds the urethral meatus and extends proximal along the urethra for

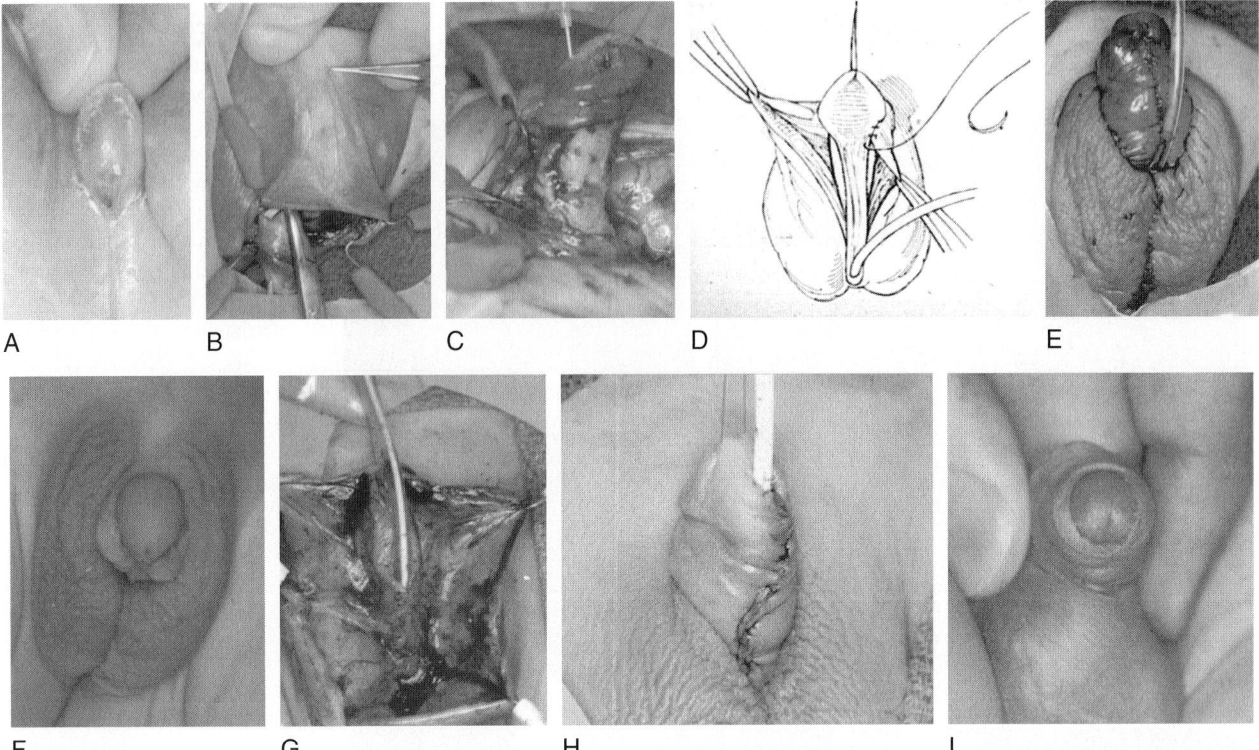

Figure 119–22 Two-stage hypospadias repair. The first stage includes correction of penile chordee and transfer of dorsal foreskin to the ventral aspect of the penis. *A,* Scrotal hypospadias with chordee and penoscrotal transposition. *B,* Foreskin attached to the scrotal skin. *C,* Penile straightening with removal of the ventral tethering urethral plate. *D,* In select cases, the urethral plate can be preserved and the dorsal skin split and wrapped to the ventrum. *E,* First stage complete. *F,* Second-stage urethroplasty is done 6 months after the first-stage surgery. *G,* Urethroplasty. *H,* Completed repair. *I,* Six-month follow-up.

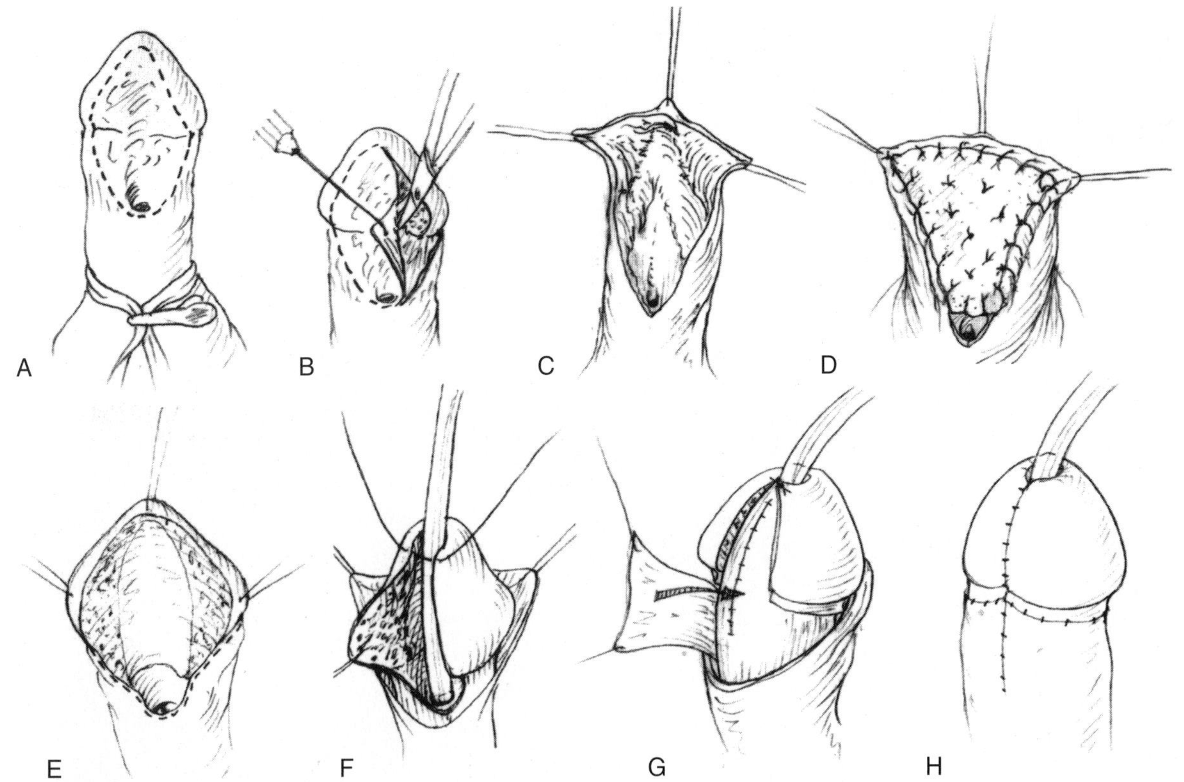

Figure 119–23 Two-stage Bracka buccal hypospadias repair. First stage: *A,* Patient with midshaft hypospadias and a paucity of available skin after multiple previous hypospadias repairs. *B,* Resection of scar tissue. *C,* Mobilization of glans wings. *D,* Buccal free graft quilted into the resected scar. The second stage is done after 6 months of healing: *E,* Exposure of the glans mesenchyme, and trimming of the buccal graft for subsequent urethroplasty. *F,* Meatal stitch for start of urethroplasty. *G,* Secondary de-epithelialized pedicle coverage of the urethroplasty. *H,* Two-layer glansplasty and completed repair.

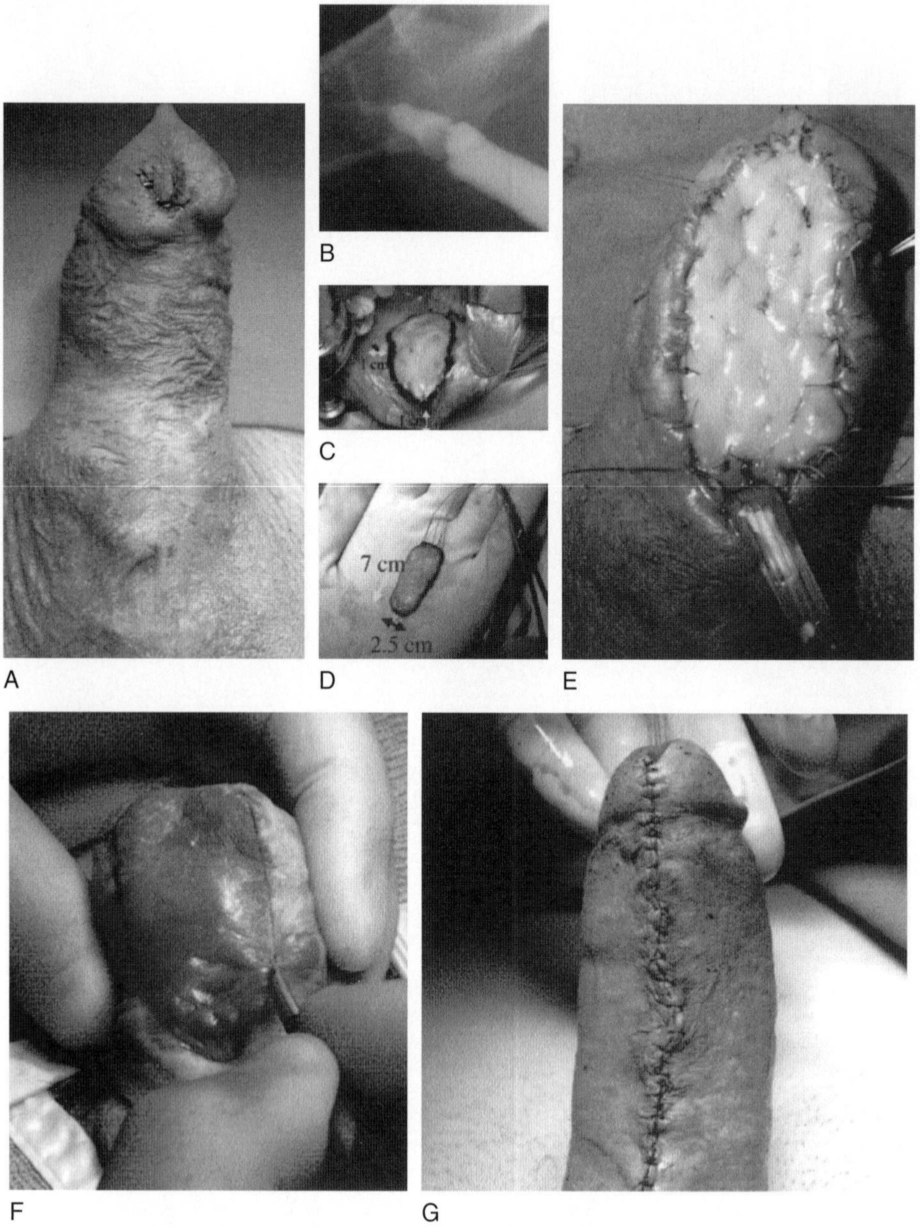

Figure 119–24 *A,* Patient with a distal urethral stricture after multiple previous hypospadias repairs. *B,* Urethrogram. *C,* Outline of buccal mucosa graft harvest. *D,* Free buccal harvest prepared for grafting. *E,* Quilted buccal mucosa graft applied to the ventral penis after resection of scar tissue. *F,* Healed buccal mucosa 6 months after grafting. *G,* Completed repair.

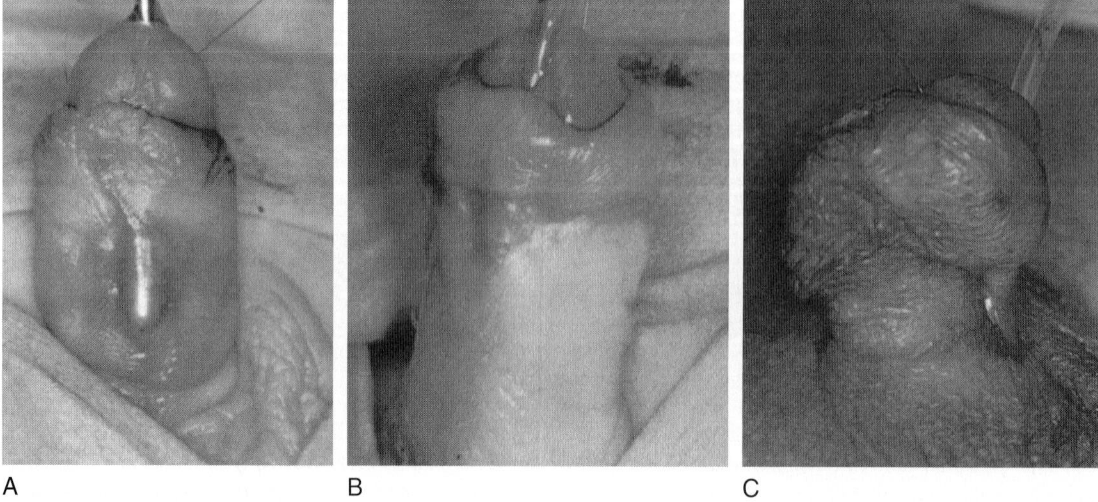

Figure 119–25 *A,* Congenital fistula. *B* and *C,* Chordee without hypospadias. Abnormal development of the urethral spongiosum necessitates urethroplasty and causes penile curvature.

a distance. This tissue should be freed completely down to the penoscrotal junction and often into the scrotal or perineal area. Once this urethral mobilization is accomplished, the shaft of the penis should be stripped of any fibrous tissue, extending out to the lateral aspect of the penis. Careful tangential cuts are made with the convex curve of iris scissors. Artificial erection is used to check the success of this excision.

Several other maneuvers have been suggested to release the last bit of bend. Lateral incisions of the outer tunica albuginea in the groove between the dorsal corpora and the ventral segment of corpora in a stepwise manner may be effective. Corporal rotation as described by Koff and Eakins[99] for epispadias may be useful in hypospadias curvature. A theoretical concern with this method arises from the fact that the permanent suture may impinge on the neurovascular bundle, causing pressure necrosis or subsequent erectile dysfunction. Unlike epispadias, in which the neurovascular bundle is lateral and out of harm's way, in hypospadias, the neurovascular bundle lies in an unstrategic position directly under the plication sutures. A midline incision along the septum between the two corpora cavernosa has been effective in some cases.[43]

If, after adequate excision of all abnormal fibrous tissue, artificial erection continues to demonstrate curvature, corporal disproportion may be the cause. Historically, chordee was corrected by a modification of Nesbit's dorsal plication, taking out wedges of tunica albuginea in an ellipse and closing this with permanent suture.[113] This technique was first described by Syng Physick, the father of American surgery, in the early 19th century; he treated chordee by shortening the dorsal tunica albuginea.[116] When the arc of maximal curvature is identified during artificial erection, wedges of tunica albuginea are excised in a stepwise fashion. These diamond wedges are closed transversely with permanent suture until the penis is straight. Nesbit's technique has been modified into dorsal tunica albuginea plication for the correction of penile curvature in the setting of corporal disproportion as well as hypospadias.[14] Based on anatomic studies of the human fetal penis, a simpler approach—placing dorsal midline plication sutures in the nerve-free zone at the 12 o'clock position—is now advocated.[18] Midline dorsal plication avoids the need for mobilization of the neurovascular bundle (Fig. 119-26).[19] Midline plication can be applied to mild to severe degrees of curvature (Fig. 119-27). If more than two rows of plication sutures or more than four permanent sutures are necessary, however, an alternative approach, such as complete resection of the urethral plate and possible dermal grafting, should be considered. During artificial erection, if the chordee cannot be corrected with the surgeon's finger, midline dorsal plication is not advised. A glans tilt may also be removed by permanent sutures on the dorsum, but care must be taken to avoid the neurovascular structures supplying the glans.[18]

In rare cases, the tunica albuginea is so deficient on the ventrum that excision of the tunica is required, with replacement by an elastic graft. I prefer the use of dermis, as described by Horton and Devine[80] (Fig. 119-28).

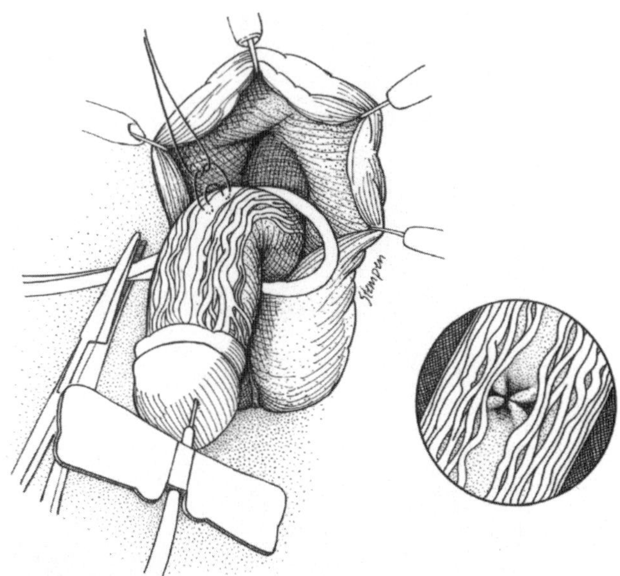

Figure 119–26 Midline dorsal plication technique. In this technique, parallel plication sutures are placed in the tunica albuginea in the 12 o'clock position, which is free of both nerves and vascular structures. This technique requires a minimal amount of manipulation of the penis. It is not necessary to incise into the corporal body or extensively mobilize Buck's fascia. If the curvature is severe, a maximum of two rows of parallel plications can be placed for correction.

About 5% of patients need ancillary penile straightening procedures after the release of skin chordee by aggressive dissection to the penoscrotal junction.[16,17] Of those requiring ancillary procedures, well over 90% can be corrected by dorsal midline plication without the need for resection of the urethral plate. This leaves a small minority of severe cases requiring resection of the urethral plate, dermal grafting, or both.

Patients with Multiple Failures

Some patients undergo multiple hypospadias repairs that fail; this unfortunate outcome can occur even in skilled hands. In such patients, it is often necessary to discard the previously created problem-plagued urethra and start anew. The penis may be further straightened, if necessary. In some cases, it may be appropriate to place a meshed split-thickness skin graft and go back later for tubularization[7,140] or to place a free graft of buccal mucosa or skin where the scarred urethra was resected.[30-32] In the past, bladder mucosa was used for the neourethra,[92] because the long-term results with free skin grafts were not as good as previously reported.[75] Unfortunately, bladder mucosa grafts were complicated by eversion at the meatus in up to 30% of patients.[92] Meatal dilatation on a daily basis could not avoid this problem. More recently, buccal mucosa grafts have been used for urethral replacement in these difficult patients.[15,53] I presently advocate the two-stage approach of Bracka (see Fig. 119-23).[10,31,32]

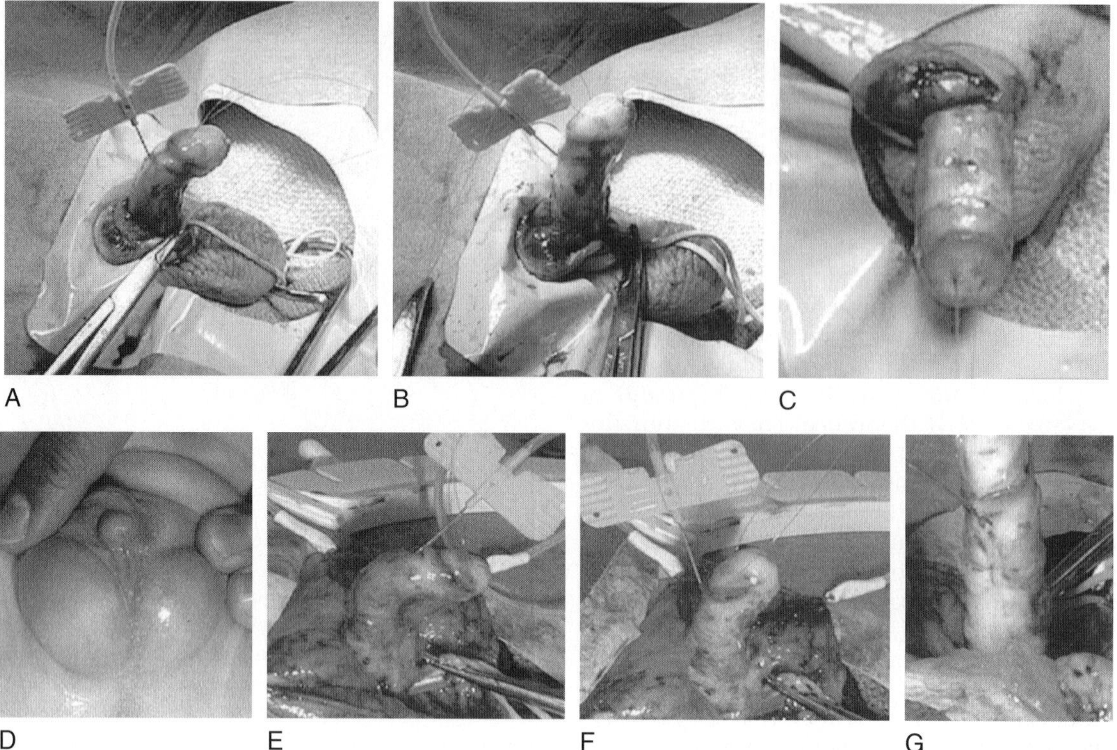

Figure 119-27 Midline dorsal plication technique. *A* to *C*, Correction of mild curvature. *D* to *G*, Correction of moderate to severe curvature. Note the two permanent 5-0 Prolene plication sutures in the midline nerve-free zone.

In the future, it may be possible to treat difficult cases of hypospadias with autologous grafts of cultured urethral epithelium.[134,135] Finding the ideal support matrix to scaffold the urothelial cells may make this technique widely applicable.

TECHNICAL CONSIDERATIONS

The principles of hypospadiology have been enhanced over the years by the precise, delicate tissue handling taught by plastic surgeons and the use of optical magnification. Sharp-pointed iris scissors and delicate-toothed forceps are the principal tools. Castroviejo needle holders and 0.5-mm forceps are useful for delicate maneuvers with 7-0 sutures. Bougie à boule probes are useful as the procedure progresses for calibrating the sizes of tubes and the anastomosis, as well as the meatus. Fine lacrimal duct probes are useful for identifying fistulas and periurethral ducts.

Hemostasis

Control of bleeding from the vascular penis and glans can be achieved in a number of ways. Placing a tourniquet at the base of the penis is simplest.[115,126] Recommended tourniquet

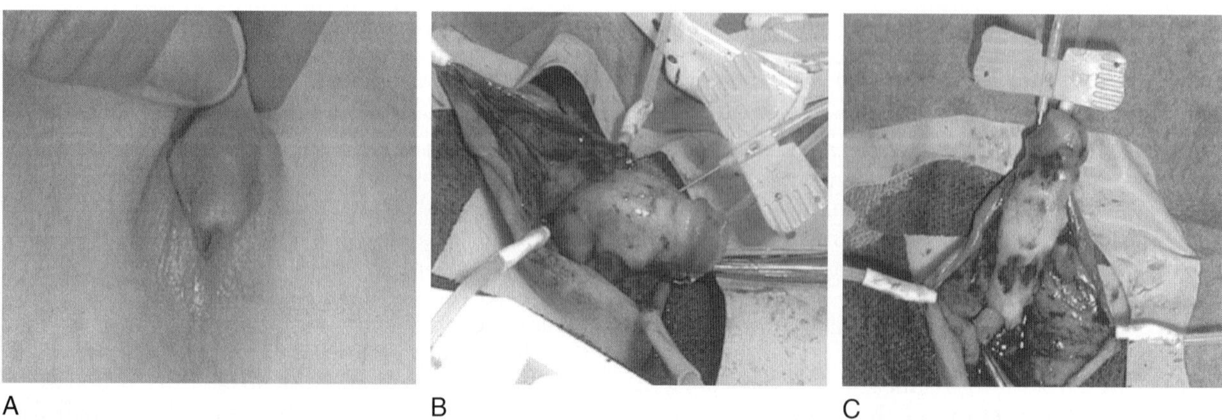

Figure 119-28 Dermal graft for severe ventral penile curvature. *A*, Scrotal hypospadias. *B*, Severe right-angle curvature after aggressive skin and subcutaneous dissection. *C*, Ventral incisions for placement of dermal graft. (From Hinman F Jr: Atlas of Urologic Surgery. Philadelphia, WB Saunders, 1989, pp 91-92.)

times vary from 20 minutes to 1 hour. I prefer the injection of 1:100,000 epinephrine in 1% lidocaine (Xylocaine) using a 29-gauge needle. Infiltration around the urethra and into the glans is helpful for developing glans wings. Usually, only 1.0 to 1.5 mL is required. There is a wide margin of safety before epinephrine sensitizes the myocardium to arrhythmias with the use of inhalational anesthetics.[91] A safe dose is 1 mL/kg of a 1:100,000 solution. I do not believe that epinephrine compromises the vascularity of the flaps. Various methods of coagulation have been recommended; I prefer a low-current electrocautery (Bovie) applied to the 0.5-mm forceps.

Analgesia

In anticipation of postoperative discomfort, the anesthesia team places a long-acting caudal nerve block before the procedure.[85] If the repair takes longer than 2 hours, the block can be repeated at the completion of the procedure. Evidence suggests that the caudal block also reduces the amount of bleeding.[72] Alternatively, a supplemental local block with 3 mL of 0.5% bupivacaine (Marcaine) is placed just beneath the symphysis to infiltrate the dorsal penile nerve bundle.[160] Penile blocks also reduce the general anesthetic needs and prevent erections, which can be bothersome and cause extra bleeding.

Dressing

For distal hypospadias repair performed without urinary diversion, I currently use a Tegaderm wrap. The parents remove the dressing at home in 24 to 48 hours. For hypospadias repair with urinary diversion, a "sandwich" dressing allows the application of more diffuse pressure by placing the penis onto the abdominal wall. A layer of Telfa followed by a 4- by 4-inch gauze folded three times on the ventrum of the penis is secured with a medium Tegaderm sheet of sticky plastic. The dressing is removed at home after 48 to 72 hours. I encourage bathing twice a day with the stent in place after 48 hours to allow the dressing to soak off. Warm bathwater allows the repair to remain clean and facilitates healing.

Diversion

Bladder spasms caused by irritation of the trigone with a catheter can be an aggravating problem. Oral oxybutynin chloride may be of help. Another problem relates to connections between tubing and a drainage bag. I avoid a Foley catheter, except in adults, and prefer a "dripping stent" in infants aged 6 to 18 months. Kendall manufactures a prepackaged 6 French hypospadias catheter; alternatively, 5 and 8 French feeding tubes are effective. The temporary stents can be sutured to the glans with 5-0 polypropylene on a noncutting needle. I have had good success with this technique, which allows the overwhelming majority of hypospadias repairs to be done on an outpatient basis. Urethral diversions are used for 3 to 10 days. If the diversion is used for 5 days or less, the family is advised to allow the stent to fall out when the dressing comes off. Patients are followed at 6 months to 1 year after surgery, after toilet training, and after puberty. The urethra is not instrumented during follow-up visits. A flow rate is obtained after bladder control is achieved to rule out occult urethral stricture.

Age for Repair

Hypospadias repair is being performed at progressively younger ages. Schultz et al.[139] pointed out that an ideal age might be 6 to 18 months to minimize the emotional effect of this traumatic experience. The consensus statement on the timing of genital surgery from the American Academy of Pediatrics also supports early surgery before 18 months of age.[6] Gender identity does not seem to be defined until after 18 months. I now prefer to operate when patients are between 4 and 9 months old; at that age, the penis is of sufficient size to achieve success comparable to that obtained by waiting until age 2 to 5 years, which was previously popular.[42] For many reasons (medical and social), however, surgery may be delayed. Kaplan et al.[90] studied 69 boys aged 6 to 10 years who had had hypospadias repair in infancy and found no increase in significant psychopathology during childhood.

Testosterone Stimulation

Enlargement of the infant penis is possible by testosterone stimulation. The recommended dose is 25 to 50 mg of testosterone propionate (2 mg/kg) intramuscularly given at three-week intervals for up to three preoperative doses.[38,64] I have not found the routine use of testosterone stimulation to be beneficial. In severe cases when the penis is small, such as partial androgen insensitivity syndrome, or for diagnostic purposes, testosterone is helpful. A patient with a small glans may benefit from presurgical testosterone stimulation. There is a suggestion in animal models that testosterone stimulation may be detrimental to the later maturation of prostatic tissue[111] and penile growth.[83] To date, clinical practice has not documented any untoward effects in humans.

COMPLICATIONS

Meatal Stenosis

Meatal stenosis is caused by technical errors in operative design or poor vascularization of the urethroplasty or glansplasty. Postoperative dilatation is seldom therapeutic and often traumatic for the patient and family. Internal urethrotomy also has poor long-term results. If the stenosis is clinically significant (fistula, infection, diverticulum), formal repair is required. In some cases, a two-stage approach (Bracka) is necessary.[31,32] If meatal stenosis persists as a long-term complication, it can be repaired by elevating a glans flap, excising the scar beneath, and interdigitating a skin flap. More extensive scarring of the glanular urethra and meatus may be due to poor vascularization of a perimeatal flap (Mathieu or Mustarde procedure).

Urethrocutaneous Fistula

Urethrocutaneous fistulas are the most common late complication of hypospadias repair, and their incidence has been used to evaluate the effectiveness of the surgical procedure.[129] The expected fistula rate is between 10% and 15% for most one-stage hypospadias surgery. Often, distal obstruction is related to persistent fistulas. Once a fistula has matured, closure procedures may be ineffective because of a discouraging rate of fistula recurrence. Therefore, some have suggested repairing urethrocutaneous fistulas using the principles of wide mobilization, adjacent skin flaps, multilayered closures, and use of urinary diversion.[24,81,154,156] I recommend using magnification and delicate instruments for fistula repair. A lacrimal duct probe is placed through the fistulous track to help identify its epithelial lining. Dissection is carried down to the urethra, and a 7-0 polyglycolic suture is used to close the urethral edges in an inverting fashion. Watertight closure is ensured by irrigating the urethra with proximal compression. Two layers of closure are obtained, and "super glue" is used as a wound sealant. No urinary diversion is used. The patient is allowed to void through his urethra and goes home on the same day.

It is extremely important to recognize a concomitant urethral stricture or diverticulum at the time of fistula closure. These should be repaired to ensure the success of the fistula closure. Occasionally, a meatoplasty may be necessary at the time of fistula repair. A fistula near the glans is best repaired by opening the bridge between the meatus and fistula, mobilizing the inner urethral edges, and closing in two layers with good glans approximation (Fig. 119-29).

Stricture

Strictures result from technical problems during the initial hypospadias repair. Proximal anastomotic strictures may result from either a luminal calibration miscalculation, resulting in a narrow neourethra, or an anastomotic overlap. The overlap problem can be avoided by lateral fixation of the oblique anastomosis to the tunica albuginea. A meatal stricture may result from chronic balanitis xerotica obliterans. This reaction is located at the meatus or may extend into the more proximal urethroplasty. This may be caused by a poorly vascularized meatoplasty, especially the Mathieu procedure. The most likely cause of meatal stenosis is vascular compromise of the urethra at the apex of the meatus. It may be secondary to an inadequate glans channel that compresses the vascularity of the pedicle. Once a stricture has developed, it can be repaired by excision and reanastomosis, a vascularized pedicle graft, or a two-stage buccal graft using the technique of Bracka.[31,32,138] I have had little success treating strictures secondary to hypospadias surgery with optical internal urethrotomy.[102]

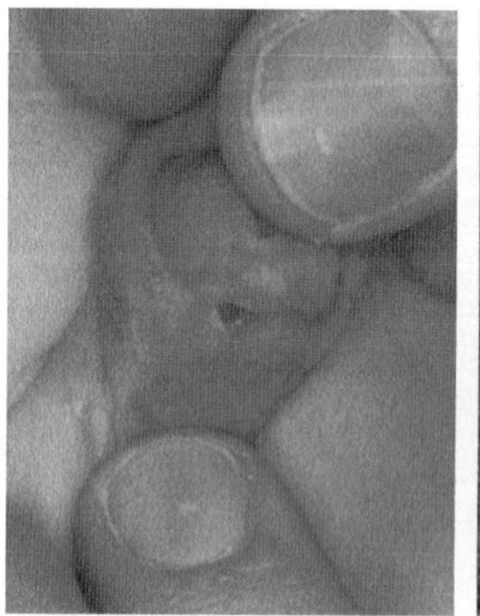
A

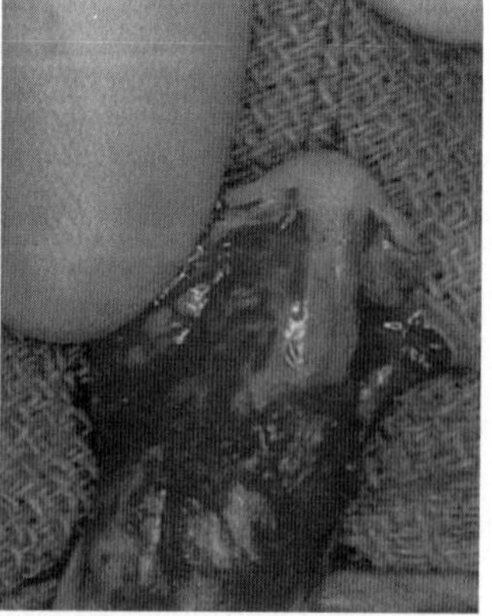
B

Figure 119-29 Hypospadias fistula. *A,* Coronal fistula requiring redo glansplasty. *B,* Preservation of the urethral plate with eccentric vascularized onlay flap preparation.

Diverticulum

A fusiform urethral diverticulum may form because the neourethra was made too wide and meatal stenosis allowed ballooning of the proximal urethra.[1] Reduction of a diverticulum may be necessary and should be done in a longitudinal fashion. Most often, a circumcising incision is used, and the penile skin is dropped to the penoscrotal junction, which allows for longitudinal repair of the diverticulum without overlying suture lines. Care must be taken to evaluate the neourethra for an associated fistula. A discrete diverticulum may develop from urinary extravasation into the tissues adjacent to the anastomosis. Usually a cutaneous fistula overlies it. Winslow et al.[159] described using diverticular tissue to reconstruct a urethroplasty.

RESULTS

Long-term follow-up reflects the older age at which repair was undertaken and the difficulties of hypospadias surgery in the past.[27,28,119,151] Although discouraging outcomes have been reported, they may not be a true reflection of modern methods.[94] Eberle et al.[57] reported a long-term review that was most disturbing. Of 42 posterior hypospadias patients followed into adulthood, 13 (30%) still had complex problems with sexual ambiguity, micropenis, small testes, no palpable prostate, and gynecomastia. There were six cases of Reifenstein's syndrome with severe AR defects. We must find better ways of identifying these patients as babies.

Today's results are much better both cosmetically and functionally than those in the past. The use of one-stage hypospadias repair at an early age with a low complication rate encourages our current positive outlook for patients with this condition. Curvature correction with the aid of an artificial erection is extremely important for ensuring satisfactory sexual function. With the placement of the urinary meatus at the tip of the glans, the fertility potential has been improved, unless the patient has other coexisting testicular problems. Evidence shows that the neourethra grows with the child, and subsequent repairs are seldom necessary.

Early hypospadias repair with minimal hospitalization helps avoid separation anxiety and castration fears. We can now counsel parents confidently that there is an excellent chance of a good cosmetic, functional, and emotional result in boys with all degrees of hypospadias.

SUMMARY

1. Hypospadias should be repaired within the first year of life, preferably at 4 to 6 months of age. Pain and catheters seem to be better tolerated at this age, and the baby's lack of mobility simplifies postoperative care.
2. A terminal slitlike meatus should be the goal, with or without preservation of the foreskin, depending on parental preference.
3. Preservation of the urethral plate provides the best possible chance of re-creating normal urethral anatomy by incorporating the abortive spongiosum into the repair.
4. Midline dorsal plication is safe and effective for the correction of penile curvature in the majority of patients. (Placing more than two rows of sutures is a sign that another technique, such as dermal grafting, is indicated.)
5. In the small percentage of patients who require resection of the urethral plate, a two-stage approach is generally warranted.
6. Vascularized pedicle onlay flaps are successful in primary and redo hypospadias surgery.
7. De-epithelialized vascular flaps should be used as a second layer for all urethroplasties.
8. Patients with a paucity of skin are best managed with the Bracka two-stage buccal repair.
9. Coronal fistulas require a redo glansplasty.

REFERENCES

1. Aigen AB, Khawand N, et al: Acquired megalourethra: An uncommon complication of the transverse preputial island flap urethroplasty. J Urol 1987;137:712-713.
2. Akman Y, Li YW, et al: Penile anatomy under the pubic arch: Reconstructive implications. J Urol 2001;166:225-230.
3. Albers N, Ulrichs C, et al: Etiologic classification of severe hypospadias: Implications for prognosis and management. J Pediatr 1997;131:386-392.
4. Allen TD, Spence HM: The surgical treatment of coronal hypospadias and related problems. J Urol 1968;100:504-508.
5. Allera A, Herbst MA, et al: Mutations of the androgen receptor coding sequence are infrequent in patients with isolated hypospadias. J Clin Endocrinol Metab 1995;80: 2697-2699.
6. American Academy of Pediatrics: Timing of elective surgery on the genitalia of male children with particular reference to the risks, benefits, and psychological effects of surgery and anesthesia. Pediatrics 1996;97:590-594.
7. Angermeier KW, Jordan GH, et al: Complex urethral reconstruction. Urol Clin North Am 1994;21:567-581.
8. Asopa H, Elhence I, et al: One-stage correction of penile hypospadias using a foreskin tube: A preliminary report. Int Surg 1971;55:435-440.
9. Avellan L: The incidence of hypospadias in Sweden. Scand J Plast Reconstr Surg 1975;9:129-138.
10. Barbagli G, Palminteri E, et al: Penile urethral reconstruction: Concepts and concerns. Arch Esp Urol 2003;56: 549-556.
11. Barcat J: Plastic and Reconstructive Surgery of the Genital Area. Boston, Little, Brown, 1973.
12. Baskin LS: Hypospadias and urethral development. J Urol 2000;163:951-956.
13. Baskin LS, Colborn T, et al: Hypospadias and endocrine disruption: Is there a connection? Environ Health Perspect 2001;109:1175-1183.
14. Baskin LS, Duckett JW: Dorsal tunica albuginea plication for hypospadias curvature. J Urol 1994;151:1668-1671.
15. Baskin LS, Duckett JW: Buccal mucosa grafts in hypospadias surgery. Br J Urol 1995;76(Suppl 3):23-30.
16. Baskin LS, Duckett JW, et al: Changing concepts of hypospadias curvature lead to more onlay island flap procedures. J Urol 1994;151:191-196.
17. Baskin LS, Duckett JW, et al: Penile curvature. Urology 1996;48:347-356.
18. Baskin LS, Erol A, et al: Anatomical studies of hypospadias. J Urol 1998;160:1108-1115.
19. Baskin LS, Erol A, et al: Anatomy of the neurovascular bundle: Is safe mobilization possible? J Urol 2000;164:977-980.
20. Baskin LS, Lee YT, et al: Neuroanatomical ontogeny of the human fetal penis. Br J Urol 1997;79:628-640.
21. Baskin LS, Liu W, et al: Anatomical studies of the mouse genital tubercle. In Baskin LS (ed): Hypospadias and Genital Development. Philadelphia, Kluwer Academic/Plenum, 2004, pp 103-120.
22. Beck C: Hypospadias and its treatment. Surg Gynecol Obstet 1917;24:511-532.
23. Bellinger M: Embryology of the male external genitalia. Urol Clin North Am 1981;8:375-382.
24. Belman AB: De-epithelialized skin flap coverage in hypospadias repair. J Urol 1988;140:1273-1276.
25. Benson GV, Lim H, et al: Mechanisms of reduced fertility in Hoxa-10 mutant mice: Uterine homeosis and loss of maternal Hoxa-10 expression. Development 1996;122:2687-2696.
26. Bentvelsen FM, Brinkmann AO, et al: Decreased immunoreactive androgen receptor levels are not the cause of isolated hypospadias. Br J Urol 1995;76:384-388.
27. Berg R, Berg G: Penile malformation, gender identity and sexual orientation. Acta Psychiatr Scand 1983;68:154-166.
28. Berg R, Svensson J, et al: Social and sexual adjustment of men operated on for hypospadias during childhood: A controlled study. J Urol 1981;125:313-317.
29. Bergstrom R, Adami HO, et al: Increase in testicular cancer incidence in six European countries: A birth cohort phenomenon. J Natl Cancer Inst 1996;88:727-733.
30. Bracka A: A long-term view of hypospadias. Br J Plast Surg 1989;42:251-255.
31. Bracka A: Hypospadias repair: The two-stage alternative. Br J Urol 1995;76(Suppl 3):31-41.
32. Bracka A: A versatile two-stage hypospadias repair. Br J Plast Surg 1995;48:345-352.
33. Carlsen E, Giwercman A, et al: Declining semen quality and increasing incidence of testicular cancer: Is there a common cause? Environ Health Perspect 1995;103(Suppl 7):137-139.
34. Cerasaro TS, Brock WA, et al: Upper urinary tract anomalies associated with congenital hypospadias: Is screening necessary? J Urol 1986;135:537-538.
35. Cheng EY, Vemulapalli SN, et al: Snodgrass hypospadias repair with vascularized dartos flap: The perfect repair for virgin cases of hypospadias? J Urol 2002;168:1723-1726.
36. Cheng W, Mya GH, et al: Associated anomalies in patients with undescended testes. J Trop Pediatr 1996;42:204-206.

37. Colborn T, Short P, et al: Health effects of contemporary-use pesticides: The wildlife/human connection. Toxicol Ind Health 1999;15:61-67.
38. Conte F, Grumbach M: Pathogenesis, classification, diagnosis and treatment of anomalies of sex. In DeGroot (ed): Endocrinology. Philadelphia, WB Saunders, 1995.
39. Cunha G, Baskin L: Development of the penile urethra. In Baskin LS (ed): Hypospadias and Genital Development. Philadelphia, Kluwer Academic/Plenum, 2004, pp 87-100.
40. Daskalopoulos EI, Baskin L, et al: Congenital penile curvature (chordee without hypospadias). Urology 1993;42:708-712.
41. de Sy WA, Hoebeke P: Urethral advancement for distal hypospadias: 14 years' experience. Eur Urol 1994;26:90-92.
42. Devine CJ Jr: Chordee and hypospadias. In Glenn J, Boyce W (eds): Urologic Surgery. Philadelphia, JB Lippincott, 1983, pp 775-797.
43. Devine CJ Jr, Blackley SK, et al: The surgical treatment of chordee without hypospadias in men. J Urol 1991;146: 325-329.
44. Devine CJ Jr, Gonzales-Serva L, et al: Utricular configuration in hypospadias and intersex. J Urol 1980;123:407-411.
45. Devine CJ Jr, Horton C: Chordee without hypospadias. J Urol 1973;110:264-267.
46. Dewan PA: Distal hypospadias repair with preputial reconstruction. J Paediatr Child Health 1993;29:183-184.
47. de Zegher F, Francois I, et al: Androgens and fetal growth. Horm Res 1998;50:243-244.
48. Dolle P, Izpisua-Belmonte JC, et al: HOX-4 genes and the morphogenesis of mammalian genitalia. Genes Dev 1991; 5:1767.
49. Donnenfeld AE, Schrager DS, et al: Update on a family with hand-foot-genital syndrome: Hypospadias and urinary tract abnormalities in two boys from the fourth generation. Am J Med Genet 1992;44:482-484.
50. Duckett JW: Transverse preputial island flap technique for repair of severe hypospadias. Urol Clin North Am 1980; 7:423-431.
51. Duckett JW: MAGPI (meatal advancement and glanuloplasty): A procedure for subcoronal hypospadias. Urol Clin North Am 1981;8:513-520.
52. Duckett JW: The current hype in hypospadiology. Br J Urol 1995;76(Suppl 3):1-7.
53. Duckett JW, Coplen D, et al: Buccal mucosa in urethral reconstruction. J Urol 1995;153:1660-1663.
54. Duckett JW, Keating MA: Technical challenge of the megameatus intact prepuce hypospadias (MIP) variant: The pyramid procedure. J Urol 1989;141:1407-1409.
55. Duckett JW, Snyder HD: Meatal advancement and glanuloplasty hypospadias repair after 1000 cases: Avoidance of meatal stenosis and regression. J Urol 1992;147:665-669.
56. Duckett JW, Keating MA: Technical challenge of the megameatus intact prepuce hypospadias variant: the pyramid procedure. J Urol 1989;141:1407-1409.
57. Eberle J, Uberreiter S, et al: Posterior hypospadias: Long-term followup after reconstructive surgery in the male direction. J Urol 1993;150:1474-1477.
58. Elder JS, Duckett JW, et al: Onlay island flap in the repair of mid and distal penile hypospadias without chordee. J Urol 1987;138:376-379.
59. Environmental Protection Agency, Endocrine Disruptor Screening and Testing Advisory Committee (EDSTAC): Final Report, 1998. Washington, DC, EPA.
60. Erol A, Baskin LS, et al: Anatomical studies of the urethral plate: Why preservation of the urethral plate is important in hypospadias repair. BJU Int 2000;85:728-734.
61. Fredell L, Lichtenstein P, et al: Hypospadias is related to birth weight in discordant monozygotic twins. J Urol 1998; 160:2197-2199.
62. Fritz G, Czeizel AE: Abnormal sperm morphology and function in the fathers of hypospadiacs. J Reprod Fertil 1996;106:63-66.
63. Fryns JP, Vogels A, et al: The hand-foot-genital syndrome: On the variable expression in affected males. Clin Genet 1993;43:232-234.
64. Gearhart JP, Jeffs RD: The use of parenteral testosterone therapy in genital reconstructive surgery. J Urol 1987;138: 1077-1078.
65. Gearhart JP, Linhard HR, et al: Androgen receptor levels and 5 alpha-reductase activities in preputial skin and chordee tissue of boys with isolated hypospadias. J Urol 1988;140: 1243-1246.
66. Gilpin D, Clements WD, et al: GRAP repair: Single-stage reconstruction of hypospadias as an out-patient procedure. Br J Urol 1993;71:226-229.
67. Gittes R, McLaughlin AI: Injection technique to induce penile erection. Urology 1974;4:473-475.
68. Glenister T: The origin and fate of the urethral plate in man. J Anat 1954;288:413-418.
69. Goldman A: Abnormal organogenesis in the reproductive system. In Wilson J, Fraser F (eds): Handbook of Teratology, vol 2. New York, Plenum Press, 1977, pp 391-419.
70. Griffin J, McPhau LM, et al: The androgen resistance syndromes: Steroid 5 alpha-reductase deficiency, testicular feminization and related disorders. In Scriver C (ed): The Metabolic and Molecular Bases of Inherited Disease, vol 3. Philadelphia, McGraw-Hill, 1995, pp 2967-2998.
71. Groshart C, Okkerman P, et al: Report to the European Commission: Identification of Endocrine Disruptors. First Draft Interim Report. Delft, the Netherlands, BKH Consulting Engineers, 1999.
72. Gunter JB, Forestner JE, et al: Caudal epidural anesthesia reduces blood loss during hypospadias repair. J Urol 1990; 144:517-519, 530.
73. Gupta C, Goldman A: Arachidonic acid cascade is involved in the masculinization of embryonic external genitalia in mice. Proc Natl Acad Sci U S A 1986;83: 4346-4349.
74. Harris EL: Genetic epidemiology of hypospadias. Epidemiol Rev 1990;12:29-40.
75. Hendren WH, Keating MA: Use of dermal graft and free urethral graft in penile reconstruction. J Urol 1988;140: 1265-1269.
76. Hinman F Jr: The blood supply to preputial island flaps. J Urol 1991;145:1232-1235.
77. Hinman F Jr: Penis and male urethra. In Hinman FJ (ed): UroSurgical Anatomy. Philadelphia, WB Saunders, 1993, pp 418-470.
78. Hiort O, Klauber G, et al: Molecular characterization of the androgen receptor gene in boys with hypospadias. Eur J Pediatr 1994;153:317-321.
79. Holmes NM, Miller WL, et al: Lack of defects in androgen production in children with hypospadias. J Clin Endocrinol Metab 2004;89:2811-2816.
80. Horton C, Devine C: Peyronie's disease. Plast Reconstr Surg 1973;52:503.
81. Horton C, Devine C, et al: Fistulas of the penile urethra. Plast Reconstr Surg 1980;66:407-418.
82. Hsieh-Li HM, Witte DP, et al: Hoxa 11 structure, extensive antisense transcription, and function in male and female fertility. Development 1995;121:1373-1385.
83. Hussman D, Cain M: Eventual phallic size is dependent on the timing of androgen administration. J Urol 1994;152: 734-739.
84. Jayanthi VR: The modified Snodgrass hypospadias repair: Reducing the risk of fistula and meatal stenosis. J Urol 2003;170:1603-1605.

85. Jensen B: Caudal block for postoperative pain relief in children after genital operations: A comparison between bupivacaine and morphine. Acta Anesthesiol Scand 1981; 25:373-375.
86. Jensen K: European Parliament's Committee on the Environment, Public Health and Consumer Protection. Report on Endocrine Disrupting Chemicals. Rapporteur, 1998.
87. Jirasek J, Raboch J, et al: The relationship between the development of gonads and external genitals in human fetuses. Am J Obstet Gynecol 1968;101:830.
88. Juskiewenski S, Vaysse P, et al: A study of the arterial blood supply to the penis. Anat Clin 1982;4:101-107.
89. Kaplan GW, Lamm DL: Embryogenesis of chordee. J Urol 1975;114:769-772.
90. Kaplan S, Hensle T, et al: Hypospadias: Associated behavior problems and male gender role development. J Urol 1989;141:45-A.
91. Karl H, Swedlow D, et al: Epinephrine-halothane interactions in children. Anesthesiology 1983;58:142-145.
92. Keating MA, Cartwright PC, et al: Bladder mucosa in urethral reconstructions. J Urol 1990;144:827-834.
93. Kelce WR, Wilson EM: Environmental antiandrogens: Developmental effects, molecular mechanisms, and clinical implications. J Mol Med 1997;75:198-207.
94. Kenawi M: Sexual function in hypospadias. Br J Urol 1975;47:883-890.
95. Khuri F, Hardy B, et al: Urologic anomalies associated with hypospadias. Urol Clin North Am 1981;8:565-571.
96. Kim KS, Torres CR, et al: Induction of hypospadias in a murine model by maternal exposure to synthetic estrogens. Environ Res 2004;94:267-275.
97. Koff S: Mobilization of the urethra in the surgical treatment of hypospadias. J Urol 1981;125:395-397.
98. Koff S, Brinkman J, et al: Extensive mobilization of the urethral plate and urethra for repair of hypospadias: The modified Barcat technique. J Urol 1994;151:466-469.
99. Koff S, Eakins M: The treatment of penile chordee using corporal rotation. J Urol 1984;131:931-934.
100. Kurzrock E, Baskin L, et al: Epithelial-mesenchymal interactions in development of the mouse fetal genital tubercle. Cells Tissues Organs 1999;164:1015-1020.
101. Kurzrock E, Baskin L, et al: Ontogeny of the male urethra: Theory of endodermal differentiation. Differentiation 1999;64:115-122.
102. Lofti A, Snyder H, et al: The treatment of urethral strictures: The contribution of clean intermittent catheterization to direct vision urethrotomy. J Urol 1991;145:810A.
103. Ma L, Benson GV, et al: Abdominal B (AbdB) Hoxa genes: Regulation in adult uterus by estrogen and progesterone and repression in mullerian duct by the synthetic estrogen diethylstilbestrol (DES). Dev Biol 1998;197:141-154.
104. Mathieu P: Traitement en un temps de l'hypospadias balanique et juxtabalanique. J Chir 1932;39:481.
105. McArdle F, Lebowitz R: Uncomplicated hypospadias and anomalies of upper urinary tract: Need for screening? Urology 1975;5:712-716.
106. McPhaul MJ, Marcelli M, et al: Genetic basis of endocrine disease. 4. The spectrum of mutations in the androgen receptor gene that causes androgen resistance. J Clin Endocrinol Metab 1993;76:17-23.
107. Mettauer JP: Practical observations on those malformations of the male urethra and penis, termed hypospadias and epispadias, with an anomalous case. Am J Med Sci 1842;4:43-47.
108. Mollard P, Mouriquand P, et al: Application of the onlay island flap urethroplasty to penile hypospadias with severe chordee. Br J Urol 1991;68:317-319.
109. Mortlock DP, Innis JW: Mutation of HOXA13 in hand-foot-genital syndrome. Nat Genet 1997;15:179-180.
110. Mouriquand PD, Persad R, et al: Hypospadias repair: current principles and procedures. Br J Urol 1995;76 Suppl 3:9-22.
111. Nasland M, Coffee D: The hormonal imprinting of the prostate and the regulation of stem cells in prostate growth. Proceedings of the 2nd NIADDK Symposium on the Study of Benign Prostatic Hyperplasia. Washington, DC, US Government Printing Office, 1985.
112. Nasrallah P, Minott H: Distal hypospadias repair. J Urol 1984;131:928-930.
113. Nesbit R: Plastic procedure for correction of hypospadias. J Urol 1941;45:699-702.
114. North K, Golding J: A maternal vegetarian diet in pregnancy is associated with hypospadias. The ALSPAC Study Team. Avon Longitudinal Study of Pregnancy and Childhood. BJU Int 2000;85:107-113.
115. Ossandon F, Ransley P: Lasso tourniquet for artificial erection in hypospadias. Urology 1982;19:656-657.
116. Pancoast J: Treatise on Operative Surgery. Philadelphia, Carrey & Hart, 1844.
117. Paulozzi L: International trends in rates of hypospadias and cryptorchidism. Environ Health Perspect 1999;107: 297-302.
118. Paulozzi L, Erickson D, et al: Hypospadias trends in two US surveillance systems. Pediatrics 1997;100:831-834.
119. Pegoraro V, Dal Poz R, et al: Controllo a lungo termine dell'pospadico operato. Estratto Urol 1979;46:1-9.
120. Podlasek CA, Barnett DH, et al: Prostate development requires Sonic hedgehog expressed by the urogenital sinus epithelium. Dev Biol 1999;209:28-39.
121. Podlasek CA, Duboule D, et al: Male accessory sex organ morphogenesis is altered by loss of function of Hoxd-13. Dev Dyn 1997;208:454-465.
122. Polus J, Lotte S: Chirurgie des hypospades: Une nouvelle technique esthetique et fonctionnelle. Ann Chir Plast 1965;10:3-9.
123. Price K, Fenwick G: Naturally occurring oestrogens in foods—a review. Food Addit Contam 1985;2:73-106.
124. Quartey J: One stage penile/preputial cutaneous island flap urethroplasty for urethral stricture: A preliminary report. J Urol 1983;129:284-287.
125. Raman-Wilms L, Tseng AL, et al: Fetal genital effects of first-trimester sex hormone exposure: A meta-analysis. Obstet Gynecol 1995;85:141-149.
126. Redman J: Tourniquet as hemostatic aid in repair of hypospadias. Urology 1986;28:241.
127. Redman J: The balanic groove technique of Barcat. J Urol 1987;137:83-85.
128. Retik AB, Bauer SB, et al: Management of severe hypospadias with a two-stage repair. J Urol 1994;152: 749-751.
129. Retik AB, Keating M, et al: Complications of hypospadias repair. Urol Clin North Am 1988;15:223-236.
130. Ritchey ML, Benson RJ, et al: Management of mullerian duct remnants in the male patient. J Urol 1988;140: 795-799.
131. Ritchey ML, Sinha A, et al: Congenital fistula of the penile urethra. J Urol 1993;151:1061-1062.
132. Rogers B: History of external genital surgery. In Horton C (ed): Plastic and Reconstructive Surgery of the Genital Area. Boston, Little, Brown, 1973, pp 3-47.
133. Rolland R, Gilbertson M, et al: Environmentally induced alterations in development: A focus on wildlife. Environ Health Perspect 1995;103(Suppl 4).
134. Romagnoli G, DeLuca M, et al: Treatment of posterior hypospadias by the autologous graft of cultured urethral epithelium. N Engl J Med 1990;323:527-530.

135. Romagnoli G, DeLuca M, et al: One-step treatment of proximal hypospadias by the autologous graft of cultured urethral epithelium. J Urol 1993;150:1204-1207.
136. Ross F, Farmer A, et al: Hypospadias—a review of 230 cases. Plast Reconstr Surg 1959;24:357-368.
137. Rushton H, Belman A: The split prepuce in situ onlay hypospadias repair. J Urol 1998;160:1134-1136.
138. Scherz HC, Kaplan GW, et al: Post-hypospadias repair urethral strictures: A review of 30 cases. J Urol 1988;140: 1253-1255.
139. Schultz J, Klykylo W, et al: Timing of elective hypospadias repair in children. Pediatrics 1983;71:342-351.
140. Secrest CL, Jordan GH, et al: Repair of the complications of hypospadias surgery. J Urol 1993;150:1415-1418.
141. Shelton TB, Noe HN: The role of excretory urography in patients with hypospadias. J Urol 1985;134:97-99.
142. Shima H, Ikoma F, et al: Developmental anomalies associated with hypospadias. J Urol 1979;122:619-621.
143. Skakkebaek NE, Rajpert-De Meyts E, et al: Germ cell cancer and disorders of spermatogenesis: An environmental connection? APMIS 1998;106:3-11.
144. Snodgrass W: Tubularized, incised plate urethroplasty for distal hypospadias. J Urol 1994;151:464-465.
145. Snodgrass W, Koyle M, et al: Tubularized incised plate hypospadias repair: Results of a multicenter experience. J Urol 1996;156:839-841.
146. Snodgrass W, Koyle M, et al: Tubularized incised plate hypospadias repair for proximal hypospadias. J Urol 1998; 159:2129-2131.
147. Sommer J, Stephens F: Dorsal ureteral diverticulum of the fossa navicularis: Symptoms, diagnosis and treatment. J Urol 1980;124:94-98.
148. Standoli L: Correzione Dell'ipospadias in tempo unico: Technica dell'ipospadias con tempo ad isola prepuziale. Rass Italia Chir Pediatr 1979;21:82-91.
149. Stoll C, Alembik Y, et al: Genetic and environmental factors in hypospadias. J Med Genet 1990;27:559-563.
150. Sutherland RW, Wiener JS, et al: Androgen receptor gene mutations are rarely associated with isolated penile hypospadias. J Urol 1996;156:828-831.
151. Svensson J, Berg R: Micturition studies and sexual function in operated hypospadiacs. Br J Urol 1983;55: 422-426.
152. Sweet R, Schrott H, et al: Study of the incidence of hypospadias in Rochester, Minnesota 1940-1970, and a case-control comparison of possible etiologic factors. Mayo Clin Proc 1974;49:52-58.
153. Toppari J, Larsen JC, et al: Male reproductive health and environmental xenoestrogens. Environ Health Perspect 1996;104(Suppl 4):741-803.
154. Turner-Warwick R: The use of pedicle grafts in the repair of urinary tract fistulae. Br J Urol 1972;44:644-656.
155. Van der Meulen J: Hypospadias Monograph. Leiden, the Netherlands, AG Stenfert, Kroese, NV, 1964.
156. Walker R: Outpatient repair of urethral fistulae. Urol Clin North Am 1981;8:582-583.
157. Wilson JD, George FW, et al: The hormonal control of sexual development. Science 1981;211:1278-1284.
158. Wilson JD, Griffin JE, et al: Steroid 5 alpha-reductase 2 deficiency. Endocr Rev 1993;14:577-593.
159. Winslow BH, Vorstman B, et al: Urethroplasty using diverticular tissue. J Urol 1985;134:552-553.
160. Yeoman D, Cooke R, et al: Penile block for circumcision? A comparison with caudal block. Anesthesia 1983;38: 862-866.
161. Young H: Genital Abnormalities, Hermaphroditism and Related Adrenal Diseases. Baltimore, Williams & Wilkins, 1937.
162. Yucel S, Baskin LS: Identification of communicating branches among the dorsal, perineal and cavernous nerves of the penis. J Urol 2003;170:153-158.
163. Yucel S, Baskin LS: Neuroanatomy of the male urethra and perineum. BJU Int 2003;92:624-630.
164. Yucel S, Liu W, et al: Anatomical studies of the fibroblast growth factor-10 mutant, Sonic Hedge Hog mutant, and androgen receptor mutant mouse genital tubercle. In Baskin L (ed): Hypospadias and Genital Development. Philadelphia, Kluwer Academic/Plenum, 2004, pp 123-145.
165. Zaontz MR: The GAP (glans approximation procedure) for glanular/coronal hypospadias. J Urol 1989;141:359-361.

Chapter 120

Abnormalities of the Urethra, Penis, and Scrotum

J. Patrick Murphy and John M. Gatti

The evaluation of abnormalities of the urethra, penis, and scrotum now begins before birth. Prenatal ultrasound has become standard of care, and with it has come the early diagnosis of many congenital anomalies of the genitourinary tract. Virtually every hydronephrotic or obstructive lesion has been documented prenatally, but new controversies have been generated regarding the efficacy and appropriateness of prenatal therapy. In no area is this more apparent than in the diagnosis of posterior urethral valves. Interventions in the way of vesicoamniotic shunting and fetoscopic urethral valve ablation have been described and utilized, but a benefit in outcome has yet to be confirmed.[18,24,29]

Prenatal diagnosis has been a mixed blessing. The early diagnosis of bladder exstrophy allows for family counseling, and arrangements can be made in advance for transfer of the newborn to a center with expertise in bladder exstrophy closure. Hydronephrosis, however, is quite common and rarely requires antenatal intervention. Despite this, parental unrest and physician uncertainty often lead to the early induction of labor, placing the infant at additional risk. The families are often confused and disappointed when the infant is born, and an expectant approach is employed. Parents are left wondering why the rush in delivery without an urgent intervention post partum. Antenatal intervention and management continues to evolve but requires education and communication between obstetricians, perinatologists, and the surgeons who treat these anomalies postnatally.

POSTERIOR URETHRAL VALVES

Posterior urethral valves (PUV) are the most common obstructive anomaly of the urethra. The incidence is between 1 in 5000 and 1 in 8000 male births.[33,42] Hugh Hampton Young is credited with the first description and classification of PUV.[125] He described three types: types I, II, and III urethral valves. Type II valves are now generally considered to be nonobstructive and are of historical interest only. Type I represents 95% of PUV. They are a membrane that originates at the verumontanum and travels distally to insert in the anterior proximal membranous urethra with an opening present posteriorly at the verumontanum. The etiology is probably a result of the mesonephric ducts entering the cloaca more anteriorly than normal and fusing in the midline.[114] Type III valves represent the other 5% and consist of a ring-type membrane distal to the verumontanum with a perforation present centrally. The membrane may occasionally migrate distally, forming a windsock appearance.[27] The cause of these valves is an incomplete dissolution of the urogenital membrane.

Presently, most cases of PUV are detected prenatally by ultrasound showing hydronephrosis and/or a distended thick-walled bladder. Postnatally, the ultrasound will show a thickened bladder wall and classically a dilated and elongated posterior urethra. Hydronephrosis will vary in degree and may be unilateral or bilateral. Physical examination may exhibit a distended, firm bladder, weak urinary stream, abdominal distention, and, possibly, urinary ascites. If the fetus has been subjected to oligohydramnios, there may be respiratory distress and the stigmata of Potter's syndrome may be present. Older boys may present with urinary tract infection and voiding dysfunction, particularly daytime urge incontinence. The voiding cystourethrogram is usually diagnostic with a dilated and often elongated posterior urethra and abrupt transition to a narrower distal urethra; a thickened bladder wall, trabeculation, bladder diverticulum, and vesicoureteral reflux may also be seen (Fig. 120-1).

Fetal intervention for PUV is controversial. The diagnostic accuracy of prenatal ultrasound has improved significantly over the past 10 years, but nonobstructive disorders such as prune-belly syndrome and high-grade vesicoureteral reflux may be difficult to differentiate from PUV. Fetal intervention may involve early delivery, vesicoamniotic shunting,[29,30] amnioinfusion,[57] percutaneous fetal cystoscopy,[92,93,119] or open fetal surgery.[66] All of these have significant risks to the fetus and mother, including preterm labor, bleeding, and infection. Therefore, the consideration of fetal intervention should

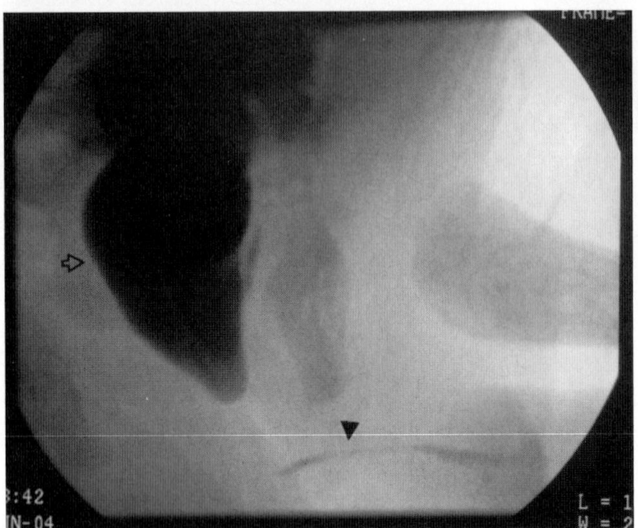

Figure 120–1 VCUG showing posterior urethral valves with dilated posterior urethra *(open arrow)* and abrupt transition to narrower anterior urethra *(solid arrow)*. The trabeculated bladder is above the posterior urethra.

be limited to centers with experienced personnel in both the diagnostic and technical skills involved. Renal dysplasia may occur early in fetal development before the time of consideration for fetal manipulation. Intervention to relieve obstruction will not reverse renal dysplasia. Therefore, most clinicians agree that a fetus with signs of severe renal dysplasia is not a candidate for prenatal treatment. Several parameters are used for determining the severity of renal dysplasia. Increased echodensity of the renal parenchyma, cystic changes of the parenchyma, and early moderate or severe oligohydramnios are all ultrasound signs of severe renal dysplasia. The character of percutaneously sampled fetal urine also predicts the degree of dysplasia.[18,24,39,112] Normal fetal urine is hypotonic and low in sodium. Fetal urine sodium greater than 100 mEq/L, osmolality greater than 210 mOsm, protein greater than 20 mg/dL, and β_2-microglobulin greater than 4 mg/L[71] all are suggestive of significant renal dysplasia. A fetus with these radiographic and urine parameters probably would not benefit from prenatal manipulation. Prenatal intervention has not been shown to improve the overall long-term renal function when compared with conventional postnatal therapy.[29,30] However, the patients who are treated prenatally likely represent the more severe degree of obstruction, and it could be argued that these patients should be predicted to have worse outcomes than those treated postnatally. Therefore, prenatal treatment may have had a beneficial effect in these higher-risk patients. The ultimate role of fetal intervention for PUV is still evolving; newer technology allowing safer and earlier treatment may improve outcomes.[105]

Postnatal management of PUV initially involves obtaining bladder drainage. Usually this can be accomplished with a small, soft No. 5 or 8 French feeding tube passed per urethra. Care must be taken to ensure it does not coil in the dilated posterior urethra. Bladder ultrasound can help confirm proper placement. Foley catheters generally should be avoided for initial drainage because the balloon may cause bladder spasm in the thick-walled bladder and affect urine drainage, or the balloon may slip into the dilated posterior urethra (Fig. 120-2). In the rare case that the urethra cannot be cannulated, percutaneous suprapubic access can be used. Fluid and electrolyte management is critical in the first 24 to 48 hours. Postobstructive diuresis may occur and both water and solute may be rapidly depleted, requiring aggressive fluid and electrolyte replacement. Acid-base balance is also important and is more of a problem in the greater degrees of renal insufficiency. Serum creatinine is monitored closely, realizing that for the first few days of life the value reflects the maternal renal function. Historically, when the creatinine stayed elevated beyond several days, supravesical diversion was considered. However, a number of studies suggest this is not necessary and subsequent renal function was not improved when supravesical diversion was compared with treatment with standard postnatal valve ablation or vesicostomy.[95,108,118] Antibiotic prophylaxis is indicated, especially in those patients presenting with hydronephrosis or vesicoureteric reflux.

When fluid electrolyte status is stable, most patients can be treated with endoscopic valve ablation. With advanced fiberoptic technology, cystoscopes of No. 7 French size are now available, allowing urethral access in all but the smallest premature infants. A Bugbee electrode with cutting current or a small-caliber laser fiber[8] can be used to incise the valves at the 5, 7, and 12 o'clock positions in a retrograde transurethral fashion. In the older child, a small resectoscope can be used. Some have advocated a percutaneous antegrade approach to fulgurate PUV.[126] In the rare case in which the valves cannot be fulgurated endoscopically, cutaneous vesicostomy is used. The Blocksom technique is favored, bringing the bladder dome to the skin to decrease the chance of bladder prolapse.[9,22] When the child has grown and stabilized medically, the valves may then be ablated endoscopically

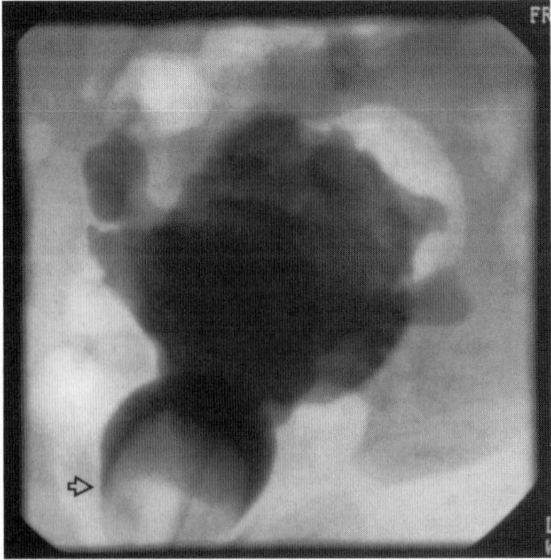

Figure 120–2 VCUG with posterior urethral valves and heavily trabeculated bladder and Foley balloon inflated in dilated posterior urethra *(arrow)*.

and the vesicostomy closed. Vesicostomy probably does not decrease long-term bladder capacity.[42,81,91]

The long-term prognosis for patients with PUV has improved over the decades and is affected mostly by three factors: (1) degree of renal dysplasia; (2) incidence of urinary infection with or without vesicoureteral reflux; and (3) bladder function. The overall infant mortality rate has improved from about 50% to 1% to 3% in the past 3 decades.[15,55] Improved neonatal critical care, along with careful attention to the treatment of the above factors, are responsible for this improvement. Renal dysplasia is irreversible, but attention to the other issues of urinary infection and bladder dysfunction can decrease or delay ongoing renal deterioration. Renal failure occurs in as high as 40% of patients treated for PUV.[95,108] Renal transplantation has improved in this group of patients owing to improved medical care and modern immunosuppressive therapy. The graft survival is comparable to patients without significant urologic pathology.[53,82] Attention to bladder dysfunction and treating these higher pressure bladders for urge incontinence with anticholinergic therapy and frequent voiding is important to delay renal deterioration or to protect the transplanted kidneys. In bladders that have progressed to myogenic failure and incomplete emptying, clean intermittent catheterization and/or overnight bladder drainage may be necessary. Urodynamics are very helpful in directing this type of bladder therapy. In rare cases, bladder augmentation may be necessary.[36,50,100,108] Vesicoureteral reflux (VUR) occurs in as many as one half of patients with PUV.[33,42,45] The high incidence is probably related to the high-pressure bladder, but anatomic studies suggest primary reflux related to ureteral position is frequent.[47] The reflux is more often bilateral, and resolution after valve fulguration occurs in one third to one half of patients.[33,45] Unilateral reflux is sometimes associated with a dilated, dysplastic, poorly functioning kidney. It has been suggested that this vesicoureteral reflux–renal dysplasia (VURD) syndrome may have a protective effect on the bladder and the opposite kidney, much like other "popoff" mechanisms such as a large bladder diverticulum or urinary ascites secondary to a ruptured renal fornix.[44,51,97]

Traditionally, it has been advocated that removal of this dilated dysplastic kidney and ureter would improve voiding efficiency and decrease potential for infection.[51] More recent evidence suggests that retaining this dysplastic unit does not affect infection or function and these units may be left in place.[58] These dilated ureters also have the potential for use as a ureterocystoplasty to augment the bladder in those rare cases of high-pressure bladder refractory to standard therapy.[14]

The presence of reflux should not change the initial overall treatment of PUV.[54] Ureteral reimplantation is generally indicated only in those patients with recurrent urinary infection despite appropriate chemoprophylaxis and after appropriate therapy to treat bladder dysfunction. The presence of VUR probably does not change long-term prognosis unless recurrent infection is an issue.[45,52] Over time, with appropriate bladder therapy, the dilation of the ureters may decrease and bladder wall thickness improve, making surgery technically easier with improved results if reimplantation is ultimately needed.

ANTERIOR URETHRAL VALVES IN BOYS

Anterior urethral valves occur much less frequently than posterior urethral valves, but their overall presentation and impact on the urinary tract are quite similar. They can occur anywhere along the anterior urethra, with a slight predominance in the bulbar urethra.[101] The etiology is most likely to be the development of a ventral urethral diverticulum. With antegrade flow of urine during voiding, the diverticulum undermines the distal urethra with the common wall becoming an obstructive flap.[116] Others postulate that this lesion develops from a primary weakness in the spongiosum or an abortive attempt at urethral duplication.[121] The diagnosis is made radiographically, with a voiding cystourethrogram revealing a dilated proximal anterior urethra, a narrow distal anterior urethra, and often a subtle flap of tissue. These valves are treated with endoscopic incision and are best visualized with minimal irrigation to prevent flattening of the valve with forceful retrograde flow. Hydronephrosis and vesicoureteral reflux are commonly associated and are generally managed in the same manner as posterior urethral valves.[41]

A similar lesion is the lacuna magna, or valve of Guérin, a dorsal urethral diverticulum located in the fossa navicularis. This is a rare entity and may require incision as described previously. The lesion can be difficult to diagnose owing to its proximity to the tip of the penis, but voiding images of the cystogram that include the glans reveal the distal lesion.[109]

URETHRAL DIVERTICULUM IN GIRLS

Urethral diverticula are rare lesions in children. They can present as dysuria, hematuria, or symptoms of obstruction. Their diagnosis can be extremely difficult because of problems of imaging the short length of the female urethra. Cystoscopy may be required for diagnosis, and treatment by excision or, if small, incision of the distal lip endoscopically may be warranted.[60]

URETHRAL STRICTURE

Urethral strictures are more common in boys than girls. They are classified as congenital, inflammatory, iatrogenic, or traumatic.[56] Congenital strictures are rare, but urethral hypoplasia can also be seen. Inflammatory strictures are uncommon in children and are more likely associated with gonococcal or chlamydial urethritis in sexually active adolescents. Inflammatory strictures related to chronic indwelling catheters are rare in the modern era. Iatrogenic strictures are encountered after urethral surgery or instrumentation.

Traumatic strictures of the anterior urethra are seen after straddle injuries in which the urethra is compressed against the pubic bone, such as falling on the crossbar of a bicycle. Posterior urethral strictures are generally seen associated with displaced fractures of the pelvis. Blood at the tip of the meatus, a high-riding bladder or prostate on abdominal and rectal examination, or a suspected pelvic fracture should all merit a retrograde urethrogram (RUG) before catheter placement to avoid converting a partial urethral disruption into a complete one. A partial injury is generally treated with endoscopic or fluoroscopic catheter placement of an indwelling catheter until the injury has healed and no extravasation of contrast agent is seen on the RUG done alongside the indwelling catheter. Controversy exists on initial management of the complete disruption. Suprapubic tube placement or vesicostomy and delayed reconstruction approximately 6 months later is generally accepted, but some advocate primary realignment of the urethra using retrograde urethroscopy and antegrade cystoscopy to place a catheter across the defect.[87]

The location and length of the stricture determine therapy. Most clinicians use antegrade cystography with retrograde urethrography to define these parameters, but others report more accurate assessments using intraoperative ultrasonography.[76] Short, filmy strictures can generally be incised or dilated with reasonable results.[85] Some authors have been quite successful with progressive urethral dilation in the setting of urethral hypoplasia.[86] Longer strictures or recurrent strictures of the bulbar urethra are generally treated by excision of the stricture and spatulated reapproximation in an end-to-end fashion. This may require an inferior pubectomy or corporal rerouting to cover a long distance.[75] The navicular and pendulous urethra are less forgiving because excision and reapproximation can result in ventral chordee. Longer strictures in these locations are generally treated with patch grafts or flaps using prepuce, penile shaft skin, or buccal mucosa.[21] These patients require long-term follow-up, although most strictures that recur do so during the first year.

URETHRAL ATRESIA

Urethral atresia is incompatible with renal development unless an alternative communication with the bladder exists such as a patent urachus. Prenatal intervention with vesicoamniotic shunting may aid in getting the fetus to delivery, but there is often significant renal dysplasia. There is a strong association with prune-belly syndrome.[43] The associated perinatal problems associated with obstructive infravesical uropathy must be dealt with initially. Further reconstruction is individualized to the degree of urethral development, but most will require some type of continent diversion ultimately.

URETHRAL STENOSIS IN GIRLS

The concept of urethral stenosis in girls has largely gone by the wayside. It was once believed that irritative or obstructive voiding symptoms or recurring urinary tract infections in girls could be related to urethral stenosis. The diagnosis was supported by the narrowed urethra at the level of the genitourinary diaphragm and sphincter on voiding cystourethrogram. It is now realized that the radiographic and clinical findings represent voiding dysfunction and its associated inappropriate sphincter activity during voiding. Although some short-term benefit of incapacitating the external sphincter muscle with dilation may be seen, urethral dilation has been largely abandoned, owing to its long-term ineffectiveness and potential for creating a true urethral stricture after overly vigorous dilation.

URETHRAL MASS IN GIRLS

Multiple lesions may present as a urethral mass in young girls. Careful attention to the lesion can often make the diagnosis by inspection. Lesions of the urethral meatus include urethral prolapse, prolapsing ureterocele, urethral cyst, or sarcoma. Lesions of the vagina may be mistaken for having a urethral origin and include Gartner's duct cysts, imperforate hymen, and sarcoma.

Urethral prolapse has classically been described in prepubertal African American girls, but white girls are also commonly affected.[26,98] The chief complaint is blood spotting in the underwear and painful urination. On physical examination, the markedly edematous urethra protrudes circumferentially at the level of the meatus and is often seen as a friable rosette that is bright red or cyanotic. A trial of sitz baths and estrogen cream is reasonable; but if this is ineffective, the redundant tissue is excised and the urethral mucosa is anastomosed to the adjacent introital epithelium in the operating room.[11] Complications are rare but can include bleeding, recurrence, or urethral stricture.

A prolapsing ureterocele can also be quite edematous, but it can usually be discerned that it is not connected to the surrounding urethral meatus. The presentation may include blood spotting in the underwear, painful urination, or urinary retention. The diagnosis is confirmed by findings of hydroureteronephrosis associated with the ectopic moiety on ultrasound. If the ureterocele cannot be manually reduced, it can be reduced and unroofed cystoscopically with definitive excision/reconstruction performed in staged fashion.

Rhabdomyosarcoma is the most common primary malignant tumor involving the uterus, vagina, or bladder in infants and children and can present in similar fashion. The botryoid type lesion is usually exophytic and commonly emanates from the vagina or urethrovaginal septum. It generally presents before 2 years of age. The urethral margins are at least partially discrete, which differentiates it from urethral prolapse. It is classically a grapelike clustered mass that extrudes through the introitus and presents as bleeding. Radiographic imaging is warranted to fully evaluate the mass and rule out metastases to the lungs, liver, or bone marrow. After tissue diagnosis, multimodal therapy including chemotherapy, radiation, and surgical excision is usually employed.[83,103]

Imperforate hymen may present as hydrocolpos or hydrometrocolpos as a bulging introital mass often with palpable distended abdominal uterus or vagina. The urethra is discretely visualized anterior to the mass. Treatment is incision and drainage.

Various cysts, including epithelial inclusion cysts, Skene's duct cysts, müllerian duct cysts, and wolffian or Gartner's duct cysts, can occur in this area, which can be incised and drained or excised if they recur. Gartner's duct cysts, which line the vaginal wall adjacent to the bladder, are worth elaboration because of their embryologic origins from the wolffian or mesonephric duct. As a result, ectopic ureters may end in a Gartner duct, and cystic rupture into the vagina results in chronic drip incontinence. Although Gartner's duct cysts are unusual in infants, they are the most common benign cause of vaginal swelling in children. They are generally asymptomatic, but when large they can protrude from the vagina and can be associated with urinary retention or dyspareunia in sexually active adolescents.[80] These are usually treated with marsupialization, but those associated with ectopic ureters require more proximal reconstruction involving ureteral reimplant or nephrectomy.

Urethral polyps are rare but present as intermittent bleeding or obstruction and are treated with excision.[59]

LABIAL ADHESIONS

Labial adhesions, or fusion of the labia minora, are believed to occur as a result of chronic inflammation related to vulvovaginitis or chronic dampness resulting from urinary incontinence. The labia may fuse near completely, causing obstructive type symptoms or incontinence with trapping of urine. More commonly they present as postmicturitional drip incontinence as small volumes of urine pool above this shelf of tissue while seated to void, only to drip into the underwear when the child assumes an upright position. This chronic dampness can also cause irritative symptoms of itching or dysuria, and an aseptic urine specimen is difficult to obtain owing to the impediment of preparing this adhesed area for culture acquisition.

Treatment of labial adhesions is not warranted in the absence of urinary tract infection, dysuria, obstruction, or drip incontinence because these adhesions commonly resolve with the physiologic estrogen surge nearing puberty.[113] If the adhesions warrant treatment, a trial of topical estrogen cream (0.01%) applied twice daily for 2 to 4 weeks may be attempted but can be unsuccessful in as many as half of patients.[79] Estrogens also carry the risk of vulvar pigmentation, development of breast buds, or breast tenderness in prepubertal patients with prolonged use. The effects reverse with the withdrawal of treatment. An effective alternative is the use of betamethasone cream (0.05%) topically twice daily for 1 month.[110]

If the adhesions are persistent or thick and well developed, surgical lysis can generally be performed in the office setting using EMLA cream. A cotton-tipped applicator or hemostat can then be used to bluntly push the adhesions apart in an anterior to posterior direction. It is imperative that the excoriated labia minora be dressed with a lubricating or antibiotic ointment to prevent the recurrence of adhesions until healed.

COWPER'S GLAND ANOMALIES

Cowper's glands are paired urethral glands that sit in the urogenital diaphragm and drain into the bulbar urethra. When the ducts draining these glands become obstructed, cysts termed *syringoceles* can form.[70] They may be seen on a urethrogram as a filling defect in the bulbar urethra or as a filling defect after rupture. Most cysts are thought to be asymptomatic; some may present as symptoms of terminal hematuria, blood spotting from the urethra, urinary tract infection, or obstructive symptoms. These are generally treated with endoscopic unroofing with incision of the leading lip to prevent obstruction such as seen with anterior urethral valves. Open resection perineally is reserved for very large cysts.[10]

URETHRAL POLYPS

Urethral polyps generally occur in the prostatic urethra and are usually fibromuscular epithelial structures with transitional epithelium covering the surface.[94] They occasionally may occur in the anterior urethra[16,88] and in either position they may cause hematuria, urgency, or obstructive symptoms. Bladder ultrasound may show the polyps in the posterior urethra (Fig. 120-3), but voiding cystourethrography and cystoscopy are diagnostic and excision through the cystoscope is usually curative.[38]

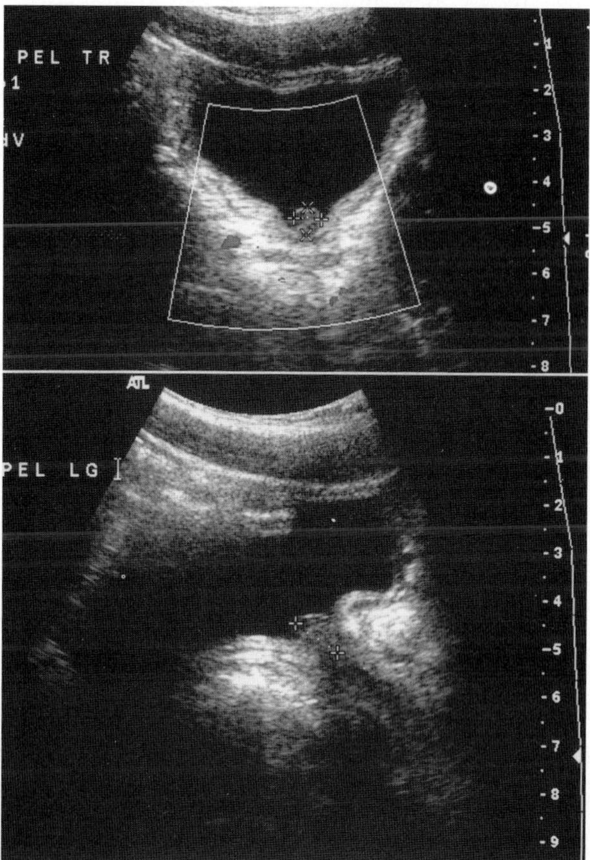

Figure 120-3 Posterior urethral polyp seen on ultrasound of bladder. Top view shows transverse image of bladder with polyp arising from urethra *(cursors)*. Bottom view shows longitudinal view of bladder with polyp seen at entry to posterior urethra *(cursors)*.

PROSTATIC UTRICLE

Prostatic utricles are müllerian duct remnants, which are common in patients with intersex disorders or with proximal hypospadias. Enlarged utricles can cause urinary symptoms including urinary tract infection, dysuria, urgency, hematuria, or epididymitis.[120] Diagnosis is usually made by voiding cystourethrogram or RUG. However, ultrasound may detect these remnants, particularly the larger ones.[61] Surgical treatment is reserved for those that are associated with recurrent symptoms. The surgical approach may be transabdominal, transvesical, perineal, posterior sagittal (transrectal or perirectal), or laparoscopic depending on the experience of the surgeon.[7,63,73,106,120,124]

URETHRAL DUPLICATION

Urethral duplication is rare but more common in males. Although embryologic explanations for the defect have been proposed, the multiple variants of the anomaly suggest that there is probably not a common etiology for all forms. Duplication of the urethra can occur along with bladder and genital duplication. In males, the duplications usually occur in the same sagittal plane on a single phallus.[23] Less often, the urethras may be side by side on the glans with either a widened or duplicate phallus (Fig. 120-4). With the sagittal-type duplications, the ventral urethra is almost always the more normal one and passes through the prostate and sphincteric mechanism. It may end anywhere from the tip of the glans to the perianal area.

The dorsal urethra may open anywhere on the shaft from an epispadiac location on the glans to the penopubic area. Dorsal chordee may be present and a widened symphysis pubis may be present, suggesting possible association with the exstrophy complex.[4,90,99,104] This dorsal urethra may communicate with the bladder or ventral urethra (Fig. 120-5) but can end blindly beneath the symphysis pubis. If it does communicate, incontinence can be an issue because it often does not traverse the sphincter. Treatment in the symptomatic patient involves excision of the dorsal accessory urethra and correction of the chordee with urethroplasty, if necessary, to bring the ventral urethra to the glans. In the extremely rare case of a dominant dorsal urethra and an accessory ventral one, the excision of the ventral tract cures the incontinence. The treatment of the even more rare side-by-side type requires an individualized approach depending on the varied anatomy. Full urinary tract evaluation radiographically is required in all forms of urethral duplication.

Female duplication may have complete bladder and genital duplication and may be associated with colonic atresia and/or cloacal anomalies.[32] A dorsal accessory urethra may occur in the pubic area and has been reported to communicate with a urachal remnant.[65]

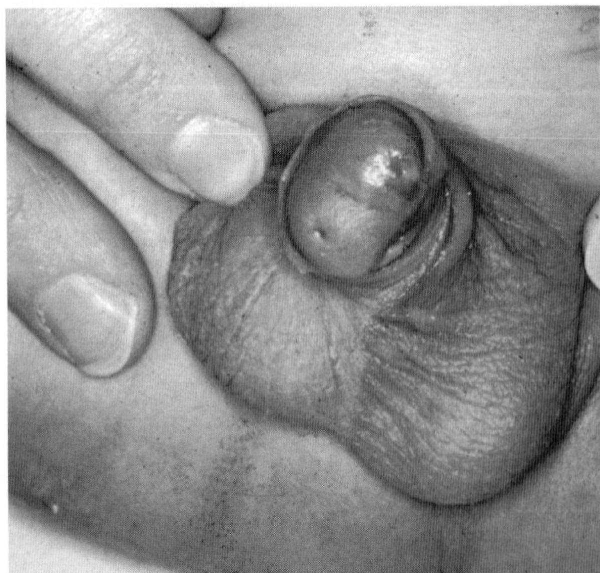

Figure 120-4 Duplicate urethra with a meatus on each side of glans and counterclockwise penile torsion.

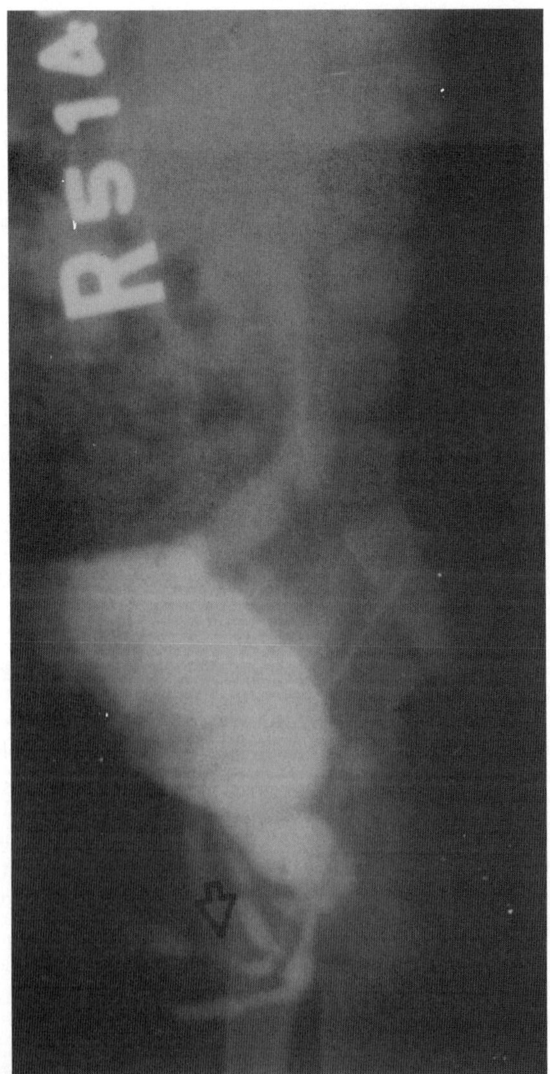

Figure 120-5 Urethral duplication with dorsal urethral duplication *(arrow)* exiting in suprapubic area.

Treatment again is individualized to the particular anatomy involved, with attempts to preserve bladder tissue and maintain continence.

MEGALOURETHRA

Megalourethra is a rare syndrome of urethral dilation. There are two types: scaphoid and fusiform. The scaphoid form is associated with abnormal development of the corpus spongiosum, and anterior bulging of the urethra is seen with voiding. In the more severe fusiform type (Fig. 120-6), the corpora cavernosa are also involved, which may have an impact on long-term potency, and the dilation during voiding is circumferential.[5] The lesion is generally discovered at birth but has also been diagnosed on prenatal ultrasound.[102]

The etiology is unclear, but it is thought to be a defect of mesodermal development, especially given its association with prune-belly syndrome.[77] A renal-bladder ultrasound is indicated to rule out other congenital anomalies. The dilation is nonobstructive, and urethroplasty with excision of the redundant tissue and tapering of the urethra is generally undertaken for cosmetic reasons.

CONGENITAL URETHRAL FISTULA

Congenital urethral fistula is rare and usually occurs in the subcoronal area of the penis. Associated hypospadias and chordee occur, suggesting this may be a form of the hypospadias anomaly. The fistula generally has a well-formed urethra distally, but it may be thinned with poor glans formation. Repair involves the techniques employed in hypospadias surgery and may involve simple multilayer closure of the fistula or more complex reconstruction of the distal urethra and glans.[12,96]

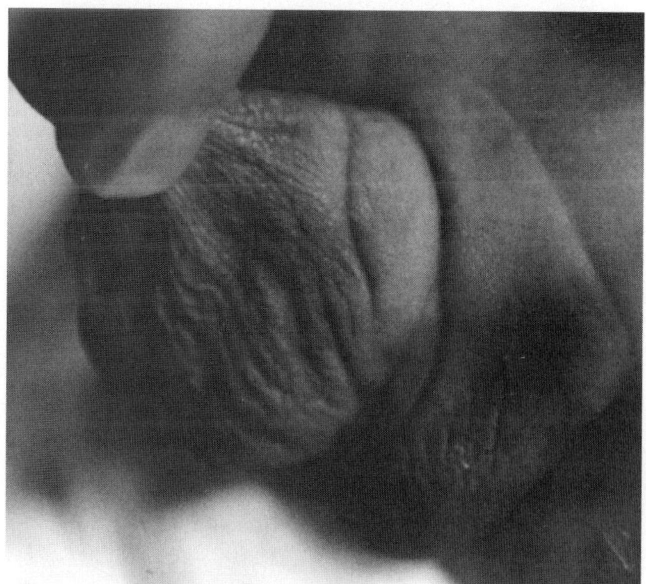

Figure 120-6 Megalourethra, fusiform type.

PHIMOSIS

Phimosis is defined as the inability to retract the foreskin. At birth, physiologic phimosis is present as adhesions between the prepuce and glans preclude retracting the foreskin. As the child grows, the two layers begin to separate as sloughed epithelial debris, or smegma, accumulates between them, defining this plane. This smegma is commonly referred to as "foreskin pearls" and can be mistaken for infection or purulence by the uneducated parent. With spontaneous erections and natural manipulation, over 90% of foreskin becomes retractable by age 3 to 4 years.[84]

Forceful retraction is not required for this to occur and may initiate the vicious cycle of tearing and scarring, which can lead to pathologic phimosis. In children older that 4 years who are unable to retract the foreskin, or who have had episodes of posthitis or balanoposthitis, a trial of betamethasone cream (0.05%) two times per day for 1 to 2 months allows the foreskin to retract in up to 90% of boys.[67] For those refractory to corticosteroid treatment or with obstructive complaints characterized by ballooning foreskin, a temporizing dorsal slit or circumcision is usually indicated.

CIRCUMCISION

Circumcision remains one of the most controversial topics in urology. The American Academy of Pediatrics issued a policy guideline in 1975 stating that there is no absolute medical indication for routine circumcision of the newborn.[117] In 1999, they offered the opinion that there are some medical benefits of the procedure but not enough to warrant routine circumcision.[2]

Circumcision advocates argue that circumcised boys have lower urinary tract infection rates, lower incidence of zipper injury or paraphimosis, and lower rates of sexually transmitted disease and penile cancer as adults.[17,64,69,123] Circumcision opponents argue the procedure is nonphysiologic and may be unnecessary or even harmful. Some more extremist groups argue that circumcised males have decreased penile sensation, less satisfaction with intercourse, and possibly even higher divorce rates.[40] Unfortunately, this issue tends to be emotionally charged and a large body of "supportive research" is highly subjective. In a cost utility analysis of circumcision, Ganiats and coworkers determined that financial and medical advantages and disadvantages of routine neonatal circumcision cancel out one another and that personal cultural or religious views rather than cost or health outcomes should be the basis of decision making.[31]

Despite the controversy, circumcision is still one of the most common elective procedures in the United States and is usually done for cosmetic and cultural reasons.

The risk of circumcision is generally low in larger series (<1%) and includes bleeding, infection, skin separation, adhesions, too much or too little skin removed, and meatal stenosis.[1,122] The two major techniques used in neonates are the Plastibell and the Gomco clamp. Similar complication rates are noted with both, the Plastibell having more problems with infection and the Gomco clamp more problems with separation.[34] The Mogan clamp carries the additional risk of glans injury, and this technique should be limited to those adequately trained in its use.

Technique

Newborn circumcisions can be carried out at the bedside or in the office safely to 2 or 3 months of age. We advocate the use of local anesthetic, either topically or subcutaneously before the procedure. With the foreskin in an unstretched position, the palpable coronal margin is marked on the overlying shaft skin to indicate the appropriate position of the clamp device. A hemostat is used to develop the plane between the glans and adherent prepuce. In the dorsal midline, the tissue is clamped with a straight hemostat and then incised with scissors to allow placement of the device. All adhesions should be taken down and smegma débrided. The appropriate size of clamp device should be chosen. The conical portion of the clamp should cover the majority of the glans. Once this portion is in position, the excess foreskin is reduced back over the clamp device and the clamp is engaged (Gomco) or the suture is tied (Plastibell) at the previously marked site. Care should be taken to draw the foreskin over the clamp at its leading edge to avoid the foreskin intussuscepting over the clamp and giving a mismatch of inner prepuce and proximal shaft skin engaged in the clamp. The amount of inner prepuce and shaft skin excised should be equal to avoid the risk of recurrent phimosis creating a hidden or buried penis due to an inappropriately large amount or residual inner prepuce. Hemostasis is usually excellent with these techniques. Electrocautery should never be applied to the metal clamp because the penis can be completely devascularized (Fig. 120-7).

In older children, the procedure is performed under a general anesthetic when the risk of anesthetic is minimized (after 6 months of age). Because the clamp devices become less reliable in older children and have a less-tailored fit, a freehand surgical technique is utilized at our institution. The proximal and distal incisions are carefully marked before cutting sharply, with the proximal mark overlying the coronal margin when any prominent prepubic fat pad is reduced. The excess shaft skin is excised at the level of the dartos pedicle with electrocautery. Hemostasis is attained by electrocautery as indicated, and larger vessels can be ligated. The edges are reapproximated with fine chromic suture in an interrupted subcuticular technique to avoid the formation of epithelialized suture sinuses. A minimal dressing of antibiotic ointment and gauze is placed with the expectation of it falling off spontaneously or being removed the following day. We also advocate early bathing on postoperative day 1 and have the family apply the ointment to the area at least three times daily for the next few weeks. A caudal block or dorsal penile nerve and ring block is usually given at the end of the procedure to help with postoperative pain management.

MEATAL STENOSIS

Meatal stenosis occurs in approximately 10% of circumcised boys.[3] It is virtually nonexistent in uncircumcised boys, with the exception of those with balanitis xerotica obliterans. It is thought to be related to chronic inflammation of the meatus after circumcision related to exposure to urine (ammoniacal dermatitis) or to relative ischemia caused by compromising the vasculature to the meatus when the frenular artery is taken during circumcision. The classic history is that of a fine-caliber urinary stream with dorsal deflection, often greater than 90 degrees. The meatus is pinpoint and tight with No. 6 or 8

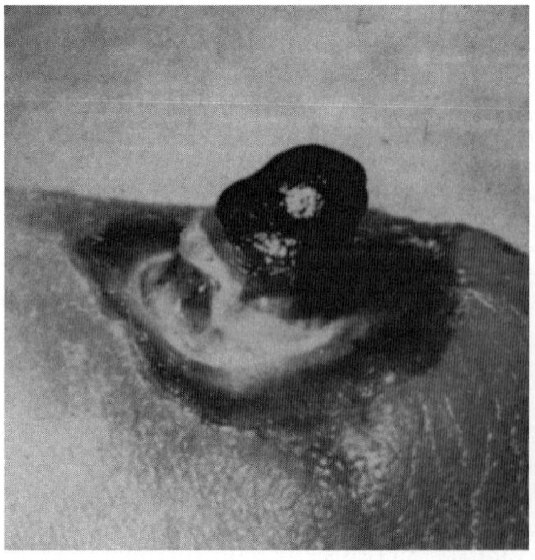
A

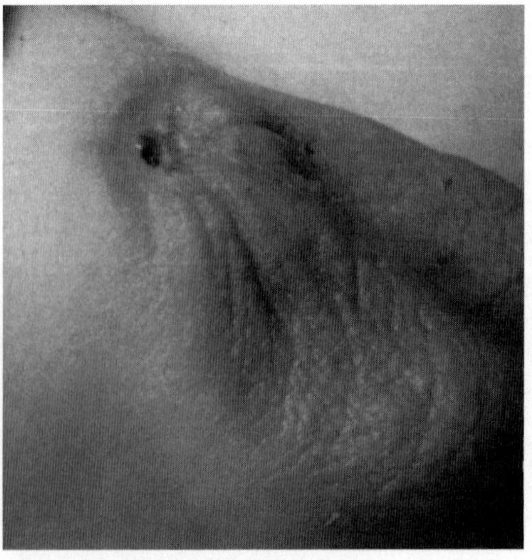
B

Figure 120-7 Neonatal circumcision injury after applying electrocautery to metal clamp. *A,* Immediate postoperative appearance. *B,* End result 3 months after surgery.

French calibration. It may or may not be associated with pain or blood spotting in the underwear. The disorder is commonly overdiagnosed, and those with painful urination who lack these physical findings often have voiding dysfunction and its associated inappropriate sphincter activity during voiding.

The treatment of meatal stenosis is a meatotomy in which the ventral parameatal tissue is engaged in a clamp or hemostat (we prefer a nontoothed bowel clamp), then incised roughly half the distance to the coronal margin. The edges are dressed with antibiotic ointment, and the family is encouraged to continue this application three times daily for at least a week to avoid recurrence, which is uncommon. This procedure can be performed safely in the office with local anesthetic or in the operating room setting.[13]

PENILE AGENESIS

Congenital aphallia is extremely rare, with an incidence of 1 in 10 million to 30 million.[46,107] It is a result of partial or complete developmental failure of the genital tubercle. The karyotype is almost always 46,XY, and the urethra usually opens into the anal verge or rectum.[46,107] Common associated anomalies can include cryptorchidism, renal anomalies, vesicoureteral reflux, anal anomalies, and cardiac anomalies.[25,46,107] The more proximal the urethral communication, the higher the incidence of associated anomalies and of neonatal mortality.[107] Female gender reassignment with orchiectomy, along with urinary tract and genital reconstruction, has traditionally been recommended for this anomaly.[46,115] However, recent evidence that persistence of male gender identity may occur despite female gender reassignment makes it imperative that careful consideration by an entire intersex assessment team, including urology, endocrinology, and psychiatry be done before full informed consent is obtained from the family.[20] Discussion of maintaining male gender assignment with later construction of a neophallus along with the cosmetic and functional limitations of this approach should be included in the informed consent.[20]

DIPHALLIA

Penile duplication has a frequency of 1 in 5 million births.[74,78] The extent of the duplication varies, and the etiology is suggested to be a failure of mesodermal banding or mesoderm encountering two urethral anlage.[49] Presentation may range from a small accessory penis to complete duplication of urethra, glans, and corporal bodies (Fig. 120-8). There is often size discrepancy, and orientation is most commonly side by side. Associated abnormalities include hypospadias, scrotal anomalies, duplicate bladder, renal anomalies, exstrophy defects, and anal and cardiac anomalies. Complete imaging of the urinary tract should be performed and ultrasound or magnetic resonance imaging may be helpful in assessment of penile anatomic development.[72] Surgical treatment must be individualized to the extent of the defect and may range from simple resection of the accessory penis to complex reconstruction.[74]

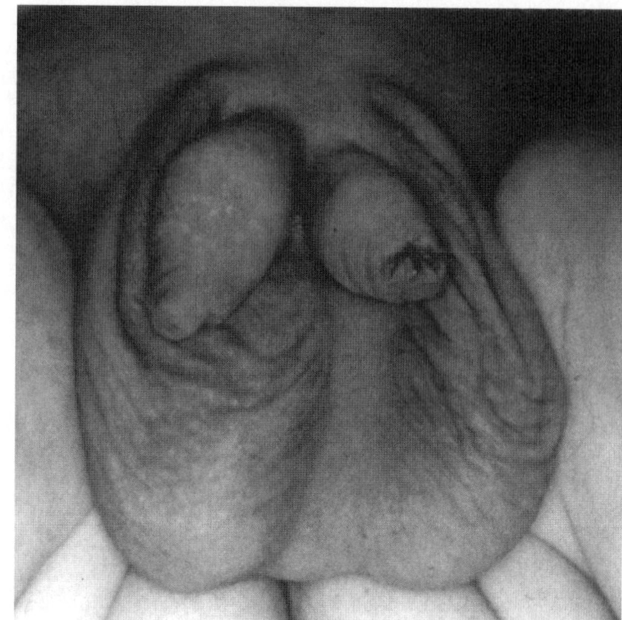

Figure 120-8 Diphallia, side-by-side configuration.

PENILE TORSION

Torsion of the penis is a rotational defect of the phallus, which is usually counterclockwise in direction and may be associated with hypospadias, chordee, and hooded dorsal foreskin. The median raphe generally courses obliquely around the shaft to the left. Rotation of less than 90 degrees often is not symptomatic and will not require correction. Surgical treatment involves degloving the penis and releasing any fibrous, dysgenic bands all the way to the base of the penis, allowing the phallus to reorient to the appropriate position.[6] In rare cases, fixation of the base of the corporal bodies to the symphysis pubis or creation of a dartos flap to rotate the corpora may be necessary to maintain proper orientation.[28]

PENOSCROTAL TRANSPOSITION AND SCROTAL ECTOPIA

The scrotum forms by migration of the labioscrotal folds inferomedial to the genital tubercle. Failure of migration possibly related to a gubernacular defect results in scrotal anomalies, such as penoscrotal transposition, bifid scrotum, or scrotal ectopia.[111] Association with hypospadias and chordee is common. The more significant the scrotal defect, the more likely other anomalies are to occur, including caudal regression, VATER syndrome, cryptorchidism, and other urinary tract abnormalities.[48,68,111]

Repair of significant forms of penoscrotal transposition require various advancement flap techniques. When associated with severe hypospadias, which requires preputial island flap type repairs, correction of penoscrotal transposition is usually done at a second stage to avoid the possibility of devascularizing the preputial flap.[35,89] Others propose combined repair of the hypospadias and scrotal transposition in one stage, but complications tend to be higher.[19,37,62] In cases of scrotal ectopia associated with cryptorchidism, scrotoplasty and orchiopexy can usually be accomplished at the same time.

REFERENCES

1. American Academy of Pediatrics: Report of the Task Force on Circumcision. Pediatrics 1989;84:388-391.
2. American Academy of Pediatrics, Task Force on Circumcision: Circumcision policy statement. Pediatrics 1999;103:686-693.
3. Allen JS, Summers JL, Wilkerson JE: Meatal calibration of newborn boys. J Urol 1972;107:498.
4. Al-Wattar KM: Congenital prepubic sinus: An epispadiac variant of urethral duplication: Case report and review of literature. J Pediatr Surg 2003;38:E10.
5. Appel RA, Kaplan GW, Brock WA, et al: Megalourethra. J Urol 1986;135:747-751.
6. Azmy A, Eckstein HB: Surgical correction of torsion of the penis. Br J Urol 1981;53:378-379.
7. Benedetto VD, Bagnara V, Guys JM, et al: A transvesical approach to mullerian duct remnants. Pediatr Surg Int 1997;12:151-154.
8. Biewald W, Schier F: Laser treatment of posterior urethral valves in neonates. Br J Urol 1992;69:425-427.
9. Blocksom BH Jr: Bladder pouch for prolonged tubeless cystostomy. J Urol 1957;78:398-401.
10. Brock WA, Kaplan GW: Lesions of Cowper's glands in children. J Urol 1979;122:121-123.
11. Brown MR, Cartwright PC, Snow BW: Common office problems in pediatric urology and gynecology. Pediatr Clin North Am 1997;44:1091-1115.
12. Caldamone AA, Chen SC, Elder JS, et al: Congenital anterior urethrocutaneous fistula. J Urol 1999;162:1430-1432.
13. Cartwright PC, Snow BW, McNees DC: Urethral meatotomy in the office using topical EMLA cream for anesthesia. J Urol 1996;156:857-858; discussion 858-859.
14. Churchill BM, Aliabadi H, Landau EH, et al: Ureteral bladder augmentation. J Urol 1993;150:716-720.
15. Churchill BM, McLorie GA, Khoury AE, et al: Emergency treatment and long-term follow-up of posterior urethral valves. Urol Clin North Am 1990;17:343-360.
16. Coleburn NH, Hensle TW: Anterior urethral polyp associated with hematuria in six-year-old child. Urology 1991;38: 143-144.
17. Cook LS, Koutsky LA, Holmes KK: Circumcision and sexually transmitted diseases. Am J Public Health 1994;84:197-201.
18. Crombleholme TM, Harrison MR, Golbus MS, et al: Fetal intervention in obstructive uropathy: Prognostic indicators and efficacy of intervention. Am J Obstet Gynecol 1990;162: 1239-1244.
19. DeFoor W, Wacksman J: Results of single staged hypospadias surgery to repair penoscrotal hypospadias with bifid scrotum or penoscrotal transposition. J Urol 2003;170: 1585-1588; discussion 1588.
20. Diamond M: Pediatric management of ambiguous and traumatized genitalia. J Urol 1999;162:1021-1028.
21. Duckett JW, Coplen D, Ewalt D, et al: Buccal mucosal urethral replacement. J Urol 1995;153:1660-1663.
22. Duckett JW Jr: Cutaneous vesicostomy in childhood: The Blocksom technique. Urol Clin North Am 1974;1: 485-495.
23. Effmann EL, Lebowitz RL, Colodny AH: Duplication of the urethra. Radiology 1976;119:179-185.
24. Elder JS, O'Grady JP, Ashmead G, et al: Evaluation of fetal renal function: Unreliability of fetal urinary electrolytes. J Urol 1990;144:574-578; discussion 593-594.
25. Evans JA, Erdile LB, Greenberg CR, et al: Agenesis of the penis: Patterns of associated malformations. Am J Med Genet 1999;84:47-55.
26. Fernandes ET, Dekermacher S, Sabadin MA, et al: Urethral prolapse in children. Urology 1993;41:240-242.
27. Field PL, Stephens FD: Congenital urethral membranes causing urethral obstruction. J Urol 1974;111:250-255.
28. Fisher C, Park M: Penile torsion repair using dorsal dartos flap rotation. J Urol 2004;171:1903-1904.
29. Freedman AL, Bukowski TP, Smith CA, et al: Fetal therapy for obstructive uropathy: Diagnosis specific outcomes [corrected]. J Urol 1996;156:720-723; discussion 723-724.
30. Freedman AL, Evans MI, Johnson MP: Complications of vesicoamniotic shunt placement for antenatal obstructive uropathy. J Urol 1997;157:3.
31. Ganiats TG, Humphrey JB, Taras HL, et al: Routine neonatal circumcision: A cost-utility analysis. Med Decis Making 1991;11:282-293.
32. Gastol P, Baka-Jakubiak M, Skobejko-Wlodarska L, et al: Complete duplication of the bladder, urethra, vagina, and uterus in girls. Urology 2000;55:578-581.
33. Gatti JM, Kirsch AJ: Posterior urethral valves: pre- and postnatal management. Curr Urol Rep 2001;2:138-145.
34. Gee WF, Ansell JS: Neonatal circumcision: A ten-year overview: with comparison of the Gomco clamp and the Plastibell device. Pediatrics 1976;58:824-827.
35. Germiyanoglu C, Ozkardes H, Altug U, et al: Reconstruction of penoscrotal transposition. Br J Urol 1994;73:200-203.
36. Ghanem MA, Wolffenbuttel KP, De Vylder A, et al: Long-term bladder dysfunction and renal function in boys with posterior urethral valves based on urodynamic findings. J Urol 2004;171:2409-2412.
37. Glassberg KI, Hansbrough F, Horowitz M: The Koyanagi-Nonomura 1-stage bucket repair of severe hypospadias with and without penoscrotal transposition. J Urol 1998;160: 1104-1107; discussion 1137.
38. Gleason PE, Kramer SA: Genitourinary polyps in children. Urology 1994;44:106-109.
39. Glick PL, Harrison MR, Golbus MS, et al: Management of the fetus with congenital hydronephrosis II: Prognostic criteria and selection for treatment. J Pediatr Surg 1985;20: 376-387.
40. Goldman R: The hidden trauma. In Circumcision. Boston, Vangard, 1997, pp 144-147.
41. Golimbu M, Orca M, Al-Askari S, et al: Anterior urethral valves. Urology 1978;12:343-346.
42. Gonzales ET: Posterior urethral valves and other urethral anomalies. In Walsh PC, et al (eds): Campbell's Urology. Philadelphia, WB Saunders, 2002, pp 2207-2330.
43. Gonzalez R, De Filippo R, Jednak R, et al: Urethral atresia: Long-term outcome in 6 children who survived the neonatal period. J Urol 2001;165:2241-2244.
44. Greenfield SP, Hensle TW, Berdon WE, et al: Unilateral vesicoureteral reflux and unilateral nonfunctioning kidney associated with posterior urethral valves—a syndrome? J Urol 1983;130:733-738.
45. Hassan JM, Pope JC 4th, Brock JW 3rd, et al: Vesicoureteral reflux in patients with posterior urethral valves. J Urol 2003;170:1677-1680; discussion 1680.

46. Hendren WH: The genetic male with absent penis and urethrorectal communication: Experience with 5 patients. J Urol 1997;157:1469-1474.
47. Henneberry MO, Stephens FD: Renal hypoplasia and dysplasia in infants with posterior urethral valves. J Urol 1980;123:912-915.
48. Hoar RM, Calvano CJ, Reddy PP, et al: Unilateral suprainguinal ectopic scrotum: The role of the gubernaculum in the formation of an ectopic scrotum. Teratology 1998;57: 64-69.
49. Hollowell JG Jr, Witherington R, Ballagas AJ, et al: Embryologic considerations of diphallus and associated anomalies. J Urol 1977;117:728-732.
50. Holmdahl G, Sillen U, Hellstrom AL, et al: Does treatment with clean intermittent catheterization in boys with posterior urethral valves affect bladder and renal function? J Urol 2003;170:1681-1685; discussion 1685.
51. Hoover DL, Duckett JW Jr: Posterior urethral valves, unilateral reflux and renal dysplasia: A syndrome. J Urol 1982;128: 994-997.
52. Hulbert WC, Duckett JW: Prognostic factors in infants with posterior urethral valves. J Urol 1986;135:121A.
53. Hyacinthe LM, Khoury AE, Churchill BM, et al: Improved outcome of renal transplant in children with posterior urethral valves. J Urol 1995;153:341A.
54. Johnston JH: Vesicoureteric reflux with urethral valves. Br J Urol 1979;51:100-104.
55. Johnston JH, Kulatilake AE: Posterior urethral valves: Results and sequelae. In Johnston JH, et al (eds): Problems in Pediatric Urology. Amsterdam, Excerpta Medica, 1972, p 161.
56. Kaplan GW, Brock WA: Urethral strictures in children. J Urol 1983;129:1200-1203.
57. Kilpatrick SJ: Therapeutic interventions for oligohydramnios: Amnioinfusion and maternal hydration. Clin Obstet Gynecol 1997;40:328-336.
58. Kim YH, Horowitz M, Combs AJ, et al: The management of unilateral poorly functioning kidneys in patients with posterior urethral valves. J Urol 1997;158:1001-1003.
59. Klee LW, Rink RC, Gleason PE, et al: Urethral polyp presenting as interlabial mass in young girls. Urology 1993;41:132-133.
60. Kohorn EI, Glickman MG: Technical aids in investigation and management of urethral diverticula in the female. Urology 1992;40:322-325.
61. Kojima Y, Hayashi Y, Maruyama T, et al: Comparison between ultrasonography and retrograde urethrography for detection of prostatic utricle associated with hypospadias. Urology 2001;57:1151-1155.
62. Koyanagi T, Nonomura K, Yamashita T, et al: One-stage repair of hypospadias: Is there no simple method universally applicable to all types of hypospadias? J Urol 1994;152: 1232-1237.
63. Krstic ZD, Smoljanic Z, Micovic Z, et al: Surgical treatment of the Mullerian duct remnants. J Pediatr Surg 2001;36: 870-876.
64. Lafferty PM, MacGregor FB, Scobie WG: Management of foreskin problems. Arch Dis Child 1991;66:696-697.
65. Liu KW, Fitzgerald RJ: An unusual case of complete urethral duplication in a female child. Aust N Z J Surg 1988;58: 587-588.
66. Longaker MT, Golbus MS, Filly RA, et al: Maternal outcome after open fetal surgery: A review of the first 17 human cases. JAMA 1991;265:737-741.
67. Lund L, Wai KH, Mui LM, et al: Effect of topical steroid on non-retractile prepubertal foreskin by a prospective, randomized, double-blind study. Scand J Urol Nephrol 2000;34: 267-269.
68. MacKenzie J, Chitayat D, McLorie G, et al: Penoscrotal transposition: A case report and review. Am J Med Genet 1994;49:103-107.
69. Maden C, Sherman KJ, Beckmann AM, et al: History of circumcision, medical conditions, and sexual activity and risk of penile cancer. J Natl Cancer Inst 1993;85:19-24.
70. Maizels M, Stephens FD, King LR, et al: Cowper's syringocele: A classification of dilatations of Cowper's gland duct based upon clinical characteristics of 8 boys. J Urol 1983;129: 111-114.
71. Mandelbrot L, Dumez Y, Muller F, et al: Prenatal prediction of renal function in fetal obstructive uropathies. J Perinatol Med 1991;19(Suppl 1):283-287.
72. Marti-Bonmati L, Menor F, Gomez J, et al: Value of sonography in true complete diphallia. J Urol 1989;142:356-357.
73. Meisheri IV, Motiwale SS, Sawant VV: Surgical management of enlarged prostatic utricle. Pediatr Surg Int 2000;16: 199-203.
74. Merrot T, Anastasescu R, Keita M, et al: [An example of diphallia in children]. Prog Urol 2003;13:509-512.
75. Morey AF, Duckett CP, McAninch JW: Failed anterior urethroplasty: Guidelines for reconstruction. J Urol 1997;158: 1383-1387.
76. Morey AF, McAninch JW: Sonographic staging of anterior urethral strictures. J Urol 2000;163:1070-1075.
77. Mortensen PH, Johnson HW, Coleman GU, et al: Megalourethra. J Urol 1985;134:358-361.
78. Mughal SA, Soomro S, Shaikh JM: Double phallus. J Coll Physicians Surg Pak 2003;13:534-535.
79. Muram D: Treatment of prepubertal girls with labial adhesions. J Pediatr Adolesc Gynecol 1999;12:67-70.
80. Muram D, Jerkins GR: Urinary retention secondary to a Gartner's duct cyst. Obstet Gynecol 1988;72:510-511.
81. Narasimhan KL, Kaur B, Chowdhary SK, et al: Does mode of treatment affect the outcome of neonatal posterior urethral valves? J Urol 2004;171:2423-2426.
82. Nguyen HT, Peters CA: The long-term complications of posterior urethral valves. BJU Int 1999;83(Suppl 3):23-28.
83. Nussbaum AR, Lebowitz RL: Interlabial masses in little girls: Review and imaging recommendations. AJR Am J Roentgenol 1983;141:65-71.
84. Oster J: Further fate of the foreskin: Incidence of preputial adhesions, phimosis, and smegma among Danish schoolboys. Arch Dis Child 1968;43:200-203.
85. Pansadoro V, Emiliozzi P: Internal urethrotomy in the management of anterior urethral strictures: Long-term followup. J Urol 1996;156:73-75.
86. Passerini-Glazel G, Araguna F, Chiozza L, et al: The P.A.D.U.A. (progressive augmentation by dilating the urethra anterior) procedure for the treatment of severe urethral hypoplasia. J Urol 1988;140:1247-1249.
87. Patterson DE, Barrett DM, Myers RP, et al: Primary realignment of posterior urethral injuries. J Urol 1983;129: 513-516.
88. Perimenis P, Panagou A: Re: Acute urinary retention caused by anterior urethral polyp. Br J Urol 1992;70:695.
89. Pinke LA, Rathbun SR, Husmann DA, et al: Penoscrotal transposition: Review of 53 patients. J Urol 2001;166:1865-1868.
90. Pippi Salle JL, Sibai H, Jacobson AI, et al: Bladder exstrophy associated with complete urethral duplication: A rare malformation with excellent prognosis. J Urol 2001;165: 2434-2437.
91. Puri A, Grover VP, Agarwala S, et al: Initial surgical treatment as a determinant of bladder dysfunction in posterior urethral valves. Pediatr Surg Int 2002;18:438-443.
92. Quintero RA, Hume R, Smith C, et al: Percutaneous fetal cystoscopy and endoscopic fulguration of posterior urethral valves. Am J Obstet Gynecol 1995;172:206-209.

93. Quintero RA, Johnson MP, Romero R, et al: In-utero percutaneous cystoscopy in the management of fetal lower obstructive uropathy. Lancet 1995;346:537-540.
94. Raviv G, Leibovitch I, Hanani J, et al: Hematuria and voiding disorders in children caused by congenital urethral polyps: Principles of diagnosis and management. Eur Urol 1993;23:382-385.
95. Reinberg Y, de Castano I, Gonzalez R: Influence of initial therapy on progression of renal failure and body growth in children with posterior urethral valves. J Urol 1992;148: 532-533.
96. Ritchey ML, Sinha A, Argueso L: Congenital fistula of the penile urethra. J Urol 1994;151:1061-1062.
97. Rittenberg MH, Hulbert WC, Snyder HM 3rd, et al: Protective factors in posterior urethral valves. J Urol 1988; 140:993-996.
98. Rudin JE, Geldt VG, Alecseev EB: Prolapse of urethral mucosa in white female children: Experience with 58 cases. J Pediatr Surg 1997;32:423-425.
99. Salle JL, Sibai H, Rosenstein D, et al: Urethral duplication in the male: Review of 16 cases. J Urol 2000;163:1936-1940.
100. Salomon L, Fontaine E, Guest G, et al: Role of the bladder in delayed failure of kidney transplants in boys with posterior urethral valves. J Urol 2000;163:1282-1285.
101. Scherz HC, Kaplan GW, Packer MG: Anterior urethral valves in the fossa navicularis in children. J Urol 1987;138:1211-1213.
102. Sepulveda W, Berry SM, Romero R, et al: Prenatal diagnosis of congenital megalourethra. J Ultrasound Med 1993;12: 761-766.
103. Shapiro E, Strother D: Pediatric genitourinary rhabdomyosarcoma. J Urol 1992;148:1761-1768.
104. Sharma SK, Kapoor R, Kumar A, et al: Incomplete epispadiac urethral duplication with dorsal penile curvature. J Urol 1987;138:585-586.
105. Shimada K, Hosokawa S, Tohda A, et al: Follow-up of children after fetal treatment for obstructive uropathy. Int J Urol 1998;5:312-316.
106. Siegel JF, Brock WA, Pena A: Transrectal posterior sagittal approach to prostatic utricle (mullerian duct cyst). J Urol 1995;153:785-787.
107. Skoog SJ, Belman AB: Aphallia: Its classification and management. J Urol 1989;141:589-592.
108. Smith GH, Canning DA, Schulman SL, et al: The long-term outcome of posterior urethral valves treated with primary valve ablation and observation. J Urol 1996;155: 1730-1734.
109. Sommer JT, Stephens FD: Dorsal urethral diverticulum of the fossa navicularis: Symptoms, diagnosis and treatment. J Urol 1980;124:94-97.
110. Sorensen C, Furness P, Koyle MA: Betamethasone Cream for Treatment of Labial Adhesions. Boston, American Urological Association, South Central Section, 2003.
111. Spears T, Franco I, Reda EF, et al: Accessory and ectopic scrotum with VATER association. Urology 1992;40:343-345.
112. Spitzer A: The current approach to the assessment of fetal renal function: Fact or fiction? Pediatr Nephrol 1996;10:230-235.
113. Starr NB: Labial adhesions in childhood. J Pediatr Health Care 1996;10:26-27.
114. Stephens FD: Congenital Malformations of the Urinary Tract. New York, Praeger, 1983, p 577.
115. Stolar CJ, Wiener ES, Hensle TW, et al: Reconstruction of penile agenesis by a posterior sagittal approach. J Pediatr Surg 1987;22:1076-1080.
116. Tank ES: Anterior urethral valves resulting from congenital urethral diverticula. Urology 1987;30:467-469.
117. Thompson HC, King LR, Knox E, et al: Report of the ad hoc task force on circumcision. Pediatrics 1975;56:610-611.
118. Tietjen DN, Gloor JM, Husmann DA: Proximal urinary diversion in the management of posterior urethral valves: Is it necessary? J Urol 1997;158:1008-1010.
119. Welsh A, Agarwal S, Kumar S, et al: Fetal cystoscopy in the management of fetal obstructive uropathy: Experience in a single European centre. Prenat Diagn 2003;23:1033-1041.
120. Willetts IE, Roberts JP, MacKinnon AE: Laparoscopic excision of a prostatic utricle in a child. Pediatr Surg Int 2003;19:557-558.
121. Williams DI, Retik AB: Congenital valves and diverticula of the anterior urethra. Br J Urol 1969;41:228-234.
122. Wiswell TE, Geschke DW: Risks from circumcision during the first month of life compared with those for uncircumcised boys. Pediatrics 1989;83:1011-1015.
123. Wiswell TE, Hachey WE: Urinary tract infections and the uncircumcised state: An update. Clin Pediatr (Phila) 1993;32:130-134.
124. Yeung CK, Sihoe JD, Tam YH, et al: Laparoscopic excision of prostatic utricles in children. BJU Int 2001;87:505-508.
125. Young H, Frantz W, Baldwin J: Congenital obstruction of the posterior urethra. J Urol 1919;3:289.
126. Zaontz MR, Firlit CF: Percutaneous antegrade ablation of posterior urethral valves in premature or underweight term neonates: An alternative to primary vesicostomy. J Urol 1985;134:139-141.

Chapter 121

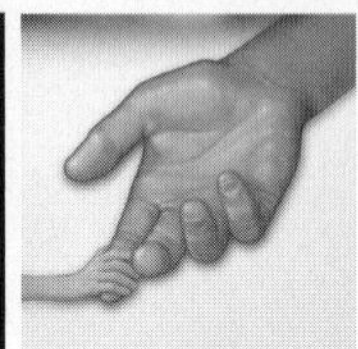

Ambiguous Genitalia

Patricia K. Donahoe, Jay J. Schnitzer, and Rafael Pieretti

DEVELOPMENTAL BIOLOGY OF MAMMALIAN SEXUAL DIFFERENTIATION

Phenotypic males and females develop as a result of a precise cascade of sequential molecular and morphologic events. The intermediate mesoderm situated between the ectoderm and the endoderm is the site that gives rise to the urogenital ridge in the early embryo (Fig. 121-1).[48] The urogenital ridge contains the undifferentiated gonad and the mesonephros, where the reproductive wolffian and müllerian ducts reside. Formation of the ridge depends on the expression of a number of important genes, including the Wilms' tumor gene *(WT1)* and a gene called steroidogenesis factor *(SF-1)*; in their absence, the gonad and adjacent structures fail to form. Mutations in *WT1* in mice result in absence of the gonad and kidney,[29] and mutations in *SF-1* result in absence of the gonad and adrenal gland[44] (see Fig. 121-1); defects in homologues of *SF-1* produce similar phenotypes in humans.[1] Other genes that are essential for development during this early process are shown in Figure 121-1. Simultaneously, genes important for wolffian and müllerian duct development are expressed. The wolffian duct requires the action of *PAX2* and possibly *PAX8*, which are paired genes important in *Drosophila* development. Müllerian duct formation requires the activity of a series of secreted factors whose expression is directed by the WNT family of proteins.[64]

During formation of the urogenital ridge, primordial germ cells must migrate from outside the embryo in the epiblast through the ectodermal layer of the embryo, the primitive streak, the base of the allantois, the wall of the hindgut, and then to the urogenital ridge, where they take up residence in the undifferentiated gonad. This complex migratory pattern is under the control of a number of genes[52] and proteins such as Fragilis, Stella, BMP4,[71] and others still being elucidated.[48] After arrival in the gonad, the mitotically active XY germ cells become arrested in G_0 under the influence of a meiosis inhibitory factor; the XX germ cells undergo the first meiotic division under the influence of factors not yet understood.

The differentiation of the gonads commences with the expression of small transcription factors such as *SRY*, a gene present on the short arm of the Y chromosome, and an SRY-related autosomal gene called *SOX 9* from 17q. The fact that testicular differentiation required a signal from the Y chromosome became evident in 1959, when the 45,X Turner phenotype was first recognized.[23] Subsequent cytogenetic studies progressively localized the male differentiation region to the short arm of the Y chromosome.[38] Much later, Page et al.[60] defined a critical region for testis determination near the pseudoautosomal region of the short arm of the Y chromosome by comparing chromosomal deletions and translocations in a series of XX phenotypic males and XY phenotypic females. Later, Sinclair et al.[77] defined a single-copy gene called the sex-determining region of the Y chromosome *(SRY)* that encodes DNA binding protein, which is expressed in the gonadal ridge immediately before testis differentiation.[43] When the *SRY* gene, which expresses a protein homologous to the high mobility group (HMG) class of nuclear proteins, was transfected into XX female mouse embryos, a substantial proportion of these transgenic animals developed testes and assumed anatomic and functional male phenotypes.[42,43]

In addition to the Y chromosome, autosomal and X factors contribute to sex differentiation. For example, mutations on the long arm of chromosome 17q, found in cases of camptomelic dysplasia associated with sex reversal,[24,80,82] caused a defect in the SRY-related gene product SOX 9, which contributes to sex differentiation. In addition, analysis of 46,XY sex-reversed females with intact *SRY* led to the discovery of the dosage-sensitive sex (DSS) reversal locus on the short arm of the X chromosome, duplication of which is required for female differentiation.[5] This region, which contains the gene *DAX-1*, may have a negative influence on testis differentiation because a double dose of the X chromosome, is associated with dysgenesis of the testis. Defects in the distal end of the short arm of chromosome 9p[7] and the distal end of the long arm of chromosome 10q[86] are also associated with sex reversal. Thus, although *SRY* orchestrates gonadal differentiation as a master genetic switch, downstream molecular signals from the X chromosome and selected autosomes contribute to the morphologic differentiation of the urogenital ridge to a sex-specific gonad. The genes responsible for differentiation of the ovary are currently being studied, but presence of the second X chromosome is probably required; thus, proper ovarian differentiation

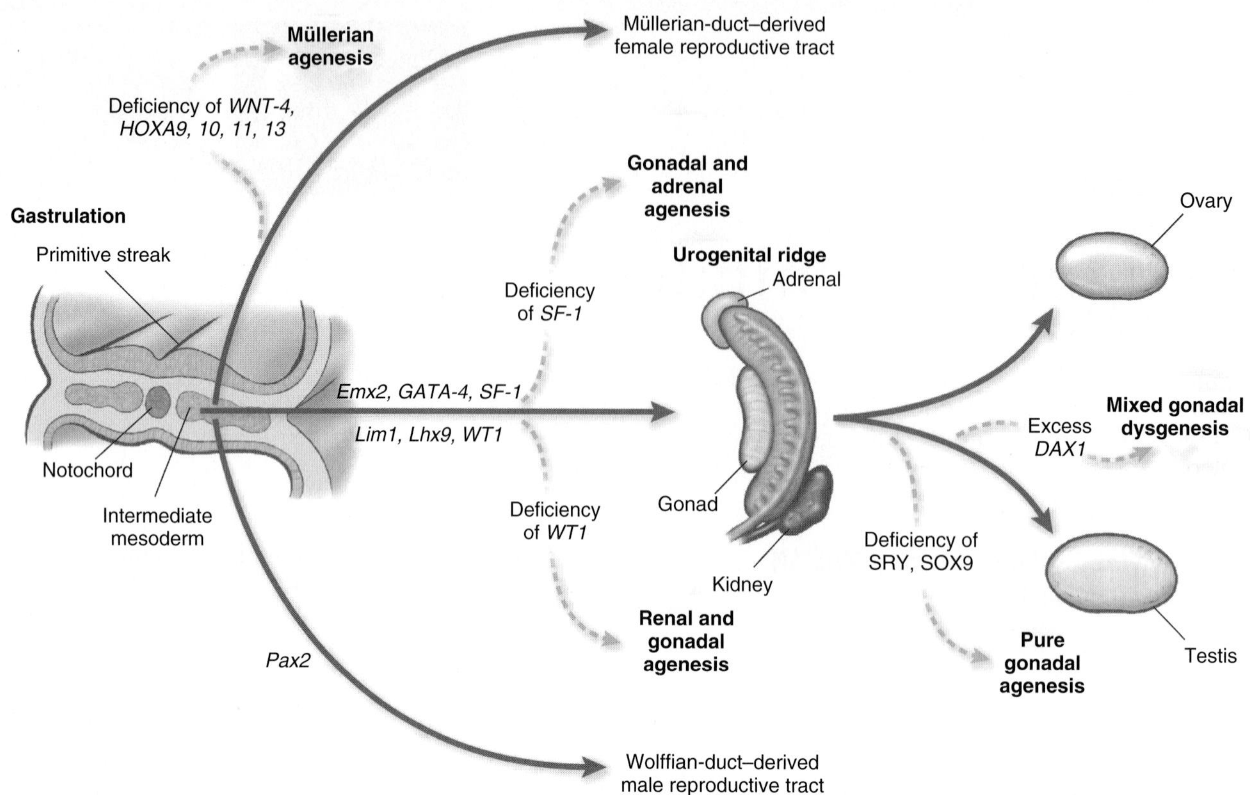

Figure 121–1 Mutations in a number of genes can lead to a variety of syndromes of dysgenesis involving the müllerian or wolffian ducts, gonads, kidneys, and adrenal glands as a result of a deficiency or excess of the proteins shown. *DAX1* denotes the gene duplicated in congenital adrenal hypoplasia on the X chromosome; *Emx2*, the empty spiracles homeobox gene; *GATA-4*, the gene encoding a protein that binds to a GATA DNA sequence; *HOXA*, homeobox protein; *Lim1*, a homeobox gene important for limb development; *Lhx9*, a lim homeobox family member; *Pax2*, a paired box homeotic gene; *SF-1*, the gene for steroidogenic factor 1; *SRY*, the sex-determining region of the Y chromosome; *SOX9*, SRY homeobox 9; *WNT-4*, a protein that induces development of the müllerian mesenchyma; and *WT1*, Wilms' tumor suppressor gene 1. (From MacLaughlin DT, Donahoe PK: Sex determination and differentiation. N Engl J Med 2004;350:367-378.)

is probably not merely the default pathway of failure of testis differentiation, as previously believed.

The testis also produces a protein that contributes to testicular descent, insulin-like growth factor 3 (Insl3).[57,89] Thus, the embryo must have the appropriate chromosomal endowment (i.e., 46,XX for females and 46,XY for males). Germ cells must then accurately migrate to the hindgut and subsequently take up residence in the retroperitoneum, where they condense in the urogenital ridge to become either a testis or an ovary. Germ cell migration into the urogenital ridge coincides with and probably induces the morphologic formation of a sex-specific gonad, which in turn produces hormones. Receptors in more distant sites subsequently respond to the secreted extracellular hormones and proteins to activate intracellular signaling pathways and somatic gene responses, which lead to morphologic and biochemical changes resulting in the appropriate male or female phenotype.[21]

Male and female primordial reproductive ducts coexist for a short period in all mammalian embryos. Müllerian ducts, the anlage for the uterus, fallopian tubes, and upper third of the vagina, develop autonomously in the female in the absence of the testis. Wolffian ducts, the anlage of the epididymis, vas deferens, and seminal vesicles, require testosterone to develop. The fetal testis, after morphogenesis into seminiferous tubules with Sertoli cells surrounding germ cells and interstitial differentiation to Leydig cells, produces two products required for male differentiation: müllerian inhibiting substance (MIS), which inhibits differentiation of the müllerian duct, and testosterone, which stimulates wolffian structures.[40] The external genital primordia develop autonomously into clitoris, labia minora, and labia majora. Complete differentiation of the external genitalia to phallus and scrotum requires reduction of testosterone to dihydrotestosterone by 5α-reductase.[35] The phallus lengthens into a penis, the urogenital folds fuse to form the penile urethra, and the labioscrotal swellings fuse in the midline to form the scrotum. The influence of testosterone is discussed in more detail later in the chapter. Autonomous female development can occur in the absence of ovaries. Although the role of estrogens in sexual differentiation is still unclear, suppression of the male pathway seems to require a duplicated locus on the short arm of the X chromosome, where the *DAX-1* gene, which transcribes a protein that blocks steroidogenesis, has been located.[5,88]

The embryonic testis also produces MIS. The existence of a müllerian inhibitor was proposed by Jost,[40] who showed that testicular implants in female rabbit embryos stimulated the wolffian duct but also caused regression of müllerian ducts. This regression is characterized morphologically by programmed cell death. Because of the importance of these events, MIS was purified,[9,67] then used to clone the *MIS* gene.[10] The bioactive C-terminal domain of MIS is homologous to a group of evolutionary conserved proteins, often referred to as the transforming growth factor-ß (TGF-ß) family, which comprises MIS, activin, inhibin, bone morphogenesis factor, *Drosophila* decapentaplagia, and *Xenopus* Vg1, among others.[10] The MIS ligand binds to a heterologous receptor composed of at least two serine-threonine kinase transmembrane units, the type II receptor,[78] which phosphorylates or activates the type I receptor,[31] which signals downstream to begin the series of molecular events that results in regression of the müllerian ducts. This substance has been developed as an antiproliferative agent for tumors of müllerian duct origin and for ovarian,[28,50] endometrial,[68] cervical,[4] breast,[34,75,76] and prostate[34] cancers. Abnormalities of the *MIS* gene itself can result in the retained müllerian duct syndrome, in which otherwise normal males, usually with undescended testes, have persistent müllerian structures that have not undergone normal regression.[6,33]

PATHOPHYSIOLOGY OF INTERSEX ABNORMALITIES

There are three major categories of developmental aberrations that are responsible for the most common forms of ambiguous genitalia in newborns (Table 121-1). In the first category, genetic females are masculinized by an overabundance of androgenic steroid production, causing a genital abnormality that requires intense medical or surgical management (or both). In the second category, intersex abnormalities occur because of deficient androgen production or action in genetic males. The third category of abnormalities results from mutations leading to absent, incomplete, or asymmetrical gonadal differentiation.[21] It is essential to understand the pathophysiology underlying these disorders in order to make a timely and accurate diagnosis and to plan optimal treatment strategies.

Overandrogenization of Genetic Females (46,XX)

The most common cause of overandrogenization or virilization is a defect in the P450 (heme pigment 450 oxidases, which metabolize multiple substrates) adrenal enzymes responsible for the conversion of progesterones to glucocorticoids and mineralocorticoids, resulting in the syndrome of congenital adrenal hyperplasia (CAH) or adrenogenital syndrome, otherwise known as female pseudohermaphroditism.[84] This syndrome affects both males and females but causes ambiguous genitalia only in females. Adrenal differentiation occurs at 11 weeks' gestation, after differentiation of the gonads and reproductive tract. Therefore, the excess androgen most severely affects the developing external genitalia, the genital tubercle, and the urogenital folds, which develop after 11 weeks. When exposed to excess androgens, the genital tubercle, instead of forming a clitoris, is stimulated to develop as a penile structure. The urogenital folds, rather than developing as labia, acquire a more fused scrotal appearance. Ovaries remain in their normal intra-abdominal position.

Mutations in the *P450c21* or 21-hydroxylase gene, now known as *CYP21* (Table 121-2), cause 90% of cases of CAH. The mutated gene, which resides on chromosome 6p in the HLA locus, results from recombination between the functional *CYP21B* and the nonfunctional pseudogene *CYP21A*. Incorporation of deletions from this pseudogene act to disable the functional gene.[27,55,58,85] The remainder of CAH cases are distributed among deficiencies of P450c11, 3ß-hydroxysteroid dehydrogenase, CYP17, or StAR, depending on the ethnic origin of the patient.[17,54,61] Rarely, CAH can result from exposure to exogenous androgens, such as those given in the past to prevent loss of pregnancy. Deficient glucocorticoids and mineralocorticoids, as a result of negative feedback on the pituitary, cause excessive production of adrenocorticotropic hormone, which in turn results in hyperplasia of the fasciculata and granulosa layers of the adrenal gland and preferential production of androgenic steroids from the reticulata layer. 17-Hydroxyprogesterone accumulates proximal to the P450c21 block, resulting in overproduction of pregnenolone and progesterone and their 17-hydroxylated derivatives, leading to the overproduction of testosterone and ultimately its reduced derivative dihydrotestosterone (Fig. 121-2). Elevations in 17-hydroxyprogesterone can be detected from a spot serum sample.[62] Polymerase chain reaction (PCR), sequencing of known genes, or fluorescent in situ hybridization (FISH) can now be used to make this diagnosis in utero.[17]

The adrenogenital syndrome defect in these 46,XX genetic females with normal ovaries resides in the adrenal glands. The uterus and fallopian tubes are also normal. The vagina, however, is foreshortened as a result of having failed to migrate to the perineum. It joins the urethra either at the position of the prostate, if masculinization is severe, or at a more distal position, if it is less severe. The external genitalia are characterized by variable clitoral enlargement, ranging from trivial to severe; some patients form an almost normal phallus. The labia can be masculinized to form either labioscrotal folds or, in the most severe cases, complete scrotal fusion. Because the ovaries are normal, the gonads never descend into these labioscrotal folds or fused scrotum.[16] Therefore, an infant with bilateral undescended testes should have a karyotype determination to identify the presence or absence of the Y chromosome. All the enzymatic defects result in deficient cortisol biosynthesis. Failure of feedback results in increased corticotropin production, which continues to stimulate the adrenal gland and leads to hyperplasia, elevated production of products proximal to the enzymatic defect, and preferential overproduction of androgenic steroids. Concomitant production of melanocyte-stimulating hormone can also darken the genitalia and breast areolae.

Underandrogenization of Genetic Males (46,XY)

Insufficient masculinization of a 46,XY genetic male can occur due to insufficient testosterone production, an androgen receptor deficiency, or an inability to convert

TABLE 121-1 Ambiguous Genitalia Syndromes: Diagnosis and Treatment

Disease	Diagnostic Features	Physical Examination	Gender Assignment	Medical Therapy	Surgical Therapy
Overandrogenized Female (Female Pseudohermaphroditism)					
Congenital adrenal hyperplasia (adrenogenital syndrome)	Karyotype 46,XX Electrolytes: K high, Na low Androgen high 17-hydroxyprogesterone high MIS 0 Sequence *CYP21* Chromosomal FISH	Symmetrical gonads Clitoral hypertrophy Sinogram: UG sinus defect Enlarged labioscrotum	F	Hydrocortisone or cortisone acetate + Florinef Embryo selection from the blastocyst Steroid replacement in utero from 6 wk gestation	Perioperative stress steroids Clitoral reduction Vaginal exteriorization Labioscrotal reduction
Underandrogenized Male (Male Pseudohermaphroditism)					
Testosterone deficiency	Karyotype 46,XY Testosterone low Sequence enzyme genes: *17-KS OH, P450scc, 3β-HSD, CYP17* FISH	Symmetrical, undescended, small testis Severe hypospadias No müllerian structures	If M	Presurgical testosterone stimulation Testosterone at adolescence	Staged hypospadias repair Prepenile scrotal repair Orchiopexy
		Predominant female phenotype	If F	Estrogen/progesterone at adolescence	Gonadectomy
Androgen receptor deficiency					
Testicular feminization (complete androgen insensitivity)	Karyotype 46,XY Testosterone high MIS high Sequence androgen receptor gene FISH	Female phenotype No müllerian structures	F	Estrogen/progesterone at adolescence	Infancy: gonadectomy, Adolescence: vaginal replacement
Reifenstein's syndrome (incomplete androgen insensitivity)	Karyotype 46,XY Testosterone normal MIS slightly elevated	As for testosterone deficiency	If F	Estrogen/progesterone at adolescence	Infancy: gonadectomy, clitoral reduction, labioscrotal reduction Adolescence: vaginal replacement
	PCR androgen receptor gene FISH CGH		If M	As for testosterone deficiency (above)	As for testosterone deficiency (above)

5α-Reductase deficiency	Karyotype 46,XY Testosterone high DHT low MIS high Sequence 5α-reductase type 2 gene FISH	Severe penoscrotal hypospadias Symmetrical, undescended, normal testes Prepenile scrotum	M	Presurgical testosterone stimulation DHT replacement	Hypospadias repair Prepenile scrotal repair
Chromosomal Abnormalities					
Pure gonadal dysgenesis	Karyotype 46,XY Sequence candidate genes: *SRY, SOX 9, DAX-1* Testosterone absent MIS absent FISH CGH	Phenotypic female Vagina present No gonads Symmetrical	F	Estrogen/progesterone at adolescence	Gonadectomy
Mixed gonadal dysgenesis	Karyotype 45,X/46,XY or 46,XY Testosterone low MIS low Sequence *DAX-1* FISH CGH	Asymmetry of gonads: streak and testis UG sinus defect Clitoral hypertrophy	If F	Estrogen/progesterone at adolescence	Clitoral recession Vaginal exteriorization Labioscrotal reduction Gonadectomy
			If M	Presurgical testosterone stimulation Testosterone at adolescence	
True hermaphrodite	Karyotype 46,XX Testosterone normal or low MIS normal or low CGH	Asymmetrical testis, ovary, or ovotestes UG sinus defect Clitoral hypertrophy	If F	Estrogen/progesterone at adolescence	Clitoral recession Vaginal exteriorization Labioscrotal reduction Preserve normal ovary or polar ovarian tissue
			If M	Presurgical testosterone stimulation Testosterone at adolescence	Staged hypospadias repair Prepenile scrotal repair Removal of müllerian structures Preserve vas and normal testis or central testicular tissue Orchiopexy? Prosthesis?

CGH, comparative genomic hybridization; DHT, dihydrotestosterone; F, female; FISH, fluorescent in situ hybridization; M, male; MIS, müllerian inhibiting substance; PCR, polymerase chain reaction; UG, urogenital.

TABLE 121-2 Steroid Biosynthetic Enzyme Nomenclature

Old	New—Protein	New—Gene
Testis		
20,22-desmolase	P450scc (side chain cleavage)	*CYP11A*
17-hydroxylase	P450c17	*CYP17*
17-lyase	P450c17	*CYP17*
3β-hydroxysteroid dehydrogenase (3ß-HSD)	Same	Same
17-ketosteroid reductase	Same	Same
Adrenal		
21-hydroxylase	P450c21	*CYP21*
11-hydroxylase	P450c11	*CYP11B1*
18-hydroxylase	P450c11	*CYP11B2*

testosterone to dihydrotestosterone. All these general categories of defects result in the syndrome of male pseudohermaphroditism.[13] Deficiency of androgen production (see Fig. 121-2) occurs because of genetic enzymatic defects, including steroid acute regulatory protein (StAR), resulting in lipoid adrenal hyperplasia (formerly thought to represent defects in cholesterol desmolase, P450scc, or $CYP11A_1$). $CYP11A_1$ (20,22 desmolase), CYP17 (17-hydroxylase or lyase), 3β-hydroxysteroid dehydrogenase (3ß-HSD), and 17β-hydroxysteroid dehydrogenase (17ß-HSD), formerly known as 17-ketosteroid reductase, together and sequentially are responsible for the cascade of metabolism from cholesterol to testosterone.[53] In these patients, stimulation of chorionic gonadotropin produces little or no testosterone; in contrast, MIS levels are normal or high for age. The testes may be undescended, small, or both. Under the influence of normal MIS, there should be no müllerian structures. Because of testosterone deficiency, the penis may be small and hypospadiac.[27]

Androgen insensitivity can occur because of receptor deficiency. Most abnormalities are caused by point mutations in the androgen receptor gene,[46,79] which can now be detected by PCR and DNA sequencing. Only rarely have large deletions been found. The phenotype can be mild or severe; the complete manifestation is often referred to as testicular feminization, a syndrome in which the patient has an almost complete female phenotype. Serum levels of testosterone may be high; MIS may be normal or, in some cases, considerably elevated; and müllerian structures are normally regressed. The gonads are symmetrical and may be intra-abdominal or descended.

Adrenal and Gonadal Biosynthesis of Steroid Hormones

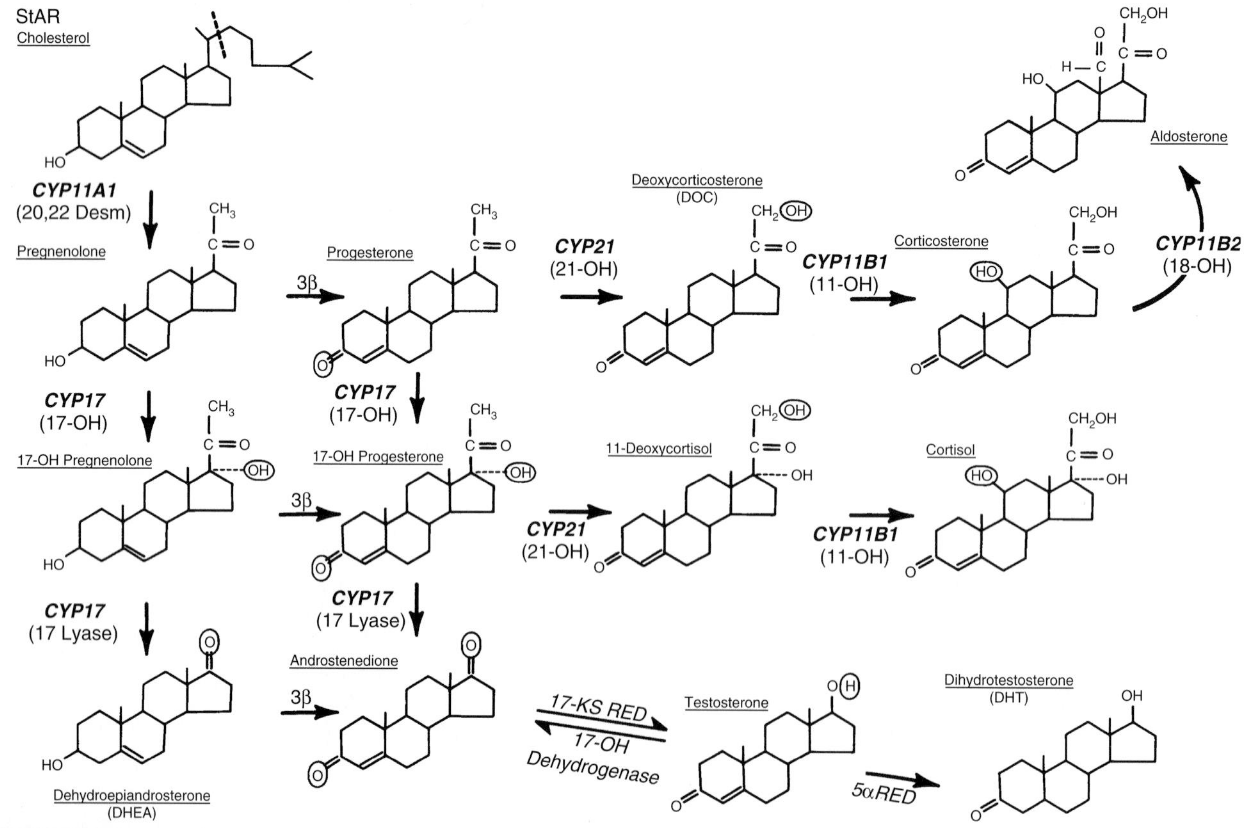

Figure 121-2 Pathways of steroid hormone biosynthesis from cholesterol. New enzyme nomenclature is in bold lettering; old nomenclature is in parentheses. Enzymatic defects of CYP21, CYP11, or 3ß-hydroxysteroid dehydrogenase can lead to congenital adrenal hyperplasia. Deficiencies in testosterone production leading to a form of male pseudohermaphroditism can result from defects in $CYP11A_1$, CYP17, 3ß-hydroxysteroid dehydrogenase, and 17-ketosteroid reductase.

However, not all patients with the 46,XY karyotype and the characteristics of male pseudohermaphroditism have a detectable molecular defect in the coding region of the androgen receptor. It is possible that the noncoding promoter, the 3′ untranslated region, or other transcription factors or their cofactors are the cause of male pseudohermaphroditism in the large subset of patients in which the molecular defect has not yet been defined.

3β-HSD acts by reducing the 3β-hydroxyl group to a 3-ketone and by isomerizing the C5-6 double bond to the C4-5 position in the conversion of pregnenolone to progesterone or 17-hydroxypregnenolone to 17-hydroxyprogesterone. All these steps are essential for the production of glucocorticoids and mineralocorticoids. The activity is also important in the testis for the conversion of dehydroepiandrosterone (DHEA) to androstenedione. Various isoforms of this enzyme have also been found in the placenta, but their functions have not been as carefully detailed. Another non-P450 enzyme in the pathway is 17β-HSD, which converts androstenedione to testosterone.

Mutations in the 5α-reductase type 2 gene cause another form of male pseudohermaphroiditism. Because of this deficiency, testosterone is not converted to dihydrotestosterone in peripheral, particularly genital, target tissues.[35,83] This non-P450 enzyme depends on the reduced form of (nicotinamide-adenine dinucleotide phosphate) NADPH. Action in the genital area results in elongation and ventral closing of the penile raphe, which encloses the urethra and displaces the urethral orifice from the perineum to the tip of the penis.[13] The labioscrotal folds are also fused in a posterior direction to create scrotal sacs. This autosomal recessive form of severe hypospadias is associated with undescended testis, prepenile scrotum, and enlarged prostatic utricle. The enzyme has binding sites for both testosterone and the NADPH cofactor, where point mutations have been associated with the defective phenotype. Two known isoforms exist[2]; however, type 2, located on chromosome 19, is the one expressed predominantly in the external genitalia. The paradoxical virilization that occurs at puberty and results in a change of sexual identity is caused by increased activity of the 5α-reductase type 1 isoform in these genetic males.

Abnormalities of Gonadal Development and Differentiation

Abnormalities of the sex chromosomes usually manifest as failed, incomplete, or asymmetrical gonadal differentiation. Patients with these disorders have either bilateral streak gonads, as in pure gonadal dysgenesis, or asymmetrical gonadal development, as in mixed gonadal dysgenesis or true hermaphroditism. Patients with pure gonadal dysgenesis and a 46,XY karyotype may have a defective Y chromosome, with either deletion in the 1A1 pseudoautosomal region[60] or a point mutation in the *SRY* gene.[41] Mutations associated with camptomelic dysplasia, a severe disorder occurring in patients with a translocation in the distal arm of chromosome 9p near the *SRY*-related *SOX 9* gene,[24,82] or mutations in *WT1* associated with Frasier's syndrome[3] also result in pure gonadal dysgenesis. These streak gonads fail to develop bilaterally, producing little or no end products of testosterone or MIS; gonadotropin levels are compensatorily high. Müllerian ducts are preserved, and the phenotype is female.

Mixed gonadal dysgenesis associated with a 45,X/46,XY karyotype is by far the most common of the chromosomal abnormalities.[20,70] The gonads are asymmetrical, most often with a small dysgenetic testis on one side and a streak gonad on the other.[15] Most patients with this defect have retained müllerian ducts. The small testis can produce sufficient testosterone to cause masculinization and hypertrophy of the clitoris. The vagina fails to migrate to the perineum and enters the urethra as a urogenital sinus defect more distal to the bladder neck than seen in severe cases of CAH. It is important to note that 40% of patients with mixed gonadal dysgenesis can have a 46,XY karyotype, and some have bilateral testes or streak ovaries. The absence of the second X chromosome is in some way related to the early ovarian dysgenesis. The mosaicism of mixed gonadal dysgenesis results from the presence of at least two gonadal germ cell lines. The degree of testicular differentiation is determined by the percentage of cells expressing the XY genotype, which may also influence the degree of asymmetry. Loss of the Y chromosome can occur because of nondisjunction, the failure of paired chromosomes to migrate to opposite poles during cell division.[18,23,48] The 45,X/46,XY karyotype is now being detected in a small percentage of cells in phenotypically normal males, because prenatal genetic testing has become more common.

True hermaphrodites are rare, except among the Bantu; the cause of this anomaly remains elusive.[14,81] More than 90% of these patients have a 46,XX karyotype. Asymmetry characterizes many of these patients, who have simultaneous and nondysgenetic ovarian and testicular differentiation that is separated on both sides or combined in one or both gonads as an ovotestis. When ovarian tissue and testicular tissue coexist in the same gonad, the testis is always central, and the ovarian tissue is polar.[59] Although the molecular cause of this disorder has not been elucidated, translocation of a fragment containing the *SRY* gene to a cryptic site on the X chromosome is occasionally observed.[8] Otherwise, *SRY* has not been detected in these patients. Although early testicular differentiation occurs, spermatogenesis is not evident,[14] which may reflect the absence of other necessary Y-directed functions. The müllerian structures are regressed on the side of the testicular tissue but retained on the side of the ovarian tissue and in the midline as well, with the vagina entering the urethra usually more distally as a urogenital sinus defect. The asymmetry associated with this disorder remains an enigma.

DIAGNOSIS

A baby born with ambiguous genitalia must have an expeditious and thoughtful evaluation to determine whether gender assignment can be made. It is important to minimize the emotional trauma to the family and later to the child. Referral to a well-organized team of endocrinologists

TABLE 121-3 Rapid Diagnostic Algorithm

Y Chromosome Absent or Abnormal		Y Chromosome Present	
Symmetry	**Asymmetry**	**Symmetry**	**Asymmetry**
Female pseudohermaphrodite (congenital adrenal hyperplasia)	True hermaphrodite	Male pseudohermaphrodite	Mixed gonadal dysgenesis

These two diagnostic criteria—presence or absence of Y chromosome and gonadal symmetry or asymmetry—allow the rapid, accurate assignment of a patient into one of the four diagnostic categories with approximately 90% accuracy.

and pediatric surgeons experienced with the complexity of these disorders often helps in this respect. Although many syndromes can affect later sexual development, only four result in sexual ambiguity at birth: female pseudohermaphroditism (also known as adrenogenital syndrome and CAH), true hermaphroditism, male pseudohermaphroditism, and mixed gonadal dysgenesis. A child with pure gonadal dysgenesis, although having a 46,XY karyotype, is phenotypically female. It is critical that the sex of rearing not be biased by the skills of the surgeons, who must be equally adept at reconstructing the infant as male or female. Two screening criteria can be used to diagnose the infant as having one of the four disorders: symmetry and the presence of a Y chromosome (Table 121-3). The diagnostic evaluation of patients with ambiguous genitalia is outlined in Table 121-1.

The first criterion is the physical finding of gonadal symmetry or asymmetry, and the second is a rapid analysis of the sex chromosomes. Probes for *SRY* can now be used to detect the distal end of Yp, the short arm of the Y chromosome, by PCR or FISH. Symmetry of the gonads is determined by the position of one gonad relative to the other, either above or below the external inguinal ring. Both gonads lie either above or below the ring, symmetrically, when a diffuse biochemical cause underlies the abnormality. For example, in female or male pseudohermaphroditism, a biochemical defect influences both gonads equally. Asymmetry occurs when one gonad lies above the inguinal ring and the other below. This asymmetry occurs in chromosomal abnormalities, such as mixed gonadal dysgenesis or true hermaphroditism, in which a predominant testis descends and a predominant ovary remains above the external ring. In cases of female pseudohermaphroditism with adrenogenital syndrome and in most cases of true hermaphroditism, the karyotype is 46,XX. Patients with male pseudohermaphroditism or mixed gonadal dysgenesis have a Y chromosome in their karyotype.

After this initial evaluation, rapid analysis for 17-hydroxyprogesterone to detect *CYP21* disorders should be done emergently in patients with 46,XX and symmetrical undescended gonads. In some states, this screening test is done on all newborns. A detailed history and physical examination can be coupled with PCR or FISH analyses to detect mutations or deletions known to cause defects in the four major categories (Table 121-4) and to further define these disorders and guide sex assignment. Subsequently, ultrasonography, magnetic resonance imaging, contrast radiography, and later cystoscopy, coupled with accurate laboratory analysis for disorders of enzymes affecting testosterone synthesis, should provide a definitive diagnosis and permit appropriate gender assignment with a high degree of accuracy.

The size and location of the penis with respect to the scrotum should be carefully noted. Although the size of the phallus varies considerably, some guidelines are helpful.[22,27] The average length of the penis is 3.5 ± 0.4 cm at term, 3.0 ± 0.4 cm at 35 weeks' gestation, and 2.5 ± 0.4 cm at 30 weeks' gestation. At term, a diameter of 1 cm is average. A penis smaller than 1.5 ± 0.7 cm in full-term infants makes the female gender assignment more compelling, except in cases of 17-ketosteroid reductase or 5α-reductase deficiencies, in which large body habitus (P. K. Donahoe, personal observation) or sex reversal at puberty, respectively, may favor or dictate male sex assignment. An early rectal examination may allow the detection of the uterus while it is still under the influence of placental human chorionic gonadotropin, before it softens. The presence of hypospadias and the position of the meatus with respect to the tip of the penis should be noted; the opening of the vaginal introitus in relation to the bladder neck and perineum and the length of the vagina should also be noted. Palpation of the gonad can help differentiate the firm testis from the softer ovotestis, and the wrapping of the epididymis around the testis can help differentiate it from an ovary in the inguinal position.[21] Often the hypospadiac phallus is displaced posteriorly behind a prepenile scrotum.

Female Pseudohermaphroditism

Female pseudohermaphroditism is a diagnostic problem if the patient is the proband for the family. If a sibling already has the disease, the level of awareness for this autosomal disorder will be high, and amniocentesis with cytogenetic analysis for the genetic defect allows early prenatal diagnosis. However, in unsuspected cases, when the child is born at term, the clitoris is hypertrophied, the gonads are symmetrical and intra-abdominal, and the vagina fails to descend to the perineum and enters the urethra quite distal to the bladder neck; however, a significant subset of patients may have a verumontanum, with the urethrovaginal confluence quite close to the bladder neck.[32] These patients can also have an enlarged, placentally stimulated, palpable prostate at the level of the verumontanum. The labioscrotal folds are rugated and enlarged and, in some cases, completely scrotalized. In addition to normal ovaries, the uterus and fallopian tubes are normal. The vagina, however, is foreshortened, as a result of having failed to migrate to the perineum.

TABLE 121-4 Mutations in Genes Involved in Sex Determination and Development and Associated with Intersex Anomalies

Gene (Locus)	Protein and Proposed Function	Mutant Phenotype
WT1 (11p13)	Transcription factor	Frasier's syndrome; Denys-Drash syndrome with Wilms' tumor
SF-1 (9q33)	Transcription factor, nuclear receptor	Gonadal and adrenal dysgenesis
SOX 9 (17q24)	High mobility group (HMG) protein transcription factor	Camptomelic dysplasia and male gonadal dysgenesis or XY sex reversal
DAX-1 (Xp21.3)	Transcriptional regulator, nuclear receptor	Gonadal dysgenesis and congenital adrenal hypoplasia
SRY (Yp11)	HMG protein transcription factor	Gonadal dysgenesis, XX sex reversal
MIS (AMH) type II receptor (12q12-13)	Serine threonine kinase receptor	Persistent müllerian duct syndrome
MIS (AMH) (19p13)	Secreted protein, fetal müllerian duct regressor, Leydig cell inhibitor	Persistent müllerian duct syndrome
AR (Xq11-12)	Androgen receptor, ligand transcription factor	Male pseudohermaphroditism, androgen insensitivity syndrome (complete or partial)
HSD17B3 (9q22)	17-hydroxysteroid dehydrogenase–17-ketosteroid reductase 3	Male pseudohermaphroditism
SRD5A2 (5p15)	5α-steroid reductase type 2	Male pseudohermaphroditism (may virilize at puberty)
CYP17 (10q24q25.)	17-hydroxylase, 20,22-lyase	Male pseudohermaphroditism
CYP21 (6q21.3)	21-hydroxylase	Congenital adrenal hyperplasia, female pseudohermaphroditism
HSD3B2 (1p13.1)	3β-hydroxysteroid dehydrogenase type 2	Congenital adrenal hyperplasia
CYP11B1 (8q24)	11β-hydroxylase	Congenital adrenal hyperplasia
StAR (8p11.2)	Steroidogenic acute regulatory protein	Congenital lipoid adrenal hyperplasia

From MacLaughlin DT, Donahoe PK: Sex determination and differentiation. N Engl J Med 2004;350:367-378.

It is essential to measure the distance from the bladder neck to the vaginal fistula at the time of cystoscopy to aid future plans for definitive reconstruction. The external genitalia are characterized by variable clitoral enlargement, ranging from trivial to severe. Some patients have a male-appearing phallus. The labia may be masculinized to form labioscrotal folds or, in severe cases, complete scrotal fusion may occur. Because the ovaries are normal, the gonads never descend into the labioscrotal folds or fused scrotum.[16,20] The karyotype is always 46,XX in females, MIS is undetectable, and a spot serum analysis reveals elevated 17-hydroxyprogesterone. Androgen levels are also elevated. Concomitant production of melanocyte-stimulating hormone can darken the genitalia and breast areolae. PCR with appropriate probes demonstrates point mutations in the *P450c21* gene.[85] Electrolytes are often normal at birth, but when maternal steroids wane after 5 to 7 days, potassium levels may become markedly elevated, and serum sodium levels may fall. As a result, electrocardiography reveals inverted T waves, which, if unattended, can lead to cardiac arrest. In rarer cases with 3ß-HSD deficiency, 17-hydroxypregnenolone, pregnenolone, and DHEA levels are elevated, and serum 11-deoxycortisol or deoxycorticosterone levels are elevated in patients with P450c11 deficiency. Gender assignment in these patients is almost always female, except when the diagnosis is delayed and the patient has already been raised as a male.[11,17]

Male Pseudohermaphroditism

Testosterone Deficiency

By definition, male pseudohermaphrodites have deficient androgenization of the external genitalia with a 46,XY karyotype. If the disorder is caused by an enzymatic defect in the testosterone-androgen pathway, patients have low basal serum testosterone, and stimulation by chorionic gonadotropin produces little or no increase in testosterone. Because the genes coding for the enzymes in the pathway have been cloned, PCR can be performed to detect deficiencies in *StAR, 3β-HSD, CYP17,* or 17-ketosteroid reductase genes. The testes may be small and are often bilaterally and symmetrically undescended. The penis is small, and hypospadias is usually severe. Under the influence of normal MIS, there are no detectable müllerian structures. In some cases, the phenotype is completely female.[25-27] Gender assignment depends on the size of the phallus. It may be better to raise those with a small phallus as females, whereas it may be preferable to raise those with a reasonably sized phallus as males because they will respond to exogenous testosterone. Special consideration should be given to those rare children with 17-ketosteroid reductase deficiency, who may be better raised as males (P. K. Donahoe, personal communication).

Androgen Receptor Deficiency

Cases in which the androgen receptor is severely dysfunctional, as occurs in testicular feminization, have been attributed to complete androgen receptor insufficiency.[87] The phenotype is female, so these children should be raised in concordance with that phenotype. No müllerian structures are present because high levels of biologically active MIS are produced. The testes are usually in the inguinal region, and their firmness and investing epididymis can be palpated to distinguish them from ovaries. The karyotype is 46,XY. Although the androgen receptor is deficient, levels of testosterone and MIS are high. PCR or sequencing of the androgen receptor gene can often pinpoint the molecular defect and provide the definitive diagnosis.

Incomplete androgen receptor insufficiency results in only partially masculinized 46,XY patients, with a wide variation from minimal to severe anomalies. As with testosterone-deficiency syndrome, the penis is small and hypospadiac. The testes may be small and are often undescended but symmetrical, and müllerian structures are not present. The testosterone levels are normal, and MIS levels are elevated. Most abnormalities are caused by point mutations in the androgen receptor gene,[46,79] which can be detected by PCR and DNA sequencing. Only rarely have large deletions been found. Gender assignment depends on the size of the phallus.

5α-Reductase Deficiency

Male pseudohermaphroditism can also result from a deficiency of 5α-reductase, which is responsible for the conversion of testosterone to dihydrotestosterone. The normal action of 5α-reductase on the genital area results in elongation and ventral closing of the penile raphe, displacing the urethral orifice from the perineum to the center of the glans penis.[13] This process is abnormal in these patients, resulting in severe penoscrotal hypospadias. Normal and symmetrical testes can be either undescended or fully descended. The labioscrotal folds are also closed in a posterior direction to create scrotal sacs. The prostatic utricle is often quite enlarged in these patients. Again, the karyotype is 46,XY. Serum levels of testosterone are high, but levels of dihydrotestosterone are low. The MIS levels are normal. PCR and full DNA sequencing can be used to genotype and to detect mutations in the 5α-reductase type 2 gene. Given the dramatic phenotypic conversion at puberty, it may be more appropriate to raise these children as males. It should be noted, however, that in this group, gender assignment involves the greatest dilemma in societies committed to two sexes, but not in societies that more readily accept assignment to a third sex.[2,35,36]

Chromosomal Abnormalities

Pure Gonadal Dysgenesis

Patients with pure gonadal dysgenesis are born as phenotypic females. Amniocentesis with a 46,XY karyotype that does not produce the expected phenotype on fetal ultrasonography now allows earlier diagnosis than was previously possible. Dorsal pedal edema and some Turner characteristics may be the only obvious somatic manifestations of the defect. Müllerian structures are present, but gonads are not palpable. Testosterone and MIS are undetectable, indicating dysgenesis of the gonad. Candidate gene mutations include *SRY, SOX 9, WT1,* and *SF-1*.[48]

Mixed Gonadal Dysgenesis

Patients with mixed gonadal dysgenesis are characterized by asymmetry, with a streak gonad on one side and a dysgenetic testis on the other. They also have retained müllerian structures.[15,20,70] The clitoris is usually quite hypertrophied. The most common karyotype is 45,X/46,XY, but 40% of patients have the 46,XY karyotype. Because the testes are dysgenetic, testosterone and MIS levels may be low. There is a propensity for neoplastic transformation to gonadoblastoma or seminoma (or both),[49,56,74] even as early as the neonatal period. These tumors can cause torsion and apparent loss of a gonad that, in rare cases, leads to a unilateral dysgenetic testis or streak ovary. Because gonadoblastomas may occur at any stage, gonadectomy and female reconstruction and rearing are the options usually chosen. The X-linked *DAX-1*, which may suppress testicular differentiation (or an inhibiting molecule), may have a role in mixed gonadal dysgenesis, which is the least understood of the intersex abnormalities at the molecular level.[37] When we identify the genes responsible for the separation of paired chromosomes during meiosis, the defects responsible for this enigmatic abnormality may be discovered.

True Hermaphroditism

The cause of true hermaphroditism remains enigmatic.[14,81] Patients with this disease also have asymmetry, with a testis on one side and an ovotestis on the other; however, various other gonadal combinations can occur. The testis is always central, and the ovarian tissue is polar.[59] Neoplastic transformation is not characteristic of these unique gonads. The müllerian structures are regressed on the side of the testicular tissue but retained on the side of the ovarian tissue and as a midline uterus as well, with the vagina entering the urethra as a urogenital sinus defect. The clitoris is hypertrophied. The karyotype is 46,XX in 90% of cases; the levels of testosterone and MIS are low or sometimes normal. Although early testicular differentiation occurs, spermatogenesis is not evident,[14] which may reflect the absence of other necessary Y-directed functions. *SRY* has not been detected in these patients[51]; both the molecular cause and the reason for the asymmetry remain an enigma. The sex of rearing is dictated by the phenotype, which is directed by the predominant gonad.

MEDICAL MANAGEMENT

Female Pseudohermaphroditism

Masculinized females with pseudohermaphroditism can be at profound risk for life-threatening complications in the neonatal period. Because maternal cortisone crosses the placenta and is released slowly from fat stores, the clinical manifestations of adrenogenital crisis may not become apparent until 5 to 7 days after birth. Heightened clinical awareness and prompt, appropriate metabolic treatment can prevent serious complications. Glucocorticoid replacement as oral hydrocortisone 8 to 10 mg/m^2 per day in two or three doses or cortisone acetate 25 mg/m^2 injected every 3 days[45] will prevent serious metabolic abnormalities associated with acute adrenal insufficiency.

Fludrocortisone (9α-fluorocortisol) 0.05 to 0.2 mg/day is started in severely virilized infants and in those less virilized with a family history of salt wasting as part of female pseudohermaphroditism. Recent evidence that even patients with milder virilizing hermaphroditism have subclinical aldosterone deficiency has led to more liberal use of fluorocortisone, although some clinicians follow electrolyte levels and plasma renin activity before starting such treatment.

An infant in adrenal crisis should be rehydrated with isotonic saline. After the first hour, half-strength saline in 5% to 10% dextrose should be administered. This regimen corrects plasma sodium and chloride imbalances rapidly, but hyperkalemia and acidosis are corrected more slowly. Dramatic elevation of plasma 17-hydroxyprogesterone can be used to monitor the effectiveness of treatment. Infants (average 0.25 m^2) in adrenal crisis are treated with 25 mg hydrocortisone sodium succinate (2 mg/kg), whereas older children receive 50 to 100 mg. This preparation has both glucocorticoid and mineralocorticoid activity; the mineralocorticoid activity is equivalent to 0.1 mg of fludrocortisone. A similar regimen is used for infants exposed to the stress of surgery. Parents are taught to recognize situations that contribute to adrenal insufficiency, such as high fever, exposure to hot environments, or surgery. Breast milk and prepared formulas are low in sodium, so table salt should be given as a supplement. Growth charts must be monitored carefully to avoid inadequate or inconsistent treatment or oversuppression and chronic adrenal insufficiency.

Prenatal diagnosis and treatment are now available.[12,63] Dexamethasone treatment, if used to suppress masculinization in utero, is initiated by the fifth or sixth week of gestation before the start of sexual differentiation. Dexamethasone crosses the placenta to suppress the fetal adrenal gland and decrease fetal androgen production, thereby minimizing in utero virilization. The sex of the fetus is determined by chromosome analysis at amniocentesis or chorionic villus sampling, and PCR and DNA sequencing can be used to analyze the *CYP21* gene. Treatment is discontinued in males and unaffected females. Affected females can be treated to term. Currently, embryo selection or genetic manipulation can be done at the early blastocyst stage. Blastocysts with a normal *CYP21* gene can be preselected for subsequent implantation if a previous pregnancy produced a child with the *CYP21* mutation.

Male Pseudohermaphroditism

Male pseudohermaphrodites with poor penile development who have testosterone biosynthetic defects or androgen resistance are usually assigned to the female gender. However, for those with 5α-reductase or 17β-hydroxysteroid reductase deficiency, it may not be appropriate to assign a gender at birth. Patients assigned to the female gender should receive early surgical correction of the external genitalia and gonadectomy but do not receive hormone therapy until puberty, at which time they will require estrogen and progesterone treatment. Vaginal replacement should be planned for late puberty.

If it is elected to assign these infants to the male gender, 10 to 25 mg of testosterone enanthate or cypionate is given intramuscularly once a month for 3 months to confirm that the penis responds to androgens or to improve the size of the penis before surgery. Repair should be done before 1 year of age if the size of the phallus permits. This approach takes advantage of an early period of presumed enhanced sensitivity to androgens. After one to three courses of monthly testosterone for 3 months, an interval of at least 1 month without testosterone must be allowed before undertaking hypospadias repair to reduce the hyperactivity that accompanies testosterone therapy. These children often require staged procedures, and testosterone therapy, if needed, can precede the second stage. Testosterone replacement is resumed at adolescence. Patients with 5α-reductase deficiency should receive dihydrotestosterone replacement, if available. Otherwise, replacement can be achieved by giving higher doses of testosterone to overcome the enzyme block.

Chromosomal Abnormalities

In patients with mixed gonadal dysgenesis or true hermaphroditism assigned to the female gender, no steroidal replacement is required in childhood. However, if the child has been assigned to the male gender, presurgical testosterone stimulation of the penis may be required before hypospadias repair. Treatment does not recommence until adolescence. If the patient is assigned to the female gender, estrogen and progesterone replacement are started at adolescence. Patients with pure gonadal dysgenesis require neither surgical nor medical therapy as newborns, and estrogen and progesterone replacement begins at adolescence. Renal function must be followed carefully in patients with the various *WT1* isoform defects. Adrenal replacement therapy may be complex in patients with *SF-1* mutations characteristic of the adrenal hypoplasia congenita syndrome. Vaginal replacement should be planned for late puberty.

SURGICAL REPAIR

Preoperative Preparation

Each reconstructive procedure is preceded by cystoscopy using either Storz or Wolff cystoscopes, which have thinner light sources and larger working channels that provide better light, increased water flow to distend the urethra, and the option to pass stents or tubes. Ballooning of the urethra with high water flow allows a better appreciation of the vaginal orifice in the back wall of the urethra (Fig. 121-3); in some cases, there may be only a pinpoint orifice.

It is necessary over the years to establish age-appropriate standards for the length of the urethra (bladder neck to urethrovaginal confluence), urogenital sinus (urethrovaginal confluence to perineum), and vagina (cervix to urethrovaginal confluence). At present, we use a simple designation based on whether the sinus confluence between the vagina and urethra appears to be at or below the verumontanum. All those at or above are considered high, and all those below are considered low. However, more accurate measurement is easy to perform. For example, one can pass a 3 or 4 French urethral catheter

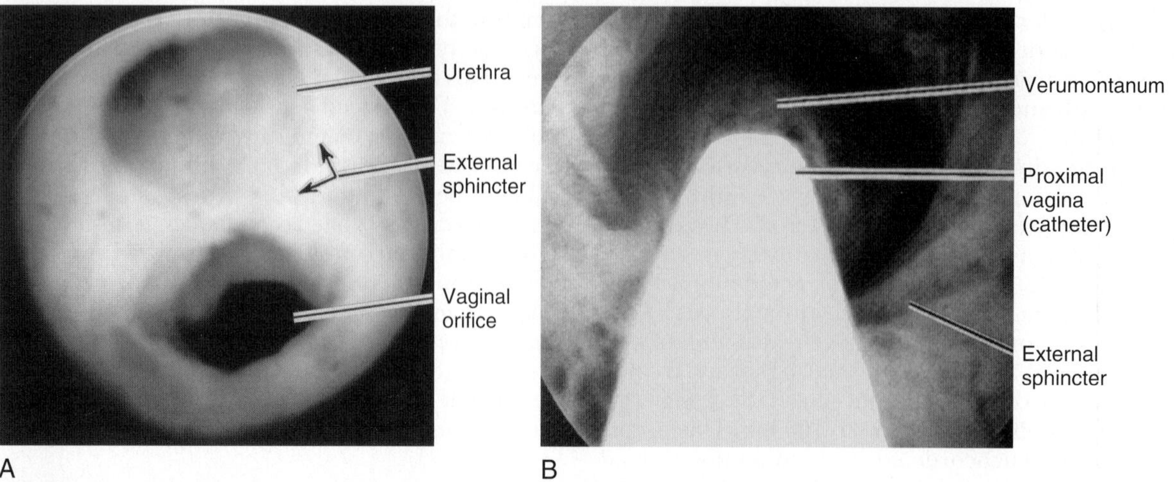

Figure 121-3 Cystoscopic examination indicates whether the vagina joins the urethra in a proximal or distal direction. *A,* The vaginal orifice is clearly distal. *B,* Catheter entering the vaginal opening at the verumontanum in a patient with severe masculinization from female pseudohermaphroditism.

with 1-cm markings alongside the cystoscope, placing its tip at the bladder neck and using the catheter markings as a ruler. The other measurements can be done the same way. These distances should be recorded, and outcomes for selected procedures can be correlated to the measurements in relation to age.

Patients with female pseudohermaphroditism, mixed gonadal dysgenesis, and true hermaphroditism have a cervix at the most proximal part of the vagina. Patients with male pseudohermaphroditism have either a small prostatic utricle or a deeper, more generous version that has no proximal cervix. This prostatic utricle is characteristically found in the center of a flattened verumontanum but has no surrounding prostatic tissue. A Fogarty catheter is secured in the vagina, a small Foley catheter is placed in the bladder, and both are tied together. The patient is then placed in the extreme lithotomy position for perineal reconstruction of the more distal fistulas or, after total body preparation, is turned prone for separation of the vagina from the urethra in some of the more proximal urogenital sinus defects.

It is important to clean the bowel adequately before repair. This should be done at home, because most children are admitted on the morning of surgery. For low repairs, magnesium citrate should be given on each of the 2 days before repair. For high repairs, GoLYTELY, a polyethylene glycol isotonic solution, is administered by mouth beginning 3 days before surgery for 2 consecutive days, followed by magnesium citrate 1 day before surgery. In some cases, ondansetron may be indicated to prevent nausea, or GoLYTELY can be administered through a small nasogastric tube. It is important to discontinue GoLYTELY at least 24 hours before surgery to prevent leakage during the procedure. Magnesium citrate, which shrinks the bowel, is given on the last day to prevent leakage. Oral administration of neomycin plus erythromycin can be used to reduce bacterial concentration.

As outlined earlier, stress doses of steroids, based on the weight of the child, are given beginning with anesthetic induction. Steroids are continued during surgery and for 2 to 3 days after surgery at double the usual oral dose, followed by a tapering of the dosage. Children on dexamethasone omit their medications, but children on prednisone take the usual morning dose on the day of surgery. Medications after surgery are worked out with pediatric endocrinology consultation. Dosing is dependent on the length and extent of surgery and the expected length of hospitalization.

Reconstruction for Female Gender Assignment

All 46,XX newborns diagnosed with female pseudohermaphroditism should be assigned to the female gender regardless of the extent of masculinization. These patients should undergo perineal reconstruction consistent with the female gender assignment. Similar repairs can be used for selected patients who are insufficiently masculinized because of male pseudohermaphroditism, mixed gonadal dysgenesis, or true hermaphroditism. The mainstays of the repair are clitoral recession, the goal of which is to minimize the clitoris while preserving sensation and erection, and exteriorization of the vagina to correct the urogenital sinus defect that results from the vagina's failure to migrate to the perineum. The more masculinized the baby, the more proximal the entry of the vagina into the urethra and the more technically demanding the repair. In addition, the labioscrotal folds need to be trimmed, thinned, and elongated to create the appearance of labia majora. Whenever possible, clitoral recession, labioscrotal reduction, and exteriorization of the vagina should be done together to take advantage of all available redundant tissue.[72,73]

The majority of children can be repaired in the lithotomy position. We reserve the posterior approach for severe anomalies in which the vagina enters the urethra close to the bladder neck. In these patients, we also consider total urogenital sinus mobilization, which can be done in the lithotomy position.

To recess the clitoris (Fig. 121-4), circumscribe immediately below the base of the glans, leaving a small cuff for later suturing (see Fig. 121-4A). Then the shaft is

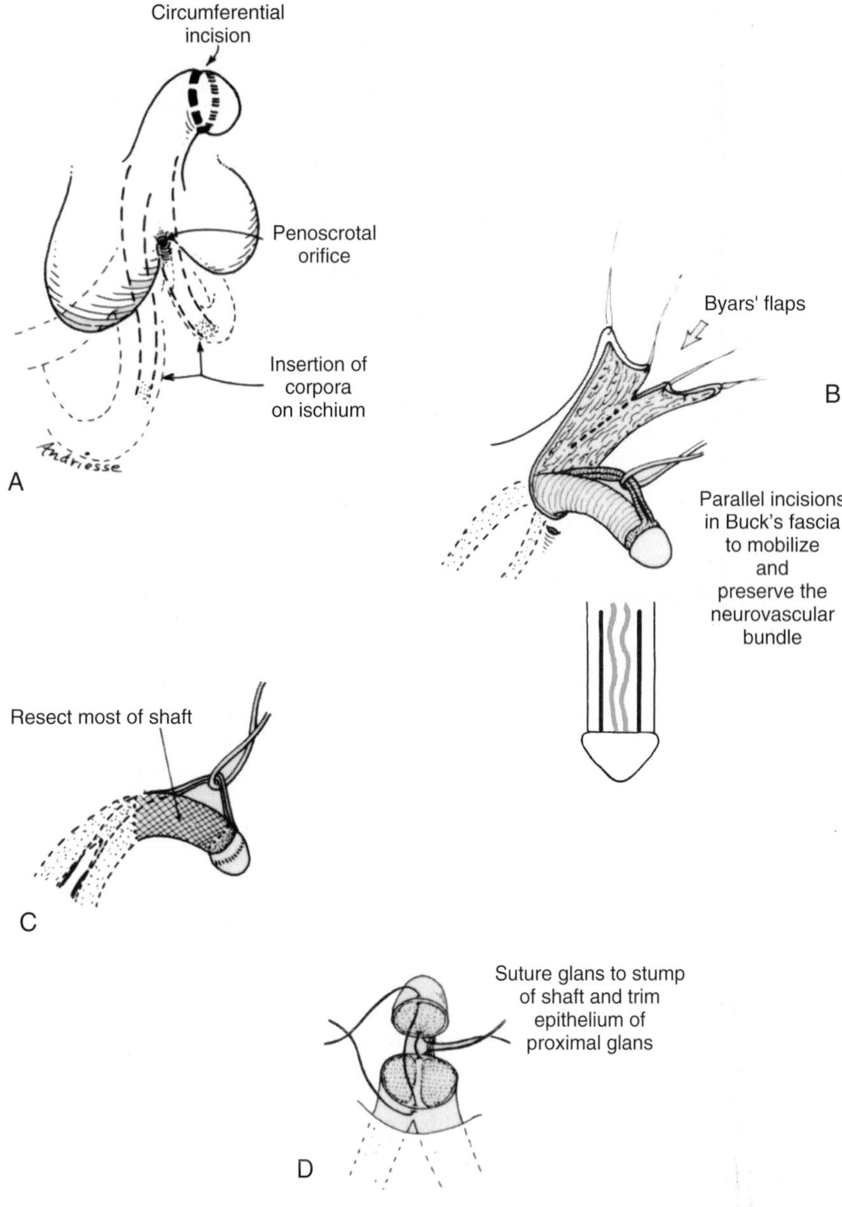

Figure 121-4 Clitoral recession. *A,* The enlarged clitoris is circumscribed below the glans. *B,* The shaft skin, which is predominantly dorsal, is mobilized and divided in the midline; the dorsal neurovascular bundle is carefully preserved by microdissection. *C,* The shaft is resected between the base of the glans and a point immediately distal to the bifurcation of the corpora cavernosa. *D,* The glans is reapproximated to the base of the shaft with fine interrupted nonabsorbable sutures.

degloved, and the shaft skin is divided in the dorsal midline to create Byars' flaps, as for hypospadias repair (see Fig. 121-4B). This dorsal midline incision is carried far enough anteriorly to allow the glans to sit comfortably at the mons pubis in the normal female clitoral position. Two parallel longitudinal incisions are made through Buck's fascia, on either side of the dorsal neurovascular bundle (see Fig 121-4B, *inset*). The dorsal artery of the penis branches from the internal pudendal artery as it egresses from Alcock's canal at the ischial tuberosity (Fig. 121-5). The dorsal artery of the penis travels on each side from the medial aspect of each corpus cavernosum to the dorsal aspect of the penis. It joins its mate from the opposite side in the midline to complete the distal course to the glans. It is not clear where the ventral to the dorsal transition occurs, but given our experience with good flow to the clitoris, we assume that the arteries conjoin proximal to the conjoining of the corpora cavernosa. Dissection is carried down to the fascial covering of the corpora (see Fig. 121-4C), using microtechnique and loupes for magnification. The neurovascular bundle and Buck's fascia are lifted off the corpora and dissected back to a point where the conjoined corpora begin to divide at the base. The midbody of the clitoris can then be resected between the base of the glans and the bifurcation of the corpora after lifting the preserved dorsal neurovascular bundle out of harm's way. Alternatively, some surgeons use two parallel longitudinal incisions on the ventral aspect of the clitoris and excise the cavernous tissue. Careful hemostasis is maintained in the corpora of the clitoris, taking care to avoid the overuse of cautery, which may cause fibrosis and possibly impair future erectile function. The redundant dorsal neurovascular bundle is displaced upward while the corpora are sutured to the base of the glans with interrupted nonabsorbable 4-0, 5-0, or 6-0 sutures, depending on the age of the child and the size of the clitoris (see Fig. 121-4D). An enlarged glans can then be trimmed, preserving the exposed tissue

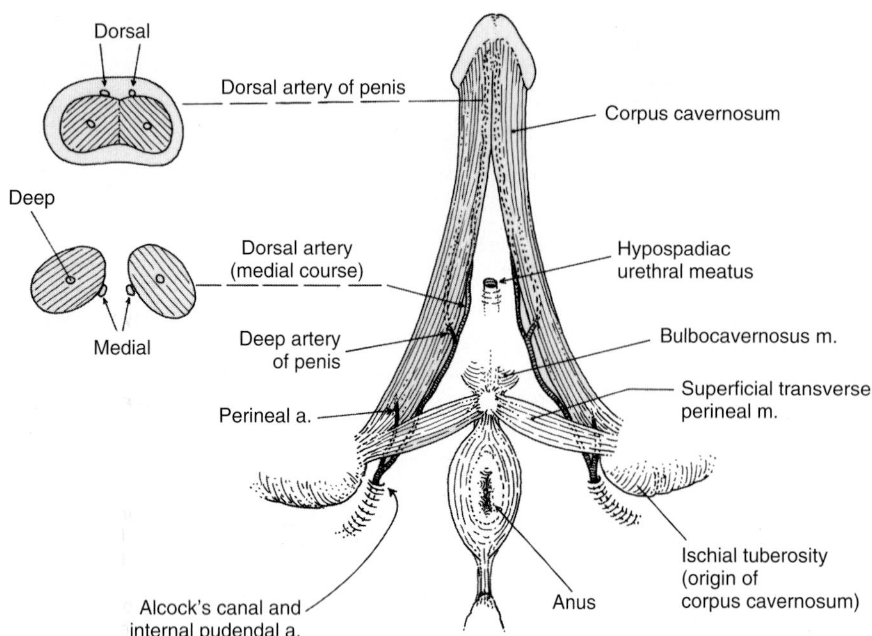

Figure 121-5 Neurovascular anatomy of the penis. The internal pudendal artery exits from Alcock's canal at the ischial tuberosity and bifurcates. The perineal artery courses in a ventral direction toward the scrotum. The dorsal artery of the penis travels in a medial direction, with one branch penetrating to become the deep artery of the penis. Each medial branch curves around the corresponding bifurcated corpus cavernosum in a medial and dorsal direction to become the dorsal artery of the penis at the point where the corpora conjoin.

as the neoclitoris. This can be performed in most cases by removing a wedge from the ventral and lateral aspect of the clitoris. This preserved or reduced glans is then sutured at its subcoronal edge to the proximal, separated Byars' flaps (see Fig. 121-4D).

Figure 121-6A depicts the incisions and flaps needed to reduce the labioscrotal folds and exteriorize the vagina. A posterior U-flap based on the rectum is advanced inward and cephalad to meet the posterior wall of the mobilized vagina opened in the midline. These maneuvers are used to create a new introitus on the perineum. In patients with a high urethrovaginal confluence, an anterior island flap, originating from the base of the glans and extending in a posterior direction, is rotated inward to meet the anterior wall of the mobilized vagina to create the new anterior wall of the new introitus. This can be split in the midline and re-formed if the posterior approach is used.

Figure 121-6B shows the anatomy as viewed from the sagittal plane. The vagina enters the urethra as a urogenital sinus; this occurs close to the bladder neck in the most severely masculinized patients with female pseudohermaphroditism from CAH and more distally in those with mixed gonadal dysgenesis, true hermaphroditism, and less severe masculinization in female pseudohermaphroditism. The principles of repair are the same for all disorders, although patients with the rare high urogenital sinus require a much more complicated repair and are more prone to subsequent narrowing. Figure 121-6C shows a finger in the rectum, which allows the surgeon to appreciate the thinness of the plane separating the vagina and the rectum and to stretch the plane posteriorly to avoid angulation and allow safer dissection.

If the urethrovaginal junction fistula is high or close to the bladder neck, and if the wall of the urethra and the vagina are conjoined as a single structure, the posterior approach without division of the rectum, as described by Rink et al.,[69] provides the exposure necessary for safe dissection in those cases with a high confluence. This procedure can be done in early infancy regardless of the location of the vagina, as can the other techniques described. The entire lower half of the body is prepared from the xiphoid process to the toes so that the child can be rotated from prone to supine and back again, if necessary.

In patients with a high confluence, we recommend that the vagina be mobilized first. After endoscopy, the patient is turned to the prone position, and a posterior inverted U-flap is fashioned, with its corners in either side of the perineal body. Dissection is undertaken in the midline to mobilize the urogenital sinus from the posterior rectum (Fig. 121-7A). The rectum can then be easily separated and displaced upward with an inserted narrow retractor, without the need for incision or division. The urogenital sinus is opened posteriorly in the midline from the meatus to the vaginal confluence (Fig. 121-7B), and the distal vagina is opened on its posterior aspect into the more proximal wider vagina. A retractor is then placed in the opened vagina and lifted upward to facilitate the exposure of the anterior vaginal confluence. Injection of a 1:200,000 epinephrine solution facilitates the separation of the vagina from the urethra (see Fig. 121-7B); a small Beaver blade is helpful in carrying the meticulous dissection proximally to the bladder neck (Fig. 121-7C). This is the most difficult part of the operation because the urethra and anterior vagina share the same thin mesenchymal tissue between each of the respective epithelial layers. The posterior inverted U-flap is sutured into the posterior vagina (Fig. 121-7D). Tubularization of the urethra is completed, with the addition of a second layer of sutures to reduce the incidence of subsequent urethrovaginal fistula. If possible, the labioscrotal fat can be placed over the suture line as an additional precaution against fistula. A labial flap or an anterior island flap, which for this procedure must be reconstructed in the midline, can now easily reach the anterior vagina. The labioscrotal tissue is widely mobilized, defatted, trimmed, and moved posteriorly as a Y-V plasty to create labia majora lateral to the vaginal orifice (see Fig. 121-6A). If there is significant clitoral hypertrophy, a clitoroplasty is undertaken after the

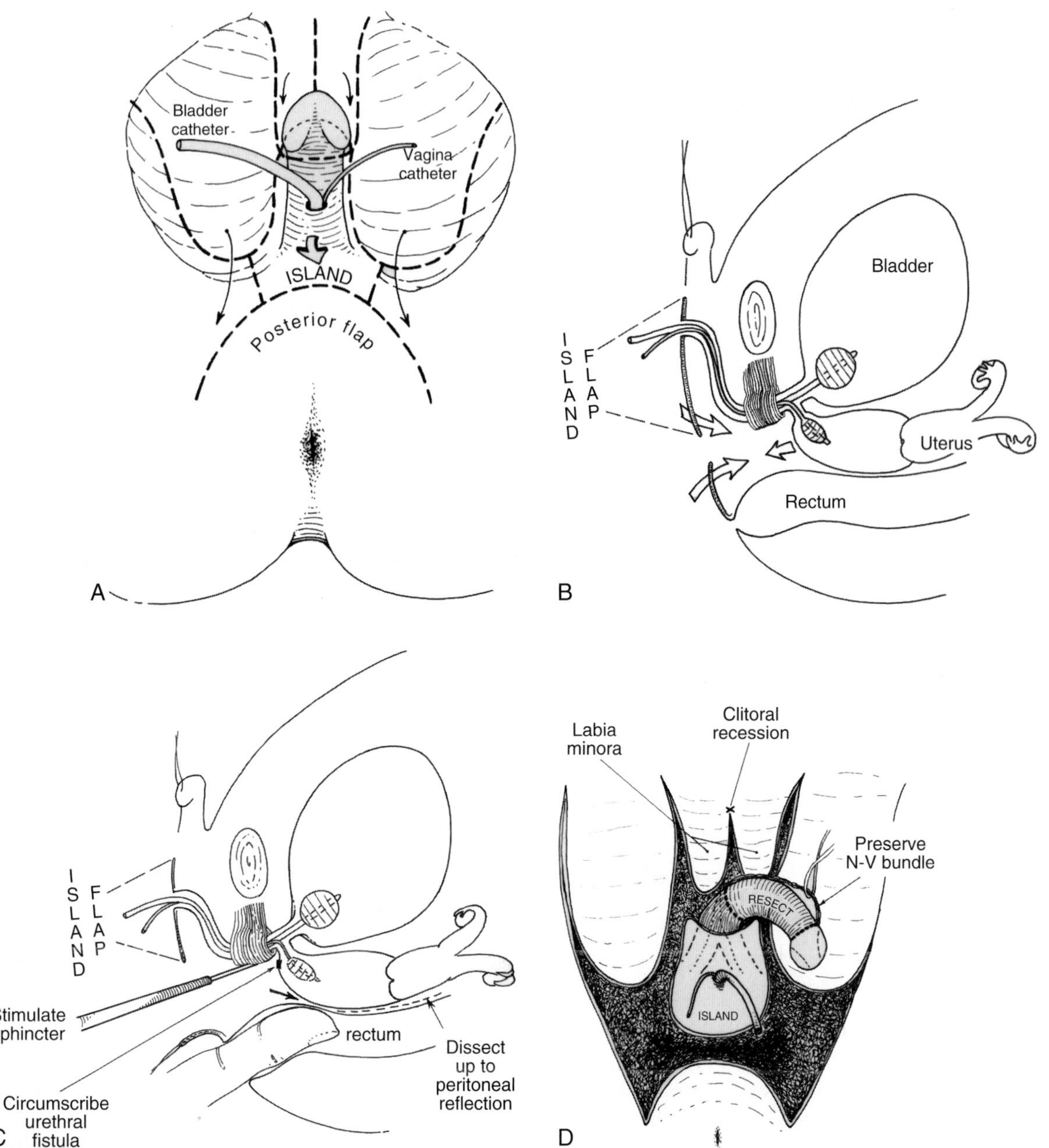

Figure 121–6 Surgical reconstruction for female gender assignment. *A,* Locations of incisions as viewed from the surgeon's perspective from the perineum with the patient in the lithotomy position. *B,* Sagittal view, showing the downward and inward direction of movement of the anterior island flap *(right-pointing arrows)* and the inward position of the posterior flap. The smaller arrow shows the distance that must be traversed by the vagina, which has been separated from the urethra. *C,* Dissection between the vagina and the rectum in a posterior direction and the beginning of the anterior separation of the vagina from the urethra. *D,* Completely dissected flaps.

Continued

patient is turned to the supine position; this is done after vaginal mobilization but before the vagina is exteriorized, because turning the patient could disrupt that fragile anastomosis. The excess clitoral skin is brought around posteriorly to fill the gap created by the anterior island flap (see Fig. 121-6G). If the neourethra is long, the neourethral meatus can be placed in a more normal perineal position, and the distal urogenital sinus can be opened to create a wet introitus. A small Foley catheter remains indwelling during the early postoperative course; however, a suprapubic percutaneous diversion catheter combined with a small Silastic urethral catheter may be a better option to prevent fistulas.

Another surgical alternative for patients with a high vagina is total urogenital sinus mobilization (TUM), described by Pena[66] in 1997 for the repair of urogenital sinus defects. The urogenital sinus can be mobilized circumferentially to help separate the sinus from the pubis (Fig. 121-8). This maneuver releases the avascular fibrous ligaments that hold the urethra and vagina anteriorly, which raises some concern about possible damage to the innervation of the external sphincter and its effect

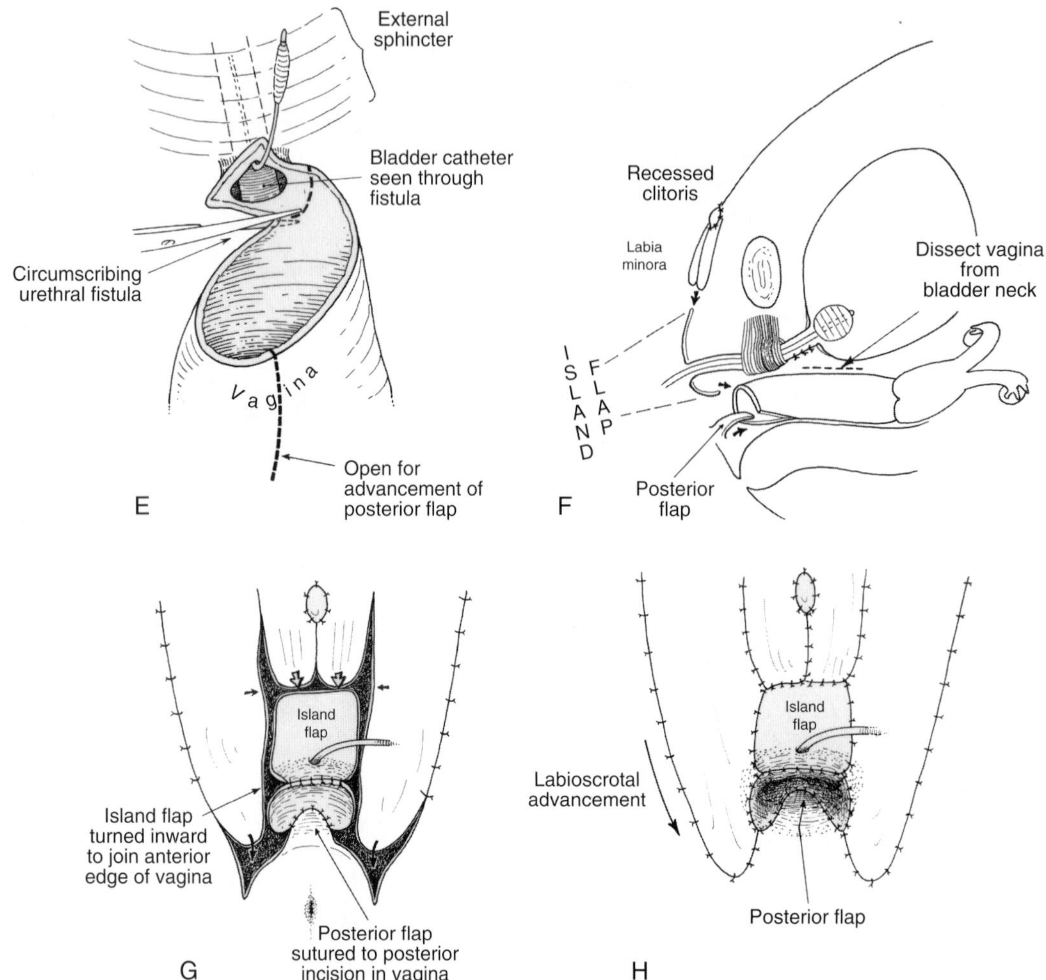

Figure 121-6—Cont'd *E,* Separation of the vagina from the urethra. *F,* Anterior plane of dissection behind the urethra and bladder. *G,* Advancement of the labioscrotal flaps to cover defects, and inward rotation of the anterior island flap and the posterior U-flap to augment the introitus. *H,* Completed reconstruction.

on urinary incontinence. The mobilization continues circumferentially until the urethrovaginal confluence has reached the perineum without tension. A partial urogenital sinus mobilization up to the level of the pubovesical ligament can be used to lessen the chance of damaging the external sphincter innervation.

We consider the posterior sagittal approach a major advance in the surgical treatment of CAH. Also, experience seems to indicate that TUM, which can be done in the lithotomy position, is a safe procedure; however, it is essential to follow these patients for a long time to evaluate their urinary continence. A number of groups reporting their experience with TUM indicated that none of their patients developed subsequent urinary incontinence.[19,30,39,47] Jenak et al.[39] recommended opening the excess urogenital sinus ventrally and using it to construct a mucosa-lined vestibule. Farkas et al.[19] recommended partially opening the redundant urogenital sinus on its dorsal aspect. Those authors leave a sufficient length of urethra but invert the opened strip of sinus to create anterior and lateral vaginal walls for the exteriorized vagina.

Another technique used for a high-confluence urogenital sinus is the clitorovaginoplasty described by Passerini-Glazel.[65] In this technique, the clitoral reduction is done with preservation of the neurovascular supply to the glans. The vagina is exteriorized by suturing the penile skin longitudinally, divided both dorsally and ventrally; it is rotated downward and posteriorly and sutured on each side of the opened distal urogenital sinus. Then a cylinder of penile and neourethral tissue is fashioned, inserted into the perineum, and anastomosed to the mobilized true vagina.

Reconstruction for Male Gender Assignment

The perineum is undermasculinized if testosterone production is deficient, if there is androgen insensitivity because of defects in the testosterone receptor, or if the 5α-reductase enzyme that converts testosterone to dihydrotestosterone is defective. An undermasculinized perineum can also be seen in patients with mixed gonadal dysgenesis and true hermaphroditism. The treatment strategy is similar for all patients assigned to the male gender. Most of these patients have a micropenis associated with severe chordee, a urethral meatus situated at the

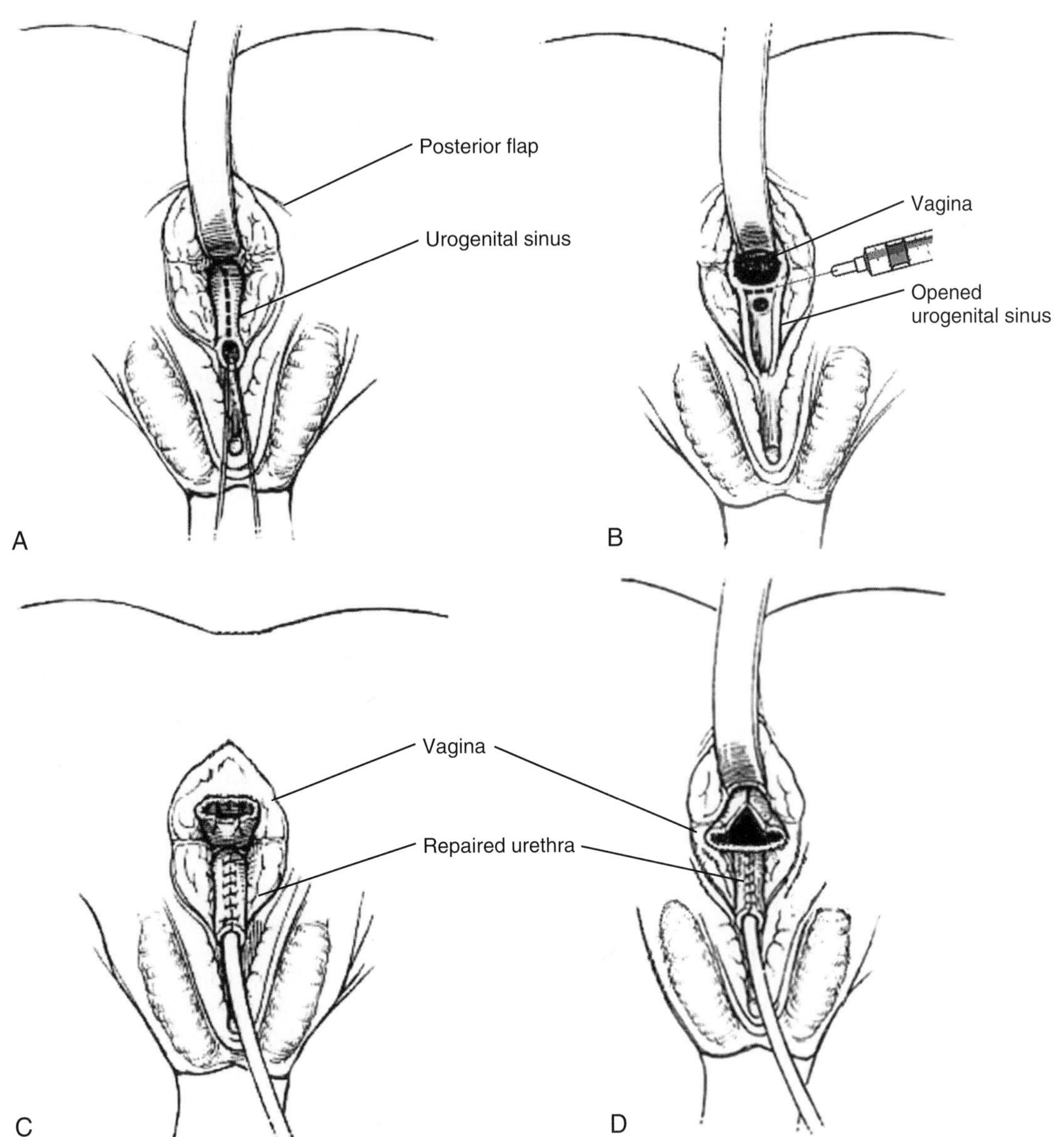

Figure 121–7 Posterior approach. *A,* A posteriorly based inverted U-flap is fashioned. The urogenital sinus is opened longitudinally on its posterior or dorsal surface up to the vaginal confluence. *B,* A narrow malleable retractor is placed inside the vagina, which has been opened posteriorly to accommodate the instrument. The vagina is then lifted upward, which facilitates the separation of the vagina from the urethra and bladder neck. Injection of diluted epinephrine (1:200,000) helps the dissection of this fragile, thin plane. A small Beaver blade is useful for this difficult step. *C,* The urethra is tubularized after the vagina has been separated. *D,* The vagina is opened, and the U-flap is inserted to create an enlarged introitus.

penoscrotal junction between a bifid scrotum, and sometimes a prepenile scrotum with an abundance of rugated scrotal skin anterior to the micropenis (Fig. 121-9A). The incomplete foreskin is present as a redundant dorsal hood, which must be preserved for repair. Pretreatment with testosterone is helpful in the repair of the micropenis and indicates whether response to testosterone is possible. Because of the micropenis and severe chordee in this group of patients, we recommend that these repairs be staged.

In the first stage of hypospadias repair, the major objective is to straighten the chordee and shift the redundant dorsal hooded foreskin ventrally, both to close the ventral defect and to supply sufficient tissue for the creation of a neourethra at the second stage. Once the foreskin is circumferentially mobilized up to the penoscrotal junction, an erection is induced by pressing down on either side of the shaft to assess the severity of the chordee. Then, all ventral scarring, which represents residual atretic corpora spongiosa, must be removed from immediately beneath the glans to the more proximal bifurcation of the corpora cavernosa (Fig. 121-9B). Because the chordee in this small subset of hypospadiac patients extends very proximally into the bifurcation, bleeding is usually considerable and places the neourethral graft at risk—hence our recommendation to stage the repair. Figure 121-9C depicts the unfurling of the dorsal hooded foreskin into a single layer to provide adequate skin to cover the ventral shaft. A longitudinal rather than a transverse incision is made to avoid dividing the blood supply to the distal tip

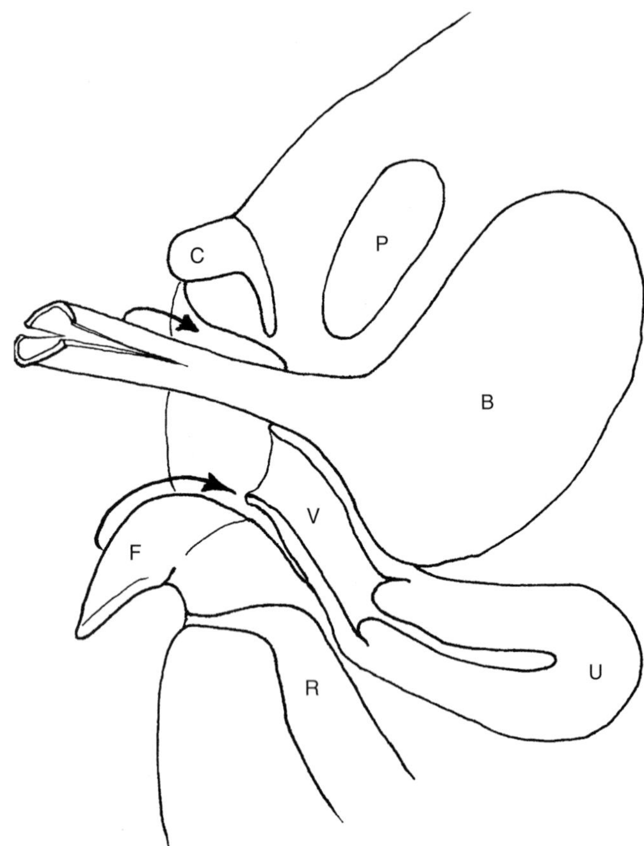

Figure 121-8 Total urogenital sinus mobilization (TUM). The urogenital sinus can be mobilized circumferentially up to the level of the inferior aspect of the pubis, then moved downward as a single unit until the urethrovaginal confluence is at the perineum. The urogenital sinus is opened posteriorly and sutured up toward the clitoris so that it can be used to create a wet introitus. The posterior inverted U-flap will be sutured to the opened back wall of the vagina. No attempt is made to separate the vagina from the urethra. C, clitoris; F, flap; P, pubis; R, rectum; U, uterus; V, vagina. (Adapted from Pena.[66])

and to allow the dorsal tissue to be positioned to cover the ventral defect. As shown in the figure, C is sutured to C′, and the distal unfurled foreskin is rotated over the top of the glans. B is sutured to B′ on the ventral surface, and the transposed skin is draped in a proximal direction to the perineum, where A is sutured to A′. This gives adequate skin coverage to the ventral shaft of the penis, with sufficient redundancy for use as a free urethral graft at a later stage of the overall reconstruction. It is important that this flap fit without re-creating the chordee (Fig. 121-9D). A Foley catheter is left in the perineal meatus to drain the bladder. The remainder of the shifted foreskin is closed, and the urine remains diverted for 4 to 5 days while the patient recovers (Fig. 121-9E).

After a hiatus of 4 to 6 months, when all edema has subsided and the shifted ventral skin feels soft and pliant, a second-stage hypospadias repair, consisting of the creation of a neourethra from the perineoscrotal meatus to the tip, is planned. It is important to take into consideration the small size of the glans, which may need to be augmented. If the penis is still small, two or three doses of testosterone are given once a month, followed by at least a 4-week interval without testosterone to avoid hyperactivity after surgery, when bed rest is required. As seen in Figure 121-10A, the redundant foreskin, now in a ventral position, is stretched to outline a graft to be tubularized. Proximally, the midscrotal skin, which tends to be hairless, is tubularized to extend the proximal meatus. Jackson-Pratt tubing with multiple holes is used to stent the proximal midscrotal neourethra and the distal free neourethral graft created from the dorsal hooded foreskin at the first stage of the reconstruction (Fig. 121-10B). A subcuticular running suture of absorbable polyglactin 910 (Vicryl), which slides well, tubularizes the midscrotal skin. The repositioned foreskin is stretched, and a skin graft of the required length and width is fashioned to provide the distal portion of the neourethra from the tubularized midscrotum, to which the free graft is anastomosed. In a child younger than 1 year, a 12-mm width is optimal. After removal, the graft is defatted and placed under saline in a depressed Silastic receptacle to prevent desiccation. This is particularly important if a bladder mucosal or buccal mucosal graft must be used. Running Vicryl sutures are used again. The graft is beveled to prevent stenosis at the interrupted anastomosis to the tubularized midscrotum, which is also beveled in the opposite orientation. The suture line of the neourethral graft from the dorsal hooded foreskin is placed inward, facing the corpora cavernosa, and is slipped over the proximal stent before the proximal anastomosis is completed. Because even a small Foley catheter tends to angulate at the proximal anastomosis, we avoid its use in a small phallus and instead use a perineal urethrostomy and a small distal Jackson-Pratt stent with multiple holes, placed just across the anastomosis.

Depending on the degree of splaying of the glans, either the neourethral graft is placed into the split glans, which is then wrapped around the graft, or the graft is tunneled to the midpoint of the glans (Fig. 121-10C). During tunneling, it is important not to twist the graft. The distal epithelium of the glans is then sutured in an interrupted fashion to the graft, taking care to fashion a wide meatus to avoid narrowing, and the stent is sutured to the glans to prevent dislodgment during the early phases of healing. It is important to cover the neourethra, particularly at the proximal anastomosis, with two to three additional layers of tissue mobilized from the side of the shaft. This creates a bulky mesenchymal layer over the proximal anastomosis, the midscrotal graft (particularly where the suture line faces out), and the more distal neourethral graft. The remainder of the ventral skin is closed with multiple Z suture lines, individualized for each patient (Fig. 121-10D). It is important not to close the glans too tightly and to select the Silastic stent carefully so that the micropenis is not stretched over too much bulk at this precarious point. If necessary, a No. 7 Silastic stent can be split longitudinally to fit the smallest glans.

The bladder is drained by either a perineal urethrostomy or a suprapubic catheter placed before surgery begins. Closure of the proximal shaft and scrotal skin over the tubularized midscrotal neourethra also tends to partially correct the bifid scrotum. Any redundant tissue should be left in place for use if a later fistula or stricture occurs. To drain this area, we simply leave a small dependent

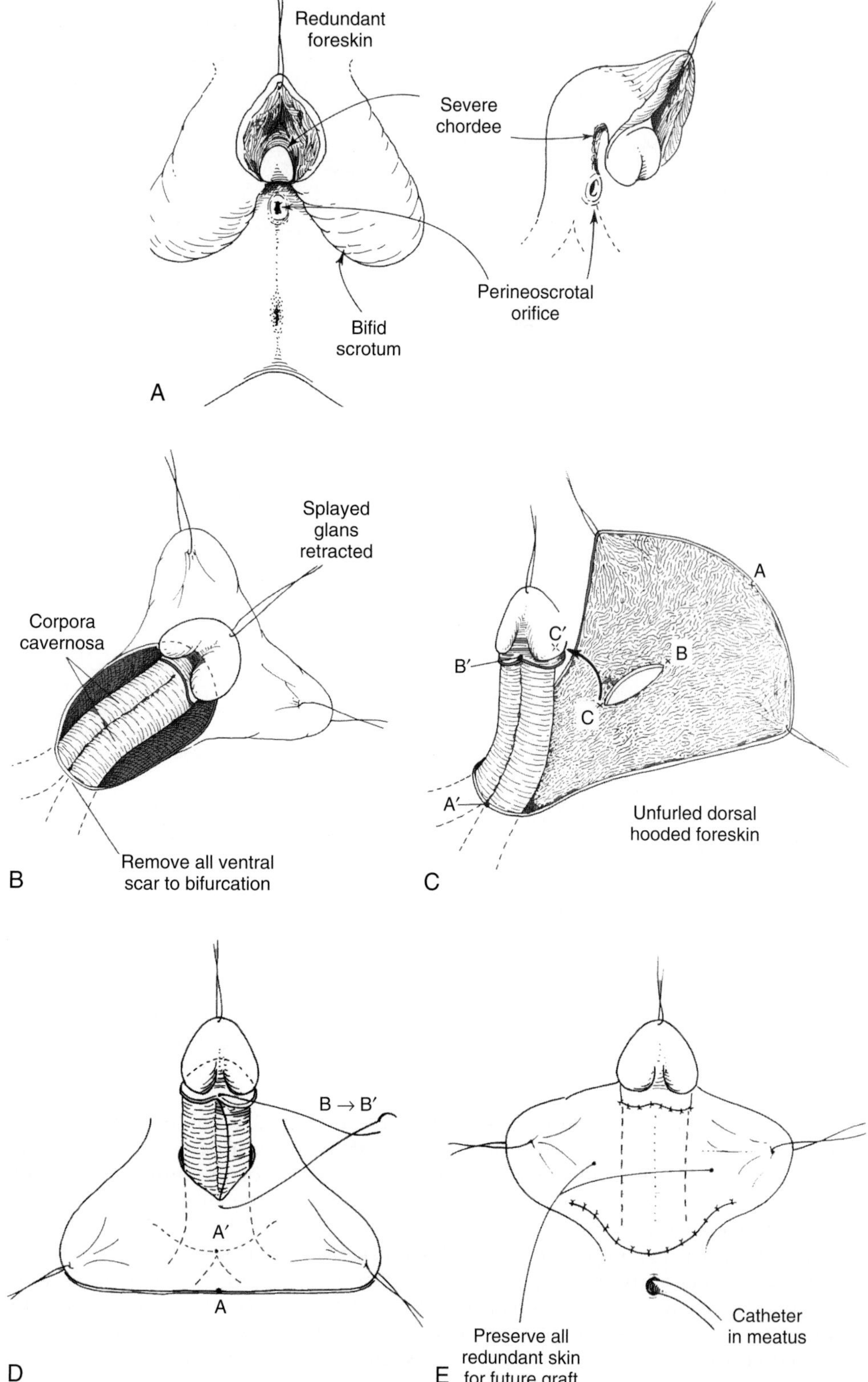

Figure 121–9 Stage 1 of surgical reconstruction for male gender assignment. *A,* The phenotype of micropenis with severe chordee, penoscrotal hypospadias, and bifid scrotum. *B,* After correction of chordee, the corpora cavernosa are straightened. *C,* The dorsal hooded foreskin is unfolded. *D,* The shaft is passed through the dorsal longitudinal incision, and the unfolded skin is transferred in a ventral direction over the shaft in a capelike fashion. *E,* Completion of stage 1 repair.

portion of the Z-plasty open. Trimming can be done after the risks of fistula or stricture have passed. If the glans is splayed and small, a 5-mm cusp of ventral distal shaft skin can be preserved and rotated distally to relieve pressure over the neourethral stented graft. Postoperative edema and swelling can be somewhat minimized by using a Tegaderm dressing placed directly over the shaft of the penis and at the base of the scrotum to provide mild tamponade. A suture in the glans fixes the stent.

In the rare event that insufficient tissue is available for both a neourethral graft and ventral coverage, it is possible to use a tubularized graft of bladder mucosa. Although such a graft is often effective, it has the disadvantage of stretching or desiccating (or both). It is important to do

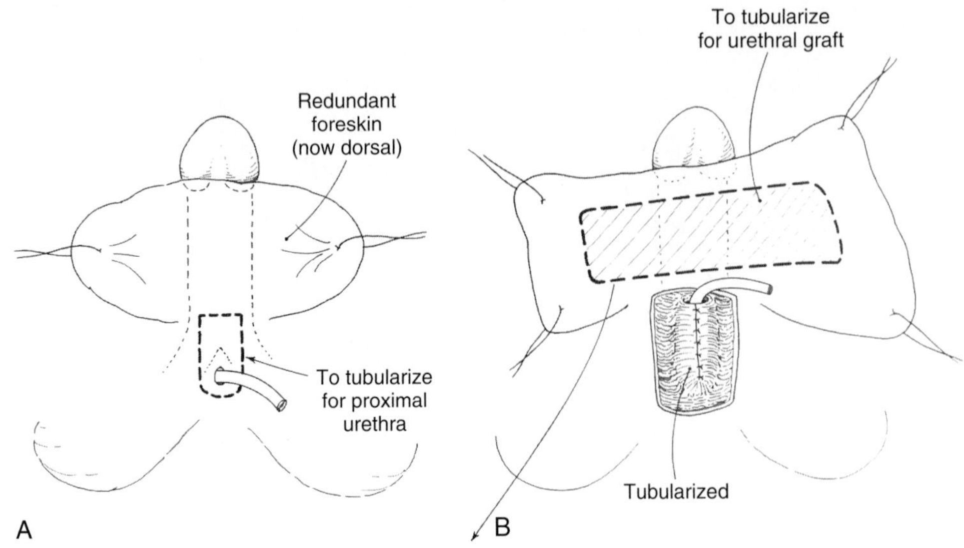

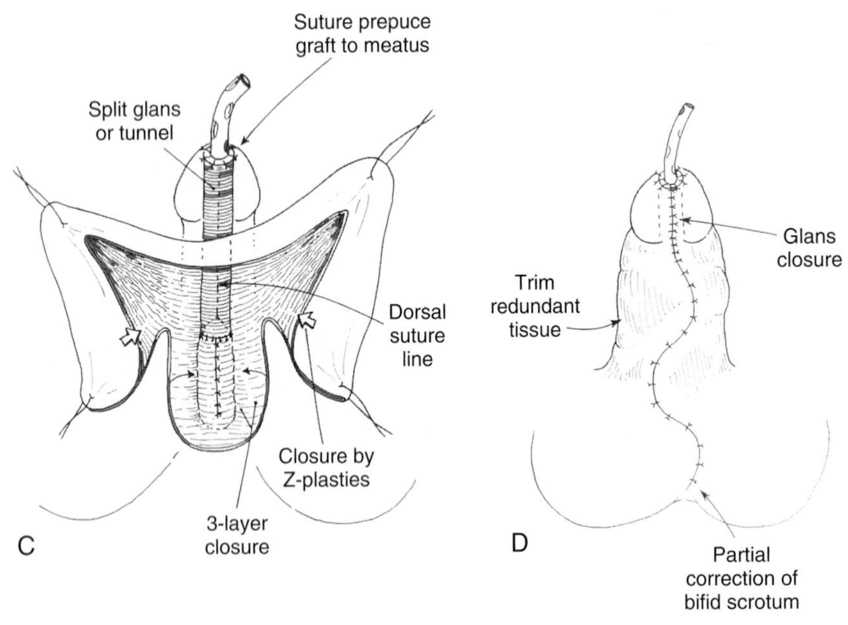

Figure 121–10 Stage 2 of surgical reconstruction for male gender assignment. *A,* Plan for a composite urethral graft. *B,* Tubularized scrotal tissue for the proximal urethra, and outline of the neourethral graft from redundant ventral skin. *C,* Completion of the distal graft, placement of a thin Silastic stent, and tunneling to the meatus. *D,* Final closure and completed external, three-layer repair using excess ventral tissue transposed from the dorsal hooded foreskin.

these anastomoses under continuous irrigation and to avoid creating a graft that is too wide. Soon after the stent is removed from the bladder neourethra, it is important to dilate the very distal neourethra daily to keep the meatus from sealing, which occurs when the bladder mucosa is exposed to air. A parent is asked to insert a Hegar dilator for only 1 cm into the meatus once or twice a day beginning 10 to 14 days after the repair.

In the rare case of a patient with true hermaphroditism or mixed gonadal dysgenesis who has been assigned the male gender, the retained müllerian ducts can become quite enlarged (Fig. 121-11A). This can occur after a second-stage neourethral graft creates more distal resistance, leading to backwash of urine and, in difficult cases, recurrent urinary tract infections, epididymitis, or both. In such cases, the müllerian duct should be removed. We attempt to preserve the vas deferens as it courses within the outer wall of the dilated vagina. Its position must be estimated until it exits at the site of the verumontanum. Lateral incisions are made on both sides of the predicted course of the vas deferens (Fig. 121-11B). The remainder of the müllerian structures are removed, including the sometimes markedly dilated vagina. The strip of vaginal wall containing the vas deferens is then tubularized, with its mucosa internalized from the urogenital sinus to the point of entry of the vas deferens (Fig. 121-11C). Running absorbable suture can be used; one layer usually suffices. In patients with mixed gonadal dysgenesis, the ovarian structure, which is discordant with the assigned sex, can be removed.

In patients in whom the penile shaft is distally displaced, prepenile rugated scrotal tissue can be found anterior to the penis (Fig. 121-12A). It is appropriate to correct this anomaly, which is often associated with a bifid scrotum. It is important, however, to delay this repair until after complete healing of the neourethral graft and the ventral closures on the shaft, because the base of the flaps needed for the hypospadias repair must be divided and displaced

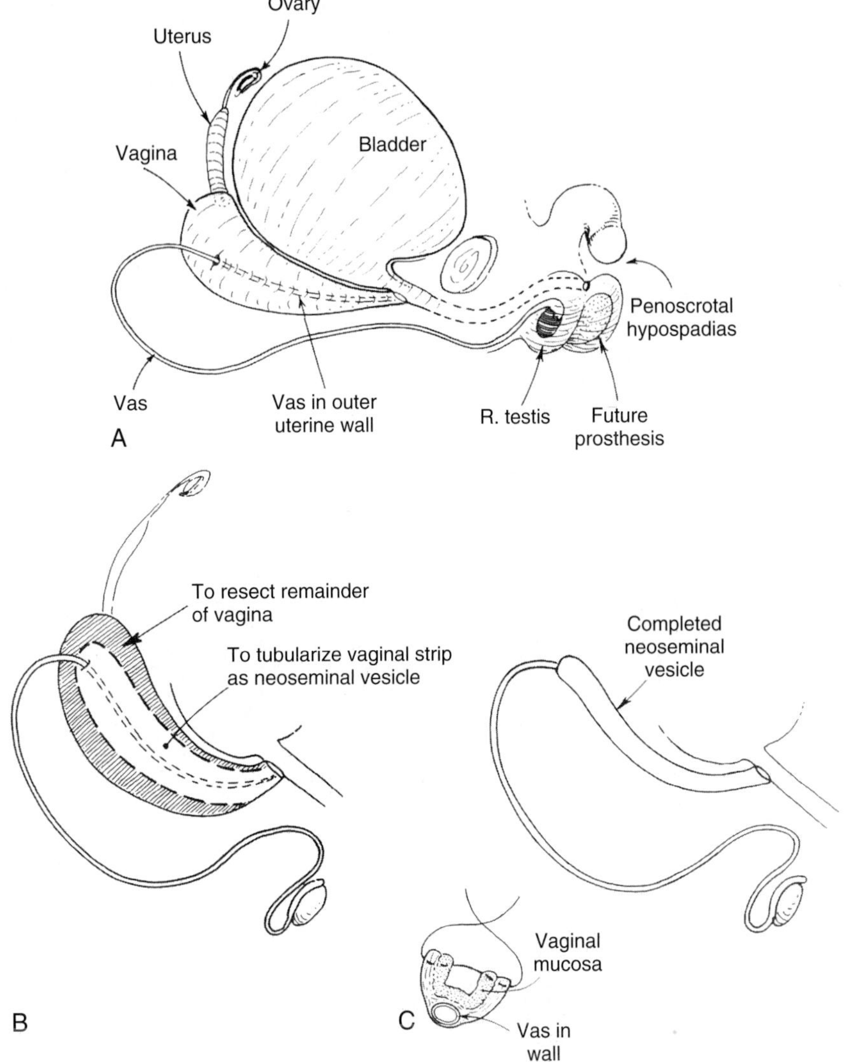

Figure 121–11 Surgical management of retained müllerian ducts. *A,* In males with retained müllerian structures, every attempt is made to preserve the vas deferens, which often enters the side wall of the enlarged vagina and travels between the mucosa and muscularis or in the muscularis, as shown. *B,* A strip of vaginal wall containing the vas is preserved and tubularized, and the remainder of the vagina and uterus are removed. *C,* The remaining strip of vagina is closed from the entrance of the vas into the wall of the vagina to the narrowed neck, where the vas deferens joins the urethra.

during correction of the prepenile scrotum. Six months or more should elapse between reconstruction of the neourethra and correction of the prepenile deformity. A square flap that circumscribes the base of the penis is displaced in a caudal direction, where it serves to lengthen the scrotum and further correct the bifid scrotal defect. The base of the penis is then advanced and held in place in a cephalad direction while the abdominal flaps are rotated in a posterior direction to the ventral base of the penis (B to B′ in Fig. 121-12B to F). During the forward, upward displacement of the penis, which is done to give it a more erect appearance, rotation of the abdominal flaps posteriorly and caudally is extremely important. Otherwise, the base of the shaft skin will simply pull away from the apical position on the mons, creating an unacceptable tented appearance. The rotated abdominal flap must be of sufficient length to create half a diameter around the base of the penis to meet the flap from the other side without tension. Midline and lateral closure of the now-lengthened scrotum completes the repair and corrects the bifid scrotum. It is important that these patients stay on bed rest with urine diversion until the ventral base of the penis has effectively healed.

SUMMARY

Intersex abnormalities are caused by several pathophysiologic entities, each of which must be systematically considered by pediatric surgeons working in collaboration with pediatric endocrinologists. All decisions must be made with the participation of the parents, with the goal of giving the child the best quality of life possible. Meticulous attention to detail is required to achieve the best technical results. The ultimate goal of these procedures is to give the patient favorable, functional intercourse, even if fertility cannot be achieved.

ACKNOWLEDGMENTS

We thank Rafael Pieretti Vanmarcke, MD, for his invaluable skills in updating the original diagrams done by Paul Andreissi, and for adapting the drawings that Richard Rink, MD, kindly gave us permission to use. We also thank David MacLaughlin, PhD, for his inestimable contributions to our understanding of the molecular mechanisms of sex differentiation. This chapter is dedicated to W. Hardy Hendren, MD, and John D. Crawford, MD, for all they taught us about the care of these children over the years.

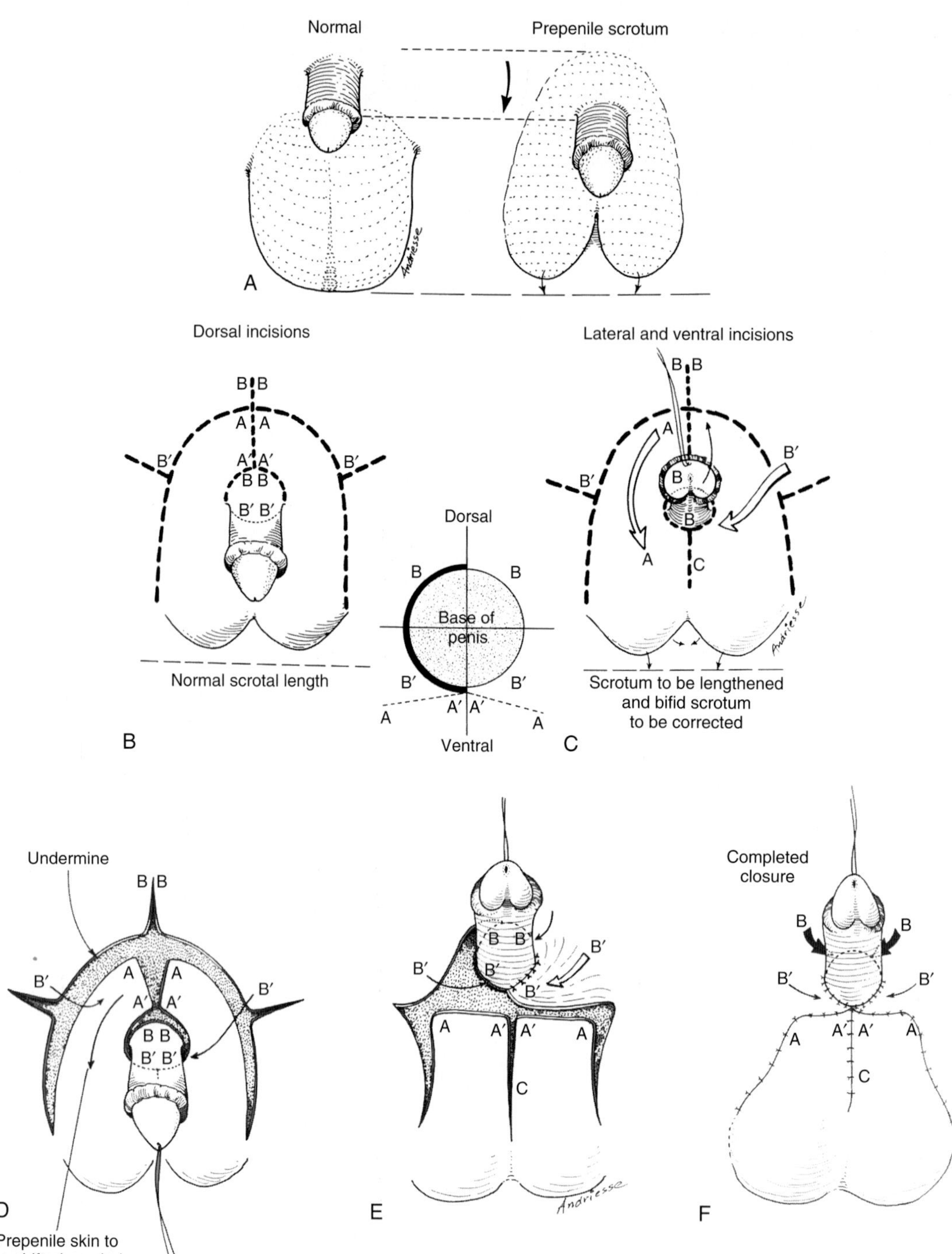

Figure 121–12 Surgical correction of prepenile and bifid scrotum. *A,* Correction is reserved for phenotypic patients in whom abundant scrotal tissue lies in an anterior direction to the dorsal base of the penis in association with a bifid scrotum. *B* and *C,* Posterior transposition of the scrotum and anterior transposition of the penis are accomplished through a series of dorsal, lateral, and ventral incisions and the movement of anterior tissue. *D,* Generous abdominal skin flaps are raised with broad bases to retain blood supply. *E,* The anterior abdominal wall flaps are mobilized sufficiently to advance to the ventral base of the penis with no tension. This is necessary to prevent unsatisfactory tenting of the anterior or dorsal base of the penis. *F,* The remaining incisions are closed using fine absorbable suture. The transposed scrotalized skin, now in a caudal position, lengthens the scrotum and corrects the bifid appearance.

REFERENCES

1. Achermann JC, Ito M, Hindmarsh PC, Jameson JL: A mutation in the gene encoding steroidogenic factor-1 causes XY sex reversal and adrenal failure in humans. Nat Genet 1999;22:125-126.
2. Andersson S, Berman DM, Jenkins EP, Russell DW: Deletion of steroid 5 alpha-reductase 2 gene in male pseudohermaphroditism. Nature 1991;354:159-161.
3. Barbaux S, Niaudet P, Gubler MC, et al: Donor splice-site mutations in WT1 are responsible for Frasier syndrome. Nat Genet 1997;17:467-470.

4. Barbie TU, Barbie DA, MacLaughlin DT, et al: Müllerian inhibiting substance inhibits cervical cancer cell growth via a pathway involving p130 and p107. Proc Natl Acad Sci U S A 2003;100:15601-15606.
5. Bardoni B, Zanaria E, Guioli S, et al: A dosage sensitive locus at chromosome Xp21 is involved in male to female sex reversal. Nat Genet 1994;7:497-501.
6. Belville C, Josso N, Picard JY: Persistence of müllerian derivatives in males. Am J Med Genet 1999;89:218-223.
7. Bennett CP, Docherty Z, Robb SA, et al: Deletion 9p and sex reversal. J Med Genet 1993;30:518-520.
8. Berkovitz GD, Fechner PY, Marcantonio SM, et al: The role of the sex-determining region of the Y chromosome (SRY) in the etiology of 46,XX true hermaphroditism. Hum Genet 1992;88:411-416.
9. Budzik GP, Powell SM, Kamagata S, Donahoe PK: Müllerian inhibiting substance fractionation by dye affinity chromatography. Cell 1983;34:307-314.
10. Cate RL, Donahoe PK, MacLaughlin DT: Müllerian inhibitory substance. In Sporn MB, Roberts AB (eds): Handbook of Experimental Pharmacology. Berlin, Springer-Verlag, 1990.
11. Dasgupta R, Schnitzer JJ, Hendren WH, Donahoe PK: Congenital adrenal hyperplasia: Surgical considerations required to repair a 46,XX patient raised as a male. J Pediatr Surg 2003;38:1269-1273.
12. David M, Forest MG: Prenatal treatment of congenital adrenal hyperplasia resulting from 21-hydroxylase deficiency. J Pediatr 1984;105:799-803.
13. Donahoe PK, Crawford JD, Hendren WH: Management of neonates and children with male pseudohermaphroditism. J Pediatr Surg 1977;12:1045-1057.
14. Donahoe PK, Crawford JD, Hendren WH: True hermaphroditism: A clinical description and a proposed function for the long arm of the Y chromosome. J Pediatr Surg 1978; 13:293-301.
15. Donahoe PK, Crawford JD, Hendren WH: Mixed gonadal dysgenesis, pathogenesis and management. J Pediatr Surg 1979;14:287-300.
16. Donahoe PK, Schnitzer JJ: Evaluation of the infant who has ambiguous genitalia, and principles of operative management. Semin Pediatr Surg 1996;5:1-12.
17. Donohoue PA, Parker K, Migeon CJ: Congenital adrenal hyperplasia. In Scriver CR, Beaudet AL, Sly WS, Valle D (eds): The Metabolic and Molecular Bases of Inherited Disease. New York, McGraw-Hill, 1995, pp 2929-2966.
18. Engle E, Forbes A: Cytogenetic and clinical findings in 48 patients with congenitally defective or absent ovaries. Medicine 1965;44:135-164.
19. Farkas A, Chertin B, Hadas-Halpren I: 1-Stage feminizing genitoplasty: 8 years of experience with 49 cases. J Urol 2001;165:2341-2346.
20. Federman DD: Abnormal Sexual Development: A Genetic and Endocrine Approach to Differential Diagnosis. Philadelphia, WB Saunders, 1967.
21. Federman DD, Donahoe PK: Ambiguous genitalia—etiology, diagnosis, and therapy. In Kreigsberg RA (ed): Advances in Endocrinology and Metabolism. Chicago, Mosby, 1995, pp 91-116.
22. Flatau E, Josefsberg Z, Reisner SH, et al: Penile size in the newborn. J Pediatr 1975;87:663-664.
23. Ford CE, Jones KW, Polani PE, et al: A sex-chromosome anomaly in a case of gonadal dysgenesis (Turner's syndrome). Lancet 1959;1:711-713.
24. Foster JW, Dominguez-Steglich MA, Guioli S, et al: Campomelic dysplasia and autosomal sex reversal caused by mutations in an SRY-related gene. Nature 1994;372:525-530.
25. Grumbach MM, Conte FA: Disorders of sexual differentiation. In Wilson JD, Foster DW (eds): Williams Textbook of Endocrinology. Philadelphia, WB Saunders, 1985, pp 312-401.
26. Grumbach MM, Conte FE: Disorders of sex differentiation. In Wilson JD, Foster DW, Kronenberg HM, Larsen PR (eds): Williams Textbook of Endocrinology, 9th ed. Philadelphia, WB Saunders, 1998, pp 1303-1425.
27. Grumbach M, Hughes I, Conte F: Disorders of sex differentiation. In Larsen PR, Kronenberg HM, Melmed S, Polonsky KS (eds): Williams Textbook of Endocrinology, 10th ed. Philadelphia, WB Saunders, 2003, pp 842-1002.
28. Ha TU, Segev DL, Barbie D, et al: Müllerian inhibiting substance inhibits ovarian cell growth through an Rb-independent mechanism. J Biol Chem 2000;275:37101-37109.
29. Hammes A, Guo JK, Lutsch G, et al: Two splice variants of the Wilms' tumor 1 gene have distinct functions during sex determination and nephron formation. Cell 2001;106:319-329.
30. Hamza AF, Soliman HA, Abdel Hay SA, et al: Total urogenital sinus mobilization in the repair of cloacal anomalies and congenital adrenal hyperplasia. J Pediatr Surg 2001; 36:1656-1658.
31. He WW, Gustafson ML, Hirobe S, Donahoe PK: The developmental expression of four novel serine/threonine kinase receptors homologous to the activin/TGF-beta receptor family. Dev Dyn 1993;196:133-142.
32. Hendren WH, Crawford JD: Adrenogenital syndrome: The anatomy of the anomaly and its repair. Some new concepts. J Pediatr Surg 1969;4:49-58.
33. Hoshiya M, Christian BP, Cromie WJ, et al: Persistent müllerian duct syndrome caused by both a 27-bp deletion and a novel splice mutation in the MIS type II receptor gene. Birth Defects Res Part A Clin Mol Teratol 2003;67:868-874.
34. Hoshiya Y, Gupta V, Segev DL, et al: Müllerian inhibiting substance induces NFκB signaling in breast and prostate cancer cells. Mol Cell Endocrinol 2003;211:43-49.
35. Imperato-McGinley J, Guerrero L, Gautier T, Peterson RE: Steroid 5alpha-reductase deficiency in man: An inherited form of male pseudohermaphroditism. Science 1974; 186:1213-1215.
36. Imperato-McGinley J, Zhu YS: Androgens and male physiology in the syndrome of 5alpha-reductase-2 deficiency. Mol Cell Endocrinol 2002;198:51-59.
37. Ito M, Yu R, Jameson JL: DAX-1 inhibits SF-1-mediated transactivation via a carboxy-terminal domain that is deleted in adrenal hypoplasia congenita. Mol Cell Biol 1997;17:1476-1483.
38. Jacobs PA, Ross A: Structural abnormalities of the Y chromosome in man. Nature 1966;210:352-354.
39. Jenak R, Ludwikowski B, Gonzalez R: Total urogenital sinus mobilization: A modified perineal approach for feminizing genitoplasty and urogenital sinus repair. J Urol 2001;165: 2347-2349.
40. Jost A: Recherches sur la differenciation sexuelle de l'embryon du lapin. Arch Anat Microsc Morphol Exp 1947;36:271-315.
41. Koopman P: SRY and SOX9: Mammalian testis-determining genes. Cell Mol Life Sci 1999;55:839-856.
42. Koopman P, Gubbay J, Vivian N, et al: Male development of chromosomally female mice transgenic for SRY. Nature 1991;351:117-121.
43. Koopman P, Munsterberg A, Capel B, et al: Expression of a candidate sex-determining gene during mouse testis differentiation. Nature 1990;348:450-452.
44. Lala DS, Rice DA, Parker KL: Steroidogenic factor I, a key regulator of steroidogenic enzyme expression, is the mouse homolog of fushi tarazu-factor I. Mol Endocrinol 1992;6:1249-1258.
45. Lee MM, Donahoe PK: Ambiguous genitalia. In Bardin W (ed): Current Therapy in Endocrinology and Metabolism. Toronto, BC Decker, 1992, pp 232-240.
46. Lubahn DB, Joseph DR, Sullivan PM, et al: Cloning of human androgen receptor complementary DNA and localization to the X chromosome. Science 1988;240:327-330.

47. Ludwikowski B, Oesch Hayward I, Gonzalez R: Total urogenital sinus mobilization. BJU Int 1999;83:820-822.
48. MacLaughlin DT, Donahoe PK: Sex determination and differentiation. N Engl J Med 2004;350:367-378.
49. Manuel M, Katayama KP, Jones HW: The age of occurrence of gonadal tumors in intersex patients with a Y chromosome. Am J Obstet Gynecol 1976;124:293-300.
50. Masiakos PT, MacLaughlin DT, Maheswaran S, et al: Human ovarian cancer, cell lines, and primary ascites cells express the human müllerian inhibiting substance (MIS) type II receptor, bind, and are responsive to MIS. Clin Cancer Res 1999;5:3488-3499.
51. McElreavey K, Vilain E, Abbas N, et al: XY sex reversal associated with a deletion 5′ to the SRY HMG box in the testis-determining region. Proc Natl Acad Sci U S A 1992; 89:11016-11020.
52. McLaren A: Mammalian germ cells: Birth, sex, and immortality. Cell Struct Funct 2001;26:119-122.
53. Miller WL: Molecular biology of steroid hormone synthesis. Endocr Rev 1988;9:295-318.
54. Miller WL: Steroid 17alpha-hydroxylase deficiency—not rare everywhere. J Clin Endocrinol Metab 2004;89:40-42.
55. Mornet E, Boue J, Raux-Demay M, et al: First trimester prenatal diagnosis of 21-hydroxylase deficiency by linkage analysis to HLA-DNA probes and by 17-hydroxyprogesterone determination. Hum Genet 1986;73:358-364.
56. Muller J, Skakkebaek NE, Nielsen OH, Graem N: Cryptorchidism and testis cancer: Atypical infantile germ cells followed by carcinoma in situ and invasive carcinoma in adulthood. Cancer 1984;54:629-634.
57. Nef S, Parada LF: Cryptorchidism in mice mutant for Insl3. Nat Genet 1999;22:295-299.
58. New MI, Wilson RC: Steroid disorders in children: Congenital adrenal hyperplasia and apparent mineralocorticoid excess. Proc Natl Acad Sci U S A 1999;96:12790-12797.
59. Nihoul-Fekete C, Lortat-Jacob S, Cachin O, Josso N: Preservation of gonadal function in true hermaphroditism. J Pediatr Surg 1984;19:50-55.
60. Page DC, Mosher R, Simpson E, et al: The sex-determining region of the human Y chromosome encodes a finger protein. Cell 1987;51:1091-1104.
61. Pang S: Congenital adrenal hyperplasia. Endocrinol Metab Clin North Am 1997;26:853-891.
62. Pang S, Pollack MS, Loo M, et al: Pitfalls of prenatal diagnosis of 21-hydroxylase deficiency congenital adrenal hyperplasia. J Clin Endocrinol Metab 1985;61:89-97.
63. Pang SY, Pollack MS, Marshall RN, Immken L: Prenatal treatment of congenital adrenal hyperplasia due to 21-hydroxylase deficiency. N Engl J Med 1990;322:111-115.
64. Parker KL, Schimmer BP, Schedl A: Genes essential for early events in gonadal development. Cell Mol Life Sci 1999;55:831-838.
65. Passerini-Glazel G: A new 1-stage procedure for clitorovaginoplasty in severely masculinized female pseudohermaphrodites. J Urol 1989;142:565-568.
66. Pena AJ: Total urogenital mobilization—an easier way to repair cloacas. J Pediatr Surg 1997;32:263-268.
67. Picard JY, Josso N: Purification of testicular anti-müllerian hormone allowing direct visualization of the pure glycoprotein and determination of yield and purification factor. Mol Endocrinol 1984;34:23-29.
68. Renaud EJ, MacLaughlin DT, Oliva E, et al: Endometrial cancer is a receptor-mediated target for müllerian inhibiting substance. Proc Natl Acad Sci U S A 2005;102:111-116.
69. Rink RC, Pope JC, Kropp BP, et al: Reconstruction of the high urogenital sinus: Early perineal prone approach without division of the rectum. J Urol 1997;158:1293-1297.
70. Robboy SJ, Miller T, Donahoe PK, et al: Dysgenesis of testicular and streak gonads in the syndrome of mixed gonadal dysgenesis: Perspective derived from a clinicopathologic analysis of twenty-one cases. Hum Pathol 1982;13:700-716.
71. Saitou M, Barton SC, Surani MA: A molecular programme for the specification of germ cell fate in mice. Nature 2002; 418:293-300.
72. Schnitzer JJ, Donahoe PK: Surgical treatment of congenital adrenal hyperplasia. Endocrinol Metab Clin North Am 2001;30:137-154.
73. Schnitzer JJ, Donahoe PK, Tash J, Poppas DP: Single stage reconstruction for infants with congenital adrenal hyperplasia. Endocrinologist 2003;13:190-194.
74. Scully RE: Gonadoblastoma: A review of 74 cases. Cancer 1970;25:1340-1356.
75. Segev DL, Ha TU, Tran TT, et al: Müllerian inhibiting substance inhibits breast cancer cell growth through an NFkappa B-mediated pathway. J Biol Chem 2000;275: 28371-28379.
76. Segev DL, Hoshiya Y, Stephen AE, et al: Müllerian inhibiting substance regulates NFkappaB signaling and growth of mammary epithelial cells in vivo. J Biol Chem 2001;276: 26799-26806.
77. Sinclair AH, Berta P, Palmer MS, et al: A gene from the human sex-determining region encodes a protein with homology to a conserved DNA-binding motif. Nature 1990; 346:240-244.
78. Teixeira J, Shah P, Donahoe PK: Developmental expression of a candidate müllerian inhibiting substance type II receptor. Endocrinology 1996;137:160.
79. Tilley WD, Marcelli M, Wilson JD, McPhaul MJ: Characterization and expression of a cDNA encoding the human androgen receptor. Proc Natl Acad Sci U S A 1989; 86:327-331.
80. Tommerup N, Schempp W, Meinecke P, et al: Assignment of an autosomal sex reversal locus (SRA1) and campomelic dysplasia (CMPD1) to 17q24.3-q25.1. Nat Genet 1993;4:170-174.
81. van Niekerk W: True hermaphroditism. Am J Obstet Gynecol 1976;126:890-907.
82. Wagner T, Wirth J, Meyer J, et al: Autosomal sex reversal and campomelic dysplasia are caused by mutations in and around the SRY-related gene SOX9. Cell 1994;79:1111-1120.
83. Walsh PC, Madden JD, Harrod MJ, et al: Familial incomplete male pseudohermaphroditism, type 2: Decreased dihydrotestosterone formation in pseudovaginal perineoscrotal hypospadias. N Engl J Med 1974;291:944-949.
84. White PC, New MI: Molecular genetics of congenital adrenal hyperplasia. Baillieres Clin Endocrinol Metab 1988;2: 941-965.
85. White PC, New MI: Genetic basis of endocrine disease 2: Congenital adrenal hyperplasia due to 21-hydroxylase deficiency. J Clin Endocrinol Metab 1992;74:6-11.
86. Wilkie AOM, Campbell FM, Daubeney P, et al: Complete and partial XY sex reversal associated with terminal deletion of 10q: Report of 2 cases and literature review. Am J Med Genet 1993;46:597-600.
87. Wilson JD, Harrod MJ, Goldstein JL, et al: Familial incomplete male pseudohermaphroditism, type 1: Evidence for androgen resistance and variable clinical manifestations in a family with Reifenstein syndrome. N Engl J Med 1974;290:1098-1103.
88. Zazopoulos E, Lalli E, Stocco DM, Sassone-Corsi P: DNA binding and transcriptional repression by DAX-1 blocks steroidogenesis. Nature 1997;390:311-315.
89. Zimmermann S, Steding G, Emmen JM, et al: Targeted disruption of the Insl3 gene causes bilateral cryptorchidism. Mol Endocrinol 1999;13:681-691.

Chapter 122  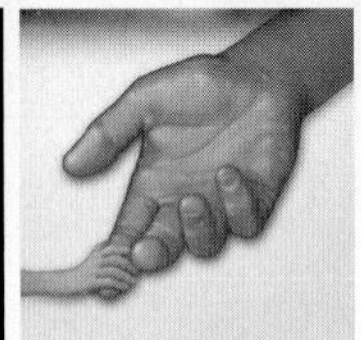

Abnormalities of the Female Genital Tract

Jay L. Grosfeld and Arnold G. Coran

Most genital anomalies in female infants present at birth and are congenital. In some instances, the abnormalities are discovered during evaluation of coexisting urologic problems or as the result of an association with a specific pattern of anomalies. A smaller number of patients present at the time of puberty with primary amenorrhea. Some have acquired conditions related to infection, foreign bodies, trauma, and neoplasia, In the past 2 decades, advances in perinatology, obstetrics, neonatology, and pediatric radiology have impacted on the recognition and subsequent care of female infants with genital tract anomalies. Many of these conditions are now being diagnosed during fetal life by prenatal maternal ultrasonography. A thorough appreciation of the embryologic development of the female urogenital tract is necessary to understand the multiplicity of congenital anomalies that may occur.

EMBRYOLOGY

The female reproductive system is derived primarily from the müllerian or paramesonephric ducts. The ureteral bud arises from the mesonephric (wolffian) duct during the 3rd week of gestation, interacting with the metanephric blastema to ultimately form the kidney and ureter. In the absence of a fetal testis, there is no production of androgen or müllerian-inhibiting substance (MIS), and consequently the wolffian duct distal to the ureteral bud is absorbed into the urogenital sinus. During the 6th week the paired paramesonephric (müllerian) ducts appear alongside the wolffian ducts with which they are intimately related. Between the 6th and 8th weeks of gestation, the paired müllerian ducts develop lateral to the wolffian ducts and then cross over the mesonephric ducts medially to fuse in the midline. Fusion occurs in a caudal to cranial direction, forming a single lumen. These fused müllerian ducts then join the urogenital sinus at the müllerian tubercle. By the 10th week of gestation, the ducts form a single midline tubular structure called the uterovaginal canal. The lateral aspect of the müllerian ducts, which remain separate (unfused), ultimately become the fallopian tubes. The caudal fused portion thickens and forms the uterus (fundus and body) and cervix.

The exact embryologic origin of the vagina is somewhat uncertain. Koff[72] suggested that the upper two thirds to four fifths of the vagina are probably formed from the fused müllerian duct, whereas the lower one third to one fifth is formed from the urogenital sinus. Although evidence supports the dual origin of the vagina, the exact contribution from each source is still unknown. By the 9th week of gestation, the fused müllerian ducts push the urogenital sinus caudad, creating Müller's tubercle. Vaginal development begins at the müllerian tubercle, where the uretovaginal canal joins the urogenital sinus. The tubercle thickens and elongates during the 3rd to 5th months of gestation, forming bilateral endodermal invaginations called the sinovaginal bulbs. The bulbs grow, the müllerian tubercle regresses, and the distance between the uterovaginal lumen and the urogenital sinus increases. The sinovaginal bulb completes its growth by the 15th to 26th weeks of gestation, giving rise to a solid cord of tissue called the primitive vaginal plate. Canalization of this cord of cells begins at the urogenital sinus and progresses in a cephalad direction to form the distal third of the vagina. By the 5th month of gestation, continuity between the proximal and distal vaginal lumens is complete. Defects can occur during development, fusion, and canalization. Failure of development may result in agenesis, failure of fusion leads to a variety of anomalies including duplication, and failure of the canalization phase results in formation of vaginal septa.[45] The close association and interaction between the müllerian and wolffian duct structures during embryogenesis may lead to associated anomalies between the genital and urinary systems.

Differentiation of the female external genitalia occurs between 12 and 16 weeks of gestation. In the absence of fetal androgen (particularly, dihydrotestosterone), the genital anlage develops passively into the external genitalia of the female. The genital tubercle elongates slightly and becomes the clitoris. The urethral folds form the labia minora and do not fuse; the unfused genital swellings form the labia majora. The urogenital groove remains open and forms the vestibule of the vagina.[68]

VAGINAL AGENESIS

Complete absence or agenesis of the vagina (also known as Mayer-Rokitansky syndrome) probably results from a failure of the müllerian ducts to reach the urogenital sinus due to a disorder involving the ureterovaginal canal or the vaginal plate. The condition appears to be a sporadic polygenic multifactorial disorder occurring between the 4th and 12th weeks of gestation.[36] No specific genetic abnormality has been identified. Mayer[81] first reported vaginal agenesis in stillborn infants with multiple birth defects in 1829. Rokitansky[112] (in 1838) and Küster[74] (in 1910) further described this clinical entity and recognized the presence of a rudimentary uterus with normal ovaries and normal external genitalia (Fig. 122-1A). Subsequently, in 1961, Hauser and coworkers[52] described the frequent association of renal and skeletal anomalies.

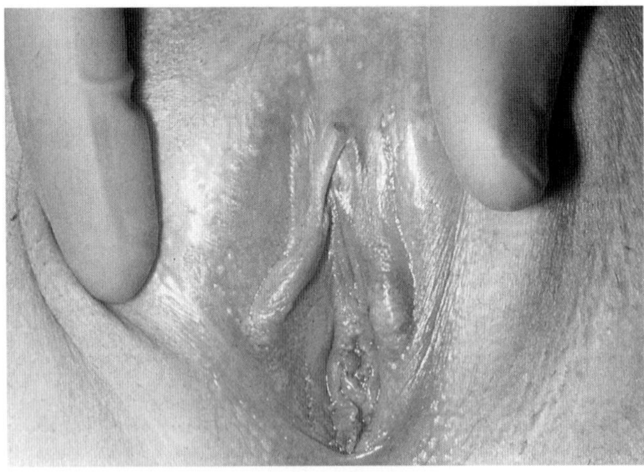

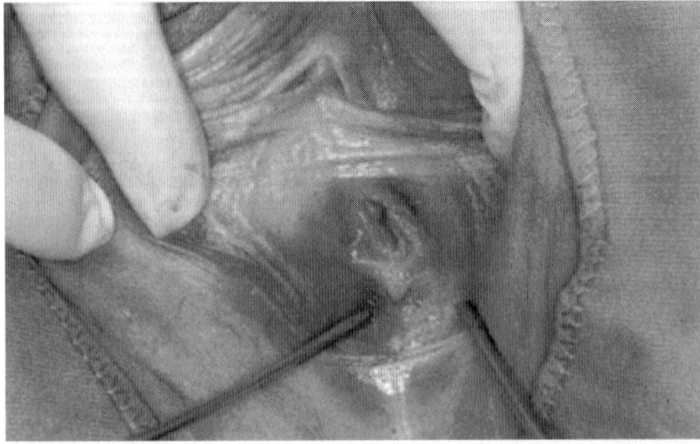

B

Figure 122-1 *A,* External genitalia of a 13-year-old girl with vaginal agenesis. The normal appearance indicates how readily this diagnosis can be overlooked. *B,* Small dilators in primitive müllerian pits. The vaginal remnant depth was 2.0 cm.

Thus, the combination of names as Mayer-Rokitansky-Küster-Hauser (MRKH) syndrome is used to describe this disorder. The incidence of vaginal agenesis varies from 1 in 4000 to 1 in 5000 live female births.[18] The patients are typically 46,XX females with normal secondary sex characteristics that commonly present at puberty with amenorrhea.[114] Uterine development in these patients may vary from normal to the more characteristic rudimentary bicornate structure without a lumen. They rarely have menstrual bleeding but may present with cyclic cramping abdominal pain because of rudimentary functioning endometrium. The vagina is completely absent in 75% of cases, whereas 25% have a very short vaginal pouch (often less than 2.5 cm) (see Fig. 122-1B). Most patients have both fallopian tubes and ovaries. However, unilateral[70] and bilateral gonadal agenesis[100] has occasionally been observed in MRKH syndrome. Plevraki and colleagues[100] noted the presence of a testis-specific protein 1-Y linked gene in one child with absent ovaries.

The association between congenital absence of the vagina and anomalies of the urinary tract is very common, with approximately one third of these patients having renal abnormalities.[37,47] The most common abnormality is agenesis of one kidney or ectopia of one or both kidneys. Fusion anomalies, such as horseshoe kidney and crossed renal ectopia, are also commonly observed.

Griffin and colleagues[47] reported skeletal anomalies in approximately 12% of MRKH patients. Two thirds of the patients with skeletal anomalies have spine, limb, or rib anomalies. Six percent of the skeletal malformations were of the Klippel-Feil type, which reflects an aberration in cervical thoracic somite development.[49] In 1979, Duncan and coworkers[30] reported on the frequency of these associated events and suggested that this combination of malformations be called the MURCS association. This is an acronym for müllerian duct aplasia, renal aplasia, and cervicothoracic somite association. MRKH syndrome may also occur in association with the TAR syndrome (thrombocytopenia–absent radius)[8,47] and rarely with anorectal malformations.[121] Radiographic abnormalities of the hand and hearing loss also have been observed.[129,130]

The McKusick-Kaufman syndrome (MKS) was described in 1964 in an Amish population and includes hydrometrocolpos due to vaginal atresia or aplasia, postaxial polydactyly, and congenital heart disease.[83,117,123] This is inherited in an autosomal recessive pattern, and a mutation in the *MKKS* gene has been identified in these cases.[122,128] Patients with MKS may have an overlap with the Bardet-Biedl syndrome (BBS).[123] Children with BBS have genital abnormalities and polydactyly in addition to retinitis pigmentosa, learning disabilities, central obesity, and cardiac abnormalities. Mutations in the *MKKS* gene occur in 10% to 15% of BBS patients. BBS can also be caused by the *BBS6* gene on chromosome 20p12, demonstrating heterogeneity.

Diagnosis

Diagnosis of vaginal agenesis is most frequently made at the time of puberty in association with amenorrhea. Approximately 15% of girls presenting with amenorrhea will have MRKH syndrome. The diagnosis should be suspected when commonly associated defects (e.g., skeletal, renal) are identified in a young girl with amenorrhea. In recent years, instances of hydrocolpos have been noted on prenatal ultrasound studies. Prenatal magnetic resonance imaging (MRI) may also document such cases. Occasionally, the disorder can be diagnosed in the neonatal period in infants with an associated abdominal mass. In infants and older patients, a complete physical examination including vaginoscopy and cystoscopy, pelvic ultrasonography, computed tomography (CT), MRI,[110] and laparoscopy are the best means of making an accurate diagnosis and identifing associated urinary tract abnormalities. Ultrasound, MRI, and endoscopy avoid unnecessary exposure to radiation.

Treatment

Treatment of vaginal agenesis depends on the anatomy of the individual patient. Functional, reproductive, and psychological issues must be carefully evaluated and addressed, taking into account both the physical and intellectual maturity of the patient.[31,32] The goal of therapy is to provide adequate sexual function and deal with the psychological impact that the patient has no uterus or vagina. Fertility is possible and is an option that should be offered to these patients because both ovaries are usually normal and successful in vitro fertilization with surrogate pregnancy has been achieved.[41,98] Psychological studies have shown that infertility rather than expected difficulty with intercourse was the most problematic issue for MRKH syndrome patients to deal with.[31,101] Proper preoperative counseling of the patient and family members is essential. The timing of the procedure is also important. If a uterus is present and the vaginal remnant is too short to reach the perineum, construction of a vagina that will communicate with the uterus should be undertaken before the onset of menses.[22] If only the distal portion of the vagina is absent, posterior or lateral skin flaps can be mobilized and rotated into the proximal portion of the vagina to provide an introitus. This, however, is difficult to accomplish in most instances, and long-term results vary. If no uterus is present, construction of a vagina should be undertaken just before the initiation of sexual activity.

Although creation of a new uterus is not yet feasible, a variety of techniques have been employed to develop a neovagina. In the normal female, the vagina is lined with stratified nonkeratinized squamous epithelium, is inclined posterosuperiorly, and has an average length of 9.0 cm on the posterior wall and 7.5 cm on the anterior wall. There are no glands in the vaginal mucous membrane, and it is lubricated by mucus derived from the cervical glands. Ideally, the neovagina should be located appropriately (posterosuperiorly), be of adequate dimensions, be lined by elastile tissue (either mucosa or skin), neither be constantly moist nor malodorous, be hairless, and be sensate at least at the introitus.[102] The method of vaginoplasty employed should be a simple, one-staged, easily reproducible procedure, with low morbidity and good outcomes (i.e., achieving painless sexual satisfaction). The ideal procedure has been elusive, and there are differences of opinion among various specialists concerning the most suitable technique for neovaginal construction in patients with MRKH.[31,45,58,60,75]

Nonoperative Management

In 1938, Frank described the use of daily dilatation of the vaginal dimple for 20 minutes using Pyrex tubes in six patients with MRKH syndrome.[38] In 1983, Rock and colleagues reported that only 43% of patients were successfully managed by forceful (passive) dilatation.[111] Lack of patient compliance affected the results. Edmonds noted improved results using graduated dilators in well-motivated patients managed in an organized treatment program influenced by ongoing support from clinical nurse specialists.[31] A policy statement from the American College of Obstetrics and Gynecology in 2002 suggested that nonoperative management using vaginal dilators is the first line of treatment.[1] However, a careful assessment of outcomes after dilatation and a comparison to other methods of treatment in prospective randomized studies are lacking. Dilatation may be beneficial in patients in whom the vaginal dimple measures more than 2.5 cm (see Fig. 122-1B).[108,111] Concerns regarding adequate length of the vagina, poor lubrication, and dyspareunia during intercourse remain.

Operative Management

A number of operative procedures have been advocated for creation of the neovagina, including insertion of a skin-covered vaginal mold (Abbe-McIndoe procedure),[71,82] various fasciocutaneous[120] and myocutaneous flaps (gluteal-thigh flap, gracilis, rectus abdominis,[78] Malaga flap,[40] and Singapore flap,[67,141] vulvovaginoplasty of Williams,[144] vulvovaginal flap (lotus petal labia majora flap),[148] horseshoe flap using labia minora,[103] labial flaps using tissue expanders,[9] full-thickness skin grafts with vacuum-assisted wound closure,[50] and the use of amnion[3,87] and peritoneum.[24] Soong and associates,[125] Rangaswamy and colleagues,[107] and Templeman and coworkers[132] described the laparoscopic approach to fashion a neovagina with peritoneum. The Vecchietti[140] procedure consists of intra-abdominal traction on the perineal membrane causing invagination of the shallow vaginal dimple. This requires either a laparotomy or laparoscopic approach and long-term dilatation. Wharton's procedure[119,143] simply places a condom-covered mold that is left in place for many months. Bowel vaginoplasty using cecum, small bowel, and sigmoid colon has been recommended as an alternative to these other procedures.[45,58,60,89] Some of the more popular procedures are presented here in more detail.

The most popular tissue for vaginal replacement during the past 3 decades has been the split-thickness skin graft as described by McIndoe.[82] The McIndoe procedure uses several split-thickness skin grafts, which are usually harvested from the buttocks or upper thigh. The grafts are then refashioned over a vaginal mold that serves as a stent to form a neovagina. Occasionally a meshed graft is employed (Fig. 122-2). The neovagina is

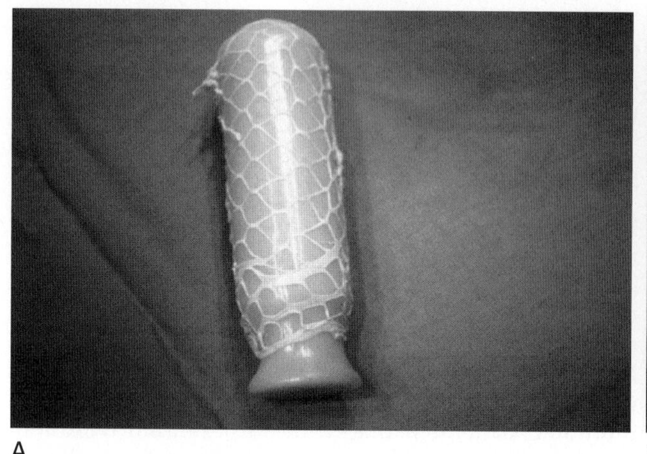

A

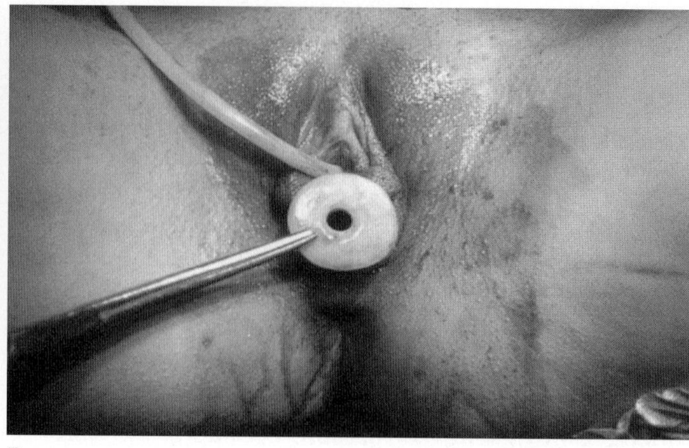

B

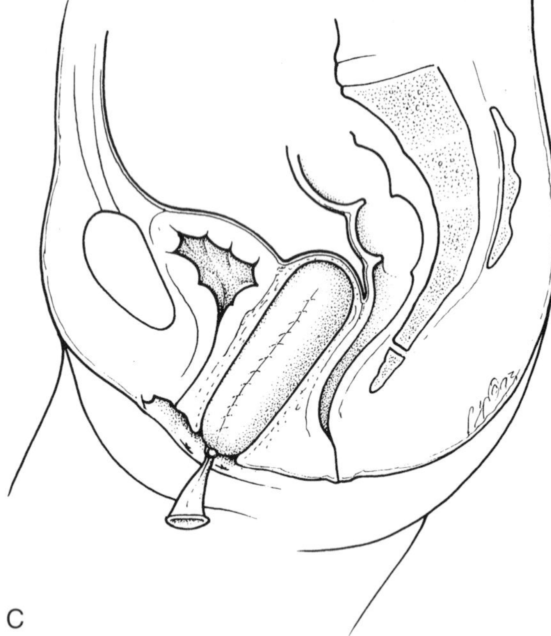

C

Figure 122–2 The McIndoe procedure. *A,* Meshed split-thickness skin graft sutured over a vaginal mold. *B,* The mold is placed in a surgically created space between the bladder and rectum. *C,* Lateral view showing the location of the mold.

then transferred to its normal anatomic position in a space surgically created through an incision in the apex of the vaginal dimple with dissection superiorly between the urethra and bladder anteriorly and the rectum posteriorly. The dissection is carried up to the pelvic peritoneum to provide length and to avoid postoperative contracture. The mold is sutured to the edge of perineal skin to hold it in position. Postoperative hematoma and fistula due to pressure necrosis related to the mold are early complications. Use of an inflatable soft vaginal mold reduces these risks. The reported complication rate is less than 10%. Despite scattered encouraging reports,[7,21] this technique is usually hampered by the need for regular and long-term home dilatation. Lubricants are required, and a significant incidence of inadequate vaginal length, vaginal stenosis, and dyspareunia due to contraction of the split-thickness skin graft are drawbacks of this procedure.[25] Antibiotics and analgesics are necessary, and the mold requires changing under an anesthetic and replacement with a larger-sized stent. There are no specific outcome studies surveying sexual satisfaction after this procedure.[32] Amnion is the preferred graft material in the United Kingdom because it avoids the need for autologous graft sites. However, acquiring amnion requires scheduled cesarean section and tissue banking and donors must be carefully screened for HIV infection and Creutzfeldt-Jakob disease.[32] The peritoneum has been used in Russia and the United States to line the neovaginal space, but this requires laparotomy or laparoscopy.[24,115,132] As noted earlier, a variety of full-thickness skin flaps have been employed to obviate the problem of contracture noted with split-thickness grafts. The disadvantage of using hair-bearing areas as the donor source of the flap for vaginal reconstruction is that hair growth results in neovaginal discharge and is associated with dyspareunia. These procedures also result in additional wounds at the donor sites. Use of vulval tissues to create a vagina may disturb the appearance of the external genitalia; and in the Williams vulvovaginoplasty, an abnormal angle for intercourse is problematic, resulting in dyspareunia and making this operation undesirable.[32,144] Use of tissue expanders to create more tissue for a labia minora graft may prove useful, but late results are not yet available to ensure that labia minora flaps will result in adequate vaginal length and will endure.[9,103] Autologous buccal mucosa has been used successfully for vaginoplasty.[92] Lin and associates[76] described eight cases using buccal mucosal grafts. This technique requires a vaginal stent mold and dilatation. Complications included vaginal bleeding presumably from granulation tissue in one patient and a bladder injury in another. Artificial dermis and recombinant basic fibroblast growth factor (bFGF) have also been used to create a neovagina in hopes of accelerating epithelialization and reducing the incidence of bloody discharge from granulation tissue.[88] Because of the small numbers of patients involved in these studies, no conclusions can be made at this time regarding the efficacy of these techniques.

In the Vecchietti procedure,[140] at laparotomy (or laparoscopy[34]) a suture is passed through the perineal membrane from above and then through a plastic olive and back up through the abdomen. The abdomen is closed and the suture is then attached to a traction device strapped to the patient's abdomen for a week to 10 days, with pressure on the olive causing invagination of the vaginal dimple, creating a vaginal vault. Claims of early vaginal length of 10 to 12 cm and a 100% anatomic and functional success rate have been reported.[16] Complications include bladder and rectal fistula in a small percentage of cases. The traction method is associated with some degree of patient discomfort, is cumbersome, still requires long-term vaginal dilatation, and has not been widely adopted in the United States. Wharton's procedure[143] involves placing a condom-covered mold in the neovagina to epithelialize vaginal granulation tissue. The process is lengthy because epithelialization may take from 3 to 6 months to occur and is associated with prolonged bloody vaginal discharge owing to the presence of granulation tissue. Schätz and colleagues[118] described initial dilatation of rudimentary müllerian ducts in three patients by gradually increasing the Hegar dilator size. The two cavities formed were joined into one by diathermy, and the resultant space is lined by smooth tissue. The dome of the space is composed of the peritoneum reflected from the bladder to the rectum. Sheares' modification of Wharton's technique[119] was applied, and an adjustable vaginal stent was placed in the space. Antibiotics and analgesics were administered for 8 days, and a Foley catheter left in place for 1 week to avoid urinary retention. The vaginal mold was changed under anesthesia after 1 week, and a new mold was inserted. The mold remained in place 24 hours per day for 3 months and then at night thereafter until regular sexual intercourse was initiated. Periodic changing of the mold required general anesthesia. Subsequent neovaginal length was 7 to 10 cm and the width was described as 2 fingerbreadths. Insufficient lubrication and dyspareunia were noted initially with sexual intercourse but resolved using lubricating gels. The two girls who experienced sexual relations expressed satisfaction with the procedure.[118] The extended period of time required to maintain the mold in place, the need for general anesthesia to repeatedly change the mold, inadequate lubrication, and lack of long-term follow-up data are drawbacks of this procedure.

Bowel Vaginoplasty

Because of the many disadvantages noted earlier, use of isolated bowel segments for vaginal replacement has gained popularity. The use of isolated segments of small intestine for vaginal replacement was first described by Baldwin[5] in 1904 and performed in 1907.[6] Ruge was the first to use the sigmoid colon to replace the vagina in 1914.[116] Experience with this technique was reported by Fall[33] in 1940, but efforts were abandoned because of an unacceptably high mortality rate in the preantibiotic era. Attention was refocused on the use of small bowel and colon for vaginal replacement in 1972 by Pratt,[102] and there have been scattered reports in the literature since that time.*

Currently, an interposed segment of the sigmoid colon is preferred for vaginal replacement. When the use of this segment is unavailable because of previous surgery, the cecum is an acceptable alternative. Although small intestine has occasionally been used, results are not as gratifying because of excessive mucus formation and friability of small bowel mucosa with intercourse.

Patients require mechanical bowel preparation for 24 hours before surgery using GoLYTELY. Perioperative systemic antibiotics are administered 30 to 45 minutes before the incision. The operation is accomplished with the patient in the lithotomy position with the legs positioned in stirrups so that the abdomen and perineum can be prepared in the same field. A Foley catheter is placed in the bladder, and the abdomen and pelvis can be approached through a Pfannenstiel or lower midline abdominal incision. In recent years, the procedure has been carried out using a minimally invasive laparoscopic approach.[106,134,138] The peritoneal cavity is explored and the genital organs evaluated. If small rudimentary bicornuate uteri are noted, these are excised. Uncommonly, if a relatively normal uterus is observed, this is maintained and can be attached to the reconstructed vagina. The ovaries should be left in place to avoid the need for external hormonal replacement and maintain the potential for in vitro fertilization surrogate pregnancy should the patient desire to pursue this in the future.[31,41]

A 10- to 15-cm sleeve of sigmoid colon, based on the left colic or superior hemorrhoidal vessels, is sufficient to provide a capacious neovagina. Keeping the segment short avoids excess mucus production, which can be associated with longer segments. The sigmoid segment is divided between Bainbridge bowel clamps, and intestinal continuity is reestablished with either a stapled or hand-sewn end-to-end colocolostomy (Fig. 122-3). In patients with Mayer-Rokitansky syndrome or those with a hypoplastic vagina, an incision is made in the vertex of the vaginal dimple and a space created between the bladder anteriorly and the rectum posteriorly up to the peritoneal reflection. Depending on the length of mesentery, the isolated segment is usually brought down to the perineum

*See references 20, 27, 39, 45, 59, 60, 89, 104, 106, 134, and 142.

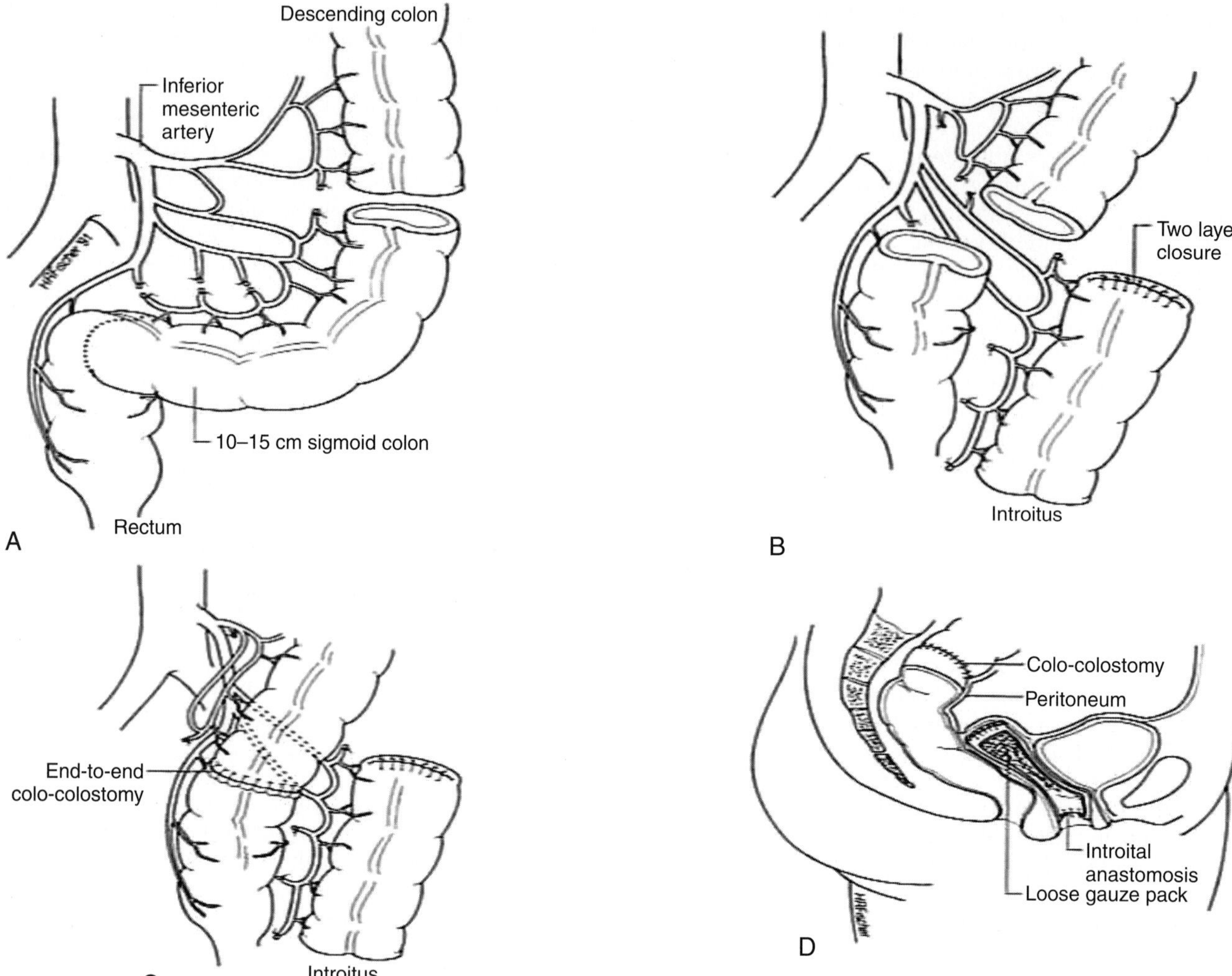

Figure 122-3 The patient is placed in a lithotomy position with the feet in stirrups. The procedure is performed through a Pfannenstiel incision or laparoscopically. *A*, A 10- to 15-cm sigmoid colon segment is isolated. *B* and *C*, The proximal portion of the sigmoid neovagina is closed in two layers and bowel continuity is restored by an end-to-end colon anastomosis. *D*, The isolated neovagina is then brought into the cul-de-sac and the distal end of the sigmoid vagina is anastomosed to the vaginal remnant if present or small introital cuff with one layer of interrupted absorbable sutures. The interposed colon is sutured to the retroperitoneal tissues to prevent prolapse. A Vaseline gauze pack is placed in the new orifice.

in an isoperistaltic fashion or rotated 180 degrees. The proximal end of the neovagina is then closed in two layers, with absorbable suture to form the vertex of the neovagina. An unrestricted one-layer anastomosis of the perineal opening to the distal end of the interposed colon segment using interrupted absorbable sutures (3-0 Vicryl or PDS) is then performed. A three-point fixation of the interposed segment to the retroperitoneum with nonabsorbable suture is essential to prevent prolapse.

Perioperative systemic antibiotics are discontinued after 24 hours. Analgesics are administered for 48 hours and discontinued after that time. Oral pain medication is available upon request. The neovagina is stented for 5 days after the procedure with petrolatum gauze. A Foley catheter drains the bladder during the period of vaginal stenting. Patients are discharged when they are ambulating and tolerating a diet, usually on the fifth postoperative day. Patients are examined at 3 weeks and 3 months. If a stenosis is evident, dilatation under anesthesia is performed. Home dilatation is usually unnecessary. Bicycling should be avoided for a 6-week period. Other exercises are permitted as tolerated.

Results

We (A.G.C.) have performed colovaginoplasty in 36 patients for a variety of conditions, including 14 patients with MRKH syndrome. The diagnoses in the other 22 patients included testicular feminization syndrome (10), cloacal anomalies (8), vaginal tumors (3), and mixed gonadal dysgenesis (1). No strictures were encountered. All of the patients who are sexually active have expressed satisfaction with the procedure and did not require lubricants or complain of dyspareunia or excess mucus production. Follow-up examination shows a widely patent vaginal introitus. No major complications were observed.

Hensle and Reiley decribed their experience with intestinal-vaginal replacement in 30 patients ranging in age from 1 to 20 years.[26,60] Long-term results were assessed by questionnaires mailed to 14 of the 20 original patients who had reached childbearing age. Ten of the women (71%) were sexually active. Four (29%) were married, and another three (21%) had been married but were divorced. Only one patient described dyspareunia; she had received an ileal vagina that required home dilatation because of stenosis and required reoperation. The other 13 patients required no home dilatation. They concluded that the ileum was not good as an interposition segment and suggested use of the sigmoid colon for intestinal-vaginoplasty in all cases. One patient had prolapse of the bowel and required retroperitoneal fixation. Burger[20] also described a stenotic segment in a patient treated by ileocecal vaginoplasty. Wesley and Coran[142] reported on six sigmoid vaginoplasties, four in adolescents and two in infants. Three of these patients were sexually active at the time of their report, and none required lubrication. Turner-Warwick and Kirby[137] described 13 patients who had colocecal vaginoplasty. Three patients required minor revisions to adjust the introitus, and 1 patient had a protrusion of the neovagina that required a simple circumferential resection of redundant intestine. Seven of the 13 patients in this series were sexually active. Novak[89] described two instances of interposition necrosis and two of prolapse among 63 patients with sigmoid colovaginoplasty. Fifty-nine of the 63 patients had a successful outcome. Syed and associates[131] described the occurrence of diversion colitis in 3 of 18 children who had undergone sigmoid vaginoplasty between 18 months and 8 years of age. We have generally not performed this procedure in very young children nor have seen this complication among our cases. Based on the report by Syed and associates,[131] Edmonds[32] has suggested that the procedure not be performed in this young age group. Hiroi and associates[63] in Japan described the only case of malignancy occurring in a sigmoid vaginoplasty. A mucinous adenocarcinoma of the colovaginoplasty was observed 30 years after the procedure.

Based on our own experience and that of many others, we believe that the sigmoid colon is an ideal tissue for vaginal replacement. Unlike other methods of vaginoplasty, this procedure creates a more normal, capacious vagina that is capable of providing natural lubrication during sexual activity and avoids the need for chronic dilatation of the neovagina in most cases. Limiting the length of the interposed segment to the usual vaginal length of 9.0 to 10.0 cm will reduce the risk of excessive mucus production. Recognized complications such as prolapse can be avoided by retroperitoneal fixation of the sigmoid segment. Use of the sigmoid colon rather than the small intestine will obviate some of the other complications, including stenosis and excessive mucus production, seen in the past. The fact that the procedure can be performed laparoscopically will reduce the risk of wound complications and intra-abdominal adhesions and make this procedure a more attractive alternative in the future.[106,135,138]

CONGENITAL VAGINAL OBSTRUCTION

Congenital vaginal obstruction is probably caused by incomplete canalization of the vagina that occurs during the fifth month of gestation. The hymen occurs at the junction of the sinovaginal bulbs with the urogenital sinus and is usually perforated during fetal life. Failure of perforation to occur results in an imperforate hymen.[32] An imperforate hymen can result in gross distention of the vagina, which is termed *hydrocolpos,* or in distention of both the vagina and uterus, which is termed *hydrometrocolpos.* Congenital vaginal obstruction is most commonly caused by a simple imperforate hymen (Fig. 122-4A).[134] Less commonly, vaginal obstruction results from more proximal lesions, such as a high transverse septum (see Fig. 122-4B).[15] A high transverse vaginal septum can be associated with partial anterior vaginal agenesis as well as with persistence of a common urogenital sinus.

Diagnosis

The diagnosis of imperforate hymen can be made on prenatal ultrasound.[145] In the fetus, the imperforate hymen appears as a thin membrane associated with a distended vagina (sonolucent mass) and spread labia majora. Imperforate hymen and hydrocolpos can be diagnosed as early as the second trimester.[146] Neonates with vaginal obstruction usually present with a lower midline abdominal mass. Frequently, these infants have associated urinary tract obstruction. The abdominal mass is the distended vagina, which results from continued collection of cervical gland secretions in response to maternal estrogens. Abdominal ultrasonography reveals a large midline sonolucent mass. This mass causes forward displacement of the bladder and posterior displacement of the rectum. Percutaneous needle aspiration and injection of contrast medium may aid in the diagnosis and can be done through the perineum or the anterior abdominal wall (Fig. 122-5). If no abdominal mass is present at birth, the condition is often not detected until early adolescence. At the time of puberty, symptoms may include amenorrhea, cyclic abdominal pain, and an abdominal mass secondary to hematocolpos or

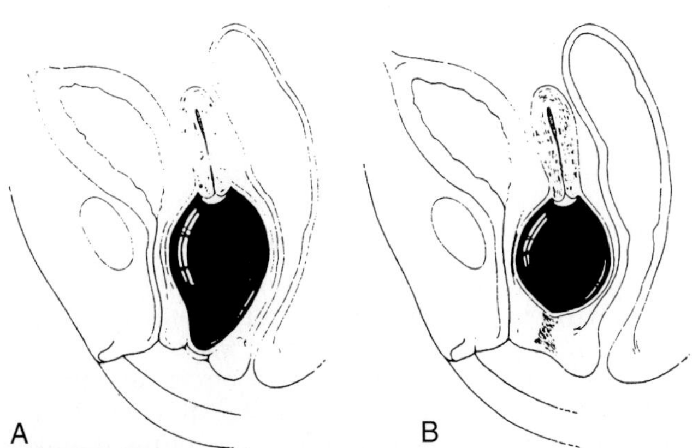

Figure 122-4 Congenital vaginal obstruction. *A,* Imperforate hymen. *B,* High transverse septum.

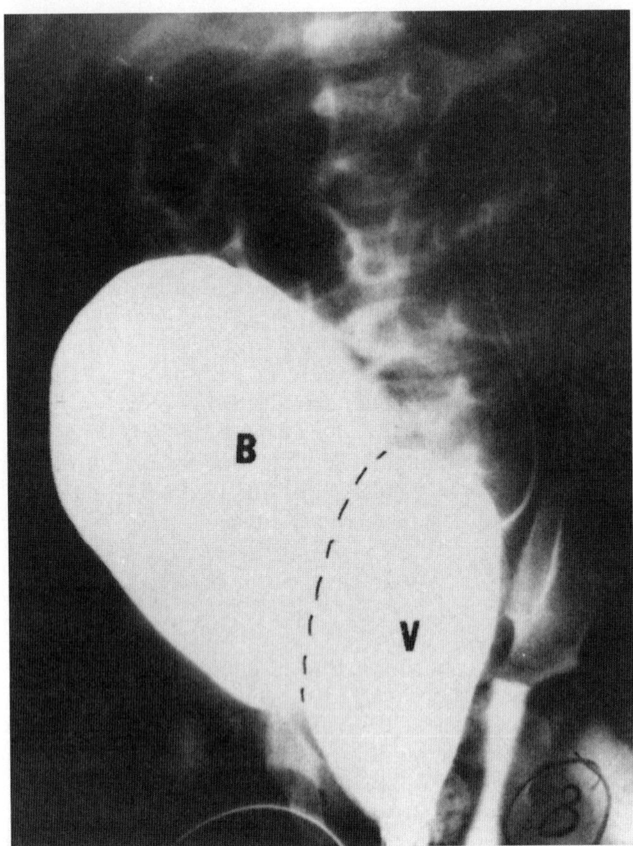

Figure 122-5 Percutaneous injection of an obstructed vagina (V) in a newborn, with simultaneous cystogram of bladder (B) and retrograde catheterization of a solitary left ureter and kidney.

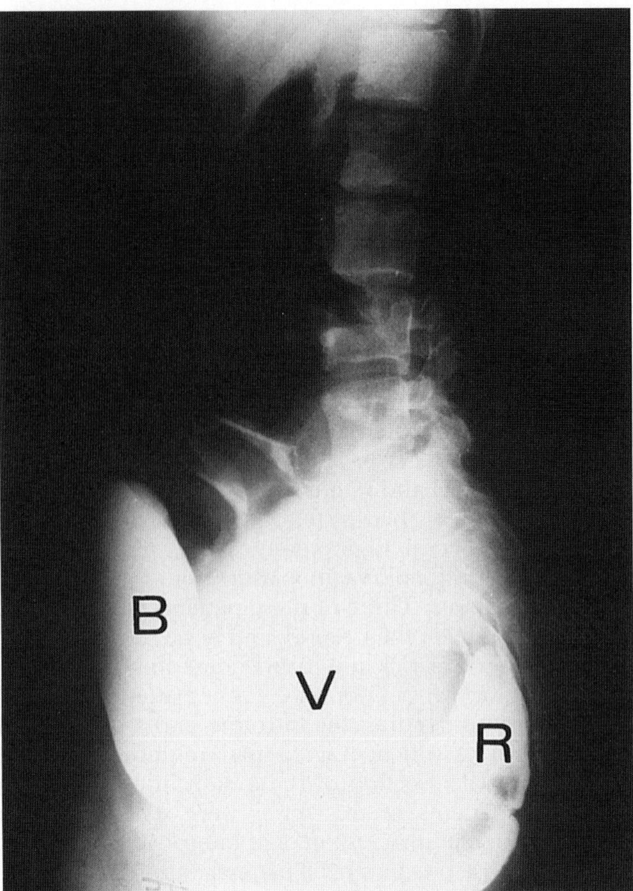

Figure 122-6 Lateral view of a contrast study in a patient with a midline mass pushing the bladder (B) forward and the rectum (R) in a posterior direction. V indicates the obstructed vagina.

hydrometrocolpos (Fig. 122-6). Introital examination may show a bulging membrane with bluish discoloration behind it due to hematocolpos.

Labial fusion is a common finding in infants and young children. Labial fusion may present as a primary skin bridge and may be associated with urinary tract infection because of obstruction. Division of the skin bridge may require a general anesthetic. More commonly, vaginal synechiae are observed in girls between age 1 and 5 years and may be the result of chronic irritation or a relative lack of estrogen stimulation. The membrane can usually be divided in the outpatient setting, revealing otherwise normal introital structures. Daily topical application of conjugated estrogen (Premarin) cream prevents re-adherence of the labial edges.

Treatment

Treatment of vaginal obstruction depends on the anatomy. An imperforate hymen in neonates that bulges at the introitus can be easily incised without anesthesia. In older patients, a cruciate incision is an effective method of achieving adequate drainage. It is necessary to clearly identify the anatomy at the time of the drainage procedure to ensure that a common urogenital sinus or other urinary tract anomaly is not associated with the lower vaginal septum.

Obstruction due to a high transverse vaginal septum and partial agenesis of the anterior portion of the vagina are less common but can be more difficult to correct. The defect results from incomplete fusion between the müllerian duct component of the vagina and the urogenital sinus component.[32] This incomplete vertical fusion results in a vaginal septum that varies in both the level of occurrence and thickness. Rock and associates[111] divided these anomalies into upper (46%), mid (35% to 40%), and lower (15% to 20%) vaginal defects. The greater the absence of the vagina, the higher the location of the septal defect. This abnormality may be associated with other malformations affecting the urinary tract, uterus, anus, and rectum. Presenting symptoms include cyclic abdominal pain in the absence of menstruation at the time of puberty.[32] Patients are often first recognized during emergency evaluation for acute abdominal pain that may be associated with an abdominal mass and urinary retention due to hematometrocolpos. Occasionally they have peritoneal irritation from oozing of blood into the peritoneal cavity from the fimbriated ends of the fallopian tubes due to hematosalpinx. A thorough evaluation of these children must occur before treatment. Pelvic ultrasonography is usually diagnostic of hematocolpos. The high transverse vaginal septum, with or without a common urogenital sinus, is best treated by draining the vagina in an anterior direction, resecting the septum, and performing a simultaneous transperineal vaginal pull-through procedure attaching the upper and lower vagina using absorbable sutures. If the rectum and anus are displaced in an anterior direction, it may be difficult to perform a definitive vaginoplasty (especially in infants). It may be more appropriate to initially drain the obstructed vagina through the common urogenital sinus and delay the vaginal reconstruction. The results with lower septum defect repair are much better than outcomes achieved with high vaginal septum defects.[32] Postoperative vaginal dilatation is necessary to prevent vaginal stenosis, which often requires a revision. Endometriosis is more frequently seen after repair of high vaginal obstruction, and the fertility rate for patients with a high transverse vaginal septum is only 20%.[111]

ANOMALIES OF FUSION

Vaginal Duplication

Disorders of embryogenesis that produce duplication anomalies of the vagina and uterus occur at approximately 9 weeks of gestation and involve a complete or partial failure of union of the two lateral müllerian ducts. These anomalies[28] are very common and can include two uteri and two cervices with two separate vaginas (uterus didelphys) or a single vagina (uterus duplex bicollis). They may also consist of two uteri fused with a single cervix and a single vagina (uterus duplex unicollis or bicornuate uterus) (Fig. 122-7).

In cases of complete vaginal duplication, one vagina can be obstructed and the other can be patent (Fig. 122-8).[15,134] Urinary tract anomalies may confound the situation with an ectopic ureter inserting into a duplicated imperforate hemivagina resulting in a mass.[73,85] The external genitalia will usually appear normal. The diagnosis of uterus didelphys and a unilateral obstructed vagina should be entertained as part of the differential diagnosis in a newborn with a sonolucent abdominal mass. The mass usually pushes the bladder forward and the normal vagina in a posterior direction (Fig. 122-9). Vaginoscopy is helpful in this situation and may reveal a bulging mass high in the vaginal side wall. A simple incision of the obstructing septum often provides adequate drainage; however, further division of the septum is usually necessary to prevent possible collection of bacteria on the abnormal side and abscess formation.[19,32] Formal laparotomy is occasionally required to provide adequate drainage and to confirm the diagnosis. Division of the vaginal septum is all that is warranted in most of these patients, because successful term pregnancies have been reported in both uterine horns, suggesting that fertility is not impaired on the obstructed side. Duplication anomalies should also be considered in pubertal girls who, despite menses, present with cyclic pelvic discomfort and a pelvic mass. Ultrasonography reveals a sonolucent mass that may have some scattered internal echos. A vaginogram shows a bladder and a normal vagina pushed apart by the mass. Pelvic MRI typically shows a normal uterine horn above a dilated, blood-filled vagina. The blood gives off a very bright signal on the T1-weighted image (Fig. 122-10).

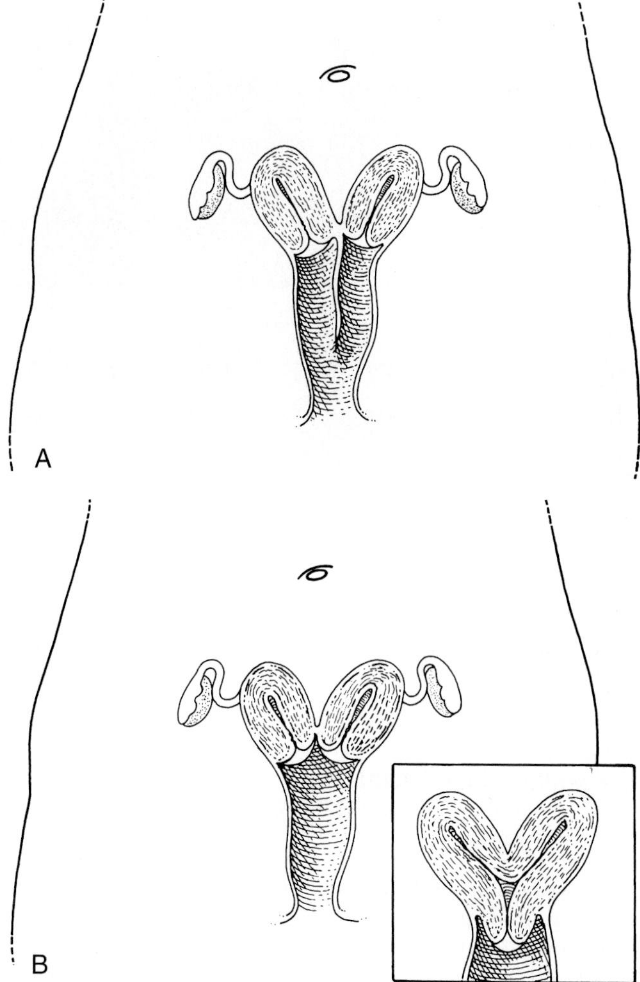

Figure 122-7 Fusion anomalies of the uterus (*A*) and vagina (*B*).

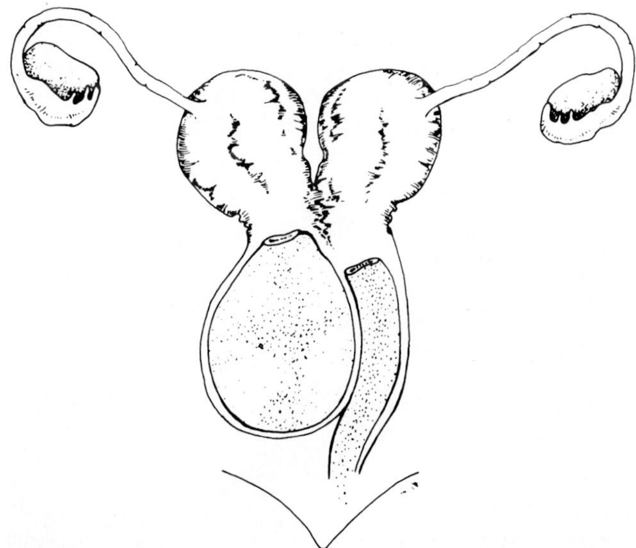

Figure 122-8 Unilateral obstruction of a duplex vagina in a patient with uterus didelphys. This disorder is usually associated with renal agenesis on the side where the atresia occurs.

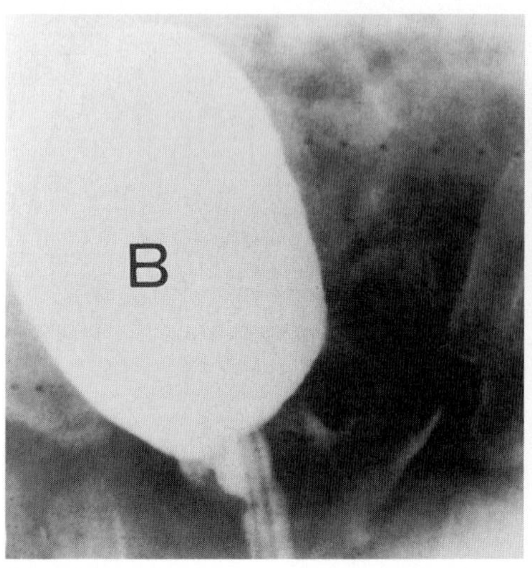

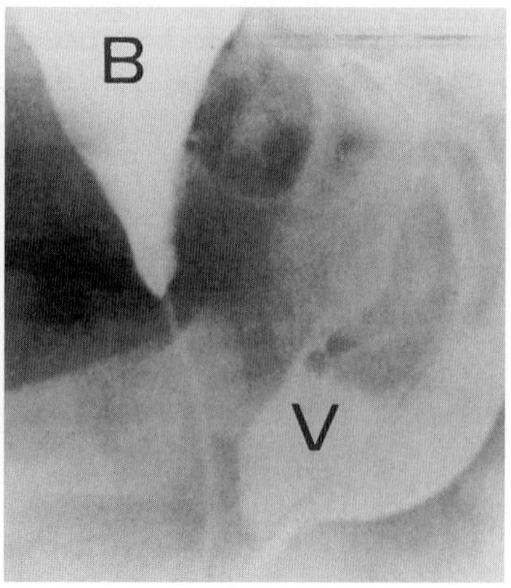

Figure 122-9 Simultaneous cystogram (*A*) and vaginogram (*B*) in a patient with uterus didelphys and unilateral obstruction of a duplex vagina showing separation of the bladder (B) and the normal vagina (V).

Treatment in the pubertal girls is identical to that of younger patients and can be easily accomplished vaginally.

Urogenital Sinus Anomalies

The urogenital sinus is defined as a common channel into which both the urinary and genital tracts open. The common urogenital sinus is a normal stage of embryonic development in both sexes. In normal females, an arrest in development of the müllerian ducts at 9 weeks of gestation, after fusion with the urogenital sinus, manifests as a urovaginal confluence or common urogenital sinus.[146] An arrest of vaginal differentiation at a slightly later date can lead to varying degrees of persistence of the urogenital sinus seen clinically (Fig. 122-11). A long urogenital sinus with a short vagina and high urethral opening will result if the defect occurs at an early stage. Conversely, a short urogenital sinus with an almost-normal vaginal vestibule and low urethral orifice will occur if the arrest occurs late in development.[79] Early defects with a high insertion of the vagina and urethra into the urogenital sinus are frequently associated with an anteriorly displaced anus. This indicates poor formation of the urorectal septum.

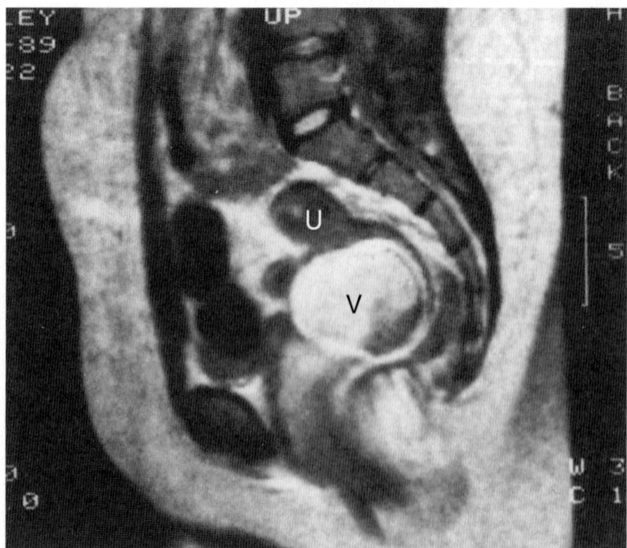

Figure 122-10 Pelvic magnetic resonance image showing a normal uterine horn (U) and an obstructed vagina (V).

Diagnosis

Adequate definition of the patient's anatomy is essential for proper evaluation of any urogenital sinus anomaly. A retrograde genitogram (Fig. 122-12) can assist in the definition of the urogenital sinus by delineating the length of the common channel and identifying the anatomic relationship of the vagina and urethra.[56] This procedure is best done with a blunt adaptor placed against the perineal opening to instill the contrast agent. Cystoscopy and vaginoscopy should be performed in each case.

Treatment

Once the anatomy of the defect has been clearly identified, various treatment options can be considered. A simple U-flap vaginoplasty[53] can be done if the urogenital sinus is low and the common channel is short. In the cases of a urogenital sinus with a high confluence of the bladder and vagina, Donahoe and Gustafson[29] advocate an inverted perineal U-flap in combination with bilateral buttock flaps to augment the vagina. However, the urogenital sinus is frequently associated with an anteriorly placed anus, which requires posterior relocation of the anus before the perineal skin flap vaginoplasty is done.[57] If the vagina enters the urogenital sinus too far proximally, a division of the vaginal moiety from the urogenital sinus in conjunction with a pull-through vaginoplasty will be necessary. A confluence of both the vagina and

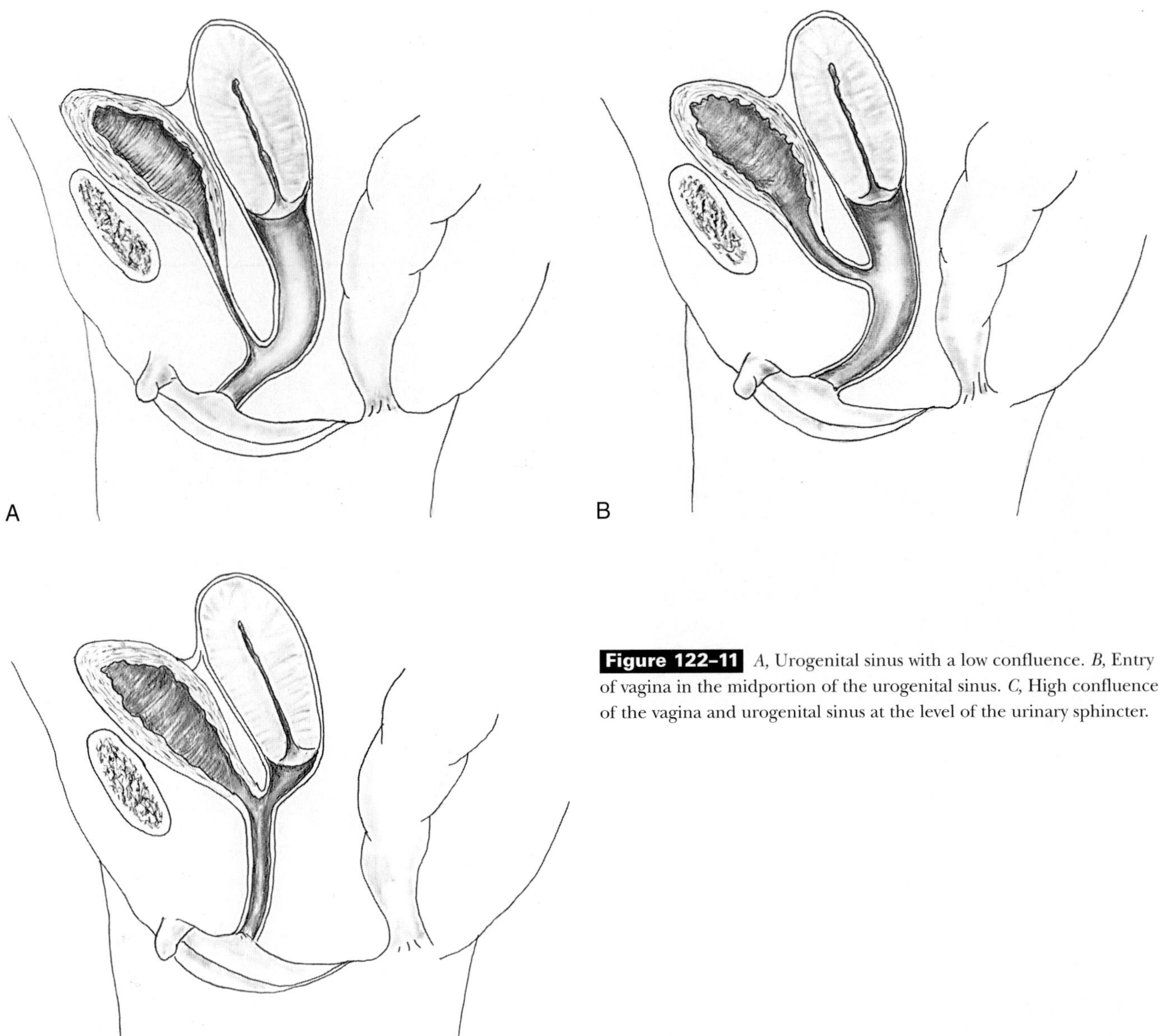

Figure 122–11 *A*, Urogenital sinus with a low confluence. *B*, Entry of vagina in the midportion of the urogenital sinus. *C*, High confluence of the vagina and urogenital sinus at the level of the urinary sphincter.

the bladder high in the urogenital sinus requires a pull-through vaginoplasty and often requires the creation of a neourethra from the anterior vaginal wall.[55] The Passerini genitovaginoplasty procedure may be useful in some cases of persistent urogenital sinus with a very high insertion of the vagina.[93] Peña has advocated total urogenital advancement for cases with a long common channel greater than 3.0 cm.[97] This maneuver has improved the ease of repair and reduced the incidence of postoperative vaginal and urethral strictures and urethrovaginal fistula (Fig. 122-13).[97]

Cloacal Malformations

Cloacal malformations result from the combination of a urogenital sinus with an anorectal anomaly.[44] In the early embryo there is a cloacal stage during which the allantois and hindgut are confluent.[127] At 4 to 6 weeks of gestation, the urorectal septum divides the allantois from the hindgut. If this separation does not take place, a common cloaca will result. Infants with this defect present at birth with abdominal distention and an abnormal perineum. They usually have no anus or vagina but possess a single perineal opening. The phallus-like structure frequently has a hooded appearance, which gives a masculinized gender appearance (Fig. 122-14). The bladder may enter the cloaca immediately inside the perineal opening and may be associated with a relatively normal length urethra. Conversely, the bladder may enter the cloaca very high and be located in proximity to the bladder neck. The entrance of the rectum into the cloaca can similarly be either high or low (Fig. 122-15).[65] Vaginal anomalies are common in patients with a cloaca, and

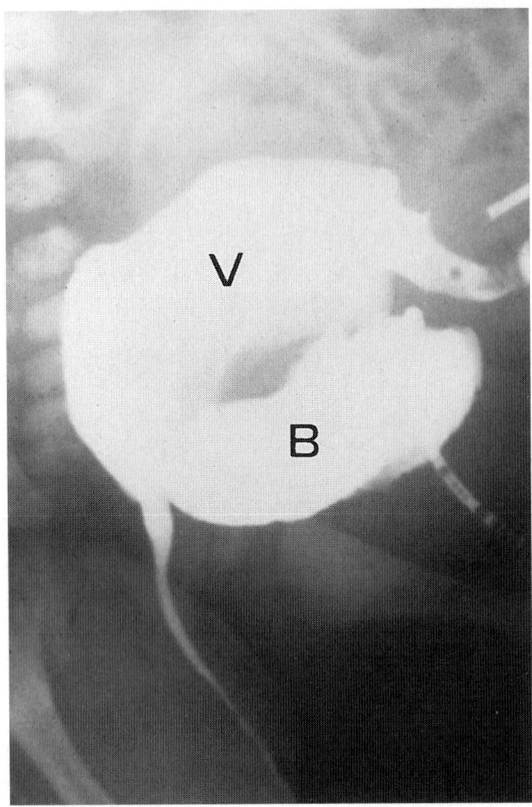

Figure 122–12 Retrograde genitogram of a urogenital sinus showing a high confluence of the bladder (B) and vagina (V) into a long urogenital sinus.

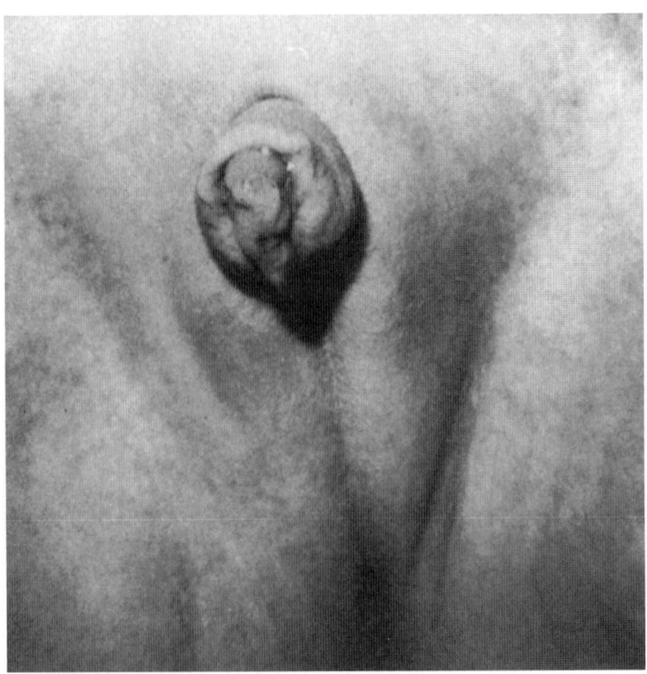

Figure 122–14 Perineum of a patient with a cloacal anomaly.

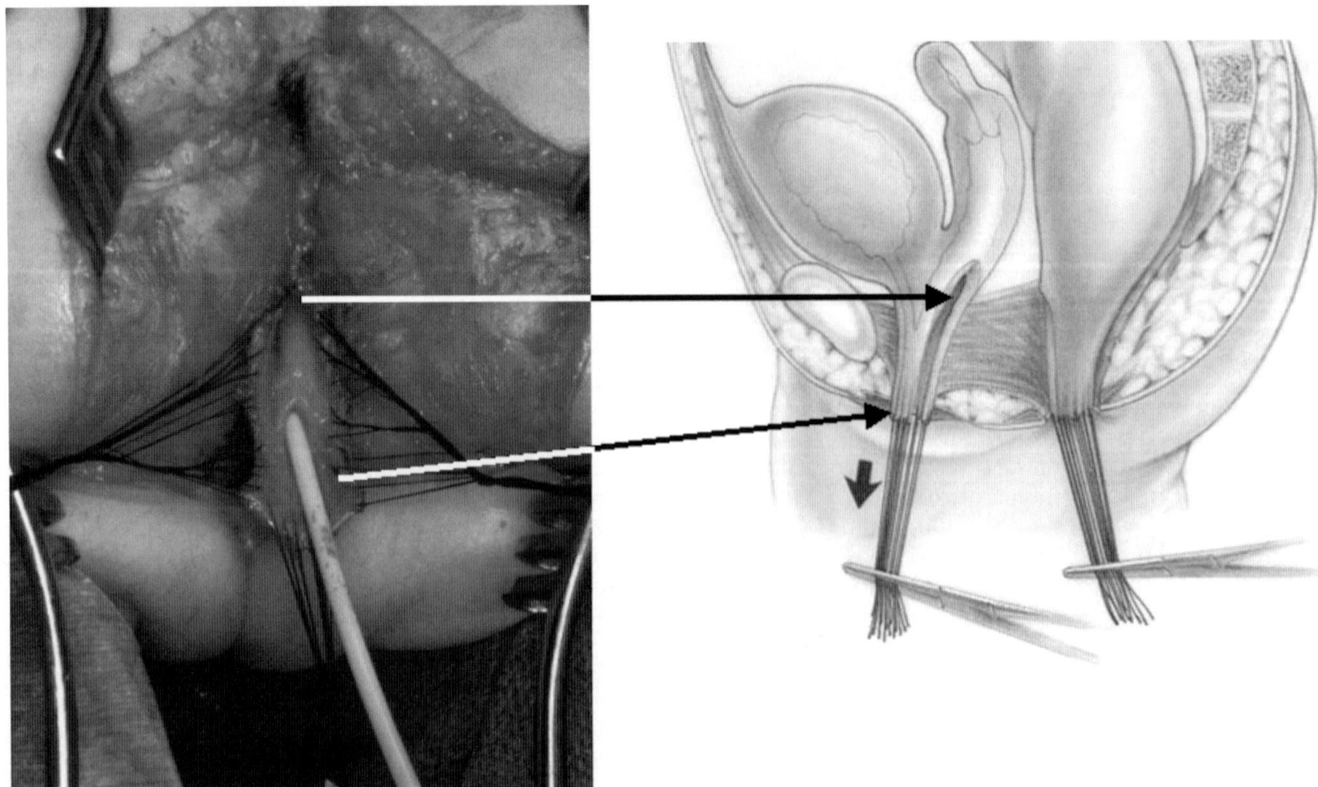

Figure 122–13 Illustration of the total urogenital advancement technique as advocated by Peña. The *upper arrow* demonstrates the level of the vagina, the *lower arrow* documents the distalmost part of the urogenital sinus. A catheter is seen in the urethra. (Courtesy of Dr. Alberto Peña.)

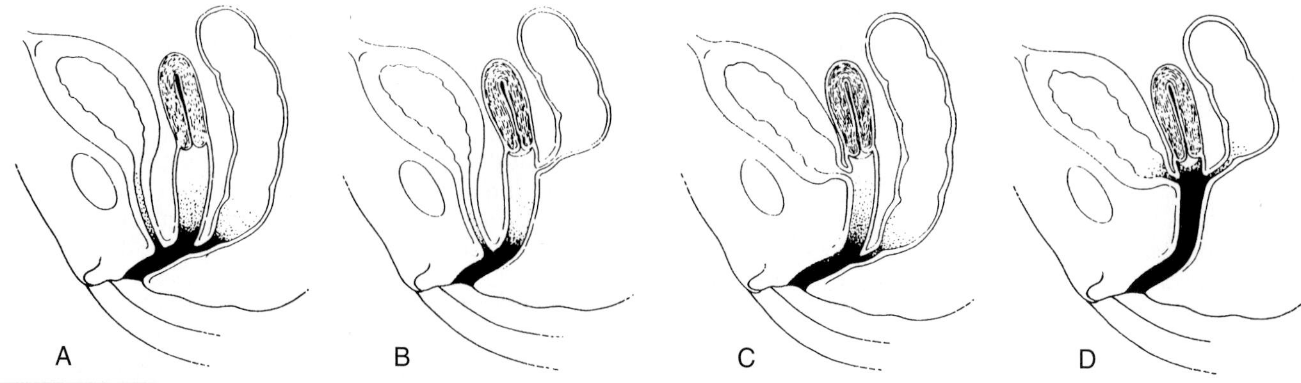

Figure 122–15 *A* to *D*, Various forms of the cloacal anomaly demonstrating proximal and distal forms.

vaginal duplication is seen most often. There may also be significant perineal obstruction in these neonates, resulting in both hydrocolpos and an obstructive uropathy (Fig. 122-16).

Diagnosis

Diagnosis of a cloacal anomaly is confirmed by a retrograde contrast study through the single perineal opening. Frequently, these studies demonstrate a confluence of both the genitourinary and gastrointestinal systems. Recently, Blask and colleagues[12] reported on the usefulness of ultrasonography in nine neonates who had either an obstructed urogenital sinus or a cloacal anomaly. On abdominopelvic ultrasonography, the bladder was often compressed by the distended vagina and difficult to visualize. Typically, the vagina was markedly distended with urine and a vaginal fluid-debris level distinguished the vagina from a distended bladder. However, all the components of the cloacal anomaly are often not identified on ultrasonography or retrograde studies. Therefore, it is only at the time of panendoscopy or an open surgical procedure that the exact anatomy can be defined. Complete definition of the patient's anatomy is the first principle of treatment.[69] Information concerning cloacal exstrophy can be found in Chapter 116.

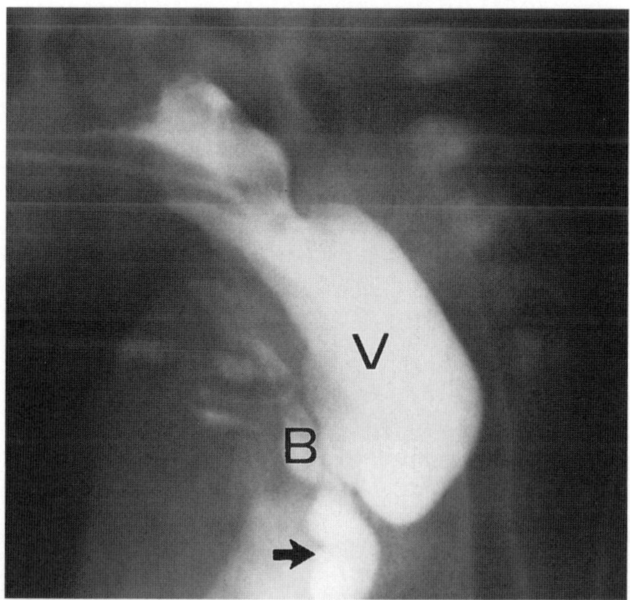

Figure 122–16 Antegrade study of the bladder (B) and vagina (V) in a patient with a cloacal anomaly. A dilated urogenital sinus (*arrow*) and relative obstruction at the perineal outlet are shown.

Treatment

Treatment of the various forms of cloacal anomalies is complex and presents one of the greatest challenges for both the pediatric surgeon and the pediatric urologist. Clearly, problems of the gastrointestinal tract must be addressed initially. If the opening of the rectum into the urogenital sinus is low, then a simple cutback anoplasty in the perineum may be possible.[54] More frequently, a supralevator opening is present, necessitating a primary colostomy followed by a later rectal pull-through procedure. If urine obstruction is not significant, specific treatment may not be necessary in the immediate perinatal period. If, however, significant urine obstruction does exist, a simple cutback of the urogenital sinus may afford adequate egress of urine to relieve the obstruction.

Definitive reconstruction of the cloacal anomaly is technically easier in later infancy and should be delayed until the patient is nearly 1 year of age.[105] Surgery should be done only when other major associated malformations will not significantly interfere with anesthesia or postoperative recovery. Reconstruction should be done in one stage, if possible. When cutback anoplasty or a pull-through procedure is done, placing the anus far enough posteriorly to allow for an adequate vaginal introitus and urethral meatus is imperative. The location of the site of the anus should be determined by electrical stimulation to define the position of the anal sphincter. Once detachment of the rectum has been accomplished, the operative approach to the anterior portion of the cloacal anomaly is very similar to that of a urogenital sinus anomaly.[53] In most high anomalies, a posterior sagittal approach is best (see Chapter 101). Peña and colleagues indicate that the length of the common urogenital channel is important in deciding what approach to take. Patients with a common channel length of more than 3.0 cm required a laparotomy, whereas those with an average length of 2.3 cm did not.[97] Patients with a long common channel have a higher incidence of associated urinary tract problems and require more complex procedures.

Results

Peña and de Vries[94,95] have reported the usefulness of simultaneous repair of the three defects of the cloacal anomaly using the posterior sagittal approach (Fig. 122-17). They described the early results of this approach in a series of 54 patients with cloaca.[94] Postoperative follow-up in 26 of the patients revealed voluntary bowel movements in 21 patients with only minor episodes of fecal soiling. Of the 19 patients with a normal sacrum, only 5 had urinary incontinence, whereas 5 of the 7 patients with an incomplete sacrum had urinary incontinence. Twenty of these patients had late postoperative vaginoscopy; 14 had an adequate introitus and vagina, and 5 had varying degrees of narrowing of the introitus. Six patients required a secondary surgical procedure for postoperative urethrovaginal fistula. A more recent review by Peña and associates involving 339 patients with cloaca included 265 children who underwent primary repair and 74 patients referred after an unsuccessful operation elsewhere.[97] Functional outcomes in patients with higher defects and a long common channel (>3.0 cm) were not as good. Overall, 54% were

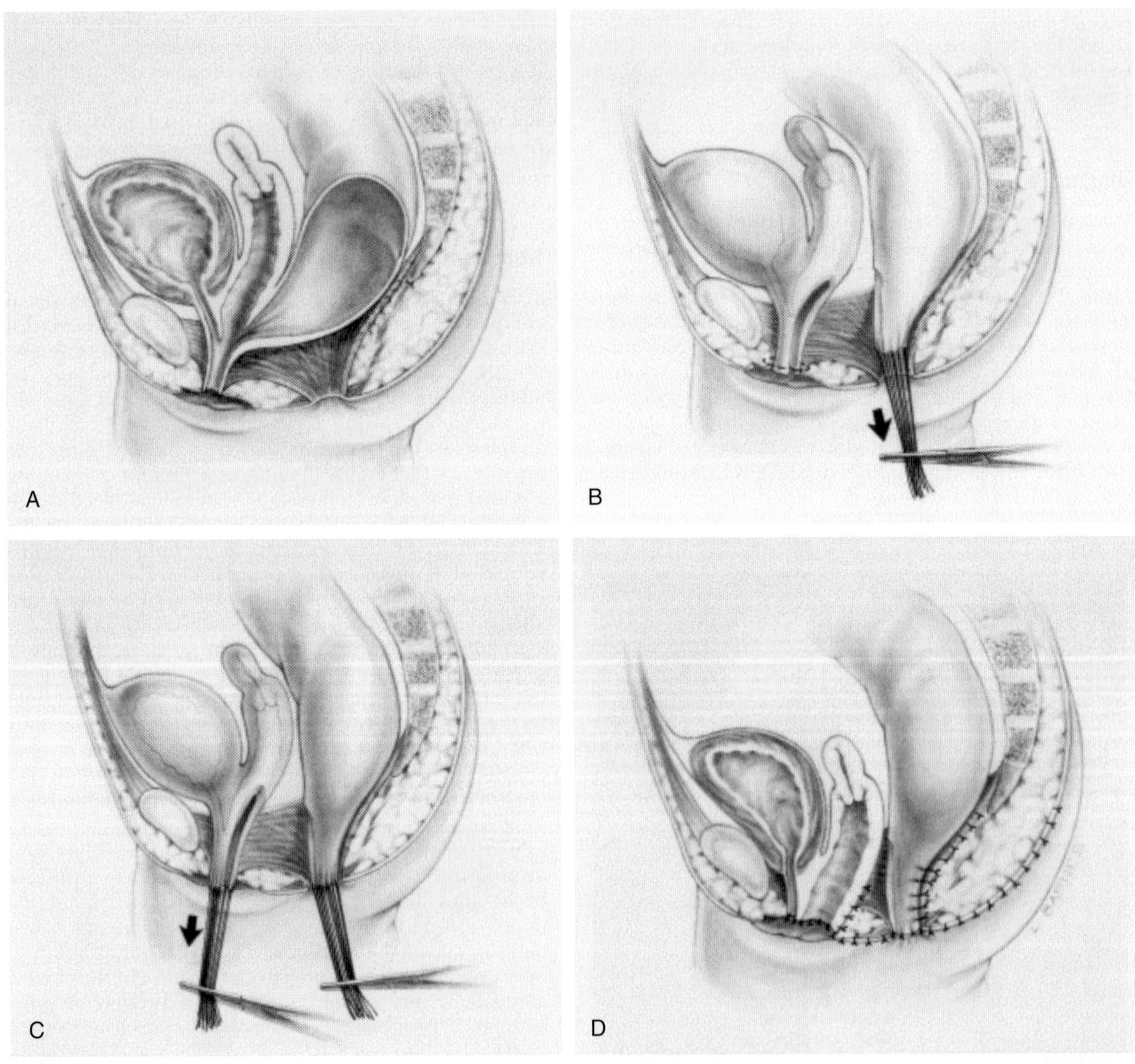

Figure 122-17 Repair of cloacal anomaly through the posterior sagittal approach recommended by Peña. *A*, Illustration depicts the single perineal opening with vesicocloacal and rectocloacal fistulas joining the cloaca. *B*, The rectal fistula is separated and the anoplasty accomplished. *C*, The urogenital sinus is mobilized. *D*, Separate urethral and vaginal orifices are created. (Courtesy of Dr. Alberto Peña.)

continent of urine, with 24% remaining dry with intermittent catheterization of their native urethra and 22% through a Mitrofanoff appendicostomy. Seventy-eight percent of those with a long common channel required intermittent urinary catheterization compared with only 28% with a common channel less than 3.0 cm. Sixty percent of all the cases have voluntary bowel motions with no soiling in 28%, and 72% soiled occasionally. Forty percent were incontinent but responded well to a bowel management program.[97]

MASSES OF THE INTROITUS

A mass presenting at the introitus between the labia is often a diagnostic dilemma. The differential diagnosis includes prolapse of the urethra, prolapsed ectopic ureterocele, prolapsed yolk-sac tumor, and rhabdomyosarcoma (sarcoma botryoides). It is important to recognize each of these clinical entities and to understand the diagnostic and treatment criteria for each.

Urethral Prolapse

Prolapse of the urethra (Fig. 122-18) occurs almost exclusively in black girls between the ages of 3 and 9 years.[135] Affected children frequently present with blood spotting on the underwear and a necrotic mass at the introitus. The tissue appears inflamed and friable and represents a prolapsed and infarcted portion of the anterior urethra.[91] Although these lesions have a close histologic resemblance to the capillary hemangioma pattern of a urethral caruncle seen in the adult, their cause remains unclear. An accurate diagnosis depends on recognition of the entity. No special diagnostic studies are needed. Medical treatment with sitz baths, topical estrogen cream, and antibiotics is successful in only one third of the cases.[139] Medically treated patients are prone to recurrence of prolapse. Operative treatment usually involves simple excision of the prolapsed segment, with suturing of the normal urethra to the meatus.[108] Complications are uncommon except for mild degrees of meatal stenosis after excision of the prolapsed segment. Valerie and colleagues[139] noted recurrence of prolapse in 1 of 20 patients treated by excision.

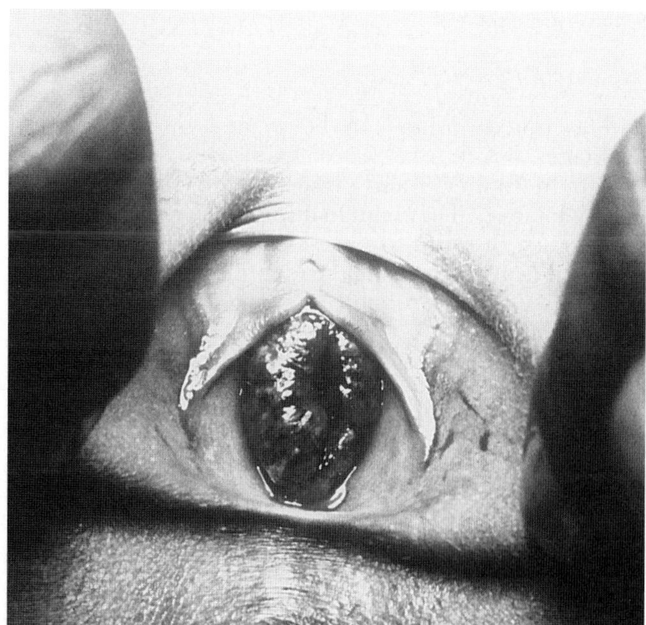

Figure 122-18 Prolapsed urethra in a 9-year-old girl. Note the congested, necrotic appearance of the prolapsed tissue.

Prolapsed Ectopic Ureterocele

Prolapsed ectopic ureteroceles can present as an intralabial introital mass (Fig. 122-19).[77] They are usually smooth and white or slightly edematous lesions that extrude from the urethral meatus. The urethral meatus can often be seen above the lesion. The diagnosis can usually be made on intravenous urography, which demonstrates a lower pole collecting system that is pushed laterally and inferiorly (i.e., drooping lily sign). The ureter is displaced away from the midline on the affected side, and the bladder has a filling defect (see Fig. 122-19).[90] Current management of these lesions in neonates consists of transurethral incision of the ectopic ureterocele. In 1993 a series from Children's Hospital of Philadelphia reported the outcome of endoscopic incision in 24 patients.[13] This method resulted in decompression in 75% of cases with upper pole function preserved in 50%. Vesicoureteral reflux occurred in 47% of the cases, requiring a secondary surgical procedure to correct the reflux in half of those patients. If renal function of the upper pole of the affected kidney is poor, traditional surgical therapy consisting of upper pole heminephrectomy with or without ureterectomy is undertaken.

Sarcoma Botryoides

Sarcoma botryoides, or rhabdomyosarcoma of the bladder or vagina, is the most common malignant condition of the lower genitourinary system presenting in infancy.[62] The tumor may be observed protruding from the introitus. It often presents as blood spotting on the undergarments with the diagnosis then achieved by vaginoscopy and biopsy.[124] The lesion, as the name denotes, appears as a lobulated, grapelike mass. The extent of the lesion is best determined by pelvic ultrasonography and CT. Rhabdomyosarcoma occurring at this primary site (vulvovaginal) is associated with an excellent outcome, with more than 90% of patients surviving with limited fertility-preserving surgery (including vaginoscopic resection) and multimodal chemotherapy.[2,10,80,124] Further details concerning management can be found in Chapter 32.

Yolk Sac Tumor

The vagina is an usual primary site for yolk sac tumors. These neoplasms can present protruding from the introitus or with vaginal spotting or bleeding.[14] These lesions

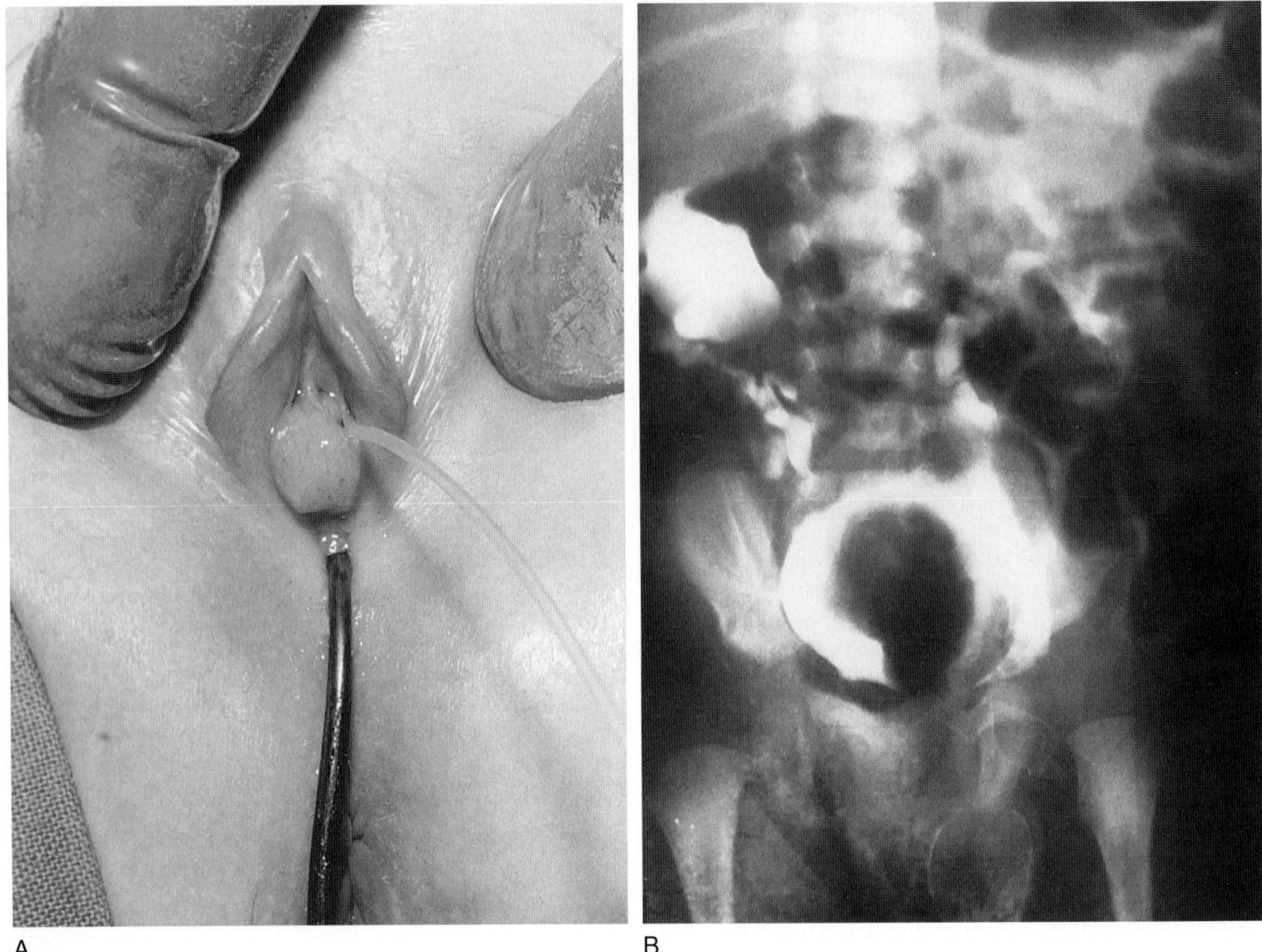

Figure 122–19 *A*, Prolapsed ureterocele in a 3-year-old girl. Note the white, healthy appearance of the cyst-like structure. *B*, Intravenous urogram in a patient with an ectopic ureterocele demonstrating a right lower pole collecting system being pushed in a lateral and inferior direction (drooping lily sign) along with a filling defect in the bladder.

are classified as endodermal sinus tumors (germ cell tumors), and affected patients frequently have an elevated serum alpha-fetoprotein level. Germ cell tumors are treated with platinum-based chemotherapy programs and often have an excellent outcome (85% survival). Fertility-sparing vaginal surgery and adjuvant chemotherapy has been successful in these cases.[4,51] In fact, cases are recorded that demonstrate resolution of the tumor with chemotherapy alone.[86] This topic is presented in depth in Chapter 34.

Miscellaneous Introital Lesions

Other lesions that can present as intralabial masses may include a low, simple imperforate hymen. This disorder can appear as a bulging intralabial mass in newborn girls (Fig. 122-20)[109] and is often simply an imperforate hymen with some degree of hydrocolpos caused by maternal estrogen stimulation. These lesions are easily recognized and as noted earlier can be treated by incision and drainage.

Paraurethral cysts also present as interlabial masses in female infants.[11] They tend to displace the urethral meatus and vaginal introitus to one side. A normal urethra and vaginal introitus can usually be identified (see Fig. 122-20). These cysts are probably embryologic remnants of Skene's glands or Gartner's duct. Most of these cysts rupture spontaneously; however, some must be incised and drained. Gartner's duct cysts are remnants of the wolffian duct and may be associated with unilateral renal dysplasia[64] and duplicated collecting system with ectopic ureter emptying into the vagina or rarely the cyst wall.[42,113] Goldstein and colleagues[42] were the first to describe the relationship of Gartner's duct cyst and ipsilateral renal agenesis in 1973. Both patients in that report had a bicornuate uterus. Patients often present with urinary tract infection and incontinence due to the ectopic ureter emptying into the vagina or Gartner's cyst wall.[23,43] Once the urinary tract abnormalities have been

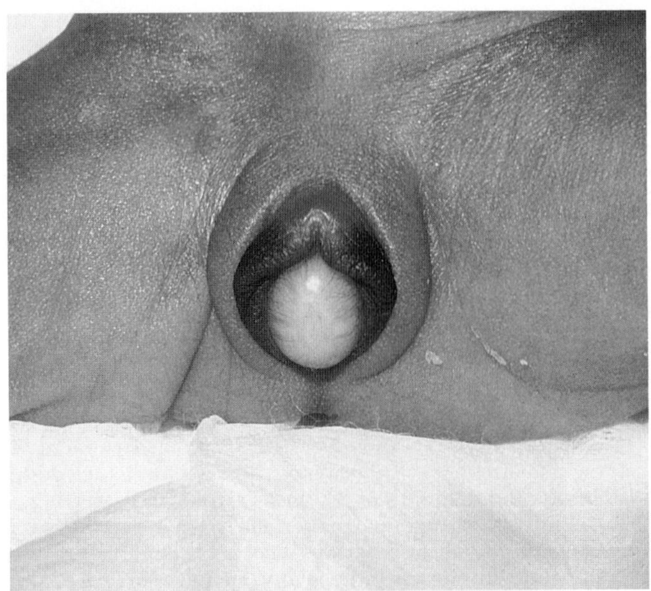

A

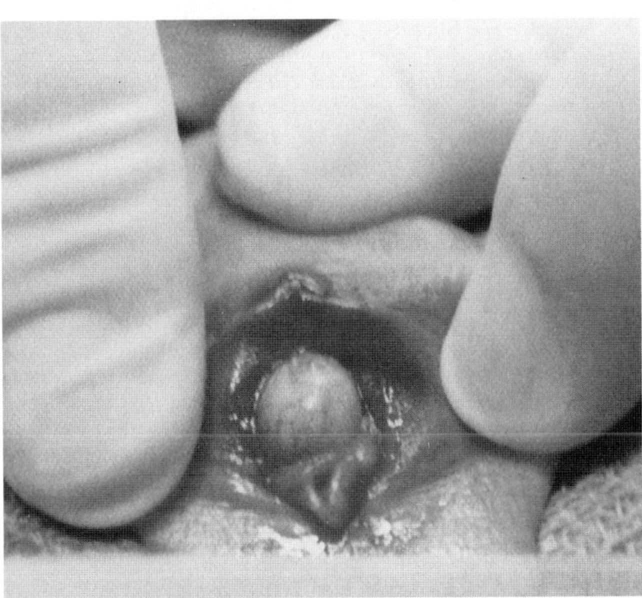

B

Figure 122-20 *A*, Bulging hymen in a newborn girl. Note the midline location. *B*, Paraurethral cyst in a 1-year-old girl. In these cases, the urethral and vaginal openings are displaced to the side, but they can be identified through careful inspection.

addressed, the Gartner's cyst can either be excised or marsupialized.

OTHER VAGINAL TUMORS

Hemangioma

Hemangiomas can occur in the vagina as they can in many other tissues. Vaginal hemangiomas are occasional extensive and coexist with hemangiomas affecting the skin and subcutaneous tissues of the perineum and perianal areas and rectal wall.[17] Conservative management is usually recommended because the natural history of these lesions suggests that spontaneous resolution will occur over a period of months to years. Ulceration and bleeding are complications that may require treatment with corticosteroids and interferon-α.[17] Failure of conservative treatment may require excision. Further information regarding hemangiomas is available in Chapter 130.

Adenocarcinoma of the Cervix and Vagina

Adenocarcinoma of the cervix and vagina is rare in children. Sexually active adolescents occasionally (<3%) may show evidence of cervical intraepithelial neoplasia and annual Papanicolaou smears have been recommended. In 1971, Herbst and associates[61] described the occurrence of clear cell adenocarcinoma of the vagina in young adolescent girls who were progeny of mothers who had received diethylstilbestrol during pregnancy. Offspring of women with this history are recommended to have a gynecologic examination by age 14 or after menarche and then annually thereafter. Vaginal clear cell adenocarcinoma has been observed in an infant who presented with hematuria.[147] In 2004, McNall and associates[84] reviewed 37 patients 18 years of age or younger with vaginal or cervical mesonephric adenocarcinoma and clear cell adenocarcinoma. The patients' ages ranged from 7 months to 18 years. The most common presenting symptoms were vaginal bleeding (89%) and/or discharge (16%). Sixty-two percent were exposed to diethylstilbestrol. Eight of 27 girls (21%) with vaginal tumors had metastases at diagnosis. Delay in diagnosis was common, owing to lack of an appropriate pelvic examination in patients younger than 13 years old. Nine patients (36%) had not reached menarche. Seventy-six percent had FIGO (early stage) stage I or II disease, whereas 24% had stage III or IV (advanced stage) disease. Twenty-two girls (58%) underwent a radical operative procedure (radical hysterectomy or pelvic exenteration): 19 had stage I or II disease and in 3 the stage was undocumented. Seven of these patients received radiation therapy. Seven girls (18%) had tumor excision alone combined with radiation therapy in 3 and chemotherapy and radiation in 1. Seven patients with advanced disease had no surgery. Three received radiation therapy, 3 had chemotherapy, and 1 had both. Overall, the 3-year disease-free survival was 71% (27/38). Ten patients died of progressive or recurrent disease. Relapse was an ominous finding. Sites of recurrence were the lungs in 6 patients, the lymph nodes or soft tissues in 2, and the brain in 1. The 3-year survival estimate for those undergoing surgical removal of tumor was 85%. Girls with tumor excision (conservative surgery) did better than those with radical surgery (100% 3-year survival vs. 78%), although there were only 7 patients with tumor excision and 4 received adjuvant therapy. The study did not evaluate tumor size. Two of the 7 patients with tumor excision had stage III disease, whereas all of those undergoing radical surgery had stage I or II disease. The only statistically significant predictors of survival were surgical resection and the presence of metastases at diagnosis. The data suggest that conservative surgical treatment with adjuvant therapy may obviate the need for radical surgery. A prospective randomized study in a larger number of patients is needed to confirm these observations. Because of the rarity of the tumor, this may be difficult to achieve. Long-term follow-up is important in these patients because late recurrences have been observed.[35,66]

REFERENCES

1. American College of Obstetrics and Gynecology: Committee Opinion: Nonsurgical diagnosis and management of vaginal agenesis. No. 274, July 2002. Int J Gynaecol Obstet 2002;79:167.
2. Andrassy RJ, Hays DM, Raney RB, et al: Conservative surgical management of vaginal and vulvar pediatric rhabdomyosarcoma: A report from the Intergroup Rhabdomyosarcoma Study III. J Pediatr Surg 1995;30:1034.
3. Ashworth MF, Morton KE, Dewhurst J, et al: Vaginoplasty using amnion. Obstet Gynecol 1986;67:443.
4. Arora M, Shrivastav RK, Jaiprakash MP: A rare germ-cell tumor site: Vaginal endodermal sinus tumor. Pediatr Surg Int 2002;18:521.
5. Baldwin JF: The formation of an artificial vagina by intestinal transplantation. Ann Surg 1904;40:398.
6. Baldwin JF: Formation of an intestinal transplantation. Am J Obstet Dis Woman Child 1907;56:636.
7. Beemer W, Hopkins MP, Morley GW: Vaginal reconstruction in gynecologic oncology. Obstet Gynecol 1988;72:911.
8. Behera M, Couchman G, Walmer D, Prfice TM: Mullerian agenesis and thrombocytopenia absent radius syndrome: A case report and review of syndromes associated with Müllerian agenesis. Obstet Gynecol Surv 2005;60:453.
9. Belloli G, Campobasso P, Musi L: Labial skin-flap vaginoplasty using tissue expanders. Pediatr Surg Int 1997;12:168.
10. Bernal KL, Fahmy L, Remmenga S, et al: Embryonal rhabdomyosarcoma (sarcoma botryoides) of the cervix presenting as a cervical polyp treated with fertility-sparing surgery and adjuvant chemotherapy. Gynecol Oncol 2004;95:243.
11. Blaivas JG, Pais VM, Retik AB: Paraurethral cysts in female neonate. Urology 1976;7:504.
12. Blask AR, Sanders RC, Gearhart JP: Obstructed ureterovaginal anomalies: Demonstration with sonography. Radiology 1991;179:79.
13. Blyth B, Passerini-Glazel G, Camuffo C, et al: Endoscopic incision of ureteroceles: Intravesical versus ectopic. J Urol 1993;149:556.
14. Bochner BH, De Filippo RE, Hardy BE: Endodermal sinus tumor of the vagina. J Urol 2000;163:1293.
15. Bowman J, Scott R: Transverse vaginal septum. Obstet Gynecol 1954;3:441.
16. Borruto F: Mayer-Rokitansky-Küster syndrome: Vecchietti's personal series. Clin Exp Obstet Gyencol 1992;19:273.
17. Bouchard S, Yazbeck S, Lallier M: Perineal hemangioma, anorectal malformation, and genital anomaly: A new association? J Pediatr Surg 1999;34:1133.
18. Bryan AL, Nigro JA, Counseller VS: One hundred cases of congenital absence of the vagina. Surg Gynecol Obstet 1949;88:79.
19. Burbige KA, Hensle TW: Uterus didelphys and vaginal duplication with unilateral obstruction presenting as a newborn abdominal mass. J Urol 1984;132:1195.
20. Burger RA, Riedmiller H, Knapstein PG, et al: Ileocecal vaginal construction. Am J Obstet Gynecol 1989;161:162.
21. Buss JG, Lee RA: McIndoe procedure for vaginal agenesis: Results and complications. Mayo Clin Proc 1989;64:758.
22. Counseller VS, Flor FS: Congenital absence of the vagina: Further results of treatment and a new technique. Surg Clin North Am 1957;37:1107.
23. Currarino G: Single vaginal ectopic ureter and Gartner's duct cyst with ipsilateral renal hypoplasia and dysplasia (or agenesis). J Urol 1982;123:988.
24. Davydov SN, Zhvitiashvili OD: Formation of vagina (colpopoiesis) from peritoneum of Douglas pouch. Acta Chir Plast 1974;16:35.
25. de Souza AZ, Maluf M, Perin PM, et al: Surgical treatment of congenital uterovaginal agenesis: Mayer-Rokitansky-Küster-Hauser syndrome. Int Surg 1987;72:45.
26. Dean GE, Hensle TW: Intestinal vaginoplasty. Curr Surg Tech Urol 1994;7:1.
27. Del Rossi C, Attanasio A, Del Curto S, et al: Treatment of vaginal atresia at a missionary hospital in Bangladesh: Results and follow up of 20 cases. J Urol 2003;170:864.
28. Dewhurst CJ: Congenital malformations of the genital tract in childhood. Br J Obstet Gynaecol 1968;75:377.
29. Donahoe PK, Gustafson ML: Early one stage surgical reconstruction of the extremely high vagina in patients with congenital adrenal hyperplasia. J Pediatr Surg 1994;29:352.
30. Duncan PA, Shapiro LR, Stanzel JJ, et al: The MURCS association: Müllerian duct aplasia, renal aplasia, and cervicothoracic somite dysplasia. J Pediatr 1979;95:399.
31. Edmonds DK: Congenital malformations of the genital tract. Obstet Gynecol Clin North Am 2000;27:49.
32. Edmonds DK: Congenital malformations of the genital tract and their management. Best Pract Res Clin Obstet Gynaecol 2003;17:19.
33. Fall FH: A simple method for making an artificial vagina. Am J Obstet Gynecol 1940;40:906.
34. Fedele L, Bianchi S, Zanconato G, Raffaelli R: Laparoscopic creation of a neovagina in patients with Rokitansky syndrome: Analysis of 52 cases. Fertil Steril 2000;74:384.
35. Fishman DA, Williams S, Small W Jr, et al: Late recurrences of vaginal clear cell adenocarcinoma. Gynecol Oncol 1996; 62:128.
36. Folche M, Pigem I, Konje JC: Müllerian agenesis: Etiology, diagnosis, and management. Obstet Gynecol Surv 2000; 55:644.
37. Fore SR, Hammond CB, Parkes RT, Anderson EE: Urologic and genital anomalies in patients with congenital absence of the vagina. Obstet Gynecol 1975;46:410.
38. Frank RT: The formation of an artificial vagina without operation. Am J Obstet Gynecol 1938;35:1053.
39. Freundt I, Toolenaar TA, Huikeshoven FJ, et al: A modified technique to create a neovagina with an isolated segment of sigmoid colon. Surg Gynecol Obstet 1992;174:11.
40. Giraldo F, Solano MJ, Mora M, et al: The Malaga flap for vaginoplasty in the Mayer-Rokitansky-Küster-Hauser syndrome: Experience and early term results. Plast Reconstr Surg 1996;98:305.
41. Goldfarb JM, Austin C, Peskin B, et al: Fifteen years experience with an in-vitro fertilization surrogate gestational pregnancy programme. Hum Reprod 2000;15:1075.
42. Goldstein AI, Ackerman ES, Woodruff R, Poyas J: Vaginal and cervical communication with mesonephric duct remnants: Relationship to unilateral renal agenesis. Am J Obstet Gynecol 1973;116:101.
43. Gotoh T, Koyanagi T: Clinicopathological and embryological considerations of single ectopic ureters opening into Gartner's duct cyst: A unique subtype of single vaginal ectopia. J Urol 1987;137:969.
44. Gough MH: Anorectal agenesis with persistence of cloaca. Proc R Soc Med 1959;52:886.

45. Graziano K, Teitelbaum DH, Hirschl RB, Coran AG: Vaginal reconstruction for ambiguous genitalia and congenital absence of the vagina: A 27-year experience. J Pediatr Surg 2002;37:955.
46. Griesinger G, Dafopoulos K, Schultze-Mosgau A, et al: Mayer-Rokitansky-Küster-Hauser syndrome associated with thrombocytopenia–absent radius syndrome. Fertil Steril 2005;83:452.
47. Griffin JE, Edwards C, Madden JD, et al: Congenital absence of the vagina. Ann Intern Med 1976;85:224.
48. Grio R, Ambroggio GP, D'Addato F, et al: A new method of neovagina in Rokitansky's syndrome: A review of the literature and description of a series. Min Ginecol 2002;54:161.
49. Gunderson CH, Greenspan RH, Glaser GH, Lubs HA: The Klippel-Feil syndrome: Genetic and clinical reevaluation of cervical fusion. Medicine (Baltimore) 1967;46:491.
50. Hallberg H, Hollstrom H: Vaginal reconstruction with skin grafts and vacuum-assisted closure. Scand J Plast Reconstruct Surg Hand Surg 2003;37:97.
51. Handel LN, Scott SM, Giller RH: New perspectives on therapy for vaginal endodermal sinus tumors. J Urol 2002; 168:687.
52. Hauser GA, Keller M, Koller T, Wenner R: Das Rokitansky-Küster syndrome: Uterus bipartitus solidus rudimentarius cum Vagina solida. Gynaecologia 1961;151:11.
53. Hendren WH: Surgical management of urogenital sinus abnormalities. J Pediatr Surg 1977;12:339.
54. Hendren WH: Construction of female urethra from vaginal wall and a perineal flap. J Urol 1980;123:657.
55. Hendren WH: Urogenital sinus and anorectal malformation: Experience with 22 cases. J Pediatr Surg 1980;15:628.
56. Hendren WH, Crawford JD: Adrenogenital syndrome: The anatomy of the anomaly and its repair. Some new concepts. J Pediatr Surg 1969;4:49.
57. Hendren WH, Donahoe PK: Correction of congenital abnormalities of the vagina and perineum. J Pediatr Surg 1980;15:751.
58. Hendren WH, Atala A: Use of bowel for vaginal reconstruction. J Urol 1994;152:752.
59. Hensle TW, Dean GE: Vaginal replacement in children. J Urol 1992;148:677.
60. Hensle TW, Reiley EA: Vaginal replacement in children and young adults. J Urol 1998;159:1035.
61. Herbst AL, Ulfelder H, Poskanzer DC: Adenocarcinoma of the vagina. Association of maternal stilbestrol therapy with tumor appearance in young women. N Engl J Med 1971; 284:878.
62. Hilgers RD, Malkasian GD Jr, Soule EH: Embryonal rhabdomyosarcoma (botryoid type) of the vagina. Am J Obstet Gynecol 1970;107:484.
63. Hiroi H, Yasugi T, Matsumoto K, et al: Mucinous adenocarcinoma arising in a neovagina using the sigmoid colon 30 years after operation: A case report. J Surg Oncol 2001; 77:61.
64. Holmes M, Upadhyay V, Pease P: Gartner's duct cyst with unilateral renal dysplasia presenting as an introital mass in a new born. Pediatr Surg Int 1999;15:277.
65. Johnson RJ, Palken M, Derrick W, Bill AH: The embryology of high anorectal and associated genitourinary anomalies in the female. Surg Gynecol Obstet 1972;135:759.
66. Jones WB, Tan LK, Lewis JL Jr: Late recurrence of clear cell adenocarcinoma of the vagina and cervix: A report of three cases. Gynecol Oncol 1993;51:266.
67. Joseph VT: Pudendal-thigh flap vaginoplasty in the reconstruction of genital anomalies. J Pediatr Surg 1997; 32:62.
68. Jost A: Embryonic sexual differentiation. In Jones HW Jr, Scott WW (eds): Hermaphroditism, Genital Anomalies and Related Endocrine Disorders, 2nd ed. Baltimore, Williams & Wilkins, 1971.
69. Kay R, Tank ES: Principles of management of the persistent cloaca in the female newborn. J Urol 1977;117:102.
70. Kaya H, Sezik M, Ozkaya O, Kose SA: Mayer-Rokitansky-Küster-Hauser syndrome associated with unilateral gonadal agenesis: A case report. J Reprod Med 2003;48:902.
71. Keser A, Bozkurt N, Taner OF, Sensoz O: Treatment of vaginal agenesis with modified Abbe-McIndoe technique: Long-term follow up in 22 patients. Eur J Obstet Gynecol Reprod Biol 2005;121:110.
72. Koff AK: Development of the vagina in the human fetus. Contemp Embryol 1933;24:61.
73. Krishnan A, Baez L, Kirsh A: Single ectopic ureter inserting into a duplicated imperforate hemivagina: A rare cause of fetal abdominal mass. Urology 2003;62:144.
74. Küster H: Uterus bipartitus solidus rudimentarius cum Vagina solida. Z Geburtshife Perinatol 1910;67:692.
75. Laufer MR: Congenital absence of the vagina: In search of the perfect solution. When, and by what technique, should a vagina be created? Curr Opin Obstet Gynecol 2002; 14:441.
76. Lin WC, Chang CY, Shen YY, Tsai HD: Use of autologous buccal mucosa for vaginoplasty: A study of eight cases. Hum Reprod 2003;18:604.
77. Mandell J, Colodny AH, Lebowitz R, et al: Ureteroceles in infants and children. J Urol 1980;123:921.
78. Marcos R, Perez-Brayfield EA, Smith EA, et al: Vaginal reconstruction using a vertical rectus abdominis myocutaneous flap in a child: A case report. J Pediatr Surg 2001; 36:1070.
79. Marshall FF, Jeffs RD, Sarafyan WK: Urogenital sinus abnormalities in the female patient. J Urol 1979;122:568.
80. Martelli H, Oberlin O, et al: Conservative treatment for girls with nonmetastatic rhabdomyosarcoma of the genital tract: A report from the study committee of the International Society of Pediatric Oncology. Eur J Cancer 1999;34:1050.
81. Mayer CAJ: Uber Verdoppelungen des Uterus und ihre Arten, nebst Bemerkungen uber Hasenscharte und Wolfsrachen. J Chir Auger 1829;13:525.
82. McIndoe AH: Treatment of congenital absence and obliterative conditions of vagina. Br J Plast Surg 1950; 2:254.
83. McKusick VA, Bauer RL, Koop CE, Scott RB: Hydrometrocolpos as a simply inherited malformation. JAMA 1964;189:813.
84. McNall RY, Nowicki PD, Miller B, et al: Adenocarcinoma of the cervix and vagina in pediatric patients. Pediatr Blood Cancer 2004;43:289.
85. Mirza M, Moriquand P: Ectopic ureter entering a uterovaginal duplication. Br J Urol 1993;72:250.
86. Neels NJJ, Tissing WJE, Pieters R, et al: Treatment of an infant with a vaginal yolk sac tumor and distant metastases with chemotherapy only. Pediatr Blood Cancer 2004; 43:296.
87. Nisolle M, Donnez J: Vaginoplasty using amnionic membranes in cases of agenesis of the vagina. J Gynecol Surg 1992;8:25.
88. Noguchi S, Nakatsuka M, Sugiyama Y, et al: Use of artificial dermis and recombinant basic fibroblast growth factor for creating a neovagina in a patient with Mayer-Rokitansky-Küster-Hauser syndrome. Hum Reprod 2004;19:1629.
89. Novak F, Kos L, Plesko F: The advantages of the artificial vagina derived from sigmoid colon. Acta Obstet Gynecol Scand 1978;57:95.
90. Nussbaum AR, Lebowitz RL: Interlabial masses in little girls. Am J Res 1983;141:65.

91. Owens SB, Morse WH: Prolapse of the female urethra in children. J Urol 1968;100:171.
92. Ozgenel GY, Ozcan M: Neovaginal reconstruction with buccal mucosal grafts. Plast Reconstr Surg 2003;111:2250.
93. Passerini-Glazel G: A new one-stage procedure for clitorovaginoplasty in severely masculinized female pseudohermaphrodites. J Urol 1989;142:565.
94. Peña A: The surgical management of persistent cloaca: Results in 54 patients treated with a posterior sagittal approach. J Pediatr Surg 1989;24:590.
95. Peña A: Atlas of Surgical Management of Anorectal Malformation. New York, Springer-Verlag, 1990.
96. Peña A, deVries PA: Posterior sagittal anorectoplasty: Important technical considerations and new applications. J Pediatr Surg 1982;17:796.
97. Peña A, Levitt MA, Hong A, Midulla P: Surgical management of cloacal malformations: A review of 339 patients. J Pediatr Surg 2004;39:470.
98. Petrozza JC, Gary MR, Davis AJ, Reindollar RH: Congenital absence of the uterus and vagina is not commonly transmitted as a dominant genetic trait: Outcomes of surrogate pregnancies. Fertil Steril 1997;67:387.
99. Pittock ST, Babovic-Vuksanovic D, Lteif A: Mayer-Rokitansky-Küster-Hauser anomaly and its associated malformations. Am J Med Genet A 2005;135A:314.
100. Plevraki E, Kita M, Goulis DG, et al: Bilateral ovarian agenesis and the presence of the testis-specific protein 1-Y-linked gene: Two new features of Mayer-Rokitansky-Küster-Hauser syndrome. Fertil Steril 2004;81:689.
101. Poland ML, Evans TN: Psychologic aspects of vaginal agenesis. J Reprod Med 1985;30:340.
102. Pratt JH: Vaginal atresia corrected by the use of small and large bowel. Clin Obstet Gynecol 1972;96:639.
103. Purushothaman V: Horse shoe flap vaginoplasty—a new technique of vaginal reconstruction with labia minora flaps for primary vaginal agenesis. Br J Plast Surg 2005; Epub July 22.
104. Radhakrishnan J: Colon interposition vaginoplasty: A modification of the Wagner-Baldwin technique. J Pediatr Surg 1987;22:1175.
105. Raffensperger JG, Ramenofsky ML: The management of a cloaca. J Pediatr Surg 1973;8:647.
106. Rajimwale A, Furness PD III, Brant WO, Koyle MA: Vaginal reconstruction using sigmoid colon in children and young adults. BJU Int 2004;94:1143.
107. Rangaswamy M, Macado NO, Kaur S, Machado L: Laparoscopic vaginoplasty using a sliding peritoneal flap for correction of complete vaginal agenesis. Eur J Obstet Gynecol Reprod Biol 2001;98:244.
108. Redman JF: Conservative management of urethral prolapse in female children. Urology 1982;19:509.
109. Reed MH, Griscom WT: Hydrometrocolpos in infancy. Am J Res 1973;118:1.
110. Reinhold C, Hricak H, Forstner R, et al: Primary amenorrhea evaluation with MR imaging. Radiology 1997;203:383.
111. Rock JA, Reeves LA, Retto H, et al: Success following vaginal creation for müllerian agenesis. Fertil Steril 1983;39:809.
112. Rokitansky K: Uber die sogenannten Verdoppelungen des Uterus. Med Jb Ost Staat 1938;26:39.
113. Rosenfeld DL, Barone JG, Lis E, et al: A "flipped" kidney in utero in an infant with a double collecting system and a Gartner's duct cyst with a vaginal ectopic ureter. Pediatr Radiol 1995;25:466.
114. Ross GT, Vande Weile RL: The ovaries. In Williams RH (ed): Textbook of Endocrinology, 5th ed. Philadelphia, WB Saunders, 1974.
115. Rothman D: The use of peritoneum in the construction of a vagina. Obstet Gynecol 1972;40:835.
116. Ruge E: Ersatz der Vagina durch die flexur mittels Laparotomie. Dtsch Med Wochenschr 1914;40:120.
117. Schaap C, de Die-Smulders CE, Kuijten RH, Fryns JP: McKusick-Kaufman syndrome: The diagnostic challenge of abdominal distension in the neonatal period. Eur J Pediatr 1992;151:583.
118. Schätz T, Huber J, Wenzl R: Creation of a neovagina according to Wharton-Sheares-George in patients with Mayer-Rokitansky-Küster-Hauser syndrome. Fertil Steril 2005;83:437.
119. Sheares BH: Congenital atresia of the vagina—a technique for tunneling the space between the bladder and rectum and construction of a new vagina by a modified Wharton technique. J Obstet Gynecol Br Emp 1960;67:24.
120. Selvaggi G, Monstrey S, Depypere H, et al: Creation of a neovagina with use of a pudendal thigh fasciocutaneous flap and restoration of uterovaginal continuity. Fertil Steril 2003;80:607.
121. Shreeprasad P, Kalrao V, Patankar SS: Mayer-Rokitansky syndrome and anorectal malformation. Indian J Pediatr 2004;71:1133.
122. Slavotinek AM, Biesecker LG: Phenotypic overlap of McKusick-Kaufman syndrome with Bardet-Biedl syndrome: A literature review. Am J Med Genet 2000;95:208.
123. Slavotinek AM, Dutra A, Kpodzo D, et al: A female with complete lack of mullerian fusion, postaxial polydactyly and tetralogy of Fallot: Genetic heterogeneity of McKusick-Kaufman syndrome or a unique syndrome? Am J Med Genet 2004;129:69.
124. Solomon LA, Zurawin RK, Edwards CL: Vaginoscopic resection for rhabdomyosarcoma of the vagina: A case report and review of the literature. Pediatr Adolesc Gynecol 2003; 16:139.
125. Soong YK, Chang FH, Lai YM, et al: Results of modified laparoscopically assisted neovaginoplasty in 18 patients with congenital absence of vagina. Hum Reprod 1996;11:200.
126. Stenchever MA, et al: Comprehensive Gynecology, 4th ed. St. Louis, CV Mosby, 2001.
127. Stephens FD, Smith ED: Anorectal Malformations in Children. Chicago, Year Book Medical, 1971.
128. Stone DL, Slavotinek A, Bouffard GG, et al: Mutation of a gene encoding a putative chaperonin causes McKusick-Kaufman syndrome. Nat Genet 2000;25:79.
129. Strubbe EH, Thijn CJ, Willemsen WN, Lappohn R: Evaluation of radiographic abnormalities of the hand in patients with Mayer-Rokitansky-Küster-Hauser syndrome. Skel Radiol 1987;16:227.
130. Strubbe EH, Cremers CW, Dikkers FG, Willemsen WN: Mayer-Rokitansky-Küster-Hauser syndrome. Am J Otol 1994;15:431.
131. Syed HA, Malone PS, Hitchcock RJ: Diversion colitis in children with colovaginoplasty. BJU Int 2001;87:857.
132. Templeman C, Hertweck P, Levine R, Reich H: A new technique for the creation of a neovagina. J Pediatr Adolesc Gynecol 2000;13:99.
133. Therrell BL, et al: Results of screening 1.9 million Texas newborns for 21-hydroxylase deficient congenital adrenal hyperplasia. Pediatrics 1998;101:583.
134. Tompkins P: Imperforate hymen and hematocolpos. JAMA 1939;113:913.
135. Thoury A, Detchev R, Darai E: Sigmoid neovagina by combined laparoscopic-perineal route for Rokitansky syndrome. Gynecol Obstet Fertil 2002;30:938.
136. Trotman M, Brewster E: Prolapse of the urethral mucosa in prepubertal West Indian girls. Br J Urol 1993;73:503.
137. Turner-Warwick R, Kirby RS: The construction and reconstruction of the vagina with the colocecum. Surg Gynecol Obstet 1990;170:132.

138. Urbanowicz W, Starzyk J, Sulislawski J: Laparoscopic vaginal reconstruction using a sigmoid colon segment: A preliminary report. J Urol 2004;171:2632.
139. Valerie E, Gilchrist HF, Frischer J, et al: Diagnosis and treatment of urethral prolapse in children. Urology 1999; 54:1082.
140. Vecchietti G: Neovagina nella syndrome di Rokitansky-Küster-Hauser. Attuat Ostet Ginecol 1965;11:131.
141. Wee JT, Joseph VT: A new technique of vaginal reconstruction using neurovascular pudendal-thigh flaps: A preliminary report. Plast Reconstr Surg 1989;83:701.
142. Wesley JR, Coran AG: Intestinal vaginoplasty for congenital absence of the vagina. J Pediatr Surg 1992; 27:885.
143. Wharton LR: A simple method of constructing a vagina: Report of four cases. Ann Surg 1938;107:842.
144. Williams EA: Congenital absence of the vagina—a simple operation for its relief. J Obstet Gynaecol Br Emp 1964; 71:511.
145. Winderl LM, Silverman RK: Prenatal diagnosis of congenital imperforate hymen. Obstet Gynecol 1995;85:857.
146. Witschi F: Development and differentiation of the uterus. In Mack HC (ed): Prenatal Life. Detroit, Wayne State University Press, 1970.
147. Yavuz H, Arslan A, Avsaz AF: Vaginal clear cell adenocarcinoma in an infant. Pediatr Hematol Oncol 1996;13:577.
148. Yii NW, Niranjan NS: Lotus petal flaps in vulvo-vaginal reconstruction. Br J Plast Surg 1996;49:547.

Part IX

Special Areas of Pediatric Surgery

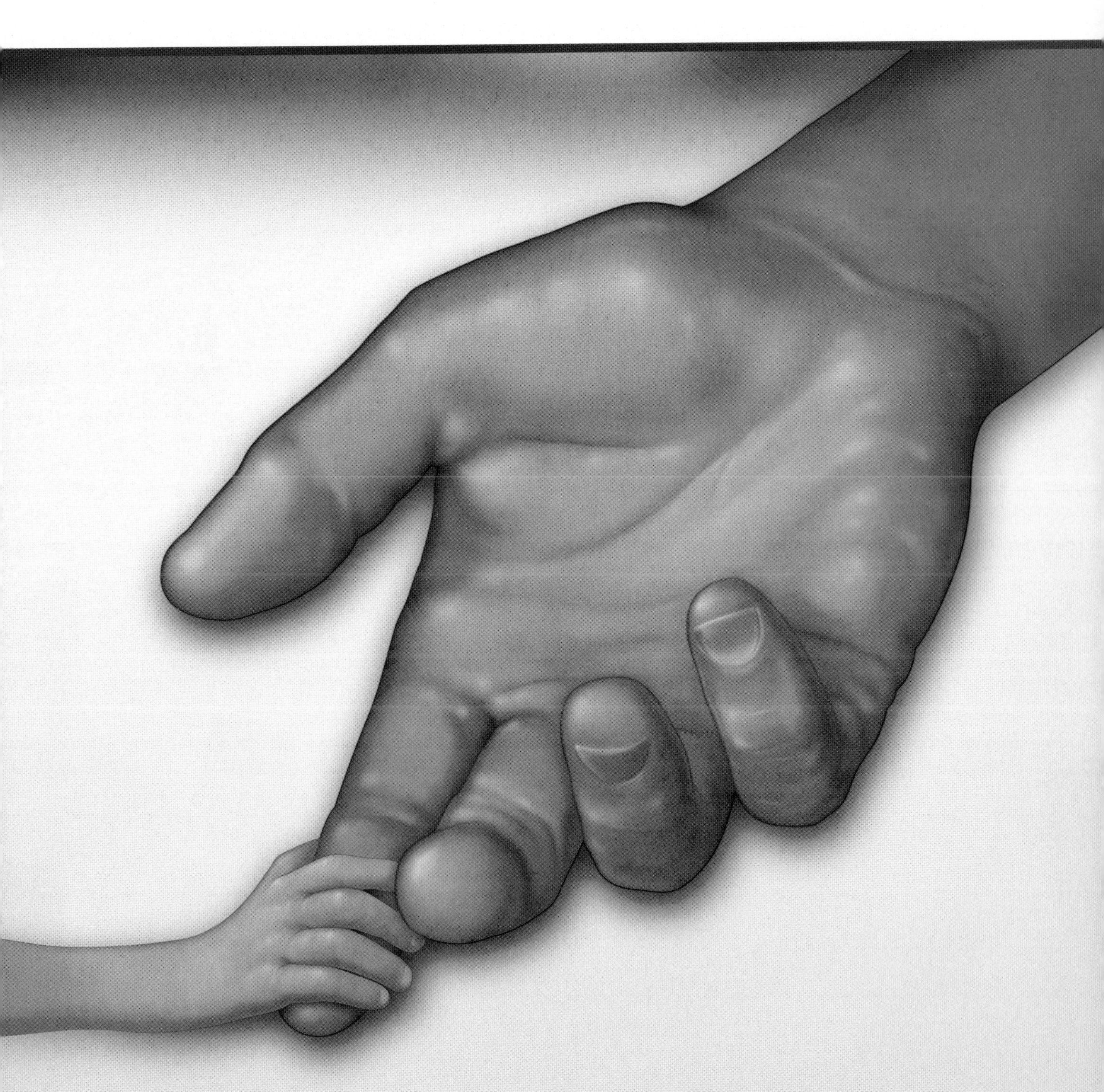

Chapter 123

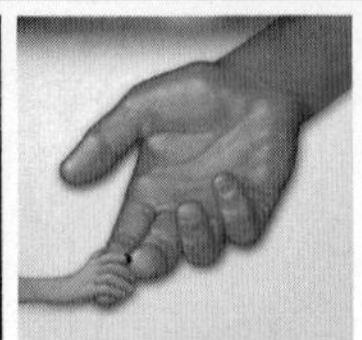

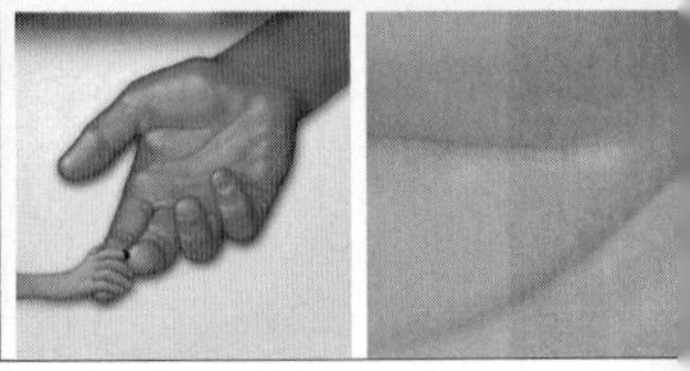

Congenital Heart Disease and Anomalies of the Great Vessels

Eric Devaney, Richard Ohye, and Edward L. Bove

PATENT DUCTUS ARTERIOSUS

The ductus arteriosus is a normal fetal structure that communicates between the pulmonary trunk or proximal left pulmonary artery (PA) and the proximal descending thoracic aorta (Fig. 123-1). During fetal development, this vessel provides a pathway for blood leaving the right ventricle (RV) to bypass the high resistance pulmonary vascular bed and traverse the systemic circulation instead. Histologically, the media of the aorta and PA contains circumferentially arranged elastic fibers, whereas the media of the ductus is composed mostly of smooth muscle cells. Normally after birth, the rise in oxygen tension that accompanies ventilation of the lungs signals closure of the ductus. In a full-term infant, closure of the ductus is usually complete by 12 to 24 hours. Closure of the ductus creates a fibrous cord called the ligamentum arteriosum. Failure of closure of the ductus leads to the condition known as patent ductus arteriosus (PDA). The incidence of isolated PDA is approximately 1 in 1200 live births and accounts for about 7% of all congenital heart defects.[39] The incidence is higher in preterm infants (greater than 20%).[68] This defect may occur in isolation or in association with a number of other anomalies. In some heart defects in which there is inadequate pulmonary blood flow (e.g., pulmonary atresia) or inadequate systemic blood flow (e.g., severe coarctation of the aorta) persistent patency of the ductus is desirable. The discovery of prostaglandins to maintain ductal patency has played a significant role in improving the survival of such patients.[28]

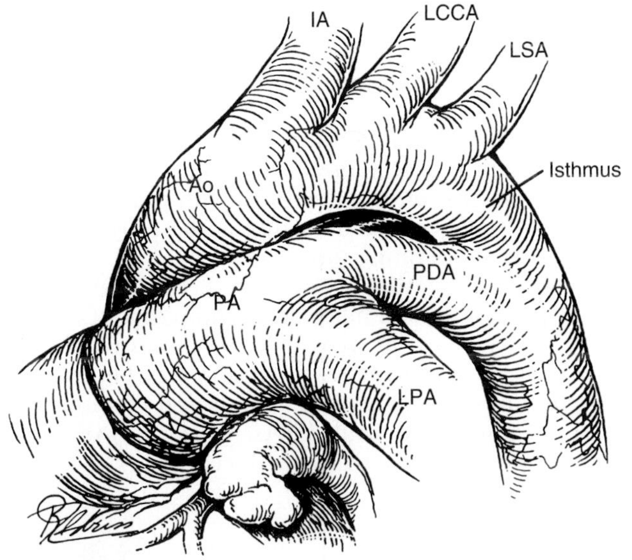

Figure 123-1 Anatomy of patent ductus arteriosus (PDA) as seen from a left thoracotomy. The ductus extends from the main pulmonary artery (PA) and enters the proximal descending thoracic aorta distal to the left subclavian artery (LSA). Ao, aorta; IA, innominate artery; LCCA, left common carotid artery; LPA, left pulmonary artery. (From Hillman ND, Mavroudis C, Backer CL: Patent ductus arteriosus. In Mavroudis C, Backer CL [eds]: Pediatric Cardiac Surgery, 3rd ed. Philadelphia, Mosby, 2003.)

Natural History and Diagnosis

The pathophysiology of PDA involves shunting of blood across the ductus. The shunt volume is determined by the size of the ductus as well as the ratio of pulmonary to systemic vascular resistance. Pulmonary vascular resistance drops dramatically at birth and continues to decrease over the first weeks of life. This leads to left-to-right flow across the ductus. Excessive pulmonary blood flow typically leads to congestive heart failure, and, in extreme cases, hypotension and systemic malperfusion may also occur. For patients with a large PDA who survive infancy there is a risk of developing pulmonary vascular obstructive disease. In these cases, Eisenmenger's physiology may develop when pulmonary vascular resistance exceeds systemic vascular resistance, leading to a reversal of shunting across the ductus (from left-to-right to right-to-left), causing cyanosis and, eventually, RV failure. Some patients with a small PDA may remain asymptomatic until adulthood. Endocarditis (and endarteritis) have also been reported as long-term complications of PDA.[16]

The clinical manifestations of PDA are determined by the shunt volume and the presence of associated cardiac defects. Left-to-right shunt flow leads to volume overload of the left side of the heart. Signs of congestive heart failure in infants commonly include tachypnea, tachycardia, and poor feeding. Older children may present with recurrent respiratory infections, fatigue, and failure to thrive. Physical findings include a widened pulse pressure and an active precordium. Auscultation reveals a continuous "machinery" murmur heard best along the left upper sternal border. Radiographic findings include increased pulmonary vascular markings and left-sided heart enlargement generally in proportion to the degree of shunting. Electrocardiography may demonstrate left ventricular (LV) hypertrophy and left atrial (LA) enlargement. Echocardiography is currently the diagnostic method of choice and can additionally rule out the presence of associated defects. Cardiac catheterization is reserved for two principal indications. First, in older patients with suspected pulmonary hypertension, it can be used to evaluate for pulmonary vascular obstructive disease. Second, transcatheter techniques have been developed to occlude the ductus in selected cases.

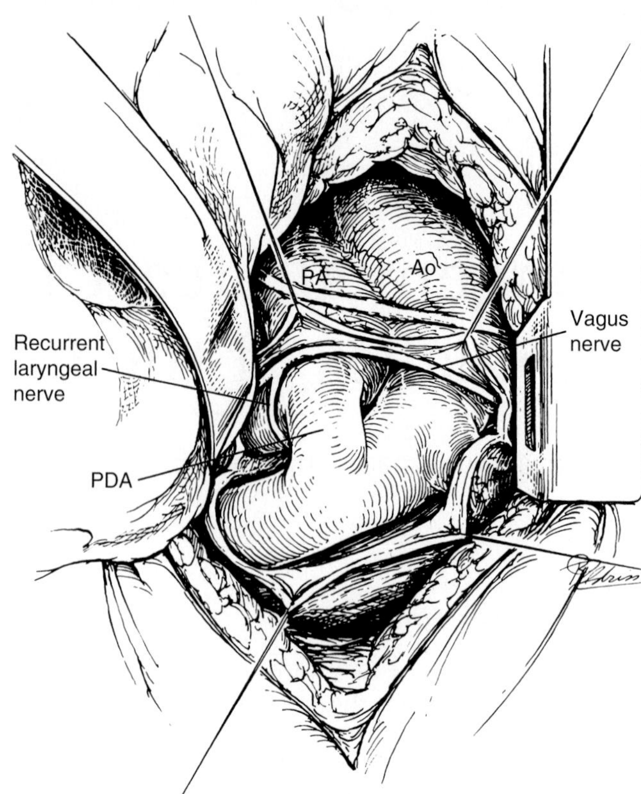

Figure 123–2 Exposure of patent ductus arteriosus (PDA) by left thoracotomy. The mediastinal pleura has been divided and reflected with preservation of the vagus and recurrent laryngeal nerves. Ao, aorta; PA, pulmonary artery. (From Hillman ND, Mavroudis C, Backer CL: Patent ductus arteriosus. In Mavroudis C, Backer CL [eds]: Pediatric Cardiac Surgery, 3rd ed. Philadelphia, Mosby, 2003.)

Management

There are three management schemes for the closure of a PDA: pharmacologic therapy, surgical closure, and endovascular device closure. Indomethacin, a prostaglandin inhibitor, is useful for stimulating PDA closure in premature infants.[36] It is rarely effective in full-term infants. A regimen of three doses of 0.1 to 0.2 mg/kg is given intravenously at 12- or 24-hour intervals. This approach is successful in nearly 80% of premature infants.[30] Indomethacin is known to have a number of possible side effects, including hypertension, decreased gastrointestinal blood flow, decreased renal blood flow, and interference with platelet function. Contraindications to indomethacin therapy include sepsis, renal insufficiency, and bleeding disorders. Failure of indomethacin after two complete courses results in referral for surgical closure.

The surgical approach to the PDA is usually via a left posterolateral thoracotomy through the third or fourth intercostal space (Fig. 123-2). The pleura is divided longitudinally over the proximal descending thoracic aorta. The vagus nerve is thereby lifted medially. Dissection is then carried out to demonstrate unequivocally the distal transverse aortic arch and ductus. In some cases the ductus may be the largest vascular structure present, so it is critical that it not be confused with the aorta. Once the anatomy is confirmed, the ductus is gently dissected. Ductal tissue is extremely friable, especially in premature infants, so direct manipulation is not recommended. The recurrent laryngeal nerve curves behind the ductus and must be preserved during the dissection. The ductus may be occluded with a surgical clip or silk ligature, or it may be divided between ligatures (Fig. 123-3). The latter is preferred in most cases; however, in premature infants, the safest approach is clip occlusion. The surgical procedure is commonly performed in the neonatal intensive care unit, which avoids problems associated with patient transfer.[18,72]

Recently, PDA ligation has been performed using video-assisted thoracoscopy.[15] This approach has the potential benefits of decreased pain and shorter hospital stay. Disadvantages include a substantial learning curve and increased operating time.

Several endovascular devices have been developed for the purpose of transcatheter occlusion of the PDA.[19,31,58] These devices have proved to be so successful that, at most centers, transcatheter occlusion has become the treatment of choice for older infants and children with small- to moderate-sized PDAs. Surgical therapy is reserved for patients with larger ducts.

Results

Closure of the PDA by surgical or transcatheter approach can be performed with a mortality of close to zero.[18] Potential morbidity from surgical therapy may include pneumothorax, recurrent laryngeal nerve injury, and chylothorax. Most patients should experience a normal life expectancy after PDA ligation. Long-term survival in

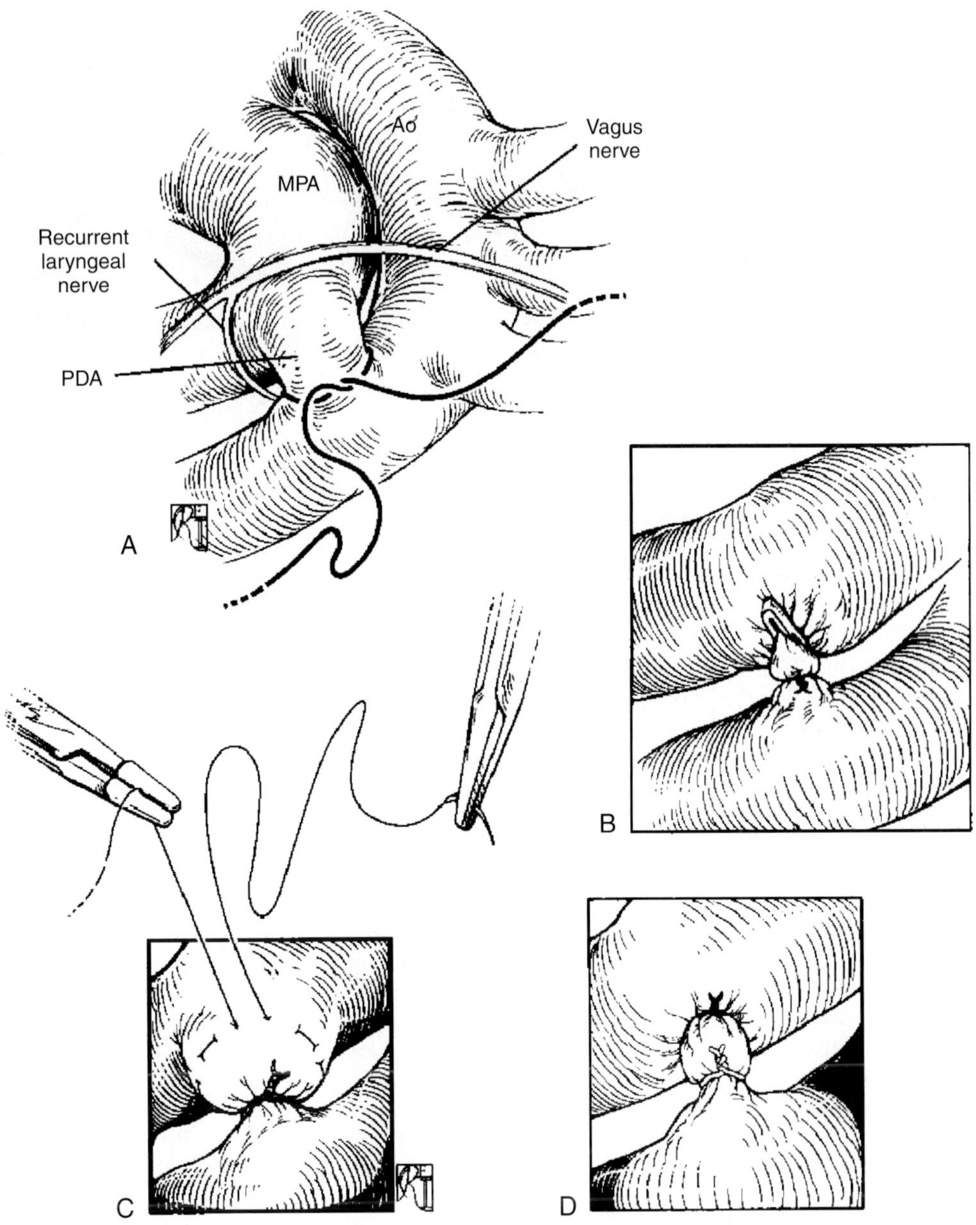

Figure 123–3 Various techniques for control of the patent ductus arteriosus (PDA). *A*, Simple ligation. *B*, Ligation and hemoclip application. *C* and *D*, Ligation and adventitial purse-string. Ao, aorta; MPA, main pulmonary artery. (From Hillman ND, Mavroudis C, Backer CL: Patent ductus arteriosus. In Mavroudis C, Backer CL [eds]: Pediatric Cardiac Surgery, 3rd ed. Philadelphia, Mosby, 2003.)

premature infants depends primarily on the extent of prematurity and the presence of associated anomalies.

COARCTATION OF THE AORTA

Coarctation of the aorta is a congenital narrowing of the proximal descending thoracic aorta near the insertion of the ductus arteriosus (or ligamentum arteriosum). This creates obstruction to blood flow and results in a pressure load on the LV. The incidence of coarctation is about 0.5 per 1000 live births, and its prevalence is 5% of congenital heart defects.[39] Coarctation is commonly associated with other heart defects, including bicuspid aortic valve (in more than 50% of cases), PDA, and ventricular septal defect (VSD). Other left-sided obstructive lesions may be present, including aortic arch hypoplasia, aortic stenosis, mitral stenosis, and LV hypoplasia.

Natural History and Diagnosis

There are two patterns of presentation, based on anatomy, age, and symptoms (Fig. 123-4). In infantile coarctation, patients develop symptoms in the first week of life. These infants have such severe aortic obstruction that perfusion of the lower body is dependent on flow from the ductus arteriosus. Spontaneous ductal closure (which also tends to worsen the aortic obstruction) then precipitates ischemia to tissues beyond the coarctation. The resultant pressure load on the LV may lead to congestive heart failure. Patients may exhibit shock with severe acidosis, oliguria, and diminished distal pulses. Survival for these patients is unlikely without therapy.

The second pattern of presentation is sometimes called adult coarctation. Patients with adult coarctation are usually asymptomatic during infancy and present later in life with hypertension. These patients generally develop

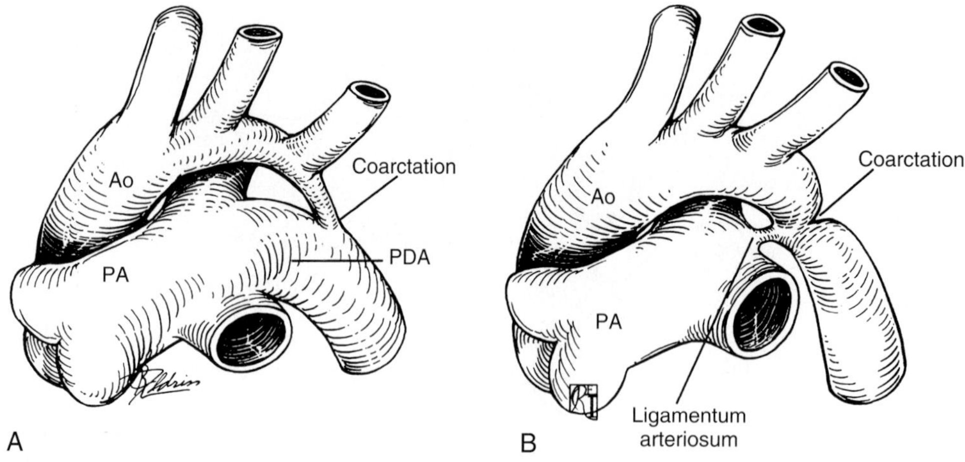

Figure 123–4 *A*, Infantile coarctation of the aorta (Ao). The isthmus (segment of the aorta between the left subclavian artery and ductal insertion) is hypoplastic, and the descending aorta receives most of its flow from the ductus. *B*, Adult coarctation with juxtaductal narrowing of the aorta and a prominent posterior shelf. The ductus has contracted to form the ligamentum arteriosum. PA, pulmonary artery. (From Backer CL, Mavroudis C: Coarctation of the aorta. In Mavroudis C, Backer CL [eds]: Pediatric Cardiac Surgery, 3rd ed. Philadelphia, Mosby, 2003.)

extensive collaterals that serve to bypass the obstruction. Life expectancy for these patients is limited owing to the development of heart failure later in life and the cumulative risk of endocarditis (frequently involving a bicuspid aortic valve) or endarteritis (in the post-stenotic aorta at the site of the turbulent jet), aortic rupture, or intracranial hemorrhage (from berry aneurysms, which are more common in patients with coarctation).[65]

Coarctation can usually be diagnosed clinically. The newborn with significant coarctation may appear normal at birth but after ductal closure will develop signs of heart failure, such as irritability, tachypnea, and poor feeding. Lower extremity pulses are absent, and upper extremity pulses may be weak. Chest radiography may show cardiomegaly and pulmonary venous congestion. There is an LV strain pattern on the electrocardiogram. Echocardiography is usually diagnostic, demonstrating anatomic narrowing at the coarctation site with a loss of pulsatility in the descending aorta; additional cardiac defects are also demonstrable.

In older children and adults there is usually a pressure gradient between the arms and legs that can be identified by measuring cuff pressures in all four extremities. Radiography may demonstrate rib notching, which is secondary to the development of large intercostal collaterals that erode into the inferior aspects of the ribs. Echocardiography is usually sufficient to confirm the diagnosis in older patients, but computed tomography (CT) and magnetic resonance imaging (MRI) provide excellent anatomic detail, which may aid in therapeutic strategy. Cardiac catheterization is usually not necessary.

Management

The diagnosis of coarctation usually mandates surgical correction, but the acute medical management of the sick neonate demands careful attention. Prostaglandin E_1 is usually effective for reopening the ductus when administered within 7 to 10 days after birth; its effectiveness wanes when initiated after 2 weeks of life. Intravenous fluids, inotropic agents, and correction of anemia may also be important for the resuscitation of the patient with coarctation.

Surgical exposure of coarctation is performed by left posterolateral thoracotomy through the third or fourth intercostal space. The mediastinal pleura overlying the left subclavian artery and proximal descending thoracic aorta is incised and the descending aorta, transverse arch, brachiocephalic vessels, and ductus (or ligamentum) are mobilized. Care is taken to avoid injury to the vagus nerve and its recurrent branch. The coarctation is usually evident externally by narrowing or posterior indentation, but the degree of internal narrowing is usually much more severe. A dose of heparin (100 units/kg) may be given intravenously for patients younger than 2 years. Proximal and distal control of the aorta is achieved using clamps. Usually the proximal clamp is positioned on the transverse arch between the innominate and left carotid vessels with concomitant occlusion of the left carotid and left subclavian. In infants and children, the preferred surgical approach to coarctation is resection with extended end-to-end repair (Fig. 123-5).[7] A generous resection of the coarctation segment is performed. The proximal aorta is then spatulated along the lesser curvature and the distal aorta along the greater curvature. An extended end-to-end anastomosis is then performed.

In older children and adults, it may not be possible to perform a resection with primary repair without creating excessive tension on the anastomosis, which might lead to hemorrhage or scarring with recurrent coarctation. In these cases, an alternative strategy is indicated. In children, in whom further growth is expected, the coarctation may be repaired by patch aortoplasty.[6,24] Less initial dissection is required. After achieving proximal and distal control, a longitudinal aortotomy is made across the area of narrowing. A patch of polytetrafluoroethylene (PTFE) is then sewn in place to augment the coarctation. By avoiding circumferential prosthetic material, growth potential

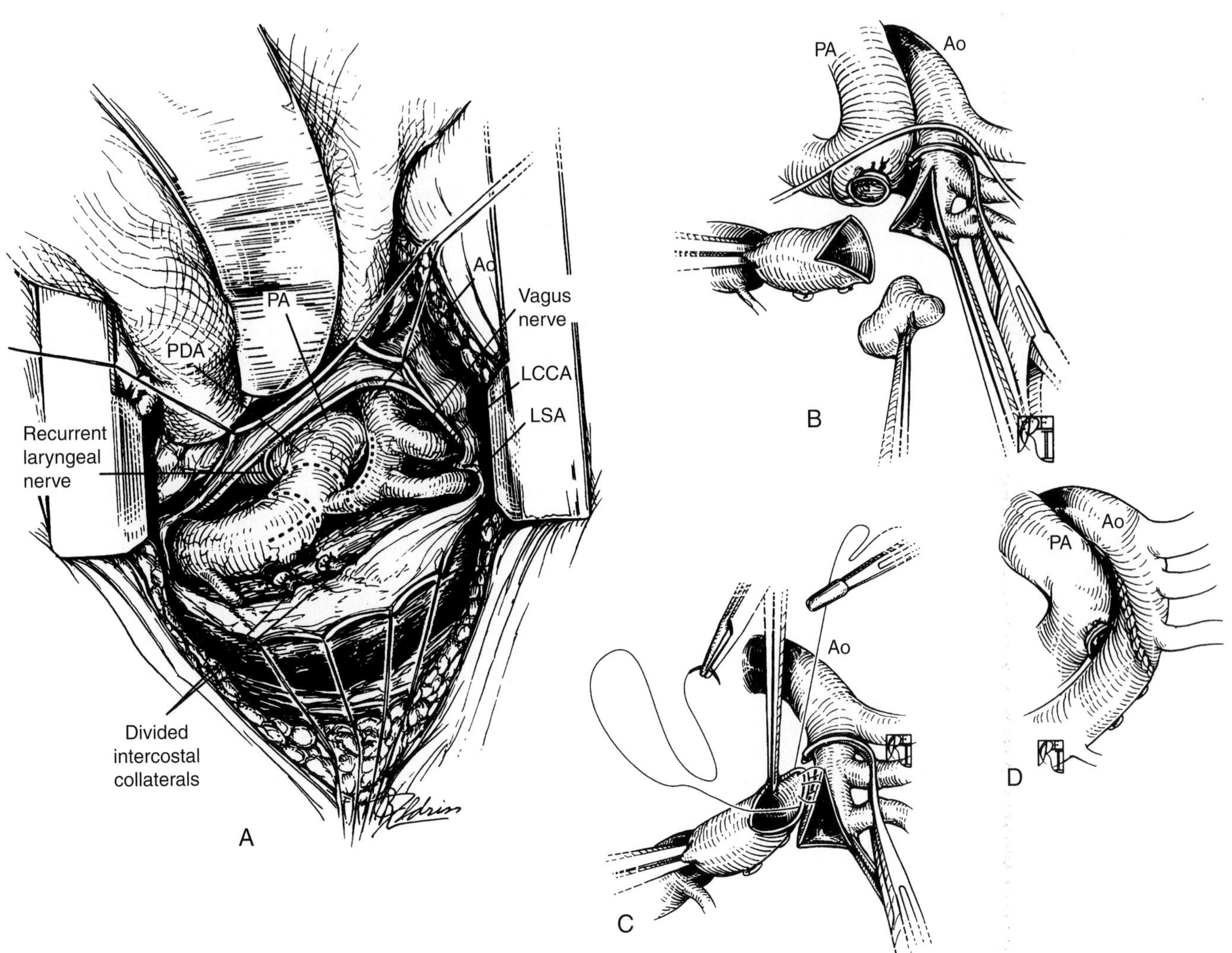

Figure 123-5 Resection with extended end-to-end anastomosis. *A*, Exposure by left posterolateral thoracotomy. Vessels are mobilized and intercostals divided when necessary. *B*, The ductus is ligated and divided. Proximal and distal control is achieved, and the coarctation segment is resected. The proximal and distal aortic segments are spatulated along the lesser and greater curvatures, respectively. *C*, The anastomosis is performed using a running technique. *D*, The completed repair. Ao, aorta; LCCA, left common carotid artery; LSA, left subclavian artery; PA, pulmonary artery. (From Backer CL, Mavroudis C: Coarctation of the aorta. In Mavroudis C, Backer CL [eds]: Pediatric Cardiac Surgery, 3rd ed. Philadelphia, Mosby, 2003.)

of the native aortic tissue is preserved. In adults, growth is no longer an issue and resection of the coarctation may be performed with subsequent placement of an interposition graft (either PTFE or Dacron).

During the operative repair of coarctation, injury to the spinal cord is a major concern. In patients who do not have well-formed collaterals, ischemia of the spinal cord may be precipitated by aortic cross-clamping and paraplegia may result. Standard protective measures include induction of mild hypothermia (35°C), maintenance of a high proximal aortic pressure, and minimization of cross-clamp time. In older children and adults with inadequate collateral flow, distal aortic perfusion may be maintained by the technique of left heart bypass (in which the LA is cannulated for drainage of oxygenated blood, which is then delivered to the femoral artery or distal aorta using a centrifugal pump).[78] Overall, the incidence of paraplegia after coarctation repair is less than 1%.[12]

After repair, patients may develop severe hypertension. This can be managed using intravenous beta blockers (e.g., esmolol) or vasodilators (e.g., sodium nitroprusside). Uncontrolled hypertension may lead to the complication of mesenteric arteritis. Hypertension usually resolves within days to weeks after repair, although older children and adults may require permanent antihypertensive therapy. Repair of coarctation during infancy is thought to minimize the risk of late hypertension.[67]

Transcatheter therapy has been attempted as primary therapy for coarctation, but this approach is controversial.[17,57,73] Limitations of this approach include the incidence of recurrent coarctation, potential need for multiple interventions, injury to the femoral vasculature (for access), and incidence of aneurysm formation. Balloon angioplasty is generally recommended for the treatment of recurrent coarctation after surgery, in which its efficacy is on the order of 90%.[35,37,80]

Results

The early mortality after repair of coarctation in neonates is 2% to 10%, whereas the risk in older children and adults is about 1%.[7,74] The incidence of recurrent coarctation after resection and end-to-end repair is 4% to 8%.[7,61] The long-term survival after coarctation repair is determined by the presence of associated defects and persistence of hypertension.

ATRIAL SEPTAL DEFECTS

Atrial septal defects (ASDs) are the third most common congenital heart defect, occurring in 1 in 1000 live births and representing 10% of congenital heart defects.[39] To understand the terminology of ASDs a review of normal atrial septation is useful. During embryologic development, the septum primum initially divides the common atrium. The ostium primum, which exists at the inferior edge of the septum primum, is obliterated as the septum primum fuses with the endocardial cushions. The ostium secundum forms in the midportion of the septum primum and is then covered by the septum secundum, which descends from the roof of the atrium along the right side of the septum primum. This arrangement creates a flap valve whereby blood from the inferior vena cava may preferentially stream beneath the edge of the septum secundum and through the ostium secundum into the LA. After birth, the septum secundum fuses with the septum primum, thereby sealing the interatrial communication (Fig. 123-6).

ASDs may be classified based on this embryology. The most common defect is the secundum ASD (80%), which occurs when the ostium secundum is too large for complete coverage by the septum secundum (Fig. 123-7). Failure of postnatal fusion of the septum secundum to the septum primum results in a persistent slit-like communication known as a patent foramen ovale (PFO). A primum ASD (10%) represents persistence of the ostium primum that occurs as a result of failure of fusion of the septum primum with the endocardial cushions. This defect is discussed in the section on atrioventricular septal defects (AVSDs). Sinus venosus ASDs (10%) are caused by abnormal fusion of the venous pathways with the atrium; these defects can be located high in the atrial septum near the orifice of the superior vena cava, or, less commonly, they may be low in the atrial septum near the inferior vena cava (Fig. 123-8). Sinus venosus ASDs occur commonly with partial anomalous pulmonary venous return, usually with the right upper pulmonary vein draining into the superior vena cava near the cavoatrial junction. An uncommon type of ASD is the unroofed coronary sinus septal defect. This occurs when there is loss of the common wall between the coronary sinus and LA adjacent to the atrial septum. This unroofing of the coronary sinus results in a communication between the RA and LA at the site of the coronary sinus.

Natural History and Diagnosis

Shunting at the atrial level occurs primarily during diastole and is determined in part by the size of the atrial

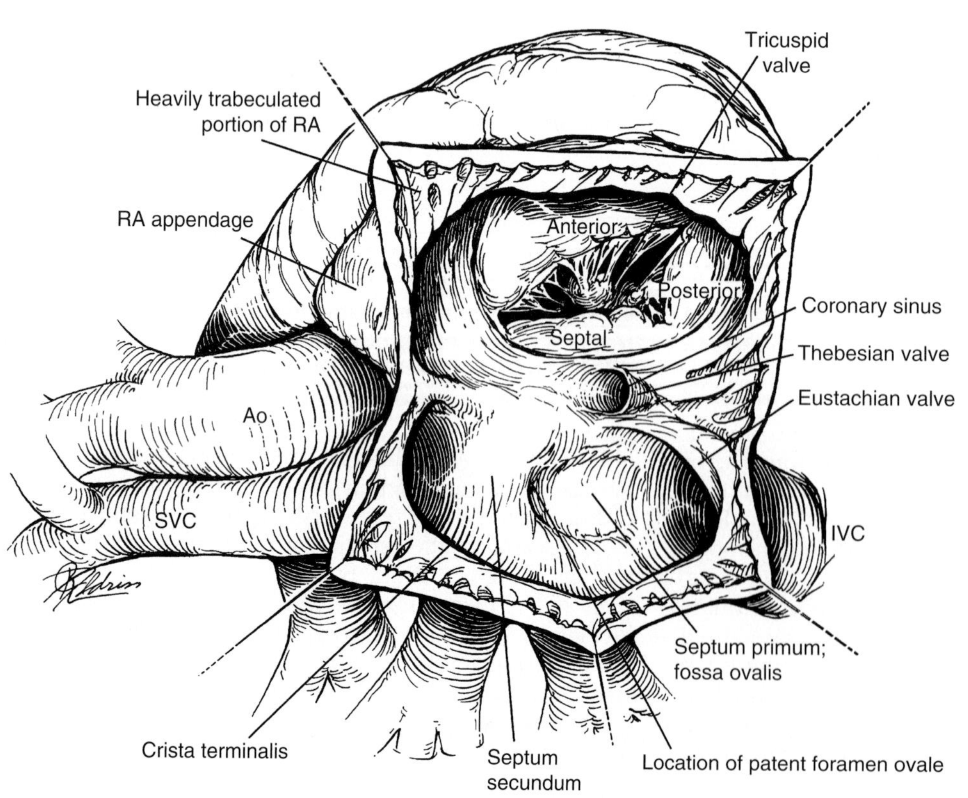

Figure 123-6 Normal intra-atrial anatomy as viewed by the surgeon through a right atriotomy. Ao, aorta; IVC, inferior vena cava; SVC, superior vena cava; RA, right atrium. (From Backer CL, Mavroudis C: Atrial septal defect, partial anomalous pulmonary venous connection, and scimitar syndrome. In Mavroudis C, Backer CL [eds]: Pediatric Cardiac Surgery, 3rd ed. Philadelphia, Mosby, 2003.)

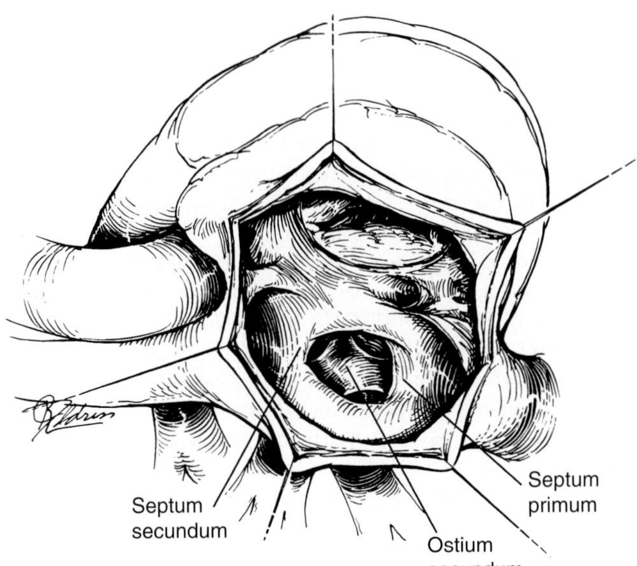

Figure 123–7 Ostium secundum atrial septal defect. Note the deficiency of the septum primum in the region of the normal fossa ovalis. (From Backer CL, Mavroudis C: Atrial septal defect, partial anomalous pulmonary venous connection, and scimitar syndrome. In Mavroudis C, Backer CL [eds]: Pediatric Cardiac Surgery, 3rd ed. Philadelphia, Mosby, 2003.)

defect and, more importantly, by relative ventricular compliance. In other words, blood preferentially fills the more compliant chamber. At birth, both chambers are equally compliant, but as pulmonary vascular resistance falls, the RV remodels and becomes more compliant. As a result, shunting across an ASD in postnatal life is from left to right. This results in a volume load on the right side of the heart. Recall that a volume load is a burden created by additional venous return to a chamber during diastole.

The volume overload created by an ASD is usually well tolerated. As a result, patients are frequently asymptomatic. Congestive heart failure is rare in infants. Children may develop symptoms of exertional dyspnea, exercise intolerance, or recurrent respiratory infections. Older patients with untreated ASDs tend to develop atrial dysrhythmias, and adults may develop congestive heart failure and right ventricular dysfunction. Pulmonary vascular obstructive disease may develop as a late complication of untreated ASD; severe pulmonary hypertension has been shown to develop in 14% of adults with untreated large ASDs between the ages of 20 and 40 years.[21] Paradoxical embolization is also an important potential complication of ASD.

On physical examination, a patient with an ASD has fixed splitting of the second heart sound and a systolic ejection murmur at the left upper sternal border due to relative pulmonary stenosis (increased flow across a normal pulmonary valve). A chest radiograph shows cardiomegaly, and electrocardiography frequently demonstrates incomplete right bundle branch block. Echocardiography confirms the clinical diagnosis of ASD and clarifies the anatomy. Cardiac catheterization is rarely needed for diagnostic purposes (to evaluate pulmonary vascular resistance in older patients) but instead is widely used with therapeutic intent (device closure).

Management

Because of the long-term complications associated with ASD, repair is recommended for all patients with symptomatic defects and in asymptomatic patients in whom the ratio of pulmonary to systemic blood flow (Qp/Qs) is greater than 1.5. Repair is usually performed in children before school age. Closure of ASDs may be accomplished surgically or using a device deployed in the cardiac catheterization laboratory.

Surgical repair of ASDs is relatively straightforward (Fig. 123-9). Surgical closure is recommended for large secundum defects and most other types of ASD. The heart is exposed by median sternotomy. Cardiopulmonary bypass

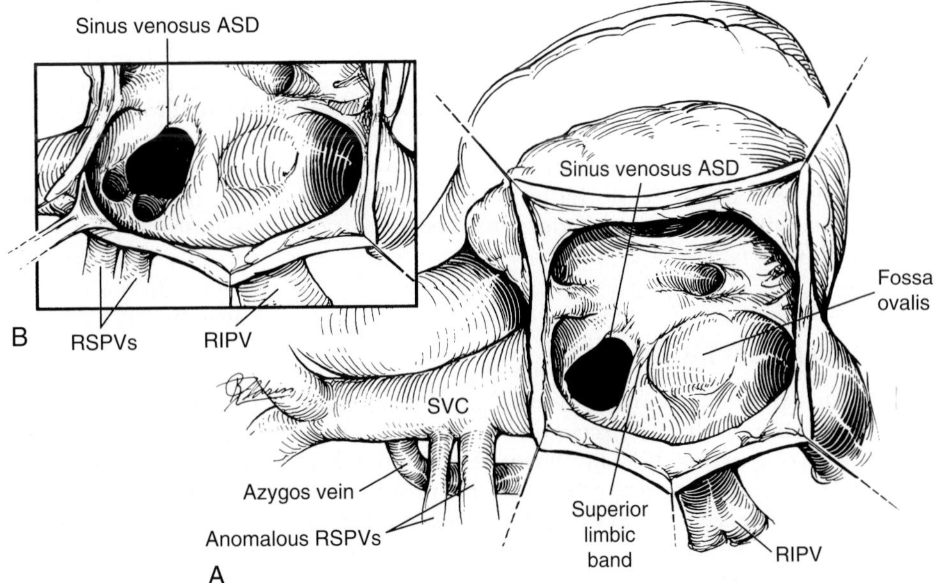

Figure 123–8 Sinus venosus atrial septal defect. *A*, Defect near the superior cavoatrial junction cephalad to the superior limbic band. Note the anomalous drainage of right superior pulmonary veins (RSPVs) to the superior vena cava (SVC) and normal drainage of the right inferior pulmonary veins (RIPVs). *B*, Another type of sinus venosus ASD with anomalous RSPVs draining adjacent to the defect. (From Backer CL, Mavroudis C: Atrial septal defect, partial anomalous pulmonary venous connection, and scimitar syndrome. In Mavroudis C, Backer CL [eds]: Pediatric Cardiac Surgery, 3rd ed. Philadelphia, Mosby, 2003.)

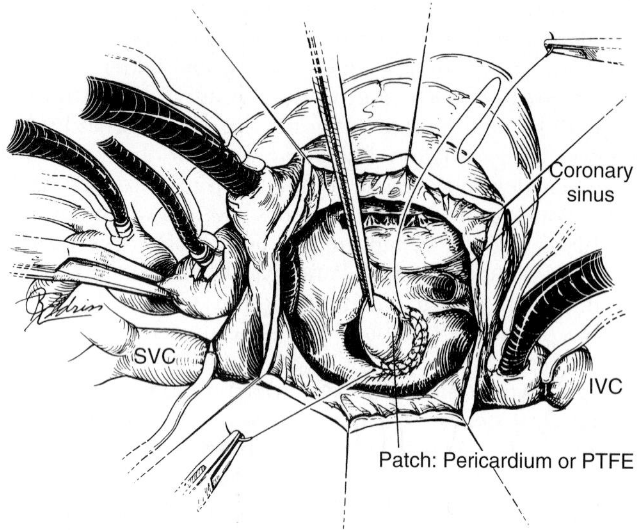

Figure 123-9 Patch closure of an ostium secundum atrial septal defect. Bicaval cannulation is utilized, and cardioplegia is infused through the aortic root to arrest the heart after application of the aortic cross-clamp. SVC, superior vena cava; IVC, inferior vena cava. PTFE, polytetrafluoroethylene. (From Backer CL, Mavroudis C: Atrial septal defect, partial anomalous pulmonary venous connection, and scimitar syndrome. In Mavroudis C, Backer CL [eds]: Pediatric Cardiac Surgery, 3rd ed. Philadelphia, Mosby, 2003.)

is necessary using bicaval cannulation and mild hypothermia. After aortic clamping and arrest of the heart with cardioplegia, the atrial septum is exposed through a right atriotomy. The defect is then closed using a patch (PTFE or autologous pericardium) and a running polypropylene suture. If there is anomalous pulmonary venous return, a baffle may be created to redirect the flow across the atrial septal defect. Small defects and PFOs can be closed primarily without a patch. In all cases, care is taken to de-air the LA to avoid the complication of air embolization.

Small- to moderate-sized secundum ASDs and PFOs can now be closed using transcatheter techniques.[63] Device closure of these defects has now become the standard of care at most centers.

Results

ASD closure by either approach is very successful.[20] Mortality is less than 1%. Morbidity is infrequent. The long-term survival for patients undergoing ASD repair in childhood is normal.[49]

VENTRICULAR SEPTAL DEFECTS

Ventricular septal defects are the most common congenital heart anomalies (with the exception of bicuspid aortic valve), occurring in 4 of 1000 live births and representing about 40% of congenital heart defects.[39] There is heterogeneity with respect to the location, size, and number of defects present. Associated cardiac defects are common. VSDs occur as a result of failure of ventricular septation. They are most commonly classified based on their location: perimembranous (80%), inlet (5%), outlet (10%), or trabecular (5%) (Fig. 123-10). The most common, perimembranous, are located in the area of the membranous septum, near the point of contact of the tricuspid, mitral, and aortic valve annuli. Inlet defects are located beneath the septal leaflet of the tricuspid valve. Outlet defects are also known as supracristal or doubly committed subarterial. These defects are bordered superiorly by both semilunar valves. Outlet defects are more common in the Asian population. Trabecular (or muscular) VSDs are completely bordered by muscle. They are frequently multiple and may be associated with perimembranous or outlet defects. The size of VSDs varies. A VSD is defined as nonrestrictive when its size (or the cumulative size of multiple defects) approximates that of the aortic annulus.

Natural History and Diagnosis

The physiology of a VSD involves left-to-right shunting primarily during systole. This creates a volume load on the left side of the heart (the LA and LV receive the increased venous return during diastole). The RV is not volume loaded (blood is ejected from the LV through the VSD and directly into the pulmonary circulation), but it does experience a pressure load. Shunt volume across a VSD is determined by the size of the defect and by the ratio of pulmonary to systemic vascular resistance. As pulmonary vascular resistance decreases during the first few weeks of life, the shunting across a VSD tends to increase. Therefore, a VSD that was asymptomatic at birth may eventually cause severe congestive heart failure.

The natural history of patients with VSD is variable. Most VSDs are restrictive and tend to close spontaneously during the first year of life.[52] Patients with large VSDs develop symptoms due to congestive heart failure. If the VSD is not treated, excessive pulmonary blood flow leads to pulmonary vascular obstructive disease by 1 to 2 years of life. Smaller VSDs may remain asymptomatic. In patients with outlet VSDs, proximity of the aortic valve may lead to prolapse of a valve cusp and aortic insufficiency.[53]

Signs of heart failure in infants with large VSDs include tachypnea, hepatomegaly, poor feeding, and failure to thrive. On examination, there is a holosystolic murmur at the left sternal border. The precordium is active. Usually, the murmur is louder with smaller defects. In patients with pulmonary vascular obstructive disease there may be no murmur present but the pulmonary component of the second heart sound is prominent. Chest radiography shows increased pulmonary vascular markings and cardiomegaly. Electrocardiography is significant for RV hypertrophy.

Patients with small VSDs have little shunting and are usually asymptomatic, having only a pansystolic murmur. Patients with moderate VSDs manifest symptoms and signs that are proportional to the degree of shunting.

Echocardiography is diagnostic in most cases. The anatomy can be accurately defined, and the presence of associated abnormalities can be excluded. Cardiac catheterization is used selectively in older children and

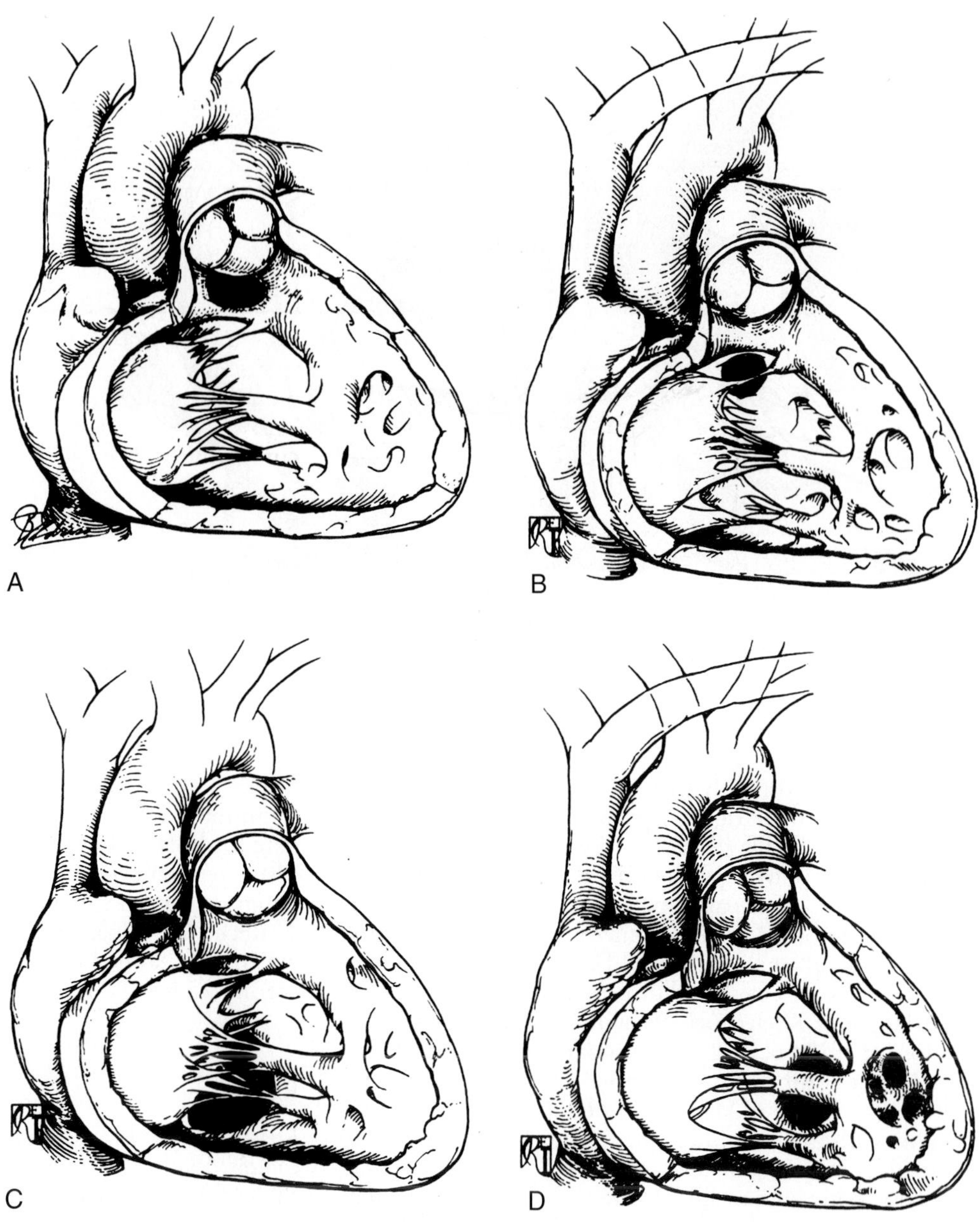

Figure 123–10 Types of ventricular septal defects (VSDs) based on location. *A*, Outlet (supracristal, doubly committed subarterial). *B*, Perimembranous. *C*, Inlet. *D*, Trabecular (muscular). (From Mavroudis C, Backer CL, Jacobs JP: Ventricular septal defect. In Mavroudis C, Backer CL [eds]: Pediatric Cardiac Surgery, 3rd ed. Philadelphia, Mosby, 2003.)

adults with VSDs to determine pulmonary vascular resistance and assess reactivity to pulmonary vasodilators.

Management

Treatment of a patient with a VSD depends on the size of the defect, the type of defect, the shunt volume, and the pulmonary vascular resistance. In general, patients with large defects who demonstrate intractable congestive heart failure or failure to thrive should undergo early surgical repair. If the congestive symptoms can be moderated by medical therapy, surgery can be delayed to 6 months of age. Patients with moderate defects may be safely followed. If spontaneous closure has not occurred by school age, then surgery may be considered. Very small VSDs with a Qp/Qs of less than 1.5 do not require closure. In these patients there is a small long-term risk of endocarditis, but this is minimized by appropriate antibiotic prophylaxis.[22] As noted previously, patients with outlet VSDs have a significant risk of developing aortic insufficiency secondary to leaflet prolapse; as a result, all outlet defects should be referred for closure.[5] Older children and adults with large VSDs who present late must undergo catheterization to evaluate the pulmonary vasculature. A fixed pulmonary vascular resistance greater than 8 to 10 Woods units · m^2 represents a contraindication to surgical closure of the VSD.

Surgical closure is performed through a median sternotomy (Fig. 123-11). Cardiopulmonary bypass is required, using bicaval cannulation. After delivery of cardioplegia, a right atriotomy is performed. Exposure of the ventricular septum is achieved through the tricuspid valve. This provides access to perimembranous, inlet, and most outlet defects. Most trabecular defects may also be exposed in this fashion. Some outlet VSDs are best exposed via a pulmonary arteriotomy, as the defect sits just beneath the valve. Trabecular VSDs located near the ventricular apex

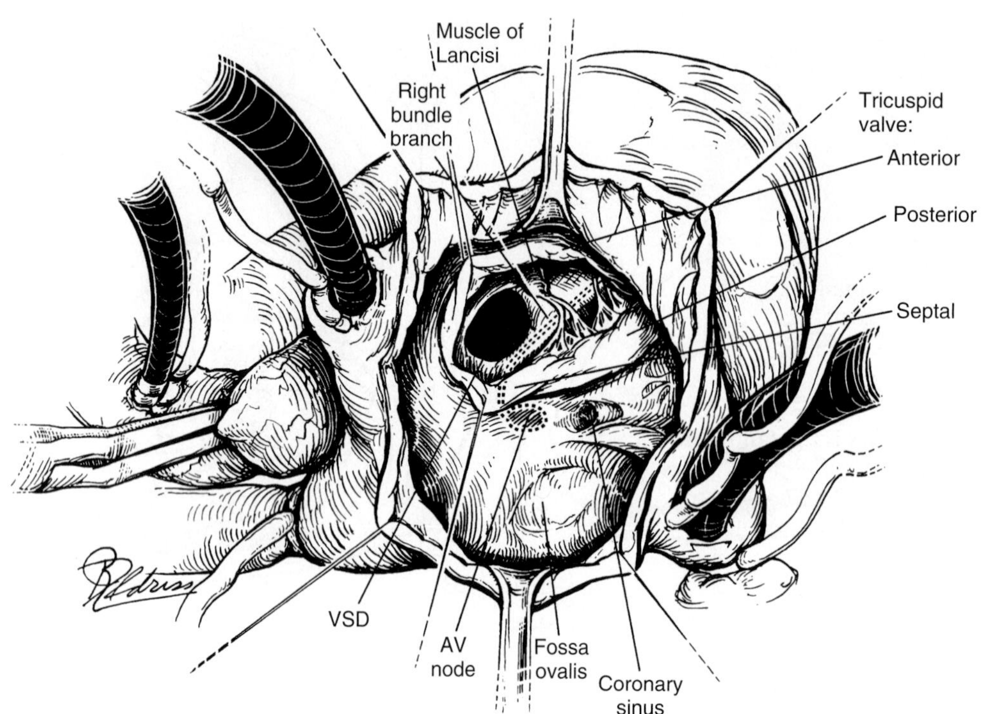

Figure 123–11 Transatrial exposure of a perimembranous ventricular septal defect (VSD) as viewed by the surgeon. The septal and anterior leaflets of the tricuspid valve are retracted to expose the VSD. The conduction tissue is demonstrated by *dashed lines* leading from the atrioventricular (AV) node along the posterior and inferior margin of the VSD. When closing these defects, sutures are placed a few millimeters away from the edge of the defect on the right ventricular side of the septum to avoid conduction injury. (From Mavroudis C, Backer CL, Jacobs JP: Ventricular septal defect. In Mavroudis C, Backer CL [eds]: Pediatric Cardiac Surgery, 3rd ed. Philadelphia, Mosby, 2003.)

are notoriously difficult to expose, and an apical ventriculotomy (left or right) may be necessary. Once the defect is exposed, it is generally closed using a PTFE patch and a running polypropylene suture, although other centers may prefer other patch material or interrupted suture technique. Knowledge of the anatomy of the conduction tissue is critical when closing VSDs. The atrioventricular (AV) node is an atrial structure that lies in the apex of the triangle of Koch (formed by the coronary sinus, the tendon of Todaro, and the annular attachment of the septal leaflet of the tricuspid valve). The node then gives rise to the bundle of His, which penetrates the AV junction beneath the membranous septum. The bundle then bifurcates into right and left bundle branches that descend along either side of the muscular ventricular septum. When a perimembranous VSD is present, the bundle of His traverses the posterior and inferior rim of the defect, generally on the LV side. In this danger area, sutures must be placed superficially on the RV side of the defect and a few millimeters away from the edge of the defect. The bundle of His also tends to run along the posterior and inferior margin of inlet VSDs, whereas in outlet and trabecular defects the conduction tissue is remote.

Banding of the PA is a palliative maneuver that is designed to protect the pulmonary circulation from excessive flow in circumstances in which the patient is not a candidate for a surgical closure, owing to either associated illness or anatomic complexity (e.g., multiple trabecular VSDs). Placement of a PA band may be accomplished via sternotomy or thoracotomy. The band is tightened, and pressures are measured proximally and distally with a goal of achieving a distal pulmonary pressure of approximately one-half systemic. The band should then be secured to the adventitia of the main PA to prevent its migration. Distal migration may result in narrowing (and poor growth) of one or both branch pulmonary arteries, whereas proximal migration may lead to deformity of the pulmonary valve. Ultimately, when the patient is a candidate for VSD closure, the band must be removed. In most cases, a repair (scar resection and primary closure or patch repair) of the main PA will also be necessary.

Recently, transcatheter technology has evolved and closure of some VSDs may be accomplished in the cardiac catheterization laboratory.

Results

Repair of a VSD is associated with a mortality of approximately 1%.[48] The main complications include injury to the conduction tissue and injury to the tricuspid valve or aortic valves. Transient heart block may develop as a result of tissue swelling, but permanent heart block occurs in only 1% to 2% of cases.[48] Patients who develop heart block after surgery are observed for a period of 7 to 10 days. If normal conduction has not occurred, then pacemaker implantation is indicated. Tricuspid insufficiency may be precipitated by annular distortion or chordal restriction by the VSD patch or sutures. The aortic valve may also be injured by inaccurate suturing (especially in perimembranous and outlet defects). A residual VSD may be observed in 5% of cases, and reoperation is indicated when significant shunting persists (Qp/Qs > 1.5). Intraoperative echocardiography is utilized routinely to identify valvular dysfunction and residual shunting.

ATRIOVENTRICULAR SEPTAL DEFECT

Atrioventricular septal defects represent a group of congenital abnormalities bound by a variable deficiency of the AV septum immediately above and below the AV valves.

Other terms commonly applied to an AVSD include AV canal defects, endocardial cushion defects, and AV communis. These resulting septal defects are invariably associated with AV valve abnormalities. AVSDs include incomplete AVSDs, also termed *ostium primum ASDs*, which have only a deficiency of the atrial septum immediately superior to the AV valves and two separate valve orifices. The far end of the spectrum encompasses complete AVSDs with both an ASD and a VSD and a single common AV valve. AVSDs represent approximately 4% of congenital cardiac anomalies and are frequently associated with other cardiac malformations. AVSDs comprise 30% to 40% of the cardiac abnormalities seen in patients with Down syndrome.[69]

The embryologic abnormality in AVSDs is the failure of the proper development of the endocardial cushions, which results in variable deficiency of the atrial and ventricular septa and malformation of the AV valves. AVSDs are generally categorized into incomplete and complete based on the AV valve morphology. Incomplete, or partial, defects have two separate AV valve orifices (Fig. 123-12). The mitral valve in an incomplete AVSD is invariably associated with a cleft in the anterior leaflet. Although most incomplete AVSDs have no ventricular level shunting, the classification of AVSDs as complete and incomplete depends only on the valve anatomy, not on the presence or absence of a VSD. Incomplete defects without associated ventricular level shunting have also been referred to as ostium primum ASDs, whereas those with a VSD have been described as intermediate or transitional AVSDs. Complete AVSDs have a single common AV valve orifice resulting in a single five-leaflet valve overlying both the RV and LV (Fig. 123-13).

Rastelli and associates[64] further subclassified complete AVSDs into types A, B, and C based on the morphology

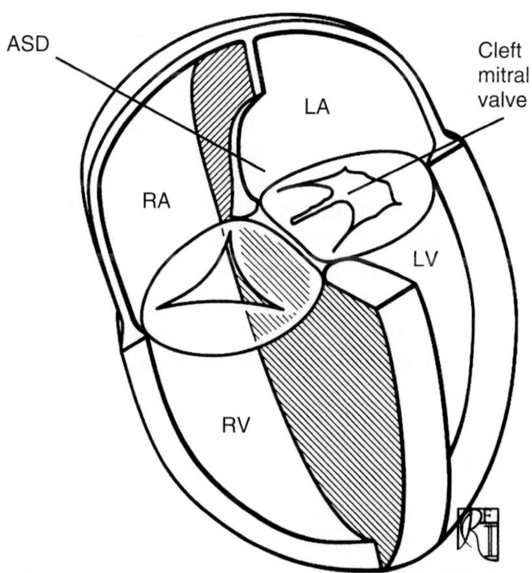

Figure 123-12 Incomplete atrioventricular septal defect. LA, left atrium; RA, right atrium; RV, right ventricle; LV, left ventricle; ASD, primum atrial septal defect. (From Backer CL, Mavroudis C: Atrioventricular canal defects. In Mavroudis C, Backer CL [eds]: Pediatric Cardiac Surgery, 3rd ed. Philadelphia, Mosby, 2003.)

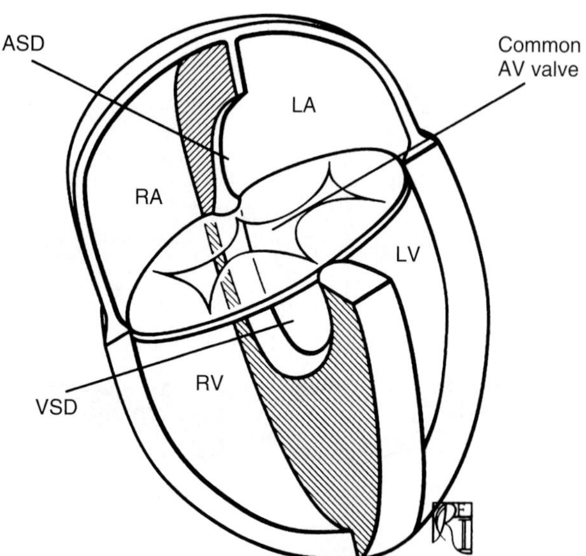

Figure 123-13 Complete atrioventricular septal defect. LA, left atrium; RA, right atrium; RV, right ventricle; LV, left ventricle; ASD, primum atrial septal defect; VSD, inlet ventricular septal defect; AV, atrioventricular. (From Backer CL, Mavroudis C: Atrioventricular canal defects. In Mavroudis C, Backer CL [eds]: Pediatric Cardiac Surgery, 3rd ed. Philadelphia, Mosby, 2003.)

of the superior bridging leaflet of the common valve (Fig. 123-14). In a Rastelli type A defect, the leaflet is divided at the plane of the interventricular septum and attached to the crest of the VSD by numerous chordae. Type B complete AVSDs, which are rare, are characterized by chordal attachments from the left AV valve to papillary muscles in the RV. In a Rastelli type C defect, the superior bridging leaflet is said to be "free floating" because it is undivided and unattached to the crest of the VSD.

If both left and right AV valves equally share the common AV valve orifice, the AVSD is termed a *balanced defect*. Occasionally the orifice of the valve may be unbalanced, with one side being dominant. In marked right dominance, the left AV valve and LV are hypoplastic and frequently coexist with other left-sided abnormalities, including aortic stenosis, hypoplasia of the aorta, and coarctation. Conversely, marked left dominance is associated with hypoplasia of the RV, pulmonary stenosis or atresia, and tetralogy of Fallot (TOF).

The location of the conduction tissue is of importance in the surgical treatment of AVSDs because this tissue is at risk during the repair. The AV node is displaced posteriorly and inferiorly toward the coronary sinus. The bundle of His courses anteriorly and superiorly to run along the leftward aspect of the crest of the VSD, giving off the left bundle branch before continuing as the right bundle branch.

Cardiac anomalies are associated with AVSDs, including a PDA (10%) and TOF (10%).[10] Important abnormalities of the left AV valve include single papillary muscle (parachute mitral valve) (2% to 6%) and double-orifice mitral valve (8% to 14%).[27] A persistent left superior vena cava with or without an unroofed coronary sinus is

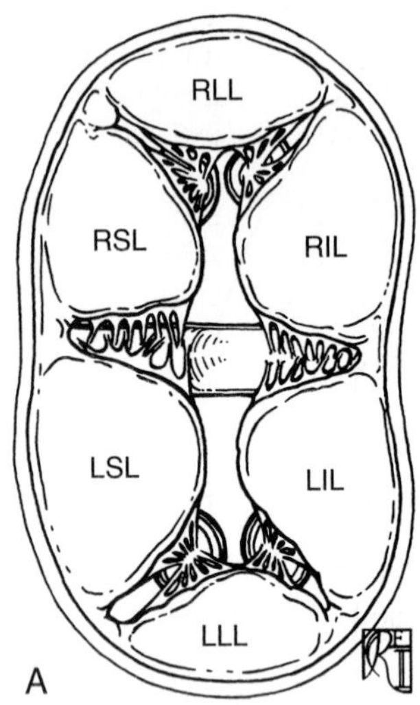

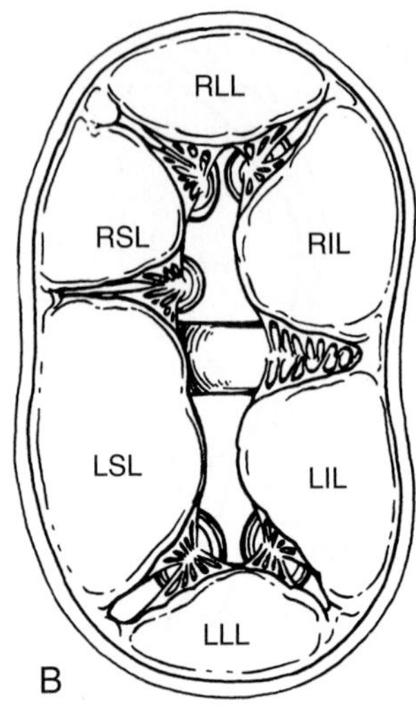

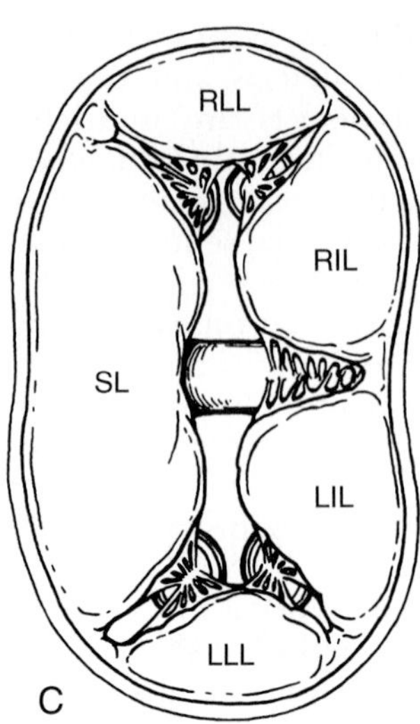

Figure 123–14 Rastelli classification. RSL, right superior leaflet; RIL, right inferior leaflet; RLL, right lateral leaflet; LSL, left superior leaflet; LIL, left inferior leaflet; LLL, left lateral leaflet; SL, superior bridging leaflet. (From Backer CL, Mavroudis C: Atrioventricular canal defects. In Mavroudis C, Backer CL [eds]: Pediatric Cardiac Surgery, 3rd ed. Philadelphia, Mosby, 2003.)

encountered in 3% of patients with an AVSD. Double-outlet RV (2%) significantly complicates or may even preclude complete surgical correction.[10] As mentioned previously, LV outflow tract obstruction from subaortic stenosis or redundant AV valve tissue occurs in 4% to 7%.[59,71] Associated transposition of the great arteries and LV inflow obstruction have been rarely reported.[10,59]

Natural History and Diagnosis

The predominant hemodynamic features of an AVSD are the result of left-to-right shunting at the atrial and ventricular levels. In the absence of ventricular level shunting, the hemodynamics and clinical presentation resemble that of a typical secundum ASD with right atrial (RA) and RV volume overload. On physical examination, there is an active precordium, a pulmonary outflow murmur, and a fixed, widely split second heart sound. Electrocardiogram reveals left-axis deviation, prominent P waves associated with atrial enlargement, and a prolonged PR interval. Chest radiograph generally shows mild cardiomegaly and increased pulmonary vascular markings. Doppler echocardiography is diagnostic of the atrial defect, the absence of ventricular level shunting, and the presence of any AV valve abnormalities. Cardiac catheterization is only indicated in patients diagnosed in adulthood or manifesting physical or radiologic signs of decreased pulmonary blood flow. The decreased PA blood flow may be a result of pulmonary vascular disease or concurrent right-sided obstructive lesions. A fixed pulmonary vascular resistance of greater than 10 units · m^2 is a contraindication to surgical closure.

As with an uncomplicated ASD, the natural history of decades of chronic volume overload results in atrial dilatation and arrhythmias, ventricular dysfunction, and potentially pulmonary vascular disease. Therefore, repair is indicated and generally undertaken by age 2 to 4 years.

Patients with a complete AVSD have both atrial and ventricular level shunting. These patients generally present early in infancy with signs and symptoms of congestive heart failure. Moderate or greater left AV valve regurgitation may occur with a complete AVSD, worsening the clinical picture. On physical examination, the precordium is hyperactive, with auscultatory findings of a systolic murmur along the left sternal border, a high-pitched murmur at the apex from left AV valve regurgitation, and a mid-diastolic flow murmur across the common AV valve. Chest radiograph demonstrates significant cardiomegaly and pulmonary overcirculation. The electrocardiogram reveals biventricular hypertrophy, atrial enlargement, prolonged PR interval, leftward axis, and counterclockwise frontal plane loop. Doppler echocardiography is diagnostic, defining the atrial and ventricular level shunting, valvular anatomy, and any associated anomalies. Cardiac catheterization should be performed for patients older than the age of 1 year, patients with signs or symptoms of increased pulmonary vascular resistance, or in some cases to further evaluate other associated major cardiac anomalies.

Up to 90% of untreated individuals with a complete AVSD develop pulmonary vascular disease by 1 year of age owing to the large left-to-right shunt, potentially exacerbated by the associated AV valve regurgitation.[54] Patients with trisomy 21 tend to develop pulmonary vascular obstructive disease earlier than chromosomally normal infants due to small airway disease, chronic hypoventilation, and elevated P_{CO_2}. Initial aggressive medical management is undertaken to relieve the symptoms of congestive heart failure. Elective surgical correction should be performed by age 3 to 6 months. Earlier intervention is indicated for failure of medical management.

Management

The treatment of choice for an incomplete or complete AVSD is complete surgical repair. Currently, PA banding for palliation has a very limited role in the management of these lesions. Indications for PA banding may include those patients with associated complex cardiac anomalies, functional single ventricle anatomy necessitating ultimate Fontan procedure, and poor clinical condition precluding major cardiac surgery.

A median sternotomy approach is employed, with routine conduct of cardiopulmonary bypass for the majority of patients. Rarely, deep hypothermic circulatory arrest may be required for the repair in very low birth weight neonates. Repair of an incomplete AVSD with only atrial level shunting is similar to the approach employed for a secundum-type ASD.

There are two techniques widely employed for the repair of complete AVSDs: a one-patch technique and a two-patch technique. Regardless of which approach is selected, the goals are to close the ASD and VSD and to separate the common AV valve into two nonstenotic, competent valves. The cleft in the anterior leaflet of the mitral valve is generally closed to lessen the risks of long-term mitral regurgitation.

For the two-patch technique, separate patches are used for the ASD and VSD (Fig. 123-15A). For the one-patch technique, the superior and inferior bridging leaflets are divided along a line separating them into right and left components. A single patch is utilized to close both the ventricular and atrial septal defects. The cut edges of the leaflets are then resuspended to the patch (see Fig. 123-15B). For defects with a small VSD component, a modified single patch technique may be employed. For this method, a single patch is sewn directly to the rim of the VSD, sandwiching the bridging leaflets between the patch and the crest of the VSD (see Fig. 123-15C).

Results

Operative mortality is largely related to any associated cardiac anomalies and left AV valve regurgitation. Mortality for repair of uncomplicated incomplete AVSDs is 0% to 0.6%. The addition of left AV valve regurgitation increases mortality to 4% to 6%.[70,71] For complete AVSDs, the mortality without left AV valve regurgitation is approximately 5%, compared with 13% when significant degrees of regurgitation are present.[71]

The difference in operative mortality between patients with and without regurgitation underscores the importance of careful management of the left AV valve. In addition, the majority of reoperations after repair of AVSD are due to left AV valve regurgitation. Significant postoperative AV valve regurgitation occurs in 10% to 15% of patients, necessitating reoperation for valve repair or replacement in 7% to 12%.[34,50,62]

The incidence of permanent complete heart block is approximately 1%.[40,71] Heart block encountered in the immediate postoperative period may be transient due to edema of or trauma to the AV node or bundle of His. However, right bundle branch block is common (22%).[40]

TETRALOGY OF FALLOT

Tetralogy of Fallot was described by Etienne Fallot in 1888. The pathologic anatomy is frequently described as having four components: VSD, overriding aorta, pulmonary stenosis, and RV hypertrophy (Fig. 123-16). The anatomy of TOF has also been related to a single embryologic defect: anterior malalignment of the infundibular septum.[75] The infundibular septum normally separates the primitive outflow tracts and fuses with the ventricular septum. Anterior malalignment of the infundibular septum creates a VSD from failure of fusion with the ventricular septum and also displaces the aorta over the VSD and RV. The malaligned infundibular septum crowds the RV outflow tract, producing pulmonary stenosis and, secondarily, RV hypertrophy. Prominent muscle bands also extend from the septal insertion of the infundibular septum to the RV free wall and contribute to the obstruction of the RV outflow tract. The pulmonary valve is usually stenotic with thickened leaflets that are bicuspid in the majority of cases. Abnormalities of coronary artery anatomy may be present, with origin of the left anterior descending from the right coronary artery in 5% of cases. In 25% of cases, there is a right aortic arch. Associated defects may include ASD, complete AVSD, PDA, or multiple VSDs.

TOF is the most common cyanotic congenital heart defect. It occurs in 0.6 per 1000 live births and has a prevalence of 5% among all patients with congenital heart disease.[39]

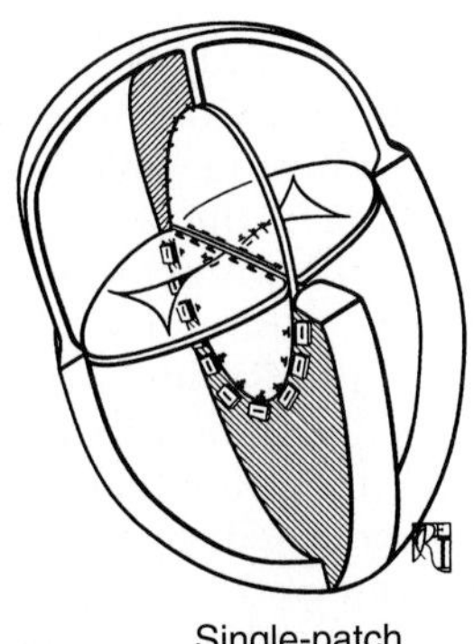

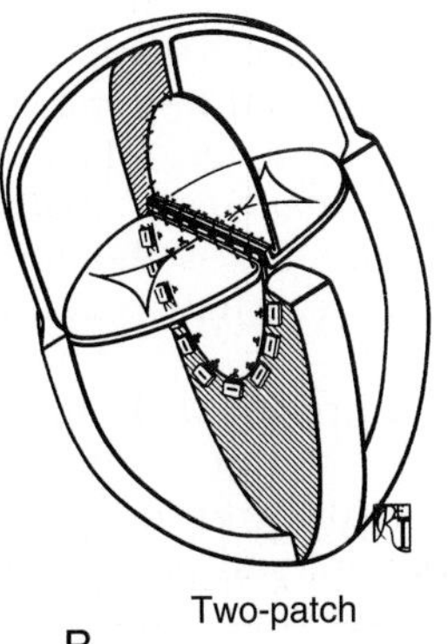

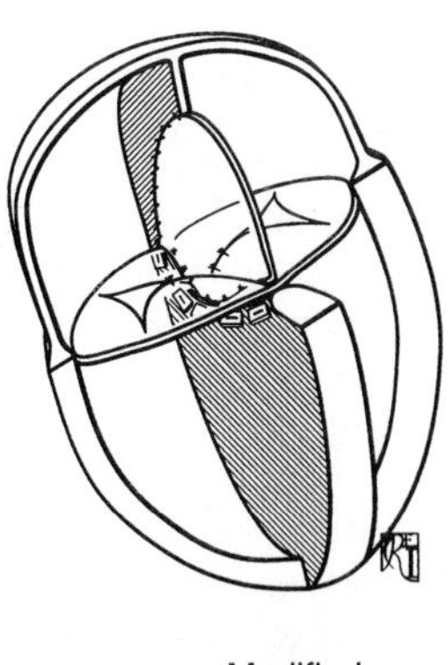

Figure 123–15 Surgical repair of an atrioventricular septal defect using a one-patch (*A*), two-patch (*B*), and modified one-patch (*C*) technique. (From Backer CL, Mavroudis C: Atrioventricular canal defects. In Mavroudis C, Backer CL [eds]: Pediatric Cardiac Surgery, 3rd ed. Philadelphia, Mosby, 2003.)

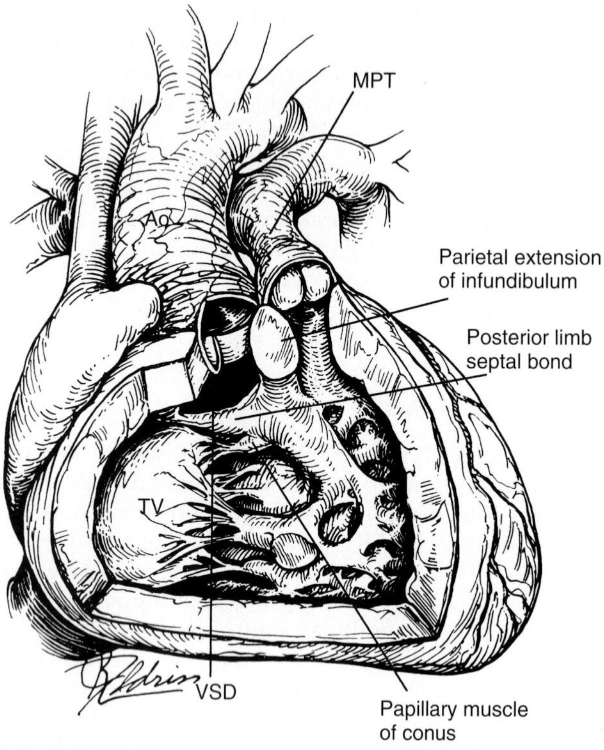

Figure 123-16 Pathologic anatomy of tetralogy of Fallot. The ventricular septal defect (VSD) is nonrestrictive. The infundibular septum is malaligned, leading to aortic override and crowding of the right ventricular outflow tract. Note the hypoplastic main pulmonary trunk (MPT). Ao, aorta; TV, tricuspid valve. (From Hirsch JC, Bove EL: Tetralogy of Fallot. In Mavroudis C, Backer CL [eds]: Pediatric Cardiac Surgery, 3rd ed. Philadelphia, Mosby, 2003.)

Natural History and Diagnosis

Patients with TOF develop cyanosis as a result of shunting from right to left across the ventricular septal defect. The degree of cyanosis is proportional to the degree of obstruction of the RV outflow tract. There is a spectrum of severity, with some patients developing symptoms as neonates and others remaining asymptomatic. The occurrence of intermittent cyanotic spells is a well-known clinical feature of tetralogy. The etiology of a spell is still controversial, but is clearly related to a transient imbalance between pulmonary and systemic blood flow. A spell may be triggered by hypovolemia, peripheral vasodilation (after a bath, for example), or infundibular spasm. Spells have been reported in neonates but tend to occur most frequently between 3 and 18 months of age. Older children have been observed to spontaneously squat to terminate spells. The squatting position is thought to increase systemic vascular resistance, which thereby favors pulmonary blood flow.

Long-term complications of untreated TOF include clubbing of the fingers and toes, severe dyspnea on exertion, brain abscesses (secondary to right-to-left shunting), paradoxical embolization, and polycythemia (which may lead to cerebral thrombosis). Long-term survival is unlikely for most patients with untreated TOF.

Cyanosis is the most frequent physical examination finding. There is usually a normal first heart sound and a single second heart sound. A systolic pulmonary ejection murmur is present at the left upper sternal border. Older children and adults may exhibit clubbing. Chest radiography characteristically demonstrates a boot-shaped heart due to elevation of the cardiac apex from RV hypertrophy. Also the presence of a right aortic arch may be evident. An electrocardiogram shows RV hypertrophy. Echocardiography is definitive, and catheterization is unnecessary in most cases.

Management

The medical management of TOF is directed at the treatment and prevention of cyanotic spells. A patient having spells should be given oxygen and sedation, and acidosis, if present, should be corrected. Transfusion may be indicated in anemic infants. Alpha agonists can be administered to increase systemic vascular resistance, which favors pulmonary blood flow. Some centers have used long-term therapy with beta blockers to reduce the incidence of cyanotic spells.

All patients with TOF should undergo surgical repair. In general, asymptomatic patients should be repaired electively between 4 and 6 months of age. Early repair is indicated for neonates with severe cyanosis as well as for infants who have had a documented spell.

Classically, the repair of TOF was performed in two stages. The first stage involved creation of a systemic-to-pulmonary shunt to relieve cyanosis. The second stage was a complete repair. Currently, one-stage complete repair is preferred by most centers. In some patients (e.g., those with multiple congenital anomalies, severe concurrent illness, or an anomalous coronary artery crossing a hypoplastic infundibulum), initial palliation with a shunt may still be indicated. The modified Blalock-Taussig shunt is the most common type of shunt used today and consists of an interposition graft (PTFE) between the innominate or subclavian artery and the ipsilateral PA. Creation of a shunt may be performed with or without the use of cardiopulmonary bypass.

Complete repair of TOF is performed using a median sternotomy and cardiopulmonary bypass with bicaval cannulation (Fig. 123-17). Via a transatrial approach, the muscle bundles obstructing the RV outflow tract are resected or divided. The VSD is closed using a patch. Depending on the status of the pulmonary valve, pulmonary valvotomy may be appropriate. In cases of severe hypoplasia of the pulmonary annulus or infundibulum, an RV outflow tract transannular patch may be required to relieve obstruction (Fig. 123-18). Our philosophy is to minimize RV incisions whenever possible to preserve RV function. When an anomalous coronary artery crosses the RV infundibulum, a transannular incision may be contraindicated; in these cases, placement of a conduit (cryopreserved homograft or bioprosthetic heterograft) between the RV (via a separate ventriculotomy) and main PA may be necessary. Patients requiring a transannular

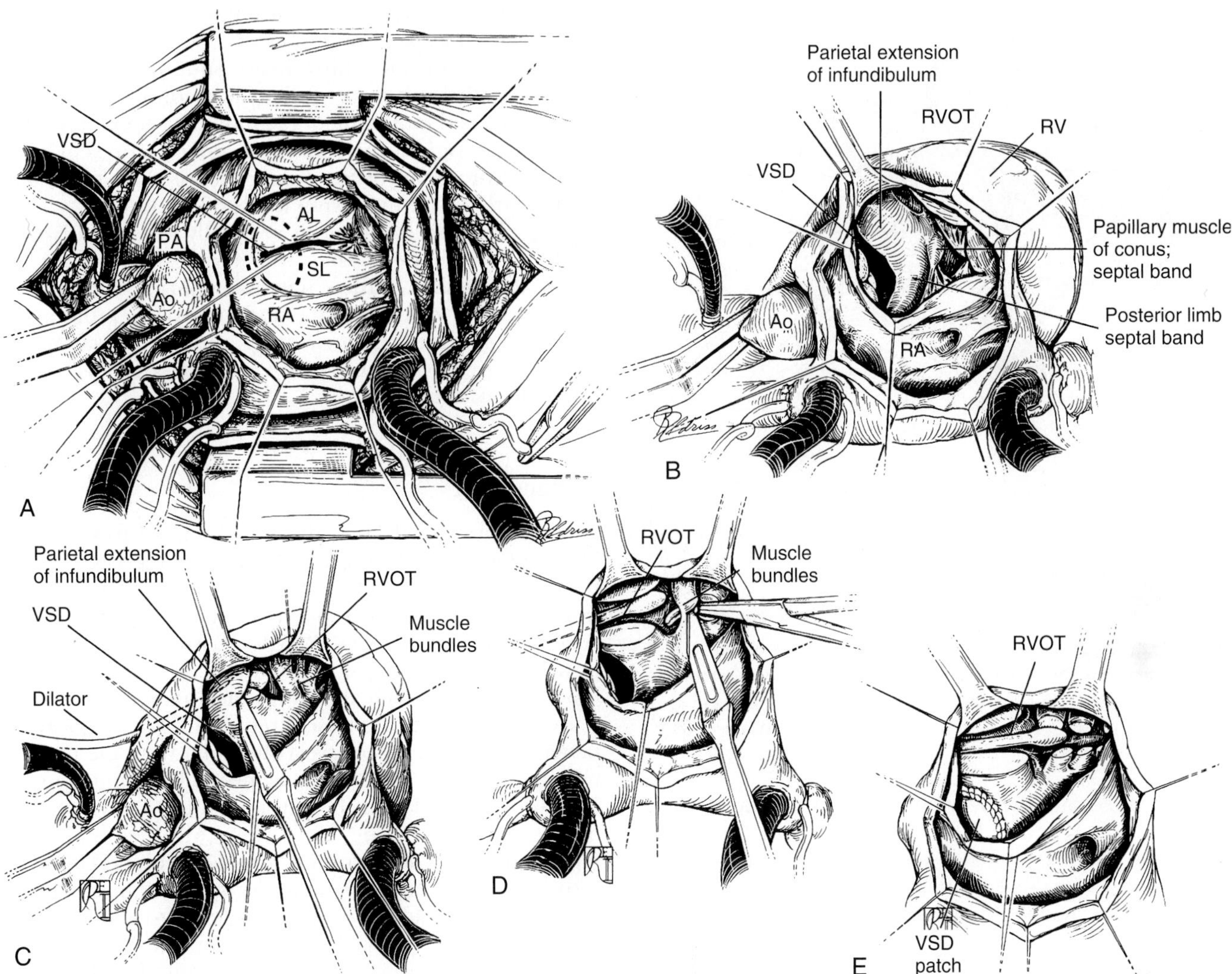

Figure 123–17 Transatrial repair of tetralogy of Fallot. *A*, The location of the ventricular septal defect (VSD) is denoted by the *dashed line*. *B*, Stay sutures on the septal and anterior leaflets of the tricuspid valve allow for exposure of the VSD. *C* and *D*, Using a dilator to demonstrate the course of the right ventricular outflow tract (RVOT), hypertrophied muscle bundles may be divided or resected. *E*, The VSD is closed with a patch. AL, anterior leaflet of tricuspid valve; SL, septal leaflet of tricuspid valve; Ao, aorta; PA, pulmonary artery; RA, right atrium. (From Hirsch JC, Bove EL: Tetralogy of Fallot. In Mavroudis C, Backer CL [eds]: Pediatric Cardiac Surgery, 3rd ed. Philadelphia, Mosby, 2003.)

patch will develop free pulmonary insufficiency. This is surprisingly well tolerated in most infants, as long as the tricuspid valve is competent. As adults, some of these patients may develop RV failure owing to chronic pulmonary insufficiency, and pulmonary valve implantation may be necessary.[23,25]

Results

The early mortality after repair of TOF is between 1% and 5%.[38,41] Long-term complications include recurrent obstruction of the RV outflow tract, conduit failure, and development of RV dysfunction due to chronic pulmonary insufficiency. Actuarial survival is 86% at 20 years with excellent functional status.[2]

TRANSPOSITION OF THE GREAT ARTERIES

Transposition of the great arteries (TGA) is a common congenital cardiovascular malformation in which there is ventriculoarterial discordance. This discordant anatomy is a result of the aorta arising from the morphologic RV and the PA arising from the morphologic LV. TGA is divided into *dextro-* or d-TGA, and *levo-* or l-TGA. l-TGA is associated with both AV discordance (RA attaches to LV and LA attaches to RV) and ventriculoarterial discordance and is also termed *congenitally corrected TGA*. l-TGA is a rare variant of TGA and its discussion is beyond the scope of this chapter.

d-TGA is the most common cause of cyanosis in the infant and accounts for approximately 10% of all congenital cardiovascular malformations.[29] The defect can

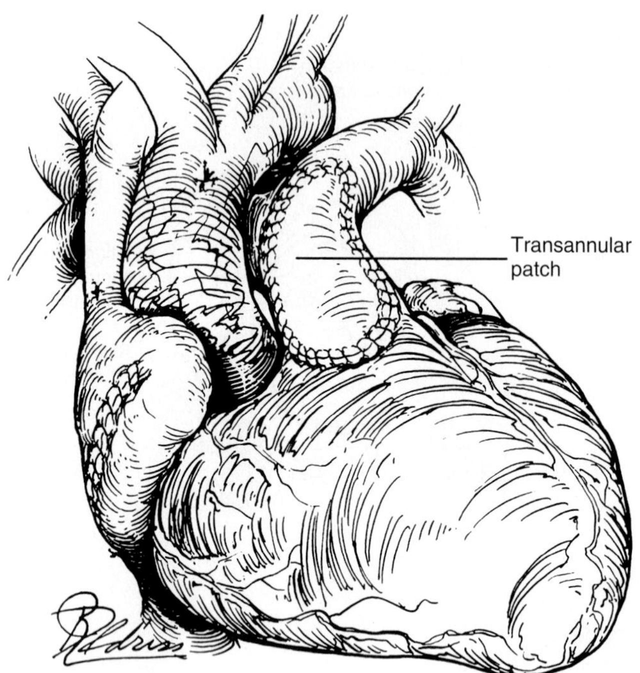

Figure 123-18 A transannular patch is used to enlarge a hypoplastic pulmonary annulus and main pulmonary trunk. (From Hirsch JC, Bove EL: Tetralogy of Fallot. In Mavroudis C, Backer CL [eds]: Pediatric Cardiac Surgery, 3rd ed. Philadelphia, Mosby, 2003.)

be subdivided into d-TGA with intact ventricular septum (55% to 60%) and d-TGA with VSD (40% to 45%); Pulmonic stenosis, causing significant LV outflow tract obstruction, occurs rarely with an intact ventricular septum and in approximately 10% of cases of d-TGA/VSD.[42]

Natural History and Diagnosis

Without intervention, d-TGA is universally fatal: without treatment, 30% of neonates will die in the first week of life, 50% by the first month, 70% within 6 months, and 90% by 1 year.[45]

Clinical characteristics are dependent on the degree of mixing and the amount of pulmonary blood flow. These factors relate to the specific anatomic subtype of d-TGA.

Neonates with d-TGA with an intact ventricular septum (or small VSD) have mixing limited to the atrial level and PDA. The ASD may be restrictive and the PDA generally will close over the first days to week of life. As the degree of mixing decreases, the patient becomes increasingly cyanotic and will eventually suffer cardiovascular collapse. Fortunately, the majority of these neonates will manifest cyanosis early in life, which is recognized by nurse or physician within the first hour in 56% and in the first day in 92%.[44]

In d-TGA with a large VSD, there is additional opportunity for mixing and increased pulmonary blood flow. The neonate with d-TGA/VSD may only manifest mild cyanosis, which may be initially overlooked. However, generally within 2 to 6 weeks signs and symptoms of congestive heart failure will emerge. Tachypnea and tachycardia become prominent, whereas cyanosis may remain mild. Auscultatory findings are consistent with congestive heart failure with increased pulmonary blood flow, including a pansystolic murmur, third heart sound, mid-diastolic rumble, gallop, and narrowly split second heart sound with increased pulmonary component. Neonates with d-TGA and significant pulmonic stenosis present with severe cyanosis at birth. Lesser degrees of pulmonic stenosis will result in varying levels of cyanosis.

The diagnosis of d-TGA is generally suspected by the clinical presentation. The chest radiograph reveals an egg-shaped heart with a narrow superior mediastinal shadow, mild cardiomegaly, and increased pulmonary vascular markings. Echocardiography is the diagnostic modality of choice. Cardiac catheterization is rarely necessary in the current era.

Management

With all forms of d-TGA, there is the need to maintain adequate mixing of oxygenated and deoxygenated blood between the right and left sides of the heart. The circulation in d-TGA is of two separate circuits, pulmonary and systemic, in parallel (Fig. 123-19). Without communication between the two sides of the heart, deoxygenated blood does not reach the lungs and oxygenated blood does not reach the systemic circulation. The majority of patients will require two levels of mixing until the time of repair. In d-TGA/IVS, this is achieved by maintaining a PDA with prostaglandin E_1 infusion and ensuring an adequate ASD, including performing a balloon atrial septostomy when necessary. Occasionally, with d-TGA/VSD with mild or no pulmonic stenosis, there will be adequate mixing at the atrial and ventricular levels to allow for discontinuation of prostaglandin E_1. In the presence of significant pulmonic stenosis, prostaglandin E_1 will be necessary to provide sufficient pulmonary blood flow. These management strategies are utilized to palliate the patient

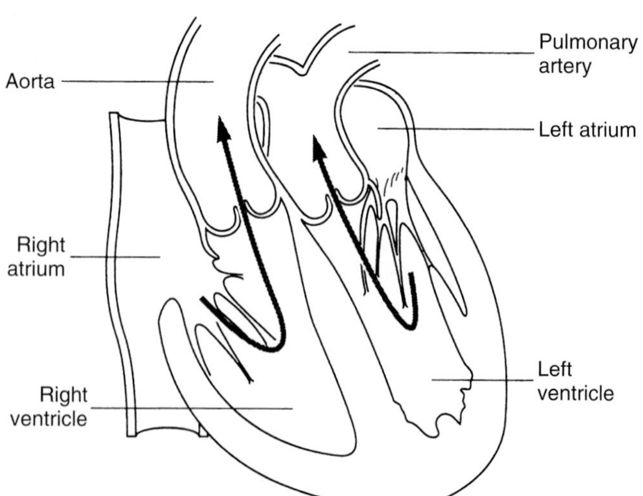

Figure 123-19 The anatomy of d-transposition of great arteries with intact ventricular septum. (From Bove EL, Lupinetti FM: Congenital heart disease and cardiac tumors. In Greenfield LJ, Mulholland MW, Oldham KT, Zelenock GB [eds]: Surgery: Scientific Principles and Practice. Philadelphia, JB Lippincott, 1993.)

until definitive surgical correction can be undertaken. In the absence of mitigating factors such as poor clinical condition preventing major open heart surgery, the current treatment of all forms of d-TGA is neonatal complete repair.

d-Transposition of the Great Arteries Without Pulmonic Stenosis

The current treatment for d-TGA is an arterial switch operation (ASO). The repair is performed via a median sternotomy with standard techniques of cardiopulmonary bypass. The aorta and main PA are divided (Fig. 123-20A). The PA is translocated anterior to the aorta using the Lecompte maneuver, and the distal aorta is anastomosed to the proximal PA (see Fig. 123-20B). The coronary arteries are removed from the aorta with buttons of adjacent artery and transferred to the proximal PA (see Fig. 123-20C). The proximal aorta is reconstructed using a pantaloon-shaped patch of autologous pericardium (see Fig. 123-20D) and anastomosed to the distal PA. The ASD and, if present, the VSD are closed.

d-Transposition of the Great Arteries with Ventricular Septal Defect and Pulmonic Stenosis

In the presence of significant pulmonic stenosis, a Rastelli procedure is performed, as an ASO will result in systemic LV outflow tract obstruction. The Rastelli operation utilizes the VSD to allow the LV to eject out of the aorta. The PA is ligated and divided at the level of the pulmonary annulus. The VSD patch is constructed to incorporate both the VSD and the aortic valve, creating a tunnel from the LV to the aorta (Fig. 123-21). RV-to-PA continuity is established using a conduit from the RV infundibulum to the distal PA.

Results

Current hospital survival for the ASO ranges from 90% to 95%.[13,33,42,46] d-TGA/IVS generally has a lower mortality than d-TGA/VSD or d-TGA/VSD/pulmonic stenosis. Hospital mortality for d-TGA/IVS ranges from 3.5% to 7.6%, compared with 9.4% to 13.1% for d-TGA/VSD.[13,33] Long-term survivals at 5 to 10 years and 15 years range from 87.9% to 93% and 86% to 88%, respectively.[13,33,46] The most common cause for re-intervention is supravalvar pulmonic stenosis, occurring in 3.9% to 16%.[33,46]

A recent study of 101 patients undergoing a Rastelli operation over a 25-year period revealed a hospital mortality of 7%, with no deaths in the last 7 years of the study.[43] Actuarial survival at 5, 10, 15, and 20 years was 82%, 80%, 68%, and 52%, respectively.

SINGLE VENTRICLE AND THE HYPOPLASTIC LEFT HEART SYNDROME

A variety of congenital cardiovascular malformations may result in a functional single ventricle anatomy, most commonly tricuspid atresia, pulmonary atresia, unbalanced AVSD, and hypoplastic left heart syndrome (HLHS). The most common lesion is HLHS. There are approximately 1000 infants with HLHS born in the United States each year. It is the most common severe congenital heart defect, comprising 7% to 9% of all anomalies diagnosed within the first year of life.[29] All single ventricle lesions share the common physiology of only a single ventricle capable of supporting cardiac output. They also share the need for a two- or three-step staged approach to reconstruction, ultimately resulting in a Fontan procedure. The goal of the initial procedure is to maintain adequate cardiac output and oxygen saturation while optimizing the patient for the ultimate Fontan procedure. Characteristics for an optimal candidate for a Fontan procedure include good ventricular function, low PA vascular resistance, no outflow tract obstruction, and no significant AV valve or semilunar valve regurgitation. Another option is cardiac transplantation.

Natural History and Diagnosis

The natural history of these lesions is dependent on the amount of pulmonary blood flow and the degree of systemic outflow tract obstruction. Patients with severely limited pulmonary blood flow or significant systemic outflow tract obstruction will succumb rapidly as the ductus arteriosus closes. Excessive pulmonary blood flow without systemic outflow tract obstruction will result in death owing to pulmonary vascular obstructive disease at months to decades of age, depending on the degree of pulmonary overcirculation. Occasionally, patients may be “balanced” with an appropriate ratio of systemic and pulmonary blood flow, which in rare cases may allow survival into adulthood. However, the treatment of choice for these patients is still staged reconstruction to a Fontan procedure, because even a perfectly balanced circulation leaves the heart volume overloaded and subject to ultimate failure. More commonly, this scenario simply allows the patient to avoid the need for an initial stage to control pulmonary blood flow in the neonatal period.

Management

Owing to the limited number of suitable donors, the uncertain effects of long-term immunosuppression, and the limited life span of transplanted hearts, the majority of centers have pursued a policy of staged reconstruction as the primary therapy for single ventricle lesions. Staged reconstruction involves a series of two or three procedures. An initial neonatal operation may or may not be necessary. This is followed at 4 to 6 months of age by a bidirectional Glenn or hemi-Fontan procedure and the Fontan procedure at 18 to 24 months of age.

Initial Palliation

Patients who do not have balanced systemic and PA flow ratios require an initial operation in the neonatal period. The goal of this first stage of reconstruction is to provide

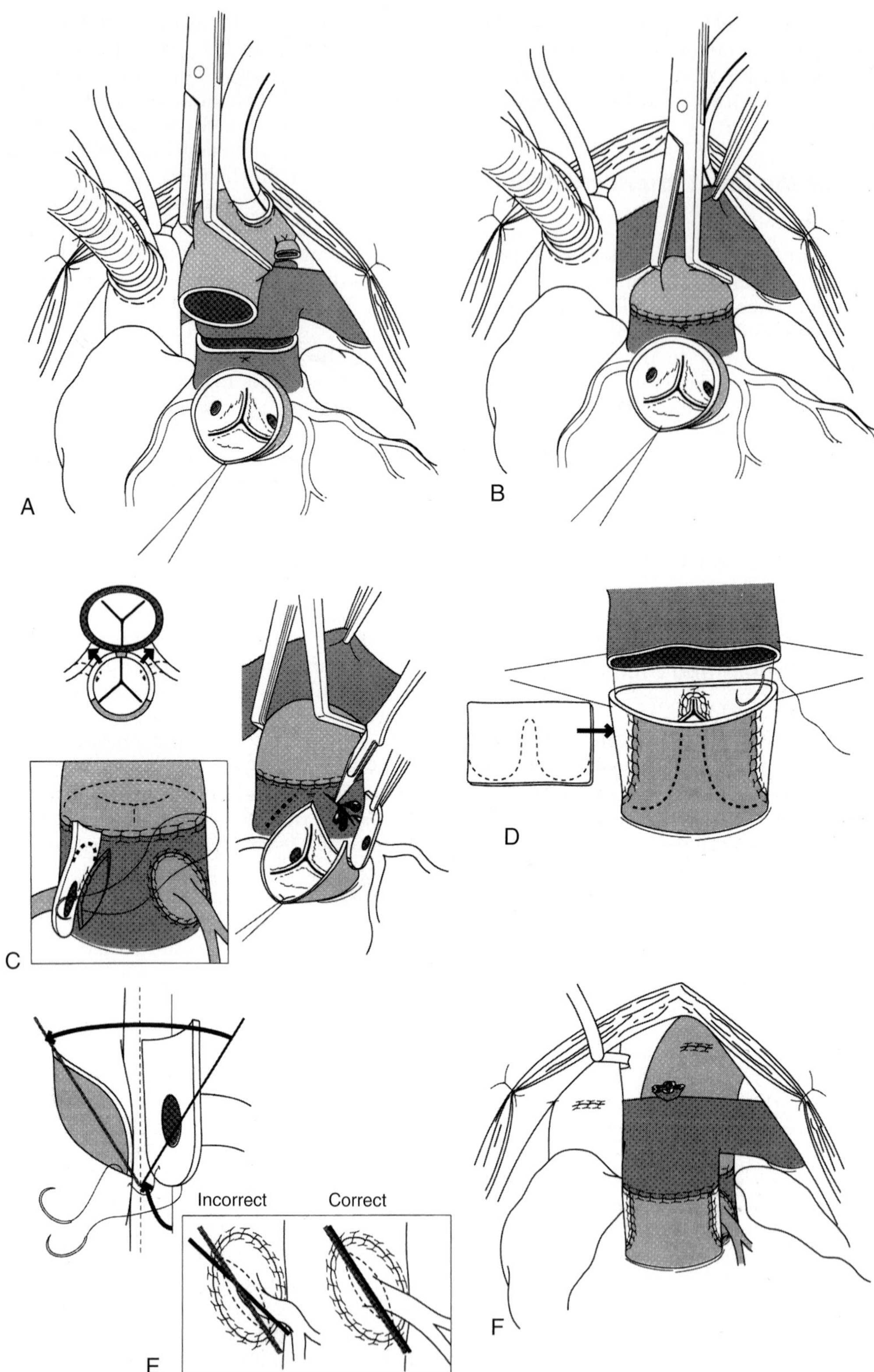

Figure 123–20 The arterial switch operation. *A,* Division of the aorta and pulmonary artery (PA). *B,* The Lecompte maneuver with the distal aorta anastomosed to the PA. *C,* Translocation of the coronary arteries. *D,* Reconstruction of the aorta with a pantaloon-shaped patch of autologous pericardium. *E,* Proper alignment of the coronary arteries. *F,* The completed repair. (From Bove EL, Lupinetti FM: Congenital heart disease and cardiac tumors. In Greenfield LJ, Mulholland MW, Oldham KT, Zelenock GB [eds]: Surgery: Scientific Principles and Practice. Philadelphia, JB Lippincott, 1993.)

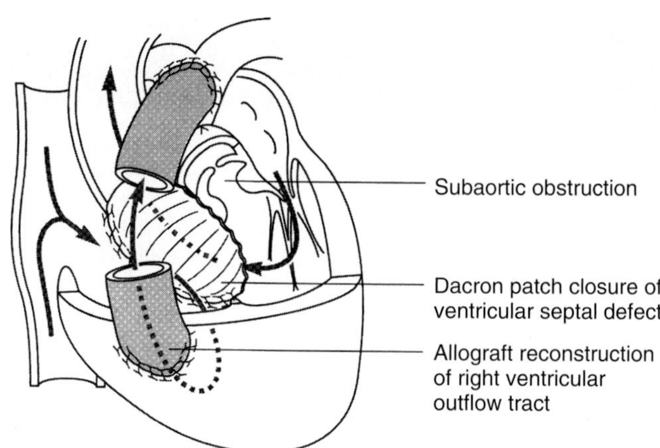

Figure 123–21 The Rastelli procedure. (From Bove EL, Lupinetti FM: Congenital heart disease and cardiac tumors. In Greenfield LJ, Mulholland MW, Oldham KT, Zelenock GB [eds]: Surgery: Scientific Principles and Practice. Philadelphia, JB Lippincott, 1993.)

unobstructed blood flow to the systemic and coronary circulations, nonrestrictive pulmonary venous return, and a controlled amount of flow to the lungs. For patients with unobstructed system blood flow and excessive pulmonary blood flow, the PA may be banded or disconnected with the placement of a systemic-to-PA shunt to control the pulmonary overcirculation. For patients with unobstructed system blood flow and inadequate pulmonary blood flow, a systemic-to-PA shunt is placed. The most common single ventricle lesion, HLHS, results in systemic outflow tract obstruction and excessive pulmonary blood flow and requires an initial Norwood operation. During the Norwood procedure, the aorta is reconstructed, incorporating the proximal PA to allow the single RV to eject out of the aorta. A systemic-to-PA shunt is then placed to provide PA blood flow (Fig. 123-22). This shunt may originate at the innominate artery (modified Blalock-Taussig shunt) or from the RV.

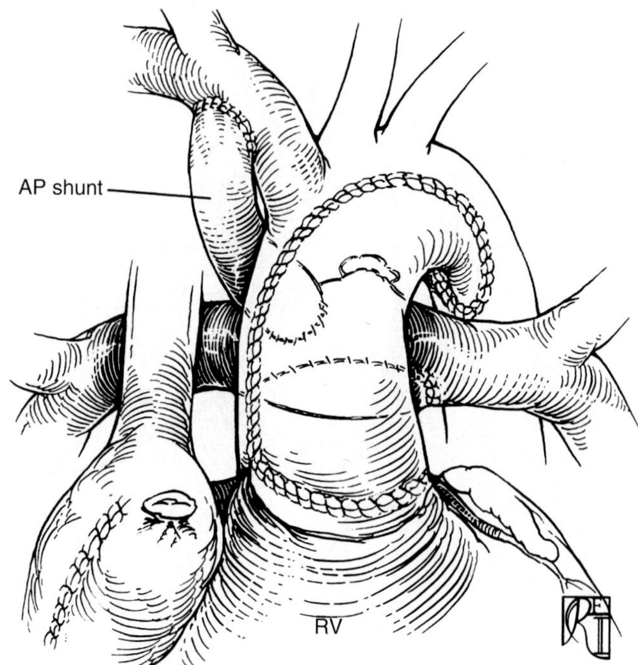

Figure 123–22 The completed Norwood procedure. RV, right ventricle; AP, aortopulmonary. (From Ohye RG, Mosca RM, Bove EL, et al: Hypoplastic left heart syndrome. In Mavroudis C, Backer CL [eds]: Pediatric Cardiac Surgery. Philadelphia, Mosby, 2003.)

The Bidirectional Glenn or Hemi-Fontan Procedure

To minimize the period of time during which the RV is subject to volume overload, the hemi-Fontan operation or a bidirectional Glenn (BDG) anastomosis is typically performed between 4 to 6 months of age. The BDG anastomosis entails removing the systemic-to-PA shunt and connecting the superior vena cava directly to the right PA by an end-to-side anastomosis. The pulmonary blood flow after this second stage is provided solely by the superior vena cava. The hemi-Fontan is a modification of the BDG procedure. The hemi-Fontan involves a side-to-side connection between the superior vena cava/RA junction and the pulmonary arteries, routine augmentation of the branch pulmonary arteries, and temporary patch closure between the pulmonary arteries and the RA (Fig. 123-23).

The Fontan Procedure

The completion Fontan procedure is usually performed at 18 to 24 months of age. The Fontan technique that we have employed for HLHS anatomy is the total cavopulmonary connection with a lateral tunnel (Fig. 123-24). During the Fontan procedure, the inferior vena caval venous return is directed to the PA. Other centers utilize an extracardiac conduit from the IVC to the right PA.

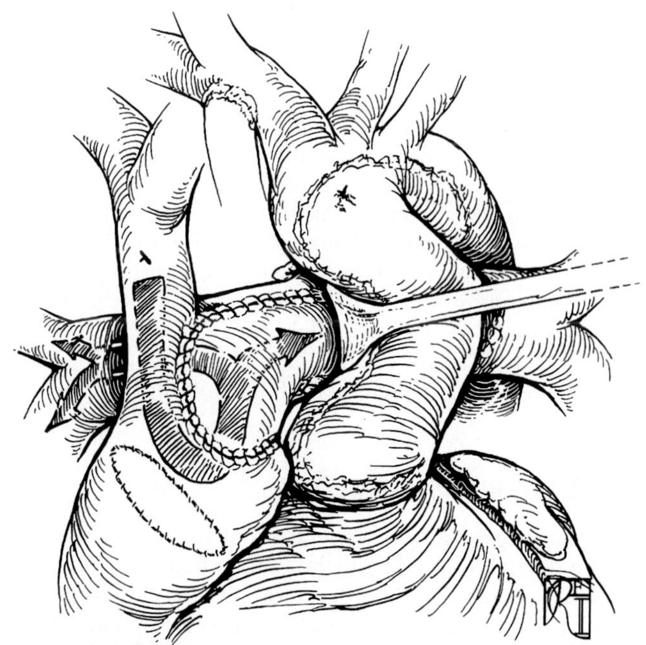

Figure 123–23 The completed hemi-Fontan procedure. (From Ohye RG, Mosca RM, Bove EL, et al: Hypoplastic left heart syndrome. In Mavroudis C, Backer CL [eds]: Pediatric Cardiac Surgery. Philadelphia, Mosby, 2003.)

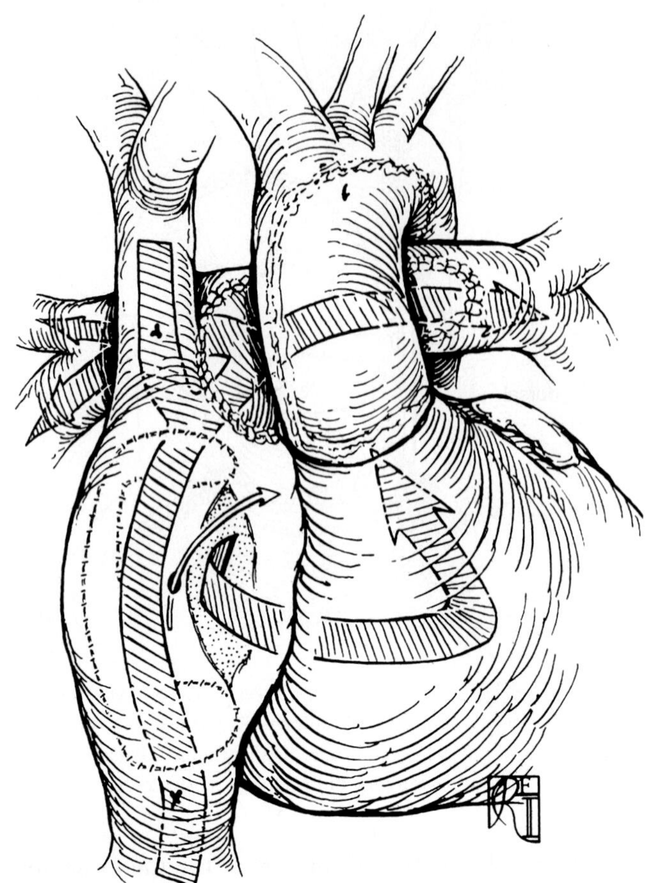

Figure 123-24 The completed Fontan procedure. (From Ohye RG, Mosca RM, Bove EL, et al: Hypoplastic left heart syndrome. In Mavroudis C, Backer CL [eds]: Pediatric Cardiac Surgery. Philadelphia, Mosby, 2003.)

Results

Recently, tremendous strides have been made in the outcomes for patients with single ventricle anatomy. Most notably, survival for patients with HLHS, universally fatal only 2 decades ago, has drastically improved. The highest risk stage of the repair remains the Norwood operation. During the 1990s, the hospital survival for the Norwood procedure across the United States was approximately 40%.[32] Currently, several select centers are reporting hospital survivals of approximately 90% or greater.[1,47,60,66] Reported survivals for the hemi-Fontan and Fontan procedures have been excellent at 98% for both operations.[11,26]

VASCULAR RINGS AND SLINGS

Vascular rings comprise a spectrum of vascular anomalies of the aortic arch, PA, and brachiocephalic vessels. The clinically significant manifestation of these lesions is a varying degree of tracheoesophageal compression. These vascular anomalies can be divided into complete vascular rings and partial vascular rings. Complete vascular rings can be divided into double aortic arch and right aortic arch with left ligamentum arteriosum. These two categories can be further subdivided based on the specific

TABLE 123-1 Anatomic Classification and Distribution of Vascular Anomalies

Anomaly Prevalence[70,71,74,79,80]	%
Complete vascular rings	65-82
Double aortic arch	38-55
Right dominant	73-81
Left dominant	15-20
Co-dominant	3-11
Right arch, left ligamentum/ductus	24-55
Aberrant left subclavian	65-92
Mirror-image branching	8-35
Right ligamentum	0-3
Incomplete vascular rings	14-29
Innominate artery compression	80-87
Aberrant right subclavian	13-20
Pulmonary sling	2-9

From Ohye RG, Wild LC, Mutabagani K, Bove EL: Vascular rings and slings. In Franco KL, Putman JB (eds): Advanced Therapy in Thoracic Surgery. Hamilton, Ontario, BC Decker, 2004.

anatomy (Table 123-1). Incomplete vascular rings include aberrant right subclavian artery, innominate artery compression, and PA sling. Other rare variations include a left aortic arch with right descending aorta and right ligamentum and a left aortic arch with aberrant right subclavian artery and right ligamentum. The incidence of clinically significant vascular rings is 1% to 2% of all congenital heart defects.

Vascular rings and pulmonary slings have been described in conjunction with other cardiac defects, including TOF, ASD, branch PA stenosis, coarctation, AVSD, VSD, interrupted aortic arch, and aortopulmonary window. Significant associated cardiac anomalies occur in 11% to 20% of patients with a vascular ring.[4,76,79] A right aortic arch is generally associated with a greater incidence of coexisting anomalies.

By the end of the fourth week of embryonic development, the six aortic or branchial arches have formed between the dorsal aortas and ventral roots. Subsequent involution and migration of the arches results in the anatomically normal or abnormal development of the aorta and its branches. The majority of the first, second, and fifth arches regress. The third arch forms the common carotid artery and proximal internal carotid artery. The right fourth arch forms the proximal right subclavian artery. The left fourth arch contributes to the portion of the aortic arch from left carotid to left subclavian arteries. The proximal portion of the right sixth arch becomes the proximal portion of the right PA, while the distal segment involutes. Similarly, the proximal left sixth arch contributes to the proximal left PA, and the distal sixth arch becomes the ductus arteriosus (Fig. 123-25).

The PA is formed from two vascular precursors, as well as through a combination of angiogenesis, the de novo development of new blood vessels, and vasculogenesis, the budding and migration of existing vessels. As stated earlier, the proximal pulmonary arteries are based on the sixth arches, whereas the primitive lung buds initially derive their blood supply from the splanchnic plexus.

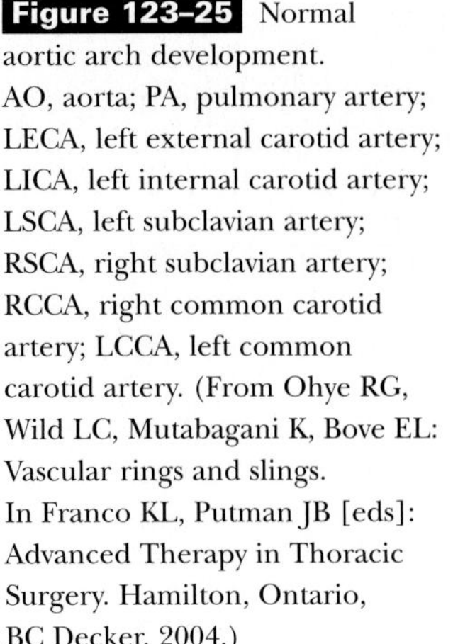

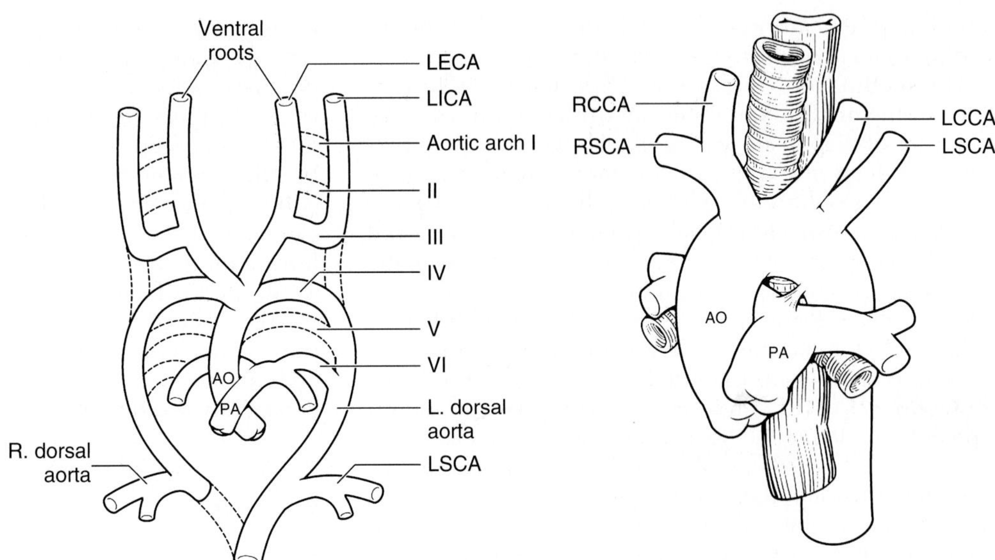

Figure 123–25 Normal aortic arch development. AO, aorta; PA, pulmonary artery; LECA, left external carotid artery; LICA, left internal carotid artery; LSCA, left subclavian artery; RSCA, right subclavian artery; RCCA, right common carotid artery; LCCA, left common carotid artery. (From Ohye RG, Wild LC, Mutabagani K, Bove EL: Vascular rings and slings. In Franco KL, Putman JB [eds]: Advanced Therapy in Thoracic Surgery. Hamilton, Ontario, BC Decker, 2004.)

Ultimately, these two segments of the PA join to form the vascular network of the lung parenchyma (Fig. 123-26).

Natural History and Diagnosis

Children with a complete vascular ring generally present within the first weeks to months of life. Typically, children with a double aortic arch present earlier in life than those with a right arch and left ligamentum. In the younger age group, respiratory symptoms predominate, as liquids are generally well tolerated. Respiratory symptoms may include stridor, nonproductive cough, apnea, or frequent respiratory infections. The cough is classically described as a "seal bark" or "brassy." These symptoms may mimic asthma, respiratory infection, or reflux, and children with vascular rings are often initially misdiagnosed. With the transition to solid food, dysphagia becomes more apparent.

The presentation of a patient with an incomplete vascular ring is variable. Children with innominate artery compression usually present within the first 1 to 2 years of life with respiratory symptoms. Although aberrant right subclavian artery is the most common arch abnormality, occurring in 0.5% to 1% of the population, it rarely causes symptoms. Classically, when symptoms do occur, they present in the seventh and eighth decades, as the aberrant vessel becomes ectatic and calcified, causing *dysphagia lusoria* owing to impingement of the artery on the posterior esophagus. An aberrant right subclavian rarely causes symptoms in children except when it is of an abnormally large caliber or associated with tracheomalacia.

Children with PA slings generally present with respiratory symptoms within the first few weeks to months of life. As with complete rings, respiratory symptoms may include stridor, nonproductive cough, apnea, or frequent respiratory infections and may mimic other conditions leading to misdiagnosis. PA slings are associated with

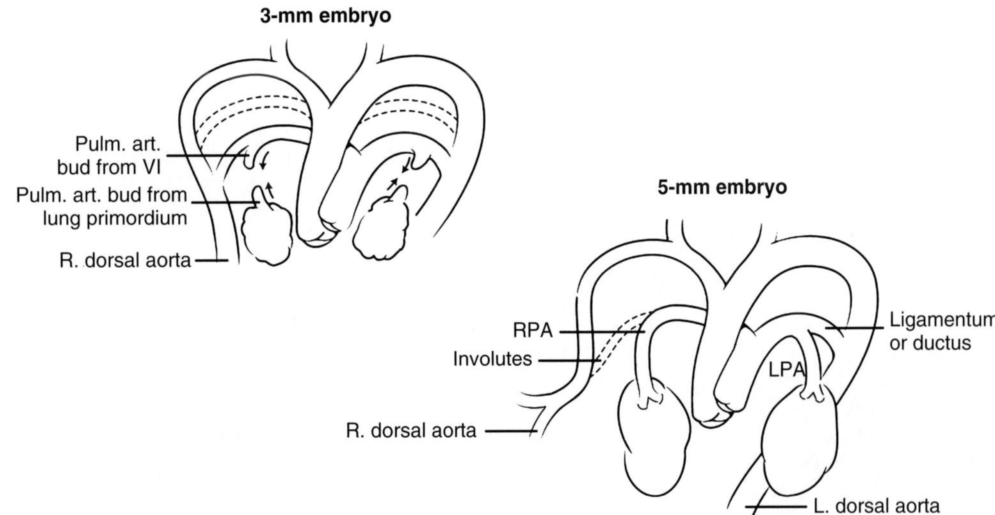

Figure 123–26 Normal pulmonary artery development. RPA, right pulmonary artery; LPA, left pulmonary artery. (From Ohye RG, Wild LC, Mutabagani K, Bove EL: Vascular rings and slings. In Franco KL, Putman JB [eds]: Advanced Therapy in Thoracic Surgery. Hamilton, Ontario, BC Decker, 2004.)

complete tracheal rings in 30% to 40% of patients, leading to focal or diffuse tracheal stenosis.[9]

The methods for diagnosing a vascular ring are variable, owing to the variability in presentation and the spectrum of diagnostic tests available. A child with a presumptive diagnosis of asthma or tracheomalacia may be referred to a pulmonologist and a diagnosis of vascular ring made or suspected initially by chest radiography and bronchoscopy. In some situations, the diagnosis is made by echocardiography during evaluation for concurrent cardiac defects. Regardless, the diagnosis generally begins with a chest radiograph. Complementary studies may include barium esophagography, CT, MRI, and bronchoscopy. CT, MRI, and bronchoscopy are important modalities to define the tracheal anatomy in a patient with a PA sling. Echocardiography may be diagnostic and may be used to rule out other cardiac anomalies. Tracheograms and cardiac catheterizations, which have been used extensively in the past, are rarely currently indicated.

Management

Complete Vascular Rings

Double Aortic Arch

A double aortic arch occurs when the distal portion of the right dorsal aorta fails to regress (Fig. 123-27). The two arches form a complete ring, encircling the trachea and esophagus. The right arch is dominant in the majority of the cases, followed by left dominant, with co-dominant arches being the least common (see Table 123-1). The left and right carotid and subclavian arteries generally arise from their respective arches. The ligamentum arteriosum and descending aorta usually remain on the left.

The approach to repair of a double aortic arch is via a left posterolateral thoracotomy. The procedure can easily be accomplished through a limited, muscle-sparing incision through the third or fourth intercostal space. The lung is retracted anteriorly and inferiorly, exposing the posterior mediastinum. The pleura is incised, after identifying the vagus and phrenic nerves. The ligamentum or ductus arteriosum is divided, while preserving the recurrent laryngeal nerve. The nondominant arch is then divided between two vascular clamps at the point where brachiocephalic flow is optimally preserved. If there is concern regarding the location for division, the arches can be temporarily occluded at various points, while monitoring pulse and blood pressure in each limb. If there is an atretic segment, the division is done at the point of the atresia. Dissection around the esophagus and trachea in the regions of the ligamentum/ductus and nondominant arch allows for retraction of the vascular structures and lysis of any residual obstructing adhesions.

Right Aortic Arch with Left Ligamentum Arteriosum

There are three anatomic variations for a right arch with a left ligamentum. If the left fourth arch regresses between the aorta and left subclavian, a right aortic arch with aberrant left subclavian artery results. The ligamentum arteriosum is retroesophageal, bridging the left PA and aberrant left subclavian, forming a complete vascular ring (Fig. 123-28). If the left fourth arch regresses after the origin of the left subclavian artery, but before the arch reaches the dorsal aorta to communicate with the left sixth arch (which becomes the ductus arteriosum), there is mirror-image branching. The retroesophageal ligamentum arteriosum arises directly from the descending aorta, or from Kommerell's diverticulum off of the descending aorta, forming the complete ring (Fig. 123-29). If communication is maintained between the left fourth and sixth arches, there is mirror image branching with the ligamentum arising from the anterior, mirror image left subclavian and a ring is not formed (Fig. 123-30).

The surgical approach for a right aortic arch with retroesophageal left ligamentum arteriosum is the same as for a double arch. The ligamentum is divided, and any adhesions around the esophagus and trachea are lysed.

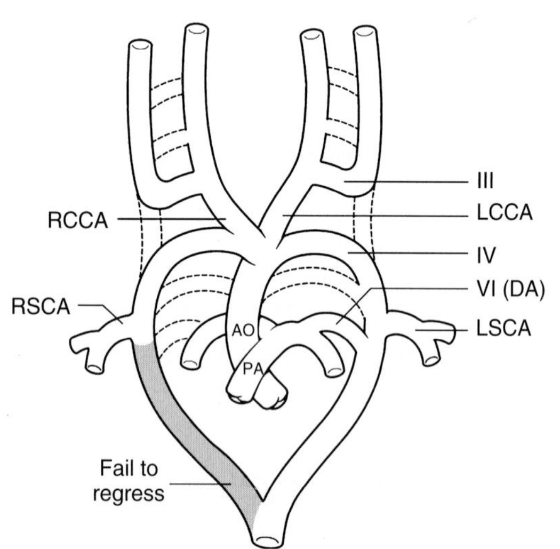

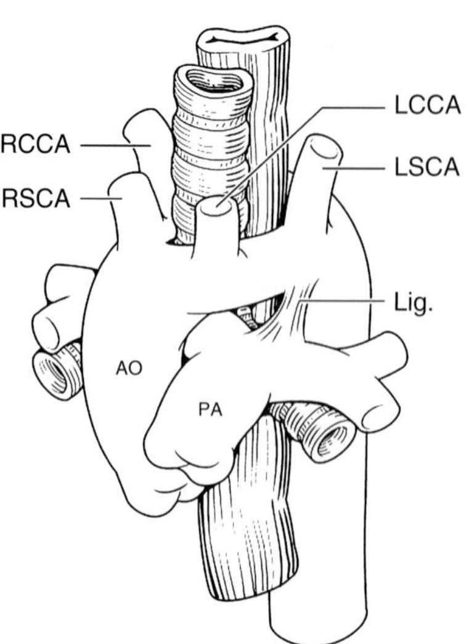

Figure 123-27 Formation of a double aortic arch. AO, aorta; PA, pulmonary artery; LSCA, left subclavian artery; RSCA, right subclavian artery; RCCA, right common carotid artery; LCCA, left common carotid artery; DA, ductus arteriosum; Lig., ligamentum arteriosum. (From Ohye RG, Wild LC, Mutabagani K, Bove EL: Vascular rings and slings. In Franco KL, Putman JB [eds]: Advanced Therapy in Thoracic Surgery. Hamilton, Ontario, BC Decker, 2004.)

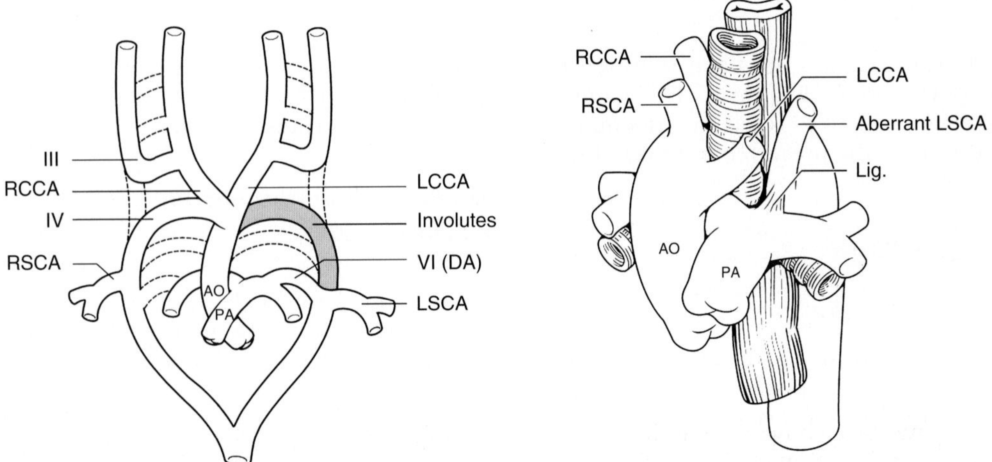

Figure 123–28 Formation of a right aortic arch with aberrant left subclavian and retroesophageal left ligamentum arteriosum. AO, aorta; PA, pulmonary artery; LSCA, left subclavian artery; RSCA, right subclavian artery; RCCA, right common carotid artery; LCCA, left common carotid artery; DA, ductus arteriosus; Lig., ligamentum arteriosum. (From Ohye RG, Wild LC, Mutabagani K, Bove EL: Vascular rings and slings. In Franco KL, Putman JB [eds]: Advanced Therapy in Thoracic Surgery. Hamilton, Ontario, BC Decker, 2004.)

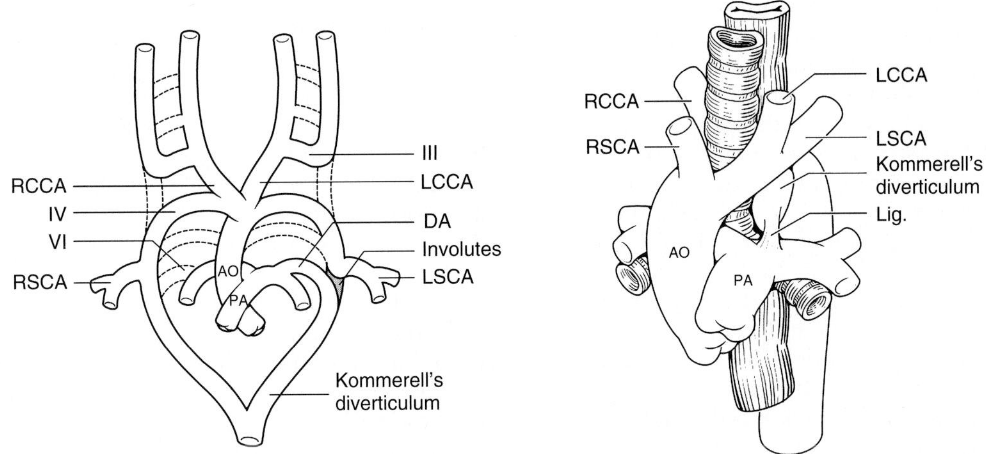

Figure 123–29 Formation of a right aortic arch with mirror image branching and retroesophageal left ligamentum arteriosum. AO, aorta; PA, pulmonary artery; LSCA, left subclavian artery; RSCA, right subclavian artery; RCCA, right common carotid artery; LCCA, left common carotid artery; DA, ductus arteriosum; Lig., ligamentum arteriosum. (From Ohye RG, Wild LC, Mutabagani K, Bove EL: Vascular rings and slings. In Franco KL, Putman JB [eds]: Advanced Therapy in Thoracic Surgery. Hamilton, Ontario, BC Decker, 2004.)

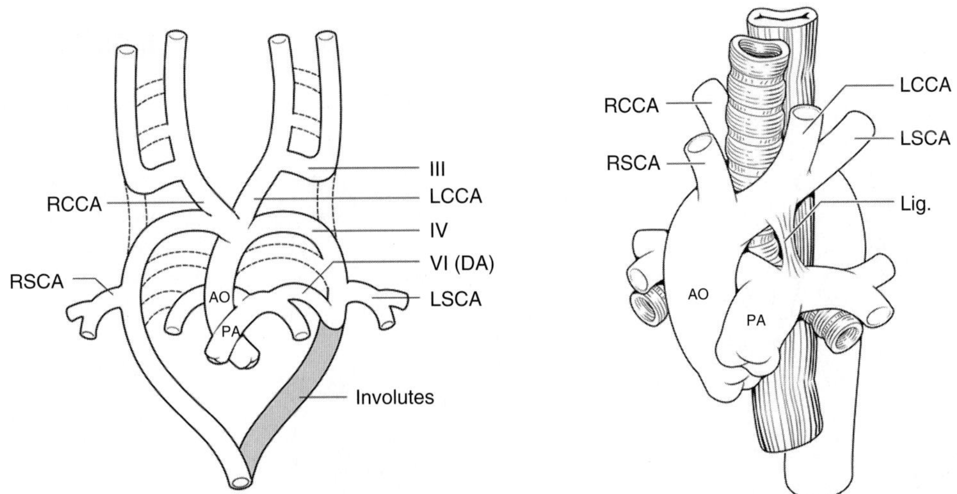

Figure 123–30 Formation of a right aortic arch with mirror image branching and left ligamentum arteriosum, which does not form a vascular ring. AO, aorta; PA, pulmonary artery; LSCA, left subclavian artery; RSCA, right subclavian artery; RCCA, right common carotid artery; LCCA, left common carotid artery; DA, ductus arteriosum; Lig., ligamentum arteriosum. (From Ohye RG, Wild LC, Mutabagani K, Bove EL: Vascular rings and slings. In Franco KL, Putman JB [eds]: Advanced Therapy in Thoracic Surgery. Hamilton, Ontario, BC Decker, 2004.)

Rarely, Kommerell's diverticulum has been reported to cause compression even after division of the ligamentum. As such, it may be prudent to resect or suspend the diverticulum posteriorly to the prevertebral fascia, if it is particularly prominent.

Incomplete Vascular Rings

Innominate Artery Compression

In innominate artery compression syndrome, the aortic arch and ligamentum are in their normal leftward position. However, the innominate artery arises partially or totally to the left of midline (Fig. 123-31). As the artery courses from left to right anterior to the trachea, it causes tracheal compression. The symptoms of innominate artery compression may be mild to severe. With mild symptoms and minimal tracheal compression on bronchoscopy, children can be observed expectantly because the symptoms may resolve with growth. Indications for surgery include apnea, severe respiratory distress, significant stridor, or recurrent respiratory tract infection.

Several approaches for the correction of innominate artery compression syndrome have been described. These include simple division, division with reimplantation into the right side of the ascending aorta, and suspension to the overlying sternum. Suspension is currently the most widely used technique. Exposure is obtained through a limited left anterior, right anterior, or right inframammary anterolateral thoracotomy. Once the innominate artery is exposed, no dissection of the artery is undertaken. By not performing a circumferential dissection of the innominate artery, the suspension of the vessel will also pull up on the anterior trachea. Pledged polypropylene sutures are passed partial thickness through both the innominate artery and the aorta at the origin of the innominate. Temporary distraction on the sutures under bronchoscopic guidance aids in the optimal placement of the sutures in the vessels and overlying sternum. Once satisfactory reestablishment of tracheal patency is confirmed by bronchoscopy, the sutures are brought through the sternum and secured.

Left Aortic Arch with Aberrant Right Subclavian Artery

An aberrant right subclavian artery occurs when there is regression of the right fourth arch between the right common carotid and right subclavian arteries (Fig. 123-32). The right subclavian then arises from the leftward descending aorta, lying posterior to the esophagus as it crosses from left to right. Although the artery can compress the esophagus posteriorly, it is rarely the cause of symptoms in children. Surgical treatment involves simple division via a left posterolateral thoracotomy. Rarely, reimplantation or grafting from the right carotid or aortic arch may be necessary.

Pulmonary Artery Sling

Normally, the right and left sixth aortic arches contribute to the proximal portions of their respective pulmonary arteries. If the proximal left sixth arch involutes and the bud from the left lung migrates rightward to meet the right PA, a PA sling is formed (Fig. 123-33). PA slings are associated with complete tracheal rings and tracheal stenosis in 30% to 40% of patients.[9] Origin of the right upper lobe bronchus from the trachea has been reported in frequent association with PA sling.[3]

Initial attempts at the repair of a PA sling involved reimplantation after division of the left PA and translocation of the trachea without cardiopulmonary bypass. In these early reports there was a high incidence of left PA thrombosis. This has led some authors to advocate division of the trachea and translocation of the left PA. This approach would seem sensible if the trachea were being divided in the course of tracheal reconstruction.

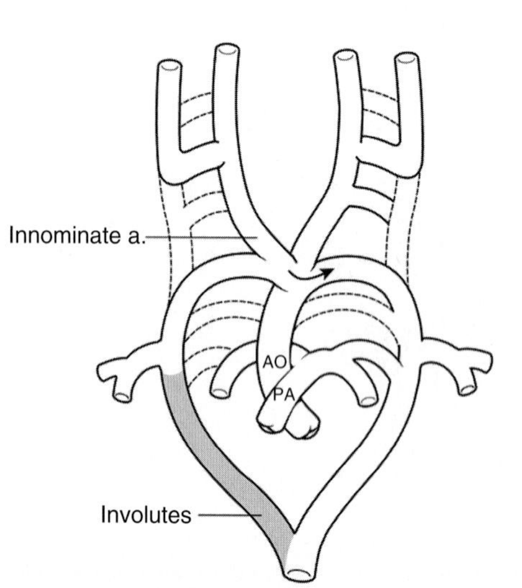

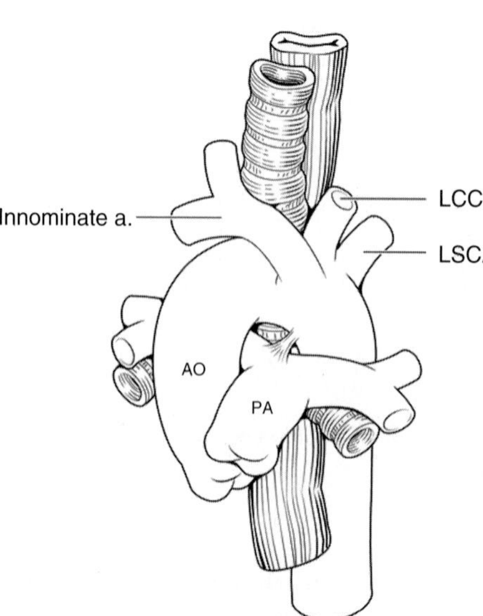

Figure 123-31 Embryologic origin of innominate artery compression syndrome. AO, aorta; PA, pulmonary artery; LCCA, left common carotid artery; LSCA, left subclavian artery. (From Ohye RG, Wild LC, Mutabagani K, Bove EL: Vascular rings and slings. In Franco KL, Putman JB [eds]: Advanced Therapy in Thoracic Surgery. Hamilton, Ontario, BC Decker, 2004.)

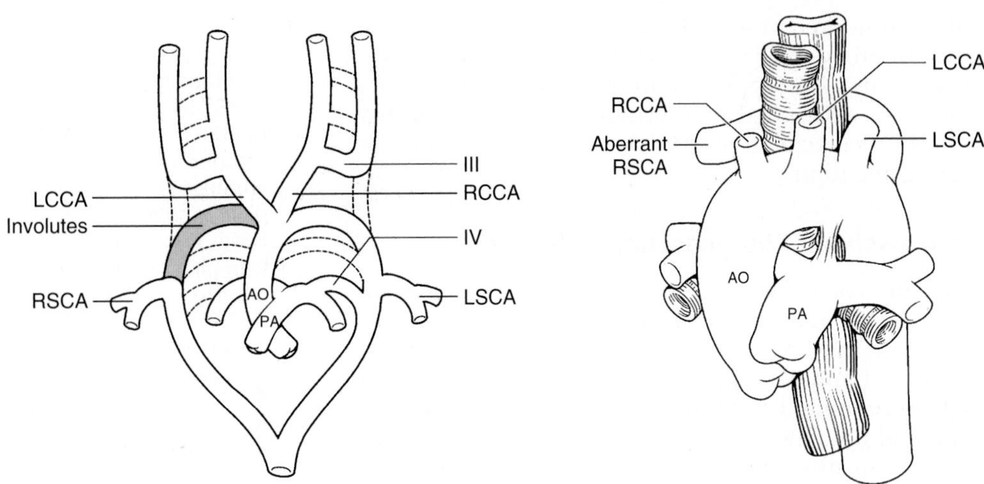

Figure 123–32 Formation of a left aortic arch with aberrant right subclavian artery. AO, aorta; PA, pulmonary artery; LSCA, left subclavian artery; RSCA, right subclavian artery; RCCA, right common carotid artery; LCCA, left common carotid artery. (From Ohye RG, Wild LC, Mutabagani K, Bove EL: Vascular rings and slings. In Franco KL, Putman JB [eds]: Advanced Therapy in Thoracic Surgery. Hamilton, Ontario, BC Decker, 2004.)

However, currently most authors advocate the reimplantation of the left PA, which has resulted in excellent results.[8,77] The procedure is done via a median sternotomy on cardiopulmonary bypass to ensure optimal visualization of the repair. Aortic cross-clamping is not necessary. The left PA is divided off of the right PA, translocated anterior to the trachea, and reimplanted into the main PA.

Any necessary reconstruction of the trachea is done concurrently with bronchoscopic assistance. Many techniques for tracheal reconstruction have been described, the most common of which are resection with primary reanastomosis and sliding tracheoplasty for short-segment stenosis and rib cartilage or pericardial patch for long areas of narrowing.

Vascular Rings Requiring a Right Thoracotomy

Over 95% of vascular rings without concurrent cardiac defects can be performed through a left thoracotomy. A right thoracotomy is indicated for the rare cases where there is a right ligamentum arteriosum. A right ligamentum occurs in the setting of a left aortic arch with right descending aorta, where the ligamentum bridges from the descending aorta to the right PA forming a complete ring. Right ligamentum arteriosum has also been described with a left aortic arch with aberrant right subclavian artery. In this case, the ligamentum may arise from the aberrant subclavian artery, from a diverticulum off of the arch, or directly from the left arch to the right PA. In addition, a

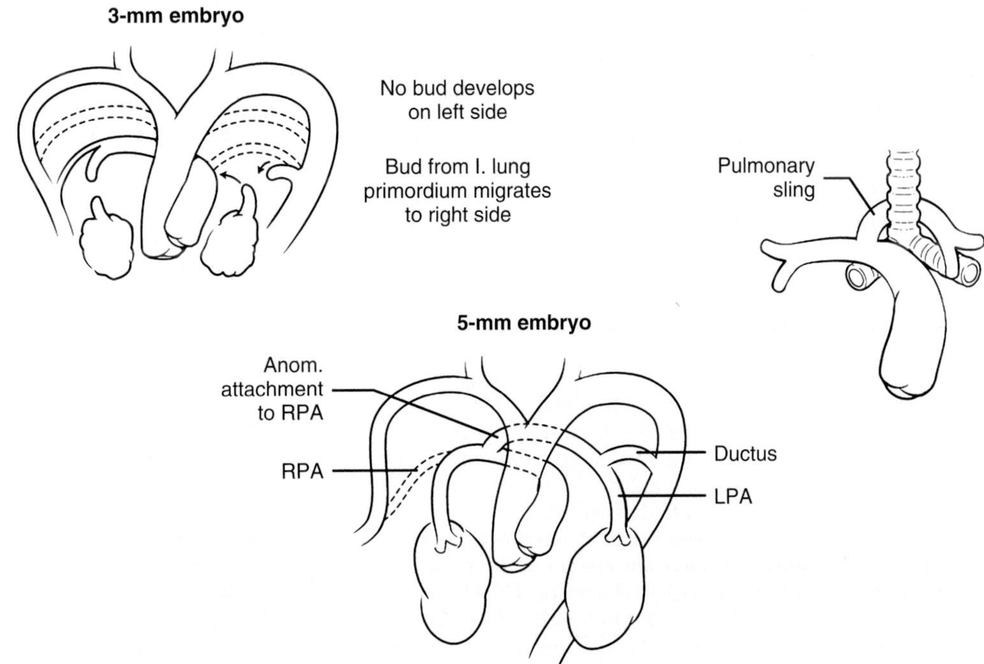

Figure 123–33 Formation of a pulmonary artery sling. RPA, right pulmonary artery; LPA, left pulmonary artery. (From Ohye RG, Wild LC, Mutabagani K, Bove EL: Vascular rings and slings. In Franco KL, Putman JB [eds]: Advanced Therapy in Thoracic Surgery. Hamilton, Ontario, BC Decker, 2004.)

double aortic arch with an atretic segment proximal to the right carotid artery is more easily divided through a right thoracotomy. The approach to these anomalies is the same as for a left-sided ring division, with the caveat that the right recurrent laryngeal nerve will loop around the right ligamentum.

Video-assisted Thoracoscopic Surgery

Burke and colleagues and our center have reported the repair of vascular rings using video-assisted thoracoscopic surgery (VATS) both with[55] and without[14] robotic assistance. Candidates for thoracoscopic division in both series were limited to those patients requiring only the division of nonpatent vascular structures. There were no operative deaths, and all procedures were completed by VATS.

Results

Mortality for the repair of a vascular ring is 0.5% to 7.6%, with improved survival occurring in more recent series.[3,51,76,79] The majority of deaths are related to other cardiac defects or respiratory infection and failure. Backer and colleagues[8] reported a series of 16 patients repaired utilizing left PA division and reimplantation for PA sling, all of whom also required tracheal reconstruction. There were no operative mortalities and one late death due to respiratory complications. The major source of morbidity, as well as mortality, in this and other series is related to the tracheal reconstruction.[8,77]

REFERENCES

1. Azakie A, Martinez D, Sapru A, et al: Impact of right ventricle to pulmonary artery conduit on outcome of the modified Norwood procedure. Ann Thorac Surg 2004;77: 1727-1733.
2. Bacha EA, Scheule AM, Zurakowski D, et al: Long-term results after early primary repair of tetralogy of Fallot. J Thorac Cardiovasc Surg 2001;122:154-161.
3. Backer C: Vascular rings and pulmonary artery sling. In Mavroudis C (ed): Pediatric Cardiac Surgery, 2nd ed. St. Louis, Mosby, 1994.
4. Backer CL, Ilbawi MN, Idriss FS, DeLeon SY: Vascular anomalies causing tracheoesophageal compression: Review of experience in children. J Thorac Cardiovasc Surg 1989; 97:725-731.
5. Backer CL, Idriss FS, Zales VR, et al: Surgical management of the conal (supracristal) ventricular septal defect. J Thorac Cardiovasc Surg 1991;102:288-295; discussion 295-296.
6. Backer CL, Paape K, Zales VR, et al: Coarctation of the aorta: Repair with polytetrafluoroethylene patch aortoplasty. Circulation 1995;92(9 Suppl):II132-II136.
7. Backer CL, Mavroudis C, Zias EA, et al: Repair of coarctation with resection and extended end-to-end anastomosis. Ann Thorac Surg 1998;66:1365-1370; discussion 1370-1371.
8. Backer CL, Mavroudis C, Dunham ME, Holinger LD: Pulmonary artery sling: Results with median sternotomy, cardiopulmonary bypass, and reimplantation. Ann Thorac Surg 1999;67:1738-1744; discussion 1744-1745.
9. Berdon WE, Baker DH, Wung JT, et al: Complete cartilage-ring tracheal stenosis associated with anomalous left pulmonary artery: The ring-sling complex. Radiology 1984; 152:57-64.
10. Bharati S, Kirklin JW, McAllister HA Jr, Lev M: The surgical anatomy of common atrioventricular orifice associated with tetralogy of Fallot, double outlet right ventricle and complete regular transposition. Circulation 1980;61:1142-1149.
11. Bove EL: Current status of staged reconstruction for hypoplastic left heart syndrome. Pediatr Cardiol 1998;19: 308-315.
12. Brewer LA 3rd, Fosburg RG, Mulder GA, Verska JJ: Spinal cord complications following surgery for coarctation of the aorta: A study of 66 cases. J Thorac Cardiovasc Surg 1972;64: 368-381.
13. Brown JW, Park HJ, Turrentine MW: Arterial switch operation: Factors impacting survival in the current era. Ann Thorac Surg 2001;71:1978-1984.
14. Burke RP, Wernovsky G, van der Velde M, et al: Video-assisted thoracoscopic surgery for congenital heart disease. J Thorac Cardiovasc Surg 1995;109:499-507; discussion 508.
15. Burke RP, Jacobs JP, Cheng W, et al: Video-assisted thoracoscopic surgery for patent ductus arteriosus in low birth weight neonates and infants. Pediatrics 1999;104:227-230.
16. Campbell M: Natural history of persistent ductus arteriosus. Br Heart J 1968;30:4-13.
17. Cooper RS, Ritter SB, Rothe WB, et al: Angioplasty for coarctation of the aorta: Long-term results. Circulation 1987;75:600-604.
18. Coster DD, Gorton ME, Grooters RK, et al: Surgical closure of the patent ductus arteriosus in the neonatal intensive care unit. Ann Thorac Surg 1989;48:386-389.
19. Cowley CG, Lloyd TR: Interventional cardiac catheterization advances in nonsurgical approaches to congenital heart disease. Curr Opin Pediatr 1999;11:425-432.
20. Cowley CG, Lloyd TR, Bove EL, et al: Comparison of results of closure of secundum atrial septal defect by surgery versus Amplatzer septal occluder. Am J Cardiol 2001;88:589-591.
21. Craig RJ, Selzer A: Natural history and prognosis of atrial septal defect. Circulation 1968;37:805-815.
22. Dajani AS, Taubert KA, Wilson W, et al: Prevention of bacterial endocarditis. Recommendations by the American Heart Association. Circulation 1997;96:358-366.
23. de Ruijter FT, Weenink I, Hitchcock FJ, et al: Right ventricular dysfunction and pulmonary valve replacement after correction of tetralogy of Fallot. Ann Thorac Surg 2002;73:1794-1800; discussion 1800.
24. del Nido PJ, Williams WG, Wilson GJ, et al: Synthetic patch angioplasty for repair of coarctation of the aorta: Experience with aneurysm formation. Circulation 1986;74:I32-I36.
25. Discigil B, Dearani JA, Puga FJ, et al: Late pulmonary valve replacement after repair of tetralogy of Fallot. J Thorac Cardiovasc Surg 2001;121:344-351.
26. Douglas WI, Goldberg CS, Mosca RS, et al: Hemi-Fontan procedure for hypoplastic left heart syndrome: Outcome and suitability for Fontan. Ann Thorac Surg 1999;68: 1361-1367; discussion 1368.
27. Draulans-Noe HA, Wenink AC, Quaegebeur J: Single papillary muscle ("parachute valve") and double-orifice left ventricle in atrioventricular septal defect convergence of chordal attachment: Surgical anatomy and results of surgery. Pediatr Cardiol 1990;11:29-35.
28. Elliott RB, Starling MB, Neutze JM: Medical manipulation of the ductus arteriosus. Lancet 1975;1:140-142.
29. Fyler D: Report of the New England Regional Infant Cardiac Program. Pediatrics 1980;65:375-461.
30. Gersony WM, Peckham GJ, Ellison RC, et al: Effects of indomethacin in premature infants with patent ductus

arteriosus: Results of a national collaborative study. J Pediatr 1983;102:895-906.

31. Goyal VS, Fulwani MC, Ramakantan R, et al: Follow-up after coil closure of patent ductus arteriosus. Am J Cardiol 1999;83:463-466.
32. Gutgesell HP, Gibson J: Management of hypoplastic left heart syndrome in the 1990s. Am J Cardiol 2002;89: 842-846.
33. Haas F, Wottke M, Poppert H, Meisner H: Long-term survival and functional follow-up in patients after the arterial switch operation. Ann Thorac Surg 1999;68:1692-1697.
34. Hanley FL, Fenton KN, Jonas RA, et al: Surgical repair of complete atrioventricular canal defects in infancy: Twenty-year trends. J Thorac Cardiovasc Surg 1993;106:387-394; discussion 394-397.
35. Hellenbrand WE, Allen HD, Golinko RJ, et al: Balloon angioplasty for aortic recoarctation: Results of Valvuloplasty and Angioplasty of Congenital Anomalies Registry. Am J Cardiol 1990;65:793-797.
36. Heymann MA, Rudolph AM, Silverman NH: Closure of the ductus arteriosus in premature infants by inhibition of prostaglandin synthesis. N Engl J Med 1976;295: 530-533.
37. Hijazi ZM, Fahey JT, Kleinman CS, Hellenbrand WE: Balloon angioplasty for recurrent coarctation of aorta: Immediate and long-term results. Circulation 1991;84:1150-1156.
38. Hirsch JC, Bove EL: Tetralogy of Fallot. In Mavroudis C, Backer CL (eds): Pediatric Cardiac Surgery, 3rd ed. Philadelphia, Mosby, 2003.
39. Hoffman JI, Kaplan S: The incidence of congenital heart disease. J Am Coll Cardiol 2002;39:1890-1900.
40. Kadoba K, Jonas RA, Mayer JE, Castaneda AR: Mitral valve replacement in the first year of life. J Thorac Cardiovasc Surg 1990;100:762-768.
41. Karl TR, Sano S, Pornviliwan S, Mee RB: Tetralogy of Fallot: Favorable outcome of nonneonatal transatrial, transpulmonary repair. Ann Thorac Surg 1992;54:903-907.
42. Kirklin J: Complete transposition of the great arteries. In Kirklin J (ed): Cardiac Surgery. New York, Churchill Livingstone, 1993, pp 1383-1467.
43. Kreutzer C, De Vive J, Oppido G, et al: Twenty-five-year experience with Rastelli repair for transposition of the great arteries. J Thorac Cardiovasc Surg 2000;120: 211-223.
44. Levin DL, Paul MH, Muster AJ, et al: d-Transposition of the great vessels in the neonate: A clinical diagnosis. Arch Intern Med 1977;137:1421-1425.
45. Liebman J: Natural history of transposition of the great arteries: Anatomy and birth and death characteristics. Circulation 1969;40:237-262.
46. Losay J, Touchot A, Serraf A, et al: Late outcome after arterial switch operation for transposition of the great arteries. Circulation 2001;104(12 Suppl 1):I121-I126.
47. Mair R, Tulzer G, Sames E, et al: Right ventricular to pulmonary artery conduit instead of modified Blalock-Taussig shunt improves postoperative hemodynamics in newborns after the Norwood operation. J Thorac Cardiovasc Surg 2003;126:1378-1384.
48. Mavroudis C, Backer CL, Jacobs JP: Ventricular septal defect. In Mavroudis C, Backer CL (eds): Pediatric Cardiac Surgery, 3rd ed. Philadelphia, Mosby, 2003.
49. Meijboom F, Hess J, Szatmari A, et al: Long-term follow-up (9 to 20 years) after surgical closure of atrial septal defect at a young age. Am J Cardiol 1993;72:1431-1434.
50. Minich LL, Tani LY, Pagotto LT, et al: Size of ventricular structures influences surgical outcome in Down syndrome infants with atrioventricular septal defect. Am J Cardiol 1998;81:1062-1065.
51. Mitchell J: Vascular rings, slings and other arch anomalies. In Kaiser L (ed): Mastery of Cardiothoracic Surgery. Philadelphia, Lippincott-Raven, 1998.
52. Moe DG, Guntheroth WG: Spontaneous closure of uncomplicated ventricular septal defect. Am J Cardiol 1987;60: 674-678.
53. Momma K, Toyama K, Takao A, et al: Natural history of subarterial infundibular ventricular septal defect. Am Heart J 1984;108:1312-1317.
54. Newfeld EA, Sher M, Paul MH, Nikaidoh H: Pulmonary vascular disease in complete atrioventricular canal defect. Am J Cardiol 1977;39:721-726.
55. Ohye R: Robotics in pediatric cardiac surgery. Presented before the 40th annual meeting of the Society of Thoracic Surgeons, San Antonio, Texas, 2004.
56. Ohye R: Vascular rings and slings. In Franco KL, Putman JB (eds): Advanced Therapy in Thoracic Surgery. Hamilton, Ontario, BC Decker, 2004.
57. Ovaert C, McCrindle BW, Nykanen D, et al: Balloon angioplasty of native coarctation: Clinical outcomes and predictors of success. J Am Coll Cardiol 2000;35: 988-996.
58. Patel HT, Cao QL, Rhodes J, Hijazi ZM: Long-term outcome of transcatheter coil closure of small to large patent ductus arteriosus. Cathet Cardiovasc Interv 1999;47:457-461.
59. Piccoli GP, Ho SY, Wilkinson JL, et al: Left-sided obstructive lesions in atrioventricular septal defects: An anatomic study. J Thorac Cardiovasc Surg 1982;83:453-460.
60. Pizarro C, Malec E, Maher KO, et al: Right ventricle to pulmonary artery conduit improves outcome after stage I Norwood for hypoplastic left heart syndrome. Circulation 2003;108(Suppl 1):II155-II160.
61. Presbitero P, Demarie D, Villani M, et al: Long term results (15–30 years) of surgical repair of aortic coarctation. Br Heart J 1987;57:462-467.
62. Puga FJ: Reoperation after repair of atrioventricular canal defects. Semin Thorac Cardiovasc Surg Pediatr Card Surg Annu 1998;1:123-128.
63. Purcell IF, Brecker SJ, Ward DE: Closure of defects of the atrial septum in adults using the Amplatzer device: 100 consecutive patients in a single center. Clin Cardiol 2004;27: 509-513.
64. Rastelli G, Kirklin JW, Titus JL: Anatomic observations on complete form of persistent common atrioventricular canal with special reference to atrioventricular valves. Mayo Clin Proc 1966;41:296-308.
65. Reifenstein GH, Levine SA, Gross RE: Coarctation of the aorta: A review of 104 autopsied cases of the "adult type," 2 years of age or older. Am Heart J 1947;33:146-168.
66. Sano S, Ishino K, Kawada M, et al: Right ventricle-pulmonary artery shunt in first-stage palliation of hypoplastic left heart syndrome. J Thorac Cardiovasc Surg 2003;126:504-509; discussion 509-510.
67. Seirafi PA, Warner KG, Geggel RL, et al: Repair of coarctation of the aorta during infancy minimizes the risk of late hypertension. Ann Thorac Surg 1998;66:1378-1382.
68. Siassi B, Blanco C, Cabal LA, Coran AG: Incidence and clinical features of patent ductus arteriosus in low-birth-weight infants: A prospective analysis of 150 consecutively born infants. Pediatrics 1976;57:347-351.
69. Spicer RL: Cardiovascular disease in Down syndrome. Pediatr Clin North Am 1984;31:1331-1343.
70. Stewart S, Alexson C, Manning J: Partial atrioventricular canal defect: The early and late results of operation. Ann Thorac Surg 1987;43:527-529.
71. Studer M, Blackstone EH, Kirklin JW, et al: Determinants of early and late results of repair of atrioventricular septal (canal) defects. J Thorac Cardiovasc Surg 1982;84:523-542.

72. Taylor RL, Grover FL, Harman PK, et al: Operative closure of patent ductus arteriosus in premature infants in the neonatal intensive care unit. Am J Surg 1986;152: 704-708.
73. Tynan M, Finley JP, Fontes V, et al: Balloon angioplasty for the treatment of native coarctation: Results of Valvuloplasty and Angioplasty of Congenital Anomalies Registry. Am J Cardiol 1990;65:790-792.
74. van Heurn LW, Wong CM, Spiegelhalter DJ, et al: Surgical treatment of aortic coarctation in infants younger than three months: 1985 to 1990. Success of extended end-to-end arch aortoplasty. J Thorac Cardiovasc Surg 1994;107:74-85; discussion 85-86.
75. Van Praagh R, Van Praagh S, Nebesar RA, et al: Tetralogy of Fallot: Underdevelopment of the pulmonary infundibulum and its sequelae. Am J Cardiol 1970;26:25-33.
76. van Son JA, Julsrud PR, Hagler DJ, et al: Surgical treatment of vascular rings: The Mayo Clinic experience. Mayo Clin Proc 1993;68:1056-1063.
77. van Son JA, Hambsch J, Haas GS, et al: Pulmonary artery sling: Reimplantation versus antetracheal translocation. Ann Thorac Surg 1999;68:989-994.
78. Wong CH, Watson B, Smith J, et al: The use of left heart bypass in adult and recurrent coarctation repair. Eur J Cardiothorac Surg 2001;20:1199-1201.
79. Woods RK, Sharp RJ, Holcomb GW 3rd, et al: Vascular anomalies and tracheoesophageal compression: A single institution's 25-year experience. Ann Thorac Surg 2001;72:434-438; discussion 438-439.
80. Yetman AT, Nykanen D, McCrindle BW, et al: Balloon angioplasty of recurrent coarctation: A 12-year review. J Am Coll Cardiol 1997;30:811-816.

Chapter 124

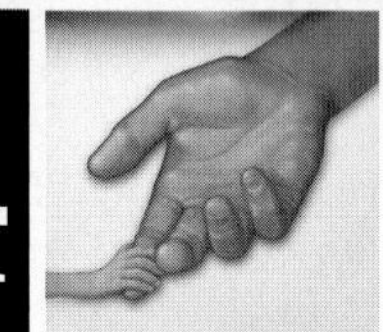

Management of Neural Tube Defects, Hydrocephalus, Refractory Epilepsy, and Central Nervous System Infections

Jodi L. Smith

NEURAL TUBE DEFECTS

Neurulation, one of the earliest and most crucial events in human development, generates the neural tube (NT), the rudiment of the entire adult central nervous system (CNS) (i.e., the brain and spinal cord [SC]). The NT forms during primary and secondary neurulation. Primary neurulation encompasses the formation of a neural plate (NP) and the subsequent morphogenetic movements that transform it into a NT. Secondary neurulation involves the formation of an epithelial cord (i.e., the medullary cord) and its subsequent cavitation to form a NT. In humans, the brain and SC, probably as far caudally as the S2 level, form by primary neurulation, whereas the SC caudal to the S2 level and the filum terminale form by secondary neurulation. For well over a century, investigators have used many different animal models and experimental paradigms to determine the mechanisms underlying primary and secondary neurulation. When these processes go awry in humans, neural tube defects (NTDs) result.

NTDs are among the most common of all human birth defects. These complex congenital malformations occur when the NT, which ultimately forms the brain and SC, fails to close during the first few weeks of embryonic development. NTDs are commonly classified as open or closed based on the presence or absence of exposed neural tissue. In open NTDs, which occur as a consequence of failed primary neurulation, the NT and its membranous coverings are abnormal and the overlying skin is lacking. In closed NTDs, which occur because of faulty secondary neurulation, the NT and its membranous coverings are abnormal but the overlying skin is intact. Open NTDs include anencephaly, spinal rachischisis or spina bifida aperta/cystica (i.e., myeloschisis, myelomeningocele, and meningocele), iniencephaly, and encephalocele. Closed NTDs include spina bifida occulta, lipomatous malformations (e.g., lipomas and lipomyelomeningoceles), split cord malformations (diastematomyelia, diplomyelia), neurenteric cysts, dermal sinuses, and sacral agenesis (caudal regression).

Anencephaly, or absence of the brain, is invariably fatal and results when the cephalic part of the NT fails to close. Infants born with this condition typically die at birth or within the first few days after birth. Spina bifida aperta or cystica (i.e., myeloschisis, myelomeningocele, and meningocele) results from incomplete development of the NT more caudally, with protrusion of the malformed neural tissue, meninges, or both through an opening in the vertebral arches, muscle, and skin (Fig. 124-1).

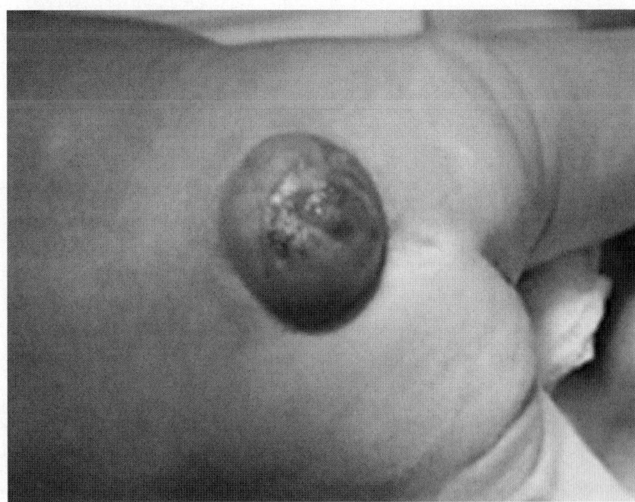

Figure 124–1 Three-hour-old male infant with an L5-S1 myelomeningocele diagnosed prenatally by ultrasound.

Open NTDs range in severity from craniorachischisis, in which the entire NT remains open, to a lesion limited to a single vertebral level. Recent studies have suggested that periconceptional folic acid supplementation reduces the occurrence and recurrence risk of NTDs by 50% to 70%[34,98]; however, these serious birth defects continue to affect approximately 1 per 1000 live-born infants. In other words, including pregnancies that are electively terminated, approximately 4000 pregnancies per year, or 11 to 12 pregnancies per day, in the United States are affected by a NTD. These devastating birth defects are associated with fetal wastage, infant mortality, lifelong disability, and substantial health care costs. To eradicate NTDs, we must continue to advance our understanding regarding the cellular and molecular mechanisms responsible for normal NT formation through dedicated research efforts.

Embryology

Most of what is already known concerning the mechanisms of normal human NT development comes from extensive descriptive studies on both human and nonhuman embryos and from experimental studies on nonhuman animal models, such as the chick and mouse, from which much of our current understanding of neurulation is derived. Such studies, which provide insight into the mechanisms underlying early human neural development, have revealed that primary neurulation occurs in four spatially and temporally overlapping stages: (1) formation of the NP, (2) shaping of the NP, (3) bending of the NP, and (4) fusion of the neural folds (Fig. 124-2A to E).[126,132]

Formation of the NP occurs early in the course of embryogenesis as the chordamesoderm/rostral endoderm induces the overlying ectoderm to thicken. This localized area of thickened ectoderm constitutes the developing flat NP, which is made up of pseudostratified columnar epithelial cells. Shortly after it forms, the flat NP begins to undergo shaping—specifically, rostrocaudal lengthening, mediolateral narrowing, and further apicobasal thickening (Fig. 124-3A to E). These form-shaping events modify the flat NP so that subsequent bending produces a longitudinal tube instead of a spherical vesicle.

Bending of the NP begins during shaping and involves three key morphogenetic events: (1) hinge point formation, (2) neural fold formation, and (3) folding of the NP (Fig. 124-4).[132] Bending commences with the formation of one median hinge point (MHP) and two dorsolateral hinge points (DLHPs).[127] Each hinge point consists of a localized area of NP that becomes anchored to adjacent tissue (i.e., prechordal plate mesoderm beneath the forebrain and notochord more caudally for the MHP and epidermal ectoderm on each side for the DLHPs) and simultaneously forms a longitudinal furrow (see Fig. 124-2C,2E). Furrowing of the NP within the hinge points occurs as a consequence of changes in neuroepithelial cell shape. In the MHP or future floor plate of the NT, the midline NP becomes anchored to prechordal plate mesoderm beneath the forebrain and to notochord further caudally. As a result of inductive interactionsbetween these tissues, midline neuroepithelial cells shorten and become wedge shaped.[131] Notochordal-induced wedging of midline neuroepithelial cells, in turn, causes the midline longitudinal furrow to form. Likewise, in the paired DLHPs, the dorsolateral NP becomes anchored to the epidermal ectoderm of the neural folds bilaterally, and the dorsolateral neuroepithelial cells become wedge shaped, which causes the dorsolateral longitudinal furrows to form. Next, bilateral, bilaminar neural folds form

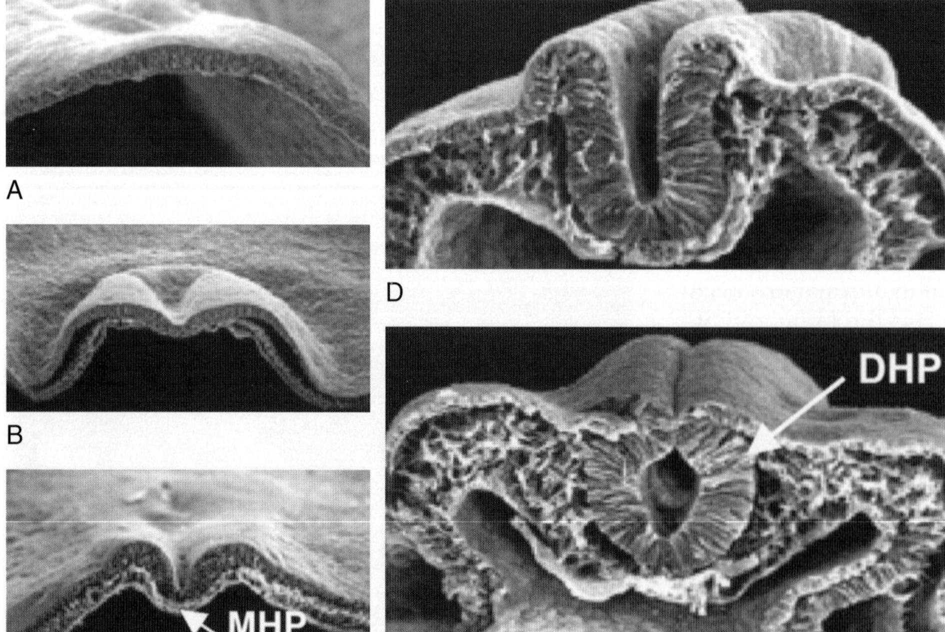

Figure 124-2 *A-E,* Scanning electron micrographs of transverse sections through the chick blastoderm demonstrating the four stages of primary neurulation—formation, shaping, and bending of the neural plate and fusion of the neural folds. During primary neurulation, the neural tube, the precursor of the entire adult central nervous system, develops from the ectodermal flat neural plate. MHP, median hinge point; DHP, dorsolateral hinge point. (Adapted from Smith JL, Schoenwolf GC: Neurulation: Coming to closure. Trends Neurosci 1997;20:510.)

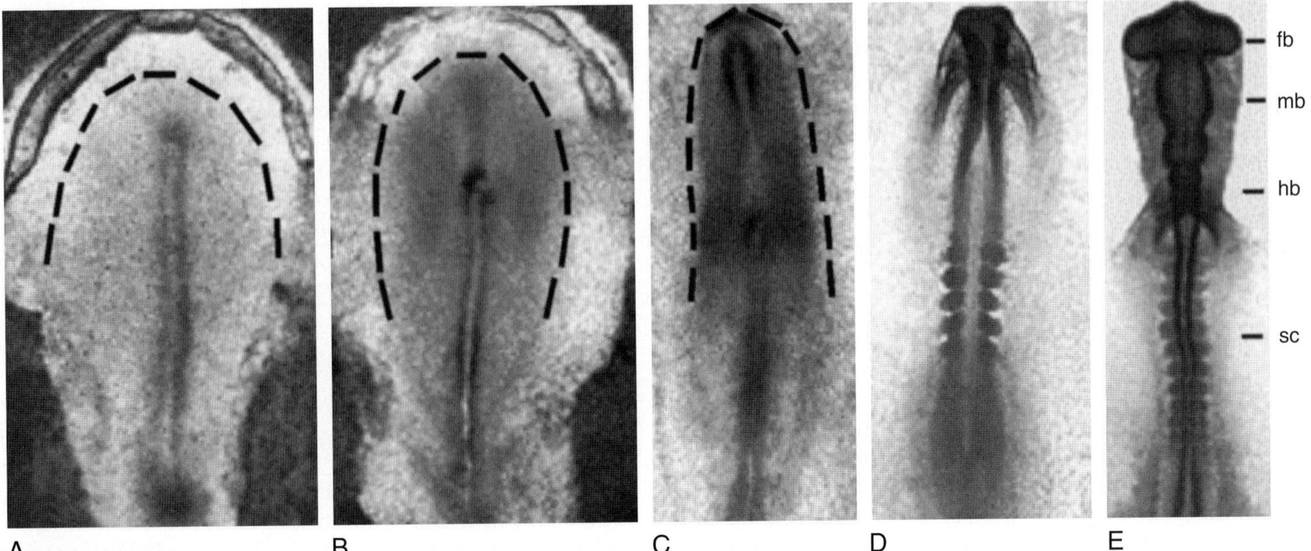

Figure 124–3 Light micrographs of dorsal views of chick blastoderms at Hamburger and Hamilton stages 4 to 10+.[54] *A*, Flat neural plate (stage 4) shortly after its formation. *B*, Flat neural plate with a notochord (head process; stage 5). *C*, Neural groove stage (stage 6) showing rostrocaudal lengthening and mediolateral narrowing characteristic of shaping of the neural plate. The *broken line* in *A* to *C* indicates approximate rostrolateral boundaries of the neural plate. *D*, Incipient neural tube (stage 8+). *E*, Definitive neural tube (stage 10+). fb, forebrain; hb, hindbrain; mb, midbrain; sc, spinal cord. (Adapted from Smith JL, Schoenwolf GC: Neurulation: Coming to closure. Trends Neurosci 1997;20:510.)

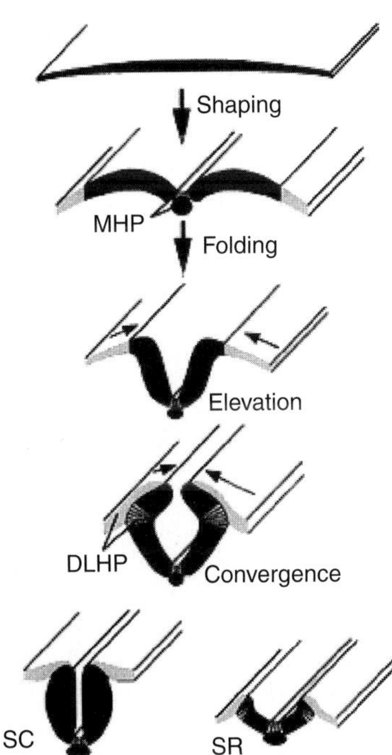

Figure 124–4 Schematic diagram illustrating the major morphogenetic events of primary neurulation at the future midbrain/hindbrain level and differing morphologies at the spinal cord (SC) and sinus rhomboidalis (SR) levels. DLHP, dorsolateral hinge point; MHP, median hinge point. (Adapted from Smith JL, Schoenwolf GC: Neurulation: Coming to closure. Trends Neurosci 1997;20:510.)

as the basal surface/basement membrane of the lateral edge of the NP on each side becomes attached to the adjacent basal surface/basement membrane of the medial edge of the epidermal ectoderm. Finally, folding of the NP, which is related both temporally and spatially to formation of the hinge points, involves elevation and convergence of the neural folds.

After the MHP forms, the lateral unfurrowed segments of NP on each side of the MHP elevate dorsad and rotate around a longitudinal axis centered at the midline furrow. This generates the incipient neural folds and circumscribed neural groove (i.e., the V-shaped space extending the length of the NP during neural fold elevation). At future brain levels, the definitive neural folds (i.e., bilaminar ectodermal structures at the lateral margins of the NP, each composed of an inner layer of neuroepithelium and an outer layer of epidermal ectoderm) then converge toward the dorsal midline, each rotating around a longitudinal axis centered at its corresponding dorsolateral furrow. Convergence brings the neural folds into close proximity in the dorsal midline. In contrast, throughout the future SC, the dorsolateral NP becomes anchored to adjacent epidermal ectoderm as the definitive neural folds form, but the dorsolateral neuroepithelial cells do not become wedge shaped, and as a result, dorsolateral furrows do not form. Consequently, as the neural folds elevate, each lateral half of the NP comes into apposition, which results in temporary occlusion of the lumen of the NT. Finally, at the level of the sinus rhomboidalis in the region of the closing caudal neuropore, folding of the NP, like that at the future brain level, involves formation of the MHP and paired DLHPs around which the neural folds elevate and converge, respectively. Closure of the neural groove and cranial and caudal neuropores then occurs as the neural folds undergo fusion in the dorsal midline. This process culminates in formation of the roof plate of the NT, associated neural crest, and overlying epidermal ectoderm (or epidermis).

The human NP is visible by postovulatory day 16 as pseudostratified columnar epithelium that is anchored in the midline to the underlying notochord. Laterally, the neuroepithelium is contiguous with the squamous epithelium of the epidermal (i.e., cutaneous) ectoderm. The midline neural groove is visible on postovulatory days 17 to 19, with the laterally flanking neural folds becoming obvious by postovulatory days 19 to 21. The neural folds then elevate and converge toward the dorsal midline. The neural groove closes to form the NT as the neural folds fuse in the dorsal midline. Initially, the neural folds fuse in the region of the caudal rhombencephalon or cranial SC. Closure of the entire neural groove and cranial and caudal neuropores occurs during a 4- to 6-day period, with closure of the caudal neuropore occurring during postovulatory days 25 to 27.

For many years, neurulation was viewed as a simple, intrinsic force–driven, all-or-none process in which the NP either rolled up into a tube or did not. Moreover, a change in neuroepithelial cell shape from column-like to wedge-like by contraction of apical microfilaments was the intrinsic force proposed to drive this process. However, through recent advances in research we now know that this "traditional view of neurulation" is incorrect. Instead, neurulation is a highly complex, multifactorial process that requires not only intrinsic forces generated by neuroepithelial cells but also extrinsic forces generated by epidermal ectoderm cells, with the intrinsic and extrinsic forces acting in concert.[126,132]

A "multifactorial model of neurulation" has been proposed to explain how the intrinsic and extrinsic morphogenetic forces generated by fundamental cell behavior, such as changes in cell shape, position, and number, interact during neurulation to transform a flat pseudostratified sheet of ectodermal cells, the NP, into an elongated NT, the precursor of the entire adult CNS.[132] According to this model, intrinsic forces generated by elongation, rearrangement, and nonrandomly oriented rostrocaudal division of neuroepithelial cells drive shaping of the NP, and intrinsic forces generated by neuroepithelial cell wedging drive furrowing of the NP. Extrinsic forces are generated by changes in epidermal ectoderm cell shape from low cuboidal to squamous, rearrangement of epidermal ectoderm cells with caudal-to-medial convergent extension, and nonrandomly oriented rostrocaudal and mediolateral cell division. Such changes in epidermal ectoderm cell behavior drive rostrocaudal lengthening of the epidermal ectoderm, as well as medial epidermal ectoderm expansion, which in turn drives neural fold elevation, convergence, and fusion.

Epidemiology

The incidence of spina bifida is estimated at one to two cases per 1000 population, with certain populations having a significantly higher incidence based on genetic predilection. There is also a marked geographic variation in incidence. For instance, the highest rates occur in parts of the British Isles, mainly Ireland and Wales, where the incidence of myelomeningocele is as high as three to four cases per 1000 population and the incidence of anencephaly is more than six cases per 1000 population for both live births and stillbirths. In the United States, the prevalence is declining, with African Americans having a rate of 0.1 to 0.4 per 1000 live births versus 1 per 1000 live births in the white population.

Etiology

The precise etiology and specific genes responsible for the generation of NTDs, such as myelomeningocele, have not yet been elucidated. The cause of such defects is probably multifactorial, with both genetic and environmental factors playing a role. Besides problems occurring during neurulation that prevent NT closure, problems in the postneurulation period (e.g., as a result of exposure of the unprotected nervous system to amniotic fluid) may also have a deleterious effect on NT development and subsequent neural function. In addition, numerous teratogens have been implicated in the etiology of NTDs. Of all the teratogens evaluated thus far, carbamazepine, valproic acid, and folic acid deficiency have been most strongly tied to the development of NTDs. In support of this association, periconceptional folic acid supplementation has been shown to reduce the occurrence *and* recurrence risks of NTDs,[34,98] suggesting that NTDs result, at least in part, from folic acid deficiency. However, the precise role of folic acid in preventing NTDs remains unclear. Nevertheless, the U.S. Public Health Service made a strong recommendation in September 1992 that all women of childbearing age in the United States who are capable of becoming pregnant should consume 0.4 mg of folic acid per day for the purpose of reducing the risk of having a pregnancy affected with a NTD. Furthermore, valproic acid (a known folate antagonist), if taken during pregnancy, results in a 1% to 2% estimated risk of having a child with a NTD.

Pathology

The two most common types of open NTDs seen with spina bifida aperta or cystica are myelomeningocele and meningocele. Myelomeningocele, the most common NTD compatible with life, consists of an open neural placode surrounded by an intermediate zone of thin epithelium, which in turn is surrounded by normal skin (see Fig. 124-1). The dorsal (i.e., exposed) surface of the neural placode constitutes the everted interior of the NT and is continuous with the central canal of the SC rostrally. In contrast, the ventral surface constitutes the outside of what should have been a closed NT. Ventral or motor roots exit from the ventral surface of the placode just lateral to the midline on both sides; dorsal or sensory roots enter the periphery of the placode lateral to the motor roots. An arachnoid sac and subarachnoid space underlie the neural placode, and the junction between the skin and dura underlies the skin within a few millimeters from the skin edge. Subjacent to the dura is an epidural space that contains fat. The spinous processes are absent, and the paraspinous muscle masses, hypoplastic laminae, and pedicles are everted. In most cases, the SC rostral to the neural placode is normal; however, additional anomalies such as a split cord malformation (i.e., diastematomyelia), arteriovenous malformation, epidermoid, or lipoma may be present. In addition, most neonates with myelomeningocele have associated neurologic malformations such as hydrocephalus and Chiari II malformation, as well as orthopedic anomalies of their lower extremities and urogenital anomalies caused by involvement of the sacral nerve roots. A meningocele is a skin-covered anomaly characterized by herniation of just the meninges through a dorsal bony defect (spina bifida). However, unlike myelomeningocele, the SC and nerve roots do not herniate into the skin-covered dural sac, and neonates with these lesions typically do not have associated neurologic malformations.

Diagnosis of Neural Tube Defects

Open NTDs, such as anencephaly and myelomeningocele, can be diagnosed prenatally by measuring alpha fetoprotein (AFP) in the amniotic fluid or maternal bloodstream. AFP, the major serum protein in early embryonic life, can leak into the amniotic fluid from an open NTD. The first step in prenatal screening for open NTDs is drawing blood to measure maternal serum AFP between 15 and 20 weeks of gestation. A patient-specific risk is then calculated on the basis of gestational age and AFP level. For example, at an estimated gestational age of 20 weeks, a maternal serum AFP concentration higher than 1000 ng/mL would be consistent with the diagnosis of an open NTD. Measurement of maternal serum AFP is more than 75% accurate in detecting an open NTD when gestational age is greater than 15 weeks. If the diagnosis is uncertain with maternal serum AFP, an amniotic AFP level can be obtained, which will detect approximately 98% of all open NTDs. Moreover, fetal ultrasound can be used to detect open and sometimes closed NTDs prenatally, especially in the hands of a skilled ultrasonographer. If the diagnosis of myelomeningocele is made prenatally, the parent or parents undergo extensive prenatal counseling and cesarean delivery is planned.

Evaluation and Treatment

Neonates with myelomeningocele have a saclike protrusion containing a neural placode bathed in cerebrospinal fluid (CSF) (see Fig. 124-1). The size of the sac on the child's back at the time of birth depends on the amount of CSF that has collected ventral to the neural placode. These children may also have other associated CNS abnormalities, including Chiari II malformation, hydrocephalus, syringomyelia, brainstem malformations, agenesis of the corpus callosum, and polymicrogyria. Shortly after birth, a thorough physical examination is performed that includes measurement of head circumference and assessment of general vigor (especially cry and suck), anal sphincter function, upper and lower extremity motor and sensory function, and the site, level, and size of the myelomeningocele defect. In addition, the neonate should be evaluated for signs and symptoms of hydrocephalus and Chiari II malformation, as well as for associated orthopedic deformities such as clubfeet and kyphoscoliosis.

Before repair, the neonate is maintained prone to prevent rupture of the sac and avoid trauma to the neural placode. In addition, the myelomeningocele is covered with sterile saline-soaked gauze to prevent desiccation of the exposed neural tissue. An intravenous catheter is placed and systemic antibiotics are started. Head ultrasonography or computed tomography (CT) is performed to evaluate the extent of ventricular enlargement and determine the need for shunt placement. Initially, the ventricles may be normal or only slightly enlarged. However, after the NTD is closed, the ventricles often enlarge. The incidence of hydrocephalus associated with myelomeningocele ranges from 80% to 95%.

A myelomeningocele is typically closed within 24 to 48 hours after birth unless the infant has associated medical conditions that prevent administration of a general anesthetic or surgery.[52] The goal of surgery is to close the neural placode into a NT to establish a microenvironment conducive to neuronal function.[93] Closure involves (1) separation of the neural placode from the intermediate zone and reconstruction of the placode into a tube with preservation of all neural tissue; (2) separation of the dura from the epidural space at the lateral margins of the defect and closure of the dura in a watertight, but patulous fashion around the newly created NT; (3) surgical correction of any significant kyphotic deformity; (4) mobilization and midline approximation of the paraspinal muscles and fascia; and (5) tension-free closure of the skin in the midline, which often requires mobilization of the skin and subcutaneous tissue from the underlying fascia rostrally, caudally, and bilaterally.

Common postoperative complications include CSF leak, wound-healing problems, and a tethered SC. The incidence of CSF leak may be reduced by careful closure of the dura and by placement of a shunt to treat associated hydrocephalus. Wound-healing problems may occur, especially in patients with large myelomeningoceles, and can be managed by keeping the patient prone and performing moist-to-dry dressing changes. Currently, no techniques are available to reduce the incidence of SC tethering after myelomeningocele repair.

Fetal Surgery for the Treatment of Neural Tube Defects

Intrauterine repair of myelomeningocele has been advocated as a means of improving the neurologic outcome in infants with myelomeningocele. This is based on the idea that secondary damage and resultant disability, which may occur when exposed neural tissue is in contact with amniotic fluid, may be reduced or even completely eliminated by closing the defect as early as possible in utero. In addition, it has been suggested that halting CSF loss by in utero closure of the neural placode may reverse some of the potentially devastating neurologic sequelae of NTDs, such as shunt-dependent hydrocephalus and Chiari II malformation.

A single-institution, nonrandomized observational study conducted between 1990 and 1999 compared outcomes, including the requirement for ventriculoperitoneal shunt placement, obstetric complications, gestational age at delivery, and birth weight, in 29 patients who underwent intrauterine myelomeningocele repair between 24 and 30 weeks of gestation with 23 lesion-matched controls who underwent standard postnatal repair.[24] The results of this study suggested that intrauterine repair decreased the incidence of hindbrain herniation and shunt-dependent hydrocephalus. However, this study also demonstrated an increased risk for oligohydramnios and admission to the hospital for preterm uterine contractions, an earlier estimated gestational age at delivery (33.2 versus 37.0 weeks), and a smaller birth weight (2171 versus 3075 g) in patients who underwent intrauterine repair. Other problems with this study included relatively short follow-up times and small sample size.

Although preliminary evidence suggests that intrauterine myelomeningocele repair may reduce the severity of hindbrain herniation and decrease the incidence of hydrocephalus, these benefits remain unproven. A recent study has also demonstrated that intrauterine repair between 20 and 28 weeks of gestation does not statistically improve lower extremity function when compared with that in patients undergoing traditional postnatal closure.[142] Furthermore, the procedure involves substantial risks not associated with standard postnatal repair. A randomized controlled trial of intrauterine and conventional therapies is currently under way in an attempt to more clearly establish the risks and benefits of intrauterine repair.[138,145] Until the procedure-related risks and benefits have been established, it is not prudent to advocate intrauterine repair of myelomeningocele as the preferred therapy.

Associated Anomalies

Children with myelomeningocele often have other anomalies of the CNS that require attention. For example, more than 90% of children with myelomeningocele have a Chiari II malformation and hydrocephalus. Chiari II malformation is a complex deformity involving the calvarium, dura, and hindbrain. The spectrum of abnormalities observed in Chiari II malformation includes a lacunar skull (i.e., thinning and scalloping of the calvaria producing a "copper-beaten" appearance), small posterior fossa, low-lying transverse sinuses and torcular Herophili, fenestrated falx, heart-shaped tentorial incisura with upward herniation of the cerebellum, medullary kinking, beaking of the tectal plate, prominence of the massa intermedia, enlargement of the suprapineal recess, elongation of the fourth ventricle, syringomyelia, and downward displacement of the cerebellar vermis, fourth ventricle, medulla, and pons through the foramen magnum (Fig. 124-5A and B). Neonates with symptomatic Chiari II malformation

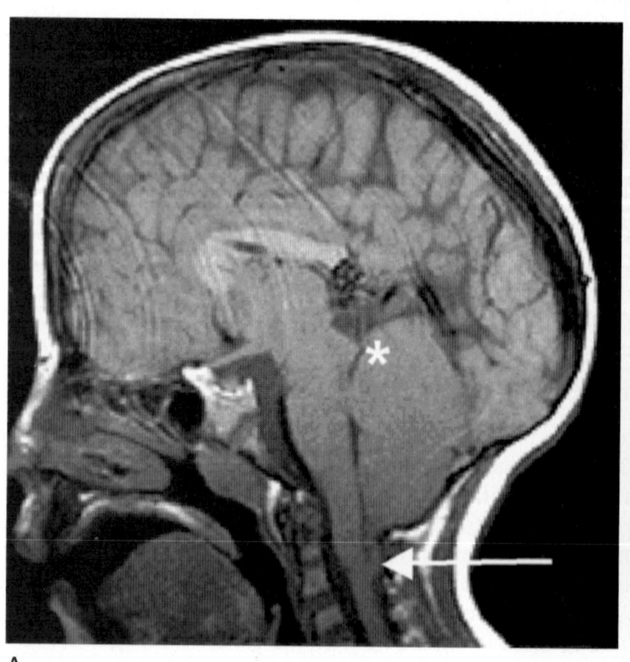

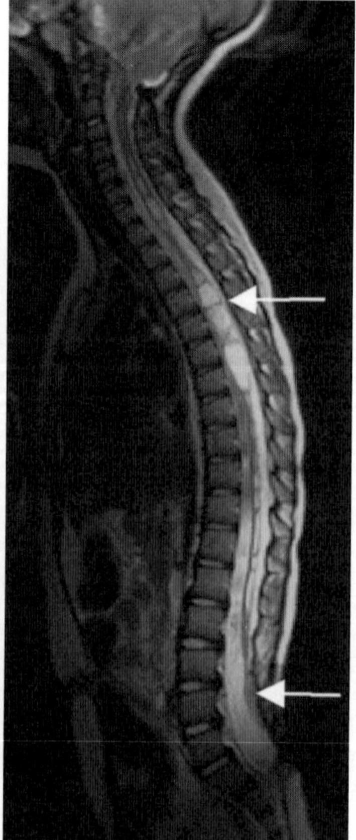

Figure 124-5 Five-year-old girl with myelomeningocele repaired in utero. *A,* Sagittal brain magnetic resonance image (MRI) showing a Chiari II malformation with upward herniation of the cerebellum and tectal plate beaking (*asterisk*), as well as downward displacement of the cerebellar tonsils through the foramen magnum (*arrow*). *B,* Sagittal spine MRI showing syringomyelia extending from C5 to L2 (*upper arrow*). The spinal cord and conus end at L4 (*lower arrow*), consistent with a tethered spinal cord.

commonly have inspiratory stridor, apnea, dysphagia or nasal regurgitation, aspiration, weak or absent cry, weakness/spasticity in the upper or lower extremities (or both), and opisthotonic posturing. Older children and adolescents have a more insidious manifestation consisting of syncopal episodes, nystagmus, oscillopsia, lower cranial nerve palsies, hyperreflexia, and spastic quadriparesis. Radiologic diagnosis of Chiari II malformation is best made by brain magnetic resonance imaging (MRI).

Treatment of patients with symptomatic Chiari II malformation (i.e., those with signs and symptoms of brainstem compression) involves decompression of the posterior fossa or cervical SC, or both, which can be surgically challenging because of the fact that the torcular Herophili and transverse sinuses are low lying (i.e., near the foramen magnum), the cerebellum is often adherent to the medulla, and the fourth ventricle is displaced caudally and dorsally. Before subjecting the patient to a Chiari decompression, one must make certain that the patient has a functioning shunt because shunt malfunction can produce signs and symptoms of brainstem compression similar to those observed in a Chiari II malformation. When evaluating shunt function, it is important to remember that CT findings can be misleading because the ventricles may remain small or fail to show an increase in size despite high-grade shunt obstruction. Therefore, a shunt tap, radionuclide shunt injection, or shunt exploration should be performed to evaluate shunt function before decompressing a Chiari II malformation in a patient with myelomeningocele.

Hydrocephalus, which is discussed in this chapter in greater detail later, is present in 80% to 95% of children with myelomeningocele. Factors contributing to the development of hydrocephalus in this patient population include the Chiari type II malformation, aqueductal stenosis, fourth ventricle outlet obstruction, anomalous venous drainage in the posterior fossa caused by compression of the dural venous sinuses, open myelomeningocele with associated CSF leak, and the presence of other CNS malformations. Hydrocephalus is usually treated with a ventriculoperitoneal shunt, which diverts CSF from the brain to the peritoneal cavity for reabsorption. Shunting can be performed at the time of myelomeningocele closure in patients with severe symptomatic hydrocephalus or several days later under separate anesthesia to reduce the risk of shunt infection.

Occult Spinal Dysraphism—Closed Neural Tube Defects

During secondary neurulation, the caudal aspect of the NT develops from the tail bud, a mesenchymal mass of cells derived from remnants of the cranial portion of the primitive streak. Secondary neurulation occurs in three stages: (1) formation of the medullary cord from the tail bud; (2) cavitation of the central portion of the medullary cord, which results in the formation of multiple lumina; and (3) coalescence of the lumina into a single, central cavity surrounded by a peripheral layer of radially oriented medullary cord cells.[125] When secondary neurulation goes awry, *closed* NTDs result in which the overlying skin is intact but the caudal NT and its membranous coverings develop abnormally. Developmental anomalies of the caudal SC—which include spina bifida occulta; tight or thickened filum terminale; lipomatous malformations such as lumbosacral lipoma, leptomyelolipoma, lipomyelomeningocele, and fatty filum; split cord malformations (also known as diastematomyelia, diplomyelia); neurenteric cysts; dermal sinuses; and sacral agenesis/caudal regression—may lead to tethering of the SC.[153] SC tethering, in turn, can cause progressive neurologic deterioration secondary to traction on the conus medullaris and resultant ischemic injury.

Cutaneous stigmata are often found in association with occult spinal dysraphism and thus serve as markers for SC tethering, especially when they are found *above* the gluteal crease. Examples of such skin lesions include lumbosacral hypertrichosis (i.e., hairy patch), dermal sinus tract, sacral dimple, capillary hemangioma, caudal appendage, and subcutaneous lipoma. Patients with one or more of these lesions *above* the gluteal crease should undergo further evaluation, including a full spine MRI, to look for SC tethering. In contrast, a skin lesion, such as a dimple or pit, *below* the gluteal crease most likely represents a benign, non-neurologic finding such as a pilonidal sinus, which requires no further workup.

Besides cutaneous stigmata, children with tethered cord syndrome and occult spinal dysraphism frequently have (1) dysraphic posterior spinal elements and vertebral anomalies; (2) orthopedic abnormalities such as scoliosis, lower extremity atrophy or asymmetry, and foot deformities; (3) progressive neurologic dysfunction such as lower extremity weakness, loss of sensation, radiculopathy, spasticity, hyperreflexia, and abnormal gait; (4) urologic dysfunction such as neurogenic bladder and urinary incontinence; and (5) bowel dysfunction. In addition, there is a high incidence of caudal SC abnormalities and associated SC tethering in patients with anorectal and urogenital malformations, including cloacal exstrophy, persistent cloaca, penoscrotal transposition, imperforate anus, and the VATER association (vertebral defects, imperforate anus, tracheoesophageal fistula with esophageal atresia, and radial and renal dysplasia).[154] Although the explanation for the simultaneous development of cloacal and caudal SC malformations remains unknown, it is probably related at least in part to the intimate temporospatial relationship of urogenital, anorectal, and caudal NT development. Because of the high incidence of coexistent malformations and associated SC tethering, patients with anorectal and urogenital malformations should undergo routine screening MRI to evaluate for asymptomatic tethering of the SC.

Lipomatous malformations of the SC, such as a fatty filum, lipomyelomeningocele, and leptomyelolipoma, cause tethering of the SC and are the most common types of closed NTDs requiring neurosurgical treatment.[55,72,153] A fatty filum consists of a short, thick filum terminale in which there is partial or complete fatty infiltration. A lipomyelomeningocele consists of a skin-covered subcutaneous lipoma that extends through a defect in the lumbosacral fascia, lamina, dura, and pia into a low-lying SC. Leptomyelolipoma, a type of lipomyelomeningocele, consists of a conus lipoma. Most children with lipomatous malformations have intact neurologic function at birth and are brought to medical attention for evaluation of a superficial lipoma or other cutaneous stigmata as described earlier.

The natural history of tethered SC is that of progressive neurologic deterioration with deficits in sensory, motor, bowel, and bladder function arising during periods of rapid growth and weight gain.[55] Consequently, early prophylactic untethering is recommended for all patients to stabilize neurologic function and prevent irreversible neurologic injury. Surgery is performed by microsurgical technique with monitoring of anal sphincter electromyography and somatosensory evoked potentials. Intraoperative stimulation of nerve roots helps distinguish functional from nonfunctional roots. In the case of a fatty filum, surgical treatment consists of a partial laminectomy at L4-L5 or L5-S1 through a short posterior midline incision and opening of the dura in the midline to expose the filum. After stimulating the filum to ensure that no neural function is present, the filum is sectioned at the rostral and caudal ends of the exposure and the intervening segment is sent to pathology for evaluation. In the case of lipomyelomeningocele or leptomyelolipoma, surgical treatment involves detaching the subcutaneous lipoma from the SC or conus lipoma at the point where it emerges through the defect in the lumbosacral fascia. It is unnecessary to resect the subcutaneous fatty mass completely because doing so can result in devascularization of the overlying skin, which in turn can compromise wound healing.[72] A laminectomy is performed rostral to the dural defect to identify normal anatomy, and then careful dissection is carried out progressively more caudally to the region where the lipoma traverses the dural defect and enters the SC or conus. The following steps are then performed: (1) untethering of the conus from its attachments to the lipoma, leptomeninges, and dura; (2) decompression of the SC and conus by debulking the intramedullary lipomatous mass with the laser or ultrasonic aspirator; (3) sectioning of the filum; (4) watertight, but patulous closure of the dura; and (5) meticulous closure of the paraspinal muscles, lumbosacral fascia, and skin. Surgery-related complications include anesthesia-related risks, worsening of neurologic or urologic function (or both), CSF leak, and infection.

Other types of occult spinal dysraphism include split cord malformations (i.e., diastematomyelia), dermal sinus tracts, and neurenteric cysts. In split cord malformations, the SC is split into two halves in the sagittal plane, with each hemicord residing either in a separate dural tube (type II malformation) or together in a single dural tube (type I malformation).[107] A hairy patch typically overlies the region of the split cord malformation, and tethering of the SC may occur as a consequence of a thickened filum or a midline bony spur, or both, in the case of type II malformations or dorsal tethering bands/fibrous median septum between the dura and hemicords in the case of type I malformations. To prevent neurologic and urologic deterioration, the SC is untethered by resecting the midline bony spur or sectioning the dorsal bands/fibrous septum between the dura and hemicords, as well as by sectioning the filum.

Dermal sinus tracts often present in childhood with cutaneous findings, neurologic deficits, or infectious or chemical meningitis, or any combination of these findings.[1,45] Dermal sinus tracts, which represent remnants of incomplete NT closure, develop as a consequence of localized failure of dysjunction, the process whereby the surface ectoderm and dermal elements separate from the neuroectoderm. Failure of dysjunction leads to the formation of an epithelial-lined tract that extends from an opening on the surface of the skin to the fascia, dura, or SC. Dermal sinus tracts can be found anywhere along the midline of the neuraxis and may be associated with drainage of CSF, intradural dermoid or epidermoid cysts, split cord malformations,[107] and tethering of the SC. Skin lesions associated with dermal sinus tracts are typically found over the midline neuraxis above the gluteal cleft and include a dimple, pit, capillary hemangioma, hairy patch, skin tag, and subcutaneous lipoma. In the case of a dimple or pit, there may be drainage of cyst contents or CSF or local signs of infection, such as erythema or induration. MRI is the neurodiagnostic tool of choice because it enables visualization of the dermal sinus tract and associated pathology, such as a tethered SC, inclusion tumor, syrinx, or split cord malformation. However, some dermal sinus tracts may not be well visualized on MRI if they are small or out of the plane of imaging.[1] Consequently, if a patient has a cutaneous finding overlying the midline neuraxis that is above the gluteal crease, surgical exploration may be warranted even if the MRI appearance is normal. Treatment consists of complete excision of the dimple and tract, intradural exploration with complete resection of any intradural connections or masses, and untethering of the SC. Timely diagnosis and appropriate surgical intervention with intradural exploration are essential in preventing infection, including meningitis, and preserving or improving neurologic function.

Spinal neurenteric cysts are rare congenital malformations lined by alimentary tract mucosa.[153] They form as a consequence of a persistent abnormal connection between the primitive ectoderm and endoderm[115] and are often accompanied by vertebral abnormalities and other forms of occult spinal dysraphism, such as split cord malformation, lipoma, dermal sinus tract, and tethered SC. Patients with spinal neurenteric cysts may have cutaneous stigmata or signs of SC compression such as pain and neurologic deficits. Treatment involves complete excision of the neurenteric cyst, as well as appropriate surgical management of other associated congenital abnormalities, including untethering of the SC. Gross total resection is essential because there is a high incidence of cyst recurrence associated with subtotal resection of neurenteric cysts.[115]

In patients with occult spinal dysraphism and tethered SC who have previously undergone an untethering procedure, progressive neurologic or urologic deterioration may signal recurrent tethering of the SC, which can occur in up to 15% of patients.[73] Consequently, long-term neurologic and urologic follow-up is warranted to determine patients who may benefit from reoperation.

Outcome and Prognosis

Treatment of NTDs has evolved over the past 50 years. Previously, neonates with NTDs either were left untreated or were treated selectively; however, most of them died of meningitis, hydrocephalus, or sepsis, or any combination of the three. In contrast, during the past 3 decades, neonates with NTDs have received prompt, aggressive treatment in almost all pediatric centers in the United States. Such treatment, including early closure of open NTDs and aggressive shunting of hydrocephalus, leads to survival with nearly normal intelligence in most patients.

Initial closure of an open NTD is just the beginning of the medical care typically required. In general, such patients require frequent and consistent follow-up at a comprehensive multidisciplinary clinic where they can be evaluated by a team of pediatric specialists, including a developmental pediatrician, neurosurgeon, urologist, orthopedic surgeon, physiatrist, physical therapist, occupational therapist, nurse, and nutritionist. The multidisciplinary team approach is critical to the ultimate success and long-term management of these patients. With proper medical care, children with open NTDs can lead active and productive lives. For example, in a recent 20- to 25-year follow-up study of children with open spina bifida who were treated aggressively in a nonselective, prospective manner, these children entered college in the same proportion as the general population, and many were actively employed.[21] With aggressive treatment and a multidisciplinary clinical approach, long-term survival into adulthood and advanced age is now common.

Neurosurgeons must always be on the alert for neurologic deterioration in children and adults with myelomeningocele. Besides shunt malfunction, the most common cause of neurologic deterioration is symptomatic SC tethering. In almost all patients with myelomeningocele, the SC is low lying and ends in the lumbar or sacral region. This may be observed in patients without any new neurologic complaints. However, symptomatic tethering of the SC develops in at least 20% of all patients with myelomeningocele despite careful surgical closure of the original neural placode. Such patients often have one or more of the following signs/symptoms: gait difficulty, back pain, leg weakness, sensory loss, a new foot deformity, a change in urodynamic data, or urinary incontinence. When one or more of these signs/symptoms occur in patients with shunted hydrocephalus, the shunt must be evaluated first to confirm that it is functioning adequately. After this has been established, surgery is performed to free the neural placode and nerve roots from the dorsal surface of the dura and untether the SC. In contrast, asymptomatic patients who demonstrate SC tethering on routine MRI do not require reoperation.

HYDROCEPHALUS

Hydrocephalus is a common pediatric disorder in which there is an increase in CSF volume, which in turn causes enlargement of the ventricles, thinning of the cortical mantle (Fig. 124-6A and B), and elevation of intracranial pressure (ICP). The incidence of congenital hydrocephalus is approximately 0.9 to 1.8 per 1000 births,[81] and the mortality rate is approximately 1% per year. To prevent neurologic deterioration associated with increased ICP, CSF diversion is required. Treatment with CSF diversion techniques such as valve-regulated CSF shunt systems and endoscopic third ventriculostomy increases life expectancy in pediatric patients with hydrocephalus and improves their intellectual outcome.

Hydrocephalus results from a disparity between CSF production and absorption, with most cases occurring as a consequence of impaired CSF absorption. The exception to this rule is hydrocephalus in patients with a choroid plexus papilloma, which results, at least in part,

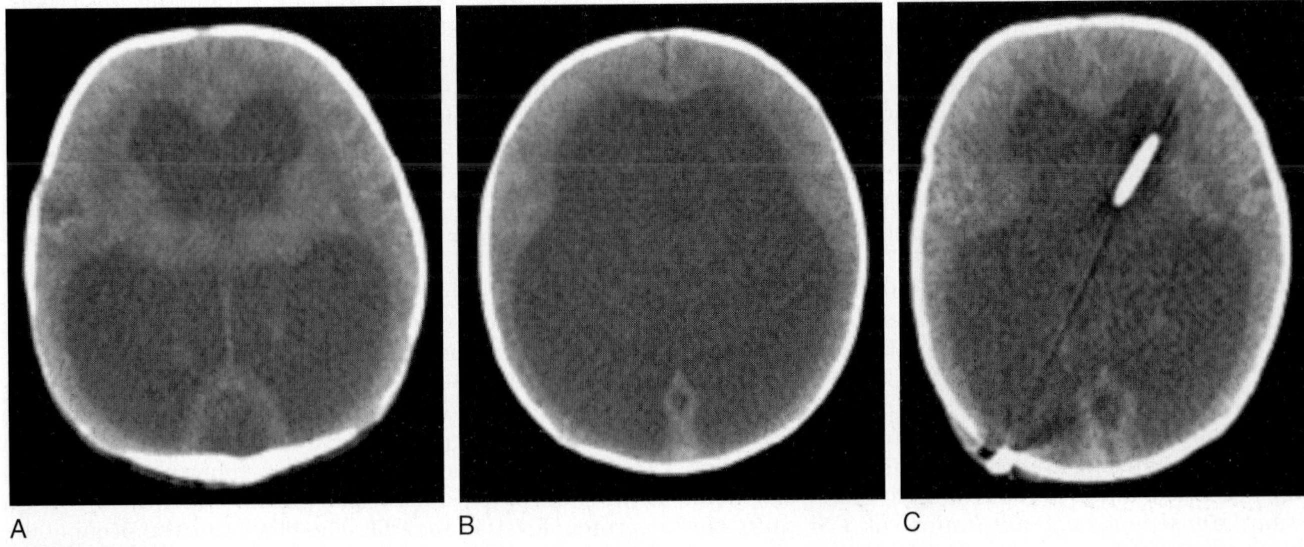

Figure 124-6 One-day-old girl with severe obstructive hydrocephalus secondary to congenital aqueductal stenosis. *A* and *B*, Head computed tomography (CT) scan showing severe ventriculomegaly. *C*, Head CT scan 1 day after shunt placement.

from overproduction of CSF. Increased CSF volume secondary to impaired absorption or increased production (or both) leads to progressive ventricular dilatation. In some children, CSF absorption can occur through alternative pathways, thereby resulting in stabilization of their ventricular enlargement. This, in turn, leads to arrested or compensated hydrocephalus. In support of this, a detailed analysis of the natural history of unoperated hydrocephalus has shown that arrest of the progressive ventricular enlargement eventually occurs in up to 45% of children with hydrocephalus.[79] Children with compensated hydrocephalus do not require CSF diversion; however, many factors, such as fever and infection, can upset this balance and cause sudden decompensation of the hydrocephalus and elevated ICP. Therefore, children with suspected shunt-independent "compensated" hydrocephalus must be monitored closely for signs and symptoms suggesting decompensation, such as headaches, vomiting, ataxia, and visual symptoms.

Formation of CSF is an energy-dependent, ICP-independent process that requires carbonic anhydrase and occurs at a rate of approximately 450 mL/day, or 0.3 mL/min. Choroid plexus in the lateral, third, and fourth ventricles produces 50% to 80% of the CSF; the remaining 20% to 50% of CSF is produced by ventricular ependyma and brain parenchyma as a by-product of cerebral metabolism. After it is produced, CSF flows in a caudal direction through the ventricular system and exits through the foramina of Luschka and Magendie into the cortical and spinal subarachnoid space. CSF then travels through the tentorial incisura, passes over the hemispheric convexity, and is absorbed into the venous system at the level of the arachnoid villi.

In contrast to CSF formation, CSF absorption is an energy-independent process that occurs predominantly by bulk flow through the arachnoid villi, which represent the interface between the cortical subarachnoid space and the intradural venous sinuses. The rate of CSF absorption depends on a pressure gradient from the subarachnoid space across the arachnoid villi to the venous space in the dural venous sinuses. When ICP is normal (i.e., <7 cm H_2O or 5 mm Hg), CSF is produced at a rate of 0.3 mL/min, but no CSF absorption occurs. When ICP increases, CSF absorption occurs in direct proportion to increases in ICP. Other pathways for CSF absorption have been proposed. Such pathways, including the lymphatic system, nasal mucosa, paranasal sinuses, and the nerve root sleeves of cranial and spinal nerves, are probably recruited for CSF absorption when ICP is elevated; however, definitive evidence for these alternative pathways is currently lacking.

Obstruction of the ventricular pathway or impaired absorption generates increased intraventricular pressure, which in turn results in progressive dilatation of the ventricular system proximal to the block. The pathologic effects of ventricular obstruction or impaired CSF absorption include ventricular dilatation, which is often more pronounced initially in the occipital horns, thinning of the cortical mantle, disruption of the ependymal membrane, transependymal absorption of CSF into the periventricular white matter, white matter injury and scarring, elevation of ICP, brain herniation, coma, and ultimately, death.

Etiology

The etiology of hydrocephalus depends on the site of the obstruction. If the block is proximal to the arachnoid villi, there is selective enlargement of the ventricles proximal to the block, and the resultant hydrocephalus is termed noncommunicating or obstructive hydrocephalus. For example, obstruction of the aqueduct of Sylvius results in enlargement of the lateral and third ventricles out of proportion to the fourth ventricle. In contrast, when there is impaired CSF absorption at the level of the arachnoid villi, the lateral, third, and fourth ventricles are dilated and the volume of CSF in the subarachnoid space is increased. The resultant hydrocephalus is referred to as communicating or nonobstructive hydrocephalus. Hydrocephalus ex vacuo, a condition in which the ventricles become enlarged as a consequence of cerebral atrophy, is not true hydrocephalus.

Obstructive hydrocephalus can be caused by blockage at the foramen of Monro. Common causes include congenital atresia or stenosis; intracranial cysts such as arachnoid cysts within the subarachnoid space or ventricle, porencephalic cysts within the brain adjacent to the ventricle, and colloid cysts; tumors such as hypothalamic gliomas, craniopharyngiomas, and subependymal giant cell astrocytomas; and cavernous malformations. Obstruction at the level of the aqueduct of Sylvius is another common cause of obstructive hydrocephalus (see Fig. 124-6A and B). Causes of aqueductal obstruction include upward herniation of the cerebellum through the tentorial incisura in patients with myelomeningocele and associated Chiari II malformation, vein of Galen vascular malformations, gliosis of the aqueduct from infection or hemorrhage, tumors of the pineal region, and tectal plate gliomas. In addition, obstructive hydrocephalus can occur as a consequence of fourth ventricle outflow obstruction from posterior fossa and fourth ventricle tumors such as medulloblastomas, ependymomas, and pilocytic astrocytomas; a Dandy-Walker malformation, in which there is a large posterior fossa cyst that communicates with an enlarged fourth ventricle and atresia of the outlet foramina (i.e., lateral foramina of Luschka and midline foramen of Magendie); and a Chiari II malformation, in which there is herniation of the fourth ventricle through the foramen magnum because of a small posterior fossa.

In communicating or nonobstructive hydrocephalus, the block can occur at the level of the basal cisterns. When this occurs, CSF flow is blocked between the spinal and cortical subarachnoid spaces and it cannot reach the arachnoid villi for absorption. As a consequence, the lateral, third, and fourth ventricles become dilated. Common causes include congenital infections; meningitis from acquired pyogenic, tuberculous, and fungal infections; subarachnoid hemorrhage from aneurysm rupture, vascular malformations, or trauma; intraventricular hemorrhage associated with germinal matrix hemorrhages in preterm infants; basal arachnoiditis; leptomeningeal carcinomatosis; neurosarcoidosis; and tumors producing high protein levels in the CSF. The block can also occur at the level of the arachnoid villi from occlusion or atresia of the arachnoid villi, which results in dilatation of the subarachnoid space and ventricles. Furthermore, the block can occur at the level of the dural venous sinus from venous outflow obstruction. Such a block can be seen in patients with achondroplasia or multisutural craniosynostosis who have stenosis of the jugular foramina, in patients with high right atrial pressure from congenital heart disease, and in those with thrombosis of the dural venous sinuses or superior vena cava. Venous outflow obstruction causes increased venous pressure, which in turn results in decreased drainage of cortical veins, increased cerebral blood volume, elevated ICP, increased brain stiffness, and decreased CSF absorption. In infants with an open anterior fontanelle and cranial sutures, increased venous pressure and decreased CSF absorption result in macrocephaly, with splitting of the cranial sutures, and ventricular enlargement. In contrast, when the cranial sutures and anterior fontanelle are closed, the elevated venous pressure produces venous engorgement, which in turn raises ICP. In such patients, the ventricular system is compressed despite decreased CSF absorption, and the clinical entity known as pseudotumor cerebri is produced.

Maximal hydrocephalus is characterized by massive ventricular enlargement with only a very thin rim of cortical mantle, the presence of background cortical activity throughout the brain on electroencephalography (EEG), and at least some restitution of the cerebral mantle with CSF diversion (see Fig. 124-6A and B). In contrast, hydranencephaly is a condition in which the intracranial cavity is filled with CSF instead of brain because of a total or nearly total loss of brain tissue supplied by the anterior and middle cerebral arteries bilaterally (Fig. 124-7A and B). The cranial vault and meninges remain intact along with the thalamus, brainstem, and a small amount of occipital lobe supplied by the posterior cerebral artery. The most common causes of hydranencephaly are bilateral internal carotid artery infarcts and infection. Cortical activity is absent on EEG. Such infants cry, suck, and feed, and they are typically hyperirritable, retain primitive reflexes, and rarely progress beyond spontaneous vowel production or a social smile. CSF shunting may be performed to control head size in the face of progressive head enlargement; however, shunting does not improve neurologic function.

Clinical Features

Hydrocephalus in infants may be manifested as irritability, lethargy, failure to thrive (with or without vomiting), delayed development, apnea, bradycardia, hyperreflexia, hypertonia, increasing head circumference, bulging anterior fontanelle, splaying of the cranial sutures, thin scalp with distended scalp veins, frontal bossing, impaired upward gaze with eyelid retraction (i.e., "setting sun" sign from pressure on the tectal plate), decreased levels of consciousness, and papilledema, as well as third, fourth, and sixth nerve palsies. In older children with a rigid cranial vault, hydrocephalus may be manifested as headache (especially in the morning), nausea, vomiting, lethargy, papilledema, deterioration in vision, decline in cognitive function or behavior, memory problems, decreased attention span, worsening of school performance, gait changes, upgaze palsy, diplopia (especially from sixth nerve palsy), and seizures.

Radiologic Features of Hydrocephalus

Plain skull films from patients with hydrocephalus often demonstrate a beaten-copper appearance and splitting of the coronal sutures. CT and MRI frequently reveal dilated temporal horns; obliteration of the sylvian and interhemispheric fissures, sulci, and basilar cisterns; ballooning of the frontal horns and third ventricle; upward bowing or atrophy of the corpus callosum, or both; and periventricular edema related to transependymal absorption of CSF.

Benign external hydrocephalus (also known as benign extra-axial fluid of infancy), a condition that rarely requires CSF diversion, is characterized by enlargement of the anterior cortical subarachnoid spaces (i.e., sulci and cisterns) bilaterally; normal or mildly dilated ventricles;

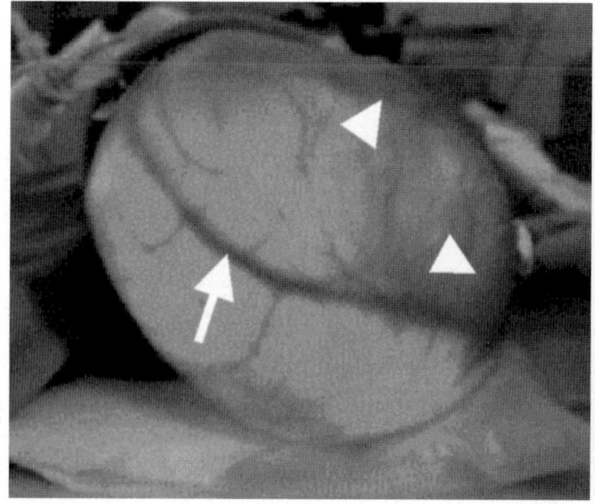
A

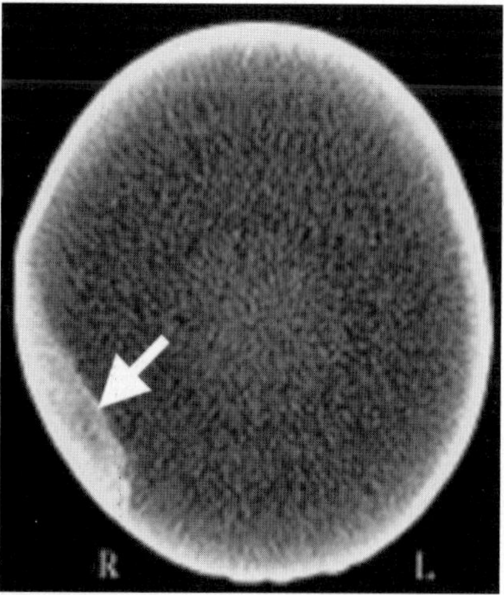

B

Figure 124–7 Two-day-old girl with hydranencephaly. *A*, Transcranial illumination showing the superior sagittal sinus (*arrow*) and a scant amount of right inferior temporal and occipital cortex (*arrowheads*). *B*, Head computed tomographic scan shortly after birth revealing a scant amount of right cerebral cortex posteriorly (*arrow*). The cerebral hemispheres are replaced almost entirely by cerebrospinal fluid.

a prominent pulsatile anterior fontanelle; and progressive enlargement of head circumference, with crossing of percentile lines when head circumference is plotted with respect to age. Infants with benign external hydrocephalus have large heads and may demonstrate slight delays in motor development related to their large head size. The etiology of this clinical entity is unclear; however, defective CSF absorption has been proposed. Frequently, the family history is significant for large heads. At roughly 12 to 18 months of age, the enlarging head circumference tends to plateau, which allows the child's body growth to catch up with head growth, and the hydrocephalus typically resolves spontaneously by 2 years of age without a need for shunting. Although shunting is not usually required, these children should be monitored closely with serial head circumference measurements and head CT or ultrasound to evaluate for abnormal ventricular enlargement.

Management

The goal of treatment is to achieve optimum neurologic function and prevent or reverse the neurologic damage caused by distortion of the brain from ventricular enlargement. The best predictor of a good outcome is postoperative reconstitution of the cerebral mantle to at least 2.8 cm.[166] This is more likely to occur if a hydrocephalic infant undergoes shunting by 5 months of age.

Treatment of hydrocephalus is surgical, and the type of surgery depends on the cause of the hydrocephalus. For example, in patients with obstructive hydrocephalus, surgery is performed to remove the obstruction (e.g., tumor). In patients with communicating hydrocephalus or obstructive hydrocephalus in which the obstruction cannot be removed, CSF is shunted from the site of its secretion within the ventricle proximal to the obstruction to a distal site capable of reabsorption. The most commonly used distal sites include the peritoneal cavity, right atrium, pleural cavity, gallbladder, bladder/ureter, and basilar cisterns (i.e., third ventriculostomy). At present, the peritoneal cavity is the preferred site for the distal catheter (i.e., ventriculoperitoneal shunt), unless there is a problem with absorption or abdominal sepsis. When abdominal abnormalities are present, such as extensive postsurgical abdominal adhesions, peritonitis, morbid obesity, and necrotizing enterocolitis in preterm infants, a ventriculoatrial shunt is the treatment of choice. Alternatively, if the peritoneum and atrium are not available, a ventriculopleural shunt can be placed in children who are 7 years or older.

CSF shunt systems consist of at least three components: a ventricular catheter, which is usually placed in the occipital or frontal horn of the lateral ventricle (see Fig. 124-6C); distal shunt tubing to drain CSF into a distal site for reabsorption; and a valve. Conventional differential pressure shunt valves control unidirectional CSF flow by opening at a fixed pressure differential across the valve. This pressure differential is determined by the characteristics of the valve and is designated as low, medium, or high (typically 5, 10, and 15 cm H_2O, respectively). Once the valve is open, it provides very little resistance to CSF flow. Consequently, the gravitational effects of an upright posture can lead to high CSF flow rates, which in turn can generate a large negative ICP, a process referred to as "siphoning."

Because siphoning can result in slit ventricles, which in turn are associated with a higher incidence of proximal shunt obstruction, some shunt valves have been designed to limit excess CSF flow, particularly in the upright position.[152] For example, the *Delta valve* (Medtronic PS Medical, Goleta, CA) is a standard diaphragm-type, differential pressure shunt valve with an integral siphon control device to diminish overdrainage in upright positions. The *Orbis-Sigma valve* (Cordis, Miami) contains a variable-resistance, flow-limiting component that limits excess CSF flow by progressively narrowing the flow orifice with increasing pressure. Although these newer valves have been advocated as a means of preventing overdrainage and improving treatment results, a recent randomized trial comparing three different shunt valve designs (i.e., standard differential pressure valve, Delta valve, and Orbis-Sigma valve) in the treatment of children with newly diagnosed hydrocephalus showed no significant difference in shunt failure rates among the valves tested.[40] Currently, there are also two types of programmable differential pressure shunt valves. Such valves, which allow the pressure setting to be altered after implantation, are commonly used in the treatment of pediatric hydrocephalus. Despite the vast array of shunt systems available to treat hydrocephalus, no prospective, randomized, double-blind, multicenter trial has ever proved a particular shunt system to be more effective than any other.

Ventriculoperitoneal shunting is the preferred method for CSF diversion in childhood hydrocephalus. Placement of a ventriculoperitoneal shunt is performed under general endotracheal anesthesia after prophylactic intravenous antibiotics are administered. The role of antibiotic prophylaxis has been studied by meta-analysis, and antibiotic coverage is recommended.[41,78] The patient is positioned at the top edge of the operating table in close proximity to the surgeon, and the head is placed on a gel donut and turned to the side opposite the shunt insertion. The neck and trunk are extended with a gel roll under the shoulders to facilitate subcutaneous tunneling of the shunt. Skin incisions are delineated before skin preparation, depending on the desired location of the bur hole for placement of the ventricular catheter (e.g., frontal or occipital). A meticulous skin preparation (e.g., with povidone-iodine scrub and paint solution) is performed, and the incisions are marked again. The abdominal incision is typically marked in the right upper quadrant or in the midline approximately two to three fingerbreadths below the xiphoid process. Surgical drapes, including an iodine-impregnated sterile adhesive drape, are placed over the incisions and tunneling site. A curvilinear incision is made in the scalp overlying the proposed bur hole site, and the scalp is retracted. The pericranium is opened at the base of the incision and a bur hole is drilled. The dura, arachnoid, and pia are then coagulated and opened.

Next, the abdominal incision is opened, and entrance into the peritoneal cavity is achieved and confirmed by gently probing the opening into the peritoneal cavity.

A shunt tunneling device is then used to create a subcutaneous tunnel extending between the two incisions. The shunt components are removed from their sterile packages just before shunt placement and placed in antibiotic solution. The distal shunt system, including the valve, is passed within the subcutaneous tunnel, and the ends are covered with sponges soaked in antibiotic solution. Care is taken to prevent contact of the shunt tubing with the skin during this portion of the procedure. Next, the ventricular catheter is passed on a wire stylet into the ventricle. Intraoperative ultrasound or ventricular endoscopy, or both, can be used to accurately place the catheter within the ventricle. Ventriculoscopy can also be used to fenestrate intraventricular cysts and provide communication between loculated ventricles.

Once the catheter is in the ventricle and CSF flow has been confirmed, the catheter is cut to the desired length, guided by measurements obtained from the preoperative head CT scan, and then connected to the distal shunt system, usually by way of a reservoir. Silk ties (2-0 or 3-0) are used to secure the catheter to the reservoir. After this, the distal shunt tubing is evaluated for CSF flow. Once confirmed, the distal shunt tubing is passed into the peritoneal cavity; it should pass freely without resistance. The incisions are then irrigated with antibiotic solution, closed in a meticulous, two-layered fashion with good approximation of the skin edges, and covered with sterile dressings.

Most children become shunt dependent after they undergo shunting. Consequently, children with shunts require lifelong follow-up to make certain that their shunt is functioning adequately, especially in light of the high incidence of failure over the life of a shunt. For example, in a previous retrospective study in which 1719 hydrocephalic children were evaluated in an attempt to understand why shunts fail,[122] the actuarial probability of the occurrence of shunt failure was 70% at 10 years after the initial shunt insertion, with the highest risk for shunt failure occurring in the immediate postoperative period (i.e., a 30% risk of shunt failure during the first year and a 2% to 5% risk per year thereafter). In addition, the actuarial probability of the occurrence of a shunt infection was 9% over the same 10-year period, and the time of shunt failure varied significantly according to the cause of the shunt failure. Other studies have reported shunt failure rates of approximately 40% within the first year for standard CSF shunts implanted for the treatment of pediatric hydrocephalus.[16,111] Moreover, in a randomized trial of CSF shunt valve design,[40] the shunt failure rate was 40% at 1 year and 60% at 2 years, and the infection rate was 8% in the hands of experienced pediatric neurosurgeons working in centers where many shunts are implanted each year.

CSF shunt system malfunction is due to three main factors: (1) mechanical failure, (2) infection, and (3) overdrainage or underdrainage (i.e., "functional" failure). Proximal obstruction (i.e., obstruction of the ventricular catheter) is the most frequent cause of mechanical shunt failure.[122] Other causes include obstruction of the distal catheter or any accessory part of the shunt (e.g., antisiphon device); formation of a peritoneal pseudocyst, which usually is associated with infection and causes obstruction of the peritoneal catheter; ascites resulting from failure of intraperitoneal reabsorption of CSF; fracture of the shunt; disconnection of the shunt at a junction point of shunt components (e.g., proximal or distal to a straight connector); migration of the shunt; inadequate length of the distal catheter; improper proximal or distal catheter placement; infection; and overdrainage, which can lead to the formation of subdural fluid collections, slit ventricles, craniosynostosis, or intracranial hypotension. In a study by Sainte-Rose and coworkers,[122] two thirds of the shunt failures were due to obstruction or fracture, with obstruction responsible for 56.1% of shunt failures and fractures occurring almost exclusively at sites of connectors. Moreover, they found that a significantly higher percentage of shunt failure was due to proximal obstruction in patients with slit ventricles than in those with normal or enlarged ventricles and to distal obstruction in patients with slit-ended peritoneal catheters than in those with open-ended catheters.

Repeated shunt failures are common in pediatric patients and are associated with significant morbidity and occasionally death. A prospective, single-institution, observational study designed to identify risk factors predisposing pediatric patients to repeated shunt failures[144] revealed that the timing of the previous shunt procedure is significant, with shunt revisions performed within less than 6 months from the time of the preceding implantation having a significantly increased risk for failure. Furthermore, in this study the age of the patient at the time of first shunt insertion was a significant risk factor for subsequent shunt failure, with patients younger than 40 weeks as well as those between 40 weeks and 1 year of age at the time of shunt insertion having a higher risk for subsequent shunt failure than those older than 1 year. With respect to the effect of the cause of hydrocephalus on repeated shunt failure, this study showed a higher risk for recurrent shunt failure in patients with intraventricular hemorrhage, meningitis, and tumor. Finally, concurrent surgical procedures also increased the risk for shunt failure in this study.

In most cases of shunt malfunction, the diagnosis is obvious because the child has acute and overt signs and symptoms of elevated ICP, such as irritability, headache, vomiting, and lethargy, and will progress to stupor, coma, and death if the shunt is not revised promptly. In the study by Sainte-Rose and colleagues,[122] there was a 1.05% mortality rate directly related to shunt failure. Alternatively, some children with shunt failure will have more subtle signs of deterioration, such as a decline in school performance, change in attention span, or change in behavior. These "subtle deteriorators" often demonstrate a gradual increase in ventricular size over time and may have a marked increase in ventricular size at the time of presentation. In contrast, acute deteriorators often have only a slight increase in ventricular size. When a child has a suspected shunt malfunction, a head CT is performed to evaluate for interval enlargement of the ventricles. This must be compared with a previous scan obtained when the patient was doing well. A shunt series is also performed to look for continuity of the shunt, especially at sites of connectors, the position of the ventricular catheter or catheters, and the length of the distal shunt tubing.

When a shunt malfunction is suspected, the site of shunt failure must be determined. The most common cause of shunt failure is obstruction of the ventricular catheter by choroid plexus, glial tissue, connective tissue, leptomeninges, ependyma, or brain tissue (or any combination of these tissues), especially in those with slit-like ventricles.[122] Proximal obstruction is typically associated with precipitous development of elevated ICP, which necessitates immediate shunt revision. To reduce the incidence of proximal catheter obstruction, surgeons attempt to place the ventricular catheter with the use of external anatomic landmarks either within the frontal horn of the lateral ventricle anterior to the foramen of Monro or within the occipital horn to keep the catheter away from choroid plexus.[122] With the introduction of fiber-optic endoscopes in the early 1990s, surgeons began using ventricular endoscopy to insert the ventricular catheter away from choroid plexus under direct visualization. Although evidence from uncontrolled series suggested that endoscopic insertion of the ventricular catheter decreased the incidence of shunt failure,[140] a multicenter randomized trial evaluating time to first shunt failure after endoscopic versus nonendoscopic placement of the ventricular catheter in children with hydrocephalus showed no reduction in the incidence of shunt failure with endoscopically assisted placement of the ventricular catheter.[75] However, in this trial, ventricular catheters that were thought by surgeons to be placed away from choroid plexus at the time of shunt insertion were actually found to be located away from choroid plexus on postoperative imaging studies only two thirds of the time in both endoscopic and nonendoscopic insertions. This suggests that the endoscope did not help achieve the goal of placing ventricular catheters away from choroid plexus in this trial. However, a secondary analysis of catheter position in this trial did demonstrate a reduced incidence of shunt failure if the ventricular catheter was positioned away from choroid plexus based on postoperative imaging studies.

Distal shunt malfunctions can occur as a consequence of shunt fracture, inadequate length of the distal shunt tubing, shunt infection, and impaired absorption of CSF at the distal site. Shunt tubing is made of silicone elastomers, which can calcify and break over time. Breakage often occurs above the clavicle, where there is increased motion, or in the region of a connector. Consequently, the shunt series should be evaluated carefully to look for a discontinuity in the shunt system, particularly at sites of connectors. If a shunt fracture is found, the shunt should be revised. The shunt series can also detect whether the distal shunt tubing is too short and a distal lengthening procedure is needed.

Shunt infection can also cause a distal shunt malfunction and is the second leading cause of shunt failure after mechanical obstruction. With each shunt operation, there is a 2% to 8% incidence of shunt infection,[40] with 5% to 15% of shunts becoming infected over the life of a shunt. The consequences of shunt infection are devastating and can include intellectual and focal neurologic deficits, enormous health care costs, and death. Most shunt infections occur within the first 6 months after a shunt operation,[41] with approximately 70% of shunt infections diagnosed within the first month after surgery and 90% by 6 months. The most common pathogens include staphylococci (*Staphylococcus epidermidis*, 40%; *Staphylococcus aureus*, 20%). Other species seen include coryneforms, streptococci, enterococci, aerobic gram-negative rods, and yeasts. Although shunt infections can occur after 6 months, they are quite rare and almost always result from indolent bacteria that are a normal part of skin flora, such as *S. epidermidis* or *Propionibacter acnes*. The fact that most shunt infections occur as a consequence of contamination with the patient's own skin flora underscores the need for meticulous attention to surgical technique.

Shunt infections can range from isolated wound infections and colonization of the shunt tubing to ventriculitis, peritonitis, and an infected pseudocyst. Risk factors implicated in shunt infection include young age of patient, poor skin condition, prolonged surgery, an open NTD, CSF leakage from an incision or wound breakdown postoperatively, increased number of shunt revisions, and concomitant infection. Patients with a shunt infection typically have a low-grade fever (i.e., between 100° F and 102° F) or evidence of shunt malfunction. However, they can also have signs of meningitis, ventriculitis, peritonitis, or cellulitis, or any combination of such signs. Symptoms include irritability, headache, nausea and vomiting, lethargy, decreased appetite, abdominal pain, erythema and tenderness along the shunt tract, photophobia, and neck stiffness. Head CT may or may not show a change in ventricular size.

If shunt infection is suspected, the patient should undergo a radiologic evaluation that includes a shunt series (i.e., anteroposterior and lateral skull, chest, and abdominal radiographs) and a head CT scan. The shunt series provides information regarding the continuity of the shunt tubing and location of the shunt reservoir for tapping, possible sources of shunt-related problems, and other potential sources of infection such as pneumonia. Head CT reveals ventricular catheter location, size, and contents, including loculations and purulent fluid collections, which can be seen in cases of severe gram-negative ventriculitis. If the patient complains of abdominal pain or abdominal distention is present, abdominal CT or ultrasound should be performed to evaluate for a CSF pseudocyst. In addition, a peripheral white blood cell count and blood cultures should be obtained because patients with shunt infections often have leukocytosis and positive blood cultures. Finally, a multisystem fever workup should be performed to evaluate for concurrent infections.

If the initial evaluation suggests possible shunt infection, a shunt tap is performed to obtain CSF for study. To do this, the area over the shunt reservoir is shaved and prepared with povidone-iodine solution. A 25-gauge butterfly needle is then passed percutaneously into the reservoir with sterile technique. Proximal and distal shunt flow dynamics are tested and CSF obtained and sent for cell count and differential, protein, glucose, Gram stain, and culture and sensitivity studies. After CSF is obtained, broad-spectrum intravenous antibiotics are started.

If CSF studies demonstrate a shunt infection (i.e., isolation of bacteria in CSF obtained from the shunt tap, elevated neutrophils and protein in CSF, or decreased CSF glucose), the entire shunt is removed and an external ventricular drain and central venous line are placed. The patient is treated with the appropriate systemic antibiotics (i.e., antibiotics that have good activity against the isolated organism and adequate CSF penetration) until the shunt infection has cleared, at which time a new shunt may be placed. Monitoring of CSF during treatment is essential. At present, significant variation exists in the duration of antibiotic therapy, with treatment regimens ranging from 2 days to 3 weeks.[155] Studies are currently under way to determine the most effective duration of antibiotic therapy in an effort to shorten hospitalization and minimize complications without sacrificing efficacy. It is the practice at the author's institution to treat with antibiotics until at least two consecutive CSF cultures, at least 48 hours apart, are negative and the inflammatory component of the infection has resolved. Aside from the practical problems associated with their treatment, shunt infections have been linked to an increase in the development of loculated CSF compartments, impaired intellectual outcome (with as high as an 8- to 10-point decrease in IQ), an increased risk for seizures, and an increased mortality rate.[41]

Shunt overdrainage, or "overshunting," can also be associated with shunt failure. Most shunts with differential pressure valves will overdrain regardless of whether the valve pressure is high or low.[152] Overdrainage can lead to the formation of subdural hematomas, a low-ICP syndrome, or a slit ventricle syndrome. Subdural hematomas result from the tearing of bridging veins as the ventricles collapse and the cortical surface pulls away from the dura. Although they often resolve without treatment, symptomatic or progressive subdural hematomas from overshunting may require a reduction in the degree of shunting to allow the ventricles to re-expand and the subdural space to become obliterated. Alternatively, drainage of the subdural space either by placing bur holes or by shunting the subdural space with a low-pressure valve may be required. Besides the formation of subdural hematomas, overshunting can lead to a low-ICP syndrome with symptoms such as headache, nausea, vomiting, tachycardia, and lethargy that are very sensitive to changes in position. In patients with low-ICP syndrome, overdrainage occurs when the patient assumes an upright position. This produces a very negative ICP, which in turn leads to intense postural headaches that are relieved by recumbency.[48,112] If symptoms persist and are frequent or recurrent enough to interfere with daily activities, especially school, the shunt should be revised by placing a higher-resistance valve or by adding an antisiphon device, or both.

Overshunting can also lead to the formation of slit-like ventricles. Ventricles commonly become very small or slit-like after placement of a shunt. In a previous retrospective study, slit ventricles developed in 80% of the total population of shunted patients.[152] Interestingly, 88.5% of the patients in whom slit-like ventricles developed were completely asymptomatic. Moreover, of the 11.5% of patients with slit ventricles who were symptomatic, only 6.5% required surgical intervention. Symptomatic slit ventricle syndrome occurs infrequently and is associated with intermittent episodes of vomiting, headache, and lethargy. Patients with symptomatic slit ventricle syndrome tend to have very small ventricles, diminished extraventricular CSF spaces, a thick skull, and no room for intracranial accumulation of CSF. In this syndrome, the ventricular walls collapse around the ventricular catheter, the catheter becomes obstructed, and the shunt fails to drain.[152] Eventually, intraventricular pressure builds up, the ventricles dilate slightly, and the shunt begins to drain. These patients often experience acute neurologic deterioration related to waves of elevated ICP that occur during periods of intermittent shunt obstruction. Moreover, because of the tight intracranial space in these patients, there is no room for any increase in intracranial volume, including cerebral blood volume. Consequently, any event that leads to cerebral vasodilatation, such as migraine headaches, or to an increase in cerebral blood flow, such as exercise or playing outside in the hot summer sun, will cause symptoms of elevated ICP.[152] Patients with slit ventricle syndrome become symptomatic very early in the phase of shunt obstruction, and head CT scans obtained in symptomatic patients frequently reveal no change in ventricular size when compared with their usual slit-like state.

Patients with acute neurologic deterioration in the face of a functioning shunt may benefit from treatment with medications such as furosemide (Lasix) or acetazolamide (Diamox) to lower ICP until the elevated pressure waves subside. Some patients may also benefit from taking antimigraine medications, such as cyproheptadine (Periactin) or propranolol (Inderal). If symptoms persist despite conservative treatment, surgical intervention may be necessary. Such interventions include ventricular catheter revision, shunt valve upgrade to increase resistance, addition of an antisiphon or flow control device, decompressive subtemporal craniectomy, usually ipsilateral to the ventricular catheter, or any combination of these interventions. ICP monitoring is useful to differentiate between high-pressure headaches caused by waves of elevated ICP in the face of a functioning shunt and low-pressure headaches caused by negative ICP in patients with true overdrainage.[117] ICP monitoring can also be helpful in identifying children with normal ICP physiology who are having headaches unrelated to shunt function.

Trapping of the fourth ventricle can occur in children with chronic shunting of the lateral ventricles, especially in those with a history of posthemorrhagic hydrocephalus from intraventricular hemorrhage related to prematurity, postinfectious hydrocephalus, or repeated shunt infections/ventriculitis. In this condition, overdrainage of CSF leads to slit ventricles or aqueductal narrowing, or to both. When aqueductal stenosis occurs, the fourth ventricle does not communicate with the third ventricle because of functional or anatomic occlusion of the aqueduct. Likewise, the fourth ventricle does not communicate with the basilar cisterns because of occlusion of the outlets (i.e., foramina of Luschka and Magendie). Production of CSF by choroid plexus in the trapped fourth ventricle results in progressive ventricular enlargement, which may lead to headache, swallowing difficulty, lower cranial nerve palsies, ataxia, lethargy, spastic quadriparesis, and nausea/vomiting. Infants may have apneic spells and bradycardia. In symptomatic patients, the isolated fourth ventricle can be shunted with a separate shunt system or by adding a fourth ventricular catheter into an existing supratentorial shunt system above the valve. However, as the ventricle is decompressed with CSF drainage, the brainstem moves posteriorly into a more normal position and the fourth ventricular catheter can damage the brainstem.[53] In addition, approximately 40% of patients require a shunt revision within 1 year.[80] Alternatively, a suboccipital craniotomy and open fenestration of the fourth ventricle to the subarachnoid space and basal cisterns may be performed with or without placement of a shunt from the fourth ventricle to the spinal subarachnoid space.[37,148] More recently, endoscopic aqueductoplasty and interventriculostomy with stent placement have been proposed as treatment options to re-establish communication between the supratentorial ventricular system and the isolated fourth ventricle.[49]

Endoscopic third ventriculostomy (ETV) can be performed to treat certain types of obstructive hydrocephalus, such as primary untreated aqueductal stenosis from tectal plate and pineal region tumors. This technique, if successful, eliminates the need for a shunt and avoids the complications of shunting. It is contraindicated in those with communicating hydrocephalus, and the success rate is poorer in patients younger than 1 year. The highest success rate occurs in older children and adults with acquired obstructive hydrocephalus, with approximately 70% of patients achieving shunt independence.[30,121] In children younger than 3 years, the success rate ranges from 40% to 50%. The success rate is also lower in patients with preexisting pathology, such as a tumor, previous shunt, prior subarachnoid hemorrhage, previous whole-brain irradiation, and significant scarring of the third ventricle floor, with as few as 20% of third ventriculostomies remaining patent in such patients.[53]

ETV is performed through a frontal bur hole that is made approximately 2.5 to 3 cm lateral to the midline, just anterior to the coronal suture.[121] A peel-away sheath is passed through the foramen of Monro to protect bordering structures from damage caused by repeated passage of the endoscope. A rigid or flexible endoscope is passed by way of the peel-away sheath through the foramen of Monro into the third ventricle, and the floor of the third ventricle is fenestrated in the midline just anterior to the cleavage plane of the mammillary bodies, which comprise the posterior border of the third ventricular floor. The fenestration is then dilated with a 2-French Fogarty balloon catheter by means of repeated inflation and deflation of the balloon. Once the third ventricular floor has been fenestrated, the endoscope is passed into the interpeduncular cistern to evaluate the arachnoid membranes and make certain that no redundant arachnoid membranes are impeding CSF flow into the subarachnoid cistern.

The complication rate associated with ETV is now becoming apparent. Failure to complete the procedure for technical reasons has been reported in up to 26% of patients,[23] and the main complication is hemorrhage secondary to vascular injury.[143] Other reported complications include cardiac arrest, diabetes insipidus, the syndrome of inappropriate antidiuretic hormone secretion, subdural hematoma, meningitis, cerebral infarction, transient third and sixth nerve palsies, and disturbances in short-term memory.[23,143] Risks of ETV include infection, injury to adjacent neural structures (e.g., hypothalamus, pituitary gland, optic chiasm), and arterial injury with intraoperative rupture or delayed hemorrhage related to traumatic aneurysm formation. In a small number of patients, delayed failure of ETV has been described. In patients with recurrent symptoms of intracranial hypertension, cine-MRI can be performed to assess the patency of the third ventriculostomy by evaluating CSF flow across the floor of the third ventricle. If the floor of the third ventricle is no longer adequately fenestrated, endoscopic exploration with an attempt at repeat fenestration is reasonable. If postoperative scarring precludes safe repeat fenestration of the third ventricular floor, a ventricular shunt system should be placed.

Outcome and Prognosis

The natural history of *untreated* hydrocephalus is poor, with 50% of children dying before 3 years of age[165] and only 20% to 23% reaching adult life. Of the survivors, only 38% had normal intelligence.[79] The development of CSF diversion techniques has improved the prognosis for children with hydrocephalus. Many patients with shunted hydrocephalus have normal intelligence and participate in all aspects of social life, with cognitive development and life expectancy determined primarily by the nature of the underlying condition. Overall, about 50% to 55% of shunted hydrocephalic children will achieve an IQ of greater than 80, with verbal cognitive skills being superior to nonverbal ones.[27,38,63] Not surprisingly, epilepsy appears to be an important predictor of poor intellectual outcome in shunted hydrocephalic children, with an IQ higher than 90 being seen in 66% of children without epilepsy versus 24% of children with epilepsy.[20] Unfortunately, repeated shunt complications in pediatric patients with hydrocephalus carry significant morbidity.

EPILEPSY SURGERY IN CHILDREN

Epilepsy is a common disorder in childhood.[57] It affects approximately 0.5% to 1.0% of the population in the United States and Canada,[9,57,58] and up to 50% of epilepsy cases begin before 5 years of age.[32,57] Typically, children with epilepsy are managed initially with antiepileptic medications. However, 20% to 25% of children with epilepsy have inadequate control of their seizures with pharmacotherapy,[22,101] and it is now recognized that seizures starting in childhood that are caused by known structural lesions and are not controlled by medication rarely remit spontaneously as the child matures.[2] Repeated seizures and the side effects of seizure medications have a negative impact on the developing brain and can lead to severe impairment of neurocognitive function.[2,3,25,59,61,147,150] Moreover, chronic seizures can have a negative impact on a child's education as a consequence of learning difficulties and the associated psychosocial effects, such as poor peer relationships, behavioral difficulties, poor school performance, depression, anxiety, and poor self-esteem.[61,62,67] Because intractable epilepsy in childhood is a progressive, debilitating condition associated with eventual deterioration in both intellectual and behavioral function, aggressive treatment is warranted. Seizure surgery provides an effective alternative therapeutic option for children who suffer from intractable seizures. The goal of surgery is to remove the seizure focus as completely as possible without creating a new neurologic deficit or worsening an existing one.

Epilepsy surgery is indicated when (1) a child's seizures persist despite an adequate trial of at least two to three appropriate anticonvulsants, alone or in combination, with each drug pushed to the maximum tolerated dosage; (2) the seizures significantly reduce the child's quality of life; (3) there is a unilateral, localized seizure focus that can be reliably and reproducibly identified; and (4) resection of the seizure focus does not cause unacceptable neurologic deficits.[2,15,97,105] A preoperative workup is initiated as soon as a child fails medical therapy because early operative intervention is paramount to a good functional outcome.[2,6,105]

Preoperative Evaluation

The main goal of preoperative evaluation is to identify the area of seizure onset (i.e., the seizure focus) and its relationship to eloquent cortex.[2,147] A child with intractable disabling epilepsy undergoes an initial evaluation that involves noninvasive characterization of the seizure syndrome and optimization of medical management. Patients undergo a thorough neurologic history and physical examination, baseline EEG, and high-resolution MRI of the brain with thin coronal cuts through the temporal lobe (e.g., three-dimensional spoiled gradient echo [3D-SPGR] scan), fluid-attenuated inversion recovery (FLAIR) sequences, and MR spectroscopy. EEG can provide important information by confirming the presence of an epileptogenic focus, by helping characterize the seizures and epilepsy syndrome, and by helping localize the seizure focus.[103] Helpful localizing features on EEG include focal slowing, focal attenuation of fast activity, and focal epileptiform discharges (e.g., spikes or sharp waves). A good prognostic factor for success with focal resective surgery is the presence of a single focus of epileptiform activity.[103] MRI is evaluated for focal structural abnormalities (e.g., cytoarchitectural) or abnormal lesions (e.g., neoplastic) that could be causing or contributing to the child's seizures. The presence of a focal abnormality on MRI, when it corresponds to the location of seizure onset on EEG, increases confidence that the epileptogenic region has been identified and also increases the likelihood of achieving seizure control with surgery.[17,103,105] Structural abnormalities that can be visualized on MRI and that are associated with medically intractable seizures include low-grade tumors, such as a ganglioglioma (Fig. 124-8A to C), dysembryoplastic neuroepithelial tumor (DNET), astrocytoma, oligodendroglioma, and pleomorphic xanthoastrocytoma; developmental abnormalities, such as cortical dysplasia and focal neuronal

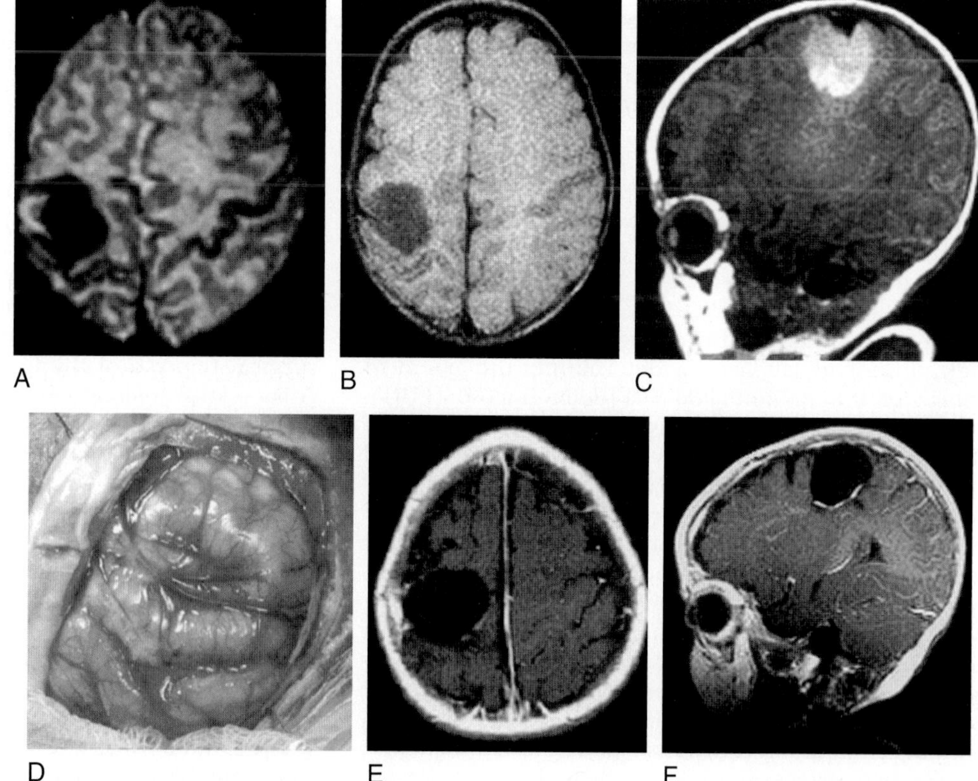

Figure 124-8 Three-month-old girl with 30 to 60 seizures per day on three anticonvulsants. *A* to *C*, Brain magnetic resonance image (MRI) showing a 2.5 × 2.5 × 2-cm right posterior frontal mass. Preoperative video electroencephalographic studies localized her seizures to the region of the abnormality on MRI. She underwent complete resection of the mass and adjacent epileptogenic zone, which was localized via intraoperative electrocorticography. The final pathology was a ganglioglioma. She is now 33 months of age with no evidence of tumor recurrence, has mild residual spastic left hemiparesis, and is completely seizure free and off all anticonvulsants.

migration abnormalities (e.g., gray matter heterotopia); vascular malformations, such as cavernomas and arteriovenous malformations; secondary post-traumatic or postischemic encephalomalacia lesions; and mesial temporal sclerosis.[103]

If the initial evaluation suggests a possible seizure focus, additional studies are performed to define the seizure focus further, including prolonged video-EEG monitoring with surface (i.e., scalp) electrodes, functional neuroimaging studies (positron emission tomography [PET] or single-photon computed emission tomography [SPECT], or both), and neuropsychological testing, with or without intracarotid injection of sodium amobarbital (i.e., Wada testing). Prolonged video-EEG monitoring involves the simultaneous recording of brain activity and clinical behavior and is the cornerstone of presurgical evaluation.[60,103] It combines the technology of simultaneous EEG recording via scalp electrodes with a synchronized, continuous real-time audio/video recording of a child's typical seizures, thereby enabling lateralization and localization of the child's seizure focus. When a temporal focus is suspected, sphenoidal electrodes can be placed to record activity from the mesial temporal lobes. In addition, antiepileptic medications can be withdrawn gradually while continuously monitoring for seizures until several "typical" seizures are recorded. In the majority of cases, the video-EEG study enables one to determine whether a patient has epilepsy, whether the patient has partial or generalized seizures, and where the partial seizures arise.[15,105] When considering a child for epilepsy surgery, the ideal circumstance is to find that the seizures are highly stereotyped on EEG and that all seizures arise from the same region.[105] Occasionally, video-EEG recording will demonstrate the presence of independent, bilateral seizure onset, especially in children with epilepsy secondary to multifocal abnormalities, as seen in tuberous sclerosis.[14] In such cases, a child may still be considered a candidate for epilepsy surgery if a majority of the seizures come from one side; however, it must be understood that complete seizure control may not be possible.[105]

Functional neuroimaging with PET[28,29,33] and SPECT[102] also provides valuable localizing information by detecting generalized and focal functional brain abnormalities. This information can then be compared with the electrophysiologic dysfunction observed on EEG and the anatomic abnormalities on MRI. PET is a noninvasive functional imaging study that measures regional cerebral glucose utilization or metabolism by determining the extent of uptake of the radionuclide [^{18}F]deoxyglucose (FDG). Interictally, an epileptic focus is seen on PET as an area of glucose hypometabolism. This study is especially helpful in localizing focal areas of cortical dysplasia, mesial temporal sclerosis, and other structural abnormalities that correspond to surface EEG localization of epileptogenic regions. SPECT is another noninvasive functional imaging study that measures regional cerebral blood flow by using perfusion radiotracers such as technetium Tc 99m hexamethylpropyleneamine oxine (^{99m}Tc-HMPAO). It provides a snapshot of local cerebral blood flow at a specific point in time.[3] Between seizures, a seizure focus is hypometabolic and receives less blood flow. Consequently, relative hypoperfusion is observed in this region on a SPECT scan.[99] In contrast, hyperperfusion is observed in the region of the seizure focus on an ictal SPECT study if the tracer is injected at the time of seizure onset because local blood flow to the seizure focus increases significantly during a seizure as a consequence of increased metabolic demands. Ictal SPECT is more reliable than interictal SPECT in localizing the epileptogenic zone,[56,86,135] and ictal SPECT is more feasible than ictal PET because unlike the ictal PET scan, which must be performed shortly after the tracer is given, the ictal SPECT scan can be performed at a convenient time after the tracer is injected.[105] Functional imaging studies, such as PET and SPECT, have reduced the need for invasive intracranial monitoring in children by up to 90%.[28,56,86]

Another important component of presurgical evaluation is the identification of areas of brain function relative to the location of the seizure focus. This helps predict the risks associated with removal of the seizure focus. Neuropsychological testing plays an important role in this part of the presurgical evaluation.[103] Such testing can provide lateralizing and localizing information by identifying areas of neurologic dysfunction that correlate with the patient's underlying lesion.[71] For example, patients with seizures arising from their dominant temporal lobe may have deficits in verbal memory or language acquisition, whereas deficits in visuospatial memory suggest seizure onset in the nondominant temporal lobe. Significant deficits in both verbal and visuospatial memory suggest bilateral temporal lobe damage and probable bilateral seizure foci. In addition, preoperative neuropsychological testing can help predict the prognosis for cognitive functioning after surgery and be used as a baseline to monitor disease progression, successful therapy, and the adverse effects of treatment.[3,103] Moreover, postoperative neuropsychological testing can be performed to identify residual or resultant cognitive deficits and to assist in planning psychoeducational interventions to address any impairments.

Intracarotid amobarbital injection (i.e., Wada testing) can also be used, especially in older children, to determine which cerebral hemisphere is dominant for language and to ascertain the relative contributions of each cerebral hemisphere to memory function.[3,15,83,139] During this study, a cerebral angiogram is performed and amobarbital is injected into each internal carotid artery individually. Intracarotid injection of amobarbital results in arrest of ipsilateral cerebral function, which mimics the effect of surgical removal of the ipsilateral cerebral hemisphere. A successful injection is demonstrated by contralateral hemiparesis and ipsilateral slowing of the EEG. Speech and memory are then tested to determine whether the hemisphere contralateral to a planned resection can adequately support language and memory function. Wada testing is the most reliable means of ascertaining lateralization of language dominance and assessing residual memory capacity after temporal lobectomy; however, it is often difficult to perform in young children because it is necessary for them to be awake and cooperative.

Results from the preoperative investigation determine whether a patient is a candidate for epilepsy surgery or whether additional studies are required to more accurately pinpoint the location of the seizure focus and areas of eloquent cortex. The results of the aforementioned studies are reviewed in a multidisciplinary clinical conference attended by epileptologists, neurosurgeons, neuroradiologists, neuropsychologists, and other members of the epilepsy surgery team to determine whether the patient is a candidate for surgery. The pediatric neurosurgeon discusses the risks and benefits of surgery, determines the surgical approach, and makes the final decision on whether to proceed.[103] Results obtained from video-EEG, MRI, and PET are typically given the strongest consideration,[15] and surgery is recommended when there is a clearly defined focal area of seizure onset that is consistent with EEG, radiographic, neuropsychological, and clinical evidence.[97] The likelihood of a successful outcome from seizure surgery increases with the number of independent elements that converge toward a single localization.[15,46,84,135]

In some patients, surgery appears to be a good option, but the data are inconclusive or discordant. Such patients include those with normal or nonlocalizing imaging studies and a video-EEG that regionalizes the seizure onset without sufficiently localizing it, patients with a seizure focus that is more extensive than the structural lesion observed on imaging studies, and those with a seizure focus in the vicinity of eloquent cortex. For these patients, prolonged, invasive intracranial EEG monitoring may be required to obtain more precise localizing information.[4,5,15,68,69,97] Intracranial EEG monitoring has the following advantages: (1) it helps define the boundaries of the epileptogenic zone around the lesion, which in turn guides the extent of resection; (2) it helps determine whether children with multiple structural lesions and multifocal interictal spike discharges are surgical candidates by ascertaining whether their seizures arise from a single operable epileptogenic zone; and (3) it enables mapping of areas of eloquent cortex that are contiguous to the seizure focus to determine whether resection of the seizure focus can be performed safely without creating new deficits or worsening existing ones.

This technique involves placing surface electrodes, such as grid and strip electrodes embedded in a thin pliable sheet of plastic, directly onto the cortical surface through a craniotomy and dural opening in the case of subdural grids or through bur holes in the case of subdural strips.[146] Before closing the dura, an ICP monitor can be placed in patients with subdural grids to facilitate postoperative monitoring and management of elevated ICP related to grid placement. ICP monitoring is particularly beneficial in the case of a prolonged postictal state because it can help differentiate postictal lethargy from neurologic deterioration as a result of hemorrhage or edema.[97] In addition, the strips and grids are sutured to the dura to minimize the risk of postoperative movement, and the electrode leads are tunneled to a distant exit site to minimize the risk of infection. Duraplasty is performed in cases in which the subdural space must be enlarged to accommodate the electrodes, the bone flap is replaced loosely, and the scalp incision is closed in a two-layered fashion. The skin around the exiting leads is closed tightly to avoid a CSF leak, and the leads are secured to the scalp with 4-0 nylon suture to minimize movement of the electrodes. If necessary, multicontact depth electrodes can be placed stereotactically with a frame-based system to achieve accurate EEG recordings from structures located deep to the cortical surface. Depth electrodes survey very restricted areas of cortex and are not helpful in delineating large epileptogenic zones. However, monitoring with depth electrodes can be advantageous in children when the seizures are thought to arise from mesial temporal lobe structures, such as the hippocampus and amygdala, but the side of origin is uncertain.[5]

After implanting the surface electrodes, a postoperative skull radiograph is obtained to document electrode position, prophylactic intravenous antibiotics and low-dose corticosteroids are administered, and continuous video-EEG monitoring is performed. The child is monitored until several typical seizures are recorded. Once an adequate number of the child's typical seizures have been recorded, cortical stimulation studies are carried out to map functional cortex and induce auras or seizures that can be of further help in localizing the seizure focus.[3,15,97] A surgical plan is then formulated on the basis of the electrical, structural, and functional data, and the child is taken back to the operating room where the craniotomy is reopened and the planned resection is performed. A repeat skull radiograph is performed before the second operation and compared with the initial skull film to document electrode position and evaluate for electrode movement. Rarely, an epileptogenic focus cannot be found or resection of the epileptogenic focus may lead to an unacceptable neurologic deficit. In such cases, the subdural electrodes are removed and the craniotomy is closed without performing resective surgery.[97]

Although intracranial EEG monitoring can help determine the feasibility and safety of epilepsy surgery, it is an invasive procedure associated with a number of possible risks, including hemorrhage, infection, CSF leak, electrode migration, increased ICP, and even death.[69,164] The complication rate for strips is 1% to 3%,[161] whereas that for depth electrodes is 3% to 10%.[136] Complications occur more commonly with grids than with strips. The risk of infection increases with the duration of invasive monitoring and may be decreased by administering prophylactic intravenous antibiotics. In many cases, extraoperative electrode grid placement is unnecessary.[5,68,106] Instead, intraoperative electrocorticography can be carried out at the time of surgery to define the precise limits of the cortical resection based on the location of interictal spike discharges, differences in background EEG patterns, and identification of critical functional cortex (e.g., primary sensorimotor cortex) by intraoperative somatosensory evoked potentials.[5,123]

Types of Epilepsy Surgery

Three main types of surgery are used to treat intractable seizures in children: (1) resections, in which the epileptogenic cortex is removed; (2) disconnections, in which critical pathways involved in the propagation of epileptiform discharges are interrupted; and (3) implantations, in which electrical stimulation is used.[103,104,147] The type of surgery performed is determined by the results of the presurgical workup.

Resection Surgery

Specific types of resection surgery include anterior temporal lobectomy with amygdalohippocampectomy for intractable complex partial seizures; extratemporal resections for nonlesional epilepsy[97]; multilobar, lobar, and focal cortical resections for intractable seizures caused by structural lesions such as cortical malformations, intracerebral hamartomas, tumors (see Fig. 124-8A to F), and vascular malformations[147]; and hemispherectomy, the extreme of resection surgery, which involves either complete removal (anatomic) or isolation (functional) of the abnormal cerebral hemisphere and is reported to be one of the most successful of all operations for the relief of epilepsy.[104,110,114] Hemispherectomy is reserved for patients who have severe damage to one hemisphere and a relatively intact contralateral hemisphere; it is particularly effective in children with severe unilateral motor seizures who already have contralateral hemiparesis and hemianopsia. Candidates for hemispherectomy include patients with Rasmussen's syndrome,[149] Sturge-Weber syndrome,[47] hemimegalencephaly,[151] diffuse hemispheric cortical dysplasia, infantile hemiplegia, and cerebral infarction. When the presurgical workup reveals that a child's seizures are arising from the entire hemisphere and that hemisphere is removed with sparing of the ipsilateral basal ganglia (anatomic hemispherectomy) or disconnected with removal of less cortical tissue (functional hemispherectomy or hemispherotomy), 75% to 80% of patients have a marked reduction (80% or more) in seizure frequency with improvement in cognitive function.[36,147,149,159]

Temporal lobe epilepsy (TLE) is the most common localization-related epilepsy in adult and adolescent surgical candidates but is less common than extratemporal epilepsy in infants and children.[43,82] In TLE, patients generally experience complex partial seizures with oral and gestural automatisms, which may be preceded by an aura.[15] Although the most common cause of TLE in adults and adolescents is mesial temporal sclerosis, such is not the case for infants and children.[42,162] Instead, TLE in this age group is more commonly caused by congenital abnormalities in cerebral development, such as cortical dysplasia, low-grade neoplasms, and vascular malformations.[6,44] In patients with lesion-related TLE, which occurs as a result of a temporal lobe mass, the source of the seizures is not generally the lesion itself but the margins around the lesion,[39] and a successful outcome in such patients depends on adequately defining the extent of the epileptogenic zone around the lesion and resecting this region along with the lesion.

When the results of diagnostic studies indicate that the seizures are arising from a single temporal lobe, surgery is recommended. Both the lateral neocortex and the medial basal portion of the temporal lobe can cause temporal lobe seizures in children.[2,3] The medial basal portion of the temporal lobe consists of the fusiform and parahippocampal gyri and the amygdalohippocampal complex. Several surgical approaches have been described for resecting epileptic foci arising from the medial temporal lobe in children with medically refractory mesial TLE of unilateral origin.[147] For example, an anterior temporal lobectomy with amygdalohippocampectomy can be performed.[3,104,134] This two-step approach involves the initial removal of approximately 3.5 cm of anterolateral temporal lobe (measured with a ruler from the temporal tip along the middle temporal gyrus) below the superior temporal gyrus with a subpial dissection technique. This results in exposure of the temporal horn and mesial temporal lobe structures, including the hippocampus, amygdala, and parahippocampal gyrus. The mesial structures are then removed by subpial dissection under the operating microscope, with the posterior limit of the dissection extending to the level of the tectal plate. In children with medically refractory mesial TLE of unilateral origin, removal of the affected mesial temporal lobe, with complete removal of the medial temporal structures, has a greater than 75% chance of markedly reducing a child's seizures or rendering a child seizure free off medication.[2,3,6,94,147]

Extratemporal epilepsy is found more frequently than TLE in pediatric epilepsy surgery candidates.[43] The epileptiform abnormalities can be frontal, parietal, or occipital and are often poorly localized.[156-158] Moreover, it is not uncommon for more than one lobe to be involved in children with intractable epilepsy.[97] When the seizure focus is outside the temporal lobe and is not associated with a lesion on imaging studies (nonlesional, extratemporal epilepsy), patients often require invasive intracranial monitoring and stimulation studies to define and accurately localize the seizure focus, as well as to map areas of eloquent brain function relative to the epileptogenic cortex.[15,97] Such seizures may be clinically silent and suggest a parietal or lateral frontal focus, complex partial and suggest a frontal lobe focus, or associated with amaurosis and suggest an occipital lobe focus. Resection margins are defined on the basis of the epileptogenic gyri identified during preoperative intracranial monitoring and stimulation studies with implanted subdural electrodes, as well as by intraoperative electrocorticography and functional cortical mapping. Corticectomy is then carried out under the operating microscope and the entire epileptogenic focus is resected en bloc with a subpial dissection technique. Roughly two thirds of children with extratemporal (both lesional and nonlesional) epilepsy derive significant improvement from surgical intervention.[7,129]

The risks associated with resection procedures are generally related to the area or areas of brain resected and include visual field cuts (e.g., contralateral superior quadrantanopsia or "pie-in-the-sky" defect caused by an injury to Meyer's loop/optic radiation during posterior temporal lobe resection), manipulation hemiplegia, speech and memory deficits, stroke from injury to nearby blood vessels (e.g., sylvian branches of the middle cerebral artery during temporal lobectomy), and cranial nerve palsies (e.g., injury to the third nerve during resection of the hippocampus). The incidence of major complications, such as stroke or paresis, ranges from 2% to 5%.[128,129]

Disconnection Surgery

Resection of an epileptogenic focus is the mainstay of epilepsy surgery. However, in some children, the epileptogenic area is in a functionally critical cortical region (e.g., sensorimotor, language, or visual cortex, or more than one of these regions) and cannot be resected safely. Such children may be candidates for disconnection surgery—surgery in which the seizure focus is isolated from the rest of the brain.[104] For example, if the presurgical workup reveals that a child has a seizure focus in an area of eloquent brain, such as the motor cortex, resection of the focus might cause unacceptable deficits, such as contralateral paralysis or weakness. To prevent this, children with seizures arising in eloquent cortex can undergo a type of "disconnection" procedure called multiple subpial transection.[95,97,104] The efficacy of this type of surgery is based on the observation that normal cortical function is transmitted vertically, whereas seizures are transmitted through horizontal pathways. A small ball-tipped probe is used to transect the horizontal fibers in regions of eloquent cortex, thereby interrupting horizontal spread of the ictal discharge without damaging the vertical columns of functional cortex. The cuts are made within the superficial convexity of the cortex under direct vision through the operating microscope, with each cut occurring at a right angle to the long axis of the gyrus at 5-mm intervals in a parallel fashion until the entire epileptogenic zone has been covered. With this technique, selected patients can achieve a substantial reduction in seizure frequency, without sustaining any persistent neurologic deficits. In extratemporal epilepsy, seizure control with multiple subpial transection is comparable to that achieved with resective surgery.[133]

Corpus callosotomy is another type of disconnection surgery that can be performed in the absence of an identifiable seizure focus or in the presence of multiple foci. During this procedure, the anterior two thirds or the entire corpus callosum is sectioned through a bifrontal craniotomy approach.[88,107,147] It is typically reserved for patients who have symptomatic generalized epilepsy with multiple seizure types and foci of epileptogenicity, as well as some degree of developmental delay or mental retardation.[15,103] Sectioning of the corpus callosum results in separation of the cerebral hemispheres and prevents rapid bilateral generalization of epileptic discharges. Candidates for operative intervention include patients with atonic seizures ("drop attacks") who are prone to violent falls and closed head injuries and patients with Lennox-Gastaut syndrome. In appropriate patients, this type of procedure can be very effective. For example, in patients with atonic seizures, up to 80% may experience complete or nearly complete cessation of attacks.[103] However, rarely do seizures totally remit, and patients with absence or myoclonic seizures either derive no benefit or experience an inconsistent response with corpus callosotomy. In addition, corpus callosotomy is associated with a number of possible adverse effects, some of which can be quite devastating, including language disturbances (e.g., complete mutism versus slowness in initiating speech), weakness, increased frequency or intensity of partial seizures, and a disconnection syndrome in patients with a dominant left hemisphere that consists of left tactile anomia, left-sided dyspraxia, pseudohemianopsia, right-sided anomia for smell, impaired spatial synthesis of the right hand resulting in difficulty copying complex figures, decreased spontaneity of speech, and incontinence.[147]

Outcome

Successful outcome from epilepsy surgery depends on (1) proper and timely patient selection guided by a thorough presurgical evaluation; (2) good correlation among clinical, electrophysiologic, and neuroradiologic data; (3) complete or nearly complete resection of the seizure focus; and (4) lack of surgically related injury. Patients undergo routine EEG, MRI, and neuropsychological testing postoperatively and are graded in terms of percentage of seizure reduction and length of time since surgery. Results from preoperative neuropsychological testing can also be compared with those from postoperative testing to ascertain the effects of surgery on the child's behavior and cognition. In this manner, postoperative neuropsychological testing can help identify residual or resultant cognitive deficits and assist in planning psychoeducational interventions to address these deficits. Patients continue taking anticonvulsants for 1 to 2 years postoperatively. Those who are seizure free at that time, with a relatively benign-appearing EEG, are gradually weaned from their seizure medications.

It has been shown in some studies that outcome after epilepsy surgery (especially in the case of multilobar, lobar, and focal cortical resections for intractable seizures caused by structural lesions) is related to the pathology and location of the lesion.[103,147] Structural lesions associated with intractable epilepsy in children include developmental lesions, such as focal cortical dysplasia and hamartomas; vascular lesions, such as cavernomas and arteriovenous malformations; low-grade tumors, such as DNET, ganglioglioma, ganglioneuroma, astrocytoma, pleomorphic xanthoastrocytoma, and oligodendroglioma; ischemic or hypoxic lesions; traumatic lesions; and mesial temporal sclerosis.[103,147] With focal cortical dysplasia, an important cause of intractable epilepsy in children, the outcome after surgical intervention is quite good within the first 2 years after surgery; however, the percentage of patients who remain seizure free declines over time. For example, in one series,[90] although 65% of patients with cortical dysplasia were seizure free at 2 years, only 40% remained seizure free at 5 years and just 33% were seizure free at 10 years. In another series with a mean follow-up period of 3.6 years, children with cortical dysplasia had seizure-free rates of 52%.[163] With mesial temporal sclerosis, a relatively rare pathologic entity in children, seizure-free rates are excellent for the vast majority of children and adolescents, with surgical results comparable to those observed in adults.[90,163] DNET is a benign cortical lesion that has cystic or microcystic components and is frequently associated with cortical dysplasia.[103] In contrast to cortical dysplasia, the epileptogenic area associated with DNET resides within the cortex immediately adjacent to the lesion rather than within the DNET itself.[50] Total resection of these lesions, aided by preresection electrocorticography to identify adjacent epileptogenic cortex, can result in complete seizure freedom in about 75% of patients.[116] In patients with ganglioglioma who have seizures (see Fig. 124-8A to F), complete surgical resection is the preferred management and the most important factor predicting a seizure-free outcome,[76] with about 78% of patients becoming seizure free off anticonvulsants.[70]

The goal of surgical management is complete elimination of seizures or excellent seizure control with seizure medications and an improvement in the child's long-term cognitive, behavioral, and social development. Surgical treatment of epilepsy in children can reduce seizure frequency and limit the cognitive and psychological impairment that often occurs as a consequence of chronic uncontrolled seizures. However, surgical intervention must be timed appropriately to enable children to develop their maximal potential and reach their educational, vocational, and social goals.[103]

As with any surgical procedure, epilepsy ablative procedures are not risk free, and the risk of creating a new permanent neurologic deficit or worsening an existing deficit must be balanced against the potential benefit of completely eliminating a patient's seizures or significantly reducing the frequency of seizures. Risks of epilepsy surgery include removal of or injury to eloquent cortex; injury to projection fibers, association fibers, or commissural fibers underlying the cortical resection; injury to Meyer's loop causing a contralateral "pie-in-the-sky" visual field defect; injury to vessels in the area of the resection causing ischemic damage or stroke in the areas of vascular distribution; and injury to nearby cranial nerves. Despite the risks of the procedure, early surgical intervention in appropriate cases can arrest progressive deleterious changes in the developing brain, including progressive psychological and intellectual impairment, allow for optimum brain development, reduce the undesirable side effects of medical therapy, and allow many children with seizures to lead normal, productive lives. Currently, surgery is the *only* therapy that offers the chance of a cure, and early identification of appropriate surgical candidates by means of a comprehensive preoperative evaluation is paramount to achieving a successful outcome.[103]

Vagus Nerve Stimulation

Vagus nerve stimulation by means of the implantable Neurocybernetic Prosthesis (NCP; Cyberonics, Houston) is a relatively recent development in the surgical treatment of childhood epilepsy and is gaining increasing popularity as an effective treatment option for children with medically refractory epilepsy who have failed multiple medications and are not candidates for resection or disconnection procedures. Such children often have many generalized or focal seizures (or both) every day that arise from multiple areas on both sides of the brain, and they are not candidates for or have already failed previous cortical resection. Placement of a vagal nerve stimulator involves wrapping helical, platinum, bifurcated ribbon electrodes around the left vagus nerve in the cervical region and connecting the bifurcated helical lead to a pulse generator, which in turn is inserted into a subcutaneous or submuscular pocket in the left pectoral region.[10,104] Together, they deliver intermittent electrical stimulation to the left cervical vagus nerve—usually for 30 seconds every 5 minutes. Electrical impulses, which travel to the cerebral cortex by way of ascending sensory nuclei (e.g., nucleus tractus solitarius), exert widespread effects on neuronal excitability throughout the CNS.[11] Although it has been postulated that these rostral impulses stop seizure activity by disrupting the abnormal electrical activity caused by abnormal groups of neurons firing in an uncontrolled synchronous fashion, the exact mechanism of seizure modulation remains unknown.[9,8,120]

The pulse generator has eight programmable parameters that are adjusted noninvasively through the skin by a telemetry programming wand controlled by a laptop or hand-held computer. The stimulation parameters are adjusted according to patient tolerance and seizure frequency, and seizure medications are weaned as tolerated. An additional benefit of vagus nerve stimulation is the ability to control seizure activity with the use of a hand-held magnet. For example, at the beginning of an aura or seizure, the patient or a family member may briefly pass a hand-held magnet across the chest pocket where the generator resides. This triggers a train of stimulation superimposed on the baseline output that can attenuate or even abort an impending seizure.[11] Other advantages of vagus nerve stimulation include guaranteed treatment compliance, sustained efficacy over time,[96] and global improvement in quality of life and cognitive function.[11] Adverse effects of vagus nerve stimulation can occur and include hoarseness, throat pain, cough, dyspnea, and paresthesias. Such effects tend to occur intermittently, concomitantly with stimulus delivery, and are typically transient.[96,124] Surgical complications of vagus nerve stimulation are rare and include left vocal cord injury, lower facial paresis, bradycardia, and infection requiring explantation in 1.1%.[11] Although the vagus nerve is the principal efferent component of the parasympathetic nervous system, vagus nerve stimulation by the NCP system has not been shown to adversely influence cardiac rhythm, pulmonary function, gastrointestinal motility, or secretion.[124]

Previous studies have shown that children and adolescents with medically and surgically refractory epilepsy derive substantial benefit from vagus nerve stimulation, with many patients achieving a significant reduction in seizure frequency and some being able to reduce the number of anticonvulsants.[100,109] Patients with idiopathic epilepsy, as well as those with seizures arising from a structural etiology, are considered appropriate candidates.[11] In particular, vagal nerve stimulation has been shown to be highly effective in patients with Lennox-Gastaut syndrome, with five of six children in one series achieving a 90% reduction in seizure frequency.[64] Moreover, use of the magnet in pediatric patients has been shown to reduce seizure duration in some patients and improve postictal lethargy in others.[109] In a previous retrospective analysis of seizure frequency and quality of life in pediatric patients with medically refractory epilepsy,[109] 29% of children achieved a greater than 90% reduction in seizure frequency, 39% had a 50% to 90% reduction, and 13% had less than a 50% reduction with vagus nerve stimulation. Although complete seizure control is possible with vagus nerve stimulation, the likelihood of complete control is quite low.[11]

SUPPURATIVE CENTRAL NERVOUS SYSTEM INFECTIONS

Suppurative infections of the CNS include intracranial infections such as brain abscess, subdural empyema, epidural abscess, osteomyelitis of the skull, Pott's puffy tumor, and acute pyogenic meningitis,[74] as well as intraspinal infections such as SC abscess, spinal epidural abscess, diskitis, and vertebral osteomyelitis. Intracranial infections can be life threatening and must be considered in the differential diagnosis in children with fever, headache, and cranial wounds or sinus disease. Similarly, intraspinal infections can result in devastating neurologic impairment, especially if the diagnosis is delayed, and must be considered in the differential diagnosis in children with back pain, spinal tenderness, and fever. The remainder of this chapter discusses suppurative CNS infections, treatment of which requires the involvement of a pediatric neurosurgeon.

Intracranial Infections

Suppurative processes in the epidural and subdural spaces and brain parenchyma are classic neurosurgical complications of otorhinologic, middle ear, and post-traumatic infections, as well as immunosuppression, and they are commonly manifested as neurosurgical emergencies.[31] An epidural abscess refers to suppuration in the epidural space between the dura and calvaria or skull base, a subdural empyema refers to suppuration in the subdural space between the dura and arachnoid, and a brain abscess refers to a circumscribed focus of suppurative tissue necrosis within the brain parenchyma.

Incidence

The reported incidence of intracranial infections in children remains quite low. In busy pediatric neurosurgical centers, the incidence of an isolated epidural abscess is about one case per year and that of subdural empyema is one to two cases per year.[108,130] The incidence of brain abscess is less than one to three cases per year.[31] Although intracranial infections are relatively uncommon in children, they can be rapidly fatal if not recognized promptly and managed appropriately. Successful treatment requires early diagnosis, guided by CT or MRI (or both), aggressive antibiotic therapy, and timely and adequate surgical intervention targeted to maximal areas of suppuration. Response to treatment must also be monitored neuroradiographically to ensure that the infection is resolving.

Etiology

Intracranial infections occur as a consequence of (1) direct extension from contiguous infection, such as paranasal sinusitis, otitis media, or mastoiditis, or propagation through venous channels; (2) direct inoculation of the brain after penetrating cranial trauma or a neurosurgical procedure; and (3) hematogenous spread from a distant focus of infection. Contiguous infection in the paranasal sinuses, mastoid air cells, orbit, or skull is the most commonly reported cause of suppuration in the epidural space.[51] Epidural abscess can also occur as a complication of a congenital dermal sinus, trauma (especially penetrating wounds), craniotomy, application of skull pins or tongs, and paranasal sinus and skull base operative procedures.[77] Subdural empyema commonly occurs as a result of infection in the frontal and ethmoidal sinuses, middle ear, and mastoid air cells.[18,92] Other causes of subdural empyema include spread from contiguous infections of the scalp, subgaleal space, calvaria, or epidural space (or any combination of these regions); meningitis; hematogenous infection of a preexisting subdural effusion or hematoma[13]; rupture of a parenchymal brain abscess into the subdural space; and subdural puncture or subdural shunt placement.

In the pediatric population, the most common cause of brain abscess is direct or indirect spread from infection in the paranasal sinuses, middle ear, and teeth.[160] In adolescent boys, frontal lobe abscess is a relatively common complication of acute frontal sinusitis.[31] In children with congenital cardiac abnormalities or pulmonary right-to-left shunt disease, hematogenous spread from remote sources of infection, such as pulmonary infections, cutaneous infections, osteomyelitis, and bacterial endocarditis, remains an important pathogenic mechanism of brain abscess formation.[141] In neonates, bacterial meningitis caused by *Citrobacter, Proteus, Serratia,* or *Enterobacter* is complicated by the formation of brain abscesses in a high percentage of patients.[118] Moreover, direct inoculation of the brain after penetrating cranial trauma, penetrating wounds of the orbit, compound skull fractures, scalp wounds, facial sepsis, CSF fistula, and post-traumatic meningitis can lead to the development of brain abscesses in children. The location of the abscess is dependent on the portal of entry. For example, otogenic abscesses or those resulting from mastoiditis often develop in the temporal lobe or cerebellar hemisphere adjacent to the infected ear or mastoid air cells, paranasal sinusitis commonly gives rise to abscess formation in the frontal lobe, and brain abscesses arising from hematogenous spread tend to occur in the distribution of the middle cerebral artery.

Aerobic organisms commonly isolated from suppurative intracranial infections include *Staphylococcus, Streptococcus,* Enterobacteriaceae, and *Haemophilus.* Anaerobic organisms include *Bacteroides, Peptostreptococcus, Fusobacterium, Veillonella, Propionibacterium,* and *Actinomyces.* In many cases, culture of pus obtained from intracranial infections reveals multiple organisms, including both anaerobic and aerobic organisms.[31] However, in some cases, no organisms are isolated despite proper handling of specimens. With regard to the causative organisms, the bacteriologic diagnosis often points to the source of the intracranial infection. For example, aerobic or anaerobic streptococci (or both) are often cultured from intracranial infections complicating paranasal sinus infection, gram-negative organisms such as *Bacteroides* and *Haemophilus* are cultured from intracranial infections complicating otogenic infections, and *S. aureus* is cultured from intracranial infections complicating compound skull fractures and neurosurgical procedures. Fungal organisms, such as *Candida, Aspergillus, Nocardia,* and *Cryptococcus,* commonly cause intracranial infections in children who are immunologically suppressed after organ transplantation or chemotherapy for malignancy or who have impaired host defenses.[137]

Pathogenesis

Spread of infection from the paranasal sinuses, mastoid air cells, or middle ear to the epidural and subdural spaces or to the brain parenchyma occurs as a consequence of infective thrombophlebitis of the diploic vessels or nutrient vessels that supply the outer layer of the dura.[31] Once infection enters the diploic space, it spreads rapidly through this space to involve widespread areas of the skull. Occasionally, a subperiosteal abscess (Pott's puffy tumor) forms as a result of the osteomyelitis and leads to swelling of the overlying scalp (Fig. 124-9A and B). Once the inflammatory process reaches the subdural space, it can spread rapidly throughout the subdural space because this space is in continuity over the surface of the brain, on each side of the falx and tentorium, and through the foramen magnum with the spinal subdural space. Direct exposure of the brain to subdural infection can lead to cortical vein occlusion and septic thrombophlebitis. This, in turn, can cause cerebral infarction and edema, and the edema can produce a significant mass effect and associated cerebral compression and herniation.

Seeding of bacteria in areas of preexisting necrosis or direct traumatic injury, hemorrhage, or infarction from septic thrombophlebitis leads to the formation of a brain abscess. Once a nidus of bacteria is established within the brain parenchyma, the organisms produce an acute inflammatory response that results in polymorphonuclear infiltration and edema. The central area eventually undergoes necrosis and liquefaction and becomes surrounded by a peripheral zone of inflammatory cells, neovascularization, and fibroblasts.[31] The fibroblasts, in turn, create a dense collagenous capsule that is surrounded by edema and reactive gliosis. An abscess with its surrounding edema can lead to significantly elevated ICP and cause brain herniation and death. Moreover, sudden deterioration and death can occur from rupture of a brain abscess into the ventricular system[141] or through the cortex into the subarachnoid space.[167]

Clinical Features

Children with intracranial infection often have a history of cerebral trauma, purulent nasal or aural discharge, fever, or headache. If there is suppuration within the epidural space, the child typically appears acutely ill with fever, headache, or earache at the initial evaluation. If the epidural abscess is associated with a subperiosteal abscess, patients also commonly have tender, fluctuant swelling in the scalp overlying the involved frontal sinus, mastoid air cells, or affected area of the diploic space (see Fig. 124-9A and B). As infection spreads within the epidural space, the mass effect on the subjacent dura and brain increases and causes escalating headaches. Eventually, focal neurologic signs and a decreased level of consciousness develop as the abscess increases in size and brain herniation occurs.[130]

With spread of infection into the subdural space, rapid neurologic deterioration occurs as a result of cerebral edema, infarction, and herniation. Patients typically have signs and symptoms of a systemic febrile illness and raised ICP, including malaise, fever, chills, meningismus, vomiting, headache, focal neurologic deficits, and altered mental status.[51] In addition, children with subdural empyema can have localized tenderness and swelling overlying the affected sinus or mastoid secondary to subperiosteal abscess formation (Pott's puffy tumor; see Fig. 124-9A and B), and focal seizures may be observed in 25% to 50% of patients.[31] Depending on the underlying cause, suppuration within the subdural space may be supratentorial or infratentorial, or both (Fig. 124-10A to C). With subdural empyema in the posterior fossa, children typically have a systemic febrile illness, headaches, and a stiff neck, but focal neurologic signs and seizures are generally lacking.[19]

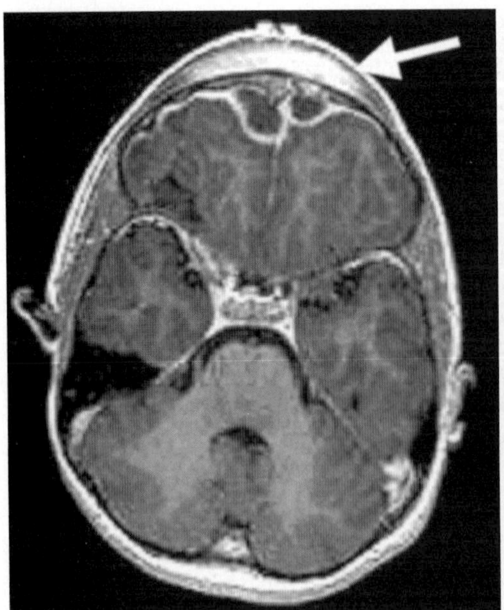
A

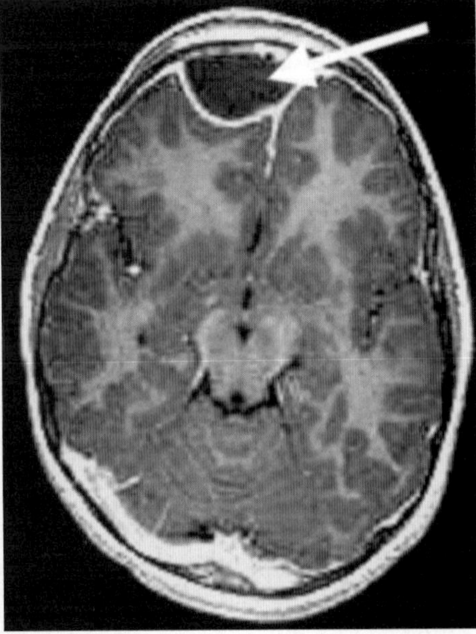
B

Figure 124-9 *A* and *B*, Axial magnetic resonance images from a 5-year-old boy with a history of strep throat, treated with 2 weeks of oral antibiotics, followed by fever, malaise, headaches, progressive swelling in the midline of his forehead, vomiting, and lethargy. A frontal subperiosteal abscess (i.e., Pott's puffy tumor; *A, arrow*) and an epidural abscess (*B, arrow*) are evident. He was managed by surgical evacuation and aggressive antibiotic therapy; the bone flap was left in place. The infection resolved completely with no neurologic sequelae.

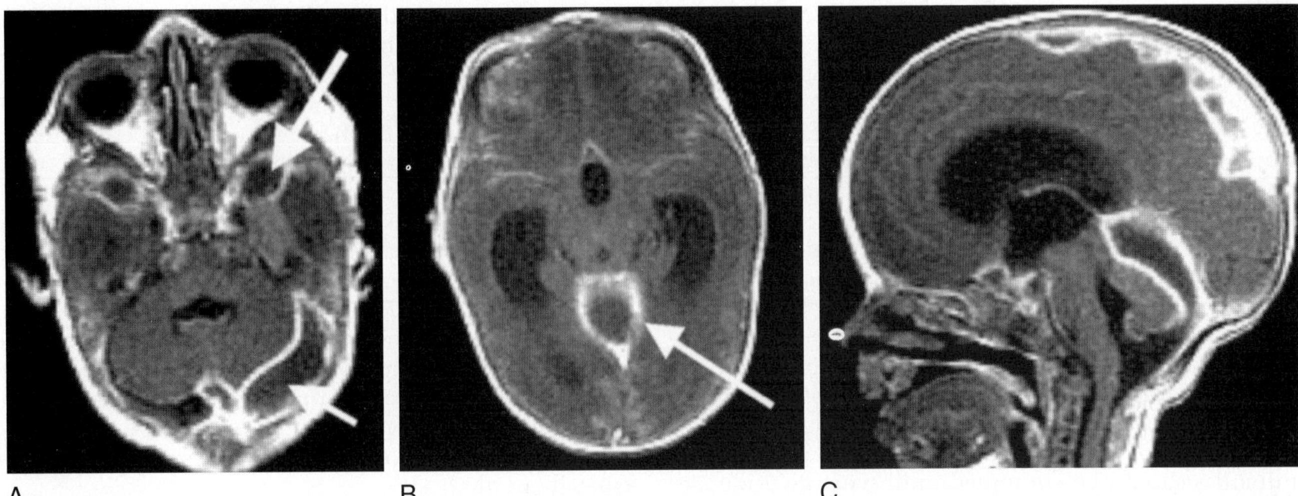

Figure 124–10 Axial (*A* and *B*) and sagittal (*C*) brain magnetic resonance imaging (MRI) in a 35-week preterm male infant with a history of meningitis, organism unknown, who was on multiple antibiotics, but not metronidazole. He began having seizures and respiratory difficulty and required intubation. MRI showed extensive subdural empyema extending bilaterally, both above and below the tentorium (*arrows*). Cultures at the time of drainage grew *Bacteroides fragilis*. The infection eventually cleared with a prolonged course of antibiotics, including metronidazole. He is now almost 4 years old, is no longer taking anticonvulsants, and has no neurologic sequelae.

The clinical manifestations of a brain abscess are influenced by the size and location of the abscess, as well as the number of abscesses present, the virulence of the organism or organisms, and the patient's age and host defenses.[31] Children and adolescents with a brain abscess exhibit signs and symptoms of (1) systemic infection, including malaise, fever, chills, and neck stiffness; (2) raised ICP as a result of the mass effect of the abscess and surrounding cerebral edema, including headache, vomiting, and a declining level of consciousness; and (3) focal neurologic deficits reflecting the location of the abscess, such as hemiparesis with an abscess in the posterior frontal region or as a consequence of uncal herniation, difficulty with speech with an abscess in the dominant temporal lobe, a visual field cut with a posterior temporal or occipital lobe abscess, and nystagmus, defective conjugate eye movements, ataxia, and hypotonia with a cerebellar abscess.[31] Infants with a brain abscess have signs and symptoms of increased ICP, including irritability, lethargy, vomiting, a bulging anterior fontanelle, frontal bossing, and increasing head circumference. At least 25% to 50% of pediatric patients with a supratentorial brain abscess also manifest focal or generalized seizures during the course of their disease.[65]

Diagnostic Studies

If intracranial infection is suspected, the patient should undergo a contrast-enhanced head CT or brain MRI study (or both). A head CT scan with contrast enhancement enables rapid diagnosis, whereas MRI provides accurate preoperative localization and is beneficial for monitoring resolution of infection. Depending on the type, extent, and stage of the intracranial infection, these studies may reveal dural enhancement, an empyema wall, an abscess capsule, and hypodense areas of cerebral edema, venous infarction, and early cerebritis. Sagittal and coronal views are also helpful for visualizing affected sinuses and suppurative collections at the vertex and skull base. In patients with a brain abscess, contrast-enhanced CT and MRI demonstrate a characteristic ring-enhancing lesion with surrounding edema. In particular, on MRI a brain abscess appears as an area of central hypointensity surrounded by a ring of enhancement after gadolinium administration on T1 weighting and as a hyperintense area of suppuration surrounded by a hypointense capsule and an outer layer of edema on T2 weighting.[113]

Laboratory studies helpful in the diagnosis of intracranial infection include a peripheral white blood cell count, erythrocyte sedimentation rate, and C-reactive protein, all of which may be mildly elevated.[65] Blood cultures may reveal the causative organism, especially in cases of epidural abscess and subdural empyema.[65] Because of the risk for herniation and the low diagnostic yield of CSF studies, a lumbar puncture should not be performed before neuroimaging, especially if a mass-occupying lesion is suspected. Identification of the causative organism or organisms is accomplished by culturing purulent material obtained at the time of surgical drainage.[31] Such cultures determine the antibiotic sensitivity of the causative organism or organisms, which in turn guides antimicrobial therapy. Proper handling of specimens and appropriate aerobic and anaerobic culture techniques are required to achieve positive culture results.

Treatment

A high index of suspicion is essential to ensure prompt diagnosis. Successful treatment requires surgical drainage, appropriate antimicrobial therapy, and close coordination of care between pediatric neurosurgeons and infectious disease specialists. Systemic antibiotics should be initiated as soon as the diagnosis is considered.[31] Although preoperative antibiotics may achieve some bone penetration, it is unlikely that they will interfere with culture results.

The initial choice of antibiotics is contingent on the microbial spectrum, which varies according to the primary site of infection.[31] Hence, knowledge of the primary infection site can be used to guide antimicrobial therapy. For example, if frontal sinusitis is the primary site, the most likely infective agent is a streptococcal species, and antibiotic coverage should include metronidazole and penicillin or a third-generation cephalosporin. If the primary site is unknown, the initial choice of antibiotics should include a penicillinase-resistant synthetic penicillin, a third-generation cephalosporin, and metronidazole to provide coverage of aerobic and anaerobic streptococci, other anaerobes, and staphylococci. Although the optimal duration of therapy remains unknown, intravenous antibiotics should be continued until systemic evidence of the infection has resolved and the intracranial infection appears to be diminishing in size.[18,130] An additional 2 to 3 months of oral antibiotics is recommended by some to prevent recurrence.[91]

Besides systemic antibiotics, children with intracranial infections may also require treatment with corticosteroids and anticonvulsants. Corticosteroids, such as dexamethasone, are effective in reducing the cerebral edema associated with intracranial infection and have not been shown to exacerbate the inflammatory response. Consequently, corticosteroids can be administered during the acute phase of the illness to reduce intracranial hypertension and prevent herniation. Because 25% to 50% of pediatric patients with intracranial infections exhibit seizures during the course of their illness, prophylactic anticonvulsants should also be started as soon as the diagnosis is made.

Besides enabling bacteriologic diagnosis and guiding antimicrobial therapy, surgical treatment permits evacuation of sizable collections of liquefied pus and reduces ICP.[31] If the primary site of infection is known and the patient's clinical condition permits, surgical intervention should also address the primary infection source. Surgical drainage of intracranial pus can be performed through a limited craniotomy, craniectomy, or bur hole. The bone removed should be just large enough to provide access to the abscess or empyema. If an epidural abscess occurs in the face of a previously devascularized bone flap, the devitalized bone is frequently left out and a delayed cranioplasty performed. However, if epidural infection complicates an extensive craniofacial reconstruction in which bone removal would probably generate irreparable defects, the bone is replaced after extensive irrigation of the epidural space with antibiotic solution and débridement, and systemic antibiotics are administered until the infection clears.[31] Follow-up neuroimaging studies are performed on all patients to monitor the progress of treatment.

For subdural empyema, the subdural space is exposed by craniotomy, craniectomy, or a bur hole, often using stereotactic CT or MRI guidance to accurately localize the purulent collection and keep the bone removal and dural opening to a minimum. Once the dura is opened, specimens are obtained for aerobic and anaerobic culture, the empyema is evacuated, and the subdural space is irrigated thoroughly with antibiotic solution. If a craniotomy has been performed and neither osteomyelitis nor epidural abscess is observed, the bone flap may be replaced. However, healing of the bone flap should be monitored closely because failure of healing can occur and result in reabsorption or sequestration of the bone flap.[85] Repeated drainage may also be necessary if the subdural empyema recurs. Infants in whom subdural fluid collections develop as a complication of *Haemophilus influenzae* meningitis typically do not require surgical intervention unless the fluid collection causes a mass effect and the patient becomes symptomatic from elevated ICP. If surgery is warranted, needle drainage through the lateral aspect of the anterior fontanelle or through a bur hole can be performed to remove the subdural fluid, which is typically sterile.[31]

Conservative management of brain abscesses with intravenous antibiotics, with or without neurosurgical intervention, has been reported. However, antibiotic treatment alone must be accompanied by frequent neuroradiographic follow-up to determine the effectiveness of the treatment. Careful monitoring of the patient's neurologic findings and level of consciousness is also essential. Immediate neurosurgical intervention is required if (1) the patient demonstrates any evidence of neurologic decline, (2) the abscess shows a significant mass effect on CT or MRI, or (3) the abscess fails to respond to antibiotics within 2 weeks of the initiation of treatment.

Two surgical options are available to treat brain abscesses, including needle aspiration, with or without catheter drainage, and excision. Ultrasound guidance or guidance with frameless or framed stereotaxy can be used to accurately localize an abscess and place a drainage needle or catheter within the abscess cavity. Ultrasound can also be used to visualize decompression of the abscess cavity as the pus is aspirated. After gentle aspiration with a syringe and irrigation with normal saline, a catheter may be left in the abscess cavity for several days until drainage of purulent fluid ceases. If aspiration fails, as frequently occurs in the case of multiloculated abscesses, surgical excision may be required. To accomplish this, a limited craniotomy bone flap is turned, the dura is opened, a small corticectomy is generated in the closest noneloquent parenchymal area, and the abscess is excised en bloc while leaving the surrounding white matter intact. The craniotomy is closed in the usual fashion after thorough irrigation with saline, and the patient is treated with long-term antibiotics.

Outcome

Outcome is determined by the rapidity of the diagnosis and initiation of treatment. Moreover, the prognosis for survival and neurologic recovery is contingent on the patient's level of consciousness at the time of diagnosis and institution of treatment. Consequently, early diagnosis and prompt aggressive therapy, with appropriate systemic antibiotics and surgical removal of suppurative collections, are paramount to minimizing the morbidity and mortality associated with suppurative intracranial infections. In support of this, the mortality associated with a brain abscess in older series approached 32% but has decreased to 10% in recent years as a consequence of more rapid diagnosis and treatment with appropriate antibiotics.[31] In contrast, the mortality rates associated with intraventricular rupture of a brain abscess remain quite high, ranging from 23.8% to 80%.[141,167] Long-term neurologic deficits occur in about 44% of patients who survive surgical treatment of brain abscess.[26] Moreover, children who survive are commonly left with learning disabilities[118] and seizures.[91]

Intraspinal Infections

Spinal epidural abscess in children is a rare clinical entity[66] that often escapes diagnosis until significant neurologic deficits develop.[119] It is a rapidly progressive, compressive lesion of the SC that often requires rapid decompression to prevent permanent paraplegia. Hematogenous spread of bacteria from cutaneous or mucosal sources of infection, such as furuncles, pharyngitis, and dental abscesses, is the most commonly reported cause of spinal epidural abscess.[12,66,87] Other potential causes include direct extension from vertebral osteomyelitis, a paraspinal abscess, or a septic focus in the pelvis, retroperitoneum, or posterior mediastinum. Such extension can occur by way of veins passing through the intervertebral foramina or bacterial seeding of an epidural hematoma that forms as a result of blunt trauma.[66] The most common pathogen of a spinal epidural abscess in children is *S. aureus*, although anaerobic and gram-negative bacteria have also been isolated.

Spinal epidural abscesses occur posterior to the SC in about 80% of cases. Posteriorly, the dura is adherent to the posterior longitudinal ligament from C1 to S2. Consequently, pus that accumulates posterior or posterolateral to the dura can spread extensively rostrocaudally but is restricted dorsally by the laminae and ligamenta flava. Although epidural infection can occur anywhere along the spinal axis, lower thoracic and lumbar abscesses are most commonly reported in the literature.[87] Once infection is established in the epidural space, pus collects deep to the laminae and ligamenta flava and is surrounded by thrombosed veins and granulation tissue. The dura provides a formidable barrier to infection. Consequently, meningitis is uncommon unless a spinal tap is performed. However, the SC is defenseless against compression and may be injured as a result of vascular compromise from arterial or venous thrombosis.[87]

Clinically, children with spinal epidural abscess may have fever and malaise, and they typically complain of deep-seated back pain, spinal tenderness, or radicular pain. The back pain is usually midthoracic and radiates around the chest wall. The pain is constant and can be exacerbated by coughing or movement. Patients often exhibit nuchal rigidity and exquisite tenderness to percussion over the involved spinal segments. A primary source of infection may be evident. Symptomatic SC compression is manifested by rapidly progressive weakness and sensory loss in the legs and evidence of bladder or bowel dysfunction, or both.

If a child is suspected of having a spinal epidural abscess, a peripheral white blood cell count, erythrocyte sedimentation rate, and C-reactive protein level are obtained and are usually elevated. Moreover, blood cultures are performed because they may reveal the offending organism. A total spine MRI with and without gadolinium enhancement enables visualization of the extent and location of a spinal epidural abscess and is the diagnostic procedure of choice. A spinal tap should not be performed. If a myelogram must be performed as part of the diagnostic workup (e.g., if MRI is not available), the spinal puncture site should be placed as far away from the suspected position of the abscess as possible.

After the diagnosis of spinal epidural abscess is made, treatment must commence immediately to prevent long-term neurologic disability. Aggressive antimicrobial therapy is initiated with intravenous antibiotics that have good coverage against staphylococci, anaerobes, and gram-negative organisms. Parenteral antibiotics are continued for at least 4 to 8 weeks. Although there are a few reports in the literature of neurologically intact children being treated successfully with antibiotics alone,[12] in the majority of cases, successful treatment requires appropriate antibiotic therapy *and* emergency evacuation of the abscess with decompression of the SC and nerve roots, especially if the abscess is widespread. This is typically performed by means of a posterior decompressive laminectomy with drainage of the purulent material. A one- or two-level laminectomy at one or both ends of the abscess with catheter irrigation and drainage is usually sufficient. If a multilevel laminectomy is required for surgical decompression, the child must be monitored carefully postoperatively for kyphosis and spinal instability, which can occur as a complication of multiple-level laminectomies in children.[12]

The prognosis is related to the patient's preoperative neurologic condition.[89] If the infection is recognized early and the patient receives appropriate treatment, recovery is expected to be excellent. If mild motor weakness has been present for less than 36 hours, a good outcome is also possible.[35] However, once a child becomes paraplegic, recovery is highly unlikely. Thus, early diagnosis and appropriate treatment are paramount to achieving a good outcome in children with a spinal epidural abscess. Mortality from spinal epidural abscess, which is unquestionably related to a delay in instituting appropriate therapy, has remained stable over the past several decades at about 14%.[35]

REFERENCES

1. Ackerman LL, Menezes AH: Spinal congenital dermal sinuses: A 30-year experience. Pediatrics 2003;112:641.
2. Adelson PD: The surgical treatment of temporal lobe epilepsy in children. In Albright AL, Pollack IF, Adelson PD (eds): Principles and Practice of Pediatric Neurosurgery. New York, Thieme, 1999, p 1111.
3. Adelson PD: Temporal lobectomy in children with intractable seizures. Pediatr Neurosurg 2001;34:268.

4. Adelson PD, Black PM, Madsen JR, et al: Use of subdural grids and strip electrodes to identify a seizure focus in children. Pediatr Neurosurg 1995;22:174.
5. Adelson PD, O'Rourke DK, Albright AL: Chronic invasive monitoring for identifying seizure foci in children. Neurosurg Clin N Am 1995;6:491.
6. Adelson PD, Peacock WJ, Chugani HT, et al: Temporal and extended temporal resections for the treatment of intractable seizures in early childhood. Pediatr Neurosurg 1992;18:169.
7. Adler J, Guisseppe E, Winston K, et al: Results of surgery for extratemporal partial epilepsy that began in childhood. Arch Neurol 1991;48:133.
8. Amar AP, Heck CN, DeGiorgio CM, et al: Experience with vagus nerve stimulation for intractable epilepsy: Some questions and answers. Neurologia Med Chir 1999;39:489.
9. Amar AP, Heck CN, Levy ML, et al: An institutional experience with cervical vagus nerve trunk stimulation for medically refractory epilepsy: Rationale, technique, and outcome. Neurosurgery 1998;43:1265.
10. Amar AP, Levy ML, Apuzzo MLJ: Vagus nerve stimulation for intractable epilepsy. In Rengachary SS (ed): Neurosurgical Operative Atlas, vol 9. Chicago, American Association of Neurological Surgeons, 2000, p 179.
11. Amar AP, Levy ML, McComb JG, et al: Vagus nerve stimulation for control of intractable seizures in childhood. Pediatr Neurosurg 2001;34:218.
12. Bair-Merritt MH, Chung C, Collier A: Spinal epidural abscess in a young child. Pediatrics 2000;106:1.
13. Bakker S, Kluytmans J, den Hollander JC, et al: Subdural empyema caused by *Escherichia coli*: Hematogenous dissemination to a preexisting chronic subdural hematoma. Clin Infect Dis 1995;21:458.
14. Bebin EM, Kelly PJ, Gomez MR: Surgical treatment for epilepsy in cerebral tuberous sclerosis. Epilepsia 1993; 34:651.
15. Benbadis SR, Wyllie E: Evaluation of intractable seizures in children. In Albright AL, Pollack IF, Adelson PD (eds): Principles and Practice of Pediatric Neurosurgery. New York, Thieme, 1999, p 1095.
16. Bierbauer KS, Storrs BB, McLone DG, et al: A prospective, randomized study of shunt function and infection as a function of shunt placement. Pediatr Neurosurg 1990;16:287.
17. Blume WT, Girvin JP, McLachlan RS, et al: Effective temporal lobectomy in childhood without invasive EEG. Epilepsia 1997;38:164.
18. Bok A, Peter J: Subdural empyema: Burr holes or craniotomy? A retrospective computerized tomography–era analysis of treatment in 90 cases. J Neurosurg 1993;78:574.
19. Borovich B, Johnston E, Spagnuoloa E: Infratentorial subdural empyema: Clinical and computerized tomography findings. Report of three cases. J Neurosurg 1990;72:299.
20. Bourgeois M, Sainte-Rose C, Cinalli G, et al: Epilepsy in children with shunted hydrocephalus. J Neurosurg 1999;90:274.
21. Bowman RM, McLone DG, Grant JA, et al: Spina bifida outcome: A 25-year prospective. Pediatr Neurosurg 2001;34:114.
22. Braathen G, Theorell K: A general hospital population of childhood epilepsy. Acta Paediatr 1995;84:1143.
23. Brockmeyer D, Abtin K, Carey L, et al: Endoscopic third ventriculostomy: An outcome analysis. Pediatr Neurosurg 1998;28:236.
24. Bruner JP, Tulipan N, Paschall RL, et al: Fetal surgery for myelomeningocele and the incidence of shunt-dependent hydrocephalus, JAMA 1999;282:1819.
25. Camfield CS, Chaplin S, Doyle A-B, et al: Side effects of phenobarbital in toddlers; behavioral and cognitive aspects. J Pediatr 1979;95:361.
26. Carey ME, Chou SN, French LA: Long-term neurological residua in patients surviving brain abscess with surgery. J Neurosurg 1971;34:652.
27. Casey AT, Kimmings EJ, Kleinlugtebeld AD, et al: The long-term outlook for hydrocephalus in childhood. Pediatr Neurosurg 1997;27:63.
28. Chugani HT: PET in preoperative evaluation of intractable epilepsy. Pediatr Neurol 1994;9:411.
29. Chugani HT, Chugani DC: Basic mechanisms of childhood epilepsies: Studies with positron emission tomography. Adv Neurol 1999;79:883.
30. Cinalli G, Sainte-Rose C, Chumas PD, et al: Failure of third ventriculostomy in the treatment of aqueductal stenosis in children. J Neurosurg 1999;90:448.
31. Cochrane DD, Dobson SR, Steinbok P: Intracranial suppuration: Epidural abscess, subdural empyema, and brain abscess. In McLone DG (editor-in-chief): Pediatric Neurosurgery: Surgery of the Developing Nervous System, 4th ed. Philadelphia, WB Saunders, 2001, p 973.
32. Cowan LD, Bodensteiner JB, Leviton A, et al: Prevalence of the epilepsies in children and adolsescents. Epilepsia 1989; 30:94.
33. Cummings TJ, Chugani DC, Chugani HT: Positron emission tomography in pediatric epilepsy. Neurosurg Clin N Am 1995;6:465.
34. Czeizel AE, Dudas I: Prevention of the first occurrence of neural-tube defects by periconceptional vitamin supplementation, N Engl J Med 1992;327:1832.
35. Danner RL, Hartman BJ: Update of spinal epidural abscess: 35 cases and review of the literature. Rev Infect Dis 1987;9:265.
36. Davies KG, Maxwell RE, French LA, et al: Hemispherectomy for intractable seizures: Long-term results in 17 patients followed for up to 38 years. J Neurosurg 1993;78:733.
37. Dollo C, Kanner A, Siomin V, et al: Outlet fenestration for isolated fourth ventricle with and without an internal shunt. Childs Nerv Syst 2001;17:483.
38. Donders J, Canady AI, Rourke BP: Psychometric intelligence after infantile hydrocephalus. Childs Nerv Syst 1990;6:148.
39. Drake JM, Hoffman HJ, Kobiashi J, et al: Surgical management of children with temporal lobe epilepsy and mass lesions. Neurosurgery 1987;2:92.
40. Drake JM, Kestle JRW, Milner R, et al: Randomized trial of cerebrospinal fluid shunt valve design in pediatric hydrocephalus. Neurosurgery 1998;43:294.
41. Drake JM, Sainte-Rose C: The Shunt Book. New York, Blackwell Scientific, 1995.
42. Duchowny M: The syndrome of partial seizures in infancy. J Child Neurol 1992;7:66.
43. Duchowny M: Epilepsy surgery in children. Curr Opin Neurol 1995;8:112.
44. Duchowny M, Lewin B, Jayakar P, et al: Temporal lobectomy in early childhood. Epilepsia 1992;33:298.
45. Elton S, Oakes WJ: Dermal sinus tracts of the spine. Neurosurgical Focus [serial online], January 10(1), Article 4, 2001. Available at http://www.aans.org/education/journal/neurosurgical/jan01/10-1-4.pdf.
46. Engel J Jr, Rausch R, Lieb JP, et al: Correlation of criteria used for localizing epileptic foci in patients considered for surgical therapy of epilepsy. Ann Neurol 1981;9:215.
47. Erba G, Cavazutti V: Sturge-Weber syndrome: Natural history and indications for surgery. J Epilepsy 1990;3(Suppl 1):287.
48. Foltz EL, Blanks JP: Symptomatic low intracranial pressure in shunted hydrocephalus. J Neurosurg 1988;68:401.
49. Fritsch MJ, Kienke S, Manwaring KH, et al: Endoscopic aqueductoplasty and interventriculostomy for the treatment of isolated fourth ventricle in children. Neurosurgery 2004; 55:372.

50. Fukuda M, Kameyama S, Tomikawa M, et al: Epilepsy surgery for focal cortical dysplasia and dysplasia and dysembryoplastic neuroepithelial tumor. No Shinkei Geka 2000;28:135.
51. Galbraith J, Barr V: Epidural abscess and subdural empyema. Adv Neurol 1974;6:257.
52. Gaskill SJ: Primary closure of open myelomeningocele. Neurosurgical Focus [serial online], February 16(2), Article 3, 2004. Available at http://www.aans.org/education/journal/neurosurgical/feb04/16-2-3.pdf.
53. Greenberg, MS: Handbook of Neurosurgery, 5th ed. New York, Thieme, 2001, p 175.
54. Hamburger V, Hamilton HL: A series of normal stages in the development of the chick embryo. J Morphol 1951;88:49.
55. Harrison MJ, Mitnick RJ, Rosenblum BR, et al: Leptomyelolipoma: Analysis of 20 cases. J Neurosurg 1990; 73:360.
56. Harvey AS, Bowe JM, Hopkins IJ, et al: Ictal ^{99m}Tc-HMPAO single photon emission computed tomography in children with temporal lobe epilepsy. Epilepsia 1993;34:869.
57. Hauser W: Seizure disorders: The changes with age. Epilepsia 1992;4:S6.
58. Hauser WA: Epidemiology of epilepsy in children. Neurosurg Clin N Am 1995;6:419.
59. Herranz JL, Armijo JA, Artega R: Clinical side effects of phenobarbital, primidone, phenytoin, carbamazepine, and valproate during monotherapy in children. Epilepsia 1988;29:794.
60. Holmes GL: Partial complex seizures in children: An analysis of 69 seizures in 24 patients using EEG FM radiotelemetry and videotape recording, Electroencephalogram Clin Neurophysiol 1984;57:13.
61. Holmes G: The long-term effects of seizures on the developing brain: Clinical and laboratory issues. Brain Dev 1991;13:393.
62. Holmes G: Epilepsy in the developing brain: Lessons from the laboratory and clinic. Epilepsia 1997;38:12.
63. Hoppe-Hirsch E, Laroussinie F, Brunet L, et al: Late outcome of the surgical treatment of hydrocephalus. Childs Nerv Syst 1998;14:97.
64. Hornig G, Murphy JV, Schallert G, et al: Left vagus nerve stimulation in children with refractory epilepsy: An update. South Med J 1997;90:484.
65. Idriss ZH, Gutman LT, Kronfol NM: Brain abscesses in infants and children: Current status of clinical findings, management and prognosis. Clin Pediatr (Phila) 1978;17:738.
66. Jacobsen FS, Sullivan B: Spinal epidural abscess in children. Orthopedics 1994;17:1131.
67. Jalava M, Sillanpaa M, Camfield C, et al: Social adjustment and competence 35 years after onset of childhood epilepsy: A prospective controlled study. Epilepsia 1997;38:708.
68. Jayakar P: Invasive EEG monitoring in children: When, where, and what? J Clin Neurophysiol 1999;16:408.
69. Jayakar P, Duchowny M, Resnick TJ: Subdural monitoring in the evaluation of children for epilepsy surgery. J Child Neurol 1994;9(Suppl 2):S61.
70. Johnson JH Jr, Hariharan S, Berman J, et al: Clinical outcome of pediatric gangliogliomas: Ninety-nine cases over 20 years. Pediatr Neurosurg 1997;27:203.
71. Jones-Gotman M, Smith ML, Zatorre RJ: Neuropsychological testing for localizing and lateralizing the epileptogenic region. In Engel J Jr (ed): Surgical Treatment of the Epilepsies, 2nd ed. New York, Raven Press, 1993, p 245.
72. Kanev PM, Lemire RJ, Loeser JD, et al: Management and long-term follow-up review of children with lipomyelomeningocele, 1952-1987. J Neurosurg 1990;73:48.
73. Kanev PM, Nierbrauer KS: Reflections on the natural history of lipomyelomeningocele. Pediatr Neurosurg 1995;22:137.
74. Katz BZ, Yogev R: Bacterial and viral meningitis and encephalitis. In McLone DG (editor-in-chief): Pediatric Neurosurgery: Surgery of the Developing Nervous System, 4th ed. Philadelphia, WB Saunders, 2001, p 991.
75. Kestle JRW, Drake JM, Cochrane DD, et al: Lack of benefit of endoscopic ventriculoperitoneal shunt insertion: A multicenter randomized trial. J Neurosurg 2003; 98:284.
76. Khajavi K, Comair YG, Prayson RA, et al: Childhood ganglioglioma and medically intractable epilepsy. A clinicopathological study of 15 patients and a review of the literature. Pediatr Neurosurg 1995;22:181.
77. Krauss WE, McCormick PC: Infections of the dural spaces. Neurosurg Clin N Am 1992;3:421.
78. Langley JM, LeBlanc JC, Drake JM, et al: Efficacy of antimicrobial prophylaxis in placement of cerebrospinal fluid shunts: Meta-analysis. Clin Infect Dis 1993;17:98.
79. Laurence KM, Coates S: The natural history of hydrocephalus. Detailed analysis of 182 unoperated cases. Arch Dis Child 1962;37:345.
80. Lee M, Leahu D, Weiner HL, et al: Complications of fourth ventricular shunts. Pediatr Neurosurg 1995;22:309.
81. Lemire RJ: Neural tube defects. JAMA 1988;259:558.
82. Lobel DA, Park YD, Lee MR: Surgical treatment of epilepsy in children. Contemp Neurosurg 2004;26:1.
83. Loring DW, Meador KJ, Lee GP, et al: Amobarbital Effects and Lateralized Brain Function: The Wada Test. New York, Springer-Verlag, 1992.
84. Luders H, Dinner DS, Morris HH, et al: EEG evaluation for epilepsy surgery in children. Clev Clin J Med 1989;56 (Suppl 1):S53.
85. Luken MG, Whelan MA: Recent diagnostic experience with subdural empyema. J Neurosurg 1980;52:764.
86. Lynch BJ, O'Tuama L, Holmes GL, et al: Correlation of Tc99-m HMPAO SPECT with EEG monitoring: Prognostic value for outcome of epilepsy surgery in children. Ann Neurol 1992;32:433.
87. Mackenzie AR, Laing RBS, Smith CC, et al.: Spinal epidural abscess: The importance of early diagnosis and treatment. J Neurol Neurosurg Psychiatry 1998;65:209.
88. Madsen JR, Black PM: Corpus callosotomy. In Albright AL, Pollack IF, Adelson PD (eds): Principles and Practice of Pediatric Neurosurgery. New York, Thieme, 1999, p 1147.
89. Maslen DR, Jones SR, Crisplin MA, et al: Spinal epidural abscess: Optimizing patient care. Arch Intern Med 1993;153:1713.
90. Mathern GW, Giza CC, Yudovin S, et al: Postoperative seizure control and antiepileptic drug use in pediatric epilepsy surgery patients: The UCLA experience, 1986-1997. Epilepsia 1999;40:1740.
91. Mathisen GE, Johnson JP: Brain abscess. Clin Infect Dis 1997;25:763.
92. Mauser HW, Van Houwelingen H, Tulleken CA: Factors affecting the outcome in subdural empyema. J Neurol Neurosurg Psychiatry 1987;50:1136.
93. McLone DG: Repair of the myelomeningocele. In Rengachary SS, Wilkins RH (eds): Neurosurgical Operative Atlas, vol 3. Chicago, American Association of Neurological Surgeons, 1993, p 38.
94. Meyer FB, Marsh WR, Laws ER, et al: Temporal lobectomy in children with epilepsy. J Neurosurg 1986;64:371.
95. Morrell F, Whisler WW, Bleck TP: Multiple subpial transection: A new approach to the surgical treatment of focal epilepsy. J Neurosurg 1989;70:231.
96. Morris GL, Mueller WM: Vagus nerve stimulation study group E01-E05: Long-term treatment with vagus nerve stimulation in patients with refractory epilepsy. Neurology 1999;53:1731.

97. Morrison G: Extratemporal epilepsy surgery in children. In Albright AL, Pollack IF, Adelson PD (eds): Principles and Practice of Pediatric Neurosurgery. New York, Thieme, 1999, p 1127.
98. MRC Vitamin Study Research Group: Prevention of neural tube defects: Results of the Medical Research Council Vitamin Study. Lancet 1991;338:131.
99. Mullan BP, O'Connor MK, Hung JC: Single photon emission computed tomography. Neuroimaging Clin N Am 1995; 5:647.
100. Murphy JV, Hornig G, Schallert G: Left vagal nerve stimulation in children with refractory epilepsy: Preliminary observations. Arch Neurol 1995;52:886.
101. National Institutes of Health: Surgery for epilepsy. Consensus Statement 1990;8:1.
102. Newton MR, Berkovic SF, Austin MC, et al: SPECT in the localization of extratemporal and temporal seizure foci. J Neurol Neurosurg Psychiatry 1995;59:26.
103. Nordli DR Jr, Kelley KR: Selection and evaluation of children for epilepsy surgery. Pediatr Neurosurg 2001; 34:1.
104. Ojemann SG, Peacock WJ: Surgical treatment of epilepsy. In McLone DG (editor-in-chief): Pediatric Neurosurgery: Surgery of the Developing Nervous System, 4th ed. Philadelphia, WB Saunders, 2001, p 1025.
105. Olson DM: Evaluation of children for epilepsy surgery. Pediatr Neurosurg 2001;34:159.
106. Olson DM, Chugani HT, Shewmon DA, et al: Electrocorticographic confirmation of focal positron emission tomographic abnormalities in children with intractable epilepsy. Epilepsia 1990;31:731.
107. Pang D, Dias MS, Ahab-Barmada M: Split cord malformation. Part I: A unified theory of embryogenesis for double SC malformations. Neurosurgery 1992;31:451.
108. Pattisapu J, Parent A: Subdural empyemas in children. Pediatr Neurosci 1987;13:251.
109. Patwardhan RV, Stong V, Bebin EM, et al: Efficacy of vagal nerve stimulation in children with medically refractory epilepsy. Neurosurgery 2000;47:1353.
110. Peacock WJ: Hemispherectomy. In McLone DG (editor-in-chief): Pediatric Neurosurgery: Surgery of the Developing Nervous System, 4th ed. Philadelphia, WB Saunders, 2001, p 1035.
111. Piatt JH Jr, Carlson CV: A search for determinants of cerebrospinal fluid shunt survival: Retrospective analysis of a 14-year institutional experience. Pediatr Neurosurg 1993;19:233.
112. Pudenz RH, Foltz EL: Hydrocephalus: Overdrainage by ventricular shunts. Surg Neurol 1991;35:200.
113. Pyhtinen J, Paakko E, Jartti P: Cerebral abscess with multiple rims of MRI. Neuroradiology 1997;39:857.
114. Rasmussen T: Hemispherectomy for seizures revisited. Can J Neurol Sci 1983;10:71.
115. Rauzzino MJ, Tubbs RS, Alexander E, et al: Spinal neurenteric cysts and their relation to more common aspects of occult spinal dysraphism. Neurosurgical Focus [serial online], January 10(1), Article 2, 2001. Available at http://www.aans.org/education/journal/neurosurgical/jan01/10-1-2.pdf.
116. Raymond AA, Halpin SF, Alsanjari N, et al: Dysembryoplastic neuroepithelial tumor. Features in 16 patients. Brain 1994;117:461.
117. Rekate HL: Classification of slit-ventricle syndromes using intracranial pressure monitoring. Pediatr Neurosurg 1993;19:15.
118. Renier D, Flandin C, Hirsch E, et al: Brain abscesses in neonates: A study of 30 cases. J Neurosurg 1988;69:877.
119. Rubin G, Michowiz SD, Ashkenasi A, et al: Spinal epidural abscess in the pediatric age group: Case report and review of the literature. Pediatr Infect Dis J 1993;12:1007.
120. Rutecki P: Anatomical, physiological, and theoretical basis for the antiepileptic effect of vagus nerve stimulation. Epilepsia 1990;31(Suppl 2):S1.
121. Sainte-Rose C, Chumas PD: Endoscopic third ventriculostomy. Tech Neurosurg 1995;1:176.
122. Sainte-Rose C, Piatt JH, Renier D, et al: Mechanical complications in shunts. Pediatr Neurosurg 1991;17:2.
123. Salanova V, Morris HHD, Van Ness PC, et al: Comparison of scalp electroencephalogram with subdural electrocorticogram recordings and functional mapping in frontal lobe epilepsy. Arch Neurol 1993;50:294.
124. Schachter SC, Saper CB: Progress in epilepsy research: Vagus nerve stimulation. Epilepsia 1998;39:677.
125. Schoenwolf GC, DeLongo J: Ultrastructure of secondary neurulation in the chick embryo. Am J Anat 1980;158:43.
126. Schoenwolf GC, Smith JL: Mechanisms of neurulation: Traditional viewpoint and recent advances. Development 1990;109:243.
127. Schoenwolf GC, Smith JL: Epithelial cell wedging: A fundamental cell behavior contributing to hinge point formation during epithelial morphogenesis. In Keller RE, Fristrom D (eds): Control of Morphogenesis by Specific Cell Behaviors, vol 1, Seminars in Developmental Biology. London, WB Saunders, 1990, p 325.
128. Sinclair DB, Aronyk K, Snyder T, et al: Pediatric epilepsy surgery at the University of Alberta: 1988-2000. Pediatr Neurol 2003;29:302.
129. Sinclair DB, Aronyk K, Snyder T, et al: Extratemporal resection for childhood epilepsy. Pediatr Neurol 2004;30:177.
130. Smith H, Hendrick E: Subdural empyema and epidural abscess in children. J Neurosurg 1983;58:392.
131. Smith JL, Schoenwolf GC: Notochordal induction of cell wedging in the chick neural plate and its role in neural tube formation. J Exp Zool 1989;250:49.
132. Smith JL, Schoenwolf GC: Neurulation: Coming to closure. Trends Neurosci 1997;20:510.
133. Smith MC: Multiple subpial transection in patients with extratemporal epilepsy. Epilepsia 1998;39(Suppl 4):S81.
134. Spencer DD, Spencer SS, Mattson RH, et al: Access to the posterior medial temporal lobe structures in the surgical treatment of temporal lobe epilepsy. Neurosurgery 1984;15:667.
135. Spencer S: The relative contributions of MRI, SPECT, PET imaging in epilepsy. Epilepsia 1994;35(Suppl 6):S72.
136. Sperling MR, O'Connor MJ: Comparison of depth and subdural electrodes in recording temporal lobe seizures. Neurology 1989;39:1497.
137. Storrs BB: Intracranial tuberculous, fungal, and parasitic infections of the central nervous system. In McLone DG (editor-in-chief): Pediatric Neurosurgery: Surgery of the Developing Nervous System, 4th ed. Philadelphia, WB Saunders, 2001, p 1009.
138. Sutton LN: Fetal neurosurgery for myelomeningocele. Contemp Neurosurg 2003;25.
139. Szabo CA, Wyllie E: Intracarotid amobarbital testing for language and memory dominance in children. Epilepsy Res 1993;15:239.
140. Taha JM, Crone KR: Endoscopically guided shunt placement. Tech Neurosurg 1996;1:159.
141. Takeshita M, Kagawa M, Yato S, et al: Current treatment of brain abscess in patients with congenital heart disease. Neurosurgery 1997;41:1270.
142. Tubbs RS, Chambers MR, Smyth MD, et al: Late gestational intrauterine myelomeningocele repair does not

improve lower extremity function. Pediatr Neurosurg 2003;38:128.

143. Tuli S, Alshail E, Drake JM: Third ventriculostomy versus cerebrospinal fluid shunt as a first procedure in pediatric hydrocephalus. Pediatr Neurosurg 1999;30:11.
144. Tuli S, Drake JM, Lawless J, et al: Risk factors for repeated cerebrospinal shunt failures in pediatric patients with hydrocephalus. J Neurosurg 2000;92:31.
145. Tulipan N: Intrauterine closure of myelomeningocele: an update. Neurosurgical Focus [serial online], February 16(2), Article 2, 2004. Available at http://www.aans.org/education/journal/neurosurgical/feb04/16-2-2.pdf.
146. Uematsu S: Detection of an epileptic focus and cortical mapping using a subdural grid. In Rengachary SS, Wilkins RH (eds): Neurosurgical Operative Atlas, vol 2. Chicago, American Association of Neurological Surgeons, 1992, p 67.
147. Villarejo F, Comair YG: Surgical treatment of pediatric epilepsy. In Choux M, Di Rocco C, Hockley AD, Walker ML (eds): Pediatric Neurosurgery. London, Churchill Livingstone, 1999, p 1717.
148. Villavicencio AT, Wellons JC, George TM: Avoiding complicated shunt systems by open fenestration of symptomatic fourth ventricular cysts associated with hydrocephalus. Pediatr Neurosurg 1998;29:314.
149. Vining EPG, Freeman JM, Brandt J, et al: Progressive unilateral encephalopathy of childhood (Rasmussen's syndrome): A reappraisal. Epilepsia 1993;34:639.
150. Vining EPG, Mellits D, Dorsen M, et al: Psychological and behavioral effects of antiepileptic drugs in children: A double blind comparison between phenobarbital and valproic acid. Pediatrics 1987;80:165.
151. Vivegano F, Bertini E, Boldrini C, et al: Hemimegalencephaly and intractable epilepsy: Benefits of hemispherectomy. Epilepsia 1989;30:833.
152. Walker ML, Fried A, Petronio J: Diagnosis and treatment of the slit ventricle syndrome. Neurosurg Clin N Am 1993;4:707.
153. Warder DE: Tethered cord syndrome and occult spinal dysraphism, Neurosurgical Focus [serial online], January 10(1), Article 1, 2001. Available at http://www.aans.org/education/journal/neurosurgical/jan01/10-1-1.pdf.
154. Warf BC, Scott RM, Barnes PD, et al: Tethered SC in patients with anorectal and urogenital malformations. Pediatr Neurosurg 1993;19:25.
155. Whitehead WE, Kestle JR: The treatment of cerebrospinal fluid shunt infections. Results from a practice survey of the American Society of Pediatric Neurosurgeons. Pediatr Neurosurg 2001;35:205.
156. Williamson PD, Boon PA, Thadani VM, et al: Parietal lobe epilepsy: Diagnostic consideration and results of surgery. Ann Neurol 1992;31:193.
157. Williamson PD, Spencer DD, Spencer SS, et al: Complex partial seizures of frontal lobe origin. Ann Neurol 1985;18:497.
158. Williamson PD, Spencer SS: Clinical and EEG features of complex partial seizures of extratemporal origin. Epilepsia 1986;27(Suppl 2):S46.
159. Winston KR, Welch K, Adler JR, et al: Cerebral hemicorticectomy for epilepsy. J Neurosurg 1992;77:889.
160. Wong TT, Lee LS, Wang HS, et al: Brain abscesses in children—a cooperative study of 83 cases. Childs Nerv Syst 1989;5:19.
161. Wyler AR, Walker G, Richey ET, et al: Chronic subdural strip electrodes recordings for difficult epileptic problems. J Epilepsy 1988;1:171.
162. Wyllie E, Chee M, Granstrom ML, et al: Temporal lobe epilepsy in early childhood. Epilepsia 1993;34:859.
163. Wyllie E, Comair YG, Kotagal P, et al: Seizure outcome after epilepsy surgery in children and adolescents. Ann Neurol 1998;44:740.
164. Wyllie E, Luders H, Morris HH III, et al: Subdural electrodes in the evaluation for epilepsy surgery in children and adults. Neuropediatrics 1988;19:80.
165. Yashon D, Jane JA, Sugar O: The course of severe untreated infantile hydrocephalus. Prognostic significance of cerebral mantle. J Neurosurg 1965;23:509.
166. Young HF, Nulsen FB, Weiss MH, et al: The relationship of intelligence and cerebral mantle in treated infantile hydrocephalus (IQ potential in hydrocephalic children). Pediatrics 1973;52:38.
167. Zeidman SM, Geisler FH, Olivi A: Intraventricular rupture of a purulent brain abscess: Case report. Neurosurgery 1995;36:189.

Chapter 125  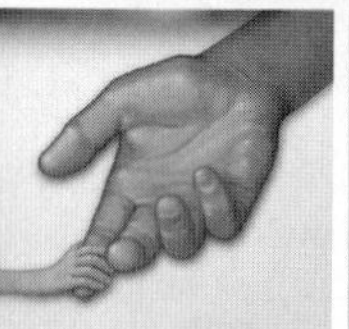

Major Congenital Orthopedic Deformities

Kosmas Kayes and William Didelot

DEVELOPMENTAL DYSPLASIA OF THE HIP

Terminology/Incidence/Etiology

Hip dysplasia in a child involves a wide spectrum of pathology, but all cases have some type of incongruity of the femoral head and acetabulum. It can vary from minimal acetabular dysplasia, in which the acetabulum has not developed fully (with a femoral head that may be normal in position or slightly subluxated), to complete dislocation of the femoral head, in which there is no contact with the acetabulum. In between these extremes are an unstable hip that is fully reduced within the acetabulum but can be gently subluxated or fully dislocated and a hip that is subluxated partially out of the acetabulum and may or may not dislocate.[1,6] Another type of dislocation, called a teratologic hip dislocation, usually occurs with some type of neuromuscular problem such as myelomeningocele, arthrogryposis, or another syndrome. This type of dislocation is a rigid, fixed dislocation that occurs prenatally and will not respond to nonoperative methods of treatment as the more common types of hip dislocation will. Most cases of hip dysplasia are evident at birth by physical examination or ultrasound, but instability may not develop until later in the first year of life and may have different findings. Still other types will be unidentifiable until adolescence, when they are often manifested as pain but no other physical examination findings. A change in terminology has occurred in the last 15 years from "congenital dislocation" to "developmental dysplasia" of the hip (DDH). This change reflects more accurate information about the less apparent types of dysplasia not identifiable at birth and the variations that are not always complete dislocations of the joint but rather abnormal development or "dysplasia."[7,31]

Hip dysplasia is the most common hip disorder in children. One in 1000 newborns has a dislocated hip, and 10 in 1000 will have some form of subluxation or dysplasia. The majority of hips will tighten up on their own, usually within the first 2 weeks of life. Approximately 4 in 10,000 will eventually have problems of dislocation, subluxation, or acetabular dysplasia. Females have a higher incidence than males do by a ratio of 4:1, which is thought to be due to sensitivity to the relaxin hormone produced by the mother during pregnancy; relaxin causes transient ligamentous laxity in females and not males (because males are not sensitive to the hormone). The left hip is affected 60% of the time, probably because of pressure on the hip from the mother's sacrum since most birth presentations are left occiput anterior. The incidence is also higher in Native Americans and other cultures that tend to swaddle or strap their infants.[6]

The cause of hip dysplasia is multifactorial. Genetics, physiologic factors, and mechanical factors such as prenatal and postnatal positioning all play a role. Genetics is a factor because babies with a positive family history have a higher incidence of DDH, as do siblings and twins. Mechanical factors are also involved as any form of intrauterine crowding or abnormal positioning, such as a first pregnancy, breech presentation, oligohydramnios, or multiple births, put the infant at higher risk. This is also true postnatally because cultures that swaddle, strap, or papoose their babies have a higher incidence of DDH as well.[33,46,53,54]

Diagnosis

History and Screening

Early detection of DDH is crucial; the sooner treatment is initiated, the better the expected outcome. Pertinent history of the newborn consists of whether the newborn is the first child, the presentation in utero, whether there is a family history of DDH, the presence of any associated orthopedic or genitourinary abnormalities, multiple births, and the presence of oligohydramnios. The biggest risk factor is breech presentation, and second is a positive family history.

Most cases are detected early as a result of the screening protocol for pediatricians developed by the American Academy of Pediatrics; the protocol consists of serial physical examinations at birth, at 2 weeks, and then at every well-baby follow-up visit at 1, 2, 4, 6, 9, and 12 months of age. The schedule should be followed closely with any child who has risk factors. For these infants, imaging is optional. If the child is a girl and is delivered breech, imaging is recommended. A child at risk should have either an ultrasound before 4 months or radiographs of the hip taken after 4 months of age. Screening of the entire newborn population has not been necessary, although some cases of late dislocation and dysplasia are not detected until later in life.[3,4,15,20] Not all cases of hip dysplasia are present at birth, and a few will not exhibit abnormal physical examination findings in the first few months of life. Some cases of DDH will not occur until "late" and may not be detectable except with imaging techniques; such children may subsequently have symptoms of pain in the early teenage years.

Physical Examination

Findings on physical examination will vary with the age of the child. From birth to about 3 months of age the most reliable findings are a positive Barlow or Ortolani maneuver. In the Barlow test the hip is held flexed 90 degrees with neutral adduction, and the knee is flexed 90 degrees. The first web space and the palm of the hand should cradle the knee and be outside the thigh with the long finger down the length of the thigh. The hand should *gently* push the thigh posteriorly while adducting the hip in an attempt to dislocate a reduced hip out the back of the socket. The Ortolani maneuver is the same but instead of pushing posteriorly, the thigh is abducted with pressure on the femur toward the middle of the socket while pulling it up anteriorly and trying to reduce a dislocated hip. Symmetrical abduction is also important during the evaluation. Any asymmetry of abduction on examination should be evaluated further. Asymmetric skin folds have been shown to be less reliable.

After 3 years of age the hip is usually dislocated and no longer reducible. It may occasionally be reduced but is subluxatable. The Barlow and Ortolani maneuvers will no longer be useful. Asymmetric abduction is the best indicator, as is leg-length inequality, or Galeazzi's sign, which is positive when both hips and both knees are flexed to 90 degrees and one knee is higher than the other, giving an apparent limb-length inequality. Actually, the dislocated hip is more posterior in position, thus making it look like the leg is shorter. At walking age the most obvious findings are apparent leg-length inequality with pelvic obliquity. The child will have a Trendelenburg gait from shortened (weak) abductors and hip flexion contracture. If the dislocation is bilateral, the child will have increased lumbar lordosis.

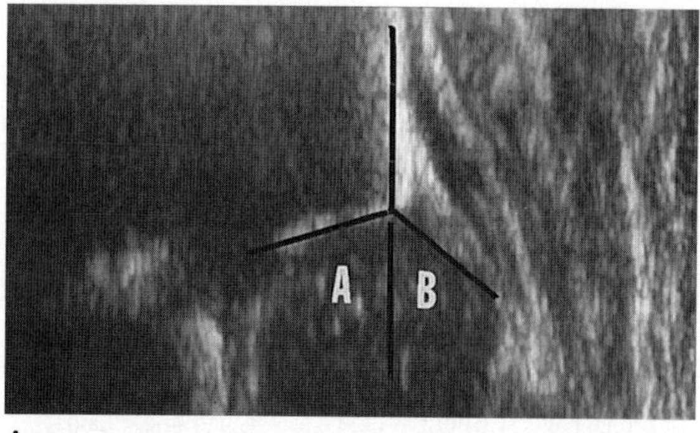

A

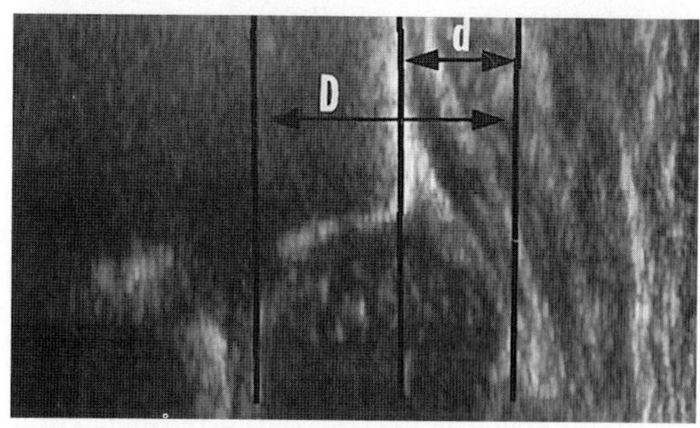

B

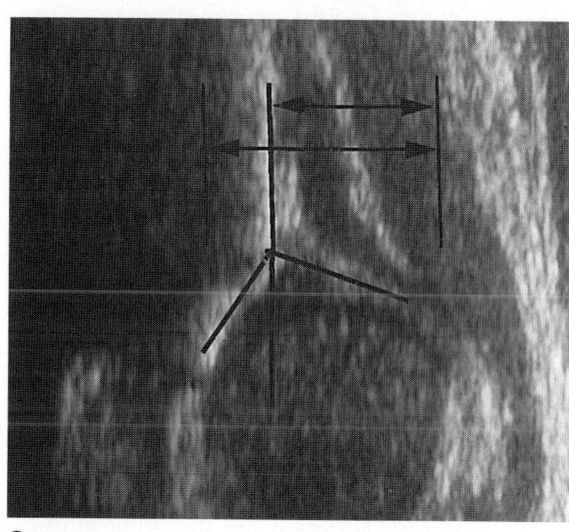

C

Figure 125-1 *A,* Standard coronal plane ultrasonogram of a normal infant's hip. The alpha angle (A) corresponds to the bony acetabular roof (normal, >60 degrees). The beta angle (B) represents the cartilaginous roof (normal, <50 degrees). *B,* Method for determining percent coverage of the femoral head: d/D × 100 (normal, 0.50%). *C,* Coronal plane ultrasonogram of a dysplastic hip. The alpha angle was 40 degrees; the femoral head was subluxated with only 25% coverage.

Imaging

Ultrasound and plain radiographs are both useful tools for assessment of hip dysplasia, but their timing is different. In a 3-week to 4-month-old child, ultrasound is very reliable in the diagnosis of hip dysplasia. It is highly dependent on the technician performing the scan and the radiologist interpreting it. General screening of all newborns is not recommended in the United States. Ultrasound can assess the amount of subluxation by identifying the position of the cartilaginous femoral head, as well as evaluate acetabular development by measuring the alpha angle of the posterior wall in relation to the ilium (Fig. 125-1). It can also provide visualization of

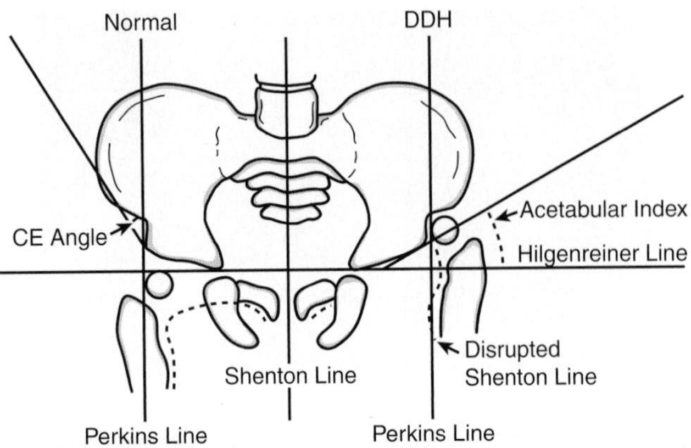

Figure 125-2 Diagram of radiographic measurements. CE, center edge angle; DDH, developmental dysplasia of the hip.

the labrum, capsule, iliopsoas, and femoral head ossific nucleus. The alpha angle is measured on a coronal image. It is the angle formed by the intersection of a line drawn vertically through the ilium and a line drawn parallel to the osseous roof of the acetabulum. An alpha angle greater than 60 degrees is considered normal. The beta angle is a measure of the labrum and indirectly measures the amount of coverage of the femoral head, but it is not used as much in assessment of the amount of dysplasia. There is also a dynamic examination that is performed in the transverse plane and measures the amount of subluxation or instability of the femoral head while performing the Barlow maneuver.

Plain radiographs of the hip are not reliable before about 3 to 4 months of age when the ossific nucleus of the acetabulum is starting to ossify and be apparent radiographically. After this age it is the standard means of diagnosis and best way to monitor progression of a dysplastic hip.[18] An anteroposterior (AP) view and a "frog-leg" view are both required when ordering any hip radiographs on a child (referred to as "AP and frog pelvis"). Several important parameters should be measured on the AP film (Fig. 125-2). Shenton's line is the continuation of a semicircle drawn on the superior portion of the obturator foramen and should be at the same level as the femoral neck. If the line is disrupted, the femur is too superior in the acetabulum. *H*ilgenreiner's line is a *h*orizontal line drawn through the level of the triradiate cartilage on each side. A perpendicular line is then drawn at the lateral edge of the acetabulum and intersects Hilgenreiner's line to form four quadrants around the hip. The medial metaphyseal beak of the femur should be in the inferior/medial quadrant, or it is not in a reduced position. The acetabular index is the angle formed by Hilgenreiner's line and a line drawn from the triradiate cartilage to the lateral edge of the acetabulum. This angle should be less than about 25 degrees by 1 year of age to indicate normal acetabular development. The higher the acetabular index, the more dysplastic (more vertical) the acetabulum.

The best way to assess a dysplastic hip is by injection of contrast material into the hip joint under general anesthesia (hip arthrography). Contrast outlines the cartilaginous femoral head and shows the exact relationship to the acetabulum. It can also show the position of the labrum and ligamentum teres and whether there is a pooling of dye in the medial joint space, which is indicative of laxity of the hip and a less then ideal reduction. Although ultrasound is very helpful in assessing the position of the hip, arthrography can be performed if there is any question regarding stability and position of the hip. It is also extremely useful in assessing a closed reduction and in preoperative planning for any reconstructive surgery. Computed tomography (CT) is useful postoperatively to check the position of the hip in the cast after closed or open reduction with immediate casting. Magnetic resonance imaging (MRI) has had limited use in DDH, but recent studies show that it may be as useful as CT in postoperative assessment and without the radiation exposure.

Anatomy/Pathoanatomy

Hip development starts with the femoral head and acetabulum being formed as a block of cartilaginous cells. At 7 to 8 weeks a cleft develops between the head and acetabulum and forms the joint. So the hip starts "reduced" in the socket, and other factors previously discussed contribute to the later instability. The hip joint is completely developed by 11 weeks of gestation. The femoral head remains totally cartilaginous until 4 months of age, when the ossific nucleus starts to form bone. The femoral head and acetabulum are dependent on each other maintaining concentric reduction for continued normal development until growth ceases. A socket without a reduced femoral head will not form normally. If the hip stabilizes early, the joint will most likely remodel any dysplasia and form a normal joint. The longer the femoral head is not concentrically reduced, the less chance of the hip having normal anatomy at maturity. The acetabulum undergoes the most remodeling and development in the first year of life, but some remodeling continues until year 4 or 5, after which time there is minimal remodeling potential.

The anatomic structures involved in hip dysplasia (Table 125-1) contribute differently in each case. The adductor muscle becomes contracted. The iliopsoas muscle can be a major block to reduction of a completely dislocated hip. It becomes contracted and can exert a powerful block to reduction by forming an hourglass-shaped constriction of the anterior medial capsule. The ligamentum teres connecting the fovea of the femoral

TABLE 125-1 Blocks to Reduction

Blocks to Reduction
Adductor tendon
Iliopsoas tendon
Medial capsule
Infolded labrum
Ligamentum teres
Pulvinar
Transverse acetabular ligament

head to deep inside the acetabulum can hypertrophy and pose a block to a good concentric reduction as well. The pulvinar is an accumulation of fat and fibrous tissue in the space next to the medial wall of the acetabulum and can keep the femoral head lateralized during a reduction attempt. The labrum or cartilaginous rim of the acetabulum can become infolded and blunted and also block the femoral head. The anterior-medial joint capsule can become constricted. The transverse acetabular ligament spanning the inferior portion of the hip between the medial and posterior walls can also block reduction inferiorly. All these problems may become more marked as the child gets older and pose more difficulty in achieving an adequate reduction.

Treatment

There are two goals of treatment. The first is to reduce the hip and allow it to stabilize in a reduced position within the acetabulum. The second goal is to ensure remodeling of any acetabular dysplasia. If the first goal is met and concentric reduction is achieved, the acetabulum will be able to remodel with further growth. Because the remodeling potential of the acetabulum is greatest in the first year of life, it is important to begin treatment as soon as possible. Treatment protocols depend on the age of the child and the amount of dysplasia of the hip joint. The following are all possible treatments to help achieve reduction and stability:

Pavlik harness
Closed reduction and casting
Open reduction and capsulorrhaphy
Femoral shortening osteotomy
Acetabular procedures

Treatment will be discussed as it relates to the age of the child. Some of the aforementioned treatments are useful only in certain age groups, whereas others span the entire age range.

0 to 6 Months

If a positive examination is recorded at birth (positive Barlow or Ortolani maneuver), immediate orthopedic referral is recommended. There is evidence to suggest that most hips will tighten up and stabilize within the first 2 weeks of life; therefore, initiation of treatment before 2 weeks is controversial, but most authors recommend immediate treatment. Either way, close follow-up is mandatory. A Pavlik harness is the gold standard of treatment at this age and can often be used in children up to 6 months of age or less than 20 lb (Fig. 125-3). When the hip is still dislocatable or reducible, the harness is the best choice. It is an active method of treatment that allows the baby to still have motion while encouraging the hip to remain in a position of stability. The harness maintains hip flexion of 90 to 100 degrees and abduction to keep the hip reduced in the most stable position. It is worn 24 hours a day, and correct placement and adjustment are crucial to help lower the incidence of complications. The harness can cause avascular necrosis (AVN; discussed later), which is thought to be due to hyperflexion of the hip or overtightening of the abduction straps. Once treatment is initiated, the harness should be checked in 1 week to ensure proper fit and use by the family. The length of treatment is generally twice as many weeks as the child's age at diagnosis, with some authors recommending a minimum of 3 months' treatment regardless of age at initiation of treatment. It can be weaned when the examination and imaging studies have normalized. It is effective in 90% or more children with Barlow-positive hips (reduced but dislocatable).[28,35,36] If the hip is Ortolani positive (dislocated but reducible), the harness may not be effective and should be discontinued after 3 weeks of treatment.

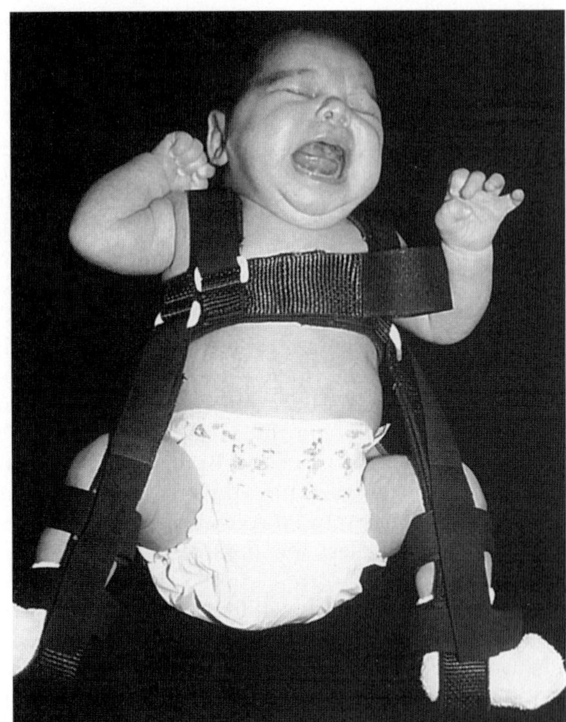

Figure 125-3 Infant being treated with a Pavlik harness. Hip flexion of approximately 100 degrees is maintained by anterior straps. Posterior straps (not seen) limit hip adduction.

The harness is positioned by placing the baby's arms through the upper straps and ensuring that the chest strap across the body is at nipple level. The feet are then placed into the stirrup straps and the Velcro is fastened. The straps in the front extending down from the chest strap to the foot strap should be loosened so that the femur is at a 90-degree angle to the long axis of the body. The hip should not be flexed any further for fear of increasing the risk for AVN or causing transient femoral nerve palsy. The abduction straps in the back should not be too tight and should limit adduction no less than to the midline.

Closed reduction may also be necessary in this time frame if the hip will not easily reduce with gentle manipulation or does not respond to treatment in the Pavlik harness within 2 weeks. Arthrography is usually performed under general anesthesia and the stability of the hip is checked. The child can then be placed in a hip spica cast if certain criteria are met during arthrography. The hip must be stable within the safe zone of 30 to 60 degrees of abduction and 90 degrees of hip flexion. If excessive abduction is required for stability, open reduction should be performed. The hip is at risk for AVN if extreme abduction is needed to keep the hip reduced in the cast. There must also be only minimal (<3 to 5 mm) pooling of contrast in the medial aspect of the joint or the closed reduction will be less successful. These impediments to reduction must be gently overcome, or careful consideration must be given to open reduction. Prereduction traction is controversial, with studies both supporting and refuting its use in reducing the incidence of AVN.[34,36,48] The babies are typically placed in Bryant's traction (hips flexed 90 degrees with the knees flexed 10 to 20 degrees) for 1 to 2 weeks before closed reduction. They are slowly abducted during the last few days of traction to try to facilitate reduction.

After closed reduction the child is placed in a hip spica cast in the human position for 6 to 8 weeks. A CT (or MRI) scan is usually checked postoperatively to ensure successful reduction. Another arthrogram is often obtained at the 6- to 8-week mark to assess progress of the hip. Casting may last 6 to 12 weeks, and then abduction bracing is used all day or nighttime only to encourage remodeling of the acetabulum. Some authors recommend some type of abduction bracing until radiographs have normalized.[41]

6 to 12 Months

As the child gets older, if the hip has not been reduced (Fig. 125-4), the compensatory changes become more severe, and more invasive treatment is often needed to overcome the blocks to reduction. At this age a Pavlik harness is not indicated. Closed reduction is still the preferred method if a gentle, concentric, stable reduction can be obtained. If too aggressive abduction or pressure is needed to keep the hip reduced easily in the cast, the chance of complications, mainly AVN, increases. At this point surgical open reduction should be considered. Some authors think that unless a closed reduction gives nearly perfect concentricity and is very stable, care should proceed immediately to open reduction, which they believe is safer than a forced, incongruous closed reduction. The goal of open reduction is the same as that of closed reduction, to achieve concentric stable reduction of the femoral head in the acetabulum. During open reduction, as many of the blocks to reduction as possible are corrected. There are two approaches that are used most frequently to achieve this goal, and each has its own advantages.

The Smith-Peterson anterior approach uses the interval between the sartorius and tensor fascia superficially. It is the more common approach and through it all the blocks to reduction can be addressed. The adductor and the iliopsoas can be lengthened, the labrum incised and relieved, and the ligamentum teres and pulvinar removed. The transverse acetabular ligament is deep in the socket but, with care, can be sectioned. Tightening of the capsule anteriorly (capsulorrhaphy) can be performed to help stability. Some authors believe that this is the most important part of the procedure, but some evidence exists that it may not be as important in achieving stability as previously believed. The patient remains in a cast for 6 to 8 weeks postoperatively. This is a better approach in older children, and an acetabular procedure can be performed through the same incision.

The medial approach of Ludloff is technically more demanding. It is often used in younger children, which is even more difficult because of the smaller size of the child. The procedure is carried out through an incision in the groin crease between the adductor muscles, either superficial or deep to the adductor brevis. It provides good access and visualization of the medial blocks to reduction. The labrum and anterior lateral capsule cannot be accessed, and therefore capsulorrhaphy is not possible through this approach. Some studies suggest that the rate of AVN is higher with this approach because of the risk of injury to the medial circumflex vessels. If the femoral head has migrated much higher than the acetabulum, it will be difficult to achieve reduction through this approach.

If the femoral head is superior to the acetabulum on radiographs and the soft tissue is significantly contracted, a femoral shortening osteotomy may be helpful to achieve a more stable reduction with less pressure on the femoral head. It helps decrease the possibility of AVN and improves the stability of the hip. If excessive coxa valga or femoral anteversion is present, the osteotomy can be readily modified to correct these deformities as well. The incision is made at the subtrochanteric level and the bone is then fixed with a plate and screws to hold the alignment while bony union is achieved. Femoral shortening is almost always needed in an older child of walking age.

Walking Age, Older Than 12 Months

Once children have been bearing weight on the hip, adaptive changes occur and closed reduction becomes less successful. More of these hips will need open reduction and many will need femoral shortening osteotomy (Fig. 125-5).[14,43] The remodeling potential of the acetabulum decreases as the child gets older, and some children

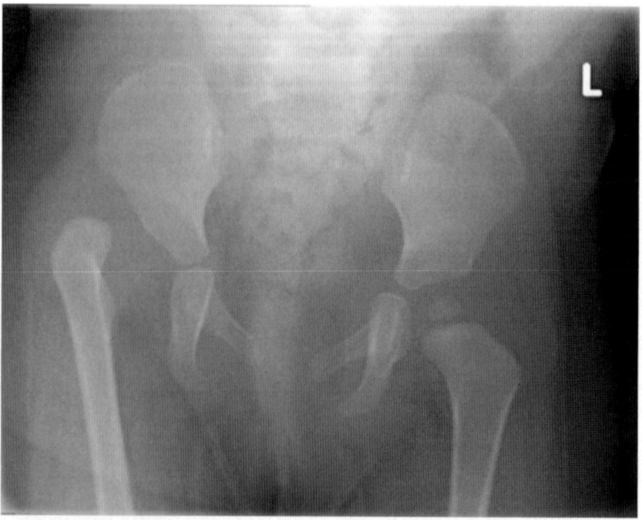

Figure 125–4 Right hip dislocation. Left hip is normal.

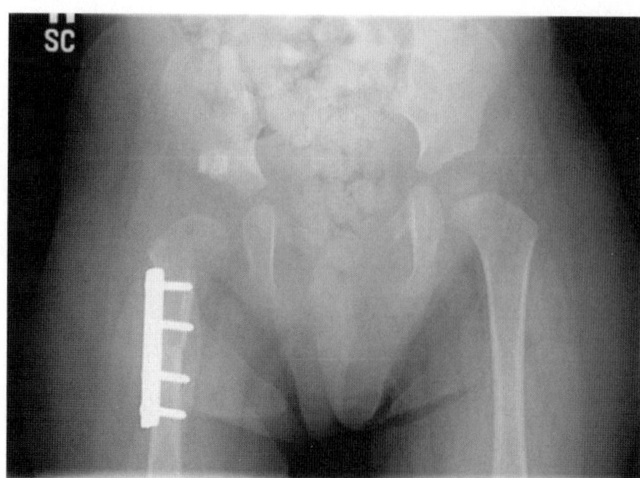

Figure 125-5 Femoral osteotomy fixed with plate and screws. Pelvic osteotomy (*arrow*).

may need to undergo pelvic osteotomy to help gain coverage of the femoral head and provide a more stable reduction (Fig. 125-5). A pelvic osteotomy can be performed in several ways, with most aimed at redirecting the socket to provide more anterior and lateral coverage of the femoral head. If more coverage is obtained and better congruency of the hip is achieved, there is more potential for the hip to form a more normal joint with time.[10,17]

Some cases of hip dysplasia will go undetected until later in life. After 4 years of age the risks of reducing a hip surgically increase. Some authors recommend attempting reduction up to the age of 8 years. If both hips are dislocated in older children, one must consider leaving them dislocated because they may do well for a long time before osteoarthritis develops. Other variations of DDH will be manifested in the early to late teens as hip pain, and acetabular dysplasia will be detected on radiographs. These hips are not dislocated, but the acetabulum is deficient in coverage of the femoral head, and the femoral head may be subluxated to varying degrees. These children will benefit from redirectional acetabuloplasty of some type to provide a more congruous joint and better coverage. This is done in the hope of delaying further arthritic changes in the hip. There is good evidence to support the natural history of DDH in that any residual dysplasia of the joint will lead to osteoarthritis, which will eventually require total hip replacement. All treatment of DDH is directed at delaying this process for as long as possible.*

Complications

Avascular Necrosis

AVN of the femoral head can occur in up to 60% of treated hips if the long-term results are looked at critically. All forms of treatment put the blood supply at risk. The exact cause is unknown but is suspected to be a pressure phenomenon on the femoral head during closed reduction and injury to the medial circumflex vessels surgically. In younger children the cartilaginous femoral head is thought to be protective, and younger kids with AVN have a good chance of healing and doing well. AVN can cause growth arrest of the physis as well and give rise to shorter femoral necks or varus or valgus position of the neck at maturity. The final outcome, however, is unpredictable at any age.[13]

Recurrent Dislocation

Some hips will not stabilize with conventional treatment whether it is the Pavlik harness or surgical intervention. Even after open reduction and bony procedures the hip may again subluxate over time or even dislocate again. This will necessitate another surgical procedure, which increases the risk for AVN even more and also bodes for a poorer result in the long term.[13,29]

CONGENITAL ABNORMALITIES OF THE FEET

Metatarsus Adductus

Terminology/Incidence/Etiology

Metatarsus adductus is a deformity in which an adducted forefoot gives the medial border of the foot a concave appearance and the lateral border looks convex (Fig. 125-6). The hindfoot is normal and has normal range of motion. It occurs in about 1 in 1000 births and has no gender predisposition.[59] The most likely cause is intrauterine positioning. There is a positive association with hip dysplasia.

Diagnosis/Imaging

The deformity is best identified with the child prone, and on examination the lateral border of the foot will

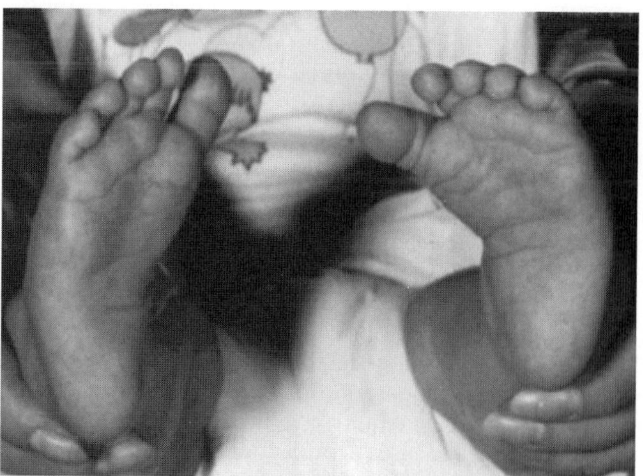

Figure 125-6 Metatarsus adductus.

*References 4, 8, 11-13, 16, 26-28, 32, 35, 38-40, 45, 47.

deviate inward and look convex. Its severity is measured by a line called the heel bisector, which passes through the heel and is drawn out to the toes. Normally, this line bisects the second and third toe. In mild metatarsus adductus it bisects the third toe and in severe forms it will bisect the fourth or fifth. The rest of the foot is normal. The hindfoot is normal, and there is normal ankle dorsiflexion. The abductor hallucis muscles may be overactive and pull the big toe into adduction as well (atavistic great toe). Radiographs may be obtained to assess the foot structurally but are not necessary unless there are other concerns.

Treatment

The natural history is that most feet with metatarsus adductus will correct spontaneously if they are supple and correctable past neutral.[57] If the deformity is more severe and left untreated, it may cause problems with shoe wear later from a prominent base of the fifth metatarsal and medial deviation of the foot. It can also be a source of in-toeing in a child. Most deformities resolve without any treatment or with the parents manipulating the feet. If the deformity persists or the feet are stiff and not passively correctable, stretching casts may fix the deformity. If the problem persists past 5 years of age, consideration may be given to surgery. Correction at a young age by joint release may leave the foot stiff. In the past, metatarsal osteotomies were performed for correction and are still used at times. Waiting until after 5 years of age and then performing opening wedge cuneiform and closing wedge cuboid osteotomies is more reliable.[55,56,58]

Flexible Flatfoot

Terminology/Incidence/Etiology

A flatfoot deformity occurs when the medial longitudinal arch is absent. This finding is very common in younger children, especially when they first begin walking. Many of these children have ligamentous laxity that contributes to the arch being depressed because the ligaments that support the arch are also lax and unable to support the foot in the weight-bearing position. The posterior tibial tendon may be incompetent and contribute to the deformity.

Diagnosis/Imaging

Diagnosis is by clinical examination. The medial arch is absent in the weight-bearing position and gives it the "flat foot" appearance. The foot is very flexible and an arch will be re-established when the foot is hanging free or the patient stands on tiptoes. As the patient goes up on toes, the heel will normally rotate into varus and the arch will become apparent. Radiographs will show a talus that is plantar-flexed and not lined up with the first metatarsal on the lateral projection; however, they are normally unnecessary unless other foot pathology is suspected.

Treatment

No treatment is necessary if the foot is flexible. The parents need to be reassured that it does not need to be treated and an orthotic will not help re-establish the arch. Many patients will tighten up over time as the ligamentous laxity improves and re-establish a medial arch as they get older. Arthroereisis or stabilization of the subtalar joint by an implant of some type (usually a Silastic or metal screw or staple) may be considered if the patient is symptomatic. An opening wedge osteotomy of the calcaneus or cuboid can be considered as well.[66-68] Fusion of the subtalar joint is reserved for patients with the most severe cases who continue to have pain despite other treatment options.

If the foot is not flexible and the arch does reconstitute when the patient goes up on tiptoes, it is considered a rigid flatfoot. This deformity may cause problems later in life, and surgery may be indicated in those with pain or significant deformity. Results are variable, and some patients may eventually undergo fusion of the subtalar joint for pain relief.

Clubfoot

Terminology/Incidence/Etiology

Clubfoot is a condition in which the foot has varying degrees of the following deformities: metatarsus adductus, supination of the forefoot, heel or hindfoot varus, and equinus (Fig. 125-7). Hence it is also called talipes equinovarus. The severity of the deformity is quite variable and ranges from a positional clubfoot that responds with minimal stretching and casting to rigid deformities often uncorrectable without surgery. The exact cause of clubfoot is unknown, but it is multifactorial and involves positioning and genetics. Positioning problems can be anything that decreases the in utero space for the fetus,

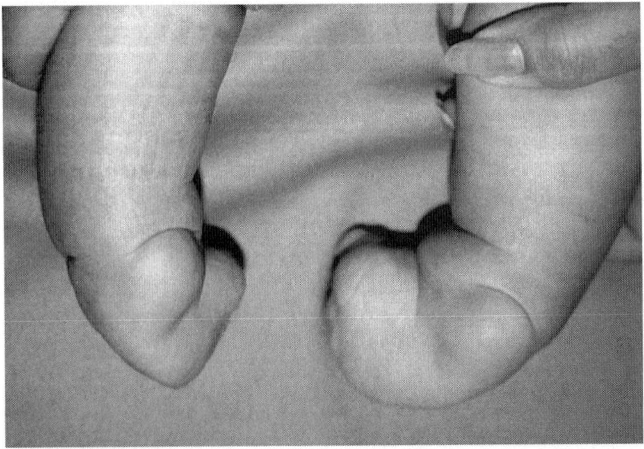

Figure 125–7 An infant with bilateral clubfeet demonstrates the deformities that are part of clubfeet. The infant is prone, a position that reveals the varus deformity of the hindfeet. The crease in the arch shows that these feet have a cavus deformity. The feet are internally rotated and are in equinus.

such as oligohydramnios, being the first baby, and multiple births. Many of the rigid, resistant feet are associated with neuromuscular problems or syndromes such as spina bifida, diastrophic dysplasia, sacral agenesis, and arthrogryposis. Those that are not associated with one of these conditions are thought to result from a defect in formation. Classification has been difficult because of the wide variation in manifestations.[71,73,80]

Diagnosis/Imaging

The diagnosis is usually apparent from the findings on physical examination discussed earlier. The forefoot is medially deviated as a result of the metatarsus adductus and supinated, which causes the forefoot to be almost touching the tibia. The calcaneus will be rotated into varus and will be very high in the calf and not palpable in the heel pad. There will be a medial crease of varying depth in the area of the medial arch. Finally, the Achilles tendon will be very tight, which is causing the high-riding calcaneus. Occasionally, the diagnosis will be subtle if most of these deformities are very mild, but such cases are rare. If the foot does not lack dorsiflexion and the heel is not in varus, it is probably not a true clubfoot.

Radiographs are not necessary at birth because most of the midtarsal bones are not yet ossified. The talocalcaneal index, or the angle formed by the intersection of a line drawn through the axis of the calcaneus and a line drawn through the axis of the talus, is measured on both AP and lateral projections. It should be greater than 30 degrees on both projections. An angle less than 30 degrees indicates parallelism of the two bones. In a normal foot they should be divergent in both projections. Radiographs are helpful as the child gets older to monitor the progress of treatment.

Anatomy/Pathoanatomy

The calcaneus and talus are normally divergent both in the axial and sagittal planes. In a clubfoot they are more parallel because of the varus deformity of the heel. This, along with the metatarsus adductus, is the major bony deformity. The first ray is also plantar-flexed and the navicular is subluxated medially and dorsally on the talar head. The talus is often smaller and misshapen with a short neck. The soft tissue deformities consist of a severe contracture of the Achilles tendon, as well as contractures of the posterior tibial tendon, flexor hallucis longus, and flexor digitorum longus. Where these tendons cross in the medial aspect of the foot they are occasionally confluent with abnormal slips of other tendons. These tendons are often entrapped in scar tissue and form what is called the knot of Henry. The plantar fascia is also tight.[70]

Treatment

Treatment of a clubfoot usually requires some type of manipulation and casting, and many feet require surgery. A technique of manipulation and casting advocated by Ponseti has been around for over 30 years, but only in the last 5 to 10 years has it been gaining widespread popularity among pediatric orthopedists. There have been good short-term results, and now older patients are showing maintenance of the correction.[72,74,77,78] The process consists of the application of a series of six to eight long leg casts with manipulation before each casting. The first step is to correct the plantar-flexed first ray and line it up with the other metatarsals in the foot. This cast does not produce much correction but is serving to improve the plantar-flexed first ray and eliminate the medial crease. The next several casts bring the foot out of supination and adduction and over into neutral alignment with the tibia and finally mild overcorrection into valgus. The last casts try to improve the Achilles contracture by slowly dorsiflexing the foot. Care should be taken to not dorsiflex the foot too quickly or before complete correction of the varus or a rocker-bottom foot deformity may be created. A tenotomy of the Achilles tendon is required in the majority of feet to release the heel cord contracture, allow the calcaneus to come down into the heel pad, and permit the foot to dorsiflex. This can be done in the office with or without sedation, and then a final long leg cast is applied with the foot slightly dorsiflexed and externally rotated. The cast is worn for 3 weeks, and then the patient goes into straight last shoes with a Denis Browne bar to keep the deformities from recurring. These shoes are worn full-time until 9 months of age and then at night and naptime until 4 years of age. Recurrence usually occurs after failure to fully correct the foot or inability to wear the bar and shoes.

If supination persists or the heel cord contracture recurs, the patient may need to undergo posterior release with open heel cord lengthening and a transfer of all or half of the anterior tibialis tendon to the lateral side of the foot. This technique is usually successful in keeping the foot in a functional position.

Surgical options are still preferred by some orthopedists who believe that manipulation and casting are not enough to correct the foot. To achieve correction, extensive release of the subtalar joint is required. The Achilles, posterior tibialis, flexor hallucis longus, and flexor digitorum tendons require lengthening, and the spring and interosseus ligaments require sectioning. The talonavicular joint is released and the navicular reduced laterally onto the head of the talus. Laterally, the peroneal tendon sheath is released. Release of the joint capsule is associated with significant joint scarring resulting in a stiff foot. Correction can be achieved, but overcorrection and undercorrection are both possible, and over time recurrence or overcorrection of the foot may develop.[79,81,82] The Ponseti method appears to produce a better foot clinically, both cosmetically and functionally.

In France, a technique developed by Dimeglio has produced good results. The feet are manipulated daily by the therapist and placed in a machine to give passive range of motion to the foot. It is very labor intensive and has not been extremely practical in the United States. In the long term recurrence is rare after the age of 5 years, but no foot, no matter what treatment protocol is used, will ever look completely normal radiographically or clinically.

CONGENITAL DISLOCATION OF THE KNEE

Congenital knee dislocation covers a spectrum of deformity ranging from simple positional contractures that

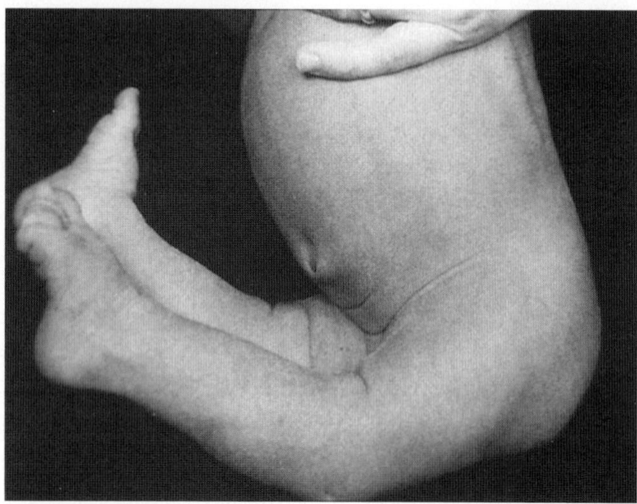

Figure 125-8 Congenital knee dislocation.

correct spontaneously to rigid dislocation of the knee joint requiring surgical intervention (Fig. 125-8). The problem often occurs in children with myelomeningocele, arthrogryposis, or other syndromes such as Larsen's. This deformity is frequently associated with DDH, clubfoot, and metatarsus adductus. It is extremely important to look for associated hip dysplasia when a knee dislocation is present. The deformity is recognized at birth in an infant with a knee that is hyperextended and a foot that is up by the infant's head because of a flexed hip. The pathology consists of one or all of the following: contracture of the quadriceps tendon, absent suprapatellar pouch, tight collateral ligaments, and anterior subluxation of the hamstring tendons.

If the problem has resulted from positioning in utero, the deformity is often mild and the knee is still fairly flexible. The knee will correct spontaneously within a few weeks or can be assisted by gentle range of motion to accelerate correction. Serial casting may also be helpful, and if hip dysplasia is present, a Pavlik harness can be worn once knee range of motion increases enough to allow the harness to fit properly.

A more severe contracture or true dislocation will be apparent fairly early in the course of treatment because there will be minimal response to stretching and casting. It is usually evident within the first 3 months of treatment. If 30 degrees of knee flexion has not been gained by this time, surgery is indicated. Surgery may consist of one or more of the following procedures, depending on the severity of the condition. The first step is V-Y quadricepsplasty or Z-lengthening of the tendon, followed as needed by release of the anterior joint capsule, posterior transposition of the hamstring tendons, and mobilization of the collateral ligaments. Ninety degrees of knee flexion should be achieved, and then the knee is cast in 45 to 60 degrees of flexion for 3 to 4 weeks.

CONGENITAL DISLOCATION OF THE PATELLA

True congenital dislocation of the patella is rare. This entity must be distinguished from a recurrent dislocation that occurs later in life. In congenital dislocation of the patella, the patella is very hypoplastic or absent and the femoral trochlea is often much flattened. The lateral retinaculum is tight and the patella is completely dislocated laterally. The patella is frequently adherent to the iliotibial band and is often irreducible over the condyle. Genu valgus is frequently present, as is a flexion contracture of the knee. Surgical intervention is required and involves extensive lateral retinacular release, often to the greater trochanter, medial plication, and either hamstring tenodesis or transfer of half of the patellar tendon.

CONGENITAL DEFORMITIES OF THE SPINE

Congenital scoliosis is relatively uncommon. It is a malformation in vertebral column development, typically a failure of formation or a failure of segmentation.[101] Congenital implies that the deformity is present at birth. The vertebral deformity is present at birth; however, the clinical deformity may not be recognized until years later, depending on the amount of growth imbalance that occurs. Isolated anomalies are usually sporadic, but multiple anomalies can be hereditary.[103] The true incidence is not known because some vertebral anomalies produce little deformity and go unrecognized.

Embryologic development of the spine occurs during the fourth to sixth weeks of gestation. By the sixth week the mesenchymal spinal anlage is complete. Defects in vertebral development occur at this time. They typically stem from failure of segmentation, failure of formation, or a mixed lesion. The resultant clinical deformity is determined by the type and location of vertebral deformity and the potential for asymmetric spinal growth.

Failure of segmentation most commonly occurs in the thoracic or thoracolumbar region. It can be unilateral or bilateral. Unilateral failure of segmentation, or a "bar," results in asymmetric growth of the spine (Fig. 125-9). It may not be evident on initial radiographs; however, there may be associated rib fusions that should raise suspicion.

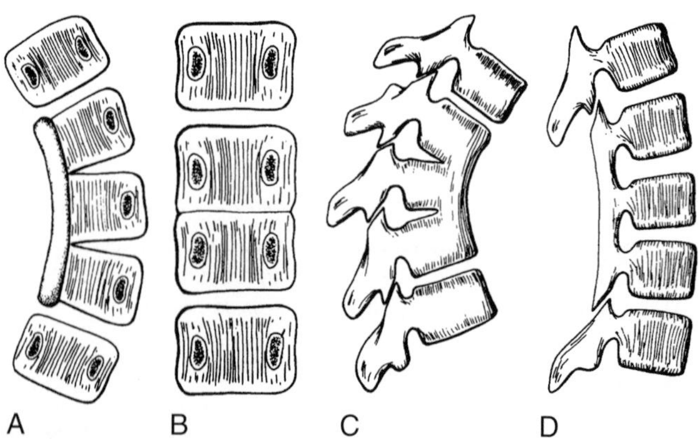

Figure 125-9 Defects of segmentation. *A*, Unilateral unsegmented bar causing scoliosis, which is usually progressive. *B*, Block vertebra caused by bilateral failure of segmentation. *C*, Anterior segmentation defect causing kyphosis. *D*, Failure of segmentation posteriorly causing lordosis. (Adapted with permission from Winter RB: Congenital Deformities of the Spine. New York, Thieme-Stratton, 1983.)

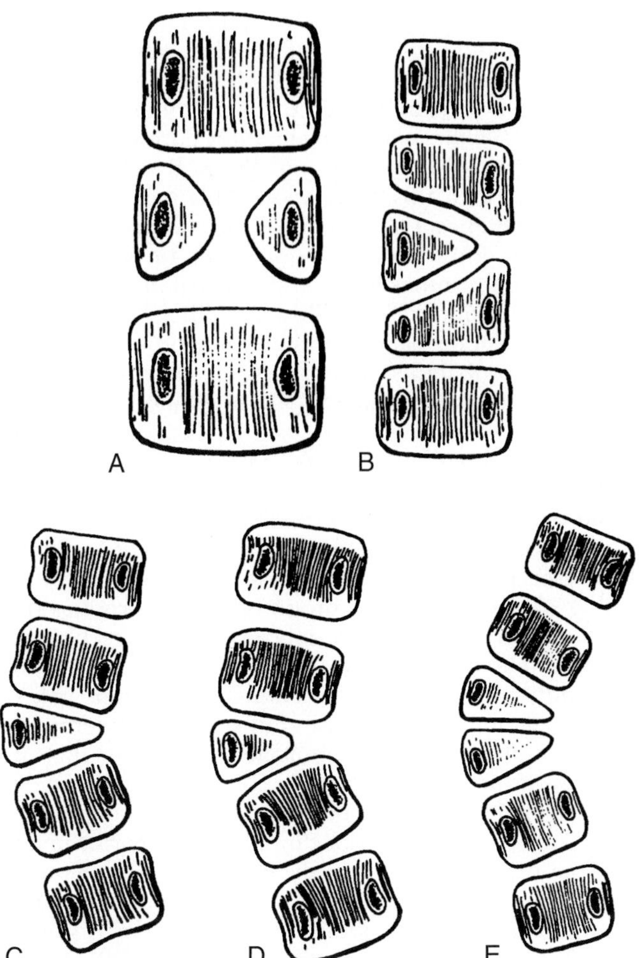

Figure 125–10 Defects of formation. *A*, Anterior central defect ("butterfly vertebra"), usually nonprogressive. *B*, Incarcerated hemivertebra. Note the accommodation by adjacent vertebrae and minimal deformity. *C* to *E*, Wedge, free, and multiple hemivertebra, respectively, demonstrating variation in the degree of vertebral wedging and increasing tendency for progression. (Adapted with permission from Bradford DS, Hensinger RM: The Pediatric Spine. New York, Thieme, 1985.)

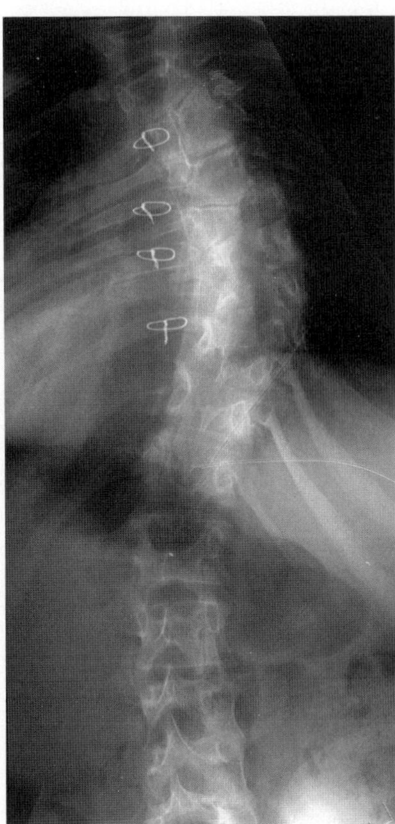

Figure 125–11 Multiple anomalies with combined failure of formation and failure of segmentation. Note the fused ribs in a concavity suggestive of a "bar."

It is often rapidly progressive. The resultant deformity depends on the location of the bony tether. A lateral bar results in scoliosis, an anterior bar results in kyphosis, and a posterior bar results in lordosis. It can also occur in combination and result in kyphoscoliosis or lordoscoliosis. By far the most common is scoliosis, followed by kyphosis. Lordosis is quite rare. Bilateral involvement creates a block vertebra with minimal deformity.

Failure of formation can range from mild wedging to complete absence of half of the vertebra (hemivertebra) (Fig. 125-10). It can occur anywhere along the spinal axis. A hemivertebra is the most common. If present in the thoracic spine, there will be an associated extra rib. The extent of the clinical deformity depends on the location of the hemivertebra and on the potential for growth of the hemivertebra. A lateral hemivertebra will result in scoliosis, whereas a posterior hemivertebra will produce kyphosis.

The remaining deformities are either mixed or cannot be classified because of the extent of their pathology (Fig. 125-11). The amount of clinical deformity is variable, depending on the defect. The most progressive deformity, however, is a combination of a hemivertebra with a contralateral unsegmented bar.[98] Such deformities rapidly progress and will require intervention, usually at the time of diagnosis.

The neural axis forms in conjunction with the bony canal, and the frequency of intraspinal anomalies has been reported to be as high as 40%.[90,100] Abnormality of the overlying skin such as a dimple, lipoma, hairy patch, or nevus may be present 70% of the time. Diastematomyelia is believed to be the most common associated defect.[94] It is a sagittal split in the spinal cord or cauda equina by an osseous or fibrocartilaginous spur protruding posteriorly from the vertebral body. It should be removed if symptomatic or before any corrective spinal surgery. Other intraspinal anomalies include tethered cord, syringomyelia, epidermoid cyst, lipoma, and teratoma. A thorough neurologic examination must be performed, and any clinical suspicion of neurologic abnormality requires imaging with MRI.

Associated anomalies occur in other systems up to 60% of the time,[87] including genitourinary, 25%; Klippel-Feil syndrome (cervical spine fusions), 25%; and cardiac, 10%. Abnormalities of the gastrointestinal system can also be seen, as well as tracheoesophageal fistulas and anal

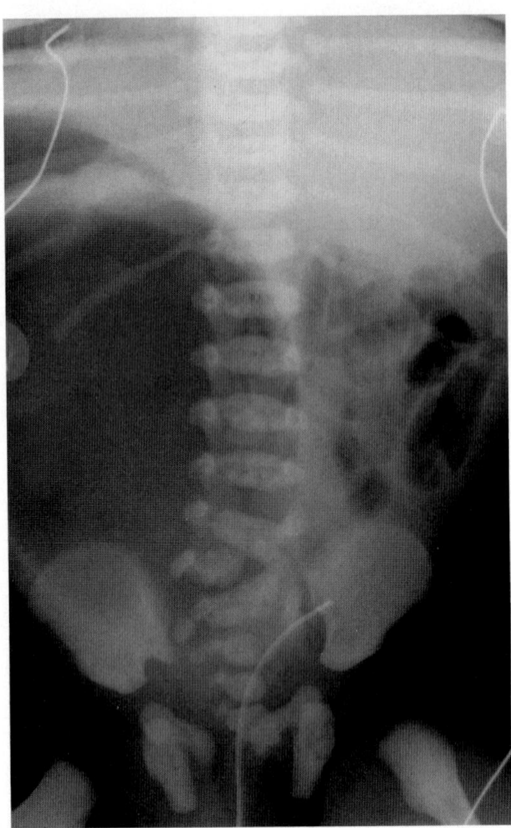

Figure 125–12 Incidental finding on a kidney-ureter-bladder radiographic workup for anal atresia. Note the S1 hemivertebra.

atresia in connection with the VATER association (in addition to vertebral defects and radial and renal dysplasia).[88] Other musculoskeletal deformities such as Sprengel's deformity (congenital elevated scapula), pectus abnormalities, and appendicular skeletal deficiencies are less common. All patients should undergo renal ultrasound screening to exclude underlying abnormalities because the genitourinary system is difficult to assess by physical examination alone.

An infant with congenital scoliosis may or may not have a spinal deformity at birth. If a deformity is present, it is typically a lateral deviation of the spine. It can be confused with congenital muscular torticollis (see Chapter 57) or infantile idiopathic scoliosis (thoracic spinal curvature). Both these conditions can cause clinical deformity at birth, but radiographs will fail to show vertebral anomalies. Most often, vertebral anomalies are incidental findings during the workup for other conditions (Fig. 125-12), and initial detection can occur at any age. The diagnosis is made with radiographs, but MRI or CT may be necessary to better delineate the pathology.

There is little nonoperative treatment to offer other than observation. Unlike other types of scoliosis that may respond to bracing, it is not routinely indicated for congenital scoliosis. The ideal therapeutic modality is surgical stabilization before spinal deterioration.

The surgical treatment of congenital scoliosis depends on the type of deformity present, the location of the deformity, and the amount of growth remaining. The goal of treatment is to halt progression and achieve spinal balance at maturity. The most rapid vertebral growth occurs up to the age of 2 years and again during adolescence. Thus, clinical deformities can change rapidly during these times and require close monitoring. Surgical complications are increased in this population. This type of scoliosis carries the highest risk for neurologic complications with attempts at intraoperative correction. Ideally, patients who have deformities with a high probability of progression should undergo stabilization when their curves are small.[95] Other patients with a lower probability or an unknown probability of progression are managed by close follow-up with serial radiographs. Surgical intervention is delayed as long as the curve is not progressing and the spine remains in balance. Overall, 50% of curves will be stable, 25% will progress slowly, and 25% will have rapid progression.

Surgery is the definitive treatment of congenital scoliosis. It is indicated for rapidly progressive curves, deformities with a high propensity to progress, and deformities that cause spinal imbalance. Numerous surgical techniques are available, depending on the type and location of the deformity. Attempts at correction carry a high risk of neurologic impairment. Fusion in situ is considered the "gold standard"[102] and is indicated for curves that are progressive or prone to progress but still within a range where spinal balance can be maintained. In younger children, anterior and posterior fusion must be performed to balance the remaining growth. Posterior fusion alone is adequate for older children with little remaining spinal growth. Hemiepiphyseodesis is a variation of fusion in situ. It involves fusion of only the convex side of the curve, thus permitting the concave side to continue unopposed growth and allow correction to occur. Because the correction is gradual, the risk for neurologic impairment is decreased. Hemivertebra excision is typically reserved for deformities in the lumbar spine where spinal imbalance is more pronounced and the cauda equina is safer to retract (Fig. 125-13). Excision has been performed in the thoracic and thoracolumbar spine less often, but with favorable results.[91] An anterior and posterior approach is usually necessary. Spinal osteotomy or vertebrectomy is reserved for the most severe curves with imbalance that are not amenable to other more standard techniques. It carries the highest risk for neurologic injury because of the acute correction and is considered a "salvage" procedure by most.

Anterior approaches to the spine require the traditional thoracotomy or thoracoabdominal approaches. Postoperative morbidity can be significant in this population because of other coexisting abnormalities, and pulmonary function may be further diminished after these approaches. Video-assisted thoracoscopic surgery can be useful in some instances.[99] Visualization of the spine is adequate and the instrumentation continues to improve to allow for more complete diskectomy and anterior fusion. Postoperative pulmonary morbidity should be lessened.

Congenital kyphosis is a variant of congenital scoliosis and usually occurs secondary to failure of formation of the anterior body (Fig. 125-14).[96] It can also result from

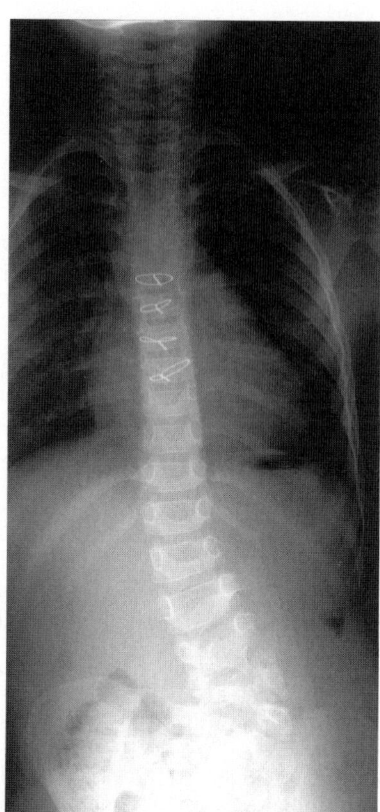

Figure 125–13 Left L5 hemivertebra causing spinal imbalance. This is the ideal location for hemivertebra excision.

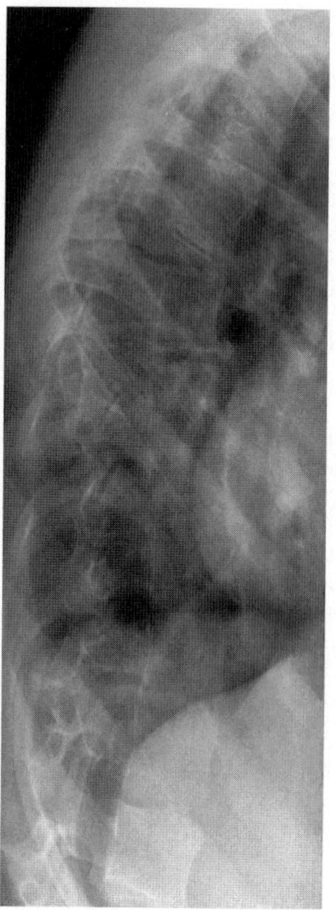

Figure 125–14 Posterior hemivertebra with anterior failure of formation resulting in kyphosis.

failure of segmentation with an anterior or, more commonly, an anterolateral bar. This type of deformity has a poor prognosis for progression and neurologic involvement. If unrecognized, it can result in paraplegia. Congenital kyphosis requires surgical stabilization at the time of diagnosis to prevent further deterioration. Bracing is of no value. Because of the variability in deformity, no single surgical approach can be applied to all. Typically, if the patient is younger than 5 years and the kyphosis is less than 50 degrees, posterior fusion will suffice. If older than 5 years or more severe kyphosis exists, anterior and posterior fusion is required.[97]

Sacral agenesis, or complete or partial absence of the sacrum, is another type of congenital spinal anomaly. It has been associated with maternal insulin-dependent diabetes,[89] although this relationship has more recently been questioned.[93] It is often associated with gastrointestinal and genitourinary abnormalities. Neurologic involvement is variable and often results in hip, knee, and foot deformities. The prognosis and treatment depend on the degree of malformation, the stability of the spine, the level of neurologic involvement, and any other associated anomalies. Typically, only patients with stability of the spinal attachment to the pelvis are able to ambulate.[92] They may require surgical procedures to correct their lower extremity deformities. Most others with spinal instability at the spinal-pelvic junction will not ambulate functionally and require treatments aimed at improved sitting balance and positioning.

REFERENCES

Developmental Dysplasia of the Hip

1. Bennett JT, MacEwen GD: Congenital dislocation of the hip. Recent advances and current problems. Clin Orthop 1989; 247:15.
2. Bialik V, Fishman J, Katzir J, Zeltzer M: Clinical assessment of hip instability in the newborn by an orthopaedic surgeon and a pediatrician. J Pediatr Orthop 1986;6:703.
3. Boeree NR, Clarke NMP: Ultrasound imaging and secondary screening for congenital dislocation of the hip. J Bone Joint Surg Br 1994;76:525.
4. Castelein RM, Sauter AJ, de Vlieger M, van Linge B: Natural history of ultrasound hip abnormalities in clinically normal newborns. J Pediatr Orthop 1992;12:423.
5. Cheng JC, Chan YL, Hui PW, et al: Ultrasonographic hip morphometry in infants. J Pediatr Orthop 1994; 14:24.
6. Coleman SS: Congenital dysplasia of the hip in the Navajo Indian. Clin Orthop 1968;56:179.
7. Coleman SS: Developmental dislocation of the hip: Evolutionary changes in diagnosis and treatment. J Pediatr Orthop 1994;14:1.
8. Drummond DS, O'Donnell J, Breed A, et al: Arthrography in the evaluation of congenital dislocation of the hip. Clin Orthop 1989;243:148.
9. Eggli KD, King SH, Boal DK, Quiogue T: Low-dose CT of developmental dysplasia of the hip after reduction: Diagnostic accuracy and dosimetry. AJR Am J Roentgenol 1994; 163:1441.

10. Faciszewski T, Kiefer GN, Coleman SS: Pemberton osteotomy for residual acetabular dysplasia in children who have congenital dislocation of the hip. J Bone Joint Surg Am 1993;75:643.
11. Fish DN, Herzenberg JE, Hensinger RN: Current practice in use of pre-reduction traction for congenital dislocation of the hip. J Pediatr Orthop 1991;11:149.
12. Fleissner PR Jr, Ciccarelli CJ, Eilert RE, et al: The success of closed reduction in the treatment of complex developmental dislocation of the hip. J Pediatr Orthop 1994; 14:631.
13. Gabuzda GM, Renshaw TS: Reduction of congenital dislocation of the hip. J Bone Joint Surg Am 1992;74:624.
14. Galpin RD, Roach JW, Wenger DR, et al: One-stage treatment of congenital dislocation of the joint in older children, including femoral shortening. J Bone Joint Surg Am 1989; 71:734.
15. Garvey M, Donoghue VB, Gorman WA, et al: Radiographic screening at four months of infants at risk for congenital hip dislocation. J Bone Joint Surg Br 1992;74:704.
16. Grill F, Benshael H, Canadell J, et al: The Pavlik harness in the treatment of congenital dislocating hip: Report of a multicenter study of the European Paediatric Orthopaedic Society. J Pediatr Orthop 1988;8:1.
17. Gulman B, Tuncay IC, Dabak N, Karaismailoglu N: Salter's innominate osteotomy in the treatment of congenital hip dislocation: A long-term review. J Pediatr Orthop 1994; 14:662.
18. Harcke HT: Imaging in congenital dislocation and dysplasia of the hip. Clin Orthop 1992;281:2.
19. Hensinger RN: Congenital dislocation of the hip. CIBA Clin Symp 1979;31:1.
20. Hernandez RJ, Cornell RG, Hensinger RN, et al: Ultrasound diagnosis of neonatal congenital dislocation of the hip. J Bone Joint Surg Br 1994;76:539.
21. Herring JA, Cummings DR: The limb-deficient child. In Morrissy RT, Weinstein SL (eds): Lovell and Winter's Pediatric Orthopaedics, 4th ed. Philadelphia, Lippincott-Raven, 1996.
22. Hinderaker T, Daltveit AK, Irgens LM, et al: The impact of intra-uterine factors on neonatal hip instability: An analysis of 1,059,479 children in Norway. Acta Orthop Scand 1994; 65:239.
23. Hummer CD, MacEwen GD: The coexistence of torticollis and congenital dysplasia of the hip. J Bone Joint Surg Am 1972;54:1255.
24. Ilfeld FW, Westin GW, Makin M: Missed or developmental dislocation of the hip. Clin Orthop 1986;203:276.
25. Ishii Y, Weinstein SL, Ponsetti IV: Correlation between arthrograms and operative findings in congenital dislocation of the hip. Clin Orthop 1980;153:138.
26. Jones GT, Schoenecker PL, Dias LS: Developmental hip dysplasia potentiated by inappropriate use of the Pavlik harness. J Pediatr Orthop 1992;12:722.
27. Kahle WK, Anderson MB, Alpert J, et al: The value of preliminary traction in the treatment of congenital dislocation of the hip. J Bone Joint Surg Am 1990;72:1043.
28. Kalamchi A, MacFarlane R 3rd: The Pavlik harness: Results in patients over three months of age. J Pediatric Orthop 1982;2:3.
29. Kasser JR, Bowen JR, MacEwen GD: Varus derotation osteotomy in the treatment of persistent dysplasia in congenital dislocation of the hip. J Bone Joint Surg Am 1985; 67:195.
30. Kershaw CJ, Ware HE, Pattison R, Fixsen JA: Revision of failed open reduction of congenital dislocation of the hip. J Bone Joint Surg Br 1993;75:744.
31. Klisic PJ: Congenital dislocation of the hip: A misleading term. J Bone Joint Surg Br 1989;71:136.
32. Malvitz TA, Weinstein SL: Closed reduction for congenital dysplasia of the hip. J Bone Joint Surg Am 1994;76:1777.
33. McKinnon B, Bosse MJ, Browning WH: Congenital dysplasia of the hip: The lax (subluxatable) newborn hip. J Pediatr Orthop 1984;4:422.
34. Mubarak SJ, Beck LR, Sutherland D: Home traction in the management of congenital dislocation of the hips. J Pediatr Orthop 1986;6:721.
35. Mubarak S, Garfin S, Vance R, et al: Pitfalls in the use of the Pavlik harness for treatment of congenital dysplasia, subluxation, and dislocation of the hip. J Bone Joint Surg Am 1981;63:1239.
36. Mubarak SJ, Leach J, Wenger DR: Management of congenital dislocation of the hip in the infant. Contemp Orthop 1987;15:29.
37. Pavlik A: Stirrups as an aid in the treatment of congenital dysplasias of the hip in children. J Pediatr Orthop 1989; 9:157.
38. Quinn RH, Renshaw TS, DeLuca PA: Preliminary traction in the treatment of developmental dislocation of the hip. J Pediatr Orthop 1994;14:636.
39. Race C, Herring JA: Congenital dislocation of the hip: An evaluation of closed reduction. J Pediatr Orthop 1983; 3:166.
40. Ramsey PL, Lasser S, MacEwen GD: Congenital dislocation of the hip: Use of the Pavlik harness in the child during the first six months of life. J Bone Joint Surg Am 1976;58:1000.
41. Rachbauer F, Sterzinger W, Klestil T, et al: Acetabular development following early treatment of hip dysplasia by Pavlik harness. Acta Orthop Trauma Surg 1994;113:281.
42. Rosendahl K, Markestad T, Lie RT: Ultrasound screening for developmental dysplasia of the hip in the neonate: The effect on treatment rate and prevalence of late cases. Pediatrics 1995;96:982.
43. Schoenecker PL, Strecker WB: Congenital dislocation of the hip in children. Comparison of the effects of femoral shortening and of skeletal traction in treatment. J Bone Joint Surg Am 1984;66:21.
44. Stanton RP, Capecci R: Computed tomography for early evaluation of developmental dysplasia of the hip. J Pediatr Orthop 1992;12:727.
45. Tavares JO, Gottwald DH, Rochelle JR: Guided abduction traction in the treatment of congenital hip dislocation. J Pediatr Orthop 1994;14:643.
46. Tredwell SJ: Neonatal screening for hip joint instability: Its clinical and economical relevance. Clin Orthop 1992; 281:63.
47. Viere RG, Birch JG, Herring JA, et al: Use of the Pavlik harness in congenital dislocation of the hip. J Bone Joint Surg Am 1990;72:238.
48. Weinstein SL: Traction in developmental dislocation of the hip. Is its use justified? Clin Orthop 1997;338:79.
49. Weinstein SL: Developmental hip dysplasia and dislocation. In Morissy RT, Weinstein SL (eds): Lovell and Winter's Pediatric Orthopedics, vol 2, 5th ed. Philadelphia, Lippincott Williams and Wilkins, 2001, p 905.
50. Weinstein SL, Mubarak SJ, Wenger DR: Developmental hip dysplasia and dislocation: Part 1. J Bone Joint Surg Am 2003;85:1824.
51. Weinstein SL, Mubarak SJ, Wenger DR: Developmental hip dysplasia and dislocation: Part 2. J Bone Joint Surg Am 2003;85:2024.
52. Weintroub S, Grill F: Ultrasonography in developmental dysplasia of the hip. J Bone Joint Surg Am 2000;82:1004.
53. Wilkinson JA: Etiologic factors in congenital displacement of the hip and myelodysplasia. Clin Orthop 1992; 281:75.

54. Yngve D, Gross R: Late diagnosis of hip dislocation in infants. J Pediatr Orthop 1990;10:777.

Metatarsus Adductus

55. Bleck EE: Metatarsus adductus: Classification and relationship to outcome of treatment. J Pediatr Orthop 1983;3:2.
56. Brink DS, Levitsky DR: Cuneiform and cuboid wedge osteotomies for correction of residual metatarsus adductus: A surgical review. J Foot Ankle Surg 1995;34:371.
57. Farsetti P, Weinstein SL, Ponseti IV: The long-term functional and radiographic outcomes of untreated and non-operatively treated metatarsus adductus. J Bone Joint Surg Am 1994;76:257.
58. Ghali NN, Abberton MJ, Silk FF: The management of metatarsus adductus et supinatus. J Bone Joint Surg Br 1984;66:376.
59. Harley BD, Fritzhand AJ, Little JM, et al: Abductory midfoot osteotomy procedure for metatarsus adductus. J Foot Ankle Surg 1995;34:153.
60. Heyman CH, Herndon CH, Strong JM: Mobilization of the tarsometatarsal and intermetatarsal joints for the correction of resistant adduction of the fore part of the foot in congenital clubfoot or congenital metatarsus varus. J Bone Joint Surg Am 1958;40:299.
61. Jacobs JE: Metatarsus varus and hip dysplasia. Clin Orthop 1960;16:203.
62. Katz K, David R, Soudry M: Below-knee plaster cast for the treatment of metatarsus adductus. J Pediatr Orthop 1999; 19:49.
63. Kite JH: Congenital metatarsus varus. J Bone Joint Surg Am 1967;49:388.
64. Ponseti IV, Becker JR: Congenital metatarsus adductus: The results of treatment. J Bone Joint Surg Am 1966; 48:702.
65. Smith JT, Bleck EE, Gamble JG, et al: Simple method of documenting metatarsus adductus. J Pediatr Orthop 1991; 11:679.

Flexible Flatfoot

66. Bruyn JM, Cerniglia MW, Chaney DM: Combination of Evans calcaneal osteotomy and STA-peg arthrodesis for correction of the severe pes valgus planus deformity. J Foot Ankle Surg 1999;38:339.
67. Giannini BS, Caccarelli F, Benedetti MG, et al: Surgical treatment of flexible flatfoot in children, a four-year follow up study. J Bone Joint Surg Am 2001;83(Suppl 2):73.
68. Roye DP Jr, Raimondo RA: Surgical treatment of the child's and adolescent's flexible flatfoot. Clin Podiatr Med Surg 2000;17:515.
69. Wenger DR, Maudlin D, Speck G, et al: Corrective shoes and inserts as treatment for flexible flatfoot in infants and children. J Bone Joint Surg Am 1989;71:800.

Clubfoot

70. Carroll NC: Pathoanatomy and surgical treatment of the resistant clubfoot. Instr Course Lect 1988;37:93.
71. Cowell HR, Wein BK: Current concepts review: Genetic aspects of clubfoot. J Bone Joint Surg Am 1980;62:1381.
72. Dobbs MB, Rudzki JR, Purcell DB, et al: Factors predictive of outcome after use of Ponseti method for the treatment of idiopathic clubfeet. J Bone Joint Surg Am 2004;86:22.
73. Goldner JL: Congenital talipes equinovarus—fifteen years of surgical treatment. Curr Pract Orthop Surg 1969; 4:61.
74. Ippolito E, Farsetti P, Caterini R, Tudisco C: Long-term comparative results in patients with congenital clubfoot treated with two different protocols. J Bone Joint Surg Am 2003:85:1286.
75. McKay DW: New concept of and approach to clubfoot treatment, I: Principles and morbid anatomy. J Pediatr Orthop 1982;2:347.
76. McKay DW: New concept of and approach to clubfoot treatment, Section III: Evaluation and results. Correction of the clubfoot. J Pediatr Orthop 1983;3:141.
77. Morcuende JA, Dolan LA, Dietz FR, Ponseti IV: Radical reduction in the rate of extensive corrective surgery for clubfoot using the Ponseti method. Pediatrics 2004;113:376.
78. Noonan KJ, Richards BS: Nonsurgical management of idiopathic clubfoot. J Am Acad Orthop Surg 2003;11:392.
79. Ryoppy S, Sairanen H: Neonatal operative treatment of clubfoot. J Bone Joint Surg Br 1983;65:320.
80. Simons GW: A standardized method for the radiographic evaluation of clubfeet. Clin Orthop 1978;135:107.
81. Thompson GH, Richardson AB, Westin GW: Surgical management of resistant congenital talipes equinovarus deformities. J Bone Joint Surg Am 1982;64:652.
82. Turco VJ: Resistant congenital clubfoot—one stage posteromedial releases with internal fixation. J Bone Joint Surg Am 1979;61:805.

Congenital Dislocation of the Knee and Patella

83. Curtis BH, Fisher RL: Congenital hyperextension with anterior subluxation of the knee. J Bone Joint Surg Am 1969;51:255.
84. Ferris B, Aichroth P: The treatment of congenital knee dislocation. Clin Orthop 1987;216:135.
85. Nogi J, MacEwen GD: Congenital dislocation of the knee. J Pediatr Orthop 1982;2:509.
86. Ooishi T, Sugioka Y, Matsumoto S, Fujii T: Congenital dislocation of the knee. Clin Orthop 1993;287:189.
87. Beals RK, Robbins JR, Rolfe B: Anomalies associated with vertebral malformations. Clin Orthop 1993;1:99.
88. Beals RK, Rolfe B: VATER association: A unifying concept of multiple anomalies. J Bone Joint Surg Am 1989; 71:948.
89. Blumel J, Evans EB, Eggers GWN: Partial and complete agenesis or malformation of the sacrum with associated anomalies; etiologic and clinical study with special reference to heredity; a preliminary report. J Bone Joint Surg Am 1959;41:497.
90. Bradford DS, Heithoff KB, Cohen M: Intraspinal abnormalities and congenital spine deformities: A radiographic and MRI study. J Pediatr Orthop 1991;11:36.
91. Deviren V, Berven S, Smith JA, et al: Excision of hemivertebrae in the management of congenital scoliosis involving the thoracic and thoracolumbar spine. J Bone Joint Surg Br 2001;83:496.
92. Guille JT, Benevides R, DeAlba LCC, et al: Lumbosacral agenesis: A new classification correlating spinal deformity and ambulatory potential. J Bone Joint Surg Am 2002;84:32.
93. Kalter H: Case reports of malformations associated with maternal diabetes: History and critique. Clin Genet 1993; 43:174.
94. McMaster MJ: Occult intraspinal anomalies and congenital scoliosis. J Bone Joint Surg Am 1984;66:588.

95. McMaster MJ, Ohtsuka K: The natural history of congenital scoliosis: A study of 251 patients. J Bone Joint Surg Am 1982;64:1128.
96. McMaster MJ, Singh H: Natural history of congenital kyphosis and kyphoscoliosis. A study of one hundred and twelve patients. J Bone Joint Surg Am 1999;81:1367.
97. McMaster MJ, Singh H: The surgical management of congenital kyphosis and kyphoscoliosis. Spine 2001;26:2146.
98. Nasca RJ, Stelling FH, Steel HH: Progression of congenital scoliosis due to hemivertebrae and hemevertebrae with bars. J Bone Joint Surg Am 1975;57:456.
99. Regan JJ, Mack MJ, Picetti GD: A technical report on video-assisted thoracoscopy in thoracic spinal surgery. Spine 1995;20:831.
100. Winter RB, Lonstein JE, Denis F, et al: Prevalence of spinal canal or cord anomalies in idiopathic, congenital, and neuromuscular scoliosis. Orthop Trans 1992;16:135.
101. Winter RB, Moe JH, Eilers VE: Congenital scoliosis: A study of 234 patients treated and untreated. J Bone Joint Surg Am 1968;50:1.
102. Winter RB, Moe J, Lonstein J: Posterior spinal arthrodesis for congenital scoliosis: An analysis of the cases of 290 patients 5-19 years old. J Bone Joint Surg Am 1984; 66:1187.
103. Wynne-Davies R: Congenital vertebral anomalies: Aetiology and relationship to spina bifida cystica. J Med Genet 1975;12:280.

Chapter 126

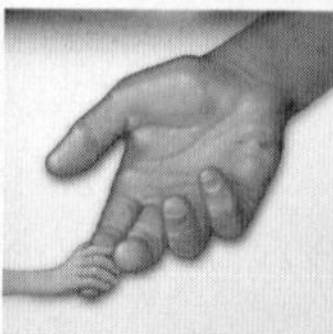

Bone and Joint Infections

Robert M. Kay and William L. Oppenheim

Prior to the antibiotic era, musculoskeletal sepsis frequently resulted in chronic drainage, repetitive infections, and even death.[121] Unfortunately, despite modern medical and surgical approaches, bone and joint infections still pose a significant threat to children. The goal of treatment remains early eradication of the infection to minimize destruction of normal tissue and thus limit long-term sequelae. The precise therapeutic regimen must be individualized for each patient based on the duration of symptoms, the site of involvement, the pathogen involved, the patient's host response to infection, and the patient's innate immunocompetence.

ACUTE HEMATOGENOUS OSTEOMYELITIS

Pathophysiology

Acute hematogenous osteomyelitis is the most common pediatric musculoskeletal infection.[23,35,100,147,162] In the preantibiotic era, such infections commonly resulted in death.[121] In the skeletally immature the infection is believed to be caused by a combination of bacteremia and local trauma. The presence of simply one of these factors alone generally does not result in the classic picture of osteomyelitis.[102,119,130,158] Children have unique anatomic and circulatory circumstances on the metaphyseal side of the growth plate of a long bone that predispose them to infections localized to this area. In adults, by comparison, infection can occur anywhere in the bone, frequently as a result of traumatic contamination.

The usual sources of bacteremia are recent or concurrent infections, such as upper respiratory tract infections, urinary tract infections, otitis media, and skin infections (e.g., impetigo).[38,61] Although the source of bacteremia is generally distant, contiguous spread is sometimes the cause of acute osteomyelitis. Osteomyelitis has also been described after closed fractures, although this circumstance is rare.[18] Overall, the incidence of acute osteomyelitis may be decreasing owing to the prompt, effective treatment of many childhood infections before they can spread to bone.[26]

As noted, the infection has a predilection for the metaphyseal regions of long bones, especially those of the leg. This predilection is presumably due to the sluggish blood flow seen in the terminal loops of the arterioles in the metaphyseal region in the growing child along with less efficient function of the reticuloendothelial system at these sites (Fig. 126-1).[35,38,102] Septic emboli appear to localize in traumatic hematomas, in part because of enhanced microbial adhesion at these locations.[58] Premature infants are especially at risk because of their less developed immune systems and the frequency with which they can be potentially colonized from indwelling catheters used in their care.[46] In children younger than 12 to 18 months of age, the infection may extend across and injure the physis. Later in childhood, such spread does not occur because the vasculature is then segmented into separate circulations proximal and distal to the physis.[22,107]

Once bacteria have localized in the metaphyseal region, the host's defense system attempts to eradicate them. The result can be complete resolution of the infection, partial resolution, or the establishment of chronic infection. If the process is locally controlled within the bone but not eradicated, Brodie's abscess results, visualized on a radiograph as a lucent area adjacent to the growth plate. In the absence of local control the infection may spread transversely through Volkmann canals, permeating the metaphysis and forming a subperiosteal abscess. In bones with intra-articular metaphyses, infection penetrating through the metaphysis may result in septic arthritis. The elevation of the periosteum by pus propagating under pressure further compromises the blood supply, resulting in a vicious cycle of devascularization, destruction of bone, and continuing spread of the infection.

The pathogens involved vary with patient age, although *Staphylococcus aureus* is the most common organism across all age groups.* *S. aureus* has been reported in 44% to 88% of positive cultures in various series.[26,35,100,132,162] Group B streptococci and gram-negative bacteria are common in neonates. *Haemophilus influenzae* is common until age 4 or 5 in children who have not received a series of *H. influenzae* type B (HIB) vaccines. In such populations, *H. influenzae* accounts for approximately 10% of all

*See references 26, 30, 35, 37, 38, 61, 66, 100, 105, 132, 138, and 162.

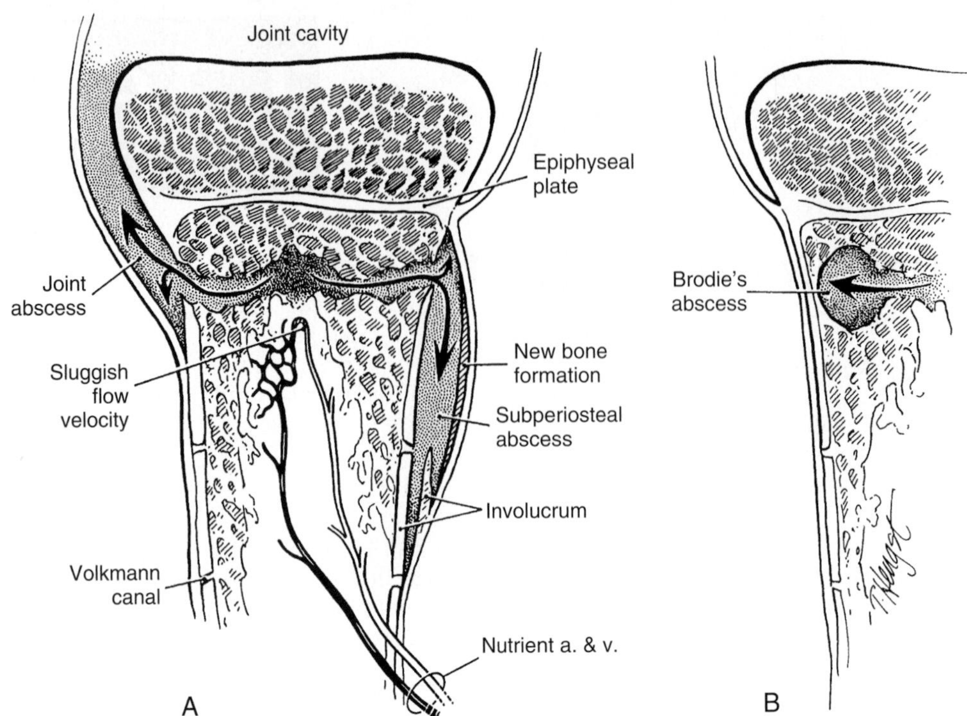

Figure 126-1 *A*, The pathogenesis of pediatric bone and joint infections: hematogenous spread of infection generally results in the infection lodging in the metaphyseal region of long bones, in part because of the sluggish blood flow found there. The infection can then spread through Volkmann's canals to the subperiosteal space, where it can form an abscess. Old, necrotic bone may be incompletely resorbed (involucrum). Subperiosteal new bone may also be seen. If the metaphysis is within the joint capsule (as in the pediatric hip and knee), the infection may spread into the joint itself, resulting in septic arthritis. *B*, Brodie's abscess results if the infection is contained within the metaphysis without being eradicated.

osteomyelitis in children up to age 2 years and for 5% of all cases in children up to age 5 years.[35,105] Inadequately treated cases of *H. influenzae* infection may be complicated by subsequent meningitis. In patients and populations immunized against HIB, *Kingella kingae* has been increasingly identified as a pathogen.[48,90,166]

Less frequent opportunistic organisms are observed in specific high-risk groups. For example, patients in the pediatric intensive care unit are often exposed to nosocomial pathogens.[61,66] Patients with sickle cell disease are at risk for *Salmonella* (in addition to *S. aureus*).[36,41,52,61,95] Athletic shoe punctures are associated with *Pseudomonas* infections.[15,45,77] *Mycobacterium tuberculosis* is more frequent in densely populated cities, developing countries, and those areas with increased prevalence of human immunodeficiency virus infection. Coccidioidomycosis is endemic to the southwestern United States, whereas Lyme disease is common in the northeastern United States and portions of the Midwest.

Presentation

Children with acute osteomyelitis usually present with fever, localized pain, and the refusal to bear weight or otherwise use the affected extremity. Children 10 years old and younger account for 65% to 85% of pediatric cases.[23,35,100,105,162] Boys outnumber girls by as much as 2:1, although this ratio may approach 4:1 in children older than 10 years of age.[37,38,61,100,105,132] In neonates, the only signs or symptoms of acute osteomyelitis may be malaise, listlessness, or failure to suck. Refusal to move the affected limb (pseudoparalysis) is also a common finding in neonates and infants (Fig. 126-2).

The femur and tibia are the sites of 50% to 70% of cases of pediatric osteomyelitis (Fig. 126-3).[23,26,35,131,162] Although involvement is generally monostotic, polyostotic involvement occurs in 2% to 7% of cases.[23,26,35,132,162]

The clinical evaluation begins with a thorough history and physical examination. The physician should ask about potential sources of infection, including recent skin lesions, and infections of the ear, respiratory tract, and urinary tract. Risk factors for infection should be sought, including underlying medical conditions, immunologic compromise, and recent disease exposures. The duration of symptoms should be determined.

During the physical examination, local pain, swelling, tenderness, and warmth are often evident. These findings may be difficult to elicit in a young and frightened child, although a change in the character and/or intensity of crying is often helpful during a careful physical examination.

Imaging

After the history and physical examination, plain radiographs should be obtained if a specific site of concern is identified.[55,86,129] Early in the course of acute osteomyelitis,

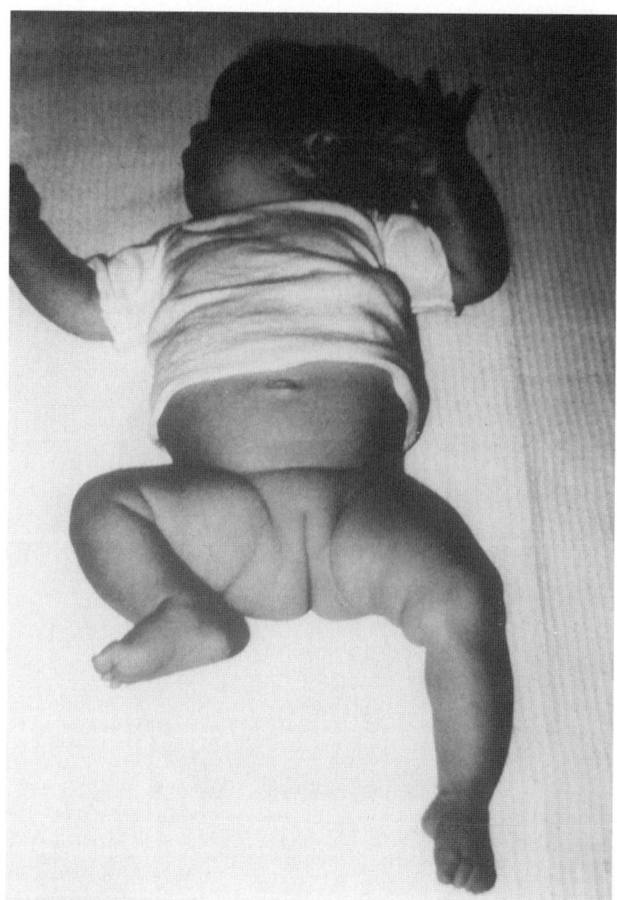

Figure 126-2 Pseudoparalysis in a neonate demonstrating asymmetrical movement of the lower extremities because of the child's unwillingness to move the affected left lower extremity.

deep soft tissue swelling accompanied by obliteration of the usual soft tissue planes is the only abnormal finding on plain radiographs. After 1 to 2 weeks, the more classic findings of osteolysis, periosteal elevation, periosteal new bone, or Brodie's abscess may be seen (Fig. 126-4).

Ultrasound findings that parallel these radiographic changes have been described.[1,67,68,85,92,93,109,117] Ultrasound can be useful for identifying a subperiosteal abscess.[1,68]

Three-phase bone scanning is helpful when trying to localize the site of involvement in neonates and toddlers as well as in the evaluation of deep infections in the spine and pelvis affecting children of all ages. Sensitivity of bone scanning has been reported from 84% to 100%, whereas specificity has been reported as 70% to 96%.[14,24,25] Bone scans are particularly important in evaluating musculoskeletal infections in neonates, because multiple sites may be involved in up to half of such neonatal cases ("metastatic" osteomyelitis).[37,105] If infection is advanced and associated with bone infarction, a "cold spot" may be seen rather than the typical "hot spot." Patients with "cold" osteomyelitis appear to have more severe infections than do those with the more typical "hot" scans.[112] A prior needle aspiration site should not affect the bone scan interpretation if the scan is done within 24 hours of the aspiration.[17] Therefore, aspiration should not be delayed while waiting for results of a bone scan.

Although useful in adults, white blood cell scans do not appear to be of value in the evaluation of children with suspected musculoskeletal infections.[83]

Cross-sectional imaging is rarely needed in the evaluation of children with acute hematogenous osteomyelitis, although it may be helpful in confirming the diagnosis and determining the extent of involvement. Computed tomography (CT) demonstrates late sequestra and bony destruction well, but frequently these can be spotted on plain films as well.[55] As a result, CT does not play a large role in the evaluation of children with suspected acute hematogenous osteomyelitis. It may be more helpful later in the disease to identify an occult sequestrum, not visualized on plain radiographs, and can be beneficial in planning a surgical procedure when draining a bone abscess.

Magnetic resonance imaging (MRI) is highly sensitive and specific for osteomyelitis and may be used to confirm the diagnosis and to assess the extent of bony and soft tissue involvement.[33,55,80,84,86] MRI is superior to CT in the delineation of the soft tissues, including sinus tracts and soft tissue abscesses, and plays a larger role in the evaluation of children with acute hematogenous osteomyelitis. MRI is often helpful in the imaging of pelvic osteomyelitis, especially when the infection involves the posterior pelvis. Because of the high association of soft tissue infections, including abscess formation, in children with pelvic osteomyelitis, MRI is often recommended to complete the workup of these children.[64,156] In addition, MRI readily distinguishes osteomyelitis from cellulitis.

Laboratory Findings

A leukocyte count with differential should be obtained; although leukocytosis and/or a left shift are common, a normal count does not rule out osteomyelitis.[37,38,132] Both the C-reactive protein (CRP) levels and the erythrocyte sedimentation rate (ESR) are usually elevated in acute osteomyelitis. An acute phase reactant, the CRP rises more rapidly in response to infection and falls more rapidly as the infection is treated than does the ESR.[111,123,138,154] Failure of the CRP to decrease rapidly after initiation of antibiotic therapy appears to be an indicator of a higher risk patient.[123]

Cultures should be obtained so that antibiotic therapy can be tailored to the individual pathogen. Aspiration of the subperiosteal space should first be performed if fluid can be obtained; if subperiosteal fluid is not obtained, then aspiration of the bone itself should be performed with the patient under conscious sedation or general anesthesia.

Aspirated fluid should be sent for Gram stain, cultures, and antimicrobial sensitivity studies for aerobic organisms, anaerobic organisms, mycobacteria, and fungi. Blood cultures and cultures of likely sources (e.g., throat, sputum, and urine) should also be obtained because these are often positive in patients with osteomyelitis, even if bone aspirates fail to grow bacteria.[35,61,138] Positive blood cultures are often the only positive cultures and may be invaluable in guiding antibiotic therapy.[35,61,138]

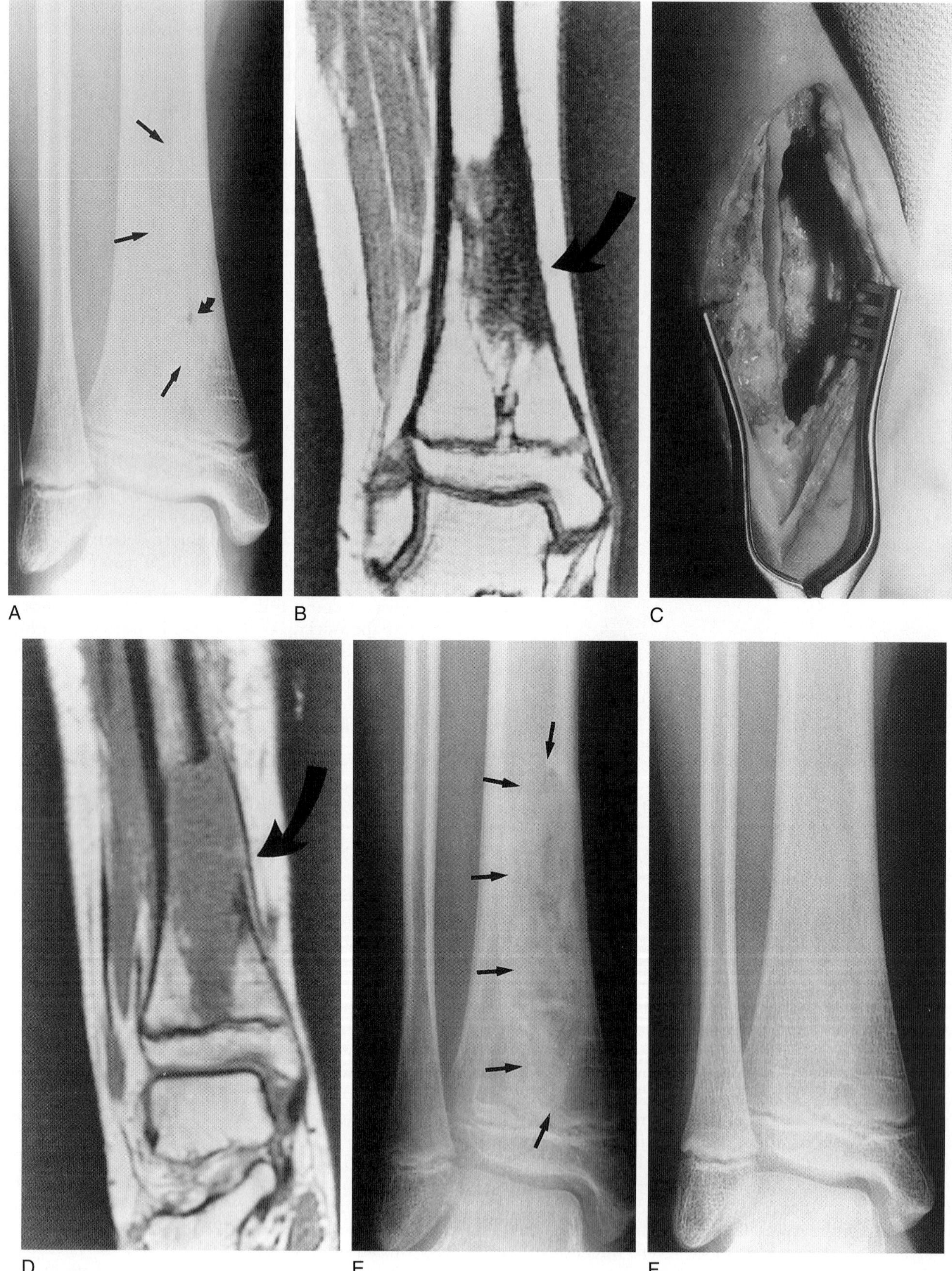

Figure 126–3 This 11-year-old boy had a history of osteomyelitis at age 10 and recurrent pain approximately 1 year later. *A,* Plain radiography of the distal tibia demonstrated osteosclerotic osteomyelitis *(straight arrows)*, with a lucent area *(curved arrow)* appearing similar to the nidus of an osteoid osteoma. *B,* A T1-weighted MR image depicts the area of involvement *(arrow)*. *C,* Intraoperative picture showing thorough débridement of the distal tibia. *D,* This was confirmed by postoperative MRI. *E,* One month after two surgical débridements, the tibial defect was bone grafted *(arrows)*. *F,* Essentially normal-appearing tibia 9 months after bone grafting.

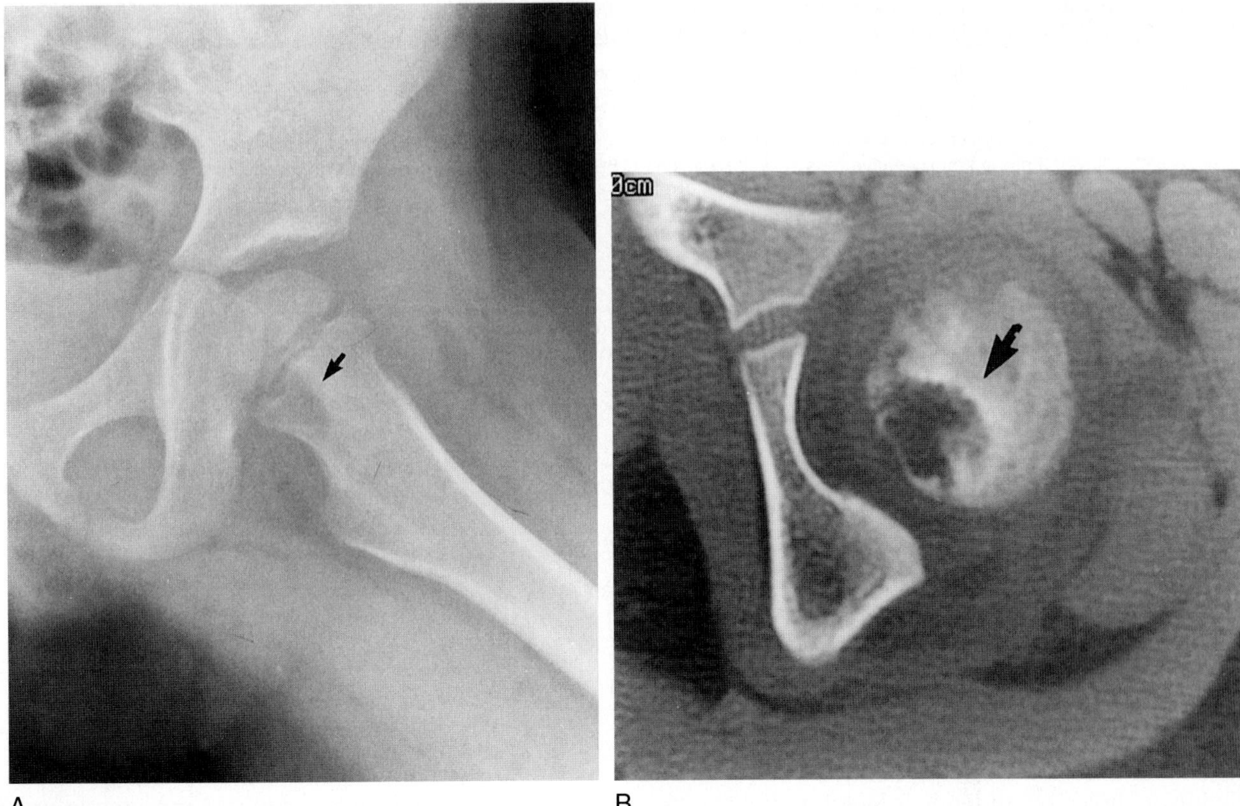

Figure 126–4 Brodie's abscess in the left proximal femur of a 3-year-old girl. At presentation, the child had had a limp for several weeks. Plain radiography (*A*) and CT scan (*B*) were consistent with Brodie's abscess. Open biopsy was consistent with osteomyelitis; curettage and fat grafting (because of physeal involvement) were performed. The patient received antibiotics for a total of 6 weeks postoperatively.

Microbiology

S. aureus is the most common pathogen in all age groups and must be covered by initial antibiotics.[61,138] In addition to *S. aureus*, common pathogens in neonates include group B streptococci and enteric gram-negative rods.

In fully immunized children 1 month to 5 years old, the most common pathogens are *S. aureus*, *Streptococcus pneumoniae*, and *Streptococcus pyogenes*.[61,101,138] *K. kingae* has become increasingly common (up to 17% of osteoarticular infections in children younger than 3 years old in one series) as *H. influenzae* infections have decreased; fortunately, *K. kingae* is sensitive to the vast majority of antibiotics used empirically in the treatment of pediatric musculoskeletal infections.[48,90,166] HIB infections typically accounted for 10% to 15% of cases of acute hematogenous osteomyelitis in this age group before the advent of HIB vaccine. *H. influenzae* remains a significant pathogen in children up to age 4 years who have not received the complete vaccination course with HIB. Children with septic arthritis caused by *H. influenzae* have up to a 30% risk of developing meningitis.[125,133]

In children older than 5 years, *S. aureus* is responsible for the vast majority of cases of acute hematogenous osteomyelitis.

Community-acquired methicillin-resistant *S. aureus* (CA-MRSA) has become increasingly common.[62,70,71,97,104,128] Two recent studies have identified CA-MRSA colonization in 0.6% to 0.8% of healthy children.[71,104] Sattler and associates reported that 63 of 144 patients (44%) admitted to their hospital with community-acquired *S. aureus* infections had methicillin-resistant strains.[128] CA-MRSA now accounts for 15% to 20% of community-acquired musculoskeletal *S. aureus* infections.[62,128] Fortunately, to date CA-MRSA infections are generally more sensitive to antibiotics than are the strains responsible for nosocomial MRSA infections.[62,70,71,97,104,128] CA-MRSA has been reported to be sensitive to clindamycin in 70% to 100% of cases, to gentamicin in 90% to 100%, and to trimethoprim-sulfamethoxazole in 90% to 100%.[62,70,128] Many strains are resistant to erythromycin; and even though the vast majority are sensitive to clindamycin,[62,97] clindamycin resistance may develop during the course of antibiotic treatment.[97]

Treatment

The goal of therapy is the prompt eradication of infection, with minimization of morbidity and long-term sequelae. Antibiotics remain a mainstay of all regimens.* Splinting of the affected extremity for a few days often provides symptomatic relief.

*See references 49, 61, 101, 105, 106, 126, 136, 138, 149, and 150.

TABLE 126–1 Common Organisms and Initial Antibiotic Treatment for Acute Osteomyelitis

Patient Age	Common Pathogens	Antibiotics and Dosages
<1 mo	Group B streptococci	Oxacillin* (150-200 mg/kg/day) and gentamicin (6.0-7.5 mg/kg/day)
	Staphylococcus aureus†	*or*
	Enteric gram-negative rods	Oxacillin* (150-200 mg/kg/day) and cefotaxime (150 mg/kg/day)
1 mo-5 yr	*S. aureus*†	Non-HIB Immunized
	Haemophilus influenzae type B (HIB)‡	Oxacillin* (150-200 mg/kg/day) and cefotaxime (100-150 mg/kg/day)
		or
	Pneumococci	Cefuroxime (100-150 mg/kg/day)
	Streptococci	
	Kingella kingae	HIB Immunized
		Cefazolin (100 mg/kg/day)
		or
		Oxacillin* (150-200 mg/kg/day)
		or
		Clindamycin (30-40 mg/kg/day)
>5 yr	*S. aureus*†	Cefazolin (100 mg/kg/day)
		or
		Oxacillin* (150-200 mg/kg/day)
		or
		Clindamycin (30-40 mg/kg/day)

*May use nafcillin instead of oxacillin.

†Consider adding either vancomycin or clindamycin in areas with high rates of methicillin-resistant *S. aureus.*

‡HIB infections rare in fully immunized child.

The initial choice of antibiotic is based on the results of the Gram stain when organisms are seen. Otherwise, the decision is an empirical one based on the patient's age and immunization status and the suspected pathogen(s) (Table 126-1). Consultation with a local infectious disease specialist should be considered in areas with high rates of MRSA infection to determine optimal antibiotic regimens.

Initial antibiotic treatment for neonates should provide coverage against *S. aureus*, group B streptococci, and enteric gram-negative rods. Appropriate antibiotics include the combination of a semi-synthetic penicillin (oxacillin or nafcillin) and gentamicin.[61,101,138] Alternatively, treatment with a semi-synthetic penicillin and cefotaxime could be undertaken. In areas with high rates of MRSA infection, it may be necessary to add vancomycin or clindamycin to the aforementioned regimens.

In children 1 month to 4 years old, immunization status plays an important role in the determination of empirical antibiotic treatment. Children who have not received the full course of HIB vaccinations need to receive empirical coverage for *H. influenzae* in addition to coverage for *S. aureus*, pneumococci, and streptococci. Antibiotic choices include the combination of a semi-synthetic penicillin (nafcillin or oxacillin) with cefotaxime or the use of single-agent therapy with cefuroxime.[61,101,138] In children who are fully immunized, cefazolin is an appropriate empirical choice. In areas with high rates of MRSA infection, it may be necessary to add vancomycin or clindamycin to the regimen.

In children older than age 4 years, *S. aureus* is easily the most common pathogen encountered in musculoskeletal infection. Single-agent treatment may be initiated with a semi-synthetic penicillin (nafcillin or oxacillin) or with cefazolin.[61,101,138] In areas with high rates of MRSA infection, it may be necessary to add vancomycin or clindamycin to the aforementioned regimens.

Surgery is rarely indicated when children first present with acute hematogenous osteomyelitis thought to be of recent onset. If clinical improvement is not seen during the first 24 to 48 hours of empirical antibiotic therapy, then further radiologic evaluation as outlined previously is indicated. Common indications for surgery include subperiosteal abscess or extensive bony involvement. Surgery consists of irrigation and débridement, with removal of necrotic tissue. Intraoperative cultures should be obtained. Swiontkowski has recommended the use of laser Doppler flowmetry to more precisely determine the extent of osseous débridement necessary, although few practitioners find this technology necessary.[146]

Initial antibiotic treatment is intravenous. The time at which antibiotic administration may be switched from parenteral to enteral is still debated. Only children and families who have a very high likelihood of complying with the oral antibiotic regimen are candidates for such treatment. In a series of acute staphylococcal osteomyelitis, Peltola and colleagues reported changing to oral antibiotics within 4 days and had no long-term sequelae.[111]

A total antibiotic course of 4 to 6 weeks is generally recommended.* An antibiotic course of less than 3 weeks has previously been reported to result in significantly higher rates of recurrence than result from longer courses.[35]

The oral antibiotic doses used to treat musculoskeletal infections are significantly higher than those routinely used to treat soft tissue infections (see Table 126-1). As an outpatient, the complete blood cell count, ESR, and CRP

*See references 49, 61, 101, 105, 106, 126, 136, 138, 149, and 150.

are monitored weekly. Serum bactericidal titers are not routinely checked currently.

Complications

Complications of acute hematogenous osteomyelitis are related to the patient's age, ability to fight infection, the affecting organism, and any delay in diagnosis and treatment of the infection.[121] As noted previously, in those younger than 12 to 18 months of age at the time of infection, the physis and epiphysis are at risk because of the persistence of the transphyseal blood supply.[22,107] Physeal damage can result in limb-length discrepancy and/or angular deformity of the affected extremity.

Perlman and colleagues reported that one third of their patients with osteomyelitis had sepsis of the adjacent joint.[113] Failure to recognize adjacent septic arthritis can lead to joint destruction. Septic arthritis is more of an emergency than osteomyelitis owing to an inability to restore the cartilage, once damaged.

Meningitis is a risk, especially with *H. influenzae* infections, and high doses of intravenous antibiotics are therefore recommended for at least 3 to 5 days. Failure to fully eradicate the acute infection leads to chronic osteomyelitis, which can result in decades of pain, intermittent drainage, and even amputation.[105] Chronically draining wounds can be complicated by squamous cell carcinoma.

Maraqa and coworkers reported the complications associated with outpatient parenteral antibiotic treatment for pediatric musculoskeletal infections.[96] Four of 172 patients (2.2%) had either persistent or recurrent infection. Complications were deemed "catheter related" in 30%, "non–catheter related" in 32%, and "unknown" in 5% during antibiotic courses of treatment. Adverse drug reactions occurred in 32% of patients, and 26% required rehospitalization during their course of outpatient treatment. Outpatient parenteral antibiotic courses were completed without interruption in 64% of patients.

SEPTIC ARTHRITIS

Pathophysiology

Septic arthritis in children may result from hematogenous bacterial spread, direct inoculation, or the contiguous spread of infection from the metaphysis of a long bone through its cortex and into the adjacent joint.* In a review of multiple series, 41% of septic arthritis occurred in the knee, 25% in the hip, 13% in the ankle, and 10% in the elbow.[60]

Presentation

The presentation of septic arthritis is similar to that of acute osteomyelitis, except for the younger age range. Children younger than 2 years old account for 40% to 50% of cases of septic arthritis.[11,75,91] Males are affected twice as often as females. Toddlers may present with refusal to walk, pain, and fever, whereas neonates simply appear ill, with vague symptoms, a normal leukocyte count, and, often, no fever.[46]

In older children, the physical findings may mimic those of acute osteomyelitis, but joint irritability and restriction of motion are the most prominent features. Usually the patient holds the affected hip or knee in a flexed position and strongly resists the practitioner's attempt to move the septic joint. The knee and hip account for about 70% of cases.[11,60,75,133,147] The ankle accounts for another 10% of cases.

CRP appears to range somewhat higher in septic arthritis than in acute osteomyelitis, although there is significant overlap between the two groups.[154] In cases of osteomyelitis, if the CRP nearly doubles in 24 hours, septic arthritis may be present as well.[154] The leukocyte count with differential and the ESR are routinely obtained but are often normal early in the course of the disease. The CRP rises within hours of the onset of pediatric musculoskeletal infection. It increases more quickly than the ESR to the infection initially and returns to normal more quickly with adequate treatment of the infection.

Septic arthritis may be difficult to differentiate from toxic synovitis, a noninfectious effusion of the hip. Septic arthritis generally results in a higher leukocyte count, higher CRP, higher ESR, higher fever, and a more toxic-appearing child than does toxic synovitis.[34] However, there is significant overlap in many clinical and laboratory parameters. Children with toxic synovitis are also more likely to bear weight on the affected extremity than are those with septic arthritis.[88] In a study done before CRP was widely available, Kocher and colleagues reported that significant risk factors for septic arthritis (compared with synovitis) included refusal to bear weight, ESR greater than or equal to 40 mm/hr, leukocyte count greater than 12,000/mL, and a fever. The combination of these risk factors was highly reliable in differentiating between the two conditions.[88]

The symptoms of toxic synovitis often plateau or begin to abate within 12 to 24 hours of seeing the physician. If a child with presumed synovitis does not follow such a course, then further evaluation for septic arthritis is warranted.

Hip ultrasound is able to detect the presence of a hip effusion. However, neither the size of the effusion nor its echogenicity can reliably differentiate a septic from a sterile effusion.[168] Although "power" Doppler can be used to detect differences in blood flow to the femoral head, it cannot reliably differentiate between a sterile and septic effusion in the laboratory or in clinical practice.[143,144]

If the diagnosis is in doubt or if septic arthritis is suspected, then joint fluid is aspirated and sent for Gram stain, cell count, and glucose. The joint fluid in toxic synovitis has a lower cell count, fewer neutrophils, and a more normal glucose level (Table 126-2). If organisms are seen on Gram stain, the diagnosis of septic arthritis is confirmed and the antibiotics may be tailored to the organism(s).

In the child, aspiration of the hip may require general anesthesia or conscious sedation; aspiration of the knee

*See references 2, 11, 30, 46, 60, 75, 91, 99, 113, and 147.

TABLE 126-2 Typical Synovial Fluid Values in Toxic Synovitis and Septic Arthritis

Variable	Toxic Synovitis	Septic Arthritis
Leukocyte count (cells/mL)	<15,000	>50,000
Polymorphonuclear cells (%)	<25	>90
Glucose (% of serum glucose)	>65	~30

can generally be accomplished at the bedside or in the clinic. If a hip tap is dry, an arthrogram should be performed to ensure that the joint capsule was indeed penetrated. A heparinized syringe is recommended to prevent the blood from clotting, which might preclude an accurate cell count in the joint fluid. If additional fluid is available after fluid is sent for cell count, differential, and cultures, then a drop may be placed between two gloved fingertips. As the fingers are separated, a "string" of fluid is normally seen between the fingertips, owing to the polymerized hyaluronic acid. If there is no "string sign," infection is likely present.

Synovial fluid cultures are positive in 50% to 80% of cases of septic arthritis.[145] As in acute osteomyelitis, blood cultures and cultures of any other likely source of infection should be obtained to maximize the chances of identifying the causative agent. In patients with clinical and laboratory evidence of septic arthritis, as well as positive blood cultures, joint aspirates may be sterile in up to 30% of cases.[147]

Staphylococcus and *Streptococcus* species account for up to 50% to 70% of septic arthritis; *H. influenzae* accounts for up to 25% of cases in children who have not received the series of HIB vaccinations.[60,75,147] *Neisseria gonorrhoeae* should be considered in neonates, sexually active adolescents, and victims of sexual abuse.[44,60,73,74,110,118,122,159,163]

Septic arthritis may also be confused with a psoas abscess.[137,138] In a child with a psoas abscess, flexion of the hip may alleviate the pain associated with hip rotation in extension (the psoas sign). Psoas abscess can at times lead to pain in the spine, abdomen, or genitourinary system. Ultrasound, CT, or MRI can easily differentiate between septic arthritis and psoas abscess.

Microbiology

In septic arthritis, *S. aureus* is the most common pathogen in all age groups and must be covered by initial antibiotics. In addition to *S. aureus*, the most common pathogens in neonates include group B streptococci and enteric gram-negative rods.

In fully immunized children 1 month to 5 years old, the most common pathogens are *S. aureus*, *K. kingae*, group A streptococci, and *Streptococcus pneumoniae*.[60,145] Although now rare due to the widespread use of the vaccine, HIB is a serious threat to children who are not fully immunized.

In children older than 5 years, *S. aureus* and group A streptococci are responsible for the vast majority of cases of acute hematogenous osteomyelitis. As noted earlier, sexually active adolescents and victims of sexual abuse of any age are at risk for gonococcal arthritis.

As with osteomyelitis, CA-MRSA is an increasingly common cause of septic arthritis.[62,70,97,128] CA-MRSA infections have been responsible for 15% to 20% of *S. aureus* musculoskeletal infections in two recent series.[62,128] The details of the infections are as described previously. Once again, consultation with a local infectious disease specialist should be considered in areas with high rates of MRSA infection to determine optimal antibiotic regimens.

Treatment

Therapy is aimed at decompressing the joint infection as promptly as possible while minimizing morbidity. Articular cartilage destruction has been demonstrated both in laboratory and clinical settings and may occur within hours of the onset of septic arthritis.* Prompt drainage of the site of infection is necessary to maximize outcome. Unlike osteomyelitis, in which damaged bone may regenerate, the joint surface is irreparably damaged after articular cartilage destruction from septic arthritis.

Drainage can consist either of surgical drainage (open or arthroscopic) or repeated joint aspirations. Surgical drainage ensures thorough drainage and irrigation of the infected joint. The physician should break up loculations when present. A drain should be used in the initial postoperative period to allow ongoing drainage of the joint. Repeated aspirations of accessible joints (e.g., the knee or ankle) have been advocated by some authors, although such a regimen likely results in less thorough initial drainage and subjects the child to multiple painful procedures and/or multiple episodes of conscious sedation or anesthesia.

Antibiotics are always used in combination with drainage, whatever the technique chosen.[60,87] Once again, the Gram stain is used to guide initial therapy, but if no organisms are seen, or identified on subsequent cultures, empirical treatment should be comparable to that for acute osteomyelitis. In neonates, this consists of treatment with a semi-synthetic penicillin (oxacillin or nafcillin) and an aminoglycoside (Table 126-3).[60,101] In children up to age 5 years, empirical treatment consists of oxacillin or nafcillin in combination with cefotaxime; alternatively, cefuroxime may be used as a single agent.[60,101] Children 5 years of age and older may be treated empirically with either oxacillin or nafcillin.

In areas with high rates of MRSA infection, consideration should be given to adding vancomycin or clindamycin to the aforementioned regimens in all children with suspected musculoskeletal infection.

Complications

Because of the rapid onset of cartilage destruction in septic joints, complications of septic arthritis are common.[7,27-29,142] The ultimate prognosis depends on the duration of symptoms before treatment, the age of the

*See references 2, 7, 11, 27-29, 46, 56, 75, 76, 114, 133, and 136.

TABLE 126-3 Common Organisms and Initial Antibiotic Treatment for Septic Arthritis

Patient Age	Common Pathogens	Antibiotics and Dosages
<1 mo	Group B streptococci *Staphylococcus aureus*† Enteric gram-negative rods	Oxacillin* (150-200 mg/kg/day) and gentamicin (6.0-7.5 mg/kg/day) *or* Oxacillin*(150-200 mg/kg/day) and cefotaxime (150 mg/kg/day)
1 mo-5 yr	*S. aureus*† *Haemophilus influenzae* type B (HIB)† *Kingella kingae* Group A streptococci Pneumococci	Non-HIB Immunized Oxacillin* (150-200 mg/kg/day) and cefotaxime (100-150 mg/kg/day) *or* Cefuroxime (100-150 mg/kg/day) HIB Immunized Cefazolin (100 mg/kg/day) *or* Oxacillin* (150-200 mg/kg/day) *or* Clindamycin (30-40 mg/kg/day)
>5 yr	*S. aureus*†	Cefazolin (100 mg/kg/day) *or* Oxacillin* (150-200 mg/kg/day)

*May use nafcillin instead of oxacillin.
†Consider adding either vancomycin or clindamycin in areas with high rates of methicillin-resistant *S. aureus.*
‡HIB infections rare in fully immunized child.

patient, and the infecting organism.[114,142,145,147] Patients younger than 1 year of age tend to have a poorer prognosis, as do patients with a longer duration of symptoms before starting treatment. The poor prognosis in young patients may be due to delayed diagnosis and/or concurrent physeal involvement.[22,107] Patients infected with *Staphylococcus* and *Enterobacter* organisms tend to have a worse prognosis than do those with *Haemophilus* species.[147] Destruction of the joint surfaces is common, although radiographs may appear much worse than the patient appears clinically.[7] Meningitis (especially with *H. influenzae*) can be catastrophic. Limb-length discrepancy and angular and rotational deformities of the extremities may also be seen as long-term sequelae of physeal involvement.[7,108,114,142,145] *K. kingae* infections are generally more benign than their counterparts and do not appear to lead to severe complications.[48,90,166]

OTHER INFECTIONS

Subacute Osteomyelitis

Subacute osteomyelitis refers to a syndrome of insidious onset in which affected patients appear relatively well.[3,38,54,65,120] Subacute infections result from a low-virulence organism or the partial eradication of the disease by the patient. Involvement may be in the epiphysis, metaphysis, or diaphysis of long bones and may cross the physis. This process lasts weeks to months before the patient presents to the physician, and plain radiographic changes are evident at presentation. These bony changes may be confused with primary bone tumors, including small round cell tumors; thus, open biopsy must sometimes be performed for diagnosis. *S. aureus* is the most common organism identified, although cultures are frequently negative.

Sacroiliac Osteomyelitis

Sacroiliac osteomyelitis accounts for 1% to 2% of pediatric osteomyelitis.[6,10] Patients may present with isolated hip pain, and the diagnosis may be mistaken for a septic hip. Beaupre and Carroll described three additional presentations in children: lumbar disk syndrome, gluteal syndrome, or abdominal syndrome.[6] Patients with lumbar disk syndrome present similarly to those with herniated lumbar disk, with back pain that often radiates to the buttock and/or leg. Those with gluteal syndrome have gluteal pain, and a gluteal mass is sometimes palpable. Patients presenting with abdominal syndrome can clinically mimic patients with an acute abdomen, and unnecessary appendectomies in such patients have been reported.[6,10] Regardless of presentation, the physical examination is remarkable for tenderness over the sacroiliac region, pain with FABER testing (hip *F*lexion, *AB*duction, and *E*xternal *R*otation), and lateral pelvic compression. Radiographs may be normal or may reveal sclerotic and/or lytic changes at the sacroiliac joint. Bone scans and/or MRI are often useful in confirming the diagnosis.[24,63] The bone scan may clearly show abnormalities only with pinhole collimation techniques. Haliloglu and associates noted that MRI was sensitive for sacroiliac infections but could not differentiate such infections from sacroiliitis.[63] Cultures grow *S. aureus* in the vast majority of cases. Treatment is generally with antibiotics alone, although surgical drainage may be required for resistant cases.

Chronic Recurrent Multifocal Osteomyelitis

Chronic recurrent multifocal osteomyelitis (CRMO) is a rare form of osteomyelitis only recognized over the past few decades.[8,13,40,47,103,141] It may initially present in a fashion indistinguishable from acute osteomyelitis. Two to 10 sites are often involved (many of which may be asymptomatic), and females are more commonly affected than males. Skin lesions, including palmoplantar pustulosis, may be evident.[40,81] Average age at presentation is generally 10 to 15 years. Common sites of involvement include the metaphyses of the lower extremity, the long bones, the clavicles, and the spine.[40]

Initial radiographs often demonstrate a lytic metaphyseal lesion, and this generally becomes progressively sclerotic with time[81]; however, at times a tumor cannot be ruled out. Bone scans often help demonstrate the extent of involvement and may show increased uptake in asymptomatic sites.[81,103] As with acute osteomyelitis, CT shows bony destruction and MRI shows marrow involvement.[81] Open biopsy with tissue being sent for microbiologic and pathologic evaluation is usually recommended initially. Cultures should be negative, and pathology should be consistent with osteomyelitis. A waxing and waning course with exacerbations and ameliorations over the course of months to years is common; exacerbations do not require repeat operation and/or culture. Antibiotics do not alter disease course. Symptomatic treatment with nonsteroidal anti-inflammatory medications may relieve symptoms.

Vertebral Osteomyelitis

Vertebral osteomyelitis accounts for 0% to 3% of pediatric osteomyelitis and typically occurs during the first decade of life.[37,43,105,132,148,152] Patients often present with low back pain, local tenderness, fever, and refusal to walk.[53] These patients resist any attempt at spine range of motion and often have loss of the normal sagittal contour of the spine. Bone scan or MRI will confirm the diagnosis, although MRI is more sensitive for early infections and more accurately reflects the extent of bony and soft tissue involvement.[94,152] The usual pathogen is *S. aureus*. Blood cultures should be performed, although they are often negative. Intravenous antibiotics for 4 to 6 weeks with bracing is generally sufficient for treatment. Needle biopsy of the disc space is not usually necessary.

Diskitis

There is disagreement as to whether diskitis and vertebral osteomyelitis are distinct entities or different points along the continuum of a single disease.[53] Patients with diskitis present similarly to those with vertebral osteomyelitis, with low back pain, local tenderness, fever, and refusal to walk.[12,39,43,53,59] Refusal to bear weight and to allow range of motion of the spine are common. Diskitis most commonly affects children 2 to 3 years old.[43,152] Whether or not diskitis is infectious remains unresolved. Radiographs demonstrate disk narrowing, with advanced cases revealing erosion of end plates. Disks may even herniate into the vertebral body. *S. aureus* is the most common pathogen. Although many patients improve with immobilization alone, antibiotics are often used in severe cases.

Infections in Patients with Sickle Cell Anemia

Patients with sickle cell anemia are at increased risk for osteomyelitis.[36,41,52,135] This may be due to sluggish blood flow, anemia, low oxygen tension, and local ischemia. It is often quite difficult to differentiate between a sickle crisis and a musculoskeletal infection in these patients. In both instances the children present with bone pain and fever, along with laboratory findings of leukocytosis and elevated inflammatory markers (ESR and CRP). In some instances, musculoskeletal infections can result in severe anemia in patients with sickle cell anemia.[82]

In a series of 247 consecutive admissions for musculoskeletal complaints in children with sickle cell disease, Dalton and coworkers reported a 1.6% incidence of musculoskeletal infection.[32] The combination of a bone scan and a bone marrow scan has been shown to be highly effective in differentiating between sickle crises and musculoskeletal infection in these children.[134] Ultrasound, bone marrow scans, and MRI have been reported to assist in this differentiation as well.[127,153,164] *Salmonella* has been reported to be the most common infecting organism in osteomyelitis in patients with sickle cell arthritis, although *S. aureus* is also common.[21,36,41,52,95] Treatment should be as for other cases of acute osteomyelitis, although the frequency of *Salmonella* infections should be kept in mind when choosing antibiotics. Pathologic fractures have been reported as complications of osteomyelitis in sickle cell patients and are more commonly seen in acute cases than in chronic ones.[21,36,41,52,95]

Foot Punctures

Infection occurs in up to 15% of foot puncture wounds, including deep infection of bone and/or cartilage in 1% to 2% of cases (Fig. 126-5).[45] Deep infection is often confused with an osteochondritis of the calcaneal apophysis and is caused by *Pseudomonas* organisms in more than 90% of cases.[61,72,77,115,147] These organisms are often found in athletic shoes in the absence of infection. The patient generally presents several days to weeks after the puncture injury with local swelling, erythema, pain, and difficulty walking. Surgical débridement and intravenous antibiotics are required in established cases of osteomyelitis. Antibiotic treatment should consist of a minimum 1- to 3-week course of aminoglycoside therapy.[61,72,77]

Tuberculosis of Bone and Joints

Tuberculosis remains a major health problem throughout the world. Worldwide, 8 million people become newly infected and 2 million die of tuberculosis each year. Most of these cases occur in developing nations.[160] In 2002, more than 15,000 cases were reported in the United States, nearly 1000 of which occurred in children younger than 15 years old.[20] Between 2% and 5% of patients with tuberculosis have bone or joint involvement.[19] Musculoskeletal tuberculosis infection involves the spine in 50% of cases.[116,157] Rasool reported polyostotic disease in 5 of

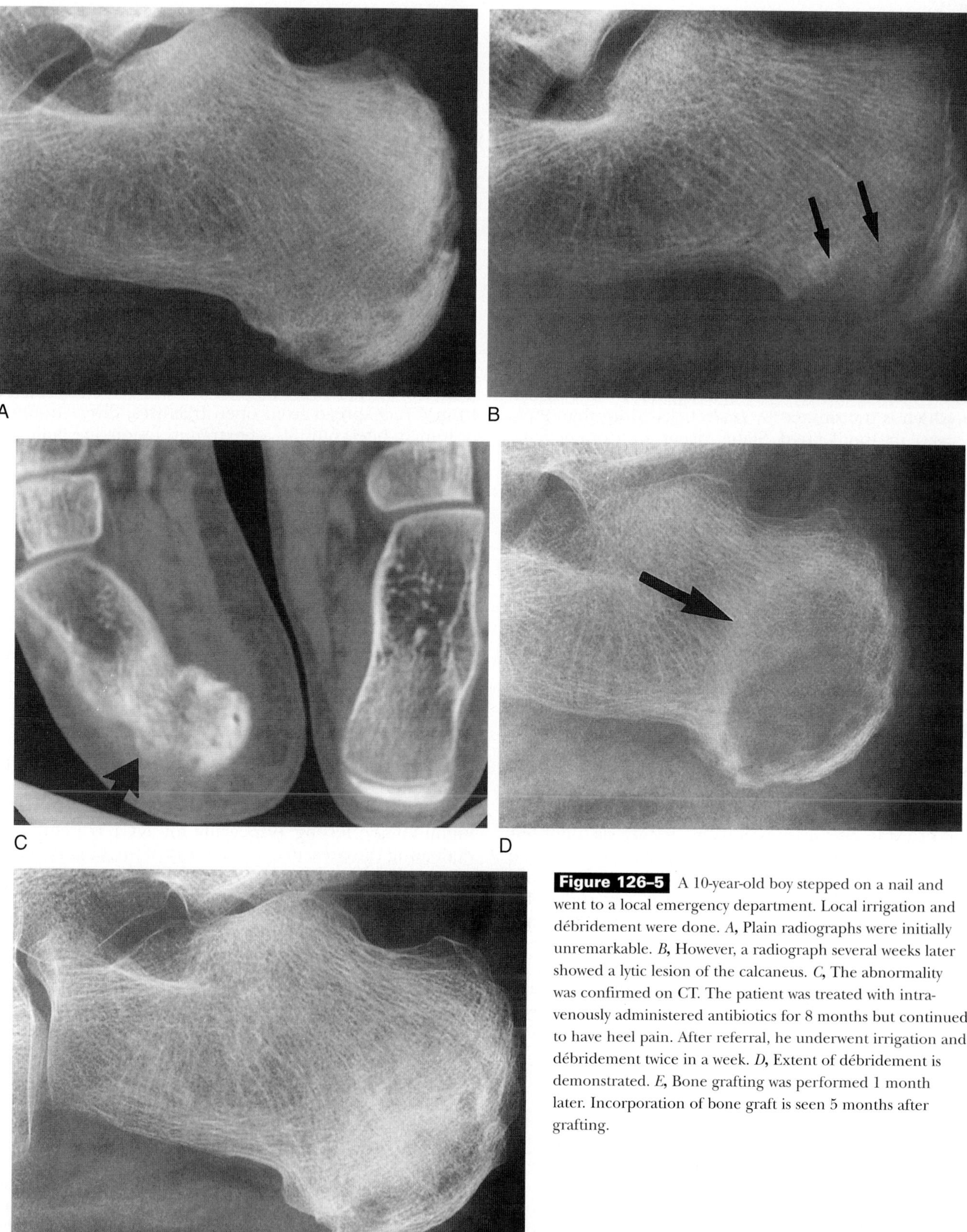

Figure 126–5 A 10-year-old boy stepped on a nail and went to a local emergency department. Local irrigation and débridement were done. *A*, Plain radiographs were initially unremarkable. *B*, However, a radiograph several weeks later showed a lytic lesion of the calcaneus. *C*, The abnormality was confirmed on CT. The patient was treated with intravenously administered antibiotics for 8 months but continued to have heel pain. After referral, he underwent irrigation and débridement twice in a week. *D*, Extent of débridement is demonstrated. *E*, Bone grafting was performed 1 month later. Incorporation of bone graft is seen 5 months after grafting.

42 children (12%) and growth disturbance in 6 of 50 bones (12%) with osseous tuberculous lesions.[116] Smears and cultures should be taken to confirm the diagnosis and to check for susceptibility to antimicrobial agents.[157] The destruction and deformity that may be seen on plain radiographs are not pathognomonic for tuberculosis.[42,116,157] MRI is an excellent imaging modality and may help differentiate tuberculosis from other disease processes.[4,57] The mainstay of treatment is antituberculous medication. Curettage may be needed for cystic lesions of the extremities.[42,116] Spinal surgery may be indicated for multiple-level involvement, neurologic deterioration, or progressive deformity.[78,79,157]

Lyme Arthritis

Lyme disease is caused by the spirochete *Borrelia burgdorferi*, which is transmitted by *Ixodes* ticks. More than 90% of cases in the United States occur in Connecticut, Rhode Island, New York, New Jersey, Pennsylvania, Wisconsin, Maryland, and Massachusetts.[140] Nearly 90% of children with Lyme disease present with either single or multiple lesions of erythema migrans.[50] The frequency of Lyme arthritis varies by series but appears less common with early detection and treatment. In a large series of pediatric Lyme disease patients, arthritis was reported in 6% of affected children, many of whom did not have cutaneous lesions.[50] Involvement of the heart and nervous system is also well described.[50,51,140]

Joint involvement may include either periodic involvement or continuous involvement (less than 4 weeks) of one to four joints.[124] Rose and associates also noted pauciarticular, polyarticular, and migratory forms of the disease.[124] The knee is the involved joint in 90% of cases with joint involvement.[5,139,140,161] Lyme arthritis can be confused with bacterial septic arthritis.[51,161] For nonclassic cases of Lyme disease, immunologic testing via a two-test approach is used to confirm the diagnosis. Synovial white blood cell counts often exceed 40,000 to 50,000/mL, with more than 75% neutrophils.[51,161] In one series, 4% (3 of 84 children) with Lyme arthritis were noted to have ocular inflammation; all three of these patients had visual symptoms associated with the inflammatory changes.[69]

Amoxicillin or doxycycline offers appropriate antibiotic coverage. With prompt antibiotic administration, chronic joint symptoms appear to affect fewer than 5% of those presenting with arthritis.[51]

Gonococcal Arthritis

N. gonorrhoeae is common in sexually active adolescents and in the victims of child abuse.[44,60,73,74,110,118,122,159,163] Approximately 1% of those with gonococcal infections will have a systemic infection characterized by fevers, rash, arthralgias, and tenosynovitis.[60] The knee and hands are most commonly involved, although any joint may be affected.[163] Irrigation and débridement of the infected joint are most commonly performed, although serial aspirations of accessible joints may be considered. Cultures of synovial fluid have low yields; and cervical, vaginal, anal, oral, skin, and/or blood cultures may help increase the yield.[60] Special culture media (e.g., chocolate agar and Thayer-Martin agar) are needed. Parenteral antibiotic treatment with third-generation cephalosporins is generally recommended for 1 to 2 weeks.

Actinomycotic Osteomyelitis

Actinomyces israelii is commonly found in the oropharynx and generally is a commensal organism.[167] This organism can become a pathogen after soft tissue trauma. More than 50% of cases of actinomycotic osteomyelitis occur in the face and neck, most commonly in the jaw after local infection.[9,98,147,151,167] Actinomycotic osteomyelitis involves the vertebral bodies in 40% of cases, nearly all of which are associated with other disease foci. Osseous involvement of the extremities is rare, usually resulting from direct spread from open fractures, direct trauma, or human bites; only 3% of extremity lesions are believed to be due to hematogenous spread.[9,98,147,151]

Coccidioidomycotic Osteomyelitis

Coccidioides immitis is a soil fungus endemic to the southwestern United States. Immunocompetent hosts generally have a mild upper respiratory tract infection and eradicate the infection in weeks or months.[155] In 5% to 10% of affected people, chronic pulmonary or disseminated disease results.[155] The disseminated disease can affect the musculoskeletal system, skin, or meninges. Polyostotic involvement was reported in 9 of 14 patients (64%) in one series.[31] Accurate diagnosis of musculoskeletal coccidioidomycosis is often delayed. Leukocyte counts and sedimentation rates are often normal. Skin testing can indicate prior exposure to *C. immitis*, and immunologic testing (especially for IgG) is helpful in evaluating the presence and severity of ongoing systemic disease. However, a local culture from either an aspirate or biopsy specimen is necessary to confirm the disease.

Surgical débridement is necessary in the vast majority of cases and should be combined with intravenous administration of amphotericin B (Fig. 126-6). Previous authors have reported better outcomes with combined medical and surgical therapy than with medical therapy alone.[16] Despite appropriate treatment, mortality rates of 12% to 17% have been reported in recent studies of musculoskeletal coccidioidomycosis.[89,165]

SUMMARY

Bone and joint infections remain an important problem encountered in the care of children. These are serious infections that resulted in high mortality rates before the advent of antibiotics. Today, early detection and treatment are of paramount importance in limiting the potential for chronic sequelae. Antibiotic treatment, although initially empirical, should be guided by specific culture results for each individual organism. (Frequently used antibiotics and dosing regimens are listed in Table 126-4.)

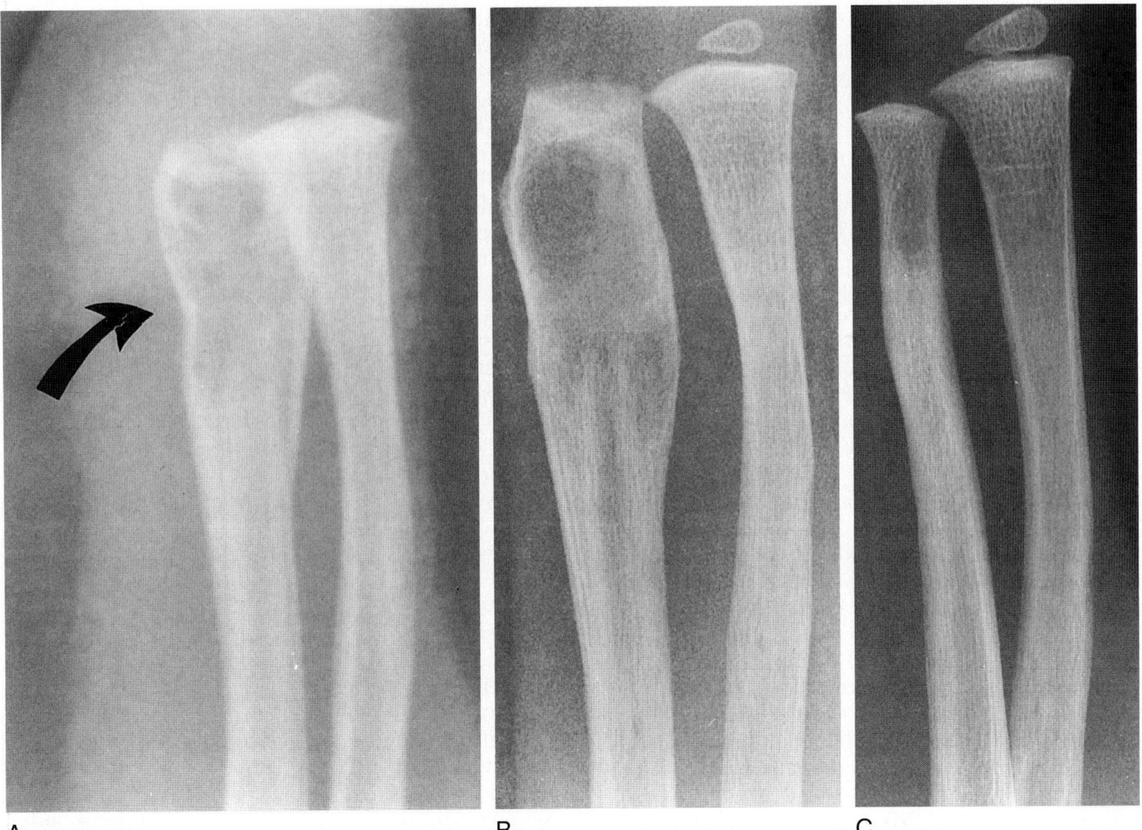

Figure 126–6 A 14-month-old boy presented with a 1-month history of swelling in the right distal forearm and an erythrocyte sedimentation rate of 41 mm/hr. *A*, A lytic lesion of the distal ulna was evident on plain radiographs. Differential diagnosis included infection and tumor, and the child underwent open biopsy and curettage. Pathologic examination demonstrated coccidioidomycosis. The patient was treated with a 6-month course of amphotericin followed by oral fluconazole. *B*, Radiograph obtained 2 months postoperatively. *C*, Radiograph obtained 12 months postoperatively reveals healing and remodeling of the ulna.

TABLE 126–4 Common Antibiotics in Pediatric Musculoskeletal Infection

Drug	Route	Dosage	Dosing Interval	Maximum Dosage
Amikacin	IV/IM	15-20 mg/kg/day	q 8-12 h	1.5 g/day
Amoxicillin	PO	80-100 mg/kg/day	q 6-8 h	
Ampicillin	PO	100-200 mg/kg/day	q 6 h	12 g/day
Cefazolin	IV	100 mg/kg/day	q 8 h	6.0 g/day
Cefotaxime	IV	100-200 mg/kg/day	q 6-8 h	12 g/day
Ceftazidime	IV/IM	150 mg/kg/day	q 6-8 h	6.0 g/day
Ceftriaxone	IV/IM	50-100 mg/kg/day	q 12-24 h	4.0 g/day
Cefuroxime	IV/IM	75-150 mg/kg/day	q 6-8 h	6.0 g/day
Cephalexin	PO	100-150 mg/kg/day	q 6 h	4.0 g/day
Ciprofloxacin*	IV	30 mg/kg/day	q 12 h	800 mg/day
	PO	30 mg/kg/day	q 12 h	1.5 g/day
Clindamycin*	IV	30-40 mg/kg/day	q 6-8 h	4.8 g/day
	PO	20-40 mg/kg/day	q 6-8 h	1.8 g/day
Dicloxacillin	PO	75-100 mg/kg/day	q 6 h	
Gentamicin	IV/IM	5.0-7.5 mg/kg/day	q 8 h	
Methicillin	IV/IM	200 mg/kg/day	q 6 h	
Nafcillin	IV	100-150 mg/kg/day	q 6 h	
Oxacillin	IV	150 mg/kg/day	q 6 h	12 g/day
Penicillin*	IV	150,000 U/kg/day	q 6 h	24 million units/day
	PO	125 mg/kg/day	q 4-6 h	3.0 g/day
Sulfamethoxazole/trimethoprim	IV/PO	10 mg/kg/day (of trimethoprim)	q 12 h	
Vancomycin	IV	40 mg/kg/day	q 6 h	4.0 g/day

*Indicates different enteral and parenteral daily and/or maximum dosages.
Data from references 60, 61, 101, 138, and 145.

Débridement is often needed in cases that present late. Even with prompt diagnosis and treatment, long-term sequelae such as late arthritis, chronic osteomyelitis, growth arrest, limb-length discrepancy, and angular deformity may be seen.

REFERENCES

1. Abernethy LJ, Lee YC, Cole WG: Ultrasound localization of subperiosteal abscesses in children with late-acute osteomyelitis. J Pediatr Orthop 1993;13:766-768.
2. Almquist EE: The changing epidemiology of septic arthritis in children. Clin Orthop 1970;68:96-99.
3. Andrew TA, Porter K: Primary subacute epiphyseal osteomyelitis: A report of three cases. J Pediatr Orthop 1985;5:155-157.
4. Andronikou S, Jadwat S, Douis H: Patterns of disease on MRI in 53 children with tuberculous spondylitis and the role of gadolinium. Pediatr Radiol 2002;32:798-805.
5. Bachman DT, Srivastava G: Emergency department presentations of Lyme disease in children. Pediatr Emerg Care 1998;14:356-361.
6. Beaupre A, Carroll N: The three syndromes of iliac osteomyelitis in children. J Bone Joint Surg Am 1979; 61:1087-1092.
7. Betz RR, Cooperman DR, Wopperer JM, et al: Late sequelae of septic arthritis of the hip in infancy and childhood. J Pediatr Orthop 1990;10:365-372.
8. Bjorksten B, Gustavson KH, Eriksson B, et al: Chronic recurrent multifocal osteomyelitis and pustulosis palmoplantaris. J Pediatr 1978;93:227-231.
9. Blinkhorn RJ Jr, Strimbu V, Effron D, et al: "Punch" actinomycosis causing osteomyelitis of the hand. Arch Intern Med 1988;148:2668-2670.
10. Bohay DR, Gray JM: Sacroiliac joint pyarthrosis. Orthop Rev 1993;22:817-823.
11. Borella L, Goobar JE, Summitt RL, et al: Septic arthritis in childhood. J Pediatr 1963;62:742-747.
12. Boston HC Jr, Bianco AJ Jr, Rhodes KH: Disk space infections in children. Orthop Clin North Am 1975;6: 953-964.
13. Bousvaros A, Marcon M, Treem W, et al: Chronic recurrent multifocal osteomyelitis associated with chronic inflammatory bowel disease in children. Dig Dis Sci 1999;44: 2500-2507.
14. Boutin RD, Brossmann J, Sartoris DJ, et al: Update on imaging of orthopedic infections. Orthop Clin North Am 1998;29:41-66.
15. Brand RA, Black H: *Pseudomonas* osteomyelitis following puncture wounds in children. J Bone Joint Surg Am 1974; 56:1637-1642.
16. Bried JM, Galgiani JN: *Coccidioides immitis* infections in bones and joints. Clin Orthop 1986;235-243.
17. Canale ST, Harkness RM, Thomas PA, et al: Does aspiration of bones and joints affect results of later bone scanning? J Pediatr Orthop 1985;5:23-26.
18. Canale ST, Puhl J, Watson FM, et al: Acute osteomyelitis following closed fractures: Report of three cases. J Bone Joint Surg Am 1975;57:415-418.
19. Centers for Disease Control and Prevention: Reported tuberculosis in the United States, 2002. Atlanta, U.S. Department of Health and Human Services, CDC, September 2003.
20. Centers for Disease Control and Prevention: Trends in tuberculosis morbidity—United States, 1992-2002. MMWR Morb Mortal Wkly Rep 2003;52:217-220, 222.
21. Chambers JB, Forsythe DA, Bertrand SL, et al: Retrospective review of osteoarticular infections in a pediatric sickle cell age group. J Pediatr Orthop 2000;20:682-685.
22. Chung SM: The arterial supply of the developing proximal end of the human femur. J Bone Joint Surg Am 1976;58: 961-970.
23. Cole WG, Dalziel RE, Leitl S: Treatment of acute osteomyelitis in childhood. J Bone Joint Surg Br 1982;64:218-223.
24. Connolly LP, Connolly SA, Drubach LA, et al: Acute hematogenous osteomyelitis of children: Assessment of skeletal scintigraphy-based diagnosis in the era of MRI. J Nucl Med 2002;43:1310-1316.
25. Connolly LP, Treves ST, Connolly SA, et al: Pediatric skeletal scintigraphy: Applications of pinhole magnification. Radiographics 1998;18:341-351.
26. Craigen MA, Watters J, Hackett JS: The changing epidemiology of osteomyelitis in children. J Bone Joint Surg Br 1992;74:541-545.
27. Curtiss PH Jr: Cartilage damage in septic arthritis. Clin Orthop 1969;64:87-90.
28. Curtiss PH Jr, Klein L: Destruction of articular cartilage in septic arthritis: I. In vitro studies. Am J Orthop 1963;45A: 797-806.
29. Curtiss PH Jr, Klein L: Destruction of articular cartilage in septic arthritis: II. In vivo studies. J Bone Joint Surg Am 1965;47:1595-1604.
30. Dagan R: Management of acute hematogenous osteomyelitis and septic arthritis in the pediatric patient. Pediatr Infect Dis J 1993;12:88-92.
31. Dalinka MK, Dinnenberg S, Greendyk WH, et al: Roentgenographic features of osseous coccidioidomycosis and differential diagnosis. J Bone Joint Surg Am 1971;53:1157-1164.
32. Dalton GP, Drummond DS, Davidson RS, et al: Bone infarction versus infection in sickle cell disease in children. J Pediatr Orthop 1996;16:540-544.
33. Dangman BC, Hoffer FA, Rand FF, et al: Osteomyelitis in children: Gadolinium-enhanced MR imaging. Radiology 1992;182:743-747.
34. Del Beccaro MA, Champoux AN, Bockers T, et al: Septic arthritis versus transient synovitis of the hip: The value of screening laboratory tests. Ann Emerg Med 1992;21: 1418-1422.
35. Dich VQ, Nelson JD, Haltalin KC: Osteomyelitis in infants and children: A review of 163 cases. Am J Dis Child 1975; 129:1273-1278.
36. Diggs LW: Bone and joint lesions in sickle-cell disease. Clin Orthop 1967;52:119-143.
37. Dirschl DR: Acute pyogenic osteomyelitis in children. Orthop Rev 1994;23:305-312.
38. Dormans JP, Drummond DS: Pediatric hematogenous osteomyelitis: new trends in presentation, diagnosis, and treatment. J Am Acad Orthop Surg 1994;2:333-341.
39. Early SD, Kay RM, Tolo VT: Childhood diskitis. J Am Acad Orthop Surg 2003;11:413-420.
40. Earwaker JW, Cotten A: SAPHO: Syndrome or concept? Imaging findings. Skeletal Radiol 2003;32:311-327.
41. Ebong WW: Pathological fracture complicating long bone osteomyelitis in patients with sickle cell disease. J Pediatr Orthop 1986;6:177-181.
42. Eren A, Atay EF, Omeroglu H, et al: Solitary cystic tuberculosis of long tubular bones in children. J Pediatr Orthop B 2003;12:72-75.
43. Fernandez M, Carrol CL, Baker CJ: Discitis and vertebral osteomyelitis in children: An 18-year review. Pediatrics 2000;105:1299-1304.
44. Feroli KL, Burstein GR: Adolescent sexually transmitted diseases: New recommendations for diagnosis, treatment,

and prevention. MCN Am J Matern Child Nurs 2003;28: 113-118.
45. Fitzgerald RH Jr, Cowan JD: Puncture wounds of the foot. Orthop Clin North Am 1975;6:965-972.
46. Frederiksen B, Christiansen P, Knudsen FU: Acute osteomyelitis and septic arthritis in the neonate, risk factors and outcome. Eur J Pediatr 1993;152:577-580.
47. Gamble JG, Rinsky LA: Chronic recurrent multifocal osteomyelitis: A distinct clinical entity. J Pediatr Orthop 1986;6:579-584.
48. Gamble JG, Rinsky LA: *Kingella kingae* infection in healthy children. J Pediatr Orthop 1988;8:445-449.
49. Gentry LO: Antibiotic therapy for osteomyelitis. Infect Dis Clin North Am 1990;4:485-499.
50. Gerber MA, Shapiro ED, Burke GS, et al: Lyme disease in children in southeastern Connecticut. Pediatric Lyme Disease Study Group. N Engl J Med 1996;335:1270-1274.
51. Gerber MA, Zemel LS, Shapiro ED: Lyme arthritis in children: Clinical epidemiology and long-term outcomes. Pediatrics 1998;102:905-908.
52. Givner LB, Luddy RE, Schwartz AD: Etiology of osteomyelitis in patients with major sickle hemoglobinopathies. J Pediatr 1981;99:411-413.
53. Glazer PA, Hu SS: Pediatric spinal infections. Orthop Clin North Am 1996;27:111-123.
54. Gledhill RB: Subacute osteomyelitis in children. Clin Orthop 1973;96:57-69.
55. Gold RH, Hawkins RA, Katz RD: Bacterial osteomyelitis: Findings on plain radiography, CT, MR, and scintigraphy. AJR Am J Roentgenol 1991;157:365-370.
56. Goldstein WM, Gleason TF, Barmada R: A comparison between arthrotomy and irrigation and débridement and multiple aspirations in the treatment of pyogenic arthritis: A histological study in a rabbit model. Orthopedics 1983; 6:1309.
57. Griffith JF, Kumta SM, Leung PC, et al: Imaging of musculoskeletal tuberculosis: A new look at an old disease. Clin Orthop 2002:32-39.
58. Gristina AG, Naylor PT, Myrvik QN: Musculoskeletal infection, microbial adhesion, and antibiotic resistance. Infect Dis Clin North Am 1990;4:391-408.
59. Gutierrez KM: Diskitis. In Long SS, Pickering LK, Prober CG (eds): Principles and Practice of Pediatric Infectious Diseases. New York, Churchill Livingstone, 2003, pp 481-484.
60. Gutierrez KM: Infectious and inflammatory arthritis. In Long SS, Pickering LK, Prober CG (eds): Principles and Practice of Pediatric Infectious Diseases. New York, Churchill Livingstone, 2003, pp 475-481.
61. Gutierrez KM: Osteomyelitis. In Long SS, Pickering LK, Prober CG (eds): Principles and Practice of Pediatric Infectious Diseases. New York, Churchill Livingstone, 2003, pp 467-474.
62. Gwynne-Jones DP, Stott NS: Community-acquired methicillin-resistant *Staphylococcus aureus:* A cause of musculoskeletal sepsis in children. J Pediatr Orthop 1999;19:413-416.
63. Haliloglu M, Kleiman MB, Siddiqui AR, et al: Osteomyelitis and pyogenic infection of the sacroiliac joint: MRI findings and review. Pediatr Radiol 1994;24:333-335.
64. Hammond PJ, Macnicol MF: Osteomyelitis of the pelvis and proximal femur: Diagnostic difficulties. J Pediatr Orthop B 2001;10:113-119.
65. Hoffman EB, de Beer JD, Keys G, et al: Diaphyseal primary subacute osteomyelitis in children. J Pediatr Orthop 1990; 10:250-254.
66. Holzel H, de Saxe M: Septicaemia in paediatric intensive-care patients at the Hospital for Sick Children, Great Ormond Street. J Hosp Infect 1992;22:185-195.
67. Howard CB, Einhorn M, Dagan R, et al: Ultrasound in diagnosis and management of acute haematogenous osteomyelitis in children. J Bone Joint Surg Br 1993;75:79-82.
68. Howard CB, Einhorun MS: Ultrasound in the detection of subperiosteal abscesses. J Bone Joint Surg Br 1991;73: 175-176.
69. Huppertz HI, Munchmeier D, Lieb W: Ocular manifestations in children and adolescents with Lyme arthritis. Br J Ophthalmol 1999;83:1149-1152.
70. Hussain FM, Boyle-Vavra S, Bethel CD, et al: Current trends in community-acquired methicillin-resistant *Staphylococcus aureus* at a tertiary care pediatric facility. Pediatr Infect Dis J 2000;19:1163-1166.
71. Hussain FM, Boyle-Vavra S, Daum RS: Community-acquired methicillin-resistant *Staphylococcus aureus* colonization in healthy children attending an outpatient pediatric clinic. Pediatr Infect Dis J 2001;20:763-767.
72. Inaba AS, Zukin DD, Perro M: An update on the evaluation and management of plantar puncture wounds and *Pseudomonas* osteomyelitis. Pediatr Emerg Care 1992;8:38-44.
73. Ingram DL: *Neisseria gonorrhoeae* in children. Pediatr Ann 1994;23:341-345.
74. Ingram DM, Miller WC, Schoenbach VJ, et al: Risk assessment for gonococcal and chlamydial infections in young children undergoing evaluation for sexual abuse. Pediatrics 2001;107:E73.
75. Jackson MA, Burry VF, Olson LC: Pyogenic arthritis associated with adjacent osteomyelitis: Identification of the sequela-prone child. Pediatr Infect Dis J 1992;11:9-13.
76. Jackson MA, Nelson JD: Etiology and medical management of acute suppurative bone and joint infections in pediatric patients. J Pediatr Orthop 1982;2:313-323.
77. Jacobs RF, McCarthy RE, Elser JM: *Pseudomonas* osteochondritis complicating puncture wounds of the foot in children: A 10-year evaluation. J Infect Dis 1989;160:657-661.
78. Jain AK: Treatment of tuberculosis of the spine with neurologic complications. Clin Orthop 2002;75-84.
79. Jain AK, Sinha S: Tuberculosis of the thoracic spine. J Bone Joint Surg Br 2003;85:150; author reply 150.
80. Jaramillo D, Treves ST, Kasser JR, et al: Osteomyelitis and septic arthritis in children: Appropriate use of imaging to guide treatment. AJR Am J Roentgenol 1995;165:399-403.
81. Jurriaans E, Singh NP, Finlay K, et al: Imaging of chronic recurrent multifocal osteomyelitis. Radiol Clin North Am 2001;39:305-327.
82. Juwah AI, Nlemadim A, Kaine W: Clinical presentation of severe anemia in pediatric patients with sickle cell anemia seen in Enugu, Nigeria. Am J Hematol 2003;72:185-191.
83. Kaiser S, Jacobsson H, Hirsch G: Specific or superfluous? Doubtful clinical value of granulocyte scintigraphy in osteomyelitis in children. J Pediatr Orthop B 2001;10: 109-112.
84. Kaiser S, Jorulf H, Hirsch G: Clinical value of imaging techniques in childhood osteomyelitis. Acta Radiol 1998;39: 523-531.
85. Kaiser S, Rosenborg M: Early detection of subperiosteal abscesses by ultrasonography: A means for further successful treatment in pediatric osteomyelitis. Pediatr Radiol 1994;24:336-339.
86. Kleinman PK: A regional approach to osteomyelitis of the lower extremities in children. Radiol Clin North Am 2002;40:1033-1059.
87. Kocher MS, Mandiga R, Murphy JM, et al: A clinical practice guideline for treatment of septic arthritis in children: Efficacy in improving process of care and effect on outcome of septic arthritis of the hip. J Bone Joint Surg Am 2003; 85:994-999.

88. Kocher MS, Zurakowski D, Kasser JR: Differentiating between septic arthritis and transient synovitis of the hip in children: An evidence-based clinical prediction algorithm. J Bone Joint Surg Am 1999;81:1662-1670.
89. Kushwaha VP, Shaw BA, Gerardi JA, et al: Musculoskeletal coccidioidomycosis: A review of 25 cases. Clin Orthop 1996:190-199.
90. Lundy DW, Kehl DK: Increasing prevalence of *Kingella kingae* in osteoarticular infections in young children. J Pediatr Orthop 1998;18:262-267.
91. Lunseth PA, Heiple KG: Prognosis in septic arthritis of the hip in children. Clin Orthop 1979:81-85.
92. Mah ET, LeQuesne GW, Gent RJ, et al: Ultrasonic features of acute osteomyelitis in children. J Bone Joint Surg Br 1994;76:969-974.
93. Mah ET, LeQuesne GW, Gent RJ, et al: Ultrasonic signs of pelvic osteomyelitis in children. Pediatr Radiol 1994;24: 484-487.
94. Mahboubi S, Morris MC: Imaging of spinal infections in children. Radiol Clin North Am 2001;39:215-222.
95. Mallouh A, Talab Y: Bone and joint infection in patients with sickle cell disease. J Pediatr Orthop 1985;5:158-162.
96. Maraqa NF, Gomez MM, Rathore MH: Outpatient parenteral antimicrobial therapy in osteoarticular infections in children. J Pediatr Orthop 2002;22:506-510.
97. Marcinak JF, Frank AL: Treatment of community-acquired methicillin-resistant *Staphylococcus aureus* in children. Curr Opin Infect Dis 2003;16:265-269.
98. Mesgarzadeh M, Bonakdarpour A, Redecki PD: Case report 395: Hematogenous *Actinomyces* osteomyelitis (calcaneus). Skeletal Radiol 1986;15:584-588.
99. Morrey BF, Bianco AJ Jr, Rhodes KH: Septic arthritis in children. Orthop Clin North Am 1975;6:923-934.
100. Morrey BF, Peterson HA: Hematogenous pyogenic osteomyelitis in children. Orthop Clin North Am 1975; 6:935-951.
101. Morrissy RT: Bone and joint sepsis. In Morrissy RT, Weinstein SL (eds): Lovell and Winter's Pediatric Orthopaedics. Philadelphia, Lippincott Williams & Wilkins, 2001, pp 459-505.
102. Morrissy RT, Haynes DW: Acute hematogenous osteomyelitis: A model with trauma as an etiology. J Pediatr Orthop 1989;9:447-456.
103. Mortensson W, Edeburn G, Fries M, et al: Chronic recurrent multifocal osteomyelitis in children: A roentgenologic and scintigraphic investigation. Acta Radiol 1988;29:565-570.
104. Nakamura MM, Rohling KL, Shashaty M, et al: Prevalence of methicillin-resistant *Staphylococcus aureus* nasal carriage in the community pediatric population. Pediatr Infect Dis J 2002;21:917-922.
105. Nelson JD: Acute osteomyelitis in children. Infect Dis Clin North Am 1990;4:513-522.
106. Nelson JD, Bucholz RW, Kusmiesz H, et al: Benefits and risks of sequential parenteral-oral cephalosporin therapy for suppurative bone and joint infections. J Pediatr Orthop 1982;2:255-262.
107. Ogden JA, Lister G: The pathology of neonatal osteomyelitis. Pediatrics 1975;55:474-478.
108. Ono CM, Albertson KS, Reinker KA, et al: Acquired radial clubhand deformity due to osteomyelitis. J Pediatr Orthop 1995;15:161-168.
109. Oudjhane K, Azouz EM: Imaging of osteomyelitis in children. Radiol Clin North Am 2001;39:251-266.
110. Palusci VJ, Reeves MJ: Testing for genital gonorrhea infections in prepubertal girls with suspected sexual abuse. Pediatr Infect Dis J 2003;22:618-623.
111. Peltola H, Unkila-Kallio L, Kallio MJ: Simplified treatment of acute staphylococcal osteomyelitis of childhood. The Finnish Study Group. Pediatrics 1997;99:846-850.
112. Pennington WT, Mott MP, Thometz JG, et al: Photopenic bone scan osteomyelitis: A clinical perspective. J Pediatr Orthop 1999;19:695-698.
113. Perlman MH, Patzakis MJ, Kumar PJ, et al: The incidence of joint involvement with adjacent osteomyelitis in pediatric patients. J Pediatr Orthop 2000;20:40-43.
114. Peters W, Irving J, Letts M: Long-term effects of neonatal bone and joint infection on adjacent growth plates. J Pediatr Orthop 1992;12:806-810.
115. Puffinbarger WR, Gruel CR, Herndon WA, et al: Osteomyelitis of the calcaneus in children. J Pediatr Orthop 1996;16:224-230.
116. Rasool MN: Osseous manifestations of tuberculosis in children. J Pediatr Orthop 2001;21:749-755.
117. Riebel TW, Nasir R, Nazarenko O: The value of sonography in the detection of osteomyelitis. Pediatr Radiol 1996; 26:291-297.
118. Rimsza ME, Niggemann EH: Medical evaluation of sexually abused children: A review of 311 cases. Pediatrics 1982;69: 8-14.
119. Rissing JP: Animal models of osteomyelitis: Knowledge, hypothesis, and speculation. Infect Dis Clin North Am 1990;4:377-390.
120. Roberts JM, Drummond DS, Breed AL, et al: Subacute hematogenous osteomyelitis in children: A retrospective study. J Pediatr Orthop 1982;2:249-254.
121. Robertson DE: Acute hematogenous osteomyelitis. J Bone Joint Surg 1938;20:35.
122. Robinson AJ, Watkeys JE, Ridgway GL: Sexually transmitted organisms in sexually abused children. Arch Dis Child 1998;79:356-358.
123. Roine I, Arguedas A, Faingezicht I, et al: Early detection of sequela-prone osteomyelitis in children with use of simple clinical and laboratory criteria. Clin Infect Dis 1997; 24:849-853.
124. Rose CD, Fawcett PT, Eppes SC, et al: Pediatric Lyme arthritis: Clinical spectrum and outcome. J Pediatr Orthop 1994;14:238-241.
125. Rotbart HA, Glode MP: *Haemophilus influenzae* type b septic arthritis in children: Report of 23 cases. Pediatrics 1985;75:254-259.
126. Sabath LD, Garner C, Wilcox C, et al: Effect of inoculum and of beta-lactamase on the anti-staphylococcal activity of thirteen penicillins and cephalosporins. Antimicrob Agents Chemother 1975;8:344-349.
127. Sadat-Ali M, al-Umran K, al-Habdan I, et al: Ultrasonography: Can it differentiate between vaso-occlusive crisis and acute osteomyelitis in sickle cell disease? J Pediatr Orthop 1998; 18:552-554.
128. Sattler CA, Mason EO Jr, Kaplan SL: Prospective comparison of risk factors and demographic and clinical characteristics of community-acquired, methicillin-resistant versus methicillin-susceptible *Staphylococcus aureus* infection in children. Pediatr Infect Dis J 2002;21:910-917.
129. Schauwecker DS, Braunstein EM, Wheat LJ: Diagnostic imaging of osteomyelitis. Infect Dis Clin North Am 1990; 4:441-463.
130. Scheman RJ, Janota M, Lewin P: The production of experimental osteomyelitis. JAMA 1941;117:1525.
131. Schutzman SA, Teach S: Upper-extremity impairment in young children. Ann Emerg Med 1995;26:474-479.
132. Scott RJ, Christofersen MR, Robertson WW Jr, et al: Acute osteomyelitis in children: A review of 116 cases. J Pediatr Orthop 1990;10:649-652.
133. Shaw BA, Kasser JR: Acute septic arthritis in infancy and childhood. Clin Orthop 1990;212-225.
134. Skaggs DL, Kim SK, Greene NW, et al: Differentiation between bone infarction and acute osteomyelitis in children with sickle-cell disease with use of sequential

radionuclide bone-marrow and bone scans. J Bone Joint Surg Am 2001;83:1810-1813.
135. Smith JA: Bone disorders in sickle cell disease. Hematol Oncol Clin North Am 1996;10:1345-1356.
136. Smith JW: Infectious arthritis. Infect Dis Clin North Am 1990;4:523-538.
137. Song J, Letts M, Monson R: Differentiation of psoas muscle abscess from septic arthritis of the hip in children. Clin Orthop 2001;258-265.
138. Song KM, Sloboda JF: Acute hematogenous osteomyelitis in children. J Am Acad Orthop Surg 2001;9:166-175.
139. Sood SK: Lyme disease. Pediatr Infect Dis J 1999;18: 913-925.
140. Sood SK, Ilowite NT: Lyme arthritis in children: Is chronic arthritis a common complication? J Rheumatol 2000;27: 1836-1838.
141. Stanton RP, Lopez-Sosa FH, Doidge R: Chronic recurrent multifocal osteomyelitis. Orthop Rev 1993;22:229-233.
142. Strong M, Lejman T, Michno P, et al: Sequelae from septic arthritis of the knee during the first two years of life. J Pediatr Orthop 1994;14:745-751.
143. Strouse PJ, DiPietro MA, Adler RS: Pediatric hip effusions: Evaluation with power Doppler sonography. Radiology 1998;206:731-735.
144. Strouse PJ, DiPietro MA, Teo EL, et al: Power Doppler evaluation of joint effusions: Investigation in a rabbit model. Pediatr Radiol 1999;29:617-623.
145. Sucato DJ, Schwend RM, Gillespie R: Septic arthritis of the hip in children. J Am Acad Orthop Surg 1997;5: 249-260.
146. Swiontkowski MF: Surgical approaches in osteomyelitis: Use of laser Doppler flowmetry to determine nonviable bone. Infect Dis Clin North Am 1990;4:501-512.
147. Syriopoulou VP, Smith AL: Osteomyelitis and septic arthritis. In Feigen RD, Cherry JD (eds): Textbook of Pediatric Infectious Diseases. Philadelphia, WB Saunders, 1992.
148. Tay BK, Deckey J, Hu SS: Spinal infections. J Am Acad Orthop Surg 2002;10:188-197.
149. Tetzlaff TR, Howard JB, McCraken GH, et al: Antibiotic concentrations in pus and bone of children with osteomyelitis. J Pediatr 1978;92:135-140.
150. Tetzlaff TR, McCracken GH Jr, Nelson JD: Oral antibiotic therapy for skeletal infections of children: II. Therapy of osteomyelitis and suppurative arthritis. J Pediatr 1978;92: 485-490.
151. Thisted E, Poulsen P, Christensen PO: Actinomycotic osteomyelitis in a child. J Laryngol Otol 1987;101:746-748.
152. Turpin S, Lambert R: Role of scintigraphy in musculoskeletal and spinal infections. Radiol Clin North Am 2001;39:169-189.
153. Umans H, Haramati N, Flusser G: The diagnostic role of gadolinium enhanced MRI in distinguishing between acute medullary bone infarct and osteomyelitis. Magn Reson Imaging 2000;18:255-262.
154. Unkila-Kallio L, Kallio MJ, Peltola H: The usefulness of C-reactive protein levels in the identification of concurrent septic arthritis in children who have acute hematogenous osteomyelitis: A comparison with the usefulness of the erythrocyte sedimentation rate and the white blood-cell count. J Bone Joint Surg Am 1994;76:848-853.
155. Vaz A, Pineda-Roman M, Thomas AR, et al: Coccidioidomycosis: An update. Hosp Pract (Off Ed) 1998;33: 105-108, 113-115, 119-120.
156. Viani RM, Bromberg K, Bradley JS: Obturator internus muscle abscess in children: Report of seven cases and review. Clin Infect Dis 1999;28:117-122.
157. Watts HG, Lifeso RM: Tuberculosis of bones and joints. J Bone Joint Surg Am 1996;78:288-298.
158. Whalen JL, Fitzgerald RH Jr, Morrissy RT: A histological study of acute hematogenous osteomyelitis following physeal injuries in rabbits. J Bone Joint Surg Am 1988;70: 1383-1392.
159. White BD: Red eyes and red rash with fever: An uncommon initial presentation for staphylococcal obturator abscess with adjacent ischial osteomyelitis. J Am Osteopath Assoc 1991;91:807-812.
160. WHO: Tuberculosis: Fact Sheet No. 104. Geneva, World Health Organization, 2002.
161. Willis AA, Widmann RF, Flynn JM, et al: Lyme arthritis presenting as acute septic arthritis in children. J Pediatr Orthop 2003;23:114-118.
162. Winters JL, Cahen I: Acute hematogenous osteomyelitis: A review of sixty-six cases. J Bone Joint Surg Am 1960; 42:691.
163. Wise CM, Morris CR, Wasilauskas BL, et al: Gonococcal arthritis in an era of increasing penicillin resistance: Presentations and outcomes in 41 recent cases (1985-1991). Arch Intern Med 1994;154:2690-2695.
164. Wong AL, Sakamoto KM, Johnson EE: Differentiating osteomyelitis from bone infarction in sickle cell disease. Pediatr Emerg Care 2001;17:60-63; quiz 64.
165. Wrobel CJ, Chappell ET, Taylor W: Clinical presentation, radiological findings, and treatment results of coccidioidomycosis involving the spine: Report on 23 cases. J Neurosurg 2001;95:33-39.
166. Yagupsky P, Dagan R: *Kingella kingae:* An emerging cause of invasive infections in young children. Clin Infect Dis 1997;24:860-866.
167. Yung BC, Cheng JC, Chan TT, et al: Aggressive thoracic actinomycosis complicated by vertebral osteomyelitis and epidural abscess leading to spinal cord compression. Spine 2000;25:745-748.
168. Zawin JK, Hoffer FA, Rand FF, et al: Joint effusion in children with an irritable hip: US diagnosis and aspiration. Radiology 1993;187:459-463.

Chapter 127

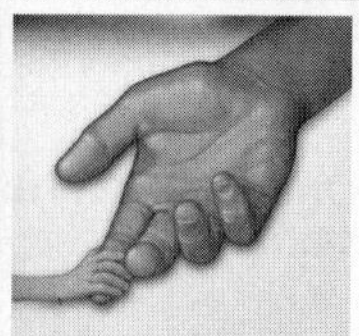

Amputations in Children

Randall T. Loder

The care of a child amputee crosses all pediatric surgical disciplines, as well as physical and psychosocial pediatric rehabilitation. A child amputee is markedly different from an adult amputee in etiology, surgical principles, and rehabilitation. Not only is the physical rehabilitation different, but psychosocial rehabilitation is also often as important if not more important than physical rehabilitation. As with all pediatric orthopedic conditions, growth is the fourth dimension and must be continuously remembered when caring for a child amputee.

Pediatric amputations consist of two main types: congenital and acquired. Congenital amputations include those that occur in utero and are noted at birth or, more commonly, those that occur as a result of definitive treatment of a particular congenital limb deficiency. Acquired amputations are usually due to trauma or disease (tumor, sepsis).

Children with amputations differ from adults in many ways.[43] The most common causes of amputation in children are congenital deficiencies, trauma, infection, and neoplasia; in adults, amputation is most commonly performed for a dysvascular limb (e.g., small-vessel disease secondary to diabetes mellitus). Multiple limb deficiencies are more frequent in children than adults because of differences in etiology (e.g., congenital deficiency, purpura fulminans, and trauma in children versus vascular disease in adults). As a result of continuing growth in a child, the residual limb in children also continues to grow. This continuing growth requires new prosthetics much more frequently than in adults; just as children need larger-sized clothes with growth, so do they need larger prostheses. Similarly, damage to the physis (growth plate) must be considered when contemplating surgical interventions. A condition unique to children is stump overgrowth as a result of continuous appositional bone formation at the end of a transosseous stump; it is for this reason that joint disarticulations are preferable to transosseous amputations in children. The activity level of most children is greater than that of adults with a dysvascular amputation. Consequently, the expected mechanical and functional demands on the residual limb and prosthetic fittings are different. The psychosocial challenges are different in the pediatric amputee than in an adult. The phantom phenomenon, however, is less common in children than in adults.

The guiding principles in pediatric amputations are to retain as much length as possible, preserve growth plates, perform disarticulations rather than transosseous amputations, and preserve as many joints as possible.

AMPUTATIONS RESULTING FROM CONGENITAL LIMB DEFICIENCY

Many congenital limb deficiencies are now diagnosed prenatally.[16,28] The expecting parents often consult the orthopedic surgeon before birth to learn about the limb deficiency, its prognosis, and therapeutic options. The classic classification system of congenital limb deficiency is that of Frantz and O'Rahilly[24] (Fig. 127-1).[34] Limb deficiencies are either terminal or intercalary. Terminal deficiencies are defined as no unaffected parts distal to or in line with the deficient portion. Intercalary deficiencies are defined as a middle part of the limb being deficient with the proximal and distal portions present. Both types are classified as transverse or paraxial. Transverse deficiencies occur across the entire width of the limb, whereas paraxial deficiencies involve only a medial or lateral limb deficiency. Paraxial deficiencies (congenital absence of a longitudinal element) are further denoted as preaxial (e.g., radial or tibial deficiency) or postaxial (e.g., ulnar or fibular deficiency).

Femoral Deficiency (Proximal Femoral Focal Deficiency)

Proximal femoral focal deficiency (PFFD), as it was known in the past, is now more properly termed congenital femoral deficiency. This term better reflects the wide spectrum of deformity that can occur, from minimal femoral shortening to complete femoral absence. Two classification schemes are used: the traditional scheme of Aitken[3] and the more recent classification of Gillespie and Torode[26,27] (Fig. 127-2A and B).[72] In children with classic PFFD, the thigh is shortened, abducted, externally rotated, and flexed (Fig. 127-3). Fibular deficiency is a common association.

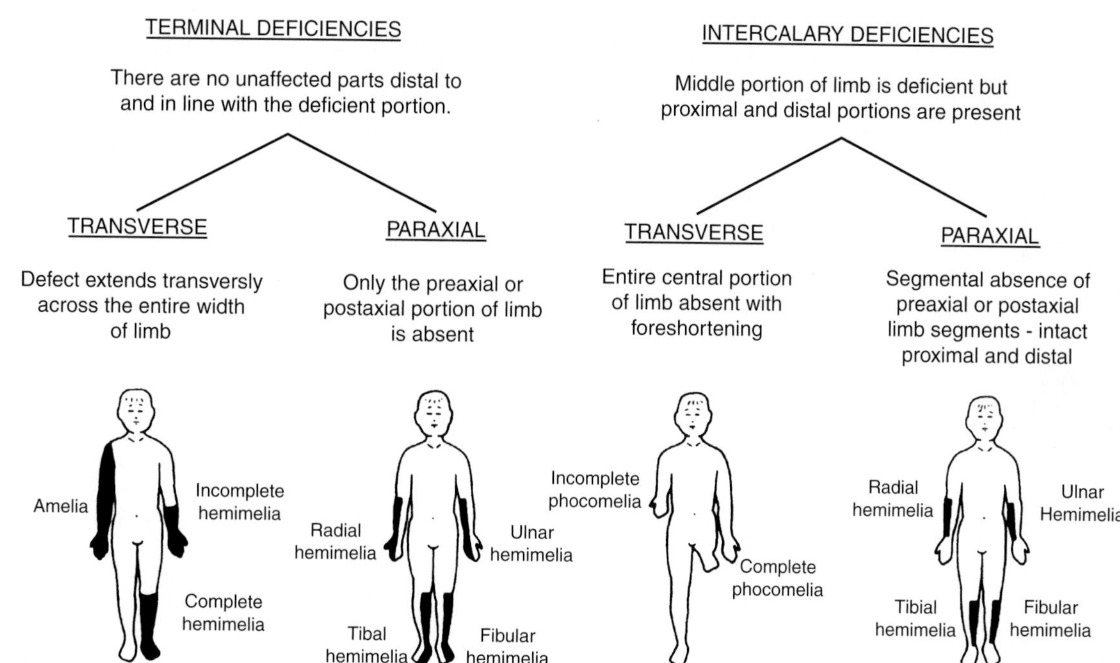

Figure 127–1 Frantz and O'Rahilly classification of congenital limb deficiencies. (From Herring JA, Cummings DR: The limb-deficient child. In Morrissy RT, Weinstein SL [eds]: Lovell and Winter's Pediatric Orthopaedics. Philadelphia, Lippincott-Raven, 1996, with permission.)

The foot is typically plantar-flexed and often deformed if associated with fibular deficiency.

Factors involved in determining treatment are the height of the foot relative to the opposite side, hip stability, and unilateral or bilateral involvement. In children with a Gillespie A deficiency, leg-lengthening/equalization procedures are often the selected treatment.[61] In children with a Gillespie B deficiency, prosthetic fitting is selected. A nonstandard prosthesis that accommodates the child's plantar-flexed foot is prescribed; if the foot is deformed, foot ablation (Syme amputation) may be performed to allow for easier, standard prosthetic fitting. However, patient satisfaction and function may be better with a nonconventional prosthesis[41] without amputation. When the overall length of the limb places the foot well below the contralateral knee and the foot has excellent motor function, a Van Nes rotationplasty is an option.[42,74] In this operation, the foot is rotated 180 degrees and the limb shortened through the knee or tibia (or both) such that the backward-appearing foot is at the level of the contralateral knee. The shortening allows rotation without tension on the neurovascular structures and simultaneously places the foot at the level of the contralateral knee. The "foot" then becomes a functional knee and the limb is fit with a below-knee prosthesis instead of a nonconventional above-knee prosthesis. The advantage of this procedure is reduced energy expenditure and better function than with foot ablation and an above-knee prosthesis.[23] The disadvantages are cosmetic, and it is often not accepted by the family or child. For those with a Gillespie C deficiency, prosthetic fitting is prescribed, with or without iliofemoral fusion.[70] Children with bilateral PFFD typically need no surgery or prosthetic fitting unless there is a marked discrepancy in leg length.

Fibular Deficiency

Fibular deficiency is the most common congenital lower extremity deficiency. This limb deficiency[2,71] is frequently associated with absent lateral rays, tarsal coalition, and fixed equinovalgus position of the foot[29]; a ball-and-socket ankle joint; a kyphotic tibia with overlying skin dimples; and absence of the knee cruciate ligaments (Fig. 127-4).[65] There are also varying degrees of femoral hypoplasia ranging from mild lateral femoral condylar hypoplasia to a congenitally short femur and PFFD. These patients may also have upper extremity anomalies, typically ulnar deficiency syndromes.

The most common classification scheme is that of Achterman and Kalamchi[2] (Fig. 127-5); a newer classification system takes into account both foot function and limb-length discrepancy (Table 127-1).[6] Treatment is based on the function of the foot, its potential for reconstruction, and severity of the limb-length discrepancy. With newer techniques for limb lengthening, it is now often possible to salvage feet and lengthen limbs that before would have undergone foot ablation and prosthetic fitting.[13,18,32,50,53,56] However, in a severe deformity, limb lengthening plus foot reconstruction does not restore ankle stability or subtalar joint function. Most surgical techniques used to achieve a plantigrade foot and equalization of limb length have been unsatisfactory in many series. The initial results are good, but longer-term follow-up demonstrates significant problems.[12] Thus, foot ablation (Syme or Boyd amputation) along with prosthetic fitting is still commonly selected for severe fibular deficiency. Limb lengthening is best suited for children who already have a plantigrade foot and stable hip, knee, and ankle joints.[13] Children with milder degrees of fibular

Type		Femoral head	Acetabulum	Femoral segment	Relationship among components of femur and acetabulum at skeletal maturity
A		Present	Normal	Short	Bony connection between components of femur Femoral head in acetabulum Subtrochanteric varus angulation, often with pseudarthrosis
B		Present	Adequate or moderately dysplastic	Short, usually proximal bony tuft	No osseous connection between head and shaft Femoral head in acetabulum
C		Absent or represented by ossicle	Severely dysplastic	Short, usually proximally tapered	May be osseous connection between shaft and proximal ossicle No articular relation between femur and acetabulum
D		Absent	Absent Obturator foramen enlarged Pelvis squared in bilateral cases	Short, deformed	(none)

A

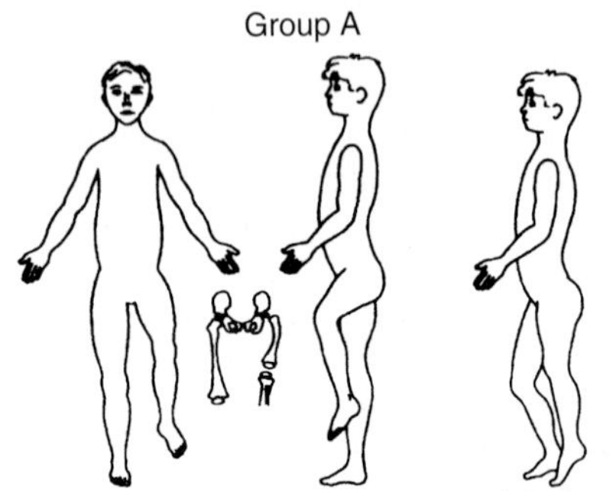
Group A
Child can extend hip and knee to weight bear

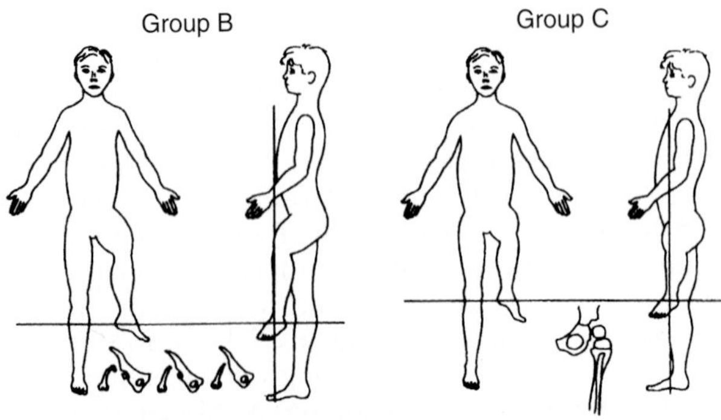
Group B
Group C
Horizontal line indicates length relationship to contralateral limb
Vertical line indicates anterior displacement of weight-bearing axis of tibia

B

Figure 127-2 Classifications of congenital femoral deficiency. *A*, Aitken classification of proximal femoral focal deficiency. There are four types of deficiency, A to D. *B*, Gillespie and Torode classification of femoral deficiency. Group A consists of those with simply a congenital short femur. Group B consists of those who are Aitken A, B, and C. Group C consists of those who are Aitken D (subtotal absence of the femur). (*A*, From Tachdjian MO: Pediatric Orthopedics. Philadelphia, WB Saunders, 1990; *B*, from Gillespie R: Classification of congenital abnormalities of the femur. In Herring JA, Birch JG [eds]: The Child with a Limb Deficiency. Rosemont, IL, American Academy of Orthopaedic Surgeons, 1998, p 63, with permission.)

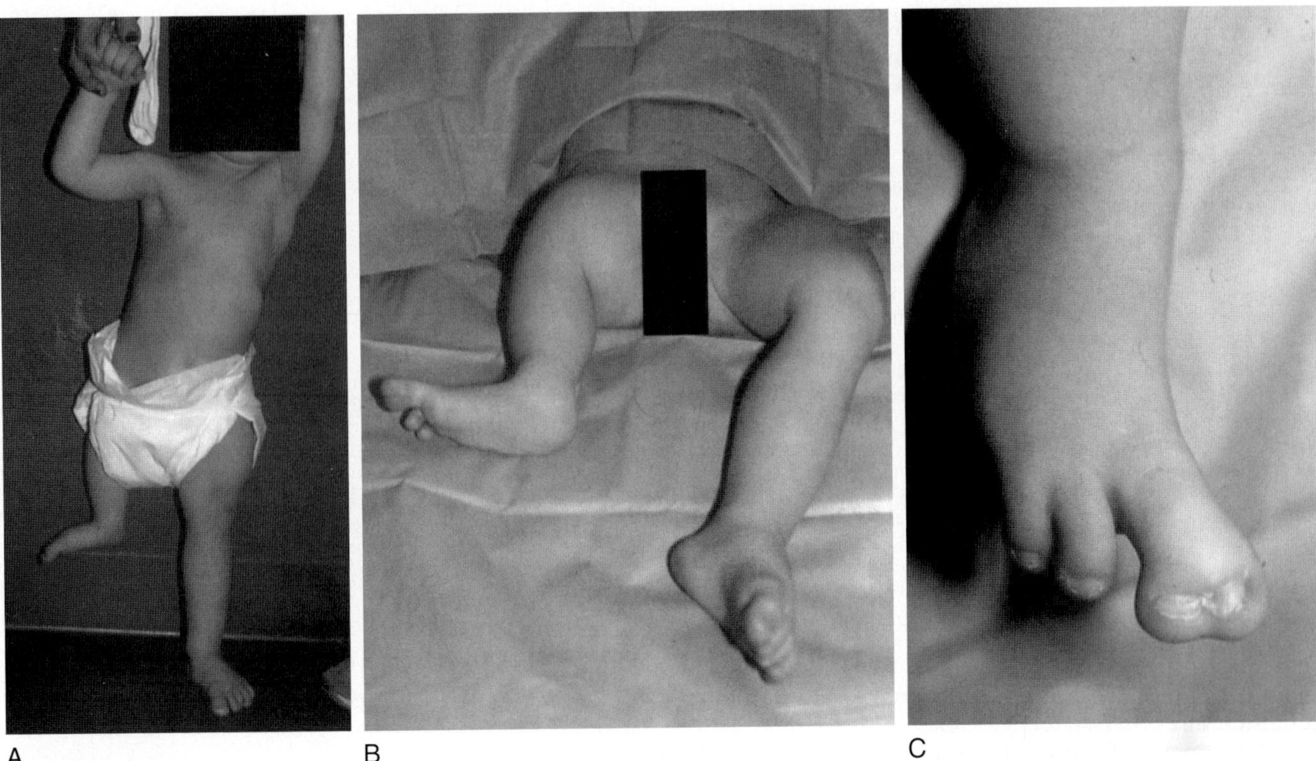

Figure 127–3 Clinical photograph of a child with a proximal femoral focal deficiency. *A*, When the child is standing, note the markedly shortened thigh, which is externally rotated, and the ankle nearly at the level of the opposite knee. When a child has this configuration and good active motor function of the ankle, the child is an excellent candidate for the Van Nes rotationplasty. *B*, When supine, note the marked flexion and abduction of the hip joint. *C*, Note the short foot with four rays, one demonstrating complex polysyndactyly of the great toe.

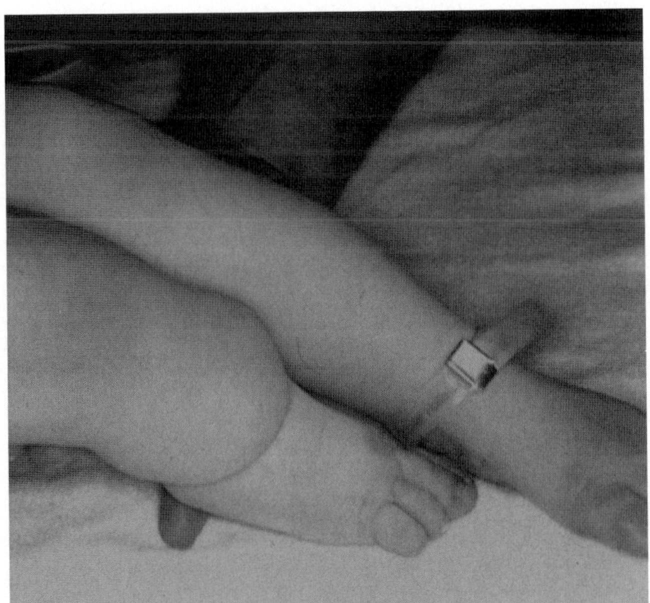

Figure 127–4 A child with fibular hemimelia. Note the shortened leg, kyphotic tibia, and three-rayed foot in the equinovalgus position.

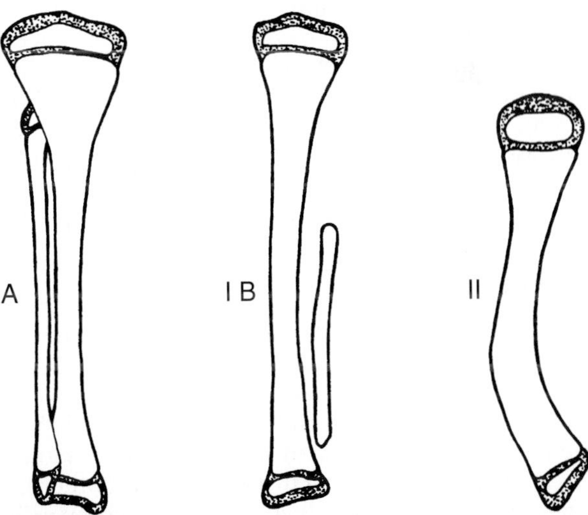

Figure 127–5 Achterman and Kalamchi classification of fibular deficiency. Type I includes all limbs in which a portion of the fibula is present. In type IA, the proximal fibular epiphysis is distal to the level of the tibial growth plate, and the distal fibular growth plate is proximal to the dome of the talus. In type IB, there is partial absence of the fibula, at least 30% to 50% of its length, and the distal end of the fibula does not support the ankle. In type II, there is complete absence of the fibula. (From Herring JA, Cummings DR: The limb-deficient child. In Morrissy RT, Weinstein SL [eds]: Lovell and Winter's Pediatric Orthopaedics. Philadelphia, Lippincott-Raven, 1996, with permission.)

TABLE 127-1 Functional Classification of Fibular Deficiency with Treatment Guidelines

Classification	Treatment
Type I: Functional Foot	
IA: 0% to 5% inequality	Orthosis/epiphyseodesis
IB: 6% to 10% inequality	Epiphyseodesis ± lengthening
IC: 11% to 30% inequality	1 to 2 lengthening procedures (or amputation)
ID: >30% inequality	>2 lengthening procedures versus amputation
Type II: Nonfunctional Foot	
IIA: Functional upper extremity	Early amputation
IIB: Nonfunctional upper extremity	Consider salvage

From Birch JG, Lincoln TL, Mack PW: Functional classification of fibular deficiency. In Herring JA, Birch JG (eds): The Child with a Limb Deficiency. Rosemont, IL, American Academy of Orthopaedic Surgeons, 1998, p 161, adapted with permission.)

deficiency typically have good functional results with limb lengthening.[39]

Traditional indications for foot ablation are ankle instability, greater than 30% shortening of the limb, rigid equinovalgus foot deformity, and abnormal ankle or subtalar joint motion (or both). In most cases of severe deformity, the results of amputation are superior to those of limb lengthening and foot reconstruction.[50] With amputation, children are more active, the leg is less painful, and they have fewer complications. The advantages of early foot ablation plus early prosthetic fitting are that fewer secondary operations are needed and the child grows up knowing nothing else, with excellent functional results.[18,33] In summary, the choice of treatment of fibular deficiency is often difficult for both the family and physician and dependent on many factors: condition of the foot, associated anomalies, family desires, and cultural perception/acceptance regarding amputation.

Tibial Deficiency

Tibial deficiency is much less common than fibular deficiency; it occurs in approximately 1 in 1 million live births and is the only skeletal deficiency with known genetic transmission.[14] Although children with fibular deficiency often have other associated musculoskeletal anomalies (e.g., femoral and ulnar deficiency) without other major organ system involvement (e.g., cardiac), children with tibial deficiency frequently have involvement of other major organ systems without associated skeletal anomalies except for congenital anomalies of the hand or spine.[67,69] Like femoral deficiency, the deformities exhibit a wide spectrum. The fibula is often normal, with varying degrees of tibial and foot deficiency. Typically, the leg is short with a flexed knee and equinovarus foot (Fig. 127-6).[18,22,67] The foot may have either fewer or more than five toes; tarsal coalitions are often present.[76]

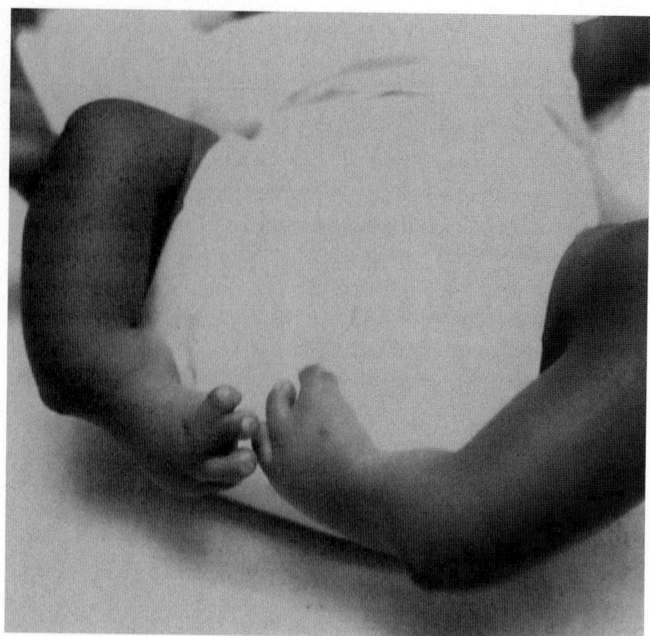

Figure 127-6 A child with bilateral complete tibial hemimelia. Note the shortened leg and equinovarus feet.

The most common classification scheme is that of Jones et al.[40] (Fig. 127-7).[34] Treatment is dependent on the presence or absence of a knee flexion contracture, active quadriceps function, and foot function/deformity. In those with complete absence of the tibia (Jones type I), centralization of the fibula to reconstruct a tibia, along with foot ablation and prosthetic fitting, has been attempted in the past. However, the results in most series have been an abysmal failure. Early knee disarticulation plus prosthetic fitting is therefore recommended for a type I Jones tibial deficiency.[19,47,67] In other types, various reconstructive options may have better success rates.[69]

AMPUTATIONS RESULTING FROM TRAUMA

Trauma is the leading cause of amputation in children. In a recent review of 256 traumatic amputations in 235 children from the Twin Cities Shriners Hospital for Children,[46] the mean age at amputation was 7.9 ± 5.0 years. The amputation involved one extremity in 92%, with the remaining 8% having amputations in two to four extremities. The lower extremity was involved in 63% and the upper extremity in 37%. The cause of these traumatic amputations was a lawnmower in 30%, farming injury in 24%, motor vehicle crash in 16%, trains in 9%, other machines in 6%, explosive devices (firecracker or bomb) in 4%, burns in 3%, gunshot wounds in 3%, and miscellaneous trauma in 5%. In a similar review of 74 children with traumatic amputations at Harborview Medical Center, 22% were due to lawnmowers, 16% to motor vehicle injuries, 14% to farming injuries, and 8% to gunshot wounds.[75]

Although explosive devices accounted for only 4% of the traumatic amputations in the United States,[46] it is probably the most common cause of traumatic amputations in

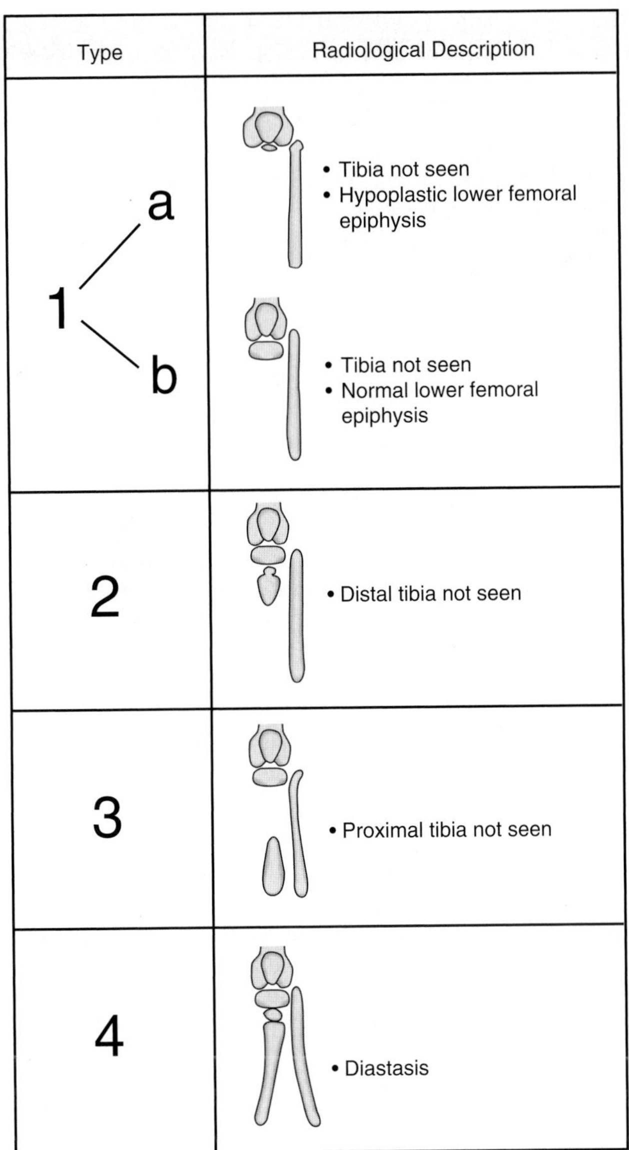

Type
Radiological Description
1
a
• Tibia not seen
• Hypoplastic lower femoral epiphysis
b
• Tibia not seen
• Normal lower femoral epiphysis
2
• Distal tibia not seen
3
• Proximal tibia not seen
4
• Diastasis

Figure 127-7 Jones classification of tibial hemimelia. (From Herring JA, Cummings DR: The limb-deficient child. In Morrissy RT, Weinstein SL [eds]: Lovell and Winter's Pediatric Orthopaedics. Philadelphia, Lippincott-Raven, 1996, with permission.)

children worldwide because of the huge burden of residual buried land mines from previous wars. There are presently 110 million buried landmines in 60 countries that maim or kill 26,000 people a year[45,59]; half of these victims are children.[5,77] This large number of land mine injuries is a significant additional burden on the health care systems of these already struggling economies, and it creates considerable problems in rehabilitation.[57,77] Injuries from land mines are so prevalent that the entity "land mine foot" has been described.[15,37]

When is a limb so severely injured that it cannot be saved and amputation should be performed? Factors to consider are the ability to technically perform a limb salvage procedure and the long-term functional outcome of such limb salvage if successful versus the function of a prosthesis. The primary issues to consider are active muscle/motor function, sensation, joint motion/stability, and in a growing child, limb-length issues. Failed efforts at limb salvage are associated with significant cost, multiple surgeries, and prolonged hospitalization, as well as psychosocial costs (to both the patient and family).[8] To help the surgeon predict which limb may not be a candidate for salvage, lower extremity injury severity scores have been developed. The most frequently one used is the Mangled Extremity Severity Score (MESS) (Table 127-2).[31,35,38] The MESS evaluates four injury characteristics: degree of tissue injury, severity of limb ischemia, presence and duration of shock, and patient age. A MESS greater than 7 is a positive predictor of amputation. However, most of these scoring systems apply to adults, and there are no gradations for different ages of children. The MESS may, however, still have some predictive ability for children,[20] but this area requires further research.

The care of a child with a mangled extremity and near amputation involves standard surgical principles. Immediate irrigation and debridement along with appropriate skeletal stabilization is paramount. Fracture stabilization is critical and may consist of external fixation (e.g., external fixators), internal fixation, or both, depending on the particular fracture characteristics. Fracture stabilization reduces the risk for infection and improves the management of soft tissue injury, including neural and vascular injury. Multiple, sequential irrigation and debridement sessions are frequently necessary every 2 to 3 days until the wounds are clean. Coverage of soft tissue defects often requires plastic surgical assistance for local or vascularized free flaps when simple split-thickness skin grafts are inadequate.

When a traumatic injury has resulted in immediate amputation or it is clear that the limb cannot be salvaged, irrigation, debridement, and delayed closure are indicated. In children all attempts at maintaining the most distal amputation level is usually warranted. If there are subsequent problems with the initial level, revision to a more proximal level can be performed in an elective fashion after functional evaluation of the child in a prosthesis at the initial injury level.

Replantation/Revascularization in Children

As the technology of microvascular techniques has improved, the ability to perform replantation/revascularization procedures now exists. However, the technical ability to successfully perform replantation/revascularization should not be confused with the functional outcome. When presented with a child who has a traumatic amputation, the surgeon is frequently asked whether the limb can be replanted. This most frequently occurs with upper extremity amputations. In children with traumatic injuries to the upper extremity that result in amputation or vascular loss, the rate of survival of the amputated part is higher for those needing only revascularization than for those needing replantation (88% versus 63%) because of the presence of intact bridging tissue and the potential for more adequate venous drainage after revascularization

TABLE 127-2 Mangled Extremity Severity Score (MESS) Variables

Variable	Description	Points
Skeletal/soft tissue injury	Low energy (stab, simple fracture, "civilian" GSW)	1
	Medium energy (open or multiple fractures, dislocation)	2
	High energy (close-range shotgun or "military" GSW, crush injury)	3
	Very high energy (above + gross contamination, soft tissue avulsion)	4
Limb ischemia*	Pulse reduced or absent but perfusion normal	1*
	Pulseless; paresthesias, diminished capillary refill	2*
	Cool, paralyzed, insensate, numb	3*
Shock	Systolic BP always >90 mm Hg	0
	Transient hypotension	1
	Persistent hypotension	2
Age (yr)	<30	0
	30-50	1
	>50	2

The MESS is simple summation of the four parameter scores.
*The score is doubled for ischemia longer than 6 hours.
BP, blood pressure; GSW, gunshot wound.
From Johansen K, Daines M, Howey T, et al: Objective criteria accurately predict amputation following lower extremity trauma. J Trauma 1990;30:568, adapted with permission.

than after replantation. Similarly, amputations resulting from lacerations have a higher survival rate after replantation than do those caused by a crush injury (72% versus 53%). Limb survival after revascularization is not dependent on age, whereas survival after replantation is. Children younger than 9 years have a better limb survival rate after replantation than do those older than 9 years (77% versus 52%).[66] In very young children, however, the survival rate may actually be less because of the increased technical difficulty of anastomosing smaller vessels and the larger proportion of crush and avulsion injuries.[9] Regarding amputations of a digit, active motion and function are much better if the amputation is distal to the insertion of the flexor digitorum superficialis tendon, at the base of the middle phalanx.

In children it is generally agreed that any amputated part should be replanted if at all possible.[4,62,66] Specifically, effort should be made to salvage an upper extremity whenever the thumb is involved, multiple digits are involved, or the amputation is proximal (wrist and forearm). Certain cultures view limb deficiency negatively and desire replantation even though the functional outcome will be poor.[10] Relative contraindications to replantation are a prolonged warm ischemia time (>12 hours for digits when muscle is absent and >6 hours for more proximal sites when muscle is present), a single border digit, a crush or avulsion injury, multilevel-segmental injury, concomitant life-threatening injuries, inability to comply with the necessary postoperative rehabilitation, and inadvertent freezing of the amputated part. Placement of the amputated part directly on ice may result in freezing, which precludes a successful result. Proper care of the amputated part is to wrap it in gauze moistened with saline or lactated Ringer's solution and place it inside a plastic bag or sterile container. This bag or container should then be placed in a larger receptacle containing ice, thereby avoiding direct contact of the amputated part with ice. Dry ice should *never* be used.[9]

AMPUTATIONS RESULTING FROM DISEASE

Neoplasia

When a surgeon is confronted with a child who has a potential limb malignancy, the issue of biopsy arises. Though a seemingly simple procedure, the biopsy must be carefully planned so that it can be incorporated into subsequent surgery, whether limb salvage or amputation.[48,49] Failure to do so may result in either an inability to perform a limb salvage procedure because of contamination of the local area with tumor or, in some cases, even actually reduced life expectancy. For this reason, the biopsy should be performed by the surgeon who will also perform the definitive surgical procedure.

As with all tumors, malignancies of the limbs are staged. Staging is extremely important in planning the biopsy. The most commonly used staging classification is that of Enneking et al.[17] Histologic grade is classified as low (G1) or high (G2), and location is classified as intracompartmental (T1), extracompartmental (T2), or metastatic (M) (Table 127-3). The term "compartment" refers to known

TABLE 127-3 Enneking System of Staging Limb Malignancy

Stage	Grade	Site
IA	Low (G1)	Intracompartmental (T1)
IB	Low (G1)	Extracompartmental (T2)
IIA	High (G2)	Intracompartmental (T1)
IIB	High (G2)	Extracompartmental (T2)
III	Any G with regional or distant metastasis	Any T

From Mirra JM: Bone Tumors. Philadelphia, Lea & Febiger, 1989, adapted with permission.

anatomic limb compartments defined by structures or spaces bounded by natural barriers to tumor extension. Such boundaries are cortical bone or fascia. For instance, an osteogenic sarcoma completely contained within the cortex of its originating bone is designated IA (high grade and intracompartmental). Similarly, a synovial sarcoma originating in the quadriceps muscle and extending beyond the quadriceps fascia into subcutaneous tissue is designated IIB (high grade and extracompartmental).

Differentiation between stages is critical in determining the appropriate level of surgical resection and associated margin. The four different margins for excision are intralesional, marginal, wide, and radical (Fig. 127-8).[11] Intralesional excision removes only a portion of the lesion and leaves behind part of the lesion, the reactive zone, and skip lesions in the surrounding normal tissue. Marginal excision removes the lesion en bloc through an extracapsular plane of dissection in the reactive inflammatory zone; satellite and skip lesions are left behind. Wide excision is an en bloc excision of the entire lesion in a plane of normal tissue beyond the reactive zone. Radical excision *requires* removal of the entire compartment in which the tumor has extended. During any musculoskeletal tumor procedure, the tumor should never be visualized; this makes it highly likely that the entire tumor with a surrounding cuff of normal tissue is removed and results in a wide margin at the minimum.

In the past, amputation was the most common surgical method to treat children with limb malignancy. Advances in technology such as imaging (magnetic resonance imaging, computed tomography), improved chemotherapy, including the use of neoadjuvant chemotherapy, and improved surgical techniques of both biopsy and later reconstruction (large allografts, newer techniques of internal fixation, and improved prosthetic joints) have made limb salvage technically possible. Similarly, the overall life expectancy and survival of children with extremity sarcomas have markedly improved because of these technical advances. For these reasons, most children with a limb malignancy today undergo limb salvage rather than amputation.

When amputation is selected as opposed to a limb salvage procedure or rotationplasty, the overall survival is similar.[60] Complications are more frequent, but quality of life and overall functional results are generally better in those who have undergone limb salvage.[25,30,55,63,64] The functional results with rotationplasty are exceptionally good,[51] and it is highly recommended if the anatomy of the tumor is appropriate and the parents/child are accepting of the cosmetic issues of a rotationplasty. In summary, the decision to proceed with amputation or limb salvage

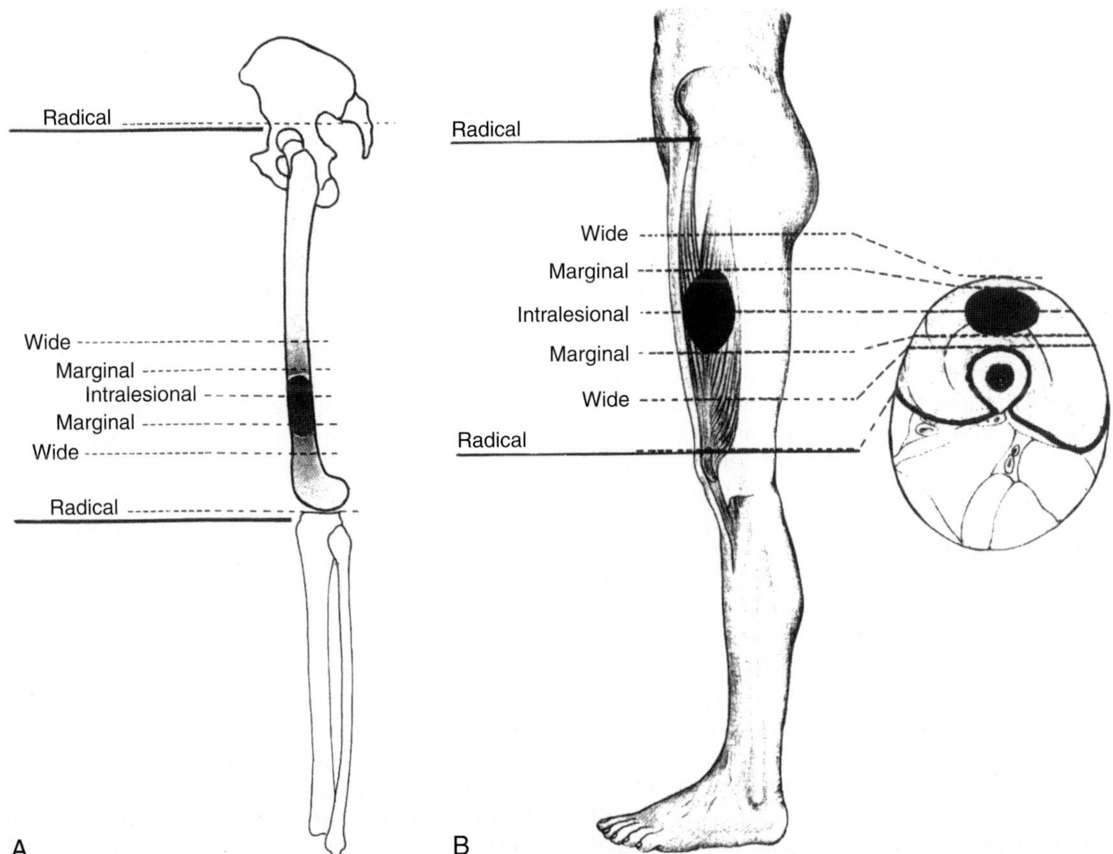

Figure 127-8 The four levels of surgical margin in resection of limb malignancies according to Enneking. *A*, For a bony tumor. *B*, For a soft tissue tumor. (From Campanacci M: Bone and Soft Tissue Tumors. New York, Springer-Verlag, 1990, with permission.)

depends on the tumor grade, tumor stage, ability to obtain a tumor-free resection, and the tumor's response to neoadjuvant therapy.[44]

Sepsis/Purpura Fulminans

Purpura fulminans is a rare, but devastating complication of septic shock and disseminated intravascular coagulopathy that results in skin and soft tissue hemorrhage and subsequent necrosis. It is first noted as a spreading petechial rash that rapidly evolves into full-thickness skin necrosis when overwhelming sepsis ensues. The associated deep soft tissue necrosis may be extensive and result in amputation. The majority of cases are caused by *Neisseria meningitidis*, but it may also be due to *Streptococcus* or other pathogens.[36,78] Acute management of children with purpura fulminans involves intravenous antibiotics (including coverage for both *Streptococcus* and *N. meningitidis*), volume resuscitation, and ventilatory and inotropic support. Fasciotomy should be considered early and performed liberally; it often reduces the depth of soft tissue involvement with a similar reduction in the extent of amputation. Purpura fulminans frequently results in dry gangrene; in these instances definitive amputation should be postponed until the margins have clearly demarcated, thereby maintaining as much limb length as possible.[36,79] Long-term complications are soft tissue coverage of transosseous stumps and growth or angular deformities (or both) of the long bones because of partial or premature physeal arrest.

Vascular Disease

Besides trauma and microvascular disease caused by purpura fulminans, other vascular conditions can also result in limb loss. Limb ischemia in a newborn child results from many different causes, with the underlying pathologic event being arterial occlusion. Premature children are at especially high risk for arterial occlusion.[7,21] Arterial occlusion can occur as a result of a hypercoagulable state or thromboembolic disease. Neonates have a diminished fibrinolytic system, thus making them more susceptible to thrombosis than adults. Arterial catheterization may also lead to thrombus formation and embolism with arterial occlusion. Children with arterial occlusion secondary to hypercoagulable states are typically seen 1 week after birth, whereas occlusion because of arterial catheterization is generally manifested 8 weeks after birth.[7] Regardless of the age or etiology, limb ischemia and secondary gangrene result in amputation. As with purpura fulminans, it is generally recommended that the injured/ischemic tissue be allowed to demarcate and progress to dry gangrene before amputation. This period of observation minimizes tissue loss before definitive amputation. The eventual amputation level is often more distal than originally expected, which preserves limb length. Earlier amputation or limb debridement is performed only when sepsis develops. Long-term sequelae are not usually significant, and the children function well with prostheses.

STUMP OVERGROWTH AND PHANTOM PHENOMENON

Overgrowth of the residual limb is a phenomenon unique to pediatric amputees. The cause of stump overgrowth is production of bone by the local environment under physiologically normal conditions. Metaphyseal transosseous amputations have the highest likelihood of bony overgrowth; the metaphysis is an extremely active site with considerable bone turnover, as well as significant endochondral and membranous bone formation. This combination probably produces a highly osteogenic environment after amputation or injury. Overgrowth at both the metaphyseal and diaphyseal stumps is due to the osteogenic periosteum and possibly activation of osteogenic bone marrow precursor cells. The active osseous-producing tissues are not present in the local environment surrounding joint disarticulations.

When stump overgrowth is sufficiently problematic, stump revision may be required to enable continued prosthetic wear. The most obvious situation is when the bone actually penetrates the skin. Other indications for stump revision are cyst formation and painful bony overgrowth.[1] In a series of 1015 skeletally immature amputees, approximately 6% needed revision because of overgrowth.[1] A more recent series reported an overall incidence of revision as high as 27%.[58] The need for stump revision is dependent on three main factors: age at initial amputation, type of amputation (congenital versus acquired), and level of amputation (transosseous versus joint disarticulation). Children older than 12 years at the time of the initial amputation are unlikely to need revision.[1] Acquired amputations are more likely to need revision, with the most frequent amputation needing revision being an acquired below-knee amputation (50%), and children with congenital amputations rarely need revisions (4%).[1] The amputation level is also important; the most common transosseous amputations needing revision, in order of frequency, are the tibia, humerus, fibula, and femur.[1] Joint disarticulations have a 0% revision rate.[1,58] Stump revision requires excision of the surrounding bursa/cyst, accompanied by generous excision of the bony overgrowth, often up to 2 or 3 cm to allow better soft tissue coverage.

The phantom phenomenon (either phantom limb sensation or phantom limb pain) is a common occurrence in adult amputees. In children, it has traditionally been believed to be much less frequent. However, recent studies in children and adolescents demonstrate that it is not at all unusual. In one series of pediatric amputees, 42% reported phantom limb sensation and 29% reported phantom limb pain.[80] Phantom phenomena are more common in children with surgical amputations than in those with congenital amputations.[80] In children with amputations secondary to burns, electrical burns are associated with a much higher incidence of phantom pain than flame burns are.[73] Up to 20% of children with congenital amputations may have phantom limb sensations.[52] Phantom limb pain is higher in children with amputations performed because of malignancy (48%) than in those resulting from trauma (12%)[68]; the chemotherapy associated with the malignancy is probably a risk factor for the development of phantom limb pain in these children.

REFERENCES

1. Abraham E, Pellicore RJ, Hamilton RC, et al: Stump overgrowth in juvenile amputees. J Pediatr Orthop 1986;6:66.
2. Achterman C, Kalamchi A: Congenital deficiency of the fibula. J Bone Joint Surg Br 1979;61:133.
3. Aitken GT: Proximal femoral focal deficiency: Definition, classification and management. In Aitken GT (ed): Proximal Femoral Focal Deficiency: A Congenital Anomaly. Washington, DC, National Academy of Sciences, 1969, p 1.
4. Beris AE, Soucacos PN, Malizos KN: Microsurgery in children. Clin Orthop 1995;314:112.
5. Bilukha OO, Brennan M, Woodruff BA: Death and injury from landmines and unexploded ordnance in Afghanistan. JAMA 2003;290:650.
6. Birch JG, Lincoln TL, Mack PW: Functional classification of fibular deficiency. In Herring JA, Birch JG (eds): The Child with a Limb Deficiency. Rosemont, IL, American Academy of Orthopaedic Surgeons, 1998, p 161.
7. Blank JE, Dormans JP, Davidson RS: Perinatal limb ischemia: Orthopaedic implications. J Pediatr Orthop 1996;16:90.
8. Bosse MJ, MacKenzie EJ, Kellam JF, et al: A prospective evaluation of the clinical utility of the lower-extremity injury-severity scores. J Bone Joint Surg Am 2001;83:3.
9. Boulas HJ: Amputations of the fingers and hands: Indications for replantation. J Am Acad Orthop Surg 1998;6:100.
10. Buncke GM, Buntic RF, Romeo O: Pediatric mutilating hand injuries. Hand Clin 2003;19:121.
11. Campanacci M: Bone and Soft Tissue Tumors. New York, Springer-Verlag, 1990.
12. Cheng JCY, Cheung KW, Ng BKW: Severe progressive deformities after limb lengthening in type-II fibular hemimelia. J Bone Joint Surg Br 1998;80:772.
13. Choi IH, Kumar SJ, Bowen JR: Amputation or limb-lengthening for partial or total absence of the fibula. J Bone Joint Surg Am 1990;72:1391.
14. Clark MW: Autosomal dominant inheritance of tibial meromelia. J Bone Joint Surg Am 1975;57:262.
15. Coupland RM, Korver A: Injuries from antipersonnel mines: The experience of the International Committee of the Red Cross. BMJ 1991;303:1509.
16. Dreyfus M, Baldauf J-J, Rigaut E, et al: Prenatal diagnosis of unilateral tibial hemimelia. Ultrasound Obstet Gynecol 1996; 7:205.
17. Enneking WF, Spanier SS, Goodman MA: A system for surgical staging of musculoskeletal sarcoma. Clin Orthop 1980;153:106.
18. Epps CH Jr, Schneider PL: Treatment of the hemimelias of the lower extremity. J Bone Joint Surg Am 1989; 71:273.
19. Epps CH Jr, Tooms RE, Edholm CD, et al: Failure of centralization of the fibula for congenital longitudinal deficiency of the tibia. J Bone Joint Surg Am 1991; 73:858.
20. Fagelman MF, Epps HR, Rang M: Mangled extremity severity score in children. J Pediatr Orthop 2002;22:182.
21. Farrar MJ, Bennet GC, Wilson NIL, et al: The orthopaedic implications of peripheral limb ischaemia in infants and children. J Bone Joint Surg Br 1996;78:6.
22. Fernandez-Palazzi F, Bendaham J, Rivas S: Congenital deficiency of the tibia: A report on 22 cases. J Pediatr Orthop B 1998;7:298.
23. Fowler E, Zernicke R, Setoguchi Y, et al: Energy expenditure during walking by children who have proximal femoral focal deficiency. J Bone Joint Surg Am 1996;78:1857.
24. Frantz CH, O'Rahilly R: Congenital skeletal limb deficiencies. J Bone Joint Surg Am 1961;43:1022.
25. Fuchs B, Kotajarvi BR, Kaufman KR, et al: Functional outcome of patients with rotationplasty about the knee. Clin Orthop 2003;415:52.
26. Gillespie R: Classification of congenital abnormalities of the femur. In Herring JA, Birch JG (eds): The Child with a Limb Deficiency. Rosemont, IL, American Academy of Orthopaedic Surgeons, 1998, p 63.
27. Gillespie R, Torode IP: Classification and management of congenital abnormalities of the femur. J Bone Joint Surg Br 1983;65:557.
28. Goncalves LF, De Luca GR, Vitorello DA, et al: Prenatal diagnosis of bilateral proximal femoral hypoplasia. Ultrasound Obstet Gynecol 1996;8:127.
29. Grogan DP, Holt GR, Ogden JA: Talocalcaneal coalition in patients who have fibular hemimelia or proximal femoral focal deficiency. J Bone Joint Surg Am 1994;76:1363.
30. Ham SJ, Koops HS, Veth RPH, et al: Limb salvage surgery for primary bone sarcoma of the lower extremities: Long-term consequences of endoprosthetic reconstructions. Ann Surg Oncol 1998;5:423.
31. Helfet DL, Howey T, Sanders R, et al: Limb salvage versus amputation: Preliminary results of the Mangled Extremity Severity Score. Clin Orthop 1990;256:80.
32. Herring JA: Symes amputation for fibular hemimelia: A second look in the Ilizarov era. Instr Course Lect 1992: 41:435.
33. Herring JA, Barnhill B, Gaffney C: Syme amputation: An evaluation of the physical and psychological function in young patients. J Bone Joint Surg Am 1986;68:573.
34. Herring JA, Cummings DR: The limb-deficient child. In Morrissy RT, Weinstein SL (eds): Lovell and Winter's Pediatric Orthopaedics. Philadelphia, Lippincott-Raven, 1996.
35. Howe HR Jr, Poole GV, Hansen KJ, et al: Salvage of lower extremities following combined orthopaedic and vascular trauma. A predictive salvage index. Am Surg 1987;53:205.
36. Huang DB, Price M, Pokorny J, et al: Reconstructive surgery in children after meningococcal purpura fulminans. J Pediatr Surg 1999;34:595.
37. Jacobs LGH: The landmine foot: Its description and management. Injury 1991;22:463.
38. Johansen K, Daines M, Howey T, et al: Objective criteria accurately predict amputation following lower extremity trauma. J Trauma 1990;30:568.
39. Johnston CE II, Haideri NF: Comparison of functional outcome in fibular deficiency treated by limb salvage versus Syme's amputation. In Herring JA, Birch JG (eds): The Child with a Limb Deficiency. Rosemont, IL, American Academy of Orthopaedic Surgeons, 1998, p 173.
40. Jones D, Barnes J, Lloyd-Roberts GC: Congenital aplasia and dysplasia of the tibia with intact fibula. J Bone Joint Surg Br 1978;60:31.
41. Kant P, Koh SH-Y, Neumann V, et al: Treatment of longitudinal deficiency affecting the femur: Comparing patient mobility and satisfaction outcomes of Syme amputation against extension prosthesis. J Pediatr Orthop 2003; 23:236.
42. Kostuik JP, Gillespie R, Hall JE, et al: Van Nes rotational osteotomy for treatment of proximal femoral focal deficiency and congenital short femur. J Bone Joint Surg Am 1975;57:1039.
43. Krajbich JI: Lower-limb deficiencies and amputations in children. J Am Acad Orthop Surg 1998;6:358.

44. Kumta SM, Cheng JCY, Li CK, et al: Scope and limitations of limb-sparing surgery in childhood sarcoma. J Pediatr Orthop 2002;22:244.
45. Letts M, Davidson D: Epidemiology and prevention of traumatic amputations in children. In Herring JA, Birch JG (eds): The Child with a Limb Deficiency. Rosemont, IL, American Academy of Orthopaedic Surgeons, 1998.
46. Loder RT: Demographics of traumatic amputations in children. Implications for prevention strategies. J Bone Joint Surg Am 2004;86:923.
47. Loder RT, Herring JA: Fibular transfer for congenital absence of the tibia: A reassessment. J Pediatr Orthop 1987;7:8.
48. Mankin HJ, Lange TA, Spanier SS: The hazards of biopsy in patients with malignant primary bone and soft tissue tumors. J Bone Joint Surg Am 1982;64:1121.
49. Mankin HJ, Mankin CJ, Simon MA: The hazards of the biopsy, revisited. J Bone Joint Surg Am 1996;78:656.
50. McCarthy JJ, Clancy GL, Chang FM, et al: Fibular hemimelia: Comparison of outcome measurements after amputation and lengthening. J Bone Joint Surg Am 2000;82:1732.
51. McClenaghan BA, Krajbich JI, Pirone AM, et al: Comparative assessment of gait after limb salvage procedures. J Bone Joint Surg Am 1989;71:1178.
52. Melzack R, Israel R, Lacroix R, et al: Phantom limbs in people with congenital limb deficiency or amputation in early childhood. Brain 1997;120:1603.
53. Miller LS, Bell DF: Management of congenital fibular deficiency by Ilizarov technique. J Pediatr Orthop 1992;12:651.
54. Mirra JM: Bone Tumors. Philadelphia, Lea & Febiger, 1989.
55. Nagarajan R, Neglia JP, Clohisy DR, et al: Limb salvage and amputation in survivors of pediatric lower-extremity bone tumors: What are the long-term implications? J Clin Oncol 2002;20:4493.
56. Naudie D, Hamdy RC, Fassier F, et al: Management of fibular hemimelia. Amputation or limb lengthening. J Bone Joint Surg Br 1997;79:58.
57. O'Connell C: The aftermath of war: In the minefields of Mozambique. Can Med Assoc J 2000;163:1590.
58. O'Neal ML, Bahner R, Ganey TM, et al: Osseous overgrowth after amputation in adolescents and children. J Pediatr Orthop 1996;16:78.
59. Pearn J: Children and war. J Paediatr Child Health 2003; 39:166.
60. Postma A, Kingma A, de Ruiter JH, et al: Quality of life in bone tumor patients comparing limb salvage and amputation of the lower extremity. J Surg Oncol 1992;51:47.
61. Price CT, Noonan KJ: Femoral lengthening with monolateral half-pin devices. In Herring JA, Birch JG (eds): The Child with a Limb Deficiency. Rosemont, IL, American Academy of Orthopaedic Surgeons, 1998, p 133.
62. Raimondi PL, Petrolati M, Delaria G: Replantation of large segments in children. Hand Clin 2000;16:547.
63. Renard AJ, Veth RP, Schreuder HWB, et al: Function and complications after ablative and limb-salvage therapy in lower extremity sarcoma of bone. J Surg Oncol 2000; 73:198.
64. Rödl RW, Pohlmann U, Gosheger G, et al: Rotationplasty—quality of life after 10 years in 22 patients. Acta Orthop Scand 2002;73:85.
65. Roux MO, Carlioz H: Clinical examination and investigation of the cruciate ligaments in children with fibular hemimelia. J Pediatr Orthop 1999;19:247.
66. Saies AD, Urbaniak JD, Nunley JA, et al: Results after replantation and revascularization in the upper extremity in children. J Bone Joint Surg Am 1994;76:1766.
67. Schoenecker PL, Capelli AM, Millar EA, et al: Congenital longitudinal deficiency of the tibia. J Bone Joint Surg Am 1989;71:278.
68. Smith J, Thompson JM: Phantom limb pain and chemotherapy in pediatric amputees. Mayo Clin Proc 1995;70:357.
69. Spiegel DA, Loder RT, Crandall RC: Congenital longitudinal deficiency of the tibia. Int Orthop 2003;27:338.
70. Steel HH, Lin PS, Betz RR, et al: Iliofemoral fusion for proximal femoral focal deficiency. J Bone Joint Surg Am 1987;69:837.
71. Stevens PM, Arms D: Postaxial hypoplasia of the lower extremity. J Pediatr Orthop 2000;20:166.
72. Tachdjian MO: Pediatric Orthopedics. Philadelphia, WB Saunders, 1990.
73. Thomas CR, Brazeal BA, Rosenberg L, et al: Phantom limb pain in pediatric burn survivors. Burns 2003;29:139.
74. Torode IP, Gillespie R: Rotationplasty of the lower limb for congenital defects of the femur. J Bone Joint Surg Br 1983; 65:569.
75. Trautwein LC, Smith DG, Rivara FP: Pediatric amputation injuries: Etiology, cost, and outcome. J Trauma 1996;41:831.
76. Turker R, Mendelson S, Ackman J, et al: Anatomic considerations of the foot and leg in tibial hemimelia. J Pediatr Orthop 1996;16:445.
77. Walsh NE, Walsh WS: Rehabilitation of landmine victims—the ultimate challenge. Bull World Health Org 2003;81:665.
78. Warner PM, Kagan RJ, Yakuboff KP, et al: Current management of purpura fulminans: A multicenter study. J Burn Care Rehabil 2003;24:119.
79. Wheeler JS, Anderson BJ, De Chalain TMB: Surgical intervention in children with meningococcal purpura fulminans—a review of 117 procedures in 21 children. J Pediatr Surg 2003; 38:597.
80. Wilkins KL, McGrath PJ, Finley GA, et al: Phantom limb sensations and phantom limb pain in child and adolescent amputees. Pain 1998;78:7.

Chapter 128

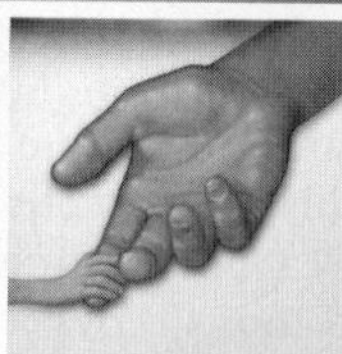

Congenital Defects of the Skin, Connective Tissues, Muscles, Tendons, and Hands

Edward P. Miranda and Stephen J. Mathes

The sequence of cellular proliferation, differentiation, and regression that is characteristic of human embryogenesis and subsequent development is complex and possesses little tolerance for error. Errors and injury during gestation do, however, occur quite often as evidenced by spontaneous abortion rates of up to 33% when implantation is detected by measurement of human chorionic gonadotropin.[49,86,87] "Failure" of these gestations can also be viewed as "success" inasmuch as embryos with errors incompatible with life (e.g., major chromosomal abnormalities) are culled out.[30] This selection for major errors is not precise because many gestations progress to delivery with sublethal abnormalities.

GENERAL INCIDENCE AND RISK

A major malformation has been defined as a structural anomaly with medical and social consequences. The incidence of major malformations has been estimated to be 2% to 3% of live births.[14,31,38,83] Minor malformations have been defined as structural alterations that pose no significant medical or social burden. At least one malformation is identifiable in about 15% of newborns. The distinction between a major and a minor anomaly is arbitrary because all human deformities exist on a continuum. However, even the most minor physical aberration can predispose the afflicted person to psychosocial isolation and thus justifies surgical therapy.

SKIN AND SOFT TISSUES

Embryology

The developmental origins of the skin, muscle, connective tissue, and tendons commence during the third week of embryonic life. During this period, a primitive streak appears and facilitates formation of the trilaminar embryo (ectoderm, mesoderm, and endoderm), notochord, and somites.[53]

Development of the Epidermis

The skin is the largest organ in the body and is composed of two layers: the dermis and the epidermis. The skin serves a variety of functions beyond simply providing an interface between the body and the environment.[53] The cutaneous interface also provides temperature regulation, sensory perception, and a barrier against water loss and microbial invasion and is a major neuroregulated immune organ.[50] The cutaneous system is also a medium for nonverbal communication, and the appearance of the skin contributes to interpersonal recognition and one's sense of self.

The epidermis itself originates from a monolayer of ectodermal cells that form the periderm at about 4 weeks of gestation.[62] The early epidermis is a monolayer that is exposed to amniotic fluid and with which it participates in significant salt and water exchange. Over time, the epidermis expands and by the third month it becomes three cell layers thick (the basal, intermediate, and superficial layers). The epidermis continues to develop, and by the sixth month differentiation has progressed far enough to achieve effective barrier function. On microscopy, the skin is similar to newborn epidermis with several observable layers: the strata basale (innermost layer), spinosum, granulosum, and corneum (outermost layer). Keratinocytes progress over their lifetime from the stratum basale to ultimate sloughing from the stratum corneum. This migration is characterized by progressive differentiation and accumulation of keratin granules in the stratum granulosum and the intermediate filament fillagrin in the stratum corneum to maintain an effective barrier to the environment. The stratum basale retains the keratinocyte stem cells that will repopulate the other layers of the skin.[53]

Several other cell types migrate into the epidermis to assist in its function. Melanocytes are neural crest–derived cells that first migrate into the dermis and then into the epidermis. These cells produce the pigment melanin for defense against ultraviolet photodamage. At approximately 3 months of gestation, Langerhans cells are found in the epidermis. Langerhans cells are bone marrow–derived, professional antigen-presenting cells that arrange themselves in the epidermis to form an immunologic net to detect and present foreign antigens to T cells.[53]

Development of the Dermis and Other Mesodermal Tissues

During the third week of embryogenesis a primitive knot appears at the cranial end of the primitive streak. Mesenchymal cells migrate cranially from the knot and form a midline cellular cord known as the notochordal process. This process grows until it reaches the oropharyngeal membrane; at this point it can extend no further because of the densely adherent ectoderm and endoderm. The notochord gives rise to the vertebral column and induces the overlying ectoderm to form the neural plate—the primordium of the nervous system.[53]

As the notochord forms, the intraembryonic mesoderm thickens on each side of it to form paired longitudinal columns of paraxial mesoderm. At the end of the third week, these columns of paraxial mesoderm divide into paired cuboidal bodies called somites. Eventually, 42 to 44 pairs of somites develop in a craniocaudal sequence. Somites are the segmental precursors to most of the axial skeleton, musculature, and its associated dermis of the skin.[53,59,78]

The emergence of mesenchyme at 3 weeks of embryonic life is essential to organogenesis. By 8 weeks of life, the face and hands are recognizably human. At 12 weeks of life, the palate has formed and the sex can be determined by visual inspection of the external genitalia. Interruptions in the development and differentiation of mesodermal events (mesenchymal migration, notochord, somites) accurately reflect the wider diversity of congenital malformations found in the skin, connective tissues, muscles, and tendons. With such an expansive array of deformities, systematic analysis and anatomic regionalization of the defect are necessary to formulate an effective treatment plan.[53]

ANALYSIS OF DEFECTS AND TECHNICAL ASPECTS OF TREATMENT

The structural aspect of any defect can be subdivided into malpositioning of otherwise normal structures, regional absence of normal tissue, and aberrations in tissue composition.

Malpositioning of Otherwise Normal Structures

Congenital malpositioning of normal structures can occur from persistence of embryonic lines of fusion, displacement of anatomic landmarks as a result of abnormal growth of adjacent tissues, or developmental malrotation. Visceral malpositioning may be entirely inconsequential to the affected individual. Dextrocardia with situs inversus is an incidental finding in asymptomatic patients. In most cases, however, malpositioning has more deleterious effects. The magnitude of the mishap depends on the cascade of events resulting from the derailment of normal development. Spina bifida is a caudal dorsal trunk defect with variable soft tissue and vertebral skeletal deficiencies that arise during the fourth week of life. When vertebral canal closure is derailed, the spinal cord may herniate through the trunk defect and give rise to meningomyelocele. A cascade of mishaps follows.[47,81] The malpositioned spinal cord degenerates and the lower extremities do not innervate, thereby leading to fibrofatty replacement of the musculature. The results are malformed, irreversibly paralyzed lower extremities.

Timely surgical intervention performed to reposition normal structures to anatomic native sites can interrupt the sequence of mishaps and possibly salvage function and body image. In utero repair of spinal canal defects has been shown in experimental animals to arrest the progression of neurologic abnormalities.[48] This approach is currently being studied in humans and has the potential to correct a wide variety of abnormalities.

Physiologically less devastating malformations, such as facial clefting, are subject to the pressures of conformation to social standards.[35,66,80] These stresses should not be underestimated. Even when function is minimally impaired, body form is still subject to grotesque deformity and social rejection. Historically, newborns with facial clefting were at increased risk for infanticide. Although this threat has almost been eliminated with modern treatment, social integration of the affected person still depends on the ability to restore normal facial anatomy and promote such skills as speech.[20,26] Defect analysis usually shows minor volume deficiencies of soft tissue in congenital cleft lip. The magnitude of the visual deformity is proportional to the degree of malpositioning of the facial landmarks. Surgical repositioning of the malpositioned structures to native anatomic sites optimally corrects the malformation. In addition to the technical aspect of the repair, performing the procedure in a timely manner is critical for social acceptance and the development of speech. Palatal repair performed before 18 months of age has consistently yielded better speech results in infants with cleft palate malformations.

Regional Absence of Normal Tissue

Structural anomalies resulting from a deficiency or absence of tissue have taxed the ingenuity of plastic surgeons. Either alloplastic or autologous materials may be used in the reconstruction of congenital defects that are caused by deficient or absent tissues. Benefits of reconstruction with alloplastic materials include unlimited supply, no donor defect, and ease of use. However, reconstruction with autologous tissues is superior for congenital malformations because such tissues can fully integrate with living structures, maintain the potential for growth and wound healing, and resist infection after healing. Nevertheless, alloplastic surgical implants, judiciously placed during adolescence, remain an excellent reconstructive standard in special clinical circumstances, such as congenital hypoplastic breast deformities.[3]

A wide spectrum of surgical procedures has evolved to optimize the use of autologous tissues. The use of nonvascularized tissue grafts is a simple and effective way to replace skin, muscle, connective tissue, and tendons. This technique is justifiable only when the gain at the recipient site will compensate for the loss sustained at the donor site. Furthermore, a well-vascularized recipient bed is necessary to nourish the graft until neovascularization occurs. When the bed is not suitable for a graft or specialized tissue is desired in the reconstruction, en bloc (composite) flap transfer of specialized tissue with its own intrinsic vascular supply should be used in the reconstruction.[15,44] The method of tissue transfer depends on the proximity of the donor and recipient sites. Free microvascular flap transfer is an elegant method of moving tissue when the distance from the donor to the recipient site is too great for local rearrangement.

Tissue expansion is an excellent way to create composite soft tissue for use with fewer donor site demands. Hair-bearing replacement of deficient scalp in conditions such as aplasia cutis (see later) best illustrates the potential dividends gained from tissue expansion.[67] Distraction osteogenesis is the analogous procedure for bone. The use of this powerful technique for bone lengthening, first described by Ilizarov for lengthening of long bones, is now being used in the facial skeleton. Gradual facial bone lengthening without donor deformity has been effective in treating the mandibular hypoplasia that is found in disorders such as hemifacial microsomia.[52]

Aberrations in Tissue Composition

An imbalance in the relative cellular composition of a tissue may lead to significant malformation without a deficiency in tissue mass. Skin lesions, such as congenital giant hairy nevus (see later) and port-wine stains, are anomalies that express an excess of a specific cell or tissue type. In congenital giant hairy nevus, the melanocyte-related nevus cell has excessively proliferated in the dermis. After birth, these cells have an increased risk of degenerating into melanomas, thus leading to the rationale for surgical ablation. Cutaneous port-wine stains result from an excessive developmental accumulation of abnormal microvascular tissue in the dermis. These lesions are not mitotically active and have no neoplastic potential. However, they are disfiguring and socially disturbing. Direct excision is generally undesirable because of subsequent scarring and deformity. Selective ablation of vascular tissue with laser light is an effective method for treating this disorder.

Many localized congenital malformations are inconsequential and can be considered normal variants. For example, congenital absence of the palmaris longus tendon has a prevalence of 15% to 20%. Such anomalies require no treatment. However, when function or body image is threatened, careful analysis of the magnitude of malpositioning of normal structure, the degree of tissue deficiency, and the composition of the aberrant tissue is essential in planning the reconstruction. Judicious timing of the operation can often interrupt a cascade of predictable secondary deformities.

SPECIFIC ANATOMIC REGIONS

Skin

Aplasia Cutis Congenita

Aplasia cutis congenita (ACC) is a rare congenital disorder characterized by full-thickness absence of the skin and underlying tissues over a section of the body. The scalp is involved in approximately 85% of cases, with occasional loss of all cranial tissues, including the calvaria and dura. The true incidence is unknown, and fewer than 300 cases have been reported in the medical literature. The diagnosis of ACC is clinical and the condition is generally discovered at birth, although diagnosis by prenatal ultrasound has been reported. The lesion is generally manifested as either a thin transparent membrane or a dried cicatrix in place of normal skin; no hair follicles are present. The vertex of the scalp is the most common area involved. For small defects, the natural history is that of epithelialization from the lateral edges, but larger defects may not close and generally warrant treatment. The mortality for extensive scalp defects is 20% to 30%.[36,85]

The etiology of ACC is not well established. ACC has been reported to be associated with other defects, including limb deformities, omphalocele, and clefts. Treatment is usually indicated immediately for larger defects and those with a bony defect. Bony involvement at the vertex of the scalp places the patient at risk for hemorrhage from the sagittal sinus and also mandates operative treatment.[36] The defect is generally repaired with flaps or skin grafts, or both. Bony skull reconstruction is typically delayed until 2 years of age; occasionally, the osteogenic dura may spontaneously generate new bone to replace the defect. Reconstruction of a normal hair pattern is accomplished via tissue expansion of the scalp and subsequent coverage of the affected area with local flaps at about 5 to 7 years of age.[69,79,85]

Congenital Melanocytic Nevus and Giant Hairy Nevus

Congenital nevi are composed of large clusters of pigment-producing cells of melanocyte lineage that are clustered in the dermis and produce pigment at birth. When compared with the more common acquired nevi, congenital nevi are larger, have increased cellularity, and lie deeper in the dermis. The incidence of congenital nevi has been estimated to be 1 in 100 births for small lesions and 1 in 20,000 for large lesions.[7] After birth it is difficult to distinguish congenital from acquired nevi even by histology. Congenital melanocytic nevi are classified according to size: small, less than 1.5 cm in diameter; medium, 1.5 to 19.9 cm; and large (giant), greater than 20 cm.[10,11]

The potential for congenital nevi to transform into melanoma is the prime reason that these lesions come to surgical attention. However, considerable uncertainty surrounds estimation of the true risk for malignant degeneration. Rates of 1% to 31% have been reported for giant congenital nevi (GCN), although these data may be even less reliable than the large range suggests because the total number of patients with GCN is unknown. A recent metareview calculates an overall melanoma risk of 8.2% in GCN, which is high enough to make surgical ablation a priority. The risk for malignant melanoma is also immediate; 60% of observed GCN-related melanomas occurred in the first decade of life, with several studies suggesting that many malignancies occur by 3 years of age. Melanoma has also been reported in small congenital nevi, and melanoma rates of 2.6% to 4.9% have been estimated.[88]

Giant hairy nevi (GHN) are a special subset of congenital nevi. These melanocytic cutaneous lesions are extensive and encompass entire anatomic regions that may exceed 20% of the body surface area (Fig. 128-1). These nevi are often hairy with benign surface nodularity consisting of focal growths of neuroectodermal tissue.[34] When the head or upper part of the trunk is involved, neurologic abnormalities have been observed in up to 20% of patients. Neurologic findings of leptomeningeal melanosis, hydrocephalus, seizures, and myelopathy in association with GHN are consistent with the developmental origin of the neuroectoderm.[34]

GHN are disfiguring and easily identifiable at birth.[74] Parents of patients with GHN often seek treatment early. Some neonates with GHN have been found to have malignant melanoma shortly after birth, thus justifying early surgical ablation. Serial resection of GHN lesions with the use of subcutaneous tissue expanders is indicated to improve aesthetic appearance and diminish the risk for malignancy.[39] The increased compliance and elasticity of infant skin provide the first opportunity to debulk a large portion of the giant nevus in the first 6 months of life.[43] At this time areas of nodularity or increased pigment are resected. The timing of subsequent resections is based on changes in appearance of the nevus and the parents' decision to proceed with complete resection. Repeated excisions may expedite lesion removal with completion in early childhood. Complete excision of the nevus with skin grafts results in scar and contracture deformities both at the site of nevus resection and at the skin graft donor site. The use of sequential excision with expansion of normal adjacent skin allows coverage of areas of nevus excision with normal skin and does not cause additional scarring.

Nevus Sebaceus of Jadassohn

Sebaceous nevus (SN) is a solitary, well-circumscribed, plaque-like raised lesion of epidermal origin. SN is commonly found on the scalp, temple, or the preauricular region and is sometimes diagnosed at birth. Histologic analysis in children reveals epidermal hyperplasia with hypoplastic hair follicles and sebaceous glands. At puberty, the sebaceous glands mature and progression of the epithelial hyperplasia ensues. Progression to basal cell carcinoma (BCC) has been reported in up to 6% to 50% of adults.[71]

Controversy exists in the management of SN in children. Early reports of BCC formation in 10% to 15% of adolescents have been refuted by large retrospective studies that have shown a low incidence of benign epithelioid lesions and no incidence of BCC in excised lesions from children up to 16 years of age. However, there is still a well-documented incidence of SN-related BCC in adults. The management of choice is excision, but delaying the resection until later in adolescence is not unreasonable.[71,82]

Congenital Webs

Congenital webs (pterygia) are most commonly found in the neck (pterygium colli). In the neck, thick folds of skin and subcutaneous tissue extend from the mastoid process laterally to the acromion. The lesions are generally bilateral and can distort local structures, including the posterior hairline, the border of which is often displaced laterally on the neck and thus causes a short-necked appearance. Webs have been identified similarly in the axillary folds and crural regions.

Congenital webbing may occur in isolation or in conjunction with other congenital deformities; however, the etiology is unknown.[27] Certain regional deformities such as Klippel-Feil syndrome can display this developmental lesion. Neck webbing is often a manifestation of Turner's syndrome. The webs can cause functional or aesthetic disabilities (or both). Correction is accomplished by lengthening with multiple Z-plasties, generally between the ages of 1 and 6 years.[70]

Congenital Deformities of the Breasts

Embryology

The breast develops in the fetus from ectodermal tissue during the fifth week of gestation. Bilateral *mammary ridges* extend from the axillae to the groins. During the seventh to eighth weeks of gestation, the mammary ridges undergo involution in all areas except on the anterior thoracic wall and axillae. After 10 to 14 weeks of gestation, the primordial breast tissue penetrates the thoracic mesenchymal tissue and begins to form glands. The mesenchyme envelops the breast and forms layers in continuity with Camper's fascia (outermost layer) and a second layer separating the breast from the underlying thoracic musculature. Camper's fascia surrounds the anterior aspect of the breast in all areas except just deep to the areola. A network of connective tissue running through the mammary gland forms Cooper's ligaments, which suspend the breast. Milk ducts begin to form at about 20 weeks of gestation, and the glandular tissue continues to develop until the end of puberty.[51,54,61]

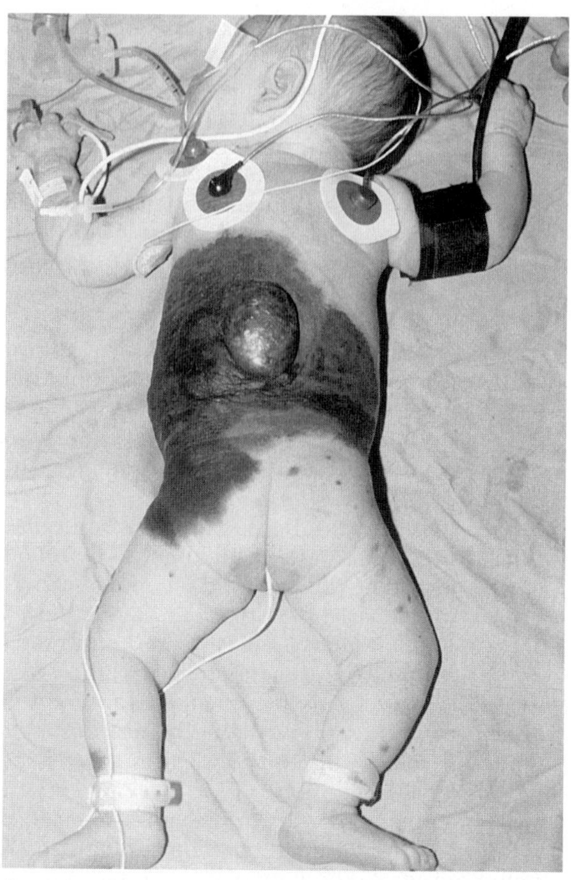

A

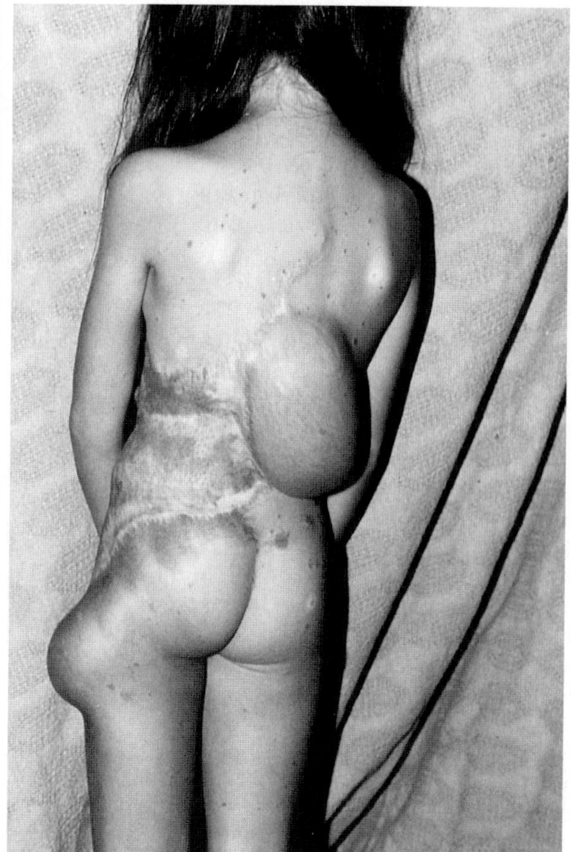

B

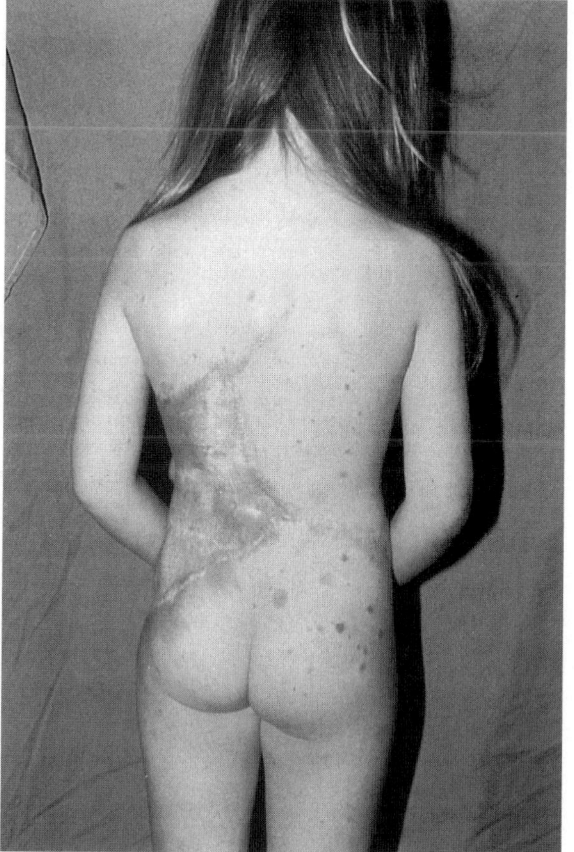

C

Figure 128-1 *A*, Congenital giant hairy nevus of the trunk. The large midline mass in this infant proved to be a malignant neural crest cell tumor already present at birth. *B*, The malignant tumor was completely resected. Multiple implanted tissue expanders have been inflated to facilitate wound coverage after excision of the nevus. *C*, Most of the nevus has been excised.

Polythelia and Polymastia

Supernumerary nipples (*polythelia*) and supernumerary breasts (*polymastia*) are relatively common congenital abnormalities with an incidence of approximately 0.2% to 2.5% (polythelia) and 0.1% to 1.0% (polymastia). Both these deformities are observed to form along the milk lines that track from the axillae to the groin. Both supernumerary nipples and supernumerary breasts form as a result of failure of normal apoptotic regression of the mammary ridges during gestation. The diagnosis of supernumerary nipples can often be made at birth. The most common site for polythelia is just inferior to a normal breast; the most common site for an accessory breast is in the axilla.[1,51]

Supernumerary nipples and breasts typically come to medical attention as an aesthetic complaint, but they can also respond to hormonal changes similar to a normal breast, including enlargement during puberty and milk production after pregnancy. Treatment of these lesions is generally simple excision, but it is important to consider that diseases that afflict the normal breast can also affect supernumerary ones. Breast masses must be excluded. Furthermore, several other anomalies have been associated with polythelia and polymastia, including a higher rate of testicular tumors in boys. Other more controversial associations include genitourinary tract abnormalities and renal cell carcinoma.[13,25,84]

Congenital Absence of the Breast

Complete absence of one or both breasts is an extremely rare anomaly that can occur in isolation or with a variety of other developmental syndromes, including Poland's syndrome, Ullrich-Turner syndrome, and AREDYLD syndrome (acrorenal field defect, ectodermal dysplasia, lipoatrophic diabetes) (Fig. 128-2A to E). Bilateral congenital absence is extremely rare, with few cases reported in the literature. Mendelian inheritance is possible, but this etiology has not been definitively established; teratogen exposure has also been implicated. Because of the rarity of this condition, optimal treatment has not been adequately investigated. The successful use of autogenous tissues, including the use of a transverse rectus abdominis muscle (TRAM) flap for construction of a breast de novo, has been reported. Tissue expansion and implant placement may also be a reasonable option.[51]

Tuberous Breast Disease

The breast anomaly known as the "tuberous breast" was initially described in 1976 by Rees and Aston for its likeness in appearance to a tuber root (Fig. 128-3A to D).[65] Although there has been much confusion in the literature about both the nomenclature and the description of a tuberous breast and breast asymmetry in general, the following facts are known: 88% of women undergoing augmentation mammaplasty have breast asymmetry and 29% have breast base constriction.[68] A true tuberous breast is much less common and is defined not simply by asymmetry or constriction, but by herniation of mammary tissue through a constricting fascial ring deep to the areola. The true incidence is uncertain, and there seems to be no heritable genetic component to the disorder.[51]

The presence of the tight fascial ring causes the breast to become asymmetric during pubertal development and ultimately herniate glandular tissue through it, thereby causing areolar enlargement. This may be associated with hypoplasia of one or more quadrants, with the deficiency being most common in the inferior pole. The inferior mammary fold is often variably elevated.[63]

A tuberous breast is often first evaluated in the early teen years because of aesthetic concern. Differentiation of this disorder from more common asymmetries is essential because the treatment is generally different. Nearly 90% of cases are bilateral, and significant hypoplasia of breast tissue is present in approximately a quarter of patients.[51]

Treatment for a tuberous breast is somewhat controversial, although several principles can be relied on. The patient should not be operated on until late in the second decade when breast development has finished. In nearly all cases, the herniated breast tissue causes enlargement of the areola and thus mandates a circumareolar incision to reduce its size. This incision also allows for access to the fascial ring, whose constricting bands must be released. Operative plans subsequent to these two steps are less definitive, although local tissue rearrangement is generally recommended with the establishment of a normal position of the inframammary fold and a natural inferior pole contour.[28] For hypoplastic or asymmetric breasts, tissue expansion, implant placement, or both can be a useful adjunct to tissue rearrangement, but the use of an implant alone has been shown to be unsatisfactory, with abnormalities of the inframammary crease being common.[42,51]

Gynecomastia (Infantile and Adolescent)

Gynecomastia, or the abnormal presence of breast tissue in males, is a common, but complex disorder with both congenital and acquired features (Fig. 128-4A to D).[9,51,56] The overall incidence is 32% to 40% with a reported incidence of 65% in adolescent boys.[56] Gynecomastia is generally bilateral (25% to 75% of reported cases).[18,55]

Although numerous individual causes of gynecomastia have been identified, breast development in males generally occurs secondary to an excess of estrogens relative to testosterone—either from an absolute estrogen excess, a testosterone deficiency, or receptor resistance. A full discussion of the causes of gynecomastia is beyond the scope of this section and is reviewed elsewhere.[24] Gynecomastia can be classified as congenital or acquired, as well as physiologic or pathologic. In boys, most cases are congenital and physiologic and occur either in the neonatal period or during adolescence. In utero, exposure to high maternal estrogen levels can cause the development of mammary tissue (neonatal gynecomastia), which regresses within a few weeks after birth. In adolescents, elevation of the estradiol-testosterone ratio causes detectable gynecomastia in as many as 65% of boys; however, in most it is not noticeable without a focused

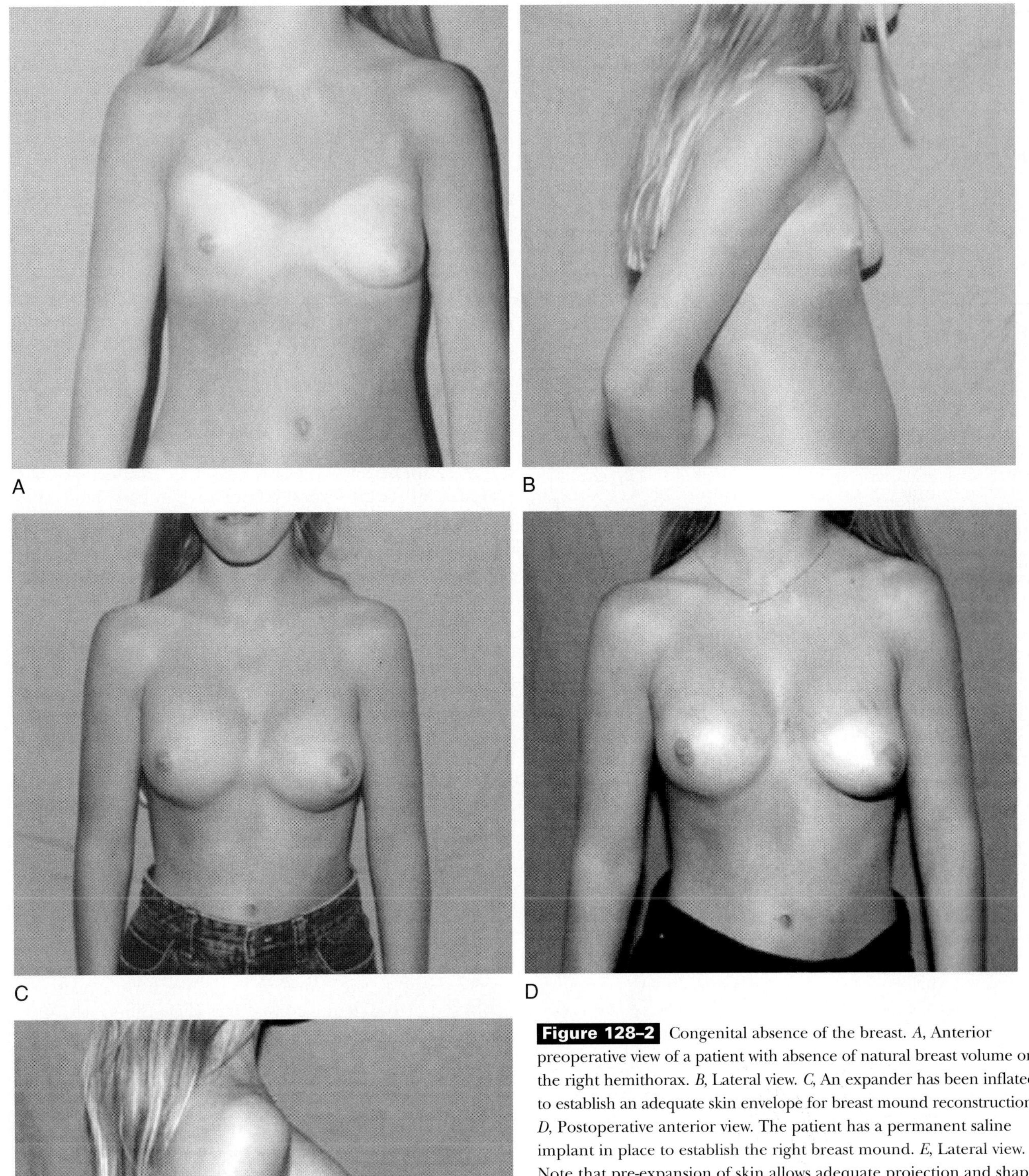

Figure 128–2 Congenital absence of the breast. *A*, Anterior preoperative view of a patient with absence of natural breast volume on the right hemithorax. *B*, Lateral view. *C*, An expander has been inflated to establish an adequate skin envelope for breast mound reconstruction. *D*, Postoperative anterior view. The patient has a permanent saline implant in place to establish the right breast mound. *E*, Lateral view. Note that pre-expansion of skin allows adequate projection and shape after the permanent implant is inserted.

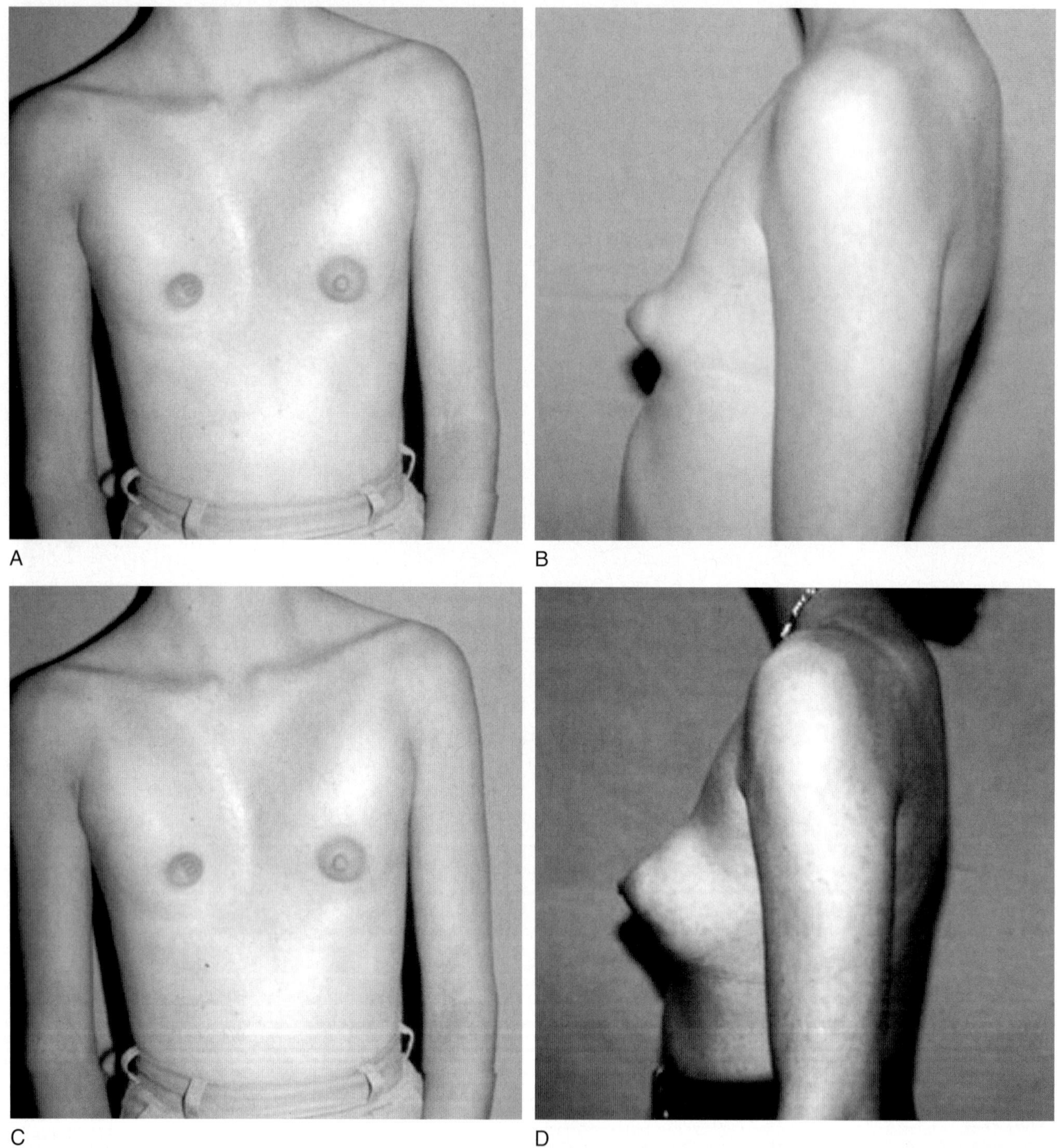

Figure 128-3 Tuberous left breast with mild pectus excavatum. *A*, Preoperative anterior view of a congenital breast and central chest deformity. *B*, Lateral view. Note the tuberous breast deformity. *C*, Postoperative release of periareolar congenital constricting bands and the use of an implant to establish the breast mound. *D*, Postoperative lateral view.

physical examination. Nearly all cases regress by the end of puberty.[18,51] Pathologic gynecomastia in children and adolescents is relatively rare, but requires special attention, especially in the case of Klinefelter's syndrome, which is associated with a 60-fold increased risk for breast cancer (unlike gynecomastia in general, which has no elevated risk).[33]

Although gynecomastia in adolescents is typically self-limited and resolves by the end of puberty, persistent gynecomastia (present for more than a year *and* beyond puberty) generally does not resolve without surgical treatment because the abnormal breast inevitably becomes fibrotic.[6] The gynecomastia for which a plastic surgeon is initially contacted is usually an aesthetic complaint;

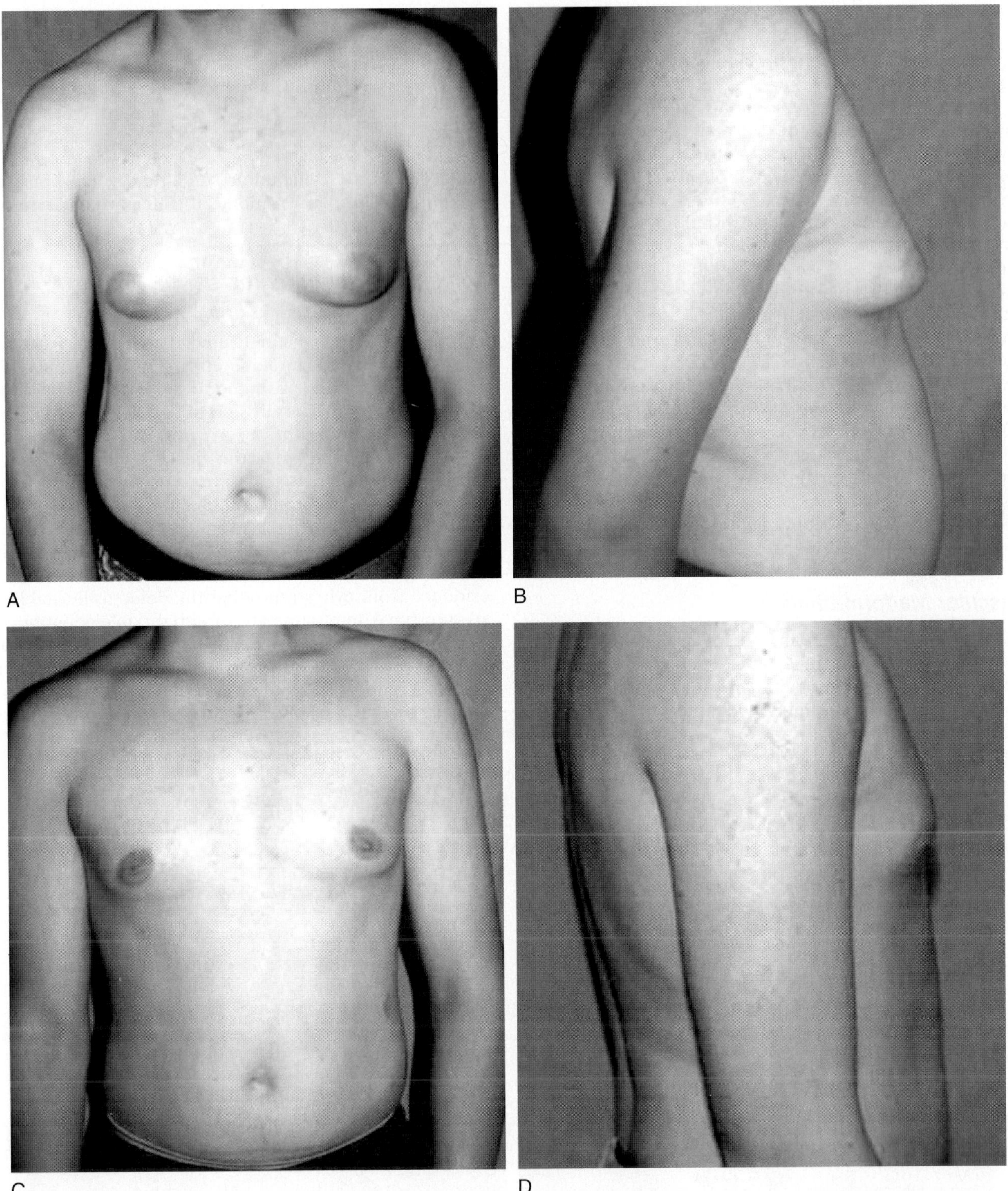

Figure 128–4 Gynecomastia. *A*, Preoperative anterior view of an adolescent with abnormal breast development. *B*, Lateral view. Note the excessive breast tissue with the development of early breast ptosis. *C*, Postoperative view after the use of liposuction. *D*, Lateral view. A contour deformity caused by over-resection was avoided by combining direct excision and liposuction.

however, this does not obviate the need for a detailed history and physical examination. Although gynecomastia in the general population and even cases examined by a pediatrician are generally uncomplicated and benign, there is good evidence that gynecomastia needing surgical treatment is a more complicated subset of the disorder. In particular, several large studies have shown an increased incidence of testicular and nonmelanoma skin cancer in males with gynecomastia requiring operative treatment. The risk for testicular cancer is particularly elevated in young men and may have a standardized incidence ratio as high as 6.7.[19,60] Examination of the testicles and skin, as well as education regarding skin cancer prevention, is mandatory.

For adolescent gynecomastia, a trial of nonoperative treatment is the rule because nearly all cases resolve within 2 years.[45] For persistent cases, treatment depends on the size of the breast and the degree of ptosis. Treatment of gynecomastia is varied and includes mastectomy via intra-areolar incisions, suction-assisted lipectomy (SAL), and ultrasound-assisted lipectomy (UAL). Drug-based therapy has had little success. For small breasts, simple excision through an intramammary incision is useful, although SAL and UAL have been used. For larger, broader-based breasts with minimal or no ptosis, a combination of excision via an intra-areolar approach and SAL/UAL is generally optimal. All the breast tissue can be removed through the incision, but the addition of suction lipectomy techniques permits better chest contouring and avoidance of a concave deformity. The approach for large breasts with significant ptosis is controversial. Often, a significant excess of skin needs to be removed and mastectomy with free nipple grafting is performed; however, a satisfactory aesthetic result is harder to achieve.[51]

Vascular Malformations

Discussions of hemangiomas, capillary malformations (port-wine stain), telangiectasia, lymphatic malformations (cystic hygroma), and venous and complex malformations are presented in Chapters 130 to 133.

Muscles, Tendons, and Connective Tissue

Information regarding Ehlers-Danlos and Marfan's syndrome is found in Chapters 59, 74, and 123.

Clefts

Cleft deformities, including unilateral cleft lip, cleft palate, and complex craniofacial clefts, are discussed in Chapters 50 and 51.

Congenital Blepharoptosis

Congenital maldevelopment of the levator palpebrae superioris muscle is distinguished at birth by drooping of one or both of the upper eyelids (Fig. 128-5A and B). This defect has been proposed to follow abnormal development of the superior division of the oculomotor nerve, although this theory has been controversial, with some evidence suggesting that the developmental defect is within the muscle itself. Its presence with a superior rectus weakness indicates a more proximal maldevelopment of the third cranial nerve, although normal papillary and accommodation reflexes suggest that the oculomotor nucleus itself is not involved. There is good evidence from twin studies that the defect is heritable in an autosomal dominant pattern with variable penetrance.[5]

Severe blepharoptosis with a risk for amblyopia demands early correction. Replacement of levator function by using redirected frontalis muscular forces through a fascial brow suspension is recommended in severe cases.

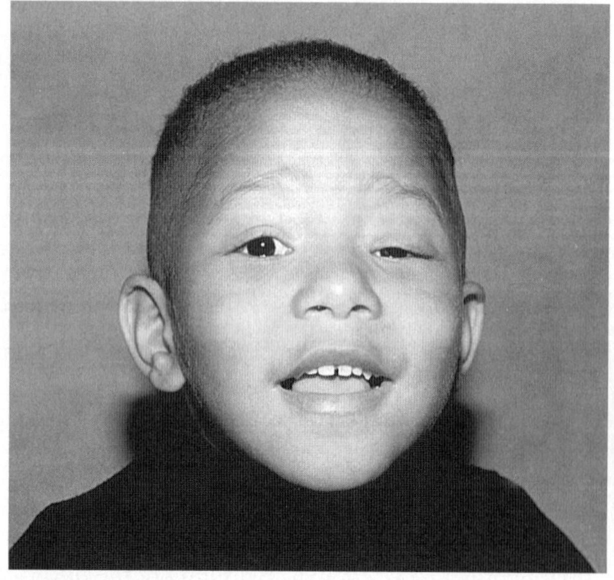

A

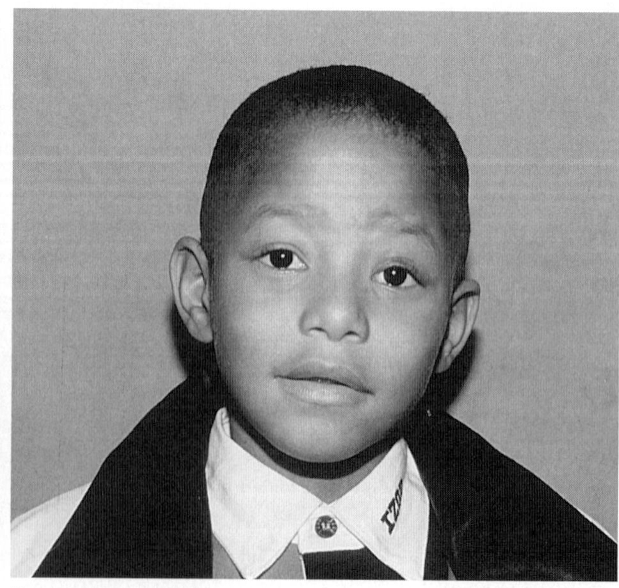

B

Figure 128–5 *A*, Congenital blepharoptosis of the left upper eyelid. *B*, Excellent correction of a ptotic upper lid with a fascial sling from the tarsus to the frontalis muscle.

Milder cases should be delayed until 3 or 4 years of age, when the delicate lid structures are easier to see and manipulate. If sufficient levator muscle is present, resection with shortening of its aponeurosis may yield adequate correction.[29,64]

Poland's Syndrome

In 1841 Alfred Poland, a medical student, reported some unusual anatomic findings on his cadaver: unilateral hypoplasia of the pectoralis musculature, upper limb, and hand. Expression of the various components of this trait varies widely. The incidence has been most frequently estimated to be 1 in 30,000 with a predilection in females of approximately 2:1 to 3:1.[22,32]

The etiology of Poland's syndrome has been theorized to be obstruction of the subclavian blood supply during the sixth to seventh weeks of gestation. During this time, the ribs grow anteriorly and medially and depress the subclavian artery into a U-shaped configuration. Tension on the arterial wall may cause kinking and obstruction. The site of diminished blood flow may determine the tissues involved in the defect, which can include the thoracic wall, the pectoralis muscle, and the breast, as well as the upper extremity and hand. Vascular studies have shown diminished blood flow in the subclavian artery on the affected side. More proximal arterial involvement of the subclavian or vertebral systems has been shown to give rise to the bony cervical anomalies found in Klippel-Feil syndrome and the congenital palsies of cranial nerves VI and VII in Möbius' syndrome. The synchronous presence of Poland's, Klippel-Feil, and Möbius' syndromes supports a common embryologic event (i.e., vascular accident) in their genesis.[16,17,23,46]

The essential feature of Poland's syndrome is absence of the sternal head of the pectoralis major muscle. Other features are hypoplasia or aplasia of the breast or nipple, deficiency of subcutaneous fat and hair across the chest and axilla, and abnormalities of the ipsilateral limb, including shortening and brachysyndactyly. Other muscles may also be involved to variable degrees, including absence of the pectoralis muscle (Fig. 128-6A to F) and hypoplasia of the serratus anterior, supraspinatus, latissimus dorsi, and external oblique muscles. The thoracic cage itself may be involved with absence of the anterolateral ribs and possible lung herniation or symptomatic depressions in the chest wall. The hand deformities can be more involved, with symphalangism occurring with syndactyly and hypoplasia or absence of the middle phalanges. Detection of syndactyly in a patient should make Poland's syndrome a consideration because 10% of all cases of syndactyly have been reported to have features of this syndrome.[2,22]

Despite the hand deformities, the functional disability is generally mild and related to the presence of syndactyly. In milder forms of Poland's syndrome, treatment is primarily for aesthetic reasons. For more severe manifestations, particularly those in which the thoracic cage is involved, stabilization of the protective chest wall is warranted first because all other chest reconstructions will be placed on top of this foundation. Minor chest wall deformities are generally reconstructed with an ipsilateral latissimus dorsi muscle flap. Major chest wall deformities require better stabilization with either bone or prosthetic mesh. Split-rib homografts and Marlex mesh have been used for moderate and severe defects and are covered with a latissimus dorsi muscle transfer. The transferred latissimus dorsi muscle replicates the missing anterior axillary fold of the pectoralis muscle and improves soft tissue coverage. The remaining major contour irregularities may be treated with a custom alloplastic implant.[4,22,58]

Reconstruction of the female breast in patients with Poland's syndrome often presents a challenging problem. In severe cases the breast reconstruction generally occurs as a second-stage procedure late in adolescence, years after stabilization of the chest wall. Placement of an implant behind a latissimus dorsi muscle transposition has been effective. Successful use of free tissue transfer has also been reported. In cases in which the cutaneous envelope is hypoplastic, tissue expansion early in puberty will augment the soft tissues for later final repair and may guard against the psychological distress of an absent breast.[3,40,72]

Torticollis

For a discussion of torticollis please refer to Chapter 57.

The Hand

Embryology

Arm buds appear at 31 days, the 14th stage in embryonic development, coincident with formation of the marginal vein beneath the surface ectoderm. The paddle-like hand segment forms on approximately day 33. Finger rays are evident at 41 days but do not begin to separate until day 47. Interdigital zones destined for apoptosis determine the separation of the fingers. The median artery supplying the embryonic hand is replaced by the radial and ulnar arteries between the fifth and sixth weeks. The reduced median artery maintains only the median nerve and interosseous blood supply. Dorsal and ventral blastemas differentiate into the dorsal and volar forearm musculature, respectively, from the fifth to eighth week and are formed superficially and deeply. Intrinsic hand muscles arise from five embryonic layers; the deep hypothenar and thenar muscles in the seventh week are the last to separate. Condensation and then chondrification of the mesenchyme begin in the fifth week and end with chondrification of the phalanges at week 6 and the sesamoids at week 7. The eighth week marks the end of embryogenesis; much of the final form is in place. Growth dominates the rest of fetal development, during which the fingernail fields develop and the cartilaginous bones ossify.[53]

Incidence

The estimated incidence of upper limb deformities ranges from 18 per 10,000 population to 1 per 626 live births.[8,37]

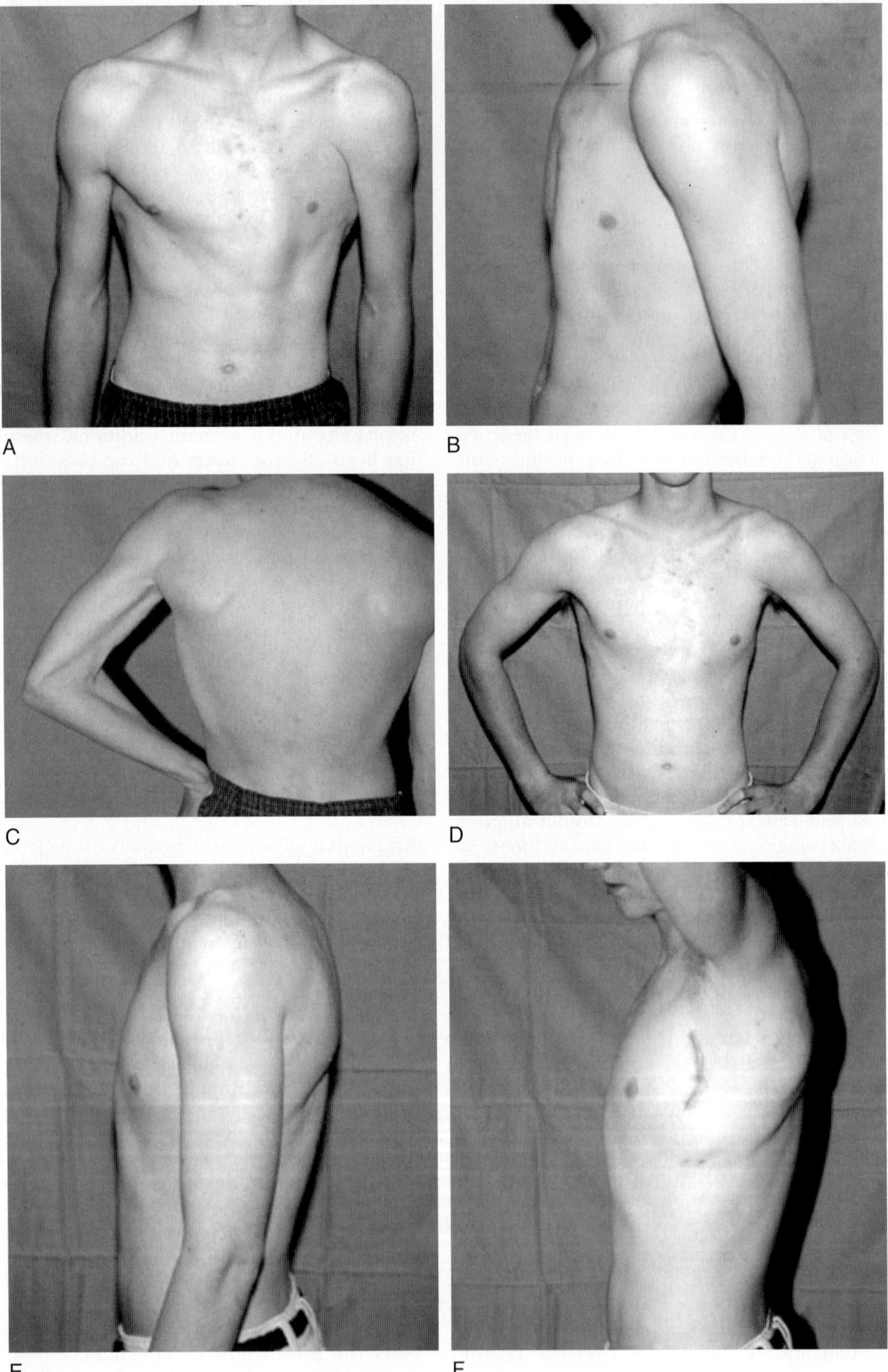

Figure 128–6 Poland's syndrome on the left side of the chest with an associated asymmetric pectus carinatum deformity. *A*, Preoperative anterior view. Note the absence of the left pectoralis muscle. *B*, Lateral view. *C*, Posterior view of the chest with the patient testing for the presence of the left latissimus dorsi muscle. Note the lateral edge of the muscle is visible with isotonic contraction. *D*, Postoperative anterior view. Note that functional transfer of the latissimus dorsi muscle to the anterior hemithorax provides contour correction and maintains latissimus dorsi function. *E*, Postoperative lateral view. The incision is concealed beneath the upper extremity. Note that the contour of the latissimus dorsi on the anterior aspect of the chest simulates the absent pectoralis muscle without contour deformity at the posterior chest donor site. *F*, A postoperative lateral view with the upper extremity abducted reveals the incision used for muscle harvest.

The Centers for Disease Control and Prevention reports the following rates per *1000* live births: 0.8 for transverse deficiencies, 0.9 for syndactyly, 0.2 for polydactyly in white persons, and 0.12 for polydactyly in black persons.[12] In 40% to 50% of cases no clear cause can be determined. It is estimated that environmental factors account for 10% of limb anomalies.[75] Rubella, cytomegalovirus, *Toxoplasma*, and varicella infections in the first trimester have been linked to longitudinal deficiencies. Chemicals affecting limb development include thalidomide, ethanol, phenytoin, and warfarin. Many genetic syndromes (of mendelian inheritance patterns or otherwise) have been associated with skeletal anomalies. Brachydactyly, clinodactyly, syndactyly, and polydactyly have been noted in trisomy 21; camptodactyly in trisomy 18; and polydactyly in trisomy 13.

Congenital Hand Deformities: Classification and Treatment

The International Federation for Surgery of the Hand has established a seven-category classification system for hand deformities, as shown in Table 128-1.[76]

Failure of Formation

Failure of formation is further divided into transverse and longitudinal arrest of development. Transverse deficiencies are congenital amputations, the most severe of which occur at the shoulder level and result in amelia. The short below-elbow defect, a common transverse deficiency, ends at the upper part of the forearm. Prosthetic fitting should begin in infancy. Wrist disarticulation defects occur more often in girls than in boys. In this condition, the skeleton is absent beyond the distal radial and ulnar epiphyses, but pronation and supination abilities are generally maintained. In bilateral defects, the Krukenberg procedure may be indicated on the dominant arm with a prosthesis worn only on the nondominant arm. The Krukenberg procedure separates the forearm bones into opposing prehensile forceps. Progressive length reduction defines longitudinal deficiencies that may be preaxial (radial), postaxial (ulnar), central or complete (phocomelia).

TABLE 128-1 International Federation for Surgery of the Hand Classification System for Congenital Hand Anomalies

1. Failure of formation
2. Failure of differentiation
3. Duplication
4. Overgrowth
5. Undergrowth
6. Congenital constriction band syndrome
7. Generalized skeletal abnormalities

Radial Deficiencies: Radial deficiencies variably affect the radius, scaphoid, trapezius, trapezoid, and thumb, as well as associated musculotendinous, neural, and vascular structures. In the classic radial clubhand, the forearm is short, the hand is radially deviated, and the thumb is absent or floating. The defect begins in the first weeks of fetal life. Radial shaft development coincides with development of the cardiac septum, which may explain the association of radial ray defects with the atrial septal defect found in Holt-Oram syndrome. Radial defects are also associated with vertebral defects, imperforate anus, tracheoesophageal fistula with esophageal atresia, radial and renal dysplasia (VATER syndrome) and with blood dyscrasias such as Fanconi's anemia and thrombocytopenia with absent radii (TAR syndrome). Treatment begins shortly after birth; traditional methods stretch the hand over the ulna by serial castings. Distraction lengthening and free fibula transfers have also been investigated.

Ulnar Defects: Ulnar ray deficiencies are rare and can be associated with defects of the ring or little finger, elbow, humerus, or shoulder girdle (Poland's syndrome). Unlike the radius, which functions as a buttress for the wrist, the ulna may be deficient without any accompanying ulnar wrist deviation. Severity varies from hypoplasia, to partial or total defects with or without humeroradial synostosis, to ulnar deficiency with amputation at the level of the wrist. Prostheses such as an elbow disarticulation device can improve limb use. In selected patients, fusion of the ulnar remnant to the radius provides stability at the elbow.

Thumb Defects: Management of thumb defects depends on their severity. In total aplasia of the thumb, pollicization of the first finger is the most successful method of achieving functional opposition. Toe-to-thumb transfer is not successful because recipient nerve and tendon structures are absent and the brain lacks the motor and sensory homunculus for the thumb. Short thumbs can be lengthened by distraction osteogenesis. Widening of the first web space and tendon transfer to establish opposition may improve function. Floating thumbs are generally amputated and opposition accomplished by pollicization of the index finger.

Cleft Hand: Cleft hand, lobster claw, and split hand are descriptive terms for defects of the central (second, third, or fourth) rays. Typical deficiencies involve partial or complete loss of the central digit or digits. Atypical deficiencies are syndactylous (the central finger remnants fuse to the second or fourth ray) or polydactylous. The polydactylous type contains supernumerary bony elements. Function determines treatment; appearance is a secondary consideration. Resection of the remnant third metacarpal assists closure of a deep cleft. Osteotomies correct rotatory deformities of the adjacent fingers.

Failure of Differentiation

Failure of differentiation includes soft tissue and skeletal failure of separation of parts, as well as congenital tumors.

Synostosis of the phalanges (symphalangism) is uncommon and usually occurs with syndactyly. Syndactyly itself is common and most often occurs between the middle and ring fingers. True failure of differentiation is distinguished from the brachysyndactyly (short, webbed fingers) of Poland's syndrome and from acrosyndactyly with fusion of the distal digits secondary to a constriction band. Syndromes featuring syndactyly include Apert's syndrome (acrocephalosyndactyly), Chotzen's syndrome (cephalodactyly), Pfeiffer's and Goltz's syndromes, oculodentogenital syndrome, and trisomy 13.

Digits with acrosyndactyly should be separated before 1 year of age if the digits are of discrepant length or the phalangeal bones are fused. In the absence of these features, separation can be performed at 2 to 3 years. The complexity of Apert's "mitten" hand presents a challenge to provide a functional hand with both prehensile function and fingertip sensation (Fig. 128-7). To this end, a three-fingered hand is often preferable to four fingers and a thumb.[21] The thumb and small fingers are released before 1 year of age. The remaining digits are separated within 6 to 9 months. Another feature of Apert's syndrome is radioclinodactyly of the thumb (radial curvature of the thumb). Thumb osteotomy and bone grafting are performed at 4 to 7 years of age, along with Z-plasty of the web space between the thumb and index finger.

Congenital Flexion Deformities: Failure of soft tissue differentiation can lead to congenital flexion deformities. In the clasped thumb or thumb-in-palm contracture, the extensor pollicis longus, extensor pollicis brevis, and abductor pollicis longus musculotendon units are absent or attenuated. Splinting and manipulation begin in infancy; surgical correction is delayed until 3 years of age. A clasped thumb must be differentiated from a trigger thumb, wherein a flexor pollicis longus nodule proximal to the first (A1) pulley of the flexor apparatus of the hand interferes with interphalangeal and metacarpophalangeal extension. Because of a 30% spontaneous resolution rate, surgical trigger finger release is recommended for contractures that persist beyond 3 years of age.

Clinodactyly most often affects the middle phalanx of the little finger and is seen in many syndromes (e.g., Treacher Collins and Silver-Russell syndromes, as well as orofaciodigital and oculodentodigital dysplasia). Camptodactyly refers to congenital proximal interphalangeal flexion contracture, usually of the little finger, and is associated with such syndromes as Marfan's, popliteal pterygium, and orofaciodigital and oculodentodigital dysplasia. If disabling or deforming, the contracture is released by dividing the flexor digitorum superficialis tendon and lengthening the volar skin with a full-thickness skin graft. In more severe cases, arthroplasty or arthrodesis is performed. Arthrogryposis multiplex congenita features multiple congenital nonprogressive joint contractures and affects all extremities and the spine. In the upper extremity the shoulder may be flexed and internally rotated, the elbow flexed or extended, the wrist flexed and ulnarly deviated or extended and radially

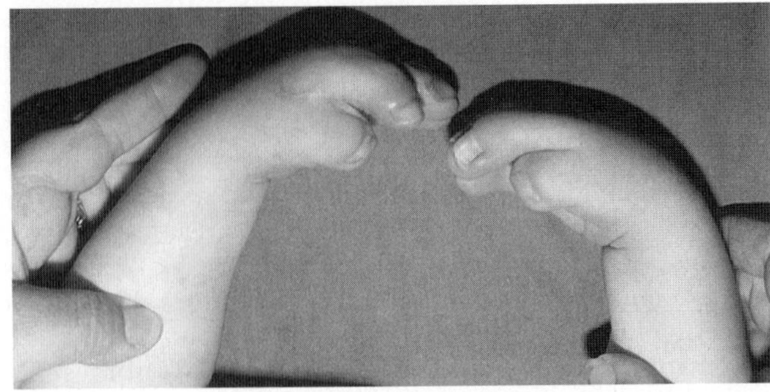
A

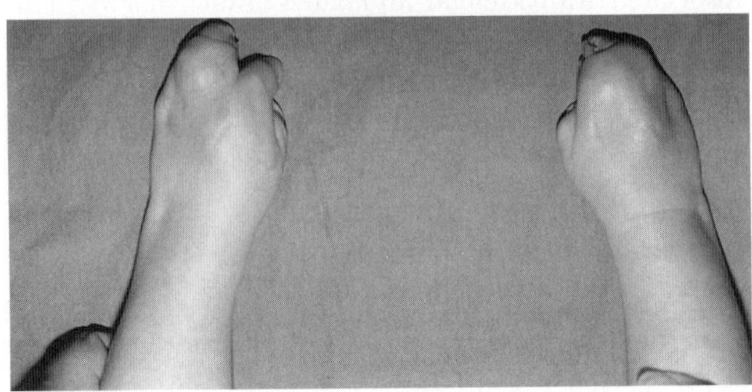
B

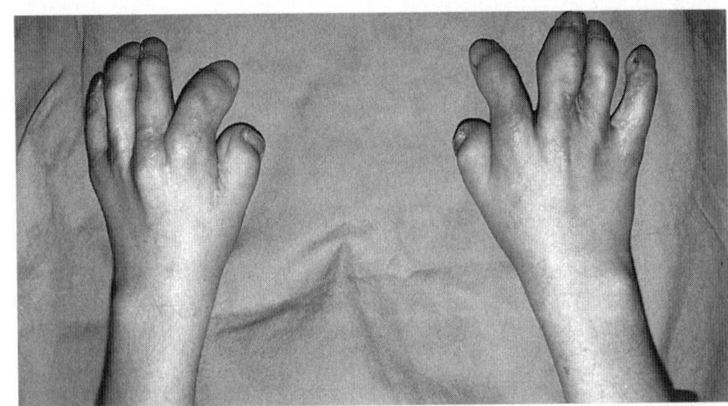
C

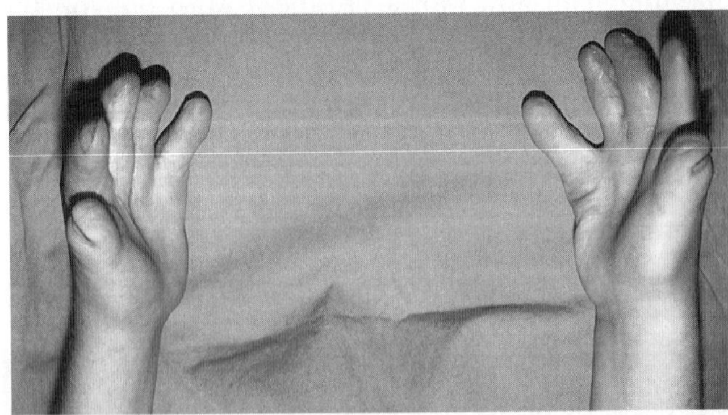
D

Figure 128–7 *A*, Infant with Apert's syndrome afflicted with the typical acrosyndactyly deformity of the hand. *B*, Complex bilateral acrosyndactyly. *C* and *D*, Postoperative appearance after release of syndactyly.

deviated, and the thumb and fingers flexed and ulnarly deviated.

Arthrogryposis isolated to the hand is manifested as the "wind-blown hand," with metacarpophalangeal flexion and ulnar deviation caused by malformation of the palmar fascia and retaining ligaments, with or without involvement of tendons and capsules. Thick fibrous subcutaneous bands and shortened digitopalmar skin contribute to this malformation. Secondary metacarpal head deformation occurs with time. The thumb is flexed, and abduction is limited by a retracted volar carpal ligament and carpal skin.

Splinting and manipulation begin in infancy. If the deformity progresses, as often happens during the adolescent growth spurt, operative intervention is indicated. Corrective procedures include release of the metacarpophalangeal joint capsule, ligament, and intrinsic tendon; relocation of the extrinsic tendon; and metacarpal osteotomy and division of palmar skin and fibrous bands, followed by skin grafting for coverage.

Duplication of Parts

Duplication of parts occurs early in embryonic development. Polydactyly is a common hand malformation. Postaxial little finger duplication occurs more often than preaxial thumb duplication. Central duplications are rare. A flail, poorly attached appendage should be amputated early. Operative correction of preaxial polydactyly is sometimes delayed until 12 months of age, when functional evaluation is possible and the dominant (usually ulnar) thumb can be identified and preserved. The collateral ligaments, even tendons and bony elements, of the ablated digit are salvaged for reconstruction of the retained digit. Alternatively, the Bilhaut-Cloquet procedure consisting of excision of a central wedge from adjacent parts of both thumbs and then joining the remaining lateral portions can be performed. If the thumb resembles an index finger and cannot be opposed, treatment consists of rotational osteotomy, tendon transfer (e.g., Huber transfer of the abductor digiti minimi across the palm), and widening of the first web space.

A mirror hand possesses seven or eight digits, one or two index with two ring and middle fingers, two ulnae, absent radius, absent thumb, and weak or absent extensor tendons. The hand loses its ability to pinch or grasp. An opposing digit needs to be constructed and excess fingers discarded; the filleted skin is used to create a wide web space. Wrist arthrodesis may be required in early adolescence. Elbow motion may be improved by excising the olecranon off one of the ulnae.

Overgrowth

Digital gigantism involves the overgrowth of bone and soft tissues. Classic type I macrodactyly is associated with lipofibromatous hamartoma of the median or (less frequently) the ulnar nerve. Phalangeal involvement is constant, and metacarpal involvement varies. Soft tissue overgrowth can affect skin and lymphatic or nerve structures, although the flexor tendons and blood vessels may be spared. Gigantism of several adjacent digits is more prevalent than single-digit macrodactyly. Median nerve hamartoma can compress structures in the carpal tunnel. Type II macrodactyly is part of von Recklinghausen's disease (neurofibromatosis). The distribution follows the path of a major peripheral nerve, most frequently the median nerve. Contrary to types I and II, type III macrodactyly (hyperostotic) is not associated with nerve enlargement but does follow the course of the sensory branches of the median nerve. Treatment has included epiphyseodesis, epiphyseal arrest, epiphyseal plat excision, multiple defatting procedures, longitudinal phalangeal osteotomies, soft tissue debulking, excision of distal nerves, and partial or ray amputation. Skin flap necrosis is not an uncommon complication after repair of macrodactyly.

Undergrowth

Undergrowth malformations vary in the structures affected and the degree of the hypoplasia. Brachydactyly (shortened digits) is commonly seen in association with syndromic disorders, generally of autosomal dominant transmission. Ectrodactyly is complete absence of the phalanx or phalanges or metacarpals. Short metacarpals are uncommon and often go unrecognized until the adolescent growth spurt; associated syndromes include pseudohyperparathyroidism, Turner's syndrome, and cri du chat. Treatment is usually unnecessary, but lengthening the affected ulnar metacarpals does increase palm size and improve grip. Lengthening procedures involve either bone grafting or distraction osteogenesis.[41,57,73] Short phalanges are the major cause of brachydactyly. The middle phalanx of the little finger is the hand bone whose length varies the most, particularly in girls. Other than osteotomies to correct deviations, there is little role for operative intervention. Phalangeal lengthening procedures rarely improve function.

Constriction Band Deformities

Constriction band deformities occur in fetal development. The predominating theory is that amniotic bands wrapped around a limb cause local ischemia and necrosis. An alternative explanation proposes an intrinsic defect wherein hemorrhage or a local defect in the limb leads to necrosis of the superficial tissues. The necrotic area heals as a circumferential scar, and amniotic bands appear secondary to the limb injury.[77] The distal regions of the extremities are affected more often than the proximal regions. Compression neuropathy distal to the constriction band scar has been reported. In the digits, acrosyndactyly results from tissue necrosis and fusion. Separations between the digits proximal to the fusion and distal transverse grooves or amputations characterize acrosyndactyly. For most constriction rings, simple or staged excision and Z-plasty suffice. Broad rings may require local flap coverage of large defects. Treatment of fused digits is individualized; separation may include cross-finger flaps, completion amputation, distraction lengthening, or free toe transfer.

SUMMARY

A wide spectrum of anomalies of varying severity can result from the congenital absence of skin, muscles, connective tissues, and tendons. Any anatomic region of the body can be affected. In determining the indications and timing for surgical correction, the severity of functional impairment, the degree of disfigurement, and the social pressures associated with the malformation must be considered. A sound plan of management relies on an accurate diagnosis and analysis of the defect. Almost all defects can be systematically evaluated by the degree of malpositioned normal structures, absence of tissues, and aberrations in tissue composition. Surgical correction can then be formulated to specifically address each component of the deformity. Using a systematic approach simplifies and optimizes a safe treatment plan for even the most complex malformations.

REFERENCES

1. Abramson DJ: Bilateral intra-areolar polythelia. Arch Surg 1975;110:1255.
2. Al-Qattan MM: Classification of hand anomalies in Poland's syndrome. Br J Plast Surg 2001;54:132.
3. Argenta LC, VanderKolk C, Friedman RJ, Marks M: Refinements in reconstruction of congenital breast deformities. Plast Reconstr Surg 1985;76:73.
4. Avci G, Misirlioglu A, Eker G, Akoz T: Mild degree of Poland's syndrome reconstruction with customized silicone prosthesis. Aesthetic Plast Surg 2003;27:112.
5. Baldwin HC, Manners RM: Congenital blepharoptosis: A literature review of the histology of levator palpebrae superioris muscle. Ophthalm Plast Reconstr Surg 2002; 18:301.
6. Bannayan GA, Hajdu SI: Gynecomastia: Clinicopathologic study of 351 cases. Am J Clin Pathol 1972;57:431.
7. Bauer BS, Corcoran J: Treatment of large and giant nevi. Clin Plast Surg 2005;32:11.
8. Bowe J, Conway H: Congenital deformities of the hands. Plast Reconstr Surg 1956;18:286.
9. Carlson HE: Gynecomastia. N Engl J Med 1980; 303:795.
10. Castilla EE, da Graca Dutra M, Orioli-Parreiras IM: Epidemiology of congenital pigmented naevi: I. Incidence rates and relative frequencies. Br J Dermatol 1981;104:307.
11. Castilla EE, da Graca Dutra M, Orioli-Parreiras IM: Epidemiology of congenital pigmented naevi: II. Risk factors. Br J Dermatol 1981;104:421.
12. Centers for Disease Control and Prevention: Congenital Malformation Surveillance Report. Atlanta, US Public Health Service, US Department of Health and Human Services, 1984.
13. Cheong JH, Lee BC, Lee KS: Carcinoma of the axillary breast. Yonsei Med J 1999;40:290.
14. Chung CS, Myrianthopoulos NC: Congenital anomalies: Mortality and morbidity, burden and classification. Am J Med Genet 1987;27:505.
15. Ciresi KF, Mathes SJ: The classification of flaps. Orthop Clin North Am 1993;24:383.
16. Cobben JM, Robinson PH, van Essen AJ, et al: Poland anomaly in mother and daughter. Am J Med Genet 1989; 33:519.
17. Cobben JM, van Essen AJ, McParland PC, et al: A boy with Poland anomaly and facio-auriculo-vertebral dysplasia. Clin Genet 1992;41:105.
18. Cohen IK, Pozez AL, McKeown JE: Gynecomastia. In Courtiss EH (ed): Male Aesthetic Surgery. St Louis, CV Mosby, 1991.
19. Daniels IR, Layer GT: Testicular tumours presenting as gynaecomastia. Eur J Surg Oncol 2003;29:437.
20. Elmendorf EN 3rd, D'Antonio LL, Hardesty RA: Assessment of the patient with cleft lip and palate. A developmental approach. Clin Plast Surg 1993;20:607.
21. Flatt A: The Care of Congenital Hand Anomalies. St Louis, CV Mosby, 1977.
22. Fokin AA, Robicsek F: Poland's syndrome revisited. Ann Thorac Surg 2002;74:2218.
23. Fraser FC, Ronen GM, O'Leary E: Pectoralis major defect and Poland sequence in second cousins: Extension of the Poland sequence spectrum. Am J Med Genet 1989; 33:468.
24. Glass AR: Gynecomastia. Endocrinol Metab Clin North Am 1994;23:825.
25. Goedert JJ, McKeen EA, Javadpour N, et al: Polythelia and testicular cancer. Ann Intern Med 1984;101:646.
26. Goldberg R, Motzkin B, Marion R, et al: Velo-cardio-facial syndrome: A review of 120 patients. Am J Med Genet 1993; 45:313.
27. Graham JM Jr, Smith DW: Dominantly inherited pterygium colli. J Pediatr 1981;98:664.
28. Grolleau JL, Lanfrey E, Lavigne B, et al: Breast base anomalies: Treatment strategy for tuberous breasts, minor deformities, and asymmetry. Plast Reconstr Surg 1999; 104:2040.
29. Han K, Kang J: Tripartite frontalis muscle flap transposition for blepharoptosis. Ann Plast Surg 1993; 30:224.
30. Hassold T, Chen N, Funkhouser J, et al: A cytogenetic study of 1000 spontaneous abortions. Ann Hum Genet 1980; 44:151.
31. Holmes LB, Kleiner BC, Leppig KA, et al: Predictive value of minor anomalies: II. Use in cohort studies to identify teratogens. Teratology 1987;36:291.
32. Hurwitz DJ, Stofman G, Curtin H: Three-dimensional imaging of Poland's syndrome. Plast Reconstr Surg 1994; 94:719.
33. Jackson AW, Muldal S, Ockey CH, O'Connor PJ: Carcinoma of male breast in association with the Klinefelter syndrome. BMJ 1965;5429:223.
34. Jerdan MS, Cohen BA, Smith RR, Hood AF: Neuroectodermal neoplasms arising in congenital nevi. Am J Dermatopathol 1985;7(Suppl):41.
35. Kapp-Simon KA: Psychological interventions for the adolescent with cleft lip and palate. Cleft Palate Craniofac J 1995;32:104.
36. Kim CS, Tatum SA, Rodziewicz G: Scalp aplasia cutis congenita presenting with sagittal sinus hemorrhage. Arch Otolaryngol Head Neck Surg 2001;127:71.
37. Lamb DW, Wynne-Davies R, Soto L: An estimate of the population frequency of congenital malformations of the upper limb. J Hand Surg [Am] 1982;7:557.
38. Leppig KA, Werler MM, Cann CI, et al: Predictive value of minor anomalies. I. Association with major malformations. J Pediatr 1987;110:531.
39. Llaneras MR, Morgan RF, Pham ST, et al: Congenital giant hairy nevus: Implications for treatment. J Emerg Med 1989;7:25.
40. Longaker MT, Glat PM, Colen LB, Siebert JW: Reconstruction of breast asymmetry in Poland's chest-wall

deformity using microvascular free flaps. Plast Reconstr Surg 1997;99:429.
41. Magnan B, Bragantini A, Regis D, Bartolozzi P: Metatarsal lengthening by callotasis during the growth phase. J Bone Joint Surg Br 1995;77:602.
42. Mandrekas AD, Zambacos GJ, Anastasopoulos A, et al: Aesthetic reconstruction of the tuberous breast deformity. Plast Reconstr Surg 2003;112:1099, discussion 1109.
43. Marchac D, Weston J: Abdominoplasty in infants for removal of giant congenital nevi: A report of three cases. Plast Reconstr Surg 1985;75:155.
44. Mathes SJ, Nahai F: Reconstructive Surgery: Principles, Anatomy and Technique. St Louis, Quality Medical, 1997.
45. McGrath MH: Gynecomastia. In Jurkiewicz MJ, Mathes SJ, Krizek TJ, Ariyan S (eds): Plastic Surgery: Principles and Practice. St Louis, CV Mosby, 1990.
46. Mentzel HJ, Seidel J, Sauner D, et al: Radiological aspects of the Poland syndrome and implications for treatment: A case study and review. Eur J Pediatr 2002; 161:455.
47. Meuli M, Meuli-Simmen C, Yingling CD, et al: Creation of myelomeningocele in utero: A model of functional damage from spinal cord exposure in fetal sheep. J Pediatr Surg 1995;30:1028, discussion 1032.
48. Meuli-Simmen C, Meuli M, Hutchins GM, et al: Fetal reconstructive surgery: Experimental use of the latissimus dorsi flap to correct myelomeningocele in utero. Plast Reconstr Surg 1995;96:1007.
49. Miller JF, Williamson E, Glue J, et al: Fetal loss after implantation. A prospective study. Lancet 1980;2:554.
50. Miranda E, Granstein RD: Neuropeptide and cytokine mediated regulation of Langerhans cell function. Excerpta Medica International Congress Series 1998;1159:101.
51. Mathes SJ, Seyfer AE, Miranda EP: Congenital anomalies of the chest wall. In Mathes SJ (ed): Plastic Surgery. Vol. 6. Philadelphia, Saunders/Elsevier, 2006; p. 457.
52. Mofid MM, Manson PN, Robertson BC, et al: Craniofacial distraction osteogenesis: A review of 3278 cases. Plast Reconstr Surg 2001;108:1103, discussion 1115.
53. Moore K: The Developing Human: Clinically Oriented Embryology, 4th ed. Philadelphia, Saunders, 1988.
54. Nelson MM, Cooper CK: Congenital defects of the breast—an autosomal dominant trait. S Afr Med J 1982; 61:434.
55. Neuman JF: Evaluation and treatment of gynecomastia. Am Fam Physician 1997;55:1835.
56. Nuttall FQ: Gynecomastia as a physical finding in normal men. J Clin Endocrinol Metab 1979;48:338.
57. Ogino T, Kato H, Ishii S, Usui M: Digital lengthening in congenital hand deformities. J Hand Surg [Br] 1994; 19:120.
58. Ohmori K, Takada H: Correction of Poland's pectoralis major muscle anomaly with latissimus dorsi musculocutaneous flaps. Plast Reconstr Surg 1980;65:400.
59. Olivera-Martinez I, Thelu J, Dhouailly D: Molecular mechanisms controlling dorsal dermis generation from the somitic dermomyotome. Int J Dev Biol 2004;48:93.
60. Olsson H, Bladstrom A, Alm P: Male gynecomastia and risk for malignant tumours—a cohort study. BMC Cancer 2002;2(1):26.
61. Osbourne M: Breast development and anatomy. In Harris J (ed): Breast Diseases, 2nd ed. Philadelphia, Lippincott, 1991, p 1.
62. O'Shaughnessy RF, Christiano AM: Inherited disorders of the skin in human and mouse: From development to differentiation. Int J Dev Biol 2004;48:171.
63. Panettiere P, Del Gaudio GA, Marchetti L, et al: The tuberous breast syndrome. Aesthetic Plast Surg 2000; 24:445.
64. Pearl RM: Improved technique for fascial sling reconstruction of severe congenital ptosis. Plast Reconstr Surg 1995; 95:920.
65. Rees TD, Aston SJ: The tuberous breast. Clin Plast Surg 1976;3:339.
66. Richman LC: Neuropsychological development in adolescents: Cognitive and emotional model for considering risk factors for adolescents with cleft. Cleft Palate Craniofac J 1995;32:99.
67. Rivera R, LoGiudice J, Gosain AK: Tissue expansion in pediatric patients. Clin Plast Surg 2005;32:35.
68. Rohrich RJ, Hartley W, Brown S: Incidence of breast and chest wall asymmetry in breast augmentation: A retrospective analysis of 100 patients. Plast Reconstr Surg 2003; 111:1513, discussion 1520.
69. Ross DA, Laurie SW, Coombs CJ, Mutimer KL: Aplasia cutis congenita: Failed conservative treatment. Plast Reconstr Surg 1995;95:124.
70. Rossillon D, De Mey A, Lejour M: Pterygium colli: Surgical treatment. Br J Plast Surg 1989;42:178.
71. Santibanez-Gallerani A, Marshall D, Duarte AM, et al: Should nevus sebaceus of Jadassohn in children be excised? A study of 757 cases, and literature review. J Craniofac Surg 2003;14:658.
72. Shamberger RC, Welch KJ, Upton J 3rd: Surgical treatment of thoracic deformity in Poland's syndrome. J Pediatr Surg 1989;24:760, discussion 766.
73. Smith RJ, Gumley GJ: Metacarpal distraction lengthening. Hand Clin 1985;1:417.
74. Straker H: Giant pigmented hairy nevi. Arch Dermatol 1968; 98:93.
75. Swanson AB, Swanson GD: Flynn's hand surgery. In Jupiter JJ (ed): Congenital Limb Malformations: Classification and Treatment, 4th ed. Baltimore, Williams & Wilkins, 1983.
76. Swanson AB, Swanson GD, Tada K: A classification for congenital limb malformation. J Hand Surg [Am] 1983; 8:693.
77. Tada K, Yonenobu K, Swanson AB: Congenital constriction band syndrome. J Pediatr Orthop 1984;4:726.
78. Tajbakhsh S, Sporle R: Somite development: Constructing the vertebrate body. Cell 1998;92:9.
79. Theile RJ, Lanigan MW, McDermant GR: Reconstruction of aplasia cutis congenita of the scalp by split rib cranioplasty and a free latissimus dorsi muscle flap in a nine month old infant. Br J Plast Surg 1995; 48:507.
80. Tobiasen JM, Hiebert JM: Clefting and psychosocial adjustment. Influence of facial aesthetics. Clin Plast Surg 1993; 20:623.
81. Urui S, Oi S: Experimental study of the embryogenesis of open spinal dysraphism. Neurosurg Clin North Am 1995;6:195.
82. van der Putte SC: Apoeccrine glands in nevus sebaceus. Am J Dermatopathol 1994;16:23.
83. Van Regemorter N, Dodion J, Druart C, et al: Congenital malformations in 10,000 consecutive births in a university hospital: Need for genetic counseling and prenatal diagnosis. J Pediatr 1984;104:386.
84. Velanovich V: Ectopic breast tissue, supernumerary breasts, and supernumerary nipples. South Med J 1995; 88:903.
85. Verhelle NA, Heymans O, Deleuze JP, et al: Abdominal aplasia cutis congenita: Case report and review of the literature. J Pediatr Surg 2004;39:237.

86. Whittaker PG, Taylor A, Lind T: Unsuspected pregnancy loss in healthy women. Lancet 1983;1:1126.
87. Wilcox AJ, Weinberg CR, O'Connor JF, et al: Incidence of early loss of pregnancy. N Engl J Med 1988; 319:189.
88. Zaal LH, Mooi WJ, Sillevis Smitt JH, van der Horst CM: Classification of congenital melanocytic naevi and malignant transformation: A review of the literature. Br J Plast Surg 2004;57:707.

Chapter 129  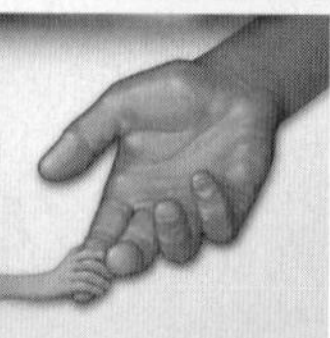

Conjoined Twins

James A. O'Neill, Jr.

Societal attitudes toward conjoined twinning have evolved over the centuries from these normal individuals being ostracized from society on religious grounds to the present day, where such individuals are considered in a much more humane fashion. Conjoined twinning is one of the rarest, most complicated, and most challenging of congenital malformations and requires the most creative aspects of all surgical specialties. In a historical review, Spitz and Kiely pointed out that the earliest references to conjoined twinning were in artistic artifacts such as a double-goddess sculpture dating from 6000 BC depicting parapagus twins.[68] A statue of female twins is displayed at the museum in Ankara, Turkey, and another early stone carving of pygopagus twins from 80 BC may be seen in the San Marco Museum in Florence, Italy. The first historical reference to conjoined twinning may be found in the writings of Pliny, but the earliest, fully described case is probably that of the Maids of Biddenden in England in 1100. Their memory has been perpetuated in the form of a yearly charity in which cakes purporting to represent their anatomy are sold. The image on the cake demonstrates junction at the shoulders and hips; most teratologists would not accept this junction, however, and the twins were probably of the pygopagus type. Their history, as well as several other historical cases, has been reviewed in detail by Bondeson.[6] The earliest attempt at separation of conjoined twins is recorded as occurring in Armenia in 970 AD.[66] This was a futile attempt to separate male ischiopagus twins at the age of 30 years after the death of one of the twins. In 1678, Paré published the first scientific report on the subject of conjoined twins in a thorough analysis of anatomy and etiology.[49] In 1670, Durston described isolated esophageal atresia in one member of a set of conjoined twins.[17]

This type of developmental asynchrony has been suggested by Seller to be an indication that conjoined twinning itself is a malformation and that other discordant malformations represent individual anomalies in individual twins, which is seen at least half the time.[56] In 1689, Koenig reported the first successful separation of omphalopagus twins by ligation of a small bridge of tissue at the level of the umbilicus, but the operation was actually performed by Johannes Fatio in Basel, Switzerland, and Koenig was only an observer.[35,52]

Interesting historical reviews have also been published by Sills et al., Anderson, Spencer, and others, and these reviews provide interesting information regarding the lives of unseparated conjoined twins and how they adapted to society at the time.[2,25,58,62]

The famous Bunker twins, born in Siam in 1811, gave rise to the term Siamese twins.[25] The fact that the twins worked in the P.T. Barnum Circus for many years strengthened the societal impression that such persons are curiosities or freaks when in truth, they are normal individuals who have potentially correctable malformations. The Bunker twins were never separated, even though successful separation would have been a simple undertaking, even at the time that they lived. To date, over 1200 cases of conjoined twinning and approximately 250 successful separations in which one or both twins have survived over the long term have been reported. Most of the latter cases have been reported since 1960.

INCIDENCE AND EMBRYOLOGY

The typical form of monozygotic twinning occurs at a constant rate of 4 per 1000 live births, although it appears to be higher when the mother is taking fertility drugs. The incidence of dizygotic, fraternal twins is approximately 10 to 15 per 1000, so overall, twin births occur in approximately 1 in 90 live births. Conjoined twinning probably occurs with a frequency of approximately 1 in 50,000 live births, but reported rates range from 1 in 100,000 live births in the United States to 1 in 50,000 in South Africa.[13,47] Clusters of more frequent occurrence of conjoined twinning are periodically reported.[18,46] Parasitic or heterotopic conjoined twins are exceedingly rare and occur in about 1 or 2 per 1,000,000 live births; this form of twinning has also been shown to be monozygotic.[24]

Spencer has reported that 1% of conjoined twins are stillborn, 40% to 60% survive only a day, and the remainder are potentially separable.[62] In stillborn conjoined twins, males predominate, which is of interest because conventional monozygotic twins are more frequently male. Recent reports reviewing prenatally diagnosed conjoined twins indicate that more than a fourth of cases die in utero and over half die immediately after birth, thus leaving only about 20% potential survivors.[39] These would appear to be more realistic figures, with survival being based primarily on the type and extent of union. However, conjoined twins who survive long enough to be candidates for separation are female at a ratio of approximately 3:1 over males.

In 1948, Rock and Hertig demonstrated that by the sixth day after fertilization, the cluster of cells constituting the human zygote becomes the so-called blastocyst.[53] The inner cell mass from which the embryo, amnion, and yolk sac develop forms from an aggregation of cells at one pole of the blastocyst. During this first week of gestation, the cells of the inner cell mass are totipotent, able to split to form two germinal disks. In turn, these disks can develop into two identical persons. Thus, division of the zygote within the first 7 days of gestation yields monozygotic twins who are identical in sex and karyotype, and they share an amnion and yolk sac. Dizygotic or fraternal twins result from the fertilization of two separate ova, and each fetus has its own amnion, yolk sac, and umbilical cord. Such twins may be of the same or opposite sex and have different karyotypes.

Although conjoined twinning obviously represents an alteration in early embryologic development, the exact cause is not known. Zimmerman described the classic theory on the embryology of conjoined twins.[77] His studies suggest that conjoined twins result when the inner cell mass incompletely divides after the first 7 days of the time that monozygotic twinning is thought to occur, that is, between 13 and 16 days after fertilization. The exact reason that complex fusion results from such late cleavage is still unknown; the range of complex fusion is broad, and incomplete division of the embryo seems to be associated with inhibition of complete differentiation of various organ systems. This latter theory of incomplete fission of a doubly fertilized embryo is accepted by most workers. On the other hand, Spencer has proposed an alternative theory in which conjoined twins might result from the secondary fusion of two originally separate monozygotic embryonic disks.[60] However, it is likely that fusion could not occur in areas where there is adjacent ectoderm. Spencer has also proposed that parasitic twins, fetuses in fetu, teratomas, and acardiacs all result from the deterioration or death of one embryo.[61] Although Spencer's meta-analysis makes great sense, both the fusion and fission theories remain unproved.

CLASSIFICATION

The most commonly applied clinical classification is an adaptation of that proposed by Potter and Craig, simplified to include the most common forms of conjoined twinning (Fig. 129-1).[50] This classification has been used almost universally in the literature as described in Table 129-1. In all descriptions, the term *pagus*, a Greek word meaning "that which is fixed," is used. In order of frequency, the most commonly used terms are thoracopagus, omphalopagus, pygopagus, ischiopagus, craniopagus, and heteropagus, and some combine the first two as thoracoomphalopagus because they commonly occur together. Alternatively, Spencer has described a classification useful from the standpoint of research that is based on an analysis of embryologic data and a collection of over 1200 cases in which the teratology was carefully analyzed.[59,62] She divided conjoined twinning into ventral and dorsal forms of junction joined in one of only eight anatomic sites. Her classification includes many rare forms of conjoined twinning, but it is not reflected broadly in the literature.

PRENATAL DIAGNOSIS AND OBSTETRIC MANAGEMENT

Various authors have described ultrasound (US) findings in conjoined twins.[7,30,33] Some reports indicate that the diagnosis can be made as early as the 10th week of gestation with this technique.[4] A large number of cases have been described over time with numerous technical improvements, including three-dimensional (3-D) reconstruction.[7] US findings indicative of conjoined twinning include a fixed position of twin bodies on serial examinations, lack of a separating membrane between the twins, and inability to demonstrate two urinary bladders, especially when associated with hydrops or polyhydramnios, which occurs half the time (Fig. 129-2). Although computed tomography (CT) with 3-D reconstruction has been used, it involves radiation and adds little to what can be shown by US.[33,37] On the other hand, ultrafast magnetic resonance imaging (MRI) with 3-D reconstruction has proved to be a valuable complementary study, particularly for cardiac evaluation.[11,22,41,65] Prenatal echocardiography (ECHO) has been shown to be extremely useful, often being more accurate than ECHO after birth. Prenatal US, ECHO, and 3-D MRI usually provide sufficient information to help families decide whether to continue the pregnancy.[73] In our experience with prenatal studies, accurate delineation of conjoined cardiac anatomy has been achieved as early as the 20th week of gestation, even though studies performed in the third trimester are probably the most reliable. Prenatal US is capable of demonstrating not only the presence of conjoined twins but also the unique complications that occur in multifetal gestations, such as twin-to-twin transfusion syndrome, acardiac twins, co-twin demise, and oligohydramnios-polyhydramnios sequence.[31,40] First-trimester color Doppler imaging is very useful for the study of vascular anatomy.[41] The usual approach is to use two-dimensional abdominal and transvaginal US during the first trimester, subsequently supplemented with color Doppler, MRI, and 3-D US.[73] Prenatal MRI has been helpful for diagnosing heteropagus forms of twins as well.[12]

The appropriate obstetric management of conjoined twins has been reviewed extensively by Sills et al. and many others.[48,58] Conjoined twins are high-risk pregnancies in which breech presentation is frequent, so prenatal US is important in planning obstetric management. Although the literature recounts a number of conjoined twin births by vaginal delivery, the safest and preferable approach is cesarean section. Cesarean section also provides an opportunity for ex utero intrapartum therapy for the management of twins expected to have rapid cardiac deterioration because of a rudimentary heart in one twin or a single heart and the twin reversed-arterial-perfusion sequence.[8,45]

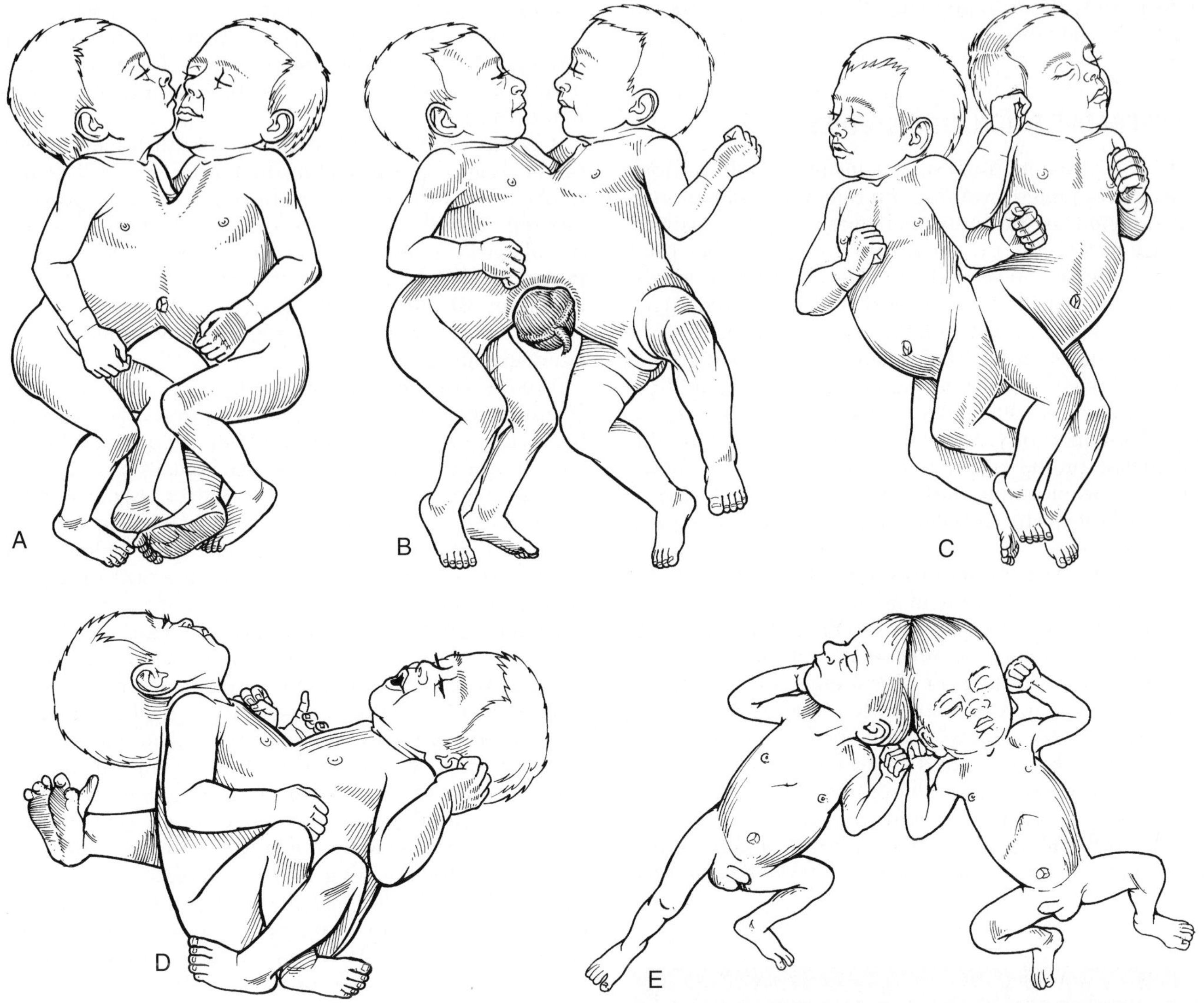

Figure 129–1 The various forms of conjoined twins. *A*, Thoracopagus. *B*, Omphalopagus, sometimes also called thoracoomphalopagus. *C*, Pygopagus; there is also a tripus form. *D*, Ischiopagus tripus; there is also a tetrapus form. *E*, Craniopagus.

Because intrauterine distress is common in conjoined twins, premature labor may need to be inhibited to permit fetuses to reach pulmonary maturity as guided by amniocentesis. At the time of birth, the condition of the infants determines how aggressive supportive care must

TABLE 129–1 Classification of Conjoined Twins

Type	Incidence (%)	Organs Potentially Involved
Thoracopagus	74	Heart, liver, intestine
Omphalopagus	1	Liver, biliary tree, intestine
Pygopagus	17	Spine, rectum, genitourinary tract
Ischiopagus	6	Pelvis, liver, intestine, genitourinary tract
Craniopagus	2	Brain, sagittal sinus

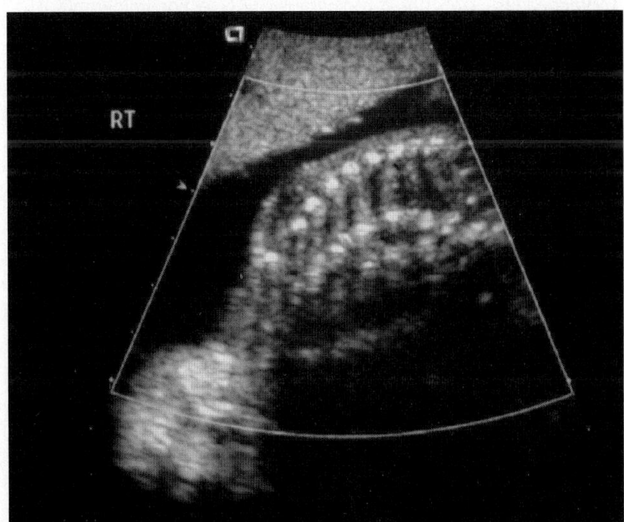

Figure 129–2 This prenatal ultrasound image demonstrates two vertebral columns, and additional images showed ventral junction of thoracopagus twins with shared hearts.

be to permit them to undergo the necessary series of diagnostic evaluations.

PREOPERATIVE DIAGNOSTIC STUDIES

Table 129-1 lists the usual organs involved in the various forms of conjoined twinning. Preoperative evaluation is best directed at the individual organ systems involved because in general, the reconstructive approaches used are the standard ones for the various anomalies encountered, modified to the degree that the involved structures are shared and incompletely developed. Beyond standard radiography, performance of invasive procedures must be timed according to the infants' condition and ability to withstand stress. Additionally, the timing of performance of diagnostic studies is related to the anticipated timing of separation because such studies may be more accurate and associated with less physiologic insult if performed later than the immediate perinatal period.

Table 129-2 lists the various studies that we and others have found to be helpful in evaluation of the various forms of twinning. The goal is to obtain as much information as possible about the precise anatomy and function to guide the planning of therapeutic efforts. Every organ system that is not obviously understood must be thoroughly investigated. In all conjoined twins, one twin is smaller than the other, and in half the instances, one infant has more anomalies than the other.[40,48,62,68] These distinctions must be identified because it is generally best to favor the more normal of the two infants when performing reconstruction, particularly when structures cannot be equally distributed. This is particularly true with regard to the status of the central nervous system, which may be incompletely formed in one infant or one infant may have had an intraventricular hemorrhage.

Cranial US, CT, and MRI are helpful for evaluation of the brains and any abnormalities.[11,33,37] MRI is particularly indicated in craniopagus and pygopagus junction for thorough assessment of the brain and spinal cord.[19,41] Although cerebral angiography has been thought to be necessary in cases of craniopagus twinning, MR angiography (MRA) and ultrafast helical CT have made conventional angiography unnecessary in many instances.

Preoperative evaluation of the vascular system is essential in all conjoined twins, regardless of whether the hearts are joined. As mentioned before, prenatal ECHO and electrocardiography (ECG) may actually provide more accurate information about the hearts than postnatal studies because of the difficulty with probe placement over the frequently encountered omphalocele. Nonetheless, these studies are performed postnatally to determine the presence of anomalies in the case of separate hearts and to determine the size and location of the cardiac junction and the presence of intracardiac and extracardiac anomalies in the case of conjoined hearts. In the past, cardiac catheterization was the only study capable of defining the exact nature of intracardiac anomalies and connections, direction of flow, and nature of all inflow and outflow vessels. However, Fogel et al. have progressively refined the technique of 3-D cardiac MRA to the point where it can provide precise anatomic information that may serve as the basis for deciding whether cardiac separation is possible.[22] Fogel and colleagues' studies have been confirmed by Spielmann et al., Norwitz et al., and Kingston and coworkers.[33,45,65] At the present time, multiplanar 3-D reconstructed MRI with or without MRA is the most useful and least invasive study for the evaluation of conjoined hearts, as demonstrated by Fogel et al. in an analysis of 139 patients with complex cardiac defects and reconstructions.[22] To date, the presence of a single QRS complex on ECG has indicated that successful cardiac separation would not be possible. Unfortunately, our studies, as well as those of others, indicate that the presence of two separate complexes does not necessarily indicate that successful separation of a conjoined heart can be accomplished.

Although radionuclide cardioangiography was used in the past because of its ability to demonstrate the direction of flow and degree of cross-circulation, this study has been supplanted by 3-D MRA. Because most twins who are candidates for surgical separation share a liver that must be divided, it is critical to determine whether one or two inferior venae cavae are present. In many instances of conjoined hearts, one inferior vena cava drains both livers; this constitutes a key element in planning separation.

Because of the high incidence of early gestational birth in conjoined twins, impaired pulmonary function is common. Oxygenation may be deficient as well in the case of intracardiac or extracardiac shunts, if portions of the thorax are shared, and if one twin's chest is smaller

TABLE 129-2 Useful Diagnostic Studies in Conjoined Twins

Type of Conjoining	Studies
Thoracopagus	Chest radiography, ECG, echocardiography, 3-D MRA, cardiac catheterization in selected patients, measurement of blood gases
Omphalopagus	Chest and abdominal radiography, upper gastrointestinal series, DISIDA liver scanning, 3-D MRI
Pygopagus, ischiopagus	Chest, abdominal, and limb radiography, upper and lower gastrointestinal series; cystoscopy; cystography; intravenous pyelography; renal scanning; vaginography, helical CT with 3-D reconstruction; spinal MRI; aortography as needed
Craniopagus	CT with 3-D reconstruction, MRA
Heropagus	Chest and abdominal radiography, gastrointestinal contrast studies in some cases

CT, computed tomography; 3-D, three-dimensional; DISIDA, diisopropylimidodiacetic acid; ECG, electrocardiography; MRA, magnetic resonance angiography; MRI, magnetic resonance imaging.

than the other's. Chest radiography, measurement of arterial blood gases, differential oximetry, and thorough evaluation of physical findings are important in the evaluation of pulmonary function. The latter studies must be integrated with information obtained from cardiac evaluation.

Most conjoined twins share a liver and may share a pancreaticobiliary system, particularly when duodenal junction is present.[43,47,68] This is a key portion of the preoperative evaluation because we have documented instances in which omphaloischiopagus twins have shared a single biliary tree and pancreas. US and radionuclide biliary scanning with separately timed injections into each twin are the most helpful studies. 3-D MRI/MRA may provide additional information, so angiography is now rarely necessary for evaluation of the liver.

With the exception of craniopagus twins, all other forms of conjoined twins may share portions of the gastrointestinal tract. This is best evaluated by upper and lower gastrointestinal contrast studies; differential injections are frequently needed to precisely define which structures are shared, in which case it is helpful to keep in mind the common patterns of intestinal sharing. In thoracopagus and omphalopagus twins, the gastrointestinal junction is frequently at the level of the duodenum. When the junction is apparent in the region of the second portion of the duodenum, only one pancreas and extrahepatic biliary system are likely to be present. In ischiopagus and pygopagus twinning, the site of intestinal junction is usually in the terminal ileum in the region of Meckel's diverticulum. In the latter case, a single colon may be shared. On occasion, the intestinal tracts are separate except for a shared rectosigmoid colon.

Genitourinary (GU) evaluation (see Fig. 129-7) is best approached by imaging studies supplemented by endoscopy. These evaluations should include US, pyelography, cystography, CT with contrast, and functional radionuclide studies as indicated.[46,75] The goal is to determine the status of renal function and the number and location of the kidneys, ureters, and bladders. Because most conjoined twins are female, accurate vaginal or urogenital sinus examinations are critically important. US, vaginoscopy, and vaginography help determine whether there is a single or duplex vaginas, as well as the presence or absence of a cervix, urogenital sinus, or hydrocolpos. Determination of the number, size, and location of these cavities is critical for planning the staged reconstructive procedures required in these cases of complex caudal junction. In males, it is important to evaluate the external genitalia and gonads before separation to determine whether a sex change will be required.

With caudal junction, as seen with ischiopagus and pygopagus twinning, degrees of sharing of the vertebral column, pelvis, and lower extremities vary.[64] Conventional radiography, CT, and MRI are needed. 3-D reconstruction of MRI and CT scans is probably the most helpful technique for surgical decision making (Fig. 129-3). When a lower extremity is shared, as in ischiopagus tripus twins, aortography is occasionally needed to determine the exact nature of the blood supply to the shared limb, the twin to which it is primarily related, and to what degree the limb can be salvaged or possibly shared by the infants, unless color Doppler studies clearly demonstrate the vascular anatomy.

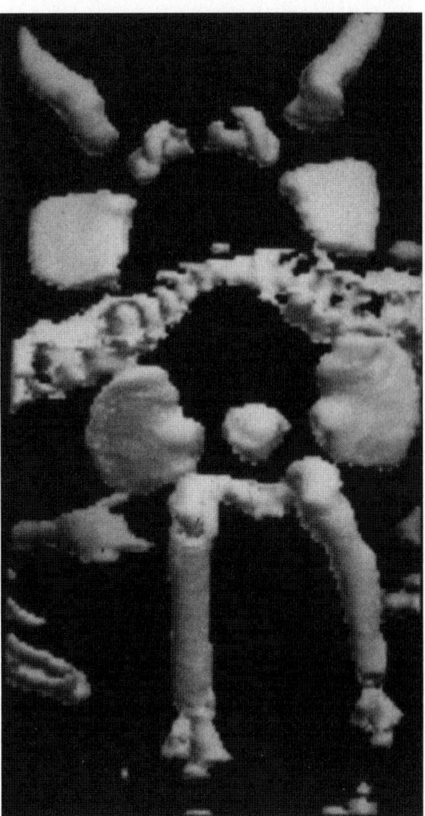

Figure 129-3 This three-dimensional reconstruction of a computed tomography scan of ischiopagus tripus twins clearly demonstrates the anatomy of the shared pelvis and extremities. The images may be viewed from a variety of perspectives when planning approaches to separation and reconstruction.

Since the advent of skin expanders and their liberal use in conjoined twins before separation, it has not been necessary to accurately determine the extent to which skin territories are shared by conjoined twins (Fig. 129-4). We developed an accurate method of evaluating the degree of skin sharing with perfusion fluorometry and the use of separately timed injections, but this technique is now used only in emergency situations when placement of skin expanders is not feasible or thought to be necessary.

Early reports on conjoined twins stress the importance of preoperative evaluation of adrenal and thyroid function; however, we have found these studies to be unnecessary except in extremely rare instances.

ETHICAL CONSIDERATIONS

As technology has improved and more separations have been performed, ethical discussions and analyses have increased remarkably in the literature. Public debate was intense regarding the Lakeberg twins, who had conjoined hearts and survival of only one twin was possible.[15,72] A similar intense debate involving Maltese conjoined twins

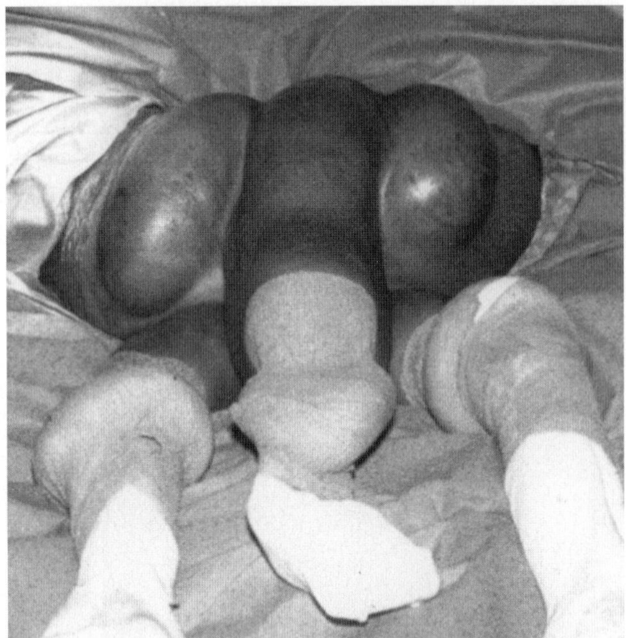

Figure 129-4 Note how the subcutaneous placement of skin expanders provides sufficient skin for closure of the abdomen and pelvis in these ischiopagus tripus twins.

who shared a heart occurred in Manchester, England, until the British Appeals Court made the determination that separation should be attempted.[5,14,34,38,43] It is well for surgeons and others involved in the management of conjoined twins to be thoroughly familiar with the ethics literature on this subject.

The section on prenatal diagnosis and imaging describes how accurate information can be based on prenatal studies, which are known to be quite reliable. A pediatric surgeon who is experienced with separation of conjoined twins is probably the best person to counsel the prospective parents about the likelihood of successful separation, as well as what the outcome for the twins is likely to be given the many advancements made in surgical technique, postoperative care, reconstruction, and rehabilitation.[67] This information puts the parents in the best position to determine whether they wish to continue the pregnancy. Both before and after the infants are born, the family's right to privacy should be respected and protected. The pediatric surgical team must develop a close and trusting relationship with the family because of the nature of the complicated decisions that must be made and the need for informed consent. Detailed and repeated discussions are necessary, particularly if it is evident, after the preoperative evaluations are performed, that only one twin can survive or that one of the two is likely to be left with a serious disability. In addition, it is realistic to expect that some degree of disability is to be expected in all but a very few separated conjoined twins. Only solitary survivors may be possible in twins with conjoined hearts, those with only one inferior vena cava draining the shared liver, and those with a single extrahepatic biliary tree. It is difficult and heart-rending for the surgeon and the parents to consider sacrificing one twin so that the other may survive. This terrible dilemma has been considered in detail by Annas, Thomasma et al., Dougherty, and others.[3,15,71,72] The decision can be aided by the knowledge that both children will usually die without separation under these circumstances, and the situation has been made more rational with the understanding that the operation itself does not determine which twin will survive but rather the nature of the anatomy involved. The analysis by Thomasma et al. discusses not only the latter ethical considerations but also societal considerations, cost factors, and other contemporary issues.[50,72]

If a reasonable degree of quality survival is possible, we have recommended that twins be separated, even if only one twin can survive, rather than an inevitable early death of both infants. Such judgments are best made on the basis of extensive experience. Organs and shared structures are best allocated on the basis of the anatomy and available data. Management and allocation of organs at the time of separation are individual considerations, with the intent of maximizing both twins when there are no medical differences between the two. However, if one twin is significantly mentally or physically impaired, we have recommended that allocation be directed toward the more healthy twin. Although we have held the view that it is preferable to intervene to save one life if possible rather than permit the loss of both, it is important to emphasize that the parents have the ultimate right to accept or refuse surgical separation. In the Manchester case, the British court held that as the representatives of society, the court had the right to make the choice. Every case is different and must be approached with utmost sensitivity for the rights and feelings of the parents and their children.

TIMING OF SEPARATION

Emergency separation is associated with high mortality because of serious organ dysfunction and physiologic deterioration in subjects with immature organ systems. We have found that urgent or emergency separation before 6 months of age is associated with higher mortality than separation performed after that age.[48] A review of our experience, as well as information available in the literature, suggests that when possible, separation is best performed on an elective basis when the twins are 9 to 12 months of age. However, Spitz and Kiely have indicated that elective separation is safe between 2 and 4 months of age, and that is probably correct.[68,69] It is understandable why anesthetic management is easier and blood loss and physiologic derangement are better tolerated in older infants than in the immediate postnatal period. If surgery is delayed much beyond 1 year of age, conjoined twins may have difficulty developing an independent personality, but even then, we have found that favorable adaptation occurs within a few months. Emergency conditions that may force separation, even in the newborn, include the presence of a stillborn twin, intestinal obstruction, rupture of an omphalocele, heart failure, obstructive uropathy, or respiratory failure.

Undertaking separation when conjoined infants are 4 months or older also provides ample time to permit thorough preoperative assessment and integration of all of the specialists who will be required for a successful operation.

PREOPERATIVE PLANNING AND ANESTHETIC MANAGEMENT

Successful separation of conjoined twins is best performed by an experienced team of pediatric surgical specialists and anesthesiologists. Team conferences are necessary for review of all gathered information and include preoperative and postoperative caretakers; all surgical, anesthetic, and diagnostic specialists; and nurses and others involved in the operation and care of the infants. We have found it helpful to construct models and drawings of the various organ systems based on the diagnostic studies performed to understand the nature of the organ sharing and to facilitate the anticipated separation, but more recently we have found that computerized 3-D MRI and MRA, which are capable of being viewed from different perspectives, are even more useful. A mock preoperative drill involving all team members has routinely been conducted to expedite the procedure so that everyone knows what the next step will be. Although some decisions are necessarily made during the separation procedure, such planning allows the team to anticipate most issues ahead of time.

Two complete surgical teams involving all appropriate specialties must be available, and there must also be two experienced teams of anesthesiologists who know how to integrate their efforts. Because exsanguinating hemorrhage, hypovolemia, and hypothermia are the primary risks that the anesthesiology teams must handle, we have routinely placed radial artery and central venous catheters and additional intravenous access lines in both twins. Both twins are monitored separately, including arterial and venous pressure, ECG, pulse oximetry, capnography, esophageal temperature, urinary output, and regular blood gas analysis. The only exception is when just one conjoined twin is expected to survive; in this case, only the twin anticipated to live is monitored. Depending on the degree of shared circulation, judiciously modified doses of intravenously administered sedatives and paralytic agents are used in an incremental fashion, particularly because it is usually possible to perform endotracheal intubation in only one twin at a time. In general, drugs and intravenous fluids are calculated according to the total weight of the twins, with half given to each. Only very experienced individuals should participate in anesthetic management, including endotracheal intubation. We have found that short-acting inhalational anesthetics with high concentrations of oxygen are the easiest to manage. In many instances, separation procedures are lengthy and special management techniques are required, such as those described by Wong et al. for a 5-day separation of craniopagus twins.[76]

Once all monitoring and intravenous lines and the endotracheal tubes have been carefully secured, the two anesthesiology teams can lift the infants into the air so that thorough total-body sterile preparation and draping can be performed. In most instances, we have found it helpful to elevate the infants on bolsters at a 30-degree angle to facilitate surgery and maximize access to the infants by the anesthesia teams. Although it is permissible to have one operative nursing team for the initial part of the separation, two complete nursing teams are required once the separation has been accomplished. The nature of the reconstruction anticipated in each twin before surgery governs the instruments and setup provided to each of the operative nursing teams. Each surgical specialty team is integrated into the operation as the separation proceeds and its participation is needed. The lead surgeon must remain available throughout the separation procedure because that surgeon is responsible for integrating everyone's efforts and for approving any changes in the planned course of the procedure. The side of the operative approach is based on the anatomy involved, the planned order of the procedure, and the side that provides maximum exposure.

APPROACHES TO ORGAN SYSTEM RECONSTRUCTION

In general, standard approaches to organ reconstruction are in order once decisions have been made relative to the distribution of the various structures. At times, innovative techniques or specially tailored reconstructive techniques are required, especially with regard to management of the skin and GU tract.

Skin

Whenever there is extensive sharing of skin and anticipation of a deficiency for closure after separation, as in thoracopagus, ischiopagus, pygopagus, and craniopagus twins, it is helpful to use skin expanders to increase the amount of skin available for coverage. The scalp, the chest and abdominal walls, the extremities, and the perineum usually pose a problem for skin coverage and body cavity closure. Filler described the use of expanders in the peritoneal cavity to enlarge the abdominal wall in ischiopagus twins.[20] However, we and others have preferred to use subcutaneous skin expanders and place as many expanders as possible on the dorsal and ventral surfaces of the body and on the upper part of the lower extremities (see Fig. 129-4).[47,48] Placement of skin expanders in the peritoneal cavity carries an inherent risk for infection and may limit gastrointestinal function.

Placement of skin expanders in the subcutaneous position in the early postnatal period is frequently complicated by erosion through the skin, even if the expanders are placed under the skin from remote small incisions. We prefer to wait a minimum of 4 weeks, preferably longer, to place expanders because by this time the infants will better tolerate the frequent injections required for sequential expansion. It generally takes 6 to 8 weeks or longer to gain the maximum advantage of skin expansion from these devices. Their placement is therefore best timed according to the scheduled time of separation.

Central Nervous System

Two forms of central nervous system sharing are encountered: the craniopagus form, in which there are varying degrees of brain sharing, and forms in which portions of the spinal cord are shared.

Pygopagus and some ischiopagus twins may share varying portions of the vertebral column and spinal cord. Our group and Fieggen et al. have reported twins with a shared sacrum and separate spinal cords but a partially shared filum requiring complicated dissection.[19,48] In such instances, it is our preference to stage the separation procedure, first undertaking division of the posterior portion of the sacrum, with careful division of the shared filum, and leaving the anterior portion of the sacrum for stability, with division at a second-stage operation. Varying degrees of bladder and anal sphincter dysfunction should be anticipated in these circumstances.

Craniopagus twinning occurs in only about 2% of conjoined twins and may be classified into partial and complete forms. The structures involved depend on whether the union is at the vertex, occiput, or parietal portions of the skull. Bucholz et al. devised a more practical classification based on the site and degree of fusion of brain tissue and the venous structures involved that would require interruption at surgery.[9] Over 30 attempts at separation have been reported, including a number recently. Most attempts have failed, and the long-term outcome in a few survivors has thus far been satisfactory only when minimal amounts of brain tissue have been shared.[36] Recent attempts to separate craniopagus twins with separate brains but a shared superior sagittal sinus have had some success, such as the cases reported by Campbell et al., Drummond et al., and press reports from Los Angeles, Dallas, and New York.[10,16] Numerous problems have been encountered in all instances, and long-term outcomes are as yet unknown. Although some limited success has been achieved in the separation of partial forms of craniopagus sharing, essentially no success has been achieved with complete forms of brain sharing. Accurate imaging is obviously critical in the differentiation of complete from partial craniopagus sharing.

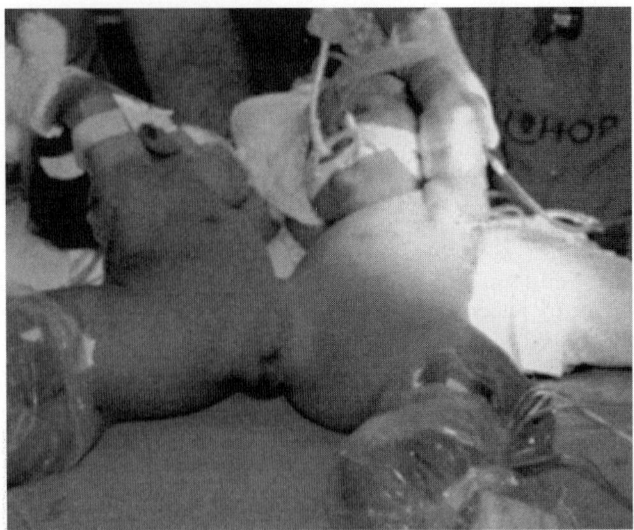

Figure 129-5 These omphalopagus twins shared only a sizable portion of liver. However, some omphalopagus twins also share duodenum and portions of the biliary tree.

Liver and Pancreaticobiliary System

With the exception of craniopagus twinning, the liver is shared in almost all anterior or ventral forms of conjoined twinning (Fig. 129-5). With regard to the liver, the most critical preoperative determination is whether each liver has an outflow to its own heart or whether a single inferior vena cava drains both livers. Survival is not possible without hepatic venous drainage. Once it has been determined that each twin has its own hepatic venous drainage, separation of the livers is feasible. The central area of the livers selected for division is first dissected free circumferentially over sufficient distance so that wide clamps or Penrose drains can be placed as tourniquets and tightened down. A double row of large overlapping mattress sutures of absorbable suture are placed so that the division can be performed between them. However, as the division is performed, individual bleeding vessels and bile ducts should be suture-ligated so that excessive bleeding can be controlled. If the infants are undergoing cardiopulmonary bypass for the management of cardiac anomalies, hepatic division under cold arrest is expeditious.

Two pitfalls may be encountered during hepatic division. The first is that although most shared livers have only one or two large, transverse portal venous connections, the venous connections are sometimes in the form of a lacework of multiple venous channels that can be difficult to control. Intraoperative use of Doppler may be helpful in this regard if preoperative studies have not clarified the nature of the portal venous connections between the shared livers. The second pitfall occurs when there is a single extrahepatic biliary tree. This must be determined ahead of time to decide where the liver should be divided on its undersurface. In twins with one extrahepatic biliary tree, intraoperative cholangiography may be necessary so that one infant can be given the extrahepatic bile duct while the other is left with a single hepatic duct that may be drained externally or into a Roux limb of jejunum. If twins with a single biliary tree also share a pancreas, the pancreas is best left with the extrahepatic biliary tree. If there are two small pancreatic anlagen, each infant should receive one. The latter consideration then determines how the shared duodenum should be reconstructed. In a few cases with a single extrahepatic biliary tree, nothing is available for one of the twins.

Gastrointestinal System

Intestinal sharing generally follows two patterns, although there are variations of each. The first pattern is sharing of the duodenum at the second or third portions; the fourth portion of the duodenum and the rest of the gastrointestinal tract are separate. Whenever there is proximal sharing of the duodenum, a single biliary tree is usually encountered. Some degree of pancreatico-biliary conjunction may also be present when the junction is in the third portion of the duodenum. If the biliary structures are separate with duodenal conjunction, the method of reconstruction must be based on identifying and preserving an ampulla of Vater for each infant. We have found that bile duct reimplantation is sometimes needed for one twin if there is only a single ampulla.

The second pattern of gastrointestinal sharing is ileocolonic or, occasionally, only colonic. In the ileocolonic form, the primary point of conjunction is at the point of Meckel's diverticulum, with sharing of the terminal ileum and the entire colon. A dual blood supply to these latter shared structures comes from each twin. In this form, it has been our preference to provide one twin with the ileocecal valve and the other with the anus, which is usually singular, with both infants getting half of the shared colon and thus both having at least one sphincter.[29,32] Although colostomy had been performed in infants without an anus in the past, we have performed immediate anorectal reconstruction since 1983 in all such instances because the pelvis is open and widely exposed at the time of separation. The overall functional results with this approach have been excellent, and it has made skin closure less of a problem than when a colostomy was performed. In another variation in which the entire small intestine and the majority of the colon are separate, the rectosigmoid is shared. Again, there is usually only a single anus, so one infant receives the anus and shared rectosigmoid and the other twin ends up with a slightly foreshortened colon and immediate reconstruction through the sphincter at the imperforate anus site. An excellent degree of continence has resulted in most instances with this approach.

Heart

Because the majority of conjoined twins born alive are thoracopagus, conjoined hearts is a common problem encountered. Additionally, it is important to note that intracardiac and extracardiac malformations are usually present as well.[23] In 1979, Synhorst et al. reported successful separation of conjoined hearts with the junction point at the level of the atria.[70] One of the twins treated by the latter group died 7 days postoperatively as a result of severe right hypoplastic heart syndrome, and the other has survived for several years. Unfortunately, cases involving only an atrial bridge are extraordinarily rare. On the other hand, a ventricular junction is common, and ventricular division has thus far not been possible.[60] We have attempted ventricular division but without success. Another method is to sacrifice one twin, disconnect the major vessels, and reconstruct the entire heart for the infant selected to survive. A third method of repair that we have used on one occasion is excision of the conjoined hearts, extracorporeal reconstruction, and autotransplantation, depending on the anatomy. We have not performed cardiac allotransplantation for conjoined twins and do not believe that it is a reasonable option to offer parents. As far as the author is aware, giving all of the cardiac tissue to one of the twins with ventricular-level conjoined hearts is the only feasible approach, and even this is rarely successful. As far as the author is aware, there have been only two short-term survivals with the latter approach and one long-term survival.

Genitourinary System

In ischiopagus and pygopagus forms of conjoined twins, numerous anatomic variations occur, and staged reconstruction has proved to be the most satisfactory approach for the GU system. Immediate reconstruction has been preferable for the gastrointestinal tract because many such infants who also have GU sharing require bladder augmentation and staged reconstructive procedures to promote continence, as well as vaginal and genital reconstruction. Our experience with GU reconstruction in ischiopagus twins has been summarized by Hsu et al.[28] In that publication we divided the planned dual reconstructions into primary and secondary reconstructive procedures, and the patients were separated according to whether one or two bladders were present (Fig. 129-6). This approach has continued to be useful in our experience. If one bladder is present but there is a urogenital sinus, the latter structure can be used as a substitute bladder and a new vagina made as reported by Holcomb and our group.[26] In the case of a single urinary bladder shared by the two infants, the decision to give each infant a portion of the bladder is made on the basis of the nerve and blood supply to the bladder base. If a shared bladder cannot be divided into two equal parts because of cystoscopic findings of limited trigonal anatomy, one twin is given the major portion of the bladder with satisfactory volume and the other receives a small part that is brought out as a temporary vesicostomy with subsequent augmentation cystoplasty and construction of a continent, catheterizable stoma.

Most female ischiopagus or pygopagus twins have single external genitalia and double vaginas (Fig. 129-7). Fertility may be preserved in both female twins. If the twins share single normal external genitalia, one twin needs secondary genitoplasty. If a urogenital sinus or common cloaca exists, the connection between the vagina and cloaca or urogenital sinus should be repaired. Male conjoined twins may have one or two sets of external genitalia that must be appropriately separated. One of the twins we treated also had penile transposition that required repositioning (see Fig. 129-7). Hypospadias is common and amenable to standard repair. In cases with only one phallus, one twin undergoes male reconstruction and the other undergoes female reconstruction, during which labia are created from available scrotal tissue.

It should be emphasized that urinary reconstruction of ischiopagus twins in particular usually requires multiple stages and close long-term follow-up if complications are to be avoided.[28,57,75] With careful observation and judicious, but aggressive intervention, it is generally possible to maintain normal renal function and reasonable bladder continence. Provided that females who have undergone vaginal reconstruction are monitored until they have achieved full growth, normal sexual activity and fertility are reasonable and achievable goals. It is in this category

Primary Reconstruction

- Conjoined Twins
  - 2 bladders
    - 4 kidneys
      - TUU
      - Reimplantation of crossed ureters
    - 2 kidneys
      - 4 ureters
        - TUU
        - Ureteropyelostomy
      - 2 ureters
        - Separation with bladder
  - 1 bladder
    - Separable (→ 2 bladders)
    - Nonseparable
      - Baby has bladder
      - Baby has no bladder
        - Ureterostomy
        - Reimplantataion to dilated hydrocolpos (female)

Secondary Reconstruction

- Continent reservoir with appendicovesicostomy and ileal augmentation

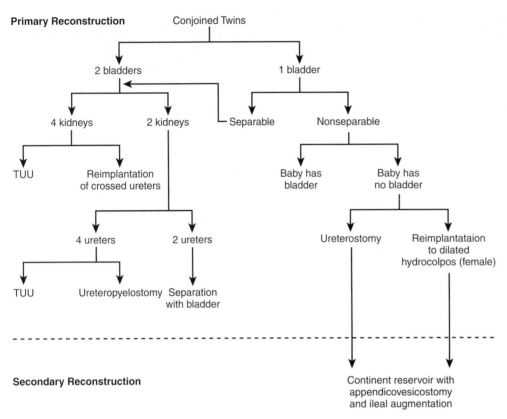

Figure 129–6 Plan for genitourinary (GU) reconstruction in ischiopagus and pygopagus twins who share portions of the GU tract. TUU, transureteroureterostomy. (From Hsu H-S, Duckett JW, Templeton JM, O'Neill JA: Experience with urogenital reconstruction of ischiopagus conjoined twins. J Urol 1995;154:563.)

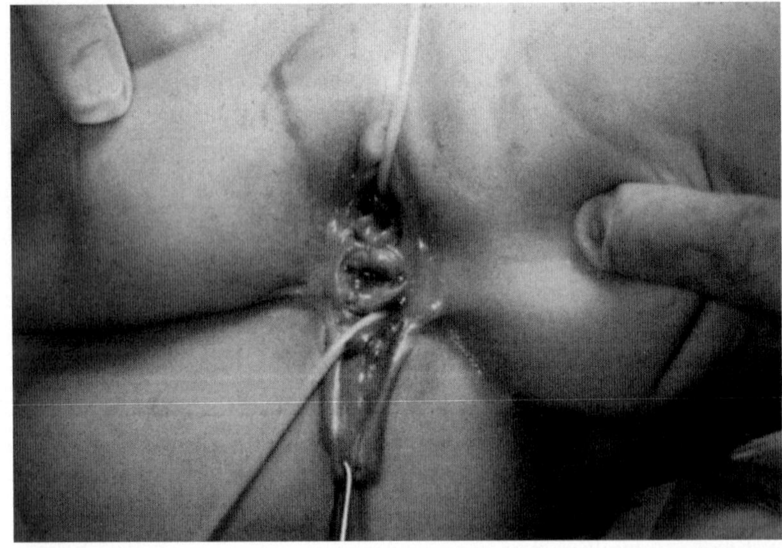

A

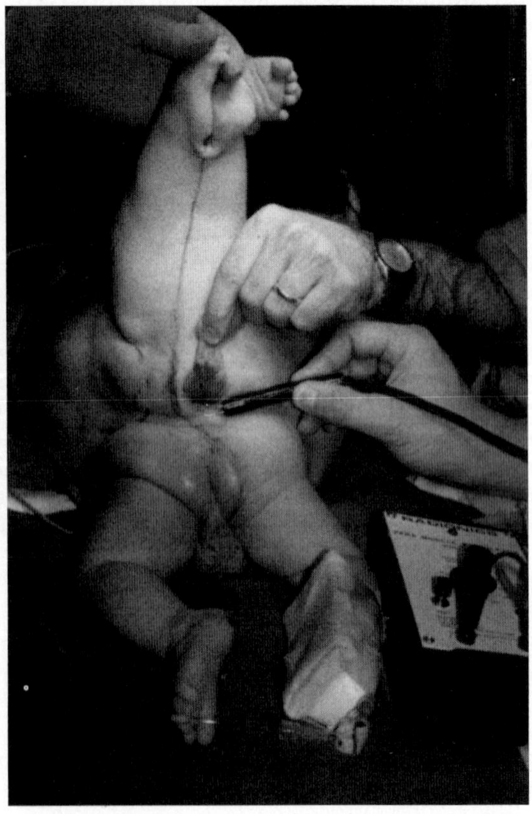

B

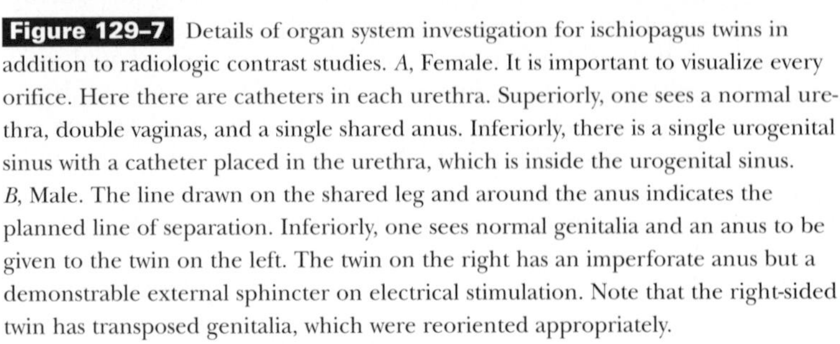

Figure 129–7 Details of organ system investigation for ischiopagus twins in addition to radiologic contrast studies. *A*, Female. It is important to visualize every orifice. Here there are catheters in each urethra. Superiorly, one sees a normal urethra, double vaginas, and a single shared anus. Inferiorly, there is a single urogenital sinus with a catheter placed in the urethra, which is inside the urogenital sinus. *B*, Male. The line drawn on the shared leg and around the anus indicates the planned line of separation. Inferiorly, one sees normal genitalia and an anus to be given to the twin on the left. The twin on the right has an imperforate anus but a demonstrable external sphincter on electrical stimulation. Note that the right-sided twin has transposed genitalia, which were reoriented appropriately.

particularly that such infants may be provided with a high-quality life and good adjustment to society.[27] It should also be pointed out that successful genital reconstruction frequently requires secure pelvic repair and sometimes bilateral iliac osteotomies.[32]

Abdominal Wall

Even with the use of skin expanders, which stretch not only the overlying skin but also the underlying abdominal wall, closure of the abdominal fascia may be difficult. In these instances, we have used absorbable mesh in the midline fascia and also to cover the lateral side of the pelvis in ischiopagus tripus twins when there has been a large defect after separation. It appears on follow-up that the absorbable mesh serves as a framework for fibrosis because herniation through the mesh site has not been encountered. We have also used such mesh for reconstruction of the chest wall.

Skeletal System

The largest contribution to long-term morbidity and disability in conjoined twins with pelvic junction relates to the skeletal system. Therefore, the orthopedic considerations related to conjoined twins are important from the standpoint of long-term function and rehabilitation. Albert et al. have reported our experience with the orthopedic management of conjoined twins, and the ongoing experience with these patients indicates that they usually require multiple operations and revisions throughout childhood and adolescence.[1,64] Whether there is ventral, lateral, or dorsal junction, the potential for scoliosis deformities exists.[19,42] We have also reported a high incidence of vertebral abnormalities in patients such as these, which likewise contributes to spinal deformities.[64] In addition, one twin or the other may have a diminutive or asymmetric chest wall that may potentiate scoliosis. If gait disturbances are related to absent limbs or pelvic deformities, scoliosis is usual. Because the potential for scoliosis exists throughout childhood, yearly follow-up is essential. Whenever there is any degree of thoracic cage sharing, later revision of initial chest wall closure will be required as noted in our experience.[21,47,48,55]

The main orthopedic challenges relate to the management of ischiopagus conjoined twins, although some pygopagus twins require orthopedic and neurosurgical care because of problems related to sacral sharing. Ischiopagus patients can be divided according to the number of legs present into bipus, tripus, or tetrapus. The latter is most common, and these types of twins have been successfully separated most often. Most of our experience has been with ischiopagus tripus twins, in which each twin has a normal leg and they share a deformed, fused third leg. Part of our experience with the latter has been summarized by Albert et al.[1] The first challenge is thorough evaluation of the pelvis and shared third lower extremity. In early reports, the third, shared leg was usually amputated and the skin used for pelvic and abdominal wall closure. However, with the current use of skin expanders, it has been possible to consider preserving as much of that extremity as possible for better function. We have used the latter approach since 1980. Only after thorough evaluation of 3-D reconstructed CT images of the pelvis can the appropriate site for division of the pelvis be determined. This method also facilitates the decision about whether the acetabulum of the shared third leg will be given to one or a portion to both twins; this decision depends on whether the shared extremity can be split or necessarily must be given to only one of the twins. Anterior division of the pelvis is usually performed first as one of the early phases of the separation procedure related to division and dissection of the perineum and pelvic organs, and the posterior division is usually performed last. As mentioned previously, a critical part of the evaluation and separation procedure is assessment of the blood supply to the shared limb by one of the several imaging techniques currently available. This evaluation determines whether one or both twins provide the main vascular supply, which guides the site of pelvic division.

In these situations, in which the pelvis is wide open after completion of the separation procedure, we believe that some attempt should be made to close the pelvis as much as possible, so we prefer to perform posterior iliac osteotomies at the time of initial separation rather than later. Not only does iliac osteotomy provide some opportunity to close the pelvic ring, it also potentiates better skin closure and stability of the perineum. Because one twin in a set of ischiopagus twins often has only one lower extremity, better pelvic closure improves the eventual ability to fit an appropriate bucket-type prosthesis.

Careful and frequent orthopedic follow-up is critical for appropriate long-term rehabilitation and function. Postoperative issues that must be addressed include problems related to the deformed shared leg, as well as to the normal leg. Hip dislocation and foot deformities are almost always associated problems, and hip dislocation may occur repeatedly over time. Thus, staged repairs are usually needed. We have encountered such problems as equinus deformity, rotational deformities of the hip, recurrent dislocation of the hip, flexion and abduction contractures of the hip, and acetabular deformities. Standard orthopedic corrective procedures have been used and for the most part have been successful, but makeshift approaches have often been required. After monitoring this group of patients for over 20 years, we have observed that careful prosthetic fitting is key to providing good long-term function and that revisions are needed throughout the growth period. It is clear that with persistence and close observation, good long-term ambulatory function can be achieved in these patients, but some degree of disability in adulthood is usual. Modern rehabilitation techniques and prosthetic appliances have made an enormous difference, however. With better preoperative imaging, increased surgical experience, and improved rehabilitative techniques, it has been possible to preserve a longer and more functional shared leg with a functional knee, and skin expanders have been central in making this possible.

CLINICAL EXPERIENCE

Twenty-four complete and 3 incomplete conjoined twins have been managed since 1957, and all but 3 have been encountered in the past 20 years. Eighteen operations have been performed in these 27 sets of twins, and 24 of these patients survived. Unfortunately, seven children died 1 month to 10 years after separation, the majority because of congenital heart disease that is probably correctable now. This experience has led to an aggressive early approach to correction of significant cardiac anomalies.

Craniopagus

We continue to care for a single set of female twins joined at the lateral aspect of the cranium; the left forehead of one is attached to the right temporo-occipital area of the other. They are now 35 years of age. Separation has been considered impossible on several evaluations over the years because of the degree of brain sharing, shared vascularity, and a small common superior sagittal sinus. These women live on their own and are completely independent, and it is surprising how well they have adapted to their environment even though their condition was certainly difficult when they were children. One of the twins is essentially normal; the other is smaller and has required several operative procedures for a complex GU malformation and intestinal obstruction on one occasion. Separation is not anticipated unless terminal illness occurs in one of the twins. We have also consulted on a newborn set of craniopagus twins with complex junction of the brains in which one was significantly deformed. Separation was not advised and the infants expired.

Thoracopagus

Thirteen sets of thoracopagus twins have been evaluated. Separation was not attempted in seven sets demonstrated to have very complex conjoined hearts and limited ventricular mass, and congestive heart failure developed in all and they died shortly after birth. Six cardiac separations have been attempted in the remaining six thoracopagus twins since 1971.[48] In one set of female thoracopagus conjoined twins, the hearts were joined at the ventricular level, with one twin having very limited ventricular mass. An attempt to separate the ventricles by amputating the rudimentary heart failed; the infant who retained the heart lived approximately 12 hours but died of myocardial insufficiency. In another instance of male conjoined twins, the hearts were joined at both the atrial and ventricular levels. The shared liver had only one hepatic venous drainage system emptying into a single inferior vena cava. Unfortunately, that inferior drainage system entered the diminutive heart in one twin, and the other twin had an essentially normal heart connected to it. Because of intractable congestive heart failure, separation was performed at 3½ weeks of age with the expectation that only one twin could survive. At separation, the twin with hepatic venous drainage was preserved and a reverse cardiac autotransplantation procedure performed. Although this heart functioned well initially, the infant died about 10 hours later of myocardial failure. This latter approach was appealing because it also provided an opportunity to reconstruct an explanted heart, which is so often abnormal.

In four sets of female thoracopagus conjoined twins, the great vessels were disconnected and one twin was sacrificed. Varying degrees of resection and reconstruction of the donor side of the heart were performed, and the main cardiac mass was left in the surviving twin in all instances. The first such procedure was performed in 1977 when the infants were 1 month of age because of severe congestive heart failure. No reconstruction other than vascular division was performed. The surviving infant lived almost 4 months but died of hepatic failure. It is noteworthy that cardiac function was satisfactory and long-term survival was considered to have been possible if biliary obstruction had not intervened. From 1992 and beyond, three additional procedures were performed in like fashion. Two sets of female thoracopagus twins underwent vascular disconnection and placement of the entire cardiac mass in the twin selected for survival. The surviving twin was selected in each instance because the heart was more normal and to some degree correctable. Detailed observations were made in these instances, and it was evident on retrospective analysis of both these infants who died 8 and 10 hours postoperatively that coronary flow to the donor side of the heart was inadequate to permit continuing function. In other words, the hearts behaved as though they each had massive myocardial infarctions. On the basis of this experience, a different approach was used in the sixth set of female thoracopagus twins. In these twins, vascular disconnection from the twin estimated to not be capable of survival was performed, and an aorto-aortic bypass was constructed from the side of the recipient aorta to the end of the donor aorta to ensure better coronary flow to the residual donor heart. Anomalous pulmonary venous drainage was also corrected. As with the other cases in which all of the cardiac mass was left in one twin, the chest wall was reconstructed partially from the donor twin so that mediastinal closure and diaphragmatic reconstruction could be accomplished. This latter infant lived 10.5 months. She was slowly being weaned from the ventilator when pneumonia developed and she expired. It is of interest that this aorto-aortic bypass approach has also been attempted at the Red Cross Hospital in Capetown, with one long-term survivor.

There is no question that most thoracopagus conjoined twins with shared hearts at the ventricular level are incapable of surviving separation because of the presence of associated complex cardiac anomalies.[23] On the other hand, occasional sets of thoracopagus twins will consist of at least one twin with an essentially normal or easily correctable heart with normal inflow and outflow vessels. In this case, attempted separation may be reasonable. The limited degrees of success achieved thus far suggest that continued efforts in this regard may be appropriate only in certain specialty centers that have experience.

Most of the reconstructive techniques used are fairly standard methods of intracardiac repair.

Omphalopagus

Two sets of omphalopagus female twins have been managed. Some of the thoracopagus twins have also had omphalopagus components. In the first set, the anatomy was much like that of the Bunker twins, and simple hepatic division was performed with primary abdominal wall closure (see Fig. 129-5). These infants are now 12 years of age and are doing well. In a second set of female twins with a large omphalopagus connection, separation took place at 6 months of age because the smaller of the twins had such severe respiratory problems that survival was threatened. We were attempting to have the infants grow while receiving mechanical ventilation because they were premature and had respiratory distress syndrome. Because these infants had only a single extrahepatic biliary duct system, that system and the common duodenum and jejunum had to be given to one infant; in the other infant, a drain was placed at the cut edge of the liver to stimulate the formation of a biliary-cutaneous fistula, which did occur. Unfortunately, the infant given the entire biliary tree died of clostridial peritonitis and bronchopulmonary dysplasia 1 month after separation. The other infant died at the age of 6 months of continued respiratory failure and subaortic stenosis.

Pygopagus

In 1957, a set of female pygopagus twins was separated at 2 weeks of age. Each twin had her own rectum, bladder, and kidneys, but a common vagina had to be divided between them.[48] The larger of the two twins is now an adult and has rectal and bladder continence, and she is married. The other, smaller twin died at 10 years of age because of complications related to the tetralogy of Fallot, a correctable entity today.

In addition, we have had some debate about whether one of our ischiopagus twins is really pygopagus because they share a sacrum, but other aspects led us to classify them as ischiopagus tripus.

Ischiopagus

We have encountered six sets of ischiopagus twins: one tetrapus type and five tripus types. The ischiopagus tetrapus twins were separated at 1 year of age, and both did very well. One is now 22 years of age and is essentially normal, but the other died at 3 years of age after aspiration of a bean. Three of the five ischiopagus tripus twins have been described previously.[47] All five sets of ischiopagus tripus twins were successfully separated, but one infant died of a tight thoracic wall closure in 1978. Since that time, skin expansion and other measures have eliminated this as a problem. The details of reconstruction of the gastrointestinal, urinary, and genital tracts in these infants have already been discussed. The results in these ischiopagus tripus twins have been most gratifying, and follow-up ranges from 6 to 24 years.

Incomplete or Heteropagus Twins

We have seen three partially conjoined twins, all with extra portions of a pelvis and lower extremity, duplicated genitalia, and portions of the intestinal tract. All were attached at the lower part of the chest and epigastrium. These are also referred to as asymmetrically conjoined twins, in contrast to the symmetrical types described earlier. An omphalocele was present in two of the three instances, and two of the three had congenital heart disease. All underwent separation shortly after birth, and all survived initially. A common feature encountered at surgery was that the vascular connections were located adjacent to the falciform ligament. In one case, venous drainage was through a large vessel going directly into the liver substance by way of the falciform ligament; in the other two cases, a large venous channel entered the suprahepatic inferior vena cava adjacent to the hepatic veins. In one of the three sets of twins, evidence indicated that the incomplete twin was monozygotic with the normal twin. One of the three heteropagus survivors died at 4 months of age because of complex congenital heart disease that was thought to be uncorrectable at the time.

OTHER COMMENTS

Separation of conjoined twins is a demanding and challenging undertaking that requires careful and detailed planning, as well as integration of many specialists, particularly surgical specialists. Modern imaging is critical, much of it very specialized and available only in a few selected centers. It should be noted that no single discipline can expect to have all the necessary talents or completely up-to-date information on every conceivable reconstructive technique. Although it is critical to have a coordinating surgeon familiar with all aspects of surgical management, no single individual can or should do it all. Particularly complex undertakings such as management of conjoined hearts and single biliary trees should be performed only in a few specialized centers that have experience with these particular problems. Additionally, long-term follow-up should be performed at these centers because this is the only way that information can be gathered regarding the validity of reconstructive techniques and the quality of life after separation. Resources for psychological management and ethical analysis must also be available so that the best can be offered to these special patients.

REFERENCES

1. Albert MJ, Drummond DS, O'Neill JA, Watts H: The orthopedic management of conjoined twins: A review of 13 cases and report of four cases. J Pediatr Orthop 1992;2:300.

2. Anderson T: Documentary and artistic evidence for conjoined twins from sixteenth century England. Am J Med Genet 2002;109:155.
3. Annas GJ: Siamese twins: Killing one to save the other. Hastings Cent Rep 1987;17:27.
4. Bega G, Wapner R, Lev-Toaff A, Kulhman K: Diagnosis of conjoined twins at 10 weeks using three-dimensional ultrasound: A case report. Ultrasound Obstet Gynecol 2000; 16:388.
5. Bennett J: Siamese twins: Both lives must be equally respected. Br J Nurs 2000;9:1122.
6. Bondeson J: The Biddenden Maids: A curious chapter in the history of conjoined twins. J R Soc Med 1992;85:217.
7. Bonilla-Musoles F, Machado LE, Osborne NG, et al: Two-dimensional and three-dimensional sonography of conjoined twins. J Clin Ultrasound 2002;30:68.
8. Bouchard S, Johnson MP, Flake AW, et al: The EXIT procedure: Experience and outcome in 31 cases. J Pediatr Surg 2002;37:418.
9. Bucholz RD, Yoon KW, Shively RE: Temporoparietal craniopagus: Case report and review of the literature. J Neurosurg 1987;66:72.
10. Campbell S, Theile R, Stuart G, et al: Separation of craniopagus joined at the occiput. Case report. J Neurosurg 2002;97:983.
11. Casele HL, Meyer JR: Ultrafast magnetic resonance imaging of cephalopagus conjoined twins. Obstet Gynecol 2000; 95:1015.
12. Chen PL, Choe KA: Prenatal MRI of heteropagus twins. AJR Am J Roentgenol 2003;181:1676.
13. Cywes S, Millar AJW, Rode H, Brown RA: Conjoined twins: The Cape Town experience. Pediatr Surg Int 1997;12:234.
14. Dominic C: Separating the twins Jodie and Mary. Ethics Medics 2001;26:2.
15. Dougherty CJ: Joining in life and death: On separating the Lakeberg twins. Bioethics Forum 1995;11:9.
16. Drummond G, Scott T, Mackay D, Lipschitz R: Separation of the Baragwanath craniopagus twins. Br J Plast Surg 1991; 44:49.
17. Durston W: A narrative of monstrous birth in Plymouth, October 22, 1670: Together with the anatomical observations thereupon by William Durston, Doctor of Physics, and communication to Dr. Tim Clerk. Philos Trans R Soc 1670;5:2096.
18. El-Gohary MD: Siamese twins in the United Arab Emirates. Pediatr Surg Int 1998;13:154.
19. Fieggen G, Millar A, Rode H, et al: Spinal cord involvement in pygopagus conjoined twins: Case report and review of the literature. Childs Nerv Syst 2003;19:183.
20. Filler RM: Conjoined twins and their separation. Semin Perinatol 1986;10:82.
21. Fishman SJ, Puder M, Geva T, et al: Cardiac relocation and chest wall reconstruction after separation of thoracopagus conjoined twins with a single heart. J Pediatr Surg 2002; 37:515.
22. Fogel MA, Hubbard A, Weinberg PM: A simplified approach for assessment of intracardiac baffles and extracardiac conduits in congenital heart surgery with two- and three-dimensional magnetic resonance imaging. Am Heart J 2001;142:1028.
23. Gerlis LM, Seo JW, Ho SY, Chi JG: Morphology of the cardiovascular system in conjoined twins: Spatial and sequential arrangements in 36 cases. Teratology 1993; 47:91.
24. Gupta DK, Lal A, Bajpai M: Epigastric heteropagus twins—a report of four cases. Pediatr Surg Int 2001;17:481.
25. Guttmacher AF: Biographical notes on some famous conjoined twins. Birth Defects (OAS) 1967;3:10.
26. Holcomb GW, Keating MA, Hollowell JG, et al: Continent urinary reconstruction in ischiopagus tripus conjoined twins. J Urol 1989;141:100.
27. Hoyle RM, Thomas CG: Twenty-three-year follow-up of separated ischiopagus tetrapus conjoined twins. Ann Surg 1989;210:673.
28. Hsu H-S, Duckett JW, Templeton JM, O'Neill JA: Experience with urogenital reconstruction of ischiopagus conjoined twins. J Urol 1995;154:563.
29. Janik JS, Hendrickson RJ, Janik JP, et al: Spectrum of anorectal anomalies in pygopagus twins. J Pediatr Surg 2003;38:608.
30. Johnson DD, Pretorius DH, Budorick N: Three-dimensional ultrasound of conjoined twins. Obstet Gynecol 1997;90:701.
31. Kim JA, Cho JY, Lee YH, et al: Complications arising in twin pregnancy: Findings of prenatal ultrasonography. Korean J Radiol 2003;4:54.
32. Kim SS, Waldhausen JH, Weidener BC, et al: Perineal reconstruction of female conjoined twins. J Pediatr Surg 2002;37:1740.
33. Kingston CA, McHugh K, Kumaradevan J, et al: Imaging in the preoperative assessment of conjoined twins. Radiographics 2001;21:1187.
34. Knowles LP: The Maltese conjoined twins. Hubris in the court. Hastings Cent Rep 2001;31:47.
35. Koenig E: Sibi invicem adnati feliciter separate. Ephemerid Natur Curios 1689;2:145.
36. Lansdell H: Intelligence test scores from infancy to adulthood for a craniopagus twin pair neurosurgically separated at 4 months of age. Psychol Rep 1999;84:209.
37. Loller LP, Spevak T, Fishman EK: Conjoined twins: Multiorgan system evaluation by multidector CT and 3D volume rendering. J Comput Assist Tomogr 2001;25:870.
38. London AJ: The Maltese conjoined twins. Two views of their separation. Hastings Cent Rep 2001;31:49.
39. MacKenzie TC, Crombleholme TM, Johnson MP, et al: The natural history of prenatally diagnosed conjoined twins. J Pediatr Surg 2002;37:303.
40. Malone FD, D'Alton ME: Anomalies peculiar to multiple gestations. Clin Perinatol 2000;37:1033.
41. Martinez L, Fernandez J, Pastor I, et al: The contribution of modern imaging to planning separation strategies in conjoined twins. Eur J Pediatr Surg 2003;13:120.
42. McDowell BC, Morton BE, Janik JS, et al: Separation of conjoined pygopagus twins. Plast Reconstr Surg 2003; 111:1998.
43. Meyers RL, Matlak ME: Biliary tract anomalies in thoracoomphalopagus conjoined twins. J Pediatr Surg 2002;37:1716.
44. Moraczewkis AS: Against the separation of Jodie and Mary. Ethics Medics 2001;26:1.
45. Norwitz ER, Hoyle LP, Jenkins KJ, et al: Separation of conjoined twins with the twin reversed-arterial-perfusion sequence after prenatal planning with three-dimensional modeling. N Engl J Med 2000;343:399.
46. Omokhodion SI, Ladipo JK, Odebode TO, et al: The Ibadan coinjoined twins: A report of omphalopagus twins and a review of cases reported in Nigeria over 60 years. Ann Trop Paediatr 2001;21:263.
47. O'Neill JA: Conjoined twins. In O'Neill JA, Rowe MI, Grosfeld JG, et al (eds): Pediatric Surgery, 5th ed. St Louis, Mosby–Year Book, 1998, p 1925.
48. O'Neill JA, Holcomb GW, Schnaufer L, et al: Surgical experience with thirteen conjoined twins. Ann Surg 1988;208:299.
49. Paré A: The collected works of Ambroise Paré, London, 1634, Translated by Johnson T. Poundridge. New York, Milford House, 1968.
50. Potter EL, Craig JM: Pathology of the Fetus and Infant, 3rd ed. Chicago, Year Book, 1975.

51. Ratiu P, Singer P: The ethics and economics of heroic surgery. Hastings Cent Rep 2001;31:47.
52. Rickham PP: The dawn of paediatric surgery: Johannes Fatio (1649-1691): His life, his work and his horrible end. Prog Pediatr Surg 1986;20:94.
53. Rock J, Hertig A: The human conceptus during the first two weeks of gestation. Am J Obstet Gynecol 1948;55:6.
54. Ross AJ, O'Neill JA, Silverman DG, et al: A new technique for evaluating cutaneous vascularity in complicated conjoined twins. J Pediatr Surg 1985;20:743.
55. Saing H, Mok C-K, Lau JTK, Tam PKH: A method of repair of thoracic cage defects after separation of thoraco-omphalopagus twins. Pediatr Surg Int 1987;2:113.
56. Seller MJ: Conjoined twins discordant for cleft lip and palate. Am J Med Genet 1990;37:530.
57. Shapiro E, Fair WR, Ternberg JL, et al: Ischiopagus tetrapus twins: Urological aspects of separation and 10-year follow up. J Urol 1991;145:120.
58. Sills ES, Vrbikova J, Kastratovic-Kotlica B: Conjoined twins, conception, pregnancy, and delivery: A reproductive history of the pygopagus Blazek sisters (1878-1922). Am J Obstet Gynecol 2001;185:1396.
59. Spencer R: Anatomic description of conjoined twins: A plea for standardized terminology. J Pediatr Surg 1996; 31:941.
60. Spencer R: Theoretical and analytical embryology of conjoined twins, parts I and II. Clin Anat 2000;13:36.
61. Spencer R: Parasitic conjoined twins: External, internal (fetuses in fetu and teratomas) and detached (acardiacs). Clin Anat 2001;14:428.
62. Spencer R: Conjoined Twins: Developmental Malformations and Clinical Implications. Baltimore, Johns Hopkins University Press, 2003.
63. Spencer R, Robichaux WH, Superneau DW, Lucas VW: Unusual cardiac malformations in conjoined twins: Thoracopagus twins with conjoined pentalogy of Cantrell and an omphalopagus twin with atretic ventricles. Pediatr Cardiol 2002;23:631.
64. Spiegel DA, Ganley TJ, Akbarnia H, Drummond DS: Congenital vertebral anomalies in ischiopagus and pygopagus conjoined twins. Clin Orthop 2000;381:137.
65. Spielmann AL, Freed KS, Spritzer CE: MRI of conjoined twins illustrating advances in fetal imaging. J Comput Assist Tomogr 2001;25:88.
66. Spitz L: Surgery for conjoined twins. Ann R Coll Surg Engl 2003;85:230.
67. Spitz L, Kiely E: Success rate for surgery of conjoined twins. Lancet 2000;356:1765.
68. Spitz L, Kiely EM: Experience in the management of conjoined twins. Br J Surg 2002;89:1188.
69. Spitz L, Kiely EM: Conjoined twins. JAMA 2003;289:1307.
70. Synhorst D, Matlak M, Roan Y, et al: Separation of conjoined thoracopagus twins joined at the right atrium. Am J Cardiol 1979;43:662.
71. Tendler MD: Siamese twins—the surgery: So one may live. Assia Jew Med Ethics 2001;4:22.
72. Thomasma DC, Muraskas J, Marshall PA, et al: The ethics of caring for conjoined twins. The Lakeberg twins. Hastings Cent Rep 1996;26:4.
73. Turner RJ, Hankins JDW, Weintraub JC, et al: Magnetic resonance imaging and ultrasonography in the antenatal evaluation of conjoined twins. Am J Obstet Gynecol 1986;155:645.
74. Watanatittan S, Niramis R, Suwatanaviroj A, Havanonda S: Conjoined twins: Surgical separation in eleven cases. J Med Assoc Thai 2003;3(Suppl):S633.
75. Wilcox DT, Quin PM, Spitz L, et al: Urological problems in conjoined twins. Br J Urol 1998;81:905.
76. Wong TG, Ong BC, Ang C, Chee HL: Anesthetic management for a five-day separation of craniopagus twins. Anesth Analg 2003;97:999.
77. Zimmerman AA: Embryologic and anatomic considerations of conjoined twins. National Foundation 1967;3:18.

Chapter 130  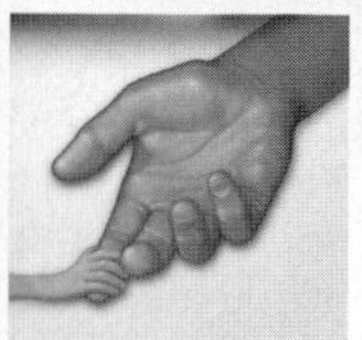

Vascular Anomalies: Hemangiomas and Malformations

Giannoula Klement and Steven J. Fishman

CLASSIFICATION

Vascular anomalies are manifested clinically by a large and varying clinical spectrum of lesions ranging from small skin discolorations to large debilitating lesions that can compromise a limb or an organ and result in a life-threatening condition.[64,67] Historically, the development of any consistent classification system was hindered by the fact that vascular anomalies have been treated inconsistently by various medical specialties, with few clinicians focused on their care. The confusing nomenclature is, in large part, responsible for misunderstanding, improper diagnosis, and inappropriate treatment of vascular anomalies. These disorders have long been described by vernacular terms, although physicians have always preferred Latin names. When the mother's emotions were blamed for her infant's vascular birthmark, the lesion was called "naevus maternus."[63] Virchow, father of cellular (and surgical) pathology, designated all vascular anomalies "angioma" and categorized them, on the basis of microscopic channel architecture, as angioma simplex, cavernosum, or racemosum.[85] Wegener, an erstwhile student of Virchow, proposed a similar histomorphic division for "lymphangioma."[86] These 19th-century histopathologic systems, admixed with popular descriptive terms, have been perpetuated in the medical texts of this century. Virchow's "angioma simplex" became synonymous with "capillary hemangioma," also known as "strawberry hemangioma," and his term "cavernous hemangioma" unfortunately came to be used for vascular anomalies that invariably regress and for those that never regress. Strictly histopathologic classification, without clinical correlation, has not been useful in the diagnosis or management of children with vascu-lar anomalies. Antiquated, conflicting, and inaccurate nosology should be abandoned.

The first comprehensive biologic classification based on the cellular features of vascular anomalies as correlated with the clinical characteristics and natural history was proposed by Mulliken and Glowacki in 1982,[65] and it has since been validated by numerous clinical and basic research studies.[29,40] In 1996 the Mulliken classification was adopted by the International Society for the Study of Vascular Anomalies (ISSVA). It divides vascular anomalies into tumors and malformations based on their cellular features and clinical behavior (Table 130-1). These two biologic categories can be distinguished by clinical, radiologic, histopathologic, and hemodynamic evaluation.[58,59] Precise terminology is essential because the prognosis and appropriate therapy for the various lesions are quite different.

Vascular tumors include infantile hemangioma, rapidly involuting congenital hemangioma, noninvoluting congenital hemangioma, tufted angioma, and kaposiform hemangioendothelioma, as well as other rarer varieties. All the vascular tumors are encountered far less frequently than the common infantile hemangioma. Hemangioma exhibits cellular proliferation. These benign tumors grow during infancy, involute in childhood, and never appear in adolescence or adulthood. The other vascular tumors also exhibit dynamic life cycles.

In contrast, vascular malformations are developmental errors composed of dysmorphic vessels and lined by

TABLE 130–1 Biologic Classification of Vascular Anomalies

Vascular Tumors
Hemangioma (common infantile)
Rapidly involuting congenital hemangioma (RICH)
Noninvoluting congenital hemangioma (NICH)
Kaposiform hemangioendothelioma (KHE)
Tufted angioma
Rare others
Vascular Malformations
Capillary (CM)
Venous (VM)
Lymphatic (LM)
Arteriovenous (AVM)
Klippel-Trenaunay syndrome (CLVM)
Other combined (CVM, LVM, CAVM, etc.)

quiescent endothelium; they almost never regress, and some even expand. Vascular malformations can be subcategorized according to channel structure and rheology. Slow-flow lesions are either capillary, lymphatic, or venous in nature. Fast-flow lesions include arterial and arteriovenous anomalies. There are also complex-combined vascular malformations that are often associated with soft tissue and skeletal overgrowth; many of these disorders are known by eponyms.

Vascular anomalies of all types can permeate any organ system. Although they are usually manifested superficially, they can also involve the thoracoabdominal walls and cavities, solid organs, hollow viscera, and brain. They may develop in multiple locations. Even though the initial manifestation is often cosmetic, vascular anomalies can give rise to endangering clinical symptoms as diverse as pain, bleeding, mass effect, and congestive heart failure.

Accurate diagnosis of a vascular anomaly, the bane of the general pediatrician, has until recently been plagued by confusing classifications and lack of referral centers. Depending on the location of the lesion, children may have been referred to a dermatologist, plastic surgeon, general surgeon, otorhinolaryngologist, orthopedic surgeon, neurosurgeon, interventional radiologist, or oncologist. The result was a multiplicity of confusing diagnoses with varied nomenclatures. These approaches, based on an uncertain diagnosis, resulted in inappropriate or inadequate treatment in the majority of cases. A number of tertiary centers have now established multidisciplinary vascular anomaly treatment centers, and significant improvements have been achieved in both diagnostic accuracy and standardization of treatment. In more than 90% of patients, the type of vascular anomaly can be correctly diagnosed by correlating the history and findings on physical examination.[29] Deep subcutaneous, intramuscular, or visceral lesions can be difficult to identify; radiologic and endoscopic evaluation is often needed in these cases to establish the diagnosis and extent of anatomic involvement.

PATHOGENESIS

Hemangiomas

A rapidly growing hemangioma is composed of plump, rapidly dividing endothelial cells (proliferative phase). With spontaneous regression, endothelial activity gradually diminishes (involuting phase).[65] The concept that tumors are "angiogenesis dependent," first proposed by Folkman and Klagsbrun,[35] suggests insight into the life cycle of hemangiomas. Angiogenic molecules are known to act on endothelial cells and pericytes to initiate the formation of capillary networks.[35,61] This process is tightly regulated by inhibitors of endothelial cell growth that help maintain the normal microvasculature in a quiescent state. Hemangioma is a model of pure, unopposed angiogenesis. Hemangiomas could result from a localized diminution in normal angiogenic inhibitors or increased production of angiogenic stimulators. Spontaneous regression of the tumor may be mediated by an increase in angiogenic inhibitors or down-regulation of angiogenic factors.

Common expression of immunohistochemical markers, including glut-1, Fcγ RII, Lewis Y antigen, merosin, and type 3 iodothyronine deiodinase, has raised speculation whether hemangioma may either derive from or share a common precursor with placenta.[47,69]

Immunohistochemical cellular markers have elucidated the clinical phases of the life cycle of hemangioma.[82] Rapid growth of hemangioma is biochemically characterized by expression of proliferating cell nuclear antigen, which is mediated, in part, by the angiogenic peptides vascular endothelial growth factor (VEGF) and basic fibroblast growth factor (bFGF).[56] Type IV collagenase is also seen in proliferating hemangiomas, thus suggesting that collagen breakdown is necessary to provide space for proliferating capillaries. Angiogenic peptides could act to induce differentiation of proliferating cells and autocrine induction of tissue inhibitor of metalloproteinases (TIMP-I), a suppressor of new blood vessel formation. Mast cells, known to be present in late proliferation and early involution, could secrete modulators that down-regulate hemangiogenesis.[39,72] Whatever factors induce the transition from proliferation to involution, the tumor differentiates, its endothelium becomes senescent, and its parenchyma is replaced by fibrosis and fat.[22,46,82]

Vascular Malformations

Each of the four major categories of vascular malformation has a particular histopathologic appearance. The complex-combined forms are often difficult to specify by light microscopy. The determinant cellular characteristic of all dysmorphic vascular anomalies is a quiescent lining of endothelium. If thrombosis occurs, however, as it commonly does within lymphatic, venous, or combined lymphaticovenous anomalies, there may be exuberant ingrowth of new capillary channels in the thrombus.

Capillary lesions are composed of regular, ectatic, thin-walled capillary- to venular-sized channels located in the papillary and upper reticular dermis.

Both lymphatic and venous anomalies exhibit walls of variable thickness. Skeletal and smooth muscle are both present in the walls of the former, and nodular collections of lymphocytes are often seen in the connective tissue stroma. Venous malformations are generally thin walled with sparse, irregular islands of smooth muscle. Pale acidophilic fluid is typically seen in the channels of lymphatic anomalies, whereas blood, thrombi, and phleboliths characterize venous malformations. The misformed venous network drains to adjacent veins, which may be varicose and lack valves. Clinically and histologically, combined lymphaticovenous malformations can occur.

The arterial vessels of an arteriovenous malformation (AVM) are dysmorphic and consist of thickened walls with hyperplastic smooth muscle fibers within the media. The veins of an immature AVM appear "arterialized" (reactive muscular hyperplasia).

Although most vascular malformations are sporadic, uncommon familial cases and varieties have led to the recent discovery of specific genetic mutations that will probably provide clues to the etiology of even sporadic cases.[13] One of several genes responsible for hereditary hemorrhagic telangiectasia (Rendu-Osler-Weber disease) is located on chromosome 9q. A locus for an autosomal dominant cutaneous and mucosal form of a venous malformation has been mapped to chromosome 9p in a three-generation family, and another locus for familial intracranial venous anomalies is located on chromosome 7q.[12] Families with a mutation in the *RASA1* gene were found to have either multiple small capillary malformations, AVMs, arteriovenous fistulas, or Parkes Weber syndrome.[24]

DIFFERENTIATION BETWEEN HEMANGIOMAS AND VASCULAR MALFORMATIONS

Clinical Features

Hemangioma

Hemangiomas are the most common tumors of infancy and early childhood. They are not usually present at birth but appear in the neonatal period, usually in the first 2 weeks of life. Approximately 30% to 40% are seen at birth as a premonitory cutaneous mark: a barely visible "anemic nevus," a telangiectatic or macular red stain, or an ecchymotic spot mimicking a bruise (Fig. 130-1A). A deep (subcutaneous) or visceral hemangioma may not be manifested until 2 to 3 months of life. The skin overlying a deep hemangioma may be only slightly raised with a bluish hue. Dilated local draining veins are often present. The old adjectives "cavernous" for a deep hemangioma and "capillary" for a superficial lesion are confusing and should not be used. In fact, there is no such entity as a "cavernous" hemangioma. The lesion is either a deep hemangioma or a mislabeled venous malformation.

Approximately 80% of hemangiomas grow as a single tumor; 20% proliferate in multiple sites.[54] These tumors occur far more commonly in females than in males (ratio of 3:1 to 5:1). The female preponderance is even higher whenever a facial hemangioma is associated with various thoracic deformities.[40] The incidence is 10% to 12% in white infants[27] and lower in dark-skinned infants. Hemangiomas develop in 22% of preterm infants weighing less than 1000 g.[2,45]

The hallmark of hemangioma is rapid growth during the first 6 to 8 months of infancy (proliferative phase). As the tumor grows in the superficial dermis, the skin becomes raised, bosselated, and bright crimson (Fig. 130-1B).

Hemangioma growth reaches a plateau by the end of the first year; the tumor then seems to grow proportionately with the child. By this time, the first signs of the involuting phase can be seen. The once crimson color fades to a dull purplish hue, the skin gradually pales as a patchy gray matte forms, and the tumor feels less tense on palpation. Regression of a typical hemangioma continues until the child is 5 to 10 years of age (Fig. 130-1C).

The rate at which a particular hemangioma regresses is not influenced by or related to its site, size, or appearance. Most hemangiomas are small harmless tumors, and normal skin is restored in about 50% of children.[15] Even an extensive and protrusive cutaneous hemangioma can completely regress. With regression of large tumors, however, the skin can have evidence of telangiectasia, crepe-like loose folds, yellowish hypoelastic patches, scarring (if ulceration occurred during the proliferative phase), or a fibrofatty residuum.

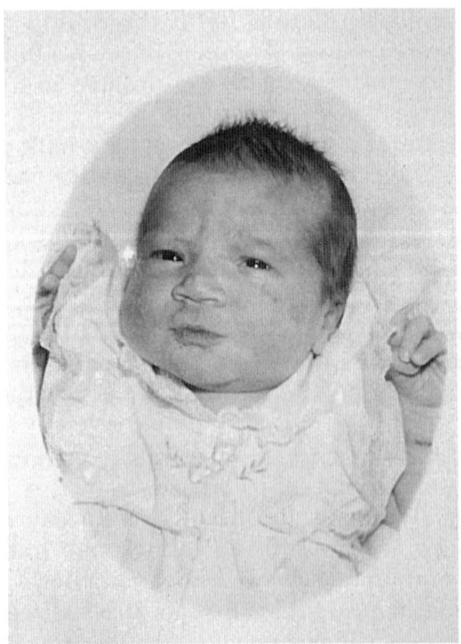
A

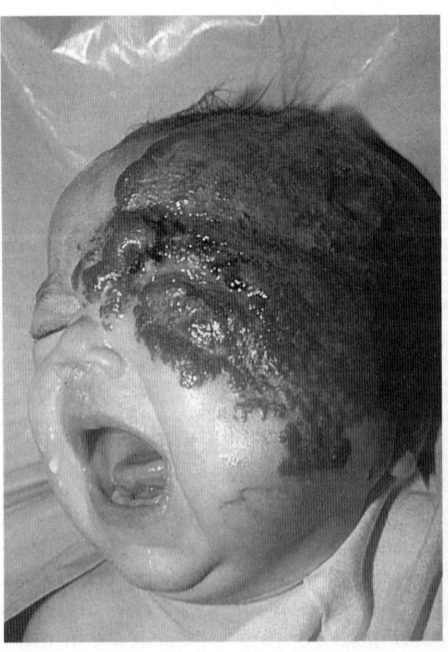
B

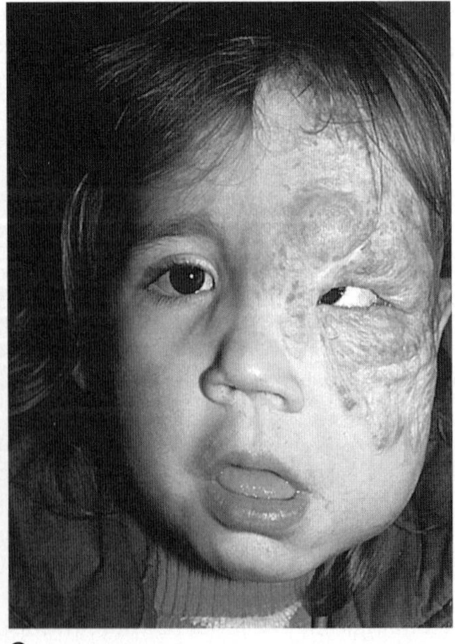
C

Figure 130–1 Natural history of hemangioma. *A*, A neonatal photograph shows a faint macular stain on the left side of the forehead, head, and cheek. *B*, Age 4 months, aggressive facial hemangioma (proliferating phase) with spontaneous ulceration, complete ocular occlusion, and no response to corticosteroids. *C*, Age 4 years, involuting phase with residual periorbital scarring, strabismus, and impaired vision in the left eye.

Unlike vascular malformations, hemangiomas rarely produce bony distortion or hypertrophy. However, a large facial hemangioma can cause cartilaginous or bony overgrowth, presumably secondary to increased blood flow or a localized mass effect on the facial skeleton. Axial skeletal overgrowth in an extremity is almost never seen, even with an extensive hemangioma of the limb.[16]

An important caveat is that not all hemangiomas look like strawberries.[58,67] A deep (subcutaneous) hemangioma, particularly in the neck and trunk, can be confused with a lymphatic malformation but can be differentiated by ultrasonography or magnetic resonance imaging (MRI). Hemangioma can also mimic a port-wine stain (capillary malformation); the true nature of the hemangioma is betrayed by the prominent draining veins and subsequent regression.[31]

A corollary caveat is that not all strawberry lesions are hemangiomas. A frequently confused lesion is pyogenic granuloma. These extremely common lesions rarely appear before the age of 6 months (mean age of onset, 6.7 years),[73] whereas hemangiomas develop earlier in infancy. Patients with pyogenic granuloma usually have no history of or preexisting dermatologic condition (although these lesions can occur in areas of port-wine stain). Pyogenic granulomas are typically single, small lesions (mean diameter, 6.5 mm). They grow rapidly, erupt through the skin, and form a stalk or pedicle. Epidermal breakdown and crusting are commonplace, but it is recurrent bleeding (often copious) that usually initiates the first visit to a physician or emergency department. A venous malformation can also be mistaken for hemangioma. Although the skin is smooth, the color can be similar. A lymphatic malformation or lymphaticovenous malformation, especially with intralesional hemorrhage at birth or appearance in infancy, can likewise be misdiagnosed as hemangioma. Physical examination is usually sufficient for diagnosis; ultrasonography is confirmatory. Infantile fibrosarcoma, rhabdomyosarcoma, and protuberant glioma can also masquerade as congenital or neonatal hemangioma.[11] MRI is usually diagnostic. Biopsy should be performed on any vascular lesion in which malignancy is suspected.

Other Tumors

A rapidly involuting congenital hemangioma (RICH) is present and fully grown at birth.[10] These rare tumors do not grow after birth and fully regress by 8 to 14 months. A RICH is typically raised, dome shaped, and red to violaceous and often has a pale peripheral halo (Fig. 130-2). Unlike typical hemangiomas, they may be seen on antenatal imaging studies. By contrast, the even more rare noninvoluting congenital hemangioma (NICH)[27] does not regress and may require resection. Congenital hemangiomas are high-flow lesions that may on occasion induce high-output heart failure. However, it is uncommon for a RICH to require therapy. In fact, families and clinicians typically marvel at their remarkably rapid spontaneous disappearance. Until their recent recognition as a distinct entity, RICHs were included with typical hemangiomas in clinical reports, thereby resulting in unjustified conclusions of apparent "miracle cures."

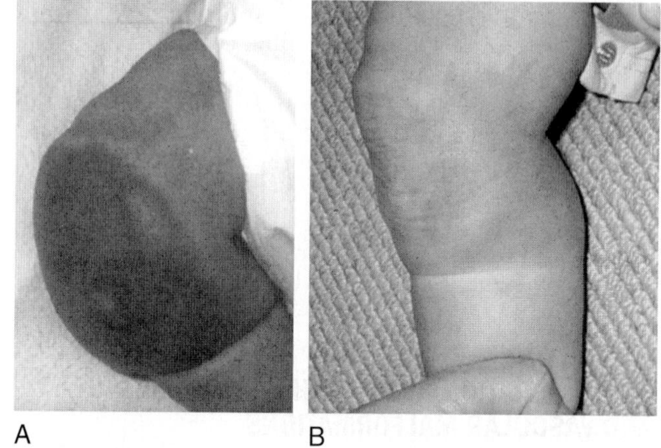

Figure 130-2 Rapidly involuting congenital hemangioma. *A*, Fully grown at birth. Note the dome shape and pale halo. *B*, Nearly completely regressed without therapy before 1 year of age.

Kaposiform hemangioendothelioma (KHE) had previously been considered an "aggressive" hemangioma. However, it also has clear histopathologic and clinical distinction from the common hemangioma of infancy. KHE can be present at birth or develop early in the postnatal period, and it is far more invasive. It occurs with equal frequency in males and females. The mass is usually purpuric with ill-defined borders and shiny tense overlying skin (Fig. 130-3). It occurs most commonly on the trunk, shoulder, or thigh or in the retroperitoneum, but it can occur more peripherally. KHE generally permeates multiple tissues, including the skin, subcutis, and muscle. Unlike hemangiomas, KHE can cause destructive changes in adjacent bones. Histologically, spindle-shaped endothelial cells are prominent, with cleft-like intercellular spaces.[87] Most importantly, KHE is often associated with the Kasabach-Merritt phenomenon (KMP), a severe consumptive thrombocytopenia caused by platelet trapping.

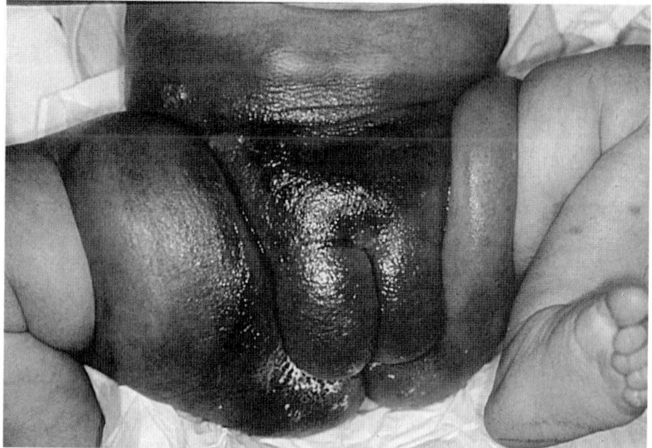

Figure 130-3 Kaposiform hemangioendothelioma with the Kasabach-Merritt phenomenon (platelet count, 6000 cells/mm^3). Note the ecchymosis and edema of the lower part of the abdomen and perineum.

The thrombocytopenia is profound (platelet count, <10,000 cells/mm^3), thereby leading to a risk for gastrointestinal, pleuropulmonic, peritoneal, or intracranial hemorrhage. The mortality rate in children with this lesion can be as high as 20% to 30%, and early treatment is essential.[23] Retrospectively, the reports of hemangiomas being associated with KMP are reflective of the past difficulty with classification of these lesions rather than an overlap of the two lesions.[76] Indeed, the typical hemangiomas of infancy *never* cause KMP. Although KHE may improve spontaneously, it may also remain prominent throughout early childhood, and even though it may be quiescent in midchildhood, it persists throughout life.[6] Musculoskeletal pain syndromes may occur in their distribution as late as adulthood.

Tufted angioma (also referred to as "angioblastoma of Nagakawa") can be congenital or acquired. The location distribution is similar to that of KHE, although tufted angiomas tend to be smaller. They are ill-defined, tender, dull red/purple patches, papules, or plaques. On histologic examination the hallmark is widely separated bluish nodules or tufts of capillaries called "cannonballs" located in the middle and lower third of the dermis.[49] These lobules are more widely spaced than hemangioma lobules. The lesion is highly cellular, and the numerous endothelial cells are spindle shaped.

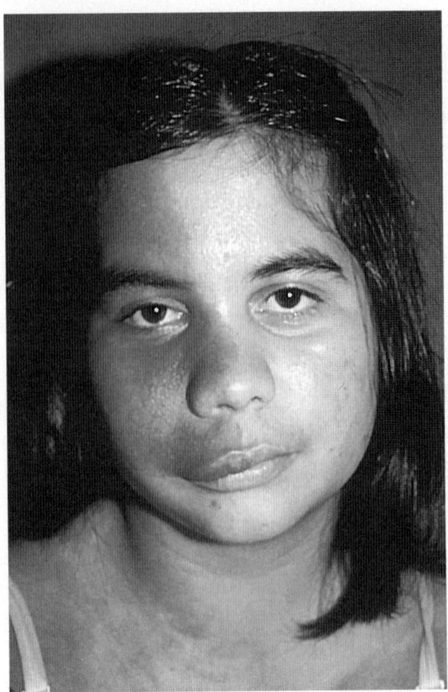

Figure 130–4 Teenage girl with a capillary malformation (port-wine stain) on the right side of her face and chest. Periodic ophthalmic studies and magnetic resonance imaging are needed in patients with a meningeal vascular anomaly (Sturge-Weber syndrome).

Capillary Malformation

A capillary malformation (also known by the 19th-century term "port-wine stain") is a macular red vascular stain that is present at birth and persists throughout life. Capillary malformations can be localized or extensive and occur on the face, trunk, or limbs. These lesions must be differentiated from the common fading macular stains, which occur in 50% of neonates and are commonly located on the glabella, eyelids, nose, upper lip, and nuchal area. These stains are variously known as nevus flammeus neonatorum, stork bite, or angel's kiss.

Sturge-Weber syndrome consists of a facial capillary malformation in association with ipsilateral leptomeningeal and ocular anomalies. The leptomeningeal vascular anomaly can cause recurrent seizures and contralateral hemiplegia, as well as developmental delay of motor and cognitive skills to varying degrees. The ophthalmic neurosensory cutaneous area (V1) is usually involved; patients with maxillary (V2) or mandibular (V3) capillary malformations are at low risk for brain involvement.[26] The risk for glaucoma is higher when the malformation occurs in both the V1 and V2 dermatomic areas (Fig. 130-4).

Facial capillary malformations are prone to darkening color and hyperplastic skin changes; thickened purple nodules can begin to develop by adolescence. These skin changes very rarely occur in malformations of the limbs. Facial capillary malformations are sometimes associated with gradual hypertrophy of the soft tissues and underlying skeleton. Extensive capillary malformation of a limb is often associated with axial and transverse hypertrophy, usually present at birth. Venous varicosities do not develop during childhood, and the limb hypertrophy does not worsen as the child grows. Capillary malformations of the limb can be associated with complex-combined vascular anomalies, such as Klippel-Trenaunay and Parkes Weber syndromes. A midline dorsal capillary malformation can be a red flag signaling an underlying occipital encephalocele and cervical or lumbar spinal dysraphism.

Lymphatic Malformation

Lymphatic malformations are manifested early in childhood and are usually apparent at birth. These lesions, as well as other vascular anomalies, are increasingly being detected by antenatal imaging.[55] They occur as localized small lesions or as diffuse involvement of a whole extremity, trunk, or region. They can be microcystic, macrocystic, or mixed. The term "cystic hygroma," which refers to a macrocystic lymphatic malformation of the neck and "lymphangioma" (in fact a microcystic lymphatic malformation), should no longer be used in modern medical terminology. The suffix "-oma" connotes a tumor, thus adding to the general terminologic confusion in this field. Clinically, macrocystic lesions are typically ballotable, flesh-colored, gravity-dependent lesions, whereas microcystic lesions are less compressible. As with all malformations, the endothelial and smooth muscle constituents of lymphatic malformations are quiescent. The connective tissue, however, contains nodular collections of lymphocytes, including follicles with germinal centers.

Lymphatic malformations may expand or contract, depending on the ebb and flow of lymphatic fluid, the presence of inflammation, and the occurrence of intralesional bleeding. Most are evident at birth or

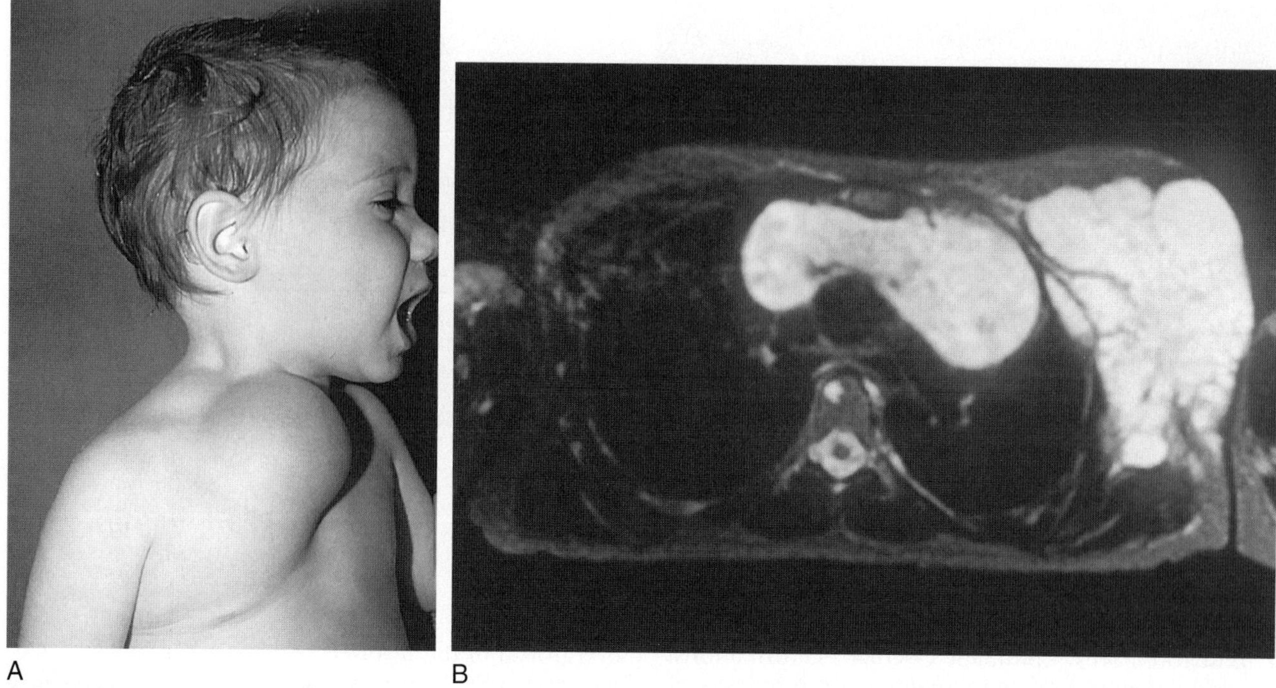

Figure 130–5 *A*, Macrocystic lymphatic malformation on the chest and axilla with involvement of the brachial plexus; mediastinal extension is likely. *B*, Lymphatic malformation of the mediastinum in a 33-year-old woman who has undergone more than 30 cervical resections since childhood.

detected before 2 years of age; some, however, are suddenly manifested in an older child (rarely in an adolescent). Prenatal ultrasonography can detect macrocystic lymphatic malformations as early as the end of the first trimester of pregnancy.[53] These malformations can occur anywhere but are most common in the cervicofacial, axillary, and back regions (Fig. 130-5A). The skin may display puckering and dimpling because of dermal involvement. Infantile fibrosarcoma can masquerade as a cervicotruncal lymphatic malformation.[44]

Macrocystic lymphatic malformations often occur in the neck and axilla. Malformations in the forehead, orbit, and cheek are frequently a combination of microcystic and macrocystic and cause facial asymmetry and distorted features. Soft tissue and bony overgrowth is a characteristic feature of lymphatic anomalies. The malformations are the most common basis for macrocheilia, macroglossia, macrotia, and macromala.[67] A cervicofacial lymphatic malformation is associated with mandibular overgrowth and malocclusion.[71] A bulky tongue, typically covered with vesicles, impairs speech and is complicated by recurrent infection, swelling, bleeding, poor dental hygiene, and caries. In the cervicofacial region, microcystic and macrocystic malformations can cause airway obstruction, sometimes necessitating tracheostomy. Cervical and axillary lymphatic malformations often involve the thorax and mediastinum and may cause life-threatening recurrent pleural and pericardial effusion (Fig. 130-5B). Pulmonary lymphatic abnormalities may lead to fatal pulmonary edema. Extensive malformation in the limbs is associated with lymphedema (even elephantiasis). Skeletal distortion and hypertrophy are also common features of malformations in a limb. The rare entity of "disappearing bone disease" (Gorham-Stout syndrome) may be a lymphatic malformation involving bone that results in progressive osteolysis. Pelvic lymphatic malformations may be manifested as perineal lymphangiectasia, bladder outlet obstruction, constipation, or recurrent infections. Gastrointestinal malformations (previously called "lymphangiomatosis") can result in hypoalbuminemia secondary to protein-losing enteropathy.

Venous Malformation

Venous malformations are present at birth but are not always evident. They are frequently mislabeled in both medical parlance and the literature as "cavernous hemangioma." These slow-flow anomalies appear as either a faint blue patch or a soft blue mass. Venous malformations can be localized or extensive. They occur in any location: the face, limbs, trunk, oronasopharynx, genitalia, bladder, brain, spinal cord, liver, spleen, hollow viscera, lungs, skeletal muscles, and bones (Fig. 130-6). They can be cosmetically inconsequential or tragically distorting. These malformations are easily compressible and exhibit increased swelling when dependent. Episodic thrombosis occurs, and phleboliths can be present as early as 2 years of age. Venous malformations grow proportionately with the child, slowly worsen, and often enlarge during puberty. Venous malformations represent

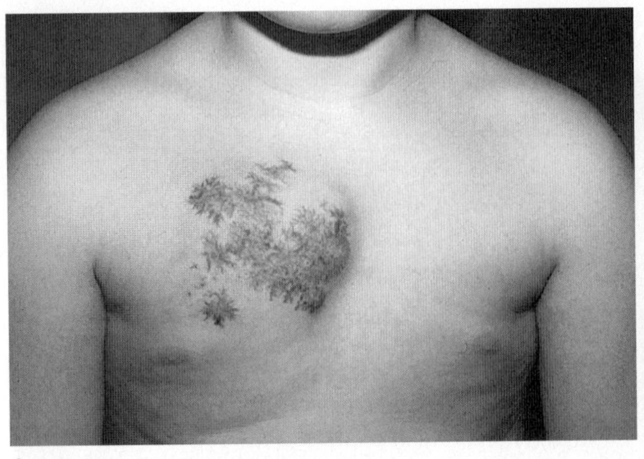

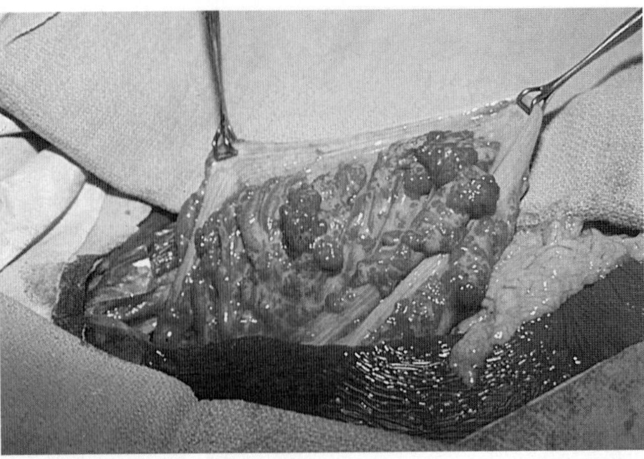

A B

Figure 130-6 *A*, Venous malformation of the chest wall. *B*, Extensive venous malformation throughout the large bowel with gastrointestinal bleeding.

the most common symptomatic vascular malformations. Discomfort results from engorgement or intralesional thrombosis, or both. Hemarthrosis and hemosiderin arthropathy may result from joint involvement.

Most venous malformations are single, but multiple cutaneous lesions can occur. The latter malformations may be inherited.[12] Familial glomuvenous malformations (glomangiomatosis) is an uncommon autosomal dominant syndrome with high penetrance that consists of multiple nodular dermal venous anomalies occurring anywhere on the skin.[14] Histologically, these lesions differ from typical venous malformations by the presence of numerous glomus cells lining the ectatic venous channels. They are often tender to palpation.

Arteriovenous Malformation

Most fast-flow malformations in childhood are AVMs. Pure arterial malformations (e.g., aneurysm, stenosis, and ectasia) or arteriovenous fistulas rarely occur alone as symptomatic lesions; they can be associated with AVMs. The epicenter of such malformations, the nidus, consists of arterial feeding vessels, micro- and macro-arteriovenous fistulas, and enlarged veins. AVMs are present at birth and become evident in infancy or childhood. They are thought to form by embryonal dysmorphogenesis and abnormal arterial determination. The resultant formation of multiple abnormal connections between a hyperdynamic arterial bed and a languid venous network causes excess blood to be shunted into the veins and thus creates a fragile, highly expansile lesion.

These malformations are often underappreciated in childhood and mistaken for hemangioma or port-wine stain. Puberty and trauma seem to trigger expansion, which causes the AVM to exhibit cutaneous signs of its fast-flow nature. The skin becomes red or violaceous, a mass appears beneath the vascular stain, and there is local warmth, thrill, and bruit (Fig. 130-7). The clinical course is often characterized by fluctuating degrees of pain related to decreased local oxygen delivery (ischemia), as well as overgrowth of the involved body part, probably related to increased blood flow. Whatever the site of an AVM, the eventual consequences may include ischemic skin changes, ulceration, intractable pain, and intermittent bleeding, even in childhood.

The clinical diagnosis is confirmed by ultrasonography and color Doppler examination. Pulsed Doppler quantification of arterial output (as compared with the normal side) can be used to monitor the progression of an AVM. MRI best documents the anatomic extent of the malformation. Schobinger's staging system is commonly used to describe the status of an AVM:

1. Stage I—a pink-bluish stain and warmth. Doppler ultrasonography reveals arteriovenous shunting.
2. Stage II—pulsations, thrill, and bruit.
3. Stage III—dystrophic skin changes, ulceration, bleeding, and pain.
4. Stage IV—high-output cardiac failure.

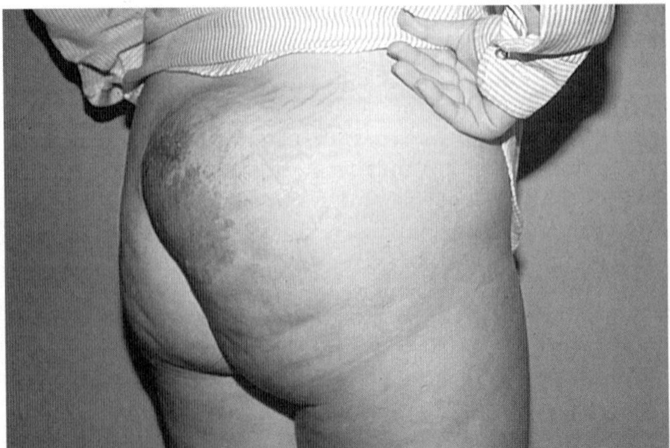

Figure 130-7 Teenage girl born with a blush over right buttock that expanded during puberty to reveal an arteriovenous malformation.

Complex-Combined Vascular Malformations

Eponyms have been applied to many of the complex vascular anomalies, usually those associated with soft tissue and skeletal hypertrophy (see Table 130-1). These eponyms are often misused and misleading and indicate nothing of pathogenesis. Nosology, based on flow characteristics and dysmorphic channel architecture, permits separation into two categories: slow flow and fast flow.

Slow-flow, complex-combined anomalies include capillary-venous malformations and capillary-lymphatic-venous malformations. The later condition corresponds to Klippel-Trenaunay syndrome, originally used to describe complex-combined anomalies associated with limb hypertrophy. The skin lesions are multiple and often occur in a geographic pattern; they may or may not have hemolymphatic vesicles and frequently occur on the anterior-lateral aspect of the thigh, buttock, and trunk. Venous anomalies may include a hypoplastic or absent deep venous system causing drainage through dilated, valveless, superficial veins. The anomalous, valveless, embryonal marginal vein of Servelle is often located in the lateral aspect of the calf and thigh and communicates variably with the deep venous system.[78] Lymphatic hypoplasia is also a primary defect; lymphatic cysts are common. Limb hypertrophy can be minor to grotesque (Fig. 130-8). The combined slow-flow anomalies often involve the ipsilateral buttock, perineum, and retroperitoneum. Extension into the pelvis can cause hematuria, hematochezia, constipation, and bladder outlet obstruction.[5] Thrombophlebitis and pulmonary embolism may occur at an increased incidence in patients with Klippel-Trenaunay syndrome.[68] Unlike some other hemihypertrophy syndromes, patients with Klippel-Trenaunay syndrome are not at increased risk for Wilms' tumor, and screening ultrasonography is unnecessary.[41]

Fast-flow, complex-combined anomalies (e.g., capillary-arteriovenous or capillary-arterial-lymphatic-venous malformations) are less common. The eponym Parkes Weber syndrome applies to these anomalies. Cutaneous warmth, bruit, and thrill are present. Arteriovenous fistulas are multiple and occur throughout the affected limb, particularly near the joints. MRI or arteriography in young children may show only diffuse hypervascularity of the limb; arteriovenous fistulas become obvious later.

Hereditary hemorrhagic telangiectasia (HHT), also called Rendu-Osler-Weber disease, is a genetic condition that begins with telangiectatic capillary lesions and progresses to capillary-venous shunts in the skin, mucous membranes, liver, lungs, and brain, usually during the third or fourth decade of life.[42] Cerebral and pulmonary AVMs and hepatic vascular anomalies develop. Two genes involving transforming growth factor-β signaling have been found. HHT1 is due to a mutation in endoglin, which encodes an endothelial glycoprotein. HHT2 is caused by a mutation in activin receptor–like kinase.

Proteus syndrome is an exceedingly rare disorder characterized by a variety of cutaneous and subcutaneous lesions, including vascular malformations, lipomas, hyperpigmentation, and several types of nevi, as well as macrocephaly, asymmetric limbs with partial gigantism of the hands and feet, and cerebriform plantar thickening. It is the partial gigantism with limb or digital overgrowth that is most typical. Hemihyperplasia and soft tissue overgrowth lead to skeletal deformities such as scoliosis and kyphoscoliosis, possibly resulting in respiratory compromise.

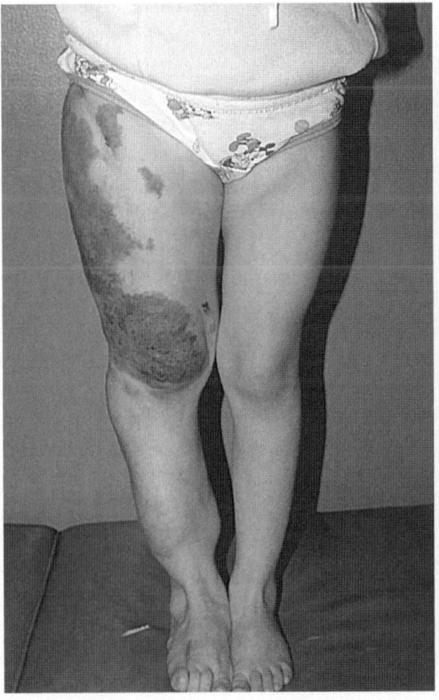

A

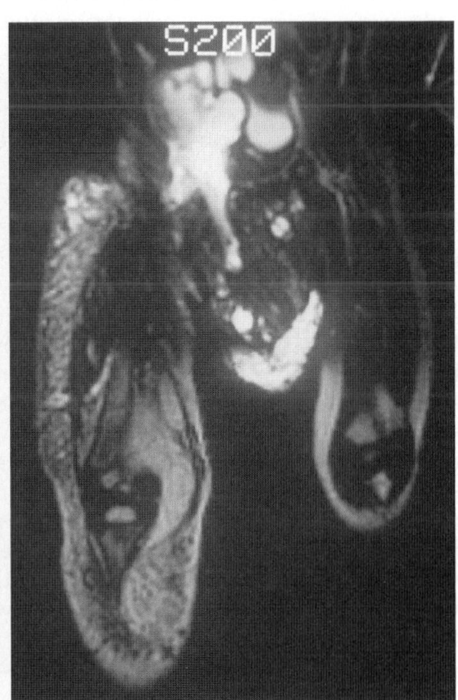

B

Figure 130-8 *A*, Complex-combined capillary-lymphatic-venous malformation with hypertrophy (Klippel-Trenaunay syndrome). *B*, Magnetic resonance image of this malformation showing macrocystic lymphatic anomalies extending into the pelvis.

Joseph Merrick (also known as "the elephant man"), once thought to have had neurofibromatosis, is now, in retrospect, thought to actually have suffered from Proteus syndrome. An increased risk for thrombotic events such as deep vein thrombosis or pulmonary embolism, particularly in males, contributes to the overall morbidity and mortality, even in young children. The diagnosis is complex and based on a multitude of specific diagnostic criteria. Proteus syndrome is probably overdiagnosed inasmuch as the moniker is often applied to patients with other poorly defined overgrowth conditions.

Bannayan-Riley-Ruvalcaba syndrome is an autosomal dominant disorder of the *PTEN* gene characterized by macrocephaly, multiple lipomas, hamartomatous polyps of the ileum and colon, Hashimoto's thyroiditis, macules on the penile glans, and vascular malformations.[57] Vascular anomalies, including capillary, venous, and arteriovenous malformations, are sometimes components of the syndrome.

Associated Anomalies

Although textbooks often list hemangiomas as occurring in association with syndromes that have dysmorphic features, these appellations are usually incorrect. The common infantile fading macular stains, or true vascular malformations (capillary, lymphatic, venous, or arterial), are not associated with dysmorphic syndromes.[19]

There are, however, well-documented examples of true hemangiomas associated with malformations. The acronym PHACE has recently been proposed to describe the association of posterior fossa malformations, hemangiomas, arterial anomalies, coarctation of the aorta and cardiac defects, and eye abnormalities. Midline defects such as sternal nonunion and supraumbilical raphe can also be seen. A spectrum of anomalies have been described, only some of which are present in affected infants.[36,74] Lumbosacral hemangioma is one of several cutaneous lesions (e.g., port-wine stain, achordoma [fawn tail], hairy patch) known to signal underlying occult spinal dysraphism (i.e., lipomeningocele, tethered cord, and diastematomyelia).[67]

Visceral Manifestations

An infant with multiple cutaneous hemangiomas is at high risk for harboring visceral (particularly intrahepatic) hemangiomas.[18,81] The cutaneous lesions are typically small (<3 to 5 mm in diameter), dark red, and dome shaped. Liver lesions may also be present in the absence of skin lesions. When symptomatic, visceral hemangiomas typically lead to evaluation of the infant 1 to 16 weeks after birth. The "classic" triad of congestive heart failure, hepatomegaly, and anemia is rarely present. Rather, hepatic vascular tumors are heterogeneous in their manifestation and clinical course.[50] Many infants will have one or multiple asymptomatic lesions detected by screening ultrasonography performed because of the presence of multiple cutaneous lesions. Lesions that cause high-output cardiac failure demonstrate macrovascular arteriovenous, arterioportal, or portosystemic shunting within the lesions. An uncommon, but feared, pattern is nearly complete replacement of the liver with multiple lesions resulting in massive hepatomegaly. These lesions will not cause high-output cardiac failure but, instead, may cause organ failure secondary to abdominal compartment syndrome. In addition, infants with large liver hemangiomas may have secondary hypothyroidism,[47] and any infant with clinically significant lesions should undergo repeat analysis even if the results of neonatal thyroid-stimulating hormone screening were normal. The hypothyroidism results from inactivation of thyroid hormone by a deiodinase expressed by hemangiomas. Clinical hypothyroidism results only when the hemangioma mass is large enough to inactivate hormone faster than the thyroid gland can produce it. A hemangioma in any location could theoretically cause hypothyroidism, but all reported cases to date have involved hepatic lesions. Large singular hepatic vascular lesions detected antenatally or shortly after birth, often associated with mild transient thrombocytopenia, are probably not classic infantile hemangioma but rather RICH. They will generally involute rapidly without manifesting other severe symptoms. The earlier reported mortality rates of 30% to 80% for hepatic hemangiomas are probably greatly overstated because of the lack of inclusion of previously undetected asymptomatic lesions and lack of appreciation of the clinical heterogeneity of these tumors.[8,20]

AVMs of the liver are probably quite rare. Diagnostic confusion may result from the high-flow macrovascular shunts seen coursing through the parenchyma of some hepatic hemangiomas.[9,50] Rarely, it may not be possible to differentiate intrahepatic hemangioma from hepatoblastoma, angiosarcoma, metastatic neuroblastoma, or mesenchymal hamartoma without biopsy or excision.

Hollow visceral hemangiomas are associated with chronic, episodic bleeding. As with hepatic lesions, they are often accompanied by multiple cutaneous hemangiomas.

Vascular malformations can also involve the viscera, particularly the gastrointestinal tract (see Fig. 130-6).[32,34] Venous lesions are most prevalent. They may be focal, multifocal, or diffuse. Flexible fiber-optic esophagoduodenoscopy and colonoscopy are invaluable in the assessment of vascular lesions of the gastrointestinal tract. Wireless capsule endoscopy, recently introduced, has revolutionized minimally invasive visualization of the small intestine. Endoscopic studies are far more useful than gastrointestinal contrast studies in demonstrating and characterizing vascular anomalies.

The association of vascular malformations of the skin and similar lesions in the gastrointestinal tract was first described by Gascoyen in 1860,[38] but the term blue rubber bleb nevus syndrome was coined by Bean in 1958.[7] This syndrome is a rare disorder with most cases being sporadic, but autosomal dominant inheritance has been reported.[51] The gastrointestinal venous malformations are sessile or polypoid and are located in the esophagus, stomach, small and large bowel, and mesentery; they are best seen by endoscopy. These patients can also have venous malformations in the parotid, brain, liver, spleen, and other organs. Recurrent intestinal bleeding can be severe and, once significant, generally continues throughout life. Some patients require blood transfusions as frequently as weekly. Although some patients will receive hundreds of transfusions over time, sudden hemodynamically severe hemorrhage is not common.[30] A venous malformation can serve as a lead point for intestinal intussusception. In cases in which lesions involve the bones and joints, the discomfort and loss of function may be so severe that an amputation is required.

Vascular malformations of the gastrointestinal tract can also occur in Turner's syndrome or as isolated vascular anomalies.[17]

Venous malformations frequently occur in the liver. In fact, the common vascular lesion seen in an adult liver and usually termed hemangioma is not a hemangioma at all, but rather a venous malformation. Hemangiomas of infancy do not persist or occur in adulthood.

Radiologic Characteristics

Radiologic imaging is used to delineate the type, rheologic nature, and anatomic extent of vascular anomalies. Ultrasonography with color Doppler differentiates slow-flow from fast-flow anomalies. A proliferative-phase hemangioma produces a remarkable to-and-fro signal that even an experienced ultrasonographer can have trouble distinguishing from the signal of an AVM. The major handicap of ultrasonography is that it is highly operator dependent and limited in its ability to display the size of the anomaly and its relationship to adjacent structures.

MRI is generally the most informative study because it provides rheologic information and shows the extent of involvement. This test shows that hemangiomas are composed of parenchymatous (solid) tissue and are of intermediate intensity on T1-weighted images and moderate hyperintensity on T2-weighted images.[48,59] Flow voids are seen around and within the tumor mass and indicate rapid flow through feeding arteries into dilated draining veins. In the late involuting phase, a regressing hemangioma becomes a slow-flow mass in which fatty tissue can be prominent.

MRI delineates all types of vascular malformation except for cutaneous capillary stains. Venous malformations have high signal intensity on T2-weighted images, brighter than that of fatty tissue. Phleboliths, seen as discrete round signal voids on T1- and T2-weighted images, are convincing evidence of a venous anomaly. On T1-weighted sequences venous malformations enhance inhomogeneously with gadolinium, and lymphatic malformations show no enhancement or just ring enhancement.[59]

To avoid exposure to radiation, contrast-enhanced computed tomography (CT) is infrequently used, although it accurately differentiates lymphatic, venous, and lymphaticovenous malformations. Phleboliths are more clearly seen on CT than on MRI. CT may be more valuable in the evaluation of some intraosseous vascular malformations and secondary bony changes.

Arteriography, the most invasive technique, is rarely used exclusively for the diagnosis of vascular anomalies. Instead, it is used in association with therapeutic superselective embolization. Venous angiography (phlebography) still has a place in the evaluation and treatment of certain venous anomalies.

MANAGEMENT OF HEMANGIOMAS

Observation

Most hemangiomas do not require treatment, but this does not mean that nothing should be done. The parents deserve a thorough explanation of the natural history of hemangioma. Photographs to illustrate involution are very helpful. Scheduled follow-up visits are needed to assess the evolution of the tumor. Frequent visits are necessary whenever the hemangioma is large, ulcerated, multiple, or located in an anatomically critical area.

Local Complications: Ulceration and Bleeding

Spontaneous ulceration occurs in 5% of cutaneous hemangiomas, most commonly in tumors of the lip or anogenital area. Frequent diaper changes and liberal use of barrier creams can help prevent ulceration. Treatment consists of cleansing and daily application of topical antibiotics. Dressing changes may be indicated if an eschar forms. An ulcerated hemangioma usually re-epithelializes within 2 weeks. Deep necrotic tissue requires debridement. Flashlamp pulsed dye laser treatment has been reported to relieve pain and possibly accelerate healing.[1,62]

Punctate bleeding from hemangioma is uncommon but frightening to parents. They should be instructed to compress the area with a clean gauze pad and hold the pressure for 10 minutes. Placement of a mattress suture is rarely necessary.

Pharmacologic Therapy for Endangering Complications

Serious or life-threatening complications are indications for pharmacologic therapy for hemangiomas. Although approximately 20% of hemangiomas cause destructive, obstructive, or endangering complications, less than 1% are truly life threatening. Potentially fatal complications include congestive heart failure, airway compromise, and gastrointestinal bleeding.

Cervicofacial hemangiomas can cause circumferential upper airway obstruction or difficulty swallowing. Subglottic hemangioma is usually manifested insidiously as biphasic stridor at 6 to 8 weeks, often in the presence of cervicofacial hemangioma. Large facial tumors grow to expand the skin and distort normal anatomic structures. Even a small hemangioma in the upper eyelid can distort the cornea and produce astigmatism and consequent amblyopia. Lesions involving edge structures, such as the eyelid, lips, nares, columella, and pinna, that may leave sequelae difficult to correct surgically are considered for therapy as well.

Corticosteroid Therapy

Corticosteroids remain the principal drug for the treatment of endangering hemangioma to impede proliferation and enhance involution. Corticosteroids accelerate the involution of hemangiomas through differentiation and inhibition of angiogenesis. Their main antiangiogenic action is inhibition of macrophage production of the proangiogenic proteins VEGF and bFGF. In addition, corticosteroids inhibit phospholipase A_2, the enzyme that releases arachidonic acid, the precursor to the proangiogenic prostaglandins.[21] Finally, corticosteroids inhibit metalloproteinases, which facilitate angiogenesis by breaking down the extracellular matrix.[49]

We use an initial regimen of prednisone or prednisolone, 2 to 3 mg/kg of body weight per day. A steroid-sensitive hemangioma begins to respond within 1 week. In general, 30% of tumors show accelerated regression, 40% respond equivocally (stabilization response), and 30% do not respond at all.[25] If no effect occurs, such as lightening of color, softening, or diminished growth, even higher doses of corticosteroid therapy, up to 5 mg/kg/day, may be considered for a short time or alternative agents used. If the hemangioma responds, the duration and dosage depend on the tumor's location and maturity. After 4 to 6 weeks of treatment, the dose can be decreased. Later in therapy, alternate-day administration can be effective and may minimize complications such as growth failure and cushingoid facies. Rebound growth can occur if the dose is lowered or the drug is withdrawn too rapidly. Corticosteroid therapy must be continued until involution is well under way, on average until 8 to 10 months of age (Fig. 130-9). Patients should be monitored closely for side effects such as temporary slowing of physical growth, cushingoid facies, behavioral changes (e.g., irritability, crying), gastrointestinal ulcerations, weight gain, infection, hypertension, or hypertrophic cardiomyopathy.

Intralesional corticosteroid is preferred for well-localized facial hemangiomas, particularly those situated in the upper eyelid, nose, cheek, or lips. Two cases of blindness that may have been due to embolic occlusion of the retinal artery have been reported with the injection of periorbital hemangioma, so caution and slow injection are warranted.[75] Triamcinolone is injected slowly, with low pressure and no more than 3 to 5 mg/kg given per procedure. Three to five injections are usually needed at 6- to 8-week intervals. The response rate is similar to that for systemic corticosteroid therapy.[52,80]

Other Agents

Interferon alfa-2a or alfa-2b (IFN-α2) should be reserved as an alternative for steroid unresponsive lesions.[28] The dose of IFN is 2 to 3 million U/m^2 subcutaneously once daily. The response appears to be slower than that of steroids, but direct comparison is difficult because the agent is rarely given as first-line therapy and may be used

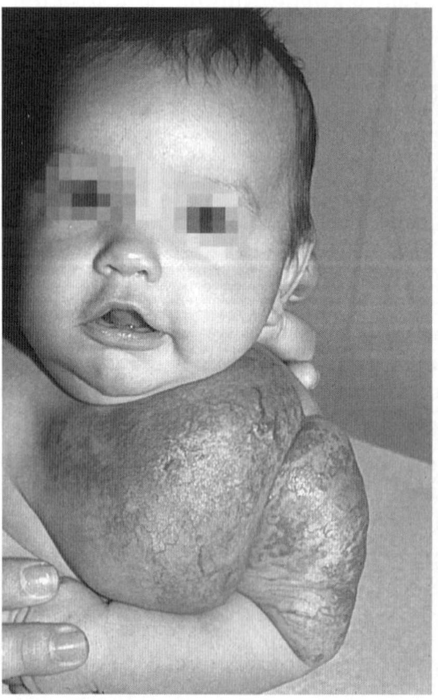
A

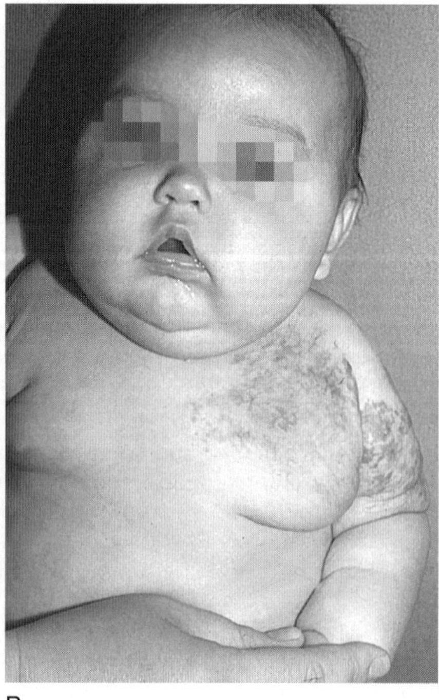
B

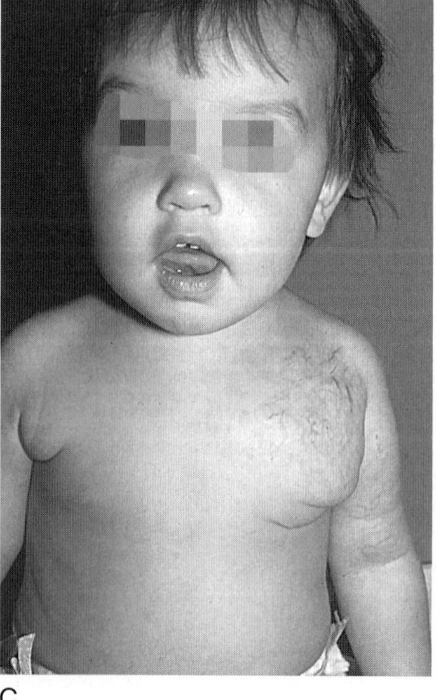
C

Figure 130-9 *A*, Large proliferating-phase hemangioma on the chest and arm in a 3-month-old girl. *B*, One month after oral corticosteroid therapy began (treatment continued for a total of 5 months). Note the accelerated regression and cushingoid facies. *C*, At age 1.5 years, natural regression continues.

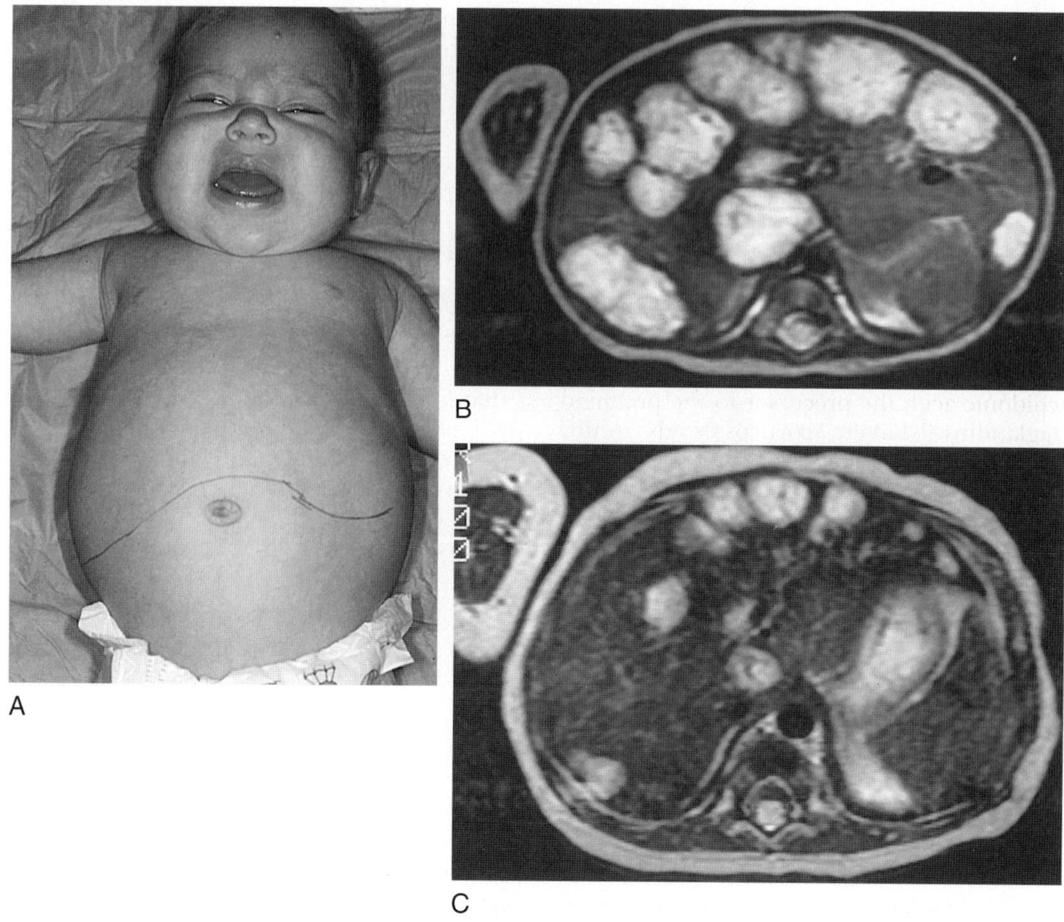

Figure 130–10 *A*, Infant with multiple intrahepatic hemangiomas causing congestive heart failure. *B*, Magnetic resonance image before pharmacologic therapy in another child (age 4 months) with multiple hepatic hemangiomas. *C*, Magnetic resonance image in the second infant obtained after 8 months of pharmacologic therapy.

for more recalcitrant lesions. IFN-α2 accelerates regression in almost all hemangiomas, as well as most KHEs, with platelet trapping.[8,28] Six to 12 months of sustained IFN-α2 therapy is generally required (Fig. 130-10). Because of the significant risk for spastic diplegia with IFN therapy, particularly in children younger than 1 year,[4,84] it should be used only after careful consideration of alternatives. Careful neurologic and developmental assessment should be performed in children receiving IFN-α. As an alternative to interferon for steroid-unresponsive lesions, low-dose weekly intravenous administration of vincristine (0.5 mg/m^2 or 0.025 mg/kg in children less than 20 kg) has recently been used at several centers.[43]

Laser Therapy

Subglottic hemangiomas can be debulked with laser therapy while corticosteroids are given time to take effect.[79] There is a popular belief that laser surgery is effective treatment of cutaneous hemangioma. Some investigators think that photocoagulation, used early for a nascent hemangioma, will prevent spread of the tumor and subsequent complications. The flashlamp pulsed dye laser penetrates no more than 0.75 to 1.0 mm into the dermis, which can result in superficial lightening of a hemangioma.[37] Although some superficial hemangiomas respond to laser treatment, these are the very tumors that do not cause problems and eventually regress to leave nearly normal skin. No evidence suggests that repeated laser therapy diminishes bulk or accelerates involution of hemangiomas in the deep dermis or subcutaneous tissue.[77] Overzealous use of the laser can result in second-degree skin loss and permanent scarring. Time and cost restraints also argue against repeated use of the laser. Laser treatment may have a role in speeding recovery of an ulcerated hemangioma.[62] There is no question that photocoagulation has a role in treatment of the tiny telangiectases that often remain after regression of cutaneous hemangioma.

Surgical Therapy

Localized, pedunculated lesions, particularly those that bleed repeatedly or are deeply ulcerated, may be considered for prompt surgical excision even during the proliferative phase (Fig. 130-11). Eyelid tumors that cause

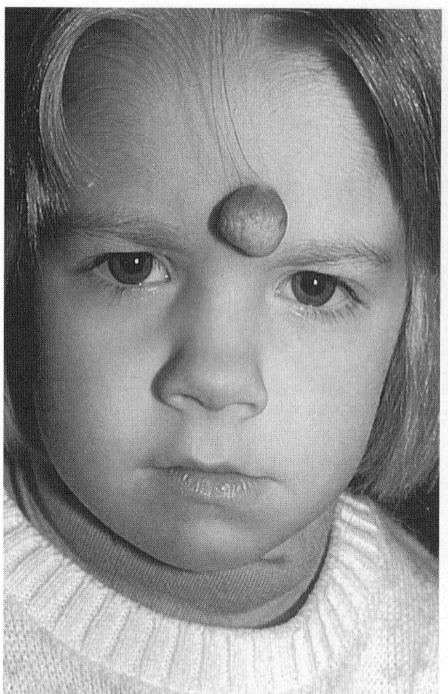

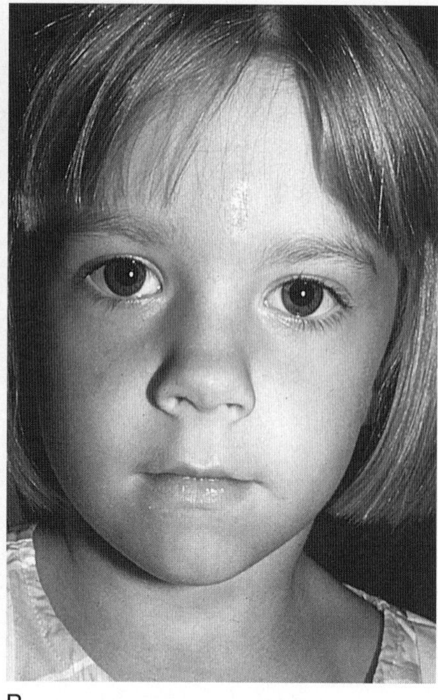

A B

Figure 130–11 *A*, Five-year-old girl with a pedunculated, involuting-phase hemangioma on her forehead. *B*, Two months after excision.

astigmatism and fail to respond to pharmacologic therapy can be surgically "debulked" to relieve pressure on the cornea.

Excision during the involuting phase, either staged or total, is sometimes warranted because of psychological concerns. For example, a bulky labial tumor or a bulbous hemangioma of the nasal tip in a preschool child can be particularly disturbing. The extent of scarring must be weighed against the degree of the child's potential emotional distress. Excision is indicated if resection is inevitable, if the scar will be the same with later removal, or if the scar is easily concealed.

Ideally, removal of the fibrofatty tissue and scarred or loose skin is best scheduled when regression is relatively complete (involuted phase). A protrusive hemangioma usually causes skin expansion, so skin excision is possible without distortion of the normal anatomic contour. Scarring and actual tissue loss occur infrequently; these adverse events require more complicated reconstructive strategies.

Nearly circular lesions, regardless of the stage at which the tumor is excised, may be best addressed by circular excision immediately adjacent to the lesion, with a purse-string closure, rather than the traditional lenticular excision and linear closure. Although a second stage may be desired 6 to 12 months later, the ultimate scar may be far preferable to the longer linear scar.[66]

Hepatic hemangiomas virtually never require resection. Asymptomatic lesions can be carefully observed with serial physical and ultrasound evaluations. Large singular RICH-type lesions will regress quickly. High-output cardiac failure, if unresponsive to steroids, can be ameliorated with superselective embolization of the macrovascular shunts by an interventional radiologist experienced at this technique in infants. There is no surgical option in patients with a massive liver diffusely replaced by tumor that is causing abdominal compartment syndrome other than liver transplantation, which may be a reasonable consideration if pharmacotherapy is ineffective and long-term profound hypothyroidism has not been present.

MANAGEMENT OF VASCULAR MALFORMATIONS

Capillary Malformations

The flashlamp pulsed dye laser is the standard treatment of a capillary malformation in infancy and childhood.[3,83] Significant lightening is achieved in 70% to 80% of patients; the best results occur in younger children. Facial lesions respond better than those on the limbs.

Lymphatic Malformations

The two reasons for sudden enlargement of a lymphatic malformation are infection and intralesional bleeding. Cellulitis in a lymphatic malformation requires immediate antibiotic therapy. Nonsteroidal anti-inflammatory drugs can also help during these flare-ups. Analgesics, rest, and time are all that is required for bleeding within a lymphatic malformation.

Surgical resection is the only way to "cure" these malformations. The strategy should be to perform as thorough a resection as possible in a single anatomic region at each operative procedure. Extensive lesions cannot usually be removed completely, even with multiple procedures.

Unfortunately, delicate normal structures frequently traverse malformations. Furthermore, deep cisterns have numerous microscopic communications. Immediate postoperative complications include long-lasting serous drainage, hematoma, and cellulitis. Wart-like lymphatic vesicles can appear in or near the operative scar. Expansion of a persistent lymphatic malformation is all too common in the late postoperative period or even years afterward.

Macrocystic lesions can sometimes be nearly obliterated or at least diminished by aspiration of lymphatic fluid and instillation of sclerosing agents such as 100% ethanol, sodium tetradecyl sulfate, bleomycin, and OK-432 (a killed strain of group A streptococcus).[60,70] Persistent malformation and recurrent swelling are unfortunately common after sclerotherapy.

Lymphatic anomalies involving the mediastinal structures and lungs can be particularly vexing. Some mass lesions of the mediastinum may remain asymptomatic for many years. Large lesions can be resected or sclerosed. A much greater challenge is encountered if pleural or pericardial effusions or ascites develop, particularly if they are chylous. There may be some benefit in performing contrast lymphangiography of the thoracic duct and central conducting lymphatic channels because innovative individualized therapy may be possible in some circumstances.[33]

Venous Malformations

Elastic support stockings are indispensable in the management of venous malformations in the extremities. Low-dose aspirin seems to minimize painful thrombotic episodes. Venous malformations may be reduced by sclerotherapy or resection.

Direct injection of sclerosant into a venous malformation is dangerous and must be done by a skilled and experienced interventional clinician. General anesthesia and real-time fluoroscopic monitoring are usually necessary. Local compression and other maneuvers prevent high levels of sclerosant from entering the systemic circulation. Local complications (such as cutaneous or mucosal blistering, full-thickness necrosis, or nerve deficit) and systemic complications (such as renal toxicity, transient pulmonary hypertension, and even cardiac arrest) have been reported. Multiple sclerotherapy sessions are generally required, often at intervals of several months. Venous anomalies have a propensity to recanalize and "recur."

Surgical resection is usually considered for bulky or extensive soft tissue lesions. Contour resection is particularly of benefit for venous malformations of the hand or foot. Blood loss can be significant and rapid. Preoperative sclerotherapy may be of use in reducing operative bleeding in some cases. A tourniquet is useful in extremity resections. Multiple large-bore intravenous catheters, as well as a prepared blood bank and anesthesia team, are essential. It is not usually possible to arrest bleeding before wound closure. However, a modicum of hemostasis can generally be achieved by skin closure. Postoperative hematoma and wound breakdown are common but manageable if the patient and family have been properly forewarned.

Diffuse coloanal venous malformations causing severe bleeding can be addressed by partial colectomy, anorectal mucosectomy, and coloanal pull-through.[31] Care must be taken to avoid injuring any surrounding pelvic venous malformation because hemostasis will probably be impossible.

Bleeding resulting from the multifocal venous malformations of the blue rubber bleb nevus syndrome may be addressed by individual eradication of each lesion, as identified by intraoperative endoscopy of the entire gastrointestinal tract from mouth to anus.[30] Though tedious and extremely time consuming, this aggressive approach was successful in eradicating bleeding in 9 of the first 10 patients, with up to 9-year follow-up. None of these nine patients have needed any transfusions postoperatively despite having received up to hundreds before surgery.

Arteriovenous Malformations

AVMs are usually quiescent in infancy and early childhood. Early embolic or surgical management of an asymptomatic AVM is debatable but probably should be undertaken if resection is easily achievable without serious deformity. Generally, AVMs are treated in late childhood or adolescence when endangering signs and symptoms arise (e.g., ischemic pain, recalcitrant skin ulceration, bleeding, or high-output congestive heart failure).

Superselective arterial embolization of the nidus of an AVM can be used as palliation for pain, bleeding, or cardiac failure, particularly in cases in which surgical excision would result in mutilation or disfigurement. Embolization can permanently cure an AVM only in occasional circumstances. A single direct arteriovenous communication provides the greatest optimism. Ligation or proximal embolization of arterial feeding vessels must never be done. Rapid recruitment of nearby arterioles will resupply the nidus, and arterial ligation limits access for later proper therapeutic subselective arterial embolization of the nidus.

Surgical resection can be used in an attempt to remove or debulk an AVM. Arterial embolization performed 24 to 72 hours before surgical resection temporarily occludes the nidus. Embolization reduces intraoperative bleeding but does not change the limits of resection. The nidus of the malformation must be widely resected, usually with overlying skin. The principles of surgery are similar to those for resecting venous malformations. After combined embolization and surgical excision, the patient must be monitored by clinical examination, ultrasonography, or MRI for years. Definitive cure is uncommon, but possible.

Complex-Combined Vascular Malformations

Management of complex lesions is fundamentally conservative. Children with these malformations should be seen annually. For lesions involving the limbs, clinical evaluation should be done by the age of 2 years and leg length should be radiologically measured. If the discrepancy is more than 1.5 cm, a shoe lift is needed to prevent limping and back disorders. Epiphysiodesis can be performed to interrupt growth of the longer extremity to have it match the opposite extremity in ultimate adult length. MRI and magnetic resonance angiography can be useful to detect arterial feeders, identify the anomalous veins, and determine whether the deep venous system is functional. Elastic compression stockings are recommended for limbs with venous insufficiency and a functioning deep system. Varicose veins are sometimes surgically treated in childhood if they are grossly incompetent. Reconstruction of the deep system has been described in some patients,[78] but it is of dubious benefit. In cases of grotesque hypertrophy that prevents fitting of shoes or ambulation, staged surgical contour resection and possibly selected amputation are needed. Large complex-combined vascular malformations of the torso and genitalia can be managed by staged resection.

REFERENCES

1. Achauer BM, Vander Kam VM: Ulcerated anogenital hemangioma of infancy. Plast Reconstr Surg 1991; 87:861.
2. Amir J, Metzker A, Krikler R, et al: Strawberry hemangioma in preterm infants. Pediatr Dermatol 1986;3:331.
3. Ashinoff R, Geronemus RG: Flashlamp-pumped pulsed dye laser for port-wine stains in infancy: Earlier versus later treatment. J Am Acad Dermatol 1991;24:467.
4. Barlow CF, Priebe CJ, Mulliken JB, et al: Spastic diplegia as a complication of interferon alfa-2a treatment of hemangiomas of infancy. J Pediatr 1998;132:527.
5. Baskerville PA, Ackroyd JS, Lea Thomas M, et al: The Klippel-Trenaunay syndrome: Clinical, radiological and haemodynamic features and management. Br J Surg 1985; 72:232.
6. Bean WB: Blue Rubber-Bleb Nevi of the Skin and Gastrointestinal Tract. Springfield, IL, Charles C Thomas, 1958.
7. Beaubien ER, Ball NJ, Storwick GS: Kaposiform hemangioendothelioma: A locally aggressive vascular tumor. J Am Acad Dermatol 1998;38:799.
8. Berman B, Lim H: Concurrent cutaneous and hepatic hemangiomata in infancy: Report of a case and a review of the literature. J Dermatol Surg Oncol 1978;4:869.
9. Boon LM, Burrows PE, Paltiel HJ, et al: Hepatic vascular anomalies in infancy: A twenty-seven-year experience. J Pediatr 1996;129:346.
10. Boon LM, Enjolras O, Mulliken JB: Congenital hemangioma: Evidence of accelerated involution. J Pediatr 1996;128:329.
11. Boon LM, Fishman SJ, Lund DP, et al: Congenital fibrosarcoma masquerading as congenital hemangioma: Report of two cases. J Pediatr Surg 1995;30:1378.
12. Boon LM, Mulliken JB, Vikkula M, et al: Assignment of a locus for dominantly inherited venous malformations to chromosome 9p. Hum Mol Genet 1994;3:1583.
13. Bowers R, Graham, EA, Tomlinson KM: The natural history of strawberry nevus. Arch Dermatol 1960;82:667.
14. Boyd JB, Mulliken JB, Kaban LB, et al: Skeletal changes associated with vascular malformations. Plast Reconstr Surg 1984;74:789.
15. Brouillard P, Boon LM, Mulliken JB, et al: Mutations in a novel factor, glomulin, are responsible for glomuvenous malformations ("glomangiomas"). Am J Hum Genet 2002; 70:866.
16. Brouillard P, Vikkula M: Vascular malformations: Localized defects in vascular morphogenesis. Clin Genet 2003; 63:340.
17. Burge DM, Middleton AW, Kamath R, et al: Intestinal haemorrhage in Turner's syndrome. Arch Dis Child 1981; 56:557.
18. Burman D, Mansell PW, Warin RP: Miliary haemangiomata in the newborn. Arch Dis Child 1967;42:193.
19. Burns AJ, Kaplan LC, Mulliken JB: Is there an association between hemangioma and syndromes with dysmorphic features? Pediatrics 1991;88:1257.
20. Cohen RC, Myers NA: Diagnosis and management of massive hepatic hemangiomas in childhood. J Pediatr Surg 1986;21:6.
21. Crum R, Szabo S, Folkman J: A new class of steroids inhibits angiogenesis in the presence of heparin or a heparin fragment. Science 1985;230:1375.
22. Dethlefsen SM, Mulliken JB, Glowacki J: An ultrastructural study of mast cell interactions in hemangiomas. Ultrastruct Pathol 1986;10:175.
23. Eerola I, Boon LM, Mulliken JB, et al: Capillary malformation–arteriovenous malformation, a new clinical and genetic disorder caused by *RASA1* mutations. Am J Hum Genet 2003;73:1240.
24. el-Dessouky M, Azmy AF, Raine PA, et al: Kasabach-Merritt syndrome. J Pediatr Surg 1988;23:109.
25. Enjolras O, Mulliken JB, Boon LM, et al: Noninvoluting congenital hemangioma: A rare cutaneous vascular anomaly. Plast Reconstr Surg 2001;107:1647.
26. Enjolras O, Riche MC, Merland JJ: Facial port-wine stains and Sturge-Weber syndrome. Pediatrics 1985;76:48.
27. Enjolras O, Riche MC, Merland JJ, et al: Management of alarming hemangiomas in infancy: A review of 25 cases. Pediatrics 1990;85:491.
28. Ezekowitz RA, Mulliken JB, Folkman J: Interferon alfa-2a therapy for life-threatening hemangiomas of infancy. N Engl J Med 1992;326:1456.
29. Finn MC, Glowacki J, Mulliken JB: Congenital vascular lesions: Clinical application of a new classification. J Pediatr Surg 1983;18:894.
30. Fishman SJ, Burrows PE, Leichtner AM, et al: Gastrointestinal manifestations of vascular anomalies in childhood: Varied etiologies require multiple therapeutic modalities. J Pediatr Surg 1998;33:1163.
31. Fishman SJ, Burrows PE, Upton J, et al: Life-threatening anomalies of the thoracic duct: Anatomic delineation dictates management. J Pediatr Surg 2001;36:1269.
32. Fishman SJ, Fox VL: Visceral vascular anomalies. Gastrointest Endosc Clin N Am 2001;11:813.
33. Fishman SJ, Shamberger RC, Fox VL, et al: Endorectal pull-through abates gastrointestinal hemorrhage from colorectal venous malformations. J Pediatr Surg 2000; 35:982.
34. Fishman SJ, Smithers CJ, Folkman J, et al: Blue rubber bleb nevus syndrome: Surgical eradication of gastrointestinal bleeding. Ann Surg 2005;241:528.
35. Folkman J, Klagsbrun M: Angiogenic factors. Science 1987; 235:442.
36. Frieden IJ, Reese V, Cohen D: PHACE syndrome. The association of posterior fossa brain malformations, hemangiomas, arterial anomalies, coarctation of the aorta and cardiac defects, and eye abnormalities. Arch Dermatol 1996; 132:307.
37. Garden JM, Bakus AD, Paller AS: Treatment of cutaneous hemangiomas by the flashlamp-pumped pulsed dye laser: Prospective analysis. J Pediatr 1992;120:555.

38. Gascoyen M: Case of naevus involving the parotid gland, and causing death from suffocation. Trans Pathol Soc 1860;11:267.
39. Glowacki J, Mulliken JB: Mast cells in hemangiomas and vascular malformations. Pediatrics 1982;70:48.
40. Gorlin RJ, Kantaputra P, Aughton DJ, et al: Marked female predilection in some syndromes associated with facial hemangiomas. Am J Med Genet 1994;52:130.
41. Greene AK, Kieran M, Burrows PE, et al: Wilms tumor screening is unnecessary in Klippel-Trenaunay syndrome. Pediatrics 2004;113:e326.
42. Guttmacher AE, Marchuk DA, White RI Jr: Hereditary hemorrhagic telangiectasia. N Engl J Med 1995;333:918.
43. Haisley-Royster C, Enjolras O, Frieden LT, et al: Kasabach-Merritt phenomenon: A retrospective study of treatment with vincristine. J Pediatr Hematol Oncol 2002; 24:459.
44. Hayward PG, Orgill DP, Mulliken JB, et al: Congenital fibrosarcoma masquerading as lymphatic malformation: Report of two cases. J Pediatr Surg 1995;30:84.
45. Holmdahl K: Cutaneous hemangiomas in premature and mature infants. Acta Paediatr 1955;44:370.
46. Hopfel-Kreiner I: Histogenesis of hemangiomas—an ultrastructural study on capillary and cavernous hemangiomas of the skin. Pathol Res Pract 1980;170:70.
47. Huang SA, Tu HM, Harney JW, et al: Severe hypothyroidism caused by type 3 iodothyronine deiodinase in infantile hemangiomas. N Engl J Med 2000;343:185.
48. Huston J III, Forbes GS, Ruefenacht DA, et al: Magnetic resonance imaging of facial vascular anomalies. Mayo Clin Proc 1992;67:739.
49. Jones EW, Orkin M: Tufted angioma (angioblastoma). A benign progressive angioma, not to be confused with Kaposi's sarcoma or low-grade angiosarcoma. J Am Acad Dermatol 1989;20:214.
50. Kassarjian A, Zurakowski D, Dubois J, et al: Infantile hepatic hemangiomas: Clinical and imaging findings and their correlation with therapy. AJR Am J Roentgenol 2004;182:785.
51. Kisu T, Yamaoka K, Uchida Y, et al: A case of blue rubber bleb nevus syndrome with familial onset. Gastroenterol Jpn 1986;21:262.
52. Kushner BJ: The treatment of periorbital infantile hemangioma with intralesional corticosteroid. Plast Reconstr Surg 1985;76:517.
53. Langer JC, Fitzgerald PG, Desa D, et al: Cervical cystic hygroma in the fetus: Clinical spectrum and outcome. J Pediatr Surg 1990;25:58.
54. Margileth AM, Museles M: Cutaneous hemangiomas in children. Diagnosis and conservative management. JAMA 1965;194:523.
55. Marler JJ, Fishman SJ, Kilroy SM, et al: Increased expression of urinary matrix metalloproteinases parallels the extent and progression of vascular anomalies. Pediatrics 2005;116:35.
56. Marler JJ, Fishman SJ, Upton J, et al: Prenatal diagnosis of vascular anomalies. J Pediatr Surg 2002;37:318.
57. Marsh DJ, Kum JB, Lunetta KL, et al: PTEN mutation spectrum and genotype-phenotype correlations in Bannayan-Riley-Ruvalcaba syndrome suggest a single entity with Cowden syndrome. Hum Mol Genet 1999;8:1461.
58. Martinez-Perez D, Fein NA, Boon LM, et al: Not all hemangiomas look like strawberries: Uncommon presentations of the most common tumor of infancy. Pediatr Dermatol 1995;12:1.
59. Meyer JS, Hoffer FA, Barnes PD, et al: Biological classification of soft-tissue vascular anomalies: MR correlation. AJR Am J Roentgenol 1991;157:559.
60. Molitch HI, Unger EC, Witte CL, et al: Percutaneous sclerotherapy of lymphangiomas. Radiology 1995; 194:343.
61. Montesano R, Vassalli JD, Baird A, et al: Basic fibroblast growth factor induces angiogenesis in vitro. Proc Natl Acad Sci U S A 1986;83:7297.
62. Morelli JG, Tan OT, Weston WL: Treatment of ulcerated hemangiomas with the pulsed tunable dye laser. Am J Dis Child 1991;145:1062.
63. Mulliken JB: Cutaneous vascular anomalies. Semin Vasc Surg 1993;6:204.
64. Mulliken JB, Fishman SJ, Burrows PE: Vascular anomalies. Curr Probl Surg 2000;37:517.
65. Mulliken JB, Glowacki J: Hemangiomas and vascular malformations in infants and children: A classification based on endothelial characteristics. Plast Reconstr Surg 1982;69:412.
66. Mulliken JB, Rogers GF, Marler JJ: Circular excision of hemangioma and purse-string closure: The smallest possible scar. Plast Reconstr Surg 2002;109:1544.
67. Mulliken JB, Young AE: Vascular Birthmarks: Hemangiomas and Malformations. Philadelphia, WB Saunders; 1988.
68. Noel AA, Gloviczki P, Cherry KJ Jr, et al: Surgical treatment of venous malformations in Klippel-Trenaunay syndrome. J Vasc Surg 2000;32:840.
69. North PE, Waner M, Mizeracki A, et al: A unique microvascular phenotype shared by juvenile hemangiomas and human placenta. Arch Dermatol 2001;137:559.
70. Ogita S, Tsuto T, Deguchi E, et al: OK-432 therapy for unresectable lymphangiomas in children. J Pediatr Surg 1991; 26:263.
71. Padwa BL, Hayward PG, Ferraro NF, et al: Cervicofacial lymphatic malformation: Clinical course, surgical intervention, and pathogenesis of skeletal hypertrophy. Plast Reconstr Surg 1995;95:951.
72. Pasyk KA, Cherry GW, Grabb WC, et al: Quantitative evaluation of mast cells in cellularly dynamic and adynamic vascular malformations. Plast Reconstr Surg 1984; 73:69.
73. Patrice SJ, Wiss K, Mulliken JB: Pyogenic granuloma (lobular capillary hemangioma): A clinicopathologic study of 178 cases. Pediatr Dermatol 1991;8:267.
74. Reese V, Frieden LT, Paller AS, et al: Association of facial hemangiomas with Dandy-Walker and other posterior fossa malformations. J Pediatr 1993;122:379.
75. Ruttum MS, Abrams GW, Harris GJ, et al: Bilateral retinal embolization associated with intralesional corticosteroid injection for capillary hemangioma of infancy. J Pediatr Ophthalmol Strabismus 1993;30:4.
76. Sarkar M, Mulliken JB, Kozakewich HP, et al: Thrombocytopenic coagulopathy (Kasabach-Merritt phenomenon) is associated with kaposiform hemangioendothelioma and not with common infantile hemangioma. Plast Reconstr Surg 1997;100:1377.
77. Scheepers JH, Quaba AA: Does the pulsed tunable dye laser have a role in the management of infantile hemangiomas? Observations based on 3 years' experience. Plast Reconstr Surg 1995;95:305.
78. Servelle M: Klippel and Trenaunay's syndrome. 768 operated cases. Ann Surg 1985;201:365.
79. Sie KC, McGill T, Healy GB: Subglottic hemangioma: Ten years' experience with the carbon dioxide laser. Ann Otol Rhinol Laryngol 1994;103:167.
80. Sloan GM, Reinisch JF, Nichter LS, et al: Intralesional corticosteroid therapy for infantile hemangiomas. Plast Reconstr Surg 1989;83:459.
81. Stenninger E, Schollin J: Diffuse neonatal haemangiomatosis in a newborn child. Acta Paediatr 1993;82:102.

82. Takahashi K, Mulliken JB, Kozakewich HP, et al: Cellular markers that distinguish the phases of hemangioma during infancy and childhood. J Clin Invest 1994;93:2357.
83. Tan OT, Sherwood K, Gilchrest BA: Treatment of children with port-wine stains using the flashlamp-pulsed tunable dye laser. N Engl J Med 1989;320:416.
84. Vesikari T, Nuutila A, Cantell K: Neurologic sequelae following interferon therapy of juvenile laryngeal papilloma. Acta Paediatr Scand 1988;77:619.
85. Virchow R: Angiome. In Die Krankhaften Geshwulste. Berlin, Hirschwald, 1863.
86. Wegner G: Ueber Lymphangiome. Arch Klin Chir 1877;20:641.
87. Zukerberg LR, Nickoloff BJ, Weiss SW: Kaposiform hemangioendothelioma of infancy and childhood. An aggressive neoplasm associated with Kasabach-Merritt syndrome and lymphangiomatosis. Am J Surg Pathol 1993;17:321.

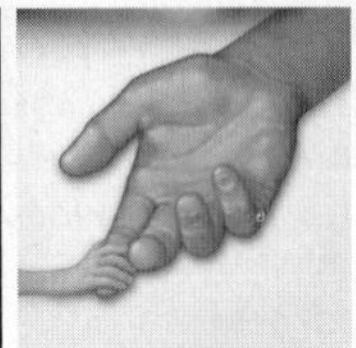

Chapter 131

Arterial Disorders

James A. O'Neill, Jr.

Many disorders may affect the arterial system. Although individual entities are rare, when taken together, arterial disorders are fairly common. Table 131-1 lists the most common disorders that affect the arterial tree with a useful classification of origin including congenital malformations, connective tissue disorders, and acquired disorders.

CONGENITAL MALFORMATIONS

Congenital Aneurysms

Congenital aneurysms are rare, are usually discovered incidentally, and may involve any artery, but the visceral arteries are the most commonly affected.[58] Rupture of a congenital aneurysm is even more unusual, although hypertension is common when renal artery branches are involved because of disturbed flow or compression of adjacent renal artery branches. Kim and colleagues have reported a congenital abdominal aortic aneurysm associated with renovascular hypertension in a 3-week-old infant.[33] Latter and associates described an abdominal aortic aneurysm in a 34-week fetus on prenatal ultrasound.[36] Prenatal diagnosis of such cases is now common.[41] Such cases prove the congenital nature of some aneurysms, differentiating them from acquired types. Sarkar and associates indicated that most children with congenital aneurysms are younger than age 5 years at presentation and that such lesions are usually found in the abdominal aorta or one of its primary branches and not in an extremity.[66] However, we and others have encountered occasional infants and young children with congenital aneurysms of proximal arterial branches to the extremities and various cerebral arteries. These lesions are either saccular or fusiform (Fig. 131-1). Histologic examination of such aneurysms usually shows only ectasia related to medial dysplasia with no further indication of cause. Senzaki and colleagues have published their observations on age-associated changes in arterial elastic properties in children.[69] These studies indicated that both peripheral and proximal arterial wall distensibility in children declined after birth, so the question is raised about whether some infants have precocious loss of elastic tissue in some arterial sites. Although congenital aneurysms are usually isolated findings in the child, occasional reports describe multiple visceral aneurysms.[67] In our experience as well as that of Guzzetta, in the order of frequency, congenital visceral aneurysms most commonly occur in the splenic, hepatic, and renal arteries, followed by the abdominal aorta.[27] We have encountered renal artery aneurysms in children as young as 8 years of age.

Congenital arterial aneurysms would appear to be quiescent in most instances unless they are associated with clinical signs such as hypertension, headache, or a palpable pulsatile mass. The diagnosis may be confirmed by magnetic resonance angiography (MRA), computed tomographic angiography (CTA), or standard arteriography.[46]

Because congenital visceral aneurysms are so uncommon and because rupture has rarely been reported, the indications for operation are uncertain. However, based on the size of congenital aneurysms that have ruptured that we have encountered and those reported in the literature, we believe that repair is indicated for patients with visceral aneurysms larger than 2 cm in diameter and those that are enlarging. Appropriate treatment is resection and arterial reconstruction with either autogenous or prosthetic material. Although arterial ligation has occasionally been reported, reconstruction is preferable from the standpoint of growth and development. Whenever possible, we prefer to perform reconstruction with autogenous tissue because of the needs of growth. However, successful aortic reconstruction with prosthetic material has been reported by Latter and associates[36] and by Saad and May.[62] We have successfully treated a patient with a lower pole splenic artery aneurysm by embolization, relying on the short gastric vessels for collateral blood supply. We have treated patients with renal artery aneurysms outside the kidney by resection and reconstruction with autogenous vein. Konan and coworkers have described transarterial embolization of aneurysms associated with spinal cord arteriovenous malformations (AVMs).[35] Redekop and coworkers have described a variety of approaches to treatment of arterial aneurysms associated with cerebral AVMs.[59]

TABLE 131-1 Classification of Disorders of the Arterial System

Congenital Malformations
Aneurysms
Congenital absence
Anomalies
Arteriovenous malformations
Connective Tissue Disorders
Marfan syndrome
Ehlers-Danlos syndrome
Familial cystic medial necrosis
Turner syndrome
Cystinosis
Melorheostosis
Acquired Disorders
Aneurysms related to Ehlers-Danlos syndrome
Kawasaki disease
Dysplasia
Trauma
Infection
Thrombosis
Embolism
Inflammatory and immunologic occlusive syndromes
Williams syndrome
Subacute bacterial endocarditis
Midaortic syndrome
Renovascular hypertension
Small artery disease

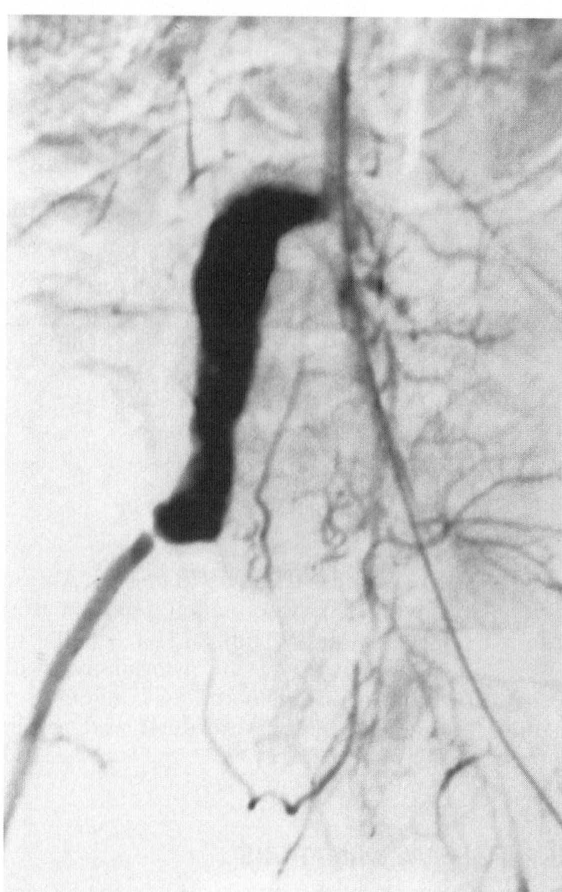

Figure 131-1 This angiogram demonstrates a congenital fusiform aneurysm of the common iliac artery in a 4-year-old boy that eventually required resection and reconstruction with an interposition graft.

Arteriovenous Malformations

The majority of AVMs are peripheral and localized (see Chapter 130). Szilagyi and coworkers described the classification of AVM into microfistulous and macrofistulous types based on the degree of embryologic differentiation (Fig. 131-2).[78] Upton and colleagues refer to such malformations as either slow flow or fast flow depending on the size and quantity of the arterial component.[85] The slow flow or microfistulous type is difficult to demonstrate angiographically, and the signs and symptoms are subtle, whereas the macrofistulous forms are clinically obvious and easily demonstrable on arteriography (see Fig. 131-2). Although congenital AVMs are relatively common, the extensive, life-threatening forms are fortunately quite rare. Tice and associates[81] and Upton and colleagues[85] have found that half of congenital AVMs occur in the extremities, most commonly in the lower limbs. Although most reports indicate that AVMs of the upper extremities and neck are more likely to have physiologic consequences, we have treated two children, 8 and 12 years of age, with severe congestive heart failure related to extensive AVMs of the pelvis and thigh. Surface AVMs may present clinically as variants of hemangioma, vascular nevi, or even aneurysmal varices on an extremity, usually a leg. The latter was originally described in 1907 by Parkes Weber, when he reported the association of such malformations with hemihypertrophy of a limb.[54] In the latter instances, limb overgrowth is independent of the microfistulous AVMs associated with this disorder. However, in the case of isolated macrofistulous AVMs in an extremity, late overgrowth of the affected limb is presumed to be the result of enhanced blood flow, with increased core temperature leading to accelerated epiphyseal growth. Knudsen and Alden reported a broad review of AVMs in infants younger than 6 months of age; AVMs were encountered in the head and neck, intestine, liver, lung, and central nervous system, usually associated with serious local and systemic physiologic effects.[34]

Signs and Symptoms

The most frequent signs and symptoms of AVMs are pain, skin disfigurement, and limb or facial swelling. Varicose veins associated with pulsations, skin ulceration, and bleeding, as well as overgrowth of the affected adjacent bones and soft tissues, are commonly seen in extremity lesions. The signs and symptoms related to AVMs in other parts of the body vary. For example, in the intestine, bleeding is the most common manifestation and the lesions are usually multiple.[16] In the liver, where the lesions are often categorized as hemangioendotheliomas, refractive congestive heart failure from massive shunt is common, particularly in the newborn. Lung AVMs may

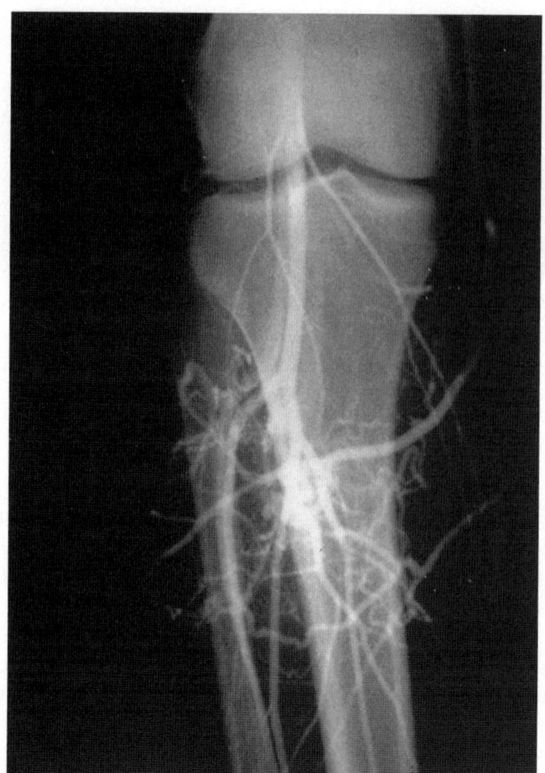

Figure 131–2 A child presented with leg pain and swelling and a few dilated superficial veins. The arteriogram shown here demonstrates a macrofistulous arteriovenous malformation with early venous filling. Most lesions of this type are not completely resectable.

be asymptomatic or associated with embolic infectious complications to the brain. Malformations of the central nervous system produce seizures or symptoms from intracranial hemorrhage or compression of associated vital structures. The report by Knudsen and Alden stressed the common occurrence of refractory high-output congestive heart failure in infants younger than 6 months of age with symptomatic AVMs of various parts of the body.[34]

Diagnosis

Hyperhidrosis and increased warmth of the part associated with pulsating varicosities within or under the skin are obvious physical findings, and palpation and auscultation of the varicosities may uncover a thrill or bruit. Interestingly, major deep AVMs may be associated with relatively insignificant small hemangiomas of the skin. Doppler examination usually reveals a continuous signal characteristic of a macrofistulous communication. The classic angiographic features of congenital AVMs are arterial dilatation and tortuosity, early filling of dilated associated veins, demonstration of AV connections, and puddling of dye in AV channels. The latter classical findings are not present in all cases, however; they occurred in only 60% of Szilagyi's cases.[78] Angiography may not demonstrate diffuse microfistulous malformations, in which case skin and muscle blood flow determinations and comparative venous blood oxygen saturations may be required to establish a diagnosis. Tanaka and coworkers evaluated the vascular structure of AVMs of the brain and divided them angiographically into the arteriovenous fistula (AVF) type and the plexiform type.[80] They then studied the specimens of these two angiographic forms of cerebral AVMs histologically, and they were similar. It is of interest that they found that many of the individual vessels connected with the feeder vessel to the lesion on one side while the other side anastomosed with the draining vessels. The only difference noted between the AVF type and the plexiform type was that the plexiform type was fundamentally a conglomeration of AVFs. In contrast to traumatic AVFs, congenital AVMs ordinarily have a complex network of feeding arteries and draining veins, which limits the value of embolization or ligation. In the case of AVMs of the head and neck, over a third of such lesions involve the underlying bone. We have encountered patients who have had massive bleeding after dental extraction as the first manifestation of a previously unsuspected AVM.

Although Doppler examination is an excellent screening study, MRA or CTA provides more information, particularly in terms of the extent of the malformation. Arteriography is still important to acquire before attempting surgical extirpation because of its ability to demonstrate precise anatomic detail, but it may eventually be replaced by MRA or CTA. Additionally, preoperative embolization may be a useful technique for control of bleeding during operation.

Treatment

Various approaches to the treatment of AVMs are described in Chapter 130. Many AVMs are amenable to nonoperative treatment when the symptoms are limited to dilated veins or the lesion is so diffuse that excision is not likely to be effective. Under these circumstances, external elastic support is usually the best approach. With the use of compression stockings, patients will often improve or at least remain stable.

In terms of operative treatment of extensive AVMs, unfortunately, simple ligation or embolization of the major feeding vessels is ineffective and often associated with complications such as extensive tissue necrosis. After ligation, such AVMs rapidly develop collateral flow. Additionally, ligation may preempt the use of preoperative embolization for the control of bleeding. In the case of the internal carotid artery, if ligation has been performed and numerous collaterals develop, then embolization therapy is contraindicated because of the risk of cerebral infarction. We reserve the use of embolization primarily as a preoperative measure, although occasional patients may be treated in a serial fashion over time if they are poor surgical candidates or refuse an extensive extirpation procedure. We have used preoperative embolization 24 hours before performing excisional therapy because collaterals will invariably form after that time. Limited resection usually results in recurrent symptoms and development of collateral flow, so the goal should be complete excision of the malformation if reasonably possible.

For microfistulous AVMs, such as those associated with the Klippel-Trenaunay syndrome, Gloviczki and colleagues have recommended treatment with elastic compression, and it is usually successful.[24] At times, partial excision of skin lesions may be useful in association with the use of compression garment support. In their study of long-term outlook, McCullough and Kenwright showed that surgical treatment is frequently needed to manage lower limb hypertrophy.[42] Unfortunately, no ideal treatment approach is available for the treatment of extensive AVMs of the head and neck. Although temporary relief can be obtained by partial resection or angiographic embolic treatment, as shown by Iglesia and Fellows,[30] recurrence is routine, although not always as severe as in the initial presentation. We have observed significant improvement in localized lesions of the pelvis or viscera with embolization therapy. Most patients with congenital AVMs require multiple forms of treatment over time with judicious selection based on maintaining adequate function. Eventually, many patients with extensive AVMs of the extremity will unfortunately require amputation.

CONNECTIVE TISSUE DISORDERS

Probably the most common of the connective tissue disorders is Marfan's syndrome. In 1896, Marfan described an hereditary autosomal dominant disorder with a characteristic body habitus consisting of a tall, slender frame, arachnodactyly with hyperextensibility of the joints, dislocation of the lens of the eye, and pectus carinatum.[40] Subsequently, it was recognized that as individuals with Marfan's syndrome got older, they also developed problems with spontaneous pneumothorax, inguinal hernias, and dissecting aneurysms of the ascending aorta involving the aortic ring and coronary vessels. Marfan's syndrome is characterized by progressive degenerative changes that tend to reduce the life span of these individuals. The characteristic vascular pathology in these patients is cystic medial necrosis with intimal rupture due to abnormal elastic tissue. It is possible to make the diagnosis of Marfan's syndrome on skin biopsy. Studies by Wilson and associates indicate that the cardiovascular complications of Marfan's syndrome are due to alterations in the structural and functional properties of fibrillin, a major constituent of vascular connective tissues.[90] Fibrillin-containing microfibrils are associated with endothelial cells, and the latter studies demonstrated impaired flow-mediated endothelium-dependent vasodilatation in these patients.

Other disorders of collagen formation may also result in the development of medial degeneration of major arteries with aneurysm formation and rupture. One of these is Ehlers-Danlos syndrome, an hereditary disorder characterized by excessive elasticity and delicacy of the skin. Although aneurysms frequently develop in the iliac and extremity arteries in the latter syndrome, the abdominal aorta is usually affected (Fig. 131-3). The vascular form of Ehlers-Danlos syndrome most likely to be associated with aneurysms is type IV, in which type III collagen is either absent or present in an abnormal amount.[57] The latter type results from mutations in the gene for type III procollagen *(COL3A1)*. In addition to aneurysm

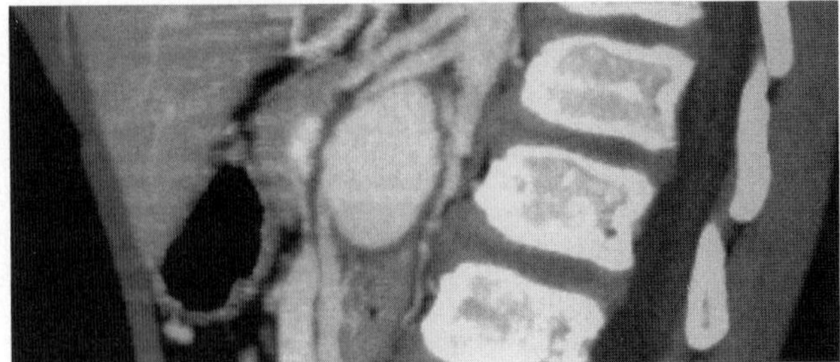

Figure 131-3 CT angiogram demonstrates an aneurysm of the superior mesenteric artery associated with abdominal pain in a child with Ehlers-Danlos syndrome. Invasive diagnostic procedures are best avoided in these patients.

formation and rupture, bowel and uterine rupture are also complications of this syndrome. It is of interest that this type of collagen type III abnormality is seen both in patients with the classical severe syndrome as well as in patients with milder phenotypes. Thus the type III collagen abnormality associated with *COL3A1* indicates a phenotypic spectrum but it does not predict the severity of the disease. Although most patients with the severe syndrome survive one or two major complications, patients with the type IV form tend to die prematurely.

Other disorders that may lead to cystic medial degeneration and aneurysm formation include tuberous sclerosis, familial cystic medial necrosis, Turner syndrome, cystinosis, and melorheostosis.[56] The last condition involves hyperostosis of one or more bones and is associated with aneurysms, particularly of the subclavian and axillary arteries.[2]

If an aneurysm is suspected, Doppler imaging studies and angiography are generally indicated, except in Ehlers-Danlos syndrome type IV, in which noninvasive studies such as MRA or CTA are preferred. Once an aneurysm has been appropriately identified and delineated, resection and replacement, usually with a prosthetic graft, may be done. This approach has usually been successful in most of these connective tissue disorders, with the exception of Ehlers-Danlos syndrome. Because the collagen matrix of the vessels in this disorder is so deficient, suture and clamp occlusion of affected vessels may result in progressive disruption of the vessel wall, making operative management difficult or impossible. The report by Cikrit and colleagues cautions about arterial repair because of the friability of the vessels.[9] When operation is unavoidable, it is sometimes better to wrap aneurysms with Teflon tape or to carefully ligate proximally and distally to peripheral aneurysms when possible. Additionally, patients with Ehlers-Danlos syndrome have a tendency for poor healing, excessive bleeding, and other complications.[22]

ACQUIRED DISORDERS

Aneurysms

Acquired aneurysms are frequently the result of trauma (see Chapter 22). The majority of traumatic aneurysms are false aneurysms that tend to have progressive enlargement.

They result from blunt trauma or iatrogenic injuries associated with arterial puncture or dialysis. False aneurysms may be treated primarily by compression or embolization, but resection and reconstruction are occasionally required. Bacterial endocarditis associated with embolism may result in degeneration of the involved vessel wall, and spontaneous rupture is common, as demonstrated by Nakayama and coworkers.[49] Emergency management is ordinarily required in addition to management of the cardiac lesion.

Kawasaki disease may produce single or multiple aneurysms anywhere in the body; the most common and the ones of most concern are coronary artery aneurysms.[61] The disease is characterized by rash, erythema, and edema of the palms and soles; pharyngitis; conjunctivitis; cervical adenopathy; and arthritis. Approximately 15% of such patients develop coronary artery aneurysms, but up to a fourth have electrocardiographic abnormalities. The manifestations of coronary artery aneurysms in children are similar to those in young adults except for the associated high incidence of hydrops of the gallbladder in affected children. Small, asymptomatic aneurysms of the coronary artery may occasionally resolve with treatment, but large ones have a high frequency of thrombosis and myocardial infarction.[1] Coronary aneurysms require coronary artery bypass because the prime problem is myocardial ischemia. Peripheral arterial aneurysms related to Kawasaki disease are usually multiple, small, fusiform, and self-limited and generally do not require treatment unless they are expanding or symptomatic. The axillary artery is the most common vessel involved.[61]

Other causes of acquired aneurysm formation are giant cell arteritis, polyarteritis nodosa, and other forms of arteritis.

TABLE 131-2 Causes of Arterial Embolism and Thrombosis

Direct Vascular Injury
Arterial and venous catheters
Inadvertent surgical injury
Injection of irritating and vasoactive drugs, narcotics
Iatrogenic diagnostic injuries
Extremity trauma
Compression
Bandages, plaster casts, and skeletal traction
Farm injuries
Fractures
Perinatal Causes
Prematurity
Sepsis
Difficult labor or delivery
Disseminated intravascular coagulation
Miscellaneous
Sepsis
Congenital heart disease
Diabetes
Vasculitis and collagen diseases
Thermal, electrical injury
Vascular anomalies
Neoplasms
Irradiation
Sickle cell disease

Thrombosis and Embolism

Table 131-2 classifies the multiple causes of arterial embolism and thrombosis. Occasional patients, primarily infants, develop spontaneous arterial thrombosis.[68] In descending order, the external iliac artery, the various visceral arteries, and the proximal upper extremity vessels are most commonly involved. Infants, who have a relatively small vascular volume, are particularly at risk when septic or with other conditions leading to low-flow states. Newborns are relatively polycythemic and have hyperviscosity as well. Some infants, particularly progeny of diabetic mothers, may demonstrate a severe hyperviscosity syndrome associated with thrombosis of various peripheral and visceral arteries, or occasionally even major aortic tributary thrombosis as reported by Colburn and colleagues.[10] Probably the earliest definitive report on this subject was by Von Khautz in 1914, which listed case reports in children up to 15 years of age.[87] Since then, many reports have described cases of spontaneous arterial thrombosis, particularly in the neonate, many associated with extremity gangrene and most associated with polycythemia or physiologic instability. In a large number of instances, however, the causes are unknown, but it is clear that in some instances the thrombotic event begins in utero.

We have found that thrombotic events generally follow a pattern. The most common presentation in infants with visceral thrombosis related to polycythemia is segmental intestinal necrosis. Thrombosis related to low-flow states and sepsis tends to produce skin necrosis of the distal portions of the extremities in a pattern of small vessel thrombosis. Clotting disorders associated with thrombosis and embolism are known to occur in sickle cell disease, leukemia, bacterial endocarditis, and other disease states.[14,82] Limited degrees of thrombosis or embolism associated with the latter disorders do not usually require operative intervention. The management of infants with hyperviscosity syndrome and polycythemia may require plasmapheresis or exchange transfusion in addition to thrombolysis, thrombectomy, or vascular repair. Intra-arterial infusion of thrombolytic agents such as tissue plasminogen activator (tPA) or urokinase should not be used if there is excessive risk related to associated coagulation defects that might predispose such infants to intracranial hemorrhage.[77] We have successfully used this technique in many instances without complications in appropriately selected patients.

Patients with bacterial endocarditis caused by *Staphylococcus aureus* and a few other organisms are particularly at risk for embolic complications. Embolism first leads to peripheral or visceral occlusion, occasionally followed by formation of a mycotic aneurysm. We have reported the treatment of eight patients with staphylococcal endocarditis of the aortic or mitral valve who developed ruptured aneurysms of the aorta or iliac vessels, all of whom required staged repair.[49] However, the majority of patients with peripheral emboli from bacterial endocarditis caused by other organisms usually require only embolectomy. In our experience, the most common site of a major peripheral embolism is the femoral artery, but occlusions of all major branch lesions have been reported. Patients with bacterial endocarditis should therefore be monitored with echocardiography; if a valve vegetation is noted to disappear, a careful search must be made for clinical evidence of peripheral embolism. Infected emboli must be extracted promptly if vascular degeneration and mycotic aneurysm formation are to be avoided. Once an infected aneurysm is recognized, it must be treated either by excision with staged repair in very small patients or, preferably, by excision and extra-anatomic bypass when feasible in older children and adolescents (Fig. 131-4).

We have also encountered patients who have sustained thrombotic or embolic complications related to umbilical artery catheters. In a few cases, these complications have been associated with staphylococcal infection that led to mycotic aneurysm formation. We previously reported on a series of 41 patients with various manifestations of thrombosis and embolism from complications associated with the use of umbilical artery catheters, most of whom were treated surgically.[53] Mendeloff and coworkers recently reported a review of 46 cases including one instance of their own of mycotic aneurysm formation in the aorta associated with umbilical artery catheterization.[44] They offered a management algorithm for patients of this sort that reflects our approach. Since our previous report, we have treated several infants with intra-arterial infusions of urokinase or tPA with an 80% success rate.

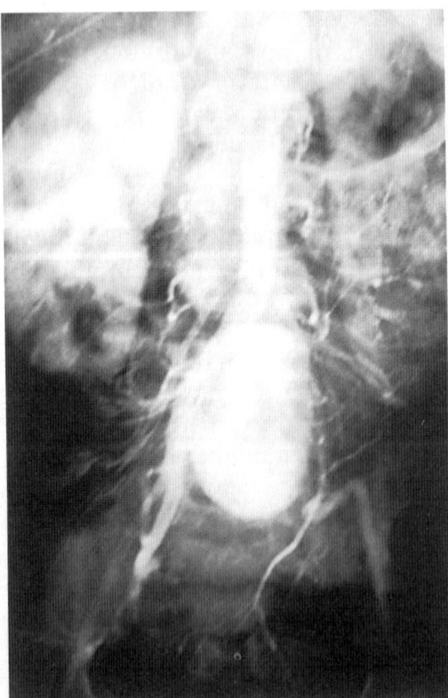

Figure 131-4 This aortogram shows an aortoiliac mycotic aneurysm in a 5-year-old boy with bacterial endocarditis on a diseased mitral valve. The aneurysm was resected because it was leaking, and later a staged prosthetic repair was successfully performed.

In instances in which the aorta or major tributary is occluded and the viability of a part is threatened, thrombectomy is indicated if thrombolysis does not immediately relieve the problem.

In addition to the above-mentioned causes of thrombosis and embolism, iatrogenic vascular insults are frequently at fault, as reported by Nehler and coworkers.[50] They point out that such injuries are increasing in frequency because of the increasing use of transluminal angioplasty and stenting, which requires a large-size arterial puncture. Furthermore, they point out that a variety of indwelling vascular devices are a source of iatrogenic vascular injury ranging from arterial rupture to thrombosis and embolism. The highest incidence would be expected to be in the pediatric age group because of the small size of the vessels and the high frequency of low-flow states as pointed out by Flanagan and colleagues.[21] The umbilical, radial, brachial, femoral, and axillary arteries are the most common sites of arterial access, and invasive procedures are often associated with arterial spasm and thrombosis. It is recognized that it is best not to infuse large volumes of fluid or to administer medications through an arterial line because of the risk for gangrene. Such drugs as sodium bicarbonate, pentobarbital, various antibiotics, or inotropic drugs may result in spasm, thrombosis, and peripheral gangrene. Although cardiac catheterization must occasionally be performed through the axillary artery, this route is associated with a significant incidence of gangrene in the upper extremity. It is safer to use the femoral artery whenever possible. If clinically significant peripheral ischemia is noted in such cases and if significant gangrene is likely to occur, infusion of thrombolytic agents, thrombectomy, or repair of an arterial injury should be considered when feasible and must be performed promptly. Anticoagulation with administration of heparin may also be useful.

Regardless of the site of vascular occlusion, whether from thrombosis, embolism, or other causes, the signs and symptoms follow predictable patterns. It is important to realize that prompt diagnosis relies primarily on clinical signs. Manifestations of an arterial occlusion include absent pulses, coolness, pallor, decreased motor function, diminished reflexes, and pain. Decreased motor function and decreased sensation tend to be late signs of ischemia. In the earlier phases of arterial compromise (less than 4 to 6 hours), the signs and symptoms may be subtle, making it difficult to differentiate between arterial occlusion and spasm. Doppler examination of peripheral vessels usually demonstrates absent pulse waves with true obstruction and attenuated waves in cases of spasm. Over time, sufficient experience has been gained on the basis of sequential Doppler and clinical examinations that indicates that spasm should not be accepted as the cause of ischemia if it lasts longer than 4 to 6 hours. Results with vascular repair or thrombolysis are best if the lesion is approached before 6 hours and certainly within 12 hours. Skin color may be preserved, in part because of collateral circulation, even when limb-threatening ischemia affects the deeper tissues, although capillary refill is usually delayed in these situations. In general, the previous approach of observation for demarcation in anticipation of amputation is no longer followed, because aggressive approaches to relieving arterial obstruction have met with success rates ranging from 75% to 90%.[21,53]

Occlusive Syndromes

Intracranial Arteries

Stroke in children is a rare but devastating occurrence. Disorders such as sickle cell disease, neurofibromatosis, cyanotic congenital heart disease, and idiopathic arteritis are the most frequent causes. In a review of 212 patients, Ganesan and colleagues performed detailed cerebral imaging and other studies to investigate risk factors for arterial ischemic stroke.[23] One hundred and fifteen of these patients were previously healthy; in this group, trauma and previous varicella-zoster infection in patients with cerebral arterial abnormalities were the most common associations. The remaining patients had known risk factors related to individual disease states. Strater and associates did a prospective assessment of risk factors for recurrent stroke during childhood in a 5-year follow-up study and identified congenital heart malformations, vasculopathies, infectious diseases, collagen tissue diseases, and metabolic disorders.[76] Previous case control studies of recurrent stroke have shown an association with hereditary prothrombotic risk factors. In these instances, the risk of recurrent stroke is as high as 10%. Chabrier and colleagues studied stroke recurrence risk by mechanism.[8] Arteriopathic stroke was the most common. Those patients with nonprogressive conditions had a generally favorable outcome with a low risk of recurrence, whereas those patients with progressive arteriopathies such as moyamoya disease had a poor outcome with a high recurrence risk. Carvalho and Garg have reviewed the treatment of arterial strokes in children and point out that treatment is supportive in most instances, but occasionally anticoagulation and thrombolysis are useful in the management of acute stroke in children.[7] In most of these disorders, the manifestations of intracranial arterial disease are mild stroke, transient ischemic attacks, and seizures. The incidence of stroke in childhood is estimated to be approximately 2.5/100,000.[7] Moyamoya disease, described in the Japanese literature, probably includes many disorders that result in the production of multiple stenoses of the intracranial arteries. The term *moyamoya* is a Japanese word that describes the angiographic pattern of the cerebral vasculature in patients with this condition; literally translated, the word means "something hazy," like a puff of cigarette smoke drifting in the air. The disorder produces major strokes but may be alleviated by superficial temporal-to-middle cerebral artery anastomosis in the rare case in which the lesions involve the proximal middle cerebral or internal carotid artery within the cranium. Caldarelli and coworkers have described the use of muscle flaps and a technique known as encephalomyosynangiosis.[6] In short-term follow-up, the authors describe improvement in cerebral circulation, but this was not associated with clinical improvement. This is probably because, in most instances, surgical treatment is applied after a major stroke has occurred.

Extracranial Arteries

In 1908, Takayasu described a patient with occlusion of the branch vessels of the ascending aorta associated with changes in the central retinal vessels.[79] Dean has reviewed the subject of arteriopathies of childhood and has pointed out that, with the exception of involvement of the origin of the arch branch vessels by Takayasu's disease, stenosing lesions of the more distal portions of the extracranial carotid and vertebral arteries are rare in children.[17] As with moyamoya disease, Takayasu's arteritis is progressive and may involve the descending aorta. Weyand and Goronzy have published an analysis of the etiology of medium- and large-vessel vasculitis.[89] They pointed out that inflammation of large arteries such as the aorta and its major branches occurs in a number of disorders, including Kawasaki's disease, Behçet's syndrome, rheumatoid arthritis, syphilis, and tuberculosis. Aortitis and large-vessel arteritis are generally of two types: giant-cell arteritis and Takayasu's arteritis. In fact, it is difficult to distinguish Takayasu's disease from fibromuscular dysplasia, also referred to as fibromuscular hyperplasia (FMH). The latter is thought to be an autoimmune disorder, whereas giant-cell arteritis and Takayasu's arteritis appear to share a different pathophysiology involving cellular immune responses involving antigen-presenting cells, T cells, and macrophages.[32] There is evidence to suggest that Takayasu's arteritis may present in Asians in a progressive fashion that involves the entire arterial tree.[31,71] On the other hand, in North America the abdominal visceral vessels are primarily involved. Whether the latter is FMH or Takayasu's disease is unclear. However, the North American form seems not to be progressive and tends to burn out, providing an opportunity for operative intervention. Aspirin and corticosteroids may attenuate the progression of giant-cell arteritis and Takayasu's disease, but there is scant evidence that they have any effect on FMH.[15]

Another disorder that may result in occlusion of extracranial vessels is Williams syndrome, which is an hereditary disorder manifested by congenital heart disease, particularly pulmonary stenosis; stenosis of a variety of arteries, among which the subclavian and renal arteries are commonly affected; and a characteristic facies.[18] Patients with Williams syndrome, like those with Takayasu's disease and FMH, ordinarily present with renovascular hypertension. They not only have a clinical phenotype but also universally have elastin hemizygosity, which manifests as stenotic arteriopathy and relatively stiff vessels.[64] The subclavian and renal arteries are particularly affected as well as the aorta.[60] We have found balloon angioplasty to be useful for the subclavian and other upper extremity stenoses, but arterial reconstruction has generally been required for renal artery lesions in our patients because of the ostial location of the stenoses.

Renovascular Hypertension

Fibromuscular Hyperplasia

As mentioned earlier, the prime cause of renovascular hypertension in children in our experience has been FMH.[51] The various causes of renovascular hypertension

TABLE 131-3 Causes of Renovascular Hypertension

Congenital
Arterial hypoplasia
Neurofibromatosis
Williams syndrome
Coarctation of the aorta
Acquired
Fibromuscular hyperplasia, renal artery stenosis
Midaortic syndrome
Takayasu's disease
Renal artery trauma, anastomotic stenosis
Renal artery occlusion after thrombosis and embolism
Nephritis, pyelonephritis, tumors, hemolytic-uremic syndrome
Obstructive uropathy

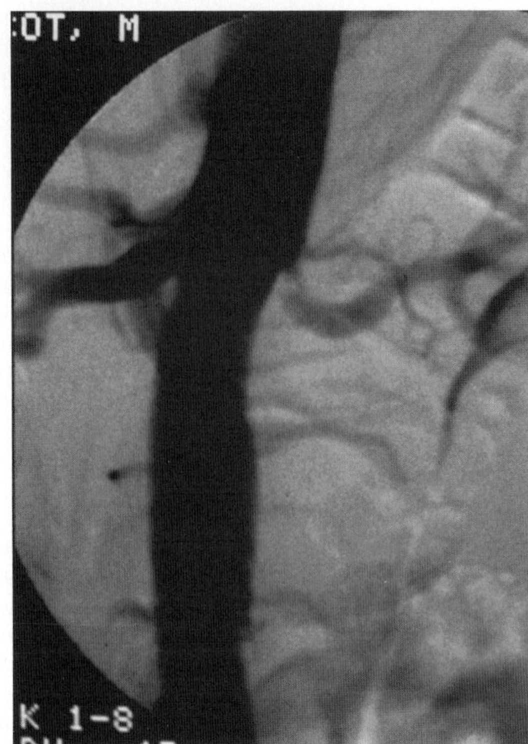

Figure 131-5 This aortogram performed on a 6-year-old boy with neurofibromatosis and hypertension shows the typical appearance of narrowing of the left renal artery at its orifice due to neural involvement of the arterial wall.

are listed in Table 131-3. The incidence of hypertension in children is estimated to be between 1% and 5%, the latter being the rate in adolescence, an incidence that approaches that of congenital heart disease. However, hypertension is diagnosed less frequently than congenital heart disease in children because blood pressure is not routinely measured in this age group. The incidence of potentially surgically correctable hypertension is approximately 80% in the birth to 5-year age group, 44% in the 6- to 10-year age group, and 20% in the 11- to 20-year age group.[51] The most common surgically correctable cause is renovascular disease. Renal artery stenosis results in renal ischemia, which in turn produces persistent elevations in systolic blood pressure, as demonstrated by Goldblatt and colleagues in 1934.[25] Subsequently, the relationship of renal ischemia to the renin-angiotensin axis was found to be the cause. Since that time, we and many others have reported large series of children who have undergone vascular reconstruction for various forms of renal artery stenosis and midaortic syndrome.[51,52]

Etiology

As indicated in Table 131-3, a specific cause of renovascular hypertension is often evident.[72] The congenital and acquired disorders include endocrine, neurologic, metabolic, renal infectious, and vascular disorders, which are the most common. Wilson and associates[90] and Dean[17] have reported congenital forms of renal artery stenosis and occlusion. Although the causes of occlusion are unknown, some of these obviously occur in utero and are associated with renal hypoplasia. The other congenital disorders resulting in renal artery stenosis include neurofibromatosis and Williams syndrome (Figs. 131-5 and 131-6).[12,18,19] The most common acquired form of renovascular hypertension is FMH. As mentioned, FMH is probably an autoimmune vasculitis encompassing more than one etiology, but the histologic appearance of involved sections of artery demonstrates varying degrees of fibrous hypertrophy of the muscularis as well as fibrous dysplasia of the intima. Renal artery stenosis is usually located at the orifice within the wall of the aorta itself, although occasionally branch vessel lesions are encountered. At times, FMH is associated with narrowing of the aorta and the major visceral arteries, a condition that has been referred to as the midaortic syndrome.[52] In cases of neurofibromatosis, we have found that the lesion responsible for occlusion of the orifice of the renal artery is a tight cuff of hypertrophied neural tissue surrounding the orifice of the renal vessel and involving both the wall of the renal artery and the adjacent aorta.

Clinical Presentation

When they are recognized, symptoms such as headache, irritability, congestive heart failure, and encephalopathy may lead to the diagnosis of hypertension. However, in a number of instances, hypertension is first noted during preanesthetic evaluation for an elective surgical procedure. In instances of bilateral renal artery stenosis, manifestations of malignant hypertension such as congestive heart failure, retinopathy, and even oliguric renal failure bring the problem to light. In our experience with more than 70 patients with renovascular hypertension of various causes, about one half of the patients are symptomatic at the time of presentation.[51] All of our patients have had elevated blood pressure, as defined by age-related norms. Blood pressures in the range of 220 to 250/120 to 100 mm Hg were common in older children, and the pressures were proportionately lower in younger patients but still elevated. Every effort has been made to

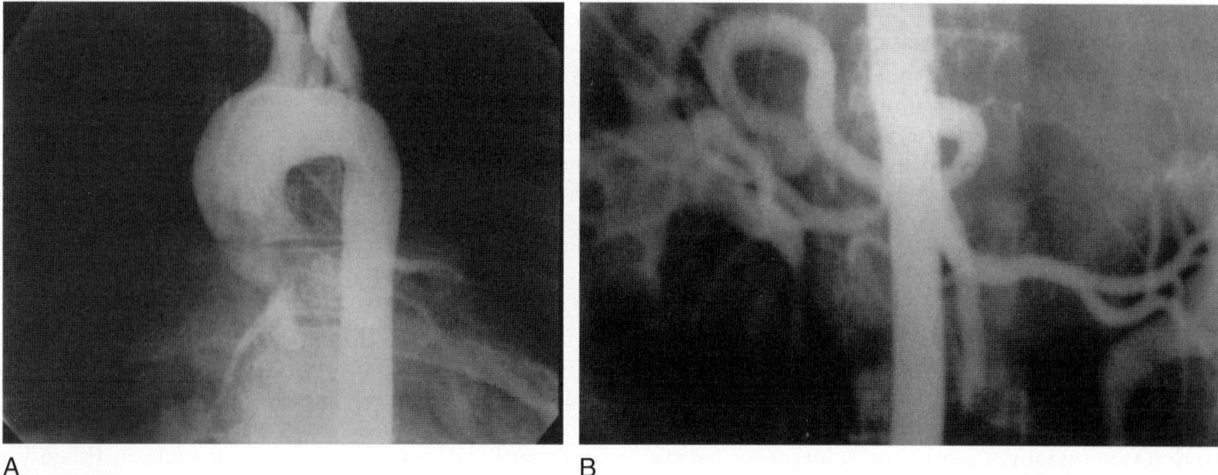

Figure 131-6 *A,* This arch aortogram in a 10-year-old girl with Williams' syndrome shows a stenotic left subclavian artery at its origin. Balloon dilatation relieved this lesion permanently but not the stenosis of the renal artery. *B,* The orificial narrowing of the right renal artery shown here required reconstruction. Because of the short length of the stenosis, it was possible to reimplant the distal vessel into the side of the aorta successfully, with relief of hypertension.

control blood pressure before performing diagnostic studies and operations, but, even after the initiation of a very intensive drug regimen, frequent elevations in blood pressure were found, especially when children were active or anxious. Abdominal bruits have been heard about half the time. Only occasional patients with midaortic narrowing have been noted to have diminished pulses in the lower extremities and blood pressure gradients ranging from 40 to 60 mm Hg between the upper and lower extremities.

Diagnostic Studies

Laboratory studies are of limited value in the evaluation and management of patients with renovascular hypertension, although several of these patients with FMH have had elevations in erythrocyte sedimentation rate and C-reactive protein. In general, sedimentation rates have fallen to normal within 6 months, so we have used this as a guide to timing repair because surgical reconstruction during an active phase of arteritis frequently fails.

Electrocardiography and chest radiography have been used to indicate the presence and severity of left ventricular failure. We have not found measurement of peripheral plasma renin levels to be of any particular value, nor have various provocative tests determined the approach to treatment. Catecholamine studies have been performed routinely to rule out pheochromocytoma but have been normal in patients with renovascular hypertension.

Imaging studies are the key to diagnosis as well as treatment. Rapid-sequence intravenous urography and radionuclide flow scanning may be useful screening studies for unilateral renal artery stenosis because they can demonstrate unilateral delay in appearance of contrast or flow on the side of the lesion. However, they are not as helpful in cases of bilateral renal artery stenosis; therefore, the overall accuracy of these studies is only about 60%. Other screening studies we have found to be helpful include MRA and particularly CTA, which is quite accurate.[86] Although CTA may eventually replace aortography, at the present time we still recommend aortography with selective renal arteriography because it is almost 100% accurate and, at times, concomitant transluminal balloon dilatation can be performed when indicated (Fig. 131-7). Limited volumes of contrast material have been used in our patients, particularly in those with impaired renal function. In patients with branch vessel lesions, local instillations of nitroglycerin are useful for showing the significance of such stenotic lesions by dilating the normal vessels and highlighting the ischemic regions supplied by the stenotic branch vessel.

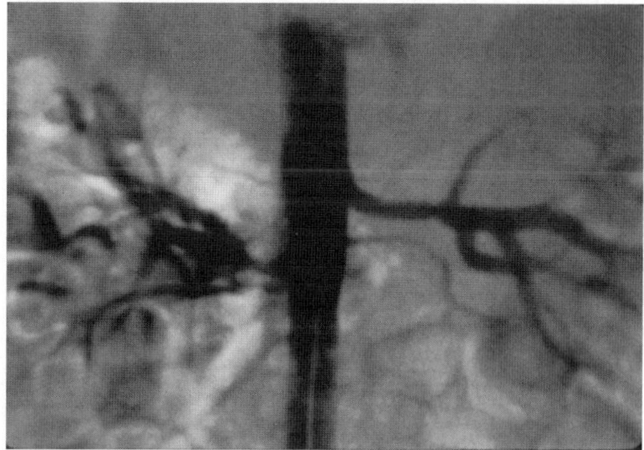

Figure 131-7 This angiogram in a 6-year-old boy shows extensive fibromuscular hyperplasia with narrowing of both renal arteries. The mild stenosis of the distal left renal artery responded to operative dilatation. The narrowing of both right renal arteries was treated with renal artery bypass with a double distal anastomosis. Hypertension has been relieved for over 8 years.

In most cases, FMH involves one or both renal arteries.[63] Usually, only the ostium is narrowed; occasionally, however, the artery is completely occluded or a long portion of the vessel is narrowed. Post-stenotic dilatation is the rule. Although FMH in young adults has a corrugated appearance on angiography, a single stenosis is usually seen in children.

Midaortic Syndrome

Midaortic syndrome is a variant of FMH that consists of more widespread vascular involvement than just the renal artery. Some authors believe that midaortic syndrome is a form of Takayasu's arteritis, but certain features distinguish the two conditions.[11,65] Another term used to describe midaortic syndrome is *subisthmic coarctation of the aorta.* We have described 17 patients with midaortic syndrome and documented their diagnosis, pathologic findings, treatment, and outcome.[52]

Most patients have been older than 5 years of age, suggesting that the lesion is acquired. The pattern of aortic narrowing has been noted to be suprarenal, infrarenal, or in a location involving the renal arteries. Lesions limited to the infrarenal aorta are very rare. Although cases of documented Takayasu's arteritis tend to be progressive, particularly in Asian populations, cases of midaortic syndrome in white populations treated successfully by reconstruction tend not to recur.

Most patients with midaortic syndrome associated with renal artery stenosis, which is usually bilateral, have severe symptoms, including malignant hypertension, congestive heart failure, and occasional oliguric renal failure and leg claudication. Despite the fact that most of our patients have had varying degrees of stenosis of the celiac and superior mesenteric arteries, none has had signs of intestinal ischemia. Signs of malignant hypertension have included severe headaches, hypertensive retinopathy, and encephalopathy.

Laboratory and other studies have confirmed renal functional impairment and congestive failure in our patients, but none had myocardial ischemia. All patients with midaortic syndrome have aortic narrowing that is variable in extent and location seen on angiography, and most instances of narrowing involve the central portion of the aorta from the aortic hiatus to a level just above the inferior mesenteric artery. Only occasionally does the disease go into the chest. Both renal arteries are usually involved; one or both renal arteries may be totally occluded with flow dependent on collateral circulation. Degrees of narrowing of the visceral mesenteric vessels characteristically stimulate the formation of extensive collateralization from the inferior mesenteric artery via the arcade of Riolan.

Treatment

Blood pressure should be controlled before diagnosis and treatment unless nephrectomy is to be undertaken or if the patient has oliguric renal failure. Even in the latter instances, blood pressure can at least be partially controlled with nitroprusside. The preferred pharmacologic method for lowering blood pressure in children is to use a combination of α- and β-adrenergic blockers plus a thiazide diuretic. The most effective drugs are minoxidil, either a short- or long-acting form of propranolol, and hydrochlorothiazide. Because the use of angiotensin-converting enzyme inhibitors is controversial because of the frequency of direct nephrotoxicity in patients with renovascular ischemia, we have avoided the use of these drugs. For short-term management of malignant hypertension, we have found nitroprusside and phenoxybenzamine to be the most effective. The same drugs have been the most useful postoperative agents for patients who have had renal revascularization. When possible, surgical repair should be deferred until manifestations of malignant hypertension can be relieved.

In the past several years, we and a number of other authors have reported the use of balloon dilatation of stenotic renal and other arteries in cases of FMH and stent insertion.[19,83] We and several others have also reported that balloon angioplasty has a lasting effect for many branch vessel lesions, but the effects appear to be transient for renal ostial lesions.[5,29,51,83] Thus, balloon angioplasty may tide a patient over impaired renal function or congestive heart failure when due to ostial renal artery stenosis, but operative repair will usually be required. Short-term success has been reported with the use of a cutting balloon catheter.[28] There has not been sufficient experience with the use of intravascular stents after balloon dilatation of renal ostial lesions in childhood, but they appear to have short- and long-term efficacy in vascular stenoses associated with congenital heart disease.[5,70] We have avoided the use of stents in small patients, although in the future there may be a role for dissolvable stents that will not interfere with growth. Surgical repair is still the preferred approach at this time.

Nephrectomy was the only surgical procedure available to manage renovascular hypertension in the past. It may be indicated in very small infants in whom vascular repair is not feasible, in the occasional patient with widespread renal artery involvement, or in patients with operative failure. Partial nephrectomy may be useful for the patient with a segmental intrarenal lesion not amenable to vascular reconstruction or dilatation or for patients with branch vessel renal artery aneurysms associated with segmental renal ischemia. In general, however, nephrectomy and partial nephrectomy should be a last-resort approach to management of renovascular hypertension.

The surgeon must necessarily be familiar with a variety of operative approaches depending on the nature of the vascular lesions encountered. The most desirable method of repair of renal artery stenosis is direct reimplantation, but this technique is impossible for patients with long-segment renal artery stenosis or midaortic syndrome. In the majority of cases of renal artery stenosis, some form of bypass graft is therefore required. In general, most surgeons prefer to use interposition grafts, end-to-side to the aorta, and end-to-end to the renal artery. Stoney and associates prefer to use autogenous hypogastric artery, but this approach is not always feasible because it may not be possible to harvest sufficient lengths of artery for interposition.[75] Additionally, FMH also sometimes involves the hypogastric artery, and harvesting both hypogastric arteries in cases of bilateral renal artery stenosis may be undesirable because of long-term concerns about impotence. We and other authors have therefore resorted to the use of autogenous saphenous vein protected with a Dacron sheath to avoid aneurysm formation in the vein graft.[4,73] This approach has been highly successful, as evidenced by long-term follow-up studies, and we have not yet encountered postoperative intimal hyperplasia. Other selectively used approaches include patch angioplasty and use of prosthetic grafts. The latter two techniques have a higher incidence of postoperative occlusion than do the standard techniques discussed earlier.

In cases of midaortic syndrome, various approaches have been described. Stanley and Fry have reported the use of patch angioplasty and bypass grafting, but they prefer extensive patch angioplasty of the aorta and renal arteries done with a prosthetic patch.[74] Messina and associates, our group, and others, have tended to use aorto-aortic bypass either from the descending thoracic aorta or the upper abdominal aorta to the level of the bifurcation with unilateral or bilateral renal artery bypass from either a normal inferior aorta or the aorto-aortic bypass graft.[45,52] Woven Dacron has been used for the aorto-aortic bypass graft in children as young as 5 years of age, although most children are older. On the other hand, we have preferred not to use prosthetic grafts for renal bypass.[55] Messina and associates[45] and Stoney and colleagues[75] prefer to perform visceral artery reconstruction even in the absence of symptoms, but we have not found this procedure to be necessary in our follow-up studies.[84] Whereas Lillehei and Shamberger have reported staged reconstruction for midaortic syndrome, most surgeons prefer immediate primary reconstruction, which is associated with good results.[38,43,45,47,74,75]

Surgical reconstruction for renal artery stenosis and the midaortic syndrome has a high degree of success and a low mortality rate. Although death after surgical repair has occasionally been reported, we and others have reported no deaths and a rate of graft failure between 5% and 10%. Unfortunately, failure has sometimes led to nephrectomy. Cure or significant improvement can be expected in more than 95% of cases, but recurrence of FMH has been reported in many studies. We encountered a patient who developed recurrent hypertension due to renal artery stenosis 14 years after treatment of the opposite renal artery for stenosis, so long-term surveillance of these patients is essential.

Small Artery Disease and Vasospastic Disorders

Athreya has nicely summarized many of the nonatherosclerotic occlusive lesions of small arteries that occur in childhood.[3] Rheumatologic diseases are prominent, including scleroderma, lupus erythematosus, dermatomyositis, juvenile rheumatoid arthritis, polyarteritis nodosa, and purpura fulminans. All these conditions have been reported to be associated with progressive occlusion of small arteries, particularly those of the fingers and toes. Patients with type I diabetes may present with a similar clinical picture when the disease is far advanced with occlusion of distal small arteries; unfortunately this usually leads to amputation. Many of the above-mentioned autoimmune diseases have vasospastic manifestations as well.

Two major syndromes, Raynaud's syndrome and reflex sympathetic dystrophy, constitute the vasospastic disorders encountered in children. Other related conditions associated with vasospasm include frostbite, cryoglobulinemia, antiphospholipid antibody syndrome, and similar vasculitic diseases. The antiphospholipid antibodies include anticardiolipin antibodies and lupus anticoagulant, the presence of which is associated with both arterial and venous thromboses.

Raynaud's Syndrome

Raynaud's syndrome involves episodic temporary spasm of the digital arteries provoked by cold and emotional stress. The typical clinical pattern is pallor, followed by cyanosis, numbness, pain, and redness of the fingers associated with a feeling of warmth and tingling. When Raynaud's syndrome has been present for a long period of time, atrophy and resorption of the tufts of the fingertips, sometimes associated with ulceration, are noted. Raynaud's syndrome varies from very mild and transient to severe. Frequently, the rheumatic and connective tissue disorders mentioned earlier are associated. Before Raynaud's syndrome is diagnosed, it is important to rule out thoracic outlet syndrome, ingestion of sympathomimetic drugs, and various viral infections.

Approaches to treatment have included treatment of any underlying rheumatic disorder, avoidance of exposure to cold, administration of nifedipine or other calcium channel blockers, infusion of prostaglandin E_1 and prostacyclin for impending gangrene, and intra-arterial reserpine or sympathectomy for severe intractable symptoms. Unfortunately, the long-term results of surgical sympathectomy are poor.

Reflex Sympathetic Dystrophy

Mitchell and coworkers first described reflex sympathetic dystrophy in 1864 as a complication of nerve injury.[48] This disorder is characterized by severe, continuous pain that is accentuated by any form of skin stimulation. Pain tends to be worse with movement. Although reflex sympathetic dystrophy frequently follows trauma, no such history is obtained on occasion. Digital atrophy is not part of this disorder, and the outlook for recovery in children is generally good. Stress and psychosomatic disorders are common associations. Treatment is primarily directed at the underlying psychological or stress problem. Physical therapy and active movement are encouraged in children, although analgesics may be needed to permit such treatment. No known drug or surgery has been found to be useful in treating this disorder.

Antiphospholipid Antibody Syndrome

Antiphospholipid or anticardiolipin antibodies occur either spontaneously or, more frequently, as part of a systemic lupus erythematosus.[37] Vascular thromboses and thrombocytopenia are associated with the presence of these antibodies.[26] The principal autoantigen has been shown to be β_2-glycoprotein I, also referred to as apolipoprotein H, a protein that binds cardiolipin and other phospholipids.[88] These autoantibodies are known to interfere with the coagulation cascade.

The only completely effective treatment is when it is possible to direct therapy at the primary manifestations of this disorder. The best treatment of the coagulation issues is warfarin.[13,39]

REFERENCES

1. Akagi T, Rose V, Benson LN, et al: Outcome of coronary artery aneurysms after Kawasaki disease. J Pediatr 1992; 121:689-694.
2. Applebaum RE, Caniano DA, Sun CC, et al: Synchronous left subclavian and axillary artery aneurysms associated with melorheostosis. Surgery 1986;99:249-253.
3. Athreya BH: Vasospastic disorders in children. Semin Pediatr Surg 1994;3:70-78.
4. Berkowitz HD, O'Neill JA. Renovascular hypertension in children. J Vasc Surg 1989;9:46-55.
5. Blum U, Krumme B, Fleugel P, et al: Treatment of ostial renal artery stenoses with vascular endoprostheses after unsuccessful balloon angioplasty. N Engl J Med 1997;336:459-465.
6. Caldarelli M, DiRocco C, Gagglini T: Surgical treatment of moyamoya disease in the pediatric age. J Neuro Surg Sci 2001;45:83-91.
7. Carvalho KS, Garg BP: Arterial strokes in children. Neurol Clin 2002;20:1079-1100.
8. Chabrier S, Husson B, Lasjaunias P, et al: Stroke in childhood: Outcome and recurrence risk by mechanism in 59 patients. J Child Neurol 2000;15:290-294.
9. Cikrit DF, Glover JR, Dalsing MC, Silver D: The Ehlers-Danlos specter revisited. Vasc Endovasc Surg 2002;36:213-217.
10. Colburn MD, Galibert HA, Quinones-Baldrich W: Neonatal aortic thrombosis. Surgery 1992;111:21-28.
11. Connolly JE, Wilson SE, Lawrence PL, Fugitani RM: Middle aortic syndrome: Distal thoracic and abdominal coarctation, a disorder with multiple etiologies. J Am Col Surg 2002; 194:774-781.
12. Criado E, Izquierdo L, Lujan S, et al: Abdominal aortic coarctation, renovascular hypertension and neurofibromatosis. Ann Vasc Surg 2002;16:363-367.
13. Crowther MA, Ginsberg JS, Julian J, et al: A comparison of two intensities of warfarin for the prevention of recurrent thrombosis in patients with the antiphospholipid antibody syndrome. N Engl J Med 2003;349:1133-1138.
14. de Chadarevine JP, Balarezo FS, Heggere M, Dampier C: Splenic artery and veins in pediatric sickle cell disease. Pediatr Dev Pathol 2001;4:538-544.
15. D'Souza SJ, Tsai Ws, Silver MM, et al: Diagnosis and management of stenotic aorto-arteriopathy in childhood. J Pediatr 1998;132:1016-1022.
16. De la Torre L, Carrasco D, More MA, et al: Vascular malformations of the colon in children. J Pediatr Surg 2002; 37:1754-1757.
17. Dean RH, Robaczewski D: Arteriopathies of childhood. Semin Pediatr Surg 1994;3:103-113.
18. Eronen M, Peippo M, Hiippala A, et al: Cardiovascular manifestations in 75 patients with Williams syndrome. J Med Genet 2002;39:554-558.
19. Estepa R, Gallego N, Orte L, et al: Renovascular hypertension in children. Scand J Urol Nephrol 2001;35:388-392.
20. Fink C, Peuster M, Hausdorf G: Endovascular stenting as an emergency treatment for neonatal coarctation. Cardiol Young 2000;10:644-646.
21. Flanagan DP, Keifer TJ, Schuler JJ, et al: Experience with iatrogenic pediatric vascular injuries: Incidence, etiology, management and results. Ann Surg 1983;198:430-442.
22. Freeman RK, Swegle J, Size MJ: The surgical complications of Ehlers-Danlos syndrome. Am Surg 1996;62:869-873.
23. Ganesan V, Prengler M, McShane MA, et al: Investigation of risk factors in children with arterial ischemic stroke. Ann Neurol 2003;53:149-150.
24. Gloviczki P, Hollier LH, Telander RL, et al: Surgical implications of Klippel-Trenaunay syndrome. Ann Surg 1983;196: 353-362.
25. Goldblatt H, Lynch J, Hanzell RF, et al: Studies on experimental hypertension: Production of persistent elevation of systolic blood pressure by means of renal ischemia. J Exp Med 1934;59:347-349.
26. Guvenc VG, Sarper N, Tuzlaci A, Gunaltay N: Transient antiphospholipid syndrome in an infant with segmental small bowel infarction. J Pediatr Surg 2004;39:124-127.
27. Guzzetta PC: Congenital and acquired aneurysmal disease. Semin Pediatr Surg 1994;3:97-102.
28. Haas NA, Ocker V, Knirsch W, et al: Successful management of a resistant renal artery stenosis in a child using a 4 mm cutting balloon catheter. Cathet Cardiovasc Interv 2002;56:227-231.
29. Hofbeck M, Singer H, Rupprecht T, et al: Successful percutaneous transluminal angioplasty for treatment of renovascular hypertension in a 15-month old child. Eur J Pediatr 1998;157:512-514.
30. Iglesia KA, Fellows KE: Contemporary interventional procedures for vascular disorders in children. Semin Pediatr Surg 1994;3:87-96.
31. Ishikawa K: Natural history and classification of occlusive thromboaortopathy (Takayasu's disease). Circulation 1978;57:27-35.
32. Johnston SL, Lock RJ, Gompels MM: Takayasu arteritis: A review. J Clin Pathol 2002;55:481-486.
33. Kim TS, Chung JW, Park JH, et al: Renal artery evaluation: Comparison of spiral CT angiography to intra-arterial DSA. J Vasc Interv Radiol 1998;9:553-559.
34. Knudson RP, Alden ER: Symptomatic arteriovenous malformation in infants less than 6 months of age. Pediatrics 1979;64:238-241.
35. Konan AV, Raymond J, Roy D: Transarterial embolization of aneurysms associated with spinal cord arteriovenous malformations: Report of four cases. J Neuro Surg 1999;90:148-154.
36. Latter D, Beland MJ, Batten A, et al: Congenital abdominal aortic aneurism. Can J Surg 1989;32:135-138.
37. Levine JS, Branch DW, Rauch J: The antiphospholipid syndrome. N Engl J Med 2002;346:752-763.
38. Lillehei CW, Shamberger RC: Staged reconstruction for middle aortic syndrome. J Pediatr Surg 2001;36:1252-1254.
39. Lockshin MD, Erkin D: Treatment of the antiphospholipid syndrome. N Engl J Med 2003;349:1177-1179.
40. Marfan BAJ: Un cas de déformation congénitale des quatre membres, bleus prononcée aux extremités, characterisée par l'allongement des os avec un certain degré d'amincissement. Bull Mem Soc Med Hop Paris 1896;13:220-221.
41. Marler JJ, Fishman SJ, Upton J, et al: Prenatal diagnosis of vascular anomalies. J Pediatr Surg 2002;37:318-326.
42. McCullough CJ, Kenwright J: The prognosis in congenital lower limb hypertrophy. Acta Orthop Scand 1979;50:307-312.
43. McTaggart SJ, Gulity S, Walker RG, et al: Evaluation and long-term outcome of pediatric renovascular hypertension. Pediatr Nephrol 2000;14:1022-1029.
44. Mendeloff J, Stallion A, Hutton M, et al: Aortic aneurysm resulting from umbilical artery catheterization: Case report, literature review, and management algorithm. J Vasc Surg 2001;33:419-424.

45. Messina LM, Riley LM, Goldstone J, et al: Middle aortic syndrome: Effectiveness and durability of complex arterial revascularization techniques. Ann Surg 1986;204:331-339.
46. Meyer JS, Fellows KE: Vascular imaging in children. Semin Pediatr Surg 1994;3:79-86.
47. Mickley V, Fleiter T: Coarctations of descending and abdominal aorta: Long-term results of surgical therapy. J Vasc Surg 1998;28;206-214.
48. Mitchell SW, Morehouse GR, Keen WW: Gunshot Wounds and Other Injuries of Nerves. Philadelphia, JB Lippincott, 1864.
49. Nakayama DK, O'Neill JA, Wagner H, et al: Management of vascular complications of bacterial endocarditis. J Pediatr Surg 1986;21:636-639.
50. Nehler MR, Taylor LM, Porter JM: Iatrogenic vascular trauma. Semin Vasc 1998;11:283-293.
51. O'Neill JA: Long-term outcome with surgical treatment of renovascular hypertension. J Pediatr Surg 1998;33:106-111.
52. O'Neill JA, Berkowitz H, Fellows KJ, Harmon CM: Midaortic syndrome and hypertension in childhood. J Pediatr Surg 1995;30:164-172.
53. O'Neill JA, Neblett WW, Born ML: Management of major thromboembolic complications of umbilical artery catheters. J Pediatr Surg 1981;16:972-978.
54. Parkes-Weber F: Angiomalformation in connection with hypertrophy of limbs or hemihypertrophy. Br J Dermatol 1907;19:231-233.
55. Paty PS, Darling RC, Lee D, et al: Is prosthetic renal artery reconstruction a durable procedure? An analysis of 489 bypass grafts. J Vasc Surg 2001;34:127-132.
56. Patzer L, Basche S, Misselwitz J: Renal artery stenosis and aneurysmatic dilatation of arteria sclerotis interna in tuberous sclerosis complex. Pediatr Nephrol 2002;17:193-196.
57. Pepin M, Schwarze U, Superti-Furga A, Byers PH: Clinical and genetic features of Ehlers-Danlos syndrome type IV, the vascular type. N Engl J Med 2000;342:673-680.
58. Rainio P, Biancar F, Leinonen S, Juvonen T: Aneurysm of the profunda femoris artery manifested as acute groin pain in a child. J Pediatr Surg 2003;38:1699-1700.
59. Redekop G, TerBurgge K, Montanera W, Willinisky R: Arterial aneurysms associated with cerebral arterial venous malformations: Classification, incidence, and risk of hemorrhage. J Neuro Surg 1998;89:539-546.
60. Rose C, Wessel A, Panku R, et al: Anomalies of the abdominal aorta in Williams-Beuren syndrome—another cause of arterial hypertension. Eur J Pediatr 2001;160:655-658.
61. Rowley AH, Gonzalez-Crussi F, Shulman ST: Kawasaki syndrome. Curr Probl Pediatr 1991;21:387-405.
62. Saad SA, May A: Abdominal aortic aneurysm in a neonate. J Pediatr Surg 1991;36:1423-1424.
63. Safian RD, Textor SC: Renal artery stenosis. N Engl J Med 2001;344:431-442.
64. Salaymeh KJ, Banerjee A: Evaluation of arterial stiffness in children with Williams syndrome: Does it play a role in evolving hypertension? Am Heart J 2001;142:549-555.
65. Sandman W, Sculte KM: Multivisceral fibromuscular dysplasia in childhood: Case report and review of the literature. Ann Vasc Surg 2000;14:496-502.
66. Sarkar R, Coran AG, Cilley RE, et al: Arterial aneurysms in children: Clinicopathologic classification. J Vasc Surg 1991;13:47-57.
67. Schiller M, Gordon R, Shifrin E, Abu-Dalu K: Mulitple arterial aneurysms. J Pediatr Surg 1983;18:27-29.
68. Schmidt B, Andrew M: Neonatal thrombosis: Report of a prospective Canadian and international registry. Pediatrics 1995;96:939-943.
69. Senzaki H, Akagi M, Hishi T, et al: Age-associated changes in arterial elastic properties in children. Eur J Pediatr 2002;161:547-551.
70. Shaffer KM, Mullens CE, Grifka RG, et al: Intravascular stents in congenital heart disease: Short- and long-term results from a large single-center experience. J Am Coll Cardiol 1998;31:661-667.
71. Sharma S, Rajani M, Talwar KK: Angiographic morphology in nonspecific aortoarteritis (Takayasu's arteritis): A study of 126 patients from North India. Cardio Vasc Intervent Radiol 1992;15:160-165.
72. Shinohara M, Shitara T, Hatakeyama S-I, et al: An infant with systemic hypertension, renal artery stenosis, and neuroblastoma. J Pediatr Surg 2004;39:103-106.
73. Stanley JC, Ernst CB, Fry WJ: Fate of 100 aortorenal vein grafts: Characteristics of late graft expansion, aneurysmal dilatation and stenosis. Surgery 1973;74:931-944.
74. Stanley JC, Fry WJ: Pediatric renal artery occlusive disease and renovascular hypertension. Surgery 1981;116: 669-675.
75. Stoney RJ, DeLuccia N, Ehrenfeld WK, Wylie EF: Aortorenal autografts: long-term assessment. Arch Surg 1981;116: 1416-1422.
76. Strater R, Becker S, von Eckardstein A, et al: Prospective assessment of risk factors for recurrent stroke during childhood—a 5-year follow-up study. Lancet 2002;360: 1540-1545.
77. Strife JL, Ball WS, Tobin RB, et al: Arterial occlusions in neonates: Use of fibrinolytic therapy. Radiology 1989;166:395-400.
78. Szilagyi DE, Smith RF, Elliott JP, Hageman JH: Congenital arteriovenous anomalies of the limbs. Arch Surg 1976; 111:422-429.
79. Takayasu M: A case with unusual changes of the central vessels in the retina. Nippon Ganka Gakkai Zasshi 1908; 12:554-556.
80. Tanaka R, Miyasaka Y, Fujii K, et al: Vascular structure of arterial venous malformations. J Clin Neurosci, 2000;7: 24-28.
81. Tice DA, Clauss RH, Keirle AM, Reed GE: Congenital arterial venous fistulae of the extremities: Observations concerning treatment. Arch Surg 1963;86:460-465.
82. Tsomi K, Karagiorga-Lagana M, Karabatsos F, et al: Arterial elastorrhexis in beta-thalassaemia intermedia, sickle cell thalassemia and hereditary spherocytosis. Eur J Haematol 2001;67:135-141.
83. Tyagi S, Kaul UA, Satsangi DK, Arora R: Percutaneous transluminal angioplasty for renovascular hypertension in children: Initial and long-term results. Pediatrics 1997;99:44-49.
84. Upchurch GR, Hanke PK, Eagleton MJ, et al: Pediatric splanchnic arterial occlusive disease: Clinical relevance and operative treatment. J Vasc Surg 2002;35:860-867.
85. Upton J, Coombs CJ, Mulliken JB, et al: Vascular malformations of the upper limb: A review of 270 patients. J Hand Surg 1999;24:1019-1035.
86. Vade A, Agarwal R, Lim-Dunham J, Hartoin D: Utility of computed tomographic renal angiogram in the management of childhood hypertension. Pediatr Nephrol 2002; 17:741-747.
87. Von Khautz A: Spontane extremitatengangran im kindersalter. Z Kinderhelkd 1914;11:35-38.
88. Von Scheven E, Athreya BH, Rose CD, et al: Clinical characteristics of antiphospholipid syndrome in children. J Pediatr 1996;129:339-345.
89. Weyand CM, Goronzy JJ: Medium- and large-vessel vasculitis. N Engl J Med 2003;349:160-169.
90. Wilson DI, Appleton RE, Coulthard MG, et al: Fetal and infantile hypertension caused by unilateral renal arterial disease. Arch Dis Child 1990;65:881-884.

Chapter 132

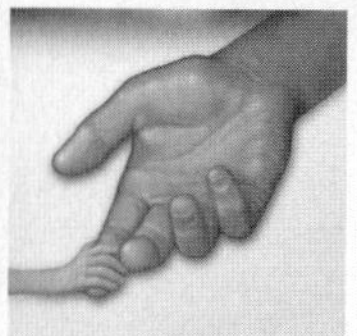

Venous Disorders in Childhood

Michael C. Dalsing and Keshav Pandurangi

Venous diseases occurring in children have an inflammatory, immunologic, infectious, or congenital origin. Such maladies are not as rare as commonly believed. In one series, they constituted more than one third of the reported 516 acute vascular problems seen in children.[125] Venous disorders can be classified into congenital abnormalities of central veins, congenital abnormalities of peripheral veins, and venous thrombosis.

This chapter is organized to reflect these three classifications with major divisions under each of particular interest to the surgeon caring for children with venous disease.

CONGENITAL ABNORMALITIES OF CENTRAL VEINS

Anomalies of Superior Vena Cava and Inferior Vena Cava

Three paired embryonic subsystems contribute to the completed systemic venous circuit: the anterior cardinal (precardinal) veins become the superior vena cava (SVC) and its tributaries, the posterior cardinal (subcardinal and supracardinal) veins form the inferior vena cava (IVC) and its tributaries, and the vitelline veins become the portal vein and its tributaries (Fig. 132-1).

Anomalies of the large venous trunks occur most often in the SVC and IVC and less frequently in the portal venous system. Duplication of the SVC with drainage into the coronary sinus is usually asymptomatic and is of no clinical significance unless open-heart surgery and cardiopulmonary bypass is being contemplated.[31,73,129] Left-sided SVC is also usually clinically silent and becomes important when the requirement of cardiopulmonary bypass arises. On the other hand, anomalous systemic venous return to the heart produces varying degrees of oxygen desaturation and complicates management of children with other intracardiac anomalies.[56] Prognosis is often dependent on the severity of associated cardiac anomalies rather than on the venous anomaly itself.

Abnormalities of the inferior vena cava are seen in up to 4% of the population.[133] Duplication or left-sided IVC, with an incidence of 0.2% to 3%, are incidental findings during abdominal imaging, cavography, or surgery of the aorta, kidney, or adrenal glands.[22,26,39] Agenesis of the IVC, a rare occurrence, may be an isolated anomaly[17] or may be associated with complex cardiac anomalies, such as in the polysplenia-asplenia syndromes. Congenital obstruction of IVC may occur secondary to a persistent eustachian valve in the right atrium[103,127] or from a suprahepatic web. Although patients may remain asymptomatic for a variable period of time, symptoms of portal hypertension eventually develop requiring surgical treatment.[87,103] Computed tomography (CT) or sonography of the abdomen is used to establish the diagnosis.[39] Once the diagnosis is made, an inferior vena cavogram can be performed to delineate the precise venous anatomy. Cavocaval bypass and transcardiac membranotomy have been performed with success.[32,58] Endovascular angioplasty and vascular stenting are promising alternatives being explored. Mid-term results reveal that vascular stenting for symptomatic central venous obstruction provides a temporary benefit but requires regular follow-up and re-interventions to maintain 79% patency at 2 years.[86]

Developmental anomalies of the renal vein are associated with IVC anomalies and can result in a retroaortic or circumaortic left renal vein. A retroaortic vein occurs with persistence of posterior left renal vein and regression of anterior left renal vein. In cases of persistence of anterior and posterior left renal veins, a circumaortic left renal vein is formed.[38] Retroaortic left renal vein has an incidence of 1.2% to 2.4%, and a circumaortic left renal vein has a reported incidence of 1.5% to 8.7%.[39] These anomalies generally are incidental findings during abdominal imaging studies for other reasons and become clinically significant only during retroperitoneal procedures or reconstruction of the abdominal aorta performed later in life.

Portal Vein Anomalies

Portal vein anomalies include branch pattern variations, absence, malposition (preduodenal position), and duplication. Variants in the normal branching pattern of the intrahepatic portal vein, reported since 1957, occur in approximately 20% of the population and are usually clinically insignificant.[36]

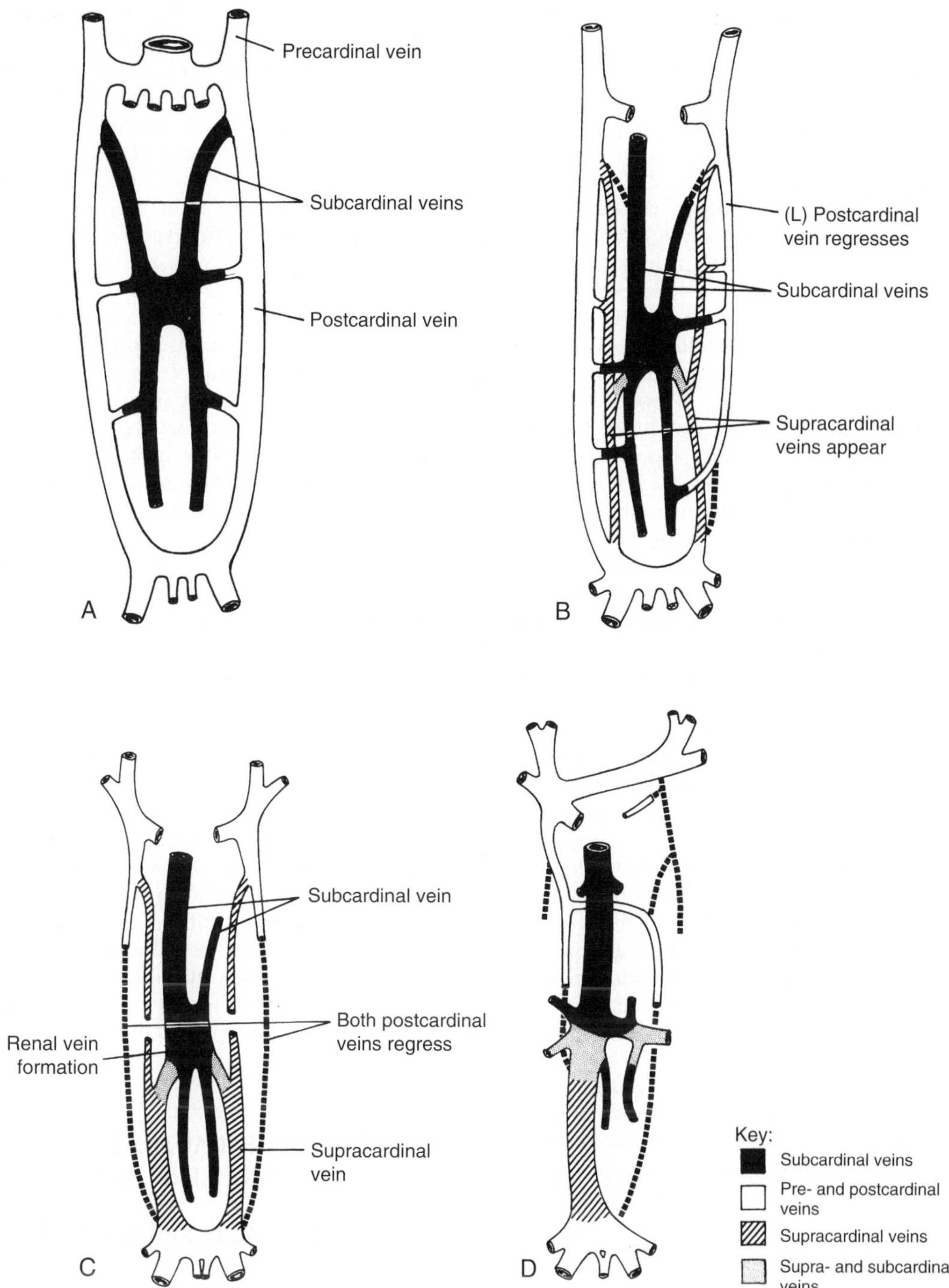

Figure 132-1 Development of the inferior vena cava. *A,* At 6 weeks of gestation, postcardinal veins are dominant. *B,* At 7 weeks of gestation, subcardinal veins are dominant and postcardinal veins begin to regress. *C,* At 8 weeks of gestation, subcardinal veins form the suprarenal inferior vena cava. Supracardinal veins form the infrarenal inferior vena cava. Postcardinal veins regress. *D,* The adult inferior vena cava. (From Giordano JM, Trout HH 3rd: Anomalies of the inferior vena cava, J Vasc Surg 1986;3:924-8, 1986, with permission.)

Congenital absence of the portal vein (CAPV) is a rare congenital malformation that occurs as a result of abnormal development during weeks 4 to 10 of gestation. Because the portal and hepatic veins originate from the vitelline and umbilical veins, CAPV is associated with the anastomosis between the splanchnic and systemic circulation. The first report of an absent portal vein and congenital mesenteric caval shunt was given by John Abernethy in 1793. Since then, only a handful of cases have been described in the literature. Anomalous mesocaval or mesorenal connections have also been described.[12,71] The majority of these anomalies are seen in girls.[93] CAPV has often been associated with other congenital abnormalities, such as cardiac defects, biliary atresia, and polysplenia. Cardiac malformations are frequently observed in patients with CAPV because the associated anomalies result from a similar embryogenic insult and compensate for the congestive effect of portal vein absence and shunting.[118] Congenital portosystemic shunting has been recognized as an important disorder in children and must be differentiated from metabolic deficiencies involving hyperammonemia or galactosemia. Newborn screening for a high level of blood galactose has been found to be useful in detecting congenital portosystemic shunts.[81]

Duplex ultrasonography is usually used as a first method in diagnosing a portal abnormality. Although this method cannot visualize the portal vein or its main branch, it does show the portocaval shunt as an abnormal pattern. CT or magnetic resonance imaging (MRI) can confirm the absence of the portal vein, and they both can visualize the portosystemic shunt. MRI can depict the vessels in multiple planes, making identification of portosystemic shunting much easier than by conventional CT.[81] Arterial portography, direct portography, and splenoportography may also be used, but these are invasive techniques that are being supplanted by MR venography (MRV).[36] Although Shinkai and colleagues reported that none of their patients ranging from newborn to adult experienced symptoms characteristic of portosystemic encephalopathy,[112] a small portion of children and more frequently adults exhibit symptoms of portosystemic encephalopathy and hepatic failure. CAPV is commonly an incidental discovery during surgery or radiologic studies for associated liver diseases such as biliary atresia or liver tumors. Liver transplantation is indicated for patients with symptomatic CAPV unresponsive to medical therapy.[112]

Preduodenal portal vein is a rare anomaly reported in 82 patients in the literature since the first description by Knight in 1921; approximately half of the patients presented clinically with high intestinal obstruction, but only in a few was the obstruction clearly caused by the anomalous portal vein.[77] In the majority of the cases, the obstruction was caused by associated anomalies such as duodenal diaphragm, intestinal malrotation, and annular pancreas. The remaining half were asymptomatic; the preduodenal portal vein was an incidental finding during surgery for other causes and did not require treatment. The preduodenal portal vein is also frequently associated with cardiac and gastrointestinal anomalies. The preferred treatment of duodenal obstruction caused by preduodenal portal vein is to bypass the obstruction by duodenoduodenostomy or gastroduodenostomy so that the portal vein will lie between the second portion of the duodenum and the anastomosis.[77] Duplicated portal vein or the preduodenal position in asymptomatic patients is hazardous during biliary, duodenal, or liver surgery performed for other reasons and must be recognized if present.

Venous Aneurysms

A venous aneurysm is best described as a solitary area of venous dilation that communicates with a main venous structure by a single channel, exclusive of an arteriovenous communication, pseudoaneurysm, or segment of varicose vein.[37] These are rare lesions in the adult and pediatric population. Aneurysms of the SVC, IVC, and visceral vessels have been described. Among the central veins, aneurysms of SVC are most common. Most SVC aneurysms are incidental findings on routine chest radiographs. Spontaneous rupture of SVC aneurysms is rare. Because of the high morbidity and mortality associated with surgical repair, nonoperative treatment is the norm for asymptomatic nonenlarging aneurysms in this location.[16]

Abdominal venous aneurysms, on the other hand, are generally symptomatic. These include aneurysms of the inferior vena cava, the superior mesenteric vein, the splenic vein, the portal vein, and the iliac veins. Presenting symptoms include abdominal pain, intestinal bleeding secondary to fistula formation, or thromboembolism. Diagnosis is confirmed by venography or the venous phase of arteriography, the latter being performed to investigate other potential causes of the child's symptoms. CT and MRI can also be used, especially for intracavitary lesions. In a literature review of venous aneurysms, Calligaro and colleagues reported that 41% of patients with abdominal venous aneurysms developed life-threatening complications if the aneurysms were managed nonoperatively, and recommended prophylactic surgical intervention consisting of complete or partial excision in low-risk patients.[16]

Portal vein aneurysms usually occur at the junction of the superior mesenteric vein and splenic veins or at the hepatic hilus at the bifurcation of the right and left portal veins. Portal vein aneurysm is a rare disorder and has been observed in approximately 0.07% of patients. Noninvasive diagnostic modalities such as duplex ultrasonography, CT, and MR can enable the diagnosis of portal vein aneurysm. However, duplex ultrasonography is the single most useful diagnostic tool, and further workup may not be necessary unless surgical procedures are planned. In the majority of patients, portal vein aneurysms are discovered incidentally.[131] Large portal vein aneurysms may cause duodenal compression, bile duct obstruction, chronic portal hypertension, rupture, and complete occlusion of the portal vein by recurrent thrombosis.[13] In the event of these complications, operative treatment is required. Portacaval shunts in the past and, more recently, prophylactic excision of the aneurysmal segment or aneurysmorrhaphy are the therapeutic options, especially when aneurysms are growing or when complications develop.[36] However, small aneurysms are usually asymptomatic and tend to remain unchanged over time, making ultrasonographic surveillance an acceptable approach to the management of these patients.

CONGENITAL ABNORMALITIES OF PERIPHERAL VEINS

Isolated Venous Malformations

Vascular malformations are present in about 1.5% of the population and result from maldevelopment of arterial, capillary, venous, or lymphatic structures.[98,132] In 1988, the "Hamburg classification" was devised that focuses on the important anatomicopathologic features and the resulting therapeutic options.[8] Depending on the vascular system predominantly involved, congenital vascular malformations are divided into the following five groups: arterial, venous (i.e., predominantly venous malformations, either localized or diffuse), arteriovenous (i.e., low or high flow), lymphatic (i.e., previously cystic hygroma and lymphangioma), and mixed or combined. Furthermore, these malformations may occur in the main trunk and in the visceral or peripheral vessels.[9]

Among the malformations, pure arterial lesions account for less than 1% of all malformations. The most common lesions, approximately half, are venous in origin. Mixed lesions with arterial and venous defects are identified in 15% to 30% of malformations.[98] In this chapter, the focus is on malformations of venous origin.

Although most of these malformations are limited to the venous system and occur sporadically in otherwise healthy individuals, associated anomalies in regional anatomic structures such as seen in the Klippel-Trenaunay syndrome have been described. The abnormalities range from asymptomatic birthmarks to life-threatening conditions. Not all vascular malformations are obvious at birth; many manifest themselves years to decades later in life. The clinical presentation depends largely on the dominant feature: arterial, capillary, venous, or lymphatic. Symptoms include palpable mass, edema, varicosities, ulceration from chronic venous insufficiency, mechanical bruit, limb-length discrepancies, or otherwise unexplained pain. Contrast medium–enhanced CT, angiography, venography, duplex ultrasonography, and MRI are techniques currently used in evaluation of malformations. Arteriography is an invasive diagnostic method but can be therapeutic in select cases in which superselective catheterization and coil embolization is utilized. Duplex ultrasonography is portable, is noninvasive, and provides functional and anatomic information regarding the lesion. But, MRI is the diagnostic imaging modality of choice in patients with vascular malformations because it identifies extension of the lesion into surrounding soft tissue and bone.[91] It also serves well as the primary diagnostic test for suspected malformations, particularly in infants and children in whom competitive tests pose additional risks. Management of venous malformations depends on the type of lesion, location, extent, and patient symptoms. Localized lesions can be observed, especially if asymptomatic. Cutaneous hemangiomas are representative of localized malformations and are discussed elsewhere.

Avalvulia

Avalvulia, or absence of venous valves, is seen in 4% to 7% of deep venous anomalies associated with congenital vascular malformations in one series.[33] This abnormality is not apparent at birth. It is an autosomal-dominant anomaly that leads to significant venous reflux, eventually resulting in chronic venous insufficiency from sustained venous hypertension as the child assumes an erect posture and begins to walk. These gravitational effects and hydrostatic loads likely lead to manifestation of symptoms later in life.[23] Severe swelling and pain of unknown origin may be the first manifestations. Symptoms of venous insufficiency in the absence of preceding deep venous thrombosis[35] or presence of varicose veins before puberty should lead to a suspicion of valvular anomalies.[133] A smooth and uniform phlebogram is diagnostic of avalvulia, in direct contradistinction to the deep veins in a normal phlebogram, which have an irregular contour because of the valve sinus dilatations.[14,124] Duplex ultrasonography is the initial screening technique of choice. Ascending and descending phlebography confirms the absence of valves and provides anatomic detail essential for surgical intervention.[99] The treatment of the sequelae of avalvulia is usually nonoperative, consisting of limb elevation and graduated compression stockings. Early experience with axillary vein valve transplantation into the deep veins of the lower extremity reported symptomatic improvement in 75% of patients and healing of the venous stasis ulcers in 94% of the patients.[116] Raju and colleagues have reported a 60% 5-year symptomatic improvement and a 60% 5-year freedom from venous ulcer recurrence.[99] Such therapy may be an option in patients with avalvulia if the symptoms become resistant to more conservative treatment.

Aplasia of Deep Veins

True aplasia of the deep veins is rare. However, longitudinal septations or "venous spurs," or simple narrowing of the origin of the left common iliac vein is seen in 20% of the population (Fig. 132-2).[133] Pseudonyms of this variant include May-Thurner syndrome, Cockett's syndrome,[24] and iliac compression syndrome. Compression of the left common iliac vein occurs between the right common iliac artery and fifth lumbar vertebra. The iliac compression syndrome is rare, and its true incidence is not known. Autopsy studies of the general population have shown a 22% incidence of iliac vein compression.[80] The majority of patients who present with symptoms are female and in their second to fourth decades of life. Symptoms range from mild unilateral lower extremity swelling and aching to deep venous thrombosis, leading to pulmonary embolism or chronic venous insufficiency. Diagnosis is suspected by duplex ultrasonography but confirmed by MRV. Treatment of symptoms starts with compression stockings and anticoagulation for DVT, but the majority of patients will need surgical intervention.[1] In adults, endovascular stenting offers a less invasive alternative, and reports of 79% to 89% 1-year patency have been published.[54,85] For younger patients in whom long-term success is optimal, operative intervention may be offered. Surgical procedures include saphenous vein femoral-femoral vein bypass graft or right iliac artery transposition followed by left common iliac vein patch angioplasty; reports suggest a 67% to 97% 3-year clinical patency.[117]

Aplasia, when present, is usually associated with anomalies of the lymphatic system. A discussion of lymphatic disorders is beyond the scope of this chapter. Aplasia or hypoplasia of the deep venous trunks that resulted in outflow obstruction, with the development of large superficial venous collaterals, has been reported in 8% of the patients with venous anomalies.[33] Sometimes the embryonal veins remain patent and provide outflow to the affected limb. These patients are prone to swelling, aching, venous claudication, thrombosis of collateral veins, and ulcerations. Venography can be used in diagnosis, but MRI is superior in defining the anatomy and extent of abnormality.[124] Once the anatomy is defined, treatment should be directed toward ligation of perforating branches of the embryonal vein that communicate with the superficial system (in cases of deep vein aplasia) or extirpation of the malformed venous interconnections (where principal drainage via deep veins is confirmed).[69] Note that surgical interruption of major collaterals may cause serious complications but still may need to be considered in decompensated patients.[44]

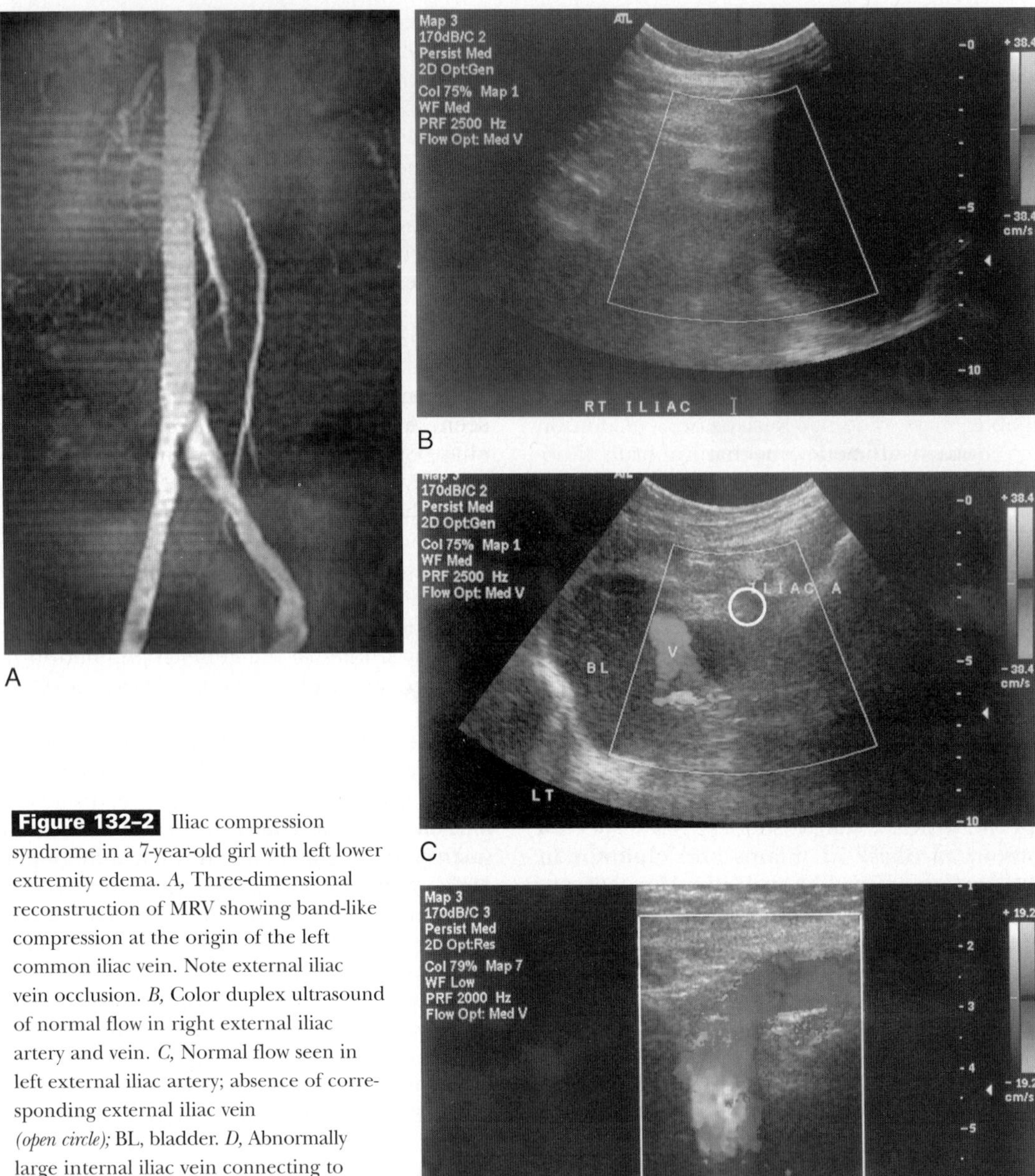

Figure 132–2 Iliac compression syndrome in a 7-year-old girl with left lower extremity edema. *A,* Three-dimensional reconstruction of MRV showing band-like compression at the origin of the left common iliac vein. Note external iliac vein occlusion. *B,* Color duplex ultrasound of normal flow in right external iliac artery and vein. *C,* Normal flow seen in left external iliac artery; absence of corresponding external iliac vein *(open circle);* BL, bladder. *D,* Abnormally large internal iliac vein connecting to large common iliac vein on the left side.

Complex Venous Malformations

Several congenital vascular malformations present clinically as a combination of arterial, venous, and lymphatic developmental abnormalities. Even though the incidence of complex malformations is rare, the severity of clinical manifestations (i.e., tissue hyperplasia and skeletal overgrowth) and magnitude of the problem are impressive and often require a multidisciplinary approach. The most common vascular malformations seen are the Klippel-Trenaunay (KTS), Parkes Weber, and Maffucci syndromes. Management of each depends on the patient's age, histologic nature of the lesion, and severity of symptoms.

The Klippel-Trenaunay syndrome is a combined capillary, venous, and lymphatic anomaly without evidence of arteriovenous shunting. Clinical symptoms are related to the extent and location of the components in this syndrome, varying from mild varicosities to massively enlarged limbs or truncal involvement.[55,106,133] In 95% of the patients the lower limb is involved, and 85% of the cases are unilateral (Fig. 132-3). Although the syndrome is present in all cases at birth, the affected children are asymptomatic. Nevertheless, 75% of all patients with Klippel-Trenaunay syndrome who become symptomatic present before the age of 10.[134] Iliofemoral vein malformations are found in approximately 20% of patients with Klippel-Trenaunay syndrome.[42] Persistent sciatic vein, although a rare anomaly, is most often associated. Mildly symptomatic patients should be managed with compressive garments. Raised verrucous capillary malformations are typically part of

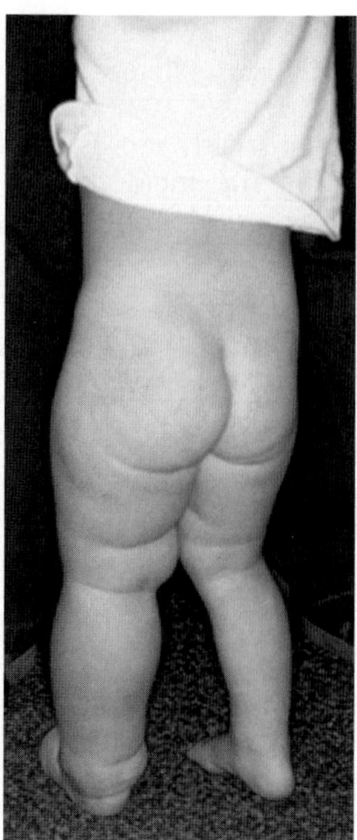

Figure 132-3 Klippel-Trenaunay syndrome. Note unilateral limb hypertrophy, edema, and limb-length discrepancy. *(See color plate.)*

this syndrome and often present as repeated bleeding. Sclerotherapy is particularly effective for these types of local, cutaneous lesions.[78,126] The most common abnormality is a lateral venous anomaly that presents as a varicose vein.[134] Symptoms (pain and edema being most common) should warrant extensive documentation of venous anatomy with phlebography and MRI. Phlebography alone has a 70% sensitivity in diagnosis of persistent sciatic vein.[21] MRI studies enhance the diagnosis of atresia of the deep veins and display the distribution of the malformations in the soft tissues exceptionally well.[124] The primary goal of diagnostic studies should be to confirm patency of the deep venous system before surgical excision of the superficial veins. Nonoperative treatment includes compression therapy and leg elevation and should be recommended to all patients. The Mayo Clinic experience notes significant clinical improvement with surgery of superficial veins in symptomatic patients despite a 50% recurrence of varicosities.[82] Although the majority of patients with Klippel-Trenaunay syndrome are managed nonoperatively, up to 10% will require surgery.[49,82] Some authors have advocated aggressive excision of varicosities in patients with patent deep veins with encouraging results on short-term follow-up.[6]

The Parkes Weber syndrome is clinically similar to Klippel-Trenaunay syndrome. The clinical distinction is determined by the presence of arteriovenous fistulas in Parkes Weber syndrome that are clinically undetectable in Klippel-Trenaunay syndrome. There are more hemodynamic complications owing to the characteristic high-flow macroarteriovenous fistulas, and thus they have become the natural focus of management in the Parkes Weber syndrome.[124] Rarely, these fistulas occur in central locations arising from major branches of the aorta or iliac arteries and present as high-output congestive heart failure.[68,124] The majority of lesions typically are surgically inaccessible or cause significant morbidity with operative intervention. Thus, embolosclerotherapy, a combination of embolization and sclerotherapy, has become the primary treatment for large symptomatic malformations and may be used as an adjunct to surgery in select cases. Recent reports of ethanol and *N*-butyl-cyanoacrylate as sclerosing agents have shown excellent results and have significantly reduced the morbidity associated with surgical excision.[66,67]

The Maffucci syndrome is the coexistence of a vascular malformation and dyschondroplasia. The most common associated lesions are complex venous anomalies that are large and subcutaneous. Deep venous anomalies are also seen. Approximately 20% of patients suffer malignant change, commonly chondrosarcoma. The risk of neoplasia in dyschondroplasia approaches 50% of the cases, and hence these patients require close follow-up. Diagnosis is established by serial radiographs and by biopsy of suspicious lesions. Surgical excision is required, and radiation therapy is of no therapeutic value.[134]

Aneurysms and Varicose Veins

Venous aneurysms of the neck and superficial veins of the extremities are generally asymptomatic but often are a concern and cause distress to the parents or the child. The differential diagnosis of internal jugular vein (IJV) aneurysm includes cavernous hemangiomas, branchial and enterogenous cysts, and lymphoceles. Most IJV aneurysms present as an asymptomatic mass with a benign natural history.[16] A Valsalva maneuver greatly enlarges IJV aneurysms and aids in diagnosis.[52] Color duplex ultrasonography is usually sufficient to diagnose the problem. The only indication to operate on an IJV aneurysm is cosmetic.[64]

Extremity venous aneurysms are categorized into deep and superficial lesions. The symptoms and suggested treatments vary with anatomic location. Aneurysms of the deep system occur most commonly in the popliteal vein and usually present as extremity pain, associated mass, or occasional swelling and are at significant risk of thromboembolic complications.[98] Simple anticoagulation therapy alone has been tried by some investigators, with poor outcome.[37] Surgical procedures described include ligation, tangential excision with lateral venorrhaphy or autologous vein patch, and complete resection and interposition grafting with patency rates of up to 76%.[16] The best long-term patency rates are obtained with tangential excision and lateral venorrhaphy techniques. Aneurysms of the superficial system usually present as a moderate degree of lower-limb swelling with or without pain. These dilations rarely rupture, and a disfiguring varicosity is generally the only indication for excision.

Congenital varicosities of peripheral veins most likely result from vein wall defects rather than valve cusp deficiency.[47,70,97,101,121] Primary varicosities have been reported in the upper extremity also, lending support to the genetic etiology of this disorder.[128] Treatment ranges from compression stockings to excision of dilated varicosities and elimination of reflux points.

Abnormalities in course and union of peripheral veins are common and of no clinical significance, although duplications of the great and small saphenous veins may present in adulthood as recurrent superficial varicosities after apparently successful vein stripping.

VENOUS THROMBOSIS

Hereditary Coagulation Disorders

Genetic anomalies of the coagulation system predispose infants and children to thrombotic and thromboembolic disease. Coagulation abnormalities identified in venous and arterial thrombotic complications include activated protein C (APC) resistance (factor V Leiden), and deficiencies of antithrombin III, protein C, and protein S. Less common are primary antiphospholipid syndrome, presence of lupus anticoagulant, hyperhomocysteinemia, and familial hyperlipidemia.[115] These prothrombotic risk factors also play an important role in thrombosis of renal and abdominal visceral veins during infancy.[51] The APC resistance is the most common congenital prothrombotic disorder yet described and was identified in 23% to 30% of children with thrombosis in one series.[5] This decreased inactivation of factor V leads to a prothrombotic state, resulting in a 7- to 10-fold increase in the risk of thrombosis for heterozygotes and a 79-fold increase in risk for homozygotes compared with the general population.[60,62,102] Among patients with prothrombotic risk factors, studies have also suggested that congenital antithrombin III deficiency predisposes to a quadruple risk of venous thrombosis when compared with congenital deficiencies of protein C and protein S (12% versus 2.8% versus 3.3%, respectively).[34]

Caval Thrombosis

Obstruction of the superior vena cava in children is most frequently caused by thrombosis from indwelling catheters and pacemakers. Thrombosis of the SVC is seen in 16% of neonates requiring central venous catheters.[92] Invasion or compression by malignant tumors or inflammatory nodes is also seen. Symptoms of swelling and cyanosis are alleviated by elevation of the head and anticoagulation.

IVC thrombosis may propagate from iliofemoral, renal, or hepatic vein thrombosis. Usually associated with severe concurrent illness or dehydration, this condition may present with dramatic symptoms consisting of edema, cyanosis, ulceration, or merely lower extremity varicosities and lower abdominal collaterals. Increased frequency of central venous catheter insertions has led to complete IVC occlusion in up to 14.5% of infants requiring this therapy.[92] Diagnosis is made by cavography, CT, or MRI. Fulminant acute cases should be treated with thrombolysis or thrombectomy and with anticoagulation. Chronic venous insufficiency of lower extremities resulting from caval occlusion is managed with elevation and compression stockings. Long-term studies indicate that prognosis after IVC thrombosis may depend predominantly on the extent of the thrombus. Varicose veins present at a young age and worsen with time. The post-thrombotic syndrome is seen in 30% of patients at 10-year follow-up.[50] Judicious use of central venous catheters is the best method yet known for reducing the incidence of IVC thrombosis and preventing long-term complications.

Renal, Mesenteric, and Portal Vein Thrombosis

Renal vein thrombosis is usually a primary process and almost always accompanies severe concurrent illness or dehydration. Treatment and prognosis will depend on the severity of the renal involvement and underlying disease process. Although renal insufficiency improves in some cases, nephrectomy may be required for late hypertension or infection.[30] Heparin anticoagulation minimizes propagation of thrombus and decreases the risk of pulmonary emboli. Compared with children and adolescents, neonates with renal vein thrombosis fare less well. Renal vein thrombosis is the most common manifestation of thrombosis in the neonate and is symptomatic in more than 40% of cases. Hematuria and thrombocytopenia are the most common symptoms and are noted in up to 50% of neonates. At least one genetic prothrombotic risk was identified in 67% to 85% of neonates with renal vein thrombosis compared with control patients.[51,61,108] Doppler ultrasonography is the most popular means of confirming the diagnosis. Contrast medium–enhanced CT and MRI have supplanted the need for routine venography. The thrombosis is usually initiated at the level of intrarenal venules and thus treatment primarily consists of supportive therapy and anticoagulation.[7,30,45] Use of systemic thrombolytics has been described in isolated cases of bilateral renal vein thrombosis with inconsistent results. The prognosis remains grave, with mortality ranging from 5% to 13% among newborns with renal vein thrombosis.[15,108]

Superior mesenteric vein thrombosis when associated with bowel ischemia also has a high mortality rate. However, as few as 5% of cases may lead to bowel necrosis.[20] Mesenteric venous thrombosis usually has a subacute, nonspecific presentation with crampy abdominal pain, abdominal distention, anorexia, and malaise. Predisposing factors include portal hypertension, congestive heart failure leading to venous stasis, intra-abdominal sepsis or pylephlebitis, obstruction caused by malignancy, and hypercoagulable states[51] (malignancy; deficiency in antithrombin III, protein C, or protein S; anticardiolipin antibodies; or deep venous thrombosis). Symptoms, in some cases, can be present for more than a month. Duplex ultrasound is readily available and noninvasive, but CT with intravenous contrast medium enhancement or MRI provides more anatomic detail. If peritoneal signs are present or if intestinal perforation is suspected, laparotomy and resection of any necrotic bowel is mandatory. A second-look laparotomy in 24 hours may be necessary if intestinal viability is of concern. Prompt heparin anticoagulation reduces the risk of further propagation of necrosis from 30% to 40% to 3% to 5%.[20] Long-term anticoagulation may be necessary if the underlying condition predisposes to venous thrombosis.

Portal vein thrombosis is rare and occurs in association with a wide variety of clinical situations. Acute portal vein thrombosis may present as nonspecific abdominal symptoms. Children with chronic portal vein thrombosis, in general, present with sequelae of portal hypertension, such as gastrointestinal bleeding. Congenital malformations, malignancies, thrombophilia, umbilical vein catheterization, abdominal operations, sepsis and omphalitis in the neonatal period, and trauma are some of the many proposed causes of portal vein thrombosis. However, in up to 40% of cases, the etiology is unknown.[89] Patients with inherited deficiencies of protein C, protein S, and antithrombin III are at a higher risk for thrombosis than the general population.[51] Interestingly, although activated protein C resistance is the most common cause of venous thrombosis, reports suggest that it is not a contributing factor in portal vein thrombosis.[111] Doppler ultrasonography may lead to early diagnosis of portal vein thrombosis, even in patients suffering from abdominal pain as the sole symptom, with a reported specificity of 90%.[46] As with diagnosis of renal and mesenteric venous thrombosis, CT with intravenous contrast medium enhancement or MRI provides better anatomic detail. Treatment involves measures directed toward the portal vein thrombosis itself, the resulting portal hypertension, and its complications. Anticoagulation has prove to be effective in treatment of acute portal vein thrombosis. A portosystemic shunt may be recommended to decompress the portal hypertension and has a success rate of up to 90%.[88]

Lower Extremity Thrombosis

Most commonly seen in those with central venous catheters, deep venous thrombosis (DVT) contributes to significant morbidity and mortality in children. From the prospective Canadian registry of venous thromboembolism, the reported incidence of DVT among children in the general population is 0.07/10,000, compared with the 2.5% to 5% seen in the adult population. The majority of these venous thromboses, up to 58%, were documented in the lower extremity veins.[3] Associated conditions (i.e., inherited prothrombotic conditions, severe dehydration, sepsis) are identified in 91% to 96% of the children with DVT and the presence of a central venous line in up to 77% of patients.[3,100] In contradistinction to DVT in adults, only 4% of DVT in children have an idiopathic etiology.[3] Deficiencies in antithrombin III, protein C, protein S, and activated protein C resistance are well-recognized risk factors for venous thrombosis in children.[120] Thrombosis resulting from inherited prothrombotic disorders is most severe and frequent in homozygous individuals.[110] Diagnosis is commonly made by duplex ultrasonography, but because of small veins and diverse locations of thrombosis in children venography may still be used in select cases. Treatment includes limb elevation, anticoagulation (heparin, then warfarin), and compression stockings. Thrombolytic therapy for central venous line–related DVT has been attempted in neonates with mixed results.[130] Acute complications include phlebitis and phlegmasia, which may require surgical intervention. Untreated DVT or residual thrombosis leads to symptoms of chronic venous insufficiency. Even with an appropriate anticoagulation regimen, DVT recurrence was seen in 8.1% to 18.5% of children.[3,74]

Upper Extremity Thrombosis

The etiology of venous thrombosis of the upper extremity can be classified as primary or secondary thrombosis. Secondary venous thrombosis is usually a result of iatrogenic instrumentation (central venous lines, pacemakers) or an underlying hypercoagulable state. Central venous lines were found to be directly associated with 36% of DVT identified in the upper extremity[3] and correlates with increasing frequency of central venous line use. Duplex evaluation is often used to confirm the diagnosis in symptomatic patients. Therapeutic anticoagulation is instituted with treatment for 3 to 6 months, and arm symptoms are treated conservatively with elevation, rest, and elastic support. Patients in whom venous access is a concern should be evaluated for the more aggressive approach of catheter-directed thrombolysis.

Primary venous thrombosis implies that no obvious cause is identified on presentation and is somewhat of a misnomer because spontaneous "effort" thrombosis (Paget-von Schroetter syndrome) as well as pathologic compression within the thoracic outlet is included in this group. Symptoms can result from bony abnormalities of thoracic outlet and subclavian vein compression or from an anomalous axillopectoral muscle that compresses the axillary vein or from muscular hypertrophy of normally situated muscle groups.[105,119] Effort thrombosis usually occurs in the dominant arm of male athletes and is not uncommon in childhood or adolescence. The usual presentation is pain and swelling in the affected arm associated with edema, cyanosis, and obvious venous collaterals. In the general population, patients with acute subclavian-axillary thrombosis present during the third to fourth decades of life and have a 10% to 15% risk of pulmonary embolism[53,75] and thus require therapeutic anticoagulation. Despite full anticoagulation, 70% to 80% of patients remain symptomatic.[28,53] An aggressive treatment approach has been advocated in the past 10 years. Although venous duplex ultrasonography may demonstrate the DVT, venography is performed to define the anatomy and to allow for thrombolysis if indicated. Because some anatomic variations compress vascular structures in certain positions, dynamic venography with extension and abduction of the affected arm is strongly recommended. The recommended treatment is catheter-directed thrombolysis and subsequent anticoagulation.[25] In addition, percutaneous transluminal balloon angioplasty with or without stent placement has been attempted in adolescents and young adults.[63] Without decompression of the thoracic outlet, these endovascular techniques have resulted in a 6% success rate at 2 years, with fracture or deformed stents noted.[41,72] Many surgical approaches to decompression of the thoracic outlet have been described, including a transaxillary, supraclavicular, and a supraclavicular approach combined with infraclavicular incision. Our preference is a combined supraclavicular and infraclavicular incision to completely decompress the thoracic outlet with removal of the first rib, scalene anticus muscle, and subclavius muscle, thereby eliminating the majority of potential sources of external vein compression. Residual venous disease may require additional venoplasty or bypass procedures. Pediatric patients present with similar symptomatology and are at risk for the same complications. Recent reports of a like treatment strategy adopted for children show excellent short-term results.[123]

Complications of Venous Thrombosis

Thrombophlebitis

Thrombophlebitis represents a spectrum of disease processes and includes (1) nonspecific, nonsuppurative thrombophlebitis manifested by pain, tenderness, and redness over the vein course; and (2) suppurative thrombophlebitis with intraluminal purulent exudate, necrosis of the vein, and periphlebitic abscess. Diagnosis is established by physical examination, blood studies, and duplex ultrasonography. Aseptic phlebitis generally responds to local therapy, including warm soaks and analgesics, and in an otherwise healthy child does not require vein excision. For superficial septic thrombophlebitis to develop, the two necessary requirements are venous thrombosis and infection of the thrombus, usually with skin flora. The most consistent clinical features are localized swelling, erythema, induration, and a palpable cord. Fever and tenderness occurred more often in older children than in neonates.[57] Approximately 90% of patients develop thrombophlebitis at an intravenous infusion site.[109] Gram-positive pathogens are the causative agents in most cases, with *Staphylococcus* species cultured most frequently. Treatment begins with removal of the catheter and empirical use of antibiotics. Definitive treatment for superficial septic thrombophlebitis is radical excision of the affected vein segment.[4,57,84,96,109]

Septic thrombophlebitis of the deep veins is rare in children. In most cases, the infection of the thrombus is caused by percutaneous insertion of a central venous line in a critically ill patient. Diagnosis requires a high index of suspicion, because physical examination can be limited in immobilized and critically ill patients. Although duplex ultrasonography can identify popliteal and femoral vein thrombus, CT with intravenous contrast medium enhancement should be performed in patients suspected of iliofemoral DVT. Not only does CT reveal intraluminal thrombus and its extension, but information regarding perivenous fluid, soft tissue abscesses, and additional organ involvement is also seen. Treatment includes prompt removal of the catheter when present, antibiotics, anticoagulation, and cultures to identify the microorganism.[59] Complications include septic pulmonary embolization, osteomyelitis, and septic arthritis.[43] In cases of sepsis refractory to conservative treatment, drainage of the identified perivenous or subcutaneous abscesses and venous thrombectomy combined with an arteriovenous fistula may be lifesaving.[59]

Thrombophlebitis of the internal jugular vein is a rare but serious complication of pharyngeal space infection. Described by Lemierre, this syndrome is seen in adolescents and young adults and presentation is usually similar to that of pharyngitis or tonsillitis. Infection of the lateral pharyngeal space leads to inflammation and subsequent damage to the endothelium of the internal jugular vein. The diagnosis is usually delayed because of a low index of suspicion due to its rarity or to atypical prodromes.[2,122] Diagnosis is confirmed by duplex ultrasound, CT with intravenous contrast, or MRI. CT and MRI are more sensitive than ultrasound, and their reported accuracy approaches that of venography.[11,79] The most common pathogen isolated is *Fusobacterium necrophorum.* Antibiotics, usually penicillin, along with heparin anticoagulation are the mainstay of treatment. Septic embolization is common.[76] Surgical drainage of the primary abscess (peritonsillar, pharyngeal space abscess) may be necessary when there is no improvement with antibiotic therapy. Internal jugular venous ligation or excision is rarely required. Despite systemic antibiotic treatment, up to 18% of patients may die.[48]

Pulmonary Embolism

Pulmonary embolism (PE) contributes significantly to morbidity and mortality of a critically ill child. The true incidence of PE is not known but is likely considerably higher than reported in the literature. Andrew and colleagues reported that pulmonary embolism was diagnosed in 70% of patients with DVT in whom ventilation-perfusion lung scans were performed. The true incidence is likely much higher because only 23% of patients at risk were evaluated for PE, possibly owing to a low index of suspicion in critically ill children. The incidence of PE was 14% from a lower extremity DVT and 6% from an upper extremity DVT.[3] The overall incidence of PE in the presence of a DVT (upper or lower extremity) was 17%, and 56% when associated with a CVL. Mortality directly attributable to PE occurred in 1.7% of children.[74]

Ventilation-perfusion scans are most often used to diagnose pulmonary embolus but are being supplanted by helical CT scans. Pulmonary angiography is still used in select cases.[29] The available options for treatment of PE are anticoagulation, thrombolysis, or surgery. Clinical trials on the management of DVT and PE in children have not been completed, so guidelines are extrapolated from studies done in adults. In children older than 2 months of age, standard heparin therapy with an activated partial thromboplastin time goal of 60 to 85 seconds should be initiated for 5 to 10 days with overlap with warfarin for 4 to 5 days. Low-molecular-weight heparin is considered an acceptable alternative.[113] Long-term anticoagulation often is necessary to prevent recurrence and is provided by administration of warfarin to a therapeutic international normalized ratio (INR) between 2 and 3.[29,114] Usually, the patients with thrombi and no underlying inherited or persistent acquired defects are treated with warfarin for 6 months after the thrombotic episode. The remaining patients should be placed on lifelong anticoagulation.[110] Surgical placement of an IVC filter should be considered in larger patients with DVT and any contraindication to anticoagulation. Consideration of thrombolytic therapy is appropriate for pulmonary embolism with hemodynamic compromise and severely symptomatic large proximal venous thrombosis. Although systemic thrombolysis resulted in complete resolution of thrombus in 81% and partial resolution in 14% of patients with thrombosis in one series,[65] catheter-directed thrombolysis is the preferred method. Long-term anticoagulation often is necessary to prevent recurrence and is provided by administration of warfarin to a therapeutic INR between 2 and 3. Recently, recombinant activated protein C has proved effective in controlling and treating both coagulopathy and inflammation during adult sepsis, with emerging pediatric applications.[40] Embolectomy must be considered on an individualized basis.

The presence of hereditary prothrombotic disorders complicates the management of DVT and PE in that the risk of recurrent embolism after the first episode of spontaneous venous thrombosis is increased significantly. In addition, the hemostatic system of the young differs from that of an adult and likely influences the formation and propagation of thrombus and the response to anticoagulation.[18,90,115] Isolated recurrent PE was found in 12.5% of patients who were initially diagnosed with femoral vein thrombosis and treated appropriately.[83]

Post-thrombotic Syndrome

Anomalies of the deep and peripheral veins can lead to symptoms of chronic venous disease. In patients with congenital peripheral venous abnormalities, complications are seen at a younger age than that of the general population. Historically, the diagnosis of chronic venous disease by physical findings (e.g., varicose veins, skin discoloration, ulceration) was sufficient and treatment was limited to external support and medications for ulcers. With newer developments allowing surgical repair of venous disease,[10,27,107] an accurate classification of chronic venous disease becomes critical to patient evaluation and management. In 1994, an ad hoc committee of the American Venous Forum developed a new classification system.[94] The CEAP classification denotes a clinical (C), etiologic (E), anatomic (A), and pathophysiologic (P) classification and is the most widely accepted schema. The C components are described in six categories (Table 132-1); the E basis of venous dysfunction as primary, secondary, or congenital; the A distribution as superficial, perforator, or deep divisions; and the P mechanisms of development as reflux, obstruction, or both as occurring in 18 defined segments of the lower extremity veins. The major value to this classification system is to standardize the key elements in a way that patients with venous disease can be either distinguished from each other or grouped in common classes and compared in a standard manner in reports from different institutions. Several modifications have since been proposed for practical assessment of response to treatment in chronic venous disease.[104]

Chronic venous insufficiency and its sequelae resulting from residual thrombus or fibrotic changes of acute DVT is termed the *post-thrombotic syndrome* and is simply one reason for chronic venous disease. Although not as common as in adults (20% to 67%), post-thrombotic syndrome is seen in up to 12% to 18% of children with prior DVT.[3,74] Symptoms include pain, swelling, brawny discoloration, and ulcers of the affected limb (CEAP classification: $C_{2\text{-}6}$). These manifestations are rare in patients whose first episode of DVT is adequately treated with anticoagulant drugs and compression elastic stockings.[95]

TABLE 132-1 Clinical Classification of Chronic Lower Extremity Venous Disease

Class 0	No visible or palpable signs of venous disease
Class 1	Telangiectases, reticular veins, malleolar flare
Class 2	Varicose veins
Class 3	Edema without skin changes
Class 4	Skin changes ascribed to venous disease (e.g., pigmentation, venous eczema, lipodermatosclerosis)
Class 5	Skin changes as defined above with healed ulceration
Class 6	Skin changes as defined above with active ulceration

SUMMARY

Venous disease in children is more heavily influenced by congenital abnormalities than in adults, but the sequelae of the malady may not be expressed until adulthood. The potential complications of the congenital abnormality generally determine the level of intervention from surveillance to surgical operation.

Venous thrombosis has some unique childhood characteristics especially as relates to renal vein thrombosis, but the goals of treatment remain prevention of clot progression (to minimize end organ damage) and prevention of pulmonary emboli. Knowledge of unique hypercoagulable states is a must for the physician caring for children with many of these disorders.

REFERENCES

1. Akers DL Jr, Creado B, Hewitt RL: Iliac vein compression syndrome: Case report and review of the literature. J Vasc Surg 1996;24:477-481.
2. Alvarez A, Schreiber JR: Lemierre's syndrome in adolescent children—anaerobic sepsis with internal jugular vein thrombophlebitis following pharyngitis. Pediatrics 1995;96:354-359.
3. Andrew M, David M, Adams M, et al: Venous thromboembolic complications (VTE) in children: First analyses of the Canadian Registry of VTE. Blood 1994;83:1251-1257.
4. Arisoy ES, Correa-Calderon A, Kaplan SL: Primary deep venous septic thrombophlebitis in a child. J Pediatr 1994;124:439-441.
5. Aschka I, Aumann V, Bergmann F, et al: Prevalence of factor V Leiden in children with thrombo-embolism. Eur J Pediatr 1996;155:1009-1014.
6. Baraldini V, Coletti M, Cipolat L, et al: Early surgical management of Klippel-Trenaunay syndrome in childhood can

prevent long-term haemodynamic effects of distal venous hypertension. J Pediatr Surg 2002;37:232-235.
7. Baum NH, Moriel E, Carlton CE Jr: Renal vein thrombosis. J Urol 1978;119:443-448.
8. Belov S: Classification of congenital vascular defects. Int Angiol 1990;9:141-146.
9. Belov S: Anatomopathological classification of congenital vascular defects. Semin Vasc Surg 1993;6:219-224.
10. Bhuller AS, Nachreiner RD, Dalsing MC: Pathophysiology of chronic venous insufficiency and new horizons in surgical management. Semin Intervent Radiol 2001;18:155-170.
11. Blomquist IK, Bayer AS: Life-threatening deep fascial space infections of the head and neck. Infect Dis Clin North Am 1988;2:237-264.
12. Braun P, Collin PP, Ducharme JC: Preduodenal portal vein: A significant entity? Report of two cases and review of the literature. Can J Surg 1974;17:316-319, 322.
13. Brock PA, Jordan PH Jr, Barth MH, et al: Portal vein aneurysm: A rare but important vascular condition. Surgery 1997;121:105-108.
14. Browse NL, Burnand KG, Thomas LM: The Klippel-Trenaunay syndrome. In Browse NL, Burnand KG, Thomas LM (eds): Diseases of the Veins: Pathology, Diagnosis and Treatment. New York, Edward Arnold, 1988, pp 609-625.
15. Brun P, Beaufils F, Pillion G, et al: Thrombosis of the renal veins in the newborn: Treatment and long-term prognosis. Ann Pediatr (Paris) 1993;40:75-80.
16. Calligaro KD, Ahmad S, Dandora R, et al: Venous aneurysms: Surgical indications and review of the literature. Surgery 1995;117:1-6.
17. Campbell M, Deuchar DC: Absent inferior vena cava, symmetrical liver, splenic agenesis, and situs inversus, and their embryology. Br Heart J 1967;29:268-275.
18. Chalmers EA, Gibson BE: Thrombolytic therapy in the management of paediatric thromboembolic disease. Br J Haematol 1999;104:14-21.
19. Chang TN, Tang L, Keller K, et al: Pylephlebitis, portal-mesenteric thrombosis, and multiple liver abscesses owing to perforated appendicitis. J Pediatr Surg 2001;36:E19.
20. Chen MC, Brown MC, Willson RA, et al: Mesenteric vein thrombosis: Four cases and review of the literature. Dig Dis 1996;14:382-389.
21. Cherry KJ, Gloviczki P, Stanson AW: Persistent sciatic vein: diagnosis and treatment of a rare condition. J Vasc Surg 1996;23:490-497.
22. Chuang VP, Mena CE, Hoskins PA: Congenital anomalies of the inferior vena cava: Review of embryogenesis and presentation of a simplified classification. Br J Radiol 1974; 47:206-213.
23. Cockett FB: The significance of absence of valves in the deep veins. J Cardiovasc Surg (Torino) 1964;15:722-727.
24. Cockett FB, Thomas ML: The iliac compression syndrome. Br J Surg 1965;52:816-821.
25. Comerota AJ: Catheter-directed thrombolysis for treatment of axillary-subclavian venous thrombosis. Perspect Vasc Surg Endovasc Ther 2001;14:51-56.
26. Crawford FA Jr, Wolfe WG: Interposition mesocaval H shunt associated with a left inferior vena cava. Surgery 1976;79: 678-681.
27. Dalsing MC: Chronic venous disease. In Greenfield LJ, Mulholland MW, Oldham KT, et al (eds): Surgery: Scientific Principles and Practice, 3rd ed. Philadelphia, Lippincott Williams & Wilkins, 2001, pp 1888-1897.
28. Donayre CE, White GH, Mehringer SM, et al: Pathogenesis determines late morbidity of axillosubclavian vein thrombosis. Am J Surg 1986;152:179-184.
29. Donnelly KM: Venous thromboembolic disease in the pediatric intensive care unit. Curr Opin Pediatr 1999;11:213-217.
30. Duncan RE, Evans AT, Martin LW: Natural history and treatment of renal vein thrombosis in children. J Pediatr Surg 1977;12:639-645.
31. Edwards JE, Du SJ, Alcott DL, et al: Thoracic venous anomalies: III. Atresia of the common pulmonary vein, the pulmonary veins draining wholly into the superior vena cava. AMA Arch Pathol 1951;51:446-460.
32. Eguchi S, Endo S, Yamaguchi A, et al: Inferior caval occlusion associated with the Budd-Chiari-syndrome: Treatment with bypass operation. J Cardiovasc Surg (Torino) 1966;7: 490-494.
33. Eifert S, Villavicencio JL, Kao TC, et al: Prevalence of deep venous anomalies in congenital vascular malformations of venous predominance. J Vasc Surg 2000;31:462-471.
34. Finazzi G, Barbui T: Different incidence of venous thrombosis in patients with inherited deficiencies of antithrombin III, protein C and protein S. Thromb Haemost 1994;71:15-18.
35. Friedman EI, Taylor LM Jr, Porter JM: Congenital venous valvular aplasia of the lower extremities. Surgery 1988;103: 24-26.
36. Gallego C, Velasco M, Marcuello P, et al: Congenital and acquired anomalies of the portal venous system. Radiographics 2002;22:141-159.
37. Gillespie DL, Villavicencio JL, Gallagher C, et al: Presentation and management of venous aneurysms. J Vasc Surg 1997;26:845-852.
38. Giordano JM: Embryology of the vascular system. In Rutherford RB (ed): Vascular Surgery, 5th ed. Philadelphia, WB Saunders, 2000, pp 46-47.
39. Giordano JM, Trout HH 3rd: Anomalies of the inferior vena cava. J Vasc Surg 1986;3:924-928.
40. Giroir BP: Recombinant human activated protein C for the treatment of severe sepsis: Is there a role in pediatrics? Curr Opin Pediatr 2003;15:92-96.
41. Glanz S, Gordon DH, Lipkowitz GS, et al: Axillary and subclavian vein stenosis: Percutaneous angioplasty. Radiology 1988;168:371-373.
42. Gloviczki P, Hollier LH, Telander RL, et al: Surgical implications of Klippel-Trenaunay syndrome. Ann Surg 1983;197: 353-362.
43. Gorenstein A, Gross E, Houri S, et al: The pivotal role of deep vein thrombophlebitis in the development of acute disseminated staphylococcal disease in children. Pediatrics 2000;106:E87.
44. Gorenstein A, Shifrin E, Gordon RL, et al: Congenital aplasia of the deep veins of lower extremities in children: The role of ascending functional phlebography. Surgery 1986; 99:414-420.
45. Gupta N, Gewertz BL: Acute occlusive events involving the renal vessels. In Rutherford RB (ed): Vascular Surgery, 5th ed. Philadelphia, WB Saunders, 2000, pp 1706-1712.
46. Gurakan F, Eren M, Kocak N, et al: Extrahepatic portal vein thrombosis in children: Etiology and long-term follow-up. J Clin Gastroenterol 2004;38:368-372.
47. Haardt B: Histochemical comparison of the enzyme profiles of healthy veins and varicose veins. Phlebologie 1986; 39:921-931.
48. Hagelskjaer Kristensen L, Prag J: Human necrobacillosis, with emphasis on Lemierre's syndrome. Clin Infect Dis 2000; 31:524-532.
49. Harris EJ Jr: Chronic venous and lymphatic diseases. In Porter JM (ed): Year Book of Vascular Surgery. St. Louis, Mosby, 2002, pp 518-520.
50. Hausler M, Hubner D, Delhaas T, et al: Long term complications of inferior vena cava thrombosis. Arch Dis Child 2001;85:228-233.
51. Heller C, Schobess R, Kurnik K, et al: Abdominal venous thrombosis in neonates and infants: Role of prothrombotic

risk factors—a multicentre case-control study. For the Childhood Thrombophilia Study Group. Br J Haematol 2000;111:534-539.
52. Hughes PL, Qureshi SA, Galloway RW: Jugular venous aneurysm in children. Br J Radiol 1988;61:1082-1084.
53. Hurlbert SN, Rutherford RB: Primary subclavian-axillary vein thrombosis. Ann Vasc Surg 1995;9:217-223.
54. Hurst DR, Forauer AR, Bloom JR, et al: Diagnosis and endovascular treatment of iliocaval compression syndrome. J Vasc Surg 2001;34:106-113.
55. Jacob AG, Driscoll DJ, Shaughnessy WJ, et al: Klippel-Trenaunay syndrome: Spectrum and management. Mayo Clin Proc 1998;73:28-36.
56. Kabbani SS, Feldman M, Angelini P, et al: Single (left) superior vena cava draining into the left atrium: Surgical repair. Ann Thorac Surg 1973;16:518-525.
57. Khan EA, Correa AG, Baker CJ: Suppurative thrombophlebitis in children: A ten-year experience. Pediatr Infect Dis J 1997;16:63-67.
58. Kimura C, Shirotani H, Hirooka M, et al: Membranous obliteration of the inferior vena cava in the hepatic portion. (Review of 6 cases with 3 autopsies). J Cardiovasc Surg (Torino) 1963;4:87-98.
59. Kniemeyer HW, Grabitz K, Buhl R, et al: Surgical treatment of septic deep venous thrombosis. Surgery 1995;118:49-53.
60. Koeleman BP, Reitsma PH, Allaart CF, et al: Activated protein C resistance as an additional risk factor for thrombosis in protein C–deficient families. Blood 1994;84:1031-1035.
61. Kosch A, Kuwertz-Broking E, Heller C, et al: Renal venous thrombosis in neonates: Prothrombotic risk factors and long-term follow-up. Blood 2004;104:1356-1360.
62. Koster T, Rosendaal FR, de Ronde H, et al: Venous thrombosis due to poor anticoagulant response to activated protein C: Leiden Thrombophilia Study. Lancet 1993;342:1503-1506.
63. Kreienberg PB, Chang BB, Darling RC 3rd, et al: Long-term results in patients treated with thrombolysis, thoracic inlet decompression, and subclavian vein stenting for Paget-Schroetter syndrome. J Vasc Surg 2001;33:S100-S105.
64. LaMonte SJ, Walker EA, Moran WB: Internal jugular phlebectasia: A clinicoroentgenographic diagnosis. Arch Otolaryngol 1976;102:706-708.
65. Leaker M, Massicotte MP, Brooker LA, et al: Thrombolytic therapy in pediatric patients: A comprehensive review of the literature. Thromb Haemost 1996;76:132-134.
66. Lee BB: Critical issues in management of congenital vascular malformation. Ann Vasc Surg 2004;18:380-392.
67. Lee BB, Bergan JJ: Advanced management of congenital vascular malformations: A multidisciplinary approach. Cardiovasc Surg 2002;10:523-533.
68. Lindenauer SM: The Klippel-Trenaunay syndrome: Varicosity, hypertrophy and hemangioma with no arteriovenous fistula. Ann Surg 1965;162:303-314.
69. Loose DA: Surgical treatment of predominantly venous defects. Semin Vasc Surg 1993;6:252-259.
70. Ludbrook J: Valvular defect in primary varicose veins: Cause or effect? Lancet 1963;41:1289-1292.
71. Marois D, van Heerden JA, Carpenter HA, et al: Congenital absence of the portal vein. Mayo Clin Proc 1979;54:55-59.
72. Meier GH, Pollak JS, Rosenblatt M, et al: Initial experience with venous stents in exertional axillary-subclavian vein thrombosis. J Vasc Surg 1996;24:974-981; discussion 981-973.
73. Miller G, Inmon TW, Pollock BE: Persistent left superior vena cava. Am Heart J 1955;49:267-274.
74. Monagle P, Adams M, Mahoney M, et al: Outcome of pediatric thromboembolic disease: A report from the Canadian Childhood Thrombophilia Registry. Pediatr Res 2000;47:763-766.
75. Monreal M, Lafoz E, Ruiz J, et al: Upper-extremity deep venous thrombosis and pulmonary embolism: A prospective study. Chest 1991;99:280-283.
76. Moore BA, Dekle C, Werkhaven J: Bilateral Lemierre's syndrome: A case report and literature review. Ear Nose Throat J 2002;81:234-236, 238-240, 242 passim.
77. Mordehai J, Cohen Z, Kurzbart E, et al: Preduodenal portal vein causing duodenal obstruction associated with situs inversus, intestinal malrotation, and polysplenia: A case report. J Pediatr Surg 2002;37:E5.
78. Mulliken JB: Cutaneous vascular anomalies. Semin Vasc Surg 1993;6:204-218.
79. Nakamura S, Sadoshima S, Doi Y, et al: Internal jugular vein thrombosis, Lemierre's syndrome; oropharyngeal infection with antibiotic and anticoagulation therapy—a case report. Angiology 2000;51:173-177.
80. Negus D, Fletcher EW, Cockett FB, et al: Compression and band formation at the mouth of the left common iliac vein. Br J Surg 1968;55:369-374.
81. Niwa T, Aida N, Tachibana K, et al: Congenital absence of the portal vein: Clinical and radiologic findings. J Comput Assist Tomogr 2002;26:681-686.
82. Noel AA, Gloviczki P, Cherry KJ Jr, et al: Surgical treatment of venous malformations in Klippel-Trenaunay syndrome. J Vasc Surg 2000;32:840-847.
83. Nowak-Gottl U, Junker R, Kreuz W, et al: Risk of recurrent venous thrombosis in children with combined prothrombotic risk factors. Blood 2001;97:858-862.
84. O'Neill JA Jr, Pruitt BA Jr, Foley FD, et al: Suppurative thrombophlebitis—a lethal complication of intravenous therapy. J Trauma 1968;8:256-267.
85. O'Sullivan GJ, Semba CP, Bittner CA, et al: Endovascular management of iliac vein compression (May-Thurner) syndrome. J Vasc Interv Radiol 2000;11:823-836.
86. Oderich GS, Treiman GS, Schneider P, et al: Stent placement for treatment of central and peripheral venous obstruction: A long-term multi-institutional experience. J Vasc Surg 2000; 32:760-769.
87. Ohara I, Ouchi H, Takahashi K: A bypass operation for occlusion of the hepatic inferior vena cava. Surg Gynecol Obstet 1963;117:151-155.
88. Orloff MJ, Orloff MS, Girard B, et al: Bleeding esophagogastric varices from extrahepatic portal hypertension: 40 years' experience with portal-systemic shunt. J Am Coll Surg 2002;194:717-728; discussion 728-730.
89. Orloff MJ, Orloff MS, Rambotti M: Treatment of bleeding esophagogastric varices due to extrahepatic portal hypertension: Results of portal-systemic shunts during 35 years. J Pediatr Surg 1994;29:142-151; discussion 151-144.
90. Patel P, Weitz J, Brooker LA, et al: Decreased thrombin activity of fibrin clots prepared in cord plasma compared with adult plasma. Pediatr Res 1996;39:826-830.
91. Pearce WH, Rutherford RB, Whitehill TA, et al: Nuclear magnetic resonance imaging: Its diagnostic value in patients with congenital vascular malformations of the limbs. J Vasc Surg 1988;8:64-70.
92. Pippus KG, Giacomantonio JM, Gillis DA, et al: Thrombotic complications of saphenous central venous lines. J Pediatr Surg 1994;29:1218-1219.
93. Pohl A, Jung A, Vielhaber H, et al: Congenital atresia of the portal vein and extrahepatic portocaval shunt associated with benign neonatal hemangiomatosis, congenital adrenal hyperplasia, and atrial septal defect. J Pediatr Surg 2003; 38:633-634.
94. Porter JM, Moneta GL: Reporting standards in venous disease: An update. International Consensus Committee on Chronic Venous Disease. J Vasc Surg 1995;21:635-645.

95. Prandoni P, Lensing AW, Prins MR: The natural history of deep-vein thrombosis. Semin Thromb Hemost 1997;23: 185-188.
96. Pruitt BA Jr, Stein JM, Foley FD, et al: Intravenous therapy in burn patients: Suppurative thrombophlebitis and other life-threatening complications. Arch Surg 1970;100: 399-404.
97. Psaila JV, Melhuish J: Viscoelastic properties and collagen content of the long saphenous vein in normal and varicose veins. Br J Surg 1989;76:37-40.
98. Rachel E, Pearce WH: Venous malformations and aneurysms: Evaluation and treatment. In Gloviczki P, Yao JST (eds): Handbook of Venous Disorders—Guidelines of the American Venous Forum, 2nd ed. New York, Arnold, 2001, pp 439-449.
99. Raju S: Venous valve reconstruction. In Raju S, Villavicencio JL (eds): Surgical Management of Venous Disease. Baltimore, Williams & Wilkins, 1997, pp 338-356.
100. Revel-Vilk S, Chan A, Bauman M, et al: Prothrombotic conditions in an unselected cohort of children with venous thromboembolic disease. J Thromb Haemost 2003;1:915-921.
101. Rose SS, Ahmed A: Some thoughts on the aetiology of varicose veins. J Cardiovasc Surg (Torino) 1986;27:534-543.
102. Rosendaal FR, Koster T, Vandenbroucke JP, et al: High risk of thrombosis in patients homozygous for factor V Leiden (activated protein C resistance). Blood 1995;85: 1504-1508.
103. Rossall RE, Caldwell RA: Obstruction of inferior vena cava by a persistent eustachian valve in a young adult. J Clin Pathol 1957;10:40-45.
104. Rutherford RB, Padberg FT Jr, Comerota AJ, et al: Venous outcomes assessment. In Gloviczki P, Yao JST (eds): Handbook of Venous Disorders—Guidelines of the American Venous Forum, 2nd ed. New York, Arnold, 2001, pp 497-508.
105. Sachatello CR: The axillopectoral muscle (Langer's axillary arch): A cause of axillary vein obstruction. Surgery 1977;81:610-612.
106. Samuel M, Spitz L: Klippel-Trenaunay syndrome: Clinical features, complications and management in children. Br J Surg 1995;82:757-761.
107. Sanders BM, Dalsing MC: Deep vein valvular incompetence: Options for reconstruction. Perspect Vasc Surg Endovasc Ther 2001;14:89-106.
108. Schmidt B, Andrew M: Neonatal thrombosis: Report of a prospective Canadian and international registry. Pediatrics 1995;96:939-943.
109. Sears N, Grosfeld JL, Weber TR, et al: Suppurative thrombophlebitis in childhood. Pediatrics 1981;68:630-632.
110. Segel GB, Francis CA: Anticoagulant proteins in childhood venous and arterial thrombosis: A review. Blood Cells Mol Dis 2000;26:540-560.
111. Seixas CA, Hessel G, Ribeiro CC, et al: Factor V Leiden is not common in children with portal vein thrombosis. Thromb Haemost 1997;77:258-261.
112. Shinkai M, Ohhama Y, Nishi T, et al: Congenital absence of the portal vein and role of liver transplantation in children. J Pediatr Surg 2001;36:1026-1031.
113. Streif W, Goebel G, Chan AK, et al: Use of low molecular mass heparin (enoxaparin) in newborn infants: A prospective cohort study of 62 patients. Arch Dis Child Fetal Neonatal Ed 2003;88:F365-F370.
114. Streif W, Mitchell LG, Andrew M: Antithrombotic therapy in children. Curr Opin Pediatr 1999;11:56-64.
115. Sutor AH, Uhl M: Diagnosis of thromboembolic disease during infancy and childhood, Semin Thromb Hemost 1997;23:237-246.
116. Taheri SA, Heffner R, Meenaghan MA, et al: Technique and results of venous valve transplantation. In Bergan JJ, Yao JST (eds): Surgery of the Veins. New York, Grune & Stratton, 1985, pp 219-231.
117. Taheri SA, Williams J, Powell S, et al: Iliocaval compression syndrome. Am J Surg 1987;154:169-172.
118. Tanaka Y, Takayanagi M, Shiratori Y, et al: Congenital absence of portal vein with multiple hyperplastic nodular lesions in the liver. J Gastroenterol 2003;38:288-294.
119. Tilney ML, Griffiths HJ, Edwards EA: Natural history of major venous thrombosis of the upper extremity. Arch Surg 1970;101:792-796.
120. Tormene D, Simioni P, Prandoni P, et al: The incidence of venous thromboembolism in thrombophilic children: A prospective cohort study. Blood 2002;100:2403-2405.
121. Travers JP, Brookes CE, Evans J, et al: Assessment of wall structure and composition of varicose veins with reference to collagen, elastin and smooth muscle content. Eur J Vasc Endovasc Surg 1996;11:230-237.
122. Venglarcik J: Lemierre's syndrome. Pediatr Infect Dis J 2003;22:921-923.
123. Vercellio G, Baraldini V, Gatti C, et al: Thoracic outlet syndrome in paediatrics: Clinical presentation, surgical treatment, and outcome in a series of eight children. J Pediatr Surg 2003;38:58-61.
124. Villavicencio JL: Congenital vascular malformations of venous predominance: Klippel-Tranaunay syndrome. In Raju S, Villavicencio JL (eds): Surgical Management of Venous Disease. Baltimore, Williams & Wilkins, 1997, pp 445-461.
125. Villavicencio JL, Gonzalez-Cerna JL: Acute vascular problems of children. Curr Probl Surg 1985;22:1-85.
126. Villavicencio JL, Scultetus A, Lee BB: Congenital vascular malformations: When and how to treat them. Semin Vasc Surg 2002;15:65-71.
127. Watkins E Jr, Fortin CL: Surgical correction of a congenital coarctation of the inferior vena cava. Ann Surg 1964;159: 536-541.
128. Welch HJ, Villavicencio JL: Primary varicose veins of the upper extremity: A report of three cases. J Vasc Surg 1994; 20:839-843.
129. Wennerstrand JR: A case with a vena cava superior on both sides. Anat Anz 1963;112:338-343.
130. Wever ML, Liem KD, Geven WB, et al: Urokinase therapy in neonates with catheter related central venous thrombosis. Thromb Haemost 1995;73:180-185.
131. Yang DM, Yoon MH, Kim HS, et al: Portal vein aneurysm of the umbilical portion: Imaging features and the relationship with portal vein anomalies. Abdom Imaging 2003; 28:62-67.
132. Young AE: Pathogenesis of vascular malformations. In Mulliken JB, Young AE (eds): Vascular Birthmarks—Hemangiomas and Malformations. Philadelphia, WB Saunders, 1988, pp 107-113.
133. Young AE: Venous and arterial malformations. In Mulliken JB, Young AE (eds): Vascular Birthmarks—Hemangiomas and Malformations. Philadelphia, WB Saunders, 1988, pp 196-214.
134. Young AE, Ackroyd J, Baskerville P: Combined vascular malformations. In Mulliken JB, Young AE (eds): Vascular Birthmarks—Hemangiomas and Malformations. Philadelphia, WB Saunders, 1988, pp 246-274.

Chapter 133

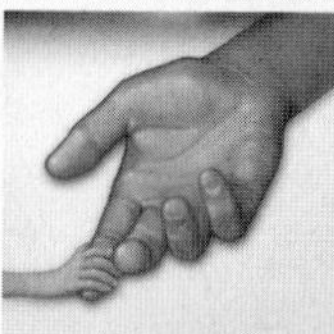

Lymphatic Disorders

Eric W. Fonkalsrud

EMBRYOLOGY AND ANATOMY

A concise history of the discovery, description, and embryology of the lymphatic system has been presented in detail by Sabin,[47] Skandalakis,[53] and others. Lymphatics develop in close relationship to venous structures and have an endothelial lining. In the sixth week of gestation, paired jugulolymphatic sacs can be identified in the developing neck region, and iliac sacs can be seen in the lumbar region.[43-46] By the eighth week of gestation, a retroperitoneal lymph sac can be identified at the base of the mesenteric root, and the cisterna chyli develops dorsal to the abdominal aorta. Paired thoracic ducts course cephalad through the chest and connect the abdominal lymphatics with the jugular system in the neck (Fig. 133-1). The final configuration of the thoracic duct leaves one major duct coursing cephalad in the right chest and then crossing over to the left side to enter the venous system at the left jugular-subclavian junction. The head, neck, and arms receive a plexus of lymphatics from the paired jugular sacs. The posterior sacs around the sciatic and femoral veins contribute to the lymphatics of the back, hips, and legs. Lymph nodes are formed by invasion of connective tissue into the lymph sacs around the ninth week of gestation.[29] Lymphocytes then enter the nodes, and lymph vessels and follicles are formed. The superficial lymphatics are valveless and compose a complex dermal network of capillary-like structures, which drain into larger subdermal channels that contain valves. These channels drain into a third, deeper layer that exists in the subcutaneous fat just above the fascia, where the lymphatics contain more valves and have a thin muscular layer for unidirectional transport.[40] There is lymphangiographic evidence of communication between the subcutaneous lymphatic system and the intramuscular lymphatics that parallel the deep arteries, particularly near regional lymph glands.[28] The superficial and deep systems are believed to function independently, except in abnormal states.[50]

Lymphatics are found throughout the body and are responsible for removing excess interstitial fluid as well as small molecules and macromolecules from tissues. Lymphatic capillaries, in contrast to blood vessels, are permeable to large molecules and cells because of an absent or vestigial basement membrane. This allows intercellular diffusion of plasma proteins and lipids, which are too large for reabsorption through the venous system.[7,38] Normally, lymphatic pressure is 0 mm H_2O or negative.[33]

The pathophysiology of lymphatic malformations is unclear, although they are believed to originate during fetal development as a result of lymphatic obstruction, hypoplasia, dysplasia, or aplasia.[60] Interference with lymphatic drainage may result from excessive fluid or a deficient drainage system. Some suggest that lymphatic malformations occur from sequestered portions of the primary lymph sacs.[46] Lymphatic obstruction results in dilated endothelium-lined spaces that range from small microscopic channels with small cysts to large cysts. Conversely, an injured or abnormal primitive lymph sac may not propagate in an orderly or complete fashion, thus causing the production of decreased or abnormal lymphatics and resulting in the clinical findings of lymphedema. A unifying concept linking disturbed lymphangiogenesis characterized by lymphedema, lymphangioma, lymphangiectasia, and lymphangiosarcoma with disorders of lymphatic dysplasia, hyperplasia, and neoplasia has been proposed.[21,27] The pathologic variants include (1) lymphangioma, a contiguous mass of dilated lymphatics resulting from a malformation of lymphatic channels; (2) lymphangiectasia, a dilatation along the course of the lymphatics caused by obstruction or hypoplasia of parenchymal or solid structures; and (3) lymphedema, related to the absence or hypoplasia of primary subcutaneous lymphatic channels.

LYMPHANGIOMA

Lymphangiomas are benign, hamartomatous lymphatic tumors characterized by multiple communicating lymphatic channels and cystic spaces. Most are less than 5 mm in diameter, and they occur in nearly all regions of the body. More than two thirds of lymphangiomas are apparent at birth, and most are present by the end of the second year of life. Prenatal ultrasonography occasionally documents the presence of lymphangiomas in the fetus.[34] In contrast to hemangiomas, spontaneous regression rarely occurs in lymphangiomas; they may enlarge and occasionally extend into adjacent tissues. Many lymphangiomas

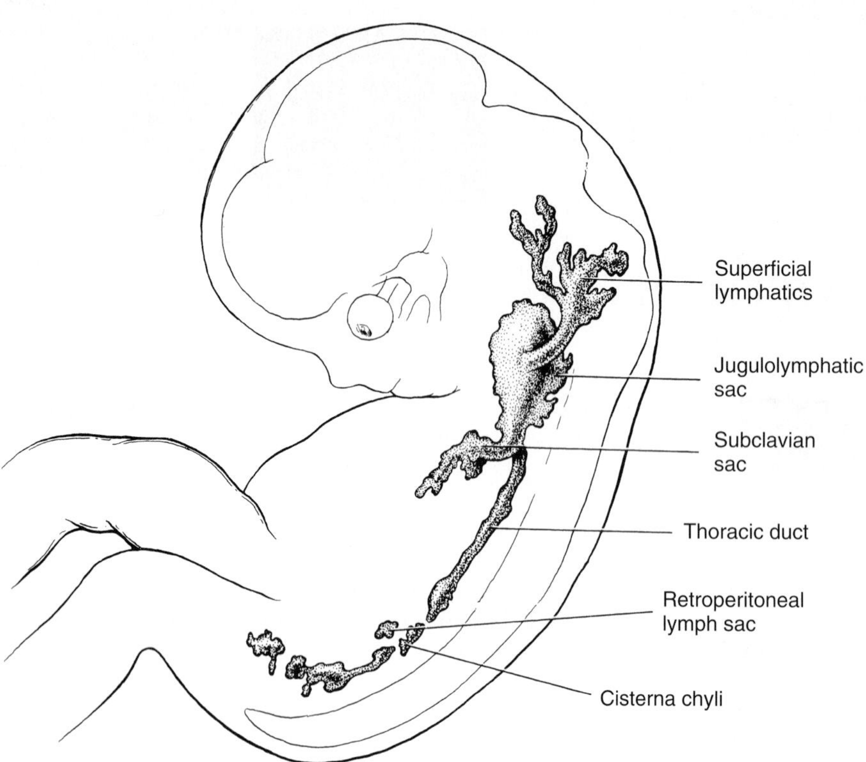

Figure 133–1 Fetal development of the lymphatics from primitive venolymphatic sacs in neck, chest, and iliac areas.

involve the skin and subcutaneous tissues and are frequently associated with other types of vascular disorders, particularly venous malformations.[33] In some patients, dilated capillaries and venous channels are interspersed with or adjacent to the lymphangioma; this is referred to as hemolymphangioma. The tumors may be localized or extensive and can involve almost any tissue.

Lymphangiomas have been classified as (1) lymphangioma simplex, composed of small, capillary-sized lymphatic channels; (2) cavernous lymphangioma, with dilated lymphatic channels, often with a fibrous adventitial covering; and (3) cystic lymphangioma, commonly referred to as cystic hygroma.[1]

The most common complication of lymphangioma is recurrent bouts of inflammation with cellulitis and lymphangitis, occasionally causing sepsis. Lymphangitis is usually associated with marked swelling and pain from compression of surrounding structures. With repetitive bouts of inflammation, these lesions tend to develop fibrosis. Rupture of lymphangiomatous cutaneous cysts, associated with leakage of lymph and blood, is often a prelude to the onset of cellulitis. Lymphangitis, which is commonly caused by streptococcal or staphylococcal organisms, is often rapidly progressive and requires prompt antibiotic therapy and moderate immobilization. Antibiotic therapy should be administered intravenously until a response is obtained, followed by weaning to oral therapy.

Lymphangiomas that infiltrate surrounding tissues by local extension may be very difficult to excise completely. These infiltrative forms tend to occur more frequently in the tongue, cheek, thorax, retroperitoneum, and extremities[37] (Fig. 133-2). They are firmer to palpation than cystic lymphangiomas and consist of tiny lymphatic spaces (microcysts) within a dense stroma of connective tissue and lymphatic channels. Respiratory distress in a neonate may be the result of a lymphangioma in the neck that is compressing the trachea. Lesions of the tongue tend to be in the midline, infiltrate into the floor of the mouth, and often cause bilateral submandibular swelling. Enlargement of the tongue frequently occurs as a result of repeated bouts of inflammation or trauma. Weeping, excess salivation, and occasionally bleeding occur when the tongue protrudes from the mouth.

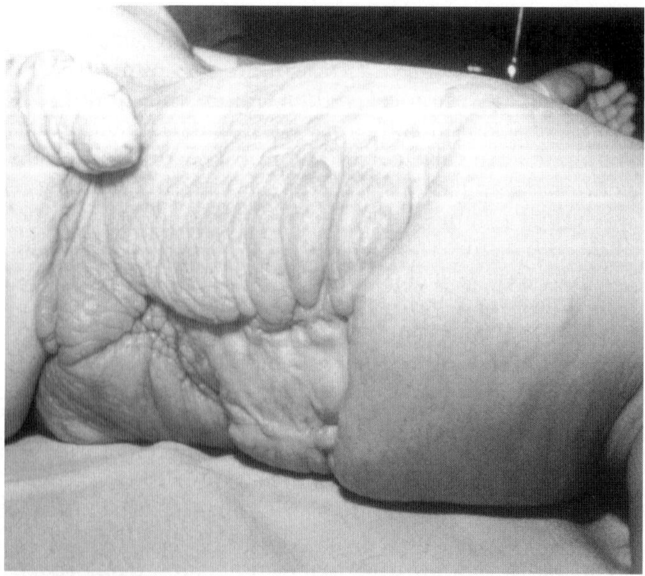

Figure 133-2 Lymphangioma of the left leg and genitalia in a 3-year-old boy who underwent staged resection of this lesion involving the skin and subcutaneous tissue.

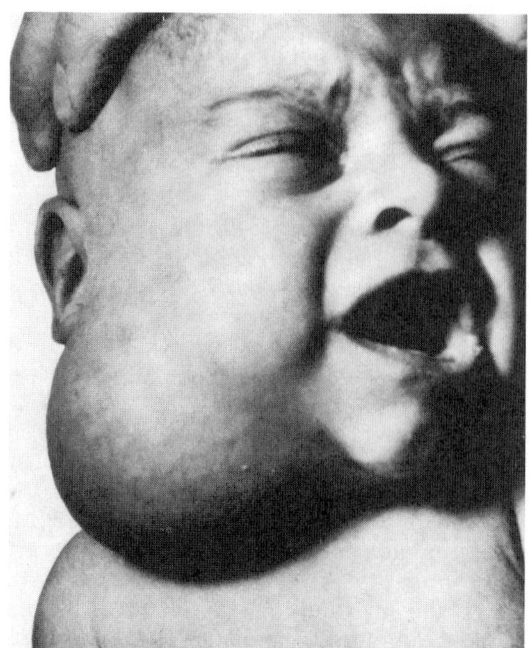

Figure 133–3 Cystic hygroma in the right anterior triangle of the neck in a 3-week-old infant.

Cystic lymphangiomas are usually soft and compressible, and they transilluminate with application of a light source. These lesions may be seen anywhere in the body but are most common in the neck (Fig. 133-3), axilla, mediastinum, and groin.[13] In some patients, the mass involves both the neck and the mediastinum or the axilla (Fig. 133-4). Occasionally, a cystic lymphangioma may occur in the liver or spleen or, rarely, the kidney. These lesions are commonly referred to as cystic hygromas.

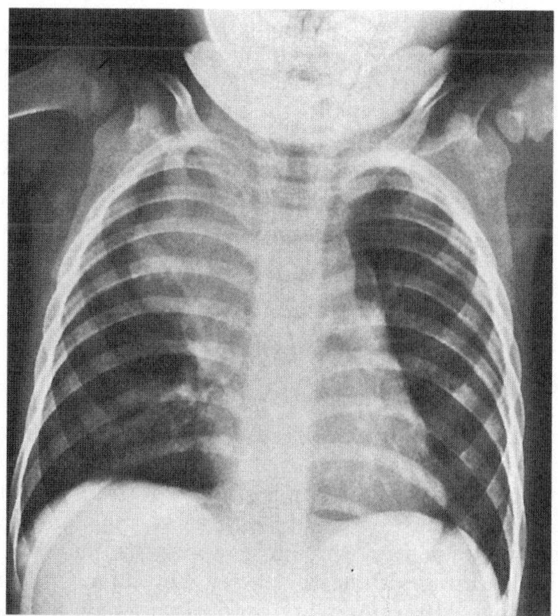

Figure 133–4 Chest radiograph of a child with a cystic hygroma of the right side of the neck, with a large mediastinal extension.

Embryologically, these lesions are believed to originate from a pinching off of the developing lymphaticovenous sacs, yielding sequestrations of lymphatic tissue that fail to communicate with the remainder of the lymphatic system. Cystic hygromas may be single, but most have multiple noncommunicating loculations present within the same lesion.[1]

The diagnosis of lymphangioma, whether cutaneous or cystic and below the skin, is generally evident on examination because of the characteristic clinical appearance. When in doubt, ultrasonography may be used to confirm the diagnosis; however, if extension of a cystic lesion into deeper structures of the body is uncertain, computed tomography (CT) with intravenous contrast enhancement can accurately show the full extent of the lesion.[1] An alternative approach is magnetic resonance imaging (MRI). Both these studies are particularly useful for the evaluation of patients with cystic lymphangiomatous lesions involving the neck, thorax, and retroperitoneum. MRI is especially valuable for the evaluation of complex vascular lesions that also involve the lymphatic system within the extremities.

Indications for the treatment of lymphangiomas include disfigurement, large size, chronic leakage of lymph fluid, and frequent bouts of inflammation.[18] The treatment of choice is operative excision when feasible.[13] These lesions are benign, so vital structures should not be sacrificed during their surgical resection. Recurrence may occur in 5% to 15% of patients after presumed complete excision and often requires reoperation. Even when complete excision of the cystic component of a lymphangioma is successful, persistent involvement of the skin in the area of resection is not uncommon. These lesions, as well as larger, weeping cutaneous lesions, may respond to topical serial laser therapy. Treatment of unresectable cystic lesions or recurrent lymphangioma with radiation, steroids, or sclerosing agents has generally been ineffective. For lesions that are difficult to resect surgically, intralesional injection of OK-432, a monoclonal antibody produced by incubation and interaction of low-virulence streptococci and penicillin, has an approximately 60% response rate.[14,17,35] Intralesional bleomycin A_5 has been used as primary therapy, with complete resolution reported in 55% of patients[36,56]; however, occasional complications, including infection, gastrointestinal disturbances, and pulmonary fibrosis, may occur. Giant lymphangiomas of the head and neck with significant microcystic components do not respond well to injection therapy. Injection of fibrin sealant has also been used, with occasional success.

Infiltrative lymphangiomas surround tissues by local extension and encase normal structures, usually splaying out and surrounding nerve branches, making excision difficult. Dissection may be lengthy and technically tedious. Familiarity with the regional anatomy is mandatory in anatomically complex areas such as the head and neck, axilla, mediastinum, and pelvis. When considering surgical treatment of lymphangiomatous lesions, it must be kept in mind that these are benign malformations and that injury to important adjacent structures should be avoided. This is especially true during the first year of life, when surgical intervention is sometimes necessary for life-threatening airway obstruction. When lesions extend into deep tissues or vital structures, the major prominent portion of the lymphangioma should be removed. Whenever possible, a lymphangioma should be completely excised, although staged resection is necessary in more than one third of cases.[18] It is rarely possible to completely remove a lymphangioma, except for localized hygromas of the neck. The desire for complete excision should not take precedence over preservation of vital function.

LYMPHANGIECTASIA

Lymphangiectasia can affect several organs and tissues, including the intestine, lung, and bone. Intestinal lymphangiectasia usually occurs in children younger than 3 years. This condition presents with diarrhea, vomiting, and growth failure and is often a cause of protein-losing enteropathy.[19] The diagnosis is made by small bowel mucosal biopsy. The bowel histology shows dilatation of lymphatic channels in the intestinal villi, with obstruction in the lamina propria alone; more generalized involvement of the lamina propria, submucosa, serosa, and mesentery; or, occasionally, involvement of the mesentery alone. The degree of protein loss may range from mild to severe. Malabsorption of fat is also present because long-chain fats cannot be absorbed by the dilated and obstructed intestinal lymphatics. Lymphopenia and hypoproteinemia are commonly present; hypogammaglobulinemia has also been noted, and coexistent pitting edema of the lower extremities is occasionally observed. Treatment of intestinal lymphangiectasia includes a high-protein, low-fat diet with the addition of medium-chain triglycerides and vitamin supplements.[42] This dietary plan usually reduces the diarrhea and improves the hypoproteinemia. Lymphangiectasia of the intestine is usually too extensive for resection, although occasionally the symptoms improve over time. Interferon-α has been used in the management of a few complex patients, with occasional improvement seen.

Pulmonary lymphangiectasia may present with respiratory distress in a newborn or in early infancy due to obstruction of the lymphatics draining the lung parenchyma. Obstruction of pulmonary lymphatics causes pulmonary edema and pleural effusion. The condition is usually bilateral and affects both lungs diffusely. Pulmonary lymphangiectasia has been observed in association with congenital heart disease; a familial occurrence has also been reported. Although some cases resolve spontaneously, many patients have rapidly progressive respiratory failure that results in early fatality. Clubbing, dyspnea, and hemoptysis may be noted in older patients. The chest radiograph often demonstrates interstitial fluid, with or without a pleural effusion. The diagnosis is confirmed by lung biopsy. The treatment is supportive, with drainage of pleural fluid as necessary by thoracentesis or a chest tube. Chemical pleurodesis with tetracycline or other sclerosing agents to prevent the recurrent accumulation of pleural fluid may assist in overall management.[13]

Children with lymphangiectasia of bone present with bone pain associated with a deformity or pathologic fracture that has a lytic radiographic appearance. Lesions have been observed in most bones except for the skull and phalanges. Lymphangiectasia of bone often coexists with other lymphangiomas, particularly in the trunk, and with chylothorax. There is a gradual increase in the size of the bone lesions, with eventual bone destruction. Lymphangiectasia of the cervical vertebrae may be lethal if vertebral collapse occurs. The diagnosis is usually confirmed radiographically by its characteristic appearance. There is no specific treatment for diffuse lymphangiectasia of bone, although curettage and filling the defects with autologous bone chips may be helpful.

CHYLOUS ASCITES

Chylous ascites may occur early in life. It is usually a result of aplastic, hypoplastic, or absent connections between the mesenteric lymphatics and the thoracic duct. Chylous ascites is probably a manifestation of generalized hypoplasia of the lymphatic system, with reflux of chyle into the intestinal lymphatics. Rupture of enlarged intestinal lymphatics into the intestinal lumen can occur, with subsequent enteral loss of protein and fat. The pathophysiology of chyluria is probably similar, with rupture into the renal pelvis.[24,39]

Chylous ascites is unrelenting and can be fatal; death results from malnutrition, hypoproteinemia, dehydration, and sepsis. Treatment consists of a low-fat or medium-chain triglyceride, high-protein enteral diet; repeated paracentesis; and total parenteral nutrition. Internal drainage by peritoneovenous shunt has occasionally been effective; however, shunt occlusion is common. Laparotomy is indicated if a correctable lesion is suspected. In these instances, radionuclide lymphangiography may be a useful method of demonstrating the approximate location of the leak within the abdomen. Some chyle leaks may be identified during surgery and then ligated; as with chylothorax, preoperative ingestion of butter and cream may demonstrate the leak.

In a few cases, a localized lymphatic obstruction in a small segment of bowel may cause diarrhea, vomiting, and loss of protein. A short intestinal resection may be curative in these cases. Biopsies of the suspected area of involved small bowel may help guide the extent of resection.

CT and radionuclide lymphangiography have been used to identify large, obstructed abdominal lymphatics that cause chyle reflux to the lower extremities. These lymphatics can occasionally be ligated, with improvement of lymphedema and correction of chyle fistulas to the scrotum.

CONGENITAL CHYLOTHORAX

Congenital chylothorax presents as effusion of chyle in one or both pleural cavities. The cause of this problem can be overproduction of chyle, failure of communication of the lymphatic vessels, minimal reabsorption of lymph, abnormalities of the pulmonary lymphatics, or injury in the newborn during a difficult delivery. The infant may have mediastinal shift, pulmonary hypoplasia, congestive heart failure, or hydrops. Associated anomalies include trisomy 21 syndrome, congenital pulmonary lymphangiectasia, esophageal atresia, extralobar pulmonary sequestration, and polyhydramnios.

A pleural effusion present prenatally or at birth may be chylothorax. The fluid may appear serous, but a fluid cell count with more than 60% lymphocytes is diagnostic of chylothorax.[4,59] If the patient has been eating fatty foods or drinking milk, the chyle will appear milky; microscopic examination will show chylomicrons that stain for fat. Chyle contains fat in the form of phospholipids, cholesterol, and long-chain triglycerides. The protein content averages 40 g/L, and electrolyte and glucose levels are similar to plasma levels. About half these children present in the first week of life.

Treatment consists of repeated thoracentesis and thoracic drainage to expand the lungs. Patients may initially receive oral feedings consisting of an elemental diet with medium-chain triglycerides. If fluid reaccumulates too rapidly, total parenteral nutrition may be required. Opinions vary about how long to continue nonoperative treatment; however, if drainage persists for 3 to 4 weeks, an attempt at surgical ligation of the thoracic duct may be necessary.[2] A meal of butter and cream before surgery may help identify the site of the leak. Ligation above and below the leak is effective in most instances.

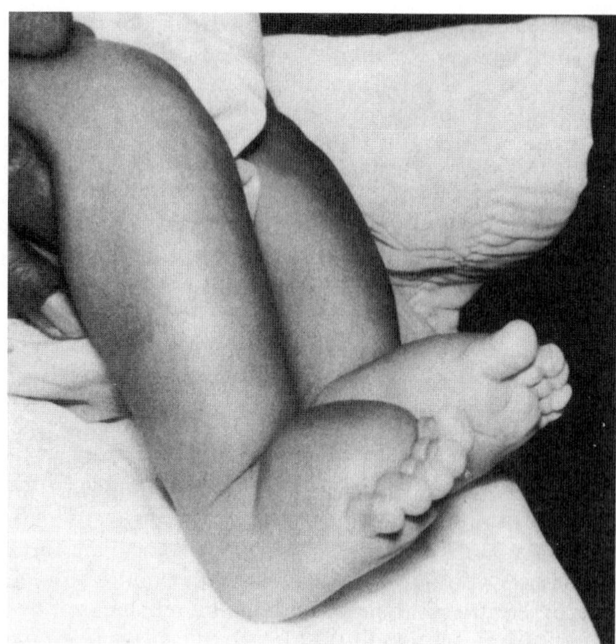

Figure 133–5 Congenital lymphedema affecting both lower extremities (dorsum of the feet and calves) in a 2-month-old infant.

LYMPHEDEMA

The exact pathogenesis of lymphedema is unclear, although in general terms, it is an abnormal collection of interstitial lymph fluid due to either congenital maldevelopment of the lymphatics or secondary lymphatic obstruction.[48] The most common cause of lymphedema in young children is a primary congenital abnormality affecting the lymphatics of the lower extremities.[26] Other causes of lower limb lymphedema include chronic infections (lymphangitis), filariasis, insect bites, neoplasms, inguinal or axillary surgery, irradiation, and trauma.[7] Unilateral leg swelling may arise (rarely) from a retroperitoneal tumor or lymphoma compressing the iliac veins. Bilateral lower extremity edema should lead to an evaluation to exclude the various causes of hypoalbuminemia, such as nephrotic syndrome, and bilateral venous obstruction, such as from intracaval Wilms' tumor. Upper extremity lymphedema is unusual in children.[12]

Primary lymphedema has been divided into three categories, based on the age of onset: (1) congenital lymphedema, which is present at birth (Fig. 133-5); (2) lymphedema praecox, which appears in early adolescence and may be influenced by hormonal factors; and (3) lymphedema tarda, which occurs spontaneously in middle age (older than 30 years).[7,16,26] Milroy's congenital familial lymphedema accounts for less than 2% of all cases of lymphedema and is associated with an autosomal inheritance of a single gene. Unlike primary lymphedema, which occurs predominantly in girls (65%),[32,48] Milroy's disease affects boys and girls equally. Affected families have single nucleotide substitutions at the chromosomal locus 5q35.3. The gene for vascular endothelial growth factor receptor 3 (VEGFR3) maps to the locus.[23] Only lymphatic endothelium expresses VEGFR3, providing further evidence that the gene is responsible for familial lymphedema. Lymphedema has also been reported in association with Turner's and Noonan's syndromes. Lower extremity edema has been observed in children with intestinal lymphangiectasia and cerebrovascular malformations.

The underlying pathology in most cases of lymphedema is an absence (aplasia) or hypoplasia of the subcutaneous lymphatic channels of the lower extremities.[25,41] With hypoplasia, lymph nodes and vessels are small and few in number. Hormonal factors have been implicated as having an influence in the development of lymphedema praecox in adolescent girls.[7,25] The "yellow nail" syndrome is caused by inadequately draining lymphatics in the nail beds, resulting in yellow discoloration and dystrophic changes in the toenails. This syndrome has been observed in children with lymphedema associated with pulmonary conditions, including chronic bronchitis and bronchiectasis.

The diagnosis of lymphedema is usually made clinically.[7,48] Noninvasive Doppler studies and plethysmography can rule out arterial or venous disease.[33] Radionuclide imaging using technetium 99m sulfur colloid within 3 hours after subcutaneous injection usually demonstrates lymphatic channels and sites of obstruction.[55] Ninety percent of children have hypoplasia of the superficial lymphatics with distal rather than proximal involvement. MRI may also be useful in differentiating lymphangioma from lymphedema. Lymphangiograms often provide helpful information but may occasionally cause lymphangitis. Complications of lymphedema include persistent swelling, brawny edema with skin thickening and discoloration, cellulitis, and lymphangitis. Prophylactic gram-positive antibiotic coverage may be required to control recurring episodes of lymphangitis.

Most observers,[41] but not all,[51] believe that the lymphatic system is divided into a valveless superficial system and a valved deep system. In cases of lymphedema, the fluid from the superficial system pools in the subcutaneous tissues; production of fluid exceeds drainage capabilities.[6] The protein-rich fluid increases the oncotic pressure, which perpetuates the edema. If the skin over the extremity has been chronically stretched, the elastic fibers lose considerable tensile strength. These fibers can no longer confine minimal edema to normal contours without the aid of external support. The deep system of lymphatics beneath the fascia and in the muscle component is separate and unaffected.[48] The universal observation that the muscles and their lymphatics are competent in all cases of lymphedema has been the key consideration in the design of procedures that attempt to deliver lymph into the valved deep system so that the fluid can move upward.

The initial conservative treatment of lymphedema of the lower extremities includes a program of attentive foot care and hygiene. Judicious use of antibiotics to treat and prevent cellulitis and the application of topical antifungal agents are important in the treatment of lymphedema.[57,58] Weight control is believed to be beneficial; however, diuretics are of little value. Other medications (e.g., pantothenic acid, hyaluronidase) are experimental and have gained little support.[48] Warfarin (Coumadin) may have a beneficial effect in the treatment of lymphedema, with a mean decrease in edema volume of approximately 50%. The benefits of warfarin may be related to its stimulatory effect on cutaneous macrophages and local proteolysis and protein absorption. Some authors advocate increasing dietary flavonoids and restricting long-chain triglycerides in an effort to protect the vascular endothelium and improve the microcirculation.[41]

Prolonged standing without compression accelerates lymph accumulation; however, walking or running appears to slow this process. The use of compression support stockings during the day and elevation of the legs at night help reduce the swelling, thus diminishing the adverse psychological impact of unsightly, swollen legs. Support stockings should be replaced every 4 to 6 months in a growing child. Pillows are usually inadequate to maintain proper leg elevation at night; placing 10- to 12-inch blocks under the foot of the bed is more effective. Pneumatic sequential pumping systems have been used to reduce the degree of lymphedema that reaccumulates when the child is standing or walking. These pumps are applied at night and intermittently compress the extremity from the toes to the groin. Approximately 85% of patients with lymphedema can be managed effectively with nonoperative treatment. Patients with distal extremity lymphatic hypoplasia and normal iliac and pelvic lymphatics seldom have severe symptoms. Children with proximal obstructive hypoplasia develop more severe lymphedema (15%) and frequently benefit from surgical intervention.

The surgical management of lymphedema in children and young adults is a challenge because the condition is uncommon and few surgeons have acquired a large experience.[26,51,57] Currently, no form of surgical treatment offers a cure for lymphedema. The indication for surgical treatment is failure of conservative measures with limitation of daily physical activities owing to the excessive size and weight of the extremity. Recurrent bouts of cellulitis and lymphangitis, often causing pain, are also indications for operation. Most patients with primary lymphedema are females, and aesthetic and psychological considerations are important in adolescents. Lymphangiosarcoma is a rare but frequently fatal complication of long-standing lymphedema.[20]

Attempts at surgical correction of lymphedema date back to 1841[53] and have included both physiologic and excisional approaches. Physiologic operations are based on the goal of reconnecting,[15,57] reconstructing,[3,9] or stimulating the growth of lymphatic pathways. These procedures include the use of an omental bridge or a defunctionalized pedicle of small bowel that has been stripped of its mucosa and placed in the affected extremity as a potential lymphatic drainage source.[15,54] These operations are rarely successful for primary lymphedema unless a large amount of subcutaneous tissue is excised during the procedure or unless the disorder is actually secondary lymphedema with local obstruction. Lymphaticovenous anastomosis using microsurgical technique has also been attempted; however, the long-term patency and effectiveness of this technique have not been established for primary lymphedema, as they have been for postmastectomy lymphedema.[9]

Because lymph is generated and collects in the subcutaneous tissues, excision of these edematous tissues is the current approach to management, based on the concept that the subfascial lymphatics are normal. In 1912 Charles[5] reported success by removing edematous skin and subcutaneous tissue down to the muscle and then covering the denuded surface with split-thickness skin grafts obtained from other areas. Drawbacks of the Charles procedure, which is now rarely used, include poor postoperative appearance, graft loss, chronic infection, exophytic keratoses, persistent weeping of lymphatic fluid, and sensory loss of the skin. In 1936 Homans[22] modified the procedure by excising the subcutaneous tissue down to the deep fascia and creating thin skin flaps to cover the excised area. Recently, liposuction to remove subcutaneous tissue, followed by compressive dressings, has been used occasionally, with limited success.

Staged subcutaneous lymphangiectomy, with pneumatic tourniquet control to minimize blood loss, has been used to significantly reduce the swelling of the extremities in patients with lymphedema praecox and tarda, as well as selected cases of congenital lymphedema.[13,52] A preoperative radionuclide lymphangiogram is advisable to ensure that there are normal subfascial lymphatics.[16,55] These operations are usually staged, with the medial side of the lower legs being excised from the ankles to slightly above the knee as the first stage; the lateral portion is resected at a second procedure at least 9 months later.[31,58] All subcutaneous tissue between the thin full-thickness skin flaps and the underlying muscular fascia is resected; strips of skin at the edges of the incision are resected (Fig. 133-6). When possible, the peroneal nerve is identified to protect it from injury. Thorough hemostasis is achieved, and drainage of the wound with suction is used for approximately 1 week. Skin staples are left in place for approximately 2 weeks because the skin flap closure heals slowly. Because the saphenous venous system is

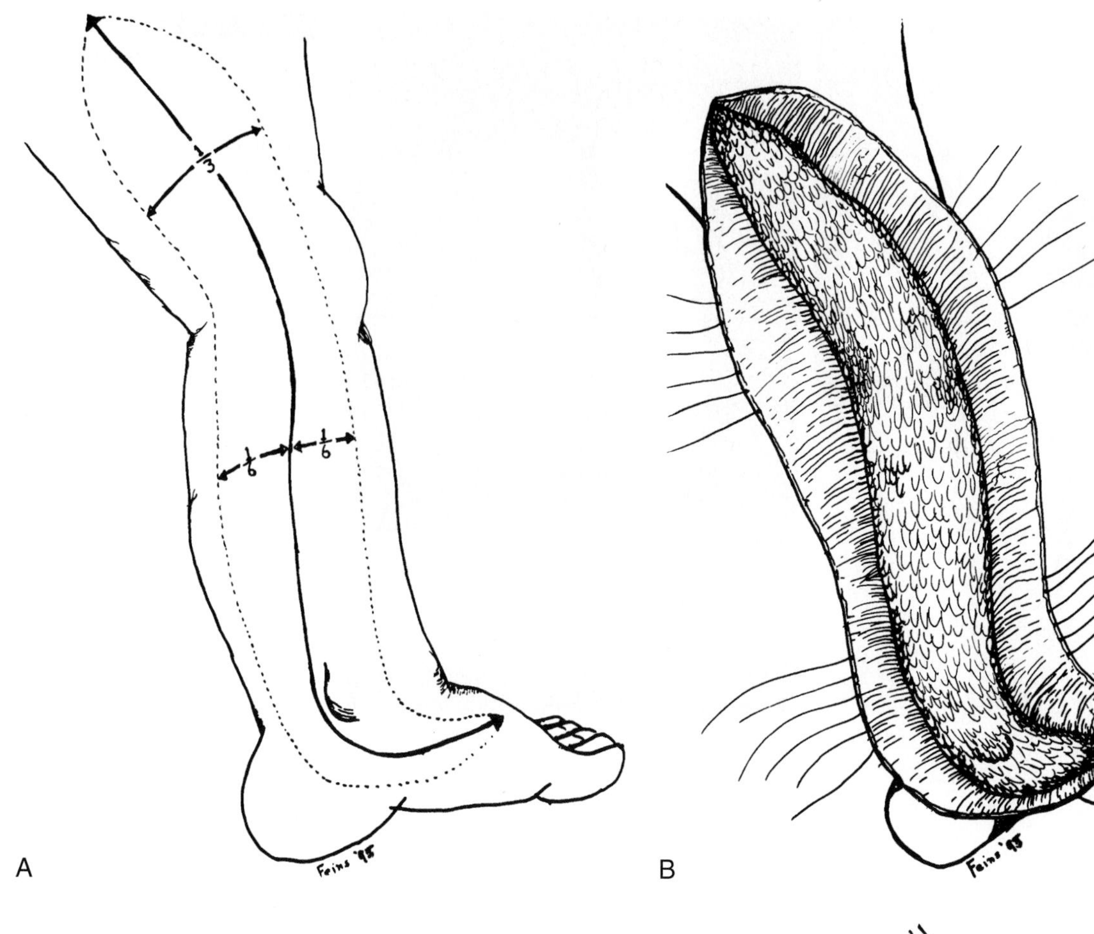

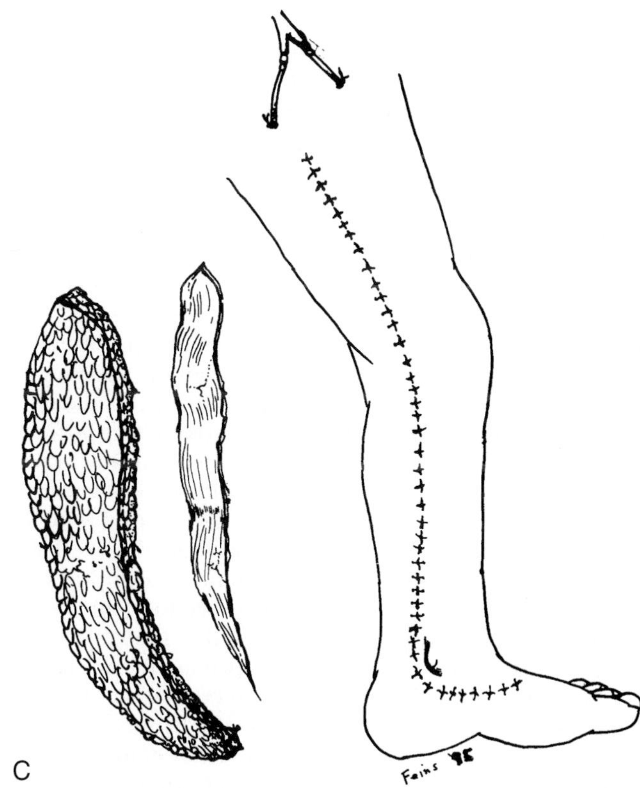

Figure 133–6 *A,* For lower extremity lymphedema praecox or tarda, the incision is made on the medial aspect of the leg. The vertical arrow indicates the length of the incision. The horizontal arrows indicate the width of the skin flap. Each flap is developed for one fourth to one sixth of the circumference of the leg, for a total exposure of one half to one third of the extremity. *B,* The flaps are thin and of full thickness. Holding sutures are placed in a subcuticular layer and are used for traction to avoid excessive manipulation of the skin. The exposed subcutaneous tissues and underlying fascia are completely removed. *C,* The subcutaneous tissue has been removed in one piece. The deep fascia has been removed as a separate specimen. The incision was closed with staples after two large Hemovac drains were placed under the flaps.

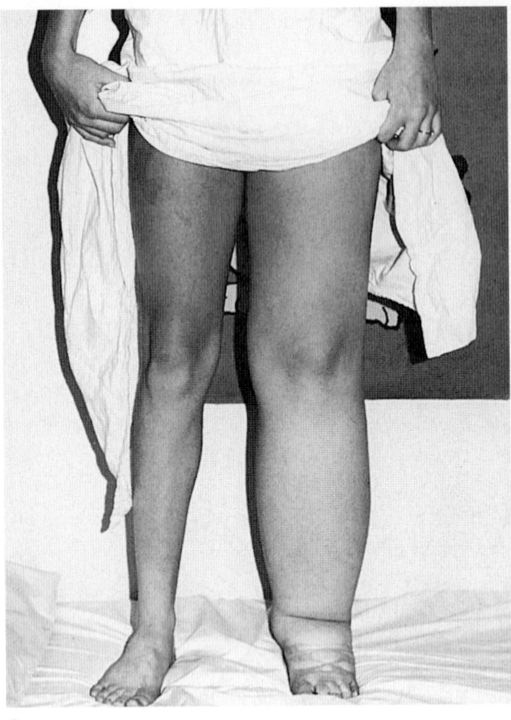

A

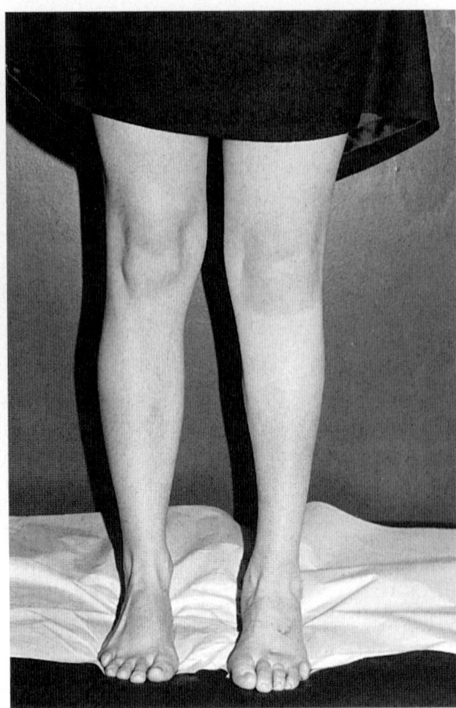

B

Figure 133–7 *A*, A 14-year-old girl with lymphedema praecox of the left lower extremity. *B*, The same patient at age 17 years, 6 months after the third serial resection.

removed during the procedure, it is imperative that the deep venous system be functioning well, as determined by a preoperative venogram. Fluffed gauze with a mild pressure dressing is used for approximately 1 week. Subsequent elastic bandage support is recommended for several weeks, followed by form-fitting elastic stockings for several months. Wound drainage may be as much as 100 mL daily; however, by the seventh postoperative day, the amount is usually less than 10 mL. Daily applications of moisturizing skin cream are helpful in reducing the dryness of the affected extremity. Although staged lymphangiectomy never produces a cure and is often followed by partial recurrence of edema, many authors believe that it is the most effective operative procedure currently available[30,49] (Fig. 133-7). Approximately 80% of patients obtain satisfactory long-term results following staged subcutaneous lymphangiectomy, although the use of support stockings indefinitely may be necessary to achieve optimal control of recurrent swelling.

Because the configuration may continue to improve for more than a year, a second-stage procedure on the same extremity is best performed after this interval.[31,58] A third-stage procedure may be necessary in an occasional patient with an unusually large extremity. For patients with lymphedema involving the upper leg as well, lymphangiectomy in this area is usually deferred until the operations on the lower leg have been completed. In managing bilateral disease, it is preferable to operate on one extremity at a time. If there are no complications with the first leg, lymphangiectomy may be performed on the contralateral extremity within several weeks.[11]

Although the basic operative technique is similar, the surgical management of congenital primary lymphedema of the upper extremities is more complex than in the legs, because each finger as well as the dorsal surface of the hand and forearm usually requires multiple staged resections.[12] Additionally, it is cumbersome for the patient to wear compression gloves or elastic bandages postoperatively. Some patients with upper extremity primary lymphedema also have lymphedema of the genitalia, although isolated swelling of the genitalia may occur. Sublabial lymphangiectomy is helpful for most affected females. For lymphedema of the penis and scrotum, almost all subcutaneous lymphatic tissue is resected through a transverse incision in the scrotum beneath the base of the penis.[8,10] The dissection is extended down to Buck's fascia on the penis and onto the tunica of the testes, with care taken to avoid injury to the spermatic cords. Excessive penile and scrotal skin is excised. Wound drains, support dressings, and a Foley catheter are used for 4 to 7 days. Antibiotics are given for 7 to 10 days.

REFERENCES

1. Alguahtani A, Nguyen LT, Flageole H, et al: Twenty-five years experience with lymphangiomas in children. J Pediatr Surg 1999;34:1164.
2. Anderson EA, Hertel J, Pedersen SA, Sorensen HR: Congenital chylothorax: Management by ligature of the thoracic duct. Scand J Thorac Cardiovasc Surg 1984;18:193.

3. Baumeister RG, Seifert J, Wiebecke B: Homologous and autologous experimental lymph vessel transplantation initial experience. Int J Microsurg 1981;3:19.
4. Benacerraf BR, Frigoletto FD: Mid-trimester fetal thoracentesis. J Clin Ultrasound 1985;13:202.
5. Charles RH: Lymphedema. In Latham A, English TC (eds): A System of Treatment, vol 3. London, Churchill, 1912.
6. Crockett DJ: Lymphatic anatomy and lymphedema. Br J Plast Surg 1965;28:12.
7. Dale WA: The swollen leg. Curr Probl Surg 1973;Sep:1.
8. Dandapat MC, Mohapatro SN, Sushanta KP: Elephantiasis of the penis and scrotum: A review of 350 cases. Am J Surg 1985;149:686.
9. Degni M: New techniques of lymphatic venous anastomosis for the treatment of lymphedema. J Cardiovasc Surg 1978; 19:577.
10. Feins NR: A new surgical technique for lymphedema of the penis and scrotum. J Pediatr Surg 1980;15:787.
11. Feins NR: Lymphatic disorders. In O'Neill JA Jr, Rowe MI, Grosfeld JL, et al (eds): Pediatric Surgery, 5th ed. St Louis, Mosby, 1998.
12. Fonkalsrud EW: A syndrome of congenital lymphedema of the upper extremity and associated systemic lymphatic malformations. Surg Gynecol Obstet 1977;145:228.
13. Fonkalsrud EW: Disorders of the lymphatic system. In Ravitch MM, Randolph JG, Welch K, et al (eds): Pediatric Surgery, 4th ed. Chicago, Mosby–Year Book, 1986.
14. Fujino A, Moriya Y, Morikawa Y, et al: A role of cytokines in OK-432 injection therapy for cystic lymphangioma: An approach to the mechanism. J Pediatr Surg 2003; 38:1806.
15. Goldsmith HS, Los Santos R, Beattie EJ Jr: Relief of chronic lymphedema by omental transposition. Ann Surg 1967; 166:572.
16. Gough MH: Primary lymphedema clinical and lymphangiographic studies. Br J Surg 1966;53:917.
17. Greinwald JH Jr, Burke DK, Sato Y, et al: Treatment of lymphangiomas in children: An update of Picibanil (OK-432) sclerotherapy. Otolaryngol Head Neck Surg 1999; 121:381.
18. Hancock BJ, St-Vil D, Luks FI, et al: Complications of lymphangiomas in children. J Pediatr Surg 1992;27:220.
19. Henzel JH, Pories WJ, Burget DE, et al: Intra-abdominal lymphangiomata. Arch Surg 1966;93:304.
20. Hermann JB, Gruhm JG: Lymphangiosarcoma of the chronically edematous extremity. Surg Gynecol Obstet 1957; 105:665.
21. Hilliard RI, McKendry JBS, Phillips MJ: Congenital abnormalities of the lymphatic system: A new clinical classification. Pediatrics 1990;86:988.
22. Homans J: The treatment of elephantiasis of the legs: Preliminary report. N Engl J Med 1936;215:1099.
23. Irrthum A, Karkkainen MJ, Devriendt K, et al: Congenital hereditary lymphedema caused by a mutation that inactivates VEGFR3 tyrosine kinase. Am J Hum Genet 2000;67:295.
24. Kelly ML Jr, Batt HR: Chylous ascites: An analysis of its etiology. Gastroenterology 1960;39:161.
25. Kinmonth JB, Taylor GW, Jantet GH: Chylous complications of primary lymphedema. J Cardiovasc Surg (Torino) 1964;5:327.
26. Kinmonth JB, Taylor GW, Tracy GD, Marsh JD: Primary lymphedema, clinical and lymphangiographic studies of a series of 107 patients in which the lower limbs were affected. Br J Surg 1957;45:1.
27. Levine C: Primary disorders of the lymphatic vessels: A unified concept. J Pediatr Surg 1989;24:233.
28. Malek P, Belan A, Kocandrle VL: The superficial and deep lymphatic system of the lower extremities and their mutual relationship under physiological and pathologic conditions. J Cardiovasc Surg 1964;5:686.
29. McClure CFW, Silvester CF: A comparative study of the lymphaticovenous communications in adult mammals. Nat Rec 1909;3:534.
30. Miller TA: A surgical approach to lymphedema. Am J Surg 1977;134:191.
31. Miller TA, Harper J, Longmire WP Jr: The management of lymphedema by staged subcutaneous excision. Surg Gynecol Obstet 1973;136:586.
32. Milroy WF: An undescribed variety of hereditary oedema. N Y Med J 1892;56:505.
33. Mulliken JB, Fishman SJ, Burrows PE: Vascular anomalies. Curr Probl Surg 2000;37:517.
34. Ogita K, Suita S, Taguchi T, et al: Outcome of fetal cystic hygromas and experience of intrauterine treatment. Fetal Diagn Ther 2001;16:105.
35. Ogita S, Tsuto T, Wakamura K, et al: OK-432 therapy in 64 patients with lymphangioma. J Pediatr Surg 1994; 29:784.
36. Okada A, Kubota, Fukuzawa M, et al: Injection of bleomycin as primary therapy of cystic hygromas. J Pediatr Surg 1992; 27:440.
37. Padwa BL, Hayward PG, Ferraro NF, et al: Cervicofacial lymphatic malformations: Clinical course, surgical intervention, and pathogenesis of skeletal hypertrophy. Plast Recontr Surg 1995;95:951.
38. Patterson RM, Ballard CL, Wasserman K, Mayerson HS: Lymphatic permeability to albumin. Am J Physiol 1958; 194:120.
39. Pomerantz M, Waldman TA: Systemic lymphatic abnormalities associated with gastrointestinal protein loss secondary to intestinal lymphangiectasia. Gastroenterology 1963; 45:703.
40. Puckett CL: Microlymphatic surgery for lymphedema. Clin Plast Surg 1983;10:133.
41. Rockson SG: Lymphedema [review]. Am J Med 2001;110:288.
42. Roisman S, Manny J, Shiloni E: Intra-abdominal lymphangioma. Br J Surg 1989;76:485.
43. Sabin FR: On the origin of the lymphatic system from the veins and the development of the lymph heart and thoracic duct in the pig. Am J Anat 1901;1:367.
44. Sabin FR: On the development of the superficial lymphatics in the skin of the pig. Am J Anat 1904;3:183.
45. Sabin FR: The development of the lymphatic nodes in the pig and their relation to the lymph hearts. Am J Anat 1905; 4:355.
46. Sabin FR: The lymphatic system in human embryos with a consideration of the morphology of the system as a whole. Am J Anat 1909;9:43.
47. Sabin FR: The development of the lymphatic system. In Keibel G, Mall FP (eds): Manual of Human Embryology, vol 2. Philadelphia, JB Lippincott, 1912, p 709.
48. Savage RC: The surgical management of lymphedema. Surg Gynecol Obstet 1985;160:283.
49. Sawhney CP: Lymphedema of the extremities; a new approach to its management. Br J Plast Surg 1980;33:445.
50. Schnur PL: Surgical treatment of lymphedema: A reappraisal. Vasc Surg 1977;11:182.
51. Serville N: Surgical treatment of lymphedema: A report of 652 cases. Surgery 1987;101:485.
52. Sistrunk WE: Further experiences with Kondolean operation for elephantiasis. JAMA 1918;71:800.
53. Skandalakis JE: I wish I had been there: Highlights in the history of lymphatics. Am Surg 1995;61:799.
54. Smith JW, Conway H: Selection of appropriate surgical procedures in lymphedema; introduction of hinged pedicle. Plast Reconstr Surg 1962;30:10.

55. Stewart G, Gaunt JI, Croft DN, et al: Isotope lymphangiography: A new method of investigating the role of the lymphatics in chronic limb edema. Br J Surg 1985;72:906.
56. Tanigawa N, Shimomatsuya T, Takahashi K, et al: Treatment of cystic hygroma and lymphangioma with the use of bleomycin fat emulsion. Cancer 1987;60:741.
57. Thompson N: Surgical treatment of chronic lymphedema of the lower limb. BMJ 1962;5319:1567.
58. Thompson N: The surgical treatment of chronic lymphedema of the extremities. Surg Clin North Am 1967; 47:445.
59. Van Aerde J, Campbell AN, Smith JA: Spontaneous chylothorax in newborns. Am J Dis Child 1984;138:961.
60. Witte MH, Witte CL: Lymphangiogenesis and lymphologic syndromes. Lymphology 1986;19:21.

Index

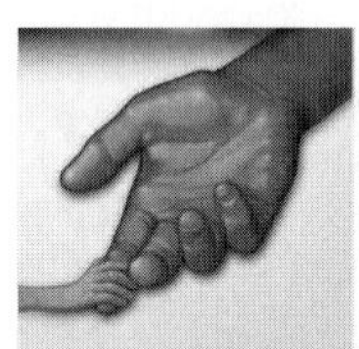

Note: Page numbers followed by the letter f refer to figures and those followed by t refer to tables.
Page numbers followed by the letter b indicate boxed material.

A

B

C

D

E

F

G

I

J

K

M

N

O

P

Q

R

S

T

U

V

W

X

Y

Z